Financial Accounting Standards Board

Original
Pronouncements

2002/2003 Edition

Accounting
Standards

as of June 1, 2002

Volume II
FASB Statements of Standards 101–145

JOHN WILEY & SONS, INC.
New York • Chichester • Brisbane • Toronto • Singapore

Published by the
Financial Accounting Standards Board

NOTICE TO USERS OF THE *ORIGINAL PRONOUNCEMENTS*

This year's edition of the Financial Accounting Standard Board's (FASB) *Original Pronouncements* has been revised and updated to include the following new pronouncements:

FAS141: Business Combinations

Statement 141, issued in June 2001, addresses financial accounting and reporting for business combinations and supersedes APB Opinion No. 16, *Business Combinations,* and FASB Statement No. 38, *Accounting for Preacquisition Contingencies of Purchased Enterprises.* Statement 141 improves the transparency of the accounting and reporting for business combinations by requiring that all business combinations be accounted for under a single method—the purchase method. Use of the pooling-of-interests method is no longer permitted.

Statement 141 requires that the purchase method be used for business combinations initiated after June 30, 2001. Statement 141 does not apply, however, to combinations of two or more not-for-profit organizations, the acquisition of a for-profit organization by a not-for-profit organization, and combinations of two or more mutual enterprises.

FAS142: Goodwill and Other Intangible Assets

Statement 142 supersedes APB Opinion No. 17, *Intangible Assets.* This Statement addresses the financial accounting and reporting for acquired goodwill and other intangible assets. It addresses how intangible assets that are acquired individually or with a group of other assets (but not those acquired in a business combination) should be accounted for in financial statements upon their acquisition. This Statement also addresses how goodwill and other intangible assets should be accounted for after they have been initially recognized in the financial statements.

Statement 142 provides that both goodwill and intangible assets that have indefinite useful lives will not be amortized but will be tested at least annually for impairment. Intangible assets that have finite useful lives will continue to be amortized over their useful lives.

FAS143: Accounting for Asset Retirement Obligations

Statement 143 addresses financial accounting and reporting for obligations associated with the retirement of tangible long-lived assets and the associated asset retirement costs. This Statement applies to all entities. Statement 143 applies to legal obligations associated with the retirement of long-lived assets that result from the acquisition, construction, development, and (or) the normal operation of a long-lived asset, except for certain obligations of lessees.

Statement 143 requires that the fair value of a liability for an asset retirement obligation be recognized in the period in which it is incurred if a reasonable estimate of fair value can be made. The associated asset retirement cost is capitalized as part of the carrying amount of the long-lived asset. Since the liability for an asset retirement obligation is recorded at its fair value, accretion expense shall be recognized each period using the credit-adjusted risk-free interest rate in effect when the liability was initially recognized. The capitalized asset retirement cost is allocated to expense using a systematic and rational method over its useful life.

FAS144: Accounting for the Impairment or Disposal of Long-Lived Assets

Statement 144, issued in August 2001, addresses financial accounting and reporting for the impairment of long-lived assets and for long-lived assets to be disposed of. Statement 144 replaces FASB Statement No. 121, *Accounting for the Impairment of Long-Lived Assets and for Long-Lived Assets to Be Disposed Of,* and institutes one accounting model, based on the framework established in Statement 121, for long-lived assets to be disposed of. This model applies to all long-lived assets to be disposed of, including discontinued operations, and replaces the provisions of APB Opinion No. 30, *Reporting the Results of Operations—Reporting the Effects of Disposal of a Segment of a Business, and Extraordinary, Unusual and Infrequently Occurring Events and Transactions,* for the disposal of components of an entity.

Statement 144 requires that long-lived assets to be disposed of by sale be measured at the lower of carrying amount or fair value less cost to sell, whether reported in continuing operations or in discontinued operations. Therefore, discontinued operations will no longer be measured at net realizable value or include amounts for operating losses that have not yet occurred. Statement 144 also broadens the reporting of discontinued operations to include all components of an entity with operations that can be distinguished from the rest of the entity and that will be eliminated from the ongoing operations of the entity in a disposal transaction.

FAS145: Rescission of FASB Statements No. 4, 44, and 64, Amendment of FASB Statement No. 13, and Technical Corrections

Statement 145, issued in April 2002, rescinds FASB Statement No. 4, *Reporting Gains and Losses from Extinguishment of Debt,* FASB Statement No. 44, *Accounting for Intangible Assets of Motor Carriers,* and FASB Statement No. 64, *Extinguishments of Debt Made to Satisfy Sinking-Fund Requirements.* Statement 145 also amends FASB Statement No. 13, *Accounting for Leases.*

Statement 4 required all gains and losses from extinguishment of debt to be aggregated and, if material, classified as an extraordinary item, net of related income tax effect. As a result of the issuance of Statement 145, the criteria in APB Opinion No. 30, *Reporting the Results of Operations—Reporting the Effects of Disposal of a Segment of a Business, and Extraordinary, Unusual and Infrequently Occurring Events and Transactions,* will now be used to classify those gains and losses.

Statement 44 was issued to establish accounting requirements for the effects of the transition to the provisions of the Motor Carrier Act of 1980 (Public Law 96-296, 96th Congress, July 1, 1980). Those transitions are completed; therefore Statement 44 is no longer necessary.

Statement 145 amends Statement 13 to require that certain lease modifications that have economic effects similar to sale-leaseback transactions be accounted for in the same manner as sale-leaseback transactions. This Statement also makes various technical corrections to existing pronouncements. Those corrections are not substantive in nature.

FTB01-1: Effective Date for Certain Financial Institutions of Certain Provisions of Statement 140 Related to the Isolation of Transferred Assets

Technical Bulletin 01-1 defers the effective date for certain provisions of FASB Statement No. 140, *Accounting for Transfers and Servicing of Financial Assets and Extinguishments of Liabilities,* for certain banks and other financial institutions and provides additional transition time for voluntary transfers to certain transferees (for example, certain master trusts).

FOREWORD

Volumes I and II contain the Statements of Financial Accounting Standards issued by the Financial Accounting Standards Board (FASB) from its inception in 1973 to June 1, 2002.

A companion volume (Volume III) contains the following materials issued by the American Institute of Certified Public Accountants or its committees through June 1973 and by the FASB to June 1, 2002:

- Accounting Research Bulletins
- Accounting Principles Board Opinions
- Interpretations of Accounting Research Bulletins and Accounting Principles Board Opinions
- FASB Interpretations
- FASB Statements of Financial Accounting Concepts
- FASB Technical Bulletins

A shading technique is used to alert the reader when paragraphs containing accounting standards have been amended or superseded. All terms and sentences that have been deleted or replaced are shaded. Paragraphs and subparagraphs that have been amended simply by the addition of terms, sentences, or new footnotes are marked with a vertical solid bar in the left margin alongside the paragraph or subparagraph.

A status page at the beginning of each pronouncement identifies (a) the source of changes to the pronouncement, (b) other pronouncements affected by that pronouncement, and (c) the principal effective date. The status page also identifies, where applicable, other interpretive pronouncements and releases that further clarify that pronouncement. In addition, the status pages of applicable pronouncements reflect either the impact of a given pronouncement on an Emerging Issues Task Force (EITF) Issue (for example, resolves, nullifies, or affects that Issue) or the relationship of an EITF Issue to a given pronouncement (for example, interpretive or related). An interpretive Issue is one in which the Task Force reached a consensus that interprets certain guidance in an existing *Original Pronouncements* document. A related Issue is one in which the topic of the Issue is related to the topic of the *Original Pronouncements* document but either there was no consensus reached or the consensus is not interpretive. Pronouncements that have been completely superseded and may no longer be applied are omitted from this volume; however, a status page is retained for those omitted pronouncements.

The appendixes and Topical Index (included in Volume III) refer to the pronouncements contained in all three volumes. Appendix A presents a current list (as of June 1, 2002) of AICPA Practice Bulletins, audit and accounting Guides, and Statements of Position. Appendix B presents a schedule of all amended and superseded standards. Appendix C lists the effective dates of all pronouncements included in the *Original Pronouncements*. That appendix also presents the transition paragraphs of more recent pronouncements whose effective dates and transition provisions are such that they might initially be applied in annual financial statements issued on or after June 1, 2002. Appendix D lists all EITF Issues discussed to date and their current status.

The Topical Index includes references to the material contained in all three volumes of the *Original Pronouncements* and, in addition, includes references to material included in the *Current Text,* the *EITF Abstracts* (a summary of proceedings of the FASB Emerging Issues Task Force), and other supplemental guidance published by the FASB in the form of question-and-answer Special Reports and published articles. (Please refer to the Introduction to the Topical Index for additional details and guidance on the use of this Index.)

Volume II

ORIGINAL PRONOUNCEMENTS

FASB Statements of Standards 101–145

(as of June 1, 2002)

TABLE OF CONTENTS

Table of Contents

Table of Contents

Statements of

Financial Accounting Standards

No. 101 through No. 140

Statement of Financial Accounting Standards No. 101
Regulated Enterprises—Accounting for the
Discontinuation of Application of FASB Statement No. 71

STATUS

Issued: December 1988

Effective Date: For discontinuations of application of Statement 71 occurring in fiscal years ending after December 15, 1988

Affects: Amends APB 30, paragraph 20

Affected by: Paragraph 6 amended by FAS 121 and FAS 144
Paragraph 19 amended by FAS 109

Issues Discussed by FASB Emerging Issues Task Force (EITF)

Affects: No Issues

Interpreted by: Paragraphs 6 and 7 interpreted by EITF Issue No. 97-4

Related Issues: No EITF Issues

SUMMARY

This Statement specifies how an enterprise that ceases to meet the criteria for application of FASB Statement No. 71, *Accounting for the Effects of Certain Types of Regulation,* to all or part of its operations should report that event in its general-purpose external financial statements.

An enterprise's operations can cease to meet those criteria for various reasons, including deregulation, a change in the method of regulation, or a change in the competitive environment for the enterprise's regulated services or products. Regardless of the reason, an enterprise whose operations cease to meet those criteria should discontinue application of that Statement and report that discontinuation by eliminating from its statement of financial position the effects of any actions of regulators that had been recognized as assets and liabilities pursuant to Statement 71 but would not have been recognized as assets and liabilities by enterprises in general. However, the carrying amounts of plant, equipment, and inventory measured and reported pursuant to Statement 71 should not be adjusted unless those assets are impaired, in which case the carrying amounts of those assets should be reduced to reflect that impairment. The net effect of the adjustments should be included in income of the period of the change and classified as an extraordinary item.

This Statement is effective for discontinuations of application of Statement 71 occurring in fiscal years ending after December 15, 1988, but its adoption may be delayed until the issuance of annual financial statements for the fiscal year that includes December 15, 1989. Retroactive application to discontinuations reported prior to fiscal years ending after December 15, 1988 by restatement of the financial statements for the period including the date of discontinuation and periods subsequent to the date of the discontinuation is permitted but not required.

Statement of Financial Accounting Standards No. 101

Regulated Enterprises—Accounting for the Discontinuation of Application of FASB Statement No. 71

CONTENTS

INTRODUCTION

1. FASB Statement No. 71, *Accounting for the Effects of Certain Types of Regulation,* requires that an enterprise's operations meet specific criteria for application of that Statement. Statement 71 does not address the accounting that should result when an enterprise's operations cease to meet those criteria. Since Statement 71 was issued, deregulation of certain industries and changes in the method of regulating others have caused several enterprises to discontinue application of Statement 71 for some or all of their operations.

2. The FASB has been informed that the methods used to account for those discontinuations have varied in practice. In its October 15, 1984 Issues Paper, *Application of Concepts in FASB Statement of Financial Accounting Standards No. 71 to Emerging Issues in the Public Utility Industry,* the AICPA Public Utility Subcommittee requested that the Board specify the appropriate accounting to reflect the discontinuation of application of Statement 71.

3. As a condition for its initial and continuing application, Statement 71 requires that an enterprise's operations meet the three criteria specified in paragraph 5 of Statement 71:

a. The enterprise's rates for regulated services or products provided to its customers are established by or are subject to approval by an independent, third-party regulator or by its own governing board empowered by statute or contract to establish rates that bind customers.

b. The regulated rates are designed to recover the specific enterprise's costs of providing the regulated services or products.

c. In view of the demand for the regulated services or products and the level of competition, direct and indirect, it is reasonable to assume that rates set at levels that will recover the enterprise's costs can be charged to and collected from customers. This criterion requires consideration of anticipated changes in levels of demand or competition during the recovery period for any capitalized costs. [Footnote reference omitted.]

4. Failure of an enterprise's operations to continue to meet the criteria in paragraph 5 of Statement 71 can result from different causes. Examples include the following:

a. Deregulation

b. A change in the regulator's approach to setting rates from cost-based rate making to another form of regulation

c. Increasing competition that limits the enterprise's ability to sell utility services or products at rates that will recover costs

d. Regulatory actions resulting from resistance to rate increases that limit the enterprise's ability to sell utility services or products at rates that will recover costs if the enterprise is unable to obtain (or chooses not to seek) relief from prior regulatory actions through appeals to the regulator or the courts.

Regardless of the reason for an enterprise's discontinuation of application of Statement 71, this Statement specifies how that discontinuation shall be reported in the enterprise's general-purpose external financial statements.

STANDARDS OF FINANCIAL ACCOUNTING AND REPORTING

Discontinuation of the Application of Statement 71

5. When an enterprise determines that its operations in a regulatory jurisdiction no longer meet the criteria for application of Statement 71, that enterprise shall discontinue application of that Statement to its operations in that jurisdiction. If a separable portion of the enterprise's operations within a regulatory jurisdiction ceases to meet the criteria for application of Statement 71, application of that Statement to that separable portion shall be discontinued. That situation creates a presumption that application of Statement 71 shall be discontinued for all of the enterprise's operations within that regulatory jurisdiction. That presumption can be overcome by establishing that the enterprise's other operations within that jurisdiction continue to meet the criteria for application of Statement 71.

Accounting to Reflect the Discontinuation of Application of Statement 71

6. When an enterprise discontinues application of Statement 71 to all or part of its operations, that enterprise shall eliminate from its statement of financial position prepared for general-purpose external financial reporting the effects of any actions of regulators that had been recognized as assets and liabilities pursuant to Statement 71 but would not have been recognized as assets and liabilities by enterprises in general. However, the carrying amounts of plant, equipment, and inventory measured and reported pursuant to Statement 71[1] shall not be adjusted unless those assets are impaired, in which case the carrying amounts of those assets shall be reduced to reflect that impairment. Whether those assets have been impaired shall be

judged in the same manner as for enterprises in general. The net effect of the adjustments required by this Statement shall be included in income of the period in which the discontinuation occurs and shall be classified as an extraordinary item.

7. An enterprise that discontinues application of Statement 71 shall no longer recognize the effects of actions of a regulator as assets or liabilities unless the right to receive payment or the obligation to pay exists as a result of past events or transactions and regardless of future transactions.

Disclosures

8. For the period in which an enterprise reflects the discontinuation of application of Statement 71 to all or a separable portion of its operations, the enterprise shall disclose the reasons for the discontinuation and identify the portion of its operations to which the application of Statement 71 is being discontinued.

9. The disclosure requirements of APB Opinion No. 30, *Reporting the Results of Operations—Reporting the Effects of Disposal of a Segment of a Business, and Extraordinary, Unusual and Infrequently Occurring Events and Transactions,* for extraordinary items apply to the net adjustment reported in the statement of operations as a result of applying this Statement.

Amendment to Opinion 30

10. This Statement amends Opinion 30 only to the extent that classification of the net effect of discontinuing the application of Statement 71 as an extraordinary item pursuant to paragraph 6 of this Statement shall be made without regard to the criteria in paragraph 20 of that Opinion.

Effective Date and Transition

11. This Statement shall be effective for discontinuations of application of Statement 71 occurring in fiscal years ending after December 15, 1988. If an enterprise has issued financial statements in which the provisions of this Statement have not been applied to a discontinuation occurring in the fiscal year that includes December 15, 1988, the financial statements for the interim period of the discontinuation and subsequent interim periods within that

---

[1]The carrying amounts of plant, equipment, and inventory for enterprises applying Statement 71 differ from those for enterprises in general only because of the allowance for funds used during construction, intercompany profit, and disallowances of costs of recently completed plants. If any other amounts that would not be includable in the carrying amounts of plant, equipment, or inventory by enterprises in general (such as postconstruction operating costs capitalized pursuant to paragraph 9 of Statement 71) are included in or netted against the carrying amounts of plant, equipment, or inventory, those amounts shall be accounted for as this Statement prescribes for the effects of actions of a regulator.

fiscal year shall be restated. For discontinuations reported in fiscal years ending prior to December 15, 1988, retroactive application by restatement of the financial statements for the period including the date of discontinuation and periods subsequent to the date of discontinuation is permitted but not required. Any financial statements restated shall disclose the nature of the restatement and its effect on income before extraordinary items, extraordinary items, net income, and related per share amounts for each period restated. Interim and annual financial statements for periods that ended prior to the date of discontinuation of application of Statement 71 shall not be restated.

12. Enterprises with discontinuations occurring in fiscal years that include December 15, 1988 or December 15, 1989 may delay adopting this Statement until the issuance of annual financial statements for the fiscal year that includes December 15, 1989. Enterprises delaying adoption of this Statement shall, when adopting this Statement, restate their interim and annual financial statements for the period including the date of discontinuation and periods subsequent to that date and shall disclose the nature of the restatement and its effect on income before extraordinary items, extraordinary items, net income, and related per share amounts for each period restated.

The provisions of this Statement need not be applied to immaterial items.

This Statement was adopted by the affirmative vote of six members of the Financial Accounting Standards Board. Mr. Lauver dissented.

Mr. Lauver dissents from the issuance of this Statement because it does not require the effects of all specialized practices followed while an enterprise applied Statement 71 to be eliminated from the balance sheet at the time the enterprise discontinues application of that Statement. Specialized practices whose effects are not required to be eliminated upon discontinuing application of Statement 71 are capitalizing an allowance for earnings on shareholders' investment, capitalizing interest on bases different from those permitted by Statement 34, and capitalizing profits on intercompany sales. The effects of those specialized practices that are permitted to remain in the balance sheet have been reported as components of asset accounts (inventory and plant) that would have existed absent those components rather than in separate asset accounts and are said, therefore, not to represent assets resulting solely from actions of regulators. Mr. Lauver believes that the effects of all specialized

practices followed while applying Statement 71 are assets (or liabilities) resulting solely from actions of regulators, are substantively the same regardless of balance sheet classification, and should be eliminated to enhance subsequent comparability with other enterprises that are not subject to Statement 71 and to enhance distinctions from enterprises that continue to be subject to Statement 71.

As indicated herein, a rationale for conclusions expressed in this Statement is that, although conceptually correct to eliminate from the balance sheet all effects of the specialized practices followed while applying Statement 71, the cost of doing so, for the practices mentioned in the preceding paragraph, would exceed the benefits derived and that elimination is prohibited by this Statement. Although Mr. Lauver believes it is appropriate for a standard setter to refrain from requiring a conceptually correct solution when costs are judged to exceed benefits, he believes it is inappropriate to preclude a conceptually correct solution in financial statements of an enterprise that concludes that the benefits it perceives will exceed the costs that it alone will bear.

Appendix A

EXAMPLES OF THE APPLICATION OF THIS STATEMENT TO SPECIFIC SITUATIONS

CONTENTS

Appendix A

EXAMPLES OF THE APPLICATION OF THIS STATEMENT TO SPECIFIC SITUATIONS

13. This appendix provides examples of the application of this Statement to some specific situations. The examples do not address all possible applications of this Statement.

Assets Recorded Based Solely on Expected Future Revenue to Be Provided by the Regulator

14. Utility A operates solely in one regulatory jurisdiction. At December 31, 19X1, Utility A concludes, based on current market conditions, that it no longer meets the criteria for the application of Statement 71. Utility A's statement of financial position at December 31, 19X1 includes the following items:

a. Deferred purchased power costs (costs of power used for operations in prior periods that were expected to be recovered from customers as a result of an automatic adjustment clause)
b. Deferred costs of abandoned plant (costs for which recovery was being provided through rates)
c. Deferred costs of repairing storm damage.

How should those items be reported at December 31, 19X1?

15. All of those items should be eliminated from the enterprise's statement of financial position when it ceases to apply Statement 71. The resulting charge to income, net of any related tax effects, should be reported as an extraordinary item in the period that includes December 31, 19X1. The enterprise should no longer defer those costs and report them as assets because they could not be reported as assets by enterprises in general. Enterprises in general would report a receivable for those items only if a right to receive payment exists as a result of past events or transactions and regardless of future transactions (such as future sales).

16. For example, a contract between a supplier and a customer for the sale of fuel oil may specify that next year's sales price will be adjusted based on the supplier's current-year cost of fuel oil. Even though it is probable that a future economic benefit (the ability to charge a higher price in the future) will result from the supplier's current-year cost of fuel oil, no asset exists at the end of the current year because the transactions (sales to the customer) that give the supplier control of the benefit are in the future. However, if the contract provides that the customer is obligated to pay additional amounts related to past purchases and regardless of future purchases, the supplier has an asset and it does not matter whether that payment is made in a single amount or when the customer will pay for next year's purchases.

Liabilities Recorded Based Solely on Actions of the Regulator

17. Utility B operates in two regulatory jurisdictions, State 1 and State 2. Forty percent of Utility B's operations are located in State 1 and 60 percent in State 2; system-wide assets, liabilities, and certain gains and losses are allocated 40 percent to State 1 and 60 percent to State 2. At December 31, 19X2, Utility B concludes, based on current and expected future market conditions in State 1, that it no longer meets the criteria for application of Statement 71 to its operations in State 1. No similar conditions exist in State 2, and actions of State 1's regulators are not expected to influence the decisions of regulators in State 2. Utility B's state-

ment of financial position at December 31, 19X2 includes the following items:

Deferred gain on restructuring debt, being amortized for rate-making purposes on an allocated basis by both states $50,000

Revenues collected subject to refund in prior years in State 1, expected to be refunded through future rates $75,000

How should those items be reported at December 31, 19X2?

18. The portion of the deferred gain allocable to State 1 (determined in the example to be 40 percent of $50,000, or $20,000), net of any related tax effects, should be eliminated from the enterprise's statement of financial position when it ceases to apply Statement 71 to its operations in State 1. No adjustment should be made for the deferred gain applicable to State 2. The regulatory-created accrual for revenues subject to refund in State 1, net of any related tax effects, should be eliminated. Whether any liability related thereto exists should be determined under generally accepted accounting principles for enterprises in general. For example, amounts that were collected in the current or prior periods for which refunds will be made *regardless of future sales* should continue to be re-

ported as liabilities after application of Statement 71 is discontinued. The credit to income resulting from the above adjustments, net of any related tax effects, should be reported as an extraordinary item in the period that includes December 31, 19X2.

Regulatory-Created Assets Resulting from the Recording of Deferred Income Taxes Not Recognized for Rate Making

19. Utility C operates solely in one regulatory jurisdiction. At June 30, 19X3, Utility C concludes, based on new legislation, that it no longer meets the criteria for application of Statement 71. Utility C had adopted FASB Statement No. 96, *Accounting for Income Taxes,* in 19X2 and because of applying Statement 71 had recorded a regulatory-created asset of $650,000 for deferred taxes resulting from temporary differences that had not been recognized in the rate-making process but that were expected to be recovered in the future. What reporting is required for that regulatory-created asset?

20. Utility C should eliminate that regulatory-created asset from its statement of financial position when the enterprise ceases to apply Statement 71. The charge to income, net of any related tax effects, should be reported as an extraordinary item in the period that includes June 30, 19X3.

Appendix B

BASIS FOR CONCLUSIONS

CONTENTS

Appendix B

BASIS FOR CONCLUSIONS

Introduction

21. This appendix summarizes considerations that were deemed significant by members of the Board in reaching the conclusions in this Statement. It in-

cludes reasons for accepting certain views and rejecting others. Individual Board members gave greater weight to some factors than to others.

22. An FASB Exposure Draft, *Regulated Enterprises—Accounting for the Discontinuation of Application of FASB Statement No. 71,* was issued for public comment on July 8, 1988. The Board received 81 letters of comment in response to the Exposure Draft. The Board concluded that it

could reach an informed decision on the basis of existing information without a public hearing.

Overall Conclusions on the Discontinuation of Application of Statement 71

23. For an enterprise with operations that meet the criteria for application of Statement 71, actions of a regulator may result in the recognition of assets and liabilities because the regulator may specify the amount and timing of recognition of allowable costs for rate-making purposes.

24. The conclusion that the criteria of Statement 71 are no longer met as a result of changes in circumstances is a significant event in terms of financial reporting for an enterprise. An objective of financial reporting is to achieve comparability of accounting information. Paragraph 119 of FASB Concepts Statement No. 2, *Qualitative Characteristics of Accounting Information,* states that this objective "is not to be attained by making unlike things look alike any more than by making like things look different." In this instance, achieving that objective requires reporting the effect of that significant event so that an enterprise that discontinues application of Statement 71 is distinguished from an enterprise that does not.

25. When an enterprise determines that it ceases to meet the criteria for application of Statement 71, assets and liabilities recognized solely because of judgments about the effects of actions of the regulator cease to meet the criteria for recognition. The Board concluded that the change in circumstances that led to the discontinuation of application of Statement 71 should be reported in financial statements. The approach set forth in the Exposure Draft required adjusting the financial statements of the enterprise so that they are comparable, at the date of the change and in future periods, with the financial statements of other enterprises that had never applied Statement 71.

26. Most respondents disagreed with the Exposure Draft's requirement to adjust the amounts recorded as plant, equipment, and inventory to the amounts that would have been recorded had the enterprise never applied Statement 71. The reasons given by those respondents for not adjusting the amounts recorded as plant, equipment, and inventory when discontinuing the application of Statement 71 included (a) viewing the allowance for funds used during construction as an acceptable substitute for interest that would have been capitalized under FASB Statement No. 34, *Capitalization of Interest Cost,* (b) the general notion, as expressed in paragraph 88 of FASB Concepts Statement No. 5, *Recognition and Measurement in Financial Statements of Business Enterprises,* that "once an asset or lia-

bility is recognized, it continues to be measured at the amount initially recognized until an event that changes the asset or liability or its amount occurs and meets the recognition criteria," (c) the precedent that the adoption of Statement 34 by enterprises in general was prospective, and (d) the assertion that the cost of obtaining the information necessary to adjust the amounts recorded as plant, equipment, and inventory exceeded the benefits derived from the adjustments.

27. Other respondents agreed with the Exposure Draft's requirement to adjust the amounts recorded as plant, equipment, and inventory to the amounts that would have been recorded had the enterprise never applied Statement 71. Those respondents viewed the differences in amounts recorded as plant, equipment, and inventory due to application of Statement 71 as no different from the separately identified effects of actions of a regulator recognized as assets and liabilities, such as deferred storm damage costs or deferred gains on reacquired debt. Those respondents agreed that those amounts should be eliminated upon the discontinuation of application of Statement 71.

28. Absent impairment, this Statement does not permit adjustment of the carrying amounts of plant, equipment, and inventory measured and recorded pursuant to Statement 71 when an enterprise discontinues application of Statement 71 to all or a portion of its operations. Some Board members agree that the allowances for funds used during construction were an acceptable substitute for the amounts of interest that would have been capitalized in accordance with Statement 34 and that once an asset is measured and recognized pursuant to generally accepted accounting principles, the cost basis of that asset, absent impairment or the occurrence of other events that change the asset or its amount, should not be adjusted. Other Board members believe that, in principle, the carrying amounts of plant, equipment, and inventory should be adjusted to the amounts that would have been recorded had Statement 71 never been applied but that the cost of determining and removing the allowance for funds used during construction and intercompany profit and of computing the interest that would have been capitalized in accordance with Statement 34 would exceed the benefits derived.

29. The Board considered permitting but not requiring enterprises that discontinue application of Statement 71 to adjust their carrying amounts of plant, equipment, and inventory to the amounts that would have been recorded had Statement 71 never been applied. Some Board members did not believe that adjustments to the carrying amounts of those assets were appropriate absent impair-

ment. Other Board members believed the advantages of prescribing a consistent method of discontinuing application of Statement 71 were sufficient to outweigh their concern about prohibiting an enterprise from using what those Board members believe to be the conceptually correct approach. For those reasons, this Statement does not permit enterprises that discontinue application of Statement 71 to adjust the carrying amounts of plant, equipment, and inventory to the amounts that would have been recorded had Statement 71 never been applied.

30. In determining the appropriate financial reporting for an enterprise that discontinues application of Statement 71, the Board considered whether the accounting for a change in circumstances should be based on the guidance contained in APB Opinion No. 20, *Accounting Changes.* The Board recognizes that the change from one accounting model to another is an unusual accounting event that is different from a discretionary change in accounting because the former is dictated by changed circumstances. That change is somewhat analogous to a "change in estimate effected by a change in accounting principle," described in paragraphs 11 and 32 of Opinion 20, that is required to be accounted for as a change in estimate. The Board concluded that, because the change in circumstances eliminates the justification for recognizing assets and liabilities whose recognition was based solely on judgments made about the effect of the rate-making process, that change should be reported as a separate component of net income of the period of the change.

31. The discontinuation of application of Statement 71 may, in some circumstances, not meet the criteria for extraordinary items in paragraph 20 of Opinion 30. The Board concluded that extraordinary-item treatment represents a practical and reasonable way to classify the adjustments resulting from the discontinuation of Statement 71 in a statement of operations. This Statement amends Opinion 30 to the extent that classification of the net effect of discontinuing the application of Statement 71 as an extraordinary item is made without regard to the criteria in paragraph 20 of that Opinion.

32. Some respondents asserted that an enterprise that discontinues the application of Statement 71 can justify continued recognition of assets and liabilities arising from the rate-making process because of judgments about the probability of their recovery from or payment to ratepayers. Those assertions were typically based on definitions of assets and liabilities in paragraphs 25 and 35 of FASB Concepts Statement No. 6, *Elements of Financial Statements,* which state:

Assets are probable future economic benefits obtained or controlled by a particular entity as a result of past transactions or events.

Liabilities are probable future sacrifices of economic benefits arising from present obligations of a particular entity to transfer assets or provide services to other entities in the future as a result of past transactions or events. [Footnote references omitted.]

33. Statement 71 recognizes that in certain circumstances the rate-making process provides a link between costs and revenues in one period and revenues in the future. When an enterprise meets the criteria for the application of Statement 71, the rate-making process can affect the recognition of assets and liabilities. The Board believes that continuing to recognize assets and liabilities based solely on judgments about the rate-making process is not appropriate when an enterprise ceases to meet the criteria for application of Statement 71. After an enterprise ceases to meet the criteria for application of Statement 71, it is in a position comparable to enterprises in a number of industries that are subject to regulation but do not apply Statement 71.

34. For enterprises that cease to meet the criteria for applying Statement 71 and continue to be subject to rate regulation, that regulation is similar to a contractual obligation to sell goods or services in the future at an established price or to other forms of price control. A contract that an enterprise in general believes is probable of generating higher than normal gross profits in the future does not provide a basis for the current recognition of an asset representing the anticipated "excess" gross profits related to that contract, nor does it provide a basis for deferring contract-related costs that would otherwise be charged to expense. Similarly, a contract that is probable of generating a lower than normal gross profit does not create a liability unless the contract meets the criteria of FASB Statement No. 5, *Accounting for Contingencies,* for accrual of a loss contingency.

35. This Statement does not provide detailed guidance for reaching judgments about whether application of Statement 71 should be discontinued. Similarly, Statement 71 does not provide detailed guidance for reaching judgments about whether it is appropriate to apply Statement 71. Because applicability of Statement 71 is and must remain a matter of judgment and because the objectives are clear, the Board decided that it was unnecessary to prescribe detailed guidance for reaching the judgments required by this Statement and by Statement 71.

36. Some respondents asked that this Statement define the term *costs* as it is used in the examples in paragraph 4. Some respondents argued it should be defined as "allowable costs" and other respondents argued it should be defined as "incurred costs." The term *costs* is used in paragraph 4 of this Statement consistent with its usage in paragraph 5 of Statement 71. As explained in paragraph 67 of the Basis for Conclusions to Statement 71, the term *costs* in paragraph 5 of Statement 71 is based on allowable costs.

Application of Overall Conclusions to Specific Items

37. The Board concluded that the approach required by this Statement would be easier to understand and implement with examples. Therefore, an appendix with examples is included.

38. The Exposure Draft included a reference to the use of estimates, averages, and computational shortcuts when implementing its provisions because of its requirement to adjust fixed assets to the amounts that would have been recorded had Statement 71 never been applied. This Statement requires significantly fewer adjustments to fixed assets than the approach in the Exposure Draft, and the Board concluded that the specific reference to the use of estimates, averages, and computational shortcuts was unnecessary.

39. Some respondents to the Exposure Draft disagreed with its application to "separable portions" of an enterprise's operation, and other respondents suggested that a separable portion of an enterprise should be no less than an enterprise's operations within a regulatory jurisdiction or a reportable segment as defined in FASB Statement No. 14, *Financial Reporting for Segments of a Business Enterprise.* Those respondents stated that discontinuing application of Statement 71 for a portion of an enterprise's operations or a portion of an enterprise's operations within a regulatory jurisdiction would not be meaningful and could be confusing to preparers and users of the financial statements. Other respondents agreed with discontinuing application of Statement 71 for separable portions of an enterprise's operations and indicated that this was consistent with the application of Statement 71. Paragraph 6 of Statement 71 states:

> If some of an enterprise's operations are regulated and meet the criteria of paragraph 5, this Statement shall be applied to only that portion of the enterprise's operations.

40. This Statement does not modify paragraph 6 of Statement 71. Statement 71 is applied to separable portions of an enterprise's operations, and therefore the discontinuation of application of Statement 71 should be applied to separable portions of an enterprise's operations. The separable portion may be an enterprise's operations within a regulatory jurisdiction or a smaller portion (such as a customer class within a regulatory jurisdiction), either of which could require the allocation of system-wide assets and liabilities.

41. This Statement does not modify FASB Statement No. 90, *Regulated Enterprises—Accounting for Abandonments and Disallowances of Plant Costs.* If the substance of the actions of the regulator for a separable portion of an enterprise's operations is an explicit, but indirect, disallowance of costs of a recently completed plant, that disallowance should be accounted for as prescribed by Statement 90. The application of Statement 71, as amended, is not optional. An enterprise's operations that meet the criteria for application of Statement 71 are required to be reported consistent with Statement 71, and an enterprise whose operations cease to meet the criteria for application of Statement 71 is required to discontinue application of Statement 71 as prescribed in this Statement.

42. This Statement requires that the carrying amounts of the plant, equipment, and inventory measured and recorded pursuant to Statement 71 not be adjusted unless those assets are impaired. Paragraph 7 of Statement 71 states:

> Authoritative accounting pronouncements that apply to enterprises in general also apply to regulated enterprises. However, enterprises subject to this Statement shall apply it instead of any conflicting provisions of standards in other authoritative pronouncements. [Footnote reference omitted.]

The carrying amounts of plant, equipment, and inventory for enterprises applying Statement 71 differ from those for enterprises in general only because of the allowance for funds used during construction, intercompany profit, and disallowances of costs of recently completed plants. If any other amounts that would not be includable in the carrying amounts of plant, equipment, or inventory by enterprises in general are included in or netted against the carrying amounts of plant, equipment, and inventory, those amounts should be separated from the carrying amounts of plant, equipment, and inventory and accounted for as prescribed in this Statement. For example, postconstruction operating costs that were capitalized pursuant to paragraph 9 of Statement 71 represent the effects of actions of a regulator regardless of their classification in the financial statements and should be accounted for as this Statement prescribes for the effects of actions of a regulator. Another example of the effect of actions of a regulator that would require adjustment is the cumulative difference, if any, between recorded depreciation and depreciation computed using a generally accepted method of depreciation.

43. Several respondents requested that this Statement address the accounting for reapplication of Statement 71 by an enterprise that had previously discontinued application of Statement 71 for all or a portion of its operations. The Board noted that the accounting for the initial application of Statement 71 has not been raised as an issue that needs to be addressed by the Board. In addition, some Board members believe that circumstances warranting reapplication of Statement 71 will occur rarely, if at all. The Board concluded that the accounting for the initial application or reapplication of Statement 71 is beyond the scope of this Statement.

44. Several respondents suggested that this Statement should require disclosures about the discontinuation of application of Statement 71, such as disclosing the reasons for the discontinuation and the portions of the enterprise's operations that do and do not apply Statement 71. In addition, for enterprises that discontinue application of Statement 71 but continue to be subject to rate regulation, some respondents suggested that the Statement require disclosure of the rate-making concepts used by the regulator and the factors that are considered in establishing rates and, to the extent that past events will be reflected in future prices, identify and quantify those regulatory actions.

45. The Board concluded that disclosure of the reasons for discontinuing application of Statement 71 and disclosure of the portion of an enterprise's operations for which the application of Statement 71 is being discontinued would provide useful information; therefore, this Statement requires disclosure of that information. The Board concluded that it would not be appropriate to require disclosure of the effects of regulation for enterprises that discontinue application of Statement 71 but continue to be subject to regulation without addressing disclosure requirements for enterprises that have never applied Statement 71 but are subject to regulation. However, the Board encourages disclo-

sures about the discontinuation of application of Statement 71 and the nature and effects of continuing regulation that would make the financial statements more informative and meaningful.

Effective Date and Transition

46. The Board considered whether this Statement should be applied retroactively to all enterprises that have previously discontinued application of Statement 71. The Board recognized that applying this Statement only to future discontinuations would diminish both comparability of financial statements among enterprises that have discontinued application of Statement 71 using different methods and consistency within an enterprise that reports discontinuations for portions of its operations in different periods using different methods. Although requiring restatement would increase comparability among companies discontinuing application of Statement 71 and consistency within a few enterprises that have previously discontinued the application of Statement 71 to a portion of their operations during fiscal years ending before December 15, 1988, the Board believes that those benefits do not justify the costs that would be incurred. Therefore, the Board decided that application of this Statement should be required for discontinuations occurring in annual periods ending after that date, with retroactive application to previously reported discontinuations permitted but not required. In no event should the interim or annual financial statements for periods that ended prior to the date of discontinuation of application of Statement 71 be restated.

47. Some respondents requested a delay of the effective date or a transition period to allow affected enterprises the time necessary to compute the effect of the discontinuation of application of Statement 71 pursuant to this Statement and, if necessary, time to resolve problems created by the accounting required by this Statement for loan indentures or other agreements. The Board believes that because plant, equipment, and inventory are not required to be restated for certain items as was required in the Exposure Draft, it would be rare that an enterprise would cease to meet the criteria for application of Statement 71 and would not know the accounting effect of the discontinuation. However, the Board concluded, primarily because this Statement is being issued late in the year in which it becomes effective, to allow for a delay in its required adoption.

Statement of Financial Accounting Standards No. 102
Statement of Cash Flows—Exemption of Certain Enterprises and Classification of Cash Flows from Certain Securities Acquired for Resale

an amendment of FASB Statement No. 95

STATUS

Issued: February 1989

Effective Date: For financial statements issued after February 28, 1989

Affects: Amends FAS 95, paragraphs 3, 15, 16(a), 16(b), 17(a), 17(b), 22(a), 23(a), 147, 148, and 149(a)

Affected by: Paragraph 8 amended by FAS 115 and FAS 145
  Paragraphs 10(b) through 10(e) amended by FAS 145
  Footnote 3 amended by FAS 135
  Footnote 4 amended by FAS 115

SUMMARY

This Statement amends FASB Statement No. 95, *Statement of Cash Flows,* to exempt from the requirement to provide a statement of cash flows (a) defined benefit pension plans covered by FASB Statement No. 35, *Accounting and Reporting by Defined Benefit Pension Plans,* and certain other employee benefit plans and (b) highly liquid investment companies that meet specified conditions.

This Statement also requires that cash receipts and cash payments resulting from acquisitions and sales of (a) securities and other assets that are acquired specifically for resale and are carried at market value in a trading account and (b) loans that are acquired specifically for resale and are carried at market value or the lower of cost or market value be classified as operating cash flows in a statement of cash flows.

This Statement is effective for financial statements issued after February 28, 1989, with earlier application encouraged.

Statement of Financial Accounting Standards No. 102

Statement of Cash Flows—Exemption of Certain Enterprises and Classification of Cash Flows from Certain Securities Acquired for Resale

an amendment of FASB Statement No. 95

CONTENTS

INTRODUCTION

1. FASB Statement No. 95, *Statement of Cash Flows,* establishes standards for cash flow reporting and requires a statement of cash flows as part of a full set of financial statements for all business enterprises. Statement 95 supersedes APB Opinion No. 19, *Reporting Changes in Financial Position.*

2. FASB Statement No. 35, *Accounting and Reporting by Defined Benefit Pension Plans,* establishes specific financial reporting requirements for those plans and states that existing generally accepted accounting principles other than those discussed in that Statement may apply. The applicability of Statement 95 to defined benefit pension plans and other employee benefit plans is not specifically addressed by Statement 95.

3. Statement 95 acknowledges that information about the cash flows of certain investment companies may be less important than similar information for other enterprises, but the Board decided when that Statement was issued that investment companies should not be exempted from the requirement to provide a statement of cash flows because information about cash flows is relevant. Several representatives of investment companies requested that the Board reconsider the applicability of Statement 95 to those companies. Discussions with those representatives and others focused primarily on the usefulness of a statement of cash flows for highly liquid investment companies with little or no debt.

4. Statement 95 requires business enterprises to present a statement of cash flows that classifies cash receipts and cash payments according to whether they result from operating, investing, or financing activities and provides a definition of each category. Statement 95 recognizes that certain cash receipts and cash payments may have aspects of more than one category of cash flows. For example, a cash payment may pertain to an item that, depending on the circumstances, could be either inventory or a productive asset. The Board was asked to address the appropriate classification of cash flows resulting from the active trading of securities in a trading account of a bank, broker and dealer in securities, or other enterprise.

STANDARDS OF FINANCIAL ACCOUNTING AND REPORTING

Exemptions from the Requirement to Provide a Statement of Cash Flows

5. A statement of cash flows is not required to be provided by a defined benefit pension plan that presents financial information in accordance with the provisions of Statement 35. Other employee benefit plans that present financial information similar to that required by Statement 35 (including

Statement of Cash Flows—Exemption of Certain Enterprises and Classification of Cash Flows from Certain Securities Acquired for Resale

FAS102

the presentation of plan investments at fair value) also are not required to provide a statement of cash flows. Employee benefit plans are encouraged to include a statement of cash flows with their annual financial statements when that statement would provide relevant information about the ability of the plan to meet future obligations (for example, when the plan invests in assets that are not highly liquid or obtains financing for investments).

6. Provided that the conditions in paragraph 7 are met, a statement of cash flows is not required to be provided by (a) an investment company that is subject to the registration and regulatory requirements of the Investment Company Act of 1940 (1940 Act), (b) an investment enterprise that has essentially the same characteristics as those subject to the 1940 Act, or (c) a common trust fund, variable annuity account, or similar fund maintained by a bank, insurance company, or other enterprise in its capacity as a trustee, administrator, or guardian for the collective investment and reinvestment of moneys.

7. For an investment enterprise specified in paragraph 6 to be exempt from the requirement to provide a statement of cash flows, all of the following conditions must be met:

a. During the period, substantially all of the enterprise's investments were highly liquid (for example, marketable securities and other assets for which a market is readily available).
b. Substantially all of the enterprise's investments are carried at market value.[1]
c. The enterprise had little or no debt, based on average debt outstanding[2] during the period, in relation to average total assets.
d. The enterprise provides a statement of changes in net assets.

Classification of Cash Flows from Acquisitions and Sales of Certain Securities and Other Assets

8. Banks, brokers and dealers in securities, and other enterprises may carry securities and other as-

sets in a trading account.[3] Cash receipts and cash payments resulting from purchases and sales of securities and other assets shall be classified as operating cash flows if those assets are acquired specifically for resale and are carried at market value in a trading account.

9. Some loans are similar to securities in a trading account in that they are originated or purchased specifically for resale and are held for short periods of time. Cash receipts and cash payments resulting from acquisitions and sales of loans also shall be classified as operating cash flows if those loans are acquired specifically for resale and are carried at market value or at the lower of cost or market value.[4] Cash receipts resulting from sales of loans that were not specifically acquired for resale shall be classified as investing cash inflows. That is, if loans were acquired as investments, cash receipts from sales of those loans shall be classified as investing cash inflows regardless of a change in the purpose for holding those loans.

Amendments to Statement 95

10. Statement 95 is amended as follows:

a. The following footnote is added to the end of the first sentence of paragraph 3:

*A statement of cash flows is not required for defined benefit pension plans and certain other employee benefit plans or for certain investment companies as provided by FASB Statement No. 102, *Statement of Cash Flows—Exemption of Certain Enterprises and Classification of Cash Flows from Certain Securities Acquired for Resale.*

b. The following sentence is added to the end of paragraph 15:

Investing activities exclude acquiring and disposing of certain loans or other debt or equity instruments that are acquired specifically for resale, as discussed in Statement 102.

---

[1]Securities for which market value is determined using matrix pricing techniques, which are described in the AICPA Audit and Accounting Guide, *Audits of Investment Companies,* would meet this condition. Other securities for which market value is not readily determinable and for which fair value must be determined in good faith by the board of directors would not.

[2]For the purpose of determining average debt outstanding, obligations resulting from redemptions of shares by the enterprise, from unsettled purchases of securities or similar assets, or from covered options written generally may be excluded. However, any extension of credit by the seller that is not in accordance with standard industry practices for redeeming shares or for settling purchases of investments shall be included in average debt outstanding.

[3]Characteristics of trading account activities are described in FASB Statement No. 89, *Financial Reporting and Changing Prices,* and in the AICPA Industry Audit Guide, *Audits of Banks,* and Audit and Accounting Guide, *Audits of Brokers and Dealers in Securities.*

[4]Mortgage loans and mortgage-backed securities held for sale are required to be reported at the lower of cost or market value in accordance with FASB Statement No. 65, *Accounting for Certain Mortgage Banking Activities.*

c. The parenthetical comment in paragraphs 16(a) and 17(a) is superseded by the following:

(other than cash equivalents and certain debt instruments that are acquired specifically for resale)

d. The following parenthetical comment is added after the word *enterprises* in paragraphs 16(b) and 17(b):

(other than certain equity instruments carried in a trading account)

e. The following footnote is added after the word *goods* in paragraphs 22(a) and 23(a):

*The term *goods* includes certain loans and other debt and equity instruments of other enterprises that are acquired specifically for resale, as discussed in Statement 102.

f. The statement of cash flows and the reconciliation of net income to net cash provided by operating activities included in paragraph 147 of Example 3 of Appendix C is superseded by the statement of cash flows and the reconciliation of net income to net cash provided by operating activities included in paragraph 30 of Appendix B of this Statement. The statement of financial position and the statement of operations included in paragraph 148 and the transactions described in paragraph 149(a) of that example are superseded by the statement of financial position and the statement of operations included in paragraph 31

and the transactions described in paragraph 32 of Appendix B of this Statement.

Effective Date and Transition

11. This Statement is effective for financial statements issued after February 28, 1989. Earlier application is encouraged. Comparative amounts in financial statements for earlier periods shall be reclassified to comply with the requirements of this Statement.

This Statement was adopted by the affirmative votes of six members of the Financial Accounting Standards Board. Mr. Lauver dissented.

Mr. Lauver dissents from the issuance of this Statement because of the manner in which it exempts certain employee benefit plans and investment companies from the requirement to issue a statement of cash flows. Although it may be defensible to exempt certain enterprises from a requirement to issue a statement of cash flows, he believes that any exemption should be made by establishing criteria believed to indicate that a statement of cash flows provides little useful information to users and exempting all enterprises satisfying those criteria. He would not establish exemptions by selectively designating industries or types of businesses because that approach inevitably produces inequities and inconsistencies. For example, in the instances covered by this Statement, employee benefit plans that own illiquid assets and finance their investments in part with debt are exempted from issuing a statement of cash flows, but investment companies in a similar position are not exempted.

Members of the Financial Accounting Standards Board:

Dennis R. Beresford,	Raymond C. Lauver	A. Clarence Sampson
Chairman	James J. Leisenring	Robert J. Swieringa
Victor H. Brown	C. Arthur Northrop	

Statement of Cash Flows—Exemption of Certain Enterprises and Classification of Cash Flows from Certain Securities Acquired for Resale

FAS102

Appendix A

BACKGROUND INFORMATION AND BASIS FOR CONCLUSIONS

CONTENTS

Appendix A

BACKGROUND INFORMATION AND BASIS FOR CONCLUSIONS

Introduction

12. This appendix discusses factors deemed significant by members of the Board in reaching the conclusions in this Statement. It discusses reasons for accepting certain views and rejecting others. Individual Board members gave greater weight to some factors than to others. The Board concluded that it could reach an informed decision on the basis of existing information without a public hearing.

13. An FASB Exposure Draft, *Statement of Cash Flows—Exemption of Certain Enterprises and Classification of Cash Flows from Certain Securities Held for Resale,* was issued for public comment on November 30, 1988. The Board received 69 letters of comment in response to the Exposure Draft. Nearly all respondents supported the Board's conclusions, although some respondents addressed only specific issues. Some respondents suggested certain modifications that generally would clarify the Board's intent.

Employee Benefit Plans

14. The financial reporting requirements of defined benefit pension plans are addressed in Statement 35. Paragraph 6 of that Statement specifies that the annual financial statements of a plan shall include:

a. A statement that includes information regarding the net assets available for benefits as of the end of the plan year
b. A statement that includes information regarding the changes during the year in the net assets available for benefits

c. Information regarding the actuarial present value of accumulated plan benefits as of either the beginning or end of the plan year
d. Information regarding the effects, if significant, of certain factors affecting the year-to-year change in the actuarial present value of accumulated plan benefits. [Footnote reference omitted.]

Statement 35 also states that existing generally accepted accounting principles other than those discussed in that Statement may apply to the financial statements of defined benefit pension plans.

15. The Board concluded that paragraph 6 of Statement 35 presents a comprehensive list of the basic financial statements that defined benefit pension plans are required to provide, although additional financial information may be provided. Furthermore, the Board concluded that Statement 95 was not intended to modify the reporting requirements for those plans.

16. Other employee benefit plans that are not covered by Statement 35, such as health and welfare plans, may have characteristics similar to those of defined benefit pension plans and may present financial information similar to that required by Statement 35 (including the presentation of plan investments at fair value). The Board believes that those plans likewise should not be required to provide a statement of cash flows.

17. The Board does not prohibit the inclusion of a statement of cash flows with the annual financial statements of an employee benefit plan. In fact, the Board encourages plans to provide a statement of cash flows when that statement would provide relevant information about the ability of the plan to meet future obligations. For example, the Board believes that a statement of cash flows would pro-

vide relevant information about a plan's ability to meet future obligations when the plan invests in assets that are not highly liquid, such as real estate, or obtains financing for its investments.

Investment Companies

18. Before the issuance of Statement 95, the Board considered whether investment companies should be required to provide a statement of cash flows as part of a full set of financial statements. The Board recognized that information about the cash flows of certain investment companies may be less important than similar information for other enterprises, but the Board decided that information about cash flows is relevant and that investment companies should not be exempted from a requirement to provide a statement of cash flows.

19. While the Board continues to believe that information about cash flows is relevant for investment companies, the Board readdressed the need for highly liquid investment companies to provide a statement of cash flows under certain conditions. Highly liquid investment companies are those whose assets consist predominantly of cash, securities, and other assets for which a market is readily available. For example, open-end investment companies hold themselves out as being able to redeem their outstanding shares within seven days; therefore, they are required to maintain a portfolio of investments that enables them to fulfill that obligation.

20. For highly liquid investment companies that do not finance investments with debt, the Board concluded that the financial statements other than a statement of cash flows generally would provide sufficient information for users to assess the enterprises' liquidity, financial flexibility, profitability, and risk. However, for investment companies that invest in assets for which a market is not readily available or that finance investments with debt, the Board believes that a statement of cash flows would provide relevant information about the enterprises' investing and financing activities to assist users in those assessments.

21. Investment companies were not required to provide a statement of changes in financial position. Investment companies that are subject to the reporting requirements of the 1940 Act are required to provide a statement of changes in net assets. Net assets and changes in those net assets are relevant because net asset value per share is used by many investment companies to determine the price of shares redeemed and sold. Although the purpose and format of a statement of changes in net assets are different from those of a statement of cash flows, much of the information contained in those statements is similar. The Board concluded that for investment companies that meet the conditions specified in paragraph 7, the cost of providing a statement of cash flows would exceed the benefits.

22. Certain investment enterprises may not be subject to the registration requirements of the 1940 Act either because the number of stockholders is limited or because they are otherwise exempted from the 1940 Act (for example, offshore funds, commodity pools, certain common trust funds of banks, or variable annuity accounts of life insurance companies). Because those investment enterprises have essentially the same characteristics as investment companies that are subject to the requirements of the 1940 Act, the Board concluded that the exemption also should apply to them provided they meet the conditions specified in paragraph 7.

Classification of Cash Flows from Acquisitions and Sales of Certain Securities and Other Assets

23. Statement 95 requires that cash flows be classified as investing, financing, or operating and provides a definition of each category. Paragraph 15 of Statement 95 defines investing activities to include:

> . . . making and collecting loans and acquiring and disposing of debt or equity instruments and property, plant, and equipment and other productive assets, that is, assets held for or used in the production of goods or services by the enterprise (other than materials that are part of the enterprise's inventory).

Operating activities include all transactions and other events that are not defined as investing or financing activities. Paragraph 21 of that Statement states that operating activities generally involve producing and delivering goods and providing services. Cash flows from operating activities are generally the cash effects of transactions and other events that enter into the determination of net income.

24. Paragraph 24 of Statement 95 recognizes that certain cash receipts and payments may have aspects of more than one category of cash flows. For example, a cash payment may pertain to an item that, depending on the circumstances, could be either inventory or a productive asset. Furthermore, paragraph 86 states that the three categories of operating, investing, and financing are not clearly mutually exclusive. For items at the margin, a reasonable case may be made for alternative classifications. Paragraph 87 notes that the Board recognizes that the most appropriate classification of items will not always be clear.

Statement of Cash Flows—Exemption of Certain Enterprises and Classification of Cash Flows from Certain Securities Acquired for Resale

FAS102

25. The definitions of operating and investing activities in Statement 95 provide flexibility for the appropriate classification of cash receipts and payments for assets that generally are productive assets but in certain cases may be inventory. For example, real estate generally is considered a productive asset, and a cash payment to purchase real estate generally is an investing cash outflow. However, if real estate is acquired by a real estate developer to be subdivided, improved, and sold in individual lots, then the cash payment to purchase that real estate would be classified as an operating cash flow because the real estate is acquired specifically for resale and is similar to inventory in other businesses.

26. For certain enterprises, purchases and sales of trading account assets have characteristics of both investing activities and operating activities. However, purchases and sales of debt and equity instruments of other enterprises are defined by Statement 95 as investing activities. The Board was asked to address the appropriate classification of cash flows from purchases and sales of securities in a trading account of a bank or a broker and dealer in securities. Because trading account assets are similar to inventory in other businesses in that they generally are acquired specifically for resale and are turned over very rapidly, the Board concluded that cash receipts and cash payments resulting from purchases and sales of securities and other assets that are acquired specifically for resale and are carried at market value in a trading account should be reported as operating cash flows.

27. Loans that are originated or purchased specifically for resale, are turned over rapidly, and are carried at market value or at the lower of cost or market value also are similar to inventory in other businesses. Therefore, the Board concluded that cash receipts and cash payments resulting from originations or purchases and sales of those loans also should be reported as operating cash flows.

28. The Board decided to require rather than permit cash flows from the activities described in paragraphs 26 and 27 to be classified as operating cash flows in order to achieve greater comparability among enterprises in classifying similar items.

29. When the Board addressed the issue of classification of cash flows resulting from the active trading of assets in a trading account, the Board also discussed whether additional net reporting of cash receipts and cash payments might be appropriate. The Board received several requests primarily from banks to reconsider the requirements of Statement 95 to report gross cash flows for various items for which they believe that the costs of accumulating the data exceed the benefits of the additional disclosures. Gross cash flows from trading activities were identified as particularly costly to accumulate. The Board concluded that the possibility of additional net reporting should be considered but that further research was required before a decision could be reached about the circumstances, if any, in which additional net reporting might be appropriate. That issue will be considered by the Board at a later date.

Appendix B

**AMENDMENTS TO APPENDIX C
OF STATEMENT 95**

30. The statement of cash flows and the reconcilia- tion of net income to net cash provided by operating activities for Financial Institution, Inc., provided in paragraph 147 of Statement 95 are superseded by the following:

**FINANCIAL INSTITUTION, INC.
STATEMENT OF CASH FLOWS
FOR THE YEAR ENDED DECEMBER 31, 19X1**
Increase (Decrease) in Cash and Cash Equivalents

Cash flows from operating activities:		
Interest received	$ 5,350	
Fees and commissions received	1,320	
Proceeds from sales of trading securities	20,550	
Purchase of trading securities	(21,075)	
Financing revenue received under leases	60	
Interest paid	(3,925)	
Cash paid to suppliers and employees	(795)	
Income taxes paid	(471)	
Net cash provided by operating activities		$ 1,014
Cash flows from investing activities:		
Proceeds from sales of investment securities	2,225	
Purchase of investment securities	(4,000)	
Net increase in credit card receivables	(1,300)	
Net decrease in customer loans with maturities of 3 months or less	2,250	
Principal collected on longer term loans	26,550	
Longer term loans made to customers	(36,300)	
Purchase of assets to be leased	(1,500)	
Principal payments received under leases	107	
Capital expenditures	(450)	
Proceeds from sale of property, plant, and equipment	260	
Net cash used in investing activities		(12,158)
Cash flows from financing activities:		
Net increase in demand deposits, NOW accounts, and savings accounts	3,000	
Proceeds from sales of certificates of deposit	63,000	
Payments for maturing certificates of deposit	(61,000)	
Net increase in federal funds purchased	4,500	
Net increase in 90-day borrowings	50	
Proceeds from issuance of nonrecourse debt	600	
Principal payment on nonrecourse debt	(20)	
Proceeds from issuance of 6-month note	100	
Proceeds from issuance of long-term debt	1,000	
Repayment of long-term debt	(200)	
Proceeds from issuance of common stock	350	
Payments to acquire treasury stock	(175)	
Dividends paid	(240)	
Net cash provided by financing activities		10,965
Net decrease in cash and cash equivalents		(179)
Cash and cash equivalents at beginning of year		6,700
Cash and cash equivalents at end of year		$ 6,521

Reconciliation of net income to net cash provided by operating activities:

Net income		$1,056
Adjustments to reconcile net income to net cash provided by operating activities:		
Depreciation	$100	
Provision for probable credit losses	300	
Provision for deferred taxes	58	
Loss on sales of investment securities	75	
Gain on sale of equipment	(50)	
Increase in trading securities (including unrealized appreciation of $25)	(700)	
Increase in taxes payable	175	
Increase in interest receivable	(150)	
Increase in interest payable	75	
Decrease in fees and commissions receivable	20	
Increase in accrued expenses	55	
Total adjustments		(42)
Net cash provided by operating activities		$1,014

31. The statement of financial position and the statement of operations for Financial Institution, Inc., provided in paragraph 148 of Statement 95 are superseded by the following:

FINANCIAL INSTITUTION, INC.
STATEMENT OF FINANCIAL POSITION

	1/1/X1	12/31/X1	Change
Assets:			
Cash and due from banks	$ 4,400	$ 3,121	$ (1,279)
Federal funds sold	2,300	3,400	1,100
Total cash and cash equivalents	6,700	6,521	(179)
Trading securities	4,000	4,700	700
Investment securities	5,000	6,700	1,700
Credit card receivables	8,500	9,800	1,300
Loans	28,000	35,250	7,250
Allowance for credit losses	(800)	(850)	(50)
Interest receivable	600	750	150
Fees and commissions receivable	60	40	(20)
Investment in direct financing lease	–	421	421
Investment in leveraged lease	–	392	392
Property, plant, and equipment, net	525	665	140
Total assets	$52,585	$64,389	$11,804
Liabilities:			
Deposits	$38,000	$43,000	$ 5,000
Federal funds purchased	7,500	12,000	4,500
Short-term borrowings	1,200	1,350	150
Interest payable	350	425	75
Accrued expenses	275	330	55
Taxes payable	75	250	175
Dividends payable	–	80	80
Long-term debt	2,000	2,300	300
Deferred taxes	–	58	58
Total liabilities	49,400	59,793	10,393
Stockholders' equity:			
Common stock	1,250	2,100	850
Treasury stock	–	(175)	(175)
Retained earnings	1,935	2,671	736
Total stockholders' equity	3,185	4,596	1,411
Total liabilities and stockholders' equity	$52,585	$64,389	$11,804

FINANCIAL INSTITUTION, INC.
STATEMENT OF OPERATIONS
FOR THE YEAR ENDED DECEMBER 31, 19X1

Revenues:

Interest income	$5,500	
Fees and commissions	1,300	
Net gain on sales of trading and investment securities	75	
Unrealized appreciation of trading securities	25	
Lease income	60	
Gain on sale of equipment	50	
Total revenues		$7,010

Expenses:

Interest expense	4,000	
Provision for probable credit losses	300	
Operating expenses	850	
Depreciation	100	
Total expenses		5,250
Income before income taxes		1,760
Provision for income taxes		704
Net income		$1,056

32. The transactions of Financial Institution, Inc., described in paragraph 149(a) of Statement 95 are superseded by the following:

Financial Institution sold trading securities with a carrying value of $20,400 for $20,550 and purchased trading securities for $21,075. Financial Institution recorded unrealized appreciation of trading securities of $25. Financial Institution also sold investment securities with a carrying value of $2,300 for $2,225 and purchased investment securities for $4,000.

(This page intentionally left blank.)

Statement of Financial Accounting Standards No. 103
Accounting for Income Taxes—Deferral of the Effective Date of FASB Statement No. 96

an amendment of FASB Statement No. 96

STATUS

Issued: December 1989

Effective Date: December 15, 1989

Affects: Amends FAS 96, paragraph 32
      Supersedes FAS 100

Affected by: Superseded by FAS 108 and FAS 109

(This page intentionally left blank.)

Statement of Financial Accounting Standards No. 104
Statement of Cash Flows—Net Reporting of Certain Cash Receipts and Cash Payments and Classification of Cash Flows from Hedging Transactions

an amendment of FASB Statement No. 95

STATUS

Issued: December 1989

Effective Date: For fiscal years ending after June 15, 1990

Affects: Amends FAS 95, paragraph 13
Supersedes FAS 95, footnote 4

Affected by: No other pronouncements

SUMMARY

This Statement amends FASB Statement No. 95, *Statement of Cash Flows,* to permit banks, savings institutions, and credit unions to report in a statement of cash flows certain net cash receipts and cash payments for (a) deposits placed with other financial institutions and withdrawals of deposits, (b) time deposits accepted and repayments of deposits, and (c) loans made to customers and principal collections of loans.

This Statement also amends Statement 95 to permit cash flows resulting from futures contracts, forward contracts, option contracts, or swap contracts that are accounted for as hedges of identifiable transactions or events to be classified in the same category as the cash flows from the items being hedged provided that accounting policy is disclosed.

This Statement is effective for annual financial statements for fiscal years ending after June 15, 1990, with earlier application permitted. Separate early adoption of either the netting or hedging provisions is permitted. If the provisions of this Statement are elected, restatement or reclassification of comparative amounts in financial statements for earlier periods is required.

Statement of Financial Accounting Standards No. 104

Statement of Cash Flows—Net Reporting of Certain Cash Receipts and Cash Payments and Classification of Cash Flows from Hedging Transactions

an amendment of FASB Statement No. 95

CONTENTS

INTRODUCTION

Net Reporting of Certain Cash Receipts and Cash Payments

1. In FASB Statement No. 95, *Statement of Cash Flows,* the Board concluded that information about the gross amounts of cash receipts and cash payments during a period generally is more relevant than information about the net amounts of cash receipts and cash payments. However, for certain items, the net amount of cash receipts and cash payments may provide sufficient information. For example, Statement 95 provides that gross cash flows need not be reported for demand deposits of a bank or for investments, loans receivable, and debt of any enterprise if the original maturity of the asset or liability is three months or less.

2. The Board received several requests to reconsider the requirements of Statement 95 as they relate to banks. Those requests included assertions that the requirements of Statement 95 produce data that are of little or no value and are difficult and costly to accumulate. In particular, because deposit and lending activities generally involve high volumes of transactions, some assert that the cost incurred by the preparer to report gross cash flow information exceeds the benefit to users of the statement of cash flows.

3. This Statement modifies Statement 95 so that banks, savings institutions, and credit unions are not required to report gross amounts of cash receipts and cash payments for (a) deposits placed with other financial institutions and withdrawals of deposits, (b) time deposits accepted and repayments of deposits, and (c) loans made to customers and principal collections of loans. When those enterprises constitute part of a consolidated enterprise, net amounts of cash receipts and cash payments for deposit or lending activities of those enterprises shall be reported separate from gross amounts of cash receipts and cash payments for other investing and financing activities of the consolidated enterprise.

Classification of Cash Flows from Hedging Transactions

4. The Board received requests from various enterprises to reconsider the classification of cash flows from an item that is intended as a hedge of another item. Those requests generally focused on cash flows from a futures contract or forward contract that is accounted for as a hedge of an inventory transaction.

5. Footnote 4 of Statement 95 specified the classification of cash flows from a hedging instrument as follows:

> Each cash receipt or payment is to be classified according to its nature without regard to whether it stems from an item intended as a hedge of another item. For example, the

Statement of Cash Flows—Net Reporting of Certain Cash Receipts and Cash Payments and Classification of Cash Flows from Hedging Transactions

FAS104

proceeds of a borrowing are a financing cash inflow whether or not the debt is intended as a hedge of an investment, and the purchase or sale of a futures contract is an investing activity without regard to whether the contract is intended as a hedge of a firm commitment to purchase inventory.

6. This Statement modifies Statement 95 to permit cash flows resulting from futures contracts, forward contracts, option contracts, or swap contracts that are accounted for as hedges of identifiable transactions or events (for example, a cash payment from a futures contract that hedges a purchase or sale of inventory), including anticipatory hedges, to be classified in the same category as the cash flows from the items being hedged provided that accounting policy is disclosed. If for any reason hedge accounting for an instrument that hedges an identifiable transaction or event is discontinued, then any cash flows subsequent to the date of discontinuance shall be classified consistent with the nature of the instrument.

STANDARDS OF FINANCIAL ACCOUNTING AND REPORTING

Amendments to Statement 95

7. Statement 95 is amended as follows:

a. The following paragraph is added after paragraph 13:

Banks, savings institutions, and credit unions are not required to report gross amounts of cash receipts and cash payments for (a) deposits placed with other financial institutions and withdrawals of deposits, (b) time deposits accepted and repayments of deposits, and (c) loans made to customers and principal collections of loans. When those enterprises constitute part of a consolidated enterprise, net amounts of cash receipts and cash payments for deposit or lending activities of those enterprises shall be reported separate from gross amounts of cash receipts and cash payments for other investing and financing activities of the consolidated enterprise, including those of a subsidiary of a bank, savings institution, or credit union that is not itself a bank, savings institution, or credit union.

b. Footnote 4 is superseded by the following:

Generally, each cash receipt or payment is to be classified according to its nature without regard to whether it stems from an item intended as a hedge of another item. For example, the

proceeds of a borrowing are a financing cash inflow even though the debt is intended as a hedge of an investment, and the purchase or sale of a futures contract is an investing activity even though the contract is intended as a hedge of a firm commitment to purchase inventory. However, cash flows from futures contracts, forward contracts, option contracts, or swap contracts that are accounted for as hedges of identifiable transactions or events (for example, a cash payment from a futures contract that hedges a purchase or sale of inventory), including anticipatory hedges, may be classified in the same category as the cash flows from the items being hedged provided that accounting policy is disclosed. If for any reason hedge accounting for an instrument that hedges an identifiable transaction or event is discontinued, then any cash flows subsequent to the date of discontinuance shall be classified consistent with the nature of the instrument.

Effective Date and Transition

8. The provisions of this Statement are effective for annual financial statements for fiscal years ending after June 15, 1990, with earlier application permitted. Separate early adoption of either paragraph 7(a) or paragraph 7(b) is permitted. If the provisions of this Statement are elected, restatement or reclassification of comparative amounts in financial statements for earlier periods is required.

This Statement was adopted by the affirmative votes of five members of the Financial Accounting Standards Board. Messrs. Lauver and Swieringa dissented.

Messrs. Lauver and Swieringa dissent from the provision of this Statement that permits banks, savings institutions, and credit unions to report net cash receipts and cash payments for certain deposit and lending activities (paragraph 7(a) of this Statement). They continue to support the conclusion in paragraph 11 of Statement 95 that "generally, information about the gross amounts of cash receipts and cash payments during a period is more relevant than information about the net amounts of cash receipts and payments." Statement 95's permitted use of the indirect method is inconsistent with that conclusion because major classes of gross operating cash flows are not required to be reported separately. That permitted exception is now used to justify reporting net cash flows for certain investing and financing activities.

It is asserted that gross cash flow amounts for certain deposit and lending activities may be no more relevant than net cash flow amounts. Messrs. Lauver and Swieringa do not believe that that assertion is supportable. Consider, for example, one bank that adopted Statement 95 in 1988 and reported gross cash payments for loans originated or acquired of $14.9 billion, $10.8 billion, and $8.8 billion for 1988, 1987, and 1986, respectively. That bank also reported gross cash receipts for principal collected on loans of $14.3 billion, $10.4 billion, and $8.1 billion, respectively. Those gross cash flow amounts indicate a compound annual growth in those loan activities of over 30 percent over the 2-year period. Reporting gross amounts for lending activities provides information about events that occurred during a period that is not provided by reporting net cash flows for those activities and is not provided elsewhere in the financial statements.

Moreover, Messrs. Lauver and Swieringa believe that reporting gross cash flow amounts is no less useful for banks, savings institutions, and credit unions than for finance companies, insurance companies, and other financial intermediaries. Paragraph 7(a) permits different cash flow reporting for enterprises that engage in essentially identical lending activities. Paragraph 7(a) also permits a consolidated enterprise to report net cash flows for the lending activities of its bank and savings institution subsidiaries even though it is required to report gross cash flows for the essentially identical lending activities of its finance, leasing, and insurance subsidiaries. Because paragraph 7(a) distinguishes among enterprises that engage in essentially identical lending transactions, Messrs. Lauver and Swieringa believe that exemption is inconsistent with the Board's stated mission to develop "neutral standards that result in accounting for similar transactions and circumstances similarly."

The Board's justification for the exemption provided to banks, savings institutions, and credit unions is that the costs of accumulating and reporting gross cash flow amounts are perceived to be larger for those enterprises than for finance companies, insurance companies, and other financial intermediaries that already voluntarily incur many of those costs as part of their reporting systems. The observation that "little incremental cost is required to develop gross cash flow information" by finance companies does not take into consideration the costs that those companies have already incurred to implement data-gathering systems that can be used to accumulate gross cash flow amounts. Messrs. Lauver and Swieringa believe that if cost-benefit judgments are to be used to justify an exemption, it is important to measure and consider all costs that are attributable to meeting a reporting requirement assuming equivalent data-gathering systems have been installed. Otherwise, individual enterprises or industries that have already installed those systems will be subjected to a

reporting requirement, and enterprises or industries that have not already installed those systems will be exempted.

Mr. Lauver dissents from the provision of this Statement that permits classification of cash flows from certain hedging instruments in the same category as the cash flows from the items being hedged (paragraph 7(b) of this Statement). He believes that alternative does not enhance the objective of a statement of cash flows but has the objective of establishing net cash flow from operating activities as an alternative performance indicator, an objective that he believes is undesirable. Hedge accounting is an accounting technique whose objective is the reporting of entity performance. It is an optional accounting technique that associates two separate economic transactions, which in the aggregate are expected to mitigate the risk to the entity of either one alone, for the purpose of permitting the results of the two transactions to be reported in the statement of operations of a single fiscal period. In that way any gain on one transaction will counteract an anticipated loss on the other and vice versa.

Statement 95 states that the primary purpose of a statement of cash flows is to provide relevant information about cash receipts and cash payments of an enterprise during a period. Mr. Lauver finds it difficult to see how this purpose is enhanced, for example, by permitting cash flows from a futures contract for gold, an optional transaction, to be classified in the same category as the cash flows from the operation of a gold mine when hedge accounting is optionally elected. He believes that the ongoing activity of operating a mine and the optional, occasional entry of a position in a futures market based on anticipated future prices are not integral; that conclusion is especially clear because they are only regarded as being related when an accounting election is made. He believes that the objective of reporting cash flows should not be confused with the objective of reporting entity performance and that hedge accounting should not be used as a basis for establishing standards for providing a statement of cash flows whatever its merits for use in the statement of operations.

Further, Mr. Lauver believes, independent of the foregoing, that interest rate swap contracts should not be included in paragraph 7(b). He believes that when the objective of those contracts is to hedge net interest rate spreads, they do not hedge an identifiable transaction or event, and when the objective is that expressed in the last sentence of paragraph 40, the conclusion therein is inconsistent with paragraph 7(b) because that conclusion is not conditioned on the existence of a hedge.

Appendix

BACKGROUND INFORMATION AND BASIS FOR CONCLUSIONS

CONTENTS

Appendix

BACKGROUND INFORMATION AND BASIS FOR CONCLUSIONS

Introduction

9. This appendix summarizes considerations that were deemed significant by members of the Board in reaching the conclusions in this Statement. It includes reasons for accepting certain views and rejecting others. Individual Board members gave greater weight to some factors than to others.

10. In response to requests that additional net reporting of cash receipts and cash payments be permitted under FASB Statement No. 95, *Statement of Cash Flows,* the Exposure Draft leading to FASB Statement No. 102, *Statement of Cash Flows—Exemption of Certain Enterprises and Classification of Cash Flows from Certain Securities Acquired for Resale,* invited interested parties to submit information about the circumstances in which additional net reporting might be appropriate. Requests for additional net reporting of cash flows focused generally on the banking industry and specifically on (a) deposits placed with banks, (b) deposits taken, (c) loans to customers, and (d) investment securities. There also were requests that the Board reexamine the classification requirement for cash flows resulting from an instrument that is intended as a hedge of another item. This Statement responds to those requests.

11. An FASB Exposure Draft, *Statement of Cash Flows—Net Reporting of Certain Cash Receipts and Cash Payments and Classification of Cash Flows from Hedging Transactions,* was issued for public comment on July 25, 1989. The Board received 112 letters of comment in response to the Exposure Draft. The Board concluded that it could reach an informed decision on the basis of existing information without a public hearing.

Net Reporting of Certain Cash Receipts and Cash Payments

12. In Statement 95, the Board concluded that information about gross amounts of cash receipts and cash payments during a period generally is more relevant than information about net amounts of cash receipts and cash payments. However, paragraph 76 of Statement 95 acknowledges that in certain circumstances, information about both cash receipts and cash payments may be no more relevant than information about only the net change.

13. Specifically, Statement 95 permits the reporting of net cash flows for (a) cash equivalents, (b) operating activities when the indirect method is used to report cash flows, (c) items in which the enterprise is substantively holding or disbursing cash on behalf of its customers, such as demand deposits of a bank and customer accounts payable of a broker-dealer, and (d) items for which the turnover is quick, the amounts are large, and the maturities are short. However, (d) above is limited to investments (other than cash equivalents), loans receivable, and debt providing that the original maturity of the asset or liability is three months or less.

14. The Exposure Draft proposed to amend Statement 95 to permit banks, savings institutions, and credit unions to report net cash flows for certain deposit and lending activities. Most respondents agreed with that proposal and contended that the requirements of Statement 95 for reporting cash flows for deposit and lending activities are costly for those enterprises to apply and that information about the gross cash flows for those activities is not useful. Representatives of the banking industry asserted that banks have had to spend an inappropriate amount of time and money to comply with the requirements for reporting cash flow information and that the additional costs include not only start-up costs or costs of modifying systems to adopt the standard but also ongoing costs of periodic reporting.

15. The Board concluded that for a bank, savings institution, or credit union information about gross cash flows for certain activities may be more difficult and costly to provide than for other enterprises, and the usefulness of this information may be questionable. The Board noted that major banking activities, such as deposit taking and lending, are required to be reported as investing or financing activities, while major activities of other enterprises, such as purchasing and selling goods and services, are reported as operating activities. Enterprises that report cash flows from operating activities using the indirect method are not required to report gross amounts of cash flows from those transactions. As noted in paragraph 109 of Statement 95, preparers of financial statements said that it would be costly for their enterprises to report gross operating cash receipts and cash payments and that they do not presently collect information in a manner that would allow them to determine amounts such as cash received from customers or cash paid to suppliers directly from their accounting systems. The Board gave particular consideration to that factor in deciding whether to permit use of the indirect method.

16. In addition, gross amounts of cash flows for certain banking activities may be difficult and costly to accumulate because of numerous noncash transactions. To report cash receipts and cash payments in a statement of cash flows, transactions that do not involve either a cash receipt or a cash payment must be eliminated from any totals. For example, when a loan is renewed or its terms are otherwise modified, the accounting records may indicate that the loan is repaid and a new loan is made. However, that transaction does not involve a cash flow and should not be reported in the statement of cash flows. The amount of effort currently required to separate cash transactions from noncash transactions is compounded by the high volume of transactions.

17. In determining the relevance of reporting gross cash flows, the Board considered comments from various users of banks' financial statements. Those users included financial analysts and individuals involved in mergers and acquisitions of financial institutions. While some users noted that a statement of cash flows for a bank may be important, particularly when determining whether an acquisition is economically sound, they generally agreed that the value of certain historical gross cash flow information is limited. Information about gross cash flows may provide a starting point or reference, but other information would be more relevant for analyzing liquidity or estimating future cash flows.

18. The high volume of transactions common to banks results in reporting gross amounts of cash flows that are large in relation to other cash flows. For example, gross cash flows pertaining to time deposits reported in the statement of cash flows of one major bank totaled more than 600 times the year-end balance of cash and cash equivalents. Banks generally have asserted that reporting gross cash flows of that magnitude tends to obscure more relevant data that may be included in the statement of cash flows. The Board generally believes that the size of a gross cash flow amount does not affect its relevance provided that amount is fairly reported.

19. Comparability of certain gross cash flow amounts among banks may be limited. Although Statement 95 permits the reporting of net cash flows when the original maturity of an asset or liability is three months or less, for practical reasons some enterprises have chosen to report gross cash flows for all such items rather than to separate them into those that qualify for net reporting and those that do not. In effect, gross cash flows and net cash flows may be reported differently, resulting in a lack of comparability.

20. Comparability also may be affected by internal accounting procedures because banks, savings institutions, and credit unions have the ability to create a reported cash flow through a debit or credit to a customer's demand deposit account. For example, if a customer rolls over a certificate of deposit upon maturity, a bank can record that transaction with or without making an entry to the customer's demand deposit account (that is, the bank may or may not debit and credit the demand deposit account), yet by definition one procedure results in a reported cash flow and the other does not. Thus, a bank that debits and credits a customer's demand deposit account when a loan or a certificate of deposit is renewed would report higher gross cash flow amounts relative to a bank that does not.

21. This Statement restricts the net reporting of lending activities to loans made to customers and to principal collections of loans. The Board believes that permitting net reporting of cash flows for all lending activities of banks would result in the loss of certain relevant gross cash flow information. For example, information about cash payments for purchases of loan portfolios or cash receipts from sales of loan portfolios provides relevant information about a bank's activities.[1] Furthermore, the Board believes that reporting gross cash flows for purchases or sales of loan portfolios should not be as difficult or costly as reporting gross cash flows for loans made or principal collections of loans. Purchases and sales of loan portfolios generally occur less frequently and are more centrally controlled. As a result, the Board concluded that net reporting of cash flows for lending activities of banks should be limited to cash payments for loans made to customers and principal collections of loans.

22. Some respondents stated that the Exposure Draft was not clear about whether a bank would be permitted to report net cash flows for principal collections attributable to purchased loans or for loans made to customers if those loans are subsequently sold. The amendment to Statement 95 in paragraph 7(a) of this Statement has been revised to clarify that net reporting of inflows of principal collections from purchased and originated loans and outflows for loan originations to customers irrespective of whether those loans are subsequently sold is permitted. (Refer to footnote 1.)

23. Statement 95 precludes reporting net cash flows for purchases and sales or maturities of investment securities. Some respondents to the Exposure Draft requested that the Board allow banks to classify cash flows from investment securities as operating activities or otherwise allow net reporting of those cash flows. However, investing in securities is not an activity that is unique to banks; similar activities occur in many other enterprises. These activities have been defined by Statement 95 as investing activities. The Board concluded that the cost and difficulty of reporting gross cash flow information for investment security transactions are less than for deposit and lending activities. Generally, investment activities are more centralized within the enterprise, the volume of transactions is smaller, and noncash transactions are less prevalent. Gross cash flow amounts may be useful because those amounts may enable users to assess investment portfolio turnover or to observe changes in an enterprise's investment strategies. The Board concluded that the benefit from reporting those amounts generally would exceed the cost.

24. Based on the factors discussed in paragraphs 14-20, the Board concluded that the cost for a bank, savings institution, or credit union to report gross amounts of cash receipts and cash payments for certain deposit and lending activities generally would exceed the benefit to users of the statement of cash flows. In response to comments, the Board also considered whether to permit finance companies, insurance companies, and other financial intermediaries to report net cash flows for their lending activities. A significant difference between those enterprises and banks, savings institutions, and credit unions is that generally finance companies, insurance companies, and other financial intermediaries cannot create reported cash flows by debiting and crediting customers' demand deposit accounts as discussed in paragraph 20. In addition, most finance companies presently accumulate loan origination or loan volume statistics for operating or other internal purposes. Accordingly, little incremental cost is required to develop gross cash flow information for external reporting. Because insurance companies generally do not engage in lending activities to the extent of banks, savings institutions, and credit unions, reporting gross cash flows for their lending activities should not be as costly. Thus, the Board concluded that for enterprises other than banks, savings institutions, and credit unions, the cost of reporting gross cash flows for lending activities generally would not exceed the benefit.

25. Some respondents requested that the Board define the transactions for which reporting net cash flows might be appropriate and allow that reporting for all enterprises that have those transactions. The Board concluded that while similar transactions generally should be accorded similar accounting treatment, in this circumstance cost-benefit considerations support different reporting based on the type of entity confronted with the transaction.

26. Consolidated enterprises frequently are engaged in various businesses in different industries. For example, a consolidated enterprise may include an industrial company, a finance company, a savings institution, and a leasing company. The Exposure Draft proposed that net cash flows may be reported for the specified activities of only a bank, savings institution, or credit union and not for those activities elsewhere within the consolidated enterprise. For example, net cash flow reporting of loans made to customers and principal collections of loans would not be permitted for a

---

[1] Statement 102, paragraph 9, specifies the reporting in a statement of cash flows for those loans acquired specifically for resale and carried at market value or at the lower of cost or market value.

finance company or leasing subsidiary of a bank, savings institution, or credit union. Furthermore, net cash flow amounts for deposit or lending activities of a subsidiary that is a bank or a savings institution should be reported separate from gross cash flow amounts for other investing and financing activities of the consolidated enterprise.

27. Some respondents to the Exposure Draft requested that the Board extend the net reporting of cash flows for deposit or lending activities to all similar activities within a consolidated reporting entity. In particular, they suggested that subsidiaries engaged in bank-related activities should be allowed to report on a basis consistent with that of a bank parent; otherwise, the financial statements would be inconsistent and confusing to users. However, bank-related subsidiaries often apply generally accepted accounting principles that differ from those of a bank subsidiary included in a consolidated group. For example, a bank may carry its investment securities at amortized cost, a broker-dealer subsidiary may carry its investment securities at market, and a venture capital subsidiary may carry its investment securities at fair value as determined by its board of directors. The Board noted that subsidiaries of a consolidated group often apply different, yet appropriate, accounting principles for similar transactions.

28. In response to requests by some respondents, the Board also considered whether the criteria for classifying cash flows should be modified to require that certain deposit and lending activities now classified as investing or financing activities be classified as operating activities. Although deposit and lending activities may be a bank's principal activities, they are not operating activities as described in Statement 95. Cash flows from operating activities include cash receipts and cash payments for purchases and sales of goods and services (inventory transactions), returns on investments, and all other cash receipts and payments not specifically defined as investing or financing activities.

29. The Board believes that a bank's deposit and lending activities are not analogous to inventory transactions in other business enterprises but are more analogous to the issuance of bonds by those enterprises to finance the construction of a new plant or the acquisition of a business. Similarly, gathering deposits is a financing activity. Cash received from customers is fungible and is commingled with the bank's other funds. Those deposits are available for a variety of purposes—to purchase trading or investment securities, to make loans, to pay operating expenses, or to redeem debt. Although deposit and lending activities may be a bank's principal activities, the Board believes

that they are appropriately classified as financing or investing activities.

Classification of Cash Flows from Hedging Transactions

30. Prior to the issuance of Statement 95, the Board addressed the classification of cash flows resulting from an instrument that is intended as a hedge of another item. The Board concluded that the cash flows from a hedging instrument should always be classified according to the nature of that instrument rather than in the same category as the cash flows of the item being hedged. The Board believed that the purchase or sale of a hedging instrument, such as a futures contract or a forward contract, is an investing activity. The Board also believed that implementation of an approach that classified the cash flows from a hedging instrument in the same category as the cash flows of the item being hedged would be more difficult and would require enterprises to maintain additional records.

31. After Statement 95 was issued, the Board received several inquiries about that classification requirement. Enterprises were particularly concerned about classifying cash flows from futures contracts or forward contracts that are accounted for as hedges of inventory transactions in a manner different from the cash flows from the purchase or sale of inventory. They indicated that the hedging transaction is integral to the inventory transaction and that the decision to purchase or sell futures contracts with the sole objective of reducing exposure to inventory price increases, establishing a profit floor, or locking in a gross margin is an operating decision by the enterprise to reduce the risks associated with its normal commercial operations of buying and selling goods. They urged the Board to allow cash flows from those types of hedges to be classified as operating cash flows and not as investing cash flows. They view that activity as being substantially different from an enterprise's typical investing activities. Some asserted that less effort would be required to classify the cash flows in the same category as the hedged item.

32. The Board readdressed the classification of cash flows from hedging instruments and reviewed examples from enterprises that engage in extensive hedging activities, primarily purchases or sales of futures contracts, related to their inventory transactions. The Board also considered foreign currency forward contracts related to a commitment to purchase or sell inventory or to a borrowing denominated in a foreign currency.

33. The Exposure Draft for this Statement proposed that cash flows from a futures contract, forward contract, or option contract that is accounted

Statement of Cash Flows—Net Reporting of Certain
Cash Receipts and Cash Payments and Classification   FAS104
of Cash Flows from Hedging Transactions

for as a hedge of an identifiable transaction or event be classified in the same category as the cash flows from the item being hedged.

34. The majority of the respondents to the Exposure Draft agreed that the cash flows of a hedging instrument that is accounted for as a hedge of an identifiable transaction or event should be classified in the same category as the cash flows from the item being hedged. They stated that a contract designed to lock in the future cost of a commodity is substantially different from an investment transaction. The objective of the hedging contract is to reduce the risk of price fluctuations and not to realize a profit. They asserted that the hedging contract is an integral part of the transaction and that reporting the cash flows of the hedge in the same category as the item being hedged would result in a more meaningful and understandable presentation.

35. However, some respondents opposed classifying cash flows from hedging instruments in the same category as the cash flows from the items being hedged. They cited increased cost in linking the two transactions together and commented that the hedging of a transaction is not a single economic event but two indirectly related transactions.

36. The Board believes that while generally each cash receipt or payment should be classified consistent with its nature, in some circumstances it may be appropriate to classify the cash flows from a hedging instrument in the same category as the cash flows from the item being hedged. For example, an enterprise may purchase a futures contract for the sole purpose of reducing exposure to increases in the price of a planned inventory purchase. The purchase of the hedging instrument may be considered integral to the subsequent purchase of the inventory. For this and similar instances when the hedging instrument is considered integral to the underlying transaction and is accounted for as a hedge, the Board believes that it may be appropriate to link the cash flows. The Board concluded that cash flows from certain contracts that are accounted for as hedges of identifiable transactions or events should be permitted to be classified in the same category as the cash flows from the items being hedged provided that accounting policy is disclosed. Changes in that policy are accounting changes to be reported in accordance with APB Opinion No. 20, *Accounting Changes*.

37. Hedge accounting reports gains or losses on the hedging instrument in the same period as the offsetting gains or losses of the item hedged. However, the cash flows from the hedging instrument may occur in a period different from the cash flows of the item hedged regardless of the amount of gain or loss that is hedged in a given year. In addition, a hedging instrument may be accounted for as a hedge for only a portion of the time that it is outstanding. Requiring the cash flows of an instrument designated as a hedge for a specified period to be linked with the item being hedged could entail significant costs. The Board is concerned that a requirement to classify the cash flows from a hedging instrument in the same category as the item being hedged may be difficult and costly.

38. For some hedging transactions, the cash flows cannot clearly be classified in the same category as the cash flows from the item being hedged. For example, an enterprise may hedge a net investment in a foreign operation with a borrowing that is denominated in the same currency as the net investment being hedged. Accounting for the borrowing as a hedge does not change the basic nature of the transaction; that is, it is still a borrowing. Furthermore, the cash flows from that foreign operation may include some cash flows that are properly classified as operating activities, some as investing activities, and some as financing activities. Accordingly, the cash receipts and payments from that borrowing cannot be identified with any specific cash flows from that operation and should be classified as financing activities.

39. Several respondents to the Exposure Draft suggested that the amendment to Statement 95 should encompass cash flows from hedging instruments other than futures contracts, forward contracts, and option contracts. Some requested that the amendment include cash flows from any instrument that would be considered a hedge of another transaction or event, while others specified that only cash flows from those instruments that qualify as hedges under current generally accepted accounting principles should be included. A few commented that the amendment should include cash flows from hedging instruments that may evolve in the future, and others requested that the Board clarify whether cash flows from swap contracts would be included.

40. The Board concluded that cash flows from swap contracts should be included within the scope of this Statement. Paragraph 17 of FASB Statement No. 52, *Foreign Currency Translation,* indicates that currency swaps are, in substance, essentially the same as forward contracts and should be accounted for the same as forward contracts. The Board also concluded that cash flows from an interest rate swap intended to effectively convert the interest rate of an asset or liability from variable to fixed or fixed to variable may be classified as operating cash flows consistent with the interest cash flows relating to the underlying asset or liability.

41. The Board believes the scope of this Statement should not be extended beyond the instruments named and conditions specified in paragraph 7(b). Otherwise, some may infer that the Board would endorse hedge accounting for any instrument that could be considered to reduce exposure to price or interest rate risk. This Statement does not address hedge accounting in the statement of financial position or the statement of operations. The Board is addressing the broader issues of hedge accounting as part of its project on financial instruments and off-balance-sheet financing.

Effective Date and Transition

42. The Exposure Draft would have been effective for annual financial statements for fiscal years ending after December 15, 1989, and would have required comparative amounts in financial statements for earlier periods to be reclassified. Because this Statement permits additional net reporting of certain cash flows, most of those responding to the Exposure Draft encouraged the Board to adopt the early effective date and commented that it would reduce cost and effort necessary to provide the information required to prepare the statement of cash flows. However, some requested that the Board delay the effective date to provide preparers of financial statements additional time to accumulate necessary information to modify the classification of cash flows from certain hedging transactions. The Board concluded, primarily because this Statement is being issued late in the year, to delay the effective date,

while allowing early adoption of either or both of the major provisions.

43. Some respondents suggested that reclassification of cash flows from hedging transactions for earlier periods should not be required. They indicated that the cost of reclassifying could exceed the benefits of additional comparability and that some enterprises may not have systems in place to accumulate the necessary information. Many of the concerns regarding requiring reclassification were in the context of an early implementation date and a requirement to modify the classification of cash flows from certain hedging transactions. Many of the respondents who agreed with the proposal to require consistent classification of cash flows from hedging transactions said that it would not be costly to report in that manner because their accounting records already link those transactions together.

44. Because modification of the classification of cash flows from certain hedging transactions is permitted and not required, the Board believes that when the option is elected, hedging cash flows for earlier periods should be reclassified to improve comparability. Also, hedging instruments and the items being hedged are linked for accounting purposes, and enterprises would have had to track them together for statement of financial position and statement of operations purposes. In addition, the Board believes that banks, savings institutions, and credit unions can restate without difficulty cash flows for the deposit and lending activities that this Statement allows to be reported net.

Statement of Financial Accounting Standards No. 105
Disclosure of Information about Financial Instruments with Off-Balance-Sheet Risk and Financial Instruments with Concentrations of Credit Risk

STATUS

Issued: March 1990

Effective Date: For fiscal years ending after June 15, 1990

Affects: Amends FAS 77, paragraph 9

Affected by: Paragraph 6 and footnotes 2 and 3 amended by FAS 107
Paragraph 14(c) amended by FAS 111 and FAS 123
Paragraph 14(e) superseded by FAS 125
Paragraphs 17 and 18 and footnote 12 amended by FAS 119
Superseded by FAS 133

Other Interpretive Pronouncement: FIN 39

Other Interpretive Release: FASB Special Report, *Illustrations of Financial Instrument Disclosures* (Nullified by FAS 133)

Issues Discussed by FASB Emerging Issues Task Force (EITF)

Affects: Partially resolves EITF Issue No. 84-23

(The next page is 1273.)

(This page intentionally left blank.)

Statement of Financial Accounting Standards No. 106
Employers' Accounting for Postretirement Benefits
Other Than Pensions

STATUS

Issued: December 1990

Effective Date: For fiscal years beginning after December 15, 1992

Affects: Amends APB 12, paragraph 6
Supersedes APB 12, footnote 1
Amends APB 16, paragraph 88
Supersedes FAS 81
Amends FAS 87, paragraph 8
Supersedes FAS 87, footnote 3
Supersedes FTB 87-1

Affected by: Paragraph 65 amended by FAS 135
Paragraphs 74, 77, 78, 82, 106, and 479 through 483 superseded by FAS 132
Paragraphs 86 and 444 amended by FAS 141
Paragraph 96(a) amended by FAS 144
Paragraphs 103, 107, 392, 417, and 461 amended by FAS 135
Paragraph 103 superseded by FAS 144
Paragraphs 464, 467, and 471 superseded by FAS 135
Footnote 23 superseded by FAS 135

Other Interpretive Releases: FASB Special Report, *A Guide to Implementation of Statement 106 on Employers' Accounting for Postretirement Benefits Other Than Pensions: Questions and Answers*
FASB Special Report, *A Guide to Implementation of Statement 87 on Employers' Accounting for Pensions: Questions and Answers*
FASB Special Report, *A Guide to Implementation of Statement 88 on Employers' Accounting for Settlements and Curtailments of Defined Benefit Pension Plans and for Termination Benefits: Questions and Answers*

Note: Although the Special Reports for Statements 87 and 88 do not specifically refer to postretirement benefits other than pensions, the user is referred to them because of the similarity in accounting.

Issues Discussed by FASB Emerging Issues Task Force (EITF)

Affects: Nullifies EITF Issue No. 86-20
Partially resolves EITF Issue No. 84-35
Resolves EITF Issue No. 86-19

Interpreted by: Paragraph 105 interpreted by EITF Issue No. 86-27
Paragraph 186 interpreted by EITF Topic No. D-36
Paragraphs 308 and 518 interpreted by EITF Issue No. 93-3

Related Issues: EITF Issues No. 88-23, 92-12, 92-13, and 96-5 and Topics No. D-27 and D-92

SUMMARY

This Statement establishes accounting standards for employers' accounting for postretirement benefits other than pensions (hereinafter referred to as postretirement benefits). Although it applies to all forms of post-retirement benefits, this Statement focuses principally on postretirement health care benefits. It will significantly change the prevalent current practice of accounting for postretirement benefits on a pay-as-you-go (cash) basis by requiring accrual, during the years that the employee renders the necessary service, of the expected cost of providing those benefits to an employee and the employee's beneficiaries and covered dependents.

The Board's conclusions in this Statement result from the view that a defined postretirement benefit plan sets forth the terms of an exchange between the employer and the employee. In exchange for the current services provided by the employee, the employer promises to provide, in addition to current wages and other benefits, health and other welfare benefits after the employee retires. It follows from that view that postretirement benefits are not gratuities but are part of an employee's compensation for services rendered. Since payment is deferred, the benefits are a type of deferred compensation. The employer's obligation for that compensation is incurred as employees render the services necessary to earn their postretirement benefits.

The ability to measure the obligation for postretirement health care benefits and the recognition of that obligation have been the subject of controversy. The Board believes that measurement of the obligation and accrual of the cost based on best estimates are superior to implying, by a failure to accrue, that no obligation exists prior to the payment of benefits. The Board believes that failure to recognize an obligation prior to its payment impairs the usefulness and integrity of the employer's financial statements.

The Board's objectives in issuing this Statement are to improve employers' financial reporting for post-retirement benefits in the following manner:

a. To enhance the relevance and representational faithfulness of the employer's reported results of operations by recognizing net periodic postretirement benefit cost as employees render the services necessary to earn their postretirement benefits

b. To enhance the relevance and representational faithfulness of the employer's statement of financial position by including a measure of the obligation to provide postretirement benefits based on a mutual understanding between the employer and its employees of the terms of the underlying plan

c. To enhance the ability of users of the employer's financial statements to understand the extent and effects of the employer's undertaking to provide postretirement benefits to its employees by disclosing relevant information about the obligation and cost of the postretirement benefit plan and how those amounts are measured

d. To improve the understandability and comparability of amounts reported by requiring employers with similar plans to use the same method to measure their accumulated postretirement benefit obligations and the related costs of the postretirement benefits.

Similarity to Pension Accounting

The provisions of this Statement are similar, in many respects, to those in FASB Statements No. 87, *Employers' Accounting for Pensions,* and No. 88, *Employers' Accounting for Settlements and Curtailments of Defined Benefit Pension Plans and for Termination Benefits*. To the extent the promise to provide pension benefits and the promise to provide postretirement benefits are similar, the provisions of this Statement are similar to those prescribed by Statements 87 and 88; different accounting treatment is prescribed only when the Board has concluded that there is a compelling reason for different treatment. Appendix B identifies the major similarities and differences between this Statement and employers' accounting for pensions.

Basic Tenets

This Statement relies on a basic premise of generally accepted accounting principles that accrual accounting provides more relevant and useful information than does cash basis accounting. The importance of information about cash flows or the funding of the postretirement benefit plan is not ignored. Amounts funded or paid are given accounting recognition as uses of cash, but the Board believes that information about cash flows alone is insufficient. Accrual accounting goes beyond cash transactions and attempts to recognize the financial effects of noncash transactions and events as they occur. Recognition and measurement of the accrued obligation to provide postretirement benefits will provide users of financial statements with the opportunity to assess the financial consequences of employers' compensation decisions.

In applying accrual accounting to postretirement benefits, this Statement adopts three fundamental aspects of pension accounting: delayed recognition of certain events, reporting net cost, and offsetting liabilities and related assets.

Delayed recognition means that certain changes in the obligation for postretirement benefits, including those changes arising as a result of a plan initiation or amendment, and certain changes in the value of plan assets set aside to meet that obligation are not recognized as they occur. Rather, those changes are recognized systematically over future periods. All changes in the obligation and plan assets ultimately are recognized unless they are first reduced by other changes. The changes that have been identified and quantified but not yet recognized in the employer's financial statements as components of net periodic postretirement benefit cost and as a liability or asset are disclosed.

Net cost means that the recognized consequences of events and transactions affecting a postretirement benefit plan are reported as a single amount in the employer's financial statements. That single amount includes at least three types of events or transactions that might otherwise be reported separately. Those events or transactions—exchanging a promise of deferred compensation in the form of postretirement benefits for employee service, the interest cost arising from the passage of time until those benefits are paid, and the returns from the investment of plan assets—are disclosed separately as components of net periodic postretirement benefit cost.

Offsetting means that plan assets restricted for the payment of postretirement benefits offset the accumulated postretirement benefit obligation in determining amounts recognized in the employer's statement of financial position and that the return on those plan assets offsets postretirement benefit cost in the employer's statement of income. That offsetting is reflected even though the obligation has not been settled, the investment of the plan assets may be largely controlled by the employer, and substantial risks and rewards associated with both the obligation and the plan assets are borne by the employer.

Recognition and Measurement

The Board is sensitive to concerns about the reliability of measurements of the postretirement health care benefit obligation. The Board recognizes that limited historical data about per capita claims costs are available and that actuarial practice in this area is still developing. The Board has taken those factors into consideration in its decisions to delay the effective date for this Statement, to emphasize disclosure, and to permit employers to phase in recognition of the transition obligation in their statements of financial position. However, the Board believes that those factors are insufficient reason not to use accrual accounting for postretirement benefits in financial reporting. With increased experience, the reliability of measures of the obligation and cost should improve.

An objective of this Statement is that the accounting reflect the terms of the exchange transaction that takes place between an employer that provides postretirement benefits and the employees who render services in exchange for those benefits. Generally the extant written plan provides the best evidence of that exchange transaction. However, in some situations, an employer's cost-sharing policy, as evidenced by past practice or by communication of intended changes to a plan's cost-sharing provisions, or a past practice of regular increases in certain monetary benefits may indicate that the substantive plan—the plan as understood by the parties to the exchange transaction—differs from the extant written plan. The substantive plan is the basis for the accounting.

This Statement requires that an employer's obligation for postretirement benefits expected to be provided to or for an employee be fully accrued by the date that employee attains full eligibility for all of the benefits expected to be received by that employee, any beneficiaries, and covered dependents (the full eligibility date), even if the employee is expected to render additional service beyond that date. That accounting reflects the fact that at the full eligibility date the employee has provided all of the service necessary to earn the right to receive all of the benefits that employee is expected to receive under the plan.

The beginning of the attribution (accrual) period is the employee's date of hire unless the plan only grants credit for service from a later date, in which case benefits are generally attributed from the beginning of that credited service period. An equal amount of the expected postretirement benefit obligation is attributed to each year of service in the attribution period unless the plan attributes a disproportionate share of the expected benefits to employees' early years of service. The Board concluded that, like accounting for other deferred compensation agreements, accounting for postretirement benefits should reflect the explicit or implicit contract between the employer and its employees.

Single Method

The Board believes that understandability, comparability, and usefulness of financial information are improved by narrowing the use of alternative accounting methods that do not reflect different facts and circumstances. The Board has been unable to identify circumstances that would make it appropriate for different employers to use fundamentally different accounting methods or measurement techniques for similar postretirement benefit plans or for a single employer to use fundamentally different methods or measurement techniques for different plans. As a result, a single method is prescribed for measuring and recognizing an employer's accumulated postretirement benefit obligation.

Amendment to Opinion 12

An employer's practice of providing postretirement benefits to selected employees under individual contracts, with specific terms determined on an individual-by-individual basis, does not constitute a postretirement benefit *plan* under this Statement. This Statement amends APB Opinion No. 12, *Omnibus Opinion—1967,* to explicitly require that an employer's obligation under deferred compensation contracts be accrued following the terms of the individual contract over the required service periods to the date the employee is fully eligible for the benefits.

Transition

Unlike the effects of most other accounting changes, a transition obligation for postretirement benefits generally reflects, to a considerable extent, the failure to accrue the accumulated postretirement benefit obligation in earlier periods as it arose rather than the effects of a change from one acceptable accrual method of accounting to another. The Board believes that accounting for transition from one method of accounting to another is a practical matter and that a major objective of that accounting is to minimize the cost and mitigate the disruption to the extent possible without unduly compromising the ability of financial statements to provide useful information.

This Statement measures the transition obligation as the unfunded and unrecognized accumulated postretirement benefit obligation for all plan participants. Two options are provided for recognizing that transition obligation. An employer can choose to immediately recognize the transition obligation as the effect of an accounting change, subject to certain limitations. Alternatively, an employer can choose to recognize the transition obligation in the statement of financial position and statement of income on a delayed basis over the plan participants' future service periods, with disclosure of the unrecognized amount. However, that delayed recognition cannot result in less rapid recognition than accounting for the transition obligation on a pay-as-you-go basis.

Effective Dates

This Statement generally is effective for fiscal years beginning after December 15, 1992, except that the application of this Statement to plans outside the United States and certain small, nonpublic employers is delayed to fiscal years beginning after December 15, 1994. The amendment of Opinion 12 is effective for fiscal years beginning after March 15, 1991.

* * *

The Board appreciates the contributions of the many people and organizations that assisted the Board in its research on this project.

Statement of Financial Accounting Standards No. 106

Employers' Accounting for Postretirement Benefits Other Than Pensions

CONTENTS

INTRODUCTION

1. This Statement establishes standards of financial accounting and reporting for an employer that offers **postretirement benefits other than pensions**[1] (hereinafter referred to as **postretirement benefits**) to its employees.[2] The Board added a project on postemployment **benefits** other than pensions to its agenda in 1979 as part of its project on accounting for pensions and other postemployment benefits. In 1984, the subject of accounting for postemployment benefits other than pensions was identified as a separate project. As interim measures, FASB Statement No. 81, *Disclosure of Postretirement Health Care and Life Insurance Benefits,* was issued in November 1984, and FASB Technical Bulletin No. 87-1, *Accounting for a Change in Method of Accounting for Certain Postretirement Benefits,* was issued in April 1987.

2. Most employers have accounted for postretirement benefits on a pay-as-you-go (cash) basis. As the prevalence and magnitude of employers' promises to provide those benefits have increased, there has been increased concern about the failure of financial reporting to identify the financial effects of those promises.

3. The Board views a **postretirement benefit plan** as a deferred compensation arrangement whereby an employer promises to exchange future benefits for employees' current services. Because the obligation to provide benefits arises as employees render the services necessary to earn the benefits pursuant to the terms of the **plan,** the Board believes that the cost of providing the benefits should be recognized over those employee service periods.

4. This Statement addresses, for the first time, the accounting issues related to measuring and recognizing the exchange that takes place between an employer that provides postretirement benefits and the employees who render services in exchange for those benefits. The Board believes the accounting recognition required by this Statement should result in more useful and representationally faithful financial statements. However, this Statement is not likely to be the final step in the evolution of more useful accounting for postretirement benefit arrangements.

5. The Board's objectives in issuing this Statement are to improve employers' financial reporting for postretirement benefits in the following manner:

a. To enhance the relevance and representational faithfulness of the employer's reported results of operations by recognizing **net periodic postretirement benefit cost**[3] as employees render the services necessary to earn their postretirement benefits

b. To enhance the relevance and representational faithfulness of the employer's statement of financial position by including a measure of the obligation to provide postretirement benefits based on a mutual understanding between the employer and its employees of the terms of the underlying plan

c. To enhance the ability of users of the employer's financial statements to understand the extent and effects of the employer's undertaking to provide postretirement benefits to its employees by disclosing relevant information about the obligation and cost of the postretirement benefit plan and how those amounts are measured

d. To improve the understandability and comparability of amounts reported by requiring employers with similar plans to use the same method to measure their **accumulated postretirement benefit obligations** and the related costs of the postretirement benefits.

STANDARDS OF FINANCIAL ACCOUNTING AND REPORTING

Scope

6. This Statement applies to *all* postretirement benefits expected to be provided by an employer to current and former employees (including **retirees,** disabled employees,[4] and other former employees who are expected to receive postretirement benefits), their beneficiaries, and covered dependents, pursuant to the terms of an employer's undertak-

---

[1] Words that appear in the glossary are set in **boldface type** the first time they appear.

[2] The accounting for benefits paid after employment but before retirement (for example, layoff benefits) is a separate phase of the Board's project on accounting for postemployment benefits other than pensions. The fact that this Statement does not apply to those benefits should not be construed as discouraging the use of accrual accounting for those benefits.

[3] This Statement uses the term *net periodic postretirement benefit cost* rather than *net postretirement benefit expense* because part of the cost recognized in a period may be capitalized along with other costs as part of an asset such as inventory.

[4] The determination of disability benefits to be accrued pursuant to this Statement is based on the terms of the postretirement benefit plan defining when a disabled employee is entitled to postretirement benefits.

ing to provide those benefits. Postretirement benefits include, but are not limited to, postretirement health care;[5] life insurance provided outside a pension plan to retirees; and other welfare benefits such as tuition assistance, day care, legal services, and housing subsidies provided after retirement. Often those benefits are in the form of a reimbursement to plan participants or direct payment to providers for the cost of specified services as the need for those services arises, but they may also include benefits payable as a lump sum, such as death benefits. This Statement also applies to **settlement** of all or a part of an employer's accumulated postretirement benefit obligation or **curtailment** of a postretirement benefit plan and to an employer that provides postretirement benefits as part of a special **termination benefits** offer.

7. For the purposes of this Statement, a postretirement benefit plan is an arrangement that is mutually understood by an employer and its employees, whereby an employer undertakes to provide its current and former employees with benefits after they retire in exchange for the employees' services over a specified period of time, upon attaining a specified age while in service, or both. Benefits may commence immediately upon termination of service or may be deferred until retired employees attain a specified age.

8. An employer's practice of providing postretirement benefits may take a variety of forms and the obligation may or may not be funded. This Statement applies to any arrangement that is in substance a postretirement benefit plan, regardless of its form or the means or timing of its funding. This Statement applies both to written plans and to unwritten plans whose existence is discernible either from a practice of paying postretirement benefits or from oral representations made to current or former employees. Absent evidence to the contrary, it shall be presumed that an employer that has provided postretirement benefits in the past or is currently promising those benefits to employees will continue to provide those future benefits.

9. This Statement applies to deferred compensation contracts with individual employees if those contracts, taken together, are equivalent to a plan that provides postretirement benefits. It does not apply to an employer's practice of providing post-

retirement benefits to selected employees under individual contracts with specific terms determined on an individual-by-individual basis. Those contracts shall be accounted for individually, following the terms of the contract. To the extent the contract does not attribute the benefits to individual years of service, the expected future benefits should be accrued over the period of service required to be rendered in exchange for the benefits. (Refer to paragraph 13.)

10. A postretirement benefit plan may be part of a larger plan or arrangement that provides benefits currently to active employees as well as to retirees. In those circumstances, the promise to provide benefits to present and future retirees under the plan shall be segregated from the promise to provide benefits currently to active employees and shall be accounted for in accordance with the provisions of this Statement.

11. This Statement does not apply to pension or life insurance benefits provided through a pension plan. The accounting for those benefits is set forth in FASB Statements No. 87, *Employers' Accounting for Pensions,* and No. 88, *Employers' Accounting for Settlements and Curtailments of Defined Benefit Pension Plans and for Termination Benefits.*[6]

12. This Statement supersedes FASB Statement No. 81, *Disclosure of Postretirement Health Care and Life Insurance Benefits.* Paragraphs 13 and 114 of this Statement amend APB Opinion No. 12, *Omnibus Opinion—1967;* paragraph 14 amends Statement 87; and paragraph 89 amends APB Opinion No. 16, *Business Combinations.* Paragraph 115 rescinds FASB Technical Bulletin No. 87-1, *Accounting for a Change in Method of Accounting for Certain Postretirement Benefits.*

Amendment to Opinion 12

13. The following paragraphs and footnote replace the first four sentences and footnote of paragraph 6 of Opinion 12:

> FASB Statement No. 87, *Employers' Accounting for Pensions,* or Statement No. 106, *Employers' Accounting for Postretirement Benefits Other Than Pensions,* applies to deferred

---

[5]Postretirement health care benefits are likely to be the most significant in terms of cost and prevalence, and certain of the issues that arise in measuring those benefits are unique. Therefore, much of the language of this Statement focuses on postretirement health care plans. Nevertheless, this Statement applies equally to all postretirement benefits.

[6]Two Special Reports prepared by the FASB staff, *A Guide to Implementation of Statement 87 on Employers' Accounting for Pensions,* and *A Guide to Implementation of Statement 88 on Employers' Accounting for Settlements and Curtailments of Defined Benefit Pension Plans and for Termination Benefits,* provide accounting guidance on implementation questions raised in connection with Statements 87 and 88. Many of the provisions in this Statement are the same as or are similar to the provisions of Statements 87 and 88. Consequently, the guidance provided in those Special Reports should be useful in understanding and implementing many of the provisions of this Statement.

compensation contracts with individual employees if those contracts, taken together, are equivalent to a postretirement income plan or a postretirement health or welfare benefit plan, respectively. Other deferred compensation contracts shall be accounted for individually on an accrual basis in accordance with the terms of the underlying contract.

To the extent the terms of the contract attribute all or a portion of the expected future benefits to an individual year of the employee's service, the cost of those benefits shall be recognized in that year. To the extent the terms of the contract attribute all or a portion of the expected future benefits to a period of service greater than one year, the cost of those benefits shall be accrued over that period of the employee's service in a systematic and rational manner. At the end of that period the aggregate amount accrued shall equal the then present value of the benefits expected to be provided to the employee, any beneficiaries, and covered dependents in exchange for the employee's service to that date.*

---

*The amounts to be accrued periodically shall result in an accrued amount at the full eligibility date (as defined in Statement 106) equal to the then present value of all of the future benefits expected to be paid. Paragraphs 413-416 of Statement 106 illustrate application of this paragraph.

Amendment to Statement 87

14. The following sentences replace the first two sentences and footnote of paragraph 8 of Statement 87:

This Statement does not apply to life insurance benefits provided outside a pension plan or to other postretirement health and welfare benefits. The accounting for those benefits is set forth in FASB Statement No. 106, *Employers' Accounting for Postretirement Benefits Other Than Pensions.*

Use of Reasonable Approximations

15. This Statement is intended to specify accounting objectives and results rather than computational means of obtaining those results. If estimates, averages, or computational shortcuts can reduce the cost of applying this Statement, their use is appropriate, provided the results are reasonably expected not to be materially different from the results of a detailed application.

Single-Employer Defined Benefit Postretirement Plans

16. This Statement primarily focuses on an em-

ployer's accounting for a **single-employer plan** that defines the postretirement benefits to be provided to retirees. For purposes of this Statement, a **defined benefit postretirement plan** is one that defines the postretirement benefits in terms of (a) monetary amounts (for example, $100,000 of life insurance) or (b) benefit coverage to be provided (for example, up to $200 per day for hospitalization, 80 percent of the cost of specified surgical procedures, and so forth). (Specified monetary amounts and benefit coverage are hereinafter collectively referred to as *benefits.*)

17. In some cases, an employer may limit its obligation through an individual or an aggregate "cap" on the employer's cost or benefit obligation. For example, an employer may elect to limit its annual postretirement benefit obligation for each retired plan participant to a maximum of $5,000. Or, an employer may elect to limit its share of the aggregate cost of covered postretirement health care benefits for a period to an amount determined based on an average per capita cost per retired plan participant. Plans of that nature are considered to be defined benefit postretirement plans. Paragraphs 472-478 illustrate measurement considerations for defined-dollar capped plans.

18. A postretirement benefit is part of the compensation paid to an employee for services rendered. In a defined benefit plan, the employer promises to provide, in addition to current wages and benefits, future benefits during retirement. Generally, the amount of those benefits depends on the **benefit formula** (which may include factors such as the number of years of service rendered or the employee's compensation before retirement or termination), the longevity of the retiree and any beneficiaries and covered dependents, and the incidence of events requiring benefit payments (for example, illnesses affecting the amount of health care required). In most cases, services are rendered over a number of years before an employee retires and begins to receive benefits or is entitled to receive benefits as a need arises. Even though the services rendered by the employee are complete and the employee has retired, the total amount of benefits the employer has promised and the cost to the employer of the services rendered are not precisely determinable but can be estimated using the plan's benefit formula and estimates of the effects of relevant future events.

Basic Elements of Accounting for Postretirement Benefits

19. Any method of accounting that recognizes the cost of postretirement benefits over employee service periods (before the payment of benefits to retirees) must deal with two factors that stem from the

nature of the arrangement. First, estimates or **assumptions** must be made about the future events that will determine the amount and timing of the benefit payments. Second, an **attribution** approach that assigns benefits and the cost of those benefits to individual years of service must be selected.

20. The **expected postretirement benefit obligation** for an employee is the **actuarial present value** as of a particular date of the postretirement benefits expected to be paid by the employer's plan to or for the employee, the employee's beneficiaries, and any covered dependents pursuant to the terms of the plan. Measurement of the expected postretirement benefit obligation is based on the expected amount and timing of future benefits, taking into consideration the expected future cost of providing the benefits and the extent to which those costs are shared by the employer, the employee (including consideration of contributions required during the employee's active service period and following retirement, deductibles, coinsurance provisions, and so forth), or others (such as through governmental programs).

21. The accumulated postretirement benefit obligation[7] as of a particular date is the actuarial present value of all future benefits attributed to an employee's service rendered to that date pursuant to paragraphs 43 and 44 and 52-55, assuming the plan continues in effect and that all assumptions about future events are fulfilled. Prior to the date on which an employee attains **full eligibility** for the benefits that employee is expected to earn under the terms of the postretirement benefit plan (the **full eligibility date**), the accumulated postretirement benefit obligation for an employee is a portion of the expected postretirement benefit obligation. On and after the full eligibility date, the accumulated postretirement benefit obligation and the expected postretirement benefit obligation for an employee are the same. Determination of the full eligibility date is affected by plan terms that provide incremental benefits expected to be received by or on behalf of an employee for additional years of service, unless those incremental benefits are trivial. Determination of the full eligibility date is not affected by plan terms that define when benefit payments commence or by an employee's current **dependency status.** (Paragraphs 397-408 illustrate determination of the full eligibility date.)

22. Net periodic postretirement benefit cost com-

prises several components that reflect different aspects of the employer's financial arrangements. The **service cost** component of net periodic postretirement benefit cost is the actuarial present value of benefits attributed to services rendered by employees during the period (the portion of the expected postretirement benefit obligation attributed to service in the period). The service cost component is the same for an unfunded plan, a plan with minimal funding, and a well-funded plan. The other components of net periodic postretirement benefit cost are **interest cost**[8] (interest on the accumulated postretirement benefit obligation, which is a discounted amount), **actual return on plan assets, amortization** of **unrecognized prior service cost,** amortization of the **transition obligation** or **transition asset,** and the **gain or loss component.**

Measurement of Cost and Obligations

Accounting for the substantive plan

23. An objective of this Statement is that the accounting reflect the terms of the exchange transaction that takes place between an employer that provides postretirement benefits and the employees who render services in exchange for those benefits, as those terms are understood by both parties to the transaction. Generally, the extant written plan provides the best evidence of the terms of that exchange transaction. However, in some situations, an employer's **cost-sharing** policy, as evidenced by past practice or by communication of intended changes to a plan's cost-sharing provisions (paragraphs 24 and 25), or a past practice of regular increases in certain monetary benefits (paragraph 26) may indicate that the **substantive plan**—the plan as understood by the parties to the exchange transaction—differs from the extant written plan. The substantive plan shall be the basis for the accounting.

24. Except as provided in paragraph 25, an employer's cost-sharing policy, as evidenced by the following past practice or communication, shall constitute the cost-sharing provisions of the substantive plan if either of the following conditions exist. Otherwise, the extant written plan shall be considered to be the substantive plan.

a. The employer has a past practice of (1) maintaining a consistent level of cost sharing between the employer and its retirees through

---

[7]The accumulated postretirement benefit obligation generally reflects a ratable allocation of expected future benefits to employee service already rendered in the attribution period; the accumulated benefit obligation under Statement 87 generally reflects the future benefits allocated to employee service in accordance with the benefit formula. In addition, unlike Statement 87, this Statement implicitly considers salary progression in the measurement of the accumulated postretirement benefit obligation of a pay-related plan.

[8]The interest cost component of postretirement benefit cost shall not be considered interest for purposes of applying FASB Statement No. 34, *Capitalization of Interest Cost.*

changes in deductibles, coinsurance provisions, retiree contributions, or some combination of those changes or (2) consistently increasing or reducing the employer's share of the cost of the covered benefits through changes in retired or **active plan participants'** contributions toward their retiree health care benefits, deductibles, coinsurance provisions, out-of-pocket limitations, and so forth, in accordance with the employer's established cost-sharing policy

b. The employer has the ability, and has communicated to affected **plan participants** its intent, to institute different cost-sharing provisions at a specified time or when certain conditions exist (for example, when health care cost increases exceed a certain level).

25. An employer's past practice of maintaining a consistent level of cost sharing with its retirees or consistently increasing or reducing its share of the cost of providing the covered benefits shall not constitute provisions of the substantive plan if accompanied by identifiable offsetting changes in other benefits or compensation[9] or if the employer incurred significant costs, such as work stoppages, to effect that cost-sharing policy.[10] Similarly, an employer's communication of its intent to institute cost-sharing provisions that differ from the extant written plan or the past cost-sharing practice shall not constitute provisions of the substantive plan (a) if the plan participants would be unwilling to accept the change without adverse consequences to the employer's operations or (b) if other modifications of the plan, such as the level of benefit coverage, or providing offsetting changes in other benefits, such as pension benefits, would be required to gain plan participants' acceptance of the change to the cost-sharing arrangement.

26. A past practice of regular increases in postretirement benefits defined in terms of monetary amounts may indicate that the employer has a present commitment to make future *improvements* to the plan and that the plan will provide monetary benefits attributable to prior service that are greater than the monetary benefits defined by the extant written plan. In those situations, the substantive commitment to increase those benefits shall be the basis for the accounting. Changes in the benefits, other than benefits defined in terms of monetary amounts, covered by a postretirement health care plan or by other postretirement benefit plans shall not be anticipated.

27. Contributions expected to be received from active employees toward the cost of their postretirement benefits and from retired plan participants are treated similarly for purposes of measuring an employer's expected postretirement benefit obligation. That obligation is measured as the actuarial present value of the benefits expected to be provided under the plan, reduced by the actuarial present value of contributions expected to be received from the plan participants during their remaining active service and postretirement periods. In determining the amount of the contributions expected to be received from those participants toward the cost of their postretirement benefits, consideration is given to any related substantive plan provisions, such as an employer's past practice of consistently increasing or reducing the contribution rates as described in paragraphs 24 and 25. An obligation to return contributions received from employees who do not attain eligibility for postretirement benefits and, if applicable, any interest accrued on those contributions shall be recognized as a component of an employer's postretirement benefit obligation.

28. Automatic benefit changes[11] specified by the plan that are expected to occur shall be included in measurements of the expected and accumulated postretirement benefit obligations and the service cost component of net periodic postretirement benefit cost. Also, **plan amendments** shall be included in the computation of the expected and accumulated postretirement benefit obligations once they have been contractually agreed to, even if

---

[9]For example, a past practice of increasing retiree contributions annually based on a specified index or formula may appear to indicate that the substantive plan includes a determinable indexing of the retirees' annual contributions to the plan. However, if that past practice of increasing retiree contributions is accompanied by identifiable offsetting changes in other benefits or compensation, those offsetting changes would indicate that the substantive plan incorporates only the *current* cost-sharing provisions. Therefore, future increases or reductions of those cost-sharing provisions should not be incorporated in measuring the expected postretirement benefit obligation.

[10]By definition, an employer does not have the unilateral right to change a collectively bargained plan. Therefore, if the postretirement benefits are the subject of collective bargaining, the extant written plan shall be the substantive plan unless the employer can demonstrate its ability to maintain (a) a consistent level of cost sharing or (b) a consistent practice of increasing or reducing its share of the cost of the covered benefits in past negotiations without making offsetting changes in other benefits or compensation of the affected plan participants or by incurring other significant costs to maintain that cost-sharing arrangement.

[11]For purposes of this Statement, a plan that promises to provide retirees a benefit in kind, such as health care benefits, rather than a defined dollar amount of benefit, is considered to be a plan that specifies automatic benefit changes. (The assumed rate of change in the future cost of providing health care benefits, the assumed health care cost trend rate, is discussed in paragraph 39.) Because automatic benefit changes are not conditional on employees rendering additional years of service, the full eligibility date is not affected by those changes. A benefit in kind includes the direct rendering of services, the payment directly to others who provide the services, or the reimbursement of the retiree's payment for those services.

some provisions take effect only in future periods. For example, if a plan amendment grants a different benefit level for employees retiring after a future date, that increased or reduced benefit level shall be included in current-period measurements for employees expected to retire after that date.

Assumptions

29. The Board believes that measuring the net periodic postretirement benefit cost and accumulated postretirement benefit obligation based on best estimates is superior to implying, by a failure to accrue, that no cost or obligation exists prior to the payment of benefits. This Statement requires the use of **explicit assumptions,** each of which individually represents the best estimate of a particular future event, to measure the expected postretirement benefit obligation. A portion of that expected postretirement benefit obligation is attributed to each period of an employee's service associated with earning the postretirement benefits, and that amount is accrued as service cost for that period.

30. The service cost component of postretirement benefit cost, any **prior service cost,** and the accumulated postretirement benefit obligation are measured using actuarial assumptions and present value techniques to calculate the actuarial present value of the expected future benefits attributed to periods of employee service. Each assumption used shall reflect the best estimate solely with respect to that individual assumption. All assumptions shall presume that the plan will continue in effect in the absence of evidence that it will not continue. Principal actuarial assumptions include the time value of money (**discount rates**); participation rates (for **contributory plans**); retirement age; factors affecting the amount and timing of future benefit payments, which for **postretirement health care benefits** consider past and present **per capita claims cost by age, health care cost trend rates, Medicare reimbursement rates,** and so forth; salary progression (for **pay-related plans**); and the probability of payment (turnover, dependency status, mortality, and so forth).

31. Assumed discount rates shall reflect the time value of money as of the **measurement date** in determining the present value of future cash outflows currently expected to be required to satisfy the postretirement benefit obligation. In making that assumption, employers shall look to rates of return on high-quality fixed-income investments cur-

rently available whose cash flows match the timing and amount of expected benefit payments. If settlement of the obligation with third-party insurers is possible (for example, the purchase of nonparticipating life insurance contracts to provide death benefits), the interest rates inherent in the amount at which the postretirement benefit obligation could be settled are relevant in determining the assumed discount rates. Assumed discount rates are used in measurements of the expected and accumulated postretirement benefit obligations and the service cost and interest cost components of net periodic postretirement benefit cost.

32. The **expected long-term rate of return on plan assets** shall reflect the average rate of earnings expected on the existing assets that qualify as **plan assets** and contributions to the plan expected to be made during the period. In estimating that rate, appropriate consideration should be given to the returns being earned on the plan assets currently invested and the rates of return expected to be available for reinvestment. If the return on plan assets is taxable to the trust or other fund under the plan, the expected long-term rate of return shall be reduced to reflect the related income taxes expected to be paid under existing law. The expected long-term rate of return on plan assets is used with the **market-related value of plan assets** to compute the **expected return on plan assets.** (Refer to paragraph 57.) There is no assumption of an expected long-term rate of return on plan assets for plans that are unfunded or that have no assets that qualify as plan assets pursuant to this Statement.

33. The service cost component of net periodic postretirement benefit cost and the expected and accumulated postretirement benefit obligations shall reflect future compensation levels to the extent the postretirement benefit formula defines the benefits wholly or partially as a function of future compensation levels.[12] For pay-related plans, assumed compensation levels shall reflect the best estimate of the actual future compensation levels of the individual employees involved, including future changes attributed to general price levels, productivity, seniority, promotion, and other factors. All assumptions shall be consistent to the extent that each reflects expectations about the same future economic conditions, such as future rates of inflation. Measuring service cost and the expected and accumulated postretirement benefit obligations based on estimated future compensation levels entails considering any indirect effects, such as

---

[12]For pay-related plans, salary progression is included in measuring the expected postretirement benefit obligation. For example, a postretirement health care plan may define the deductible amount or copayment, or a postretirement life insurance plan may define the amount of death benefit, based on the employee's average or final level of annual compensation.

benefit limitations, that would affect benefits provided by the plan.[13]

Assumptions unique to postretirement health care benefits

34. Measurement of an employer's postretirement health care obligation requires the use of several assumptions unique to health care benefits. Most significantly, it includes several assumptions about factors that will affect the amount and timing of future benefit payments for postretirement health care. Those factors include consideration of historical per capita claims cost by age, health care cost trend rates (for plans that provide a benefit in kind), and medical coverage to be paid by governmental authorities and other providers of health care benefits.

35. In principle, an employer's share of the expected future postretirement health care cost for a plan participant is developed by reducing the **assumed per capita claims cost** at each age at which the plan participant is expected to receive benefits under the plan by (a) the effects of coverage by Medicare and other providers of health care benefits, and (b) the effects of the cost-sharing provisions of the plan (deductibles, copayment provisions, out-of-pocket limitations, caps on the limits of the employer-provided payments, and retiree contributions).[14] The resulting amount represents the assumed **net incurred claims cost** at each age at which the plan participant is expected to receive benefits under the plan. If contributions are required to be paid by active plan participants toward their postretirement health care benefits, the actuarial present value of the plan participants' future contributions reduces the actuarial present value of the aggregate assumed net incurred claims costs.

36. The assumed per capita claims cost by age is the annual per capita cost, for periods after the measurement date, of providing the postretirement health care benefits covered by the plan from the earliest age at which an individual could begin to receive benefits under the plan through the remainder of the individual's life or the covered period, if shorter. The assumed per capita claims cost

shall be the best estimate of the expected future cost of the benefits covered by the plan.[15] It may be appropriate to consider other factors in addition to age, such as sex and geographical location, in developing the assumed per capita claims cost.

37. Past and present claims data for the plan, such as a historical pattern of gross claims by age (claims curve), should be used in developing the current per capita claims cost to the extent that those data are considered to be indicative of the current cost of providing the benefits covered by the plan. Those current claims data shall be adjusted by the assumed health care cost trend rate. The resulting assumed per capita claims cost by age, together with the **plan demographics,** determines the amount and timing of expected future **gross eligible charges.**

38. In the absence of sufficiently reliable plan data about the current cost of the benefits covered by the plan, the current per capita claims cost should be based, entirely or in part, on the claims information of other employers to the extent those costs are indicative of the current cost of providing the benefits covered by the plan. For example, the current per capita claims cost may be based on the claims experience of other employers derived from information in data files developed by insurance companies, actuarial firms, or employee benefits consulting firms. The current per capita claims cost developed on those bases shall be adjusted to best reflect the terms of the employer's plan and the plan demographics. For example, the information should be adjusted, as necessary, for differing demographics, such as the age and sex of plan participants, health care utilization patterns by men and women at various ages, and the expected geographical location of retirees and their dependents, and for significant differences between the nature and types of benefits covered by the employer's plan and those encompassed by the underlying data.

39. The assumption about health care cost trend rates represents the expected annual rates of change in the cost of health care benefits currently provided by the postretirement benefit plan, due to factors other than changes in the demographics of

---

[13]For example, a plan may define the maximum benefit to be provided under the plan (a fixed cap). In measuring the expected postretirement benefit obligation under that plan, the projected benefit payments would be limited to that cap. For a plan that automatically adjusts the maximum benefit to be provided under the plan for the effects of inflation (an adjustable cap), the expected postretirement benefit obligation would be measured based on adjustments to that cap consistent with the assumed inflation rate reflected in other inflation-related assumptions.

[14]In some cases, retiree contributions are established based on the average per capita cost of benefit coverage under an employer's health care plan that provides coverage to both active employees and retirees. However, the medical cost of the retirees may cause the average per capita cost of benefit coverage under the plan to be higher than it would be if only active employees were covered by the plan. In that case, the employer has a postretirement benefit obligation for the portion of the expected future cost of the retiree health care benefits that are not recovered through retiree contributions, Medicare, or other providers of health care benefits.

[15]If significant, the internal and external costs directly associated with administering the postretirement benefit plan also should be accrued as a component of assumed per capita claims cost.

the plan participants, for each year from the measurement date until the end of the period in which benefits are expected to be paid. Past and current health care cost trends shall be used in developing an employer's assumed health care cost trend rates, which implicitly consider estimates of health care inflation, changes in health care utilization or delivery patterns, technological advances, and changes in the health status of plan participants.[16] Differing services, such as hospital care and dental care, may require the use of different health care cost trend rates. It is appropriate for that assumption to reflect changes in health care cost trend rates over time. For example, the health care cost trend rates may be assumed to continue at the present level for the near term, or increase for a period of time, and then grade down over time to an estimated health care cost trend rate ultimately expected to prevail.

40. Certain medical claims may be covered by governmental programs under existing law or by other providers of health care benefits.[17] Benefit coverage by those governmental programs shall be assumed to continue as provided by the present law and by other providers pursuant to their present plans. Presently enacted changes in the law or amendments of the plans of other health care providers that take effect in future periods and that will affect the future level of their benefit coverage shall be considered in current-period measurements for benefits expected to be provided in those future periods. Future changes in laws concerning medical costs covered by governmental programs and future changes in the plans of other providers shall not be anticipated.

41. In some cases, determining the assumed per capita claims cost by age as described in paragraphs 36-38 may not be practical because credible historical information about the gross per capita cost of covered benefits may not be available or determinable to satisfy the stated measurement approach. However, credible historical information about **incurred claims costs** may be available. In those cases, an alternative method of developing the assumed per capita claims cost may be used provided the method results in a measure that is the best estimate of the expected future cost of the benefits covered by the plan. For example, the assumed health care cost trend rates may be determined by adjusting the expected change in the employer's share of per capita incurred claims cost by age by a factor that reflects the effects of the plan's cost-sharing provisions. However, an approach that projects net incurred claims costs using unadjusted assumed health care cost trend rates would implicitly assume changes in the plan's cost-sharing provisions at those assumed rates and, therefore, is not acceptable unless the plan's cost-sharing provisions are indexed in that manner or the substantive plan (paragraphs 24-26) operates in that manner.

42. Assumed discount rates include an inflationary element that reflects the expected general rate of inflation. Assumed compensation levels include consideration of future changes attributable to general price levels. Similarly, assumed health care cost trend rates include an element that reflects expected general rates of inflation for the economy overall and an element that reflects price changes of health care costs in particular. To the extent that those assumptions consider similar inflationary effects, the assumptions about those effects shall be consistent.

Attribution

43. An equal amount of the expected postretirement benefit obligation for an employee generally shall be attributed to each year of service in the **attribution period** (a benefit/years-of-service approach). However, some plans may have benefit formulas that attribute a disproportionate share of the expected postretirement benefit obligation to employees' early years of service. For that type of plan, the expected postretirement benefit obligation shall be attributed in accordance with the plan's benefit formula.

44. The beginning of the attribution period generally shall be the date of hire. However, if the plan's benefit formula grants credit only for service from a later date and that **credited service period** is not nominal in relation to employees' total years of service prior to their full eligibility dates, the expected postretirement benefit obligation shall be attributed from the beginning of that credited service period. In all cases, the end of the attribution period shall be the full eligibility date. (Paragraphs 409-412 illustrate the attribution provisions of this Statement.)

---

[16]An assumption about changes in the health status of plan participants considers, for example, the probability that certain claims costs will be incurred based on expectations of future events, such as the likelihood that some retirees will incur claims requiring technology currently being developed or that historical claims experience for certain medical needs may be reduced as a result of participation in a wellness program.

[17]For example, a retiree's spouse also may be covered by the spouse's present (or former) employer's health care plan. In that case, the spouse's employer (or former employer) may provide either primary or secondary postretirement health care benefits to the retiree's spouse or dependents.

Recognition of Net Periodic Postretirement Benefit Cost

45. As with other forms of deferred compensation, the cost of providing postretirement benefits shall be attributed to the periods of employee service rendered in exchange for those future benefits pursuant to the terms of the plan. That cost notionally represents the change in the **unfunded accumulated postretirement benefit obligation** for the period, ignoring employer contributions to the plan, plan settlements, and payments made by the employer directly to retirees. However, changes in that unfunded obligation that arise from experience gains and losses and the effects of changes in assumptions may be recognized as a component of net periodic postretirement benefit cost on a delayed basis. In addition, the effects of a plan initiation or amendment generally are recognized on a delayed basis.

46. The following components shall be included in the net postretirement benefit cost recognized for a period by an employer sponsoring a defined benefit postretirement plan:

a. Service cost (paragraph 47)
b. Interest cost (paragraph 48)
c. Actual return on plan assets, if any (paragraph 49)
d. Amortization of unrecognized prior service cost, if any (paragraphs 50-55)
e. **Gain or loss** (including the effects of changes in assumptions) to the extent recognized (paragraphs 56-62)
f. Amortization of the unrecognized obligation or asset existing at the date of initial application of this Statement, hereinafter referred to as the **unrecognized transition obligation**[18] or **unrecognized transition asset** (paragraphs 110 and 112).

Service cost

47. The service cost component recognized in a period shall be determined as the portion of the expected postretirement benefit obligation attributed to employee service during that period. The measurement of the service cost component requires identification of the substantive plan and the use of assumptions and an attribution method, which are discussed in paragraphs 23-44.

Interest cost

48. The interest cost component recognized in a period shall be determined as the increase in the accumulated postretirement benefit obligation to recognize the effects of the passage of time. Measuring the accumulated postretirement benefit obligation as a present value requires accrual of an interest cost at rates equal to the assumed discount rates.

Actual return on plan assets

49. For a funded plan, the actual return on plan assets shall be determined based on the **fair value** of plan assets (refer to paragraphs 65 and 66) at the beginning and end of the period, adjusted for contributions and benefit payments. If the fund holding the plan assets is a taxable entity, the actual return on plan assets shall reflect the tax expense or benefit for the period determined in accordance with generally accepted accounting principles. Otherwise, no provision for taxes shall be included in the actual return on plan assets.

Prior service cost

50. Plan amendments (including initiation of a plan) may include provisions that attribute the increase or reduction in benefits to employee service rendered in prior periods or only to employee service to be rendered in future periods. For purposes of measuring the accumulated postretirement benefit obligation, the effect of a plan amendment on a plan participant's expected postretirement benefit obligation shall be attributed to each year of service in that plan participant's attribution period, including years of service already rendered by that plan participant, in accordance with the attribution of the expected postretirement benefit obligation to years of service as discussed in paragraphs 43 and 44. If a plan is initiated that grants benefits solely in exchange for employee service after the date of the plan initiation or a future date, no portion of the expected postretirement benefit obligation is attributed to prior service periods because, in that case, the credited service period for the current employees who are expected to receive benefits under the plan begins at the date of the plan initiation or the future date.

51. Plan amendments that improve benefits are granted with the expectation that the employer will realize economic benefits in future periods. Consequently, except as discussed in paragraph 54, this Statement does not permit the cost of benefit improvements (that is, prior service cost) to be included in net periodic postretirement benefit cost entirely in the year of the amendment. Rather, paragraph 52 provides for recognition of prior service

---

[18]Amortization of the unrecognized transition obligation or asset will be adjusted prospectively to recognize the effects of (a) a negative plan amendment pursuant to paragraph 55, (b) a constraint on immediate recognition of a net gain or loss pursuant to paragraph 60, (c) settlement accounting pursuant to paragraphs 92 and 93, (d) plan curtailment accounting pursuant to paragraphs 97-99, and (e) a constraint on delayed recognition of the unrecognized transition obligation pursuant to paragraph 112.

cost arising from benefit improvements during the remaining years of service to the full eligibility dates of those plan participants active at the date of the plan amendment. (Refer to paragraph 55 for plan amendments that reduce benefits.)

52. The cost of benefit improvements (including improved benefits that are granted to **fully eligible plan participants**) is the increase in the accumulated postretirement benefit obligation as a result of the plan amendment, measured at the date of the amendment. Except as specified in the next sentence and in paragraphs 53 and 54, that prior service cost shall be amortized by assigning an equal amount to each remaining year of service to the full eligibility date of each plan participant active at the date of the amendment who was not yet fully eligible for benefits at that date. If all or almost all of a plan's participants are fully eligible for benefits, the prior service cost shall be amortized based on the remaining life expectancy of those plan participants rather than on the remaining years of service to the full eligibility dates of the active plan participants.

53. To reduce the complexity and detail of the computations required, consistent use of an alternative amortization approach that more rapidly reduces unrecognized prior service cost is permitted. For example, a straight-line amortization of the cost over the average remaining years of service to full eligibility for benefits of the active plan participants is acceptable.

54. In some situations, a history of regular plan amendments and other evidence may indicate that the period during which the employer expects to realize economic benefits from an amendment that grants increased benefits is shorter than the remaining years of service to full eligibility for benefits of the active plan participants. Identification of those situations requires an assessment of the individual circumstances of the particular plan. In those circumstances, the amortization of prior service cost shall be accelerated to reflect the more rapid expiration of the employer's economic benefits and to recognize the cost in the periods benefited.

55. A plan amendment can reduce, rather than increase, the accumulated postretirement benefit obligation. A reduction in that obligation shall be used first to reduce any existing unrecognized prior service cost, then to reduce any remaining unrecognized transition obligation. The excess, if any, shall be amortized on the same basis as specified in paragraph 52 for prior service cost. Immediate recognition of the excess is not permitted.

Gains and losses

56. Gains and losses are changes in the amount of either the accumulated postretirement benefit obligation or plan assets resulting from experience different from that assumed or from changes in assumptions. This Statement generally does not distinguish between those sources of gains and losses. Gains and losses include amounts that have been realized, for example, by the sale of a security, as well as amounts that are unrealized. Because gains and losses may reflect refinements in estimates as well as real changes in economic values and because some gains in one period may be offset by losses in another or vice versa, this Statement does not require recognition of gains and losses as components of net postretirement benefit cost in the period in which they arise, except as described in paragraph 61. (Gain and loss recognition in accounting for settlements and curtailments is addressed in paragraphs 90-99.)

57. The expected return on plan assets shall be determined based on the expected long-term rate of return on plan assets (refer to paragraph 32) and the market-related value of plan assets. The market-related value of plan assets shall be either fair value or a calculated value that recognizes changes in fair value in a systematic and rational manner over not more than five years. Different methods of calculating market-related value may be used for different classes of assets (for example, an employer might use fair value for bonds and a five-year-moving-average value for equities), but the manner of determining market-related value shall be applied consistently from year to year for each class of plan assets.

58. Plan asset gains and losses are differences between the actual return on plan assets during a period and the expected return on plan assets for that period. Plan asset gains and losses include both (a) changes reflected in the market-related value of plan assets and (b) changes not yet reflected in the market-related value of plan assets (that is, the difference between the fair value and the market-related value of plan assets). Plan asset gains and losses not yet reflected in market-related value are not required to be amortized under paragraphs 59 and 60.

59. As a minimum, amortization of an **unrecognized net gain or loss** (excluding plan asset gains and losses not yet reflected in market-related value) shall be included as a component of net postretirement benefit cost for a year if, as of the beginning of the year, that unrecognized net gain

or loss exceeds 10 percent of the greater of the accumulated postretirement benefit obligation or the market-related value of plan assets. If amortization is required, the minimum amortization[19] shall be that excess divided by the average remaining service period of active plan participants. If all or almost all of a plan's participants are inactive, the average remaining life expectancy of the inactive participants shall be used instead of the average remaining service period.

60. Any systematic method of amortization of unrecognized gains and losses may be used in place of the minimum amortization specified in paragraph 59 provided that (a) the minimum amortization is recognized in any period in which it is greater (reduces the unrecognized amount by more) than the amount that would be recognized under the method used, (b) the method is applied consistently, (c) the method is applied similarly to both gains and losses, and (d) the method used is disclosed. If an enterprise uses a method of consistently recognizing gains and losses immediately, any gain that does not offset a loss previously recognized in income pursuant to this paragraph shall first offset any unrecognized transition obligation; any loss that does not offset a gain previously recognized in income pursuant to this paragraph shall first offset any unrecognized transition asset.

61. In some situations, an employer may forgive a retrospective adjustment of the current or past years' cost-sharing provisions of the plan as they relate to benefit costs *already incurred* by retirees[20] or may otherwise deviate from the provisions of the substantive plan to increase or decrease the employer's share of the benefit costs *incurred in the current or past periods*. The effect of a decision to temporarily deviate from the substantive plan shall be immediately recognized as a loss or gain.

62. The gain or loss component of net periodic postretirement benefit cost shall consist of (a) the difference between the actual return on plan assets and the expected return on plan assets, (b) any gain or loss immediately recognized or the amortization of the unrecognized net gain or loss from previous periods, and (c) any amount immediately recog-

nized as a gain or loss pursuant to paragraph 61.

Measurement of Plan Assets

63. Plan assets are assets—usually stocks, bonds, and other investments (except certain **insurance contracts** as noted in paragraph 67)—that have been segregated and restricted (usually in a trust) to be used for postretirement benefits. The amount of plan assets includes amounts contributed by the employer, and by plan participants for a contributory plan, and amounts earned from investing the contributions, less benefits, income taxes, and other expenses incurred. Plan assets ordinarily cannot be withdrawn by the employer except under certain circumstances when a plan has assets in excess of obligations and the employer has taken certain steps to satisfy existing obligations. Securities of the employer held by the plan are includable in plan assets provided they are transferable.

64. Assets not segregated in a trust, or otherwise effectively restricted, so that they cannot be used by the employer for other purposes are not plan assets for purposes of this Statement, even though the employer may intend that those assets be used to provide postretirement benefits. Those assets shall be accounted for in the same manner as other employer assets of a similar nature and with similar restrictions. Amounts accrued by the employer but not yet paid to the plan are not plan assets for purposes of this Statement.

65. For purposes of the disclosures required by paragraph 74, plan investments, whether equity or debt securities, real estate, or other, shall be measured at their fair value as of the measurement date. The fair value of an investment is the amount that the plan could reasonably expect to receive for it in a current sale between a willing buyer and a willing seller, that is, other than in a forced or liquidation sale. Fair value shall be measured by the market price if an active market exists for the investment. If no active market exists for an investment but an active market exists for similar investments, selling prices in that market may be helpful in estimating fair value. If a market price is not available, a forecast of expected cash flows may aid in estimating

---

[19]The amortization must always reduce the beginning-of-the-year balance. Amortization of an unrecognized net gain results in a decrease in net periodic postretirement benefit cost; amortization of an unrecognized net loss results in an increase in net periodic postretirement benefit cost.

[20]For example, the terms of a substantive postretirement health care plan may provide that any shortfall resulting from current year benefit payments in excess of the employer's stated share of incurred claims cost and retiree contributions for that year is to be recovered from increased retiree contributions in the subsequent year. The employer may subsequently determine that increasing retiree contributions for the shortfall in the prior year would be onerous and make a decision to bear the cost of the shortfall for that year. The employer's decision to bear the shortfall represents a change in intent and the resulting loss shall be recognized immediately. Future decisions by the employer to continue to bear the shortfall suggest an amendment of the substantive plan that should be accounted for as described in paragraphs 50-55.

fair value, provided the expected cash flows are discounted at a current rate commensurate with the risk involved.[21] (Refer to paragraph 71.)

66. Plan assets used in plan operations (for example, buildings, equipment, furniture and fixtures, and leasehold improvements) shall be measured at cost less accumulated depreciation or amortization for all purposes.

Insurance Contracts

67. For purposes of this Statement, an insurance contract is defined as a contract in which an insurance company unconditionally undertakes a legal obligation to provide specified benefits to specific individuals in return for a fixed consideration or premium; an insurance contract is irrevocable and involves the transfer of significant risk from the employer (or the plan) to the insurance company.[22] Benefits covered by insurance contracts shall be excluded from the accumulated postretirement benefit obligation. Insurance contracts shall be excluded from plan assets, except as provided in paragraph 69 for the cost of **participation rights.**

68. Some insurance contracts (**participating insurance contracts**) provide that the purchaser (either the plan or the employer) may participate in the experience of the insurance company. Under those contracts, the insurance company ordinarily pays dividends to the purchaser, the effect of which is to reduce the cost of the plan. If the participating insurance contract causes the employer to remain subject to all or most of the risks and rewards associated with the benefit obligation covered or the assets transferred to the insurance company, that contract is not an insurance contract for purposes of this Statement, and the purchase of that contract does not constitute a settlement pursuant to paragraphs 90-95.

69. The purchase price of a participating insurance contract ordinarily is higher than the price of an equivalent contract without a participation right. The difference is the cost of the participation right. The cost of the participation right shall be recognized at the date of purchase as an asset. In subsequent periods, the participation right shall be measured at its fair value if the contract is such that fair value is reasonably estimable. Otherwise the participation right shall be measured at its amortized cost (not in excess of its net realizable value), and the cost

shall be amortized systematically over the expected dividend period under the contract.

70. To the extent that insurance contracts are purchased during the period to cover postretirement benefits attributed to service in the current period (such as life insurance benefits), the cost of those benefits shall be the cost of purchasing the coverage under the contracts, except as provided in paragraph 69 for the cost of a participation right. If all the postretirement benefits attributed to service in the current period are covered by **nonparticipating insurance contracts** purchased during that period, the cost of the contracts determines the service cost component of net postretirement benefit cost for that period. Benefits attributed to current service in excess of benefits provided by nonparticipating insurance contracts purchased during the current period shall be accounted for according to the provisions of this Statement applicable to plans not involving insurance contracts.

71. Other contracts with insurance companies may not meet the definition of an insurance contract because the insurance company does not unconditionally undertake a legal obligation to provide specified benefits to specified individuals. Those contracts shall be accounted for as investments and measured at fair value. If a contract has a determinable cash surrender value or conversion value, that is presumed to be its fair value. For some contracts, the best available estimate of fair value may be contract value.

Measurement Date

72. The measurements of *plan assets and obligations* required by this Statement shall be as of the date of the financial statements or, if used consistently from year to year, as of a date not more than three months prior to that date. Even though the postretirement benefit measurements are required as of a particular date, all procedures are not required to be performed after that date. As with other financial statement items requiring estimates, much of the information can be prepared as of an earlier date and projected forward to account for subsequent events (for example, employee service).

73. Measurements of *net periodic postretirement benefit cost* for both interim and annual financial statements generally shall be based on the assump-

---

[21]For an indication of factors to be considered in determining the discount rate, refer to paragraphs 13 and 14 of APB Opinion No. 21, *Interest on Receivables and Payables.* If significant, the fair value of an investment shall reflect the brokerage commissions and other costs normally incurred in a sale.

[22]If the insurance company providing the contract does business primarily with the employer and related parties (a **captive insurer**) or if there is any reasonable doubt that the insurance company will meet its obligations under the contract, the contract is not an insurance contract for purposes of this Statement.

tions at the beginning of the year (assumptions used for the previous year-end measurements of plan assets and obligations) unless more recent measurements of both plan assets and the accumulated postretirement benefit obligation are available. For example, if a significant event occurs, such as a plan amendment, settlement, or curtailment, that ordinarily would call for remeasurement, the assumptions used for those later measurements shall be used to remeasure net periodic postretirement benefit cost from the date of the event to the year-end measurement date.

Disclosures

74. This Statement requires disclosures about an employer's obligation to provide postretirement benefits and the cost of providing those benefits that are intended to enhance the usefulness of the financial statements to investors, creditors, and other users of financial information. An employer sponsoring one or more defined benefit postretirement plans (refer to paragraphs 77 and 78) shall disclose, if applicable, the following information about those plans:

a. A description of the substantive plan(s) that is the basis for the accounting (refer to paragraphs 23-28), including the nature of the plan, any modifications of the existing cost-sharing provisions that are encompassed by the substantive plan(s) (refer to paragraphs 24 and 25), and the existence and nature of any commitment to increase monetary benefits provided by the postretirement benefit plan (refer to paragraph 26), employee groups covered, types of benefits provided, **funding policy,** types of assets held and significant nonbenefit liabilities, and the nature and effect of significant matters affecting the comparability of information for all periods presented, such as the effect of a business combination or divestiture

b. The amount of net periodic postretirement benefit cost showing separately the service cost component, the interest cost component, the actual return on plan assets for the period, amortization of the unrecognized transition obligation or transition asset, and the net total of other components[23]

c. A schedule reconciling the funded status of the plan(s) with amounts reported in the employer's statement of financial position, showing separately:

(1) The fair value of plan assets
(2) The accumulated postretirement benefit obligation, identifying separately the portion attributable to retirees, other fully eligible plan participants, and other active plan participants
(3) The amount of unrecognized prior service cost
(4) The amount of unrecognized net gain or loss (including plan asset gains and losses not yet reflected in market-related value)
(5) The amount of any remaining unrecognized transition obligation or transition asset
(6) The amount of net postretirement benefit asset or liability recognized in the statement of financial position, which is the net result of combining the preceding five items

d. The assumed health care cost trend rate(s) used to measure the expected cost of benefits covered by the plan (gross eligible charges) for the next year and a general description of the direction and pattern of change in the assumed trend rates thereafter, together with the ultimate trend rate(s) and when that rate is expected to be achieved

e. The weighted-average of the assumed discount rate(s) and rate(s) of compensation increase (for pay-related plans) used to measure the accumulated postretirement benefit obligation and the weighted-average of the expected long-term rate(s) of return on plan assets and, for plans whose income is segregated from the employer's investment income for tax purposes, the estimated income tax rate(s) included in that rate of return

f. The effect of a one-percentage-point increase in the assumed health care cost trend rates for each future year on (1) the aggregate of the service and interest cost components of net periodic postretirement health care benefit cost and (2) the accumulated postretirement benefit obligation for health care benefits (For purposes of this disclosure, all other assumptions shall be held constant and the effects shall be measured based on the substantive plan that is the basis for the accounting.)

g. The amounts and types of securities of the employer and related parties included in plan assets, and the approximate amount of future an-

---

[23]The net total of other components is generally the net effect during the period of certain delayed recognition provisions of this Statement. That net total includes:

a. The net asset gain or loss during the period deferred for later recognition (in effect, an offset or a supplement to the actual return on plan assets)
b. Amortization of unrecognized prior service cost
c. Amortization of the net gain or loss from earlier periods
d. Any gain or loss recognized due to a temporary deviation from the substantive plan (paragraph 61).

nual benefits of plan participants covered by insurance contracts issued by the employer and related parties

h. Any alternative amortization method used pursuant to paragraphs 53 or 60

i. The amount of gain or loss recognized during the period for a settlement or curtailment and a description of the nature of the event(s) (Refer to paragraphs 90-99.)

j. The cost of providing special or contractual termination benefits recognized during the period and a description of the nature of the event(s). (Refer to paragraphs 101 and 102.)

Employers with Two or More Plans

75. Postretirement benefits offered by an employer may vary in nature and may be provided to different groups of employees. As discussed in paragraph 76, in some cases an employer may aggregate data from unfunded plans for measurement purposes in lieu of performing separate measurements for each unfunded plan (including plans whose designated assets are not appropriately segregated and restricted and thus have no plan assets as that term is used in this Statement). Net periodic postretirement benefit cost, the accumulated postretirement benefit obligation, and plan assets shall be determined for each separately measured plan or aggregation of plans by applying the provisions of this Statement to each such plan or aggregation of plans.

76. The data from all unfunded postretirement health care plans may be aggregated for measurement purposes if (a) those plans provide different benefits to the same group of employees or (b) those plans provide the same benefits to different groups of employees. Data from other unfunded postretirement welfare benefit plans may be aggregated for measurement purposes in similar circumstances, such as when an employer has a variety of welfare benefit plans that provide benefits to the same group of employees. However, a plan that has plan assets (as defined herein) shall not be aggregated with other plans but shall be measured separately.

77. Disclosures for plans with plan assets in excess of the accumulated postretirement benefit obligation generally may be aggregated with disclosures for plans that have accumulated postretirement benefit obligations that exceed plan assets. However, for purposes of the disclosures required by paragraph 74(c), the aggregate plan assets and the aggregate accumulated postretirement benefit obligation of the underfunded plans shall be separately disclosed. Otherwise, except as described in paragraph 78, the disclosures required by this Statement may be aggregated for all of an employ-

er's single-employer defined benefit plans, or plans may be disaggregated in groups to provide more useful information.

78. The disclosures required by this Statement shall be presented separately for the following:

a. Plans that provide primarily postretirement health care benefits and plans that provide primarily other postretirement welfare benefits if the accumulated postretirement benefit obligation of the latter plans is significant relative to the aggregate accumulated postretirement benefit obligation for all of the plans

b. Plans inside the United States and plans outside the United States if the accumulated postretirement benefit obligation of the latter plans is significant relative to the aggregate accumulated postretirement benefit obligation for all of the plans.

Multiemployer Plans

79. For purposes of this Statement, a **multiemployer plan** is a postretirement benefit plan to which two or more unrelated employers contribute, usually pursuant to one or more collective-bargaining agreements. A characteristic of multiemployer plans is that assets contributed by one participating employer may be used to provide benefits to employees of other participating employers since assets contributed by an employer are not segregated in a separate account or restricted to provide benefits only to employees of that employer.

80. A multiemployer plan usually is administered by a board of trustees composed of management and labor representatives and may also be referred to as a "joint trust" or "union plan." Generally, many employers participate in a multiemployer plan, and an employer may participate in more than one plan. The employers participating in multiemployer plans usually have a common industry bond, but for some plans the employers are in different industries, and the labor union may be their only common bond. Some multiemployer plans do not involve a union. For example, local chapters of a not-for-profit organization may participate in a plan established by the related national organization.

81. An employer participating in a multiemployer plan shall recognize as net postretirement benefit cost the required contribution for the period, which shall include both cash and the fair market value of noncash contributions, and shall recognize as a liability any unpaid contributions required for the period.

82. An employer that participates in one or more

multiemployer plans shall disclose the following separately from disclosures for a single-employer plan:

a. A description of the multiemployer plan(s) including the employee groups covered, the type of benefits provided (defined benefits or defined contribution), and the nature and effect of significant matters affecting comparability of information for all periods presented
b. The amount of postretirement benefit cost recognized during the period, if available. Otherwise, the amount of the aggregate required contribution for the period to the general health and welfare benefit plan that provides health and welfare benefits to both active employees and retirees shall be disclosed.

83. In some situations, withdrawal from a multiemployer plan may result in an employer's having an obligation to the plan for a portion of the plan's unfunded accumulated postretirement benefit obligation. If it is either probable or reasonably possible that (a) an employer would withdraw from the plan under circumstances that would give rise to an obligation or (b) an employer's contribution to the fund would be increased during the remainder of the contract period to make up a shortfall in the funds necessary to maintain the negotiated level of benefit coverage (a "maintenance of benefits" clause), the employer shall apply the provisions of FASB Statement No. 5, *Accounting for Contingencies.*

Multiple-Employer Plans

84. Some postretirement benefit plans to which two or more unrelated employers contribute are not multiemployer plans. Rather, those **multiple-employer plans** are in substance aggregations of single-employer plans, combined to allow participating employers to pool plan assets for investment purposes or to reduce the costs of plan administration. Those plans ordinarily do not involve collective-bargaining agreements. They may also have features that allow participating employers to have different benefit formulas, with the employer's contributions to the plan based on the benefit formula selected by the employer. Those plans shall be considered single-employer plans rather than multiemployer plans for purposes of this Statement, and each employer's accounting shall be based on its respective interest in the plan.

Postretirement Benefit Plans outside the United States

85. Except for its effective date (paragraph 108), this Statement includes no special provisions applicable to postretirement benefit arrangements outside the United States. Those arrangements are subject to the provisions of this Statement for purposes of preparing financial statements in accordance with accounting principles generally accepted in the United States. The applicability of this Statement to those arrangements is determined by the nature of the obligation and by the terms or conditions that define the amount of benefits to be paid, not by whether or how a plan is funded, whether benefits are payable at intervals or as a single amount, or whether the benefits are required by law or custom or are provided under a plan the employer has elected to sponsor.

Business Combinations

86. When an employer is acquired in a business combination that is accounted for by the purchase method under Opinion 16 and that employer sponsors a single-employer defined benefit postretirement plan, the assignment of the purchase price to individual assets acquired and liabilities assumed shall include a liability for the accumulated postretirement benefit obligation in excess of the fair value of the plan assets or an asset for the fair value of the plan assets in excess of the accumulated postretirement benefit obligation. The accumulated postretirement benefit obligation assumed shall be measured based on the benefits attributed by the acquired entity to employee service prior to the date the business combination is consummated, adjusted to reflect (a) any changes in assumptions based on the purchaser's assessment of relevant future events (as discussed in paragraphs 23-42) and (b) the terms of the substantive plan (as discussed in paragraphs 23-28) to be provided by the purchaser to the extent they differ from the terms of the acquired entity's substantive plan.

87. If the postretirement benefit plan of the acquired entity is amended as a condition of the business combination (for example, if the change is required by the seller as part of the consummation of the acquisition), the effects of any improvements attributed to services rendered by the participants of the acquired entity's plan prior to the date of the business combination shall be accounted for as part of the accumulated postretirement benefit obligation of the acquired entity. Otherwise, if improvements to the postretirement benefit plan of the acquired entity are not a condition of the business combination, credit granted for prior service shall be recognized as a plan amendment as discussed in paragraphs 50-55. If it is expected that the plan will be terminated or curtailed, the effects of those actions shall be considered in measuring the accumulated postretirement benefit obligation. Otherwise, no future changes to the plan shall be anticipated.

88. As a result of applying the provisions of para-

graphs 86 and 87, any previously existing unrecognized net gain or loss, unrecognized prior service cost, or unrecognized transition obligation or transition asset is eliminated for the acquired employer's plan. Subsequently, to the extent that the net obligation assumed or net assets acquired are considered in determining the amounts of contributions to the plan, differences between the purchaser's net periodic postretirement benefit cost and amounts it contributes will reduce the liability or asset recognized at the date of the combination.

Amendment to Opinion 16

89. The following footnote is added to the end of the last sentence of paragraph 88 of Opinion 16:

> *Paragraphs 86-88 of FASB Statement No. 106, *Employers' Accounting for Postretirement Benefits Other Than Pensions,* specify how the general guidelines of this paragraph shall be applied to assets and liabilities related to plans that provide postretirement benefits other than pensions.

Accounting for Settlement of a Postretirement Benefit Obligation

90. For purposes of this Statement, a settlement is defined as a transaction that (a) is an irrevocable action, (b) relieves the employer (or the plan) of primary responsibility for a postretirement benefit obligation, and (c) eliminates significant risks related to the obligation and the assets used to effect the settlement.[24] Examples of transactions that constitute a settlement include making lump-sum cash payments to plan participants in exchange for their rights to receive specified postretirement benefits and purchasing long-term nonparticipating insurance contracts for the accumulated postretirement benefit obligation for some or all of the plan participants.

91. A transaction that does not meet the three criteria of paragraph 90 does not constitute a settlement for purposes of this Statement. For example, investing in a portfolio of high-quality fixed-income securities with principal and interest payment dates similar to the estimated payment dates of benefits may avoid or minimize certain risks. However, that investment decision does not constitute a settlement because that decision can be reversed, and investing in that portfolio does not relieve the employer (or the plan) of primary responsibility for a postretirement benefit obligation nor does it eliminate significant risks related to that obligation.

92. For purposes of this Statement, the maximum gain or loss subject to recognition in income when a postretirement benefit obligation is settled is the unrecognized net gain or loss defined in paragraphs 56-60 plus any remaining unrecognized transition asset. That maximum gain or loss includes any gain or loss resulting from remeasurements of plan assets and the accumulated postretirement benefit obligation at the time of settlement.

93. If the entire accumulated postretirement benefit obligation is settled and the maximum amount subject to recognition is a gain, the settlement gain shall first reduce any remaining unrecognized transition obligation;[25] any excess gain shall be recognized in income.[26] If the entire accumulated postretirement benefit obligation is settled and the maximum amount subject to recognition is a loss, the maximum settlement loss shall be recognized in income. If only part of the accumulated postretirement benefit obligation is settled, the employer shall recognize in income the excess of the pro rata portion (equal to the percentage reduction in the accumulated postretirement benefit obligation) of the maximum settlement gain over any remaining unrecognized transition obligation or a pro rata portion of the maximum settlement loss.

94. If the purchase of a participating insurance contract constitutes a settlement (refer to paragraphs 67 and 90), the maximum gain (but not the maximum loss) shall be reduced by the cost of the participation right before determining the amount to be recognized in income.

---

[24]If an insurance contract is purchased from an insurance company controlled by the employer, the purchase of the contract does not constitute a settlement.

[25]As discussed in paragraph 112, in measuring the gain or loss subject to recognition in income when a postretirement benefit obligation is settled, it shall first be determined whether recognition of an additional amount of any unrecognized transition obligation is required.

[26]Because the plan is the unit of accounting, the determination of the effects of a settlement considers only the unrecognized net gain or loss and unrecognized transition obligation or asset related to the plan for which all or a portion of the accumulated postretirement benefit obligation is being settled.

95. If the cost of all settlements[27] in a year is less than or equal to the sum of the service cost and interest cost components of net postretirement benefit cost for the plan for the year, gain or loss recognition is permitted but not required for those settlements. However, the accounting policy adopted shall be applied consistently from year to year.

Accounting for a Plan Curtailment

96. For purposes of this Statement, a curtailment is an event that significantly reduces the expected years of future service of active plan participants or eliminates the accrual of defined benefits for some or all of the future services of a significant number of active plan participants. Curtailments include:

a. Termination of employees' services earlier than expected, which may or may not involve closing a facility or discontinuing a segment of a business
b. Termination or suspension of a plan so that employees do not earn additional benefits for future service. In the latter situation, future service may be counted toward eligibility for benefits accumulated based on past service.

97. The unrecognized prior service cost associated with the portion of the future years of service that had been expected to be rendered, but as a result of a curtailment are no longer expected to be rendered, is a loss. For purposes of measuring the effect of a curtailment, unrecognized prior service cost includes the cost of plan amendments and any remaining unrecognized transition obligation. For example, a curtailment may result from the termination of a significant number of employees who were plan participants at the date of a prior plan amendment.[28] The loss associated with that curtailment is measured as (a) the portion of the remaining unrecognized prior service cost related to that (and any prior) plan amendment attributable to the previously expected remaining future years of service of the employees who were terminated and (b) the portion of the remaining unrecognized transition obligation attributable to the previously

expected remaining future years of service of the terminated employees who were plan participants at the date of transition.

98. The accumulated postretirement benefit obligation may be decreased (a gain) or increased (a loss) by a curtailment.[29] That (gain) loss shall reduce any unrecognized net loss (gain).

a. To the extent that such a gain exceeds any unrecognized net loss (or the entire gain, if an unrecognized net gain exists), it is a curtailment gain.
b. To the extent that such a loss exceeds any unrecognized net gain (or the entire loss, if an unrecognized net loss exists), it is a curtailment loss.

For purposes of applying the provisions of this paragraph, any remaining unrecognized transition asset shall be treated as an unrecognized net gain and shall be combined with the unrecognized net gain or loss arising subsequent to transition to this Statement.

99. If the sum of the effects identified in paragraphs 97 and 98 is a net loss, it shall be recognized in income when it is probable that a curtailment will occur and the net effect is reasonably estimable. If the sum of those effects is a net gain, it shall be recognized in income when the related employees terminate or the plan suspension or amendment is adopted.

Relationship of Settlements and Curtailments to Other Events

100. A settlement and a curtailment may occur separately or together. If benefits expected to be paid in future periods are eliminated for some plan participants (for example, because a significant portion of the work force is dismissed or a plant is closed) but the plan remains in existence and continues to pay benefits, to invest assets, and to receive contributions, a curtailment has occurred but not a settlement. If an employer purchases nonparticipating insurance contracts for the accumulated postretirement benefit obligation and continues to

---

[27]For the following types of settlements, the cost of the settlement is:

a. For a cash settlement, the amount of cash paid to plan participants
b. For a settlement using nonparticipating insurance contracts, the cost of the contracts
c. For a settlement using participating insurance contracts, the cost of the contracts less the amount attributed to participation rights. (Refer to paragraphs 68 and 69.)

[28]A curtailment also may result from terminating the accrual of additional benefits for the future services of a significant number of employees. The loss in that situation is (a) a proportionate amount of the remaining unrecognized prior service cost based on the portion of the remaining expected years of service in the amortization period that originally was attributable to those employees who were plan participants at the date of the plan amendment and whose future accrual of benefits has been terminated and (b) a proportionate amount of the remaining unrecognized transition obligation based on the portion of the remaining years of service of all participants active at the date of transition that originally was attributable to the remaining expected future years of service of the employees whose future accrual of benefits has been terminated.

[29]Increases in the accumulated postretirement benefit obligation that reflect termination benefits are excluded from the scope of this paragraph. (Refer to paragraphs 101 and 102.)

provide defined benefits for future service, either in the same plan or in a successor plan, a settlement has occurred but not a curtailment. If a **plan termination** occurs (that is, the obligation is settled and the plan ceases to exist) and the plan is not replaced by a successor defined benefit plan, both a settlement and a curtailment have occurred (whether or not the employees continue to work for the employer).

Measurement of the Effects of Termination Benefits

101. Postretirement benefits offered as special or contractual termination benefits shall be recognized in accordance with paragraph 15 of Statement 88. That is, an employer that offers special termination benefits to employees shall recognize a liability and a loss when the employees accept the offer and the amount can be reasonably estimated. An employer that provides contractual termination benefits shall recognize a liability and a loss when it is probable that employees will be entitled to benefits and the amount can be reasonably estimated. A situation involving special or contractual termination benefits may also result in a curtailment to be accounted for under paragraphs 96-99 of this Statement.

102. The liability and loss recognized for employees who accept an offer of special termination benefits to be provided by a postretirement benefit plan shall be the difference between (a) the accumulated postretirement benefit obligation for those employees, assuming that those employees (active plan participants) not yet fully eligible for benefits would terminate at their full eligibility date and that fully eligible plan participants would retire immediately, without considering any special termination benefits and (b) the accumulated postretirement benefit obligation as measured in (a) adjusted to reflect the special termination benefits.

Disposal of a Segment

103. If the gain or loss measured in accordance with paragraphs 92-94, 97-99, or 101 and 102 is directly related to disposal of a segment of a business or a portion of a line of business, it shall be included in determining the gain or loss associated with that event. The net gain or loss attributable to the disposal shall be recognized pursuant to the requirements of APB Opinion No. 30, *Reporting the Results of Operations—Reporting the Effects of Disposal of a Segment of a Business, and Extraor-*

dinary, Unusual and Infrequently Occurring Events and Transactions.

Defined Contribution Plans

104. For purposes of this Statement, a **defined contribution postretirement plan** is a plan that provides postretirement benefits in return for services rendered, provides *an individual account* for each participant, and has terms that specify how contributions to the individual's account are to be determined rather than the amount of postretirement benefits the individual is to receive.[30] Under a defined contribution plan, the postretirement benefits a plan participant will receive are limited to the amount contributed to the plan participant's account, the returns earned on investments of those contributions, and forfeitures of other plan participants' benefits that may be allocated to the plan participant's account.

105. To the extent a plan's defined contributions to an individual's account are to be made for periods in which that individual renders services, the net postretirement benefit cost for a period shall be the contribution called for in that period. If a plan calls for contributions for periods after an individual retires or terminates, the estimated cost shall be accrued during the employee's service period.

106. An employer that sponsors one or more defined contribution plans shall disclose the following separately from its defined benefit plan disclosures:

a. A description of the plan(s) including employee groups covered, the basis for determining contributions, and the nature and effect of significant matters affecting comparability of information for all periods presented
b. The amount of cost recognized during the period.

107. A postretirement benefit plan having characteristics of both a defined benefit plan and a defined contribution plan requires careful analysis. If the *substance* of the plan is to provide a defined benefit, as may be the case with some "target benefit" plans, the accounting and disclosure requirements shall be determined in accordance with the provisions of this Statement applicable to a defined benefit plan.

Effective Dates and Transition

108. Except as noted in the following sentences of this paragraph and in paragraphs 114 and 115, this

---

[30]For example, an employer may establish individual postretirement health care accounts for each employee, each year contributing a specified amount to each active employee's account. The balance in each employee's account may be used by that employee after the employee's retirement to purchase health care insurance or for other health care benefits. Rather than providing for defined health care benefits, the employer is providing a defined amount of money that may be used by retirees toward the payment of their health care costs.

Statement shall be effective for fiscal years beginning after December 15, 1992. For plans outside the United States and for defined benefit plans of employers that (a) are **nonpublic enterprises** and (b) sponsor defined benefit postretirement plan(s) with no more than 500 plan participants in the aggregate, this Statement shall be effective for fiscal years beginning after December 15, 1994. Earlier application is encouraged. Restatement of previously issued annual financial statements is not permitted. If a decision is made in other than the first interim period of an employer's fiscal year to apply this Statement early, previous interim periods of that year shall be restated.

109. If at the transition date an employer has excluded assets in a **postretirement benefit fund** from its statement of financial position and some or all of the assets in that fund do not qualify as plan assets as defined herein, the employer shall recognize in the statement of financial position the fair value of those nonqualifying assets as the employer's assets (not prepaid postretirement benefit cost) and an equal amount as an accrued postretirement benefit obligation pursuant to the transition to this Statement and before applying paragraph 110. Thereafter, those assets shall be accounted for in accordance with generally accepted accounting principles applicable to those types of assets, including their presentation in the employer's statement of financial position based on any restrictions on their use. The fair value of those assets at the transition date shall be used as their cost.

110. For a defined benefit plan, an employer shall determine as of the measurement date (paragraph 72) for the beginning of the fiscal year in which this Statement is first applied (the transition date), the amounts of (a) the accumulated postretirement benefit obligation and (b) the fair value of plan assets plus any recognized accrued postretirement benefit cost or less any recognized prepaid postretirement benefit cost. The difference between those two amounts, whether it represents a transition obligation or a transition asset, may be recognized either immediately in net income of the period of the change (paragraph 111) as the effect of a change in accounting principle,[31] or on a delayed basis (paragraph 112) as a component of net periodic postretirement benefit cost. Any transition obligation related to a defined contribution plan shall be recognized in the same manner. A single method of transition shall be elected at the date this Statement is initially applied for all defined benefit and defined contribution postretirement plans.

111. If immediate recognition of the transition obligation or asset is elected, the amount attributable to the effects of a plan initiation or any benefit improvements adopted after December 21, 1990 shall be treated as unrecognized prior service cost and excluded from the transition amount immediately recognized. In addition, an employer who chooses to immediately recognize the transition obligation or asset shall, at the date of transition, adjust as necessary the accounting for purchase business combinations consummated subsequent to December 21, 1990 to include in the assignment of the purchase price to assets acquired and liabilities assumed, recognition of the difference between the accumulated postretirement benefit obligation and the fair value of the plan assets, as described in paragraphs 87 and 88. If reliable information on which to base measurement of the assumed postretirement benefit obligation as of the date the business combination is consummated is not available, the purchaser shall retroactively adjust the purchase price allocation to recognize the obligation assumed or the asset acquired, using the best information available at the date of transition to this Statement. The cumulative effect on prior periods' income of that retroactive adjustment of the purchase price allocation, for example, increased amortization of goodwill associated with the business combination, and the amortization of prior service cost related to a plan initiation or amendment adopted after December 21, 1990, shall be recognized as part of the effect of the accounting change to adopt this Statement.

112. If delayed recognition is elected, the transition obligation or asset shall be amortized on a straight-line basis over the average remaining service period of active plan participants, except that (a) if the average remaining service period is less than 20 years, the employer may elect to use a 20-year period, and (b) if all or almost all of the plan participants are inactive, the employer shall use the average remaining life expectancy period of those plan participants. However, amortization of the transition obligation shall be accelerated if the cumulative benefit payments subsequent to the transition date to all plan participants exceed the cumulative postretirement benefit cost accrued subsequent to the transition date. In that situation, an additional amount of the unrecognized transition obligation shall be recognized equal to the excess cumulative benefit payments. For purposes of applying this provision, cumulative benefit payments shall be reduced by any plan assets or any recognized accrued postretirement benefit obligation at the transition date. Payments made pursuant to a settlement, as discussed in

---

[31]The effect of the accounting change and the related income tax effect shall be presented in the statement of income between the captions "extraordinary items" and "net income." The per share information presented on the statement of income shall include the per share effect of the accounting change.

paragraphs 90-94, shall be included in the determination of cumulative benefit payments made subsequent to the transition date.

113. If at the measurement date for the beginning of an employer's fiscal year it is expected that additional recognition of any remaining unrecognized transition obligation will be required pursuant to paragraph 112, amortization of the transition obligation for interim reporting purposes shall be based on the amount expected to be amortized for the year, except for the effects of applying paragraph 112 for any settlement required to be accounted for pursuant to paragraphs 90-94. Those effects shall be recognized when the related settlement is recognized. The effects of changes during the year in the initial assessment of whether additional recognition of the unrecognized transition obligation will be required for the year shall be recognized over the remainder of the year. The amount of the unrecognized transition obligation to be recognized for a year shall be finally determined at the measurement date for the end of the year based on the constraints on delayed recognition discussed in paragraph 112; any difference between the amortization of the transition obligation recognized during interim periods and the amount required to be recognized for the year shall be recognized immediately.

Effective Date and Transition—Amendment to Opinion 12

114. Paragraph 6 and the related footnote of APB Opinion No. 12, *Omnibus Opinion—1967,* are amended effective for fiscal years beginning after March 15, 1991. The effect of the amendment on existing individual deferred compensation contracts, other than those providing postretirement health or welfare benefits, shall be recognized as the effect of a change in accounting principle in accordance with paragraphs 17-21 of APB Opinion No. 20, *Accounting Changes.* Individual deferred compensation contracts that provide postretirement health or welfare benefits shall be subject to the general transition provisions and effective dates of this Statement.

Rescission of Technical Bulletin 87-1

115. Effective with the issuance of this Statement, FASB Technical Bulletin No. 87-1, *Accounting for a Change in Method of Accounting for Certain Postretirement Benefits,* is rescinded. If a change in method of accounting for postretirement benefits is adopted subsequent to the issuance of this Statement, the new method shall comply with the provisions of this Statement.

> **The provisions of this Statement need not be applied to immaterial items.**

This Statement was adopted by the unanimous vote of the seven members of the Financial Accounting Standards Board:

Dennis R. Beresford, *Chairman*	Raymond C. Lauver	A. Clarence Sampson
Victor H. Brown	James J. Leisenring	Robert J. Swieringa
	C. Arthur Northrop	

Appendix A

BASIS FOR CONCLUSIONS

CONTENTS

Appendix A

BASIS FOR CONCLUSIONS

Introduction

116. This appendix summarizes considerations that were deemed significant by members of the Board in reaching the conclusions in this Statement. It includes reasons for accepting certain approaches and rejecting others. Individual Board members gave greater weight to some factors than to others.

117. This Statement addresses the accounting issues related to measuring and recognizing the exchange that takes place between an employer that promises to provide postretirement health care or other welfare benefits (postretirement benefits) and the employees who render services in exchange for those benefits. The Board's conclusion to recognize postretirement benefit promises on an accrual basis over employee service periods is not a new notion; rather, it is fundamental to accounting for all deferred compensation contracts.

Benefits and Costs

118. The mission of the FASB is to "establish and improve standards of financial accounting and reporting for the guidance and education of the public, including issuers, auditors, and users of financial statements" (FASB *Rules of Procedure,* page 2). In fulfilling that mission the Board follows certain precepts, including the precept to promulgate standards only when the expected benefits of the resulting information exceed the perceived costs. The Board strives to determine that a proposed standard will fill a significant need and that the costs imposed to meet that standard, as compared with other alternatives, are justified in relation to the overall benefits of the resulting information.

119. The objective, and implicit benefit, of issuing an accounting standard is the increased credibility and representational faithfulness of financial reporting as a result of the new or revised accounting. However, the value of that incremental improvement to financial reporting is impossible to quantify. Consequently, the Board's assessment of the benefit to preparers, creditors, investors, and other users of issuing an accounting standard is, unavoidably, subjective. Like the incremental benefit of issuing an accounting standard, the incremental costs imposed by a new accounting standard are diffuse. They are borne by users and attesters as well as preparers of financial statements. Some of those costs can be quantified, albeit imprecisely and with difficulty; but, most of the benefits and many of the costs of adopting a new accounting standard cannot be quantified. How does one measure the benefit of improved financial reporting? Or stated another way, how does one assess the cost of the failure to accrue an obligation?

120. FASB Concepts Statement No. 2, *Qualitative Characteristics of Accounting Information,* discusses the benefits and costs of accounting information. It states:

> The costs and benefits of a standard are both direct and indirect, immediate and deferred. They may be affected by change in circumstances not foreseen when the standard was promulgated. There are wide variations in the estimates that different people make about the dollar values involved and the rate of discount to be used in reducing them to a present value. . . . [It has been observed that] "the merits of any Standard, or of the Standards as a whole, can be decided finally only by judgments that are largely subjective. They cannot be decided by scientific test." [paragraph 142]

The Board believes those observations remain pertinent and accurately describe its process of considering benefits and costs.

121. An assessment of the benefits and costs of issuing an accounting standard is integral to the Board's decision-making process. Consideration of each individual issue includes the subjective weighing of the incremental improvement in financial reporting against the incremental cost of implementing the identified alternatives. At the end

of that process, the Board considers the accounting provisions in the aggregate and must conclude that issuance of the standard is a sufficient improvement in financial reporting to justify the perceived costs. Paragraphs 122-132 address the Board's overall assessment of possible benefits and costs. Various benefits and costs that were deemed significant in reaching the conclusions in this Statement are described in later paragraphs of this basis for conclusions.

122. The Board believes that this Statement will fill a significant need for information about the financial effects of postretirement benefits that have been exchanged for employee service. Those financial effects are currently omitted from most general-purpose financial statements. Pay-as-you-go (cash) basis accounting delays the recognition and measurement of those effects until postretirement benefits are paid; as a result, costs incurred currently are not recognized until future periods.

123. General-purpose financial statements imply completeness of information within the bounds of what is material and feasible. A material omission can rob financial statements of their credibility. Continuation of the present accounting practice for postretirement benefits would represent a material omission from the financial statements of many employers. That practice led some respondents to the February 1989 Exposure Draft, *Employers' Accounting for Postretirement Benefits Other Than Pensions,* to suggest immediate recognition of the currently existing obligation as the correction of an error.

124. This Statement fulfills a significant need for information by requiring the use of accrual accounting for postretirement benefits. Accrual accounting will more appropriately reflect the financial effects of an employer's existing promise to provide those benefits and the events that affect that promise in financial statements, as those events occur. That accounting will subject the employer's estimates and assumptions about the future events that will determine the amount and timing of future benefit payments to the discipline of accounting recognition and measurement, and to the independent review of auditors and others, thereby enhancing the utility of the information provided.

125. This Statement also fills the need for information by requiring descriptive disclosures about the postretirement benefit plan, current measures of the plan assets, obligations, and costs, and the effect on the employer's financial statements of the provisions for delayed recognition of certain events affecting those measures. Fulfilling the significant need for information comes at a cost—

namely, the incremental cost of developing, implementing, and maintaining a measurement and reporting system to support the required accrual accounting and disclosures and the cost of learning how to use the new information.

126. Many employers have not monitored and managed their postretirement benefit obligations and costs. Consequently, a significant portion of the incremental system's cost reflects costs that a prudent employer would incur in monitoring and managing the consequences of its postretirement benefit arrangement. The Board believes that those costs should be associated with the existence of those arrangements, rather than with the requirements of this Statement. The Board also believes that there will be relatively little incremental systems cost incurred to satisfy the disclosure requirements of this Statement because the necessary information already will be developed in order to meet the basic recognition and measurement requirements.

127. The incremental cost of the accounting and disclosure requirements of this Statement has been reduced by following, to a significant extent, the precedents in Statement 87 for pension accounting. Moreover, the general approach is similar in many respects to that used by consulting actuaries who have estimated postretirement benefit costs and obligations as part of special health care cost containment studies, employee termination incentive programs, restructurings, and mergers and business combinations.

128. The incremental cost of implementing the requirements of this Statement has been increased by alternative approaches that provide for the delayed recognition of employers' transition obligations and the effects of subsequent plan amendments and gains and losses. Those provisions generally increase the complexity of the requirements, reduce understandability and comparability, and create the need for additional disclosures. However, those provisions enhance the acceptability of this Statement to the extent they reflect the views of some constituents and minimize disruption.

129. This Statement provides both general objectives and provisions and detailed guidance and illustrations. Some respondents indicated that providing detailed guidance might increase the incremental cost of the requirements of this Statement. However, a lack of detailed guidance can result in incremental costs being incurred by employers, auditors, regulators, and others by implicitly requiring that they define issues, identify and debate alternatives, assess possible effects, and select and implement solutions. Those costs are often not readily apparent but, nevertheless, are sig-

nificant. Moreover, if different employers select different solutions in similar situations, with effects that are materially different, the resulting information lacks comparability, thereby reducing the benefits to investors and other users. Inevitably, critics, regulators, and other users demand elimination of alternatives, and additional costs would be incurred as those actions are taken.

130. Some believe that employers will change the designs of postretirement benefit plans or the way those plans are financed as a result of the new information about the financial effects of postretirement benefits. In addition, some believe that the new information may provide an additional impetus to federal legislation covering employers' obligations for those plans or the deductibility of employers' advance funding of those plans. Those actions, if taken, are not the direct result of a requirement to accrue postretirement benefits, but rather, may result from more relevant and useful information on which to base decisions.

131. The Board is sensitive to the consequences that are likely to occur as a result of the new information. However, the nature and extent of those consequences are highly uncertain and are difficult to isolate from the effects of other events that will occur independent of that new information. For example, the costs of providing health care benefits are significant and are increasing. Expected future changes in those costs are likely to affect the design and funding of postretirement benefit plans and federal legislation covering those plans, regardless of the issuance of this Statement.

132. Even if the Board could isolate the likely consequences of the information provided pursuant to this Statement from other events that produce change, enhancing or diminishing the possibility of those consequences is not the Board's objective. The information provided by general-purpose financial statements is a public good. That information is shared by many interested parties with disparate interests and forms the basis for contracts and for monitoring contract performance. Both the benefits and costs of the information provided pursuant to this Statement will be recognized over time and will affect many parties differently. Those parties and the contracts they enter into will benefit from more relevant and reliable information about the incidence of postretirement benefit costs. But improved financial information comes at a cost, and while some of those parties may not pay directly for the benefits they derive from that information, they are likely to bear indirectly some of its cost.

Scope

133. In considering the scope of the project, the Board discussed various benefits provided after retirement, such as postretirement health care benefits, and benefits offered after employment but before retirement, such as temporary benefits after a layoff. Postemployment benefits provided to non-retirees may have many of the same characteristics as postretirement benefits—they may be defined in kind rather than in fixed amounts and their legal status may be uncertain. However, while most postretirement benefits are provided for the lifetime of an eligible retiree and for some covered dependents, many nonretiree postemployment benefits are provided for a specified period of time, often based on years of service. But the most important difference may lie in the fundamentally different nature of the employer's promise. Nonretiree postemployment benefits are generally more like termination compensation—a payment for not working—than deferred compensation—a delayed payment of compensation for working.

134. The Board concluded that postretirement benefits, because of their prevalence and magnitude, should be addressed in the initial stages of the project. Upon completion of this first phase, the Board will consider the need to provide guidance for accounting for other benefits offered after employment but not pursuant to retirement.

135. This Statement covers all benefits, other than cash benefits and life insurance benefits paid by pension plans, provided to current or former employees, their beneficiaries, and covered dependents during the period following the employees' retirement. Benefits encompassed include, but are not limited to, postretirement health care; life insurance provided outside a pension plan; and other welfare benefits such as tuition assistance, day care, legal services, and housing subsidies provided after retirement. The Board's conclusion about accrual of an obligation over the period of employee service rendered in exchange for that benefit is applicable to all forms of compensation.

136. Health and other welfare benefits expected to be provided to employees deemed to be on a disability retirement are within the scope of this Statement. In many cases those employees will have permanently ceased active employment because of their disabilities and retired under the disability provisions of a postretirement benefit (pension) plan. In other cases those employees may have ceased permanent active employment because of their disabilities but not yet gone through formal

"retirement" procedures and are carried on nonretired status under the disability provisions of the plan solely to continue earning additional postretirement benefits such as pensions.

137. The determination of disability benefits to be accrued pursuant to this Statement is based on the terms of the postretirement benefit plan that define when a disabled employee is entitled to postretirement benefits. For example, the provisions of the postretirement health care plan may provide postretirement health care coverage after a disabled employee attains a specified number of years of credited service (which may include credit for periods after the employee is disabled), with a separate disability plan that provides health benefits prior to that date.[32] Or, the postretirement health care plan may have special provisions for disabled employees that entitle them to benefit coverage under the postretirement benefit plan at a date earlier than that coverage would commence for other employees who are not disabled. Including disability health and other welfare benefits provided to employees on a disability retirement within the scope of this Statement is consistent with past practice, most notably in the pension area. Disability benefits offered through a pension plan are covered by Statement 87 and FASB Statement No. 35, *Accounting and Reporting by Defined Benefit Pension Plans.*

138. The Board concluded that all promises to provide postretirement benefits should be accrued whether they are provided through a plan or through individual contracts. For purposes of this Statement, the Board has defined a plan as an arrangement whereby an employer undertakes to provide its employees with benefits after they retire (terminate their service after meeting specified age, service, or age and service requirements defined by the postretirement benefit plan) in exchange for their services over a specified period of time, upon attaining a specified age, or both. The amount of the benefits can be determined or estimated in advance from the provisions of a document or document ments or from the employer's current and past practices. The plan may be written or unwritten. An employer's practice of providing postretirement benefits pursuant to informal guidelines is considered to be a plan for purposes of this Statement.

139. This Statement applies to deferred compensation contracts with individual employees if those contracts, taken together, are equivalent to a postretirement benefit plan. However, an employer's practice of providing postretirement benefits to selected employees under individual contracts, with specific terms determined on an individual-by-individual basis, does not constitute a postretirement benefit plan under this Statement. This Statement amends Opinion 12 to explicitly require that the employer's obligation under those contracts be accrued following the terms of the individual contract.

Evolutionary Changes in Accounting Principles

140. The Board concluded that the changes required by this Statement represent a significant improvement in financial reporting. Paragraph 2 of FASB Concepts Statement No. 5, *Recognition and Measurement in Financial Statements of Business Enterprises,* states that "the Board intends future change [in practice] to occur in the gradual, evolutionary way that has characterized past change." The Board realizes that the evolutionary change may have to be slower in some areas than in others.

141. Some Board members believe that it would be conceptually appropriate and preferable to (a) recognize an obligation for postretirement benefits that would not be less than the vested benefit obligation,[33] (b) immediately recognize the effects of plan initiations and amendments that are retroactive, and (c) immediately recognize gains and losses, perhaps with gains and losses reported currently in comprehensive income but not in earnings. However, the Board concluded that those alternatives should not be adopted at this time. Those alternatives would be a major change from current practice and from the standards adopted by the Board for employers' accounting for pensions.

---

[32]For example, an employer may promise to provide postretirement health care coverage to all employees who render 30 or more years of service. The employer may carry active employees who become disabled on active status so a disabled employee continues to accumulate credit toward postretirement benefits. Measurement of the expected postretirement benefit obligation should include an assumption that some employees who are expected to receive benefits under the postretirement benefit plan will become disabled and cease working prior to the date at which they otherwise would have been eligible for post-retirement health care benefits. The measurement of the postretirement benefits expected to be paid to disabled employees would encompass only those benefits expected to be paid during the period following what otherwise would have been their full eligibility date; in this case, the date at which the employee would have completed 30 years of service. That amount is attributed to an employee's service to the date the disability is assumed to occur.

[33]As used herein, *vested postretirement benefit obligation* refers to the actuarial present value as of a particular date of the benefits expected to be paid to or for retirees, former employees, and active employees assuming they terminated immediately, including benefits expected to be paid to or for beneficiaries and any covered dependents of those plan participants.

Improvements in Financial Reporting

142. This Statement represents the first authoritative accounting pronouncement that requires current recognition of the exchange transaction between an employer that promises to provide postretirement benefits and the employees who render service in exchange for the benefits promised. Employers have generally recognized the obligation and related costs arising from the exchange as the obligation was satisfied rather than when it was incurred. The Board concluded that the recognition required by this Statement should result in a more meaningful representation of the employer's financial position and results of operations at any point in time.

143. Certain aspects of the delayed recognition features of this Statement cause the obligation that is recognized to differ from the current measure of the unfunded obligation attributed to service in the current and prior years. However, that current measure of the obligation and the effect of delayed recognition in deriving the amount of that obligation that has been recognized are required to be disclosed.

144. This Statement requires recognition of a service cost component of net periodic postretirement benefit cost based on the actuarial present value of the portion of the expected postretirement benefit obligation attributed to service during the period. This Statement also requires disclosure of the other compensatory and financial components of postretirement benefit cost for the period in order to reflect the employer's net cost of the benefit promise. The Board concluded that disclosure of the components should significantly assist users in understanding the economic events that have occurred. Those disclosures also make it easier to understand why reported amounts change from period to period.

145. Some respondents argued that the uncertainties inherent in quantifying the obligation for postretirement benefits lead to the conclusion that the measurements are not sufficiently reliable for recognition in financial statements. They would prefer to disclose rather than recognize that obligation and the related cost. The Board does not find those arguments persuasive. The Board concluded that it is possible for employers to produce an estimate of that obligation that is sufficiently reliable and relevant to justify recognition in financial statements. The Board expects that with experience, the reliability of the measurement will be enhanced. The Board concluded that employers' current practice of not recognizing their postretirement benefit obligations and the related costs results in less reliable

financial statements and impairs the usefulness and integrity of those financial statements.

Conclusions on Basic Issues—Single-Employer Defined Benefit Postretirement Plans

The Exchange

146. The Board's conclusions in this Statement derive from the view that a defined postretirement benefit is part of an exchange between the employer and the employee. In exchange for services provided by the employee, the employer promises to provide, in addition to current wages and other current and deferred benefits (such as a pension), health care and other welfare benefits during the employee's retirement period. Postretirement benefits are not gratuities but instead are part of an employee's compensation for services rendered. Since payment is deferred, the benefit is a type of deferred compensation. The employer's obligation for that compensation is incurred when the services exchanged for that benefit are rendered, not when an employee terminates or when a retiree receives benefits.

147. Postretirement benefits are a form of pension benefits in kind. Unlike traditional cash pension benefits, the employer promises to provide defined benefits or services as the need for those benefits or services arises or on the occurrence of a specified event. Typically, those postretirement benefits supplement cash benefits paid after retirement. Regardless of the form of the benefit—in cash or in kind—the underlying promise is the same. In exchange for service over a specified period, the employer will provide the employee and any covered dependents or beneficiaries with the defined postretirement benefits.

Funding and Accrual Accounting

148. This Statement relies on a basic premise of generally accepted accounting principles that accrual accounting provides more relevant and useful information than cash basis accounting. Accrual accounting goes beyond cash transactions and recognizes the financial effects on an entity of transactions and other events and circumstances that have future cash consequences as those events and transactions occur, rather than only when cash is received or paid by the entity. In particular, accrual accounting provides a link between an entity's operations (and other transactions, events, and circumstances that affect it) and its cash receipts and outlays. It provides information about an entity's assets and liabilities and changes in those amounts that cannot be obtained from information produced by accounting only for cash re-

ceipts and outlays. Because the Board views the event obligating the employer as the rendering of employee service in exchange for future (postretirement) benefits, this Statement rejects terminal accrual (accrual at retirement) and cash basis accounting. The Board concluded that for postretirement benefits, as in other areas, the information resulting from accrual accounting is more representationally faithful and more relevant to financial statement users than accounting information prepared solely on the basis of cash transactions.

149. This Statement reaffirms Board decisions that funding should not be used as the basis for accounting recognition of cost. However, the Board's conclusion that accounting information on an accrual basis is needed does not mean that accounting information and funding decisions are unrelated. Measurement and recognition of the accrued obligation to provide postretirement benefits will provide management and other users of financial statements with better information to assess the financial consequences of management's actions. That information about the postretirement benefit obligation will be a factor in determining the amount and timing of future contributions to the plan.

150. The decision of how or when to fund the obligation is not an accounting issue. It is a financing decision that is properly influenced by many factors (such as tax considerations and the availability of attractive investment alternatives) that are unrelated to how or when the postretirement benefit obligation is incurred. The amount funded (however determined) is, of course, given accounting recognition as a use of cash, but the Board concluded that this is one of many areas in which information about cash flows alone is not sufficient.

The Principal Issues

151. Among the many issues considered by the Board in this project, three stand out as central to the Board's extensive deliberations and to public debate. Those issues are (a) whether a postretirement benefit plan results in an obligation that meets the definition of a liability, (b) how and when the obligation and related cost should be measured and recognized, and (c) how and when any net obligation or net asset that exists when this Statement is first applied should be measured and recognized.

The liability

152. Liabilities are defined in paragraph 35 of FASB Concepts Statement No. 6, *Elements of Financial Statements,* as "probable future sacrifices of economic benefits arising from present obliga-

tions of a particular entity to transfer assets or provide services to other entities in the future as a result of past transactions or events" (footnote references omitted). Liabilities reflect the residual of certain transactions or events affecting an entity. For example, a liability for postretirement benefits reflects the interrelationship of the cumulative cost to an employer of an exchange transaction and the ultimate payment of benefits to the [former] employees—the other party to the exchange transaction.

153. The first characteristic of a liability is that it "embodies a present duty or responsibility to one or more entities that entails settlement by probable future transfer or use of assets at a specified or determinable date, on occurrence of a specified event, or on demand" (Concepts Statement 6, paragraph 36). The employer has a duty or requirement to sacrifice assets in the future—the essence of the first characteristic of a liability. That duty exists even though a benefit obligation may be satisfied by providing goods and services rather than cash and the amount and timing of the benefit payments are estimated.

154. An employer that promises to provide postretirement benefits almost certainly has assumed a responsibility to make future payments because at least some of the present employees will receive those benefits in the future. Measurement of the postretirement benefit obligation considers the likelihood that some employees will work to or beyond the date eligibility for some or all of the postretirement benefits is attained, while others will terminate prior to that date and forego any right to postretirement benefits.

155. The second characteristic of a liability is that "the duty or responsibility obligates a particular entity, leaving it little or no discretion to avoid the future sacrifice" (Concepts Statement 6, paragraph 36). Paragraph 36 also states that ". . . although most liabilities rest generally on a foundation of legal rights and duties, existence of a legally enforceable claim is not a prerequisite for an obligation to qualify as a liability if for other reasons the entity has the duty or responsibility to pay cash, to transfer other assets, or to provide services to another entity." Some respondents indicated that postretirement benefits do not meet this characteristic of a liability and consequently, in their view, need not be recognized. Some of those respondents argued that only legally enforceable claims should be reported as liabilities. Others noted that most employers have retained the right to terminate or amend their postretirement benefit promises and therefore believe those employers can avoid the obligation at their discretion.

156. Case law has not been unequivocal about the le-

gal enforceability or lack thereof of promises to provide postretirement benefits, although legal enforceability of certain claims has been demonstrated. However, in accordance with Concepts Statement 6, the Board has looked beyond the legal status of the promise to consider whether the liability is effectively binding on the employer because of past practices, social or moral sanctions, or customs.

157. An entity is not obligated to sacrifice assets in the future if it can avoid the future sacrifice at its discretion without significant penalty. The penalty to the employer need not be in the form of another liability but could be in the form of a reduction in the value of assets. Concepts Statement 6, paragraph 203, illustrates that notion as follows: "The example of an entity that binds itself to pay employees vacation pay or year-end bonuses by paying them every year even though it is not contractually bound to do so and has not announced a policy to do so has already been noted. . . . It could refuse to pay only by risking substantial employee-relations problems." As a practical matter, it is unlikely that an employer could terminate its existing obligations under a postretirement benefit plan without incurring some cost. Therefore, the Board concluded that in the absence of evidence to the contrary, an employer is presumed to have accepted responsibility to provide the promised benefits. Consequently, the accounting for postretirement benefit arrangements generally is based on the presumption that the plan will continue and that the benefits promised by the employer will be provided.

158. The third characteristic of a liability is that "the transaction or other event obligating the entity has already happened" (Concepts Statement 6, paragraph 36). This characteristic is met when the employee renders service in exchange for the future benefits. The Board concluded that, conceptually, compensation cost should be recognized in the period in which it is earned under the plan—that is, when the employee renders the required service, not when the need for the benefit arises (which is factored into measurement of the obligation). An objective of this Statement is to recognize the compensation cost of an employee's postretirement benefits over the employee's credited service period, even though the complexity of the postretirement benefit arrangement and the uncertainty of the amount and timing of the future payments may preclude complete recognition of the precise postretirement benefit cost and obligation over that period.

Criteria for recognition

159. Paragraph 63 of Concepts Statement 5, states that an item should be recognized when four fundamental recognition criteria are met:

> *Definitions*—The item meets the definition of an element of financial statements.
> *Measurability*—It has a relevant attribute measurable with sufficient reliability.
> *Relevance*—The information about it is capable of making a difference in user decisions.
> *Reliability*—The information is representationally faithful, verifiable, and neutral.

160. Most respondents indicated that employee service pursuant to a postretirement benefit plan creates an obligation that meets the definition of a liability. Some of those respondents expressed concerns about an employer's ability to measure its obligation with sufficient reliability, while others questioned whether the costs outweigh the benefits of recognizing the liability and the related cost in the financial statements. However, a majority of the respondents supported recognizing an obligation for postretirement benefits. They indicated that reasonable estimates of the measure of an employer's postretirement benefit obligation can be developed and that recognition of a liability based on that best estimate is preferable to no recognition or to footnote disclosure in lieu of recognition.

161. Paragraph 46 of Concepts Statement 6 acknowledges that the effects of economic events are often uncertain and that the existence and amount of items need not be certain for them to qualify as assets and liabilities. Estimates and approximations are commonplace in financial statements. Paragraph 74 of Concepts Statement 5 states that "relevance should be evaluated in the context of the principal objective of financial reporting: providing information that is useful in making rational investment, credit, and similar decisions." Paragraph 59 of Concepts Statement 2 states that the reliability of a measurement of accounting information is dependent on the extent to which users can depend on it to represent the economic conditions or events that it purports to represent. That concepts Statement acknowledges that that is seldom a clear choice; rather, the issue is whether the accounting information is so relevant that some allowance ought to be made for some lack of reliability because the information provides a better representation of economic conditions than would be portrayed without the information.

162. Reliability may affect the timing of recognition. Paragraphs 76 and 77 of Concepts Statement 5 state:

> Information about some items that meet a definition may never become sufficiently reliable at a justifiable cost to recognize the item. For other items, those uncertainties

are reduced as time passes, and reliability is increased as additional information becomes available.

. . . waiting for virtually complete reliability or minimum cost may make the information so untimely that it loses its relevance. At some intermediate point, uncertainty may be reduced at a justifiable cost to a level tolerable in view of the perceived relevance of the information.

163. The Board concluded that the obligation to provide postretirement benefits meets the definition of a liability (paragraphs 152-158), is representationally faithful, is relevant to financial statement users, and can be measured with sufficient reliability at a justifiable cost. To imply by a failure to accrue that no obligation exists prior to the payment of benefits is not a faithful representation of what the financial statements purport to represent. The Board concluded that failure to recognize the existence of the obligation significantly impairs the usefulness and credibility of the employer's financial statements.

Recognition versus disclosure

164. Some respondents agreed that better information about the cost of and obligation for postretirement benefits is needed but argued that the information would be just as useful if it were disclosed in the footnotes. In the Board's view, it is important that elements that qualify for recognition be recognized in the basic financial statements. Footnote disclosure is not an adequate substitute for recognition. The argument that the information is equally useful regardless of how it is presented could be applied to any financial statement element. The usefulness and integrity of financial statements are impaired by each omission of an element that qualifies for recognition. The incremental systems cost of recognition is insignificant. All of the costs of measuring the postretirement benefit obligation would be incurred to provide useful disclosures.

165. If disclosures and recognition are equally useful, then any asset or liability, or revenue or expense, could be reported with equal effect in either manner. Few would argue that disclosure is an alternative to recognition when discussing an entity's trade payables or cost of sales. If one accepts the view that an employer has a liability and cost for postretirement benefits exchanged for employees' current and past services, there is no substantive difference between postretirement benefits and other costs and liabilities other than the difficulty of measurement and the longer period of time over which the liability is paid. Although the "equal usefulness" argument may be valid for some so-

phisticated users, it may not hold for all or even most users. Those who assert that footnote disclosure or recognition would be equally useful, but argue only for disclosure, must believe that recognition and disclosure have different consequences.

Measurement of cost and obligations

166. The Board believes that the understandability, comparability, and usefulness of financial information are improved by narrowing the use of alternative accounting methods that do not reflect different facts and circumstances. Consequently, the Board has attempted to improve financial reporting by accounting for similar transactions similarly and by measuring enterprises' resources and claims to or interest in those resources on similar bases. Any method of accounting for postretirement benefits that recognizes the expected future cost during the service period must deal with two problems that stem from the nature of the arrangement. First, estimates or assumptions must be made about the future events that will determine the amount and timing of the benefit payments. Second, an approach must be selected for attributing the cost of those benefits to individual years of service.

167. The Board recognizes that uncertainty in measuring the benefit obligation for a single employee is greater than for a group because the future events that affect the amount and timing of future benefits, such as retirement date and life expectancy, can be more reliably estimated on a group basis. However, that uncertainty does not change the nature of the promise. Actuarial computations consider that some existing or future retirees will live longer than others and that some individuals will terminate employment before becoming eligible for the benefits or die before receiving any benefits. Those factors are appropriately considered in measuring the probable future sacrifice that will result from the present existing promise of benefits to former and current employees.

168. This Statement uses the term *expected postretirement benefit obligation* (a term not used in Statement 87) to describe the obligation for benefits expected to be received by plan participants. The expected postretirement benefit obligation is used as the basis for determining the benefit cost to be attributed to credited years of service. The term *accumulated postretirement benefit obligation* is used to describe the portion of the expected postretirement benefit obligation attributed to service to a measurement date. Since measurement of the expected postretirement benefit obligation includes an assumed salary progression for a pay-related plan, salary progression is, by definition, included in the accumulated benefit obligation for a pay-related postretirement benefit plan. Thus, the ac-

cumulated postretirement benefit obligation disclosed pursuant to this Statement is defined in terms notionally more comparable to the projected benefit obligation under Statement 87.

169. Since the accumulated benefit obligation defined by Statement 87 excludes assumed salary progression, the accumulated benefit obligation for a pay-related pension plan has no counterpart in this Statement. The Board concluded that it would be more confusing to define an additional measure of a benefit obligation, in addition to the expected and accumulated postretirement benefit obligations, under this Statement to compare with the accumulated benefit obligation for pay-related plans under Statement 87 than to measure the accumulated benefit obligation for those plans differently under the two Statements.

170. Despite that difference in the definition of the accumulated benefit obligation for a postretirement benefit plan and for a pension plan, service cost and interest cost are defined and measured in a similar fashion under both this Statement and Statement 87. Service cost under both Statements is the actuarial present value of benefits attributed to services rendered by plan participants during the period and includes consideration of salary progression for pay-related plans. Interest cost under this Statement is defined as the increase in the *accumulated* postretirement benefit obligation to recognize the effects of the passage of time; under Statement 87 interest cost is defined as the increase in the *projected* benefit obligation to recognize the effects of the passage of time.

171. In considering postretirement benefit plans, neither respondents nor the Board was able to identify fundamentally different circumstances that would make it appropriate for different employers to adopt different accounting methods or measurement techniques for similar plans or for a single employer to adopt different methods or measurement techniques for different plans. As a result, a single method is prescribed for measuring and recognizing an employer's obligation and the related net periodic cost. That method attributes the expected postretirement benefit obligation to employee service rendered to the date full eligibility for the postretirement benefits is attained. The method is intended to improve comparability and understandability of employers' financial statements in reporting the financial consequences of providing postretirement benefits. It generally is also consistent with accounting for other forms of deferred compensation earned by employees that are paid during retirement, such as pensions.

Accounting for the substantive plan

172. Many respondents to the Exposure Draft observed that employers' postretirement benefit promises (particularly for health care benefits) are evolving. They stated that employers will change their promises in reaction to expected future health care costs. They believe that because future costs are considered in postretirement benefit measurements, employers should be permitted to anticipate the changes to the plan that the employer would be likely to make in reaction to the expected future cost of the benefits currently covered by the plan. Some respondents suggested that a designated health care cost trend rate, such as the general inflation rate, be used to consider implicitly the future actions employers might take to control their postretirement health care costs. Other respondents suggested the use of more explicit approaches that would anticipate future plan amendments if certain conditions were met.

173. In response to those suggestions, the Board considered whether there are situations in which future plan changes should be anticipated for measurement purposes. Board members generally believed that when an employer has a present commitment to amend the plan, the extant written plan, amended to reflect that commitment, should be the basis for the accounting. The Board believed that evidence of an employer's commitment to amend the plan should include an employer's past practices of amending the plan, identification of strategies to effect future changes, and the assessment of the feasibility and likelihood of making those changes in light of the expected economic and social costs. Because the transaction that is the basis for the accounting is the result of an exchange between an employer and its employees, Board members believed that the substantive plan that is the basis for the accounting should be communicated to and understood by the plan participants as representing that exchange agreement.

174. Some Board members supported permitting the anticipation of changes, including changes in a plan's covered benefits, if certain conditions were met. The Board noted, however, that unlike changes in cost-sharing provisions, there would be no past practice of changing covered benefits that could be considered representative of the substantive plan. Once a benefit is eliminated, it cannot be eliminated again. In addition, given a choice of benefit changes that might occur, it is unlikely that employers could determine which would be most likely to occur. And, since different health care benefits may have different assumed health care

cost trend rates, the inability to determine the most likely change in the covered benefits would affect an employer's ability to measure its expected postretirement benefit obligation. The Board noted that those measurement concerns do not arise when benefits are defined solely in terms of monetary amounts. The Board concluded that changes in in-kind benefits covered by a postretirement health care plan or by other postretirement benefit plans should not be anticipated. The Board noted, however, that if an employer amends the benefits to be provided by the plan, the effect of the amendment is recognized immediately in measuring the employer's expected and accumulated postretirement benefit obligations, even if the effective date of the change in benefits is delayed until a specified date in the future.

175. Some Board members do not favor anticipating any future plan changes for purposes of measuring and recognizing an employer's postretirement benefit obligations. They note that financial statements are intended to present the financial effects of events and transactions that have already happened. In their view, future actions that change the promise should be recognized when the change occurs; to anticipate future changes is not a representationally faithful portrayal of the employer's current obligation. Therefore, they believe the obligation and cost to provide postretirement benefits should be measured as defined by the plan at the measurement date. Further, they believe the criteria to limit those plan changes that may be anticipated will prove to be unworkable, just as other attempts to account for management's intent have been unworkable. Other Board members believe that a plan's existing terms do not necessarily establish the substance of the current or past exchange transaction and therefore may not always provide the best basis for measuring an employer's current obligation.

176. The Board concluded that measures of an employer's postretirement benefit obligations should reflect the terms of the exchange transaction understood by an employer and its employees. To the extent that an employer has a past practice of maintaining a consistent level of cost sharing or consistently increasing or reducing the cost-sharing provisions of the plan that reflects the employer's cost-sharing policy, without offsetting identifiable changes in other benefits or compensation or other significant costs, that policy represents the substantive terms of the exchange transaction. Such a past practice would be indicated when the nature of the change and duration of the past practice are sufficient to warrant a presumption that it is understood by the plan participants. Similarly, if an employer has communicated its intent to institute different cost-sharing provisions of the plan at a specified time or when specified conditions are met and those changes are likely to occur without adverse consequences to the employer's operations or offsetting changes in the plan participants' other benefits, those changes should be anticipated. The Board notes, however, that in most cases collectively bargained plans will be unable to anticipate plan changes because the employer does not have the unilateral ability to amend the plan and would most likely be unable to demonstrate a consistent past practice of cost-sharing changes without offsetting changes in other benefits. For that reason, some Board members believe there should be no possibility of an exception.

Contributory plans

177. Some employers may require that active employees contribute toward the cost of their postretirement benefits. Those contributions may be adjusted throughout the service period and may vary depending on the number of an employee's dependents. In addition, postretirement benefit plans may have cost-sharing provisions that require retired employees to share a portion of the cost of the benefits through contributions, copayment provisions, or deductibles. Because an employer's postretirement benefit obligation is measured as of a defined measurement date, the Exposure Draft proposed that for purposes of measuring the expected postretirement benefit obligation, employee contributions or cost-sharing provisions should be assumed using the rates or provisions required by the current plan benefit formula. Unless an employer had a history of regular increases in benefits indicative of a commitment to make future improvements to the plan, anticipating future changes to the plan would have been precluded for purposes of measuring the expected postretirement benefit obligation and net periodic postretirement benefit cost.

178. Contributions expected to be received from active employees toward the cost of their postretirement benefits and from retired plan participants are treated similarly for purposes of measuring an employer's expected postretirement benefit obligation. An employer's obligation to return contributions received from employees who do not attain eligibility for postretirement benefits, and, if applicable, any interest accrued on those contributions, should be recognized as a component of an employer's postretirement benefit obligation. Thus, an employer's statement of financial position should reflect an accrued obligation for postretirement benefits that includes (a) the accrued obligation to provide benefits to plan participants who are eligible for benefits or are expected to become eligible for benefits under the postretirement benefit plan and (b) the obligation to return accumulated contributions, plus any

interest thereon, to employees who are expected to terminate without attaining eligibility for the postretirement benefits.

Assumptions

179. Measurements of the actuarial present value of the expected and accumulated postretirement benefit obligations require actuarial assumptions. Those assumptions include discount rates, retirement age, the timing and amount of future benefits (which for postretirement health care benefits consider past and present per capita claims cost, health care cost trend rates, and medical coverage by governmental authorities and other providers of health care benefits), and the probability of payment (turnover, dependency status, mortality, and so forth). Measurement of the expected postretirement benefit obligation and the accumulated postretirement benefit obligation also considers salary progression when applicable. Many of the assumptions used in postretirement benefit measurements are similar to assumptions used in pension measurements.

180. This Statement requires that each significant assumption reflect the best estimate of the plan's future experience, solely with respect to that individual assumption (an "explicit" approach). All assumptions should assume that the plan will continue, absent compelling evidence to the contrary. The Board believes that an explicit approach results in more understandable and useful information about changes in the benefit obligation and the choice of significant assumptions used to determine the various measurements required by this Statement.

181. Some respondents argued that an implicit approach to assumptions, that combines the effect of two or more assumptions to approximate future experience, would improve comparability by reducing variability in employers' assumptions. Under an implicit approach, reliability of assumptions is judged in the aggregate, not individually. However, some respondents who supported an implicit approach seemed to favor uniformity of certain assumptions, such as the use of designated health care cost trend rates, rather than favoring the combination of two or more assumptions. Other respondents who supported an implicit approach seemed to support that approach because it would implicitly consider how the plan might be amended in the future to achieve a desired limit on cost increases. For example, some respondents supported measuring the employer's share of future incurred claims costs by projecting the increase in health care costs using the expected general inflation rate. They stated that applying the expected general inflation rate to the employer's share of per capita incurred claims costs (current cost) best reflects management's intent to control

those costs in the future within that limit. However, the Board believes that such an approach cannot be characterized as measuring the current promise or as being generally representative of a trend to limit an employer's commitment. If an employer has historically amended its plan to achieve a trend equal to the general inflation rate, the Board believes that that past practice is better considered explicitly in determining the substantive plan than implicitly through a surrogate health care cost trend rate.

182. The Board considered an implicit approach as an alternative for certain individual assumptions—for example, by measuring an employer's postretirement benefit obligation and cost using an assumed spread between the health care cost trend rate and the discount rate. An implicit approach was rejected because the Board concluded that users of financial statements are better able to make judgments about the measures presented if they are given the opportunity to compare employers' individual assessments of specific future events. Consequently, the Board concluded that employers should be required to measure their obligations using the best information and estimates available based on existing information and circumstances.

183. Measurement of an employer's postretirement benefit obligation is based on the current plan participants (a "closed group" approach) because it better recognizes the benefit obligation over the period in which employees render service in exchange for benefits. Accounting on the basis of an ongoing employee group (an "open group" approach) often defers recognition of part of the cost of employees' current service to later periods. That open group view provides no basis for recognizing the cost of benefits over the service periods related to the current work force and suggests by its application that employers have a cost and obligation for employees not yet hired.

184. The Board concluded that application of accrual accounting to postretirement benefit accounting requires that the cost of the benefits be recognized in the period in which the employer receives the associated economic benefits—as employee services are rendered. Employee compensation, whether paid currently or deferred, should be recognized when the services are rendered. The Board concluded that, in concept, the employer's obligation to an existing employee group is the sum of its obligations to individual employees, adjusted to reflect the present value of the amount of the obligation and the probability of payment (the actuarial present value).

185. Employers' postretirement benefit obligations will differ to the extent that their promises

are different. For example, some employers may fully reimburse the cost of nursing home care, while others may not provide for that care. Or, some employers may carve out Medicare benefits and provide a low level of supplementary health care coverage, while others may provide a more generous plan that coordinates benefits with Medicare. No standard plan design or package of postretirement benefits or a static set of circumstances exists that would call for all employers to use the same assumptions. Different types of benefits may have differing trend rate assumptions, and different employers may have differing expectations about benefit utilization. Because of differences in plan design and employer circumstances, including the expected demographics of the plan population, measurement assumptions about the timing and amount of future benefits should represent an employer's best estimate with respect to the factors affecting its particular promise.

186. The objective of selecting assumed discount rates is to measure the single amount that, if invested at the measurement date in a portfolio of high-quality debt instruments, would provide the necessary future cash flows to pay the accumulated benefits when due. Notionally, that single amount, the accumulated postretirement benefit obligation, would equal the current market value of a portfolio of high-quality zero coupon bonds whose maturity dates and amounts would be the same as the timing and amount of the expected future benefit payments. Because cash inflows would equal cash outflows in timing and amount, there would be no reinvestment risk in the yields to maturity of the portfolio. However, in other than a zero coupon portfolio, such as a portfolio of long-term debt instruments that pay semiannual interest payments or whose maturities do not extend far enough into the future to meet expected benefit payments, the assumed discount rates (the yield to maturity) need to incorporate expected reinvestment rates available in the future. Those rates should be extrapolated from the existing yield curve at the measurement date. Assumed discount rates should be reevaluated at each measurement date. If the general level of interest rates rises or declines, the assumed discount rates should change in a similar manner.

187. The Board concluded that, conceptually, the basis for determining the assumed discount rates for measuring the present value of the postretirement benefit obligation and the service cost component should be the same as the basis for determining the assumed discount rates for pension measurements. That is, conceptually, the selection of assumed discount rates should be based on the single sum that, if invested at the measurement date, would generate the necessary cash flows to pay the benefits when due.

188. Consistent with Statement 87, the Exposure Draft referred to "the interest rates inherent in the amount at which the postretirement benefit obligation could be effectively settled." Many respondents found that notion confusing because postretirement benefit obligations generally cannot be settled at the current time. However, as opposed to "settling" the obligation, which incorporates the insurer's risk factor, "effectively settling" the obligation focuses only on the time value of money and ignores the insurer's cost for assuming the risk of experience losses. Because of the misunderstanding of the meaning of "effectively settled," the Board concluded that reference to that phrase should be eliminated in order to clarify that the objective of the discount rate is to measure the time value of money. However, elimination of that phrase from this Statement is not intended to reflect a substantive difference between the requirements of Statement 87 and this Statement.

189. Some respondents to the Exposure Draft suggested that an indebtedness model approach that would consider the risk of default by an employer be used to discount an employer's postretirement benefit obligation. That approach suggests that the extent to which an employer chooses to fund its obligation in a trust or similar arrangement changes the value of the promise to retirees because the existence of the plan assets enhances the security of their benefit payments. Using that approach, two employers with identical postretirement benefit promises and plan demographics, but with different funding policies, would measure their expected postretirement benefit obligations differently.

190. The Board rejected the indebtedness model for postretirement benefit measurements. Measurement of pension obligations is not dependent on the level of plan assets, and the Board finds no reason for using different approaches to measure pension and postretirement benefit obligations. In addition, the Board notes that acceptance of the indebtedness model for discounting those obligations raises a broader issue that is beyond the scope of this Statement. The Board currently has a project on its agenda on present-value-based measurements; consideration of an indebtedness model will be encompassed by that project.

191. Most respondents who disagreed with the proposed discount rate favored basing assumed discount rates on company-specific rates, such as an entity's cost of capital or internal rate of return on assets or on shareholders' equity or a financing rate such as its incremental borrowing rate, or on "normalized" long-term interest rates. Generally, those respondents stated that the source of assets that will be used to satisfy an obligation should de-

termine the discount rate. Because most employers currently pay for postretirement benefits with cash generated from current operations or financing transactions, those respondents stated that the rate used to discount the obligation should be based on an employer's rate of return on shareholders' equity or its cost of financing. However, implementation of that approach would be difficult because there is no uniform method for determining a company's cost of capital and a negative rate of return on shareholders' equity would produce inexplicable results. Using a financing rate such as an entity's incremental borrowing rate for discounting purposes also would be difficult because the duration of existing debt is unlikely to be the period over which the postretirement benefits are expected to be paid.

192. Those respondents who advocated a "normalized" long-term rate stated that the use of a current rate for discounting introduces volatility into the measurement process that is unrelated to the postretirement benefit obligation. They recommended that some form of smoothing be used to reduce that volatility. However, the Board noted that smoothing only one assumption would not necessarily make the measurement less volatile because all of the other data and assumptions used in measuring an employer's postretirement benefit obligation and cost are updated annually and represent the best estimate of conditions at that point in time. Concerns about the volatility introduced by all assumptions are mitigated by the delayed recognition provisions provided for gains and losses, including the permitted use of a "corridor" to shield certain gains and losses from recognition. Furthermore, it is not the Board's intent to eliminate all volatility, particularly when it is representationally faithful of the phenomenon being reported.

193. The discounting approach prescribed by this Statement for employers' postretirement benefit obligations is consistent with the approach prescribed by Statement 87 for discounting employers' pension obligations. The Board's project on present-value-based measurements will consider alternative methods for discounting all of the obligations of an employer. In the interim, the approach required by this Statement should result in more comparable measures of the accumulated postretirement benefit obligation and of the service and interest cost components among employers than the other discounting alternatives considered.

194. Many of the other assumptions used in postretirement benefit measurements also are similar to assumptions used in pension measurements, but the sensitivity of the measures to changes in the assumptions may be more significant. For example, the turnover assumption may have a more signifi-

cant effect for postretirement benefits than for pension benefits because, in many cases, eligibility for postretirement benefits is an all-or-nothing proposition, while most pension plans provide reduced benefits for relatively short periods of service. The dependency status assumption also may have a more significant effect on postretirement benefit measurements than on pension measurements. Plan provisions that entitle an employee's spouse and other dependents to health care and other welfare benefits may substantially increase an employer's cost and obligation for postretirement benefits.

195. Postretirement benefit measurements are more sensitive to assumptions about retirement ages and the probability of retiring at each age than are pension measurements. For example, employer-provided postretirement health care benefits are significantly more expensive before Medicare coverage begins than after. Many pension arrangements provide for an actuarially reduced pension benefit for employees retiring before the normal retirement age; however, for an employee retiring early, there typically is no reduction in the postretirement benefit levels, and those benefits will be paid over a longer period of time and at a higher annual cost to the employer than if the employee retired at the normal retirement age. Similarly, postretirement benefit measurements are more sensitive than pension measurements to the life expectancy assumption. In particular, health care benefits are sensitive to that assumption because health care costs generally increase with age.

196. Postretirement health care and life insurance benefits may be based on an employee's final compensation. For example, an employer's postretirement health care plan may require retiree contributions based on the retiree's level of compensation at retirement, or a postretirement life insurance plan may provide a death benefit that is a multiple of final pay. As in employers' accounting for pensions, the Board concluded that assumed compensation levels should reflect the best estimate of participants' actual future compensation levels and should be consistent with assumed discount rates to the extent that both incorporate expectations about the same future economic conditions.

Assumptions unique to postretirement health care benefits

197. Measuring the expected postretirement benefit obligation for postretirement health care benefits includes making assumptions about the amount and timing of postretirement health care benefits expected to be paid in the future for current plan participants. Recent claims cost experience and the claims cost experience of other em-

ployers in the same industry or geographical location may provide useful information in developing the assumed per capita claims cost by age from the earliest age at which a plan participant could receive benefits under the plan to the longest life expectancy. Data files developed and maintained by insurers or benefits consultants about employers' claims costs for similar benefits programs and national or regional statistics about claims cost patterns also may provide information that may be used for developing the per capita claims cost by age.

198. The assumed health care cost trend rates consider the expected annual change in per capita claims costs due to all factors other than changes in the composition of the plan participants by age or dependency status. Changes in the cost of health care are influenced by numerous factors including changes in the cost of health care services, changes in the utilization pattern for health care services, changes in the nature and type of those services as medical practices change and new technology is developed, sociodemographic changes, and changes in public and private policy. Thus, in developing the assumed health care cost trend rates, the effects of medical care inflation, changes in medical care utilization or delivery patterns, technological advances, and changes in the health status of the covered population are all implicitly incorporated in the estimates. The effects of changes in enacted legislation are recognized as those changes occur.

199. Some respondents suggested that the health care cost trend rate would be more costly to develop than other estimates of future trends in costs, such as the general inflation rate. Consulting actuaries informed the Board that the health care cost trend rate per se is not significantly more costly to develop than other estimates of future costs. The more potentially significant cost is in the accumulation of the claims cost data to which any trend rate would be applied for measuring an employer's postretirement health care obligation and cost. (The measurement provisions of this Statement take into account employers' data limitations and the cost of measuring the employer's obligation and cost as described in paragraphs 38 and 41.) Consulting actuaries noted that the application of health care cost trend rates to the claims cost data produces a more relevant and representationally faithful measure of an employer's expected future cash outflows for postretirement health care benefits than would the use of alternative rates, at little or no incremental cost.

Attribution method

200. In the context of this Statement, attribution is the process of assigning the expected cost of ben-

efits to periods of employee service. The general objective is to assign to each year of service the cost of benefits earned or assumed to have been earned in that year. There are two broad groups, or families, of attribution methods—benefit approaches and cost approaches—and there are different attribution methods within those families.

201. Under Statement 87, pension benefits are attributed to employee service on the basis of the plan's benefit formula. A pension benefit formula is defined in paragraph 264 of that Statement as "the basis for determining payments to which participants may be entitled under a pension plan. Pension benefit formulas usually refer to the employee's service or compensation or both." For example, a benefit formula may be stated as: $Y\% \times$ number of years of service $\times$ final pay. The benefit formula method assigns benefits to periods of employee service based on the terms of the plan that define the benefits an employee will receive; the cost is calculated as the actuarial present value of the benefits assigned.

202. The Board believes that, normally, the terms of a plan (benefit formula) provide the most relevant basis for relating benefits promised to services rendered. The Board also believes that a single attribution method, normally based on the terms of the plan, should be prescribed to enhance comparability and understandability of financial statements. However, the Board considered whether the measurement approach should differ for plans that do not have a benefit formula that defines benefits in terms of the specific periods of service that must be rendered in exchange for the benefits. Noting that a difference in method might be warranted for those plans, the Board considered a variety of measurement approaches.

203. Arguments for a particular attribution method are usually based on which approach is perceived to best represent the underlying exchange between the employer and employee. The benefit approaches view the cost of the plan in terms of the benefits being earned each year, generally based on the terms of the plan (benefit formula). A distinct unit of retirement benefit is associated with each year of credited service; that is, those approaches assign benefits directly to years of service. The obligation measured under the benefit approaches is the actuarial present value of the benefits attributed to past and current employees' service to the reporting date, generally based on the terms of the plan.

204. The cost approaches view measurement of the obligation and cost on an annual basis as less important than the pattern of cost recognition from one period to another. Proponents of the

cost approaches generally take the view that an employer has career contracts with its employees. Thus, the cost of the plan is viewed in terms of the benefits expected to be earned over the entire working lives of the plan participants. That cost is allocated to years of service as a level amount that, if invested at the assumed discount rates, would equal the actuarial present value of those benefits at retirement, assuming no experience gains or losses. The costs assigned to each year may be level in dollar amounts or as a percentage of compensation. Proponents of cost approaches view the liability for an individual as measurable only at the date of hire or plan initiation (as zero) and at the retirement date (as the expected postretirement benefit obligation); at any interim date, only an arbitrary allocation is possible. The cost approaches produce an obligation for a group of employees with differing retirement dates that, at any point in time, can be described only as the result of the allocation that produced it. The accrued liability does not represent a measure of the benefits "earned" to date pursuant to the terms of the plan.

205. Because cost approaches assign a level amount of cost to each period, either as a percentage of compensation or in terms of dollars, they generally assign a greater percentage of the total cost of the benefit to earlier years of service in the attribution period than do benefit approaches. For postretirement benefit plans that have a level benefit formula, the benefit approaches assign a service cost to earlier periods of service in the attribution period that, when discounted, is less than that assigned during later years of service. Consequently, for those plans the benefit approaches typically result in lower charges than the cost approaches in early service periods offset by higher charges in later periods, and, in the absence of plan amendments, they generally result in a lower accrued liability at any point prior to the end of the attribution period.

206. For postretirement benefit plans that have a variable benefit formula,[34] cost approaches and benefit approaches may account for the benefit cost differently. Cost approaches generally project the expected postretirement benefit obligation at retirement and allocate an amount to each service period that is level in terms of dollars or percentage of compensation and that, together with interest at the assumed discount rates, will accumulate to the expected postretirement benefit obligation. Benefit approaches generally attribute different costs to different service periods when the benefit formula assigns different benefits to different periods of service.

207. The Board considered six methods for attributing postretirement benefits that are undefined in terms of the specified period of service to be rendered in exchange for the benefits. Those methods are described in paragraphs 180-186 of the Exposure Draft. Four of the methods were traditional approaches that incorporate the use of present value techniques, while the other two methods allocate the total benefit or cost on an undiscounted basis. The latter approaches attribute the expected postretirement benefits or cost to periods of service either as a level amount of benefit or cost or as a level percentage of compensation. Undiscounted approaches produce identical results under the benefit and cost methods.

208. The Board rejected the undiscounted approaches. Because the obligation is to provide benefits in the future, not currently, the Board concluded that the present value of the obligation expected to be paid is the most relevant and reliable measure of the obligation and of the cost of the services received. Discounting explicitly recognizes that the present value of an obligation payable in the future is less than that of an equal obligation payable currently. The Board concluded that recording an obligation at its ultimate cost without discounting is overly conservative and does not provide the information most relevant for decision making.

209. The Board rejected attribution on the basis of compensation because it does not faithfully represent how the cost is incurred under the terms of the plan. In cases in which compensation levels are a factor, years of service generally are also a consideration in determining the benefits to be provided because an employee would not be eligible for the benefits unless some period of service had been provided.

210. The Board was unable to identify a basis for attributing postretirement benefits that would be more appropriate, in most cases, than measurement of the current benefit cost and accumulated postretirement benefit obligation based on years of service. Statement 87 prescribes the attribution of pension benefits on the basis of years of service; compensation is considered for measuring the amount of the benefit to be attributed to each year of service when compensation levels are a factor in determining the amount of the pension benefit. The Board found no compelling reason to prescribe a different basis for attributing postretirement benefits than the basis used for attributing pension benefits.

---

[34]For example, the terms of the plan may state that retirees will receive an annual benefit that is equal to (a) 2.5 percent of covered benefits for each year of service through year 10, (b) 3.0 percent of covered benefits for each year of service in years 11-20, and (c) 3.5 percent of covered benefits for each year of service in years 21-30.

211. The Board's consideration therefore focused on two attribution approaches: a benefit/years-of-service approach and a cost/years-of-service approach. A benefit approach attributes benefits on the basis of individual plan participants; a cost approach may attribute either on an individual or on an aggregate basis. Of those alternative cost approaches, the Board focused on an aggregate approach. Since the objective of a cost method is the allocation of benefit costs, there is no reason to burden that method unnecessarily with complexities and computations that could not be supported as enhancing measurement of either the obligation at a point in time or the cost incurred for a period.

212. A benefit/years-of-service approach is viewed by the Board as more consistent with its conceptual framework's focus on measurement of assets and liabilities. An objective of a benefit approach is to fully accrue the expected postretirement benefit obligation for an employee by the end of the credited service period for that employee. Under an aggregate cost approach, cost is attributed based on the average remaining years of service of all active plan participants; consequently, the cost of the expected postretirement benefit obligation for an employee generally would be attributed to a period beyond the end of the credited service period for that employee.

213. The Board considers the benefit attribution pattern under a benefit approach to be more representative of how benefits are earned than the pattern under a cost approach. Assume, for example, that postretirement benefits are provided in exchange for 20 years of service. A benefit approach results in a level attribution of the *future* benefits, implying that the benefits are earned equally over the attribution period. An aggregate cost approach implicitly results in a declining *future* benefit attributed to years of service with the passing of time and approaching retirement, implying that proportionately more benefits are attributable to the early years of service than to the later years. Under both approaches, absent funding considerations, the cost of providing benefits rises with the passing of time as retirement is approached, although the increase is lower under the aggregate cost approach because the service cost component is a level amount or percentage.

214. When it began deliberations on the attribution method, the Board considered present plan designs as well as possible future plan designs. Because postretirement health care and other welfare benefits generally supplement pension benefits, the Board considered the likelihood that future postretirement benefit plan formulas will become more similar to pension plan formulas. That is, employers may promise postretirement benefits that vary

based on individual years of service rather than promise the same benefits to all employees who become eligible for benefits. Since that time, various surveys have documented a trend in plan designs in that direction.

215. The Board noted that one particular aggregate cost approach is computationally less complex than a benefit approach because it does not attempt to differentiate between the causes of any unexpected changes in the unfunded accumulated benefit obligation; any unexpected change is recognized prospectively. The effects of plan amendments and gains and losses are incorporated into the unfunded expected postretirement benefit obligation for prospective recognition. However, the Board concluded that the computational advantages of that somewhat less complex aggregate cost approach did not outweigh the other considerations favoring a benefit/years-of-service approach.

216. A few respondents suggested that the Board not require the use of a single method of attributing the cost of postretirement benefits to periods of employee service but, rather, allow a choice among a number of acceptable actuarial methods. They noted that choices among accounting methods are allowed in other areas, including accounting for inventory and depreciation. They also suggested that a standardized method would not achieve comparability because of differences in assumptions or would impair comparability because it would obscure different circumstances that call for different approaches.

217. The Board is not convinced that differences in circumstances among employers require different methods for measuring the service cost component of net periodic postretirement benefit cost. Similar arguments were made about employers' accounting for pensions. However, respondents were unable to identify, and the Board was unable to develop, any basis to support the use of different methods. Differences in circumstances require the use of different assumptions or different attribution periods that appropriately result in different patterns of recognizing the cost of providing postretirement benefits.

218. Most respondents preferred a single attribution method based on the terms of the plan, similar to the approach prescribed by Statement 87. They maintained that that method would be more understandable and more useful than a less familiar method and would be less costly to implement than a new method. The Board agreed and concluded that a benefit/years-of-service approach should be prescribed. When a benefit formula does not define the specific years of service to be rendered in exchange for the benefits, the Board acknowledges

that an allocation of benefits to individual years of service in the attribution period has to be assumed. However, the Board believes that it would be inappropriate to develop an approach that is inconsistent with the benefit approach underlying Statement 87 unless that approach would significantly reduce implementation costs without unduly compromising the more conceptually appropriate approach, particularly since the Board views the promise for postretirement benefits to be similar to the promise for pension benefits.

Attribution period

219. A plan's benefit formula is the basis for determining the benefits to which plan participants may be entitled. The benefit formula specifies how plan participants attain eligibility for those benefits—the years of service to be rendered, the age to be attained while in service, or a combination of those factors. Consequently, a plan's benefit formula provides the most relevant and reliable basis for measuring the expected postretirement benefit obligation and for determining the period over which those benefits should be accrued.

220. The Board concluded that if the expected postretirement benefits promised pursuant to a plan are similar to a deferred vested pension benefit,[35] the benefit obligation should not be attributed beyond the date an employee has rendered the required service for full eligibility for the future benefits expected to be received by that employee. Full eligibility is attained by meeting specified age, service, or age and service requirements of the plan. The full eligibility date is the date at which an employee attains eligibility for all of the benefits that are expected to be received by that employee, including any benefits expected to be received by any beneficiaries or covered dependents.

221. For example, if a plan provides a postretirement health care or life insurance benefit to an employee who renders 10 years of service, the actuarial present value of that benefit should be fully accrued at the end of 10 years of service. Similarly, if a plan provides a postretirement benefit to an employee who attains age 55 while in service, the actuarial present value of that benefit should be fully accrued when the employee attains age 55. Whether benefits commence immediately or in the future does not change the employee's eligibility for postretirement benefits. The Board concluded that postretirement benefits should not be attrib-

uted beyond the date *full* eligibility for those benefits is attained.

222. The Exposure Draft proposed that, consistent with Statement 87, determination of the full eligibility date not be affected by measurement assumptions such as when benefit payments commence, dependency status, salary progression, and so forth. During its redeliberations, the Board again considered whether the full eligibility date should be affected by certain measurement assumptions. For example, for pay-related plans that define the benefit earned as a fixed percentage of final pay, an incremental benefit is earned each year for the effect of the change in an employee's pay rate for that year. Similarly, for plans that provide an indexed benefit that is "capped" at the indexed amount of the benefit at an employee's retirement, an incremental benefit equal to the effect of the annual change in that index is earned for each year of service. Board members believed the attribution period should include all employee service periods for which a nontrivial incremental postretirement benefit is earned. The Board recognized that consideration of those measurement assumptions in determining the full eligibility date would be inconsistent with how Statement 87 applies to certain pension plans with maximum credited service periods. Those situations are limited.

223. The Board concluded that it is willing to accept that inconsistency because considering all years of service that provide an incremental benefit in determining an employee's full eligibility date is both more understandable and more consistent with the accounting for other deferred compensation contracts under Opinion 12. Consequently, the full eligibility date is determined by plan terms that provide incremental benefits for additional service, such as benefits based on final pay or benefits that are indexed through an employee's active service period, unless those incremental benefits are trivial. Determination of the full eligibility date is *not* affected by plan terms that define when benefit payments commence or by an employee's current dependency status. (Paragraphs 397–408 illustrate determination of the full eligibility date.)

224. Respondents to the Exposure Draft generally disagreed with ending the attribution period at an employee's full eligibility date. Those respondents supported attributing benefits to an employee's full service period—ending with the expected retirement date—whether or not the benefit formula

---

[35]This Statement uses the term *vested benefits* in the accounting sense, not in the legal context. For accounting purposes, vesting refers to an employee's right to receive present or future benefits whether or not the employee remains in the service of the employer. The fact that the benefits do not commence until after the employee retires or that additional benefits may be earned by rendering additional service does not change the right to the benefits that have been earned and to which the employee would be entitled if the employee terminated.

defines the specific years of service to be rendered in exchange for the benefits. Many respondents indicated that, irrespective of the terms of the plan, attributing benefits to employees' full service periods reflects the employer's intent, asserting that the postretirement benefits promised to employees are substantially independent of their compensation levels or years of service. Other respondents indicated that attributing postretirement benefits to an employee's expected retirement date is more consistent with the attribution period for most pension benefits.

225. In its redeliberation of the attribution period, the Board observed the results of the field test of the Exposure Draft. Those results suggested that, for many employers who elect delayed recognition of the transition obligation, the difference in net periodic cost that results from attributing the expected postretirement benefit obligation to an employee's full eligibility date rather than the employee's expected retirement date is minimal. That is because, in those situations, net periodic cost reflects the interplay of service cost, interest cost, and amortization of an employer's transition obligation. If the expected postretirement benefit obligation is attributed to an employee's full eligibility date, the transition obligation that is recognized on a delayed basis in future periods is greater than if the benefit obligation is attributed over a longer period. In addition, if the benefit obligation is attributed to an employee's full eligibility date, there is no service cost for fully eligible plan participants. As a result of those effects, and the relative magnitude of interest cost, regardless of the attribution period, the net periodic cost for most employers is not likely to be significantly affected by attributing the expected postretirement benefit obligation over service to employees' full eligibility dates rather than over service to employees' expected retirement dates.

226. The Board observes that the terms of most pension plans result in attributing the pension benefits to the years of service to an employee's expected retirement date. Because most pension plans provide an incremental benefit for each year of service, the full eligibility date and retirement date are the same. Recent surveys suggest a trend among employers to amend their postretirement benefit plans to define the amount of benefits employees will receive based on the length of their service, similar to most pension plans. If that trend continues, the full eligibility date for many or most postretirement benefit plans also may be the employee's retirement date.

227. For postretirement benefit plans that are not pay-related or otherwise indexed during an employee's service period (most existing postretire-

ment health care plans), attributing the benefits to an employee's full eligibility date *is* consistent with the attribution period for pension benefits; what may make the periods appear to be different is different plan terms that define when the benefits are earned. For postretirement benefit plans that are pay-related or that otherwise index benefits during employees' service periods to their retirement date, the full eligibility date and retirement date generally will be the same. The attribution period for those benefits will differ from the attribution period for a similarly defined pension benefit with a capped credited service period. (Refer to paragraphs 222 and 223.)

228. Ending the attribution period at an employee's full eligibility date is consistent with the plan terms, which, in the Board's view, provide the best evidence of the exchange transaction. The accounting for an exchange transaction should reflect the understanding of both parties to the transaction. If an employer were to change the eligibility requirements for postretirement benefits from 10 years of service and attainment of age 55 while in service to a requirement of 15 years of service and attainment of age 62 while in service, that would be a fundamentally different promise with an economic consequence for the employer and at least some employees. The Board believes it would not be representationally faithful to ignore the difference between those promises in determining the attribution period.

229. The Board considered attributing benefits beyond the full eligibility date in some, but not all, cases. Several criteria were considered in defining the conditions under which that should occur, such as whether eligibility for benefits is attained gradually or all at once, whether the benefit formula unambiguously defines the specific years of service to be rendered, whether a specific age must be attained while in service, and whether retirement from the company is required.

230. The Board considered an approach that would require attribution of benefits beyond a plan participant's full eligibility date to the participant's expected retirement date if all eligible plan participants receive the same benefit and if eligibility for the benefits is attained all at once upon attaining a specified age while in service, upon rendering a specified number of years of service, or a combination of both. However, the Board rejected that approach because it was troubled by the arbitrary nature of the resulting attribution period. For example, if a plan provides 60 percent of the cost of postretirement health care benefit coverage to all employees who render 25 or more years of service, that approach would require attribution over a 30-year period for an employee expected to

retire after 30 years of service. However, if a plan provides 40 percent of the cost of postretirement health care benefit coverage to all employees who render 20 years of service and an additional benefit of 4 percent for service in each of the following 5 years, the expected postretirement benefit obligation for an employee expected to render 30 years of service would be attributed to that employee's first 25 years of service. The accounting would attribute the benefits over different periods even though, in both cases, the benefit promise would be vested after 25 years of service and service beyond 25 years would not result in an incremental benefit.

231. The Board also considered an approach that would require attribution of benefits beyond the full eligibility date for those benefits if a plan's benefit formula does not unambiguously define the specific period of service to be rendered in exchange for the benefits. The Board rejected that condition because of the inconsistent results that would occur. For example, if one plan provides 75 percent of the cost of postretirement health care coverage to employees who render 30 years of service and a different plan provides the same benefits to employees who attain age 55 while in service and render at least 10 years of service, benefits would be attributed beyond the full eligibility date in the latter case but not the former. For an employee hired at age 25 who is expected to render 40 years of service, the benefits under the first plan would be attributed to the employee's first 30 years of service and the benefits under the second plan would be attributed to the employee's full service period, even though the same benefit is earned upon meeting the age and service conditions of the respective plans.

232. The Board also considered an approach that would require attribution of benefits beyond the full eligibility date if a plan's benefit formula requires attaining a specified age while in service. In that case, the credited service period is not unambiguously defined. The Board noted that the approach creates anomalies and rejected it as arbitrary for the reasons discussed in paragraphs 230 and 231.

233. The Board also considered an approach that would require attribution of benefits beyond the full eligibility date if an employee must meet the employer's criteria for retirement before termina-

tion in order to receive the benefits.[36] Under that approach, the benefit promise is viewed as an exchange for service over an employee's career, and retirement is viewed as the recognizable event. The Board rejected that approach for several reasons. While meeting the employer's criteria for retirement may define when postretirement benefit coverage is expected to commence, the act of retirement in and of itself does not reflect the exchange that takes place between the employer and an employee. It is the required employee service that is exchanged for postretirement benefits. In addition, an approach that attributes benefits beyond the full eligibility date based on the act of retirement would be inconsistent with accruing other deferred compensation contracts, including pensions, to the full eligibility date.

234. The need to be "retired" in order to receive benefits is not unique to other postretirement benefit plans. At the full eligibility date the employee has completed the contractual requirements for eligibility for all the postretirement benefits that employee is expected to receive and can terminate with entitlement to those benefits when a specified event occurs or the need for those benefits arises. An objective of accounting for deferred compensation contracts is to measure the accrued liability defined by the contract as reliably as possible and, therefore, to recognize cost over the periods in which the benefits are earned and the exchange takes place. Although for some contracts it may not be possible to determine the portion of the expected future benefits earned by an employee before that employee attains full eligibility for the benefits, no uncertainty remains at the full eligibility date. The total expected postretirement benefits have been earned at that date.

235. Attribution of postretirement benefits beyond the date full eligibility for the benefits is attained would suggest that there is a difference between "fully vested" pension benefits and "full eligibility" for other postretirement benefits. At the full eligibility date, the *right* to the benefits is not contingent upon rendering future service. Both vesting in pension benefits and attaining full eligibility for postretirement benefits are rights that are "earned" (exchanged) for meeting specified age, service, or age and service requirements. In both cases, an employee is not entitled to *receive* the benefits until after the employer-employee rela-

---

[36]For example, an employer may promise to provide postretirement health care coverage to all employees who retire from the company (terminate after meeting the age or service requirements that entitle an employee to immediate pension benefits); under the terms of the retirement plan, an employee may retire from the company early with 30 years of service or at the normal retirement age with less than 30 years of service. Consequently, for an employee hired at age 25 who renders 30 years of consecutive service, the employer has promised to provide postretirement benefit coverage upon that employee's termination (retirement) on or after rendering 30 years of service. Although that employee will render service beyond age 55, eligibility for the benefits is not conditional upon rendering additional service, and no incremental benefit is provided for doing so.

tionship is terminated. The Board saw no significant distinction between the two.

236. Paragraph 42(a) of Statement 87 states that "for benefits of a type includable in vested benefits,[9] [the benefits shall be considered to accumulate] in proportion to the ratio of the number of completed years of service to the number that will have been completed *when the benefit is first fully vested*" (emphasis added). Footnote 9 of Statement 87 describes a supplemental early retirement benefit that is vested after a stated number of years as an example of a benefit of a type includable in vested benefits. Paragraph 42(b) of Statement 87 states that "for benefits of a type not includable in vested benefits,[10] [the benefits shall be considered to accumulate] in proportion to the ratio of completed years of service to total projected years of service." Footnote 10 of Statement 87 describes a death or disability benefit that is payable only if death or disability occurs during active service as an example of a benefit of a type *not* includable in vested benefits. Most postretirement benefits are of a type includable in vested benefits.

237. The Board was unable to identify any approach that would, in its opinion, appropriately attribute benefits beyond the date full eligibility for those benefits is attained. Accordingly, the Board concluded that postretirement benefits should not be attributed to service beyond the date an employee attains full eligibility for those benefits. The Board also concluded that if the benefit formula defines the beginning of the credited service period, benefits generally should be attributed from that date. If the beginning of the credited service period is not defined, the beginning of the credited service period is deemed to be the date of hire, and benefits should be attributed from that date.

238. Some Board members disagree with ending the attribution period at the full eligibility date as defined in this Statement. They support attributing the expected postretirement benefit obligation from an employee's date of hire (or beginning of the credited service period, if later) to the date beyond which the employee's additional service will not change (neither increase nor decrease) the amount of benefits to which the employee will be entitled—usually the employee's retirement date. That approach would extend the attribution period to include any years of employee service during which the employer conceptually incurs a negative service cost because the employee, by electing to continue service after earning a vested postretirement benefit, gives back benefits that have been earned (refer to paragraphs 240-242). This Statement attributes the expected postretirement benefit obligation, rather than the vested postretirement benefit obligation, to years of credited

service and assigns no service cost to the years of service beyond the full eligibility date. Those Board members would attribute the expected postretirement benefit obligation on a pro rata basis to *all* years of service that change the amount of benefits an employee is entitled to receive, *including* those years in the giveback period.

239. Those Board members recognize that, depending on a plan's terms, an employee's full eligibility date may be the same as the employee's retirement date. In those instances there is no period during which the employer conceptually incurs a negative service cost. But for many existing plans, an employee's full eligibility date and retirement date differ. Those Board members are concerned with those latter plans. They observe that many existing plans provide benefits to employees "upon retirement" or "upon retiring from the company" without defining the specific years of service to be rendered in exchange for the benefits. Those Board members believe that, for those plans, ending the attribution period at the expected retirement date more appropriately reflects the understanding that postretirement benefits are exchanged for *all* years of employee service. Those Board members believe that attributing benefits to the date beyond which an employee's service will not change the amount of benefits to be received by the employee is a preferable, practical, and understandable approach to attributing the expected postretirement benefit obligation to years of service.

Amount attributed

240. Implicit in the Board's conclusion is the view that at the full eligibility date the employer has a measurable obligation to provide benefits in the future. The Board considered whether measurement of that obligation for a plan that provides benefits immediately after retirement should be based on (a) benefits the employee is expected to receive given the employee's expected retirement date (the expected postretirement benefit obligation) or (b) benefits the employee would be eligible to receive were the employee to retire (terminate) immediately (a vested postretirement benefit obligation). Under the latter approach, if the vested postretirement benefit obligation for an employee were attributed to service to the full eligibility date and that employee continued to render service rather than retire, a negative service cost would be recognized (for the reduction in the vested postretirement benefit obligation) during the subsequent service period as the employee foregoes a portion of the benefits that had been earned at the full eligibility date. Under either approach the same obligation—the expected postretirement benefit obligation—would be recognized at the employee's retirement date.

241. Attributing the vested postretirement benefit obligation to service to the full eligibility date is viewed as conceptually appropriate by some Board members. At that date, an obligation exists to provide postretirement benefits; that obligation is no longer contingent upon the employee rendering future service. Those Board members believe it is inconsistent to measure an obligation to which an employee is immediately eligible as the expected postretirement benefit obligation, which considers that benefits commence after additional future service, because no future service is required. They believe that a measurement based on rendering future service is not representationally faithful when a greater benefit has been earned that is not dependent upon the rendering of future service.

242. The ability to satisfy the benefit obligation at less than the "vested" amount is outside the control of an employer. Further, to attribute benefits on the basis of the expected postretirement benefit obligation anticipates an employee's election to remain in service and consequently give back a benefit. Certain Board members believe that, conceptually, that election should be accounted for as it is made. In their view, recognition of the vested postretirement benefit obligation at the full eligibility date and the subsequent giveback of benefits in the intervening period until retirement better reflects the exchange that has occurred. That is, the employer has promised to provide a specified level of benefit coverage in exchange for a minimum period of employee service or service to a specified attained age. During the service period subsequent to the full eligibility date, the economic benefit to the employee for continuing to work (and the employer's compensation cost) is the excess of the amount the employee receives for working over the amount the employee would have received had the employee not continued to work.

243. Despite the conceptual support that some Board members believe exists for attributing the vested postretirement benefit obligation over the service period to the full eligibility date, Board members recognized the difficulty of conveying to preparers and users of financial statements the notion of a negative service cost for some employees. Therefore, the Board concluded that the expected postretirement benefit obligation, rather than the vested postretirement benefit obligation, should be attributed to service to the full eligibility date.

244. The Board acknowledges that attribution of the expected postretirement benefit obligation to the full eligibility date may be viewed as being internally inconsistent because recognition and measurement are on different bases. Whereas recognition is based on service to the full eligibility date, measurement of the obligation considers service beyond that date because an employer must consider when benefit payments are likely to commence in order to measure the expected postretirement benefit obligation that is to be attributed to employees' service periods. The Board notes that although some future events do not provide a basis for recognition of elements of financial statements, they may affect the measurement of recognized past events. The Board concluded that, absent a reconsideration of fundamental measurement and recognition concepts, attribution of the expected postretirement benefit obligation, rather than the vested postretirement benefit obligation, to the full eligibility date is preferable given the evolutionary state of accounting for postretirement benefits.

Attribution pattern

245. The Exposure Draft proposed attributing the expected postretirement benefit obligation to employee service using the benefit formula. That is, if the benefit formula attributes certain benefits to individual years or groups of years of service in the credited service period, the benefit formula generally would have been followed for attribution purposes. Otherwise, an equal amount of the expected benefits would have been assigned to each year of service in the attribution period. The Board believed then and continues to believe that the benefit formula is the most relevant basis for attributing benefits to years of service. However, it is particularly difficult to attribute benefits to years of service in accordance with the present terms of many postretirement health care plans. Frequently, the plan terms are ambiguous and quite difficult to apply at interim dates. For example, a plan may define different benefits for different years of service and have a separate age and service requirement that must be met to attain eligibility for any benefits.

246. Following a plan's benefit formula for attributing postretirement benefits to individual years of service in the attribution period adds a degree of complexity that the Board concluded was unnecessary. The Board believes that the primary objective of attribution is to have fully accrued the actuarial present value of the cost of the postretirement benefits expected to be provided to an employee pursuant to the terms of the contract (the expected postretirement benefit obligation) at the date the employee attains full eligibility for those benefits. Although following the benefit formula for attribution purposes would be more representationally faithful and consistent with Statement 87, the Board concluded that because postretirement benefits do not typically vest at interim dates during an employee's service period in the same manner as pension benefits, and because the terms of postretirement benefit plans generally are more complex than the terms of pension plans, the obligation ac-

crued at an interim date is not as relevant and reliable as the obligation accrued at the full eligibility date. Consequently, in order to reduce complexity, the Board concluded that the expected postretirement benefit obligation should be recognized by assigning an equal amount to each year of service in the attribution period, unless the plan's benefit formula attributes a disproportionate share of the expected postretirement benefit obligation to employees' early years of service.

Transition

247. The issues of how and when the transition amount should be recognized are sensitive ones to employers who face, for the first time, the prospect of accruing the cost of postretirement benefits exchanged for current service as well as accounting for the cost of those benefits exchanged for prior service. Unlike the effects of most other accounting changes, a transition obligation for postretirement benefits generally reflects, to some extent, the failure to accrue the obligation in the earlier periods in which it arose rather than the effects of a change from one accrual method of accounting to another.

248. An employer changing from the cash basis of accounting for postretirement benefits to the accrual basis required by this Statement has not recognized any of the cost of the benefits for active plan participants and only some portion of the cost of the benefits for retired plan participants— amounts that would have been recognized as the service and interest cost components of net periodic postretirement benefit cost in earlier periods. In addition, an indeterminate portion of the transition obligation may represent unrecognized prior service cost arising from a plan initiation or amendment, an unrecognized net gain or loss, or an unrecognized obligation from a prior business combination.

249. Determining the portion of the transition obligation that represents unrecognized service cost and interest cost of prior periods would require retroactively measuring the amount of benefit obligation that would have been recognized for each prior period by the employer had this Statement always been applied. To do that, an employer would have to determine the historical data and assumptions about the economic environment that would have been made at the date of plan adoption and at each subsequent measurement date. It is unlikely that the data necessary to measure the obligation at those dates exist, and it would be difficult, if not impossible, to develop assumptions that ignore the benefit of hindsight.

250. The Board concluded that transition is, to a significant extent, a practical matter. A major ob-

jective of transition is to minimize implementation costs and to mitigate disruption to the extent possible without unduly compromising the ability of financial statements to provide useful information. The Board also concluded that it would be confusing, complex, and inconsistent to measure the transition obligation differently from other measurements in accounting for postretirement benefits. The transition obligation is measured as the unrecognized unfunded accumulated postretirement benefit obligation, which is based on the portion of the expected postretirement benefit obligation attributed to each year of service rendered prior to a plan participant's full eligibility date. That measurement is consistent with the attribution of benefits to years of service, measurement of the effects of a plan initiation that grants retroactive benefits or a plan amendment, and the measurement of a postretirement benefit obligation assumed in a business combination accounted for as a purchase.

251. Changes from cash basis to accrual basis accounting are usually made retroactively. If the components of the transition obligation (asset) could be separately determined, it would be consistent with other provisions of this Statement to treat the unrecognized current service and interest cost as the cumulative effect of an accounting change (that is, to immediately recognize those components when this Statement is first applied), and retroactively remeasure prior purchase business combinations for postretirement benefit obligations assumed but not recognized. It also would be consistent to recognize at least some of the unrecognized prior service cost and unrecognized gain or loss prospectively, based on the delayed recognition afforded those components of postretirement benefit cost by this Statement. However, if the cumulative effect of the accounting change were required to be estimated, the cost of doing so could be prohibitive and the results questionable for the reasons discussed in paragraph 249.

252. Several alternatives to immediate recognition of the transition obligation or asset were considered. The Board believed that, conceptually, immediate recognition of the cumulative effect of the accounting change (as described in paragraph 251) would be most appropriate. The potential magnitude of the accumulated postretirement benefit obligation, particularly the obligation for postretirement health care benefits, suggests that any omission of that obligation would detract from the usefulness of the statement of financial position. However, the Board recognized that the magnitude of that obligation and the limited availability of historical data on which to base its measurement suggest the need for a more pragmatic approach. Those considerations led the Board to conclude in

the Exposure Draft that the initial emphasis of this Statement should be on disclosure of the transition obligation and that the subsequent recognition of that amount in the statement of financial position and in the statement of income should be phased in over future periods.

253. Respondents generally favored a transition period longer than the 15-year period proposed in the Exposure Draft. Some maintained that the magnitude of employers' transition obligations argues for a longer transition period to minimize disruption of current practice. Others noted that a longer transition period would better reflect the average remaining service period of the employee work force that will be entitled to the benefits. Because most existing plans do not give employees postretirement health care benefits unless they meet the company's criteria for retirement with an immediate pension benefit, the remaining service periods of participants in a postretirement health care plan is typically longer than the remaining service periods of participants in a pension plan. Employees who are eligible for postretirement health care benefits are generally only long-service employees, while employees are often entitled to a deferred vested pension benefit if they terminate at younger ages with shorter service periods. For a majority of the companies that participated in the field test of the Exposure Draft, the average remaining service period of the active participants in their postretirement benefit plans was between 18 years and 21 years; previous surveys of employers' pension plans indicated an average remaining service period of those plan participants that is several years shorter.

254. The Board concluded that employers whose plan participants' average remaining years of service is less than 20 years could elect to recognize their transition obligation or asset over 20 years, reflecting the average remaining service periods for participants in many other employers' postretirement benefit plans. However, the Board also concluded that phasing in recognition of a transition obligation should not result in slower recognition of an employer's postretirement benefit obligation than would result from continuation of the pay-as-you-go (cash basis) method. The Exposure Draft proposed that amortization of the transition obligation be accelerated if (a) cumulative benefit payments subsequent to the transition date to fully eligible plan participants at the transition date exceeded the sum of (1) the cumulative amortization of the entire transition obligation and (2) the cumulative interest on the unpaid transition obligation or (b) cumulative benefit payments subsequent to the transition date to all plan participants exceeded the cumulative postretirement benefit cost accrued subsequent to the transition date. As a result of the complexity associated with applying the first of those constraints, the Board concluded that recognition of the transition obligation should be accelerated only if the second constraint applies.

255. Although respondents to the Exposure Draft supported delayed recognition of the transition obligation as a practical approach to transition, most of those respondents also favored permitting (but not requiring) immediate recognition of the transition obligation or asset. They noted that FASB Technical Bulletin No. 87-1, *Accounting for a Change in Method of Accounting for Certain Postretirement Benefits,* permitted immediate recognition of the transition obligation in certain circumstances. They also noted that immediate recognition provides the simplest method of recognition that would most significantly improve financial reporting. Because a significant portion of the transition obligation is likely to relate to service and interest costs for prior periods, they argued that the Board should permit an employer to immediately recognize its transition obligation for postretirement benefits.

256. The Board's consideration of permitting immediate recognition of the transition obligation or asset focused on whether financial reporting would be enhanced by limiting alternatives, recognizing that in doing so, a conceptually defensible, and in some cases preferable, alternative might be eliminated. Some Board members believe that immediate recognition of the transition obligation or asset should not be permitted. They believe that the understandability and comparability of financial reporting, both in the year of adoption and in subsequent periods, would be improved by uniformly phasing in recognition of the transition obligation or asset for postretirement benefits for all employers. They also note that the actuarial techniques for measuring postretirement health care benefit obligations are still developing and should become more sophisticated and reliable with time and experience. They observe that near-term measures of the accumulated postretirement benefit obligation from which the transition obligation is derived will reflect the deficiencies of insufficient data collection in the past and the evolving actuarial practice in this area. They also note that subsequent adjustments to measures of the accumulated postretirement benefit obligation will be recognized in income through the gain or loss component of net periodic postretirement benefit cost.

257. Because an indeterminate portion of the transition obligation may relate to unrecognized prior service cost, an unrecognized net gain or loss, or the effects of a prior purchase business combination, immediate recognition of the transition obligation in its entirety would result in premature recognition of those amounts. Under the recogni-

tion provisions of this Statement, those effects are properly recognized in the results of operations for subsequent periods. Some Board members were troubled by that result. This Statement delays recognition of the effects of plan improvements, because they are granted with the expectation that the employer will realize economic benefits in the future, and of plan reductions and permits the delayed recognition of gains and losses. Opinion 16, as amended by this Statement, requires recognition of postretirement benefit obligations assumed in a purchase business combination in determining the cost of the assets acquired, including goodwill related to the purchase; that increase in the cost of the assets acquired is recognized as a charge against operations in future periods.

258. The Board concluded that an employer's transition obligation or asset may be recognized either on a delayed basis or immediately, subject to certain constraints. In reaching that conclusion, the Board recognized that complete comparability would not be achieved by proscribing immediate recognition of the transition obligation. A few companies have already adopted accrual accounting for postretirement benefits pursuant to Technical Bulletin 87-1 and have immediately recognized their transition obligations. Others would have the opportunity to do so before issuance of this Statement. Despite concerns about the availability and reliability of data on which to base measurement of an employer's accumulated postretirement benefit obligation, the Board believes that the delayed effective date of this Statement should provide for further development of actuarial techniques and the accumulation of more reliable data on which to base the measurements at the date of transition. The Board concluded that employers should not be precluded from recognizing their transition obligations in the manner that some believe most significantly improves financial reporting.

259. The Board considered limiting the immediate recognition of the postretirement benefit transition obligation to the amount in excess of any remaining unrecognized transition asset for pensions because the transition amounts result from similar standards for similar costs. Some Board members are concerned about the credibility of financial statements if income from the transition to one standard is included in income over time, while expense from the transition to a related standard is recognized all at once. Others believe that because the two standards relate to different subjects, credibility is not affected. The Board concluded that immediate recognition of the transition obligation for postretirement benefits should not be limited by any remaining transition asset for pensions. The Board observes that because transition is largely a practical matter, consideration should be

given to the facts and circumstances surrounding the issues addressed by the standard. In the case of postretirement benefits other than pensions, some Board members believe that a change from cash basis to accrual accounting is a circumstance sufficiently different from a change from one accrual method to another to justify a unique transition provision. They also believe that the transition obligation for postretirement benefits reflects service cost and interest cost attributable to prior periods to a much greater degree than the transition obligation for pensions.

260. Immediate recognition of an employer's transition obligation or asset is permitted only at the date of initial application of this Statement. The Board concluded that to permit immediate recognition at any subsequent time would result in too much variability in financial reporting for a long period of time. That option also would be inconsistent with some of the arguments in favor of immediate recognition and would introduce additional complexities in determining the amount that could be subsequently recognized.

261. The effect of immediately recognizing a transition obligation or asset and any related tax effect are to be reported separately in the statement of income as the effect of a change in accounting. To more closely approximate the measure of the cumulative effect of the accounting change, the amount immediately recognized in income is required to exclude certain effects that should, more appropriately, be reflected in determining future periods' income. Thus, the amount immediately recognized in income as the effect of the change in accounting is required to exclude the effects of (a) any previously unrecognized postretirement benefit obligation assumed in a business combination accounted for as a purchase, (b) a plan initiation, and (c) any plan amendment that improved benefits, to the extent that those events occur after the issuance of this Statement.

262. The Board considered excluding from the amount immediately recognized in income any significant portion of the transition obligation attributable to obligations assumed in past purchase business combinations or the effects of past plan initiations or amendments that improved benefits, in order to more reliably measure the effect of the accounting change. However, the Board believes that the data on which those measurements would be based for those past events are generally not available and would be costly, if not impossible, to develop. Some Board members believe that, at a minimum, the amounts related to any of those events that are known or are readily available should be excluded from any transition obligation immediately recognized in income. For primarily

practical reasons, the Board concluded that only the constraints identified in paragraph 261 should be applied.

263. The Board considered whether the effects of recognizing an employer's transition obligation or asset should be included in determining net income, as an adjustment of retained earnings, or as a component of comprehensive income, but not net income. Opinion 20 states that most changes in accounting should be recognized by including the cumulative effect of the change in accounting in net income of the period of change. The correction of an error and certain changes in accounting principles identified in that Opinion are recognized by restating prior periods, resulting in an adjustment of beginning retained earnings for the current period.

264. Some respondents favored recognizing the transition obligation (or asset) through a direct charge (or credit) to retained earnings because the amount relates primarily to past periods. However, recognition of the cumulative effect of an accounting change through income, as specified in Opinion 20, is a well-established principle. In addition, implementation issues would arise in recognizing the future effects of changes in the measure of the accumulated benefit obligation that is included in the transition obligation. One such issue would be how the effects of plan amendments that reduce benefits that existed at the transition date or the effects of settlements or curtailments and gains from experience different from that assumed should be reflected.

265. A few respondents supported a comprehensive income approach. Concepts Statement 5 discusses comprehensive income as a broad measure of the effects of all changes in an enterprise's equity for a period, other than from transactions resulting from investments by or distributions to owners. Earnings are described as a measure of performance for a period. Following a comprehensive income approach would include the effects of changes in accounting principles in comprehensive income but not in earnings. Respondents suggested establishing a separate, permanent component of equity to report the effect of recognizing the transition obligation either immediately or on a delayed basis. The suggested approach differs from certain existing separate components of equity (as described in FASB Statements No. 12, *Accounting for Marketable Securities,* and No. 52, *Foreign Currency Translation,* and Statement 87), that ultimately are reflected in determining net income of subsequent periods, if not offset by other events. The comprehensive income approach suggested by respondents would require separate Board consideration of how comprehensive income would be displayed, since Concepts State-

ment 5 does not address that issue. That consideration is beyond the scope of this Statement.

266. The Board concluded that, if an employer's transition obligation or asset is recognized immediately, the effect of that change in accounting should be recognized in a manner consistent with recognition of the effects of other changes in accounting. The Board believes that recognition of the effects of an accounting change through income is widely understood and accepted. To immediately recognize the effects of adopting this Statement in a different manner would be inconsistent with how subsequent adjustments of the transition obligation are recognized and would diminish the understandability and usefulness of the financial statements. Therefore, the Board concluded that the effects of an employer's election to immediately recognize its transition obligation or asset for postretirement benefits should be reported as the effect of an accounting change; employers that elect delayed recognition of the transition obligation or asset should report the recognition of that amount as a component of net periodic postretirement benefit cost, consistent with the manner of reporting the transition effects of Statement 87.

267. The Board also concluded that for individual deferred compensation contracts, the effects of a change in the measurement and recognition of an employer's obligation at the date the change in accounting is adopted should be recognized in a manner consistent with the nature of the benefit provided by the contract. Consequently, the effect of the change in accounting for individual contracts that provide postretirement health or other welfare benefits, measured at the date of the change, is subject to the general transition provisions and effective dates of this Statement (paragraphs 108-114). However, the effect of a change in accounting for other individual deferred compensation contracts is to be recognized as the cumulative effect of a change in accounting in accordance with Opinion 20, effective for fiscal years beginning after March 15, 1991. The Board believed that that delay in the effective date for those contracts should provide sufficient time for communication of the amendment of Opinion 12 to affected employers.

Components of Net Periodic Postretirement Benefit Cost

268. The Board concluded that an understanding of postretirement benefit accounting is facilitated by separately considering the components of net periodic postretirement benefit cost. Those components are service cost, interest cost, actual return on plan assets, amortization of unrecognized prior service cost, gain or loss recognition, and amorti-

zation of the transition obligation or asset for employers who elect delayed recognition of the unrecognized obligation or asset existing at the date of initial application of this Statement.

269. A plan with no plan assets, no plan amendments, no gains or losses, and no unrecognized transition amount would have two components of cost—service cost and interest cost. As employees work during the year in exchange for promised benefits, a *service cost* (compensation cost) accrues. Measurement of that component is discussed in the section on measurement of cost and obligations (paragraphs 166-246). Since the service cost component and the related obligation are measured on a present value basis under this Statement, a second component—*interest cost*—also must be accounted for. Measurement of that component is straightforward once the discount rates are determined; selection of appropriate discount rates is discussed in paragraphs 186-193.

270. A third component of cost exists for a funded plan—the *return* (or possibly loss) *on plan assets.* That component ordinarily reduces net periodic postretirement benefit cost. The interest cost and return on plan assets components represent financial items rather than employee compensation cost and are affected by changes in the employer's financing arrangements. For example, an employer can increase the return on plan assets by making additional contributions to a fund that is segregated and restricted for the payment of the postretirement benefits. An employer can decrease interest cost (and return on plan assets) by using plan assets to purchase nonparticipating life insurance contracts to settle part of the accumulated postretirement benefit obligation of a postretirement life insurance plan.

271. The fourth component of cost is the *amortization of unrecognized prior service cost,* which reflects the increase or decrease in compensation cost as a result of granting, improving, or reducing postretirement benefits attributed, pursuant to this Statement, to periods prior to the plan initiation or amendment. The amortization of unrecognized prior service cost that results from a plan initiation that grants retroactive benefits will increase net periodic postretirement benefit cost; amortization of prior service cost that results from a plan amendment will increase or decrease the net periodic postretirement benefit cost depending on whether the amendment increases or reduces (a negative plan amendment) benefits.

272. The fifth component of cost is the *gain or loss component.* That component either decreases or increases postretirement benefit cost depending on whether the net unrecognized amount is a gain or a loss, whether the actual return on plan assets for a particular period is less than or greater than the expected return on plan assets, and whether an employer makes a decision to temporarily deviate from the substantive plan. That component combines gains and losses of various types and therefore includes both compensation and financial items that are not readily separable.

Conclusions on Other Issues—Single-Employer Defined Benefit Postretirement Plans

Fundamentals of Postretirement Benefit Accounting

273. In applying accrual accounting to postretirement benefits, this Statement accepts three fundamental ideas that are common to pension accounting: delayed recognition of certain events, reporting net cost, and offsetting liabilities and related assets. Those three features of practice have shaped financial reporting for pensions for many years even though they conflict in some respects with accounting principles applied elsewhere.

274. Delayed recognition means that certain changes in the obligation for postretirement benefits, including those changes that result from a plan initiation or amendment, and certain changes in the value of plan assets set aside to meet that obligation are not recognized as they occur. Rather, those changes are recognized systematically over future periods. All changes in the obligation and plan assets are ultimately recognized unless they are first offset by future changes. The changes that have been quantified but not yet recognized in the employer's financial statements as components of net periodic postretirement benefit cost and as a liability or asset are disclosed.

275. Net cost means that the recognized consequences of events and transactions that affect a postretirement benefit plan are reported as a single amount in the employer's financial statements. That net cost comprises at least three types of events or transactions that might otherwise be reported separately. Those events or transactions—exchanging a promise of deferred compensation in the form of postretirement benefits for employee service, the interest cost arising from the passage of time until those benefits are paid, and the returns from the investment of plan assets—are disclosed separately as components of net periodic postretirement benefit cost.

276. Offsetting means that the postretirement benefit obligation recognized in the employer's statement of financial position is reported net of amounts contributed to a plan specifically for the payment of that obligation and that the return on plan assets is offset in the employer's statement of

income against other components of net periodic postretirement benefit cost. That offsetting is reflected even though the obligation has not been settled, the investment of the plan assets may be largely controlled by the employer, and substantial risks and rewards associated with both the obligation and the plan assets are borne by the employer.

Recognition and Measurement of a Plan Initiation or Amendment

277. When a postretirement benefit plan is initiated or amended to increase benefits, credit may be explicitly granted for employee service rendered prior to the date of the plan initiation or amendment. However, a plan initiation or amendment may not explicitly grant prior service credit. Thus it may be unclear whether an obligation for prior service arises for all or some of the participants.

278. A plan initiation or amendment that provides benefits to current retirees can only grant the retirees credit for their prior service, since no future service can be required for them to be entitled to the new or amended benefits. Consequently, an obligation for prior service arises to the extent a plan initiation or amendment provides new or increased benefits to current retirees. A similar assessment can be made for a plan initiation or amendment that provides benefits to other plan participants who have rendered sufficient service to be fully eligible to receive the new or amended benefits. However, since some of those plan participants have not yet retired and are expected to render additional future service, some respondents argued that a plan initiation or amendment affecting active plan participants fully eligible for benefits may be viewed as prospective. That view acknowledges no obligation for prior service; any obligation would arise as the employees render future service in exchange for the benefits. As applied to active plan participants who are fully eligible for benefits, the latter argument appears to be consistent only with the use of an attribution period that would end at an active plan participant's retirement date, not with an attribution period ending at an active plan participant's full eligibility date.

279. When new or amended benefits are granted to active plan participants who are not yet fully eligible for benefits, the determination of whether those benefits are granted in exchange for past or future service is unclear unless specified by the plan initiation or amendment. Some respondents argued that because eligibility for the new or amended benefits is contingent on rendering future service, the plan initiation or amendment should be viewed only as prospective. Others argued that, consistent with the attribution approach that allocates an equal amount of benefit to each year of

service in the attribution period and assuming the plan's benefit formula does not specify the benefits earned for specific years of service, the granting of new or amended benefits should be viewed as partially retroactive, to the extent the benefits are attributable to prior service periods, and partially prospective.

280. The Board noted that if a plan initiation or amendment does not explicitly state whether the new or amended benefits are granted prospectively or retroactively, but affects retirees as well as active plan participants, the plan could be viewed as implicitly granting prior service credit to active plan participants expected to receive the new or amended benefits. Assigning new or amended benefits to prior periods acknowledges that benefits are provided in exchange for employee service over the total credited service period.

281. The Board considered whether a plan initiation should be given the same accounting treatment as a plan amendment. If a plan initiation is viewed as retroactive, presumably any subsequent plan amendment also should be viewed as retroactive unless the plan specifically ignores prior service in determining eligibility for the new or amended benefit. However, if a plan initiation is viewed as prospective, one could view a subsequent amendment to that plan either as retroactive to the date of plan initiation or as prospective.

282. In considering whether plan initiations and amendments should be viewed similarly (that is, both as retroactive or both as prospective), the Board acknowledged the potential difficulty in distinguishing between a plan initiation and plan amendment. For example, if an employer has a health care plan for retirees and decides to provide dental benefits to retirees, one can view the action as an amendment of the postretirement health care plan or as the initiation of a postretirement dental care plan. The Board also was concerned about accounting for other amendments that might be viewed as plan initiations. For example, if a plan providing nominal benefits was initiated on January 1 and then was amended a few months later to increase benefits, the amended plan could be viewed as the plan that was contemplated when initiated on January 1. The Board concluded that a plan initiation should be accounted for in a manner similar to a plan amendment, unless the plan specifically provides benefits solely in exchange for service after the date of the plan initiation or a future date.

283. The Board also considered whether the effects of a plan initiation or amendment on retirees and other fully eligible plan participants should be viewed as retroactive and the effects on other ac-

tive plan participants as prospective. In granting new or amended benefits to retirees and other fully eligible plan participants, an employer is implicitly, if not explicitly, granting credit for prior service. However, for active plan participants who have not yet attained full eligibility for those benefits, the new or amended benefits could be provided in exchange for their remaining service to full eligibility for benefits. Some interested parties, particularly consulting actuaries, advised the Board of the difficulties in measuring the service cost component of net periodic postretirement benefit cost and gains and losses if plan amendments were viewed as prospective for some plan participants.

284. Under a prospective approach, the benefits granted at plan initiation and with each subsequent amendment would need to be layered, requiring a repricing of each layer at each measurement date to determine service cost and gains or losses. That repricing could be particularly difficult when the plan does not define the specific periods of service to be rendered in exchange for the benefits and the benefits are defined in kind, rather than in terms of a fixed value or amount of benefit. In addition to the concerns expressed with prospective treatment of a plan initiation or amendment that affects certain active plan participants, the Board noted that negative plan amendments cannot logically be viewed as prospective for those plan participants. Given those factors, and the decision to reduce complexity by attributing the expected postretirement benefit obligation ratably to employees' years of service in the attribution period, the Board concluded that all plan amendments should be viewed as retroactive for all plan participants. Similarly, plan initiations generally should be viewed as retroactive unless the plan initiation specifically disregards prior service in determining eligibility for the new benefits.

Recognition of prior service cost

285. When a plan is amended to increase benefits or a plan is initiated and grants credit for prior service, the accumulated postretirement benefit obligation, based on retroactive allocation of benefits to service in prior years, is greater than before the plan initiation or amendment. As a result, the incremental obligation created by a plan initiation or amendment is reflected immediately as an increase in the accumulated postretirement benefit obligation. Whether that increase should be recognized (a) immediately as postretirement benefit cost for the year of the plan initiation or amendment or (b) on a delayed basis as part of postretirement benefit cost for future periods is arguable, particularly when the plan's terms attribute the increase to employees' prior service.

286. Some Board members support immediate recognition of prior service cost as an expense, particularly the portion related to existing retirees. Although some intangible economic benefits of a plan initiation or amendment may be received in future periods from benefit improvements for active plan participants, they believe that those intangible benefits do not qualify for recognition as an asset. Therefore, they believe there is little basis for delaying recognition of the underlying prior service cost to future periods. Other Board members believe that a plan initiation or amendment is made with a view to benefiting the employer's future operations through reduced employee turnover, improved productivity, or reduced demands for increases in cash compensation.

287. In its deliberations on Statement 87, the Board concluded that it is reasonable to assume that a plan amendment is the result of an economic decision and that a future economic benefit to the employer exists when benefit increases are granted to active plan participants and retirees. They observed that amortizing the cost of acquiring a future economic benefit over future periods is consistent with accounting practice in other areas. The Board also concluded that a requirement to charge the cost of a retroactive plan initiation or amendment immediately to net periodic pension cost would be an unacceptable change from prior practice. Accordingly, the Board concluded that the increase in the obligation resulting from a pension plan initiation or amendment should be recognized as a component of net periodic pension cost over a number of future periods as the anticipated benefit to the employer is expected to be realized.

288. In considering postretirement benefits, the Board found no compelling reason to recognize the cost of a retroactive plan initiation or amendment in a manner fundamentally different from that required by Statement 87. Thus, this Statement requires recognizing an equal amount of the prior service cost in each remaining year of service to the full eligibility date of each plan participant active at the date of the plan initiation or amendment who is not yet fully eligible for benefits at that date. Other alternatives provided under Statement 87 that recognize the prior service cost more rapidly, such as over the average remaining years of service to full eligibility for benefits of the active plan participants, also are permitted.

289. The Board recognizes that treating any plan amendment as retroactive, even if the new or amended benefits are provided solely in exchange for future service, results in a measure of the accumulated postretirement benefit obligation and of unrecognized prior service cost that may exceed

the measure that would result from following the plan terms. The effect of retroactive treatment, however, is consistent with the pattern of ratably attributing the expected postretirement benefit obligation to each year of service in the attribution period. The effects of a higher measure of the accumulated postretirement benefit obligation and unrecognized prior service cost in some cases, as a result of treating prospective changes as retroactive, are consequences that offset the benefits of the simpler methodology provided by a ratable attribution pattern. However, delayed recognition of prior service cost mitigates those effects and net periodic postretirement benefit cost is not expected to be significantly affected.

Recognition of the effect of a plan amendment that reduces benefits (negative plan amendment)

290. A plan amendment may reduce rather than increase benefits attributed to prior service. The Board concluded that, consistent with Statement 87, any decrement in the obligation for benefits attributable to prior service should first reduce any existing unrecognized prior service cost arising from the plan's initiation or subsequent benefit increases. Further, the Board concluded that any remaining effects of a negative plan amendment should next reduce any unrecognized transition obligation with any remaining credit generally recognized in a manner consistent with prior service cost; that is, over remaining years of service to full eligibility for benefits of the active plan participants. The Board concluded that those constraints on recognition of the effects of a negative plan amendment are necessary because the effects of reducing a plan promise should not be recognized before the original promise, including the unrecognized transition obligation, is recognized. Immediate recognition of the effects of a negative plan amendment also is precluded because future periods may be affected by an employer's decision to reduce benefits provided under the plan.

Delayed Recognition of Gains and Losses

291. Gains and losses, sometimes called actuarial gains and losses, are changes in either the accumulated postretirement benefit obligation or the fair value of plan assets arising from changes in assumptions and from experience different from that incorporated in the assumptions. For example, gains and losses include the effects on measurement of the accumulated postretirement benefit obligation that result from changes in the assumed health care cost trend rates for postretirement health care plans and actual returns on plan assets greater than or less than the expected rates of return.

292. Some respondents expressed concern about

the volatility of a measure of an unfunded postretirement benefit obligation and the practical effects of incorporating that volatility into financial statements. The Board does not believe that volatility in financial statements is necessarily undesirable. If a financial measure purports to represent a phenomenon that is volatile, that measure must reflect the volatility or it will not be representationally faithful.

293. The Board acknowledges that, in the case of the accumulated postretirement benefit obligation, reported volatility may not be entirely a faithful representation of changes in the status of the obligation (the phenomenon represented). It also may reflect an unavoidable inability to predict accurately the future events that are anticipated in making period-to-period measurements. That may be particularly true for postretirement health care plans in light of the current inexperience in measuring the accumulated postretirement benefit obligation for those plans. The difference in periodic measures of the accumulated benefit obligation for a postretirement health care plan, and therefore the funded status of the plan, results partly from the inability to predict accurately for a period, or over several periods, annual expected claims costs, future trends in the cost of health care, turnover rates, retirement dates, dependency status, life expectancy, and other pertinent events. As a result, actual experience often differs significantly from what was estimated, which leads to changes in the estimates for future measurements. Recognizing the effects of revisions in estimates in full in the period in which they occur may produce financial statements that portray more volatility than is inherent in the employer's obligation.

294. The Board considered those views and concluded that, similar to employers' accounting for pensions, gains and losses should not be required to be recognized immediately as a component of net periodic postretirement benefit cost. Accordingly, this Statement provides for delayed recognition of gains (losses) over future periods to the extent they are not reduced by subsequent losses (gains). The effects of changes in the fair value of plan assets, including the indirect effect of those changes on the return-on-assets component of net periodic postretirement benefit cost, are recognized on a basis intended to reduce volatility. The method used was developed in Statement 87. Both the extent of reduction in volatility and the mechanism adopted to effect it are essentially practical decisions without conceptual basis. The Board believes that the market-related value of plan assets used in this Statement as a device to reduce the volatility of net periodic postretirement benefit cost is not as relevant as the fair value of those assets.

295. Unlike most pension plans, the return on postretirement benefit plan assets may be subject to income tax because of the lack of tax-exempt vehicles for funding those benefits. At present, even if postretirement benefit plan assets are restricted and segregated within a trust, the income generated by those assets generally is taxable. If the plan has taxable income, the assessed tax will reduce the returns available for payment of benefits or reinvestment. The Board concluded that when the trust or other entity holding the plan assets is taxed as a separate entity on the return on *plan assets* (as defined herein), the expected long-term rate of return should be determined by giving consideration to anticipated income taxes under enacted tax law. However, if the tax on income generated by plan assets is not a liability of the plan, but of the employer, the expected long-term rate of return should not anticipate a tax on those earnings, because that tax will be reflected in the employer's accounting for income taxes.

296. The Board had several reasons for adopting the approach required in this Statement for measuring and incorporating the return on plan assets into net periodic postretirement benefit cost. First, it is the same as that used in Statement 87 and is similar, mechanically, to actuarial practices intended to reflect the return on plan assets. As a result, it should be easier for those familiar with pension accounting or actuarial practices to understand and apply. Second, the use of explicit estimates of the return on plan assets avoids the use of discount rates, which are primarily relevant for measuring the accumulated postretirement benefit obligation, as part of a calculation related to the return on plan assets. Therefore, it reflects more clearly the Board's basic conclusion that information about a deferred compensation plan is more understandable if asset-related or financial features of the arrangement are distinguished from the liability-related and compensation cost features.

297. If assumptions prove to be accurate estimates of experience over a number of years, gains or losses in one year will be offset by losses or gains in subsequent periods. In that situation, all gains and losses would be offset over time, and amortization of unrecognized gains and losses would be unnecessary. The Board was concerned that the uncertainties inherent in assumptions could lead to gains or losses that increase rather than offset, and concluded that gains and losses should not be ignored completely. Actual experience will determine the final net cost of a postretirement benefit plan. The Board concluded that some amortization, at least when the net unrecognized gain or loss becomes significant, should be required.

298. Consistent with Statement 87, this Statement uses a "corridor" approach as a minimum amortization approach. That approach allows a reasonable opportunity for gains and losses to offset each other without affecting net periodic postretirement benefit cost. The Board also noted that the corridor approach is similar in some respects to methods used by some to deal with gains and losses on plan assets for funding purposes. The width of that corridor is related to the market-related value of plan assets and the amount of the accumulated postretirement benefit obligation because the gains and losses subject to amortization are changes in those two amounts. The Exposure Draft proposed that a net gain or loss equal to 10 percent of the greater of those two amounts should not be required to be amortized (and thus included in net periodic postretirement benefit cost). Thus, the width of the resulting corridor would be 20 percent (from 90 percent to 110 percent of the greater balance).

299. Respondents generally agreed with the proposal to shield from recognition gains and losses falling within a defined corridor. However, many of the respondents suggested a wider corridor. They stated that they believe there will be greater volatility of measurement of postretirement benefit obligations than of pension obligations. They suggested that that consideration and the inability to fund postretirement benefit plans (which they believed would provide offsetting asset-related gains and losses) warrant a wider corridor to further mitigate potential swings in net postretirement benefit cost from one period to the next.

300. The effects of widening the corridor to 20 percent of the greater of the accumulated postretirement benefit obligation or market-related value of plan assets were tested in a number of different scenarios. The results of that study showed that widening the corridor would have little effect on mitigating the volatility of net periodic postretirement benefit cost; the significant factor in mitigating that volatility is the period over which unrecognized gains or losses in excess of the corridor are recognized. The Board concluded that understandability and comparability would be enhanced by retaining the approach followed for pension accounting.

301. Gains and losses also may be recognized immediately or on a delayed basis using any systematic method of amortizing unrecognized gains and losses, provided the method is consistently followed and that it does not result in less rapid recognition of gains and losses than the minimum amortization discussed in paragraph 298. Amortization of unrecognized net gains or losses is based on beginning-of-year balances. If an employer elects to recognize gains and losses immediately, the amount of any net gain in excess of a net loss previously recognized in income shall first offset any

unrecognized transition obligation, and the amount of any net loss in excess of a net gain previously recognized in income shall first offset any unrecognized transition asset. That constraint was added because Board members believe that gains (losses) should not be recognized before the underlying unfunded (overfunded) accumulated postretirement benefit obligation is recognized.

302. In some cases an employer may assume a benefit obligation for current and past benefit payments that differs from the substance of the employer's commitment. For example, on the basis of the mutually understood terms of the substantive plan, an employer may anticipate for accounting purposes that any shortfall resulting from current year benefit payments in excess of the employer's substantive plan cost and participant contributions for the year will be recovered from increased participant contributions in the subsequent year. However, the employer may subsequently determine that increasing participant contributions for the prior year's shortfall is onerous and make a decision to bear the cost of the shortfall for that year. That is, an employer may make a decision not to retrospectively adjust participants' contributions to recover the shortfall. The Board concluded that the gain or loss from such a temporary deviation from the substantive plan should be immediately recognized as a gain or loss, without the benefit of the corridor or other delayed recognition alternatives. Because the effect of the deviation from the substantive plan has no future economic benefit to the employer, and relates to benefits already paid, the Board believes that delayed recognition of that effect would be inappropriate.

Minimum Liability

303. The Exposure Draft proposed that, similar to Statement 87, a minimum liability should be prescribed to limit the extent to which the delayed recognition of the transition obligation, plan amendments, and losses could result in omission of liabilities from an employer's statement of financial position. The minimum liability was defined as the unfunded accumulated postretirement benefit obligation for retirees and other fully eligible plan participants. The Board believed that that measurement represented a threshold below which the recognized liability would not be sufficiently representationally faithful. The proposed minimum liability provisions would have been effective five years after the effective date of this Statement.

304. Respondents generally disagreed with prescribing the minimum liability that should be recognized. They believed that the proposed minimum liability provision represented a departure from accrual accounting and was inconsistent with the provisions of this Statement that provide for delayed recognition of gains and losses, prior service cost, and an employer's transition obligation. Respondents stated that unlike pensions, postretirement benefit obligations do not vest, as that term is used in its legal sense. They observed that the minimum liability provisions in Statement 87 approximate the statutory liability a U.S. employer would face if its pension plan were terminated. Currently, there are no similar statutory requirements for postretirement health care or welfare benefits. Some respondents also believed that the minimum liability provision would be confusing because it introduces an alternative measure of an employer's postretirement benefit obligation.

305. The Board concluded that this Statement should not require recognition of a minimum liability. The field test of the Exposure Draft provisions suggested that, ignoring the effects of gains and losses and plan amendments, the minimum liability provision for mature companies as defined in that study (companies with a ratio of one retiree to two to six active employees) generally would be inoperative after eight years. For companies with a higher retiree to active employee ratio, the field test suggested that the minimum liability provisions might be operative for more than 10 years. In other words, for possibly 10 or more years the minimum liability provisions could be effective solely as a result of phasing in recognition of the transition obligation. The Board concluded that the transition provisions of this Statement that provide for the delayed recognition of an employer's obligation for postretirement benefits at the date this Statement is initially applied should not be overridden by a requirement to recognize a liability that would accelerate recognition of that obligation in the statement of financial position.

306. The Board considered and decided not to amend Statement 87 to eliminate its minimum liability provision. Because most pension plans were thought to be adequately funded when Statement 87 was issued, the minimum liability provision served to identify those exceptional situations in which the pension plan was underfunded. However, it is widely acknowledged that postretirement benefit plans are significantly or totally underfunded. As a result, recognition of a minimum liability for such plans would be commonplace rather than an exception.

307. Some Board members believe that a liability that reflects only the accrued and unfunded postretirement benefit cost, in and of itself, is not a relevant or reliable representation of an employer's probable future sacrifice if recognition of significant losses, prior service costs, or the transition obliga-

tion has been delayed. They support retaining the minimum liability provision proposed in the Exposure Draft for the reasons described in paragraph 303. They observe that the liability for accrued and unfunded postretirement benefit cost does not purport to be a measure of the employer's present obligation in most cases; rather, it is the residual resulting from an allocation process. To the extent that one assumes that the employer is a going concern and that a postretirement benefit plan will continue, the employer's probable future sacrifice is represented by benefits to which retirees and other fully eligible plan participants are entitled and the portion of expected future benefits earned by other active plan participants. That probable future sacrifice can only be determined by considering the current funded status of the plan.

Measurement of Plan Assets

308. The Board considered whether employer assets intended to be used for the payment of postretirement benefits, including funds set aside in a separate trust or similar funding vehicle, should be included in plan assets. The Board concluded that if those assets can be used for other purposes at the employer's discretion, they should not be considered to be plan assets. In measuring the funded status of a postretirement benefit plan, the Board concluded that it is appropriate and consistent with pension accounting to include in plan assets only those assets that are restricted for the purpose of paying the plan's postretirement benefit obligations. Some respondents questioned whether certain funding vehicles can be restricted solely for the provision of postretirement benefits, as opposed to funding both active employees' and retirees' benefits, and would, therefore, qualify as plan assets. Whether a funding vehicle can be restricted solely for the payment of retirees' benefits is subject to legal, not accounting, interpretation.

309. The Board concluded that plan investments should be measured at fair value for purposes of this Statement, except as provided in paragraph 57 for purposes of determining the extent of delayed recognition of gains and losses. Fair value is the most relevant information that can be provided for assessing both the plan's ability to pay benefits as they come due and the future contributions necessary to provide for benefits already promised to employees. The relevance of fair value outweighs objections to its use based on difficulty of measurement. The same reasons led to a similar decision in Statements 35 and 87.

310. Measuring investments at fair value could introduce volatility into the financial statements as a result of short-term changes in fair values. Some respondents indicated that that volatility would be meaningless or even misleading, particularly because of the long-run nature of the postretirement benefit commitment or because plan investments are often held for long periods, thus providing the opportunity for some gains or losses to reverse. As noted in paragraphs 58-60, the Board concluded that the difference between the actual return on plan assets and the expected return on plan assets could be recognized in net periodic postretirement benefit cost on a delayed basis. That conclusion was based on (a) the probability that at least some gains would be offset by subsequent losses, and vice versa, and (b) arguments that immediate recognition would produce unacceptable volatility and would be inconsistent with the present accounting model.

311. The Board also concluded that, similar to the conclusion in Statement 87, including accrued postretirement benefit costs as plan assets for purposes of the disclosure of funded status (paragraph 74(c)) (a) would be inappropriate because that amount has not been funded (contributed) and (b) would unnecessarily complicate the recognition and disclosure requirements of this Statement. Similarly, the Board concluded that elimination from plan assets of all securities of the employer held by the plan would be impractical and might be inappropriate absent a decision that the financial statements of the plan should be consolidated with those of the employer. However, the Board concluded that disclosure of the amount of those securities held is appropriate and should be required.

Measurement Date

312. The Board concluded that the prescribed measurement date should be responsive to the difficulties inherent in measurement of the accumulated postretirement benefit obligation as well as the time required to obtain actuarial valuation reports. The Board believed those considerations justified some flexibility in selecting the date at which the accumulated postretirement benefit obligation and plan assets should be measured.

313. Measuring plan assets as of the date of the financial statements does not present very significant or unusual problems; the difficulty arises primarily with measurement of the accumulated postretirement benefit obligation. The Board concluded that it should be feasible to provide information about the accumulated postretirement benefit obligation as of the date of the financial statements based on a valuation performed at an earlier date with adjustments for relevant subsequent events (especially employee service) after that date.

314. The Board concluded that the benefits of

having information on a timely basis and measured consistently with other financial information will usually outweigh the incremental costs. The Board acknowledges that practical problems may sometimes make it costly to obtain information, especially information about the accumulated postretirement benefit obligation and related components of net periodic postretirement benefit cost, as of the date of the financial statements. The Board concluded that the information required by this Statement should be as of a date not earlier than three months before the date of the financial statements. That measurement date is consistent with the measurement date prescribed by Statement 87. Measurements of postretirement benefit cost for interim and annual financial statements should be based on the assumptions used for the previous year-end financial reporting unless more recent measures of both plan assets and the accumulated postretirement benefit obligation are available, for example, as a result of a significant event, such as a plan amendment.

Settlements and Curtailments

315. This Statement provides for delayed recognition of the effects of plan initiations and amendments and gains and losses arising in the ordinary course of operations. In certain circumstances, however, recognition of some or all of those delayed effects may be appropriate. Paragraphs 316-332 discuss the basis for the Board's conclusions on settlement and curtailment accounting for postretirement benefit plans, which draw on the basis for conclusions in Statement 88. Except as discussed in paragraph 325, the Board's conclusions are the same as those prescribed in Statement 88 for a settlement or a curtailment of a defined benefit pension plan.

316. Settlements and curtailments are events that require income or expense recognition of previously unrecognized amounts and adjustments to liabilities or assets recognized in the employer's statement of financial position. The Board concluded that, similar to employers' accounting for pensions, previously unrecognized prior service cost, including any unrecognized transition obligation, and the previously unrecognized net gain (including any unrecognized transition asset) or loss should be recognized in the period when all of the following conditions are met:

a. All postretirement health care or other welfare benefit obligations under the plan are settled.
b. Defined benefits are no longer accrued under the plan.
c. The plan is not replaced by another defined benefit plan.
d. No plan assets remain.
e. The employees are terminated.
f. The plan ceases to exist as an entity.

317. It is not uncommon for some, but not all, of the above conditions to exist in a particular situation. For example, the accumulated postretirement benefit obligation may be settled without terminating the plan, or a plan may be suspended so that no further benefits will accrue for future services but its obligations are not settled. In other situations one or more of the above conditions may apply to only part of a plan. For example, one plan may be divided into two plans, one of which is then terminated, or one-half of the employees in a plan may terminate employment and the obligation for their benefits may be settled.

318. If recognition of previously unrecognized prior service cost and net gain or loss were required only when a plan is completely terminated and settled and if no recognition occurred when a plan is partially curtailed or an obligation is partially settled, anomalies and implementation problems would result. For example, if one employer had two plants with separate plans and another employer had two plants with a single plan, the accounting result of closing one plant and settling the related obligation would be a recognizable event for one employer but not for the other. If recognition were an all-or-nothing proposition, it would be necessary to determine when the extent of settlement or curtailment is sufficient for recognition. If all employees but one from a large group are terminated and obligations to the terminated employees are settled, presumably the accounting should reflect a plan termination. But it is not clear whether that accounting should apply if 5 percent, 10 percent, or 25 percent of the original group were to remain. The Board concluded in Statement 88 and reconfirmed in this Statement that a complete plan termination and settlement need not occur to recognize previously unrecognized amounts.

Settlement of the obligation

319. The Board concluded that settlement of all or part of the accumulated postretirement benefit obligation should be the event that requires recognition of all or part of the previously unrecognized net gain (including any unrecognized transition asset) or loss. Delayed recognition of gains and losses under this Statement is based in part on the possibility that gains or losses occurring in one period will be offset by losses or gains in subsequent periods. To the extent that the accumulated postretirement benefit obligation has been settled, the possibility of future gains and losses related to that obligation and the assets used to effect the settlement is eliminated.

320. Settlement of all or a large portion of the accumulated postretirement benefit obligation also may be viewed as realization of past gains or losses associated with that portion of the obligation and

the assets used to effect the settlement. That realization would not be affected by the employer's subsequent decision to undertake or not to undertake future defined benefit obligations.

321. The Board acknowledges that other actions an employer can take, especially those related to plan assets, can affect the possibility of a subsequent net gain or loss. For example, an employer may avoid or minimize certain risks by investing in a portfolio of high-quality fixed-income securities with principal and interest payment dates similar to the estimated payment dates of benefits, as with a dedicated bond portfolio.

322. Settlement differs from other actions in that (a) it is irrevocable, (b) it relieves the employer (or the plan) of primary responsibility for the obligation, and (c) it eliminates significant risks related to the obligation, such as the risk that participants will live longer than assumed, and to the assets used to effect the settlement. The decision to have a dedicated bond portfolio can be reversed, it does not relieve the employer of primary responsibility for the obligation, and such a strategy does not eliminate various risks, such as mortality risk and the escalating cost of providing the benefits. The Board concluded that the circumstances requiring gain or loss recognition should be defined narrowly.

323. The Board recognizes that changes in the previously estimated values of the accumulated postretirement benefit obligation and the plan assets may become evident at the time the obligation is settled. For example, the interest rates inherent in the price actually paid for insurance contracts that settle an obligation may be different from the assumed discount rates. Some respondents suggested that those changes should be recognized immediately in income as a gain or loss directly resulting from the settlement. The Board concluded that, based on the measurement principles adopted in this Statement, those changes reflect factors expected to be considered in the measurement of the postretirement benefit obligation and plan assets. The Board also concluded that those amounts should be included with the previously unrecognized net gain or loss before a pro rata portion of that amount is recognized.

324. This Statement requires measurement of a pro rata portion of the unrecognized net gain or loss based on the decrease in the accumulated postretirement benefit obligation resulting from a settlement. The Board acknowledges that a decrease in the amount of plan assets also can affect the possibility of future gains and losses. However, the Board concluded that it would be simpler and more practical to base the measurement only on the obligation settled.

325. Under Statement 88, a gain resulting from settlement of a pension obligation is measured without regard to any remaining unrecognized transition obligation. In contrast with the nature of the transition obligation that may arise under Statement 87, any unrecognized transition obligation for postretirement benefits is likely to include a significant amount of previously unrecognized current service cost and interest cost. For an ongoing plan, this Statement requires that for an employer that elects immediate recognition of gains or losses, any net gain for the year that does not offset a loss previously recognized in income must first reduce any remaining unrecognized transition obligation. Similarly, the Board has concluded that any gain arising from a settlement should be reduced by any unrecognized transition obligation; only the excess is recognized as a settlement gain. The Board concluded that an employer should not be permitted to accelerate recognition of gains if the underlying obligation that was remeasured, causing those gains to arise, has not yet been recognized.

Curtailment of the plan

326. One basis for delayed recognition of prior service cost is the likelihood of future economic benefits to the employer as a result of a plan initiation or amendment. Those benefits, in the Board's view, are derived from the future services of active plan participants, and the amortization of unrecognized prior service cost is based on those services. A curtailment, as defined in this Statement, is an event that significantly reduces the expected years of future service of present active plan participants or eliminates for a significant number of active plan participants the accrual of defined benefits for some or all of their future services.

327. The Board concluded that reduction of the expected years of future service of the work force or elimination of the accrual of defined postretirement benefits for a significant number of active plan participants raises doubt about the continued existence of the future economic benefits of unrecognized prior service cost. Therefore, the Board concluded that any remaining unrecognized prior service cost, including any unrecognized transition obligation, should be recognized when it is probable that a curtailment will occur, the effects are reasonably estimable, and the net result of the curtailment (as described in paragraphs 97 and 98) is a loss.

328. The Board also considered whether either the settlement or the termination of one plan and the adoption of a substantially equivalent replacement plan should trigger recognition of prior service cost. The Board concluded that neither of those events, absent a curtailment, raises sufficient

doubt as to the existence of future economic benefits to trigger that recognition.

329. A curtailment may directly cause a decrease in the accumulated postretirement benefit obligation (a gain) or an increase in the accumulated postretirement benefit obligation (a loss). For example, the accumulated postretirement benefit obligation may decline if active plan participants who are not yet eligible for benefits are terminated (a gain). On the other hand, the accumulated postretirement benefit obligation may increase if an event occurs that causes active plan participants fully eligible for benefits to leave earlier than previously expected (a loss).

330. Conceptually, the Board concluded that it would be appropriate to recognize those gains or losses immediately to the extent they do not represent the reversal of previously unrecognized losses or gains. However, the obligation eliminated or created by a curtailment may not be independent of previously unrecognized losses or gains. For example, part of that obligation could relate to past changes in actuarial assumptions about the discount rates that produced gains or losses not yet fully recognized. To illustrate, if in year 1 the employer reduces the assumed weighted-average discount rate from 9 percent to 8 percent, any accumulated postretirement benefit obligation is increased, resulting in an unrecognized loss. If in year 2 the employer terminates active plan participants, the obligation related to their nonvested accumulated benefits is eliminated and a gain arises, which is, at least in part, a reversal of the previously unrecognized loss.

331. The Board concluded that, similar to Statement 88, a curtailment gain or loss as defined in paragraph 97 (which does not include recognition of prior service cost) should first be offset to the extent possible against the plan's previously existing unrecognized net loss or gain. Any remainder of the curtailment gain or loss cannot, at least in an overall sense, be a reversal of unrecognized amounts, and, therefore, recognition of that remainder is appropriate.

332. The Board considered whether curtailment gains should be recognized before the curtailment occurs. It concluded that continuing the delayed recognition feature of this Statement for a curtailment gain should be retained until the related active plan participants terminate or the plan suspension or amendment is adopted. That is consistent with Statement 88 and Opinion 30 and avoids the inconsistent results that would otherwise occur if

the curtailment gain is directly related to a disposal of a segment of a business.

Measurement of Special Termination Benefits

333. FASB Statement No. 74, *Accounting for Special Termination Benefits Paid to Employees,* acknowledged that other benefits, in addition to pensions, may be offered pursuant to a special termination arrangement and should be included in measuring the termination expense. Statement 88, which superseded Statement 74, retains that scope and therefore applies to other benefits in addition to pensions. However, the Board concluded that reiterating the applicability of Statement 88 is necessary, since practice may have been to exclude postretirement health care costs from the measurement of termination benefits.

334. The primary conclusion of the Board in Statement 74 was that the cost of special termination benefits should be recognized as a liability and a loss when the employees accept the offer and the amount can be reasonably estimated. That conclusion is incorporated in Statement 88. The cost of other contractual termination benefits provided by the existing terms of a plan that are payable only in the event of employees' involuntary termination of service due to a plant closing or a similar event should be recognized when it is probable that employees will be entitled to benefits and the amount can be reasonably estimated.

335. Paragraph 3 of Statement 74 stated:

> The termination of employees under a special termination benefit arrangement may affect the estimated costs of other employee benefits, such as pension benefits, because of differences between past assumptions and actual experience. If reliably measurable, the effects of any such changes on an employer's previously accrued expenses for those benefits that result directly from the termination of employees shall be included in measuring the termination expense. [Footnote reference omitted.]

Statement 88 superseded that paragraph and provides that a gain or loss in a plan arising as a direct result of a curtailment, including a curtailment resulting from an offer of special termination benefits, is first offset against any previously existing unrecognized net loss or gain for that plan and any excess is then recognized (paragraph 13).

336. The Board considered the following three alternative measures of the termination expense[37]

---

[37]The cost of any related curtailment would be determined separately pursuant to paragraphs 97-99.

arising from the acceptance of an offer of special postretirement health care or other welfare termination benefits:

a. The difference between (1) the accumulated postretirement benefit obligation under the existing plan that would have been attributed to service to date assuming that active plan participants not yet fully eligible for benefits would terminate at their full eligibility date and that fully eligible active plan participants would retire immediately, without considering any special termination benefits, and (2) the remeasured accumulated postretirement benefit obligation based on the special termination benefits
b. The difference between (1) the accumulated postretirement benefit obligation attributed to service to date and (2) the remeasured accumulated postretirement benefit obligation based on the special termination benefits
c. The difference between (1) the actuarial present value of the postretirement benefits an employee would have received if the employee had terminated voluntarily immediately before the offer and (2) the actuarial present value of the postretirement benefits the employee is expected to receive after accepting the offer.

337. The Board concluded that the first alternative was appropriate because it better reflects the exchange. Unlike the second alternative, it recognizes the incentive offered in exchange for termination earlier than expected. The first alternative becomes more compelling when one considers the offer of special termination benefits for fully eligible active plan participants. For those employees, there may be no incentive in the form of benefits not already available. Under the first alternative, the effects of the change in the expected retirement dates for employees who accept the offer may be a curtailment loss pursuant to paragraphs 97-99.

338. In contrast, the third alternative ignores the notion that the obligation to provide postretirement benefits arises with the rendering of employee service. That notion underlies the accounting for all deferred compensation contracts. The Board also noted that the third alternative fails to recognize that the termination benefit incentive for an employee one year away from eligibility for retirement differs from the incentive for an employee five years away.

Disclosure

General considerations

339. Decisions on disclosure requirements require

evaluating and balancing considerations of relevance, reliability, and cost. Relevance and reliability are characteristics that make information useful for making decisions and that make it beneficial to require disclosure of some information. Benefits to users that are expected to result from required disclosures must be compared with the costs of providing and assimilating that information. Evaluating individual disclosures relative to those criteria is generally a matter of judgment. Cost, for example, is affected by several factors, such as the number of different plans and the difficulty of aggregating or meaningfully summarizing some disclosures. As the total amount of disclosure increases, consideration must be given to whether the incremental cost to both preparers and users of additional disclosure may be greater than the benefit of the additional information. Conversely, there is also a cost of not disclosing information. The absence of certain disclosures may directly affect the ability of financial statement users to make well-informed decisions.

340. Many of the disclosure requirements arise as a result of provisions of this Statement that reflect practical, rather than conceptual, decisions. For example, the components of net periodic postretirement benefit cost are disclosed because the recognized consequences of events and transactions affecting a postretirement benefit plan are reported as a single amount that includes at least three types of transactions that conceptually should be reported separately. The effects of those events or transactions—the exchange of employee service for deferred compensation in the form of postretirement benefits, interest cost reflecting the passage of time until those benefits are paid, and the returns from the investment of plan assets—are therefore disclosed. Similarly, the reconciliation of the funded status of the plan(s) is disclosed as a result of the decision to exclude certain obligations and assets from the statement of financial position due to provisions that permit delayed recognition of (a) the transition obligation, (b) the effect of certain changes in the measure of an employer's accumulated postretirement benefit obligation, and (c) the effect of certain changes in the value of plan assets set aside to meet that obligation. Although those effects are identified and measured, they are not required to be recognized in the financial statements as they arise.

341. Many of the disclosures required by this Statement are similar to required disclosures for pension plans. Some studies of the pension disclosures required by Statement 87 have suggested they are valuable because of the information provided.

Specific disclosure requirements

Descriptive information

342. Respondents generally agreed with disclosure of information about plan provisions and employee groups. The Board concluded that a brief description of the plan that is the basis for the accounting (the substantive plan), including any modifications of the existing cost-sharing provisions or increases in monetary benefits that are encompassed by the substantive plan, the employee groups covered, and the types of benefits provided, could assist users in understanding the reported effects of the plan on the employer's financial statements. The Board also concluded that financial statements should disclose the nature and effects of significant changes in the factors affecting the computation of the accumulated postretirement benefit obligation and related cost recognized in the financial statements. Any other significant or unusual matters, such as the effect of a business combination, also should be disclosed to enhance a user's understanding of the impact of those matters on an employer's financial position and results of operations.

343. Many postretirement benefit plans currently in existence are unfunded. For those that are funded, the Board concluded that disclosure of the funding policy would be useful in understanding differences between funding and accounting for that plan. Information that highlights any changes in funding policies also can be useful in assessing future cash flows.

Net periodic postretirement benefit cost information

344. Most respondents indicated that information about an employer's net periodic postretirement benefit cost would be useful. As with pensions, the cost of providing postretirement benefits comprises several components. Disclosure of the components will, over time, increase the general understanding of the nature of postretirement benefit cost, the reasons for changes in that cost, and the relationship between financing activities and employee compensation cost.

Information about obligations and assets

345. Most respondents who addressed the proposed disclosures agreed with disclosures about the funded status of the postretirement benefit plan. They stated that it provides information that is important to an understanding of the economics of the plan. Some respondents indicated that as part of that disclosure, it is important to present the components of the accumulated postretirement

benefit obligation. The Exposure Draft proposed disclosure of the vested postretirement benefit obligation to provide information about the employer's obligation to retirees and other former employees, and active employees assuming they terminated immediately. The Board believed the information required to measure the vested postretirement benefit obligation would be available and that no significant incremental cost would be associated with providing that disclosure.

346. Most respondents opposed disclosure of the vested postretirement benefit obligation. They said the disclosure would be misleading because the term *vested,* although used in its accounting sense, could be misunderstood to imply a legal obligation. Although an employer may have a social or moral obligation to provide the postretirement benefits that have been earned, employers indicated that they currently do not have a statutory requirement to provide those promised benefits, unlike their legal obligation to provide certain vested pension benefits. In addition, respondents observed that if a postretirement benefit plan were terminated, the actual liability would very likely differ from the amount proposed to be measured as the vested obligation.

347. The Board accepted those arguments and concluded that disclosure of the vested postretirement benefit obligation should not be required. However, the Board added paragraph 74(c)(2), which requires disaggregated information about the accumulated benefit obligation for retirees, other fully eligible plan participants, and other active plan participants. Respondents suggested those disclosures would be more useful.

348. Management has a stewardship responsibility for efficient use of plan assets just as it does for operating assets. The Board concluded that disclosure of general information about the major types of any plan assets (and nonbenefit liabilities, if any) and the actual amount of return on plan assets for the period is useful in assessing the profitability of investment policies and the degree of risk assumed.

349. The Board concluded that a reconciliation of the amounts included in the employer's statement of financial position to the funded status of the plan's accumulated postretirement benefit obligation is essential to understanding the relationship between the accounting for and the funded status of the plan. The Board acknowledges that the amount recognized in the financial statements as a net postretirement benefit liability or asset pursuant to this Statement generally will not fully reflect the underlying funded status of the plan, that is, the plan assets and the accumulated postretirement benefit obligation for an overfunded or underfunded plan.

Information about assumptions

350. The Exposure Draft proposed disclosure, if applicable, of the weighted-average assumed discount rate, rate of compensation increase, health care cost trend rate, expected long-term rate of return on plan assets, and, for plans whose income is segregated from the employer's income for tax purposes, the estimated income tax rate on the expected return on plan assets. Most respondents who addressed the disclosure issues supported disclosure of the significant assumptions used in measuring an employer's postretirement benefit obligation and cost. A few respondents, however, maintained that a more descriptive disclosure about the assumed health care cost trend rates would be more useful. They noted that a weighted-average rate can mask differences in an employer's assumptions about year-by-year health care cost trend rates. For example, two employers could report the same weighted-average health care cost trend rate even though they made significantly different assumptions about future trends in health care costs and have very different expected payment schedules.

351. The Board concluded that descriptive information about an employer's assumed health care cost trend rates would be more useful than disclosure of a weighted-average rate. Therefore, this Statement requires disclosure of the assumed health care cost trend rate(s) used to measure the expected cost of benefits covered by the plan (gross eligible charges) for the year following the measurement date and a more general description of the direction and pattern of change in the assumed trend rates thereafter. The Board believes that disclosure will result in more comparable and understandable information about the assumptions used by employers in measuring their postretirement benefit obligations and costs.

352. The Board concluded that the weighted-average assumed discount rate, rate of compensation increase, and long-term rate of return on plan assets should be required to be disclosed as proposed in the Exposure Draft. In determining those weighted averages, employers should consider both the timing and amount of the expected benefit payments, compensation increases, or return on plan assets. The weighted-average discount rate reflects an assumption that significantly affects the computation of the accumulated postretirement benefit obligation and net periodic postretirement benefit cost, as might the weighted-average rate of compensation increase for pay-related plans. Those disclosures assist in assessing the comparability of that information among employers. Because the weighted-average assumed long-term rate of return on plan assets is expected to differ from the weighted-average discount rate, the Board concluded that disclosure of that assumption should be required. As proposed in the Exposure Draft, disclosure of the estimated income tax rate on the return on plan assets is required for plans whose income is segregated from the employer's income for tax purposes.

353. This Statement also requires disclosure of the effect on the current measurement of the accumulated benefit obligation for postretirement health care benefits and the combined service cost and interest cost components of net periodic postretirement benefit cost, assuming a one-percentage-point increase in the health care cost trend rates for each year following the measurement date, holding all other assumptions constant. Respondents generally did not support disclosure of the sensitivity of reported amounts to particular assumptions. Some respondents asserted that disclosure of sensitivity information would diminish the credibility of the amounts reported in the financial statements and would ignore the effects of changes in other assumptions. They also noted that the effects of a one-percentage-point change are not linear, reducing, therefore, the predictive value of the information and its usefulness. Other respondents who supported sensitivity disclosures stated that the information would assist users in judging the sensitivity of the measures of an employer's postretirement benefit obligation and cost to changes in one of its significant underlying assumptions and would provide information about the potential impact of subsequent events different from that assumed.

354. Measuring the sensitivity of the accumulated postretirement benefit obligation and the combined service and interest cost components to a change in the assumed health care cost trend rates requires remeasuring the accumulated postretirement benefit obligation as of the beginning and end of the year. That measurement should be possible at minimal incremental cost as part of the actuarial valuation needed to develop the basic information required by this Statement. The Board concluded that requiring that sensitivity information will assist users in assessing the comparability of information reported by different employers as well as the extent to which future changes in assumptions or actual experience different from that assumed may affect the measurement of the obligation and cost. In addition, the sensitivity information may assist users in understanding the relative significance of an employer's cost-sharing policy as encompassed by the employer's substantive plan.

355. Sensitivity disclosures were initially proposed in accounting for pension costs. However, the Board ultimately decided not to require those disclosures for pensions because the cost of providing that information was viewed as outweighing the

benefits to users. The Board concluded that the need for sensitivity information is more compelling for postretirement health care measurements. Financial statement users are considerably less familiar with postretirement health care measurements than with pension measurements and with the subjectivity of the health care cost trend rate and the significant effect that assumption may have on measurement of the postretirement health care obligation. The Board acknowledges that the effects of percentage-point changes are not linear but concluded that the significance of the sensitivity disclosure outweighs concerns about users erroneously extrapolating from the amounts disclosed.

356. Some Board members believe the volume of disclosures required by this Statement is excessive and further contributes to the already extensive disclosures required in general-purpose financial statements. They believe that at some point the sheer volume of all required disclosures may overwhelm users' ability to assimilate information and focus on the more important matters. In particular, those Board members do not support the required sensitivity disclosures because they highlight only one aspect of the postretirement benefit obligation and cost. Similar sensitivity requirements could be imposed for other aspects of this Statement's requirements and, for that matter, any accounting estimate. They are also concerned that sensitivity disclosures may confuse or mislead users who attempt to use the information to make their own estimates of measures of the obligation and cost in different scenarios, without realizing the limitations of the disclosure.

Two or More Plans

357. Under certain circumstances, this Statement permits combining two or more *unfunded* plans for financial accounting and reporting purposes. Plans that provide different benefits to the same group of participants may be combined. For example, an employer may have separate medical care, dental care, and eye care plans that provide benefit coverage to all retirees of the company. Similarly, an employer may combine two or more unfunded plans that provide the same benefits to different groups of plan participants. For example, an employer may have identical postretirement medical care plans at each of its operating locations. This Statement permits combining plans in those situations because the differences in the plans are not substantive. Combining information in those cases results in combined measurements for accounting and disclosure purposes.

358. The Board concluded that an employer with one well-funded plan and another less well funded or unfunded plan is in a different position than an employer with similar obligations and assets in a single plan. Netting the plan assets of one plan against the net unfunded obligation of another would be an inappropriate disclosure of the unfunded obligation if those assets cannot be used to settle that obligation. That conclusion is consistent with existing generally accepted accounting principles that generally preclude offsetting assets and liabilities unless a right of setoff exists. The Exposure Draft proposed separate disclosure by over- and underfunded plans. However, the Board concluded that limiting the requirement for separate disclosure to the accumulated postretirement benefit obligation and the fair value of plan assets for plans with assets less than the accumulated postretirement benefit obligation (underfunded plans) would provide satisfactory information about the financial condition of an employer's plans and would reduce the cost of providing the required disclosures.

Different Accounting for Certain Small Employers

359. The 1985 FASB Exposure Draft, *Employers' Accounting for Pensions,* recognized that the cost of compliance with a pension standard was relatively greater for small employers than for large employers and more likely to exceed the perceived benefits. In that Exposure Draft, the Board tentatively concluded that the different relative costs and benefits might justify reduced disclosure requirements.

360. However, the Board ultimately concluded that the measurement of pension costs and recognition of pension liabilities should not differ for small or nonpublic employers, in part because evidence from users of financial statements of those employers did not support a different approach. Further, in the Board's view, the existence of a separate set of measurement requirements or a range of alternatives for certain employers probably would not reduce costs significantly, but would add complexity and reduce the comparability and usefulness of financial statements.

361. Similarly, the Board does not believe that postretirement benefit plans for small employers are sufficiently different from the plans of larger employers to warrant fundamentally different measurement and recognition or disclosure requirements. Although the costs of applying this Statement may be relatively higher for small employers, the postretirement benefit obligations of those employers are no different in nature from the postretirement benefit obligations of larger employers. The measurement provisions and effective date of this Statement take into account the data limitations of certain employers and the cost of measuring expected postretirement benefit

costs. Paragraph 38 provides for the use of claims experience of other employers in developing current per capita claims cost. Paragraph 41 permits the use of certain alternative approaches to developing assumed per capita claims cost. Therefore, the Board concluded that the requirements of this Statement should apply to all employers.

362. The Exposure Draft proposed a 2-year delay in the effective date for nonpublic employers whose plans all had fewer than 100 participants. Respondents generally agreed with the proposed delay in the effective date, although some suggested that the size criterion be increased to encompass larger groups of plan participants. Those respondents were concerned about the availability of data and the general lack of experience in measuring the postretirement benefit obligations for smaller plan populations.

363. The effective date of this Statement is delayed 2 years for those nonpublic employers whose plans in the aggregate have fewer than 500 participants. The size criterion was increased in response to the concerns expressed by respondents. The Board concluded that small employers and the professionals serving those employers may need additional time to obtain and evaluate the necessary data including, perhaps, tailoring data collected by actuaries or insurers for use in developing the assumed per capita claims cost by age. The Board concluded that a delayed effective date is a practical and appropriate means for facilitating adoption of this Statement by those employers.

Different Accounting for Certain Industries

364. For some employers subject to certain types of regulation (rate-regulated enterprises) or for employers that have certain types of government contracts for which reimbursement is a function of cost based on cash disbursements, the effects of the requirement to accrue the cost of postretirement benefits (the difference between the cost accrued and the pay-as-you-go cost for a period) may not be recoverable currently. The Board recognizes the practical concerns of those employers but concluded that the cost of a promise to provide postretirement benefits to qualifying employees is not changed by the circumstances described. The Board concluded that this Statement should include no special provisions for those employers. For some rate-regulated enterprises, FASB Statement No. 71, *Accounting for the Effects of Certain Types of Regulation,* may require that the difference between net periodic postretirement benefit cost as defined in this Statement and amounts of postretirement benefit cost considered for rate-making purposes be recognized as an asset or a liability created by the actions of the regulator.

Those actions of the regulator change the timing of recognition of net periodic postretirement benefit cost as an expense; they do not otherwise affect the requirements of this Statement.

Other Situations and Types of Plans

Contracts with Insurance Companies

365. The Board concluded that some contracts with insurance companies are in substance forms of investments and that the use of those funding arrangements should not affect the accounting principles for determining an employer's net periodic postretirement benefit cost. If those contracts have features linked with the insurance company's possible future obligation to pay benefits, their fair values may be difficult or impossible to determine. Although the Board concluded that fair value should be the measurement basis for all types of investments, it acknowledges that for some contracts the best available estimate of fair value may be contract value.

366. The Board recognizes that, except for single-premium life insurance contracts, there are few, if any, contracts at the present time that unconditionally obligate an insurance company to provide most forms of postretirement benefits. However, some insurance contracts, such as single-premium, nonparticipating life insurance contracts, do effectively transfer the primary obligation for payment of benefits from the employer (or the plan) to the insurance company. In those circumstances, the premium paid for the benefits attributed to the current period is an appropriate measure of postretirement benefit cost for that period. The Board concluded that the purchase of a nonparticipating insurance contract is a settlement of a postretirement benefit obligation rather than an investment.

367. Under some insurance contracts, the purchaser (either the plan or the employer) acquires the right to participate in the investment performance or experience of the insurance company (participating contracts). Under those contracts, if the insurance company has favorable experience, the purchaser receives dividends. For example, if the insurance company's investment return is better than anticipated, or perhaps if actual experience related to mortality or other assumptions is favorable, the purchaser will receive dividends that reduce the cost of the contract.

368. Participating contracts have some of the characteristics of an investment. However, the employer is as fully relieved of the obligation as with a nonparticipating contract, and a separate actuarial computation ordinarily would not be performed. The Board concluded that, except as indicated in

paragraphs 369, 370, and 374, it would be appropriate to treat a participating contract the same as a nonparticipating contract and to exclude the benefits covered from measures of the accumulated postretirement benefit obligation.

369. The Board was concerned that a participating contract could be structured in such a way that the premium would be significantly in excess of the cost of nonparticipating contracts because of the expectation of future dividends. If the full amount of the premium were recognized as service cost in the year paid and dividends were recognized as return on plan assets when received, the resulting measures of postretirement benefit cost would be unrelated to benefits earned by employees. If the employer had the ability to influence the timing of dividends, it would then be possible to shift cost among periods without regard to underlying economic events. The Board concluded that part of a participating contract (the participation right) is in substance an investment that should be recognized as an asset.

370. The Board concluded that, consistent with the measurement of other assets, the participation right should be measured at fair value in periods subsequent to its acquisition to the extent that fair value can be reasonably determined. The Board recognizes, however, that some participating contracts may not provide a basis for a better estimate of fair value than that provided by amortized cost and concluded that, in that situation, amortized cost should be used. That conclusion is not intended to permit use of amortized cost if that amount is in excess of net realizable value.

371. When it addressed employers' accounting for pensions, the Board was advised that the information needed to treat insurance contracts purchased from an insurance company affiliated with the employer as investments (that is, to include those contracts and covered benefits in plan assets and the accumulated postretirement benefit obligation, respectively) was not available and would not be cost beneficial to develop. The Board expects that also to be true for postretirement benefits. Therefore, this Statement requires only contracts purchased from a captive insurance subsidiary, and contracts purchased from an insurance company when there is reasonable doubt whether the insurance company will meet its obligations under the contract, to be treated as investments. However, because an employer remains indirectly at risk if insurance contracts are purchased from an affiliate, the Board concluded that disclosure of the approximate amount of annual benefits covered by those contracts should be required.

Insurance contracts used in settlements

372. As discussed in paragraph 368, an employer is as fully relieved of the accumulated postretirement benefit obligation by the purchase of a participating contract as it is by the purchase of a nonparticipating contract. Consequently, except as discussed in paragraphs 369 and 374, the Board concluded that it would be appropriate to treat a participating contract the same as a nonparticipating contract and to consider purchases of participating contracts as settlements of accumulated postretirement benefit obligations.

373. The Board recognizes that it is difficult to determine the extent to which a participating contract exposes the purchaser to the risk of unfavorable experience, which would be reflected in lower than expected future dividends or failure to recover the cost of the participation right. The Board also recognizes that under some insurance contracts described as participating, the purchaser might remain subject to all or most of the same risks and rewards of future experience that would have existed had the contract not been purchased. The Board also is aware that some participating contracts may require or permit payment of additional premiums if experience is unfavorable. The Board concluded that if a participating contract requires or permits payment of additional premiums because of experience losses, or if the substance of the contract is such that the purchaser retains all or most of the related risks and rewards, the purchase of that contract does not constitute a settlement.

374. If the purchase of a participating contract constitutes a settlement for purposes of this Statement, recognition of a previously unrecognized net gain or loss is required (paragraphs 93 and 94) except for settlement of a small portion of the accumulated postretirement benefit obligation (paragraph 95). However, the possibility of a subsequent loss is not completely eliminated with a participating contract because realization of the participation right is not assured. Because of the continuing risk of the participation right, this Statement requires that the maximum gain subject to recognition from a settlement (paragraph 94) be reduced by an amount equal to the cost of the participation right before determining the full or pro rata portion of that maximum gain (paragraph 93) to be recognized.

Multiemployer Plans

375. Generally, the employers that participate in multiemployer postretirement benefit plans are similar, in terms of both nature and industry affiliation, to employers that participate in multiem-

ployer pension plans. Although the plans provide defined benefits, they typically require a defined contribution from participating employers. Consequently, an employer's obligation to a multiemployer plan may be changed by events affecting other participating employers and their employees.

376. At present in the United States, the consequences of an employer's withdrawal from a multiemployer postretirement benefit plan are different from an employer's withdrawal from a multiemployer pension plan. In addition to any contractual requirements, withdrawal from a multiemployer pension plan is governed by the Multiemployer Pension Plan Amendments Act of 1980. An employer withdrawing from a multiemployer postretirement benefit plan is currently only subject to any contractual requirements.

377. In a multiemployer setting, eligibility for benefits is defined by the plan; retired employees continue to receive benefits whether or not their former employers continue to contribute to the plan. On the other hand, plan participants not yet eligible for benefits may lose accumulated postretirement benefits if their current or former employer withdraws from a plan unless they take or have a job with other employers who participate in the plan. While the plan may have the option of cancelling the accrued service credits that apply toward the required service, within the bargaining unit, of plan participants who were employed by a withdrawing employer and who become or are employed by another participating employer, that rarely occurs because of the difficulty of matching employees to specific employers. For example, in certain industries, an employee may work for more than one employer in a single day and different employers on different days, making it difficult to associate any portion of that employee's past service with a specific employer.

378. The Board considered the substantive differences between a multiemployer plan and a single-employer plan and concluded that separate disclosure for the two types of plans would enhance the understandability and usefulness of the information. This Statement requires disclosures that provide descriptive information about multiemployer plans and the cost recognized for the period. In some situations, employers participating in a multiemployer plan that provides health and welfare benefits to active employees and retirees may be unable to distinguish the portion of their required contribution that is attributable to postretirement benefits. In those situations, the amount of the aggregate contribution to the general health and welfare benefit plan is to be disclosed. The Board also noted that the provisions of FASB Statement No. 5, *Accounting for Contingencies,*

apply when additional liabilities, such as a withdrawal liability or increased contribution pursuant to a plan's "maintenance of benefits" clause, are probable and should be recognized, or are reasonably possible and, therefore, should be disclosed.

Multiple-Employer Plans

379. Some plans to which two or more unrelated employers contribute are not multiemployer plans. Rather, they are in substance more like aggregations of single-employer plans than like multiemployer plans. In a multiple-employer plan, the plan terms are defined by each participating employer. Whereas an employer's obligation to a multiemployer plan may be changed by events affecting other participating employers and their employees, an employer's accumulated postretirement benefit obligation in a multiple-employer plan is unchanged by those events. Therefore, the Board concluded that for purposes of this Statement, multiple-employer plans should be considered single-employer plans rather than multiemployer plans and each employer's accounting should be based on its respective interest in the plan.

Postretirement Benefit Plans outside the United States

380. The Board understands that employer-provided postretirement benefits currently are not prevalent outside the United States. In countries where those plans are provided, the Board believes that this Statement should be applied. The Board is not aware of extraordinary problems arising from the application of Statement 87 to foreign plans, and those requirements are based on actuarial calculations and assumptions similar to those needed to apply this Statement. Therefore, the provisions of this Statement are equally applicable to postretirement benefit plans in the United States and in other countries.

381. The Board concluded, however, that practical problems could arise in communicating the requirements of and obtaining the information necessary for initial application of this Statement to plans outside the United States. The Board concluded that allowing an extra two years before application is required would give employers time to make necessary arrangements in an orderly manner and would reduce the cost of transition. Unless the accumulated postretirement benefit obligation of the plans outside the United States is significant relative to the accumulated postretirement benefit obligation for all of an employer's postretirement benefit plans, the Board concluded that disclosures for those plans could be combined with disclosures for plans in the United States.

Defined Contribution Plans

382. The Board concluded that in most cases the formula in a defined contribution plan unambiguously assigns contributions to periods of employee service. The employer's present obligation under the terms of the plan is fully satisfied when the contribution for the period is made, provided that costs (defined contributions) are not being deferred and recognized in periods after the related service period of the individual to whose account the contributions are to be made. The Board concluded that defined contribution plans are sufficiently different from defined benefit plans that disclosures about the two types of plans should not be combined. The disclosures about defined contribution plans required by this Statement are limited to a description of the plan, the basis for determining contributions, the nature and effect of significant matters affecting comparability of information presented, and the cost recognized during the period.

Business Combinations

383. Opinion 16 requires that, in a business combination accounted for as a purchase, an acquiring company allocate the cost of an acquired company to the assets acquired and the obligations assumed. Paragraph 88 of that Opinion sets forth general guides for assigning amounts to the individual assets acquired and liabilities assumed, and includes in that list liabilities and accruals, such as deferred compensation, measured at the present value of the amounts to be paid determined at appropriate current interest rates. Practice has been mixed, with most acquiring companies assigning no value to those postretirement benefit obligations.

384. This Statement amends Opinion 16 to clarify that, in a business combination accounted for as a purchase, the purchaser recognize a postretirement benefit obligation (asset) for any assumed accumulated postretirement benefit obligation in excess of (less than) plan assets. That obligation (asset) is to be measured using the assumptions that reflect the purchaser's assessment of relevant future events. The terms of the substantive plan as determined by the purchaser may differ from the acquired company's plan if the criteria set forth in paragraph 24 for defining the substantive plan that is the basis of the accounting are satisfied. The Board concluded that those criteria apply equally in establishing an obligation that is assumed and an obligation that arises from the exchange of benefits for employee service.

385. Improvements to the acquired company's plan that are attributed to employee service prior to the date the business combination is consummated and that are conditions of the purchase

agreement are not to be accounted for as prior service cost, but as part of the purchase agreement. Other improvements to the plan that are not part of the purchase agreement are to be accounted for as prior service cost to the extent they are attributable to employees' prior service pursuant to this Statement. If it is expected that the plan will be terminated or curtailed, the effects of those actions should be reflected in measuring the accumulated postretirement benefit obligation.

386. The Board concluded that measurement of the unfunded or overfunded accumulated postretirement benefit obligation defined by this Statement generally is consistent with measurement of a pension benefit obligation (or asset) assumed in a business combination accounted for as a purchase pursuant to paragraph 88 of Opinion 16, as amended by paragraph 75 of Statement 87. One result of the accounting required by this Statement is that the effects of plan amendments and gains and losses of the acquired company's plan that occurred before the acquisition are not a part of future postretirement benefit cost of the acquiring company. That is consistent with purchase accounting as defined by Opinion 16, which specifies that a new basis of accounting reflect the bargained (fair) value of assets acquired and liabilities assumed whether or not those values were previously reflected in the acquired company's financial statements.

387. The Board concluded that no recognition of additional liabilities for multiemployer plans should be required under Opinion 16 unless conditions exist that make an additional liability probable. The Board was not convinced that there ordinarily is an obligation for future contributions to a multiemployer plan or that recognition of any contractual withdrawal liability would provide useful information about such an obligation, absent a probable withdrawal.

Effective Dates

388. The Exposure Draft proposed that this Statement generally be effective for fiscal years beginning after December 15, 1991. Most respondents urged the Board to delay the proposed effective date for at least one year because of their concerns about the availability and reliability of data necessary to measure employers' postretirement benefit obligations and cost. Other respondents noted the significant improvement to financial statements resulting from adoption of the accounting required by this Statement and suggested accelerating the effective date.

389. The Board decided to allow more than the normal amount of time between issuance of this Statement and its required application to give employers

and their advisors time to assimilate the requirements and to obtain the information required. The Board concluded that an additional one-year delay in the general effective date to fiscal years beginning after December 15, 1992, is adequate for those purposes. As noted previously, the Board also allowed an addi- tional two years before employers are required to ap- ply the provisions of this Statement to plans outside the United States and before certain small employers are required to apply those provisions. Paragraph 267 discusses the effective date for the amendment of Opinion 12.

Appendix B

COMPARISON OF EMPLOYERS' ACCOUNTING FOR OTHER POSTRETIREMENT BENEFITS WITH EMPLOYERS' ACCOUNTING FOR PENSIONS

390. This appendix provides a summary comparison of the major provisions of this Statement with the provisions of FASB Statement No. 87, *Employers' Accounting for Pensions.*

	Other Postretirement Benefit Plan	Non-pay-related Pension Plan
Basis for accounting	Extant written plan unless (a) past practice of maintaining a consistent level of cost sharing or consistently increasing or decreasing the cost-sharing provisions of the plan, (b) communication of intended changes to cost-sharing policy,* or (c) past practice of regular increases in monetary benefits indicates substantive plan differs from extant written plan; substantive plan is basis for accounting	Extant written plan unless a past practice of regular increases in non-pay-related benefits or benefits under career-average-pay plan indicates substantive commitment differs from extant written plan, then substantive commitment is basis for accounting
Attribution method and period	Benefit/years-of-service approach that attributes expected benefit obligation (EBO)† for postretirement benefits to years of service to date employee attains full eligibility for benefits expected to be provided to employee; beginning of attribution period is employee's date of hire unless plan only grants credit for service from a later date, in which case benefits are generally attributed from beginning of that credited service period; equal amount of EBO attributed to each year of service in attribution period	Benefit/years-of-service approach that attributes EBO to years of service in accordance with plan benefit formula If plan benefit formula results in disproportionate attribution to later years of service, equal amount of EBO attributed to years of service to date employee attains full eligibility for those benefits

---

Note: This appendix compares employers' accounting for a *postretirement benefit plan* with employers' accounting for a *non-pay-related pension plan* because most postretirement benefit plans (in particular, postretirement health care plans) do not have benefit formulas that are pay related.

*Conditions (a) and (b) are subject to the criteria in paragraph 25.

†*Expected benefit obligation (EBO)*—actuarial present value (APV) as of a particular date of postretirement benefits expected to be paid to or for a current plan participant.

Recognition of net cost	Other Postretirement Benefit Plan	Non-pay-related Pension Plan
Service cost	Actuarial present value (APV) of EBO allocated to a period of employee service during attribution period	Same as for other postretirement benefits
Interest cost	Accrual of interest to reflect effects of passage of time on the accumulated benefit obligation (ABO)‡	Same as for other postretirement benefits
Actual return on plan assets	Actual return based on fair value (FV) of plan assets at beginning and end of period, adjusted for contributions and benefit payments	Same as for other postretirement benefits
Prior service cost	Plan initiations and amendments treated as retroactive except for plan initiations that specifically provide new benefits only in exchange for future service	Retroactive benefits defined by plan initiation or amendment
Measurement	Change in ABO for new or amended benefits granted to plan participants	Same as for other postretirement benefits
Amortization	Delayed; equal amount assigned to each future year of service to full eligibility date of each active plan participant	Delayed; equal amount assigned to each future year of service of each active plan participant
	Presumption of economic benefit in future years; can overcome presumption if evidence that *increasing* plan benefits has no future economic benefit for the employer	Same as for other postretirement benefits
	If all or almost all participants are fully eligible for benefits, their remaining life expectancy used, rather than future service period	If all or almost all participants are inactive, their remaining life expectancy used, rather than remaining service period
	Alternative approaches permitted that more rapidly reduce unrecognized cost	Same as for other postretirement benefits
Negative plan amendment	Immediate recognition of effect precluded; initially offsets existing unrecognized prior service cost and unrecognized transition obligation, balance is amortized	Same treatment as pension benefit increase

Gains and losses	Changes in ABO and plan assets from experience different from that assumed or from changes in assumptions	Same as for other postretirement benefits
	Gain-loss component of net cost consists of (a) differences between actual and expected return on plan assets, (b) amortization of unrecognized net gain or loss, and (c) amount immediately recognized as a gain or loss due to decision to temporarily deviate from substantive plan; asset gains/losses not reflected in market-related value (MRV)§ not required to be amortized	Except for (c), same as for other postretirement benefits
Recognition	Either immediate or delayed; if immediate, gains (losses) that do not offset previously recognized losses (gains) first reduce any unrecognized transition obligation (asset)	Either immediate (without offsetting any unrecognized transition obligation or asset) or delayed
Minimum amortization	Unrecognized net gain or loss in excess of 10 percent of greater of ABO or MRV of plan assets, amortized over average remaining service period of active plan participants	Same as for other postretirement benefits
	If all or almost all participants are inactive, amortized over their average remaining life expectancy rather than over remaining service period	Same as for other postretirement benefits
Definition of plan assets	Assets segregated and restricted for sole purpose of providing the defined benefit	Same as for other postretirement benefits
Recognition of minimum liability	Recognition of minimum liability not required	ABO (for all plan participants) in excess of FV of plan assets
		If additional liability recognized, contra amount recognized first as intangible asset up to amount of unrecognized prior service cost and unrecognized transition obligation, with any excess reported as reduction of equity

‡ *Accumulated benefit obligation (ABO)*—the portion of EBO attributed to service rendered to a specified date. That portion for a pension plan with a benefit formula that is pay related is referred to as the *projected benefit obligation*. However, for a pension plan with a benefit formula that excludes the effects of future compensation levels, the accumulated benefit obligation is the appropriate measure of the pension obligation for comparative purposes throughout this appendix.

§ *Market-related value (MRV)*—either fair market value or a calculated value that recognizes changes in fair value in a systematic and rational manner over not more than five years.

	Other Postretirement Benefit Plan	Non-pay-related Pension Plan
Business combinations	Measure obligation assumed as unfunded ABO for all plan participants, using purchaser's assumptions	Same as for other postretirement benefits
Transition		
Measurement	Over- or underfunded ABO for all plan participants	Same as for other postretirement benefits
Recognition	Either immediate or delayed	Delayed recognition required
	If immediate, amount attributable to plan initiation or benefit improvements adopted after December 21, 1990 treated as unrecognized prior service cost and amount attributable to purchase business combinations consummated after December 21, 1990 treated as retroactive adjustment of purchase price allocation	Immediate recognition precluded
	If delayed, amortized on straight-line basis over average remaining service period of active plan participants; cannot be less rapid than pay-as-you-go cost	Amortized on a straight-line basis over average remaining service period of active plan participants
	If amortization period determined above is less than 20 years, may use a 20-year period	If amortization period determined above is less than 15 years, may use a 15-year period
	If all or almost all participants are inactive, their average remaining life expectancy used	Same as for other postretirement benefits
Disclosure	Similar to disclosures required by Statement 87, supplemented by disclosure of descriptive information about the substantive plan, amortization of transition obligation or asset, assumed health care cost trend rate, and the effect on the measure of the ABO and aggregate of service and interest cost components of net periodic cost of a one-percentage-point increase in the health care cost trend rate, holding all other assumptions constant	Disclosures required by Statement 87
	Disclosures for plans in and outside the United States may be combined unless ABO for plans outside the United States is significant relative to aggregate ABO	Disclosures for plans in and outside the United States may not be combined unless those plans use similar economic assumptions

Appendix C

ILLUSTRATIONS

CONTENTS

Appendix C

ILLUSTRATIONS

Introduction

391. This appendix provides additional discussion and examples that illustrate the application of certain requirements of this Statement to specific aspects of employers' accounting for postretirement benefits other than pensions. The illustrations are referenced to the applicable paragraph(s) of the standards section of this Statement where appropriate. Certain illustrations have been included to facilitate the understanding and application of certain provisions of this Statement that apply in specific circumstances that may not be encountered frequently by employers. The fact patterns shown may not be representative of actual situations but are presented only to illustrate those requirements.

392. Throughout these illustrations the accumulated postretirement benefit obligation and service cost are assumed as inputs rather than calculated based on some underlying population. For simplicity, benefit payments are assumed to be made at the end of the year, service cost is assumed to include interest on the portion of the expected postretirement benefit obligation attributed to the current year, and interest cost is based on the accumulated postretirement benefit obligation as of the beginning of the year. For unfunded plans, benefits are assumed to be paid directly by the employer and are reflected as a reduction in the accrued postretirement benefit cost. The required disclosure of the reconciliation of the funded status of the plan is illustrated in many of the cases; however, for simplicity, the components of the accumulated postretirement benefit obligation are not included in those reconciliations as required by paragraph 74(c)(2). In many of the cases, application of the underlying concepts has been simplified by focusing on a single employee for purposes of

illustration. In practice, the determination of the full eligibility date and the measurement of postretirement benefit cost and obligation are based on employee groups and consider various possible retirement dates and the probabilities associated with retirement at each of those dates.

Illustration 1—Illustration of Terms

Case 1A—Expected Postretirement Benefit Obligation and Accumulated Postretirement Benefit Obligation

393. This Statement uses two terms to describe certain measures of the obligation to provide postretirement benefits: *expected postretirement benefit obligation* and *accumulated postretirement benefit obligation.* The expected postretirement benefit obligation for an employee is the actuarial present value as of a measurement date of the postretirement benefits expected to be paid to or for the employee, the employee's beneficiaries, and any covered dependents. Prior to the date on which an employee attains full eligibility for the benefits that employee is expected to earn under the terms of the postretirement benefit plan (the full eligibility date), the accumulated postretirement benefit obligation for an employee is a portion of the expected postretirement benefit obligation. On and after the full eligibility date, the accumulated postretirement benefit obligation and the expected postretirement benefit obligation for an employee are the same. (Refer to paragraphs 20 and 21.) The following example illustrates the notion of the expected postretirement benefit obligation and the relationship between that obligation and the accumulated postretirement benefit obligation at various dates.

394. Company A's plan provides postretirement health care benefits to all employees who render at least 10 years of service and attain age 55 while in service. A 50-year-old employee, hired January 1, 1973 at age 30 and eligible for benefits upon attain-

ing age 55, is expected to terminate employment at age 62 and is expected to live to age 77. A discount rate of 8 percent is assumed.

At December 31, 1992, Company A estimates the expected amount and timing of benefit payments for that employee as follows:

Age	Expected Future Claims	Present Value at Age		
		50	53	55
63	$ 2,796	$1,028	$1,295	$1,511
64	3,093	1,052	1,326	1,547
65	856	270	339	396
66	947	276	348	406
67	1,051	284	357	417
68	1,161	291	366	427
69	1,282	297	374	436
70	1,425	306	385	449
71	1,577	313	394	460
72	1,744	321	404	471
73	1,934	329	415	484
74	2,137	337	424	495
75	2,367	346	435	508
76	2,620	354	446	520
77	3,899	488	615	717
	$28,889	$6,292	$7,923	$9,244

395. The expected and accumulated postretirement benefit obligations at December 31, 1992 (age 50) are $6,292 and $5,034 (20/25 of $6,292), respectively. An equal amount of the expected postretirement benefit obligation is attributed to each year of service from the employee's date of hire to the employee's full eligibility date (age 55) (paragraphs 43 and 44). Therefore, when the employee is age 50, the accumulated postretirement benefit obligation is measured as 20/25 of the expected postretirement benefit obligation, as the employee has rendered 20 years of the 25-year credited service period. Refer to Case 1B (paragraphs 397-408) for additional illustrations on the full eligibility date and Case 1C (paragraphs 409-412) for additional illustrations on attribution.

396. Assuming no changes in health care costs or other circumstances, the accumulated postretirement benefit obligation at December 31, 1995 (age 53) is $7,289 (23/25 of $7,923). At the end of the employee's 25th year of service and thereafter, the expected postretirement benefit obligation and the accumulated postretirement benefit obligation are equal. In this example, at December 31, 1997, when the employee is 55 and fully eligible for benefits, the accumulated and expected postretirement benefit obligations are $9,244. At the end of the 26th year of service (December 31, 1998) when the employee is 56, those obligations are $9,984 ($9,244 plus interest at 8 percent for 1 year).

Case 1B—Full Eligibility Date

397. The *full eligibility date* (paragraph 21) is the date at which an employee has rendered all of the service necessary to have earned the right to receive all of the benefits expected to be received by that employee under the terms of the postretirement benefit plan. Therefore, the present value of all of the benefits expected to be received by or on behalf of an employee is attributed to the employee's credited service period, which ends at the full eligibility date. Determination of an employee's full eligibility date is affected by plan terms that provide incremental benefits expected to be received by the employee for additional years of service, unless those incremental benefits are trivial. Determination of the full eligibility date is *not* affected by an employee's current dependency status or by plan terms that define when benefit payments commence. The following examples (paragraphs 398-408) are presented to assist in understanding the full eligibility date.

Plans that provide incremental benefits for additional years of service

Graded benefit formula

398. Some plans have benefit formulas that define different benefits for different years of service. To illustrate, assume a plan in which the percentage of

postretirement health care coverage to be provided by an employer is defined by groups of years of service. The plan provides 20 percent postretirement health care coverage for 10 years of service after age 35, 50 percent for 20 years of service after age 35, 70 percent for 25 years of service after age 35, and 100 percent for 30 years of service after age 35. The full eligibility date for an employee who was hired at age 35 and is expected to retire at age 62 is at age 60. At that date the employee has rendered 25 years of service after age 35 and is eligible to receive a benefit of 70 percent health care coverage after retirement. The employee receives no additional benefits for the last two years of service.

Pay-related plans

399. Some plans may base the amount of benefits or level of benefit coverage on employees' compensation, for example, as a percentage of their final pay. To the extent the plan's postretirement benefit formula defines benefits wholly or partially as a function of future compensation (that is, the plan provides incremental benefits for additional years of service when it is assumed that final pay will increase), determination of the full eligibility date for an employee is affected by those additional years of service the employee is expected to render (paragraph 21). In addition, measurements of the postretirement benefit obligation and service cost reflect the best estimate of employees' future compensation levels (paragraph 33).

400. For example, assume a plan provides life insurance benefits to employees who render 20 years of service and attain age 55 while in service; the benefit is equal to 20 percent of final pay. A 55-year-old employee, who currently earns a salary of $90,000, has worked 22 years for the company. The employee is expected to retire at age 60 and is expected to be earning $120,000 at that time. The employee is eligible for life insurance coverage under the plan at age 55, when the employee has met the age and service requirements. However, because the employee's salary continues to increase each year, the employee is not *fully eligible* for benefits until age 60 when the employee retires because the employee earns an incremental benefit for each additional year of service beyond age 55. That is, the employee earns an additional benefit equal to 20 percent of the increase in salary each year from age 55 to retirement at age 60 for service during each of those years.

Spousal coverage

401. Some postretirement benefit plans provide spousal or dependent coverage or both if the em-

ployee works a specified number of years beyond the date at which the employee attains eligibility for single coverage. For example, a postretirement health care plan provides single coverage to employees who work 10 years and attain age 50 while in service; the plan provides coverage for dependents if the employee works 20 years and attains age 60 while in service. Because the additional 10 years of service may provide an incremental benefit to employees, for employees expected to satisfy the age and service requirements and to have covered dependents during the period following the employee's retirement, their full eligibility date is the date at which they have both rendered 20 years of service and attained age 60 while in service. For employees not expected to have covered dependents after their retirement or who are not expected to render at least 20 years of service or attain age 60 while in service, or both, their full eligibility date is the date at which they have both rendered 10 years of service and attained age 50 while in service.

Single plan provides health care and life insurance benefits

402. Some postretirement benefit plans may have different eligibility requirements for different types of benefits. For example, assume a plan provides a postretirement death benefit of $100,000 to employees who render 20 or more years of service. Fifty percent health care coverage is provided to eligible employees who render 10 years of service, 70 percent coverage to those who render 20 years of service, and 100 percent coverage to those who render 30 years of service. Employees are eligible for the health care and death benefits if they attain age 55 while in service.

403. The full eligibility date for an individual hired at age 30 and expected to terminate employment at age 62 is the date on which that employee has rendered 30 years of service and attained age 55 while in service (age 60 in this example). At that date the employee is eligible for all of the benefits expected to be paid to or on behalf of that employee under the postretirement benefit plan ($100,000 death benefits and 100 percent health care coverage). The full eligibility date for an employee hired at age 37 and expected to retire at age 62 is the date on which that employee has rendered 20 years of service and attained age 55 while in service (age 57 in this example). At that date the employee is eligible for all of the benefits expected to be paid to or on behalf of that employee under the postretirement benefit plan ($100,000 death benefits and 70 percent health care coverage).

Plans that provide benefits based on status at date of termination

404. Some postretirement benefit plans provide coverage for the spouse to whom an employee is married when the employee terminates service; that is, the marital status of an employee upon termination of employment determines whether single or spousal coverage is to be provided. In measuring the expected postretirement benefit obligation, consideration is given to factors such as when benefit coverage will commence, who will receive benefits (employee and any covered dependents), and the expected need for and utilization of benefit coverage. However, determination of an employee's full eligibility date is not affected by plan terms that define when payments commence or by an employee's current marital (or dependent) status (paragraph 21).

405. For example, assume a plan provides postretirement health care coverage to employees who render at least 10 years of service and attain age 55 while in service; health care coverage also is provided to employees' spouses at the date of the employees' retirement. A 55-year-old employee is single, has worked for the company for 30 years, and is expected to marry at age 59 and to retire at age 62. Although the employee is entitled to spousal coverage only if married at retirement, at age 55 the employee has earned the right to spousal coverage. The probability that the employee will be married when the employee retires is included in the actuarial assumptions developed to measure the expected postretirement benefit obligation for that plan participant. The full eligibility date (age 55 in this example) is not affected by that measurement assumption.

Postretirement benefits to be received by disabled plan participants

406. Some plans provide postretirement benefits to disabled employees. For example, Company B provides disability income and health care benefits to employees who become disabled while in service and have rendered 10 or more years of service. Retiree health care benefits are provided to employees who render 20 or more years of service and attain age 55 while in service. Employees receiving disability benefits continue to accrue "credit" toward their eligibility for retiree health care benefits. Under this plan, an employee hired at age 25, who becomes permanently disabled at age 40, is entitled to receive retiree health care benefits commencing at age 55 (in addition to any disability income benefits commencing at age 40) because that employee worked for Company B for more than 10 years before becoming disabled. Under the terms of the plan the employee is given credit for working to age 55 even though no actual service is rendered by the employee after the disabling event occurs.

407. Because the employee is permanently disabled, the full eligibility date is accelerated to recognize the shorter period of service required to be rendered in exchange for the retiree health care benefits—in this case the full eligibility date is age 40, the date of the disabling event. For a similar employee who is temporarily disabled at age 40 but returns to work and attains age 55 while in service, the full eligibility date is age 55. Company B's expected postretirement benefit health care obligation for the permanently disabled employee is based on the employee's expected health care costs commencing at age 55 and is attributed ratably to that employee's active service to age 40.

408. Only some employees become and remain disabled. Therefore, in measuring the expected postretirement benefit obligation and in determining the attribution period for plan participants expected to become disabled, the probability and timing of a disabling event is considered in determining whether employees are likely to become disabled and whether they will be entitled to receive postretirement benefits.

Case 1C—Attribution

Attribution period

409. Paragraph 44 states that the beginning of the *attribution period* shall be the date of hire unless the plan's benefit formula grants credit only for service from a later date, in which case benefits generally shall be attributed from the beginning of that credited service period. For example, for a plan that provides benefit coverage to employees who render 30 or more years of service or who render at least 10 years of service and attain age 55 while in service, without specifying when the credited service period begins, the expected postretirement benefit obligation is attributed to service from the date of hire to the earlier of the date at which a plan participant has rendered 30 years of service or has rendered 10 years of service and attained age 55 while in service. However, for a plan that provides benefit coverage to employees who render at least 20 years of service after age 35, the expected postretirement benefit obligation is attributed to a plan participant's first 20 years of service after attaining age 35 or after the date of hire, if later than age 35.

410. For a plan with a benefit formula that attributes benefits to a credited service period that is nominal in relation to employees' total years of service prior to their full eligibility dates, an equal

amount of the expected postretirement benefit obligation for an employee is attributed to each year of that employee's service from date of hire to date of full eligibility for benefits. For example, a plan with a benefit formula that defines 100 percent benefit coverage for service for the year in which employees attain age 60 has a 1-year credited service period. If plan participants are expected to have rendered an average of 20 years of service at age 60, the credited service period is nominal in relation to their total years of service prior to their full eligibility dates. In that case, the service cost is recognized from date of hire to age 60.

Attribution pattern

411. For all plans, except those that "frontload" benefits, the expected postretirement benefit obligation is attributed ratably to each year of service in the attribution period (paragraph 43). That is, an equal amount of the expected postretirement benefit obligation is attributed to each year of service from the employee's date of hire or beginning of the credited service period, if later, to the employee's full eligibility date unless (a) the credited service period is nominal relative to the total years of service prior to the full eligibility date (paragraph 410) or (b) the benefit formula frontloads benefits (paragraph 412).

Frontloaded plans

412. Some plans may have a benefit formula that defines benefits in terms of specific periods of service to be rendered in exchange for those benefits but attributes all or a disproportionate share of the expected postretirement benefit obligation to employees' early years of service in the credited service period. An example would be a life insurance plan that provides postretirement death benefits of $250,000 for 10 years of service after age 45 and $5,000 of additional death benefits for each year of service thereafter up to age 65 (maximum benefit of $300,000). For plans that frontload the benefit, the expected postretirement benefit obligation is attributed to employee service in accordance with the plan's benefit formula (paragraph 43). In this example, the actuarial present value of a $25,000 death benefit is attributed to each of the first 10 years of service after age 45, and the actuarial present value of an additional $5,000 death benefit is attributed to each year of service thereafter up to age 65.

Case 1D—Individual Deferred Compensation Contracts

413. An employer may provide postretirement benefits to selected employees under individual contracts with specific terms determined on an individual-by-individual basis. Paragraph 13 of this Statement amends APB Opinion No. 12, *Omnibus Opinion—1967,* to attribute those benefits to the individual employee's years of service following the terms of the contract. Paragraphs 414-416 illustrate the application of paragraph 13 for individual deferred compensation contracts.

Contract provides only prospective benefits

414. A company enters into a deferred compensation contract with an employee at the date of hire. The contract provides for a payment of $150,000 upon termination of employment following a minimum 3-year service period. The contract provides for a compensation adjustment for each year of service after the third year determined by multiplying $150,000 by the company's return on equity for the year. Also, each year after the third year of service, interest at 10 percent per year is credited on the amount due under the contract at the beginning of that year. Accordingly, a liability of $150,000 is accrued in a systematic and rational manner over the employee's first 3 years of service. Following the third year of service, the accrued liability is adjusted annually for accrued interest and the increased or decreased compensation based on the company's return on equity for that year. At the end of the third year and each subsequent year of the employee's service, the amount accrued equals the then present value of the benefit expected to be paid in exchange for the employee's service rendered to that date.

Contract provides retroactive benefits

415. A company enters into a contract with a 55-year-old employee who has worked 5 years for the company. The contract states that in exchange for past and future services and for serving as a consultant for 2 years after the employee retires, the company will pay an annual pension of $20,000 to the employee, commencing immediately upon the employee's retirement. It is expected that the future benefits to the employer from the consulting services will be minimal. Consequently, the actuarial present value of a lifetime annuity of $20,000 that begins at the employee's expected retirement date is accrued at the date the contract is entered into because the employee is fully eligible for the pension benefit at that date.

416. If the terms of the contract described in paragraph 415 had stated that the employee is entitled to the pension benefit only if the sum of the employee's age and years of service equal 70 or more at the date of retirement, the employee would be fully eligible for the pension benefit at age 60, after rendering 5 more years of service. The actuarial present value of a lifetime annuity of $20,000 that

begins at the expected retirement date would be accrued in a systematic and rational manner over the 5-year period from the date the contract is entered into to the date the employee is fully eligible for the pension benefit.

Illustration 2—Delayed Recognition and Reconciliation of Funded Status

417. Pursuant to the provisions of this Statement, the recognition of certain changes affecting measurement of the accumulated postretirement benefit obligation or the fair value of plan assets may be delayed. Those changes include plan amendments (paragraph 51) and gains and losses due to experience different from that assumed or from changes in assumptions (paragraph 56). Information about the effect of the changes that have been afforded delayed recognition is provided through disclosure of the reconciliation of the funded status of a plan to the accrued or prepaid postretirement benefit cost recognized in the employer's statement of financial position (paragraph 74(c)). The following cases (2A-2E, paragraphs 418-429) show how events that change the accumulated postretirement benefit obligation are reflected in that reconciliation.

Case 2A—Unrecognized Obligation at Date of Transition

418. For an unfunded plan with an accumulated postretirement benefit obligation of $600,000 at the date of transition (January 1, 1993), the reconciliation of the funded status of the plan with the

amount shown in the statement of financial position as of that date is as follows:

Accumulated postretirement benefit obligation	$(600,000)[a]
Plan assets at fair value	0
Funded status	(600,000)
Transition obligation at January 1, 1993	600,000
(Accrued)/prepaid postretirement benefit cost	$ 0

---

[a]The actuarial present value of the obligation for fully eligible plan participants' expected postretirement benefits and the portion of the expected postretirement benefit obligation for other active plan participants attributed to service to December 31, 1992. For example, assume a plan provides benefits to employees who render at least 20 years of service after age 35. For employees age 45 with 10 years of service at December 31, 1992, the accumulated postretirement benefit obligation is 50% of the expected postretirement benefit obligation for those employees. For employees age 55 or older who have rendered 20 or more years of service at December 31, 1992 and retirees (collectively referred to as fully eligible plan participants), the accumulated postretirement benefit obligation is the full amount of the expected postretirement benefit obligation for those employees.

419. The transition obligation or asset is the difference between (a) the accumulated postretirement benefit obligation and (b) the fair value of plan assets plus any recognized accrued postretirement benefit cost or less any recognized prepaid postretirement benefit cost at the date of transition (paragraph 110). If, as in this case, advance contributions were not made and postretirement benefit cost was not accrued in prior periods, there is no

accrued or prepaid postretirement benefit cost recognized in the statement of financial position, and, therefore, the transition obligation is equal to the unfunded status ($600,000).

Unrecognized amounts after date of transition

420. After the date of transition, any change in the accumulated postretirement benefit obligation or the plan assets (other than contributions and benefit payments) either is unrecognized, due to the delayed recognition provisions of this Statement, or is included in net periodic postretirement benefit cost. Contributions by the employer increase plan assets and decrease the accrued postretirement benefit cost or increase the prepaid postretirement benefit cost, subject to the provision of paragraph 112 requiring recognition of an addi-

tional amount of the unrecognized transition obligation in certain situations. All changes in the accumulated postretirement benefit obligation and plan assets are reflected in the reconciliation. Using Case 2A as the starting point, the following reconciliations (Cases 2B-2E) illustrate the effect of changes in assumptions or changes in the plan on measurement of the accumulated postretirement benefit obligation.

Case 2B—Employer Accrual of Net Periodic Postretirement Benefit Cost

421. Benefit payments of $42,000 are made at the end of 1993. Changes in accrued postretirement benefit cost, accumulated postretirement benefit obligation, and unrecognized transition obligation in 1993 are summarized as follows:

	Accrued Postretirement Benefit Cost	Accumulated Postretirement Benefit Obligation	Unrecognized Transition Obligation
Beginning of year	$ 0	$(600,000)	$600,000
Recognition of components of net periodic postretirement benefit cost:			
Service cost	(32,000)	(32,000)	
Interest cost[a]	(48,000)	(48,000)	
Amortization of transition obligation[b]	(30,000)		(30,000)
	(110,000)	(80,000)	(30,000)
Benefit payments	42,000	42,000	
Net change	(68,000)	(38,000)	(30,000)
End of year	$ (68,000)	$(638,000)	$570,000

[a]Assumed discount rate of 8% applied to the accumulated postretirement benefit obligation at the beginning of the year.

[b]The transition obligation of $600,000 is amortized on a straight-line basis over 20 years. Illustration 3, Case 3B, (paragraphs 435-442) illustrates the constraint on delayed recognition of the transition obligation pursuant to paragraph 112.

422. The funded status of the plan at January 1, 1993 and December 31, 1993 is reconciled with the amount shown in the statement of financial position at those dates as follows:

	1/1/93	Net Change	12/31/93
Accumulated postretirement benefit obligation	$(600,000)	$(38,000)	$(638,000)
Plan assets at fair value	0		0
Funded status	(600,000)	(38,000)	(638,000)
Unrecognized transition obligation	600,000	(30,000)	570,000
Accrued postretirement benefit cost	$ 0	$(68,000)	$ (68,000)

*Case 2C—Plan Amendment That Increases
Benefits*

423. The plan is amended on January 2, 1994,
resulting in a $90,000 increase in the accumu-
lated postretirement benefit obligation. The
effects of plan amendments are reflected immediately in measurement of the accumulated
postretirement benefit obligation; however,
the effects of the amendment are not recog-

nized immediately in the financial statements,
but rather are recognized on a delayed basis
(paragraph 52).

424. Benefit payments of $39,000 are made at the
end of 1994. Changes in accrued postretirement
benefit cost, accumulated postretirement benefit
obligation, unrecognized transition obligation,
and unrecognized prior service cost in 1994 are
summarized as follows:

	Accrued Postretirement Benefit Cost	Accumulated Postretirement Benefit Obligation	Unrecognized Transition Obligation	Unrecognized Prior Service Cost
Beginning of year	$ (68,000)	$(638,000)	$570,000	$ 0
Plan amendment		(90,000)		90,000
Recognition of components of net periodic postretirement benefit cost:				
Service cost	(30,000)	(30,000)		
Interest cost[a]	(58,240)	(58,240)		
Amortization of transition obligation	(30,000)		(30,000)	
Amortization of prior service cost[b]	(9,000)			(9,000)
	(127,240)	(178,240)	(30,000)	81,000
Benefit payments	39,000	39,000		
Net change	(88,240)	(139,240)	(30,000)	81,000
End of year	$(156,240)	$(777,240)	$540,000	$81,000

[a]Assumed discount rate of 8% applied to the accumulated postretirement benefit obligation at the beginning of the year and to the increase in
that obligation for the unrecognized prior service cost at the date of the plan amendment [($638,000 × 8%) + ($90,000 × 8%)].

[b]As permitted by paragraph 53, prior service cost of $90,000 is amortized on a straight-line basis over the average remaining years of service to
full eligibility for benefits of the active plan participants (10 years in this example).

425. The funded status of the plan at December
31, 1993 and 1994 is reconciled with the amount

shown in the statement of financial position at
those dates as follows:

	12/31/93	Net Change	12/31/94
Accumulated postretirement benefit obligation	$(638,000)	$(139,240)	$(777,240)
Plan assets at fair value	0		0
Funded status	(638,000)	(139,240)	(777,240)
Unrecognized prior service cost	0	81,000	81,000
Unrecognized transition obligation	570,000	(30,000)	540,000
Accrued postretirement benefit cost	$ (68,000)	$ (88,240)	$(156,240)

Case 2D—Negative Plan Amendment

426. The plan is amended on January 4, 1995, resulting in a $99,000 reduction in the accumulated postretirement benefit obligation. As with a plan amendment that increases benefits, the effect of a negative plan amendment (an amendment that decreases benefits) is reflected immediately in the measurement of the accumulated postretirement benefit obligation. The effects of the negative plan amendment are recognized by first reducing any existing unrecognized prior service cost and then any existing unrecognized transition obligation; the remainder is recognized in the financial statements on a delayed basis.

427. Benefit payments in 1995 are $40,000. Changes in accrued postretirement benefit cost, accumulated postretirement benefit obligation, unrecognized transition obligation, and unrecognized prior service cost in 1995 are summarized as follows:

	Accrued Postretirement Benefit Cost	Accumulated Postretirement Benefit Obligation	Unrecognized Transition Obligation	Unrecognized Prior Service Cost
Beginning of year	$(156,240)	$(777,240)	$540,000	$ 81,000
Plan amendment[a]		99,000	(18,000)	(81,000)
Recognition of components of net periodic postretirement benefit cost:				
Service cost	(30,000)	(30,000)		
Interest cost[b]	(54,259)	(54,259)		
Amortization of transition obligation[c]	(29,000)		(29,000)	
Amortization of prior service cost	0			0
	(113,259)	14,741	(47,000)	(81,000)
Benefit payments	40,000	40,000		
Net change	(73,259)	54,741	(47,000)	(81,000)
End of year	$(229,499)	$(722,499)	$493,000	$ 0

---

[a]Paragraph 55 requires that the effects of a plan amendment that reduces the accumulated postretirement benefit obligation be used first to reduce any existing unrecognized prior service cost, then any unrecognized transition obligation. Any remaining effects are recognized on a delayed basis over the remaining years of service to full eligibility for those plan participants who were active at the date of the amendment. If all or almost all of the plan participants were fully eligible at that date, the remaining effects should be recognized over the remaining life expectancy of those plan participants.

[b]Assumed discount rate of 8% applied to the accumulated postretirement benefit obligation at the beginning of the year and to the decrease in that obligation at the date of the plan amendment [($777,240 × 8%) − ($99,000 × 8%)].

[c]Unrecognized transition obligation of $522,000 ($540,000 − $18,000) is amortized on a straight-line basis over the 18 years remaining in the transition period.

428. The funded status of the plan at December 31, 1994 and 1995 is reconciled with the amount shown in the statement of financial position at those dates as follows:

	12/31/94	Net Change	12/31/95
Accumulated postretirement benefit obligation	$(777,240)	$ 54,741	$(722,499)
Plan assets at fair value	0		0
Funded status	(777,240)	54,741	(722,499)
Unrecognized prior service cost	81,000	(81,000)	0
Unrecognized transition obligation	540,000	(47,000)	493,000
Accrued postretirement benefit cost	$(156,240)	$(73,259)	$(229,499)

Case 2E—Change in Assumption

429. The assumed health care cost trend rates are changed at December 31, 1995, resulting in a $55,000 increase in the accumulated postretirement benefit obligation. The net loss that results from a change in the health care cost trend rates assumption is reflected immediately in the measurement of the accumulated postretirement benefit obligation. However, as with most other gains and losses, the effect of a change in assumption may be recognized in the financial statements either immediately or on a delayed basis, as long as the recognition method is applied consistently.

	Before Change	Net Loss	After Change
Accumulated postretirement benefit obligation	$(722,499)	$(55,000)	$(777,499)
Plan assets at fair value	0		0
Funded status	(722,499)	(55,000)	(777,499)
Unrecognized net loss[a]	0	55,000	55,000
Unrecognized transition obligation	493,000		493,000
Accrued postretirement benefit cost	$(229,499)	$ 0	$(229,499)

[a]This Statement generally does not require recognition of gains and losses in the period in which they arise (paragraphs 56-61). However, at a minimum, amortization of an unrecognized net gain or loss is required to be recognized as a component of net periodic postretirement benefit cost for a year if, as of the beginning of the year, the unrecognized net gain or loss exceeds 10 percent of the greater of the accumulated postretirement benefit obligation or the market-related value of plan assets. Applications of those provisions are included in Illustration 5 (paragraphs 455-471).

Illustration 3—Transition—Determination of Amount and Timing of Recognition

430. This Statement provides two options for recognizing the transition obligation or asset in the statement of financial position and in the statement of income. An employer can phase in recognition of the transition obligation (asset) over future periods, as illustrated in Case 3A (paragraphs 432-434). However, phasing in recognition of a transition obligation should not result in less rapid recognition than would have resulted under pay-as-you-go accounting. That is, after the transition date, the cumulative postretirement benefit cost accrued should not be less than cumulative benefit payments (paragraph 112). Case 3B (paragraphs 435-442) illustrates a situation in which recognition of the transition obligation is accelerated as a result of that constraint.

431. Alternatively, an employer can recognize the transition obligation (asset) immediately in net income of the period of the change. However, if immediate recognition is elected, the amount attributable to the effects of a plan initiation or any benefit improvements adopted after December 21, 1990 is treated as prior service cost and excluded from the transition amount immediately recognized. In addition, an employer who chooses to immediately recognize its transition obligation shall, in accounting for any purchase business combination consummated after December 21, 1990, include in the purchase price allocation the unfunded accumulated postretirement benefit ob-

ligation assumed (paragraph 111). Case 3C (paragraphs 443-448) illustrates a situation in which those limitations apply.

Case 3A—Measuring the Transition Obligation and Delayed Recognition

432. Company C adopts this Statement for its financial statements for the year beginning January 1, 1993. Prior to adopting this Statement, Company C accrued postretirement benefit costs and made contributions to the plan to the extent those contributions were tax deductible. At January 1, 1993, the company had accrued postretirement benefit cost of $150,000 and plan assets of $180,000.

433. The transition obligation or asset is measured as the difference between (a) the accumulated postretirement benefit obligation and (b) the fair value of plan assets plus any recognized accrued postretirement benefit cost or less any recognized prepaid postretirement benefit cost as of the date of transition (paragraph 110). Company C's transition obligation is determined as follows:

Accumulated postretirement benefit obligation	$(465,000)
Plan assets at fair value	180,000
Accumulated postretirement benefit obligation in excess of plan assets	(285,000)
Accrued postretirement benefit cost	150,000
Transition obligation	$(135,000)

434. Company C elects to delay recognition of its transition obligation. Paragraph 112 permits straight-line amortization of the transition obligation or asset over the average remaining service period of plan participants or 20 years, if longer. Company C estimates the average remaining service period of its active employees who are plan participants at the date of transition to be 10 years. Therefore, Company C can elect to amortize its transition obligation of $135,000 on a straight-line basis over either the average remaining service period of 10 years or 20 years. That amortization (either $13,500 for 10 years or $6,750 for 20 years) is included as a component of net periodic postretirement benefit cost. However, amortization of the transition obligation is accelerated when the constraint on delayed recognition described in paragraph 112 applies. (Refer to Case 3B, paragraphs 435-442.)

Case 3B—Constraint on Delayed Recognition of Transition Obligation

435. At December 31, 1992, the accumulated (and unrecognized) postretirement benefit obligation and plan assets of a defined benefit postretirement plan sponsored by Company D are as follows:

Accumulated postretirement benefit obligation	$(255,000)
Plan assets at fair value	0
Transition obligation	$(255,000)

436. Company D adopts this Statement for the year beginning January 1, 1993. At December 31, 1992, Company D has no prepaid or accrued postretirement benefit cost (postretirement benefit cost in prior years was accounted for on a pay-as-you-go basis). The average remaining service period of active plan participants at the date of transition is 17 years. Since the average remaining service period is less than 20 years, Company D may elect to amortize the transition obligation over 20 years

rather than 17 years (paragraph 112); Company D elects the 17-year period.

437. Benefit payments in 1993 are $45,000.

Changes in accrued postretirement benefit cost, accumulated postretirement benefit obligation, and unrecognized transition obligation in 1993 are summarized as follows:

	Accrued Postretirement Benefit Cost	Accumulated Postretirement Benefit Obligation	Unrecognized Transition Obligation
Beginning of year	$ 0	$(255,000)	$255,000
Recognition of components of net periodic postretirement benefit cost:			
Service cost	(30,000)	(30,000)	
Interest cost[a]	(20,400)	(20,400)	
Amortization of transition obligation[b]	(15,000)		(15,000)
	(65,400)	(50,400)	(15,000)
Benefit payments	45,000	45,000	
Net change	(20,400)	(5,400)	(15,000)
End of year	$(20,400)	$(260,400)	$240,000

[a]An 8% discount rate is assumed.

[b]$255,000 ÷ 17 years = $15,000 per year.

438. The funded status of the plan at January 1, 1993 and December 31, 1993 is reconciled with the amount shown in the statement of financial position at those dates as follows:

	1/1/93	Net Change	12/31/93
Accumulated postretirement benefit obligation	$(255,000)	$ (5,400)	$(260,400)
Plan assets at fair value	0		0
Funded status	(255,000)	(5,400)	(260,400)
Unrecognized transition obligation	255,000	(15,000)	240,000
Accrued postretirement benefit cost	$ 0	$(20,400)	$ (20,400)

439. In 1994, benefit payments increase to $95,000 and service cost increases to $35,000. Changes in accrued postretirement benefit cost, accumulated postretirement benefit obligation, and unrecognized transition obligation in 1994 are summarized as follows:

	Accrued Postretirement Benefit Cost	Accumulated Postretirement Benefit Obligation	Unrecognized Transition Obligation
Beginning of year	$(20,400)	$(260,400)	$240,000
Recognition of components of net periodic postretirement benefit cost:			
Service cost	(35,000)	(35,000)	
Interest cost	(20,832)	(20,832)	
Amortization of transition obligation[c]	(18,768)		(18,768)
	(74,600)	(55,832)	(18,768)
Benefit payments	95,000	95,000	
Net change	20,400	39,168	(18,768)
End of year	$ 0	$(221,232)	$221,232

[c]Amortization of the transition obligation in 1994 includes straight-line amortization of $15,000 plus additional recognition of $3,768. The additional recognition is required because in 1994 cumulative benefit payments subsequent to the January 1, 1993 transition date exceed cumulative postretirement benefit cost accrued subsequent to that date (paragraph 112). The additional transition obligation required to be recognized ($3,768) is determined as follows:

	1993	1994
Benefit payments:		
1/1/93 to beginning of current year		$ 45,000
Current year	$45,000	95,000
Cumulative 1/1/93 to end of current year	$45,000	$140,000
Postretirement benefit cost recognized:		
1/1/93 to beginning of current year		$ 65,400
Current year prior to recognition of any additional amount pursuant to paragraph 112	$65,400	70,832
Cumulative 1/1/93 to end of current year before applying paragraph 112 constraint	65,400	136,232
Additional amount required to be recognized pursuant to paragraph 112	0	3,768
Cumulative 1/1/93 to end of current year	$65,400	$140,000

440. The objective of the constraint on delayed recognition of the transition obligation (paragraph 112) is to preclude slower recognition of postretirement benefit cost (as a result of applying the delayed recognition provisions of this Statement) than would have resulted under pay-as-you-go accounting for costs. An indication that the constraint may apply is the existence of a prepaid post-retirement benefit cost after the date of transition for an enterprise that prior to the application of this Statement was on a pay-as-you-go basis of accounting for other postretirement benefits. For example, in paragraph 439, if the employer had not recognized the additional $3,768 of transition obligation, the employer would have had a prepaid postretirement benefit cost equal to that amount.

441. The funded status of the plan at December 31, 1993 and 1994 is reconciled with the amount shown in the statement of financial position at those dates as follows:

	12/31/93	Net Change	12/31/94
Accumulated postretirement benefit obligation	$(260,400)	$ 39,168	$(221,232)
Plan assets at fair value	0		0
Funded status	(260,400)	39,168	(221,232)
Unrecognized transition obligation	240,000	(18,768)	221,232[d]
Accrued postretirement benefit cost	$ (20,400)	$ 20,400	$ 0

[d]In 1995, the straight-line amortization of the unrecognized transition obligation will be $14,749 ($221,232 ÷ 15 years remaining in the transition period).

442. Paragraph 113 states that if at the measurement date for the beginning of an employer's fiscal year it is expected that additional recognition of any remaining unrecognized transition obligation will be required pursuant to paragraph 112, amortization of the transition obligation for interim reporting purposes shall be based on the amount expected to be amortized for the year, except for the effects of applying the constraint in paragraph 112 for any settlement required to be accounted for pursuant to paragraphs 90-94. Those effects shall be recognized when the related settlement is recognized. The effects of changes during the year in the initial assessment of whether additional recognition of the unrecognized transition obligation will be required for the year shall be recognized over the remainder of the year. The amount of the unrecognized transition obligation to be recognized for a year shall be finally determined at the end of the year (or the measurement date, if earlier) based on the constraints on delayed recognition discussed in paragraph 112; any difference between the amortization of the transition obligation recognized during interim periods and the amount required to be recognized for the year shall be recognized immediately.

Case 3C—Limitation on Immediate Recognition of Transition Obligation

443. Company F plans to adopt this Statement for its financial statements for the year beginning January 1, 1993. Company F's postretirement defined benefit health care plan is presently accounted for on a pay-as-you-go basis.

444. On January 1, 1991, Company F acquires Company G and accounts for the business combination as a purchase pursuant to APB Opinion No. 16, *Business Combinations*. Company G has a postretirement health care plan that Company F agrees to combine with its own plan. Company F assumes the accumulated postretirement benefit obligation of Company G's plan as part of the acquisition agreement. However, at the date the business combination is consummated, no liability is recognized for the postretirement benefit obligation assumed.

445. On July 3, 1992, Company F amends its postretirement benefit plan to provide postretirement life insurance benefits to its employees; employees are given credit for their service prior to that date. At the date of the plan amendment, prior service cost is estimated at $250,000. Average remaining years of service to the full eligibility dates of the plan participants active at the date of the amendment is 25 years.

446. At December 31, 1992, the accumulated postretirement benefit obligation is $2,000,000; there are no plan assets or accrued postretirement benefit cost. On January 1, 1993, when Company F adopts this Statement, it elects to recognize immediately the transition obligation. Because the plan amendment occurred after December 21, 1990, Company F must treat the effect of the amendment as unrecognized prior service cost (paragraph 111). Company F elects to recognize prior service cost on a straight-line basis over the average remaining years of service to full eligibility of the active plan participants as permitted by paragraph 53. Therefore, at December 31, 1992, the remaining prior service cost to be recognized over those plan participants' *future* years of service to their full eligibility dates is $245,000 ($250,000 less $5,000 retroactively recognized for the period from July 3, 1992 to December 31, 1992).

447. Because the purchase business combination also occurred after December 21, 1990, Company F must retroactively reallocate the purchase price to the assets acquired and obligations assumed to reflect the postretirement benefit obligation assumed. Company F determines that the postretirement benefit obligation it assumed with the acquisition of Company G, measured as of the date of the acquisition, was $800,000. The cumulative effect on statements of income for the period January 1, 1991 to December 31, 1992 is the amortization of additional goodwill ($40,000), which Company F recognizes in

1993 as part of the effect of the change in accounting (paragraph 111).

448. On January 1, 1993, Company F recognizes on its statement of financial position goodwill of $760,000 and an obligation for postretirement benefits of $1,755,000 ($2,000,000 unfunded postretirement benefit obligation less $245,000 unrecognized prior service cost). The difference of $995,000 ($1,755,000 − $760,000) is recognized in the statement of income as the effect of an accounting change and comprises the following:

Consequences of events affecting accumulated postretirement benefit obligation other than the business combination and plan amendment	$950,000
Amortization of goodwill for prior purchase business combination	40,000
Amortization of prior service cost for prior plan amendment	5,000
Effect of accounting change	$995,000

The unrecognized prior service cost ($245,000) will be recognized on a delayed basis over the remaining 24.5-year amortization period for the plan participants active at the date of the amendment.

Illustration 4—Plan Amendments and Prior Service Cost

449. This Statement requires that, at a minimum, prior service cost arising from a plan initiation or plan amendment be recognized by assigning an equal amount of the prior service cost to each remaining year of service to the full eligibility date of each plan participant active at the date of the plan initiation or amendment (paragraph 52). Consistent use of an alternative amortization method that more rapidly reduces the unrecognized prior service cost is permitted (paragraph 53).

450. Company H has a postretirement benefit plan that provides benefits to employees who render at least 20 years of service after age 35. On January 2, 1994, Company H amends its postretirement benefit plan to increase the lifetime cap on benefits provided, resulting in unrecognized prior service cost of $750,000 (the increase in the accumulated postretirement benefit obligation as a result of the plan amendment). Amortization of that unrecognized prior service cost is illustrated in

Cases 4A and 4B (paragraphs 451-454).

Case 4A—Equal Amount Assigned to Each Future Year of Service to Full Eligibility Date

451. The determination of the amortization of prior service cost is based on remaining years of service prior to the full eligibility date of each plan participant active at the date of the amendment but not yet fully eligible for benefits. (Refer to the glossary for the definition of plan participant.) Future years of service of active employees who are not plan participants are excluded. Each remaining year of service prior to the full eligibility date of each active plan participant not yet fully eligible for benefits is assigned an equal share of the prior service cost (paragraph 52). Thus, the portion of prior service cost to be recognized in each of those future years is weighted based on the number of those plan participants expected to render service in each of those future years.

452. At the date of the amendment (January 2, 1994), Company H has 165 employees of whom 15 are fully eligible for benefits, 10 are under age 35, and 40 are expected to terminate before becoming eligible for any benefits. Because the 10 employees under age 35 have not met the age requirements to participate in the plan (only service after age 35 is credited) and 40 employees are not expected to receive benefits under the plan, those 50 employees are not considered to be plan participants and, therefore, are excluded from the calculation. The 15 fully eligible plan participants also are excluded from the calculation because they do not have to render any additional service to earn the added benefits. The remaining 100 employees have not yet earned the full amount of the benefits they are expected to earn under the plan. Those employees are expected to become fully eligible for those benefits over the next 20 years. Their remaining years of service to full eligibility for benefits is the basis for amortization of the prior service cost.

453. The following schedules illustrate the calculation of the expected remaining years of service prior to full eligibility (Schedule 1) and the amortization schedule for recognizing the prior service cost (Schedule 2). Employees hired after the date of the plan amendment or who attain age 35 after the date of the plan amendment do not affect the amortization nor do revised estimates of remaining years of service, except those due to a curtailment.

Schedule 1—Determination of expected remaining years of service prior to full eligibility as of January 2, 1994

Indiv.	Remaining Years of Service Prior to Full Elig.	Year																				Total Remaining Years of Service Prior to Full Elig.
		1994	1995	1996	1997	1998	1999	2000	2001	2002	2003	2004	2005	2006	2007	2008	2009	2010	2011	2012	2013	
A1-A4	1	4																				4
B1-B6	2	6	6																			12
C1-C5	3	5	5	5																		15
D1-D5	4	5	5	5	5																	20
E1-E7	5	7	7	7	7	7																35
F1-F5	6	5	5	5	5	5	5															30
G1-G9	7	9	9	9	9	9	9	9														63
H1-H7	8	7	7	7	7	7	7	7	7													56
I1-I5	9	5	5	5	5	5	5	5	5	5												45
J1-J5	10	5	5	5	5	5	5	5	5	5	5											50
K1-K4	11	4	4	4	4	4	4	4	4	4	4	4										44
L1-L8	12	8	8	8	8	8	8	8	8	8	8	8	8									96
M1-M8	13	8	8	8	8	8	8	8	8	8	8	8	8	8								104
N1-N5	14	5	5	5	5	5	5	5	5	5	5	5	5	5	5							70
O1-O4	15	4	4	4	4	4	4	4	4	4	4	4	4	4	4	4						60
P1-P3	16	3	3	3	3	3	3	3	3	3	3	3	3	3	3	3	3					48
Q1-Q4	17	4	4	4	4	4	4	4	4	4	4	4	4	4	4	4	4	4				68
R1-R3	18	3	3	3	3	3	3	3	3	3	3	3	3	3	3	3	3	3	3			54
S1-S2	19	2	2	2	2	2	2	2	2	2	2	2	2	2	2	2	2	2	2	2		38
T1	20	1	1	1	1	1	1	1	1	1	1	1	1	1	1	1	1	1	1	1	1	20
Service Years Rendered		100	96	90	85	80	73	68	59	52	47	42	38	30	22	17	13	10	6	3	1	932
Amortization Fraction		$\frac{100}{932}$	$\frac{96}{932}$	$\frac{90}{932}$	$\frac{85}{932}$	$\frac{80}{932}$	$\frac{73}{932}$	$\frac{68}{932}$	$\frac{59}{932}$	$\frac{52}{932}$	$\frac{47}{932}$	$\frac{42}{932}$	$\frac{38}{932}$	$\frac{30}{932}$	$\frac{22}{932}$	$\frac{17}{932}$	$\frac{13}{932}$	$\frac{10}{932}$	$\frac{6}{932}$	$\frac{3}{932}$	$\frac{1}{932}$	$\frac{932}{932}$

Note: To determine total remaining years of service prior to full eligibility, consideration is given to the remaining number of years of service to the full eligibility date of each plan participant or group of plan participants active at the date of the plan amendment who is not yet fully eligible for benefits. For example, in 1994, individuals A1-A4 meet the company's age and service requirements for full eligibility for the benefits they are expected to receive under the plan. Although it may be expected that those employees will work beyond 1994, benefits are not attributed to years of service beyond their full eligibility date (paragraph 21). Refer to Case 4B, paragraph 454, for less complex amortization approaches.

Schedule 2—Amortization of unrecognized prior service cost

Year	Beginning-of-Year Balance	Amortization Rate	Amortization	End-of-Year Balance
1994	$750,000	100/932	$80,472	$669,528
1995	669,528	96/932	77,253	592,275
1996	592,275	90/932	72,425	519,850
1997	519,850	85/932	68,401	451,449
1998	451,449	80/932	64,378	387,071
1999	387,071	73/932	58,745	328,326
2000	328,326	68/932	54,721	273,605
2001	273,605	59/932	47,479	226,126
2002	226,126	52/932	41,845	184,281
2003	184,281	47/932	37,822	146,459
2004	146,459	42/932	33,798	112,661
2005	112,661	38/932	30,579	82,082
2006	82,082	30/932	24,142	57,940
2007	57,940	22/932	17,704	40,236
2008	40,236	17/932	13,680	26,556
2009	26,556	13/932	10,461	16,095
2010	16,095	10/932	8,047	8,048
2011	8,048	6/932	4,828	3,220
2012	3,220	3/932	2,414	806
2013	806	1/932	806	0

Case 4B—Straight-Line Amortization over Average Remaining Years of Service to Full Eligibility Date

454. To reduce the complexity and detail of the computations shown in Case 4A (paragraph 453, Schedules 1 and 2), alternative amortization approaches that recognize prior service cost related to plan amendments more rapidly may be applied if used consistently (paragraph 53). For example, if Company H (Case 4A) elects to use straight-line amortization of prior service cost over the average remaining years of service prior to full eligibility for benefits of the active plan participants (932 future service years ÷ 100 employees = 9.32 years), the amortization would be as follows:

Year	Beginning-of-Year Balance	Amortization	End-of-Year Balance
1994	$750,000	$80,472[a]	$669,528
1995	669,528	80,472	589,056
1996	589,056	80,472	508,584
1997	508,584	80,472	428,112
1998	428,112	80,472	347,640
1999	347,640	80,472	267,168
2000	267,168	80,472	186,696
2001	186,696	80,472	106,224
2002	106,224	80,472	25,752
2003	25,752	25,752	0

[a]$750,000 ÷ 9.32 years = $80,472.

Note: Under this approach, the first year's amortization is the same as the first year's amortization under the weighted remaining years of service method illustrated in Case 4A (paragraph 453, Schedule 2). Thereafter, the amortization pattern will differ.

Illustration 5—Accounting for Gains and Losses and Timing of Measurements

455. Gains and losses include changes in the amount of the accumulated postretirement benefit obligation or plan assets resulting from experience different from that assumed or changes in assumptions (paragraph 56). This illustration demonstrates the effects of gains and losses in accounting for postretirement benefits for Company I from 1993 to 1995. Case 5A (paragraphs 457-461) illustrates the accounting for a loss resulting from changes in assumptions in measuring the accumulated postretirement benefit obligation. Case 5B

(paragraphs 462-464) illustrates the effect of a gain when the return on plan assets exceeds projections. Case 5C (paragraphs 465-467) illustrates the accounting in a year when both gains and losses are experienced.

456. Company I adopts this Statement for the fiscal year beginning January 1, 1993 and elects a December 31 measurement date (date at which the accumulated postretirement benefit obligation and plan assets are measured). Alternatively, as discussed in paragraph 72, the company could

choose a measurement date not earlier than September 30. The company's accumulated postretirement benefit obligation on December 31, 1992 is $6,000,000, and the plan is unfunded. Beginning in 1993, and unless otherwise noted, the company funds at the end of each year an amount equal to the benefits paid that year plus the service cost and interest cost for that year. For illustrative purposes, the following assumptions are used to project changes in the accumulated postretirement benefit obligation and plan assets during the period 1993-1995:

	1993	1994	1995
Discount rate	9.5%	9.0%	9.0%
Expected long-term rate of return on plan assets		10.0%	10.0%
Average remaining years of service of active plan participants	12	12	12

Case 5A—Loss on Obligation

457. The reconciliation of the funded status of Company I's postretirement benefit plan with the amount shown in the statement of financial position at the date of transition (January 1, 1993) follows:

	Actual 1/1/93
Accumulated postretirement benefit obligation	$(6,000,000)
Plan assets at fair value	0
Funded status	(6,000,000)
Unrecognized transition obligation	6,000,000
(Accrued)/prepaid postretirement benefit cost	$ 0

458. Pursuant to paragraph 112, Company I elects to amortize the unrecognized transition obligation over a 20-year period rather than the average remaining service period of active plan participants at the date of transition (12 years).

Projected changes in prepaid postretirement benefit cost, accumulated postretirement benefit obligation, unrecognized transition obligation, and plan assets in 1993 are summarized as follows:

	Prepaid Postretirement Benefit Cost	Accumulated Postretirement Benefit Obligation	Unrecognized Transition Obligation	Plan Assets
Beginning of year	$ 0	$(6,000,000)	$6,000,000	$ 0
Recognition of components of net periodic postretirement benefit cost:				
Service cost	(300,000)	(300,000)		
Interest cost	(570,000)	(570,000)		
Amortization of transition obligation	(300,000)		(300,000)	
	(1,170,000)	(870,000)	(300,000)	
Assets contributed to plan	1,500,000			1,500,000
Benefit payments from plan		630,000		(630,000)
Net change	330,000	(240,000)	(300,000)	870,000
End of year—projected	$ 330,000	$(6,240,000)	$5,700,000	$ 870,000

459. When Company I's plan assets and obligations are measured at December 31, 1993, the accumulated postretirement benefit obligation is $760,000 greater than had been projected (a loss occurs) because the discount rate declined to 9 percent and for various other reasons not specifically identified. Company I elects to amortize amounts in excess of the "corridor" over the average remaining service period of active plan participants.[a]

460. The change in the funded status of the plan at December 31, 1993 from amounts projected and the reconciliation of the funded status of the plan with the amount shown in the statement of financial position at that date follow:

	Projected 12/31/93	Net Loss	Actual 12/31/93
Accumulated postretirement benefit obligation	$(6,240,000)	$(760,000)	$(7,000,000)
Plan assets at fair value	870,000		870,000
Funded status	(5,370,000)	(760,000)	(6,130,000)
Unrecognized net loss		760,000	760,000
Unrecognized transition obligation	5,700,000		5,700,000
Prepaid postretirement benefit cost	$ 330,000	$ 0	$ 330,000

461. In addition to the funded status reconciliation, the 1993 financial statements include the following disclosure of the components of net periodic postretirement benefit cost (as required by paragraph 74(b)):

Service cost	$ 300,000
Interest cost	570,000
Amortization of transition obligation	300,000
Net periodic postretirement benefit cost	$1,170,000

Case 5B—Gain on Assets

462. Changes in prepaid postretirement benefit cost, accumulated postretirement benefit obligation, unrecognized transition obligation, unrecognized net loss, and plan assets are projected at the beginning of the year. That projection serves as the basis for interim accounting until a subsequent event occurs requiring remeasurement. The projection at the beginning of 1994 follows:

[a]Paragraph 59 states that, at a minimum, amortization of an unrecognized net gain or loss is included as a component of net periodic postretirement benefit cost if, as of the beginning of the year, that unrecognized net gain or loss exceeds 10 percent of the greater of the accumulated postretirement benefit obligation or market-related value of plan assets. As used herein, *amounts in excess of the corridor* refers to the portion of the unrecognized net gain or loss in excess of the greater of those defined amounts.

	Prepaid Postretirement Benefit Cost	Accumulated Postretirement Benefit Obligation	Unrecognized Transition Obligation	Unrecognized Net Loss	Plan Assets
Beginning of year	$ 330,000	$(7,000,000)	$5,700,000	$760,000	$ 870,000
Recognition of components of net periodic postretirement benefit cost:					
Service cost	(320,000)	(320,000)			
Interest cost	(630,000)	(630,000)			
Amortization of transition obligation	(300,000)		(300,000)		
Amortization of unrecognized net loss[a]	(5,000)			(5,000)	
Expected return on plan assets[b]	87,000				87,000
	(1,168,000)	(950,000)	(300,000)	(5,000)	87,000
Assets contributed to plan	1,650,000				1,650,000
Benefit payments from plan		700,000			(700,000)
Net change	482,000	(250,000)	(300,000)	(5,000)	1,037,000
End of year—projected	$ 812,000	$(7,250,000)	$5,400,000	$755,000	$1,907,000

[a]Refer to Schedule 2 (paragraph 469) for computation.

[b]Refer to Schedule 1 (paragraph 468) for computation.

463. When Company I's plan assets and obligations are measured at December 31, 1994, the fair value of the plan assets is $150,000 greater than expected (an experience gain) because market performance was better than the 10 percent return that was assumed. The change in the funded status of the plan at December 31, 1994 from amounts projected and the reconciliation of the funded status of the plan with the amount shown in the statement of financial position at that date follow:

	Projected 12/31/94	Net Gain	Actual 12/31/94
Accumulated postretirement benefit obligation	$(7,250,000)		$(7,250,000)
Plan assets at fair value	1,907,000	$ 150,000[c]	2,057,000
Funded status	(5,343,000)	150,000	(5,193,000)
Unrecognized net (gain) or loss	755,000	(150,000)	605,000
Unrecognized transition obligation	5,400,000		5,400,000
Prepaid postretirement benefit cost	$ 812,000	$ 0	$ 812,000

[c]Refer to Schedule 1 (paragraph 468) for computation.

464. The 1994 financial statements include the following disclosure of the components of net periodic postretirement benefit cost:

Service cost	$ 320,000
Interest cost	630,000
Actual return on plan assets[d]	(237,000)
Amortization of transition obligation	300,000
Net amortization and deferral[e]	155,000
Net periodic postretirement benefit cost	$1,168,000

[d]Refer to Schedule 3 (paragraph 470) for computation.

[e]Refer to Schedule 4 (paragraph 471) for computation.

Case 5C—Loss on Assets and Gain on Obligation

465. Projected changes in prepaid postretirement benefit cost, accumulated postretirement benefit obligation, unrecognized transition obligation, unrecognized net loss, and plan assets for 1995 are summarized as follows:

	Prepaid Postretirement Benefit Cost	Accumulated Postretirement Benefit Obligation	Unrecognized Transition Obligation	Unrecognized Net Loss	Plan Assets
Beginning of year	$ 812,000	$(7,250,000)	$5,400,000	$605,000	$2,057,000
Recognition of components of net periodic postretirement benefit cost:					
Service cost	(360,000)	(360,000)			
Interest cost	(652,500)	(652,500)			
Amortization of transition obligation	(300,000)		(300,000)		
Amortization of unrecognized net loss[a]	0			0	
Expected return on plan assets[b]	193,700				193,700
	(1,118,800)	(1,012,500)	(300,000)	0	193,700
Assets contributed to plan	1,912,500				1,912,500
Benefit payments from plan		900,000			(900,000)
Net change	793,700	(112,500)	(300,000)	0	1,206,200
End of year—projected	$1,605,700	$(7,362,500)	$5,100,000	$605,000	$3,263,200

[a]Refer to Schedule 2 (paragraph 469) for computation.

[b]Refer to Schedule 1 (paragraph 468) for computation.

466. When Company I's plan assets and obligations are measured at December 31, 1995, both an asset loss of $220,360 and a liability gain of $237,260 are determined. The change in the funded status of the plan at December 31, 1995 from amounts projected and the reconciliation of the funded status of the plan with the amount shown in the statement of financial position at that date follow:

	Projected 12/31/95	Net Gain/Loss	Actual 12/31/95
Accumulated postretirement benefit obligation	$(7,362,500)	$ 237,260	$(7,125,240)
Plan assets at fair value	3,263,200	(220,360)c	3,042,840
Funded status	(4,099,300)	16,900	(4,082,400)
Unrecognized net (gain) or loss	605,000	(16,900)	588,100
Unrecognized transition obligation	5,100,000		5,100,000
Prepaid postretirement benefit cost	$ 1,605,700	$ 0	$ 1,605,700

cRefer to Schedule 1 (paragraph 468) for computation.

467. The 1995 financial statements include the following disclosure of the components of net periodic postretirement benefit cost:

Service cost	$ 360,000
Interest cost	652,500
Actual loss on plan assetsd	26,660
Amortization of transition obligation	300,000
Net amortization and deferrale	(220,360)
Net periodic postretirement benefit cost	$1,118,800

dRefer to Schedule 3 (paragraph 470) for computation.

eRefer to Schedule 4 (paragraph 471) for computation.

Supporting Schedules

Schedule 1—Plan assets

468. This Statement requires use of an assumption about the long-term rate of return on plan assets and a market-related value of plan assets to calculate the expected return on plan assets. If the fund holding plan assets is a taxable entity, the expected long-term rate of return on plan assets is net of estimated income taxes, and the nonbenefit liability for accrued income taxes reduces plan assets. This Statement defines market-related asset value as either fair value or a calculated value that recognizes changes in fair value in a systematic and rational manner over not more than five years (paragraph 57). This schedule reflects the calculation of market-related value, the fair value of plan assets, the actual return on plan assets, and the deferred asset gain or loss for the year (the difference between actual and expected return on plan assets included in the net amortization and deferral component of net periodic postretirement benefit cost).

	1993	1994	1995
Expected long-term rate of return on plan assets		10.0%	10.0%
Beginning balance, market-related value[a]	$ 0	$ 870,000	$1,937,000
Contributions to plan (end of year)	1,500,000	1,650,000	1,912,500
Benefits paid by plan	(630,000)	(700,000)	(900,000)
Expected return on plan assets		87,000	193,700
	870,000	1,907,000	3,143,200
20% of each of last 5 years' asset gains (losses)		30,000	(14,072)
Ending balance, market-related value	$ 870,000	$1,937,000	$3,129,128
Beginning balance, fair value of plan assets	$ 0	$ 870,000	$2,057,000
Contributions to plan	1,500,000	1,650,000	1,912,500
Benefits paid	(630,000)	(700,000)	(900,000)
Actual return (loss) on plan assets[b]	0	237,000	(26,660)
Ending balance, fair value of plan assets	$ 870,000	$2,057,000	$3,042,840
Deferred asset gain (loss) for year[c]	$ 0	$ 150,000	$ (220,360)
Gain (loss) not included in ending balance market-related value[d]	$ 0	$ 120,000	$ (86,288)

[a]This example uses an approach that adds in 20% of each of the last 5 years' gains or losses.

[b]Refer to Schedule 3 (paragraph 470) for computation.

[c](Actual return on plan assets) − (expected return on plan assets).

[d](Ending balance, fair value of plan assets) − (ending balance, market-related value of plan assets).

Schedule 2—Test for amortization of unrecognized net gain or loss

469. This Statement generally does not require recognition of any of the gain or loss in the period in which it arises and permits a minimum amortization of an unrecognized net gain or loss whereby the net amount in excess of the "corridor" is amortized over the average remaining service period of active plan participants (paragraph 59 and paragraph 459, footnote a). That allows a reasonable opportunity for gains and losses to offset each other without affecting net periodic postretirement benefit cost.

	1993	1994	1995
10% of beginning balance of accumulated postretirement benefit obligation	$600,000	$700,000	$725,000
10% of beginning balance of market-related value of plan assets[e]	$ 0	$ 87,000	$193,700
Greater of the above	$600,000	$700,000	$725,000
Unrecognized net (gain) loss at beginning of year		$760,000	$605,000
Asset gain (loss) not included in beginning balance of market-related value[f]		0	120,000
Amount subject to amortization		$760,000	$725,000
Amount in excess of the corridor subject to amortization		$ 60,000	$ 0
Divided by average remaining service period (years)		12	
Required amortization		$ 5,000	

[e]Refer to Schedule 1 (paragraph 468) for calculation of market-related value of plan assets.

[f]Refer to Schedule 1 (paragraph 468) for calculation of gain or loss not included in prior year's ending balance market-related value.

Schedule 3—Determination of actual return or loss on plan assets

470. The determination of the actual return or loss on plan assets component of net periodic postretirement benefit cost is as follows:

	1993	1994	1995
Plan assets at fair value, beginning of year	$ 0	$ 870,000	$2,057,000
Plus: assets contributed to plan	1,500,000	1,650,000	1,912,500
Less: benefit payments from plan	(630,000)	(700,000)	(900,000)
	870,000	1,820,000	3,069,500
Less: plan assets at fair value, end of year	(870,000)	(2,057,000)	(3,042,840)
Actual (return) loss on plan assets	$ 0	$ (237,000)	$ 26,660

Schedule 4—Determination of net amortization and deferral

471. The net amortization and deferral component of net periodic postretirement benefit cost required to be disclosed pursuant to paragraph 74(b) is determined as follows:

	1994	1995
Amortization of unrecognized net (gain) or loss[g]	$ 5,000	$ 0
Deferred asset gain (loss) for year[h]	150,000	(220,360)
Net amortization and deferral	$155,000	$(220,360)

[g]Refer to Schedule 2 (paragraph 469) for computation.

[h]Refer to Schedule 1 (paragraph 468) for computation.

Illustration 6—Defined-Dollar Capped Plans

472. The following cases (6A and 6B, paragraphs 473-478) demonstrate the operation of defined-dollar capped plans and the possible effect of the "cap" on projecting costs for purposes of measuring the accumulated postretirement benefit obligation and net periodic postretirement benefit

cost. The examples are simplified and illustrate only one aspect of the measurement process (paragraph 17 and paragraph 33, footnote 13).

Case 6A—Dollar Cap Defined on Individual Coverage

473. Company J sponsors a postretirement health care plan for its salaried employees. The plan has an annual limitation (a "cap") on the dollar amount of the employer's share of the cost of covered benefits incurred by a plan participant. The retiree is responsible, therefore, for the amount by which the cost of the benefit coverage under the plan incurred during a year exceeds that cap. The company adjusts the cap annually for the effects of inflation. For 1993, the cap is $1,500; the inflation adjustment in 1994 and 1995 is assumed to be 4 percent. The employer's health care cost trend rate assumption is 13 percent for 1994 and 12 percent for 1995.

474. The employer's projected cost of providing benefit coverage in 1993-1995 for a 67-year-old retiree follows. Similar projections are made for each age at which a plan participant is expected to receive benefits under the plan. In this example, the incurred claims cost exceeds the cap on the employer's share of the cost in each year.

	Expected Cost for 67-Year-Old Retiree		
	1993	1994	1995
Gross eligible charges	$3,065	$3,463	$3,879
Medicare[a]	(890)	(1,003)	(1,125)
Deductible/coinsurance	(325)	(340)	(355)
Incurred claims cost	$1,850	$2,120	$2,399
Annual cap on employer's cost	$1,500	$1,560	$1,622
Employer's share of incurred claims cost	$1,500	$1,560	$1,622
Retiree's share of gross eligible charges[b]	$ 675	$ 900	$1,132

[a]The change in Medicare reflects the portion of the gross eligible charges for which Medicare is responsible under enacted Medicare legislation.

[b]Deductible/coinsurance plus share of incurred claims: 1993—[$325 + ($1,850 − $1,500)]; 1994—[$340 + ($2,120 − $1,560)]; 1995—[$355 + ($2,399 − $1,622)].

475. If, based on the health care cost trend rate assumptions, the employer's share of costs for each plan participant is not expected to be less than the cap in the future, Company J could measure its expected postretirement benefit obligation by projecting the annual cap. However, if per capita claims data for some plan participants or estimates of the health care cost trend rate indicate that in the future the employer's share of the incurred claims cost will be less than the cap for at least some plan participants, the employer's obligation is to be measured as described in paragraphs 34-42.

Case 6B—Dollar Cap Defined in the Aggregate for the Retiree Group

476. Company K sponsors a contributory postretirement health care plan for its hourly employees. The plan has an annual limitation (a "cap") on the dollar amount of the employer's share of the cost of covered benefits incurred by the retiree group as a whole. The company agrees to bear annual costs equal to a specified dollar amount ($1,500 in 1993) multiplied by the number of retired plan participants (the employer contribution); participating retirees are required to contribute a stated amount each year ($1,000 in 1993). The cap on the employer's share of annual costs and the retirees' contribution rates are increased 5 percent annually. The shortfall in a year (the amount by which incurred claims cost exceeds the combined employer and retiree contributions) is initially borne by the employer but is passed back to retirees in the subsequent year through supplemental retiree contributions for that year (a retrospective adjustment).

477. The employer projects the aggregate cost of benefits expected to be paid to current plan participants (40 retirees) in each future period as follows:

	1993	1994	1995
Gross eligible charges	$160,000	$215,000	$197,000
Medicare	(46,500)	(62,350)	(57,300)
Deductible/coinsurance	(20,750)	(27,440)	(24,700)
Incurred claims cost	$ 92,750	$125,210	$115,000
Retiree contributions[a]	$ 40,000	$ 42,000	$ 44,080
Maximum employer contribution[b]	60,000	63,000	66,160
	$100,000	$105,000	$110,240
Shortfall (to be recovered by additional retiree contributions in subsequent year)		$ 20,210	$ 4,760
Supplemental contribution from retirees due to shortfall in prior year			$ 20,210

[a]Per retiree: 1993—$1,000; 1994—$1,050; 1995—$1,102.

[b]Per retiree: 1993—$1,500; 1994—$1,575; 1995—$1,654.

478. If, as in this example, retirees absorb the entire shortfall in annual contributions and if there is a projected shortfall for all future years, the employer could measure its expected postretirement benefit obligation by projecting its annual contribution (contribution rate × expected number of retirees = expected obligation for the year).

Illustration 7—Disclosure Requirements

479. This Statement requires an employer to disclose information in its financial statements about the obligation to provide postretirement benefits and the cost of providing those benefits. Paragraph 74 describes the disclosures required for defined benefit postretirement plans (paragraphs 77 and 78 describe how those disclosures may be aggregated by an employer with more than one postretirement benefit plan), paragraph 106 describes the disclosures required for defined contribution plans, and paragraph 82 describes the disclosures required for multiemployer plans. The following cases (7A-7C, paragraphs 480-483) illustrate those disclosure requirements. For simplicity, comparative financial statements are assumed not to be presented.

Case 7A—Single-Employer Defined Benefit Postretirement Plan

480. Paragraph 78(a) permits an employer to combine the disclosures for health and other welfare benefit plans unless the accumulated postretirement benefit obligation of the plans that provide primarily other postretirement welfare benefits is significant relative to the aggregate accumulated postretirement benefit obligation of all the employer's postretirement benefit plans. For an employer that provides more than one defined benefit postretirement plan, the disclosure for the year ended December 31, 1993 would be as follows. Because the life insurance plan is not significant, it is combined with the health care plan for disclosure purposes as permitted by paragraph 78.

Note X: The company sponsors two defined benefit postretirement plans that cover both salaried and nonsalaried employees. One plan provides medical and dental benefits, and the other provides life insurance benefits. The postretirement health care plan is contributory, with retiree contributions adjusted annually; the life insurance plan is noncontributory. The accounting for the health care plan anticipates future cost-sharing changes to the written plan that are consistent with the company's expressed intent to increase retiree contributions each year by 50 percent of the excess of the expected general inflation rate over 6 percent. On July 24, 1993, the company amended its postretirement health care plan to provide vision coverage. Beginning in 1993, the company adopted a funding policy for its postretirement health care plan similar to its funding policy for its life insurance plan—an amount equal to a level percentage of the employees' salaries is contributed to the plan annually. For 1993, that percentage was 4.25, and the aggregate contribution for both plans was $34,000.

The following table sets forth the plans' combined funded status reconciled with the amount shown in the company's statement of financial position at December 31, 1993:

Accumulated postretirement benefit obligation:	
Retirees	$(187,000)
Fully eligible active plan participants	(100,000)
Other active plan participants	(297,400)
	(584,400)
Plan assets at fair value, primarily listed U.S. stocks and bonds	87,960
Accumulated postretirement benefit obligation in excess of plan assets	(496,440)
Unrecognized net gain from past experience different from that assumed and from changes in assumptions	(40,000)
Prior service cost not yet recognized in net periodic postretirement benefit cost	19,000
Unrecognized transition obligation	470,250
Accrued postretirement benefit cost	$ (47,190)

The company's postretirement health care plan is underfunded; the accumulated postretirement benefit obligation and plan assets for that plan are $552,400 and $36,800, respectively.

Net periodic postretirement benefit cost for 1993 included the following components:

Service cost—benefits attributed to service during the period	$15,000
Interest cost on accumulated postretirement benefit obligation	44,400
Actual return on plan assets	(3,960)
Amortization of transition obligation over 20 years	24,750
Net amortization and deferral	1,000
Net periodic postretirement benefit cost	$81,190

For measurement purposes, a 16 percent annual rate of increase in the per capita cost of covered health care benefits was assumed for 1994; the rate was assumed to decrease gradually to 6 percent for 2020 and remain at that level thereafter. The health care cost trend rate assumption has a significant effect on the amounts reported. To illustrate, increasing the assumed health care cost trend rates by 1 percentage point in each year would increase the accumulated postretirement benefit obligation as of December 31, 1993 by $73,000 and the aggregate of the service and interest cost components of net periodic postretirement benefit cost for the year then ended by $13,000.

The weighted-average discount rate used in determining the accumulated postretirement benefit obligation was 8 percent. The trust holding the plan assets is subject to federal income taxes at a 34 percent tax rate. The expected long-term rate of return on plan assets after estimated taxes was 6.6 percent.

Case 7B—Defined Contribution Plan

481. An illustration of the disclosure for a defined contribution plan follows:

Note X: The company sponsors a defined contribution postretirement health care plan covering substantially all of its employees in both its chemicals and automotive subsidiaries. The company's contributions and cost are determined annually as

1.5 percent of each covered employee's salary and totaled $569,000 in 1993.

Case 7C—Multiemployer Plan

482. An illustration of the disclosure for a multiemployer plan follows:

Note X: The company's trucking subsidiary participates in a multiemployer plan that provides defined postretirement health care benefits to substantially all unionized workers in that subsidiary. Amounts charged to postretirement benefit cost and contributed to the plan totaled $319,000 in 1993.

483. If the information regarding the amount of postretirement benefit cost recognized during the period (disclosed in paragraph 482) is not available and the postretirement health and welfare benefits are provided through a general health and welfare plan, the amount of the aggregate required contribution to the general health and welfare benefit plan should be disclosed as follows (paragraph 82(b)):

Note X: The company's trucking subsidiary participates in a multiemployer plan that provides substantially all unionized workers in that subsidiary with health care and other welfare benefits during their working lives and after retirement. Amounts charged to benefit cost and contributed to the health and welfare plan for those benefits totaled $400,000 in 1993.

Illustration 8—Accounting for Settlements

484. This Statement provides for delayed recognition of the effects of a plan initiation or a plan amendment, the transition obligation or transition asset, and gains or losses arising in the ordinary course of operations. In certain circumstances, however, recognition of some or all of those previously delayed amounts is appropriate. Settlements are events that may require income or expense recognition of certain previously unrecognized amounts and adjustments to liabilities or assets recognized in the employer's statement of financial position. The settlement of all or part of the accumulated postretirement benefit obligation is the event that requires recognition of all or part of a previously unrecognized net gain or loss and unrecognized transition asset. A settlement also may accelerate recognition of a transition obligation under the constraint in paragraph 112 (paragraphs 92 and 93). The following cases (8A-8C, paragraphs 485-495) illustrate the accounting for settlements in various circumstances.

Case 8A—Settlement When an Unrecognized Transition Obligation Exists

485. Company L sponsors a postretirement life insurance plan. On January 1, 1993, the company adopts this Statement; prior to that date it accounted for postretirement benefits on a pay-as-you-go (cash) basis. On December 31, 1994, Company L settles the accumulated postretirement benefit obligation for its current retirees ($70,000) through the purchase of nonparticipating life insurance contracts.

486. In accounting for the settlement, Company L must determine whether recognition of an additional amount of any unrecognized transition obligation is required pursuant to the constraint on delayed recognition of the transition obligation (paragraphs 112 and 113). At December 31, 1994, the cumulative postretirement benefit cost accrued subsequent to the date of transition exceeds the cumulative benefits payments subsequent to that date (including payments made pur-

suant to the settlement); thus, the constraint on delayed recognition of the transition obligation is not operative. The results of the settlement are as follows:

| | December 31, 1994 | | |
	Before Settlement	Settlement	After Settlement
Accumulated postretirement benefit obligation	$(257,000)	$70,000	$(187,000)
Plan assets at fair value	73,000	(70,000)[a]	3,000
Funded status	(184,000)	0	(184,000)
Unrecognized net gain	(44,575)	12,124[a]	(32,451)
Unrecognized prior service cost	33,000		33,000
Unrecognized transition obligation	195,000	(12,124)[a]	182,876
Accrued postretirement benefit cost	$ (575)	$ 0	$ (575)

[a]The maximum settlement gain subject to recognition is the unrecognized net gain subsequent to transition plus any unrecognized transition asset ($44,575 + $0 = $44,575) (paragraph 92). If, as in this case, only part of the accumulated postretirement benefit obligation is settled, a pro rata portion of the maximum gain based on the relationship of the accumulated postretirement benefit obligation settled to the total accumulated postretirement benefit obligation ($70,000 ÷ $257,000 or 27.2%) is subject to recognition. That amount ($44,575 × 27.2% = $12,124) must first reduce any unrecognized transition obligation; any excess is recognized in income in the current period (paragraph 93). In this case, the settlement gain is entirely offset against the unrecognized transition obligation.

Case 8B—Settlement When an Unrecognized Transition Asset Exists

487. Company M sponsors a postretirement life insurance plan. On January 2, 1995, Company M settles the accumulated postretirement benefit obligation for its current retirees ($200,000) through the purchase of nonparticipating life insurance contracts.

488. Pursuant to paragraphs 92 and 93, a settlement gain of $78,506 is recognized, determined as follows:

| | January 2, 1995 | | |
	Before Settlement	Settlement	After Settlement
Accumulated postretirement benefit obligation	$(257,000)	$200,000	$(57,000)
Plan assets at fair value	350,900	(200,000)	150,900
Funded status	93,900	0	93,900
Unrecognized net gain	(44,575)	34,679[a]	(9,896)
Unrecognized prior service cost	33,000		33,000
Unrecognized transition asset	(56,333)	43,827[a]	(12,506)
Prepaid postretirement benefit cost	$ 25,992	$ 78,506	$104,498

[a]The maximum settlement gain is measured as the unrecognized net gain subsequent to transition plus the unrecognized transition asset ($44,575 + $56,333 = $100,908) (paragraph 92). Since only a portion of the accumulated postretirement benefit obligation is settled, a pro rata portion of the maximum gain based on the relationship of the accumulated postretirement benefit obligation settled to the total accumulated postretirement benefit obligation ($200,000 ÷ $257,000 or 77.8%) is subject to recognition. That amount ($100,908 × 77.8% = $78,506) must first reduce any unrecognized transition obligation ($0); any excess is recognized in income in the current period (paragraph 93). In this case, the entire settlement gain of $78,506 is recognized in income. The transition constraint of paragraph 112 that requires additional recognition of a *transition obligation* in certain circumstances is not applicable because there is an unrecognized *transition asset*.

Case 8C—Effect of Mid-Year Settlement on Transition Constraint

489. A settlement is an event that requires remeasurement of the accumulated postretirement benefit obligation prior to the settlement. This case illustrates the accounting for a settlement of part of the accumulated postretirement benefit obligation that occurs mid-year and the interaction between that event and other provisions of the Statement, such as the constraint on delayed recognition of the transition obligation.

490. Company N adopts this Statement for the fiscal year beginning January 1, 1993 and elects a year-end (December 31) measurement date. At the date of transition, the company's accumulated postretirement benefit obligation for its

postretirement life insurance plan is $6,000,000, and there are no plan assets. In 1993, the company establishes a policy of funding at the end of each year an amount equal to the benefits paid during the year plus the service and interest cost for the year. Benefits are paid at the end of each year and in 1993 are $630,000, which is less than the net periodic postretirement benefit cost accrued for the year ($1,170,000); thus, no additional transition obligation is recognized pursuant to paragraph 112. Company N elects to amortize net unrecognized gains and losses in excess of the "corridor" over the average remaining service period of plan participants (paragraph 59 and paragraph 459, footnote a).

491. At the beginning of 1994, Company N projects the life insurance benefits expected to be paid in 1994 to retirees' beneficiaries to determine whether recognition of an additional amount of

the unrecognized transition obligation will be required (paragraph 113). Although Company N is considering settling a portion of the accumulated postretirement benefit obligation, the effects of the settlement are not included in the projection because plan settlements are not anticipated for measurement or recognition prior to their occurrence. The projection indicates that no additional amount is required to be recognized. On June 30, 1994, Company N contributes additional funds ($1,430,000) and settles a portion ($1,900,000) of the accumulated postretirement benefit obligation for its current retirees through the purchase of nonparticipating life insurance contracts.

492. The changes in the funded status of the plan during the first six months of the year and a reconciliation of the funded status of the plan with the amount shown in the statement of financial position immediately prior to the settlement are as follows:

	Actual 12/31/93	Six Months Postretirement Benefit Cost	Assets Contributed to Plan	Effects of Remeasurement Immediately before Settlement	Before Settlement 6/30/94
Accumulated postretirement benefit obligation	$(6,600,000)	$(457,000)[a]		$420,000[b]	$(6,637,000)
Plan assets at fair value	870,000	43,500[c]	$1,430,000	0[b]	2,343,500
Funded status	(5,730,000)	(413,500)	1,430,000	420,000	(4,293,500)
Unrecognized net (gain) or loss	360,000	0		(420,000)[b]	(60,000)
Unrecognized transition obligation	5,700,000	(150,000)			5,550,000
Prepaid postretirement benefit cost	$ 330,000	$(563,500)	$1,430,000	$ 0	$ 1,196,500[d]

[a]Represents 6 months' service cost of $160,000 and interest cost of $297,000 on the accumulated postretirement benefit obligation for 1994, assuming a 9% discount rate.

[b]A gain results from the remeasurement of the accumulated postretirement benefit obligation immediately prior to the settlement as a result of a change in the assumed discount rates based on the interest rates inherent in the price at which the accumulated postretirement benefit obligation for the retirees will be settled. No gain or loss results from remeasurement of plan assets.

[c]Represents 6 months' return on plan assets, assuming a 10% return.

[d]Because there is a settlement (treated as a benefit payment) and a prepaid asset exists as a result of providing the funds to effect that settlement, the constraint on delayed recognition of the transition obligation pursuant to paragraph 112 may be applicable. The test to determine whether additional recognition is necessary should be done based on amounts for the full year (paragraph 494).

493. In accounting for a settlement, an employer must determine whether recognition of an additional amount of any unrecognized transition obligation is required pursuant to the constraint on delayed recognition (paragraph 112). Any additional

transition obligation required to be recognized as a result of a settlement is recognized when the related settlement is recognized (paragraph 113) as illustrated in the following table. Detailed calculations are presented in paragraph 494.

	June 30, 1994		
	Before Settlement	**Settlement**	**Recognition of Transition Obligation**	**After Settlement**
Accumulated postretirement benefit obligation	$(6,637,000)	$1,900,000		$(4,737,000)
Plan assets at fair value	2,343,500	(1,900,000)		443,500
Funded status	(4,293,500)	0		(4,293,500)
Unrecognized net (gain) or loss	(60,000)	17,160e		(42,840)
Unrecognized transition obligation	5,550,000	(17,160)e	$(718,822)	4,814,018
Prepaid postretirement benefit cost	$ 1,196,500	$ 0	$(718,822)	$ 477,678

eThe maximum settlement gain subject to recognition is the unrecognized net gain subsequent to transition plus any unrecognized transition asset ($60,000 + $0 = $60,000). If, as in this case, only part of the accumulated postretirement benefit obligation is settled, a pro rata portion of the maximum gain based on the relationship of the accumulated postretirement benefit obligation settled to the total accumulated postretirement benefit obligation ($1,900,000 ÷ $6,637,000 or 28.6%) is subject to recognition. That amount ($60,000 × 28.6% = $17,160) must first reduce any unrecognized transition obligation (paragraph 93); any excess is recognized. In this situation, the settlement gain is entirely offset against the unrecognized transition obligation.

494. When a settlement occurs in the middle of the year, as in this example, the additional transition obligation to be recognized, if any, pursuant to the constraint in paragraph 112 is determined based on projected amounts for the full year. In this case, at June 30, 1994, cumulative benefit payments from the date of transition (January 1, 1993) to December 31, 1994 are projected to exceed cumulative postretirement benefit cost accrued for that same period as illustrated in the following table. The additional transition obligation to be recognized is the amount by which cumulative benefit payments exceed cost accrued, or $718,822.

	Projected 12/31/94
Benefit payments:	
1/1/93 to beginning of 1994	$ 630,000
1994 excluding settlement	410,000
Settlement	1,900,000
Cumulative benefit payments	$2,940,000
Postretirement benefit cost recognized:	
1/1/93 to beginning of 1994	$1,170,000
1994	1,051,178f
Cumulative cost recognized	$2,221,178
Benefit payments in excess of cost recognized	$ 718,822

f$563,500 for period 1/1/94-6/30/94 plus $487,678 for period 7/1/94-12/31/94. The net postretirement benefit cost of $487,678 recognized in the second half of 1994 (paragraph 495) includes amortization ($130,108) of the unrecognized transition obligation that remains after recognizing an additional portion ($718,822) of the unrecognized transition obligation pursuant to paragraph 112. Because determination of the additional portion of the transition obligation to be recognized and the transition obligation amortized in the second half of 1994 are interrelated, those amounts are determined in a single computation that is intended to result in unrecognized transition obligation at the end of the year that appropriately reflects the constraint of paragraph 112.

495. After the settlement, net periodic postretirement benefit cost for the remainder of the year is remeasured. The projected funded status of the plan reconciled to the projected amount to be shown in the statement of financial position follows:

	After Settlement 6/30/94	Six Months Postretirement Benefit Cost	Benefit Payments	Assets Contributed to Plan	Projected 12/31/94
Accumulated postretirement benefit obligation	$(4,737,000)	$(379,745)g	$410,000		$(4,706,745)
Plan assets at fair value	443,500	22,175h	(410,000)	$1,246,745	1,302,420
Funded status	(4,293,500)	(357,570)	0	1,246,745	(3,404,325)
Unrecognized net gain	(42,840)	0			(42,840)
Unrecognized transition obligation	4,814,018	(130,108)i			4,683,910
(Accrued)/prepaid postretirement cost	$ 477,678	$(487,678)	$ 0	$1,246,745	$ 1,236,745

gRepresents 6 months' service cost of $150,000 and interest cost of $229,745 on the accumulated postretirement benefit obligation, assuming a 9.7% discount rate.

hRepresents 6 months' return on plan assets, assuming a 10% return.

iUnrecognized transition obligation at 6/30/94 of $4,814,018 ÷ 18.5 years remaining in amortization period = $260,217; half-year amortization = $130,108.

Illustration 9—Accounting for Curtailments

496. This Statement provides for delayed recognition of the effects of a plan initiation or a plan amendment, the transition obligation or transition asset, and gains or losses arising in the ordinary course of operations. In certain circumstances, however, recognition of some or all of those previously delayed amounts is appropriate. Curtailments are events that may require income or expense recognition of certain previously unrecognized amounts and adjustments to liabilities or assets recognized in the employer's statement of financial position.

497. A curtailment is an event that significantly reduces the expected years of future service of active plan participants or eliminates the accrual of defined benefits for some or all of the future services of a significant number of active plan participants. Such a reduction or elimination raises doubt about the continued existence of the future economic benefits of prior plan amendments. Therefore, an appropriate portion of the remaining unrecognized prior service cost should be recognized when it is probable that a curtailment will occur, the effects are reasonably estimable, and the estimated effects of the curtailment are a net loss. When the estimated effects of a curtailment are a net gain, the gain should be recognized in income when the related employees terminate or the plan suspension or amendment is adopted (paragraphs 97-99). For purposes of measuring those effects, any remaining unrecognized transition obligation is treated as unrecognized prior service cost. The following cases (9A and 9B, paragraphs 498-501) illustrate the accounting for curtailments.

Case 9A—Curtailment When an Unrecognized Gain and an Unrecognized Transition Obligation Exist

498. Company P sponsors a postretirement benefit plan. On October 29, 1994, Company P decides to reduce its operations by terminating a significant number of employees effective December 31, 1994. On October 29, 1994, it is expected that a curtailment gain will result from the termination. A consequence of the curtailment is a significant reduction in the number of employees accumulating benefits under the plan. The *remaining years of expected service* associated with those terminated employees who were plan participants at the date of transition is 22 percent of the remaining years of service of all plan participants at the date of transition. The *remaining years of service prior to full eligibility* associated with those terminated employees who were plan participants at the date of a prior plan amendment is 18 percent of the remaining years of service of all plan participants at the date of that plan amendment.

499. The sum of the effects of the plan curtailment is a gain of $5,160 that should be recognized in income when the related employees terminate (paragraph 99). That gain is determined as follows:

| | December 31, 1994 | | |
	Before Curtailment	Curtailment	After Curtailment
Accumulated postretirement benefit obligation	$(257,000)	$54,000[a]	$(203,000)
Plan assets at fair value	73,000		73,000
Funded status	(184,000)	54,000	(130,000)
Unrecognized net gain	(44,575)		(44,575)
Unrecognized prior service cost	33,000	(5,940)[a]	27,060
Unrecognized transition obligation	195,000	(42,900)[a]	152,100
(Accrued)/prepaid postretirement benefit cost	$ (575)	$ 5,160	$ 4,585

[a]The effect of the curtailment consists of two components:

1. The unrecognized transition obligation and unrecognized prior service cost associated with remaining years of service no longer expected to be rendered—measured as 22% (reduction in the remaining years of expected service associated with those terminated employees who were plan participants at the date of transition) of the unrecognized transition obligation of $195,000 ($42,900) and 18% (reduction in the remaining years of service prior to full eligibility for benefits associated with those terminated employees who were plan participants at the date of a prior plan amendment) of the unrecognized prior service cost of $33,000 related to that amendment ($5,940) (paragraph 97)

2. The gain from the decrease in the accumulated postretirement benefit obligation of $54,000 (due to the termination of employees whose accumulated benefits were not vested under the plan) in excess of the unrecognized net loss of $0, or $54,000 (paragraph 98(a)).

Case 9B—Curtailment Related to a Disposal of a Portion of the Business and an Unrecognized Loss and Unrecognized Transition Obligation Exist

500. Company R sponsors a postretirement benefit plan. On December 31, 1994, Company R sells a portion of its business at a gain of $100,000 before considering the effect of the related curtailment of its postretirement benefit plan. In connection with the sale, the number of employees accumulating benefits under the plan is significantly reduced; thus, a curtailment occurs. The *remaining years of expected service* associated with the terminated employees who were plan participants at the date of transition is 22 percent of the remaining years of service of all plan participants at the date of transition. The *remaining years of service prior to full eligibility* associated with the terminated employees who were plan participants at the date of that prior plan amendment is 18 percent of the remaining years of service of all plan participants at the date of that plan amendment.

501. The sum of the effects of the plan curtailment is a loss of $36,265 that should be recognized with the gain of $100,000 associated with Company R's sale of a portion of its business. The loss is determined as follows:

| | December 31, 1994 | | |
	Before Curtailment	Curtailment	After Curtailment
Accumulated postretirement benefit obligation	$(343,000)	$ 54,000[a]	$(289,000)
Plan assets at fair value	73,000		73,000
Funded status	(270,000)	54,000	(216,000)
Unrecognized net loss	41,425	(41,425)[a]	0
Unrecognized prior service cost	33,000	(5,940)[a]	27,060
Unrecognized transition obligation	195,000	(42,900)[a]	152,100
Accrued postretirement benefit cost	$ (575)	$(36,265)	$ (36,840)

[a]The effect of the curtailment consists of two components:

1. The unrecognized transition obligation and unrecognized prior service cost associated with remaining years of service no longer expected to be rendered—measured as 22% (reduction in the remaining years of expected service associated with those terminated employees who were plan participants at the date of transition) of the unrecognized transition obligation of $195,000 ($42,900) and 18% (reduction in the remaining years of service prior to full eligibility for benefits associated with those terminated employees who were plan participants at the date of a prior plan amendment) of the unrecognized prior service cost of $33,000 related to that amendment ($5,940) (paragraph 97)

2. The gain from the decrease in the accumulated postretirement benefit obligation of $54,000 (due to the termination of employees whose accumulated benefits were not vested under the plan) in excess of the unrecognized net loss of $41,425, or $12,575 (paragraph 98(a)).

Illustration 10—Accounting for a Partial Settlement and a Full Curtailment That Occur as a Direct Result of a Sale of a Line of Business

502. Company S sells a line of business on December 31, 1994; prior to that date, the company had no formal plan for disposal of those operations. Company S has a separate postretirement benefit plan that provides health care benefits to retirees of the division that is sold. In connection with that sale, (a) all of the employees of that division are terminated by Company S resulting in no further accumulation of benefits under the postretirement benefit plan (a full curtailment), (b) most of the terminated employees are hired by the acquiring company (some terminated employees fully eligible for benefits elect to retire immediately), (c) an accumulated postretirement benefit obligation of $80,000 for postretirement benefits related to the hired employees is assumed by the acquiring company (a partial settlement, since the obligation for current retirees is retained by Company S), and (d) plan assets of $100,000, representing $80,000 for the settlement of the accumulated postretirement benefit obligation and $20,000 as an excess contribution, are transferred from the plan to the acquiring company. A $300,000 gain from the sale is calculated before considering the related effects on the plan.

503. The employer's accounting policy is to determine the effects of a curtailment before determining the effects of a settlement when both events occur simultaneously. Pursuant to paragraph 97, the unrecognized prior service cost associated with the portion of the future years of service that had been expected to be rendered, but as a result of a curtailment are no longer expected to be rendered, is a loss. When a full curtailment occurs, the entire remaining unrecognized prior service cost and unrecognized transition obligation is a loss because there are no future years of service to be rendered.

504. The net loss from the curtailment is $228,000, which is recognized with the $300,000 gain resulting from the disposal of the division. The effect of the curtailment is determined as follows:

	December 31, 1994		
	Before Curtailment	Curtailment-Related Effects Resulting from Sale	After Curtailment
Accumulated postretirement benefit obligation	$(257,000)	$ (10,000)[a]	$(267,000)
Plan assets at fair value	110,000		110,000
Funded status	(147,000)	(10,000)	(157,000)
Unrecognized net gain	(49,575)	10,000[a]	(39,575)
Unrecognized prior service cost	33,000	(33,000)[b]	0
Unrecognized transition obligation	195,000	(195,000)[c]	0
(Accrued)/prepaid postretirement benefit cost	$ 31,425	$(228,000)	$(196,575)

[a]The increase in the accumulated postretirement benefit obligation as a result of the fully eligible employees retiring earlier than expected is a loss of $10,000. That loss reduces the unrecognized net gain of $49,575; any excess (none in this case) would be recognized as the effect of a curtailment (paragraph 98).

[b]Measured as 100% (reduction in the remaining years of service prior to full eligibility for benefits associated with those terminated employees who were plan participants at the date of a prior plan amendment) of the unrecognized prior service cost of $33,000 related to that amendment (paragraph 97).

[c]Measured as 100% (reduction in the remaining years of expected service associated with those terminated employees who were plan participants at the date of transition) of the unrecognized transition obligation of $195,000 (paragraph 97).

505. The $8,128 loss related to the settlement and transfer of plan assets that is recognized with the gain from the sale is determined as follows:

	December 31, 1994		
	After Curtailment	Settlement and Transfer of Plan Assets	After Settlement
Accumulated postretirement benefit obligation	$(267,000)	$ 80,000[d]	$(187,000)
Plan assets at fair value	110,000	(100,000)[d]	10,000
Funded status	(157,000)	(20,000)	(177,000)
Unrecognized net gain	(39,575)	11,872[e]	(27,703)
Unrecognized prior service cost	0		0
Unrecognized transition obligation	0		0
Accrued postretirement benefit cost	$(196,575)	$ (8,128)	$(204,703)

[d]The accumulated postretirement benefit obligation for the employees hired by the purchaser is determined to be $80,000 and is settled when Company S transfers plan assets of an equal amount to the purchaser. In connection with the purchase agreement, Company S transfers an additional $20,000 of plan assets.

[e]Represents a pro rata amount of the maximum gain based on the relationship of the accumulated postretirement benefit obligation settled to the total accumulated postretirement benefit obligation ($80,000 ÷ $267,000 or 30%). The maximum gain is measured as the unrecognized net gain subsequent to transition plus any unrecognized transition asset ($39,575 + $0 = $39,575). The settlement gain is, therefore, 30% of $39,575, or $11,872; recognition of that gain is subject to first reducing any remaining unrecognized transition obligation. As there is no remaining unrecognized transition obligation (the remainder was recognized in connection with the curtailment), the gain of $11,872 is recognized together with the excess $20,000 transfer of plan assets as part of the net gain from the sale (paragraphs 92 and 93).

506. The sum of the effects related to postretirement benefits resulting from the sale is a loss of $236,128, the components of which are as follows:

Curtailment loss (paragraph 504)	$228,000
Settlement gain and loss from transfer of plan assets (paragraph 505)	8,128
Effects of sale	$236,128

Illustration 11—Accounting for the Effects of an Offer of Special Termination Benefits

507. The measurement of the effects of an offer of special termination benefits pursuant to paragraphs 101 and 102 and the accounting for the related curtailment are illustrated in the following paragraphs.

508. On January 16, 1995, Company T offers for a short period of time (until January 30, 1995) special benefits to its employees who elect voluntary termination of employment during that period (special termination benefits). As part of the offer, employees who voluntarily terminate will be credited with an additional five years of service and five years of age to determine eligibility for postretirement health care benefits. Employees are normally eligible for those benefits upon attaining age 55 and rendering at least 20 years of service.

509. On January 30, 1995, employees representing 18 percent of the work force accept the offer of special termination benefits. For those employees,

the accumulated postretirement benefit obligation attributed to prior service periods based on their previously expected retirement dates (without consideration of the special offer) is $280,000. If those employees were assumed to terminate (retire) immediately upon attaining full eligibility for benefits (age 55 with 20 years of service), the accumulated postretirement benefit obligation for those employees would be $450,000. The accumulated postretirement benefit obligation for those employees after they accept the offer of the special termination benefits (full eligibility date accelerated, benefit coverage begins immediately) is $630,000.

510. The *remaining years of expected service* associated with the terminated employees who were plan participants at the date of transition is 24 percent of the remaining years of service of all plan participants at the date of transition. In addition, the portion of the unrecognized prior service cost arising from a prior plan amendment associated with the *remaining years of service prior to full eligibility* that are no longer expected to be rendered by the terminated employees is $25,000.

511. Pursuant to paragraph 99, if the sum of the effects resulting from a curtailment is a net loss, it shall be recognized in income when it is probable that a curtailment will occur and the effects are reasonably estimable. In this illustration, the effects resulting from the curtailment are not reasonably estimable until January 30, 1995, the acceptance date of the offer of special termination benefits. Consequently, at January 30, 1995, the

employer recognizes a loss of $453,400 that includes the cost of the special termination benefits ($180,000) and the net loss from the curtailment ($273,400) determined as follows:

	Before Employee Terminations	Special Termination Benefits	Effect of Curtailment	After Employee Terminations
	January 30, 1995			
Accumulated postretirement benefit obligation:				
Employees accepting offer	$(280,000)	$(180,000)[a]	$(170,000)[b]	$ (630,000)
Other employees	(633,000)			(633,000)
	(913,000)	(180,000)	(170,000)	(1,263,000)
Plan assets at fair value	141,000			141,000
Funded status	(772,000)	(180,000)	(170,000)	(1,122,000)
Unrecognized net gain	(88,000)		88,000[b]	0
Unrecognized prior service cost	148,500		(25,000)[c]	123,500
Unrecognized transition obligation	693,333		(166,400)[c]	526,933
Accrued postretirement benefit cost	$ (18,167)	$(180,000)	$(273,400)	$ (471,567)

[a]The loss from acceptance of the special termination benefits is $180,000 ($450,000 − $630,000), representing the difference between (1) the accumulated postretirement benefit obligation measured assuming that active plan participants not yet fully eligible for benefits would terminate employment at their full eligibility date and that fully eligible plan participants would retire immediately and (2) the accumulated postretirement benefit obligation reflecting the special termination benefits (paragraph 102).

[b]The increase in the accumulated postretirement benefit obligation as a result of the employees (fully eligible plan participants and other active plan participants not yet fully eligible for benefits) retiring at a date earlier than expected is a loss of $170,000 ($280,000 − $450,000). That amount is reduced by the unrecognized net gain of $88,000 (paragraph 98(b)) as part of the accounting for the curtailment.

[c]Additional effects of the curtailment are (1) the reduction of $25,000 in the unrecognized prior service cost (arising from a prior plan amendment) associated with the remaining years of service prior to full eligibility that are no longer expected to be rendered by the terminated employees and (2) the reduction of $166,400 in the unrecognized transition obligation associated with remaining years of service no longer expected to be rendered—measured as 24% (reduction in the remaining years of expected service associated with those employees affected by the early retirement who were plan participants at the date of transition) of the unrecognized transition obligation of $693,333 (paragraph 97).

Appendix D

BACKGROUND INFORMATION

512. In 1979, the Board added other postemployment benefits to its project on employers' accounting for pensions. The Board was concerned about the lack of information in financial statements about the cost of and obligation for other postemployment benefits. Evidence suggested that most large employers, as well as many smaller ones, provided health care and life insurance benefits to their retirees and were accounting for those benefits on a pay-as-you-go (cash) basis. Existing accounting pronouncements did not cover postretirement benefits provided outside a pension plan.

513. Other postemployment benefits were first considered in a 1981 FASB Discussion Memorandum, *Employers' Accounting for Pensions and Other Postemployment Benefits.* In its 1982 Preliminary Views, *Employers' Accounting for Pensions and Other Postemployment Benefits,* the Board tentatively concluded that the cost of postemployment health care and life insurance provided to retirees should be accrued during the service lives of the employees expected to receive benefits under those plans. The Board did not consider the cash basis and terminal accrual (accrual at retirement) methods to be acceptable methods for recognizing the cost of those benefits.

514. The Board based its tentative conclusion on its view that an employer has an obligation for promised postretirement benefits to the extent that future payments are probable and the service required of retirees and future retirees in exchange for those benefits has been rendered. That view led to the conclusion that postemployment benefits are a form of deferred compensation. Those views were reiterated in a 1983 FASB Discussion Memorandum, *Employers' Accounting for Pensions and Other Postemployment Benefits,* that addressed additional issues not raised in the 1981 Discussion Memorandum. However, in considering comments on that second Discussion Memorandum, the Board concluded that the accounting issues related to other postemployment benefits were being overshadowed by pension issues.

515. In February 1984, the Board concluded that

it should address employers' accounting for post-employment benefits other than pensions as a separate project. As an interim measure, in 1984 the Board issued FASB Statement No. 81, *Disclosure of Postretirement Health Care and Life Insurance Benefits.* In April 1987, FASB Technical Bulletin No. 87-1, *Accounting for a Change in Method of Accounting for Certain Postretirement Benefits,* was issued to provide temporary guidance to employers making a voluntary change in their method of accounting for postretirement health care benefits and postretirement life insurance benefits provided outside a pension plan.

516. A task force was appointed in December 1986. Employers' accounting for postretirement benefits was addressed at 29 public Board meetings and 3 public task force meetings between February 1987 and October 1988. In February 1989, the Board issued an Exposure Draft, *Employers' Accounting for Postretirement Benefits Other Than Pensions.* The Exposure Draft proposed standards of financial accounting and reporting for an employer that offers postretirement benefits other than pensions to its employees. Twenty-five companies participated in a field test of the Exposure Draft that was sponsored by the Financial Executives Research Foundation.

517. The Board received more than 475 comment letters in response to the Exposure Draft. Public hearings on the Exposure Draft were conducted in October and November 1989. Sixty-two organizations and individuals presented their views at the 5 days of hearings. Based on the information received in the comment letters and at the public hearings, the Board reconsidered its proposals in the Exposure Draft at 28 public Board meetings during the remainder of 1989 and 1990. The task force met at a public meeting in June 1990 to discuss the Board's tentative conclusions on employers' accounting for postretirement benefits. Appendix A discusses the basis for the Board's conclusions, including reasons for changes made to the provisions of the 1989 Exposure Draft.

Appendix E

GLOSSARY

518. This appendix contains definitions of certain terms used in accounting for postretirement benefits.

Accumulated postretirement benefit obligation
The actuarial present value of benefits attributed to employee service rendered to a particular date. Prior to an employee's full eligibility date, the accumulated postretirement benefit

obligation as of a particular date for an employee is the portion of the expected postretirement benefit obligation attributed to that employee's service rendered to that date; on and after the full eligibility date, the accumulated and expected postretirement benefit obligations for an employee are the same.

Active plan participant
Any active employee who has rendered service during the credited service period and is expected to receive benefits, including benefits to or for any beneficiaries and covered dependents, under the postretirement benefit plan. Also refer to **Plan participant.**

Actual return on plan assets (component of net periodic postretirement benefit cost)
The change in the fair value of the plan's assets for a period including the decrease due to expenses incurred during the period (such as income tax expense incurred by the fund, if applicable), adjusted for contributions and benefit payments during the period.

Actuarial present value
The value, as of a specified date, of an amount or series of amounts payable or receivable thereafter, with each amount adjusted to reflect (a) the time value of money (through discounts for interest) and (b) the probability of payment (for example, by means of decrements for events such as death, disability, or withdrawal) between the specified date and the expected date of payment.

Amortization
Usually refers to the process of reducing a recognized liability systematically by recognizing revenues or of reducing a recognized asset systematically by recognizing expenses or costs. In accounting for postretirement benefits, amortization is also used to refer to the systematic recognition in net periodic postretirement benefit cost over several periods of previously *unrecognized* amounts, including unrecognized prior service cost, unrecognized net gain or loss, and any unrecognized transition obligation or asset.

Assumed per capita claims cost (by age)
The annual per capita cost, for periods after the measurement date, of providing the postretirement health care benefits covered by the plan from the earliest age at which an individual could begin to receive benefits under the plan through the remainder of the individual's life or the covered period, if shorter. To determine the assumed per capita claims cost, the per capita claims cost by age based on histori-

cal claims costs is adjusted for assumed health care cost trend rates. The resulting assumed per capita claims cost by age reflects expected future costs and is applied with the plan demographics to determine the amount and timing of future gross eligible charges. Also refer to **Gross eligible charges** and **Per capita claims cost by age.**

Assumptions

Estimates of the occurrence of future events affecting postretirement benefit costs, such as turnover, retirement age, mortality, dependency status, per capita claims costs by age, health care cost trend rates, levels of Medicare and other health care providers' reimbursements, and discount rates to reflect the time value of money.

Attribution

The process of assigning postretirement benefit cost to periods of employee service.

Attribution period

The period of an employee's service to which the expected postretirement benefit obligation for that employee is assigned. The beginning of the attribution period is the employee's date of hire unless the plan's benefit formula grants credit only for service from a later date, in which case the beginning of the attribution period is generally the beginning of that credited service period. The end of the attribution period is the full eligibility date. Within the attribution period, an equal amount of the expected postretirement benefit obligation is attributed to each year of service unless the plan's benefit formula attributes a disproportionate share of the expected postretirement benefit obligation to employees' early years of service. In that case, benefits are attributed in accordance with the plan's benefit formula. Also refer to **Credited service period.**

Benefit formula

The basis for determining benefits to which participants may be entitled under a postretirement benefit plan. A plan's benefit formula specifies the years of service to be rendered, age to be attained while in service, or a combination of both that must be met for an employee to be eligible to receive benefits under the plan. A plan's benefit formula may also define the beginning of the credited service period and the benefits earned for specific periods of service.

Benefits

The monetary or in-kind benefits or benefit coverage to which participants may be entitled under a postretirement benefit plan, including health care benefits, life insurance not provided through a pension plan, and legal, educational, and advisory services.

Captive insurer

An insurance company that does business primarily with related entities.

Contributory plan

A plan under which retirees or active employees contribute part of the cost. In some contributory plans, retirees or active employees wishing to be covered must contribute; in other contributory plans, participants' contributions result in increased benefits.

Cost-sharing (provisions of the plan)

The provisions of the postretirement benefit plan that describe how the costs of the covered benefits are to be shared between the employer and the plan participants. Cost-sharing provisions describe retired and active plan participants' contributions toward their postretirement health care benefits, deductibles, coinsurance, out-of-pocket limitations on participant costs, caps on employer costs, and so forth.

Credited service period

Employee service period for which benefits are earned pursuant to the terms of the plan. The beginning of the credited service period may be the date of hire or a later date. For example, a plan may provide benefits only for service rendered after a specified age. Service beyond the end of the credited service period does not earn any additional benefits under the plan. Also refer to **Attribution period.**

Curtailment (of a postretirement benefit plan)

An event that significantly reduces the expected years of future service of active plan participants or eliminates the accrual of defined benefits for some or all of the future services of a significant number of active plan participants.

Defined benefit postretirement plan

A plan that defines postretirement benefits in terms of monetary amounts (for example, $100,000 of life insurance) or benefit coverage to be provided (for example, up to $200 per day for hospitalization, 80 percent of the cost of specified surgical procedures, and so forth). Any postretirement benefit plan that is not a defined contribution postretirement plan is, for purposes of this Statement, a defined benefit postretirement plan.

Defined contribution postretirement plan

A plan that provides postretirement benefits in return for services rendered, provides an individual account for each plan participant, and specifies how contributions to the individual's account are to be determined rather than specifies the amount of benefits the individual is to receive. Under a defined contribution postretirement plan, the benefits a plan participant will receive depend solely on the amount contributed to the plan participant's account, the returns earned on investments of those contributions, and the forfeitures of other plan participants' benefits that may be allocated to that plan participant's account.

Dependency status
The status of a current or former employee having dependents (for example, a spouse or other relatives) who are expected to receive benefits under a postretirement benefit plan that provides dependent coverage.

Discount rates
The rates used to reflect the time value of money. Discount rates are used in determining the present value as of the measurement date of future cash flows currently expected to be required to satisfy the postretirement benefit obligation. Also refer to **Actuarial present value.**

Expected long-term rate of return on plan assets
An assumption about the rate of return on plan assets reflecting the average rate of earnings expected on existing plan assets and expected contributions to the plan during the period.

Expected postretirement benefit obligation
The actuarial present value as of a particular date of the benefits expected to be paid to or for an employee, the employee's beneficiaries, and any covered dependents pursuant to the terms of the postretirement benefit plan.

Expected return on plan assets
An amount calculated as a basis for determining the extent of delayed recognition of the effects of changes in the fair value of plan assets. The expected return on plan assets is determined based on the expected long-term rate of return on plan assets and the market-related value of plan assets.

Explicit (approach to) assumptions
An approach under which each significant assumption used reflects the best estimate of the plan's future experience solely with respect to that assumption.

Fair value
The amount that a plan could reasonably expect to receive for an investment in a current sale between a willing buyer and a willing seller, that is, other than a forced or liquidation sale.

Full eligibility (for benefits)
The status of an employee having reached the employee's full eligibility date. Full eligibility for benefits is achieved by meeting specified age, service, or age and service requirements of the postretirement benefit plan. Also refer to **Full eligibility date.**

Full eligibility date
The date at which an employee has rendered all of the service necessary to have earned the right to receive all of the benefits expected to be received by that employee (including any beneficiaries and dependents expected to receive benefits). Determination of the full eligibility date is affected by plan terms that provide incremental benefits expected to be received by or on behalf of an employee for additional years of service, unless those incremental benefits are trivial. Determination of the full eligibility date is *not* affected by plan terms that define when benefit payments commence or by an employee's current dependency status.

Fully eligible plan participants
Collectively, that group of former employees (including retirees) and active employees who have rendered service to or beyond their full eligibility date and who are expected to receive benefits under the plan, including benefits to their beneficiaries and covered dependents.

Funding policy
The program regarding the amounts and timing of contributions by the employer(s), plan participants, and any other sources to provide the benefits a postretirement benefit plan specifies.

Gain or loss
A change in the value of either the accumulated postretirement benefit obligation or the plan assets resulting from experience different from that assumed or from a change in an actuarial assumption, or the consequence of a decision to temporarily deviate from the substantive plan. Also refer to **Unrecognized net gain or loss.**

Gain or loss component (of net periodic postretirement benefit cost)
The sum of (a) the difference between the actual return on plan assets and the expected return on plan assets, (b) any gain or loss immediately recognized or the amortization of the unrecognized net gain or loss from previous periods, and (c) any amount immediately recognized as a gain or loss pursuant to a decision to

temporarily deviate from the substantive plan. The gain or loss component is generally the net effect of delayed recognition of gains and losses (the net change in the unrecognized net gain or loss) except that it does not include changes in the accumulated postretirement benefit obligation occurring during the period and deferred for later recognition.

Gross eligible charges

The cost of providing the postretirement health care benefits covered by the plan to a plan participant, before adjusting for expected reimbursements from Medicare and other providers of health care benefits and for the effects of the cost-sharing provisions of the plan.

Health care cost trend rates

An assumption about the annual rate(s) of change in the cost of health care benefits currently provided by the postretirement benefit plan, due to factors other than changes in the composition of the plan population by age and dependency status, for each year from the measurement date until the end of the period in which benefits are expected to be paid. The health care cost trend rates implicitly consider estimates of health care inflation, changes in health care utilization or delivery patterns, technological advances, and changes in the health status of the plan participants. Differing types of services, such as hospital care and dental care, may have different trend rates.

Incurred claims cost (by age)

The cost of providing the postretirement health care benefits covered by the plan to a plan participant, after adjusting for reimbursements from Medicare and other providers of health care benefits and for deductibles, coinsurance provisions, and other specific claims costs borne by the retiree. Also refer to **Net incurred claims cost (by age)**.

Insurance contract

A contract in which an insurance company unconditionally undertakes a legal obligation to provide specified benefits to specific individuals in return for a fixed consideration or premium. An insurance contract is irrevocable and involves the transfer of significant risk from the employer (or the plan) to the insurance company. If the insurance company providing the contract is a captive insurer, or if there is any reasonable doubt that the insurance company will meet its obligations under the contract, the contract is not an insurance contract for purposes of this Statement.

Interest cost (component of net periodic postretirement benefit cost)

The accrual of interest on the accumulated postretirement benefit obligation due to the passage of time.

Market-related value of plan assets

A balance used to calculate the expected return on plan assets. Market-related value can be either fair value or a calculated value that recognizes changes in fair value in a systematic and rational manner over not more than five years. Different methods of calculating market-related value may be used for different classes of plan assets, but the manner of determining market-related value shall be applied consistently from year to year for each class of plan asset.

Measurement date

The date of the financial statements or, if used consistently from year to year, a date not more than three months prior to that date, as of which plan assets and obligations are measured.

Medicare reimbursement rates

The health care cost reimbursements expected to be received by retirees through Medicare as mandated by currently enacted legislation. Medicare reimbursement rates vary by the type of benefits provided.

Multiemployer plan

A postretirement benefit plan to which two or more unrelated employers contribute, usually pursuant to one or more collective-bargaining agreements. A characteristic of multiemployer plans is that assets contributed by one participating employer may be used to provide benefits to employees of other participating employers since assets contributed by an employer are not segregated in a separate account or restricted to provide benefits only to employees of that employer. A multiemployer plan is usually administered by a board of trustees composed of management and labor representatives and may also be referred to as a "joint trust" or "union plan." Generally, many employers participate in a multiemployer plan, and an employer may participate in more than one plan. The employers participating in multiemployer plans usually have a common industry bond, but for some plans the employers are in different industries and the labor union may be their only common bond.

Multiple-employer plan

A postretirement benefit plan maintained by more than one employer but not treated as a multiemployer plan. Multiple-employer plans are generally not collectively bargained and are intended to allow participating employers, commonly in the same industry, to pool their plan assets for investment purposes and to reduce the cost of plan administration. A multiple-employer plan maintains separate accounts for each employer so that contributions provide benefits only for employees of the contributing employer. Multiple-employer plans may have features that allow participating employers to have different benefit formulas, with the employer's contributions to the plan based on the benefit formula selected by the employer.

Net incurred claims cost (by age)
The employer's share of the cost of providing the postretirement health care benefits covered by the plan to a plan participant; incurred claims cost net of retiree contributions. Also refer to **Incurred claims cost (by age).**

Net periodic postretirement benefit cost
The amount recognized in an employer's financial statements as the cost of a postretirement benefit plan for a period. Components of net periodic postretirement benefit cost include service cost, interest cost, actual return on plan assets, gain or loss, amortization of unrecognized prior service cost, and amortization of the unrecognized transition obligation or asset.

Nonparticipating insurance contract
An insurance contract that does not provide for the purchaser to participate in the investment performance or in other experience of the insurance company. Also refer to **Insurance contract.**

Nonpublic enterprise
An enterprise other than one (a) whose debt or equity securities are traded in a public market, either on a stock exchange or in the over-the-counter market (including securities quoted only locally or regionally), or (b) whose financial statements are filed with a regulatory agency in preparation for the sale of any class of securities.

Participating insurance contract
An insurance contract that provides for the purchaser to participate in the investment performance and possibly other experience (for example, morbidity experience) of the insurance company. Also refer to **Insurance contract.**

Participation right
A purchaser's right under a participating insurance contract to receive future dividends or retroactive rate credits from the insurance company.

Pay-related plan
A plan that has a benefit formula that bases benefits or benefit coverage on compensation, such as a final-pay or career-average-pay plan.

Per capita claims cost by age
The current cost of providing postretirement health care benefits for one year at each age from the youngest age to the oldest age at which plan participants are expected to receive benefits under the plan. Also refer to **Assumed per capita claims cost (by age).**

Plan
An arrangement that is mutually understood by an employer and its employees, whereby an employer undertakes to provide its employees with benefits after they retire in exchange for their services over a specified period of time, upon attaining a specified age while in service, or a combination of both. A plan may be written or it may be implied by a well-defined, although perhaps unwritten, practice of paying postretirement benefits or from oral representations made to current or former employees. Also refer to **Substantive plan.**

Plan amendment
A change in the existing terms of a plan. A plan amendment may increase or decrease benefits, including those attributed to years of service already rendered.

Plan assets
Assets—usually stocks, bonds, and other investments—that have been segregated and restricted (usually in a trust) to provide for postretirement benefits. The amount of plan assets includes amounts contributed by the employer (and by plan participants for a contributory plan) and amounts earned from investing the contributions, less benefits, income taxes, and other expenses incurred. Plan assets ordinarily cannot be withdrawn by the employer except under certain circumstances when a plan has assets in excess of obligations and the employer has taken certain steps to satisfy existing obligations. Assets not segregated in a trust, or otherwise effectively restricted, so that they cannot be used by the employer for other purposes are not plan assets, even though it may be intended that those assets be used to provide postretirement benefits. Amounts accrued by the employer as net periodic postretirement benefit cost but not yet paid to the plan are not plan assets. Securities of the employer held by the plan are includable in plan assets provided they are transferable. If a plan has liabilities other than for benefits, those nonbenefit obligations are considered as reductions of plan assets.

Plan demographics
The characteristics of the plan population including geographical distribution, age, sex, and marital status.

Plan participant
Any employee or former employee who has rendered service in the credited service period *and is expected to receive employer-provided benefits* under the postretirement benefit plan, including benefits to or for any beneficiaries and covered dependents. Also refer to **Active plan participant.**

Plan termination
An event in which the postretirement benefit plan ceases to exist and all benefits are settled by the purchase of insurance contracts or by other means. The plan may or may not be replaced by another plan. A plan termination with a replacement plan may or may not be in substance a plan termination for accounting purposes.

Postretirement benefit fund
Assets accumulated in the hands of a funding agency for the sole purpose of paying postretirement benefits when the claims are incurred or benefits are due. Those assets may or may not qualify as plan assets. Also refer to **Plan assets.**

Postretirement benefit plan
Refer to **Plan.**

Postretirement benefits
All forms of benefits, other than retirement income, provided by an employer to retirees. Those benefits may be defined in terms of specified benefits, such as health care, tuition assistance, or legal services, that are provided to retirees as the need for those benefits arises, such as certain health care benefits, or they may be defined in terms of monetary amounts that become payable on the occurrence of a specified event, such as life insurance benefits.

Postretirement benefits other than pensions
Refer to **Postretirement benefits.**

Postretirement health care benefits
A form of postretirement benefit provided by an employer to retirees for defined health care services or coverage of defined health care costs, such as hospital and medical coverage, dental benefits, and eye care.

Prior service cost
The cost of benefit improvements attributable to plan participants' prior service pursuant to a plan amendment or a plan initiation that provides benefits in exchange for plan participants' prior service. Also refer to **Unrecognized prior service cost.**

Retirees
Collectively, that group of plan participants that includes retired employees, their beneficiaries, and covered dependents.

Service cost (component of net periodic postretirement benefit cost)
The portion of the expected postretirement benefit obligation attributed to employee service during a period.

Settlement (of a postretirement benefit plan)
An irrevocable action that relieves the employer (or the plan) of primary responsibility for a postretirement benefit obligation and eliminates significant risks related to the obligation and the assets used to effect the settlement. Examples of transactions that constitute a settlement include (a) making lump-sum cash payments to plan participants in exchange for their rights to receive specified postretirement benefits and (b) purchasing nonparticipating insurance contracts for the accumulated postretirement benefit obligation for some or all of the plan participants.

Single-employer plan
A postretirement benefit plan that is maintained by one employer. The term also may be used to describe a plan that is maintained by related parties such as a parent and its subsidiaries.

Substantive plan
The terms of the postretirement benefit plan as understood by an employer that provides postretirement benefits and the employees who render services in exchange for those benefits. The substantive plan is the basis for the accounting for that exchange transaction. In some situations an employer's cost-sharing policy, as evidenced by past practice or by communication of intended changes to a plan's cost-sharing provisions, or a past practice of regular increases in certain monetary benefits may indicate that the substantive plan differs from the extant written plan.

Termination benefits
Benefits provided by an employer to employees in connection with their termination of employment. They may be either special termination benefits offered only for a short period of

time or contractual benefits required by the terms of a plan only if a specified event, such as a plant closing, occurs.

Transition asset

The unrecognized amount, as of the date this Statement is initially applied, of (a) the fair value of plan assets plus any recognized accrued postretirement benefit cost or less any recognized prepaid postretirement benefit cost in excess of (b) the accumulated postretirement benefit obligation.

Transition obligation

The unrecognized amount, as of the date this Statement is initially applied, of (a) the accumulated postretirement benefit obligation in excess of (b) the fair value of plan assets plus any recognized accrued postretirement benefit cost or less any recognized prepaid postretirement benefit cost.

Unfunded accumulated postretirement benefit obligation

The accumulated postretirement benefit obligation in excess of the fair value of plan assets.

Unrecognized net gain or loss

The cumulative net gain or loss that has not been recognized as a part of net periodic postretirement benefit cost or as a part of the accounting for the effects of a settlement or a curtailment. Also refer to **Gain or loss.**

Unrecognized prior service cost

The portion of prior service cost that has not been recognized as a part of net periodic postretirement benefit cost, as a reduction of the effects of a negative plan amendment, or as a part of the accounting for the effects of a curtailment.

Unrecognized transition asset

The portion of the transition asset that has not been recognized either immediately as the effect of a change in accounting or on a delayed basis as a part of net periodic postretirement benefit cost, as an offset to certain losses, or as a part of accounting for the effects of a settlement or a curtailment.

Unrecognized transition obligation

The portion of the transition obligation that has not been recognized either immediately as the effect of a change in accounting or on a delayed basis as a part of net periodic postretirement benefit cost, as an offset to certain gains, or as a part of accounting for the effects of a settlement or a curtailment.

Statement of Financial Accounting Standards No. 107
Disclosures about Fair Value of Financial Instruments

STATUS

Issued: December 1991

Effective Date: For fiscal years ending after December 15, 1992

Affects: Amends FAS 105, paragraph 6 and footnotes 2 and 3

Affected by: Paragraph 4 superseded by FAS 133
Paragraph 7 amended by FAS 126
Paragraph 8(a) amended by FAS 112 and FAS 123
Paragraph 8(b) superseded by FAS 125 and FAS 140
Paragraphs 10 and 13 amended by FAS 119 and FAS 133
Paragraphs 15A through 15D added after paragraph 15 by FAS 133
Paragraph 28 amended by FAS 125 and FAS 140
Paragraph 31 amended by FAS 133

Other Interpretive Release: FASB Special Report, *Illustrations of Financial Instrument Disclosures* (Nullified by FAS 133)

Issues Discussed by FASB Emerging Issues Task Force (EITF)

Affects: No EITF Issues

Interpreted by: Paragraph 10 interpreted by EITF Topic No. D-69
Paragraph 16 interpreted by EITF Topic No. D-29

Related Issue: EITF Issue No. 98-10

SUMMARY

This Statement extends existing fair value disclosure practices for some instruments by requiring all entities to disclose the fair value of financial instruments, both assets and liabilities recognized and not recognized in the statement of financial position, for which it is practicable to estimate fair value. If estimating fair value is not practicable, this Statement requires disclosure of descriptive information pertinent to estimating the value of a financial instrument. Disclosures about fair value are not required for certain financial instruments listed in paragraph 8.

This Statement is effective for financial statements issued for fiscal years ending after December 15, 1992, except for entities with less than $150 million in total assets in the current statement of financial position. For those entities, the effective date is for fiscal years ending after December 15, 1995.

Statement of Financial Accounting Standards No. 107

Disclosures about Fair Value of Financial Instruments

CONTENTS

INTRODUCTION

1. The FASB added a project on financial instruments and off-balance-sheet financing to its agenda in May 1986. The project is expected to develop broad standards to aid in resolving existing financial accounting and reporting issues and other issues likely to arise in the future about various financial instruments and related transactions.

2. Because of the complexity of the issues about how financial instruments and transactions should be recognized and measured, the Board decided that, initially, improved disclosure of information about financial instruments is necessary. The first disclosure phase was completed in March 1990 with the issuance of FASB Statement No. 105, *Disclosure of Information about Financial Instruments with Off-Balance-Sheet Risk and Financial Instruments with Concentrations of Credit Risk.* The second phase, which resulted in this Statement, considers disclosures about fair value of all financial instruments, both assets and liabilities recognized and not recognized in the statement of financial position, except those listed in paragraph 8.

STANDARDS OF FINANCIAL ACCOUNTING AND REPORTING

Definitions and Scope

3. A financial instrument is defined as cash, evidence of an ownership interest in an entity, or a contract that both:

a. Imposes on one entity a contractual obligation[1] (1) to deliver cash or another financial instrument[2] to a second entity or (2) to exchange other financial instruments on potentially unfavorable terms with the second entity

b. Conveys to that second entity a contractual right[3] (1) to receive cash or another financial instrument from the first entity or (2) to exchange other financial instruments on potentially favorable terms with the first entity.

4. The definition in paragraph 3 is essentially the same as that in paragraph 6 of Statement 105, which is hereby amended to conform to this Statement. Appendix A of Statement 105 provides examples of instruments that are included in and

---

[1]*Contractual obligations* encompass both those that are conditioned on the occurrence of a specified event and those that are not. All contractual obligations that are financial instruments meet the definition of *liability* set forth in FASB Concepts Statement No. 6, *Elements of Financial Statements,* although some may not be recognized as liabilities in financial statements—may be "off-balance-sheet"—because they fail to meet some other criterion for recognition. For some financial instruments, the obligation is owed to or by a group of entities rather than a single entity.

[2]The use of the term *financial instrument* in this definition is recursive (because the term *financial instrument* is included in it), though it is not circular. The definition requires a chain of contractual obligations that ends with the delivery of cash or an ownership interest in an entity. Any number of obligations to deliver financial instruments can be links in a chain that qualifies a particular contract as a financial instrument.

[3]*Contractual rights* encompass both those that are conditioned on the occurrence of a specified event and those that are not. All contractual rights that are financial instruments meet the definition of *asset* set forth in Concepts Statement 6, although some may not be recognized as assets in financial statements—may be "off-balance-sheet"—because they fail to meet some other criterion for recognition. For some financial instruments, the right is held by or the obligation is due from a group of entities rather than a single entity.

excluded from the definition of a financial instrument.

5. For purposes of this Statement, the fair value of a financial instrument is the amount at which the instrument could be exchanged in a current transaction between willing parties, other than in a forced or liquidation sale. If a quoted market price is available for an instrument, the fair value to be disclosed for that instrument is the product of the number of trading units of the instrument times that market price.

6. Under the definition of fair value in paragraph 5, the quoted price for a single trading unit in the most active market is the basis for determining market price and reporting fair value. This is the case even if placing orders to sell all of an entity's holdings of an asset or to buy back all of a liability might affect the price, or if a market's normal volume for one day might not be sufficient to absorb the quantity held or owed by an entity.

7. This Statement requires disclosures about fair value for all financial instruments, whether recognized or not recognized in the statement of financial position, except for those specifically listed in paragraph 8. It applies to all entities. It does not change any requirements for recognition, measurement, or classification of financial instruments in financial statements.

8. The disclosures about fair value prescribed in paragraphs 10-14 are not required for the following:

a. Employers' and plans' obligations for pension benefits, other postretirement benefits including health care and life insurance benefits, employee stock option and stock purchase plans, and other forms of deferred compensation arrangements, as defined in FASB Statements No. 35, *Accounting and Reporting by Defined Benefit Pension Plans,* No. 87, *Employers' Accounting for Pensions,* No. 106, *Employers' Accounting for Postretirement Benefits Other Than Pensions,* and No. 43, *Accounting for Compensated Absences,* and APB Opinions No. 25, *Accounting for Stock Issued to Employees,* and No. 12, *Omnibus Opinion—1967*
b. Substantively extinguished debt subject to the disclosure requirements of FASB Statement No. 76, *Extinguishment of Debt,* and assets held in trust in connection with an in-substance defeasance of that debt
c. Insurance contracts, other than financial guarantees and investment contracts, as discussed in FASB Statements No. 60, *Accounting and Reporting by Insurance Enterprises,* and No. 97, *Accounting and Reporting by Insurance Enterprises for Certain Long-Duration Contracts*

and for Realized Gains and Losses from the Sale of Investments
d. Lease contracts as defined in FASB Statement No. 13, *Accounting for Leases* (a contingent obligation arising out of a cancelled lease and a guarantee of a third-party lease obligation are not lease contracts and are included in the scope of this Statement)
e. Warranty obligations and rights
f. Unconditional purchase obligations as defined in paragraph 6 of FASB Statement No. 47, *Disclosure of Long-Term Obligations*
g. Investments accounted for under the equity method in accordance with the requirements of APB Opinion No. 18, *The Equity Method of Accounting for Investments in Common Stock*
h. Minority interests in consolidated subsidiaries
i. Equity investments in consolidated subsidiaries
j. Equity instruments issued by the entity and classified in stockholders' equity in the statement of financial position.

9. Generally accepted accounting principles already require disclosure of or subsequent measurement at fair value for many classes of financial instruments. Although the definitions or the methods of estimation of fair value vary to some extent, and various terms such as market value, current value, or mark-to-market are used, the amounts computed under those requirements satisfy the requirements of this Statement and those requirements are not superseded or modified by this Statement.

Disclosures about Fair Value of Financial Instruments

10. An entity shall disclose, either in the body of the financial statements or in the accompanying notes, the fair value of financial instruments for which it is practicable to estimate that value. An entity also shall disclose the method(s) and significant assumptions used to estimate the fair value of financial instruments.

11. Quoted market prices, if available, are the best evidence of the fair value of financial instruments. If quoted market prices are not available, management's best estimate of fair value may be based on the quoted market price of a financial instrument with similar characteristics or on valuation techniques (for example, the present value of estimated future cash flows using a discount rate commensurate with the risks involved, option pricing models, or matrix pricing models). Appendix A of this Statement contains examples of procedures for estimating fair value.

12. In estimating the fair value of deposit liabilities, a financial entity shall not take into account the

value of its long-term relationships with depositors, commonly known as core deposit intangibles, which are separate intangible assets, not financial instruments. For deposit liabilities with no defined maturities, the fair value to be disclosed under this Statement is the amount payable on demand at the reporting date. This Statement does not prohibit an entity from disclosing separately the estimated fair value of any of its nonfinancial intangible and tangible assets and nonfinancial liabilities.

13. For trade receivables and payables, no disclosure is required under this Statement when the carrying amount approximates fair value.

14. If it is not practicable for an entity to estimate the fair value of a financial instrument or a class of financial instruments, the following shall be disclosed:

a. Information pertinent to estimating the fair value of that financial instrument or class of financial instruments, such as the carrying amount, effective interest rate, and maturity
b. The reasons why it is not practicable to estimate fair value.

15. In the context of this Statement, *practicable* means that an estimate of fair value can be made without incurring excessive costs. It is a dynamic concept: what is practicable for one entity might not be for another; what is not practicable in one year might be in another. For example, it might not be practicable for an entity to estimate the fair value of a class of financial instruments for which a quoted market price is not available because it has not yet obtained or developed the valuation model necessary to make the estimate, and the cost of obtaining an independent valuation appears excessive considering the materiality of the instruments to the entity. Practicability, that is, cost considerations, also may affect the required precision of the estimate; for example, while in many cases it might seem impracticable to estimate fair value on an individual instrument basis, it may be practicable for a class of financial instruments in a portfolio or on a portfolio basis. In those cases, the fair value of that class or of the portfolio should be disclosed. Finally, it might be practicable for an entity to estimate the fair value only of a subset of a class of financial instruments; the fair value of that subset should be disclosed.

Effective Dates and Transition

16. This Statement shall be effective for financial statements issued for fiscal years ending after December 15, 1992, except for entities with less than $150 million in total assets in the current statement of financial position. For those entities, the effective date shall be for financial statements issued for fiscal years ending after December 15, 1995. Earlier application is encouraged. In the initial year of application of this Statement, it need not be applied to complete interim financial statements.

17. Disclosures required by paragraphs 10-14 that have not previously been reported need not be included in financial statements that are being presented for comparative purposes for fiscal years ending before the applicable effective date of this Statement for an entity. For all subsequent fiscal years, the information required to be disclosed by this Statement shall be included for each year for which a statement of financial position is presented for comparative purposes.

The provisions of this Statement need not be applied to immaterial items.

This Statement was adopted by the unanimous vote of the six members of the Financial Accounting Standards Board:

Dennis R. Beresford,	Victor H. Brown	A. Clarence Sampson
Chairman	James J. Leisenring	Robert J. Swieringa
Joseph V. Anania		

Appendix A

EXAMPLES OF PROCEDURES FOR ESTIMATING FAIR VALUE

18. This appendix provides examples of procedures for estimating the fair value of financial instruments. The examples are illustrative and are not meant to portray all possible ways of estimating the fair value of a financial instrument in order to comply with the provisions of this Statement.

19. Fair value information is frequently based on information obtained from market sources. In broad terms, there are four kinds of markets in which financial instruments can be bought, sold, or originated; available information about prices differs by kind of market:

a. *Exchange market.* An exchange or "auction" market provides high visibility and order to the trading of financial instruments. Typically, closing prices and volume levels are readily available in an exchange market.
b. *Dealer market.* In a dealer market, dealers stand ready to trade—either buy or sell—for their own account, thereby providing liquidity to the market. Typically, current bid and asked prices are more readily available than information about closing prices and volume levels. "Over-the-counter" markets are dealer markets.
c. *Brokered market.* In a brokered market, brokers attempt to match buyers with sellers but do not stand ready to trade for their own account. The broker knows the prices bid and asked by the respective parties, but each party is typically unaware of another party's price requirements; prices of completed transactions are sometimes available.
d. *Principal-to-principal market.* Principal-to-principal transactions, both originations and resales, are negotiated independently, with no intermediary, and little, if any, information is typically released publicly.

Financial Instruments with Quoted Prices

20. As indicated in paragraph 11 of this Statement, quoted market prices, if available, are the best evidence of fair value of financial instruments. Prices for financial instruments may be quoted in several markets; generally, the price in the most active market will be the best indicator of fair value.

21. In some cases, an entity's management may decide to provide further information about the fair value of a financial instrument. For example, an entity may want to explain that although the fair value of its long-term debt is less than the carrying amount, settlement at the reported fair value may not be possible or may not be a prudent management decision for other reasons; or the entity may want to state that potential taxes and other expenses that would be incurred in an actual sale or settlement are not taken into consideration.

Financial Instruments with No Quoted Prices

22. For financial instruments that do not trade regularly, or that trade only in principal-to-principal markets, an entity should provide its best estimate of fair value. Judgments about the methods and assumptions to be used in various circumstances must be made by those who prepare and attest to an entity's financial statements. The following discussion provides some examples of how fair value might be estimated.

23. For some short-term financial instruments, the carrying amount in the financial statements may approximate fair value because of the relatively short period of time between the origination of the instruments and their expected realization. Likewise, for loans that reprice frequently at market rates, the carrying amount may normally be close enough to fair value to satisfy these disclosure requirements, provided there is no significant change in the credit risk of those loans.

24. Some financial instruments (for example, interest rate swaps and foreign currency contracts) may be "custom-tailored" and, thus, may not have a quoted market price. In those cases, an estimate of fair value might be based on the quoted market price of a similar financial instrument, adjusted as appropriate for the effects of the tailoring. Alternatively, the estimate might be based on the estimated current replacement cost of that instrument.

25. Other financial instruments that are commonly "custom-tailored" include various types of options (for example, put and call options on stock, foreign currency, or interest rate contracts). A variety of option pricing models that have been developed in recent years (such as the Black-Scholes model and binomial models) are regularly used to value options. The use of those pricing models to estimate fair value is appropriate under the requirements of this Statement.

26. For some predominantly financial entities, loans receivable may be the most significant category of financial instruments. Market prices may be more readily available for some categories of loans (such as residential mortgage loans) than for others. If no quoted market price exists for a category of loans, an estimate of fair value may be based on (a) the market prices of similar traded loans with similar credit ratings, interest rates, and

maturity dates, (b) current prices (interest rates) offered for similar loans in the entity's own lending activities, or (c) valuations obtained from loan pricing services offered by various specialist firms or from other sources.

27. An estimate of the fair value of a loan or group of loans may be based on the discounted value of the future cash flows expected to be received from the loan or group of loans. The selection of an appropriate current discount rate reflecting the relative risks involved requires judgment, and several alternative rates and approaches are available to an entity. A single discount rate could be used to estimate the fair value of a homogeneous category of loans; for example, an entity might apply a single rate to each aggregated category of loans reported for regulatory purposes. An entity could use a discount rate commensurate with the credit, interest rate, and prepayment risks involved, which could be the rate at which the same loans would be made under current conditions. An entity also could select a discount rate that reflects the effects of interest rate changes and then make adjustments to reflect the effects of changes in credit risk. Those adjustments could include (a) revising cash flow estimates for cash flows not expected to be collected, (b) revising the discount rate to reflect any additional credit risk associated with that group of loans, or some combination of (a) and (b).

28. A fair value for financial liabilities for which quoted market prices are not available can generally be estimated using the same techniques used for estimating the value of financial assets. For example, a loan payable to a bank could be valued at the discounted amount of future cash flows using an entity's current incremental rate of borrowing for a similar liability; alternatively, the discount rate could be the rate that an entity would have to pay to a creditworthy third party to assume its obligation, with the creditor's legal consent (sometimes referred to as the "settlement rate"), or the rate that an entity would have to pay to acquire essentially risk-free assets to extinguish the obligation in accordance with the requirements of Statement 76.

29. For deposit liabilities with defined maturities, such as certificates of deposit, an estimate of fair value might also be based on the discounted value of the future cash flows expected to be paid on the deposits. The discount rate could be the current rate offered for similar deposits with the same remaining maturities. For deposit liabilities with no defined maturities, paragraph 12 of this Statement requires that the fair value to be disclosed be the amount payable on demand at the reporting date.

Appendix B

ILLUSTRATIONS APPLYING THE DISCLOSURE REQUIREMENTS ABOUT FAIR VALUE OF FINANCIAL INSTRUMENTS

30. The examples that follow are guides to implementation of the disclosure requirements of this Statement. Entities are not required to display the information contained herein in the specific manner illustrated. Alternative ways of disclosing the information are permissible as long as they satisfy the disclosure requirements of this Statement. Paragraphs 12 and 21 of this Statement describe possible additional voluntary disclosures that may be appropriate in certain circumstances.

Example 1—Financial Entity

31. Bank A might disclose the following:

Note V: Disclosures about Fair Value of Financial Instruments

The following methods and assumptions were used to estimate the fair value of each class of financial instruments for which it is practicable to estimate that value:

Cash and short-term investments
For those short-term instruments, the carrying amount is a reasonable estimate of fair value.

Investment securities and trading account assets
For securities and derivative instruments held for trading purposes (which include bonds, interest rate futures, options, interest rate swaps, securities sold not owned, caps and floors, foreign currency contracts, and forward contracts) and marketable equity securities held for investment purposes, fair values are based on quoted market prices or dealer quotes. For other securities held as investments, fair value equals quoted market price, if available. If a quoted market price is not available, fair value is estimated using quoted market prices for similar securities.

Loan receivables
For certain homogeneous categories of loans, such as some residential mortgages, credit card receivables, and other consumer loans, fair value is estimated using the quoted market prices for securities backed by similar loans, adjusted for differences in loan characteristics. The fair value of other types of loans is estimated by discounting the future cash flows using the current rates at which similar loans would be made to borrowers with similar credit ratings and for the same remaining maturities.

Deposit liabilities
The fair value of demand deposits, savings accounts, and certain money market deposits is the amount payable on demand at the reporting date. The fair value of fixed-maturity certificates of deposit is estimated using the rates currently offered for deposits of similar remaining maturities.

Long-term debt
Rates currently available to the Bank for debt with similar terms and remaining maturities are used to estimate fair value of existing debt.

Interest rate swap agreements
The fair value of interest rate swaps (used for hedging purposes) is the estimated amount that the Bank would receive or pay to terminate the swap agreements at the reporting date, taking into account current interest rates and the current credit-worthiness of the swap counterparties.

Commitments to extend credit, standby letters of credit, and financial guarantees written
The fair value of commitments is estimated using the fees currently charged to enter into similar agreements, taking into account the remaining terms of the agreements and the present creditworthiness of the counterparties. For fixed-rate loan commitments, fair value also considers the difference between current levels of interest rates and the committed rates. The fair value of guarantees and letters of credit is based on fees currently charged for similar agreements or on the estimated cost to terminate them or otherwise settle the obligations with the counterparties at the reporting date.

The estimated fair values of the Bank's financial instruments are as follows:

	19X9		19X8	
	Carrying Amount	Fair Value	Carrying Amount	Fair Value
Financial assets:				
Cash and short-term investments	$XXX	$XXX	$XXX	$XXX
Trading account assets	XXX	XXX	XXX	XXX
Investment securities	XXX	XXX	XXX	XXX
Loans	XXX		XXX	
Less: allowance for loan losses	(XXX)		(XXX)	
Loans, net of allowance	XXX	XXX	XXX	XXX
Financial liabilities:				
Deposits	XXX	XXX	XXX	XXX
Securities sold not owned	XXX	XXX	XXX	XXX
Long-term debt	XXX	XXX	XXX	XXX
Unrecognized financial instruments:*				
Interest rate swaps:				
In a net receivable position	XXX	XXX	XXX	XXX
In a net payable position	(XXX)	(XXX)	(XXX)	(XXX)
Commitments to extend credit	(XXX)	(XXX)	(XXX)	(XXX)
Standby letters of credit	(XXX)	(XXX)	(XXX)	(XXX)
Financial guarantees written	(XXX)	(XXX)	(XXX)	(XXX)

*The amounts shown under "carrying amount" represent accruals or deferred income (fees) arising from those unrecognized financial instruments. Interest rate swaps and other derivative instruments entered into as trading activities are included in "trading account assets" or "securities sold not owned."

Example 2—Nonfinancial Entity

[In this example, it is assumed that the carrying amounts of the short-term trade receivables and payables approximate their fair values.]

32. Corporation B might disclose the following:

Note X: Disclosures about Fair Value of Financial Instruments

The following methods and assumptions were used to estimate the fair value of each class of financial instruments for which it is practicable to estimate that value:

Cash and short-term investments
The carrying amount approximates fair value because of the short maturity of those instruments.

Long-term investments
The fair values of some investments are estimated based on quoted market prices for those or similar investments. For other investments for which there are no quoted market prices, a reasonable estimate of fair value could not be made without incurring excessive costs. Additional information pertinent to the value of an unquoted investment is provided below.

Long-term debt
The fair value of the Corporation's long-term debt is estimated based on the quoted market prices for the same or similar issues or on the current rates offered to the Corporation for debt of the same remaining maturities.

Foreign currency contracts
The fair value of foreign currency contracts (used for hedging purposes) is estimated by obtaining quotes from brokers.

The estimated fair values of the Corporation's financial instruments are as follows:

	19X9		19X8	
	Carrying Amount	Fair Value	Carrying Amount	Fair Value
Cash and short-term investments	$XXX	$XXX	$XXX	$XXX
Long-term investments for which it is:				
• Practicable to estimate fair value	XXX	XXX	XXX	XXX
• Not practicable	XXX	—	XXX	—
Long-term debt	(XXX)	(XXX)	(XXX)	(XXX)
Foreign currency contracts	XXX	XXX	(XXX)	(XXX)

It was not practicable to estimate the fair value of an investment representing 12 percent of the issued common stock of an untraded company; that investment is carried at its original cost of $XXX (19X8, $XXX) in the statement of financial position. At year-end, the total assets reported by the untraded company were $XXX (19X8, $XXX) and the common stockholders' equity was $XXX (19X8, $XXX), revenues were $XXX (19X8, $XXX), and net income was $XXX (19X8, $XXX).

Example 3—Small Nonfinancial Entity

33. Corporation C, whose only financial instruments are cash, short-term trade receivables and payables for which their carrying amounts approximate fair values, and long-term debt, might disclose the following:

Note Z: Long-Term Debt

Based on the borrowing rates currently available to the Corporation for bank loans with similar terms and average maturities, the fair value of long-term debt is $XXX (19X8, $XXX).

Appendix C

BACKGROUND INFORMATION AND BASIS FOR CONCLUSIONS

CONTENTS

Appendix C

BACKGROUND INFORMATION AND BASIS FOR CONCLUSIONS

Introduction

34. This appendix summarizes considerations that Board members deemed significant in reaching the conclusions in this Statement. It includes reasons for accepting certain views and rejecting others. Individual Board members gave greater weight to some factors than to others.

Background Information

35. Following the issuance of Statement 105 in March 1990, the Board decided to focus primarily on disclosures about fair value as the second phase in the disclosure part of the financial instruments project. Background information on the financial instruments project and on the purposes of disclosure is provided in Appendix D of Statement 105.

36. On December 31, 1990, after discussing the issues in five public Board meetings and two public task force meetings, the Board issued the Exposure Draft, *Disclosures about Market Value of Financial Instruments* (1990 Exposure Draft). The Board re-

ceived 204 comment letters on that Exposure Draft and 19 organizations and individuals presented their views during public hearings held on May 29 and 30, 1991. Also, eight entities participated in a field test of the disclosures proposed in the 1990 Exposure Draft. The field test results, which are kept confidential at the entities' request, were used by the Board during its deliberations on scope, display, and other issues addressed by this Statement.

Terminology

37. Some respondents to the 1990 Exposure Draft suggested that use of the term *market value* did not reflect adequately the broad range of financial instruments covered by this Statement. Those respondents associate the term *market value* only with items that are traded on active secondary markets (such as exchange and dealer markets). As highlighted by the discussion in paragraph 19 of this Statement, the Board does not make that distinction. The term *market value,* as defined in paragraph 5 of the 1990 Exposure Draft, is applicable whether the market for an item is active or inactive, primary or secondary. The Board decided, however, to use the term *fair value* in this Statement to avoid further confusion and also to be consistent with the terminology used in similar disclosure proposals made recently by other national and international standard-setting organiza-

tions. The concept of fair value is the same as that of market value in the 1990 Exposure Draft; those who associate the term *market value* only with items that are traded in active secondary markets may however prefer to consider fair value as a broader concept that includes prices and rates obtained from both secondary and primary markets.

Disclosures about Fair Value of Financial Instruments

38. The Board decided to proceed with the second phase of the disclosure project because it has concluded that fair value provides a relevant measure for unrecognized financial instruments and another relevant measure for recognized financial instruments that are measured on other bases. The Board also concluded that the benefits of disclosing information about fair value, when practicable, justify the costs involved, except for certain financial instruments for which that information is not required by this Statement.

Relevance of Fair Value Information

39. Many respondents to the 1990 Exposure Draft questioned the relevance of measures of financial assets and liabilities based on fair values. The Board concluded that information about fair value of financial instruments meets the first objective of financial reporting stated in FASB Concepts Statement No. 1, *Objectives of Financial Reporting by Business Enterprises,* that is, to provide information that is useful to present and potential investors, creditors, and other users in making rational investment, credit, and similar decisions.

40. Fair values of financial instruments depict the market's assessment of the present value of net future cash flows directly or indirectly embodied in them, discounted to reflect both current interest rates and the market's assessment of the risk that the cash flows will not occur. Investors and creditors are interested in predicting the amount, timing, and uncertainty of future net cash inflows to an entity, as those are the primary sources of future cash flows from the entity to them. Periodic information about the fair value of an entity's financial instruments under current conditions and expectations should help those users both in making their own predictions and in confirming or correcting their earlier expectations.

41. Information about fair value better enables investors, creditors, and other users to assess the consequences of an entity's investment and financing strategies, that is, to assess its performance. For example, information about fair value shows the effects of a decision to borrow using fixed-rate rather than floating-rate financial instruments or

of a decision to invest in long-term rather than short-term instruments. Also, in a dynamic economy, information about fair value permits continuous reassessment of earlier decisions in light of current circumstances.

42. Finally, several articles and reports in recent years have indicated the potential usefulness of information about market value of financial instruments, particularly as an indicator of the solvency of financial institutions. For example, a report issued by the U.S. Department of the Treasury in February 1991, *Modernizing the Financial System,* discusses the possible advantages of market value information for regulatory supervision of financial institutions.

43. Some respondents to the 1990 Exposure Draft argued that information about fair value of financial instruments is not relevant if an entity intends to hold them for the long term. They contend that, in those cases, the only relevant measure for a financial instrument is carrying value based on the amount initially paid or received (or perhaps a lower recoverable amount for an asset). They further argue that carrying value based on historical cost or proceeds provides relevant information because it focuses on the decision that creates the asset or liability, the earning effects of that decision that will be realized over time, and the ultimate recoverable or settlement value of the financial asset or liability. They also question the relevance of fair value measures because those measures focus on the effects of transactions and events that do not involve the entity. They reflect only "opportunity" gains and losses; "opportunities" that are not relevant unless they are intended to be realized.

44. The Board concluded that information about fair value of financial instruments, combined with information about carrying value, is relevant in part because it reflects the effects of management's decisions to buy a financial asset or incur a financial liability at a specific time, and then to continue to hold an asset or owe a liability. Deciding first on the best timing, based on existing market conditions, to acquire an asset or incur a liability and then when and how to realize gains or losses are important parts of management's stewardship responsibility to an entity's owners. Movements in fair values, and thus in market returns, during the period that a financial asset is held or a financial liability is owed provide a benchmark with which to assess the results of management's decisions and its success in maximizing the profitable use of an entity's economic resources and in minimizing financing costs.

45. Some respondents to the 1990 Exposure Draft argued that the subjectivity inherent in estimating

the fair value of some financial assets and liabilities renders the information irrelevant and potentially misleading. Some also mentioned that many financial assets and liabilities are not readily marketable and that since it might be difficult or impossible to sell or settle them, information about their fair value is not useful.

46. The Board concluded that those arguments pertain more to the reliability of the estimates than to their relevance. In some cases, it may not be practicable to make a reasonable estimate of fair value. However, the Board expects that, in most cases, it will be practicable for an entity to make a reasonable estimate of fair value even of financial instruments that are not readily marketable.

47. Some have suggested that most or all financial instruments should be recognized and measured at their fair value in financial statements. The Board is considering recognition and measurement issues in other parts of the project on financial instruments. This Statement requires only disclosures about fair value.

48. The disclosures about fair value required by this Statement build on current practice and requirements. For example, FASB Statement No. 12, *Accounting for Certain Marketable Securities,* requires lower of cost or market measures and disclosure of the market value of certain equity securities traded on exchanges or in the over-the-counter markets, and FASB Statement No. 15, *Accounting by Debtors and Creditors for Troubled Debt Restructurings,* provides guidance on determining the fair value of assets without active markets when transferred in settlement of troubled debt.

49. Other accounting standard-setting organizations have also concluded that fair value information about financial instruments is relevant. In September 1991, the International Accounting Standards Committee (IASC) issued an Exposure Draft, *Financial Instruments,* which, among other things, proposes disclosures about fair value for all financial instruments. The Exposure Draft is the result of a joint effort with the Canadian Institute of Chartered Accountants (CICA), which also issued an Exposure Draft, *Financial Instruments,* in September 1991.

50. The disclosures about fair value proposed in the IASC Exposure Draft are essentially the same as those required by this Statement. The CICA Exposure Draft also proposes disclosures about fair value, but only for financial assets; however, disclosures about fair value of financial liabilities are encouraged.

Benefits and Costs

51. One of the precepts of the Board's mission is to promulgate standards only when the expected benefits of the resulting information exceed the perceived costs. The Board strives to determine that a proposed standard will fill a significant need and that the costs entailed in satisfying that need, as compared with other alternatives, are justified in relation to the overall benefits of the resulting information. The benefits of providing fair value information are discussed in paragraphs 38-46 of this Statement.

52. The benefits of providing fair value information about financial instruments come at a cost—principally, the incremental cost of developing, implementing, and maintaining a measurement and reporting system to generate the required disclosures. The Board believes that many entities already have some systems in place to monitor and manage the market risk of their portfolios of financial instruments. The Board also believes that the incremental costs of the disclosure requirements of this Statement have been reduced in various ways: by introducing a notion of practicability to ensure that excessive costs will not be incurred solely to comply with the provisions of this Statement; by giving only general guidance on how to estimate fair value, so that an entity can exercise judgment in determining the most cost-efficient way of obtaining the information; by excluding certain financial instruments from the scope of the Statement because the benefits of providing fair value information about those instruments are at least uncertain in relation to the costs involved; and by delaying the effective date of application of this Statement for smaller entities that may need more time to be able to comply with the provisions of this Statement.

53. The Board realizes that by reducing some of the incremental costs of the requirements of this Statement in those ways, it also has reduced some of the benefits and possibly increased other costs of those requirements. For example, by providing general rather than detailed guidance, it has potentially reduced the comparability of the fair value information among entities. At the same time, general guidance may increase the costs that will be incurred by preparers, auditors, regulators, and others as they evaluate and select appropriate approaches to assessing and disclosing fair value. Also, there will be a cost to users of financial statements as they attempt to make comparisons among entities of fair value information based on different methods and assumptions.

54. The Board is sensitive to the consequences that may occur as a result of the new information. For example, some respondents to the 1990 Exposure Draft and the 1987 Exposure Draft, *Disclosures about Financial Instruments,* mentioned that entities could possibly refrain from investing in financial instruments with significant market value volatility or in long-term instruments as a result of the required disclosures. Others mentioned that disclosing periodic changes in the fair value of all financial instruments of financial institutions might jeopardize the safety and soundness of the banking system as a whole. However, the nature and extent of those consequences are highly uncertain and are difficult to isolate from the effects of other events that will occur independent of that new information. For example, regulatory agencies for banks and thrifts recently have made and currently are considering further changes in regulations that may affect considerably the costs of doing business for those entities in the future. The Board's objective is not to enhance or diminish the possibility of those consequences but to improve disclosure of information about financial instruments so that users of financial statements may make better informed decisions.

Level of Guidance

55. Disclosures about fair value were originally proposed as part of a comprehensive set of disclosures about financial instruments included in the 1987 Exposure Draft. Some respondents to that Exposure Draft were concerned about the lack of specific guidance on how to estimate fair value. They maintained that different entities would disclose different market value estimates for similar financial instruments by using varying methods and assumptions, resulting in a lack of comparability between those entities' financial statements. Similar comments were made by some respondents to the 1990 Exposure Draft.

56. After considering those concerns, the Board reaffirmed its preference for general rather than detailed guidance in this Statement even though general guidance may result in disclosures that are less comparable from entity to entity. The Board concluded that the benefits to investors and creditors of having some timely information about fair value outweigh the disadvantage of that information being less than fully comparable. The Board noted that information about financial instruments based on historical prices also is not comparable from entity to entity. The Board also is aware that the current practices followed by entities that estimate fair value (as defined in this Statement) for internal management purposes vary and to impose specific methods or assumptions could increase the cost of compliance for at least some enti-

ties. Furthermore, those entities will be using methods they consider to be most pertinent to their situation. Finally, financial instruments have such diverse characteristics that the Board believes that it is not practicable at this time to prescribe detailed methods and assumptions to be used in estimating fair value.

Financial Instruments with Quoted Prices

57. The Board concluded that quoted market prices provide the most reliable measure of fair value. Quoted market prices are easy to obtain and are reliable and verifiable. They are used and relied upon regularly and are well understood by investors, creditors, and other users of financial information. In recent years, new markets have developed and some existing markets have evolved from thin to active markets, thereby increasing the ready availability of reliable fair value information.

58. Although many respondents to the 1990 and 1987 Exposure Drafts agreed with the usefulness of disclosing quoted market prices derived from active markets, some argued that quoted prices from thin markets do not provide relevant measures of fair value, particularly when an entity holds a large amount of a thinly traded financial instrument that could not be absorbed by the market in a single transaction. The Board considered this issue and reiterated its belief that quoted prices, even from thin markets, provide useful information because investors and creditors regularly rely on those prices to make their decisions. The Board noted that providing the liquidation value of a block of financial instruments is not the objective of this Statement. The Board also concluded that requiring the use of available quoted market prices would increase the comparability of the disclosures among entities.

Financial Instruments with No Quoted Prices

59. The Board realizes that estimating fair value when quoted market prices are unavailable may, in some cases, require considerable judgment. However, the Board noted that a considerable degree of judgment also is needed when complying with other longstanding accounting and reporting requirements.

60. Many respondents to the 1990 and 1987 Exposure Drafts commented that some valuation techniques require sophisticated assumptions (for example, expected prepayments on a portfolio of loans assuming various future levels of interest rates) that would force entities, particularly smaller ones, to incur significant additional costs. The Board believes that simplified assumptions may sometimes be used (with appropriate disclo-

sure) by an entity to provide a reliable estimate of fair value at a reasonable cost.

61. Paragraph 28 of the 1990 Exposure Draft stated that "an entity could also estimate market value by calculating separately (a) changes in market value due to changes in overall general interest rates and (b) changes in market value due to cash flows not expected to be collected and due to changes in market premiums for credit risk." Some respondents questioned whether that wording permitted the use of the allowance for loan losses in estimating the fair value of loans. Although the Board did not consider that specific issue at the Exposure Draft stage, some Board members believe that the use of the allowance for loan losses would not provide an acceptable estimate of fair value in most cases because, according to current accounting literature, the allowance does not take into account the timing of the expected losses and all the potential losses due to credit risk. On the other hand, the factors considered in determining an appropriate allowance for loan losses are considered in determining the effects of changes in credit risk when estimating fair value. The Board decided to provide general rather than detailed guidance by stating, in paragraph 27 of Appendix A of this Statement, that adjustments to reflect the effects of changes in credit risk could be made by revising cash flow estimates, revising the discount rate, or some combination of both.

62. The Board is aware that it is not always practicable for an entity to estimate the fair value of a financial instrument or a category of financial instruments. The Board concluded that, in such cases, an entity should disclose the reasons fair value was not estimated and certain descriptive information pertinent to the value of those financial instruments that would help investors and creditors make their decisions. Examples of that information are the carrying amount of a financial instrument, the expected maturity, and the effective interest rate of the instrument.

63. Paragraph 14(c) of the 1990 Exposure Draft would have required an entity to state whether it believes the carrying amount approximates fair value or is significantly higher or lower than fair value. Many respondents objected to that requirement because they believe that, in most situations where it is not practicable to estimate fair value, it also would not be practicable to make such a statement. Also, they mentioned the risk of litigation arising from such a subjective disclosure. Based on those arguments, the Board decided not to include that disclosure requirement in this Statement.

Financial Liabilities

64. Some respondents to the 1990 Exposure Draft proposed excluding all financial liabilities from the scope of this Statement. Although most existing disclosures about fair value, and most discussion of the need for additional disclosures, have focused on the values of assets, the Board concluded that disclosures about the fair value of financial liabilities are important because market price volatility, which creates economic gains and losses, affects financial liabilities as well as assets. For example, a decline in the market price of an entity's bonds may give the entity an opportunity to settle the debt at a price below the carrying amount and, thus, to recognize a gain.

65. Some respondents to the 1990 Exposure Draft questioned the relevance of fair value information for liabilities when an entity does not have the intent or the ability to settle the debt. Some respondents argued that even when an entity intends to settle a debt to realize a gain due to an increase in market interest rates, there would be no economic gain if the cash needed for settlement is obtained through issuance of other debt at current higher rates. The Board believes that fair value information also is relevant in those cases because it helps users of financial statements assess the effects on the entity of interest rate changes and the entity's ability to manage the related risk. The fair value of liabilities also provides information about the entity's success in minimizing financing costs on a continuing basis (for example, by timing borrowing decisions to take advantage of favorable market conditions). The Board noted that an entity does not necessarily need to settle a debt financed at a rate below prevailing market rates to realize a gain; the gain could be realized over the period of repayment of that debt. The Board also noted that under longstanding provisions of APB Opinion No. 26, *Early Extinguishment of Debt,* a gain is recognized in income if a debt is settled for less than its carrying amount, regardless of the source of the cash used to settle the debt.

66. Information about the fair values of both assets and liabilities is essential to permit an assessment of a financial institution's success in managing its financial assets and liabilities in a coordinated way. To limit potential net loss, financial institutions often seek to balance their asset and liability positions so that a decrease in the fair value of a financial asset is accompanied by a decrease in the fair value of a financial liability.

67. Some respondents, however, suggested that fair value information for liabilities of predominantly nonfinancial entities is not useful because

those entities hold relatively few financial assets. Also, those liabilities are often incurred to finance the acquisition of nonfinancial assets; disclosing the changes in the fair value of financial liabilities without the corresponding changes in the fair value of nonfinancial assets may be misleading. The Board considered those arguments and reiterated its belief that fair value information for liabilities in itself is relevant information and should be provided. The Board acknowledges that the usefulness of the fair value information for liabilities would be enhanced by fair value information for nonfinancial assets but those assets are outside the scope of this Statement. This Statement, however, emphasizes that an entity may voluntarily disclose information about the fair value of its nonfinancial assets and liabilities (paragraph 12).

68. The Board acknowledges that, as for assets with no quoted prices, variations in the methods used to estimate the fair value of liabilities with no quoted prices might reduce the comparability of fair value information among entities. Some entities will estimate fair value by using an incremental rate of borrowing that considers changes in an entity's own credit risk, while others will use a settlement rate that ignores at least part of those credit risk changes. However, the Board concluded that it should not, at this time, prescribe a single method to be used for all unquoted liabilities. The Board currently has a project on its agenda on the uses of interest methods of accounting that examines questions about accounting measurements based on the present value of future economic benefits or sacrifices, and it will consider the question of a single method as part of that project.[4]

Core Deposits

69. Some respondents to the 1990 Exposure Draft commented that a financial institution should consider the value of its long-term customer relationships (core deposit intangibles) in estimating the fair value of its deposits. The Board concluded that core deposit intangibles are separate intangible assets, not financial instruments, and are therefore outside the scope of this Statement. The Board noted that the accounting treatment for intangible assets similar to those identified by respondents as core deposit intangibles is partially addressed in FASB Statement No. 72, *Accounting for Certain Acquisitions of Banking or Thrift Institutions,* and the arguments used in Statement 72 support the conclusion reached by the Board in this Statement. The Board also noted that accounting standards do not prohibit voluntary disclosures about fair value of core deposit intangibles or any

other assets or liabilities that are not included in the scope of this Statement.

70. Some respondents asked whether the Board's intention, in the 1990 Exposure Draft, was to prescribe the disclosure of the carrying amount of deposit liabilities as an estimate of their fair value. Others mentioned that the fair value of deposit liabilities may differ from their carrying amount even when, as required by paragraph 12 of this Statement, the value of core deposit intangibles is not taken into consideration; they suggested that those deposits represent an inexpensive source of funds that will be available for a considerable period of time. The Board decided that for deposit liabilities with no defined maturities, the fair value to be disclosed should be the amount payable on demand at the reporting date. The Board disagreed with the view that deposit liabilities should be valued using the rates available on more expensive alternative sources of funds because those rates are not relevant to the markets for deposits; also, that approach does not consider all the costs related to servicing the deposits.

Exclusion of Certain Financial Instruments

71. This Statement does not require disclosures about fair value for (a) employers' and plans' obligations for pension benefits, employers' and plans' obligations for other postretirement benefits including health care and life insurance benefits, employee stock option and stock purchase plans, and other forms of deferred compensation arrangements, (b) substantively extinguished debt subject to the disclosure requirements of Statement 76 and assets held in trust in connection with an in-substance defeasance of that debt, (c) insurance contracts, other than financial guarantees and investment contracts, (d) lease contracts, (e) warranty obligations and rights, (f) unconditional purchase obligations as defined in Statement 47, (g) investments accounted for under the equity method, (h) minority interests in consolidated subsidiaries, (i) equity investments in consolidated subsidiaries, and (j) equity instruments issued by the entity and classified in stockholders' equity in the statement of financial position.

72. Some disclosures about fair value are already required by existing generally accepted accounting principles for some items included in category (a) of the previous paragraph. In addition, a project on employee stock compensation plans is currently on the Board's agenda. In Statement 76, the Board concluded that meeting specified conditions effectively immunizes the obligation against market risk.

---

[4]The Discussion Memorandum, *Present-Value-Based Measurements in Accounting,* was issued on December 7, 1990.

73. This Statement uses a definition of a financial instrument based on the definition contained in Statement 105. During the Board's deliberations on this phase of the disclosure project, some questions arose about the application of the definition to contracts that involve the future delivery of goods or services. For example, Statement 105 excludes from the definition a contract that either requires the exchange of a financial instrument for a nonfinancial commodity (a forward contract) or permits settlement of an obligation by delivery of a nonfinancial commodity (an option), because those contracts involve the required or optional future exchange or delivery of an item that is not a financial instrument. An alternative approach would separate those contracts into financial and nonfinancial components; for example, a forward contract to purchase goods could be viewed as both an obligation to pay cash—a financial instrument—and a right to receive goods—not a financial instrument. If the financial component of that contract were subject to the disclosure requirements of this Statement, a further question would be whether the estimate of the fair value of the financial component should take into account changes in value caused by changes in the price of the underlying commodity. If not, difficulties would arise in distinguishing between changes in the fair value of the financial component and changes in the fair value of the nonfinancial component of the contract.

74. The Board concluded that disclosures about fair value should not be required for insurance contracts, lease contracts, warranty obligations, and unconditional purchase obligations (such as take-or-pay contracts). The Board believes that definitional and valuation difficulties are present to a certain extent in those contracts and obligations, and that further consideration is required before decisions can be made about whether to apply the definition to components of those contracts and whether to require disclosures about fair value for the financial components. The Board noted that issues about the application of the definition of a financial instrument are addressed more comprehensively in the November 1991 FASB Discussion Memorandum, *Recognition and Measurement of Financial Instruments*.

75. The other instruments listed in paragraph 71(g)-(j) were added as a result of comments received from respondents on the scope of the Statement. The disclosures were intended to apply only to financial assets and liabilities; therefore, minority interests in consolidated subsidiaries and an entity's own equity instruments classified in stockholders' equity are exempt from the disclosure requirements. The Board also decided to clarify that there is no requirement to disclose the fair value of investments in consolidated subsidiaries. Finally, the Board decided to exempt investments accounted for under the equity method from the disclosure requirements. The market value of those investments for which a quoted market price is available is already required to be disclosed under the provisions of Opinion 18, and the Board believes that the incremental benefits of estimating fair value for unquoted investments accounted for under the equity method do not outweigh the related costs.

76. Respondents to the 1990 Exposure Draft who proposed exempting other types of financial instruments from the disclosures required by this Statement were concerned about the difficulty or cost of estimating fair value. The Board concluded that no other type of financial instrument needs to be specifically excluded from the scope of this Statement because an entity will not be required to provide an estimate of fair value for a financial instrument if it is not practicable to do so.

Application in Comparative Financial Statements

77. The Board decided that, in the initial year of applying the provisions of this Statement, disclosures about fair value should be required as of the date of the latest statement of financial position. Obtaining prior-year fair value information not previously required might be difficult for many entities, and the Board believes the benefits would likely not justify the costs.

78. Although some respondents to the 1990 Exposure Draft suggested that the volume of disclosures would be unduly increased, the Board concluded that, after transition, comparative information about fair value should be provided for each year for which a statement of financial position is presented because that information is useful in assessing the management of market risk and pertinent trends.

Applicability to Small, Nonpublic, or Nonfinancial Entities

79. The Board considered whether certain entities should be excluded from the scope of this Statement. In particular, the Board considered the usefulness of the disclosures about fair value required by this Statement for small, nonpublic, or predominantly nonfinancial entities; a number of respondents to the 1990 Exposure Draft suggested exclusions on one or more of those bases. After considering the costs and benefits of those disclosures, the Board concluded that the disclosures are important and should be required for all entities, including small and nonpublic entities. The Board believes that the notion of "practicability" discussed in paragraph 15 ensures that excessive costs do not have to be incurred to comply with the dis-

closure requirements. In addition, the Board's decision to allow smaller entities additional time to apply the provisions of this Statement recognizes the fact that the costs of compliance can be reduced for those entities because the overall benefits of the information might be less than for larger entities.

80. The Board also concluded that while this Statement would likely have its greatest effect on the financial reporting of entities whose assets and liabilities are primarily financial instruments, financial instruments constitute an important part of the assets and liabilities of many predominantly nonfinancial entities as well, and disclosures about their fair value are useful and should be required. Furthermore, distinctions between financial and nonfinancial entities are becoming less pronounced.

81. The Board acknowledges that, for predominantly nonfinancial entities that have relatively few financial instruments, the benefits of disclosures about fair value might be less than for financial entities for which financial instruments are the most important part of their activities. However, the Board noted that the costs of compliance are relatively lower for those entities and that there are comparability benefits associated with having similar disclosure requirements apply to similar financial instruments. Accordingly, the Board decided that the disclosures required by this Statement should apply to all entities.

Location of Information within Financial Reports

82. The Board considered whether the disclosures required by this Statement should be part of the basic financial statements or should be provided as supplementary information. FASB Concepts Statement No. 5, *Recognition and Measurement in Financial Statements of Business Enterprises,* distinguishes between information that should be part of the basic financial statements and that which should be provided as supplementary information. Paragraph 7 of Concepts Statement 5 emphasizes that information disclosed as part of the basic financial statements amplifies or explains information recognized in financial statements and is essential to understanding that information.

83. Some respondents to the 1990 Exposure Draft suggested that the fair value information required by this Statement be disclosed as supplementary information because of the subjectivity associated with some estimates and to reduce the costs of compliance. Other respondents supported the Board's position in the Exposure Draft to allow entities enough flexibility to select the best way to disclose the information as part of the basic financial statements. Some also mentioned that the disclosures would be more credible if they are made as part of the basic financial statements.

84. The disclosures required by this Statement build on disclosures already included in basic financial statements and, like them, serve the major purposes of disclosure summarized in Appendix D of Statement 105; that is, to provide descriptions, to provide measures, and to help in assessing risks and potentials. In the past, requiring information to be supplementary has been done in conjunction with excluding certain entities from the scope of the requirements; however, as discussed in paragraphs 79-81, the Board concluded that the disclosures required by this Statement should be provided by all entities. The Board also concluded that all the disclosures about fair value of financial instruments should be included within the basic financial statements. The Board noted that having some fair value disclosures outside and others as part of the basic financial statements could potentially confuse the users of financial statements.

85. Some respondents believed that this Statement should require the fair value information to be disclosed in a tabular format in a single note to the financial statements. They believed that that approach would make the information more readily available and easier to understand by users of financial statements, thereby increasing the benefits of the disclosures. However, the Board concluded that entities should be allowed to determine the most appropriate way to disclose the fair value information in their financial statements.

Applicability to Interim Financial Statements

86. Some respondents to the 1990 Exposure Draft questioned whether the provisions of this Statement apply to interim financial statements. Paragraph 16 clarifies that disclosures about fair value are required to be made in all complete sets of interim financial statements, except in the initial year of application of this Statement. The minimum disclosure requirements for summarized interim financial information issued by publicly traded entities are established by APB Opinion No. 28, *Interim Financial Reporting.* Since the provisions of this Statement do not amend Opinion 28, summarized interim financial information need not include the disclosures required by this Statement.

Effective Dates and Transition

87. Some respondents to the 1987 Exposure Draft mentioned that completion of the disclosure part of the financial instruments project would be desirable as soon as practicable so that the Board could proceed to focus entirely on recognition and measure-

ment issues. On the other hand, many respondents expressed concern that some entities, particularly smaller ones, may not currently have in place the systems necessary to provide the required disclosures. After considering those comments, the Board proposed in the 1990 Exposure Draft that the effective date for larger entities, defined as entities with more than $100 million in total assets at the date of the latest statement of financial position, should be for financial statements issued for fiscal years ending after December 15, 1991. The Board also proposed to delay for one year the application of this Statement's requirements for entities that fall below that size criterion.

88. Many respondents to the 1990 Exposure Draft were concerned that they would not have sufficient time to prepare the required fair value information if a final Statement were issued late in 1991. Others suggested that the size criterion used to determine which entities would have additional time to implement the provisions of this Statement should be increased; some noted that bank regulators require less extensive information for banks with less than $150 million in total assets. After considering those comments, the Board concluded that larger entities, defined as entities with more than $150 million in total assets in the current statement of financial position, should apply the provisions of this Statement in financial statements issued for fiscal years ending after December 15, 1992. The Board decided to delay the effective date for smaller entities by an additional three years to provide sufficient time for those entities to develop the systems necessary to provide the required disclosures, in light of the experience gained by larger entities on the use of various methods and assumptions for estimating fair value.

Statement of Financial Accounting Standards No. 108 Accounting for Income Taxes—Deferral of the Effective Date of FASB Statement No. 96

an amendment of FASB Statement No. 96

STATUS

Issued: December 1991

Effective Date: December 16, 1991

Affects: Amends FAS 96, paragraph 32
   Supersedes FAS 100
   Supersedes FAS 103

Affected by: Superseded by FAS 109

(The next page is 1412.)

Statement of Financial Accounting Standards No. 109
Accounting for Income Taxes

STATUS

Issued: February 1992

Effective Date: For fiscal years beginning after December 15, 1992

Affects: Amends ARB 43, Chapter 9C, paragraph 5
     Supersedes ARB 43, Chapter 9C, paragraphs 11 through 13
     Supersedes ARB 43, Chapter 10B
     Supersedes ARB 43, Chapter 11B, paragraph 8
     Supersedes ARB 44 (Revised) and related letter dated April 15, 1959
     Supersedes APB 1
     Supersedes APB 2, paragraph 16
     Supersedes APB 6, paragraphs 20 through 23 and footnotes 7 and 8
     Supersedes APB 11
     Amends APB 16, paragraphs 87 and 88
     Supersedes APB 16, paragraph 89
     Amends APB 17, paragraph 30
     Amends APB 21, footnote 8*
     Amends APB 23, paragraphs 9, 13,* 21, and 23 and footnotes 7* and 9
     Supersedes APB 23, paragraphs 10, 11, 14, and 24 and footnotes 3, 4, 6, and 10
     Supersedes APB 24
     Amends APB 25, paragraph 17
     Amends APB 28, paragraphs 19* and 20 and footnotes 2 and 3
     Amends APB 29, paragraph 27*
     Amends APB 30, paragraph 7
     Supersedes AIN-APB 4, Interpretations No. 4 and 6
     Supersedes AIN-APB 11, Interpretations No. 1 through 25
     Supersedes AIN-APB 15, Interpretations No. 13 and 16
     Amends AIN-APB 18, Interpretations No. 1 and 2*
     Supersedes AIN-APB 23, Interpretation No. 1
     Amends AIN-APB 25, Interpretation No. 1
     Amends FAS 12, paragraph 22*
     Amends FAS 13, paragraph 47
     Supersedes FAS 16, paragraph 11 and footnote 5
     Amends FAS 16, paragraph 13 and footnotes 3 and 4
     Amends FAS 19, paragraphs 61 and 62
     Supersedes FAS 31
     Supersedes FAS 37, paragraphs 4, 17, 18, and 26 through 29 and footnotes 1 through 3 and footnotes
       (*) and (†) of paragraph 4
     Amends FAS 37, paragraphs 19,* 20, 21,* 22,* 23, 24,* and 25*
     Amends FAS 38, paragraphs 2 and 5
     Supersedes FAS 38, footnote 2
     Amends FAS 44, paragraph 6*
     Amends FAS 52, paragraphs 22,* 23,* 24,* and 48
     Amends FAS 57, paragraph 2
     Supersedes FAS 60, paragraphs 55 through 58, 60(i), and 60(j) and footnote 8

---

*Result of the amendment, at least in part, described in paragraph 287.

Amends FAS 60, paragraph 59

Amends FAS 69, paragraphs 26, 30(c), 40, and 41

Supersedes FAS 71, paragraph 18 and footnote 12

Amends FAS 71, paragraph 46

Amends FAS 87, paragraph 37*

Amends FAS 89, paragraphs 33* and 96

Amends FAS 90, paragraphs 14 and 27*

Supersedes FAS 96

Supersedes FAS 100

Amends FAS 101, paragraph 19*

Supersedes FAS 103

Supersedes FAS 108

Amends FIN 18, paragraphs 6,* 8, 16, 18, 40 through 43, 46 through 55, 58, 65, 66, and 68 and
footnotes 2,* 19, and footnote (*) of paragraph 47

Supersedes FIN 18, paragraphs 14, 15, 20, 23, 59 through 61, and 70 and footnotes 9 through 14, 18,
21 through 23, and 25

Supersedes FIN 22

Supersedes FIN 25

Supersedes FIN 29

Amends FIN 30, paragraph 5*

Amends FIN 31, footnote 1

Supersedes FIN 32

Amends FTB 79-9, paragraph 3

Amends FTB 79-16 (Revised), paragraph 4

Supersedes FTB 81-2

Supersedes FTB 82-1, paragraph 5

Amends FTB 82-1, paragraph 7*

Supersedes FTB 83-1

Supersedes FTB 84-2

Supersedes FTB 84-3

Supersedes FTB 86-1

Supersedes FTB 87-2, paragraphs 9 through 11, 13, and 22 through 33 and footnotes 4 and 8

Amends FTB 87-2, paragraphs 14,* 18,* 34,* 35,* 36,* 40,* 45,* and 46*

Amends FTB 88-2, paragraph 4*

Affected by: Paragraphs 11(h), 13, and 30 amended by FAS 141
Paragraphs 35 and 36 amended by FAS 130
Paragraph 36(b) amended by FAS 115
Paragraphs 36(d), 259, and 270 amended by FAS 141
Paragraph 36(e) amended by FAS 123
Paragraph 276 amended by FAS 135

Other Interpretive Release: FASB Special Report, *A Guide to Implementation of Statement 109 on*
Accounting for Income Taxes: Questions and Answers

Issues Discussed by FASB Emerging Issues Task Force (EITF)

Affects: Nullifies EITF Issues No. 84-43, 85-3, 85-15, 85-33, 86-1, 86-4, 86-37, 86-41, and 86-42
Partially nullifies EITF Issues No. 86-3 and 87-8
Resolves EITF Issues No. 84-1, 84-2, 84-27, 85-5, 86-11, 87-28, and 91-3 and Topic No. D-7
Partially resolves EITF Issues No. 85-41 and 88-5
Affects EITF Issues No. 86-31, 88-19, and 91-8

---

*Result of the amendment, at least in part, described in paragraph 287.

Interpreted by: Paragraph 9 interpreted by EITF Topic No. D-31
Paragraph 9(f) interpreted by EITF Issues No. 92-8 and 93-9 and Topic No. D-56
Paragraph 11 interpreted by EITF Issue No. 93-9
Paragraphs 15 and 31 interpreted by EITF Issue No. 93-16
Paragraph 17 interpreted by EITF Issue No. 94-1 and Topic No. D-31
Paragraph 18 interpreted by EITF Issue No. 95-10
Paragraph 19 interpreted by EITF Issue No. 95-20
Paragraph 26 interpreted by EITF Issue No. 94-10
Paragraph 27 interpreted by EITF Issues No. 93-12, 93-13, and 99-15 and Topic No. D-30
Paragraph 30 interpreted by EITF Issues No. 93-7 and 99-15
Paragraph 34 interpreted by EITF Issue No. 93-17
Paragraph 35 interpreted by EITF Issue No. 95-9 and Topic No. D-32
Paragraph 36 interpreted by EITF Issue No. 94-10 and Topic No. D-32
Paragraph 36(f) interpreted by EITF Issue No. 92-3
Paragraphs 37 and 38 interpreted by EITF Topic No. D-32
Paragraph 268 interpreted by EITF Topic No. D-33

Related Issues: EITF Issues No. 85-31, 86-9, 88-4, 96-7, 98-11, and 00-15

SUMMARY

This Statement establishes financial accounting and reporting standards for the effects of income taxes that result from an enterprise's activities during the current and preceding years. It requires an asset and liability approach for financial accounting and reporting for income taxes. This Statement supersedes FASB Statement No. 96, *Accounting for Income Taxes,* and amends or supersedes other accounting pronouncements listed in Appendix D.

Objectives of Accounting for Income Taxes

The objectives of accounting for income taxes are to recognize (a) the amount of taxes payable or refundable for the current year and (b) deferred tax liabilities and assets for the future tax consequences of events that have been recognized in an enterprise's financial statements or tax returns.

Basic Principles of Accounting for Income Taxes

The following basic principles are applied in accounting for income taxes at the date of the financial statements:

a. A current tax liability or asset is recognized for the estimated taxes payable or refundable on tax returns for the current year.
b. A deferred tax liability or asset is recognized for the estimated future tax effects attributable to temporary differences and carryforwards.
c. The measurement of current and deferred tax liabilities and assets is based on provisions of the enacted tax law; the effects of future changes in tax laws or rates are not anticipated.
d. The measurement of deferred tax assets is reduced, if necessary, by the amount of any tax benefits that, based on available evidence, are not expected to be realized.

Temporary Differences

The tax consequences of most events recognized in the financial statements for a year are included in determining income taxes currently payable. However, tax laws often differ from the recognition and measurement requirements of financial accounting standards, and differences can arise between (a) the amount of taxable income and pretax financial income for a year and (b) the tax bases of assets or liabilities and their reported amounts in financial statements.

APB Opinion No. 11, *Accounting for Income Taxes,* used the term *timing differences* for differences between the years in which transactions affect taxable income and the years in which they enter into the determination of pretax financial income. Timing differences create differences (sometimes accumulating over more than one year) between the tax basis of an asset or liability and its reported amount in financial statements. Other events such as business combinations may also create differences between the tax basis of an asset or liability and its reported amount in financial statements. All such differences collectively are referred to as *temporary differences* in this Statement.

Deferred Tax Consequences of Temporary Differences

Temporary differences ordinarily become taxable or deductible when the related asset is recovered or the related liability is settled. A deferred tax liability or asset represents the increase or decrease in taxes payable or refundable in future years as a result of temporary differences and carryforwards at the end of the current year.

Deferred Tax Liabilities

A deferred tax liability is recognized for temporary differences that will result in taxable amounts in future years. For example, a temporary difference is created between the reported amount and the tax basis of an installment sale receivable if, for tax purposes, some or all of the gain on the installment sale will be included in the determination of taxable income in future years. Because amounts received upon recovery of that receivable will be taxable, a deferred tax liability is recognized in the current year for the related taxes payable in future years.

Deferred Tax Assets

A deferred tax asset is recognized for temporary differences that will result in deductible amounts in future years and for carryforwards. For example, a temporary difference is created between the reported amount and the tax basis of a liability for estimated expenses if, for tax purposes, those estimated expenses are not deductible until a future year. Settlement of that liability will result in tax deductions in future years, and a deferred tax asset is recognized in the current year for the reduction in taxes payable in future years. A valuation allowance is recognized if, based on the weight of available evidence, it is *more likely than not* that some portion or all of the deferred tax asset will not be realized.

Measurement of a Deferred Tax Liability or Asset

This Statement establishes procedures to (a) measure deferred tax liabilities and assets using a tax rate convention and (b) assess whether a valuation allowance should be established for deferred tax assets. Enacted tax laws and rates are considered in determining the applicable tax rate and in assessing the need for a valuation allowance.

All available evidence, both positive and negative, is considered to determine whether, based on the weight of that evidence, a valuation allowance is needed for some portion or all of a deferred tax asset. Judgment must be used in considering the relative impact of negative and positive evidence. The weight given to the potential effect of negative and positive evidence should be commensurate with the extent to which it can be objectively verified. The more negative evidence that exists (a) the more positive evidence is necessary and (b) the more difficult it is to support a conclusion that a valuation allowance is not needed.

Changes in Tax Laws or Rates

This Statement requires that deferred tax liabilities and assets be adjusted in the period of enactment for the effect of an enacted change in tax laws or rates. The effect is included in income from continuing operations.

Effective Date

This Statement is effective for fiscal years beginning after December 15, 1992. Earlier application is encouraged.

Statement of Financial Accounting Standards No. 109

Accounting for Income Taxes

CONTENTS

INTRODUCTION

1. This Statement addresses financial accounting and reporting for the effects of **income taxes**[1] that result from an enterprise's activities during the current and preceding years.

2. FASB Statement No. 96, *Accounting for Income Taxes,* which was issued in December 1987, superseded APB Opinion No. 11, *Accounting for Income Taxes.* The effective date of Statement 96 was delayed to fiscal years that begin after December 15, 1992. In March 1989, the Board began consideration of requests to amend Statement 96 to (a) change the criteria for recognition and measurement of deferred tax assets and various other requirements of Statement 96 and (b) reduce complexity. This Statement is the result of that reconsideration.

STANDARDS OF FINANCIAL ACCOUNTING AND REPORTING

Scope

3. This Statement establishes standards of financial accounting and reporting for income taxes that are currently payable and for the tax consequences of:

a. Revenues, expenses, gains, or losses that are included in **taxable income** of an earlier or later year than the year in which they are recognized in financial income
b. Other **events** that create differences between the tax bases of assets and liabilities and their amounts for financial reporting
c. Operating loss or tax credit **carrybacks** for re-

---

[1]Words that appear in the glossary are set in **boldface type** the first time they appear.

funds of taxes paid in prior years and **carryforwards** to reduce taxes payable in future years.

This Statement supersedes Statement 96 and supersedes or amends other accounting pronouncements listed in Appendix D.

4. The principles and requirements of this Statement are applicable to:

a. Domestic federal (national) income taxes (U.S. federal income taxes for U.S. enterprises) and foreign, state, and local (including franchise) taxes based on income
b. An enterprise's[2] domestic and foreign operations that are consolidated, combined, or accounted for by the equity method
c. Foreign enterprises in preparing financial statements in accordance with U.S. generally accepted accounting principles.

5. This Statement does not address:

a. The basic methods of accounting for the U.S. federal investment tax credit (ITC) and for foreign, state, and local investment tax credits or grants (The deferral and flow-through methods as set forth in APB Opinions No. 2 and No. 4, *Accounting for the "Investment Credit,"* continue to be acceptable methods to account for the U.S. federal ITC.)
b. Discounting (Paragraph 6 of APB Opinion No. 10, *Omnibus Opinion—1966,* addresses that subject.)
c. Accounting for income taxes in interim periods (other than the criteria for recognition of tax benefits and the effect of enacted changes in tax laws or rates and changes in valuation allowances). (APB Opinion No. 28, *Interim Financial Reporting,* and other accounting pronouncements address that subject.)

Objectives and Basic Principles

6. One objective of accounting for income taxes is to recognize the amount of taxes payable or refundable for the current year. A second objective is to recognize **deferred tax liabilities and assets** for the future **tax consequences** of events[3] that have been recognized in an enterprise's financial statements or tax returns.

7. Ideally, the second objective might be stated more specifically to recognize the *expected* future tax consequences of events that have been recognized in the financial statements or tax returns. However, that objective is realistically constrained because (a) the tax payment or refund that results from a particular tax return is a joint result of all the items included in that return, (b) taxes that will be paid or refunded in future years are the joint result of events of the current or prior years and events of future years, and (c) information available about the future is limited. As a result, attribution of taxes to individual items and events is arbitrary and, except in the simplest situations, requires estimates and approximations.

8. To implement the objectives in light of those constraints, the following basic principles (the only exceptions are identified in paragraph 9) are applied in accounting for income taxes at the date of the financial statements:

a. A current tax liability or asset is recognized for the estimated taxes payable or refundable on tax returns for the current year.
b. A deferred tax liability or asset is recognized for the estimated future tax effects attributable to **temporary differences** and carryforwards.
c. The measurement of current and deferred tax liabilities and assets is based on provisions of the enacted tax law; the effects of future changes in tax laws or rates are not anticipated.
d. The measurement of deferred tax assets is reduced, if necessary, by the amount of any tax benefits that, based on available evidence, are not expected to be realized.

9. The only exceptions in applying those basic principles are that this Statement:

a. Continues certain exceptions to the requirements for recognition of deferred taxes for the areas addressed by APB Opinion No. 23, *Accounting for Income Taxes—Special Areas,* as amended by this Statement (paragraphs 31-34)
b. Provides special transitional procedures for temporary differences related to deposits in statutory reserve funds by U.S. steamship enterprises (paragraph 32)
c. Does not amend accounting for leveraged leases as required by FASB Statement No. 13, *Accounting for Leases,* and FASB Interpretation No. 21, *Accounting for Leases in a Business Combination* (paragraphs 256-258)
d. Prohibits recognition of a deferred tax liability or asset related to goodwill (or the portion

---

[2]The term *enterprise* is used throughout this Statement because accounting for income taxes is primarily an issue for business enterprises. However, the requirements of this Statement apply to the activities of a not-for-profit organization that are subject to income taxes.

[3]Some events do not have tax consequences. Certain revenues are exempt from taxation and certain expenses are not deductible. In the United States, for example, interest earned on certain municipal obligations is not taxable and fines are not deductible.

thereof) for which amortization is not deductible for tax purposes (paragraph 30)

e. Does not amend Accounting Research Bulletin No. 51, *Consolidated Financial Statements,* for income taxes paid on intercompany profits on assets remaining within the group, and prohibits recognition of a deferred tax asset for the difference between the tax basis of the assets in the buyer's tax jurisdiction and their cost as reported in the consolidated financial statements

f. Prohibits recognition of a deferred tax liability or asset for differences related to assets and liabilities that, under FASB Statement No. 52, *Foreign Currency Translation,* are remeasured from the local currency into the functional currency using historical exchange rates and that result from (1) changes in exchange rates or (2) indexing for tax purposes.

Temporary Differences

10. **Income taxes currently payable**[4] for a particular year usually include the tax consequences of most events that are recognized in the financial statements for that year. However, because tax laws and financial accounting standards differ in their recognition and measurement of assets, liabilities, equity, revenues, expenses, gains, and losses, differences arise between:

a. The amount of taxable income and pretax financial income for a year
b. The tax bases of assets or liabilities and their reported amounts in financial statements.

11. An assumption inherent in an enterprise's statement of financial position prepared in accordance with generally accepted accounting principles is that the reported amounts of assets and liabilities will be recovered and settled, respectively. Based on that assumption, a difference between the tax basis of an asset or a liability and its reported amount in the statement of financial position will result in taxable or deductible amounts in some future year(s) when the reported amounts of assets are recovered and the reported amounts of liabilities are settled. Examples follow:

a. *Revenues or gains that are taxable after they are recognized in financial income.* An asset (for example, a receivable from an installment sale) may be recognized for revenues or gains that will result in future taxable amounts when the asset is recovered.

b. *Expenses or losses that are deductible after they are recognized in financial income.* A liability (for example, a product warranty liability) may be recognized for expenses or losses that will result in future tax deductible amounts when the liability is settled.

c. *Revenues or gains that are taxable before they are recognized in financial income.* A liability (for example, subscriptions received in advance) may be recognized for an advance payment for goods or services to be provided in future years. For tax purposes, the advance payment is included in taxable income upon the receipt of cash. Future sacrifices to provide goods or services (or future refunds to those who cancel their orders) will result in future tax deductible amounts when the liability is settled.

d. *Expenses or losses that are deductible before they are recognized in financial income.* The cost of an asset (for example, depreciable personal property) may have been deducted for tax purposes faster than it was depreciated for financial reporting. Amounts received upon future recovery of the amount of the asset for financial reporting will exceed the remaining tax basis of the asset, and the excess will be taxable when the asset is recovered.

e. *A reduction in the tax basis of depreciable assets because of tax credits.*[5] Amounts received upon future recovery of the amount of the asset for financial reporting will exceed the remaining tax basis of the asset, and the excess will be taxable when the asset is recovered.

f. *ITC accounted for by the deferral method.* Under Opinion 2, ITC is viewed and accounted for as a reduction of the cost of the related asset (even though, for financial statement presentation, deferred ITC may be reported as deferred income). Amounts received upon future recovery of the reduced cost of the asset for financial reporting will be less than the tax basis of the asset, and the difference will be tax deductible when the asset is recovered.

g. *An increase in the tax basis of assets because of indexing whenever the local currency is the functional currency.* The tax law for a particular tax jurisdiction might require adjustment of the tax basis of a depreciable (or other) asset for the effects of inflation. The inflation-adjusted tax basis of the asset would be used to compute future tax deductions for depreciation or to compute gain or loss on sale of the asset. Amounts received upon future recovery of the local currency historical cost of the asset will be

---

[4]References in this Statement to income taxes currently payable and (total) **income tax expense** are intended to include also **income taxes currently refundable** and (total) **income tax benefit,** respectively.

[5]The Tax Equity and Fiscal Responsibility Act of 1982 provided taxpayers with the choice of either (a) taking the full amount of Accelerated Cost Recovery System (ACRS) deductions and a reduced tax credit (that is, investment tax credit and certain other tax credits) or (b) taking the full tax credit and a reduced amount of ACRS deductions.

less than the remaining tax basis of the asset, and the difference will be tax deductible when the asset is recovered.

h. *Business combinations accounted for by the purchase method.* There may be differences between the assigned values and the tax bases of the assets and liabilities recognized in a business combination accounted for as a purchase under APB Opinion No. 16, *Business Combinations.* Those differences will result in taxable or deductible amounts when the reported amounts of the assets and liabilities are recovered and settled, respectively.

12. Examples (a)-(d) in paragraph 11 illustrate revenues, expenses, gains, or losses that are included in taxable income of an earlier or later year than the year in which they are recognized in pretax financial income. Those differences between taxable income and pretax financial income also create differences (sometimes accumulating over more than one year) between the tax basis of an asset or liability and its reported amount in the financial statements. Examples (e)-(h) in paragraph 11 illustrate other events that create differences between the tax basis of an asset or liability and its reported amount in the financial statements. For all eight examples, the differences result in taxable or deductible amounts when the reported amount of an asset or liability in the financial statements is recovered or settled, respectively.

13. This Statement refers collectively to the types of differences illustrated by those eight examples and to the ones described in paragraph 15 as *temporary differences.* Temporary differences that will result in taxable amounts in future years when the related asset or liability is recovered or settled are often referred to in this Statement as **taxable temporary differences** (examples (a), (d), and (e) in paragraph 11 are taxable temporary differences). Likewise, temporary differences that will result in deductible amounts in future years are often referred to as **deductible temporary differences** (examples (b), (c), (f), and (g) in paragraph 11 are deductible temporary differences). Business combinations accounted for by the purchase method (example (h)) may give rise to both taxable and deductible temporary differences.

14. Certain basis differences may not result in taxable or deductible amounts in future years when the related asset or liability for financial reporting is recovered or settled and, therefore, may not be temporary differences for which a deferred tax liability or asset is recognized. One example under current U.S. tax law is the excess of cash surrender value of life insurance over premiums paid. That excess is a temporary difference if the cash surrender value is expected to be recovered by surrendering the policy, but is not a temporary difference if the asset is expected to be recovered without tax consequence upon the death of the insured (there will be no taxable amount if the insurance policy is held until the death of the insured).

15. Some temporary differences are deferred taxable income or tax deductions and have balances only on the income tax balance sheet and therefore cannot be identified with a particular asset or liability for financial reporting. That occurs, for example, when a long-term contract is accounted for by the percentage-of-completion method for financial reporting and by the completed-contract method for tax purposes. The temporary difference (income on the contract) is deferred income for tax purposes that becomes taxable when the contract is completed. Another example is organizational costs that are recognized as expenses when incurred for financial reporting and are deferred and deducted in a later year for tax purposes. In both instances, there is no related, identifiable asset or liability for financial reporting, but there is a temporary difference that results from an event that has been recognized in the financial statements and, based on provisions in the tax law, the temporary difference will result in taxable or deductible amounts in future years.

Recognition and Measurement

16. An enterprise shall recognize a deferred tax liability or asset for all temporary differences[6] and operating loss and tax credit carryforwards in accordance with the provisions of paragraph 17. **Deferred tax expense or benefit** is the change during the year in an enterprise's deferred tax liabilities and assets.[7] For deferred tax liabilities and assets acquired in a purchase business combination during the year, it is the change since the combination date. Total income tax expense or benefit for the year is the sum of deferred tax expense or benefit and income taxes currently payable or refundable.

Annual Computation of Deferred Tax Liabilities and Assets

17. Deferred taxes shall be determined separately for each tax-paying component (an individual en-

---

[6]Refer to paragraph 9. A deferred tax liability shall be recognized for the temporary differences addressed by Opinion 23 in accordance with the requirements of this Statement (paragraphs 31-34) and that Opinion, as amended.

[7]Paragraph 230 addresses the manner of reporting the transaction gain or loss that is included in the net change in a deferred foreign tax liability or asset when the reporting currency is the functional currency.

tity or group of entities that is consolidated for tax purposes) in each tax jurisdiction. That determination includes the following procedures:

a. Identify (1) the types and amounts of existing temporary differences and (2) the nature and amount of each type of operating loss and tax credit carryforward and the remaining length of the carryforward period
b. Measure the total deferred tax liability for taxable temporary differences using the applicable tax rate (paragraph 18)
c. Measure the total deferred tax asset for deductible temporary differences and operating loss carryforwards using the applicable tax rate
d. Measure deferred tax assets for each type of tax credit carryforward
e. Reduce deferred tax assets by a **valuation allowance** if, based on the weight of available evidence, it is *more likely than not* (a likelihood of more than 50 percent) that some portion or all of the deferred tax assets will not be realized. The valuation allowance should be sufficient to reduce the deferred tax asset to the amount that is more likely than not to be realized.

18. The objective is to measure a deferred tax liability or asset using the enacted tax rate(s) expected to apply to taxable income in the periods in which the deferred tax liability or asset is expected to be settled or realized. Under current U.S. federal tax law, if taxable income exceeds a specified amount, all taxable income is taxed, in substance, at a single flat tax rate. That tax rate shall be used for measurement of a deferred tax liability or asset by enterprises for which graduated tax rates are not a significant factor. Enterprises for which graduated tax rates are a significant factor shall measure a deferred tax liability or asset using the average graduated tax rate applicable to the amount of estimated annual taxable income in the periods in which the deferred tax liability or asset is estimated to be settled or realized (paragraph 236). Other provisions of enacted tax laws should be considered when determining the tax rate to apply to certain types of temporary differences and carryforwards (for example, the tax law may provide for different tax rates on ordinary income and capital gains). If there is a phased-in change in tax rates, determination of the applicable tax rate requires knowledge about when deferred tax liabilities and assets will be settled and realized.

19. In the U.S. federal tax jurisdiction, the applicable tax rate is the regular tax rate, and a deferred tax asset is recognized for alternative minimum tax credit carryforwards in accordance with the provisions of paragraph 17(d) and (e) of this Statement. If alternative tax systems exist in jurisdictions other than the U.S. federal jurisdiction, the applicable tax rate is determined in a manner consistent with the tax law after giving consideration to any interaction (that is, a mechanism similar to the U.S. alternative minimum tax credit) between the two systems.

20. All available evidence, both positive and negative, should be considered to determine whether, based on the weight of that evidence, a valuation allowance is needed. Information about an enterprise's current financial position and its results of operations for the current and preceding years ordinarily is readily available. That historical information is supplemented by all currently available information about future years. Sometimes, however, historical information may not be available (for example, start-up operations) or it may not be as relevant (for example, if there has been a significant, recent change in circumstances) and special attention is required.

21. Future realization of the tax benefit of an existing deductible temporary difference or carryforward ultimately depends on the existence of sufficient taxable income of the appropriate character (for example, ordinary income or capital gain) within the carryback, carryforward period available under the tax law. The following four possible sources of taxable income may be available under the tax law to realize a tax benefit for deductible temporary differences and carryforwards:

a. Future reversals of existing taxable temporary differences
b. Future taxable income exclusive of reversing temporary differences and carryforwards
c. Taxable income in prior carryback year(s) if carryback is permitted under the tax law
d. **Tax-planning strategies** (paragraph 22) that would, if necessary, be implemented to, for example:
   (1) Accelerate taxable amounts to utilize expiring carryforwards
   (2) Change the character of taxable or deductible amounts from ordinary income or loss to capital gain or loss
   (3) Switch from tax-exempt to taxable investments.

Evidence available about each of those possible sources of taxable income will vary for different tax jurisdictions and, possibly, from year to year. To the extent evidence about one or more sources of taxable income is sufficient to support a conclusion that a valuation allowance is not necessary, other sources need not be considered. Consideration of each source is required, however, to determine the amount of the valuation allowance that is recognized for deferred tax assets.

22. In some circumstances, there are actions (including elections for tax purposes) that (a) are prudent and feasible, (b) an enterprise ordinarily might not take, but would take to prevent an operating loss or tax credit carryforward from expiring unused, and (c) would result in realization of deferred tax assets. This Statement refers to those actions as *tax-planning strategies*. An enterprise shall consider tax-planning strategies in determining the amount of valuation allowance required. Significant expenses to implement a tax-planning strategy or any significant losses that would be recognized if that strategy were implemented (net of any recognizable tax benefits associated with those expenses or losses) shall be included in the valuation allowance. Refer to paragraphs 246-251 for additional guidance.

23. Forming a conclusion that a valuation allowance is not needed is difficult when there is negative evidence such as cumulative losses in recent years. Other examples of negative evidence include (but are not limited to) the following:

a. A history of operating loss or tax credit carryforwards expiring unused
b. Losses expected in early future years (by a presently profitable entity)
c. Unsettled circumstances that, if unfavorably resolved, would adversely affect future operations and profit levels on a continuing basis in future years
d. A carryback, carryforward period that is so brief that it would limit realization of tax benefits if (1) a significant deductible temporary difference is expected to reverse in a single year or (2) the enterprise operates in a traditionally cyclical business.

24. Examples (not prerequisites) of positive evidence that might support a conclusion that a valuation allowance is not needed when there is negative evidence include (but are not limited to) the following:

a. Existing contracts or firm sales backlog that will produce more than enough taxable income to realize the deferred tax asset based on existing sales prices and cost structures
b. An excess of appreciated asset value over the tax basis of the entity's net assets in an amount sufficient to realize the deferred tax asset
c. A strong earnings history exclusive of the loss that created the future deductible amount (tax loss carryforward or deductible temporary difference) coupled with evidence indicating that the loss (for example, an unusual, infrequent,

or extraordinary item) is an aberration rather than a continuing condition.

25. An enterprise must use judgment in considering the relative impact of negative and positive evidence. The weight given to the potential effect of negative and positive evidence should be commensurate with the extent to which it can be objectively verified. The more negative evidence that exists (a) the more positive evidence is necessary and (b) the more difficult it is to support a conclusion that a valuation allowance is not needed for some portion or all of the deferred tax asset.

A Change in the Valuation Allowance

26. The effect of a change in the beginning-of-the-year balance of a valuation allowance that results from a change in circumstances that causes a change in judgment about the realizability of the related deferred tax asset in future years ordinarily shall be included in income from continuing operations. The only exceptions are the initial recognition (that is, by elimination of the valuation allowance) of certain tax benefits that are allocated as required by paragraph 30 and paragraph 36 (items (c) and (e)-(g)). The effect of other changes in the balance of a valuation allowance are allocated among continuing operations and items other than continuing operations as required by paragraph 35.

An Enacted Change in Tax Laws or Rates

27. Deferred tax liabilities and assets shall be adjusted for the effect of a change in tax laws or rates. The effect shall be included in income from continuing operations for the period that includes the enactment date.

A Change in the Tax Status of an Enterprise

28. An enterprise's tax status may change from nontaxable to taxable or from taxable to nontaxable. An example is a change from a partnership to a corporation and vice versa. A deferred tax liability or asset shall be recognized for temporary differences in accordance with the requirements of this Statement at the date that a nontaxable enterprise becomes a taxable enterprise. A deferred tax liability or asset shall be eliminated at the date an enterprise ceases to be a taxable enterprise. In either case, the effect of (a) an election for a voluntary change in tax status is recognized on the approval date or on the filing date if approval is not necessary and (b) a change in tax status that results from a change in tax law is recognized on the enactment date. The effect of recognizing or elimi-

nating the deferred tax liability or asset shall be included in income from continuing operations.

Regulated Enterprises

29. Regulated enterprises that meet the criteria for application of FASB Statement No. 71, *Accounting for the Effects of Certain Types of Regulation*, are not exempt from the requirements of this Statement. Specifically, this Statement:

a. Prohibits net-of-tax accounting and reporting
b. Requires recognition of a deferred tax liability (1) for tax benefits that are flowed through to customers when temporary differences originate and (2) for the equity component of the allowance for funds used during construction
c. Requires adjustment of a deferred tax liability or asset for an enacted change in tax laws or rates.

If, as a result of an action by a regulator, it is probable that the future increase or decrease in taxes payable for items (b) and (c) above will be recovered from or returned to customers through future rates, an asset or liability is recognized for that probable future revenue or reduction in future revenue pursuant to paragraphs 9-11 of Statement 71. That asset or liability also is a temporary difference for which a deferred tax liability or asset shall be recognized.

Business Combinations

30. A deferred tax liability or asset shall be recognized in accordance with the requirements of this Statement for differences between the assigned values and the tax bases of the assets and liabilities (except the portion of goodwill for which amortization is not deductible for tax purposes, unallocated "negative goodwill," leveraged leases, and acquired Opinion 23 differences[8]) recognized in a purchase business combination (refer to paragraphs 259-272 for additional guidance). If a valuation allowance is recognized for the deferred tax asset for an acquired entity's deductible temporary differences or operating loss or tax credit carryforwards at the acquisition date, the tax benefits for those items that are first recognized (that is, by elimination of that valuation allowance) in financial statements after the acquisition date shall be applied (a) first to reduce to zero any goodwill related to the acquisition, (b) second to reduce to zero other noncurrent intangible assets related to the acquisition, and (c) third to reduce income tax expense.

Opinion 23 and U.S. Steamship Enterprise Temporary Differences

31. A deferred tax liability is not recognized for the following types of temporary differences unless it becomes apparent that those temporary differences will reverse in the foreseeable future:

a. An excess of the amount for financial reporting over the tax basis of an investment in a foreign subsidiary or a foreign corporate joint venture as defined in APB Opinion No. 18, *The Equity Method of Accounting for Investments in Common Stock,* that is essentially permanent in duration
b. Undistributed earnings of a domestic subsidiary or a domestic corporate joint venture that is essentially permanent in duration that arose in fiscal years beginning on or before December 15, 1992[9]
c. "Bad debt reserves" for tax purposes of U.S. savings and loan associations (and other "qualified" thrift lenders) that arose in tax years beginning before December 31, 1987 (that is, the base-year amount)
d. "Policyholders' surplus" of stock life insurance companies that arose in fiscal years beginning on or before December 15, 1992.

The indefinite reversal criterion in Opinion 23 shall not be applied to analogous types of temporary differences.

32. A deferred tax liability shall be recognized for the following types of taxable temporary differences:

a. An excess of the amount for financial reporting over the tax basis of an investment in a domestic subsidiary that arises in fiscal years beginning after December 15, 1992
b. An excess of the amount for financial reporting over the tax basis of an investment in a 50-percent-or-less-owned investee except as provided in paragraph 31(a) and (b) for a corporate joint venture that is essentially permanent in duration
c. "Bad debt reserves" for tax purposes of U.S. savings and loan associations (and other "qualified" thrift lenders) that arise in tax years beginning after December 31, 1987 (that is, amounts in excess of the base-year amount).

The tax effects of temporary differences related to deposits in statutory reserve funds by U.S. steamship enterprises that arose in fiscal years beginning on or before December 15, 1992 and that were not

---

[8]Acquired Opinion 23 differences are accounted for in accordance with the requirements of Opinion 23, as amended by this Statement.

[9]A last-in, first-out (LIFO) pattern determines whether reversals pertain to differences that arose in fiscal years beginning on or before December 15, 1992.

previously recognized shall be recognized when those temporary differences reverse or in their entirety at the beginning of the fiscal year for which this Statement is first applied.

33. Whether an excess of the amount for financial reporting over the tax basis of an investment in a more-than-50-percent-owned domestic subsidiary is a taxable temporary difference must be assessed. It is not a taxable temporary difference if the tax law provides a means by which the reported amount of that investment can be recovered tax-free and the enterprise expects that it will ultimately use that means. For example, under current U.S. federal tax law:

a. An enterprise may elect to determine taxable gain or loss on the liquidation of an 80-percent-or-more-owned subsidiary by reference to the tax basis of the subsidiary's net assets rather than by reference to the parent company's tax basis for the stock of that subsidiary.

b. An enterprise may execute a statutory merger whereby a subsidiary is merged into the parent company, the minority shareholders receive stock of the parent, the subsidiary's stock is cancelled, and no taxable gain or loss results if the continuity of ownership, continuity of business enterprise, and certain other requirements of the tax law are met.

Some elections for tax purposes are available only if the parent company owns a specified percentage of the subsidiary's stock. The parent company sometimes may own less than that specified percentage, and the price per share to acquire a minority interest may significantly exceed the per share equivalent of the amount reported as minority interest in the consolidated financial statements. In those circumstances, the excess of the amount for financial reporting over the tax basis of the parent's investment in the subsidiary is not a taxable temporary difference if settlement of the minority interest is expected to occur at the point in time when settlement would not result in a significant cost. That could occur, for example, toward the end of the life of the subsidiary, after it has recovered and settled most of its assets and liabilities, respectively. The fair value of the minority interest ordinarily will approximately equal its percentage of the subsidiary's net assets if those net assets consist primarily of cash.

34. A deferred tax asset shall be recognized for an excess of the tax basis over the amount for financial reporting of an investment in a subsidiary or corporate joint venture that is essentially permanent in duration only if it is apparent that the temporary difference will reverse in the foreseeable future. The need for a valuation allowance for that deferred tax asset and other deferred tax assets related to Opinion 23 temporary differences (for example, a deferred tax asset for foreign tax credit carryforwards or for a savings and loan association's bad-debt reserve for financial reporting) shall be assessed. Paragraph 21 identifies four sources of taxable income to be considered in determining the need for and amount of a valuation allowance for those and other deferred tax assets. One source is future reversals of temporary differences. Future reversals of taxable differences for which a deferred tax liability has not been recognized based on the exceptions cited in paragraph 31, however, shall not be considered. Another source is future taxable income exclusive of reversing temporary differences and carryforwards. Future distributions of future earnings of a subsidiary or corporate joint venture, however, shall not be considered except to the extent that a deferred tax liability has been recognized for existing undistributed earnings or earnings have been remitted in the past.

Intraperiod Tax Allocation

35. Income tax expense or benefit for the year shall be allocated among continuing operations, discontinued operations, extraordinary items, and items charged or credited directly to shareholders' equity (paragraph 36). The amount allocated to continuing operations is the tax effect of the pretax income or loss from continuing operations that occurred during the year, plus or minus income tax effects of (a) changes in circumstances that cause a change in judgment about the realization of deferred tax assets in future years (paragraph 26), (b) changes in tax laws or rates (paragraph 27), (c) changes in tax status (paragraph 28), and (d) tax-deductible dividends paid to shareholders (except as set forth in paragraph 36 for dividends paid on unallocated shares held by an employee stock ownership plan [ESOP] or any other stock compensation arrangement). The remainder is allocated to items other than continuing operations in accordance with the provisions of paragraph 38.

36. The tax effects of the following items occurring during the year are charged or credited directly to related components of shareholders' equity:

a. Adjustments of the opening balance of retained earnings for certain changes in accounting principles or a correction of an error

b. **Gains and losses included in comprehensive income but excluded from net income** (for example, translation adjustments under Statement 52 and changes in the carrying amount of marketable securities under FASB Statement No. 12, *Accounting for Certain Marketable Securities*)

c. An increase or decrease in contributed capital (for example, deductible expenditures reported as a reduction of the proceeds from issuing capital stock)

d. An increase in the tax basis of assets acquired in a taxable business combination accounted for as a pooling of interests and for which a tax benefit is recognized at the date of the business combination

e. Expenses for employee stock options recognized differently for financial reporting and tax purposes (refer to paragraph 17 of APB Opinion No. 25, *Accounting for Stock Issued to Employees*)

f. Dividends that are paid on unallocated shares held by an ESOP and that are charged to retained earnings

g. Deductible temporary differences and carryforwards that existed at the date of a quasi reorganization (except as set forth in paragraph 39).

37. The tax benefit of an operating loss carryforward or carryback (other than those carryforwards referred to at the end of this paragraph) shall be reported in the same manner as the source of the income or loss in the current year and not in the same manner as (a) the source of the operating loss carryforward or taxes paid in a prior year or (b) the source of expected future income that will result in realization of a deferred tax asset for an operating loss carryforward from the current year. The only exceptions are as follows:

a. Tax effects of deductible temporary differences and carryforwards that existed at the date of a purchase business combination and for which a tax benefit is initially recognized in subsequent years in accordance with the provisions of paragraph 30

b. Tax effects of deductible temporary differences and carryforwards that are allocated to shareholders' equity in accordance with the provisions of paragraph 36 (items (c) and (e)-(g)).

38. If there is only one item other than continuing operations, the portion of income tax expense or benefit for the year that remains after the allocation to continuing operations is allocated to that item. If there are two or more items other than continuing operations, the amount that remains after the allocation to continuing operations shall be allocated among those other items in proportion to their individual effects on income tax expense or benefit for the year. When there are two or more items other than continuing operations, the sum of the separately calculated, individual effects of each item sometimes may not equal the amount of income tax expense or benefit for the year that remains after the allocation to continuing operations. In those circumstances, the procedures to allocate the remaining amount to items other

than continuing operations are as follows:

a. Determine the effect on income tax expense or benefit for the year of the total net loss for all net loss items

b. Apportion the tax benefit determined in (a) ratably to each net loss item

c. Determine the amount that remains, that is, the difference between (1) the amount to be allocated to all items other than continuing operations and (2) the amount allocated to all net loss items

d. Apportion the tax expense determined in (c) ratably to each net gain item.

Refer to paragraphs 273-276 for additional guidance.

Certain Quasi Reorganizations

39. The tax benefits of deductible temporary differences and carryforwards as of the date of a quasi reorganization as defined and contemplated in ARB No. 43, Chapter 7, "Capital Accounts," ordinarily are reported as a direct addition to contributed capital if the tax benefits are recognized in subsequent years. The only exception is for enterprises that have previously both adopted Statement 96 and effected a quasi reorganization that involves only the elimination of a deficit in retained earnings by a concurrent reduction in contributed capital prior to adopting this Statement. For those enterprises, subsequent recognition of the tax benefit of prior deductible temporary differences and carryforwards is included in income and reported as required by paragraph 37 (without regard to the referenced exceptions) and then reclassified from retained earnings to contributed capital. Those enterprises should disclose (a) the date of the quasi reorganization, (b) the manner of reporting the tax benefits and that it differs from present accounting requirements for other enterprises and (c) the effect of those tax benefits on income from continuing operations, income before extraordinary items, and on net income (and on related per share amounts).

Separate Financial Statements of a Subsidiary

40. The consolidated amount of current and deferred tax expense for a group that files a consolidated tax return shall be allocated among the members of the group when those members issue separate financial statements. This Statement does not require a single allocation method. The method adopted, however, shall be systematic, rational, and consistent with the broad principles established by this Statement. A method that allocates current and deferred taxes to members of the group by applying this Statement to each member

as if it were a separate taxpayer[10] meets those criteria. Examples of methods that are not consistent with the broad principles established by this Statement include:

a. A method that allocates only current taxes payable to a member of the group that has taxable temporary differences
b. A method that allocates deferred taxes to a member of the group using a method fundamentally different from the asset and liability method described in this Statement (for example, the Opinion 11 deferred method)
c. A method that allocates no current or deferred tax expense to a member of the group that has taxable income because the consolidated group has no current or deferred tax expense.

Certain disclosures are also required (paragraph 49).

Financial Statement Presentation

41. In a classified statement of financial position, an enterprise shall separate deferred tax liabilities and assets into a current amount and a noncurrent amount. Deferred tax liabilities and assets shall be classified as current or noncurrent based on the classification of the related asset or liability for financial reporting. A deferred tax liability or asset that is not related to an asset or liability for financial reporting (paragraph 15), including deferred tax assets related to carryforwards, shall be classified according to the expected reversal date of the temporary difference pursuant to FASB Statement No. 37, *Balance Sheet Classification of Deferred Income Taxes.* The valuation allowance for a particular tax jurisdiction shall be allocated between current and noncurrent deferred tax assets for that tax jurisdiction on a pro rata basis.

42. For a particular tax-paying component of an enterprise and within a particular tax jurisdiction, (a) all current deferred tax liabilities and assets shall be offset and presented as a single amount and (b) all noncurrent deferred tax liabilities and assets shall be offset and presented as a single amount. However, an enterprise shall not offset deferred tax liabilities and assets attributable to different tax-paying components of the enterprise or to different tax jurisdictions.

Financial Statement Disclosure

43. The components of the net deferred tax liability or asset recognized in an enterprise's statement of financial position shall be disclosed as follows:

a. The total of all deferred tax liabilities measured in procedure (b) of paragraph 17
b. The total of all deferred tax assets measured in procedures (c) and (d) of paragraph 17
c. The total valuation allowance recognized for deferred tax assets determined in procedure (e) of paragraph 17.

The net change during the year in the total valuation allowance also shall be disclosed. A **public enterprise** shall disclose the approximate tax effect of each type of temporary difference and carryforward that gives rise to a significant portion of deferred tax liabilities and deferred tax assets (before allocation of valuation allowances). A **nonpublic enterprise** shall disclose the types of significant temporary differences and carryforwards but may omit disclosure of the tax effects of each type. A public enterprise that is not subject to income taxes because its income is taxed directly to its owners shall disclose that fact and the net difference between the tax bases and the reported amounts of the enterprise's assets and liabilities.

44. The following information shall be disclosed whenever a deferred tax liability is not recognized because of the exceptions to comprehensive recognition of deferred taxes for any of the areas addressed by Opinion 23 (as amended by this Statement) or for deposits in statutory reserve funds by U.S. steamship enterprises:

a. A description of the types of temporary differences for which a deferred tax liability has not been recognized and the types of events that would cause those temporary differences to become taxable
b. The cumulative amount of each type of temporary difference
c. The amount of the unrecognized deferred tax liability for temporary differences related to investments in foreign subsidiaries and foreign corporate joint ventures that are essentially permanent in duration if determination of that lia-

---

[10]In that situation, the sum of the amounts allocated to individual members of the group may not equal the consolidated amount. That may also be the result when there are intercompany transactions between members of the group. The criteria are satisfied, nevertheless, after giving effect to the type of adjustments (including eliminations) normally present in preparing consolidated financial statements.

bility is practicable or a statement that determination is not practicable

d. The amount of the deferred tax liability for temporary differences other than those in (c) above (that is, undistributed domestic earnings, the bad-debt reserve for tax purposes of a U.S. savings and loan association or other qualified thrift lender, the policyholders' surplus of a life insurance enterprise, and the statutory reserve funds of a U.S. steamship enterprise) that is not recognized in accordance with the provisions of paragraphs 31 and 32.

45. The significant components of income tax expense attributable to continuing operations for each year presented shall be disclosed in the financial statements or notes thereto. Those components would include, for example:

a. **Current tax expense or benefit**
b. Deferred tax expense or benefit (exclusive of the effects of other components listed below)
c. Investment tax credits
d. Government grants (to the extent recognized as a reduction of income tax expense)
e. The benefits of operating loss carryforwards
f. Tax expense that results from allocating certain tax benefits either directly to contributed capital or to reduce goodwill or other noncurrent intangible assets of an acquired entity
g. Adjustments of a deferred tax liability or asset for enacted changes in tax laws or rates or a change in the tax status of the enterprise
h. Adjustments of the beginning-of-the-year balance of a valuation allowance because of a change in circumstances that causes a change in judgment about the realizability of the related deferred tax asset in future years.

46. The amount of income tax expense or benefit allocated to continuing operations and the amounts separately allocated to other items (in accordance with the provisions of paragraphs 35-39) shall be disclosed for each year for which those items are presented.

47. A public enterprise shall disclose a reconciliation using percentages or dollar amounts of (a) the reported amount of income tax expense attributable to continuing operations for the year to (b) the amount of income tax expense that would result from applying domestic federal statutory tax rates to pretax income from continuing operations. The "statutory" tax rates shall be the regular tax rates if there are alternative tax systems. The estimated amount and the nature of each significant reconciling item shall be disclosed. A nonpublic enterprise shall disclose the nature of significant reconciling items but may omit a numerical

reconciliation. If not otherwise evident from the disclosures required by this paragraph and paragraphs 43-46, all enterprises shall disclose the nature and effect of any other significant matters affecting comparability of information for all periods presented.

48. An enterprise shall disclose (a) the amounts and expiration dates of operating loss and tax credit carryforwards for tax purposes and (b) any portion of the valuation allowance for deferred tax assets for which subsequently recognized tax benefits will be allocated to reduce goodwill or other noncurrent intangible assets of an acquired entity or directly to contributed capital (paragraphs 30 and 36).

49. An entity that is a member of a group that files a consolidated tax return shall disclose in its separately issued financial statements:

a. The aggregate amount of current and deferred tax expense for each statement of earnings presented and the amount of any tax-related balances due to or from affiliates as of the date of each statement of financial position presented
b. The principal provisions of the method by which the consolidated amount of current and deferred tax expense is allocated to members of the group and the nature and effect of any changes in that method (and in determining related balances to or from affiliates) during the years for which the disclosures in (a) above are presented.

Effective Date and Transition

50. This Statement shall be effective for fiscal years beginning after December 15, 1992. Earlier application is encouraged. Financial statements for any number of consecutive fiscal years before the effective date may be restated to conform to the provisions of this Statement. Initial application of this Statement shall be as of the beginning of an enterprise's fiscal year (that is, if the Statement is adopted prior to the effective date and during an interim period other than the first interim period, all prior interim periods of that fiscal year shall be restated). Application of the requirements for recognition of a deferred tax liability or asset for a restated interim or annual period shall be based on the facts and circumstances as they existed at that prior date and without the benefit of hindsight.

51. The effect of initially applying this Statement shall be reported as the effect of a change in accounting principle in a manner similar to the cumulative effect of a change in accounting principle

(APB Opinion No. 20, *Accounting Changes,* paragraph 20) except for initially recognized tax benefits of the type required by this Statement to be excluded from comprehensive income. If the earliest year restated is not presented in the financial statements, the beginning balance of retained earnings and, if necessary, any other components of shareholders' equity for the earliest year presented shall be adjusted for the effect of the restatement as of that date. Paragraph 30 addresses the manner of reporting acquired tax benefits initially recognized subsequent to a business combination and paragraph 36 identifies five items ((c)-(g)) for which tax benefits are excluded from comprehensive income and allocated directly to contributed capital or retained earnings. Pro forma effects of retroactive application (Opinion 20, paragraph 21) are not required if statements of earnings presented for prior years are not restated.

52. When initially presented, the financial statements for the year this Statement is first adopted shall disclose:

a. The effect, if any, of adopting this Statement on pretax income from continuing operations (for example, the effect of adjustments for prior purchase business combinations and for regulated enterprises) for the year of adoption if restated financial statements for the prior year are not presented
b. The effect of any restatement on income from continuing operations, income before extraordinary items, and net income (and on related per share amounts) for each year for which restated financial statements are presented.

Prior Business Combinations

53. If financial statements for prior years are restated, all purchase business combinations that were consummated in those prior years shall be remeasured in accordance with the requirements of this Statement.

54. For a purchase business combination consummated prior to the beginning of the year for which this Statement is first applied, any balance remaining as of that date for goodwill or negative goodwill shall not be adjusted to equal the amount it would be if financial statements for the year of the combination and subsequent years were restated. However, except for leveraged leases and except as provided in paragraph 55, (a) remaining balances as of the date of initially applying this Statement for assets and liabilities acquired in that combination shall be adjusted from their net-of-tax amounts to their pretax amounts and (b) any differences between those adjusted remaining balances and their tax bases are temporary differences. A deferred tax liability or asset shall be recognized for those temporary differences pursuant to the requirements of this Statement as of the beginning of the year for which this Statement is first applied.

55. If, for a particular business combination, determination of the adjustment for any or all of the assets and liabilities referred to in paragraph 54 is impracticable, either because the necessary information is no longer available or because the cost to develop that information is excessive, none of the remaining balances of any assets and liabilities acquired in that combination shall be adjusted to pretax amounts, that is, all remaining amounts that were originally assigned on a net-of-tax basis pursuant to paragraph 89 of Opinion 16 shall not be adjusted. Any differences between those unadjusted remaining balances and their tax bases are temporary differences, and a deferred tax liability or asset shall be recognized for those temporary differences pursuant to the requirements of this Statement as of the beginning of the year for which this Statement is first applied.

56. The net effect of the adjustments required by paragraphs 54 and 55 shall be included in the effect of initially applying this Statement and reported in accordance with the provisions of paragraph 51.

Assets of Regulated Enterprises Reported on a Net-of-Tax or After-Tax Basis

57. Some regulated enterprises that apply Statement 71 have accounted for certain components of construction in progress on either a net-of-tax or after-tax basis, or both. Upon initial application of this Statement, those enterprises shall make appropriate adjustments required by this Statement to account for the net-of-tax and after-tax components of construction in progress as if the requirements of this Statement were applied to that construction in progress in all prior years. Except as provided in paragraph 58, the reported amount of plant in service at the beginning of the year for which this Statement is first applied shall be similarly adjusted.

58. If determination of the adjustment to plant in service referred to in paragraph 57 is impracticable, either because the necessary information is no longer available or because the cost to develop that information is excessive, any difference between the reported amount and the tax basis of that plant in service is a temporary difference, and a deferred tax liability shall be recognized for that temporary difference. If, as a result of an action by a regulator, it is probable that amounts required

for settlement of that deferred tax liability will be recovered from customers through future rates, an asset and the related deferred tax liability for that additional temporary difference shall be recognized for that probable future revenue.

59. The net effect of the adjustments required by paragraphs 57 and 58 shall be included in the effect of initially applying this Statement and reported in accordance with the provisions of paragraph 51.

> **The provisions of this Statement need not be applied to immaterial items.**

This Statement was adopted by the unanimous vote of the six members of the Financial Accounting Standards Board:

Dennis R. Beresford, *Chairman* Joseph V. Anania	Victor H. Brown James J. Leisenring	A. Clarence Sampson Robert J. Swieringa

Appendix A

BASIS FOR CONCLUSIONS

CONTENTS

Appendix A

BASIS FOR CONCLUSIONS

Introduction

60. This appendix summarizes considerations that members of the Board deemed significant in reaching the conclusions in this Statement. It includes reasons for accepting certain views and rejecting others. Individual Board members gave greater weight to some factors than to others.

61. The tax consequences of most events affect taxable income for the year the events are recognized in the financial statements. The tax consequences of some events are deferred and will affect taxable income in future years. Events that have **deferred tax consequences** give rise to temporary differences. Paragraphs 10-15 discuss examples of temporary differences and describe how they originate and how they result in taxable or deductible amounts in future years.

62. The basic accounting issues about the effects of income taxes to be recognized in the financial statements for a period are as follows:

a. Whether the effects of income taxes recognized in the financial statements should be:
  (1) The amount of taxes payable for the period as determined by the tax return
  (2) The above plus the effect of all (comprehensive recognition) or at least some (partial recognition) temporary differences
  (3) The above plus the future tax benefit of operating loss and tax credit carryforwards

b. If recognized, whether the tax effects of temporary differences are:
  (1) Tax assets or liabilities to be recovered or settled in the future (the asset and liability approach)
  (2) Reductions in related assets and liabilities (the net-of-tax approach)
  (3) Deferred charges or deferred credits (the deferred approach)
  (4) A combination of the above based on the nature of the temporary differences

c. Whether measurement of the tax effects of temporary differences should be:
  (1) The incremental effect in the current year or the incremental effect in future years
  (2) Discounted

d. Whether deferred tax calculations are too complex, burdensome, and costly for:
  (1) Private and small public enterprises
  (2) All enterprises.

Conclusions on Basic Issues

63. The Board concluded that the financial statements should reflect the current and deferred tax consequences of all events[11] that have been recognized in the financial statements or tax returns. The Board believes that the asset and liability approach to accounting for income taxes is most consistent with the definitions in FASB Concepts Statement No. 6, *Elements of Financial Statements,* and with other parts of the conceptual framework. It also believes that the asset and liability approach produces the most useful and understandable information and that it is no more complex than any other approach to accounting for income taxes.

---
[11]Refer to paragraph 9.

64. The Board concluded that a current tax liability or asset should be recognized for taxes payable or refundable for the current year, and that a deferred tax liability or asset should be recognized for the deferred tax consequences of temporary differences and operating loss or tax credit carryforwards. The Board's reasons for rejecting partial or no recognition of deferred taxes are explained in paragraphs 200-205, and the reasons for rejecting the net-of-tax, deferred, and combination approaches are explained in paragraphs 206-222.

65. The Board believes that it would be desirable to measure a deferred tax liability or asset as the incremental effect on future cash flows for income taxes that will result from existing temporary differences and carryforwards. As a practical matter, however, the Board notes that the information needed for precise predictions about the future is not available. The Board concluded that certain simplifying assumptions and procedures are necessary.

66. Under the requirements of this Statement:

a. The enacted tax rate(s) expected to apply to taxable income in future years is used to measure:
   (1) The total deferred tax liability for taxable temporary differences
   (2) The total deferred tax asset for deductible temporary differences and operating loss carryforwards.
b. The total deferred tax asset is reduced by a valuation allowance if it is more likely than not that some portion or all of the asset will not be realized.
c. Deferred tax liabilities and assets are not discounted.

67. Measurement of current and deferred tax liabilities and assets is based on provisions of the enacted tax law; the effects of future changes in tax laws or rates are not anticipated. Calculations may often be complicated, but the Board believes that most of those complications are primarily attributable to applying the complexities in the tax law to complex business transactions. The Board concluded that complexities in the tax law do not justify different accounting for income taxes depending on an enterprise's size or ownership.

Benefits and Costs

68. The Board follows certain precepts, including the precept to promulgate standards only when the expected benefits of the resulting information exceed the perceived costs. The Board strives to determine that a proposed standard will fill a significant need and that the costs imposed to meet that standard, as compared with other alternatives, are justified in relation to the overall benefits of the resulting information.

69. Accounting for income taxes is a pervasive subject that affects most enterprises. Income taxes must be computed for complex business transactions within the context of voluminous, complicated, and constantly changing tax laws, rules, and regulations. Accounting requirements add additional complexities.

70. Opinion 11 was issued in 1967. Criticisms and concerns set forth in the accounting literature and in letters to the Board that requested reconsideration of Opinion 11 focused both on the complexity of the accounting requirements and on the relevance of the results of applying the requirements.

71. Numerous accounting pronouncements amended, interpreted, or supplemented Opinion 11 for areas that were not addressed or were not clear in that Opinion and for changes in the tax law. One criticism was that the various accounting requirements were inconsistent and that the results of applying them could only be described in terms of a mechanical process. Another criticism was that the time devoted to coping with the complexities and ambiguities of the requirements was not cost-beneficial when compared with the usefulness of the resulting information.

72. Criticisms and concerns also focused on the effect of applying Opinion 11 on the statement of financial position and on the increasing amounts of deferred tax credits reported by many enterprises. As measured and recognized under the requirements of Opinion 11, deferred tax credits and charges were not payables or receivables. Because those items were often considered to be only "bookkeeping" entries, some users of financial statements added deferred tax credits to shareholders' equity, and they also added the provision for deferred taxes back to earnings. Others did not. Uncertainty about the nature of those amounts created confusion for users.

73. Statement 96 was issued in December 1987. After it was issued, the Board received numerous requests to amend Statement 96. Those requests primarily focused on (a) changing the restrictive Statement 96 requirements for recognition of deferred tax assets to permit, in more instances, recognition of tax benefits that are expected to be realized and (b) reducing the complexity of scheduling the future reversals of temporary differences and considering hypothetical tax-planning strategies. The Board carefully considered the criticisms and concerns about the complexity of the requirements of Statement 96

and the understandability of the results of applying those requirements.

74. This Statement is the result of a comprehensive reconsideration of Opinion 11, Statement 96, and other related authoritative pronouncements. The Board believes that the requirements of this Statement produce results that are understandable and relevant. The Board also believes that the requirements are less complex than those of either Opinion 11 or Statement 96. Practical decisions, such as eliminating the proposal in the June 1991 FASB Exposure Draft, *Accounting for Income Taxes,* to recognize deferred taxes for certain temporary differences that are not timing differences, may reduce the cost and complexity of computing deferred taxes for many enterprises. Application of judgment to assess whether a valuation allowance is needed for deferred tax assets may sometimes be complex, but that complexity is the unavoidable result of the need for an informed decision about the effect of income taxes on an enterprise's financial position and results of operations.

A Deferred Tax Liability for Taxable Temporary Differences

75. The Board considered whether the deferred tax consequences of taxable temporary differences are a liability. Liabilities are defined in paragraph 35 of Concepts Statement 6 as "probable future sacrifices of economic benefits arising from present obligations of a particular entity to transfer assets or provide services to other entities in the future as a result of past transactions or events" (footnote references omitted).

76. The first characteristic of a liability is that it "embodies a present duty or responsibility to one or more other entities that entails settlement by probable future transfer or use of assets at a specified or determinable date, on occurrence of a specified event, or on demand" (Concepts Statement 6, paragraph 36). Taxes are a legal obligation imposed by a government, and an obligation for the deferred tax consequences of taxable temporary differences stems from the requirements of the tax law.

77. A government levies taxes on net taxable income. Temporary differences will become taxable amounts in future years, thereby increasing taxable income and taxes payable, upon recovery or settlement of the recognized and reported amounts of an enterprise's assets or liabilities.

78. The second characteristic of a liability is that "the duty or responsibility obligates a particular entity, leaving it little or no discretion to avoid the future sacrifice" (Concepts Statement 6, paragraph 36). An enterprise might be able to delay the future reversal of taxable temporary differences by delaying the events that give rise to those reversals, for example, by delaying the recovery of related assets or the settlement of related liabilities. A contention that those temporary differences will never result in taxable amounts, however, would contradict the accounting assumption inherent in the statement of financial position that the reported amounts of assets and liabilities will be recovered and settled, respectively; thereby making that statement internally inconsistent. For that reason, the Board concluded that the only question is when, not whether, temporary differences will result in taxable amounts in future years.

79. The third characteristic of a liability is that "the transaction or other event obligating the entity has already happened" (Concepts Statement 6, paragraph 36). Deferred tax liabilities result from the same past events that create taxable temporary differences.

A Deferred Tax Asset for Deductible Temporary Differences and Carryforwards

80. The Board considered whether the deferred tax consequences of deductible temporary differences and carryforwards are an asset. Assets are defined in paragraph 25 of Concepts Statement 6 as "probable future economic benefits obtained or controlled by a particular entity as a result of past transactions or events" (footnote reference omitted).

81. The first characteristic of an asset is that it "embodies a probable future benefit that involves a capacity, singly or in combination with other assets, to contribute directly or indirectly to future net cash inflows" (Concepts Statement 6, paragraph 26). Deductible temporary differences and carryforwards at the end of the current year that reduce taxable income and taxes payable in future years contribute indirectly to future net cash inflows. Alternatively, if loss carryback is permitted by the tax law, deductible temporary differences at the end of the current year that increase taxes refundable in future years contribute directly to future net cash inflows. In both circumstances, the first characteristic of an asset is met.

82. The second characteristic of an asset is that "a particular entity can obtain the benefit and control others' access to it" (Concepts Statement 6, paragraph 26). To the extent permitted by tax law, an enterprise has the ability to obtain the benefit that may result from existing deductible temporary differences and carryforwards by reducing taxes payable either for future years or for the current or preceding years by carryback refund. The enterprise has an exclusive right to that future benefit and therefore can control others' access to it.

83. The third characteristic of an asset is that "the transaction or other event giving rise to the entity's right to or control of the benefit has already occurred" (Concepts Statement 6, paragraph 26). The Board's conclusion in Statement 96 was that the critical past event is earning the income that permits realization of the benefit. Prior to earning income, deductible temporary differences and carryforwards were considered to be future tax benefits that are not yet recognizable in the financial statements.

84. The Statement 96 requirements for recognition of the tax benefit of deductible temporary differences and carryforwards were criticized by the Board's constituents. Many constituents stated that Statement 96 sometimes produced results that were not understandable or relevant. Some constituents were particularly concerned about the nonrecognition of tax benefits that are expected to be realized.

85. Upon reconsidering the requirements of Statement 96, the Board decided that the critical recognition event is the event that gives rise to deductible temporary differences and carryforwards. The Exposure Draft proposed, and most respondents agreed, that that event is the event that gives the enterprise a right to or control over the future tax benefits. Once that event has occurred, those tax benefits are recognizable in the financial statements.

86. A tax benefit will be realized, however, only if there is sufficient taxable income in particular future years. The existence or absence of future taxable income is critical to measurement of the amount of tax benefit that is recognized for deductible temporary differences and carryforwards at the end of the current year. The Board concluded that earning taxable income in future years (a) is the event that confirms the existence of a recognizable tax benefit at the end of the current year and (b) is not the prerequisite event that must occur before a tax benefit may be recognized as was the case under the requirements of Statement 96.

The Asset and Liability Approach to Accounting for Income Taxes

87. In concept, a deferred tax liability or asset represents the increase or decrease in taxes payable or refundable in future years as a result of temporary differences and carryforwards at the end of the current year. That concept is an incremental concept. A literal application of that concept would require measurement of:

a. The amount of taxes that *will* be payable or refundable in future years *inclusive* of reversing temporary differences and carryforwards

b. The amount of taxes that *would* be payable or refundable in future years *exclusive* of reversing temporary differences and carryforwards.

The incremental tax effect is the difference between those measurements.

88. As a practical matter, the Board believes that determination of the incremental difference between all future income tax cash flows with and without reversing temporary differences and carryforwards is impossible except in the simplest situations. For that reason, the Board decided to establish procedures (a) to measure deferred tax liabilities and assets using a tax rate convention and then (b) to assess whether a valuation allowance should be established for deferred tax assets.

Measurement

89. The Exposure Draft proposed that deferred tax liabilities and assets should be measured using the enacted tax rate expected to apply to the *last* dollars of taxable income in the periods in which the deferred tax liability or asset is expected to be settled or realized. Some respondents to the Exposure Draft disagreed. In their view, that approach would often overstate deferred tax liabilities and assets for enterprises for which graduated tax rates are a significant factor. For example, if the highest graduated tax rate is for taxable income in excess of $1,000, that tax rate would be the tax rate for measurement of deferred taxes if future annual taxable income is expected to be $1,001. However, lower graduated tax rates would actually apply to all but the last dollar of annual reversals of temporary differences in future years. For that reason, the Board decided to adopt the average graduated tax rate approach required by this Statement for enterprises for which graduated tax rates are a significant factor.

90. A few respondents to the Exposure Draft suggested measurement of deferred taxes using the lower alternative minimum tax (AMT) rate if an enterprise currently is an AMT taxpayer and expects to "always" be an AMT taxpayer. The Board believes that no one can predict whether an enterprise will always be an AMT taxpayer. Furthermore, it would be counterintuitive if the addition of AMT provisions to the tax law were to have the effect of reducing the amount of an enterprise's income tax expense for financial reporting, given that the provisions of AMT may be either neutral or adverse but never beneficial to an enterprise. It also would be counterintuitive to assume that an enterprise would permit its AMT credit carryforward to expire unused at the end of the life of the enterprise, which would have to occur if that enterprise was "always" an AMT taxpayer.

91. The Board concluded that all enterprises should measure deferred taxes for temporary differences using regular tax rates and assess the need for a valuation allowance for an AMT credit carryforward deferred tax asset using the guidance in this Statement. Otherwise, an enterprise's deferred tax liability could be understated for either of two reasons:

a. It could be understated if the enterprise currently is an AMT taxpayer because of temporary differences. Temporary differences reverse and, over the entire life of the enterprise, cumulative income will be taxed at regular tax rates.
b. It could be understated if the enterprise currently is an AMT taxpayer because of preference items but does not have enough AMT credit carryforward to reduce its deferred tax liability from the amount of regular tax on regular tax temporary differences to the amount of tentative minimum tax (TMT) on AMT temporary differences. In those circumstances, measurement of the deferred tax liability using AMT rates would anticipate the tax benefit of future special deductions, such as statutory depletion, which have not yet been earned.

Realizability of Deferred Tax Assets

92. The Board considered two basic approaches to the measurement of deferred tax assets. Under one approach, the "affirmative judgment" approach, a deferred tax asset is recognized for deductible temporary differences and carryforwards *if,* based on an affirmative judgment, that asset will be realized. Under the other approach, the "impairment" approach, a deferred tax asset is recognized for deductible temporary differences and carryforwards *unless* that asset is deemed to be impaired.

93. The Board also considered whether the criterion for either (a) future realization of the asset (under the affirmative judgment approach) or (b) impairment of the asset should be (1) "probable," (2) "more likely than not," or (3) something else.

94. Concepts Statement 6 defines assets and liabilities, in part, as *probable* future economic benefits and *probable* future sacrifices of economic benefits, respectively. But footnotes 18 and 21 explain that probable refers to "that which can reasonably be expected or believed on the basis of available evidence or logic but is neither certain nor proved" and is not used "in a specific accounting or technical sense (such as that in FASB Statement No. 5, *Accounting for Contingencies,* par. 3)."

95. For purposes of measurement of a deferred tax asset, the Board rejected *probable* as that term is used in Statement 5. The limited amount of information available about the future contributes to the following results of using that criterion in conjunction with each basic approach:

a. *Affirmative judgment approach.* A deferred tax asset would be recognized if it is probable that the asset *will* be realized. The problem is that recognition of a deferred tax asset that is *expected* to be realized is prohibited when the likelihood of realizing that asset is considered to be less than probable. The Board believes that result is unacceptable.
b. *Impairment approach.* A deferred tax asset would be recognized unless it is probable that the asset *will not* be realized. The problem is that recognition of a deferred tax asset that is not *expected* to be realized is nevertheless required when the likelihood of not realizing that asset is considered to be less than probable. The Board believes that result also is unacceptable.

96. The Board believes that the criterion required for measurement of a deferred tax asset should be one that produces accounting results that come closest to the expected outcome, that is, realization or nonrealization of the deferred tax asset in future years. For that reason, the Board selected *more likely than not* as the criterion for measurement of a deferred tax asset. Based on that criterion, (a) recognition of a deferred tax asset that is expected to be realized is required, and (b) recognition of a deferred tax asset that is not expected to be realized is prohibited.

97. The Board intends *more likely than not* to mean a level of likelihood that is more than 50 percent. Selection of more likely than not as the criterion for measurement of a deferred tax asset is intended to virtually eliminate any distinction between the impairment and affirmative judgment approaches. In practice, there should be no substantive difference between the accounting results of either:

a. Recognition of a deferred tax asset if the likelihood of realizing the future tax benefit is more than 50 percent (the affirmative judgment approach)
b. Recognition of a deferred tax asset unless the likelihood of not realizing the future tax benefit is more than 50 percent (the impairment approach).

98. The Board acknowledges that future realization of a tax benefit sometimes will be expected for a portion but not all of a deferred tax asset, and that the dividing line between the two portions may be unclear. In those circumstances, application of judgment based on a careful assessment of all available evidence is required to determine the

portion of a deferred tax asset for which it is more likely than not a tax benefit will not be realized. Most respondents to the Exposure Draft supported the impairment approach based on the criterion of more likely than not and believed that the guidance for exercise of judgment as provided in paragraphs 20-25 is sufficient.

Cumulative Losses in Recent Years

99. The Board considered whether there should be different requirements for recognition of a deferred tax asset for (a) deductible temporary differences and (b) tax loss carryforwards. The Board believes that, in substance, both are the same—both are amounts deductible on tax returns in future years. For example, a decision about whether to fund accrued pension costs currently will determine whether an enterprise has a tax loss carryforward or a deductible temporary difference if that enterprise otherwise has zero taxable income in the current year. The Board concluded that there should not be different requirements for recognition of a deferred tax asset for deductible temporary differences and tax loss carryforwards.

100. The Board also considered whether the criterion for recognition of a deferred tax asset should be at a higher level such as *assured beyond a reasonable doubt* when there is a cumulative pretax loss for financial reporting for the current and two preceding years. The rationale for that sort of requirement would be that cumulative losses in recent years is significant negative evidence about an enterprise's profitability that creates significant uncertainty about an enterprise's ability to earn taxable income and realize tax benefits in future years. When that condition exists, a more restrictive criterion for recognition of a deferred tax asset might be warranted to offset potential undue optimism concerning an enterprise's future profitability.

101. The Board is concerned, however, about the numerous implementation issues that would arise in applying a three-year cumulative loss test or some other similar test on a taxable entity by entity basis within consolidated financial statements. Implementation issues would include matters such as intercompany transactions, foreign operations, and business combinations accounted for by the purchase method. Numerous and detailed implementation rules for a three-year cumulative loss test would significantly increase the complexity of understanding and applying the requirements of this Statement.

102. The Board also is concerned about the effect on earnings when an enterprise moves into or out of a three-year cumulative loss status. When an enterprise moves into a three-year cumulative loss status, the assured beyond a reasonable doubt criterion ordinarily would (a) prohibit recognition of a tax benefit for the current year loss and (b) require recognition of a valuation allowance for deferred tax assets originally recognized in prior years. In those circumstances, deferred tax expense from elimination of the deferred tax asset would be added to a pretax loss to produce a larger net loss. Similarly, when an enterprise moves out of a three-year cumulative loss status, the more likely than not criterion might remove the need for a valuation allowance. In those circumstances, a deferred tax benefit from reinstatement of the deferred tax asset would be added to pretax income to produce a larger net income.

103. The Board believes that the more likely than not criterion required by this Statement is capable of appropriately dealing with all forms of negative evidence, including cumulative losses in recent years. That criterion requires positive evidence of sufficient quality and quantity to counteract negative evidence in order to support a conclusion that, based on the weight of *all* available evidence, a valuation allowance is not needed. A cumulative loss in recent years is a significant piece of negative evidence that is difficult to overcome. For that reason, the Board concluded that a more restrictive criterion such as assured beyond a reasonable doubt is not necessary.

Tax-Planning Strategies

104. Statement 96 prohibited anticipation of taxable income expected to be earned in future years for purposes of recognizing a tax benefit for deductible temporary differences and carryforwards at the end of the current year. Within the bounds of that constraint, however, Statement 96 required consideration of tax-planning strategies that maximize the amount of tax benefits recognizable in the current year. As a result, an enterprise was required to identify and recognize the effect of strategies that the enterprise did not expect to implement if it expected to be profitable in future years. Many of the Board's constituents believed that requirement for "hypothetical" strategies was complex and confusing.

105. This Statement requires consideration of future taxable income and other available evidence when assessing the need for a valuation allowance. Various assumptions and strategies (including elections for tax purposes) are implicit in estimates of expected future taxable income. The Board concluded that it should not try to establish detailed criteria and other rules and requirements for those types of assumptions and strategies.

106. A tax-planning strategy, as that term is used in this Statement, is a possible source of taxable in-

come that must be considered only in determining the amount of valuation allowance required. It is an action that an enterprise ordinarily might not implement but would implement, if necessary, to realize a tax benefit for an operating loss or tax credit carryforward before it expires. The existence of a tax-planning strategy demonstrates that a valuation allowance is not needed for some portion or all of a deferred tax asset.

107. A tax-planning strategy must be prudent and feasible. If an action is not prudent, management probably would not do it. If an action is not feasible, management does not have the ability to do it. Implementation of the tax-planning strategy must be primarily within the control of management but need not be within the unilateral control of management.

108. Statement 96 prohibited any tax-planning strategy that is expected to result in a significant cost. That requirement was consistent with the Statement 96 requirement to not anticipate any future events that are not inherently assumed in the financial statements. That requirement is not consistent, however, with this Statement's requirement to assess all available evidence to determine whether a valuation allowance is needed.

109. The Board concluded that tax-planning strategies that are expected to result in a significant cost should not be prohibited. The tax benefit recognized as a result of a tax-planning strategy, however, should be net of any significant expenses to implement that tax-planning strategy or any significant losses that would be recognized if that tax-planning strategy is implemented. The Board believes that it would be inappropriate to recognize a tax benefit in the current year and postpone recognition of any expenses or losses necessary to generate that tax benefit to a later year.

Change in Valuation Allowance

110. Some respondents to the Exposure Draft proposed that the current-year tax effect of a change in the valuation allowance for a deferred tax asset related to prior-year losses or expenses that were charged direct to equity pursuant to Statement 12, 52, or FASB Statement No. 60, *Accounting and Reporting by Insurance Enterprises,* also should be allocated direct to equity rather than to continuing operations. In effect, those respondents recommend a current-year correction of the after-tax amount of those losses or expenses originally reported in a prior year. But no respondent recommended current-year corrections of the after-tax amount of prior-year extraordinary gains or prior-year gains that were credited direct to equity. That situation could arise, for example, if the current-year loss from continuing operations

(a) offsets a deferred tax liability for a prior-year Statement 52 hedging gain or (b) results in a refund of taxes paid on a prior-year extraordinary gain.

111. The Board believes that there is no conceptual basis to require current-year corrections for the after-tax amount of prior-year losses or expenses while not requiring the same treatment of prior-year gains. Furthermore, current-year corrections of the after-tax amount of both gains and losses that occurred in prior years would be very complex. For those reasons, the Board decided that this Statement should retain the proposals in the Exposure Draft.

Changes in Tax Law and Tax Status

112. A change in tax law or rate or a change in the tax status of an enterprise is an event that has economic consequences for an enterprise in the year that the change occurs, that is, in the year that a change in tax law or rate is enacted or a change in tax status is approved. As a result of the change, deferred tax consequences become larger or smaller. Conceptually, it could be argued that an enterprise should anticipate the tax effect of an expected future change in tax law or rate or a change in tax status on its deferred tax liability or asset at the end of the current year. The Board believes, however, that recognition of those tax consequences in the year that a change occurs permits a more reliable measurement of the economic effects of an enacted change in tax law or rate or a change in the tax status of an enterprise.

113. Some respondents to the Exposure Draft proposed that the tax effect of an enacted change in tax rates on temporary differences related to a prior-year gain or loss that was reported as an extraordinary item, discontinued operations, or an item of comprehensive income excluded from net income should be reported in the same manner as that gain or loss was reported in the prior year. The Board concluded that it should not require reporting portions of the tax effect of an enacted change in tax rates (or a change in a valuation allowance as discussed above) as extraordinary items, and so forth, to remeasure in the current year the after-tax amount of gains and losses that occurred and were reported in prior years. The Board decided that the entire tax effect of a change in enacted tax rates should be allocated to continuing operations in order to avoid the sometimes complex problems of tracing back to events of prior years in conjunction with:

a. Many different types of temporary differences
b. Incremental tax rates (used for intraperiod allocation) that may be different from statutory tax rates

c. Operating loss and tax credit carrybacks and carryforwards.

Temporary Differences That Are Not Timing Differences

114. This Statement, and Statement 96 before it, requires recognition of a deferred tax liability or asset for temporary differences that are not timing differences under Opinion 11. Some of the Board's constituents objected to that requirement of Statement 96 for three particular types of temporary differences because of a perceived "conflict of concepts" with some other authoritative accounting pronouncement. The three types of differences and the perceived conflict of concepts for each are as follows:

a. *Deferred ITC.* Under Opinion 2, ITC is deferred and amortized over the life of the related asset, but Statement 96 required immediate recognition of a deferred tax asset for the difference between the book and tax basis of the related asset that results from deferral of ITC.
b. *Foreign nonmonetary assets.* Under Statement 52, exchange gains and losses are not recognized for foreign nonmonetary assets when the U.S. dollar is the functional currency, but Statement 96 required recognition of a deferred tax liability or asset for the difference between the book and tax basis of the related nonmonetary asset that results from a change in exchange rates.
c. *Intercompany sale of inventory or other assets.* Under ARB 51, taxes paid on intercompany profits are deferred, but Statement 96 required recognition of a deferred tax asset for the difference between the book and tax basis of the related asset that results from an intercompany sale.

115. The Board reconsidered whether to require recognition of deferred taxes for each of those three types of differences. The Board's reasons for continuing the requirement for deferred ITC and eliminating the requirement for foreign nonmonetary assets and intercompany sales are discussed below.

Deferred investment tax credit

116. The requirements for accounting for investment tax credits are contained in Opinions 2 and 4. In Opinion 2, the Accounting Principles Board (APB) concluded that:

a. The investment tax credit reduces the cost of the related asset, and for that reason, it should be deferred and amortized over the productive life of the related asset.
b. Display of the deferral in the statement of financial position as a reduction of the cost of the asset ordinarily is preferable.
c. Display of the deferral as deferred income is also permitted provided that the investment tax credit is accounted for as a reduction of the cost of the asset, that is, amortized over the productive life of the asset.

In Opinion 4, the APB concluded that:

(1) The essential nature of the investment tax credit is that it reduces the cost of the related asset, and the method of accounting for it in Opinion 2 is preferable.
(2) The flow-through method to account for the investment tax credit is also acceptable.

117. Accounting for an investment tax credit as required by Opinion 2 reduces the cost of the asset to less than its tax basis. The excess of tax basis over cost for financial reporting will be deductible in future years when the asset is recovered. Deferred tax accounting for that temporary difference does not change the accounting for the investment tax credit required by Opinion 2. The entire amount of the investment tax credit is still deferred at the outset and subsequently amortized over the life of the asset. The Board concluded that accounting for this temporary difference (a) is consistent with the basic principles of the Board's asset and liability approach to accounting for deferred *income taxes* and (b) is not a change in the deferred method of accounting for *investment tax credits* under Opinion 2.

Foreign nonmonetary assets

118. Statement 52 requires use of the U.S. dollar to measure the cost of foreign nonmonetary assets such as inventory, land, and depreciable assets when the U.S. dollar is the functional currency.[12] When exchange rates change, the amount of foreign currency revenues needed to recover the U.S. dollar cost of those assets also changes—but the foreign currency tax basis of those assets does not change. After a change in exchange rates, there will be a difference between (a) the amount of foreign currency needed to recover the U.S. dollar cost of those assets and (b) the foreign currency tax basis of those assets. Some believe that deferred taxes for those differences should be recognized in the period in which exchange rates change.

---

[12]Under Statement 52, another foreign currency could be the functional currency when the local currency is not the functional currency for a foreign entity. The requirements of this Statement and the basis for the Board's conclusions are the same for those situations as for when the U.S. dollar is the functional currency for a foreign entity.

119. Under Statement 96, that difference between the foreign currency equivalent of the U.S. dollar cost and the foreign tax basis of nonmonetary assets is accounted for as a temporary difference. Although that difference technically meets the definition of a temporary difference, the Board concluded that the substance of accounting for it as such is to recognize deferred taxes on exchange gains and losses that are not recognized under Statement 52. The Board decided to resolve that conflict between the requirements of Statements 96 and 52 by prohibiting recognition of deferred taxes for those differences. The Board believes that decision will significantly reduce complexity by eliminating cross-currency (U.S. dollar cost versus foreign tax basis) computations of deferred taxes for those differences.

120. The Board also considered indexing of foreign nonmonetary assets for tax purposes (to counter the effects of inflation) when the U.S. dollar is the functional currency. In most countries, indexing is "too little, too late." As a result, at least in part, of the Board's decision about Statement 52 differences discussed above, however, a comparison of indexed tax basis to local currency historical cost ordinarily would indicate an excess of tax over book basis and a potential deferred tax asset—a counterintuitive result in highly inflationary economies. For that reason, the Board decided to prohibit deferred tax accounting for differences that result from indexing for tax purposes whenever the U.S. dollar is the functional currency for a foreign entity.

Intercompany transfers of assets

121. An intercompany transfer of assets such as the sale of inventory or depreciable assets between tax jurisdictions is a taxable event that establishes a new tax basis for those assets in the buyer's tax jurisdiction. The new tax basis of those assets is deductible on the buyer's tax return when the cost of those assets as reported in the consolidated financial statements is recovered.

122. Paragraph 17 of ARB 51 requires deferral of income taxes paid by the seller on intercompany profits on assets remaining within the consolidated group. Under Statement 96, however, the tax paid by the seller is charged to expense, and a deferred tax asset is potentially recognizable for the excess of the buyer's tax basis over the cost of the assets as reported in the consolidated financial statements. As a result, under Statement 96, a tax benefit or tax expense attributable to transferred inventory may be recognized in a period before that inventory is sold to an unrelated third party.

123. This Statement changes that requirement of Statement 96. Some argued that the Board's con-clusion to recognize a deferred tax asset for the seller's tax payments and to not recognize a deferred tax asset for the buyer's deductible temporary difference reflects a deferred approach that is inconsistent with the asset and liability approach to accounting for income taxes. An intercompany sale of inventory between tax jurisdictions changes the tax basis of the inventory and thereby creates a temporary difference that will result in tax deductions on the buyer's tax return when the cost of the inventory as reported in the consolidated financial statements is recovered. In this view, those deferred tax consequences should be recognized in the year they occur (usually the year of the intercompany sale) and not in the year that the inventory is sold to an unrelated third party.

124. The Board concluded that although the excess of the buyer's tax basis over the cost of transferred assets as reported in the consolidated financial statements technically meets the definition of a temporary difference, the substance of accounting for it as such is to recognize income taxes related to intercompany gains that are not recognized under ARB 51. The Board decided to resolve that conflict between the requirements of Statement 96 and ARB 51 by prohibiting recognition of a deferred tax asset in the buyer's tax jurisdiction for those differences. As a result, ARB 51 is unchanged, and the income taxes paid by the seller including the tax effect, in the seller's tax jurisdiction, of any reversing temporary differences as a result of that intercompany sale are deferred. The Board believes that that decision together with the decisions for Statement 52 and certain Opinion 23 differences should eliminate the need for complex cross-currency deferred tax computations for most enterprises.

Regulated Enterprises

125. When Statement 71 was issued, accounting for income taxes was a project on the Board's agenda, and the Board decided not to change regulated enterprises' accounting for income taxes until that project was completed. The general standards of accounting for the effects of regulation set forth in Statement 71 require recognition of a deferred tax liability or asset for the tax consequences of temporary differences because a regulator cannot relieve a regulated enterprise of a liability or asset that was not created by rate actions of the regulator. Those general standards require (a) recognition of an asset when a deferred tax liability is recognized if it is probable that future revenue will be provided for the payment of those deferred tax liabilities and (b) recognition of a liability when a deferred tax asset is recognized if it is probable that a future reduction in revenue will result when that deferred tax asset is realized. The Board concluded that this Statement should be ap-

plied to regulated enterprises consistent with the general standards of accounting for the effects of regulation set forth in Statement 71.

Leveraged Leases

126. The Board acknowledges that the accounting for income taxes related to leveraged leases set forth in Statement 13 and Interpretation 21 is not consistent with the requirements of this Statement. However, the Board concluded that it should not change the accounting for income taxes related to leveraged leases without considering the need to change leveraged lease accounting, and decided not to reopen the subject of leveraged lease accounting as part of this project. Therefore, this Statement does not change the requirements of Statement 13 or Interpretation 21. The Board also considered whether there should be any integration of (a) the results of accounting for income taxes related to leveraged leases with (b) the other results of accounting for income taxes as required by this Statement. Integration is an issue when all of the following exist:

(1) The accounting for a leveraged lease requires recognition of deferred tax credits.
(2) The requirements of this Statement limit the recognition of a tax benefit for deductible temporary differences and carryforwards not related to the leveraged lease.
(3) Unrecognized tax benefits in (b) could offset taxable amounts that result from future recovery of the net investment in the leveraged lease.

The Board concluded that, in those circumstances, integration should be required. However, consistent with the decision not to change leveraged lease accounting, the Board decided that integration should not override any results that are unique to income tax accounting for leveraged leases, for example, the manner of recognizing the tax effect of an enacted change in tax rates.

Business Combinations

127. Values are assigned to identified assets and liabilities when a business combination is accounted for as a purchase. The assigned values frequently will be different from the tax bases of those assets and liabilities. The Board concluded that a liability or asset should be recognized for the deferred tax consequences of differences between the assigned values and the tax bases of the assets and liabilities (other than nondeductible goodwill and leveraged leases) recognized in a purchase business combination.

128. The Board considered and rejected the approach that assigns net-of-tax values to those assets and liabilities. That approach mixes the nor-

mal amounts of expenses and revenues with their tax effects and thereby confuses the relationship between various items on the statement of earnings in subsequent years. For example, the relationship between sales and cost of sales is affected if cost of sales includes amounts that reflect the net-of-tax values assigned to acquired inventory or depreciable assets. Likewise, the relationship between pretax income from continuing operations and income tax expense is affected to the extent that pretax income from continuing operations includes any net-of-tax amounts.

129. Paragraph 89 of Opinion 16 stated that ". . . the fair value of an asset to an acquirer is less than its market or appraisal value if all or a portion of the market or appraisal value is not deductible for income taxes." The Board believes that the net result is the same whether amounts assigned to the individual assets acquired and liabilities assumed are pretax or net-of-tax. For example, assume (a) that the pretax market or appraisal value of depreciable assets acquired in a purchase business combination is $1,000, (b) that the tax basis of those assets is zero, and (c) that the enacted tax rate is 40 percent for all years. If net-of-tax, the assigned value of those assets would be $600. If pretax, the assigned value of those assets would be $1,000, and there would be a $400 deferred tax liability. Under either approach, the net result of allocating the purchase price is the same. The Board concluded that the amounts assigned to assets and liabilities in a purchase business combination should not be net of any related deferred tax liability or asset.

130. Paragraph 89 of Opinion 16 also stated that "the impact of tax effects on amounts assigned to individual assets and liabilities depends on numerous factors, including imminence or delay of realization of the asset value and the possible timing of tax consequences." That sentence has been interpreted to permit discounting the deferred tax effects of differences between the assigned amounts and the tax bases of the assets and liabilities in a purchase business combination. The issue of discounting a deferred tax liability or asset, however, has been excluded from the scope of this project. The Board decided that discounting deferred tax assets or liabilities should be prohibited for temporary differences (except for leveraged leases) related to business combinations as it is for other temporary differences.

131. Goodwill is recognized in a business combination accounted for as a purchase if the purchase price exceeds the assigned value of the identifiable net assets acquired. Conceptually, a deferred tax liability or asset always should be recognized for the deferred tax consequences of a difference between

the reported amount and the tax basis of goodwill. The requirements of this Statement differ, however, depending on whether amortization of goodwill is deductible for tax purposes. In tax jurisdictions where amortization of goodwill is not deductible, the Board believes that adjusting goodwill by an amount equal to the deferred tax liability or asset for the deferred tax consequences of recovering goodwill would not provide information that is particularly relevant. Furthermore, the computation of that adjustment often is very complex. For those reasons, the Board decided that a deferred tax liability or asset should not be recognized for goodwill temporary differences if amortization is not deductible.

132. Amortization of goodwill is deductible in certain tax jurisdictions. Nonrecognition of a deferred tax liability or asset would result in an uneven effective tax rate for financial reporting if the annual amount of amortization is different for financial reporting and tax purposes. For that reason, the Board concluded that a deferred tax liability or asset should be recognized for goodwill temporary differences in those tax jurisdictions.

133. Goodwill is not the only type of intangible asset for which amortization is not deductible in certain tax jurisdictions. The Board considered whether the exception to comprehensive recognition of deferred taxes that pertains to temporary differences related to goodwill should be extended to temporary differences related to other types of intangible assets. The Board decided that the exception should not be extended. Goodwill is a residual. It is the excess of purchase price over the assigned values of the identifiable net assets acquired. Other types of intangibles are not residuals. One reason for not recognizing deferred taxes related to goodwill is to avoid the gross-up of both sides of the statement of financial position that occurs because goodwill and the related deferred tax liability are mutually dependent on each other. That relationship does not exist for other types of intangible assets.

134. The other reason for not recognizing deferred taxes related to nondeductible goodwill is complexity. That complexity does not exist for other types of intangible assets. Furthermore, if amounts assigned to intangible assets, depreciable assets, or other types of assets acquired in a business combination exceed the tax basis of those assets, that excess will be taxable when those assets are recovered. The Board concluded that a deferred tax liability should be recognized for those taxable temporary differences regardless of whether the related assets are intangible assets or some other type of assets.

135. The tax law may permit operating loss or tax credit carryforwards of the acquiring or the acquired enterprise to reduce future taxable income or taxes payable attributable to the other enterprise if consolidated tax returns are filed subsequent to the acquisition. In those circumstances, the Board decided that any tax benefits recognizable by either enterprise as a result of the business combination should be included in accounting for the business combination. Goodwill is reduced, thereby reducing the annual charge to income for amortization of goodwill in subsequent years.

136. An acquired enterprise's deductible temporary differences and carryforwards are not included in measuring a purchase transaction if the criteria for recognition of tax benefits are not met. The Board decided against retroactive restatement of the purchase transaction and results of operations for intervening years if the criteria for recognition of tax benefits are met in subsequent periods. Recognition of a tax benefit in subsequent years is a consequence of either (a) earning income or (b) some other significant change in circumstances that causes a change in judgment about the need for a valuation allowance in those subsequent years. For that reason, the Board decided that (1) tax benefits should be accounted for in financial statements for the year in which the criteria for recognition of tax benefits are met, (2) the tax benefits should be applied first to reduce goodwill to zero and then to reduce other noncurrent intangible assets acquired in that business combination to zero, and (3) any additional tax benefits should be recognized as a reduction of income tax expense.

137. The Board decided that any noncurrent intangible assets other than goodwill should be reduced to zero before reducing income tax expense for acquired tax benefits that are recognized after the acquisition date for two reasons. One reason is that some of the Board's constituents were concerned that the opportunity to reduce income tax expense in future years for a portion of acquired tax benefits might sometimes influence purchase price allocations for business combinations. If amounts allocated to other noncurrent assets are increased, goodwill is reduced, thereby increasing the portion of acquired tax benefits that could reduce income tax expense in future years. Moreover, reliable fair values are sometimes difficult to obtain for noncurrent assets, particularly intangible assets. For those reasons, the Board concluded that both goodwill and other noncurrent intangible assets should be reduced to zero before the tax benefit of acquired deductible temporary differences and carryforwards are recognized as a reduction of income tax expense in future years.

138. Paragraph 72 of Statement 96 and the proposals in the Exposure Draft that preceded this Statement would have required, in certain limited circumstances, recognition of a tax benefit for the excess of an acquiring enterprise's tax basis of the stock of an acquired enterprise over the tax basis of the net assets of the acquired enterprise. The Board decided to eliminate that requirement because of changes in the U.S. federal tax law and the complexity of determining whether that requirement would be applicable in other tax jurisdictions.

Intraperiod Tax Allocation

139. The amount of tax expense or benefit for the year is allocated between pretax income or loss from continuing operations and other items that gave rise to the tax expense or benefit. Under Statement 96, the amount of tax expense or benefit allocated to continuing operations was determined without regard to any items that are reported apart from income or loss from continuing operations. Items reported apart from continuing operations were viewed as incremental, and their tax consequences were not considered in determining the amount of tax expense or benefit to be allocated to continuing operations.

140. This Statement, however, requires consideration of the tax consequences of events for which consideration was prohibited under Statement 96. Under this Statement, for example, taxable income expected in future years is considered for measurement of a deferred tax asset for the carryforward of a current-year loss from continuing operations. For that reason, the Board believes that it is also appropriate to consider an extraordinary gain in the current year for purposes of allocating a tax benefit to a current-year loss from continuing operations. The Board concluded that all items (for example, extraordinary items, discontinued operations, and so forth) should be considered for purposes of determining the amount of tax benefit that results from a loss from continuing operations and that should be allocated to continuing operations.

141. The Board concluded that the tax benefit of a loss or tax credit carryforward, if not recognized when the item arose, is not an extraordinary item when subsequently recognized because the tax benefit is neither unusual in nature nor infrequent in occurrence. That tax benefit results from both (a) earning income in the current year or the expectation of earning income in a future year and (b) incurring a loss in a prior year. The Board also considered whether the tax benefit should be reported in the same manner as the prior-year loss that gave rise to the carryforward. The Board decided that reporting the benefit of a loss or tax credit carryforward based on the event that occurred in the prior year would (1) produce less understandable results and (2) create the sometimes complex problem of tracing back to events of prior years.

142. The Board concluded that the amount of income taxes allocated to the beginning balance of retained earnings for a change in accounting principles should be measured as if the newly adopted accounting principles had been followed in prior years. If prior years are restated for a change in accounting principles or for a correction of an error, the related tax consequences also should be restated for those prior years.

143. The Board believes that the tax consequences of an event that increases or decreases contributed capital should be allocated directly to contributed capital. A tax deduction may be received for the difference between the exercise price of employee stock options and the fair value of the stock at the date of exercise. Because that difference between the exercise price and the fair value of the stock is not presently recognized as compensation expense in the financial statements, the Board believes that reporting the related tax benefit as a reduction of income tax expense would not be appropriate. Pending completion of the Board's project on accounting for employee stock options, the Board decided to make no changes to the requirements of Opinion 25 for reporting the tax effects of stock compensation plans.

144. The requirements of this Statement for reporting the tax benefit of tax-deductible dividends paid on allocated shares (that is, shares already earned by employees) of an employee stock ownership plan (ESOP) are the same as the requirements of Statement 96 for tax-deductible dividends paid to other shareholders. The Board also believes that the requirements of this Statement for tax-deductible dividends paid on shares held by an ESOP but not yet earned by employees are consistent with the requirements of Statement 96 and Opinion 25. An ESOP and a stock option plan are analogous. Both are compensatory arrangements and both sometimes result in tax deductions for amounts that are not presently recognized as compensation expense in the financial statements under existing generally accepted accounting principles. The tax benefits of both are reported as a credit to shareholders' equity.

145. The Board believes that a tax deduction received for the payment of dividends (exclusive of dividends paid on unallocated shares held by an ESOP) represents, in substance, an exemption from taxation of an equivalent amount of earnings. For that reason, the Board concluded that the tax benefit should be recognized as a reduction of tax expense and should not be allocated directly to

shareholders' equity. A tax benefit should not be recognized, however, for tax deductions or favorable tax rates attributable to future dividends of undistributed earnings for which a deferred tax liability has not been recognized under the requirements of Opinion 23. Favorable tax treatment would be reflected in measuring that unrecognized deferred tax liability for disclosure purposes.

146. The Board reconsidered the Statement 96 requirements for reporting tax benefits after a quasi reorganization. Statement 96 had different requirements for (a) quasi reorganizations that are only an elimination of a deficit in retained earnings by a concurrent reduction in contributed capital and (b) other quasi reorganizations. The Board concluded that after any quasi reorganization, including those that are only a deficit reclassification, the enterprise's accounting should be substantially similar to that appropriate for a new enterprise. The income reported by a new enterprise would not include tax benefits attributable to deductible temporary differences and carryforwards that arose prior to its organization date. Therefore, those tax benefits should be reported as a direct addition to contributed capital when recognized subsequent to the date of the quasi reorganization.

147. The Board is aware, however, that some enterprises effected a quasi reorganization that involved only a deficit reclassification and adopted Statement 96 based, at least in part, on reliance on the requirements for the manner of reporting those tax benefits under Statement 96. For that reason, although some noted that other changes to more restrictive requirements than Statement 96 have not received special treatment in this Statement and that this exception is inconsistent with other requirements of this Statement, the Board concluded that it is appropriate to provide an exception for those enterprises.

148. Statement 96 required and the Exposure Draft proposed that interest and penalities assessed on income tax deficiencies should not be reported as income tax expense. Some respondents cited the difficulty of separating the total accrual for an income tax "cushion" between taxes, interest, and penalties. Some financial statement users stated a preference for excluding interest on income tax deficiencies from other types of interest expense. Upon reconsideration, the Board decided to eliminate that proposed requirement.

Classification in a Statement of Financial Position

149. Statement 96 required that the current portion of a deferred tax liability or asset should be the deferred tax consequences of temporary differences that will result in taxable or deductible

amounts during the following year or operating cycle if longer than one year. Some of the Board's constituents believe that requirement increased complexity because it required a detailed analysis to determine the amount of next year's reversing temporary differences. For that reason, the Board considered two alternatives to the requirements of Statement 96. One alternative was to classify all deferred taxes as noncurrent. The other was to continue the requirements of Opinion 11 and Statement 37 and to allocate a valuation allowance between current and noncurrent deferred tax assets on a pro rata basis.

150. Some prefer the requirements of Statement 96. They believe that those requirements are consistent with the overall objective of and reinforce the concepts underlying an asset and liability approach to accounting for income taxes. Furthermore, application of those requirements would produce the information needed to determine the current and noncurrent portions of a valuation allowance so that allocation on a pro rata basis would be unnecessary. They also believe that most enterprises would spend very little time and effort on classification of deferred taxes because classification is not a significant issue for those enterprises. When classification is a significant issue, they believe any additional time and effort is entirely appropriate.

151. The first alternative, classify all deferred taxes as noncurrent, was not adopted because the Board believes that a deferred tax liability or asset should be classified as current or noncurrent in a classified statement of financial position. An inappropriate current ratio would result from noncurrent classification of the deferred tax consequences of temporary differences related to current assets and liabilities. The results of applying that alternative would be confusing for the users of financial statements.

152. The Board concluded, and most respondents to the Exposure Draft agreed, that the requirements for classification of deferred taxes in a classified statement of financial position should be the same as under Opinion 11 and Statement 37. The Board also concluded that a valuation allowance should be allocated on a pro rata basis. The reasons for those conclusions are:

a. The results from applying that alternative ordinarily should not be significantly different from the results from applying the requirements of Statement 96.
b. The requirements of that alternative are easier to understand and apply.
c. That alternative does not create the impression that detailed scheduling is required for situations in which it otherwise could be avoided.

153. The Board considered whether deferred tax assets and liabilities should be offset or presented separately. The Board decided to permit offset of deferred tax liabilities and assets for the same tax jurisdiction for purposes of presentation in the statement of financial position to avoid the detailed analyses necessary to determine whether reversing taxable and deductible temporary differences offset each other on a particular future tax return or in carryback or carryforward years. However, the Board decided to prohibit offset of deferred tax liabilities and assets attributable to different tax jurisdictions. Detailed analyses are not necessary to determine, for example, that a tax asset for German income taxes does not offset a tax liability for French income taxes.

Disclosures

154. The Board believes that the financial statement disclosures required by this Statement provide information that is useful in understanding the general effect of income taxes on a particular enterprise and that those disclosures can be prepared without encountering undue complexities or significant incremental costs.

155. Some respondents to the Exposure Draft recommended disclosure of additional information that might enable financial statement users to estimate the potential future effect of a change in tax laws or rates for each tax jurisdiction in which an enterprise has significant operations. The Board decided that this would require too much detail. In response to a similar recommendation by users of financial statements, however, the Board decided that a public enterprise should disclose the approximate total tax effect (not the separate tax effect for each tax jurisdiction) for each type of temporary difference and carryforward that gives rise to a significant portion of the enterprise's deferred tax liabilities and assets. The Board believes that this summarized information is useful and that it does not impose significant additional costs. This Statement also requires disclosure of the effect of enacted changes in tax laws or rates.

156. Some respondents to the Exposure Draft stated that disclosure of the amount of an enterprise's total deferred tax liabilities, deferred tax assets, and valuation allowances is of little value and potentially misleading. It might be misleading, for example, to continue to disclose a deferred tax asset and valuation allowance of equal amounts for a loss carryforward after operations are permanently terminated in a particular tax jurisdiction. The Board believes that it need not and should not develop detailed guidance for when to cease disclosure of the existence of a worthless asset. Some financial statement users, on the other hand, stated that disclosure of the total liability, asset, and valuation allowance as proposed in the Exposure Draft is essential for gaining some insight regarding management's decisions and changes in decisions about recognition of deferred tax assets. Other respondents recommended significant additional disclosures such as the extent to which net deferred tax assets are dependent on (a) future taxable income exclusive of reversing temporary differences or even (b) *each* of the four sources of taxable income cited in paragraph 21. After reconsideration, the Board concluded that disclosure of the total amounts as proposed in the Exposure Draft is an appropriate level of disclosure.

157. The Board considered and rejected a requirement for disclosure of the future maturities of a long-term deferred tax liability or asset. Disclosure of future maturities would require all enterprises with deferred tax liabilities or assets to analyze the distribution of taxable and deductible amounts among particular future years.

158. This Statement requires certain disclosures for an unrecognized deferred tax liability for temporary differences related to the areas addressed in Opinion 23 and deposits in statutory reserve funds by U.S. steamship enterprises. Those disclosure requirements are a result of the Board's decision to continue, in certain circumstances, the exception to comprehensive recognition of deferred taxes for those temporary differences.

159. This Statement does not prescribe a single method for recognition and measurement of income taxes in the separately issued financial statements of an entity that is a member of a group that files a consolidated tax return. It does, however, require certain criteria for the allocation method adopted (paragraph 40) and certain disclosures (paragraph 49) that previously were not required under Opinion 11 about the accounting for income taxes by such an entity. Some would have preferred to not require criteria for the allocation method because generally accepted accounting principles normally rely on disclosures under FASB Statement No. 57, *Related Party Disclosures,* and do not specify accounting requirements for related party transactions. The Board concluded, however, that those requirements are necessary (a) because an entity's reported results of operations and financial position can be significantly affected by those related-party transactions and (b) to obtain reported results that are closer to those that would be reported if the entity were an independent enterprise.

Effective Date and Transition

160. The Board considered and rejected a solely prospective application of the accounting stan-

dards required by this Statement. Continued recognition of deferred tax assets or liabilities computed under Opinion 11 or Statement 96 is inconsistent with the Board's present decisions about the deferred tax consequences of temporary differences. Furthermore, the cost and complexity of maintaining two systems of accounting for income taxes would not be justified.

161. The Exposure Draft proposed disclosure of the effect of adopting this Statement for the year of adoption if financial statements for the prior year are not restated. Some respondents to the Exposure Draft stated that the cost to develop that information would exceed the benefit of providing it. Two sets of deferred tax computations would be required for the year of adoption—one under the requirements of this Statement and another under the requirements of either Statement 96 or Opinion 11.

162. Upon reconsideration, the Board decided that it should not require two sets of deferred tax computations for a single year. However, this Statement does require disclosure of either (a) the current-year effect on pretax income (from adjustments for prior year business combinations and regulated enterprises) if prior-year financial statements are not restated or (b) the prior-year effect of restatement if prior-year financial statements are restated. Some users of financial statements study changes in the trend of pretax income, and the disclosure required in (a) above will identify the current-year impact on that trend as a result of adopting this Statement. The Board believes that the disclosures required in (b) above should not require excessive cost because that information already will have been developed as a result of restating prior-year financial statements.

163. The Board believes that restatement of financial statements for prior years would be desirable to provide useful information about income taxes for purposes of comparing financial data after the effective date of this Statement with data presented for earlier years. The Board recognizes, however, that the procedures required by this Statement sometimes would differ significantly from procedures followed in previous years and that restatement could be particularly complex and time-consuming for some enterprises. In addition, restatement requires the availability of records or information that an enterprise may no longer have or that its past procedures did not require. Therefore, the Board decided that restatement should be permitted but not required.

164. For similar reasons, the Board decided that the initial and subsequent accounting for purchase business combinations consummated in years prior to the year for which this Statement is first applied should not be restated.

165. For those purchase business combinations, the Board also considered whether to require adjustment of the remaining balances of assets (except for leveraged leases) and liabilities to pretax rather than net-of-tax amounts and recognition of a deferred tax liability or asset for the related temporary differences. The Board understands that for some prior business combinations, determination of those adjustments is impracticable, either because the necessary information is no longer available or because the cost to develop that information is excessive.

166. Statement 96 prohibited those adjustments in all instances. The purpose of that requirement was to eliminate the lack of comparability between the financial statements of enterprises that could and could not compute those adjustments. In reconsidering Statement 96, however, the Board decided to require those adjustments, if practicable, so that statements of financial position and statements of earnings will be more useful and representationally faithful (for both display and measurement) in future years. The Exposure Draft description of impracticable as involving "prohibitive" costs was changed to "excessive" costs to clarify that this is intended to be a "reasonable hurdle."

167. If determination of those adjustments is impracticable for a particular business combination, this Statement requires (except for leveraged leases) that any differences between the remaining balances of the assets and liabilities and their tax bases should be considered to be temporary differences and that a deferred tax liability or asset should be recognized for those temporary differences. For that calculation, the only information required for transition is the amounts of an enterprise's assets and liabilities for financial reporting and for tax purposes. That information should be available.

168. Similar considerations affected the Board's decisions about the method of transition for regulated enterprises. Upon initial application of this Statement, the reported amount of construction in progress is adjusted to the amount that would have resulted from applying this Statement to account for that construction in progress in all prior years. If construction is still in progress, the information needed to make that adjustment should be available. The information needed for plant that is already in service, however, might not be available. Upon initial application of this Statement, the reported amount of plant in service is adjusted to the amount that would have resulted from applying

this Statement in all prior years, if practicable. Otherwise, any difference between the reported amount and the tax basis of plant in service is accounted for as the temporary difference.

Exceptions to Comprehensive Recognition of Deferred Taxes

Opinion 23 and U.S. Steamship Enterprise Temporary Differences

169. Under Opinion 11 and Statement 96, there were certain exceptions to comprehensive recognition of deferred tax liabilities. A deferred tax liability was not recognized for the areas addressed by Opinion 23 and for deposits in statutory reserve funds by U.S. steamship enterprises. At the time of issuing Statement 96, the Board concluded that those temporary differences give rise to a recognizable deferred tax liability. However, the Board decided to continue those exceptions because of (a) the complexity of measuring the deferred tax liability for foreign undistributed earnings, (b) the need to compromise, and (c) the omission of discounting.

170. In reconsidering the requirements of Statement 96, the Board reconsidered whether the Opinion 23 and U.S. steamship enterprise temporary differences give rise to a recognizable deferred tax liability. The Board concluded that those temporary differences give rise to a recognizable deferred tax liability. Opinion 23 required partial recognition of deferred taxes—an approach to accounting for income taxes that the Board has rejected. The underlying rationale for Opinion 23 is based on an enterprise's ability and intent to control the timing of the events that cause temporary differences to reverse and result in taxable amounts in future years. The Board concluded that management's ability to determine the particular future year(s) in which a deferred tax liability will be settled does not eliminate the existence of that liability at the end of the current year.

171. Not recognizing a liability for the deferred tax consequences of Opinion 23 and U.S. steamship enterprise temporary differences overstates the shareholders' residual ownership interest in an enterprise's net earnings and net assets. The government has a claim (a right to collect taxes) that precludes shareholders from ever realizing a portion of the enterprise's net assets. A tax obligation is not a component of shareholders' equity.

172. The Board considered whether payment of income taxes for the Opinion 23 and U.S. steamship enterprise temporary differences might be a *contingency* as that term is used in Statement 5. The Board concluded that there is no uncertainty that a tax obligation has been incurred for those

temporary differences. The amount of the government's claim will never revert to the benefit of the shareholders unless there is a change in the tax law. The possibility of a change in the tax law in some future year is not an *uncertainty* as that term is used in Statement 5.

173. Complexity was one reason Statement 96 did not require recognition of a deferred tax liability for Opinion 23 and U.S. steamship enterprise temporary differences. Information received from constituents has convinced the Board that calculation of a deferred tax liability for undistributed foreign earnings that are or will be invested in a foreign entity indefinitely may sometimes be extremely complex. The hypothetical nature of those calculations introduces significant implementation issues and other complexities that occur less frequently in calculations of a deferred tax liability for an *expected* remittance of earnings from a foreign entity. For that reason, the Exposure Draft proposed to not require recognition of a deferred tax liability for undistributed earnings that are or will be invested in a foreign entity indefinitely. Based on respondents' concerns about complexity, however, the Board decided to extend that exception for foreign undistributed earnings to include the entire amount of a temporary difference between the book and tax basis of an investment in a foreign subsidiary or foreign corporate joint venture that is essentially permanent in duration regardless of the underlying reason(s) for that temporary difference.

174. A deferred tax liability is recognized for exempted taxable temporary differences if those temporary differences will reverse in the foreseeable future, and the Board decided that the same criterion should apply for recognition of a deferred tax asset for an excess of tax over the book basis of an investment in a foreign or domestic subsidiary or corporate joint venture that is essentially permanent in duration. The Exposure Draft proposed to prohibit recognition of a deferred tax asset for foreign tax credit carryforwards in excess of the amount by which those credits reduce the deferred tax liability recognized for undistributed foreign earnings and other foreign source income. Many respondents to the Exposure Draft objected to that limitation. After considering respondents' views, the Board decided to modify that limitation to permit recognition of the entire deferred tax asset so long as its future realization does not depend on either past or future Opinion 23 items (for example, undistributed earnings) for which a deferred tax liability either has not or will not be recognized.

175. Statement 96 required, in certain circumstances, disclosure of the amount of withholding taxes that would be payable upon remittance of

foreign earnings. Payment of withholding taxes may be avoided in many foreign jurisdictions if the parent's investment in the foreign entity is recovered by some means other than dividends, for example, by sale of the stock of that foreign entity. For that reason, the Board decided to eliminate the Statement 96 requirement for disclosure of withholding taxes.

176. The need to compromise was the second reason cited in Statement 96 for not requiring recognition of a deferred tax liability for Opinion 23 temporary differences. The Statement 96 requirements for recognition of deferred tax assets created the overriding reason for the need to compromise. The requirements of this Statement result in the recognition of deferred tax assets that could not be recognized under the requirements of Statement 96.

177. The omission of discounting was the third reason cited in Statement 96. This Statement prohibits discounting either deferred tax assets or deferred tax liabilities. The Board acknowledges that some of the types of deductible temporary differences that potentially give rise to the largest deferred tax assets are related to estimated liabilities (for example, other postretirement benefits) that are already discounted amounts. The Board notes, however, that an undiscounted deferred tax asset will sometimes be recognized for operating loss and tax credit carryforwards that may not be realized for up to 15 years into the future. Furthermore, discounting would usually require scheduling the reversals of temporary differences in future years.

178. Paragraph 2 of FASB Concepts Statement No. 5, *Recognition and Measurement in Financial Statements of Business Enterprises,* states that "the Board intends future change [in practice] to occur in the gradual, evolutionary way that has characterized past change." Thus, evolutionary change may have to be slower in some areas than in others. The Board concluded that, in this area, recognition of a deferred tax liability for *all* Opinion 23 and U.S. steamship enterprise temporary differences should not be required at this time. That requirement would be too great a change from present practice under either Opinion 11 or Statement 96. The Board also concluded that recognition of a deferred tax liability for those temporary differences on a *prospective* basis as required by this Statement is an evolutionary change in practice that results in a significant improvement in financial reporting.

179. The Board considered the cost and complexity that would result from recognition of a deferred tax liability for Opinion 23 and U.S. steamship enterprise temporary differences on a

prospective basis. The Board concluded that, except for temporary differences between the book and tax basis of investments in foreign subsidiaries and foreign corporate joint ventures, any increase in cost or complexity as a result of that requirement would be minimal. For that reason, the Board decided to require recognition of a deferred tax liability for those temporary differences on a prospective basis.

180. Over the years, as a result of changes in the tax law, the particular tax benefits that gave rise to Opinion 23 temporary differences have been reduced for savings and loan associations (and other qualified thrift lenders) and have been eliminated for life insurance companies. Thus, eliminating those exceptions on a prospective basis should not have a significant effect for many of those enterprises. The tax law for recapture of a savings and loan association's bad-debt reserve for tax purposes changed for tax years beginning after December 31, 1987 and, for that reason, the Board chose that date for prospective recognition of a deferred tax liability for this type of temporary difference. The Exposure Draft proposed a limitation on recognition of a deferred tax asset for a savings and loan association's bad-debt reserve for financial reporting. Respondents disagreed because the effect of that limitation sometimes would be, in substance, the same as recognizing a deferred tax liability for tax bad-debt reserves that arose prior to tax years beginning after December 31, 1987. The Board decided to eliminate that limitation.

181. The Board sees little similarity between Opinion 23 differences and U.S. steamship enterprise differences. Opinion 23 differences reverse in indefinite future periods. U.S. steamship enterprise differences reverse in predictable future periods and, in substance, are no different from depreciation differences for which recognition of deferred taxes is required. For those reasons, the Exposure Draft proposed to eliminate the exception for U.S. steamship enterprises on a prospective basis. After consideration of responses to the Exposure Draft, however, the Board decided that recognition of the entire deferred tax liability for those temporary differences that exist at the beginning of the year for which this Statement is first applied also should be permitted.

182. A few respondents to the Exposure Draft proposed extending the Opinion 23 exception to comprehensive recognition of deferred taxes to certain analogous types of temporary differences, such as LIFO inventory temporary differences. The Board's reasons for concluding that Opinion 23 temporary differences give rise to a recognizable deferred tax liability equally apply to analogous types of temporary differences. The Board concluded that nonrecogni-

tion of a deferred tax liability for analogous types of temporary differences should be prohibited.

Tax Holidays

183. The Board considered whether a deferred tax asset ever should be recognized for the expected future reduction in taxes payable during a tax holiday. In most tax jurisdictions that have tax holidays, the tax holiday is "generally available" to any enterprise (within a class of enterprises) that chooses to avail itself of the holiday. The Board views that sort of exemption from taxation for a class of enterprises as creating a nontaxable status (somewhat analogous to S-corporation status under U.S. federal tax law) for which a deferred tax asset should not be recognized.

184. Some tax jurisdiction(s) may have a "unique" type of tax holiday that is *controlled* by the enterprise that qualifies for it (that is, a tax holiday that is not generally available to any enterprise within a class of enterprises that chooses to avail itself of the holiday). In those circumstances, conceptually, a deferred tax asset might be recognizable so long as (a) the enterprise has done whatever is necessary to qualify for the holiday and (b) the deferred tax asset recognized is net of the incremental cost of special requirements for future performance under the tax holiday agreement. The Board decided to prohibit recognition of a deferred tax asset for *any* tax holiday because of the practical problems in (1) distinguishing "unique" tax holidays (if any exist) for which recognition of a deferred tax asset might be appropriate from "generally available" tax holidays and (2) measuring the deferred tax asset.

The Incremental Effect of Future Losses

185. Conceptually, under an incremental approach, the tax consequences of tax losses expected in future years would be anticipated for purposes of:

a. Nonrecognition of a deferred tax liability for taxable temporary differences if there will be no future sacrifice because of future tax losses that otherwise would expire unused
b. Recognition of a deferred tax asset for the carryback refund of taxes paid for the current or a prior year because of future tax losses that otherwise would expire unused.

Nevertheless, the Board decided to prohibit anticipation of the tax consequences of future tax losses. That decision reduces the complexity of understanding and applying the requirements of this Statement.

Private and Small Public Enterprises

186. An issue in the August 1983 FASB Discussion Memorandum, *Accounting for Income Taxes,* is whether accounting requirements for income taxes should differ for private or small public enterprises. Most respondents to the Discussion Memorandum who addressed this issue opposed differential recognition or measurement. Respondents who could be identified as having a small enterprise perspective were rather evenly divided on this issue.

187. Under the asset and liability approach required by this Statement, measurement of a deferred tax liability or asset is based on the provisions of the tax law. Calculations may often be complicated, but the Board believes that many of those complications are primarily attributable to the tax law. Complexities in the tax law are applicable to small as well as to large enterprises. Those complexities must be dealt with for tax purposes regardless of what the accounting requirements might be. The Board believes that complexities in the tax law do not give rise to a need for different accounting requirements based on an enterprise's size or ownership.

188. The Board believes that accounting standards should establish requirements that result in accounting for similar transactions and circumstances similarly and for different transactions and circumstances differently. Different accounting standards for income taxes based on an enterprise's size or ownership would affect how financial statement amounts (for example, net income, total assets, and total liabilities) and relationships (for example, debt-to-equity ratio and times interest earned) are determined. The Board believes that the deferred tax consequences of temporary differences are recognizable liabilities or assets and nonrecognition of deferred taxes by some enterprises would deny the existence of deferred tax liabilities and assets. The Board believes that result would significantly reduce the credibility and usefulness of general-purpose external financial reporting.

189. The Board believes that the disclosure requirements of this Statement generally do not create significant new complexities or significant incremental costs. Paragraph 47 generally requires a numerical reconciliation between the reported amount of income tax expense and the amount that would result from applying domestic federal statutory tax rates. A numerical reconciliation was previously required only for public enterprises. The Board decided that nonpublic enterprises should disclose the reasons for significant differences but that a numerical reconciliation should

not be required. Similarly, paragraph 43 requires that nonpublic enterprises disclose the types of temporary differences, but not the tax effect of each, that give rise to significant portions of deferred tax liabilities and assets. In addition, the disclosures required when an enterprise's income is taxed directly to owners are applicable only for public enterprises. The Board decided that there should be no other differences between the disclosures required by this Statement for public enterprises and the disclosures required for nonpublic enterprises.

Interim Financial Reporting

190. The accounting requirements of Opinion 28 are based on a view that each interim period is primarily an integral part of the annual period. Tax expense for interim periods is measured using an estimated annual effective tax rate for the annual period. Opinion 28 rejects the discrete approach to interim reporting whereby the results of operations for each interim period would be determined as if the interim period were an annual period. The Board's asset and liability approach to accounting for income taxes for annual periods, however, is a discrete approach that measures a deferred tax liability or asset at a particular time.

191. The Board decided not to reopen the subject of interim accounting as part of this project and did not reconsider the general approach in Opinion 28 to accounting for income taxes in interim periods. As a result, most of the requirements in Opinion 28 remain unchanged. The Board concluded, however, that some changes were necessary because of the basic principles encompassed in this Statement.

192. In certain circumstances, Opinion 28 prohibits recognition of tax benefits unless future realization is assured beyond a reasonable doubt. That provision in Opinion 28 creates a conflict with the accounting requirements to be applied at the end of the year for annual reporting, and the Board decided to eliminate that provision.

193. Under the requirements of this Statement for annual reporting, the tax benefit of an operating loss carryforward is not reported as an extraordinary item unless realization of the carryforward results from an extraordinary gain. If realization of an operating loss carryforward that is attributable to losses in prior years is expected because of estimated "ordinary" income in the current year, the operating loss carryforward is included in the computation of the estimated annual effective tax rate the same as, for example, tax credit carryforwards.

194. Measurements of a deferred tax liability or asset for annual reporting are subject to change when enacted tax laws or rates change. Likewise, a valuation allowance is subject to change when a change in circumstances causes a change in judgment about the realizability of the related deferred tax asset in *future* years. For interim reporting, the Board believes that the effects of those changes should be recognized as of the enactment date for a change in tax law or rate or as of the date of a change in circumstances for a change in valuation allowance and should not be allocated to subsequent interim periods by an adjustment of the estimated annual effective tax rate for the remainder of the year. Thus, in effect, there is a catch-up adjustment for the cumulative effect as of the date of the change. The effect of changes in tax laws or rates and changes in judgment about the need for a valuation allowance on income or losses for future interim periods, however, is reflected by an adjustment of the estimated annual effective tax rate for the remainder of the year.

195. Paragraph 13 of FASB Statement No. 16, *Prior Period Adjustments,* identifies four items for which the results of prior interim periods should be restated. One of them encompasses the effects of new retroactive tax legislation. Subsequent to the issuance of Statement 16, however, restatement of prior interim periods has not been adopted in Board pronouncements addressing the tax effects of the 1979 U.K. tax legislation or the 1984 and 1986 U.S. tax legislation. Furthermore, that requirement of Statement 16 conflicts with the Board's decision that enactment of tax legislation is a discrete event and that the effects should be recognized in the period of enactment. The Board decided to amend Statement 16 to prohibit restatement of prior interim periods for the enactment of new tax legislation.

Issues Removed from the Scope of This Project

Accounting for the Investment Tax Credit

196. An issue in the 1983 Discussion Memorandum that preceded Statement 96 was the basic method for recognition of investment tax credits in financial income. The basic nature of the U.S. investment tax credit has been viewed in three different ways. Each view leads to different accounting for the investment tax credit. The three possibilities are that the investment tax credit:

a. Reduces the cost of the related asset (The investment tax credit is recognized in financial income as a reduction of depreciation over the productive life of the asset.)

b. Results in a liability because of the provision for recapture upon early disposal of the related asset (The investment tax credit is recognized in financial income as a reduction of tax expense for the years that the recapture periods lapse or ratably over the recapture period.)

c. Results in a reduction of tax expense. (The investment tax credit is recognized in financial income as a reduction of tax expense of the year that taxes payable are reduced.)

197. The Board believes that it would be desirable to have only one method to account for the investment tax credit. However, the Board decided not to address the issue of accounting for the investment tax credit for practical reasons including the Revenue Act of 1971.[13] As a result, the conclusions of the APB remain unchanged and both the deferral method (Opinion 2) and the flow-through method (Opinion 4) continue to be acceptable methods to account for the investment tax credit.

Discounting

198. Another issue in the 1983 Discussion Memorandum was whether measurement of a deferred tax liability or asset should reflect the time value of money, that is, whether a deferred tax liability or asset should be determined on a present value or discounted basis. Most respondents to the Discussion Memorandum opposed discounting deferred income taxes.

199. Conceptual issues, such as whether discounting income taxes is appropriate, and implementation issues associated with discounting income taxes are numerous and complex. Implementation issues include selection of the discount rate(s) and determination of the future years in which amounts will become taxable or deductible. The Board decided not to consider those issues at this time. If deferred income taxes were discounted, however, a detailed analysis of the future reversals of temporary differences would be routinely required and a frequent criticism of Statement 96 was the need for scheduling.

Proposals for Partial or No Recognition of Deferred Taxes That Were Rejected

Taxes Payable As Determined by the Tax Return

200. Some respondents to the Discussion Memorandum advocated that income tax expense for financial reporting should be the amount of taxes payable for the year as determined by the tax return. The rationale most frequently cited to support that proposal is summarized as follows:

a. The tax return determines the legal liability for income taxes.

b. Taxes are levied on aggregate taxable income, and individual events are merely indistinguishable pieces of the overall determination of aggregate taxable income.

c. Any tax payments for future years will be solely a consequence of generating taxable income in those future years.

d. Notional tax calculations based on the recognition and measurement of events for financial reporting are not appropriate.

e. All other approaches to accounting for income taxes are too complex.

201. The Board believes that the tax consequences of an individual event are separable from aggregate taxable income. For example, if the gain on an installment sale is taxable, both the sale and the tax consequences of the gain on the sale should be recognized in financial income for the same year. The tax law may permit an election to include some or all of the gain in the determination of taxable income in future years. That election, however, only affects when and not whether the gain will be included in determining taxable income. The tax consequences arose at the time of the sale and result from the gain on the sale.

202. As the installment sale receivable is collected, pro rata amounts of the gain are included in determining taxable income. Reporting the uncollected balance of the receivable at its net realizable value in the statement of financial position reflects an assumption that the receivable will be recovered and, therefore, that the gain will become taxable. Recognition of the sale and the gain on the sale on an accrual basis requires concurrent recognition of the tax consequences of the gain on the sale. For example, commission expense attributable to the installment sale is recognized on an accrual basis even if the commissions are paid as the receivable is collected and, likewise, income tax expense should also be recognized on an accrual basis. To do otherwise would result in accounting for the sale and the gain on an accrual basis and the related tax consequences on a cash basis—a result that the Board believes is inconsistent and inappropriate.

Partial Recognition of Deferred Taxes

203. Some respondents to the Discussion Memorandum suggested that the tax consequences of some events may never be paid and, therefore, should not be recognized as a tax liability. They

---

[13]The Revenue Act of 1971 states that no particular method to account for investment tax credit shall be required in taxpayers' reports to any federal agency.

stated that the aggregate of all timing differences or of timing differences for a particular type of recurring item such as depreciation usually keeps getting larger because new originating differences more than offset reversing differences. Their view is that since the cumulative amount of differences does not reverse, no future tax payment will arise, and a deferred tax liability should not be recognized.

204. The Board does not agree. The Board believes that a deferred tax liability will result in a future sacrifice even if the aggregate amount of temporary differences increases in future years.

205. Depreciation differences resulting from accelerated depreciation for tax purposes may be used as an example. The aggregate amount of depreciation differences may become larger in future years because of general price inflation, expansion of enterprise activities, or for other reasons. Nevertheless, the deferred tax consequences of a depreciation difference for a particular depreciable asset ordinarily will result in a sacrifice in future years. There will be a future sacrifice because an *individual* difference results in a taxable amount when revenue that recovers the reported amount of the depreciable asset exceeds its remaining tax basis. That taxable amount for a future year will result in a sacrifice in one of the following ways:

a. Increase taxable income and taxes payable if the enterprise earns net taxable income for that year
b. Reduce a tax loss and a loss carryback refund if the enterprise incurs a tax loss that offsets net taxable income of an earlier year
c. Reduce an operating loss carryforward, thereby increasing taxes payable if net taxable income is earned during the carryforward period.

The depreciation difference results in a future sacrifice in each of the three situations described above. The only circumstance in which there would be no future sacrifice is if, in situation (c) above, the enterprise does not pay taxes during the carryforward period.

Methods of Accounting for Income Taxes That Were Rejected

206. The Discussion Memorandum identified four basic approaches to accounting for income taxes. The conceptual nature of the resulting item in the statement of financial position is an important distinction among the four approaches. That item is viewed as:

a. A tax asset or liability under the asset and liability approach
b. A deferred credit or a deferred charge under the deferred approach

c. A reduction in related assets or liabilities under the net-of-tax approach
d. Either (b) or (c) above in combination with (a), depending on whether a difference between financial and taxable income results from an item that is recognized in financial income after or before it is included in determining taxable income.

This Statement requires the asset and liability approach to accounting for income taxes. The Board's reasons for rejecting the other approaches are discussed below.

The Deferred Approach to Accounting for Income Taxes

207. Opinion 11 required a deferred approach to accounting for income taxes. The objective was to match tax expense with related revenues and expenses for the year in which those revenues and expenses were recognized in pretax financial income. Differential calculations were used to measure the incremental effect on income tax expense resulting from either individual or groups of similar timing differences. Those calculations were based on either the gross change or the net change method. No adjustment was made to reflect changes in tax rates or laws in subsequent years. Deferred tax credits and charges in the statement of financial position represented the cumulative effect of interperiod tax allocation and were not receivables or payables.

208. The deferred method produces different results depending on whether the calculations are made by the gross change or the net change method in the following circumstances:

a. When tax rates change
b. When tax credits have statutory limitations
c. When an enterprise is significantly affected by graduated income tax rates
d. When originating timing differences affect one type of taxable income (for example, ordinary income) and the reversal affects a different type of taxable income (for example, capital gains).

209. Under the net change method, deferred tax balances may remain after the individual timing differences that gave rise to those balances have reversed if one of the situations described in paragraph 208 occurs. Those balances may continue to be reported in an enterprise's statement of financial position for as long as the particular type of timing difference exists. Those balances are not eliminated earlier than that because the objective of the deferred method is to measure the incremental effect on income tax expense as a result of tim-

ing differences in the year they originate; the objective is not to measure the cumulative amount of taxes payable or refundable when timing differences reverse in future years.

210. A criticism of the deferred method is its failure to recognize the consequences of an enacted change in tax laws or rates. The use of accelerated depreciation for taxes and straight-line depreciation for financial reporting is sometimes cited by advocates of the deferred approach as an example illustrating why that approach is appropriate. Advocates of the deferred approach state that a realized tax benefit for accelerated depreciation deductions cannot change as a result of a change in future tax rates. Under the deferred method, the realized benefit is reported in the statement of financial position pending allocation to reduce income tax expense in future years when the depreciation differences reverse. Measured and reported in that manner, deferred tax credits and charges do not meet the Board's definition of liabilities and assets in Concepts Statement 6.

211. A realized tax benefit for accelerated depreciation does not subsequently change if tax rates change. Depreciation differences, however, affect income taxes in two years—once in the year they originate and once again in the year they reverse. Revenues received in later years that recover the amount of depreciable assets reported in the financial statements are taxable. Taxable income as determined by the tax return is larger in later years because depreciation deductions for tax purposes have been used up. Taxes payable on that increased amount of taxable income will be determined by enacted tax rates for the year(s) the depreciation differences reverse and not for the year(s) that they originated. In the Board's opinion, measurements using enacted future tax rates provide more relevant information.

212. Other situations are not satisfactorily dealt with under a deferred approach that focuses on the statement of earnings and timing differences between financial and taxable income. Examples include:

a. A business combination gives rise to differences between the assigned values and the tax bases of an acquired enterprise's assets and liabilities that are not "timing" differences.
b. Deferred amounts may be affected by a change in the tax law such as the 1979 U.K. tax legislation regarding stock relief or the 1984 U.S. Tax Reform Act regarding taxation of Domestic International Sales Corporations and stock life insurance companies.

c. Deferred amounts may be affected when an enterprise changes its tax status and becomes or ceases to be a taxable entity.
d. Alternative minimum tax.

On the other hand, under a deferred approach that focuses on the statement of earnings and timing differences between financial and taxable income, the Board can see no reason for not recognizing the tax effects of timing differences for the areas addressed by Opinion 23 and for deposits in statutory reserve funds by U.S. steamship enterprises.

213. Some respondents to the Discussion Memorandum criticized the complexity of multiple with-and-without calculations particularly when deferred tax credits are eliminated and reinstated because of operating loss and tax credit carrybacks and carryforwards. The Board believes that the complexities arise because the issues pertain to amounts, deferred tax credits and charges, that can be described only in terms of the procedures by which the amounts were computed.

The Net-of-Tax Approach to Accounting for Income Taxes

214. The net-of-tax approach accounts for the effects of taxability and deductibility on assets and liabilities as reductions of the reported amounts of those assets and liabilities. The amount of accounts receivable from installment sales, for example, is reduced for the taxability of the cash receipts in the future years in which the receivables are collected. Depreciable assets, on the other hand, are viewed as providing future benefits from tax deductions and from use of the assets to provide a product or service. The cost of depreciable assets is allocated between the cost of future tax benefits and the cost of future benefits from use of the assets. As the tax deductibility of the assets is used up, a portion of the cost of the assets is used up and the reported amount of the assets is reduced.

215. Allocations of the cost of depreciable assets between tax benefits and benefits from use of the assets are subjective. Advocates of the net-of-tax approach propose that the portion of the cost of depreciable assets allocated to future tax benefits should be the amount of the tax benefits. The remaining cost of the assets is allocated to the future benefits from use of the assets. That approach appears to allocate too much cost to tax benefits and too little cost to benefits from use of the asset, but there may not be a workable solution to the problem that provides a better answer. An example of applying the net-of-tax method when there are depreciable assets is presented below. Equipment that costs $1,000 has a 4-year life. The tax rate is

40 percent. Tax deductions and their tax benefit are as follows:

	Tax Depreciation	Tax Benefit at 40 Percent
Year 1	$ 400	$160
Year 2	300	120
Year 3	200	80
Year 4	100	40
	$1,000	$400

Allocation of the cost of the equipment between the cost of future tax benefits and the cost of future benefits from use of the equipment, and the annual expiration of each of those components are as follows:

	Cost of Tax Benefits	Cost of Operation Benefits	Annual Expiration
Year 1	$160	$150	$ 310
Year 2	120	150	270
Year 3	80	150	230
Year 4	40	150	190
	$400	$600	$1,000

The reported amount of the equipment is reduced by $310 the first year, an additional $270 the second year, and so forth.

216. Straight-line depreciation for financial reporting would be $250 each year. In year 1, deferred tax expense would be $60 under either the deferred or the liability approach. An issue under the net-of-tax approach is whether the $310 expiration of the cost of depreciable assets in year 1 should be reported as $310 of depreciation or, alternatively, whether depreciation should be $250 and tax expense $60. The latter approach is recommended by most net-of-tax advocates. They cite some precedents for their approach and practical reasons why the other approach does not make sense. Nevertheless, application of the net-of-tax approach to depreciable assets is viewed as a cost allocation process.

217. Valuation accounts would be used to reduce assets and liabilities for the effects of their taxability or deductibility. The additional special procedures that are necessary to determine the amount of timing differences and their tax effects for each different asset or liability would be a practical problem. Another problem is that some timing differences cannot be identified with a specific asset or liability, for example, timing differences that result from (a) cash basis accounting for tax purposes and accrual accounting for financial reporting and (b) completed-contract accounting for tax purposes and percentage-of-completion accounting for financial reporting.

218. Reporting an enterprise's assets and liabilities net of their tax effects would make it difficult to understand an enterprise's overall tax situation, and those tax effects would have to be combined in financial statement disclosures. Financial statement disclosures that refer to income taxes that become payable or refundable in future years, however, would appear to contradict the underlying net-of-tax accounting. The Board believes that if recovery of an asset or settlement of a liability will result in amounts that are taxable or deductible, that fact is better communicated by reporting a deferred tax liability or asset rather than by reducing other assets and liabilities.

A Combination of Approaches to Accounting for Income Taxes

219. The net-of-tax or the deferred approach is sometimes proposed in combination with the asset and liability approach. Advocates believe that timing differences for items not yet included in the tax return give rise to an estimated future sacrifice or benefit that is a liability or an asset. Settlement of the estimated tax liability or asset occurs when the item enters the tax return. If the item has already been included in the tax return, advocates believe that the tax sacrifice or benefit has already occurred and that the tax effects should be deferred or applied to reduce a related asset or liability until the timing difference reverses.

220. The Board rejected use of either the deferred or the net-of-tax approach in combination with the asset and liability approach for the same reasons that the deferred and net-of-tax approaches were rejected as a single overall approach. The Board believes that the deferred tax consequences of temporary differences are recognizable liabilities and assets regardless of whether the item that created the temporary difference was first recognized in financial income or first included in taxable income.

221. Any combination of methods increases complexity. All of an enterprise's timing differences would have to be analyzed and sorted into two different groups. Different tax calculation procedures would then have to be applied to each group. In some instances, a single type of timing difference might have to be analyzed and sorted into both groups. For example, depreciation for some classes of assets is sometimes faster for financial reporting than for tax purposes. The underlying rationale for a combination of approaches does not permit offsetting those depreciation differ-

ences against excess tax depreciation in the early years for other classes of depreciable assets.

222. Amounts reported in the statement of financial position under a combination of approaches would be confusing. The tax effects of some differ-

ences would be reported as deferred tax liabilities or assets. The tax effects of other differences would be reported as deferred tax credits or charges, or as reductions of other assets and liabilities. Some sort of financial statement disclosure of an enterprise's overall tax status would be required.

Appendix B

APPLICATION OF THE STANDARDS TO SPECIFIC ASPECTS OF ACCOUNTING FOR INCOME TAXES

CONTENTS

Appendix B

APPLICATION OF THE STANDARDS TO SPECIFIC ASPECTS OF ACCOUNTING FOR INCOME TAXES

Introduction

223. This appendix provides additional discussion and examples[14] that illustrate application of the

standards to specific aspects of accounting for income taxes.

Recognition of Deferred Tax Assets and Deferred Tax Liabilities

224. A deferred tax liability is recognized for all taxable temporary differences,[15] and a deferred tax asset is recognized for all deductible temporary differences and operating loss and tax credit carryforwards. A valuation allowance is recognized if it

---

[14]The discussion and examples in this appendix assume that the tax law requires offsetting net deductions in a particular year against net taxable amounts in the 3 preceding years and then in the 15 succeeding years. Assumptions in this appendix about the tax law are for illustrative purposes only. The enacted tax law for a particular tax jurisdiction should be used for recognition and measurement of deferred tax liabilities and assets.

[15]Refer to paragraph 9.

is more likely than not that some portion or all of the deferred tax asset will not be realized.

225. The following example illustrates recognition of deferred tax assets and liabilities. At the end of year 3 (the current year), an enterprise has $2,400 of deductible temporary differences and $1,500 of taxable temporary differences.

A deferred tax liability is recognized at the end of year 3 for the $1,500 of taxable temporary differences, and a deferred tax asset is recognized for the $2,400 of deductible temporary differences. All available evidence, both positive and negative, is considered to determine whether, based on the weight of that evidence, a valuation allowance is needed for some portion or all of the deferred tax asset. If evidence about one or more sources of taxable income (refer to paragraph 21) is sufficient to support a conclusion that a valuation allowance is not needed, other sources of taxable income need not be considered. For example, if the weight of available evidence indicates that taxable income will exceed $2,400 in each future year, a conclusion that no valuation allowance is needed can be reached without considering the pattern and timing of the reversal of the temporary differences, the existence of qualifying tax-planning strategies, and so forth.

Similarly, if the deductible temporary differences will reverse within the next 3 years and taxable income in the current year exceeds $2,400, nothing needs to be known about future taxable income exclusive of reversing temporary differences because the deferred tax asset could be realized by carryback to the current year. A valuation allowance is needed, however, if the weight of available evidence indicates that some portion or all of the $2,400 of tax deductions from future reversals of the deductible temporary differences will not be realized by offsetting:

a. The $1,500 of taxable temporary differences and $900 of future taxable income exclusive of reversing temporary differences
b. $2,400 of future taxable income exclusive of reversing temporary differences

c. $2,400 of taxable income in the current or prior years by loss carryback to those years
d. $2,400 of taxable income in one or more of the circumstances described above and as a result of a qualifying tax-planning strategy (refer to paragraphs 246-251).

To the extent that evidence about one or more sources of taxable income is sufficient to eliminate any need for a valuation allowance, other sources need not be considered. Detailed forecasts, projections, or other types of analyses[16] are unnecessary if expected future taxable income is more than sufficient to realize a tax benefit. Detailed analyses are not necessary, for example, if the enterprise earned $500 of taxable income in each of years 1-3 and there is no evidence to suggest it will not continue to earn that level of taxable income in future years. That level of future taxable income is more than sufficient to realize the tax benefit of $2,400 of tax deductions over a period of at least 19 years (the year(s) of the deductions, 3 carryback years, and 15 carryforward years) in the U.S. federal tax jurisdiction.

226. The following example illustrates recognition of a valuation allowance for a portion of a deferred tax asset in one year and a subsequent change in circumstances that requires adjustment of the valuation allowance at the end of the following year. The assumptions are as follows:

a. At the end of the current year (year 3), an enterprise's only temporary differences are deductible temporary differences in the amount of $900.
b. Pretax financial income, taxable income, and taxes paid for each of years 1-3 are all positive, but relatively negligible, amounts.
c. The enacted tax rate is 40 percent for all years.

A deferred tax asset in the amount of $360 ($900 at 40 percent) is recognized at the end of year 3. If management concludes, based on an assessment of all available evidence (refer to guidance in paragraphs 20-25), that it is more likely than not that future taxable income will not be sufficient to realize a tax benefit for $400 of the $900 of deductible temporary differences at the end of the current year, a $160 valuation allowance ($400 at 40 percent) is recognized at the end of year 3.

---

[16]The terms *forecast* and *projection* refer to any process by which available evidence is accumulated and evaluated for purposes of estimating whether future taxable income will be sufficient to realize a deferred tax asset. Judgment is necessary to determine how detailed or formalized that evaluation process should be. Furthermore, information about expected future taxable income is necessary only to the extent positive evidence available from other sources (refer to paragraph 21) is not sufficient to support a conclusion that a valuation allowance is not needed. This Statement does not require either a *financial forecast* or a *financial projection* within the meaning of those terms in the Statements on Standards for Accountants' Services on Prospective Financial Information issued by the Auditing Standards Board of the American Institute of Certified Public Accountants.

Assume that pretax financial income and taxable income for year 4 turn out to be as follows:

Pretax financial loss	$ (50)
Reversing deductible temporary differences	(300)
Loss carryforward for tax purposes	$(350)

The $50 pretax loss in year 4 is additional negative evidence that must be weighed against available positive evidence to determine the amount of valuation allowance necessary at the end of year 4. Deductible temporary differences and carryforwards at the end of year 4 are as follows:

Loss carryforward from year 4 for tax purposes (see above)	$350
Unreversed deductible temporary differences ($900 − $300)	600
	$950

The $360 deferred tax asset recognized at the end of year 3 is increased to $380 ($950 at 40 percent) at the end of year 4. Based on an assessment of all evidence available at the end of year 4, management concludes that it is more likely than not that $240 of the deferred tax asset will not be realized and, therefore, that a $240 valuation allowance is necessary. The $160 valuation allowance recognized at the end of year 3 is increased to $240 at the end of year 4. The $60 net effect of those 2 adjustments (the $80 increase in the valuation allowance less the $20 increase in the deferred tax asset) results in $60 of deferred tax expense that is recognized in year 4.

Offset of Taxable and Deductible Amounts

227. The tax law determines whether future reversals of temporary differences will result in taxable and deductible amounts that offset each other in future years. The tax law also determines the extent to which deductible temporary differences and carryforwards will offset the tax consequences of income that is expected to be earned in future years. For example, the tax law may provide that capital losses are deductible only to the extent of capital gains. In that case, a tax benefit is not recognized for temporary differences that will result in future deductions in the form of capital losses unless those deductions will offset either (a) other existing temporary differences that will result in future capital gains, (b) capital gains that are expected to occur in future years, or (c) capital gains of the current year or prior years if carryback (of those capital loss deductions from the future reversal years) is expected.

Pattern of Taxable or Deductible Amounts

228. The particular years in which temporary differences result in taxable or deductible amounts generally are determined by the timing of the recovery of the related asset or settlement of the related liability. However, there are exceptions to that general rule. For example, a temporary difference between the tax basis and the reported amount of inventory for which cost is determined on a LIFO basis does not reverse when present inventory is sold in future years if it is replaced by purchases or production of inventory in those same future years. A LIFO inventory temporary difference becomes taxable or deductible in the future year that inventory is liquidated and not replaced.

229. For some assets or liabilities, temporary differences may accumulate over several years and then reverse over several years. That pattern is common for depreciable assets. Future originating differences for existing depreciable assets and their subsequent reversals are a factor to be considered when assessing the likelihood of future taxable income (paragraph 21(b)) for realization of a tax benefit for existing deductible temporary differences and carryforwards.

Change in Deferred Foreign Tax Assets and Liabilities

230. When the reporting currency (not the foreign currency) is the functional currency, remeasurement of an enterprise's deferred foreign tax liability or asset after a change in the exchange rate will result in a transaction gain or loss that is recognized currently in determining net income. Statement 52 requires disclosure of the aggregate transaction gain or loss included in determining net income but does not specify how to display that transaction gain or loss or its components for financial reporting. Accordingly, a transaction gain or loss that results from remeasuring a deferred foreign tax liability or asset may be included in the reported amount of deferred tax benefit or expense if that presentation is considered to be more useful. If reported in that manner, that transaction gain or loss is still included in the aggregate transaction gain or loss for the period to be disclosed as required by Statement 52.

Special Deductions

231. Statement 96 amended FASB Statement No. 19, *Financial Accounting and Reporting by Oil and Gas Producing Companies*, to require recognition of statutory depletion that would result from generating fu-

ture revenues exactly equal to the amount of the related assets (that is, the assets subject to statutory depletion) to the extent that the statutory depletion offsets a deferred tax liability for taxable temporary differences attributable to those assets. This Statement eliminates that amendment of Statement 19. The Board concluded that, under the basic approach to recognition of deferred tax benefits required by this Statement, the necessary past event for recognition of the tax benefit of statutory depletion is producing oil, mining copper, and so forth (or its subsequent sale). The tax benefit of statutory depletion and other types of special deductions such as those for Blue Cross-Blue Shield and small life insurance companies in future years should not be anticipated for purposes of offsetting a deferred tax liability for taxable temporary differences at the end of the current year.

232. As required above, the tax benefit of special deductions ordinarily is recognized no earlier than the year in which those special deductions are deductible on the tax return. However, some portion of the future tax effects of special deductions are implicitly recognized in determining (a) the average graduated tax rate to be used for measuring deferred taxes when graduated tax rates are a significant factor and (b) the need for a valuation allowance for deferred tax assets. In those circumstances, implicit recognition is unavoidable because (1) those special deductions are one of the determinants of future taxable income and (2) future taxable income determines the average graduated tax rate and sometimes determines the need for a valuation allowance.

Measurement of Deferred Tax Liabilities and Assets

233. The tax rate that is used to measure deferred tax liabilities and deferred tax assets is the enacted tax rate(s) expected to apply to taxable income in the years that the liability is expected to be settled or the asset recovered. Measurements are based on elections (for example, an election for loss carryforward instead of carryback) that are expected to be made for tax purposes in future years. Presently enacted changes in tax laws and rates that become effective for a particular future year or years must be considered when determining the tax rate to apply to temporary differences reversing in that year or years. Tax laws and rates for the current year are used if no changes have been enacted for future years. An asset for deductible temporary differences that are expected to be realized in future years through carryback of a future loss to the current or a prior year (or a liability for taxable temporary differences that are expected to reduce the refund claimed for the carryback of a future loss to the current or a prior year) is measured using tax laws and rates for the current or a prior year, that is, the year for which a

refund is expected to be realized based on loss carryback provisions of the tax law.

234. The following example illustrates determination of the tax rate for measurement of a deferred tax liability for taxable temporary differences when there is a phased-in change in tax rates. At the end of year 3 (the current year), an enterprise has $2,400 of taxable temporary differences, which are expected to result in taxable amounts of approximately $800 on the future tax returns for each of years 4-6. Enacted tax rates are 35 percent for years 1-3, 40 percent for years 4-6, and 45 percent for year 7 and thereafter.

The tax rate that is used to measure the deferred tax liability for the $2,400 of taxable temporary differences differs depending on whether the tax effect of future reversals of those temporary differences is on taxes payable for years 1-3, years 4-6, or year 7 and thereafter. The tax rate for measurement of the deferred tax liability is 40 percent whenever taxable income is expected in years 4-6. If tax losses are expected in years 4-6, however, the tax rate is:

a. 35 percent if realization of a tax benefit for those tax losses in years 4-6 will be by loss carryback to years 1-3
b. 45 percent if realization of a tax benefit for those tax losses in years 4-6 will be by loss carryforward to year 7 and thereafter.

235. The following example illustrates determination of the tax rate for measurement of a deferred tax asset for deductible temporary differences when there is a change in tax rates. The assumptions are as follows:

a. Enacted tax rates are 30 percent for years 1-3 and 40 percent for year 4 and thereafter.
b. At the end of year 3 (the current year), an enterprise has $900 of deductible temporary differences, which are expected to result in tax deductions of approximately $300 on the future tax returns for each of years 4-6.

The tax rate is 40 percent if the enterprise expects to realize a tax benefit for the deductible temporary differences by offsetting taxable income earned in future years. Alternatively, the tax rate is 30 percent if the enterprise expects to realize a tax benefit for the deductible temporary differences by loss carryback refund.

Assume that (a) the enterprise recognizes a $360 ($900 at 40 percent) deferred tax asset to be realized by offsetting taxable income in future years and (b) taxable income and taxes payable in each of years 1-3 were $300 and $90, respectively. Realization of a tax benefit of at least $270 ($900 at 30 percent) is assured because carryback refunds totalling $270 may be realized even if no taxable income is earned in future years. Recognition of a valuation allowance for the other $90 ($360 − $270) of the deferred tax asset depends on management's assessment of whether, based on the weight of available evidence, a portion or all of the tax benefit of the $900 of deductible temporary differences will not be realized at 40 percent tax rates in future years.

Alternatively, if enacted tax rates are 40 percent for years 1-3 and 30 percent for year 4 and thereafter, measurement of the deferred tax asset at a 40 percent tax rate could only occur if tax losses are expected in future years 4-6.

236. The following example illustrates determination of the average graduated tax rate for measurement of deferred tax liabilities and assets by an enterprise for which graduated tax rates ordinarily are a significant factor. At the end of year 3 (the current year), an enterprise has $1,500 of taxable temporary differences and $900 of deductible temporary differences, which are expected to result in net taxable amounts of approximately $200 on the future tax returns for each of years 4-6. Enacted tax rates are 15 percent for the first $500 of taxable income, 25 percent for the next $500, and 40 percent for taxable income over $1,000. This example assumes that there is no income (for example, capital gains) subject to special tax rates.

The deferred tax liability and asset for those reversing taxable and deductible temporary differences in years 4-6 are measured using the average graduated tax rate for the estimated amount of annual taxable income in future years. Thus, the average graduated tax rate will differ depending on the expected level of annual taxable income (including reversing temporary differences) in years 4-6. The average tax rate will be:

a. 15 percent if the estimated annual level of taxable income in years 4-6 is $500 or less
b. 20 percent if the estimated annual level of taxable income in years 4-6 is $1,000
c. 30 percent if the estimated annual level of taxable income in years 4-6 is $2,000

Temporary differences usually do not reverse in equal annual amounts as in the example above, and a different average graduated tax rate might apply to reversals in different future years. However, a detailed analysis to determine the net reversals of temporary differences in each future year usually is not warranted. It is not warranted because the other variable (that is, taxable income or losses exclusive of reversing temporary differences in each of those future years) for determination of the average graduated tax rate in each future year is no more than an estimate. For that reason, an

aggregate calculation using a single estimated average graduated tax rate based on estimated average annual taxable income in future years is sufficient. Judgment is permitted, however, to deal with unusual situations, for example, an abnormally large temporary difference that will reverse in a single future year, or an abnormal level of taxable income that is expected for a single future year. The lowest graduated tax rate should be used whenever the estimated average graduated tax rate otherwise would be zero.

237. Deferred tax liabilities and assets are measured using enacted tax rates applicable to capital gains, ordinary income, and so forth, based on the expected type of taxable or deductible amounts in future years. For example, evidence based on all facts and circumstances should determine whether an investor's liability for the tax consequences of temporary differences related to its equity in the earnings of an investee should be measured using enacted tax rates applicable to a capital gain or a dividend. Computation of a deferred tax liability for undistributed earnings based on dividends should also reflect any related dividends received deductions or foreign tax credits, and taxes that would be withheld from the dividend.

Alternative Minimum Tax

238. Temporary differences such as depreciation differences are one reason why TMT may exceed regular tax. Temporary differences, however, ultimately reverse and, absent a significant amount of preference items, total taxes paid over the entire life of the enterprise will be based on the regular tax system. Preference items are another reason why TMT may exceed regular tax. If preference items are large enough, an enterprise could be subject, over its lifetime, to the AMT system; and the cumulative amount of AMT credit carryforwards would expire unused. No one can know beforehand which scenario will prevail because that determination can only be made after the fact. In the meantime, this Statement requires procedures that provide a practical solution to that problem.

239. Under the requirements of this Statement, an enterprise should:

a. Measure the total deferred tax liability and asset for regular tax temporary differences and carryforwards using the regular tax rate
b. Measure the total deferred tax asset for all AMT credit carryforward
c. Reduce the deferred tax asset for AMT credit carryforward by a valuation allowance if, based on the weight of available evidence, it is more likely than not that some portion or all of that deferred tax asset will not be realized.

Paragraph 21 identifies four sources of taxable income that should be considered in determining the need for and amount of a valuation allowance. No valuation allowance is necessary if the deferred tax asset for AMT credit carryforward can be realized:

1. Under paragraph 21(a), by reducing a deferred tax liability from the amount of regular tax on regular tax temporary differences to not less than the amount of TMT on AMT temporary differences
2. Under paragraph 21(b), by reducing taxes on future income from the amount of regular tax on regular taxable income to not less than the amount of TMT on AMT income
3. Under paragraph 21(c), by loss carryback
4. Under paragraph 21(d), by a tax-planning strategy such as switching from tax-exempt to taxable interest income.

Operating Loss and Tax Credit Carryforwards and Carrybacks

Recognition of a Tax Benefit for Carrybacks

240. An operating loss, certain deductible items that are subject to limitations, and some tax credits arising but not utilized in the current year may be carried back for refund of taxes paid in prior years or carried forward to reduce taxes payable in future years. A receivable is recognized for the amount of taxes paid in prior years that is refund-able by carryback of an operating loss or unused tax credits of the current year.

Recognition of a Tax Benefit for Carryforwards

241. A deferred tax asset is recognized for an operating loss or tax credit carryforward.[17] In assessing the need for a valuation allowance, provisions in the tax law that limit utilization of an operating loss or tax credit carryforward are applied in determining whether it is more likely than not that some portion or all of the deferred tax asset will not be realized by reduction of taxes payable on taxable income during the carryforward period.

242. The following example illustrates recognition of the tax benefit of an operating loss in the loss year and in subsequent carryforward years when a valuation allowance is necessary in the loss year. The assumptions are as follows:

a. The enacted tax rate is 40 percent for all years.
b. An operating loss occurs in year 5.
c. The only difference between financial and taxable income results from use of accelerated depreciation for tax purposes. Differences that arise between the reported amount and the tax basis of depreciable assets in years 1-7 will result in taxable amounts before the end of the loss carryforward period from year 5.
d. Financial income, taxable income, and taxes currently payable or refundable are as follows:

	Year 1	Years 2-4	Year 5	Year 6	Year 7
Pretax financial income (loss)	$2,000	$5,000	$(8,000)	$2,200	$7,000
Depreciation differences	(800)	(2,200)	(800)	(700)	(600)
Loss carryback	—	—	2,800	—	—
Loss carryforward	—	—	—	(6,000)	(4,500)
Taxable income (loss)	$1,200	$2,800	$(6,000)	$(4,500)	$1,900
Taxes payable (refundable)	$ 480	$1,120	$(1,120)	$ —	$ 760

e. At the end of year 5, profits are not expected in years 6 and 7 and later years, and it is concluded that a valuation allowance is necessary to the extent realization of the deferred tax asset for the operating loss carryforward depends on taxable income (exclusive of reversing temporary differences) in future years.

---

[17]This requirement pertains to all ITC carryforwards regardless of whether the flow-through or deferral method is used to account for ITC.

The deferred tax liability for the taxable temporary differences is calculated at the end of each year as follows:

	Year 1	Years 2-4	Year 5	Year 6	Year 7
Unreversed differences:					
Beginning amount	$ —	$ 800	$3,000	$3,800	$4,500
Additional amount	800	2,200	800	700	600
Total	$800	$3,000	$3,800	$4,500	$5,100
Deferred tax liability (40 percent)	$320	$1,200	$1,520	$1,800	$2,040

The deferred tax asset and related valuation allowance for the loss carryforward are calculated at the end of each year as follows:

	Year 1	Years 2-4	Year 5	Year 6	Year 7
Loss carryforward for tax purposes	$—	$—	$6,000	$4,500	$—
Deferred tax asset (40 percent)	$—	$—	$2,400	$1,800	$—
Valuation allowance equal to the amount by which the deferred tax asset exceeds the deferred tax liability	—	—	(880)	—	—
Net deferred tax asset	$—	$—	$1,520	$1,800	$—

Total tax expense for each period is as follows:

	Year 1	Years 2-4	Year 5	Year 6	Year 7
Deferred tax expense (benefit):					
Increase in deferred tax liability	$320	$ 880	$ 320	$280	$ 240
(Increase) decrease in net deferred tax asset	—	—	(1,520)	(280)	1,800
	320	880	(1,200)	—	2,040
Currently payable (refundable)	480	1,120	(1,120)	—	760
Total tax expense (benefit)	$800	$2,000	$(2,320)	$ —	$2,800

In year 5, $2,800 of the loss is carried back to reduce taxable income in years 2-4, and $1,120 of taxes paid for those years is refunded. In addition, a $1,520 deferred tax liability is recognized for $3,800 of taxable temporary differences, and a $2,400 deferred tax asset is recognized for the $6,000 loss carryforward. However, based on the conclusion described in assumption (e), a valuation allowance is recognized for the amount by which that deferred tax asset exceeds the deferred tax liability.

In year 6, a portion of the deferred tax asset for the loss carryforward is realized because taxable income is earned in that year. The remaining balance of the deferred tax asset for the loss carryforward at the end of year 6 equals the deferred tax liability for the taxable temporary differences. A valuation allowance is not needed.

In year 7, the remaining balance of the loss carryforward is realized, and $760 of taxes are payable on net taxable income of $1,900. A $2,040 deferred tax liability is recognized for the $5,100 of taxable temporary differences.

243. An operating loss or tax credit carryforward from a prior year (for which the deferred tax asset was reduced by a valuation allowance) may sometimes reduce taxable income and taxes payable that are attributable to certain revenues or gains that the tax law requires be included in taxable income for the year that cash is received. For financial reporting, however, there may have been no revenue or gain and a liability is recognized for the cash received. Future sacrifices to settle the liability will result in deductible amounts in future years. Under those circumstances, the reduction in taxable income and taxes payable from utilization of the operating loss or tax credit carryforward gives no cause for recognition of a tax benefit because, in effect, the operating loss or tax credit carryforward has been replaced by temporary differences that will result in deductible amounts when a nontax liability is settled in future years. The requirements for recognition of a tax benefit for de-

ductible temporary differences and for operating loss carryforwards are the same, and the manner of reporting the eventual tax benefit recognized (that is, in income or as required by paragraph 37) is not affected by the intervening transaction reported for tax purposes.

244. The following example illustrates the interaction of loss carryforwards and temporary differences that will result in net deductible amounts in future years. The assumptions are as follows:

a. The financial loss and the loss reported on the tax return for an enterprise's first year of operations are the same.
b. In year 2, a gain of $2,500 from a transaction that is a sale for tax purposes but a sale and leaseback for financial reporting is the only difference between pretax financial income and taxable income.

	Financial Income	Taxable Income
Year 1: Income (loss) from operations	$(4,000)	$(4,000)
Year 2: Income (loss) from operations	$ —	$ —
Taxable gain on sale		2,500
Taxable income before loss carryforward		2,500
Loss carryforward from year 1		(4,000)
Taxable income		$ —

The $4,000 operating loss carryforward at the end of year 1 is reduced to $1,500 at the end of year 2 because $2,500 of it is used to reduce taxable income. The $2,500 reduction in the loss carryforward becomes $2,500 of deductible temporary differences that will reverse and result in future tax deductions when lease payments are made. The enterprise has no deferred tax liability to be offset by those future tax deductions, the future tax deductions cannot be realized by loss carryback because no taxes have been paid, and the enterprise has had pretax losses for financial reporting since inception. Unless positive evidence exists that is sufficient to overcome the negative evidence associated with those losses, a valuation allowance is recognized at the end of year 2 for the full amount of the deferred tax asset related to the $2,500 of deductible temporary differences and the remaining $1,500 of operating loss carryforward.

Reporting the Tax Benefit of Operating Loss Carryforwards or Carrybacks

245. Except as noted in paragraph 37, the manner of reporting the tax benefit of an operating loss carryforward or carryback is determined by the source of the income or loss in the current year and not by (a) the source of the operating loss carryforward or taxes paid in a prior year or (b) the source of expected future income that will result in realization of a deferred tax asset for an operating loss carryforward from the current year. Deferred tax expense or benefit that results because a change in circumstances causes a change in judgment about the future realization of the tax benefit of an operating loss carryforward is allocated to continuing operations (refer to paragraph 26). Thus, for example:

a. The tax benefit of an operating loss carryforward that resulted from an extraordinary loss in a prior year and that is first recognized in the financial statements for the current year:
   (1) Is allocated to continuing operations if it offsets the current or deferred tax consequences of income from continuing operations
   (2) Is allocated to an extraordinary gain if it offsets the current or deferred tax consequences of that extraordinary gain
   (3) Is allocated to continuing operations if it results from a change in circumstances that causes a change in judgment about future realization of a tax benefit
b. The current or deferred tax benefit of a loss from continuing operations in the current year is allocated to continuing operations regardless of whether that loss offsets the current or deferred tax consequences of an extraordinary gain that:
   (1) Occurred in the current year
   (2) Occurred in a prior year (that is, if realization of the tax benefit will be by carryback refund)
   (3) Is expected to occur in a future year.

Tax-Planning Strategies

246. Expectations about future taxable income incorporate numerous assumptions about actions, elections, and strategies to minimize income taxes in future years. For example, an enterprise may have a practice of deferring taxable income whenever possible by structuring sales to qualify as installment sales for tax purposes. Actions such as that are not *tax-planning strategies*, as that term is used in this Statement, because they are actions that management takes in the normal course of business. For purposes of applying the require-

ments of this Statement, a *tax-planning strategy* is an action that management ordinarily might not take but would take, if necessary, to realize a tax benefit for a carryforward before it expires. For example, a strategy to sell property and lease it back for the expressed purpose of generating taxable income to utilize a carryforward before it expires is not an action that management takes in the normal course of business. A qualifying tax-planning strategy is an action that:

a. *Is prudent and feasible.* Management must have the ability to implement the strategy and expect to do so unless the need is eliminated in future years. For example, management would not have to apply the strategy if income earned in a later year uses the entire amount of carryforward from the current year.
b. *An enterprise ordinarily might not take, but would take to prevent an operating loss or tax credit carryforward from expiring unused.* All of the various strategies that are expected to be employed for business or tax purposes other than utilization of carryforwards that would otherwise expire unused are, for purposes of this Statement, implicit in management's estimate of future taxable income and, therefore, are not tax-planning strategies as that term is used in this Statement.
c. *Would result in realization of deferred tax assets.* The effect of qualifying tax-planning strategies must be recognized in the determination of the amount of a valuation allowance. Tax-planning strategies need not be considered, however, if positive evidence available from other sources (refer to paragraph 21) is sufficient to support a conclusion that a valuation allowance is *not* necessary.

247. Tax-planning strategies may shift estimated future taxable income between future years. For example, assume that an enterprise has a $1,500 operating loss carryforward that expires at the end of next year and that its estimate of taxable income exclusive of the future reversal of existing temporary differences and carryforwards is approximately $1,000 per year for each of the next several years. That estimate is based, in part, on the enterprise's present practice of making sales on the installment basis and on provisions in the tax law that result in temporary deferral of gains on installment sales. A tax-planning strategy to increase taxable income next year and realize the full tax benefit of that operating loss carryforward might be to structure next year's sales in a manner that does not meet the tax rules to qualify as installment sales. Another strategy might be to change next year's depreciation procedures for tax purposes.

248. Tax-planning strategies also may shift the estimated pattern and timing of future reversals of temporary differences. For example, if an operating loss carryforward otherwise would expire unused at the end of next year, a tax-planning strategy to sell the enterprise's installment sale receivables next year would accelerate the future reversal of *taxable* temporary differences for the gains on those installment sales. In other circumstances, a tax-planning strategy to accelerate the future reversal of *deductible* temporary differences if they otherwise would reverse and provide no tax benefit in some later future year(s). Examples of actions that would accelerate the future reversal of deductible temporary differences include:

a. An annual payment that is larger than an enterprise's usual annual payment to reduce a long-term pension obligation (recognized as a liability in the financial statements) might accelerate a tax deduction for pension expense to an earlier year than would otherwise have occurred.
b. Disposal of obsolete inventory that is reported at net realizable value in the financial statements would accelerate a tax deduction for the amount by which the tax basis exceeds the net realizable value of the inventory.
c. Sale of loans at their reported amount (that is, net of an allowance for bad debts) would accelerate a tax deduction for the allowance for bad debts.

249. A significant expense might need to be incurred to implement a particular tax-planning strategy, or a significant loss might need to be recognized as a result of implementing a particular tax-planning strategy. In either case, that expense or loss (net of any future tax benefit that would result from that expense or loss) reduces the amount of tax benefit that is recognized for the expected effect of a qualifying tax-planning strategy. For that purpose, the future effect of a differential in interest rates (for example, between the rate that would be earned on installment sale receivables and the rate that could be earned on an alternative investment if the tax-planning strategy is to sell those receivables to accelerate the future reversal of related taxable temporary differences) is not considered.

250. The following example illustrates recognition of a deferred tax asset based on the expected effect of a qualifying tax-planning strategy when a signif-

icant expense would be incurred to implement the strategy. The assumptions are as follows:

a. A $900 operating loss carryforward expires at the end of next year.
b. Based on historical results and the weight of other available evidence, the estimated level of taxable income exclusive of the future reversal of existing temporary differences and the operating loss carryforward next year is $100.
c. Taxable temporary differences in the amount of $1,200 ordinarily would result in taxable amounts of approximately $400 in each of the next 3 years.
d. There is a qualifying tax-planning strategy to accelerate the future reversal of all $1,200 of taxable temporary differences to next year.
e. Estimated legal and other expenses to implement that tax-planning strategy are $150.
f. The enacted tax rate is 40 percent for all years.

Without the tax-planning strategy, only $500 of the $900 operating loss carryforward could be realized next year by offsetting (a) $100 of taxable income exclusive of reversing temporary differences and (b) $400 of reversing taxable temporary differences. The other $400 of operating loss carryforward would expire unused at the end of next year. Therefore, the $360 deferred tax asset ($900 at 40 percent) would be offset by a $160 valuation allowance ($400 at 40 percent), and a $200 net deferred tax asset would be recognized for the operating loss carryforward.

With the tax-planning strategy, the $900 operating loss carryforward could be applied against $1,300 of taxable income next year ($100 of taxable income exclusive of reversing temporary differences and $1,200 of reversing taxable temporary differences). The $360 deferred tax asset is reduced by a $90 valuation allowance recognized for the net-of-tax expenses necessary to implement the tax-planning strategy. The amount of that valuation allowance is determined as follows:

Legal and other expenses to implement the tax-planning strategy	$150
Future tax benefit of those legal and other expenses—$150 at 40 percent	60
	$ 90

In summary, a $480 deferred tax liability is recognized for the $1,200 of taxable temporary differences, a $360 deferred tax asset is recognized for the $900 operating loss carryforward, and a $90 valuation allowance is recognized for the net-of-

tax expenses of implementing the tax-planning strategy.

251. Under this Statement, the requirements for consideration of tax-planning strategies pertain only to the determination of a valuation allowance for a deferred tax asset. A deferred tax liability ordinarily is recognized for all taxable temporary differences. The only exceptions are identified in paragraph 9. Certain seemingly taxable temporary differences, however, may or may not result in taxable amounts when those differences reverse in future years. One example is an excess of cash surrender value of life insurance over premiums paid (paragraph 14). Another example is an excess of the book over the tax basis of an investment in a domestic subsidiary (paragraph 33). The determination of whether those differences are taxable temporary differences does not involve a tax-planning strategy as that term is used in this Statement.

Regulated Enterprises

252. Paragraph 9 of Statement 71 requires a regulated enterprise that applies Statement 71 to capitalize an incurred cost that would otherwise be charged to expense if the following criteria are met:

a. It is probable that future revenue in an amount at least equal to the capitalized cost will result from inclusion of that cost in allowable costs for rate-making purposes.
b. Based on available evidence, the future revenue will be provided to permit recovery of the previously incurred cost rather than to provide for expected levels of similar future costs.

If the income taxes that result from recording a deferred tax liability in accordance with this Statement meet those criteria, an asset is recognized for those income taxes when the deferred tax liability is recognized. That asset and the deferred tax liability are not offset for general-purpose financial reporting; rather, each is displayed separately.

253. The following example illustrates recognition of an asset for the probable future revenue to recover future income taxes related to the deferred tax liability for the equity component of the allowance for funds used during construction (AFUDC). The assumptions are as follows:

a. During year 1, the first year of operations, total construction costs for financial reporting and tax purposes are $400,000 (exclusive of AFUDC).

b. The enacted tax rate is 34 percent for all future years.

c. AFUDC (consisting entirely of the equity component) is $26,000. The asset for probable future revenue to recover the related income taxes is calculated as follows:

34 percent of ($26,000 + A) = A (where A equals the asset for probable future revenue)

A = $13,394

At the end of year 1, the related accounts[18] are as follows:

Construction in progress	$426,000
Probable future revenue	$ 13,394
Deferred tax liability [34 percent of ($26,000 + $13,394)]	$ 13,394

254. The following example illustrates adjustment of a deferred tax liability for an enacted change in tax rates. The assumptions are the same as for the example in paragraph 253 except that a change in the tax rate from 34 percent to 30 percent is enacted on the first day of year 2. As of the first day of year 2, the related accounts are adjusted so that the balances are as follows:

Construction in progress	$426,000
Probable future revenue	$ 11,143
Deferred tax liability [30 percent of ($26,000 + $11,143)]	$ 11,143

255. The following example illustrates adjustment of a deferred tax liability for an enacted change in tax rates when that deferred tax liability represents amounts already collected from customers for the future payment of income taxes. In that case, there would be no asset for "probable future revenue." The assumptions are as follows:

a. Amounts at the end of year 1, the current year, are as follows:

Construction in progress for financial reporting	$400,000
Tax basis of construction in progress	$300,000
Deferred tax liability (34 percent of $100,000)	$ 34,000

b. A change in the tax rate from 34 percent to 30 percent is enacted on the first day of year 2. As a result of the reduction in tax rates, it is probable that $4,000 of the $34,000 (previously collected from customers for the future payment of income taxes) will be refunded to customers, together with the tax benefit of that refund, through a future rate reduction. The liability for the future rate reduction to refund a portion of the deferred taxes previously collected from customers is calculated as follows:

$4,000 + (30 percent of R) = R (where R equals the probable future reduction in revenue)

R = $5,714

As of the first day of year 2, the related accounts are adjusted so that the balances are as follows:

Construction in progress	$400,000
Probable reduction in future revenue	$ 5,714
Deferred tax liability [30 percent of ($100,000 − $5,714)]	$ 28,286

Leveraged Leases

256. This Statement does not change (a) the pattern of recognition of after-tax income for leveraged leases as required by Statement 13 or (b) the allocation of the purchase price in a purchase business combination to acquired leveraged leases as required by Interpretation 21. Integration of the results of income tax accounting for leveraged leases with the other results of accounting for income taxes under this Statement is required when deferred tax credits related to leveraged leases are the only source (refer to paragraph 21) for recognition of a tax benefit for deductible temporary differences and carryforwards not related to leveraged leases. A valuation allowance is not necessary if deductible temporary differences and carryforwards will offset taxable amounts from future recovery of the net investment in the leveraged lease. However, to the extent that the amount of deferred tax credits for a leveraged lease as determined under Statement 13 differs from the amount of the deferred tax liability related to the leveraged lease that would otherwise result from applying the requirements of this Statement, that difference is preserved and is not a source of taxable income for recognition of the tax benefit of deductible temporary differences and operating loss or tax credit carryforwards.

---

[18]In this example, if AFUDC had consisted entirely of a net-of-tax debt component in the amount of $26,000, the related accounts and their balances at the end of year 1 would be construction in progress in the amount of $439,394 and a deferred tax liability in the amount of $13,394.

257. Interpretation 21 requires that the tax effect of any difference between the assigned value and the tax basis of a leveraged lease at the date of a business combination not be accounted for as a deferred tax credit. This Statement does not change that requirement. Any tax effects included in unearned and deferred income as required by Interpretation 21 are not offset by the deferred tax consequences of other temporary differences or by the tax benefit of operating loss or tax credit carryforwards. However, deferred tax credits that arise after the date of a business combination are accounted for in the same manner as described above for leveraged leases that were not acquired in a purchase business combination.

258. The following example illustrates integration of the results of income tax accounting for leveraged leases with the other results of accounting for income taxes as required by this Statement.

a. At the end of year 1, the current year, an enterprise has two temporary differences. One temporary difference is for a leveraged lease that was entered into in a prior year. During year 1, the enacted tax rate for year 2 and thereafter changed from 40 percent to 35 percent. After adjusting for the change in estimated total net income from the lease as a result of the change in tax rates as required by Statement 13, the components of the investment in the leveraged lease at the end of year 1 are as follows:

Net rentals receivable plus residual value less unearned pretax income		$150,000
Reduced by:		
Deferred ITC	$ 9,000	
Deferred tax credits	39,000	48,000
Net investment in leveraged lease for financial reporting		$102,000

b. The other temporary difference is for a $120,000 estimated liability for warranty expense that will result in a tax deduction in year 5 when the liability is expected to be paid. Absent consideration of the deferred tax credits attributable to the leveraged lease, the weight of available evidence indicates that a valuation allowance is needed for the entire amount of the deferred tax asset related to that $120,000 deductible temporary difference.

c. The tax basis of the investment in the leveraged lease at the end of year 1 is $41,000. The amount of the deferred tax liability for that lev-

eraged lease that would otherwise result from the requirements of this Statement is determined as follows:

Net rentals receivable plus residual value less unearned pretax income	$150,000
Temporary difference for deferred ITC	9,000
	141,000
Tax basis of leveraged lease	41,000
Temporary difference	$100,000
Deferred tax liability (35 percent)	$ 35,000

d. Loss carryback (to year 2) and loss carryforward (to year 20) of the $120,000 tax deduction for warranty expense in year 5 would offset the $100,000 of taxable amounts resulting from future recovery of the net investment in the leveraged lease over the remainder of the lease term.

e. At the end of year 1, the enterprise recognizes a $42,000 ($120,000 at 35 percent) deferred tax asset and a related $7,000 valuation allowance. The effect is to recognize a $35,000 net deferred tax benefit for the reduction in deferred tax credits attributable to the leveraged lease. Deferred tax credits attributable to the leveraged lease determined under the requirements of Statement 13 are $39,000. However, the deferred tax liability determined under the requirements of this Statement is only $35,000. The $4,000 difference is not available for offsetting.

Business Combinations

259. This Statement requires recognition of deferred tax liabilities and deferred tax assets (and related valuation allowances, if necessary) for the deferred tax consequences of differences between the assigned values and the tax bases of the assets and liabilities recognized in a business combination accounted for as a purchase under Opinion 16. A deferred tax liability or asset is not recognized for a difference between the reported amount and the tax basis of goodwill or the portion thereof for which amortization is not deductible for tax purposes (paragraphs 262 and 263), unallocated "negative" goodwill, and leveraged leases (paragraphs 256-258). Acquired Opinion 23 differences are accounted for in accordance with the requirements of Opinion 23, as amended by this Statement (paragraphs 31-34).

Nontaxable Business Combinations

260. The following example illustrates recognition and measurement of a deferred tax liability and as-

set in a nontaxable business combination. The assumptions are as follows:

a. The enacted tax rate is 40 percent for all future years, and amortization of goodwill is not deductible for tax purposes.
b. An enterprise is acquired for $20,000, and the enterprise has no leveraged leases.
c. The tax basis of the net assets acquired is $5,000, and the assigned value (other than goodwill) is $12,000. Future recovery of the assets and settlement of the liabilities at their assigned values will result in $20,000 of taxable amounts and $13,000 of deductible amounts that can be offset against each other. Therefore, no valuation allowance is necessary.

The amounts recorded to account for the purchase transaction are as follows:

Assigned value of the net assets (other than goodwill) acquired	$12,000
Deferred tax liability for $20,000 of taxable temporary differences	(8,000)
Deferred tax asset for $13,000 of deductible temporary differences	5,200
Goodwill	10,800
Purchase price of the acquired enterprise	$20,000

Taxable Business Combinations

261. In a taxable business combination, the purchase price is assigned to the assets and liabilities recognized for tax purposes as well as for financial reporting. However, the amounts assigned to particular assets and liabilities may differ for financial reporting and tax purposes. A deferred tax liability and asset are recognized for the deferred tax consequences of those temporary differences in accordance with the recognition and measurement requirements of this Statement. For example, a portion of the amount of goodwill for financial reporting may be allocated to some other asset for tax purposes, and amortization of that other asset may be deductible for tax purposes. If a valuation allowance is recognized for that deferred tax asset at the acquisition date, recognized benefits for those tax deductions after the acquisition date should be applied (a) first to reduce to zero any

goodwill related to that acquisition, (b) second to reduce to zero other noncurrent intangible assets related to that acquisition, and (c) third to reduce income tax expense.

262. Amortization of goodwill is deductible for tax purposes in some tax jurisdictions. In those tax jurisdictions, the reported amount of goodwill and the tax basis of goodwill are each separated into two components as of the combination date for purposes of deferred tax calculations. The first component of each equals the lesser of (a) goodwill for financial reporting or (b) tax-deductible goodwill. The second component of each equals the remainder of each, that is, (1) the remainder, if any, of goodwill for financial reporting or (2) the remainder, if any, of tax-deductible goodwill. Any difference that arises between the book and tax basis of that first component of goodwill in future years is a temporary difference for which a deferred tax liability or asset is recognized based on the requirements of this Statement. No deferred taxes are recognized for the second component of goodwill. If that second component is an excess of tax-deductible goodwill over the reported amount of goodwill, the tax benefit for that excess is recognized when realized on the tax return, and that tax benefit is applied first to reduce to zero the goodwill related to that acquisition, second to reduce to zero other noncurrent intangible assets related to that acquisition, and third to reduce income tax expense.

263. The following example illustrates accounting for the tax consequences of goodwill when amortization of goodwill is deductible for tax purposes. The assumptions are as follows:

a. At the combination date, the reported amount and tax basis of goodwill are $600 and $800, respectively.
b. For tax purposes, amortization of goodwill will result in tax deductions of $400 in each of years 1 and 2. Those deductions result in a current tax benefit in years 1 and 2.
c. For financial reporting, amortization of goodwill is straight-line over years 1-4.
d. For purposes of simplification, the consequences of other temporary differences are ignored for years 1-4.
e. Income before amortization of goodwill and income taxes in each of years 1-4 is $1,000.
f. The tax rate is 40 percent for all years.

Income taxes payable for years 1-4 are:

	Year			
	1	2	3	4
Income before amortization of goodwill	$1,000	$1,000	$1,000	$1,000
Amortization of goodwill	400	400	—	—
Taxable income	$ 600	$ 600	$1,000	$1,000
Income taxes payable (40 percent)	$ 240	$ 240	$ 400	$ 400

At the combination date, goodwill is separated into two components as follows:

	Reported Amount	Tax Basis
First component	$600	$600
Second component	—	200
Total goodwill	$600	$800

A deferred tax liability is recognized at the end of years 1-3 for the excess of the reported amount over the tax basis of the first component of goodwill. A deferred tax asset is not recognized for the second component of goodwill; the tax benefit is allocated to reduce goodwill when realized on the tax returns for years 1 and 2.

The second component of goodwill is deductible $100 per year in years 1 and 2. Those tax deductions provide $40 ($100 at 40 percent) of tax benefits that are realized in years 1 and 2. Allocation of those realized tax benefits to reduce the first component of goodwill produces a deferred tax benefit by reducing the taxable temporary difference related to that component of goodwill. Thus, the total tax benefit allocated to reduce the first component of goodwill in each of years 1 and 2 is the sum of (a) the $40 realized tax benefit allocated to reduce goodwill and (b) the deferred tax benefit from reducing the deferred tax liability related to goodwill. That total tax benefit (TTB) is determined as follows:

TTB = realized tax benefit plus (tax rate times TTB)
TTB = $40 + (.40 × TTB)
TTB = $67

Goodwill for financial reporting for years 1-4 is:

	Year			
	1	2	3	4
Balance at beginning of year	$600	$383	$188	$94
Amortization:				
$600 ÷ 4 years	150			
$383 ÷ 3 years		128		
$188 ÷ 2 years			94	94
Total tax benefit allocated to reduce goodwill	67	67	—	—
Balance at end of year	$383	$188	$ 94	$—

The deferred tax liability for the first component of goodwill and the related amount of deferred tax expense (benefit) for years 1-4 are:

	Year			
	1	2	3	4
Reported amount of goodwill at end of year	$383	$188	$ 94	$ —
Tax basis of goodwill (first component)	300	—	—	—
Taxable temporary difference	$ 83	$188	$ 94	$ —
Deferred tax liability:				
At end of year (40 percent)	$ 33	$ 75	$ 38	$ —
At beginning of year	—	33	75	38
Deferred tax expense (benefit) for the year	$ 33	$ 42	$(37)	$(38)

Income for financial reporting for years 1-4 is:

	Year			
	1	**2**	**3**	**4**
Income before amortization of goodwill and income taxes	$1,000	$1,000	$1,000	$1,000
Amortization of goodwill	150	128	94	94
Pretax income	850	872	906	906
Income tax expense (benefit):				
Current	240	240	400	400
Deferred	33	42	(37)	(38)
Benefit applied to reduce goodwill	67	67	—	—
Income tax expense	340	349	363	362
Net income	$ 510	$ 523	$ 543	$ 544

Carryforwards—Purchase Method

264. Accounting for a business combination should reflect any provisions in the tax law that restrict the future use of either of the combining enterprises' deductible temporary differences or carryforwards to reduce taxable income or taxes payable attributable to the other enterprise subsequent to the business combination. For example, the tax law may limit the use of the acquired enterprise's deductible temporary differences and carryforwards to subsequent taxable income of the acquired enterprise in a consolidated tax return for the combined enterprise. In that circumstance, or if the acquired enterprise will file a separate tax return, the need for a valuation allowance for some portion or all of the acquired enterprise's deferred tax assets for deductible temporary differences and carryforwards is assessed based on the acquired enterprise's *separate* past and expected future results of operations.

265. The following example illustrates (a) recognition of a deferred tax asset and the related valuation allowance for acquired deductible temporary differences at the date of a nontaxable business combination and in subsequent periods when (b) the tax law limits the use of an acquired enterprise's deductible temporary differences and carryforwards to subsequent taxable income of the acquired enterprise in a consolidated tax return. The assumptions are as follows:

a. The enacted tax rate is 40 percent for all future years.
b. The purchase price is $20,000, and the assigned value of the net assets acquired is also $20,000.
c. The tax basis of the net assets acquired is $60,000. The $40,000 ($60,000 − $20,000) of deductible temporary differences at the combination date is primarily attributable to an allowance for loan losses. Provisions in the tax law limit the use of those future tax deductions

to subsequent taxable income of the acquired enterprise.
d. The acquired enterprise's actual pretax results for the two preceding years and the expected results for the year of the business combination are as follows:

Year 1	$(15,000)
Year 2	(10,000)
Year 3 to the combination date	(5,000)
Expected results for the remainder of year 3	(5,000)

e. Based on assessments of all evidence available at the date of the business combination in year 3 and at the end of year 3, management concludes that a valuation allowance is needed at both dates for the entire amount of the deferred tax asset related to the acquired deductible temporary differences.

The acquired enterprise's pretax financial income and taxable income for year 3 (after the business combination) and year 4 are as follows:

	Year 3	Year 4
Pretax financial income	$15,000	$10,000
Reversals of acquired deductible temporary differences	(15,000)	(10,000)
Taxable income	$ —	$ —

At the end of year 4, the remaining balance of acquired deductible temporary differences is $15,000 ($40,000 − $25,000). The deferred tax asset is $6,000 ($15,000 at 40 percent). Based on an assessment of all available evidence at the end of year 4, management concludes that no valuation allowance is needed for that $6,000 deferred tax asset. Elimination of the $6,000 valuation allowance results in a $6,000 deferred tax benefit that is reported as a reduction of deferred income tax expense because there is no goodwill or other noncurrent intangible assets related to the acquisition. For the same reason, tax benefits realized in years 3 and 4 attributable to reversals of acquired deductible temporary differences are reported as a zero current income tax expense. The consolidated statement of earnings would include the following amounts attributable to the acquired enterprise for year 3 (after the business combination) and year 4:

	Year 3	Year 4
Pretax financial income	$15,000	$10,000
Income tax expense (benefit):		
Current	—	—
Deferred	—	(6,000)
Net income	$15,000	$16,000

266. The tax law in some tax jurisdictions may permit the future use of either of the combining enterprises' deductible temporary differences or carryforwards to reduce taxable income or taxes payable attributable to the other enterprise subsequent to the business combination. If the combined enterprise expects to file a consolidated tax return, a deferred tax asset (net of a valuation allowance, if necessary) is recognized for deductible temporary differences or carryforwards of either combining enterprise based on an assessment of the *combined* enterprise's past and expected future results of operations as of the acquisition date. This either reduces goodwill or noncurrent assets (except long-term investments in marketable securities) of the acquired enterprise or creates or increases negative goodwill.

267. The following example illustrates (a) elimination of the need for a valuation allowance for the deferred tax asset for an acquired loss carryforward based on offset against taxable temporary differences of the acquiring enterprise in a nontaxable business combination when (b) the tax law permits use of an acquired enterprise's deductible temporary differences and carryforwards to reduce taxable income or taxes payable attributable to the acquiring enterprise in a consolidated tax return. The assumptions are as follows:

a. The enacted tax rate is 40 percent for all future years.
b. The purchase price is $20,000. The tax basis of the identified net assets acquired is $5,000, and the assigned value is $12,000, that is, there are $7,000 of taxable temporary differences. The acquired enterprise also has a $16,000 operating loss carryforward, which, under the tax law, may be used by the acquiring enterprise in the consolidated tax return.

c. The acquiring enterprise has temporary differences that will result in $30,000 of net taxable amounts in future years.
d. All temporary differences of the acquired and acquiring enterprises will result in taxable amounts before the end of the acquired enterprise's loss carryforward period.

In assessing the need for a valuation allowance, future taxable income exclusive of reversing temporary differences and carryforwards (paragraph 21(b)) need not be considered because the $16,000 operating loss carryforward will offset (a) the *acquired* enterprise's $7,000 of taxable temporary differences and (b) another $9,000 of the *acquiring* enterprise's taxable temporary differences. The amounts recorded to account for the purchase transaction are as follows:

Assigned value of the identified net assets acquired	$12,000
Deferred tax liability recognized for the acquired company's taxable temporary differences ($7,000 at 40 percent)	(2,800)
Deferred tax asset recognized for the acquired loss carryforward based on offset against the acquired company's taxable temporary differences ($7,000 at 40 percent)	2,800
Deferred tax asset recognized for the acquired loss carryforward based on offset against the acquiring company's taxable temporary differences ($9,000 at 40 percent)	3,600
Goodwill	4,400
Purchase price of the acquired enterprise	$20,000

Subsequent Recognition of Carryforward Benefits—Purchase Method

268. If a valuation allowance is recognized for some portion or all of an acquired enterprise's deferred tax asset for deductible temporary differences and operating loss or tax credit carryforwards at the acquisition date, tax benefits for those items recognized in financial statements for a subsequent year(s) are:

a. First applied to reduce to zero any goodwill related to the acquisition
b. Second applied to reduce to zero other noncurrent intangible assets related to the acquisition
c. Third applied to reduce income tax expense.

Additional amounts of deductible temporary differences and operating loss or tax credit carryforwards may arise after the acquisition date and before recognition of the tax benefit of amounts existing at the acquisition date. Tax benefits are recognized in later years as follows:

a. The tax benefit of amounts existing at the acquisition date is first applied to reduce goodwill and other noncurrent intangible assets to zero. Any additional tax benefit reduces income tax expense.
b. The tax benefit of amounts arising after the acquisition date is recognized as a reduction of income tax expense.

Whether a tax benefit recognized in later years is attributable to an amount (for example, an operating loss carryforward) existing at or arising after the acquisition date is determined for financial reporting by provisions in the tax law that identify the sequence in which those amounts are utilized for tax purposes. If not determinable by provisions in the tax law, a tax benefit recognized for financial reporting is prorated between a reduction of (a) goodwill and other noncurrent intangible assets and (b) income tax expense.

269. The following example illustrates recognition of tax benefits subsequent to a business combination. The assumptions are as follows:

	Year 1	Year 2	Year 3
Pretax financial income (loss)	$(3,000)	$2,500	$1,500
Disposal of acquired identified net assets	(1,000)	—	—
Taxable income (loss) before loss carryforward	(4,000)	2,500	1,500
Loss carryforward (loss carryback not permitted)	4,000	(2,500)	(1,500)
Taxable income after loss carryforward	$ —	$ —	$ —

c. The tax rate is 40 percent for all years.
d. Based on an assessment of all available evidence, management reaches the following conclusions at the acquisition date and at the end of years 1 and 2:
(1) At the acquisition date, the portion of the $1,000 of deductible temporary differences ($6,000 − $5,000) for which it is more likely than not that a tax benefit will not be realized is $500.
(2) At the end of year 1, the portion of the $4,000 loss carryforward for which it is

a. A nontaxable business combination occurs on the first day of year 1. Before considering any acquired deferred tax assets, the purchase transaction is summarized as follows:

	Assigned Value	Tax Basis
Net assets acquired	$5,000	$6,000
Excess of purchase price over the fair value of the net assets acquired*	1,500	
Purchase price	$6,500	

*There are no other noncurrent intangible assets.

b. The only difference between pretax financial income and taxable income (amortization of goodwill is disregarded for this example) for years 1-3 is a $1,000 loss for tax purposes in year 1 from disposal of the acquired identified net assets at amounts equal to their $5,000 assigned value on the acquisition date.

more likely than not that a tax benefit will not be realized is $1,750.
(3) At the end of year 2, it is more likely than not that a tax benefit will be realized for all of the remaining $1,500 of loss carryforward.

At the acquisition date, a $400 ($1,000 at 40 percent) deferred tax asset and a $200 ($500 at 40 percent) valuation allowance are recognized. The $200 net tax benefit reduces the excess of purchase price over the fair value of the net assets acquired from $1,500 to $1,300. Thus, the amount of goodwill recognized at the acquisition date is $1,300.

During year 1, the $1,000 of net deductible temporary differences at the acquisition date reverse and

are part of the $4,000 loss carryforward for tax purposes at the end of year 1. An analysis of the components of that $4,000 loss carryforward follows:

	Acquired Deductions	Loss in Year 1	Total
Tax loss carryforward	$1,000	$3,000	$4,000
Portion for which a tax benefit was recognized at the acquisition date	500	—	500
Remainder available for recognition of a tax benefit at the end of year 1	$ 500	$3,000	$3,500

Provisions in the tax law do not distinguish between those two components of the $3,500, and the component that is used first for tax purposes is indeterminable. However, the $500 of acquired deductions for which a tax benefit has not been recognized is one-seventh of the $3,500 total, and the $3,000 loss in year 1 is six-sevenths of the $3,500 total. The tax benefit of that $3,500 is prorated one-seventh to reduce goodwill and six-sevenths to reduce income tax expense when recognized in years 1 and 2.

At the end of year 1, a $1,600 ($4,000 at 40 percent) deferred tax asset and a $700 ($1,750 at 40 percent) valuation allowance are recognized. The tax benefit for the $700 increase in the net deferred

tax asset (from $200 at the acquisition date to $900 at the end of year 1) is prorated as follows:

a. One-seventh or $100 to reduce goodwill
b. Six-sevenths or $600 to reduce tax expense.

During year 2, $1,000 ($2,500 at 40 percent) of the deferred tax asset recognized at the end of year 1 is realized. In addition, a tax benefit is recognized for the remaining $1,750 of future tax deductions by eliminating the $700 valuation allowance. That tax benefit is prorated $100 to reduce goodwill and $600 to reduce tax expense. The combined effect of the changes in the deferred tax asset and the related valuation allowance during year 2 is illustrated below:

	Deferred Tax Asset Year 1	Year 2	Tax Expense or (Benefit)
Deferred tax asset	$1,600	$600	$1,000
Valuation allowance	(700)	—	(700)
	$ 900	$600	300
Portion of $700 tax benefit allocated to reduce goodwill			100
Deferred tax expense for year 2			$ 400

The $600 deferred tax asset at the end of year 2 is realized in year 3, resulting in $600 of deferred tax expense for year 3. The consolidated statement of earnings would include the following amounts attributable to the acquired enterprise:

	Year 1	Year 2	Year 3
Pretax financial income (loss)	$(3,000)	$2,500	$1,500
Net deferred tax expense (benefit)	(600)	400	600
Net income (loss)	$(2,400)	$2,100	$ 900

Carryforwards—Pooling-of-Interests Method

270. The separate financial statements of combining enterprises for prior periods are restated on a combined basis when a business combination is accounted for by the pooling-of-interests method. For restatement of periods prior to the combination date, a combining enterprise's operating loss carryforward does not offset the other enterprise's taxable income because consolidated tax returns cannot be filed for those periods. However, provisions in the tax law may permit an operating loss carryforward of either of the combining enter-

prises to offset combined taxable income subsequent to the combination date.

271. If the combined enterprise expects to file consolidated tax returns, a deferred tax asset is recognized for either combining enterprise's operating loss carryforward in a prior period. A valuation allowance is necessary to the extent it is more likely than not that a tax benefit will not be realized for that loss carryforward through offset of either (a) the other enterprise's deferred tax liability for taxable temporary differences that will reverse subsequent to the combination date or (b) combined taxable income subsequent to the combination date. Determined in that manner, the valuation allowance may be less than the sum of the valuation allowances in the separate financial statements of the combining enterprises prior to the combination date. That tax benefit is recognized as part of the adjustment to restate financial statements on a combined basis for prior periods. The same requirements apply to deductible temporary differences and tax credit carryforwards.

272. A taxable business combination may sometimes be accounted for by the pooling-of-interests method. The increase in the tax basis of the net assets acquired results in temporary differences. The deferred tax consequences of those temporary differences are recognized and measured the same as for other temporary differences. As of the combination date, recognizable tax benefits attributable to the increase in tax basis are allocated to contributed capital. Tax benefits attributable to the increase in tax basis that become recognizable after the combination date (that is, by elimination of a valuation allowance) are reported as a reduction of income tax expense.

Intraperiod Tax Allocation

273. If there is only one item other than continuing operations, the portion of income tax expense or benefit for the year that remains after the allocation to continuing operations is allocated to that item. If there are two or more items other than continuing operations, the amount that remains after the allocation to continuing operations is allocated among those other items in proportion to their individual effects on income tax expense or benefit for the year.

274. The following example illustrates allocation of income tax expense if there is only one item

other than income from continuing operations. The assumptions are as follows:

a. The enterprise's pretax financial income and taxable income are the same.
b. The enterprise's ordinary loss from continuing operations is $500.
c. The enterprise also has an extraordinary gain of $900 that is a capital gain for tax purposes.
d. The tax rate is 40 percent on ordinary income and 30 percent on capital gains. Income taxes currently payable are $120 ($400 at 30 percent).

Income tax expense is allocated between the pretax loss from operations and the extraordinary gain as follows:

Total income tax expense	$120
Tax benefit allocated to the loss from operations	(150)
Incremental tax expense allocated to the extraordinary gain	$270

The effect of the $500 loss from continuing operations was to offset an equal amount of capital gains that otherwise would be taxed at a 30 percent tax rate. Thus, $150 ($500 at 30 percent) of tax benefit is allocated to continuing operations. The $270 incremental effect of the extraordinary gain is the difference between $120 of total tax expense and the $150 tax benefit from continuing operations.

275. The following example illustrates allocation of the tax benefit of a tax credit carryforward that is recognized as a deferred tax asset in the current year. The assumptions are as follows:

a. The enterprise's pretax financial income and taxable income are the same.
b. Pretax financial income for the year comprises $300 from continuing operations and $400 from an extraordinary gain.
c. The tax rate is 40 percent. Taxes payable for the year are zero because $330 of tax credits that arose in the current year more than offset the $280 of tax otherwise payable on $700 of taxable income.
d. A $50 deferred tax asset is recognized for the $50 ($330 − $280) tax credit carryforward. Based on the weight of available evidence, management concludes that no valuation allowance is necessary.

Income tax expense or benefit is allocated between pretax income from continuing operations and the extraordinary gain as follows:

Total income tax benefit		$ (50)
Tax expense (benefit) allocated to income from continuing operations:		
Tax (before tax credits) on $300 of taxable income at 40 percent	$120	
Tax credits	(330)	(210)
Tax expense allocated to the extraordinary gain		$ 160

Absent the extraordinary gain and assuming it was not the deciding factor in reaching a conclusion that a valuation allowance is not needed, the entire tax benefit of the $330 of tax credits would be allocated to continuing operations. The presence of the extraordinary gain does not change that allocation.

276. Income taxes are sometimes allocated directly to shareholders' equity. The following example illustrates the allocation of income taxes for translation adjustments under Statement 52 directly to shareholders' equity.

a. A foreign subsidiary has earnings of FC600 for year 2. Its net assets (and unremitted earnings) are FC1,000 and FC1,600 at the end of years 1 and 2, respectively.
b. The foreign currency is the functional currency. For year 2, translated amounts are as follows:

	Foreign Currency	Exchange Rate	Dollars
Unremitted earnings, beginning of year	1,000	FC1 = $1.20	1,200
Earnings for the year	600	FC1 = $1.10	660
Unremitted earnings, end of year	1,600	FC1 = $1.00	1,600

c. A $260 translation adjustment ($1,200 + $660 − $1,600) is charged to the cumulative translation adjustment account in shareholders' equity for year 2.
d. The U.S. parent expects that all of the foreign subsidiary's unremitted earnings will be remitted in the foreseeable future, and under Opinion 23, a deferred U.S. tax liability is recognized for those unremitted earnings.
e. The U.S. parent accrues the deferred tax liability at a 20 percent tax rate (that is, net of foreign tax credits, foreign tax credit carryforwards, and so forth). An analysis of the net investment in the foreign subsidiary and the related deferred tax liability for year 2 is as follows:

	Net Investment	Deferred Tax Liability
Balances, beginning of year	$1,200	$240
Earnings and related taxes	660	132
Translation adjustment and related taxes	(260)	(52)
Balances, end of year	$1,600	$320

f. For year 2, $132 of deferred taxes are charged against earnings, and $52 of deferred taxes are credited directly to the cumulative translation adjustment account in shareholders' equity.

Appendix C

BACKGROUND INFORMATION

277. Opinion 11 was issued in 1967. Over the years that followed, it was the frequent subject of numerous criticisms and concerns that focused both on the complexity of the accounting requirements and on the meaningfulness of the results of applying the requirements.

278. In January 1982, the Board added a project to its agenda to reconsider accounting for income taxes, and a task force was appointed to advise the Board during its deliberations on this project. An FASB Research Report, *Accounting for Income Taxes: A Review of Alternatives,* prepared by Ernst & Whinney, was published in July 1983. The report discusses the accounting and reporting alternatives advanced in the accounting literature on income taxes.

279. The Discussion Memorandum on accounting for income taxes was issued in August 1983, and more than 400 comment letters were received. The Board conducted a public hearing on the Discussion Memorandum in April 1984, and 43 organizations and individuals presented their views at the 3-day

hearing. In May 1984, the FASB sponsored three regional meetings to obtain the views of preparers, users, and auditors associated with the financial statements of small companies.

280. Accounting for income taxes was addressed at 20 public Board meetings and at 2 public task force meetings and, in September 1986, the Board issued an Exposure Draft, *Accounting for Income Taxes.* It proposed an asset and liability approach to account for the effects of income taxes that result from an enterprise's activities during the current and preceding years. The Board received more than 400 comment letters in response to the Exposure Draft.

281. In January 1987, the Board conducted a public hearing on the Exposure Draft. Fifty-one organizations and individuals presented their views at the 3-day hearing. Based on the information received in the comment letters and at the public hearing, the Board reconsidered its proposals in the Exposure Draft at 21 public Board meetings during 1987.

282. FASB Statement No. 96, *Accounting for Income Taxes,* was issued in December 1987 and the FASB Special Report, *A Guide to Implementation of Statement 96 on Accounting for Income Taxes,* was issued in March 1989. As issued, Statement 96 was effective for financial statements for fiscal years beginning after December 15, 1988, but the effective date was deferred three times, the last of which was to fiscal years beginning after December 15, 1992.

283. After the issuance of Statement 96, the Board received (a) requests for about 20 different limited-scope amendments to that Statement, (b) requests to change the criteria for recognition and measurement of deferred tax assets to anticipate, in certain circumstances, the tax consequences of future income, and (c) requests to reduce the complexity of scheduling the future reversals of temporary differences and considering hypothetical tax-planning strategies. The Board considered the requests to amend Statement 96 at 41 public Board meetings and 3 Implementation Group meetings starting in March 1989.

284. In June 1991, the Board issued an Exposure Draft, *Accounting for Income Taxes.* The Exposure Draft retained the asset and liability approach for financial accounting and reporting for income taxes as in Statement 96, but reduced the complexity of the standard and changed the criteria for recognizing and measuring deferred tax assets. During the comment period for the Exposure Draft, a limited-scope field test of the proposals in the Exposure Draft was completed, and an FASB-prepared seminar that explained

and analyzed the proposals was presented by Board and staff members at nine locations throughout the country.

285. The Board received more than 250 comment letters in response to the Exposure Draft. In October 1991, the Board held a 3-day public hearing on the Exposure Draft, and 25 organizations and individuals presented their views. Based on the information received in the comment letters and at the public hearing, the Board reconsidered its proposals in the Exposure Draft at 12 public Board meetings. The basis for the Board's conclusions, including reasons for changes made to the provisions of the Exposure Draft, is set forth in Appendix A.

Appendix D

AMENDMENTS TO EXISTING PRONOUNCEMENTS

286. This Statement supersedes the following pronouncements:

a. Accounting Research Bulletin No. 44 (Revised), *Declining-balance Depreciation*
b. APB Opinion No. 1, *New Depreciation Guidelines and Rules*
c. APB Opinion No. 11, *Accounting for Income Taxes*
d. APB Opinion No. 24, *Accounting for Income Taxes—Investments in Common Stock Accounted for by the Equity Method (Other than Subsidiaries and Corporate Joint Ventures)*
e. FASB Statement No. 31, *Accounting for Tax Benefits Related to U.K. Tax Legislation concerning Stock Relief*
f. FASB Statement No. 96, *Accounting for Income Taxes*
g. FASB Statement No. 100, *Accounting for Income Taxes—Deferral of the Effective Date of FASB Statement No. 96*
h. FASB Statement No. 103, *Accounting for Income Taxes—Deferral of the Effective Date of FASB Statement No. 96*
i. FASB Statement No. 108, *Accounting for Income Taxes—Deferral of the Effective Date of FASB Statement No. 96*
j. AICPA Accounting Interpretations 4, "Change in Method of Accounting for Investment Credit," and 6, "Investment Credit in Consolidation," of APB Opinion No. 4, *Accounting for the "Investment Credit"*
k. AICPA Accounting Interpretations of APB Opinion No. 11, *Accounting for Income Taxes*

l. AICPA Unofficial Accounting Interpretations 13, "Subchapter S Corporations," and 16, "EPS for Extraordinary Items," of APB Opinion No. 15, *Earnings per Share*

m. AICPA Accounting Interpretations of APB Opinion No. 23, *Accounting for Income Taxes—Special Areas*

n. FASB Interpretation No. 22, *Applicability of Indefinite Reversal Criteria to Timing Differences*

o. FASB Interpretation No. 25, *Accounting for an Unused Investment Tax Credit*

p. FASB Interpretation No. 29, *Reporting Tax Benefits Realized on Disposition of Investments in Certain Subsidiaries and Other Investees*

q. FASB Interpretation No. 32, *Application of Percentage Limitations in Recognizing Investment Tax Credit*

r. FASB Technical Bulletin No. 81-2, *Accounting for Unused Investment Tax Credits Acquired in a Business Combination Accounted for by the Purchase Method*

s. FASB Technical Bulletin No. 83-1, *Accounting for the Reduction in the Tax Basis of an Asset Caused by the Investment Tax Credit*

t. FASB Technical Bulletin No. 84-2, *Accounting for the Effects of the Tax Reform Act of 1984 on Deferred Income Taxes Relating to Domestic International Sales Corporations*

u. FASB Technical Bulletin No. 84-3, *Accounting for the Effects of the Tax Reform Act of 1984 on Deferred Income Taxes of Stock Life Insurance Enterprises*

v. FASB Technical Bulletin No. 86-1, *Accounting for Certain Effects of the Tax Reform Act of 1986.*

287. Other pronouncements issued by the Accounting Principles Board and the Financial Accounting Standards Board refer to Opinion 11, Opinion 24, or Statement 96 or use the term *timing differences* as defined in Opinion 11. All such references appearing in paragraphs that establish standards or the scope of a pronouncement are hereby amended to refer instead to FASB Statement No. 109, *Accounting for Income Taxes,*[19] or to use the term *temporary differences.*

288. This Statement amends the following pronouncements:

a. Accounting Research Bulletin No. 43, *Restatement and Revision of Accounting Research Bulletins.* The following is added to the end of paragraph 5 of Chapter 9C:

The declining-balance method is one that meets the requirements of being systematic and rational.[2] If the expected productivity or revenue-earning power of the asset is relatively greater during the earlier years of its life, or where maintenance charges tend to increase during later years, the declining-balance method may provide the most satisfactory allocation of cost. That conclusion also applies to other methods, including the sum-of-the-years'-digits method, that produce substantially similar results.

---

[2]Accounting Terminology Bulletin No. 1, *Review and Résumé,* paragraph 56.

Paragraphs 11-13 of Chapter 9C are replaced by the following:

11. Refer to FASB Statement No. 109, *Accounting for Income Taxes.*

Chapter 10B is deleted.

Paragraph 8 of Chapter 11B is deleted.

b. APB Opinion No. 2, *Accounting for the "Investment Credit."* Paragraph 16 is replaced by the following:

An investment credit should be reflected in the financial statements to the extent it has been used as an offset against income taxes otherwise currently payable or to the extent its benefit is recognizable under the provisions of FASB Statement No. 109, *Accounting for Income Taxes.* Refer to paragraph 48 of Statement 109 for required disclosures related to (a) tax credit carryforwards for tax purposes and (b) tax credit carryforwards for which a tax benefit has not been recognized for financial reporting.

c. APB Opinion No. 6, *Status of Accounting Research Bulletins.* Paragraphs 20-23 and footnotes 7 and 8 are deleted.

d. APB Opinion No. 16, *Business Combinations.* The last sentence in paragraph 87 is replaced by the following:

The tax basis of an asset or liability shall not be a factor in determining its fair value.

The last sentence in paragraph 88 is replaced by the following:

FASB Statement No. 109, *Accounting for Income Taxes,* paragraph 30, addresses accounting for the deferred tax consequences of the differences between the assigned values and the tax

---

[19]Except as in paragraph 288(dd).

bases of assets and liabilities of an enterprise acquired in a purchase business combination.

Paragraph 89 is deleted.

e. APB Opinion No. 17, *Intangible Assets.* The last sentence in paragraph 30 is deleted.

f. APB Opinion No. 23, *Accounting for Income Taxes—Special Areas.* In paragraph 9, all words following *equity method* are deleted and replaced by *results in a temporary difference.*

Paragraph 10 is replaced by the following:

Temporary Difference. The Board believes it should be presumed that all undistributed earnings of a subsidiary will be transferred to the parent company. Accordingly, the undistributed earnings of a subsidiary included in consolidated income should be accounted for as a temporary difference unless the tax law provides a means by which the investment in a domestic subsidiary can be recovered tax free. However, for reasons described in FASB Statement No. 109, *Accounting for Income Taxes,* a deferred tax liability is not recognized for (a) an excess of the amount for financial reporting over the tax basis of an investment in a foreign subsidiary that meets the criteria in paragraph 12 of this Opinion and (b) undistributed earnings of a domestic subsidiary that arose in fiscal years beginning on or before December 15, 1992 and that meet the criteria in paragraph 12 of this Opinion. The criteria in paragraph 12 of this Opinion do not apply to undistributed earnings of domestic subsidiaries that arise in fiscal years beginning after December 15, 1992, and a deferred tax liability shall be recognized if the undistributed earnings are a taxable temporary difference.

Footnotes 3 and 4 are deleted.

Paragraph 11 is replaced by the following:

A deferred tax asset shall be recognized for an excess of the tax basis over the amount for financial reporting of an investment in a subsidiary in accordance with the requirements of paragraph 34 of Statement 109.

The last sentence of paragraph 13 is replaced by the following:

If a parent company recognizes a deferred tax liability for the temporary difference arising from its equity in undistributed earnings of a subsidiary and subsequently reduces its investment in the subsidiary through a taxable sale or other transac-

tion, the amount of the temporary difference and the related deferred tax liability will change. An investment in common stock of an investee (other than a subsidiary or corporate joint venture) may change so that the investee becomes a subsidiary because the investor acquires additional common stock, the investee acquires or retires common stock, or other transactions affect the investment. A temporary difference for the investor's share of the undistributed earnings of the investee prior to the date it becomes a subsidiary shall continue to be treated as a temporary difference for which a deferred tax liability shall continue to be recognized to the extent that dividends from the subsidiary do not exceed the parent company's share of the subsidiary's earnings subsequent to the date it became a subsidiary.

Paragraph 14 is replaced by the following:

Disclosure. Statement 109 specifies the requirements for financial statement disclosures.

Footnote 6 is deleted.

In the second sentence in paragraph 21, *permanent differences* is replaced with *events that do not have tax consequences.*

The first and second sentences of paragraph 23 are deleted.

The first and second sentences in footnote 9 are deleted.

The third sentence of paragraph 23 is replaced by the following:

As described in Statement 109, a savings and loan association[9] should not provide deferred taxes on taxable temporary differences related to bad-debt reserves for tax purposes that arose in tax years beginning before December 31, 1987 (the base-year amount).

Paragraph 24 is replaced by the following:

Disclosure. Statement 109 specifies the requirements for financial statement disclosures.

Footnote 10 is deleted.

g. APB Opinion No. 25, *Accounting for Stock Issued to Employees.* In the second sentence of paragraph 17, (1) *are timing differences* is replaced by *result in temporary differences* and (2) *(APB Opinion No. 11, paragraphs 34 to 37)* is deleted and *in accordance with the provisions of FASB Statement No. 109, Accounting for Income Taxes* is added to the end of that sentence.

h. APB Opinion No. 28, *Interim Financial Reporting.* In footnote 2, *(see APB Opinion No. 11, paragraph 63)* is replaced by *(refer to FASB Statement No. 109, Accounting for Income Taxes, paragraph 47).*

In the first sentence of paragraph 20, (1) *(in the event carryback of such losses is not possible)* is deleted and (2) *realization is assured beyond any reasonable doubt (paragraph 45 of APB Opinion No. 11)* is replaced by *the tax benefits are expected to be (a) realized during the year or (b) recognizable as a deferred tax asset at the end of the year in accordance with the provisions of Statement 109.* In the second and third sentences of paragraph 20, *assured beyond reasonable doubt* is replaced by *more likely than not.* In footnote 3, *as is provided for in annual periods in paragraph 45 of APB Opinion No. 11* is deleted.

The last sentence in paragraph 20 is replaced by the following:

The tax effect of a valuation allowance expected to be necessary for a deferred tax asset at the end of the year for originating deductible temporary differences and carryforwards during the year should be included in the effective tax rate. The effect of a change in the beginning-of-the-year balance of a valuation allowance as a result of a change in judgment about the realizability of the related deferred tax asset in future years shall not be apportioned among interim periods through an adjustment of the effective tax rate but shall be recognized in the interim period in which the change occurs. The effects of new tax legislation shall not be recognized prior to enactment. The tax effect of a change in tax laws or rates on taxes currently payable or refundable for the current year shall be reflected after the effective dates prescribed in the statutes in the computation of the annual effective tax rate beginning no earlier than the first interim period that includes the enactment date of the new legislation. The effect of a change in tax laws or rates on a deferred tax liability or asset shall not be apportioned among interim periods through an adjustment of the annual effective tax rate. The tax effect of a change in tax laws or rates on taxes payable or refundable for a prior year shall be recognized as of the enactment date of the change as tax expense (benefit) for the current year.

i. APB Opinion No. 30, *Reporting the Results of Operations—Reporting the Effects of Disposal of a Segment of a Business, and Extraordinary, Unusual and Infrequently Occurring Events and Transactions.* In paragraph 7, *APB Opin-*

ion No. 11, Accounting for Income Taxes, paragraphs 45 and 61 is replaced by *FASB Statement No. 109, Accounting for Income Taxes, paragraph 37.*

j. AICPA Accounting Interpretations of APB Opinion No. 18, *The Equity Method of Accounting for Investments in Common Stock.* In the fourth sentence of the fifth paragraph of the interpretation section of Interpretation 1, the second half of the sentence beginning with *; for example* is deleted.

k. AICPA Accounting Interpretations of APB Opinion No. 25, *Accounting for Stock Issued to Employees.* In the last sentence of the last paragraph, the reference to paragraph 89 of Opinion 16 is deleted.

l. FASB Statement No. 12, *Accounting for Certain Marketable Securities.* The last sentence of paragraph 22 is deleted.

m. FASB Statement No. 13, *Accounting for Leases.* In paragraph 47, , *as prescribed in APB Opinion No. 11, "Accounting for Income Taxes," paragraphs 57, 59, and 64* is deleted.

n. FASB Statement No. 16, *Prior Period Adjustments.* Paragraph 11 is replaced by the following:

An item of profit and loss related to the correction of an error in the financial statements of a prior period[3] shall be accounted for and reported as a prior period adjustment[4] and excluded from the determination of net income for the current period.

Footnotes 3 and 4 are renumbered 4 and 3, respectively, and their positions are reversed. Footnote 5 is deleted. In the first sentence of paragraph 13, *(except for the effects of retroactive tax legislation)* is added after *taxes.* In the third sentence of paragraph 13, *new retroactive tax legislation or* is deleted.

o. FASB Statement No. 19, *Financial Accounting and Reporting by Oil and Gas Producing Companies.* In paragraph 61, *by the deferred method, as described in APB Opinion No. 11, "Accounting for Income Taxes,"* is replaced by *as described in FASB Statement No. 109, Accounting for Income Taxes,.* In the first sentence of paragraph 62, *the amount of income taxes otherwise payable shall not be taken into account* is replaced by *taxable income in future years shall be considered in determining whether it is more likely than not that the tax benefits of deferred tax assets will not be realized.* The second sentence is deleted. In the third sentence, (1) *Accordingly, the* is replaced by *However, the tax benefit of the*, (2) *shall be accounted for as a permanent difference in* is replaced by *shall not be recognized until*, and (3) *; it shall not be anticipated by recognizing interaction* is deleted.

p.　FASB Statement No. 37, *Balance Sheet Classification of Deferred Income Taxes*. Paragraph 4 and the preceding caption and related footnotes are replaced by the following:

> 4.　A temporary difference is related to an asset or liability if reduction* of the asset or liability causes the temporary difference to reverse. A deferred tax liability or asset for a temporary difference that is related to an asset or liability shall be classified as current or noncurrent based on the classification of the related asset or liability. A deferred tax liability or asset for a temporary difference not related to an asset or liability because (a) there is no associated asset or liability or (b) reduction of an associated asset or liability will not cause the temporary difference to reverse shall be classified based on the expected reversal date of the specific temporary difference. Such classification disregards any additional temporary differences that may arise and is based on the criteria used for classifying other assets and liabilities.

---

*As used here, the term *reduction* includes amortization, sale, or other realization of an asset and amortization, payment, or other satisfaction of a liability.

Paragraphs 17 and 18, the preceding caption, and footnote 1 are deleted.

In paragraph 19, the first and second references to *deferred income taxes* are replaced by *The deferred tax liability or asset* and *deferred tax liability or asset*, respectively.

In the illustration at the end of paragraph 20, *Accumulated Deferred Income Tax Debits Related to Accounting Change . . . $2,357,500* is replaced by *Deferred Tax Asset (40 percent is the enacted tax rate—no valuation allowance deemed necessary) . . . $2,050,000*.

In the first sentence of paragraph 21, *deferred income taxes do* is replaced by *deferred tax asset does*. In the second and third sentences, *deferred income tax debits* is replaced by *deferred tax asset*. At the end of the third sentence, *($261,944)* is replaced by *($227,778)*.

In the second sentence of paragraph 22, *deferred income tax credits* is replaced by *temporary differences*. In the fourth and fifth sentences, *deferred income tax credits* is replaced by *deferred tax liability* and *deferred tax liabilities*, respectively.

In paragraphs 23-25, references to *deferred income tax credits* are changed to *deferred tax liability*. In the first sentence of paragraph 24, *do* is replaced by *does*.

Paragraphs 26-29, the captions preceding paragraphs 26 and 28, and footnotes 2 and 3 are deleted.

q.　FASB Statement No. 38, *Accounting for Preacquisition Contingencies of Purchased Enterprises*. In the fourth sentence of paragraph 2, *benefits of preacquisition net operating loss carryforwards* is replaced by *effects of (a) temporary differences and carryforwards of the acquired enterprise that exist at the acquisition date and (b) income tax uncertainties related to the acquisition (for example, an uncertainty related to the tax basis of an acquired asset that will ultimately be agreed to by the taxing authority)*. The last sentence of paragraph 2 is deleted. In the first sentence of paragraph 5, *tax benefit of a loss carryforward[2]* is replaced by *income tax effects referred to in paragraph 2 of this Statement[2]*.

The first sentence of footnote 2 is replaced by the following:

> Those potential income tax effects shall be accounted for in accordance with the provisions of FASB Statement No. 109, *Accounting for Income Taxes*.

The second and third sentences of footnote 2 are deleted.

r.　FASB Statement No. 52, *Foreign Currency Translation*. In paragraph 48, *deferred income taxes and* is deleted from the table in both places.

s.　FASB Statement No. 57, *Related Party Disclosures*. The following item is added to the end of paragraph 2:

> (e)　The information required by paragraph 49 of FASB Statement No. 109, *Accounting for Income Taxes*.

t. FASB Statement No. 60, *Accounting and Reporting by Insurance Enterprises.* Paragraph 55 is replaced by the following:

> Except as noted in paragraph 59, a deferred tax liability or asset shall be recognized for the deferred tax consequences of temporary differences in accordance with FASB Statement No. 109, *Accounting for Income Taxes.*

Paragraphs 56-58 and footnote 8 are deleted.

The first and second sentences of paragraph 59 are deleted.

The third sentence of paragraph 59 is replaced by the following:

> As described in Statement 109, a life insurance enterprise should not provide deferred taxes on taxable temporary differences related to "policyholders' surplus" that arose in fiscal years beginning on or before December 15, 1992.

Paragraph 60(i) is replaced by the following:

> Statement 109 specifies the requirements for financial statement disclosures about income taxes.

Paragraph 60(j) is deleted.

u. FASB Statement No. 69, *Disclosures about Oil and Gas Producing Activities.* In the second sentence of paragraph 26 and the second sentence of paragraph 30(c), *permanent differences* is deleted and *tax deductions* is inserted before *tax credits and allowances.* In paragraphs 40 and 41 of Appendix A, *permanent differences* is replaced by *tax deductions.*

v. FASB Statement No. 71, *Accounting for the Effects of Certain Types of Regulation.* Paragraph 18 is replaced by the following:

> A deferred tax liability or asset shall be recognized for the deferred tax consequences of temporary differences in accordance with FASB Statement No. 109, *Accounting for Income Taxes.*

Footnote 12 is deleted. In paragraph 46, (1) *as amended* is inserted after *Statement 16* and (2) , *adjustments that result from realization of income tax benefits of preacquisition operating loss carryforwards of purchased subsidiaries,* is deleted.

w. FASB Statement No. 89, *Financial Reporting and Changing Prices.* In paragraph 96, *Deferred income tax charges[a]—Offsets to prospective monetary liabilities* and *Deferred income tax credits[a]—Cash requirements will not vary materially due to changes in specific prices.* are replaced by *Deferred tax assets[a]* and *Deferred tax liabilities[a],* respectively.

x. FASB Statement No. 90, *Regulated Enterprises—Accounting for Abandonments and Disallowances of Plant Costs.* The fifth and sixth sentences of paragraph 14 are replaced by the following:

> Under FASB Statement No. 109, *Accounting for Income Taxes,* the tax effects of temporary differences are measured based on enacted tax laws and rates and are recognized based on specified criteria.

y. FASB Interpretation No. 18, *Accounting for Income Taxes in Interim Periods.* The following sentence is inserted after the second sentence in paragraph 8:

> It also includes the effect of any valuation allowance expected to be necessary at the end of the year for deferred tax assets related to originating deductible temporary differences and carryforwards during the year.

Paragraph 14 is replaced by the following:

> *Recognition of the tax benefit of a loss.* Paragraph 20 of Opinion 28 (as amended by Statement 109) provides that a tax benefit is recognized for a loss that arises early in a fiscal year if the tax benefits are expected to be (a) realized during the year or (b) recognizable as a deferred tax asset at the end of the year in accordance with the provisions of Statement 109. Paragraph 17(e) of Statement 109 requires that a valuation allowance be recognized if it is more likely than not that the tax benefit of some portion or all of a deferred tax asset will not be realized. Those limitations shall be applied in determining the estimated tax benefit of an "ordinary" loss for the fiscal year, used to determine the estimated annual effective tax rate described in paragraph 8 above, and the year-to-date tax benefit of a loss.

Footnotes 9-11 are deleted.

Paragraph 15 is replaced by the following:

> *Reversal of taxable temporary differences.* A deferred tax liability related to existing taxable temporary differences is a source of evidence for recognition of a tax benefit when (a) an enterprise anticipates an "ordinary"

loss for the fiscal year or has a year-to-date "ordinary" loss in excess of the anticipated "ordinary" loss for the fiscal year, (b) the tax benefit of that loss is not expected to be realized during the year, and (c) recognition of a deferred tax asset for that loss at the end of the fiscal year is expected to depend on taxable income from the reversal of existing taxable temporary differences (that is, a higher valuation allowance [paragraph 17(e) of Statement 109] would be necessary absent the existing taxable temporary differences). If the tax benefit relates to an estimated "ordinary" loss for the fiscal year, it shall be considered in determining the estimated annual effective tax rate described in paragraph 8 above. If the tax benefit relates to a year-to-date "ordinary" loss, it shall be considered in computing the maximum tax benefit that shall be recognized for the year-to-date.

Footnotes 12-14 are deleted.

In paragraph 16, the following sentence is inserted after the first sentence:

Paragraph 20 of Opinion 28 (as amended) excludes the effects of changes in judgment about beginning-of-year valuation allowances and effects of changes in tax laws or rates from the estimated annual effective tax rate calculation.

The reference to *Paragraph 52 of APB Opinion No. 11*[18] in the third sentence is replaced by *Paragraphs 35-38 of Statement 109*. The fourth sentence and footnote 18 are deleted.

In the first sentence of paragraph 18, *shall not be recognized until it is realized or realization is assured beyond any reasonable doubt* is replaced by *shall be recognized when the tax benefit of the loss is expected to be (a) realized during the year or (b) recognizable as a deferred tax asset at the end of the year in accordance with the provisions of Statement 109*. The second sentence of paragraph 18 is deleted.

The third sentence of paragraph 18 is replaced by the following:

Realization would appear to be more likely than not if future taxable income from (ordinary) income during the current year is expected based on an established seasonal pattern of loss in early interim periods offset by income in later interim periods.[19]

In footnote 19, *paragraph 47 of APB Opinion No. 11 (see Appendix A, paragraph 31) and* is deleted.

The fourth sentence in paragraph 18 is replaced by the following:

If recognition of a deferred tax asset at the end of the fiscal year for all or a portion of the tax benefit of the loss depends on taxable income from the reversal of existing taxable temporary differences, refer to paragraph 15 above.

In the fifth sentence, *assured beyond any reasonable doubt* is replaced by *more likely than not* in all three places.

Paragraph 20 is replaced by the following:

Paragraph 37 of Statement 109 requires that the manner of reporting the tax benefit of an operating loss carryforward recognized in a subsequent year generally is determined by the source of the income in that year and not by (a) the source of the operating loss carryforward or (b) the source of expected future income that will result in realization of a deferred tax asset for the operating loss carryforward. The tax benefit is allocated first to reduce tax expense from continuing operations to zero with any excess allocated to the other source(s) of income that provides the means of realization, for example, extraordinary items, discontinued operations, and so forth. That requirement also pertains to reporting the tax benefit of an operating loss carryforward in interim periods. The tax benefit of an operating loss carryforward from prior years shall be included in the effective tax rate computation if the tax benefit is expected to be realized as a result of "ordinary" income in the current year. Otherwise, the tax benefit shall be recognized in the manner described above in each interim period to the extent that income in the period and for the year to date is available to offset the operating loss carryforward or, in the case of a change in judgment about realizability of the related deferred tax asset in future years, the effect shall be recognized in the interim period in which the change occurs.

Footnotes 21-23 are deleted.

Paragraph 23 is replaced by the following:

Paragraph 20 of Opinion 28 (as amended by Statement 109) sets forth the requirements for recognition of the tax effects of a change in tax laws or rates. That paragraph refers to effective dates prescribed in the statutes. Paragraph 24 below describes the determination of when new legislation becomes effective.

Footnote 25 is deleted.

In the assumed facts for the examples in Appendix C, references in paragraphs 41, 43, 48, 49, 65, and 68 to *permanent differences* are replaced by references to *events that do not have tax consequences*. In the second sentence of the last subparagraph of paragraph 43, *assured of future realization beyond any reasonable doubt at year-end* is replaced by *recognizable at the end of the current year in accordance with the provisions of Statement 109*. The third and fourth sentences of that subparagraph are deleted.

The third sentence of paragraph 46 is replaced by the following:

Established seasonal patterns provide evidence that realization in the current year of the tax benefit of the year-to-date loss and of anticipated tax credits is more likely than not.

The third sentence of paragraph 47 is replaced by the following:

There is no established seasonal pattern and it is more likely than not that the tax benefit of the year-to-date loss and the anticipated tax credits will not be realized in the current or future years.

In footnote *, *realization of* is deleted and *assured beyond any reasonable doubt* is replaced by *expected to be (a) realized during the current year or (b) recognizable as a deferred tax asset at the end of the current year in accordance with the provisions of Statement 109*.

In the third subparagraph of paragraph 49, *If realization of the tax benefit of the loss and realization of tax credits were assured beyond any reasonable doubt* is replaced by *If there is a recognizable tax benefit for the loss and the tax credits pursuant to the requirements of Statement 109*. In the last sentence of paragraph 49, *assured beyond any reasonable doubt* is replaced by *expected to be (a) realized during the current year or (b) recognizable as a deferred*

tax asset at the end of the current year in accordance with the provisions of Statement 109.

The third sentence of paragraph 50 is replaced by the following:

The full tax benefit of the anticipated "ordinary" loss and the anticipated tax credits will be realized by carryback.

In paragraph 51, the third and fourth sentences are replaced by the following:

The full tax benefit of the anticipated "ordinary" loss and the anticipated tax credits will be realized by carryback. The full tax benefit of the maximum year-to-date "ordinary" loss can also be realized by carryback.

In the first sentence of paragraph 52, (1) *realization of*, *nor realization of*, and *assured beyond any reasonable doubt* are deleted, and (2) *nor* is added directly before, and *recognizable pursuant to Statement 109* is added directly after, *anticipated tax credits were*.

In the third sentence of paragraphs 53 and 54, (1) *Realization of* is replaced by *It is more likely than not that*, (2) *is assured beyond any reasonable doubt only to the extent* is replaced by *in excess*, and (3) *will not be realized* is added to the end of each sentence.

In the second sentence of paragraph 55, *are not assured beyond any reasonable doubt* is replaced by *exclusive of reversing temporary differences are unlikely*. In the third and fourth sentences of paragraph 55, (1) *credits* is replaced by *liabilities* and (2) *timing differences* is replaced by *existing net taxable temporary differences*. In the fifth sentence of paragraph 55, *(refer to paragraph 15 of this Interpretation)* is added after *to be used*. In the computation at the end of paragraph 55, (1) *credits* is replaced by *liabilities* and (2) *amortized* is replaced by *settled*.

The third sentence of paragraph 58 is replaced by the following:

The loss cannot be carried back, and available evidence indicates that a valuation allowance is needed for all of the deferred tax asset.

In the fourth sentence of paragraph 58, (1) *realization of* is deleted and (2) *not assured beyond any reasonable doubt except* is replaced by *recognized only*. Paragraphs 59-61 and the heading *Using a Prior Year Operating Loss Carryforward* are deleted.

In the fifth sentence of paragraph 66, (1) *Realization of* is replaced by *It is expected that* and (2) *is not assured beyond any reasonable doubt* is replaced by *will not be recognizable as a deferred tax asset at the end of the current year pursuant to Statement 109.*

Paragraph 70 and all references thereto are deleted.

z. FASB Interpretation No. 31, *Treatment of Stock Compensation Plans in EPS Computations.* In the last sentence of footnote 1, *as described in paragraph 36 of APB Opinion No. 11, Accounting for Income Taxes* is deleted.

aa. FASB Technical Bulletin No. 79-9, *Accounting in Interim Periods for Changes in Income Tax Rates.* The last sentence in paragraph 3 is deleted.

bb. FASB Technical Bulletin No. 79-16 (Revised), *Effect of a Change in Income Tax Rate on the Accounting for Leveraged Leases.* In paragraph 4, *paragraph 63 of APB Opinion No. 11, Accounting for Income Taxes* is replaced by *paragraph 47 of FASB Statement No. 109, Accounting for Income Taxes.*

cc. FASB Technical Bulletin No. 82-1, *Disclosure of the Sale or Purchase of Tax Benefits through Tax Leases.* Paragraph 5 is replaced by the following:

Paragraph 47 of FASB Statement No. 109, *Accounting for Income Taxes,* requires that (a) the reported amount of income tax expense attributable to continuing operations for the year be reconciled to the amount of income tax expense that would result from applying domestic federal statutory tax rates to pretax income from continuing operations and (b) the estimated amount and the nature of each significant reconciling item be disclosed. Transactions involving the sale or purchase of tax benefits through tax leases may give rise to a significant reconciling item that should be disclosed pursuant to the requirements of Statement 109.

dd. FASB Technical Bulletin No. 87-2, *Computation of a Loss on an Abandonment.* Paragraphs 9-11 and 13 and footnote 4 are deleted. The first sentence of paragraph 18 is deleted. Appendix A is deleted. In Appendix B, in the second sentence of paragraph 36, the reference to *Opinion 11* should remain. In paragraph 40, the fifth, sixth, and seventh sentences should be deleted.

Appendix E

GLOSSARY

289. This appendix contains definitions of certain terms or phrases used in this Statement.

Carrybacks
Deductions or credits that cannot be utilized on the tax return during a year that may be carried back to reduce taxable income or taxes payable in a prior year. An operating loss carryback is an excess of tax deductions over gross income in a year; a tax credit carryback is the amount by which tax credits available for utilization exceed statutory limitations. Different tax jurisdictions have different rules about whether excess deductions or credits may be carried back and the length of the carryback period.

Carryforwards
Deductions or credits that cannot be utilized on the tax return during a year that may be carried forward to reduce taxable income or taxes payable in a future year. An operating loss carryforward is an excess of tax deductions over gross income in a year; a tax credit carryforward is the amount by which tax credits available for utilization exceed statutory limitations. Different tax jurisdictions have different rules about whether excess deductions or credits may be carried forward and the length of the carryforward period. The terms *carryforward, operating loss carryforward,* and *tax credit carryforward* refer to the amounts of those items, if any, reported in the tax return for the current year.

Current tax expense or benefit
The amount of income taxes paid or payable (or refundable) for a year as determined by applying the provisions of the enacted tax law to the taxable income or excess of deductions over revenues for that year.

Deductible temporary difference
Temporary differences that result in deductible amounts in future years when the related asset or liability is recovered or settled, respectively. Also refer to **Temporary difference.**

Deferred tax asset
The deferred tax consequences attributable to deductible temporary differences and carryforwards. A deferred tax asset is measured using the applicable enacted tax rate and provisions of the enacted tax law. A deferred tax asset is reduced by a valuation allowance if, based on the weight of evidence available, it is more likely than not that some portion or all of a deferred tax asset will not be realized.

Deferred tax consequences

The future effects on income taxes as measured by the applicable enacted tax rate and provisions of the enacted tax law resulting from temporary differences and carryforwards at the end of the current year.

Deferred tax expense or benefit

The change during the year in an enterprise's deferred tax liabilities and assets. For deferred tax liabilities and assets acquired in a purchase business combination during the year, it is the change since the combination date. Income tax expense or benefit for the year is allocated among continuing operations, discontinued operations, extraordinary items, and items charged or credited directly to shareholders' equity.

Deferred tax liability

The deferred tax consequences attributable to taxable temporary differences. A deferred tax liability is measured using the applicable enacted tax rate and provisions of the enacted tax law.

Event

A happening of consequence to an enterprise. The term encompasses both transactions and other events affecting an enterprise.

Gains and losses included in comprehensive income but excluded from net income

Under present practice, gains and losses included in comprehensive income but excluded from net income include certain changes in market values of investments in marketable equity securities classified as noncurrent assets, certain changes in market values of investments in industries having specialized accounting practices for marketable securities, adjustments from recognizing certain additional pension liabilities, and foreign currency translation adjustments. Future changes to generally accepted accounting principles may change what is included in this category.

Income taxes

Domestic and foreign federal (national), state, and local (including franchise) taxes based on income.

Income taxes currently payable (refundable)

Refer to **Current tax expense or benefit.**

Income tax expense (benefit)

The sum of current tax expense (benefit) and deferred tax expense (benefit).

Nonpublic enterprise

An enterprise other than one (a) whose debt or equity securities are traded in a public market, including those traded on a stock exchange or in the over-the-counter market (including securities quoted only locally or regionally), or

(b) whose financial statements are filed with a regulatory agency in preparation for the sale of any class of securities.

Public enterprise

An enterprise (a) whose debt or equity securities are traded in a public market, including those traded on a stock exchange or in the over-the-counter market (including securities quoted only locally or regionally), or (b) whose financial statements are filed with a regulatory agency in preparation for the sale of any class of securities.

Taxable income

The excess of taxable revenues over tax deductible expenses and exemptions for the year as defined by the governmental taxing authority.

Taxable temporary difference

Temporary differences that result in taxable amounts in future years when the related asset or liability is recovered or settled, respectively. Also refer to **Temporary difference.**

Tax consequences

The effects on income taxes—current or deferred—of an event.

Tax-planning strategy

An action (including elections for tax purposes) that meets certain criteria (paragraph 22) and that would be implemented to realize a tax benefit for an operating loss or tax credit carryforward before it expires. Tax-planning strategies are considered when assessing the need for and amount of a valuation allowance for deferred tax assets.

Temporary difference

A difference between the tax basis of an asset or liability and its reported amount in the financial statements that will result in taxable or deductible amounts in future years when the reported amount of the asset or liability is recovered or settled, respectively. Paragraph 11 cites 8 examples of temporary differences. Some temporary differences cannot be identified with a particular asset or liability for financial reporting (paragraph 15), but those temporary differences (a) result from events that have been recognized in the financial statements and (b) will result in taxable or deductible amounts in future years based on provisions of the tax law. Some events recognized in financial statements do not have tax consequences. Certain revenues are exempt from taxation and certain expenses are not deductible. Events that do not have tax consequences do not give rise to temporary differences.

Valuation allowance

The portion of a deferred tax asset for which it is more likely than not that a tax benefit will not be realized.

Statement of Financial Accounting Standards No. 110
Reporting by Defined Benefit Pension Plans of
Investment Contracts

an amendment of FASB Statement No. 35

STATUS

Issued: August 1992

Effective Date: For financial statements for fiscal years beginning after December 15, 1992

Affects: Amends FAS 35, paragraph 11
        Supersedes FAS 35, paragraph 12 and footnote 6

Affected by: No other pronouncements

Issues Discussed by FASB Emerging Issues Task Force (EITF)

    Affects: Resolves EITF Issue No. 89-1

    Interpreted by: No EITF Issues

    Related Issues: No EITF Issues

SUMMARY

    This Statement requires a defined benefit pension plan to report an investment contract issued by either an insurance enterprise or other entity at fair value. This Statement amends FASB Statement No. 35, *Accounting and Reporting by Defined Benefit Pension Plans,* to permit a defined benefit pension plan to report only contracts that incorporate mortality or morbidity risk at contract value.

    This Statement is effective for fiscal years beginning after December 15, 1992. It need not be applied to deposit administration and immediate participation guarantee contracts entered into before March 20, 1992. Restatement of financial statements of prior years is required only if those statements are presented with statements for plan years beginning after December 15, 1992.

Statement of Financial Accounting Standards No. 110

Reporting by Defined Benefit Pension Plans of Investment Contracts

an amendment of FASB Statement No. 35

CONTENTS

INTRODUCTION

1. FASB Statement No. 35, *Accounting and Reporting by Defined Benefit Pension Plans,* establishes standards of financial accounting and reporting for the annual financial statements of a defined benefit pension plan. Paragraph 11 of Statement 35 states that "plan investments, whether equity or debt securities, real estate, or other (excluding contracts with insurance companies) shall be presented at their fair value at the reporting date." Paragraph 12 of that Statement states that "contracts with insurance companies shall be presented in the same manner as that contained in the annual report filed by the plan with certain governmental agencies pursuant to ERISA" (footnote reference omitted). The instructions to Forms 5500 and 5500-C permit unallocated contracts recognized as plan assets to be reported either at fair value or at amounts determined by the insurance company (that is, contract value).

2. Some have interpreted the exception in Statement 35 for contracts with insurance companies to allow guaranteed interest contracts, also referred to as "guaranteed investment contracts" or "GICs," to be reported at contract value. A GIC is a negotiated contract generally between an insurance enterprise (issuer) and an investor, typically a pension plan or savings and investment plan. GICs held by defined benefit pension plans generally provide for a specified return on principal invested over a specified period. Entities other than insurance enterprises have also offered instruments with similar characteristics. However, paragraph 11 of Statement 35 refers only to contracts with insurance companies. That reference raised questions about whether defined benefit pension plans that hold investments with characteristics similar to those of a GIC but issued by entities other than insurance enterprises may be permitted to report those investments at contract value.

3. The Emerging Issues Task Force (EITF) discussed the issue in EITF Issue No. 89-1, "Accounting by a Pension Plan for Bank Investment Contracts and Guaranteed Investment Contracts," but did not reach a consensus. As a result, the FASB added a project on pension plan accounting for investment contracts to its agenda.

**STANDARDS OF FINANCIAL
ACCOUNTING AND REPORTING**

Reporting of Contracts

4. A defined benefit pension plan shall report investment contracts at fair value. A defined benefit pension plan shall report insurance contracts in the same manner as they are reported in the annual report filed by the plan with certain governmental agencies pursuant to the Employee Retirement Income Security Act of 1974 (ERISA). For purposes of this Statement, the terms *insurance contract* and *investment contract* are used as those terms are described for accounting purposes in FASB Statements No. 60, *Accounting and Reporting by Insurance Enterprises,* and No. 97, *Accounting and Reporting by Insurance Enterprises for Certain Long-Duration Contracts and for Realized Gains and Losses from the Sale of Investments.*

5. Paragraph 1 of Statement 60 describes insurance contracts:

> The primary purpose of insurance is to provide economic protection from identified risks occurring or discovered within a specified period. Some types of risks insured include death, disability, property damage, injury to others, and business interruption. Insurance transactions may be characterized generally by the following:
>
> a. The purchaser of an insurance contract makes an initial payment or deposit to the insurance enterprise in advance of the possible occurrence or discovery of an insured event.
> b. When the insurance contract is made, the insurance enterprise ordinarily does not know if, how much, or when amounts will be paid under the contract.

6. Paragraphs 7 and 8 of Statement 97 describe insurance and investment contracts:

> Long-duration contracts that do not subject the insurance enterprise to risks arising from policyholder mortality or morbidity are referred to in this Statement as investment contracts. A mortality or morbidity risk is present if, under the terms of the contract, the enterprise is required to make payments or forego required premiums contingent upon the death or disability (in the case of life insurance contracts) or the continued survival (in the case of annuity contracts) of a specific individual or group of individuals. A contract provision that allows the holder of a long-duration contract to purchase an annuity at a guaranteed price on settlement of the contract does not entail a mortality risk until the right to purchase is executed. If purchased, the annuity is a new contract to be evaluated on its own terms.
>
> Annuity contracts may require the insurance enterprise to make a number of payments that are not contingent upon the survival of the beneficiary, followed by payments that are made if the beneficiary is alive when the payments are due (often referred to as *life-contingent payments*). Such contracts are considered insurance contracts under this Statement and Statement 60 unless (a) the

probability that life-contingent payments will be made is remote or (b) the present value of the expected life-contingent payments relative to the present value of all expected payments under the contract is insignificant. [Footnote references omitted.]

Amendment to Statement 35

7. Statement 35 is amended as follows:

a. The parenthetical comment (*excluding contracts with insurance companies*) in paragraph 11 is replaced by (*excluding insurance contracts*).
b. Paragraph 12 is replaced by the following:

> Insurance contracts shall be presented in the same manner as specified in the annual report filed by the plan with certain governmental agencies pursuant to ERISA; that is, either at fair value or at amounts determined by the insurance enterprise (contract value). A plan not subject to ERISA shall present its insurance contracts as if the plan were subject to the reporting requirements of ERISA.

Effective Date and Transition

8. This Statement is effective for financial statements for fiscal years beginning after December 15, 1992. Earlier adoption is encouraged. This Statement is not required to be applied to deposit administration and immediate participation guarantee contracts (as described in paragraphs 114-119 of Statement 35) entered into before March 20, 1992. Those contracts may continue to be presented in the same manner as insurance contracts as set forth in paragraph 12 of Statement 35 as amended by this Statement.

9. Accounting changes adopted to conform to the provisions of this Statement shall be made retroactively by restating the beginning balance of net assets available for plan benefits for the earliest period presented. Financial statements of prior plan years shall be restated to comply with the provisions of this Statement only if presented with financial statements for plan years beginning after December 15, 1992. If accounting changes are necessary to conform to the provisions of this Statement, the effect on the beginning balance of net assets available for benefits shall be disclosed in the financial statements for the year in which this Statement is first applied.

> **The provisions of this Statement need not be applied to immaterial items.**

This Statement was adopted by the unanimous vote of the seven members of the Financial Accounting Standards Board:

Dennis R. Beresford, *Chairman*	Victor H. Brown	A. Clarence Sampson
Joseph V. Anania	James J. Leisenring	Robert J. Swieringa
	Robert H. Northcutt, Jr.	

Appendix

BACKGROUND INFORMATION AND BASIS FOR CONCLUSIONS

CONTENTS

Appendix

BACKGROUND INFORMATION AND BASIS FOR CONCLUSIONS

Introduction

10. This appendix summarizes considerations that Board members deemed significant in reaching the conclusions in this Statement. It includes reasons for accepting certain views and rejecting others. Individual Board members gave greater weight to some factors than to others.

11. An FASB Exposure Draft, *Reporting by Defined Benefit Pension Plans of Investment Contracts,* was issued for public comment on March 20, 1992. The Board received 48 comment letters in response to that Exposure Draft. The Board concluded that it could reach an informed decision on the basis of existing information without a public hearing.

Background

12. Paragraph 5 of Statement 35 states that "the primary objective of a pension plan's financial statements is to provide financial information that is useful in assessing the plan's present and future ability to pay benefits when due" (footnote reference omit-

ted). The Board concluded that the reporting of plan investments at fair value provides the most relevant information about the resources of a plan. Statement 35 requires that defined benefit pension plans report investments at their fair value.

13. Although the Board recognized that there might be practical problems in determining the fair value of certain types of investments, it initially concluded that the relevance of fair value was sufficient to require its use. As a result, the July 1979 FASB Exposure Draft, *Accounting and Reporting by Defined Benefit Pension Plans,* that preceded Statement 35 required contracts with insurance companies to be reported at fair value. However, many respondents to that Exposure Draft expressed concerns about the complexity and feasibility of determining fair value for contracts with insurance companies.

14. Because the Board was concerned about delaying the issuance of Statement 35 to address those concerns, it concluded that contracts with insurance companies should be reported in the same manner as that required for filings under ERISA. The instructions to Form 5500 permit contracts with insurance companies to be reported at contract value. Therefore, in Statement 35, the Board permitted for practical reasons an exception to fair value reporting for contracts with insurance companies.

Application of Fair Value Exclusion to Insurance Contracts

15. Paragraph 74 of FASB Statement No. 107, *Disclosures about Fair Value of Financial Instruments,* states:

> The Board concluded that disclosures about fair value should not be required for insurance contracts. . . . The Board believes that definitional and valuation difficulties are present to a certain extent in those contracts and obligations, and that further consideration is required before decisions can be made about whether to apply the definition to components of those contracts and whether to require disclosures about fair value for the financial components.

16. The Board recognized in its discussions about investments held by defined benefit pension plans that it may be difficult to determine the fair value of an insurance contract that, as discussed in paragraph 1 of Statement 60 and paragraphs 7 and 8 of Statement 97, incorporates either a mortality or morbidity risk. The Board decided the fair value exclusion in Statement 35 should continue for insurance contracts as a result of the definitional and valuation difficulties.

17. Some respondents to the 1992 Exposure Draft argued that investment contracts with benefit-responsive provisions are insurance contracts or have valuation difficulties similar to insurance contracts with mortality or morbidity risk. Benefit-responsive investment contracts typically transfer investment-yield risk (that is, uncertainty as to the ultimate amount of investment income that will be earned on the net funds invested in the contract) and some principal payment timing risk to the issuer of the contract. However, the plan remains at risk for the ultimate amount of benefit payments. The Board concluded that a contract with benefit-responsive provisions should be reported as an investment contract if it cannot otherwise be considered an insurance contract as discussed in this Statement.

Reporting Investment Contracts at Fair Value

18. The Board considered whether the exception to fair value in Statement 35 should apply to investment contracts held by defined benefit pension plans. Paragraph 15 of Statement 97 states that "investment contracts issued by an insurance enterprise . . . do not incorporate significant insurance risk as that concept is contemplated in Statement 60 and shall not be accounted for as insurance contracts." Further, paragraph 39 of Statement 97 states that ". . . the Board concluded

that the accounting for investment contracts issued by insurance enterprises should be consistent with the accounting for interest-bearing and other financial instruments." Statement 107 requires holders of investment contracts, including defined benefit pension plans, to disclose the fair value of those contracts.

19. Several respondents to the 1992 Exposure Draft argued that contract value provides the most relevant information about a plan's ability to pay benefits when due because it represents the amount the plan will receive at the contract's maturity. Several respondents also questioned the relevance of reporting investment contracts at fair value. Because an established secondary market for investment contracts does not currently exist, the plan will be unable to realize fair value.

20. The Board continues to believe that fair value is more relevant as explained in paragraphs 105 and 107 of Statement 35 as follows:

> Plan administrators or other fiduciaries who manage plan assets are accountable not only for the custody and safekeeping of those [plan] assets but also for their efficient and profitable use in producing additional assets for use in paying benefits. Investment performance is an essential element of stewardship responsibility. Measuring changes in fair value provides information necessary for assessing annual investment performance and stewardship responsibility. Historical cost provides that information only when investments are sold.

> For fixed-income investments held to maturity, the Board recognizes that market fluctuations will reverse before maturity (assuming no defaults). However, at the reporting date, it is the fair value, not the historical cost or the expected value at maturity, that is relevant to an assessment of the plan's ability to pay benefits. Changes in value from period to period are relevant to an assessment of investment performance and discharge of stewardship responsibility. Presenting fixed-income investments at historical cost (whether or not the intent is to hold them to maturity) does not provide essential information about the effect on investment performance of the decision to hold. Further, it may be difficult to determine whether the plan has both the intent and ability to hold a particular fixed-income investment to maturity.

21. The Board understands that the lack of an active secondary market limits the ability of the

holder of an investment contract to realize fair value through a sale. However, it is inconsistent to require fixed-income investments that the plan has the ability and intent to hold to maturity to be reported at fair value and to allow investment contracts that generally have similar characteristics to be reported at contract value. In addition, reporting investment contracts at fair value based on current, not historical, interest rates is consistent with how the actuarial present value of accumulated plan benefits is measured.

22. The Board reaffirmed its belief that fair value provides the most relevant information about the resources of the plan and concluded it should require defined benefit pension plans to report investment contracts at fair value. The Board also concluded that investments with similar terms should be measured in a consistent manner whether an insurance enterprise or another entity issues the investment.

23. Several respondents to the 1992 Exposure Draft suggested that the Board provide additional guidance for determining the fair value of investment contracts. Those respondents expressed concern that the lack of an established secondary market would result in the determination of fair value based on subjective estimates that would result in inconsistent measurements. Other respondents suggested that if additional guidance is not provided by the Board, many plan trustees may inappropriately conclude that contract value equals fair value. The Board believes that the broad guidance provided in Statements 35 and 107, as noted in paragraph 26 of this Statement, should be sufficient to determine fair value. The Board realizes that it cannot anticipate the variety of terms that can be included in an investment contract and that application of this Statement may, in some cases, require considerable judgment. However, the Board noted, as it did when it issued Statement 107, that considerable judgment also is needed when complying with other longstanding accounting and reporting requirements.

Defined Contribution Plans

24. The Board discussed whether the project should include the reporting of investments held by defined contribution plans since a significant number of investment contracts are held by those plans. The Board has not previously addressed issues related to financial statements of defined contribution plans. The current authoritative guidance on the issue is the AICPA Audit and Accounting Guide, *Audits of Employee Benefit Plans*. That Guide follows the requirements of Statement 35 by requiring that investments held by defined contribution plans be reported at fair value except for contracts with insurance companies, which are permitted to be reported at contract value.

25. The Board decided not to address the measurement of plan assets held by defined contribution plans in this project. Pursuing the differences between defined benefit pension plans and defined contribution plans would significantly expand the project. The issues that would have to be resolved before the Board could reach a conclusion about the appropriate measurement attribute would include the following: Who are the principal users of financial statements of defined contribution plans, what information is most relevant to their needs, and what are plan assets? Resolving those questions for all types of defined contribution plans, including those in which all investment decisions are made by the individual participants, would be time-consuming. The Board asked the AICPA, in view of its experience with defined contribution plans, to further address the appropriate reporting of investments held by defined contribution plans. The AICPA has undertaken a project to review the appropriate reporting for investment contracts held by defined contribution plans and health and welfare benefit plans.

Cost-Benefit Considerations

26. The benefits of this Statement are twofold. First, investment contracts held by defined benefit pension plans will be reported at fair value so that changes in the economic value of those contracts will be reflected in amounts reported to financial statement users. Second, the AICPA will be able to address defined contribution plan issues in light of the requirements of this Statement. However, those benefits have a cost; that is, the incremental cost of developing, implementing, and maintaining a system to generate the required valuations. The Board believes the cost of implementing this Statement is reduced by retaining the general guidance provided in paragraph 11 of Statement 35:

> If there is not an active market for an investment but there is such a market for similar investments, selling prices in that market may be helpful in estimating fair value. If a market price is not available, a forecast of expected cash flows may aid in estimating fair value, provided the expected cash flows are discounted at a rate commensurate with the risk involved. [Footnote reference omitted.]

In addition, Appendix A of Statement 107 provides examples of procedures for estimating fair value that are consistent with the general guidance provided in paragraph 11 of Statement 35.

Credit Quality Issues

27. The Board also discussed how to incorporate the credit quality of the issuer in determining the fair value for an investment that is not actively traded. Some plans may receive less than the amount that the issuer is legally obligated to pay due to the issuer's financial difficulties. The Board believes that the guidance provided in paragraph 11 of Statement 35 and by Statement 107 is appropriate for estimating fair value.

28. The credit quality of the issuer also must be evaluated when using contract value to report a contract with significant insurance risk. FASB Statement No. 5, *Accounting for Contingencies,* requires the accrual of a loss when both criteria of paragraph 8 of that Statement are met. The need to recognize a contingent loss always should be considered when there is an existing condition, situation, or set of circumstances involving uncertainty as to possible loss.

29. The Board noted that financial instruments held by a defined benefit pension plan are subject to the disclosure requirements of FASB Statement No. 105, *Disclosure of Information about Financial Instruments with Off-Balance-Sheet Risk and Financial Instruments with Concentrations of Credit Risk.*

Effective Date and Transition

30. The Board decided that some plans may need time to implement procedures necessary to determine fair value. Accordingly, this Statement is effective for fiscal years beginning after December 15, 1992.

31. In the basis for conclusions of Statement 35, the Board discussed the characteristics of both deposit administration and immediate participation guarantee contracts. Plan sponsors may have reported those contracts at contract value based on their discussion in Statement 35. The Board decided, for practical reasons, not to require the application of the provisions of this Statement to those contracts entered into before March 20, 1992. The 1992 Exposure Draft required deposit administration and immediate participation guarantee contracts entered into after March 19, 1992 to be reported at fair value. Several respondents to the 1992 Exposure Draft said that a few deposit administration and immediate participation guarantee contracts are still being issued and that some of those contracts may have significant insurance risk. The Board decided that any contract entered into after March 19, 1992 should be classified as either an insurance or investment contract pursuant to the requirements of this Statement and reported by the defined benefit pension plan accordingly.

Statement of Financial Accounting Standards No. 111
Rescission of FASB Statement No. 32 and Technical Corrections

STATUS

Issued: November 1992

Effective Date: November 30, 1992

Affects: Amends ARB 43, Chapter 1A, paragraph 1; Chapter 3A, paragraph 6(g); Chapter 7A, paragraph 10; Chapter 10A, paragraph 19; and Chapter 11B, paragraph 9
Supersedes ARB 43, Chapter 11B, footnotes 3 and 4
Supersedes ARB 51, footnote 1
Amends APB 6, paragraph 16
Amends APB 9, paragraph 17
Amends APB 10, paragraph 11(b)
Supersedes APB 12, footnote 1
Amends APB 15, paragraph 5 and Exhibit B of Appendix C
Amends APB 20, paragraphs 4, 7, 9, and 16 and footnote 4
Supersedes APB 20, footnotes 2 and 5
Amends APB 22, footnote 2
Supersedes AIN-ARB 51, Interpretation No. 1
Supersedes AIN-APB 4, Interpretation No. 5
Supersedes AIN-APB 7, Interpretation No. 1
Supersedes AIN-APB 8, Interpretations No. 1 through 28
Supersedes AIN-APB 9, Interpretation No. 2
Amends AIN-APB 15, Part I and Interpretations No. 2, 26, 30, 33, 56, and 92
Supersedes AIN-APB 15, Interpretations No. 10 and 38 and footnote 22
Amends AIN-APB 16, Interpretation No. 30
Amends AIN-APB 18, Interpretation No. 2
Supersedes AIN-APB 22, Interpretation No. 1
Amends AIN-APB 26, Interpretation No. 1
Amends FAS 5, paragraph 18
Amends FAS 14, paragraph 27(c)
Supersedes FAS 15, footnote 20
Amends FAS 15, footnote 26
Supersedes FAS 25, paragraphs 6 and 8
Supersedes FAS 32
Supersedes FAS 55
Supersedes FAS 56
Amends FAS 67, paragraph 2(b) and footnote 10
Amends FAS 76, paragraph 7
Supersedes FAS 83
Amends FAS 105, paragraph 14(c)
Supersedes FIN 18, footnote 5
Amends FIN 20, paragraph 5
Amends FTB 79-8, paragraphs 5 and 6
Amends FTB 80-1, paragraphs 1 through 4
Supersedes FTB 81-3
Supersedes FTB 85-2, footnote 9

Affected by: No other pronouncements

Issues Discussed by FASB Emerging Issues Task Force (EITF)

Affects: No EITF Issues

Interpreted by: No EITF Issues

Related Issue: EITF Topic No. D-1

SUMMARY

This Statement rescinds FASB Statement No. 32, *Specialized Accounting and Reporting Principles and Practices in AICPA Statements of Position and Guides on Accounting and Auditing Matters,* and its related pronouncements. The guidance in Statement 32, which specifies that the specialized accounting principles and practices contained in AICPA Statements of Position and Guides are preferable for purposes of justifying a change in accounting principles as required by APB Opinion No. 20, *Accounting Changes,* is no longer needed with the issuance of the AICPA's Statement on Auditing Standards (SAS) No. 69, *The Meaning of "Present Fairly in Conformity With Generally Accepted Accounting Principles" in the Independent Auditor's Report.* In general, SAS 69 *requires* an entity to adopt the accounting principles in pronouncements whose effective date is after March 15, 1992. An entity initially applying an accounting principle after that date (including those making an accounting change) must follow the applicable hierarchy set forth in SAS 69. An entity following an established accounting principle that was effective as of March 15, 1992 need not change its accounting until a new pronouncement is issued. This Statement also amends other existing authoritative literature to make various technical corrections.

This Statement is effective November 30, 1992.

Statement of Financial Accounting Standards No. 111

Rescission of FASB Statement No. 32 and Technical Corrections

CONTENTS

INTRODUCTION

Rescission of Statement 32

1. FASB Statement No. 32, *Specialized Accounting and Reporting Principles and Practices in AICPA Statements of Position and Guides on Accounting and Auditing Matters,* states that the specialized accounting principles contained in the AICPA Statements of Position (SOPs) and Guides on accounting and auditing matters listed in Appendix A of that Statement are preferable for the purpose of adopting a change in accounting principle under paragraphs 15 and 16 of APB Opinion No. 20, *Accounting Changes.*

2. The Board has amended that list twice with the issuance of FASB Statements No. 56, *Designation of AICPA Guide and Statement of Position (SOP) 81-1 on Contractor Accounting and SOP 81-2 concerning Hospital-Related Organizations as Preferable for Purposes of Applying APB Opinion 20* (issued February 1982), and No. 83, *Designation of AICPA Guides and Statement of Position on Accounting by Brokers and Dealers in Securities, by Employee Benefit Plans, and by Banks as Preferable for Purposes of Applying APB Opinion 20* (issued March 1985). Statements 56 and 83 added new AICPA audit and accounting Guides and SOPs to the Statement 32 list and eliminated those that had been superseded.

3. In January 1992, the AICPA Auditing Standards Board issued Statement on Auditing Standards (SAS) No. 69, *The Meaning of "Present Fairly in Conformity With Generally Accepted Ac-counting Principles"* in the Independent Auditor's Report. That Statement supersedes AU section 411 of the AICPA *Professional Standards.* SAS 69 revises the generally accepted accounting principles (GAAP) hierarchy by (a) adding a new category, (b) changing some of the sources of established accounting principles in two categories, and (c) designating which category is to be used when there is a conflict between categories. A summary of those categories is provided in paragraph 25.

4. The provisions of SAS 69 require that an affected entity must apply the provisions of pronouncements contained in categories *(b)-(d)* with an effective date after March 15, 1992. This will require a change in accounting principles by an entity not following such accounting. An entity initially applying an accounting principle after March 15, 1992 must follow the applicable hierarchy set forth in SAS 69. Special transition provisions apply to FASB Emerging Issues Task Force (EITF) consensus positions (refer to paragraph 18). An entity following an established accounting principle (in categories *(b)* and *(c)* under the previous GAAP hierarchy) that was effective as of March 15, 1992 need not change its accounting unless it chooses to make a change or unless a new pronouncement in categories *(b)-(d)* (under SAS 69) becomes effective after March 15, 1992. Since category *(b)* in SAS 69 contains the AICPA Guides and SOPs, the Board no longer needs to designate the specialized accounting and reporting principles and practices in AICPA Guides and SOPs that are preferable for the purpose of adopting a change in accounting principle under Opinion 20. This Statement rescinds Statement 32 and related pronouncements.

Technical Corrections

5. When the Board issues a pronouncement that contains amendments to prior pronouncements, the proposed amendments are reviewed by the Board and exposed for comment as part of the due process procedures. Over the years, the FASB staff and various constituents have identified instances where additional amendments should have been made explicit in certain pronouncements. Although, in general, those "effective" amendments have been appropriately indicated in the various editions of the FASB's *Original Pronouncements* and *Current Text* publications, those effective amendments were not subjected to the Board's review and due process procedures. This Statement identifies those effective amendments and establishes them as Board-approved amendments. In addition, this Statement amends existing authoritative literature (a) to correct references to AICPA guidance that has been revised or superseded since the issuance of that literature and (b) to extend certain provisions to reflect established practice.

STANDARDS OF FINANCIAL ACCOUNTING AND REPORTING

Rescission of Statement 32 and Related Pronouncements

6. This Statement rescinds the following pronouncements:

a. FASB Statement No. 32, *Specialized Accounting and Reporting Principles and Practices in AICPA Statements of Position and Guides on Accounting and Auditing Matters*
b. FASB Statement No. 56, *Designation of AICPA Guide and Statement of Position (SOP) 81-1 on Contractor Accounting and SOP 81-2 concerning Hospital-Related Organizations as Preferable for Purposes of Applying APB Opinion 20*
c. FASB Statement No. 83, *Designation of AICPA Guides and Statement of Position on Accounting by Brokers and Dealers in Securities, by Employee Benefit Plans, and by Banks as Preferable for Purposes of Applying APB Opinion 20.*

Amendments to Opinion 20

7. This Statement amends Opinion 20 as follows:

a. The second and third sentences of paragraph 4 are replaced by the following:

Each Statement and Interpretation of the Financial Accounting Standards Board (FASB), Opinion of the Accounting Principles Board, and AICPA Accounting Research Bulletin specifies its effective date and the manner of reporting a change to conform with the conclusions of that pronouncement. Other pronouncements of the FASB or other designated bodies as described in categories *(b)-(d)* of AICPA Statement on Auditing Standards (SAS) No. 69, *The Meaning of "Present Fairly in Conformity With Generally Accepted Accounting Principles" in the Independent Auditor's Report,* may also prescribe the manner of reporting a change in accounting principle.

b. Footnote 5 is deleted and the penultimate sentence of paragraph 16 is replaced by the following:

The issuance of a new pronouncement by the FASB or by other designated bodies as described in categories *(a)-(d)* of SAS 69 that creates a new accounting principle, interprets an existing principle, expresses a preference for an accounting principle, or rejects a specific principle *may require* an entity to adopt a change in accounting principle. The issuance of such a pronouncement is considered to constitute sufficient support for making a change in accounting principle provided that the hierarchy established by SAS 69 is followed.

Technical Corrections

8. This Statement amends the following pronouncements to make technical corrections to existing authoritative literature:

a. Accounting Research Bulletin No. 43, *Restatement and Revision of Accounting Research Bulletins.*

(1) The following is added after the second sentence of paragraph 1 of Chapter 1A (effectively amended by APB Opinion No. 10, *Omnibus Opinion—1966,* paragraph 12, which reaffirms that the installment method of recognizing revenue is generally not acceptable):

In the absence of the circumstances referred to above or other specific guidance, such as in FASB Statement No. 66, *Accounting for Sales of Real Estate,* the installment method is not acceptable.

(2) In paragraph 6 of Chapter 3A, *and certain types of research and development costs* is deleted from the last sentence (effectively superseded by FASB Statement No. 2, *Accounting for Research and Development*

Costs, paragraph 12, which requires that research and development costs be charged to expense when incurred).

(3) The following is added to the end of paragraph 10 of Chapter 7A (effectively amended by ARB No. 46, *Discontinuance of Dating Earned Surplus,* paragraph 2, which provides guidance as to when the dating of earned surplus should be discontinued):

> The dating of earned surplus following a quasi reorganization would rarely, if ever, be of significance after a period of 10 years. There may be exceptional circumstances in which the discontinuance of the dating of earned surplus could be justified at the conclusion of a period less than 10 years.

(4) The last sentence of paragraph 19 of Chapter 10A is deleted (effectively superseded by FASB Statement No. 16, *Prior Period Adjustments,* paragraph 16(a), which amends the accounting for prior period adjustments).

(5) In paragraph 9 of Chapter 11B, everything following *income statement* in the second sentence through the end of that paragraph and footnotes 3 and 4 are deleted (effectively amended by Statement 16, paragraph 16(a), which amends the accounting for prior period adjustments).

b. ARB No. 51, *Consolidated Financial Statements.* Footnote 1 is deleted (effectively superseded by APB Opinion No. 16, *Business Combinations,* paragraph 7, which supersedes ARB No. 48, *Business Combinations*—referenced in footnote 1).

c. APB Opinion No. 6, *Status of Accounting Research Bulletins.* The last sentence of paragraph 16 is amended to refer to APB Opinion No. 18, *The Equity Method of Accounting for Investments in Common Stock* (effectively amended by FASB Statement No. 94, *Consolidation of All Majority-owned Subsidiaries,* paragraph 14, which supersedes paragraph 19 of ARB 51—referenced in paragraph 16).

d. APB Opinion No. 9, *Reporting the Results of Operations.* In paragraph 17, *described below* is deleted from the end of the second sentence (effectively superseded by Statement 16, paragraph 16(a), which deletes paragraphs 23 and 24 of Opinion 9—referenced by paragraph 17).

e. APB Opinion No. 10, *Omnibus Opinion—1966.* In paragraph 11(b), *as called for by paragraph 35 of APB Opinion No. 9,* is deleted

(effectively amended by APB Opinion No. 15, *Earnings per Share,* paragraph 3, which supersedes paragraph 35 of Opinion 9).

f. APB Opinion No. 12, *Omnibus Opinion—1967.* In paragraph 7, footnote 1 is replaced by the following (effectively superseded by FASB Statement No. 106, *Employers' Accounting for Postretirement Benefits Other Than Pensions,* paragraph 13):

> The amounts to be accrued periodically shall result in an accrued amount at the full eligibility date (as defined in Statement 106) equal to the then present value of all of the future benefits expected to be paid. Paragraphs 413-416 of Statement 106 illustrate application of this paragraph.

g. APB Opinion No. 15, *Earnings per Share.*

(1) In paragraph 5, *and as described in paragraph 12 of FASB Statement No. 21, Suspension of the Reporting of Earnings per Share and Segment Information by Nonpublic Enterprises* is added at the end of the first sentence (effectively amended by Statement 21, paragraph 15, which amends the scope of Opinion 15).

(2) In Exhibit B of Appendix C, *bank prime rate* is replaced by *average Aa corporate bond yield as defined in FASB Statement No. 85, Yield Test for Determining whether a Convertible Security Is a Common Stock Equivalent* (effectively amended by Statement 85, paragraph 3, which amends the yield test for determining whether a convertible security is a common stock equivalent).

(3) Also in Exhibit B, *cash* is deleted from the term *cash yield* (effectively superseded by Statement 85, paragraph 4, which deletes *cash* from the term *cash yield* in paragraph 35 of Opinion 15).

h. APB Opinion No. 20, *Accounting Changes.* In paragraph 9, *; and a change in accounting for research and development expenditures, such as from recording as expense when incurred to deferring and amortizing the costs* is deleted (effectively amended by Statement 2, paragraph 12, which requires that research and development costs be expensed when incurred).

i. AICPA Accounting Interpretation 1, "Tax Allocation for DISCs," of ARB 51 is deleted (effectively superseded by paragraph 3 of APB Opinion No. 23, *Accounting for Income Taxes—Special Areas,* which supersedes paragraph 16 of ARB 51, the basis for the Interpretation, and by footnote 2 of Opinion 23, which addresses DISCs).

j. AICPA Accounting Interpretation 5, "Investment Credit Is Prior Period Adjustment," of APB Opinion No. 4, *Accounting for the "Investment Credit,"* is deleted (effectively superseded by Statement 16, paragraph 16(a), which amends the accounting for prior period adjustments).

k. AICPA Accounting Interpretation 1, "Accounting for Leases by Manufacturer or Dealer Lessors," of APB Opinion No. 7, *Accounting for Leases in Financial Statements of Lessors,* is deleted (effectively superseded by APB Opinion No. 27, *Accounting for Lease Transactions by Manufacturer or Dealer Lessors,* and Statement 13, paragraph 2, which supersedes Opinions 7 and 27).

l. AICPA Accounting Interpretations 1-28 of APB Opinion No. 8, *Accounting for the Cost of Pension Plans,* are deleted (effectively superseded by FASB Statement No. 87, *Employers' Accounting for Pensions,* paragraph 9, which supersedes Opinion 8).

m. AICPA Accounting Interpretation 2, "Revenue Ruling on LIFO Inventory of Subsidiary," of Opinion 9 is deleted (effectively superseded by Opinion 20, paragraph 5(c), which supersedes paragraph 25 of Opinion 9, which is the basis for the Interpretation).

n. AICPA Accounting Interpretations of Opinion 15.

　(1) In Part I and Interpretations 2, 26, 30, 33, and 92, the phrases *bank prime rate, bank prime interest rate,* and *the prime rate* are replaced with *average Aa corporate bond yield as defined in FASB Statement No. 85, Yield Test for Determining whether a Convertible Security Is a Common Stock Equivalent* (effectively amended by Statement 85, paragraph 3, which amends the yield test for determining whether a convertible security is a common stock equivalent).

　(2) Interpretation 10, "Closely Held Corporations," of Opinion 15 is deleted (effectively superseded by FASB Statement No. 21, *Suspension of the Reporting of Earnings per Share and Segment Information by Nonpublic Enterprises,* paragraph 12, which eliminates the requirements of Opinion 15 for nonpublic enterprises).

　(3) Interpretation 38, "Prime Rate Used in Yield Test," of Opinion 15 is deleted (effec-

tively superseded by Statement 85, paragraph 3, which deletes the use of the bank prime interest rate in yield tests).

o. AICPA Accounting Interpretation 30, "Representations in a Pooling," of Opinion 16. In the second sentence of the sixth paragraph, *paragraph 2 of ARB No. 50* is replaced by *paragraph 3(b) of FASB Statement No. 5, Accounting for Contingencies* (effectively amended by Statement 5, paragraph 7, which supersedes ARB No. 50, *Contingencies*).

p. AICPA Accounting Interpretation 2, "Investments in Partnerships and Ventures," of Opinion 18. In the fourth paragraph, *contrary to the provisions of paragraph 19-j (income taxes on undistributed earnings of subsidiaries),* is deleted (effectively amended by Opinion 23, paragraph 3, which supersedes paragraph 19-j of Opinion 18).

q. AICPA Accounting Interpretation 1, "Disclosure of 'Leveraged Lease' Transactions by Lessors," of APB Opinion No. 22, *Disclosure of Accounting Policies,* is deleted (effectively superseded by paragraphs 41-47 of Statement 13, which specify the accounting and disclosure requirements for lessors in leveraged lease transactions).

r. AICPA Accounting Interpretation 1, "Debt Tendered to Exercise Warrants," of APB Opinion No. 26, *Early Extinguishment of Debt.*

　(1) In the first paragraph, *before its scheduled maturity* is deleted (effectively amended by FASB Statement No. 76, *Extinguishment of Debt,* paragraph 9, which deletes this phrase from Opinion 26).

　(2) In the second paragraph, *"pursuant to the existing conversion privileges of the holder" (see paragraph 2 of the Opinion)* is deleted (effectively amended by Statement 76, paragraph 7, which supersedes paragraph 2 of Opinion 26).

s. FASB Statement No. 5, *Accounting for Contingencies.* The second sentence in paragraph 18 is replaced by the following (effectively amended because the documents referenced have been superseded):

Subsequent Opinions issued by the Accounting Principles Board and Statements issued by the Financial Accounting Standards Board established more explicit disclosure requirements for a number of those items.

t. FASB Statement No. 14, *Financial Reporting for Segments of a Business Enterprise.* In paragraph 27(c), *unconsolidated subsidiaries and other* is deleted (effectively amended by Statement 94, paragraph 15, which deletes this phrase from Opinion 18).

u. FASB Statement No. 25, *Suspension of Certain Accounting Requirements for Oil and Gas Producing Companies.* Paragraphs 6 and 8 are deleted (effectively superseded by FASB Statement No. 69, *Disclosures about Oil and Gas Producing Activities,* paragraph 5, which deletes paragraphs in FASB Statement No. 19, *Financial Accounting and Reporting by Oil and Gas Producing Companies,* relating to disclosure requirements).

v. FASB Statement No. 55, *Determining whether a Convertible Security Is a Common Stock Equivalent,* is superseded (effectively superseded by Statement 85, paragraph 3, which amends the yield test for determining whether a convertible security is a common stock equivalent).

w. FASB Statement No. 67, *Accounting for Costs and Initial Rental Operations of Real Estate Projects.*

(1) In paragraph 2(b), the reference to FASB Statement No. 17, *Accounting for Leases—Initial Direct Costs,* and the last sentence are deleted and replaced by the following:

> FASB Statement No. 91, *Accounting for Nonrefundable Fees and Costs Associated with Originating or Acquiring Loans and Initial Direct Costs of Leases.* The accounting for initial direct costs is prescribed in FASB Statement No. 13, *Accounting for Leases,* as amended by Statement 91 and FASB Statement No. 98, *Accounting for Leases: Sale-Leaseback Transactions Involving Real Estate, Sales-Type Leases of Real Estate, Definition of the Lease Term, and Initial Direct Costs of Direct Financing Leases.*

(Paragraph 2(b) is effectively amended by Statement 91, paragraphs 24 and 25, which supersede Statement 17, amend the definition of initial direct costs, and amend the accounting for initial direct costs of direct financing leases, and by Statement 98, subparagraphs 22(h) and (i), which reflect the intent of the amendment made by Statement 91.)

(2) In footnote 10, the reference to Statement 17 is replaced by a reference to Statement 91

and *as amended by Statements 91 and 98* is added to the end of the second sentence.

x. FASB Statement No. 76, *Extinguishment of Debt.* The following is added to the end of paragraph 7 (effectively amended by FASB Statement No. 84, *Induced Conversions of Convertible Debt,* paragraph 5, which amends paragraph 2 of Opinion 26—referenced in paragraph 7):

> Also, this Opinion does not apply to a conversion of convertible debt when conversion privileges provided in the terms of the debt at issuance are changed (including changes that involve payment of consideration) to induce conversion of the debt to equity securities in accordance with the conditions of paragraph 2 of FASB Statement No. 84, *Induced Conversions of Convertible Debt.*

y. FASB Statement No. 105, *Disclosure of Information about Financial Instruments with Off-Balance-Sheet Risk and Financial Instruments with Concentrations of Credit Risk.* In paragraph 14(c), *No. 81, Disclosure of Postretirement Health Care and Life Insurance Benefits* is replaced by *No. 106, Employers' Accounting for Postretirement Benefits Other Than Pensions* (effectively amended by Statement 106, paragraph 12, which supersedes Statement 81).

z. FASB Interpretation No. 18, *Accounting for Income Taxes in Interim Periods.* Footnote 5 is deleted (effectively superseded by FASB Statement No. 97, *Accounting and Reporting by Insurance Enterprises for Certain Long-Duration Contracts and for Realized Gains and Losses from the Sale of Investments,* paragraph 28).

aa. FASB Technical Bulletin No. 79-8, *Applicability of FASB Statements 21 and 33 to Certain Brokers and Dealers in Securities.* In paragraphs 5 and 6, *statement of changes in financial position* is replaced by *statement of cash flows* (effectively amended by FASB Statement No. 95, *Statement of Cash Flows,* paragraph 152, which requires this change in other pronouncements).

bb. FASB Technical Bulletin No. 80-1, *Early Extinguishment of Debt through Exchange for Common or Preferred Stock.*

(1) In paragraphs 1-4, *early* is deleted (effectively amended by Statement 76, paragraph 9, which requires this change in Opinion 26).

(2) In the last sentence of paragraph 2, *before the scheduled maturity of the debt* and *early* is deleted (effectively amended by Statement 76, paragraph 8, which replaces the concept of early extinguishment).

(3) In the last sentence of paragraph 3, *as amended by FASB Statements No. 76, Extinguishment of Debt, and No. 84, Induced Conversions of Convertible Debt,* is added after *Opinion 26* (effectively amended by Statement 76, paragraph 7, and Statement 84, paragraph 5, which amend the applicability of Opinion 26).

(4) In paragraph 4, *a conversion by the holder pursuant to conversion privileges contained in the original debt issue* is replaced by the following (effectively amended by Statement 76, paragraph 7, and Statement 84, paragraph 5, which amend the applicability of Opinion 26):

a conversion of debt to equity securities of the debtor (a) pursuant to conversion privileges provided in the terms of the debt at issuance or (b) when conversion privileges provided in the terms of the debt at issuance are changed (including changes that involve payment of consideration) to induce conversion of the debt to equity securities in accordance with the conditions of paragraph 2 of Statement 84.

cc. FASB Technical Bulletin No. 81-3, *Multiemployer Pension Plan Amendments Act of 1980.* This Technical Bulletin is superseded (effectively superseded by Statement 87, paragraph 9, which supersedes Opinion 8).

dd. FASB Technical Bulletin No. 85-2, *Accounting for Collateralized Mortgage Obligations (CMOs).* Footnote 9 is deleted (effectively superseded by Statement 94, paragraph 13, which amends ARB 51 to require consolidation of all majority-owned subsidiaries).

9. This Statement amends the following pronouncements to delete or amend references to AICPA pronouncements that have been revised or superseded:

a. APB Opinion No. 20, *Accounting Changes.*

(1) In paragraph 7, the quotation marks in the second sentence and footnote 2 are deleted.

(2) In footnote 4, *Statement on Auditing Procedure No. 41, Subsequent Discovery of Facts Existing at the Date of the Auditor's Report* is replaced by *Section 561 of Statement on Auditing Standards No. 1, Codification of Auditing Standards and Procedures.*

b. APB Opinion No. 22, *Disclosure of Accounting Policies.* In footnote 2, *(see Statement on Auditing Procedure No. 38, paragraphs 5 and 6)* and *(see Statement on Auditing Procedure No. 33, Chapter 13, paragraphs 9 and 10)* are deleted.

c. AICPA Accounting Interpretation 56, "Fair Value Used If No Market Price," of Opinion 15. In the fourth paragraph, *Audits of Personal Financial Statements (an AICPA Industry Audit Guide published by the American Institute of CPAs in 1968)* is replaced by *Personal Financial Statements Guide (an Audit and Accounting Guide published by the American Institute of CPAs).*

d. FASB Statement No. 15, *Accounting by Debtors and Creditors for Troubled Debt Restructurings.*

(1) Footnote 20 is deleted (effectively superseded for finance companies by the AICPA Audit and Accounting Guide, *Audits of Finance Companies (Including Independent and Captive Financing Activities of Other Companies),* and for other entities by Statement 91).

(2) The last sentence in footnote 26 is deleted.

10. FASB Interpretation No. 20, *Reporting Accounting Changes under AICPA Statements of Position,* is amended to reflect established practice that has extended the provisions of Interpretation 20 to include AICPA Practice Bulletins, FASB Technical Bulletins, and EITF consensuses.

a. In the first sentence of paragraph 5, *or practice bulletin, an FASB technical bulletin, or a consensus of the FASB Emerging Issues Task Force (EITF)* is added after *statement of position* and at the end of the sentence *statement* is replaced by *pronouncement.*

b. The second sentence is replaced by the following:

If the pronouncement does not specify the manner of reporting a change in accounting principle to conform with its recommendations, an enterprise making a change in accounting principle to conform with the recommendations of the pronouncement shall report the change as specified by Opinion 20, except that EITF consensuses may be applied prospectively to future transactions unless otherwise stated.

The paragraph will then read as follows:

For purposes of applying *APB Opinion No. 20,* an enterprise making a change in accounting principle to conform with the recommendations of an AICPA statement of position or practice bulletin, an FASB technical bulletin, or a consensus of the FASB Emerging Issues Task Force (EITF) shall report the change as specified in the pronouncement. If the pronouncement does not

specify the manner of reporting a change in accounting principle to conform with its recommendations, an enterprise making a change in accounting principle to conform with the recommendations of the pronouncement shall report the change as specified by Opinion 20, except that EITF consensuses may be applied prospectively to future transactions unless otherwise stated.

Effective Date

11. This Statement is effective November 30, 1992.

This Statement was adopted by the unanimous vote of the seven members of the Financial Accounting Standards Board:

Dennis R. Beresford,	Victor H. Brown	A. Clarence Sampson
Chairman	James J. Leisenring	Robert J. Swieringa
Joseph V. Anania	Robert H. Northcutt	

Appendix

BACKGROUND INFORMATION AND BASIS FOR CONCLUSIONS

Rescission of Statement 32

12. In 1979, the Board decided to exercise responsibility for all specialized accounting and reporting principles and practices in AICPA SOPs and Guides on accounting and auditing matters by extracting the specialized principles and practices from those documents and, after appropriate due process, issuing them as FASB Statements. That decision, made after extensive public comment, responded to a statement by the Securities and Exchange Commission in its 1978 report to Congress on its oversight of the accounting profession that "in the long run, the FASB should develop a mechanism for dealing . . . with accounting matters related to particular industries that are now covered by SOPs."

13. To clarify any uncertainty about the ongoing status of those specialized principles and practices and alleviate concern that those accounting principles would not be followed pending release of final FASB Statements, the Board in September 1979 is-

sued Statement 32. Statement 32 designated the specialized[1] accounting and reporting principles in AICPA Guides and SOPs as preferable for purposes of justifying a change in accounting principles as required by Opinion 20.

14. Under the GAAP hierarchy that existed at the time Statement 32 was issued, as established by the AICPA in July 1975 in Statement on Auditing Standards No. 5, *The Meaning of "Present Fairly in Conformity With Generally Accepted Accounting Principles" in the Independent Auditor's Report,*[2] AICPA Guides, Interpretations, and SOPs together with FASB Technical Bulletins and widely recognized industry practice were considered secondary sources of established accounting principles— categories *(b)* and *(c)*. If the accounting treatment of a transaction or event was not specified by a pronouncement covered by Rule 203 of the AICPA *Code of Professional Conduct,*[3] an established principle from any of those secondary sources could be used for financial reporting as long as it fairly presented the substance of the transaction.

15. Statement 32 did not require entities to change their specialized accounting and reporting practices to those contained in the AICPA Guides and SOPs. Statement 32 did, however, provide preferability status to the AICPA Guides and SOPs for

---

[1]The term *specialized* was used to refer to those current accounting and reporting principles and practices in existing AICPA Guides and SOPs that were neither superseded by nor contained in FASB Statements, FASB Interpretations, APB Opinions, and AICPA Accounting Research Bulletins.

[2]SAS 5 is codified in AICPA *Professional Standards,* Volume 1, in AU section 411 and was superseded in January 1992 by SAS 69.

[3]Pronouncements covered by Rule 203—category *(a)*—of the AICPA *Code of Professional Conduct* include FASB Statements, FASB Interpretations, APB Opinions, and AICPA Accounting Research Bulletins.

the purpose of applying Opinion 20 so an entity electing to change its accounting treatment did not have to justify changing to the accounting specified by an AICPA Guide or SOP and an entity applying that accounting could not adopt a change to something less preferable. Likewise, an entity proposing a change to something other than a specialized accounting principle contained in an AICPA Guide or SOP had to justify that change.

16. Statement 32 lists the AICPA Guides and SOPs that contain specialized accounting and reporting principles considered preferable by the Board for the purpose of applying Opinion 20. The Board has amended Statement 32 twice, with the issuance of Statements 56 and 83, to add new audit and accounting Guides and SOPs issued by the AICPA and to delete those that have been superseded. The Board last amended Statement 32 in March 1985 (with the issuance of Statement 83) and has postponed subsequent amendments pending completion by the AICPA of its reexamination of the GAAP hierarchy. That reexamination resulted in SAS 69, issued in January 1992, which revises the GAAP hierarchy.

17. The revised GAAP hierarchy under SAS 69 (as summarized in paragraph 25) clearly indicates the accounting treatment required for a specific event or transaction when that event or transaction is not covered by Rule 203 guidance. SAS 69, paragraph 7, states:

> If the accounting treatment of a transaction or event is not specified by a pronouncement covered by rule 203, the auditor should consider whether the accounting treatment is specified by another source of established accounting principles. If an established accounting principle from one or more sources in category *(b), (c),* or *(d)* is relevant to the circumstances, the auditor should be prepared to justify a conclusion that another treatment is generally accepted. If there is a conflict between accounting principles relevant to the circumstances from one or more sources in category *(b), (c),* or *(d),* the auditor should follow the treatment specified by the source in the higher category—for example, follow category *(b)* treatment over category *(c)*— or be prepared to justify a conclusion that a treatment specified by a source in the lower category better presents the substance of the transaction in the circumstances.

18. SAS 69 requires an entity to adopt a new pronouncement in categories *(b)-(d)* (as summarized in paragraph 25) that becomes effective after March 15, 1992. An entity following an established

accounting principle (in categories *(b)* and *(c)* under the previous GAAP hierarchy) as of March 15, 1992 need not change its accounting treatment unless it chooses to make a change or unless a new pronouncement becomes effective in categories *(b)-(d)* (under SAS 69) after March 15, 1992. The transition provisions of SAS 69 state that an entity initially applying an accounting principle or making a change in accounting principle after March 15, 1992 must follow the applicable hierarchy as set forth in categories *(b)-(d)* except when initially applying FASB Emerging Issues Task Force consensus positions issued before March 16, 1992. Those consensuses "become effective in the hierarchy for initial application of an accounting principle after March 15, 1993."

19. With the issuance of SAS 69 the Board believes that there is no longer any uncertainty regarding the ongoing status of the specialized accounting and reporting principles and practices in AICPA Guides and SOPs. Consequently, the Board decided that the guidance provided by Statement 32 and related pronouncements is no longer needed and that those Statements should be rescinded.

Technical Corrections

20. At the time a pronouncement is developed by the Board, part of the process requires that a determination be made of the effect this new guidance will have on existing authoritative accounting pronouncements. If there is an effect, then the new pronouncement should amend or supersede the existing authoritative literature in detail so that there is (a) no doubt about what the amendment changes and (b) no conflict between the requirements of prior pronouncements and the requirements of the new pronouncement.

21. In the past, certain detailed amendments that could have been explicitly made to the authoritative literature were omitted. Those omissions occurred for various reasons. For example, because of a difference in style some pronouncements made general rather than specific amendments to prior pronouncements, and some needed technical amendments were overlooked when the new pronouncement was prepared.

22. As those omissions were discovered by the FASB staff or members of the accounting profession, corrections were made to the various editions of the FASB's *Original Pronouncements* and *Current Text* publications through effective amendments. However, those effective technical amendments have not been subjected to the Board's usual due process procedures. With the decision to issue a Statement to rescind Statement 32, the Board also decided to take this opportunity to identify

those effective amendments and issue them as Board-approved amendments.

23. The Board considered what parts of previously issued pronouncements to amend and decided that only the official guidance sections should be amended. The Board believes that the introduction, background information, and basis for conclusions paragraphs provide historical information that should not be amended or superseded unless the entire pronouncement is superseded. Those paragraphs are considered historical because they document the circumstances surrounding the development of a pronouncement. For example, they record (a) the reasons why the accounting requirements were considered to be necessary at that time, (b) what alternative guidance was considered, and (c) what the public comments were regarding the proposed requirements and how those comments were resolved.

24. In addition to the accounting guidance and historical paragraphs (described above), a pronouncement sometimes contains other paragraphs or appendixes. Those paragraphs or appendixes are ones that (a) state the scope of the pronouncement, (b) indicate substantive amendments to other existing pronouncements, (c) present examples or illustrations of application of the requirements of the pronouncement, and (d) present a glossary of the terms used in the pronouncement. The Board discussed the content of those various paragraphs and appendixes and decided that that material is part of the accounting guidance of the pronouncement and should be amended if the pronouncement is amended by a subsequent pronouncement. The Board further decided that when a pronouncement is superseded, the amendments made by that superseded pronouncement remain in effect unless they are explicitly amended.

Summary of GAAP Hierarchy under SAS 69

25. The chart below summarizes the GAAP hierarchy for financial statements of nongovernmental entities[4] under SAS 69.

Established Accounting Principles

Category *(a)*— FASB Statements and Interpretations, APB Opinions, and AICPA Accounting Research Bulletins

Category *(b)*— FASB Technical Bulletins, cleared[5] AICPA Industry Audit and Accounting Guides, and cleared AICPA Statements of Position

Category *(c)*— Consensus positions of the FASB Emerging Issues Task Force and cleared AICPA AcSEC Practice Bulletins

Category *(d)*— AICPA Accounting Interpretations, FASB Implementation Guides (Q&As), and widely recognized and prevalent industry practices

Other Accounting Literature

Other accounting literature, including FASB concepts Statements; APB Statements; AICPA Issues Papers; International Accounting Standards Committee Statements; GASB Statements, Interpretations, and Technical Bulletins; pronouncements of other professional associations or regulatory agencies; AICPA *Technical Practice Aids;* and accounting textbooks, handbooks, and articles.

Comments on Exposure Draft

26. The Board issued an Exposure Draft of a proposed Statement, *Rescission of FASB Statement No. 32 and Technical Corrections,* for comment on June 30, 1992 and received 21 letters of comment. Most of the respondents agreed that Statement 32 and related pronouncements should be rescinded.

27. Several respondents said that the guidance in Opinion 20, paragraph 4, which addresses scope, and paragraph 16 and footnote 5, which address the support needed to make a change in accounting principle, were confusing in view of the guidance

---

[4]"Rules and interpretive releases of the Securities and Exchange Commission (SEC) have an authority similar to category *(a)* pronouncements for SEC registrants. In addition, the SEC staff issues Staff Accounting Bulletins that represent practices followed by the staff in administering SEC disclosure requirements. Also, the Introduction to the FASB's *EITF Abstracts* states that the Securities and Exchange Commission's Chief Accountant has said that the SEC staff would challenge any accounting that differs from a consensus of the FASB Emerging Issues Task Force, because the consensus position represents the best thinking on areas for which there are no specific standards" (quoted from footnote 3 of SAS 69).

[5]As used in SAS 69, *cleared* means that the FASB has indicated that it does not object to the issuance of the proposed pronouncement. Footnote 4 of SAS 69 states that it should be assumed that such pronouncements have been cleared by the FASB unless the pronouncement indicates otherwise.

set forth in SAS 69. The Board agreed and has revised the amendment to Opinion 20 in paragraph 7 of this Statement to address this concern. In addition, the amendment to Interpretation 20 in paragraph 10 of this Statement was revised to clarify the application of EITF consensuses. Unless a consensus specifies the manner of reporting a change in accounting principle, an enterprise making a change in accounting principle to conform with an EITF consensus may apply the consensus prospectively to future transactions or may apply the provisions of Opinion 20 to prior transactions.

28. A majority of respondents agreed with the technical corrections. Several respondents indicated support for the practice of making needed technical corrections when they are identified and then formally issuing those corrections as Board-approved amendments after due process. A few respondents had suggestions for additional amendments. Because those suggested amendments were considered to be more substantive than technical corrections or were to sections of pronouncements that are not normally amended, they are not included in this Statement.

Statement of Financial Accounting Standards No. 112
Employers' Accounting for Postemployment Benefits

an amendment of FASB Statements No. 5 and 43

STATUS

Issued: November 1992

Effective Date: For fiscal years beginning after December 15, 1993

Affects: Amends FAS 5, paragraph 7
Amends FAS 43, paragraph 1
Supersedes FAS 43, paragraph 2
Amends FAS 107, paragraph 8(a)

Affected by: Paragraph 5(d) amended by FAS 123
Paragraph 9 amended by FAS 144

Issues Discussed by FASB Emerging Issues Task Force (EITF)

Affects: No EITF Issues

Interpreted by: No EITF Issues

Related Issue: EITF Issue No. 96-5

SUMMARY

This Statement establishes accounting standards for employers who provide benefits to former or inactive employees after employment but before retirement (referred to in this Statement as *postemployment benefits*). Postemployment benefits are all types of benefits provided to former or inactive employees, their beneficiaries, and covered dependents. Those benefits include, but are not limited to, salary continuation, supplemental unemployment benefits, severance benefits, disability-related benefits (including workers' compensation), job training and counseling, and continuation of benefits such as health care benefits and life insurance coverage.

This Statement requires employers to recognize the obligation to provide postemployment benefits in accordance with FASB Statement No. 43, *Accounting for Compensated Absences,* if the obligation is attributable to employees' services already rendered, employees' rights to those benefits accumulate or vest, payment of the benefits is probable, and the amount of the benefits can be reasonably estimated. If those four conditions are not met, the employer should account for postemployment benefits when it is probable that a liability has been incurred and the amount can be reasonably estimated in accordance with FASB Statement No. 5, *Accounting for Contingencies.* If an obligation for postemployment benefits is not accrued in accordance with Statements 5 or 43 only because the amount cannot be reasonably estimated, the financial statements shall disclose that fact.

This Statement is effective for fiscal years beginning after December 15, 1993.

Statement of Financial Accounting Standards No. 112

Employers' Accounting for Postemployment Benefits

an amendment of FASB Statements No. 5 and 43

CONTENTS

INTRODUCTION

1. This Statement establishes standards of financial accounting and reporting for the estimated cost of benefits provided by an employer to former or inactive employees after employment but before retirement (referred to in this Statement as *postemployment benefits*). Postemployment benefits are all types of benefits provided to former or inactive employees, their beneficiaries, and covered dependents. Inactive employees are those who are not currently rendering service to the employer and who have not been terminated. They include those who have been laid off and those on disability leave, regardless of whether they are expected to return to active status. Postemployment benefits include, but are not limited to, salary continuation, supplemental unemployment benefits, severance benefits, disability-related benefits (including workers' compensation), job training and counseling, and continuation of benefits such as health care benefits and life insurance coverage.

2. Prior to this Statement, employers' accounting for the cost of postemployment benefits varied. Some employers accrued the estimated cost of those benefits over the related service periods of active employees. Other employers applied a terminal accrual approach and recognized the estimated cost of those benefits at the date of the event giving rise to the payment of the benefits (for example, the death of an active employee, the temporary or permanent disability of an active employee, or the layoff of an employee). Still other employers recognized the cost of postemployment benefits when they were paid (cash basis). Some employers may have used different methods of accounting for different types of benefits.

3. The Board concluded that postemployment benefits are part of the compensation provided to an employee in exchange for service. FASB Statement No. 43, *Accounting for Compensated Absences,* addresses amounts paid to active employees while on a compensated absence, such as for vacation, occasional sick days, and holidays. Other long-term fringe benefits and postemployment benefits, however, are specifically excluded from the scope of that Statement. In addition, all employment-related costs are excluded from the scope of FASB Statement No. 5, *Accounting for Contingencies.* This Statement affirms the Board's view that generally accepted accounting principles require recognition of the cost of postemployment benefits on an accrual basis and amends Statements 5 and 43 to include the accounting for postemployment benefits. Therefore, Statement 43 will (a) continue to specify the accounting for amounts paid to active employees while on a compensated absence, such as for vacation, occasional sick days, and holidays, (b) continue to not address other long-term fringe benefits provided to active employees, and (c) specify the accounting for postemployment benefits provided to former or inac-

tive employees prior to retirement that meet the conditions in paragraph 6. Statement 5 will specify the accounting for postemployment benefits that are not addressed by Statement 43 or by other FASB Statements or APB Opinions.

STANDARDS OF FINANCIAL ACCOUNTING AND REPORTING

Scope

4. This Statement applies to all types of postemployment benefits provided to former or inactive employees, their beneficiaries, and covered dependents after employment but before retirement, except as noted in the following paragraph. Benefits may be provided in cash or in kind and may be paid as a result of a disability, layoff, death, or other event. Benefits may be paid immediately upon cessation of active employment or over a specified period of time. Employees' rights to benefits may accumulate or vest as they render service.

5. This Statement does not apply to:

a. Postemployment benefits provided through a pension or postretirement benefit plan (FASB Statements No. 87, *Employers' Accounting for Pensions,* No. 88, *Employers' Accounting for Settlements and Curtailments of Defined Benefit Pension Plans and for Termination Benefits,* and No. 106, *Employers' Accounting for Postretirement Benefits Other Than Pensions,* specify the accounting for those costs.)
b. Individual deferred compensation arrangements that are addressed by APB Opinion No. 12, *Omnibus Opinion—1967,* as amended by Statement 106
c. Special or contractual termination benefits covered by Statements 88 and 106
d. Stock compensation plans that are addressed by APB Opinion No. 25, *Accounting for Stock Issued to Employees.*

Accounting for Postemployment Benefits

6. Postemployment benefits that meet the conditions in paragraph 6 of Statement 43 shall be accounted for in accordance with that Statement. Paragraph 6 of Statement 43 states:

An employer shall accrue a liability for employees' compensation for future absences if *all* of the following conditions are met:

a. The employer's obligation relating to employees' rights to receive compensa-

tion for future absences is attributable to employees' services already rendered,
b. The obligation relates to rights that vest or accumulate,
c. Payment of the compensation is probable, and
d. The amount can be reasonably estimated. [Footnote references omitted.]

Postemployment benefits that are within the scope of this Statement and that do not meet those conditions shall be accounted for in accordance with Statement 5. Paragraph 8 of Statement 5 states:

An estimated loss from a loss contingency (as defined in paragraph 1) shall be accrued by a charge to income if *both* of the following conditions are met:

a. Information available prior to issuance of the financial statements indicates that it is probable that an asset had been impaired or a liability had been incurred at the date of the financial statements. It is implicit in this condition that it must be probable that one or more future events will occur confirming the fact of the loss.
b. The amount of loss can be reasonably estimated. [Footnote references omitted.]

Disclosures

7. If an obligation for postemployment benefits is not accrued in accordance with Statements 5 or 43 only because the amount cannot be reasonably estimated, the financial statements shall disclose that fact.

Amendments to Existing Pronouncements

8. The following sentences are added to the end of paragraph 1 of Statement 43:

This Statement also applies to all forms of postemployment benefits, as defined in FASB Statement No. 112, *Employers' Accounting for Postemployment Benefits,* that meet the conditions in paragraph 6 of this Statement, except as noted in the following paragraph. Postemployment benefits that do not meet the conditions in paragraph 6 of this Statement shall be accounted for in accordance with FASB Statement No. 5, *Accounting for Contingencies,* as amended by Statement 112. This Statement does not address the accounting for benefits paid to active employees other than compensated absences.

9. The following paragraph replaces paragraph 2 of Statement 43:

This Statement does not apply to:

a. Postemployment benefits provided through a pension or postretirement benefit plan (FASB Statements No. 87, *Employers' Accounting for Pensions,* No. 88, *Employers' Accounting for Settlements and Curtailments of Defined Benefit Pension Plans and for Termination Benefits,* and No. 106, *Employers' Accounting for Postretirement Benefits Other Than Pensions,* specify the accounting for those costs.)
b. Individual deferred compensation arrangements that are addressed by APB Opinion No. 12, *Omnibus Opinion—1967,* as amended by Statement 106
c. Special or contractual termination benefits covered by Statements 88 and 106
d. Stock compensation plans that are addressed by APB Opinion No. 25, *Accounting for Stock Issued to Employees.*

This Statement does not address the allocation of costs of compensated absences to interim periods. The cost of postemployment benefits as determined under this Statement that is directly related to the disposal of a segment of a business or a portion of a line of business shall be recognized pursuant to the requirements of APB Opinion No. 30, *Reporting the Results of Operations—Reporting the Effects of Disposal of a Segment of a Business, and Extraordinary, Unusual and Infrequently Occurring Events and Transactions,* and included in determining the gain or loss associated with that event.

10. The last two sentences of paragraph 7 of Statement 5 are deleted and replaced by the following sentence:

Accounting for other employment-related costs is also excluded from the scope of this Statement except for postemployment benefits that become subject to this Statement through application of FASB Statement No. 112, *Employers' Accounting for Postemployment Benefits.*

11. In paragraph 8(a) of FASB Statement No. 107, *Disclosures about Fair Value of Financial Instruments,* the words *postemployment benefits,* are inserted after *other postretirement benefits including health care and life insurance benefits,* and No. 112, *Employers' Accounting for Postemployment Benefits,* is inserted after No. 106, *Employers' Accounting for Postretirement Benefits Other Than Pensions,* to exclude an employer's obligation for postemployment benefits from the requirements for disclosures about fair value.

Effective Date and Transition

12. This Statement shall be effective for fiscal years beginning after December 15, 1993. Earlier application is encouraged. The effect of initially applying this Statement shall be reported as the effect of a change in accounting principle in a manner similar to the cumulative effect of a change in accounting principle (APB Opinion No. 20, *Accounting Changes,* paragraph 20). Pro forma effects of retroactive application (Opinion 20, paragraph 21) are not required. Previously issued financial statements shall not be restated.

The provisions of this Statement need not be applied to immaterial items.

This Statement was adopted by the unanimous vote of the seven members of the Financial Accounting Standards Board:

Dennis R. Beresford, *Chairman*
Joseph V. Anania

Victor H. Brown
James J. Leisenring
Robert H. Northcutt

A. Clarence Sampson
Robert J. Swieringa

Appendix

BACKGROUND INFORMATION AND BASIS FOR CONCLUSIONS

CONTENTS

Introduction

13. This appendix summarizes considerations that were deemed significant by Board members in reaching the conclusions in this Statement. It discusses reasons for accepting certain views and rejecting others. Individual Board members gave greater weight to some factors than to others.

14. The Board issued the Exposure Draft, *Employers' Accounting for Postemployment Benefits,* for public comment on May 12, 1992. Fifty-nine comment letters were received and most respondents agreed with the Board that the cost of postemployment benefits should be accounted for on an accrual basis. The Board concluded that it could reach an informed decision on the basis of existing information without a public hearing.

Background

15. The project on employers' accounting for pensions and other postemployment benefits was initially added to the Board's agenda in 1979. In 1984, the Board concluded that it should address employers' accounting for postemployment benefits other than pensions as a separate project. In 1987, the Board deferred consideration of issues relating to benefits provided after employment but before retirement to focus its resources on postretirement benefits other than pensions. The Board excluded postemployment benefits from the scope of Statement 106:

> The accounting for benefits paid after employment but before retirement (for example, layoff benefits) is a separate phase of the Board's project on accounting for postemployment benefits other than pensions. The fact that this Statement does not apply to those benefits should not be construed as discouraging the use of accrual accounting for those benefits. [footnote 2]

Consequently, accounting for postemployment benefits other than retirement benefits is the final phase of the Board's project on employers' accounting for pensions and other postemployment benefits.

Applicability of Other Pronouncements

16. Certain postemployment benefits are covered by existing Statements or Opinions. Accounting for deferred compensation contracts is covered by Opinion 12 (as amended by Statement 106). Accounting for contractual and special termination benefits is covered by Statements 88 and 106. Accounting for the disposal of a segment of a business is covered by Opinion 30. Accounting for benefits paid after retirement is covered by Statements 87, 88, and 106. This Statement does not change the accounting for those benefits.

17. The Board considered whether guidance is needed in addressing employers' accounting for postemployment benefits. In the Board's view, Statements 5 and 43 specify appropriate accounting for postemployment benefits. However, postemployment benefits were specifically excluded from the scope of those Statements because at the time those Statements were issued the Board had a project on its agenda to address the accounting for pensions and other postemployment benefits. Since that time, the Board issued Statements that address postretirement benefits but none that address the accounting for postemployment benefits. The Board, therefore, concluded that it is appropriate to amend Statements 5 and 43 to include the accounting for postemployment benefits.

18. Several respondents to the Exposure Draft commented that it would be inappropriate to account for postemployment benefits by applying the criteria in Statement 43. They stated that postemployment benefits generally do not vest and if postemployment benefits do not vest, an employer does not have an obligation to provide benefits un-

til a future event occurs. The Board considered whether an employer's liability to provide nonvesting postemployment benefits arises only when a future event, such as termination or disability, occurs. If the rights to nonvesting postemployment benefits accumulate over the service period, then the event that creates a liability and affects the amount of benefits is the rendering of service by employees. If the payment of those benefits is probable and can be reasonably estimated, then the cost of those benefits should be recognized as they are earned by the employees. The Board concluded that if postemployment benefits meet the conditions in paragraph 6 of Statement 43, then the estimated cost of those benefits should be recognized in accordance with that Statement.

19. Some respondents noted that Statement 43 does not require employers to accrue a liability for nonvesting accumulating rights to receive sick pay benefits and questioned whether that exception would apply to nonvesting accumulating rights to receive postemployment benefits. In developing Statement 43, the Board concluded that probable payments for accumulating sick pay benefits would rarely be material unless they vest or are paid without an illness-related absence. The Board also noted that the lower degree of reliability associated with estimates of future sick pay and the cost of making and evaluating those estimates did not justify a requirement for an accrual.

20. Unlike nonvesting sick pay, nonvesting postemployment benefits may be material for certain employers, especially in certain industries, depending on many factors including, but not limited to, the duration of benefit payments and the incidence of events giving rise to the payment of benefits. In addition, the fact that there are employers currently accruing the estimated cost of those benefits, some over applicable employee service periods and others using a terminal accrual approach, suggests that sufficient information is available to many employers on which to develop a reliable estimate without significant cost. Accordingly, the Board concluded that the exception in Statement 43 should not be extended to postemployment benefits.

21. If postemployment benefits do not meet the conditions in paragraph 6 of Statement 43, then employers should recognize the estimated cost of those benefits in accordance with Statement 5. Statement 5 requires recognition of a loss contingency when it is probable that an asset has been impaired or a liability has been incurred and the amount of the loss can be reasonably estimated. Paragraph 59 of Statement 5 further clarifies the recognition of loss contingencies:

. . . even losses that are reasonably estimable should not be accrued if it is not probable that an asset has been impaired or a liability has been incurred at the date of an enterprise's financial statements because those losses relate to a future period rather than the current or a prior period.

22. For example, an employer may provide any former employee on permanent disability with continued medical insurance coverage until that employee meets the requirements for participation in the employer's postretirement medical plan. If the level of benefits provided is the same for any disabled employee regardless of years of service, the cost of those benefits should be recognized when the event causing a permanent disability occurs and a reasonable estimate can be made as specified by Statement 5.

23. Several respondents requested that this Statement provide guidance on how to measure an employer's postemployment benefit obligation. FASB Statements 87 and 106 discuss measurement issues extensively. To the extent that similar issues apply to postemployment benefit plans, employers may refer to those Statements for guidance in measuring their obligations in compliance with the requirements of this Statement. Respondents also asked the Board to provide explicit guidance on the applicability and use of discounting. Statements 5 and 43 do not provide explicit guidance and readdressing those Statements is beyond the intended scope of this project. In addition, discounting is being addressed in the Board's existing project on present-value-based measurements. Accordingly, the Board decided not to provide explicit guidance on discounting in this Statement. As a result, the Board understands that the use of discounting in measuring postemployment benefit obligations will continue to be permitted but not required.

Disclosures

24. Statements 5 and 43 require disclosure if it is probable that an obligation has been incurred but it cannot be reasonably estimated. Statement 5 requires additional disclosures in other situations including when it is reasonably possible that a liability has been incurred. The Board decided not to apply the additional Statement 5 disclosures to postemployment benefit obligations because it believes that the additional cost of compliance is not warranted. Thus, this Statement requires disclosure only if an obligation for postemployment benefits is not accrued in accordance with Statements 5 or 43 solely because the amount cannot be reasonably estimated.

Effective Date and Transition

25. The effect of initially applying this Statement is to be reported as the effect of a change in accounting principle. Some respondents recommended that an option be provided to recognize that effect over future periods. The Board considered whether a provision for delayed recognition of the transition amount was needed. A major objective of transition is to minimize implementation costs and mitigate disruption without unduly compromising the ability of financial statements to provide useful information. An important factor considered by the Board was the potential magnitude of the unrecorded postemployment benefit obligation. Information made available to the Board indicated that postemployment benefits are generally not as significant as pension or other postretirement benefits. The Board concluded that a provision for delayed recognition was not needed to mitigate the financial statement impact of immediately recognizing the transition amount when this Statement is adopted. That provision would have added unnecessary complexity to the application of this Statement, reduced financial statement comparability, and been inconsistent with Statements 5 and 43, which do not provide for delayed recognition at transition.

Statement of Financial Accounting Standards No. 113
Accounting and Reporting for Reinsurance of Short-Duration and Long-Duration Contracts

STATUS

Issued: December 1992

Effective Date: For financial statements for fiscal years beginning after December 15, 1992

Affects: Amends FAS 5, paragraph 44
Supersedes FAS 60, paragraphs 38, 39, 40, and 60(f)
Supersedes FAS 97, paragraph 27
Amends FIN 39, paragraph 7

Affected by: Paragraph 6 amended by FAS 120
Paragraph 28 amended by FAS 133

Other Interpretive Pronouncement: FIN 40

Other Interpretive Release: FASB Viewpoints, "Accounting for Reinsurance: Questions and Answers about Statement 113, " FASB *Status Report,* February 26, 1993

Issues Discussed by FASB Emerging Issues Task Force (EITF)

Affects: No EITF Issues

Interpreted by: Paragraph 21 interpreted by EITF Issue No. 93-6
Paragraphs 22 through 24 interpreted by EITF Issue No. 93-6 and Topic No. D-54
Paragraph 25 interpreted by EITF Issue No. 93-6

Related Issues: EITF Topics No. D-35 and D-79

SUMMARY

This Statement specifies the accounting by insurance enterprises for the reinsuring (ceding) of insurance contracts. It amends FASB Statement No. 60, *Accounting and Reporting by Insurance Enterprises,* to eliminate the practice by insurance enterprises of reporting assets and liabilities relating to reinsured contracts net of the effects of reinsurance. It requires reinsurance receivables (including amounts related to claims incurred but not reported and liabilities for future policy benefits) and prepaid reinsurance premiums to be reported as assets. Estimated reinsurance receivables are recognized in a manner consistent with the liabilities relating to the underlying reinsured contracts.

This Statement establishes the conditions required for a contract with a reinsurer to be accounted for as reinsurance and prescribes accounting and reporting standards for those contracts. The accounting standards depend on whether the contract is long duration or short duration and, if short duration, on whether the contract is prospective or retroactive. For all reinsurance transactions, immediate recognition of gains is precluded unless the ceding enterprise's liability to its policyholder is extinguished. Contracts that do not result in the reasonable possibility that the reinsurer may realize a significant loss from the insurance risk assumed generally do not meet the conditions for reinsurance accounting and are to be accounted for as deposits.

This Statement requires ceding enterprises to disclose the nature, purpose, and effect of reinsurance transactions, including the premium amounts associated with reinsurance assumed and ceded. It also requires disclosure of concentrations of credit risk associated with reinsurance receivables and prepaid reinsurance premiums under the provisions of FASB Statement No. 105, *Disclosure of Information about Financial Instruments with Off-Balance-Sheet Risk and Financial Instruments with Concentrations of Credit Risk.*

This Statement applies to financial statements for fiscal years beginning after December 15, 1992, with earlier application encouraged.

Statement of Financial Accounting Standards No. 113

Accounting and Reporting for Reinsurance of Short-Duration and Long-Duration Contracts

CONTENTS

INTRODUCTION

1. Insurance provides indemnification against loss or liability from specified events and circumstances that may occur or be discovered during a specified period. In exchange for a payment from the policyholder (a premium), an insurance enterprise agrees to pay the policyholder if specified events occur or are discovered. Similarly, the insurance enterprise may obtain indemnification against claims[1] associated with contracts it has written by entering into a reinsurance contract with another insurance enterprise (the **reinsurer**[2] or **assuming enterprise**). The insurer (or **ceding enterprise**) pays (cedes) an amount to the reinsurer, and the reinsurer agrees to reimburse the insurer for a specified portion of claims paid under the reinsured contracts. However, the policyholder usually is unaware of the reinsurance arrangement, and the insurer ordinarily is not relieved of its obligation to the policyholder. The reinsurer may, in turn, enter into reinsur-

ance contracts with other reinsurers, a process known as retrocession.

2. FASB Statement No. 60, *Accounting and Reporting by Insurance Enterprises* (issued in 1982), specified the accounting by insurance enterprises for reinsurance contracts. Statement 60 is an extraction of requirements of the AICPA Industry Audit Guides, *Audits of Fire and Casualty Insurance Companies* and *Audits of Stock Life Insurance Companies* (1979 editions). It continued the long-established practice that originated in statutory accounting whereby ceding enterprises reported insurance activities net of the effects of reinsurance. If a reinsurance contract indemnified the ceding enterprise against loss or liability, Statement 60 required the ceding enterprise to reduce unpaid claim liabilities by related estimated amounts recoverable from reinsurers (ceded reserves or reinsurance recoverables) and to reduce

---

[1]The term *claim* is used in this Statement in the sense used in FASB Statement No. 60, *Accounting and Reporting by Insurance Enterprises,* to describe a demand for payment of a policy benefit because of the occurrence of an event insured by a long-duration or short-duration insurance contract.

[2]Words that appear in the glossary are set in **boldface type** the first time they appear.

unearned premiums by related amounts paid to re-insurers (ceded unearned premiums or prepaid re-insurance premiums).

3. APB Opinion No. 10, *Omnibus Opinion—1966,* paragraph 7, states, "It is a general principle of ac-counting that the offsetting of assets and liabilities in the balance sheet is improper except where a right of setoff exists." FASB Interpretation No. 39, *Offset-ting of Amounts Related to Certain Contracts,* spec-ifies criteria for determining whether a right of set-off exists but does not change the offsetting permitted or required by existing accounting pro-nouncements. Amounts payable to the policyholder and amounts receivable from the reinsurer do not meet the criteria for offsetting in Opinion 10 or In-terpretation 39. Those criteria include the require-ment that the reporting party have the legal right to set off the amount owed to one party with an amount receivable from that same party.

4. The issues of (a) whether net reporting of the ef-fects of reinsurance is appropriate and (b) what is meant by indemnification against loss or liability under a reinsurance contract (generally referred to as risk transfer) have been studied by the insurance industry and the accounting and actuarial profes-sions for some time. Interest in those issues has grown in recent years as a result of widespread public attention focused on failures of insurance enterprises. Risks associated with reinsurance have been cited as a contributing factor in several of those failures. Some commentators have observed that the offsetting of reinsurance-related assets and liabilities and inadequate reinsurance disclosures obscure risks associated with reinsurance. Others have observed that the accounting guidance in Statement 60 allows the use of reinsurance to accel-erate the recognition of income relating to the rein-sured contracts.

5. The increasing concerns about the effect of rein-surance accounting for contracts that do not indem-nify the ceding enterprise against loss or liability, the limited accounting guidance on reinsurance in State-ment 60, the lack of disclosure requirements for rein-surance transactions, and the inconsistency between the net accounting for reinsurance-related assets and liabilities and the established criteria for offsetting led the Board to reconsider the accounting and reporting for reinsurance required by Statement 60.

STANDARDS OF FINANCIAL ACCOUNTING AND REPORTING

Applicability and Scope

6. This Statement applies to all insurance enter-prises to which Statement 60 applies. Insurers may

enter into various types of contracts described as re-insurance, including those commonly referred to as **fronting arrangements.** This Statement provides guidance in paragraphs 8-13 on determining whether those contracts indemnify the ceding enter-prise against loss or liability and therefore meet the conditions for reinsurance accounting. Contracts that meet those conditions shall be accounted for ac-cording to the provisions of paragraphs 14-26 of this Statement; other contracts with reinsurers are ac-counted for as deposits. The accounting provisions for reinsurance depend on whether the contract is long duration or short duration and, if short dura-tion, on whether the contract is considered **prospec-tive reinsurance** or **retroactive reinsurance.** Regard-less of its form, any transaction that indemnifies an insurer against loss or liability relating to **insurance risk** shall be accounted for according to the provi-sions of this Statement.

7. This Statement does not address or change ex-isting practice in accounting for reinsurance as-sumed, other than to provide guidance on indem-nification against loss or liability relating to insurance risk in paragraphs 8-13 and require cer-tain disclosures in paragraph 27.

Indemnification against Loss or Liability Relating to Insurance Risk

8. Determining whether a contract with a rein-surer provides indemnification against loss or lia-bility relating to insurance risk requires a complete understanding of that contract and other contracts or agreements between the ceding enterprise and related reinsurers. A complete understanding in-cludes an evaluation of all contractual features that (a) limit the amount of insurance risk to which the reinsurer is subject (such as through experience refunds, cancellation provisions, adjustable fea-tures, or additions of profitable lines of business to the reinsurance contract) or (b) delay the timely re-imbursement of claims by the reinsurer (such as through payment schedules or accumulating reten-tions from multiple years).

Reinsurance of Short-Duration Contracts

9. Indemnification of the ceding enterprise against loss or liability relating to insurance risk in reinsur-ance of short-duration contracts requires both of the following, unless the condition in paragraph 11 is met:

a. The reinsurer assumes significant insurance risk under the reinsured portions of the underlying insurance contracts.
b. It is reasonably possible that the reinsurer may realize a significant loss from the transaction.

A reinsurer shall not be considered to have assumed significant insurance risk under the reinsured contracts if the probability of a significant variation in either the amount or timing of payments by the reinsurer is remote. Contractual provisions that delay timely reimbursement to the ceding enterprise would prevent this condition from being met.

10. The ceding enterprise's evaluation of whether it is reasonably possible for a reinsurer to realize a significant loss from the transaction shall be based on the present value of all cash flows between the ceding and assuming enterprises under reasonably possible outcomes, without regard to how the individual cash flows are characterized. The same interest rate shall be used to compute the present value of cash flows for each reasonably possible outcome tested.

11. Significance of loss shall be evaluated by comparing the present value of all cash flows, determined as described in paragraph 10, with the present value of the amounts paid or deemed to have been paid[3] to the reinsurer. If, based on this comparison, the reinsurer is not exposed to the reasonable possibility of significant loss, the ceding enterprise shall be considered indemnified against loss or liability relating to insurance risk only if substantially all of the insurance risk relating to the reinsured portions of the underlying insurance contracts has been assumed by the reinsurer.[4]

Reinsurance of Long-Duration Contracts

12. Indemnification of the ceding enterprise against loss or liability relating to insurance risk in reinsurance of long-duration contracts requires the reasonable possibility that the reinsurer may realize significant loss from assuming insurance risk as that concept is contemplated in Statement 60 and FASB Statement No. 97, *Accounting and Reporting by Insurance Enterprises for Certain Long-Duration Contracts and for Realized Gains and Losses from the Sale of Investments*. Statement 97 defines long-duration contracts that do not subject the insurer to mortality or morbidity risks as investment contracts. Consistent with that definition, a contract that does not subject the reinsurer to the reasonable possibility of significant loss from the events insured by the underlying insur-

ance contracts does not indemnify the ceding enterprise against insurance risk.

13. The evaluation of mortality or morbidity risk in contracts that reinsure policies subject to Statement 97 shall be consistent with the criteria in paragraphs 7 and 8 of that Statement. Evaluation of the presence of insurance risk in contracts that reinsure other long-duration contracts (such as those that reinsure ordinary life contracts or contracts that provide benefits related only to illness, physical injury, or disability) also shall be consistent with those criteria.

Reporting Assets and Liabilities Related to Reinsurance Transactions

14. Reinsurance contracts that are legal replacements of one insurer by another (often referred to as assumption and novation) extinguish the ceding enterprise's liability to the policyholder and result in removal of related assets and liabilities from the financial statements of the ceding enterprise. Reinsurance contracts in which a ceding enterprise is not relieved of the legal liability to its policyholder do not result in removal of the related assets and liabilities from the ceding enterprise's financial statements. Ceding enterprises shall report estimated **reinsurance receivables** arising from those contracts separately as assets. Amounts paid to the reinsurer relating to the unexpired portion of reinsured contracts (prepaid reinsurance premiums) also shall be reported separately as assets.

15. Amounts receivable and payable between the ceding enterprise and an individual reinsurer shall be offset only when a right of setoff exists, as defined in Interpretation 39.

16. The amounts of earned premiums ceded and recoveries recognized under reinsurance contracts either shall be reported in the statement of earnings, as separate line items or parenthetically, or those amounts shall be disclosed in the footnotes to the financial statements.

Recognition of Revenues and Costs

17. The financial reporting for a contract with a reinsurer depends on whether the contract is considered to be reinsurance for purposes of applying

---

[3]Payments and receipts under a reinsurance contract may be settled net. The ceding enterprise may withhold funds as collateral or may be entitled to compensation other than recovery of claims. Determining the amounts paid or deemed to have been paid (hereafter referred to as "amounts paid") for reinsurance requires an understanding of all contract provisions.

[4]This condition is met only if insignificant insurance risk is retained by the ceding enterprise on the reinsured portions of the underlying insurance contracts. The term *insignificant* is defined in paragraph 8 of FASB Statement No. 97, *Accounting and Reporting by Insurance Enterprises for Certain Long-Duration Contracts and for Realized Gains and Losses from the Sale of Investments*, to mean "having little or no importance; trivial" and is used in the same sense in this Statement.

this Statement. Paragraphs 8-13 identify the conditions necessary for a contract to be accounted for as reinsurance. Financial reporting for a reinsurance contract also depends on whether the contract reinsures short-duration or long-duration insurance contracts and, for short-duration contracts, on whether the contract is prospective or retroactive. Paragraphs 18-20 prescribe accounting standards applicable to all reinsurance contracts. Paragraphs 21-25 prescribe accounting standards specifically applicable to reinsurance of short-duration contracts, and paragraph 26 prescribes accounting standards for reinsurance of long-duration contracts.

18. This Statement does not specify the accounting for contracts that do not meet the conditions for reinsurance accounting, other than to incorporate the following provisions from paragraphs 39 and 40 of Statement 60, which continue in effect:

a. To the extent that a reinsurance contract does not, despite its form, provide for indemnification of the ceding enterprise by the reinsurer against loss or liability, the premium paid less the premium to be retained by the reinsurer shall be accounted for as a deposit by the ceding enterprise. A net credit resulting from the contract shall be reported as a liability by the ceding enterprise. A net charge resulting from the contract shall be reported as an asset by the reinsurer.
b. Proceeds from reinsurance transactions that represent recovery of acquisition costs shall reduce applicable unamortized acquisition costs in such a manner that net acquisition costs are capitalized and charged to expense in proportion to net revenue recognized.[5] If the ceding enterprise has agreed to service all of the related insurance contracts without reasonable compensation, a liability shall be accrued for estimated excess future servicing costs under the reinsurance contract. The net cost to the assuming enterprise shall be accounted for as an acquisition cost.

19. Reinsurance contracts do not result in immediate recognition of gains unless the reinsurance contract is a legal replacement of one insurer by another and thereby extinguishes the ceding enterprise's liability to the policyholder.

20. Reinsurance receivables shall be recognized in a manner consistent with the liabilities (including estimated amounts for claims incurred but not reported

and future policy benefits) relating to the underlying reinsured contracts. Assumptions used in estimating reinsurance receivables shall be consistent with those used in estimating the related liabilities.

Recognition of Revenues and Costs for Reinsurance of Short-Duration Contracts

21. Amounts paid for prospective reinsurance that meets the conditions for reinsurance accounting shall be reported as prepaid reinsurance premiums and amortized over the remaining **contract period** in proportion to the amount of insurance protection provided. If the amounts paid are subject to adjustment and can be reasonably estimated, the basis for amortization shall be the estimated ultimate amount to be paid.

22. Amounts paid for retroactive reinsurance that meets the conditions for reinsurance accounting shall be reported as reinsurance receivables to the extent those amounts do not exceed the recorded liabilities relating to the underlying reinsured contracts. If the recorded liabilities exceed the amounts paid, reinsurance receivables shall be increased to reflect the difference and the resulting gain deferred. The deferred gain shall be amortized over the estimated remaining **settlement period.** If the amounts and timing of the reinsurance recoveries can be reasonably estimated, the deferred gain shall be amortized using the effective interest rate inherent in the amount paid to the reinsurer and the estimated timing and amounts of recoveries from the reinsurer (the interest method). Otherwise, the proportion of actual recoveries to total estimated recoveries (the recovery method) shall determine the amount of amortization.

23. If the amounts paid for retroactive reinsurance exceed the recorded liabilities relating to the underlying reinsured contracts, the ceding enterprise shall increase the related liabilities or reduce the reinsurance receivable or both at the time the reinsurance contract is entered into, so that the excess is charged to earnings.

24. Changes in the estimated amount of the liabilities relating to the underlying reinsured contracts shall be recognized in earnings in the period of the change. Reinsurance receivables shall reflect the related change in the amount recoverable from the reinsurer, and a gain to be deferred and amortized, as described in paragraph 22, shall be adjusted or established as a result.[6] When changes in the estimated

---

[5]Paragraph 29 of Statement 60 addresses recognition of acquisition costs.

[6]Decreases in the estimated amount of the liabilities shall reduce the related amount recoverable from the reinsurer and accordingly reduce previously deferred gains. However, if the revised estimate of the liabilities is less than the amounts paid to the reinsurer, a loss shall not be deferred. The resulting difference shall be recognized in earnings immediately, as described in paragraph 23.

amount recoverable from the reinsurer or in the timing of receipts related to that amount occur, a cumulative amortization adjustment shall be recognized in earnings in the period of the change so that the deferred gain reflects the balance that would have existed had the revised estimate been available at the inception of the reinsurance transaction.

25. When practicable,[7] prospective and retroactive provisions included within a single contract shall be accounted for separately. If separate accounting for prospective and retroactive provisions included within a single contract is impracticable, the contract shall be accounted for as a retroactive contract provided the conditions for reinsurance accounting are met.

Recognition of Revenues and Costs for Reinsurance of Long-Duration Contracts

26. Amortization of the estimated cost of reinsurance of long-duration contracts that meets the conditions for reinsurance accounting depends on whether the reinsurance contract is long duration or short duration. The cost shall be amortized over the remaining life of the underlying reinsured contracts if the reinsurance contract is long duration, or over the contract period of the reinsurance if the reinsurance contract is short duration. Determining whether a contract that reinsures a long-duration insurance contract is long duration or short duration in nature is a matter of judgment, considering all of the facts and circumstances. The assumptions used in accounting for reinsurance costs shall be consistent with those used for the reinsured contracts. The difference, if any, between amounts paid for a reinsurance contract and the amount of the liabilities for policy benefits relating to the underlying reinsured contracts is part of the estimated cost to be amortized.

Disclosure

27. All insurance enterprises shall disclose the following in their financial statements:

a. The nature, purpose, and effect of ceded reinsurance transactions on the insurance enterprise's operations (Ceding enterprises also shall disclose the fact that the insurer is not relieved of its primary obligation to the policyholder in a reinsurance transaction.[8])
b. For short-duration contracts, premiums from direct business, reinsurance assumed, and reinsurance ceded, on both a written and an earned basis; for long-duration contracts, premiums and amounts assessed against policyholders from direct business, reinsurance assumed and ceded, and premiums and amounts earned
c. Methods used for income recognition on reinsurance contracts.

28. A ceding enterprise shall disclose concentrations of credit risk associated with reinsurance receivables and prepaid reinsurance premiums under the provisions of FASB Statement No. 105, *Disclosure of Information about Financial Instruments with Off-Balance-Sheet Risk and Financial Instruments with Concentrations of Credit Risk.*

Amendments to Other Pronouncements

29. This Statement supersedes paragraphs 38-40 and 60(f) of Statement 60, which address reinsurance, and incorporates the provisions of paragraphs 39 and 40 of Statement 60 in paragraph 18 of this Statement.

30. This Statement amends FASB Statement No. 5, *Accounting for Contingencies,* to include the following footnote at the end of paragraph 44:

> *Paragraphs 8-13 of FASB Statement No. 113, *Accounting and Reporting for Reinsurance of Short-Duration and Long-Duration Contracts,* identify conditions that are required for a reinsurance contract to indemnify the ceding enterprise against loss or liability and to be accounted for as reinsurance. Any transaction between enterprises to which FASB Statement No. 60, *Accounting and Reporting by Insurance Enterprises,* applies must meet those conditions to be accounted for as reinsurance.

31. Paragraph 27 of Statement 97, which refers to the reinsurance guidance in Statement 60, is amended to read as follows:

> The provisions of Statement 60 addressing loss recognition (premium deficiency) and financial statement disclosure, and the provisions of FASB Statement No. 113, *Accounting and Reporting for Reinsurance of Short-Duration and Long-Duration Contracts,* addressing reinsurance shall apply to limited-payment and universal life-type contracts addressed by this Statement.

---

[7]This term is used in the sense used in paragraph 15 of FASB Statement No. 107, *Disclosures about Fair Value of Financial Instruments,* to mean that the prospective and retroactive provisions can be accounted for separately without incurring excessive costs.

[8]As indicated in paragraph 16, the amount of recoveries recognized under reinsurance contracts also must be disclosed by the ceding enterprise if not reported separately in the statement of earnings.

32. Interpretation 39 does not modify the accounting prescribed by authoritative pronouncements in specific circumstances that result in offsetting or in a presentation that is similar to the effect of offsetting. Paragraph 7 of Interpretation 39 includes examples of that accounting and is amended to delete the reference to reinsurance in Statement 60.

Effective Date and Transition

33. This Statement is effective for financial statements for fiscal years beginning after December 15, 1992, with earlier application encouraged. The provisions of paragraphs 8-13 that establish the conditions for reinsurance accounting and paragraphs 17-26 that address recognition of revenues and costs of reinsurance need not be applied in financial statements for interim periods in the year of initial application, but amounts reported for those interim periods shall be restated if they are reported with annual financial statements for that fiscal year. Restatement of financial statements for earlier years to apply the provisions of paragraphs 8-13 and 17-26 is prohibited. Restatement of financial statements for earlier years to apply paragraphs 14-16 relating to gross reporting is encouraged but not required. The provisions of this Statement that establish the conditions for reinsurance accounting and address recognition of revenues and costs apply to reinsurance contracts entered into, renewed, amended,[9] or having an anniversary date in the year of adoption.

> **The provisions of this Statement need not be applied to immaterial items.**

This Statement was adopted by the unanimous vote of the seven members of the Financial Accounting Standards Board:

Dennis R. Beresford,
 Chairman
Joseph V. Anania

Victor H. Brown
James J. Leisenring
Robert H. Northcutt

A. Clarence Sampson
Robert J. Swieringa

---

[9]Any change or adjustment of contractual terms is considered an amendment for purposes of applying this Statement.

Appendix A

BASIS FOR CONCLUSIONS

CONTENTS

Appendix A

BASIS FOR CONCLUSIONS

Introduction

34. This appendix summarizes considerations deemed significant by Board members in reaching the conclusions in this Statement. It includes reasons for accepting certain approaches and rejecting others. Individual Board members gave greater weight to some factors than to others.

35. An FASB Exposure Draft, *Accounting and Reporting for Reinsurance of Short-Duration and Long-Duration Contracts,* was issued for public comment in March 1992 and distributed to members of various industry organizations, in addition to the standard distribution, to encourage comment by those most affected by the proposal. Fifty-three comment letters were received in response to the Exposure Draft. The Board concluded that it could reach an informed decision without holding a public hearing. However, those who responded to the Exposure Draft were invited to participate in a public Board meeting, which took place in September 1992.

Background Information

36. For reinsurance contracts that indemnified the ceding enterprise against risk of loss or liability, Statement 60 continued the long-established practice that originated in statutory accounting whereby ceding enterprises reported insurance activities net of the effects of reinsurance. Unearned premiums and unpaid claim liabilities represent an insurance enterprise's obligation to policyholders at different times during the period of an insurance contract. Similarly, prepaid reinsurance premiums and reinsurance receivables represent probable future economic benefits to be received from a reinsurer. Statement 60 required insurance liabilities to be reported net of the related reinsurance amounts and also allowed reporting of earned premiums and claims costs net of reinsurance amounts in the statement of earnings.

37. Whether this offsetting of reinsurance amounts in financial statements of insurance enterprises should continue has been a recurring issue. Opinion 10 states, "It is a general principle of accounting that the offsetting of assets and liabilities in the balance sheet is improper except where a right of setoff exists." In issuing Interpretation 39, the FASB did not modify accounting treatments specified in

existing FASB and AICPA accounting pronouncements that result in offsetting, including the accounting for reinsurance under Statement 60.

38. How to determine whether a reinsurance contract indemnifies the ceding enterprise against loss or liability has been another recurring issue. Statement 5 requires deposit accounting for insurance and reinsurance contracts that do not indemnify the insured or ceding enterprise against loss or liability. Statement 60 incorporates that guidance for reinsurance contracts without specifying further the conditions under which loss or liability is indemnified. At the time Statement 60 was issued, the insurance industry and the accounting and actuarial professions were studying what circumstances constitute indemnification against loss or liability in a reinsurance transaction.

39. Many have expressed concern about the appropriateness of reporting the effects of reinsurance on a net basis, the effect of reinsurance accounting for contracts written as reinsurance that do not indemnify the ceding enterprise against loss or liability, the adequacy of reinsurance disclosures, and the limited accounting guidance for reinsurance contracts in Statement 60. In response to those concerns, the Board decided to reconsider the reinsurance provisions of Statement 60.

40. The Board had two objectives in adding this project to its agenda. The first objective was to consider the inconsistency between accounting for reinsurance and the established criteria for offsetting and to address the perceived deficiencies in the reporting of reinsurance transactions. Amounts recoverable from reinsurers are a very significant asset for some insurance enterprises. However, the netting provisions of Statement 60 and the exclusion of insurance contracts from Statement 105 have resulted in limited reporting about the amounts receivable from reinsurers, the effects of reinsurance on the reporting enterprise's operations, and the resulting exposure to credit risk. The second objective was to address the recognition of revenues and costs resulting from reinsurance transactions. The Board concluded that it was necessary to consider the lack of guidance in Statement 60 on recognition issues relating to reinsurance because of the increasing diversity and complexity of reinsurance arrangements and the proliferation of nontraditional reinsurance contracts. There also was an apparent inconsistency between the practice of immediately recognizing gains and losses on reinsurance contracts and the premise that reinsurance does not result in extinguishment of the related liabilities.

Benefits and Costs

41. The FASB's mission statement calls for the Board to determine whether a proposed standard will fill a significant need and whether the costs it imposes, compared with the possible alternatives, will be justified in relation to the overall benefits. The costs to implement an accounting standard and the benefits of reporting consistent, comparable, and reliable information in financial statements ordinarily must be assessed in general terms and cannot be quantified. There also is no common measure for objectively comparing those costs and benefits. Moreover, implementation costs are borne primarily by the preparers of financial statements rather than the broader constituency that also benefits from improved reporting. In establishing standards that are cost-effective, the Board must balance the diverse and often conflicting needs of a variety of constituents.

42. In addressing this project, the Board determined that the information provided to users about the effects of reinsurance transactions could be improved by (a) eliminating the industry practice of offsetting reinsurance assets and liabilities, (b) requiring disclosures about the credit risk associated with reinsurance receivables, and (c) limiting diversity among ceding enterprises in recognizing revenues and costs from reinsurance contracts.

43. The Board concluded that not all accounting issues relating to reinsurance contracts could be effectively addressed in this Statement. However, information provided to users about the effects of reinsurance could be improved and inconsistencies could be reduced by providing guidance for both short-duration and long-duration contracts. The Exposure Draft provided only general implementation guidance and did not attempt to identify and address all issues that could arise. Some respondents recommended that the Statement provide far more extensive implementation guidance and additional examples, particularly on applying the conditions for reinsurance accounting. Those requests were evaluated individually and, in certain instances, the Board concluded that additional guidance was warranted. However, because the Board believes that the cost of implementing very detailed standards for reinsurance accounting would outweigh the benefits, the overall approach of providing general rather than detailed guidance was retained. The Board believes the increased usefulness of the information provided on the effects of reinsurance transactions will exceed the costs of complying with this Statement.

44. The information required by this Statement should be readily available to the reporting enterprise because of similar regulatory reporting guidelines. Modification of existing systems may be required to facilitate reporting concentrations of credit risk and to comply with the provisions for recognizing revenues and costs required by this Statement. The Exposure Draft would have required prospective and retroactive elements of all reinsurance contracts to be accounted for separately. Respondents indicated that the cost of allocating amounts related to these provisions could be significant and that allocation might not always be practicable. To address these concerns, the Board concluded that contracts containing both prospective and retroactive elements should be accounted for as retroactive contracts when allocation is impracticable.

Scope

45. After reviewing current practice and the nature of reinsurance contracts, the Board concluded that an extensive reconsideration of the accounting for reinsurance is not necessary at this time; concerns could be addressed by modifying the standards of financial accounting and reporting for reinsurance in Statement 60 and by providing limited additional guidance. The guidance in paragraphs 39 and 40 of Statement 60 was not reconsidered and continues in effect. The provisions of those paragraphs have been incorporated in this Statement for convenience.

46. This Statement applies to any transaction that indemnifies an insurer against loss or liability relating to insurance risk. All transactions must meet the conditions in paragraphs 8-13 of this Statement to be accounted for as reinsurance. The Exposure Draft would have amended paragraph 44 of Statement 5 to indicate that similar conditions are required for an insurance policy to indemnify the insured against loss or liability. While that amendment was not expected to have a significant effect in practice, some respondents indicated its effect would be greater than anticipated. The Board decided not to extend the provisions in paragraphs 8-13 to primary insurance transactions. This potential inconsistency was accepted, even though paragraph 44 of Statement 5 suggests it is appropriate to apply a uniform concept of indemnification to both insurance and reinsurance, because the Board's intention was to not significantly change the accounting for primary insurance transactions in this narrow-scope project.

47. Likewise, the Board concluded that it was not necessary to address the accounting for reinsurance by the assuming enterprise. An assuming enterprise generally accounts for a reinsurance contract in the same manner as an insurance contract sold to an individual or noninsurance enterprise, as prescribed in Statements 60 and 97. Some constituents recommended that the Board specify the accounting by assuming enterprises and require symmetrical accounting by both parties to a reinsurance transaction. Those recommendations were not adopted because addressing the accounting for assuming enterprises would inevitably require a reconsideration of the accounting for primary insurance, which was beyond this project's scope. However, the conditions for reinsurance accounting in paragraphs 8-13 and certain disclosure requirements apply to both ceding and assuming enterprises.

48. Some respondents to the Exposure Draft asked that certain types of entities or transactions be excluded from the scope. The Board was urged to limit the scope to loss portfolio transfers or other transactions that some consider prone to abusive accounting under current standards. The Board considered and rejected that approach because it perceived the need for improved accounting and reporting guidance for reinsurance in general. The transactions in question also could not be distinguished conceptually from other reinsurance transactions. Insurers may enter into various transactions with reinsurers that serve legitimate business purposes but do not meet the conditions for reinsurance accounting in this Statement. The Board's objective was only to specify the accounting standards for reinsurance, as distinct from other transactions.

49. For similar reasons, fronting arrangements are included within the scope of this Statement. Some insurance enterprises currently do not report fronting arrangements as reinsurance contracts. However, the ceding enterprise in a fronting arrangement retains the same risks associated with any other type of reinsurance contract and is not relieved of its obligation to the policyholders.

50. Several respondents questioned whether servicing carriers for involuntary risk pools should be included in the Statement's scope. Servicing carriers generally retain the primary obligation to the policyholder and have no right to offset claim liabilities against amounts due from other pool participants. Although the credit risk associated with involuntary pools may be reduced because of the pool membership's joint and several liability, the servicing carrier is still dependent on the ability of other pool members to pay their proportionate share of claims. State authorities oversee such pools and may act to support the solvency of a pool, but that action generally is voluntary. The Board concluded that it was unable to effectively distinguish servicing carrier business from other types of reinsurance for accounting purposes. Separate presentation or disclosure of servicing carrier activity is not precluded by this Statement.

51. Some respondents asked the Board to limit the Statement's scope to short-duration contracts, citing a perceived lack of accounting abuse related to long-duration contracts and the differences between the long-duration and short-duration insurance models. However, reinsurance of long-duration contracts sometimes is used to accelerate income recognition by effectively unlocking the assumptions used in estimating benefit reserves. In addition, reinsurance of long-duration contracts is not unique and the specific questions raised by respondents about how the standard would be applied to long-duration contracts were not so complex or difficult as to justify a separate project to develop additional detailed guidance for reinsurance of long-duration contracts.

52. Reinsurance contracts sometimes are used to "sell" a line of business by coinsuring all or substantially all of the risks related to the line. Some respondents asked that those contracts be exempt from the requirements of this Statement. The Board concluded that unless the ceding enterprise is legally relieved of its liability to the policyholder, as described in paragraph 19, such reinsurance does not constitute a sale and immediate recognition of a gain should be precluded.

53. Some respondents asked whether structured settlement transactions are included within the scope of this Statement. Structured settlements may, in some circumstances, legally replace one insurer by another and thereby extinguish the primary insurer's liability to the policyholder. This Statement requires that an immediate gain or loss be recognized when such an extinguishment occurs. A structured settlement transaction that does not constitute an extinguishment is accounted for as reinsurance if the annuity funding the settlement meets the conditions for reinsurance accounting. Otherwise, the transaction is accounted for in accordance with paragraph 18 of this Statement. Whether a ceding enterprise has been legally relieved of its entire obligation to the policyholder under a structured settlement is a factual question that depends on the settlement's terms.

54. This Statement applies only to enterprises to which Statement 60 applies and, thus, continues the exemption in Statement 60 for mutual life insurance enterprises. The Board specifically considered whether that exemption is appropriate in accounting and reporting for reinsurance. Mutual life insurance enterprises are included within the scope of Interpretation 39 and Opinion 10, suggesting that they also should be required to separately report assets and liabilities arising from reinsurance. However, the Board observed that this Statement's provisions on reporting revenues and costs are closely linked to the accounting model for

long-duration contracts found in Statement 60. Determining how those provisions would apply to enterprises that do not follow the Statement 60 model might be time-consuming and could involve considering the appropriate accounting for insurance contracts by mutual life insurance enterprises.

55. The Board also noted that it has asked the AICPA to expeditiously complete its project on the accounting for insurance activities, including reinsurance, by mutual life insurance enterprises. Accordingly, the Board did not expand this Statement's scope to encompass those topics, and concluded that this Statement should apply only to enterprises to which Statement 60 applies.

Indemnification against Loss or Liability Relating to Insurance Risk

56. This Statement incorporates the provisions of paragraph 40 of Statement 60 that require deposit accounting for reinsurance contracts that do not indemnify the ceding enterprise against loss or liability. Those provisions incorporate without change the guidance in paragraph 44 of Statement 5. Determining whether a reinsurance contract indemnifies the ceding enterprise against loss or liability has been controversial and problematic in practice. The Board concluded that this Statement should provide general guidance on the circumstances under which reinsurance contracts provide indemnification against loss or liability and therefore meet the conditions for reinsurance accounting.

57. Transactions other than reinsurance may provide indemnification against various types of loss or liability. Under this Statement, the distinguishing characteristic of reinsurance is indemnification against loss or liability related to insurance risk. As contemplated in Statements 60 and 97, insurance risk is the risk associated with the occurrence of insured events under an insurance contract. Those risks include the uncertainties relating to both the ultimate amount of payments and the timing of those payments. Risks other than those associated with the occurrence of insured events under an insurance contract, such as the risk that investment income will vary from expectations, are not elements of insurance risk. Although insurers may face significant exposure to risks other than insurance risk, indemnification against loss or liability in a reinsurance transaction is a function of the insurance risk assumed by the reinsurer.

58. Determining whether a reinsurance contract indemnifies the ceding enterprise against loss or liability relating to insurance risk requires a complete understanding of all contracts or agreements with related reinsurers. Although an individual contract may appear to indemnify the ceding enterprise, the risk assumed

by the reinsurer through one reinsurance contract may have been offset by other contracts or agreements. A contract does not meet the conditions for reinsurance accounting if features of the reinsurance contract or other contracts or agreements directly or indirectly compensate the reinsurer or related reinsurers for losses. That compensation may take many forms, and an understanding of the substance of the contracts or agreements is required to determine whether the ceding enterprise has been indemnified against loss or liability relating to insurance risk. For example, contractual features may limit the reinsurer's exposure to insurance risk or delay the reimbursement of claims so that investment income mitigates exposure to insurance risk. Examples of those contractual features, which are not intended to be all-inclusive, are included in paragraph 8 of this Statement.

59. Reinsurance programs often entail the reinsurance of various layers of exposure through multiple reinsurance contracts. The Board concluded that indemnification against loss or liability relating to insurance risk should be determined in relation to the provisions of the individual reinsurance contract being evaluated. That is, to meet the conditions for reinsurance accounting, the terms of the individual reinsurance contract must indemnify the ceding enterprise against loss or liability relating to insurance risk.

60. Several respondents to the Exposure Draft observed that this requirement could result in different accounting for similar transactions depending on the contractual structure of the transactions. Those respondents recommended that the conditions for reinsurance accounting be evaluated based on whether a reinsurance program, taken as a whole, indemnifies the insurer against loss or liability related to insurance risk. That approach was rejected because it would not have been practicable to define what constitutes a reinsurance program. Further, contracts that are not, in substance, reinsurance could meet the conditions for reinsurance accounting by being designated as part of a program that, as a whole, met those conditions.

Reinsurance of Short-Duration Contracts

61. A short-duration insurance contract requires that an insurer make payments to the policyholder because insured events occurred during the contract period. However, an insurer's exposure to risk does not end with the close of the contract period. Exposure to risk extends beyond that date to the date when the last claim is settled and paid. During that period, many factors may affect the ultimate claims paid. Policyholders may discover and assert more claims than expected or may assert them more quickly than expected. The costs of individual claims may exceed the insurer's expectations. Courts and legislative bodies may extend the insurer's exposure beyond that originally contemplated. A reinsurance contract may limit the insurer's exposure to some or all of those circumstances. The extent of protection provided may range from very little to a considerable amount.

62. The Board concluded that two conditions must be met for reinsurance of a short-duration contract to indemnify the ceding enterprise against loss or liability relating to insurance risk. First, the reinsurer must assume significant insurance risk under the reinsured portions[10] of the underlying contracts. Implicit in this condition is the requirement that both the amount and timing of the reinsurer's payments depend on and directly vary with the amount and timing of claims settled under the reinsured contracts. Contractual features that delay timely reimbursement to the ceding enterprise prevent the reinsurer's payments from directly varying with the claims settled under the reinsured contracts.

63. Second, even if the first condition is met, the contract does not indemnify the ceding enterprise against loss or liability relating to insurance risk unless either (a) it is reasonably possible that the assuming enterprise may realize a significant loss[11] from the transaction or (b) the contract fulfills the condition described in paragraph 11.

64. The Exposure Draft did not specify how to determine exposure to significant loss, and a number of respondents asked for additional guidance in this area. Paragraph 10 requires that significance be determined based on the present value of all cash flows between the ceding and assuming enterprise under reasonably possible outcomes. All cash flows are included because payments that effectively represent premiums or refunds of premiums may be described in various ways under the terms of a reinsurance contract. The way a cash flow is characterized does not affect whether it should be included in determining the reinsurer's exposure to loss. Consistent with Statement 5, an outcome is reasonably possible if its probability is more than remote.

---

[10]A ceding enterprise may reinsure only part of the risks associated with the underlying contracts. For example, a proportionate share of all risks or only specified risks may be reinsured. The conditions for reinsurance accounting are evaluated in relation to the reinsured portions of the underlying insurance contracts, rather than all aspects of those contracts.

[11]The Exposure Draft would have required the possibility of significant gain or loss. Based on comments received, the Board concluded that possibility of loss is the essential condition for indemnification and deleted the reference to gain from this Statement.

65. Respondents asked for more guidance about the benchmark for measuring significance. The Board clarified this provision to indicate that significance of loss is evaluated in relation to the present value of the amounts paid to the reinsurer.

66. The cash flows between the ceding and assuming enterprise and the amounts paid to the reinsurer are compared at their present values to achieve a consistent temporal frame of reference. A constant interest rate is used in determining those present values because the possibility of investment income varying from expectations is not an element of insurance risk. The Board concluded that it was not necessary to specify in detail the interest rate used in the calculation; judgment is required to identify a reasonable and appropriate rate.

67. Under very limited circumstances, the reinsurer need not be exposed to the reasonable possibility of significant loss for a contract to meet the conditions for reinsurance accounting. For example, applying the "reasonable possibility of significant loss" condition is problematic when the underlying insurance contracts themselves do not result in the reasonable possibility of significant loss to the ceding enterprise.[12] The Board concluded that, when the reinsurer has assumed substantially all of the insurance risk in the reinsured portions of the underlying policies,[13] even if that risk does not result in the reasonable possibility of significant loss, the transaction meets the conditions for reinsurance accounting. In this narrow circumstance, the reinsurer's economic position is virtually equivalent to having written the insurance contract directly. The risks retained by the ceding enterprise are insignificant, so that the reinsurer's exposure to loss is essentially the same as the insurer's.

Reinsurance of Long-Duration Contracts

68. The Board considered the concept of insurance risk as it relates to certain long-duration contracts when it deliberated Statement 97 and concluded that, to be considered insurance, those contracts must subject the insurance enterprise to mortality or morbidity risk. Indemnification of a ceding enterprise against loss or liability relating to insurance risk under a related reinsurance contract requires that the reinsurer be subject to those same risks. Even though other risks, such as investment yield risk, are significant business elements of a long-duration insurance contract, those risks are not unique to insurance or reinsurance. Consistent with Statement 97, reinsurance of long-duration contracts that does not subject the reinsurer to mortality or morbidity risks associated with the underlying reinsured contracts is, in substance, an investment contract. The Board also concluded that for a long-duration contract to meet the conditions for reinsurance accounting, the contract must subject the reinsurer to the reasonable possibility of significant loss from the insurance risk assumed.

69. Statement 97 focuses on certain life insurance-type contracts and excludes various other types of long-duration contracts, such as health and disability insurance contracts. The Board concluded that the conditions for reinsurance accounting for other types of long-duration contracts should be consistent with those described in paragraph 68 of this Statement. To be accounted for as reinsurance, the contract must subject the reinsurer to the risks insured by the underlying reinsured contracts.

Reporting Assets and Liabilities Related to Reinsurance Transactions

70. The Actuarial Standards Board's Actuarial Standard of Practice No. 11, *The Treatment of Reinsurance Transactions in Life and Health Insurance Company Financial Statements,* acknowledges the need to evaluate the gross liability to policyholders in establishing an appropriate net liability under a reinsurance contract. Auditing guidance issued by the AICPA identifies reinsurance as an area with potential for increased audit risk and emphasizes the exposure associated with the gross insurance liability. However, some observers have expressed concern that actuarial and audit practices sometimes focus on net exposures and may fail to adequately assess and analyze gross exposures.

71. The Board determined that the net reporting of assets and liabilities related to reinsurance is inconsistent with the established conditions for offsetting and does not result in a meaningful presentation in financial statements of insurance enterprises. Some respondents to the Exposure Draft objected to gross reporting on the basis that disclosure is adequate to ensure a meaningful presentation. However, disclosure of offsetting amounts is not equivalent to the recognition of assets and liabilities in the statement of financial position. In addition, some reinsurance disclosures are not easily understood or comparable with disclosures of other insurance enterprises.

72. The net accounting for reinsurance prescribed in Statement 60 also may obscure the required ac-

---

[12]Most commonly, this arises when an individual risk or insurance contract, rather than a group of risks or contracts, is reinsured. The probability of loss from any individual short-duration insurance contract generally is considered to be remote. Therefore, outcomes that would expose the assuming enterprise to risk of significant loss ordinarily could not be characterized as reasonably possible.

[13]It is presumed that those policies qualify as insurance for accounting purposes.

counting for the underlying reinsured contracts. A number of constituents indicated that the current practice of reporting insurance net of reinsurance activity is consistent with the way insurers view and manage their businesses. These constituents maintained that reporting the net exposure from the reinsured contracts appropriately reflects the role of reinsurance in mitigating risk. However, the existence of a reinsurance contract does not alter the measurement of the liabilities that should be recognized on the underlying reinsured contracts. The Board concluded that separate reporting of reinsurance receivables and the related liabilities will provide a more relevant and representationally faithful presentation of the effects of reinsurance. The additional disclosures required for reinsurance transactions in paragraph 27 should provide users of financial statements with information about the purpose of reinsurance and its role in mitigating risk.

73. The Board also concluded that reinsurance receivables should be recognized consistent with recognition of the liabilities related to the underlying reinsured contracts. Because the valuation of reinsurance receivables depends on the terms of the reinsurance contract and on estimates used in measuring the liabilities relating to the reinsured contracts, the Board chose not to stipulate a specific valuation method. However, the ceding enterprise must assess the collectibility of those receivables in accordance with Statement 5.

74. Some respondents to the Exposure Draft disputed the Board's characterization of reinsurance receivables on unpaid claims as assets. In their view, the reporting of a claim is the event triggering asset recognition; otherwise, the reinsurer has no contractual obligation to the ceding enterprise. However, reinsurance receivables on unpaid claims represent probable future economic benefits controlled by the ceding enterprise as a result of the payment of a reinsurance premium and the occurrence of an insured event. The entity that controls the economic benefit need not have the ability to convert it to cash or another asset immediately, through sale or assertion of a contractual right, to meet the established criteria for recognition. Reporting and settlement of claims relate to measurement of the asset rather than the criteria for recognition. Those events represent the conditions[14] necessary to establish the ultimate amount of the asset and the timing of its collection.

75. Some respondents suggested that reinsurance recoverables be reported as valuation accounts associated with the claim liability. FASB Concepts Statement No. 6, *Elements of Financial Statements,* paragraph 43, describes a liability valuation account:

> A separate item that reduces or increases the carrying amount of a liability is sometimes found in financial statements. For example, a bond premium or discount increases or decreases the face value of a bond payable to its proceeds or present value. Those "valuation accounts" are part of the related liability and are neither liabilities in their own right nor assets.

Reinsurance receivables are an asset, not a liability valuation account. Valuation accounts exist only as part of a measurement of a liability, not as a complete measurement of a liability.

76. Amounts recoverable from reinsurers on unasserted claims may be included with other reinsurance receivables in the statement of financial position. Some respondents objected to the combined presentation because users of financial statements might find that presentation confusing. However, similar concerns could be expressed about other balances typically reported in an insurer's financial statements. For example, claim liabilities generally include amounts relating to both reported and unreported claims. Although this Statement requires amounts recoverable on unasserted claims to be reported as reinsurance receivables, it does not preclude separate presentation or disclosure of various types of receivables.

77. Statement 60 requires that unearned premiums received by an insurance enterprise relating to the unexpired portion of short-duration contracts be reported separately from other liabilities. The Board concluded that a ceding enterprise should likewise report amounts paid to reinsurers relating to the unexpired portion of short-duration contracts (referred to in Statement 60 as ceded unearned premiums) separately from reinsurance receivables. Those amounts represent prepaid premiums on prospective reinsurance contracts.

78. Several balances may arise between the ceding and assuming enterprise in a reinsurance contract, including funds withheld on ceded premiums, commissions, unsettled claims, and funds advanced by the assuming enterprise. Those items may qualify for offsetting under the conditions established by Interpretation 39, and this Statement does not preclude offsetting when appropriate.

---

[14]Among the transactions specifically addressed by Interpretation 39 is the offsetting of amounts related to conditional contracts, whose obligations or rights depend on the occurrence of some specified future event that is not certain to occur.

However, an insurance enterprise must evaluate each situation in light of the conditions required for offsetting in determining the appropriate financial statement presentation.

79. Some respondents suggested that gross reporting of amounts related to reinsurance would result in less useful financial statements. Those respondents generally maintained that users of financial statements are more interested in the net exposure, consistent with the way management views its business. Some were concerned that enterprises engaging heavily in reinsurance transactions will be perceived as being financially stronger because of the correspondingly larger assets and liabilities that will be reported. Others stated that financial ratios and trend data used by analysts will be adversely affected by the change. Respondents also suggested that commingling assets and liabilities related to servicing carrier business with other types of reinsurance will diminish the usefulness of financial statements. However, a number of respondents indicated that gross information would be more useful than net information.

80. The comments on usefulness often referred to the perceived relevance and representational faithfulness of net reporting. The Board carefully considered those comments and concluded that financial statements from which significant amounts of assets and liabilities are omitted generally lack relevance and are not representationally faithful. Offsetting reinsurance assets against the related liabilities implies a relationship between those assets and liabilities that does not exist unless the established criteria for offsetting are met. Further, offsetting reinsurance receivables against the related liabilities obscures the credit risk associated with reinsurance.

81. Examples of other accounting literature in which net reporting is permitted, such as pension accounting and leveraged leases, were cited by some respondents as a basis for continuing the practice of net reporting of reinsurance transactions. Interpretation 39 did not modify the accounting treatment of those transactions. The Board decided to include the exemptions in Interpretation 39 as a practical matter to avoid disturbing certain longstanding accounting practices without full exploration of the issues involved. Having addressed those issues for reinsurance, the Board concluded that the benefits of reporting reinsurance assets and liabilities separately are sufficient to justify the change.

82. A number of respondents asked the Board to consider allowing reinsurance recoverables on unpaid claims to be reported as a contraliability against claim reserves, rather than as an asset. Many of the same arguments made against gross reporting were provided as reasons for a contraliability presentation.

83. Advocates of a contraliability presentation also observed that the amount recoverable from the reinsurer and the related claim liabilities are difficult to measure. In their view, the volatile nature of the reinsured risks renders the gross amounts unreliable, but the presence of reinsurance permits measurement of a net exposure with more reliability. Contraliability presentation would minimize the effect of that volatility by presenting the reinsurance recoverable and the related liabilities together.

84. Advocates of a contraliability presentation also cited the linkage between the reinsured liabilities and the amounts recoverable from the reinsurer. In reinsurance, the asset arises from and is dependent on the same transaction as the liability for both the amount and timing of its realization. These respondents believe that relationship is more faithfully represented by displaying those amounts together rather than as a separate asset and liability.

85. The Board acknowledged the potential volatility of the estimates and the close linkage between the asset and liability but rejected the contraliability approach. Reinsurance recoverables on unpaid claims meet the qualifications for recognition as an asset and should be reported as such. Contraliabilities are not considered a financial statement element under the Board's conceptual framework. The Board also was not persuaded that the characteristics of a reinsurance transaction are sufficiently different from other transactions to justify a presentation other than that prescribed in Interpretation 39. The additional disclosure requirements this Statement prescribes, including the requirement to disclose the nature, purpose, and effect of reinsurance on the enterprise's operations, should provide users of financial statements with additional information to assess the effect of volatility and the ability of reinsurance to mitigate it.

86. Paragraph 38 of Statement 60 allowed, but did not require, amounts paid to reinsurers and reinsurance recoveries to be netted against related earned premiums and incurred claim costs in the statement of earnings. Most enterprises report those amounts on a net basis consistent with the presentation in the statement of financial position. The Board determined that reporting gross amounts in the statement of earnings would be preferable. However, the Board acknowledged that the reasons for gross reporting in the statement of earnings are less compelling. Opinion 10 and Interpretation 39 address only the offsetting of assets and liabilities. Further, unlike the statement of financial position, the statement of earnings does not convey information about credit risk.

87. As proposed in the Exposure Draft, enterprises could have reported the effects of reinsurance on earned premiums and claim costs (that is, the amount by which earned premiums are reduced by amounts paid or payable to reinsurers, and the amount by which claim costs are reduced by amounts received or receivable from reinsurers) either as separate line items or parenthetically within the statement of earnings. Appendix B illustrates those presentations. Respondents recommended that the Board also allow those amounts to be reported net, with appropriate footnote rather than parenthetical disclosure. The Board agreed that earned premiums ceded and reinsurance recoveries may be disclosed rather than reported separately in the statement of earnings.

Recognition of Revenues and Costs

88. Accounting for the effects of reinsurance contracts on the revenues and costs of the ceding enterprise is complicated because reinsurance contracts serve various objectives. An insurance enterprise may purchase reinsurance to reduce exposure to losses from the events it has agreed to insure, similar to a direct insurance contract purchased by an individual or noninsurance enterprise. The insurance enterprise also may contract with a reinsurer to facilitate the writing of contracts larger than those normally accepted, to obtain or provide assistance in entering new types of business, or to accomplish tax or regulatory objectives. It is not practicable to identify and separately account for each individual element of a reinsurance contract, and the guidance in Statement 60 is inadequate to result in consistent accounting for the payments and proceeds resulting from reinsurance contracts. The Board determined that this Statement should prescribe in more detail the accounting for revenues and costs of reinsurance contracts.

89. Although a contract may meet the conditions for reinsurance accounting, the difference between the amount paid to the reinsurer and the liabilities related to the reinsured contracts may result from underwriting, investment, service, sales, or financing activities. Varying applications of the provisions of Statement 60 have sometimes resulted in immediate recognition of a gain or loss equal to that difference. The Exposure Draft concluded that immediate recognition of gains or losses from reinsurance contracts generally is inappropriate and inconsistent with the premise that the insurance enterprise has not been relieved of its obligations to the holders of the reinsured contracts.[15]

90. Some constituents stated that it would be appropriate to recognize the effects of reinsurance in income immediately, referring to reinsurance as a sale or a form of extinguishment of debt. Others stated that, when the ceding enterprise has been indemnified against loss or liability relating to insurance risk, sufficient risk has been transferred to the reinsurer to result in immediate recognition. However, in the Board's view, immediate recognition is not appropriate unless an extinguishment has taken place. The conditions necessary for indemnification against insurance risk are considerably less stringent than those required for extinguishment, which occurs only when the ceding enterprise has been entirely relieved of its obligations to the policyholder.

91. A few respondents stated that the reinsurance transaction is a significant event that should result in remeasurement of the related liabilities and recognition of the effects of remeasurement in income. The Board concluded that reinsurance does not alter the nature or amount of the obligations owed to the policyholder. Rather, the ceding enterprise has acquired a separate asset—the right to recoveries from the reinsurer.

92. Some respondents said that the significant gains sometimes recognized by ceding enterprises under the current standards result from an accounting anomaly, and the Board's proposed accounting would not resolve that anomaly. The amounts paid to the reinsurer may reflect the time value of money as an element of pricing. The ceding enterprise's gains occur at least partly because the related liabilities are not stated at present value under current accounting standards. Several constituents recommended that the Board defer reaching a conclusion about reinsurance until the fundamental question of the role of discounting in measuring assets and liabilities is resolved. Those constituents correctly described the nature of the issue, but the Board decided that delaying resolution of the inconsistencies in reinsurance accounting would not be appropriate.

93. The Board concluded that estimated reinsurance receivables should be recognized in a manner consistent with the related liability. The accounting for amounts that represent recovery of acquisition costs is addressed in paragraph 39 of Statement 60 and incorporated in paragraph 18 of this Statement. Other amounts paid or received, other than advances or forms of collateral, are presumed to be part of the net cost of reinsurance discussed in paragraphs 94-109.

---

[15]The Board decided, as a number of respondents to the Exposure Draft recommended, that losses relating to retroactive contracts should be distinguished from other gains and losses arising from reinsurance transactions. The accounting for retroactive contracts is described in paragraphs 22-24.

*Recognition of Revenues and Costs for
Reinsurance of Short-Duration Contracts*

94. Contracts that meet the conditions for reinsurance accounting also may include elements of a financing arrangement. Existing accounting pronouncements do not provide guidance that would allow an insurer to identify the separate elements and costs of reinsurance. If a reinsurance contract is prospective, reinsurance activities affect the results of the ceding enterprise while the reinsured contracts are in force (the contract period) and during the subsequent period over which claims are settled. If a reinsurance contract is retroactive, the coverage period is closed and the reinsurance contract can affect only the remaining settlement period.

95. The distinction between prospective and retroactive reinsurance contracts is based on whether the contract reinsures future or past insured events covered by the underlying contracts. For example, in occurrence-based insurance, the insured event is the occurrence of a loss covered by the insurance contract. In claims-made insurance, the insured event is the reporting to the insurer, within the period specified by the policy, of a claim for a loss covered by the insurance contract. A claims-made reinsurance contract that reinsures claims asserted to the reinsurer in a future period as a result of insured events that occurred prior to entering into the reinsurance contract is a retroactive contract.

96. Some constituents stated that, in their view, the distinction between prospective and retroactive contracts is unnecessary because all reinsurance transactions that indemnify the ceding enterprise against loss or liability relating to insurance risk should be treated alike. However, the Board was not prepared to impose settlement period accounting on all reinsurance transactions without a more complete exploration of the insurance accounting model.

97. Some would prefer that the distinction between prospective and retroactive contracts be based on the event covered by the reinsurance contract rather than the insured event under the insurance contract. Others recommended using management's intentions to determine whether the contract is prospective or retroactive. The Board concluded that the significant distinction in reinsurance is whether an insured event has occurred under the underlying insurance contracts. The nature of the risks assumed by the reinsurer is fundamentally different when an insured event has already occurred. The Board also believes that management's intentions do not determine whether a contract is retroactive or prospective.

98. Reinsurance contracts may include both prospective and retroactive provisions. For example, a reinsurance contract that reinsures liabilities relating to contracts written during one or more prior years also may reinsure losses on contracts to be written during one or more future years. Reinsurance also may be acquired some time after the reinsured contract has been written, but before the close of the coverage period for that contract, and be made effective as of the beginning of the contract period. This may result in a reinsurance contract with prospective and retroactive provisions that relate to a single contract year.[16]

99. A troublesome issue for the Board was deciding whether and how to separate the various elements of such mixed contracts. The Exposure Draft proposed separate accounting for the prospective and retroactive elements of all contracts having elements of both. Respondents observed that the cost to separate these elements could be significant and separation would not be practicable in all circumstances. They generally would have resolved this problem by making the classification based on the contract's predominant characteristics. The Board rejected that approach because the criterion for making the determination was vague and could require extremely detailed implementation guidance. When practicable, separate accounting is required for the prospective and retroactive provisions of the contract. Otherwise, the contract is classified as retroactive.

100. The Board concluded that amounts paid for prospective reinsurance should be amortized over the contract period in proportion to the amount of insurance protection provided. This approach ignores the protection provided by reinsurance over the remaining settlement period but is consistent with the basic insurance accounting model in Statement 60 for short-duration contracts, which recognizes estimated revenues and costs over the contract period. Subsequent changes in estimates are recognized in income of the period in which the estimates are changed.

101. The amounts paid for retroactive reinsurance are made up of various elements of the reinsurance contract. The primary elements are the implicit discounting of the related liabilities and a premium for indemnification against loss from adverse development on the reinsured contracts. It generally is not practicable to identify the effect of each element, and the Board has not required these elements to be accounted for separately. However, the amount paid to the reinsurer for retroactive reinsurance may ex-

---

[16]It is not uncommon for a reinsurance arrangement to be initiated before the beginning of a policy period but not finalized until after the policy period begins. Whether there was agreement in principle at the beginning of the policy period and, therefore, the contract is substantively prospective must be determined based on the facts and circumstances.

ceed the recorded liabilities relating to the reinsured contracts. In the Exposure Draft, the Board concluded that amounts paid for a reinsurance contract in excess of the related liabilities either may result from significant risk of future adverse development under the reinsured contracts or may indicate that the liabilities are understated. The Exposure Draft would have permitted amounts in excess of the recorded liabilities to be recognized as an asset to the extent they represented protection against future adverse development.

102. Respondents who addressed this issue generally disagreed with the Board's conclusion. Some pointed out that, when such differences arise from retroactive transactions, the reinsured events have already occurred. The uncertainty that is being reinsured is the estimation of the liabilities relating to those past events, and the amount paid to the reinsurer in excess of the recorded liabilities may be viewed as representing at least the minimum liability that should be accrued. Otherwise, the amount does not reflect anticipated future recoveries from the reinsurer and should not be recorded as an asset. The Board concluded that amounts paid for retroactive reinsurance in excess of recorded liabilities should be charged to expense at the inception of the reinsurance contract. The offsetting adjustment may increase the liability, reduce the amount recoverable from the reinsurer, or both, depending on the facts and circumstances. Recognizing an appropriate liability for the claims relating to the underlying reinsured contracts may require a charge to expense greater than the amount paid in excess of the recorded liabilities, but the charge to expense will not be less than that amount.

103. The Board concluded that costs and revenues of retroactive reinsurance other than amounts in excess of the recorded liabilities should be accounted for over the settlement period of the underlying insurance contracts. Unlike prospective reinsurance, a retroactive reinsurance contract cannot provide protection over the coverage period. That period is past, and any protection provided by retroactive reinsurance must relate to the remaining settlement period.

104. Some respondents objected to the inconsistency between settlement period accounting for retroactive contracts and the contract period accounting required by the insurance accounting model. However, the Board observed that resolving that inconsistency would entail a comprehensive review of insurance accounting, including reconsideration of revenue and expense recognition, measurement (discounting), and financial statement presentation. One solution to the inconsistency that likely would be considered if such a

comprehensive review were undertaken is accounting for all insurance and reinsurance contracts over the settlement period. Although the Board has not deliberated this issue, some believe that the settlement period best represents the period over which services are provided by insurers and reinsurers and, therefore, is the appropriate period over which all revenues and costs should be recognized. The Board concluded that the concerns raised in this project are not sufficient to expand the scope to a general reconsideration of insurance accounting and that users would be better served by a more timely resolution of concerns specific to reinsurance reporting.

105. The Board faced similar issues in defining the amortization method for gains deferred for retroactive reinsurance contracts. To the extent the deferred gain arises from the implicit discounting of liabilities, amortization using the interest method would appear appropriate. However, the difference being amortized is the net accounting effect of all elements of the reinsurance contract, including the effects of discounting and of the premium paid for indemnification against loss or liability relating to insurance risk. Separate identification and accounting for each element is not considered feasible and would have greatly increased the complexity of this Statement. The interest method also requires estimates of the amount and timing of payments, which may not be practicable in some circumstances. Consequently, the Exposure Draft would have permitted ratable recognition as amounts are recovered under the reinsurance contract (the recovery method) or on a straight-line basis.

106. The Board's decision to eliminate the deferral of amounts in excess of recorded liabilities (as described in paragraph 23) made the straight-line method unnecessary. Many respondents to the Exposure Draft found that method objectionable on conceptual grounds. A number of respondents also recommended that the interest method be required when practicable. Upon reconsideration, the Board agreed to require the interest method when the amount and timing of the recoveries can be reasonably estimated and require the recovery method in other circumstances.

107. Amortization of deferred amounts arising from retroactive reinsurance under both the interest method and the recovery method is based on the ceding enterprise's estimates of the expected timing and total amount of cash flows. The Board concluded that the timing of changes in those estimates should not alter the recognition of the revenues and costs of reinsurance. Therefore, this Statement requires changes in estimates of the amount recoverable from the reinsurer to be ac-

counted for consistently both at the inception of and after the reinsurance transaction.

108. Establishing an amount recoverable from a reinsurer may result in a deferred gain, reflecting the amount by which the recorded liabilities exceed the amounts paid to the reinsurer. Likewise, a change in the estimate of the amount recoverable from a reinsurer after the inception of the reinsurance transaction results in or adjusts the amount of a deferral. Previously deferred amounts are reduced when the estimate is decreased. However, if the revised estimate of the related liabilities is less than the amounts paid to the reinsurer, a loss is not deferred. The resulting difference is charged to expense, as described in paragraph 23.

109. Changes in the estimated amount recoverable from a reinsurer or the timing of receipts related to those amounts affect amortization through a catch-up adjustment. When the change in estimate is recognized, the deferral is adjusted to the balance that would have existed had the revised estimate been available at the inception of the reinsurance transaction, with an offsetting charge or credit to income.

Recognition of Revenues and Costs for Reinsurance of Long-Duration Contracts

110. When a long-duration contract is reinsured, there may be a difference between the amounts paid for the reinsurance contract and the amount of liabilities related to the underlying reinsured contracts. That difference results from differences between the assumptions used by the ceding enterprise and those used by the reinsurer in estimating the future performance of the reinsured contracts.

111. The Board concluded that the difference between the amounts paid for a reinsurance contract and the amount of liabilities related to the underlying long-duration contracts should be considered part of the net cost of the reinsurance at the time it is acquired. The cost of reinsurance should be recognized over the remaining life of the underlying reinsured contracts unless the reinsurance contract is short duration in nature, when the cost should be recognized over the period of the reinsurance contract. Determining whether reinsurance of a long-duration contract is short duration in nature is a matter of judgment. For example, some contracts described as yearly renewable term may be, in substance, long-duration contracts, depending on their terms and how they are priced. Paragraphs 7 and 8 of Statement 60 provide guidance on distinguishing between short-duration and long-duration contracts.

Disclosure

112. Statement 60 required disclosure of the nature and significance of reinsurance transactions to the enterprise's operations, including total reinsurance premiums assumed and ceded, and estimated amounts recoverable from reinsurers, which are offset against claim liabilities. Current reinsurance disclosures are not comparable, are often difficult to understand, and are not as useful as they could be in assessing the effect of reinsurance on the operating results of an insurance enterprise. Moreover, disclosures about the credit risk associated with reinsurance receivables currently are not provided.

113. This Statement supersedes the disclosure requirements in paragraph 60(f) of Statement 60. Because of the complexities of reinsurance, the Board concluded that the gross amounts reported in the financial statements should be supplemented by disclosure about the nature, purpose, and effect of reinsurance transactions on the ceding enterprise. However, because the uses of reinsurance are varied, the Board did not specify what information is useful in assessing the effect of reinsurance, other than to require an indication by ceding enterprises that reinsurance does not relieve the insurer of its obligation to the policyholder. Appendix B provides some illustrations of disclosures required by this Statement. The Board determined that information about the significance of reinsurance, as reflected in the total amount of reinsurance premiums ceded and assumed, should be provided, including information about both written and earned premiums relating to short-duration contracts (if the difference is significant).

114. In reviewing current disclosure practices, the Board observed that credit risk associated with amounts due from reinsurers, although significant to some insurance enterprises, is not disclosed. Insurance contracts were among the financial instruments excluded from the scope of Statement 105, because the significant business risks involved generally are other than credit and market risk, namely, uncertainty about the ultimate timing and amount of claims. Because receivables and payables that result from insurance contracts are not subject to the same insurance risks that persuaded the Board to exclude insurance contracts from Statement 105, the Board concluded that Statement 105 disclosures are required for concentrations of credit risk for reinsurance receivables and prepaid reinsurance premiums.

115. The Board considered whether disclosures about the extent to which reinsurance contracts indemnify the ceding enterprise against loss or liability relating to insurance risk would be useful in as-

sessing the viability of an insurance enterprise and the objectives of reinsurance. The Board decided that a specific disclosure requirement should not be imposed in this Statement. The extent to which risk is transferred between enterprises has broader implications than reinsurance. For example, those disclosures would be relevant for insurance purchased by any enterprise and for transactions that purport to hedge financial positions. Developing verifiable and reliable disclosures may be difficult, but the Board encourages appropriate disclosure of indemnification policies as part of this Statement's required disclosure about the nature and effect of reinsurance transactions.

116. Some respondents asked the Board to consider requiring numerous additional disclosures other than those included in the Exposure Draft. Several of these would have imposed more stringent requirements on insurers than are imposed on other enterprises in the same circumstances. For example, a number of respondents suggested additional disclosures about credit risk that would have effectively amended Statement 105 to result in stricter requirements for insurers. The Board rejected these suggestions because it believes disclosures applicable to all enterprises should be applied consistently across industries. In considering requests for additional disclosures, the Board also balanced concerns about "disclosure overload" with requests from some respondents for additional disclosures that financial statement users might find useful. The Board concluded that the disclosures required in this Statement achieve an appropriate balance between those concerns.

Effective Date and Transition

117. The Board concluded that this Statement should be applied in a manner that will minimize the accounting changes that must be made for existing reinsurance contracts. The Board discussed effective dates intended to allow insurance enterprises sufficient time to gather the required information for restatement of assets and liabilities of prior periods, if desired. Because information similar to that required by this Statement must be reported under current regulatory requirements and should be available to the reporting enterprise and because constituents indicated that improved reporting in this area is needed as soon as is practicable, the Board concluded that this Statement should be effective for fiscal years beginning after December 15, 1992. However, to allow more time for adoption, the provisions of this Statement relating to indemnification against loss or liability relating to insurance risk and recognition of revenues and costs need not be applied in financial statements for interim periods in the year of adoption.

If those interim amounts are reported with annual financial statements for that fiscal year, restatement is required.

118. The Exposure Draft would have allowed restatement of previously reported revenues and costs if the financial statements also were restated to report gross amounts. Upon reconsideration, the Board concluded that restatement was not appropriate because of the significance of management's intentions in determining whether and when to enter into a reinsurance transaction. Prohibiting restatement of revenues and costs also will result in more consistent reporting during the transition period and will lessen implementation costs for some enterprises.

119. The Exposure Draft would have applied to transactions entered into or renewed in the year of adoption. Respondents asked how this provision should be applied to continuous and multiple-year contracts and to contract amendments. The Board concluded that this Statement should apply to transactions having an anniversary date in the year of adoption, effectively subjecting all in-force reinsurance contracts to its provisions. The Board also concluded that this Statement should apply to all contract amendments, including amendments of contracts that were otherwise excluded from this Statement under the transition provisions. However, because financial statements will not be restated to reflect the provisions on recognition of revenues and costs, previously recognized amounts relating to existing contracts are not affected by this Statement.

Appendix B

ILLUSTRATIONS

Introduction

120. This appendix contrasts reporting of gross amounts for reinsurance contracts, as required by this Statement, and reporting of net amounts for those contracts, as previously required by Statement 60. The requirements of this Statement are applied to a property-casualty insurance enterprise that issues short-duration contracts in Illustration 1 and to a life insurance enterprise that issues long-duration contracts in Illustration 2. The illustrations include examples of reinsurance disclosures that would be appropriate under the provisions of this Statement. Significant judgment is required in assessing the adequacy of disclosures. These examples are not intended to incorporate all possible types of disclosure that may be relevant.

Illustration 1

The Property-Casualty Insurance Company
Statement of Financial Position (in millions)

	Gross	Net[a]
Assets:		
Investments	$ 8,500	$ 8,500
Cash	20	20
Receivables:		
Reinsurance[b]	1,400	100
Other	1,900	1,900
Deferred policy acquisition costs	300	300
Prepaid reinsurance premiums[c]	250	—
Other assets	1,400	1,400
Total assets	$13,770	$12,220
Liabilities and equity:		
Liabilities for claims and claim settlement expenses	$ 7,600	$ 6,300
Unearned premiums	1,700	1,450
Other liabilities	2,300	2,300
Equity	2,170	2,170
Total liabilities and equity	$13,770	$12,220

The Property-Casualty Insurance Company
Statement of Earnings (in millions)

	Gross	Net[a]
Revenues:		
Premiums earned	$3,350	$2,900
Premiums ceded[d]	(450)	—
Net premiums earned	2,900	2,900
Net investment income	1,700	1,700
Other revenues	400	400
Total revenues	5,000	5,000
Expenses:		
Claims and claim settlement expenses	2,200	1,900
Reinsurance recoveries[d]	(300)	—
Net claims and claim settlement expenses	1,900	1,900
Policy acquisition costs	1,450	1,450
Other expenses	1,150	1,150
Total expenses	4,500	4,500
Earnings before tax	$ 500	$ 500

[a]Net numbers are presented for illustrative comparison and are not required by this Statement.

[b]Under Statement 60 requirements, typically only the amount receivable for paid claims and claim settlement expenses would be reported as a reinsurance receivable. This Statement requires that estimated amounts receivable from reinsurers include amounts related to paid and unpaid claims and claims incurred but not reported. Details of the amounts comprising reinsurance receivables may be presented separately.

[c]Prepaid reinsurance premiums include amounts paid to reinsurers relating to the unexpired portion of reinsured policies, often referred to as ceded unearned premiums.

[d]Alternatively, the effect of reinsurance on premiums earned and claim costs may be shown parenthetically or may be disclosed. For example, following is an illustration of a parenthetical presentation:

Premiums earned (net of premiums ceded totaling $450) $2,900

Claims and claim settlement expenses (net of reinsurance recoveries totaling $300) $1,900

The Property-Casualty Insurance Company
Notes to Financial Statements

Summary of Significant Accounting Policies

In the normal course of business, the Company seeks to reduce the loss that may arise from catastrophes or other events that cause unfavorable underwriting results by reinsuring certain levels of risk in various areas of exposure with other insurance enterprises or reinsurers.

Amounts recoverable from reinsurers are estimated in a manner consistent with the claim liability associated with the reinsured policy. The amount by which the liabilities associated with the reinsured policies exceed the amounts paid for retroactive reinsurance contracts is amortized in income over the estimated remaining settlement period using the interest method. The effects of subsequent changes in estimated or actual cash flows are accounted for by adjusting the previously deferred amount to the balance that would have existed had the revised estimate been available at the inception of the reinsurance transactions, with a corresponding charge or credit to income.

Reinsurance

Reinsurance contracts do not relieve the Company from its obligations to policyholders. Failure of reinsurers to honor their obligations could result in losses to the Company; consequently, allowances are established for amounts deemed uncollectible. The Company evaluates the financial condition of its reinsurers and monitors concentrations of credit risk arising from similar geographic regions, activities, or economic characteristics of the reinsurers to minimize its exposure to significant losses from reinsurer insolvencies. At December 31, 19X3, reinsurance receivables with a carrying value of $260 million and prepaid reinsurance premiums of $45 million were associated with a single reinsurer. The Company holds collateral under related reinsurance agreements in the form of letters of credit totaling $150 million that can be drawn on for amounts that remain unpaid for more than 120 days.

The effect of reinsurance on premiums written and earned is as follows (in millions):

	Written	Earned
Direct	$2,880	$2,730
Assumed	630	620
Ceded	(470)	(450)
Net premiums	$3,040	$2,900

Illustration 2

The Life Insurance Company
Statement of Financial Position (in millions)

	Gross	Net[a]
Assets:		
Investments	$13,100	$13,100
Cash	20	20
Receivables:		
Reinsurance[b]	1,400	100
Other	1,900	1,900
Deferred policy acquisition costs	300	300
Other assets	1,400	1,400
Total assets	$18,120	$16,820
Liabilities and equity:		
Liability for policy benefits	$ 7,200	$ 6,300
Policyholders' contract deposits	5,000	4,600
Other liabilities	3,750	3,750
Equity	2,170	2,170
Total liabilities and equity	$18,120	$16,820

The Life Insurance Company
Statement of Earnings (in millions)

	Gross	Net[a]
Revenues:		
Premiums and policyholder fees earned	$3,350	$2,900
Premiums ceded[c]	(450)	—
Net premiums and policyholder fees earned	2,900	2,900
Net investment income	1,700	1,700
Other revenues	400	400
Total revenues	5,000	5,000
Expenses:		
Policyholder benefits	2,200	1,900
Reinsurance recoveries[c]	(300)	—
Net policyholder benefits	1,900	1,900
Amortization of deferred policy acquisition costs	950	950
Other expenses	1,650	1,650
Total expenses	4,500	4,500
Earnings before tax	$ 500	$ 500

---

[a]Net numbers are presented for illustrative comparison and are not required by this Statement.

[b]Under Statement 60 requirements, typically only the amount receivable for benefits and expenses paid would be reported as a reinsurance receivable. This Statement requires that estimated amounts receivable from reinsurers include amounts related to paid and unpaid benefits, including amounts related to liabilities recognized for future policy benefits. Details of the amounts comprising reinsurance receivables may be presented separately.

[c]Alternatively, the effect of reinsurance on premiums earned and benefit costs may be shown parenthetically or may be disclosed. For example, following is an illustration of a parenthetical presentation:

Premiums and policyholder fees earned (net of premiums ceded totaling $450) $2,900

Benefits (net of reinsurance recoveries totaling $300) $1,900

The Life Insurance Company
Notes to Financial Statements

Summary of Significant Accounting Policies

In the normal course of business, the Company seeks to limit its exposure to loss on any single insured and to recover a portion of benefits paid by ceding reinsurance to other insurance enterprises or reinsurers under excess coverage and coinsurance contracts. The Company retains a maximum of $500,000 of coverage per individual life.

Amounts paid or deemed to have been paid for reinsurance contracts are recorded as reinsurance receivables. The cost of reinsurance related to long-duration contracts is accounted for over the life of the underlying reinsured policies using assumptions consistent with those used to account for the underlying policies.

Reinsurance

Reinsurance contracts do not relieve the Company from its obligations to policyholders. Failure of reinsurers to honor their obligations could result in losses to the Company; consequently, allowances are established for amounts deemed uncollectible. The Company evaluates the financial condition of its reinsurers and monitors concentrations of credit risk arising from similar geographic regions, activities, or economic characteristics of the reinsurers to minimize its exposure to significant losses from reinsurer insolvencies. At December 31, 19X3, reinsurance receivables with a carrying value of $260 million were associated with a single reinsurer. The Company holds collateral under related reinsurance agreements in the form of letters of credit totaling $150 million that can be drawn on for amounts that remain unpaid for more than 120 days.

The effect of reinsurance on premiums and amounts earned is as follows (in millions):

Direct premiums and amounts assessed against policyholders	$2,730
Reinsurance assumed	620
Reinsurance ceded	(450)
Net premiums and amounts earned	$2,900

Appendix C

GLOSSARY

121. This appendix defines certain terms as they are used in this Statement. Various other terms common to the insurance industry are defined in Appendix A of Statement 60.

Assuming enterprise
The party that receives a reinsurance premium in a reinsurance transaction. The assuming enterprise (or reinsurer) accepts an obligation to reimburse a ceding enterprise under the terms of the reinsurance contract.

Ceding enterprise
The party that pays a reinsurance premium in a reinsurance transaction. The ceding enterprise receives the right to reimbursement from the assuming enterprise under the terms of the reinsurance contract.

Contract period
The period over which insured events that occur are covered by the reinsured contracts. Commonly referred to as the coverage period or period that the contracts are in force.

Fronting arrangements
Reinsurance arrangements in which the ceding enterprise issues a policy and reinsures all or substantially all of the insurance risk with the assuming enterprise.

Insurance risk
The risk arising from uncertainties about both (a) the ultimate amount of net cash flows from premiums, commissions, claims, and claim settlement expenses paid under a contract (often referred to as underwriting risk) and (b) the timing of the receipt and payment of those cash flows (often referred to as timing risk). Actual or imputed investment returns are not an element of insurance risk. Insurance risk is fortuitous—the possibility of adverse events occurring is outside the control of the insured.

Prospective reinsurance
Reinsurance in which an assuming enterprise agrees to reimburse a ceding enterprise for losses that may be incurred as a result of future insurable events covered under contracts subject to the reinsurance. A reinsurance contract may include both prospective and retroactive reinsurance provisions.

Reinsurance receivables
All amounts recoverable from reinsurers for paid and unpaid claims and claim settlement expenses, including estimated amounts receivable

for unsettled claims, claims incurred but not reported, or policy benefits.

Reinsurer
Refer to **Assuming enterprise.**

Retroactive reinsurance
Reinsurance in which an assuming enterprise agrees to reimburse a ceding enterprise for liabilities incurred as a result of past insurable events covered under contracts subject to the reinsurance. A reinsurance contract may include both prospective and retroactive reinsurance provisions.

Settlement period
The estimated period over which a ceding enterprise expects to recover substantially all amounts due from the reinsurer under the terms of the reinsurance contract.

Statement of Financial Accounting Standards No. 114
Accounting by Creditors for Impairment of a Loan

an amendment of FASB Statements No. 5 and 15

STATUS

Issued: May 1993

Effective Date: For fiscal years beginning after December 15, 1994

Affects: Amends FAS 5, paragraph 23
   Amends prospectively FAS 15, paragraphs 1, 33, 34, and 42
   Supersedes prospectively FAS 15, paragraphs 30 through 32, 35 through 37, 40(a), and 41 and
    footnotes 18, 19, 21, 24, and 25
   Amends FAS 60, paragraph 47
   Amends FAS 91, paragraph 14
   Supersedes FTB 79-6
   Supersedes FTB 79-7

Affected by: Paragraphs 8 and 11 through 15 amended by FAS 118
    Paragraphs 17 through 20 and 65 superseded by FAS 118

Other Interpretive Pronouncement: FTB 94-1

Other Interpretive Release: FASB *Viewpoints,* "Application of FASB Statements 5 and 114 to a Loan Portfolio,"
    April 12, 1999

Issues Discussed by FASB Emerging Issues Task Force (EITF)

 Affects: Nullifies EITF Issues No. 87-5 and 89-9 and Topic No. D-37

 Interpreted by: Paragraph 13 interpreted by EITF Issue No. 98-13

 Related Issues: EITF Issues No. 84-4, 84-19, 85-44, 87-18, 87-19, 94-8, 96-22, and 99-20 and Topic No.
    D-80

SUMMARY

This Statement addresses the accounting by creditors for impairment of certain loans. It is applicable to all creditors and to all loans, uncollateralized as well as collateralized, except large groups of smaller-balance homogeneous loans that are collectively evaluated for impairment, loans that are measured at fair value or at the lower of cost or fair value, leases, and debt securities as defined in FASB Statement No. 115, *Accounting for Certain Investments in Debt and Equity Securities.* It applies to all loans that are restructured in a troubled debt restructuring involving a modification of terms.

It requires that impaired loans that are within the scope of this Statement be measured based on the present value of expected future cash flows discounted at the loan's effective interest rate or, as a practical expedient, at the loan's observable market price or the fair value of the collateral if the loan is collateral dependent.

This Statement amends FASB Statement No. 5, *Accounting for Contingencies,* to clarify that a creditor should evaluate the collectibility of both contractual interest and contractual principal of all receivables when assessing the need for a loss accrual. This Statement also amends FASB Statement No. 15, *Accounting by Debtors and Creditors for Troubled Debt Restructurings,* to require a creditor to measure all loans that are restructured in a troubled debt restructuring involving a modification of terms in accordance with this Statement.

This Statement applies to financial statements for fiscal years beginning after December 15, 1994. Earlier application is encouraged.

Statement of Financial Accounting Standards No. 114

Accounting by Creditors for Impairment of a Loan

an amendment of FASB Statements No. 5 and 15

CONTENTS

INTRODUCTION

1. The FASB was asked by the AICPA's Accounting Standards Executive Committee (AcSEC), the Federal Deposit Insurance Corporation (FDIC), and others to address in what circumstances, if any, a creditor should measure impairment of a loan based on the present (discounted) value of expected future cash flows related to the loan. AcSEC originally addressed the issue of accounting for loan impairment in an effort to reconcile certain AICPA Audit and Accounting Guides for different types of financial institutions, which provide inconsistent guidance for the application of FASB Statement No. 5, *Accounting for Contingencies,* to the loan portfolio of a financial institution. That inconsistent guidance has resulted in significant differences in when and how different types of financial institutions recognize losses for impaired loans.

2. This Statement amends Statement 5 to clarify that a creditor should evaluate the collectibility of both contractual interest and contractual principal of all receivables when assessing the need for a loss accrual.

3. This Statement also amends FASB Statement No. 15, *Accounting by Debtors and Creditors for Troubled Debt Restructurings,* to require creditors to measure all loans that are restructured in a trou-

bled debt restructuring involving a modification of terms in accordance with this Statement.

STANDARDS OF FINANCIAL ACCOUNTING AND REPORTING

Definitions and Scope

4. For purposes of this Statement, a loan is a contractual right to receive money on demand or on fixed or determinable dates that is recognized as an asset in the creditor's statement of financial position. Examples include but are not limited to accounts receivable (with terms exceeding one year) and notes receivable.

5. This Statement applies to all creditors. It addresses the accounting by creditors for impairment of a loan by specifying how allowances for credit losses related to certain loans should be determined. This Statement also addresses the accounting by creditors for all loans that are restructured in a troubled debt restructuring involving a modification of terms of a receivable, except restructurings of loans excluded from the scope of this Statement in paragraph 6(b)-(d), including those involving a receipt of assets in partial satisfaction of a receivable. The term *troubled debt restructuring* is used in this Statement consistent with its use in Statement 15.

Accounting by Creditors for
Impairment of a Loan
FAS114

6. This Statement applies to all loans that are identified for evaluation, uncollateralized as well as collateralized, except:

a. Large groups of smaller-balance homogeneous loans that are collectively evaluated for impairment. Those loans may include but are not limited to credit card, residential mortgage, and consumer installment loans.
b. Loans that are measured at fair value or at the lower of cost or fair value, for example, in accordance with FASB Statement No. 65, *Accounting for Certain Mortgage Banking Activities,* or other specialized industry practice.
c. Leases as defined in FASB Statement No. 13, *Accounting for Leases.*
d. Debt securities as defined in FASB Statement No. 115, *Accounting for Certain Investments in Debt and Equity Securities.*

7. This Statement does not specify how a creditor should identify loans that are to be evaluated for collectibility.[1] A creditor should apply its normal loan review procedures in making that judgment. This Statement does not address when a creditor should record a direct write-down of an impaired loan, nor does it address how a creditor should assess the overall adequacy of the allowance for credit losses. In addition to the allowance calculated in accordance with this Statement, a creditor should continue to recognize an allowance for credit losses necessary to comply with Statement 5.

Recognition of Impairment

8. A loan is impaired when, based on current information and events, it is probable that a creditor will be unable to collect all amounts due according to the contractual terms of the loan agreement. As used in this Statement and in Statement 5, as amended, *all amounts due according to the contractual terms* means that both the contractual interest payments and the contractual principal payments of a loan will be collected as scheduled in the loan agreement. This Statement does not specify how a creditor should determine that it is probable that it will be unable to collect all amounts due according to the contractual terms of a loan. A creditor should apply its normal loan review procedures in making that judgment. An insignificant delay or insignificant

shortfall in amount of payments does not require application of this Statement. A loan is not impaired during a period of delay in payment if the creditor expects to collect all amounts due including interest accrued at the contractual interest rate for the period of delay. Thus, a demand loan or other loan with no stated maturity is not impaired if the creditor expects to collect all amounts due including interest accrued at the contractual interest rate during the period the loan is outstanding.

9. Usually, a loan whose terms are modified in a troubled debt restructuring already will have been identified as impaired because the condition specified in paragraph 8 will have existed before a formal restructuring. However, if a loan is excluded from the scope of this Statement under paragraph 6(a), a creditor may not have accounted for that loan in accordance with this Statement before the loan was restructured. The creditor shall apply the provisions of this Statement to that loan when it is restructured.

10. The term *probable* is used in this Statement consistent with its use in Statement 5, which defines probable as an area within a range of the likelihood that a future event or events will occur confirming the fact of the loss. That range is from probable to remote, as follows:

> *Probable.* The future event or events are likely to occur.
> *Reasonably possible.* The chance of the future event or events occurring is more than remote but less than likely.
> *Remote.* The chance of the future event or events occurring is slight.

The term probable is further described in paragraph 84 of Statement 5, which states:

> The conditions for accrual in paragraph 8 [of Statement 5] are not inconsistent with the accounting concept of conservatism. *Those conditions are not intended to be so rigid that they require virtual certainty before a loss is accrued.* [Emphasis added.] They require only that it be *probable* that an asset has been impaired or a liability has been incurred and that the amount of loss be *reasonably* estimable. [Emphasis in original.]

---

[1] Sources of information useful in identifying loans for evaluation that are listed in the AICPA's Auditing Procedure Study, *Auditing the Allowance for Credit Losses of Banks,* include a specific materiality criterion; regulatory reports of examination; internally generated listings such as "watch lists," past due reports, overdraft listings, and listings of loans to insiders; management reports of total loan amounts by borrower; historical loss experience by type of loan; loan files lacking current financial data related to borrowers and guarantors; borrowers experiencing problems such as operating losses, marginal working capital, inadequate cash flow, or business interruptions; loans secured by collateral that is not readily marketable or that is susceptible to deterioration in realizable value; loans to borrowers in industries or countries experiencing economic instability; and loan documentation and compliance exception reports.

Measurement of Impairment

11. Measuring impaired loans requires judgment and estimates, and the eventual outcomes may differ from those estimates. Creditors should have latitude to develop measurement methods that are practical in their circumstances. Paragraphs 12-16 address those measurement methods.

12. Some impaired loans have risk characteristics that are unique to an individual borrower, and the creditor will apply the measurement methods described in paragraphs 13-16 on a loan-by-loan basis. However, some impaired loans may have risk characteristics in common with other impaired loans. A creditor may aggregate those loans and may use historical statistics, such as average recovery period and average amount recovered, along with a composite effective interest rate as a means of measuring those impaired loans.

13. When a loan is impaired as defined in paragraph 8 of this Statement, a creditor shall measure impairment based on the present value of expected future cash flows discounted at the loan's effective interest rate, except that as a practical expedient, a creditor may measure impairment based on a loan's observable market price, or the fair value of the collateral if the loan is collateral dependent. Regardless of the measurement method, a creditor shall measure impairment based on the fair value of the collateral when the creditor determines that foreclosure is probable. A loan is collateral dependent if the repayment of the loan is expected to be provided solely by the underlying collateral. The creditor may choose a measurement method on a loan-by-loan basis. A creditor shall consider estimated costs to sell, on a discounted basis, in the measure of impairment if those costs are expected to reduce the cash flows available to repay or otherwise satisfy the loan. If the measure of the impaired loan is less than the recorded investment in the loan[2] (including accrued interest, net deferred loan fees or costs, and unamortized premium or discount), a creditor shall recognize an impairment by creating a valuation allowance with a corresponding charge to bad-debt expense or by adjusting an existing valuation allowance for the impaired loan with a corresponding charge or credit to bad-debt expense.

14. If a creditor measures an impaired loan using a present value amount, the creditor shall calculate that present value amount based on an estimate of the expected future cash flows of the impaired loan, discounted at the loan's effective interest rate. The effective interest rate of a loan is the rate of return implicit in the loan (that is, the contractual interest rate adjusted for any net deferred loan fees or costs, premium, or discount existing at the origination or acquisition of the loan).[3] The effective interest rate for a loan restructured in a troubled debt restructuring is based on the original contractual rate, not the rate specified in the restructuring agreement. If the loan's contractual interest rate varies based on subsequent changes in an independent factor, such as an index or rate (for example, the prime rate, the London interbank offered rate, or the U.S. Treasury bill weekly average), that loan's effective interest rate may be calculated based on the factor as it changes over the life of the loan or may be fixed at the rate in effect at the date the loan meets the impairment criterion in paragraph 8. The creditor's choice shall be applied consistently for all loans whose contractual interest rate varies based on subsequent changes in an independent factor. Projections of changes in the factor should not be made for purposes of determining the effective interest rate or estimating expected future cash flows.

15. If a creditor measures an impaired loan using a present value calculation, the estimates of expected future cash flows shall be the creditor's best estimate based on reasonable and supportable assumptions and projections. All available evidence, including estimated costs to sell if those costs are expected to reduce the cash flows available to repay or otherwise satisfy the loan, should be considered in developing the estimate of expected future cash flows. The weight given to the evidence should be commensurate with the extent to which the evidence can be verified objectively. If a creditor estimates a range for either the amount or timing of possible cash flows, the likelihood of the possible outcomes shall be considered in determining the best estimate of expected future cash flows.

16. Subsequent to the initial measurement of impairment, if there is a significant change (increase or decrease) in the amount or timing of an impaired loan's expected future cash flows, or if actual cash flows are significantly different from the cash flows previously projected, a creditor shall recalculate the impairment by applying the procedures specified in paragraphs 12-15 and by adjust-

---

[2]The term *recorded investment in the loan* is distinguished from *net carrying amount of the loan* because the latter term is net of a valuation allowance, while the former term is not. The recorded investment in the loan does, however, reflect any direct write-down of the investment.

[3]A loan may be acquired at a discount because of a change in credit quality or rate or both. When a loan is acquired at a discount that relates, at least in part, to the loan's credit quality, the effective interest rate is the discount rate that equates the present value of the investor's estimate of the loan's future cash flows with the purchase price of the loan.

ing the valuation allowance. Similarly, a creditor that measures impairment based on the observable market price of an impaired loan or the fair value of the collateral of an impaired collateral-dependent loan shall adjust the valuation allowance if there is a significant change (increase or decrease) in either of those bases. However, the net carrying amount of the loan shall at no time exceed the recorded investment in the loan.

Income Recognition

17. The present value of an impaired loan's expected future cash flows will change from one reporting period to the next because of the passage of time and also may change because of revised estimates in the amount or timing of those cash flows. A creditor shall recognize the change in present value in accordance with either (a) or (b) as follows:

a. The increase in present value of the expected future cash flows that is attributable to the passage of time shall be reported as interest income accrued on the net carrying amount of the loan at the effective interest rate used to discount the impaired loan's estimated future cash flows. The change in present value, if any, that is attributable to changes in the amount or timing of expected future cash flows shall be reported as bad-debt expense in the same manner in which impairment initially was recognized or as a reduction in the amount of bad-debt expense that otherwise would be reported.
b. The entire change in present value shall be reported as bad-debt expense in the same manner in which impairment initially was recognized or as a reduction in the amount of bad-debt expense that otherwise would be reported.

18. A creditor that recognizes income in accordance with paragraph 17(a) shall apply that method to all loans for which impairment is measured based on the present value of expected future cash flows discounted at the loan's effective interest rate and shall apply that method consistently from one reporting period to the next.

19. The observable market price of an impaired loan or the fair value of the collateral of an impaired collateral-dependent loan may change from one reporting period to the next. A creditor that measures impairment on either of those bases shall report a decrease in the measure of the impaired loan as bad-debt expense in the same manner in which impairment initially was recognized. An increase in the measure of the impaired loan shall be reported as a reduction in the amount of bad-debt expense that otherwise would be reported.

Disclosures

20. A creditor shall disclose, either in the body of the financial statements or in the accompanying notes, the following information:

a. As of the date of each statement of financial position presented, the recorded investment in the loans for which impairment has been recognized in accordance with this Statement and the total allowance for credit losses related to those impaired loans
b. For each period for which results of operations are presented, the activity in the allowance for credit losses account, including the balance in the allowance for credit losses account at the beginning and end of each period, additions charged to operations, direct write-downs charged against the allowance, and recoveries of amounts previously charged off
c. The creditor's income recognition policy (paragraph 17(a) or (b)). A creditor that recognizes income in accordance with paragraph 17(a) also shall disclose the amount of interest income recognized in accordance with that paragraph.

Amendments to Existing Pronouncements

21. The first sentence of paragraph 23 of Statement 5 is replaced by the following:

If, based on current information and events, it is probable that the enterprise will be unable to collect all amounts due according to the contractual terms of the receivable, the condition in paragraph 8(a) is met. As used here, *all amounts due according to the contractual terms* means that both the contractual interest payments and the contractual principal payments will be collected as scheduled according to the receivable's contractual terms. However, a creditor need not consider an insignificant delay or insignificant shortfall in amount of payments as meeting the condition in paragraph 8(a).

22. Statement 15 is amended prospectively as follows:

a. The second sentence in paragraph 1 is replaced by:

A creditor in a troubled debt restructuring involving a modification of terms shall account for the restructured loan in accordance with the provisions of FASB Statement No. 114, *Accounting by Creditors for Impairment of a Loan,* except that a troubled debt restructuring involving a modification of terms before the effective date of Statement 114 may continue to be accounted for and disclosed in accordance with this Statement as long as the restructured loan is not impaired based on the terms of the restructuring agreement.

b. Paragraph 30 is replaced by the following:

A creditor in a troubled debt restructuring involving only a modification of terms of a receivable—that is, not involving receipt of assets (including an equity interest in the debtor)—shall account for the troubled debt restructuring in accordance with the provisions of Statement 114.

c. In the second sentence of paragraph 33, *paragraphs 30-32* is deleted and replaced by *Statement 114.* The third and fourth sentences are deleted.

d. In paragraph 34, the following is added after *foreclosure by the creditor,*:

that is, the creditor receives physical possession of the debtor's assets regardless of whether formal foreclosure proceedings take place,

e. In the third sentence of paragraph 42, *according to the provisions of paragraphs 30-32* is replaced by *as prescribed in Statement 114.* In the fourth sentence, *Those paragraphs* is replaced by *That Statement.*

f. Paragraphs 31, 32, 35-37, 40(a), 41, and footnotes 18, 19, 21, 24, and 25 are superseded prospectively. (Refer to paragraph 27 of this Statement.)

23. In the last sentence of paragraph 47 of FASB Statement No. 60, *Accounting and Reporting by Insurance Enterprises,* the phrase *realized gains and losses* is replaced by *income as prescribed in FASB Statement No. 114, Accounting by Creditors for Impairment of a Loan.*

24. In the first sentence of paragraph 14 of FASB Statement No. 91, *Accounting for Nonrefundable Fees and Costs Associated with Originating or Acquiring Loans and Initial Direct Costs of Leases,* the phrase *for purposes of applying paragraph 30 of that Statement* is deleted.

25. FASB Technical Bulletins No. 79-6, *Valuation Allowances Following Debt Restructuring,* and No. 79-7, *Recoveries of a Previous Writedown under a Troubled Debt Restructuring Involving a Modification of Terms,* are superseded by this Statement.

Effective Date and Transition

26. This Statement shall be effective for financial statements for fiscal years beginning after December 15, 1994. Earlier application is encouraged. Previously issued annual financial statements shall not be restated. Initial application of this Statement shall be as of the beginning of an enterprise's fiscal year (that is, if the Statement is adopted prior to the effective date and during an interim period other than the first interim period, all prior interim periods of that fiscal year shall be restated).

27. This Statement applies to all troubled debt restructurings involving a modification of terms. However, if a loan that was restructured in a troubled debt restructuring involving a modification of terms before the effective date of this Statement is not impaired based on the terms specified by the restructuring agreement, a creditor may continue to account for the loan in accordance with the provisions of Statement 15 prior to its amendment by this Statement.

> **The provisions of this Statement need not be applied to immaterial items.**

This Statement was adopted by the affirmative votes of five members of the Financial Accounting Standards Board. Messrs. Leisenring and Swieringa dissented.

Messrs. Leisenring and Swieringa disagree with the measurement of impaired loans required by paragraphs 13 and 14 of this Statement. They believe that if a loan is impaired, a new direct measurement of the loan at fair value should be recognized. That fair value should be measured by the market value of the loan or similar asset if an ac-

tive market exists. If no market value is readily available, a creditor should use a forecast of expected future cash flows to estimate the fair value of the impaired loan, provided that those cash flows are discounted at a rate or rates commensurate with the risk involved.

Messrs. Leisenring and Swieringa disagree that this Statement has improved the information provided to users about impaired loans by eliminating inconsistencies in the accounting for those loans by different types of creditors for similar loans (paragraph 33). Paragraph 13 permits three different measures of impairment to be used by a given creditor for similar loans. The measures based on an observable market price of the loan or the fair value of the collateral of an impaired collateral-dependent loan are inconsistent with the Board's objective to measure only the loss due to credit deterioration (paragraph 51). Those two measurements reflect changes in market rates of interest or other factors that may cause a change in the fair value of an impaired loan. Messrs. Leisenring and Swieringa believe that a fair value objective or notion should underlie the measurement of all loan impairments. An impaired loan is a risky asset. Not only are expected future cash flows likely to differ from contractual amounts, there is risk that they will differ from actual future cash flows, in some cases dramatically. They believe that measuring that risky asset at its fair value provides the most relevant information about expected future cash flows and the riskiness of those cash flows.

Messrs. Leisenring and Swieringa also disagree with the requirement in paragraph 14 to discount expected future cash flows at the loan's effective interest rate if a creditor chooses to measure an impaired loan using a present value amount. As suggested above, they believe that expected future cash flows of an impaired loan should be discounted at market interest rates that reflect current economic events and conditions and that are commensurate with the risks involved; that is, current rates that would be charged under current conditions for a new loan with similar terms and expected future cash flows rather than at the loan's historical effective interest rate. The historical ef-

fective interest rate reflects the risk characteristics of the loan at the time it was originated or acquired, but not at the time it is impaired. In addition, they believe that use of an historical effective interest rate would overstate the charge to bad-debt expense if the effective rate is higher than current market rates. They believe that the charge to income for impairment losses should not exceed the charge to income that would be necessary for the net carrying amount to equal the loan's fair value.

Messrs. Leisenring and Swieringa disagree with the Board's conclusions about a troubled debt restructuring involving a modification of terms as defined in paragraph 5(c) of Statement 15. They believe that if a troubled loan is formally restructured, the terms of the original loan agreement and the loan's historical effective interest rate cease to be relevant and that the loan should be remeasured at fair value to reflect the risk characteristics of the loan and the market conditions at the time of the restructuring.

Finally, Mr. Leisenring disagrees with the conclusion in paragraph 27 that allows loans that were restructured before the effective date of this Statement and are not impaired based on the terms of the restructuring agreement to be accounted for in accordance with Statement 15. Mr. Leisenring believes that loans that were restructured prior to the effective date of this Statement should be remeasured at the market rate of interest in effect at the time the loan was restructured. If it is not practicable to determine the market rate in effect at that time, the current market rate of interest could be used.

Members of the Financial Accounting Standards Board:

Dennis R. Beresford,
Chairman
Joseph V. Anania

Victor H. Brown
James J. Leisenring
Robert H. Northcutt

A. Clarence Sampson
Robert J. Swieringa

Appendix

BACKGROUND INFORMATION AND BASIS FOR CONCLUSIONS

CONTENTS

Appendix

BACKGROUND INFORMATION AND BASIS FOR CONCLUSIONS

Introduction

28. This appendix summarizes considerations that were deemed significant by Board members in reaching the conclusions in this Statement. It includes reasons for accepting certain approaches and rejecting others. Individual Board members gave greater weight to some factors than to others.

29. An FASB Exposure Draft, *Accounting by Creditors for Impairment of a Loan,* was issued for public comment in June 1992. The Board received approximately 160 comment letters, and 17 organizations and individuals presented their views during a public hearing held on November 3 and 9, 1992. Also, four entities participated in a field test of the provisions of the Exposure Draft. Members of the Board visited six other entities to discuss the provisions of the Exposure Draft with chief executive officers, chief financial officers, and credit officers. The field test results and the results of the meetings, which are confidential at the entities' request, were useful to the Board during its deliberations of the issues addressed by this Statement.

Background Information

30. The Board accelerated part of the financial instruments project to address in what circum-stances, if any, a creditor should measure the impairment of a loan based on the present value of expected future cash flows related to the loan. This acceleration was undertaken in part at the urging of AcSEC. AcSEC had previously considered this issue as part of a proposed Statement of Position that also considered how to determine whether collateral for a loan has been in-substance foreclosed and how to account for foreclosed assets. (AcSEC's consideration resulted in Practice Bulletin No. 7, *Criteria for Determining Whether Collateral for a Loan Has Been In-Substance Foreclosed,* and AICPA Statement of Position 92-3, *Accounting for Foreclosed Assets.*) However, AcSEC informed the Board that it could not develop a solution to the loan impairment issue that would achieve consensus and requested the Board to resolve the issue.

31. AcSEC originally undertook its deliberations in an effort to reconcile the inconsistent guidance existing in certain AICPA Audit and Accounting Guides. The Guides address, among other things, the application of Statement 5 to a financial institution's loan portfolio. The most significant inconsistency in the guidance relates to the inclusion of interest in the valuation of troubled loans. The AICPA Audit and Accounting Guide, *Audits of Savings Institutions,* and AICPA Statement of Position 75-2, *Accounting Practices of Real Estate Investment Trusts,* call for interest to be included in the measurement of troubled loans—a discounted cash flow concept—but other AICPA Guides are silent on that point. This inconsistent guidance led to different accounting among the different types

of financial institutions. The Securities and Exchange Commission, the Federal Home Loan Bank Board, and the FDIC also urged reconciliation of this diverse guidance.

Benefits and Costs

32. The FASB's mission statement charges the Board to determine that a proposed standard will fill a significant need and that the costs it imposes, compared with possible alternatives, will be justified in relation to the overall benefits. Fulfilling that charge can be problematic since there is no common gauge by which to judge objectively the costs to implement a standard against the need to report consistent, comparable, and reliable information in financial statements. The challenge is amplified because the costs to implement a new standard are not borne directly by some of those who derive the benefits of improved reporting. In establishing standards that are cost-effective, the Board must balance the diverse and often conflicting needs of a wide cross section of constituents.

33. The Board determined that the information provided to users about impaired loans could be improved by eliminating inconsistencies in the accounting among different types of creditors for similar loans. As discussed in FASB Concepts Statement No. 2, *Qualitative Characteristics of Accounting Information,* providing comparable financial information enables users to identify similarities in and differences between two sets of economic events. Therefore, to the extent that similar loans are subject to the same requirements for measuring impaired loans, financial reporting would be improved.

34. The benefits of eliminating inconsistencies in the accounting among different types of creditors come with a cost to some creditors—principally, the incremental cost of developing, implementing, and maintaining a measurement and reporting system to generate the required present values, observable market prices, or fair value of the collateral of collateral-dependent loans. However, the Board believes the cost of implementing this standard will be minimized because the Statement does not specify how a creditor should identify loans that are to be evaluated for collectibility or how a creditor should determine that it is probable that it will be unable to collect all amounts due according to the loan's contractual terms. Rather, the Statement provides that a creditor should apply its normal loan review procedures in making those judgments. In addition, the Board believes that prescribing a loan's effective interest rate as the appropriate discount rate will minimize implementation costs because that rate is readily available.

35. Application of judgment to determine expected future cash flows may be complex, but that complexity is the unavoidable result of the need for information about the effect of impaired loans on a creditor's financial position and results of operations. Practical decisions, such as permitting a creditor to recognize an observable market price of the loan or the fair value of the collateral of a collateral-dependent loan as alternatives to discounting and eliminating the proposed requirement in the Exposure Draft to recognize separately the two components of the change in present value, were made to reduce the cost and complexity of applying this Statement. Additionally, permitting a creditor to aggregate loans and use historical experience in calculating the present value of expected future cash flows also may reduce the cost and complexity of applying this Statement. The Board believes that the benefits of this Statement will exceed the costs of implementation.

Definitions and Scope

36. The Board believes that accounting for impaired loans should be consistent among all creditors and for all types of lending except for loans that are measured at fair value or at the lower of cost or fair value in accordance with specialized industry practice. (For example, Statement 65 specifies that mortgage loans held for sale should be accounted for at the lower of cost or market value, and venture capital investment companies generally account for loans at fair value.) Fair value accounting or the lower of cost or fair value accounting obviates the need for accounting guidance for impairment associated with those loans.

37. The Board was unable to identify any compelling reasons to support a conclusion that the lending process for consumer, mortgage, commercial, and other loans, whether uncollateralized or collateralized, is fundamentally different. Neither was the Board able to identify any compelling reasons to suggest that different types of creditors should account for impaired loans differently or that financial statement users for a particular industry or size of entity would be better served by accounting that differs from that of other creditors.

38. The Board concluded that this Statement should not apply to large groups of smaller-balance homogeneous loans that are collectively evaluated for impairment. In situations in which all or a portion of a loan portfolio consists of a large number of small-dollar-value homogeneous loans (such as consumer installment loans, residential mortgages, or credit card loans), creditors typically use a formula based on various factors to estimate an allowance for loan losses. Those factors include past loss

experience, recent economic events and current conditions, and portfolio delinquency rates. The Board recognizes the established practice of using a formula approach for estimating losses related to these types of loans and does not intend for this Statement to change that approach. The Board presumes that while a formula approach does not explicitly discount expected future cash flows, it results in a measure of impairment that implicitly discounts expected future cash flows.

39. The Exposure Draft would have applied to all loans that are individually and specifically evaluated for impairment but not to loans that are accounted for at fair value or at the lower of cost or fair value. It also did not address large groups of smaller-balance homogeneous loans that are collectively evaluated for impairment. Some respondents said that it was unclear whether the Exposure Draft applied to medium-balance loans. By deleting the reference to loans that are individually and specifically evaluated for impairment, the Board clarified that the only loans it did not intend to address were large groups of smaller-balance loans that are collectively evaluated for impairment. This Statement does not apply to leases or debt securities.

Recognition of Impairment

Discounted or Undiscounted Measurement of Impairment

40. An assumption inherent in a creditor's statement of financial position prepared in accordance with generally accepted accounting principles is that the reported amounts of assets will be recovered. However, as discussed in paragraph 31, different types of creditors have applied the guidance in Statement 5 about collectibility of receivables differently in measuring the amount of loan impairment. Some creditors have recognized impairment of a loan only when *undiscounted* expected future cash inflows are less than the loan's net carrying amount. Others have recognized impairment when *discounted* expected future cash inflows are less than the loan's net carrying amount.

41. The threshold issue is whether impaired loans should be carried at discounted or undiscounted amounts. The Board observed that a creditor's recorded investment in a loan both at origination and subsequently during the life of the loan, as long as the loan performs according to its contractual terms, is the sum of the present values of the future cash flows that are designated as interest and the future cash flows that are designated as principal, including any amount due at maturity, discounted at the effective interest rate implicit in the loan. The effective interest rate implicit in the loan may be the same as or may differ from the in-

terest rate stated in the agreement. If the effective interest rate differs from the stated interest rate, the recorded investment in the loan is the face amount plus net deferred loan costs and unamortized premium or less net deferred loan fees and unamortized discount.

42. The Board concluded that a loan that becomes impaired should continue to be carried at an amount that considers the present value of all expected future cash flows, in a manner consistent with the loan's measurement before it became impaired. The Board concluded that because loans are recorded originally at discounted amounts, the ongoing assessment for impairment should be made in a similar manner.

43. The Board recognizes that expected future cash flows from impaired loans are usually uncertain and creditors will be required to exercise significant judgment in developing the estimates of expected future cash flows. The Board believes that existing methods of measuring impaired loans and determining the adequacy of the allowance for credit losses already consider the uncertainty of expected future cash flows. The Board concluded that this uncertainty of expected future cash flows is not a valid reason to ignore discounting and that failure to measure impaired loans on a discounted basis would not only be inconsistent with the manner in which unimpaired loans are measured but also would inappropriately ignore the time value of money. If impaired loans were measured on an undiscounted basis, two loans could be carried at the same amount although one is performing fully and the other is a loan for which no cash flows are expected to be received for several years. In the Board's view, this is an unreasonable result both in terms of the appropriate measure of the two loans in the statement of financial position and in terms of the appropriate measurement of the event of impairment.

44. Some respondents interpreted the Exposure Draft to require an estimate of a specific amount of expected future cash flows for each impaired loan for each reporting period. The Board clarified this Statement to indicate that estimates of expected future cash flows may represent a creditor's best estimate within a range of possibilities.

45. Some respondents suggested that impaired loans could be aggregated as a means of measuring the present value of the expected future cash flows. In the Board's view, some impaired loans have risk characteristics that are unique to the borrower, and it is appropriate to measure those impaired loans on a loan-by-loan basis. However, some impaired loans may have risk characteristics in common with other impaired loans. The Board concluded that it is appropriate to use aggregation techniques

in measuring those impaired loans at the present value of the expected future cash flows. Past experience with loans with similar risk characteristics may provide an indication of the average time it takes to work out an impaired loan and the average amount the creditor will recover. The Board concluded that making estimates of the expected future cash flows and calculating the present value of the expected future cash flows based on the creditor's experience with loans with similar risk characteristics is consistent with the requirement for a creditor to make its best estimate of expected future cash flows. The Board acknowledges that actual cash flows will seldom, if ever, be exactly the same in timing and amount as the projections of expected future cash flows.

46. This Statement requires that a creditor consider estimated costs to sell, on a discounted basis, in the creditor's measure of impairment if those costs are expected to reduce the cash flows available to repay or otherwise satisfy the loan. For example, if repayment of a loan is dependent on the sale of the collateral, a creditor that uses a discounted cash flow method to measure impairment should reduce its estimate of expected future cash flows by its estimates of costs to sell. Likewise, if a creditor uses the fair value of the collateral to measure impairment of a collateral-dependent loan and repayment or satisfaction of a loan is dependent on the sale of the collateral, the fair value of the collateral should be adjusted to consider estimated costs to sell. However, if repayment or satisfaction of the loan is dependent only on the operation, rather than the sale, of the collateral, the measure of impairment would not incorporate estimated costs to sell the collateral.

47. The Board's conclusion that impaired loans should be carried at discounted amounts is not intended to signal a similar conclusion in the Board's project on accounting for impairment of long-lived assets. Loans and long-lived assets are similar in that both are intended to be cash-generating assets and both are subject to impairment. However, basic differences between loans and long-lived assets may or may not lead the Board to different conclusions about discounting in the project on impairment of long-lived assets.

48. The Board observed that other standard-setting organizations also have concluded that it is appropriate to measure impaired loans based on discounted expected future cash flows. In November 1992, the Canadian Institute of Chartered Accountants issued an Exposure Draft, *Impaired Loans,* which proposes that an impaired loan or group of loans be measured as the estimated future cash flows discounted at the effective interest rate

inherent in the loan agreement. At its March 1993 meeting, the International Accounting Standards Committee (IASC) considered comments received on E40, *Financial Instruments.* The IASC concluded that its final standard on financial instruments should indicate that the carrying amount of an impaired financial asset (including impaired and restructured loans) should be the present value of the estimated future cash flows discounted at the effective interest rate.

49. The Board also considered whether the loss threshold for recognition of loan impairment should be changed from the Statement 5 definition of probable to some other threshold. The United States General Accounting Office asserted in its April 1991 report, *Failed Banks: Accounting and Auditing Reforms Urgently Needed,* that "'probable' . . . has, in the case of banks, come to mean 'virtually certain,' rather than 'more likely than not,'" and "the 'probable' requirement as it is sometimes applied has unduly delayed loss recognition . . . of problem assets." The Board did not intend "probable" to mean "virtually certain to occur." The Statement 5 definition of probable states that "the future event or events are *likely to occur*" (emphasis added). The Board recognizes that application of the term probable in practice requires judgment, and to clarify its intent the Board has reiterated the guidance in paragraph 84 of Statement 5 in paragraph 10 of this Statement. The term probable is used in this Statement consistent with its use in Statement 5. This Statement does not specify how a creditor should determine that it is probable that it will be unable to collect all amounts due according to a loan's contractual terms.

Appropriate Discount Rate

50. This Statement specifies that when a loan is impaired, a creditor should measure impairment based on the present value of expected future cash flows discounted at the loan's effective interest rate. As a practical expedient, a creditor may measure impairment based on the loan's observable market price or the fair value of the collateral if the loan is collateral dependent. The Board understands that estimates of expected future cash flows from impaired loans require judgment and that the eventual outcomes may differ from those estimates. The Board does not believe that the judgment inherent in the estimates is a valid reason to ignore discounting. However, the Board does believe that the judgment inherent in the estimates is sufficient to permit the use of observable market price or fair value of the collateral of a collateral-dependent loan as practical alternatives to the present value of expected future cash flows discounted at the loan's effective rate.

51. The Board concluded that a loan impairment measurement should reflect only a deterioration of credit quality, which is evidenced by a decrease in the estimate of expected future cash flows to be received from the loan. The Board believes that the measure of an impaired loan should recognize the change in the net carrying amount of the loan based on new information about expected future cash flows rather than record a new direct measurement. The Board, therefore, concluded that the loan impairment measurement should not reflect changes in market rates of interest that may cause a change in the fair value of an impaired loan.

52. Because the Board believes that only the loss due to credit deterioration should be measured, the Board concluded that the expected future cash flows should be discounted at the loan's effective interest rate. The effective interest rate of a loan is the rate of return implicit in the loan (that is, the contractual interest rate adjusted for any net deferred loan fees or costs, premium, or discount). The Board observed that the recorded amount of an unimpaired loan, as long as the loan performs according to its contractual terms, is the present value of the contractual future cash inflows—both those designated as principal and as interest—discounted at the loan's historical or effective interest rate. Thus, the measurement basis for an impaired loan will be the same as the measurement basis for the same loan before it became impaired. As a practical expedient, the Board concluded that for a loan whose stated rate varies based on subsequent changes in an independent factor, creditors should be permitted to fix the rate at the rate in effect at the date the loan meets the impairment criterion.

53. Some respondents suggested that creditors be permitted to recognize an observable market price of the loan or the fair value of the collateral of an impaired collateral-dependent loan as alternatives to discounting. Some respondents suggested that creditors be required to recognize the fair value of the collateral if a loan is collateral dependent. For regulatory reporting purposes, banks and other depository institutions are required to recognize the fair value of the collateral of an impaired collateral-dependent loan. As a practical expedient, the Board decided to permit a creditor to recognize an observable market price for the loan or the fair value of the collateral of a collateral-dependent loan as alternatives to estimating and discounting the expected future cash flows for the loan. The Board expects that the measurement method for an individual impaired loan would be applied consistently to that loan and that a change in method would be justified by a change in circumstance.

54. The Board concluded that impairment of a loan is not an event that should result in a new di-

rect measurement of the loan at fair value at the date impairment is recognized. Under that approach, an impaired loan's expected future cash flows would be discounted at a market interest rate commensurate with the risks involved to arrive at a measure of the loan's fair value. Noting that unimpaired loans are not carried at fair value after origination, the Board concluded that loan impairment should be recognized based solely on deterioration of credit quality evidenced by a decrease in expected future cash flows rather than on changes in both expected future cash flows and other current economic events, such as changes in interest rates. In addition, the Board observed that if a market rate were specified, questions could be raised about whether a new measurement would be[^] required if the creditor's estimate of expected future cash flows remained constant but current market interest rates changed.

55. Some respondents observed that fair value is widely used in a variety of situations and could be implemented with minimal cost to financial statement preparers because it is consistent with the values disclosed in accordance with FASB Statement No. 107, *Disclosures about Fair Value of Financial Instruments.* The Board noted that many creditors make the disclosures required under Statement 107 on a portfolio basis; they do not make separate disclosures for impaired loans. Furthermore, the Board understands that there are practical difficulties in determining a market rate for an impaired loan.

56. The Board also considered whether an impaired loan's expected future cash flows should be discounted at the creditor's cost-of-funds interest rate. A cost-of-funds interest rate would reflect the time value of money to a specific creditor and would reflect the creditor's cost to carry an impaired loan (a cost-recovery notion). Under that approach, interest would be one of a creditor's costs to carry an impaired loan. This method is consistent with current requirements of the AICPA Guide on savings institutions and SOP 75-2, which require discounting at a rate that would correspond to an expected average rate to be paid during the estimated holding period. The Board believes that impairment should be measured by looking only at the loan and that a loan's net carrying amount should not be affected by the credit standing of the creditor and the interest rate it pays on its debt or by whether the creditor has outstanding debt.

57. The Board also considered whether an impaired loan's expected future cash flows should be discounted at a risk-free interest rate. A risk-free interest rate would reflect at least the minimum interest that could have been earned if the funds were not invested in the impaired loan. The Board concluded that the risk-free rate has no relationship to

the impaired loan being measured and, therefore, would be an irrelevant discount rate to use in measuring an impaired loan.

Income Recognition

58. When an asset is carried on a discounted basis, the present value of expected future cash flows will increase from one reporting period to the next as a result of the passage of time (assuming that the timing and amount of expected future cash flows remain constant). The change in present value from one reporting period to the next may result not only from the passage of time but also from changes in estimates of the timing or amount of expected future cash flows. Similarly, the observable market price of an impaired loan or the fair value of the collateral of an impaired collateral-dependent loan may change from one reporting period to the next. Because the Board believes that the net carrying amount of an impaired loan should be the present value of expected future cash flows (or the observable market price or the fair value of the collateral) not only at the date at which impairment initially is recognized but also at each subsequent reporting period, the Board concluded that changes in that measure should be recognized.

59. The Exposure Draft would have required the change in present value attributable to the passage of time to be reported as interest income and the change in present value, if any, attributable to changes in the amount or timing of expected future cash flows to be reported as bad-debt expense or as a reduction in the amount of bad-debt expense that otherwise would be reported. Some respondents stated that the change in present value attributable to the passage of time should be reported as a reduction of bad-debt expense because that approach could be implemented with less cost to financial statement preparers. The Board concluded that a creditor that measures impairment based on the present value of expected future cash flows should be permitted to report the entire change in present value as bad-debt expense but that a creditor that wishes to report the change in present value attributable to the passage of time as interest income should not be proscribed from doing so. Because some financial analysts indicated that knowing that information is important, the Board concluded that creditors that choose the latter alternative should disclose the amount of interest income that represents the change in present value attributable to the passage of time. For practical reasons, the Board concluded that changes in observable market prices or the fair value of the collateral should be reported as bad-debt expense or a reduction in bad-debt expense.

60. The Board considered and rejected an approach under which the change in present value would be reported as a separate amount such as "accrual of interest on impaired loans" because that presentation does not identify the reason for the change in present value. The Board reasoned that changes in a present-value-based measurement of loan impairment must be either interest or part of bad-debt expense.

61. The Board also considered whether loan impairment should be recorded through a valuation allowance or through a direct write-down that would establish a new cost basis for the impaired loan. The Board concluded that because of the subjectivity inherent in the valuation of an impaired loan and because estimates of the timing and amount of an impaired loan's cash flows, an observable market price, or the fair value of the collateral may change, impairment should be recorded through a valuation allowance that subsequently may change to reflect changes in the measure of the impaired loan. However, the net carrying amount of the loan shall at no time exceed the recorded investment in the loan.

Troubled Debt Restructurings

62. The Exposure Draft would have required a formal loan restructuring (a troubled debt restructuring involving a modification of terms as defined in paragraph 5(c) of Statement 15) to be remeasured at a current fair value to recognize that the terms of the original loan agreement cease to be relevant. Some respondents indicated that a troubled debt restructuring does not result in a new loan but rather represents part of a creditor's ongoing effort to recover its investment in the original loan. Therefore, the interest rate used to discount expected future cash flows on a restructured loan should be the same interest rate used to discount expected future cash flows on an impaired loan. Some respondents stated that requiring a different interest rate to discount the expected future cash flows on impaired loans and restructured loans would give creditors the incentive to accelerate or delay the timing of a troubled debt restructuring to achieve an accounting result. Some respondents stated that the Board would have to provide guidance on when a restructuring had occurred in substance. Based on those considerations, the Board concluded that it is appropriate to use the effective interest rate in the original loan agreement to discount the expected future cash flows on an impaired loan and a restructured loan.

63. The Board recognizes that this Statement introduces asymmetry between creditors' and

debtors' accounting for troubled debt restructurings involving a modification of terms. However, the Board concluded that this Statement should address only creditors' accounting and that debtors' accounting should not be considered because expanding the scope of this Statement to address debtors' accounting likely would delay issuance of the final Statement.

Disclosures

64. The Board believes that the financial statement disclosures required by this Statement provide information that is useful in understanding a creditor's accounting for impaired loans. The Board concluded that the recorded investment in the impaired loans, the total allowance for credit losses related to those impaired loans, an analysis of the activity in a creditor's allowance for credit losses account, and the creditor's income recognition policy are information relevant to financial statement users. The Board also concluded that the disclosures previously required by paragraphs 40(a) and 41 of Statement 15 are no longer necessary because all loans that are restructured in troubled debt restructurings will meet the definition of impairment and, therefore, will be subject to the disclosure requirements of paragraph 20 of this Statement except as discussed in the following paragraph.

65. Some respondents asked whether the requirement in paragraph 20(a) to disclose the recorded investment in the loans for which impairment has been recognized in accordance with this Statement applies to a restructured loan if the creditor has written down the loan and the present value of the expected future cash flows, or the observable market price, or the fair value of the collateral is equal to or greater than the recorded investment in the loan. As noted in paragraph 9, usually a loan whose terms are modified in a troubled debt restructuring already will be impaired because the condition specified in paragraph 8 will have existed before a formal restructuring. However, if the creditor has written down a loan and the measure of the restructured loan under paragraph 13 is equal to or greater than the recorded investment in the loan, there would be no impairment to be recognized in accordance with this Statement. The creditor is not required to disclose the recorded investment in that loan in years after the write-down but is required under paragraph 20(b) to disclose the amount of the write-down and is required under paragraph 20(a) to disclose the recorded investment in the year of the write-down. Some respondents asked a similar question for loans that have not been restructured, but for which the creditor has taken a direct write-down. In that situation, if the measure of the loan under paragraph 13 is equal to or greater than the recorded investment in the loan, there is no impairment to be recognized in accordance with this Statement, and the creditor is not required to disclose the recorded investment in the loan in years after the write-down.

66. The Exposure Draft would have required a creditor to disclose reversals of the allowance for interest (that is, the change in present value attributable to the passage of time) and reversals of the allowance attributable to increases in estimates of expected future cash flows. The Board agreed with respondents who indicated that the information might be excessive for a creditor that recognizes income in accordance with paragraph 17(b) and should not be required. The Board agreed with respondents who said that a creditor that recognizes interest income in accordance with paragraph 17(a) should disclose the amount of interest income that is accrued on the net carrying amount of an impaired loan.

67. Additionally, paragraph 21 of the Exposure Draft reiterated a disclosure requirement that already exists under paragraph 32 of FASB Statement No. 95, *Statement of Cash Flows;* that paragraph, but not the requirement in Statement 95, was deleted and is not repeated in this Statement.

Amendments to Existing Pronouncements

68. The impairment recognition criterion in paragraph 8 of this Statement is similar to that of paragraph 23 of Statement 5, which describes the application of the Statement 5 conditions for accrual of loss contingencies to the collectibility of all receivables. That paragraph states that ". . . based on available information, it is probable that the enterprise will be unable to collect all amounts due." The Board recognizes that in practice, "all amounts due" has not always been interpreted to include both the future contractual interest and the contractual principal of a loan. Thus, this Statement amends paragraph 23 of Statement 5 to clarify that "all amounts due" refers to both principal and interest. The Board believes this is the appropriate interpretation because, as illustrated in Appendix A of APB Opinion No. 21, *Interest on Receivables and Payables,* the recorded amount of a loan is the present value of the contractual principal and interest cash flows discounted at the loan's effective interest rate. While this Statement requires a creditor to consider collectibility of both principal and interest for all receivables, it specifies the method to be used to measure impairment only for impaired loans that are within the scope of this Statement.

69. After considering comments received, the Board decided that when a creditor determines that foreclosure is probable, a creditor should remeasure

the loan at the fair value of the collateral so that loss recognition is not delayed until actual foreclosure. The Board believes that the requirement in this Statement to discount expected future cash flows will reduce the amount of loss that would be recognized when foreclosure is probable compared with the loss that would be recognized for the same loan under the current undiscounted measure of loan losses. However, the requirement to discount may not preclude the need to recognize additional loss when foreclosure is probable because estimates of expected future cash flows are not remeasured using a market rate and because estimates of expected future cash flows may change when a creditor determines that foreclosure is probable.

70. This Statement amends paragraph 34 of Statement 15 to clarify the applicability of that paragraph. Paragraph 34 was intended to apply to a narrow set of circumstances; that is, a troubled debt restructuring or other circumstance in which a debtor surrendered property to the creditor and the creditor was in possession of the asset with or without having to go through formal foreclosure procedures. Paragraph 84 of the basis for conclusions in Statement 15 states, "The Board agreed that a restructuring may be in substance a foreclosure, repossession, or other transfer of assets even though formal foreclosure or repossession proceedings are not involved." The amendment to paragraph 34 of Statement 15 clarifies that intent.

71. The Board recognizes that in practice paragraph 34 of Statement 15 and the term *in-substance foreclosure* are applied in situations other than troubled debt restructurings or situations in which a debtor surrenders property to the creditor. Under the SEC's Financial Reporting Release No. 28, *Accounting for Loan Losses by Registrants Engaged in Lending Activities,* and Practice Bulletin 7, a creditor is required to account for the operations of the collateral underlying some loans, even though the creditor has not taken possession of collateral, as if foreclosure had occurred. The Board recognizes the practical problems of accounting for the operations of an asset the creditor does not possess and concluded, therefore, that a loan for which foreclosure is probable should continue to be accounted for as a loan.

Effective Date and Transition

72. The Board decided to prohibit retroactive application of the Statement. Because the measurement of impaired loans is based on estimates that are likely to change, the Board questioned the relevance of restatement. The Board recognizes the benefits of comparative financial statements, but it questions the ability of a creditor to "re-create"

historical estimates of the timing and amounts of cash flows, the observable market price, or the fair value of the collateral that would be necessary for restatement. For those reasons, the Board concluded that retroactive application of the Statement should be prohibited. The Board also discussed accounting for loans that were restructured in troubled debt restructurings before the effective date of this Statement. The Exposure Draft would have applied to all loans restructured before the effective date. Some respondents indicated that the final Statement should not apply to restructurings before the effective date because those transactions were entered into based on the accounting rules at the time. Some respondents said that previously restructured loans should be accounted for under the final Statement only if they are currently or subsequently impaired based on the restructured terms or subsequently are restructured again. The Board concluded that troubled debt restructurings before the effective date of this Statement are required to be accounted for in accordance with this Statement only if the restructured loans are impaired; that is, if they are not performing in accordance with the contractual terms of the restructuring agreement.

73. Some respondents requested a one-year delay in the effective date to give them time to develop techniques for estimating expected future cash flows and to develop systems to calculate present value. Bank regulators also requested a one-year delay so that their examiners could be adequately trained. The Board believes that changes made to the provisions of the Exposure Draft—in particular, permitting creditors to recognize the observable market price of the loan or the fair value of the collateral of a collateral-dependent loan and permitting use of aggregation techniques—will minimize the implementation burden. However, the Board decided to delay the effective date proposed in the Exposure Draft.

74. The Exposure Draft would have required a creditor to report the effect of initially applying this Statement as the effect of a change in accounting principle in a manner similar to the cumulative effect of a change in accounting principle as described in paragraph 20 of APB Opinion No. 20, *Accounting Changes.* The Board decided that the cost of isolating a "cumulative effect" would exceed the related benefit of that information and that a creditor should report the effect of initially applying this Statement as bad-debt expense or as an adjustment to bad-debt expense in accordance with paragraph 13. This Statement does not preclude a creditor from disclosing in the notes to the financial statements the effect of initially applying this Statement if the creditor believes it is practical to do so.

Statement of Financial Accounting Standards No. 115
Accounting for Certain Investments in Debt and Equity Securities

STATUS

Issued: May 1993

Effective Date: For fiscal years beginning after December 15, 1993

Affects: Amends ARB 43, Chapter 3A, paragraph 4
Amends APB 18, paragraph 19(l)
Supersedes FAS 12
Supersedes FAS 60, paragraphs 45 and 46 and footnote 7
Amends FAS 60, paragraphs 50 and 51
Amends FAS 65, paragraphs 4 through 8, 9(a), 9(c), 12, 17, 28, and 29
Amends FAS 80, paragraph 5
Amends FAS 91, paragraphs 3 and 27(a)
Amends FAS 97, paragraph 28
Amends FAS 102, paragraph 8 and footnote 4
Amends FAS 109, paragraph 36(b)
Supersedes FIN 11
Supersedes FIN 12
Supersedes FIN 13
Supersedes FIN 16
Amends FIN 40, paragraphs 4 and 5
Amends FTB 79-19, paragraph 1
Supersedes FTB 79-19, paragraph 6
Amends FTB 85-1, paragraph 3

Affected by: Paragraph 4 amended by FAS 124 and FAS 133
Paragraph 7 amended by FAS 125, FAS 135, and FAS 140
Paragraph 8(c) amended by FAS 144
Paragraph 12(a) amended by FAS 134
Paragraph 13 amended by FAS 130 and FAS 133
Paragraph 15(b) amended by FAS 133
Paragraphs 15(c) and 15(d) amended by FAS 130
Paragraph 16 amended by FAS 130 and FAS 133
Paragraph 17 superseded by FAS 135
Paragraphs 19 through 22 amended by FAS 133
Paragraphs 115 and 137 amended by FAS 133
Footnote 4 amended by FAS 135 and FAS 145

Other Interpretive Pronouncement: FTB 94-1

Other Interpretive Release: FASB Special Report, *A Guide to Implementation of Statement 115 on Accounting for Certain Investments in Debt and Equity Securities: Questions and Answers*

Issues Discussed by FASB Emerging Issues Task Force (EITF)

Affects: EITF Issues No. 85-25, 86-40, 89-18, and 91-5

Interpreted by: Paragraph 3 interpreted by EITF Topic No. D-39
Paragraph 7 interpreted by EITF Issue No. 96-10 and Topic No. D-39
Paragraph 9 interpreted by EITF Topic No. D-51
Paragraph 12 interpreted by EITF Issue No. 98-13
Paragraph 13 interpreted by EITF Topic No. D-41
Paragraph 16 interpreted by EITF Topic No. D-44
Paragraph 115 interpreted by EITF Issues No. 96-15 and 97-7

Related Issues: EITF Issues No. 84-20, 85-23, 85-39, 94-8, 96-11, 96-12, 97-14, 98-2, 98-5, 98-15, 99-4, 99-20, 00-8, 00-18, 00-27, 01-1, and 02-2 and Topics No. D-11, D-40, D-73, and D-74

SUMMARY

This Statement addresses the accounting and reporting for investments in equity securities that have readily determinable fair values and for all investments in debt securities. Those investments are to be classified in three categories and accounted for as follows:

- Debt securities that the enterprise has the positive intent and ability to hold to maturity are classified as *held-to-maturity securities* and reported at amortized cost.
- Debt and equity securities that are bought and held principally for the purpose of selling them in the near term are classified as *trading securities* and reported at fair value, with unrealized gains and losses included in earnings.
- Debt and equity securities not classified as either held-to-maturity securities or trading securities are classified as *available-for-sale securities* and reported at fair value, with unrealized gains and losses excluded from earnings and reported in a separate component of shareholders' equity.

This Statement does not apply to unsecuritized loans. However, after mortgage loans are converted to mortgage-backed securities, they are subject to its provisions. This Statement supersedes FASB Statement No. 12, *Accounting for Certain Marketable Securities,* and related Interpretations and amends FASB Statement No. 65, *Accounting for Certain Mortgage Banking Activities,* to eliminate mortgage-backed securities from its scope.

This Statement is effective for fiscal years beginning after December 15, 1993. It is to be initially applied as of the beginning of an enterprise's fiscal year and cannot be applied retroactively to prior years' financial statements. However, an enterprise may elect to initially apply this Statement as of the end of an earlier fiscal year for which annual financial statements have not previously been issued.

(This page intentionally left blank.)

Statement of Financial Accounting Standards No. 115

Accounting for Certain Investments in Debt and Equity Securities

CONTENTS

INTRODUCTION

1. This Statement addresses the accounting and reporting for certain investments in **debt securities**[1] and **equity securities**. It expands the use of **fair value** accounting for those securities but retains the use of the amortized cost method for investments in debt securities that the reporting enterprise has the positive intent and ability to hold to maturity.

2. This Statement was undertaken mainly in response to concerns expressed by regulators and others about the recognition and measurement of investments in debt securities, particularly those held by financial institutions. They questioned the appropriateness of using the amortized cost method for certain investments in debt securities in light of certain trading and sales practices. Their concerns also were prompted by the existence of inconsistent guidance on the reporting of debt securities held as assets in various AICPA Audit and Accounting Guides. The AICPA's Accounting Standards Executive Committee (AcSEC) and the major CPA firms, among others, urged the Board

to reexamine the accounting for certain investments in **securities.**

STANDARDS OF FINANCIAL ACCOUNTING AND REPORTING

Scope

3. Except as indicated in paragraph 4, this Statement establishes standards of financial accounting and reporting for investments in equity securities that have readily determinable fair values and for all investments in debt securities.

a. The fair value of an equity security is readily determinable if sales prices or bid-and-asked quotations are currently available on a securities exchange registered with the Securities and Exchange Commission (SEC) or in the over-the-counter market, provided that those prices or quotations for the over-the-counter market are publicly reported by the National Association of Securities Dealers Automated Quotations

---

[1]Words that appear in the glossary in Appendix C are set in **boldface type** the first time they appear.

systems or by the National Quotation Bureau. Restricted stock[2] does not meet that definition.

b. The fair value of an equity security traded only in a foreign market is readily determinable if that foreign market is of a breadth and scope comparable to one of the U.S. markets referred to above.

c. The fair value of an investment in a mutual fund is readily determinable if the fair value per share (unit) is determined and published and is the basis for current transactions.

4. This Statement does not apply to investments in equity securities accounted for under the equity method nor to investments in consolidated subsidiaries. This Statement does not apply to enterprises whose specialized accounting practices include accounting for substantially all investments in debt and equity securities at market value or fair value, with changes in value recognized in earnings (income) or in the change in net assets. Examples of those enterprises are brokers and dealers in securities, defined benefit pension plans, and investment companies. This Statement also does not apply to not-for-profit organizations; however, it does apply to cooperatives and mutual enterprises, including credit unions and mutual insurance companies.

5. This Statement supersedes FASB Statement No. 12, *Accounting for Certain Marketable Securities,* and supersedes or amends other accounting pronouncements listed in Appendix B.

Accounting for Certain Investments in Debt and Equity Securities

6. At acquisition, an enterprise shall classify debt and equity securities into one of three categories: held-to-maturity, available-for-sale, or trading. At each reporting date, the appropriateness of the classification shall be reassessed.

Held-to-Maturity Securities

7. Investments in debt securities shall be classified as *held-to-maturity* and measured at amortized cost in the statement of financial position only if the reporting enterprise has the positive intent and ability to hold those securities to maturity.

8. The following changes in circumstances, however, may cause the enterprise to change its intent to hold a certain security to maturity without calling into question its intent to hold other debt securities to maturity in the future. Thus, the sale or transfer of a held-to-maturity security due to one of the following changes in circumstances shall not be considered to be inconsistent with its original classification:

a. Evidence of a significant deterioration in the issuer's creditworthiness

b. A change in tax law that eliminates or reduces the tax-exempt status of interest on the debt security (but not a change in tax law that revises the marginal tax rates applicable to interest income)

c. A major business combination or major disposition (such as sale of a segment) that necessitates the sale or transfer of held-to-maturity securities to maintain the enterprise's existing interest rate risk position or credit risk policy

d. A change in statutory or regulatory requirements significantly modifying either what constitutes a permissible investment or the maximum level of investments in certain kinds of securities, thereby causing an enterprise to dispose of a held-to-maturity security

e. A significant increase by the regulator in the industry's capital requirements that causes the enterprise to downsize by selling held-to-maturity securities

f. A significant increase in the risk weights of debt securities used for regulatory risk-based capital purposes.

In addition to the foregoing changes in circumstances, other events that are isolated, nonrecurring, and unusual for the reporting enterprise that could not have been reasonably anticipated may cause the enterprise to sell or transfer a held-to-maturity security without necessarily calling into question its intent to hold other debt securities to maturity. All sales and transfers of held-to-maturity securities shall be disclosed pursuant to paragraph 22.

9. An enterprise shall not classify a debt security as held-to-maturity if the enterprise has the intent to hold the security for only an indefinite period. Consequently, a debt security should not, for example, be classified as held-to-maturity if the enterprise anticipates that the security would be available to be sold in response to:

a. Changes in market interest rates and related changes in the security's prepayment risk

b. Needs for liquidity (for example, due to the withdrawal of deposits, increased demand for loans, surrender of insurance policies, or payment of insurance claims)

---

[2]*Restricted stock,* for the purpose of this Statement, means equity securities for which sale is restricted by governmental or contractual requirement (other than in connection with being pledged as collateral) except if that requirement terminates within one year or if the holder has the power by contract or otherwise to cause the requirement to be met within one year. Any portion of the security that can be reasonably expected to qualify for sale within one year, such as may be the case under Rule 144 or similar rules of the SEC, is not considered restricted.

c. Changes in the availability of and the yield on alternative investments

d. Changes in funding sources and terms

e. Changes in foreign currency risk.

10. Although its asset-liability management may encompass consideration of the maturity and repricing characteristics of all investments in debt securities, an enterprise may decide that it can accomplish the necessary adjustments under its asset-liability management without having all of its debt securities available for disposition. In that case, the enterprise may choose to designate certain debt securities as unavailable to be sold to accomplish those ongoing adjustments deemed necessary under its asset-liability management, thereby enabling those debt securities to be accounted for at amortized cost on the basis of a positive intent and ability to hold them to maturity.

11. Sales of debt securities that meet either of the following two conditions may be considered as maturities for purposes of the classification of securities under paragraphs 7 and 12 and the disclosure requirements under paragraph 22:

a. The sale of a security occurs near enough to its maturity date (or call date if exercise of the call is probable) that interest rate risk is substantially eliminated as a pricing factor. That is, the date of sale is so near the maturity or call date (for example, within three months) that changes in market interest rates would not have a significant effect on the security's fair value.

b. The sale of a security occurs after the enterprise has already collected a substantial portion (at least 85 percent) of the principal outstanding at acquisition due either to prepayments on the debt security or to scheduled payments on a debt security payable in equal installments (both principal and interest) over its term. For variable-rate securities, the scheduled payments need not be equal.

Trading Securities and Available-for-Sale Securities

12. Investments in debt securities that are not classified as held-to-maturity and equity securities that have readily determinable fair values shall be classified in one of the following categories and measured at fair value in the statement of financial position:

a. *Trading securities.* Securities that are bought and held principally for the purpose of selling them in the near term (thus held for only a short period of time) shall be classified as *trading securities.* Trading generally reflects active and frequent buying and selling, and trading securities are generally used with the objective of generating profits on short-term differences in price. Mortgage-backed securities that are held for sale in conjunction with mortgage banking activities, as described in FASB Statement No. 65, *Accounting for Certain Mortgage Banking Activities,* shall be classified as trading securities. (Other mortgage-backed securities not held for sale in conjunction with mortgage banking activities shall be classified based on the criteria in this paragraph and paragraph 7.)

b. *Available-for-sale securities.* Investments not classified as trading securities (nor as held-to-maturity securities) shall be classified as *available-for-sale securities.*

Reporting Changes in Fair Value

13. Unrealized **holding gains and losses** for trading securities shall be included in earnings. Unrealized holding gains and losses for available-for-sale securities (including those classified as current assets) shall be excluded from earnings and reported as a net amount in a separate component of shareholders' equity until realized. Paragraph 36 of FASB Statement No. 109, *Accounting for Income Taxes,* provides guidance on reporting the tax effects of unrealized holding gains and losses reported in a separate component of shareholders' equity.

14. Dividend and interest income, including amortization of the premium and discount arising at acquisition, for all three categories of investments in securities shall continue to be included in earnings. This Statement does not affect the methods used for recognizing and measuring the amount of dividend and interest income. Realized gains and losses for securities classified as either available-for-sale or held-to-maturity also shall continue to be reported in earnings.

Transfers between Categories of Investments

15. The transfer of a security between categories of investments shall be accounted for at fair value.[3] At the date of the transfer, the security's

---

[3]For a debt security transferred into the held-to-maturity category, the use of fair value may create a premium or discount that, under amortized cost accounting, shall be amortized thereafter as an adjustment of yield pursuant to FASB Statement No. 91, *Accounting for Nonrefundable Fees and Costs Associated with Originating or Acquiring Loans and Initial Direct Costs of Leases.*

unrealized holding gain or loss shall be accounted for as follows:

a. For a security transferred from the trading category, the unrealized holding gain or loss at the date of the transfer will have already been recognized in earnings and shall not be reversed.
b. For a security transferred into the trading category, the unrealized holding gain or loss at the date of the transfer shall be recognized in earnings immediately.
c. For a debt security transferred into the available-for-sale category from the held-to-maturity category, the unrealized holding gain or loss at the date of the transfer shall be recognized in a separate component of shareholders' equity.
d. For a debt security transferred into the held-to-maturity category from the available-for-sale category, the unrealized holding gain or loss at the date of the transfer shall continue to be reported in a separate component of shareholders' equity but shall be amortized over the remaining life of the security as an adjustment of yield in a manner consistent with the amortization of any premium or discount. The amortization of an unrealized holding gain or loss reported in equity will offset or mitigate the effect on interest income of the amortization of the premium or discount (discussed in footnote 3) for that held-to-maturity security.

Consistent with paragraphs 7-9, transfers from the held-to-maturity category should be rare, except for transfers due to the changes in circumstances identified in subparagraphs 8(a)-8(f). Given the nature of a trading security, transfers into or from the trading category also should be rare.

Impairment of Securities

16. For individual securities classified as either available-for-sale or held-to-maturity, an enterprise shall determine whether a decline in fair value below the amortized cost basis is other than temporary. For example, if it is probable that the investor will be unable to collect all amounts due according to the contractual terms of a debt security not impaired at acquisition, an other-than-temporary impairment shall be considered to have occurred.[4] If the decline in fair value is judged to be other than temporary, the cost basis of the individual security shall be written down to fair value as a new cost basis and the amount of the write-down shall be included in earnings (that is, accounted for as a realized loss). The new cost basis shall not be changed for subsequent recoveries in fair value. Subsequent increases in the fair value of available-for-sale securities shall be included in the separate component of equity pursuant to paragraph 13; subsequent decreases in fair value, if not an other-than-temporary impairment, also shall be included in the separate component of equity.

Financial Statement Presentation

17. An enterprise that presents a classified statement of financial position shall report all trading securities as current assets and shall report individual held-to-maturity securities and individual available-for-sale securities as either current or noncurrent, as appropriate, under the provisions of ARB No. 43, Chapter 3A, "Working Capital—Current Assets and Current Liabilities."[5]

18. Cash flows from purchases, sales, and maturities of available-for-sale securities and held-to-maturity securities shall be classified as cash flows from investing activities and reported gross for each security classification in the statement of cash flows. Cash flows from purchases, sales, and maturities of trading securities shall be classified as cash flows from operating activities.

Disclosures

19. For securities classified as available-for-sale and separately for securities classified as held-to-maturity, all reporting enterprises shall disclose the aggregate fair value, gross unrealized holding gains, gross unrealized holding losses, and amortized cost basis by major security type as of each date for which a statement of financial position is

---

[4]A decline in the value of a security that is other than temporary is also discussed in AICPA Auditing Interpretation, *Evidential Matter for the Carrying Amount of Marketable Securities,* which was issued in 1975 and incorporated in Statement on Auditing Standards No. 1, *Codification of Auditing Standards and Procedures,* as Interpretation 20, and in SEC Staff Accounting Bulletin No. 59, *Accounting for Noncurrent Marketable Equity Securities.*

[5]Chapter 3A of ARB 43 indicates in paragraph 4 that "the term *current assets* is used to designate cash and other assets or resources commonly identified as those which are reasonably expected to be realized in cash or sold or consumed during the normal operating cycle of the business." That paragraph further indicates that the term also comprehends "marketable securities representing the investment of cash available for current operations." Paragraph 5 indicates that "a one-year time period is to be used as a basis for the segregation of current assets in cases where there are several operating cycles occurring within a year."

presented. In complying with this requirement, financial institutions[6] shall include in their disclosure the following major security types, though additional types also may be included as appropriate:

a. Equity securities
b. Debt securities issued by the U.S. Treasury and other U.S. government corporations and agencies
c. Debt securities issued by states of the United States and political subdivisions of the states
d. Debt securities issued by foreign governments
e. Corporate debt securities
f. Mortgage-backed securities
g. Other debt securities.

20. For investments in debt securities classified as available-for-sale and separately for securities classified as held-to-maturity, all reporting enterprises shall disclose information about the contractual maturities of those securities as of the date of the most recent statement of financial position presented. Maturity information may be combined in appropriate groupings. In complying with this requirement, financial institutions shall disclose the fair value and the amortized cost of debt securities based on at least 4 maturity groupings: (a) within 1 year, (b) after 1 year through 5 years, (c) after 5 years through 10 years, and (d) after 10 years. Securities not due at a single maturity date, such as mortgage-backed securities, may be disclosed separately rather than allocated over several maturity groupings; if allocated, the basis for allocation also shall be disclosed.

21. For each period for which the results of operations are presented, an enterprise shall disclose:

a. The proceeds from sales of available-for-sale securities and the gross realized gains and gross realized losses on those sales
b. The basis on which cost was determined in computing realized gain or loss (that is, specific identification, average cost, or other method used)
c. The gross gains and gross losses included in earnings from transfers of securities from the available-for-sale category into the trading category
d. The change in net unrealized holding gain or loss on available-for-sale securities that has been included in the separate component of shareholders' equity during the period
e. The change in net unrealized holding gain or loss on trading securities that has been included in earnings during the period.

22. For any sales of or transfers from securities classified as held-to-maturity, the amortized cost amount of the sold or transferred security, the related realized or unrealized gain or loss, and the circumstances leading to the decision to sell or transfer the security shall be disclosed in the notes to the financial statements for each period for which the results of operations are presented. Such sales or transfers should be rare, except for sales and transfers due to the changes in circumstances identified in subparagraphs 8(a)-8(f).

Effective Date and Transition

23. This Statement shall be effective for fiscal years beginning after December 15, 1993. Except as indicated in the following paragraph, initial application of this Statement shall be as of the beginning of an enterprise's fiscal year; at that date, investments in debt and equity securities owned shall be classified based on the enterprise's current intent. Earlier application as of the beginning of a fiscal year is permitted only in financial statements for fiscal years beginning after issuance of this Statement. This Statement may not be applied retroactively to prior years' financial statements.

24. For fiscal years beginning prior to December 16, 1993, enterprises are permitted to initially apply this Statement as of the end of a fiscal year for which annual financial statements have not previously been issued. This Statement may not be applied retroactively to the interim financial statements for that year.

25. The effect on retained earnings of initially applying this Statement shall be reported as the effect of a change in accounting principle in a manner similar to the cumulative effect of a change in accounting principle as described in paragraph 20 of APB Opinion No. 20, *Accounting Changes.* That effect on retained earnings includes the reversal of amounts previously included in earnings that would be excluded from earnings under this Statement (refer to paragraph 13). The unrealized holding gain or loss, net of tax effect, for securities classified as available-for-sale as of the date that this Statement is first applied shall be an adjustment of the balance of the separate component of equity. The pro forma effects of retroactive application (discussed in paragraph 21 of Opinion 20) shall not be disclosed.

The provisions of this Statement need not be applied to immaterial items.

---

[6]For purposes of the disclosure requirements of paragraphs 19 and 20, the term *financial institutions* includes banks, savings and loan associations, savings banks, credit unions, finance companies, and insurance companies, consistent with the usage of that term in AICPA Statement of Position 90-11, *Disclosure of Certain Information by Financial Institutions About Debt Securities Held as Assets.*

This Statement was adopted by the affirmative votes of five members of the Financial Accounting Standards Board. Messrs. Sampson and Swieringa dissented.

Messrs. Sampson and Swieringa disagree with the accounting treatment prescribed in paragraphs 6-18 of this Statement because it does not resolve two of the most important problems that caused the Board to address the accounting for certain investments in debt and equity securities—namely, accounting based on intent, and gains trading. They believe that those problems can only be resolved by reporting all securities that are within the scope of this Statement at fair value and by including unrealized changes in fair value in earnings.

This Statement requires that debt securities be classified as held-to-maturity, available-for-sale, or trading and that securities in each classification be accounted for differently. As a result, three otherwise identical debt securities could receive three different accounting treatments within the same enterprise. Moreover, classification of debt securities as held-to-maturity is based on management's positive intent and ability to hold to maturity. The notion of intent to hold to maturity (a) is subjective at best, (b) is not likely to be consistently applied, (c) given the provisions in paragraphs 8-11, is not likely to be descriptive of actual transactions and events, and (d) disregards the best available information about the present value of expected future cash flows from a readily marketable debt security—namely, its observable market price. Effective management of financial activities increasingly requires a flexible approach to asset and liability management that is inconsistent with a hold-to-maturity notion.

This Statement also requires that certain debt securities classified as held-to-maturity be reported at amortized cost and that certain debt and equity securities classified as available-for-sale be reported at fair value with unrealized changes in fair value excluded from earnings. Those requirements provide the opportunity for the managers of an enterprise to manage its earnings by selectively selling securities and thereby selectively including realized gains in earnings and selectively excluding unrealized losses from earnings. An impressive amount of empirical evidence indicates that many financial institutions have engaged in that behavior. That behavior undermines the relevance and reliability of accounting information.

The Board concluded that unrealized changes in fair value for trading securities should be reported in earnings because that reporting reflects the economic consequences of the events of the enterprise (such as changes in fair values) as well as the transactions (such as sales of securities) when those events and transactions occur and results in more relevant reporting (paragraph 92). However, the Board concluded that similar reporting of unrealized changes in fair value for available-for-sale securities has the potential for significant earnings volatility that is unrepresentative of both the way enterprises manage their businesses and the impact of economic events on the overall enterprise and, therefore, decided that those changes should be excluded from earnings (paragraphs 93 and 94). Those conclusions do not alleviate the potential for volatility in reported earnings; rather, they provide the opportunity for selective volatility in reported earnings—that is, the volatility in reported earnings that results from the recognition of unrealized changes in fair value in earnings through selective sales of securities.

Reporting all securities that are within the scope of this Statement at fair value and including unrealized changes in fair value in earnings would result in reflecting the consequences of economic events (price changes) in the periods in which they occur rather than when managers wish to selectively recognize those consequences in earnings. Messrs. Sampson and Swieringa believe that this reporting is the only way to resolve the problems of accounting based on intent and gains trading that have raised concerns about the relevance and credibility of accounting for certain investments in debt and equity securities.

In addition, Mr. Sampson is concerned that the conclusions adopted in this Statement may, in some cases, portray unrepresentative volatility in capital because enterprises are not permitted to recognize the unrealized changes in fair value of the liabilities that are related to investments accounted for as available-for-sale securities.

Appendix A

BACKGROUND INFORMATION AND BASIS FOR CONCLUSIONS

CONTENTS

Appendix A

BACKGROUND INFORMATION AND BASIS FOR CONCLUSIONS

Introduction and Overview

26. This appendix summarizes considerations that Board members deemed significant in reaching the conclusions in this Statement. It includes reasons for accepting certain views and rejecting others. Individual Board members gave greater weight to some factors than to others.

27. The Board tried to resolve several problems with the current accounting and reporting practices for debt and equity securities. Those problems, which are discussed in greater detail in this appendix, are summarized as follows:

a. *Inconsistent literature.* The authoritative literature on investments in debt securities is incon-sistent among different industries and has resulted in diversity in reporting.

b. *LOCOM not evenhanded.* The current requirement to use the lower-of-cost-or-market (LOCOM) method for debt securities held for sale and for noncurrent marketable equity securities is not evenhanded because it recognizes the net diminution in value but not the net appreciation in the value of those securities.

c. *Greater relevance of fair value information.* Some believe that fair value information about debt securities is more relevant than amortized cost information in helping users and others assess the effect of current economic events on the enterprise.

d. *Gains trading.* The current requirement to use the amortized cost method permits the recognition of holding gains through the selective sale of appreciated securities but does not require the concurrent recognition of holding losses.

e. *Accounting based on intent.* Current accounting for a debt security is based not on the characteristics of the asset but on management's plans for holding or disposing of the investment. Intent-based accounting impairs comparability.

28. After concluding that the project would not prescribe the comprehensive use of fair value accounting for all securities and related liabilities, the Board supported an approach that resolves the first two problems listed in paragraph 27. It partially addresses the third issue and leaves the last two problems unresolved, although required disclosures will at least highlight situations where gains trading exists. Nevertheless, because the disparities among industries and the differences in recognizing unrealized gains and unrealized losses are eliminated, the Board considers this standard to be an improvement in financial reporting.

Background Information

29. In May 1986, the Board added to its agenda a project to reexamine the accounting for financial instruments, including issues involving off-balance-sheet financing. The Board focused initially on disclosures, resulting in the issuance of FASB Statements No. 105, *Disclosure of Information about Financial Instruments with Off-Balance-Sheet Risk and Financial Instruments with Concentrations of Credit Risk,* in March 1990 and No. 107, *Disclosures about Fair Value of Financial Instruments,* in December 1991.

30. Regulators and others have expressed concerns about the recognition and measurement of investments in debt securities, particularly those held by financial institutions. In 1988, the Office of the Comptroller of the Currency issued a banking circular that identified certain investment practices deemed to be unsuitable and specified that securities acquired in connection with those practices generally should not be classified in the investment portfolio. That same year the Federal Home Loan Bank Board released a proposed statement of policy that addressed the classification of securities as held for investment, held for sale, and held for trading.

31. Those regulators questioned the appropriateness of using the amortized cost method rather than the LOCOM method when trading and sales practices were inconsistent with the amortized cost method. They expressed specific concerns about "gains trading" by financial institutions, an activity implying that decisions to sell certain securities are based on being able to report gains in the financial statements. In gains trading, appreciated securities are sold to recognize gains, but securities with unrealized losses are held and, because the amortized cost method is used, unrealized losses are not recognized. Those practices suggest that, rather than being held for investment, the securities in the portfolio are being held for sale, in which case the

LOCOM method is usually considered to be more appropriate. Some regulators also expressed concern about an institution's ability to "defer" the recognition of losses by using the amortized cost method even though they did not engage in gains-trading activities.

32. Those concerns, along with inconsistent guidance on the reporting of debt securities held as assets in the AICPA Audit and Accounting Guides, prompted AcSEC to undertake a project on the measurement and reporting of debt securities held as assets by financial institutions. That project led to the exposure for comment of a proposed Statement of Position (SOP), *Reporting by Financial Institutions of Debt Securities Held as Assets,* in May 1990.

33. In September 1990, the chairman of the SEC emphasized some of the shortcomings of reporting investments at amortized cost and indicated that, for banks and thrift institutions, "serious consideration must be given to reporting all investment securities at market value." In October 1990, AcSEC concluded that the project on debt securities held as assets by financial institutions could be most effectively dealt with by the FASB and urged the FASB to undertake a limited-scope project on the recognition and measurement of investment securities. AcSEC indicated that "an objective standard, such as one based on market value measurements, may be more appropriate. . . ." AcSEC noted that current economic developments suggested that, in addition to depository institutions, it might be desirable to include insurance companies, mortgage bankers, finance companies, and other commercial enterprises in the scope of any FASB Statement. In November 1990, the major CPA firms advised the FASB that they endorsed AcSEC's recommendations.

34. As an interim measure, AcSEC issued Statement of Position 90-11, *Disclosure of Certain Information by Financial Institutions About Debt Securities Held as Assets,* in November 1990. That SOP requires disclosure of, among other things, the estimated market values, gross unrealized gains, and gross unrealized losses, by pertinent category, for debt securities held as assets by financial institutions. That SOP was initially effective for 1990 calendar-year reporting.

35. Although AcSEC's focus was on the accounting for investments in debt securities, AcSEC also suggested that the FASB could conform the accounting for debt securities and equity securities by amending Statement 12 to include debt securities.

36. Early in the development of the project, the Board and staff members held meetings with repre-

sentatives of banks, thrifts, insurance enterprises, industrial enterprises, and regulators to better understand why investments in debt and equity securities are held and how they are used in managing interest rate risk. During the course of the project, the Board and staff members consulted frequently with the Financial Accounting Standards Advisory Council (FASAC), the Financial Instruments Task Force, professional groups, regulators, users of financial statements, and other interested parties.

37. In September 1992, the Board issued an Exposure Draft, *Accounting for Certain Investments in Debt and Equity Securities,* for a 90-day comment period. Approximately 600 organizations and individuals responded to the Exposure Draft, many with multiple letters. In November and December 1992, members of the Board and staff also conducted eight field visits to constituents to discuss the Exposure Draft. The results of those visits were useful to the Board during its deliberations of the issues addressed by this Statement.

38. In December 1992 and January 1993, the Board held a public hearing on the proposals in the Exposure Draft. Twenty-eight individuals and firms presented their views at the 3-day public hearing. In March 1993, the Board's Financial Instruments Task Force met and discussed, among other things, the Exposure Draft and a staff draft of possible revisions to reflect the Board's redeliberations to that date.

Relevance of Fair Values of Investments in Securities

39. Some Board members believe that measuring all investments in debt and equity securities at fair value in the financial statements is relevant and useful to present and potential investors, creditors, and others in making rational investment, credit, and similar decisions—the first objective of financial reporting, as discussed in FASB Concepts Statement No. 1, *Objectives of Financial Reporting by Business Enterprises.* Other Board members are uncertain about the relevance of measuring those investments at fair value and believe that the relevance of that information should be evaluated after the results of applying Statement 107 are analyzed.

40. Some Board members believe the fair value of debt and equity securities is useful because it assists investors, creditors, and other users in evaluating the performance of an enterprise's investment strategies. Investors are interested in assessing the amounts, timing, and uncertainty of prospective net cash inflows to an enterprise, since those are also the main source of cash flows from the enter-

prise to them. Fair value portrays the market's estimate of the present value of the net future cash flows of those securities, discounted to reflect both the current interest rate and the market's estimate of the risk that the cash flows will not occur. Other Board members believe that fair value information is less relevant for debt securities that will be held to maturity.

41. Several articles and reports in recent years have indicated the potential usefulness of information about the market value of investment securities, particularly as an indicator of the solvency of financial institutions. Those articles indicate that some depository institutions have failed, or experienced impairment of earnings or capital, because of speculative securities activities and that other institutions have experienced an erosion of the liquidity of their securities portfolios as a result of decreases in the market value of those securities. In a liquidity shortage, the fair value of investments, rather than their amortized cost, is the amount available to cover an enterprise's obligations.

42. Some persons question the relevance of fair value measures for investments in securities, arguing in favor of reporting based on amortized cost. They believe that amortized cost provides relevant information because it focuses on the decision to acquire the asset, the earning effects of that decision that will be realized over time, and the ultimate recoverable value of the asset. They argue that fair value ignores those concepts and focuses instead on the effects of transactions and events that do not involve the enterprise, reflecting opportunity gains and losses whose recognition in the financial statements is, in their view, not appropriate until they are realized.

43. Opponents of fair value reporting also challenge the subjectivity that may be necessary in estimating fair values and question the usefulness of reporting fair values for securities if they are not readily marketable. They argue that the questionable reliability impairs the relevance of the fair value information. The Board understands that reliability is an important factor in financial reporting and, therefore, decided that for equity securities the scope be limited to those that have readily determinable fair values. The scope of this Statement includes only those debt instruments that are securities. The Board believes that sufficiently reliable estimates of fair value can be made for those instruments. The Board also believes that the increased use of fair values in financial reporting, partially reflecting the requirements in Statement 107 and SOP 90-11, will result in increased availability and reliability of fair value information.

Scope and Project Approach

44. The Board decided to limit the scope of the project because of its desire to expedite resolution of the problems with the current accounting and reporting practices for investment securities. Accordingly, the Board decided to address the accounting for only certain financial assets and not to change the accounting for financial liabilities nor include other assets.

Financial Assets

45. In deciding which assets to include in the scope of the Statement, the Board excluded receivables that are not securities because of concerns about the effort and cost required in some cases to make a reasonable estimate of fair value. Examples of receivables that are not securities include commercial accounts receivable, consumer installment loans, commercial real estate loans, residential mortgage loans, and checking account overdraft advances.

46. The Board decided to model the definition of *security* (paragraph 137) after the definition provided in the Uniform Commercial Code. The Board decided not to use the definition provided in the Securities Exchange Act of 1934 because that definition is too broad; it encompasses instruments that the Board concluded should not be included in the scope of this Statement, such as notes for routine personal bank loans.

47. The Board decided to include certain equity securities in the scope of this Statement because the relevance of fair value is at least as great for those equity securities as for debt securities, since equity securities can be converted to cash only through sale at fair value. The Board decided the scope should include only equity securities with readily determinable fair values because a broader scope would include equity instruments that would present significant valuation problems, such as investments in closely held companies and partnerships. By including only equity securities with readily determinable fair values, this Statement addresses the same investments in marketable equity securities as addressed in Statement 12.

48. Some respondents noted that the definition of *equity security* in Statement 12 included stock warrants and other options to acquire or dispose of equity securities, whereas the definition in the Exposure Draft did not. Those respondents suggested that the definition be consistent with Statement 12. The Board agreed and has revised the definition of *equity security* to include those options.

Financial Liabilities

49. Some enterprises, particularly financial institutions, manage their interest rate risk by coordinating their holdings of financial assets and financial liabilities. This practice would suggest that, in order for the financial statements to present a more accurate view of an enterprise's exposure to risk, some liabilities should be reported at fair value if some investments are required to be reported at fair value. The Board considered in significant detail whether enterprises should be permitted the option of reporting at fair value the liabilities that are related to the investments in debt securities that are reported at fair value.

50. The valuation of liabilities was considered as an option rather than as a requirement because the Board understood that many enterprises that typically invest their resources primarily in physical assets or intangible assets rather than in financial assets do not manage interest rate risk by relating their financial assets and liabilities.

51. The Board believes it would be preferable to permit certain related liabilities to be reported at fair value especially if all investments in debt securities were required to be reported at fair value. However, the Board was unable to identify, and respondents did not propose, any approach for valuing liabilities that the Board considered workable and not unacceptably complex or permissive. Because many enterprises manage interest rate risk on an overall basis for all financial assets and liabilities rather than for specific financial assets and specific liabilities, difficulties arose in trying to identify which liabilities should be considered as related to the debt securities being reported at fair value.

52. The Board also was unable to agree on how deposit liabilities of banks and thrifts should be valued. Some Board members believe that the fair value of a deposit liability should be based on the terms of the obligation, that is, if the deposit is payable on demand, the fair value cannot be less than the amount that could be withdrawn. That amount represents the settlement amount with the counterparties and is consistent with the Board's decision in Statement 107 that the unit of measure for financial instruments generally should be the individual instrument rather than the portfolio. Other Board members would anticipate the depositor's probable forbearance in exercising its right to withdraw the funds on deposit; thus, in their view, the fair value of the deposit liability should be based on the probable timing of the expected future cash outflows—which essentially incorporates

the institution's core deposit intangible into the valuation of deposit liabilities. The value associated with the probable timing of those expected cash flows is currently recognized in purchase business combinations, but as an intangible asset.

53. Similar difficulties exist for the valuation of certain liabilities of life insurance companies. Differing views exist about how the fair value of liabilities would be determined. For example, some respondents believe the fair value of an insurer's liabilities depends on what assets it holds, whereas others believe the fair value of the insurer's obligations to make future cash outflows should be determined independent of the composition of its assets. In addition, some believe that a life insurer's liabilities for policy reserves should not be less than the amount payable on demand at the policyholder's option for the cash surrender value, particularly since most life insurance policies result in the payment of the cash value at surrender rather than in the payment of death benefits. Others believe the cash surrender value should not be a minimum level for the fair value of the liabilities.

54. Because the Board was unable to develop a workable approach for identifying specific related liabilities and determining their fair value once identified, it decided not to require that all investments in debt securities be reported at fair value and, in replacing the LOCOM method with fair value for certain securities, decided not to include their unrealized changes in fair value in earnings. Instead, the Board agreed to an approach that would introduce more fair value into the financial reporting for investments in debt and equity securities but not change the valuation of related liabilities. The Board believes that the approach in this standard is appropriate because it is built on existing practice, which does not involve the valuation of liabilities.

55. Many respondents, principally bankers and insurers, commented that the approach in the Exposure Draft was unfair because it was one-sided, applying fair value to only some financial assets and no liabilities. Those respondents indicated that if the Board requires that securities be reported at fair value, it should also require (or at least permit) enterprises to report the related liabilities at fair value to avoid unrepresentative volatility in their financial statements. The Board believes that unrepresentative volatility (as well as unrepresentative smoothing) may also result from the use of historical cost accounting when securities are selectively sold and gains or losses are recognized. That volatility may be more acceptable to some because management can control it by deciding which securities to sell and when.

56. As indicated previously, the Board believes it would be preferable to permit certain related liabilities to be reported at fair value if all investments in debt securities were required to be reported at fair value. But this Statement does not broadly expand the use of fair value in reporting securities, and current practice recognizes the net diminution in fair value of securities held for sale (through the LOCOM method) without considering changes in the value of any liabilities. Consequently, the Board believes it is not essential to address the valuation of liabilities in this Statement and that the changes required by this Statement will provide more relevant, reliable, and useful information.

The Approach in This Statement

57. In developing this Statement, the Board considered two frequently heard criticisms of fair value accounting for debt and equity securities: (a) fair values are not as relevant for debt securities that are held to maturity and (b) the valuation of only some assets, without related liabilities, could result in inappropriate volatility of reported earnings. Those two criticisms prompted the Board to consider both retaining the use of amortized cost accounting for debt securities that are held to maturity and reporting the unrealized holding gains and losses on securities available for sale outside earnings.

Investments being held to maturity

58. Some persons believe that amortized cost is a more relevant measure of debt securities because, if a debt security is held to maturity, that cost will be realized, absent default, and any interim unrealized gains and losses will reverse. The Board concluded that amortized cost is most likely to be relevant for those debt securities that will be held to maturity and decided to prescribe different accounting for those debt securities. This criterion is consistent with the provisions of the AICPA Audit and Accounting Guide, *Audits of Savings Institutions,* which requires "the intent and ability to hold to maturity" as a prerequisite for use of the amortized cost method. The use of the amortized cost method in FASB Statement No. 60, *Accounting and Reporting by Insurance Enterprises,* also is based on the ability and intent to hold debt securities to maturity, whereas the guidance for banks is based on the ability and intent to hold securities on a long-term basis.

59. The Board deliberately chose to make the *held-to-maturity* category restrictive because it believes that the use of amortized cost must be justified for each investment in a debt security. At acquisition, an enterprise should determine if it has the positive intent and ability to hold a security to *maturity,*

which is distinct from the mere absence of an intent to sell. The Board believes that, if management's intention to hold a debt security to maturity is uncertain, it is not appropriate to carry that investment at amortized cost; amortized cost is relevant only if a security is actually held to maturity. In establishing intent, an enterprise should consider pertinent historical experience, such as sales and transfers of debt securities classified as held-to-maturity. A pattern of sales or transfers of those securities is inconsistent with an expressed current intent to hold similar debt securities to maturity.

60. The Board decided that a debt security that is available to be sold in response to changes in market interest rates, changes in the security's prepayment risk, the enterprise's need for liquidity, changes in foreign exchange risk, or other similar factors should not be included in the held-to-maturity category because the possibility of a sale is indicative that the enterprise does not have a positive intent and ability to hold the security to maturity. A debt security that is considered available to be sold as part of an enterprise's asset-liability management activities should not be classified as held-to-maturity. Similarly, an enterprise that maintains a dynamic hedging program in which changes in external factors require that certain securities be sold to maintain an effective hedge would not have the intent and ability to hold those securities to maturity.

61. In articulating the views expressed in the preceding paragraph, the Exposure Draft used the phrase *might be sold*. Many respondents misunderstood the Board's intended meaning of that phrase, extracting it from its context and emphasizing the uncertainty of future events—that anything "might" happen. The Board expects that extremely remote "disaster scenarios" (such as a run on a bank or an insurance company) would not be anticipated by an enterprise in deciding whether it had the positive intent and ability to hold a debt security to maturity. This Statement does not use the phrase *might be sold* to avoid the potential for misunderstanding.

62. The Board believes that an enterprise's decision to classify a security as held-to-maturity implies that during the term of the security the enterprise's decisions about continuing to hold that security will not be affected by changes in market interest rates or the security's prepayment risk. That decision is consistent with the view that a change in fair value, which would reflect a change in market interest rates or prepayment risk, is not relevant for a security that will be held to maturity. The Board believes that the classification of a debt security as held-to-maturity is theoretically incompatible with the subsequent designation of a futures contract or other financial instrument as a hedge of that debt security's interest rate risk. That designation is the basis for hedge accounting (that is, deferring and amortizing the change in value due to changes in market interest rates), which effectively reflects an alteration in the characteristics of the debt security (as though a new synthetic instrument has been created).

63. Because of that theoretical incompatibility, the Board proposed in the Exposure Draft that, subsequent to a debt security's classification as held-to-maturity, hedge accounting could not be achieved by designating a futures contract as a hedge of that security. Respondents generally opposed the proposed restriction on the use of hedge accounting as unnecessary and contrary to the Board's current efforts to address hedging issues on a comprehensive basis. The Board decided that, even though a theoretical incompatibility may exist for subsequent hedges of held-to-maturity securities, the proposed restriction on using hedge accounting should not be included in the final standard because the accounting for all hedging transactions is currently being addressed by the Board in a separate project. The Board also noted that hedge accounting does not provide the same accounting results as the sale of the security because it does not result in immediate recognition of the security's unrealized holding gain or loss.

64. The Exposure Draft indicated that "the sale of a debt security near enough to its maturity (for example, within 30 days) that interest rate risk is substantially eliminated as a pricing factor shall be considered in substance held to maturity." A number of respondents requested that the example of 30 days be changed to 90 days, many noting that the guidance regarding cash equivalents in FASB Statement No. 95, *Statement of Cash Flows,* applies a 3-month cutoff in determining whether securities are "so near their maturity that they present insignificant risk of changes in value because of changes in interest rates." The Board agreed with the suggestion and changed the example of "30 days" to "three months."

65. Some respondents commented that interest rate risk is also substantially eliminated as a pricing factor near to a call date when the issuer is expected to exercise the call option. Those respondents suggested that the standard also address the sale of a callable debt security near to the call date if exercise of the call is probable. The Board agreed with that suggestion.

66. A few respondents reported that many banks routinely sell their investments in mortgage-backed securities after a substantial portion of the principal has been recovered through prepayments. They

explained that the "tail" portion of a mortgage-backed security is sold because it no longer represents an efficient investment to the enterprise mainly due to the economic costs of accounting for remnants of the original issue. They requested that the Board consider permitting enterprises to sell securities classified as held-to-maturity prior to their maturity when prepayments have reduced the remaining principal to low levels. The Board decided for practical reasons that selling a debt security after a substantial portion of the principal has been collected should be considered equivalent to holding the security to maturity. The Board decided that the collection of 85 percent of the principal outstanding at acquisition (not the principal outstanding at issuance for securities purchased in the secondary market) constituted a reasonable threshold of what represents a "substantial portion of the principal." However, the Board limited application of this practical exception to collections of principal due either to prepayments on the debt security or to scheduled payments on a security payable in equal installments (both principal and interest) over its term (except that the scheduled payments need not be equal for variable-rate debt).

67. Some respondents indicated that, although they have the intent to hold the vast majority of their investments to maturity, they do not know at acquisition which specific securities will or will not be sold. Having to classify securities upon acquisition does not, in their opinion, provide the desired degree of flexibility to manage their portfolio. The Board considered two approaches that would potentially address those concerns.

68. The Board considered an approach that would eliminate the need to classify specific debt securities as available-for-sale or held-to-maturity. Instead, enterprises would designate the percentage of the securities acquired each year that would not be held to maturity and, at each reporting date, recognize a pro rata portion of the unrealized holding gain or loss on all securities. The Board rejected that approach because it would obscure the reporting of discrete investments. Under that approach, no specific debt security would be reported at fair value; instead, the carrying amount of the available-for-sale securities would be a blended amount—an allocation of portfolio totals—that, in the Board's view, would not be useful to users of financial statements. The Board also noted that the approach would continue to limit management's discretion in selling securities.

69. The Board also considered whether the standard should permit enterprises to sell without justification some specified amount of held-to-maturity securities without calling into question the enterprise's intent to hold other debt securities

to maturity. The Board rejected that approach as being inconsistent with the premise underlying the use of amortized cost—that management intends to hold all such securities to maturity. However, the Board decided that the sale of a held-to-maturity security due to events that are isolated, nonrecurring, and unusual for the reporting enterprise that could not have been reasonably anticipated should not necessarily call into question the enterprise's intent to hold other debt securities to maturity. But if the sale of a held-to-maturity security occurs without justification, the materiality of that contradiction of the enterprise's previously asserted intent must be evaluated.

70. The Board recognizes that the intent to hold a security to maturity is not absolute and that in some circumstances management's intent could change for certain securities. The Exposure Draft acknowledged that, for example, management might decide to sell a security because of either an increase in the security's credit risk or a change in the tax law that eliminates the tax-exempt status of interest on that security. Respondents identified a variety of other circumstances that they believed should justify the sale of a security classified as held-to-maturity.

71. Some respondents believed that enterprises should be permitted to sell held-to-maturity securities to generate taxable gains to offset existing taxable losses, or vice versa. Some respondents also desired to be able to sell those securities in response to changes in the enterprise's anticipated future profitability. It was suggested, for example, that if taxable losses were expected for the next several years, the enterprise should be permitted to sell tax-exempt securities classified as held-to-maturity. The Board rejected those suggested reasons for selling held-to-maturity securities. Securities that may need to be sold to implement tax-planning strategies should be classified as available-for-sale, not held-to-maturity.

72. Some respondents suggested that the standard permit the sale of a held-to-maturity security in advance of any deterioration in the creditworthiness of the issuer, perhaps based solely on industry statistics. The Board believes that the sale must be in response to an actual deterioration, not mere speculation. That deterioration should be supported by evidence about the issuer's creditworthiness; however, the enterprise need not await an actual downgrading in the issuer's published credit rating or inclusion on a "credit watch" list.

73. Some respondents suggested that major business combinations and major dispositions should be identified as circumstances that would justify being able to sell a held-to-maturity security. The

Board agreed that, following a pooling of interests, the continuing management may need to sell or transfer some held-to-maturity securities to maintain the enterprise's existing credit risk policy, foreign exchange risk exposure, or interest rate risk position under its asset-liability management policy. Similarly, following a major purchase acquisition, some of the acquiring enterprise's held-to-maturity securities may need to be transferred or sold because of the nature of the liabilities assumed—even though all of the acquired securities are classified anew following such a business combination.

74. The Board acknowledged that, after a major disposition, some held-to-maturity securities may need to be transferred or sold to maintain the interest rate risk exposure that predated the disposition. In considering those issues, the Board rejected a suggestion to automatically permit investment portfolio restructurings after a business combination or disposition. The Board believes that held-to-maturity securities should be transferred or sold only when the transfer or sale is necessary to maintain a particular risk exposure consistent with the enterprise's risk posture prior to the business combination or disposition. Furthermore, the Board believes those necessary transfers or sales should occur concurrent with or shortly after the business combination or disposition.

75. Some respondents suggested that the transfer or sale of a held-to-maturity security should be permitted in response to changes in the regulatory environment. The Board believes that if an enterprise is forced to dispose of a held-to-maturity security because a change in statutory or regulatory requirements significantly modifies what constitutes a permissible investment, that disposition should not call into question management's intent to hold the remaining securities in that category to maturity. Similarly, if a change in statutory or regulatory requirements significantly reduces the maximum level of investment that the enterprise can make in certain kinds of securities or in securities with a specified low credit quality, the sale of held-to-maturity securities to comply with that newly imposed maximum also should not call into question the classification of other held-to-maturity securities. The Board also agreed that if regulators significantly increase the risk weights of certain debt securities used for risk-based capital purposes, the sale of held-to-maturity securities with those recently increased risk weights should not call into question the classification of other held-to-maturity securities.

76. Some respondents suggested that the sale of held-to-maturity securities should always be permitted to meet regulatory capital requirements.

The Board rejected blanket approval for those sales. It noted that an enterprise's ability and intent to hold securities to maturity would be called into question by the sale of held-to-maturity securities to realize gains to replenish regulatory capital that had been reduced by a provision for loan losses. The Board believes that gains trading with held-to-maturity securities to meet an enterprise's capital requirements is inconsistent with the held-to-maturity notion. In contrast, if an enterprise chooses to downsize to comply with a significant increase in the industry's capital requirements, the sale of one or more held-to-maturity securities in connection with that downsizing would not call into question the classification of other held-to-maturity securities.

77. In some circumstances it may not be possible to hold a security to its original stated maturity, such as when the security is called by the issuer prior to maturity. The issuer's exercise of the call option effectively accelerates the security's maturity and should not be viewed as inconsistent with classification in the held-to-maturity category.

Investments not being held to maturity

78. For investments in debt securities that management does not have the positive intent and ability to hold to maturity, and for investments in equity securities with readily determinable fair values, the Board concluded that fair value information is more relevant than amortized cost information, in part because it reflects the effects of management's decision to buy a financial asset at a specific time and then continue to hold it for an unspecified period of time. For example, if an enterprise invests in a fixed-rate security and interest rates fall, the enterprise is in a better position than if it had invested in a variable-rate security. Movements in fair values, and thus market returns, during the period that a debt or equity security is held also provide a benchmark from which to assess the results of management's decisions and its success in maximizing the profitable use of the enterprise's economic resources. That success, or failure, is relevant and should be reflected in the financial statements in the period that the event (that is, the change in interest rates) occurs.

79. The Board decided that those investments in debt and equity securities should be reported at fair value. However, because of concerns about the potential volatility that would result from reporting the fair value changes of only some assets, and no liabilities, in earnings, the Board determined that the unrealized holding gains and losses for available-for-sale securities should be excluded from earnings. The basis for that conclusion is discussed in paragraphs 90-95.

80. The Board concluded that investments that are bought and held principally for the purpose of selling them in the near term should be classified as *trading* securities. Trading generally reflects active and frequent buying and selling, and trading securities generally are used with the objective of generating profits on short-term differences in price. The designation of trading securities under this Statement is the same as present practice by depository institutions.

81. Some respondents suggested that the criteria for classifying assets as current or noncurrent be used to distinguish between trading securities and available-for-sale securities. The Board disagreed because that suggestion is inconsistent with the character of trading securities, which are acquired generally with the objective of generating profits on short-term differences in price. Other respondents suggested that all securities classified as current should be classified as trading securities. The Board believes that available-for-sale securities should not be automatically transferred to the trading category because the passage of time has caused the maturity date to be within one year or because management intends to sell the security within one year.

82. All investments in debt and equity securities that are valued at fair value and are not classified as trading securities would be classified as *available-for-sale securities*. This category would include marketable equity securities previously covered by Statement 12, except to the extent that the investor classifies some of them as trading securities. Additionally, the available-for-sale category will include debt securities that are being held for an unspecified period of time, such as those that the enterprise would consider selling to meet liquidity needs or as part of an enterprise's risk management program.

83. At acquisition, an investor should determine and document the classification of debt and equity securities into one of the three categories—held-to-maturity, available-for-sale, or trading. At each reporting date, the appropriateness of the classification must be reassessed. For example, if an enterprise no longer has the ability to hold securities to maturity, their continued classification as held-to-maturity would not be appropriate.

Transfers between categories of investments

84. Many respondents noted that the Exposure Draft's proposed requirement to account for transfers at fair value and recognize in earnings any unrealized holding gains and losses existing at the date of a transfer would facilitate gains trading; a change in management's intent would cause an ap-

preciated security to be transferred, resulting in immediate recognition of the gain in earnings. Respondents urged the Board not to provide that opportunity, especially in a standard that they expected would help resolve the gains trading issue, not aggravate it. Some respondents suggested that all unrealized holding gains or losses on transferred securities be deferred in a separate component of equity. Others supported an approach that reported unrealized holding gains and losses in a manner consistent with the category into which the security has been transferred.

85. The Board acknowledged that the proposed accounting for transfers would have permitted discretionary adjustments to earnings that could weaken the credibility of reported earnings. To avoid that potential consequence, the Board decided that unrealized holding gains and losses would be recognized in earnings only if the security were transferred into the trading category. Otherwise, the unrealized holding gains and losses that had not yet been recognized in earnings would be reported in a separate component of equity. In certain respects, this approach is similar to the notion of recognizing unrealized gains and losses in a manner consistent with the category into which the security has been transferred. Because the Board expects transfers from the held-to-maturity category to be rare, special disclosures about the circumstances that resulted in the transfers are required.

Comments on the approach in this statement

86. As stated previously, some Board members would have preferred to require the use of fair value for all investments in debt and equity securities, even if the Board was unable to resolve at this time how to deal with the option to account for related liabilities at their fair values. Other Board members would have preferred to require the use of fair value for all securities, but only if it were practicable to permit the valuation of liabilities at their fair values. Other Board members, as well as many respondents, believe that consideration of the use of fair value for all investments in debt and equity securities should be delayed until the results of applying Statement 107 can be analyzed.

87. Despite those various views, Board members believe that the existing diversity in guidance must be addressed and that an interim solution is appropriate at this point, given the present status of the overall project on the recognition and measurement of financial instruments. The Board expects that the use of fair value measurements for financial instruments will be reassessed at an appropriate future point in the financial instruments project. This reassessment would likely include an evaluation of the relevance, reliability, and use of

fair values based on experience from applying Statement 107 and this Statement. The Board has no preconceived views about the outcome of that consideration.

88. The Board also recognizes that the classification of investments in debt securities into three categories and the use of management intent as a criterion to distinguish among the categories present some difficulties. The classification of debt securities into three categories, each of which has different accounting, could result in comparability problems among enterprises. Enterprises with virtually identical securities may account for those securities differently. Additionally, basing the distinction in accounting treatment on management intent could result in an inconsistent application of the standard and contribute to comparability difficulties. Some constituents as well as some Board members question the relevance of accounting that results from using the intent of management as a criterion.

89. While the Board recognizes that there are some difficulties associated with the use of management intent as a criterion, and with the classification of identical instruments into several categories, it believes that this standard will improve financial reporting overall because it will standardize for all enterprises the criterion for when a debt security should be reported at amortized cost and specify a more evenhanded approach for recognizing unrealized gains and unrealized losses.

Reporting Changes in Fair Value

90. This Statement provides requirements for reporting changes in the fair value of investments in securities. The total change in fair value consists of both the unpaid interest income earned on a debt security (or the unpaid accrued dividends on an equity security) and the remaining change in fair value that results from holding a security, known as the *unrealized holding gain or loss*. The reporting requirements for unrealized holding gains and losses depend on the classification of securities as trading or available-for-sale, as outlined in paragraph 13. This Statement does not change the current practice of including interest income in earnings, regardless of a security's classification.

91. For trading securities, the Board decided that unrealized holding gains and losses should be included in the determination of earnings, consistent with present accounting. The Board also decided that unrealized holding gains and losses on available-for-sale securities should be excluded from the determination of earnings. The unrealized holding gains and losses should be reported as a net amount in a separate component of shareholders'

equity until the holding gains and losses are realized or a provision for impairment is recognized.

92. For securities that are actively managed, the Board believes that financial reporting is improved when earnings reflect the economic consequences of the events of the reporting enterprise (such as changes in fair value) as well as the transactions (such as purchases and sales of securities) that occur. Including changes in fair value in the determination of earnings results in more relevant financial information to current shareholders, whose composition typically changes to some degree from one reporting period to the next. Including unrealized changes in fair value in earnings provides a more equitable reporting of results and changes in shareholders' equity among the different shareholder groups over the period that a security is held by recognizing in each reporting period the effects of economic events occurring in those periods. Thus, the Board concluded that unrealized changes in value on trading securities should be reported in earnings.

93. However, some enterprises, particularly financial institutions, that consider both their investments in securities and their liabilities in managing interest rate risk contend that reporting unrealized holding gains and losses on only the investments, and not related liabilities, in earnings has the potential for significant volatility that is unrepresentative of both the way they manage their business and the impact of economic events on the overall enterprise.

94. Based principally on those concerns, the Board decided that unrealized holding gains and losses on debt and equity securities that are available for sale but that are not actively managed in a trading account should be reported outside earnings—a method of reporting currently used for some securities under Statement 12. That reporting would alleviate the potential for volatility in reported earnings resulting from a requirement to value some assets at fair value without at least permitting fair-value-based accounting for related liabilities. It also would mitigate concerns about reporting the fluctuation in fair value of long-term investments in earnings. However, the Board recognizes that volatility in earnings can still result from the sale of securities. Furthermore, the approach does not resolve concerns about gains trading.

95. Many respondents, particularly bankers and insurers, emphasized that reporting the unrealized holding gains and losses for available-for-sale securities in a separate component of equity would create volatility in reported capital. The Board acknowledges that reporting those securities at fair

value will cause greater volatility in total share-holders' equity than use of the amortized cost method would, but believes that the greater relevance of fair value for those securities significantly outweighs the disadvantages of that potential volatility in equity. Furthermore, the Board believes those disadvantages are mitigated by the supplemental disclosures of fair value for other financial assets and liabilities pursuant to Statement 107.

Benefits and Costs

96. In accomplishing its mission, the Board follows certain precepts, including the precept to promulgate standards only when the expected benefits of the information exceed the perceived costs. The Board endeavors to determine that a proposed standard will fill a significant need and that the costs imposed to meet that standard, as compared to other alternatives, are justified in relation to the overall benefits of the resulting information.

97. The benefits of reporting debt and equity securities at fair value are discussed in paragraphs 39-43 of this Statement. Furthermore, in eliminating the inconsistencies in the existing authoritative literature, this Statement is beneficial in avoiding the diversity and confusion resulting from the current accounting guidance. It also eliminates the unevenhandedness of LOCOM, which recognizes the net diminution in value of securities but not the net appreciation in value.

98. The incremental costs of the accounting and disclosure requirements of this Statement have been minimized in several ways. The Board has been informed that many enterprises already have systems in place to manage the market risk of their portfolios and that those systems provide much of the information that is necessary to comply with this Statement. Additionally, the required disclosures in Statement 107 provide much of the information required in this Statement. For financial institutions, the incremental burden is further minimized by the existing disclosure requirements of SOP 90-11 and regulatory reporting requirements. Furthermore, because the LOCOM method is not used, enterprises will not be required to combine portfolios of investments of various subsidiaries.

99. The Board is sensitive to the economic consequences that may result from the new information. For example, many respondents commented that enterprises may no longer invest in long-term instruments, such as long-term U.S. Treasury securities and corporate bonds, to reduce the potential for volatility in reported capital. They further suggested that such discontinued investment could jeopardize the market for those long-term securities. Some respondents also predicted that this

Statement would exacerbate the credit crunch by causing financial institutions to make fewer loans, particularly long-term loans.

100. However, the nature and extent of those consequences are highly uncertain and are difficult to isolate from the effects of other events that will occur independent of that new information. For example, regulatory agencies are continuing to make changes in regulations that may affect the future costs of doing business for certain enterprises. Even if the Board could isolate the likely consequences of the information provided pursuant to this Statement from other events that produce change, it is outside the Board's role to deal with those possible consequences. The Board's objective in this pronouncement is to improve the consistency in how information about investments in securities is determined so that users of financial statements may make better-informed decisions.

Enterprises Included in Scope

101. Although the issues that gave rise to the Board's consideration of this Statement were raised in the context of financial institutions, particularly depository institutions, the Board believes that this Statement should not be limited to the accounting by those institutions. The Board's approach to standard setting generally has been to consider the accounting for a specific transaction or financial instrument and not to try to develop specialized accounting methods for different industries, particularly for transactions that are not unique to a specific industry.

102. The Board considered whether certain enterprises should be excluded from the scope of this Statement based on industry, size, or nonpublic status and concluded that any enterprise that chooses to invest in marketable securities should be able to make or gain access to a reasonable estimate of fair value. Deregulation and market forces have blurred the distinction between industries and have heightened desires for greater comparability between financial statements of enterprises nominally in different industries. Those factors reinforced the Board's belief that all enterprises with identical financial instruments should account for those instruments in the same manner.

103. Some respondents suggested that nondepository financial institutions (particularly life insurance companies) be exempted from this Statement. The Board believes that distinguishing between nondepository financial institutions and other financial institutions is not warranted because both types of institutions invest their resources primarily in financial assets and the fair value of invest-

ments in debt and equity securities of all financial institutions is similarly affected by changes in market interest rates. Furthermore, Statement 60 already requires that the use of amortized cost in accounting for debt securities held by insurance companies be based on the ability and intent to hold the securities to maturity.

104. Other respondents suggested that nonfinancial institutions be exempted from this Statement. The Board believes that a distinction between financial and nonfinancial institutions is not warranted even though commercial and industrial companies invest their resources primarily in physical assets rather than financial assets. To the extent that those enterprises invest in debt and equity securities, those financial assets have the same future economic benefits as when held by a financial institution.

105. Respondents, principally bankers, also suggested that smaller and nonpublic enterprises be exempted because they lack the capabilities or resources necessary to provide estimates of fair values. The Board believes that prudent investment management normally warrants knowledge of market estimates, and smaller enterprises should have access to those estimates. Additionally, the fair value of investments in debt and equity securities owned by smaller or nonpublic enterprises is affected by changes in market interest rates in the same manner as those owned by large or public enterprises. The Board notes that even small, nonpublic banks have been required for many years to disclose the market value of their investments in securities.

106. The Board also considered exempting not-for-profit organizations, such as health and welfare organizations, hospitals, colleges and universities, religious institutions, trade associations, and private foundations, from the scope of this Statement. The Board believes that for those organizations not currently reporting their investments at fair value, the measurement standards in this Statement would probably be an improvement to the current accounting for investments in debt and equity securities, such as those held in endowment funds. At issue is whether those requirements should be articulated in this Statement or in a later Statement after the Board resolves its agenda project on financial statement display by not-for-profit organizations. The Board decided it was more efficient to solicit and consider comments only on the accounting by enterprises other than not-for-profit organizations. Accordingly, not-for-profit organizations are not required to apply the provisions in this Statement. The Board intends to address the issue of accounting for investments by not-for-profit organizations within its separate overall project on not-for-profit organizations.

107. Some respondents questioned whether a credit union was included in the scope as a financial institution or excluded as a not-for-profit organization. FASB Concepts Statement No. 4, *Objectives of Financial Reporting by Nonbusiness Organizations,* states in paragraph 7, "Examples of organizations that clearly fall outside the focus of this Statement include all investor-owned enterprises and other types of organizations, such as mutual insurance companies and other mutual cooperative entities that provide dividends, lower costs, or other economic benefits directly and proportionately to their owners, members, or participants." Accordingly, because credit unions, like mutual insurance companies, provide economic benefits to their members, they are not considered nonbusiness or not-for-profit organizations and, thus, are *not* excluded from the scope of this Statement.

108. The Board understands that enterprises in certain industries apply specialized accounting practices that include accounting for substantially all investments in debt and equity securities at market value or fair value, with the changes in those values recognized in earnings or in changes in net assets. The Board decided not to change the accounting by those enterprises because it believes that, for those enterprises, that accounting provides more relevant information for users of their financial statements. Consequently, those enterprises, such as brokers and dealers in securities, defined benefit pension plans, and investment companies, are excluded from the scope of this Statement.

Other Issues

Terminology

109. The Board decided to use the term *fair value* in this Statement to avoid confusion between the terms *fair value* and *market value;* some constituents associate the term *market value* only with items that are traded on active secondary markets (such as exchange and dealer markets). However, the Board does not make that distinction, intending the term to be applicable whether the market for an item is active or inactive, primary or secondary. The Board decided to use the term *fair value* also to maintain consistency with the terminology in Statement 107 and the financial instrument proposals made recently by the International Accounting Standards Committee and the Canadian Institute of Chartered Accountants. Those proposals would require disclosures of fair value for financial assets and financial liabilities.

Determining Fair Values

110. The Board concluded that quoted market prices, if available, provide the most reliable meas-

ure of fair value. Quoted market prices are easy to obtain and are reliable and verifiable. They are used and relied upon regularly and are well understood by investors, creditors, and other users of financial information.

111. Although quoted market prices are not available for all debt securities, the Board believes that a reasonable estimate of fair value can be made or obtained for the remaining debt securities required to be valued at fair value by this Statement. Some respondents mentioned the difficulty of reliably estimating the fair value of local municipal bonds; however, because municipal bonds are often intended to be held to maturity, to that extent, they are not reported at fair value. For debt securities that do not trade regularly or that trade only in principal-to-principal markets, a reasonable estimate of fair value can be made using a variety of pricing techniques, including, but not limited to, discounted cash flow analysis, matrix pricing, option-adjusted spread models, and fundamental analysis. The Board realizes that estimating fair value may require judgment but noted that a considerable degree of judgment is also needed when complying with other long-standing accounting and reporting requirements.

Impairment of Securities

112. The Board concluded that it is important to recognize in earnings all declines in fair value below the amortized cost basis that are considered to be other-than-temporary; a loss inherent in an investment security should be recognized in earnings even if it has not been sold. This is consistent with the other-than-temporary-impairment notion that was included in Statement 12.

113. The Board recognizes that the impairment provisions of this Statement differ from those in FASB Statement No. 114, *Accounting by Creditors for Impairment of a Loan*, which indicates that a loan is impaired when it is probable that the creditor (investor) will be unable to collect all amounts due according to the contractual terms of the loan agreement. This Statement requires that the measure of impairment be based on the fair value of the security, whereas Statement 114 permits measurement of an unsecuritized loan's impairment based on either fair value (of the loan or the collateral) or the present value of the expected cash flows discounted at the loan's effective interest rate. The Board recognizes that a principal difference between securities and unsecuritized loans is the relatively greater and easier availability of reliable market prices for securities, which makes it more practical and less costly to require use of a fair value approach. In addition, some Board members believe that securities are distinct from receivables

that are not securities and that securities warrant a different measure of impairment—one that reflects both current estimates of the expected cash flows from the security and current economic events and conditions.

114. During the course of this project, some have urged the Board to develop guidance that would resolve recent practice problems about the application of other-than-temporary impairment. Although the Board believes that other-than-temporary impairment exists if it is probable that the investor will be unable to collect all amounts due according to the contractual terms of the security, the Board believes that providing comprehensive guidance on other-than-temporary impairment involves issues beyond the scope of this Statement.

Financial Instruments Used to Hedge Investments at Fair Value

115. This Statement does not address the accounting for other financial instruments used to hedge investments in securities. However, the accounting for those instruments may be affected if they are hedges of securities whose accounting is changed by this Statement. Gains and losses on instruments that hedge securities classified as trading would be reported in earnings, consistent with the reporting of unrealized gains and losses on the trading securities. Gains and losses on instruments that hedge available-for-sale securities are initially reported in a separate component of equity, consistent with the reporting for those securities, but then should be amortized as a yield adjustment. The reporting of available-for-sale securities at fair value does not change the recognition and measurement of interest income.

Amendment of Statement 91

116. Some respondents noted that the change from LOCOM to fair value for reporting available-for-sale securities would cause FASB Statement No. 91, *Accounting for Nonrefundable Fees and Costs Associated with Originating or Acquiring Loans and Initial Direct Costs of Leases*, to no longer apply to those securities. Paragraph 3 of Statement 91 indicates that it does not apply to loans and securities reported at fair value. The Board noted that the intent of that provision was to exclude only the loans and securities whose changes in value were included in earnings, not those loans and securities whose changes in value are reported in a separate component of shareholders' equity. Consequently, the Board agreed to amend Statement 91 to clarify that only loans and securities reported at fair value with changes in value reported in earnings are excluded from that Statement's scope. Thus, Statement 91 would continue to apply to available-for-sale securi-

ties that previously were reported at amortized cost or LOCOM.

Financial Statement Presentation and Disclosure

117. The Board decided not to require the presentation of individual amounts for the three categories of investments on the face of the statement of financial position, provided the information is presented in the notes. Thus, enterprises that report certain investments in debt securities as *cash equivalents* in accordance with the provisions of Statement 95 can continue that practice, provided that the notes reconcile the reporting classifications used in the statement of financial position.

118. Some respondents asked how the cash flows from purchases, sales, and maturities of trading and available-for-sale securities should be classified in the statement of cash flows. Because trading securities are bought and held principally for the purpose of selling them in the near term, the cash flows from purchases and sales of trading securities should be classified as cash flows from operating activities. However, available-for-sale securities are not acquired for that purpose. The Board believes that cash flows from purchases, sales, and maturities of available-for-sale securities should be classified as cash flows from investing activities and reported gross in the statement of cash flows.

119. The Board believes that the financial statement disclosures required by this Statement provide information that is useful in analyzing an enterprise's investment strategies and exposures to risk. Gross unrealized gains and losses may indicate the results of hedging activities. Information about the sale or transfer of securities, including information on realized gains and losses, would reveal reallocations of the enterprise's resources and would help identify gains-trading activity. In considering the disclosures to be required, the Board consulted with representative organizations of users of financial statements. Respondents were generally supportive of the disclosures proposed in the Exposure Draft.

Effective Date and Transition

120. The Board proposed that this Statement should be effective for fiscal years beginning after December 15, 1993 for all enterprises. The Board considered whether to permit a delayed effective date for smaller enterprises (as provided in Statement 107) but decided that extra time was not required to develop the fair value information required by this Statement. In contrast, Statement 107 required disclosure of the fair value of all financial instruments, some of which are more difficult to value. The Board noted that smaller financial insti-

tutions are already required by SOP 90-11 to disclose the market value of their investments in debt securities. Respondents generally concurred with the proposed effective date, indicating that no deferral of the effective date was needed.

121. Some respondents requested that application of the new standard in 1993 financial statements be permitted, in part to enable them to include the cumulative effect of the accounting change in the income statement for 1993 rather than 1994. The Board decided to permit enterprises, for fiscal years beginning prior to December 16, 1993, to initially apply this Statement as of the end of a fiscal year for which annual financial statements have not previously been issued.

122. Because the classification of securities among the three categories is based on the enterprise's current intent, the Board decided that retroactive application of the provisions of this Statement is inappropriate. Except as permitted in the preceding paragraph, this Statement should be applied prospectively as of the beginning of the fiscal year.

123. As indicated in paragraph 23, at the date of initial application of this Statement, the enterprise's investments in debt and equity securities shall be classified based on the enterprise's current intent. The classification at initial application should not be considered a transfer between categories; thus, the accounting for transfers in paragraph 15 is not relevant to the initial application of this Statement. At the date of initial application, the unrealized holding gain or loss, net of tax effect, for securities classified as available-for-sale should be reported in the separate component of shareholders' equity. The unrealized holding gains and losses, net of tax effect, previously included in earnings that would be excluded from earnings under this Statement would be reversed in the income statement as the cumulative effect of a change in accounting principle.

Appendix B

AMENDMENTS TO EXISTING PRONOUNCEMENTS

124. This Statement supersedes Statement 12 and related FASB Interpretations No. 11, *Changes in Market Value after the Balance Sheet Date,* No. 12, *Accounting for Previously Established Allowance Accounts,* No. 13, *Consolidation of a Parent and Its Subsidiaries Having Different Balance Sheet Dates,* and No. 16, *Clarification of Definitions and Accounting for Marketable Equity Securities That Become Nonmarketable.*

125. The following is added to paragraph 4 of Chapter 3A of ARB 43 following *operations* in subitem (f):

, including investments in debt and equity securities classified as trading securities under FASB Statement No. 115, *Accounting for Certain Investments in Debt and Equity Securities*

126. The following sentence is added to the end of paragraph 19(l) of APB Opinion No. 18, *The Equity Method of Accounting for Investments in Common Stock:*

FASB Statement No. 115, *Accounting for Certain Investments in Debt and Equity Securities,* addresses the accounting for investments in equity securities with readily determinable fair values that are not consolidated or accounted for under the equity method.

127. FASB Statement 60 is amended as follows:

a. Paragraph 45 is replaced by the following:

All investments in debt securities and investments in equity securities that have readily determinable fair values, as defined by FASB Statement No. 115, *Accounting for Certain Investments in Debt and Equity Securities,* shall be accounted for in accordance with the provisions of that Statement.

b. Paragraph 46 is replaced by the following:

Investments in equity securities that are not addressed by Statement 115 because they do not meet the criteria in paragraph 3 of that Statement shall be reported at fair value, and changes in fair value shall be recognized as unrealized gains and losses and reported, net of applicable income taxes, in a separate component of equity.

c. The last two sentences of paragraph 50 and footnote 7 to that paragraph are deleted.

d. The first sentence of paragraph 51 is replaced by the following:

If a decline in the fair value of an equity security that is not addressed by Statement 115 because it does not meet the criteria in paragraph 3 of that Statement is considered to be other than temporary, the investment shall be reduced to its net realizable value, which becomes its new cost basis.

128. Statement 65 is amended as follows:

a. In paragraph 4, *and mortgage-backed securities* is deleted and the following is added at the end of the paragraph:

Mortgage-backed securities held for sale in conjunction with mortgage banking activities shall be classified as trading securities and reported at fair value in accordance with the provisions of FASB Statement No. 115, *Accounting for Certain Investments in Debt and Equity Securities.*

b. In paragraph 5, *and mortgage-backed securities* is deleted.

c. In the first sentence of paragraph 6, *or mortgage-backed security* is deleted. In the last sentence of paragraph 6, *or mortgage-backed security* and *or security* are deleted. The following is added to paragraph 6 immediately after the first sentence:

The securitization of a mortgage loan held for sale shall be accounted for as the sale of the mortgage loan and the purchase of a mortgage-backed security classified as a trading security at fair value.

d. In paragraph 7, all references to *or mortgage-backed security* and *or security* are deleted.

e. In the last sentence of paragraph 8, *as being held for sale* is replaced by *as being either mortgage loans held for sale or mortgage-backed securities classified as trading securities under Statement 115.*

f. In the first sentence of paragraph 9(a), *and mortgage-backed securities* is deleted. The following is added to the end of paragraph 9(a):

If the fair value of a mortgage-backed security subject to an investor purchase commitment exceeds the commitment price, the implicit loss on the commitment shall be recognized.

g. In each sentence of paragraph 9(c), the first usage of *market value* is replaced by *fair value.*

h. In paragraph 12, all references to *or mortgage-backed securities* and *or securities* are deleted.

i. The following is added to the penultimate sentence in paragraph 17 after *investor*:

(or fair value of the mortgage loan at the time it is securitized)

j. In paragraphs 28 and 29, *and mortgage-backed securities* is deleted.

129. In the last sentence of paragraph 5 of FASB Statement No. 80, *Accounting for Futures Contracts,* the phrase *until it is amortized or* is added after *equity.*

130. Statement 91 is amended as follows:

a. In paragraph 3, *if the changes in market value are included in earnings* is added at the end of the last sentence.

b. In paragraph 27(a), which amends paragraph 6 of Statement 65, *or security* is deleted.

131. In paragraph 28 of FASB Statement No. 97, *Accounting and Reporting by Insurance Enterprises for Certain Long-Duration Contracts and for Realized Gains and Losses from the Sale of Investments,* the phrase *investments that are classified as trading securities and* is added after *except* in the parenthetical expression of the amendment of Statement 60 in the fourth sentence of that paragraph.

132. FASB Statement No. 102, *Statement of Cash Flows—Exemption of Certain Enterprises and Classification of Cash Flows from Certain Securities Acquired for Resale,* is amended as follows:

a. The following sentence is added to the end of paragraph 8:

Cash flows from purchases, sales, and maturities of available-for-sale securities shall be classified as cash flows from investing activities and reported gross in the statement of cash flows.

b. In footnote 4 to paragraph 9, *and mortgage-backed securities* is deleted.

133. In paragraph 36(b) of Statement 109, *changes in the carrying amount of marketable securities under FASB Statement No. 12, Accounting for Certain Marketable Securities* is replaced by *changes in the unrealized holding gains and losses of securities classified as available-for-sale under FASB Statement No. 115, Accounting for Certain Investments in Debt and Equity Securities.*

134. In paragraphs 4 and 5 of FASB Interpretation No. 40, *Applicability of Generally Accepted Accounting Principles to Mutual Life Insurance and Other Enterprises,* the references to Statement 12 are deleted.

135. FASB Technical Bulletin No. 79-19, *Investor's Accounting for Unrealized Losses on Marketable Securities Owned by an Equity Method Investee,* is amended as follows:

a. In paragraph 1, *accumulated changes in the valuation allowance for marketable equity securities* is replaced by *unrealized holding gains or losses on investments in debt and equity securities.*

b. Paragraph 6 is replaced by the following:

If a subsidiary or other investee that is accounted for by the equity method is required to include unrealized holding gains and losses on investments in debt and equity securities in the stockholders' equity section of the balance sheet pursuant to the provisions of Statement 115, the parent or investor shall adjust its investment in that investee by its proportionate share of the unrealized gains and losses and a like amount shall be included in the stockholders' equity section of its balance sheet.

136. In paragraph 3 of FASB Technical Bulletin No. 85-1, *Accounting for the Receipt of Federal Home Loan Mortgage Corporation Participating Preferred Stock,* the phrase *a marketable equity security that subsequently should be reported in accordance with Statement 12 (at the lower of cost or market)* is replaced by *an equity security that subsequently should be reported at fair value in accordance with FASB Statement No. 115, Accounting for Certain Investments in Debt and Equity Securities.*

Appendix C

GLOSSARY

137. This appendix contains definitions of terms or phrases as used in this Statement.

Debt security
Any security representing a creditor relationship with an enterprise. It also includes (a) preferred stock that by its terms either must be redeemed by the issuing enterprise or is redeemable at the option of the investor and (b) a collateralized mortgage obligation (CMO) (or other instrument) that is issued in equity form but is required to be accounted for as a nonequity instrument regardless of how that instrument is classified (that is, whether equity or debt) in the issuer's statement of financial position. However, it excludes option contracts, financial futures contracts, forward contracts, and lease contracts.

• Thus, the term *debt security* includes, among other items, U.S. Treasury securities, U.S. government agency securities, municipal securities, corporate bonds, convertible debt, commercial paper, all securitized debt instruments, such as CMOs and real estate mortgage investment conduits (REMICs), and interest-only and principal-only strips.
• Trade accounts receivable arising from sales on credit by industrial or commercial enterprises and loans receivable arising from consumer,

commercial, and real estate lending activities of financial institutions are examples of receivables that do not meet the definition of *security;* thus, those receivables are not debt securities (unless they have been securitized, in which case they would meet the definition).

Equity security

Any security representing an ownership interest in an enterprise (for example, common, preferred, or other capital stock) or the right to acquire (for example, warrants, rights, and call options) or dispose of (for example, put options) an ownership interest in an enterprise at fixed or determinable prices. However, the term does not include convertible debt or preferred stock that by its terms either must be redeemed by the issuing enterprise or is redeemable at the option of the investor.

Fair value

The amount at which a financial instrument could be exchanged in a current transaction between willing parties, other than in a forced or liquidation sale. If a quoted market price is available for an instrument, the fair value to be used in applying this Statement is the product of the number of trading units of the instrument times its market price.

Holding gain or loss

The net change in fair value of a security exclusive of dividend or interest income recognized but not yet received and exclusive of any write-downs for other-than-temporary impairment.

Security

A share, participation, or other interest in property or in an enterprise of the issuer or an obligation of the issuer that (a) either is represented by an instrument issued in bearer or registered form or, if not represented by an instrument, is registered in books maintained to record transfers by or on behalf of the issuer, (b) is of a type commonly dealt in on securities exchanges or markets or, when represented by an instrument, is commonly recognized in any area in which it is issued or dealt in as a medium for investment, and (c) either is one of a class or series or by its terms is divisible into a class or series of shares, participations, interests, or obligations.

Statement of Financial Accounting Standards No. 116
Accounting for Contributions Received and
Contributions Made

STATUS

Issued: June 1993

Effective Date: For fiscal years beginning after December 15, 1994

Affects: No other pronouncements

Affected by: No other pronouncements

Other Interpretive Pronouncement: FIN 42 (Superseded by FAS 136)

Other Interpretive Release: FASB *Highlights*, "Time for a Change—Implementing FASB Statements 116 and 117," January 1995

SUMMARY

This Statement establishes accounting standards for contributions and applies to all entities that receive or make contributions. Generally, contributions received, including unconditional promises to give, are recognized as revenues in the period received at their fair values. Contributions made, including unconditional promises to give, are recognized as expenses in the period made at their fair values. Conditional promises to give, whether received or made, are recognized when they become unconditional, that is, when the conditions are substantially met.

This Statement requires not-for-profit organizations to distinguish between contributions received that increase permanently restricted net assets, temporarily restricted net assets, and unrestricted net assets. It also requires recognition of the expiration of donor-imposed restrictions in the period in which the restrictions expire.

This Statement allows certain exceptions for contributions of services and works of art, historical treasures, and similar assets. Contributions of services are recognized only if the services received (a) create or enhance nonfinancial assets or (b) require specialized skills, are provided by individuals possessing those skills, and would typically need to be purchased if not provided by donation. Contributions of works of art, historical treasures, and similar assets need not be recognized as revenues and capitalized if the donated items are added to collections held for public exhibition, education, or research in furtherance of public service rather than financial gain.

This Statement requires certain disclosures for collection items not capitalized and for receipts of contributed services and promises to give.

This Statement is effective for financial statements issued for fiscal years beginning after December 15, 1994, except for not-for-profit organizations with less than $5 million in total assets and less than $1 million in annual expenses. For those organizations, the Statement is effective for fiscal years beginning after December 15, 1995. Earlier application is encouraged. This Statement may be applied either retroactively or by recognizing the cumulative effect of the change in the year of the change. The provisions for recognition of expirations of restrictions may be applied prospectively.

Statement of Financial Accounting Standards No. 116

Accounting for Contributions Received and Contributions Made

CONTENTS

INTRODUCTION

1. This Statement establishes standards of financial accounting and reporting for **contributions**[1] received and contributions made. Accounting for contributions is an issue primarily for **not-for-profit organizations** because contributions are a significant source of revenues for many of those organizations. However, this Statement applies to all entities (not-for-profit organizations and business enterprises) that receive or make contributions. This Statement also establishes standards for recognizing expirations of restrictions on contributions received and for accounting for **collections** of works of art, historical treasures, and similar assets acquired by contribution or by other means.

2. Guidance for accounting for contributions received by not-for-profit organizations is currently provided primarily by the AICPA Guides and Statement of Position (SOP) listed in Appendix A. This Statement is part of a broader FASB agenda project that considers several inconsistencies in that guidance. Because this Statement establishes standards for accounting for contributions, provisions in the Guides and SOP that are inconsistent with this Statement are no longer acceptable *specialized*[2] accounting and reporting principles and practices. This Statement's consideration of the classification of receipts of donor-restricted contributions and the recognition and display of expirations of donor restrictions is within the general framework for financial reporting

---

[1]Words that appear in the glossary are set in **boldface type** the first time they appear.

[2]The term *specialized* is used to refer to those current accounting and reporting principles and practices in the existing AICPA Guides and SOPs that are neither superseded by nor contained in the Accounting Research Bulletins, APB Opinions, FASB Statements, and FASB Interpretations.

as set forth in FASB Statement No. 117, *Financial Statements of Not-for-Profit Organizations.*

STANDARDS OF FINANCIAL ACCOUNTING AND REPORTING

Scope

3. This Statement applies to contributions[3] of cash and other assets, including **promises to give**. It does not apply to transfers of assets that are in substance purchases of goods or services—exchange transactions in which each party receives and sacrifices commensurate value. However, if an entity voluntarily transfers assets to another or performs services for another in exchange for assets of substantially lower value and no unstated rights or privileges are involved, the contribution inherent in that transaction is within the scope of this Statement.

4. This Statement does not apply to transfers of assets in which the reporting entity acts as an agent, trustee, or intermediary, rather than as a donor or donee. It also does not apply to tax exemptions, tax incentives, or tax abatements, or to transfers of assets from governmental units to business enterprises.

Definitions

5. A contribution is an unconditional transfer of cash or other assets to an entity or a settlement or cancellation of its liabilities in a voluntary **nonreciprocal transfer** by another entity acting other than as an owner. Other assets include securities, land, buildings, use of facilities or utilities, materials and supplies, intangible assets, services, and **unconditional promises to give** those items in the future.

6. A promise to give is a written or oral agreement to contribute cash or other assets to another entity; however, to be recognized in financial statements there must be sufficient evidence in the form of verifiable documentation that a promise was made and received. A communication that does not indicate clearly whether it is a promise is considered an unconditional promise to give if it indicates an unconditional intention to give that is legally enforceable.

7. A **donor-imposed condition** on a transfer of assets or a promise to give specifies a future and uncer-

tain event whose occurrence or failure to occur gives the promisor a right of return of the assets transferred or releases the promisor from its obligation to transfer assets promised. In contrast, a **donor-imposed restriction** limits the use of contributed assets; it specifies a use that is more specific than broad limits resulting from the nature of the organization, the environment in which it operates, and the purposes specified in its articles of incorporation or bylaws or comparable documents for an unincorporated association.

Contributions Received

8. Except as provided in paragraphs 9 and 11, contributions received shall be recognized as revenues or gains in the period received and as assets, decreases of liabilities, or expenses depending on the form of the benefits received. Contributions received shall be measured at their fair values. Contributions received by not-for-profit organizations shall be reported as **restricted support** or **unrestricted support** as provided in paragraphs 14-16.

Contributed Services

9. Contributions of services shall be recognized if the services received (a) create or enhance nonfinancial assets or (b) require specialized skills, are provided by individuals possessing those skills, and would typically need to be purchased if not provided by donation. Services requiring specialized skills are provided by accountants, architects, carpenters, doctors, electricians, lawyers, nurses, plumbers, teachers, and other professionals and craftsmen. Contributed services and promises to give services that do not meet the above criteria shall not be recognized.

10. An entity that receives contributed services shall describe the programs or activities for which those services were used, including the nature and extent of contributed services received for the period and the amount recognized as revenues for the period. Entities are encouraged to disclose the fair value of contributed services received but not recognized as revenues if that is practicable.

Contributed Collection Items

11. An entity need not recognize contributions of works of art, historical treasures, and similar assets if

---

[3]This Statement also uses terms such as *gift* and *donation* to refer to a contribution; however, it generally avoids terms such as *awards, grants, sponsorships,* and *appropriations* that often are more broadly used to refer not only to contributions but also to assets transferred in exchange transactions in which the *grantor, sponsor,* or *appropriator* expects to receive commensurate value.

the donated items are added to collections that meet all of the following conditions:

a. Are held for public exhibition, education, or research in furtherance of public service rather than financial gain
b. Are protected, kept unencumbered, cared for, and preserved
c. Are subject to an organizational policy that requires the proceeds from sales of collection items to be used to acquire other items for collections.

12. For purposes of initial application of this Statement, entities are encouraged either to capitalize retroactively collections acquired in previous periods[4] or to capitalize collections on a prospective basis. Capitalization of selected collections or items is precluded.

13. Contributed collection items shall be recognized as revenues or gains if collections are capitalized and shall not be recognized as revenues or gains if collections are not capitalized. An entity that does not recognize and capitalize its collections or that capitalizes collections prospectively shall disclose the additional information required by paragraphs 26 and 27.

Reporting by Not-for-Profit Organizations

14. A not-for-profit organization shall distinguish between contributions received with **permanent restrictions**, those received with **temporary restrictions**, and those received without donor-imposed restrictions. A restriction on an organization's use of the assets contributed results either from a donor's explicit stipulation or from circumstances surrounding the receipt of the contribution that make clear the donor's implicit restriction on use. Contributions with donor-imposed restrictions shall be reported as restricted support; however, donor-restricted contributions whose restrictions are met in the same reporting period may be reported as unrestricted support provided that an organization reports consistently from period to period and discloses its accounting policy. Restricted support increases **permanently restricted net assets** or **temporarily restricted net assets**.

Contributions without donor-imposed restrictions shall be reported as unrestricted support that increases **unrestricted net assets**.

15. Receipts of unconditional promises to give with payments due in future periods shall be reported as restricted support unless explicit donor stipulations or circumstances surrounding the receipt of a promise make clear that the donor intended it to be used to support activities of the current period. For example, receipts of unconditional promises to give cash in future years generally increase temporarily restricted net assets.

16. Gifts of long-lived assets received without stipulations about how long the donated asset must be used shall be reported as restricted support if it is an organization's accounting policy to imply a time restriction that expires over the useful life of the donated assets. Organizations that adopt a policy of implying time restrictions also shall imply a time restriction on long-lived assets acquired with gifts of cash or other assets restricted for those acquisitions. In the absence of that policy and other donor-imposed restrictions on use of the asset, gifts of long-lived assets shall be reported as unrestricted support. An organization shall disclose its accounting policy.

Expiration of Donor-imposed Restrictions

17. A not-for-profit organization shall recognize the expiration of a donor-imposed restriction on a contribution in the period in which the restriction expires. A restriction expires when the stipulated time has elapsed, when the stipulated purpose for which the resource was restricted has been fulfilled, or both.[5] If an expense is incurred for a purpose for which both unrestricted and temporarily restricted net assets are available, a donor-imposed restriction is fulfilled to the extent of the expense incurred unless the expense is for a purpose that is directly attributable to another specific external source of revenue. For example, an expense does not fulfill an existing donor restriction if that expense is incurred for a purpose that is directly attributable to and reimbursed by a sponsored exchange agreement or a conditional

---

[4]Collections of works of art, historical treasures, and similar assets acquired in previous periods but not capitalized as assets may be retroactively capitalized at their cost or fair value at date of acquisition, current cost, or current market value, whichever is deemed most practical.

[5]If two or more temporary restrictions are imposed on a contribution, the effect of the expiration of those restrictions is recognized in the period in which the last remaining restriction has expired. Temporarily restricted net assets with time restrictions are not available to support expenses until the time restrictions have expired. Time restrictions implied on gifts of long-lived assets expire as the economic benefits of the acquired assets are used up; that is, over their estimated useful lives. In the absence of donor stipulations specifying how long donated assets must be used or an organization's policy of implying time restrictions, restrictions on long-lived assets, if any, or cash to acquire long-lived assets expire when the assets are placed in service.

award from a government agency, private foundation, or others. Pursuant to paragraph 19 of Statement 117, expirations of donor-imposed restrictions that simultaneously increase one class of net assets and decrease another (reclassifications) are reported separately from other transactions.

Contributions Made

18. Contributions made shall be recognized as expenses in the period made and as decreases of assets or increases of liabilities depending on the form of the benefits given. For example, gifts of items from inventory held for sale are recognized as decreases of inventory[6] and contribution expenses, and unconditional promises to give cash are recognized as payables and contribution expenses. Contributions made shall be measured at the fair values of the assets given or, if made in the form of a settlement or cancellation of a donee's liabilities, at the fair value of the liabilities canceled.

Measurement at Fair Value

19. Quoted market prices, if available, are the best evidence of the fair value of monetary and nonmonetary assets, including services. If quoted market prices are not available, fair value may be estimated based on quoted market prices for similar assets, independent appraisals, or valuation techniques, such as the present value of estimated future cash flows. Contributions of services that create or enhance nonfinancial assets may be measured by referring to either the fair value of the services received or the fair value of the asset or of the asset enhancement resulting from the services. A major uncertainty about the existence of value may indicate that an item received or given should not be recognized.[7]

20. The present value of estimated future cash flows using a discount rate commensurate with the risks involved is an appropriate measure of fair value of unconditional promises to give cash.[8] Subsequent accruals of the interest element shall be accounted for

as contribution income by donees and contribution expense by donors. Not-for-profit organizations shall report the contribution income as an increase in either temporarily or permanently restricted net assets if the underlying promise to give is donor restricted.

21. Unconditional promises to give that are expected to be collected or paid in less than one year may be measured at net realizable value (net settlement value) because that amount, although not equivalent to the present value of estimated future cash flows, results in a reasonable estimate of fair value.

Conditional Promises to Give

22. **Conditional promises to give**, which depend on the occurrence of a specified future and uncertain event to bind the promisor, shall be recognized when the conditions on which they depend are substantially met, that is, when the conditional promise becomes unconditional. A conditional promise to give is considered unconditional if the possibility that the condition will not be met is remote. For example, a stipulation that an annual report must be provided by the donee to receive subsequent annual payments on a multiyear promise is not a condition if the possibility of not meeting that administrative requirement is remote. A transfer of assets with a conditional promise to contribute them shall be accounted for as a refundable advance until the conditions have been substantially met.

23. Determining whether a promise is conditional or unconditional can be difficult if it contains donor stipulations that do not clearly state whether the right to receive payment or delivery of the promised assets depends on meeting those stipulations. It may be difficult to determine whether those stipulations are conditions or restrictions. In cases of ambiguous donor stipulations, a promise containing stipulations that are not clearly unconditional shall be presumed to be a conditional promise.

---

[6]If the fair value of an asset transferred differs from its carrying amount, a gain or loss should be recognized on the disposition of the asset (APB Opinion No. 29, *Accounting for Nonmonetary Transactions*, paragraph 18).

[7]Contributed tangible property worth accepting generally possesses the common characteristic of all assets—future economic benefit or service potential. The future economic benefit or service potential of a tangible item usually can be obtained by exchanging it for cash or by using it to produce goods or services. However, if an item is accepted solely to be saved for its potential future use in scientific or educational research and has no alternative use, it may have uncertain value, or perhaps no value, and should not be recognized.

[8]An entity may estimate the future cash flows of a portfolio of short-term promises resulting from a mass fund-raising appeal by using experience it gained from similar appeals.

Disclosures of Promises to Give

24. Recipients of unconditional promises to give shall disclose the following:

a. The amounts of promises receivable in less than one year, in one to five years, and in more than five years
b. The amount of the allowance for uncollectible promises receivable.

25. Recipients of conditional promises to give shall disclose the following:

a. The total of the amounts promised
b. A description and amount for each group of promises having similar characteristics, such as amounts of promises conditioned on establishing new programs, completing a new building, and raising matching gifts by a specified date.

Financial Statement Presentation and Disclosure for Collections

26. An entity that does not recognize and capitalize its collections shall report the following on the face of its statement of activities, separately from revenues, expenses, gains, and losses:

a. Costs of collection items purchased as a decrease in the appropriate class of net assets
b. Proceeds from sale of collection items as an increase in the appropriate class of net assets
c. Proceeds from insurance recoveries of lost or destroyed collection items as an increase in the appropriate class of net assets.

Similarly, an entity that capitalizes its collections prospectively shall report proceeds from sales and insurance recoveries of items not previously capitalized separately from revenues, expenses, gains, and losses.

27. An entity that does not recognize and capitalize its collections or that capitalizes collections prospectively shall describe its collections, including their relative significance, and its accounting and stewardship policies for collections. If collection items not capitalized are deaccessed during the period, it also shall (a) describe the items given away, damaged, destroyed, lost, or otherwise deaccessed during the pe-

riod or (b) disclose their fair value. In addition, a line item shall be shown on the face of the statement of financial position that refers to the disclosures required by this paragraph. That line item shall be dated if collections are capitalized prospectively, for example, "Collections acquired since January 1, 1995 (Note X)."

Effective Date and Transition

28. This Statement shall be effective for financial statements issued for fiscal years beginning after December 15, 1994 and interim periods within those fiscal years, except for not-for-profit organizations with less than $5 million in total assets and less than $1 million in annual expenses. For those organizations, the effective date shall be for fiscal years beginning after December 15, 1995. Earlier application is encouraged.

29. Unless this Statement is applied retroactively under the provisions of paragraph 30, the effect of initially applying this Statement shall be reported as the effect of a change in accounting principle in a manner similar to the cumulative effect of a change in accounting principle (APB Opinion No. 20, *Accounting Changes,* paragraph 19). The amount of the cumulative effect shall be based on a retroactive computation, except that the provisions of paragraph 17 for recognition of expirations of restrictions may be applied prospectively. A not-for-profit organization shall report the cumulative effect of a change in accounting on each class of net assets in the statement of activities between the captions "extraordinary items," if any, and "change in unrestricted net assets," "change in temporarily restricted net assets," and "change in permanently restricted net assets." A business enterprise shall report the amount of the cumulative effect in the income statement between the captions "extraordinary items" and "net income" (Opinion 20, paragraph 20).

30. This Statement may be applied retroactively by restating opening net assets for the earliest year presented or for the year this Statement is first applied if no prior years are presented. The provisions of paragraph 17 for recognition of expirations of restrictions may be applied prospectively. In the period that this Statement is first applied, a not-for-profit organization shall disclose the nature of any restatement and its effect on the change in net assets

for each period presented. A business enterprise shall account for any restatement as a change in account- ing principle applied retroactively (Opinion 20, paragraphs 27 and 28).

> **The provisions of this Statement need not be applied to immaterial items.**

This Statement was adopted by the affirmative votes of six members of the Financial Accounting Standards Board. Mr. Beresford dissented.

Mr. Beresford dissents from the issuance of this Statement because it requires recipients of unconditional promises to give to recognize assets and revenues in the period the promise is received. In particular, he questions whether the recognition of revenues for restricted gifts, especially for promises collectible in the distant future, results in more meaningful financial reporting. Further, Mr. Beresford believes there is too much subjectivity involved in distinguishing between promises to give and other communications of intentions to give. He suggests that, until these matters are satisfactorily resolved, improving disclosures about promises and precluding their recognition would be a better step.

Mr. Beresford is troubled by the potential for misunderstanding of financial information resulting from the requirement. Currently, most organizations that recognize promises to give also recognize deferred revenue. Organizations, particularly those that rely heavily on annual pledge drives, will report large increases in net assets if promises are recorded. He is concerned that the amounts will be regarded as surplus resources or otherwise misinterpreted by financial statement users.

It is not clear to Mr. Beresford that the distinction between a promise to give and a communication of intention to give is an appropriate basis for distinguishing an asset from a "nonasset." Both are communications that a donor will provide cash in the future for the support of the organization. The only difference may be in the percentage of the communications that ultimately results in future cash receipts, and this difference may be slight in many cases.

Mr. Beresford believes that it will be difficult to differentiate between promises and intentions in many cases. He is troubled that the subjectivity involved in making the distinction will result in an unacceptable level of inconsistency and that the motivations of some preparers of financial statements will increase that level of inconsistency. That inconsistency, when combined with the requirement to recognize revenues for unconditional promises to give, would make it difficult, if not impossible, for donors and other users of financial statements to compare different organizations' statements of activities and make informed resource allocation decisions. Therefore, Mr. Beresford would preclude recognition of promises to give to enhance comparability. He believes a period of experience with improved disclosures would allow time to resolve implementation concerns and to gain experience in using the information.

Members of the Financial Accounting Standards Board:

Dennis R. Beresford, *Chairman*	Victor H. Brown	A. Clarence Sampson
Joseph V. Anania	James J. Leisenring	Robert J. Swieringa
	Robert H. Northcutt	

Appendix A

BACKGROUND INFORMATION

31. In March 1986, the Board added a project to its agenda to establish standards needed to resolve certain inconsistent accounting and reporting practices of not-for-profit organizations. The project has three parts: accounting for contributions, display of infor- mation in financial statements, and accounting for depreciation. The Board completed the part on depreciation in 1987 when it issued FASB Statement No. 93, *Recognition of Depreciation by Not-for-Profit Organizations.*

32. In October 1990, the Board issued an Exposure Draft of a proposed Statement, *Accounting for Contributions Received and Contributions Made and Capitalization of Works of Art, Historical Treasures,*

and Similar Assets. Many respondents to that Exposure Draft suggested that because the parts on accounting for contributions and on financial statement display are interrelated, it would be more productive if they were combined or more closely coordinated. The Board agreed and coordinated this Statement with Statement No. 117, *Financial Statements of Not-for-Profit Organizations.*

33. Accounting for contributions is described in the following AICPA documents:

a. *Audits of Colleges and Universities,* 1973
b. *Audits of Voluntary Health and Welfare Organizations,* 1974
c. SOP 78-10, *Accounting Principles and Reporting Practices for Certain Nonprofit Organizations,* 1978
d. *Audits of Providers of Health Care Services,* 1990.

The requirements for accounting for contributions in those documents are similar in some respects. In other respects they differ from each other and from generally accepted accounting principles applicable to other entities.

34. For example, guidance for recognizing restricted contributions is inconsistent. The colleges and universities Guide and the health care services Guide suggest accounting for those contributions as direct additions to restricted fund balances (net assets). Both Guides suggest that temporarily restricted contributions be recognized as "revenues" when the restrictions are met. The health and welfare Guide suggests accounting for purpose-restricted contributions as revenues of a restricted fund and time-restricted contributions as deferred revenues. SOP 78-10 suggests accounting for current restricted contributions as liabilities until the restrictions on the gifts are met.

35. Guidance for recognizing certain other contributions also has been inconsistent. For example, page 14 of the health and welfare Guide says, "In the absence of clear evidence as to a specified program period, donations and pledges should be recorded as support when received." However, paragraph 65 of SOP 78-10 says, "In the absence of a specified support period, . . . [legally enforceable] pledges scheduled to be received over a future period should be assumed to be support for that period and should be accounted for as deferred support in the balance sheet." Paragraph 7.18 of the health care services Guide provides similar guidance for unrestricted

pledges. The colleges and universities Guide differs significantly, since it permits but does not require recognition of a pledge as an asset or as revenue.

36. Criteria for recognition of contributed services also differ among the Guides. The health and welfare Guide requires recognition of revenue and expense under certain specified conditions and does not preclude recognition of other services received. The health care services Guide provides similar guidance. In contrast, SOP 78-10 precludes recognition of services other than those meeting conditions similar to the other Guides. The colleges and universities Guide does not provide criteria for recognition of contributed services.

37. Although generally accepted accounting principles require recognition of contributions of tangible assets at their fair value at date of receipt, SOP 78-10 permits an exception. Paragraph 114 of SOP 78-10 says the ". . . contributed value of current-period accessions . . . should be disclosed in the financial statements." SOP 78-10 has been interpreted as allowing disclosure as an alternative to recognition of revenues in financial statements of museums, art galleries, botanical gardens, libraries, and similar entities that receive contributions of property for their "inexhaustible collections."

38. Further, the specialized industry guidance of SOP 78-10, paragraph 113, encourages but does not require capitalization of "inexhaustible collections owned by museums, art galleries, botanical gardens, libraries, and similar entities." The Board added this issue to the scope of this Statement as a result of responses to the Exposure Draft that led to Statement 93. In paragraph 39 of Statement 93, the Board indicated that the Statement on recognition of depreciation need not cover recognition of assets but that the Board would consider recognition of "collections," both contributed and purchased, as part of its project on accounting for contributions. Accordingly, in addition to addressing recognition of contributions, this Statement considers accounting for works of art, historical treasures, and similar assets whether acquired by contribution or by other means.

39. The Board discussed how to resolve the inconsistencies in accounting for contributions at public Board meetings and public meetings of the FASB Task Force on Accounting Issues for Not-for-Profit Organizations. In October 1990, the Board issued its first Exposure Draft on contributions. More than 1,000 organizations and individuals provided written

comments. Forty respondents presented their views at a public hearing in July 1991, and most agreed that there is a need to establish consistent standards for accounting for contributions.

40. The Board reconsidered the proposals in that Exposure Draft at public meetings of the Board and of the task force. The major changes resulting from the Board's redeliberations were:

a. Works of art, historical treasures, and similar items need not be capitalized if they are added to collections that are held for public exhibition, education, or research in furtherance of public service rather than financial gain. Disclosures about collections that are not capitalized are required.
b. Criteria for recognition of contributed services were made more restrictive, and recognition of contributed services that do not meet the revised criteria is precluded rather than encouraged.
c. Provisions for recognizing expirations of donor-imposed restrictions may be applied prospectively
d. Disclosures about receipts of promises to give are required.

41. In November 1992, the Board issued a revised Exposure Draft, *Accounting for Contributions Received and Contributions Made,* which incorporated the above changes and certain other revisions. The Board received more than 280 comment letters on that revised Exposure Draft. In October 1992, the Board also issued a related Exposure Draft, *Financial Statements of Not-for-Profit Organizations.* Twenty-four organizations and individuals presented their views at a 2-day public hearing held in February 1993. That hearing was held to obtain additional information from participants about the proposals for financial statements of not-for-profit organizations; however, participants also were encouraged to comment on the revised proposals for contributions. Most participants commented on provisions in both Exposure Drafts.

42. Twenty organizations also participated in a field test of the proposed Statements on financial statements and on accounting for contributions. Those organizations shared their recasted financial statements with 39 users of financial statements who also participated in the field test. The field test results, the details of which are confidential at the request of some participants, and the written comments and public hearing testimony of respondents to both proposed Statements were considered by the Board during its deliberations of the issues addressed by this Statement. The major issues and concerns raised by respondents and field test participants and the basis for the Board's conclusions on those issues and concerns are discussed in Appendix B.

Appendix B

BASIS FOR CONCLUSIONS

CONTENTS

Appendix B

BASIS FOR CONCLUSIONS

Introduction

43. This appendix summarizes considerations that Board members deemed significant in reaching the conclusions in this Statement. It includes reasons for accepting certain views and rejecting others. Individual Board members gave greater weight to some factors than to others.

Objectives

44. To accomplish its mission, the FASB strives to improve the usefulness of financial reporting by fo-

cusing on the primary characteristics of relevance and reliability and on the qualities of comparability and consistency. The usefulness of information about an entity increases if that information can be compared with similar information about other entities or about the same entity in other periods. To the extent that similar contributions are subject to the same requirements for recognition and disclosure, financial reporting will be improved. In return for some sacrifice of freedom of choice, adherence to externally imposed standards brings a gain from greater comparability and consistency and also a gain in credibility (FASB Concepts Statement No. 2, *Qualitative Characteristics of Accounting Information,* paragraph 16).

Benefits and Costs

45. A major benefit of this Statement is the increased comparability, consistency, and credibility of financial reporting that will result from eliminating some of the inconsistencies in current guidance (Appendix A). The Board believes that financial reporting of not-for-profit organizations will significantly improve by consistently recognizing (a) restricted contributions as revenues, (b) unconditional promises to give as assets and revenues or as liabilities and expenses, and (c) certain contributed services. Increased disclosure of information about receipts of contributed services and conditional promises to give and about collections also will improve financial reporting.

46. The Board believes that consistent standards for recognizing contributions are needed. However, the value of the incremental improvement to financial reporting is impossible to quantify. Because there is no common gauge by which to judge objectively the costs to implement a standard against the need to improve information in financial statements, the Board's assessment of the costs and benefits is unavoidably subjective. Moreover, because the costs to implement a new standard are not borne directly by those who derive the benefits of the improved reporting, the Board must balance the diverse and often conflicting needs of preparers, investors, donors, creditors, and others who use financial statements.

47. The Board believes that the incremental costs of the requirements of this Statement have been reduced in various ways: by not requiring contributions of works of art, historical treasures, and similar items to be capitalized if they are held in collections as defined; by restricting the criteria for recognition of contributed services; by allowing prospective appli-

cation of provisions for expirations of restrictions; by extending the effective date of this Statement; and by allowing an additional one-year extension for small not-for-profit organizations. Reducing some of the incremental costs of the requirements of this Statement in those ways may reduce some of the benefits and possibly increase other costs. For example, allowing alternatives to capitalization of collections may increase the costs incurred by users of financial statements as they evaluate differing information about those items. The Board concluded that the overall benefits of the information provided by applying this Statement justify the costs of complying with these standards.

Distinguishing Contributions from Other Transactions

48. The Board focused on three characteristics that help distinguish contributions from other transactions—contributions (a) are nonreciprocal transfers, (b) are transfers to or from entities acting other than as owners, and (c) are made or received voluntarily. Those characteristics distinguish contributions from exchange transactions, which are reciprocal transfers in which each party receives and sacrifices approximately equal value; from investments by owners and distributions to owners, which are nonreciprocal transfers between an entity and its owners; and from other nonreciprocal transfers, such as impositions of taxes or fines and thefts, which are not voluntary transfers.

Distinguishing Contributions from Exchange Transactions

49. Because some exchange transactions may appear to be much like contributions, a careful assessment of the characteristics of the transaction is required to determine whether the recipient of a transfer of assets has given up an asset or incurred a liability of commensurate value. The Board believes that assessing the characteristics of transactions from the perspectives of both the resource provider and the recipient is necessary to determine whether a contribution has occurred.

50. For example, a resource provider may sponsor research and development activities at a research university and retain proprietary rights or other privileges, such as patents, copyrights, or advance and exclusive knowledge of the research outcomes. The research outcomes may be intangible, uncertain, or difficult to measure, and may be perceived by the

university as a sacrifice of little or no value; however, their value often is commensurate with the value that a resource provider expects in exchange. Similarly, a resource provider may sponsor research and development activities and specify the protocol of the testing so the research outcomes are particularly valuable to the resource provider. Those transactions are not contributions if their potential public benefits are secondary to the potential proprietary benefits to the resource providers.

51. Moreover, a single transaction may be in part an exchange and in part a contribution. For example, if a donor transfers a building to an entity at a price significantly lower than its market value and no unstated rights or privileges are involved, the transaction is in part an exchange of assets and in part a contribution to be accounted for as required by this Statement.

Distinguishing Contributions from Agency and Similar Transactions

52. A transfer of assets also may appear to be a contribution when a donor uses an intermediary organization as its agent or trustee to transfer assets to a third-party donee, particularly if the agent indirectly achieves its mission by disbursing the assets. Although the transaction between the donor and the donee may be a contribution, the transfer of assets from the donor is not a contribution received by the agent, and the transfer of assets to the donee is not a contribution made by the agent.

53. The recipient of assets who is an agent or trustee has little or no discretion in determining how the assets transferred will be used. For example, if a recipient receives cash that it must disburse to *any* who meet guidelines specified by a resource provider or return the cash, those receipts may be deposits held by the recipient as an agent rather than contributions received as a donee. Similarly, if a recipient receives cash that it must disburse to individuals identified by the resource provider or return the cash, neither the receipt nor the disbursement is a contribution for the agent, trustee, or intermediary.

54. In contrast, if the resource provider allows the recipient to establish, define, and carry out the programs that disburse the cash, products, or services to the recipient's beneficiaries, the recipient generally is involved in receiving and making contributions.

Exclusion of Certain Transactions

55. Some respondents to the 1990 Exposure Draft asked whether the scope of this Statement was intended to include accounting for certain transfers that might be considered both voluntary and nonreciprocal, such as tax incentives, tax abatements, and transfers of land, buildings, or other assets by governments to entice businesses to their communities. The Board concluded that those transactions present specific complexities that may need special study and therefore excluded them from the scope of this Statement.

56. Some respondents to the 1992 Exposure Draft asked the Board to exclude all governmental transfers. Many colleges and universities, in particular, said determining whether specific grants, appropriations, loan guarantees, and similar governmental transfers are exchange transactions or are voluntary and nonreciprocal transfers—contributions—is difficult and often arbitrary. Some asserted that governmental transfers are never voluntary contributions. They suggested that all governmental transfers be reported as a separate category of revenue and be excluded from the scope of this Statement to allow their industry associations or the AICPA to provide industry-specific guidance. The Board believes that whether a grant is from a government agency, private foundation, or corporation, the difficulties in determining whether a transfer is an exchange transaction or a contribution are substantially the same. The Board acknowledges that to apply the provisions of this Statement requires a careful assessment of the characteristics of the transfers as discussed in paragraphs 48-54; however, it concluded that excluding all governmental transfers is neither necessary nor desirable because that would further delay improvements to practice.

Distinguishing Donor-imposed Restrictions from Conditions

57. This Statement distinguishes between unrestricted gifts, restricted gifts, and transfers of cash or other assets with conditions, which are similar to conditional promises to give. A donor-imposed restriction limits the use of donated assets; however, a condition creates a barrier that must be overcome before assets transferred or promised become contributions received or made. The distinction between a restriction and a condition, although clear in concept, sometimes is obscure in practice.

58. The Board concluded that a donor-imposed restriction, which limits or directs the use of donated assets, is not fundamentally different from an explicit or implied stipulation that donated assets be used to

support an organization's broad charitable, educational, religious, or similar purposes. Both are expressions or directives that the donated assets be used to support an organization's activities, and both are gifts that increase the organization's capacity to provide services. A donor's directive may be more prescriptive; for example, that donated assets be used to support a particular program service, to support the acquisition of long-lived assets, or to create a permanent endowment or term-endowment fund. That prescription, however, does not change the fundamental and underlying event—the voluntary nonreciprocal transfer of economic benefits from a donor to a donee.

59. The Board also concluded that although an unrestricted gift and a restricted gift are similar events, information about the nature and extent of donor-imposed restrictions is relevant to users of financial statements (paragraphs 145-148). A donor-imposed restriction imposes special responsibilities on the management of an organization to ensure that it uses donated assets as stipulated. The limits imposed by those restrictions may impinge upon an organization's performance and its ability to provide a satisfactory level of services.

60. The Board concluded that a transfer of cash or other assets with a stipulation that the assets be returned if a specified future and uncertain event occurs or fails to occur is fundamentally different from both an unrestricted gift and a restricted gift. Imposing a condition creates a barrier that must be overcome before the recipient of the transferred assets has an unconditional right to retain those promised assets. For example, a transfer of cash with a promise to contribute that cash if a like amount of new gifts are raised from others within 30 days and a provision that the cash be returned if the gifts are not raised imposes a condition on which a promised gift depends.

61. By imposing a condition, the transferor of assets not only retains a right of return of the transferred assets, but also casts doubt on whether the intent of the transfer was to make a gift, to conditionally promise a gift, or, at the extreme, not to make a gift. Because donors impose very different kinds of conditions, the likelihood of meeting a condition can range from probable to remote. The Board concluded that if a transferor imposes a condition, a reasonable possibility exists that the condition will not occur and the transferred assets will be returned and, thus, should be accounted for as a refundable advance.

62. Some respondents to the 1992 Exposure Draft, particularly foundations, said this Statement should make clear whether imposing administrative requirements, such as requiring routine annual reporting as a "condition" of a multiyear grant, would preclude recognition of an otherwise unconditional promise to give. Some also expressed concern that donors and donees may avoid recognition of unconditional promises to give by adding *trivial* conditions or requesting that they be added. Paragraph 22 clarifies that a promise to give is considered unconditional if the possibility that the condition will not be met is remote. Conditions on transfers of assets as described in this Statement are similar to those described in federal income tax laws and regulations. Title 26 of the Code of Federal Regulations says that if "a transfer for charitable purposes is dependent upon the performance of some act or the happening of a precedent event in order that it might become effective, no deduction is allowable unless the possibility that the charitable transfer will not become effective is so remote as to be negligible" (26 CFR Sec.1.170A-1(e)).

63. Private foundations, governmental agencies, and some business enterprises transfer cash or other assets with both donor-imposed restrictions and stipulations that impose a condition on which a gift depends. Certain not-for-profit organizations use fund accounting and reporting methods that emphasize accountability for all funds received but may not distinguish between transfers of cash received with donor-imposed restrictions and those with conditions. This Statement, however, makes that distinction and provides that when a restriction and a condition exist, the transfer be accounted for as a refundable advance until the condition on which it depends is substantially met.

64. Some respondents to the 1990 and 1992 Exposure Drafts said that the distinction between a donor-imposed restriction and a condition is not significant. Many of those respondents said because donated assets received with a restriction would be returned if a restriction was not met, those transfers also should be accounted for as refundable advances (liabilities) until the restrictions are met. Others said that transfers of assets with restrictions are similar to advance payments for services to be rendered and should be accounted for as "deferred revenues" (liabilities). A few respondents that would not distinguish between restrictions and conditions said that transfers of assets with donor-imposed restrictions or conditions should be accounted for as refundable advances but that both should be recognized as contributions received when it becomes *probable* that the restrictions or conditions will be met.

65. Failures to comply with donors' restrictions, although rare, do occur, sometimes as a result of events occurring subsequent to receiving a contribution. The Board continues to believe that a presumption that an organization will use donated assets in accordance with the limitations specified is inherent in the acceptance of a contribution. Donors and donees both expect donors' directives will be carried out.

66. The Board concluded that to require ongoing assessments of the probability of meeting a restriction in order to determine when to recognize a restricted gift is neither necessary nor practical. FASB Statement No. 5, *Accounting for Contingencies,* applies if a subsequent event raises the possibility that an organization may not satisfy a restriction. Paragraph 8 of Statement 5 requires that an estimated loss be recognized if information available prior to issuance of the financial statements indicates that it is probable an asset had been impaired or a liability had been incurred at the date of the financial statements and the amount of the loss can be reasonably estimated.

67. The Board believes that a gift of cash or other assets given to increase an organization's ability to carry out its charitable purposes differs significantly from an advance payment for services to be rendered in exchange. A donor's restriction may emphasize specific program services that the donor wishes to support; however, designating that donated assets be used to support services provided to an organization's beneficiaries, although viewed as "deferred revenues" by some respondents to the Exposure Drafts, is not the equivalent of an advance payment in exchange for services to be received. FASB Concepts Statement No. 6, *Elements of Financial Statements,* states that a restricted contribution involves a fiduciary responsibility, not an obligation:

The essence of a not-for-profit organization is that it obtains and uses resources to provide specific types of goods or services, and the nature of those goods or services is often critical in donors' decisions to contribute cash or other assets to a particular organization. Most donors contribute assets (restricted as well as unrestricted) to an organization to increase its capacity to provide those goods or services, and receipt of donated assets not only increases the assets of the organization but also imposes a fiduciary responsibility on its management to use those assets effectively and efficiently in pursuit of those service objectives.

That responsibility pertains to all of the organization's assets and does not constitute an equitable or constructive obligation . . . . In other words, a not-for-profit organization's fiduciary responsibility to use assets to provide services to beneficiaries does not itself create a duty of the organization to pay cash, transfer other assets, or provide services to one or more creditors. Rather, an obligation to a creditor results when the organization buys supplies for a project, its employees work on it, and the like, and the organization therefore owes suppliers, employees, and others for goods and services they have provided to it.

A donor's restriction focuses that fiduciary responsibility on a stipulated use for specified contributed assets but does not change the basic nature of the organization's fiduciary responsibility to use its assets to provide services to beneficiaries. A donor's gift . . . imposes a responsibility to spend the cash or use the asset in accordance with the donor's instructions. In its effect on the liabilities of the organization, a donor's restriction is essentially the same as management's designating a specified use for certain assets. That is, the responsibility imposed by earmarking assets for specified uses is fundamentally different, both economically and legally, from the responsibility imposed by incurring a liability, which involves a creditor's claim. [Paragraphs 56-58, footnote reference omitted.]

68. The Board concluded that the distinction between donor-imposed restrictions and conditions is relevant to users of financial statements. The Board reaffirmed its conclusion that donor-imposed restrictions place limits on the use of contributed resources, but those limits do not create liabilities. To treat all restricted contributions as liabilities merely because a few may be returned would overstate an organization's liabilities. The Board also concluded that conditions cast significant doubts that assets will be retained, and those doubts are a cause for delaying recognition of a gift (paragraphs 75-81). The Board believes that consistent application of this distinction will result in a significant improvement over the current inconsistent accounting practices for restricted gifts and transfers of assets with conditional promises to contribute them.

Ambiguous Donor Stipulations

69. The distinction between a condition and a restriction, although clear in concept, may not be clear in practice because of ambiguous donor stipulations. For example, a restricted contribution may appear to also be conditional if it contains stipulations that do not clearly state whether the right to retain assets transferred or to receive the promised assets is dependent on fulfilling the stipulation.

70. To minimize implementation problems, the Board concluded that a presumption is necessary when ambiguous donor stipulations cannot be resolved by a review of facts and circumstances surrounding the gift or communications with the donor. Paragraph 23 of this Statement provides that a promise that contains stipulations that are not clearly unconditional shall be presumed to be a conditional promise. A few respondents to the 1992 Exposure Draft requested further clarification for promises to give services. The Board believes promises to give services generally involve personal services that, if not explicitly conditional, are often implicitly conditioned upon the future and uncertain availability of specific individuals whose services have been promised. The Board also clarified that organizations may not recognize the receipt of an unconditional promise to give services of the kind that do not meet the criteria in paragraph 9.

71. Absence of a specified time for transfer of cash or other assets, by itself, does not necessarily lead to a determination that a promise to give is ambiguous. If the parties fail to express the time or place of performance and performance is unconditional, performance within a reasonable time after making a promise is an appropriate expectation; similarly, if a promise is conditional, performance within a reasonable time after fulfilling the condition is an appropriate expectation. The Board concluded that promises to give that are silent about payment terms but otherwise are clearly unconditional should be accounted for as unconditional promises to give.

Recognition, Measurement, and Disclosure of Contributions

72. Some not-for-profit organizations have disclosed information about certain noncash contributions and unconditional promises to give in notes to financial statements but have not recognized those gifts as revenues. The Board believes that nonrecognition or delayed recognition generally omits relevant information about an entity's economic resources and obligations and about its activities during a period, making financial statements unnecessarily incomplete. The Board concluded that disclosures about contributions are not a satisfactory substitute for financial statement recognition.

Criteria for Recognition

73. The Board considered when contributions should be recognized. Paragraph 63 of FASB Concepts Statement No. 5, *Recognition and Measurement in Financial Statements of Business Enterprises,* states that an item should be recognized in financial statements when four fundamental criteria are met:

> *Definitions*—The item meets the definition of an element of financial statements.
> *Measurability*—It has a relevant attribute measurable with sufficient reliability.
> *Relevance*—The information about it is capable of making a difference in user decisions.
> *Reliability*—The information is representationally faithful, verifiable, and neutral.

All four criteria are subject to a pervasive cost-benefit constraint. To be useful and worth providing, the expected benefits of information should justify the perceived costs of providing and using it.

74. Difficulty in measuring reliably and uncertainty of realization are sometimes cited as reasons for not recognizing certain contributions received. It is sometimes suggested that accounting and financial reporting should reflect "conservatism" whenever uncertainties exist. Those arguments suggest that if significant doubt exists about whether to recognize an item, financial reporting should err on the side of understating assets or overstating liabilities. However, accounting procedures that deliberately err in the direction of understatement of net assets introduce a bias into financial reporting. Deliberate bias conflicts with representational faithfulness, neutrality, and comparability. Thus, the doctrine of conservatism cannot be used to justify deferring recognition of revenues or gains beyond the time that adequate evidence of their existence becomes available, or to justify recognizing expenses or losses before adequate evidence that they have been incurred becomes available.

Effects of Conditions on Timing of Recognition

75. In certain circumstances, uncertainties may be so significant that recognition of an asset or liability must be delayed until there is adequate evidence that it exists, has value, and can be reliably measured. If an asset or liability is recognized before uncertainty is sufficiently resolved, the resulting information may be unreliable. Paragraph 76 of Concepts Statement 5 states:

> Reliability may affect the timing of recognition. The first available information about an event that may have resulted in an asset, liability, or change therein is sometimes too uncertain to be recognized: it may not yet be clear whether the effects of the event meet one or more of the definitions or whether they are measurable, and the cost of resolving those uncertainties may be excessive. Information about some items that meet a definition may never become sufficiently reliable at a justifiable cost to recognize the item. For other items, those uncertainties are reduced as time passes, and reliability is increased as additional information becomes available.

76. Uncertainty is inherent in a transfer of assets with a conditional promise to contribute those assets. Until the specified condition occurs, it is uncertain whether the transfer will become a right to retain those assets or an obligation to relinquish them. Several factors affect whether a condition will be met. They include whether the condition of the promise is an event outside the organization's control and whether work necessary to meet the condition requires additional funding from other sources. These factors make it difficult to determine reliably when, if at all, the conditional promise will become a right giving the promisee sufficient control of the promised asset and a duty making the promisor unable to avoid future sacrifice.

77. Uncertainties about meeting a condition typically diminish over time. Makers of conditional promises generally can avoid a future sacrifice of assets if they provide promisees with timely notification of the cancellation of their conditional promise. However, as time passes that ability diminishes. Case law and public policy suggest that once a promisee has begun efforts in reliance on a conditional promise, both parties should be held to their promises. Promisors generally are not allowed to escape their promises until and unless a reasonable period of time has elapsed for the promisee to meet the condition, and promisees generally are held to their part of the agreement, which includes meeting the condition. However, until the specified future and uncertain event that is the subject of the condition occurs or fails to occur, a promisee does not have an unconditional right to retain the assets transferred or to demand payment.

78. Some respondents to the 1990 and 1992 Exposure Drafts said delaying recognition until a conditional right becomes unconditional defers recognition of conditional transfers of assets and conditional promises to give beyond the time that adequate evidence of the existence of the asset is available. They said that evidence of a probable future economic benefit is sufficient to recognize an asset. Some said that at a minimum, recognition of an asset on a percentage-of-completion basis should be allowed.

79. The Board believes that until the condition is substantially met, there is insufficient basis to make a presumption about the expected outcome. Doubt remains about whether all or none of the promised assets will be realized. Presently, there are no cost-effective techniques to measure with sufficient reliability the value of a conditional right to receive a promised gift or a conditional obligation to deliver a promised gift. The Board concluded that substantially meeting the condition is the underlying event resulting in a contribution to the promisee from the promisor and until that event occurs a contribution should not be recognized, regardless of whether the promisor has already transferred the assets or has promised to transfer the assets in the future.

80. The Board noted, however, that certain promises become unconditional in stages because they are dependent on several or a series of conditions—milestones—rather than on a single future and uncertain event and are recognized in increments as each of the conditions is met. Similarly, other promises are conditioned on promisees' incurring certain qualifying expenses (or costs). Those promises become unconditional and are recognized to the extent that the expenses are incurred. The accounting for that type of conditional promise results in recognition of assets and revenues as allowable costs are incurred, which resembles contractor accounting for government cost plus fixed fee arrangements where the contractor's right to partial payment becomes unconditional in advance of delivery of a finished product.

81. The Board considered whether a waiver of a condition is implicit in a promisor's decision to transfer assets after a conditional promise was made but before the condition is substantially met. It concluded that a change in the original conditions of the agreement between promisor and promisee should not be implied without an explicit waiver. A transfer of assets after a conditional promise to give is made and before the conditions are met is the same as a transfer of assets with a conditional promise to contribute those assets. By imposing a condition, a promisor retains its right of return of its assets if the condition is not met. It is reasonable to believe that by imposing a condition rather than promising unconditionally, a promisor has evidenced a strong and continuing interest in seeing that the specified condition occurs.

Basic Conclusions about Recognition and Measurement

82. Information about contributions of assets generally is relevant and should be recognized in financial statements. To be recognized in financial statements an item also must have a relevant attribute that is measurable with reasonable reliability and information about it must be representationally faithful, verifiable, and neutral.

83. The Board concluded that the fair value of the asset transferred, liability incurred, or liability canceled or settled is the relevant attribute for measuring contributions received or made. That conclusion reaffirms the conclusion reached in APB Opinion No. 29, *Accounting for Nonmonetary Transactions,* and the relevant AICPA Guides and SOP 78-10.[9] Specifically, Opinion 29 provides that

> . . . a nonmonetary asset received in a nonreciprocal transfer should be recorded at the fair value of the asset received. A transfer of a nonmonetary asset . . . in a nonreciprocal transfer should be recorded at the fair value of the asset transferred, and a gain or loss should be recognized on the disposition of the asset. [paragraph 18]

The Board also concluded that contributions generally are measurable with sufficient reliability. Contributions of monetary assets generally do not cause measurability problems, and although contributions of nonmonetary assets may present difficulties, they generally are measurable by both donors and donees.

84. However, a major uncertainty about the existence of value may indicate that a specific item received or given should not be recognized. If an item is accepted solely for a potential educational value or historical significance and has no alternative use, it may have uncertain value, or no value, and should not be recognized. For example, contributions of flora, fauna, photographs, and objects that are identified with historic persons, places, or events often have no value or have highly restricted alternative uses. The benefits of information about items, received or given, that may not have values are negligible.

85. Based on its considerations about the relevance of information about contributions and the measurability of contributed assets, the Board reached the following basic conclusions:

a. A contribution made and a corresponding contribution received should be recognized by both the donor and the donee at the same time, that is, upon occurrence of the underlying event—the nonreciprocal transfer of an economic benefit.
b. Donor-imposed restrictions place limits on the use of contributed resources and may affect an entity's performance and its ability to provide services. However, limitations on the use of donated resources do not change the fundamental nature of the contribution transaction or conclusions about when to recognize the underlying event.
c. Certain forms of contributed resources may be more difficult to measure reliably than others, but the form of the contributed resources alone should not change conclusions about whether to recognize the underlying event.

86. The Board considered whether those basic conclusions about recognition and measurement should be applied to all contributions received or whether certain exceptions permitted by the Guides and SOP 78-10 should continue. The Board specifically considered the recognition of promises to give, contributed services, and contributed works of art, historical treasures, and similar assets.

Promises to Give

87. This Statement defines the term *promise to give* using the common meaning of the word promise—a

---

[9] The AICPA's health care services Guide, paragraph 2.07, the colleges and universities Guide, page 48, the health and welfare Guide, page 20, and SOP 78-10, paragraph 71, generally specify that gifts of nonmonetary assets received should be measured at the fair value of the item received at the date of gift.

written or oral agreement to do (or not to do) something. A promise to give is a written or oral agreement to contribute cash or other assets to another entity. A promise carries rights and obligations—the recipient of a promise to give has a right to expect that the promised assets will be transferred in the future, and the maker has a social and moral obligation, and generally a legal obligation, to make the promised transfer.

88. Other sources have used other terms to describe promises to give. For example, legal treatises often use the term *subscription,* as in *charitable subscription,* as does the colleges and universities Guide. A similar promise made by corporate and governmental entities has sometimes been described as a *grant agreement, grant award,* or *sponsored agreement;* however, those terms have also been used for exchange contracts.

89. The 1990 Exposure Draft used the term *pledge* to describe a promise to give, as do the health care services and health and welfare Guides and SOP 78-10. However, some respondents to that Exposure Draft said that they use that term to describe promises as well as other indications of intentions to give that are not promises. Although the Board continues to believe that most pledges are promises to give, this Statement avoids use of the term *pledge* because it may be misinterpreted.

90. Paragraph 6 of this Statement provides additional guidance to minimize implementation concerns raised by respondents to the Exposure Drafts. First, it clarifies that sufficient evidence in the form of verifiable documentation must exist to recognize a promise to give. That clarification is intended to mitigate concerns that accounting results may be manipulated by recognizing potentially nonexistent assets; however, it does not preclude recognition of verifiable oral promises, such as those documented by tape recordings, written registers, or other means that permit subsequent verification. This Statement also clarifies that a written or oral communication that does not indicate clearly whether it is a promise is considered an unconditional promise to give if it indicates an unconditional intention to give that is legally enforceable. The Board decided that presumption is necessary to resolve ambiguities that cannot otherwise be resolved by a review of the facts and circumstances or by communications with the other party. The Board believes that in those circumstances it is reasonable to assume that a communication is a promise if it is legally enforceable.

91. The Board concluded that promises to give should be recognized on a basis consistent with recognition of other contributions. The making or receiving of an unconditional promise to give is an event that meets the fundamental recognition criteria. Accordingly, this Statement requires the promisee to recognize the promise as an asset and a contribution revenue or gain and the promisor to recognize the promise as a liability and a contribution expense. A conditional promise to give, like a transfer of assets with a conditional promise to contribute them, is recognized as a contribution at the time the condition is substantially met.

Meeting the definition of an asset or a liability

92. The Board concluded that an unconditional promise to give meets the definition of an asset when received and the definition of a liability when made. Concepts Statement 6 says that "assets are probable future economic benefits obtained or controlled by a particular entity as a result of past transactions or events" and "liabilities are probable future sacrifices of economic benefits arising from present obligations of a particular entity to transfer assets or provide services to other entities in the future as a result of past transactions or events" (paragraphs 25 and 35, footnote references omitted). Concepts Statement 6 discusses the three essential characteristics of assets and liabilities.

93. The first essential characteristic of an asset is that "it embodies a probable future benefit that involves a capacity, singly or in combination with other assets, to contribute directly or indirectly to future net cash inflows" (Concepts Statement 6, paragraph 26). Similarly, the first essential characteristic of a liability is that "it embodies a present duty or responsibility to one or more other entities that entails settlement by probable future transfer or use of assets at a specified or determinable date, on occurrence of a specified event, or on demand" (Concepts Statement 6, paragraph 36).

94. A promise by one entity to make a nonreciprocal transfer of assets to another entity in the future has the first essential characteristic of an asset and of a liability. That promise reflects a clear duty or requirement of the promisor to transfer promised assets in the future at a specified or determinable date or, if conditional, upon occurrence of a specified event.

95. In addition, an unconditional promise clearly is a precursor of a probable future benefit to the promisee. Inherent in that promise to give is a reasonable

expectation that the promisor will deliver and the promisee will receive, and evidence suggests that promises to give generally are kept. A conditional pledge, which involves future and uncertain events, raises significant uncertainties about obtaining the economic benefits promised.

96. The second essential characteristic of an asset is that "a particular entity can obtain the benefit and control others' access to it"; the second essential characteristic of a liability is that "the duty or responsibility obligates a particular entity, leaving it little or no discretion to avoid the future sacrifice" (Concepts Statement 6, paragraphs 26 and 36).

97. The Board believes that because of social and moral sanctions promisors commonly feel bound by their unconditional promises, regardless of their legal status. Paragraph 40 of Concepts Statement 6 states:

> . . . although most liabilities stem from legally enforceable obligations, some liabilities rest on equitable or constructive obligations. . . . Liabilities stemming from equitable or constructive obligations are commonly paid in the same way as legally binding contracts, but they lack the legal sanction that characterizes most liabilities and may be binding primarily because of social or moral sanctions or custom. An equitable obligation stems from ethical or moral constraints rather than from rules of common or statute law, that is, from a duty to another entity to do that which an ordinary conscience and sense of justice would deem fair, just, and right—to do what one ought to do rather than what one is legally required to do.

The equitable obligation that results from making a promise gives the promisee the ability to obtain the future benefit of the promised assets regardless of the legal status of the promise.

98. The availability of legal remedies provides another means of obtaining control over the promised assets, even if those legal remedies are seldom exercised. The Board consulted lawyers and reviewed the research of others[10] about the legal enforceability of promises to give. It understands that charitable promises generally have been enforced in this country, with the courts often applying the principles of con-

tract law. Promises are universally enforced if some consideration exists; some courts go far in their efforts to discover consideration sufficient to support a promise to give. Other courts, to make a promise enforceable, adopt the doctrine of promissory estoppel as the equivalent of consideration; that is, the promisor is estopped from raising the defense of lack of consideration if the promisor makes a promise that should reasonably be expected to induce action or forbearance of a substantial character on the part of a promisee. Still other courts will uphold a promise to give as valid and enforceable as a matter of public policy.

99. The Board concluded that unconditional promises result in equitable or legal obligations; conditional promises may not. Promisors may not feel bound by their conditional promises until the promisee begins meeting the condition or until the condition has been met.

100. The third essential characteristic of an asset is that "the transaction or other event giving rise to the entity's right to or control of the benefit has already occurred"; the third essential characteristic of a liability is that "the transaction or other event obligating the entity has already happened" (Concepts Statement 6, paragraphs 26 and 36). For unconditional promises, the Board concluded that the transaction or other event—the promise—giving rise to the entity's right to the benefit has already occurred. For conditional promises, the Board concluded that the event that should result in recognition is substantially meeting the condition.

Measurability, relevance, and reliability

101. The Board concluded that unconditional promises to give also meet the criteria of measurability, relevance, and reliability. The Board concluded that promises to give generally are measurable with sufficient reliability and, consistent with measuring contributions received at their fair value at date of gift, those receivables and payables should be measured at their fair value at the date the promise is received.

102. The Board concluded that information about promises to give, whether received or made, is relevant. Donors, creditors, and other users are interested in information about probable future transfers

[10]M. F. Budig, G. T. Butler, and L. M. Murphy, *Pledges to Non-Profit Organizations: Are They Enforceable and Must They Be Enforced?* New York University. In press.

of cash or other economic resources. That information is useful in assessing an entity's financial position and ability to generate public support and continue to operate. If the promisor is a not-for-profit organization whose primary purpose is to make contributions to others in the furtherance of its own mission, information about promises made is helpful in assessing the organization's performance. Thus, information about promises to give meets the test of relevance since it is "capable of making a difference in a decision by helping users to form predictions about the outcomes of past, present, and future events or to confirm or correct expectations" (Concepts Statement 2, paragraph 47).

Respondents' comments about recognition of promises to give

103. Most respondents to the 1990 Exposure Draft, including users of financial statements, said that not-for-profit organizations should not be required to recognize promises to give. Some of those respondents suggested that the Board establish standards to improve the disclosures of information about receipts of promises to give (pledges) and permit rather than require recognition of those promises as assets in financial statements.

104. The Board concluded that to permit rather than require recognition of unconditional promises to give would not improve existing practice. Since the 1970s, the Guides have required recognition of pledges by hospitals, voluntary health and welfare organizations, and most organizations other than colleges and universities. In 1979, the FASB designated that guidance as the preferred specialized industry practices for organizations considering a change in their accounting practice. The Board is aware that large numbers of colleges and universities and religious organizations do not recognize pledges receivable as assets although most maintain records of their pledges.[11] The Board believes that to permit, rather than require, recognition of pledges receivable would not further comparability between organizations and thus would not improve practice. The Board also concluded that disclosures that provide relevant in-

formation about an organization's future cash flows would be a useful improvement to practice and the 1992 Exposure Draft proposed that all organizations that receive promises to give provide the information required by paragraphs 24 and 25 of this Statement. Considerably fewer comments were received on the 1992 Exposure Draft; however, most of those respondents also disagreed with this Statement's required recognition of unconditional promises.

105. The Board also considered whether, as a few respondents suggested, it should preclude recognition of unconditional promises to give. The Board concluded that precluding recognition of unconditional promises to give would not faithfully represent an entity's assets or liabilities at the end of a period or its revenues or expenses during a period. That omission of relevant information about an entity's assets or liabilities and its revenues or expenses would make financial statements of all organizations unnecessarily incomplete. Furthermore, precluding recognition of unconditional promises to give would not improve comparability; rather, that would make unlike circumstances appear the same.

106. Some respondents said that promises to give that are binding primarily because of social and moral sanctions are indistinguishable from statements of intent to give and that making a distinction between the two will result in similar transactions being accounted for differently. Most would not recognize promises or statements of intent; a few would recognize both. Because social and moral sanctions obligate a promisor, the Board concluded that if a communication of intention to give is in substance a promise, it should be recognized. The Board does not intend, however, that entities recognize communications that clearly are not promises.

107. Several other respondents to the 1990 Exposure Draft said that only legally enforceable promises to give should be recognized. Many of those respondents contended that promises to give generally are not legally enforceable. The 1992 Exposure Draft noted that research examined by the Board indicates

---

[11]A 1985 survey and review of college and university annual reports found that of the 344 private institutions reviewed, only 10 percent recognized pledges receivable as assets in their balance sheet, 37 percent disclosed information about their pledges in notes to their financial statements, and more than 50 percent did neither, possibly because the pledges were not material (*Principles & Presentation: Higher Education,* [New York, Peat, Marwick, Mitchell & Co.: 1985], 39). A September 1987 survey conducted by the FASB staff had similar findings for colleges and universities and for religious organizations (9 percent and 18 percent, respectively, recognizing unrestricted pledges as assets) but noted that most (67 percent) hospitals recognized their unrestricted pledges and almost all organizations (more than 94 percent) maintained records of their pledges (Adams, Bossio, and Rohan, FASB Special Report, *Accounting for Contributed Services: Survey of Preparers and Users of Financial Statements of Not-for-Profit Organizations,* 52).

that most courts enforce promises to give, although in a few states promises are not enforceable except under the doctrine of promissory estoppel. The Board considered whether *only* legally enforceable promises to give should be recognized, and concluded that doing so would result in recognizing transactions with the same economic substance differently because of the differences in states' laws.

108. Many of the respondents to the 1990 Exposure Draft said that unconditional promises to give are not assets because donees would not use legal remedies to enforce a promise. They said that legal remedies are inconsistent with the nature of a contribution or that enforcement would jeopardize future fund raising. The Board acknowledges that legal remedies are often impractical; however, legal remedies seldom are necessary because promises generally are kept. Further, it is the *availability* of legal remedies, rather than the intent to use them, that provides an entity with an additional means of obtaining the future benefit. Although few respondents to the 1992 Exposure Draft asserted that unconditional promises are not assets, many respondents continued to recommend limiting recognition to only legally enforceable promises.

109. A few respondents to the 1990 and 1992 Exposure Drafts said an unconditional promise to give is similar to a purchase order. They said that both are legally enforceable and are indications of future cash flows. They suggested that, like purchase orders, promises to give should not be recognized before they are partially executed. The critical difference is that a promise to give is a nonreciprocal transfer, while a purchase order is part of an exchange transaction. To a seller, a purchase order involves a right to receive cash and an obligation to deliver goods or services in the future in approximately offsetting amounts. An unconditional promise to give involves a right to receive assets without an obligation to deliver assets or services.

110. Some respondents to the 1990 Exposure Draft contended that complying with recognition requirements for promises to give would hinder fund-raising efforts. This was the most frequently cited concern of respondents to the 1992 Exposure Draft. Some said recognition of unconditional promises to give would make entities appear to have excess spendable funds and, thus, have a reduced need for contributions. Others said that documenting information so that promises to give can be distinguished from other communications would damage trusting relationships

between an entity and its donors. Still others asserted that requiring donors to recognize multiyear unconditional promises would discourage that kind of long-term giving. The extent of those consequences is highly uncertain. The Board concluded that donors and other users need information about promises to give to make informed decisions about allocation of resources to not-for-profit organizations and the information must report promises as faithfully as possible without coloring the image it communicates for the purpose of influencing behavior in any particular direction.

Measurement of unconditional promises to give

111. The Board considered whether, as suggested by respondents to the 1990 Exposure Draft, it should provide further guidance on measuring the fair value of unconditional promises to give. The 1990 Exposure Draft said that APB Opinion No. 21, *Interest on Receivables and Payables,* provides the relevant standards for discounting future receipts or payments. Several respondents to that Exposure Draft said further guidance on measuring the fair value of unconditional promises to give is necessary or would be helpful. The 1992 Exposure Draft proposed and the Board concluded in this Statement that the present value of estimated future cash flows using a discount rate commensurate with the risks involved is an appropriate measure of fair value for unconditional promises to give cash.

112. Several respondents to the Exposure Drafts said that the undiscounted amount of cash promised should be used to measure all promises to give or all promises due within a period of no more than 5 years. Some of those respondents said that although a zero percent interest rate is unreasonable in a bargained-for exchange, that rate is appropriate to measure a promise to give because it is a voluntary nonreciprocal transfer. Others said the sum of the undiscounted promised cash flows is consistent with the amount the donor intended as a contribution. Still others said discounting would add costs and complexities without providing sufficiently useful information for promises that are due within relatively short periods (up to five years). The Board believes that failure to discount a promise to give does not faithfully represent its fair value. Cash to be received or paid in the future does not have the same value or utility as cash that is available now.

113. This Statement permits measuring unconditional promises to give that are expected to be collected or paid within one year at their net realizable

value because that amount, although not equivalent to the present value of estimated future cash flows, results in a reasonable estimate of fair value. That provision, which was not in the 1990 Exposure Draft, was added for practical reasons. The Board concluded that the requirements for measuring promises to give should be no more stringent than requirements for measuring trade receivables.

114. This Statement also permits measuring a portfolio of short-term promises to give that result from mass fund-raising appeals by using estimates of future cash flows based on experience gained from similar appeals. Annual campaigns, mail solicitations, telethons, or phonathons generally result in many promises of small dollar amounts that are due in less than one year and are unconditional. To measure individually the present value of estimated cash flows for promises to give resulting from those campaigns generally is impracticable. Measurement difficulties are compounded because the solicitation process may result in some spurious promises. The Board concluded that an entity may estimate the cash flows of a portfolio of short-term promises from mass fund-raising appeals using collection experience gained in previous similar appeals and that the promises may be measured at net realizable value because that measurement results in a reasonable estimate of fair value.

115. The 1992 Exposure Draft proposed that, consistent with guidance in Opinion 21, the subsequent accrual of the interest element on a multiyear promise to give should be reported as interest income by the donee and interest expense by the donor. A significant majority of respondents commenting on that proposal disagreed, including those that support recognition of promises to give at their present value. Some said that the interest element is a component of the contribution or that donors perceive it as part of their contribution. They contend that reporting that component as interest would add confusion that would exceed any potential benefit. The Board reconsidered its decision and concluded that the interest element should be accounted for as contribution income by donees and contribution expense by donors. The Board agreed that is likely to result in more understandable reporting. It also notes that reporting the interest element as a component of contribution income or contribution expense is consistent with accounting for the element of interest involved in certain other transactions; such as, the costs of pensions or of other postretirement benefits.

Disclosures

116. The 1992 Exposure Draft proposed that recipients be required to provide information about both promises to give and unrecognized communications that indicate an intention to give. The Board concluded that information about both would be useful in assessing a not-for-profit organization's ability to provide services in the future. The Board also concluded that this Statement should not require disclosures for makers of promises and indications of intentions to give because Statement 5 and Statement No. 47, *Disclosure of Long-Term Obligations,* provide the relevant standards.

117. Many respondents to the 1992 Exposure Draft said that the proposed disclosures for intentions to give would provide information of dubious value that would not justify the costs to provide that information. The Board continues to believe that information about intentions to give may be helpful to users of financial statements, especially if significant difficulties and uncertainties are encountered in distinguishing intentions to give from receipts of promises to give or when intentions to give are regularly solicited. However, the Board is sensitive to concerns raised about the costs of quantifying and verifying amounts of intentions to give, including negative consequences that might result from required audit procedures imposed during a delicate gift solicitation (precommitment) phase. The Board decided that this Statement should neither require nor preclude disclosures for intentions to give because it is not clear, at this time, that the potential benefits of information about the amount of intentions to give would justify the costs to provide that information.

Contributed Services

118. Most not-for-profit organizations receive and use contributed services in their operations, but few recognize them as revenues and expenses. The health and welfare Guide says that "because of the difficulty of placing a monetary value on donated services, and the absence of control over them, the value of these services often is not recorded as contributions [revenue] and expense" (page 21). However, the Guide requires recognition of revenue and expense under certain specified conditions, and although it does not encourage recognition of services received under other conditions, it does not preclude their recognition. In contrast, SOP 78-10, paragraph 67, precludes recognition of services not meeting similar conditions, and it has been interpreted by some as permitting rather than requiring recognition of contributed services meeting its conditions.

119. The Board considered that guidance, and the 1990 Exposure Draft proposed conditions for recognition of contributed services that generally are measurable with sufficient reliability. That Exposure Draft also encouraged recognition of other contributed services if they could be measured with sufficient reliability and at a reasonable cost. Permitting entities to recognize other measurable services was believed to be a reasonable step to allow practice to continue to evolve.

120. Some respondents to the 1990 Exposure Draft said that recognition of contributed services should not be required under any circumstances because the benefits of reporting information about their fair values would not exceed the cost to provide that information. Some respondents suggested recognizing only services that are donated by qualified entities if they would normally be purchased or suggested other conditions that focused on services integral to an organization's mission. Still other respondents, including users of financial statements, expressed concern about encouraging recognition of measurable services that did not meet the conditions. They questioned whether those services would be measured reliably and said standards are necessary to limit rather than encourage diverse recognition practices.

121. Because of user skepticism about the information provided by recognizing most contributed services and concerns raised about the cost to provide that information, the Board decided to revise the recognition criteria proposed by the 1990 Exposure Draft. The Board believes the conditions of paragraph 9 of this Statement limit recognition to only those services that will provide information that is clearly relevant, clearly measurable, and obtainable at a cost that does not exceed the benefits of the information provided. By drawing on existing industry guidance, the revised criteria should help minimize disruption to practice yet also should improve practice by eliminating certain inconsistencies in the existing guidance.

122. The Board also decided, for practical reasons, to preclude recognition of contributed services received that do not meet the conditions of paragraph 9 of this Statement. Respondents to the 1990 Exposure Draft expressed strong concerns about any permissive recognition. They said that methods of measurement and assumptions would vary considerably between entities, that resulting financial information often would not be reliable, or that discretionary recognition would lead to differing accounting practices or perhaps practices biased toward presenting favorable ratios of program or fund-raising cost to total expenses. The Board believes that the disadvantages of inconsistent recognition practices outweigh the advantages of permitting discretionary recognition as a means for practice to evolve.

123. The Board also concluded that nonmonetary information about the nature and extent of contributed services received is useful in understanding an organization's operations, including its dependence on contributed services. Accordingly, the Board decided that organizations should describe the programs or activities for which contributed services are received and used. Nonmonetary information, such as the number and trends of donated hours received or service outputs provided by volunteer efforts, may be helpful in assessing the success and long-term viability of the organization. Other monetary information about contributed services received also may be helpful, such as the fair values of contributed services not recognized or the dollar amount of contributions raised by volunteers.

124. Views of respondents to the 1992 Exposure Draft differed on recognition of contributed services. Some said that the revised criteria are a significant improvement over the original proposal. Others said the criteria are too restrictive and preclude recognition of some contributed services that are both relevant and measurable with sufficient reliability. Some reiterated concerns raised in paragraph 120. The Board considered those comments and concluded that the criteria in paragraph 9 are necessary to limit recognition to only those services that are clearly relevant and measurable at a cost that does not exceed the benefits of the information provided.

Collection Items

125. This Statement considers certain specialized industry practices that permit but do not require certain organizations to capitalize works of art, historical treasures, and similar items held in their inexhaustible collections (paragraphs 37 and 38). In 1978, the accounting standards division of the AICPA said:

> . . . it is often impracticable to determine a value for [inexhaustible] collections [owned by museums, art galleries, botanical gardens, libraries, and similar entities] and accordingly [the division] has concluded that they need not be capitalized. If records and values do exist for the collections, the division encourages capitalization, at cost, if purchased, and

at a fair value, if acquired by donation. If historical cost is indeterminable, the alternative methods of valuing described in the section on fixed assets should be used. . . .

The nature and the cost or contributed value of current-period accessions and the nature of and proceeds from deaccessions should be disclosed in the financial statements. [SOP 78-10, paragraphs 113 and 114]

Some museums and similar entities recognize their "inexhaustible collections" as assets; however, most do not.

126. The 1990 Exposure Draft generally would have required all entities to recognize works of art, historical treasures, and similar items as assets in the period acquired and retroactively capitalize those items. The few respondents that supported that proposal generally said that recognition of these items as assets in financial statements is necessary to provide users of financial statements with information to assess an entity's financial position, the results of its operations, and how its managers have discharged their responsibilities for the custody and safekeeping of the entity's assets. However, almost all of the other respondents said that for most museums and similar entities that hold collections, the costs to capitalize works of art, historical treasures, and similar assets would outweigh the benefits of the information that capitalization would provide.

127. The Board reaffirmed its conclusion that works of art, historical treasures, and similar items are assets, regardless of the owner or the owner's intent to sell or hold the items as part of a collection. The Board also concluded, however, that because information necessary to recognize those items was not compiled in the past and may no longer be available or may be too costly to obtain, the incremental benefits of the information gained by recognizing works of art, historical treasures, and similar items held in "collections" as assets often would not justify the cost to provide that information. Accordingly, the 1992 Exposure Draft proposed that under certain specific circumstances entities need not recognize as assets works of art, historical treasures, and similar items held as part of a collection.

Definition of a collection

128. The Board's objective in defining collections (paragraph 11) is to exempt from recognition only those works of art, historical treasures, and similar assets that are held for public exhibition, education, or research in furtherance of public service and that are to be preserved and protected. Collections, as used in this Statement, generally are held by museums, botanical gardens, libraries, aquariums, arboretums, historic sites, planetariums, zoos, art galleries, nature, science and technology centers, and similar educational, research, and public service organizations that have those divisions; however, the definition is not limited to those entities nor does it apply to all items held by those entities.

129. This Statement's definition of a collection is based on the American Association of Museums' *Code of Ethics for Museums* (1991) and its "Accreditation: Self-Study" (1989). The definitions in those documents are widely used by the kinds of organizations for which the Board believes the relevant cost and benefit problem exists. The Board decided that having an organizational policy that requires that the proceeds from collection items sold be used to acquire other items for collections demonstrates a commitment and a probability that the collections will and can be maintained. The Board believes that commitment is particularly relevant to its considerations about both the benefits and costs of providing information about those assets.

Collection items are assets

130. Collection items, although generally held for long periods of time and seldom sold, are assets that continue to provide economic benefit or service potential through their use. In a not-for-profit organization, that service potential or future economic benefit is used to provide desired or needed goods or services to beneficiaries. Those items also provide future cash flows from admissions, rentals, and royalties, and often are the reason for contributions in support of the entity's mission. The Board concluded that collection items have the common characteristics possessed by all assets—the scarce capacity to provide services or benefits to the entity that uses those items (Concepts Statement 6, paragraph 28).

131. Some respondents said that works of art, historical treasures, and similar assets that are part of "collections" are "held in trust" for the public and are not assets of the collectors. Many equated the "inability" to sell items from collections with forgoing the economic benefit inherent in those items. The Board concluded, however, that holders of collection items continue to reap economic benefits from those assets and it would be inappropriate to preclude their recognition and capitalization as assets.

Benefits and costs of capitalizing collections

132. Respondents to the 1990 Exposure Draft provided information useful to the Board in considering the benefits and costs of recognizing collection items. Most respondents said that they had experienced little or no demand for information about the value of collections held by museums and similar entities. Many also said that because of the extraordinarily long lives of most collection items, measures of their cost or fair value at date of gift are irrelevant. Although current values for collections or selected items may be of interest to an organization's managers, particularly in relation to decisions about the level of protection or insurance for assets, most respondents said to maintain current values on an annual basis would be cost prohibitive. The Board believes that information about the existence of collection items and changes in the nature of those assets is relevant to many, if not most, users of financial statements. However, the Board is unaware of a significant demand among external users of general-purpose financial statements for dollar-value information about collection items.[12]

133. Almost all respondents to the 1990 Exposure Draft said that the cost to retroactively capitalize collections would be excessive because records of the cost of purchased items or of the fair value at the date of contribution of donated items generally do not exist. They also said that the extraordinary human resources required to value the large collections of most organizations are neither currently available nor likely to be affordable in the future. Further, some said that galleries would have to be closed to the public to appraise objects on display and that removing objects from storage and returning them to storage would require additional cost and involve risk of damage.

134. The Board concluded that the cost of retroactively capitalizing collections often would exceed the incremental benefit of the information gained, especially for entities that have been in existence for several decades or more. The Board also concluded that the disclosures required by paragraphs 26 and 27 of this Statement, which were proposed by the 1992 Exposure Draft, will provide information that is useful in assessing how managers of an entity are discharging their responsibilities for the custody and safekeeping of collections without imposing significant costs to provide that information. The Board believes that this disclosure alternative to required recognition is a practical step that will improve current reporting practices.

135. The Board also concluded that works of art, historical treasures, and similar items that are not part of a collection should be recognized as assets in financial statements. Some entities that hold these items do not espouse the mission of public education, exhibition, and research and the attendant responsibilities to protect, keep unencumbered, care for, and preserve the items, and some entities that do maintain collections have some items that are not part of its collections. The Board found no reason to exempt items that are not part of a collection from recognition as assets.

Capitalization of collections is encouraged

136. The Board believes that, although often not practical, retroactive capitalization is conceptually the proper accounting for works of art, historical treasures, and similar assets and encourages entities that have capitalized their collections to continue that practice. However, the Board also believes that it would be inappropriate and potentially confusing to users of financial statements if entities selectively capitalize or omit some gifts or some purchases of collection items. Accordingly, an entity that has capitalized only a portion of its collections should assess the costs and benefits of capitalization and determine whether (a) recognition of all gifts and purchases either retroactively or prospectively from a date of adoption or (b) no capitalization and no recognition of gifts is most appropriate.

137. To assist entities that are considering retroactive capitalization, the Board decided to permit entities to measure collection items acquired in previous periods at their cost or fair value at date of acquisition, current cost, or current market value, whichever is deemed most practical. The Board expects that individual entities will use the measure that is most readily determinable with reasonable reliability. Additionally, the Board decided to permit entities to

---

[12]In response to a 1989 FASB survey of users and potential users of financial statements, some users said that information about the dollar amount of donated collection items could be useful in evaluating a museum; however, most did not believe the usefulness of information gained by retroactive capitalization of prior acquisitions would exceed the costs to provide that information.

Interviews of users conducted by others "uncovered no evidence of the usefulness of dollar-value information about collections" (Henry R. Jaenicke and Alan S. Glazer, *Accounting for Museum Collections and Contributions of Collection Items* [Washington, D.C.: American Association of Museums, 1991], 4 and 75-78).

measure one attribute of some collection items or groups of items and a different attribute of other collection items or groups of items if that would be practical. Flexibility in the attributes used to measure the amount to be capitalized will reduce the usefulness of the information provided; however, the Board decided that allowing entities a one-time option to capitalize collection items at the measure they deem most practical is a reasonable step to help reduce the costs of retroactive capitalization.

138. Many, if not most, respondents to the 1990 Exposure Draft that hold collections said they are unwilling to retroactively capitalize their collections because the costs of doing so would outweigh the benefits of information gained. However, the substantial one-time costs and disruptions that often make retroactive capitalization impracticable generally do not exist at the time donated items are received, and no costs or disruptions are associated with capitalizing purchased items. Because the Board believes that collection items are assets and are measurable and that information about collections generally is relevant and reliable, it decided to permit prospective recognition provided an entity capitalizes all collection items acquired after the date of initial adoption of this Statement.

139. The Board also considered whether to permit or preclude recognition of revenues for contributed collection items if an entity does not capitalize collections. The Board believes recognition of revenues for contributed collection items would be confusing if the amount recognized is also reported as a decrease in net assets rather than as an asset. Further, the Board believes that if an entity decides to incur the costs necessary to report contribution revenues, that entity should capitalize its collections, either prospectively or retroactively. Thus, the Board concluded that contributed collection items shall be recognized as revenues or gains if collections are capitalized and shall not be recognized as revenues or gains if collections are not capitalized.

Disclosures required if collections are not capitalized retroactively

140. Several respondents to the 1990 Exposure Draft, including the American Association of Museums' Accounting for Contributions Task Force, suggested disclosures that might compensate for weaknesses in financial reporting that result from not capitalizing collections. The Board concluded that the disclosures required by paragraphs 26 and 27 of this Statement are necessary to overcome financial reporting weaknesses and anomalies that result from not capitalizing collections. For example, an entity that does not capitalize collections reports its purchases of collection items as a decrease to its net assets in the statement of activities, but that decrease is neither an expense nor a loss. Under generally accepted accounting principles, an expenditure for the acquisition of a long-lived tangible asset does not result in a decrease in net assets. Further, an entity might fail to report information about gifts made to other entities and uninsured losses from fires, thefts, or impairments of assets because the items have no carrying value.

141. The Board decided that certain transactions involving collection items should be reported separately from items of revenues, gains, expenses, and losses to reduce confusion resulting from the anomalies that result from not capitalizing collection items. The following illustrates one possible format[13] that may be used to satisfy the financial disclosure provisions of this Statement.

---

[13]Appendix C of Statement 117 contains illustrations of several formats of statements of activities that might be adapted to comply with the provisions of this Statement.

Organization M
Statement of Activities
For the Year Ended June 30, 19XX

	Unrestricted	Temporarily Restricted	Permanently Restricted	Total
Revenues and other support	XXX	XXX	XXX	XXX
Gain on sale of art that is not held in a collection	1			1
Net assets released from restrictions	XXX	(XXX)		
Total revenues, gains, and other support	XXX	XX	XXX	XXX
Expenses	XXX			XXX
Change in net assets before changes related to collection items not capitalized	XX	XX	XXX	XXX
Change in net assets related to collection items not capitalized:				
Proceeds from sale of collection items	5		10	15
Proceeds from insurance recoveries on destroyed collection items			1	1
Collection items purchased but not capitalized			(25)	(25)
	5		(14)	(9)
Change in net assets	XX	XX	XXX	XXX

142. The Board concluded that users need additional disclosures if collections are not capitalized. To increase users' understanding of the size and significance of the collections and management's responsibilities for the collections, the Board decided to require a general description of the collection and its significance and a description of management's stewardship efforts. To ensure that users of the financial statements understand that significant assets of the entity are omitted, the Board decided to require disclosure of accounting policies for collections and a line item on the face of the statement of financial position that refers to all required note disclosures. To provide information about losses or impairments of collection items if those items were not capitalized, the Board decided to require a description of items given away, damaged, destroyed, lost, or otherwise deaccessed or disclosure of their fair value.

143. The Board also considered the suggestion by some respondents that the Board require all entities that do not capitalize their collections to provide a schedule that reconciles from period to period the number of items held in each of their major collections. The Board decided not to require that reconciliation because it believes that other forms of disclosure may be more useful than item counts.

144. Most museums and other respondents to the 1992 Exposure Draft that commented on the provisions for recognition of and disclosures about collections supported the provisions in this Statement. Some museums that endorse the provisions of paragraphs 11(a) and (b) but are not committed to reinvesting proceeds from sales of collection items to acquire other items for collections (paragraph 11(c)) asked the Board to allow nonrecognition of their collection items. Having an organizational policy and demonstrated commitment to reinvest in collection items is particularly relevant to the Board's conclusions about collection assets.

Reporting Information about Donor-imposed Restrictions

145. Contributions are a primary source of revenues for many not-for-profit organizations; often they are donor restricted. Donor-imposed restrictions place limits on the use of assets received that affect the types and levels of service that an organization can provide. Because those limitations generally are pervasive, recurring, and sometimes permanent, the Board believes that financial reporting should reflect the extent and nature of donor-imposed limits and changes in them.

Information about Three Classes of Net Assets

146. Some restrictions limit the organization's ability to sell or exchange the asset received; more commonly, the restriction applies to an amount of net assets. Some donor-imposed restrictions impose limits that are permanent, for example, stipulating that resources be invested in perpetuity (not used up). Others are temporary, for example, stipulating that resources may be used only after a specified date, for particular programs or services, or to acquire buildings and equipment. The nature and extent of the limits resulting from donor-imposed restrictions are relevant to donors and other users, as well as management, when making their resource allocation decisions. The Board concluded that not-for-profit organizations should distinguish between contributions received that increase permanently restricted net assets, that increase temporarily restricted net assets, and that increase unrestricted net assets (paragraph 14).

147. Donors, creditors, and other resource providers are interested in knowing not only that an organization's net assets have increased (or decreased) but also how and why. Concepts Statement 6 says:

> Since donor-imposed restrictions affect the types and levels of service a not-for-profit organization can provide, whether an organization has maintained certain classes of net assets may be more significant than whether it has maintained net assets in the aggregate. For example, if net assets were maintained in a period only because permanently restricted endowment contributions made up for a decline in unrestricted net assets, information focusing on the aggregate change might obscure the fact that the organization had not maintained the part of its net assets that is fully available to support services in the next period. [paragraph 106]

148. The Board believes that information about a minimum of three classes of net assets, based on the presence or absence of donor-imposed restrictions and their nature, generally is necessary to gain an adequate understanding of the financial position and results of operations of a not-for-profit organization. Information about permanent restrictions is useful in determining the extent to which an organization's net assets are not a source of cash for payments to present or prospective lenders, suppliers, or employees and thus are not expected to be directly available for providing services or paying creditors. Information about the extent of unrestricted net assets and of temporarily restricted net assets is useful in assessing an organization's ability and limitations on its ability to allocate resources to provide services or particular kinds of services or to make cash payments to creditors in the future.

Implicit Donor Restrictions

149. The 1990 Exposure Draft said that donor-imposed restrictions result from either a donor's explicit stipulation or a donee's explicit representation to donors. Some respondents noted that certain contributions contain implicit donor restrictions and asked whether those contributions would be reported as donor restricted. The Board clarified that donor-imposed restrictions also may result from circumstances at the time a gift is received that make clear a donor's implicit restriction of the use of contributed assets. The Board identified two situations in which it believes implied donor restrictions exist—contributions of unconditional promises to give with payments due in future periods and contributions of long-lived assets.

150. The Board concluded that a time restriction is implicit in an unconditional promise to give with payments due in future periods. That time restriction is implied unless a donor explicitly states that the gift is to support current activities or other circumstances make that clear. The Board believes that it is reasonable to assume that by specifying future payment dates donors indicate that their gift is to support activities in each period in which a payment is scheduled.

151. The 1992 Exposure Draft also proposed that time restrictions be implied on gifts of long-lived assets unless the donor explicitly states that the donated asset is to be sold to provide proceeds for unrestricted use or other circumstances make that clear. A significant majority of the respondents to the 1992 Exposure Draft did not comment on whether a time restriction is implicit in a gift of a long-lived asset, perhaps indicating tacit agreement with the proposal. However, nearly all of the minority of respondents commenting on this matter disagreed with the Exposure Draft.

152. Some respondents said that implying a time restriction is inconsistent with the Board's fundamental conclusion that donor-imposed restrictions result from either a donor's explicit stipulation or a donee's

explicit representation to donors. Those respondents agreed that a donor restriction exists on gifts of cash or other assets to acquire long-lived assets; however, they said those are explicit restrictions that are satisfied when the stipulated acquisition occurs. Others said that implying a time restriction adds unnecessary recordkeeping costs for long-lived assets that are acquired with multiple sources of funding and raises other accounting complexities for the gifted portion. Still others said the Board should make clear that the implied time restriction is required only in circumstances where donor-restricted amounts are material in relation to total funding sources for long-lived assets.

153. The Board continues to believe that it is reasonable to assume that by contributing long-lived assets without saying they may be sold immediately, donors indicate that those assets are to be used to provide services in future periods and that a similar implicit restriction exists for gifts of cash or other assets restricted to acquisition of long-lived assets. However, in light of the implementation concerns raised and the lack of a compelling legal basis or general acceptance for implying a time restriction on gifts of long-lived assets, the Board concluded that without further study it would be inappropriate to require or preclude organizations from applying that accounting convention. Accordingly, paragraph 16 of this Statement permits but does not require organizations to adopt a policy of implying a time restriction for donations of long-lived assets and because that choice is allowed, organizations must disclose the policy adopted.

Exception to Reporting Gifts as Donor Restricted

154. Some respondents to the 1992 Exposure Draft suggested that broadly restricted contributions—for activities that ordinarily occur in the normal course of operations—should be classified as unrestricted revenues. They said information about *restricted* gifts would be more meaningful if only donor-restricted gifts that permit the organization to undertake activities it would not otherwise conduct were separately reported as restricted gifts. They also said defining donor restrictions in that way would avoid reporting of virtually automatic reclassifications for expirations of restrictions that they contend provides information of little value and adds unnecessary bookkeeping.

155. The Board concluded there is no need to redefine donor restrictions. However, it decided, for practical reasons, to permit contributions with restrictions that are met in the same reporting period to be re-

ported as unrestricted support provided that an organization reports consistently from period to period and discloses its accounting policy (paragraph 14). That reporting, if elected, would not affect the reported amounts for change in temporarily restricted net assets for the period or temporarily restricted net assets at the end of a period. Thus, the expected benefits from applying the basic provisions of this Statement are not reduced significantly by the allowed exception, which the Board believes could help reduce the costs of implementing this Statement.

Expiration of Restrictions

Recognition of the Expiration

156. The Board concluded that an expiration of a donor-imposed restriction on a not-for-profit organization's net assets is an event that affects the entity and that financial statements should recognize the effects of that event in the period in which it occurs (paragraph 17). Information about the expiration of restrictions is useful in assessing the extent to which a not-for-profit organization used resources obtained in past periods for activities of the current period. Additionally, recognizing expirations of restrictions is necessary in determining the nature and extent to which net assets remain restricted at the end of the period.

157. Some respondents to the 1990 Exposure Draft asked the Board to clarify whether its intent was to specify that temporarily restricted net assets should be decreased when both unrestricted and purpose-restricted net assets are available for the same expenditure. Some, but not all of those respondents said that if both unrestricted and purpose-restricted net assets are available, restrictions expire when management identifies an expense with a restricted gift. They said that this method reflects the way that the organization's managers have discharged their stewardship responsibilities. The Board rejected that method of reporting, which it believes would result in different accounting for similar events because of differences in management objectives.

158. Other respondents said that donors assume that their gifts will be spent after unrestricted funds allocated to the same purpose have been exhausted, that is, that they have given incremental funds. The Board believes that restrictions should not be implied unless circumstances make clear that the donor restricted use of the contribution. The Board does not believe that it is reasonable to imply that a donor prevents use of contributed resources until unrestricted resources are exhausted.

159. The 1992 Exposure Draft retained the provision of the 1990 Exposure Draft that would require recognition of the expiration of a donor-imposed restriction when that event occurs and clarified that the recognition of an expense that satisfies a donor-imposed restriction decreases temporarily restricted net assets. The 1992 Exposure Draft also noted that this Statement would not specify or limit management discretion in determining which source of temporarily restricted net assets is decreased if an expense is incurred for a purpose for which more than one source of temporarily restricted net assets is available.

160. A minority of respondents to the 1992 Exposure Draft, mostly colleges and universities, said that the additional guidance provided about when donor restrictions expire is inadequate, too prescriptive, or too difficult to implement. Generally, they repeated previous suggestions that organizations be allowed to recognize expirations of donor restrictions when the institutional fiduciary charged with executing the terms of the gift determines an expense has been incurred for the specified purpose. The Board continues to reject that suggestion. The Board believes that this Statement's permitted exception for gifts with restrictions received and met in the same period may help reduce implementation concerns raised by those respondents.

161. Paragraph 17 of this Statement also provides that if an expense is incurred for a purpose for which both unrestricted and temporarily restricted net assets are available, a donor-imposed restriction is fulfilled to the extent of the expense incurred *unless the expense is for a purpose that is directly attributable to another specific external source of revenue.* The latter provision and an example were added to avoid unintended negative economic consequences that could result from the more prescriptive guidance of the 1992 Exposure Draft.

Reporting Expiration of Restrictions

162. This Statement specifies when to recognize expirations of donor-imposed restrictions, and Statement 117 specifies how to report the effects of those expirations in financial statements. The latter Statement specifies that expirations of restrictions that simultaneously decrease restricted net assets and increase unrestricted net assets (reclassifications) are reported separately from other transactions.

163. Some respondents to the 1990 Exposure Draft said that reporting expirations of restrictions in financial statements is unnecessary or potentially confusing. Generally, those respondents suggested reporting restricted contributions as deferred revenue until the restriction is met, thereby avoiding the need for reclassifications among classes of net assets. They also said that delaying recognition of the revenue from restricted contributions would achieve a better "match" of revenues and expenses. Some respondents to the 1992 Exposure Draft reiterated those comments.

164. The Board concluded that information about the relationship between inflows and outflows of a period and the relationship between restricted resources and the expenses or other activities they support generally is useful in assessing whether activities during a period have drawn upon, or contributed to, past or future periods. The Board also concluded that delaying recognition of revenue from a restricted gift is not necessary to provide information about those relationships. Further, as discussed in paragraphs 57-68, restricted contributions do not result in deferred revenues. Nonreciprocal transfers seldom involve matching procedures because "nonreciprocal transfers to an entity rarely result directly and jointly from the same transactions as expenses [and] most contributions and expenses are much more closely related to time periods than to each other" (Concepts Statement 6, paragraph 151).

165. The Board believes that reporting the relationship between gifts restricted to support specific program expenses and the expenses they support can be achieved by reporting expirations of donor-imposed restrictions. First, reporting the relationship of gifts to periods is achieved by recognizing contributions in the period received. Second, the relationship between the restricted contribution and the expense it supports is reported because a restriction generally expires in the period when the specified expense occurs. For example, an expiration of a purpose restriction decreases temporarily restricted net assets and increases unrestricted net assets at the same time as the expense that satisfies the restriction is reported as a decrease in unrestricted net assets. Thus, the relationship is reported in the unrestricted class of net assets in the period the restricted resources are used to support expenses.

166. That same type of relationship is reported with gifts that are time restricted. For example, a gift of a term endowment that is to be invested for five years is recognized as restricted support (revenue or gain) in the period it is received. In year 5, when that term

endowment becomes unrestricted, a reclassification is reported to reflect the decrease in temporarily restricted net assets and the increase in unrestricted net assets. Thus, the related effects of that time-restricted gift are reported in the period of receipt as well as the period in which the nature of the restriction changes.

167. The Board also believes that its clarification of expirations of restrictions and its conclusions about implicit restrictions on unconditional promises to give and on gifts of long-lived assets may help eliminate-other "matching" concerns raised by some respondents. Most unconditional promises to give with payments due in future periods will be recognized as temporarily restricted support with time restrictions that expire in the periods those payments are due. That recognition should avoid misunderstandings that some respondents said would occur if promises to give due in future periods were recognized as unrestricted revenue and were perceived by users of financial statements as currently available funds.

168. Some respondents said misunderstanding would occur if gifts of long-lived assets (or long-lived assets acquired with restricted gifts of cash) were reported as current revenues or perceived to result in currently available funds. Some of those respondents would initially report those gifts as so-called capital contributions, or report the contributions and assets in a discrete fund group, or both. The Board believes that with appropriate labeling of land, buildings, equipment, and other long-lived assets in statements of financial position, users of financial statements will understand that those assets differ from cash and other liquid assets, whether or not they are initially reported as contributions that increase unrestricted net assets. The Board also concluded reporting long-lived assets in a separate fund group is not necessary. Nonetheless, this Statement allows organizations the option to recognize most gifts of long-lived assets as temporarily restricted support with implied time restrictions and report the expirations of those restrictions over the useful life of the assets. That reporting option provides a means to avoid the potential misunderstandings that are of concern to some respondents.

Effective Date and Transition

169. The 1992 Exposure Draft proposed that this Statement generally be effective for annual financial statements issued for fiscal years beginning after December 15, 1994. The Board believes that providing ample time before this Statement becomes effective is desirable so organizations can coordinate its implementation with Statement 117.

170. The Board also concluded that a delay to fiscal years beginning at least one year (and up to 18 months) after the date of this Statement's issuance would be reasonable for most not-for-profit organizations. The Board believes that this Statement's effective date (fiscal years beginning after December 15, 1994) would allow many small not-for-profit organizations and their external advisors sufficient time to assimilate the requirements of this Statement, obtain information that may be required, and put in place the systems necessary to gather required information.

171. Nonetheless, a national association representing more than 400 human services organizations (and a few other respondents) requested an additional one-year delay for small not-for-profit organizations. About one-third of the association's members have annual budgets of less than $1 million and the association said the extended transition period would allow them sufficient time to utilize the initial experience gained by larger organizations and CPAs. They believe that experience could help them find cost-effective ways to implement this Statement and Statement 117. Board members believe a further delay generally is not necessary. However, because small organizations are often dependent on outside volunteers and are particularly sensitive to any incremental one-time costs, the Board decided to grant a one-year delay for organizations with less than $5 million in total assets and less than $1 million in annual expenses.

172. Earlier application of this Statement is encouraged where practicable. Applying this Statement early may result in some loss of comparability of reporting among organizations during the transition period; however, the Board concluded that the benefits of the information gained by permitting early application outweigh its disadvantages. Because retroactive application of the provisions of paragraph 17 may be difficult, and perhaps impossible, if an organization no longer has the necessary records or past procedures did not require those records, the Board decided to permit rather than require retroactive application of the provisions of that paragraph. Respondents to the 1992 Exposure Draft generally agreed with its proposed effective date and transition provisions.

Appendix C

EXAMPLES OF THE APPLICATION OF THIS STATEMENT TO SPECIFIC SITUATIONS

CONTENTS

Appendix C

EAMPLES OF THE APPLICATION OF THIS STATEMENT TO SPECIFIC SITUATIONS

Introduction

173. This appendix provides additional discussion and examples that illustrate application of this Statement to some specific situations. The examples do not address all possible applications of this Statement and assume that all items addressed are material.

Scope and Definition

174. Some transfers of assets that are exchange transactions may appear to be contributions if the services or other assets given in exchange are perceived to be a sacrifice of little value and the exchanges are compatible with the recipient's mission. Furthermore, a single transaction may be in part an exchange and in part a contribution. A careful assessment of the characteristics of the transaction, from the perspectives of both the resource provider and the recipient, is necessary to determine whether a contri-

bution has occurred. Examples 1 and 2 illustrate the need to assess the relevant facts and circumstances to distinguish between the receipt of resources in an exchange and the receipt of resources in a contribution.

175. A transfer of assets also may appear to be a contribution when a donor uses an agent, a trustee, or an intermediary to transfer assets to a donee. Receipts of resources as an agent, trustee, or intermediary of a donor are not contributions received to the agent. Deliveries of resources as an agent, trustee, or intermediary of a donor are not contributions made by the agent. Similarly, contributions of services (time, skills, or expertise) between donors and donees that are facilitated by an intermediary are not contributions received or contributions made by the intermediary. Examples 3-5 illustrate the need to assess the relevant facts and circumstances to distinguish between the receipt of resources as a donee and the receipt of resources as an agent, a trustee, or an intermediary organization.

Example 1—Receipt of Resources in an Exchange

176. University A, a large research university with a cancer research center, regularly conducts research to

discover more effective methods of treating cancer and often receives contributions to support its efforts. University A receives resources from a pharmaceutical company to finance the costs of a clinical trial of an experimental cancer drug the company developed. The pharmaceutical company specifies the protocol of the testing, including the number of participants to be tested, the dosages to be administered, and the frequency and nature of follow-up examinations. The pharmaceutical company requires a detailed report of the test outcome within two months of the test's conclusion. Because the results of the clinical trial have particular commercial value for the pharmaceutical company, receipt of the resources is not a contribution received by University A, nor is the disbursement of the resources a contribution made by the pharmaceutical company.

Example 2—Receipt of Resources Partially in Exchange and Partially as a Contribution

177. Charitable Organization B receives $100,000 in cash from a donor under a charitable remainder annuity trust agreement designating Organization B as the trustee and charitable remainder beneficiary—a donee. The terms of the trust agreement require that Organization B, as trustee, invest the trust assets and pay $5,000 each year to an annuitant (an income beneficiary specified by the donor) for the remainder of the annuitant's life. Upon death of the annuitant, Organization B may use its remainder interest for any purpose consistent with its mission.

178. Organization B, as a donee, would recognize the contribution received as revenue in the period the trust is established. The transfer is partially an exchange transaction—an agreement for annuity payments to a beneficiary over time—and partially a contribution. The contribution received by Organization B is the unconditional right to receive the remainder interest of the annuity trust. The amount of the contribution received by Organization B is the fair value of the trust assets ($100,000 cash transferred) less the fair value of the estimated annuity payments (the present value of $5,000 to be paid annually over the expected life of the annuitant). Because Organization B must invest the underlying donated assets until the annuitant's death, the revenue recognized for this type of contribution—temporarily restricted support—should be distinguished from revenues from gifts that are either unrestricted or permanently restricted (paragraph 14). The death of the annuitant determines when the required annuity payments cease and when the trust expires and effec-

tively removes all restrictions on the net assets of Organization B. If the terms of this agreement had specified that upon death of the annuitant Organization B is to use its remainder interest to establish a permanent endowment, the revenue would be recognized as permanently restricted support rather than temporarily restricted support.

Example 3—Receipt of Resources as an Agent Rather Than as a Donee

179. Organization C receives relief supplies from Individual D with instructions to deliver the supplies to specified third-party beneficiaries. Organization C accepts responsibility for delivering those supplies because it has a distribution network and a mutual interest in serving the needs of the specified beneficiaries. Organization C has no discretion in determining the parties to be benefited; it must deliver the resources to the specified beneficiaries. Receipt of those goods is not a contribution received to Organization C, nor is the delivery of those goods to the beneficiaries a contribution made by Organization C. Rather, a contribution of goods is made by Individual D and received by the third-party beneficiaries.

Example 4—Intermediary between Donor and Donee

180. Organization E develops and maintains a list of lawyers and law firms that are interested in providing services without charge to charitable organizations and certain individuals. Organization E encourages individuals in need of free legal services to contact Organization E for referral to lawyers in the individual's community that may be willing to serve them. The decision about whether and how to serve a specific individual rests with the lawyer. Under those circumstances, Organization E merely acts as an intermediary in bringing together a willing donor and donee. The free legal services are not a contribution received by Organization E.

Example 5—Intermediary between Government Provider and Its Beneficiary

181. Hospital F provides health care services to patients that are entitled to Medicaid assistance under a joint federal and state program. The program sets forth various administrative and technical requirements covering provider participation, payment mechanisms, and individual eligibility and benefit provisions. Medicaid payments made to Hospital F on behalf of the program beneficiaries are third-party

payments for patient services rendered. Hospital F provides patient care for a fee—an exchange transaction—and acts as an intermediary between the government provider of assistance and the eligible beneficiary. The Medicaid payments are not contributions to Hospital F.

Contributions Received

182. Contributions are received in several different forms. Most often the item contributed is an asset, but it also can be forgiveness of a liability. The types of assets commonly contributed include cash, marketable securities, land, buildings, use of facilities or utilities, materials and supplies, other goods or services, and unconditional promises to give those items in the future. This Statement requires entities receiving contributions to recognize them at the fair values of the assets received. However, recognition of contributions of works of art, historical treasures, and similar assets is not required if the donated items are added to collections (paragraph 11). Recognition of contributions of services is required for those contributed services received that meet one of the specified conditions of paragraph 9 of this Statement and is precluded for contributed services that do not. Examples 6-16 illustrate application of the recognition and measurement principles in this Statement.

Example 6—Contribution of Real Property

183. Mission G, a religious organization, receives a building (including the land on which it was constructed) as a gift from a local corporation with the understanding that the building will be used principally as an education and training center for organization members or for any other purpose consistent with the organization's mission. Educating and training its members is an important activity of the mission.

184. Mission G would recognize the contributed property as an asset and as support and measure that property at its fair value (paragraph 8). Information necessary to estimate the fair value of that property could be obtained from various sources, including (a) amounts recently paid for similar properties in the locality, (b) estimates of the market value of the property by local appraisers or real estate brokers, (c) an estimate of the fair value of the property by the local tax assessor's office, or (d) estimates of its replacement cost (paragraph 19). This contribution is unrestricted support because the donated assets may be used for any purpose and Mission G does not have a

policy of implying time restrictions on gifts of long-lived assets (paragraph 16). If Mission G's policy is to imply a time restriction, the contribution is temporarily restricted support and the restriction expires over the useful life of the building.

Example 7—Contribution of a Work of Art

185. Museum H, which preserves its collections as described in paragraph 11, receives a gift of a valuable painting from a donor. The donor obtained an independent appraisal of the fair value of the painting for tax purposes and furnished a copy to the museum. The museum staff evaluated the painting to determine its authenticity and worthiness for addition to the museum's collection. The staff recommended that the gift be accepted, adding that it was not aware of any evidence contradicting the fair value provided by the donor and the donor's appraiser.

186. If Museum H capitalizes its collections, Museum H would recognize the fair value of the contributed work of art received as revenue and capitalize it as an asset at its fair value (paragraphs 13 and 19). The staff of Museum H is qualified to estimate the fair value of the contributed painting and evidence of its fair value exists. If Museum H does not capitalize its collections, Museum H is precluded from recognizing the contribution (paragraph 13) and would provide the information required by paragraphs 26 and 27.

187. If Museum H accepted the painting with the donor's understanding that it would be sold rather than added to its collection, Museum H would recognize the contribution of the painting received as unrestricted revenue and as an asset at its fair value (paragraphs 8 and 16).

Example 8—Contribution of Historical Objects

188. Historical Society I receives several old photographs as a gift from a long-time local resident. The photographs depict a particular area as it was 75 years ago. After evaluating whether the photographs were worthy of addition to the historical society's collection, the staff concluded the photographs should be accepted solely because of their potential historical and educational use; that is, the photographs may be of interest to future researchers, historians, or others interested in studying the area. The photographs are not suitable for display and no alternative use exists.

189. Regardless of whether Historical Society I capitalizes its collections, Historical Society I would

not recognize the contributed photographs in this example as assets because there is major uncertainty about the existence of value and no alternative use exists (paragraph 19).

Example 9—Contribution of Utilities

190. Foundation J operates from a building it owns in City K. The holding company of a local utility has been contributing electricity on a continuous basis subject to the donor's cancellation.

191. The simultaneous receipt and use of electricity or other utilities is a form of contributed assets and not services. Foundation J would recognize the fair value of the contributed electricity as both revenue and expense in the period it is received and used (paragraph 8). Foundation J could estimate the fair value of the electricity received by using rates normally charged to a consumer of similar usage requirements.

Example 10—Contribution of Use of Property

192. Charity L receives the free use of 10,000 square feet of prime office space provided by a local company. The local company has informed Charity L that it intends to continue providing the space as long as it is available, and although it expects it would be able to give the charity 30 days advance notice, it may discontinue providing the space at any time. The local company normally rents similar space for $14 to $16 annually per square foot, the going market rate for office space in the area. Charity L decides to accept this gift—the free use of office space—to conduct its daily central administrative activities.

193. The simultaneous receipt and use of facilities is a form of contributed assets and not services. Charity L would recognize the fair value of the contributed use of facilities as both revenue and expense in the period it is received and used (paragraph 8).

194. If the local company explicitly and unconditionally promises the use of the facility for a specified period of time (for example, five years), the promise would be an unconditional promise to give. In that case, Charity L would recognize the receipt of the unconditional promise as a receivable and as restricted support at its fair value. The donor would recognize the unconditional promise when made as a payable and an expense at its fair value (paragraph 18).

Example 11—Contribution of Services

195. Institute M decides to construct a building on its property. It obtains the necessary architectural plans

and specifications and purchases the necessary continuing architectural services, materials, permits, and so forth at a total cost of $400,000. A local construction company contributes the necessary labor and equipment. An independent appraisal of the building (exclusive of land), obtained for insurance purposes, estimates its fair value at $725,000.

196. Institute M would recognize the services contributed by the construction company because the contributed services received meet condition (a)—the services received create or enhance nonfinancial assets—or because the services meet condition (b)—the services require specialized skills, are provided by individuals possessing those skills, and would typically need to be purchased if not provided by donation (paragraph 9). Contributions of services that create or enhance nonfinancial assets may be measured by referring to either the fair value of the services received or the fair value of the asset or of the asset enhancement resulting from the services (paragraph 19). In this example, the fair value of the contributed services received could be determined by subtracting the cost of the purchased services, materials, and permits ($400,000) from the fair value of the asset created ($725,000), which results in contributed services received of $325,000. Alternatively, the amount the construction company would have charged could be used if more readily available.

197. If some of the labor did not require specialized skills and was provided by volunteers, those services still would be recognized because they meet condition (a).

Example 12—Contribution of Services

198. Faculty salaries are a major expense of University N. The faculty includes both compensated faculty members (approximately 80 percent) and uncompensated faculty members (approximately 20 percent) who are associated with religious orders and contribute their services to the university. The performance of both compensated and uncompensated faculty members is regularly and similarly evaluated; both must meet the university's standards and both provide services in the same way.

199. University N would recognize both revenue and expense for the services contributed by the uncompensated faculty members because the contribution meets condition (b) of paragraph 9. Teaching requires specialized skills; the religious personnel are qualified and trained to provide those skills; and University N typically would hire paid instructors if the

religious personnel did not donate their services. University N could refer to the salaries it pays similarly qualified compensated faculty members to determine fair value of the services received.

200. Similarly, if the uncompensated faculty members in this example were given a nominal stipend to help defray certain of their out-of-pocket expenses, University N still would recognize both revenue and expense for the services contributed. The contribution received would be measured at the fair value of the services received less the amount of the nominal stipend paid.

Example 13—Contribution of Services

201. A member of the Board of Trustees of Civic Organization O is a lawyer and from time to time in the capacity of a trustee provides advice on general business matters, including questions about business opportunities and risks and ethical, moral, and legal matters. The advice provided on legal matters is provided as a trustee in the role of a trustee, not as a lawyer, and the opinions generally are limited to routine matters. Generally, the lawyer suggests that Civic Organization O seek the opinion of its attorneys on substantive or complex legal questions. All of the organization's trustees serve without compensation, and most trustees have specialized expertise (for example, a chief executive officer, a minister, a physician, a professor, and a public accountant) that makes their advice valuable to Civic Organization O. The trustee-lawyer also serves without compensation as a trustee for two other charitable organizations.

202. Civic Organization O would be precluded from recognizing the contributed services it receives from its trustee-lawyer or its other trustees because the services contributed do not meet either of the conditions of paragraph 9 of this Statement. Condition (a) is not relevant. The trustee-lawyer's services do not meet condition (b) because the substantive or complex legal questions that require the specialized skills of a lawyer are referred to the organization's attorneys or because the advice provided by trustees typically would not be purchased if not provided by donation.

Example 14—Contribution of Services

203. Hospital P provides short-term inpatient and outpatient care and also provides long-term care for the elderly. As part of the long-term care program, the hospital has organized a program whereby local high school students may contribute a minimum of 10 hours a week, from 3:00 p.m. to 6:00 p.m., to the hospital. These students are assigned various duties, such as visiting and talking with the patients, distributing books and magazines, reading, playing chess, and similar activities. The hospital does not pay for these services or similar services. The services are accepted as a way of enhancing or supplementing the quality of care and comfort provided to the elderly long-term care patients.

204. Hospital P would be precluded from recognizing the contributed services because the services contributed do not meet either of the conditions of paragraph 9 of this Statement. Condition (a) is not relevant. Condition (b) has not been met because the services the students provide do not require specialized skills nor would they typically need to be purchased if not provided by donation.

Example 15—Contribution of Services

205. College Q conducts an annual fund-raising campaign to solicit contributions from its alumni. In prior years, College Q recruited unpaid student volunteers to make phone calls to its alumni. This year, a telemarketing company, whose president is an alumnus of College Q, contributed its services to College Q for the annual alumni fund-raising campaign. The company normally provides telemarketing services to a variety of clients on a fee basis. College Q provided the company with a list of 10,000 alumni, several copies of a typed appeal to be read over the phone, and blank contribution forms to record pledges received. The company contacted most of the 10,000 alumni.

206. College Q would be precluded from recognizing the contributed services of the telemarketing company. Condition (a) of paragraph 9 is not relevant. Condition (b) has not been met because the services do not require specialized skills or because College Q typically would not need to purchase the services if they were not provided by donation. College Q normally conducts its campaign with untrained students in a manner similar to the manner used by the telemarketing firm.

*Example 16—Contribution of an Interest
in an Estate*

207. In 19X0, Individual R notifies Church S that she has remembered the church in her will and provides a written copy of the will. In 19X5, Individ-

ual R dies. In 19X6, Individual R's last will and testament enters probate and the probate court declares the will valid. The executor informs Church S that the will has been declared valid and that it will receive 10 percent of Individual R's estate, after satisfying the estate's liabilities and certain specific bequests. The executor provides an estimate of the estate's assets and liabilities and the expected amount and time for payment of Church S's interest in the estate.

208. The 19X0 communication between Individual R and Church S specified an intention to give. The ability to modify a will at any time prior to death is well established; thus in 19X0 Church S did not receive a promise to give and did not recognize a contribution received. When the probate court declares the will valid, Church S would recognize a receivable and revenue for an unconditional promise to give at the fair value of its interest in the estate (paragraphs 8 and 19-21). If the promise to give contained in the valid will was instead conditioned on a future and uncertain event, Church S would recognize the contribution when the condition was substantially met. A conditional promise in a valid will would be disclosed in notes to financial statements (paragraph 25).

Appendix D

GLOSSARY

209. This appendix contains definitions of certain terms used in this Statement.

Collections

Works of art, historical treasures, or similar assets that are (a) held for public exhibition, education, or research in furtherance of public service rather than financial gain, (b) protected, kept unencumbered, cared for, and preserved, and (c) subject to an organizational policy that requires the proceeds of items that are sold to be used to acquire other items for collections.

Conditional promise to give

A promise to give that depends on the occurrence of a specified future and uncertain event to bind the promisor.

Contribution

An unconditional transfer of cash or other assets to an entity or a settlement or cancellation of its liabilities in a voluntary nonreciprocal transfer by another entity acting other than as an owner.

Donor-imposed condition

A donor stipulation that specifies a future and uncertain event whose occurrence or failure to occur gives the promisor a right of return of the assets it has transferred or releases the promisor from its obligation to transfer its assets.

Donor-imposed restriction

A donor stipulation that specifies a use for the contributed asset that is more specific than broad limits resulting from the nature of the organization, the environment in which it operates, and the purposes specified in its articles of incorporation or bylaws or comparable documents for an unincorporated association. A restriction on an organization's use of the asset contributed may be temporary or permanent.

Nonreciprocal transfer

A transaction in which an entity incurs a liability or transfers an asset to another entity (or receives an asset or cancellation of a liability) without directly receiving (or giving) value in exchange.

Not-for-profit organization

An entity that possesses the following characteristics that distinguish it from a business enterprise: (a) contributions of significant amounts of resources from resource providers who do not expect commensurate or proportionate pecuniary return, (b) operating purposes other than to provide goods or services at a profit, and (c) absence of ownership interests like those of business enterprises. Not-for-profit organizations have those characteristics in varying degrees (Concepts Statement 4, paragraph 6). Organizations that clearly fall outside this definition include all investor-owned enterprises and entities that provide dividends, lower costs, or other economic benefits directly and proportionately to their owners, members, or participants, such as mutual insurance companies, credit unions, farm and rural electric cooperatives, and employee benefit plans (Concepts Statement 4, paragraph 7).

Permanent restriction

A donor-imposed restriction that stipulates that resources be maintained permanently but permits the organization to use up or expend part or all of the income (or other economic benefits) derived from the donated assets.

Permanently restricted net assets

The part of the net assets of a not-for-profit organization resulting (a) from contributions and other inflows of assets whose use by the organization is limited by donor-imposed stipulations that neither expire by passage of time nor can be fulfilled or otherwise removed by actions of the organization, (b) from other asset enhancements and diminishments subject to the same kinds of stipulations, and (c) from reclassifications from (or to) other classes of net assets as a consequence of donor-imposed stipulations (Concepts Statement 6, paragraph 92).

Promise to give

A written or oral agreement to contribute cash or other assets to another entity. A promise to give may be either conditional or unconditional.

Restricted support

Donor-restricted revenues or gains from contributions that increase either temporarily restricted net assets or permanently restricted net assets. Also refer to **Unrestricted support**.

Temporarily restricted net assets

The part of the net assets of a not-for-profit organization resulting (a) from contributions and other inflows of assets whose use by the organization is limited by donor-imposed stipulations that either expire by passage of time or can be fulfilled and removed by actions of the organization pursuant to those stipulations, (b) from other asset enhancements and diminishments subject to the same kinds of stipulations, and (c) from reclassifications to (or from) other classes of net assets as a consequence of donor-imposed stipulations, their expiration by passage of time, or their fulfillment and removal by actions of the organization pursuant to those stipulations (Concepts Statement 6, paragraph 93).

Temporary restriction

A donor-imposed restriction that permits the donee organization to use up or expend the donated assets as specified and is satisfied either by the passage of time or by actions of the organization.

Unconditional promise to give

A promise to give that depends only on passage of time or demand by the promisee for performance.

Unrestricted net assets

The part of net assets of a not-for-profit organization that is neither permanently restricted nor temporarily restricted by donor-imposed stipulations (Concepts Statement 6, paragraph 94).

Unrestricted support

Revenues or gains from contributions that are not restricted by donors. Also refer to **Restricted support.**

Statement of Financial Accounting Standards No. 117
Financial Statements of Not-for-Profit Organizations

STATUS

Issued: June 1993

Effective Date: For fiscal years beginning after December 15, 1994

Affects: Amends FAS 95, paragraphs 3, 18, 19, 27(b), 28 through 30, 32, and 130 and footnote 12

Affected by: Paragraph 164 amended by FAS 144
Paragraph 168 amended by FAS 124

Other Interpretive Release: FASB *Highlights,* "Time for a Change—Implementing FASB Statements 116 and 117," January 1995

Issues Discussed by FASB Emerging Issues Task Force (EITF)

Affects: No EITF Issues

Interpreted by: Paragraph 22 interpreted by EITF Topic No. D-49

Related Issues: No EITF Issues

SUMMARY

This Statement establishes standards for general-purpose external financial statements provided by a not-for-profit organization. Its objective is to enhance the relevance, understandability, and comparability of financial statements issued by those organizations. It requires that those financial statements provide certain basic information that focuses on the entity as a whole and meets the common needs of external users of those statements.

This Statement requires that all not-for-profit organizations provide a statement of financial position, a statement of activities, and a statement of cash flows. It requires reporting amounts for the organization's total assets, liabilities, and net assets in a statement of financial position; reporting the change in an organization's net assets in a statement of activities; and reporting the change in its cash and cash equivalents in a statement of cash flows.

This Statement also requires classification of an organization's net assets and its revenues, expenses, gains, and losses based on the existence or absence of donor-imposed restrictions. It requires that the amounts for each of three classes of net assets—permanently restricted, temporarily restricted, and unrestricted—be displayed in a statement of financial position and that the amounts of change in each of those classes of net assets be displayed in a statement of activities.

This Statement amends FASB Statement No. 95, *Statement of Cash Flows,* to extend its provisions to not-for-profit organizations and to expand its description of cash flows from financing activities to include certain donor-restricted cash that must be used for long-term purposes. It also requires that voluntary health and welfare organizations provide a statement of functional expenses that reports expenses by both functional and natural classifications.

This Statement is effective for annual financial statements issued for fiscal years beginning after December 15, 1994, except for organizations with less than $5 million in total assets and less than $1 million in annual expenses. For those organizations, the Statement is effective for fiscal years beginning after December 15, 1995. Earlier application is encouraged.

Statement of Financial Accounting Standards No. 117

Financial Statements of Not-for-Profit Organizations

CONTENTS

INTRODUCTION

1. This Statement establishes standards for general-purpose external financial statements provided by a **not-for-profit organization**.[1] It specifies that those statements include a statement of financial position, a statement of activities, and a statement of cash flows. This Statement also amends FASB Statement No. 95, *Statement of Cash Flows,* to extend its provisions to not-for-profit organizations. It also specifies that **voluntary health and welfare organizations** continue to provide a statement of functional expenses, which is useful in associating expenses with service efforts and accomplishments of not-for-profit organizations.

2. Not-for-profit organizations currently provide financial statements that differ in their form and content. For example, most hospitals, trade associations, and membership organizations provide a statement of financial position and a statement of activities (or statement of revenues and expenses) that report their financial position and results of operations for the entity as a whole. In contrast, universities, museums, religious organizations, and certain other not-for-profit organizations often provide financial statements that report the financial position and changes in financial position of individual fund groups, but many do not report financial position and results of operations for the entity as a whole. Recently, some not-for-profit organizations have begun reporting cash flow information, but most do not. Further, voluntary health and welfare organizations and certain other charitable organizations generally provide a statement that reports expenses by **functional classification** and by

---

[1]Words that appear in the glossary are set in **boldface type** the first time they appear.

natural classification, but most other not-for-profit organizations do not.

3. This Statement is part of a project that has been considering those and other inconsistent practices of not-for-profit organizations, including accounting and reporting principles and practices that are incorporated in several of the audit Guides of the American Institute of Certified Public Accountants (Appendix A). Because this Statement now establishes standards for reporting certain basic information in financial statements that are applicable to all not-for-profit organizations, provisions in AICPA Guides and Statements of Position that are inconsistent with this Statement are no longer acceptable *specialized*[2] accounting and reporting principles and practices. Within the parameters of this Statement, the AICPA or another appropriate body, following the process described in AICPA Statement on Auditing Standards (SAS) No. 69, *The Meaning of "Present Fairly in Conformity With Generally Accepted Accounting Principles" in the Independent Auditor's Report,* may provide more specific reporting guidance for certain not-for-profit organizations.

STANDARDS OF FINANCIAL ACCOUNTING AND REPORTING

Purpose of a Set of Financial Statements

4. The primary purpose of financial statements is to provide relevant information to meet the common interests of donors, members, creditors, and others who provide resources to not-for-profit organizations. Those external users of financial statements have common interests in assessing (a) the services an organization provides and its ability to continue to provide those services and (b) how managers discharge their stewardship responsibilities and other aspects of their performance.

5. More specifically, the purpose of financial statements, including accompanying notes, is to provide information about:

a. The amount and nature of an organization's assets, liabilities, and net assets
b. The effects of transactions and other events and circumstances that change the amount and nature of net assets

c. The amount and kinds of inflows and outflows of economic resources during a period and the relation between the inflows and outflows
d. How an organization obtains and spends cash, its borrowing and repayment of borrowing, and other factors that may affect its liquidity
e. The service efforts of an organization.

Individual financial statements provide different information, and the information each statement provides generally complements information in other financial statements.

Scope

6. A complete set of financial statements of a not-for-profit organization shall include a statement of financial position as of the end of the reporting period, a statement of activities and a statement of cash flows for the reporting period, and accompanying notes to financial statements.

7. This Statement specifies certain basic information to be reported in financial statements of not-for-profit organizations. Its requirements generally are no more stringent than requirements for business enterprises. A set of financial statements includes, either in the body of financial statements or in the accompanying notes, that information required by generally accepted accounting principles that do not specifically exempt not-for-profit organizations and required by applicable specialized accounting and reporting principles and practices. For example, not-for-profit organizations should apply the disclosure and display provisions for financial instruments; loss contingencies; extraordinary, unusual, and infrequently occurring events; and accounting changes.

8. This Statement discusses how to report assets, liabilities, net assets, revenues, expenses, gains, and losses in financial statements; however, it does not specify when to recognize or how to measure those elements. The degree of aggregation and order of presentation of items of assets and liabilities in statements of financial position or of items of revenues and expenses in statements of activities of not-for-profit organizations, although not specified by this Statement, generally should be similar to those required or permitted for business enterprises. Appendix C includes financial statements that illustrate some of the ways that the requirements of this Statement may be met.

---

[2] The term *specialized* is used to refer to those current accounting and reporting principles and practices in existing AICPA Guides and Statements of Position that are neither superseded by nor contained in the Accounting Research Bulletins, APB Opinions, FASB Statements, and FASB Interpretations.

Statement of Financial Position

Purpose and Focus of a Statement of Financial Position

9. The primary purpose of a statement of financial position is to provide relevant information about an organization's assets, liabilities, and net assets and about their relationships to each other at a moment in time. The information provided in a statement of financial position, used with related disclosures and information in other financial statements, helps donors, members, creditors, and others to assess (a) the organization's ability to continue to provide services and (b) the organization's liquidity, financial flexibility,[3] ability to meet obligations, and needs for external financing.

10. A statement of financial position shall focus on the organization as a whole and shall report the amounts of its total assets, liabilities, and net assets.

Classification of Assets and Liabilities

11. A statement of financial position, including accompanying notes to financial statements, provides relevant information about liquidity, financial flexibility, and the interrelationship of an organization's assets and liabilities. That information generally is provided by aggregating assets and liabilities that possess similar characteristics into reasonably homogeneous groups. For example, entities generally report individual items of assets in homogeneous groups, such as cash and cash equivalents; accounts and notes receivable from patients, students, members, and other recipients of services; inventories of materials and supplies; deposits and prepayments for rent, insurance, and other services; marketable securities and other investment assets held for long-term purposes; and land, buildings, equipment, and other long-lived assets used to provide goods and services. Cash or other assets received with a **donor-imposed restriction** that limits their use to long-term purposes should not be classified with cash or other assets that are unrestricted and available for current use.[4]

12. Information about liquidity shall be provided by one or more of the following:

a. Sequencing assets according to their nearness of conversion to cash and sequencing liabilities according to the nearness of their maturity and resulting use of cash

b. Classifying assets and liabilities as current and noncurrent, as defined by Accounting Research Bulletin No. 43, Chapter 3A, "Working Capital—Current Assets and Current Liabilities"

c. Disclosing in notes to financial statements relevant information about the liquidity or maturity of assets and liabilities, including restrictions on the use of particular assets.

Classification of Net Assets as Donor Restricted or Unrestricted

13. A statement of financial position provided by a not-for-profit organization shall report the amounts for each of three classes of net assets—**permanently restricted net assets, temporarily restricted net assets**, and **unrestricted net assets**—based on the existence or absence of donor-imposed restrictions.

14. Information about the nature and amounts of different types of **permanent restrictions** or **temporary restrictions** shall be provided either by reporting their amounts on the face of the statement or by including relevant details in notes to financial statements. Separate line items may be reported within permanently restricted net assets or in notes to financial statements to distinguish between permanent restrictions for holdings of (a) assets, such as land or works of art, donated with stipulations that they be used for a specified purpose, be preserved, and not be sold or (b) assets donated with stipulations that they be invested to provide a permanent source of income. The latter result from gifts and bequests that create permanent **endowment funds**.

15. Similarly, separate line items may be reported within temporarily restricted net assets or in notes to financial statements to distinguish between temporary restrictions for (a) support of particular operating

---

[3]Liquidity reflects an asset's or liability's nearness to cash. Financial flexibility is the ability of an entity to take effective actions to alter amounts and timing of cash flows so it can respond to unexpected needs and opportunities. Information about the nature and amount of restrictions imposed by donors on the use of contributed assets, including their potential effects on specific assets and on liabilities or classes of net assets, is helpful in assessing the financial flexibility of a not-for-profit organization.

[4]ARB No. 43, Chapter 3A, "Working Capital—Current Assets and Current Liabilities," paragraph 6, says that the "concept of the nature of current assets contemplates the exclusion from that classification of . . . cash and claims to cash which are restricted as to withdrawal or use for other than current operations, are designated for expenditure in the acquisition or construction of noncurrent assets, or are segregated[1] for the liquidation of long-term debts," and footnote 1 explains that "even though not actually set aside in special accounts, funds that are clearly to be used in the near future for the liquidation of long-term debts, payments to sinking funds, or for similar purposes should also . . . be excluded from current assets."

activities, (b) investment for a specified term, (c) use in a specified future period, or (d) acquisition of long-lived assets. Donors' temporary restrictions may require that resources be used in a later period or after a specified date (time restrictions), or that resources be used for a specified purpose (purpose restrictions), or both. For example, gifts of cash and other assets with stipulations that they be invested to provide a source of income for a specified term and that the income be used for a specified purpose are both time and purpose restricted. Those gifts often are called *term endowments*.

16. Unrestricted net assets generally result from revenues from providing services, producing and delivering goods, receiving unrestricted contributions, and receiving dividends or interest from investing in income-producing assets, less expenses incurred in providing services, producing and delivering goods, raising contributions, and performing administrative functions. The only limits on the use of unrestricted net assets are the broad limits resulting from the nature of the organization, the environment in which it operates, and the purposes specified in its articles of incorporation or bylaws and limits resulting from contractual agreements with suppliers, creditors, and others entered into by the organization in the course of its business. Information about those contractual limits that are significant, including the existence of loan covenants, generally is provided in notes to financial statements. Similarly, information about self-imposed limits that may be useful, including information about voluntary resolutions by the governing board of an organization to designate a portion of its unrestricted net assets to function as an endowment (sometimes called a *board-designated endowment*), may be provided in notes to or on the face of financial statements.

Statement of Activities

Purpose and Focus of a Statement of Activities

17. The primary purpose of a statement of activities is to provide relevant information about (a) the effects of transactions and other events and circumstances that change the amount and nature of net assets, (b) the relationships of those transactions and

other events and circumstances to each other, and (c) how the organization's resources are used in providing various programs or services. The information provided in a statement of activities, used with related disclosures and information in the other financial statements, helps donors, creditors, and others to (1) evaluate the organization's performance during a period, (2) assess an organization's service efforts and its ability to continue to provide services, and (3) assess how an organization's managers have discharged their stewardship responsibilities and other aspects of their performance.

18. A statement of activities provided by a not-for-profit organization shall focus on the organization as a whole and shall report the amount of the change in net assets for the period. It shall use a descriptive term such as *change in net assets* or *change in equity*.[5] The change in net assets should articulate to the net assets or equity reported in the statement of financial position.

Changes in Classes of Net Assets

19. A statement of activities shall report the amount of change in permanently restricted net assets, temporarily restricted net assets, and unrestricted net assets for the period. Revenues, expenses, gains, and losses increase or decrease net assets and shall be classified as provided in paragraphs 20-23. Other events, such as expirations of donor-imposed restrictions, that simultaneously increase one class of net assets and decrease another (reclassifications) shall be reported as separate items. Information about revenues, expenses, gains, losses, and reclassifications generally is provided by aggregating items that possess similar characteristics into reasonably homogeneous groups.

Classification of Revenues, Expenses, Gains, and Losses

20. A statement of activities shall report revenues as increases in unrestricted net assets unless the use of the assets received is limited by donor-imposed restrictions. For example, fees from rendering services and income from investments generally are unrestricted; however, income from donor-restricted permanent or term endowments may be donor restricted

---

[5]This Statement does not use the terms *fund balance* or *changes in fund balances* because in current practice those terms are commonly used to refer to individual groups of assets and related liabilities rather than to an entity's net assets or changes in net assets taken as a whole. Reporting by fund groups is not a necessary part of external financial reporting; however, this Statement does not preclude providing disaggregated information by fund groups.

and increase either temporarily restricted net assets or permanently restricted net assets. A statement of activities shall report expenses as decreases in unrestricted net assets.

21. Pursuant to FASB Statement No. 116, *Accounting for Contributions Received and Contributions Made,* in the absence of a donor's explicit stipulation or circumstances surrounding the receipt of the contribution that make clear the donor's implicit restriction on use, contributions are reported as unrestricted revenues or gains (**unrestricted support**), which increase unrestricted net assets. Donor-restricted contributions are reported as restricted revenues or gains (**restricted support**), which increase temporarily restricted net assets or permanently restricted net assets depending on the type of restriction. However, donor-restricted contributions whose restrictions are met in the same reporting period may be reported as unrestricted support provided that an organization reports consistently from period to period and discloses its accounting policy.

22. A statement of activities shall report gains and losses recognized on investments and other assets (or liabilities) as increases or decreases in unrestricted net assets unless their use is temporarily or permanently restricted by explicit donor stipulations or by law. For example, net gains on investment assets, to the extent recognized in financial statements, are reported as increases in unrestricted net assets unless their use is restricted to a specified purpose or future period. If the governing board determines that the relevant law requires the organization to retain permanently some portion of gains on investment assets of endowment funds, that amount shall be reported as an increase in permanently restricted net assets.

23. Classifying revenues, expenses, gains, and losses within classes of net assets does not preclude incorporating additional classifications within a statement of activities. For example, within a class or classes of changes in net assets, an organization may classify items as *operating* and nonoperating, expendable and nonexpendable, earned and unearned, recurring and nonrecurring, or in other ways. This Statement neither encourages nor discourages those further classifications. However, because terms such as *operating income, operating profit, operating surplus, operating deficit,* and *results of operations* are used with different meanings, if an intermediate measure of *operations* (for example, excess or deficit of *operating* revenues over expenses) is reported, it shall be in a fi-

nancial statement that, at a minimum, reports the change in unrestricted net assets for the period. If an organization's use of the term *operations* is not apparent from the details provided on the face of the statement, a note to financial statements shall describe the nature of the reported measure of operations or the items excluded from operations.

Information about Gross Amounts of Revenues and Expenses

24. To help explain the relationships of a not-for-profit organization's ongoing major or central operations and activities, a statement of activities shall report the gross amounts of revenues and expenses. However, investment revenues may be reported net of related expenses, such as custodial fees and investment advisory fees, provided that the amount of the expenses is disclosed either on the face of the statement of activities or in notes to financial statements.

25. A statement of activities may report gains and losses as net amounts if they result from peripheral or incidental transactions or from other events and circumstances that may be largely beyond the control of the organization and its management. Information about their net amounts generally is adequate to understand the organization's activities. For example, an entity that sells land and buildings no longer needed for its ongoing activities commonly reports that transaction as a net gain or loss, rather than as gross revenues for the sales value and expense for the carrying value of the land and buildings sold. The net amount of those peripheral transactions, used with information in a statement of cash flows, usually is adequate to help assess how an entity uses its resources and how managers discharge their stewardship responsibilities.

Information about an Organization's Service Efforts

26. To help donors, creditors, and others in assessing an organization's service efforts, including the costs of its services and how it uses resources, a statement of activities or notes to financial statements shall provide information about expenses reported by their functional classification such as major classes of program services and supporting activities. Voluntary health and welfare organizations shall report that information as well as information about expenses by their natural classification, such as salaries, rent, electricity, interest expense, depreciation, awards and

grants to others, and professional fees, in a matrix format in a separate financial statement. Other not-for-profit organizations are encouraged, but not required, to provide information about expenses by their natural classification.

27. Program services are the activities that result in goods and services being distributed to beneficiaries, customers, or members that fulfill the purposes or mission for which the organization exists. Those services are the major purpose for and the major output of the organization and often relate to several major programs. For example, a large university may have programs for student instruction, research, and patient care, among others. Similarly, a health and welfare organization may have programs for health or family services, research, disaster relief, and public education, among others.[6]

28. Supporting activities are all activities of a not-for-profit organization other than program services. Generally, they include management and general, fund-raising, and membership-development activities. Management and general activities include oversight, business management, general recordkeeping, budgeting, financing, and related administrative activities, and all management and administration except for direct conduct of program services or fund-raising activities. Fund-raising activities include publicizing and conducting fund-raising campaigns; maintaining donor mailing lists; conducting special fund-raising events; preparing and distributing fund-raising manuals, instructions, and other materials; and conducting other activities involved with soliciting contributions from individuals, foundations, government agencies, and others. Membership-development activities include soliciting for prospective members and membership dues, membership relations, and similar activities.

Statement of Cash Flows

Purpose of a Statement of Cash Flows

29. The primary purpose of a statement of cash flows is to provide relevant information about the cash receipts and cash payments of an organization during a period. Statement 95 discusses how that in-

formation helps investors, creditors, and others and establishes standards for the information to be provided in a statement of cash flows of a business enterprise.

Amendments to Statement 95

30. Statement 95 is amended to extend its provisions to not-for-profit organizations as follows:

a. In the first sentence of paragraph 3, *or not-for-profit organization* is added after *business enterprise.*

b. In paragraph 3, the following is added after the first sentence:

> In this Statement *enterprise* encompasses both business enterprises and not-for-profit organizations, and the phrase *investors, creditors, and others* encompasses donors. The terms *income statement* and *net income* apply to a business enterprise; the terms *statement of activities* and *change in net assets* apply to a not-for-profit organization.

c. In paragraph 18, the following is added after *investment;* :

> receiving restricted resources that by donor stipulation must be used for long-term purposes;

d. In paragraph 19, the following is added to the end of the list:

> c. Receipts from contributions and investment income that by donor stipulation are restricted for the purposes of acquiring, constructing, or improving property, plant, equipment, or other long-lived assets or establishing or increasing a permanent endowment or term endowment.

e. In paragraph 27(b), the following footnote is added after *received*:

> *Interest and dividends that are donor restricted

---

[6]Information about an organization's major programs (or segments) can be enhanced by reporting the interrelationships of program expenses and program revenues. For example, a university might report expenses for its instruction and other academic services with related revenues from student tuition and expenses for its housing and food services with related revenues from room and board fees. Related nonmonetary information about program inputs, outputs, and results also is helpful; for example, information about applications, acceptances, admissions, enrollment and occupancy rates, and degrees granted. Generally, reporting that kind of information is feasible only in supplementary information or management explanations or by other methods of financial reporting.

for long-term purposes as noted in paragraphs 18 and 19(c) are not part of operating cash receipts.

f. In paragraphs 28, 29, and 30 and in footnote 12, the following is added after each reference to *net income*:

of a business enterprise or change in net assets of a not-for-profit organization

g. In the third sentence of paragraph 32, the following is added after *lease;*:

obtaining a building or investment asset by receiving a gift;

h. In paragraph 130, the following is added to the end of the first sentence:

of business enterprises. Appendix C of Statement No. 117, *Financial Statements of Not-for-Profit Organizations,* provides illustrations for the preparation of statements of cash flows for a not-for-profit organization.

Effective Date and Transition

31. This Statement shall be effective for annual financial statements issued for fiscal years beginning after December 15, 1994, except for organizations with less than $5 million in total assets and less than $1 million in annual expenses. For those organizations, the effective date shall be for fiscal years beginning after December 15, 1995. Earlier application is encouraged. This Statement need not be applied in financial statements for interim periods in the initial year of application, but information for those interim periods shall be reclassified if reported with annual financial statements for that fiscal year. If comparative annual financial statements are presented for earlier periods, those financial statements shall be reclassified (or restated) to reflect retroactive application of the provisions of this Statement. In the year that this Statement is first applied, the financial statements shall disclose the nature of any restatements and their effect, if any, on the change in net assets for each year presented.

The provisions of this Statement need not be applied to immaterial items.

This Statement was adopted by the unanimous vote of the seven members of the Financial Accounting Standards Board:

Dennis R. Beresford, *Chairman*	Victor H. Brown	A. Clarence Sampson
Joseph V. Anania	James J. Leisenring	Robert J. Swieringa
	Robert H. Northcutt	

Appendix A

BACKGROUND INFORMATION

32. This Statement considers and sets standards to resolve inconsistencies in financial statement display practices of not-for-profit organizations and has been coordinated with Statement 116 that considers accounting for contributions. This Statement also considers the specialized accounting and reporting principles of not-for-profit organizations that are described in the following AICPA documents:

a. *Audits of Colleges and Universities,* 1973
b. *Audits of Voluntary Health and Welfare Organizations,* 1974

c. Statement of Position 78-10, *Accounting Principles and Reporting Practices for Certain Nonprofit Organizations,* 1978
d. *Audits of Providers of Health Care Services,* 1990.

33. In March 1986, the Board added a project to its agenda to establish standards needed to resolve certain inconsistent accounting and reporting practices of not-for-profit organizations. Initially the project had two major parts: accounting for contributions and accounting for depreciation. The Board completed the depreciation part in 1987 when it issued FASB Statement No. 93, *Recognition of Depreciation by Not-for-Profit Organizations.*

34. In April 1986, with the Board's encouragement, the AICPA agreed to undertake a project to study

matters of financial statement display. The AICPA's Accounting Standards Executive Committee (AcSEC) established a Not-for-Profit Organizations Task Force to prepare a report on display issues. In December 1988, AcSEC submitted its task force's report, *Display in the Financial Statements of Not-for-Profit Organizations,* to the Board. In February 1989, the Board added financial statement display as a third part of its project to establish standards for not-for-profit organizations.

35. In August 1989, the Board issued an Invitation to Comment, *Financial Reporting by Not-for-Profit Organizations: Form and Content of Financial Statements,* that included the AICPA task force report and requested comments on issues raised by that report. It identified 26 issues, many of which included one or more subordinate issues. The Board received more than 150 written responses to the Invitation to Comment. The AICPA task force report and the responses to the issues it raised provided useful information that assisted the Board in its deliberations. The major issues and the basis for the Board's conclusions on those issues are discussed in Appendix B.

36. In October 1992, the Board issued the Exposure Draft, *Financial Statements of Not-for-Profit Organizations.* The Board received more than 280 comment letters on that Exposure Draft, and 24 organizations and individuals presented their views during a public hearing held on February 25 and 26, 1993. In November 1992, the Board also issued a related revised Exposure Draft, *Accounting for Contributions Received and Contributions Made.* Twenty organizations participated in a field test of these proposed Statements. Those organizations shared their recasted financial statements with 39 users of financial statements who also participated in this field test. The field test results, the details of which are confidential at the request of some participants, and the written comments and public hearing testimony of respondents to both proposed Statements were considered by the Board at a number of public Board meetings and at public meetings of the FASB Task Force on Accounting Issues for Not-for-Profit Organizations. That 17-member task force has provided advice on technical matters and about the priorities of the issues considered during all stages of the project.

Appendix B

BASIS FOR CONCLUSIONS

CONTENTS

Appendix B

BASIS FOR CONCLUSIONS

Introduction

37. This appendix summarizes considerations that Board members deemed significant in reaching the conclusions in this Statement. It includes reasons for accepting certain views and rejecting others. Individual Board members gave greater weight to some factors than to others.

Benefits and Costs

38. The mission of the FASB is to establish and improve standards of financial accounting and reporting for the guidance and education of the public, including issuers, auditors, and users of financial information. In fulfilling that mission the Board strives to determine that a proposed standard will fill a significant need and that the costs imposed to meet that standard, as compared with other alternatives, are justified in relation to the overall benefits of the resulting information. Because there is no common gauge by which to judge objectively the costs to implement a standard against the need to improve information in financial statements, the Board's assessment of the costs and benefits of issuing an accounting standard is unavoidably subjective. Moreover, because the costs to implement a new standard are not borne directly by those who derive the benefits of the improved reporting, the Board must balance the diverse and often conflicting needs of preparers, investors, donors, creditors, and others who use financial statements.

39. The Board's objective in issuing this Statement is to improve the relevance, understandability, and comparability of general-purpose financial statements issued by not-for-profit organizations. Those organizations currently provide financial statements that differ in their form and content. The Board believes that this Statement fills a significant need by requiring information that meets the objectives of financial reporting for not-for-profit organizations, by defining what constitutes a complete set of general-purpose financial statements for those organizations, and by requiring methods of reporting that information that are comprehensive, understandable, useful for decisions by present and potential resource providers, and consistent with the Board's conceptual framework.

40. The Board concluded that the overall benefits of the information provided by applying this Statement justify the costs that this Statement may impose. Although there will be transitional costs as not-for-profit organizations apply the requirements of this Statement, the Board believes that those organizations generally have the information systems that are needed to meet those requirements and that the ongoing costs should not be significantly greater than for existing requirements. The Board also believes that some of the costs this Statement imposes have been reduced in various ways: by limiting the provisions of this Statement to requirements that are generally no more stringent than those for business enterprises, by providing broad guidance and allowing some latitude in how information is reported in financial statements, and by extending the effective date of application of this Statement.

Framework for Considering Issues on Financial Statement Display

41. The Board's consideration about what information should be reported in financial statements provided by not-for-profit organizations and how it should be displayed benefited from initial research contained in the report of the AICPA task force, which was included in the Invitation to Comment. The issues identified in that report, as well as the comments received, provided a framework for considering the kind of information that might be required or permitted to be reported or precluded from being reported in financial statements.

42. Several respondents to the Invitation to Comment suggested that the Board focus its efforts on fundamental issues and the Board agreed. It concluded that the reporting standards in this Statement generally should focus on information that is essential in meeting the financial reporting objectives applicable to all not-for-profit organizations and should be no more stringent than requirements for business enterprises.

Objectives of General-Purpose External Financial Reporting

43. The Board reaffirms that general-purpose external financial reporting should focus on the interests of present and potential resource providers. Paragraph 9 of FASB Concepts Statement No. 4, *Objectives of Financial Reporting by Nonbusiness Organizations,* says:

> The objectives [of financial reporting by not-for-profit organizations] stem from the

common interests of those who provide resources to [not-for-profit] organizations in the services those organizations provide and their continuing ability to provide services. In contrast, the objectives of financial reporting [of business enterprises] stem from the interests of resource providers in the prospects of receiving cash as a return of and return on their investment. Despite different interests, resource providers of all entities look to information about economic resources, obligations, net resources, and changes in them for information that is useful in assessing their interests. All such resource providers focus on indicators of organization performance and information about management stewardship. [Footnote reference omitted.]

44. Thus, financial reporting by both not-for-profit organizations and business enterprises focuses on providing information that is useful to resource providers in deciding whether to provide resources to an entity. More specifically, Concepts Statement 4 says:

Financial reporting should provide information about an organization's economic resources, obligations, and net resources. That information helps resource providers and others identify the organization's financial strengths and weaknesses, evaluate information about the organization's performance during the period . . . , and assess its ability to continue to render services. [paragraph 44]

Periodic measurement of the changes in the amount and nature of the net resources of a [not-for-profit] organization and information about the service efforts and accomplishments of an organization together represent the information most useful in assessing its performance. [paragraph 47]

Financial reporting should provide information about the amounts and kinds of inflows and outflows of resources during a period. It should distinguish resource flows that change net resources, such as inflows of fees or contributions and outflows for wages and salaries, from those that do not change net resources, such as borrowings or purchases of buildings. It also should identify inflows and outflows of restricted resources. [paragraph 48]

Financial reporting should provide information about the relation between inflows and outflows of resources during a period. [paragraph 49]

Financial reporting should provide information about the service efforts of a [not-for-profit] organization. Information about service efforts should focus on how the organization's resources . . . are used in providing different programs or services. [paragraph 52]

Financial reporting should provide information about how an organization obtains and spends cash or other liquid resources, about its borrowing and repayment of borrowing, and about other factors that may affect its liquidity. [paragraph 54]

45. The objectives and capabilities of general-purpose external financial statements are limited; they do not and cannot satisfy all potential users equally well. They are useful to groups of external users, such as donors and creditors, that generally have similar needs. Regulatory bodies, such as departments of health, education, and consumer affairs, although interested in financial information, often have special-purpose needs that general-purpose financial statements cannot provide. They also have the authority to require information to meet their needs.

46. Individual financial statements also have practical limits. Generally, dissimilar information cannot be combined in a single statement without complicating the information, obscuring the statement's purpose, or both. For example, a single statement of "funds flows" might report and measure changes in economic resources of current funds as well as changes in other economic resources; however, that statement might unnecessarily confuse items of revenue with transfers from noncurrent funds or items of expense with expenditures to acquire noncurrent assets. This Statement considers whether that information is essential and should be presented in a single financial statement or in separate financial statements.

Broad Standards for Basic Information

47. Several respondents to the Invitation to Comment urged the Board to establish broad standards directed at the "critical" issues and to allow organizations sufficient latitude to report relevant information

in ways they believe are most useful to present and potential users of their financial statements. Some respondents also suggested that that approach might allow more possibility for certain not-for-profit organizations, such as hospitals and universities, to report in ways that are comparable to similar profit-making or governmental entities. The Board agreed that broad standards that allow, within certain parameters, the exercise of judgment in determining how to best communicate meaningful information have certain advantages.

48. The Board believes that this Statement's broad general standards for reporting information in financial statements provided by not-for-profit organizations represent a significant step toward improving the comparability of those financial statements. Those standards also allow for future changes in financial statement display practices to occur in the gradual, evolutionary way that has characterized past changes in practices of both business enterprises and not-for-profit organizations. The Board believes that, at this time, broad general standards are preferable to narrow prescriptive standards that could unnecessarily inhibit the evolutionary development of meaningful financial reporting. Those respondents to the Exposure Draft who commented on this matter generally supported this fundamental approach and the reporting flexibility that this Statement permits.

49. The AICPA and other respondents, including members of the FASB's task force, asked the Board to clarify whether future Guides could establish more specific guidance than the broad reporting standards established by this Statement. Paragraph 3 of this Statement indicates that within the parameters of this Statement, the AICPA or another appropriate body, following the process described in AICPA Statement on Auditing Standards (SAS) No. 69, *The Meaning of "Present Fairly in Conformity With Generally Accepted Accounting Principles" in the Independent Auditor's Report,* may provide more specific reporting guidance for certain not-for-profit organizations. SAS 69 requires that an entity adopt *cleared* AICPA Industry Audit and Accounting Guides, and *cleared* AICPA Statements of Position that become effective after March 15, 1992. As used in SAS 69, *cleared* means that the FASB has indicated that it does not object to the issuance of the proposed pronouncement.

50. A national association representing colleges and universities and other respondents also asked the Board to clarify whether existing fund accounting re-

quirements in Chapters 3-10 of *Audits of Colleges and Universities* are superseded by this Statement. Footnote 5 to paragraph 18 clarifies that reporting by fund groups is not required or precluded for purposes of external financial reporting. However, how an organization maintains its internal accounting and recordkeeping systems is a matter outside the purview of the FASB.

Complete Set of Financial Statements

51. The Invitation to Comment asked what basic financial statements, at a minimum, should be required parts of a complete set of general-purpose external financial statements for a not-for-profit organization. Most respondents agreed with the advisory recommendation of the AICPA task force that a balance sheet (statement of financial position), a statement of changes in net assets (statement of activities), and a statement of cash flows should be required parts of a complete set of financial statements.

52. The Board agreed; it concluded that three financial statements are necessary to provide the variety of information needed to meet the financial reporting objectives of a not-for-profit organization and to report that information in ways that are both comprehensive and understandable. A statement of financial position, a statement of activities, and a statement of cash flows, used with related disclosures, provide information that is useful in assessing (a) the services an organization provides and its ability to continue to provide those services and (b) how managers discharge their stewardship responsibilities and other aspects of their performance. A majority of respondents agreed that the three basic financial statements should be required. However, some respondents to the Exposure Draft said that a statement of cash flows should not be a required part of a set of financial statements. They said that the additional information it provides may not be sufficiently useful to justify the added cost or may add confusion. However, most users of financial statements that participated in the field test found the statement of cash flows helpful or said the statement enhanced their understanding of the organization.

53. The Board concluded that the changes required by this Statement will result in greater comparability, completeness, and clarity in the financial statements issued by not-for-profit organizations, which should enhance significantly the understanding of the information provided by their financial statements. The direct beneficiaries of that information are likely to

be present and potential donors, members, and creditors of not-for-profit organizations, which include individuals, foundations, and government granting agencies. Indirectly, not-for-profit organizations and society are likely to benefit from improved information that may lead to more efficient and effective decisions about how resources are allocated. The Board believes that not-for-profit organizations generally have management information systems that provide the basic information needed to prepare a set of financial statements that conform to the provisions of this Statement and that the benefits of the information provided generally exceed the costs to provide that information.

54. The Board continues to believe that "ideally, financial reporting also should provide information about the service accomplishments of a [not-for-profit] organization" (Concepts Statement 4, paragraph 53). However, this Statement emphasizes information to be reported in financial statements. Since information about service accomplishments generally is not measurable in units of money, it cannot be included and reported in the totals of the financial statements.

Other Financial Statements

55. Some respondents to the Invitation to Comment and to the Exposure Draft said that one or more additional financial statements are necessary to report or measure other essential information. Some respondents said that a statement that reports expenses by both functional and natural classifications is necessary. Others said that a statement that reports operating revenues and expenses separate from other revenues and expenses should be required. Still others said that comparative financial statements for the prior period should be a required part of a complete set of financial statements.

Statement of Functional Expenses

56. The Board considered whether all not-for-profit organizations should provide information about expenses by (a) functional classification, (b) natural classification, (c) either functional or natural classification at the option of the organization, or (d) both functional and natural classification. It also considered whether they should provide that information in a financial statement or in notes to financial statements.

Reporting expenses by functional classification

57. The Board concluded that information about expenses by function, such as major programs or services and major classes of supporting services, is necessary to an understanding of a not-for-profit organization's service efforts and that a set of financial statements should include that information. Requiring that information also is a step toward providing information that may be useful in associating an organization's expenses with its accomplishments. The Board concluded that information about an organization's expenses by function may be meaningfully communicated either in a statement of activities or in notes to financial statements.

58. The Board also concluded that information about the costs of significant programs or services are both relevant and measurable with sufficient reliability. Many costs are directly related to a major program or service or to a supporting activity. Some costs relate to two or more major programs and may require allocations. Techniques for allocating costs among significant programs or services are reasonably well developed; allocating costs among segments, products or services, and accounting periods are common in general-purpose accounting and reporting, managerial accounting, tax accounting, and contract accounting of all entities.

59. This Statement provides latitude for organizations to define their major programs and determine the degree of aggregation used when reporting expenses of major programs. That latitude has several advantages. Foremost, it allows organizations to report in ways that they believe are meaningful, related to their service efforts, and consistent with internal management information systems. That latitude allows organizations to use existing cost-allocation systems to provide the information necessary to comply with this Statement.

60. This Statement describes program services (paragraph 27) and supporting activities (paragraph 28) broadly. The Board believes those descriptions are consistent with functional reporting practices commonly used by most not-for-profit organizations for general-purpose reporting, regulatory filings, or sometimes both. By conforming to predominant existing practices of classification, this Statement should minimize disruption to the continuity of financial reporting by not-for-profit organizations and minimize transitional costs.

61. Some respondents to the Exposure Draft said reporting expenses by function should not be required because that would be more stringent than reporting required of business enterprises. The Board concluded, however, that this difference, which stems

from different indicators of performance of not-for-profit organizations and business enterprises, is appropriate and necessary. Paragraph 9 of Concepts Statement 4 explains that not-for-profit organizations "generally have no single indicator of performance comparable to a business enterprise's profit. Thus, other indicators of performance are usually needed." It adds that those indicators are "information about the nature of and relation between inflows and outflows of resources and information about *service efforts* and accomplishments" (emphasis added). Furthermore, the Board observes that a requirement for information about a not-for-profit organization's expenses by function is similar to standards that require information about a business enterprise's industry segments.

Reporting expenses by natural classification

62. The Board decided not to require not-for-profit organizations to provide an analysis of expenses by natural classification. Some respondents said that information about expenses by natural classification may be essential in understanding the ability of an organization to continue to provide services and about the nature of the costs of providing those services. They noted that information about relatively fixed costs, such as salaries, versus discretionary costs, such as grants to subrecipients or awards to others, can be particularly useful. The Board agrees that information about expenses by natural classification often is useful and encourages organizations to provide that information. However, it also believes that information about expenses by natural classification may not be essential in understanding the service efforts of all not-for-profit organizations or in assessing the ability of all organizations to continue to provide services.

Reporting by voluntary health and welfare organizations

63. The Board indicated in the Exposure Draft that it believes that current specialized accounting and reporting principles and practices that require certain organizations to provide information about their expenses by both functional and natural classifications are not inconsistent with the requirements of this Statement. Thus, those specialized requirements continue in effect. It also noted that not-for-profit organizations often provide that information in regulatory filings to the Internal Revenue Service and certain state agencies, which are available to the public. Nonetheless, some respondents said the status of current AICPA requirements was unclear because this Statement encourages but does not require information about expense by natural classification. Respondents who use the financial statements of voluntary health and welfare organizations and other not-for-profit organizations expressed strong concern that they might lose meaningful information that currently is available to them if the Board did not clarify the status of the statement of functional expenses.

64. This Statement requires that voluntary health and welfare organizations continue to provide a statement that reports expenses by their functional and natural classifications in a matrix format. The Board believes that requirement is appropriate to prevent the loss of information that voluntary health and welfare organizations and users of their financial statements generally have found to be useful. The Board concluded that before extending that requirement to other organizations, further study is necessary to determine whether other cost-beneficial means of reporting information useful in associating expenses with service efforts might be developed.

Operating Statement

65. Some respondents to both the Invitation to Comment and the Exposure Draft suggested that a statement of activities should be divided into two parts, a statement of "operations" and a statement of other changes in net assets. They generally suggested that the first statement would report "operating" revenues and expenses and would be accompanied by another statement that would report all other revenues, gains, expenses, and losses and the change in net assets for the organization as a whole. They said that a separate operating statement is needed with a "bottom line" different from change in net assets. However, the respondents who expressed that view differed on how to define an operating measure and on which revenues and expenses would be included in or excluded from "operations." For example, some would include in "operations" all gifts that are available for current period use, whether restricted or not. Others would exclude gifts restricted to specified operating purposes if those purposes were not met in the current period. Some would exclude from "operations" revenues, gains, or losses from nonrecurring, unexpected, or unusual events such as a very large bequest, an insurance gain on a fire loss, or an unexpected loss contingency. Others would include some or all of those items.

66. The AICPA task force also considered whether a distinction should be made between operating and

nonoperating activities and, if so, whether it should be accomplished within a statement of changes in net assets or through separate statements. In paragraph 124 of its report, the task force said that as it "tried to find a universal definition of 'operations' in a not-for-profit environment, differences in the use of that term became more apparent. In fact, it became clear that distinctions based on operations tend to be arbitrary." That observation is not limited to the not-for-profit sector. To define "operations" for business enterprises has proved equally problematic.

67. The Board decided to neither require nor preclude a not-for-profit organization from classifying its revenues, expenses, gains, and losses as operating or nonoperating within its statement of activities. Present standards neither require nor preclude a business enterprise from classifying its revenues, expenses, gains, and losses in that way, and the Board found no compelling reason to prescribe more specific display standards for not-for-profit organizations.

68. The Board believes that within the parameters of this Statement, not-for-profit organizations should have the same latitude as a business enterprise to make distinctions that they believe will provide meaningful information. Most respondents to the Exposure Draft that commented on this matter agreed that this Statement should not preclude making so-called operating or nonoperating or other distinctions within each of this Statement's required classes of net assets. A few respondents and FASB task force members suggested, however, that because terms such as *operating income, operating profit, operating surplus, operating deficit,* and *results of operations* are used with different meanings, some constraints are necessary to avoid focusing on undefined measures that may be misunderstood. The Board decided that if an intermediate measure of *operations* is reported, it should be in a financial statement that, at a minimum, reports the change in unrestricted net assets for the period. This Statement also specifies that if an organization's use of the term *operations* is not apparent from the details provided on the face of the statement, a note to financial statements should describe the nature of the reported measure of operations or

the items excluded from operations. Appendix C illustrates how an intermediate measure of operations might be presented in financial statements.

Comparative Financial Statements

69. The Invitation to Comment asked whether a complete set of financial statements should include prior-year comparative information in essentially the same form as financial statements for the current period. Most respondents agreed with the AICPA task force advisory conclusion that prior-year comparative information should be encouraged but not required and that if presented, prior-year information should comply with the minimum requirements for a set of financial statements.

70. The Board concluded that the existing standard provided by ARB No. 43, Chapter 2A, "Form of Statements—Comparative Financial Statements," which encourages but does not require comparative financial statements, is relevant to all entities. The usefulness of information about an entity increases if that information can be compared with similar information for other periods, but at times it may be impractical or impossible to provide comparative information on a fully consistent basis of accounting. For example, if a business enterprise or not-for-profit organization changes from a cash basis to an accrual basis of accounting, comparable information for periods before the change may be impossible or too expensive to obtain because of the way accounts were kept. The Board found no reason to impose a more stringent standard for reporting by not-for-profit organizations. Most respondents to the Exposure Draft agreed; others generally said that comparative financial statements should be required.

Aggregation and Classification of Information

71. The Board believes that if financial statements are to be useful, data must be simplified, condensed, and aggregated into meaningful totals.[7] Many not-for-profit organizations are complex entities with multiple program services and diverse, complex, and sometimes unpredictable sources of funding. Their transactions and events are voluminous and must be

---

[7]"It is a very fundamental principle indeed that knowledge is always gained by the *orderly* loss of information, that is, by condensing and abstracting and indexing the great buzzing confusion of information that comes from the world around us into a form which we can appreciate and comprehend" (Kenneth E. Boulding, *Economics as a Science* [New York: McGraw-Hill Book Company, 1970], 2, emphasis added).

combined and condensed to be reported in financial statements in ways that are understandable to external resource providers and others. That fact leads to a number of considerations.

Aggregated Information Focusing on an Entity

72. The Board believes that aggregated information about an entity as a whole facilitates an overall understanding of its financial position, results of its operations, and its cash flows. It concluded that reporting certain basic totals, such as total assets, liabilities, net assets, change in net assets, cash and cash equivalents, and change in cash and cash equivalents, will improve the understandability, usefulness, and completeness of financial reporting by not-for-profit organizations. It also believes that that basic information is necessary to an overall understanding of the entity's financial position, results of its operations, and its cash flows.

73. Summary amounts also are useful in assessing an entity's financial strengths and weaknesses over periods of time, and they provide a basis for further inquiry and analysis of the reasons why its net assets increased or decreased, the causes of the changes in its cash and other liquid assets, and so forth. Summary amounts also are helpful in comparing a not-for-profit organization with other organizations, including similar entities in the profit-making or governmental sectors.

74. In assessing the financial position or performance of a not-for-profit organization, however, the Board believes it is important to avoid focusing attention almost exclusively on net assets, change in net assets, total assets, or other highly simplified and aggregated amounts. For example, in Concepts Statement No. 6, *Elements of Financial Statements,* paragraph 106, the Board says, "Since donor-imposed restrictions affect the types and levels of service a not-for-profit organization can provide, whether an organization has maintained certain classes of net assets may be more significant than whether it has maintained net assets in the aggregate." Similarly, it is important to avoid focusing attention almost exclusively on "the bottom line" or other highly simplified and condensed information about business enterprises. Accordingly, this Statement requires not only summary amounts that focus on a not-for-profit organization as a whole but also information about items and components of those amounts; for example, it generally requires reporting information about the gross amounts of items of revenues and expenses and of cash receipts and cash payments.

Classification of Information

75. The Board concluded that the usefulness of information provided by financial statements of not-for-profit organizations could be vastly improved if certain basic information is classified in comparable ways. The Board decided that all not-for-profit organizations should:

a. Report assets and liabilities in reasonably homogeneous groups and sequence or classify them in ways that provide relevant information about their interrelationships, liquidity, and financial flexibility.

b. Classify and report net assets in three groups—permanently restricted, temporarily restricted, and unrestricted—based on the existence or absence of donor-imposed restrictions and the nature of those restrictions.

c. Aggregate items of revenues, expenses, gains, and losses into reasonably homogeneous groups and classify and report them as increases or decreases in permanently restricted, temporarily restricted, or unrestricted net assets.

d. Classify and report cash receipts and cash payments as resulting from investing, financing, or operating activities.

The Board concluded that those broad classifications are among the minimum requirements necessary to meet the objectives of financial reporting by not-for-profit organizations (paragraphs 43 and 44).

76. Classifying and aggregating items with similar characteristics into reasonably homogeneous groups and separating items with differing characteristics is a basic reporting practice that increases the usefulness of information. For example, cash collections of receivables from patients, students, or other service recipients may differ significantly in continuity, stability, and risk from cash collections of pledges made to a special-purpose fund-raising campaign. Classifying and reporting those receivables and collections of receivables as separate groups of assets and of cash inflows facilitates financial statement analysis aimed at objectives such as predicting amounts, timing, and uncertainty of future cash flows.

77. Perhaps the most prevalent problem in current practice is that not-for-profit organizations report their financial position and the effects of transactions, events, and circumstances that change the amount and nature of their net assets in significantly different ways. Many not-for-profit organizations report information for groups of assets and related liabilities of

four or more individual fund groups, either in several columns on a single page or in statements on separate pages. Some also include a total column or measures of total assets, liabilities, and net assets of the organization; however, many do not.

78. Although disaggregated information can be useful, differing definitions and terminology for reporting disaggregated fund groups make current financial reporting by not-for-profit organizations difficult to understand. Some organizations use internally defined fund groups that focus on measures of importance to an organization's managers rather than on the common information needs of external users of its financial statements. Other organizations focus on measures or fund groups unique to their particular industry.

79. Differing definitions and fund groups often result in financial statements with objectives or measurement focuses that are unclear, misunderstood, or both. For example, the Guide for colleges and universities explicitly says, "The statement of current funds revenues, expenditures, and other changes is a statement unique to educational and similar institutions. . . . It does not purport to present the results of operations or the net income or loss for the period as would a statement of income or a statement of revenues and expenses" (pages 55 and 56). That statement of current funds revenues, expenditures, and other changes measures the change in current funds, which is similar to a measure of change in working capital. Nonetheless, it often is said to be an "operating statement" or said to present the operating surplus, deficit, or "bottom line" for the period.

80. The Board believes this Statement's basic requirements for classifying information in financial statements will lead to more relevant, comparable, and understandable financial reporting by not-for-profit organizations. More prescriptive standards that require information to be classified in ways that go beyond the minimum requirements of this Statement may result in further improvements. However, because not-for-profit organizations are diverse and many are complex entities, the Board decided that it is best at this time to allow sufficient latitude for financial reporting practices to continue to evolve. The Board also believes that AICPA Guides and industry groups are likely, as in the past, to provide guidance to meet more specific needs for disaggregated information that may arise in practice.

Format of Financial Statements

81. The Invitation to Comment raised several questions about whether specified financial statement formats should be required, permitted, or precluded. For example, the AICPA task force suggested that information about revenues, expenses, gains, and losses for each of three classes of net assets should be allowed to be reported on a single page with no organization-wide totals for each item. That task force also suggested that a standardized format should not be required. Views of respondents to the Invitation to Comment were divided. Most would require columnar formats, although a large minority would not. Many would require totals for items of an entity's revenues, expenses, gains, and losses, but many would not. Many of those that would require or preclude particular formats are concerned that unstructured disaggregated information may obscure other essential and meaningful information.

82. Except as noted in paragraph 68, the Board decided to neither prescribe nor prohibit particular formats for a statement of financial position, a statement of activities, or a statement of cash flows, in part because similar prescriptions and proscriptions do not exist for business enterprises. The Board also concluded that standards for reporting financial information should focus on the content of financial statements, that is, on the basic information to be provided in financial statements. Most respondents to the Exposure Draft agreed. The Board expects this Statement's focus on certain basic aggregated information will place practical limits on the number of differing ways information is formatted and that those practical limits will eliminate most concerns about highly disaggregated information. The Board also expects that, as in the past, industry associations will encourage their member organizations to adopt, within the parameters of this Statement, reasonably common and preferable practices for reporting information in financial statements.

Statement of Financial Position

83. The Board concluded that a statement of financial position (balance sheet) should provide relevant information about an organization's assets, liabilities, and net assets. Information that helps resource providers and others identify the organization's financial strengths and weaknesses, evaluate its performance during the period, and assess its ability to continue to render services is relevant.

Display of Aggregated Totals

84. The Board concluded that a statement of financial position should report the aggregated totals for an organization's assets, liabilities, and net assets. These totals are helpful in assessing the interrelationship of an organization's assets and liabilities and, together with information about the components of assets, liabilities, and net assets, are necessary to an understanding of an organization's financial position. In paragraph 103 of its report, the AICPA task force explicitly recommended that the aggregated total of an organization's net assets be presented in a statement of financial position. Respondents to the Invitation to Comment generally agreed.

85. The Invitation to Comment did not ask whether not-for-profit organizations should report aggregated totals for assets and liabilities. However, the AICPA task force recommended that amounts for items of assets, liabilities, and net assets be presented as a self-balancing group of amounts in a single column, which suggests that highly aggregated totals would be presented. A single group of amounts also implies exclusion or elimination of interfund amounts that could overstate an organization's total assets and total liabilities.[8] Most respondents to the Invitation to Comment and to the Exposure Draft supported reporting assets, liabilities, and net assets in one self-balancing group of amounts in a single column.

86. This Statement emphasizes the need for information about both aggregated totals for assets, liabilities, and net assets and about reasonably homogeneous groups of items of assets and liabilities. Because the Board decided not to emphasize or preclude specific statement formats, this Statement permits a left-to-right or top-to-bottom "balanced" format as well as single-column, multicolumn, single-page, or multipage formats. The Board believes that the provisions of this Statement applied with other generally accepted accounting principles will provide relevant information about the amounts and nature of differing kinds of assets and liabilities, either through disclosures in a statement of financial position or in accompanying notes to financial statements.

Classification of Assets and Liabilities

87. The Invitation to Comment asked whether not-for-profit organizations should classify items of assets and liabilities as current or long-term or should use another classification method, such as nearness to cash, to provide information about liquidity. The AICPA task force recommended that not-for-profit organizations be required to either provide a classified statement of financial position (current and noncurrent assets and liabilities) or highlight illiquid assets by displaying in the net asset section the amount of the entity's fixed assets less related liabilities (sometimes called the *net investment in plant* or *net equity invested in property, plant, and equipment*). A significant majority of respondents disagreed with that recommendation. Some respondents said that the requirements should be more permissive, but many others said that they should be more prescriptive. For example, many agreed that a classified statement of financial position should be permitted but they would not require that or the alternative breakout of the net asset section. Many others said a classified statement should be required. Others said that a nearness to cash method of classification should be required.

88. The Board concluded that reporting the net equity invested in property, plant, and equipment within the net asset section is not a substitute for arranging or classifying items of assets and liabilities in ways that provide information about liquidity. The Board believes that essential information about liquidity and an organization's financial flexibility can be provided either by classifying assets and liabilities as current and noncurrent or by sequencing assets according to their nearness of conversion to cash and liabilities according to the nearness of their maturity and resulting use of cash. Each method has advantages and practical limitations.

---

[8]This Statement does not preclude display of interfund items in a statement of financial position; rather, its requirement to display total assets and liabilities results in certain practical limits on how interfund items are displayed in a financial statement. For example, because receivables and payables between fund groups are not organizational assets or liabilities, a statement of financial position must clearly label and arrange those interfund items to eliminate their amounts when displaying total assets or liabilities.

89. Classifying assets and liabilities as current and noncurrent, although not required by generally accepted accounting principles, is a common reporting practice of both business enterprises and not-for-profit organizations. As others have noted,[9] this classification alone generally does not provide users of financial statements with the liquidity information they need. Thus, other disclosures must be added to the financial statement or notes to financial statements. More recently, financial reporting has emphasized information about changes in cash and cash equivalents, and that new emphasis obviates the need for a rigid requirement to classify and report amounts of current assets and current liabilities.

90. For many small or less-complex organizations, grouping homogeneous items of assets and liabilities and sequencing them according to nearness of cash or maturity is sufficient. Further distinctions at higher degrees of aggregation, such as current and noncurrent assets and liabilities, generally would be unnecessary. Board members also noted that since the issuance of FASB Statement No. 94, *Consolidation of All Majority-Owned Subsidiaries,* many entities have been experimenting with differing degrees of aggregating and displaying information about their assets and liabilities. They believe that at this time it is best to avoid prescriptive standards that might stand in the way of those evolving reporting practices.

91. Some relevant information about the liquidity or maturity of assets and liabilities cannot be adequately communicated solely by classification methods, such as current and noncurrent, or by sequencing information in financial statements. This Statement and generally accepted accounting principles provide latitude, in those circumstances, to disclose information in notes to financial statements. For example, organizations that receive significant amounts of multiyear pledges or that finance their cash needs by borrowing long term generally must use notes to their statements to provide information about expected cash inflows from receivables or expected cash outflows to satisfy long-term borrowings. The Board decided that to report relevant information about liquidity and the interrelationship of assets and liabilities, not-for-profit organizations should have latitude to select classification methods, levels of aggregation, and disclosure techniques that are most meaningful and practical for their circumstances.

92. The Board also considered whether more specific standards are necessary to provide information about the nature and amount of donor-imposed restrictions on the use of contributed assets. A majority of respondents to the Invitation to Comment agreed with the AICPA task force advisory recommendation that not-for-profit organizations be permitted but not required to disaggregate and report assets and liabilities by their related classes of net assets. Respondents that disagreed were divided. Some would preclude that kind of disaggregation and others would require it. A few respondents to the Invitation to Comment and to the Exposure Draft said restrictions on gifts that create permanent endowments or that require acquisition of land, buildings, and other long-lived assets differ significantly from other donor restrictions and that those assets must be reported in a separate statement of financial position.

93. Donor-imposed restrictions may influence the liquidity or cash flow patterns of certain assets and that kind of information may be helpful in assessing the financial flexibility of a not-for-profit organization. For example, a donor stipulation that donated cash be used to acquire land and buildings limits an organization's ability to take effective actions to respond to unexpected opportunities or needs, such as emergency disaster relief. On the other hand, some donor-imposed restrictions have little or no influence on cash flow patterns or an organization's financial flexibility. For example, a gift of cash with a donor stipulation that it be used for emergency-relief efforts has a negligible impact on an organization if emergency relief is one of its major ongoing programs.

94. The Board decided to permit but not require not-for-profit organizations to disaggregate and report assets and liabilities by donor-restricted and unrestricted classes or fund groups. It believes that not-for-profit organizations generally can provide relevant information about liquidity and financial flexibility by aggregating assets and liabilities into reasonably homogeneous groups that include the effects of donor-imposed restrictions as well as other contractual restrictions. Classifying and labeling assets in ways that include the effects of restrictions on

---

[9]"New business practices, new methods of financing, and new methods of accounting have resulted in balance sheet accounts that defy classification as current or noncurrent.

"Perhaps one of the most significant changes that has occurred is the change in attitudes toward disclosure of financial information. Financial statement users demand, and companies are willing to disclose, much more detailed information about their financial affairs in supporting schedules and notes to financial statements than at the time accountants began to classify assets and liabilities as current or noncurrent" (Loyd C. Heath, Accounting Research Monograph 3, *Financial Reporting and the Evaluation of Solvency* [New York, AICPA, 1978], 74).

liquidity is a long-established practice. For example, cash and claims to cash restricted as to withdrawal or use for other than current operations, whether actually set aside in a special account or not, are excluded from current assets of a business enterprise. Similarly, amounts of cash restricted to a permanent endowment should be excluded from aggregated amounts of cash and cash equivalents for current operations of a not-for-profit organization because they are not homogeneous items.

Classification of Net Assets

95. The Invitation to Comment asked if not-for-profit organizations should report amounts for classes of net assets and, if so, how they should label those amounts. The AICPA task force recommended that not-for-profit organizations report three classes of net assets (or equity)—unrestricted, temporarily restricted, and permanently restricted—as defined by Concepts Statement 6. It also said organizations should use those terms in their financial statements. Respondents generally agreed with the first recommendation; however, views differed about how to label the three classes of net assets.

96. The Board concluded that information about the effects of donor-imposed restrictions on net assets is relevant to users of financial statements of not-for-profit organizations. Donors' restrictions impose special responsibilities on management of an organization to ensure that it uses donated assets as stipulated. Because they also place limits on the use of resources, donors' restrictions may impinge upon an organization's performance and its ability to provide a satisfactory level of services. Information about how managers discharge their stewardship responsibilities for donor-restricted resources also is useful in assessing an organization's performance.

97. Although respondents to the Invitation to Comment generally supported requiring a minimum of three classes of net assets, the Board also considered whether fewer or more classes of net assets would be appropriate. For example, the Board considered whether reporting unrestricted net assets and donor-restricted net assets would suffice. The Board also considered the present practices of not-for-profit organizations that provide disaggregated information through the use of several fund groups. The Board believes that aggregation in financial statements at a level higher than that commonly found in practice would improve financial reporting by not-for-profit organizations and an understanding of the financial

position of those organizations. Important details about differing kinds of donor-restricted classes of net assets also can be provided in notes to financial statements.

98. The Board concluded that consistent with Concepts Statement 6, information about a minimum of three classes of net assets, based on the presence or absence of donor-imposed restrictions and their nature, generally is necessary to gain an adequate understanding of the financial position of a not-for-profit organization, including its financial flexibility and ability to continue to render services. Information about permanent restrictions is useful in determining the extent to which an organization's net assets are not a source of cash for payments to present or prospective lenders, suppliers, or employees and thus are not expected to be directly available for providing services or paying creditors. Information about the extent of unrestricted net assets and of temporarily restricted net assets is useful in assessing an organization's ability and limitations on its ability to allocate resources to provide services or particular kinds of services or to make cash payments to creditors in the future. The Board believes that aggregated information about the three component parts of an organization's net assets is especially important to both donors and creditors and that that information is best provided by display of their amounts in a statement of financial position. Most respondents to the Exposure Draft expressed similar views; others said that amounts for fund balances should be required for fund groups, such as operating, plant, endowment, and other funds.

99. The Board also considered comments raised about how to label the three classes of net assets. Several representatives of health care providers said that single equity line items, identified as unrestricted, temporarily restricted, and permanently restricted are sufficient but that specific terms should not be required. Other respondents said organizations should have sufficient latitude to use other terms, such as unrestricted fund balance, temporarily restricted fund balance, and permanently restricted fund balance.

100. The Board concluded that while definitions are necessary to make the distinctions required by this Statement, stringent requirements to use specific terms are not necessary to faithfully represent those distinctions. As illustrated in Appendix C, this Statement encourages the use of the terms unrestricted, temporarily restricted, and permanently restricted net assets; however, the Board knows that other labels

exist. For example, *equity* may be used for net assets, and *other* or *not donor-restricted* may be used with care to distinguish unrestricted net assets from the temporarily and permanently restricted classes of net assets. For example, the net asset section might be arranged as follows:

Donor restricted:		
Permanently	$XXX	
Temporarily	XXX	
Other:		
Designated by the Board		
for [*purpose*]	$XXX	
Undesignated	XXX	XXX
Net assets		$XXX

At a minimum, the amounts for each of the three classes of net assets and the total of net assets must be reported in a statement of financial position and the captions used to describe those amounts must correspond with their meanings, as defined by this Statement. A few respondents to the Exposure Draft suggested that organizations should be required to report separate amounts of unrestricted net assets designated by the governing board for long-term investment or for investment in plant. The Board concluded that those disclosures are not essential and that organizations should be permitted but not required to provide those or other disclosures on the face of financial statements or in notes to financial statements.

Disclosures about Composition of Assets in Accordance with Donor Restrictions

101. The Invitation to Comment asked whether an organization that does not maintain an appropriate composition of assets (usually cash and marketable securities) in amounts needed to comply with all donor restrictions should report that noncompliance. It also asked if that reporting should be accomplished by (a) explicit disclosure in notes to financial statements, (b) displaying self-balancing fund groups for each significant type of donor restriction, or (c) other means. The AICPA task force recommended that if an organization does not maintain an appropriate composition of assets in amounts needed to comply with all donor restrictions, the amounts and circumstances involved should be disclosed. Respondents to the Invitation to Comment generally agreed; however, some respondents suggested that existing ac-

counting and auditing standards adequately address this matter.

102. In their May 7, 1992 letter responding to a request of the FASB about the adequacy of existing accounting and auditing standards, the AICPA's Not-for-Profit Organizations Committee and Not-for-Profit Organizations Guide Task Force said:

> We believe [FASB Statement No. 5, *Accounting for Contingencies,* AICPA Statements on Auditing Standards No. 47, *Audit Risk and Materiality in Conducting an Audit,* and No. 54, *Illegal Acts by Clients*] require that noncompliance with donor-imposed restrictions be disclosed if there is a reasonable possibility that a material contingent liability has been incurred at the date of the financial statements or there is at least a reasonable possibility that the noncompliance could lead to a material loss of revenue, or can cause an entity not to be able to continue as a going concern.

They also said that existing AICPA Guides for not-for-profit organizations provide relevant guidance and they will consider developing further guidance as part of a Guide revision project to be completed after the FASB issues this Statement. Accordingly, the Board concluded that this Statement, which emphasizes how and what information to provide in financial statements, need not explicitly consider this matter of compliance and related disclosure issues raised by the Invitation to Comment.

Statement of Activities

103. The Board concluded that a statement of activities should provide relevant information about the effects of transactions and other events and circumstances that change the amount and nature of an organization's net assets. This Statement affirms that information about revenues, expenses, gains, and losses is relevant and emphasizes four measures of their effects—change in the amount of an organization's net assets and change in the amounts of an organization's permanently restricted net assets, temporarily restricted net assets, and unrestricted net assets. The Board believes those measures together with information about their components are essential to resource providers and others in evaluating an organization's performance during the period. Respondents to the Exposure Draft generally agreed.

Display of Aggregated Totals

104. The Invitation to Comment requested comments about the appropriate level of aggregation or disaggregation in reporting the amounts for items of revenues, expenses, gains, and losses, and the change in net assets. Several interrelated questions asked whether certain disaggregated information and certain aggregated totals about those items should be required or permitted to be reported or precluded from being reported in a statement of changes in net assets (statement of activities). It also raised several questions about how to format those items in a statement of changes in net assets.

105. In paragraph 225 of its report, the AICPA task force said that among other things it "believes that the statement of changes in net assets should . . . include . . . revenues, expenses, gains, and losses and their components classified into the appropriate class of net assets—permanently restricted, temporarily restricted, and unrestricted [and] the change for the period in each of the three classes of net assets. . . ." In paragraph 226 the task force also said that "a total for each element [revenues, expenses, gains, and losses] should not be required to be displayed" and it summarized more specifically the ways it believes the content of a statement of changes in net assets should be presented, including how specific line items should be sequenced and how statements should be formatted, to best achieve the objectives of financial reporting by not-for-profit organizations. The Board decided that at this time it would be preferable to focus on requirements for reporting certain basic and essential information by all not-for-profit organizations rather than how specific line items are sequenced or how statements are formatted.

Change in net assets and change in classes of net assets

106. The AICPA task force recommended that a statement of changes in net assets include measures of change in permanently restricted net assets, change in temporarily restricted net assets, and change in unrestricted net assets. The task force was divided on whether change in net assets for the organization as a whole should be displayed; the majority of its members said display of that measure should be permitted and a significant minority said it should be required. A majority of respondents supported the AICPA recommendation to classify revenues, expenses, gains, and losses and their components into permanently restricted, temporarily restricted, and unrestricted net assets and report the change for each of the three classes of net assets. Some respondents who disagreed would require totals for the activity of the organization as a whole or would classify revenues, expenses, gains, and losses in other ways, such as by an "operating" and nonoperating classification or by "managed fund groups" as defined by the organization.

107. The Board concluded that not-for-profit organizations should report the amounts for the change in net assets for the organization as a whole and the change in permanently restricted net assets, temporarily restricted net assets, and unrestricted net assets. The Board concluded that those four measures of the effects of revenues, expenses, and other transactions, events, and circumstances are necessary to evaluate an organization's performance during the period and they are useful in assessing its ability to continue to render services. This Statement also affirms the conclusions in paragraphs 9 and 47 of Concepts Statement 4 that not-for-profit organizations "generally have no single indicator of performance comparable to a business enterprise's profit" and that "periodic measurement of the changes in the amount and nature of the net resources of a [not-for-profit] organization and information about the service efforts and accomplishments of an organization together represent the information most useful in assessing its performance."

108. Measures of the change in an organization's net assets and its classes of net assets are useful individually and collectively. Paragraphs 103-106 of Concepts Statement 6 explain that a measure of the amount of periodic change in net assets is useful in assessing whether an organization is maintaining its net assets, drawing upon resources received in past periods, or adding resources that can be used to support future periods. That measure provides information useful in assessing an organization's overall ability to continue to provide satisfactory levels of services. Periodic measures of change in net assets are also useful in assessing trends over time.

109. Moreover, not-for-profit organizations receive significant amounts of contributed resources and because donor-imposed restrictions often affect the types and level of service they can provide, information about changes in the nature of net assets of not-for-profit organizations is useful, particularly in assessing their ability to respond to short-term needs for differing types or higher levels of services. For example, if an organization maintained its net assets

solely because it received a significant permanently restricted endowment contribution that made up for a significant decrease in unrestricted net assets, measures of the change in the permanently restricted and unrestricted classes of net assets would be informative in assessing the organization's long-run and short-run ability to provide comparable types or levels of services in the future. Similarly, if the organization received significant restricted contributions in response to a building campaign, a measure of the change in the temporarily restricted class of net assets may be useful in assessing the extent to which the organization maintained the part of net assets that is restricted to specific uses and is not fully available to support services of the next period. While each of the four required measures provide useful information, because of their interrelationships, they also provide information by complementing each other.

110. Furthermore, the Board believes that requiring not-for-profit organizations to distinguish between transactions and other events without donor-imposed restrictions and those with temporary or permanent restrictions imposes no more stringent standards on those organizations than exist for business enterprises. Rather, the distinctions required of not-for-profit organizations and of business enterprises reflect differences in their characteristics and objectives of financial reporting. Business enterprises must distinguish between owner and nonowner transactions that change their net assets, a distinction that generally is not relevant to not-for-profit organizations, and not-for-profit organizations must distinguish between transactions without donor-imposed restrictions and those with permanent and temporary restrictions, a distinction that generally is not relevant to business enterprises.

A measure of "operating income" or similar measures

111. As discussed in paragraphs 65-68, the Board also considered whether to require distinctions between "operating" revenues, expenses, gains, and losses and other transactions that change an organization's net assets. Some respondents to the Invitation to Comment and to the Exposure Draft said that there is a strong need for a measure of how an organization is managing or maintaining the resources available for its "operations" or its "current operations." Others characterized that as a need for a measure similar to a business enterprise's "net income," "operating income," or "income from continuing operations." A

few others said that unusually large gifts should be classified as nonoperating revenues or capital contributions if the organization's governing board designates those gifts for long-term investment. However, most respondents to the Exposure Draft suggested that the Board not define or proscribe a so-called operating measure for all or specific types of not-for-profit organizations.

112. The Board believes that change in unrestricted net assets, which measures whether an organization has maintained the part of its net assets that is fully available to support services in the next period, may serve as an *operating measure* as that term is used by some respondents. The Board also believes that this Statement provides ample latitude to sequence items of revenues and expenses in ways that permit organizations to report subtotals similar to other respondents' descriptions of "operating income" or "current operating income." Thus, this Statement should not inhibit an evolution toward reporting the so-called operating measure if all or certain kinds of not-for-profit organizations or industries find that measure desirable for their specific circumstances.

113. The Board also considered whether to preclude or limit the use of terms such as *operating income* or *operating surplus or deficit.* Some FASB task force members and others said that this Statement allows too much flexibility and that the term *operating income* may be used inconsistently. They suggested specifying that if an *operating* label is used, it should only be used for the measure of unrestricted net assets as defined by this Statement or for an intermediate component of unrestricted net assets that excludes a few specified items, such as extraordinary items, the effects of discontinued operations, the cumulative effect of accounting changes, and perhaps certain gains and losses on investment assets.

114. The Board concluded that there is no compelling reason to prescribe the display of another measure similar to but not identical to a measure of change in unrestricted net assets. The Board observes that generally accepted accounting principles and the application of paragraph 7 of this Statement require display of an appropriately labeled subtotal for change in a class of net assets before the effects of an extraordinary item, the discontinuance of an operating segment, or an accounting change. For example, using the columnar Format B in Appendix C, a statement of activities would report the effects of an extraordinary item as follows:

	Unrestricted	Temporarily Restricted	Permanently Restricted	Total
Change in net assets before extraordinary items	$11,558	$(1,128)	$5,020	$15,450
Extraordinary items (Note X)	xxx	xxx	xxx	xxx
Change in net assets	$xx,xxx	$(x,xxx)	$x,xxx	$xx,xxx

Because generally accepted accounting principles require that these captions be modified appropriately when an organization reports the cumulative effect of an accounting change or the effects of disposal of a segment of its operations that may affect any one or more classes of its net assets, there is no need for this Statement to require the use of a specific label for the unrestricted or any one class of net assets. That would impose a standard more stringent than those that exist for business enterprises. The results of the Board's field test revealed that about half of the participants chose to report an intermediate measure of operations; however, they differed significantly in how they defined and described that measure. In its redeliberations of the Exposure Draft, the Board decided to add the disclosure and reporting requirements of paragraph 23 of this Statement.

115. The Board also reaffirmed its decision not to prescribe, at this time, whether to report gains and losses from investments in a particular sequence, in an intermediate measure of net assets, or as a specified component of change in net assets. The Board intends to consider the issue of accounting for investments by not-for-profit organizations, including how to measure investment assets and whether to recognize unrealized gains and losses, in a subsequent part of its project on not-for-profit organizations. The Board considered similar accounting and reporting issues for business enterprises in Statement No. 115, *Accounting for Certain Investments in Debt and Equity Securities.*

Totals for revenues, expenses, gains, and losses

116. The AICPA task force recommended that organizations be permitted but not required to display totals for the aggregated amounts of their revenues, expenses, gains, or losses. Most respondents to the Invitation to Comment agreed with that recommendation; almost all of the respondents that disagreed with that recommendation would require display of those totals. The Board concluded that totals for each element are not essential. That requirement would be more stringent than display requirements for business enterprises and could inhibit meaningful financial re-

porting by not-for-profit organizations. The Board believes that the measures of change in net assets and classes of net assets required by this Statement provide the necessary and relevant aggregated information about the effects of a not-for-profit organization's revenues, expenses, gains, and losses.

117. The Invitation to Comment also asked if the activity for the three classes of net assets is reported separately, whether organization-wide totals should be required for each line item of revenues, expenses, gains, and losses. Almost half of the respondents to the Invitation to Comment would require those totals; others were nearly evenly divided between precluding and permitting totals.

118. The Board concluded, and most respondents to the Exposure Draft agreed, that organization-wide totals are not necessary for individual line items of revenues, expenses, gains, or losses. It believes information about reasonably homogeneous components of revenues, such as unrestricted contributions available to support current expenses and restricted contributions to be used to acquire land and buildings, generally is more meaningful than the aggregated total of those components. Disaggregated information that permits users of financial information to relate components of revenues to components of expenses also is often preferable to information provided by their aggregated amounts. For example, information that permits analysis of the levels of revenues from tuition in relation to expenses for instruction and other academic services and of revenues from room and board fees in relation to expenses for housing and food services generally is more meaningful than totals of aggregated items of revenues, such as student tuition and fees, or aggregated items of expenses, such as salaries, heat, electricity, or supplies. The Board believes that those who prepare financial statements generally are best able to make judgments about the extent to which financial statements or notes to financial statements should provide disaggregated information about various items of revenues or expenses and that this Statement need not limit those judgments.

Classification of Items as Donor Restricted or Unrestricted

119. This Statement generally specifies reporting an item of revenue, expense, gain, or loss as an increase or decrease in unrestricted net assets unless the use of the asset received is limited by donor-imposed restrictions. That provision is consistent with and stems from decisions reached in Statement 116, which establishes the standards for recognizing, measuring, and classifying contributions received. Paragraph 21 of this Statement describes the basic guidance for classifying donor-restricted and unrestricted contributions. Paragraphs 120-137 discuss considerations about two classification issues that were raised by the Invitation to Comment: classifying net appreciation on endowments and classifying expenses.

Classification of net appreciation on investments of donor-restricted endowments

120. The Invitation to Comment requested comments about the classification of net appreciation on investments of donor-restricted endowments. It asked whether not-for-profit organizations should initially display gains and losses as permanently restricted or initially display net appreciation in excess of original principal as unrestricted or temporarily restricted, depending on the purposes and uses specified by the donor.

121. In paragraph 187 of its report, the AICPA task force recommended that "gains and losses on investments of permanently restricted net assets should be displayed initially as permanently restricted, and the amount of net gains available for use by the organization should be disclosed in the notes to the financial statements." It also said, "To the extent that accumulated net gains are appropriated for use by the organization in accordance with the law, such amounts should be displayed as capital reclassifications." Most respondents to the Invitation to Comment agreed with the recommendation for initial display and disclosure, but some of those respondents and others said certain amounts subsequently appropriated by the organization's governing board are "operating reclassifications" rather than "capital reclassifications."

122. Respondents who disagreed with the AICPA recommendation to initially display net gains as permanently restricted challenged the appropriateness of that classification and necessity for a subsequent reclassification. Those respondents generally said that

if net gains are available for use by the organization, those gains are not permanently restricted and classifying those gains as permanently restricted would be misleading. The Board agreed and concluded that there is no need to delay recognizing available net gains in unrestricted or temporarily restricted net assets until such time as the organization's governing board acts to appropriate them for use. Decisions about when to spend resources generally do not bear on the issue, which is whether the resources are available for spending.

123. The Board concluded that not-for-profit organizations should classify gains and losses on permanent endowments consistent with the Board's fundamental conclusions for contributions received. That is, restricted net assets result only from a donor's stipulation that limits the organization's use of net assets or from a law that extends the donor's stipulation to enhancements (including holding gains) and diminishments of those net assets.

124. The Board believes that there is general agreement that, for example, if a donor stipulates that net gains be added to the principal of its gift until that endowed gift plus accumulated gains increases to a specified dollar level, the gains are permanently restricted. Support for that view also exists in the comments to Section 3 of the Uniform Management of Institutional Funds Act (Uniform Act), which since its development in 1972 has been adopted in varying forms in at least 29 states and the District of Columbia. The Uniform Act says, "If a gift instrument expresses or otherwise indicates the donor's intention that the governing board may not appropriate the net appreciation in the value of the fund, his wishes will govern." Section 3 also prohibits implying a restriction on the expenditure of net appreciation from a common set of words often used in gift instruments:

> A restriction upon the expenditure of net appreciation may not be implied from a designation of a gift as an endowment, or from a direction or authorization in the applicable gift instrument to use only "income," "interest," "dividends," or "rents, issues or profits," or "to preserve the principal intact," or a direction which contains other words of similar import.

125. The Board believes that the relevant issue is one of fact. Do donor-imposed restrictions exist that preclude the use of gains and losses (net appreciation) on permanent endowments, either as a result of

explicit or clear implicit donor stipulations or by law? The Board believes that because donor stipulations and laws vary, not-for-profit organizations must assess the relevant facts and circumstances for their endowment gifts and their relevant laws to determine if net appreciation on endowments is available for spending or is permanently restricted.

126. Some business officers of colleges and universities have expressed strong concern that institutions in the same state will interpret the state laws differently. They attribute that concern to differing interpretations about the provisions of the Uniform Act, particularly those of Section 2, "Appropriation of Appreciation," and Section 6, "Standard of Conduct." The Board considered that concern and it specifically considered the Uniform Act. Sections 2 and 6 of the Uniform Act provide that:

> The governing board may appropriate for expenditure for the uses and purposes for which an endowment fund is established so much of the net appreciation, realized and unrealized, in the fair value of the assets of an endowment fund over the historic dollar value of the fund as is prudent under the standard established by Section 6.
>
> In the administration of the powers to appropriate appreciation, . . . members of a governing board shall exercise ordinary business care and prudence under the facts and circumstances prevailing at the time of the action or decision. In so doing they shall consider long and short term needs of the institution in carrying out its educational, religious, charitable, or other eleemosynary purposes, its present and anticipated financial requirements, expected total return on its investments, price level trends, and general economic conditions.

127. Interpretations differ about the extent to which, if at all, the standard of ordinary business care and prudence precludes an institution's use of net appreciation. Some constituents believe that the Uniform Act supports the traditional view that gains on investments of endowments are not expendable unless the governing board makes an affirmative judgment that it is prudent to spend those gains. Others, including Board members, believe that the responsibility to exercise ordinary business care and prudence in determining whether to spend net appreciation is similar to the fiduciary responsibilities that exist for all charitable resources under an organization's control. That

latter view is consistent with page 5 of the Prefatory Note to the Uniform Act, which says:

> The Uniform Act authorizes expenditure of appreciation subject to a standard of business care and prudence. It seems unwise to fix more exact standards in a statute. To impose a greater constriction would hamper adaptation by different institutions to their particular needs.
>
> The standard of care is that of a reasonable and prudent director of a nonprofit corporation—similar to that of a director of a business corporation—which seems more appropriate than the traditional Prudent Man Rule applicable to private trustees. . . .

128. Some states have adopted modified forms of the Uniform Act and in some cases those modifications may be substantive and relevant to the classification of net gains. For example, at least one state (Rhode Island) provides that the "historic dollar value" of an endowment fund, as defined in the Uniform Act, shall be adjusted to reflect the change, if any, in the purchasing power of the historic dollar value of the fund. This modification is substantive because it requires changes to the measure of the original historic dollar value. Thus, the portion of net appreciation in excess of the original historic dollar value that is necessary to cover the purchasing power adjustments must be retained and, considering past economic history and prospects for continued inflation, interpreting and classifying that amount as permanently restricted would be a fair representation. Most states, however, have not adopted explicit provisions that fix more exacting standards or impose a greater constriction than the standard of ordinary business care and prudence quoted above.

129. The Board concluded that a definitive interpretation of the Uniform Act is not necessary or critical to the issue. The Board decided that this Statement should require reporting of gains and losses on endowments that faithfully represents the relevant facts and circumstances. Accordingly, the Board concluded that if the law of the relevant jurisdiction, as interpreted by an organization's governing board, places permanent restrictions on some part of the net appreciation, that amount should be reported as permanently restricted net assets in the organization's financial statements. In the absence of such a law or a donor's explicit or clear implicit permanent restriction, net appreciation should be reported as unrestricted if the endowment's income is unrestricted or

temporarily restricted if the endowment's income is temporarily restricted by the donor.

130. The Board also concluded that to implement the provisions of this Statement, latitude for interpretation by an institution's governing board is necessary for both conceptual and practical reasons, especially for institutions in Uniform Act states. Section 1(5) of the Uniform Act defines the "historic dollar value" of an endowment fund and includes comments that provide additional guidance. It also provides that "the determination of historic dollar value made in good faith by the institution is conclusive." Accordingly, the Board believes that it is appropriate that this Statement provide that net appreciation be classified in accordance with those conclusive good-faith determinations made by an institution's governing board.

131. Respondents to the Exposure Draft that commented on the provisions of paragraph 22 of this Statement expressed differing views; although most agreed, many continue to believe that the Uniform Act requires retention of some gains or that interpretations of the Uniform Act will be inconsistent. At this time, the Board has no reason to believe that governing boards will interpret similar facts and circumstances, including state statutes, in significantly differing ways. Rather, the Board believes that ample opportunities exist for the directors and officers of colleges, universities, museums, and other organizations to avoid that perceived problem. Consultations with others, including corporate counsel, outside auditors, industry associations, attorneys general, state societies of CPAs, and other institutions generally result in common understandings and conclusions about matters of state and local law.

132. Some respondents raised questions about reporting losses on investments and requested guidance for display if the law requires repatriation from unrestricted assets of previously appropriated earnings. Their questions generally relate to specific facts and circumstances and the display generally would follow from the requirements, if any, of the relevant laws. The Board plans to consider those and other issues of accounting for investments in a subsequent part of its project on not-for-profit organizations.

Classification of expenses as unrestricted

133. The Invitation to Comment asked whether all expenses should be classified as decreases in unrestricted net assets or, if not, whether expenses financed by restricted resources should be reported as decreases in the permanently or temporarily restricted class of net assets. The AICPA task force recommended that all expenses be shown in the unrestricted class of net assets. Paragraph 193 of its report said, "Some members believe all expenses should be presented in the unrestricted [class of net assets] because expenses are the using up of resources, causing any restrictions related to them to expire." The task force also noted that a reclassification of resources from temporarily restricted net assets to unrestricted net assets could be presented when restricted resources are used to finance expenses of a restricted grant.

134. Respondents to the Invitation to Comment expressed mixed views. Although many agreed with the AICPA task force advisory recommendation, most did not. Those who disagreed generally said that (a) the related reclassifications are confusing and that a direct decrease to temporarily restricted net assets is easy to understand, (b) the revenues and expenses relate to each other and should be presented together, or (c) certain specific exceptions should be allowed.

135. The Board concluded that not-for-profit organizations should report expenses as decreases in unrestricted net assets. Identifying or designating sources of donor-restricted revenues to be used to finance specific expenses does not make an expense donor restricted. Rather, expenses result from the decisions of an organization's managers about the activities to be carried out and about how and when particular resources are to be used. The Board believes that the perceived confusion about reclassifications can be avoided by appropriate labeling in financial statements and by reporting those items separately and in reasonably homogeneous groups as required by paragraph 19.

136. Further, although some respondents to the Invitation to Comment and the Exposure Draft said reporting certain expenses as a decrease in the restricted class of net assets is simpler or more understandable, the Board believes that reporting has disadvantages that outweigh the perceived simplicity. Because expenses often occur months or years after the related restricted support is received and recognized in financial statements, reporting an expense in the restricted class of net assets would not necessarily achieve the "match" of revenues and expenses that some respondents desire. Moreover, reporting current period expenses in the temporarily restricted

class of net assets with restricted support for gifts restricted for use in a future period may cause greater confusion, particularly for those users of financial statements that believe revenues and expenses of a period are necessarily directly related to each other.

137. A few respondents to the Exposure Draft said that certain information currently available to them may be lost if all expenses are reported in the unrestricted class of net assets. Generally, they expressed concern that the extent to which an organization's expenses are dependent on restricted contributions may no longer be clear from its financial statements. The Board believes those concerns generally are satisfied by this Statement's requirements to distinguish between donor-restricted and unrestricted revenues and gains and present those and other items in reasonably homogeneous groups.

Reporting Gross Amounts of Revenues for Special Events

138. Paragraph 24 of this Statement requires reporting of gross amounts of revenues and expenses. The Board concluded that information about those amounts is essential to "provide information about the amounts and kinds of inflows and outflows of resources during a period" (Concepts Statement 4, paragraph 48). That information is helpful to users of financial statements in understanding and assessing an organization's ongoing major or central operations and activities. A few respondents to the Exposure Draft said that the current practice of netting the revenues and direct costs of *special events* should be permitted. As paragraph 25 explains, organizations may report net amounts for their special events if they result from peripheral or incidental transactions. However, so-called special events often are ongoing and major activities; if so, organizations should report the gross revenues and expenses of those activities.

Statement of Cash Flows

139. The Board concluded that a statement of cash flows should provide relevant information about the cash receipts and cash payments of an organization during a period. Statement 95 established standards for the information to be provided in a statement of cash flows of a business enterprise. Paragraph 69 of Statement 95 says the "exclusion of not-for-profit organizations from the scope of [Statement 95] means only that the Board has not yet decided whether not-for-profit organizations should be re-

quired to provide a statement of cash flows." The Board concluded, in this Statement, that the provisions of Statement 95 generally are applicable to not-for-profit organizations.

140. The Invitation to Comment requested comments on provisions of Statement 95 and whether to apply or amend those provisions to make them applicable to not-for-profit organizations. The AICPA task force recommended applying most of the provisions of Statement 95. Respondents to the Invitation to Comment generally agreed as did most respondents to the Exposure Draft.

Amendment to Description of Financing Cash Flows

141. The Invitation to Comment asked whether items identified by the AICPA task force as "capital cash flows" should be reported as operating, investing, or as a separate category of cash flows. The AICPA task force recommended that a fourth category be created to display capital cash flows, which it defined in paragraph 255 of its report to "include all permanently restricted gifts and temporarily restricted cash receipts from donors for property, plant, and equipment, and those that are not immediately available for operations, such as term endowments, and gifts subject to a life interest." Most respondents to the Invitation to Comment agreed; however, several respondents, including an organization representing institutional lending officers, said that a new category could be misinterpreted and confusing, and is not necessary.

142. In paragraph 254 of its report, the AICPA task force said that "transactions involving changes in permanently restricted and temporarily restricted net assets for which the restrictions are likely to last for an extended period of time . . . may not easily fit into the categories prescribed in FASB Statement No. 95." Those who disagreed with the task force's recommendation generally said that "capital cash flows" can be appropriately reported as financing activities. Some also suggested that the financing cash flows could be presented in two sections: debt financing cash flows and capital cash flows.

143. The Board concluded that creating a fourth category of cash flows to accommodate the cash inflows of not-for-profit organizations described by the AICPA task force as capital cash flows is neither necessary nor desirable. The Board believes that a new

category would create new differences in terminology and definitions between not-for-profit organizations and business enterprises, and between not-for-profit organizations and governmental entities, and those differences could cause more confusion than clarity. Paragraph 15 of GASB Statement No. 9, *Reporting Cash Flows of Proprietary and Nonexpendable Trust Funds and Governmental Entities That Use Proprietary Fund Accounting,* which requires governmental entities to classify cash receipts and cash payments as resulting from operating, noncapital financing, capital and related financing, or investing activities, uses similar terms that have definitions that differ from those in Statement 95 and those recommended by the AICPA task force.

144. The Board concluded that comparability of reporting will be enhanced if both business enterprises and not-for-profit organizations report their cash flows using the same classifications and definitions. Common definitions and reporting will help enhance users' understandings of information provided in statements of cash flows. Although GASB Statement 9 provides different definitions, colleges, universities, hospitals, and other organizations may, under this Statement, subdivide categories of cash flows to provide information in their statement of cash flows that is reasonably comparable to if not the same as governmental entities.

145. To implement the Board's conclusion, this Statement amends Statement 95 to extend its scope to not-for-profit organizations and to expand the description of financing activities in paragraph 18 of Statement 95 to encompass receipts of resources that by donor stipulation must be used for long-term purposes. That category of transactions was not considered when Statement 95 was issued. This Statement also amends paragraph 19 to include among its list of cash inflows from financing activities receipts from contributions and investment income that by donor stipulation are restricted for the purposes of acquiring, constructing, or improving property, plant, equipment, or other long-lived assets or establishing or increasing a permanent endowment or term endowment.

Reporting Net Cash Flows from Operating Activities

146. The Invitation to Comment asked whether not-for-profit organizations should be required to report cash flows from operating activities using the direct method and, if so, whether they should provide a rec-

onciling statement. The AICPA task force discussed the advantages of the direct method and the indirect method of presenting cash flows from operating activities and, in paragraph 260, the task force said that it "believes that the direct method of reporting would be more useful to preparers and users of not-for-profit organization's financial statements." It recommended that not-for-profit organizations be required to present their statements of cash flows using the direct method of presentation. A significant majority of respondents disagreed. Respondents generally said that the option of presenting net cash flows from operating activities using the indirect method as permitted for business enterprises should be allowed for not-for-profit organizations for reasons similar to those discussed in Statement 95.

147. The Board agreed with those respondents and concluded that, consistent with Statement 95, not-for-profit organizations should be encouraged to use the direct method of reporting net cash flows from operating activities and allowed to use the indirect method. The advantages and disadvantages of each method and the Board's considerations of each are discussed in paragraphs 106-121 of Statement 95. More specifically, paragraph 119 says:

> The Board believes that both the direct and the indirect methods provide potentially important information. The more comprehensive and presumably more useful approach would be to use the direct method in the statement of cash flows and to provide a reconciliation of net income and net cash flow from operating activities in a separate schedule—thereby reaping the benefits of both methods while maintaining the focus of the statement of cash flows on cash receipts and payments. This Statement therefore encourages enterprises to follow that approach. But most providers and users of financial statements have little or no experience and only limited familiarity with the direct method, while both have extensive experience with the indirect method. Not only are there questions about the ability of enterprises to determine gross amounts of operating cash receipts and payments, . . . but also little information is available on which specific categories of operating cash receipts and payments would be most meaningful.

148. The Board concluded that those observations also apply to not-for-profit organizations, which generally have little experience presenting statements of

cash flows. This Statement also clarifies that not-for-profit organizations that present a reconciling schedule when using the direct method or that use the indirect method should reconcile the change in net assets as reported in a statement of activities to net cash flows from operating activities. The Board believes that reconciling from the change in net assets is consistent with reporting information that focuses on cash flows for the entity as a whole.

Reporting Cash Flows from Purchases and Sales of Investment Securities

149. A few respondents to the Exposure Draft said that the reporting of gross amounts of cash from purchasing and selling securities, particularly those of endowment funds, may be misleading, inappropriate, or both. Some suggested that because permanent endowments require reinvestment of cash inflows from selling securities, the cash outflows, which are nondiscretionary expenditures to maintain the existing endowment, are not available and the appearance of those inflows and outflows in a statement of cash flows can easily mislead users. The Board believes that reporting those cash flows as investing activities—not operating activities—is appropriate and is generally understood by users of financial statements. Furthermore, the Board believes that, for reasons similar to those discussed in paragraphs 97-99 of Statement 95, allocating transactions for pooled investments between nondiscretionary transactions to maintain or expand the permanent endowments and discretionary expenditures to maintain or expand board-designated endowment funds would necessarily be arbitrary and add additional costs that would exceed the benefits provided.

Effective Date and Transition

150. The Exposure Draft proposed that this Statement generally be effective for annual financial statements issued for fiscal years beginning after December 15, 1994. The Board decided to provide ample time before this Statement becomes effective primarily to coordinate its implementation with Statement 116. The Board also noted that that extended time may be helpful to organizations that have not determined the historic dollar value of their permanent endowment funds. Most respondents agreed that the proposed effective date would provide adequate time for organizations to update systems and gather information necessary to report the basic information required by this Statement.

151. Nonetheless, a national association representing over 400 human services organizations (and a few other respondents) requested an additional one-year delay for small not-for-profit organizations. About one-third of the association's members have annual budgets of less than $1 million and the association said an extended transition period would allow them sufficient time to utilize the initial experience gained by larger organizations and CPAs. They believe that experience could help them find cost-effective ways to implement this Statement and Statement 116. Board members believe a further delay generally is not necessary. However, because small organizations are often dependent on outside volunteers and are particularly sensitive to any incremental one-time costs, the Board decided to grant a one-year delay for organizations with less than $5 million in total assets and less than $1 million in annual expenses.

152. Earlier application of this Statement is encouraged. Applying this Statement early may result in some erosion in comparability of reporting during the transition period; however, the Board concluded that the benefits of the information gained by permitting early application outweigh its disadvantages. Respondents to the Exposure Draft generally agreed.

Appendix C

ILLUSTRATIVE EXAMPLES

153. This appendix provides illustrations of statements of financial position, statements of activities, and statements of cash flows. These illustrations are intended as examples only; they present only a few of the permissible formats. Other formats or levels of detail may be appropriate for certain circumstances. Organizations are encouraged to provide information in ways that are most relevant and understandable to donors, creditors, and other external users of financial statements. The Board encourages organizations to provide comparative financial statements; however, for simplicity, the illustrative statements of activities and statements of cash flows provide information for a single period.

154. The illustrations also include certain notes to the financial statements for matters discussed in this Statement. The illustrative notes are not intended to illustrate compliance with all generally accepted accounting principles and specialized accounting and reporting principles and practices.

155. Shading* is used to highlight certain basic totals that must be reported in financial statements to comply with the provisions of this Statement. This Statement requires not only reporting those certain basic totals but also reporting components of those aggregates; for example, it requires reporting information about the gross amounts of items of revenues and expenses and cash receipts and payments.

Statement of Financial Position

156. A statement of financial position that sequences assets and liabilities based on their relative liquidity is presented. For example, cash and contributions receivable restricted by donors to investment in land,

buildings, and equipment are not included with the line items "cash and cash equivalents" or "contributions receivable." Rather, those items are reported as "assets restricted to investment in land, buildings, and equipment" and are sequenced closer to "land, buildings, and equipment"; cash and cash equivalents of permanent endowment funds held temporarily until suitable long-term investment opportunities are identified are included in the classification "long-term investments." Assets and liabilities also may be arrayed by their relationship to net asset classes, classified as current and noncurrent, or arranged in other ways. Comparative statements of financial position are provided to facilitate understanding of the statement of cash flows.

Not-for-Profit Organization
Statements of Financial Position
June 30, 19X1 and 19X0
(in thousands)

	19X1	19X0
Assets:		
Cash and cash equivalents	$ 75	$ 460
Accounts and interest receivable	2,130	1,670
Inventories and prepaid expenses	610	1,000
Contributions receivable	3,025	2,700
Short-term investments	1,400	1,000
Assets restricted to investment in land, buildings, and equipment	5,210	4,560
Land, buildings, and equipment	61,700	63,590
Long-term investments	218,070	203,500
Total assets	$292,220	$278,480
Liabilities and net assets:		
Accounts payable	$ 2,570	$ 1,050
Refundable advance		650
Grants payable	875	1,300
Notes payable		1,140
Annuity obligations	1,685	1,700
Long-term debt	5,500	6,500
Total liabilities	10,630	12,340
Net assets:		
Unrestricted	115,228	103,670
Temporarily restricted (Note B)	24,342	25,470
Permanently restricted (Note C)	142,020	137,000
Total net assets	281,590	266,140
Total liabilities and net assets	$292,220	$278,480

*Editor's Note: In this edition, the totals are highlighted by being enclosed in brackets rather than by shading.

Statement of Activities

157. Three formats of statements of activities are presented. Each format has certain advantages. Format A reports information in a single column. That format most easily accommodates presentation of multiyear comparative information. Format B reports the same information in columnar format with a column for each class of net assets and adds an optional total column. That format makes evident that the effects of expirations on donor restrictions result in reclassifications between classes of net assets. It also accommodates presentation of aggregated information about contributions and investment income for the entity as a whole. Format C reports information in two statements with summary amounts from a statement of revenues, expenses, and other changes in unrestricted net assets (Part 1 of 2) articulating with a statement of changes in net assets (Part 2 of 2). Alternative formats for the statement of changes in net assets—a single column and a multicolumn—are illustrated. The two-statement approach of Format C focuses attention on changes in unrestricted net assets. That format may be preferred by organizations that view their *operating* activities as excluding receipts of donor-restricted revenues and gains from contributions and investment income. To facilitate comparison of the formats, the same level of aggregation is used in each of the statements of activities.

158. The three illustrative statements of activities show items of revenues and gains first, then expenses, then losses; reclassifications, which must be shown separately, are reported with revenues and gains. Those items could be arranged in other ways and other subtotals may be included. For example, the items may be sequenced as (a) revenues, expenses, gains and losses, and reclassifications shown last or (b) certain revenues, less directly related expenses, followed by a subtotal, then other revenues, other expenses, gains and losses, and reclassifications. Paragraph 167 provides an example that shows how items may be sequenced to distinguish between operating and nonoperating activities or to make other distinctions, if desired.

159. Although the illustrative statements of activities report expenses by function, expenses may be reported by natural classification in the statements with functional classification disclosed in the notes.

Format A

Not-for-Profit Organization
Statement of Activities
Year Ended June 30, 19X1
(in thousands)

Changes in unrestricted net assets:
Revenues and gains:

Contributions	$ 8,640
Fees	5,400
Income on long-term investments (Note E)	5,600
Other investment income (Note E)	850
Net unrealized and realized gains on long-term investments (Note E)	8,228
Other	150
Total unrestricted revenues and gains	28,868

Net assets released from restrictions (Note D):

Satisfaction of program restrictions	11,990
Satisfaction of equipment acquisition restrictions	1,500
Expiration of time restrictions	1,250
Total net assets released from restrictions	14,740
Total unrestricted revenues, gains, and other support	43,608

Expenses and losses:

Program A	13,100
Program B	8,540
Program C	5,760
Management and general	2,420
Fund raising	2,150
Total expenses (Note F)	31,970
Fire loss	80
Total expenses and losses	32,050
[Increase in unrestricted net assets	11,558]

Changes in temporarily restricted net assets:

Contributions	8,110
Income on long-term investments (Note E)	2,580
Net unrealized and realized gains on long-term investments (Note E)	2,952
Actuarial loss on annuity obligations	(30)
Net assets released from restrictions (Note D)	(14,740)
[Decrease in temporarily restricted net assets	(1,128)]

Changes in permanently restricted net assets:

Contributions	280
Income on long-term investments (Note E)	120
Net unrealized and realized gains on long-term investments (Note E)	4,620
Increase in permanently restricted net assets	5,020]
Increase in net assets	15,450]
Net assets at beginning of year	266,140
Net assets at end of year	$281,590

Format B

Not-for-Profit Organization
Statement of Activities
Year Ended June 30, 19X1
(in thousands)

	Unrestricted	Temporarily Restricted	Permanently Restricted	Total
Revenues, gains, and other support:				
Contributions	$ 8,640	$ 8,110	$ 280	$ 17,030
Fees	5,400			5,400
Income on long-term investments (Note E)	5,600	2,580	120	8,300
Other investment income (Note E)	850			850
Net unrealized and realized gains on long-term investments (Note E)	8,228	2,952	4,620	15,800
Other	150			150
Net assets released from restrictions (Note D):				
Satisfaction of program restrictions	11,990	(11,990)		
Satisfaction of equipment acquisition restrictions	1,500	(1,500)		
Expiration of time restrictions	1,250	(1,250)		
Total revenues, gains, and other support	43,608	(1,098)	5,020	47,530
Expenses and losses:				
Program A	13,100			13,100
Program B	8,540			8,540
Program C	5,760			5,760
Management and general	2,420			2,420
Fund raising	2,150			2,150
Total expenses (Note F)	31,970			31,970
Fire loss	80			80
Actuarial loss on annuity obligations		30		30
Total expenses and losses	32,050	30		32,080
[Change in net assets	11,558	(1,128)	5,020	15,450]
Net assets at beginning of year	103,670	25,470	137,000	266,140
Net assets at end of year	$115,228	$ 24,342	$142,020	$281,590

Format C, Part 1 of 2

Not-for-Profit Organization
Statement of Unrestricted Revenues, Expenses, and
Other Changes in Unrestricted Net Assets
Year Ended June 30, 19X1
(in thousands)

Unrestricted revenues and gains:	
Contributions	$ 8,640
Fees	5,400
Income on long-term investments (Note E)	5,600
Other investment income (Note E)	850
Net unrealized and realized gains on long-term investments (Note E)	8,228
Other	150
Total unrestricted revenues and gains	28,868
Net assets released from restrictions (Note D):	
Satisfaction of program restrictions	11,990
Satisfaction of equipment acquisition restrictions	1,500
Expiration of time restrictions	1,250
Total net assets released from restrictions	14,740
Total unrestricted revenues, gains, and other support	43,608
Expenses and losses:	
Program A	13,100
Program B	8,540
Program C	5,760
Management and general	2,420
Fund raising	2,150
Total expenses (Note F)	31,970
Fire loss	80
Total unrestricted expenses and losses	32,050
[Increase in unrestricted net assets	$11,558]

Format C, Part 2 of 2

Not-for-Profit Organization
Statement of Changes in Net Assets
Year Ended June 30, 19X1
(in thousands)

Unrestricted net assets:	
Total unrestricted revenues and gains	$ 28,868
Net assets released from restrictions (Note D)	14,740
Total unrestricted expenses and losses	(32,050)
[Increase in unrestricted net assets	11,558]
Temporarily restricted net assets:	
Contributions	8,110
Income on long-term investments (Note E)	2,580
Net unrealized and realized gains on long-term investments (Note E)	2,952
Actuarial loss on annuity obligations	(30)
Net assets released from restrictions (Note D)	(14,740)
[Decrease in temporarily restricted net assets	(1,128)]
Permanently restricted net assets:	
Contributions	280
Income on long-term investments (Note E)	120
Net unrealized and realized gains on long-term investments (Note E)	4,620
Increase in permanently restricted net assets	5,020]
[Increase in net assets	15,450]
Net assets at beginning of year	266,140
Net assets at end of year	$281,590

Format C, Part 2 of 2 (Alternate)

Not-for-Profit Organization
Statement of Changes in Net Assets
Year Ended June 30, 19X1
(in thousands)

	Unrestricted	Temporarily Restricted	Permanently Restricted	Total
Revenues, gains, and other support:				
Unrestricted revenues, gains, and other support	$ 28,868			$ 28,868
Restricted revenues, gains, and other support:				
Contributions		$ 8,110	$ 280	8,390
Income on long-term investments (Note E)		2,580	120	2,700
Net unrealized and realized gains on long-term investments (Note E)		2,952	4,620	7,572
Net assets released from restrictions (Note D)	14,740	(14,740)		
Total revenues, gains, and other support	43,608	(1,098)	5,020	47,530
Expenses and losses:				
Unrestricted expenses and losses	32,050			32,050
Actuarial loss on annuity obligations		30		30
Total expenses and losses	32,050	30		32,080
[Change in net assets	11,558	(1,128)	5,020	15,450]
Net assets at beginning of year	103,670	25,470	137,000	266,140
Net assets at end of year	$115,228	$ 24,342	$142,020	$281,590

(This page intentionally left blank.)

Statement of Cash Flows

160. Statements of cash flows are illustrated using both the direct and indirect methods of reporting cash flow from operating activities.

Direct Method

Not-for-Profit Organization
Statement of Cash Flows
Year Ended June 30, 19X1
(in thousands)

Cash flows from operating activities:	
Cash received from service recipients	$ 5,220
Cash received from contributors	8,030
Cash collected on contributions receivable	2,615
Interest and dividends received	8,570
Miscellaneous receipts	150
Interest paid	(382)
Cash paid to employees and suppliers	(23,808)
Grants paid	(425)
[Net cash used by operating activities	(30)]
Cash flows from investing activities:	
Insurance proceeds from fire loss on building	250
Purchase of equipment	(1,500)
Proceeds from sale of investments	76,100
Purchase of investments	(74,900)
[Net cash used by investing activities	(50)]
Cash flows from financing activities:	
Proceeds from contributions restricted for:	
Investment in endowment	200
Investment in term endowment	70
Investment in plant	1,210
Investment subject to annuity agreements	200
	1,680
Other financing activities:	
Interest and dividends restricted for reinvestment	300
Payments of annuity obligations	(145)
Payments on notes payable	(1,140)
Payments on long-term debt	(1,000)
	(1,985)
Net cash used by financing activities	(305)
Net decrease in cash and cash equivalents	(385)
Cash and cash equivalents at beginning of year	460
Cash and cash equivalents at end of year	$ 75

Reconciliation of change in net assets to net cash used by operating activities:

[Change in net assets	$ 15,450]
Adjustments to reconcile change in net assets to net cash used by operating activities:	
Depreciation	3,200
Fire loss	80
Actuarial loss on annuity obligations	30
Increase in accounts and interest receivable	(460)
Decrease in inventories and prepaid expenses	390
Increase in contributions receivable	(325)
Increase in accounts payable	1,520
Decrease in refundable advance	(650)
Decrease in grants payable	(425)
Contributions restricted for long-term investment	(2,740)
Interest and dividends restricted for long-term investment	(300)
Net unrealized and realized gains on long-term investments	(15,800)
[Net cash used by operating activities	$ (30)]

Supplemental data for noncash investing and financing activities:

Gifts of equipment	$140
Gift of paid-up life insurance, cash surrender value	80

Indirect Method

Not-for-Profit Organization
Statement of Cash Flows
Year Ended June 30, 19X1
(in thousands)

Cash flows from operating activites:

[Change in net assets $ 15,450]

Adjustments to reconcile change in net assets to net cash used by operating activities:

Depreciation	3,200
Fire loss	80
Actuarial loss on annuity obligations	30
Increase in accounts and interest receivable	(460)
Decrease in inventories and prepaid expenses	390
Increase in contributions receivable	(325)
Increase in accounts payable	1,520
Decrease in refundable advance	(650)
Decrease in grants payable	(425)
Contributions restricted for long-term investment	(2,740)
Interest and dividends restricted for long-term investment	(300)
Net unrealized and realized gains on long-term investments	(15,800)
[Net cash used by operating activities	(30)]

Cash flows from investing activities:

Insurance proceeds from fire loss on building	250
Purchase of equipment	(1,500)
Proceeds from sale of investments	76,100
Purchase of investments	(74,900)
[Net cash used by investing activities	(50)]

Cash flows from financing activities:

Proceeds from contributions restricted for:

Investment in endowment	200
Investment in term endowment	70
Investment in plant	1,210
Investment subject to annuity agreements	200
	1,680

Other financing activities:

Interest and dividends restricted for reinvestment	300
Payments of annuity obligations	(145)
Payments on notes payable	(1,140)
Payments on long-term debt	(1,000)
	(1,985)
Net cash used by financing activities	(305)]
Net decrease in cash and cash equivalents	(385)
Cash and cash equivalents at beginning of year	460
Cash and cash equivalents at end of year	$ 75]

Supplemental data:

Noncash investing and financing activities:

Gifts of equipment	$140
Gift of paid-up life insurance, cash surrender value	80
Interest paid	382

Notes to Financial Statements

161. Illustrative Note A provides required policy disclosures (paragraphs 14 and 16 of Statement 116) that bear on the illustrated statements and Notes B and C provide information required by this Statement. Notes D through F provide information that not-for-profit organizations are encouraged to disclose. However, paragraph 26 requires voluntary health and welfare organizations to provide the information in Note F in a statement of functional expenses. All amounts are in thousands.

Note A

The Organization reports gifts of cash and other assets as restricted support if they are received with donor stipulations that limit the use of the donated assets. When a donor restriction expires, that is, when a stipulated time restriction ends or purpose restriction is accomplished, temporarily restricted net assets are reclassified to unrestricted net assets and reported in the statement of activities as net assets released from restrictions.

The Organization reports gifts of land, buildings, and equipment as unrestricted support unless explicit donor stipulations specify how the donated assets must be used. Gifts of long-lived assets with explicit restrictions that specify how the assets are to be used and gifts of cash or other assets that must be used to acquire long-lived assets are reported as restricted support. Absent explicit donor stipulations about how long those long-lived assets must be maintained, the Organization reports expirations of donor restrictions when the donated or acquired long-lived assets are placed in service.

Note B

Temporarily restricted net assets are available for the following purposes or periods:

Program A activities:	
Purchase of equipment	$ 3,060
Research	4,256
Educational seminars and publications	1,520
Program B activities:	
Disaster relief	2,240
Educational seminars and publications	2,158
Program C activities: general	2,968
Buildings and equipment	2,150
Annuity trust agreements	2,850
For periods after June 30, 19X1	3,140
	$24,342

Note C

Permanently restricted net assets are restricted to:

Investment in perpetuity, the income from which is expendable to support:	
Program A activities	$ 27,524
Program B activities	13,662
Program C activities	13,662
Any activities of the organization	81,972
	136,820
Endowment requiring income to be added to original gift until fund's value is $2,500	2,120
Paid-up life insurance policy that will provide proceeds upon death of insured for an endowment to support general activities	80
Land required to be used as a recreation area	3,000
	$142,020

Note D

Net assets were released from donor restrictions by incurring expenses satisfying the restricted purposes or by occurrence of other events specified by donors.

Purpose restrictions accomplished:

Program A expenses	$ 5,800
Program B expenses	4,600
Program C expenses	1,590
	11,990
Program A equipment acquired and placed in service	1,500
Time restrictions expired:	
Passage of specified time	850
Death of annuity beneficiary	400
	1,250
Total restrictions released	$14,740

Note E

Investments are carried at market or appraised value, and realized and unrealized gains and losses are reflected in the statement of activities. The Organization invests cash in excess of daily requirements in short-term investments. At June 30, 19X1, $1,400 was invested short term, and during the year short-term investments earned $850. Most long-term investments are held in two investment pools. Pool A is for permanent endowments and the unappropriated net appreciation of those endowments. Pool B is for amounts designated by the board of trustees for long-term investment. Annuity trusts, term endowments, and certain permanent endowments are separately invested. Long-term investment activity is reflected in the table below:

	Pool A	Pool B	Other	Total
Investments at beginning of year	$164,000	$32,800	$6,700	$203,500
Gifts available for investment:				
Gifts creating permanent endowment	200		80	280
Gifts creating term endowments			70	70
Gifts creating annuity trusts			200	200
Amount withdrawn at death of annuitant			(400)	(400)
Investment returns (net of expenses of $375):				
Dividends, interest, and rents	6,000	2,000	300	8,300
Realized and unrealized gains	12,000	3,800		15,800
Total return on investments	18,000	5,800	300	24,100
Amounts appropriated for current operations	(7,500)	(2,000)		(9,500)
Annuity trust income for current and future payments			(180)	(180)
Investments at end of year	$174,700	$36,600	$6,770	$218,070

The participation in the pools and ownership of the other investments at June 30, 19X1 is shown in the table below:

	Pool A	Pool B	Other	Total
Permanently restricted net assets	$136,820		$2,200	$139,020
Temporarily restricted net assets	10,752		4,570	15,322
Unrestricted net assets	27,128	$36,600		63,728
	$174,700	$36,600	$6,770	$218,070

The board of trustees has interpreted state law as requiring the preservation of the purchasing power (real value) of the permanent endowment funds unless explicit donor stipulations specify how net appreciation must be used. To meet that objective, the Organization's endowment management policies require that net appreciation be retained permanently in an amount necessary to adjust the historic dollar value of original endowment gifts by the change in the Consumer Price Index. After maintaining the real value of the permanent endowment funds, any remainder of total return is available for appropriation. In 19X1, the total return on Pool A was $18,000 (10.6 percent), of which $4,620 was retained permanently to preserve the real value of the original gifts. The remaining $13,380 was available for appropriation by the board of trustees. State law allows the board to appropriate so much of net appreciation as is prudent

considering the Organization's long- and short-term needs, present and anticipated financial requirements, expected total return on its investments, price level trends, and general economic conditions. Under the Organization's endowment spending policy, 5 percent of the average of the market value at the end of the previous 3 years is appropriated, which was $7,500 for the year ended June 30, 19X1.

Note F

Expenses incurred were for:

		Program			Management	Fund
	Total	**A**	**B**	**C**	**and General**	**Raising**
Salaries, wages, and benefits	$15,115	$ 7,400	$3,900	$1,725	$1,130	$ 960
Grants to other organizations	4,750	2,075	750	1,925		
Supplies and travel	3,155	865	1,000	490	240	560
Services and professional fees	2,840	160	1,490	600	200	390
Office and occupancy	2,528	1,160	600	450	218	100
Depreciation	3,200	1,440	800	570	250	140
Interest	382				382	
Total expenses	$31,970	$13,100	$8,540	$5,760	$2,420	$2,150

Transactions Reported in the Illustrative Financial Statements

162. The following facts and transactions are reflected in the illustrative financial statements. The transactions are presented by class of net assets to facilitate locating their effects in the statements and notes.

The following transactions affect unrestricted net assets:

a. The organization invested cash in excess of daily requirements in short-term investment instruments. Interest earned on these investments totaled $850. The governing board has designated a portion of unrestricted net assets for long-term investment. Those assets earned $2,000.

b. The organization received unrestricted contributions of the following: cash, $5,120; recognizable contributed services, $300; other consumable

assets, $1,410; equipment, $140; and unconditional promises to give to support activities of 19X1, $1,020.

c. Equipment with an original cost of $660 and accumulated depreciation of $330 was destroyed in a fire. Insurance proceeds of $250 were received. The equipment was originally purchased with unrestricted assets.

d. All conditions of a prior year's grant of $650 were substantially met. The grant proceeds were originally recorded as a refundable advance.

e. The organization made a payment of $425 on its prior year unconditional grant to an unrelated agency.

f. The organization repaid $1,140 of its notes payable. Interest of $32 was incurred and paid on these notes.

g. The organization repaid $1,000 of its long-term debt. Interest of $350 was incurred and paid on the debt.

h. Depreciation amounted to $3,200.

The following transactions affect temporarily restricted net assets:

i. The organization received temporarily restricted contributions as follows:

Restricted to:	Cash	Consumable Assets	Promises to Give
Program purposes	$2,170	$960	$ 990
Use in future periods	740		930
Acquisition of land, buildings, and equipment	770		1,380

j. In addition, a donor transferred cash of $200 to set up an annuity trust having a related annuity obligation with a present value of $100. Upon the death of the beneficiary, the remaining interest will be used for a donor-stipulated purpose.

k. In addition, a donor contributed cash of $70 to create a term endowment. At the end of 15 years the endowment assets can be used to support the organization's operations.

l. The organization made payments of $145 to beneficiaries of annuity trust agreements.

The following transactions affect permanently restricted net assets:

m. A donor contributed a paid-up life insurance policy with a cash surrender value of $80. Upon the death of the insured, the death benefit must be used to create a permanent endowment. There was no change in the cash surrender value between the date of the gift and the end of the fiscal year.

n. A donor contributed cash of $200 to create a permanent endowment fund. The income is restricted to use for Program A activities.

The following transactions affect more than one class of net assets:

o. The organization collected promises to give of $3,055: $980 of amounts for unrestricted purposes, $610 of amounts restricted to future periods, $1,025 of amounts restricted to program purposes, and $440 of amounts for acquisition of land, buildings, and equipment.

p. The organization utilized all of the $1,410 consumable assets contributed for unrestricted purposes, and $350 of the $960 consumable assets contributed for program purposes.

q. A trust annuitant died and the $400 remainder interest became available for the unrestricted use of the organization. Management decided to invest the remainder interest in short-term investments. The actuarial gain on death of the annuitant is included in the actuarial loss on annuity obligations.

r. The organization acquired and placed in service $1,500 of equipment for Program A; temporarily restricted net assets were available at the time the equipment was purchased.

s. The net gain, unrealized and realized, on unrestricted net assets designated by the governing board for long-term investment of $3,800 was recognized. The net gain, unrealized and realized, on permanent endowments and the unappropriated net appreciation of those endowments of $12,000 was recognized. The governing board has interpreted the law in its jurisdiction as requiring preservation of purchasing power. The governing board has selected the CPI as the measure of changes in purchasing power. The CPI has changed by 3.5 percent over the year. The index-adjusted original gift amount of the endowment at the end of the previous year was $132,000.

t. The organization reinvested the yield of $120 on a permanent endowment that requires income to be added to the original gift until the fund's value is $2,500.

Statement of Activities with Additional Classifications

163. This Statement neither encourages nor discourages organizations from classifying items of revenues, expenses, and other changes in net assets as operating and nonoperating, expendable and nonexpendable, earned and unearned, recurring and nonrecurring, or in other ways. Rather, the requirements of this Statement provide a few broad constraints for a statement of activities and allow not-for-profit organizations latitude to make distinctions that they believe will provide meaningful information to users of their financial statements. Like business enterprises, that latitude allows organizations to report an undefined intermediate measure of operations. That latitude also allows reporting practices to develop in an evolutionary manner for all or certain kinds of not-for-profit organizations.

164. Entities that use terms such as *operating income, operating profit, operating surplus, operating*

deficit, and *results of operations* often use those terms with different meanings. Business enterprises that choose to make an operating and nonoperating distinction do so within an income statement (statement of earnings) that at a minimum reports net income for the period as well as an intermediate measure of income before the effects of a discontinued operating segment, extraordinary items, or an accounting change, if any.

165. Paragraph 23 imposes a similar constraint on not-for-profit organizations that choose to use similar terms. If an organization reports an intermediate measure of *operations,* it must do so within a financial statement that, at a minimum, reports the change in unrestricted net assets for the period. Paragraph 23 also specifies that if an organization's use of the term *operations* is not apparent from the details provided on the face of the statement, a note to financial statements should describe the nature of the reportedmeasure of operations or the items excluded from operations.

166. A statement of unrestricted revenues, expenses, and other changes in unrestricted net assets that subdivides all transactions and other events and circumstances to make an operating and nonoperating distinction is illustrated. This example uses part 1 of 2 of Format C of the previously illustrated statements of activities to show a measure of operations—change in unrestricted net assets from operations.

167. The shaded* areas depict the constraints imposed by this Statement and by generally accepted accounting principles to report appropriately labeled subtotals for changes in classes of net assets before the effects of discontinued operating segments, extraordinary items, or accounting changes, if any. The unshaded areas depict areas within the statement for which there is latitude to sequence and classify items of revenues and expenses. Other formats also may be used. For example, the single-statement approach of Format B may be helpful in describing an organiza-

tion's ongoing major or central operations if that organization's view of operating activities includes receiving donor-restricted revenues from contributions and investment income.

Other Not-for-Profit Organization
Statement of Unrestricted Revenues, Expenses, and
Other Changes in Unrestricted Net Assets
Year Ended June 30, 19X1
(in thousands)

Operating revenues and support:	
Fees from providing services	$ X,XXX
Operating support	X,XXX
Net assets released from restrictions	X,XXX
Total operating revenues and support	XX,XXX
Operating expenses:	
Programs	XX,XXX
Management and general	X,XXX
Fund raising	X,XXX
Total operating expenses	XX,XXX
Change in unrestricted net assets from operations	X,XXX
Other changes:	
[Items considered to be nonoperating	X,XXX
(paragraphs 65-68 and 111-115).]	X,XXX
Change in net assets before effects of discontinued operations,	
extraordinary items, and changes in accounting principles	XX,XXX
Discontinued operations	X,XXX
Extraordinary items	X,XXX
Changes in accounting principles	X,XXX
Change in net assets	XX,XXX
Net assets at beginning of year	XXX,XXX
Net assets at end of year	$XXX,XXX

---
*Editor's Note: In this edition, the areas are highlighted by being enclosed in brackets rather than by shading.

Appendix D

GLOSSARY

168. This appendix contains definitions of certain terms or phrases used in this Statement.

Donor-imposed restriction

A donor stipulation that specifies a use for a contributed asset that is more specific than broad limits resulting from the nature of the organization, the environment in which it operates, and the purposes specified in its articles of incorporation or bylaws or comparable documents for an unincorporated association. A restriction on an organization's use of the asset contributed may be temporary or permanent.

Endowment fund

An established fund of cash, securities, or other assets to provide income for the maintenance of a not-for-profit organization. The use of the assets of the fund may be permanently restricted, temporarily restricted, or unrestricted. Endowment funds generally are established by donor-restricted gifts and bequests to provide a permanent endowment, which is to provide a permanent source of income, or a term endowment, which is to provide income for a specified period. The principal of a permanent endowment must be maintained permanently—not used up, expended, or otherwise exhausted—and is classified as permanently restricted net assets. The principal of a term endowment must be maintained for a specified term and is classified as temporarily restricted net assets. An organization's governing board may earmark a portion of its unrestricted net assets as a board-designated endowment (sometimes called funds functioning as endowment or quasi-endowment funds) to be invested to provide income for a long but unspecified period. The principal of a board-designated endowment, which results from an internal designation, is not donor restricted and is classified as unrestricted net assets.

Functional classification

A method of grouping expenses according to the purpose for which costs are incurred. The primary functional classifications are program services and supporting activities.

Not-for-profit organization

An entity that possesses the following characteristics that distinguish it from a business enterprise: (a) contributions of significant amounts of resources from resource providers who do not expect commensurate or proportionate pecuniary return, (b) operating purposes other than to provide goods or services at a profit, and (c) absence of ownership interests like those of business enterprises. Not-for-profit organizations have those characteristics in varying degrees (Concepts Statement 4, paragraph 6). Organizations that clearly fall outside this definition include all investor-owned enterprises and entities that provide dividends, lower costs, or other economic benefits directly and proportionately to their owners, members, or participants, such as mutual insurance companies, credit unions, farm and rural electric cooperatives, and employee benefit plans (Concepts Statement 4, paragraph 7).

Permanent restriction

A donor-imposed restriction that stipulates that resources be maintained permanently but permits the organization to use up or expend part or all of the income (or other economic benefits) derived from the donated assets.

Permanently restricted net assets

The part of the net assets of a not-for-profit organization resulting (a) from contributions and other inflows of assets whose use by the organization is limited by donor-imposed stipulations that neither expire by passage of time nor can be fulfilled or otherwise removed by actions of the organization, (b) from other asset enhancements and diminishments subject to the same kinds of stipulations, and (c) from reclassifications from (or to) other classes of net assets as a consequence of donor-imposed stipulations (Concepts Statement 6, paragraph 92).

Restricted support

Donor-restricted revenues or gains from contributions that increase either temporarily restricted net assets or permanently restricted net assets. Also refer to **Unrestricted support**.

Temporarily restricted net assets

The part of the net assets of a not-for-profit organization resulting (a) from contributions and other inflows of assets whose use by the organization is limited by donor-imposed stipulations that either expire by passage of time or can be fulfilled and removed by actions of the organization pursuant to those stipulations, (b) from other asset enhancements and diminishments subject to the same kinds of stipulations, and (c) from reclassifications to (or from) other classes of net assets as a consequence of donor-imposed stipulations, their expiration by passage of time, or their fulfillment and removal by actions of the organization pursuant to those stipulations (Concepts Statement 6, paragraph 93).

Temporary restriction

A donor-imposed restriction that permits the donee organization to use up or expend the donated assets as specified and is satisfied either by the passage of time or by actions of the organization.

Unrestricted net assets

The part of net assets of a not-for-profit organization that is neither permanently restricted nor temporarily restricted by donor-imposed stipulations (Concepts Statement 6, paragraph 94).

Unrestricted support

Revenues or gains from contributions that are not restricted by donors. Also refer to **Restricted support**.

Voluntary health and welfare organizations

Organizations formed for the purpose of performing voluntary services for various segments of society. They are tax exempt (organized for the benefit of the public), supported by the public, and operated on a "not-for-profit" basis. Most voluntary health and welfare organizations concentrate their efforts and expend their resources in an attempt to solve health and welfare problems of our society and, in many cases, those of specific individuals. As a group, voluntary health and welfare organizations include those not-for-profit organizations that derive their revenue primarily from voluntary contributions from the general public to be used for general or specific purposes connected with health, welfare, or community services (*Audits of Voluntary Health and Welfare Organizations,* preface).

Statement of Financial Accounting Standards No. 118
Accounting by Creditors for Impairment of a Loan—Income Recognition and Disclosures

an amendment of FASB Statement No. 114

STATUS

Issued: October 1994

Effective Date: For fiscal years beginning after December 15, 1994

Affects: Amends FAS 114, paragraphs 8 and 11 through 15
Supersedes FAS 114, paragraphs 17 through 20 and 65

Affected by: No other pronouncements

Issues Discussed by FASB Emerging Issues Task Force (EITF)

Affects: No EITF Issues

Interpreted by: Paragraph 6(g) interpreted by EITF Issue No. 98-13
Paragraph 6(i) interpreted by EITF Issue No. 96-22

Related Issue: EITF Issue No. 99-20

SUMMARY

This Statement amends FASB Statement No. 114, *Accounting by Creditors for Impairment of a Loan*, to allow a creditor to use existing methods for recognizing interest income on an impaired loan. To accomplish that, it eliminates the provisions in Statement 114 that described how a creditor should report income on an impaired loan (paragraphs 17-19).

This Statement does not change the provisions in Statement 114 that require a creditor to measure impairment based on the present value of expected future cash flows discounted at the loan's effective interest rate, or as a practical expedient, at the observable market price of the loan or the fair value of the collateral if the loan is collateral dependent.

This Statement amends the disclosure requirements in Statement 114 to require information about the recorded investment in certain impaired loans and about how a creditor recognizes interest income related to those impaired loans.

This Statement is effective concurrent with the effective date of Statement 114, that is, for financial statements for fiscal years beginning after December 15, 1994, with earlier application encouraged.

Statement of Financial Accounting Standards No. 118

Accounting by Creditors for Impairment of a Loan—Income Recognition and Disclosures

an amendment of FASB Statement No. 114

CONTENTS

INTRODUCTION AND BACKGROUND

1. FASB Statement No. 114, *Accounting by Creditors for Impairment of a Loan,* was issued in May 1993 and addresses the accounting by creditors for impairment of certain loans. Statement 114 is effective for financial statements for fiscal years beginning after December 15, 1994.

2. The Board received several requests to delay the effective date of Statement 114 and to clarify how that Statement should be implemented. A delay was requested to allow more time to resolve implementation questions about the application of the income recognition provisions in paragraphs 17-19 of Statement 114 and to make the necessary changes to accounting systems.

3. This Statement amends Statement 114 to allow a creditor to use existing methods for recognizing interest income on impaired loans. To accomplish this, it eliminates the income recognition provisions in paragraphs 17-19 of Statement 114. As amended, Statement 114 does not address how a creditor should recognize, measure, or display interest income on an impaired loan. This Statement amends the disclosure requirements in Statement 114 to require information about the recorded investment in certain impaired loans and about how a creditor recognizes interest income related to those impaired loans.

4. Prior to the issuance of this Statement, Statement 114 provided for two alternative income recognition methods to be used to account for changes in the net carrying amount of an impaired loan subsequent to the initial measure of impairment. Under the first income recognition method, a creditor would accrue interest on the net carrying amount of the impaired loan and report other changes in the net carrying amount of the loan as an adjustment to bad-debt expense. Under the second income recognition method, a creditor would recognize all changes in the net carrying amount of the loan as an adjustment to bad-debt expense. While those income recognition methods are no longer required, this Statement does not preclude a creditor from using either of those methods.

5. Statement 114 requires that a creditor recognize impairment of a loan *if* the present value of expected future cash flows discounted at the loan's effective interest rate (or, alternatively, the observable market price of the loan or the fair value of the collateral) is less than the recorded investment in the impaired loan. If the present value of expected future cash

flows (or, alternatively, the observable market price of the loan or the fair value of the collateral) is equal to or greater than the recorded investment in the impaired loan, no impairment is recognized. This Statement does not change those requirements. When the net carrying amount of an impaired loan equals the present value of expected future cash flows (or, alternatively, the observable market price of the loan or the fair value of the collateral), this Statement will affect only the *classification* of income (or expense) that results from changes in the measure of an impaired loan, not the total *amount* of income (or expense) recognized within a given reporting period. However, when a creditor's policies for recognizing interest income and for charging off loans result in a recorded investment in an impaired loan that is less than the present value of expected future cash flows discounted at the loan's effective interest rate (or, alternatively, the observable market price of the loan or the fair value of the collateral), this Statement will cause both the classification and the total amount of income (or expense) recognized within a given reporting period to be different from that which would have been determined in accordance with paragraphs 17-19 of Statement 114.

STANDARDS OF FINANCIAL ACCOUNTING AND REPORTING

Amendments to Statement 114

6. Statement 114 is amended as follows:

a. The following sentence is added after the second sentence of paragraph 8:

> For a loan that has been restructured in a troubled debt restructuring, *the contractual terms of the loan agreement* refers to the contractual terms specified by the original loan agreement, not the contractual terms specified by the restructuring agreement.

b. In the first sentence of paragraph 11, *impaired loans* is replaced by *impairment of a loan.*

c. In the last sentence of paragraph 12, *those impaired loans* is replaced by *impairment of those loans.*

d. In the last sentence of paragraph 13, *measure of the impaired loan* is replaced by *present value of expected future cash flows (or, alternatively, the observable market price of the loan or the fair value of the collateral).*

e. In the first sentence of paragraph 14, *measures an impaired loan using* is replaced by *bases its measure of loan impairment on.*

f. In the first sentence of paragraph 15, *measures an impaired loan using* is replaced by *bases its measure of loan impairment on.*

g. Paragraph 17 is replaced by the following:

> This Statement does not address how a creditor should recognize, measure, or display interest income on an impaired loan. Some accounting methods for recognizing income may result in a recorded investment in an impaired loan that is less than the present value of expected future cash flows (or, alternatively, the observable market price of the loan or the fair value of the collateral). In that case, while the loan would meet the definition of an impaired loan in paragraph 8, no additional impairment would be recognized. Those accounting methods include recognition of interest income using a cost-recovery method, a cash-basis method, or some combination of those methods. The recorded investment in an impaired loan also may be less than the present value of expected future cash flows (or, alternatively, the observable market price of the loan or the fair value of the collateral) because the creditor has charged off part of the loan.

h. Paragraphs 18 and 19 are deleted.

i. Paragraph 20 is replaced by the following paragraphs:

> A creditor shall disclose, either in the body of the financial statements or in the accompanying notes, the following information about loans that meet the definition of an impaired loan in paragraph 8 of this Statement:

> a. As of the date of each statement of financial position presented, the total recorded investment in the impaired loans at the end of each period and (1) the amount of that recorded investment for which there is a related allowance for credit losses determined in accordance with this Statement and the amount of that allowance and (2) the amount of that recorded investment for which there is no related allowance for credit losses determined in accordance with this Statement

b. The creditor's policy for recognizing interest income on impaired loans, including how cash receipts are recorded

c. For each period for which results of operations are presented, the average recorded investment in the impaired loans during each period, the related amount of interest income recognized during the time within that period that the loans were impaired, and, unless not practicable, the amount of interest income recognized using a cash-basis method of accounting during the time within that period that the loans were impaired.

Information about an impaired loan that has been restructured in a troubled debt restructuring involving a modification of terms need not be included in the disclosures required by paragraphs 20(a) and 20(c) in years after the restructuring if (i) the restructuring agreement specifies an interest rate equal to or greater than the rate that the creditor was willing to accept at the time of the restructuring for a new loan with comparable risk and (ii) the loan is not impaired based on the terms specified by the restructuring agreement. That exception shall be applied consistently for paragraphs 20(a) and 20(c) to all loans restructured in a troubled debt restructuring that meet the criteria in (i) and (ii).

For each period for which results of operations are presented, a creditor also shall disclose the activity in the total allowance for credit losses related to loans, including the balance in the allowance at the beginning and end of each period, additions charged to operations, direct write-downs charged against the allowance, and recoveries of amounts previously charged off. The total allowance for credit losses related to loans includes those amounts that have been determined in accordance with FASB Statement No. 5, *Accounting for Contingencies,* and with this Statement.

j. Paragraph 65 is deleted.

Effective Date and Transition

7. This Statement is effective concurrent with the effective date of Statement 114. Statement 114 is effective for financial statements for fiscal years beginning after December 15, 1994, with earlier application encouraged.

> **The provisions of this Statement need not be applied to immaterial items.**

This Statement was adopted by the affirmative votes of five members of the Financial Accounting Standards Board. Messrs. Leisenring and Swieringa dissented.

Messrs. Leisenring and Swieringa disagree that paragraphs 17-19 of Statement 114 should have been eliminated. Those paragraphs permitted a choice between two methods for recognizing income on impaired loans. They do not believe that those methods are complex or that complex guidance would have been necessary to implement those methods. The Board was aware that changes in accounting systems would be needed to implement those methods when it issued Statement 114 and that the accounting for impaired loans required by bank and thrift regulators was inconsistent with the income recognition provisions in paragraphs 17-19.

Messrs. Leisenring and Swieringa agree that the elimination of the income recognition provisions in Statement 114 will affect only the classification of income and not the total amount of income recognized within a given reporting period if the recorded investment in an impaired loan is equal to or greater than the present value of expected future cash flows (or, alternatively, the observable market price of the loan or the fair value of the collateral). However, the accounting for impaired loans currently required by bank and thrift regulators includes recognition of interest income using a cost-recovery method, a cash-basis method, or some combination of those accounting methods. Those methods can result in a recorded investment in an impaired loan that is less than the present value of expected future cash flows (or, alternatively, the observable market price of the loan or the fair value of the collateral). In that circumstance, income effects of the passage of time and changes in estimates, that otherwise would be recognized currently, are recognized in later periods. Messrs. Leisenring and Swieringa believe that that result is inconsistent with the fundamental premise in Statement 114 that loans should be carried at the present value of expected future cash flows (or, alternatively, the observable market price of the loan or the fair value of the collateral).

The cost-recovery method is intended to address the uncertainty of expected future cash flows from impaired loans by delaying income recognition. The measure of impairment under Statement 114 takes into account the uncertainty of expected future cash flows. The Board concluded in Statement 114 that impairment of a loan should be based on the present value of expected future cash flows (or, alternatively, the observable market price of the loan or the fair value of the collateral) and that changes in estimates (or, alternatively, in market prices or fair values) should be recognized currently (paragraphs 40-43 and 58 of Statement 114). As a result, Messrs. Leisenring and Swieringa believe that the cost-recovery method is not acceptable under Statement 114, and they disagree with the amendment because it would permit the use of that method under that Statement.

Messrs. Leisenring and Swieringa are concerned that the amendment will allow the net carrying amount of a loan to be any amount as long as it does not exceed the present value of expected cash flows (or, alternatively, the observable market price of the loan or the fair value of the collateral). They believe that paragraphs 17-19 of Statement 114 could have been amended to eliminate inconsistencies in accounting for income on impaired loans by specifying a single method for recognizing interest income on an impaired loan. They would have delayed the effective date of Statement 114 if the Board needed time to develop a single method.

Members of the Financial Accounting Standards Board:

Dennis R. Beresford,	Anthony T. Cope	Robert H. Northcutt
Chairman	John M. Foster	Robert J. Swieringa
Joseph V. Anania	James J. Leisenring	

Appendix A

BACKGROUND INFORMATION AND BASIS FOR CONCLUSIONS

8. This appendix summarizes considerations that were deemed significant by Board members in reaching the conclusions in this Statement. It includes reasons for accepting certain approaches and rejecting others. Individual Board members gave greater weight to some factors than to others. The Board concluded that it could reach an informed decision on the basis of existing information without a public hearing.

9. Statement 114 requires that a creditor measure impairment of a loan based on the present value of expected future cash flows discounted at the loan's effective interest rate or, as a practical expedient, at the observable market price of the loan or the fair value of the collateral if the loan is collateral dependent. Prior to the issuance of this Statement, Statement 114 provided for two alternative income recognition methods to be used to account for changes in the net carrying amount of the loan subsequent to the initial measure of impairment. Under the first income recognition method, a creditor would accrue interest on the net carrying amount of the impaired loan and report other changes in the net carrying amount of the loan as an adjustment to bad-debt expense. Under the second income recognition method, a creditor would recognize all changes in the net carrying amount of the loan as an adjustment to bad-debt expense. A creditor would have been precluded from using a cost-recovery or a cash-basis method of accounting. The two measurement methods that were allowed as practical expedients and the second income recognition method were not included in the Exposure Draft that resulted in Statement 114 and were added during the deliberations leading to that Statement because commentators said those provisions would facilitate implementation.

10. The Board received several requests to delay the effective date of Statement 114 and to clarify how that Statement should be implemented. The requests stated that more time was needed to resolve implementation issues about the application of the income recognition provisions in paragraphs 17-19. The requests also stated that the accounting for impaired loans currently required by bank and thrift regulators is inconsistent with the provisions in those paragraphs. The requests stated that enterprises under the jurisdiction of those regulators would be required to make significant changes to their accounting systems to comply with the income recognition provisions in paragraphs 17-19 and that the implementation issues could not be resolved in time to make the necessary changes to accounting systems.

11. Statement 114 addresses the measurement of loan impairment. While income recognition was addressed in paragraphs 17-19 of Statement 114, the Board considered those provisions to be secondary in importance to the provisions that addressed measurement of loan impairment. The requests to delay the effective date were based on implementation issues related to those income recognition provisions, not on the measurement provisions.

12. An FASB Exposure Draft, *Accounting by Creditors for Impairment of a Loan—Income Recognition,* was issued on March 31, 1994. In the deliberations that preceded that Exposure Draft, the Board considered delaying the effective date of Statement 114 and issuing guidance for implementing the provisions in paragraphs 17-19 of Statement 114. The Board concluded that the implementation guidance would be complex and that constituents might be required to make costly changes to their accounting systems to implement that guidance; those systems changes could require further modifications if regulators issued accounting guidance in response to the provisions of Statement 114. Furthermore, implementation of the income recognition provisions in paragraphs 17-19 of Statement 114 would not have eliminated inconsistencies in the accounting for income on impaired loans because those provisions permitted a choice between two methods for recognizing income on impaired loans. Accordingly, the Board concluded that, to avoid a delay in the effective date of the measurement provisions of Statement 114, it would be preferable to allow creditors to use existing accounting methods for recognizing interest income and to eliminate the income recognition provisions.

13. The Board received 57 comment letters on the Exposure Draft. Some respondents to the Exposure Draft agreed that the income recognition provisions in paragraphs 17-19 of Statement 114 should be eliminated but gave other reasons for delaying the effective date. Some stated that the effective date should be delayed to give regulators time to resolve regulatory accounting and disclosure issues related to impaired loans. Some stated that a delay would give creditors time to modify accounting systems and policies. Some stated that more time would be needed to implement the disclosure requirements proposed in the Exposure Draft. After considering those comments, the Board concluded that the most significant implementation issues would be resolved by the elimination of paragraphs 17-19 of Statement 114 and by the simplification of certain disclo-

sure requirements that were proposed in the Exposure Draft of this Statement. The Board also concluded that a creditor should implement Statement 114 for fiscal years beginning after December 15, 1994.

14. Some respondents asked whether the amendment to Statement 114 would allow a creditor to use the methods for recognizing interest income that were described in paragraphs 17-19 of Statement 114. While those income recognition methods are no longer required by Statement 114, the Board concluded that a creditor should not be precluded from using those methods.

15. Some respondents said that the elimination of the income recognition provisions in paragraphs 17-19 of Statement 114 would result in inconsistent application of that Statement. Implementation of the income recognition provisions in paragraphs 17-19 would not have eliminated inconsistencies in income recognition on impaired loans, since the provisions in those paragraphs permitted a choice between two methods for recognizing income. Moreover, because not all impaired loans are within the scope of Statement 114, creditors could recognize interest income using existing accounting methods for some impaired loans. That is, a creditor could use a cost-recovery or cash-basis method of accounting for recognizing income on impaired loans that are excluded from the scope of Statement 114 because they are smaller-balance homogeneous loans that are collectively evaluated for impairment.

16. Statement 114, as amended by this Statement, does not address how a creditor should recognize, measure, or display interest income on an impaired loan. However, users of financial statements have told the Board that it is important to know how a creditor recognizes interest and records cash receipts related to impaired loans. The Board decided that a creditor should disclose its accounting policies for recognizing interest income on impaired loans, including its policy for recording cash receipts.

17. The Exposure Draft would have required that a creditor quantify and disclose the amount of interest income recognized, including the amount of cash receipts recorded as interest on an impaired loan and the amount of interest income that would have been recognized according to the contractual terms of the original loan agreement. Some respondents indicated that the information required to make those disclosures was not readily available and that it would be

costly to develop accounting systems to gather that information. In response to those comments, the Board decided to simplify the disclosures that were proposed in the Exposure Draft by requiring that a creditor disclose the average recorded investment in the impaired loans during the reporting period and the related amount of interest income recognized during the time within that period that those loans were impaired. The Board believes that those disclosures will provide financial statement users with useful information about how a creditor recognized interest income on impaired loans. This Statement does not specify how a creditor should calculate the average recorded investment in the impaired loans during the reporting period. The Board believes that a creditor should develop an appropriate method and that averages based on month-end balances may be considered an appropriate method.

18. The Board believes that disclosure of the amount of interest income recognized on impaired loans using a cash-basis method of accounting also will provide financial statement users with valuable information about how cash receipts were recorded. The Board understands that this information generally is available and believes that a creditor should provide that information unless it is not practicable to do so.

19. Paragraph 20(a) of Statement 114 (prior to amendment) required that a creditor disclose the recorded investment in the loans for which impairment had been recognized in accordance with Statement 114 and the total allowance related to those impaired loans. Paragraph 65 of Statement 114 explained that if the creditor had written down a loan so that the present value of expected future cash flows (or, alternatively, the observable market price of the loan or the fair value of the collateral) was equal to or greater than the recorded investment in the loan, no impairment would be recognized. In those situations, the creditor would not have been required to disclose the recorded investment in the loan in years after the write-down. Respondents indicated that that disclosure would confuse financial statement users because information would not be provided about the total population of loans that meet the definition of an impaired loan in paragraph 8 of Statement 114. They said that information about the total population of impaired loans could be provided easily. This Statement eliminates paragraph 65 of Statement 114 and amends the disclosure provisions in paragraph 20 of that Statement to require that a creditor disclose the total recorded investment in loans that meet the definition of an impaired loan in paragraph 8 of State-

ment 114 at the end of the reporting period, the recorded investment in those impaired loans for which there is a related allowance for credit losses, and the recorded investment in those impaired loans for which there is no related allowance for credit losses. Those disclosures should be provided for impaired loans that have been charged off partially. Those disclosures cannot be provided for loans that have been charged off fully because both the recorded investment and the allowance for credit losses will equal zero.

20. A troubled debt restructuring need not be included in the disclosures required by paragraphs 20(a) and 20(c) of Statement 114 (as amended) if the restructuring agreement specifies an interest rate equal to or greater than the rate that the creditor was willing to accept at the time of the restructuring for a new loan with comparable risk and the loan is not impaired based on the terms specified by the restructuring agreement. Although troubled debt restructurings meet the definition of an impaired loan in paragraph 8 of Statement 114, this treatment is consistent with the disclosure requirements (prior to amendment) in paragraph 40(a) of FASB Statement No. 15, *Accounting by Debtors and Creditors for Troubled Debt Restructurings,* and should limit the cost of providing those disclosures.

21. Some respondents indicated that the scope of paragraph 20(b) of Statement 114 (prior to amendment) was unclear. Some stated that they believed that the intent of that paragraph was to require that a creditor provide information about the activity for the total allowance for credit losses, including amounts determined in accordance with Statement 5. Others stated that they believed that the scope of paragraph 20(b) was limited to the allowances determined in accordance with Statement 114. The Board believes that the creditor should provide information about the activity for the total allowance for credit losses, including amounts determined in accordance with Statement 5.

22. The Exposure Draft would have amended the scope of paragraph 20(c) of Statement 114 to apply to "loans that are impaired (or, alternatively, for all loans for which a creditor has credit concerns)." The alternative scope for the disclosures was included in the Exposure Draft to help reduce the cost of implementing the disclosure requirements. However, some respondents stated that the alternative scope would not reduce the cost of implementation and would result in inconsistent disclosure practices. The Board

decided to delete the phrase *(or, alternatively, for all loans for which a creditor has credit concerns).*

23. Some respondents asked whether a loan should be considered to meet the definition of an impaired loan in paragraph 8 of Statement 114 if it was restructured in a troubled debt restructuring and is not impaired based on the terms specified by the restructuring agreement. The Board concluded in Statement 114 that a loan restructured in a troubled debt restructuring is an impaired loan. It should not be accounted for as a new loan because a troubled debt restructuring is part of a creditor's ongoing effort to recover its investment in the original loan. A loan' usually will have been identified as impaired because the condition specified in paragraph 8 of Statement 114 will have existed before a formal restructuring. Although certain troubled debt restructurings may be excluded from the disclosures required by paragraphs 20(a) and 20(c) of Statement 114 (as amended), for a restructured loan that has not been excluded from the scope of Statement 114 because of the transition provisions in paragraph 27 of Statement 114, the measurement provisions of Statement 114 should be applied when it is probable that a creditor will be unable to collect all amounts due according to the contractual terms of the *original* loan agreement. Likewise, a creditor should use existing accounting methods for recognizing interest income on impaired loans for that loan; the income recognition provisions (prior to amendment) in paragraph 30 of Statement 15, need not be applied.

(This page intentionally left blank.)

Appendix B

THE SCOPE OF THE DISCLOSURE REQUIREMENTS IN PARAGRAPH 20(a) OF STATEMENT 114, AS AMENDED

24. The following table summarizes the scope of the disclosure requirements in paragraph 20(a) of Statement 114, as amended by this Statement.

Description of Loans	Required Disclosures about the Recorded Investment in Loans That Meet the Definition of an Impaired Loan in Paragraph 8 of Statement 114		
	(A) The Total Recorded Investment in the Impaired Loans	(B) The Amount of the Recorded Investment in (A) for Which There Is a Related Allowance for Credit Losses	(C) The Amount of the Recorded Investment in (A) for Which There Is No Related Allowance for Credit Losses
1. Loans that meet the definition of an impaired loan in paragraph 8 of Statement 114 and that have *not* been charged off fully	Included. The amount disclosed in (A) must equal the sum of (B) and (C).	Included if there is a related allowance for credit losses.	Included if there is no related allowance for credit losses.
2. Loans that meet the definition of an impaired loan in paragraph 8 of Statement 114 and that have been charged off fully	Excluded. The recorded investment and allowance for credit losses are equal to zero.		
3. Loans restructured in a troubled debt restructuring before the effective date of Statement 114 that are not impaired based on the terms specified by the restructuring agreement	Excluded. Disclosures should be provided in accordance with Statement 15.		

4. Loans restructured in a troubled debt restructuring before the effective date of Statement 114 that are impaired based on the terms specified by the restructuring agreement

Refer to items 1 and 2 above.

5. Loans restructured in a troubled debt restructuring after the effective date of Statement 114

May be excluded in years after the restructuring if (a) the restructuring agreement specifies an interest rate equal to or greater than the rate that the creditor was willing to accept at the time of the restructuring for a new receivable with comparable risk and (b) the loan is not impaired based on the terms specified by the restructuring agreement. Otherwise, refer to items 1 and 2 above.

6. Large groups of smaller-balance homogeneous loans that are collectively evaluated for impairment and other loans that are excluded from the scope of Statement 114 as defined in paragraph 6 of that Statement

Excluded unless restructured in a troubled debt restructuring (refer to items 3-5 above and paragraph 9 of Statement 114 for requirements for a restructured loan).

Statement of Financial Accounting Standards No. 119
Disclosure about Derivative Financial Instruments
and Fair Value of Financial Instruments

STATUS

Issued: October 1994

Effective Date: For fiscal years ending after December 15, 1994

Affects: Amends FAS 105, paragraphs 17 and 18 and footnote 12
Amends FAS 107, paragraphs 10 and 13

Affected by: Superseded by FAS 133

Other Interpretive Release: FASB Special Report, *Illustrations of Financial Instrument Disclosures*
(Nullified by FAS 133)

Issues Discussed by FASB Emerging Issues Task Force (EITF)

Affects: Partially nullifies EITF Issue No. 91-4

(The next page is 1692.)

(This page intentionally left blank.)

Statement of Financial Accounting Standards No. 120
Accounting and Reporting by Mutual Life Insurance Enterprises and by Insurance Enterprises for Certain Long-Duration Participating Contracts

an amendment of FASB Statements No. 60, 97, and 113 and Interpretation No. 40

STATUS

Issued: January 1995

Effective Date: For fiscal years beginning after December 15, 1995

Affects: Amends FAS 60, paragraph 6
   Amends FAS 97, paragraphs 6 and 11
   Amends FAS 113, paragraph 6
   Amends FIN 40, paragraph 7

Affected by: No other pronouncements

SUMMARY

This Statement extends the requirements of FASB Statements No. 60, *Accounting and Reporting by Insurance Enterprises,* No. 97, *Accounting and Reporting by Insurance Enterprises for Certain Long-Duration Contracts and for Realized Gains and Losses from the Sale of Investments,* and No. 113, *Accounting and Reporting for Reinsurance of Short-Duration and Long-Duration Contracts,* to mutual life insurance enterprises, assessment enterprises, and fraternal benefit societies (all of which are hereafter referred to as mutual life insurance enterprises). The AICPA has established accounting for certain participating life insurance contracts of mutual life insurance enterprises in its Statement of Position 95-1, *Accounting for Certain Insurance Activities of Mutual Life Insurance Enterprises,* that should be applied to those contracts that meet the conditions in this Statement. This Statement also permits stock life insurance enterprises to apply the provisions of the SOP to participating life insurance contracts that meet the conditions in this Statement. This Statement is effective for financial statements issued for fiscal years beginning after December 15, 1995.

This Statement also amends FASB Interpretation No. 40, *Applicability of Generally Accepted Accounting Principles to Mutual Life Insurance and Other Enterprises,* to defer the effective date of the general provisions of that Interpretation to fiscal years beginning after December 15, 1995. This Statement does not change the disclosure and other transition provisions of Interpretation 40.

Accounting and Reporting by Mutual Life Insurance   **FAS120**
Enterprises and by Insurance Enterprises for
Certain Long-Duration Participating Contracts

Statement of Financial Accounting Standards No. 120

Accounting and Reporting by Mutual Life Insurance Enterprises and by Insurance Enterprises for Certain Long-Duration Participating Contracts

an amendment of FASB Statements No. 60, 97, and 113 and Interpretation No. 40

CONTENTS

INTRODUCTION

1. FASB Statements No. 60, *Accounting and Reporting by Insurance Enterprises,* No. 97, *Accounting and Reporting by Insurance Enterprises for Certain Long-Duration Contracts and for Realized Gains and Losses from the Sale of Investments,* and No. 113, *Accounting and Reporting for Reinsurance of Short-Duration and Long-Duration Contracts,* exempted mutual life insurance enterprises from the requirements of those Statements. FASB Interpretation No. 40, *Applicability of Generally Accepted Accounting Principles to Mutual Life Insurance and Other Enterprises,* did not address or change the existing exemptions of mutual life insurance enterprises from those Statements. Because of the lack of accounting guidance for the insurance and reinsurance activities of those enterprises, the Board asked the AICPA to reactivate and expeditiously complete its project on that issue. The Board's discussions with the AICPA emphasized that any guidance should be within the parameters of Statements 60, 97, and 113.

2. This Statement extends the requirements of Statements 60, 97, and 113 to mutual life insurance enterprises, assessment enterprises, and fraternal benefit societies. The AICPA has established accounting for certain participating life insurance contracts of those

enterprises in its Statement of Position 95-1, *Accounting for Certain Insurance Activities of Mutual Life Insurance Enterprises,* that should be applied to those contracts that meet the conditions in this Statement. This Statement also permits stock life insurance enterprises to apply the provisions of the SOP to participating life insurance contracts that meet the conditions in this Statement. This Statement and the SOP are effective for fiscal years beginning after December 15, 1995.

3. This Statement also amends Interpretation 40 to defer the effective date of the general provisions of that Interpretation to fiscal years beginning after December 15, 1995, so that Interpretation 40, this Statement, and the SOP are concurrently effective. This Statement does not change the disclosure and other transition provisions of Interpretation 40.

STANDARDS OF FINANCIAL ACCOUNTING AND REPORTING

Accounting and Reporting by Mutual Life Insurance Enterprises

4. Mutual life insurance enterprises, assessment enterprises, and fraternal benefit societies (all of which

are hereafter referred to as mutual life insurance enterprises) shall apply Statements 60 and 97, except as noted in the following paragraph, and shall apply Statement 113 in reporting their insurance and reinsurance activities in financial statements prepared in conformity with generally accepted accounting principles.

Accounting and Reporting by Insurance Enterprises for Certain Long-Duration Participating Contracts

5. Mutual life insurance enterprises shall apply Statement 60 or 97, as appropriate, to participating life insurance contracts unless those contracts meet both of the following conditions:[1]

a. The contracts are long-duration participating contracts that are expected to pay dividends to policyholders based on actual experience of the insurer.
b. Annual policyholder dividends are paid in a manner that identifies divisible surplus and distributes that surplus in approximately the same proportion as the contracts are considered to have contributed to divisible surplus (commonly referred to in actuarial literature as the contribution principle).

6. Stock life insurance enterprises with participating life insurance contracts that meet the conditions in paragraph 5 of this Statement are permitted to account for those contracts in accordance with the SOP. The same accounting policy shall be applied consistently to all those participating life insurance contracts. Disclosure of the specific accounting policy applied to those contracts shall be made in accordance with APB Opinion No. 22, *Disclosure of Accounting Policies.*

Amendments to Statements 60, 97, and 113 and Interpretation 40

7. Paragraph 6 of Statement 60 is amended as follows:

a. In the first sentence, *and title insurance enterprises* is replaced by **title insurance enterprises,** *mutual life insurance enterprises,* **assessment enterprises,** *and fraternal benefit societies.*

b. The last sentence is replaced by:

FASB Statement No. 120, *Accounting and Reporting by Mutual Life Insurance Enterprises and by Insurance Enterprises for Certain Long-Duration Participating Contracts,* addresses the accounting for certain long-duration participating life insurance contracts.

8. Statement 97 is amended as follows:

a. In paragraph 6, *and FASB Statement No. 120, Accounting and Reporting by Mutual Life Insurance Enterprises and by Insurance Enterprises for Certain Long-Duration Participating Contracts,* is added to the end of the last sentence.

b. In paragraph 11, *and Statement 120* is added to the end of the second sentence.

9. The following is added at the end of the first sentence of paragraph 6 of Statement 113:

and to participating life insurance contracts that meet the conditions in paragraph 5 of FASB Statement No. 120, *Accounting and Reporting by Mutual Life Insurance Enterprises and by Insurance Enterprises for Certain Long-Duration Participating Contracts.*

10. The first sentence of paragraph 7 of Interpretation 40 is replaced by the following:

The general provisions of this Interpretation are effective for financial statements issued for fiscal years beginning after December 15, 1995, and the disclosures specified in paragraphs 5 and 6 are effective for annual statements for fiscal years beginning after December 15, 1992.

Effective Date and Transition

11. This Statement shall be effective for financial statements for fiscal years beginning after December 15, 1995, with earlier application encouraged. The effect of initially applying this Statement shall be reported retroactively through restatement of all previously issued annual financial statements presented for comparative purposes for fiscal years beginning after December 15, 1992. Previously issued financial statements for any number of consecutive annual pe-

---

[1]The AICPA's SOP establishes the accounting for those participating life insurance contracts of mutual life insurance enterprises that meet the conditions in paragraph 5 of this Statement. Because the accounting for those contracts is not specified in any of the officially established accounting principles in category (a) of AICPA Statement on Auditing Standards No. 69, *The Meaning of "Present Fairly in Conformity With Generally Accepted Accounting Principles" in the Independent Auditor's Report,* SAS 69 recognizes the SOP as generally accepted accounting principles (category (b)) for those contracts.

Accounting and Reporting by Mutual Life Insurance **FAS120**
Enterprises and by Insurance Enterprises for
Certain Long-Duration Participating Contracts

riods preceding that date may be restated to conform to the provisions of this Statement. The cumulative effect of adopting this Statement shall be included in the earliest year restated.

**The provisions of this Statement need
not be applied to immaterial items.**

This Statement was adopted by the affirmative votes of six members of the Financial Accounting Standards Board. Mr. Leisenring dissented.

Mr. Leisenring disagrees with the deferral of the effective date of Interpretation 40. He believes that by delaying the effective date of Interpretation 40 the Board is allowing a practice to continue that it observed was unacceptable for the reasons described in that Interpretation. He believes that no events or circumstances have arisen since the issuance of Interpretation 40 that warrant a delay in the effective date of that Interpretation.

Mr. Leisenring believes that users of financial statements that are described as having been prepared in conformity with generally accepted accounting principles should expect that all appropriate accounting pronouncements have been applied. Interpretation 40 does not change the accounting for transactions, events, or circumstances under generally accepted accounting principles, but clarifies that those pronouncements must be applied when the financial statements have been described as being prepared in conformity with those standards. He believes that the effective date of Interpretation 40 should not be deferred because that Interpretation will improve the comparability of financial reporting among insurance enterprises for transactions and events other than those specifically addressed in Statements 60, 97, and 113 and the SOP for mutual life insurance enterprises that decide to prepare financial statements in conformity with generally accepted accounting principles.

Members of the Financial Accounting Standards Board:

Dennis R. Beresford, *Chairman*	Anthony T. Cope	Robert H. Northcutt
	John M. Foster	Robert J. Swieringa
Joseph V. Anania	James J. Leisenring	

Appendix

BACKGROUND INFORMATION AND BASIS FOR CONCLUSIONS

CONTENTS

Appendix

BACKGROUND INFORMATION AND BASIS FOR CONCLUSIONS

Introduction

12. This appendix summarizes considerations that were deemed significant by Board members in reaching the conclusions in this Statement. It includes reasons for accepting certain views and rejecting others. Individual Board members gave greater weight to some factors than to others.

13. An FASB Exposure Draft, *Accounting and Reporting by Mutual Life Insurance Enterprises and by Insurance Enterprises for Certain Long-Duration Participating Contracts,* was issued for public comment on March 24, 1994, and distributed to members of various industry organizations, in addition to the standard distribution, to encourage comment from those most affected by the proposal. The Board received 31 comment letters in response to that Exposure Draft. The Board concluded that it could reach an informed decision on the basis of existing information without a public hearing.

Background Information

14. In 1972, the AICPA published an Industry Audit Guide, *Audits of Stock Life Insurance Companies.* That Guide did not apply to mutual life insurance enterprises. The AICPA Insurance Companies Committee subsequently formed a task force to address accounting and reporting by mutual life insurance enterprises but later suspended that project.

15. In 1982, the Board issued Statement 60 which extracted the specialized accounting practices from the Guide. Statement 60 specifically exempted mutual life insurance enterprises from its requirements because the issue of which insurance accounting and reporting principles should be applied to those entities still had not been resolved. In 1987, Statement 97 was issued and also excluded mutual life insurance enterprises for the same reason. Statement 113, issued in 1992, continued the exemption of mutual life insurance enterprises.

16. In 1993, Interpretation 40 was issued. Interpretation 40 clarified that mutual life insurance enterprises that issue financial statements described as prepared "in conformity with generally accepted accounting principles" are required to apply all applicable authoritative accounting pronouncements in preparing those statements.

17. Interpretation 40 did not address or change the existing exemptions of mutual life insurance enterprises from Statements 60, 97, and 113. Interpretation 40, originally effective for fiscal years beginning after December 15, 1994, highlighted the need to definitively resolve the accounting and reporting requirements for the insurance activities of mutual life insurance enterprises.

18. Mutual life insurance enterprises primarily issue participating life insurance contracts. Participating life insurance contracts provide policyholders with certain guaranteed benefits and allow policyholders to share in the experience of the enterprise through dividends. Dividends are paid periodically and generally reflect the experience and performance of the enterprise for investment activity, mortality experience, and contract administration for each particular class of contracts. The determination and distribution of dividends distinguish participating life insurance contracts from nonparticipating life insurance contracts.

19. The AICPA identified certain participating life insurance contracts that have features of the policies addressed by both Statements 60 and 97. Those contracts are different from other forms of participating contracts because dividends paid by those contracts are adjusted to reflect actual company experience. The features of those contracts that are similar to the contracts addressed by Statement 60 include individual contract functions that are not separately displayed to policyholders nor explicitly stated in the policy, a pattern of premiums that is specified in the policy and that is generally level and fixed over the contract's life, and the lack of an explicit policyholder account balance. Those contracts also have features that provide a measure of flexibility and discretion to the insurance enterprise that is similar to those found in universal life-type contracts addressed by Statement 97. For example, dividends on participating life insurance contracts are adjusted by the insurer to reflect actual company performance. In effect, those contracts contain similar provisions to Statement 60 contracts but function like Statement 97 contracts. Accordingly, the AICPA decided that those contracts should receive specialized accounting treatment to reflect the features of those contracts.

20. The AICPA has issued SOP 95-1 that requires mutual life insurance enterprises to apply the SOP's

Accounting and Reporting by Mutual Life Insurance **FAS120**
Enterprises and by Insurance Enterprises for
Certain Long-Duration Participating Contracts

accounting to participating life insurance contracts that meet the conditions in paragraph 5 of the SOP and to apply Statement 60 or 97 to all other life insurance policies in reporting their insurance activities in financial statements prepared in conformity with generally accepted accounting principles. Statement 113 applies to all reinsurance activities of mutual life insurance enterprises.

21. The AICPA asked the Board to remove the exemption for mutual life insurance enterprises from Statements 60, 97, and 113 and to require stock life insurance enterprises that have participating life insurance contracts that meet the conditions in paragraph 5 of the SOP to apply the accounting in the SOP to those policies in reporting their insurance activities in financial statements prepared in conformity with generally accepted accounting principles.

22. The Board considered the SOP and the AICPA's requests and decided to issue this Statement to address accounting and reporting principles for the insurance and reinsurance activities of mutual life insurance enterprises and to permit rather than require stock life insurance enterprises to apply the accounting in the SOP to participating life insurance contracts that meet the conditions in paragraph 5 of this Statement.

Applicability of Other Pronouncements

23. After considering the nature of insurance and reinsurance contracts of mutual life insurance enterprises, the AICPA concluded that Statements 60, 97, and 113 generally provide an appropriate model for the accounting and reporting of insurance and reinsurance activities of mutual life insurance enterprises. Based on that conclusion, the AICPA decided that requiring mutual life insurance enterprises to apply the provisions of those Statements to the insurance and reinsurance activities of those enterprises, except for participating life insurance contracts that meet the conditions in paragraph 5 of this Statement, would improve the comparability and understandability of financial reporting among insurance enterprises for insurance and reinsurance activities. Accordingly, the AICPA requested that the Board remove the exemptions of mutual life insurance enterprises from Statements 60, 97, and 113.

24. After considering the AICPA's conclusions, the Board decided that a general consideration of accounting and reporting by mutual life insurance enterprises was not necessary at this time. The Board agreed with the AICPA and decided to remove the exemptions of mutual life insurance enterprises from Statements 60, 97, and 113.

25. Most respondents to the March 1994 Exposure Draft supported the overall approach of applying Statements 60, 97, and 113 to mutual life insurance enterprises. A few respondents suggested that the needs of policyowners, regulators, and the accounting profession would be better served by developing a universal accounting model for mutual life insurance enterprises that incorporates the best practices of statutory and generally accepted accounting principles. Such an approach would entail a comprehensive review of insurance accounting and reporting. The Board concluded that the concerns raised by those respondents do not warrant general reconsideration of insurance accounting and reporting at this time. The Board believes that the needs of users would be better served by providing mutual life insurance enterprises that elect to adopt generally accepted accounting principles with a more timely resolution of insurance accounting and reporting issues that is based on the existing framework of those principles.

Accounting for Certain Long-Duration Participating Life Insurance Contracts

26. The AICPA also concluded that the accounting for certain long-duration participating life insurance contracts of mutual life insurance enterprises should be addressed separately. The AICPA decided that considering separately the accounting for participating life insurance contracts that meet the conditions in paragraph 5 of this Statement was warranted because of the contractual differences between those contracts and other types of participating life insurance contracts.

27. The Board believes that the accounting in the SOP is reasonable for participating life insurance contracts that meet the conditions in paragraph 5 of this Statement. The Board acknowledges that the SOP will establish accounting principles for those contracts that differ from those applied to other types of participating life insurance contracts, but the Board believes that differences in the features of those contracts justify differences in accounting. The Board believes that the accounting in the SOP reasonably reflects the features of those contracts within the parameters of Statements 60 and 97.

28. A few respondents to the Exposure Draft disagreed with the AICPA's and the Board's conclusion

on that issue. Those respondents stated that participating life insurance contracts that meet the conditions in paragraph 5 of this Statement should be accounted for using a Statement 60 methodology because those contracts are similar to other life insurance contracts accounted for in accordance with Statement 60. In its redeliberations on the SOP, the AICPA reconsidered that approach and concluded that the accounting in the SOP more closely reflects the features of those contracts than a Statement 60 methodology. The Board concurs with the AICPA that for participating life insurance contracts that meet the conditions in paragraph 5 of this Statement the accounting in the SOP is more appropriate than the accounting under a Statement 60 approach.

29. The Board considered two approaches to include the SOP's accounting for participating life insurance contracts that meet the conditions in paragraph 5 of this Statement in the framework of generally accepted accounting principles. One approach would have referred to the SOP as a source of established accounting principles for those contracts. The other approach would have included the SOP's accounting requirements (paragraphs 11-24 of the SOP) in this Statement, making this Statement the source of accounting principles for those contracts.

30. The Board decided that the SOP should be referred to in this Statement as the source of established accounting principles for those contracts. The Board understands that including the SOP's accounting in this Statement would have established that accounting as category (a) accounting principles and would have integrated the SOP's accounting into FASB literature, thereby facilitating retrieval of that information. However, including the SOP's accounting in this Statement would have required the Board to deliberate the SOP's accounting, and the Board decided that that was not warranted at this time. The Board also concluded that this Statement and AICPA Statement on Auditing Standards No. 69, *The Meaning of "Present Fairly in Conformity With Generally Accepted Accounting Principles" in the Independent Auditor's Report*, will appropriately establish the SOP's accounting in the body of generally accepted accounting principles. The Board believes that financial statement users, preparers, and auditors will have reasonable access to the SOP and that reference to the SOP will provide adequate notice about the SOP's applicability to those contracts.

31. The Board also considered whether stock life insurance enterprises with participating life insurance contracts that meet the conditions in paragraph 5 of

this Statement should be required or permitted to apply the SOP's accounting to those contracts. Stock life insurance enterprises currently are required to apply Statement 60 to those contracts. The AICPA requested that the Board amend Statement 60 to require stock life insurance enterprises having that type of contract to apply the accounting in the SOP to those contracts.

32. The Board recognizes that the information provided to users about the insurance and reinsurance activities of life insurance enterprises could be improved by limiting the diversity among insurance enterprises in accounting and reporting for those activities. The Board acknowledges that permitting stock life insurance enterprises with participating life insurance contracts that meet the conditions in paragraph 5 of this Statement to apply the accounting in the SOP to those contracts may cause inconsistencies between insurance enterprises in their accounting for those contracts. The Board believes, however, that there are likely to be only a limited number of stock life insurance enterprises with material amounts of those contracts and decided not to require those enterprises to comply with the SOP.

33. In addition, the Board agreed that requiring stock life insurance enterprises to comply with the SOP would require the Board to deliberate the SOP's accounting and include that accounting in this Statement. The Board decided that the limited inconsistencies that may arise by permitting stock life insurance enterprises to apply the accounting in the SOP do not warrant further Board consideration at this time. The Board believes that the disclosures required by this Statement and Opinion 22 will provide sufficient information to assist users in understanding differences in accounting (between insurance enterprises) for participating life insurance contracts that meet the conditions in paragraph 5 of this Statement.

34. Most respondents to the Exposure Draft that addressed that issue agreed with the Board's conclusion to permit stock life insurance enterprises to apply the SOP to participating contracts that meet the conditions in paragraph 5 of this Statement. Some respondents stated that consistency and comparability in financial reporting among insurance enterprises would be improved if stock life insurance enterprises were either precluded from applying or required to apply the accounting in the SOP to those contracts. The Board reconsidered that issue but continues to believe that the accounting in the SOP reasonably reflects the features of those contracts and should be

Accounting and Reporting by Mutual Life Insurance Enterprises and by Insurance Enterprises for Certain Long-Duration Participating Contracts

FAS120

available to stock life insurance enterprises. The Board also believes that a decision to require stock life insurance enterprises to apply the SOP's accounting to those contracts would necessitate adding the accounting conclusions in the SOP to this Statement thereby requiring time-consuming deliberations. The Board decided not to require stock life insurance enterprises to apply the provisions of the SOP because the overall benefits of providing timely guidance on the accounting and reporting of insurance activities by mutual life insurance enterprises outweigh the incremental improvement in the consistency and comparability of financial reporting among insurance enterprises that would result from requiring stock life insurance enterprises to apply the SOP's accounting. Accordingly, the Board decided to retain the provision to permit stock life insurance enterprises to apply the accounting in the SOP.

Effective Date and Transition

35. Adoption of the provisions of this Statement is likely to establish a fundamentally different basis of accounting for insurance and reinsurance activities of mutual life insurance enterprises that currently prepare financial statements based on statutory accounting practices. Therefore, the Board decided that retroactive restatement is the appropriate method of reporting the effect of initially applying this Statement. Requiring a uniform transition method will improve the understandability and comparability of financial statements of mutual life insurance enterprises, both in the year of adoption and in subsequent periods. The Board recognizes that restatement of all years may be costly and may require information that mutual life insurance enterprises may no longer have or that was not previously required. The Board concluded that transition is, to a significant extent, a practical matter and therefore limited the requirement to restate previously issued annual financial statements that are presented for comparative purposes to fiscal years beginning after December 15, 1992, consistent with reporting the effect of initially applying Interpretation 40.

36. The Exposure Draft and Interpretation 40 provided only general implementation guidance and did not attempt to identify and address all issues that could arise from the adoption of multiple accounting standards. A few respondents asked the Board to provide more detailed implementation guidance. Those respondents stated that the financial information provided to users could be improved and inconsistencies could be reduced by providing more extensive guid-

ance. The Board considered those requests but concluded that delaying timely resolution of the accounting and reporting of insurance activities of mutual life insurance enterprises to undertake the time-consuming effort to identify all potential implementation issues and provide detailed implementation guidance was not warranted. The Board decided that for practical reasons the overall approach of providing general guidance should be retained and that this Statement should not address detailed implementation issues that may result from its requirements or those of Interpretation 40.

37. The Exposure Draft would have required that this Statement be effective for fiscal years beginning after December 15, 1994. The Board had previously stated its intention to address the accounting and reporting of insurance and reinsurance activities of mutual life insurance enterprises within the parameters of Statements 60, 97, and 113. Accordingly, the Board believed that that effective date would provide sufficient time to assimilate the requirements of this Statement and the SOP and to obtain the required information. The Board also concluded that the provisions of the proposed Statement and Interpretation 40 should be concurrently effective.

38. Many respondents urged the Board to delay the proposed effective date in the Exposure Draft. They pointed out that the Statement and SOP establish a fundamentally different basis of accounting for those mutual life insurance enterprises that currently prepare financial statements based on statutory accounting practices that differ significantly from generally accepted accounting principles. Respondents indicated that applying the Statement and the SOP to 1995 financial statements would be difficult if the final pronouncements were not issued until late 1994.

39. In its redeliberations, the Board discussed effective dates that would allow mutual life insurance enterprises sufficient time to assimilate the requirements of this Statement and the SOP, obtain the required information, and develop systems to meet ongoing accounting and reporting requirements. The Board decided that a one-year delay of the proposed effective date to fiscal years beginning after December 15, 1995 would be adequate for that purpose. The AICPA similarly deferred the effective date of the SOP.

Deferral of the Effective Date of Interpretation 40

40. As issued, the general provisions of Interpretation 40 are effective for fiscal years beginning after

December 15, 1994. Most respondents to the Exposure Draft that commented on the effective date agreed with the Board that this Statement, the SOP, and Interpretation 40 should be effective concurrently. Many respondents indicated that because the initial adoption of multiple accounting pronouncements is complex, the pronouncements should be adopted in the same reporting period. That complexity is primarily attributable to the interaction of insurance and noninsurance accounting standards. Also, several respondents stated that the understandability and comparability of financial statements of enterprises affected by this Statement, the SOP, and Interpretation 40 would be improved by concurrent adoption of all applicable authoritative accounting pronouncements in preparing financial statements in accordance with generally accepted accounting principles. Some respondents stated that because of limited accounting and actuarial resources, deferral of the effective date of Interpretation 40 would allow for a more orderly implementation of the provisions of this Statement, the SOP, and Interpretation 40.

41. The Board continues to believe that the understandability and comparability of financial reporting among insurance enterprises that elect to adopt generally accepted accounting principles would be improved by concurrent initial adoption of insurance and noninsurance accounting pronouncements. The Board concluded that the disadvantages to preparers, users, and auditors that would be caused by required adoption of Interpretation 40 one year before the required adoption of this Statement and the SOP outweigh the disadvantages of a one-year delay in the effective date of that Interpretation.

42. On September 30, 1994, the Board issued the Exposure Draft, *Applicability of Generally Accepted Accounting Principles to Mutual Life Insurance and Other Enterprises—Deferral of the Effective Date of FASB Interpretation No. 40,* which proposed deferring the effective date of Interpretation 40 by one year to fiscal years beginning after December 15, 1995. The Board received 10 comment letters on that Exposure Draft. A large majority of respondents supported the deferral. A few respondents repeated suggestions that were included in their comment letters on the March 1994 Exposure Draft and that are addressed in this basis for conclusions.

43. The Board concluded that (a) it could reach an informed decision on that Exposure Draft on the basis of existing information without a public hearing, (b) deferral of the general provisions of Interpretation 40 is necessary and a one-year deferral to fiscal years beginning after December 15, 1995 is appropriate, and (c) the amendment of Interpretation 40 as specified in paragraph 10 is appropriately included in this Statement. The Board emphasized that the disclosures specified in paragraphs 5 and 6 of Interpretation 40 remain in effect.

Statement of Financial Accounting Standards No. 121
Accounting for the Impairment of Long-Lived Assets
and for Long-Lived Assets to Be Disposed Of

STATUS

Issued: March 1995

Effective Date: For fiscal years beginning after December 15, 1995

Affects: Supersedes APB 16, paragraph 88(d)
       Amends APB 17, paragraph 31
       Amends APB 18, paragraph 19(h)
       Amends AIN-APB 30, Interpretation No. 1
       Amends FAS 15, paragraphs 28 and 33
       Amends FAS 19 by adding a paragraph after paragraph 62
       Amends FAS 34, paragraph 19
       Amends FAS 51, paragraph 14
       Amends FAS 60, paragraph 48
       Amends FAS 61, paragraph 6
       Supersedes FAS 66, footnote 5
       Amends FAS 67, paragraphs 3, 24, and 28
       Supersedes FAS 67, paragraphs 16 and 25
       Amends FAS 71, paragraphs 9 and 10
       Amends FAS 101, paragraph 6

Affected by: Paragraph 3 amended by FAS 142
          Paragraph 3(b) amended by FAS 139
          Paragraphs 4, 6, and 27 amended by FAS 142
          Paragraph 12 superseded by FAS 142
          Paragraph 147 amended by FAS 139 and FAS 142
          Superseded by FAS 144

Issues Discussed by FASB Emerging Issues Task Force (EITF)

Affects: Resolves EITF Issue No. 84-28
       Partially resolves EITF Issue No. 85-36
       Affects EITF Issues No. 90-16, 93-4, and 93-11

Interpreted by: Paragraphs 6 and 10 interpreted by EITF Issue No. 95-23
             Paragraphs 15, 34, and 35 interpreted by EITF Topic No. D-45

Related Issues: EITF Issues No. 87-11, 89-13, 90-6, 94-3, 95-21, 97-4, 99-14, 01-2, and 01-5

SUMMARY

This Statement establishes accounting standards for the impairment of long-lived assets, certain identifiable intangibles, and goodwill related to those assets to be held and used and for long-lived assets and certain identifiable intangibles to be disposed of.

This Statement requires that long-lived assets and certain identifiable intangibles to be held and used by an entity be reviewed for impairment whenever events or changes in circumstances indicate that the carrying amount of an asset may not be recoverable. In performing the review for recoverability, the entity should estimate the future cash flows expected to result from the use of the asset and its eventual disposition. If the sum of the expected future cash flows (undiscounted and without interest charges) is less than the carrying amount of the asset, an impairment loss is recognized. Otherwise, an impairment loss is not recognized. Measurement of an impairment loss for long-lived assets and identifiable intangibles that an entity expects to hold and use should be based on the fair value of the asset.

This Statement requires that long-lived assets and certain identifiable intangibles to be disposed of be reported at the lower of carrying amount or fair value less cost to sell, except for assets that are covered by APB Opinion No. 30, *Reporting the Results of Operations—Reporting the Effects of Disposal of a Segment of a Business, and Extraordinary, Unusual and Infrequently Occurring Events and Transactions.* Assets that are covered by Opinion 30 will continue to be reported at the lower of carrying amount or net realizable value.

This Statement also requires that a rate-regulated enterprise recognize an impairment for the amount of costs excluded when a regulator excludes all or part of a cost from the enterprise's rate base.

This Statement is effective for financial statements for fiscal years beginning after December 15, 1995. Earlier application is encouraged. Restatement of previously issued financial statements is not permitted. Impairment losses resulting from the application of this Statement should be reported in the period in which the recognition criteria are first applied and met. The initial application of this Statement to assets that are being held for disposal at the date of adoption should be reported as the cumulative effect of a change in accounting principle.

Statement of Financial Accounting Standards No. 121

Accounting for the Impairment of Long-Lived Assets and for Long-Lived Assets to Be Disposed Of

CONTENTS

INTRODUCTION

1. This Statement establishes accounting standards for the impairment of long-lived assets, certain identifiable intangibles, and goodwill related to those assets to be held and used and for long-lived assets and certain identifiable intangibles to be disposed of.

2. Long-lived assets such as plant and equipment generally are recorded at cost, which is usually fair value at the date of acquisition. The original cost usually is reduced over time by depreciation (amortization) so that the cost of the asset is allocated to the periods in which the asset is used. That practice has been modified in some circumstances when an asset has been determined to be impaired, in which case the asset has been written down to a new carrying amount that is less than the remaining cost and a loss has been recognized. Accounting standards generally have not addressed when impairment losses should be recognized or how impairment losses should be measured. As a result, practice has been diverse.

STANDARDS OF FINANCIAL ACCOUNTING AND REPORTING

Scope

3. This Statement applies to long-lived assets, certain identifiable intangibles, and goodwill related to those assets to be held and used and to long-lived assets and certain identifiable intangibles to be disposed of. The Statement applies to all entities. This Statement does not apply to financial instruments, long-term customer relationships of a financial institution (for example, core deposit intangibles and credit cardholder intangibles), mortgage and other servicing rights, deferred policy acquisition costs, or deferred tax assets. It also does not apply to assets whose accounting is prescribed by:

a. FASB Statement No. 50, *Financial Reporting in the Record and Music Industry*
b. FASB Statement No. 53, *Financial Reporting by Producers and Distributors of Motion Picture Films*

c. FASB Statement No. 63, *Financial Reporting by Broadcasters*

d. FASB Statement No. 86, *Accounting for the Costs of Computer Software to Be Sold, Leased, or Otherwise Marketed*

e. FASB Statement No. 90, *Regulated Enterprises— Accounting for Abandonments and Disallowances of Plant Costs.*

Appendix B contains a list of certain pronouncements that refer to impairment or disposal of assets and indicates which pronouncements are amended by this Statement and which pronouncements remain as authoritative literature. All references to an asset in this Statement also refer to groups of assets representing the lowest level of identifiable cash flows as described in paragraph 8.

Assets to Be Held and Used

Recognition and Measurement of Impairment

4. An entity shall review long-lived assets and certain identifiable intangibles to be held and used for impairment whenever events or changes in circumstances indicate that the carrying amount of an asset may not be recoverable.

5. The following are examples of events or changes in circumstances that indicate that the recoverability of the carrying amount of an asset should be assessed:

a. A significant decrease in the market value of an asset

b. A significant change in the extent or manner in which an asset is used or a significant physical change in an asset

c. A significant adverse change in legal factors or in the business climate that could affect the value of an asset or an adverse action or assessment by a regulator

d. An accumulation of costs significantly in excess of the amount originally expected to acquire or construct an asset

e. A current period operating or cash flow loss combined with a history of operating or cash flow losses or a projection or forecast that demonstrates

continuing losses associated with an asset used for the purpose of producing revenue.

6. If the examples of events or changes in circumstances set forth in paragraph 5 are present or if other events or changes in circumstances indicate that the carrying amount of an asset that an entity expects to hold and use may not be recoverable, the entity shall estimate the future cash flows expected to result from the use of the asset and its eventual disposition. Future cash flows are the future cash inflows expected to be generated by an asset less the future cash outflows expected to be necessary to obtain those inflows. If the sum of the expected future cash flows (undiscounted and without interest charges) is less than the carrying amount of the asset, the entity shall recognize an impairment loss in accordance with this Statement. Otherwise, an impairment loss shall not be recognized; however, a review of depreciation policies may be appropriate.[1]

7. An impairment loss recognized in accordance with paragraph 6 shall be measured as the amount by which the carrying amount of the asset exceeds the fair value of the asset. The fair value of an asset is the amount at which the asset could be bought or sold in a current transaction between willing parties, that is, other than in a forced or liquidation sale. Quoted market prices in active markets are the best evidence of fair value and shall be used as the basis for the measurement, if available. If quoted market prices are not available, the estimate of fair value shall be based on the best information available in the circumstances. The estimate of fair value shall consider prices for similar assets and the results of valuation techniques to the extent available in the circumstances. Examples of valuation techniques include the present value of estimated expected future cash flows using a discount rate commensurate with the risks involved, option-pricing models, matrix pricing, option-adjusted spread models, and fundamental analysis.

8. In estimating expected future cash flows for determining whether an asset is impaired (paragraph 6), and if expected future cash flows are used in measuring assets that are impaired (paragraph 7), assets shall be grouped at the lowest level for which there are

---

[1]Paragraph 10 of APB Opinion No. 20, *Accounting Changes,* addresses the accounting for changes in depreciation estimates, and paragraph 32 addresses the accounting for changes in the method of depreciation. Whenever there is reason to assess the recoverability of the carrying amount of an asset under paragraphs 4 and 5 of this Statement, there may be reason to review the depreciation estimates and method under paragraphs 10 and 32 of Opinion 20. However, an impairment loss that results from applying this Statement should be recognized prior to performing that review. The provisions of Opinion 20 apply to the reporting of changes in the depreciation estimates and method regardless of whether an impairment loss is recognized under paragraph 6 of this Statement.

identifiable cash flows that are largely independent of the cash flows of other groups of assets.

9. Estimates of expected future cash flows shall be the best estimate based on reasonable and supportable assumptions and projections. All available evidence should be considered in developing estimates of expected future cash flows. The weight given to the evidence should be commensurate with the extent to which the evidence can be verified objectively. If a range is estimated for either the amount or timing of possible cash flows, the likelihood of possible outcomes shall be considered in determining the best estimate of future cash flows.

10. In limited circumstances, the test specified in paragraph 6 will be applicable at only the entity level because the asset being tested for recoverability does not have identifiable cash flows that are largely independent of other asset groupings. In those instances, if the asset is not expected to provide any service potential to the entity, the asset shall be accounted for as if abandoned or held for disposal in accordance with the provisions of paragraph 15 of this Statement. If the asset is expected to provide service potential, an impairment loss shall be recognized if the sum of the expected future cash flows (undiscounted and without interest charges) for the entity is less than the carrying amounts of the entity's assets covered by this Statement.

11. After an impairment is recognized, the reduced carrying amount of the asset shall be accounted for as its new cost. For a depreciable asset, the new cost shall be depreciated over the asset's remaining useful life. Restoration of previously recognized impairment losses is prohibited.

Goodwill

12. If an asset being tested for recoverability was acquired in a business combination accounted for using the purchase method, the goodwill that arose in that transaction shall be included as part of the asset grouping (paragraph 8) in determining recoverability. If some but not all of the assets acquired in that transaction are being tested, goodwill shall be allocated to the assets being tested for recoverability on a pro rata basis using the relative fair values of the long-lived assets and identifiable intangibles acquired at the acquisition date unless there is evidence to suggest that some other method of associating the goodwill with those assets is more appropriate. In instances where goodwill is identified with assets that are subject to an impairment loss, the carrying amount of the identified goodwill shall be eliminated before making any reduction of the carrying amounts of impaired long-lived assets and identifiable intangibles.

Reporting and Disclosure

13. An impairment loss for assets to be held and used shall be reported as a component of income from continuing operations before income taxes for entities presenting an income statement and in the statement of activities of a not-for-profit organization. Although there is no requirement to report a subtotal such as "income from operations," entities that present such a subtotal must include the impairment loss in that subtotal.

14. An entity that recognizes an impairment loss shall disclose all of the following in financial statements that include the period of the impairment write-down:

a. A description of the impaired assets and the facts and circumstances leading to the impairment
b. The amount of the impairment loss and how fair value was determined
c. The caption in the income statement or the statement of activities in which the impairment loss is aggregated if that loss has not been presented as a separate caption or reported parenthetically on the face of the statement
d. If applicable, the business segment(s) affected.

Assets to Be Disposed Of

Recognition and Measurement

15. APB Opinion No. 30, *Reporting the Results of Operations—Reporting the Effects of Disposal of a Segment of a Business, and Extraordinary, Unusual and Infrequently Occurring Events and Transactions,* requires that certain assets to be disposed of be measured at the lower of carrying amount or net realizable

value.[2] All long-lived assets and certain identifiable intangibles to be disposed of that are not covered by that Opinion and for which management, having the authority to approve the action, has committed to a plan to dispose of the assets, whether by sale or abandonment, shall be reported at the lower of carrying amount or fair value less cost to sell. The fair value of the assets to be disposed of shall be measured in accordance with paragraph 7 of this Statement.

16. Cost to sell an asset to be disposed of generally includes the incremental direct costs to transact the sale of the asset such as broker commissions, legal and title transfer fees, and closing costs that must be incurred before legal title can be transferred. Costs generally excluded from cost to sell an asset to be disposed of include insurance, security services, utility expenses, and other costs of protecting or maintaining an asset. However, if a contractual agreement for the sale of an asset obligates an entity to incur costs in the future to effect the ultimate sale, those costs shall be included as adjustments to the cost to sell an asset to be disposed of. If the fair value of an asset is measured by the current market value or by using the current selling price for a similar asset, that fair value shall be considered to be a current amount and that fair value and cost to sell shall not be discounted. If the fair value of an asset is measured by discounting expected future cash flows and if the sale is expected to occur beyond one year, the cost to sell also shall be discounted. Assets to be disposed of covered by this Statement shall not be depreciated (amortized) while they are held for disposal.

17. Subsequent revisions in estimates of fair value less cost to sell shall be reported as adjustments to the carrying amount of an asset to be disposed of, provided that the carrying amount of the asset does not exceed the carrying amount (acquisition cost or other basis less accumulated depreciation or amortization) of the asset before an adjustment was made to reflect the decision to dispose of the asset.

Reporting and Disclosure

18. An entity that holds assets to be disposed of that are accounted for in accordance with paragraphs 15-17 of this Statement shall report gains or losses resulting from the application of those paragraphs as a component of income from continuing operations before income taxes for entities presenting an income statement and in the statement of activities of a not-for-profit organization. Although entities are not required to report a subtotal such as "income from operations," entities that present such a subtotal must include the gains or losses resulting from the application of paragraphs 15-17 in that subtotal.

19. An entity that accounts for assets to be disposed of in accordance with paragraphs 15-17 shall disclose all of the following in financial statements that include a period during which those assets are held:

a. A description of assets to be disposed of, the facts and circumstances leading to the expected disposal, the expected disposal date, and the carrying amount of those assets
b. If applicable, the business segment(s) in which assets to be disposed of are held
c. The loss, if any, resulting from the application of paragraph 15 of this Statement
d. The gain or loss, if any, resulting from changes in the carrying amounts of assets to be disposed of that arises from application of paragraph 17 of this Statement
e. The caption in the income statement or statement of activities in which the gains or losses in (c) and (d) are aggregated if those gains or losses have not been presented as a separate caption or reported parenthetically on the face of the statement
f. The results of operations for assets to be disposed of to the extent that those results are included in the entity's results of operations for the period and can be identified.

[2]Paragraphs 13-16 of Opinion 30 prescribe the accounting for the disposal of a segment of a business. Paragraph 13 defines a segment of a business as "a component of an entity whose activities represent a separate major line of business or class of customer." Paragraph 15 of that Opinion prescribes the determination of a gain or loss on the disposal of a segment of a business and states:

> In the usual circumstance, it would be expected that the plan of disposal would be carried out within a period of one year from the measurement date and that such projections of operating income or loss would not cover a period exceeding approximately one year. [Footnote reference omitted.]

Amendments to Existing Pronouncements

20. Paragraph 88(d) of APB Opinion No. 16, *Business Combinations,* is replaced by the following:

> d. Plant and equipment: (1) to be used, at the current replacement cost for similar capacity[11] unless the expected future use of the assets indicates a lower value to the acquirer, and (2) to be sold, at fair value less cost to sell.

21. The following sentence is added to the beginning of paragraph 31 of APB Opinion No. 17, *Intangible Assets,* immediately following the heading:

> Identifiable intangible assets not covered by FASB Statement No. 121, *Accounting for the Impairment of Long-Lived Assets and for Long-Lived Assets to Be Disposed Of,* and goodwill not identified with assets that are subject to an impairment loss shall be evaluated as follows.

22. In the first sentence of paragraph 19(h) of APB Opinion No. 18, *The Equity Method of Accounting for Investments in Common Stock,* the phrase *the same as a loss in value of other long-term assets* is deleted.

23. The last question and its interpretation of AICPA Accounting Interpretation 1, "Illustration of the Application of APB Opinion No. 30," are superseded by this Statement.

24. FASB Statement No. 15, *Accounting by Debtors and Creditors for Troubled Debt Restructurings,* is amended as follows:

a. The following sentence is added after the first sentence in paragraph 28:

> A creditor that receives long-lived assets that will be sold from a debtor in full satisfaction of a receivable shall account for those assets at their fair value less cost to sell, as that term is used in paragraphs 15-17 of FASB Statement No. 121, *Accounting for the Impairment of Long-Lived Assets and for Long-Lived Assets to Be Disposed Of.*

b. The last sentence of paragraph 28 is replaced by the following:

> The excess of (i) the recorded investment in the receivable[17] satisfied over (ii) the fair value of assets received (less cost to sell, if required above) is a loss to be recognized. For purposes of this paragraph, losses, to the extent they are not offset against allowances for uncollectible amounts or other valuation accounts, shall be included in measuring net income for the period.

c. In the second sentence of paragraph 33, *at their fair values* is deleted and *less cost to sell* is inserted after *reduced by the fair value.*

25. The following new paragraph and heading are added after paragraph 62 of FASB Statement No. 19, *Financial Accounting and Reporting by Oil and Gas Producing Companies:*

> **Impairment Test for Proved Properties and Capitalized Exploration and Development Cost**
>
> The provisions of FASB Statement No. 121, *Accounting for the Impairment of Long-Lived Assets and for Long-Lived Assets to Be Disposed Of,* are applicable to the costs of an enterprise's wells and related equipment and facilities and the costs of the related proved properties. The impairment provisions relating to unproved properties referred to in paragraphs 12, 27-29, 31(b), 33, 40, 47(g), and 47(h) of this Statement remain applicable to unproved properties.

26. The following sentence is added to the end of paragraph 19 of FASB Statement No. 34, *Capitalization of Interest Cost:*

> The provisions of FASB Statement No. 121, *Accounting for the Impairment of Long-Lived Assets and for Long-Lived Assets to Be Disposed Of,* apply in recognizing impairment of assets held for use.

27. The first two sentences of paragraph 14 of FASB Statement No. 51, *Financial Reporting by Cable*

Television Companies, are replaced by the following:

> Capitalized plant and certain identifiable intangible assets are subject to the provisions of FASB Statement No. 121, *Accounting for the Impairment of Long-Lived Assets and for Long-Lived Assets to Be Disposed Of.*

28. FASB Statement No. 60, *Accounting and Reporting by Insurance Enterprises,* is amended as follows:

a. In the first sentence of paragraph 48, *and an allowance for any impairment in value* is deleted.

b. In the last sentence of paragraph 48, *Changes in the allowance for any impairment in value relating to real estate investments* is replaced by *Reductions in the carrying amounts of real estate investments resulting from the application of FASB Statement No. 121, Accounting for the Impairment of Long-Lived Assets and for Long-Lived Assets to Be Disposed Of.*

29. FASB Statement No. 61, *Accounting for Title Plant,* is amended as follows:

a. In the first and second sentences of paragraph 6, *value* is replaced by *carrying amount.*

b. The last sentence of paragraph 6 is replaced by the following:

> Those events or changes in circumstances, in addition to the examples in paragraph 5 of FASB Statement No. 121, *Accounting for the Impairment of Long-Lived Assets and for Long-Lived Assets to Be Disposed Of,* indicate that the carrying amount of the capitalized costs may not be recoverable. Accordingly, the provisions of Statement 121 apply.

30. Footnote 5 to paragraph 21 of FASB Statement No. 66, *Accounting for Sales of Real Estate,* is replaced by the following:

> Paragraph 24 of FASB Statement No. 67, *Accounting for Costs and Initial Rental Operations of Real Estate Projects,* as amended by FASB Statement No. 121, *Accounting for the Impairment of Long-Lived Assets and for Long-Lived Assets to Be Disposed Of,* specifies the accounting for property that has not yet been sold but is substantially complete and ready for its intended use.

31. FASB Statement No. 67, *Accounting for Costs and Initial Rental Operations of Real Estate Projects,* is amended as follows:

a. In paragraph 3, *costs in excess of estimated **net realizable value*** is replaced by *reductions in the carrying amounts of real estate assets prescribed by FASB Statement No. 121, Accounting for the Impairment of Long-Lived Assets and for Long-Lived Assets to Be Disposed Of.*

b. Paragraph 16 is deleted.

c. The first and second sentences of paragraph 24 are replaced by the following:

> A real estate project, or parts thereof, that is substantially complete and ready for its intended use* shall be accounted for at the lower of carrying amount or fair value less cost to sell as prescribed in paragraphs 15-17 of Statement 121. The recognition and measurement principles contained in paragraphs 4-7 of that Statement shall apply to real estate held for development and sale, including property to be developed in the future as well as that currently under development. Determining whether the carrying amounts of real estate projects require write-downs shall be based on an evaluation of individual projects.

> ---
> *Refer to footnote 5.

d. Paragraph 25 is replaced by the following:

> Paragraph 5 of Statement 121 provides examples of events or changes in circumstances that indicate that the recoverability of the carrying amount of an asset should be assessed. Insufficient rental demand for a rental project currently under construction is an additional example that indicates that the recoverability of the real estate project should be assessed in accordance with paragraph 6 of Statement 121.

e. In paragraph 28, the term *net realizable value* and its definition are deleted.

32. FASB Statement No. 71, *Accounting for the Effects of Certain Types of Regulation,* is amended as follows:

a. The following sentence is added to the end of paragraph 9:

> If at any time the incurred cost no longer meets the above criteria, that cost shall be charged to earnings.

b. Paragraph 10 is amended as follows:

> (1) The second and third sentences are replaced by:
>
> > If a regulator excludes all or part of a cost from allowable costs, the carrying amount of any asset recognized pursuant to paragraph 9 of this Statement shall be reduced to the extent of the excluded cost.
>
> (2) In the fourth sentence, *the asset has* is replaced by *other assets have* and the following phrase is added to the end of that sentence after the footnote added by FASB Statement No. 90, *Regulated Enterprises—Accounting for Abandonments and Disallowances of Plant Costs:*
>
> > and FASB Statement No. 121, *Accounting for the Impairment of Long-Lived Assets and for Long-Lived Assets to Be Disposed Of,* shall apply.

c. The following new paragraph is added after paragraph 10:

> If a regulator allows recovery through rates of costs previously excluded from allowable costs, that action shall result in recognition of a new asset. The classification of that asset shall be consistent with the classification that would have resulted had those costs been initially included in allowable costs.

33. The following phrase is added to the end of the third sentence of paragraph 6 of FASB Statement No. 101, *Regulated Enterprises—Accounting for the Discontinuation of Application of FASB Statement No. 71:*

> and FASB Statement No. 121, *Accounting for the Impairment of Long-Lived Assets and for Long-Lived Assets to Be Disposed Of,* shall apply, except for the provisions for income statement reporting in paragraph 13 of that Statement.

Effective Date and Transition

34. This Statement shall be effective for financial statements for fiscal years beginning after December 15, 1995. Earlier application is encouraged. Restatement of previously issued financial statements is not permitted. Impairment losses resulting from the application of this Statement shall be reported in the period in which the recognition criteria are first applied and met.

35. The initial application of this Statement to assets that are being held for disposal at the date of adoption shall be reported as the cumulative effect of a change in accounting principle, as described in APB Opinion No. 20, *Accounting Changes.* A business enterprise shall report the amount of the cumulative effect in the income statement between the captions "extraordinary items," if any, and "net income" (Opinion 20, paragraph 20). A not-for-profit organization shall report the cumulative effect of a change in accounting on each class of net assets in the statement of activities between the captions "extraordinary items," if any, and "change in unrestricted net assets," "change in temporarily restricted net assets," and "change in permanently restricted net assets." The pro forma effects of retroactive application (Opinion 20, paragraph 21) are not required to be disclosed.

> **The provisions of this Statement need not be applied to immaterial items.**

This Statement was adopted by the affirmative votes of five members of the Financial Accounting Standards Board. Messrs. Anania and Northcutt dissented.

Messrs. Anania and Northcutt disagree with this Statement's conclusion in paragraph 7 that an impairment loss should be measured as the amount by which the carrying amount of an asset exceeds the asset's fair value. The Board concluded that a decision to continue to operate rather than sell an impaired asset is economically similar to a decision to invest in that asset and, therefore, the impaired asset should be measured at its fair value. Messrs. Anania and Northcutt do not agree with the rationale of that conclusion. In their view, fair value, which is predicated on the concept of an exchange in a current transaction between willing parties, is not an appropriate measure of impairment because (1) there has been no exchange transaction with an independent party and (2) the asset will continue to be used in operations.

Mr. Anania believes that an impaired asset should be measured at its recoverable cost including the time value of money. In Mr. Anania's view, that approach is the appropriate improvement within the historical cost model to resolve the inconsistent accounting practices that currently exist. Mr. Anania would accept an incremental borrowing rate to determine the present value of estimated future cash flows from an impaired asset that does not have a quoted market price. However, he also would support a discount rate based on rates of return on high-quality, fixed-income investments, with cash flows matching the timing of the asset's expected cash flows. Mr. Anania believes that use of the latter rate would provide greater comparability when similar assets are owned by different entities that have different debt capacities. The recoverable cost including interest approach is discussed in paragraphs 82-85.

In addition, Mr. Anania believes that a forecast of expected cash flows will be the only available information to determine fair value for assets of an entity-specific nature, such as special-purpose structures and customized equipment. In Mr. Anania's view, the requirement to discount those cash flows at a rate commensurate with the risks involved, as discussed in paragraphs 92 and 93, imposes an unnecessary burden to determine that rate when there is clearly no plan or intent to sell the asset.

Mr. Northcutt believes that this Statement's requirement to measure an impaired asset at fair value is a precedent-setting departure from the transaction-based historical cost model. In Mr. Northcutt's view, the requirement to recognize an impairment loss is not an event or transaction that warrants the adoption of a new basis of accounting at fair value. He does not believe that a fair value measure provides the most relevant and reliable information for users of financial statements, and he finds little relevance in using that measure for an impaired asset that will continue to be held and used. Further, Mr. Northcutt believes that using fair value to measure an impaired

asset fails to recognize the nature of that asset, permits "fresh-start" accounting based on management's decision to keep an asset rather than sell it, and usually results in an excessive loss in the current period and an excessive profit in future periods.

Under the present accounting model, a long-lived asset is initially recognized and measured at cost, which is also presumed to be fair value. All subsequent measurements of that asset are the result of a process of allocation through depreciation or amortization. The carrying amount of the asset never purports to reflect anything other than the unallocated balance of the asset's original cost. Mr. Northcutt agrees with the impairment recognition test in paragraph 6 of this Statement and believes that when the carrying amount of an asset cannot be recovered through future operations, an impairment loss should be recognized. However, he believes that an impairment loss should reflect the cost of the asset that will not be recovered from the future operation and subsequent disposal of the asset. Thus, an impaired asset should be written down to its recoverable cost excluding interest. Mr. Northcutt views interest cost as a period cost. For the same reasons as those cited in the dissent to FASB Statement No. 34, *Capitalization of Interest Cost,* he believes that interest cost should not be included as part of an impairment loss regardless of whether the interest is an accrual of actual debt costs or the result of discounting expected future cash flows at some debt rate.

Mr. Northcutt further believes that the use of a fair value measurement, which is based on the notion of an exchange transaction between a willing buyer and a willing seller, fails to consider the nature of the asset in question. He believes that measurement at fair value is not operational. Clearly, the test for recoverability in paragraph 6 of this Statement is an entity-specific test. The estimate of future cash flows expected to result from the use of the asset reflects many aspects that are unique to the specific plans and operations of the entity. That estimate depends on assumptions about many variables, such as the efficiency of the entity's work force, the effectiveness of its marketing efforts, the creativity of its engineers, and management's willingness to invest additional capital. Estimating expected future cash flows is a very subjective process at best, but is probably within the capabilities of an entity's management if it is in the context of that entity's specific plans and operations.

Mr. Northcutt believes that while it may be possible to estimate the timing of expected future cash flows and then discount those cash flows at a rate "commensurate with the risks," it is presumptuous to believe that the result approximates fair value, as defined. In paragraph 70, the Board argues that the decision to continue to use rather than sell an impaired asset is presumably based on a comparison of expected future cash flows from alternative courses of action and is essentially a capital investment decision. The Board further presumes that no entity would decide to continue to use an asset unless that alternative was expected to produce more in terms of expected future cash flows or service potential than the alternative of selling it and reinvesting the proceeds. Mr. Northcutt believes that the Board's rationale demonstrates that the entity-specific cash flows are not the same as the market-based cash flows used to estimate fair value and that both sets of cash flows must be determined.

Mr. Northcutt believes that due to the nature of the long-lived assets subject to this Statement, quoted market prices in active markets will rarely be available and that the use of other valuation techniques will be required. Prices of similar assets, rental cash flows, and appraisals may produce reasonable fair value estimates for certain assets, such as an office building, but are unavailable for unique assets, such as manufacturing facilities or industrial equipment. Mr. Northcutt believes that cash flows used to estimate fair value must be based on some notion of "market" cash flows. He doubts the operationality of this Statement when the only available information is an entity's own cash flows expected from an asset's use and disposition. In Mr. Northcutt's view, a measure that uses entity-specific assumptions about an asset's expected future cash flows does not represent fair value.

Mr. Northcutt disagrees with the use of a fair value measurement that will yield variable results for identical assets. For example, consider two identical assets subject to different depreciation methods that result in different carrying amounts. It is possible that one asset could fail the impairment test in paragraph 6 of this Statement, whereas the other asset could pass, with the difference attributed solely to management's choice of a depreciation method. One asset would be written down to its fair value in accordance with paragraphs 7-11, whereas the other asset would remain at its carrying amount. Mr. Northcutt does not believe that those significantly different outcomes for the two assets, solely based on the depreciation method that was selected, produce decision-useful information for comparing the performance of different entities. In Mr. Northcutt's view, an asset's depreciation method does not influence management's decision to continue to use the asset or to dispose of the asset. He believes that if the recoverable cost approach was permitted, the resulting write-down would appropriately reflect a depreciation "catch-up" adjustment and that future depreciation would be based on the asset's new recoverable cost.

Mr. Northcutt also disagrees with this Statement's requirement that long-lived assets to be disposed of that are not covered by Opinion 30 be measured at the lower of carrying amount or fair value less cost to sell. Consistent with his view on assets to be held and used, Mr. Northcutt believes that a long-lived asset to be disposed of also should be written down to its recoverable cost—its net realizable value. In his view, net realizable value is a market value notion because it represents the net proceeds expected to be received when an asset is sold. The only difference between the fair value less cost to sell measure and the net realizable value measure is the consideration of the time value of money. The fair value less cost to sell measure requires that the expected net proceeds be discounted.

The Board decided to include assets to be disposed of in the scope of this Statement to preclude an entity from avoiding recognition of a larger fair value impairment loss by declaring an impaired asset as held for disposal and writing it down to its net realizable value. That decision illustrates that the measurements of impaired assets and assets to be disposed of are interrelated. Mr. Northcutt agrees that the measurements are interrelated but believes that the appropriate measure for an impaired asset is recoverable cost and, therefore, the appropriate measure for an asset to be disposed of is net realizable value.

Furthermore, Mr. Northcutt believes that measuring assets to be disposed of at the lower of carrying amount or fair value less cost to sell will not produce the best decision-useful information for users of financial statements because that measure usually results in a higher current-period loss and higher future-period income. According to paragraph 17, the carrying amount of an asset to be disposed of must be adjusted each reporting period for all revisions to the estimate of fair value less cost to sell. If the estimate of future net proceeds does not change, the passage of time will result in the carrying amount of the asset being adjusted to reflect the time value of money by a credit to income. Mr. Northcutt believes that a present decision to dispose of an asset at a loss should not result in income in future periods.

Appendix A

BACKGROUND INFORMATION AND BASIS FOR CONCLUSIONS

CONTENTS

Appendix A

BACKGROUND INFORMATION AND BASIS FOR CONCLUSIONS

Introduction

36. This appendix summarizes considerations that Board members deemed significant in reaching the conclusions in this Statement. It includes reasons for accepting certain approaches and rejecting others. Individual Board members gave greater weight to some factors than to others.

37. Accounting standards generally have not addressed when impairment losses for long-lived assets, identifiable intangibles, and goodwill related to those assets should be recognized or how those losses should be measured. As a result, practice has

been diverse. This Statement provides accounting guidance for the recognition and measurement of impairment losses for long-lived assets, certain identifiable intangibles, and goodwill related to those assets to be held and used. This Statement also addresses the accounting for long-lived assets and certain identifiable intangibles to be disposed of.

Background Information

38. In July 1980, the Accounting Standards Executive Committee of the AICPA (AcSEC) sent the Board the AICPA Issues Paper, *Accounting for the Inability to Fully Recover the Carrying Amounts of Long Lived Assets.* AcSEC urged the Board to consider issues raised in the Issues Paper and to provide specific accounting guidance for the impairment of assets.

39. In 1980, the Financial Accounting Standards Advisory Council (FASAC) also discussed accounting for impairment of long-lived assets and advised the Board to continue its work on the conceptual framework project and other agenda topics before adding a project on impairment of assets. The Board agreed and in November 1980 decided not to add a project on impairment of assets to its agenda.

40. The FASB Emerging Issues Task Force (EITF) discussed the issue of impairment at its meetings in October 1984, December 1985, and February 1986. EITF members noted that there were divergent measurement practices in accounting for impairment of assets and a significant increase in the size and frequency of write-downs of long-lived assets. However, members were not able to reach a consensus on any of the impairment issues and urged the Board to add a project on impairment of assets to its agenda.

41. In a March 1985 survey about potential new agenda issues, FASAC members cited impairment of assets as the second most important issue for the Board to address. In September 1986, responding to a similar survey, most FASAC members supported adding a project on impairment to the FASB technical agenda. Many members stated that the problem of large, "surprise" write-downs of assets was significant enough to justify consideration by the Board.

42. Also in September 1986, the Committee on Corporate Reporting of the Financial Executives Institute (FEI) published the results of its "Survey on Unusual Charges," which was conducted at the request of the Board to assist in exploring current accounting practices for impairment of long-lived assets. The study indicated divergent reporting and measurement practices. In 1991, the FEI updated the survey and found that divergent reporting and measurement practices persisted.

43. In May 1987, the Institute of Management Accountants (IMA), formerly the National Association of Accountants, with the encouragement of the Board, approved a research study to examine accounting for impairment of assets. The IMA research report, *Impairments and Writeoffs of Long-Lived Assets,* published in May 1989, noted a variety of disclosure practices and a steady increase in the number of write-downs. The report suggested that authoritative guidance on the accounting for impairment of long-lived assets was needed.

44. The Board added a project to its agenda in November 1988 to address accounting for the impairment of long-lived assets and identifiable intangibles. A task force was formed in May 1989 to assist with the preparation of a Discussion Memorandum and to advise the Board. The FASB Discussion Memorandum, *Accounting for the Impairment of Long-Lived Assets and Identifiable Intangibles,* was issued in December 1990. The Board received 146 comment letters on the Discussion Memorandum, and 20 individuals and organizations presented their views at a public hearing that was held in August 1991. In January 1992, the Board began deliberating the issues at its public meetings. The Board also discussed those issues at a public meeting of the task force.

45. In November 1993, the Board issued an Exposure Draft, *Accounting for the Impairment of Long-Lived Assets.* The Board received 147 comment letters on the Exposure Draft, and 15 individuals and organizations presented their views at a public hearing that was held in May 1994. The Board reconsidered the proposals in the Exposure Draft at its public meetings. The Board also discussed possible revisions to the Exposure Draft at a public meeting of the task force.

46. In November 1994, the results of a field test of the Exposure Draft were published in an FASB Special Report, *Results of the Field Test of the Exposure Draft on Accounting for the Impairment of Long-Lived Assets.* The field test was conducted jointly by the Asset Impairment Subcommittee of the Financial Executives Institute's Committee on Corporate Re-

porting and the FASB. Ten entities participated in the field test by completing a comprehensive questionnaire. That questionnaire asked participants to detail the accounting policies and procedures used in the recognition and measurement of previous impairment losses and adjustments to the carrying amounts of assets to be disposed of. The questionnaire also asked what the effects would have been had the provisions of the Exposure Draft been applied to the same losses and adjustments. The field test results were considered by the Board during its redeliberations of the issues addressed by this Statement.

Scope

47. The original scope of the project was limited to accounting for the impairment of long-lived assets and identifiable intangibles. The Discussion Memorandum did not address accounting for goodwill, long-lived assets to be disposed of, or depreciation. It also did not address joint or common costs, cash flow estimation techniques, or discounting. It did, however, invite comments on the tentative decision to exclude goodwill, assets to be disposed of, and depreciation from the scope of the project. Based on comments received, the Board decided to include goodwill related to impaired assets in the scope of the Exposure Draft and this Statement. It concluded that long-lived assets and identifiable intangibles could not be tested for impairment without also considering the goodwill arising from the acquisition of those assets. The Board also decided that accounting for long-lived assets and identifiable intangibles to be disposed of should be included in the scope of the Exposure Draft and this Statement. In the Board's view, if those assets were not addressed, an entity could potentially avoid the recognition of an impairment loss for assets otherwise subject to an impairment write-down by declaring that those assets are held for sale.

48. The Board decided not to expand the scope of the project to include depreciation. The choice of depreciation method and estimates of useful life and salvage value can have an impact on whether an impairment exists and, when it does, the amount. The Board believes that an asset's depreciation method, estimated useful life, and estimated salvage value should be reviewed periodically and should be changed if current estimates are significantly different from previous estimates. Paragraph 32 of Opinion 20 addresses the accounting for changes in the method of depreciation; paragraph 10 of Opinion 20 addresses the accounting for changes in estimates.

The Board agreed that a review of depreciation policies is necessary when considering impairment and included reference to that review in paragraph 6 of this Statement.

49. The Board believes that an impairment condition—the inability to recover fully the carrying amount of an asset—is different from the need to review an asset's depreciation method and estimates of useful life and salvage value. As stated in paragraph 5 of ARB No. 43, Chapter 9C, "Emergency Facilities: Depreciation, Amortization and Income Taxes," depreciation accounting is "a system of accounting which aims to distribute the cost or other basic value of tangible capital assets, less salvage (if any), over the estimated useful life of the unit (which may be a group of assets) in a systematic and rational manner. It is a process of allocation, not of valuation." It is important to recognize that depreciation accounting is used to distribute or allocate asset carrying amounts that are recoverable. Perhaps the period of recovery may be longer or shorter than previously estimated. Perhaps an alternative depreciation method may be more appropriate. Yet, in using depreciation accounting, it is inherently assumed that the carrying amount of the asset will be recovered.

50. This Statement does not apply to financial instruments, long-term customer relationships of a financial institution (for example, core deposit intangibles and credit cardholder intangibles), mortgage and other servicing rights, deferred policy acquisition costs, or deferred tax assets. Financial instruments (including investments in equity securities accounted for under the cost or equity method), mortgage servicing rights, and other servicing rights are excluded from this Statement because they are under study in other agenda projects. This Statement does not apply to core deposit intangibles and credit cardholder intangibles because they have characteristics that make their measurements similar to measurements that are used for financial instruments.

51. The Board chose not to include accounting for leases in the scope of the Exposure Draft because FASB Statement No. 13, *Accounting for Leases,* discusses leases in detail. Most respondents who commented on the treatment of leases in the Exposure Draft suggested that the scope should include all capital leases of lessees, and the Board agreed to include those leases in this Statement. The Board also agreed that assets of lessors subject to operating leases are within the scope of this Statement. The Board did not include deferred tax assets in the scope

of this Statement because they are addressed in FASB Statement No. 109, *Accounting for Income Taxes.*

52. The Exposure Draft would not have applied to assets whose accounting is prescribed by FASB Statement No. 60, *Accounting and Reporting by Insurance Enterprises.* In part, Statement 60 addresses the accounting by insurance enterprises for deferred policy acquisition costs and real estate investments. Several respondents questioned whether that scope exclusion applied to both of those types of assets. The Board intended to exclude only deferred policy acquisition costs. Deferred policy acquisition costs are often considered to be related to other assets and liabilities of insurance enterprises, and as a result, the accounting for those costs is unique to the insurance industry. Statement 60 and FASB Statement No. 97, *Accounting and Reporting by Insurance Enterprises for Certain Long-Duration Contracts and for Realized Gains and Losses from the Sale of Investments,* address the impairment of those costs. Therefore, the Board concluded that deferred policy acquisition costs, but not real estate investments or other assets covered by Statement 60, should be excluded from the scope of this Statement. The Board also decided to exclude from the scope of this Statement assets addressed in Statements that apply to certain specialized industries, specifically the record and music, motion picture, broadcasting, and software industries.

53. This Statement applies to long-lived assets and certain identifiable intangibles to be disposed of that are not covered by Opinion 30. The Board decided not to reconsider the conclusions of Opinion 30 because it did not wish to undertake an examination of all of the issues contained in that Opinion.

54. The Board decided to include impairment of regulatory assets in the scope of this Statement. The Board concluded that a distinction should be made between a regulated enterprise's plant and other fixed assets that any other enterprise would recognize as assets and its regulatory assets that any other enterprise would charge to expense as incurred.

55. Some respondents to the Exposure Draft suggested that not-for-profit organizations should not be included in the scope of the Statement because some assets may not have independent cash flows at a level lower than the total organization. The Board has provided further guidance in paragraph 10 to address those assets, whether held by business enterprises or

by not-for-profit organizations. Accordingly, not-for-profit organizations are included in the scope of this Statement.

When to Test for Impairment

56. Respondents to the Discussion Memorandum stressed that requiring a specific periodic impairment test for all assets would be unnecessary and cost prohibitive. They favored limiting impairment testing to when events or changes in circumstances indicate that an impairment test is necessary. They suggested that the impairment indicators contained in the Discussion Memorandum, which had been suggested in the Issues Paper, would be useful examples of events or changes in circumstances that indicate that an impairment assessment is warranted.

57. The Board concluded in the Exposure Draft that management has the responsibility to consider whether an asset is impaired but that to test each asset each period would be too costly. Existing information and analyses developed for management review of the entity and its operations generally will be the principal evidence needed to determine when an impairment exists. Indicators of impairment, therefore, are useful examples of events or changes in circumstances that suggest that the recoverability of the carrying amount of an asset should be assessed. The examples in paragraph 5 of this Statement were derived from the following list in the Issues Paper:

a. Reduction in the extent to which a plant is used
b. Dramatic change in the manner in which an asset is used
c. Substantial drop in the market value of an asset
d. Change in law or environment
e. Forecast showing lack of long-term profitability
f. Costs in excess of amount originally expected to acquire or construct an asset.

58. The Board considered suggestions that the list of impairment indicators should be definitive, that is, the existence of one or more indicators should determine whether an impairment exists. Because Board members were convinced that the list could never be complete, they concluded that it would best serve as examples of events or changes in circumstances that might suggest an impairment loss exists. The Board sought additional examples of impairment indicators in its review of comment letters and public hearing testimony on the Exposure Draft and during meetings with constituent organizations. Some respondents suggested that the list of examples should ad-

dress events or changes in circumstances that might suggest an impairment loss exists when past events or changes in circumstances also are considered, such as a current period operating or cash flow loss combined with a history of operating or cash flow losses. Other respondents suggested that an impairment assessment is warranted if a regulator excludes a cost from a regulated enterprise's rate base. The Board agreed and incorporated additional examples into paragraph 5 of this Statement, such as a significant physical change in an asset, an adverse action or assessment by a regulator, and a current period operating or cash flow loss combined with a history of operating or cash flow losses.

Recognition of an Impairment Loss

59. The Board considered the alternative recognition criteria identified and discussed in the Discussion Memorandum and used in practice: economic impairment, permanent impairment, and probability of impairment.

60. The economic criterion calls for loss recognition whenever the carrying amount of an asset exceeds the asset's fair value. It is an approach that would require continuous evaluation for impairment of long-lived assets similar to the ongoing lower-of-cost-or-market measurement of inventory. The economic criterion is based on the measurement of the asset. Using the same measure for recognition and measurement assures consistent outcomes for identical fact situations. However, the economic criterion presupposes that a fair value is available for every asset on an ongoing basis. Otherwise, an event or change in circumstance would be needed to determine which assets needed to be measured and in which period. Some respondents to the Discussion Memorandum indicated that the results of a measurement should not be sufficient reason to trigger recognition of an impairment loss. They favored using either the permanence or probability criterion to avoid recognition of write-downs that might result from measurements reflecting only temporary market fluctuations.

61. The permanence criterion calls for loss recognition when the carrying amount of an asset exceeds the asset's fair value and the condition is judged to be permanent. Some respondents to the Discussion Memorandum indicated that a loss must be permanent rather than temporary before recognition should occur. In their view, a high hurdle for recognition of an impairment loss is necessary to prevent premature write-offs of productive assets. Others stated that re-

quiring the impairment loss to be permanent makes the criterion too restrictive and virtually impossible to apply with any reliability. Still others noted that the permanence criterion is not practical to implement; in their view, requiring management to assess whether a loss is permanent goes beyond management's ability to apply judgment and becomes a requirement for management to predict future events with certainty.

62. The probability criterion, initially presented in the Issues Paper, calls for loss recognition based on the approach taken in FASB Statement No. 5, *Accounting for Contingencies.* Using that approach, an impairment loss would be recognized when it is deemed probable that the carrying amount of an asset cannot be fully recovered. Some respondents to the Discussion Memorandum stated that assessing the probability that an impairment loss has occurred is preferable to other recognition alternatives because it is already required by Statement 5. Most respondents to the Discussion Memorandum supported the probability criterion because, in their view, it best provides for management judgment.

63. A practical approach to implementing a probability criterion was presented at the public hearing on the Discussion Memorandum. That approach uses the sum of the expected future cash flows (undiscounted and without interest charges) to determine whether an asset is impaired. If that sum exceeds the carrying amount of an asset, the asset is not impaired. If the carrying amount of the asset exceeds that sum, the asset is impaired and the recognition of a new cost basis for the impaired asset is triggered.

64. The Exposure Draft included an undiscounted cash flows recognition criterion, and most respondents supported that criterion. Some respondents expressed concern about situations where small differences in cash flow estimates might result in a large loss being recognized in one instance and no loss being recognized in another. Other respondents suggested that the recognition criteria should be more flexible; management should be able to choose the recognition criteria to be used in impairment situations. Some respondents suggested that fair value be used for both recognition and measurement purposes. Still other respondents suggested using the present value of expected future cash flows discounted at the entity's incremental borrowing rate for both recognition and measurement purposes.

65. The Board affirmed its conclusion that an impairment loss should be recognized whenever the

sum of the expected future cash flows (undiscounted and without interest charges) resulting from the use and ultimate disposal of an asset is less than the carrying amount of the asset. The Board believes that the approach is consistent with the definition of an impairment as the inability to fully recover the carrying amount of an asset and with a basic presumption underlying a statement of financial position that the reported carrying amounts of assets should, at a minimum, be recoverable.

66. The Board adopted the recoverability test that uses the sum of the expected future cash flows (undiscounted and without interest charges) as an acceptable approach for identifying when an impairment loss must be recognized. In many cases, it may be relatively easy to conclude that the amount will equal or exceed the carrying amount of an asset without incurring the cost of projecting cash flows.

67. The recognition approach adopted by the Board must be operational in an area of significant uncertainty. The Board's approach requires the investigation of potential impairments on an exception basis. An asset must be tested for recoverability only if there is reason to believe that the asset is impaired as evidenced by events or changes in circumstances. If that test indicates that the sum of the expected future cash flows (undiscounted and without interest charges) to be generated by the asset is insufficient to recover the carrying amount of the asset, the asset is considered impaired. That approach uses information that the Board believes is generally available to an entity.

68. The Board acknowledges that some object to this approach because they believe that relatively minor changes in cash flow estimates, which may be imprecise, could result in significant differences in the carrying amount of an asset. The Board considered that objection in evaluating whether it was appropriate to use undiscounted cash flows as a recoverability test. The Board concluded that the potential usefulness, from a practical standpoint, of that test was sufficient to overcome that objection.

Measurement of an Impairment Loss

69. An impairment loss is not recognized unless the carrying amount of an asset is no longer recoverable using a test of recoverability—the sum of the expected future cash flows (undiscounted and without interest charges). When an asset's carrying amount is not recoverable using that measure, the Board be-

lieves that a new cost basis for the impaired asset is appropriate. The Board concluded that a decision to continue to operate rather than sell an impaired asset is economically similar to a decision to invest in that asset and, therefore, the impaired asset should be measured at its fair value. The amount of the impairment loss should be the amount by which the carrying amount of the impaired asset exceeds the fair value of the asset. That fair value then becomes the asset's new cost basis.

70. When an entity determines that expected future cash flows from using an asset will not result in the recovery of the asset's carrying amount, it must decide whether to sell the asset and use the proceeds for an alternative purpose or to continue to use the impaired asset in its operations. The decision presumably is based on a comparison of expected future cash flows from those alternative courses of action and is essentially a capital investment decision. In either alternative, proceeds from the sale of the impaired asset are considered in the capital investment decision. Consequently, a decision to continue to use the impaired asset is equivalent to a new asset purchase decision, and a new basis of fair value is appropriate.

71. Some respondents to the Exposure Draft disagreed with using fair value to measure impairment. The Board considered those views, but it concluded that the fair value of an impaired asset is the best measure of the cost of continuing to use that asset because it is consistent with management's decision process. Presumably, no entity would decide to continue to use an asset unless that alternative was expected to produce more in terms of expected future cash flows or service potential than the alternative of selling it and reinvesting the proceeds. The Board also believes that using fair value to measure the amount of an impairment loss is not a departure from the historical cost principle. Rather, it is a consistent application of principles practiced elsewhere in the current system of accounting whenever a cost basis for a newly acquired asset must be determined.

72. The Board believes that fair value is an easily understood notion. It is the amount at which an asset could be bought or sold in a current transaction between willing parties. The fair value measure is basic to economic theory and is grounded in the reality of the marketplace. Fair value estimates are readily available in published form for many assets, especially machinery and equipment. For some assets, multiple, on-line database services provide up-to-

date market price information. Estimates of fair value also are subject to periodic verification whenever assets are exchanged in transactions between willing parties.

73. The Exposure Draft included an approach for measuring an asset's fair value that was based on paragraph 13 of FASB Statement No. 15, *Accounting by Debtors and Creditors for Troubled Debt Restructurings*. That approach was not clear about whether the results of valuation techniques could be considered only if selling prices in an active market for similar assets did not exist. Further, some respondents to the Exposure Draft indicated that assumptions developed from selling prices for similar assets are sometimes included in valuation techniques that also consider expected future cash flows. The Board decided to include an approach for measuring the fair value of an asset that would be broadly applicable to other assets in addition to those covered by this Statement.

74. The Board concluded that quoted market prices in active markets are the most objective and relevant measure of an asset's fair value and should be used, if available. If quoted market prices are not available, the estimate of fair value should be based on the best information available in the circumstances. The estimate of fair value should consider prices for similar assets and the results of valuation techniques to the extent available in the circumstances. Valuation techniques for measuring an asset covered by this Statement should be consistent with the objective of measuring fair value and should incorporate assumptions that market participants would use in their estimates of the asset's fair value.

75. The Board recognizes that there may be practical problems in determining the fair value of certain types of assets covered by this Statement that do not have quoted market prices in active markets. While the objective of using a valuation technique is to determine fair value, the Board acknowledges that in some circumstances, the only information available without undue cost and effort will be the entity's expected future cash flows from the asset's use.

Alternative Measures of an Impairment Loss

76. The Board considered approaches other than fair value that also are possible within the historical cost framework for determining the amount of an impairment loss. Those approaches are recoverable cost and recoverable cost including interest.

Recoverable Cost

77. Recoverable cost is measured as the sum of the undiscounted future cash flows expected to be generated over the life of an asset. For example, if an asset has a carrying amount of $1,000,000, a remaining useful life of 5 years, and expected future cash flows over the 5 years of $180,000 per year, the recoverable cost would be $900,000 (5 × $180,000), and the impairment loss would be $100,000 ($1,000,000 − $900,000).

78. The Board did not adopt recoverable cost as the measure of an impairment loss. Proponents of the recoverable cost measure believe that impairment is the result of the inability to recover the carrying amount of an asset. They do not view the decision to retain an impaired asset as an investment decision; rather, they view the recognition of an impairment loss as an adjustment to the historical cost of the asset. They contend that recoverable cost measured by the sum of the undiscounted expected future cash flows is the appropriate carrying amount for an impaired asset and the amount on which the impairment loss should be determined.

79. Proponents of the recoverable cost measure do not believe that the fair value of an asset is a relevant measure unless a transaction or other event justifies a new basis for the asset at fair value. They do not view impairment to be such an event.

80. Some proponents of the recoverable cost measure assert that measuring an impaired asset at either fair value or a discounted present value results in an inappropriate understatement of net income in the period of the impairment and an overstatement of net income in subsequent periods. The Board did not agree with that view. Board members noted that measuring an impaired asset at recoverable cost could result in reported losses in future periods if the entity had incurred debt directly associated with the asset.

81. Proponents of the recoverable cost measure view interest cost as a period cost that should not be included as part of an impairment loss regardless of whether the interest is an accrual of actual debt costs or the result of discounting expected future cash flows using a debt rate.

Recoverable Cost including Interest

82. Recoverable cost including interest generally is measured as either (a) the sum of the undiscounted expected future cash flows including interest costs on actual debt or (b) the present value of expected future cash flows discounted at some annual rate such as a debt rate. For example, if an asset has a carrying value of $1,000,000, a remaining useful life of 5 years, expected future cash flows (excluding interest) over the 5 years of $180,000 per year, and a debt rate of 6 percent, recoverable cost including interest would be $758,225 (4.21236 × $180,000), and the impairment loss would be $241,775 ($1,000,000 − $758,225).

83. The Board did not adopt recoverable cost including interest as an appropriate measure of an impairment loss. Proponents of the recoverable cost including interest measure agree that the time value of money should be considered in the measure, but they view the time value of money as an element of cost recovery rather than as an element of fair value. Proponents believe that the measurement objective for an impaired asset should be recoverable cost and not fair value. However, they believe that interest should be included as a carrying cost in determining the recoverable cost. To them, the objective is to recognize the costs (including the time value of money) that are not recoverable as an impairment loss and to measure an impaired asset at the costs that are recoverable.

84. Because of the difficulties in attempting to associate actual debt with individual assets, proponents of the recoverable cost including interest measure believe that the present value of expected future cash flows using a debt rate such as an incremental borrowing rate is a practical means of achieving their measurement objective. They recognize that an entity that has no debt may be required to discount expected future cash flows. They believe that the initial investment decision would have included consideration of the debt or equity cost of funds.

85. The Board believes that use of the recoverable cost including interest measure would result in different carrying amounts for essentially the same impaired assets because they are owned by different entities that have different debt capacities. The Board does not believe that discounting expected future cash flows using a debt rate is an appropriate measure for determining the value of those assets.

Different Measures for Different Impairment Losses

86. The Board also considered but did not adopt an alternative approach that would require different measures for different impairments. At one extreme, an asset might be impaired because depreciation assumptions were not adjusted appropriately. At the other extreme, an asset might be impaired because of a major change in its use. Some believe that the first situation is similar to a depreciation "catch-up" adjustment and that an undiscounted measure should be used. They believe that the second situation is similar to a new investment in an asset with the same intended use and that a fair value measure should be used. The Board was unable to develop a workable distinction between the first and second situations that would support the use of different measures.

Cash Flows

87. The Board recognizes that judgments, estimates, and projections will be required for measuring impaired assets and that precise information about the relevant attributes of those assets seldom will be available. Partly as a result, the Board decided that the measurement guidance provided in this Statement should be general.

88. The Board agreed that one method of obtaining an appropriate measure in some situations is to project expected future cash flows and to discount those cash flows at a current rate that considers the risks inherent in those cash flows. The Board decided not to address issues about how to project cash flows or what interest rate should be associated with those cash flows. The Board currently has a separate project on present-value-based measurements in accounting on its agenda to consider the latter issue.

89. The Board acknowledges that the language in paragraph 9 allows the use of either the single most likely estimate of expected future cash flows or a range that considers the probability of the possible outcomes. The Board concluded that it would be more useful to permit entities to use cash flow estimation techniques that are currently available and to allow for the use of new techniques that may be developed in the future rather than to prescribe specific techniques in this Statement.

90. The Board considered imposing specific limits on assumptions used to estimate expected future cash flows, such as limiting volume and price assumptions to current levels. The Board decided not to include limits on assumptions because specific limits may be inconsistent with the assumptions that market participants would use in their estimates of an asset's fair value.

91. The Exposure Draft used the term *net* cash flows in certain instances to describe the expected future cash flows used to test the recoverability of an asset in paragraph 6 and to measure an impaired asset in paragraph 7. In this Statement, the reference to *net* cash flows has been eliminated to be consistent with descriptions of cash flows used to determine the fair value of an asset in other pronouncements. The Board's intended meaning of *net*—future cash inflows expected to be generated by an asset should be reduced by the future cash outflows expected to be necessary to obtain those inflows—has been added to paragraph 6 of this Statement.

Discount Rate

92. If quoted market prices for an asset are not available, paragraph 7 of this Statement allows for the consideration of the results of valuation techniques in estimating the fair value of the asset. If such techniques are used, the estimate of fair value may be based on the present value of expected future cash flows using a discount rate commensurate with the risks involved.

93. The discount rate commensurate with the risks involved is a rate that would be required for a similar investment with like risks. That rate is the asset-specific rate of return expected from the market—the return the entity would expect if it were to choose an equally risky investment as an alternative to operating the impaired asset. For some entities that have a well-developed capital budgeting process, the hurdle rate used to make investment decisions might be useful in estimating that rate.

94. Several respondents to the Exposure Draft said that disclosure of the discount rate used to determine the present value of the estimated expected future cash flows should not be required. The Board decided that disclosure of the discount rate without disclosure of the other assumptions used in estimating expected future cash flows generally would not be

meaningful to financial statement users. Therefore, this Statement does not require disclosure of the discount rate.

Grouping for Recognition and Measurement of an Impairment Loss

95. The Board concluded that for testing whether an asset is impaired and for measuring the amount of the impairment loss, assets should be grouped at the lowest level for which there are identifiable cash flows that are largely independent of the cash flows generated by other asset groups. The issue underlying the grouping of assets is when, if ever, it is appropriate to offset the unrealized losses on one asset with the unrealized gains on another. In the Board's view, for determining whether to recognize and how to measure an impairment loss, assets should be grouped when they are used together; that is, when they are part of the same group of assets and are used together to generate joint cash flows.

96. In deciding the appropriate grouping of assets for impairment consideration, the Board reviewed a series of examples that demonstrated the subjectivity of the grouping issue. Varying facts and circumstances introduced in the cases inevitably justified different groupings. Although most respondents to the Discussion Memorandum generally favored grouping at the lowest level for which there are identifiable cash flows for recognition and measurement of an impairment loss, determining that lowest level requires considerable judgment.

97. The Board considered a case that illustrated the need for judgment in grouping assets for impairment. In that case, an entity operated a bus company that provided service under contract with a municipality that required minimum service on each of five separate routes. Assets devoted to serving each route and the cash flows from each route were discrete. One of the routes operated at a significant deficit that resulted in the inability to recover the carrying amounts of the dedicated assets. The Board concluded that the five bus routes would be an appropriate level at which to group assets to test for and measure impairment because the entity did not have the option to curtail any one bus route.

98. The Board concluded that the grouping issue requires significant management judgment within certain parameters. Those parameters are that the assets

should be grouped at the lowest level for which there are cash flows that are identifiable and that those cash flows should be largely independent of the cash flows of other groupings of assets.

99. Not-for-profit organizations that rely in part on contributions to maintain their assets may need to consider those contributions in determining the appropriate cash flows to compare with the carrying amount of an asset. Some respondents to the Exposure Draft stated that the recognition criteria in paragraph 6 would be problematic for many not-for-profit organizations because it may be difficult, if not impossible, for them to identify expected future cash flows with specific assets or asset groupings. In other cases, expected future cash flows can be identified with asset groups. However, if future unrestricted contributions to the organization as a whole are not considered, the sum of the expected future cash flows may be negative, or positive but less than the carrying amount of the asset. For example, the costs of administering a museum may exceed the admission fees charged, but the organization may fund the cash flow deficit with unrestricted contributions.

100. Other respondents indicated that similar difficulties would be experienced by business enterprises. For example, the cost of operating assets such as corporate headquarters or centralized research facilities may be funded by revenue-producing activities at lower levels of the enterprise. Accordingly, in limited circumstances, the lowest level of identifiable cash flows that are largely independent of other asset groups may be the entity level. The Board concluded that the recoverability test in paragraph 6 should be performed at the entity level if an asset does not have identifiable cash flows lower than the entity level. The cash flows used in the recoverability test should be reduced by the carrying amounts of the entity's other assets that are covered by this Statement to arrive at the cash flows expected to contribute to the recoverability of the asset being tested. Not-for-profit organizations should include unrestricted contributions to the organization as a whole that are a source of funds for the operation of the asset.

101. If an impairment write-down is not required, the entity should review the asset's depreciation method, estimated useful life, and estimated salvage value to determine if any adjustments are necessary. However, if the asset does not have any future service potential to the entity, it should be accounted for at the lower of carrying amount or fair value less cost to sell as if the asset had been abandoned or will be

disposed of. Paragraph 28 of FASB Concepts Statement No. 6, *Elements of Financial Statements,* defines service potential as "the scarce capacity to provide services or benefits to the entities that use them."

102. The Exposure Draft would have required entities that follow the successful efforts method of accounting prescribed by FASB Statement No. 19, *Financial Accounting and Reporting by Oil and Gas Producing Companies,* to group, for impairment purposes, those capitalized costs of an entity's wells and related equipment and facilities and the costs of related proved properties in the same manner as those costs are grouped, for amortization purposes, under paragraphs 30 and 35 of that Statement. That provision was included in the Exposure Draft so that entities that follow the successful efforts method of accounting would not need to group cash flows at a level lower than the level at which the applicable costs are being amortized. However, many respondents to the Exposure Draft objected to singling out the oil and gas industry for special grouping provisions. Although the Board agreed to delete that requirement in this Statement because there is no reason to provide an exception to the general grouping provision, the Board did not endorse the view of many respondents that oil and gas companies should group their assets in the same manner as those assets are managed or on a country-by-country basis. The Board concluded that all entities should group assets at the lowest level for which there are identifiable cash flows that are largely independent of the cash flows of other groups of assets.

103. The Board considered requests for a limited exception to the fair value measurement for impaired long-lived assets that are subject to nonrecourse debt. Some believe that the nonrecourse provision is effectively a put option for which the borrower has paid a premium. They believe that the impairment loss on an asset subject entirely to nonrecourse debt should be limited to the loss that would occur if the asset were put back to the lender.

104. The Board decided not to provide an exception for assets subject to nonrecourse debt. The recognition of an impairment loss and the recognition of a gain on the extinguishment of debt are separate events, and each event should be recognized in the period in which it occurs. The Board believes that the recognition of an impairment loss should be based on the measurement of the asset at its fair value and that the existence of nonrecourse debt should not influence that measurement. The Board further believes

that a gain on the extinguishment of debt should be recognized in the period in which it occurs and that it should continue to be classified as an extraordinary gain in accordance with FASB Statement No. 4, *Reporting Gains and Losses from Extinguishment of Debt.*

Restoration of Impairment Losses

105. The Board considered whether to prohibit or require restoration of previously recognized impairment losses. It decided that an impairment loss should result in a new cost basis for the impaired asset. That new cost basis puts the asset on an equal basis with other assets that are not impaired. In the Board's view, the new cost basis should not be adjusted subsequently other than as provided under the current accounting model for prospective changes in the depreciation estimates and method and for further impairment losses. Most respondents to the Exposure Draft agreed with the Board's decision that restoration should be prohibited.

Goodwill

106. The Exposure Draft proposed that goodwill identified with potentially impaired long-lived assets and identifiable intangibles be combined with those assets when testing for impairment. If the test indicates that an impairment exists, the carrying amount of the identified goodwill would be eliminated before making any reduction of the carrying amounts of impaired long-lived assets and identifiable intangibles. Several respondents to the Exposure Draft objected to the allocation of goodwill to the asset groups on the basis that goodwill is a residual that results from a business combination accounted for under the purchase accounting method. Some respondents suggested that the residual should be evaluated on its own merits, without describing how that evaluation might be accomplished. Others said that goodwill should be evaluated apart from long-lived assets and identifiable intangibles. They suggested excluding goodwill completely from the scope of this Statement, leaving all goodwill subject to the provisions of APB Opinion No. 17, *Intangible Assets.*

107. The Board decided to retain the provisions of the Exposure Draft to include goodwill identified with a potentially impaired asset with the carrying amount of that asset in performing the impairment test in paragraph 6 and in measuring an impairment loss in accordance with paragraph 7. The amount of the impairment loss should equal the difference be-

tween an asset's carrying amount, including identified goodwill, and the asset's fair value. If the carrying amount of an impaired asset, excluding identified goodwill, exceeds the asset's fair value, the identified goodwill should be eliminated and the asset should be written down to its fair value. If the fair value of an impaired asset exceeds the asset's carrying amount, excluding identified goodwill, the identified goodwill should be written down to an amount equal to that excess. The Board concluded that in the absence of evidence to support a more appropriate association, goodwill should be attributed to long-lived assets and identifiable intangibles that were acquired in a business combination using a pro rata allocation based on the relative fair values of those assets at the date of acquisition. Goodwill that is not identified with impaired assets should continue to be accounted for under Opinion 17.

Reporting and Disclosure of Impairment Losses

108. The Board considered the alternative ways described in the Discussion Memorandum for reporting an impairment loss: reporting the loss as a component of continuing operations, reporting the loss as a special item outside continuing operations, or separate reporting of the loss without specifying the classification in the statement of operations. The Board concluded that an impairment loss should be reported as a component of income from continuing operations before income taxes for entities that present an income statement and in the statement of activities of a not-for-profit organization. If no impairment had occurred, an amount equal to the impairment loss would have been charged to operations over time through the allocation of depreciation or amortization. That depreciation or amortization charge would have been reported as part of continuing operations of a business enterprise or as an expense in the statement of activities of a not-for-profit organization. Further, an asset that is subject to a reduction in its carrying amount due to an impairment loss will continue to be used in operations. The Board concluded that an impairment loss does not have characteristics that warrant special treatment, for instance, as an extraordinary item.

109. The Board believes that financial statements should include information on impairment losses that would be most useful to users. After considering responses to the Exposure Draft, the Board concluded that an entity that recognizes an impairment loss should describe the assets impaired and the facts and circumstances leading to the impairment; disclose

the amount of the loss and how fair value was determined; disclose the caption in the income statement or the statement of activities in which the loss is aggregated unless that loss has been presented as a separate caption or reported parenthetically on the face of the statement; and, if applicable, disclose the business segment(s) affected. The Board decided not to require further disclosures, such as the assumptions used to estimate expected future cash flows and the discount rate used when fair value is estimated by discounting expected future cash flows.

Early Warning Disclosures

110. In 1985, the AICPA established a task force to consider the need for improved disclosures about risks and uncertainties that affect companies and the manner in which they do business. In July 1987, the task force published *Report of the Task Force on Risks and Uncertainties,* which concluded that companies should make early warning disclosures in their financial statements. In December 1994, AcSEC issued AICPA Statement of Position 94-6, *Disclosure of Certain Significant Risks and Uncertainties.* That SOP requires entities to include in their financial statements disclosures about (a) the nature of operations, (b) the use of estimates in the preparation of financial statements, (c) certain significant estimates, and (d) current vulnerability due to certain concentrations.

111. The Board observed that early warning disclosures would be useful for certain potential impairments. However, most respondents to the Exposure Draft said that the Statement should not require early warning disclosures. The Board observed that SOP 94-6 uses essentially the same events or changes in circumstances as those in paragraph 5 of this Statement to illustrate when disclosures of certain significant estimates should be made for long-lived assets. Therefore, the Board concluded that it was not necessary for this Statement to require early warning disclosures.

Assets to Be Disposed Of

112. The Board agreed that accounting for long-lived assets and certain identifiable intangibles to be disposed of should be addressed by this Statement. In the Board's view, if those assets were not addressed, an entity could potentially avoid the recognition of an impairment loss for assets otherwise subject to an impairment write-down by declaring that those assets are held for sale. Existing guidance for assets to be disposed of that constitute a segment of a business is provided by Opinion 30. Some believe that Opinion 30 requires the use of a net realizable value measure because it anticipates a relatively short holding period for the assets to be disposed of. The last sentence of paragraph 15 of the Opinion states:

> In the usual circumstance, it would be expected that the plan of disposal would be carried out within a period of one year from the measurement date and that such projections of operating income or loss would not cover a period exceeding approximately one year. [Footnote reference omitted.]

113. The net realizable value measure of Opinion 30 seems to anticipate that the disposal of an asset will be completed within approximately one year and does not consider the time value of money. However, a measurement principle for assets to be disposed of that assumes a disposal period of one year or less often is not realistic. For example, concerns about environmental liabilities, such as remediation costs that must be incurred before legal title can be transferred, often extend the period of time necessary to dispose of an asset well beyond one year. The Board considered several alternative measures. For reasons similar to the conclusions reached for assets held for use, the Board concluded that the appropriate measure for assets to be disposed of is the lower of carrying amount or fair value less cost to sell. If the fair value of an asset is measured by the current market value or by using the current selling price for a similar asset, that fair value should be considered to be a current amount and that fair value and cost to sell should not be discounted. If the fair value of an asset is measured by discounting expected future cash flows and if the sale is expected to occur beyond one year, the cost to sell also should be discounted.

114. Opinion 30 applies to assets to be disposed of in a limited context. The Board realizes that potential inconsistencies might arise if fair value is used to measure impairment losses for assets held for use and net realizable value is used to measure certain assets to be disposed of. Several respondents to the Exposure Draft suggested that the Board consider the issues related to Opinion 30 in a separate project. Others suggested that the Board modify Opinion 30 to provide consistency between the provisions for disposal of a segment of a business and those for all other assets to be disposed of.

115. The Board considered amending Opinion 30 to change the lower of carrying amount or net realizable value measure to the lower of carrying amount or fair value less cost to sell measure. However, the Board did not wish to expand the scope of this Statement and undertake an examination of all the issues contained in Opinion 30 on the expected disposal of a segment of a business. Those issues include the calculation of operating results during the holding period, the presentation of operating results in the income statement, and the netting of operating income or loss with adjustments to the carrying amounts of assets held for disposal. The Board decided not to amend Opinion 30 and concluded that long-lived assets and certain identifiable intangibles to be disposed of that are not covered by that Opinion should be measured at the lower of carrying amount or fair value less cost to sell.

116. The Board concluded that the cost to sell an asset to be disposed of generally includes the incremental direct costs to transact the sale of the asset. Cost to sell is deducted from the fair value of an asset to be disposed of to arrive at the current value of the estimated net proceeds to be received from the asset's future sale. The Board decided that costs incurred during the holding period to protect or maintain an asset to be disposed of generally are excluded from the cost to sell an asset because those costs usually are not required to be incurred in order to sell the asset. However, the Board believes that costs required to be incurred under the terms of a contract for an asset's sale as a condition of the buyer's consummation of the sale should be included in determining the cost to sell an asset to be disposed of.

117. Some respondents to the Exposure Draft objected to the elimination of the last question and its interpretation of AICPA Accounting Interpretation 1, "Illustration of the Application of APB Opinion No. 30." Those respondents said that the Interpretation's guidance for disposals of assets that do not meet the requirements of Opinion 30 has been helpful in practice. Other respondents stated that the guidance was too permissive and agreed that it should be superseded. Interpretation 1 is not specific as to the grouping of assets to which it applies, is not clear in its definitions of gains and losses and holding period, and provides no guidance on how to distinguish a portion of a segment of a business from other assets.

118. Because of the ambiguities associated with the Interpretation, the Board concluded that it was not feasible to amend the Interpretation to conform its requirements to this Statement. The Board decided that the only practical solution was to supersede the last question and its interpretation of Interpretation 1 and that all long-lived assets and certain identifiable intangibles to be disposed of not covered by Opinion 30 should be covered by this Statement. The Board agreed that applying this Statement to assets not already covered by Opinion 30, leaving that Opinion unchanged, and superseding the portion of the Interpretation that specified another accounting treatment for a portion of a line of business to be disposed of would enhance reporting and disclosure consistency for assets to be disposed of.

119. This Statement addresses the measurement of long-lived assets and certain identifiable intangibles to be disposed of not covered by Opinion 30 and whether those assets should be depreciated (amortized) during the holding period. This Statement also provides guidance on the cost to sell an asset to be disposed of, including the determination of the cost to sell an asset when a contractual obligation for an asset's sale requires an entity to incur certain costs during the holding period. This Statement does not address the general issue of accounting for the results of operations of assets to be disposed of during the holding period.

120. In March 1994, the EITF began discussing EITF Issue No. 94-3, "Liability Recognition for Certain Employee Termination Benefits and Other Costs to Exit an Activity (including Certain Costs Incurred in a Restructuring)." The EITF completed its discussion of the issues in January 1995 after reaching a number of consensuses. Certain consensuses address the issue of when an entity should recognize a liability for costs, other than employee termination benefits, that are directly associated with a plan to exit an activity. In part, the consensuses establish certain criteria that must be met in order for an entity to recognize a liability for those costs and require the results of operations of an activity that will be exited to be recognized in the periods in which the operations occur. The Board believes that the consensuses provide useful guidance about the accounting for the results of operations of an asset to be disposed of when the planned disposal also involves an exit from an activity.

Depreciation of Assets to Be Disposed Of

121. The Board considered whether assets to be disposed of that are carried at the lower of carrying amount or fair value less cost to sell should be depreciated while they are held for disposal. Depreciation

is the systematic allocation of an asset's cost over the asset's service period. Some believe that depreciation accounting is inconsistent with the notion of assets to be disposed of and with the use of the lower of carrying amount or fair value less cost to sell measure for those assets. They believe that assets to be disposed of are equivalent to inventory and should not be depreciated. Others believe that all operating assets should be depreciated and that no exception should be made for operating assets held for disposal.

122. The Board concluded that assets to be disposed of covered by this Statement should not be depreciated during the period they are held. Because the assets will be recovered through sale rather than through operations, accounting for those assets is a process of valuation rather than allocation. An asset to be disposed of will not be reported at carrying amount but at the lower of carrying amount or fair value less cost to sell and fair value less cost to sell will be evaluated each period to determine if it has changed.

Goodwill Related to Assets to Be Disposed Of

123. Goodwill related to assets to be disposed of by an entity should be accounted for under the provisions of Opinion 17, paragraph 32, which states:

> Ordinarily goodwill and similar intangible assets cannot be disposed of apart from the enterprise as a whole. However, a large segment or separable group of assets of an acquired company or the entire acquired company may be sold or otherwise liquidated, and all or a portion of the unamortized cost of the goodwill recognized in the acquisition should be included in the cost of the assets sold.

Real Estate Development

124. The Exposure Draft proposed amending FASB Statements No. 66, *Accounting for Sales of Real Estate,* and No. 67, *Accounting for Costs and Initial Rental Operations of Real Estate Projects,* to change the lower of carrying amount or net realizable value measure to the lower of carrying amount or fair value less cost to sell measure. The Board initially decided to amend those Statements to conform the measurement of assets subject to those Statements with the measurement of assets to be disposed of.

125. Some real estate development organizations objected to the proposed amendments in the Exposure Draft. They questioned why the scope of a project on long-lived assets included real estate development. They argued that real estate development assets are more like inventory and, therefore, the lower of carrying amount or net realizable value measure is more relevant. They did not address, however, why that measure would be more appropriate for real estate inventory than the lower of cost or market measure required for inventory under paragraph 4 of ARB No. 43, Chapter 4, "Inventory Pricing."

126. Others disagreed with the inventory argument, asserting that although real estate development assets will eventually be disposed of, the provisions of the Exposure Draft would have required long-term real estate projects to recognize impairments far too frequently. They said that nearly all long-term projects, regardless of their overall profitability, would become subject to write-downs in their early stages of development, only to be reversed later in the life of the project due to revised estimates of fair value less cost to sell. The Board considered alternative approaches to measuring those real estate assets. The Board decided to apply the provisions of paragraphs 4-7 to land to be developed and projects under development and to apply paragraphs 15-17 to completed projects. The Board believes that assets under development are similar to assets held for use, whereas completed projects are clearly assets to be disposed of.

Regulated Enterprises

127. FASB Statement No. 71, *Accounting for the Effects of Certain Types of Regulation,* establishes the accounting model for certain rate-regulated enterprises. Because the rates of rate-regulated enterprises generally are designed to recover the costs of providing regulated services or products, those enterprises are usually able to recover the carrying amounts of their assets. Paragraph 10 of Statement 71 states that when a regulator excludes a cost from rates, "the carrying amount of any related asset shall be reduced to the extent that the asset has been impaired. Whether the asset has been impaired shall be judged the same as for enterprises in general" (footnote reference omitted). Statement 71 does not provide any guidance about when an impairment has, in fact, oc-

curred or about how to measure the amount of the impairment.

128. The Board considered whether the accounting for the impairment of long-lived assets and identifiable intangibles by rate-regulated enterprises that meet the criteria for applying Statement 71 should be the same as for enterprises in general. In March 1993, the EITF discussed incurred costs capitalized pursuant to the criteria of paragraph 9 of Statement 71. The EITF reached a consensus in EITF Issue No. 93-4, "Accounting for Regulatory Assets," that a cost that does not meet the asset recognition criteria in paragraph 9 of Statement 71 at the date the cost is incurred should be recognized as a regulatory asset when it does meet those criteria at a later date. The EITF also reached a consensus that the carrying amount of a regulatory asset should be reduced to the extent that the asset has been impaired with impairment judged the same as for enterprises in general; the provisions of this Statement nullify that consensus.

129. The Board considered several approaches to recognizing and measuring the impairment of long-lived assets and identifiable intangibles of rate-regulated enterprises. One approach the Board considered was to apply paragraph 7 of FASB Statement No. 90, *Regulated Enterprises—Accounting for Abandonments and Disallowances of Plant Costs,* to all assets of a regulated enterprise and not just to costs of recently completed plants. That paragraph requires that an impairment loss be recognized when a disallowance is probable and the amount can be reasonably estimated. If a regulator explicitly disallows a certain dollar amount of plant costs, an impairment loss should be recognized for that amount. If a regulator explicitly but indirectly disallows plant costs (for example, by excluding a return on investment on a portion of plant costs), an impairment loss should be recognized for the effective disallowance by estimating the expected future cash flows that have been disallowed as a result of the regulator's action and then computing the present value of those cash flows. That approach would recognize a probable disallowance as an impairment loss, the amount of the loss would be the discounted value of the expected future cash flows disallowed, and the discount rate would be the same as the rate of return used to estimate the expected future cash flows.

130. A second approach the Board considered was to supersede paragraph 7 of Statement 90 and apply this Statement's requirements to all plant costs. A disallowance would result in costs being excluded from the rate base. The recognition and measurement requirements of this Statement would be applied to determine whether an impairment loss would be recognized for financial reporting purposes.

131. A third approach the Board considered was to apply the general impairment provisions of this Statement to all assets of a regulated enterprise except for disallowances of costs of recently completed plants, which would continue to be covered by paragraph 7 of Statement 90. A disallowance would result in the exclusion of costs from the rate base. That disallowance would result in an impairment loss for financial reporting purposes if the costs disallowed relate to a recently completed plant. If the costs disallowed do not relate to a recently completed plant, the recognition and measurement requirements of this Statement would be applied to determine whether and how much of an impairment loss would be recognized for financial reporting purposes.

132. A fourth approach the Board considered was to apply the general impairment standard to all assets of a regulated enterprise except (a) regulatory assets that meet the criteria of paragraph 9 of Statement 71 and (b) costs of recently completed plants that are covered by paragraph 7 of Statement 90. Impairment of regulatory assets capitalized as a result of paragraph 9 of Statement 71 would be recognized whenever the criteria of that paragraph are no longer met.

133. The Board decided that the fourth approach should be used in accounting for the impairment of all assets of a rate-regulated enterprise. The Board amended paragraph 9 of Statement 71 to provide that a rate-regulated enterprise should charge a regulatory asset to earnings if and when that asset no longer meets the criteria in paragraph 9(a) and (b) of that Statement. The Board also amended paragraph 10 of Statement 71 to require that a rate-regulated enterprise recognize an impairment for the amount of costs excluded when a regulator excludes all or part of a cost from rates, even if the regulator allows the rate-regulated enterprise to earn a return on the remaining costs allowed.

134. The Board believes that because a rate-regulated enterprise is allowed to capitalize costs that enterprises in general would otherwise have charged to expense, the impairment criteria for those assets should be different from enterprises in general. The Board believes that symmetry should exist between the recognition of those assets and the subsequent

impairment of those assets. The Board could see no reason that an asset created as a result of regulatory action could not be impaired by the actions of the same regulator. Other assets that are not regulatory assets covered by Statement 71 or recently completed plant costs covered by Statement 90, such as older plants or other nonregulatory assets of a rate-regulated enterprise, would be covered by the general provisions of this Statement.

135. Some respondents to the Exposure Draft also asked that the Board clarify the accounting for previously disallowed costs that are subsequently allowed by a regulator. The Board decided that previously disallowed costs that are subsequently allowed by a regulator should be recorded as an asset, consistent with the classification that would have resulted had those costs initially been included in allowable costs. Thus, plant costs subsequently allowed should be classified as plant assets, whereas other costs (expenses) subsequently allowed should be classified as regulatory assets. The Board amended Statement 71 to reflect this decision. The Board decided to restore the original classification because there is no economic change to the asset—it is as if the regulator never had disallowed the cost. The Board determined that restoration of cost is allowed for rate-regulated enterprises in this situation, in contrast to other impairment situations, because the event requiring recognition of the impairment resulted from actions of an independent party and not management's own judgment or determination of recoverability.

Loan Impairment

136. In May 1993, the Board issued FASB Statement No. 114, *Accounting by Creditors for Impairment of a Loan,* which requires certain impaired loans to be measured based on the present value of expected future cash flows, discounted at the loan's effective interest rate, or as a practical expedient, at the loan's observable market price or the fair value of the collateral if the impaired loan is collateral dependent. Regardless of the measurement method, a creditor should measure impairment based on the fair value of the collateral when the creditor determines that foreclosure is probable. A creditor should consider estimated costs to sell, on a discounted basis, in the measure of impairment if those costs are expected to reduce the cash flows available to repay or otherwise satisfy the loan.

137. As suggested by one commentator to the Exposure Draft, the Board decided to amend Statement 15

to make the measurement of long-lived assets that are received in full satisfaction of a receivable and that will be sold consistent with the measurement of other long-lived assets under this Statement. The amendment requires that those assets be measured at fair value less cost to sell. The Board considered amending Statement 15 to address shares of stock or equity interests in long-lived assets that are received in full satisfaction of a receivable and that will be sold, but it determined that those items are outside the scope of this Statement.

138. Loans and long-lived assets are similar in that both are cash-generating assets that are subject to impairment. However, inherent differences between monetary and nonmonetary assets have resulted in different accounting treatments for them under the current reporting model.

Benefits and Costs

139. In establishing standards that are cost-effective, the Board must balance the diverse and often conflicting needs of constituents. The Board must conclude that a proposed standard will fulfill a need and that the costs it imposes, compared with possible alternatives, will be justified in relation to the overall benefits. There is no objective way to determine the costs to implement a standard and weigh them against the need to report consistent, comparable, relevant, and reliable information in the financial statements.

140. The Board determined that the information provided to users about impaired long-lived assets could be improved by increasing comparability in the recognition, measurement, display, and disclosure of impairment among entities. As discussed in FASB Concepts Statement No. 2, *Qualitative Characteristics of Accounting Information,* comparable financial information enables users to compare one entity's response to economic or other forces with the response of another. Therefore, to the extent that similar situations for impairment of long-lived assets are subject to the same requirements for recognition, measurement, display, and disclosure, financial reporting would be improved.

141. The Board believes that using the examples provided in paragraph 5 of events or changes in circumstances that might suggest a lack of recoverability will help maximize the use of information already known by management. Comment letters and public hearing testimony on the Discussion Memorandum

and the Exposure Draft clearly indicated that a requirement to specifically test each asset or group of assets for impairment each period would not be cost-effective.

142. Determination of an asset's fair value is required only if the asset's carrying amount, including identified goodwill, cannot be recovered. The Board believes that information necessary to perform the recoverability test is generally available from budgets and projections used by management in the decision-making process. Grouping assets at the lowest level of identifiable cash flows minimizes the offsetting of unrealized losses on one asset with the unrealized gains on another without requiring the complexities and costs of attributing interdependent cash flows to individual assets.

Effective Date and Transition

143. The Exposure Draft proposed that this Statement be effective for financial statements for fiscal years beginning after December 15, 1994. Some respondents requested a delay in the effective date to allow for a reasonable amount of time for entities to develop appropriate accounting policies and procedures. The Board agreed and decided that this Statement should be effective for financial statements for fiscal years beginning after December 15, 1995. The Board believes that the effective date provides adequate time for entities to make modifications to their procedures for reviewing long-lived assets and certain identifiable intangibles to conform with this Statement. The Board encourages early adoption of this Statement.

144. The recognition provisions of this Statement should be applied based on the facts and circumstances existing at the date of adoption. The continuing effect of events or changes in circumstances that occurred prior to the Statement's adoption should be considered when this Statement is initially applied. For example, the recoverability of an asset should be tested, in accordance with paragraph 6, on the date the Statement is adopted if that asset experienced a significant decrease in market value in a prior period and the market value of that asset has not recovered.

145. The Board considered requests to provide for a cumulative effect of a change in accounting principle adjustment for impairment losses that have not been previously recognized but are recognized at the time this Statement is implemented. The Board decided to prohibit the cumulative effect adjustment and retro-active application of this Statement's requirements for assets to be held and used because measurement of an impaired asset is based on estimates that are likely to change and management's assessment of events and circumstances is subjective and not readily subject to retroactive review. Impairment losses resulting from the application of this Statement should be reported in the period in which the recognition criteria are first applied and met.

146. The initial application of this Statement to assets that are being held for disposal at the date of adoption should be reported as the cumulative effect of a change in accounting principle, as described in Opinion 20. The pro forma effects of retroactive application (Opinion 20, paragraph 21) are not required to be disclosed. The Board concluded that the effect of applying this Statement to assets to be disposed of represents a change in measurement principle and does not affect when management identifies an asset for future disposal. The Board decided to prohibit retroactive application of this Statement's requirements for assets to be disposed of because that approach would require an entity to derive fair values for assets that had been disposed of in periods prior to the Statement's initial application.

Appendix B

REFERENCES TO PRONOUNCEMENTS

147. There are many references in the existing authoritative literature to impairment of assets and disposal of assets. Paragraphs 20-33 indicate the amendments to existing pronouncements. The Board decided that the scope of this Statement should exclude financial instruments, long-term customer relationships of a financial institution (for example, core deposit intangibles and credit cardholder intangibles), mortgage and other servicing rights, deferred policy acquisition costs, and deferred tax assets. The Board also decided that assets whose accounting is specifically addressed in Statements covering certain specialized industries, specifically the record and music, motion picture, broadcasting, and software industries, would remain subject to the various requirements of the existing literature for those assets. The following table indicates (a) certain pronouncements that refer to impairment of assets and disposal of assets and (b) which of those pronouncements will apply this Statement and which will continue to apply the existing requirements.

(This page intentionally left blank.)

Pronouncement	Title	Apply General Impairment Standard	Apply Existing Requirement	Existing Requirement Paragraph Number
APB Opinion No. 17	*Intangible Assets*			
	• Identifiable intangibles specifically excluded from the scope of this Statement (long-term customer relationships of a financial institution [for example, core deposit intangibles and credit card-holder intangibles])		X	31
	• All other identifiable intangibles	X		
	• Goodwill identified with assets included in the scope of this Statement	X		
	• Goodwill identified with assets not included in the scope of this Statement		X	31
APB Opinion No. 18	*The Equity Method of Accounting for Investments in Common Stock*		X	19(h) (as amended by this Statement)
APB Opinion No. 30	*Reporting the Results of Operations—Reporting the Effects of Disposal of a Segment of a Business, and Extraordinary, Unusual and Infrequently Occurring Events and Transactions*		X	14, 15
FASB Statement No. 7	*Accounting and Reporting by Development Stage Enterprises*	X		
FASB Statement No. 13	*Accounting for Leases*			
	• Capital leases of lessees	X		
	• Sales-type, direct financing, and leveraged leases of lessors		X	17
	• Assets of lessors subject to operating leases	X		

Pronouncement			Paragraphs
FASB Statement No. 19 *Financial Accounting and Reporting by Oil and Gas Producing Companies*			
• Unproved properties	X		12, 27-29, 31(b), 33, 40, 47(g), 47(h)
• Proved properties, wells and related equipment and facilities		X	
FASB Statement No. 34 *Capitalization of Interest Cost*		X	
FASB Statement No. 44 *Accounting for Intangible Assets of Motor Carriers*	X		3-7
FASB Statement No. 50 *Financial Reporting in the Record and Music Industry*	X		11
FASB Statement No. 51 *Financial Reporting by Cable Television Companies*		X	
FASB Statement No. 53 *Financial Reporting by Producers and Distributors of Motion Picture Films*	X		16-17
FASB Statement No. 60 *Accounting and Reporting by Insurance Enterprises*			
• Deferred policy acquisition costs		X	
• All other assets	X		32-37
FASB Statement No. 61 *Accounting for Title Plant*		X	
FASB Statement No. 63 *Financial Reporting by Broadcasters*	X		7
FASB Statement No. 65 *Accounting for Certain Mortgage Banking Activities*	X		7
FASB Statement No. 66 *Accounting for Sales of Real Estate*		X	

Pronouncement	Title	Apply General Impairment Standard	Apply Existing Requirement	Existing Requirement Paragraph Number
FASB Statement No. 67	*Accounting for Costs and Initial Rental Operations of Real Estate Projects*	X		
FASB Statement No. 71	*Accounting for the Effects of Certain Types of Regulation*	X		
FASB Statement No. 86	*Accounting for the Costs of Computer Software to Be Sold, Leased, or Otherwise Marketed*		X	10
FASB Statement No. 90	*Regulated Enterprises—Accounting for Abandonments and Disallowances of Plant Costs*		X	7
FASB Statement No. 97	*Accounting and Reporting by Insurance Enterprises for Certain Long-Duration Contracts and for Realized Gains and Losses from the Sale of Investments*			
	• Deferred policy acquisition costs		X	25, 27
FASB Statement No. 101	*Regulated Enterprises—Accounting for the Discontinuation of Application of FASB Statement No. 71*	X		
FASB Statement No. 109	*Accounting for Income Taxes*		X	20-26
FASB Statement No. 114	*Accounting by Creditors for Impairment of a Loan*		X	8-16
FASB Statement No. 115	*Accounting for Certain Investments in Debt and Equity Securities*		X	16

Statement of Financial Accounting Standards No. 122
Accounting for Mortgage Servicing Rights

an amendment of FASB Statement No. 65

STATUS

Issued: May 1995

Effective Date: Prospectively for fiscal years beginning after December 15, 1995

Affects: Amends FAS 65, paragraphs 1, 10, 15, 19, and 30
        Supersedes FAS 65, paragraphs 16 through 18 and footnote 6
        Amends FAS 65 by adding paragraphs after paragraph 30
        Supersedes FTB 87-3, paragraph 9

Affected by: Superseded by FAS 125 and FAS 140

Issues Discussed by FASB Emerging Issues Task Force (EITF)

  Affects: Nullifies EITF Issues No. 86-39 and 92-10
          Partially nullifies EITF Issue No. 86-38

(The next page is 1754.)

Statement of Financial Accounting Standards No. 123
Accounting for Stock-Based Compensation

STATUS

Issued: October 1995

Effective Date: For fiscal years beginning after December 15, 1995

Affects: Amends ARB 43, Chapter 13B, paragraph 2
Supersedes ARB 43, Chapter 13B, paragraph 15
Amends APB 25, paragraph 4
Supersedes APB 25, paragraph 19 and footnote 5
Supersedes APB 29, footnote 4
Amends AIN-APB 25, Interpretation No. 1
Amends FAS 5, paragraph 7
Amends FAS 21, footnote 3
Amends FAS 43, paragraph 2
Amends FAS 105, paragraph 14(c)
Amends FAS 107, paragraph 8(a)
Amends FAS 109, paragraph 36(e)
Amends FAS 112, paragraph 5(d)
Amends FIN 28, paragraph 2
Amends FIN 31, footnote 1
Amends FIN 38, paragraph 2
Supersedes FTB 82-2

Affected by: Paragraphs 8 and 36 amended by FAS 141
Paragraph 9 amended by FAS 144
Paragraph 49 superseded by FAS 128
Paragraph 49 amended by FAS 135
Paragraphs 50 and 357 amended by FAS 128
Paragraph 358 amended by FAS 128 and FAS 135
Paragraphs 359 through 361 and footnote 26 superseded by FAS 128
Paragraph 359 amended by FAS 135

Other Interpretive Pronouncement: FTB 97-1

Issues Discussed by FASB Emerging Issues Task Force (EITF)

Affects: EITF Issue No. 84-8

Interpreted by: Paragraph 8 interpreted by EITF Issues No. 96-18 and 97-2
Paragraphs 9 and 10 interpreted by EITF Issue No. 96-18
Paragraph 11 interpreted by EITF Issue No. 97-2

Related Issues: EITF Issues No. 97-12, 00-8, 00-12, 00-15, 00-16, 00-18, and 01-1 and Topics No. D-83 and D-90

SUMMARY

This Statement establishes financial accounting and reporting standards for stock-based employee compensation plans. Those plans include all arrangements by which employees receive shares of stock or other equity instruments of the employer or the employer incurs liabilities to employees in amounts based on the price of the employer's stock. Examples are stock purchase plans, stock options, restricted stock, and stock appreciation rights.

This Statement also applies to transactions in which an entity issues its equity instruments to acquire goods or services from nonemployees. Those transactions must be accounted for based on the fair value of the consideration received or the fair value of the equity instruments issued, whichever is more reliably measurable.

Accounting for Awards of Stock-Based Compensation to Employees

This Statement defines a *fair value based method* of accounting for an employee stock option or similar equity instrument and encourages all entities to adopt that method of accounting for all of their employee stock compensation plans. However, it also allows an entity to continue to measure compensation cost for those plans using the *intrinsic value based method* of accounting prescribed by APB Opinion No. 25, *Accounting for Stock Issued to Employees.* The fair value based method is preferable to the Opinion 25 method for purposes of justifying a change in accounting principle under APB Opinion No. 20, *Accounting Changes.* Entities electing to remain with the accounting in Opinion 25 must make pro forma disclosures of net income and, if presented, earnings per share, as if the fair value based method of accounting defined in this Statement had been applied.

Under the fair value based method, compensation cost is measured at the grant date based on the value of the award and is recognized over the service period, which is usually the vesting period. Under the intrinsic value based method, compensation cost is the excess, if any, of the quoted market price of the stock at grant date or other measurement date over the amount an employee must pay to acquire the stock. Most fixed stock option plans—the most common type of stock compensation plan—have no intrinsic value at grant date, and under Opinion 25 no compensation cost is recognized for them. Compensation cost is recognized for other types of stock-based compensation plans under Opinion 25, including plans with variable, usually performance-based, features.

Stock Compensation Awards Required to Be Settled by Issuing Equity Instruments

Stock Options

For stock options, fair value is determined using an option-pricing model that takes into account the stock price at the grant date, the exercise price, the expected life of the option, the volatility of the underlying stock and the expected dividends on it, and the risk-free interest rate over the expected life of the option. Nonpublic entities are permitted to exclude the volatility factor in estimating the value of their stock options, which results in measurement at *minimum value.* The fair value of an option estimated at the grant date is not subsequently adjusted for changes in the price of the underlying stock or its volatility, the life of the option, dividends on the stock, or the risk-free interest rate.

Nonvested Stock

The fair value of a share of nonvested stock (usually referred to as restricted stock) awarded to an employee is measured at the market price of a share of a nonrestricted stock on the grant date unless a restriction will be imposed after the employee has a vested right to it, in which case fair value is estimated taking that restriction into account.

Employee Stock Purchase Plans

An employee stock purchase plan that allows employees to purchase stock at a discount from market price is not compensatory if it satisfies three conditions: (a) the discount is relatively small (5 percent or less satisfies this condition automatically, though in some cases a greater discount also might be justified as noncompensatory), (b) substantially all full-time employees may participate on an equitable basis, and (c) the plan incorporates no option features such as allowing the employee to purchase the stock at a fixed discount from the lesser of the market price at grant date or date of purchase.

Stock Compensation Awards Required to Be Settled by Paying Cash

Some stock-based compensation plans require an employer to pay an employee, either on demand or at a specified date, a cash amount determined by the increase in the employer's stock price from a specified level. The entity must measure compensation cost for that award in the amount of the changes in the stock price in the periods in which the changes occur.

Disclosures

This Statement requires that an employer's financial statements include certain disclosures about stock-based employee compensation arrangements regardless of the method used to account for them.

The pro forma amounts required to be disclosed by an employer that continues to apply the accounting provisions of Opinion 25 will reflect the difference between compensation cost, if any, included in net income and the related cost measured by the fair value based method defined in this Statement, including tax effects, if any, that would have been recognized in the income statement if the fair value based method had been used. The required pro forma amounts will not reflect any other adjustments to reported net income or, if presented, earnings per share.

Effective Date and Transition

The accounting requirements of this Statement are effective for transactions entered into in fiscal years that begin after December 15, 1995, though they may be adopted on issuance.

The disclosure requirements of this Statement are effective for financial statements for fiscal years beginning after December 15, 1995, or for an earlier fiscal year for which this Statement is initially adopted for recognizing compensation cost. Pro forma disclosures required for entities that elect to continue to measure compensation cost using Opinion 25 must include the effects of all awards granted in fiscal years that begin after December 15, 1994. Pro forma disclosures for awards granted in the first fiscal year beginning after December 15, 1994, need not be included in financial statements for that fiscal year but should be presented subsequently whenever financial statements for that fiscal year are presented for comparative purposes with financial statements for a later fiscal year.

Statement of Financial Accounting Standards No. 123

Accounting for Stock-Based Compensation

CONTENTS

INTRODUCTION

1. This Statement establishes a **fair value**[1] based method of accounting for **stock-based compensation plans.** It encourages entities to adopt that method in place of the provisions of APB Opinion No. 25, *Accounting for Stock Issued to Employees,* for all arrangements under which employees receive shares of stock or other equity instruments of the employer or the employer incurs liabilities to employees in amounts based on the price of its stock.

2. This Statement also establishes fair value as the measurement basis for transactions in which an entity acquires goods or services from nonemployees in exchange for equity instruments. This Statement uses the term *compensation* in its broadest sense to refer to the consideration paid for goods or services, regardless of whether the supplier is an employee or not. For example, employee compensation includes both cash salaries or wages and other consideration that may be thought of more as means of attracting, retaining, and motivating employees than as direct payment for services rendered.

---

[1] Terms defined in Appendix E, the glossary, are set in **boldface type** the first time they appear.

3. Opinion 25, issued in 1972, requires compensation cost[2] for stock-based employee compensation plans to be recognized based on the difference, if any, between the quoted market price of the stock and the amount an employee must pay to acquire the stock. Opinion 25 specifies different dates for the pertinent quoted market price of the stock used in measuring compensation cost, depending on whether the terms of an award[3] are fixed or variable, as those terms are defined in Opinion 25.

4. Since 1972, **stock options** and other forms of stock-based employee compensation plans have become increasingly common. Also, option-pricing models have become widely used for measuring the value of stock options and similar equity instruments other than those issued to employees as compensation. Opinion 25 has been criticized for producing anomalous results and for providing little general guidance to use in deciding how to account for new forms of stock-based employee compensation plans. Several FASB Interpretations and Technical Bulletins have dealt with specific kinds of plans, and the Emerging Issues Task Force has considered numerous related issues.

5. Because of the perceived deficiencies in Opinion 25, early in the 1980s the AICPA's Accounting Standards Executive Committee, the staff of the Securities and Exchange Commission, most of the larger accounting firms, industry representatives, and others asked the Board to reconsider the accounting specified in Opinion 25. This Statement, which is the result of that reconsideration, establishes an accounting method based on the fair value of equity instruments awarded to employees as compensation that mitigates many of the deficiencies in Opinion 25. The Board encourages entities to adopt the new method. However, this Statement permits an entity in determining its net income to continue to apply the accounting provisions of Opinion 25 to its stock-based employee compensation arrangements. An entity that continues to apply Opinion 25 must comply with the disclosure requirements of this Statement, which supersede the disclosure requirements of paragraph 19 of Opinion 25. This Statement also supersedes or amends other accounting pronouncements listed in Appendix D. Appendix A explains the reasons the Board decided not to require recognition of compensation cost for stock-based employee compensation arrangements measured in accordance with the fair value based method described in this Statement.

STANDARDS OF FINANCIAL ACCOUNTING AND REPORTING

Scope and Alternative Accounting Methods

6. This Statement applies to all transactions in which an entity acquires goods or services by issuing equity instruments[4] or by incurring liabilities to the supplier in amounts based on the price of the entity's common stock or other equity instruments. Therefore, it applies to all transactions in which an entity grants shares of its common stock, stock options, or other equity instruments to its employees, except for equity instruments held by an employee stock ownership plan.[5]

7. The accounting for all stock-based compensation arrangements with employees or others shall reflect the inherent rights and obligations, regardless of how those arrangements are described. For example, the rights and obligations embodied in a transfer of stock to an employee for consideration of a nonrecourse note are substantially the same as if the transaction were structured as the grant of a stock option, and the transaction shall be accounted for as such. The terms of the arrangement may affect the fair value of the

---

[2]This Statement refers to recognizing *compensation cost* rather than *compensation expense* because part of the amount recognized in a period may be capitalized as part of the cost to acquire an asset, such as inventory.

[3]This Statement uses the term *award* as the collective noun for multiple instruments with the same terms granted at the same time either to a single employee or to a group of employees. An award may specify multiple vesting dates, referred to as graded vesting, and different parts of an award may have different expected lives.

[4]An entity may conditionally transfer an equity instrument to another party under an arrangement that permits that party to choose at a later date or for a specified time whether to deliver the consideration for it or to forfeit the right to the conditionally transferred instrument with no further obligation. In that situation, the equity instrument is not *issued* until the issuing entity has received the consideration, such as cash, an enforceable right to receive cash, other financial instruments, goods, or services, agreed to by the parties to the transaction. For that reason, this Statement does not use the term *issued* for the grant of stock options or other equity instruments subject to service or performance conditions (or both) for vesting.

[5]AICPA Statement of Position No. 93-6, *Employers' Accounting for Employee Stock Ownership Plans,* specifies the accounting by employers for employee stock ownership plans.

stock options or other equity instruments and shall be appropriately reflected in determining that value. For example, whether an employee who is granted an implicit option structured as the exchange of shares of stock for a nonrecourse note is required to pay nonrefundable interest on the note affects the fair value of the implicit option.

Accounting for Transactions with Other Than Employees

8. Except for transactions with employees that are within the scope of Opinion 25, all transactions in which goods or services are the consideration received for the issuance of equity instruments shall be accounted for based on the fair value of the consideration received or the fair value of the equity instruments issued, whichever is more reliably measurable. The fair value of goods or services received from suppliers other than employees frequently is reliably measurable and therefore indicates the fair value of the equity instruments issued. The fair value of the equity instruments issued shall be used to measure the transaction if that value is more reliably measurable than the fair value of the consideration received.[6] A common example of the latter situation is the use of the fair value of tradable equity instruments issued in a purchase business combination to measure the transaction because the value of the equity instruments issued is more reliably measurable than the value of the business acquired.

9. This Statement uses the term *fair value* for assets and financial instruments, including both liability and equity instruments, with the same meaning as in FASB Statement No. 121, *Accounting for the Impairment of Long-Lived Assets and for Long-Lived Assets to Be Disposed Of.* Statement 121 says that the fair value of an asset is

> . . . the amount at which the asset could be bought or sold in a current transaction between willing parties, that is, other than in a forced or liquidation sale. Quoted market prices in active markets are the best evidence of fair value and shall be used as the basis for the measurement, if available. If quoted market prices are not available, the estimate of

fair value shall be based on the best information available in the circumstances. The estimate of fair value shall consider prices for similar assets and the results of valuation techniques to the extent available in the circumstances. Examples of valuation techniques include the present value of estimated expected future cash flows using a discount rate commensurate with the risks involved, option-pricing models, matrix pricing, option-adjusted spread models, and fundamental analysis. [paragraph 7]

10. If the fair value of the goods or services received is not reliably measurable, paragraph 8 of this Statement requires that the measure of the cost of goods or services acquired in a transaction with other than an employee be based on the fair value of the equity instruments issued. However, this Statement does not prescribe the **measurement date,** that is, the date of the stock price on which the fair value of the equity instrument is based, for a transaction with a nonemployee (paragraphs 70-73).

Accounting for Transactions with Employees

11. This Statement provides a choice of accounting methods for transactions with employees that are within the scope of Opinion 25. Paragraphs 16-44 of this Statement describe a method of accounting based on the fair value, rather than the **intrinsic value,** of an employee stock option or a similar equity instrument. The Board encourages entities to adopt the fair value based method of accounting, which is preferable to the Opinion 25 method for purposes of justifying a change in accounting principle under APB Opinion No. 20, *Accounting Changes.*[7] However, an entity may continue to apply Opinion 25 in accounting for its stock-based employee compensation arrangements. An entity that does so shall disclose pro forma net income and, if presented, earnings per share, determined as if the fair value based method had been applied in measuring compensation cost (paragraph 45).

12. The fair value based method described in paragraphs 16-44 of this Statement applies for (a) measuring stock-based employee compensation cost by an

---

[6]The consideration received for issuing equity instruments, like the consideration involved in a repurchase of treasury shares, may include intangible rights. FASB Technical Bulletin No. 85-6, *Accounting for a Purchase of Treasury Shares at a Price Significantly in Excess of the Current Market Price of the Shares and the Income Statement Classification of Costs Incurred in Defending against a Takeover Attempt,* provides pertinent guidance.

[7]Opinion 20, paragraph 8, provides that initial adoption of an accounting principle for a transaction that the entity has not previously had to account for is not a change in accounting principle.

entity that adopts that method for accounting purposes and (b) determining the pro forma disclosures required of an entity that measures stock-based employee compensation cost in accordance with the intrinsic value based method in Opinion 25. Neither those paragraphs (16-44) nor subsequent paragraphs (45-54) of this Statement affect application of the *accounting* provisions of Opinion 25 by an entity that continues to apply it in determining reported net income.

13. For convenience, in describing the fair value based method, paragraphs 16-44 of this Statement refer only to *recognition* or *accounting* requirements. However, those provisions apply equally in determining the pro forma amounts that must be disclosed if an entity continues to apply Opinion 25.

14. An entity shall apply the same accounting method—either the fair value based method described in this Statement or the intrinsic value based method in Opinion 25—in accounting for all of its stock-based employee compensation arrangements. Once an entity adopts the fair value based method for those arrangements, that election shall not be reversed.[8]

15. Equity instruments granted or otherwise transferred directly to an employee by a **principal stockholder** are stock-based employee compensation to be accounted for by the entity under either Opinion 25 or this Statement, whichever method the entity is applying, unless the transfer clearly is for a purpose other than compensation.[9] The substance of a transaction in which a principal stockholder directly transfers equity instruments to an employee as compensation is that the principal stockholder makes a capital contribution to the entity and the entity awards equity instruments to its employee. An example of a situation in which a direct transfer of equity instruments to an employee from a principal stockholder is not compensation cost is a transfer to settle an obligation of the principal stockholder unrelated to employment by the reporting entity.

Valuation of Equity Instruments Issued for Employee Services

Measurement Basis

16. Frequently, part or all of the consideration received for equity instruments issued to employees is past or future employee services. Equity instruments issued to employees and the cost of the services received as consideration shall be measured and recognized based on the fair value of the equity instruments issued. The portion of the fair value of an equity instrument attributed to employee services is net of the amount, if any, that employees pay for the instrument when it is granted. Paragraphs 17-25 of this Statement provide guidance on how to measure the fair value of stock-based employee compensation. Paragraphs 26-33 provide guidance on how to attribute compensation cost to the periods in which employees render the related services. Appendix B, which is an integral part of this Statement, provides additional guidance on both measurement and attribution of employee compensation cost.

Measurement Objective and Date

17. The objective of the measurement process is to estimate the fair value, based on the stock price at the **grant date,** of stock options or other equity instruments to which employees become entitled when they have rendered the requisite service and satisfied any other conditions necessary to earn the right to benefit from the instruments (for example, to exercise stock options or to sell shares of stock). Restrictions that continue in effect after employees have earned the rights to benefit from their instruments, such as the inability to transfer **vested** employee stock options to third parties, affect the value of the instruments actually issued and therefore are reflected in estimating their fair value. However, restrictions that stem directly from the forfeitability of instruments to which employees have not yet earned the right, such as the inability either to exercise a nonvested option or to sell **nonvested stock,** do not affect the value of the instruments issued at the vesting date, and their effect therefore is not included in that

---

[8]APB Opinion No. 22, *Disclosure of Accounting Policies,* requires an entity to include a description of all significant accounting policies as an integral part of the financial statements. The method used to account for stock-based employee compensation arrangements is an accounting policy to be included in that description.

[9]That accounting has been required since 1973 in accordance with AICPA Accounting Interpretation 1, "Stock Plans Established by a Principal Stockholder," of Opinion 25.

value. Instead, no value is attributed to instruments that employees forfeit because they fail to satisfy specified service- or performance-related conditions.

Measurement Methods

Awards that call for settlement by issuing equity instruments

18. The fair value of a share of nonvested stock awarded to an employee shall be measured at the market price (or estimated market price, if the stock is not publicly traded) of a share of the same stock as if it were vested and issued on the grant date. Nonvested stock granted to employees usually is referred to as **restricted stock,** but this Statement reserves that term for shares whose sale is contractually or governmentally restricted after the shares are vested and fully outstanding. The fair value of a share of restricted stock awarded to an employee, that is, a share that will be restricted after the employee has a vested right to it, shall be measured at its fair value, which is the same amount as a share of similarly restricted stock issued to nonemployees.

19. The fair value of a stock option (or its equivalent) granted by a **public entity** shall be estimated using an option-pricing model (for example, the Black-Scholes or a binomial model) that takes into account as of the grant date the exercise price and expected life of the option, the current price of the underlying stock and its expected **volatility,** expected dividends on the stock (except as provided in paragraphs 32 and 33), and the risk-free interest rate for the expected term of the option. For options that a U.S. entity grants on its own stock, the risk-free interest rate used shall be the rate currently available on zero-coupon U.S. government issues with a remaining term equal to the expected life of the options. Guidance on selecting other assumptions is provided in Appendix B. The fair value of an option estimated at the grant date shall not be subsequently adjusted for changes in the price of the underlying stock or its volatility, the life of the option, dividends on the stock, or the risk-free interest rate.

20. A **nonpublic entity** shall estimate the value of its options based on the factors described in the preceding paragraph, except that a nonpublic entity need not consider the expected volatility of its stock over the expected life of the option. The result of excluding volatility in estimating an option's value is an amount commonly termed **minimum value.**

21. It should be possible to reasonably estimate the fair value of most stock options and other equity instruments at the date they are granted. Appendix B illustrates techniques for estimating the fair values of several options with complicated features. However, in unusual circumstances, the terms of a stock option or other equity instrument may make it virtually impossible to reasonably estimate the instrument's fair value at the date it is granted. For example, it may be extremely difficult, if not impossible, to reasonably estimate the fair value of a stock option whose exercise price decreases (or increases) by a specified amount with specified changes in the price of the underlying stock. Similarly, it may not be possible to reasonably estimate the value of a convertible instrument if the conversion ratio depends on the outcome of future events.

22. If it is not possible to reasonably estimate the fair value of an option or other equity instrument at the grant date, the final measure of compensation cost shall be the fair value based on the stock price and other pertinent factors at the first date at which it is possible to reasonably estimate that value. Generally, that is likely to be the date at which the number of shares to which an employee is entitled and the exercise price are determinable. Estimates of compensation cost for periods during which it is not possible to determine fair value shall be based on the current intrinsic value of the award, determined in accordance with the terms that would apply if the option or similar instrument had been currently exercised.

Employee stock purchase plans

23. If an employee stock purchase plan satisfies all of the following criteria, the plan is not compensatory. Therefore, the discount from market price merely reduces the proceeds from issuing the related shares of stock.

a. The plan incorporates no option features other than the following, which may be incorporated:
  (1) Employees are permitted a short period of time—not exceeding 31 days—after the purchase price has been fixed to enroll in the plan.
  (2) The purchase price is based solely on the stock's market price at date of purchase, and employees are permitted to cancel participation before the purchase date and obtain a refund of amounts previously paid (such as those paid by payroll withholdings).

b. The discount from the market price does not exceed the greater of (1) a per-share discount that would be reasonable in a recurring offer of stock to stockholders or others or (2) the per-share amount of stock issuance costs avoided by not having to raise a significant amount of capital by a public offering. A discount of 5 percent or less from the market price shall be considered to comply with this criterion without further justification.

c. Substantially all full-time employees that meet limited employment qualifications may participate on an equitable basis.

24. A plan provision that establishes the purchase price as an amount based on the lesser of the stock's market price at date of grant or its market price at date of purchase is, for example, an option feature that causes the plan to be compensatory. Similarly, a plan in which the purchase price is based on the stock's market price at date of grant and that permits a participating employee to cancel participation before the purchase date and obtain a refund of amounts previously paid is a compensatory plan.

Awards that call for settlement in cash

25. Some awards of stock-based compensation result in the entity's incurring a liability because employees can compel the entity to settle the award by transferring its cash or other assets to employees rather than by issuing equity instruments. For example, an entity may incur a liability to pay an employee either on demand or at a specified date an amount to be determined by the increase in the entity's stock price from a specified level. The amount of the liability for such an award shall be measured each period based on the current stock price. The effects of changes in the stock price during the **service period** are recognized as compensation cost over the service period in accordance with the method illustrated in FASB Interpretation No. 28, *Accounting for Stock Appreciation Rights and Other Variable Stock Option or Award Plans*. Changes in the amount of the liability due to stock price changes after the service period are compensation cost of the period in which the changes occur.

Recognition of Compensation Cost

26. The total amount of compensation cost recognized for an award of stock-based employee compensation shall be based on the number of instruments that eventually vest. No compensation cost is recognized for awards that employees forfeit either because they fail to satisfy a service requirement for vesting, such as for a **fixed award,** or because the entity does not achieve a **performance condition,** unless the condition is a target stock price or specified amount of intrinsic value on which vesting or exercisability is conditioned. For awards with the latter condition, compensation cost shall be recognized for awards to employees who remain in service for the requisite period regardless of whether the target stock price or amount of intrinsic value is reached.[10] Previously recognized compensation cost shall not be reversed if a vested employee stock option expires unexercised.

27. For purposes of this Statement, a stock-based employee compensation award becomes vested when an employee's right to receive or retain shares of stock or cash under the award is not contingent on the performance of additional services. Typically, an employee stock option that is vested also is immediately exercisable. However, if performance conditions affect either the exercise price or the exercisability date, the service period used for attribution purposes shall be consistent with the assumptions used in estimating the fair value of the award. Paragraphs 309 and 310 in Appendix B illustrate how to account for an option whose exercise price depends on a performance condition.

28. An entity may choose at the grant date to base accruals of compensation cost on the best available estimate of the number of options or other equity instruments that are expected to vest and to revise that estimate, if necessary, if subsequent information indicates that actual forfeitures are likely to differ from initial estimates. Alternatively, an entity may begin accruing compensation cost as if all instruments granted that are subject only to a service requirement are expected to vest. The effect of actual forfeitures would then be recognized as they occur. Initial accruals of compensation cost for an award with a performance condition that will determine the number of options or shares to which all employees receiving the award will be entitled shall be based on the best estimate of the outcome of the performance condition, although forfeitures by individual employees

---

[10]The existence of a target stock price that must be achieved to make an option exercisable generally affects the value of the option. Option-pricing models have been adapted to value many of those *path-dependent* options.

may either be estimated at the grant date or recognized only as they occur.[11]

29. Compensation cost estimated at the grant date for the number of instruments that are expected to vest based on performance-related conditions, as well as those in which vesting is contingent only on future service for which the entity chooses to estimate forfeitures at the grant date pursuant to paragraph 28, shall be adjusted for subsequent changes in the expected or actual outcome of service- and performance-related conditions until the vesting date. The effect of a change in the estimated number of shares or options expected to vest is a change in an estimate, and the cumulative effect of the change on current and prior periods shall be recognized in the period of the change.

30. The compensation cost for an award of equity instruments to employees shall be recognized over the period(s) in which the related employee services are rendered by a charge to compensation cost and a corresponding credit to equity (paid-in capital) if the award is for future service. If the service period is not defined as an earlier or shorter period, the service period shall be presumed to be the period from the grant date to the date that the award is vested and its exercisability does not depend on continued employee service (paragraph 27). If an award is for past services, the related compensation cost shall be recognized in the period in which it is granted.

31. Compensation cost for an award with a graded vesting schedule shall be recognized in accordance with the method described in Interpretation 28 if the fair value of the award is determined based on different expected lives for the options that vest each year, as it would be if the award is viewed as several separate awards, each with a different vesting date. If the expected life or lives of the award is determined in another manner, the related compensation cost may be recognized on a straight-line basis. However, the amount of compensation cost recognized at any date must at least equal the value of the vested portion of the award at that date. Appendix B illustrates application of both attribution methods to an award accounted for by the fair value based method.

32. Dividends or dividend equivalents paid to employees on the portion of an award of stock or other equity instruments that vests shall be charged to retained earnings. Nonforfeitable dividends or dividend equivalents paid on shares of stock that do not vest shall be recognized as additional compensation cost. The choice of whether to estimate forfeitures at the grant date or to recognize the effect of forfeitures as they occur described in paragraph 28 also applies to recognition of nonforfeitable dividends paid on shares that do not vest.

33. If employees receive only the dividends declared on the class of stock granted to them after the stock becomes vested, the value of the award at the grant date shall be reduced by the present value of dividends expected to be paid on the stock during the vesting period, discounted at the appropriate risk-free interest rate. The fair value of an award of stock options on which dividend equivalents are paid to employees or are applied to reduce the exercise price pursuant to antidilution provisions shall be estimated based on a dividend payment of zero.

Additional Awards and Modifications of Outstanding Awards

34. The fair value of each award of equity instruments, including an award of **reload options,** shall be measured separately based on its terms and the current stock price and related factors at the date it is granted.

35. A modification of the terms of an award that makes it more valuable shall be treated as an exchange of the original award for a new award. In substance, the entity repurchases the original instrument by issuing a new instrument of greater value, incurring additional compensation cost for that incremental value. The incremental value shall be measured by the difference between (a) the fair value of the modified option determined in accordance with the provisions of this Statement and (b) the value of the old option immediately before its terms are modified, determined based on the shorter of (1) its remaining expected life or (2) the expected life of the modified option. Appendix B provides further guidance on and illustrates the accounting for modifications of both vested and nonvested options.

36. Exchanges of options or changes to their terms in conjunction with business combinations, spinoffs, or other equity restructurings, except for those made to reflect the terms of the exchange of shares in a

---

[11]For convenience, the remainder of this document refers to options or shares *expected to vest* because referring specifically to both acceptable methods of accounting for forfeitures by individual employees each time the point is mentioned would be too unwieldy.

business combination accounted for as a pooling of interests, are modifications for purposes of this Statement. However, a change to the terms of an award in accordance with antidilution provisions that are designed, for example, to equalize an option's value before and after a stock split or a stock dividend is not a modification of an award for purposes of this Statement.

Settlements of Awards

37. An entity occasionally may repurchase equity instruments issued to employees after the employees have vested rights to them. The amount of cash or other assets paid (or liabilities incurred) to repurchase an equity instrument shall be charged to equity, provided that the amount paid does not exceed the value of the instruments repurchased. For example, an entity that repurchases for $10 a share of stock on the date it becomes vested does not incur additional compensation cost if the market price of the stock is $10 at that date. However, if the market price of the stock is only $8 at that date, the entity incurs an additional $2 ($10 − $8) of cost. An entity that settles a nonvested award for cash has, in effect, vested the award, and the amount of compensation cost measured at the grant date but not yet recognized shall be recognized at the date of repurchase.

38. For employee stock options, the incremental amount, if any, to be recognized as additional compensation cost upon cash settlement shall be determined based on a comparison of the amount paid with the value of the option repurchased, determined based on the remainder of its original expected life at that date. As indicated in paragraph 37, if stock options are repurchased before they become vested, the amount of unrecognized compensation cost shall be recognized at the date of the repurchase.

39. The accounting shall reflect the terms of a stock-based compensation plan as those terms are mutually understood by the employer and the employees who receive awards under the plan. Generally, the written plan provides the best evidence of its terms. However, an entity's past practice may indicate that the **substantive terms** of a plan differ from its written terms. For example, an entity that grants a **tandem award** consisting of either a stock option or a cash stock appreciation right (SAR) is obligated to pay cash on demand if the choice is the employee's, and the entity thus incurs a liability to the employee. In contrast, if the choice is the entity's, it can avoid transferring its assets by choosing to settle in stock,

and the award qualifies as an equity instrument. However, if an entity that nominally has the choice of settling awards by issuing stock generally settles in cash, or if the entity generally settles in cash whenever an employee asks for cash settlement, the entity probably is settling a substantive liability rather than repurchasing an equity instrument. The substantive terms shall be the basis for the accounting.

40. To restrict control to a limited group, for example, the members of a particular family, a nonpublic entity may obligate itself to repurchase its equity instruments for their fair value at the date of repurchase. In practice, such an obligation is not deemed to convert the stock to a liability. This Statement is not intended to change that view of the effect of a fair value repurchase agreement for a nonpublic entity. Thus, a nonpublic entity may grant or otherwise issue to employees equity instruments subject to such a repurchase agreement. The repurchase agreement does not convert those equity instruments to liabilities, provided that the repurchase price is the fair value of the stock at the date of repurchase.

Accounting for Tax Consequences of Equity Instruments Awarded to Employees

41. Income tax regulations specify allowable tax deductions for stock-based employee compensation arrangements in determining an entity's income tax liability. Compensation cost recognized under this Statement is measured based on the fair value of an award to an employee. Under existing U.S. tax law, allowable tax deductions are generally measured at a specified date as the excess of the market price of the related stock over the amount the employee is required to pay for the stock (that is, at intrinsic value). The **time value** component of the fair value of an option is not tax deductible. Therefore, tax deductions generally will arise in different amounts and in different periods from compensation cost recognized in financial statements.

42. The cumulative amount of compensation cost recognized for a stock-based award that ordinarily results in a future tax deduction under existing tax law shall be considered to be a deductible temporary difference in applying FASB Statement No. 109, *Accounting for Income Taxes*. The deferred tax benefit (or expense) that results from increases (or decreases) in that temporary difference, for example, as additional service is rendered and the related cost is recognized, shall be recognized in the income statement.

Recognition of compensation cost for an award that ordinarily does not result in tax deductions under existing tax law shall not be considered to result in a deductible temporary difference in applying Statement 109. A future event, such as an employee's disqualifying disposition of stock under existing U.S. tax law, can give rise to a tax deduction for an award that ordinarily does not result in a tax deduction. The tax effects of such an event shall be recognized only when it occurs.

43. Statement 109 requires a deferred tax asset to be evaluated for future realization and to be reduced by a valuation allowance if, based on the weight of the available evidence, it is more likely than not that some portion or all of the deferred tax asset will not be realized. Differences between (a) the deductible temporary difference computed pursuant to paragraph 42 and (b) the tax deduction inherent in the current fair value of the entity's stock shall not be considered in measuring either the gross deferred tax asset or the need for a valuation allowance for a deferred tax asset recognized under this Statement.

44. If a deduction reported on a tax return for a stock-based award exceeds the cumulative compensation cost for that award recognized for financial reporting, the tax benefit for that excess deduction shall be recognized as additional paid-in capital. If the deduction reported on a tax return is less than the cumulative compensation cost recognized for financial reporting, the write-off of a related deferred tax asset in excess of the benefits of the tax deduction, net of the related valuation allowance, if any, shall be recognized in the income statement except to the extent that there is remaining additional paid-in capital from excess tax deductions from previous stock-based employee compensation awards accounted for in accordance with the fair value based method in this Statement. In that situation, the amount of the write-off shall be charged against that additional paid-in capital.

Disclosures

45. Regardless of the method used to account for stock-based employee compensation arrangements, the financial statements of an entity shall include the disclosures specified in paragraphs 46-48. In addition, an entity that continues to apply Opinion 25 shall disclose for each year for which an income statement is provided the pro forma net income and, if earnings per share is presented, pro forma earnings per share, as if the fair value based accounting method in this Statement had been used to account for stock-based compensation cost. Those pro forma amounts shall reflect the difference between compensation cost, if any, included in net income in accordance with Opinion 25 and the related cost measured by the fair value based method, as well as additional tax effects, if any, that would have been recognized in the income statement if the fair value based method had been used. The required pro forma amounts shall reflect no other adjustments to reported net income or earnings per share.

46. An entity with one or more stock-based compensation plans shall provide a description of the plan(s), including the general terms of awards under the plan(s), such as vesting requirements, the maximum term of options granted, and the number of shares authorized for grants of options or other equity instruments. An entity that uses equity instruments to acquire goods or services other than employee services shall provide disclosures similar to those required by this paragraph and paragraphs 47 and 48 to the extent that those disclosures are important in understanding the effects of those transactions on the financial statements.

47. The following information shall be disclosed for each year for which an income statement is provided:

a. The number and weighted-average exercise prices of options for each of the following groups of options: (1) those outstanding at the beginning of the year, (2) those outstanding at the end of the year, (3) those exercisable at the end of the year, and those (4) granted, (5) exercised, (6) forfeited, or (7) expired during the year.

b. The weighted-average grant-date fair value of options granted during the year. If the exercise prices of some options differ from the market price of the stock on the grant date, weighted-average exercise prices and weighted-average fair values of options shall be disclosed separately for options whose exercise price (1) equals, (2) exceeds, or (3) is less than the market price of the stock on the grant date.

c. The number and weighted-average grant-date fair value of equity instruments other than options, for example, shares of nonvested stock, granted during the year.

d. A description of the method and significant assumptions used during the year to estimate the fair values of options, including the following weighted-average information: (1) risk-free interest rate, (2) expected life, (3) expected volatility, and (4) expected dividends.

e. Total compensation cost recognized in income for stock-based employee compensation awards.

f. The terms of significant modifications of outstanding awards.

An entity that grants options under multiple stock-based employee compensation plans shall provide the foregoing information separately for different types of awards to the extent that the differences in the characteristics of the awards make separate disclosure important to an understanding of the entity's use of stock-based compensation. For example, separate disclosure of weighted-average exercise prices at the end of the year for options with a fixed exercise price and those with an indexed exercise price is likely to be important, as would segregating the number of options not yet exercisable into those that will become exercisable based solely on employees' rendering additional service and those for which an additional condition must be met for the options to become exercisable.

48. For options outstanding at the date of the latest statement of financial position presented, the range of exercise prices (as well as the weighted-average exercise price) and the weighted-average remaining contractual life shall be disclosed. If the range of exercise prices is wide (for example, the highest exercise price exceeds approximately 150 percent of the lowest exercise price), the exercise prices shall be segregated into ranges that are meaningful for assessing the number and timing of additional shares that may be issued and the cash that may be received as a result of option exercises. The following information shall be disclosed for each range:

a. The number, weighted-average exercise price, and weighted-average remaining contractual life of options outstanding

b. The number and weighted-average exercise price of options currently exercisable.

Earnings per Share Implications

49. APB Opinion No. 15, *Earnings per Share*, requires that employee stock options, nonvested stock, and similar equity instruments granted to employees be treated as common stock equivalents in computing earnings per share. The number of nonvested equity instruments used in computing primary earnings per share shall be the same as the number that are used in measuring the related compensation cost in accordance with this Statement. Fully diluted earnings per share shall continue to be based on the actual number of options or shares granted and not yet forfeited, unless doing so would be antidilutive. If vesting is contingent on other factors, such as the level of future earnings, the shares or options shall be treated as contingent shares in accordance with paragraph 62 of Opinion 15. AICPA Accounting Interpretation 91, "Earnings Conditions," of Opinion 15 provides additional guidance on applying paragraph 62 of Opinion 15 to stock-based employee compensation plans. If stock options or other equity instruments are granted during a period, the shares issuable shall be weighted to reflect the portion of the period during which the equity instruments were outstanding.

50. In applying the treasury stock method of Opinion 15, the assumed proceeds shall be the sum of (a) the amount, if any, the employee must pay, (b) the amount of compensation cost attributed to future services and not yet recognized, and (c) the amount of tax benefits, if any, that would be credited to additional paid-in capital. FASB Interpretation No. 31, *Treatment of Stock Compensation Plans in EPS Computations*, provides detailed examples of the treatment of stock compensation plans accounted for under Opinion 25 in earnings per share computations. Although the related cost and tax amounts will differ if the fair value based accounting method in this Statement is applied, the principles in Interpretation 31 remain applicable.

Effective Date and Transition

51. The requirement in paragraph 8 of this Statement shall be effective for transactions entered into after December 15, 1995.

52. The recognition provisions of this Statement may be adopted upon issuance. Regardless of when an entity initially adopts those provisions, they shall be applied to all awards granted after the beginning of the fiscal year in which the recognition provisions are first applied. The recognition provisions shall not be applied to awards granted in fiscal years before the year of initial adoption except to the extent that prior years' awards are modified or settled in cash after the beginning of the fiscal year in which the entity adopts the recognition provisions. Accounting for modifications and settlements of awards initially accounted for in accordance with Opinion 25 is discussed and illustrated in Appendix B.

53. The disclosure requirements of this Statement shall be effective for financial statements for fiscal years beginning after December 15, 1995, or for the

fiscal year for which this Statement is initially adopted for recognizing compensation cost, whichever comes first. The disclosure requirements need not be applied in an interim report unless a complete set of financial statements is presented for that period. Pro forma disclosures required by paragraph 45 of this Statement shall include the effects of all awards granted in fiscal years that begin after December 15, 1994. Pro forma disclosures for awards granted in the first fiscal year beginning after December 15, 1994 need not be included in financial statements for that fiscal year but shall be presented subsequently whenever financial statements for that fiscal year are presented for comparative purposes with financial statements for a later fiscal year.

54. During the initial phase-in period, the effects of applying this Statement for either recognizing compensation cost or providing pro forma disclosures are not likely to be representative of the effects on reported net income for future years, for example, because options vest over several years and additional awards generally are made each year. If that situation exists, the entity shall include a statement to that effect. The entity also may wish to provide supplemental disclosure of the effect of applying the fair value based accounting method to all awards made in fiscal years beginning before the date of initial adoption that were not vested at that date.

> **The provisions of this Statement need not be applied to immaterial items.**

This Statement was adopted by the affirmative votes of five members of the Financial Accounting Standards Board. Messrs. Foster and Leisenring dissented.

Messrs. Foster and Leisenring dissent from the issuance of this Statement because they believe that the compensation associated with employee stock options should be recognized as a cost in the financial statements and disagree with the decision to permit that cost to be reflected only in pro forma disclosures. They agree with the Board's conclusion that employee stock options represent compensation and that the amount of associated cost can be determined with sufficient reliability for recognition in financial statements. Messrs. Foster and Leisenring believe that, having reached those conclusions, the Board should accept the conclusion of paragraph 9 of FASB Concepts Statement No. 5, *Recognition and Measurement in Financial Statements of Business Enterprises,* that disclosure is not a substitute for recognition in financial statements for items that meet recognition criteria.

Messrs. Foster and Leisenring believe that a high level of controversy and a perceived threat to accounting standard setting in the private sector as discussed in paragraphs 57-62 are inappropriate reasons for not requiring recognition in financial statements of an item that meets the recognition criteria of Concepts Statement 5.

Messrs. Foster and Leisenring further believe that the effect of this Statement on improving disclosure of compensation cost for those entities that choose

not to adopt the fair value based method is substantially diminished because the Statement does not require disclosure of the pro forma effect on net income and earnings per share in summarized interim financial data required by APB Opinion No. 28, *Interim Financial Reporting.* They believe that comparable data presented on a quarterly basis is important to financial analysis.

While Messrs. Foster and Leisenring concur with the conclusion that fair value of employee stock options is the appropriate measure of compensation cost, they do not agree that the grant date method of accounting as described in paragraphs 16-44 results in the best measure of that cost. As discussed in paragraphs 155-160, the Board's decision to look to certain events that occur after the grant date in measuring compensation cost, by, for example, adjusting for forfeitures after that date, is inconsistent with its decision to base compensation cost on a grant date stock price. Messrs. Foster and Leisenring believe that a more understandable, representationally faithful, and consistent measure of the compensation granted in an employee stock option would be achieved by measuring the fair value of all vested options at the vesting date. As explained in paragraphs 96 and 167, employee stock options are not issued until the vesting date. At that date, the employer and employee have fulfilled their obligations under the agreement that offers the stock options and consequently the options are issued and can then be measured.

Despite their belief that vesting date measurement would result in a superior measure of compensation cost, Messrs. Foster and Leisenring would have accepted the modified grant date method and assented to issuance of this Statement if the cost determined under that method was required to be recognized rather than only disclosed. Notwithstanding the shortcomings of the modified grant date method of measuring compensation expense, it is significantly better than the continued failure to recognize compensation cost in financial statements—the result of applying Opinion 25.

Members of the Financial Accounting Standards Board:

Dennis R. Beresford,	Anthony T. Cope	Robert H. Northcutt
Chairman	John M. Foster	Robert J. Swieringa
Joseph V. Anania	James J. Leisenring	

Appendix A

BASIS FOR CONCLUSIONS

CONTENTS

Appendix A

BASIS FOR CONCLUSIONS

Introduction

55. This appendix summarizes considerations that Board members deemed significant in reaching the conclusions in this Statement. It includes reasons for accepting certain approaches and rejecting others. Individual Board members gave greater weight to some factors than to others.

56. Accounting for stock-based employee compensation plans is a pervasive subject that affects most public entities and many nonpublic entities. Opinion 25 continues to be criticized for producing anomalous results and for lacking an underlying conceptual rationale that helps in resolving implementation questions or in deciding how to account for stock-based compensation plans with new features. A frequently cited anomaly is that the requirements of Opinion 25 typically result in the recognition of compensation cost for performance options but no cost is recognized for fixed options that may be more valuable at the grant date than performance options. Critics of Opinion 25 also note that long-term fixed options granted to employees are valuable financial instruments, even though they carry restrictions that usually are not present in other stock options. Financial statements prepared in accordance with the requirements of Opinion 25 do not recognize that value. The resulting financial statements are less credible than they could be, and the financial statements of entities that use fixed employee options extensively are not comparable to those of entities that do not make significant use of fixed options. Because of the various criticisms of Opinion 25, in March 1984, the Board added a project to its agenda to reconsider accounting by employers for stock-based compensation plans.

Why the Board Decided Not to Require Fair Value Accounting

57. In June 1993, the Board issued an Exposure Draft on accounting for stock-based compensation that would have replaced Opinion 25 with an accounting method based on recognizing the fair value of equity instruments issued to employees, regardless of whether the instrument was a share of stock, a fixed or performance option, or some other instrument, with measurement based on the stock price at the date the instrument was granted. Requiring all entities to follow the fair value based method in the Exposure Draft would have (a) resulted in accounting for stock-based employee compensation that was both internally consistent and also consistent with accounting for all other forms of compensation, (b) "leveled the playing field" between fixed and variable awards, and (c) made the accounting for equity instruments issued to employees more consistent with the accounting for all other free-standing equity instruments[12] and the related consideration received.

58. That Exposure Draft was extraordinarily controversial. The Board's due process is intended to ensure that the views of all interested parties are heard and fully considered. The Board not only expects but actively encourages debate of the issues and proposals in an Exposure Draft, and the final Statement generally benefits from information the Board receives during that debate. Both the Board and its constituents usually learn from the debate, with the result that the Board's views and the views of many of its constituents generally move closer together during the debate.

59. Unlike other highly controversial topics, the controversy on accounting for stock-based compensation escalated throughout the exposure process. The main point of contention was whether compensation cost should be recognized for stock options with fixed terms that are at-the-money[13] at the date they are granted. Constituents gave different reasons for opposing cost recognition, with many expressing concerns about whether the fair value of employee stock options at the grant date can be estimated with sufficient reliability. Most respondents urged the Board to expand disclosures about stock-based employee compensation arrangements rather than to change the basic accounting method in Opinion 25. The specific comments of respondents to the Exposure Draft and later comments made as the Board redeliberated the issues are discussed later in this appendix.

60. The debate on accounting for stock-based compensation unfortunately became so divisive that it threatened the Board's future working relationship with some of its constituents. Eventually, the nature of the debate threatened the future of accounting standards setting in the private sector.

61. The Board continues to believe that financial statements would be more relevant and representationally faithful if the estimated fair value of employee stock options was included in determining an entity's net income, just as all other forms of compensation are included. To do so would be consistent with accounting for the cost of all other goods and services received as consideration for equity instruments. The Board also believes that financial reporting would be improved if all equity instruments granted to employees, including instruments with variable features such as options with performance criteria for vesting, were accounted for on a consistent basis. However, in December 1994, the Board decided that the extent of improvement in financial reporting that was envisioned when this project was added to its technical agenda and when the Exposure Draft was issued was not attainable because the deliberate, logical consideration of issues that usually leads to improvement in financial reporting was no longer present. Therefore, the Board decided to specify as preferable and to encourage but not to require recognition of compensation cost for all stock-based employee compensation, with required disclosure of the pro forma effects of such recognition by entities that continue to apply Opinion 25.

62. The Board believes that disclosure of the pro forma effects of recognizing compensation cost according to the fair value based method will provide relevant new information that will be of value to the capital markets and thus will achieve some but not all of the original objectives of the project. However, the Board also continues to believe that disclosure is not an adequate substitute for recognition of assets, liabilities, equity, revenues, and expenses in financial

---

[12]A *free-standing* equity instrument is one that is not embedded in a compound instrument with other, nonequity, components. For example, convertible debt is a compound instrument with both liability and equity components. The call option on common stock that is part of convertible debt is not a free-standing equity instrument, and it is not currently accounted for separately from the liability component.

[13]For convenience, this appendix uses the terms *at-the-money, out-of-the-money,* and *in-the-money* commonly used by option traders to denote an option with an exercise price that *equals, exceeds,* or *is less than,* respectively, the current price of the underlying stock.

statements, as discussed more fully later in this appendix. The Board chose a disclosure-based solution for stock-based employee compensation to bring closure to the divisive debate on this issue—not because it believes that solution is the best way to improve financial accounting and reporting.

Alternative Accounting Methods

63. When the Board decided not to require recognition of compensation cost determined by the fair value based method, it also decided that it was important to avoid explicitly or implicitly endorsing arguments against the Exposure Draft that the Board did not find credible. For example, endorsing the argument that an at-the-money option has no value or that financial statements should exclude the values of financial instruments that are difficult to measure would misrepresent the Board's views and likely would impede efforts to improve financial reporting in other areas—especially for other financial instruments, some of which are more complex and may be more difficult to value than employee stock options. The Board's reasons for rejecting those arguments are discussed in paragraphs 76-117 of this appendix.

64. The Board also decided that improved disclosure alone—regardless of the nature of the disclosure—is not sufficient. The Board thus encourages entities to adopt the fair value based accounting method described in this Statement. That method permits an entity to avoid in its financial statements the effects of Opinion 25 that encourage fixed plans and discourage plans with variable, performance-based features. Providing an alternative accounting method does not achieve as level a playing field for fixed and performance-based plans as the Board and some of its constituents would like. However, it establishes a mechanism that can result in a more level playing field over time if many entities eventually choose the fair value based accounting method. It also provides a means by which improved accounting for stock-based employee compensation can evolve through the voluntary actions of entities and their advisors without the Board's having to undertake another reconsideration of this topic.

65. Some respondents asked the Board to permit a plan-by-plan choice between the intrinsic value based method in Opinion 25 and the fair value based method established by this Statement. Those respondents argued that permitting a choice on a plan-by-plan basis would result in a more level playing field than this Statement does because entities could

avoid the volatility in compensation cost for performance-based awards that often results from Opinion 25's requirements while continuing to report zero expense for most fixed awards.

66. The Board decided not to permit a plan-by-plan choice of accounting method. The overriding objective of this project was to improve the accounting for stock-based employee compensation by superseding Opinion 25's inconsistent requirements for fixed and variable awards with accounting standards that would result in more relevant and representationally faithful financial statements. That overriding objective could not be achieved without developing an internally consistent accounting method for all stock-based employee compensation awards, which in turn would result in a more level playing field for fixed and performance-based awards. Providing a plan-by-plan choice would permit an entity to choose whichever method it expected to produce the lower reported cost for each award. Permitting that choice was not among the objectives of this project.

67. The Board notes that permitting a plan-by-plan choice of accounting method would still be biased in favor of fixed awards and therefore would not level the playing field because entities would continue to be required to report compensation cost for performance-based awards while reporting no cost for fixed, at-the-money stock options. Permitting a plan-by-plan choice of method also would eliminate any possibility that evolution alone, perhaps including the development of improved methods of valuing employee stock options, would eventually result in better accounting for stock-based employee compensation.

68. Permitting a plan-by-plan choice also would result in more complicated financial statements. Entities would need to explain which method was used for which plans and why, as well as provide disclosures to help users of the financial statements understand the effects of the accounting choices and to put all entities' reporting on a comparable basis.

Pro Forma Disclosure of the Effects of Applying Fair Value Based Accounting

69. Because this Statement permits an entity to choose either of two different methods of accounting for its stock-based employee compensation arrangements, pro forma disclosures of net income and earnings per share computed as if the fair value based method had been applied are required in the financial

statements of an entity that chooses to continue to apply Opinion 25. Those disclosures will give investors, creditors, and other users of the financial statements more comparable information, regardless of the accounting method chosen. The pro forma disclosures also will make available better information than Opinion 25 provides about the costs of stock-based employee compensation.

Accounting for Equity Instruments Issued for Consideration Other Than Employee Services

70. The Exposure Draft was the result of a comprehensive reconsideration of accounting issues related to the measurement and recognition of stock-based compensation paid to employees for their services. The Board's deliberations that led to the Exposure Draft also considered current accounting principles for other issuances of equity instruments. The Exposure Draft covered accounting for all issuances of equity instruments for consideration other than cash, which may consist of goods, services, or noncash financial instruments. Issuances of equity instruments for cash rarely raise significant accounting issues.

71. That the cost of employee services measured by the fair value of equity instruments issued in exchange for them should be recognized in determining the employer's net income is not a new notion. Indeed, recognition of consideration received and the cost incurred as that consideration is used in an entity's operations is fundamental to the accounting for equity instruments. Therefore, the Board decided that the choice of continuing to apply Opinion 25 should be limited to issuances of equity instruments for employee services that fall within the scope of Opinion 25. All other issuances of equity instruments should be recognized based on the fair value of the consideration received or the fair value of the equity instrument issued, whichever is more reliably measurable.

72. The appropriate date at which to measure an issuance of equity instruments for consideration other than employee services usually is a relatively minor issue. Generally, an issuer of equity instruments receives the consideration for them—whether it is cash, another financial instrument, or an enforceable right to receive financial instruments, goods, or services in the future—almost immediately after the parties agree to the transaction. If a longer time elapses between agreement and receipt of consideration, neither the issuer nor the other party may have a unilateral obligation under the contract during that period.

That is, the distinction between grant date and vesting date may not be clearly present in many situations other than stock-based employee compensation. For some transactions, such as business combinations, in which the measurement date can be a significant issue, other accounting pronouncements specify the date of the stock price on which the measurement should be based. Therefore, this Statement does not specify the measurement date for determining the fair value of equity instruments issued to other than employees.

73. An initial draft of portions of this Statement was distributed for comment to task force members and other constituents. That draft would have excluded stock options issued to independent contractors from the transactions to which an entity may apply Opinion 25 in determining net income. Some respondents objected to that exclusion because, in practice, the scope of Opinion 25 has been extended to include many option recipients treated as independent contractors for tax purposes. Some Board members believe that application of Opinion 25 to service providers that are not employees is inappropriate. However, the Board decided that resolving the issue of whether Opinion 25 has been applied correctly is outside the scope of this Statement. The Board expects to consider at a future date the need for a pronouncement about the scope of Opinion 25.

Why Stock-Based Employee Compensation Is a Cost That Should Be Recognized in Financial Statements

74. Paragraphs 75-117 of this appendix discuss the reasons for the Board's principal conclusions on recognition and measurement issues, which support the Board's belief that recognition of stock-based employee compensation cost determined according to the fair value based method is preferable to continued application of Opinion 25 with only pro forma disclosures of the effect of recognizing stock-based employee compensation cost. That discussion begins with the basic issue of why employee stock options give rise to recognizable compensation cost.

75. The Board's conclusion that recognizing the costs of all stock-based employee compensation, including fixed, at-the-money stock options, is the preferable accounting method stems from the following premises:

a. Employee stock options have value.

b. Valuable financial instruments given to employees give rise to compensation cost that is properly included in measuring an entity's net income.

c. The value of employee stock options can be estimated within acceptable limits for recognition in financial statements.

Employee Stock Options Have Value

76. An option or warrant to buy an entity's stock for a fixed price during an extended future time period is a valuable right, even if the ways in which the holder can exercise the right are limited. Investors pay cash to buy stock options and warrants that generally have fewer restrictions than employee stock options, and unrestricted options and warrants are traded daily in financial markets. The additional restrictions inherent in employee stock options, such as the inability to transfer the option to a third party for cash, cause the value of an employee stock option to be less than the value of an otherwise identical tradable option at any time before the expiration date, but the restrictions do not render employee stock options valueless.

77. Employees rarely pay cash to acquire their employee stock options. Instead, employees provide services to their employer in exchange for cash, stock options, and other employee benefits. Even if employees are required to pay a nominal amount of cash for their options, it usually is far less than the fair value of the options received. The majority of the consideration an employer receives for employee stock options is employee services. Nonrecognition of compensation cost implies either that employee stock options are free to employees or that the options have no value—neither of which is true.

78. Some respondents argued that an employee stock option has value only if the employee ultimately realizes a gain from it. The Board does not agree. Many traded options ultimately expire worthless; that does not mean that the options had no value either when they were written or at any other time before they expired. An employee stock option has value when it is granted regardless of whether, ultimately, (a) the employee exercises the option and purchases stock worth more than the employee pays for it or (b) the option expires worthless at the end of the option period. The grant date value of a stock option is the value *at that date* of the right to purchase an entity's stock at a fixed price for an extended time period. Investors pay cash to acquire that right—employees provide services to acquire it.

Valuable Financial Instruments Given to Employees Give Rise to Compensation Cost That Is Properly Included in Measuring an Entity's Net Income

79. Employees provide services for which employers pay compensation. The components of an employee's total compensation package are, to some extent, flexible. The compensation package, for example, might include more cash and less health insurance, or the package might include stock options and less cash. Some employers even offer employees a choice between predetermined amounts of cash and stock options.

80. Large employers have included stock options in the compensation packages of upper echelon management for many years, and some employers recently have adopted broad-based plans that cover most of their full-time employees. A stated objective of issuing stock options is to align employee interests with those of shareholders and thereby motivate employees to work to maximize shareholder value. In addition, many start-up and other cash-poor entities provide stock options to make up for cash wages and other benefits that are less than those available elsewhere. Many respondents from younger, rapidly growing entities said that their success was attributable in large part to their extensive use of stock options; without stock options, they could not have attracted and retained the employees they needed.

81. Some respondents said that stock options are not direct compensation for services rendered and thus are not comparable to cash salaries and wages. Rather, stock options usually have other objectives, such as to attract valuable employees and to encourage them to stay with the employer by requiring a period of service before their options vest and become exercisable. Stock options, like other forms of incentive compensation, also are intended to motivate employees to perform better than they might have without the incentive. Stock-based compensation awards often are intended to compensate employees for incremental efforts beyond the basic performance required to earn their salaries or wages. Respondents that made those points generally said that the value of stock options is not a compensation cost that should be recognized in the entity's financial statements.

82. The Board acknowledges that employee stock options, as well as other forms of stock-based compensation, usually are not direct substitutes for a

stated amount of cash salaries. That does not, however, imply that the value of options issued to employees is not a recognizable cost. Group medical and life insurance, disability insurance, employer-paid memberships in health clubs, and the like also are not direct compensation like cash salaries because the amount of benefit that an individual employee may receive does not necessarily vary directly with either the amount or the quality of the services rendered. However, virtually everyone agrees that the costs of those benefits are properly deducted in determining the entity's net income. Like employee stock options, benefits such as medical insurance and pensions are compensation in the broad sense of costs incurred to attract, retain, and motivate employees. It has long been an established practice that, even if employee benefits are paid—directly or indirectly—with shares of the employer's stock, the value of the stock issued to the employee or the service provider is a cost to be reported in the employer's income statement.

83. Some opponents of recognizing compensation cost for stock options acknowledge that stock options are recognizable compensation, but they say that a requirement to recognize that compensation would have adverse economic consequences because many entities would reduce or eliminate their stock option programs. However, some of the same respondents also said that Opinion 25's bias in favor of fixed awards at the expense of awards with performance conditions, options with indexed exercise prices, and the like should be eliminated because that bias has undesirable economic consequences. It deters employers from using more performance-based awards, which those respondents consider preferable to fixed options in many situations.

84. The Board's operating precepts require it to consider issues in an even-handed manner, without intentionally attempting to encourage or to discourage specific economic actions. That does not imply that improved financial reporting should not have economic consequences; a change in accounting standards that makes available more relevant and representationally faithful financial information often will have economic consequences. For example, the availability of the new information resulting from application of this Statement may lead an entity to reassess the costs and benefits of its existing stock option plans. If a reassessment reveals that the expected benefits of a stock option plan do not justify its costs, a rational response would be to revise or eliminate the plan. However, an entity presumably would not

restrict or eliminate a stock option program whose motivational effect on employees is expected to make a net contribution to reported results of operations. To do so would not be rational because continuing the plan would be expected to increase revenues (or to decrease other expenses) more than enough to offset the reported compensation cost. In addition, many small, emerging entities told the Board that stock options often substitute for higher cash wages or other benefits, such as pensions. Significantly reducing those option programs would not make economic sense if employees would demand equal or greater cash wages or other benefits to replace the lost stock options.

85. Some people told the Board that a requirement to recognize compensation cost might bring additional discipline to the use of employee stock options. Unless and until the stock price rises sufficiently to result in a dilutive effect on earnings per share, the current accounting for most fixed stock options treats them as though they were a "free good." Stock options have value—employee stock options are granted as consideration for services and thus are not free.

86. Some respondents said that recognizing the compensation cost stemming from stock options would, by itself, raise the cost of capital of all entities that use options extensively. An individual entity's cost of capital would rise only if its lenders or buyers and sellers of its stock had previously been misled by the accounting under Opinion 25 to believe that fixed, at-the-money employee stock options have no value and thus impose no cost on the entity. If that were the situation for an individual entity or a group of entities, any increase in cost of capital would result from new, relevant information. Making available at an acceptable cost information that is helpful in making investment, credit, and similar decisions is the overriding objective of financial reporting.

87. Some respondents that agreed with the Board's conclusion that accounting standards, by themselves, are highly unlikely to have negative economic consequences noted that the market abhors uncertainty. Reducing uncertainty can reduce the cost of capital. Therefore, recognizing in financial statements the cost of all stock-based compensation measured in a reasonable and internally consistent manner might lower rather than raise an entity's cost of capital. Financial statement users no longer would have to decide how to consider the cost of stock options in their analysis of an entity, knowing that whatever method they chose would be based on inadequate information. With amounts recognized and measured on a

reasonable and consistent basis that takes into account detailed information generally available only to the entity, users might still choose to modify or use the available information in different ways, but they would have a reasonable starting point for their analysis.

Expenses and capital transactions

88. Some respondents pointed out that the definition of expenses in FASB Concepts Statement No. 6, *Elements of Financial Statements,* says that expenses result from outflows or using up of assets or incurring of liabilities (or both). They asserted that because the issuance of stock options does not result in the incurrence of a liability, no expense should be recognized. The Board agrees that employee stock options are not a liability—like stock purchase warrants, employee stock options are equity instruments of the issuer. However, equity instruments, including employee stock options, are valuable financial instruments and thus are issued for valuable consideration, which often is cash or other financial instruments but for employee stock options is employee services. Using in the entity's operations the benefits embodied in the asset received results in an expense, regardless of whether the consideration is cash or other financial instruments, goods, or services.[14] Moreover, even if shares of stock or other equity instruments are donated to a charity, the fair value of the instruments issued is recognized together with other charitable contributions in determining the issuer's net income. The Board recently reaffirmed that general principle in FASB Statement No. 116, *Accounting for Contributions Received and Contributions Made.*

89. Others noted that the issuance of an employee stock option is a capital transaction. They contended that capital transactions do not give rise to expenses. As discussed in paragraph 88, however, issuances of equity instruments result in the receipt of cash, other financial instruments, goods, or services, which give rise to expenses as they are used in an entity's operations. Accounting for the consideration received for issuing equity instruments has long been fundamental to the accounting for all free-standing equity instruments except one—fixed stock options subject to the requirements of Opinion 25.

90. Some respondents also asserted that the issuance of an employee stock option is a transaction directly

between the recipient and the preexisting stockholders in which the stockholders agree to share future equity appreciation with employees. The Board disagrees. Employees provide services to the entity—not directly to the individual stockholders—as consideration for their options. Carried to its logical conclusion, that view would imply that the issuance of virtually any equity instrument, at least those issued for goods or services rather than cash or other financial instruments, should not affect the issuer's financial statements. For example, no asset or related cost would be reported if shares of stock were issued to acquire legal or consulting services, tangible assets, or an entire business in a business combination. Moreover, in practice today, even if a stockholder directly pays part of an employee's cash compensation (or other corporate expenses), the transaction and the related costs are reflected in the entity's financial statements, together with the stockholder's contribution to paid-in capital. To omit such costs would give a misleading picture of the entity's financial performance.

91. The Board sees no conceptual basis that justifies different accounting for the issuance of employee stock options than for all other transactions involving either equity instruments or employee services. As explained in paragraphs 57-62, the Board's decision not to require recognition of compensation expense based on the fair value of options issued to employees was not based on conceptual considerations.

Prepaid compensation

92. The Exposure Draft proposed that an asset, prepaid compensation, be recognized at the date stock-based employee compensation awards are granted; the prepaid compensation would represent the value already conveyed to employees for services to be received in the future. Later, compensation cost would have been incurred as the benefits embodied in that asset were used up; that is, as the employees rendered service during the vesting period.

93. Many respondents objected to the recognition of prepaid compensation at the grant date. They said that, unlike most other amounts paid to suppliers before services are received, the proposed prepaid compensation for nonvested stock-based employee compensation did not meet the definition of an asset in paragraph 25 of Concepts Statement 6, which defines

---

[14]Concepts Statement 6, paragraph 81, footnote 43, notes that, in concept, most expenses decrease assets. However, if receipt of an asset, such as services, and its use occur virtually simultaneously, the asset often is not recorded.

assets as "probable future economic benefits obtained or controlled by a particular entity as a result of past transactions or events" (footnote reference omitted). Prepaid fees for legal services, consulting services, insurance services, and the like represent probable future economic benefits that are controlled by the entity because the other party to the transaction has entered into a contract to provide services to earn the fees. The service provider is not entitled to walk away from its obligation to render the services that are the subject of the contract by merely foregoing collection of the fee for services not rendered. Although courts rarely enforce specific performance under a service contract, a construction contractor, for example, cannot decide unilaterally not to finish a building after digging the foundation without being subject to legal action for monetary damages by the other party to the contract. Contracts sometimes specify the damages to be paid if the contract is broken. In other circumstances, such as prepaid rent or insurance, the purchaser of the service may be able to successfully sue for specific performance—the right to occupy an office or to be reimbursed for fire damage, for example.

94. Those respondents said that employee stock options do not represent probable future benefits that are controlled by the employer at the date the options are granted because employees are not obligated to render the services required to earn their options. The contract is unilateral—not bilateral—because the entity has only conditionally transferred forfeitable equity instruments and is obligated to issue the instruments *if and when* the employee has rendered the specified service or satisfied other conditions. However, the employee is not obligated to perform the services and may leave the employer's service without being subject to damages beyond the loss of the compensation that would have been paid had the services been rendered.

95. The Board agreed that an entity does not obtain an asset for future service to be rendered at the date employee stock options are granted. Therefore, this Statement does not require recognition of prepaid compensation at the grant date. Rather, the cost of the related services is accrued and charged to compensation cost only in the period or periods in which the related services are received. At the grant date, awards of stock-based employee compensation are fully executory contracts. Once employees begin to render the services necessary to earn the compensation, execution of the contracts has begun, and recognition of the services already received is appropriate. The

Board's conclusions on how to attribute compensation cost to the periods in which the entity receives the related employee services are discussed further in paragraphs 196-203.

96. An equity instrument may be conditionally transferred to another party under an agreement that allows that party to choose at a later date whether to deliver the agreed consideration for it, which may be goods or services rather than cash or financial instruments, or to forfeit the right to the instrument conditionally transferred, with no further obligation. In that situation, the equity instrument is not *issued* for accounting purposes until the issuing entity has received consideration for it and the condition is thus satisfied. The grant of an employee stock option subject to vesting conditions is an example of such a conditional transfer. For that reason, this Statement does not use the term *issued* to refer to the grant of a stock option or other equity instrument that is subject to service or performance conditions for vesting. The Board's conclusion that the entity receives no asset at the date employee stock options are granted is consistent with that use of the term *issued*. That conclusion about the issuance date of employee stock options, in turn, has implications for the appropriate date at which to measure the value of the equity instruments issued. This Statement requires a measurement method that combines attributes of both grant date and vesting date measurement. The Board's conclusions on measurement date and method are discussed in paragraphs 149-154.

The usefulness and integrity of the income statement

97. An entity's income statement reports the revenues from and the costs of its operations. Under Opinion 25, part of a cost, compensation to employees, is not reported in the income statements of most entities that issue fixed stock options. Some entities use fixed stock options more extensively than other entities do, and reported operating expenses thus are understated to differing degrees. Comparisons between entities of profit margins, rates of return, income from operations, and the like are impaired to the extent that entities continue to account for their stock-based employee compensation according to the provisions of Opinion 25.

98. To illustrate the lack of comparability under Opinion 25, assume that Companies A, B, and C each report $6 million of total compensation cost. Company A does not grant fixed stock options to its

employees, but Companies B and C do. The value of fixed stock options as a percentage of the total compensation package for employees of Companies B and C are 20 percent and 40 percent, respectively. Total compensation cost for Company A is $6 million, as reported in its financial statements. Although Companies B and C report the same amount of compensation cost as Company A, actual compensation is $7.5 million for Company B and $10 million for Company C. The three companies are not competing for capital on a level playing field because their financial statements are not comparable.

99. Some opponents of recognizing compensation cost for stock options are concerned about the adverse effect they contend it would have on their income statements. The effect of recognizing compensation cost for employee stock options should be neither more nor less adverse than the effect of recognizing a comparable amount of depreciation (or any other) cost. Recognition of depreciation always reduces a company's profit or increases its loss. Entities would look more profitable on paper if they discontinued depreciating their assets, but no one recommends not recognizing depreciation to eliminate its adverse effect on the income statement. The Board believes that the rationale that a potentially adverse effect on income statements argues against recognition is no more compelling for compensation than it is for any other cost.

The cost of employee stock options is not "recognized" in earnings per share

100. Primary earnings per share represents the entity's earnings (the numerator) divided by the number of common and common equivalent shares outstanding (the denominator). Some respondents that opposed recognizing compensation cost for employee stock options said that to do so would "double count" the effect of issuing stock options. The dilutive effect of any in-the-money stock options is included in the denominator of earnings per share, and a reduction in net income (the numerator) would, in their view, create an inappropriate dual effect.

101. The Board disagrees. A transaction that results in an expense and also increases, actually or potentially, the number of shares outstanding properly affects both the numerator and denominator of the earnings per share calculation. If an entity issues stock, stock options, or stock purchase warrants for cash and uses the cash received to pay expenses, earnings are reduced and more common equivalent

shares are outstanding. Even in applying the requirements of Opinion 25, granting nonvested (so-called restricted) stock decreases the numerator (earnings) and increases the denominator (shares outstanding). In both of those examples, the effect on income appropriately reflects the use of the consideration received (either cash or employee services) for issuing equity instruments.

Disclosure is not a substitute for recognition

102. FASB Concepts Statement No. 5, *Recognition and Measurement in Financial Statements of Business Enterprises,* says:

> Since recognition means depiction of an item in both words and numbers, with the amount included in the totals of the financial statements, disclosure by other means is *not* recognition. Disclosure of information about the items in financial statements and their measures that may be provided by notes or parenthetically on the face of financial statements, by supplementary information, or by other means of financial reporting is not a substitute for recognition in financial statements for items that meet recognition criteria. [paragraph 9]

103. Many respondents contended that improved disclosures about employee stock options in the notes to financial statements would be as useful as recognition of compensation cost in the income statement. A specific disclosure proposal submitted by a group of providers and users of financial statements and endorsed by the largest accounting firms was illustrated in Appendix E of the Exposure Draft. Most respondents, including some that had previously endorsed that proposal, agreed that the proposed disclosures were too extensive and included some items that more properly belong in a proxy statement. The Board received several other proposals for disclosures in lieu of recognition during the exposure period and during its redeliberations of the conclusions in the Exposure Draft. Some of those proposals included a measure of the value of options granted during the year, but most focused largely on greatly expanding the detailed data disclosed about stock-based employee compensation plans.

104. As discussed in paragraphs 57-62, the Board's decision to encourage but not to require recognition of compensation cost for the fair value of stock-based

employee compensation was not based on acceptance of the view that disclosure is an adequate substitute for recognition in the financial statements. If disclosure and recognition were equal alternatives, the arguments for only disclosing either detailed information about stock-based employee compensation awards or the amount of unrecognized cost would apply equally to other costs such as depreciation, warranties, pensions, and other postretirement benefits.

105. The Board believes that the pro forma disclosures required by this Statement will mitigate to some extent the disadvantages of permitting disclosure in lieu of recognition. To disclose only additional details about options granted, vested, forfeited, exercised, expired, and the like would permit only the most sophisticated users of financial statements to estimate the income statement impact of recognizing all compensation costs. Many individual investors and other users of financial statements could not, and even the more sophisticated users would have available less information than the entity itself has on which to base estimates of value and related compensation cost related to employee stock options. The Board's continuing belief that disclosure is not an adequate substitute for recognition of items that qualify for recognition in financial statements is the reason for this Statement's establishment of the fair value based accounting method as preferable for purposes of justifying an accounting change and for encouraging entities to adopt it.

106. The Board did not specifically address during its formal deliberations whether pro forma disclosures of the effects on net income and earnings per share of applying the fair value based method should be included in summarized interim financial data required by APB Opinion No. 28, *Interim Financial Reporting*. That question arose late in the process of drafting this Statement when some Board members noted that comparable information about earnings and earnings per share presented on a quarterly basis would be important to financial analysis. Other Board members agreed but thought that it was too late in this extraordinarily controversial project to add a requirement for pro forma disclosures in summarized interim financial data. Therefore, this Statement does not require those disclosures. If a need for pro forma disclosures on a quarterly basis becomes apparent, the Board will consider at a later date whether to require those disclosures.

The Value of Employee Stock Options Can Be Estimated within Acceptable Limits for Recognition in Financial Statements

107. The value of employee services rendered is almost always impossible to measure directly. For that reason, accounting for the cost of employee services is based on the value of compensation paid, which is presumed to be an adequate measure of the value of the services received. Compensation cost resulting from employee stock options is measured based on the value of stock options granted rather than on the value of the services rendered by the employee, which is consistent with the accounting for other forms of employee compensation.

108. Trading of options in the financial markets has increased significantly in the last 20 years. During that time, mathematical models to estimate the fair value of options have been developed to meet the needs of investors. Some employers and compensation consultants have used variations of those models in considering how much of a compensation package should consist of employee stock options and in determining the total value of a compensation package that includes stock options. Many that have been using option-pricing models for those purposes said that the existing models are not sufficiently accurate for accounting purposes, although they are adequate for comparing the value of compensation packages across entities and for estimating the value of options in designing compensation packages. Those respondents generally said that a more precise measure is needed for measuring compensation cost in the income statement than for comparing the value of total compensation, including options, paid by various entities or in determining how many options to grant an employee.

109. The Board disagrees with the distinction made by those respondents. One important use of financial statements is to compare the relative attractiveness of investment and lending opportunities available in different entities. Therefore, increasing the comparability of financial statements is a worthy goal, even if all entities use a measurement method that is less precise than the Board or its constituents might prefer.

110. The derivative markets have developed rapidly with the introduction of new kinds of options and option-like instruments, many of which are long term and nontraded—or even nontransferable. For example, interest rate caps and floors, both of which are forms of options, are now common. Often, option

components are embedded in other instruments, and both the seller and the purchaser of the instrument need to evaluate the value added by each component of a compound instrument. Mathematical models that extend or adapt traditional option-pricing models to take into account new features of options and other derivative securities also continue to be developed. Sometimes decisions have been made based on inadequate analysis or incomplete models, resulting in large and highly publicized losses for one party to a contract. Those instances usually lead to additional analysis of the instruments in question and further refinement of the models. However, market participants—whether they consider themselves to be traders, investors, or hedgers—continue to commit billions of dollars to positions in options and other derivatives, based at least in part on analysis using mathematical pricing models that are not perfect.

111. The Exposure Draft noted that uncertainties inherent in estimates of the fair value of employee stock options are generally no more significant than the uncertainties inherent in measurements of, for example, loan loss reserves, valuation allowances for deferred tax assets, and pension and other postretirement benefit obligations. All estimates, because they are estimates, are imprecise. Few accrual-based accounting measurements can claim absolute reliability, but most parties agree that financial statement recognition of estimated amounts that are approximately right is preferable to the alternative—recognizing nothing—which is what Opinion 25 accounting recognizes for most employee stock options. Zero is not within the range of reasonable estimates of the value of employee stock options at the date they are granted, the date they vest, or at other dates before they expire, with the possible exception of deep-out-of-the-money options that are near expiration. Even those latter options generally have a nominal value until very shortly before expiration.

112. Many respondents said that the Exposure Draft inappropriately compared the imprecision in estimating the value of employee stock options with similar imprecisions inherent in estimating, for example, the amount of an entity's obligation to provide postretirement health care benefits. They said that because postretirement health care benefits eventually result in cash payments by the entity, the total obligation and related cost are "trued up" over the entity's life. In contrast, the value of employee stock options estimated at the grant date is not trued up to reflect the actual gain, if any, that an employee realizes from an award of employee stock options. Those respondents

asserted that the lack of true-up makes it necessary for the estimated value of employee stock options that forms the basis for recognizing the related compensation cost to be more precise than an estimate of the value of the same entity's obligation for postretirement health care benefits.

113. The Board questions that perceived distinction between the relative importance of the precision of estimates of the value of employee stock options and the precision of other estimates inherent in financial statements. Although the total amount of any expense that is ultimately paid in cash will necessarily equal the total of the amounts attributed to each of a series of years, the appropriate amount to attribute to any individual year is never trued up. Nor can the precision of the reported total obligation be determined at any date while it is being incurred. For example, the total cost of a postretirement health care plan will be trued up only if the plan is terminated. Investors, creditors, and other users of financial statements must make decisions based on a series of individual years' financial statements that covers less than the entire life of the entity. For costs such as postretirement health care benefits, the true-up period for an individual employee (or group of similar employees) may be decades, and even then the total amount cannot be separated from amounts attributed to other employees. Concern about the reliability of estimates of the value of employee stock options and the related cost seem equally applicable to annual estimates of, for example, obligations for postretirement benefits and the related cost.

114. The respondents that emphasized the importance of truing up the total cost of a stock-based employee compensation award generally were adamantly opposed to exercise date accounting—the only accounting method for employee stock options that would true up interim cost estimates to equal the total gain, if any, an employee realizes. The Board rejected exercise date accounting for conceptual reasons, as discussed in paragraph 149. However, deferring final measurement of a transaction until enough of the related uncertainties have been resolved to make reasonably reliable measurement possible is the usual accounting response to measurement difficulties for virtually all other transactions except an award to an employee of fixed stock options.

115. The standard Black-Scholes and binomial option-pricing models were designed to estimate the value of transferable stock options. The value of transferable stock options is more than the value of

employee stock options at the date they are granted primarily for two reasons. First, transferable stock options can be sold, while employee stock options are not transferable and can only be exercised. Second, an employee can neither sell nor exercise nonvested options. Nonvested employee options cannot be exercised because the employee has not yet fully paid for them and is not obligated to do so. Options other than employee options rarely include a lengthy period during which the holder may choose to walk away from the right to the options.

116. The measurement method in this Statement reduces the estimated value of employee stock options below that produced by an option-pricing model for nonforfeitable, transferable options. Under the method in this Statement, the recognized value of an employee stock option that does not vest—and thus is never issued to the employee—is zero. In addition, the estimated value of an employee stock option is based on its expected life rather than its maximum term, which may be considerably longer. Paragraphs 155-173 explain why the Board believes those adjustments are appropriate and sufficient to deal with the forfeitability and nontransferability of employee stock options.

117. The Board continues to believe that use of option-pricing models, as modified in this Statement, will produce estimates of the fair value of stock options that are sufficiently reliable to justify recognition in financial statements. Imprecision in those estimates does not justify failure to recognize compensation cost stemming from employee stock options. That belief underlies the Board's encouragement to entities to adopt the fair value based method of recognizing stock-based employee compensation cost in their financial statements.

The Major Measurement Issues

118. Having concluded that stock-based compensation awards, including fixed employee stock options, give rise to compensation cost that should be measured and recognized, the Board considered more detailed measurement and recognition issues.

Measurement Date for Compensation Cost

119. The measurement date for equity instruments awarded to employees is the date at which the stock

price that determines the measurement of the transaction is fixed. The Board decided to retain the provisions of the Exposure Draft that the measurement date for equity instruments awarded to employees (and subsequently issued to them if vesting conditions are satisfied) and the related compensation cost is to be measured based on the stock price at the grant date. The Board also decided that the measurement method for public entities should be fair value. The reasons for those conclusions are discussed in paragraphs 120-153.

Alternative measurement dates

120. Possible measurement dates[15] include the date an award of employee stock options or similar instruments is granted *(grant date)*, the date on which an employee has completed the service period necessary for the award to vest *(vesting date)*, the dates on which an employee renders the related services *(service date)*, the date on which all service-related conditions expire *(service expiration date)*, and the date an award is exercised or expires *(exercise date)*.

Grant date

121. Advocates of grant date measurement note that the employer and employee come to a mutual understanding of the terms of a stock-based compensation award at the grant date and that the employee begins to render the service necessary to earn the award at that date. They therefore consider use of the grant date stock price appropriate in measuring the transaction. In deciding whether to grant shares of stock, for example, and how many shares to award an individual employee, both parties to the agreement presumably have in mind the current stock price—not the possible stock price at a future date. If compensation cost were measured based on the stock price at a later date, such as the date at which the award vests, the amount of compensation cost that could result from an award would not be known when an entity decides how many shares to grant.

122. Advocates of grant date measurement also consider it to be consistent with generally accepted concepts and practices applied to other equity instruments. They note that changes in the price of an issuer's stock after the parties agree to the terms of a transaction in which equity instruments are issued

---

[15]The various measurement dates discussed refer to the dates of the stock price on which fair value and the related cost are based—not the date at which accounting based on estimates begins. For example, most advocates of vesting date measurement would begin accruing compensation cost as soon as employees begin to render the service necessary to earn their awards.

generally do not affect the amount at which the transaction is recognized. Grant date measurement is based on the view that equity instruments are issued to employees—not just conditionally transferred to them—at the grant date because the entity becomes unilaterally obligated at that date. To be fully consistent with that premise, application of grant date measurement would reflect at the grant date the effect of all restrictions inherent in vesting requirements in estimating the value of the instrument considered to be effectively issued at the grant date. For example, the value of an option with a performance vesting condition would be reduced to reflect both the likelihood that the performance condition will not be satisfied and the likelihood that an employee will not continue in service until the end of the vesting period. Because the option is considered to have been issued to the employee at the grant date, initial estimates would not be subsequently adjusted to reflect differences between estimates and experience.

123. To illustrate, if an employee stock option is considered to be issued at the grant date, the effects of its forfeitability, nonexercisability, and any other restrictions that are in effect during the vesting period but that are removed after the equity instrument vests would be estimated at the grant date and not subsequently adjusted. Changes in the value of an entity's equity instruments, whatever the source, are not reflected in its income statement. For example, if an entity grants 10,000 options, of which 8,000 are expected to vest, the final measurement of compensation cost in accordance with a strict application of grant date measurement would be based on the value of 8,000 options estimated at the grant date, regardless of whether all 10,000 options or only 4,000 options eventually vested.

Vesting date

124. Proponents of measuring the value of equity instruments awarded to employees and the related compensation cost based on the stock price at the date the award vests note that employees have not earned the right to retain their shares or options until that date. They suggest that a more descriptive term for the *grant date* would be *offer date* because the entity makes an offer at that date and becomes unilaterally obligated to issue equity instruments to employees if the employees render the necessary service or satisfy other conditions for vesting. Employees effectively accept the offer by fulfilling the requisite conditions (generally rendering services) for vesting. Proponents contend that the transaction between the

employer and employee should not be finally measured until both parties have fulfilled their obligations under the agreement because the employee has only a conditional right to the equity instruments and the instruments thus are not actually issued until that date.

125. Advocates of vesting date measurement consider that method to be consistent with accounting for the issuance of similar equity instruments to third parties for either cash or an enforceable right to receive cash or other assets in the future. At the date a stock purchase warrant, for example, is issued and measured, the investor need not satisfy obligations to provide further assets or services to the issuer to become eligible to retain and exercise the warrant. For the same reason, vesting date advocates do not think that measurement of the transaction should be held open after the vesting date. Once an employee stock option becomes vested, they contend that the employee is in much the same position as a third-party holder of a stock purchase warrant.

Service date

126. Service date measurement can be described as a variation of vesting date measurement because, in both methods, measurement of the transaction between an employer and its employees is held open until employees have rendered the services necessary to earn their awards. Advocates of service date measurement, however, point out that the earning of a stock-based compensation award—like the earning of other forms of compensation—is a continuous process. They say that the related compensation cost should be measured based on the stock prices during the period the service is rendered—not solely on the stock price at either the beginning or the end of that period.

127. Advocates of service date measurement prefer it to vesting date measurement because the latter adjusts the value (and related cost) of the service received in, for example, year 1 of a two-year vesting period based on stock price changes that occur in year 2. Moreover, the increment (or decrement) in value attributable to year 1's service is recognized in year 2. In their view, to retroactively adjust the value of consideration (in this situation, employee services) already received for future issuance of an equity instrument is to treat awards of equity instruments to employees as if they were liabilities until the employees have vested rights to them. Because an entity that grants stock options is obligated only to issue its own

stock, not to transfer its assets, those that favor service date accounting contend that measuring nonvested awards as if they were liabilities is inappropriate.

128. Under service date measurement, a proportionate number of the shares in a grant of shares of stock subject to vesting requirements, for example, would in concept be measured based on the stock price each day that an employee renders service. In practice, the results of daily accrual probably would be reasonably approximated by basing the amount of compensation cost recognized each accounting period on the average stock price for that period.

Service expiration date

129. The service expiration date, sometimes referred to as the *portability date,* is the date at which all service-related conditions that may change the terms under which employees may exercise their stock options expire. Awards of employee stock options generally specify a limited period of time, often 90 days but sometimes a shorter or even no period, after termination of service during which employees with vested options may exercise them. The options are canceled if they are not exercised by the end of that period. If the exercise period is 90 days after termination, the service expiration or portability date is 90 days before the maximum term of the options expires. If the options are exercised before then, the exercise date would be the measurement date. (For an award of stock subject to vesting requirements, the service expiration date is the date at which service-related restrictions on the sale of the stock lapse, which usually would be the same as the vesting date.)

130. Advocates of service expiration date measurement argue that a limitation on exercise of an option after termination of service, say to 90 days, effectively reduces the term of a vested option to 90 days. On the day that an employee's rights to that option vest, the employee holds an option whose effective term is 90 days, regardless of its stated term. Each additional day of service until the service expiration date extends the life of the option by one day. Advocates also generally note that equity of an entity arises from transactions between the entity and its owners in their role as owners, not as suppliers, employees, creditors, or some other role. Advocates of service expiration date measurement do not consider an employee stock option to be an outstanding equity instrument as long as the employee must render additional service to extend the term of the option. Until

then, the ongoing transaction is one between an entity and its employees in their role as employees in which the entity incurs a liability to pay for employee services. Thus, they say that it is appropriate to treat the option as a liability until all service-related restrictions expire (or the option is exercised, whichever comes first).

131. Supporters of service expiration date measurement also note that it would be easier to apply than earlier measurement dates. If the period after which service-related conditions expire is short, such as 90 days, most of the option's value at that time is likely to be made up of its intrinsic value, which is readily measurable. If the option has no intrinsic value at that time, its total value also is likely to be low, and concerns about how well traditional option-pricing models measure that value would be mitigated by the short life of the option.

Exercise date

132. Some that favor exercise date measurement of stock-based employee compensation awards do so because they consider call options written by an entity on its stock to be liabilities rather than equity instruments. They acknowledge that those options, including both employee stock options and stock purchase warrants, do not qualify as liabilities under the definition in paragraph 35 of Concepts Statement 6 because they do not obligate the entity to transfer its assets to the holder and thus lack an essential characteristic of a liability. Those that hold this view generally favor revising the conceptual distinction between liabilities and equity instruments so that an obligation to issue stock at a fixed price would qualify as a liability.

133. Advocates of exercise date measurement note that an obligation to issue stock at a price that may be less than its market price at the date of the transaction has the potential to transfer value from the preexisting stockholders to holders of the call options. In their view, that potential makes the obligation a liability of the entity, even though the entity is not obligated to transfer its own assets to the holders of the options. Other advocates of exercise date measurement contend that the gain, if any, that an employee realizes upon exercise of a stock option appropriately measures the total compensation paid. They are less concerned about the conceptual distinction between liabilities and equity because they see little, if any, practical difference between an employee stock option and a cash bonus indexed to the price of the entity's stock.

134. Exercise date advocates also note that measurement at that date is simple and straightforward. Concerns about how to apply option-pricing models initially developed for traded options to forfeitable, nontransferable employee options, how to estimate expected long-term volatility, and the like do not apply if final measurement is based on the gain, if any, that an employee realizes by exercising an option. The usual response to major problems in measuring the effects of a transaction is to defer final measurement until the difficulties are resolved. Exercise date measurement might be appropriate for that reason, regardless of more conceptual considerations.

Measurement Method for Compensation Cost

135. This Statement specifies fair value as the basic method for measuring awards of equity instruments, including stock options, to employees as compensation. Not only the appropriate measurement method but also the meaning of *fair value*—especially at the grant date—were contentious issues during the exposure period. Moreover, respondents' views on the measurement method often were closely linked to their views on the measurement date question. The possible measurement methods, together with differences, if any, in how they might be applied at various possible measurement dates are discussed in paragraphs 136-148. The reasons for the Board's conclusions on measurement date and method are then explained.

Intrinsic value

136. The intrinsic value of an option at any point during its term is the difference between its exercise price and the current price of the underlying stock. Intrinsic value thus excludes the value of the right to purchase the underlying stock at a fixed price for a specified future period—its time value. Respondents that favored measuring employee stock options at their intrinsic value generally said that intrinsic value is easily measured and understood. Some also noted that employees cannot convert the time value of their options to cash.

137. Intrinsic value measurement might be combined with any of the measurement dates discussed in paragraphs 120-134. However, the vast majority of the advocates of intrinsic value would accept only intrinsic value measurement at the grant date. They generally said that Opinion 25 has "worked well" and that the Board should not change its requirements but merely supplement them with additional disclosures.

However, some respondents went further and said that grant date-intrinsic value accounting—Opinion 25's method for fixed plans—should be applied to variable plans as well. Adopting that suggestion would result in recognition of no compensation cost for all options that are at-the-money when granted, implying that at-the-money options have no value. The inaccuracy of that implication already has been discussed (paragraphs 76-78).

138. Respondents that favored extending grant date-intrinsic value measurement to variable plans said that the result would be a level playing field for fixed and variable plans. The Board believes that adopting a grant date-intrinsic value method for all options would level the playing field at the cost of making financial statements even less relevant and representationally faithful than they are when Opinion 25 is the basis of measuring stock-based employee compensation cost. That is not an acceptable outcome of a project that was undertaken with the overriding objective of improving financial reporting. An *exercise date*-intrinsic value method also would level the playing field, and some Board members think that it would enhance the relevance and representational faithfulness of financial statements.

Minimum value

139. The so-called minimum value method derives its name from the theory underlying its calculation. The idea is that a person who wishes to purchase a call option on a given stock would be willing to pay *at least* (perhaps more important, the option writer would demand *at least*) an amount that represents the benefit (sacrifice) of the right to defer payment of the exercise price until the end of the option's term. For a dividend-paying stock, that amount is reduced by the present value of the expected dividends because the holder of an option does not receive the dividends paid on the underlying stock.

140. Minimum value thus can be determined by a present value calculation. It is (a) the current price of the stock reduced by the present value of the expected dividends on the stock, if any, during the option's term minus (b) the present value of the exercise price. Present values are based on the risk-free rate of return. For a 10-year option with an exercise price of $50 on a stock with a current price of $50 and expected dividends of $.25 paid at the end of each quarter—an expected annual dividend yield of 2 percent—minimum value is computed as shown below. The risk-free interest rate available for 10-year investments is 7 percent.

Current stock price	$50.00
Minus:	
Present value of exercise price[16]	24.83
Present value of expected dividends	7.21
Minimum value	$17.96

Investing $24.83 at a 7 percent risk-free interest rate for 10 years would give the investor $50, which is the amount needed to exercise the option. However, an investor who held the stock rather than the option would receive dividends during the term of the option with a present value of $7.21. The net benefit from deferring payment of the exercise price thus is $17.96.

141. Minimum value also can be computed using an option-pricing model and an expected volatility of effectively zero. (Standard option-pricing models do not work if the volatility input is zero because the models use volatility as a divisor, and zero cannot be a divisor. Using an expected volatility of, say, 0.001 avoids that problem.) In the above example, using an option-pricing model with an expected volatility of effectively zero, a risk-free rate of 7 percent, an expected dividend yield of 2 percent, and an option term of 10 years results in a minimum value of $16.11. That is lower than the amount calculated using simple present value techniques ($16.11 versus $17.96) because the calculations inherent in option-pricing models assume that both the stock price and dividends will grow at the same rate (if the dividend assumption is stated as a constant yield). The assumed growth rate is the difference between the risk-free interest rate and the dividend rate, which is 5 percent (7 percent – 2 percent) in this example.

142. For a stock that pays no dividends, minimum value is the same regardless of which method is used, and the lower the expected dividend yield, the less difference between the results of the two methods. This Statement permits only nonpublic entities to measure their options at minimum value (paragraphs 174-178 explain the Board's conclusions on nonpublic entities), and many of the nonpublic entities that use employee stock options extensively pay either no or relatively low dividends. Moreover, the expected life of employee stock options with a contractual term of 10 years often is substantially shorter, which also reduces the amount of potential difference. In addition, models are available that compute

value based on a fixed dividend amount, rather than a constant dividend yield. Therefore, the Board acceded to the request of some respondents to permit either method of computing minimum value.

Fair value

143. Because it ignores the effect of expected volatility, the minimum value method differs from methods designed to estimate the fair value of an option, such as the Black-Scholes and binomial option-pricing models and extensions or modifications of those original models. Expected volatility provides much of the value of options—especially relatively short-term options. Even for longer term options such as most employee stock options, the level of expected volatility accounts for a significant part of the difference in the values of options on different stocks. Option holders benefit from the volatility of stocks because they have the right to capture increases in the price of (and related return on) the underlying stock during the term of the option without having to bear the full risk of loss from stock price decreases. The maximum amount that the holder of a call option can lose is the premium paid to the option writer—which represents the right to benefit from price increases without the corresponding risk of loss from price decreases during the option term. In contrast, the holder of a share of the underlying stock can lose the full value of the share.

144. The fair value of the option whose minimum value was computed in paragraphs 140 and 141 thus is more than either $17.96 or $16.11. The fair value of that option depends on the expected volatility of the underlying stock. If the expected long-term volatility of the stock in the example is 35 percent, the fair value of the option is approximately $23.08. Volatility and its effect on option value are defined and explained more fully in Appendixes E and F.

What is the fair value of an employee stock option?

145. The Exposure Draft applied to employee stock options the same definition of fair value that is used elsewhere in the authoritative literature. That definition and the related guidance, which are quoted in paragraph 9, focus first on the price at which a willing buyer and a willing seller would be willing to exchange an item in other than a forced or liquidation

---

[16]Present value calculations reflect daily compounding.

sale and require the use of quoted market prices for the same or similar items if they are available. However, the definition mentions several valuation techniques, including option-pricing models, that are acceptable for estimating fair value if quoted market or other exchange prices for the item or a similar item are not available.

146. Some respondents apparently focused solely on the part of the definition that refers to the price a willing buyer would pay for an item. They said that the objective of determining the fair value of an employee stock option should be to determine the amount of cash compensation employees would be willing to trade for their stock options. Those respondents mentioned several reasons, such as the relatively large amount of most employees' personal financial wealth that is tied to the fortunes of their employer or employees' need for cash to pay current expenses, that might make most employees unwilling to pay as much as a third party might pay for a given stock option.

147. The Board rejected that view of the meaning of the *fair value* of an employee stock option. The fair values of other financial instruments do not take into account either the source of the funds with which a buyer might pay for the instrument or other circumstances affecting individual buyers. A logical extension of that view could result in a different "fair value" for identical options in a single grant for each employee who receives an award, even if the expected life is the same for each option.

148. Moreover, the definition of fair value places equal emphasis on the amount a willing (and presumably rational) seller would demand for the item. The estimated fair value of employee stock options, like the estimated fair value of other financial instruments for which market prices are not available, may not reflect all of the factors that an individual willing buyer or willing seller would consider in establishing an exchange price. That does not make it inappropriate to estimate the fair value of the item using a valuation technique that takes into account the theoretical effect on buyers and sellers as a group of the various features of the instrument. In addition, market prices are usually set at the margin. An option writer would seek the highest bidder with the capacity to buy the option. That bidder would be the pertinent "willing buyer."

Conclusions on Measurement Date and Method

149. After considering both the written responses to the Discussion Memorandum, *Distinguishing between Liability and Equity Instruments and Accounting for Instruments with Characteristics of Both,* and comments made at the public hearing on that document (refer to Appendix C), the Board decided early in 1992 not to pursue possible changes to the conceptual definitions of liabilities and equity. Instead, the Board decided to seek resolution of issues on accounting for stock-based compensation within the context of the conceptual definitions set forth in Concepts Statement 6 under which a call option written by an entity on its stock is an equity instrument rather than a liability. The Board decided not to pursue exercise date measurement on conceptual grounds because it is more consistent with viewing call options written as liabilities.

150. Each of the other possible measurement dates had advocates among the Board members in deliberations preceding issuance of the Exposure Draft. Even at that time, most Board members thought that a reasonable conceptual case could be made for either the vesting date or the service date. On balance, however, the Board agreed that a variation of grant date measurement was appropriate, and that was what the Exposure Draft proposed. In reaching that conclusion, Board members generally found persuasive the argument that measurement at the grant date bases the compensation cost stemming from a stock-based compensation award on the stock price at the date the parties agree to its terms. As discussed in paragraphs 92-96, the Board also concluded in the Exposure Draft that an asset—prepaid compensation—should be recognized at the grant date because the Board was persuaded at that time that a forfeitable equity instrument conditionally transferred to an employee could be considered "issued," which is an important part of the rationale for grant date accounting. However, Board members subsequently agreed with the majority of respondents that said that an entity that grants stock-based compensation does not receive an enforceable right to employee services at the grant date. That conclusion raises an additional question about the appropriateness of grant date accounting versus some version of vesting date accounting.

151. An overwhelming majority of respondents favored grant date measurement. They generally emphasized the importance of basing the measure of the related cost on the stock price at the date the parties

agree to the terms of an award. Most of those respondents, however, did not support the fair value based measurement method in the Exposure Draft. Most that opposed the Exposure Draft on that basis said that traditional option-pricing models, even modified to take into account the effect of forfeitability and nontransferability, did not fully reflect all of the factors that would affect the fair value of an employee stock option at the grant date. For example, an employee or a third party to whom an option is issued that is neither exercisable nor transferable for the first part of its life presumably would want to pay less for the option because of those restrictions. Similarly, many respondents pointed out that liquidity adds value and that the fair value of shares of "restricted" or "letter" stock is less than the value of unrestricted stock of the same entity.

152. Most respondents that took that view favored continued measurement of employee stock options at intrinsic value on the grounds that fair value could not be measured with reasonable reliability at the grant date. Others, however, suggested reducing the estimated fair value of both stock options and nonvested stock at the grant date to reflect additional restrictions during the vesting period. For example, some suggested a reduction in value by an arbitrary percentage, say, 10 percent for each year of the vesting period. The Board considered both that and other possible, but more complicated, ways of taking restrictions during the vesting period into account.

153. The Board reaffirmed its conclusion in the Exposure Draft that public entities should account for their stock options and other equity instruments at fair value. A fair value basis is consistent with the measurement principles applied to other issuances of equity instruments and to other forms of compensation paid to employees. Equity instruments other than employee stock options and the consideration received for them are recognized at their fair values on the dates the instruments are issued. For example, the initial recognition of debt issued with detachable stock purchase warrants is based on the relative fair values of the debt and the warrants at the date of issuance—not on a calculated minimum value of the warrants. Similarly, a share of stock or a warrant issued to settle an obligation to pay for services other than employee services would be measured at fair value. Other forms of compensation paid to employees, including cash, other assets, pension benefits, and the like are initially measured at the fair value of the asset given up or the liability incurred. The Board does not believe that concerns about measurement

are a sufficient reason to measure compensation paid in stock options on a different basis.

154. Paragraphs 165-173 discuss the modifications to standard option-pricing models to take into account the nontransferability of vested employee stock options. The Board's intent in this Statement is for the guidance in both the standards section and the guidance and illustrations in Appendix B to be sufficiently broad that employers may adopt future refinements in models that improve their application to employee stock options without requiring the Board to amend this Statement.

Restrictions that apply only during the vesting period

155. This Statement requires recognition of no compensation cost for awards that do not vest, as proposed in the Exposure Draft. Even so, some respondents said that an additional reduction in value is needed for awards of employee stock options that do vest to reflect their nonexercisability before they vested. Those respondents did not consider the use of expected life sufficient to reflect both the nontransferability and nonexercisability of nonvested options.

156. Board members generally agreed that investors who might purchase equity instruments with restrictions similar to those in a nonvested award of employee stock compensation (including nonvested shares of stock, which in effect are options for which the entire exercise price is employee services) would take those restrictions into account in determining how much they would be willing to pay for the instruments. However, employees do not pay the full value of their options at the grant date, although they may pay a nominal amount for each option granted. If they fully paid for their options at the grant date, the options would not be subsequently forfeitable, and the restrictions stemming from forfeitability would not exist. An investor who pays cash or other enforceable consideration for an option subject to restrictions similar to those in a nonvested employee stock option could not be required subsequently to forfeit entirely any benefit inherent in the instrument if the investor did not fulfill additional requirements.

157. Restrictions that apply to awards of stock-based employee compensation only during the period before they become vested stem entirely from the forfeitability of nonvested awards, which in turn stems from employees' not yet having satisfied the conditions necessary to earn their awards and having no

enforceable obligation to do so. That conclusion is consistent with not recognizing prepaid compensation at the grant date. Some Board members believe that conclusion calls for measuring both the value of the equity instrument and the related compensation cost based on the stock price at the vesting date—the date the instrument is issued. Other Board members agree that vesting date measurement may be conceptually appropriate; nevertheless, they consider it important to base the measure of compensation cost stemming from awards of employee stock options on the stock price at the date the entity decides how many options to award to an employee—the grant date.

158. Respondents' overwhelming opposition to vesting date measurement and the potential resulting volatility in reported net income during the vesting period would make it less likely that entities would voluntarily adopt the fair value based method if it were based on the stock price at the vesting date. The choice of accounting methods in this Statement provides an opportunity for entities to improve their accounting for employee stock options. Therefore, on balance, the Board decided to retain the Exposure Draft's provision that compensation cost should be measured based on the stock price at the grant date. However, the Board does not consider it necessary also to reflect in the measurement of fair value restrictions that no longer apply after employee stock options become vested and nonforfeitable. To do so would be inconsistent with the employee stock options' being issued at the vesting date (paragraph 96). The measurement method in the Exposure Draft combined features of both grant date and vesting date measurement because it adjusted for the effect of the difference, if any, between estimated and actual forfeitures due to failure to render the requisite service or to satisfy performance conditions. The measurement method in this Statement also is a hybrid of grant date and vesting date accounting for the same reason.

159. Some respondents that favored reducing the value of nonvested employee stock options for restrictions that stem from their forfeitability were opposed to similar reductions in the value of shares of nonvested stock. They noted similar situations in which the value of shares of an entity's stock that are involved in other employee compensation or benefit arrangements is not reduced below the market price of an unrestricted share at the date compensation is measured even though individual employees may not be able to realize the value of the stock for many

years. Examples are stock transferred to employee stock ownership plans, an entity's contributions of its own stock to either defined benefit or defined contribution pension plans, and deferred compensation arrangements designed to permit employees to defer payment of income taxes.

160. As mentioned earlier, the Board views shares of nonvested stock as employee stock options in which the exercise price consists entirely of employee services. Therefore, the Board believes that any reduction in the value of stock-based compensation to reflect restrictions during the vesting period would have to apply to both nonvested options and nonvested shares of stock. The Board is concerned that applying such a reduction to the stock-based employee compensation covered by this Statement would raise questions about the appropriateness of making similar value reductions in other situations in which shares of an entity's stock are used to provide employee benefits.

Option-pricing models and fair value

161. A quoted market price, if one is available, is the best measure of the fair value of an asset, liability, or equity instrument. In its deliberations leading to this Statement, the Board was not able to identify currently available quoted market prices or negotiated prices for employee stock options that would qualify as a price at which a willing buyer and a willing seller would exchange cash for an option. Some employers have offered employees a choice between a specified amount of cash or a specified number of options on the employer's stock. However, the Board understands that the terms of those arrangements generally do not result from negotiation between the employer and employee(s). The Board also was told that employers often offer a relatively low alternative cash amount to induce employees to choose options.

162. Market prices for employee stock options may become available in the future, perhaps through arrangements that permit employees to purchase their options by trading a specified amount of cash compensation for them on clearly unbiased terms. If so, the foregone cash compensation—not an estimated fair value of the options—would be recognized as compensation cost, and no adjustments for expected option forfeitures and nontransferability would be needed.

163. It also is conceivable, although unlikely, that options between parties other than employers and

employees that are subject to essentially the same restrictions as employee stock options might be developed and traded. For example, a third-party option might in concept be made forfeitable under certain conditions, and the option contract might specify that the options can only be exercised—not transferred to another party. The provisions of this Statement are not intended to preclude use of quoted market prices to determine the fair values of employee stock options if such prices become available. However, various implementation questions would need to be considered, such as how to treat options that are forfeited. Because neither quoted nor negotiated market prices existed when the Board developed this Statement, it has not considered those issues. This Statement specifies the basic method and assumptions to be used in estimating the fair values of employee stock options in the absence of a quoted market price. Specifically, this Statement requires the use of an option-pricing model, and it also specifies how to reduce the amount resulting from use of a traditional option-pricing model to reflect the unique restrictions inherent in employee stock options.

164. The Board recognizes that many entities and their auditors are not familiar with option-pricing models and the inherent mathematics. However, software to apply the models is widely available and easy to use for one who is familiar with electronic spreadsheets and similar tools. Selecting the appropriate assumptions to use as inputs to the models is not easy, but entities and their advisors must select similar assumptions about the future in many other areas of accounting. Understanding the details of the inherent mathematical formulas is not necessary, just as it is not necessary for an entity to understand the precise computations an actuary might use to estimate the amount of a liability for pension benefits.

Adapting option-pricing models for employee stock options

165. Paragraphs 166-173 explain the reasons for the specified adjustments to the results of standard option-pricing models to reflect differences between the terms of employee stock options and the traded options for which option-pricing models were initially developed.

Forfeitures before vesting

166. This Statement uses the term *forfeiture* to refer only to an employee's failure to earn a vested right to a stock-based employee compensation award be-

cause the specified vesting requirements are not satisfied. In other words, a vested award is no longer subject to forfeiture as this Statement uses that term, although the term of a vested award may be truncated by termination of service. Some respondents said that previously recognized compensation cost should be reversed to income if an option expires unexercised because its exercise price exceeds the market price of the stock. Some of those respondents interpreted the notion of forfeiture to include all situations in which employees do not realize gains on their options—for whatever reason. This Statement does not permit reversal of compensation cost in that situation because to do so would be inconsistent with the nature of an employee stock option (an equity instrument of the employer) and with both grant date and vesting date accounting. As with other equity instruments, the cost recognized for an employee stock option stems from use of the consideration received—not from subsequent changes in the value of the equity instrument. Moreover, to be internally consistent, recognizing income when an option expires out-of-the-money would call for recognizing additional compensation cost when the stock price increases as well—the result would be exercise date accounting.

167. This Statement requires that the compensation cost for an award of employee stock options reflect the number of options that actually vest. That is the same as the provision of the Exposure Draft, although the rationale is somewhat different. The Exposure Draft explained that provision as a means of adjusting the grant date value of an award of forfeitable stock-based employee compensation to reflect the risk of forfeiture. The measurement method in this Statement is intended to be consistent with an entity's having no enforceable right to future employee services or other consideration for forfeitable awards. An award of stock-based employee compensation does not result in the issuance of equity instruments until the award is vested. Recognizing compensation cost only for the number of instruments actually issued (vested) is consistent with that view of the nature of a nonvested award.

168. The Exposure Draft proposed that an entity be required to estimate expected forfeitures at the grant date, with subsequent adjustments if actual forfeitures differed from estimates. Some respondents said that permitting accrual of compensation cost for all awards not yet forfeited, with reversals of previously accrued compensation cost for subsequently forfeited awards, would reduce the implementation cost of this

Statement. The Board decided to permit that method of accounting for forfeitures for cost-benefit reasons. However, accrual of compensation cost during the service period based on expected forfeitures, with subsequent adjustments as necessary, remains an acceptable method. Respondents asked how changes in estimates of forfeitures (and performance outcomes) during the vesting period should be attributed. The Board concluded that the effects of retroactively applying a change in estimate during the vesting period should be recognized at the date of the change.

Inability to transfer vested employee stock options to third parties

169. The value of a transferable option is based on its maximum term because it rarely is economically advantageous to exercise, rather than sell, a transferable option before the end of its contractual term. Employee stock options differ from most other options in that employees cannot sell their options—they can only exercise them.[17] To reflect the effect of employees' inability to sell their vested options, this Statement requires that the value of an employee stock option be based on its expected life rather than its maximum term.

170. For example, a 10-year option with an exercise price of $50 on a stock with a market price of $50 might be valued at $25.89, assuming that the stock's volatility is 30 percent, it pays a dividend of 1 percent, and the risk-free interest rate is 7.5 percent. After 5 years, when the stock price has risen to $75, an option holder might wish to realize the gain on the option, thereby terminating exposure to future price changes. The fair value of a 5-year option with an intrinsic value of $25 ($75 - $50) on the same stock is $39.86, assuming that the stock's volatility is now 35 percent, the dividend yield remains at 1 percent, and the current risk-free rate for 5-year maturities is 7 percent. If the option is transferable, the holder could sell it for $39.86 rather than exercise it and receive only the intrinsic value of $25. An employee who does not wish to remain exposed to future price changes in the underlying stock after 5 years can only exercise the option and sell the stock obtained upon exercise—realizing only the gain of $25 in intrinsic

value. The employee is unable to realize the option's remaining time value of $14.86 ($39.86 – $25) because of its nontransferability. In other words, an employee who exercises an option with a contractual term of 10 years after only 5 years receives the benefit of only a 5-year option. Because the economic effect of holding a nontransferable rather than a transferable option is to make early exercise significantly more likely, the Board's conclusion stated in the Exposure Draft was that estimating the fair value of an employee stock option based on its expected life, later adjusted to actual life, rather than its maximum term is a logical and practical means of reducing the option's value to reflect its nontransferability.

171. Many respondents objected to the Exposure Draft's proposed subsequent adjustment of expected life to actual life. They generally pointed to the resulting counterintuitive effect that higher expense would be recognized for an option that runs for its full contractual term because its exercise price always exceeds the stock price than for an option that is exercised relatively early in its contractual term because the stock price increased rapidly.

172. As discussed in Appendix C, the Board held a roundtable discussion in April 1994. Participants were invited to submit papers and discuss with other participants, the Board, and its staff potential changes to the measurement method proposed in the Exposure Draft. The papers presented by academic researchers generally agreed that use of expected life is the appropriate way to adjust for the nontransferability of employee stock options. They also agreed with other respondents that the expected life estimated at the grant date should not be subsequently adjusted if actual life differs from expected life because that would produce a counterintuitive result. The participants in the roundtable also discussed several features that affect the expected life of an employee stock option, such as the relationship between expected life and expected volatility and the effect of the nonlinear relationship between option value and option life. Several factors considered helpful in estimating expected life are incorporated in the guidance on selecting assumptions in Appendix B.

---

[17]Some employees may be permitted to place their nontransferable options in a trust for the benefit of family members or otherwise to transfer vested options to family members. However, the options remain nontransferable in the hands of the trust or family member. The transfer thus does not affect the value of the option—both the option holder and the option writer (the employer) know it may be economically advantageous for the holder to exercise the options before maturity because exercise remains the only available means to terminate exposure to future price changes.

173. The Board reaffirmed its conclusion in the Exposure Draft that the appropriate way to reflect the effect on an option's fair value of an employee's inability to sell vested options is to use the option's expected life rather than its contractual term in estimating fair value using an option-pricing model. However, the Board also agreed with respondents and researchers that the Exposure Draft's requirement to adjust compensation cost to reflect the effect of a difference between expected life and actual life should be eliminated. The Board believes that eliminating that requirement will reduce the costs of complying with this Statement. Not adjusting option value to reflect differences between initial estimates and later estimates or outcomes—at least not after the vesting date—also is generally consistent with the Board's conclusion that equity instruments awarded to employees are issued at the vesting date. The value recognized for equity instruments issued in other situations is not changed by subsequent events. An argument could be made that changes in expected life should be reflected until the vesting date, but to do so without also reflecting changes in the price of the underlying stock during the vesting period would have the same counterintuitive results as the Exposure Draft's requirement to reflect differences between expected life and actual life.

Nonpublic Entities

Measurement

174. An emerging entity whose stock is not yet publicly traded may offer stock options to its employees. In concept, those options also should be measured at fair value at the grant date. However, the Board recognizes that estimating expected volatility for the stock of a newly formed entity that is rarely traded, even privately, is not feasible. The Board therefore decided to permit a nonpublic entity to omit expected volatility in determining a value for its options. The result is that a nonpublic entity may use the *minimum value* method discussed and illustrated in paragraphs 139-142. Options granted after an entity qualifies as a public entity must be measured using the procedures specified for public entities. Paragraphs 273-287 in Appendix B provide guidance on how to determine the assumptions required by option-pricing models, including expected volatility for a publicly traded stock that has little, if any, trading history.

175. The Exposure Draft included a provision that permitted a nonpublic entity to use the minimum value method except when its stock was traded with sufficient frequency to reasonably estimate expected volatility. Several respondents to the Exposure Draft thought that "traded with sufficient frequency" would be difficult to judge and that few nonpublic entities would likely incorporate volatility into their measurements on that basis. The Board decided to permit any nonpublic entity to exclude volatility from its measurement of option value. However, a nonpublic entity may incorporate volatility if it desires to do so.

176. Some respondents to the Exposure Draft suggested that there is no reason for different measurement methods for public and nonpublic entities. They believe all entities should use the same method and that requiring public entities to report higher compensation cost based on fair value creates a bias against them. Some respondents endorsed using minimum value for all entities. Others said that the need for special guidance for nonpublic entities was additional evidence that the Exposure Draft's proposals were flawed and that the Board should abandon its approach.

177. A solution suggested by other respondents was to require all entities to use the same expected volatility, such as the historical volatility of a market index. They believe that would ease application of the Statement, mitigate the differences in an entity's transition from nonpublic to public, and improve comparability by reducing the subjectivity of the estimate of volatility.

178. The Board believes that mandating the same estimate of expected volatility for use by all entities would impair, rather than improve, comparability because the volatilities of different entities differ. The use of minimum value by nonpublic entities is a practical solution to the difficulties of estimating expected volatility for a nonpublic entity. For a public entity, estimating the fair value of its options is practicable because an estimate of expected volatility can be made.

Definition of a public entity

179. The Exposure Draft defined a public entity consistent with definitions used in FASB Statements, except that an entity with only publicly traded debt, not equity securities, would be classified as a nonpublic entity. The Exposure Draft definition also drew from the definition in AICPA Statement on Auditing Standards No. 26, *Association with Financial Statements,* which makes it clear that a subsidiary of a

public entity also is a public entity. Some respondents objected to considering a subsidiary of a public entity that, by itself, would not meet that definition to be a public entity for purposes of this Statement. They believe that whether an entity is owned by a public entity is not relevant to the measure of a nonpublic subsidiary's options. They also said that awards related to the subsidiary's stock may be better employee incentives than awards related to the parent company's stock.

180. The Board recognizes that the accounting consequences of classifying a subsidiary as a public entity may limit the types of award that it chooses to grant. For example, an entity might choose not to grant an option on the stock of a wholly owned subsidiary combined with a repurchase agreement for the stock issued upon exercise because that award would be treated as a liability in consolidated financial statements. If classification as nonpublic were extended to subsidiaries, the effect of the provisions of paragraph 40 that permit nonpublic entities with mandatory fair value stock repurchase agreements to treat them as equity instruments even though the entity is effectively obligated to transfer its assets to the holder would be to permit a consolidated public entity to treat effective liabilities to employees of those subsidiaries as if they were equity instruments. The Board believes that would be an inappropriate result. The Board notes that an award of the parent's equity instruments could include a subsidiary performance criterion, at least partially achieving the goal of relating incentive compensation of subsidiary employees to subsidiary performance.

181. Some respondents to the Exposure Draft suggested that a newly public entity should continue to be classified as nonpublic for some period. Others suggested that a public entity whose stock is thinly traded should be classified as nonpublic. In contrast, some respondents suggested that a nonpublic entity that expected to go public within a certain period should be classified as a public entity. The Board decided that the most straightforward approach would be to determine public or nonpublic status based on an entity's characteristics at the date an award is granted.

Other Measurement Issues

Reload Options and Options with a Reload Feature

182. Reload options are granted upon exercise of previously granted options whose original terms provide for the use of shares of stock that the employee has held for a specified period of time, referred to as *mature shares,* rather than cash to satisfy the exercise price. At the time of exercise using mature shares, the employee is automatically granted a reload option for the same number of shares used to exercise the original option. The exercise price of the reload option is the market price of the stock at the date the reload option is granted; its term is equal to the remainder of the term of the original options.

183. Because a reload feature is part of the options initially awarded, the Board believes that the value added to those options by the reload feature ideally should be considered in estimating the fair value of the initial award at its grant date. However, the Board understands that no reasonable method currently exists to estimate the value added by a reload feature.

184. Some respondents to the Exposure Draft suggested that an option with a reload feature can be valued at the grant date as a "forward start option" commencing at the date or dates that the option is "reloaded." The forward start option's value would be added to the value of the option granted with a reload feature to determine the total value of the award. However, the forward start option formula calls for a number of subjective inputs, such as the number of expected reloads, the expected timing of each reload, and the expected total rate of return on the stock. Also, because an employee can take advantage of the reload feature only with shares already held, the employer would need to estimate (a) the number of employees who are expected to pay the exercise price with those shares rather than with cash and (b) their holdings of mature shares.

185. Others suggested that a reload feature be treated as if it merely extended the life of an option to its maximum term because the term of a reload option granted upon exercise of an option with mature shares cannot extend beyond the expiration date of the original option. Under that view, the fair value of an option with a reload feature would be estimated based on its maximum term, regardless of the expected life of the original option. However, that method understates the value of the reload feature because the value of an option on a dividend-paying stock is reduced by the present value of the dividends expected to be paid during the term of the option. The holder of an option subject to a reload feature, however, receives the dividends paid on stock obtained by exercising the option early and also is granted a reload option. Further, the holder of a reload option

can effectively realize a gain by selling the stock acquired on exercise without forfeiting the opportunity to benefit from future increases in the price of the underlying stock, which also makes the reload option worth more than an otherwise identical option without a reload feature even if its value is based on its contractual life.

186. The Board continues to believe that, ideally, the value of an option with a reload feature should be estimated at the grant date, taking into account all of its features. However, at this time, it is not feasible to do so. Accordingly, the Board concluded that the best way to account for an option with a reload feature is to treat both the initial grant and each subsequent grant of a reload option separately.

Modifications of Awards

187. An employer and employee may agree to modify the terms of an award of stock options or similar instruments. The Board concluded that the effects of a modification of terms are indistinguishable from the effects of an exchange of the existing equity instrument for a new instrument. For example, the same transaction might be described either as a decrease in the exercise price of an outstanding option or as the repurchase (and subsequent cancellation) of the existing option in exchange for a new option with a lower exercise price. The economics of the transaction are the same regardless of how it is described. In effect, the employee surrenders, and the employer repurchases, the existing instrument in exchange for another instrument.

188. The repurchase of an equity instrument generally is accounted for based on the fair values of the instrument repurchased and the consideration paid for it. For example, if an entity repurchases shares of common stock at an amount significantly in excess of the current market price of the shares, the excess is presumed to be attributable to stated or unstated rights the issuer receives in addition to the shares surrendered, such as an agreement that the stockholder will not purchase additional shares. The Board concluded that a modification of the terms of a stock-based compensation award should be accounted for based on a comparison of the fair value of the modified option at the date it is granted and the value at that date of the old option that is repurchased (immediately before its terms are modified) determined based on the shorter of (a) its remaining initially estimated expected life or (b) the expected life of the modified option. If the fair value of the modified option exceeds the value of the old option repurchased, the entity recognizes additional compensation cost for the difference.

189. The method in the Exposure Draft for determining the additional compensation cost arising from a modification of an award was revised based on comments received and because of changes in the proposed measurement method for measuring compensation cost. As discussed in paragraph 173, under the measurement method in this Statement, the expected life estimated at the grant date is not subsequently adjusted to the actual life in determining the value of options granted. The "true-up" approach in the Exposure Draft significantly influenced the proposed method for modifications, which based the fair value of the original option on its remaining contractual life at the date of modification. However, under this Statement's requirements, no changes are made to the value of an instrument determined at the grant date. Therefore, the Board believes that determining the value of the original option at the date of modification using the shorter of the expected life of the modified option or the remaining portion of the expected life of the original option is consistent with not truing up the initial measure of compensation cost for a change in option life. It also precludes the possibility of a counterintuitive result, namely, a reduction of compensation cost, which some respondents said could result from certain minor modifications. Using the shorter of the expected life of the modified option or the remaining portion of the expected term of the original option precludes net credits to compensation cost arising from modifications of an award.

190. An employee generally will accept a modification only if its effect is to increase the value of the instrument the employee holds. For example, the maximum term of an award of stock options may be extended or the exercise price may be lowered. Some respondents asked that the Statement address the accounting for cancellations of existing awards or for modifications of existing awards that reduce the value of the instrument held by the employee. The Board discussed those situations and believes that the circumstances under which an employer could unilaterally cancel or reduce the value of an award to an employee without substituting another form of compensation would be rare. The Board decided that it was not practical to consider the appropriate accounting for such an unusual—perhaps nonexistent—transaction except in the context of a specific set of facts.

191. Exchanges of equity instruments or changes to their terms in conjunction with a business combination accounted for as a pooling of interests are not considered modifications for purposes of this Statement. The Board recognizes that entities have essentially no discretion in revising the terms of outstanding equity awards if the business combination is to qualify as a pooling of interests. However, there are no similar criteria for other equity transactions, such as a business combination accounted for as a purchase. Therefore, an exchange or modification of an equity instrument as a result of a purchase business combination, spinoff, or other equity restructuring is considered a modification for purposes of this Statement. The terms of an equity instrument also may be modified pursuant to a stock dividend or a stock split without changing the value of the instruments that the employee holds. For example, an adjustment to an option's exercise price designed to equalize the holder's value before and after a stock split or a stock dividend is not a modification for purposes of this Statement.

192. Some respondents suggested that the criteria in EITF Issue No. 90-9, "Changes to Fixed Employee Stock Option Plans as a Result of Equity Restructuring," should be used to determine whether additional compensation should be recognized for equity restructurings under the fair value based method in this Statement. EITF Issue 90-9 is written in the context of Opinion 25's intrinsic value measurement method. The Board believes that the requirements in this Statement for accounting for modifications of awards, including those resulting from equity restructurings, are more appropriate for the fair value based method because those requirements are based on comparing fair values before and after a modification. As with all other Opinion 25-related authoritative literature, the consensus on EITF Issue 90-9 continues to apply for an entity that recognizes compensation cost based on Opinion 25.

193. Some respondents requested additional guidance on the accounting for cash settlements or modifications of nonvested awards. Paragraphs 35-40 of this Statement provide that guidance, and Appendix B illustrates the accounting for cash settlements and modifications.

194. Appendix B also illustrates accounting for cash settlements and modifications of options granted before or after initial application of this Statement. Generally, whether the entity has chosen to recognize compensation cost under the fair value based method

or to disclose the pro forma effects of that method does not affect the illustrations.

195. An entity that has disclosed the pro forma effects of adopting this Statement for several years may choose to adopt the cost recognition method in this Statement. In that situation, subsequent modifications of awards for which pro forma disclosures were made should be accounted for as if cost had been recognized under the fair value based method as shown in the illustrations for modifications of awards granted after adoption of this Statement (Illustrations 5(a)-5(d)). Doing so will make the financial statements for periods after adoption more consistent for comparative purposes with the pro forma disclosures made for any prior years presented.

Recognizing Compensation Cost over the Service Period

Attribution Period

196. This Statement continues the provisions of Opinion 25 and Interpretation 28 that stock-based compensation cost is to be recognized over the period or periods during which the employee performs the related services. If the service period is not defined as an earlier or shorter period, the service period is presumed to be the vesting period. If the award is for past service, compensation cost is recognized when the award is granted.

197. The Board considered whether the attribution period for employee stock options should extend beyond the vesting date, perhaps to the service expiration date (paragraphs 129-131), even though the measurement date is the grant date. Advocates of that method, which might be considered consistent with amortization of postretirement health care benefits over the period to *full eligibility date,* contend that employees have not earned the full benefit to which they are entitled until termination of service no longer shortens the life of the option. They would use the longer attribution period to allocate the time value of an option.

198. Most respondents that addressed this issue agreed with the Exposure Draft that the attribution period should not extend beyond the vesting date. However, some respondents suggested attribution over the option's expected life, which would be consistent with the method described in paragraph 197. They believe that the option serves as an incentive during its entire life and that attribution over the longer period "better matches" revenues and costs.

199. Although amortization of the time value of an option beyond the vesting date has some conceptual appeal, the Board concluded that no compelling reason exists to extend the attribution period beyond the period now used for stock options that give rise to compensation cost. The Board notes that the decision on when to exercise a vested option is the employee's. The right to exercise an option has been earned by the date the option becomes vested.

200. As discussed in paragraph 96, options are issued to employees at the vesting date. Some advocates of vesting date accounting say that a logical extension of that view would call for recognition of the full amount of the compensation cost at the vesting date, once the equity instrument has been fully earned and issued to the employee. However, the cost of services received in exchange for other employee benefits with a vesting period, such as pensions and other postemployment benefits, generally is recognized in the periods in which the services are received even if the benefits are not yet vested. Although those employee benefit plans generally result in the incurrence of liabilities rather than the issuance of equity instruments, the Board decided that the form of eventual settlement should not change the general principle that the costs of employee services are recognized over the periods in which employees are required to render service to earn the right to the benefit.

Awards with Graded Vesting

201. Interpretation 28 requires that compensation cost for a variable award with a graded vesting schedule, such as an award that vests 25 percent per year over 4 years, be accrued as if the grant were a series of awards rather than a single award. Each award in the series is accounted for as if it had its own separate service period and vesting date. That method attributes a higher percentage of the reported cost to the earlier years than to the later years of the service period because the early years of service are part of the vesting period for later awards in the series. For example, cost attributed to the first year of service includes not only the amount that vests in that year but also one-half of the award that vests in the second year, one-third of the award that vests in the third year, and so on.

202. The Exposure Draft acknowledged that the Interpretation 28 method of recognizing compensation cost is more complicated than others and may be considered illogical if an award with graded vesting is viewed as a single award rather than a series of linked awards. Therefore, it proposed that an award with graded vesting would be attributed ratably to individual years of service. Some respondents recommended that the cost of awards that vest in a graded pattern should be attributed using the method in Interpretation 28.

203. As noted in paragraph 31, an entity may estimate the fair value of an award of stock options with graded vesting using different estimated lives for each group of options depending on the length of the vesting period for that group. If the entity uses that method, the Board concluded that it would be logically consistent to require the attribution pattern specified by Interpretation 28. If the entity does not use different estimated lives but rather uses either an average life for the entire award or different lives based on considerations other than the vesting period for each group, it may use either the Interpretation 28 approach or an approach that ratably allocates compensation cost over the service period. However, to be consistent with the attribution pattern required for other employee benefit plans, the cumulative compensation cost recognized at any date must at least equal the value of the portion of the award that is vested. For example, if an award vests over 3 years, with 50 percent vested after the first year, and 25 percent in each of the next 2 years, cost accrued by the end of the first year must at least equal the amount attributable to 50 percent of the award.

Dividends

204. This Statement requires that dividends paid on shares of nonvested stock that are not expected to, and do not, vest be recognized as additional compensation cost during the vesting period. If an employee terminates service and forfeits nonvested stock but is not required to return dividends paid on the stock during the vesting period, the Board concluded that recognizing those dividends as additional compensation is appropriate.

205. The fair value of a share of stock in concept equals the present value of the expected future cash flows to the stockholder, which includes dividends. Therefore, additional compensation does not arise from dividends on nonvested shares that eventually vest. Because the measure of compensation cost for those shares is their fair value at the grant date, recognizing dividends as additional compensation would effectively double count the dividends.

206. The recipient of an award of nonvested stock may not receive dividends paid on the stock during the vesting period. In that situation, the Board concluded that the value of the award at the grant date should be the fair value of a dividend-paying share of the stock reduced for the present value of the dividends that will not be received during the vesting period.

207. Some employee stock options are *dividend protected,* which means that the exercise price is adjusted downward during the term of the option to take account of dividends paid on the underlying stock that the option holder does not receive. The effect of that adjustment of the exercise price is to remove the effect of dividends as a factor that reduces the value of a stock option on a dividend-paying stock. The usual method of applying an option-pricing model to estimate the value of a dividend-protected option is to assume a dividend payment of zero on the underlying stock, and this Statement requires use of that method.

Settlements of Stock-Based Compensation Awards

208. This Statement deals primarily with equity instruments, such as stock options, issued to employees as compensation. Ordinarily, an entity settles stock options upon exercise by issuing stock rather than by paying cash. However, an entity sometimes may choose to repurchase an employee stock option for a cash payment equal to the intrinsic value of the option when it is exercised.

209. Under some stock-based compensation plans, an entity incurs a liability to its employees, the amount of which is based on the price of the entity's stock. An example of the latter is a cash SAR under which an employee receives upon "exercise" a cash payment equal to the increase in the price of the employer's common stock from a specified level. For example, if the price of the stock increases from $25 to $35 per share, employees receive a $10 cash payment for each SAR held.

210. In addition, some tandem plans offer employees a choice of receiving either cash or shares of stock in settlement of their stock-based compensation awards. For example, an employee may be given an award consisting of a cash SAR and a stock SAR with the same terms. A stock SAR is the same as a cash SAR except that it calls for settlement in shares of stock with an equivalent value. Exercise of one

cancels the other. The employee can demand settlement either in cash or in shares of stock.

211. Opinion 25 provides that the amount of cash paid to settle an earlier award of stock or stock options is the final measure of the related compensation cost. An entity's repurchase of stock shortly after the employee acquired that stock upon exercise of an option is considered *cash paid to settle an earlier award,* and compensation cost is adjusted accordingly. Under Opinion 25, a stock SAR is a variable award because the number of shares to which an employee is entitled cannot be determined at the grant date. Compensation cost for a stock SAR thus is finally measured when the SAR is exercised, which produces the same compensation as for a cash SAR. However, a stock SAR and a stock option with similar terms, both of which qualify as equity instruments under the definitions in Concepts Statement 6, result in different amounts of compensation cost under Opinion 25. For example, no compensation cost is recognized for an award of 100 stock options at $25 per share if the market price of the stock is $25 at the grant date even if the stock price is $35 when the options are exercised. However, if an identical transaction involved an award of stock SARs rather than stock options, compensation cost of $1,000 [100 shares × ($35 – $25)] is recognized.

212. One reason for the Board's undertaking a comprehensive review of Opinion 25 was a concern that the differing results produced for stock-based compensation awards that call for settlement by issuing stock and those that call for settlement in cash were, at best, difficult to understand and explain. While it may be appropriate for cash plans and stock plans to result in different total charges to income, no common thread to distinguish between cash and stock plans is apparent in Opinion 25. For example, some awards that result in the entity's issuing equity instruments, such as stock SARs, are treated as if the entity had incurred a liability. Similar awards, such as stock options, are treated as equity instruments unless they are eventually settled in cash, at which time the accounting is adjusted to produce the same results as if the entity had incurred a liability rather than issued an equity instrument at the grant date.

213. Some constituents contend that the amount of compensation cost recognized for stock-based compensation awards should not differ solely because one award calls for settlement in stock and another calls for settlement in an equivalent amount of cash. Others are not concerned with differing results for

stock plans and cash plans, but they note that the provisions of Opinion 25 sometimes produce results that are inconsistent with those for similar transactions in equity instruments issued to outside parties. For example, the repurchase of stock from an investor who recently acquired it by exercising a stock purchase warrant would not be accounted for as if it were the settlement of a liability.

214. As discussed in Appendix C, late in 1988 the Board set aside work on stock compensation issues to await progress on its broader project on distinguishing between liability and equity instruments. The main reason for that decision was concern about whether applying the current distinction between liabilities and equity instruments and the different effects on income stemming from repurchase of an equity instrument versus settlement of a liability produced appropriate results for stock-based compensation plans. Because the Board subsequently decided not to pursue substantive changes to the conceptual definitions of liabilities and equity, it considered accounting for stock-based compensation awards in the context of the definitions in Concepts Statement 6.

215. Concepts Statement 6 distinguishes between liabilities and equity on the basis of whether an instrument obligates the issuer to transfer its assets (or to use its assets in providing services) to the holder. A liability embodies such an obligation, while an equity instrument does not. A call option that an entity writes on its own stock, such as an employee stock option, is an equity instrument because its settlement requires only the issuance of stock, which is not the issuer's asset. The entity's obligation under a cash SAR, on the other hand, is a liability because its settlement requires the transfer of assets to the holder.

216. Whether an instrument qualifies as a liability or an equity instrument of its issuer depends on the nature of the obligation embodied in it—not on the means by which it is actually settled. In other words, the characteristics of a liability are present from the date it is incurred. Settlement of a liability by issuing equity instruments, such as shares of stock, whose value is the same as the amount of the liability does not change the nature of the obligation settled—the transaction is the settlement of a liability. Similarly, the repurchase of an equity instrument for cash does not convert the equity instrument to a liability—the transaction still is the repurchase of an equity instrument.

217. The Board decided that the principles outlined in paragraph 216 apply to obligations incurred to employees under stock-based compensation awards as well as to similar obligations incurred to other parties. Those principles provide the basis for dealing with both awards that call for settlement in stock and awards that call for settlement in cash (or other assets of the entity). The former are equity instruments when issued, and their subsequent repurchase for cash equal to their value does not call for an adjustment to previously recognized compensation cost. The latter are liabilities, and their settlement calls for an adjustment to previously recognized compensation cost if the settlement amount differs from the carrying amount of the liability.

218. The Board also concluded that the conceptual distinctions between liabilities and equity instruments provide a reasonable way of accounting for tandem plans that offer a choice of settlement in stock or in cash. An entity that grants a tandem award consisting of either a stock option or a cash SAR, for example, is obligated to pay cash upon demand if the choice of settlement is the employee's. The contract gives the entity no discretion to avoid transferring its assets to the employee if the employee elects settlement in cash. The entity thus has incurred a liability. If the choice is the entity's, however, it can avoid transferring assets simply by electing to issue stock, and the award results in the issuance of an equity instrument. However, this Statement requires accounting for the substantive terms of a plan. If an entity nominally has the choice of settling awards under a tandem plan by issuing stock but regularly does so by paying cash, or if the entity settles awards in cash whenever employees ask for cash settlement, the instrument awarded likely is a substantive liability of the entity.

Stock Repurchase Agreements of Closely Held Entities

219. Many respondents to the Discussion Memorandum on distinguishing between liabilities and equity noted that closely held entities commonly specify that shares of stock granted or otherwise issued to employees cannot be transferred to a third party but can only be sold to the issuer. Often, the holder is required to sell, and the issuer is required to repurchase, the stock at a price that reasonably approximates fair value at the date of repurchase. In a family-owned entity, a repurchase agreement may apply to all of the

stock outstanding, or it may apply only to shares held by employees and others that are not members of the founding family.

220. In concept, stock that its issuer must repurchase for fair value at the date of repurchase is a liability rather than an equity instrument because the issuer is obligated to transfer its assets to the holder. To treat all of those instruments as liabilities, however, would be troublesome because an entity with repurchase agreements for all of its common stock would report no equity. In practice, the existence of a mandatory fair value repurchase agreement, by itself, is not considered to convert to a liability an instrument that otherwise would qualify as equity. Future work on the Board's liability-equity project will consider the effect of a mandatory fair value repurchase agreement. The Board therefore concluded that this Statement should not change current practice concerning the effect of a mandatory fair value repurchase agreement applicable to the stock of a nonpublic entity.

221. Some respondents to the Exposure Draft asked that mandatory repurchases under all formula-based plans be considered repurchases at fair value that are accounted for as the repurchase of an equity instrument. Others requested that additional criteria be provided to establish whether the formula in a plan produces a repurchase price equivalent to fair value. The Board believes that the terms of formula value repurchase plans are too diverse to specify the circumstances, if any, in which a formula-based value might be fair value. Whether the terms of a particular plan produce a repurchase price that is a reasonable estimate of fair value and whether the plan is subject to additional compensation cost needs to be assessed on a case-by-case basis (paragraphs 37-40).

Accounting for Tax Effects of Stock Compensation Awards

222. The provisions of the Exposure Draft on accounting for the tax effects of awards of stock-based employee compensation were based on recognizing an asset, prepaid compensation, for the fair value of an award at the grant date. For awards of stock options, the financial reporting basis of that asset generally would exceed its tax basis at the grant date because the time value component of an option's value is not tax deductible. Therefore, a temporary difference would arise for which a deferred tax liability would be recognized under Statement 109. Because the Board decided that prepaid compensation should not be recognized at the grant date, the proposed tax accounting no longer could be applied.

223. Statement 109 retained Opinion 25's provisions on accounting for the income tax effects of stock-based employee compensation. The Board considered whether it should fundamentally change those requirements and decided not to, for the reasons explained in paragraphs 225-231.

224. The Board believes that recognition of deferred tax benefits related to stock-based awards for financial reporting should be based on provisions in the tax law that govern the deductibility of stock-based compensation. Some stock-based compensation plans result in tax deductions. Examples under existing U.S. tax law are so-called nonstatutory stock options (which are options that do not qualify for preferential tax treatment as incentive stock options) and nonvested stock. However, under existing U.S. tax law, an entity does not receive tax deductions for so-called incentive stock options (provided that employees comply with the requisite holding periods).

225. The Board believes that the recognition of compensation cost in an entity's income statement for an award that ordinarily results in tax deductions creates a deductible temporary difference for which deferred taxes are recognized under Statement 109. Paragraph 15 of Statement 109 describes temporary differences that are not associated with a particular asset or liability for financial reporting but that result from an event that has been recognized in the financial statements and, based on the provisions in the tax law, will result in deductible amounts in future years. Normally, tax deductions ultimately recognized for a stock option accounted for under this Statement will differ in amount from the compensation cost recognized for financial reporting. Compensation cost recognized for financial reporting under this Statement is measured as the fair value of the award at the grant date, which includes a time value component that is never tax deductible. Changes in the market value of the stock after the grant date do not affect the measurement of compensation cost recognized. Tax deductions are generally based on the intrinsic value of the award measured as the excess of the market price of the stock over the price, if any, the employee pays for the stock at a specified date. Changes in the market price of the stock between the date an award is granted and the exercise date directly affect the amount of the entity's tax deduction.

226. The Board decided that the amount of the temporary difference should be determined based on the compensation cost recognized for financial reporting

rather than by reference to the expected future tax deduction (which would be estimated by the current intrinsic value of the award). The Board believes that approach is preferable because it is less complex to apply, will produce less volatility in reported net income, and will be consistent with the recognition of the tax effects of stock-based awards for those employers that continue to apply Opinion 25 for their stock-based employee compensation plans.

227. The temporary difference related to a stock-based award is measured by the cumulative compensation cost recognized rather than the expected future tax deduction based on the present intrinsic value of the award. Therefore, a deferred tax asset recognized for that temporary difference should be reduced by a valuation allowance only if, based on the weight of the available evidence, the entity expects future taxable income will be insufficient to recover the deferred tax asset in the periods the tax deduction for the stock-based award will be recognized or in an applicable carry-back or carry-forward period.

228. The amount of stock-based compensation that is deducted on the tax return may exceed the compensation cost recognized for financial reporting. This Statement requires that the tax benefits of deductions in excess of compensation cost be recognized as additional paid-in capital when they are initially recognized. The Board agrees with the conclusion of the Accounting Principles Board in Opinion 25 that the additional tax benefits are attributable to an equity transaction.

229. Alternatively, the deductible amount on the tax return may be less than the cumulative compensation cost recognized for a particular stock-based award. The Board concluded that the write-off of the related deferred tax asset in that situation should be recognized in the income statement except to the extent that there is paid-in capital arising from excess tax deductions from previous awards under stock-based employee compensation arrangements accounted for using the fair value based method described in this Statement. The Board believes that it would be inappropriate for an entity to use credits to paid-in capital from awards accounted for under Opinion 25 to offset the write-off of a deferred tax asset related to compensation cost measured using the fair value based method in this Statement because those credits generally result from awards for which no compensation cost has been recognized. To use those credits would overstate an entity's cumulative net income.

230. This Statement does not permit retroactive application to determine the fair value of stock-based awards granted before this Statement's effective date. The Board believes that it would not be practical to determine the appropriate amount of excess tax deductions that would have been credited to paid-in capital had the fair value based method been applied to awards granted before the effective date of this Statement. After the effective date of this Statement, entities that continue to apply Opinion 25 are required to determine not only the pro forma net income effects of the fair value based method but also the pro forma equity effects in determining the tax benefits for excess tax deductions that would have been recognized in paid-in capital had the fair value based method in this Statement been applied to recognize compensation cost. Paid-in capital for tax benefits resulting from awards granted before the effective date of this Statement are still available for applying paragraph 17 of Opinion 25 because this Statement does not change the accounting for tax effects under Opinion 25. Entities also are precluded from offsetting the write-off of a deferred tax asset against the tax benefits of excess deductions or tax credits reported as paid-in capital from stock-based arrangements that are outside the scope of this Statement, such as employee stock ownership plans.

231. An entity sometimes may realize tax benefits for an award that ordinarily does not result in a tax deduction because an employee receiving the stock does not comply with a holding period required by the tax law for favorable tax treatment for the recipient. The Board decided that the resulting tax benefit from such a disqualifying disposition should be recognized in the period that the event occurs. The benefit of any deduction recognized in the income statement is limited to the tax benefit for the cumulative compensation cost previously recognized for financial reporting. Any excess benefit should be recognized as an increase to paid-in capital.

Employee Stock Purchase Plans and Other Broad-Based Plans

232. The Exposure Draft applied to broad-based employee stock option plans and broad-based plans that permit employees to purchase stock at a discount from market value *(employee stock purchase plans)* the same recognition and measurement provisions as those proposed for all other stock-based plans. Many respondents said that broad-based plans should be

exempted from the proposed requirement to recognize compensation cost for the fair value of the benefit given to employees. They noted that Opinion 25, paragraph 7, considers broad-based plans that meet certain specified criteria to be *noncompensatory*, with no compensation cost recognized even if the purchase price is less than the price of the underlying stock at the measurement date. Respondents also pointed out that Opinion 25 cites an employee stock purchase plan that qualifies under Section 423 of the Internal Revenue Code as an example of a noncompensatory plan.

233. The Internal Revenue Code provides that employees will not be immediately taxed on the difference between the market price of the stock purchased and a discounted purchase price if several requirements in Section 423 are met. The requirements are generally the same as those in paragraph 7 of Opinion 25, with the following additions:

a. The option price may not be less than the lesser of (1) 85 percent of the market price when the option is granted or (2) 85 percent of the price at exercise.
b. The term of the option cannot exceed 5 years from the grant date if the purchase price is 85 percent or more of the market price at the exercise date. If the purchase price can turn out to be less than 85 percent of the stock price at exercise, the term of the option cannot exceed 27 months from the grant date. For example, 27 months is the maximum term of a *look-back option* in which the purchase price equals the lower of 85 percent of the stock price at the grant date or at the exercise date.

234. In the past few years, some employers have granted fixed, 10-year stock options to substantially all employees. Those awards differ from Section 423 employee stock purchase plans because the exercise price usually equals the stock price at the date of grant and the term is longer. Although those options generally do not qualify as *noncompensatory* under Opinion 25, no compensation cost is typically recognized for them because of the intrinsic value method specified in Opinion 25. In this Statement, the phrase *broad-based* plans includes long-term fixed stock options issued to substantially all of an entity's employees as well as Section 423 plans.

235. In supporting the noncompensatory treatment of broad-based plans, respondents said that the primary purpose of those plans is not to compensate employees for services rendered. Rather, broad-based plans are aimed at encouraging employees to become stakeholders, thereby leading to greater employee loyalty and an interest in increasing shareholder value, and at raising capital over time without incurring the stock issuance costs related to a public offering. Many respondents asserted that the purchase discount offered to employees was comparable to the stock issuance costs avoided by issuing the stock to employees rather than to the public. The purchase discount is viewed as an inducement for employees to participate in the plans or as a cost of raising capital. Some respondents suggested that the noncompensatory provisions of Opinion 25 should be not only retained but also broadened to encompass options with a 10-year term.

236. The Board found merit in the argument that a small percentage discount in a broad-based plan offered to employees is an inducement that is analogous to a discount routinely offered to stockholders and others or to avoided stock issuance cost. The Board decided that the purchase discount in a broad-based plan is noncompensatory if the discount from the market price does not exceed the greater of the following two thresholds:

a. The per-share discount that would be reasonable in a recurring offer of stock to stockholders or others. For example, some entities offer a purchase discount to shareholders participating in a dividend reinvestment program. The Board related this threshold to a recurring discount because it did not want a percentage discount justified by an isolated rights offering that might involve an above-normal discount.
b. The per-share amount of stock issuance costs avoided by not having to raise a significant amount of capital by a public offering. Some respondents suggested that this threshold should be based on the per-share avoided stock issuance costs for a public offering of only the number of shares expected to be issued to the employees. The Board rejected that suggestion. Per-share amounts would tend to be higher for a small public offering because many of the costs are more fixed than variable. The Board agreed to include this threshold in the standard because of the long-term impact of broad-based plans, which some respondents indicated provide a significant source of capital *over time*. The Board does not want this threshold used to justify a higher percentage discount as noncompensatory simply based on a short-term focus.

237. Some constituents expressed concern about the effort and related costs to justify the purchase discount granted to employees. The Board discussed whether a specified discount should be established for cost-benefit reasons as a safe harbor for a noncompensatory discount. It decided to specify that a purchase discount of 5 percent or less automatically complies with the Statement's limitations on the amount of purchase discount allowed for noncompensatory broad-based plans. The Board chose 5 percent because, based on available data, it believes that amount is closer to the average cost of most public offerings than is the 15 percent discount effectively used as a safe harbor under Opinion 25. A discount in excess of 5 percent is permitted if an entity can justify it under the criteria in paragraph 23.

238. Having decided that a reasonable percentage discount (such as 5 percent) can be included in a noncompensatory broad-based plan, the Board considered how compensation cost should be determined for a broad-based plan that includes a higher percentage discount than could be considered noncompensatory. Should the cost computation include the entire discount or only the portion that exceeds the amount that would, by itself, qualify as noncompensatory? The Board decided that if an employee stock purchase plan includes an excessively high discount that cannot be justified under the criteria in paragraph 23(b), the plan is compensatory and the entire discount should be used in determining compensation cost. The Board rejected the notion that an employee stock purchase plan could be accounted for as partially compensatory and partially noncompensatory.

239. The Board considered respondents' requests that broad-based plans with look-back options be considered noncompensatory and noted that a look-back option can have substantial value because it enables the employee to purchase the stock for an amount that could be significantly less than the market price at date of purchase. A look-back option is not an essential element of a broad-based plan aimed at promoting broad employee stock ownership; a purchase discount also provides inducement for participation. The Board concluded that broad-based plans that contain look-back options cannot be treated as noncompensatory. The consequences of other option features are discussed in paragraphs 240 and 241.

240. Under some employee stock purchase plans, the purchase price is fixed at the grant date (for example, as a percentage of the market price at the grant date) and an enrollment period is provided for employees to decide whether to participate. Technically, the availability of an enrollment period after the purchase price has been fixed constitutes an option feature that has time value. However, for practical reasons, the Board decided that an enrollment period not in excess of 31 days is not a disqualifying option feature that would otherwise preclude a plan from being treated as noncompensatory.

241. To facilitate employee participation and eliminate the need for lump-sum payments, employee stock purchase plans typically stipulate that participating employees pay for stock purchases by payroll withholding during a period preceding the date of purchase. Under some plans, employees are permitted to cancel their participation in the plan before the purchase date and obtain a refund of amounts previously withheld. If a plan permits a participating employee to cancel participation in the plan after the purchase price has been fixed, that cancellation ability is an option feature. The Board decided that a plan in which the purchase price is fixed at the grant date and participating employees may cancel their participation before the purchase date and obtain a refund of previous withholdings is indistinguishable from a fixed-price option and therefore should be treated as compensatory. In contrast, a plan in which the purchase price is based *solely* on the *purchase-date* market price embodies no valuable option feature. Even if the plan enables participating employees to cancel their participation before the purchase date and obtain a refund of previous withholdings, that plan might qualify as noncompensatory.

242. The Board considered attempting to simplify determining the fair value of an employee stock purchase plan that incorporates a look-back option by establishing a specified percentage of the stock price at the grant date, such as 20 percent, that could be considered fair value. The Board rejected that idea largely because determining an appropriate percentage that would produce a reasonable substitute for fair value for a wide variety of plans did not seem feasible. Moreover, the Board understands that, given the choice of using a specified amount or determining an amount based on its own circumstances, many entities do not select the specified amount without first determining the alternative amount.

Disclosures

243. Paragraphs 244-261 discuss the basis for the Board's conclusions on the required disclosures of

this Statement other than the pro forma disclosures required by paragraph 45. The basis for the Board's conclusions on those pro forma disclosures is discussed in paragraph 69.

244. Some respondents suggested that the Board provide percentage guidelines to specify when both the pro forma disclosures of the effects of applying the fair value based method and the disclosures in paragraphs 46-48 could be omitted on the grounds of immateriality. The Board decided not to do so because it believes an entity can best determine the materiality of the disclosures in its individual circumstances. In addition, different percentage criteria likely would be needed for different disclosures, for example, the materiality of some items might be best evaluated in terms of the effect on reported net income, while the materiality of other items might be better evaluated in the context of number of shares outstanding. Specifying those guidelines for individual disclosures could unduly complicate this Statement. The Board notes, however, that the general guidance provided at the end of each Statement on application of its provisions to immaterial items applies to both accounting and disclosure requirements.

Disclosures Similar to Those Required by Opinion 25

245. The Board concluded that the disclosures specified in paragraphs 46-48 should be required for all entities regardless of the method used to account for stock-based employee compensation. The disclosures required by Opinion 25 thus are superseded by this Statement, regardless of the method an entity uses to account for stock-based employee compensation cost.

246. The Exposure Draft proposed continuing the disclosures required by Opinion 25, including the number of shares under option, the option price, the number of shares for which options are exercisable, the number of shares exercised, and the exercise prices. In applying Opinion 25, many entities have disclosed only the range of exercise prices of options, which is not very helpful in understanding the potential increase in outstanding shares by option exercises, especially if the range is wide. The Exposure Draft proposed disclosing the weighted-average exercise prices of options outstanding, granted, and exercised.

247. Many respondents expressed support for the proposed disclosures. Others said that additional in-

formation about options outstanding at the date of the financial statements would be useful. They generally requested more information helpful in evaluating "potential future dilution," "option overhang," or potential capital contributions from outstanding options. They suggested the need for more information about options whose exercise prices are greater than, equal to, or less than the current stock price. Those respondents said that weighted-average information, although important, is not sufficient for those assessments because, by itself, it provides no information helpful in evaluating the likelihood that options will be exercised in the future. Disclosure of the number of options outstanding at each exercise price, or at least by ranges of exercise prices, was suggested.

248. The Board concurred and decided to require disclosure of the range of exercise prices (as well as the weighted-average exercise price) and the weighted-average remaining contractual life for the options outstanding as of the date of the latest statement of financial position presented. If the overall range of exercise prices is wide (for example, the highest exercise price exceeds approximately 150 percent of the lowest exercise price), the Board decided to require further segregation of those prices into narrower ranges that are meaningful for assessing the likelihood and consequences of future exercises. The Board also decided that the number and weighted-average exercise price of options that are currently exercisable at that date should be disclosed for each range.

249. The Board decided not to specify strict criteria for when further segregation should be required. The 150 percent example in paragraph 48 is meant to be a guideline. An entity should exercise its judgment in providing the most meaningful disclosures.

Disclosures of Method and Significant Assumptions Used to Determine Fair Value

250. The Exposure Draft proposed requiring disclosure of the method and significant assumptions used to estimate the fair value of options. About half of the respondents that commented on the proposed disclosures supported that requirement; others considered those disclosures unnecessary if compensation cost is recognized. Many respondents opposed disclosure of expected dividends, and a fewer number also opposed disclosure of the expected volatility. They said they feared that those disclosures raised the potential for future litigation if the disclosures were misconstrued as a commitment to declare future dividends

or a forecast of future stock prices. Others suggested that disclosure of assumptions should not be required because entities might have to reveal confidential information about possible future changes in dividend rates and the like.

251. As explained in paragraphs 273-287 of Appendix B, the assumptions about expected volatility and dividends needed to comply with this Statement generally should be based on historical experience, adjusted for *publicly available information* that may indicate ways in which the future is reasonably expected to differ from the past. In addition, required disclosures of potentially sensitive assumptions in other areas, such as expected rates of salary increases used in measuring pension cost for a period, apparently have not led to litigation or other problems. Moreover, after the Exposure Draft was issued, the SEC began requiring registrants to disclose the underlying assumptions, including expected volatility and dividends, if they choose to comply with the recently expanded proxy disclosures about the value of options granted to executives by disclosing the "present value" of the options at the grant date.

252. The Exposure Draft did not propose requiring disclosure of expected lives of stock options, principally because that assumption was required to be subsequently adjusted to actual life in measuring compensation cost. Some respondents said that disclosure of expected lives would be useful, especially should the Board decide not to require "true up" of expected life to actual life—which is the conclusion that the Board reached (paragraph 173).

253. The Board therefore concluded that disclosure of the method and significant assumptions used in estimating the fair values of stock options should be required. The assumptions used in an option-pricing model can significantly affect the estimated value of stock options, and therefore disclosure of the assumptions used will assist in understanding the information provided by entities in their financial statements.

Other Required Disclosures

254. The Exposure Draft proposed requiring entities with both fixed and indexed or performance-based plans to provide separate disclosures for the different types of plans. Some respondents to the Exposure Draft requested additional guidance on the situations in which separate disclosures would be necessary and what information should be provided separately for

fixed plans and other plans. The Board decided that separate disclosures should be provided to the extent that differences in the characteristics of the awards make those disclosures important to an understanding of the entity's use of stock-based compensation. This Statement gives examples of such circumstances rather than specifying detailed requirements. The Board recognizes that entities differ in the extent to which they use various forms of stock-based employee compensation. An entity should exercise its judgment in providing detailed information that is useful in its own situation.

255. The Exposure Draft proposed, and this Statement retains, required disclosure of the weighted-average fair values of options granted during the year, along with the weighted-average exercise prices. That disclosure will allow a reader to compute the ratio of option value to stock value at grant date, which is commonly used for comparisons between entities and in assessing the perceived reasonableness of option valuations. Reference to a ratio helps in comparing, for example, the estimated value of an option on a $20 stock with one on a $90 stock. However, that ratio generally is used only for options whose exercise prices equal the stock price at the grant date.

256. For example, if both the $20 stock and the $90 stock paid dividends of approximately 1.5 percent and other factors such as expected lives of the options, historical stock price volatility, and future prospects were similar, one might question estimated fair values of options on the 2 stocks with similar terms if the ratio of fair value to stock price is 20 percent for the $20 stock and 40 percent for the $90 stock. Those ratios might be comparable, however, if the exercise price of the first option is $20 (equal to the stock price at grant date) but the exercise price of the second option is $75 ($15 less than the stock price at grant date). To combine in the same ratio options with exercise prices that equal, exceed, and are less than the stock price at the grant date would produce a meaningless amount. Accordingly, this Statement requires separate disclosure of weighted-average fair values and exercise prices of options granted at exercise prices that equal the stock price at the grant date and those whose exercise prices differ from the grant date stock price.

257. During the Board's redeliberations of the proposals in the Exposure Draft, questions arose about whether the disclosures required by this Statement were generally consistent with current disclosures for

other potentially dilutive financial instruments. APB Opinion No. 15, *Earnings per Share,* says:

> The use of complex securities complicates earnings per share computations and makes additional disclosures necessary. The Board has concluded that financial statements should include a description, in summary form, sufficient to explain the pertinent rights and privileges of the various securities outstanding. Examples of information which should be disclosed are dividend and liquidation preferences, participation rights, call prices and dates, conversion or exercise prices or rates and pertinent dates, sinking fund requirements, unusual voting rights, etc. [paragraph 19]

That paragraph could be interpreted to apply to employee stock options, although entities generally have not done so because Opinion 25 specifically deals with stock-based awards to employees. The Board believes that the disclosures required by this Statement are generally consistent with disclosures long required for other potentially dilutive securities.

258. During its deliberations leading to the Exposure Draft, the Board received several proposals for disclosures in lieu of cost recognition for stock-based compensation, the most comprehensive of which was submitted by a group of preparers and users of financial statements and was endorsed by the six largest accounting firms. That proposal was included in the Exposure Draft as Appendix E.

259. As discussed earlier, many respondents to the Exposure Draft supported additional disclosures as a substitute for measurement and recognition of compensation cost. The notice to recipients asked whether any of the additional disclosure items in Appendix E should be added to the required disclosures, assuming that recognition of compensation cost was required. Few respondents suggested additional disclosure items, and some said that none of the additional disclosure items in Appendix E's example were warranted. The Board therefore did not expand the required disclosures to include items from Appendix E of the Exposure Draft.

260. During its deliberations, especially after the Board had initially decided to require disclosure of pro forma information rather than recognition of compensation cost determined by the fair value based method, some constituents asserted that disclosure of a single point estimate of the fair value of employee stock options was not appropriate. They said that the assumptions used in option-pricing models are too subjective or that available option-pricing models are inappropriate for estimating the fair value of employee stock options with their inherent differences from tradable options. They suggested that the Board require only disclosure of a range of possible values for employee stock options.

261. As discussed earlier in this appendix and in Appendix B, the Board believes that option-pricing models, adjusted as this Statement specifies for the differences between the typical employee stock option and a tradable option for which the models were initially developed, will produce estimated values for employee stock options that will be within acceptable limits for recognition in financial statements. The Board also believes that it has required disclosure of the basic information needed to understand the effects of stock-based compensation plans. An entity may, of course, disclose additional information it considers pertinent to readers of its financial statements. For example, an entity may disclose supplemental information, such as a range of values calculated on the basis of different assumptions, provided that the supplemental information is reasonable and does not discredit the information required by this Statement (paragraph 364).

Benefits and Costs

262. The mission of the FASB is to "establish and improve standards of financial accounting and reporting for the guidance and education of the public, including issuers, auditors, and users of financial information" (FASB *Rules of Procedure,* page 1). In fulfilling that mission the Board strives to determine that the expected benefits of the information resulting from a new standard will exceed the perceived costs. The objective and implicit benefit of issuing an accounting standard are the increased credibility and representational faithfulness of financial reporting as a result of the new or revised accounting. However, the value of that incremental improvement to financial reporting and most of the costs to achieve it are subjective and cannot be quantified. Likewise, the costs of *not* issuing an accounting standard are impossible to quantify.

263. The Board's consideration of each individual issue in a particular project includes the subjective weighing of the incremental improvement in financial reporting against the incremental cost of implementing the identified alternatives. At the end of that

process, the Board considers the accounting provisions in the aggregate and must conclude that issuance of the standard is a sufficient improvement in financial reporting to justify the related costs.

264. The Board concluded that the expected benefits resulting from this Statement will exceed the related costs. Although required recognition using the fair value based method of determining compensation cost for stock-based employee compensation would have provided greater benefits, the representational faithfulness and credibility of the information provided by the financial statements and notes, taken as a whole, will be improved even if the results of that method are only reflected in disclosure of pro forma information. Entities that choose to adopt the fair value based method will be better able to establish plans that they believe provide the best incentives with less need to "design around" accounting standards. Opinion 25's distinction between fixed and variable awards effectively encourages fixed stock options and discourages performance awards. Encouraging one form of award at the expense of another not only imposes the cost of treating accounting requirements as a significant factor in plan design but also may encourage selection of plans that an entity might not otherwise choose.

265. The Board has attempted to mitigate the incremental costs of complying with this Statement wherever possible without detracting from its objectives. For example:

a. A nonpublic entity is permitted to use the so-called minimum value method to value its options.
b. Entities may choose to estimate the number of options or other equity instruments that are expected to vest and to revise that estimate, if necessary, if subsequent information indicates that actual forfeitures are likely to differ from initial estimates. Alternatively, an entity may begin recognizing compensation cost as if all instruments granted are expected to vest, with recognition of actual forfeitures as they occur.
c. The grant-date estimate of expected option life is not adjusted to actual outstanding life, as was proposed in the Exposure Draft. The Board believes that elimination of that requirement will reduce the costs of complying with this Statement.
d. If there is a range of reasonable assumptions about the factors that are used in option-pricing models, entities are to use the low end of the range. That should somewhat simplify the decisions involved in determining appropriate assumptions.

Effective Dates and Transition

266. The Exposure Draft proposed two effective dates: one for its disclosure provisions, including pro forma disclosures of its effects on net income and earnings per share, and a later date for adopting its recognition provisions in the financial statements. Because this Statement does not require an entity to adopt the fair value based method of accounting for stock-based employee compensation (although the Board encourages entities to do so), the question of effective date pertains almost entirely to the required pro forma disclosures. An entity may adopt the fair value based method of accounting for its stock-based employee compensation cost as soon as the Statement is issued or at any date thereafter. The only restriction is that the new method must be applied *as of* the beginning of the fiscal year in which it is adopted.

267. The Board decided that a lengthy transition period for the required pro forma disclosures is not necessary. The fair value based method to be used in those disclosures has been debated and widely publicized for several years. The measurement method in this Statement is similar to the one in the Exposure Draft, and the areas of change, such as not adjusting for the effect of a difference between initially estimated expected and actual lives of options, should ease implementation. Therefore, the Board decided that the required pro forma disclosures should begin with awards granted in fiscal years beginning after December 15, 1994 (that is, awards granted in 1995 fiscal years). However, the Board recognizes that the issuance of this Statement relatively late in 1995 might make it difficult for some entities with fiscal years ending in December to gather the information necessary to disclose pro forma information in their 1995 financial statements. The Board thus decided that required presentation of pro forma information should begin with financial statements for 1996, which also should include the pro forma disclosures for 1995 if comparative financial information is presented.

268. This Statement deals separately with issuances of equity instruments to acquire employee services in transactions that are included in the scope of Opinion 25 and other issuances of equity instruments to acquire goods or services. For the latter transactions, this Statement essentially codifies current best practice, which is to measure the transaction at the fair value of the consideration received or the fair value of the equity instrument issued, whichever is more

reliably measurable. The Board decided that the effective date of that provision should be transactions entered into after December 15, 1995, because the provisions are not expected to result in a significant change in practice.

269. The Exposure Draft proposed prospective application of the new method of accounting for stock-based employee compensation plans, that is, the new method would be applied only to awards granted after a specified date. This Statement retains prospective application. Some respondents were concerned about the inherent "ramp-up" effect on compensation cost as additional awards are granted and the first awards to which the new method applies move through their vesting periods. Those respondents generally suggested either requiring or permitting retroactive application to all awards that are not vested at the effective date.

270. The Board recognizes the potential for misleading implications caused by the ramp-up effect of prospective application of a new accounting or pro forma disclosure requirement for a recurring transaction. However, the Board continues to question the feasibility of retroactive application of the fair value based method of accounting, which could involve several years depending on the length of the vesting period. (Some constituents even objected to having to apply the fair value based method to awards granted in 1995, but before this Statement was issued.) For example, field test participants reported that estimating what assumptions they might have used for expected option lives, volatility, or dividends for grants made several years in the past was problematical. The Board decided that requiring retroactive application would be excessively burdensome. Permitting either retroactive or prospective application would detract from the comparability of the information reported by different entities. Instead, the Board decided that entities should be required to alert readers of the financial statements if amounts of compensation cost determined using the fair value based method that are reflected in the pro forma disclosures or recognized are not indicative of future amounts when the new method will apply to all outstanding, nonvested awards.

Appendix B

ILLUSTRATIVE GUIDANCE FOR APPLYING THE STANDARDS

CONTENTS

Appendix B

ILLUSTRATIVE GUIDANCE FOR APPLYING THE STANDARDS

Introduction

271. This appendix, which is an integral part of the requirements of this Statement, discusses further the fair value based method of accounting for stock-based employee compensation and illustrates its application to specific awards. The examples and related assumptions in this appendix are illustrative only; they may not represent actual situations.

272. The guidance in paragraphs 273-287 on selecting assumptions for use in an option-pricing model applies equally to (a) an entity that applies the fair value based method in accounting for its stock-based employee compensation cost and (b) an entity that accounts for its stock-based employee compensation in accordance with Opinion 25 and discloses the pro forma information required by paragraph 45. Except where noted, the illustrations in paragraphs 288-356 assume that the reporting entity had adopted the fair value based method of accounting for compensation cost before the transactions illustrated. However, had the entity continued to account for its stock-based employee compensation cost in accordance with Opinion 25, it would follow the same procedures in preparing the pro forma disclosures required by this Statement.

Selecting Assumptions for Use in an Option-Pricing Model

273. This Statement requires a public entity to estimate the fair value of an employee stock option using a pricing model that takes into account the exercise price and expected life of the option, the current price of the underlying stock, its expected volatility, the expected dividends on the stock, and the current risk-free interest rate for the expected life of the option. As indicated in paragraph 19, a U.S. entity issuing an option on its own stock must use as the risk-free interest rate the implied yield currently available on zero-coupon U.S. government issues with a remaining term equal to the expected life of the option that is

being valued. Guidance on selecting the other assumptions listed in paragraph 19 is provided in the following paragraphs.[18]

274. In estimating the expected volatility of and dividends on the underlying stock, the objective is to approximate the expectations that likely would be reflected in a current market or negotiated exchange price for the option. Similarly, the objective in estimating the expected lives of employee stock options is to approximate the expectations that an outside party with access to detailed information about employees' exercise behavior likely would develop based on information available at the grant date.

275. The Board recognizes that in most circumstances there is likely to be a range of reasonable expectations about future volatility, dividends, and option life. If one amount within the range is a better estimate than any other amount, that amount should be used. If no amount within the range is a better estimate than any other amount, it is appropriate to use an estimate at the *low* end of the range for expected volatility and expected option life, and an estimate at the *high* end of the range for expected dividends. (Computed option value varies directly with expected volatility and life, but it varies inversely with expected dividends.) That approach is similar to the one used in FASB Interpretation No. 14, *Reasonable Estimation of the Amount of a Loss,* which requires accrual of the minimum amount in a range of reasonable estimates of the amount of a loss if no amount within the range is a better estimate than any other amount.

276. Expectations about the future generally are based on past experience, modified to reflect ways in which currently available information indicates that the future is reasonably expected to differ from the past. In some circumstances, identifiable factors may indicate that unadjusted historical experience is a relatively poor predictor of future experience. For example, if an entity with two distinctly different lines of business disposes of the one that was significantly less volatile and generated more cash than the other, historical volatility, dividends, and perhaps lives of stock options from the predisposition period are not likely to be the best information on which to base reasonable expectations for the future.

277. In other circumstances, historical information may not be available. For example, an entity whose common stock has only recently become publicly traded will have little, if any, historical data on the volatility of its own stock. In that situation, expected volatility may be based on the average volatilities of similar entities for an appropriate period following their going public. Similarly, an entity whose common stock has been publicly traded for only a few years and has generally become less volatile as more trading experience has been gained might appropriately place more weight on the more recent experience. It also might consider the stock price volatilities of similar entities.

278. Not all of the general guidance on selecting assumptions provided in paragraphs 273-277 is repeated in the following discussion of factors to be considered in selecting specific assumptions. However, the general guidance is intended to apply to each individual assumption. The Board does *not* intend for an entity to base option values on historical average option lives, stock volatility, or dividends (whether stated as a yield or a dollar amount) without considering the extent to which historical experience reasonably predicts future experience.

Expected Lives of Employee Stock Options

279. The value of an award of employee stock options may be based either on an appropriately weighted average expected life for the entire award or on appropriately weighted lives for subgroups of the award based on more detailed data about employees' exercise behavior. Paragraphs 281 and 282 each discuss a different way to incorporate a range of expected lives in estimating option value rather than effectively assuming that all employees hold their options for the weighted-average life.

280. Factors to consider in estimating the expected life of an award of stock options include:

a. The vesting period of the grant. The expected life must at least include the vesting period. In addition, if all other factors are equal, the length of time employees hold options after they first become exercisable may vary inversely with the length of the vesting period. For example, employees may be more likely to exercise options

---

[18]The guidance on assumptions in this Statement, especially the expected lives of employee stock options, benefited from several working papers discussed at an informal roundtable discussion on measuring the value of employee stock options the Board held on April 18, 1994. Some of those papers have subsequently been published.

shortly after the options vest if the vesting period is four years than if the vesting period is only two years.

b. The average length of time similar grants have remained outstanding in the past.

c. Expected volatility of the underlying stock. On average, employees may tend to exercise options on highly volatile stocks earlier than on stocks with low volatility.

281. Segregating options into groups for employees with relatively homogeneous exercise behavior may also be important. Option value is not a linear function of option term; value increases at a decreasing rate as the term lengthens. For example, a two-year option is worth less than twice as much as a one-year option if all other assumptions are equal. That means that calculating estimated option value based on a single weighted-average life that includes widely differing individual lives will overstate the value of the entire award. Segregating options granted into several groups, each of which has a relatively narrow range of lives included in its weighted-average life, reduces that overstatement. For example, the experience of an entity that grants options broadly to all levels of employees might indicate that top-level executives tend to hold their options longer than middle-management employees hold theirs and that hourly employees tend to exercise their options earlier than any other group. In addition, employees who are encouraged or required to hold a minimum amount of their employer's equity instruments, including options, might on average exercise options later than employees not subject to that provision. In those situations, segregating options by groups of recipients with relatively homogeneous exercise behavior and determining the related option values based on appropriate weighted-average expected lives for each group will result in an improved estimate of the fair value of the total award.

282. Rather than estimating expected life directly, an entity may wish to estimate it indirectly, using an option-pricing model that has been modified to compute an option value using an assumed stock price at which the options would be expected to be exercised. For example, an entity's experience might show a large increase in option exercises when the stock price first reaches 200 percent of the exercise price. If so, that entity might compute an option value using a pricing model that implicitly determines a weighted-average life based on exercise at an assumed price of 200 percent of the exercise price. The model would assume exercise of the option at each point on the in-herent probability distribution of possible stock prices at which the expected price at exercise is first reached. On branches of the binomial tree on which the stock price does not reach 200 percent of the exercise price but is in-the-money at the end of the contractual term, the model would assume exercise at that date. The expected life is then computed as the weighted-average life of the resulting binomial tree. That method recognizes that employees' exercise behavior is related to the path of the stock price.

283. Segregating options into groups based on the exercise behavior of the recipients also may be important if the technique in paragraph 282 is used. For example, an employer's experience might indicate that hourly employees tend to exercise for a smaller percentage gain than do more highly compensated employees.

Expected Volatility

284. Volatility is a measure of the amount by which a price has fluctuated or is expected to fluctuate during a period. The measure of volatility used in the Black-Scholes option-pricing model is the annualized standard deviation of the continuously compounded rates of return on the stock over a period of time. Generally, at least 20 to 30 price observations made at regular intervals are needed to compute a statistically valid standard deviation. For long-term options, historical volatility generally should be calculated based on more—probably many more—than 30 observations. The concept of volatility is defined more fully in the glossary. One method of calculating historical average annualized volatility based on weekly price observations is illustrated in Appendix F. As discussed further in the following paragraph, an entity may need to adjust historical average annualized volatility to estimate a reasonable expected volatility over the expected life of an option.

285. Factors to consider in estimating expected volatility include:

a. The historical volatility of the stock over the most recent period that is generally commensurate with the expected option life.

b. The length of time an entity's stock has been publicly traded. If that period is shorter than the expected life of the option, historical volatility should be computed for the longest period for which trading activity is available. A newly public entity also should consider the historical volatility of similar entities following a comparable period in their lives. For example, an entity that has been publicly traded for only one year that grants options with an average expected life of five years might consider the pattern and level of historical volatility of more mature entities in the same industry for the first six years the stocks of those entities were publicly traded.

c. The mean-reversion tendency of volatilities. For example, an entity with insufficient trading history on which to base an estimate of historical volatility might take into account mean-reversion tendencies (sometimes called *shrinkage*). A newly public entity with a trading history of only 1 year might have a historical volatility of 60 percent, while the mean volatility of an appropriate peer group is only 35 percent. Until a longer series of historical data is available, the entity might use an expected volatility of approximately 47.5 percent [(.60 + .35) ÷ 2]. A more mature entity also should consider mean-reversion tendencies and other reasons for which expected future volatility may differ from past volatility. For example, if an entity's stock was extraordinarily volatile for some identifiable period of time because of a failed takeover bid or a major restructuring, that period might be disregarded in computing historical average annual volatility.

d. Appropriate and regular intervals for price observations. In general, weekly price observations should be sufficient for computing long-term historical volatility. The price observations should be consistent from period to period. For example, an entity might use the closing price for each week or the highest price for the week, but it should not use the closing price for some weeks and the highest price for other weeks.

Expected Dividends

286. Standard option-pricing models generally call for expected dividend yield. However, the models may be modified to use an expected dividend amount rather than a yield. An entity may use either its expected yield or its expected payments. If the latter, the entity's historical pattern of increases in dividends should be considered. For example, if an entity's policy generally has been to increase dividends by approximately 3 percent per year, its estimated option value should not assume a fixed dividend amount throughout the expected life unless there is evidence that supports that assumption.

287. Generally, the assumption about expected dividends should be based on publicly available information. An entity that does not pay dividends and has no plans to do so would assume an expected dividend yield of zero. However, an emerging entity with no history of paying dividends might expect to begin paying dividends during the expected lives of its employee stock options. Those entities may use an average of their past dividend yield (zero) and the mean dividend yield of an appropriately comparable peer group. For example, it would not be appropriate for a young, rapidly growing entity to base its expected dividend yield on the average dividend yield of the entities in the Standard & Poor's 500 Index.

Illustrative Computations

Illustration 1—Fixed Stock Option

288. Company S, a public entity, grants options with a maximum term of 10 years to its employees. The exercise price of each option equals the market price of its stock on the grant date. All options vest at the end of three years (cliff vesting). The options do not qualify for tax purposes as incentive stock options. The corporate tax rate is 34 percent.

289. The following table shows assumptions and information about options granted on January 1, 2000.

Options granted	900,000
Employees granted options	3,000
Expected forfeitures per year	3%
Stock price	$50
Exercise price	$50
Expected life of options	6 years
Risk-free interest rate	7.5%
Expected volatility	30%
Expected dividend yield	2.5%

290. Using as inputs the last 6 items from the table above, the Black-Scholes option-pricing model modified for dividends determines a fair value of $17.15 for each option. Using the same assumptions, a binomial model produces a value of $17.26. A difference between a Black-Scholes model and a binomial model grant-date valuation of an option generally arises from the binomial model's fully reflecting the benefit in limited circumstances of being able to exercise an option on a dividend-paying stock before its expiration date when it is economic to do so. (If Company S paid no dividends, both the Black-Scholes and the binomial models would determine a fair value of $22.80, holding other assumptions constant.) Although some available software modifies

the Black-Scholes model to attempt to take that benefit into account, the result may not be exactly the same as a binomial model. The following illustrations use a fair value of $17.15, but $17.26 is equally acceptable.

291. Total compensation cost recognized over the vesting period will be the fair value of all options that actually vest, determined based on the stock price at the grant date. This Statement allows an entity either to estimate at the grant date the number of options expected to vest or to recognize compensation cost each period based on the number of options not yet forfeited. An adjustment to eliminate compensation cost previously recognized for options that were subsequently forfeited is recognized when the forfeitures occur. This example assumes that Company S estimates at the grant date the number of options that will vest and subsequently adjusts compensation cost for changes in the assumed rate of forfeitures and differences between expectations and actual experience. None of the compensation cost is capitalized as part of the cost to produce inventory or other assets.

292. The estimate of the expected number of forfeitures considers historical employee turnover rates and expectations about the future. Company S has experienced historical turnover rates of approximately 3 percent per year for employees at the grantees' level having nonvested options, and it expects that rate to continue. Therefore, Company S estimates the total value of the award at the grant date based on an expected forfeiture rate of 3 percent per year. Actual forfeitures are 5 percent in 2000, but no adjustments to cost are recognized in 2000 because Company S still expects actual forfeitures to average 3 percent per year over the 3-year vesting period. During 2001, however, management decides that the rate of forfeitures is likely to continue to increase through 2002, and the assumed forfeiture rate for the entire award is changed to 6 percent per year. Adjustments to cumulative cost to reflect the higher forfeiture rate are made at the end of 2001. At the end of 2002 when the award becomes vested, actual forfeitures have averaged 6 percent per year, and no further adjustment is necessary.

Cliff vesting

293. The first set of calculations illustrates the accounting for the award of options on January 1, 2000,

assuming that the entire award vests at the end of three years, that is, the award provides for cliff vesting rather than graded vesting. (Paragraphs 298-305 illustrate the accounting for an award assuming graded vesting in which a specified portion of the award vests at the end of each year.) The number of options expected to vest is estimated at the grant date to be 821,406 (900,000 × .97 × .97 × .97). Thus, as shown in Table 1, the estimated value of the award at January 1, 2000 is $14,087,113 (821,406 × $17.15), and the compensation cost to be recognized during each year of the 3-year vesting period is $4,695,704 ($14,087,113 ÷ 3). The journal entries to recognize compensation cost follow.

For 2000:

Compensation cost	4,695,704	
Additional paid-in capital— stock options		4,695,704

To recognize compensation cost.

Deferred tax asset	1,596,539	
Deferred tax expense		1,596,539

To recognize the deferred tax asset for the temporary difference related to compensation cost ($4,695,704 × .34 = $1,596,539).

The net after-tax effect on income of recognizing compensation cost for 2000 is $3,099,165 ($4,695,704 – $1,596,539).

294. In the absence of a change in estimate or experience different from that initially assumed, the same journal entries would be made to recognize compensation cost and related tax effects for 2001 and 2002, resulting in a net after-tax cost for each year of $3,099,165. However, at the end of 2001, management changes its estimated employee forfeiture rate from 3 percent to 6 percent per year. The revised number of options expected to vest is 747,526 (900,000 × .94 × .94 × .94). Accordingly, the revised total compensation cost to be recognized by the end of 2002 is $12,820,071 (747,526 × $17.15). The cumulative adjustment to reflect the effect of adjusting the forfeiture rate is the difference between two-thirds of the revised cost of the award and the cost already recognized for 2000 and 2001. The related journal entries and the computations follow.

At December 31, 2001 to adjust for new forfeiture rate:

Revised total compensation cost	$12,820,071
Revised cumulative cost as of 12/31/01 ($12,820,071 × ⅔)	$ 8,546,714
Cost already recognized in 2000 and 2001 ($4,695,704 × 2)	9,391,408
Adjustment to cost at 12/31/01	$ (844,694)

The related journal entries are:

Additional paid-in capital— stock options	844,694	
Compensation cost		844,694

To adjust compensation cost and equity already recognized to reflect a higher estimated forfeiture rate.

Deferred tax expense	287,196	
Deferred tax asset		287,196

To adjust the deferred tax accounts to reflect the tax effect of increasing the estimated forfeiture rate ($844,694 × .34 = $287,196).

For 2002:

Compensation cost	4,273,357	
Additional paid-in capital— stock options		4,273,357

To recognize compensation cost ($12,820,071 ÷ 3 = $4,273,357).

Deferred tax asset	1,452,941	
Deferred tax expense		1,452,941

To recognize the deferred tax asset for additional compensation cost ($4,273,357 × .34 = $1,452,941).

At December 31, 2002, the entity would examine its actual forfeitures and make any necessary adjustments to reflect compensation cost for the number of shares that actually vested.

Table 1—Fixed Stock Option—Cliff Vesting

Year	Total Value of Award	Pretax Cost for Year	Cumulative Pretax Cost
2000	$14,087,113 (821,406 × $17.15)	$4,695,704 ($14,087,113 ÷ 3)	$4,695,704
2001	$12,820,071 (747,526 × $17.15)	$3,851,010 [($12,820,071 × ⅔) − $4,695,704]	$8,546,714
2002	$12,820,071 (747,526 × $17.15)	$4,273,357 ($12,820,071 ÷ 3)	$12,820,071

295. For simplicity, the illustration assumes that all of the options are exercised on the same day and that Company S has already recognized its income tax expense for the year without regard to the effects of the exercise of the employee stock options. In other words, current tax expense and current taxes payable were recognized based on income and deductions before consideration of additional deductions from exercise of the employee stock options. The amount credited to common stock (or other appropriate equity account) for the exercise of the options is the sum of (a) the cash proceeds received and (b) the amounts credited to additional paid-in capital for services received earlier that were charged to compensation cost. At exercise, the stock price is assumed to be $70.

At exercise:

Cash (747,526 × $50)	37,376,300	
Additional paid-in capital—stock options	12,820,071	
Common stock		50,196,371

To recognize the issuance of stock upon exercise of options.

296. The difference between the market price of the stock and the exercise price on the date of exercise is deductible for tax purposes because the options do not qualify as incentive stock options. The benefit of tax return deductions in excess of compensation cost recognized results in a credit to additional paid-in capital. Tax return deductions that are less than compensation cost recognized result in a debit to additional paid-in capital to the extent that the benefit of tax deductions from stock-based compensation awards in excess of compensation cost recognized based on the fair value method have been previously credited to capital. To the extent that insufficient credits are available in additional paid-in capital, a charge is made to income tax expense in the period of exercise (paragraph 44). With the stock price at $70 at exercise, the deductible amount is $14,950,520 [747,526 × ($70 − $50)]. The entity has sufficient taxable income, and the tax benefit realized is $5,083,177 ($14,950,520 × .34).

At exercise:

Deferred tax expense	4,358,824	
Deferred tax asset		4,358,824

To write off deferred tax asset related to deductible stock options at exercise ($12,820,071 × .34 = $4,358,824).[19]

Current taxes payable	5,083,177	
Current tax expense		4,358,824
Additional paid-in capital—stock options		724,353

To adjust current tax expense and current taxes payable to recognize the current tax benefit from deductible compensation cost upon exercise of options. The credit to additional paid-in capital is the tax benefit of the excess of the deductible amount over the compensation cost recognized: [($14,950,520 − $12,820,071) × .34 = $724,353].

297. If instead the options had expired unexercised, the additional paid-in capital—stock options account would have been closed to other paid-in capital. Previously recognized compensation cost would not be reversed. Similar to the adjustment for the actual tax deduction realized described in paragraph 296, whether part or all of the deferred tax asset of $4,358,824 is charged to additional paid-in capital or to income tax expense is determined by applying paragraph 44.

Graded vesting

298. Paragraph 31 of this Statement provides for use of either the attribution method described in Interpretation 28 or a straight-line method for awards with graded vesting depending on the approach used to estimate the value of the option award. Both methods are illustrated and use the same assumptions that follow. Company S awards 900,000 options on January 1, 2000, that vest according to a graded schedule of 25 percent for the first year of service, 25 percent for the second year, and the remaining 50 percent for the third year. Each employee is granted 300 options.

299. Table 2 shows the calculation of the number of employees and the related number of options expected to vest. Using the expected 3 percent annual forfeiture rate, 90 employees are expected to terminate during 2000 without having vested in any portion of the award, leaving 2,910 employees to vest in 25 percent of the award. During 2001, 87 employees are expected to terminate, leaving 2,823 to vest in the second 25 percent of the award. During 2002, 85 employees are expected to terminate, leaving 2,738 employees to vest in the last 50 percent of the award. That results in a total of 840,675 options expected to vest from the award of 900,000 options with graded vesting. As provided in paragraph 28, Company S could have chosen to recognize cost based on the number of options granted and recognized forfeitures as they occur; that method is not illustrated.

---

[19]Individual entries to the deferred tax asset account do not add to $4,358,824 due to rounding differences.

Table 2—Fixed Stock Option—Graded Vesting—Expected Amounts

Year	Number of Employees	Number of Vested Options
	Total at date of grant 3,000	
2000	3,000 – 90 (3,000 × .03) = 2,910	2,910 × 75 (300 × 25%) = 218,250
2001	2,910 – 87 (2,910 × .03) = 2,823	2,823 × 75 (300 × 25%) = 211,725
2002	2,823 – 85 (2,823 × .03) = 2,738	2,738 × 150 (300 × 50%) = 410,700
		Total vested options 840,675

Circumstances in which Interpretation 28 attribution is required

300. If the value of the options that vest over the three-year period is estimated by separating the total award into three groups according to the year in which they vest because the expected life for each group differs significantly, the fair value of the award and its attribution would be determined as follows. (Paragraphs 281 and 283 discuss segregation of options into groups that vest.) The estimated weighted-average expected life of the options that vest in 2000 is assumed to be 2.5 years, resulting in a value of $11.33 per option.[20] The estimated weighted-average expected life of the options that vest in 2001 is assumed to be 4 years, resulting in a value of $14.32 per option. The estimated weighted-average expected life of the options that vest in 2002 is assumed to be 5.5 years, resulting in a value of $16.54 per option. Table 3 shows the estimated compensation cost for the options expected to vest.

Table 3—Fixed Stock Option—Graded Vesting—Expected Cost

Year	Vested Options	Expected Life	Value per Option	Compensation Cost
2000	218,250	2.5 years	$11.33	$ 2,472,773
2001	211,725	4.0 years	14.32	3,031,902
2002	410,700	5.5 years	16.54	6,792,978
	840,675			$12,297,653

301. Compensation cost is recognized over the periods of service during which each group of options is earned. Thus, the $2,472,773 cost attributable to the 218,250 options that vest in 2000 is allocated to the year 2000. The $3,031,902 cost attributable to the 211,725 options that vest at the end of 2001 is allocated over their 2-year vesting period (2000 and 2001). The $6,792,978 cost attributable to the 410,700 options that vest at the end of 2002 is allocated over their 3-year vesting period (2000, 2001, and 2002).

302. Table 4 shows how the $12,297,653 expected amount of compensation cost determined at the grant date is attributed to the years 2000, 2001, and 2002.

---

[20]To simplify the illustration, the fair value of each of the 3 groups of options is based on the same assumptions about expected volatility, expected dividend yield, and the risk-free interest rate used to determine the value of $17.15 for the cliff-vesting options (paragraph 290). In practice, each of those assumptions would be related to the expected life of the group of options being valued, which means that at least the risk-free interest rate and perhaps all three assumptions would differ for each group.

**Table 4—Fixed Stock Option—Graded Vesting—
Computation of Expected Cost**

	Pretax Cost to Be Recognized		
	2000	**2001**	**2002**
Options vesting in 2000	$2,472,773		
Options vesting in 2001	1,515,951	$ 1,515,951	
Options vesting in 2002	2,264,326	2,264,326	$ 2,264,326
Cost for the year	$6,253,050	$ 3,780,277	$ 2,264,326
Cumulative cost	$6,253,050	$10,033,327	$12,297,653

Circumstances in which straight-line attribution is permitted

303. Company S assumes a single weighted-average expected life of five years for the entire award of graded vesting options because the expected lives of each group of options that vest are not expected to be significantly different. Other assumptions except for expected life are the same as in the previous illustration. Company S elects to recognize compensation cost on a straight-line basis.

304. Using an estimated weighted-average expected life of 5 years results in a value of $15.87 per option. The same number of options are expected to vest as shown in the previous illustration, 840,675, based on estimated forfeitures. Total compensation cost to be attributed in a straight-line pattern over the 3-year vesting period is $13,341,512 (840,675 × $15.87). Compensation cost recognized at any date must be at least equal to the amount attributable to options that are vested at that date. For example, if this same option award vested 50 percent in the first year of the 3-year vesting period, at least $6,670,756 ($13,341,512 × 50%) would be recognized in the first year.

305. The estimated value of the award is adjusted to reflect differences between expected and actual forfeitures as illustrated for the cliff-vesting options, regardless of which method described in paragraph 31 is used to estimate value and attribute cost for the graded vesting options. For example, if the actual forfeiture rate is 5 percent rather than 3 percent in 2000, the compensation cost for the options that vest in 2000 (attributed under the Interpretation 28 method) is adjusted to $2,421,788 (2,850 × 75 × $11.33), reflecting the reduction in the number of employees [2,850 = 3,000 – (3,000 × .05)] whose first 75 options became vested at December 31, 2000. Compensation

cost for the options expected to vest in 2001 and 2002 also is recomputed to reflect the actual forfeitures in 2000. Similar adjustments are made to reflect differences, if any, between expected and actual forfeitures in those years. Total compensation cost at the end of 2002 reflects the number of vested options at that date.

Illustration 2—Performance-Based Stock Option

Illustration 2(a)—Option award under which the number of options to be earned varies

306. Illustration 2(a) shows the computation of compensation cost if Company S grants a performance-based stock option award instead of a fixed stock option award. Under the plan, employees vest in differing numbers of options depending on the increase in market share of one of Company S's products over a three-year period. On January 1, 2000, Company S grants to each of 1,000 employees an award of up to 300 10-year options on shares of its common stock. If by December 31, 2002, market share increases by at least 5 percentage points, each employee vests in at least 100 options at that date. If market share increases by at least 10 percentage points, another 100 options vest, for a total of 200. If market share increases by more than 20 percentage points, each employee vests in 300 options. Company S's stock price on January 1, 2000, is $50, and other assumptions are the same as in Illustration 1. The fair value at the grant date of an option expected to vest is $17.15. The estimated fair value of the entire performance-based award depends on the number of options that are expected to be earned during the vesting period. Accruals of cost are based on the best estimate of market share growth over the three-year vesting period, and adjusted for subsequent changes in the expected or actual market share growth. Paragraph 28 requires accruals of cost to be

based on the best estimate of the outcome of the performance condition. Therefore, Company S is not permitted to estimate a percentage likelihood of achieving a performance condition and base accruals on an amount that is not a possible outcome.

307. Table 5 shows the compensation cost recognized in 2000, 2001, and 2002 if Company S estimates at the grant date that it is probable that market share will increase between 10 and 20 percentage points. That estimate remains reasonable until the end of 2002, when Company S's market share has increased over the 3-year period by more than 20 percentage points. Thus, each employee vests in options on 300 shares.

308. As in Illustration 1, Company S experiences actual forfeiture rates of 5 percent in 2000, and in 2001 changes its estimate of forfeitures for the entire award from 3 percent to 6 percent per year. In 2001, cumulative compensation cost is adjusted to reflect

the higher forfeiture rate. By the end of 2002, a 6 percent forfeiture rate has been experienced, and no further adjustments for forfeitures are necessary. Through 2000, Company S estimates that 913 employees ($1,000 \times .97 \times .97 \times .97$) will remain in service until the vesting date. At the end of 2001, the number of employees estimated to vest is adjusted for the higher forfeiture rate, and the number of employees expected to vest in the award is 831 ($1,000 \times .94 \times .94 \times .94$). The value of the award is estimated initially based on the number of options expected to vest, which in turn is based on the expected level of performance, and the fair value of each option. Compensation cost is initially recognized ratably over the three-year vesting period, with one-third of the value of the award recognized each year, adjusted as needed for changes in the estimated and actual forfeiture rates and for differences between estimated and actual market share growth.

Table 5—Performance-Based Stock Option—Number of Options Varies

Year	Total Value of Award	Pretax Cost for Year	Cumulative Pretax Cost
2000	$3,131,590 ($17.15 × 200 × 913)	$1,043,863 ($3,131,590 ÷ 3)	$1,043,863
2001	$2,850,330 ($17.15 × 200 × 831)	$856,357 [($2,850,330 × ⅔) – $1,043,863]	$1,900,220
2002	$4,275,495 ($17.15 × 300 × 831)	$2,375,275 ($4,275,495 – $1,900,220)	$4,275,495

Illustration 2(b)—Option award under which the exercise price varies

309. Illustration 2(b) shows the computation of compensation cost if Company S grants a performance-based stock option award under which the exercise price, rather than the number of shares, varies depending on the level of performance achieved. On January 1, 2000, Company S grants to its chief executive officer (CEO) 10-year options on 10,000 shares of its common stock, which are immediately exercisable. The stock price at the grant date is $50, and the initial exercise price also is $50. However, that price decreases to $30 if the market share of Company S's products increases by at least 10 per-

centage points by December 31, 2001, and provided that the CEO continues to be employed by Company S.

310. Company S estimates at the grant date the expected level of market share growth, the exercise price of the options, and the expected life of the options. Other assumptions, including the risk-free interest rate and the service period over which the cost is attributed, need to be consistent with those estimates. Company S estimates at the grant date that its market share growth will be at least 10 percentage points over the 2-year performance period, which means that the expected exercise price of the options is $30, resulting in an estimated option value of

$22.64.[21] Compensation cost of $226,400 (10,000 × $22.64) would be accrued over the expected 2-year service period. Paragraph 19 of this Statement requires the value of both fixed and performance awards to be estimated as of the date of grant. Paragraph 26, however, calls for recognition of cost for the number of instruments that actually vest. For this performance award, Company S also selects the expected assumptions at the grant date if the performance goal is not met. If market share growth is not at least 10 percentage points over the 2-year period, Company S estimates that the CEO will exercise the options with a $50 exercise price in 5 years. All other assumptions would need to be consistent, resulting in an estimated option value of $15.87.[22] (For convenience, the illustration assumes that all options are expected to be exercised on the same date.) Total compensation cost to be recognized if the performance goal is not met would be $158,700 (10,000 × $15.87). During the two-year service period, adjustments to expected amounts for changes in estimates or actual experience are made and cost recognized by the end of that period reflects whether the performance goal was met.

Illustration 3—Stock Option with Indexed Exercise Price

311. Company S instead might have granted stock options whose exercise price varies with an index of the stock prices of a group of entities in the same industry. Assume that on January 1, 2000, Company S grants 100 options on its stock with a base exercise price of $50 to each of 1,000 employees. The options have a maximum term of 10 years. The exercise price of the options increases or decreases on December 31 of each year by the same percentage that the index has increased or decreased during the year. For example, if the peer group index increases by 10 percent in 2000, the exercise price of the options during 2001 increases to $55 ($50 × 1.10). The assumptions about the risk-free interest rate and expected life, dividends, volatility, and forfeiture rates are the same as in Illustration 1. On January 1, 2000, the peer group index is assumed to be 400. The dividend yield on the index is assumed to be 1.25 percent.

312. Each indexed option may be analyzed as an option to exchange 0.1250 (50 ÷ 400) "shares" of the

peer group index for a share of Company S stock, that is, to exchange one noncash asset for another noncash asset. An option to purchase stock for cash also can be thought of as an option to exchange one asset (cash in the amount of the exercise price) for another (the share of stock). The gain on a cash option equals the difference between the price of the stock upon exercise and the amount—the "price"—of the cash exchanged for the stock. The gain on an option to exchange 0.1250 "shares" of the peer group index for a share of Company S stock also equals the difference between the prices of the 2 assets exchanged.

313. To illustrate the equivalence of an indexed option and the option above, assume that an employee exercises the indexed option when Company S's stock price has increased 100 percent to $100 and the peer group index has increased 75 percent, from 400 to 700. The exercise price of the indexed option thus is $87.50 ($50 × 1.75). The employee's realized gain is $12.50.

Price of Company S stock	$100.00
Less: Exercise price of option	87.50
Gain on indexed option	$ 12.50

That is the same as the gain on an option to exchange 0.1250 "shares" of the index for one share of Company S stock:

Price of Company S stock	$100.00
Less: Price of a "share" of the peer group index (.1250 × $700)	87.50
Gain on exchange	$ 12.50

314. The Black-Scholes or binomial option-pricing models can be extended to value an option to exchange one asset for another. The principal extension is that the volatility of an option to exchange two noncash assets is based on the relationship between the volatilities of the prices of the assets to be exchanged—their **cross-volatility.** In a cash option, the amount of cash to be paid involves no risk, that is, it is not volatile, so that only the volatility of the stock needs to be considered in estimating the option's value. In contrast, the value of an option to exchange two noncash assets depends on possible movements

---

[21]Option value is determined using a $50 stock price, $30 exercise price, 3-year expected life, 6.5 percent risk-free interest rate, 2.5 percent dividend yield, and .30 volatility.

[22]Option value is determined using a $50 stock price, $50 exercise price, 5-year expected life, 7.5 percent risk-free interest rate, 2.5 percent dividend yield, and .30 volatility.

in the prices of both assets—in this example, a "share" of the peer group index and a share of Company S stock. Historical cross-volatility can be computed directly by measuring the stock price in "shares" of the peer group index. For example, the stock price was 0.1250 "shares" at the grant date and 0.1429 (100 ÷ 700) "shares" at the exercise date. Those share amounts then are used to compute cross-volatility. Cross-volatility also can be computed indirectly based on the respective volatilities of Company S stock and the peer group index and the correlation between them. The cross-volatility between Company S stock and the peer group index is assumed to be 26.5 percent.

315. In a cash option, the assumed risk-free interest rate (discount rate) represents the return on the cash that will not be paid until exercise. In this example, an equivalent "share" of the index, rather than cash, is what will not be "paid" until exercise. The dividend yield on the peer group index of 1.25 percent therefore is used in place of the risk-free interest rate as an input to the Black-Scholes model.

316. The exercise price for the indexed option is the value of an equivalent "share" of the peer group index, which is $50 (0.1250 × 400). The fair value of each option granted is $9.78 based on the following inputs:

Stock price	$50
Exercise price	$50
Dividend yield	2.50%
Discount rate	1.25%
Volatility	26.5%
Expected life	6 years

The value of the entire award would be based on the number of options expected to vest. That cost would be recognized over the service period as shown in Illustration 1.

Illustration 4—Option with Exercise Price That Increases by a Fixed Amount or a Fixed Percentage

317. Some entities grant options with exercise prices that increase by a fixed amount or a constant percentage periodically rather than by the percentage change in an index. For example, the exercise price of the options in Illustration 1 might increase by a fixed amount of $2.50 per year. Binomial option-pricing models can be adapted to accommodate exercise prices that change over time.

318. Options with exercise prices that increase by a constant percentage also can be valued using an option-pricing model that accommodates changes in exercise prices. Alternatively, those options can be valued by deducting from the discount rate the annual percentage increase in the exercise price. That method works because a decrease in the risk-free interest rate and an increase in the exercise price have a similar effect—both reduce the option value. For example, the exercise price of the options in Illustration 1 might increase at the rate of 5 percent annually. For that example, Company S's options would be valued based on a risk-free interest rate of 2.5 percent (7.5% − 5%). Holding all other assumptions constant from Illustration 1, the value of each option granted by Company S would be $12.34.

Illustration 5—Modifications and Cash Settlements

Illustration 5(a)—Modification of vested options granted after adoption of this Statement

319. The following examples of accounting for modifications of the terms of an award are based on Illustration 1, in which Company S granted its employees 900,000 options with an exercise price of $50 on January 1, 2000. At January 1, 2004, after the options have vested, the market price of Company S stock has declined to $40 per share, and Company S decides to reduce the exercise price of the outstanding options to $40. In effect, Company S issues new options with an exercise price of $40 and a contractual term equal to the remaining contractual term of the original January 1, 2000, options, which is 6 years, in exchange for the original vested options. Company S incurs additional compensation cost for the excess of the fair value of the modified options issued over the value of the original options at the date of the exchange measured as shown in paragraph 320. The modified options are immediately vested, and the additional compensation cost is recognized in the period the modification occurs.

320. The fair value on January 1, 2004, of the modified award, based on a 3-year expected life, $40 current stock price, $40 exercise price, 7 percent risk-free interest rate, 35 percent volatility, and a 2.5 percent dividend yield, is $10.82. To determine the amount of additional compensation cost arising from the modification, the value of the original vested options assumed to be repurchased is computed based on the shorter of (a) the remaining expected life of the original options or (b) the expected

life of the modified options. In this example, the remaining expected life of the original options is two years, which is shorter than the expected life of the modified options (three years). The resulting computed value at January 1, 2004, of the original options based on a $40 current stock price, a $50 exercise price, a risk-free interest rate of 7 percent, expected volatility of 35 percent, and a 2.5 percent dividend yield is $5.54 per option. Thus, the additional compensation cost stemming from the modification is $5.28 per option, determined as follows:

Fair value of modified option at January 1, 2004	$10.82
Less: Value of original option at January 1, 2004	5.54
Additional compensation cost to be recognized	$ 5.28

Compensation cost already recognized during the vesting period of the original award is $12,820,071 for 747,526 vested options (refer to Illustration 1). For simplicity, it is assumed that no options were exercised before the modification. Previously recognized cost is not adjusted. Additional compensation cost of $3,946,937 (747,526 vested options × $5.28) is recognized on January 1, 2004, because the modified options are fully vested.

Illustration 5(b)—Cash settlement of vested options granted after adoption of this Statement

321. Rather than modify the option terms, Company S offers to settle the original January 1, 2000 options for cash at January 1, 2004. The value of each option is estimated in the same way as illustrated in the preceding example, resulting in a value of $5.54. Company S recognizes the settlement as the repurchase of an outstanding equity instrument, and no additional compensation cost is recognized at the date of settlement unless the cash payment exceeds $5.54. Previously recognized compensation cost for the fair value of the original options is not adjusted.

Illustration 5(c)—Modification of nonvested options granted after adoption of this Statement

322. This example assumes that Company S granted its employees 900,000 options with an exercise price of $50, as in Illustration 1. At January 1, 2001, 1 year into the 3-year vesting period, the market price of Company S stock has declined to $40 per share, and Company S decides to reduce the exercise price of the options to $40. The 3-year cliff-vesting requirement is not changed. In effect, Company S grants new options with an exercise price of $40 and a contractual term equal to the 9-year remaining contractual term of the options granted on January 1, 2000, in exchange for the original nonvested options. The expected life of the repriced options is five years. Company S incurs additional compensation cost for the excess of the fair value of the modified options issued over the value of the original options at the date of the exchange determined in the manner set forth in paragraph 320. Company S adds that incremental amount to the remaining unrecognized compensation cost for the original options at the date of modification and recognizes the total amount over the remaining two years of the three-year vesting period.

323. The fair value at January 1, 2001, of the modified options, based on a 5-year expected life, $40 current stock price, $40 exercise price, 7 percent risk-free interest rate, 35 percent volatility, and a 2.5 percent dividend yield, is $13.60 per option. The computed value of the original options at the date of modification used to measure additional compensation cost is based on an expected life of five years because the remaining expected life of the original options and the expected life of the modified options both are five years. The resulting value of the original options, based on a current stock price of $40 and an exercise price of $50, with other assumptions the same as those used to determine the fair value of the modified options, is $10.77. Thus, the additional compensation cost stemming from the modification is $2.83, determined as follows:

Fair value of modified option at January 1, 2001	$13.60
Less: Value of original option at January 1, 2001	10.77
Incremental value of modified January 1, 2001, option	$ 2.83

324. On January 1, 2001, the remaining balance of unrecognized compensation cost for the original op-

tions is $11.43 per option.[23] The total compensation cost for each modified option that is expected to vest is $14.26, determined as follows:

Incremental value of modified option	$ 2.83
Unrecognized compensation cost for original option	11.43
Total compensation cost to be recognized	$14.26

That amount is recognized during 2001 and 2002, which are the two remaining years of the service period.

Illustration 5(d)—Cash settlement of nonvested options granted after adoption of this Statement

325. Rather than modify the option terms, Company S offers to settle the original January 1, 2000 grant of options for cash at January 1, 2001. Because the stockprice decreased from $50 at the grant date to $40 at the date of settlement, the estimated fair value of each option is the same as in Illustration 5(c), $10.77. If Company S pays $10.77 per option, it would recognize that cash settlement as the repurchase of an outstanding equity instrument and total compensation cost would not be remeasured. However, the cash payment for the options effectively vests them. Therefore, the remaining unrecognized compensation cost of $11.43 per option also would be recognized at the date of settlement.

Illustration 5(e)—Modification of vested options granted before adoption of this Statement

326. This example assumes that a modification similar to Illustration 5(a) above occurred on January 1, 1998, and that the original award was granted before Company S adopted this Statement.[24] Thus, Company S recognized no compensation cost for the original options accounted for in accordance with Opinion 25 because the exercise price equaled the stock price at the measurement (grant) date. To better illustrate the accounting distinction, all other assumptions are the same as in Illustration 5(a). Therefore, the fair value of the modified option is assumed to be $10.82, as determined in paragraph 320.

327. Because no compensation cost was recognized for the original options, the modified options are treated as a new grant. Compensation cost of $10.82 is recognized for each outstanding option at the date of the modification. However, if immediately before their terms were modified, the original options had been in-the-money and thus had intrinsic value at the date of modification, that intrinsic value would be excluded from the amount of compensation cost recognized. For example, if a modification of terms occurred in conjunction with a spinoff, the original options might have intrinsic value of, say, $2 each, just before their terms are modified. In that situation, if the fair value of a modified option is $16.50, only $14.50 ($16.50 – $2) of compensation cost would be recognized at the date of the modification. The intrinsic value is excluded from compensation cost because the employees could have exercised their options immediately before the modification and received the intrinsic value without affecting the amount of compensation cost recognized. Only the time value of the modified options is additional compensation cost.

Illustration 5(f)—Modification of nonvested options granted before adoption of this Statement

328. This example of a modification of an option assumes that an award originally accounted for according to Opinion 25 is not yet vested when it is modified. Company S grants an option with an exercise price of $47 when the stock price is $50 and the option cliff-vests after 3 years. Opinion 25 requires compensation cost of $3 ($50 – $47) to be recognized over the vesting period at the rate of $1 per year. After two years of that three-year cliff-vesting period, Company S adopts the accounting method for cost recognition encouraged by this Statement. It also decides to reduce the exercise price of the options to $40, which is the current price of the stock. For convenience, the value of the modified option on the date of the modification is again assumed to be $10.82 (paragraph 320), which consists entirely of time value.

329. Company S had recognized compensation cost of $2 under Opinion 25 at the date of modification for each option that had not been forfeited. After the

---

[23]Using a value of $17.15 for the original option as in Illustration 1 results in recognition of $5.72 ($17.15 ÷ 3) per year. The unrecognized balance at January 1, 2001 is $11.43 ($17.15 – $5.72) per option.

[24]For purposes of the pro forma disclosures required by paragraph 45 of this Statement, the method in Illustrations 5(e) through 5(g) applies only to modifications and cash settlements of awards granted before the beginning of the fiscal year for which that paragraph is initially applied. A modification or cash settlement of an award for which compensation cost has been included in pro forma disclosures since it was granted would be treated in the pro forma disclosures in the same manner as in Illustrations 5(a) through 5(d).

modification, the remaining amount of compensation cost to be recognized during the final year of the 3-year service period is $9.17 for each option that vests, determined as follows:

Fair value of modified option	$10.82
Less: Value of original option, based on 1-year remaining life[25]	2.65
Incremental value of modified option	8.17
Plus: Remaining unrecognized cost for original option	1.00
Compensation cost to be recognized	$ 9.17

The value of the original option deducted from the fair value of the modified option to determine the amount of compensation cost to recognize is based on a one-year life because that is the remaining term of the vesting period. To maintain consistency with (a) the requirements of this Statement for accounting for plan modifications and (b) the principal difference between this Statement and Opinion 25—accounting for the time value of an option—the vesting period is used as the expected life of the original option. The life of an option beyond the vesting period is not pertinent to the accounting under Opinion 25.

Illustration 5(g)—Cash settlement of vested options granted before adoption of this statement

330. This example assumes that a cash settlement of the options described in Illustration 5(a) above occurred on January 1, 1998, and that the original options were granted before Company S adopted the accounting method for cost recognition encouraged by this Statement. Thus, Company S recognized no compensation cost for the original award accounted for in accordance with Opinion 25 because the exercise price equaled the stock price at the measurement (grant) date. All other assumptions are the same as in Illustration 5(a). Therefore, the amount of the cash payment and the fair value of the out-of-the-money option at the date of cash settlement are $10.82, as determined in paragraph 320.

331. Because no cost was recognized for the original award, the cash settlement of the out-of-the-money options for $10.82 each is treated as a new grant. Compensation cost of $10.82 is recognized for each outstanding option at the date of settlement. However, if the original options had been in-the-money and thus had intrinsic value immediately before the

settlement, that intrinsic value would be excluded from the amount of compensation cost recognized for the reasons cited in Illustration 5(e), paragraph 327.

Illustration 6—Options Granted by a Nonpublic Entity

332. Company P, a nonpublic entity, grants 100 stock options on its stock to each of its 100 employees. The options cliff-vest after three years. The fair value of the stock and the exercise price of the options is $5, the expected life of the options is 8 years, and the risk-free interest rate is 7.5 percent. Company P calculates a *minimum value* for each option. The so-called minimum value does not take into account the expected volatility of the underlying stock.

Fair value of stock	$5.00
Present value of exercise price (compounded daily)	2.74
Minimum value of each option	$2.26

333. An option-pricing model can also be used to compute the minimum value of Company P's options if the volatility assumption is set to near zero (say, 0.001), resulting in the same $2.26. If Company P expected to pay dividends, the minimum value of the options would be further reduced to reflect the present value of the expected dividends that the option holder will not receive. Assuming a 1 percent dividend yield over the 8-year expected life of the options, an option-pricing model results in a minimum value of $1.87.

334. Alternatively, the present value of the expected dividends would be computed as $.30, using 32 quarterly (8-year expected life) payments of $.0125 [($5.00 × .01) ÷ 4], and a quarterly interest rate of 1.875 percent (7.5 percent annual rate). That amount would be deducted from the minimum value of an option on a stock that pays no dividends computed in paragraph 332, resulting in a minimum value of $1.96 ($2.26 − $.30). The $0.39 present value of the dividends computed using the option-pricing model ($2.26 − $1.87) differs from the $0.30 present value computed by directly discounting dividend payments because the option-pricing model assumes that dividends will grow with increases in the stock price (if

---

[25]Other assumptions are $40 stock price, $47 exercise price, expected volatility of 30 percent, risk-free interest rate of 5 percent, and dividend yield of 2.5 percent.

the dividend assumption is stated as a constant yield). The assumed growth rate is the difference between the risk-free interest rate and the dividend rate. In this example, that difference is 6.5 percent (7.5% – 1%). Either method of computing minimum value is acceptable in applying this Statement.

Illustration 7—Tandem Plan—Stock Options or Cash SARs

335. A plan in which employees are granted awards with two separate components, in which exercise of one component cancels the other, is referred to as a tandem plan. In contrast, a **combination plan** is an award with two separate components, both of which can be exercised.

336. The following illustrates the accounting for a tandem plan in which employees have a choice of either stock options or cash SARs. Company S grants to its employees an award of 900,000 stock options or 900,000 cash SARs on January 1, 2000. The award vests on December 31, 2002, and has a contractual life of 10 years. If an employee exercises the SARs, the related stock options are canceled. Conversely, if an employee exercises the options, the related SARs are canceled.

337. The tandem award results in Company S's incurring a liability because the employees can demand settlement in cash, and Company S therefore is obligated to pay cash upon demand. If Company S could choose whether to settle the award in cash or by issuing stock, the award would be an equity instrument because Company S would have the discretion to avoid transferring its assets to employees (unless Company S's past practice is to settle most awards in cash, indicating that Company S has incurred a substantive liability as indicated in paragraph 39). In this illustration, however, Company S incurs a liability to pay cash, which it will recognize over the service period. The amount of the liability will be adjusted each year to reflect the current stock price. If employees choose to exercise the options rather than the SARs, the liability is settled by issuing stock.

338. In concept, the fair value of the expected liability at the grant date is $14,087,113 as computed in Illustration 1 because the value of the SARs and the value of the stock options are equal. However, this Statement does not require accounting for the time value of the cash SARs at the grant date because compensation cost stemming from the award must be finally measured as the intrinsic value of the SARs at

the exercise (or expiration) date. Accordingly, at the end of 2000, when the stock price is $55, the amount of the liability is $4,107,030 (821,406 cash SARs expected to vest × $5 increase in stock price). One-third of that amount, $1,369,010, is recognized as compensation cost for 2000. At the end of each year during the vesting period, the expected liability is remeasured based on the current stock price. As provided in paragraph 28, Company S has the choice of estimating forfeitures at the grant date or accruing cost for the total grant and adjusting for forfeitures as they occur. After the vesting period, the expected liability is remeasured for all outstanding vested awards.

Illustration 8—Tandem Plan—Phantom Shares or Stock Options

339. The illustration that follows is for a tandem plan in which the components have different values after the grant date, depending on the movement in the price of the entity's stock. The employee's choice of which component to exercise will depend on the relative values of the components when the award is exercised.

340. Company S grants to its CEO an immediately vested award consisting of two measurable parts:

a. 1,000 phantom stock units (units) whose value is always equal to the value of 1,000 shares of Company S's common stock.
b. Options on 3,000 shares of Company S stock with an exercise price of $50 per share.

At the grant date, Company S's stock price is $50 per share. The CEO may choose whether to exercise the options or to cash in the units at any time during the next five years. Exercise of all of the options cancels all of the units, and cashing in all of the units cancels all of the options. The cash value of the units will be paid to the CEO at the end of five years if the option component of the tandem award is not exercised before then.

341. With a 3-to-1 ratio of options to units, exercise of 3 options will produce a higher gain than receipt of cash equal to the value of 1 share of stock if the stock price appreciates from the grant date by more than 50 percent. Below that point, one unit is more valuable than the gain on three options. To illustrate that relationship, the results if the stock price increases 50 percent to $75 are:

	Units		**Exercise of Options**	
Market value	$75,000	($75 × 1,000)	$225,000	($75 × 3,000)
Purchase price	0		150,000	($50 × 3,000)
Net cash value	$75,000		$ 75,000	

342. If the price of Company S's common stock increases from $50 to $75, each part of the tandem grant will produce the same net cash inflow (ignoring transaction costs) to the CEO. If the price increases only to $74, the value of 1 share of stock exceeds the gain on exercising 3 options, which would be $72 [3 × ($74 – $50)]. But if the price increases to $76, the gain on exercising 3 options, $78 [3 × ($76 – $50)], exceeds the value of 1 share of stock.

343. At the grant date, the CEO could take $50,000 cash for the units and forfeit the options. Therefore, the total value of the award at the grant date must exceed $50,000 because at stock prices above $75, the CEO receives a higher amount than would the holder of 1 share of stock. To exercise the 3,000 options, the CEO must forfeit the equivalent of 1,000 shares of stock, in addition to paying the total exercise price of $150,000 (3,000 × $50). In effect, the CEO receives only 2,000 shares of Company S stock upon exercise. That is the same as if the option component of the tandem award consisted of options to purchase 2,000 shares of stock for $75 per share.

344. The cash payment obligated by the units qualifies the award as a liability of Company S. The maximum amount of the cash liability, which is indexed to the price of Company S's common stock, is $75,000 because at stock prices above $75, the CEO will exercise the options.

345. In measuring compensation cost, the award may be thought of as a *combination*—not tandem—grant of (a) 1,000 units with a value at grant of $50,000 and (b) 2,000 options with a strike price of $75 per share. Compensation cost is measured as the combined value of the two parts.

346. The expected volatility of Company S stock is assumed to be 30 percent, the risk-free interest rate is 7 percent, Company S stock pays no dividend, and the expected life of the options is 5 years. Using those assumptions, the fair value of an option with an exercise price of $75 is $12.13 when the price of Company S's stock price is $50. Therefore, the total value of the award at the grant date is:

Units (1,000 × $50)	$50,000
Options (2,000 × $12.13)	24,260
Value of award	$74,260

347. Compensation cost recognized at the date of grant (the award is immediately vested) therefore would be $74,260. That amount is more than either of the components by itself, but less than the total cost that would be computed if both components (1,000 units and 3,000 options with an exercise price of $50) were exercisable. Because granting the units creates a liability, changes in the liability that result from increases or decreases in the price of Company S's stock price would be recognized each period until exercise, except that the amount of the liability would not exceed $75,000.

Illustration 9—"Look-Back" Options

348. Some entities offer options to employees under Section 423 of the Internal Revenue Code, which provides that employees will not be immediately taxed on the difference between the market price of the stock and a discounted purchase price if several requirements are met. One requirement is that the option price may not be less than the smaller of (a) 85 percent of the market price when the option is granted or (b) 85 percent of the price at exercise. An option that provides the employee the choice of (a) or (b) may not have a term in excess of 27 months. Options that provide for the more favorable of two (or more) exercise prices are referred to as "look-back" options. A look-back option with a 15 percent discount from the market price at either grant or exercise is worth more than a fixed option to purchase stock at 85 percent of the current market price because the holder of the look-back option cannot lose. If the price rises, the holder benefits to the same extent as if the exercise price were fixed at the grant date. If the

stock price falls, the holder still receives the benefit of purchasing the stock at a 15 percent discount from its price at the date of exercise.

349. For example, on January 1, 2000, when its stock price is $50, Company S offers its employees the opportunity to sign up for a payroll deduction to purchase its stock at either 85 percent of the stock's current price or 85 percent of the price at the end of the year when the options expire, whichever is lower. The exercise price of the options is the lesser of (a) $42.50 ($50 × .85) or (b) 85 percent of the stock price at the end of the year when the option is exercised. For simplicity, the first set of calculations assumes that Company S pays no dividends, its expected volatility is .30, and the risk-free interest rate available for the next 12 months is 6.8 percent.

350. The value of that look-back option can be estimated at the grant date by breaking it into its components and valuing the option as a combination position. In this situation, the components are:

- 0.15 of a share of nonvested stock
- 0.85 of a 1-year call option held with an exercise price of $50.

Supporting analysis for the two components is discussed below.

351. Beginning with the first component, an option with an exercise price that equals 85 percent of the value of the stock at the exercise date will always be worth 15 percent (100% − 85%) of the stock price upon exercise. For a stock that pays no dividends, that option is the equivalent of 15 percent of a share of the stock. The holder of the look-back option will receive *at least* the equivalent of 0.15 of a share of stock upon exercise, regardless of the stock price at that date. For example, if the stock price falls to $40, the exercise price of the option will be $34 ($40 × .85), and the holder will benefit by $6 ($40 − $34), which is the same as receiving 0.15 of a share of stock for each option.

352. If the stock price upon exercise is more than $50, the holder of the look-back option receives a benefit that is worth more than 15 percent of a share of stock. At prices of $50 or more, the holder receives a benefit for the difference between the stock price upon exercise and $42.50—the exercise price of the option (.85 × $50). If the stock price is $60, the holder benefits by $17.50 ($60 − $42.50). However, the holder cannot receive *both* the $17.50 value of an

option with an exercise price of $42.50 *and* 0.15 of a share of stock. In effect, the holder gives up 0.15 of a share of stock worth $7.50 ($50 × .15) if the stock price is above $50 at exercise. The result is the same as if the exercise price of the option were $50 ($42.50 + $7.50), and the holder of the look-back option held 85 percent of a 1-year call option with an exercise price of $50 in addition to 0.15 of a share of stock that will be received if the stock price is $50 or less upon exercise.

353. A standard option-pricing model can be used to value the 1-year call option on 0.85 of a share of stock represented by the second component. Therefore, the compensation cost for the look-back option at the grant date is:

- 0.15 of a share of nonvested stock ($50 × 0.15) .... $ 7.50
- Call on 0.85 of a share of stock, exercise price of $50 ($7.56 × .85) 6.43

Total grant date value $13.93

354. For a look-back option on a dividend-paying stock, both the value of the nonvested stock component and the value of the option component would be adjusted to reflect the effect of the dividends that the employee does not receive during the life of the option. The present value of the dividends expected to be paid on the stock during the life of the option, which is one year in the example, would be deducted from the value of a share that receives dividends. One way to accomplish that is to base the value calculation on shares of stock rather than dollars by assuming that the dividends are reinvested in the stock.

355. For example, if Company S pays a quarterly dividend of 0.625 percent (2.5% ÷ 4) of the current stock price, 1 share of stock would grow to 1.0252 (the future value of 1 using a return of 0.625 percent for 4 periods) shares at the end of the year if all dividends are reinvested. Therefore, the present value of 1 share of stock to be received in 1 year is only 0.9754 of a share today (again applying conventional compound interest formulas compounded quarterly) if the holder does not receive the dividends paid during the year.

356. The value of the option component is easier to compute; the appropriate dividend assumption is used in the option-pricing model in determining the

value of an option on a whole share of stock. Thus, the compensation cost for the look-back option if Company S pays quarterly dividends at the annual rate of 2.5 percent is:

- 0.15 of a share of nonvested stock
  ($50 × 0.15 × 0.9754) $ 7.32
- Call on 0.85 of a share of stock,
  $50 exercise price, 2.5% dividend
  yield ($6.78 × 0.85)   5.76

Total grant date value $13.08

The first component, which is worth $7.32 at the grant date, is the minimum amount the holder benefits regardless of the price of the stock at the exercise date. The second component, worth $5.76 at the grant date, represents the additional benefit to the holder if the stock price is above $50 at the exercise date.

Illustration of the Earnings per Share Computation

357. An illustration of the computation of earnings per share follows. Under Opinion 15 and FASB Interpretation No. 31, *Treatment of Stock Compensation Plans in EPS Computations,* stock options, stock appreciation rights, and other awards to be settled in stock are common stock equivalents for purposes of computing earnings per share. In applying the treasury stock method, all dilutive common stock equivalents, regardless of whether they are exercisable, are treated as if they had been exercised. The treasury stock method assumes that the proceeds upon exercise are used to repurchase the entity's stock, reducing the number of shares to be added to outstanding common stock in computing earnings per share. The proceeds assumed to be received upon exercise include the exercise price that the employee pays, the amount of compensation cost measured and attributed to future services but not yet recognized, and the amount of any tax benefits upon assumed exercise that would be credited to additional paid-in capital. The assumed proceeds exclude any future tax benefits related to compensation cost to be recognized in income.

358. Under paragraph 28 of this Statement, an entity has the choice of estimating forfeitures in advance or recognizing forfeitures as they occur. The same number of options used to measure compensation cost should be used in the calculation of primary earnings per share. The following computation of the number of incremental shares to be considered outstanding in computing primary earnings per share assumes that options have been granted in the current year and prior years and that the entity anticipates the effect of future forfeitures. For this illustration, a total of 4,600,000 options are assumed to be outstanding from current year's and prior years' grants, of which 4,500,000 are expected to vest. The weighted-average exercise price of outstanding options is assumed to be $40. The average stock price during 2000 is assumed to be $52. The year-end stock price is $55. To simplify the illustration, it is assumed that (a) all outstanding options are the type that upon exercise give rise to deductible compensation cost for income tax purposes, and (b) no tax benefit upon exercise would be credited to additional paid-in capital; that is, the tax deduction based on current intrinsic value is less than the amount of cost recognized for financial statement purposes.

359. Computation of assumed proceeds for primary earnings per share:

- Amount employees would pay if all
  options expected to vest were
  exercised using weighted-average
  exercise price (4,500,000 × $40) $180,000,000
- Average unrecognized
  compensation
  balance during year[26]   16,000,000

Assumed proceeds $196,000,000

360. Assumed repurchase of shares:

- Repurchase shares at average market
  price during the year
  ($196,000,000 ÷ $52)   3,769,231
- Incremental shares to be added
  (4,500,000 − 3,769,231)   730,769

361. The number of shares to be added to outstanding shares for purposes of the primary earnings per share calculation is 730,769. The computation of fully diluted earnings per share would be based on the same method illustrated above. However, the total number of options outstanding, rather than the number of options expected to vest, would be used,

---

[26]Average unrecognized compensation balance is determined by averaging the beginning-of-the-year balance of cost measured and unrecognized and the end-of-the-year balance of cost measured and unrecognized. The assumed amount is $16,000,000 based on ongoing cost recognition for stock options granted in the current year and prior years.

and the average and year-end net unrecognized compensation cost would be adjusted to reflect the inclusion of options not expected to vest. The year-end unrecognized compensation cost and the year-end stock price would be used in computing fully diluted earnings per share if they result in a more dilutive calculation than use of average unrecognized compensation and the average stock price for the year.

Illustrative Disclosures

362. An illustration of disclosures of an entity's compensation plans follows. The illustration assumes that compensation cost has been recognized in accordance with the provisions of this Statement for several years. The amount of compensation cost recognized each year includes both costs from that year's grants and from prior years' grants. The number of options outstanding, exercised, forfeited, and expired each year includes options granted in prior years. The additional disclosures that would be required if the entity had elected to continue to recognize compensation cost in accordance with Opinion 25 are presented in paragraph 363.

* * *

Stock Compensation Plans

At December 31, 2006, the Company has four stock-based compensation plans, which are described below. The Company accounts for the fair value of its grants under those plans in accordance with FASB Statement 123. The compensation cost that has been charged against income for those plans was $23.3 million, $28.7 million, and $29.4 million for 2004, 2005, and 2006, respectively.

Fixed Stock Option Plans

The Company has two fixed option plans. Under the 1999 Employee Stock Option Plan, the Company may grant options to its employees for up to 8 million shares of common stock. Under the 2004 Managers' Incentive Stock Option Plan, the Company may grant options to its management personnel for up to 5 million shares of common stock. Under both plans, the exercise price of each option equals the market price of the Company's stock on the date of grant and an option's maximum term is 10 years. Options are granted on January 1 and vest at the end of the third year under the 1999 Plan and at the end of the second year under the 2004 Plan.

The fair value of each option grant is estimated on the date of grant using the Black-Scholes option-pricing model with the following weighted-average assumptions used for grants in 2004, 2005, and 2006, respectively: dividend yield of 1.5 percent for all years; expected volatility of 24, 26, and 29 percent, risk-free interest rates of 6.5, 7.5, and 7 percent for the 1999 Plan options and 6.4, 7.4, and 6.8 percent for the 2004 Plan options; and expected lives of 6, 5, and 5 years for the 1999 Plan options and 5, 4, and 4 years for the 2004 Plan options.

A summary of the status of the Company's two fixed stock option plans as of December 31, 2004, 2005, and 2006, and changes during the years ending on those dates is presented below:

Fixed Options	2004 Shares (000)	2004 Weighted-Average Exercise Price	2005 Shares (000)	2005 Weighted-Average Exercise Price	2006 Shares (000)	2006 Weighted-Average Exercise Price
Outstanding at beginning of year	4,500	$34	4,600	$38	4,660	$42
Granted	900	50	1,000	55	950	60
Exercised	(700)	27	(850)	34	(800)	36
Forfeited	(100)	46	(90)	51	(80)	59
Outstanding at end of year	4,600	38	4,660	42	4,730	47
Options exercisable at year-end	2,924		2,873		3,159	
Weighted-average fair value of options granted during the year	$15.90		$17.46		$19.57	

The following table summarizes information about fixed stock options outstanding at December 31, 2006:

Range of Exercise Prices	Options Outstanding			Options Exercisable	
	Number Outstanding at 12/31/06	Weighted-Average Remaining Contractual Life	Weighted-Average Exercise Price	Number Exercisable at 12/31/06	Weighted-Average Exercise Price
$25 to 33	1,107,000	3.6 years	$29	1,107,000	$29
39 to 41	467,000	5.0	40	467,000	40
46 to 50	1,326,000	6.6	48	1,326,000	48
55 to 60	1,830,000	8.5	57	259,000	55
$25 to 60	4,730,000	6.5	47	3,159,000	41

Performance-Based Stock Option Plan

Under its Goals 2010 Stock Option Plan adopted in 2002, each January 1 the Company grants selected executives and other key employees stock option awards whose vesting is contingent upon increases in the Company's market share for its principal product. If at the end of 3 years market share has increased by at least 5 percentage points from the date of grant, one-third of the options under the award vest to active employees. However, if at that date market share has increased by at least 10 percentage points, two-thirds of the options under the award vest, and if mar-

ket share has increased by 20 percentage points or more, all of the options under the award vest. The number of shares subject to options under this plan cannot exceed 5 million. The exercise price of each option, which has a 10-year life, is equal to the market price of the Company's stock on the date of grant.

The fair value of each option grant was estimated on the date of grant using the Black-Scholes option-pricing model with the following assumptions for 2004, 2005, and 2006, respectively: risk-free interest rates of 6.5, 7.6, and 7.4 percent; dividend yield of 1.5 percent for all years; expected lives of 6, 6, and 7 years; and volatility of 24, 26, and 29 percent.

A summary of the status of the Company's performance-based stock option plan as of December 31, 2004, 2005, and 2006, and changes during the years ending on those dates is presented below:

Performance Options	2004		2005		2006	
	Shares (000)	Weighted-Average Exercise Price	Shares (000)	Weighted-Average Exercise Price	Shares (000)	Weighted-Average Exercise Price
Outstanding at beginning of year	830	$46	1,635	$48	2,533	$51
Granted	850	50	980	55	995	60
Exercised	0		0		(100)	46
Forfeited	(45)	48	(82)	50	(604)	51
Outstanding at end of year	1,635	48	2,533	51	2,824	55
Options exercisable at year-end	0		780	46	936	47
Weighted-average fair value of options granted during the year	$16.25		$19.97		$24.32	

As of December 31, 2006, the 2.8 million performance options outstanding under the Plan have exercise prices between $46 and $60 and a weighted-average remaining contractual life of 7.7 years. The Company expects that approximately one-third of the nonvested awards at December 31, 2006, will eventually vest based on projected market share.

Employee Stock Purchase Plan

Under the 1987 Employee Stock Purchase Plan, the Company is authorized to issue up to 10 million shares of common stock to its full-time employees, nearly all of whom are eligible to participate. Under the terms of the Plan, employees can choose each year to have up to 6 percent of their annual base earnings withheld to purchase the Company's common stock. The purchase price of the stock is 85 percent of the lower of its beginning-of-year or end-of-year market price. Approximately 75 to 80 percent of eligible employees have participated in the Plan in the last 3 years. Under the Plan, the Company sold 456,000 shares, 481,000 shares, and 503,000 shares to employees in 2004, 2005, and 2006, respectively. Compensation cost is recognized for the fair value of the employees' purchase rights, which was estimated using the Black-Scholes model with the following assumptions for 2004, 2005, and 2006, respectively: dividend yield of 1.5 percent for all years; an expected life of 1 year for all years; expected volatility of 22, 24, and 26 percent; and risk-free interest rates of 5.9, 6.9, and 6.7 percent. The weighted-average fair value of those purchase rights granted in 2004, 2005, and 2006 was $11.95, $13.73, and $15.30, respectively.

* * *

363. If compensation cost has been determined by applying Opinion 25 as permitted by this Statement (paragraph 5), the total compensation cost disclosed in the first paragraph of the illustrative disclosures would need to be revised to reflect the cost recognized under Opinion 25. The following paragraph would replace that paragraph; all other disclosures about the plans and related assumptions would be required.

* * *

At December 31, 2006, the Company has four stock-based compensation plans, which are described below. The Company applies APB Opinion 25 and related Interpretations in accounting for its plans. Accordingly, no compensation cost has been recognized for its fixed stock option plans and its stock purchase plan. The compensation cost that has been charged against income for its performance-based plan was $6.7 million, $9.4 million, and $0.7 million for 2004, 2005, and 2006, respectively. Had compensation cost for the Company's four stock-based compensation plans been determined based on the fair value at the grant dates for awards under those plans consistent with the method of FASB Statement 123, the Company's net income and earnings per share would have been reduced to the pro forma amounts indicated below:

		2004	2005	2006
Net income	As reported	$347,790	$407,300	$479,300
	Pro forma	$336,828	$394,553	$460,398
Primary earnings per share	As reported	$1.97	$2.29	$2.66
	Pro forma	$1.91	$2.22	$2.56
Fully diluted earnings per share	As reported	$1.49	$1.73	$2.02
	Pro forma	$1.44	$1.68	$1.94

* * *

Supplemental Disclosures

364. In addition to the information required by this Statement, an entity may disclose supplemental information that it believes would be useful to investors and creditors, such as a range of values calculated on the basis of different assumptions, provided that the supplemental information is reasonable and does not discredit the information required by this

Statement. The alternative assumptions should be described to enable users of the financial statements to understand the basis for the supplemental information. For example, if in the previous example the Company estimated in 2004 that its expected stock price volatility over the next 6 years was within a range of 24 to 32 percent in which no amount was a better estimate than any other amount, its use of a 24 percent volatility assumption is consistent with paragraph 275, which indicates that using an estimate at the low end of the range for expected volatility is appropriate in that circumstance. The Company could, however, choose to disclose supplementally the weighted-average fair value of stock options granted during the year (and related effect on the pro forma disclosures) based on the midpoint or the high end of the range of expected volatility. However, presenting supplemental disclosures based on, for example, an expected volatility assumption of 18 percent would not be appropriate because the Company had already concluded in making its calculations that an 18 percent assumption is below the range of reasonable assumptions. Presenting supplemental disclosures of the value of stock options based on an approach contrary to the methodology specified in this Statement, such as reflecting an additional discount related to the nontransferability of nonvested stock options, is similarly inappropriate. However, the Company's supplemental disclosures could include the intrinsic value of stock options exercised during the year.

Appendix C

BACKGROUND INFORMATION

365. In 1984, the Board added to its agenda a project to reconsider APB Opinion No. 25, *Accounting for Stock Issued to Employees.* On May 31, 1984, an FASB Invitation to Comment, *Accounting for Compensation Plans Involving Certain Rights Granted to Employees,* was issued based on the November 4, 1982, AICPA Issues Paper, *Accounting for Employee Capital Accumulation Plans.* The Board received 144 letters of comment.

366. From 1985 through 1988, the Board considered accounting for stock-based compensation and conducted research on various aspects of those plans, including how existing option-pricing models might be adapted to measure the fair value of employee stock options.

367. The issues were complex and highly controversial. Still, each time the issue was raised, Board members voted unanimously that employee stock options result in compensation cost that should be recognized in the employer's financial statements.

368. As with all FASB projects, the Board's discussions of stock compensation were open to public observation, and its tentative conclusions on individual

issues were reported in its weekly *Action Alert.* During the Board's deliberations from 1985 to 1988, more than 200 letters were received that commented on, and usually objected to, tentative conclusions reported in *Action Alert.* That was unusual because most of the Board's constituents await publication of an Exposure Draft before they submit comments.

369. Some Board members and others were troubled by the differing results of stock-based compensation plans that called for settlement in cash and those that called for settlement in stock. But exercise date accounting for all plans is the only way to achieve consistent results between cash and stock plans, and that accounting was not considered to be consistent with the definitions of liabilities and equity in FASB Concepts Statement No. 6, *Elements of Financial Statements.* It also would be inconsistent with current accounting for stock purchase warrants, which are similar to employee stock options except that warrants are issued to outsiders rather than to employees.

370. A part of the financial instruments project on the Board's agenda considers whether changes to the concepts of liabilities and equity are needed. Late in 1988, the Board decided to set aside specific work on stock compensation while it considered broader questions of how to distinguish between liabilities and equity and the implications of that distinction.

371. In August 1990, a Discussion Memorandum, *Distinguishing between Liability and Equity Instruments and Accounting for Instruments with Characteristics of Both,* was issued. The Discussion Memorandum framed and discussed numerous issues, some of which bear directly on deciding how to account for employee stock options. The Board received 104 comment letters and in March 1991 held a public hearing on the issues, at which 14 commentators appeared.

372. More than 90 percent of the respondents to the Discussion Memorandum said that an entity's obligation to issue its own stock is an equity instrument because the entity does not have an obligation to transfer its assets (an entity's own stock is not its asset), which is an essential characteristic of a liability. In February 1992, the Board decided not to pursue possible changes to the conceptual distinction between liabilities and equity and to resume work on the stock compensation project within the present conceptual framework.

373. In March 1992, the Board met with several compensation consultants and accountants to discuss

current practice in valuing employee stock options and accounting for stock compensation. The compensation consultants generally agreed that current accounting provisions heavily affect the design of stock compensation plans. They said that there were far fewer variable (or performance) plans than fixed plans because of the required accounting for variable plans. The compensation consultants also said that the Black-Scholes and other option-pricing models were used to value various types of employee stock options for purposes other than accounting. Grant date measures were relied on to provide comparisons to other compensation arrangements.

374. A task force of accountants, compensation consultants, industry representatives, and academics was formed to assist in the project. Accounting for stock compensation was addressed at 19 public Board meetings and at 2 public task force meetings in 1992 and 1993. The Board's tentative conclusions on individual issues were reported in *Action Alert.* During 1992 and the first part of 1993, more than 450 comment letters were received, mostly objecting to the tentative conclusions. Many of the letters proposed disclosure in lieu of cost recognition for stock compensation. Several of the commentators submitted alternatives to the Board; the most comprehensive disclosure proposal was included as an appendix to the Exposure Draft.

375. In June 1993, the Board issued an FASB Exposure Draft, *Accounting for Stock-based Compensation,* that would have required recognizing compensation cost for all awards of stock-based compensation that eventually vest, based on their fair value at the grant date. The Board and KPMG Peat Marwick conducted a field test of the provisions of the Exposure Draft. In addition, other organizations provided information about their own test applications of the Exposure Draft.

376. As discussed in Appendix A, the Exposure Draft was extraordinarily controversial. The Board received 1,786 comment letters, including approximately 1,000 form letters, on the Exposure Draft. The vast majority of respondents objected to the recognition of compensation cost for fixed employee stock options—sometimes for reasons that had little to do with accounting. In March 1994, the Board held six days of public hearings in Connecticut and California. Representatives from 73 organizations presented testimony at those hearings. Several legislative proposals were introduced in Congress, both opposing and supporting proposals in the Exposure

Draft. A Sense of the Senate resolution was passed that the FASB "should not at this time change the current generally accepted accounting treatment of stock options and stock purchase plans." However, a second resolution was passed that "Congress should not impair the objectivity or integrity of the FASB's decisionmaking process by legislating accounting rules."

377. In April 1994, the Board held a public round-table discussion with academic researchers and other participants on proposals the participants had submitted to improve the measure of the value of stock options. Also during 1994, the Board discussed accounting for stock-based compensation at 13 public Board meetings and at 1 public task force meeting.

378. In December 1994, the Board discussed the alternatives for proceeding with the project on accounting for stock-based compensation in light of the comment letters, public hearing testimony, and various meetings held to discuss the project. The Board decided to encourage, rather than require, recognition of compensation cost based on a fair value method and to pursue expanded disclosures. Employers would be permitted to continue to apply the provisions of Opinion 25. Employers that continued to apply Opinion 25 would be required to disclose the pro forma effects on net income and earnings per share if the new accounting method had been applied.

379. The Board discussed the details of the disclosure-based approach at six Board meetings in 1995. In 1995, 131 comment letters were received on the disclosure-based approach. In May 1995, an initial draft of the standards section and some of the other parts of this Statement were distributed to task force members and other interested parties that requested the draft; 34 comment letters were received. Appendix A discusses the basis for the Board's conclusions, including reasons for changes made to the provisions of the 1993 Exposure Draft.

Appendix D

AMENDMENTS TO EXISTING PRONOUNCEMENTS

380. FASB Technical Bulletin No. 82-2, *Accounting for the Conversion of Stock Options into Incentive Stock Options as a Result of the Economic Recovery Tax Act of 1981,* is superseded.

381. This Statement amends ARB No. 43, Chapter 13B, "Compensation Involved in Stock Option and Stock Purchase Plans," as follows:

a. The following sentences are added to the end of paragraph 2:

> FASB Statement No. 123, *Accounting for Stock-Based Compensation,* specifies a fair value based method of accounting for stock-based compensation plans and encourages entities to adopt that method for all arrangements under which employees receive shares of stock or other equity instruments of the employer or the employer incurs liabilities to employees in amounts based on the price of the employer's stock. However, Statement 123 permits an employer in determining its net income to continue to apply the accounting provisions of this section and Opinion 25 to all its stock-based employee compensation arrangements. Entities that continue to apply this section and Opinion 25 shall comply with the disclosure requirements of Statement 123.

b. Paragraph 15 is deleted.

382. APB Opinion No. 25, *Accounting for Stock Issued to Employees,* is amended as follows:

a. The following sentences are added to the end of paragraph 4:

> FASB Statement No. 123, *Accounting for Stock-Based Compensation,* specifies a fair value based method of accounting for stock-based compensation plans and encourages entities to adopt that method in place of the provisions of this Opinion for all arrangements under which employees receive shares of stock or other equity instruments of the employer or the employer incurs liabilities to employees in amounts based on the price of the employer's stock. Statement 123 permits an entity in determining its net income to continue to apply the accounting provisions of Opinion 25. If an entity makes that election, it shall apply Opinion 25 to all its stock-based employee compensation arrangements. If an entity elects to apply Statement 123, that election shall not be reversed. Entities that continue to apply Opinion 25 shall comply with the disclosure requirements of Statement 123.

b. Paragraph 19 is replaced by the following:

> *Disclosure.* Paragraphs 45-48 of FASB Statement No. 123, *Accounting for Stock-Based Compensation,* specify the disclosures related to stock-based employee compensation arrangements that shall be made in the financial statements.

c. Footnote 5 is deleted.

383. Footnote 4 of APB Opinion No. 29, *Accounting for Nonmonetary Transactions,* is replaced by the following:

> FASB Statement No. 123, *Accounting for Stock-Based Compensation,* applies to all transactions in which an entity acquires goods or services by issuing equity instruments or by incurring liabilities to the supplier in amounts based on the price of the entity's common stock or other equity instruments.

384. The following is added as a footnote to the end of the penultimate paragraph of AICPA Accounting Interpretation 1, "Stock Plans Established by a Principal Stockholder," of Opinion 25:

> *FASB Statement No. 123, *Accounting for Stock-Based Compensation,* specifies a fair value based method of accounting for stock-based compensation plans and encourages entities to adopt that method in place of the provisions of Opinion 25 for all arrangements under which employees receive shares of stock or other equity instruments of the employer or the employer incurs liabilities to employees in amounts based on the price of the employer's stock. Paragraph 15 of Statement 123 adopts the substance of this Interpretation regardless of the method chosen to account for stock-based compensation.

385. In the fourth sentence of paragraph 7 of FASB Statement No. 5, *Accounting for Contingencies,* the phrase *APB Opinion No. 25, Accounting for Stock Issued to Employees,* is replaced by *FASB Statement No. 123, Accounting for Stock-Based Compensation.*

386. In footnote 3 to paragraph 12 of FASB Statement No. 21, *Suspension of the Reporting of Earnings per Share and Segment Information by Nonpublic Enterprises,* the phrase *paragraph 15 of Chapter 13B, "Compensation Involved in Stock Option and Stock Purchase Plans," of ARB No. 43* is replaced by *paragraphs 45-48 of FASB Statement No. 123, Accounting for Stock-Based Compensation.*

387. In paragraph 2 of FASB Statement No. 43, *Accounting for Compensated Absences,* as amended by FASB Statement No. 112, *Employers' Accounting for Postemployment Benefits,* the phrase *APB Opinion No. 25, Accounting for Stock Issued to Employees,* is replaced by *FASB Statement No. 123, Accounting for Stock-Based Compensation.*

388. In paragraph 14(c) of FASB Statement No. 105, *Disclosure of Information about Financial Instruments with Off-Balance-Sheet Risk and Financial Instruments with Concentrations of Credit Risk,* the phrase *as well as APB Opinions No. 25, Accounting for Stock Issued to Employees, and No. 12* is replaced by *and No. 123, Accounting for Stock-Based Compensation, and APB Opinion No. 12.*

389. Paragraph 8(a) of FASB Statement No. 107, *Disclosures about Fair Value of Financial Instruments,* as amended by Statement 112, is amended as follows:

a. The phrase *No. 123, Accounting for Stock-Based Compensation,* is added before *and No. 43.*
b. The phrase *APB Opinions No. 25, Accounting for Stock Issued to Employees, and No. 12* is replaced by *APB Opinion No. 12.*

390. In paragraph 36(e) of FASB Statement No. 109, *Accounting for Income Taxes,* the phrase *paragraphs 41-44 of FASB Statement No. 123, Accounting for Stock-Based Compensation, and* is added after *refer to.*

391. In paragraph 5(d) of Statement 112, the phrase *APB Opinion No. 25, Accounting for Stock Issued to Employees,* is replaced by *FASB Statement No. 123, Accounting for Stock-Based Compensation.*

392. The following is added as a footnote to the end of the second sentence of paragraph 2 of FASB Interpretation No. 28, *Accounting for Stock Appreciation Rights and Other Variable Stock Option or Award Plans:*

> *FASB Statement No. 123, Accounting for Stock-Based Compensation,* specifies a fair value based method of accounting for stock-based compensation plans (including those that involve variable plan awards) and encourages entities to adopt that method in place of the provisions of Opinion 25 for all arrangements under which employees receive shares of stock or other equity instruments of the employer or the employer incurs liabilities to employees in amounts based on the price of the employer's stock. Statement 123 permits an entity in determining its net income to continue to apply the accounting provisions of Opinion 25. If an entity makes that election, it shall apply Opinion 25 (including this Interpretation) to all its stock-based employee compensation arrangements.

393. The following is added to the end of footnote 1 to paragraph 3 of FASB Interpretation No. 31, *Treatment of Stock Compensation Plans in EPS Computations:*

> FASB Statement No. 123, *Accounting for Stock-Based Compensation,* specifies a fair value based method of accounting for stock-based compensation plans (including those that involve variable plan awards) and encourages entities to adopt that method in place of the provisions of Opinion 25.

394. The following is added as a footnote at the end of paragraph 2 of FASB Interpretation No. 38, *Determining the Measurement Date for Stock Option, Purchase, and Award Plans Involving Junior Stock:*

> *FASB Statement No. 123, Accounting for Stock-Based Compensation,* specifies a fair value based method of accounting for stock-based compensation plans (including those that involve variable plan awards) and encourages entities to adopt that method in place of the provisions of Opinion 25.

Appendix E

GLOSSARY

395. This appendix contains definitions of certain terms or phrases used in this Statement.

Combination plan
An award with two (or more) separate components, all of which can be exercised. Each part of the award is actually a separate grant, and compensation cost is measured and recognized for each grant.

Cross-volatility
A measure of the relationship between the volatilities of the prices of two assets taking into account the correlation between price movements in the assets.

Fair value

The amount at which an asset could be bought or sold in a current transaction between willing parties, that is, other than in a forced or liquidation sale. Quoted market prices in active markets are the best evidence of fair value and are to be used as the basis for measurement, if available. If quoted market prices are not available, the estimate of fair value is based on the best information available in the circumstances. The estimate of fair value considers prices for similar assets and the results of valuation techniques to the extent available in the circumstances. Examples of valuation techniques include the present value of estimated expected future cash flows using a discount rate commensurate with the risks involved, option-pricing models, matrix pricing, option-adjusted spread models, and fundamental analysis.

Fixed award

An award of stock-based employee compensation for which vesting is based solely on an employee's continuing to render service to the employer for a specified period of time, that is, an award that does not specify a performance condition for vesting. This Statement uses the term *fixed award* in a somewhat different sense than Opinion 25 uses the same or similar terms because Opinion 25 distinguishes between fixed awards and variable awards, while this Statement only distinguishes between fixed awards and performance awards. For example, Opinion 25 does not consider stock appreciation rights (SARs), regardless of whether they call for settlement in stock or in cash, to be fixed awards because the number of shares to which an employee is entitled is not known until the exercise date. This Statement considers an SAR that calls for settlement in stock to be substantially the same as a fixed stock option. A cash SAR is an indexed liability pursuant to this Statement, and the measurement date is the settlement (exercise) date because that is consistent with accounting for similar liabilities—not because a cash SAR is a variable award.

Grant date

The date at which an employer and an employee have a mutual understanding of the terms of a stock-based compensation award. The employer becomes contingently obligated on the grant date to issue equity instruments or transfer assets to employees who fulfill vesting requirements. Awards made under a plan that is subject to shareholder approval are not deemed to be granted until that approval is obtained unless approval is essentially a formality, for example, management and the members of the board of directors control enough votes to approve the plan. The grant date of an award for current service may be the end of a fiscal period instead of a subsequent date when an award is made to an individual employee if (a) the award is provided for by the terms of an established formal plan, (b) the plan designates the factors that determine the total dollar amount of awards to employees for that period (for example, a percentage of net income), and (c) the award is attributable to the employee's service during that period.

Intrinsic value

The amount by which the market price of the underlying stock exceeds the exercise price of an option. For example, an option with an exercise price of $20 on a stock whose current market price is $25 has an intrinsic value of $5.

Issuance of an equity instrument

An equity instrument is issued when the issuing entity receives the agreed-upon consideration, which may be cash, an enforceable right to receive cash or another financial instrument, goods, or services. An entity may conditionally transfer an equity instrument to another party under an arrangement that permits that party to choose at a later date or for a specified time whether to deliver the consideration or to forfeit the right to the conditionally transferred instrument with no further obligation. In that situation, the equity instrument is not *issued* until the issuing entity has received the consideration. For that reason, this Statement does not use the term *issued* for the grant of stock options or other equity instruments subject to service or performance conditions (or both) for vesting.

Measurement date

The date at which the stock price that enters into measurement of the fair value of an award of employee stock-based compensation is fixed.

Minimum value

An amount attributed to an option that is calculated without considering the expected volatility of the underlying stock. Minimum value may be computed using a standard option-pricing model and a volatility of effectively zero. It also may be computed as (a) the current price of the stock reduced to exclude the present value of any expected dividends during the option's life minus (b) the present value of the exercise price. Different methods of reducing the current price of the stock for the present value of the expected dividends, if any, may result in different computed minimum values.

Nonpublic entity

Any entity other than one (a) whose equity securities trade in a public market either on a stock exchange (domestic or foreign) or in the over-the-counter market, including securities quoted only locally or regionally, (b) that makes a filing with a regulatory agency in preparation for the sale of any class of equity securities in a public market, or (c) that is controlled by an entity covered by (a) or (b).

Nonvested stock

Shares of stock that cannot currently be sold because the employee to whom the shares were granted has not yet satisfied the vesting requirements necessary to earn the right to the shares. The restriction on sale of nonvested stock is due to the forfeitability of the shares. A share of nonvested stock also can be described as a nonvested employee stock option with a cash exercise price of zero—employee services are the only consideration the employer has received for the stock when the option is "exercised," and the employer issues vested, unrestricted shares to the employee.

Performance condition or performance award

An award of stock-based employee compensation for which vesting depends on both (a) an employee's rendering service to the employer for a specified period of time and (b) the achievement of a specified performance target, for example, attaining a specified growth rate in return on assets or a specified percentage increase in market share for a specified product. A performance condition might pertain either to the performance of the enterprise as a whole or to some part of the enterprise, such as a division.

Principal stockholder

One who either owns 10 percent or more of an entity's common stock or has the ability, directly or indirectly, to control or significantly influence the entity.

Public entity

Any entity (a) whose equity securities trade in a public market either on a stock exchange (domestic or foreign) or in the over-the-counter market, including securities quoted only locally or regionally, (b) that makes a filing with a regulatory agency in preparation for the sale of any class of equity securities in a public market, or (c) that is controlled by an entity covered by (a) or (b).

Reload option and option granted with a reload feature

An option with a reload feature is one that provides for automatic grants of additional options whenever an employee exercises previously granted options using shares of stock, rather than cash, to satisfy the exercise price. At the time of exercise using shares, the employee is automatically granted a new option, called a *reload option* for the same number of shares used to exercise the previous option. The number of reload options granted is the number of shares tendered, and the exercise price of the reload option is the market price of the stock on the date the reload option is granted. All terms of the reload option, such as expiration date and vesting status, are the same as the terms of the previous option.

Restricted stock

Shares of stock for which sale is contractually or governmentally restricted for a given period of time. Most stock grants to employees are better termed *nonvested stock* because the limitation on sale stems solely from the forfeitability of the shares before employees have satisfied the necessary service or performance requirements to earn the rights to the shares. Restricted stock issued for consideration other than employee services, on the other hand, is fully paid for immediately, that is, there is no period analogous to a vesting period during which the issuer is unilaterally obligated to issue the stock when the purchaser pays for it, but the purchaser is not obligated to buy the stock. This Statement uses the term *restricted stock* to refer only to fully vested and outstanding stock whose sale is contractually or governmentally restricted. (Refer to the definition of *nonvested stock.*)

Service period

The period or periods during which the employee performs the service in exchange for stock options or similar awards. If the service period is not defined as an earlier or shorter period, the service period is presumed to be the vesting period. However, if performance conditions affect either the exercise price or the exercisability date, this Statement requires that the service period over which compensation cost is attributed be consistent with the related assumption used in estimating the fair value of the award. Doing so will require estimates at the grant date, which will be subsequently adjusted as necessary to reflect experience that differs from initial expectations.

Stock option

A contract that gives the holder the right, but not the obligation, either to purchase or to sell a certain number of shares of stock at a predetermined price for a specified period of time.

Stock-based compensation plan

A compensation arrangement under which one or more employees receive shares of stock, stock options, or other equity instruments, or the employer incurs a liability(ies) to the employee(s) in amounts based on the price of the employer's stock.

Substantive terms

The terms of a stock-based compensation plan as those terms are mutually understood by the employer and the employee who receives a stock-based award under the plan. Although the written terms of a stock-based compensation plan usually provide the best evidence of the plan's terms, an entity's past practice may indicate that some aspects of the substantive terms differ from the written terms.

Tandem plan

An award with two (or more) components in which exercise of one part cancels the other(s).

Time value

The portion of the fair value of an option that exceeds its intrinsic value. For example, an option with an exercise price of $20 on a stock whose current market price is $25 has intrinsic value of $5. If the fair value of that option is $7, the time value of the option is $2 ($7 – $5).

Vest or Vested

To earn the rights to. An employee's award of stock-based compensation becomes vested at the date that the employee's right to receive or retain shares of stock or cash under the award is no longer contingent on remaining in the service of the employer or the achievement of a performance condition (other than the achievement of a target stock price or specified amount of intrinsic value). Typically, an employee stock option that is vested also is immediately exercisable.

Volatility

A measure of the amount by which a price has fluctuated (historical volatility) or is expected to fluctuate (expected volatility) during a period. The volatility of a stock is the standard deviation of the continuously compounded rates of return on the stock over a specified period. That is the same as the standard deviation of the differences in the natural logarithms of the stock prices plus dividends, if any, over the period. The higher the volatility, the more the returns on the stock can be expected to vary—up or down. Volatility is typically expressed in annualized terms that are comparable regardless of the time period used in the calculation, for example, daily, weekly, or monthly price observations.

The *rate of return* (which may be positive or negative) on a stock for a period measures how much a stockholder has benefited from dividends and appreciation (or depreciation) of the share price. Return on a stated rate increases as compounding becomes more frequent, approaching e^{rate} as a limit as the frequency of compounding approaches continuous. For example, the continuously compounded return on a stated rate of 9 percent is $e^{(.09)}$. (The base of the natural logarithm system is e, which is a constant, transcendental number, the first 5 digits of which are 2.7183.) Stock price changes are log-normally distributed, but continuously compounded rates of return on stocks are normally distributed.

The expected annualized volatility of a stock is the range within which the continuously compounded annual rate of return is expected to fall roughly two-thirds of the time. For example, to say that a stock with an expected continuously compounded rate of return of 12 percent has a volatility of 30 percent means that the probability that the rate of return on the stock for 1 year will fall between -18 percent (12% – 30%) and 42 percent (12% + 30%) is approximately two-thirds. If the stock price is $100 at the beginning of the year and it does not pay dividends, the year-end price would be expected to fall between $83.53 ($100 × e$^{(-.18)}$) and $152.20 ($100 × e$^{(.42)}$) approximately two-thirds of the time.

For the convenience of those who are not familiar with the concept of volatility, Appendix F provides more information on volatility and shows one way in which an electronic spreadsheet may be used to calculate historical volatility based on weekly price observations.

Appendix F

CALCULATING HISTORICAL VOLATILITY

Introduction

396. As discussed in paragraphs 273-278 of Appendix B, estimating expected long-term future volatility generally begins with calculating historical volatility for a similar long-term period and then considering the effects of ways in which the future is reasonably expected to differ from the past. For some mature entities, unadjusted long-term historical volatility may be the best available predictor of future long-term volatility. However, this appendix should be read in the context of paragraphs 284 and 285 of Appendix B, which mention factors that should be considered in determining whether historical volatility is a reasonable indicator of expected future volatility.

397. The concept of volatility and the reason that it is an important factor in estimating the fair value of an option is well explained in various texts on option-pricing models and the use of derivative financial instruments. However, those texts are generally directed more at mathematicians than at accountants, and one without an extensive background in statistics and mathematics may find them difficult to understand. During the exposure process and the field test, the staff received numerous requests for help in understanding the notion of volatility, especially for an illustration of how to compute historical volatility. This appendix responds to that request.

398. The goal of this appendix is not to explain the development of traditional option-pricing models and why they are valid. Sources for that information are

available. Several currently available articles and texts that explain option-pricing models and the place of volatility in option value are listed at the end of this appendix. This appendix is intended to help someone familiar with the use of electronic spreadsheets to compute historical volatility in three common situations. The illustrations do not provide a rigorous explanation of the mathematical concepts underlying the computations. In addition, the illustrations do not illustrate the only possible way of calculating historical volatility; for example, observations at daily or monthly, rather than weekly, intervals might have been used.

399. This appendix also is not intended to deemphasize the importance of adjusting historical volatility, however computed, to reflect ways in which future volatility is reasonably expected to differ from historical volatility for entity-specific reasons.

Volatility Is a Standard Deviation

400. The needed assumption about expected volatility for use in the traditional Black-Scholes and binomial option-pricing models is the *annualized* standard deviation of the differences in the natural logarithms of the possible future stock prices. Natural logarithms are needed to compute the continuous rate of return reflected in the change from one stock price to another, plus dividends, if any. A standard deviation is a statistical method used to convert a series of natural logarithms of stock price changes into a single, usable statistic—volatility. Like rates of return, volatility can be measured over any time period. For convenience and consistency, volatility is generally expressed on an annual basis even if the measurement period is longer or shorter than one year.

Computing Historical Volatility for a Stock That Pays No Dividends

401. The first step in computing historical volatility is to gather the necessary stock prices. The expected lives of employee stock options generally are several years long, so weekly (perhaps even monthly) stock price observations generally should be sufficient. (Volatility estimates for shorter-term options, such as 30-, 60-, or 90-day options commonly traded on exchanges, generally rely on daily, or even more frequent, stock price observations). The consistency of the time intervals between observations is critical—determining the frequency of the observations is not as critical, although the frequency of observations

likely will affect the computed volatility. The time intervals between price observations should be as uniform as possible; for example, the weekly stock closing price could be used for all observations. It would not be appropriate to use the weekly closing price for some observations and, for example, the average weekly price for other observations in the same calculation.

402. The Board is not aware of any research that demonstrates conclusively how long the historical period used to estimate expected long-term future volatility should be. However, informal tests and preliminary research tends to confirm the intuitive expectation that long-term historical volatility generally predicts long-term future volatility better than short-term historical volatility predicts long-term future volatility. Paragraph 285 of this Statement says that estimates of expected future long-term volatility should be based on historical volatility for a period that approximates the expected life of the option being valued. For example, if the expected life of an employee stock option is three years, historical volatility might be based on weekly closing stock prices for the most recent three years. In that situation, approximately 157 weekly stock price observations would be needed (52 observations per year for 3 years plus the initial observation).

403. For convenience, the illustrative calculations are based on only 20 price observations, which is generally considered to be the minimum number of sample observations necessary to compute a statistically valid estimate of standard deviation. Therefore, the table shows the calculation of the annualized historical volatility based on 19 weeks of stock price activity. More than 20 price observations would be necessary for long-term employee stock options; more observations also would improve the statistical validity of the estimate of expected volatility.

404. In the following table, column B contains the 20 stock price observations for the 19-week period. Each cell in column C contains the ratio of the stock price at the end of that week to the stock price at the end of the preceding week. That is designated by the symbol P_n/P_{n-1}. For example, in week 4, the number in column C is computed as the week 4 stock closing price ($48.50) divided by the week 3 stock closing price ($51.00), or 0.95098. Column D is the natural logarithm (the mathematical expression Ln) of the amount computed in column C. The weekly volatility estimate is the standard deviation of the amounts shown in column D. Most, if not all, electronic spreadsheets include a standard deviation function that will automatically compute the standard deviation of a series of amounts.

Table 1

A	B	C	D
Date	Stock Price	P_n/P_{n-1}	$Ln(P_n/P_{n-1})$
Week 0	$50.00		
Week 1	51.50	1.030000	0.029559
Week 2	52.00	1.009709	0.009662
Week 3	51.00	0.980769	-0.019418
Week 4	48.50	0.950980	-0.050262
Week 5	46.50	0.958763	-0.042111
Week 6	45.75	0.983871	-0.016261
Week 7	50.50	1.103825	0.098782
Week 8	53.50	1.059406	0.057708
Week 9	51.75	0.967290	-0.033257
Week 10	53.25	1.028986	0.028573
Week 11	54.50	1.023474	0.023203
Week 12	56.00	1.027523	0.027151
Week 13	53.50	0.955357	-0.045670
Week 14	52.00	0.971963	-0.028438
Week 15	55.00	1.057692	0.056089
Week 16	56.25	1.022727	0.022473
Week 17	58.00	1.031111	0.030637
Week 18	55.50	0.956897	-0.044060
Week 19	56.00	1.009009	0.008969

Weekly Volatility			**0.041516**
Annualized Volatility	$0.041516\sqrt{52}$		**0.299**

405. Weekly volatility must be converted to an annualized measure of volatility before it can be used in most option-pricing models. To convert from periodic to annualized volatility, the periodic volatility is multiplied by the square root of the number of periods in a year. In this example, weekly observations are used. There are 52 weeks in a year, so weekly volatility is multiplied by the square root of 52 to convert it to annualized volatility. If monthly stock price observations were used, the monthly volatility would be multiplied by the square root of 12 to convert to annualized volatility. Likewise, daily volatility would be multiplied by the square root of the number of trading days in the year to compute annualized volatility (about 260). The annualization calculation is independent of the number of observations used to compute the periodic historical volatility. For example, whether 20 or 157 weeks of data are used to compute weekly volatility, that weekly volatility must be multiplied by the square root of 52 to convert it to annual volatility.

Computing Historical Volatility for a Dividend-Paying Stock

406. Computing volatility for a dividend-paying stock is very similar to computing volatility for a stock that does not pay dividends. The only difference is an adjustment for dividends paid. Because volatility is defined as the standard deviation of the total return on a stock, dividend payments, which are part of the total return, affect the computation. The price change resulting solely from the effect of dividend payment on the stock price must be removed from the price observations used to calculate volatility.

407. As discussed in paragraph 401, stock price observations used in the calculations should be separated by uniform time periods. When gathering data, it is important to observe the payment of dividends. If an ex-dividend date occurs between two price observations, the per-share dollar amount of the dividends should be noted. For example, if the ex-dividend date for a dividend of one dollar occurs between the third and fourth weekly price observations, that payment should be noted when gathering stock price observations. In computing historical volatility, dividends must be added to the stock price after the ex-dividend date before the ratio in column C (the price after the dividend to the price before the dividend) is computed. Note that the market reflects the effect of a dividend payment on the stock price on the ex-dividend date, not the date of the cash distribution, because the ex-dividend date is the last date that a seller, rather than a purchaser, of stock is entitled to the dividend.

408. The following table illustrates the computation of historical volatility based on weekly stock closing prices for a company that pays a dividend of $1 between both the week 3 and week 4 price observations and the week 15 and week 16 price observations.

Table 2

A	B	C	D
Date	**Stock Price**	P_n/P_{n-1}	$Ln(P_n/P_{n-1})$
Week 0	$50.00		
Week 1	51.50	1.030000	0.029559
Week 2	52.00	1.009709	0.009662
Week 3	51.00	0.980769	-0.019418
Week 4	48.50		
Dividend Adjusted	49.50	0.970588	-0.029853
Week 5	46.50	0.958763	-0.042111
Week 6	45.75	0.983871	-0.016261
Week 7	50.50	1.103825	0.098782
Week 8	53.50	1.059406	0.057708
Week 9	51.75	0.967290	-0.033257
Week 10	53.25	1.028986	0.028573
Week 11	54.50	1.023474	0.023203
Week 12	56.00	1.027523	0.027151
Week 13	53.50	0.955357	-0.045670
Week 14	52.00	0.971963	-0.028438
Week 15	55.00	1.057692	0.056089
Week 16	56.25		
Dividend Adjusted	57.25	1.040909	0.040094
Week 17	58.00	1.031111	0.030637
Week 18	55.50	0.956897	-0.044060
Week 19	56.00	1.009009	0.008969
Weekly Volatility			**0.040799**
Annualized Volatility	$.040799\sqrt{52}$		**0.294**

409. The only difference between Table 2 and Table 1 is the necessary adjustment in Table 2 for the dividend payments made between the week 3 and week 4 observations and between the week 15 and week 16 observations. In each case, the ratio of the current period stock price to the prior period stock price must be adjusted for the dividend payment. For example, the pre-dividend week 3 observation is

used in the ratio of the week 3 stock price to the week 2 stock price. Then, the post-dividend week 4 stock price must be adjusted by the amount of the dividend payment before the ratio of the week 4 stock price to the week 3 stock price is computed in column C (both stock prices in the ratio must be either pre-dividend or post-dividend). That adjustment is necessary to isolate the price change effect in the change from week 3 to week 4 that is independent from the stock price decrease caused by the dividend payment.

Computing Historical Volatility for a Stock That Has Split

410. If a stock split occurs during the historical period over which volatility is to be calculated, an adjustment much like the one for a dividend payment is required for that split. For computing the ratio of the stock prices around the period of the split, the prices must be shown in consistent form, that is, either pre-split or post-split. For example, in Table 2, if a stock split had occurred between the week 16 and week 17 stock price observations, the price observed in week 17 would be $29 instead of the $58 shown in the table. For computing column B, the ratio of the week 16 stock price to the week 15 stock price would be unchanged, but the ratio of the week 17 to the week 16 price would need adjustment. The split-adjusted week 17 stock price of $29 should be divided by the split-adjusted week 16 stock price, which is $28.125. After the adjustment is made for the stock split, the calculation of historical volatility

is the same as in Table 2. If the only difference from the Table 2 stock price changes is the stock split, the historical volatility would be the same as the volatility computed in Table 2 because the stock split would not alter the relative size of the random stock price changes that volatility measures.

Sources for Further Information about Option-Pricing Models and Volatility

411. The following sources provide further information on option-pricing models and the relationship of volatility to option value:

- Black, Fischer, and Myron Scholes. "The Pricing of Options and Corporate Liabilities." *The Journal of Political Economy 81,* 3 (May-June 1973): 637-654.
- Cox, John C., and Mark Rubinstein. *Option Markets.* Englewood Cliffs, N.J.: Prentice-Hall, Inc., 1985.
- Figlewski, Stephen, William L. Silber, and Marti G. Subrahmanyam, eds. *Financial Options: From Theory to Practice.* New York: New York University, Business One Irwin, 1990.
- Hull, John C. *Options, Futures, and Other Derivative Securities.* Englewood Cliffs, N.J.: Prentice-Hall, Inc., 1993.
- Smithson, Charles W., Clifford W. Smith, Jr., and D. Sykes Wilford. *Managing Financial Risk.* New York: Richard D. Irwin, Inc., 1995.

Those sources include the classic works in which the Black-Scholes and binomial option-pricing models were first developed and other sources that may be useful.

Statement of Financial Accounting Standards No. 124
Accounting for Certain Investments Held by Not-for-Profit Organizations

STATUS

Issued: November 1995

Effective Date: For fiscal years beginning after December 15, 1995

Affects: Amends FAS 60, paragraph 45
      Supersedes FAS 60, paragraph 46
      Amends FAS 65, paragraph 4
      Amends FAS 91, paragraph 3
      Amends FAS 115, paragraph 4
      Amends FAS 117, paragraph 168

Affected by: Paragraphs 3, 5, 6, and 112 and footnote 6 amended by FAS 133

Issues Discussed by FASB Emerging Issues Task Force (EITF)

Affects: No EITF Issues

Interpreted by: Paragraph 11 interpreted by EITF Topic No. D-49

Related Issues: No EITF Issues

SUMMARY

This Statement establishes standards for accounting for certain investments held by not-for-profit organizations. It requires that investments in equity securities with readily determinable fair values and all investments in debt securities be reported at fair value with gains and losses included in a statement of activities. This Statement requires certain disclosures about investments held by not-for-profit organizations and the return on those investments.

This Statement also establishes standards for reporting losses on investments held because of a donor's stipulation to invest a gift in perpetuity or for a specified term.

This Statement is effective for annual financial statements issued for fiscal years beginning after December 15, 1995. Earlier application is encouraged. This Statement is applied either by restating the financial statements of all prior years presented or by recognizing the cumulative effect of the change in the year of the change. The expiration of restrictions on previously unrecognized net gains may be recognized prospectively.

Statement of Financial Accounting Standards No. 124

Accounting for Certain Investments Held by Not-for-Profit Organizations

CONTENTS

INTRODUCTION

1. This Statement establishes standards of financial accounting and reporting for certain investments in **securities**[1] and establishes disclosure requirements for most investments held by not-for-profit organizations.

2. Guidance for accounting for and reporting of investments held by not-for-profit organizations is currently provided primarily by the AICPA Guides listed in paragraph 22. This Statement is part of a broader FASB agenda project that considers several inconsistencies in that guidance. In addition, this Statement considers many of the same concerns that were examined for business enterprises in FASB Statement No. 115, *Accounting for Certain Investments in Debt and Equity Securities.* Because this Statement establishes standards for certain investments, provisions in the AICPA Guides that are inconsistent with this Statement are no longer acceptable *specialized*[2] accounting and reporting principles and practices.

STANDARDS OF FINANCIAL ACCOUNTING AND REPORTING

Scope

3. The measurement standards of paragraph 7 apply to investments in **equity securities** that have readily determinable fair values, except those described in paragraph 5, and to all investments in **debt securities.** For purposes of this Statement, the **fair value** of an equity security is readily determinable if one of the following three criteria is met:

a. Sales prices or bid-and-asked quotations for the security are currently available on a securities exchange registered with the Securities and Exchange Commission (SEC) or in the over-the-counter market, provided that those prices or quotations for the over-the-counter market are publicly reported by the National Association of Securities Dealers Automated Quotations systems

---

[1]Words that appear in the glossary are set in **boldface type** the first time they appear.

[2]The term *specialized* is used to refer to the current accounting and reporting principles and practices in the existing AICPA Guides and Statements of Position that are neither superseded by nor contained in Accounting Research Bulletins, APB Opinions, FASB Statements, or FASB Interpretations.

or by the National Quotation Bureau. Restricted stock[3] does not meet that definition.

b. For an equity security traded only in a foreign market, that foreign market is of a breadth and scope comparable to one of the U.S. markets referred to above.

c. For an investment in a mutual fund, the fair value per share (unit) is determined and published and is the basis for current transactions.

4. The reporting standards of paragraphs 8-16 apply to all investments held by not-for-profit organizations, except those described in paragraph 5.

5. This Statement does not apply to investments in equity securities that are accounted for under the equity method or to investments in consolidated subsidiaries.

6. Generally accepted accounting principles other than those discussed in this Statement also apply to investments held by not-for-profit organizations. For example, not-for-profit organizations must disclose information required by FASB Statements No. 105, *Disclosure of Information about Financial Instruments with Off-Balance-Sheet Risk and Financial Instruments with Concentrations of Credit Risk,* No. 107, *Disclosures about Fair Value of Financial Instruments,* and No. 119, *Disclosure about Derivative Financial Instruments and Fair Value of Financial Instruments.*

Accounting for Investments in Debt Securities and Certain Equity Securities

7. Investments in equity securities with readily determinable fair values and all investments in debt securities shall be measured at fair value in the statement of financial position.

Reporting Investment Gains, Losses, and Income

8. Pursuant to paragraph 22 of FASB Statement No. 117, *Financial Statements of Not-for-Profit Organizations,* gains and losses on investments shall be reported in the statement of activities as increases or decreases in unrestricted net assets unless their use is temporarily or permanently restricted by explicit donor stipulations or by law.

9. Pursuant to paragraph 20 of Statement 117, dividend, interest, and other investment income shall be reported in the period earned as increases in unrestricted net assets unless the use of the assets received is limited by donor-imposed restrictions. Donor-restricted investment income is reported as an increase in temporarily restricted net assets or permanently restricted net assets, depending on the type of restriction. This Statement does not specify methods to be used for measuring the amount of dividend and interest income.

10. Gains and investment income that are limited to specific uses by donor-imposed restrictions may be reported as increases in unrestricted net assets if the restrictions are met in the same reporting period as the gains and income are recognized, provided that the organization has a similar policy for reporting contributions received, reports consistently from period to period, and discloses its accounting policy.

Donor-Restricted Endowment Funds

11. A donor's stipulation that requires a gift to be invested in perpetuity or for a specified term creates a **donor-restricted endowment fund.** Unless gains and losses are temporarily or permanently restricted by a donor's explicit stipulation or by a law that extends a donor's restriction to them, gains and losses on investments of a donor-restricted endowment fund are changes in unrestricted net assets. For example, if a donor states that a specific investment security must be held in perpetuity, the gains and losses on that security are subject to that same permanent restriction unless the donor specifies otherwise. However, if a donor allows the organization to choose suitable investments, the gains are not permanently restricted unless the donor or the law requires that an amount be retained permanently. Instead, those gains are unrestricted if the investment income is unrestricted or are temporarily restricted if the investment income is temporarily restricted by the donor.

12. In the absence of donor stipulations or law to the contrary, losses on the investments of a donor-restricted endowment fund shall reduce temporarily restricted net assets to the extent that donor-imposed temporary restrictions on net appreciation of the fund have not been met before the loss occurs. Any remaining loss shall reduce unrestricted net assets.

---

[3]For the purpose of this Statement, *restricted stock* means equity securities for which sale is restricted at acquisition by governmental or contractual requirement (other than in connection with being pledged as collateral) except if that requirement terminates within one year or if the holder has the power by contract or otherwise to cause the requirement to be met within one year. Any portion of the security that can be reasonably expected to qualify for sale within one year, such as may be the case under Rule 144 or similar rules of the SEC, is not considered restricted.

13. If losses reduce the assets of a donor-restricted endowment fund below the level required by the donor stipulations or law,[4] gains that restore the fair value of the assets of the endowment fund to the required level shall be classified as increases in unrestricted net assets.

Disclosures

14. For each period for which a statement of activities is presented, a not-for-profit organization shall disclose:

a. The composition of investment return including, at a minimum, investment income, net realized gains or losses on investments reported at other than fair value, and net gains or losses on investments reported at fair value
b. A reconciliation of investment return to amounts reported in the statement of activities if investment return is separated into operating and nonoperating amounts, together with a description of the policy used to determine the amount that is included in the measure of operations and a discussion of circumstances leading to a change, if any, in that policy.

15. For each period for which a statement of financial position is presented, a not-for-profit organization shall disclose:

a. The aggregate carrying amount of investments by major types, for example, equity securities, U.S. Treasury securities, corporate debt securities, mortgage-backed securities, oil and gas properties, and real estate
b. The basis for determining the carrying amount for investments other than equity securities with readily determinable fair values and all debt securities
c. The method(s) and significant assumptions used to estimate the fair values of investments other

than financial instruments[5] if those other investments are reported at fair value
d. The aggregate amount of the deficiencies for all donor-restricted endowment funds for which the fair value of the assets at the reporting date is less than the level required by donor stipulations or law.

16. For the most recent period for which a statement of financial position is presented, a not-for-profit organization shall disclose the nature of and carrying amount for each individual investment or group of investments that represents a significant concentration of market risk.[6]

Effective Date and Transition

17. This Statement shall be effective for fiscal years beginning after December 15, 1995, and interim periods within those fiscal years. Earlier application is encouraged.

18. Unless this Statement is applied retroactively under the provisions of paragraph 19, the effect of initially applying this Statement shall be reported as the effect of a change in accounting principle in a manner similar to the cumulative effect of a change in accounting principle (APB Opinion No. 20, *Accounting Changes,* paragraph 19). The amount of the cumulative effect shall be based on a retroactive computation, except that the expiration of restrictions on previously unrecognized gains and losses may be recognized prospectively.[7] A not-for-profit organization shall report the cumulative effect of a change in accounting on each class of net assets in the statement of activities between the captions "extraordinary items," if any, and "change in unrestricted net assets," "change in temporarily restricted net assets," and "change in permanently restricted net assets."

19. This Statement may be applied retroactively by restating the beginning net assets for the earliest year presented or, if no prior years are presented, for the

---

[4]Donors that create endowment funds can require that their gifts be invested in perpetuity or for a specified term. Some donors may require that a portion of income, gains, or both be added to the gift and invested subject to similar restrictions. It is generally understood that at least the amount of the original gift(s) and any required accumulations is not expendable, although the value of the investments purchased may occasionally fall below that amount. Future appreciation of the investments generally restores the value to the required level. In states that have enacted its provisions, the Uniform Management of Institutional Funds Act describes "historic dollar value" as the amount that is not expendable.

[5]Paragraph 10 of Statement 107 requires organizations to disclose the method(s) and significant assumptions used to estimate the fair value of *financial instruments.*

[6]Paragraph 20 of Statement 105 requires organizations to disclose all significant concentrations of *credit risk* arising from financial instruments, whether from an individual counterparty or groups of counterparties.

[7]Paragraph 17 of FASB Statement No. 116, *Accounting for Contributions Received and Contributions Made,* establishes standards for recognizing the expiration of donor-imposed restrictions. Those standards also apply to the expiration of donor-imposed restrictions on investment income, gains, and losses. A similar provision permitting prospective recognition of the expirations of restrictions is included in paragraphs 29 and 30 of Statement 116.

year this Statement is first applied. The expiration of restrictions on previously unrecognized gains and losses may be recognized prospectively. In the period that this Statement is first applied, a not-for-profit organization shall disclose the nature of any restatement and its effect on the change in net assets and on each class of net assets for each period presented.

> **The provisions of this Statement need not be applied to immaterial items.**

This Statement was adopted by the affirmative votes of five members of the Financial Accounting Standards Board. Messrs. Beresford and Northcutt dissented.

Mr. Beresford disagrees with the standard in paragraph 7 that requires all investments in debt securities to be measured at fair value. Mr. Beresford believes this Statement should require a two-category approach. Under that approach, debt securities that an organization has the positive intent and ability to hold to maturity would be reported at amortized cost. Other debt securities and equity securities with readily determinable fair values would be reported at fair value. If a debt security is held to maturity, interim changes in that security's market value do not affect either the amount or timing of net cash flows to the entity. Consequently, Mr. Beresford agrees with the Board's conclusion in paragraph 58 of Statement 115 that "amortized cost is most likely to be relevant for those debt securities that will be held to maturity," and he believes that different accounting treatment is warranted for those debt securities. He believes that not-for-profit organizations should have the same ability as business enterprises to measure those securities at amortized cost.

Mr. Beresford also believes that more restrictive display requirements are necessary when amounts computed under a spending-rate or other budgetary method are included within an organization's measure of operations. He believes that users of financial statements might be misled if the amount reported within an operating measure is greater than the actual return for the period. He would limit the amount reported within the operating measure to actual gains and losses for the period—those amounts are based on the nature of the underlying transactions rather than on spending-rate or budgetary designations.

Mr. Northcutt disagrees with the standards in paragraphs 11-13, which prescribe the accounting for losses on the investments of donor-restricted endowment funds. Mr. Northcutt believes this Statement should require the method described in paragraphs 78 and 79, in which losses on investments of perma-

nently restricted endowment funds reduce the net asset classes in which unappropriated net appreciation of the fund is reported and any additional losses reduce permanently restricted net assets. In Mr. Northcutt's view, the method required by paragraphs 11-13 has three main problems.

First, Mr. Northcutt believes that the method required by this Statement fails to acknowledge that not-for-profit organizations identify the assets of each endowment fund and the investment income earned by those assets because they have fiduciary responsibilities and must be able to demonstrate that they are complying with the donors' stipulations and applicable laws. Because the assets of an endowment fund are known, classification of the net assets related to those assets is straightforward. First, the portion of the net assets that may never be spent because of donor or legal restrictions should be classified as permanently restricted net assets. Next, net appreciation for which restrictions on expenditure have not yet been met should be classified as temporarily restricted net assets. Finally, the remaining portion of net appreciation should be classified as unrestricted net assets. If a loss reduces the value of the assets of an endowment fund, the classification of the net assets related to the remaining assets follows the same procedure. If a loss reduces the assets of an endowment fund below the amount that must be maintained in perpetuity (historic dollar value), those assets are entirely unexpendable and all the net assets of that endowment fund should be classified as permanently restricted.

Mr. Northcutt acknowledges that the method he prefers must either define the assets of the fund or tolerate the effects of differing definitions. A definition requires a method for identifying when assets are removed from the fund for spending and thus are no longer present to absorb losses. Mr. Northcutt accepts the method provided in the Uniform Management of Institutional Funds Act for removing net appreciation—appropriation. He would define the assets of an endowment fund using appropriation because he believes the effects of management's discretion on classification of net assets are limited. An appropriation for expenditure does not change the class of net assets in which the appropriated amount is reported. An appropriation does not change when restrictions on net appreciation expire. When a loss occurs, only one classification of net assets is possible because an appropriation either was made or was not made prior to the loss. An appropriation can be made only when the fund has available net appreciation, and amounts appropriated may not be returned to the fund. The appropriation determines only the amount of net appreciation of a donor-restricted endowment fund that is available to absorb a future loss.

Mr. Northcutt recognizes that attributing significance to the act of appropriation for purposes of classifying losses on endowment funds may be viewed as inconsistent with the Board's decisions in Statements 116 and 117. He would be willing to amend Statement 117 to allow an exception only for this case.

Second, Mr. Northcutt believes that the method of accounting for losses described in this Statement can result in the classification of permanently restricted net assets and unrestricted net assets in a manner that

is inconsistent with the definitions of those classes of net assets. That method can result in an overstatement of permanently restricted net assets, which could lead users to believe that there are more assets generating income for support of the organization than there actually are. That method also can result in an understatement of the net resources that an organization as a whole has available to meet current operating needs.

Third, Mr. Northcutt believes that the method described in paragraphs 11-13 of this Statement misclassifies the gains that restore the fair value of the assets of the endowment fund to the level required by donor stipulations or law. That method would report future gains as increases in unrestricted net assets, even though the amount of net resources that are expendable for current operating needs is unchanged. In effect, gains that must be retained in perpetuity because of a donor-imposed restriction will be reported as increases in unrestricted net assets, which makes sense only because it corrects the erroneous reporting of the year of the loss.

Appendix A

BACKGROUND INFORMATION

20. In March 1986, the Board added a project to its agenda to resolve certain inconsistent accounting practices of not-for-profit organizations. The Board identified five areas of inconsistency that persist, in part, because the specialized accounting principles and practices in the AICPA Guides for not-for-profit organizations contain inconsistent requirements. Accounting for investments, one of the five areas, was initially included in the financial instruments project, which was added to the Board's agenda in May 1986.

21. FASB Statement No. 115, *Accounting for Certain Investments in Debt and Equity Securities,* issued in May 1993, specifically excluded not-for-profit organizations from its scope. The Board decided to consider the issues about investments held by not-for-profit organizations after it resolved its

agenda projects on accounting for contributions and financial statement display by those organizations. FASB Statements No. 116, *Accounting for Contributions Received and Contributions Made,* and No. 117, *Financial Statements of Not-for-Profit Organizations,* were issued in June 1993. In February 1994, the Board began deliberations to establish standards for reporting investments held by not-for-profit organizations.

22. Current guidance for accounting for and reporting of investments held by not-for-profit organizations is provided by the following four AICPA Guides:

a. *Audits of Colleges and Universities*
b. *Audits of Voluntary Health and Welfare Organizations*
c. *Audits of Providers of Health Care Services*
d. *Audits of Certain Nonprofit Organizations.*

The requirements in those Guides are similar in some respects. In other respects they differ from each other and from generally accepted accounting principles applicable to other entities. The inconsistencies lead to differences in accounting practices and, hence, to comparability and understandability problems. Further, three of the Guides permit accounting alternatives that lead to further inconsistencies within the subsector they cover.

23. In addition to the inconsistencies in the Guides, the Board identified other problems that this project should attempt to resolve:

a. *Greater relevance of fair value information.* Some believe that fair value information about investments is a more relevant measure of the ability of the organization's assets to support operations than cost-based information.

b. *LOCOM is not evenhanded.* The lower-of-cost-or-market method, which is required by one Guide and permitted by another, is not even-handed because it recognizes the net diminution in value but not the net appreciation in the value of investments.

c. *Managing change in net assets.* Cost-based measures create situations in which decisions to sell certain securities may be based on the sale's effect on the change in net assets. Organizations may choose to sell appreciated securities to recognize the unrealized gains while choosing to retain other securities with unrealized losses. Similarly, organizations may choose to sell securities with unrealized losses while choosing to retain appreciated securities to reduce the change in net assets.

d. *Accounting based on intent.* Accounting standards based on the intent of management make the accounting treatment depend on the plans of management rather than the economic characteristics of an asset. Intent-based accounting impairs comparability.

24. The Board discussed the resolution of those problems at a number of public Board meetings. In March 1995, the Board issued the Exposure Draft, *Accounting for Certain Investments Held by Not-for-Profit Organizations.* The Board and staff analyzed the 86 comment letters received and obtained additional information from a field test of the proposed requirements for classification of losses on investments of endowment funds and from a meeting with rating agency analysts, officers of grant-making foundations, and others who use the financial statements of not-for-profit organizations. The concerns raised by respondents, field test participants, and users of financial statements were considered by the Board at additional public Board meetings. Throughout the project, the Board and staff consulted with the members of the FASB Task Force on Accounting Issues for Not-for-Profit Organizations, including discussing the Board's tentative decisions at a June 1994 public meeting. The Board decided that it could reach an informed decision without holding a public hearing.

Appendix B

BASIS FOR CONCLUSIONS

CONTENTS

Appendix B

BASIS FOR CONCLUSIONS

Introduction

25. This appendix summarizes considerations that Board members deemed significant in reaching the conclusions in this Statement. It includes reasons for accepting certain views and rejecting others. Individual Board members gave greater weight to some factors than to others.

Benefits and Costs

26. The mission of the Board is to establish and improve standards of financial accounting and reporting for the guidance and education of the public, including issuers, auditors, and users of financial information. In fulfilling that mission, the Board strives to determine that a proposed standard will fill a significant need and that the costs imposed to meet that standard, as compared with other alternatives, are justified in relation to the overall benefits of the resulting information. Present and potential donors, creditors, members, and others all benefit from improvements in financial reporting; however, the costs to implement a new standard may not be borne evenly by all parties. Further, the costs of not issuing a standard are impossible to quantify. Because there is no common gauge by which to judge objectively the costs to implement a standard against the need to improve information in financial statements, the Board's assessment of the costs and benefits of issuing an accounting standard is unavoidably subjective.

27. The benefits of reporting debt and certain equity securities at fair value are discussed in paragraphs 33-40. In addition to those benefits, fair value measurement resolves for those investments each of the problems discussed in paragraph 23 of Appendix A. This Statement enhances comparability by eliminating the inconsistencies in the current guidance for reporting carrying amounts of equity securities with readily determinable fair values and all debt securities. For those securities, this Statement also removes the bias implicit in LOCOM accounting, precludes opportunities for managing change in net assets through selective sale of securities, and

eliminates the subjectivity of accounting based on management's intent.

28. The Board concluded that the overall benefits of the information provided by applying this Statement justify the costs that this Statement may impose. Because the AICPA Guides and FASB Statement No. 107, *Disclosures about Fair Value of Financial Instruments,* require that not-for-profit organizations disclose fair value information for investments reported at cost, organizations generally have the information systems that are needed to meet the requirements of this Statement. Although there will be transitional costs as not-for-profit organizations apply the requirements, the Board believes that the ongoing costs of applying this Statement should not be significantly greater than for existing requirements. The Board also believes that some of the costs this Statement imposes have been reduced in various ways: by limiting the scope of the measurement standards to equity securities whose fair values are readily determinable and to debt securities, by providing broad guidance and allowing some latitude in how information is reported in financial statements, and by eliminating requirements to disclose cost-based information for investments reported at fair value.

Scope

29. This Statement provides measurement standards for most investments held by not-for-profit organizations. Some not-for-profit organizations have more complex investment portfolios that include investments that are outside the scope of this Statement. A broader scope would have included investments such as interests in trusts, joint-venture agreements, oil and gas properties, real estate, and investments in closely held companies and partnerships. Those investments could have raised significant valuation issues that might not have been resolved in time to coordinate the implementation of this Statement with the implementation of Statements 116 and 117.

30. Most respondents to the Exposure Draft agreed with the Board's decision to limit the scope of this Statement. A few of those respondents said that the Board should consider carefully any requests to expand the scope to include investments that are not readily marketable. They were troubled by the subjectivity that may be necessary in estimating fair values. The Board understands that reliability is an important factor in financial reporting and, therefore, limited the scope for equity securities to those that have readily determinable fair values. The scope of

this Statement includes all debt instruments that are securities because the Board believes that sufficiently reliable estimates of fair value can be made for those instruments.

31. A few other respondents indicated that the scope should be expanded to include either all investments or all financial instruments. Provisions of the AICPA Guides remain in effect for measuring investments that are not within the scope of this Statement, including impairment of investments reported using cost-based measures. Where permitted by the relevant AICPA Guide, the Board does not discourage not-for-profit organizations from using fair value to measure investments that are outside the scope of this Statement; the Board limited the scope for practical reasons.

32. The Board decided to use the definitions of *security, equity security, debt security,* and *readily determinable fair value* that were developed in Statement 115 to ensure that this Statement and Statement 115 apply to the same investments. In the future, the Board expects to consider the accounting for other financial instruments held by business enterprises and not-for-profit organizations within the financial instruments project that is currently on its technical agenda.

Accounting for Certain Investments in Debt and Equity Securities

Relevance of Fair Values of Investments in Securities

33. The Board concluded that measuring investments in debt and equity securities at fair value in the financial statements provides information that is relevant and useful to present and potential donors, creditors, and others in making rational decisions about the allocation of resources to not-for-profit organizations—the first objective of financial reporting discussed in FASB Concepts Statement No. 4, *Objectives of Financial Reporting by Nonbusiness Organizations.*

34. Measuring those investments at fair value also serves to achieve the second objective of financial reporting—providing information that is useful in assessing the ability of the organization to provide services. Fair value more accurately measures the resources available to provide mission-related services because it portrays the market's estimate of the net

future cash flows of those securities, discounted to reflect both time value and risk. "The assessment of cash flow potential is important because it relates directly to the organization's ability to provide the goods and services for which it exists" (Concepts Statement 4, paragraph 45).

35. Fair value information assists users in assessing management's stewardship and performance—thus helping to meet the third objective of financial reporting discussed in Concepts Statement 4. Management must continually decide whether to hold an investment or to sell the investment and redirect resources to other investments or other uses. Fair value reports information useful in evaluating the performance of management in dynamic market conditions.

36. Many respondents to the Exposure Draft agreed with the Board about the relevance of fair value information. Creditors, rating agencies, regulators, and others that use the financial statements of not-for-profit organizations said fair value measures provide information that is useful to them in comparing and evaluating organizations and their managements. Because the goal of investing is to maximize returns commensurate with the risks undertaken, the only way to evaluate performance is to compare returns, adjusted for risk, to that of other entities or to common market indicators. Those financial statement users said that comparisons are reasonable only when securities and their returns are measured using fair value measures.

37. The ability to make meaningful comparisons between organizations is enhanced when securities are measured at fair value. Cost-based measures of the same security can vary significantly from organization to organization; fair value measures vary little, if at all. The value of securities, and all financial instruments, comes from the ability to convert them to their promised cash flows and to use the resulting cash to purchase the services, goods, and long-lived assets that the organization needs to conduct its activities. The cash flows associated with the securities do not depend on which organization owns them; thus, the measures of securities should not vary from organization to organization.

38. Some respondents were concerned primarily about reporting unrealized changes in fair value in their financial statements. Some that supported fair value measures said that changes in the fair values of securities should not be reported in the statement of activities until realized. They argued that the volatility that results from reporting unrealized gains and losses in change in net assets is unrepresentative of the results of operations of the organization and presents a false picture of the organization's stewardship abilities. Other respondents that favored cost-based measures said that not-for-profit organizations invest for long-term returns that support program activities and that temporary fluctuations in market values are irrelevant to managing the organization or its investment portfolio. They argued that fair value measures ignore those considerations. In their view, fair value measures focus on the effects of transactions and events that do not involve the organization and report opportunity gains and losses that should not be recognized until realized.

39. The Board concluded that to delay recognition of gains and losses until they are realized omits relevant information from the financial statements of not-for-profit organizations. To ignore fluctuations that actually occur fails to represent faithfully the risks inherent in investing activities, and to fail to report increases and decreases in value in periods when market conditions change impairs the credibility of financial statements. Recognizing only realized gains and losses in financial statements does not eliminate volatility in the change in net assets; instead, it provides opportunities to use selective sales of securities to manage that volatility. This Statement attempts to reduce opportunities to manage the reported change in net assets by selective sales of securities.

40. The requirement to report investments in equity securities with readily determinable fair values and all debt securities at fair value builds on current and evolving practices and requirements. Three of the four AICPA Guides permit organizations to report investments at fair value, and all four Guides require disclosure of fair value if investments are reported using a cost-based measure. FASB Statement No. 35, *Accounting and Reporting by Defined Benefit Pension Plans,* requires that all plan investments be reported at fair value because that reporting provides the most relevant information about the resources of a plan and its present and future ability to pay benefits when due. Statements 107, 115, and 119 also require that entities report fair value information about their financial instruments because that information is relevant to users of financial statements.

Consideration of Whether to Amend Statement 115

41. The Board considered amending Statement 115 to include not-for-profit organizations within its

scope. In addition to not-for-profit organizations, Statement 115 excludes from its scope enterprises whose specialized accounting practices include accounting for substantially all investments in debt and equity securities at market or fair value, with changes in value recognized in earnings (income) or in change in net assets. Those enterprises (principally brokers and dealers in securities, defined benefit pension plans, and investment companies) are excluded because the Board believes that their current accounting practices provide more relevant information for users of their financial statements. The specialized accounting practices of most not-for-profit organizations permit reporting investments at fair value with changes in fair value recognized in change in net assets, and a significant number of not-for-profit organizations presently do so. Accordingly, the Board considered whether an approach similar to those specialized accounting practices or the approach used in Statement 115 would result in more relevant information for the users of the financial statements of not-for-profit organizations.

42. Statement 115 identifies three categories of investments into which an enterprise classifies its investments. The accounting and reporting differ by category. Investments in debt securities that the enterprise has the positive intent and ability to hold to maturity are classified as *held-to-maturity securities* and are reported at amortized cost. Debt and equity securities that are bought and held principally for the purpose of selling them in the near term are classified as *trading securities* and reported at fair value, with unrealized holding gains and losses included in earnings.[8] Debt and equity securities not classified as either held-to-maturity securities or trading securities are classified as *available-for-sale securities* and reported at fair value, with unrealized holding gains and losses excluded from earnings and reported in a separate component of shareholders' equity.

43. The approach in Statement 115 resulted from a need to accommodate situations that are largely nonexistent in not-for-profit organizations. Some enterprises affected by Statement 115 (principally banks, thrifts, credit unions, and insurance companies) manage their interest rate risk by coordinating the maturity and repricing characteristics of their investments and their liabilities. Reporting unrealized holding gains and losses on only the investments, and not the

related liabilities, could cause volatility in earnings that is not representative of how financial institutions are affected by economic events. The Board concluded that accommodations similar to those in Statement 115 were unnecessary for not-for-profit organizations because (a) the purposes for which not-for-profit organizations hold investments generally do not relate investments to liabilities and (b) the change in net assets is not a performance measure comparable to earnings of a business enterprise.

44. Respondents to the Exposure Draft and task force members helped the Board identify the purposes for which not-for-profit organizations hold investments. Three of the primary purposes identified were endowment, funded depreciation, and short-term investment of operating cash surpluses. Organizations usually do not relate investment assets to liabilities when investing for those purposes. However, organizations may relate investment assets to specific liabilities when investing for other purposes. For many of those other purposes, the related liability is measured and periodically remeasured at the present value of estimated future cash flows using a discount rate commensurate with the risks involved. For example, the obligation to the beneficiary of an annuity agreement is measured at the present value of the payments to be made, the obligation to employees covered by a funded postretirement benefit plan is measured at the actuarial present value of the expected benefits attributed to periods of employee service, and the obligation to provide future service in continuing care retirement communities is measured at the present value of future net cash flows. This Statement's requirement to measure investment securities at fair value will eliminate situations where the adjustment of the liability is included in the change in net assets, but the change in the value of related investments is not.

45. In other identified relationships, such as many debt service funds, this Statement requires that the investments be measured at fair value, although the related liability is reported at historical proceeds. However, most respondents that supported a Statement 115 approach or its held-to-maturity category indicated that they did not coordinate maturities of the investments with the related liabilities. The Board concluded that the possibility for volatility that is not representative of how not-for-profit organizations are

---

[8]In addition to securities that are acquired with the purpose of selling them in the near term, Statement 115 also permits an enterprise to classify securities that it plans to hold for a longer period as *trading securities*. However, the decision to classify a security as trading should occur at acquisition; transfers into or out of the trading category should be rare.

affected by economic events is limited, both in the number of not-for-profit organizations potentially affected and in the amounts of investments and liabilities involved.

46. The Board also noted that the distinctions between the three categories of investments of Statement 115 are less relevant for not-for-profit organizations because the change in net assets is not a performance measure equivalent to earnings of a business enterprise. "[Not-for-profit] organizations generally have no single indicator of performance comparable to a business enterprise's profit" (Concepts Statement 4, paragraph 9). Although the magnitude of profits is generally indicative of how successfully a business enterprise performed, the same relationship is not true of a not-for-profit organization. The magnitude of change in net assets does not indicate how successfully a not-for-profit organization performed in providing goods and services. Further, because donor-imposed restrictions affect the types and levels of service a not-for-profit organization can provide, the change in each class of net assets may be more significant than the change in net assets for the organization as a whole (FASB Concepts Statement No. 6, *Elements of Financial Statements,* paragraph 106).

47. Because change in net assets is not a performance measure, the distinction between trading securities and available-for-sale securities is less relevant for not-for-profit organizations in reporting changes in fair value than that distinction is for business enterprises. Business enterprises distinguish between components of comprehensive income,[9] reporting certain changes in equity (net assets) in an income statement and other changes in net assets in a separate component of equity. The trading and available-for-sale categories are used to make those differentiations. In contrast, the statement of activities of a not-for-profit organization is like a statement of comprehensive income; it reports all changes in net assets. Reporting in a manner similar to Statement 115 introduces unnecessary complications by introducing separate components of equity within the three classes of net assets.

48. The Board concluded that fair value is more relevant to donors and other users of a not-for-profit organization's financial statements than the approach used in Statement 115. The Board decided that use of the three categories of investments prescribed in Statement 115 would add complexity without returning sufficient benefits for measurement or reporting purposes of not-for-profit organizations.

49. Some respondents, primarily health care organizations and their auditors, said that because Statement 115 requires business enterprises to report changes in fair value of available-for-sale securities in a separate category of equity and to report held-to-maturity securities at amortized cost, users would be unable to make meaningful comparisons when not-for-profit organizations and business enterprises are engaged in the same industry. This Statement allows an organization with those comparability concerns to report in a manner similar to business enterprises by identifying securities as available-for-sale or held-to-maturity and excluding the unrealized gains and losses on those securities from an operating measure within the statement of activities.

Debt Securities Held to Maturity

50. In addition to the three-category approach used in Statement 115, the Board considered a two-category approach. Under that approach, debt securities that the organization has the positive intent and ability to hold to maturity would be reported at amortized cost. Other debt securities and equity securities with readily determinable fair values would be reported at fair value. Two of the AICPA Guides permit the use of amortized cost for debt securities if a not-for-profit organization has the intent and ability to hold those securities to maturity. The Board considered whether that practice should continue and decided that amortized cost should not be permitted.

51. Respondents to the Exposure Draft that favored a two-category approach said that fair value information is less relevant for debt securities that are being held to maturity. They said that amortized cost provides relevant information because it focuses on the decision to acquire the asset, the earning effects of that decision that will be realized over time, and the ultimate recoverable value of the asset. If a debt security is held to maturity, the face value of the security will be realized, unless the issuer defaults, and all interim unrealized gains and losses will be reversed. In their view, increases and decreases in the fair value of

---

[9]Comprehensive income includes all changes in equity during a period except those resulting from investments by owners and distributions to owners (Concepts Statement 6, paragraph 70).

the debt security are not true gains and losses in investment value because the organization's cash flows are "locked in" at purchase.

52. Other respondents said that fair value information is as relevant for debt securities that are being held to maturity as it is for other investments. Increases or decreases in fair value reflect the success or failure of the strategy of purchasing and holding a longer-term rather than a shorter-term debt security in an environment of changing interest rates. For example, if an organization invests in a fixed-rate debt security and interest rates rise, the organization generally will receive less cash than if it had invested in a variable-rate security. That success (or failure) in maximizing the return on the organization's resources is relevant and should be reflected in the financial statements in the period the event (that is, the change in interest rates) occurs. In addition, fair value also reflects the risk that the cash flows will not be received as expected.

53. Some respondents that favored fair value measures mentioned that effective management of financial activities often requires a flexible investment strategy that is inconsistent with a held-to-maturity notion. They said that although many investment policies are based on long-term strategies, market fluctuations impact decisions to buy or sell specific instruments in order to achieve the organization's overall objectives. The Board believes that if an organization would sell a debt security to achieve its investment objectives, the organization does not have the positive intent to hold the security to maturity.

54. Other respondents that favored a two-category approach said they use a buy-and-hold strategy or "ladder" the maturities of their debt securities so that the organization can hold debt securities to maturity. Many of those respondents were concerned about volatility in the change in net assets, which would result if debt securities could not be reported at amortized cost when market interest rates changed. However, respondents that expressed that concern indicated that debt securities being held to maturity represent only a small portion of their portfolios. The Board noted that unless a portfolio was composed completely of debt securities being held to maturity, a two-category approach would not resolve concerns about volatility in change in net assets.

55. Respondents also said that not-for-profit organizations should have the same ability as business enterprises to report debt securities classified as held-to-maturity securities at amortized cost. Measuring an investment at (a) amortized cost if the organization has the positive intent and ability to hold it to maturity or (b) fair value if the organization does not have that intent bases the measurement on the intent of management rather than on the economic characteristics of the asset. Measurement based on the intent of management is one of the problems that this Statement attempts to resolve.

56. Statement 115 did not resolve the problem of accounting by intent. As discussed in paragraphs 43-48 of this Statement, the approach in Statement 115 resulted from a need to accommodate situations that are largely nonexistent in not-for-profit organizations. Thus, the Board concluded that allowing a not-for-profit organization to account for investments based on management's intent is unwarranted and that investments in equity securities with readily determinable fair values and all debt securities should be reported at fair value.

Determining Fair Values

57. The Board decided to use the term *fair value* in this Statement to avoid confusion between the terms *fair value* and *market value;* some constituents associate the term *market value* only with items that are traded on active secondary markets (such as exchange and dealer markets). However, the Board does not make that distinction and intends the term to be applicable whether the market for an item is active or inactive, primary or secondary.

58. The fair value of an asset is the amount at which the asset could be bought or sold in a current transaction between willing parties, that is, other than in a forced or liquidation sale. Quoted market prices in active markets are the best evidence of fair value and should be used as the basis for measurement, if available. Quoted market prices are easy to obtain and are reliable and verifiable. They are used and relied upon regularly and are well understood by donors, creditors, and other users of financial information.

59. Although quoted market prices are not available for all debt securities, the Board believes that a reasonable estimate of fair value can be made or obtained for the remaining debt securities required to be reported at fair value by this Statement. For debt securities that do not trade regularly or that trade only in principal-to-principal markets, the estimate of fair value should be based on the best information available in the circumstances. The estimate of fair value

should consider market prices for similar debt securities and the results of valuation techniques to the extent available in the circumstances. Examples of valuation techniques include the present value of estimated expected future cash flows using a discount rate commensurate with the risks involved, option-pricing models, matrix pricing, option-adjusted spread models, and fundamental analysis. The Board realizes that estimating fair value may require judgment but notes that a considerable degree of judgment also is needed when complying with other long-standing accounting and reporting requirements.

Financial Statement Presentation

Reporting Investment Gains, Losses, and Income

60. This Statement provides requirements for reporting changes in the fair value of investments in securities. The total change in fair value consists of both the change in the unpaid interest income on a debt security (or the unpaid accrued dividends on an equity security until the ex-dividend date) and the change in fair value that results from holding a security—the gain or loss, which can be either realized or unrealized. Gains and losses are recognized as changes in net assets in the periods in which they occur, and investment income is recognized as revenue in the period earned. Delaying recognition of restricted gains, losses, and income until the restrictions are met is inappropriate. The requirements of this Statement clarify, but do not change, the requirements of Statement 117.

61. Statement 117 establishes broad standards directed at critical display issues and allows organizations latitude to present information in a form that management believes is most meaningful to financial statement users. The Board decided that display guidance in this Statement also should focus on critical information that is essential in meeting the financial reporting objectives for all not-for-profit organizations.

62. The Board concluded that the most critical information—investment gains, losses, and investment income—should be recognized and reported

in the statement of activities. Other critical information about the types of investments, their risks, and their returns should be disclosed, but organizations can decide whether that information is disclosed on the face of the statements or in the notes to financial statements.

63. The Board considered whether more restrictive display requirements were necessary for realized gains and losses, unrealized gains and losses, investment return, or the amounts computed under a spending-rate or other budgetary method for reporting endowment returns. By not prescribing specific standards in this Statement, the Board recognizes that differing financial statement display practices are probable. Statement 117 is not yet in effect for most organizations, and they are just beginning to explore reporting that complies with its requirements and responds to its flexibility. The Board believes that it is premature to conclude that reporting differences will be undesirable and that at this time it is best to allow latitude so that financial reporting practices may continue to evolve.

64. Most respondents supported the reporting flexibility that this Statement permits. However, several respondents said that users of financial statements might be misled if organizations use a spending-rate or total return policy[10] that reports in an operating measure an amount that exceeds the total investment return for the year. The Board noted that those respondents were not similarly concerned about reporting less than the total investment return in an operating measure, nor were they concerned about reporting net realized gains in an operating measure and net unrealized losses outside that measure, although the reporting in that latter case also may result in including an amount in an operating measure that exceeds the total investment return for the year. A few respondents said that distinctions between realized and unrealized amounts are acceptable because those distinctions are based on the underlying nature of the transaction, but spending-rate and total return amounts are computed using formulas. In general, the Board agrees that amounts reported in an organization's financial statements should be based on the nature of the underlying transactions

---

[10]In managing their endowment funds, some organizations use a spending-rate or total return policy. Those policies consider total investment return—investment income (interest, dividends, rents, and so forth) plus net realized and unrealized gains (or minus net losses). Typically, spending-rate or total return policies emphasize (a) the use of prudence and a rational and systematic formula to determine the portion of cumulative investment return that can be used to support operations of the current period and (b) the protection of endowment gifts from a loss of purchasing power as a consideration in determining the formula to be used.

rather than on budgetary designations—to report otherwise suggests the reported operating measure is being managed. In this case only, the Board agreed that amounts based on budgetary designations may be displayed because the necessary constraints are provided by the disclosures required by paragraph 14 of this Statement and paragraph 23 of Statement 117 (including its requirement that an operating measure, if reported, must appear in a financial statement that, at a minimum, reports the change in unrestricted net assets for the period).

Reporting Losses on Endowment Funds

65. Statement 117 requires that gains and losses be classified based on the existence or absence of donor-imposed restrictions or law that limits their use. Paragraph 129 of that Statement explains the application of that requirement to the net appreciation of endowment funds:

> . . . the Board concluded that if the law of the relevant jurisdiction, as interpreted by an organization's governing board, places permanent restrictions on some part of the net appreciation, that amount should be reported as permanently restricted net assets in the organization's financial statements. In the absence of such a law or a donor's explicit or clear implicit permanent restriction, net appreciation should be reported as unrestricted if the endowment's income is unrestricted or temporarily restricted if the endowment's income is temporarily restricted by the donor.

Some respondents to the Exposure Draft of Statement 117 raised questions about reporting losses on investments of endowments. The Board deferred consideration of those issues to this Statement.

66. The Board limited its consideration to losses on investments of endowment funds that are created by donor stipulations requiring that the gifts be invested in perpetuity or for a specified term. The classification of losses on investments of an endowment fund

created by a board designation of unrestricted funds is straightforward; the losses are classified as reductions in unrestricted net assets because all sources of that endowment fund—original amount, gains and losses, and interest and dividends—are free of donor restrictions.

67. The classification of losses on investments of an endowment fund created by a donor also is straightforward if the donor explicitly states in the gift agreement what is to occur in the event of a loss; the losses are classified in accordance with the donor stipulations. Similarly, a donor's explicit requirement that an organization hold a specific donated asset in perpetuity implies that the enhancements and diminishments of that asset (gains and losses) are subject to the same permanent restriction. In the absence of donor stipulations or law to the contrary, the Board concluded that losses on investments of a donor-restricted endowment fund should reduce temporarily restricted net assets to the extent that donor-imposed temporary restrictions on net appreciation of the fund have not been met before the loss occurs and that any remaining loss should reduce unrestricted net assets.

Fundamental conclusions about the classification of losses

68. In determining the method to be used to classify losses in the absence of explicit donor stipulations or law, the Board considered the Uniform Management of Institutional Funds Act (Uniform Act), which has been adopted in varying forms in at least 38 states and the District of Columbia. It says:

> The governing board may appropriate for expenditure for the uses and purposes for which an endowment fund[11] is established so much of the net appreciation, realized and unrealized, in the fair value of the assets of an endowment fund over the historic dollar value[12] of the fund as is prudent. . . .
> Unrealized gains and losses must be combined with realized gains and losses to insure

---

[11]The Uniform Act uses the term *endowment fund* to describe a fund with characteristics of a donor-restricted endowment fund, as defined in this Statement. Section 1(3) of the Uniform Act defines an endowment fund as:

> . . . an institutional fund, or any part thereof, not wholly expendable by the institution on a current basis under the terms of the applicable gift instrument.

[12]The Uniform Act defines *historic dollar value* in Section 1(5) as:

> . . . the aggregate fair value in dollars of (i) an endowment fund at the time it became an endowment fund, (ii) each subsequent donation to the fund at the time it is made, and (iii) each accumulation made pursuant to a direction in the applicable gift instrument at the time the accumulation is added to the fund.

that the historic dollar value is not impaired. [Section 2 and the comment to that section, footnotes added.]

Although the Uniform Act indicates that losses should be netted against gains and that realized and unrealized amounts should be considered equally in applying its provisions, the Act is silent about an organization's responsibility to restore a decrease in the value of the assets of an endowment fund. The Board concluded that a method for classifying losses of a donor-restricted endowment fund should not define an organization's fiduciary responsibilities to maintain the assets of the fund; each organization should determine its responsibilities in accordance with donor-imposed restrictions and law.

69. The Board also considered different interpretations of "the assets of an endowment fund," in part because the Uniform Act does not define that phrase. Different interpretations result in different determinations of which investment losses are losses of a donor-restricted endowment fund and how much of prior periods' appreciation can be netted with losses of the fund in the current period. Respondents' interpretations of the phrase differed. For example, some organizations that participated in the field test of the Exposure Draft interpreted the phrase to mean that assets purchased with a gift and assets purchased with its net appreciation are part of the endowment fund until a portion of the assets is removed by an appropriation for expenditure. Other participants said that in addition to those assets, assets purchased with investment income are part of the fund. Another participant said that assets purchased with net appreciation are not part of the fund at all. Without case law to help interpret the Uniform Act, the Board has no basis to adopt one interpretation and reject all others. The Board concluded that a method for classifying losses should accommodate different interpretations of "the assets of an endowment fund" but minimize the effects of differing interpretations on the classification of net assets.

70. The Board considered whether the ability to "appropriate for expenditure" granted by the Uniform Act should influence the classification of losses. Attributing significance to an act of appropriation would allow management's intent to influence the classification of net assets and is inconsistent with the Board's conclusions in Statements 116 and 117. Statement 116 requires that a restriction on temporarily restricted net appreciation expire when an expense is incurred for the restricted purpose, regard-

less of whether an amount is appropriated. In Statement 117, the Board concluded that decisions about when to appropriate resources should not influence their classification—net gains are reported in unrestricted or temporarily restricted net assets unless permanently restricted by the donor or law. The Board concluded that appropriation of a portion of net appreciation should not change the classification of a loss on an endowment fund.

71. The Board believes that inconsistent classification of net assets would result if it did not specify a method for classifying losses on investments of donor-restricted endowment funds. Donors generally are silent about losses on the investments of the funds they establish, and the Uniform Act is unclear about an organization's responsibilities when a loss occurs. Without explicit donor stipulations or law to determine the classification of losses on investments of endowment funds, organizations could arrive at different answers in similar circumstances.

72. The Board considered the three methods for classifying losses on investments of donor-restricted endowment funds that are discussed in paragraphs 73-82, as well as variations of those methods. All of the methods considered had some drawbacks. The Board believes that the method in this Statement for classifying losses is simple to apply and will result in greater comparability and consistency in classification of net assets so that users of financial statements may make better-informed decisions.

Method used in this Statement for classifying losses

73. The Board concluded that, in the absence of donor stipulations or law to the contrary, losses on the investments of a donor-restricted endowment fund reduce temporarily restricted or unrestricted net assets. The Board concluded that if a donor requires an endowment fund to be invested in perpetuity, permanently restricted net assets should equal the historic dollar value of the fund. The Uniform Act says, "Accounting entries recording realization of gains or losses to the fund have no effect upon historic dollar value. No increase or decrease in historic dollar value of the fund results from the sale of an asset held by the fund and the reinvestment of the proceeds in another asset" (comment to Section 1(5)). Unless historic dollar value changes, such as when a donor directs that gains be accumulated in the fund, neither gains nor losses affect permanently restricted net assets.

74. Whether a loss reduces temporarily restricted net assets, unrestricted net assets, or both depends on where the net appreciation of the fund is classified at the time the loss occurs. First, to the extent that donor-imposed temporary restrictions on net appreciation have not been met prior to the loss, the loss reduces temporarily restricted net assets. The remaining loss reduces unrestricted net assets, which can be viewed as reducing any net appreciation classified in that net asset class and then reducing unrestricted net assets for any excess loss (that is, the amount by which the fair value of the assets of the fund is less than the historic dollar value). In other words, when losses exceed the net appreciation classified in temporarily restricted and unrestricted net assets, the excess loss reduces unrestricted net assets.

75. The Board concluded that the method used in this Statement is most consistent with the fundamental conclusions described in paragraphs 68-72. Under that method, different interpretations of "the assets of an endowment fund," especially differences in how and when net appreciation is removed from the fund, have a lesser effect on the classification of net assets. A loss that reduces the fair value of the assets of the endowment fund to historic dollar value and a loss that reduces the fair value below historic dollar value reduce the same net asset class, unrestricted net assets, unless restrictions on net appreciation have not been met prior to the loss. The effects of appropriation are minimized because the amounts appropriated for expenditure also are classified in unrestricted net assets (or will be reclassified to that net asset class shortly because the donor-imposed restrictions will be met when the amounts are spent).

76. A drawback of that method is that excess losses decrease unrestricted net assets even if the organization is not required by a donor-imposed restriction or law to use its unrestricted resources to restore immediately the value of the endowment fund to the level required by donor stipulations or law. Some respondents said that that drawback could be mitigated by requiring organizations to disclose the amount of the deficiency when the fair value of the assets of a donor-restricted endowment fund is less than the level required by the donor's restriction or law. The Board agreed and added that requirement. However, the field test results indicated that, except in the early years of an endowment fund, incidences of excess losses will be few because organizations generally accumulate net appreciation through policies that preserve and grow their endowment funds.

77. Because unrestricted net assets are reduced for the excess loss when the fair value of the assets of the endowment fund falls below the fund's historic dollar value, this Statement requires that unrestricted net assets be restored from future gains for that reduction. Some respondents said that that classification was confusing and that they would expect those gains to be classified as increases in permanently restricted net assets because they cannot be appropriated for expenditure. However, because the prior loss did not reduce permanently restricted net assets, the classification suggested by respondents would increase the amount of permanently restricted net assets beyond the level required by donor restrictions or law. Thus, gains that restore the fair value of the assets of the endowment fund to the fund's required level (historic dollar value) should be classified as increases to the same class of net assets that was previously reduced for the excess loss—unrestricted net assets. After the fair value of the assets of the endowment fund equals the required level, gains are again available for expenditure, and those gains that are restricted by the donor are classified as increases in temporarily restricted net assets.

Other methods considered

78. The Board also considered a method in which losses would reduce temporarily restricted and unrestricted net assets to the extent that unappropriated net appreciation is classified in those net asset classes, but the excess loss would reduce permanently restricted net assets if the donor required the fund to be invested in perpetuity or would reduce temporarily restricted net assets if the donor required the fund to be invested for a specified term. Most respondents that commented on the endowment loss provisions preferred that method.

79. That method would result in the same classification of net assets as this Statement except when the fair value of the assets of the endowment fund is less than historic dollar value. However, it cannot accommodate differing interpretations of "the assets of an endowment fund." Unless all organizations interpret the phrase in the same way, the calculation of the excess loss could differ, resulting in different classifications of net assets in similar circumstances. In addition, how and when an organization removes net appreciation from the fund also can affect classification of net assets. If an organization determines that appropriated amounts are unavailable to absorb losses on the investments of an endowment fund, an action of the governing board to appropriate an

amount forces a larger reduction in permanently restricted net assets than would have occurred if that amount had not been appropriated. The Board concluded that it is unacceptable to have differing classifications of net assets result from an action of the governing board. The Board rejected that method after evaluating it in light of the fundamental conclusions in paragraphs 68-72.

80. The Board also considered a second method that would allocate income, gains, and losses between the classes of net assets based on the proportionate interests of those classes in the investment pool—or the investments of each fund if investments were not pooled. Each time the fair value of the units related to permanently restricted net assets increased beyond historic dollar value, units with a value equal to the net appreciation would be transferred to temporarily restricted net assets (or unrestricted net assets if the donor did not restrict the use of income from the endowment). Each time a restriction expired, units with a value equal to the expired amount would be transferred from temporarily restricted net assets to unrestricted net assets. Income and gains on the units related to permanently restricted net assets would be classified as increases in temporarily restricted net assets if restricted by the donor to a specific use; otherwise, they would increase unrestricted net assets in accordance with paragraphs 8 and 9 of this Statement. Losses on those units would decrease permanently restricted net assets. Income, gains, and losses on the units related to unrestricted and temporarily restricted net assets would increase or decrease those net asset classes.

81. That second method results in similar classifications of net assets regardless of the interpretation of "the assets of an endowment fund" or whether amounts were appropriated. Further, it is the only method considered by the Board that does not reduce unrestricted net assets for a loss on investments of permanently restricted net assets. The method in this Statement and the other methods considered by the Board result in restriction of previously unrestricted gains when a loss occurs.

82. However, because that method allocates gains, losses, and income based on the proportionate interests of each net asset class, it can be inconsistent with some organizations' interpretations of their fiduciary responsibilities to maintain the assets of the endowment fund and to use the income earned by those assets in accordance with the donors' stipulations. That method's classification of losses is most consistent

with an interpretation that an organization's fiduciary responsibilities do not extend to net appreciation of previous periods; that is, net appreciation is not included in "the assets of an endowment fund." The Board rejected the second method after evaluating it in light of the fundamental conclusions in paragraphs 68-72.

Disclosures

83. Using an approach of broad standards for basic information similar to that used in Statement 117, the Board determined the information that is required to be disclosed without prescribing whether it should be disclosed on the face of the statements or in the notes. That approach allows an organization's management to report the information in a manner that is most useful to users of its financial statements. The disclosure requirements are not intended to limit the amount of detail or the manner of providing information; additional classifications and subclassifications may be useful.

84. The Board developed the disclosure requirements after consulting with its task force and with users of financial statements of not-for-profit organizations. It also considered existing disclosure requirements for investments reported at fair value, especially those found in Statements 35 and 115. The Board believes that the required disclosures provide information that is useful in assessing management's stewardship and the organization's liquidity and exposure to risk.

85. Some respondents questioned the need for the information about the composition of investment return or the reconciliation required if investment return is separated into operating and nonoperating amounts. Disclosures required for investment return reinforce the requirements of Statement 117 to (a) report information about revenues, gains, and losses by aggregating items into relatively homogeneous groups and (b) disclose information about the nature of a reported measure of operations if the definition of operations is not apparent from the face of the statement of activities. Users of financial information indicated that the disclosures required by paragraph 14 were especially useful in their work. The Board retained those requirements.

86. A few respondents suggested that additional guidance should be provided for the disclosure about "significant concentration of market risk or risk of physical loss" that was proposed in the Exposure

Draft. Others suggested that the Board should quantify *significant*. The Board believes that management's judgment about concentrations and significance is in itself useful information. Therefore, the Board chose not to define further those terms. The Board concluded that an entity should review its portfolio of investments to determine if any significant concentrations of market risk result from the nature of the investments or from a lack of diversity of industry, currency, or geographic location. The Board decided to delete the requirement to disclose information about the risk of physical loss.

87. The Board concluded that disclosure of realized gains and losses is necessary when investments that are reported at measures other than fair value are sold. Without that disclosure, information about total investment return may be misleading to donors, creditors, and other users of financial statements because the realized gains or losses reported will represent the activity of more than a single period; that is, the organization's change in net assets will include unrealized gains and losses accumulated in previous periods but not recognized until the year of sale.

88. However, the Board is not convinced that information about realized gains and losses or about the historical cost of investments is relevant and useful for investments reported at fair value when the changes in their fair values are reported in a statement of activities. Most respondents agreed. Both realized and unrealized net gains on endowment funds may be prudently spent in accordance with the Uniform Act. Thus, distinguishing between them does not enhance a user's assessment of an organization's ability to provide mission-related services and to pay debtors. Both realized and unrealized gains and losses are included in a statement of activities, and opportunities for managing change in net assets through selective sale of securities are greatly reduced by the requirements of this Statement. A user, therefore, does not need information about realized and unrealized gains and losses and about the historical cost of investments to determine if selective sales are occurring. Further, a user does not need the information to determine the potential tax consequences of management's decisions to sell or hold investments; realization of gains and losses has no tax consequences for most not-for-profit organizations.

89. The Board recognizes that information about realized and unrealized gains and losses and about historical costs of investments may be useful in some circumstances. For example, if a state adopted a modified form of the Uniform Act that allows a not-for-profit organization to spend only realized gains or if an organization pays taxes on realized gains and losses, information that distinguishes between realized and unrealized amounts may be useful. Thus, this Statement does not preclude disclosing that information.

90. The Exposure Draft would have required that organizations disclose information about their investment objectives and about the contractual maturities of debt securities. Many respondents, including users of financial statements, asked the Board not to require those disclosures. Some said that information about investment objectives should not be required of not-for-profit organizations because Statement 115 does not require business enterprises to make that disclosure. Others said that organizations may have different objectives for different investment portfolios and that, as an organization's policies become more complex, investment objectives become more difficult to summarize. Still others said that the resulting disclosures might be "boilerplate" or would be meaningless without an accompanying disclosure of investment performance. A number of respondents said that information about contractual maturities was unnecessary when debt securities are reported at fair value. The Board decided that the information need not be disclosed.

Effective Date and Transition Method

91. The Board concluded that this Statement should be effective for fiscal years beginning after December 15, 1995. That effective date corresponds to the later effective date of Statements 116 and 117, which are effective for fiscal years beginning after December 15, 1995, for organizations with less than $5 million in total assets and $1 million in revenues. It was not possible to require the implementation of this Statement for the earlier effective date of Statements 116 and 117 (fiscal years beginning after December 15, 1994).

92. A few respondents said that smaller organizations might have difficulty implementing this Statement by its effective date. Because the AICPA Guides and Statement 107 require disclosure of the fair value of investments, organizations already have the necessary information systems in place. In addition, many not-for-profit organizations already report investments at fair value. Thus, the Board concluded that there is adequate time to develop the information required by this Statement. The Statement should not

be difficult to implement, except perhaps for the release of restrictions on investment appreciation.

93. The Board decided to allow prospective treatment for the release of restrictions on previously unrecognized gains and losses. Determining the expiration of restrictions may be difficult or impossible if an organization no longer has the necessary records or if past procedures did not require those records. The Board permits similar treatment for expiration of restrictions on contributions in Statement 116.

94. Early application of this Statement is encouraged whenever practicable. Some respondents said that applying this Statement early may result in some loss of comparability of reporting between organizations during the transition period; however, the Board concluded that the benefits of early application outweigh its disadvantages. In addition, allowing early implementation will allow organizations that must implement Statements 116 and 117 on the earlier effective date to implement this Statement in the same fiscal year.

Appendix C

ILLUSTRATIVE EXAMPLES

Example of Classification of an Endowment Fund Loss

95. This example illustrates the classification prescribed by this Statement of a loss on investments of a donor-restricted endowment fund. Paragraph 12 of this Statement requires that in the absence of donor stipulations or law to the contrary, losses on the investments of a donor-restricted endowment fund reduce temporarily restricted net assets to the extent that donor-imposed temporary restrictions on net appreciation of the fund have not been met before the loss occurs. Any remaining loss reduces unrestricted net assets. Paragraph 13 requires that if losses reduce the assets of a donor-restricted endowment fund below the level required by donor stipulations or law, gains that restore the fair value of the assets of the endowment fund to the required level are classified as increases in unrestricted net assets.

Year 1

96. At the beginning of year 1, NFP Organization received a gift of $1,000,000. The donor specified that the gift be used to create an endowment fund that will be invested in perpetuity with income to be used for the support of Program A. The investments purchased with the gift earned $30,000 of investment income. NFP Organization spent that income plus an additional $20,000 of unrestricted resources on Program A during the year. At the end of the year, the fair value of the investments was $1,047,000.

Transactions for year 1 are classified as increases or decreases in permanently restricted net assets, tem- porarily restricted net assets, or unrestricted net assets as follows:

| | Net Assets | | | |
Transactions	Unrestricted	Temporarily Restricted	Permanently Restricted	Total
Activity of Program A				
Board-designated resources[a]	$ 20,000			$ 20,000
Investment income		$ 30,000		30,000
Expenses	(50,000)			(50,000)
Release restriction[b]	30,000	(30,000)		
Subtotal	0	0		0
Investments				
Gift			$1,000,000	1,000,000
Gains[c]		47,000		47,000
Release restriction[b]	20,000	(20,000)		
Subtotal	20,000	27,000	1,000,000	1,047,000
End of year	$ 20,000	$ 27,000	$1,000,000	$1,047,000

a. The governing board designates $20,000 of unrestricted resources of the organization to be spent in support of Program A.

b. When $50,000 is spent in support of Program A, restrictions are released on the $30,000 of income and $20,000 of temporarily restricted gains according to the provisions of Statement 116. The restrictions on the gains expire even though the governing board chose to use unrestricted resources rather than sell some investments and use the proceeds for Program A.

c. The $47,000 gain is restricted to the same purpose as the income in accordance with the Uniform Act.

Year 2

97. On January 1, in accordance with its spending policy, the governing board of NFP Organization sold some investments for $25,000 and spent the proceeds on Program A. The remaining investments earned $30,000 of investment income, which NFP Organization also spent on Program A. At the end of the year, the fair value of the investments was $1,097,000.

Transactions for year 2 are classified as follows:

Transactions	Unrestricted	Net Assets Temporarily Restricted	Permanently Restricted	Total
Activity of Program A				
Spending policy[d]		$ 25,000		$ 25,000
Investment income		30,000		30,000
Expenses	$(55,000)			(55,000)
Release restriction	55,000	(55,000)		0
Subtotal	0	0		0
Investments				
Spending policy[d]		(25,000)		(25,000)
Gains		75,000		75,000
Beginning of year	20,000	27,000	$1,000,000	1,047,000
End of year	$ 20,000	$ 77,000	$1,000,000	$1,097,000

d. When the governing board sells investments and uses the proceeds for the donor's specified purpose, the historic dollar value of the endowment fund does not change. Neither the decision by the governing board to appropriate net appreciation nor the sale of the investments changes the class of net assets in which the appropriated amount is reported. The $25,000 is classified as temporarily restricted net assets until the restriction is met by spending on Program A.

Year 3

98. On January 1, in accordance with its spending policy, the governing board of NFP Organization sold some investments for $28,000 and spent the proceeds on Program A. The remaining investments earned $30,000 of investment income, which NFP Organization also spent on Program A. At the end of the year, the fair value of the investments was $975,000.

Transactions for year 3 are classified as follows:

	Net Assets			
	---	---	---	---
Transactions	Unrestricted	Temporarily Restricted	Permanently Restricted	Total
Activity of Program A				
Spending policy		$ 28,000		$ 28,000
Investment income		30,000		30,000
Expenses	$(58,000)			(58,000)
Release restriction	58,000	(58,000)		0
Subtotal	0	0		0
Investments				
Spending policy		(28,000)		(28,000)
Losses[e]	(45,000)	(49,000)		(94,000)
Beginning of year	20,000	77,000	$1,000,000	1,097,000
End of year[f]	$(25,000)	$ 0	$1,000,000	$ 975,000

e. According to the provisions of paragraph 12, the decline in the fair value of the assets of the endowment fund reduces temporarily restricted net assets by $49,000. The remaining loss reduces unrestricted net assets.

f. According to the provisions of paragraph 15(d), NFP Organization would disclose the $25,000 deficiency between the fair value of the investments of the endowment fund at the end of the year and the level required by donor stipulations or law. If NFP Organization had other donor-restricted endowment funds in deficit positions, it would disclose the aggregate amount of the deficiencies.

Year 4

99. On January 1, the governing board of NFP Organization could not apply its spending policy because the fair value of the investments was less than the historic dollar value of the fund; thus, no appreciation was available for expenditure. The investments earned income of $27,000, which NFP Organization spent on Program A. At the end of the year, the fair value of the investments was $1,005,000.

Transactions for year 4 are classified as follows:

Transactions	Unrestricted	Net Assets Temporarily Restricted	Permanently Restricted	Total
Activity of Program A				
Investment income		$ 27,000		$ 27,000
Expenses	$(27,000)			(27,000)
Release restriction	27,000	(27,000)		0
Subtotal	0	0		0
Investments				
Gains[g]	25,000	5,000		30,000
Beginning of year	(25,000)	0	$1,000,000	975,000
End of year	$ 0	$ 5,000	$1,000,000	$1,005,000

g. According to the provisions of paragraph 13 of this Statement, because losses have reduced the assets of a donor-restricted endowment fund below the level required by donor stipulations or law ($1,000,000), the gains ($25,000) that restore the fair value of the assets of the endowment fund to the required level are classified as increases in unrestricted net assets. The remaining gains ($5,000) are available to be spent on Program A.

Example of an Organization That Separates Investment Return into Operating and Nonoperating Amounts

100. This example illustrates the disclosures required by paragraph 14 and a statement of activities that reports a portion of investment return within a measure of operations. Paragraph 14(a) requires an organization to disclose the composition of investment return including, at a minimum, investment income, net realized gains or losses on investments reported at other than fair value, and net gains or losses on investments reported at fair value. Paragraph 14(b) requires a reconciliation of investment return to amounts reported in the statement of activities if investment return is separated into operating and nonoperating amounts, together with a description of the policy used to determine the amount that is included in the measure of operations and a discussion of circumstances leading to a change, if any, in that policy. The reconciliation need not be provided if an organization includes all investment return in its measure of operations or excludes it from that measure entirely.

101. Statement 117 neither encourages nor discourages organizations from classifying items of revenues, expenses, and other changes in net assets as operating and nonoperating, but it requires that if an organization reports an intermediate measure of operations, it must do so within a financial statement that, at a minimum, reports the change in unrestricted net assets for the period. Statement 117 also specifies that if an organization's use of the term *operations* is not apparent from the details provided on the face of the statement of activities, a note to financial statements should describe the nature of the reported measure of operations or the items excluded from operations.

102. This example is illustrative only; it does not indicate a preferred method of reporting investment return or defining operations. Organizations may separate investment return into operating and nonoperating amounts in ways that they believe will provide meaningful information to users of their financial statements. Distinctions may be based on:

a. The nature of the underlying transactions, such as classifying realized amounts as operating and unrealized amounts as nonoperating

b. Budgetary designations, such as classifying amounts computed under a spending-rate or total return policy as operating and the remainder of investment return as nonoperating

c. The reporting requirements for categories of investments used in Statement 115, such as classifying investment income, realized gains and losses, unrealized gains and losses on trading securities, and other-than-temporary impairment losses on securities (that is, all items included in net income of a business enterprise) as operating and classifying the remainder of investment return as nonoperating

d. Other characteristics that provide information that is relevant and understandable to donors, creditors, and other users of financial statements.

103. A statement of activities of Not-for-Profit Organization is illustrated below. Not-for-Profit Organization invests cash in excess of daily requirements in short-term investments; during the year, those investments earned $1,275. Most long-term investments of Not-for-Profit Organization's endowments are held in an investment pool, which earned income of $11,270 and had net gains of $15,450. Certain endowments are separately invested because of donors' requirements. The investments of those endowments earned income of $1,000 and increased in value by $1,500. One donor required that the net gains be added to the original endowment gift; that endowment's investment in the pool increased in value by $180.

Not-for-Profit Organization
Statement of Activities
Year Ended June 30, 19X1

	Unrestricted	Temporarily Restricted	Permanently Restricted	Total
Operating revenues, gains, and other support:				
Contributions	$ x,xxx	$ x,xxx		$xx,xxx
Fees	x,xxx			x,xxx
Investment return designated for current operations	11,025	4,500		15,525
Other	xxx			xxx
Net assets released from restrictions	xx,xxx	(xx,xxx)		
Total operating revenues, gains, and other support	xx,xxx	(x,xxx)		xx,xxx
Operating expenses and losses:				
Program A	xx,xxx			xx,xxx
Program B	x,xxx			x,xxx
Program C	x,xxx			x,xxx
Management and general	x,xxx			x,xxx
Fund raising	x,xxx			x,xxx
Total operating expenses	xx,xxx			xx,xxx
Change in net assets from operations	x,xxx	(x,xxx)		x,xxx
Other changes:				
Investment return in excess of amounts designated for current operations	10,992	3,798	$180	14,970
[Other items considered to be nonoperating]	x,xxx	x,xxx		x,xxx
	xxx	xxx	xxx	xxx
Change in net assets	$xx,xxx	$ x,xxx	$xxx	$xx,xxx

104. Not-for-Profit Organization would add the following illustrative text to its note to the financial statements that describes the measure of operations:

The board of trustees designates only a portion of the Organization's cumulative investment return for support of current operations; the remainder is retained to support operations of future years and to offset potential market declines. The amount computed under the endowment spending policy of the investment pool and all investment income earned by investing cash in excess of daily requirements are used to support current operations.

105. The following illustrative text and schedule would be added to a note to the financial statements about investments to provide the information about the composition of return and the reconciliation of investment return required by paragraph 14:

State law allows the board to appropriate so much of the net appreciation as is prudent considering the Organization's long- and short-term needs, present and anticipated financial requirements, expected total return on its investments, price level trends, and general economic conditions. Under the Organization's endowment spending policy, 5 percent of the average of the fair value at the end of the previous 3 years is appropriated to support current operations. The following schedule summarizes the investment return and its classification in the statement of activities:

	Unrestricted	Temporarily Restricted	Permanently Restricted	Total
Dividends, interest, and rents (net of expenses of $565)	$ 8,400	$ 3,870		$ 12,270
Net realized and unrealized gains	12,342	4,428	$180	16,950
Return on long-term investments	20,742	8,298	180	29,220
Interest on short-term investments	1,275			1,275
Total return on investments	22,017	8,298	180	30,495
Investment return designated for current operations	(11,025)	(4,500)		(15,525)
Investment return in excess of amounts designated for current operations	$ 10,992	$ 3,798	$180	$ 14,970

106. Often, as in the example above, the amount of investment return designated for current operations is less than the total return on investments for the year. An organization may be able to designate an amount for the support of operations even if the total investment return for the year is less than the amount computed under a spending-rate policy; for example, when the organization designates part of its cumulative investment return from prior years to support its current operations. In that case, the operating and nonoperating amounts should be labeled to faithfully represent their natures. For example, the amount excluded from operations, which is negative, might be labeled "Investment return reduced by the portion of cumulative net appreciation designated for current operations."

Appendix D

AMENDMENTS TO EXISTING PRONOUNCEMENTS

107. FASB Statement No. 60, *Accounting and Reporting by Insurance Enterprises,* as amended by FASB Statement No. 115, *Accounting for Certain In-* *vestments in Debt and Equity Securities,* is amended as follows:

a. The following sentence is added at the end of paragraph 45:

A not-for-profit organization that conducts insurance activities should account for those investments in accordance with FASB Statement No. 124, *Accounting for Certain Investments Held by Not-for-Profit Organizations.*

b. Paragraph 46 is replaced by the following:

Investments in equity securities that are not addressed by Statement 115 or Statement 124 because they do not have "readily determinable fair values" as defined by those Statements shall be reported at fair value. A business enterprise shall recognize changes in fair value as unrealized gains and losses reported, net of applicable income taxes, in a separate component of equity. A not-for-profit organization shall recognize the change in fair value in its statement of activities.

108. The following sentence is added at the end of paragraph 4 of FASB Statement No. 65, *Accounting*

for Certain Mortgage Banking Activities, as amended by Statement 115:

> Mortgage-backed securities held by not-for-profit organizations shall be reported at fair value in accordance with the provisions of FASB Statement No. 124, *Accounting for Certain Investments Held by Not-for-Profit Organizations.*

109. In paragraph 3 of FASB Statement No. 91, *Accounting for Nonrefundable Fees and Costs Associated with Originating or Acquiring Loans and Initial Direct Costs of Leases,* as amended by Statement 115, *of a business enterprise or change in net assets of a not-for-profit organization* is added at the end of the last sentence.

110. The last sentence of paragraph 4 of Statement 115 is replaced by the following:

> This Statement applies to cooperatives and mutual enterprises, including credit unions and mutual insurance companies, but does not apply to not-for-profit organizations. FASB Statement No. 124, *Accounting for Certain Investments Held by Not-for-Profit Organizations,* establishes standards for not-for-profit organizations.

111. In paragraph 168 of FASB Statement No. 117, *Financial Statements of Not-for-Profit Organizations,* the definition of *endowment fund* is replaced by the following:

> An established fund of cash, securities, or other assets to provide income for the maintenance of a not-for-profit organization. The use of the assets of the fund may be permanently restricted, temporarily restricted, or unrestricted. Endowment funds generally are established by donor-restricted gifts and bequests to provide a permanent endowment, which is to provide a permanent source of income, or a term endowment, which is to provide income for a specified period. The portion of a permanent endowment that must be maintained permanently—not used up, expended, or otherwise exhausted—is classified as permanently restricted net assets. The portion of a term endowment that must be maintained for a specified term is classified as temporarily restricted net assets. An organization's governing board may earmark a portion of its unrestricted net assets as a board-designated endowment (sometimes called funds functioning as endowment or quasi-endowment funds) to be invested to provide income for a long but unspecified period. A board-designated endowment, which results from an internal designation, is not donor restricted and is classified as unrestricted net assets.

Appendix E

GLOSSARY

112. This appendix contains definitions of terms or phrases as used in this Statement.

Debt security
Any security representing a creditor relationship with an enterprise. It also includes (a) preferred stock that by its terms either must be redeemed by the issuing enterprise or is redeemable at the option of the investor and (b) a collateralized mortgage obligation (CMO) (or other instrument) that is issued in equity form but is required to be accounted for as a nonequity instrument regardless of how that instrument is classified (that is, whether equity or debt) in the issuer's statement of financial position. However, it excludes option contracts, financial futures contracts, forward contracts, lease contracts, and swap contracts.

- Thus, the term *debt security* includes, among other items, U.S. Treasury securities, U.S. government agency securities, municipal securities, corporate bonds, convertible debt, commercial paper, all securitized debt instruments, such as CMOs and real estate mortgage investment conduits (REMICs), and interest-only and principal-only strips.
- Trade accounts receivable arising from sales on credit and loans receivable arising from consumer, commercial, and real estate lending activities of financial institutions and not-for-profit organizations are examples of receivables that do not meet the definition of *security;* thus, those receivables are not debt securities (unless they have been securitized, in which case they would meet the definition).

Donor-restricted endowment fund
An endowment fund that is created by a donor stipulation requiring investment of the gift in perpetuity or for a specified term. Also refer to **Endowment fund.**

Endowment fund

An established fund of cash, securities, or other assets to provide income for the maintenance of a not-for-profit organization. The use of the assets of the fund may be permanently restricted, temporarily restricted, or unrestricted. Endowment funds generally are established by donor-restricted gifts and bequests to provide a permanent endowment, which is to provide a permanent source of income, or a term endowment, which is to provide income for a specified period. The portion of a permanent endowment that must be maintained permanently—not used up, expended, or otherwise exhausted—is classified as permanently restricted net assets. The portion of a term endowment that must be maintained for a specified term is classified as temporarily restricted net assets. An organization's governing board may earmark a portion of its unrestricted net assets as a board-designated endowment (sometimes called funds functioning as endowment or quasi-endowment funds) to be invested to provide income for a long but unspecified period. A board-designated endowment, which results from an internal designation, is not donor restricted and is classified as unrestricted net assets.

Equity security

Any security representing an ownership interest in an enterprise (for example, common, preferred, or other capital stock) or the right to acquire (for example, warrants, rights, and call op-

tions) or dispose of (for example, put options) an ownership interest in an enterprise at fixed or determinable prices. However, the term does not include convertible debt or preferred stock that by its terms either must be redeemed by the issuing enterprise or is redeemable at the option of the investor.

Fair value

The amount at which an asset could be bought or sold in a current transaction between willing parties, that is, other than in a forced or liquidation sale. If a quoted market price is available for a financial instrument, the fair value to be used in applying this Statement is the product of the number of trading units of the instrument times the market price per unit.

Security

A share, participation, or other interest in property or in an enterprise of the issuer or an obligation of the issuer that (a) either is represented by an instrument issued in bearer or registered form or, if not represented by an instrument, is registered in books maintained to record transfers by or on behalf of the issuer, (b) is of a type commonly dealt in on securities exchanges or markets or, when represented by an instrument, is commonly recognized in any area in which it is issued or dealt in as a medium for investment, and (c) either is one of a class or series or by its terms is divisible into a class or series of shares, participations, interests, or obligations.

Statement of Financial Accounting Standards No. 125
Accounting for Transfers and Servicing of Financial Assets and Extinguishments of Liabilities

STATUS

Issued: June 1996

Effective Date: For transfers and servicing of financial assets and extinguishments
of liabilities occurring after December 31, 1996

Affects: Supersedes APB 26, paragraph 3(a)
Amends FAS 13, paragraph 20
Amends FAS 22, footnote 1
Amends FAS 65, paragraphs 1, 6, 9(a), 10, 15, and 34
Supersedes FAS 65, paragraphs 8, 11, 16 through 19, 30 and the paragraphs added by FAS 122,
and footnotes 4 and 6
Supersedes FAS 76
Supersedes FAS 77
Supersedes FAS 105, paragraph 14(e)
Supersedes FAS 107, paragraph 8(b)
Amends FAS 107, paragraph 28
Amends FAS 115, paragraph 7
Supersedes FAS 122
Supersedes FTB 84-4
Supersedes FTB 85-2
Supersedes FTB 86-2, paragraph 12
Supersedes FTB 87-3, paragraphs 1 through 7 and 9

Affected by: Paragraphs 4 and 14 amended by FAS 133
Paragraph 19 superseded by FAS 127
Paragraphs 31 and 243 amended by FAS 133
Superseded by FAS 140

Other Interpretive Release: FASB Special Report, *A Guide to Implementation of Statement 125 on Accounting
for Transfers and Servicing of Financial Assets and Extinguishments of Liabili-
ties: Questions and Answers* (third edition) (nullified by FAS 140)

**Note: Although superseded, this pronouncement must still be applied until the effective date of
FAS 140. See the Status page of FAS 140 for details of effective dates for FAS 140.**

Issues Discussed by FASB Emerging Issues Task Force (EITF)

Affects: Nullifies EITF Issues No. 85-40, 86-24, 86-39, 89-2, 92-10, and 94-9 and Topics No. D-13 and D-48
Partially nullifies EITF Issues No. 84-5, 85-25, 86-18, 86-38, 87-30, 88-11, 88-17, 88-22,
89-4, 90-2, 92-2, and 96-10
Resolves EITF Issues No. 84-21, 84-26, 85-26, 85-30, 85-34, 87-18, 87-25, and 94-4
Partially resolves EITF Issues No. 84-20 and 87-20 and Topic No. D-14

Interpreted by: Paragraph 4 interpreted by EITF Issues No. 98-8 and 01-2
Paragraph 9 interpreted by EITF Topics No. D-51, D-65, and D-75
Paragraph 9(a) interpreted by EITF Topic No. D-67
Paragraph 9(c) interpreted by EITF Topic No. D-63
Paragraph 10 interpreted by EITF Issue No. 98-15

Paragraph 11 interpreted by EITF Topics No. D-69 and D-75
Paragraph 16 interpreted by EITF Issue No. 96-19
Paragraph 17 interpreted by EITF Topic No. D-65
Paragraph 17(e)(2) interpreted by EITF Topic No. D-69
Paragraph 26 interpreted by EITF Topic No. D-66
Paragraphs 27 and 29 interpreted by EITF Topic No. D-65
Paragraph 43 interpreted by EITF Topic No. D-69
Paragraph 53 interpreted by EITF Topic No. D-75
Paragraphs 58 and 121 interpreted by EITF Topic No. D-67

Related Issues: EITF Issues No. 84-15, 85-13, 86-8, 86-36, 87-34, 88-18, 88-20, 90-18, 90-19, 90-21, 95-5, 95-15, 96-20, 97-3, 97-6, 97-14, 98-12, 98-14, 99-8, and 00-17

SUMMARY

This Statement provides accounting and reporting standards for transfers and servicing of financial assets and extinguishments of liabilities. Those standards are based on consistent application of a *financial-components approach* that focuses on control. Under that approach, after a transfer of financial assets, an entity recognizes the financial and servicing assets it controls and the liabilities it has incurred, derecognizes financial assets when control has been surrendered, and derecognizes liabilities when extinguished. This Statement provides consistent standards for distinguishing transfers of financial assets that are sales from transfers that are secured borrowings.

A transfer of financial assets in which the transferor surrenders control over those assets is accounted for as a sale to the extent that consideration other than beneficial interests in the transferred assets is received in exchange. The transferor has surrendered control over transferred assets if and only if all of the following conditions are met:

a. The transferred assets have been isolated from the transferor—put presumptively beyond the reach of the transferor and its creditors, even in bankruptcy or other receivership.
b. Either (1) each transferee obtains the right—free of conditions that constrain it from taking advantage of that right—to pledge or exchange the transferred assets or (2) the transferee is a qualifying special-purpose entity and the holders of beneficial interests in that entity have the right—free of conditions that constrain them from taking advantage of that right—to pledge or exchange those interests.
c. The transferor does not maintain effective control over the transferred assets through (1) an agreement that both entitles and obligates the transferor to repurchase or redeem them before their maturity or (2) an agreement that entitles the transferor to repurchase or redeem transferred assets that are not readily obtainable.

This Statement requires that liabilities and derivatives incurred or obtained by transferors as part of a transfer of financial assets be initially measured at fair value, if practicable. It also requires that servicing assets and other retained interests in the transferred assets be measured by allocating the previous carrying amount between the assets sold, if any, and retained interests, if any, based on their relative fair values at the date of the transfer.

This Statement requires that servicing assets and liabilities be subsequently measured by (a) amortization in proportion to and over the period of estimated net servicing income or loss and (b) assessment for asset impairment or increased obligation based on their fair values.

This Statement requires that debtors reclassify financial assets pledged as collateral and that secured parties recognize those assets and their obligation to return them in certain circumstances in which the secured party has taken control of those assets.

This Statement requires that a liability be derecognized if and only if either (a) the debtor pays the creditor and is relieved of its obligation for the liability or (b) the debtor is legally released from being the primary obligor under the liability either judicially or by the creditor. Therefore, a liability is not considered extinguished by an in-substance defeasance.

This Statement provides implementation guidance for assessing isolation of transferred assets and for accounting for transfers of partial interests, servicing of financial assets, securitizations, transfers of sales-type and direct financing lease receivables, securities lending transactions, repurchase agreements including "dollar rolls," "wash sales," loan syndications and participations, risk participations in banker's acceptances, factoring arrangements, transfers of receivables with recourse, and extinguishments of liabilities.

This Statement supersedes FASB Statements No. 76, *Extinguishment of Debt,* and No. 77, *Reporting by Transferors for Transfers of Receivables with Recourse.* This Statement amends FASB Statement No. 115, *Accounting for Certain Investments in Debt and Equity Securities,* to clarify that a debt security may not be classified as held-to-maturity if it can be prepaid or otherwise settled in such a way that the holder of the security would not recover substantially all of its recorded investment. This Statement amends and extends to all servicing assets and liabilities the accounting standards for mortgage servicing rights now in FASB Statement No. 65, *Accounting for Certain Mortgage Banking Activities,* and supersedes FASB Statement No. 122, *Accounting for Mortgage Servicing Rights.* This Statement also supersedes Technical Bulletins No. 84-4, *In-Substance Defeasance of Debt,* No. 85-2, *Accounting for Collateralized Mortgage Obligations (CMOs),* and No. 87-3, *Accounting for Mortgage Servicing Fees and Rights.*

This Statement is effective for transfers and servicing of financial assets and extinguishments of liabilities occurring after December 31, 1996, and is to be applied prospectively. Earlier or retroactive application is not permitted.

(This page intentionally left blank.)

Statement of Financial Accounting Standards No. 125

Accounting for Transfers and Servicing of Financial Assets and Extinguishments of Liabilities

CONTENTS

INTRODUCTION AND SCOPE

1. The Board added a project on financial instruments and off-balance-sheet financing to its agenda in May 1986. The project is intended to develop standards to aid in resolving existing financial accounting and reporting issues and other issues likely to arise in the future about various financial instruments and related transactions. The November 1991 FASB Discussion Memorandum, *Recognition and Measurement of Financial Instruments,* describes the issues to be considered. This Statement focuses on the issues of accounting for **transfers**[1] and servicing of **financial assets** and extinguishments of liabilities.

2. Transfers of financial assets take many forms. Accounting for transfers in which the **transferor** has no continuing involvement with the transferred assets or with the **transferee** has not been controversial. However, transfers of financial assets often occur in which the transferor has some continuing involvement either with the assets transferred or with the transferee. Examples of continuing involvement are **recourse,** servicing, agreements to reacquire, options written or held, and pledges of **collateral.** Transfers of financial assets with continuing involvement raise issues about the circumstances under which the transfers should be considered as sales of all or part of the assets or as secured borrowings and about how transferors and transferees should account for sales and secured borrowings. This Statement establishes standards for resolving those issues.

3. An entity may settle a liability by transferring assets to the creditor or otherwise obtaining an unconditional release. Alternatively, an entity may enter into other arrangements designed to set aside assets dedicated to eventually settling a liability. Accounting for those arrangements has raised issues about when a liability should be considered extinguished. This Statement establishes standards for resolving those issues.

---

[1] Terms defined in Appendix D, the glossary, are set in **boldface type** the first time they appear.

4. This Statement does not address transfers of custody of financial assets for safekeeping, contributions,[2] or investments by owners or distributions to owners of a business enterprise. This Statement does not address subsequent measurement of assets and liabilities, except for (a) **servicing assets** and **servicing liabilities** and (b) **interest-only strips,** securities, loans, other receivables, or retained interests in securitizations that can contractually be prepaid or otherwise settled in such a way that the holder would not recover substantially all of its recorded investment. This Statement does not change the accounting for employee benefits subject to the provisions of FASB Statement No. 87, *Employers' Accounting for Pensions,* No. 88, *Employers' Accounting for Settlements and Curtailments of Defined Benefit Pension Plans and for Termination Benefits,* or No. 106, *Employers' Accounting for Postretirement Benefits Other Than Pensions.* This Statement does not change the provisions relating to leveraged leases in FASB Statement No. 13, *Accounting for Leases,* or money-over-money and wrap lease transactions involving nonrecourse debt subject to the provisions of FASB Technical Bulletin No. 88-1, *Issues Relating to Accounting for Leases.* This Statement does not address transfers of nonfinancial assets, for example, servicing assets, or transfers of unrecognized financial assets, for example, minimum lease payments to be received under operating leases.

5. The Board concluded that an objective in accounting for transfers of financial assets is for each entity that is a party to the transaction to recognize only assets it controls and liabilities it has incurred, to **derecognize** assets only when control has been surrendered, and to derecognize liabilities only when they have been extinguished. Sales and other transfers frequently result in a disaggregation of financial assets and liabilities into components, which become separate assets and liabilities. For example, if an entity sells a portion of a financial asset it owns, the portion retained becomes an asset separate from the portion sold and from the assets obtained in exchange.

6. The Board concluded that another objective is that recognition of financial assets and liabilities should not be affected by the sequence of transactions that result in their acquisition or incurrence unless the effect of those transactions is to maintain effective control over a transferred financial asset. For example, if a transferor sells financial assets it owns and at the same time writes a put option (such as a guarantee or recourse obligation) on those assets, it should recognize the put obligation in the same manner as would another unrelated entity that writes an identical put option on assets it never owned. Similarly, a creditor may release a debtor on the condition that a third party assumes the obligation and that the original debtor becomes secondarily liable. In those circumstances, the original debtor becomes a guarantor and should recognize a guarantee obligation in the same manner as would a third-party guarantor that had never been primarily liable to that creditor, whether or not explicit consideration was paid for that guarantee. However, certain agreements to repurchase or redeem transferred assets maintain effective control over those assets and should therefore be accounted for differently than agreements to acquire assets never owned.

7. Previous accounting standards generally required that a transferor account for financial assets transferred as an inseparable unit that had been either entirely sold or entirely retained. Those standards were difficult to apply and produced inconsistent and arbitrary results. For example, whether a transfer "purported to be a sale" was sufficient to determine whether the transfer was accounted for and reported as a sale of receivables under one accounting standard or as a secured borrowing under another.

8. Previous standards did not accommodate recent innovations in the financial markets. After studying many of the complex developments that have occurred in financial markets during recent years, the Board concluded that previous approaches that viewed each financial asset as an indivisible unit do not provide an appropriate basis for developing consistent and operational standards for dealing with transfers and servicing of financial assets and extinguishments of liabilities. To address those issues adequately and consistently, the Board decided to adopt as the basis for this Statement a *financial-components approach* that focuses on control and recognizes that financial assets and liabilities can be divided into a variety of components.

---

[2]Contributions—unconditional nonreciprocal transfers of assets—are addressed in FASB Statement No. 116, *Accounting for Contributions Received and Contributions Made.*

STANDARDS OF FINANCIAL ACCOUNTING AND REPORTING

Accounting for Transfers and Servicing of Financial Assets

9. A transfer of financial assets (or all or a portion of a financial asset) in which the transferor surrenders control over those financial assets shall be accounted for as a sale to the extent that consideration other than **beneficial interests** in the transferred assets is received in exchange. The transferor has surrendered control over transferred assets if and only if all of the following conditions are met:

a. The transferred assets have been isolated from the transferor—put presumptively beyond the reach of the transferor and its creditors, even in bankruptcy or other receivership (paragraphs 23 and 24).
b. Either (1) each transferee obtains the right—free of conditions that constrain it from taking advantage of that right (paragraph 25)—to pledge or exchange the transferred assets or (2) the transferee is a qualifying special-purpose entity (paragraph 26) and the holders of beneficial interests in that entity have the right—free of conditions that constrain them from taking advantage of that right (paragraph 25)—to pledge or exchange those interests.
c. The transferor does not maintain effective control over the transferred assets through (1) an agreement that both entitles and obligates the transferor to repurchase or redeem them before their maturity (paragraphs 27-29) or (2) an agreement that entitles the transferor to repurchase or redeem transferred assets that are not readily obtainable (paragraph 30).

10. Upon completion of any transfer of financial assets, the transferor shall:

a. Continue to carry in its statement of financial position any retained interest in the transferred assets, including, if applicable, servicing assets (paragraphs 35-41), beneficial interests in assets transferred to a qualifying special-purpose entity in a **securitization** (paragraphs 47-58), and retained **undivided interests** (paragraph 33)

b. Allocate the previous carrying amount between the assets sold, if any, and the retained interests, if any, based on their relative **fair values** at the date of transfer (paragraphs 31-34).

11. Upon completion[3] of a transfer of assets that satisfies the conditions to be accounted for as a sale (paragraph 9), the transferor (**seller**) shall:

a. Derecognize all assets sold
b. Recognize all assets obtained and liabilities incurred in consideration as **proceeds** of the sale, including cash, put or call options held or written (for example, guarantee or recourse obligations), forward commitments (for example, commitments to deliver additional receivables during the revolving periods of some securitizations), swaps (for example, provisions that convert interest rates from fixed to variable), and servicing liabilities, if applicable (paragraphs 31, 32, and 35-41)
c. Initially measure at fair value assets obtained and liabilities incurred in a sale (paragraphs 42-44) or, if it is not practicable to estimate the fair value of an asset or a liability, apply alternative measures (paragraphs 45 and 46)
d. Recognize in earnings any gain or loss on the sale.

The transferee shall recognize all assets obtained and any liabilities incurred and initially measure them at fair value (in aggregate, presumptively the price paid).

12. If a transfer of financial assets in exchange for cash or other consideration (other than beneficial interests in the transferred assets) does not meet the criteria for a sale in paragraph 9, the transferor and transferee shall account for the transfer as a secured borrowing with pledge of collateral (paragraph 15).

Recognition and Measurement of Servicing Assets and Liabilities

13. Each time an entity undertakes an obligation to service financial assets it shall recognize either a servicing asset or a servicing liability for that servicing contract, unless it securitizes the assets, retains all of the resulting securities, and classifies them as debt securities held-to-maturity in accordance with FASB Statement No. 115, *Accounting for Certain*

---

[3]Although a transfer of securities may not be considered to have reached completion until the settlement date, this Statement does not modify other generally accepted accounting principles, including FASB Statement No. 35, *Accounting and Reporting by Defined Benefit Pension Plans*, and AICPA Statements of Position and audit and accounting Guides for certain industries, that require accounting at the trade date for certain contracts to purchase or sell securities.

Investments in Debt and Equity Securities. If the servicing asset or liability was purchased or assumed rather than undertaken in a sale or securitization of the financial assets being serviced, it shall be measured initially at its fair value, presumptively the price paid. A servicing asset or liability shall be amortized in proportion to and over the period of estimated net servicing income (if servicing revenues exceed servicing costs) or net servicing loss (if servicing costs exceed servicing revenues). A servicing asset or liability shall be assessed for impairment or increased obligation based on its fair value (paragraphs 35-38).

Financial Assets Subject to Prepayment

14. Interest-only strips, loans, other receivables, or retained interests in securitizations that can contractually be prepaid or otherwise settled in such a way that the holder would not recover substantially all of its recorded investment shall be subsequently measured like investments in debt securities classified as available-for-sale or trading under Statement 115, as amended by this Statement (paragraph 233).[4]

Secured Borrowings and Collateral

15. A debtor may grant a **security interest** in certain assets to a lender (the secured party) to serve as collateral for its obligation under a borrowing, with or without recourse to other assets of the debtor. An obligor under other kinds of current or potential obligations, for example, interest rate swaps, also may grant a security interest in certain assets to a secured party. If collateral is transferred to the secured party, the custodial arrangement is commonly referred to as a pledge. Secured parties sometimes are permitted to sell or repledge (or otherwise transfer) collateral held under a pledge. The same relationships occur, under different names, in transfers documented as sales that are accounted for as secured borrowings (paragraph 12). The accounting for collateral by the debtor (or obligor) and the secured party depends on whether the secured party has taken control over the collateral and on the rights and obligations that result from the collateral arrangement:

a. If (1) the secured party is permitted by contract or custom to sell or repledge the collateral and (2) the debtor does not have the right and ability to redeem the collateral on short notice, for example, by substituting other collateral or terminating the contract, then

(i) The debtor shall reclassify that asset and report that asset in its statement of financial position separately (for example, as securities receivable from broker) from other assets not so encumbered.

(ii) The secured party shall recognize that collateral as its asset, initially measure it at fair value, and also recognize its obligation to return it.

b. If the secured party sells or repledges collateral on terms that do not give it the right and ability to repurchase or redeem the collateral from the transferee on short notice and thus may impair the debtor's right to redeem it, the secured party shall recognize the proceeds from the sale or the asset repledged and its obligation to return the asset to the extent that it has not already recognized them. The sale or repledging of the asset is a transfer subject to the provisions of this Statement.

c. If the debtor defaults under the terms of the secured contract and is no longer entitled to redeem the collateral, it shall derecognize the collateral, and the secured party shall recognize the collateral as its asset to the extent it has not already recognized it and initially measure it at fair value.

d. Otherwise, the debtor shall continue to carry the collateral as its asset, and the secured party shall not recognize the pledged asset.

Extinguishments of Liabilities

16. A debtor shall derecognize a liability if and only if it has been extinguished. A liability has been extinguished if either of the following conditions is met:

a. The debtor pays the creditor and is relieved of its obligation for the liability. *Paying the creditor* includes delivery of cash, other financial assets, goods, or services or reacquisition by the debtor of its outstanding debt securities whether the securities are canceled or held as so-called treasury bonds.

---

[4]As a result of that amendment to Statement 115, securities that were previously classified as held-to-maturity may need to be reclassified. Reclassifications of interest-only strips or other securities from held-to-maturity to available-for-sale required to initially apply this Statement would not call into question an entity's intent to hold other debt securities to maturity in the future.

b. The debtor is legally released[5] from being the primary obligor under the liability, either judicially or by the creditor.

Disclosures

17. An entity shall disclose the following:

a. If the entity has entered into repurchase agreements or securities lending transactions, its policy for requiring collateral or other security
b. If debt was considered to be extinguished by in-substance defeasance under the provisions of FASB Statement No. 76, *Extinguishment of Debt*, prior to the effective date of this Statement, a general description of the transaction and the amount of debt that is considered extinguished at the end of the period so long as that debt remains outstanding
c. If assets are set aside after the effective date of this Statement solely for satisfying scheduled payments of a specific obligation, a description of the nature of restrictions placed on those assets
d. If it is not practicable to estimate the fair value of certain assets obtained or liabilities incurred in transfers of financial assets during the period, a description of those items and the reasons why it is not practicable to estimate their fair value
e. For all servicing assets and servicing liabilities:
    (1) The amounts of servicing assets or liabilities recognized and amortized during the period
    (2) The fair value of recognized servicing assets and liabilities for which it is practicable to estimate that value and the method and significant assumptions used to estimate the fair value
    (3) The risk characteristics of the underlying financial assets used to stratify recognized servicing assets for purposes of measuring impairment in accordance with paragraph 37
    (4) The activity in any valuation allowance for impairment of recognized servicing assets—including beginning and ending balances, aggregate additions charged and reductions credited to operations, and aggregate direct write-downs charged against the allowances—for each period for which results of operations are presented.

Implementation Guidance

18. Appendix A describes certain provisions of this Statement in more detail and describes their application to certain types of transactions. Appendix A is an integral part of the standards provided in this Statement.

Effective Date and Transition

19. This Statement shall be effective for transfers and servicing of financial assets and extinguishments of liabilities occurring after December 31, 1996, and shall be applied prospectively. Earlier or retroactive application of this Statement is not permitted.

20. For each servicing contract in existence before January 1, 1997, previously recognized servicing rights and "excess servicing" receivables that do not exceed **contractually specified servicing fees** shall be combined, net of any previously recognized servicing obligations under that contract, as a servicing asset or liability. Previously recognized servicing receivables that exceed contractually specified servicing fees shall be reclassified as interest-only strips receivable. Thereafter, the subsequent measurement provisions of this Statement shall be applied to the servicing assets or liabilities for those servicing contracts (paragraph 37) and to the interest-only strips receivable (paragraph 14).

21. The provisions of paragraph 14 and the amendment to Statement 115 (paragraph 233) shall be effective for financial assets held on or acquired after January 1, 1997.

> **The provisions of this Statement need
> not be applied to immaterial items.**

---

[5]If nonrecourse debt (such as certain mortgage loans) is assumed by a third party in conjunction with the sale of an asset that serves as sole collateral for that debt, the sale and related assumption effectively accomplish a legal release of the seller-debtor for purposes of applying this Statement.

This Statement was adopted by the affirmative votes of six members of the Financial Accounting Standards Board. Mr. Foster dissented.

Mr. Foster dissents from the issuance of this Statement because he believes that the notion of effective control that is applied to repurchase agreements, including dollar rolls, and securities lending transactions should be applied consistently to other transfers of financial assets, including securitization transactions. Furthermore, he believes that in those instances where the financial-components approach is applied, all rights (assets) and obligations (liabilities) that are recognized by the transferor after a sale or securitization has occurred should be measured at fair value.

Under paragraphs 9(a) and 9(b) of this Statement, control is deemed to have been surrendered if the transferred assets have been legally isolated from the transferor and the transferee has the right to pledge or exchange the transferred assets. That notion of control is the cornerstone of the financial-components approach. However, the Board considered that approach inappropriate to account for certain transactions, such as those involving repurchase agreements, including dollar rolls, and securities lending transactions, where legal control over the assets has been surrendered, but where the Board believes that effective control still exists. For those transactions, paragraph 9(c) was specifically crafted to override the criteria for transfers of legal control in paragraphs 9(a) and 9(b). Paragraph 9(c), however, was designed to provide an exception only for certain transactions resulting in inconsistent application of the control notion: one set of transfers of financial assets—securitizations—is accounted for using a narrow, legal definition of control while others are accounted for using a broad notion of effective control. Mr. Foster favors an approach that encompasses the broader notion of effective control. He questions why, if the financial-components approach is inappropriate to account for all transfers of financial assets, it is appropriate to apply it to securitizations. He believes that if the entirety of the arrangement is considered, certain securitization transactions, such as those having a revolving-period agreement, also result in effective control being retained by the transferor and accordingly those transactions should be accounted for as secured borrowings.

In securitizations having a revolving-period agreement, which are described in paragraphs 130-133, the transferor generally continues to collect the cash from the transferred receivables, commingles that cash with its own cash, invests the cash for its own benefit, and uses the cash to buy additional receiv-

ables from itself that it selects. As a result of those features, the future benefits of the receivables (the cash flows to be received from them) that inure to the transferor are little different, if at all, from the future benefits that the transferor would obtain from receivables that it holds for its own account. Mr. Foster believes that in those transactions effective control of the receivables has not been surrendered and that the transferred receivables continue to be assets of the transferor.

Paragraph 26 of FASB Concepts Statement No. 6, *Elements of Financial Statements,* states, "An asset has three essential characteristics: (a) it embodies a probable future benefit that involves a capacity, singly or in combination with other assets, to contribute directly or indirectly to future net cash inflows, (b) a particular entity can obtain the benefit and control others' access to it, and (c) the transaction or other event giving rise to the entity's right to or control of the benefit has already occurred." Mr. Foster believes that in securitizations having revolving-period agreements, the transferred receivables meet each of those criteria from the perspective of the transferor. The transferred receivables directly or indirectly contribute to the transferor's cash inflows—it generally receives and retains all of the cash inflows during the term of the arrangement subject only to payment of what amounts to interest on the investment of the holders of beneficial interests—and the transferor can and does obtain and control others' access to both the receivables and the cash inflows by its structuring of the transaction and retention of most of the cash flows until termination of the arrangement. Paragraph 131 of this Statement asserts that the cash obtained by the transferor in those securitizations is received in exchange for new receivables and is not obtained as a benefit attributable to its previous ownership of the transferred receivables. In substance, however, the transfer of new receivables is little different from the substitution of collateral prevalent in many secured loan arrangements. In short, the transferred receivables have all of the attributes of assets controlled by the transferor.

As described below, the principal criteria cited in the basis for conclusions for treating repurchase agreements and securities lending transactions as secured borrowings apply equally to many securitizations, particularly those having a revolving-period agreement.

The inability of the transferor in a transfer with a revolving-period agreement to sell new receivables elsewhere because it has contracted to sell those new receivables on prearranged terms at times that it does not determine or have much influence over is asserted to be significant in paragraph 131. However, within fairly wide latitude, the transferor in those circumstances has retained the right to change the interest rate (the price) on both the previously transferred receivables and receivables to be transferred in the future. Mr. Foster believes that that right substantially diminishes any disadvantage of not being able to sell the receivables elsewhere and substantially negates any effect, favorable or onerous, on the transferor as a result of changes in market conditions as asserted in paragraph 50. In fact, any effects on the transferor result solely from having financed the receivables at whatever rate is paid the beneficial owners of the securities. Furthermore, the transferor of assets transferred under repurchase agreements or in securities lending transactions cannot sell those assets elsewhere.

Two reasons advanced in support of the treatment of repurchase agreements and securities lending transactions as secured borrowings are that (a) those transactions are difficult to characterize because they have attributes of both borrowings and sales and (b) supporting arguments can be found for accounting for those transactions as borrowings or sales. Those two reasons are equally applicable to securitization transactions having a revolving-period agreement—they are treated as sales for purposes of marketing to investors and as borrowings for tax purposes, and legal opinions and the prospectuses for those transactions acknowledge that their treatment as sales may not be sustained in a legal dispute.

The only supporting arguments cited for the treatment of repurchase agreements and securities lending transactions as secured borrowings that are not equally applicable to certain securitizations are that (a) forward contracts that are fully secured should be treated differently than those that are unsecured and (b) making a change in existing accounting practice would have a substantial impact on the reported financial position of certain entities and on the markets in which they participate. Mr. Foster does not believe that the existence of security in support of a transaction should determine its accounting treatment and notes that extension of the reasoning in paragraph 141 would lead to lenders not recognizing loans receivable that are unsecured. While it may be necessary to consider prior accounting treatment and the effect a change in accounting practice would have

on certain entities, Mr. Foster believes that those factors should carry relatively little weight in determining what is an appropriate accounting standard.

Paragraph 18 of Opinion 29 states, "The Board concludes that in general accounting for nonmonetary transactions should be based on the fair values of the assets (or services) involved which is the same basis as that used in monetary transactions. Thus, the cost of a nonmonetary asset acquired in exchange for another nonmonetary asset is the fair value of the asset surrendered to obtain it . . ." (footnote reference omitted). The conclusion embodied in that language is that the accounting for both monetary and nonmonetary transactions acquired in an exchange should be based on the fair values of the assets (or services) involved. Mr. Foster believes that in securitization transactions in which control is deemed under this Statement to be surrendered and in partial sales of financial assets, assets (or rights) are surrendered in exchange for cash and other rights and obligations, all of which are new.[6] The new assets (rights) received are part of the proceeds of the exchange, and any liabilities (obligations) incurred are a reduction of the proceeds. As such, those new assets and liabilities should be measured at their fair values as they are in all other exchange transactions.

This Statement contends that in those transactions certain components of the original assets have not been exchanged. If that is one's view, however, it is clear that a transaction of sufficient significance to result in the derecognition of assets has occurred. Furthermore, the event of securitization results in a change in the form and value of assets— securities are generally more easily sold or used as collateral and thus are more valuable than receivables. Mr. Foster believes that a securitization transaction, like the initial recognition of an asset or liability and derecognition of assets and liabilities where it is clear an exchange has occurred, is also sufficiently significant that the resulting, or remaining components of, assets and liabilities should be recorded at fair value.

Mr. Foster also notes, as described in paragraphs 182-184, that the distinctions made in paragraphs 10 and 11 between (a) assets retained and (b) assets obtained and liabilities incurred are arbitrary. For example, one could easily argue that beneficial interests acquired in a transfer of receivables have different rights and obligations than the receivables and accordingly should be accounted for

---

[6]In the case of a partial sale of a financial asset, the transferor generally has reduced the marketability of the asset because it can no longer sell the entire asset—it can only sell part of that asset. Consequently, the partial interest in the original asset has different rights and privileges than those embodied in the original asset and, therefore, is a new asset—different from the original asset.

not as retained assets, but as new and different assets, and, arguably, the rights inherent in derivatives arising in a securitization transaction, which are considered new rights (assets) in this Statement, were embedded, albeit in an obscure form, in the transferred assets and could be as readily identified as retained portions of them. That the Board needed to make those distinctions arbitrarily begs for a consistent measurement attribute—fair value—for all of the rights and obligations held by the transferor subsequent to the transfer.

Members of the Financial Accounting Standards Board:

Dennis R. Beresford,	Anthony T. Cope	Robert H. Northcutt
Chairman	John M. Foster	Robert J. Swieringa
Joseph V. Anania	James J. Leisenring	

Appendix A

IMPLEMENTATION GUIDANCE

CONTENTS

Appendix A

IMPLEMENTATION GUIDANCE

Introduction

22. This appendix describes certain provisions of this Statement in more detail and describes how they apply to certain types of transactions. This appendix discusses generalized situations. Facts and circumstances and specific contracts need to be considered carefully in applying this Statement. This appendix is an integral part of the standards provided in this Statement.

Isolation beyond the Reach of the Transferor and Its Creditors

23. The nature and extent of supporting evidence required for an assertion in financial statements that transferred financial assets have been isolated—put presumptively beyond the reach of the transferor and its creditors, either by a single transaction or a series of transactions taken as a whole—depend on the facts and circumstances. All available evidence that either supports or questions an assertion shall be considered. That consideration includes making judgments about whether the contract or circumstances permit the transferor to revoke the transfer. It also may include making judgments about the kind of bankruptcy or other receivership into which a transferor or special-purpose entity might be placed, whether a transfer of financial assets would likely be deemed a true sale at law, whether the transferor is affiliated with the transferee, and other factors pertinent under applicable law. Derecognition of transferred assets is appropriate only if the available evidence provides reasonable assurance that the transferred assets would be beyond the reach of the powers of a bankruptcy trustee or other receiver for the transferor

or any of its affiliates, except for an affiliate that is a qualifying special-purpose entity designed to make remote the possibility that it would enter bankruptcy or other receivership (paragraph 57(c)).

24. Whether securitizations isolate transferred assets may depend on such factors as whether the securitization is accomplished in one step or two steps (paragraphs 54-58). Many common financial transactions, for example, typical repurchase agreements and securities lending transactions, isolate transferred assets from the transferor, although they may not meet the other criteria for surrender of control.

Conditions That Constrain a Transferee

25. Many transferor-imposed or other conditions on a transferee's contractual right to pledge or exchange a transferred asset constrain a transferee from taking advantage of that right. However, a transferor's right of first refusal on a bona fide offer from a third party, a requirement to obtain the transferor's permission to sell or pledge that shall not be unreasonably withheld, or a prohibition on sale to the transferor's competitor generally does not constrain a transferee from pledging or exchanging the asset and, therefore, presumptively does not preclude a transfer containing such a condition from being accounted for as a sale. For example, a prohibition on sale to the transferor's competitor would not constrain the transferee if it were able to sell the transferred assets to a number of other parties; however, it would be a constraint if that competitor were the only potential willing buyer.

Qualifying Special-Purpose Entity

26. A qualifying special-purpose entity[7] must meet both of the following conditions:

a. It is a trust, corporation, or other legal vehicle whose activities are permanently limited by the legal documents establishing the special-purpose

---

[7]The description of a special-purpose entity is restrictive. The accounting for transfers of financial assets to special-purpose entities should not be extended to any entity that does not satisfy all of the conditions articulated in this paragraph.

entity to:

(1) Holding title to transferred financial assets

(2) Issuing beneficial interests (If some of the beneficial interests are in the form of debt securities or equity securities, the transfer of assets is a securitization.)

(3) Collecting cash proceeds from assets held, reinvesting proceeds in financial instruments pending distribution to holders of beneficial interests, and otherwise servicing the assets held

(4) Distributing proceeds to the holders of its beneficial interests.

b. It has standing at law distinct from the transferor. Having standing at law depends in part on the nature of the special-purpose entity. For example, generally, under U.S. law, if a transferor of assets to a special-purpose trust holds all of the beneficial interests, it can unilaterally dissolve the trust and thereby reassume control over the individual assets held in the trust, and the transferor "can effectively assign his interest and his creditors can reach it."[8] In that circumstance, the trust has no standing at law, is not distinct, and thus is not a qualifying special-purpose entity.

Agreements That Maintain Effective Control over Transferred Assets

27. An agreement that both entitles and obligates the transferor to repurchase or redeem transferred assets from the transferee maintains the transferor's effective control over those assets, and the transfer is therefore to be accounted for as a secured borrowing, if and only if all of the following conditions are met:

a. The assets to be repurchased or redeemed are the same or substantially the same as those transferred (paragraph 28).

b. The transferor is able to repurchase or redeem them on substantially the agreed terms, even in the event of default by the transferee (paragraph 29).

c. The agreement is to repurchase or redeem them before maturity, at a fixed or determinable price.

d. The agreement is entered into concurrently with the transfer.

28. To be substantially the same,[9] the asset that was transferred and the asset that is to be repurchased or redeemed need to have all of the following characteristics:

a. The same primary obligor (except for debt guaranteed by a sovereign government, central bank, government-sponsored enterprise or agency thereof, in which case the guarantor and the terms of the guarantee must be the same)

b. Identical form and type so as to provide the same risks and rights

c. The same maturity (or in the case of mortgage-backed pass-through and pay-through securities have similar remaining weighted-average maturities that result in approximately the same market yield)

d. Identical contractual interest rates

e. Similar assets as collateral

f. The same aggregate unpaid principal amount or principal amounts within accepted "good delivery" standards for the type of security involved.

29. To be able to repurchase or redeem assets on substantially the agreed terms, even in the event of default by the transferee, a transferor must at all times during the contract term have obtained cash or other collateral sufficient to fund substantially all of the cost of purchasing replacement assets from others.

30. A call option or forward contract that entitles the transferor to repurchase, prior to maturity, transferred assets not readily obtainable elsewhere maintains the transferor's effective control, because it would constrain the transferee from exchanging those assets, unless it is only a **cleanup call**.

Measurement of Interests Held after a Transfer of Financial Assets

Assets Obtained and Liabilities Incurred as Proceeds

31. The proceeds from a sale of financial assets consist of the cash and any other assets obtained in the transfer less any liabilities incurred. Any asset obtained that is not an interest in the transferred asset is part of the proceeds from the sale. Any liability incurred, even if it is related to the transferred assets, is a reduction of the proceeds. Any **derivative financial**

---

[8]*Scott's Abridgement of the Law on Trusts,* 156 (Little, Brown and Company, 1960), 296.

[9]In this Statement, the term *substantially the same* is used consistently with the usage of that term in the AICPA Statement of Position 90-3, *Definition of the Term Substantially the Same for Holders of Debt Instruments, as Used in Certain Audit Guides and a Statement of Position.*

instrument entered into concurrently with a transfer of financial assets is either an asset obtained or a liability incurred and part of the proceeds received in the transfer. All proceeds and reductions of proceeds from a sale shall be initially measured at fair value, if practicable.

Illustration—Recording Transfers with Proceeds of Cash, Derivatives, and Other Liabilities

32. Company A sells loans with a fair value of $1,100 and a carrying amount of $1,000. Company A retains no servicing responsibilities but obtains an option to purchase from the transferee the loans sold or similar loans and assumes a recourse obligation to repurchase delinquent loans. Company A agrees to provide the transferee a return at a floating rate of interest even though the contractual terms of the loan are fixed rate in nature (that provision is effectively an interest rate swap).

Fair Values

Cash proceeds	$1,050
Interest rate swap	40
Call option	70
Recourse obligation	60

Net Proceeds

Cash received	$1,050
Plus: Call option	70
Interest rate swap	40
Less: Recourse obligation	(60)
Net proceeds	$1,100

Gain on Sale

Net proceeds	$1,100
Carrying amount of loans sold	1,000
Gain on sale	$ 100

Journal Entry

Cash	1,050	
Interest rate swap	40	
Call option	70	
Loans		1,000
Recourse obligation		60
Gain on sale		100

To record transfer

Retained Interests

33. Other interests in transferred assets—those that are not part of the proceeds of the transfer—are retained interests over which the transferor has not relinquished control. They shall be measured at the date of the transfer by allocating the previous carrying amount between the assets sold, if any, and the retained interests, based on their relative fair values. That procedure shall be applied to all transfers in which interests are retained, even those that do not qualify as sales. Examples of retained interests include securities backed by the transferred assets, undivided interests, servicing assets, and cash reserve accounts and residual interests in securitization trusts. If a transferor cannot determine whether an asset is a retained interest or proceeds from the sale, the asset shall be treated as proceeds from the sale and accounted for in accordance with paragraph 31.

Illustration—Recording Transfers of Partial Interests

34. Company B sells a pro rata nine-tenths interest in loans with a fair value of $1,100 and a carrying amount of $1,000. There is no servicing asset or liability, because Company B estimates that the **benefits of servicing** are just adequate to compensate it for its servicing responsibilities.

Fair Values

Cash proceeds for nine-tenths interest sold $990

One-tenth interest retained [($990 $\div \frac{9}{10}$) $\times \frac{1}{10}$]   110

Carrying Amount Based on Relative Fair Values

	Fair Value	Percentage of Total Fair Value	Allocated Carrying Amount
Nine-tenths interest sold	$ 990	90	$ 900
One-tenth interest retained	110	10	100
Total	$1,100	100	$1,000

Gain on Sale

Net proceeds	$990
Carrying amount of loans sold	900
Gain on sale	$ 90

Journal Entry

Cash	990	
Loans		900
Gain on sale		90
To record transfer		

Servicing Assets and Liabilities

35. Servicing of mortgage loans, credit card receivables, or other financial assets includes, but is not limited to, collecting principal, interest, and escrow payments from borrowers; paying taxes and insurance from escrowed funds; monitoring delinquencies; executing foreclosure if necessary; temporarily investing funds pending distribution; remitting fees to guarantors, trustees, and others providing services; and accounting for and remitting principal and interest payments to the holders of beneficial interests in the financial assets. Servicing is inherent in all financial assets; it becomes a distinct asset or liability only when contractually separated from the underlying assets by sale or securitization of the assets with servicing retained or separate purchase or assumption of the servicing.

36. An entity that undertakes a contract to service financial assets shall recognize either a servicing asset or a servicing liability, unless the transferor securitizes the assets, retains all of the resulting securities, and classifies them as debt securities held-to-maturity in accordance with Statement 115, in which case the servicing asset or liability may be reported together with the asset being serviced. Each sale or securitization with servicing retained or separate purchase or assumption of servicing results in a servicing contract. A servicer of financial assets commonly receives the benefits of servicing—revenues from contractually specified servicing fees, late charges, and other ancillary sources, including "float," all of which it is entitled to receive only if it performs the servicing—and incurs the costs of servicing the assets. Each servicing contract results in a servicing asset or servicing liability. Typically, the benefits of servicing are expected to be more than **adequate compensation** to the servicer for performing the servicing, and the contract results in a servicing asset. However, if the benefits of servicing are not expected to adequately compensate the servicer for performing the servicing, the contract results in a servicing liability.

37. A servicer that recognizes a servicing asset or servicing liability shall account for the contract to service financial assets separately from those assets, as follows:

a. Report servicing assets separately from servicing liabilities in the statement of financial position (paragraph 13).

b. Initially measure servicing assets retained in a sale or securitization of the assets being serviced at their allocated previous carrying amount based on relative fair values, if practicable, at the date of the sale or securitization (paragraphs 10, 33, 34, and 42-46).

c. Initially measure servicing assets purchased or servicing liabilities assumed at fair value (paragraph 13).

d. Initially measure servicing liabilities undertaken in a sale or securitization at fair value, if practicable (paragraphs 11(b), 11(c), and 42-46).

e. Account separately for rights to future interest income from the serviced assets that exceeds contractually specified servicing fees. Those rights are not servicing assets; they are financial assets, effectively interest-only strips to be accounted for in accordance with paragraph 14 of this Statement.

f. Subsequently measure servicing assets by amortizing the amount recognized in proportion to and over the period of estimated net servicing income—the excess of servicing revenues over servicing costs (paragraph 13).

g. Subsequently evaluate and measure impairment of servicing assets as follows:

(1) Stratify servicing assets based on one or more of the predominant risk characteristics of the underlying financial assets. Those characteristics may include financial asset type,[10] size, interest rate, date of origination, term, and geographic location.

(2) Recognize impairment through a valuation allowance for an individual stratum. The amount of impairment recognized shall be the amount by which the carrying amount of servicing assets for a stratum exceeds their fair value. The fair value of servicing assets that have not been recognized shall not be used in the evaluation of impairment.

(3) Adjust the valuation allowance to reflect changes in the measurement of impairment subsequent to the initial measurement of im-

pairment. Fair value in excess of the carrying amount of servicing assets for that stratum, however, shall not be recognized. This Statement does not address when an entity should record a direct write-down of recognized servicing assets (paragraph 13).

h. Subsequently measure servicing liabilities by amortizing the amount recognized in proportion to and over the period of estimated net servicing loss—the excess of servicing costs over servicing revenues. However, if subsequent events have increased the fair value of the liability above the carrying amount, for example, because of significant changes in the amount or timing of actual or expected future cash flows from the cash flows previously projected, the servicer shall revise its earlier estimates and recognize the increased obligation as a loss in earnings (paragraph 13).

38. As indicated above, transferors sometimes agree to take on servicing responsibilities when the future benefits of servicing are not expected to adequately compensate them for performing that servicing. In that circumstance, the result is a servicing liability rather than a servicing asset. For example, if in the transaction illustrated in paragraph 32 the transferor had agreed to service the loans without explicit compensation and it estimated the fair value of that servicing obligation at $50, net proceeds would be reduced to $1,050, gain on sale would be reduced to $50, and the transferor would report a servicing liability of $50.

Illustration—Sale of Receivables with Servicing Retained

39. Company C originates $1,000 of loans that yield 10 percent interest income for their estimated lives of 9 years. Company C sells the $1,000 principal plus the right to receive interest income of 8 percent to another entity for $1,000. Company C will continue to service the loans and the contract stipulates that its compensation for performing the servicing is the right to receive half of the interest income not sold. The remaining half of the interest income not sold is considered an interest-only strip receivable. At the date of the transfer, the fair value of the loans, including servicing, is $1,100. The fair value of the servicing asset is $40.

---

[10]For example, for mortgage loans, financial asset type refers to the various conventional or government guaranteed or insured mortgage loans and adjustable-rate or fixed-rate mortgage loans.

Fair Values

Cash proceeds	$1,000
Servicing asset	40
Interest-only strip receivable	60

Carrying Amount Based on Relative Fair Values

	Fair Value	Percentage of Total Fair Value	Allocated Carrying Amount
Loans sold	$1,000	91	$ 910
Servicing asset	40	3.6	36
Interest-only strip receivable	60	5.4	54
Total	$1,100	100	$1,000

Gain on Sale

Net proceeds	$1,000
Carrying amount of loans sold	910
Gain on sale	$ 90

Journal Entries

Cash	1,000	
Loans		910
Gain on sale		90
To record transfer		

Servicing asset	36	
Interest-only strip receivable	54	
Loans		90
To record servicing asset and interest-only strip receivable		

Interest-only strip receivable	6	
Equity		6
To begin to subsequently measure interest-only strip receivable like an available-for-sale security (paragraph 14)		

40. The previous illustration demonstrates how a transferor would account for a simple sale or securitization in which servicing is retained. Company C might instead transfer the financial assets to a corporation or a trust that is a qualifying special-purpose entity. If the qualifying special-purpose entity securitizes the loans by selling beneficial interests to the public, it in turn becomes a transferor of securities to investors. The qualifying special-purpose entity pays the cash proceeds to the original transferor, which accounts for the transfer as a sale and derecognizes the financial assets assuming that the criteria in paragraph 9 are met. Securitizations often combine the elements shown in paragraphs 32, 34, and 39, as illustrated below.

Illustration—Recording Transfers of Partial Interests with Proceeds of Cash, Derivatives, Other Liabilities, and Servicing

41. Company D originates $1,000 of prepayable loans that yield 10 percent interest income for their

9-year expected lives. Company D sells nine-tenths of the principal plus interest of 8 percent to another entity. Company D will continue to service the loans, and the contract stipulates that its compensation for performing the servicing is the 2 percent of the interest income not sold. Company D retains an option to purchase the loans sold or similar loans and a recourse obligation to repurchase delinquent loans.

Fair Values

Cash proceeds	$900
Call option	70
Recourse obligation	60
Servicing asset	90
One-tenth interest retained	100

Net Proceeds

Cash received	$900
Plus: Call option	70
Less: Recourse obligation	(60)
Net proceeds	$910

Carrying Amount Based on Relative Fair Values

	Fair Value	Percentage of Total Fair Value	Allocated Carrying Amount
Interest sold	$ 910	83	$ 830
Servicing asset	90	8	80
One-tenth interest retained	100	9	90
Total	$1,100	100	$1,000

Gain on Sale

Net proceeds	$910
Carrying amount of loans sold	830
Gain on sale	$ 80

Journal Entries

Cash	900	
Call option	70	
Loans		830
Recourse obligation		60
Gain on sale		80
To record transfer		
Servicing asset	80	
Loans		80
To record servicing asset		

At the time of the transfer, Company D reports its one-tenth retained interest in the loans at its allocated carrying amount of $90.

Fair Value

42. The fair value of an asset (or liability) is the amount at which that asset (or liability) could be bought (or incurred) or sold (or settled) in a current transaction between willing parties, that is, other than in a forced or liquidation sale. Quoted market prices in active markets are the best evidence of fair value and shall be used as the basis for the measurement, if available. If a quoted market price is available, the fair value is the product of the number of trading units times market price.

43. If quoted market prices are not available, the estimate of fair value shall be based on the best information available in the circumstances. The estimate of fair value shall consider prices for similar assets and liabilities and the results of valuation techniques to the extent available in the circumstances. Examples of valuation techniques include the present value of estimated expected future cash flows using a discount rate commensurate with the risks involved, option-pricing models, matrix pricing, option-adjusted spread models, and fundamental analysis. Valuation techniques for measuring financial assets and liabilities and servicing assets and liabilities shall be consistent with the objective of measuring fair value. Those techniques shall incorporate assumptions that market participants would use in their estimates of values, future revenues, and future expenses, including assumptions about interest rates, default, prepayment, and volatility. In measuring **financial liabilities** and servicing liabilities at fair value by discounting estimated future cash flows, an objective is to use discount rates at which those liabilities could be settled in an arm's-length transaction.

44. Estimates of expected future cash flows, if used to estimate fair value, shall be the best estimate based on reasonable and supportable assumptions and projections. All available evidence shall be considered in developing estimates of expected future cash flows. The weight given to the evidence shall be commensurate with the extent to which the evidence can be verified objectively. If a range is estimated for either the amount or timing of possible cash flows, the likelihood of possible outcomes shall be considered in determining the best estimate of future cash flows.

If It Is Not Practicable to Estimate Fair Values

45. If it is not practicable to estimate the fair values of assets, the transferor shall record those assets at zero. If it is not practicable to estimate the fair values of liabilities, the transferor shall recognize no gain on the transaction and shall record those liabilities at the greater of:

a. The excess, if any, of (1) the fair values of assets obtained less the fair values of other liabilities incurred, over (2) the sum of the carrying values of the assets transferred

b. The amount that would be recognized in accordance with FASB Statement No. 5, *Accounting for Contingencies,* as interpreted by FASB Interpretation No. 14, *Reasonable Estimation of the Amount of a Loss.*

Illustration—Recording Transfers If It Is Not Practicable to Estimate a Fair Value

46. Company E sells loans with a carrying amount of $1,000 to another entity for cash plus a call option to repurchase the loans sold or similar loans and incurs a recourse obligation to repurchase any delinquent loans. Company E undertakes to service the transferred assets for the other entity. In Case 1, Company E finds it impracticable to estimate the fair value of the servicing contract, although it is confident that servicing revenues will be more than adequate compensation for performing the servicing. In Case 2, Company E finds it impracticable to estimate the fair value of the recourse obligation.

Fair Values	Case 1	Case 2
Cash proceeds	$1,050	$1,050
Servicing asset	XX*	40
Call option	70	70
Recourse obligation	60	XX*
Fair value of loans transferred	1,100	1,100

*Not practicable to estimate fair value.

Net Proceeds	Case 1	Case 2
Cash received	$1,050	$1,050
Plus: Call option	70	70
Less: Recourse obligation	(60)	XX
Net proceeds	$1,060	$1,120

Carrying Amount Based on Relative Fair Values (Case 1)

	Fair Value	Percentage of Total Fair Value	Allocated Carrying Amount
Loans sold	$1,060	100	$1,000
Servicing asset	0	0	0
Total	$1,060	100	$1,000

Carrying Amount Based on Relative Fair Values (Case 2)

	Fair Value	Percentage of Total Fair Value	Allocated Carrying Amount
Loans sold	$1,120	97	$ 970
Servicing asset	40	3	30
Total	$1,160	100	$1,000

Journal Entries	Case 1		Case 2	
Cash	1,050		1,050	
Servicing asset	0*		30	
Call option	70		70	
Loans		1,000		1,000
Recourse obligation		60		150[†]
Gain on sale		60		0
To record transfer				

*Assets shall be recorded at zero if an estimate of the fair value of the assets is not practicable.
[†]The amount recorded as a liability in this example equals the sum of the known assets less the fair value of the known liabilities, that is, the amount that results in no gain or loss.

Securitizations

47. Financial assets such as mortgage loans, automobile loans, trade receivables, credit card receivables, and other revolving charge accounts are assets commonly transferred in securitizations. Securitizations of mortgage loans may include pools of single-family residential mortgages or other types of real estate mortgage loans, for example, multifamily residential mortgages and commercial property mortgages. Securitizations of loans secured by chattel mortgages on automotive vehicles as well as other equipment (including direct financing or sales-type

leases) also are common. Both financial and nonfinancial assets can be securitized; life insurance policy loans, patent and copyright royalties, and even taxi medallions also have been securitized. But securitizations of nonfinancial assets are outside the scope of this Statement.

48. An originator of a typical securitization (the transferor) transfers a portfolio of financial assets to a special-purpose entity, commonly a trust. In "pass-through" and "pay-through" securitizations, receivables are transferred to the special-purpose entity at the inception of the securitization, and no further

transfers are made; all cash collections are paid to the holders of beneficial interests in the special-purpose entity. In "revolving-period" securitizations, receivables are transferred at the inception and also periodically (daily or monthly) thereafter for a defined period (commonly three to eight years), referred to as the revolving period. During the revolving period, the special-purpose entity uses most of the cash collections to purchase additional receivables from the transferor on prearranged terms.

49. Beneficial interests in the qualifying special-purpose entity are sold to investors and the proceeds are used to pay the transferor for the assets transferred. Those beneficial interests may comprise either a single class having equity characteristics or multiple classes of interests, some having debt characteristics and others having equity characteristics. The cash collected from the portfolio is distributed to the investors and others as specified by the legal documents that established the qualifying special-purpose entity.

50. Pass-through, pay-through, and revolving-period securitizations that meet the criteria in paragraph 9 qualify for sale accounting under this Statement. All financial assets obtained or retained and liabilities incurred by the originator of a securitization that qualifies as a sale shall be recognized and measured as provided in paragraph 11; that includes the implicit forward contract to sell new receivables during a revolving period, which may become valuable or onerous to the transferor as interest rates and other market conditions change.

Revolving-Period Securitizations

51. The value of the forward contract implicit in a revolving-period securitization arises from the difference between the agreed-upon rate of return to investors on their beneficial interests in the trust and current market rates of return on similar investments. For example, if the agreed-upon annual rate of return to investors in a trust is 6 percent, and later market rates of return for those investments increased to 7 percent, the forward contract's value to the transferor (and burden to the investors) would approximate the present value of 1 percent of the amount of the investment for each year remaining in the revolving structure after the receivables already transferred have been collected. If a forward contract to sell receivables is entered into at the market rate, its value at inception may be zero. Changes in the fair value of the forward contract are likely to be greater if

the investors receive a fixed rate than if the investors receive a rate that varies based on changes in market rates.

52. Gain or loss recognition for revolving-period receivables sold to a securitization trust is limited to receivables that exist and have been sold. Recognition of servicing assets or liabilities for revolving-period receivables is similarly limited to the servicing for the receivables that exist and have been transferred. As new receivables are sold, rights to service them become assets or liabilities and are recognized.

53. Revolving-period securitizations may use either a discrete trust, used for a single securitization, or a master trust, used for many securitizations. To achieve another securitization using an existing master trust, a transferor first transfers additional receivables to the trust and then sells additional ownership interests in the trust to investors. Adding receivables to a master trust, in itself, is neither a sale nor a secured borrowing under paragraph 9, because that transfer only increases the transferor's beneficial interest in the trust's assets. A sale does not occur until the transferor receives consideration other than beneficial interests in the transferred assets. Transfers that result in an exchange of cash, that is, either transfers that in essence replace previously transferred receivables that have been collected or sales of beneficial interests to outside investors, are transfers in exchange for consideration other than beneficial interests in the transferred assets and thus are accounted for as sales (if they satisfy all the criteria in paragraph 9) or as secured borrowings.

Isolation of Transferred Assets in Securitizations

54. A securitization, carried out in one transfer or a series of transfers, may or may not isolate the transferred assets beyond the reach of the transferor and its creditors. Whether it does depends on the structure of the securitization transaction taken as a whole, considering such factors as the type and extent of further involvement in arrangements to protect investors from credit and interest rate risks, the availability of other assets, and the powers of bankruptcy courts or other receivers.

55. In certain securitizations, a corporation that, if it failed, would be subject to the U.S. Bankruptcy Code transfers financial assets to a special-purpose trust in exchange for cash. The trust raises that cash by issuing to investors beneficial interests that pass through all cash received from the financial assets, and the

transferor has no further involvement with the trust or the transferred assets. The Board understands that those securitizations generally would be judged as having isolated the assets, because in the absence of any continuing involvement there would be reasonable assurance that the transfer would be found to be a true sale at law that places the assets beyond the reach of the transferor and its creditors, even in bankruptcy or other receivership.

56. In other securitizations, a similar corporation transfers financial assets to a special-purpose entity in exchange for cash and beneficial interests in the transferred assets. That entity raises the cash by issuing to investors commercial paper that gives them a senior interest in cash received from the financial assets. The beneficial interests retained by the transferring corporation represent a junior interest to be reduced by any credit losses on the financial assets in trust. The commercial paper interests are highly rated by credit rating agencies largely because the transferor is highly rated. Depending on facts and circumstances, the Board understands that those "single-step" securitizations often would be judged in the United States as not having isolated the assets, because the nature of the continuing involvement may make it difficult to obtain reasonable assurance that the transfer would be found to be a true sale at law that places the assets beyond the reach of the transferor and its creditors in U.S. bankruptcy (paragraph 83). If the transferor fell into bankruptcy and the transfer was found not to be a true sale at law, investors in the transferred assets might be subjected to an automatic stay that would delay payments due them, and they might have to share in bankruptcy expenses and suffer further losses if the transfer was recharacterized as a secured loan.

57. Still other securitizations use two transfers intended to isolate transferred assets beyond the reach of the transferor and its creditors, even in bankruptcy. In those "two-step" structures:

a. First, the corporation transfers financial assets to a special-purpose corporation that, although wholly owned, is so designed that the possibility that the transferor or its creditors could reclaim the assets is remote. This first transfer is designed to be judged to be a true sale at law, in part because the transferor does not provide "excessive" credit or yield protection to the special-purpose corporation, and the Board understands that transferred assets are likely to be judged beyond the reach of the transferor or the transferor's creditors even in bankruptcy.

b. Second, the special-purpose corporation transfers the assets to a trust, with a sufficient increase in the credit or yield protection on the second transfer (provided by a junior retained beneficial interest or other means) to merit the high credit rating sought by third-party investors who buy senior beneficial interests in the trust. Because of that aspect of its design, that second transfer might not be judged to be a true sale at law and, thus, the transferred assets could at least in theory be reached by a bankruptcy trustee for the special-purpose corporation.

c. However, the special-purpose corporation is designed to make remote the possibility that it would enter bankruptcy, either by itself or by substantive consolidation into a bankruptcy of its parent should that occur. For example, its charter forbids it from undertaking any other business or incurring any liabilities, so that there can be no creditors to petition to place it in bankruptcy. Furthermore, its dedication to a single purpose is intended to make it extremely unlikely, even if it somehow entered bankruptcy, that a receiver under the U.S. Bankruptcy Code could reclaim the transferred assets because it has no other assets to substitute for the transferred assets.

The Board understands that the "two-step" securitizations described above, taken as a whole, generally would be judged under present U.S. law as having isolated the assets beyond the reach of the transferor and its creditors, even in bankruptcy or other receivership.

58. A securitization by an entity subject to a possible receivership under procedures different from the U.S. Bankruptcy Code may isolate transferred assets from the transferor and its creditors even though it uses only one transfer directly to a special-purpose entity that issues beneficial interests to investors and the transferor provides credit or yield protection. For example, the Board understands that assets transferred by a U.S. bank are not subject to an automatic stay under Federal Deposit Insurance Corporation (FDIC) receivership and could only be obtained by the receiver if it makes the investors completely whole, that is, the investors must be paid compensation equivalent to all the economic benefits contained in the transferred assets, including bargained-for yield, before the FDIC could obtain those assets. Those limited powers appear insufficient to place the transferred assets within reach of the receiver. The powers of other receivers for entities not subject to the U.S. Bankruptcy Code, and of bankruptcy trustees in other

jurisdictions, vary considerably, and therefore some receivers may be able to reach transferred financial assets, and others may not.

Sales-Type and Direct Financing Lease Receivables

59. Sales-type and direct financing receivables secured by leased equipment, referred to as gross investment in lease receivables, are made up of two components: minimum lease payments and residual values. Minimum lease payments are requirements for lessees to pay cash to lessors and meet the definition of a financial asset. Thus, transfers of minimum lease payments are subject to the requirements of this Statement. Residual values represent the lessor's estimate of the "salvage" value of the leased equipment at the end of the lease term and may be either guaranteed or unguaranteed; they meet the definition of financial assets *if they are guaranteed*. Thus, transfers of guaranteed residual values also are subject to the requirements of this Statement. Unguaranteed residual values do not meet the definition of financial assets, and transfers of them are not subject to the requirements of this Statement. Transfers of unguaranteed residual values continue to be subject to Statement 13, as amended. Because guaranteed residual value interests are treated as financial assets, increases to their estimated value over the life of the related lease are recognized. Entities selling or securitizing lease financing receivables shall allocate the gross investment in receivables between minimum lease payments and unguaranteed residual values using the individual carrying amounts of those components at the date of transfer. Entities also shall record a servicing asset or liability in accordance with paragraphs 10 and 13, if appropriate.

Illustration—Recording Transfers of Lease Financing Receivables with Residual Values

60. At the beginning of the second year in a 10-year sales-type lease, Company F sells for $505 a nine-tenths interest in the minimum lease payments and retains a one-tenth interest in the minimum lease payments and a 100 percent interest in the unguaranteed residual value of leased equipment. Company F receives no explicit compensation for servicing, but estimates that the other benefits of servicing are just adequate to compensate it for its servicing responsibilities, and hence records no servicing asset or liability. The carrying amounts and related gain computation are as follows:

Carrying Amounts

Minimum lease payments		$ 540
Unearned income related to minimum lease payments		370
Gross investment in minimum lease payments		910
Unguaranteed residual value	$ 30	
Unearned income related to residual value	60	
Gross investment in residual value		90
Total gross investment in financing lease receivable		$1,000

Gain on Sale

Cash received		$ 505
Nine-tenths of carrying amount of gross investment in minimum lease payments	$819	
Nine-tenths of carrying amount of unearned income related to minimum lease payments	333	
Net carrying amount of minimum lease payments sold		486
Gain on sale		$ 19

Journal Entry

Cash	505	
Unearned income	333	
Lease receivable		819
Gain on sale		19

To record sale of nine-tenths of the minimum lease
payments at the beginning of year 2

Securities Lending Transactions

61. Securities lending transactions are initiated by broker-dealers and other financial institutions that need specific securities to cover a short sale or a customer's failure to deliver securities sold. Transferees ("borrowers") of securities generally are required to provide "collateral" to the transferor ("lender") of securities, commonly cash but sometimes other securities or standby letters of credit, with a value slightly higher than that of the securities "borrowed." If the "collateral" is cash, the transferor typically earns a return by investing that cash at rates higher than the rate paid or "rebated" to the transferee. If the "collateral" is other than cash, the transferor typically receives a fee. Securities custodians or other agents commonly carry out securities lending activities on behalf of clients. Because of the protection of "collateral" (typically valued daily and adjusted frequently for changes in the market price of the securities transferred) and the short terms of the transactions, most securities lending transactions in themselves do not impose significant credit risks on either party. Other risks arise from what the parties to the transaction do with the assets they receive. For example, investments made with cash "collateral" impose market and credit risks on the transferor.

62. In some securities lending transactions, the criteria in paragraph 9 are met, including the third criterion. Those transactions shall be accounted for (a) by the transferor as a sale of the "loaned" securities for proceeds consisting of the "collateral"[11] and a forward repurchase commitment and (b) by the transferee as a purchase of the "borrowed" securities in exchange for the "collateral" and a forward resale commitment. During the term of that agreement, the transferor has surrendered control over the securities transferred and the transferee has obtained control over those securities with the ability to sell or transfer them at will. In that case, creditors of the transferor have a claim only to the "collateral" and the forward repurchase commitment.

63. However, many securities lending transactions are accompanied by an agreement that entitles and obligates the transferor to repurchase or redeem the transferred assets before their maturity under which the transferor maintains effective control over those assets (paragraphs 27-30). Those transactions shall be accounted for as secured borrowings, in which cash (or securities that the holder is permitted by contract or custom to sell or repledge) received as "collateral" is considered the amount borrowed, the securities "loaned" are considered pledged as collateral against the cash borrowed, and any "rebate" paid to the transferee of securities is interest on the cash the transferor is considered to have borrowed. Collateral provided in securities lending transactions that are accounted for as secured borrowings shall be reported in the statement of financial position like other collateral, as set forth in paragraph 15.

64. The transferor of securities being "loaned" accounts for cash received (or for securities received that may be sold or repledged and were obtained under agreements that are not subject to repurchase or redemption on short notice, for example, by substitution of other collateral or termination of the contract) in the same way whether the transfer is accounted for as a sale or a secured borrowing. The cash (or securities) received shall be recognized as the transferor's asset—as shall investments made with that cash, even if made by agents or in pools with other securities lenders—along with the obligation to return the cash (or securities).

---

[11]If the "collateral" is a financial asset that the holder is permitted by contract or custom to sell or repledge and the debtor does not have the right and ability to redeem the collateral on short notice, for example, by substituting other collateral or terminating the contract, that financial asset is proceeds of the sale of the "loaned" securities. To the extent that the "collateral" consists of letters of credit or other financial instruments that the holder is not permitted by contract or custom to sell or pledge, a securities lending transaction does not satisfy the sale criteria and is accounted for as a loan of securities by the transferor to the transferee.

Illustration—Securities Lending Transaction Treated as a Secured Borrowing

65. Accounting for a securities lending transaction treated as a secured borrowing:

Facts

Transferor's carrying amount and fair value of security loaned	$1,000
Cash "collateral"	1,020
Transferor's return from investing cash collateral at a 5 percent annual rate	5
Transferor's rebate to the borrower at a 4 percent annual rate	4

The loaned securities cannot be redeemed on short notice, for example, by substitution of other collateral. For simplicity, the fair value of the security is assumed not to change during the 35-day term of the transaction.

Journal Entries for the Transferor

At inception:

Cash	1,020	
Payable under securities loan agreements		1,020
To record the receipt of cash collateral		
Securities loaned to broker	1,000	
Securities		1,000
To reclassify loaned securities that cannot be redeemed on short notice		
Money market instrument	1,020	
Cash		1,020
To record investment of cash collateral		

At conclusion:

Cash	1,025	
Interest		5
Money market instrument		1,020
To record results of investment		
Securities	1,000	
Securities loaned to broker		1,000
To record return of security		
Payable under securities loan agreements	1,020	
Interest ("rebate")	4	
Cash		1,024
To record repayment of cash collateral plus interest		

Journal Entries for the Transferee

At inception:

Receivable under securities loan agreements	1,020	
Cash		1,020
To record transfer of cash collateral		
Securities	1,000	
Obligation to return borrowed securities		1,000
To record receipt of borrowed securities that cannot be redeemed on short notice		

At conclusion:

Obligation to return borrowed securities	1,000	
Securities		1,000
To record the return of securities		
Cash	1,024	
Receivable under securities loan agreements		1,020
Interest revenue ("rebate")		4
To record the receipt of cash collateral and rebate interest		

Repurchase Agreements and "Wash Sales"

66. Government securities dealers, banks, other financial institutions, and corporate investors commonly use repurchase agreements to obtain or use short-term funds. Under those agreements, the transferor ("repo party") transfers a security to a transferee ("repo counterparty" or "reverse party") in exchange for cash[12] and concurrently agrees to reacquire that security at a future date for an amount equal to the cash exchanged plus a stipulated "interest" factor.

67. Repurchase agreements can be effected in a variety of ways. Some repurchase agreements are similar to securities lending transactions in that the transferee has the right to sell or repledge the securities to a third party during the term of the repurchase agreement. In other repurchase agreements, the transferee does not have the right to sell or repledge the securities during the term of the repurchase agreement. For example, in a tri-party repurchase agreement, the transferor transfers securities to an independent third-party custodian that holds the securities during the term of the repurchase agreement. Also, many repurchase agreements are for short terms, often overnight, or have indefinite terms that allow either party to terminate the arrangement on short notice. However, other repurchase agreements are for longer terms, sometimes until the maturity of the transferred asset. Some repurchase agreements call for repurchase of securities that need not be identical to the securities transferred.

68. If the criteria in paragraph 9 are met, including the third criterion, the transferor shall account for the repurchase agreement as a sale of financial assets and a forward repurchase commitment, and the transferee shall account for the agreement as a purchase of financial assets and a forward resale commitment. Other transfers that are accompanied by an agreement to repurchase the transferred assets that shall be accounted for as sales include transfers with agreements to repurchase at maturity and transfers with repurchase agreements in which the transferee has not obtained collateral sufficient to fund substantially all of the cost of purchasing replacement assets.

69. Furthermore, "wash sales" that previously were not recognized if the same financial asset was purchased soon before or after the sale shall be accounted for as sales under this Statement. Unless there is a concurrent contract to repurchase or redeem the transferred financial assets from the transferee, the transferor does not maintain effective control over the transferred assets.

---

[12]Other securities or letters of credit rarely are exchanged in repurchase agreements instead of cash.

70. As with securities lending transactions, under many agreements to repurchase transferred assets before their maturity the transferor maintains effective control over those assets. Repurchase agreements that do not meet all the criteria in paragraph 9 shall be treated as secured borrowings. Fixed-coupon and dollar-roll repurchase agreements, and other contracts under which the securities to be repurchased need not be the same as the securities sold, qualify as borrowings if the return of substantially the same (paragraph 28) securities as those concurrently transferred is assured. Therefore, those transactions shall be accounted for as secured borrowings by both parties to the transfer.

71. If a transferor has transferred securities to an independent third-party custodian, or to a transferee, under conditions that preclude the transferee from selling or repledging the assets during the term of the repurchase agreement (as in most tri-party repurchase agreements), the transferor has not surrendered control over those assets. In those circumstances, the transferee does not acquire the right to sell or repledge the securities during the term of the repurchase agreement; therefore, it does not have access to the benefits embodied in those assets. The transferee shall not record those assets as its own, nor shall the transferor derecognize those assets.

Loan Syndications

72. Borrowers often borrow amounts greater than any one lender is willing to lend. Therefore, it is common for groups of lenders to jointly fund those loans. That may be accomplished by a syndication under which several lenders share in lending to a single borrower, but each lender loans a specific amount to the borrower and has the right to repayment from the borrower.

73. Each lender in the syndication shall account for the amounts it is owed by the borrower. Repayments by the borrower may be made to a lead lender that then distributes the collections to the other lenders of the syndicate. In those circumstances, the lead lender is simply functioning as a servicer and, therefore, shall not recognize the aggregate loan as an asset.

Loan Participations

74. Groups of banks or other entities also may jointly fund large borrowings through loan participations in which a single lender makes a large loan to a borrower and subsequently transfers undivided interests in the loan to other entities.

75. Transfers by the originating lender may take the legal form of either assignments or participations. The transfers are usually on a nonrecourse basis, and the transferor ("originating lender") continues to service the loan. The transferee ("participating entity") may or may not have the right to sell or transfer its participation during the term of the loan, depending upon the terms of the participation agreement.

76. If the loan participation agreement gives the transferee the right to pledge or exchange those participations and the other criteria in paragraph 9 are met, the transfers to the transferee shall be accounted for by the transferor as sales of financial assets. A transferor's right of first refusal on a bona fide offer from a third party, a requirement to obtain the transferor's permission that shall not be unreasonably withheld, or a prohibition on sale to the transferor's competitor is a limitation on the transferee's rights but presumptively does not constrain a transferee from exercising its right to pledge or exchange. However, if the loan participation agreement constrains the transferees from pledging or exchanging their participations, the transferor has not relinquished control over the loan and shall account for the transfers as secured borrowings.

Banker's Acceptances and Risk Participations in Them

77. Banker's acceptances provide a way for a bank to finance a customer's purchase of goods from a vendor for periods usually not exceeding six months. Under an agreement between the bank, the customer, and the vendor, the bank agrees to pay the customer's liability to the vendor upon presentation of specified documents that provide evidence of delivery and acceptance of the purchased goods. The principal document is a draft or bill of exchange drawn by the customer that the bank stamps to signify its "acceptance" of the liability to make payment on the draft on its due date.

78. Once the bank accepts a draft, the customer is liable to repay the bank at the time the draft matures. The bank recognizes a receivable from the customer and a liability for the acceptance it has issued to the vendor. The accepted draft becomes a negotiable financial instrument. The vendor typically sells the accepted draft at a discount either to the accepting bank or in the marketplace.

79. A risk participation is a contract between the accepting bank and a participating bank in which the

participating bank agrees, in exchange for a fee, to reimburse the accepting bank in the event that the accepting bank's customer fails to honor its liability to the accepting bank in connection with the banker's acceptance. The participating bank becomes a guarantor of the credit of the accepting bank's customer.

80. An accepting bank that obtains a risk participation shall not derecognize the liability for the banker's acceptance because the accepting bank is still primarily liable to the holder of the banker's acceptance even though it benefits from a guarantee of reimbursement by a participating bank. The accepting bank shall not derecognize the receivable from the customer because it controls the benefits inherent in that receivable and it is still entitled to receive payment from the customer. The accepting bank shall, however, record the guarantee purchased, and the participating bank shall record a liability for the guarantee issued.

Illustration—Banker's Acceptance with a Risk Participation

81. An accepting bank assumes a liability to pay a customer's vendor and obtains a risk participation from another bank. The details of the banker's acceptance are provided below:

Facts

Face value of the draft provided to vendor	$1,000
Term of the draft provided to vendor	90 days
Commission with an annual rate of 10 percent	25
Fee paid for risk participation	10

Journal Entries for Accepting Bank

At issuance of acceptance:

Receivable from customer	1,000	
Cash	25	
Time draft payable to vendor		1,000
Deferred acceptance commission revenue		25

At purchase of risk participation from a participating bank:

Guarantee purchased	10	
Cash		10

Upon presentation of the accepted time draft:

Time draft payable to vendor	1,000	
Deferred acceptance commission revenue	25	
Cash		1,000
Acceptance commission revenue		25

Upon collection from the customer (or the participating bank, if the customer defaults):

Cash	1,000	
Guarantee expense	10	
Receivable from customer		1,000
Guarantee purchased		10

Journal Entries for Participating Bank

Upon issuing the risk participation:

Cash	10	
Guarantee liability		10

Upon payment by the customer to the accepting bank:

Guarantee liability	10	
Guarantee revenue		10

OR:

In the event of total default by the customer:

Guarantee loss	990	
Guarantee liability	10	
Cash (paid to accepting bank)		1,000

Factoring Arrangements

82. Factoring arrangements are a means of discounting accounts receivable on a nonrecourse, notification basis. Accounts receivable are sold outright, usually to a transferee (the factor) that assumes the full risk of collection, without recourse to the transferor in the event of a loss. Debtors are directed to send payments to the transferee. Factoring arrangements that meet the criteria in paragraph 9 shall be accounted for as sales of financial assets because the transferor surrenders control over the receivables to the factor.

Transfers of Receivables with Recourse

83. In a transfer of receivables with recourse, the transferor provides the transferee with full or limited recourse. The transferor is obligated under the terms of the recourse provision to make payments to the transferee or to repurchase receivables sold under certain circumstances, typically for defaults up to a specified percentage. The effect of a recourse provision on the application of paragraph 9 may vary by jurisdiction. In some jurisdictions, transfers with full recourse may not place transferred assets beyond the reach of the transferor and its creditors, but transfers with limited recourse may. A transfer of receivables with recourse shall be accounted for as a sale, with the proceeds of the sale reduced by the fair value of the recourse obligation, if the criteria in paragraph 9 are met. Otherwise, a transfer of receivables with recourse shall be accounted for as a secured borrowing.

Extinguishments of Liabilities

84. If a creditor releases a debtor from primary obligation on the condition that a third party assumes the obligation and that the original debtor becomes secondarily liable, that release extinguishes the original debtor's liability. However, in those circumstances, whether or not explicit consideration was paid for that guarantee, the original debtor becomes a guarantor. As a guarantor, it shall recognize a guarantee obligation in the same manner as would a guarantor that had never been primarily liable to that creditor, with due regard for the likelihood that the third party will carry out its obligations. The guarantee obligation shall be initially measured at fair value, and that amount reduces the gain or increases the loss recognized on extinguishment.

Appendix B

BACKGROUND INFORMATION AND BASIS FOR CONCLUSIONS

CONTENTS

Appendix B

BACKGROUND INFORMATION AND BASIS FOR CONCLUSIONS

Introduction

85. This appendix summarizes considerations that were deemed significant by Board members in reaching the conclusions in this Statement. It includes reasons for accepting certain approaches and rejecting others. Individual Board members gave greater weight to some factors than to others.

Background

86. In recent years, transfers of financial assets in which the transferor has some continuing involvement with the transferred assets or with the transferee have grown in volume, variety, and complexity. Those transfers raise the issues of whether transferred financial assets should be considered to be sold and a related gain or loss recorded, whether the assets should be considered to be collateral for borrowings, or whether the transfer should not be recognized.

87. A transferor may sell financial assets and receive in exchange cash or other assets that are unrelated to the assets sold so that the transferor has no continuing involvement with the assets sold. Alternatively, an entity may borrow money and pledge financial assets as collateral, or a transferor may engage in any of a variety of transactions that transfer financial assets to another entity with the transferor having some continuing involvement with the assets transferred. Examples of continuing involvement are recourse or guarantee obligations, servicing, agreements to repurchase or redeem, and put or call options on the assets transferred.

88. Many transactions disaggregate financial assets into separate components by creating undivided interests in pools of financial assets that frequently reflect multiple participations (often referred to as tranches) in a single pool. The components created may later be recombined to restore the original assets or may be combined with other financial assets to create still different assets.

89. An entity also may enter into transactions that change the characteristics of an asset that the entity continues to hold. An entity may sell part of an asset, or an undivided interest in the asset, and retain part of the asset. In some cases, it has not been clear what the accounting should be.

90. An entity may settle a liability by transferring assets to a creditor and obtaining an unconditional release from the obligation. Alternatively, an entity may arrange for others to settle or set aside assets to settle a liability later. Those alternative arrangements have raised issues about when a liability is extinguished.

91. The Board previously provided guidance for two specific types of transfers of financial assets in FASB Statement No. 77, *Reporting by Transferors for Transfers of Receivables with Recourse,* and in FASB Technical Bulletin No. 85-2, *Accounting for Collateralized Mortgage Obligations (CMOs).* Confusion and inconsistency in accounting practices developed because the provisions of those two pronouncements provided seemingly conflicting guidance. In practice, if an entity sold financial assets to a special-purpose entity that issued debt securities, the guidance under Technical Bulletin 85-2 would be applied, and if any of those securities were obtained by the seller, the transaction would be accounted for as a borrowing. However, if the interests issued by the special-purpose entity were designated as participations instead of debt securities, the guidance in Statement 77 would be applied, and the transaction would be accounted for as a sale even if the seller retained recourse on some of the participations. Further, accounting for other types of transfers, whether developed by analogy to Statement 77 or Technical Bulletin 85-2, in industry practices codified in various AICPA audit and accounting Guides, in consensuses of the Emerging Issues Task Force (EITF), or in other ways, added to the confusion and inconsistency.

92. FASB Statement No. 76, *Extinguishment of Debt,* established accounting practices that (a) treat liabilities that are not fully settled as if they had been extinguished and (b) derecognize assets transferred to a trust even though the assets continue to benefit the transferor. Some criticized Statement 76 as being inconsistent with Statement 77; others disagreed.

93. The Board decided that it was necessary to reconsider Statements 76 and 77, Technical Bulletin 85-2, and other guidance and to develop new standards for transfers of financial assets and extinguishments of liabilities.

94. The Board added a project to its agenda in May 1986 to address those and other problems in accounting for financial instruments and off-balance-sheet financing. This Statement, as part of that

project, focuses on accounting for transfers and servicing of financial assets and extinguishments of liabilities. The Financial Instruments Task Force, which was formed in January 1989, assisted in the preparation of a Discussion Memorandum on those issues and advised the Board in its deliberations. The FASB Discussion Memorandum, *Recognition and Measurement of Financial Instruments,* was issued in November 1991. The Board received 96 comment letters on the Discussion Memorandum. During 1994 and 1995, the Board discussed issues about transfers and servicing of financial assets and extinguishments of liabilities at numerous public meetings. The Financial Instruments Task Force reviewed drafts of the proposed Statement and discussed it with the Board at a public meeting in February 1995. The Financial Accounting Standards Advisory Council discussed a draft of the proposed Statement and advised the Board at public meetings. The Board also received requests from constituents to discuss issues about credit card securitizations and securities lending transactions and repurchase agreements. The Board met with constituents interested in those issues at public meetings in November 1994 and April 1995.

95. In October 1995, the Board issued an Exposure Draft, *Accounting for Transfers and Servicing of Financial Assets and Extinguishments of Liabilities.* The Board received 112 comment letters on the Exposure Draft, and 24 individuals and organizations presented their views at a public hearing held in February 1996. In addition, 10 enterprises participated in limited field-testing of the provisions of the Exposure Draft. The comments and test results were considered by the Board during its redeliberations of the issues addressed by the Exposure Draft in public meetings in 1996. The Financial Instruments Task Force reviewed a draft of the final Statement. This Statement is a result of those Board meetings and deliberations.

Benefits and Costs

96. The Board's mission statement charges the Board to determine that a proposed standard will fill a significant need and that the costs it imposes will be justified in relation to the overall benefits.

97. Previous practices in accounting for transfers of financial assets were inconsistent about the circumstances that distinguish sales from secured borrowings. The result was confusion on the part of both users and preparers of financial statements. This Statement eliminates that inconsistency and should reduce that confusion by distinguishing sales from secured borrowings based on the underlying contractual commitments and customs that determine substance. Much of the information needed to implement the accounting required by this Statement is substantially the same as that required for previous accounting and, therefore, should be available. Some of the information may not have been collected in accounting systems but is commonly obtained by sellers and buyers for use in negotiating transactions. Although there will be one-time costs for systems changes needed to apply the accounting required by this Statement, the benefits in terms of more credible, consistent, and understandable information will be ongoing.

98. In addition, in developing this Statement, the Board considered how the costs incurred to implement the requirements of this Statement could be minimized by, for example, (a) not requiring retroactive application of the initial measurement provisions of this Statement to existing servicing rights and excess servicing receivables, (b) carrying over without change the subsequent measurement (amortization and impairment) provisions of FASB Statement No. 122, *Accounting for Mortgage Servicing Rights,* which mortgage servicers have recently implemented, (c) not requiring allocation of previous carrying amounts of assets partially sold based on relative fair values at acquisition, but rather at the date of transfer, and (d) not requiring additional disclosures for transfers such as securitizations beyond those currently presented within the financial statements. The Board is confident that the benefits derived from the accounting required by this Statement will outweigh the costs of implementation.

Approaches Considered

99. The Board noted that the most difficult questions about accounting for transfers of financial assets concern the circumstances in which it is appropriate to remove previously recognized financial assets from the statement of financial position and to recognize gain or loss. One familiar approach to those questions views each financial asset as a unit that should not be derecognized until the risks and rewards that are embodied in that asset have been surrendered. Variations on that approach attempt to choose which risks and rewards are most critical and whether all or some major portion of those risks and rewards must be surrendered to allow derecognition.

100. In addition to reviewing U.S. accounting literature, the Board reviewed the approach described

by the International Accounting Standards Committee (IASC) in its Proposed International Accounting Standard, *Financial Instruments,* Exposure Draft E40 (1992), later revised as Exposure Draft E48 (1994). In E40, derecognition of financial assets and liabilities would have been permitted only upon the transfer to others of the underlying risks and rewards, presumably all risks and rewards. That approach could have resulted in an entity's continuing to recognize assets even though it had surrendered control over the assets to a successor entity. The approach in E40 was similar to that taken in Technical Bulletin 85-2. The Board concluded that the approaches proposed in E40 and provided in Technical Bulletin 85-2 were unsatisfactory because the result does not faithfully represent the effects of the transfer of assets and because of the potential for inconsistencies.

101. In response to comments received on E40, the IASC proposal was revised in E48 to require the transfer of *substantially all* risks and rewards. That modification did not overcome the inconsistency noted in paragraphs 97 and 100 of this Statement and added the prospect of difficulties in application because of the need to identify, measure, and weigh in the balance each of possibly many and varied risks and rewards embodied in a particular financial asset. The number of different risks and rewards would vary depending on the definitions used. Questions would arise about whether each identified risk and reward should be substantially surrendered to allow derecognition, whether all risks should be aggregated separately from all rewards, and whether risks and rewards should somehow be offset and then combined for evaluation. That modification also might lead to wide variations in practice depending on how various entities interpreted *substantially all* in the necessarily subjective evaluation of the aggregated, offset, and combined risks and rewards. Moreover, viewing each financial asset as an indivisible unit is contrary to the growing practice in financial markets of disaggregating individual financial assets or pools of financial assets into components. The IASC is continuing to study that issue in its financial instruments project.

102. The Board also noted that application of a risks-and-rewards approach for derecognizing financial assets would be highly dependent on the sequence of transactions leading to their acquisition. For example,

if Entity A initially acquired an undivided subordinated interest in a pool of financial assets, it would recognize that subordinated interest as a single asset. If, on the other hand, Entity B initially acquired a pool of financial assets identical to the pool in which Entity A participates, then sold a senior interest in the pool and continued to hold a subordinated interest identical to the undivided interest held by Entity A, Entity B might be judged under a risks-and-rewards approach to have retained substantially all the risks of the entire pool. Thus, Entity B would carry in its statement of financial position the entire pool of financial assets as well as an obligation equal to the proceeds from the sale of the undivided senior interest, while Entity A would report its identical position quite differently. Those accounting results would disregard one of the fundamental tenets of the Board's conceptual framework; that is, "accountants must not disguise real differences nor create false differences."[13]

103. The Board also considered the approach required by the United Kingdom's Accounting Standards Board in Financial Reporting Standard No. 5, *Reporting the Substance of Transactions,* a variation of the risks-and-rewards approach that requires the surrender of substantially all risks and rewards for derecognition of financial assets but permits, in limited circumstances, the use of a *linked presentation.* Use of the linked presentation is restricted to circumstances in which an entity borrows funds to be repaid from the proceeds of pledged financial assets, any excess proceeds go to the borrower, and the lender has no recourse to other assets of the borrower. In those circumstances, the pledged assets remain on the borrower's statement of financial position, but the unpaid borrowing is reported as a deduction from the pledged assets rather than as a liability; no gain or loss is recognized. That approach had some appeal to the Board because it would have highlighted significant information about transactions that many believe have characteristics of both sales and secured borrowings. The Board observed, however, that the linked presentation would not have dealt with many of the problems created by the risks-and-rewards approach. Further, the Board concluded that it is not appropriate for an entity to offset restricted assets against a liability or to derecognize a liability merely because assets are dedicated to its repayment, as discussed in paragraphs 218-221.

---

[13]FASB Concepts Statement No. 2, *Qualitative Characteristics of Accounting Information,* par. 119.

104. Statement 77 based the determination of whether to derecognize receivables on transfer of control instead of on evaluation of risks and rewards. This Statement takes a similar approach. However, Statement 77 was narrowly focused on sales of receivables with recourse and did not address other transfers of financial assets. Also, the derecognition of receivables under that Statement could depend on the sequence of transactions that led to their acquisition or on whether any options were involved. The Board concluded that simply superseding Technical Bulletin 85-2 and allowing Statement 77 to remain in effect would not have dealt adequately with the issues about transfers of financial assets.

105. Statement 76 followed a risks-and-rewards approach in requiring that (a) it be probable that a debtor would not be required to make future payments with respect to the debt under any guarantees and (b) an in-substance defeasance trust be restricted to owning only monetary assets that are risk free with cash flows that approximately coincide, as to timing and amount, with the scheduled interest and principal payments on the debt being extinguished. The Board concluded (paragraphs 218-221) that that approach was inconsistent with the financial-components approach that focuses on control developed in this Statement. As a result, the Board decided to supersede Statement 76 but to carry forward those of its criteria that could be modified to conform to the financial-components approach.

106. The considerations discussed in paragraphs 99-105 led the Board to seek an alternative to the risks-and-rewards approach and variations to that approach.

Objectives of the Financial-Components Approach

107. The Board concluded that it was necessary to develop an approach that would be responsive to current developments in the financial markets to achieve consistent accounting for transfers and servicing of financial assets and extinguishments of liabilities. That approach—the financial-components approach—is designed to:

a. Be consistent with the way participants in the financial markets deal with financial assets, including the combination and separation of components of those assets

b. Reflect the economic consequences of contractual provisions underlying financial assets and liabilities

c. Conform to the FASB conceptual framework.

108. The approach analyzes a transfer of a financial asset by examining the component assets (controlled economic benefits) and liabilities (obligations for probable future sacrifices of economic benefits) that exist after the transfer. Each party to the transfer recognizes the assets and liabilities that it controls after the transfer and no longer recognizes the assets and liabilities that were surrendered or extinguished in the transfer. That approach has some antecedents in existing accounting guidance, for example, in EITF Issue No. 88-11, "Allocation of Recorded Investment When a Loan or Part of a Loan Is Sold." The Board identified the concepts set forth in paragraphs 109-111 as an appropriate basis for the financial-components approach.

Conceptual Basis for the Financial-Components Approach

109. FASB Concepts Statement No. 6, *Elements of Financial Statements,* states the following about assets:

> Assets are probable future economic benefits obtained or controlled by a particular entity as a result of past transactions or events. [Paragraph 25, footnote reference omitted.]
> *Every asset is an asset of some entity; moreover, no asset can simultaneously be an asset of more than one entity,* although a particular physical thing or other agent [e.g., contractual rights and obligations] that provides future economic benefit may provide separate benefits to two or more entities at the same time. . . . To have an asset, an entity must control future economic benefit to the extent that it can benefit from the asset and generally can deny or regulate access to that benefit by others, for example, by permitting access only at a price.
> Thus, *an asset of an entity is the future economic benefit that the entity can control and thus can, within limits set by the nature of the benefit or the entity's right to it, use as it pleases.* The entity having an asset is the one that can exchange it, use it to produce goods or services, exact a price for others' use of it,

use it to settle liabilities, hold it, or perhaps distribute it to owners.

The definition of assets focuses primarily on the future economic benefit to which an entity has access and only secondarily on the physical things and other agents that provide future economic benefits. *Many physical things and other agents are in effect bundles of future economic benefits that can be unbundled in various ways, and two or more entities may have different future economic benefits from the same agent at the same time or the same continuing future economic benefit at different times.* For example, two or more entities may have undivided interests in a parcel of land. Each has a right to future economic benefit that may qualify as an asset under the definition in paragraph 25, even though the right of each is subject at least to some extent to the rights of the other(s). Or, one entity may have the right to the interest from an investment, while another has the right to the principal. [Paragraphs 183-185; emphasis added.]

110. Concepts Statement 6 states the following about liabilities:

Liabilities are probable future sacrifices of economic benefits arising from present obligations of a particular entity to transfer assets or provide services to other entities in the future as a result of past transactions or events. [Paragraph 35, footnote references omitted.]

Most liabilities are obligations of only one entity at a time. Some liabilities are shared—for example, two or more entities may be "jointly and severally liable" for a debt or for the unsatisfied liabilities of a partnership. But most liabilities bind a single entity, and those that bind two or more entities are commonly ranked rather than shared. For example, *a primary debtor and a guarantor may both be obligated for a debt, but they do not have the same obligation—the guarantor must pay only if the primary debtor defaults and thus has a contingent or secondary obligation,* which ranks lower than that of the primary debtor.

Secondary, and perhaps even lower ranked, obligations may qualify as liabilities under the definition in paragraph 35, but recognition considerations are highly significant in deciding whether they should for-

mally be included in financial statements because of the effects of uncertainty (paragraphs 44-48). For example, the probability that a secondary or lower ranked obligation will actually have to be paid must be assessed to apply the definition. [Paragraphs 204 and 205; emphasis added.]

111. Financial assets and liabilities are assets and liabilities that qualify as financial instruments as defined in paragraph 3 of FASB Statement No. 107, *Disclosures about Fair Value of Financial Instruments:*

A financial instrument is defined as cash, evidence of an ownership interest in an entity, or a contract that both:

a. Imposes on one entity a contractual obligation (1) to deliver cash or another financial instrument to a second entity or (2) to exchange other financial instruments on potentially unfavorable terms with the second entity

b. Conveys to that second entity a contractual right (1) to receive cash or another financial instrument from the first entity or (2) to exchange other financial instruments on potentially favorable terms with the first entity. [Footnote references omitted.]

112. Based on the concepts and definitions cited in paragraphs 109-111, the Board concluded that the key to applying the financial-components approach can be summarized as follows:

a. The economic benefits provided by a financial asset (generally, the right to future cash flows) are derived from the contractual provisions that underlie that asset, and the entity that controls those benefits should recognize them as its asset.

b. A financial asset should be considered sold and therefore should be derecognized if it is transferred and control is surrendered.

c. A transferred financial asset should be considered pledged as collateral to secure an obligation of the transferor (and therefore should not be derecognized) if the transferor has not surrendered control of the financial asset.

d. Each liability should be recognized by the entity that is primarily liable and, accordingly, an entity that guarantees another entity's obligation should recognize only its obligation to perform on the guarantee.

e. The recognition of financial assets and liabilities should not be affected by the sequence of transactions that led to their existence unless as a result of those transactions the transferor maintains effective control over a transferred asset.

f. Transferors and transferees should account symmetrically for transfers of financial assets.

113. Most respondents to the Exposure Draft generally supported the financial-components approach, especially as it applies to securitization transactions.

114. The concepts underlying the financial-components approach could be applied by analogy to accounting for transfers of nonfinancial assets and thus could result in accounting that differs significantly from that required by existing standards and practices. However, the Board believes that financial and nonfinancial assets have significantly different characteristics, and it is not clear to what extent the financial-components approach is applicable to nonfinancial assets. Nonfinancial assets have a variety of operational uses, and management skill plays a considerable role in obtaining the greatest value from those assets. In contrast, financial assets have no operational use. They may facilitate operations, and financial assets may be the principal "product" offered by some entities. However, the promise embodied in a financial asset is governed by contract. Once the contract is established, management skill plays a limited role in the entity's ability to realize the value of the instrument. Furthermore, the Board believes that attempting to extend this Statement to transfers of nonfinancial assets would unduly delay resolving the issues for transfers of financial assets, because of the significant differences between financial assets and nonfinancial assets and because of the significant unresolved recognition and measurement issues posed by those differences. For those reasons, the Board concluded that existing accounting practices for transfers of nonfinancial assets should not be changed at this time. The Board further concluded that transfers of servicing assets and transfers of property subject to operating leases are not within the scope of this Statement because they are nonfinancial assets.

115. The following paragraphs discuss the application of the concepts and principles described in paragraphs 109-114. First, circumstances that require derecognition of transferred assets and recognition of assets and liabilities received in exchange are discussed in the paragraphs about sales of financial assets, transfers to special-purpose entities, and other transfers (paragraphs 116-175). Then, the measurement of assets controlled and liabilities incurred (paragraphs 176-214) and subsequent measurement (paragraphs 215-217) are discussed. Finally, extinguishments of liabilities are discussed (paragraphs 218-224).

Sales of Financial Assets

116. If an entity transfers financial assets, surrenders control of those assets to a successor entity, and has no continuing involvement with those assets, accounting for the transaction as a sale and derecognizing the assets and recognizing the related gain or loss is not controversial. However, accounting for transfers of financial assets has been controversial and inconsistent in circumstances in which an entity transfers only a partial interest in a financial asset or has some other continuing involvement with the transferred asset or the transferee.

117. Under the financial-components approach, the accounting for a transfer is based on whether a transferor surrenders control of financial assets. Paragraph 3 of Statement 77 states, "This Statement establishes standards of financial accounting and reporting by transferors for transfers of receivables with recourse that *purport to be sales* of receivables" (emphasis added). The Board believes that, while it may have some significance at law, a more exacting test than whether a transaction purports to be a sale is needed to conclude that control has been surrendered in a manner that is consistent with the definitions in Concepts Statement 6. The Board concluded that a sale occurs only if control has been surrendered to another entity or group of entities and that surrender of control depends on whether (a) transferred assets have been isolated from the transferor, (b) transferees have obtained the right to pledge or exchange either the transferred assets or beneficial interests in the transferred assets, and (c) the transferor does not maintain effective control over the transferred assets through an agreement to repurchase or redeem them before their maturity.

118. The Board developed its criterion that transferred assets must be isolated—put presumptively beyond the reach of the transferor and its creditors, even in bankruptcy or other receivership (paragraph 9(a))—in large part with reference to securitization practices. Credit rating agencies and investors in securitized assets pay close attention to (a) the possibility of bankruptcy or other receivership of the

transferor, its affiliates, or the special-purpose entity, even though that possibility may seem unlikely given the present credit standing of the transferor, and (b) what might happen in such a receivership, because those are major areas of risk for them. If certain receivers can reclaim securitized assets, investors will suffer a delay in payments due them and may be forced to accept a pro rata settlement. Credit rating agencies and investors commonly demand transaction structures that minimize those possibilities and sometimes seek assurances from attorneys about whether entities can be forced into receivership, what the powers of a receiver might be, and whether the transaction structure would withstand receivers' attempts to reach the securitized assets in ways that would harm investors. Unsatisfactory structures or assurances commonly result in credit ratings that are no higher than those for the transferor's liabilities and in lower prices for transferred assets.

119. Because legal isolation of transferred assets has substance, the Board decided that it could and should serve as an important part of the basis for determining whether a sale should be recognized. Some constituents expressed concern about the feasibility of an accounting standard based on those legal considerations, but the Board concluded that having to consider only the evidence available should make that requirement workable.

120. Respondents to the Exposure Draft raised several questions about the application of the isolation criterion in paragraph 9(a) to existing securitization structures. The questions included whether it was necessary to consider separately the accounting by the first-tier special-purpose entity, whose transfer to the second-tier trust taken by itself might not satisfy the isolation test. After considering those comments and consulting with respondents who specialize in the structure of securitization transactions, the Board concluded that related language in Appendix A should be revised to explain that that criterion can be satisfied either by a single transaction or by a series of transactions considered as a whole. As discussed in paragraphs 54-58, the Board understands that the series of transactions in a typical two-tier structure taken as a whole may satisfy the isolation test because the design of the structure achieves isolation.

121. The Board understands that a one-tier structure with significant continuing involvement by a transferor subject to the U.S. Bankruptcy Code might not satisfy the isolation test, because a trustee in bankruptcy has substantial powers that could alter

amounts that investors might receive and thus it may be difficult to conclude that control has been relinquished. Some respondents argued that a one-tier structure with continuing involvement generally should be adequate if the transferor's credit rating is sufficiently high that the chance of sudden bankruptcy is remote. The Board did not accept that view because isolation should not depend on the credit standing of the transferor. The Board believes that a one-tier structure may satisfy the isolation test despite continuing involvement if the transferor is subject to receivership by receivers with more limited powers over transferred assets, for example, the FDIC. The Board understands that the FDIC, unlike a receiver in bankruptcy, cannot impose an automatic stay. However, it can terminate the transaction by paying investors compensation equivalent to all principal and interest earned to date, in effect making the investors whole.

122. The second criterion (paragraph 9(b)) for a transfer to be a sale focuses on whether the transferee has the right—free of conditions that constrain it from taking advantage of that right—to pledge or exchange the transferred assets. That criterion is consistent with the idea that the entity that has an asset is the one that can use it in the various ways set forth in Concepts Statement 6, paragraph 184 (quoted in paragraph 109 of this Statement). A transferee may be able to use a transferred asset in some of those ways but not in others. Therefore, establishing criteria for determining whether control has been relinquished to a transferee necessarily depends in part on identifying which ways of using the kind of asset transferred are the decisive ones. In the case of transfers of financial assets, the transferee holds the assets, but that is not necessarily decisive because the economic benefits of financial assets consist primarily of future cash inflows. The Board concluded that the ways of using assets that are important in determining whether a transferee holding a financial asset controls it are the ability to exchange it or pledge it as collateral and thus obtain all or most of the cash inflows that are the primary economic benefits of financial assets. As discussed in paragraph 127, if the transferee is a special-purpose entity, the ultimate holders of the assets are the beneficial interest holders, and the important rights concern their ability to exchange or pledge their interests.

123. The Exposure Draft proposed that a transferee be required to have the right—free of transferor-imposed conditions—to pledge or exchange the transferred assets for a transfer to qualify as a sale.

Respondents to the Exposure Draft observed that some transferor-imposed conditions may not indicate that the transferor retains control over the assets transferred. The respondents suggested that some conditions are imposed for business or competitiveness purposes, not to keep control over future economic benefits of the transferred assets, and that those conditions should not preclude a transfer from being accounted for as a sale. Other respondents noted that not all conditions that might limit a transferee's ability to take advantage of a right to pledge or exchange transferred assets were necessarily imposed by the transferor. The Board decided that the criterion should not be restricted to being transferor imposed and that some conditions, described in paragraph 25, should not disqualify a transaction, so long as those conditions do not constrain the transferee from taking advantage of its right to pledge or exchange the transferred assets.

Settlement Date and Trade Date Accounting

124. Many transfers of financial assets have been and, under this Statement, will be recognized at the settlement date. During its redeliberations, the Board discussed the implications of this Statement on trade date accounting for certain securities transactions, and concluded that this project did not set out to address that issue. Therefore, the Board decided that this Statement should not modify generally accepted accounting principles, including FASB Statement No. 35, *Accounting and Reporting by Defined Benefit Pension Plans,* and AICPA Statements of Position and audit and accounting Guides for certain industries, that require accounting at the trade date for certain contracts to purchase or sell securities. The Board observes that the AICPA's Securities Contracts Task Force is currently developing a proposed Statement of Position that would clarify for all entities the date at which to recognize (or derecognize) contracts to purchase or sell securities in (or from) the statement of financial position.

Transfers to Qualifying Special-Purpose Entities, Including Securitizations

125. Many transfers of financial assets are to qualifying special-purpose entities of the type described in paragraph 26. After those transfers, the qualifying special-purpose entity holds legal title to the transferred assets but does not have the right to pledge or exchange the transferred assets. Rather, the activities of the qualifying special-purpose entity are limited to carrying out the provisions of the legal documents that established it. One significant purpose of those limitations on activities often is to make remote the possibility that a qualifying special-purpose entity could enter bankruptcy or other receivership, even if the transferor were to enter receivership.

126. Some respondents asked whether the special-purpose entity criteria apply to entities formed for purposes other than transfers of financial assets. The Board decided that the description of a special-purpose entity in paragraph 26 is restrictive. Transfers to entities that meet all of the conditions in paragraph 26 qualify for sale accounting under paragraph 9 of this Statement. Other entities with some similar characteristics also might be broadly described as "special-purpose." For example, an entity might be formed for the purpose of holding specific nonfinancial assets and liabilities or carrying on particular commercial activities. The Board decided that those entities are not qualifying special-purpose entities as the term is used in this Statement, and the accounting for transfers of financial assets to special-purpose entities should not be extended to transfers to any entity that does not satisfy all of the conditions in paragraph 26.

127. Qualifying special-purpose entities issue beneficial interests of various kinds—variously characterized as debt, participations, residual interests, and otherwise—as required by the provisions of those agreements. Holders of beneficial interests in the qualifying special-purpose entity have the right to pledge or exchange those interests but do not control the individual assets held by the qualifying special-purpose entity. The effect of establishing the qualifying special-purpose entity is to merge the contractual rights in the transferred assets and to allocate undivided interests in them—the beneficial interests. Therefore, the right of holders to pledge or exchange those beneficial interests is the counterpart of the right of a transferee to pledge or exchange the transferred assets themselves.

128. Sometimes financial assets, especially mortgage loans, are securitized and the transferor retains all of the beneficial interests in the qualifying special-purpose entity as securities. The objective is to increase financial flexibility because securities are more liquid and can more readily be sold or pledged as collateral to secure borrowings. In some cases, securitization may reduce regulatory capital requirements. The Board concluded that transfers of financial assets to a qualifying special-purpose entity, including securitizations, should qualify as sales only to the extent that consideration other than beneficial interests in the transferred assets is received.

129. The Board observes that a special-purpose entity that has distinct standing at law may still be an affiliate of the transferor, and therefore its assets and liabilities may be required to be included with those of the transferor in consolidated financial statements. That issue is dealt with in generally accepted accounting principles for consolidated financial statements. Many respondents maintained that existing principles are not clear and asked the Board to develop within this Statement additional consolidation guidance for special-purpose entities. The Board concluded that this Statement is not intended to change existing generally accepted accounting principles for consolidation issues. However, the Board acknowledges that consolidation of special-purpose entities is an issue that merits further consideration and is committed to deliberating that issue in its current project on consolidated financial statements.

Securitizations with Revolving-Period Features

130. As noted in paragraph 48, in some securitizations, short-term receivables are transferred to a special-purpose entity, and the special-purpose entity then issues long-term beneficial interests. Collections from transferred receivables are used to purchase additional receivables during a defined period called the revolving period. Thereafter, the collections are used to redeem beneficial interests in due course. Some have questioned the propriety of sales treatment in those securitizations because much of the cash collected during the revolving period is returned to the transferor. The Board decided that sales treatment was appropriate for transfers with revolving-period features because the transferor surrenders control of the assets transferred. While the revolving-period agreement requires that the transferor sell receivables to the trust in exchange for cash on prearranged terms, sales of additional receivables during the revolving period are separate transactions from the original sale.

131. The transferor in a transfer with a revolving-period agreement, such as a credit card securitization, must sell receivables to the securitization trust on prearranged terms. The transferor can perhaps predict the timing of transfers, but the actual timing depends primarily on borrower behavior. If not bound by that contract, the transferor could sell its new receivables elsewhere, possibly on better terms. The transferor obtains the cash as proceeds in exchange for new receivables transferred under the revolving-period agreement, not as benefits from its previous ownership of the receivables or its residual interest in the securitization trust.

132. The revolving-period agreement is an implicit forward contract, with rights and obligations on both sides. The transferor has little or no discretion to avoid its obligations under the revolving-period agreement and would suffer adverse consequences for failure to deliver receivables to the trust during the revolving period. For example, if the transferor were to take deliberate actions to avoid its obligations to sell receivables by triggering the agreement's "early amortization" provisions, the transferor would be exposed to litigation for not honoring its commitment. The transferor also could suffer if it later tried to sell its receivables in the securitization market: the transferor would probably have to offer wary investors a higher return. Deliberate early termination by the transferor is rare in practice because of those adverse consequences. Similarly, the securitization trust and investors cannot avoid the obligation to purchase additional receivables. For those reasons, the revolving-period agreement does not provide control over receivables previously sold but rather is an implicit forward contract for future sales of receivables.

133. Some respondents to the Exposure Draft proposed that existing revolving-period securitizations should continue to apply previous accounting standards for all transfers into an existing trust after the effective date of this Statement. Several respondents asked about the effect of the provisions of this Statement on transfers into a master trust that is used for a series of securitizations. They pointed out that it would be difficult to change the present structure of those trusts in response to new accounting standards. Others observed that because master trusts have very long or indefinite lives, "grandfathering" transfers to existing trusts would result in noncomparable financial statements for a long time to come. After considering those arguments, the Board decided to retain the proposed requirement that this Statement apply to all transfers of assets after its effective date, in order to minimize the noncomparability caused by the transition. However, the Board also responded to respondents' questions about accounting for master trusts by clarifying in paragraph 53 that a transfer into a master trust in exchange for beneficial interests is neither a sale nor a secured borrowing under the provisions of paragraph 9.

Other Transfers of Financial Assets

Repurchase Agreements and Securities Lending Transactions

134. The Exposure Draft proposed that transfers of financial assets with repurchase commitments, such as repurchase agreements and securities lending transactions, should qualify as secured borrowings only if the transfer was *assuredly temporary*—the period until repurchase is less than three months or the period is indefinite but the contracts are repriced daily at overnight market rates and can be terminated by either party on short notice. It also proposed that the assets to be repurchased had to be the same (for example, U.S. securities having the same CUSIP number) as those transferred. Respondents generally disagreed with those provisions of the Exposure Draft about these ambiguous transactions, and the Board changed those provisions in its redeliberations.

Legal and economic ambiguity of these transactions

135. Repurchase agreements and securities lending transactions are difficult to characterize because those transactions are ambiguous: they have attributes of both sales and secured borrowings. Repurchase agreements typically are documented as sales with forward purchase contracts and generally are treated as sales in bankruptcy law and receivers' procedures, but as borrowings in tax law, under court decisions that cite numerous economic and other factors. Repurchase agreements are commonly characterized by market participants as secured borrowings, even though one reason that repurchase agreements arose is that selling and then buying back securities, rather than borrowing with those securities as collateral, allows many government agencies, banks, and other active participants in the repurchase agreement market to stay "within investment and borrowing parameters that delineate what they may or may not do."[14] Securities loans are commonly documented as loans of securities collateralized by cash or by other securities or by letters of credit, but the "borrowed" securities are invariably sold, free of any conditions, by the "borrowers," to fulfill obligations under short sales or customers' failure to deliver securities they have sold; securities loans are generally treated as sales

under U.S. bankruptcy and tax laws (but only as they relate to income distributions).

136. Previous accounting practice generally has treated repurchase agreements as secured borrowings, although "repos-to-maturity" and certain other longer term repurchase agreements have been treated as sales. Previous accounting practice has not recognized some securities lending transactions, because the transactions were executed by an entity's custodian or other agent, and has treated others as secured borrowings. Supporting arguments exist for accounting for both kinds of transactions as borrowings, both kinds as sales, or some as borrowings and others as sales.

137. The American Law Institute[15] describes the legal status of a securities lending transaction as follows:

> The securities lender does not retain any property interest in the securities that are delivered to the borrower. The transaction is an outright transfer in which the borrower obtains full title . . . the borrower needs the securities to transfer them to someone else . . . if the securities borrower defaults on its redelivery obligation, the securities lender has no property interest in the original securities that could be asserted against any person to whom the securities borrower may have transferred them. . . . The securities lender's protection is its right to foreclose on the collateral given to secure the borrower's redelivery obligation. Perhaps the best way to understand securities lending is to note that the word "loan" in securities lending transactions is used in the sense it carries in loans of money, as distinguished from loans of specific identifiable chattels. Someone who lends money does not retain any property interest in the money that is handed over to the borrower.

138. While that description focuses on securities lending, much of it appears applicable to repurchase agreements as well. If judged by the criteria in paragraphs 9(a) and 9(b) and the legal reasoning in paragraph 137, financial assets transferred under typical repurchase or securities lending agreements would qualify for derecognition as having been sold for

---

[14]Marcia Stigum, *The Repo and Reverse Markets* (Homewood, Ill.: Dow Jones-Irwin, 1989), 313.

[15]*Uniform Commercial Code, Revised Article 8, Investment Securities,* Proposed Final Draft (Philadelphia: American Law Institute, 1994), 18 and 19.

proceeds consisting of cash and a forward purchase contract. During the term of the agreement, the transferred assets are isolated from the transferor, are placed in the hands of a transferee that can—and typically does—obtain their benefits by selling or pledging them, and are readily obtainable in the market.

139. The Board considered requiring sales treatment for all of those transactions. The Board also considered an approach that would have recognized the effects of the transaction in the statement of financial position (recognizing the proceeds received as cash or securities and a forward purchase contract) without characterizing the transaction as a sale. The Board ultimately decided, for both conceptual and practical reasons, that secured borrowing treatment should be retained for most of those transactions.

140. In concept, having a forward purchase contract—a right and obligation to buy an asset—is not the same as owning that asset. Dividends or interest on securities are paid by the issuer to the current security holder, that is, to whoever may now hold the securities transferred in the repurchase agreement or loan, while the transferor has at most only the contractual right to receive—from the transferee—payments in lieu of dividends or interest. In addition, the voting rights reside not with the transferor but with the current security holder, because those rights generally cannot be contractually released.

141. However, the commitments entered into in a repurchase or securities lending agreement are more extensive than a common forward purchase contract. The transferor has agreed to repurchase the security, often in as little as a day, at a fixed price that differs from the sale price by an amount that is essentially interest on the cash transferred. The transferor also commonly receives payments in lieu of interest or dividends and has protection of collateral that is valued daily and adjusted frequently for changes in the market value of the transferred asset—collateral that the transferor is entitled to use to purchase replacement securities should the transferee default, even in the event of bankruptcy or other receivership. Those arrangements are not typical of forward purchase contracts and suggest that having a repurchase agreement or securities lending contract to repurchase a transferred asset before its maturity is much like still owning that asset.

142. Practically, participants in the very large markets for repurchase agreements and securities lending transactions are, for the most part, unaccustomed to treating those transactions as sales, and a change to sale treatment would have a substantial impact on their reported financial position. Given the difficulty in characterizing those ambiguous transactions, the decision to treat all of those transactions as sales would be a close call, and the Board was not convinced that the benefits of a change based on that close call would justify the costs.

143. The Exposure Draft proposed that transfers of financial assets with repurchase commitments, such as repurchase agreements and securities lending transactions, should be accounted for as secured borrowings if the transfers were assuredly temporary, and as sales if the transfers were not assuredly temporary. As proposed, to be assuredly temporary, the period until repurchase would have had to be short enough not to diminish assurance that the contract and arrangements backing it up would prove effective, that is, with maturities either under three months or indefinite and terminable by either party on short notice. Also, to be assuredly temporary, the entity would have had to be entitled and obligated to repurchase the same assets. After considering comment letters and testimony at the public hearing, the Board decided to change both of those proposed requirements.

The period until repurchase

144. The Exposure Draft proposed that transfers of financial assets should qualify as borrowings if the period until repurchase is less than three months or the period is indefinite but the contracts are repriced daily at overnight market rates and can be terminated by either party on short notice. A three-month limit was arbitrary, but based on its initial inquiries, the Board tentatively concluded that three months would be a clear and workable time limit that should not present difficulty, because it understood that most repurchase agreements and securities loans are for periods much shorter than three months or are indefinite, and almost all of the others are for periods much longer than three months.

145. Respondents generally disagreed with that provision of the Exposure Draft. They argued that the arbitrary three-month limit would not be effective and that entities could alter the accounting for a transfer by adding or subtracting one or two days to or from the term of the agreement. While some offered other arbitrary time limits, many respondents argued that all transfers accompanied by a forward contract to repurchase the transferred assets before maturity

should be accounted for as secured borrowings. In their view, most repurchase agreements represent a temporary transfer of only some elements of control over the transferred assets.

146. After considering those comments, the Board decided to remove the proposed requirement that the period until repurchase be less than three months. Board members concluded that any distinction based on the specified time until repurchase would not be workable. As outlined in paragraph 141, the elements of control by the transferee over assets obtained in a typical securities lending or repurchase agreement are both temporary and limited. The Board concluded that the contractual obligation and right to repurchase an asset before its maturity effectively bind the asset transferred back to the transferor.

147. Some respondents suggested a distinction based on a different time period, or on the proportion of the life of the asset transferred, but the Board rejected those possibilities. Any other time period would have the same faults as the three-month limit proposed in the Exposure Draft: it would be arbitrary, with no meaningful distinction between transactions just on one side of the limit and those just on the other side. Similarly, the Board concluded that the only meaningful distinction based on required repurchase at some proportion of the life of the assets transferred is between a "repo-to-maturity," in which the typical settlement is a net cash payment, and a repurchase before maturity, in which the portion of the asset that remains outstanding is indeed reacquired in an exchange.

Substantially the same assets

148. The Exposure Draft proposed that a repurchase agreement would have to require return of the same asset (for example, U.S. securities having the same CUSIP number) for the transfer to be treated as a borrowing. In the Exposure Draft, the Board reasoned that agreements to acquire securities that—while perhaps similar—are not the same as those transferred do not maintain any kind of control over the transferred securities. Most repurchase agreements require return of the same asset. Some are less rigid. For example, some mortgage-backed instruments are transferred in a class of repurchase agreements known as *dollar rolls*. There are several procedural differences between dollar-roll transactions and ordinary repurchase agreements. However, the most significant difference is the agreement that assets returned need not be the same as those transferred.

Instead, the transferor agrees to accept back assets with characteristics that are substantially the same within limits established by the market.

149. While a few respondents supported the Exposure Draft's reasoning, most did not. Respondents argued that the economic differences between the assets initially transferred and assets to be reacquired under a dollar-roll transaction that meets the existing accounting criteria for being substantially the same are, as the term implies, not substantial and should not result in an accounting difference. They argued that existing accounting guidance found in AICPA Statement of Position No. 90-3, *Definition of the Term Substantially the Same for Holders of Debt Instruments, as Used in Certain Audit Guides and a Statement of Position,* has proven adequate to constrain the characteristics of assets that are to be reacquired. After redeliberation, the Board accepted those arguments and decided that if the assets to be repurchased are the same or substantially the same as those concurrently transferred, the transaction should be accounted for as a secured borrowing. The Board also decided to incorporate the definition in SOP 90-3 in this Statement. The Board noted that not all contracts in the dollar-roll market require that the securities involved have all of the characteristics of "substantially the same." If the contract does not require that, the transferor does not maintain effective control.

The importance of the right and *obligation to repurchase, collateral, and symmetry*

150. The Board based its decisions about agreements that maintain effective control over transferred assets in part on observation of contracts and practices that prevail in the repurchase agreement and securities lending markets. Concerns of market participants about risk of default by the parties to the contract, rights at law in the event of default, and credit risk of transferred assets, among other factors, have led to several contractual features intended to assure that the transferors indeed maintain effective control.

151. The Board decided that to maintain effective control the transferor must have *both* the contractual right *and* the contractual obligation to reacquire securities that are identical to or substantially the same as those concurrently transferred. Transfers that include only the right to reacquire, at the option of the transferor or upon certain conditions, or only the obligation to reacquire, at the option of the transferee or

upon certain conditions, generally do not maintain the transferor's control, because the option might not be exercised or the conditions might not occur. Similarly, expectations of reacquiring the same securities without any contractual commitments, as in "wash sales," provide no control over the transferred securities.

152. The Board also decided that the transferor's right to repurchase is not assured unless it is protected by obtaining collateral sufficient to fund substantially all of the cost of purchasing identical replacement securities during the term of the contract so that it has received the means to replace the assets even if the transferee defaults. Judgment is needed to interpret the term *substantially all* and other aspects of the criterion that the terms of a repurchase agreement do not maintain effective control over the transferred asset. However, arrangements to repurchase or lend readily obtainable securities, typically with as much as 98 percent collateralization (for entities agreeing to repurchase) or as little as 102 percent overcollateralization (for securities lenders), valued daily and adjusted up or down frequently for changes in the market price of the security transferred and with clear powers to use that collateral quickly in event of default, typically fall clearly within that guideline. The Board believes that other collateral arrangements typically fall well outside that guideline.

153. Some respondents argued for a continuation of previous asymmetrical practices in accounting for dollar rolls. In previous practice, transferors have accounted for dollar-roll agreements as borrowing transactions, while dealers who receive the transferred assets have accounted for them as purchases. The Board observed that the same transaction cannot in concept or simple logic be a borrowing-lending arrangement to the transferor and a purchase-sale transaction to the transferee. The Exposure Draft would have resolved that asymmetry by requiring that transferors account for the transactions as sales. In response to respondents' concerns about transferors' accounting, this Statement instead calls for transferors to account for qualifying dollar-roll transactions as secured borrowings and requires that dealers account for the same transactions as secured loans.

Agreements Entitling the Transferor to Repurchase or Redeem Assets That Are Not Readily Obtainable

154. The Board considered whether to allow sale treatment if a transferor of financial assets concur-

rently acquires from the transferee a call option on the assets sold. Some questioned whether the transferor that holds a call option has surrendered control of the assets to the transferee. Some believe that an entity that holds an option to acquire a financial asset controls that asset. However, the holder of a call option does not receive interest or dividends generated by the asset, cannot exercise any voting rights inherent in the asset, may not be aware of the location or present custody of the asset, and is not able to sell the asset and deliver it without first exercising the call. And it may never exercise the call. If an entity that holds a call option on an asset controls that asset, then it follows that the entity should recognize the asset under the call option at the time the call option is acquired. However, two parties would then recognize the same asset—the entity that holds the call option and either the writer of the call option or the party from whom the writer plans to acquire the asset if the call is exercised.

155. The Board concluded that sale treatment should not be precluded in instances in which the transferor simultaneously obtains a call option on the asset sold, provided that the asset is readily obtainable. The writer of a call option on a financial asset may choose not to own the asset under the call option if it is readily obtainable; it may instead plan to acquire that asset if the call is exercised and delivery is demanded. In those circumstances, it is realistic to assume that the transferee can sell or repledge the asset to a third party and, at the same time, in good faith write a call option on that asset.

156. The Board concluded that a sale should not be recognized in instances in which the transferor simultaneously obtains a call on a transferred asset that is not readily obtainable. The resulting accounting treatment of an option on a not-readily-obtainable asset that is obtained as part of a transfer of financial assets is different from the accounting treatment generally accorded to the same option that is purchased for cash. From the transferor's viewpoint, that difference in accounting treatment between an option purchased and an option obtained as part of a transfer of assets conflicts with the principle that the recognition of financial assets and liabilities should not be affected by the sequence of transactions that led to their existence. However, as noted in paragraph 25, if the option is a component of a transfer of financial assets, and it does not constrain the transferee from selling or repledging the asset, that should not preclude the transfer from being accounted for as a sale. If the existence of an option constrains the transferee from

selling or repledging the transferred asset (because the asset is not readily obtainable to satisfy the option if exercised), then the transferor has not relinquished effective control over the asset and thus should not derecognize it.

Assets Obtained as Collateral That Can Be Sold or Repledged

157. The Exposure Draft proposed that for transactions involving collateral, including securities lending transactions and repurchase agreements, secured parties should recognize all cash collateral received as well as all other financial instruments received as collateral that they have the ability by contract or custom to sell or repledge prior to the debtor's default, because they have important rights over that collateral. Secured parties in those positions are entitled and able to use the cash received as collateral, or the cash they can obtain by selling or repledging other collateral, for their own purposes. Therefore, in the Exposure Draft, the Board concluded that that collateral is the secured party's asset, along with an obligation to return the collateral that is the secured party's liability. In the Exposure Draft, the Board reasoned that if that collateral was permitted to be excluded from the statement of financial position, assets that secured parties can use to generate income would not be recognized. Reporting income but not the assets that generate it could understate a secured party's assets (and liabilities) as well as overstate its return on assets. In contrast, noncash collateral that secured parties are not able to sell or repledge cannot be used to generate cash or otherwise benefit the secured party (other than by reducing the credit risk on the financial asset it secures, an effect already recognized in measuring that financial asset) and is not the secured party's asset.

158. The Board noted that the accounting proposed was consistent with Governmental Accounting Standards Board (GASB) Statement No. 28, *Accounting and Financial Reporting for Securities Lending Transactions,* that was issued in May 1995. GASB Statement 28 also required, for reasons similar to those noted in this Statement, that securities lenders record noncash collateral if the contract specifically allows the governmental entity to pledge or sell the collateral before a debtor defaults.

159. Many respondents objected to recognition of collateral because they contended that the proposed accounting would result in the same asset being recognized by two entities. As discussed in para-

graph 172 and in the Exposure Draft, while the secured party reports the security as its asset, the transferor reports a different asset, a receivable for the return of the collateral from the secured party. Respondents also argued that recognizing the collateral implies that the secured party expects all the benefits of that asset, whereas it typically is not entitled to retain dividends, interest, or benefits from appreciation. Respondents who objected to recognizing collateral generally preferred that secured parties disclose collateral received. Other respondents suggested that it was not clear that the collateral provisions applied not only to a secured borrowing but also to collateral pledged in all other kinds of transactions.

160. The Board reconsidered the provisions of the Exposure Draft in light of those comments. To improve clarity and refine its conclusions, the Board focused on four circumstances in which a secured party arguably should recognize collateral it has received: (a) cash collateral, (b) collateral securing obligations in default, (c) other collateral that the secured party has sold or repledged, and (d) other collateral that the secured party can sell or repledge.

Cash collateral

161. Some respondents objected to recording any asset received as collateral, even cash, on the grounds that it remains the asset of the party posting it as collateral and is therefore not the secured party's asset. Other respondents agreed that cash collateral should be recognized because transfers of financial assets in exchange for cash collateral cannot be distinguished from borrowing cash and because cash is fungible. It is therefore impossible to determine whether it has been used by the secured party. The Board concluded for the latter reason that all cash collateral should be recorded as an asset by the secured party, together with a liability for the obligation to return it to the transferor, whose asset is a receivable.

Collateral securing obligations in default

162. Many respondents pointed out that collateral securing an obligation becomes the property of the secured party upon default on the secured obligation. A respondent argued differently, maintaining that a defaulting debtor does not relinquish control over the collateral until it no longer has an opportunity to redeem the collateral by curing the default. The Board agreed that the secured party should recognize collateral to the extent it has not already recognized the collateral if the debtor defaults and is no longer entitled to redeem it.

Other collateral that the secured party has sold or repledged

163. Some respondents who agreed that cash collateral should be recognized argued that the secured party should not recognize other collateral unless the debtor had defaulted, no matter what powers it has over that collateral, again because in their view the transferred assets remain the assets of the transferor. Others argued that while it may make sense for the secured party to recognize an obligation if collateral is sold, as is common practice in some industries, it is not common practice for broker-dealers and others to recognize an asset and a liability when they repledge collateral. Respondents from the broker-dealer community noted that they regularly repledge substantial amounts of collateral in conjunction with loans secured by customer margin balances and "borrow versus pledge" matched securities transactions and that that collateral activity has not been recognized under previous practice, although it has been disclosed. After considering those arguments, the Board concluded that collateral should be considered for recognition when it is sold or repledged, because the ability to pledge or exchange an asset is the benefit that the Board determined constitutes control over a financial asset, as set forth in paragraph 9(b) and discussed in paragraphs 122 and 123.

164. One respondent observed that the documentation supporting some transactions preserves the transferor's legal right to redeem its collateral, even though the transferee has repledged the assets to a third entity. In those instances, should the transferee default, the transferor has rights to redeem its collateral directly from the third entity to which the initial transferee repledged it. The respondent argued that a transferee with that right has not surrendered control over the assets. The Board agreed with that reasoning and adopted it. Because the status of the right to redeem may not always be clear, the Board chose to implement it by requiring recognition of collateral by the secured party if it sells or repledges collateral on terms that do not enable it to repurchase or redeem the collateral from the transferor on short notice. One result is that broker-dealers and others who obtain financial assets in reverse repurchase agreements, securities loans, or as collateral for loans and then sell or repledge those assets will in some cases recognize under this Statement assets and liabilities that previously went unrecognized. The Board noted that obligations to return to the transferor assets borrowed and then sold have sometimes been effectively recognized as part of a liability for securities sold but not yet purchased, and did not require change in that practice.

Other collateral that the secured party can sell or repledge

165. The Exposure Draft called for recognition of collateral that the secured party can repledge or exchange but has not yet used. Some argued that secured parties should not be required to recognize any unused collateral, reasoning that the collateral and related obligation did not meet the definition of an asset or a liability of the secured party. They contended that to be considered an asset of the secured party the collateral must embody a probable future economic benefit that contributes directly or indirectly to future net cash inflows and that in the case of many kinds of collateral, there is only a possible benefit that has not been realized until that collateral is sold or repledged. The Board disagreed, noting that collateral that can be sold or repledged has a capacity to contribute directly to future cash inflows—from a sale or secured borrowing—and that the obligation to return the collateral when reclaimed will require a future economic sacrifice—the relinquishing of control. The Board also observed that broker-dealers and others are able to benefit from collateral in various ways and that the right to benefit from the use of a financial asset is, in itself, an asset.

166. A respondent pointed out that the right to repledge or exchange is significantly constrained if the transferor has the right and ability to redeem the collateral on short notice, for example, by substituting other collateral or terminating the contract on short notice, and thereby demand the return of the particular security pledged as collateral. The Board agreed, reasoning that a transferor that can redeem its pledged collateral on short notice has not surrendered control of the transferred assets. The transferee will be able to use the transferred assets in certain ways to earn a return during the period of the agreement, but the value of its asset may be very limited because of the transferor's rights to substitute or cancel.

167. The Board considered an approach that would have recorded only the net value of the specific rights that the secured party has over the collateral. That approach might have been consistent with the financial-components approach, and several respondents asked the Board to consider it. However, no one, including the Board, was able to identify a method that the Board judged to be sound for separating the collateral into components.

168. Another possibility considered would have been to recognize the transfer of control over the collateral and for the two parties each to report their mutual rights and obligations under the contract net, that is, for the debtor to net its receivable for the transferred security against its obligation under the secured borrowing and for the secured creditor to net its obligation to return the security against its secured loan receivable. The only change to the statement of financial position would have been the difference in carrying amounts, if any, with a note disclosing the details. That approach is different from present practice in its details but would have produced similar total assets and liabilities. It arguably would have been more consistent with the financial-components approach that focuses on control and would have simplified the accounting. While this approach appealed to some Board members, the Board ultimately rejected it. The approach would have been inconsistent with other pronouncements that govern offsetting, because in this case there is no intent to settle net.

169. After considering comments and testimony on those matters, the Board decided that financial assets transferred as collateral in a secured borrowing should be recognized by the secured party as an asset with a corresponding liability for the obligation to return the collateral if the secured party is permitted by contract or custom to sell or repledge the collateral and the transferor does not have the right and ability to redeem the collateral on short notice, for example, by substituting other collateral or terminating the contract.

170. In addition, because there appears to be significant variation in practice, the Board decided to require entities to disclose their policies for requiring collateral or other security for securities lending transactions and repurchase agreements to inform users about the credit risk that entities assume in those transactions. Respondents did not object to that proposed disclosure.

Security Interests, Custodial Arrangements, Contributions, and Other Transfers That Do Not Qualify as Sales

171. The Board concluded that a borrower that grants a security interest in financial assets should not derecognize the financial assets during the term of the secured obligation. Although the borrower's rights to those assets are restricted because it cannot sell them until the borrowing is repaid, it has not surrendered control if the lender cannot sell or repledge the assets unless the borrower defaults. That assets subject to a security interest have been pledged, and are therefore collateral in the possession of the lender or the lender's agent, does not affect recognition by the debtor because effective control over those assets remains with the debtor in the absence of default under the terms of the borrowing.

172. To maintain symmetry in the accounting of secured parties and debtors (paragraphs 157-170), the Board decided that debtors should redesignate in their statements of financial position collateral that has been put into the hands of a secured party that is permitted by contract or custom to sell or repledge it and which they are not entitled and able to redeem on short notice, for example, by substituting other collateral or terminating the arrangement. That redesignation avoids a situation in which two or more entities report the same assets as if both held them (as could occur under previous accounting practices).

173. Under previous practice, financial assets transferred to another party for safekeeping or custody continue to be carried as assets by the transferor. The only consideration exchanged in those transfers is, perhaps, payment of a fee by the transferor to the custodian for the custodial services. The custodian does not control the assets but must follow the transferor's instructions. The Board concluded that existing practice should continue and that this Statement need not deal with transfers of custody for safekeeping.

174. Some transfers of financial assets are unconditional nonreciprocal transfers that are contributions. The Board did not address them in this Statement because accounting for contributions is addressed in FASB Statement No. 116, *Accounting for Contributions Received and Contributions Made.*

175. Some transfers of financial assets will fail to meet the criteria specified in paragraph 9 to be accounted for as sales even though they might be structured as and purport to be sales. The Board concluded that those transfers should be accounted for as secured borrowings.

Measurement under the Financial-Components Approach

176. Following a transfer of financial assets that qualifies as a sale, assets retained or obtained and liabilities incurred by the transferor could at first be measured at either (a) fair value at the date of the transfer or (b) an allocated portion of the transferor's carrying amount for the assets transferred.

177. The usual initial measure of assets and liabilities is the price in an exchange transaction or the equivalent fair value. Paragraph 88 of FASB Concepts Statement No. 5, *Recognition and Measurement in Financial Statements of Business Enterprises,* states:

> Initial recognition of assets acquired and liabilities incurred generally involves measurement based on current exchange prices at the date of recognition. Once an asset or a liability is recognized, it continues to be measured at the amount initially recognized until an event that changes the asset or liability or its amount occurs and meets the recognition criteria.

178. In APB Opinion No. 29, *Accounting for Nonmonetary Transactions,* the Accounting Principles Board, in prescribing the basis for measurement of assets received in nonmonetary exchanges, states:

> . . . in general accounting for nonmonetary transactions should be based on the fair values of the assets (or services) involved which is the same basis as that used in monetary transactions. [Paragraph 18, footnote reference omitted.]

179. The Board believes that those concepts should be applied to new interests obtained or incurred in transfers of financial assets. At issue is whether the financial assets controlled and liabilities incurred in a transfer of financial assets that qualifies as a sale are new to the transferor and thus are part of the proceeds from the transfer, subject to initial measurement using the concepts summarized in paragraphs 177 and 178, or instead are retained beneficial interests over which the transferor has not surrendered control that need not be subject to new measurement under those concepts. The Board concluded that the answer depends on the type of financial instrument or other interest held or incurred.

180. The Board decided that a distinction can and should be made between new assets and liabilities that are part of the proceeds from the transfer and continuing interests in retained assets held in a new form. Cash received as proceeds for assets sold has no continuing connection with those assets and is clearly a new asset. Unrelated assets obtained also

are clearly new assets, for example, a government bond received in exchange for transferred accounts receivable. Any asset received that is not an interest in the transferred asset is new to the transferor and thus is part of the proceeds from the sale. Any liability incurred, even if it is related to the transferred assets, is an obligation that is new to the transferor and thus a reduction of proceeds. Therefore, all of those new assets and liabilities should be initially measured at fair value. The issue becomes more challenging for assets controlled after a sale that are related to the assets sold.

Measuring Liabilities and Derivative Financial Instruments Related to Assets Sold at Fair Value

181. An entity that sells a financial asset may incur liabilities that are related to the assets sold. A common example of a liability incurred by the transferor is a recourse or guarantee obligation. Certain risks, such as recourse or guarantees, are inherent in the original financial asset before it is transferred, which might seem to support carrying over the prior carrying amount. However, before the transfer, the transferor has no obligation to another party; after the transfer, it does. The Board concluded that liabilities incurred in a transfer of financial assets are therefore new and should be initially measured at fair value.

182. An entity that sells a financial asset may enter into derivative financial instrument contracts that are related to the assets sold, for example, options, forwards, or swaps. One example of a related contract is an option that allows purchasers of receivables to put them back to the transferor, which is similar to a recourse obligation. Another example is a repurchase commitment held by the seller in a repurchase agreement that is accounted for as a sale,[16] which is a kind of forward contract. A third example is an agreement similar to an interest rate swap in which the transferor receives from a securitization trust the fixed interest amounts due on securitized receivables and pays the trust variable amounts based on a floating interest rate index. Under present practice, a party to an option or a forward purchase or sale commitment generally does not recognize the acquisition or disposition of the underlying assets until and unless delivery occurs. A party to a swap recognizes net amounts receivable or payable under the swap rather than the

---

[16]Accounting for repurchase agreements is discussed in paragraphs 66-71.

full notional amounts of the reference contracts. Options, forward commitments, swaps, and other derivative contracts are financial assets or liabilities separate and apart from the underlying asset. For that reason and because of the practical need to make a workable distinction, the Board concluded that derivative financial instruments entered into by a seller in an exchange for a financial asset are newly created in the transaction and should be considered part of the proceeds and initially measured at fair value at the date of exchange.

183. Respondents to the Exposure Draft asked the Board to provide more detailed guidance on how they should differentiate between an asset or liability that is part of the proceeds of a transfer and a retained interest in transferred assets. The Board acknowledges that, at the margin, it may be difficult to distinguish between a retained interest in the asset transferred and a newly created asset. The Board believes that it is impractical to provide detailed guidance that would cover all possibilities. A careful examination of cash flows, risks, and other provisions should provide a basis for resolving most questions. However, the Board agrees that it would be helpful to provide guidance if an entity cannot determine how to classify an instrument and decided that in that case the instrument should be considered to be a new asset and thus part of the proceeds of the sale initially measured at fair value.

Measuring Retained Interests in Assets Sold at Allocated Previous Carrying Amount

184. The Board decided that all other interests in the transferred financial assets held after a securitization or other transfer of financial assets should be measured at their previous carrying amount, allocated between the assets sold, if any, and the retained interests, if any, based on their relative fair values at the date of the transfer. Retained interests in the transferred assets continue to be assets of the transferor, albeit assets of a different kind, because they never left the possession of the transferor and, thus, a surrender of control cannot have occurred. Therefore, the retained interests should continue to be carried at their allocated previous carrying amount, with no gain or loss recognized. Defining this category as the residual set of interests in transferred instruments held after the transfer (those interests that are neither derivatives nor liabilities of the transferor) establishes a clearer distinction between assets and liabilities that are part of the proceeds of the transfer and retained interests.

Other Alternatives Considered

185. In developing the Exposure Draft, the Board considered several alternative measurement approaches including (a) measuring all assets held after a securitization or sale of a partial undivided interest (either a pro rata interest or a nonproportional interest) initially at fair value, (b) measuring interests held after a securitization at fair value and measuring retained undivided interests at allocated previous carrying amounts, and (c) measuring all interests in transferred financial assets held after a transfer at their allocated previous carrying amounts. Some respondents to the Exposure Draft supported each of those approaches. However, most respondents agreed with the Board's reasoning that a retained interest in a transferred asset represents continuing control over a previous asset, albeit in different form, and thus should not be remeasured at fair value. Most respondents also accepted the approach proposed in the Exposure Draft as workable.

186. Another possibility that was rejected by the Board was to allocate the carrying amount between the portion of an asset sold and the portion of an asset retained based on relative fair values at the date the receivable was originated or acquired by the transferor, adjusted for payments and other activity from the date of acquisition to the date of transfer. The consensus reached in EITF Issue No. 88-11, "Allocation of Recorded Investment When a Loan or Part of a Loan Is Sold," required use of that acquisition date method unless it is not practical, in which case the allocation should be based on relative fair values at the date of sale. In its deliberations on this Statement, the Board decided to require allocation based on fair values at the date of sale or securitization because it is more representative of the asset's value and the cost of re-creating the information from the date of acquisition would exceed the perceived benefits. The Board decided that the acquisition date method was not clearly superior in concept to an allocation based on fair values at the date of sale or securitization and, based in part on practices under that consensus, that that method was so often impractical because of recordkeeping difficulties that it was not useful as a general principle. No other possible methods of allocation appeared likely to produce results that were significantly more relevant.

Servicing Assets and Servicing Liabilities

187. Previously, net "mortgage servicing rights" were recognized as assets and those rights were accounted for in accordance with FASB Statements No. 65, *Accounting for Certain Mortgage Banking Activities,* and No. 91, *Accounting for Nonrefundable Fees and Costs Associated with Originating or Acquiring Loans and Initial Direct Costs of Leases,* and Statements 115 and 122. The amount recognized as net mortgage servicing rights was based on the fair value of certain expected cash inflows net of expected cash outflows. The expected cash inflows—future servicing revenues—included a normal servicing fee,[17] expected late charges, and other ancillary revenues. The expected cash outflows—future servicing costs—included various costs of performing the servicing. A separate "excess servicing fee receivable" was recognized if the servicer expected to receive cash flows in excess of a normal servicing fee, and a liability was recognized if the servicer expected to receive less than a normal servicing fee or if the entity's servicing costs were expected to exceed normal costs. The servicing rights asset was subsequently measured by amortization and assessment for impairment based on its fair value. That set of procedures has been called the mortgage servicing method.

188. Servicing assets and obligations for other assets sold or securitized were either accounted for like mortgage servicing or, more commonly, remained unrecognized until amounts were received and services were provided. Attempts have been made in practice to extend the mortgage servicing method to the servicing of other financial assets. However, identifying a normal servicing fee and other aspects of the mortgage servicing method have been difficult and disparate practices have resulted. The Board concluded it was necessary to address in this project accounting for servicing of all kinds of financial assets.

189. In October 1993, the Board decided to reconsider the accounting for mortgage servicing activities established in Statement 65. The primary thrust of that project was to resolve differences in the accounting for purchased versus originated mortgage servicing. Statement 122 was the result of that effort. In February 1995, the Board decided that accounting for excess mortgage servicing receivables and other servicing issues should be dealt with, to the extent necessary, not in that project but rather in this one, because those issues largely arise in transfers of financial assets and possible answers are necessarily interrelated. The Board considered alternative methods of accounting for servicing (the mortgage servicing method required by Statement 65, as amended by Statement 122, as well as a gross method and a right or obligation method) and chose a method that combines the best features of the mortgage servicing method and other possible methods.

Alternatives to the Mortgage Servicing Method

190. The mortgage servicing method described in paragraph 187 was required by Statement 65, as amended by Statement 122, for mortgage servicing rights. While that method was familiar to mortgage servicers and had certain advantages over other methods, the distinction between normal and excess servicing and other complexities of the method make it difficult to apply for some other kinds of servicing.

191. The Board considered a gross method that would have required that a servicer recognize both a servicing receivable asset consisting of expected future servicing revenues and a servicing obligation liability for the servicing work to be performed. The Board decided that it was questionable whether a receivable for servicing not yet rendered met the definition of an asset and that, given the conceptual questions, that method did not merit the large change in practice that it would have required.

192. The Board also considered a right or obligation method that would have recognized a single item, commonly an asset but occasionally a liability, for each servicing contract. That asset or liability would have been the net of the gross asset and liability that would have been reported separately under the gross approach. The resulting asset would have been subsequently measured like an interest-only strip, that is, at fair value with unrealized gains and losses recognized in equity if available-for-sale. Some respondents suggested that servicing rights should be subsequently measured in that way, because reporting servicing rights at fair value would be more useful to investors and other financial statement users than the historical cost amortization and impairment methods of the mortgage servicing approach. Furthermore,

---

[17]Statement 65 defined a current (normal) servicing fee rate as "a servicing fee rate that is representative of servicing fee rates most commonly used in comparable servicing agreements covering similar types of mortgage loans." FASB Technical Bulletin No. 87-3, *Accounting for Mortgage Servicing Fees and Rights,* clarified what rate a seller-servicer should use as a servicing fee rate as described in Statement 65.

under an approach like that in Statement 115, unrealized gains and losses would not have been recognized in earnings, but rather in a separate component of shareholders' equity.

193. The Board considered the right or obligation method well suited in several respects to the range of mortgage and other servicing contracts that now exist or might arise. However, the Board did not choose that method in part for the practical reason of avoiding an early change from the recently adopted provisions of Statement 122. Instead, the Board chose to combine the best features of that method—the simplicity of reporting only a single asset or liability for each servicing contract and not having to distinguish between normal and excess servicing—with the best features of the mortgage servicing method.

Recognition and Measurement of Servicing Assets and Servicing Liabilities

194. The method adopted in this Statement carries forward the amortization and impairment provisions that were required under the mortgage servicing method in Statements 65 and 122. The Board considers those subsequent measurement provisions workable. However, changes to the mortgage servicing method are necessary to adapt the accounting for mortgage servicing to all servicing assets and servicing liabilities, to reduce complexities for financial statement preparers and users, and to be compatible with the other recognition and initial measurement principles in this Statement.

195. One change is the elimination of the distinction between normal and excess servicing. The Board decided that that distinction has been too difficult to make except in markets as liquid as the market for residential mortgage servicing. The Board considered two ways in which normal and excess servicing might be retained in accounting for those liquid markets.

196. One way would have been to leave in place the accounting for servicing of mortgages as required in Statement 65, as amended by Statement 122, while using a different method that was not dependent on determining a normal servicing fee for all other servicing. However, the Board concluded that comparability of financial statements would have suffered if the accounting for essentially similar servicing activities differed depending on the type of asset serviced. Another way would have been to revise the definition of normal servicing fee rates so that servicers could

determine a normal servicing fee rate in the absence of a developed secondary market for servicing. That change would have provided servicers of other types of loans or receivables (such as auto loans and credit card balances) with an opportunity to establish normal servicing rates and apply the mortgage servicing method to other servicing rights, rather than be subject to recognizing less gain or more loss on the sale of receivables because normal servicing was unknown. The Board considered that method but concluded that that alternative might result in continuing questions about what are normal servicing fees for different types of servicing.

197. The Board also noted that the distinction between normal and excess servicing, even in liquid markets, is no longer relevant for financial reporting because under current market practices, excess and normal servicing assets, which arise from a single contract, generally cannot be sold separately after the sale or securitization of the underlying financial assets. The excess servicing receivable, like normal servicing, will be collected only if the servicing work is performed satisfactorily. In addition, accounting based on that distinction is unduly complex and often results in several assets and liabilities being recognized for one servicing contract. While excess servicing continues to resemble an interest-only strip in some respects, the Board concluded in light of the lessened distinction between normal and excess servicing that it was more useful to account for all servicing assets and servicing liabilities in a similar manner.

198. The Board chose instead to distinguish only between the benefits of servicing—amounts that will be received only if the servicing work is performed to the satisfaction of the assets' owner or trustee—and other amounts retained after a securitization or other transfer of financial assets. A consequence of that method is that interest-only strips retained in securitizations, which do not depend on the servicing work being performed satisfactorily, are subsequently measured differently from servicing assets that arise from the same securitizations. That difference in accounting could lead transferors that retain an interest in transferred assets to select a stated servicing fee that results in larger servicing assets and lower retained interests (or vice versa) with an eye to subsequent accounting. The Board believes, however, that the potential accounting incentives for selecting a higher or lower stated servicing fee largely will counterbalance each other.

199. Most respondents agreed with the Board's decision to eliminate the distinction between excess and normal servicing. Some respondents to the Exposure Draft asked for further explanation of the new terms it used for accounting for servicing and about how they differed from the terminology of the mortgage servicing approach used in prior pronouncements. In response, this Statement defines the terms *adequate compensation* for servicing, *benefits of servicing*, and *contractually specified servicing fees* in the glossary and discusses them more completely in paragraphs 36-38.

200. The Exposure Draft proposed that an entity account for all servicing assets in the same manner because rights to service financial assets, while they may differ in the particulars of the servicing, in the extent of compensation, and in liquidity, are in essence the same. As with other retained interests in transferred assets, valid arguments can be made for measuring servicing assets either at allocated previous carrying amount or at fair value. However, the Board saw no reason to treat retained servicing assets differently than other retained interests and therefore decided that they should be initially measured at their allocated previous carrying amount.

201. For similar reasons, the Board viewed servicing liabilities as new obligations arising from a transfer and decided to account for them like other liabilities incurred upon sale or securitization, at fair value.

202. Some respondents questioned how to apply the transition provisions to servicing rights and excess servicing receivables in existence as of this Statement's effective date. The Board considered those comments and as a result decided to change paragraph 20 to (a) not permit retroactive application of this Statement to ensure comparability between entities and (b) clarify how this Statement should be applied to previous balances.

Financial Assets Subject to Prepayment

203. Paragraph 233 of this Statement amends Statement 115 to eliminate the use of the *held-to-maturity* category for securities subject to substantial prepayment risk, thereby requiring that they be classified as either available-for-sale or trading and subsequently measured at fair value. Paragraph 14 extends that measurement principle to interest-only strips, loans, other receivables, and retained interests in securitizations subject to substantial prepayment risk.

204. The justification for using historical-cost-based measurement for debt securities classified as

held-to-maturity is that no matter how market interest rates fluctuate, the holder will recover its recorded investment and thus realize no gains or losses when the issuer pays the amount promised at maturity. The same argument is used to justify historical-cost-based measurement for other receivables not held for sale. That justification does not extend to receivables purchased at a substantial premium over the amount at which they can be prepaid, and it does not apply to instruments whose payments derive from prepayable receivables but have no principal balance, as demonstrated by large losses realized in recent years by many holders of interest-only strips and other mortgage derivatives. As a result, the Board concluded that those receivables must be subsequently measured at fair value with gains or losses being recognized either in earnings (if classified as trading) or in a separate component of shareholders' equity (if classified as available-for-sale). The Board, by deciding that a receivable may not be classified as held-to-maturity if it can be prepaid or otherwise settled in such a way that the holder of the asset would not recover *substantially all* of its recorded investment, left room for judgment, so that investments in mortgage-backed securities or callable securities purchased at an insubstantial premium, for example, are not necessarily disallowed from being classified as held-to-maturity.

205. Some respondents to the Exposure Draft agreed with the Board's conclusions about financial assets subject to prepayment when applied to interest-only strips but questioned the application of those conclusions to loans, other receivables, and retained interests in securitizations. They maintained that the nature of the instrument and management's intent should govern classification rather than actions that a borrower might take under the contract.

206. The Board did not agree with those arguments. A lender that holds a portfolio of prepayable loans or bonds at par will realize the carrying amount of its investment if the borrowers prepay. However, if the lender originated or acquired those loans or bonds at a substantial premium to par, it may lose some or all of that premium and thus not recover a substantial portion of its recorded investment if borrowers prepay. The potential loss is less drastic for premium loans or bonds than for interest-only strips, but it can still be substantial. The Board concluded that the rationale outlined in paragraph 204 extends to any situation in which a lender would not recover substantially all of its recorded investment if borrowers were to exercise prepayment or other rights granted to

them under the contracts. The Board also concluded that the provisions of paragraph 14 do not apply to situations in which events that are not the result of contractual provisions, for example, borrower default or changes in the value of an instrument's denominated currency relative to the entity's functional currency, cause the holder not to recover substantially all of its recorded investment.

207. Other respondents asked that the Board clarify the term *substantially all*. Some suggested that the Board use the 90 percent test found in APB Opinion No. 16, *Business Combinations*. Although applying the term *substantially all* requires judgment about how close to 100 percent is close enough, the Board decided to leave the language of paragraphs 14 and 233 unchanged rather than to require a specific percentage test that would be inherently arbitrary.

Fair Value

208. The Board decided to include an approach for measuring fair value that would be broadly applicable. The definition of fair value in paragraphs 42-44 is consistent with that included in other recent Statements.[18] The Board found no compelling reason to redefine *fair value* under the financial-components approach.

209. Many of the assets and liabilities held after a sale by a transferor with continuing involvement are not traded regularly. Because quoted market values would not be available for those assets and liabilities, fair values would need to be determined by other means in applying the financial-components approach. There was concern that, in some cases, the best estimate of fair value would not be sufficiently reliable to justify recognition in earnings of a gain following a sale of financial assets with continuing involvement, because errors in the estimate of asset value or liability value might result in recording a nonexistent gain. The Board considered requiring that fair value be verifiable to achieve a higher degree of reliability to justify recognition in earnings of a gain following a sale of financial assets with continuing involvement. However, to promote consistency between its Statements, the Board decided not to introduce a new notion of fair value based on reliability.

210. The Exposure Draft proposed that gain recognition following a sale with continuing involvement

should be allowed only to the extent that it is practicable to estimate fair values for assets obtained and liabilities incurred in sales with continuing involvement. To accomplish that, the Board concluded that if it is not practicable to estimate their fair values, assets should be measured at zero and liabilities at the greater of the amount called for under Statement 5, as interpreted by Interpretation 14, or the excess, if any, of the fair value of the assets obtained less the fair value of the other liabilities incurred over the sum of the carrying values of the assets transferred. That requirement was intended to prevent recognition of nonexistent gains through underestimating liabilities. The Board considered whether the practicability exception should be extended to the transferee's accounting and decided not to allow such an exception. The Board concluded that because the transferee is the purchaser of the assets, it should be able to value all assets and any liabilities it purchased or incurred, presumptively based on the purchase price paid. In addition, because the transferee recognizes no gain or loss on the transfer, there is no possibility of recognizing a nonexistent gain.

211. Respondents to the Exposure Draft asked the Board to clarify the meaning of the term *practicable*, especially in relation to the use of the same term in Statement 107. The comment letters also revealed a considerable range of interpretation of that provision among respondents. Some suggested that the provision would apply to all but the most common transactions. Others suggested that the provision would seldom apply and alluded to the relatively few entities that have used the practicability exception in Statement 107.

212. Because no practicability exception is used, for example, in the June 1996 FASB Exposure Draft, *Accounting for Derivative and Similar Financial Instruments and for Hedging Activities*, the Board considered whether to expand the discussion of practicability, or to remove it from the document. The Board ultimately concluded that the October 1995 Exposure Draft's practicability provisions should remain unchanged in this Statement for the reason noted in paragraphs 209 and 210.

213. Other respondents suggested that this Statement should include a limit on the amount of gain that can be recognized in a transfer of financial assets. Several suggested the limitation found in EITF

---

[18]FASB Statements No. 121, *Accounting for the Impairment of Long-Lived Assets and for Long-Lived Assets to Be Disposed Of*, par. 7, and No. 122, *Accounting for Mortgage Servicing Rights*, par. 3(f).

Issue 88-11. In that Issue, the Task Force reached a consensus that "the amount of any gain recognized when a portion of a loan is sold should not exceed the gain that would be recognized if the entire loan was sold." Respondents maintained that a limitation would meet the Board's objective of preventing recognition of nonexistent gains through underestimating liabilities.

214. The Board rejected the suggested limitation for several reasons. First, it was not clear that the limitation in Issue 88-11 could have been applied across a wide range of transactions. The limitation presumes that a market price exists for transfers of whole assets, but one reason that securitization transactions take place is because sometimes no market exists for the whole assets being securitized. Second, the limitation would have required that accountants ignore the added value that many maintain is created when assets are divided into their several parts. Third, the use of relative fair values at the date of transfer, rather than relative fair values on initial acquisition as in Issue 88-11, would have mitigated many of the concerns that appear to have prompted the Task Force to adopt a limitation. Finally, the Board was concerned that a gain limitation might have obscured the need to consider whether the transaction gives rise to a loss.

Subsequent Measurement

215. The provisions of this Statement focus principally on the initial recognition and measurement of assets and liabilities that result from transfers of financial assets. This Statement does not address subsequent measurement except for servicing assets and servicing liabilities and financial assets subject to prepayment.

216. Several respondents to the Exposure Draft asked the Board to include guidance about subsequent measurement in this Statement. They observed that the financial-components approach leads to recognition of assets and liabilities that were not recognized under previous standards. They also observed that accountants who draw analogies to existing accounting practices may find a variety of equally plausible approaches to subsequent measurement.

217. The Board is sensitive to concerns about subsequent measurement, especially to the possibility of emerging diversity in practice. However, attempting to address subsequent measurement would have expanded significantly the scope of this project. In addition, any guidance on subsequent measurement in this project would have applied only to assets and liabilities that emerge from a transfer of financial assets. Accounting for similar assets and liabilities not connected with a transfer of financial assets would have continued to follow existing practice; if so, diversity would have continued to exist. On balance, the Board concluded that it was better to complete this project without providing guidance on subsequent measurement and leave reconsideration of existing standards and practices for subsequent measurement for future segments of the Board's financial instruments project or other projects.

Extinguishments of Liabilities

218. Statement 76 required that a debtor treat a liability as if extinguished if it completed an in-substance defeasance. Under that Statement, a debtor derecognized a liability if it transferred essentially risk-free assets to an irrevocable defeasance trust and the cash flows from those assets approximated the scheduled interest and principal payments of the debt that was being extinguished. Under that Statement, the debtor also derecognized the assets that were set aside in the trust.

219. Derecognition of liabilities after an in-substance defeasance has been controversial. A number of respondents to the Exposure Drafts that led to Statement 76 and subsequent Board requests for comment have criticized the transactions as having insufficient economic substance to justify derecognition or gain recognition. Researchers and analysts have demonstrated that in-substance defeasance transactions conducted after interest rates have risen, which resulted in an accounting gain under Statement 76, have economic impact; those transactions constitute an economic loss to shareholders.[19] That research and analysis suggest that derecognition of liabilities and recognition of a gain in those circumstances may not be representationally faithful.

[19]The research referred to includes John R. M. Hand, Patricia J. Hughes, and Stephan E. Sefcik, "In-Substance Defeasances: Security Price Reactions and Motivations," *Journal of Accounting and Economics* (May 1990): 47-89; Judy Beckman, J. Ralph Byington, and Paul Munter, "Extinguishment of Debt by In-Substance Defeasance: Managerial Perspectives," *Journal of Corporate Accounting and Finance* (Winter 1989/90): 167-174; Bruce R. Gaumnitz and Joel E. Thompson, "In-Substance Defeasance: Costs, Yes; Benefits, No," *Journal of Accountancy* (March 1987): 102-105; and Abraham M. Stanger, "Accounting Developments: In-Substance Defeasance—Reality or Illusion?" *The Corporation Law Review* (Summer 1984): 274-277.

220. Under the financial-components approach, an in-substance defeasance transaction does not meet the derecognition criteria for either the liability or the asset. The transaction lacks the following critical characteristics:

a. The debtor is not released from the debt by putting assets in the trust; if the assets in the trust prove insufficient, for example, because a default by the debtor accelerates its debt, the debtor must make up the difference.
b. The lender is not limited to the cash flows from the assets in trust.
c. The lender does not have the ability to dispose of the assets at will or to terminate the trust.
d. If the assets in the trust exceed what is necessary to meet scheduled principal and interest payments, the transferor can remove the assets.
e. Neither the lender nor any of its representatives is a contractual party to establishing the defeasance trust, as holders of interests in a qualifying special-purpose entity or their representatives would be.
f. The debtor does not surrender control of the benefits of the assets because those assets are still being used for the debtor's benefit, to extinguish its debt, and because no asset can be an asset of more than one entity, those benefits must still be the debtor's assets.

221. The Board concluded that the previous treatment of in-substance defeasance was inconsistent with the derecognition criteria of the financial-components approach and that the provisions on in-substance defeasance in Statement 76 should be superseded by this Statement. Respondents to the Exposure Draft generally accepted that change, although some disagreed, citing arguments similar to those made in Statement 76 and refuted, in the Board's view, by the critical characteristics cited in paragraph 220.

222. Paragraph 3(a) of Statement 76 required derecognition of the transferred assets and the liability by the debtor if a debtor transfers assets to its creditor in exchange for a release from all further obligation under the liability. That provision has not been controversial and is consistent with the financial-components approach. Accordingly, paragraph 3(a) of Statement 76 was incorporated substantially unchanged as paragraph 16(a) of this Statement.

223. Paragraph 3(b) of Statement 76 stated, "The debtor is legally released from being the primary obligor under the debt either judicially or by the creditor

and it is probable that the debtor will not be required to make future payments with respect to that debt under any guarantees" (emphasis added; footnote references omitted). Except for the italicized portion, paragraph 3(b) was carried forward as paragraph 16(b) of this Statement. Some respondents to the Exposure Draft disagreed with that change, arguing that the revised provision was too lenient in that it might allow, for example, derecognition of liabilities and inappropriate gain recognition when entities are replaced as primary obligor by entities with little economic substance. However, the italicized phrase is omitted from this Statement because it is contrary to the financial-components approach. If an entity is released from being a primary obligor and becomes a secondary obligor and thus effectively a guarantor of that liability, it should recognize that guarantee in the same manner as a third-party guarantor that was never the primary obligor. The Board noted, however, that concerns about inappropriate gains are unwarranted: if an entity with little substance were to become a primary obligor, a guarantor of that obligation would have to recognize a liability almost as great as if it were the primary obligor. To emphasize those matters, the Board included a discussion of the secondary obligor's liability in Appendix A.

224. The Board concluded that the basic principle that liabilities should be derecognized only if the debtor pays the creditor or is legally released from its obligation applies not just to debt securities but to all liabilities. Accordingly, this Statement broadens the scope of paragraphs 3(a) and 3(b) of Statement 76 to include all liabilities not excluded from this Statement's scope by paragraph 4 and to delete the reference to sales in the public market.

Disclosures

225. The Board decided that this Statement should continue to require disclosure of debt defeased in accordance with Statement 76 before the effective date of this Statement because this Statement does not change the accounting for those defeasance transactions. The Board also decided to require that an entity disclose assets restricted to the repayment of particular debt obligations, for example, in in-substance defeasance transactions after this Statement becomes effective, because while that restriction is insufficient cause to derecognize the assets, that information is useful in determining what resources are unavailable to general creditors and for general operations. The

Board decided that an entity should disclose its policies for requiring collateral or other securities in repurchase agreements and securities lending transactions accounted for as borrowings. The Board believes that that information is useful for assessing the amount of risk that an entity assumes in repurchase agreements and securities lending transactions, which appears to vary considerably in practice.

226. The Board also decided to carry forward the disclosures required by Statement 122 and extend them to all servicing rights, because those disclosures provide information financial statement users need to make independent judgments about the value of servicing rights and obligations and the related risks.

227. In addition, the Board decided to require that an entity describe items for which it is impracticable to measure their fair value and disclose why the fair value of an asset obtained or liability incurred could not be estimated, despite the concerns of some Board members that this requirement was unnecessary and might lead to uninformative disclosures.

228. The Board decided that only those additional disclosures should be required because sufficient disclosures are currently in place for transfers and servicing of financial assets, extinguishments of liabilities, and the components resulting from those transfers and extinguishments. For example, transfers of financial assets in exchange for cash must appear in the statement of cash flows, while information about any noncash exchanges must appear in related disclosures, under the provisions of FASB Statement No. 95, *Statement of Cash Flows*. The Board also considered various disclosures now required for certain specialized industries by AICPA Guides and other pronouncements and decided that the potential benefits of requiring those disclosures in this Statement did not justify the costs involved.

Effective Date and Transition

229. The Board proposed in the Exposure Draft that this Statement should be effective for transfers and servicing of financial assets and extinguishments of liabilities occurring after December 31, 1996, and the Board did not change that effective date. While many respondents accepted and some even urged adoption on that date, some respondents expressed concern about the ability to carry out certain of this Statement's provisions by that date, including systems changes needed to keep track of supporting data efficiently. The Board concluded that some of those concerns should be ameliorated by the effects of changes from the Exposure Draft on the accounting for repurchase agreements, securities lending, loan participations, and collateral, and that in other cases data adequate for external financial reporting could be obtained in other ways while systems changes were being completed.

230. The Exposure Draft proposed that this Statement should be applied prospectively to achieve consistency in accounting for transfers of financial assets. That requirement also will ensure that all entities entering into a given transaction report that transaction under the same guidance. If entities were permitted to implement early or implement at the beginning of fiscal years that did not coincide, opportunities might arise to structure transactions in ways that result in the same assets and liabilities being reported in the financial statements of both parties or in the financial statements of neither party. The Board found that possibility undesirable. Most respondents to the Exposure Draft generally accepted that conclusion.

231. The Board also decided that retroactive implementation for all entities was not feasible and that allowing voluntary retroactive implementation was unwise because it would impair comparability of financial statements by permitting disparate accounting treatment for similar transactions reported in previous periods. The Board concluded that those considerations outweighed the lack of consistency within an entity's financial statements for transactions occurring before and after the effective date of this Statement. In addition, the Board concluded that the benefits of retroactive application of the provisions of this Statement would not justify the considerable cost of doing that. Respondents generally accepted that conclusion.

Appendix C

AMENDMENTS TO EXISTING PRONOUNCEMENTS

232. This Statement supersedes FASB Statements No. 76, *Extinguishment of Debt,* No. 77, *Reporting by Transferors for Transfers of Receivables with Recourse,* and No. 122, *Accounting for Mortgage Servicing Rights,* and FASB Technical Bulletins No. 84-4, *In-Substance Defeasance of Debt,* and No. 85-2, *Accounting for Collateralized Mortgage Obligations (CMOs).*

233. The following sentence is added to the end of paragraph 7 of FASB Statement No. 115, *Accounting for Certain Investments in Debt and Equity Securities:*

> A security may not be classified as held-to-maturity if that security can contractually be prepaid or otherwise settled in such a way that the holder of the security would not recover substantially all of its recorded investment.

234. Paragraph 3(a) of APB Opinion No. 26, *Early Extinguishment of Debt,* as amended by Statement 76, is replaced by the following:

> *Extinguishment of liabilities.* FASB Statement No. 125, *Accounting for Transfers and Servicing of Financial Assets and Extinguishments of Liabilities,* defines transactions that the debtor shall recognize as an extinguishment of a liability.

235. In the last sentence of paragraph 20 of FASB Statement No. 13, *Accounting for Leases,* as amended by Statement 77, the reference to Statement 77 is replaced with a reference to FASB Statement No. 125, *Accounting for Transfers and Servicing of Financial Assets and Extinguishments of Liabilities.*

236. The last sentence of footnote 1 of FASB Statement No. 22, *Changes in the Provisions of Lease Agreements Resulting from Refundings of Tax-Exempt Debt,* as amended by Statement 76, is deleted.

237. FASB Statement No. 65, *Accounting for Certain Mortgage Banking Activities,* is amended as follows:

a. The second sentence of paragraph 6 that was added by Statement 115 is replaced by the following:

> After the securitization of a mortgage loan held for sale, the mortgage-backed security shall be classified as a trading security.

b. Paragraph 8, as amended by Statement 115, is deleted.

c. The last sentence of paragraph 9(a) is deleted.

d. In paragraph 10, *(paragraphs 16 through 19)* is deleted and replaced by *(paragraph 13 of FASB Statement No. 125, Accounting for Transfers and Servicing of Financial Assets and Extinguishments of Liabilities).*

e. Paragraph 11 and footnote 4 are deleted.

f. In paragraph 15, the reference to paragraph 18 (as amended by Statement 122) is deleted and the following is added to the end of paragraph 15 replacing the sentence added by Statement 122:

> The rate used to determine the present value shall be an appropriate long-term interest rate. For this purpose, estimates of future servicing revenue shall include expected late charges and other ancillary revenue. Estimates of expected future servicing costs shall include direct costs associated with performing the servicing function and appropriate allocations of other costs. Estimated future servicing costs may be determined on an incremental cost basis. The amount capitalized shall be amortized in proportion to, and over the period of, estimated net servicing income—the excess of servicing revenues over servicing costs.

g. Paragraphs 16-19 and 30 and footnote 6, as amended by Statement 122, are deleted.

h. The three paragraphs added by Statement 122 to paragraph 30 are deleted.

i. In paragraph 34, the terms *current (normal) servicing fee rate* and *servicing* and their definitions are deleted.

238. This Statement carries forward certain amendments that Statement 122 made to Statement 65. Those amendments are:

a. In the first sentence of paragraph 1, *origination or acquisition* is replaced by *purchase or acquisition.*

b. In the first sentence of paragraph 10, *of existing* is replaced by *or origination of.*

239. Paragraph 14(e) of FASB Statement No. 105, *Disclosure of Information about Financial Instruments with Off-Balance-Sheet Risk and Financial Instruments with Concentrations of Credit Risk,* is replaced by the following:

> Substantively extinguished debt subject to the disclosure requirements of FASB Statement

No. 125, *Accounting for Transfers and Servicing of Financial Assets and Extinguishments of Liabilities.*

240. FASB Statement No. 107, *Disclosures about Fair Value of Financial Instruments,* is amended as follows:

a. Paragraph 8(b) of FASB Statement 107 is replaced by the following:

Substantively extinguished debt subject to the disclosure requirements of FASB Statement No. 125, *Accounting for Transfers and Servicing of Financial Assets and Extinguishments of Liabilities*

b. In the last sentence of paragraph 28, *, or the rate that an entity would have to pay to acquire essentially risk-free assets to extinguish the obligation in accordance with the requirements of Statement 76* is deleted.

241. Paragraph 12 of FASB Technical Bulletin No. 86-2, *Accounting for an Interest in the Residual Value of a Leased Asset: Acquired by a Third Party or Retained by a Lessor That Sells the Related Minimum Rental Payments,* is replaced by the following:

Yes. A residual value of a leased asset is a financial asset to the extent of the guarantee of the residual value. Accordingly, increases to its estimated value over the remaining lease term should be recognized.

242. FASB Technical Bulletin No. 87-3, *Accounting for Mortgage Servicing Fees and Rights,* is amended as follows:

a. Paragraphs 1-7 are deleted.

b. Paragraph 9, as amended by Statement 122, is replaced by the following:

An enterprise may acquire servicing assets or liabilities by purchasing or originating financial assets with servicing rights retained or by purchasing the servicing rights separately. Servicing assets and liabilities are amortized in proportion to, and over the period of, estimated net servicing income—the excess of servicing revenues over servicing costs.

Appendix D

GLOSSARY

243. This appendix defines terms or phrases used in this Statement.

Adequate compensation
The amount of benefits of servicing that would fairly compensate a substitute servicer should one be required, which includes the profit that would be demanded in the marketplace.

Beneficial interests
Rights to receive all or portions of specified cash inflows to a trust or other entity, including senior and subordinated shares of interest, principal, or other cash inflows to be "passed-through" or "paid-through," premiums due to guarantors, and residual interests.

Benefits of servicing
Revenues from contractually specified servicing fees, late charges, and other ancillary sources, including "float."

Cleanup call
An option held by the servicer, which may be the transferor, to purchase transferred financial assets when the amount of outstanding assets falls to a level at which the cost of servicing those assets becomes burdensome.

Collateral
Personal or real property in which a security interest has been given.

Contractually specified servicing fees
All amounts that, per contract, are due to the servicer in exchange for servicing the financial asset and would no longer be received by a servicer if the beneficial owners of the serviced assets or their trustees or agents were to exercise their actual or potential authority under the contract to shift the servicing to another servicer. Depending on the servicing contract, those fees may include some or all of the difference between the interest rate collectible on the asset being serviced and the rate to be paid to the beneficial owners of those assets.

Derecognize

Remove previously recognized assets or liabilities from the statement of financial position.

Derivative financial instrument

A futures, forward, swap, or option contract, or other financial instrument with similar characteristics (Statement 119, paragraph 5).

Fair value

Refer to paragraphs 42-44.

Financial asset

Cash, evidence of an ownership interest in an entity, or a contract that conveys to a second entity a contractual right (a) to receive cash or another financial instrument from a first entity or (b) to exchange other financial instruments on potentially favorable terms with the first entity (Statement 107, paragraph 3(b)).

Financial liability

A contract that imposes on one entity a contractual obligation (a) to deliver cash or another financial instrument to a second entity or (b) to exchange other financial instruments on potentially unfavorable terms with the second entity (Statement 107, paragraph 3(a)).

Interest-only strip

A contractual right to receive some or all of the interest due on a bond, mortgage loan, collateralized mortgage obligation, or other interest-bearing financial asset.

Proceeds

Cash, derivatives, or other assets that are obtained in a transfer of financial assets, less any liabilities incurred.

Recourse

The right of a transferee of receivables to receive payment from the transferor of those receivables for (a) failure of debtors to pay when due, (b) the effects of prepayments, or (c) adjustments resulting from defects in the eligibility of the transferred receivables.

Securitization

The process by which financial assets are transformed into securities.

Security interest

A form of interest in property that provides that upon default of the obligation for which the security interest is given, the property may be sold in order to satisfy that obligation.

Seller

A transferor that relinquishes control over financial assets by transferring them to a transferee in exchange for consideration.

Servicing asset

A contract to service financial assets under which the estimated future revenues from contractually specified servicing fees, late charges, and other ancillary revenues are expected to more than adequately compensate the servicer for performing the servicing. A servicing contract is either (a) undertaken in conjunction with selling or securitizing the financial assets being serviced or (b) purchased or assumed separately.

Servicing liability

A contract to service financial assets under which the estimated future revenues from stated servicing fees, late charges, and other ancillary revenues are not expected to adequately compensate the servicer for performing the servicing.

Transfer

The conveyance of a noncash financial asset by and to someone other than the issuer of that financial asset. Thus, a transfer includes selling a receivable, putting it into a securitization trust, or posting it as collateral but excludes the origination of that receivable, the settlement of that receivable, or the restructuring of that receivable into a security in a troubled debt restructuring.

Transferee

An entity that receives a financial asset, a portion of a financial asset, or a group of financial assets from a transferor.

Transferor

An entity that transfers a financial asset, a portion of a financial asset, or a group of financial assets that it controls to another entity.

Undivided interest

Partial legal or beneficial ownership of an asset as a tenant in common with others. The proportion owned may be pro rata, for example, the right to receive 50 percent of all cash flows from a security, or non–pro rata, for example, the right to receive the interest from a security while another has the right to the principal.

Statement of Financial Accounting Standards No. 126
Exemption from Certain Required Disclosures about Financial Instruments for Certain Nonpublic Entities

an amendment of FASB Statement No. 107

STATUS

Issued: December 1996

Effective Date: For fiscal years ending after December 15, 1996

Affects: Amends FAS 107, paragraph 7

Affected by: Paragraph 2(c) superseded by FAS 133

SUMMARY

This Statement amends FASB Statement No. 107, *Disclosures about Fair Value of Financial Instruments*, to make the disclosures about fair value of financial instruments prescribed in Statement 107 optional for entities that meet all of the following criteria:

a. The entity is a nonpublic entity.
b. The entity's total assets are less than $100 million on the date of the financial statements.
c. The entity has not held or issued any derivative financial instruments, as defined in FASB Statement No. 119, *Disclosure about Derivative Financial Instruments and Fair Value of Financial Instruments,* other than loan commitments, during the reporting period.

This Statement shall be effective for fiscal years ending after December 15, 1996. Earlier application is permitted in financial statements that have not been issued previously.

Statement of Financial Accounting Standards No. 126

Exemption from Certain Required Disclosures about Financial Instruments for Certain Nonpublic Entities

an amendment of FASB Statement No. 107

CONTENTS

INTRODUCTION

1. The FASB received requests that it exempt certain entities from the requirements of FASB Statement No. 107, *Disclosures about Fair Value of Financial Instruments*. The Board concluded that the disclosures required by Statement 107 should be optional for certain nonpublic entities. The basis for the Board's conclusions is presented in the appendix to this Statement.

STANDARDS OF FINANCIAL ACCOUNTING AND REPORTING

2. Disclosures about the fair value of financial instruments prescribed in Statement 107 shall be optional for an entity that meets all of the following criteria:

a. The entity is a nonpublic entity.
b. The entity's total assets are less than $100 million on the date of the financial statements.
c. The entity has not held or issued any derivative financial instruments as defined in FASB Statement No. 119, *Disclosure about Derivative Financial Instruments and Fair Value of Financial Instruments,* other than loan commitments, during the reporting period.

The criteria shall be applied to the most recent year presented in comparative financial statements to determine applicability of this Statement. If disclosures are not required in the current period, the disclosures for previous years may be omitted if financial statements for those years are presented for comparative purposes. If disclosures are required in the current period, disclosures about the fair value of financial instruments prescribed in Statement 107 that have not been reported previously need not be included in financial statements that are presented for comparative purposes.

3. For purposes of this Statement, a nonpublic entity is any entity other than one (a) whose debt or equity securities trade in a public market either on a stock exchange (domestic or foreign) or in the over-the-counter market, including securities quoted only locally or regionally, (b) that makes a filing with a regulatory agency in preparation for the sale of any class of debt or equity securities in a public market, or (c) that is controlled by an entity covered by (a) or (b).

4. This Statement does not change the requirements of FASB Statements No. 115, *Accounting for Certain Investments in Debt and Equity Securities,* and No. 124, *Accounting for Certain Investments Held by Not-for-Profit Organizations* (including disclosures about financial instruments other than equity and debt securities that are measured at fair value in the statement of financial position), or any requirements,

other than those specified in paragraph 2, for recognition, measurement, classification, or disclosure of financial instruments in financial statements.

Amendment to Statement 107

5. The following is added at the end of the second sentence of paragraph 7 of Statement 107:

> but is optional for those entities covered by FASB Statement No. 126, *Exemption from Certain Required Disclosures about Financial Instruments for Certain Nonpublic Entities.*

Effective Date

6. This Statement shall be effective for fiscal years ending after December 15, 1996. Earlier application is permitted in financial statements that have not been issued previously.

> **The provisions of this Statement need not be applied to immaterial items.**

This Statement was adopted by the unanimous vote of the seven members of the Financial Accounting Standards Board:

Dennis R. Beresford, *Chairman*	Anthony T. Cope	James J. Leisenring
	John M. Foster	Gerhard G. Mueller
Joseph V. Anania	Gaylen N. Larson	

Appendix

BACKGROUND INFORMATION AND BASIS FOR CONCLUSIONS

CONTENTS

Appendix

BACKGROUND INFORMATION AND BASIS FOR CONCLUSIONS

Introduction

7. This appendix summarizes considerations that were deemed significant by Board members in reaching the conclusions in this Statement. It discusses reasons for accepting certain views and rejecting others. Individual Board members gave greater weight to some factors than to others.

8. The Board issued an Exposure Draft, *Elimination of Certain Disclosures about Financial Instruments by Small Nonpublic Entities,* on September 20, 1996. The Exposure Draft proposed making the disclosures prescribed by Statement 107 optional for nonpublic

entities with total assets of less than $10 million that do not hold or issue derivative instruments during the reporting period. The Board received 76 comment letters. The Board considered those comments and revised the Exposure Draft by clarifying this Statement's applicability and modifying the criteria for determining if the disclosures required by Statement 107 are optional. The Board concluded that it could reach an informed decision on the basis of existing information without a public hearing.

Benefits and Costs

9. The mission of the Board is to establish and improve standards of financial accounting and reporting for the guidance and education of the public, including issuers, auditors, and users of financial information. In fulfilling that mission, the Board strives to determine that a proposed standard will fill a significant need and that the costs imposed to meet that standard, as compared with other alternatives, are justified in relation to the overall benefits of the resulting information. Present and potential investors, creditors, and others benefit from improvements in financial reporting; however, the costs to implement a new standard may not be borne evenly by all parties. Further, the costs of not issuing a standard are impossible to quantify. Because there is no common gauge by which to judge objectively the costs to implement a standard against the need to improve information in financial statements, the Board's assessment of the costs and benefits of issuing an accounting standard is unavoidably subjective.

10. The Board has a commitment to consider potential disclosure differences between small and large companies on a case-by-case basis.[1] The Board recognizes that there is an incremental cost of applying Statement 107. The Board has long acknowledged that the cost of any accounting requirement falls disproportionately on small entities because of their limited accounting resources and need to rely on outside professionals.[2]

11. In paragraph 79 of Statement 107, the Board observed:

> The Board considered whether certain entities should be excluded from the scope of this Statement. In particular, the Board con-

sidered the usefulness of the disclosures about fair value required by this Statement for small, nonpublic, or predominantly nonfinancial entities; a number of respondents to the 1990 Exposure Draft suggested exclusions on one or more of those bases. After considering the costs and benefits of those disclosures, the Board concluded that the disclosures are important and should be required for all entities, including small and nonpublic entities. The Board believes that the notion of "practicability" discussed in paragraph 15 ensures that excessive costs do not have to be incurred to comply with the disclosure requirements. In addition, the Board's decision to allow smaller entities additional time to apply the provisions of this Statement recognizes the fact that the costs of compliance can be reduced for those entities because the overall benefits of the information might be less than for larger entities.

12. Public accountants who serve smaller nonpublic entities informed the Board that the practicability provisions of Statement 107 have been useful in reducing the costs of complying with the Statement. However, they also reported that there is a cost of documenting compliance with the Statement, including the reasons why an entity concludes that estimating fair value is impracticable.

13. This Statement will result in some loss of information provided by the financial statements of certain nonpublic entities. However, the Board views that loss as temporary. The Board currently plans to address a number of issues involving the recognition and measurement of financial instruments. As those issues are resolved, the disclosures required by Statement 107 will change. The Board will have the opportunity to consider whether the entities to which this Statement applies should make the revised disclosures.

Fair Value Information in the Financial Statements of Smaller Nonpublic Entities

14. The Board has concluded in its Exposure Draft, *Accounting for Derivative and Similar Financial Instruments and for Hedging Activities,* that fair value is the most relevant measure for financial instruments. Nothing in this Statement changes that view.

---

[1] "Board Responds to Concerns about 'Standards Overload,' " FASB *Status Report,* No. 150, November 22, 1983.

[2] "FASB Analyzes Small Business Concerns about Accounting Standards," FASB *Status Report,* No. 181, November 3, 1986.

However, the Board concluded that the disclosures required by Statement 107 likely have limited utility to users of the financial statements of certain nonpublic entities. In reaching that conclusion, the Board considered (a) the types of financial instruments held by smaller nonpublic entities, (b) the extent to which those entities' financial statements already provide information about the fair value of financial instruments, and (c) the extent to which those entities make use of Statement 107's practicability provisions.

Types of Financial Instruments

15. Smaller nonpublic entities are less likely than larger entities to engage in complex financial transactions. Apart from cash and trade receivables, their financial assets tend to be traded securities, investments in other closely held entities, and balances with related parties. Their financial liabilities tend to be trade payables, variable-rate loans, and fixed-rate loans. In contrast, entities that engage in complex financial transactions or that have substantial risk associated with changes in the fair values of financial instruments are likely to use derivative financial instruments. This Statement does not apply to entities that held or issued derivative financial instruments, other than loan commitments, during the reporting period.

Information Already Provided in Financial Statements

16. The financial statements of entities covered by this Statement generally provide significant information about fair value of financial instruments, even without the requirements of Statement 107. Trade receivables and payables and variable-rate instruments are already carried at amounts that approximate fair value. Investments in securities addressed by Statements 115 and 124 are carried at fair value (as trading or available-for-sale) or, if carried at cost, the fair values are disclosed. Existing disclosures about fixed-rate long-term debt include information about interest rates and repayment terms. That information should allow users to estimate whether the fair value of the long-term debt is significantly different from the carrying amount.

Use of the Practicability Exception

17. The Board has been informed that smaller entities make frequent use of Statement 107's practicability exception when considering whether to disclose the fair value of many financial instruments, especially investments in other closely held entities and balances with related parties.

18. After considering the issues discussed in paragraphs 14-17, the Board concluded that, pending resolution of the underlying recognition and measurement issues, certain entities should have the option of not making disclosures mandated by Statement 107.

Factors Considered in Determining Scope

19. In considering which entities might be removed from the scope of Statement 107, the Board considered questions of size, financial activity, and ownership.

20. Previous FASB Statements that provided differential disclosure requirements have done so based on whether the entity is nonpublic. That criterion alone would have removed many large, nonpublic entities with complicated financial activities from the scope of Statement 107. The Board does not believe that it is appropriate to exempt those entities from the scope of Statement 107.

21. The Board decided that a size criterion was necessary to supplement the nonpublic criterion used in earlier pronouncements. The Exposure Draft proposed $10 million of total assets. The majority of the respondents to the Exposure Draft said that that amount was too low. The Board considered the nature of financial instruments in smaller nonpublic firms that do not use derivative financial instruments and decided that a higher threshold was acceptable. The Board settled on $100 million of total assets as an amount. In reaching its decision, the Board noted that exempting certain entities from current fair value disclosures is a practical matter and that the criteria used in paragraph 2 of this Statement are not meant to carry over into or influence future considerations about the usefulness of disclosures about financial instruments or other matters.

22. Some respondents said that total-asset size was not the best indicator of the relevance of disclosures about financial instruments. Some firms would not qualify for exemption as a result of having significant inventory or other physical assets. The Board considered changing the criterion to total financial instruments or to the amount of financial instruments not included within the scope of Statement 115 or Statement 124. While a criterion based on financial instruments may be more pertinent to the decision to exempt certain entities from the disclosure requirements in Statement 107, the Board decided that such

a criterion would unnecessarily complicate the standard. The objective of this Statement is to reduce complexity for certain entities, and requiring them to make decisions as to what is and what is not a financial instrument would not contribute to that objective. A total-asset criterion is easier to apply and could accomplish much of the same effect.

23. A larger total-asset criterion also exempts more financial institutions and other entities with higher concentrations of financial instruments. Some Board members were concerned that disclosures about fair values of financial instruments are particularly relevant for those entities. However, the Board decided to exempt entities with less than $100 million of total assets that meet the other criteria in this Statement. In reaching that decision, the Board considered (a) available evidence about the composition of assets at smaller financial institutions and (b) regulatory requirements for reporting fair values to the Federal Deposit Insurance Corporation.

24. The Board had concluded in the Exposure Draft that an entity that uses derivative financial instruments subject to the requirements of Statement 119 should remain within the scope of Statement 107.

Statements 119 and 107 interact with one another, and their requirements are not easily separated. More important, an entity that uses derivative financial instruments is not, by virtue of its utilization of complex financial instruments, the type of entity to which this Statement is intended to apply. Several respondents to the Exposure Draft indicated that the definition of derivative financial instruments in Statement 119 includes loan commitments and, as such, many entities would be precluded from applying this Statement. The Board agreed that loan commitments should not preclude entities from applying the provisions of this Statement.

25. Some respondents noted that the Exposure Draft was not clear on whether disclosures are required when previous periods are presented for comparative purposes. The Board determined that it would not be cost beneficial to provide information for periods presented for comparative purposes unless those disclosures were presented in prior periods and the disclosures prescribed by Statement 107 are required in the current period. The following table presents the requirements for disclosures when prior periods are presented in comparative financial statements.

If Disclosures for the Current Period Are:	And Disclosures for Prior Periods Were:	Then Disclosures for Prior Periods Presented in Comparative Statements Are:
Optional	Optional	Optional
Optional	Required	Optional
Required	Optional	Optional
Required	Required	Required

Statement of Financial Accounting Standards No. 127
Deferral of the Effective Date of Certain Provisions of FASB Statement No. 125

an amendment of FASB Statement No. 125

STATUS

Issued: December 1996

Effective Date: December 31, 1996

Affects: Supersedes FAS 125, paragraph 19

Affected by: Superseded by FAS 140

SUMMARY

FASB Statement No. 125, *Accounting for Transfers and Servicing of Financial Assets and Extinguishments of Liabilities,* was issued in June 1996 and establishes, among other things, new criteria for determining whether a transfer of financial assets in exchange for cash or other consideration should be accounted for as a sale or as a pledge of collateral in a secured borrowing. Statement 125 also establishes new accounting requirements for pledged collateral. As issued, Statement 125 is effective for all transfers and servicing of financial assets and extinguishments of liabilities occurring after December 31, 1996.

The Board was made aware that the volume and variety of certain transactions and the related changes to information systems and accounting processes that are necessary to comply with the requirements of Statement 125 would make it extremely difficult, if not impossible, for some affected enterprises to apply the transfer and collateral provisions of Statement 125 to those transactions as soon as January 1, 1997. As a result, this Statement defers for one year the effective date (a) of paragraph 15 of Statement 125 and (b) for repurchase agreement, dollar-roll, securities lending, and similar transactions, of paragraphs 9-12 and 237(b) of Statement 125.

This Statement provides additional guidance on the types of transactions for which the effective date of Statement 125 has been deferred. It also requires that if it is not possible to determine whether a transfer occurring during calendar-year 1997 is part of a repurchase agreement, dollar-roll, securities lending, or similar transaction, then paragraphs 9-12 of Statement 125 should be applied to that transfer.

All provisions of Statement 125 should continue to be applied prospectively, and earlier or retroactive application is not permitted.

Statement of Financial Accounting Standards No. 127

Deferral of the Effective Date of Certain Provisions of FASB Statement No. 125

an amendment of FASB Statement No. 125

CONTENTS

INTRODUCTION

1. FASB Statement No. 125, *Accounting for Transfers and Servicing of Financial Assets and Extinguishments of Liabilities*, was issued in June 1996. That Statement establishes, among other things, new criteria for determining whether a transfer of financial assets should be accounted for as a sale or as a pledge of collateral in a secured borrowing. Statement 125 also establishes new accounting requirements for pledged collateral.

2. As issued, Statement 125 is effective for all transfers and servicing of financial assets and extinguishments of liabilities occurring after December 31, 1996, and is to be applied prospectively. Earlier or retroactive application of Statement 125 is not permitted.

3. The Board was made aware that the volume and variety of certain transactions and the related changes to information systems and accounting processes that are necessary to comply with the requirements of Statement 125 would make it extremely difficult, if not impossible, for some affected enterprises to apply the transfer and collateral provisions of Statement 125 to those transactions as soon as January 1, 1997. As a result, this Statement defers for one year the effective date (a) of paragraph 15 of Statement 125 and (b) for repurchase agreement, dollar-roll, securities lending, and similar transactions, of paragraphs 9-12 and 237(b) of Statement 125. The provisions of Statement 125 will continue to be applied prospectively, and earlier or retroactive application is not permitted.

4. To defer the effective date of paragraphs 9-12 and 237(b) of Statement 125 only for certain transactions, the Board has grouped all transfers of financial assets into two broad categories: (a) repurchase agreement, dollar-roll, securities lending, and similar transactions and (b) all other transfers and servicing of financial assets. As discussed in paragraph 14 of this Statement, the Board recognizes that it may be difficult to determine the appropriate categorization of certain transactions for purposes of determining the effective date of Statement 125 and therefore has provided guidance for those circumstances.

STANDARDS OF FINANCIAL ACCOUNTING AND REPORTING

Amendment to Statement 125

5. Paragraph 19 of Statement 125 is replaced by the following:

> This Statement shall be effective for transfers and servicing of financial assets and extinguishments of liabilities occurring after December 31, 1996, except that:
>
> a. Paragraph 15 shall be effective for all transfers of financial assets occurring after December 31, 1997.

b. For repurchase agreement, dollar-roll, securities lending, and similar transactions, paragraphs 9-12 and 237(b) shall be effective for transfers of financial assets occurring after December 31, 1997.

If it is not possible to determine whether a transfer occurring during calendar-year 1997 is covered by paragraph 19(b), then paragraphs 9-12 and 237(b) shall be applied to that transfer. All provisions of this Statement shall be applied prospectively, and earlier or retroactive application is not permitted.

Effective Date

6. This Statement is effective December 31, 1996.

> **The provisions of this Statement need
> not be applied to immaterial items.**

This Statement was adopted by the unanimous vote of the seven members of the Financial Accounting Standards Board:

Dennis R. Beresford,	Anthony T. Cope	James J. Leisenring
Chairman	John M. Foster	Gerhard G. Mueller
Joseph V. Anania	Gaylen N. Larson	

Appendix

**BACKGROUND INFORMATION AND
BASIS FOR CONCLUSIONS**

7. Statement 125 was issued in June 1996 and as issued is effective for transfers and servicing of financial assets and extinguishments of liabilities occurring after December 31, 1996. As discussed in paragraph 229 of Statement 125, some respondents to the Exposure Draft had expressed concern about their ability to apply certain provisions of Statement 125 by that date, including making the changes to information and accounting systems needed to apply the newly established accounting requirements and efficiently track supporting data. The Board concluded that some of those concerns should be ameliorated by the effects of changes from the Exposure Draft and that in other cases data adequate for external financial reporting could be obtained in other ways while systems changes were being completed.

8. After Statement 125 was issued, however, representatives from various enterprises, particularly those representing brokers and dealers in securities, continued to express to the Board concerns about the effective date of Statement 125. On October 16, 1996, the Board met with representatives from interested enterprises to discuss those concerns, which focused on the volume and variety of repurchase agreement, dollar-roll, securities lending, and similar transactions. The Board became convinced that, for those transactions, substantial changes to information systems and accounting processes were essential for brokers and dealers in securities and other enterprises to comply with Statement 125. The requisite changes and the volume and variety of those transactions would make it extremely difficult, if not impossible, for some affected enterprises to account for those transfers of financial assets and apply the secured borrowing and collateral provisions of Statement 125 as soon as January 1, 1997.

9. The Board appreciated the concerns expressed by those enterprises that attempting to account for those types of transactions manually until appropriate modifications could be made to information systems and accounting processes might lead to a significant temporary deterioration in the financial controls over and quality of financial information reported by the affected enterprises. Those enterprises informed the Board that a one-year delay for those transactions would provide an appropriate period of time for modifying information systems and accounting processes.

10. In November 1996, the Board issued an Exposure Draft, *Deferral of the Effective Date of Certain Provisions of FASB Statement No. 125,* that proposed deferring for one year the effective date of paragraph 15 (addressing secured borrowings and collateral) of Statement 125 for all transactions and of paragraphs 9-12 (addressing transfers of financial assets) only for transfers of financial assets that are part

of repurchase agreement, dollar-roll, securities lending, and similar transactions. The Board did not believe that it was necessary or appropriate to defer the effective date of the other provisions of Statement 125 for other types of transactions because those provisions and transactions do not involve so great a volume or variety, nor do they involve such extensive changes to information systems and accounting processes. The Board received letters of comment from 29 respondents, a large majority of whom supported the Exposure Draft. The comments were considered by the Board during its redeliberations in a public meeting in December 1996, and the Board concluded that it could reach an informed decision on the basis of existing information without a public hearing.

11. The Board recognized that some enterprises that enter into repurchase agreement, dollar-roll, securities lending, and similar transactions and into collateral arrangements do so in volumes and varieties that would permit them to apply paragraphs 9-12 and 15 of Statement 125 to those transactions beginning on January 1, 1997, with little difficulty. However, the Board decided to require deferral rather than allow optional deferral because the Board continues to believe, for reasons discussed in paragraph 230 of Statement 125, that all parties should consistently apply Statement 125 to the same types of transactions and as of the same date.

12. To facilitate the deferral of the effective date of paragraphs 9-12 and 237(b) of Statement 125 for only the specified transactions, transfers of financial assets have been grouped into two broad categories. Transfers in the first category—repurchase agreement (refer to paragraphs 66-68 and 71 of Statement 125), dollar-roll (refer to paragraph 70 of Statement 125), securities lending (refer to paragraphs 61-64 of Statement 125), and similar transactions—frequently involve an agreement that both entitles and obligates the transferor to repurchase or redeem the same or substantially the same (refer to paragraphs 27 and 28 of Statement 125) financial assets before their maturity. Other similar transactions include "buy-sell" agreements and certain other transfers of financial assets that are very similar to repurchase agreement, dollar-roll, and securities lending transactions in both form and objectives.

13. Transfers in the second category include securitizations (as defined in paragraph 243 of Statement 125) and other transfers of financial assets that,

prior to the effective date of Statement 125, are accounted for in accordance with FASB Statements No. 77, *Reporting by Transferors for Transfers of Receivables with Recourse,* and No. 65, *Accounting for Certain Mortgage Banking Activities,* as amended by FASB Statement No. 122, *Accounting for Mortgage Servicing Rights,* and FASB Technical Bulletin No. 85-2, *Accounting for Collateralized Mortgage Obligations (CMOs).* Transfers in the second category also include, but are not limited to, wash sales, loan syndications and participations, bankers' acceptances, and factoring arrangements (as discussed in Appendix A to Statement 125).

14. The Board recognized that in some cases it may be difficult to determine whether a transaction is better included in one category or the other for purposes of determining the effective date of Statement 125. As indicated in paragraph 5 of this Statement, if it is not possible to determine the category in which a transfer occurring during calendar-year 1997 should be included, then paragraphs 9-12 and 237(b) of Statement 125 should be applied to that transfer. That guidance is intended to be restrictive and does not allow an enterprise the option of including a transaction in one category or the other. The Board continues to believe that the effective date of Statement 125 should be the same for similar transactions, particularly for all parties to the same transaction.

Other Possibilities Considered

15. The Board considered not deferring any portion of Statement 125 for any type of transfer of financial assets. However, the Board concluded that that option would be unresponsive to a valid concern of some of its constituents. The Board then considered several possibilities for deferring the effective date of Statement 125. One possibility was deferring the effective date of the entire Statement for all transactions. Board members noted that that approach would be simpler. However, a number of constituents desire and have incurred significant effort and expense to apply the provisions of Statement 125 to securitizations, sales of mortgages and other receivables, and other transactions occurring after December 31, 1996. For that reason, the Board concluded that prohibiting those enterprises from applying the provisions associated with transfers and servicing of financial assets to those transactions as of the original effective date of Statement 125 would be undesirable.

16. The Board also considered permitting the choice of earlier or retroactive application. However, the Board continues to believe that, for the reasons discussed in paragraphs 230 and 231 of Statement 125, that would be undesirable.

17. The Board also considered deferring the effective date of Statement 125 with earlier implementation encouraged and requiring that the cumulative effect of applying Statement 125 to all transfers of financial assets and extinguishments of liabilities occurring after December 31, 1996 be recognized in the year beginning after December 15, 1997. The Board determined, however, that an approach that includes a cumulative-effect adjustment would not sufficiently alleviate the systems and administrative problems that the Board was attempting to respond to because it would continue to be necessary for affected enterprises to capture and process accounting information beginning with transfers occurring as soon as January 1, 1997.

18. The Board also considered deferring the effective date only for paragraph 15 of Statement 125. While that solution would perhaps be simpler than the other options that were considered and would address a portion of the problems raised by the affected enterprises, it would not address the information systems and accounting process requirements for a large volume and variety of transactions. Therefore, the Board concluded that deferring the effective date of only paragraph 15 was less desirable than the approach in this Statement.

Statement of Financial Accounting Standards No. 128
Earnings per Share

STATUS

Issued: February 1997

Effective Date: For financial statements for both interim and annual periods ending after December 15, 1997

Affects: Supersedes APB 15
Amends APB 18, paragraph 18
Supersedes APB 18, footnote 8
Amends APB 20, paragraphs 20, 21, 42 through 44, and 46 through 48
Supersedes APB 28, paragraph 30(b)
Amends APB 30, paragraph 9
Supersedes APB 30, paragraph 12 and footnote 3
Supersedes AIN-APB 15, Interpretations No. 1 through 102
Supersedes AIN-APB 20, Interpretations No. 1 and 2
Amends FAS 21, paragraphs 12 and 14
Supersedes FAS 21, footnote 3
Supersedes FAS 85
Supersedes FAS 123, paragraphs 49 and 359 through 361 and footnote 26
Amends FAS 123, paragraphs 50, 357, and 358
Supersedes FIN 28, paragraph 6
Supersedes FIN 31
Supersedes FIN 38, paragraph 7
Amends FTB 79-8, paragraph 2

Affected by: Paragraph 28 amended by FAS 135
Paragraph 59 amended by FAS 141
Paragraph 171 amended by FAS 145

Issues Discussed by FASB Emerging Issues Task Force (EITF)

Affects: Partially nullifies EITF Issues No. 85-18 and 90-4
Partially resolves EITF Issue No. 96-13

Interpreted by: Paragraphs 8 and 9 interpreted by EITF Topic No. D-82
Paragraph 29 interpreted by EITF Topic No. D-72
Paragraph 46 and footnote 18 interpreted by EITF Topic No. D-62
Paragraph 61 interpreted by EITF Topic No. D-95

Related Issues: EITF Issues No. 84-22, 90-19, 92-3, 98-12, 99-7, and 00-19 and Topics No. D-15, D-42, and D-53

SUMMARY

This Statement establishes standards for computing and presenting earnings per share (EPS) and applies to entities with publicly held common stock or potential common stock. This Statement simplifies the standards for computing earnings per share previously found in APB Opinion No. 15, *Earnings per Share,* and makes them comparable to international EPS standards. It replaces the presentation of primary EPS with a presentation of basic EPS. It also requires dual presentation of basic and diluted EPS on the face of the income statement for all entities with complex capital structures and requires a reconciliation of the numerator and denominator of the basic EPS computation to the numerator and denominator of the diluted EPS computation.

Basic EPS excludes dilution and is computed by dividing income available to common stockholders by the weighted-average number of common shares outstanding for the period. Diluted EPS reflects the potential dilution that could occur if securities or other contracts to issue common stock were exercised or converted into common stock or resulted in the issuance of common stock that then shared in the earnings of the entity. Diluted EPS is computed similarly to fully diluted EPS pursuant to Opinion 15.

This Statement supersedes Opinion 15 and AICPA Accounting Interpretations 1-102 of Opinion 15. It also supersedes or amends other accounting pronouncements listed in Appendix D. The provisions in this Statement are substantially the same as those in International Accounting Standard 33, *Earnings per Share,* recently issued by the International Accounting Standards Committee.

This Statement is effective for financial statements issued for periods ending after December 15, 1997, including interim periods; earlier application is not permitted. This Statement requires restatement of all prior-period EPS data presented.

Statement of Financial Accounting Standards No. 128

Earnings per Share

CONTENTS

INTRODUCTION

1. This Statement specifies the computation, presentation, and disclosure requirements for **earnings per share**[1] (EPS) for entities with publicly held **common stock** or **potential common stock.** This Statement's objective is to simplify the computation of earnings per share and to make the U.S. standard for computing earnings per share more compatible with the EPS standards of other countries and with that of the International Accounting Standards Committee (IASC).

2. In 1969, the AICPA issued APB Opinion No. 15, *Earnings per Share,* and by 1971 had published 102 Accounting Interpretations of Opinion 15. Given the widespread use of EPS data, the objective of Opinion 15 was to provide a standard so that earnings per share would be computed on a consistent basis and presented in the most meaningful manner. That objective also underlies this Statement.

3. Opinion 15 permitted a single presentation of "earnings per common share" for entities with simple

---

[1]Terms defined in Appendix E, the glossary, are set in **boldface type** the first time they appear.

capital structures. That presentation was similar to **basic EPS,** which is a common presentation outside the United States. However, Opinion 15 required that entities with complex capital structures present both "primary" and "fully diluted" EPS on the face of the income statement. The primary EPS computation included "common stock equivalents" in the denominator (the number of common shares outstanding). Only two other countries require presentation of primary EPS; all other countries that have EPS requirements require presentation of only basic EPS or both basic and fully diluted EPS.

4. In October 1993, the IASC issued a draft Statement of Principles, *Earnings per Share,* for public comment. Because earnings per share is one of the most widely used financial statistics, the IASC's goal was to initiate a common approach to the determination and presentation of earnings per share that would permit global comparisons. Even though EPS data may have limitations because of the different national methods for determining "earnings," the IASC and the FASB believe that a consistently determined denominator will be a significant improvement in international financial reporting.

5. The Board pursued its EPS project concurrently with the IASC to help achieve international harmonization of the accounting standards for computing earnings per share. The focus of the project was on the denominator of the EPS computation, not on issues about the determination of earnings. The IASC issued IAS 33, *Earnings per Share,* concurrently with the issuance of this Statement; the provisions in that Standard are substantially the same as those in this Statement.

STANDARDS OF FINANCIAL ACCOUNTING AND REPORTING

Scope

6. This Statement requires presentation of earnings per share by all entities that have issued common stock or potential common stock (that is, **securities** such as **options, warrants, convertible securities,** or **contingent stock agreements**) if those securities

trade in a public market either on a stock exchange (domestic or foreign) or in the over-the-counter market, including securities quoted only locally or regionally. This Statement also requires presentation of earnings per share by an entity that has made a filing or is in the process of filing with a regulatory agency in preparation for the sale of those securities in a public market. This Statement does not require presentation of earnings per share for investment companies[2] or in statements of wholly owned subsidiaries. Any entity that is not required by this Statement to present earnings per share in its financial statements that chooses to present earnings per share in its financial statements shall do so in accordance with the provisions of this Statement.

7. This Statement supersedes Opinion 15, AICPA Accounting Interpretations 1-102 of Opinion 15, AICPA Accounting Interpretations 1, "Changing EPS Denominator for Retroactive Adjustment to Prior Period," and 2, "EPS for 'Catch-up' Adjustment," of APB Opinion No. 20, *Accounting Changes,* FASB Statement No. 85, *Yield Test for Determining whether a Convertible Security Is a Common Stock Equivalent,* and FASB Interpretation No. 31, *Treatment of Stock Compensation Plans in EPS Computations.* It also amends other accounting pronouncements listed in Appendix D.

Basic Earnings per Share

8. The objective of basic EPS is to measure the performance of an entity over the reporting period. Basic EPS shall be computed by dividing **income available to common stockholders** (the numerator) by the **weighted-average number of common shares outstanding** (the denominator) during the period. Shares issued during the period and shares reacquired during the period shall be weighted for the portion of the period that they were outstanding.

9. Income available to common stockholders shall be computed by deducting both the dividends declared in the period on **preferred stock** (whether or not paid) and the dividends accumulated for the period on cumulative preferred stock (whether or not earned)[3] from income from continuing operations (if

---

[2]That is, investment companies that comply with the requirements of the AICPA Audit and Accounting Guide, *Audits of Investment Companies,* to present selected per-share data.

[3]Preferred dividends that are cumulative only if earned shall be deducted only to the extent that they are earned.

that amount appears in the income statement)[4] and also from net income. If there is a loss from continuing operations or a net loss, the amount of the loss shall be increased by those preferred dividends.

10. Shares issuable for little or no cash consideration upon the satisfaction of certain conditions (**contingently issuable shares**) shall be considered outstanding common shares and included in the computation of basic EPS as of the date that all necessary conditions have been satisfied (in essence, when issuance of the shares is no longer contingent). Outstanding common shares that are contingently returnable (that is, subject to recall) shall be treated in the same manner as contingently issuable shares.[5]

Diluted Earnings per Share

11. The objective of **diluted EPS** is consistent with that of basic EPS—to measure the performance of an entity over the reporting period—while giving effect to all **dilutive** potential common shares that were outstanding during the period. The computation of diluted EPS is similar to the computation of basic EPS except that the denominator is increased to include the number of additional common shares that would have been outstanding if the dilutive potential common shares had been issued. In addition, in computing the dilutive effect of convertible securities, the numerator is adjusted to add back (a) any convertible preferred dividends and (b) the after-tax amount of interest recognized in the period associated with any convertible debt. The numerator also is adjusted for any other changes in income or loss that would result from the assumed conversion of those potential common shares, such as profit-sharing expenses. Similar adjustments also may be necessary for certain contracts that provide the issuer or holder with a choice between settlement methods.

12. Diluted EPS shall be based on the most advantageous **conversion rate** or **exercise price** from the standpoint of the security holder. Previously reported diluted EPS data shall not be retroactively adjusted for subsequent conversions or subsequent changes in the market price of the common stock.

No Antidilution

13. The computation of diluted EPS shall not assume conversion, exercise, or **contingent issuance** of securities that would have an **antidilutive** effect on earnings per share. Shares issued on actual conversion, exercise, or satisfaction of certain conditions for which the underlying potential common shares were antidilutive shall be included in the computation as outstanding common shares from the date of conversion, exercise, or satisfaction of those conditions, respectively. In determining whether potential common shares are dilutive or antidilutive, each issue or series of issues of potential common shares shall be considered separately rather than in the aggregate.

14. Convertible securities may be dilutive on their own but antidilutive when included with other potential common shares in computing diluted EPS. To reflect maximum potential dilution, each issue or series of issues of potential common shares shall be considered in sequence from the most dilutive to the least dilutive. That is, dilutive potential common shares with the lowest "earnings per incremental share" shall be included in diluted EPS before those with a higher earnings per incremental share.[6] Illustration 4 in Appendix C provides an example of that provision.

15. An entity that reports a discontinued operation, an extraordinary item, or the cumulative effect of an accounting change in a period shall use income from continuing operations[7] (adjusted for preferred dividends as described in paragraph 9) as the "control number" in determining whether those potential common shares are dilutive or antidilutive. That is, the same number of potential common shares used in computing the diluted per-share amount for income from continuing operations shall be used in computing all other reported diluted per-share amounts even

---

[4]An entity that does not report a discontinued operation but reports an extraordinary item or the cumulative effect of an accounting change in the period shall use that line item (for example, *income before extraordinary items* or *income before accounting change*) whenever the line item *income from continuing operations* is referred to in this Statement.

[5]Thus, contingently issuable shares include shares that (a) will be issued in the future upon the satisfaction of specified conditions, (b) have been placed in escrow and all or part must be returned if specified conditions are not met, or (c) have been issued but the holder must return all or part if specified conditions are not met.

[6]Options and warrants generally will be included first because use of the treasury stock method does not impact the numerator of the computation.

[7]Refer to footnote 4.

if those amounts will be antidilutive to their respective basic per-share amounts.[8]

16. Including potential common shares in the denominator of a diluted per-share computation for continuing operations always will result in an antidilutive per-share amount when an entity has a *loss* from continuing operations or a *loss* from continuing operations available to common stockholders (that is, after any preferred dividend deductions). Although including those potential common shares in the other diluted per-share computations may be dilutive to their comparable basic per-share amounts, no potential common shares shall be included in the computation of any diluted per-share amount when a loss from continuing operations exists, even if the entity reports net income.

Options and Warrants and Their Equivalents

17. The dilutive effect of outstanding **call options** and warrants (and their equivalents) issued by the reporting entity shall be reflected in diluted EPS by application of the **treasury stock method** unless the provisions of paragraphs 24 and 50-53 require that another method be applied. Equivalents of options and warrants include nonvested stock granted to employees, stock purchase contracts, and partially paid stock subscriptions.[9] Under the treasury stock method:

a. Exercise of options and warrants shall be assumed at the beginning of the period (or at time of issuance, if later) and common shares shall be assumed to be issued.
b. The proceeds from exercise shall be assumed to be used to purchase common stock at the average market price during the period.[10]
c. The incremental shares (the difference between the number of shares assumed issued and the number of shares assumed purchased) shall be included in the denominator of the diluted EPS computation.[11]

18. Options and warrants will have a dilutive effect under the treasury stock method only when the average market price of the common stock during the period exceeds the exercise price of the options or warrants (they are "in the money"). Previously reported EPS data shall not be retroactively adjusted as a result of changes in market prices of common stock.

19. Dilutive options or warrants that are issued during a period or that expire or are canceled during a period shall be included in the denominator of diluted EPS for the period that they were outstanding. Likewise, dilutive options or warrants exercised during the period shall be included in the denominator for the period prior to actual exercise. The common shares issued upon exercise of options or warrants shall be included in the denominator for the period after the exercise date. Consequently, incremental shares assumed issued shall be weighted for the period the options or warrants were outstanding, and common shares actually issued shall be weighted for the period the shares were outstanding.

Stock-based compensation arrangements

20. Fixed awards and nonvested stock (as defined in FASB Statement No. 123, *Accounting for Stock-Based Compensation*) to be issued to an employee[12]

---

[8]For example, assume that Corporation X has income from continuing operations of $2,400, a loss from discontinued operations of $(3,600), a net loss of $(1,200), and 1,000 common shares and 200 potential common shares outstanding. Corporation X's basic per-share amounts would be $2.40 for continuing operations, $(3.60) for the discontinued operation, and $(1.20) for the net loss. Corporation X would include the 200 potential common shares in the denominator of its diluted per-share computation for continuing operations because the resulting $2.00 per share is dilutive. (For illustrative purposes, assume no numerator impact of those 200 potential common shares.) Because income from continuing operations is the control number, Corporation X also must include those 200 potential common shares in the denominator for the other per-share amounts, even though the resulting per-share amounts [$(3.00) per share for the loss from discontinued operation and $(1.00) per share for the net loss] are antidilutive to their comparable basic per-share amounts; that is, the loss per-share amounts are less.

[9]Refer to paragraph 64.

[10]Refer to paragraphs 21, 47, and 48.

[11]Consider Corporation Y that has 10,000 warrants outstanding exercisable at $54 per share; the average market price of the common stock during the reporting period is $60. Exercise of the warrants and issuance of 10,000 shares of common stock would be assumed. The $540,000 that would be realized from exercise of the warrants ($54 × 10,000) would be an amount sufficient to acquire 9,000 shares ($540,000/$60). Thus, 1,000 incremental shares (10,000 − 9,000) would be added to the outstanding common shares in computing diluted EPS for the period.

A shortcut formula for that computation follows (note that this formula may not be appropriate for stock-based compensation awards [refer to paragraph 21]):

Incremental shares = [(market price − exercise price)/market price] × shares assumed issued under option; thus, [($60 − $54)/$60] × 10,000 = 1,000 incremental shares.

[12]The provisions in paragraphs 20-23 also apply to stock-based awards issued to other than employees in exchange for goods and services.

under a stock-based compensation arrangement are considered options for purposes of computing diluted EPS. Such stock-based awards shall be considered to be outstanding as of the grant date for purposes of computing diluted EPS even though their exercise may be contingent upon vesting. Those stock-based awards are included in the diluted EPS computation even if the employee may not receive (or be able to sell) the stock until some future date. Accordingly, all shares to be issued shall be included in computing diluted EPS if the effect is dilutive. The dilutive effect of stock-based compensation arrangements shall be computed using the treasury stock method. If the stock-based awards were granted during the period, the shares issuable must be weighted to reflect the portion of the period during which the awards were outstanding.

21. In applying the treasury stock method described in paragraph 17, the assumed proceeds shall be the sum of (a) the amount, if any, the employee must pay upon exercise, (b) the amount of compensation cost attributed to future services and not yet recognized,[13] and (c) the amount of tax benefits (both deferred and current), if any, that would be credited to additional paid-in capital assuming exercise of the options. Assumed proceeds shall not include compensation ascribed to past services. The tax benefit is the amount resulting from a tax deduction for compensation in excess of compensation expense recognized for financial reporting purposes. That deduction arises from an increase in the market price of the stock under option between the measurement date and the date at which the compensation deduction for income tax purposes is determinable. The amount of the tax benefit shall be determined by a "with-and-without" computation. Paragraph 17 of APB Opinion No. 25, *Accounting for Stock Issued to Employees,* states that in some instances the tax deduction for compensation may be less than the compensation expense recognized for financial reporting purposes. If the resulting difference in income tax will be deducted from capital in accordance with that paragraph, such taxes to be deducted from capital shall be treated as a reduction of assumed proceeds.

22. If stock-based compensation arrangements are payable in common stock or in cash at the election of either the entity or the employee, the determination of whether such stock-based awards are potential common shares shall be made based on the provisions in paragraph 29. If an entity has a tandem plan (as defined in Statement 123) that allows the entity or the employee to make an election involving two or more types of equity instruments, diluted EPS for the period shall be computed based on the terms used in the computation of compensation expense for that period.

23. Performance awards (as defined in Statement 123) shall be included in diluted EPS pursuant to the contingent share provisions in paragraphs 30-35 of this Statement. As discussed in paragraph 26 of Statement 123, targeted stock price options are not considered to be a performance award. However, because options with a target stock price have a market price contingency, the contingent share provisions of this Statement shall be applied in determining whether those options are included in the computation of diluted EPS.

Written put options

24. Contracts that require that the reporting entity repurchase its own stock, such as written **put options** and forward purchase contracts, shall be reflected in the computation of diluted EPS if the effect is dilutive. If those contracts are "in the money" during the reporting period (the exercise price is above the average market price for that period), the potential dilutive effect on EPS shall be computed using the **reverse treasury stock method.** Under that method:

a. Issuance of sufficient common shares shall be assumed at the beginning of the period (at the average market price during the period) to raise enough proceeds to satisfy the contract.

b. The proceeds from issuance shall be assumed to be used to satisfy the contract (that is, to buy back shares).

c. The incremental shares (the difference between the number of shares assumed issued and the

---

[13]This provision applies only to those stock-based awards for which compensation cost will be recognized in the financial statements in accordance with APB Opinion No. 25, *Accounting for Stock Issued to Employees,* or Statement 123.

number of shares received from satisfying the contract) shall be included in the denominator of the diluted EPS computation.[14]

Purchased options

25. Contracts such as purchased put options and **purchased call options** (options held by the entity on its own stock) shall not be included in the computation of diluted EPS because including them would be antidilutive. That is, the put option would be exercised only when the exercise price is higher than the market price and the call option would be exercised only when the exercise price is lower than the market price; in both instances, the effect would be antidilutive under both the treasury stock method and the reverse treasury stock method, respectively.

Convertible Securities

26. The dilutive effect of convertible securities shall be reflected in diluted EPS by application of the **if-converted method.** Under that method:

a. If an entity has convertible preferred stock outstanding, the preferred dividends applicable to convertible preferred stock shall be added back to the numerator.[15]

b. If an entity has convertible debt outstanding, (1) interest charges applicable to the convertible debt shall be added back to the numerator, (2) to the extent nondiscretionary adjustments based on income[16] made during the period would have been computed differently had the interest on convertible debt never been recognized, the numerator shall be appropriately adjusted, and (3) the numerator shall be adjusted for the income tax effect of (1) and (2).

c. The convertible preferred stock or convertible debt shall be assumed to have been converted at the beginning of the period (or at time of issuance, if later), and the resulting common shares shall be included in the denominator.

27. In applying the if-converted method, conversion shall not be assumed for purposes of computing diluted EPS if the effect would be antidilutive. Convertible preferred stock is antidilutive whenever the amount of the dividend declared in or accumulated for the current period per common share obtainable on conversion exceeds basic EPS. Similarly, convertible debt is antidilutive whenever its interest (net of tax and nondiscretionary adjustments) per common share obtainable on conversion exceeds basic EPS.

28. Dilutive convertible securities that are issued during a period in circumstances where conversion options lapse, preferred stock is redeemed, or related debt is extinguished shall be included in the denominator of diluted EPS for the period that they were outstanding. Likewise, dilutive convertible securities converted during a period shall be included in the denominator for the period prior to actual conversion. The common shares issued upon actual conversion shall be included in the denominator for the period after the date of conversion. Consequently, shares assumed issued shall be weighted for the period the convertible securities were outstanding, and common shares actually issued shall be weighted for the period the shares were outstanding.

Contracts That May Be Settled in Stock or Cash

29. If an entity issues a contract that may be settled in common stock or in cash at the election of either the entity or the holder, the determination of whether that contract shall be reflected in the computation of diluted EPS shall be made based on the facts available each period.[17] It shall be presumed that the contract will be settled in common stock and the resulting potential common shares included in diluted EPS (in accordance with the relevant provisions of this Statement) if the effect is more dilutive. A contract that is reported as an asset or liability for accounting purposes may require an adjustment to the numerator for any changes in income or loss that would result if the contract had been reported as an equity instrument for accounting purposes during the period. That

---

[14]For example, Corporation Z sells 100 put options with an exercise price of $25; the average market price for the period is $20. In computing diluted EPS at the end of the period, Corporation Z assumes it issues 125 shares at $20 per share to satisfy its put obligation of $2,500. The difference between the 125 shares issued and the 100 shares received from satisfying the put option (25 incremental shares) would be added to the denominator of diluted EPS.

[15]The amount of preferred dividends added back will be the amount of preferred dividends for convertible preferred stock deducted from income from continuing operations (and from net income) in computing income available to common stockholders pursuant to paragraph 9.

[16]Nondiscretionary adjustments include any expenses or charges that are determined based on the income (loss) for the period, such as profit-sharing and royalty agreements.

[17]An example of such a contract is a written put option that gives the holder a choice of settling in common stock or in cash. Stock-based compensation arrangements that are payable in common stock or in cash at the election of either the entity or the employee shall be accounted for pursuant to this paragraph.

adjustment is similar to the adjustments required for convertible debt in paragraph 26(b). The presumption that the contract will be settled in common stock may be overcome if past experience or a stated policy provides a reasonable basis to believe that the contract will be paid partially or wholly in cash.

Contingently Issuable Shares

30. Shares whose issuance is contingent upon the satisfaction of certain conditions shall be considered outstanding and included in the computation of diluted EPS as follows:

a. If all necessary conditions have been satisfied by the end of the period (the events have occurred), those shares shall be included as of the beginning of the period in which the conditions were satisfied (or as of the date of the contingent stock agreement, if later).
b. If all necessary conditions have not been satisfied by the end of the period, the number of contingently issuable shares included in diluted EPS shall be based on the number of shares, if any, that would be issuable if the end of the reporting period were the end of the contingency period (for example, the number of shares that would be issuable based on current period earnings or period-end market price) and if the result would be dilutive. Those contingently issuable shares shall be included in the denominator of diluted EPS as of the beginning of the period (or as of the date of the contingent stock agreement, if later).[18]

Paragraphs 31-34 provide general guidelines that shall be applied in determining the EPS impact of different types of contingencies that may be included in contingent stock agreements.

31. If attainment or maintenance of a specified amount of earnings is the condition and if that amount has been attained, the additional shares shall be considered to be outstanding for the purpose of computing diluted EPS if the effect is dilutive. The diluted EPS computation shall include those shares that would be issued under the conditions of the contract based on the assumption that the current amount of earnings will remain unchanged until the end of the agreement, but only if the effect would be dilutive. Because the amount of earnings may change in a future period, basic EPS shall not include such con-

tingently issuable shares because all necessary conditions have not been satisfied. Illustration 3 in Appendix C provides an example of that provision.

32. The number of shares contingently issuable may depend on the market price of the stock at a future date. In that case, computations of diluted EPS shall reflect the number of shares that would be issued based on the current market price at the end of the period being reported on if the effect is dilutive. If the condition is based on an average of market prices over some period of time, the average for that period shall be used. Because the market price may change in a future period, basic EPS shall not include such contingently issuable shares because all necessary conditions have not been satisfied.

33. In some cases, the number of shares contingently issuable may depend on both future earnings and future prices of the shares. In that case, the determination of the number of shares included in diluted EPS shall be based on both conditions, that is, earnings to date and current market price—as they exist at the end of each reporting period. If *both* conditions are not met at the end of the reporting period, no contingently issuable shares shall be included in diluted EPS.

34. If the contingency is based on a condition other than earnings or market price (for example, opening a certain number of retail stores), the contingent shares shall be included in the computation of diluted EPS based on the assumption that the current status of the condition will remain unchanged until the end of the contingency period. Illustration 3 in Appendix C provides an example of that provision.

35. Contingently issuable potential common shares (other than those covered by a contingent stock agreement, such as contingently issuable convertible securities) shall be included in diluted EPS as follows:

a. An entity shall determine whether the potential common shares may be assumed to be issuable based on the conditions specified for their issuance pursuant to the contingent share provisions in paragraphs 30-34.
b. If those potential common shares should be reflected in diluted EPS, an entity shall determine

---

[18]For year-to-date computations, contingent shares shall be included on a weighted-average basis. That is, contingent shares shall be weighted for the interim periods in which they were included in the computation of diluted EPS.

their impact on the computation of diluted EPS by following the provisions for options and warrants in paragraphs 17-25, the provisions for convertible securities in paragraphs 26-28, and the provisions for contracts that may be settled in stock or cash in paragraph 29, as appropriate.[19]

However, exercise or conversion shall not be assumed for purposes of computing diluted EPS unless exercise or conversion of similar outstanding potential common shares that are not contingently issuable is assumed.

Presentation on Face of Income Statement

36. Entities with simple capital structures, that is, those with only common stock outstanding, shall present basic per-share amounts for income from continuing operations[20] and for net income on the face of the income statement. All other entities shall present basic and diluted per-share amounts for income from continuing operations and for net income on the face of the income statement with equal prominence.

37. An entity that reports a discontinued operation, an extraordinary item, or the cumulative effect of an accounting change in a period shall present basic and diluted per-share amounts for those line items either on the face of the income statement or in the notes to the financial statements. Per-share amounts not required to be presented by this Statement that an entity chooses to disclose shall be computed in accordance with this Statement and disclosed only in the notes to the financial statements; it shall be noted whether the per-share amounts are pretax or net of tax.[21]

Periods Presented

38. Earnings per share data shall be presented for all periods for which an income statement or summary of earnings is presented. If diluted EPS data are reported for at least one period, they shall be reported for all periods presented, even if they are the same amounts as basic EPS. If basic and diluted EPS are

the same amount, dual presentation can be accomplished in one line on the income statement.

Terminology

39. The terms *basic EPS* and *diluted EPS* are used in this Statement to identify EPS data to be presented and are not required to be captions used in the income statement. There are no explicit requirements for the terms to be used in the presentation of basic and diluted EPS; terms such as *earnings per common share* and *earnings per common share—assuming dilution,* respectively, are appropriate.

Disclosure Requirements

40. For each period for which an income statement is presented, an entity shall disclose the following:

a. A reconciliation of the numerators and the denominators of the basic and diluted per-share computations for income from continuing operations.[22] The reconciliation shall include the individual income and share amount effects of all securities that affect earnings per share.[23] Illustration 2 in Appendix C provides an example of that disclosure.
b. The effect that has been given to preferred dividends in arriving at income available to common stockholders in computing basic EPS.
c. Securities (including those issuable pursuant to contingent stock agreements) that could potentially dilute basic EPS in the future that were not included in the computation of diluted EPS because to do so would have been antidilutive for the period(s) presented.

41. For the latest period for which an income statement is presented, an entity shall provide a description of any transaction that occurs after the end of the most recent period but before issuance of the financial statements that would have changed materially the number of common shares or potential common shares outstanding at the end of the period if the transaction had occurred before the end of the period.

---

[19]Neither interest nor dividends shall be imputed for the additional contingently issuable convertible securities because any imputed amount would be reversed by the if-converted adjustments for assumed conversions.

[20]Refer to footnote 4.

[21]Paragraph 33 of FASB Statement No. 95, *Statement of Cash Flows,* prohibits reporting an amount of cash flow per share.

[22]Refer to footnote 4.

[23]An entity is encouraged to refer to pertinent information about securities included in the EPS computations that is provided elsewhere in the financial statements as prescribed by FASB Statement No. 129, *Disclosure of Information about Capital Structure,* and other accounting pronouncements.

Examples of those transactions include the issuance or acquisition of common shares; the issuance of warrants, options, or convertible securities; the resolution of a contingency pursuant to a contingent stock agreement; and the conversion or exercise of potential common shares outstanding at the end of the period into common shares.

Computational Guidance

42. The determination of EPS data as required by this Statement considers the complexities of the capital structures of some entities. The calculations also shall give effect to matters such as stock dividends or splits and business combinations. Guidelines for dealing with some common computational matters and some complex capital structures are set forth in Appendix A. That appendix is an integral part of the requirements of this Statement.

Effective Date and Transition

43. This Statement shall be effective for financial statements for both interim and annual periods ending after December 15, 1997. Earlier application is not permitted. However, an entity is permitted to disclose pro forma EPS amounts computed using this Statement in the notes to the financial statements in periods prior to required adoption. After the effective date, all prior-period EPS data presented shall be restated (including interim financial statements, summaries of earnings, and selected financial data) to conform with the provisions of this Statement.

**The provisions of this Statement need
not be applied to immaterial items.**

This Statement was adopted by the unanimous vote of the seven members of the Financial Accounting Standards Board:

Dennis R. Beresford,	Anthony T. Cope	James J. Leisenring
Chairman	John M. Foster	Gerhard G. Mueller
Joseph V. Anania	Gaylen N. Larson	

Appendix A

COMPUTATIONAL GUIDANCE

CONTENTS

Appendix A

COMPUTATIONAL GUIDANCE

Introduction

44. This appendix, which is an integral part of the requirements of this Statement, provides general guidance to be used in the computation of earnings per share.

Computing a Weighted Average

45. The weighted-average number of shares discussed in this Statement is an arithmetical mean average of shares outstanding and assumed to be outstanding for EPS computations. The most precise average would be the sum of the shares determined on a daily basis divided by the number of days in the period. Less-precise averaging methods may be used, however, as long as they produce reasonable results. Methods that introduce artificial weighting, such as the "Rule of 78" method, are not acceptable for computing a weighted-average number of shares for EPS computations.

Applying the Treasury Stock Method

Year-to-Date Computations

46. The number of incremental shares included in quarterly diluted EPS shall be computed using the average market prices during the three months included in the reporting period. For year-to-date diluted EPS, the number of incremental shares to be included in the denominator shall be determined by computing a year-to-date weighted average of the number of incremental shares included in each quarterly diluted EPS computation. Illustration 1 (Full Year 20X1, footnote a) in Appendix C provides an example of that provision.

Average Market Price

47. In applying the treasury stock method, the average market price of common stock shall represent a meaningful average. Theoretically, every market transaction for an entity's common stock could be included in determining the average market price. As a practical matter, however, a simple average of weekly or monthly prices usually will be adequate.

48. Generally, closing market prices are adequate for use in computing the average market price. When prices fluctuate widely, however, an average of the high and low prices for the period that the price represents usually would produce a more representative price. The method used to compute the average market price shall be used consistently unless it is no longer representative because of changed conditions. For example, an entity that uses closing market prices to compute the average market price for several years of relatively stable market prices might need to change to an average of high and low prices if prices start fluctuating greatly and the closing market prices no longer produce a representative average market price.

Options and Warrants and Their Equivalents

49. Options or warrants to purchase convertible securities shall be assumed to be exercised to purchase the convertible security whenever the average prices of both the convertible security and the common stock obtainable upon conversion are above the exercise price of the options or warrants. However, exercise shall not be assumed unless conversion of similar outstanding convertible securities, if any, also is assumed. The treasury stock method shall be applied to determine the incremental number of convertible securities that are assumed to be issued and immediately converted into common stock. Interest or dividends shall not be imputed for the incremental convertible securities because any imputed amount would be reversed by the if-converted adjustments for assumed conversions.

50. Paragraphs 51-53 provide guidance on how certain options, warrants, and convertible securities should be included in the computation of diluted EPS. Conversion or exercise of the potential common shares discussed in those paragraphs shall not be reflected in diluted EPS unless the effect is dilutive. Those potential common shares will have a dilutive effect if (a) the average market price of the related common stock for the period exceeds the exercise price or (b) the security to be tendered is selling at a price below that at which it may be tendered under the option or warrant agreement and the resulting discount is sufficient to establish an effective exercise price below the market price of the common stock obtainable upon exercise. When several conversion alternatives exist, the computation shall give effect to the alternative that is most advantageous to the holder of the convertible security. Similar treatment shall be given to preferred stock that has similar provisions or

to other securities that have conversion options that permit the investor to pay cash for a more favorable conversion rate.

51. Options or warrants may permit or require the tendering of debt or other securities of the issuer (or its parent or its subsidiary) in payment of all or a portion of the exercise price. In computing diluted EPS, those options or warrants shall be assumed to be exercised and the debt or other securities shall be assumed to be tendered. If tendering cash would be more advantageous to the option holder or warrant holder and the contract permits tendering cash, the treasury stock method shall be applied. Interest (net of tax) on any debt assumed to be tendered shall be added back as an adjustment to the numerator. The numerator also shall be adjusted for any nondiscretionary adjustments based on income (net of tax). The treasury stock method shall be applied for proceeds assumed to be received in cash.

52. The underlying terms of certain options or warrants may require that the proceeds received from the exercise of those securities be applied to retire debt or other securities of the issuer (or its parent or its subsidiary). In computing diluted EPS, those options or warrants shall be assumed to be exercised and the proceeds applied to purchase the debt at its average market price rather than to purchase common stock under the treasury stock method. The treasury stock method shall be applied, however, for excess proceeds received from the assumed exercise. Interest, net of tax, on any debt assumed to be purchased shall be added back as an adjustment to the numerator. The numerator also shall be adjusted for any nondiscretionary adjustments based on income (net of tax).

53. Convertible securities that permit or require the payment of cash by the holder of the security at conversion are considered the equivalent of warrants. In computing diluted EPS, the proceeds assumed to be received shall be assumed to be applied to purchase common stock under the treasury stock method and the convertible security shall be assumed to be converted under the if-converted method.

Restatement of EPS Data

Stock Dividends or Stock Splits

54. If the number of common shares outstanding increases as a result of a stock dividend or stock split[24]

or decreases as a result of a reverse stock split, the computations of basic and diluted EPS shall be adjusted retroactively for all periods presented to reflect that change in capital structure. If changes in common stock resulting from stock dividends, stock splits, or reverse stock splits occur after the close of the period but before issuance of the financial statements, the per-share computations for those and any prior-period financial statements presented shall be based on the new number of shares. If per-share computations reflect such changes in the number of shares, that fact shall be disclosed.

Rights Issues

55. A **rights issue** whose exercise price at issuance is less than the fair value of the stock contains a bonus element that is somewhat similar to a stock dividend. If a rights issue contains a bonus element and the rights issue is offered to all existing stockholders, basic and diluted EPS shall be adjusted retroactively for the bonus element for all periods presented. If the ability to exercise the rights issue is contingent on some event other than the passage of time, the provisions of this paragraph shall not be applicable until that contingency is resolved.

56. The number of common shares used in computing basic and diluted EPS for all periods prior to the rights issue shall be the number of common shares outstanding immediately prior to the issue multiplied by the following factor: (fair value per share immediately prior to the exercise of the rights)/(theoretical ex-rights fair value per share). Theoretical ex-rights fair value per share shall be computed by adding the aggregate fair value of the shares immediately prior to the exercise of the rights to the proceeds expected from the exercise of the rights and dividing by the number of shares outstanding after the exercise of the rights. Illustration 5 in Appendix C provides an example of that provision. If the rights themselves are to be publicly traded separately from the shares prior to the exercise date, fair value for the purposes of this computation shall be established at the close of the last day on which the shares are traded together with the rights.

Prior-Period Adjustments

57. Certain APB Opinions and FASB Statements require that a restatement of the results of operations of a prior period be included in the income statement or

---

[24]Refer to ARB No. 43, Chapter 7B, "Capital Accounts—Stock Dividends and Stock Split-Ups."

summary of earnings. In those instances, EPS data given for the prior period or periods shall be restated. The effect of the restatement, expressed in per-share terms, shall be disclosed in the period of restatement.

58. Restated EPS data shall be computed as if the restated income or loss had been reported originally in the prior period or periods. Thus, it is possible that common stock assumed to be issued upon exercise, conversion, or issuance of potential common shares in accordance with the provisions of this Statement may not be included in the computation of restated EPS amounts. That is, retroactive restatement of income from continuing operations could cause potential common shares originally determined to be dilutive to become antidilutive pursuant to the control number provision in paragraph 15. The reverse also is true. Retroactive restatement also may cause the numerator of the EPS computation to change by an amount that differs from the amount of the retroactive adjustment.

Business Combinations and Reorganizations

59. When common shares are issued to acquire a business in a transaction accounted for as a purchase business combination, the computations of earnings per share shall recognize the existence of the new shares only from the acquisition date. When a business combination is accounted for as a pooling of interests, EPS computations shall be based on the aggregate of the weighted-average outstanding shares of the constituent businesses, adjusted to equivalent shares of the surviving business for all periods presented. In reorganizations, EPS computations shall be based on analysis of the particular transaction and the provisions of this Statement.

Participating Securities and Two-Class Common Stock

60. The capital structures of some entities include:

a. Securities that may participate in dividends with common stocks according to a predetermined formula (for example, two for one) with, at times, an upper limit on the extent of participation (for example, up to, but not beyond, a specified amount per share)

b. A class of common stock with different dividend rates from those of another class of common stock but without prior or senior rights.

61. The if-converted method shall be used for those securities that are convertible into common stock if the effect is dilutive. For those securities that are not convertible into a class of common stock, the "two class" method of computing earnings per share shall be used. The two-class method is an earnings allocation formula that determines earnings per share for each class of common stock and participating security according to dividends declared (or accumulated) and participation rights in undistributed earnings. Under that method:

a. Income from continuing operations (or net income) shall be reduced by the amount of dividends declared in the current period for each class of stock and by the contractual amount of dividends (or interest on participating income bonds) that must be paid for the current period (for example, unpaid cumulative dividends).[25]
b. The remaining earnings shall be allocated to common stock and participating securities to the extent that each security may share in earnings as if all of the earnings for the period had been distributed. The total earnings allocated to each security shall be determined by adding together the amount allocated for dividends and the amount allocated for a participation feature.
c. The total earnings allocated to each security shall be divided by the number of outstanding shares of the security to which the earnings are allocated to determine the earnings per share for the security.
d. Basic and diluted EPS data shall be presented for each class of common stock.

For the diluted EPS computation, outstanding common shares shall include all potential common shares assumed issued. Illustration 6 in Appendix C provides an example of that provision.

Securities of Subsidiaries

62. The effect on consolidated EPS of options, warrants, and convertible securities issued by a subsidiary depends on whether the securities issued by the subsidiary enable their holders to obtain common

---

[25]Dividends declared in the current period do not include dividends declared in respect of prior-year unpaid cumulative dividends. Preferred dividends that are cumulative only if earned are deducted only to the extent that they are earned.

stock of the subsidiary company or common stock of the parent company. The following general guidelines shall be used for computing consolidated diluted EPS by entities with subsidiaries that have issued common stock or potential common shares to parties other than the parent company:[26]

a. Securities issued by a subsidiary that enable their holders to obtain the subsidiary's common stock shall be included in computing the subsidiary's EPS data. Those per-share earnings of the subsidiary shall then be included in the consolidated EPS computations based on the consolidated group's holding of the subsidiary's securities. Illustration 7 in Appendix C provides an example of that provision.
b. Securities of a subsidiary that are convertible into its parent company's common stock shall be considered among the potential common shares of the parent company for the purpose of computing consolidated diluted EPS. Likewise, a subsidiary's options or warrants to purchase common stock of the parent company shall be considered among the potential common shares of the parent company in computing consolidated diluted EPS. Illustration 7 in Appendix C provides an example of that provision.

As noted in paragraph 18 of APB Opinion No. 18, *The Equity Method of Accounting for Investments in Common Stock,* as amended by this Statement, the above provisions are applicable to investments in common stock of corporate joint ventures and investee companies accounted for under the equity method.

63. The if-converted method shall be used in determining the EPS impact of securities issued by a parent company that are convertible into common stock of a subsidiary company or an investee company accounted for under the equity method. That is, the securities shall be assumed to be converted and the numerator (income available to common stockholders) adjusted as necessary in accordance with the provisions in paragraph 26(a) and (b). In addition to those adjustments, the numerator shall be adjusted appropriately for any change in the income recorded by the parent (such as dividend income or equity method income) due to the increase in the number of common shares of the subsidiary or equity method investee outstanding as a result of the assumed conversion. The denominator of the diluted EPS computation would not be affected because the number of shares of parent company common stock outstanding would not change upon assumed conversion.

Partially Paid Shares and Partially Paid Stock Subscriptions

64. If an entity has common shares issued in a partially paid form[27] and those shares are entitled to dividends in proportion to the amount paid, the common-share equivalent of those partially paid shares shall be included in the computation of basic EPS to the extent that they were entitled to participate in dividends. Partially paid stock subscriptions that do not share in dividends until fully paid are considered the equivalent of warrants and shall be included in diluted EPS by use of the treasury stock method. That is, the unpaid balance shall be assumed to be proceeds used to purchase stock under the treasury stock method. The number of shares included in diluted EPS shall be the difference between the number of shares subscribed and the number of shares assumed to be purchased.

---

[26]Refer to paragraphs 140 and 141.

[27]Issuing common shares that are not fully paid is permitted in some countries.

Appendix B

BACKGROUND INFORMATION AND BASIS FOR CONCLUSIONS

CONTENTS

Appendix B

BACKGROUND INFORMATION AND BASIS FOR CONCLUSIONS

Introduction

65. This appendix summarizes considerations that were deemed significant by Board members in reach-ing the conclusions in this Statement. It includes reasons for accepting certain views and rejecting others. Individual Board members gave greater weight to some factors than to others.

Background Information

66. In 1991, the Board issued a plan for international activities (which was updated in 1995) that describes

the FASB's role in international activities and proposes steps to increase the range and intensity of its international activities.[28] An objective of the plan is to make financial statements more useful for investors and creditors by increasing the international comparability of accounting standards concurrent with improving the quality of accounting standards. One element of the plan is for the FASB to work toward greater international comparability of accounting standards by identifying projects that potentially could achieve broad international agreement in a relatively short time and by initiating cooperative international standards-setting projects.

67. An FASB Prospectus, *Earnings per Share,* was distributed for public comment in June 1993. The objective of the Prospectus was to inform the Board's constituents of a potential EPS project and to obtain information from them about the scope and importance of that project. The Prospectus explained that Opinion 15, as amended and interpreted, often had been criticized for having complex and arbitrary provisions and that, over the years, the FASB had received requests to reconsider EPS issues. In addition, it mentioned that the IASC had an EPS project on its agenda that provided an opportunity for the FASB to work with that international group toward achieving greater international comparability of EPS data.

68. The Prospectus explained that an EPS project would lend itself to a relatively narrow selection of issues and would not involve profound or divisive theoretical issues; thus, the Board concluded that an EPS project was a potential candidate for a successful cooperative international project. A majority of respondents to the Prospectus favored the Board's adding the project to its agenda in light of the agenda criteria. Most respondents indicated that the potential for international comparability should be an important consideration in the Board's agenda decision.

69. In March 1994, the Board added a project on earnings per share to its technical agenda to be pursued concurrently with the similar project of the IASC. The objective of the project was twofold: (a) to improve and simplify U.S. generally accepted accounting principles and (b) to issue a standard that would be compatible with international standards.

70. The IASC added an EPS project to its agenda in 1989 and issued a draft Statement of Principles, *Earnings per Share,* for public comment in

October 1993. In June 1994, the IASC approved a Statement of Principles to be used as the basis for an IASC Exposure Draft. In November 1995, the IASC approved an Exposure Draft of a proposed International Accounting Standard, *Earnings per Share,* which was issued in January 1996.

71. In January 1996, the FASB issued an Exposure Draft, *Earnings per Share and Disclosure of Information about Capital Structure.* Part I of the Exposure Draft proposed computation, presentation, and disclosure requirements for earnings per share by entities with publicly held common stock or potential common stock, and Part II proposed disclosures about an entity's capital structure applicable to all entities. Part I was substantially the same as the IASC Exposure Draft. The Board received 104 comment letters in response to the FASB Exposure Draft. Most letters were supportive of the proposal. The IASC received 75 comment letters in response to its Exposure Draft. The concerns raised by respondents to both Exposure Drafts and the concerns expressed by the IASC were considered by the Board at public meetings in 1996. No formal field test was conducted on the FASB Exposure Draft; however, six respondents to the Exposure Draft noted that they had applied the provisions in Part I to their company's capital structure and generally had found that the requirements were not difficult to apply and resulted in minor changes, if any, from their current EPS computations.

72. The Board decided to issue the two parts of the Exposure Draft as separate Statements because of the differences in scope. That is, the Board did not want nonpublic entities that were excluded from the scope of Part I of the Exposure Draft to have to concern themselves with numerous provisions that were not applicable to them. FASB Statement No. 129, *Disclosure of Information about Capital Structure,* was issued concurrently with this Statement. The provisions of Statement 129 are essentially unchanged from those proposed in Part II of the Exposure Draft.

73. The FASB and the IASC exchanged information on the progress of their respective EPS projects during the deliberation and redeliberation processes, and the FASB considered the tentative decisions reached by the IASC on all issues. In addition, members of the IASC Steering Committee on Earnings per Share

---

[28]FASB *Highlights,* "FASB's Plan for International Activities," January 1995.

and the IASC staff participated in FASB meetings to discuss the differences between the tentative conclusions of the two standards-setting bodies. Similarly, members of the FASB and its staff participated in IASC meetings to discuss those differences. Both the FASB and the IASC agreed to modifications of their initial positions on issues that were not considered critical. In addition, some of the conclusions reached by the FASB were influenced by how those conclusions would simplify the computation of earnings per share. The FASB decided it could reach an informed decision on the project without holding a public hearing. In January 1997, the IASC approved IAS 33, *Earnings per Share,* which was issued about the same time as this Statement.

Benefits and Costs

74. One of the precepts of the Board's mission is to promulgate standards only when the expected benefits of the resulting information exceed the perceived costs of providing that information. The Board strives to determine that a proposed standard will fill a significant need and that the costs entailed in satisfying that need, as compared with other alternatives, are justified in relation to the overall benefits of the resulting information.

75. The Board concluded that EPS information provided to users in financial statements could be improved by simplifying the existing computational guidance, revising the disclosure requirements, and increasing the comparability of EPS data on an international basis. Some of the changes made to the EPS guidance in an effort to simplify the computation include (a) not considering common stock equivalents in the computation of basic EPS, (b) eliminating the modified treasury stock method and the 3 percent materiality provision, and (c) revising the contingent share provisions (including eliminating the requirement to restate prior EPS data in certain situations) and the supplemental EPS data requirements.

76. The Board expects that the costs to implement this Statement will include initial costs for education and the redesign of procedures used to compute EPS data but that any ongoing costs should be minimal. The Board believes that the benefits of simplifying the EPS computation and harmonizing with national and international standards-setting bodies will outweigh the costs of implementing this Statement.

Conclusions on Basic Issues

Scope

77. This Statement, which provides computation, presentation, and disclosure requirements for earnings per share, requires presentation of earnings per share by entities with publicly held common stock or potential common stock and by entities that are in the process of selling that stock to the public. Nonpublic entities are excluded from the scope because, generally, those entities have simple capital structures and few common stockholders; thus, EPS data may not be meaningful for users of their financial statements. In addition, nonpublic entities were excluded from the scope of Opinion 15 (as amended by FASB Statement No. 21, *Suspension of the Reporting of Earnings per Share and Segment Information by Nonpublic Enterprises*), and the Board was not aware of any new information that would suggest that those entities should be required to report EPS data. For similar reasons, the Board decided not to include in the scope of this Statement entities whose publicly traded securities include only debt. However, any entity that chooses to present EPS data should do so in accordance with this Statement.

78. Few respondents commented on the proposed scope of the Statement. Those that did suggested that the scope exemption in the Exposure Draft for investment companies registered under the Investment Company Act of 1940 be expanded to include investment companies, such as offshore mutual funds, that are not registered under the 1940 Act but that provide the same selected per-share data (in accordance with the AICPA Audit and Accounting Guide, *Audits of Investment Companies*). The Board agreed to make that change.

Objective of the Earnings per Share Computations

79. In discussing various issues about the computation of diluted EPS, the Board found it helpful to identify the objective of both basic and diluted EPS in order to reach consistent conclusions on those issues. The Board concluded that the objective of basic EPS is to measure the performance of an entity over the reporting period and that the objective of diluted EPS should be consistent with the basic EPS objective while giving effect to all dilutive potential common shares that were outstanding during the period.

80. Other objectives of diluted EPS that the Board considered and rejected were that it should be a predictor of dilution—a forward-looking number as opposed to one based on historic numbers—or that it should maximize dilution. In concluding that diluted EPS should be an extension of basic EPS—a historic, "for the period" number—the Board looked to FASB Concepts Statement No. 1, *Objectives of Financial Reporting by Business Enterprises,* which discusses the historical nature of accounting information, and FASB Concepts Statement No. 2, *Qualitative Characteristics of Accounting Information,* which discusses the "predictive value" of financial information. Concepts Statement 1 explains that users of financial statements may make predictions using financial information—information that is historical. Paragraph 53 of Concepts Statement 2 states in part:

> Users can be expected to favor those sources of information and analytical methods that have the greatest predictive value in achieving their specific objectives. Predictive value here means value as an *input* [emphasis in original] into a predictive process, *not value directly as a prediction.* [Emphasis added.]

81. The IASC initially concluded that the objective of diluted EPS should be to indicate the potential variability or risk attached to basic EPS as a consequence of the issue of potential common shares or to act as a warning signal of the potential dilution of basic EPS. Following that objective, diluted EPS would be computed using end-of-period shares and stock prices. The Board considers that objective to be relevant and useful but believes that it is preferable for diluted EPS to be computed in a manner consistent with the computation of basic EPS. After much discussion, the IASC agreed to require that diluted EPS be computed following the FASB objective because (a) diluted EPS computed following a performance objective can be presented in a time series and compared with diluted EPS of other periods and (b) a "warning signal" objective can be adequately conveyed through supplementary note disclosure.

82. To accommodate the concerns of the IASC, both the FASB and the IASC Exposure Drafts included disclosure requirements related to the IASC's warning signal objective. More than half of the respondents to the FASB Exposure Draft who commented on those disclosure requirements stated that they did not believe that the warning signal objective was relevant or useful, and some found the related disclosures confusing. Respondents to the IASC Exposure Draft made similar comments; they also encouraged the IASC to choose one objective. The FASB and the IASC decided to eliminate those disclosure requirements in response to the comments received.

Basic Earnings per Share

83. One of the main objectives of the Board's project on earnings per share was to issue a standard that would be compatible with those of the IASC and national standards-setting bodies. The biggest difference between Opinion 15 and other EPS standards is that Opinion 15 required presentation of primary EPS, which includes the dilutive effect of common stock equivalents. Currently, only two other countries require that primary EPS be presented. Thus, the first issue that the Board had to address was whether to eliminate the requirement to present primary EPS and replace it with a computation that does not consider the effects of common stock equivalents.

84. In making its decision to replace primary EPS with basic EPS, the Board considered the requirements of Opinion 15 to compute primary EPS, the criticisms about primary EPS, the arguments in favor of basic EPS, and the comments it had received from constituents prior to adding the project to its agenda.

Primary earnings per share

85. The rules used to compute primary EPS (Opinion 15 and its amendments and interpretations) had been criticized as being extremely complex and containing a number of arbitrary provisions. Those criticisms largely focused on the determination of convertible securities as common stock equivalents, specifically, the use of the Aa corporate bond rate for the common stock equivalency test, the two-thirds yield test for common stock equivalency, and the classification of a security as a common stock equivalent at issuance without regard to later events.

86. The complexity of Opinion 15 may have contributed to errors or to inconsistency in its application. Several empirical studies indicated that EPS rules often are misunderstood by preparers and auditors and are not always applied correctly. The primary EPS statistic itself had been widely criticized as not being useful. Considerable evidence showed that many users of financial statements think that primary EPS is based on an undiluted weighted-average number of common shares outstanding; that is, they think that primary EPS is computed without giving effect to common stock equivalents.

87. Because primary EPS assumes exercise and conversion of dilutive common stock equivalents, it includes a certain amount of dilution. Some said that the endpoints on the scale of dilution—from zero dilution to maximum dilution—would convey better information to financial statement users. Those critics said that the rules of Opinion 15 conceal part of the total potential dilution by presenting two numbers that include dilution rather than an undiluted and a diluted number.

88. Opinion 15 had drawn its strongest criticism from users (primarily financial analysts) and academics. Analysts' interest stemmed from the use of EPS in the computation of the price-earnings ratio, perhaps the most frequently cited statistic in the business of equity investment. In addition, analysts' earnings projections almost always are presented on a per-share basis. The Board did not receive many requests from other parties to comprehensively reconsider Opinion 15; therefore, it appeared that preparers and auditors had assimilated and accepted the rules. Most respondents to the EPS Prospectus agreed that basic EPS would be a simpler and more useful statistic than primary EPS. Most respondents to the Exposure Draft agreed that disclosing the full range of possible dilution using basic EPS and diluted EPS would reveal more useful information than the partial range of dilution disclosed with primary EPS and fully diluted EPS under Opinion 15. However, some respondents noted that that they did not find basic EPS to be a useful statistic and thought that users would focus only on diluted EPS.

89. The Board decided to replace primary EPS with basic EPS for the following reasons:

a. Presenting undiluted and diluted EPS data would give users the most factually supportable *range* of EPS possibilities. The spread between basic and diluted EPS would provide information about an entity's capital structure by disclosing a reasonable estimate of how much potential dilution exists.
b. Use of a common international EPS statistic has become even more important as a result of database-oriented financial analysis and the internationalization of business and capital markets.
c. The notion of common stock equivalents as used in primary EPS is viewed by many as not operating effectively in practice, and "repairing" it does not appear to be a feasible option.
d. The primary EPS computation is complex, and

there is some evidence that the current guidance is not well understood and may not be consistently applied.
e. If basic EPS were to replace primary EPS, the criticisms about the arbitrary methods by which common stock equivalents are determined would no longer be an issue. If entities were required to disclose the details of their convertible securities, the subjective determination of the likelihood of conversion would be left to individual users of financial statements.

Computation of basic earnings per share

Weighted-average number of shares

90. In computing basic (and diluted) EPS, the Board agreed that use of a weighted-average number of shares is necessary so that the effect of increases or decreases in outstanding shares on EPS data will be related to the portion of the period during which the related consideration affected operations.

Contingently issuable shares

91. Contractual agreements (usually associated with purchase business combinations) sometimes provide for the issuance of additional common shares contingent upon certain conditions being met. The Board concluded that (a) consistent with the objective that basic EPS should represent a measure of the performance of an entity over a specific reporting period, contingently issuable shares should be included in basic EPS only when there is no circumstance under which those shares would not be issued and (b) basic EPS should not be restated for changed circumstances.

92. A few respondents to the Exposure Draft suggested that contingently issuable shares should never be included in the computation of basic EPS because basic EPS is supposed to be an EPS ratio with no dilution. They said that the denominator should include only actual shares outstanding. The Board considered that view but decided to retain the provision that "vested" contingently issuable shares should be considered in the computation of basic EPS because consideration for those shares has been received. The Board also agreed to retain the provision that contingently returnable shares should be treated in the same manner as contingently issuable shares. The IASC agreed to include a similar provision in IAS 33 in response to the comments received on its Exposure Draft (which did not include such a provision).

Diluted Earnings per Share

93. Securities (such as options, warrants, convertible debt, and convertible preferred stock) that do not have a current right to participate fully in earnings but that may do so in the future by virtue of their option or conversion rights are referred to in this Statement as potential common shares or potentially dilutive shares. That "potential dilution" is relevant to users because it may reduce the per-share amount of current earnings to be distributed by way of dividends in the future and may increase the number of shares over which the total market value of an entity is divided.

94. Whether option or conversion rights of potential common shares actually will be exercised is usually not determinable at an entity's reporting date. However, with the use of assumptions, it is possible to arrive at a reasonable estimate of what earnings per share would have been had common stock been issued for those securities. The Board concluded that the treasury stock method and the if-converted method prescribed in Opinion 15 should continue to be used in computing diluted EPS.

No antidilution

95. In computing diluted EPS, only potential common shares that are dilutive—those that reduce earnings per share or increase loss per share—are included. Exercise of options and warrants or conversion of convertible securities is not assumed if the result would be antidilutive, such as when a loss from continuing operations is reported. The sequence in which potential common shares are considered may affect the amount of dilution that they produce. The sequence of the computation was not specifically addressed in Opinion 15, but the IASC proposed that in order to maximize the dilution of earnings per share, each issue or series of potential common shares should be considered in sequence from the most dilutive to the least dilutive. The Board agreed with the IASC that that is a reasonable approach and included a similar provision in this Statement. Most respondents to the Exposure Draft agreed that sequencing potential common shares from the most dilutive to the least dilutive is a workable approach.

96. The Board also concluded that the "control number" for determining whether including potential common shares in the diluted EPS computation would be antidilutive should be *income from continuing operations* (or a similar line item above net in-

come if it appears on the income statement). As a result, if there is a loss from continuing operations, diluted EPS would be computed in the same manner as basic EPS is computed, even if an entity has net income after adjusting for a discontinued operation, an extraordinary item, or the cumulative effect of an accounting change. Similarly, if an entity has income from continuing operations but its preferred dividend adjustment made in computing *income available to common stockholders* in accordance with paragraph 9 results in a "loss from continuing operations available to common stockholders," diluted EPS would be computed in the same manner as basic EPS.

97. If *net income* were the control number as it was under Opinion 15, diluted EPS often would be the same number as basic EPS. The Board decided to change the control number to income from continuing operations because in the United States net losses are often the result of discontinued operations, extraordinary items, or accounting changes reported by the cumulative-effect method. The Board agreed that if an entity had income from continuing operations but had an accounting change that resulted in a net loss, its diluted net loss per share *should* include potential common shares (even though their effect would be antidilutive) and should not be the same as its basic net loss per share that does not include potential common shares. With income from continuing operations as the control number, the diluted net loss per share in that case would reflect the effect of potential common shares.

98. In addition, EPS data are more comparable over time if income from continuing operations is used as the control number. That is, for an entity that reports a net loss in the period solely because of the cumulative effect of an accounting change upon adopting a new accounting standard, that period's diluted net loss per share would reflect no dilution if net income were the control number and, thus, diluted net loss per share for the period would not be comparable with past or future diluted net income per-share amounts (which would reflect some dilution). The same would be true for an entity that makes a voluntary accounting change, reports discontinued operations, or reports extraordinary items that result in a net loss.

99. Respondents to the Exposure Draft agreed with the change in the control number from *net income* under Opinion 15 to *income from continuing operations* in this Statement. The IASC did not include a

control number provision in its Exposure Draft. In response to the comments received on the FASB Exposure Draft and the few comments on the issue received in response to the IASC Exposure Draft, the IASC agreed to include a provision in IAS 33 that requires *net profit from continuing ordinary activities* to be used as the control number in establishing whether potential common shares are dilutive or antidilutive.

Options and warrants and their equivalents

100. The issuance of common stock upon exercise of options and warrants produces cash inflows for the issuing entity but does not affect income. In computing earnings per share, an assumed issuance of stock increases the denominator but does not affect the numerator. The resulting reduction in earnings per share could be considered excessive if there were no adjustment for the use of the cash proceeds. The treasury stock method was meant to adjust for that situation by assuming that the cash proceeds from issuing common stock are used to acquire treasury shares. Thus, only the *net* assumed issuance of shares (common shares issued upon exercise less treasury shares acquired) is reflected in the denominator of the diluted EPS computation. Other methods that the Board considered in determining how to reflect the potential dilution of options and warrants in the computation of diluted EPS are discussed in paragraphs 101-104.

Imputed earnings method

101. Some countries use an imputed earnings method to compute diluted EPS. That method assumes that the proceeds from exercise of options and warrants are used to repay debt or are invested, for example, in government securities, rather than used to purchase treasury shares. Following the imputed earnings method, either the amount of interest that would have been saved (if the debt were repaid) or the income that would have been earned (on the investment) is added to the numerator of the computation, and the denominator is adjusted for the number of shares assumed to have been issued upon exercise of the options or warrants. The disadvantages of that method are that it requires an arbitrary assumption about the appropriate rate of earnings, it overstates dilution because it treats antidilutive potential common shares as if they were dilutive, and it gives the

same effect to all options and warrants regardless of the current market price.

Treasury stock method with a discounted exercise price

102. Another method that the Board considered was to discount the expected proceeds from exercise of options or warrants with long exercise periods to reflect the time value of money prior to applying the treasury stock method. The argument for that method is that because contracts with long exercise periods are not likely to be exercised for a considerable period of time, the exercise price should be discounted to its fair value at the balance sheet date, reflecting "time value" as one component of the value of an option or warrant. The main disadvantage of that method is that the determination of (a) the time periods over which to discount the options or warrants and (b) the applicable discount rate is subjective.

Maximum dilution method

103. The maximum dilution method assumes that all options and warrants are exercised and that the common shares issued upon exercise are added to the denominator with no change in the numerator. The principal disadvantage of that method is that an assumption that all potential common shares will convert without a change in earnings is both counterintuitive and unrealistic. It also would give the same effect to all options and warrants regardless of the current market price.

Graham-Dodd method

104. In computing diluted EPS, the Graham-Dodd method[29] takes into consideration all options and warrants, including those whose exercise price exceeds the market price of common stock. That method assumes that options and warrants are equivalent to additional outstanding common shares with the same aggregate market value as that of the options or warrants issued. The computation divides the total market value of all options and warrants by the current market price of the common stock to determine the number of additional common shares that would be equivalent to the value of outstanding options and warrants. Those additional common shares would be included in the denominator of the diluted EPS computation. In addition to showing the dilutive

[29]The method is described in Graham, Dodd, and Cottle, *Security Analysis: Principles and Technique,* 4th ed. (New York: McGraw-Hill, 1962).

effect of "out of the money" options and warrants, the Graham-Dodd method reflects more dilution as the value of options and warrants increases relative to the value of common stock. That method requires the use of option-pricing models at each reporting period to value options and warrants that are not traded.[30]

Treasury stock method

105. The Board decided to retain the treasury stock method from Opinion 15 because of its use in present practice, its relative simplicity and lack of subjectivity, and its adoption by the IASC (although the method is described differently in IAS 33). The method also reflects more dilution as the value of options and warrants increases relative to the value of common stock. That is, as the average market price of the stock increases, the assumed proceeds from exercise will buy fewer shares, thus, increasing the EPS denominator. The Board was concerned that the treasury stock method understates potential dilution because it gives no dilutive effect to options and warrants whose exercise prices exceed current common stock prices and, therefore, are antidilutive under the treasury stock method but may be dilutive sometime in the future. However, the Board was unable to identify another method that would address that concern that did not have its own set of disadvantages. To offset that concern, the Board decided to require disclosure in the notes to the financial statements of potential common shares not included in the computation of dilutive EPS because their impact would be antidilutive based on current market prices.

106. Another common criticism of the treasury stock method that the Board considered is that it assumes a hypothetical purchase of treasury stock. The Board recognizes that the funds obtained by issuers from the exercise of options and warrants are used in many ways with a wide variety of results that cannot be anticipated. Application of the treasury stock method in EPS computations represents a practical approach to reflecting the dilutive effect that would result from the issuance of common stock under option and warrant agreements at an effective price below the current market price.

107. The Board made one change to the treasury stock method prescribed in Opinion 15. This Statement requires that the average stock price for the period always be used in determining the number of

treasury shares assumed purchased with the proceeds from the exercise of options or warrants rather than the higher of the average or ending stock price as prescribed by Opinion 15. The Board believes that use of the average stock price is consistent with the objective of diluted EPS to measure earnings per share for the period based on period information and that use of end-of-period data or estimates of the future is inconsistent with that objective. If purchases of treasury shares actually were to occur, the shares would be purchased at various prices, not at the price at the end of the period. In addition, use of an average stock price eliminates the concern that end-of-period fluctuations in stock prices could have an undue effect on diluted EPS if an end-of-period stock price were required to be used. Respondents to the Exposure Draft generally agreed with the requirement to use the average stock price.

108. Opinion 15 required that the "modified treasury stock" method be used if the number of shares of common stock obtainable upon exercise of outstanding options and warrants in the aggregate is more than 20 percent of the number of common shares outstanding at the end of the period. The Board found that the modified treasury stock method prescribed in Opinion 15 was not widely used in practice because few entities ever met the 20 percent test. For that reason, and in an effort to simplify the EPS computation and to be consistent with the IASC Standard, the Board decided not to include that method in this Statement. Respondents to the Exposure Draft generally agreed with the elimination of the modified treasury stock method.

Stock-based compensation arrangements

109. Fixed employee stock options (fixed awards) and nonvested stock (including restricted stock) are included in the computation of diluted EPS based on the provisions for options and warrants in paragraphs 17-25. Even though their issuance may be contingent upon vesting, they are not considered to be "contingently issuable shares" as that term is used in this Statement because to consider them contingently issuable shares would be a change from present practice and the provisions of IAS 33. However, because issuance of performance-based stock options (and performance-based nonvested stock) is contingent upon satisfying conditions in addition to

---

[30]Statement 123 generally requires that valuation only at the grant date.

the mere passage of time, those options and non-vested stock are considered to be contingently issuable shares in the computation of diluted EPS. The Board decided that a distinction should be made only between time-related contingencies and contingencies requiring specific achievement.

110. The guidance in paragraph 21 for determining the assumed proceeds when applying the treasury stock method to an entity that has stock-based compensation arrangements is based on similar guidance in Statement 123, which was based on the provisions in paragraph 3 of FASB Interpretation No. 31, *Treatment of Stock Compensation Plans in EPS Computations.* The Board agreed that it would be appropriate to carry forward the remainder of the relevant guidance in paragraphs 4-6 of Interpretation 31 into this Statement. That guidance has been incorporated into paragraphs 20, 22, and 29 of this Statement. Examples 1 and 2 from Appendix B of Interpretation 31 are included in Illustration 8 in Appendix C.

Written put options and purchased options

111. A number of respondents to the Exposure Draft requested that the Board address how written put options, purchased put options, and purchased call options should be included in the computation of diluted EPS. Emerging Issues Task Force (EITF) Issue No. 87-31, "Sale of Put Options on Issuer's Stock," addresses put options sold by a company for cash that enable the holder to sell shares of the company's stock at a fixed price to the company. The EITF reached a consensus that the reverse treasury stock method should be used in computing the impact of those options on earnings per share. Under that method, the incremental number of shares to be added to the denominator is computed as the excess of shares that will be issued for cash at the then current market price to obtain cash to satisfy the put obligation over the shares received from satisfying the puts. The Board agreed to include that approach in this Statement for "in the money" contracts that require that the reporting entity repurchase its own stock.

112. The Board concluded that neither purchased put options nor purchased call options should be reflected in diluted EPS because their effect would be antidilutive. A few respondents stated that entities should be permitted to aggregate the calls held by an entity on its own stock (purchased calls) with the options or warrants it is attempting to hedge. Those re-

spondents suggested that the Board modify the treasury stock method to require that proceeds assumed to be received from the exercise of options be used to pay the strike price on the call option that the entity holds on its own stock (rather than assume that the proceeds received will be used to purchase treasury shares as required by the treasury stock method). The Board confirmed its position that securities that would have an antidilutive effect should not be included in the diluted EPS computation and that securities should be considered separately rather than in the aggregate in determining whether their effect on diluted EPS would be dilutive or antidilutive.

Convertible securities

113. Other securities that could result in the issuance of common shares, in addition to options and warrants, are debt and preferred stock that are convertible into common stock. The impact of those potential common shares on diluted EPS is determined by use of the if-converted method. That method recognizes that the holders of convertible preferred stock cannot share in distributions of earnings available to common stockholders unless they relinquish their right to senior distributions. Conversion is assumed, and income available to common stockholders is determined before distributions are made to holders of those securities. Likewise, the if-converted method recognizes that convertible debt can participate in earnings through interest or dividends, either as a senior security or as common stock, but not both.

114. The Board chose to retain the if-converted method prescribed in Opinion 15 in this Statement. There have been few criticisms of that method, and it is the method used by the IASC. One common criticism of the if-converted method is that conversion may be assumed when a convertible security appears likely to remain a senior security.

Contracts that may be settled in stock or cash

115. As discussed in paragraph 110, the guidance in Interpretation 31 has been brought forward into this Statement. Paragraph 6 of that Interpretation established a rebuttable presumption that when stock appreciation rights and other variable plan awards may be settled in stock or cash (at the election of either the holder or the reporting entity), the entity should presume settlement in common stock and the dilutive potential common shares should be included in the EPS computation unless the presumption is overcome. The Board agreed that that guidance was

equally appropriate for other contracts that could be settled in stock or cash and thus included that guidance in paragraph 29 of this Statement. The Board believes that that approach is consistent with the objective of diluted EPS to reflect potential dilution that existed during the period. In circumstances in which the contract is reported as an asset or liability for accounting purposes (as opposed to an equity instrument) but the contract is presumed to be settled in common stock for EPS purposes, the Board believes it is appropriate to adjust income available to common stockholders for any changes in the fair value of the contract that had been recognized in income. Although all such contracts that provide the issuer or holder with a choice between settlement methods may not meet the definition of an option, warrant, convertible security, or contingently issuable share, they do meet the definition of potential common stock in paragraph 171 of this Statement.

Contingently issuable shares

116. In discussing the issue of the impact of contingently issuable shares on diluted EPS, the Board chose not to retain the requirements in Opinion 15 to (a) increase the numerator of the computation for possible future earnings levels and (b) restate prior EPS data for differences in actual and assumed earnings levels. The Board concluded that making assumptions about future earnings and restating for events that occur after the end of a period would be inconsistent with a "historic" objective. Thus, the Board decided to include contingently issuable shares in the computation of diluted EPS based only on current earnings (which are assumed to remain unchanged until the end of the contingency period) and to prohibit restatement.

117. The Board also was not in favor of permitting restatement of EPS data due to changes in market prices. The Board noted that restatement was prohibited for the impact of changes in market prices on the number of shares included in the denominator as a result of applying the treasury stock method. The Board decided to include shares contingent on market price in diluted EPS based on the end-of-period market price and to prohibit restatement.

118. Contingent stock agreements sometimes provide for shares to be issued in the future pending the satisfaction of conditions unrelated to earnings or market value (for example, opening a certain number of retail locations). Similar to its other conclusions, the Board decided (a) to include contingent shares in the computation of diluted EPS based on the assumption that the current status of the condition will remain unchanged until the end of the contingency period and (b) to prohibit restatement. Thus, if only half of the requisite retail locations have been opened, then no contingent shares would be included in the diluted EPS computation.

119. The Board considered including contingent shares on a pro rata basis based on the current status of the condition (such as half of the contingent shares for the example in paragraph 118). However, the Board was concerned that a pro rata approach would not be implemented easily and that it might make little sense in many instances, such as when it is readily apparent that the condition will not be met.

120. Some Board members were concerned about the inconsistency in when compensation cost for performance awards is included in the numerator of the diluted EPS computation (pursuant to Statement 123) and when the related contingent shares are included in the denominator of the same computation (pursuant to this Statement). The initial accruals of compensation cost for performance awards are based on the best estimate of the outcome of the performance condition. That is, compensation cost is estimated at the grant date for the options that are expected to vest based on performance-related conditions and that are accrued over the vesting period. However, pursuant to this Statement, diluted EPS would reflect only those shares (stock options) that would be issued if the end of the reporting period were the end of the contingency period. In most cases, performance awards will not be reflected in diluted EPS until the performance condition has been satisfied. The Board observed that (a) the focus of this Statement is the denominator of the EPS computation, not the determination of earnings, and (b) that treatment is consistent with current practice when compensation is associated with a contingent award.

121. Most respondents to the Exposure Draft agreed with the changes proposed for contingent stock agreements. A few respondents requested that the Board clarify as of what date contingently issuable shares should be included in the computations of basic and diluted EPS. The Board concluded that contingent shares should be deemed to be issued when all of the necessary conditions have been met and that those shares should be included in basic EPS on a weighted-average basis. In most cases, the shares would be included only as of the last day of the period because whether the condition has been satisfied

may not be certain until the end of the period. The Board concluded that contingent shares should be included in the denominator of the diluted EPS computation in a manner similar to other potential common shares; that is, as if the shares were issued at the beginning of the period (or as of the date of the contingent stock agreement, if later). However, for year-to-date computations, the Board agreed that contingent shares should be included on a weighted-average basis. That approach is similar to the method used for including incremental shares in year-to-date computations when applying the treasury stock method.

Presentation on Face of Income Statement

122. The Board agreed that EPS data should be presented prominently in the financial statements because of the significance attached by investors and others to EPS data and because of the importance of evaluating the data in conjunction with the financial statements. Thus, the Board concluded that both basic and diluted per-share amounts should be presented on the face of the income statement for income from continuing operations and net income. The Board agreed that, at a minimum, those per-share amounts should be presented on the face of the income statement to help users determine the impact of items reported "below-the-line."

123. The Board decided to give entities the option of presenting basic and diluted per-share amounts for discontinued operations, extraordinary items, and the cumulative effect of an accounting change either on the face of the income statement or in the notes to financial statements to address the concern that some constituents had with excessive information on the income statement. The extent of the data presented and the captions used will vary with the complexity of an entity's capital structure and the presence of transactions outside continuing operations.

124. The IASC Exposure Draft required presentation of only basic and diluted net income per share on the face of the income statement and encouraged presentation of other per-share amounts. Most respondents to the FASB Exposure Draft agreed with the requirements related to presentation of per-share amounts on the face of the income statement and in the notes to the financial statements and stated that the IASC should adopt the FASB's presentation approach. The IASC decided not to change its presentation requirements in its EPS standard but acknowledged that it will have to address presentation of per-share amounts other than net income per share as part of other related projects on its agenda.

125. The June 1996 FASB Exposure Draft, *Reporting Comprehensive Income,* would require presentation of a per-share amount for comprehensive income on the face of the statement of financial performance in which comprehensive income is reported. Per-share amounts are not required by that Exposure Draft for subtotals resulting from classifications within other comprehensive income. If that Exposure Draft is finalized as proposed, the Board will have to determine how comprehensive income per share should be computed to be in accordance with the provisions of this Statement.

126. The Board's decision to require a dual EPS presentation (basic and diluted EPS) for entities with complex capital structures regardless of the variance between basic and diluted EPS is a change from Opinion 15. Opinion 15 provided that fully diluted EPS did not have to be presented if the dilution caused by including all potential common shares in the computation was less than 3 percent of "simple" EPS, which includes no dilution. Similarly, primary EPS could be presented as simple EPS if the dilution caused by including common stock equivalents in the computation was less than 3 percent of simple EPS.

127. The Board decided to eliminate what is referred to as the "materiality threshold" for presentation of diluted EPS because (a) the requirement was used inconsistently, (b) in many cases, an entity had to compute fully diluted EPS to determine whether it met the 3 percent test, and (c) in any period that an entity's earnings per share fell out of the 3 percent range, Opinion 15 required fully diluted EPS to be shown for all periods presented. The Board concluded that requiring a dual presentation at all times by all entities with complex capital structures places all of the facts in the hands of users of financial statements at minimal or no cost to preparers and gives users an understanding of the extent and trend of potential dilution. The Board also noted that many entities currently present fully diluted EPS even when it does not differ by 3 percent from simple or primary EPS because when fully diluted EPS is compared over time, small differences may be relevant in assessing relative changes between periods.

128. Most respondents to the Exposure Draft agreed with the Board's conclusion that presenting both basic and diluted EPS on the face of the income statement would result in minimal or no additional cost to the preparer. However, many of those respondents requested that the Board retain a materiality threshold

similar to that in Opinion 15. They stated that presentation of diluted EPS when it is not materially different from basic EPS is an immaterial disclosure that could cause confusion (that is, multiple EPS amounts on the face of the income statement might be confusing to users). Some respondents also stated that the marginal costs of dual presentation would exceed the marginal benefits to the user community.

129. Because of those comments and the view of some respondents that diluted EPS is the more useful statistic, the Board initially decided that if only one per-share amount were to be required to be presented on the face of the income statement it should be diluted EPS, not basic EPS. The Board reasoned that a single presentation would eliminate any confusion that unsophisticated users might have with multiple EPS amounts and any confusion over which EPS number databases should include. In addition, presenting only diluted EPS on the face of the income statement would display the most meaningful information in the primary financial statements and would be another step toward simplification of the EPS guidance. The Board acknowledged the usefulness of providing a range of potential dilution and, therefore, agreed to retain the requirement that basic EPS should be presented in the notes to the financial statements as part of the required reconciliation of basic and diluted EPS.

130. Because of the international harmonization goal of the project, the FASB presented its initial decisions on income statement presentation to the IASC Steering Committee on Earnings per Share and the IASC Board in September 1996 as preliminary conclusions. The FASB indicated that it would reconsider those decisions based on the IASC's level of support for making similar changes to its proposed standard. The IASC decided to retain its requirement for equal prominence of basic and diluted EPS on the face of the income statement because it believes that there is valuable information content in the difference between the two numbers. The users in the United States with whom the FASB discussed its preliminary conclusions shared that view.

131. In the interest of international harmonization, the Board ultimately decided to retain the dual presentation requirement proposed in the Exposure Draft. The Board acknowledged that if it were to stay with its "diluted EPS only" preliminary conclusion, the resulting FASB and IASC EPS standards would have been substantially the same because EPS would be *computed* in the same manner even though

it would not be *presented* in the same manner. However, the Board believes it is most important to achieve harmonization in all aspects with the IASC, especially because the difference is only one of display, not one of a conceptual nature.

132. Consequently, both the FASB and the IASC agreed that dual presentation of basic and diluted EPS should be required in all instances, regardless of the difference between the two numbers. As noted in paragraph 89(a), the Board believes that, when compared with diluted EPS, basic EPS is useful as a benchmark for determining the amount of potential dilution. If basic and diluted EPS are the same amount, dual presentation can be accomplished in one line on the income statement. In response to the concerns of some respondents to the Exposure Draft that removal of the 3 percent materiality threshold will result in more variations in the concept of materiality than currently exists, the Board noted that the materiality box that states "The provisions of this Statement need not be applied to immaterial items" does not apply to the difference between two numbers.

Conclusions on Other Issues

Stock Dividends or Stock Splits

133. This Statement requires an entity that has a stock dividend, stock split, or reverse stock split after the close of the period but before issuance of the financial statements to compute basic and diluted EPS in those financial statements based on the new number of shares because those per-share amounts would have to be restated in the subsequent period. The IASC Exposure Draft proposed computing earnings per share in those situations based on the shares actually existing at the date of the financial statements. It also proposed disclosing a description of the subsequent event and pro forma EPS amounts in the financial statements of the period prior to the actual event.

134. Most respondents to the FASB Exposure Draft preferred the FASB restatement requirement over the IASC disclosure approach. Those respondents noted that reflecting the subsequent event in the current period would provide more useful, relevant, and meaningful information and would obviate the need for later restatement. In response to the comments it received on that issue and in the interest of harmonization, the IASC agreed to change from a disclosure approach to a requirement to restate, similar to that in this Statement.

Rights Issues

135. The IASC Exposure Draft proposed using the "theoretical ex-rights method" for adjusting EPS data for a bonus element contained in a rights issue offered to all existing stockholders. The FASB Exposure Draft proposed that the treasury stock method be used for making that adjustment. The Board initially decided not to use the IASC's proposed method because of the complexity of that method and the familiarity in the United States with the treasury stock method and because the treasury stock method achieves quite similar results. As noted by a few respondents to the Exposure Drafts, rights offerings are much more common outside the United States and use of the ex-rights method is established in international practice. In the interest of harmonization, the Board decided to accept the IASC's position on that issue and require use of the ex-rights method when adjusting both basic and diluted EPS for the bonus element in a rights issue.

Supplemental Earnings per Share Data

136. Opinion 15 required disclosure of supplemental EPS data. The purpose of those disclosures was to show what primary EPS would have been if the conversions or sales of securities had occurred at the beginning of the period being reported on rather than during the period. The Board concluded that requiring disclosure of similar information in this Statement was not consistent with the objective of basic and diluted EPS and, thus, decided not to include that requirement in this Statement. However, the Board agreed that it would be useful for financial statements to include a description of transactions that occur after the balance sheet date but before issuance of the financial statements that would have resulted in a material change in the number of common or potential common shares outstanding at the end of the period. Including that information will provide those that want to compute "pro forma" EPS information with the necessary data. Some respondents to the Exposure Draft suggested that information about post-balance-sheet transactions that occurred in periods other than the most recent period would not be useful. The Board decided to require disclosure of that information only for the current reporting period rather than, as proposed in the Exposure Draft, for all periods for which an income statement is presented.

Disclosure Requirements

137. The Board decided to require a reconciliation of the numerators and denominators of the basic and diluted EPS computations in this Statement because the reconciliation is simple and straightforward and will help users better understand the dilutive effect of certain securities included in the EPS computations. SEC Regulation S-K requires presentation of a statement that reasonably details the computation of earnings per share unless the computation can be clearly determined from the material contained in the annual report. The reconciliation required by this Statement should satisfy the SEC requirement and should not result in additional costs to preparers. The Board agreed that disclosing the nature and impact of each dilutive potential common share (or series of shares) included in the diluted EPS computation, as well as separately identifying those antidilutive potential common shares that could dilute earnings per share in the future, allows users to exercise their own judgment as to the "likely" EPS number.

138. Some respondents to the Exposure Draft did not support the reconciliation requirement and stated that (a) the costs to prepare it would exceed the benefit to users, (b) it would be complex and confusing, and (c) it is already required by the SEC. A number of respondents observed that the SEC has proposed eliminating its similar reconciliation requirement in Regulation S-K. The SEC has decided to postpone acting on that proposal in light of comments it has received regarding the usefulness of the reconciliation to investors and financial analysts and the similar proposed requirement in the FASB Exposure Draft. The comments received by the SEC reinforced the Board's position that the reconciliation contains information that is very useful to users of financial statements. However, in response to some of the comments it received, the Board agreed that insignificant reconciling items need not be itemized as part of the reconciliation and could be combined (aggregated).

139. The Exposure Draft would have required disclosure of information that would assist users of financial statements in assessing how basic EPS may be affected in the future due to the potential common shares still outstanding at the balance sheet date as well as the common stock price at that date. Those requirements were referred to as the "warning signal" disclosures because they were meant to address the IASC's warning signal objective for diluted EPS.

However, as noted in paragraph 82, many respondents who commented on the warning signal disclosure requirement in the Exposure Draft stated that they did not believe that the warning signal objective was relevant or useful, and some found the related disclosures confusing. Those respondents generally stated that the costs of the related disclosures would exceed the benefits and that those disclosures would be too complex. A number of respondents to the IASC Exposure Draft made similar comments, and some suggested that the disclosure requirement be made optional. Respondents also noted that some of the information is already required to be disclosed in the financial statements pursuant to other IASC standards. After reconsideration, both the FASB and the IASC agreed to eliminate the warning signal disclosure requirements from their respective standards.

Securities of Subsidiaries

140. This Statement is based on the current practice of deducting income attributable to the noncontrolling interest (minority interest) to arrive at consolidated net income in the consolidated financial statements. The October 1995 FASB Exposure Draft, *Consolidated Financial Statements: Policy and Procedures,* would change that practice to require that net income attributable to the noncontrolling interest be deducted from consolidated net income to arrive at an amount called *net income attributable to the controlling interest.* In addition, that Exposure Draft states that the computation of earnings per share in consolidated financial statements that include subsidiaries that are not wholly owned should be based on and designated as the amount of net income attributable to the controlling interest. Although consolidated net income would include the results of all consolidated operations, the EPS computation would continue to be based only on net income attributable to the controlling interest.

141. The consolidations Exposure Draft would not require disclosure of "income from continuing operations attributable to the controlling interest" if a noncontrolling interest exists. If that Exposure Draft is finalized as proposed, the Board will have to determine what the control number should be for entities that are required to present earnings per share for net income attributable to the controlling interest. Those and other related issues will be addressed before the Board finalizes its redeliberations on the proposed Statement on consolidated financial statements.

Effective Date and Transition

142. The Board decided that this Statement should be effective for financial statements issued for periods ending after December 15, 1997, including interim periods. The Board believes that that effective date provides adequate time for entities to make any needed modifications to their systems and procedures to conform with the provisions of this Statement. For comparability, the Board decided to require restatement of all prior-period EPS data presented (including interim and summary financial information) in the period of adoption.

143. Earnings per share is a widely quoted statistic; therefore, to enhance comparability among entities, the Board decided to prohibit early adoption of this Statement. Thus, entities are prohibited from presenting EPS data computed in accordance with this Statement on the face of the income statement prior to the required adoption date. However, the Board decided to permit entities to disclose pro forma EPS data in the notes to the financial statements prior to that date.

144. Most respondents to the Exposure Draft agreed with the proposed effective date; however, some respondents suggested that this Statement be effective as of the beginning of the year (for calendar-year entities) rather than as of the end of the year. Most respondents agreed with the Board that the benefits of restatement would exceed the related costs and that both the requirement to restate and the prohibition on early adoption would enhance the consistency and comparability of financial reporting. Due to the prohibition on early adoption, the Board decided to retain the effective date proposed in the Exposure Draft so that calendar-year entities will not have to wait until 1998 to adopt this Statement. That is, calendar-year entities will have to implement the Statement in the fourth quarter of 1997 (and restate back to January 1, 1997). An entity with a June 30, 1997 year-end will have to implement the Statement in its second quarter, the quarter ending December 31, 1997 (and restate its first-quarter results).

145. Some respondents indicated that restatement of all EPS data presented would be impracticable in some situations, especially for entities that present tables of 10-year selected data or that have had a number of changes in capital structure due to mergers or acquisitions. The Board acknowledged that it might be difficult to restate EPS data for 10 years, especially if there have been changes in capital structures. However, the Board decided to retain the

requirement for restatement because it believes that the benefits far outweigh the costs. In conjunction with that decision, the Board noted that this Statement does not require presentation of EPS data for 10 years. It requires only that if EPS data are presented, those data must be computed in accordance with the provisions of this Statement. Thus, entities that choose to present EPS data in summaries of earnings or selected financial data must restate that EPS data.

Other Literature on Earnings per Share

146. A number of respondents to the Exposure Draft suggested that the Board address changes to or continuation of other authoritative guidance on earnings per share, including that of the SEC and the EITF. Because one of the objectives of the EPS project was to simplify the EPS literature, the Board agreed to include in this Statement a table listing all non-FASB authoritative EPS literature and this Statement's impact, if any, on that literature. That table is presented in Appendix F as a reference tool. The Board did not deliberate any of the issues discussed in the other literature, except where specifically noted.

Appendix C

ILLUSTRATIONS

CONTENTS

Appendix C

ILLUSTRATIONS

Introduction

147. This appendix illustrates this Statement's application to entities with complex capital structures. Certain assumptions have been made to simplify the computations and focus on the issue at hand in each illustration.

Illustration 1—Computation of Basic and Diluted Earnings per Share and Income Statement Presentation

148. This example illustrates the quarterly and annual computations of basic and diluted EPS in the year 20X1 for Corporation A, which has a complex capital structure. The control number used in this illustration (and in Illustration 2) is income before extraordinary item and accounting change because Corporation A has no discontinued operations. Paragraph 149 illustrates the presentation of basic

and diluted EPS on the face of the income statement. The facts assumed are as follows:

Average market price of common stock. The average market prices of common stock for the calendar-year 20X1 were as follows:

First quarter	$59
Second quarter	$70
Third quarter	$72
Fourth quarter	$72

The average market price of common stock from July 1 to September 1, 20X1 was $71.

Common stock. The number of shares of common stock outstanding at the beginning of 20X1 was 3,300,000. On March 1, 20X1, 100,000 shares of common stock were issued for cash.

Convertible debentures. In the last quarter of 20X0, 4 percent convertible debentures with a principal amount of $10,000,000 due in 20 years were sold for cash at $1,000 (par). Interest is payable semiannually on November 1 and May 1. Each $1,000 debenture is convertible into 20 shares of common stock. No debentures were converted in 20X0. The entire issue was converted on April 1, 20X1, because the issue was called by the Corporation.

Convertible preferred stock. In the second quarter of 20X0, 600,000 shares of convertible preferred stock were issued for assets in a purchase transaction. The quarterly dividend on each share of that convertible preferred stock is $0.05, payable at the end of the quarter. Each share is convertible into one share of common stock. Holders of 500,000 shares of that convertible preferred stock converted their preferred stock into common stock on June 1, 20X1.

Warrants. Warrants to buy 500,000 shares of common stock at $60 per share for a period of 5 years were issued on January 1, 20X1. All outstanding warrants were exercised on September 1, 20X1.

Options. Options to buy 1,000,000 shares of common stock at $85 per share for a period of 10 years were issued on July 1, 20X1. No options were exercised during 20X1 because the exercise price of the options exceeded the market price of the common stock.

Tax rate. The tax rate was 40 percent for 20X1.

Year 20X1	Income (Loss) before Extraordinary Item and Accounting Change[a]	Net Income (Loss)
First quarter	$3,000,000	$ 3,000,000
Second quarter	4,500,000	4,500,000
Third quarter	500,000	(1,500,000)[b]
Fourth quarter	(500,000)	3,750,000[c]
Full year	$7,500,000	$ 9,750,000

[a]This is the control number (before adjusting for preferred dividends). Refer to paragraph 15.

[b]Corporation A had a $2 million extraordinary loss (net of tax) in the third quarter.

[c]Corporation A had a $4.25 million cumulative effect of an accounting change (net of tax) in the fourth quarter.

(This page intentionally left blank.)

First Quarter 20X1

Basic EPS Computation

Net income	$3,000,000
Less: Preferred stock dividends	(30,000)[a]
Income available to common stockholders	$2,970,000

Dates Outstanding	Shares Outstanding	Fraction of Period	Weighted- Average Shares
January 1–February 28	3,300,000	2/3	2,200,000
Issuance of common stock on March 1	100,000		
March 1–March 31	3,400,000	1/3	1,133,333
Weighted-average shares			3,333,333

Basic EPS $0.89

The equation for computing basic EPS is:

$$\frac{\text{Income available to common stockholders}}{\text{Weighted-average shares}}$$

---

[a]600,000 shares × $0.05

First Quarter 20X1

Diluted EPS Computation

Income available to common stockholders		$2,970,000
Plus: Income impact of assumed conversions		
Preferred stock dividends	$ 30,000[a]	
Interest on 4% convertible debentures	60,000[b]	
Effect of assumed conversions		90,000
Income available to common stockholders + assumed conversions		$3,060,000
Weighted-average shares		3,333,333
Plus: Incremental shares from assumed conversions		
Warrants	0[c]	
Convertible preferred stock	600,000	
4% convertible debentures	200,000	
Dilutive potential common shares		800,000
Adjusted weighted-average shares		4,133,333

Diluted EPS $0.74

The equation for computing diluted EPS is:

$$\frac{\text{Income available to common stockholders} + \text{Effect of assumed conversions}}{\text{Weighted-average shares} + \text{Dilutive potential common shares}}$$

---

[a]600,000 shares × $0.05

[b]($10,000,000 × 4%) ÷ 4; less taxes at 40%

[c]The warrants were not assumed exercised because they were antidilutive in the period ($60 exercise price > $59 average price).

Second Quarter 20X1

Basic EPS Computation

Net income	$4,500,000
Less: Preferred stock dividends	(5,000)[a]
Income available to common stockholders	$4,495,000

Dates Outstanding	Shares Outstanding	Fraction of Period	Weighted-Average Shares
April 1	3,400,000		
Conversion of 4% debentures on April 1	200,000		
April 1–May 31	3,600,000	2/3	2,400,000
Conversion of preferred stock on June 1	500,000		
June 1–June 30	4,100,000	1/3	1,366,667
Weighted-average shares			3,766,667

Basic EPS $1.19

The equation for computing basic EPS is:

$$\frac{\text{Income available to common stockholders}}{\text{Weighted-average shares}}$$

---

[a] 100,000 shares × $0.05

Second Quarter 20X1

Diluted EPS Computation

Income available to common stockholders		$4,495,000
Plus: Income impact of assumed conversions		
Preferred stock dividends	$ 5,000[a]	
Effect of assumed conversions		5,000
Income available to common stockholders + assumed conversions		$4,500,000
Weighted-average shares		3,766,667
Plus: Incremental shares from assumed conversions		
Warrants	71,429[b]	
Convertible preferred stock	433,333[c]	
Dilutive potential common shares		504,762
Adjusted weighted-average shares		4,271,429

Diluted EPS $1.05

The equation for computing diluted EPS is:

$$\frac{\text{Income available to common stockholders} + \text{Effect of assumed conversions}}{\text{Weighted-average shares} + \text{Dilutive potential common shares}}$$

---

[a]100,000 shares × $0.05

[b]$60 × 500,000 = $30,000,000; $30,000,000 ÷ $70 = 428,571; 500,000 − 428,571 = 71,429 shares **OR**
[($70 − $60) ÷ $70] × 500,000 shares = 71,429 shares

[c](600,000 shares × 2/3) + (100,000 shares × 1/3)

Third Quarter 20X1

Basic EPS Computation

Income before extraordinary item	$ 500,000
Less: Preferred stock dividends	(5,000)
Income available to common stockholders	495,000
Extraordinary item	(2,000,000)
Net loss available to common stockholders	$(1,505,000)

Dates Outstanding	Shares Outstanding	Fraction of Period	Weighted-Average Shares
July 1–August 31	4,100,000	2/3	2,733,333
Exercise of warrants on September 1	500,000		
September 1–September 30	4,600,000	1/3	1,533,333
Weighted-average shares			4,266,666

Basic EPS

Income before extraordinary item	**$ 0.12**
Extraordinary item	**$(0.47)**
Net loss	**$(0.35)**

The equation for computing basic EPS is:

$$\frac{\text{Income available to common stockholders}}{\text{Weighted-average shares}}$$

Third Quarter 20X1

Diluted EPS Computation

Income available to common stockholders		$ 495,000
Plus: Income impact of assumed conversions		
Preferred stock dividends	$ 5,000	
Effect of assumed conversions		5,000
Income available to common stockholders + assumed conversions		500,000
Extraordinary item		(2,000,000)
Net loss available to common stockholders + assumed conversions		$(1,500,000)
Weighted-average shares		4,266,666
Plus: Incremental shares from assumed conversions		
Warrants	51,643[a]	
Convertible preferred stock	100,000	
Dilutive potential common shares		151,643
Adjusted weighted-average shares		4,418,309

Diluted EPS

Income before extraordinary item	**$ 0.11**
Extraordinary item	**$(0.45)**
Net loss	**$(0.34)**

The equation for computing diluted EPS is:

$$\frac{\text{Income available to common stockholders} + \text{Effect of assumed conversions}}{\text{Weighted-average shares} + \text{Dilutive potential common shares}}$$

Note: The incremental shares from assumed conversions are included in computing the diluted per-share amounts for the extraordinary item and net loss even though they are antidilutive. This is because the control number (income before extraordinary item, adjusted for preferred dividends) was income, not a loss. (Refer to paragraphs 15 and 16.)

---

[a][($71 − $60) ÷ $71] × 500,000 = 77,465 shares; 77,465 × 2/3 = 51,643 shares

Fourth Quarter 20X1

Basic and Diluted EPS Computation

Loss before accounting change	$ (500,000)
Plus: Preferred stock dividends	(5,000)
Loss available to common stockholders	(505,000)
Accounting change	4,250,000
Net income available to common stockholders	$3,745,000

Dates Outstanding	Shares Outstanding	Fraction of Period	Weighted-Average Shares
October 1–December 31	4,600,000	3/3	4,600,000
Weighted-average shares			4,600,000

Basic and Diluted EPS

Loss before accounting change	**$(0.11)**
Accounting change	**$ 0.92**
Net income	**$ 0.81**

The equation for computing basic (and diluted) EPS is:

$$\frac{\text{Income available to common stockholders}}{\text{Weighted-average shares}}$$

Note: The incremental shares from assumed conversions are not included in computing the diluted per-share amounts for the accounting change and net income because the control number (loss before accounting change, adjusted for preferred dividends) was a loss, not income. (Refer to paragraphs 15 and 16.)

(This page intentionally left blank.)

Full Year 20X1

Basic EPS Computation

Income before extraordinary item and accounting change	$ 7,500,000
Less: Preferred stock dividends	(45,000)
Income available to common stockholders	7,455,000
Extraordinary item	(2,000,000)
Accounting change	4,250,000
Net income available to common stockholders	$ 9,705,000

Dates Outstanding	Shares Outstanding	Fraction of Period	Weighted-Average Shares
January 1–February 28	3,300,000	2/12	550,000
Issuance of common stock on March 1	100,000		
March 1–March 31	3,400,000	1/12	283,333
Conversion of 4% debenture on April 1	200,000		
April 1–May 31	3,600,000	2/12	600,000
Conversion of preferred stock on June 1	500,000		
June 1–August 31	4,100,000	3/12	1,025,000
Exercise of warrants on September 1	500,000		
September 1–December 31	4,600,000	4/12	1,533,333
Weighted-average shares			3,991,666

Basic EPS

Income before extraordinary item and accounting change	**$ 1.87**
Extraordinary item	**$(0.50)**
Accounting change	**$ 1.06**
Net income	**$ 2.43**

The equation for computing basic EPS is:

$$\frac{\text{Income available to common stockholders}}{\text{Weighted-average shares}}$$

Full Year 20X1

Diluted EPS Computation

Income available to common stockholders		$ 7,455,000
Plus: Income impact of assumed conversions		
Preferred stock dividends	$ 45,000	
Interest on 4% convertible debentures	60,000	
Effect of assumed conversions		105,000
Income available to common stockholders + assumed conversions		7,560,000
Extraordinary item		(2,000,000)
Accounting change		4,250,000
Net income available to common stockholders + assumed conversions		$ 9,810,000
Weighted-average shares		3,991,666
Plus: Incremental shares from assumed conversions		
Warrants	30,768[a]	
Convertible preferred stock	308,333[b]	
4% convertible debentures	50,000[c]	
Dilutive potential common shares		389,101
Adjusted weighted-average shares		4,380,767

Diluted EPS

Income before extraordinary item and accounting change	**$ 1.73**
Extraordinary item	**$(0.46)**
Accounting change	**$ 0.97**
Net income	**$ 2.24**

The equation for computing diluted EPS is:

$$\frac{\text{Income available to common stockholders} + \text{Effect of assumed conversions}}{\text{Weighted-average shares} + \text{Dilutive potential common shares}}$$

---

[a] (71,429 shares × 3/12) + (51,643 shares × 3/12)

[b] (600,000 shares × 5/12) + (100,000 shares × 7/12)

[c] 200,000 shares × 3/12

149. The following illustrates how Corporation A might present its EPS data on its income statement. Note that the per-share amounts for the extraordinary item and the accounting change are not required to be shown on the face of the income statement.

	For the Year Ended 20X1
Earnings per common share	
Income before extraordinary item and accounting change	$ 1.87
Extraordinary item	(0.50)
Cumulative effect of a change in accounting principle	1.06
Net income	$ 2.43
Earnings per common share—assuming dilution	
Income before extraordinary item and accounting change	$ 1.73
Extraordinary item	(0.46)
Cumulative effect of a change in accounting principle	0.97
Net income	$ 2.24

150. The following table includes the quarterly and annual EPS data for Corporation A. The purpose of this table is to illustrate that the sum of the four quarters' EPS data will not necessarily equal the annual EPS data. This Statement does not require disclosure of this information.

	First Quarter	Second Quarter	Third Quarter	Fourth Quarter	Full Year
Basic EPS					
Income (loss) before extraordinary item and accounting change	$0.89	$1.19	$ 0.12	$(0.11)	$ 1.87
Extraordinary item	—	—	(0.47)	—	(0.50)
Accounting change	—	—	—	0.92	1.06
Net income (loss)	$0.89	$1.19	$(0.35)	$ 0.81	$ 2.43
Diluted EPS					
Income (loss) before extraordinary item and accounting change	$0.74	$1.05	$ 0.11	$(0.11)	$ 1.73
Extraordinary item	—	—	(0.45)	—	(0.46)
Accounting change	—	—	—	0.92	0.97
Net income (loss)	$0.74	$1.05	$(0.34)	$ 0.81	$ 2.24

Illustration 2—Earnings per Share Disclosures

151. The following is an illustration of the reconciliation of the numerators and denominators of the basic and diluted EPS computations for "income before extraordinary item and accounting change" and other related disclosures required by paragraph 40 for Corporation A in Illustration 1. **Note:** Statement 123 has specific disclosure requirements related to stock-based compensation arrangements.

	For the Year Ended 20X1		
	Income (Numerator)	**Shares (Denominator)**	**Per-Share Amount**
Income before extraordinary item and accounting change	$7,500,000		
Less: Preferred stock dividends	(45,000)		
Basic EPS			
Income available to common stockholders	7,455,000	3,991,666	$1.87
Effect of Dilutive Securities			
Warrants		30,768	
Convertible preferred stock	45,000	308,333	
4% convertible debentures	60,000	50,000	
Diluted EPS			
Income available to common stockholders + assumed conversions	$7,560,000	4,380,767	$1.73

Options to purchase 1,000,000 shares of common stock at $85 per share were outstanding during the second half of 20X1 but were not included in the computation of diluted EPS because the options' exercise price was greater than the average market price of the common shares. The options, which expire on June 30, 20Y1, were still outstanding at the end of year 20X1.

Illustration 3—Contingently Issuable Shares

152. The following example illustrates the contingent share provisions described in paragraphs 10 and 30-35. The facts assumed are as follows:

- Corporation B had 100,000 shares of common stock outstanding during the entire year ended December 31, 20X1. It had no options, warrants, or convertible securities outstanding during the period.
- Terms of a contingent stock agreement related to a recent business combination provided the following to certain shareholders of the Corporation:
  - 1,000 additional common shares for each new retail site opened during 20X1
  - 5 additional common shares for each $100 of consolidated, after-tax net income in excess of $500,000 for the year ended December 31, 20X1.
- The Corporation opened two new retail sites during the year:
  - One on May 1, 20X1
  - One on September 1, 20X1.
- Corporation B's consolidated, year-to-date after-tax net income was:
  - $400,000 as of March 31, 20X1
  - $600,000 as of June 30, 20X1
  - $450,000 as of September 30, 20X1
  - $700,000 as of December 31, 20X1.

Note: In computing diluted EPS for an interim period, contingent shares are included as of the beginning of the period. For year-to-date computations, footnote 18 of this Statement requires that contingent shares be included on a weighted-average basis.

	First Quarter	Second Quarter	Third Quarter	Fourth Quarter	Full Year
Basic EPS Computation					
Numerator	$400,000	$200,000	$(150,000)	$250,000	$700,000
Denominator:					
Common shares outstanding	100,000	100,000	100,000	100,000	100,000
Retail site contingency	0	667[a]	1,333[b]	2,000	1,000[c]
Earnings contingency[d]	0	0	0	0	0
Total shares	100,000	100,667	101,333	102,000	101,000
Basic EPS	$ 4.00	$ 1.99	$ (1.48)	$ 2.45	$ 6.93

	First Quarter	Second Quarter	Third Quarter	Fourth Quarter	Full Year
Diluted EPS Computation					
Numerator	$400,000	$200,000	$(150,000)	$250,000	$700,000
Denominator:					
Common shares outstanding	100,000	100,000	100,000	100,000	100,000
Retail site contingency	0	1,000	2,000	2,000	1,250[e]
Earnings contingency	0[f]	5,000[g]	0[h]	10,000[i]	3,750[j]
Total shares	100,000	106,000	102,000	112,000	105,000
Diluted EPS	$ 4.00	$ 1.89	$ (1.47)[k]	$ 2.23	$ 6.67

---

[a]1,000 shares × 2/3

[b]1,000 shares + (1,000 shares × 1/3)

[c](1,000 shares × 8/12) + (1,000 shares × 4/12)

[d]The earnings contingency has no effect on basic EPS because it is not certain that the condition is satisfied until the end of the contingency period (paragraphs 10 and 31). The effect is negligible for the fourth-quarter and full-year computations because it is not certain that the condition is met until the last day of the period.

[e](0 + 1,000 + 2,000 + 2,000) ÷ 4

[f]Corporation B did not have $500,000 year-to-date, after-tax net income at March 31, 20X1. Projecting future earnings levels and including the related contingent shares are not permitted by this Statement.

[g][($600,000 − $500,000) ÷ $100] × 5 shares

[h]Year-to-date, after-tax net income was less than $500,000.

[i][($700,000 − $500,000) ÷ $100] × 5 shares

[j](0 + 5,000 + 0 + 10,000) ÷ 4

[k]Loss during the third quarter is due to a change in accounting principle; therefore, antidilution rules (paragraph 15) do not apply.

Illustration 4—Antidilution Sequencing

153. The following example illustrates the antidilution sequencing provisions described in paragraph 14 for Corporation C for the year ended December 31, 20X0. The facts assumed are as follows:

- Corporation C had income available to common stockholders of $10,000,000 for the year 20X0.
- 2,000,000 shares of common stock were outstanding for the entire year 20X0.
- The average market price of the common stock was $75.

- Corporation C had the following potential common shares outstanding during the year:
  - Options (not compensation related) to buy 100,000 shares of common stock at $60 per share.
  - 800,000 shares of convertible preferred stock entitled to a cumulative dividend of $8 per share. Each preferred share is convertible into 2 shares of common stock.
  - 5 percent convertible debentures with a principal amount of $100,000,000 (issued at par). Each $1,000 debenture is convertible into 20 shares of common stock.
- The tax rate was 40 percent for 20X0.

Determination of Earnings per Incremental Share

	Increase in Income	Increase in Number of Common Shares	Earnings per Incremental Share
Options	0	20,000[a]	—
Convertible preferred stock	$6,400,000[b]	1,600,000[c]	$4.00
5% convertible debentures	3,000,000[d]	2,000,000[e]	1.50

Computation of Diluted Earnings per Share

	Income Available	Common Shares	Per Share	
As reported	$10,000,000	2,000,000	$5.00	
Options	0	20,000		
	10,000,000	2,020,000	4.95	Dilutive
5% convertible debentures	3,000,000	2,000,000		
	13,000,000	4,020,000	3.23	Dilutive
Convertible preferred stock	6,400,000	1,600,000		
	$19,400,000	5,620,000	3.45	Antidilutive

Note: Because diluted EPS *increases* from $3.23 to $3.45 when convertible preferred shares are included in the computation, those convertible preferred shares are antidilutive and are ignored in the computation of diluted EPS. Therefore, diluted EPS is reported as $3.23.

---

[a][($75 − $60) ÷ $75] × 100,000
[b]800,000 shares × $8
[c]800,000 shares × 2
[d]($100,000,000 × 5%) less taxes at 40%
[e]100,000 debentures × 20

Illustration 5—Rights Issues

154. The following example illustrates the provisions for stock rights issues that contain a bonus element as described in paragraphs 55 and 56. The facts assumed are as follows:

- Net income was $1,100 for the year ended December 31, 20X0.
- 500 common shares were outstanding for the entire year ended December 31, 20X0.
- A rights issue was offered to all existing shareholders in January 20X1. The last date to exercise the rights was March 1, 20X1. The offer provided 1 common share for each 5 outstanding common shares (100 new shares).
- The exercise price for the rights issue was $5 per share acquired.

- The fair value of 1 common share was $11 at March 1, 20X1.
- Basic EPS for the year 20X0 (prior to the rights issuance) was $2.20.

As a result of the bonus element in the January 20X1 rights issue, basic and diluted EPS for 20X0 will have to be adjusted retroactively. The number of common shares used in computing basic and diluted EPS is the number of shares outstanding immediately prior to the rights issue (500) multiplied by an *adjustment factor*. Prior to computing the adjustment factor, the *theoretical ex-rights fair value per share* must be computed. Those computations follow:

Theoretical ex-rights fair value per share[a] $10   = $\dfrac{(500 \times \$11) + (100 \times \$5)}{(500 + 100)}$

Adjustment factor[b]   1.1   = $11 ÷ $10

Denominator for restating basic EPS   550   =   500 × 1.1

Restated basic EPS for 20X0 $2.00   = $1,100 ÷ 550

Diluted EPS would be adjusted retroactively by adding 50 shares to the denominator that was used in computing diluted EPS prior to the restatement.

---

[a]The equation for computing the theoretical ex-rights fair value per share is:

$$\frac{\text{Aggregate fair value of shares prior to exercise of rights } + \text{ Proceeds from exercise of rights}}{\text{Total shares outstanding after exercise of rights}}$$

[b]The equation for computing the adjustment factor is:

$$\frac{\text{Fair value per share immediately prior to exercise of rights}}{\text{Theoretical ex-rights fair value per share}}$$

Illustration 6—Two-Class Method

155. The two-class method of computing basic EPS for an entity that has more than one class of nonconvertible securities is illustrated in the following example. This method is described in paragraph 61; as noted in that paragraph, diluted EPS would be computed in a similar manner. The facts assumed for the year 20X0 are as follows:

- Net income was $65,000.
- 10,000 shares of $50 par value common stock were outstanding.

- 5,000 shares of $100 par value nonconvertible preferred stock were outstanding.
- The preferred stock was entitled to a noncumulative annual dividend of $5 per share before any dividend is paid on common stock.
- After common stock has been paid a dividend of $2 per share, the preferred stock then participates in any additional dividends on a 40:60 *per-share* ratio with common stock. (That is, after preferred and common stock have been paid dividends of $5 and $2 per share, respectively, preferred stock participates in any additional dividends at a rate of

two-thirds of the additional amount paid to common stock on a per-share basis.)
- Preferred stockholders have been paid $27,000 ($5.40 per share).
- Common stockholders have been paid $26,000 ($2.60 per share).

Basic EPS for 20X0 would be computed as follows:

Net income		$65,000
Less dividends paid:		
Preferred	$27,000	
Common	26,000	53,000
Undistributed 20X0 earnings		$12,000

Allocation of undistributed earnings:

To preferred:
0.4(5,000) ÷ [0.4(5,000) + 0.6(10,000)] × $12,000 = $3,000
$3,000 ÷ 5,000 shares = $0.60 per share

To common:
0.6(10,000) ÷ [0.4(5,000) + 0.6(10,000)] × $12,000 = $9,000
$9,000 ÷ 10,000 shares = $0.90 per share

Basic per-share amounts:

	Preferred Stock	Common Stock
Distributed earnings	$5.40	$2.60
Undistributed earnings	0.60	0.90
Totals	$6.00	$3.50

Illustration 7—Securities of a Subsidiary: Computation of Basic and Diluted Earnings per Share

156. The following example illustrates the EPS computations for a subsidiary's securities that enable their holders to obtain the subsidiary's common stock based on the provisions in paragraph 62. This example is based on current practice. Based on the provisions in the consolidations Exposure Draft, the presentation of earnings per share would differ from that illustrated in this example for an entity that includes subsidiaries that are not wholly owned. The facts assumed are as follows:

Parent corporation:

- Net income was $10,000 (excluding any earnings of or dividends paid by the subsidiary).
- 10,000 shares of common stock were outstanding; the parent corporation had not issued any other securities.

- The parent corporation owned 900 common shares of a domestic subsidiary corporation.
- The parent corporation owned 40 warrants issued by the subsidiary.
- The parent corporation owned 100 shares of convertible preferred stock issued by the subsidiary.

Subsidiary corporation:

- Net income was $3,600.
- 1,000 shares of common stock were outstanding.
- Warrants exercisable to purchase 200 shares of its common stock at $10 per share (assume $20 average market price for common stock) were outstanding.
- 200 shares of convertible preferred stock were outstanding. Each share is convertible into two shares of common stock.
- The convertible preferred stock paid a dividend of $1.50 per share.
- No intercompany eliminations or adjustments were necessary except for dividends.
- Income taxes have been ignored for simplicity.

Subsidiary's Earnings per Share

Basic EPS $3.30   Computed: $(\$3{,}600^a - \$300^b) \div 1{,}000^c$

Diluted EPS $2.40   Computed: $\$3{,}600^d \div (1{,}000 + 100^e + 400^f)$

Consolidated Earnings per Share

Basic EPS $1.31   Computed: $(\$10{,}000^g + \$3{,}120^h) \div 10{,}000^i$

Diluted EPS $1.27   Computed: $(\$10{,}000 + \$2{,}160^j + \$48^k + \$480^l) \div 10{,}000$

---

[a]Subsidiary's net income

[b]Dividends paid by subsidiary on convertible preferred stock

[c]Shares of subsidiary's common stock outstanding

[d]Subsidiary's income available to common stockholders ($3,300) increased by $300 preferred dividends from applying the if-converted method for convertible preferred stock

[e]Incremental shares from warrants from applying the treasury stock method, computed: $[(\$20 - \$10) \div \$20] \times 200$

[f]Shares of subsidiary's common stock assumed outstanding from conversion of convertible preferred stock, computed: 200 convertible preferred shares × conversion factor of 2

[g]Parent's net income

[h]Portion of subsidiary's income to be included in consolidated basic EPS, computed: $(900 \times \$3.30) + (100 \times \$1.50)$

[i]Shares of parent's common stock outstanding

[j]Parent's proportionate interest in subsidiary's earnings attributable to common stock, computed: $(900 \div 1{,}000) \times (1{,}000 \text{ shares} \times \$2.40 \text{ per share})$

[k]Parent's proportionate interest in subsidiary's earnings attributable to warrants, computed: $(40 \div 200) \times (100 \text{ incremental shares} \times \$2.40 \text{ per share})$

[l]Parent's proportionate interest in subsidiary's earnings attributable to convertible preferred stock, computed: $(100 \div 200) \times (400 \text{ shares from conversion} \times \$2.40 \text{ per share})$

Illustration 8—Application of the Treasury Stock Method for Stock Appreciation Rights and Other Variable Stock Option Award Plans

157. The following examples illustrate the provisions in paragraphs 20-22 for computing the effect on diluted EPS of stock appreciation rights and other variable stock option or award plans when the service period is presumed to be the vesting period. The examples do not comprehend all possible combinations of circumstances. Amounts and quantities have been rounded for simplicity. The following examples are based on the examples in Appendix B of Interpretation 31, which is superseded by this Statement. Accordingly, the terminology and compensation cost is based on the guidance in Opinion 25 and related literature.

The provisions of the agreements are as follows:

Date of grant	January 1, 1999
Expiration date	December 31, 2008
Vesting	100% at the end of 2002
Number of shares under option	1,000
Option exercise price	$10 per share
Quoted market price at date of grant	$10 per share

- Stock appreciation rights are granted in tandem with stock options for market value appreciation in excess of the option price.
- Exercise of the rights cancels the options for an equal number of shares and vice versa.
- Share appreciation is payable in stock, cash, or a combination of stock and cash at the entity's election.

The facts assumed are as follows:

- There are no circumstances in these two examples that would overcome the presumption that the rights are payable in stock (refer to paragraph 29).
- The tax deduction for compensation will equal the compensation recognized for financial reporting purposes.
- The quoted market prices of common stock on December 31 of the years 1999–2004 were as follows:

1999	$11
2000	$12
2001	$15
2002	$14
2003	$15
2004	$18

Example 1

158. The following example illustrates the annual computation of incremental shares for the above-described stock appreciation right plan. A single annual computation is shown for simplicity in this and in the following example. Normally, a computation would be done monthly or quarterly.

Date	Market Price	Compensation				Measurable Compensation Attributed to Future Periods[d]	Amount to Be Paid by Employee	Assumed Proceeds	Additional Shares for Diluted EPS		
		Per Share[a]	Aggregate[b]	Percentage Accrued[c]	Compensation Accrued to Date				Shares Issuable[e]	Treasury Shares Assumed Repurchased[f]	Incremental Shares
12/31/99	$11	$1	$1,000	25%	$ 250	$ 750	—	$ 750	47	35	12
12/31/00	12	2	2,000	50	1,000	1,000	—	1,000	130	76	54
12/31/01	15	5	5,000	75	3,750	1,250	—	1,250	259	83	176
12/31/02	14	4	4,000	100	4,000	0	—	0	310g	43g	267g
12/31/03	15	5	5,000	100	5,000	0	—	0	310	0	310
12/31/04	18	8	8,000	100	8,000	0	—	0	394	0	394

[a] Market price less exercise price ($10).

[b] Aggregate compensation for unexercised shares to be allocated to periods in which service is performed (shares under option × compensation per share).

[c] The percentage accrued is based on the four-year vesting period.

[d] Unaccrued compensation in this example.

[e] Average aggregate compensation ÷ average market price.

[f] Average assumed proceeds ÷ average market price.

[g] Illustration of computation of additional shares for one year (2002) follows:

Date	Market Price	Aggregate Compensation	Assumed Proceeds
12/31/01	$15.00	$5,000	$1,250
12/31/02	14.00	4,000	0
Average	14.50	4,500	625

Additional shares for diluted EPS:

Shares issuable	310	(4,500 ÷ $14.50)
Treasury shares	(43)	(625 ÷ $14.50)
Incremental shares	267	

Example 2

159. If the stock appreciation rights vested 25 percent per year commencing in 1999, the annual computation of incremental shares for diluted EPS in Example 1 would change as illustrated in the following example. The computation of compensation expense is explained in FASB Interpretation No. 28, *Accounting for Stock Appreciation Rights and Other Variable Stock Option or Award Plans*, Appendix B, Example 2.

The additional facts assumed are as follows:

- On December 31, 2001, the employee exercises the right to receive share appreciation on 300 shares.
- On March 15, 2002, the employee exercises the right to receive share appreciation on 100 shares; quoted market price $15 per share.
- On June 15, 2003, the employee exercises the right to receive share appreciation on 100 shares; quoted market price $16 per share.
- On December 31, 2003, the employee exercises the right to receive share appreciation on 300 shares.
- On December 31, 2004, the employee exercises the right to receive share appreciation on 200 shares.

Date	Transaction	Number of Shares under Option	Market Price	Compensation Per Share[a]	Aggregate[b]	Percentage Accrued[c]	Compensation Accrued to Date	Measurable Compensation Attributed to Future Periods[d]	Amount to Be Paid by Employee	Assumed Proceeds	Shares Issuable[e]	Treasury Shares Assumed Repurchased[f]	Incremental Shares	Weighted-Average Shares Outstanding[g]	Total Shares
12/31/99			$11	$1	$1,000	52%	$ 520	$480	—	$480	47	22	25	—	25
12/31/00			12	2	2,000	79	1,580	420	—	420	130	39	91	—	91
12/31/01			15	5	5,000	94	4,700	300	—	300	259	26	233	—	233
12/31/01	SAR	300	15	5											
3/15/02	SAR	100	15	5											
12/31/02	SAR		14	4	2,400	100	2,400	0	—	0	193	10	183	126	309
6/15/03	SAR	100	16	6											
12/31/03	SAR		15	5	2,500	100	2,500	0	—	0	170[h]	0	170	153[i]	323
12/31/03	SAR	300	15	5											
12/31/04	SAR		18	8	1,600	100	1,600	0	—	0	78	0	78	270	348
12/31/04	SAR	200	18	8											

Transaction code:
SAR—Exercise of a stock appreciation right.

[a] Market price for the year less exercise price ($10).

[b] Aggregate compensation for unexercised shares to be allocated to periods in which the service is performed (shares under option × compensation per share).

[c] Refer to the schedule in paragraph 24 of Interpretation 28.

[d] Unaccrued compensation in this example.

[e] Average aggregate compensation ÷ average market price.

[f] Average assumed proceeds ÷ average market price.

[g] Shares issued upon exercise of stock appreciation rights. These would be included in the enterprise's total weighted-average shares outstanding.

[h] Illustration of computation of shares issuable for one year (2003) follows:

	Number of Shares under Option	Average Compensation per Share	Average Aggregate Compensation	Average Market Price	Aggregate Shares Issuable	Weighing Factor	Shares Issuable
Rights outstanding:							
Entire year 2003	500	$4.50	$2,250	$14.50	155	12/12	155
1/1-6/15	100	5.00	500	15.00	33	5.5/12	15
							170

[i] Illustration of computation of weighted-average shares outstanding for one year (2003) follows:

	Number of Shares under Option	Compensation per Share	Aggregate Compensation	Market Price	Aggregate Shares Outstanding	Weighing Factor	Weighted-Average Shares Outstanding
Shares issued:							
12/31/01	300	$5	$1,500	$15	100	12/12	100
3/15/02	100	5	500	15	33	12/12	33
6/15/03	100	6	600	16	38	6.5/12	20
							153

Appendix D

AMENDMENTS TO EXISTING PRONOUNCEMENTS

160. This Statement supersedes the following pronouncements:

a. APB Opinion No. 15, *Earnings per Share*
b. AICPA Accounting Interpretations 1-102 of Opinion 15
c. AICPA Accounting Interpretations 1, "Changing EPS Denominator for Retroactive Adjustment to Prior Period," and 2, "EPS for 'Catch-up' Adjustment," of APB Opinion No. 20, *Accounting Changes*
d. FASB Statement No. 85, *Yield Test for Determining whether a Convertible Security Is a Common Stock Equivalent*
e. FASB Interpretation No. 31, *Treatment of Stock Compensation Plans in EPS Computations.*

161. This Statement also amends other pronouncements issued by either the Accounting Principles Board or the Financial Accounting Standards Board that refer to Opinion 15. All such references appearing in paragraphs that establish standards or the scope of a pronouncement are hereby amended to refer instead to FASB Statement No. 128, *Earnings per Share.*

162. The last sentence of paragraph 18 and footnote 8 of APB Opinion No. 18, *The Equity Method of Accounting for Investments in Common Stock,* are replaced by the following:

An investor's *share of the earnings or losses* of an investee should be based on the shares of *common* stock held by an investor. [8]

---
[8]Paragraph 62 of FASB Statement No. 128, *Earnings per Share,* discusses the treatment of common shares or potential common shares for purposes of computing consolidated EPS. The provisions of that paragraph also apply to investments in common stock of corporate joint ventures and investee companies accounted for under the equity method.

163. Opinion 20 is amended as follows:

a. The last sentence of paragraph 20 is replaced by the following:

Presentation of per-share amounts for the cumulative effect of an accounting change shall be made either on the face of the income statement or in the related notes.

b. The parenthetical phrase in the second sentence of paragraph 21 is replaced by the following:

(basic and diluted, as appropriate under FASB Statement No. 128, *Earnings per Share*)

c. In paragraphs 42 and 46, *(which are not common stock equivalents)* is deleted.

d. In the comparative statements in paragraphs 43, 44, and 47, in Note A in paragraph 47, and in the five-year summary in paragraph 48, *full* in *assuming full dilution* is deleted.

164. Paragraph 30(b) of APB Opinion No. 28, *Interim Financial Reporting,* is replaced by the following:

Basic and diluted earnings per share data for each period presented, determined in accordance with the provisions of FASB Statement No. 128, *Earnings per Share.*

165. APB Opinion No. 30, *Reporting the Results of Operations—Reporting the Effects of Disposal of a Segment of a Business, and Extraordinary, Unusual and Infrequently Occurring Events and Transactions,* is amended as follows:

a. Paragraph 9 is amended as follows:

(1) In the first sentence, *APB Opinion No. 15,* is replaced by *FASB Statement No. 128, Earnings per Share.*

(2) Footnote 3 is deleted.

b. Paragraph 12 is replaced by the following:

Earnings per share data for extraordinary items shall be presented either on the face of the income statement or in the related notes, as prescribed by Statement 128.

166. FASB Statement No. 21, *Suspension of the Reporting of Earnings per Share and Segment Information by Nonpublic Enterprises,* is amended as follows:

a. Paragraph 12 is amended as follows:

(1) In the first sentence, *APB Opinion No. 15*[3] *and* is deleted.

(2) In the second sentence, *Opinion No. 15 and* is deleted.

(3) Footnote 3 is deleted.

b. In paragraph 14, *earnings per share and* and *APB Opinion No. 15 and* are deleted.

167. FASB Statement No. 123, *Accounting for Stock-Based Compensation,* is amended as follows:

a. Paragraph 49 is replaced by the following:

> FASB Statement No. 128, *Earnings per Share,* requires that employee stock options, nonvested stock, and similar equity instruments granted to employees be treated as potential common shares in computing diluted earnings per share. Diluted earnings per share shall be based on the actual number of options or shares granted and not yet forfeited, unless doing so would be anti-dilutive. If vesting is contingent upon factors other than continued service, such as the level of future earnings, the shares or options shall be treated as contingently issuable shares in accordance with paragraphs 30-35 of Statement 128. If stock options or other equity instruments are granted during a period, the shares issuable shall be weighted to reflect the portion of the period during which the equity instruments were outstanding.

b. Paragraph 50 is amended as follows:

(1) In the first sentence, *Opinion 15* is replaced by *Statement 128.*

(2) In the second sentence, *FASB Interpretation No. 31, Treatment of Stock Compensation Plans in EPS Computations,* is replaced by *Statement 128.*

(3) In the third sentence, *Interpretation 31* is replaced by *Statement 128.*

c. Paragraph 357 is amended as follows:

(1) In the second sentence, *Under Opinion 15 and FASB Interpretation No. 31, Treatment of Stock Compensation Plans in EPS Computations* is replaced by *Under FASB Statement No. 128, Earnings per Share* and *common stock equivalents* is replaced by *potential common shares.*

(2) In the third sentence, *common stock equivalents* is replaced by *potential common shares.*

d. Paragraph 358 is amended as follows:

(1) The first three sentences are deleted.

(2) In the fourth sentence, , *of which 4,500,000 are expected to vest* is deleted.

(3) The seventh sentence is deleted.

e. Paragraph 359 and footnote 26 are replaced by the following:

Computation of assumed proceeds for diluted earnings per share:

• Amount employees would pay if all options outstanding were exercised using the weighted-average exercise price (4,600,000 × $40)	$184,000,000
• Average unrecognized compensation balance during year [26]	17,700,000
Assumed proceeds	$201,700,000

---

[26]Average unrecognized compensation balance is determined by averaging the beginning-of-the-year balance of cost measured and unrecognized and the end-of-the-year balance of cost measured and unrecognized. The assumed amount is $17,700,000 based on ongoing cost recognition for stock options granted in the current year and prior years.

f. Paragraph 360 is replaced by the following:

Assumed repurchase of shares:

• Repurchase shares at average market price during the year ($201,700,000 ÷ $52)	3,878,846
• Incremental shares to be added (4,600,000 – 3,878,846)	721,154

The number of shares to be added to outstanding shares for purposes of the diluted earnings per share calculation is 721,154.

g. Paragraph 361 is deleted.

168. Paragraph 6 of FASB Interpretation No. 28, *Accounting for Stock Appreciation Rights and Other Variable Stock Option or Award Plans,* is replaced by the following:

> Stock appreciation rights and other variable plan awards are included in the computation of diluted

earnings per share pursuant to the provisions of paragraphs 20-23 of FASB Statement No. 128, *Earnings per Share.*

169. Paragraph 7 of FASB Interpretation No. 38, *Determining the Measurement Date for Stock Option, Purchase, and Award Plans Involving Junior Stock,* is replaced by the following:

Paragraphs 20-23 of FASB Statement No. 128, *Earnings per Share,* provide guidance on when and how junior stock plans should be reflected in the diluted earnings per share computation.

170. In the first sentence of paragraph 2 of FASB Technical Bulletin No. 79-8, *Applicability of FASB Statements 21 and 33 to Certain Brokers and Dealers in Securities, and APB Opinion No. 15, Earnings per Share,* is deleted.

Appendix E

GLOSSARY

171. This appendix contains definitions of certain terms or phrases used in this Statement.

Antidilution (antidilutive)
An increase in earnings per share amounts or a decrease in loss per share amounts.

Basic earnings per share (basic EPS)
The amount of earnings for the period available to each share of common stock outstanding during the reporting period.

Call option
A contract that allows the holder to buy a specified quantity of stock from the writer of the contract at a fixed price for a given period. Refer to **option** and **purchased call option**.

Common stock (common shares)
A stock that is subordinate to all other stock of the issuer.

Contingent issuance
A possible issuance of shares of common stock that is dependent on the satisfaction of certain conditions.

Contingent stock agreement
An agreement to issue common stock (usually in

connection with a business combination accounted for by the purchase method) that is dependent on the satisfaction of certain conditions. Refer to **contingently issuable shares**.

Contingently issuable shares (contingently issuable stock)
Shares issuable for little or no cash consideration upon the satisfaction of certain conditions pursuant to a contingent stock agreement. Refer to **contingent stock agreement**.

Conversion rate (conversion ratio)
The ratio of the number of common shares issuable upon conversion to a unit of a convertible security. For example, $100 face value of debt convertible into 5 shares of common stock would have a conversion ratio of 5 to 1.

Convertible security
A security that is convertible into another security based on a conversion rate; for example, convertible preferred stock that is convertible into common stock on a two-for-one basis (two shares of common for each share of preferred).

Diluted earnings per share (diluted EPS)
The amount of earnings for the period available to each share of common stock outstanding during the reporting period and to each share that would have been outstanding assuming the issuance of common shares for all dilutive potential common shares outstanding during the reporting period.

Dilution (dilutive)
A reduction in earnings per share resulting from the assumption that convertible securities were converted, that options or warrants were exercised, or that other shares were issued upon the satisfaction of certain conditions.

Earnings per share (EPS)
The amount of earnings attributable to each share of common stock. For convenience, the term is used in this Statement to refer to either earnings or loss per share.

Exercise price
The amount that must be paid for a share of common stock upon exercise of an option or warrant.

If-converted method

A method of computing EPS data that assumes conversion of convertible securities at the beginning of the reporting period (or at time of issuance, if later).

Income available to common stockholders

Income (or loss) from continuing operations or net income (or net loss) adjusted for preferred stock dividends.

Option

Unless otherwise stated in this Statement, a call option that gives the holder the right to purchase shares of common stock from the reporting entity in accordance with an agreement upon payment of a specified amount. As used in this Statement, options include, but are not limited to, options granted to employees and stock purchase agreements entered into with employees. Options are considered "securities" in this Statement. Refer to **call option.**

Potential common stock

A security or other contract that may entitle its holder to obtain common stock during the reporting period or after the end of the reporting period.

Preferred stock

A security that has rights that are preferential to common stock.

Purchased call option

A contract that allows the reporting entity to buy a specified quantity of its own stock from the writer of the contract at a fixed price for a given period. Refer to **call option**.

Put option

A contract that allows the holder to sell a specified quantity of stock to the writer of the contract at a fixed price during a given period.

Reverse treasury stock method

A method of recognizing the dilutive effect on earnings per share of satisfying a put obligation. It assumes that the proceeds used to buy back common stock (pursuant to the terms of a put option) will be raised from issuing shares at the average market price during the period. Refer to **put option.**

Rights issue

An offer to existing shareholders to purchase additional shares of common stock in accordance with an agreement for a specified amount (which is generally substantially less than the fair value of the shares) for a given period.

Security

The evidence of debt or ownership or a related right. For purposes of this Statement, it includes options and warrants as well as debt and stock.

Treasury stock method

A method of recognizing the use of proceeds that could be obtained upon exercise of options and warrants in computing diluted EPS. It assumes that any proceeds would be used to purchase common stock at the average market price during the period.

Warrant

A security that gives the holder the right to purchase shares of common stock in accordance with the terms of the instrument, usually upon payment of a specified amount.

Weighted-average number of common shares outstanding

The number of shares determined by relating (a) the portion of time within a reporting period that common shares have been outstanding to (b) the total time in that period. In computing diluted EPS, equivalent common shares are considered for all dilutive potential common shares.

Appendix F

OTHER LITERATURE ON EARNINGS PER SHARE

172. The following table addresses changes to or continuation of other authoritative guidance on earnings per share, including that of the SEC and the EITF. For each item, this table either discusses the impact of this Statement, if any, or indicates reasons that specific items are beyond the scope of this Statement. This table is presented in this Statement for use as a reference tool. The Board did not deliberate any of the issues contained in the literature listed in this table, except where specifically noted.

Note: Current SEC, EITF, and AICPA guidance has been quoted, paraphrased, or restated to facilitate the reader's understanding of the effect of this Statement.

Status after Statement 128

N/A

N/A

Current Guidance

**Staff Accounting Bulletin (SAB) 64
Topic 3C: Redeemable Preferred Stock**

SAB 64 states that if the initial fair value of redeemable preferred stock is less than the mandatory redemption amount, the carrying amount of the stock should be increased to the mandatory redemption amount through periodic accretions charged against retained earnings. Those periodic accretions are treated in the same manner as a dividend on nonredeemable preferred stock for EPS computations. That is, dividends on the preferred stock and accretions of their carrying amounts cause income or loss available to common stockholders (the EPS numerator) to be less than reported income.

**Topic 6B: Accounting Series Release (ASR)
No. 280—*General Revision of Regulation S-X***

ASR 280 states that income or loss available to common stockholders should be reported on the face of the income statement when it is materially different in quantitative terms from reported net income or loss or when it is indicative of significant trends or other qualitative considerations.

Effect of Statement 128

The Board expects to address the accounting for preferred stock in its project on distinguishing between liability and equity instruments. Statement 128 does not address numerator issues relating to the EPS computation. Statement 128 permits an adjustment only for preferred dividends in computing income available to common stockholders. The SEC guidance for redeemable preferred stock continues to apply. [9]

The disclosure requirement is due, in part, to the provisions in Topic 3C; similar provisions are not included in Statement 128. Statement 128 does not require income available to common stockholders to be presented on the face of the income statement. The SEC disclosure guidance continues to apply.

SAB 68
Topic 5Q: Increasing Rate Preferred Stock

SAB 68 states that the discount resulting from the issuance of increasing rate preferred stock should be amortized over the period preceding commencement of the perpetual dividend through a charge to retained earnings and a corresponding increase in the carrying amount of the preferred stock. Those periodic increases are treated in the same manner as a dividend on nonredeemable preferred stock for EPS computations. That is, dividends on the preferred stock and accretions of their carrying amounts cause income or loss available to common stockholders (the EPS numerator) to be less than reported income.

The Board expects to address the accounting for preferred stock in its project on distinguishing between liability and equity instruments. Statement 128 does not address numerator issues relating to the EPS computation. Statement 128 permits an adjustment only for preferred dividends in computing income available to common stockholders. The SEC guidance for increasing rate preferred stock continues to apply. [9]

N/A

Status Legend:

Affirmed = Consensus is carried forward (with or without modifications).

N/A = Issue is either outside the scope of or unaffected by Statement 128.

Nullified = Consensus is overturned (either entirely or partially, as noted).

Pending = The SEC staff has indicated that it will consider amending or rescinding the guidance prior to the effective date of Statement 128.

Resolved = Guidance is provided by Statement 128 on issues previously unresolved by EITF.

Bold numbers in brackets refer to related paragraphs in Statement 128.

Status after Statement 128	Current Guidance	Effect of Statement 128
	SAB 83 **Topic 4D: Earnings per Share Computations in an Initial Public Offering**	
Pending	The guidance in SAB 83 is applicable to registration statements filed in connection with an initial public offering (IPO) of common stock. SAB 83 states that potentially dilutive instruments with exercise prices below the IPO price that are issued within a one-year period prior to the initial filing of the IPO registration statement should be treated as outstanding for all reported periods (current and prior), in the same manner as shares issued in a stock split are treated. However, in determining the dilutive effect of the issuances, a treasury stock approach may be used.	Statement 128 would permit those potentially dilutive common shares to be included only in the computation of *diluted* EPS and only from the date of issuance. In essence, SAB 83 permits an entity involved in an IPO to treat those potentially dilutive common shares as outstanding common shares in the computation of both basic and diluted EPS for all reported periods. [17]
	This method should be applied in the computation of EPS for all prior periods, including loss years in which the impact of the incremental shares is antidilutive.	Statement 128 does not permit incremental shares to be included in the computation of diluted EPS when an entity has a loss from continuing operations (as the effect is antidilutive). [13, 15, 16]
		The SEC guidance continues to apply to SEC registrants involved in an IPO that have issued such potentially dilutive common shares.

EITF Topic No. D-15—Earnings-per-Share Presentation for Securities Not Specifically Covered by APB Opinion No. 15

N/A	Topic D-15 (an SEC Observer announcement) states that when situations not expressly covered in Opinion 15 occur, they should be dealt with according to their substance. It also provides the two following general principles that must be considered in analyzing new securities in order to reflect the most appropriate EPS presentation.	Although not expressly stated, this broad concept is implicit in Statement 128.
Pending	1. Securities that enable the holder to participate with common shareholders in dividends over a significant period of time should be reflected in EPS using the two-class method if that method is more dilutive than other methods.	Statement 128 requires use of the two-class method for participating securities that are not convertible into common stock (the if-converted method should be used for all convertible securities). **[60, 61]**
Pending	2. Contingent issuances should be reflected in fully diluted EPS if those contingent issuances have at least a reasonable possibility of occurring.	The contingent-share provisions in Statement 128 are fairly specific and do not permit an entity to consider the probability of a contingent issuance occurring. **[30]**

Status after Statement 128	Current Guidance	Effect of Statement 128
N/A	**EITF Topic No. D-42—The Effect on the Calculation of Earnings per Share for the Redemption or Induced Conversion of Preferred Stock** Topic D-42 (an SEC Observer announcement) states that if a registrant redeems its preferred stock, the excess of the fair value of the consideration transferred to the holders of the preferred stock over the carrying amount of the preferred stock should be subtracted from net income to arrive at net income available to common stockholders in the computation of EPS. Similarly, if convertible preferred stock is converted to other securities issued by the registrant pursuant to an inducement offer, the excess of the fair value of all securities and other consideration transferred to the holders of the convertible preferred stock over the fair value of securities issuable pursuant to the original conversion terms should be subtracted from net income to arrive at net income available to common stockholders.	The Board expects to address the accounting for preferred stock in its project on distinguishing between liability and equity instruments. Statement 128 does not address numerator issues relating to the EPS computation. Statement 128 permits an adjustment only for preferred dividends in computing income available to common stockholders. The SEC guidance for redemption or induced conversion of preferred stock continues to apply. [9]
N/A	**EITF Topic No. D-53—Computation of Earnings per Share for a Period That Includes a Redemption or an Induced Conversion of a Portion of a Class of Preferred Stock** Topic D-53 (an SEC Observer announcement) is related to Topic D-42. Topic D-53 states that if a registrant effects a redemption or induced conversion of only a *portion* of the outstanding securities of a class of preferred stock, any excess consideration should be attributed to those shares that are redeemed or converted.	The Board expects to address the accounting for preferred stock in its project on distinguishing between liability and equity instruments. Statement 128 does not address numerator issues relating to the EPS computation. The SEC guidance for redemption or induced conversion of preferred stock continues to apply.

For purposes of determining whether the "if converted" method is dilutive for the period, the shares redeemed or converted should be considered separately from those shares that are not redeemed or converted.

The "if converted" provisions in Statement 128 do not address how to determine whether a convertible security is antidilutive when there has been a partial conversion. [26-28]

EITF Issue No. 85-18—Earnings-per-Share Effect of Equity Commitment Notes

Issue 85-18 states that shares contingently issuable under equity commitment notes and equity contracts should *not* be included in EPS computations. Those shares are considered contingently issuable because the company has an option of paying in cash or stock.

Statement 128 contradicts the consensus reached. Statement 128 states that contracts that may be settled in stock or cash should be presumed to be settled in stock and reflected in the computation of diluted EPS unless past experience or a stated policy provides a reasonable basis to believe otherwise. [29]

Nullified

Issue 85-18 states that equity contracts that specifically require the issuance of common stock to repay debt should be included in the EPS computations as potentially dilutive securities.

Statement 128 supports the consensus reached; equity contracts that require payment in stock should be considered potentially dilutive securities (convertible debt). [26-28]

Affirmed

EITF Issue No. 87-31—Sale of Put Options on Issuer's Stock

Issue 87-31 prescribes use of the reverse treasury stock method to account for the dilutive effect of written put options that are "in the money" during the period.

In computing diluted EPS, Statement 128 requires use of the reverse treasury stock method to account for the dilutive effect of written put options and similar contracts that are "in the money" during the reporting period. [24]

Affirmed

Note: The EITF combined the consensuses in this Issue with the consensuses in Issue No. 96-13, "Accounting for Derivative Financial Instruments Indexed to, and Potentially Settled in, a Company's Own Stock."

Status after Statement 128	Current Guidance	Effect of Statement 128
N/A	**EITF Issue No. 88-9—Put Warrants** The EITF superseded its consensus on this Issue for companies with publicly traded stock in Issue 96-13.	N/A
Nullified	**EITF Issue No. 90-4—Earnings-per-Share Treatment of Tax Benefits for Dividends on Stock Held by an Employee Stock Ownership Plan (ESOP)** Issue 1: Dividends on preferred stock held by an ESOP should be deducted from net income, net of any applicable income tax benefit, when computing primary EPS. Issue 2: The second issue was addressed by the EITF in Issue No. 92-3, "Earnings-per-Share Treatment of Tax Benefits for Dividends on Unallocated Stock Held by an Employee Stock Ownership Plan (Consideration of the Implications of FASB Statement No. 109 on Issue 2 of EITF Issue No. 90-4)."	Statement 128 has no provisions related to primary EPS and, thus, nullifies the consensus of Issue 90-4. However, it seems appropriate to make a similar deduction for dividends on preferred stock held by an ESOP when computing both basic and diluted EPS if that preferred stock is considered outstanding (that is, if the ESOP shares are allocated).
	EITF Issue No. 90-19—Convertible Bonds with Issuer Option to Settle for Cash upon Conversion Issue 90-19 provides EPS guidance for companies that issue debt instruments that are convertible into a fixed number of common shares. Upon conversion, the issuer either is required or has the option to satisfy all or part of the obligation in cash as follows:	

Affirmed*

Instrument A: If the issuer must satisfy the obligation entirely in cash, the instrument does not have an impact on primary or fully diluted EPS other than that the conversion spread must be recognized as a charge to income.

Statement 128 implicitly supports the consensus reached; this type of security does not meet the definition of potential common stock. [171]

Affirmed*

Instrument B: If the issuer may satisfy the entire obligation in either stock or cash equivalent to the conversion value, the instrument is treated as convertible debt for purposes of computing primary and fully diluted EPS.

Statement 128 implicitly supports the consensus reached. Contracts that may be settled in stock or cash should be presumed to be settled in stock and reflected in the computation of diluted EPS unless past experience or a stated policy provides a reasonable basis to believe otherwise. [29]

Affirmed*

Instrument C: If the issuer must satisfy the accreted value of the obligation in cash and may satisfy the conversion spread in either cash or stock, the instrument does not have an impact on primary EPS but impacts fully diluted EPS as convertible debt.

Statement 128 implicitly supports the consensus reached for diluted EPS. [29]

---

*The guidance related to primary EPS is nullified because Statement 128 eliminates the presentation of primary EPS.

Status after Statement 128	Current Guidance	Effect of Statement 128
N/A	**EITF Issue No. 92-3—Earnings-per-Share Treatment of Tax Benefits for Dividends on Inoculated Stock Held by an Employee Stock Ownership Plan (Consideration of the Implications of FASB Statement No. 109 on Issue 2 of EITF Issue No. 90-4)**

Issue 92-3 states that tax benefits related to dividends paid on unallocated common stock held by an ESOP, which are charged to retained earnings, should not be an adjustment to net income for purposes of computing EPS.

SOP 93-6 was issued in November 1993. Under SOP 93-6, dividends paid on unallocated ESOP shares are not treated as dividends for financial reporting purposes and, therefore, do not affect the if-converted EPS computations. | Statement 128 provides no guidance on common stock held by an ESOP. The guidance in AICPA Statement of Position (SOP) 93-6, *Employers' Accounting for Employee Stock Ownership Plans*, continues to apply as does the consensus in EITF Issue 92-3. AICPA Statement of Position 76-3, *Accounting Practices for Certain Employee Stock Ownership Plans*, continues to apply for "grandfathered" shares. |

EITF Issue No. 94-7—Accounting for Financial Instruments Indexed to, and Potentially Settled in, a Company's Own Stock

Resolved

Issue 94-7 addresses the classification of certain contracts (forward sales, forward purchases, purchased put options, and purchased call options) that are settled in a variety of ways (physical, net share, or net cash) as equity instruments or assets-liabilities and specifies the treatment of changes in the fair value of those instruments. The Issue does not address EPS treatment.

Note: The EITF combined the consensuses in this Issue with the consensuses in Issue 96-13.

Statement 128 states that contracts that may be settled in stock or cash should be presumed to be settled in stock and reflected in the computation of diluted EPS unless past experience or a stated policy provides a reasonable basis to believe otherwise. **[29]**

In computing diluted EPS, Statement 128 requires use of the reverse treasury stock method to account for the dilutive effect of written put options and similar contracts that are "in the money" during the reporting period. Statement 128 states that purchased options should not be reflected in the computation of diluted EPS because to do so would be antidilutive. **[24, 25]**

EITF Issue No. 96-1—Sale of Put Options on Issuer's Stock That Require or Permit Cash Settlement

Resolved

Issue 96-1 provides guidance similar to Issue 94-7 and relates only to written put options settled in a variety of ways. The Issue does not address EPS treatment.

Note: The EITF combined the consensuses in this Issue with the consensuses in Issue 96-13.

Refer to discussion on Issue 94-7.

Status after Statement 128	Current Guidance	Effect of Statement 128
Resolved	**EITF Issue No. 96-13—Accounting for Derivative Financial Instruments Indexed to, and Potentially Settled in, a Company's Own Stock** Issue 96-13 codifies the consensuses provided in Issues 87-31, 94-7, and 96-1 into a framework that can be applied to a variety of similar financial instruments settled in a variety of different ways. With the exception of the consensus on use of the reverse treasury stock method in Issue 87-31, Issue 96-13 does not address EPS treatment.	Refer to discussion on Issue 94-7.

Statement of Financial Accounting Standards No. 129
Disclosure of Information about Capital Structure

STATUS

Issued: February 1997

Effective Date: For financial statements for periods ending after December 15, 1997

Affects: Supersedes APB 10, paragraphs 10 and 11
Supersedes FAS 47, paragraph 10(c)

Affected by: No other pronouncements

Issues Discussed by FASB Emerging Issues Task Force (EITF)

Affects: No EITF Issues

Interpreted by: Paragraphs 4 and 8 interpreted by EITF Issue No. 00-19

Related Issues: EITF Issues No. 86-32, 98-5, and 00-27 and Topic No. D-98

SUMMARY

This Statement establishes standards for disclosing information about an entity's capital structure. It applies to all entities. This Statement continues the previous requirements to disclose certain information about an entity's capital structure found in APB Opinions No. 10, *Omnibus Opinion—1966,* and No. 15, *Earnings per Share,* and FASB Statement No. 47, *Disclosure of Long-Term Obligations,* for entities that were subject to the requirements of those standards. This Statement eliminates the exemption of nonpublic entities from certain disclosure requirements of Opinion 15 as provided by FASB Statement No. 21, *Suspension of the Reporting of Earnings per Share and Segment Information by Nonpublic Enterprises.* It supersedes specific disclosure requirements of Opinions 10 and 15 and Statement 47 and consolidates them in this Statement for ease of retrieval and for greater visibility to nonpublic entities.

This Statement is effective for financial statements for periods ending after December 15, 1997. It contains no change in disclosure requirements for entities that were previously subject to the requirements of Opinions 10 and 15 and Statement 47.

Statement of Financial Accounting Standards No. 129

Disclosure of Information about Capital Structure

CONTENTS

INTRODUCTION

1. In conjunction with its project to supersede the provisions for computing earnings per share (EPS) found in APB Opinion No. 15, *Earnings per Share,* the Board reviewed the disclosure requirements specified in that Opinion. The Board noted that although some of the disclosures were not necessarily related to the computation of earnings per share, they provided useful information. Because nonpublic entities were excluded from the scope of Opinion 15 and that Opinion's disclosure requirements regarding capital structure are not required elsewhere, the Board decided to include those disclosure requirements in this Statement and make them applicable to all entities. In addition, the Board decided to incorporate related disclosure requirements from other Opinions or Statements into this Statement for ease of use. The specific disclosures required by this Statement were previously required by APB Opinion No. 10, *Omnibus Opinion—1966,* Opinion 15, and FASB Statement No. 47, *Disclosure of Long-Term Obligations,* for entities that were subject to the requirements of those standards.

2. The following terms and definitions are used in this Statement:

a. *Securities*—the evidence of debt or ownership or a related right. For purposes of this Statement, the term *securities* includes options and warrants as well as debt and stock.

b. *Participation rights*—contractual rights of security holders to receive dividends or returns from the security issuer's profits, cash flows, or returns on investments.

c. *Preferred stock*—a security that has preferential rights compared to common stock.

STANDARDS OF FINANCIAL ACCOUNTING AND REPORTING

Scope

3. This Statement applies to all entities, public and nonpublic, that have issued securities addressed by this Statement.

Information about Securities

4. An entity shall explain, in summary form within its financial statements, the pertinent rights and privileges of the various securities outstanding. Examples of information that shall be disclosed are dividend and liquidation preferences, participation rights, call prices and dates, conversion or exercise prices or rates and pertinent dates, sinking-fund requirements, unusual voting rights, and significant terms of contracts to issue additional shares.[1]

---

[1]Disclosure of this information about securities previously was required by Opinion 15, paragraph 19.

5. An entity shall disclose within its financial statements the number of shares issued upon conversion, exercise, or satisfaction of required conditions during at least the most recent annual fiscal period and any subsequent interim period presented.[2]

Liquidation Preference of Preferred Stock

6. An entity that issues preferred stock (or other senior stock) that has a preference in involuntary liquidation considerably in excess of the par or stated value of the shares shall disclose the liquidation preference of the stock (the relationship between the preference in liquidation and the par or stated value of the shares).[3] That disclosure shall be made in the equity section of the statement of financial position in the aggregate, either parenthetically or "in short," rather than on a per-share basis or through disclosure in the notes.

7. In addition, an entity shall disclose within its financial statements (either on the face of the statement of financial position or in the notes thereto):

a. The aggregate or per-share amounts at which preferred stock may be called or is subject to redemption through sinking-fund operations or otherwise; and

b. The aggregate and per-share amounts of arrearages in cumulative preferred dividends.[4]

Redeemable Stock

8. An entity that issues redeemable stock shall disclose the amount of redemption requirements, separately by issue or combined, for all issues of capital stock that are redeemable at fixed or determinable prices on fixed or determinable dates in each of the five years following the date of the latest statement of financial position presented.[5]

Amendments to Existing Pronouncements

9. Paragraphs 10 and 11 of Opinion 10 are deleted as well as the heading preceding paragraph 10.

10. Paragraph 10(c) of Statement 47 is deleted.

Effective Date and Transition

11. This Statement shall be effective for financial statements for periods ending after December 15, 1997. It contains no change in disclosure requirements for entities that were previously subject to the requirements of Opinions 10 and 15 and Statement 47.

> **The provisions of this Statement need not be applied to immaterial items.**

This Statement was adopted by the unanimous vote of the seven members of the Financial Accounting Standards Board:

Dennis R. Beresford, *Chairman*	Anthony T. Cope	James J. Leisenring
Joseph V. Anania	John M. Foster	Gerhard G. Mueller
	Gaylen N. Larson	

---

[2]Disclosure of this information about changes in securities previously was required by Opinion 15, paragraph 20. Footnote 5 to Opinion 15 referred to paragraph 10 of APB Opinion No. 12, *Omnibus Opinion—1967*. That paragraph requires, among other things, disclosure of the changes in the number of shares of equity securities during at least the most recent annual fiscal period and any subsequent interim period presented to make the financial statements sufficiently informative. The disclosure required by paragraph 5 of this Statement meets that requirement.

[3]Disclosure of this information about liquidation preferences previously was required by Opinion 10, paragraph 10.

[4]Disclosure of this information about preferred stock previously was required by Opinion 10, paragraph 11.

[5]Disclosure of this information about redemption requirements previously was required by Statement 47, paragraph 10(c).

Appendix

BACKGROUND INFORMATION AND BASIS FOR CONCLUSIONS

CONTENTS

Appendix

BACKGROUND INFORMATION AND BASIS FOR CONCLUSIONS

Introduction

12. This appendix summarizes considerations that were deemed significant by Board members in reaching the conclusions in this Statement. It includes reasons for accepting certain views and rejecting others. Individual Board members gave greater weight to some factors than to others.

Background Information

13. In March 1994, the Board added a project on earnings per share to its technical agenda to be pursued concurrently with a similar project of the International Accounting Standards Committee (IASC). The objective of the Board's project was twofold: (a) to improve and simplify U.S. generally accepted accounting principles and (b) to issue a standard that would be compatible with international standards.

14. In January 1996, the Board issued an FASB Exposure Draft, *Earnings per Share and Disclosure of Information about Capital Structure.* Part I of the proposed Statement included provisions related to the computation and presentation of earnings per share and was not applicable to nonpublic entities. Part II of the proposed Statement included disclosure requirements for information about capital structure and was applicable to all entities. The Board received 104 comment letters on the Exposure Draft, most of which commented only on the earnings per share provisions in Part I. The few letters that addressed Part II generally supported the Board's intent to centralize capital structure disclosure requirements.

15. The Board decided to issue Part II as a separate Statement because of its applicability to nonpublic entities. The Board was concerned that if it included those disclosure requirements in the final Statement on computing earnings per share, nonpublic entities might not be aware of the existence of those disclosure requirements and their wider applicability.

Conclusions on Basic Issues

Scope

16. This Statement is applicable to all entities that have issued securities addressed by this Statement. The Board believes that all of the required disclosures will be useful to users of financial statements of entities that have issued any type of security covered by this Statement, whether or not those securities are publicly held. The scope of this Statement is unchanged from that of the standards that previously contained its disclosure requirements (Opinions 10 and 15 and Statement 47), except for the elimination of the exemption of nonpublic entities from the provisions of Opinion 15. That exemption was provided by FASB Statement No. 21, *Suspension of the Reporting of Earnings per Share and Segment Information by Nonpublic Enterprises,* which was amended by FASB Statement No. 128, *Earnings per Share.*

Disclosure Requirements

17. Opinion 15 required disclosure of descriptive information about securities that is not necessarily related to the computation of earnings per share. The Board considered limiting that disclosure to information about only those securities that affect or could affect the computation of basic and diluted EPS. However, the Board decided not to limit the disclosure requirement because it contains useful information about the capital structure of an entity that is not required elsewhere.

18. This Statement also requires disclosure of information about (a) the liquidation preference of preferred stock and (b) redeemable stock that previously had been required to be disclosed by Opinion 10 and Statement 47, respectively. Those disclosure requirements were incorporated into this Statement because the Board believes that it is useful to include all disclosure requirements related to an entity's capital structure in the same standard.

Effective Date

19. The Board decided that this Statement should be effective for financial statements for periods ending after December 15, 1997. That effective date corresponds to the effective date of Statement 128. This Statement contains no change in disclosure requirements for entities that were previously subject to the requirements of Opinions 10 and 15 and Statement 47.

FAS130

Statement of Financial Accounting Standards No. 130
Reporting Comprehensive Income

STATUS

Issued: June 1997

Effective Date: For fiscal years beginning after December 15, 1997

Affects: Amends APB 28, paragraphs 2 and 30(a)
 Amends FAS 52, paragraph 13
 Amends FAS 80, paragraph 5
 Amends FAS 87, paragraphs 37 and 38
 Amends FAS 109, paragraphs 35 and 36
 Amends FAS 115, paragraphs 13, 15(c), 15(d), and 16

Affected by: Paragraph 27 amended by FAS 135

SUMMARY

   This Statement establishes standards for reporting and display of comprehensive income and its components (revenues, expenses, gains, and losses) in a full set of general-purpose financial statements. This Statement requires that all items that are required to be recognized under accounting standards as components of comprehensive income be reported in a financial statement that is displayed with the same prominence as other financial statements. This Statement does not require a specific format for that financial statement but requires that an enterprise display an amount representing total comprehensive income for the period in that financial statement.
   This Statement requires that an enterprise (a) classify items of other comprehensive income by their nature in a financial statement and (b) display the accumulated balance of other comprehensive income separately from retained earnings and additional paid-in capital in the equity section of a statement of financial position.
   This Statement is effective for fiscal years beginning after December 15, 1997. Reclassification of financial statements for earlier periods provided for comparative purposes is required.

Statement of Financial Accounting Standards No. 130

Reporting Comprehensive Income

CONTENTS

INTRODUCTION

1. This Statement establishes standards for reporting and display of comprehensive income and its components in a full set of general-purpose financial statements. It does not address issues of recognition[1] or measurement for comprehensive income and its components.

2. Historically, issues about income reporting were characterized broadly in terms of a contrast between the so-called current operating performance (or dirty surplus) and the all-inclusive (or clean surplus) income concepts. Under the current operating performance income concept, extraordinary and nonrecurring gains and losses are excluded from income. Under the all-inclusive income concept, all revenues, expenses, gains, and losses recognized during the period are included in income, regardless of whether they are considered to be results of operations of the period. The Accounting Principles Board largely adopted the all-inclusive income concept when it issued APB Opinion No. 9, *Reporting the Results of Operations,* and later reaffirmed the concept when it issued APB Opinions No. 20, *Accounting Changes,* and No. 30, *Reporting the Results of Operations— Reporting the Effects of Disposal of a Segment of a Business, and Extraordinary, Unusual and Infrequently Occurring Events and Transactions.*

---

[1]"Recognition is the process of formally recording or incorporating an item in the financial statements of an entity. Thus, an asset, liability, revenue, expense, gain, or loss may be recognized (recorded) or unrecognized (unrecorded). *Realization* and *recognition* are not used as synonyms, as they sometimes are in accounting and financial literature" (Concepts Statement No. 6, *Elements of Financial Statements,* paragraph 143; footnote reference omitted).

3. Although the Board generally followed the all-inclusive income concept, occasionally it made specific exceptions to that concept by requiring that certain changes in assets and liabilities not be reported in a statement that reports results of operations for the period in which they are recognized but instead be included in balances within a separate component of equity in a statement of financial position. Statements that contain those exceptions are FASB Statements No. 12, *Accounting for Certain Marketable Securities,*[2] No. 52, *Foreign Currency Translation,* No. 80, *Accounting for Futures Contracts,* No. 87, *Employers' Accounting for Pensions,* and No. 115, *Accounting for Certain Investments in Debt and Equity Securities.*

4. Some users of financial statement information expressed concerns about the increasing number of comprehensive income items that bypass the income statement. Currently, an enterprise is required to report the accumulated balances of those items in equity. However, because of the considerable diversity as to how those balances and changes in them are presented in financial statements, some of those users urged the Board to implement the concept of comprehensive income that was introduced in FASB Concepts Statement No. 3, *Elements of Financial Statements of Business Enterprises* (which was superseded by FASB Concepts Statement No. 6, *Elements of Financial Statements*), and further described in FASB Concepts Statement No. 5, *Recognition and Measurement in Financial Statements of Business Enterprises.*

5. As a first step in implementing the concept of comprehensive income, this Statement requires that all items that meet the definition of components of comprehensive income be reported in a financial statement for the period in which they are recognized. In doing so, this Statement amends Statements 52, 80, 87, and 115 to require that changes in the balances of items that under those Statements are reported directly in a separate component of equity in a statement of financial position be reported in a financial statement that is displayed as prominently as other financial statements. Items required by accounting standards to be reported as direct adjustments to paid-in capital, retained earnings, or other nonincome equity accounts are not to be included as

components of comprehensive income. (Refer to paragraphs 108-119.)

STANDARDS OF FINANCIAL ACCOUNTING AND REPORTING

Scope

6. This Statement applies to all enterprises that provide a full set of financial statements that report financial position, results of operations, and cash flows.[3] This Statement does not apply to an enterprise that has no items of other comprehensive income in any period presented or to a not-for-profit organization that is required to follow the provisions of FASB Statement No. 117, *Financial Statements of Not-for-Profit Organizations.*

7. This Statement discusses how to report and display comprehensive income and its components. However, it does not specify when to recognize or how to measure the items that make up comprehensive income. Existing and future accounting standards will provide guidance on items that are to be included in comprehensive income and its components.

Definition of Comprehensive Income

8. Comprehensive income is defined in Concepts Statement 6 as "the change in equity [net assets] of a business enterprise during a period from transactions and other events and circumstances from nonowner sources. It includes all changes in equity during a period except those resulting from investments by owners and distributions to owners" (paragraph 70).

9. In Concepts Statement 5, the Board stated that "a full set of financial statements for a period should show: Financial position at the end of the period, earnings (net income) for the period, comprehensive income (total nonowner changes in equity) for the period, cash flows during the period, and investments by and distributions to owners during the period" (paragraph 13, footnote references omitted). Prior to issuance of this Statement, the Board had neither required that an enterprise report comprehensive income, nor had it recommended a format for displaying comprehensive income.

---

[2]Statement 12 was superseded by Statement 115.

[3]Investment companies, defined benefit pension plans, and other employee benefit plans that are exempt from the requirement to provide a statement of cash flows by FASB Statement No. 102, *Statement of Cash Flows—Exemption of Certain Enterprises and Classification of Cash Flows from Certain Securities Acquired for Resale,* are not exempt from the requirements of this Statement if they otherwise apply.

Use of the Term Comprehensive Income

10. This Statement uses the term *comprehensive income* to describe the total of all components of comprehensive income, including net income.[4] This Statement uses the term *other comprehensive income* to refer to revenues, expenses, gains, and losses that under generally accepted accounting principles are included in comprehensive income but excluded from net income. This Statement does not require that an enterprise use the terms *comprehensive income* or *other comprehensive income* in its financial statements, even though those terms are used throughout this Statement.[5]

Purpose of Reporting Comprehensive Income

11. The purpose of reporting comprehensive income is to report a measure of all changes in equity of an enterprise that result from recognized transactions and other economic events of the period other than transactions with owners in their capacity as owners. Prior to the issuance of this Statement, some of those changes in equity were displayed in a statement that reports the results of operations, while others were included directly in balances within a separate component of equity in a statement of financial position.

12. If used with related disclosures and other information in the financial statements, the information provided by reporting comprehensive income should assist investors, creditors, and others in assessing an enterprise's activities and the timing and magnitude of an enterprise's future cash flows.

13. Although total comprehensive income is a useful measure, information about the components that make up comprehensive income also is needed. A single focus on total comprehensive income is likely to result in a limited understanding of an enterprise's activities. Information about the components of comprehensive income often may be more important than the total amount of comprehensive income.

Reporting and Display of Comprehensive Income

14. All components of comprehensive income shall be reported in the financial statements in the period in which they are recognized. A total amount for comprehensive income shall be displayed in the financial statement where the components of other comprehensive income are reported.

Classifications within Comprehensive Income

15. This Statement divides comprehensive income into net income and other comprehensive income. An enterprise shall continue to display an amount for net income. An enterprise that has no items of other comprehensive income in any period presented is not required to report comprehensive income.

Classifications within net income

16. Items included in net income are displayed in various classifications. Those classifications can include income from continuing operations, discontinued operations, extraordinary items, and cumulative effects of changes in accounting principle. This Statement does not change those classifications or other requirements for reporting results of operations.

Classifications within other comprehensive income

17. Items included in other comprehensive income shall be classified based on their nature. For example, under existing accounting standards, other comprehensive income shall be classified separately into foreign currency items, minimum pension liability adjustments, and unrealized gains and losses on certain investments in debt and equity securities. Additional classifications or additional items within current classifications may result from future accounting standards.

Reclassification adjustments

18. Adjustments shall be made to avoid double counting in comprehensive income items that are displayed as part of net income for a period that also had been displayed as part of other comprehensive income in that period or earlier periods. For example, gains on investment securities that were realized and included in net income of the current period that also had been included in other comprehensive income as unrealized holding gains in the period in which they

---

[4]This Statement uses the term *net income* to describe a measure of financial performance resulting from the aggregation of revenues, expenses, gains, and losses that are not items of other comprehensive income as identified in this Statement. A variety of other terms such as *net earnings* or *earnings* may be used to describe that measure.

[5]Paragraph 40 of Concepts Statement 5 states that "just as a variety of terms are used for net income in present practice, the Board anticipates that total nonowner changes in equity, comprehensive loss, and other equivalent terms will be used in future financial statements as names for comprehensive income."

arose must be deducted through other comprehensive income of the period in which they are included in net income to avoid including them in comprehensive income twice. Those adjustments are referred to in this Statement as *reclassification adjustments.*

19. An enterprise shall determine reclassification adjustments for each classification of other comprehensive income, except minimum pension liability adjustments. The requirement for a reclassification adjustment for Statement 52 foreign currency translation adjustments is limited to translation gains and losses realized upon sale or upon complete or substantially complete liquidation of an investment in a foreign entity.

20. An enterprise may display reclassification adjustments on the face of the financial statement in which comprehensive income is reported, or it may disclose reclassification adjustments in the notes to the financial statements. Therefore, for all classifications of other comprehensive income other than minimum pension liability adjustments, an enterprise may use either (a) a gross display on the face of the financial statement or (b) a net display on the face of the financial statement and disclose the gross change in the notes to the financial statements.[6] Gross and net displays are illustrated in Appendix B. An example of the calculation of reclassification adjustments for Statement 115 available-for-sale securities is included in Appendix C.

21. An enterprise shall not determine a reclassification adjustment for minimum pension liability adjustments. Therefore, an enterprise shall use a net display for that classification.

Alternative Formats for Reporting Comprehensive Income

22. An enterprise shall display comprehensive income and its components in a financial statement that is displayed with the same prominence as other financial statements that constitute a full set of financial statements. This Statement does not require a specific format for that financial statement but requires that an enterprise display net income as a component of comprehensive income in that financial statement. Appendix B provides illustrations of the components of other comprehensive income and to-

tal comprehensive income being reported below the total for net income in a statement that reports results of operations, in a separate statement of comprehensive income that begins with net income, and in a statement of changes in equity.

23. Although this Statement does not require a specific format for displaying comprehensive income and its components, the Board encourages an enterprise to display the components of other comprehensive income and total comprehensive income below the total for net income in a statement that reports results of operations or in a separate statement of comprehensive income that begins with net income.

24. An enterprise may display components of other comprehensive income either (a) net of related tax effects or (b) before related tax effects with one amount shown for the aggregate income tax expense or benefit related to the total of other comprehensive income items.

25. An enterprise shall disclose the amount of income tax expense or benefit allocated to each component of other comprehensive income, including reclassification adjustments, either on the face of the statement in which those components are displayed or in the notes to the financial statements. Alternative formats for disclosing the tax effects related to the components of other comprehensive income are illustrated in Appendix B.

Reporting Other Comprehensive Income in the Equity Section of a Statement of Financial Position

26. The total of other comprehensive income for a period shall be transferred to a component of equity that is displayed separately from retained earnings and additional paid-in capital in a statement of financial position at the end of an accounting period. A descriptive title such as *accumulated other comprehensive income* shall be used for that component of equity. An enterprise shall disclose accumulated balances for each classification in that separate component of equity on the face of a statement of financial position, in a statement of changes in equity, or in notes to the financial statements. The classifications shall correspond to classifications used elsewhere in the same set of financial statements for components of other comprehensive income.

---

[6]If displayed gross, reclassification adjustments are reported separately from other changes in the respective balance; thus, the total change is reported as two amounts. If displayed net, reclassification adjustments are combined with other changes in the balance; thus, the total change is reported as a single amount.

Interim-Period Reporting

27. APB Opinion No. 28, *Interim Financial Reporting,* clarifies the application of accounting principles and reporting practices to interim financial information, including interim financial statements and summarized interim financial data of publicly traded companies issued for external reporting purposes. An enterprise shall report a total for comprehensive income in condensed financial statements of interim periods issued to shareholders.

Amendments to Existing Pronouncements

28. APB Opinion No. 28, *Interim Financial Reporting,* is amended as follows:

a. In the first sentence of paragraph 2, as amended by FASB Statement No. 95, *Statement of Cash Flows,* the term *comprehensive income,* is inserted before *and cash flows.*

b. In paragraph 30(a), the phrase *and net income* is replaced by *net income, and comprehensive income.*

29. In the last sentence of paragraph 13 of FASB Statement No. 52, *Foreign Currency Translation,* the phrase *separately and accumulated in a separate component of equity* is replaced by *in other comprehensive income.*

30. FASB Statement No. 80, *Accounting for Futures Contracts,* is amended as follows:

a. In the third sentence of paragraph 5, *a separate component of stockholders' (or policyholders') equity* is replaced by *other comprehensive income.*

b. In the last sentence of paragraph 5, as amended by FASB Statement No. 115, *Accounting for Certain Investments in Debt and Equity Securities,* the phrase *shall be included as part of other comprehensive income and* is inserted after *those assets.*

31. FASB Statement No. 87, *Employers' Accounting for Pensions,* is amended as follows:

a. In the last sentence of paragraph 37, as amended by FASB Statement No. 109, *Accounting for Income Taxes,* the phrase *as a separate component (that is, a reduction) of equity* is replaced by *in other comprehensive income.*

b. Paragraph 38 is amended as follows:

   (1) In the first sentence, *the balance accumulated in a* is inserted before *separate.*

   (2) The following sentence is added to the end of paragraph 38:

   > Eliminations of or adjustments to that balance shall be reported in other comprehensive income.

32. FASB Statement No. 109, *Accounting for Income Taxes,* is amended as follows:

a. In the first sentence of paragraph 35, *other comprehensive income,* is inserted after *extraordinary items.*

b. In the first sentence of paragraph 36, *to other comprehensive income or* is inserted after *credited directly.*

33. FASB Statement No. 115, *Accounting for Certain Investments in Debt and Equity Securities,* is amended as follows:

a. Paragraph 13 is amended as follows:

   (1) In the second sentence, *as a net amount in a separate component of shareholders' equity until realized* is replaced by *in other comprehensive income.*

   (2) In the last sentence, *a separate component of shareholders' equity* is replaced by *other comprehensive income.*

b. In paragraph 15(c), *recognized in a separate component of shareholders' equity* is replaced by *reported in other comprehensive income.*

c. In the first sentence of paragraph 15(d), *such as accumulated other comprehensive income,* is inserted after *shareholders' equity.*

d. In the last sentence of paragraph 16, both references to *the separate component of equity* are replaced by *other comprehensive income.*

Effective Date and Transition

34. The provisions of this Statement shall be effective for fiscal years beginning after December 15, 1997. Earlier application is permitted. If comparative financial statements are provided for earlier periods, those financial statements shall be reclassified to reflect application of the provisions of this Statement. The provisions of this Statement that require display of reclassification adjustments (paragraphs 18-21) are not required, but are encouraged, in comparative financial statements provided for earlier periods. Initial application of this Statement shall be as of the beginning of an enterprise's fiscal year; that is, if the Statement is adopted prior to the effective date and during an interim period other than the first interim period, all prior interim periods of that fiscal year shall be reclassified.

> **The provisions of this Statement need not be applied to immaterial items.**

This Statement was adopted by the affirmative votes of five members of the Financial Accounting Standards Board. Messrs. Cope and Foster dissented.

Messrs. Cope and Foster dissent from this Statement because it permits an enterprise to display the items of other comprehensive income identified in this Statement with less prominence and to characterize them differently from other items of comprehensive income that are currently included in net income. The Board's conceptual framework does not define earnings or net income, nor does it provide criteria for distinguishing the characteristics of items that should be included in comprehensive income but not in net income. The qualitative characteristics of the items currently classified as items of other comprehensive income have not been conceptually distinguished from those items included in net income. Messrs. Cope and Foster believe that items of other comprehensive income can be as significant to measurement of an enterprise's economic and financial performance as those items of comprehensive income that are currently included in measuring net income, and that the comparability and the neutrality of reported information are adversely affected if some items of comprehensive income are omitted from reports on economic and financial performance. Therefore, they have concluded that this Statement should have required that items of other comprehensive income be reported in a statement of financial performance, preferably in a single statement in which net income is reported as a component of comprehensive income.

Messrs. Cope and Foster believe that a primary objective in undertaking a project on reporting comprehensive income was to significantly enhance the visibility of items of other comprehensive income. They do not believe that this Statement will achieve that objective. Messrs. Cope and Foster think that it is likely that most enterprises will meet the requirements of this Statement by providing the required information in a statement of changes in equity, and that displaying items of other comprehensive income solely in that statement as opposed to reporting them in a statement of financial performance will do little to enhance their visibility and will diminish their perceived importance. Thus, it is their view that this Statement will inappropriately relegate certain items of comprehensive income to a lesser standing, having less visibility than other items of comprehensive income that are included in net income, and will do so for the foreseeable future.

Another objective of the project on reporting comprehensive income was to encourage users of financial statements to focus on the components that constitute comprehensive income rather than limiting their analyses solely to the amounts reported as net income and earnings per share. The current, apparent market fixation on earnings per share is evidence that some users exclude other measures of performance from their analyses. Messrs. Cope and Foster believe that permitting items of other comprehensive income to be reported solely in a statement of changes in equity does not achieve the foregoing objective and may, in fact, divert the attention of some users of financial statements from those items of comprehensive income, thereby diminishing their understanding of the economic and financial performance of the reporting enterprise. For users of financial statements to fully understand and appropriately analyze the economic and financial performance of an enterprise, all items of other comprehensive income must be reported in a statement of financial performance, as was proposed in the Exposure Draft of this Statement.

Messrs. Cope and Foster believe that the Board inappropriately failed to respond to the clear and unequivocal call from users of financial statements for the transparent presentation of all items of comprehensive income, whose request is acknowledged in paragraphs 40 and 41 of this Statement. While many respondents to the Exposure Draft asserted that users would be confused by the presentation of comprehensive income, the users that testified at the public hearing on this project categorically denied that that would be the case.

Messrs. Cope and Foster also note that, as evidenced by the basis for conclusions in the Exposure Draft, the Board held views similar to theirs when it issued that document. The stated objective in the Exposure Draft was "to issue a Statement that requires that an enterprise report all components of comprehensive income in one or two statements of financial performance for the period in which those items are recognized." Messrs. Cope and Foster believe that the basis for conclusions supporting this Statement provides little, if any, rationale as to why, having determined at the time it issued the Exposure Draft that comprehensive income is clearly a measure of financial performance, the Board subsequently concluded it should not require presentation of comprehensive income in a statement of financial performance

(paragraphs 58-67). In fact, paragraph 67 of this Statement acknowledges the conceptual superiority of displaying comprehensive income in a statement of performance.

Finally, based on the Board's tentative conclusions, at this time it seems that a future standard on accounting for hedging and derivative instruments likely will provide that certain gains and losses on transactions in derivative instruments not be included in the determination of net income when they occur, but be reported as items of other comprehensive income. Much concern recently has been expressed about derivative instruments and their effects on the financial position and performance of various enterprises. The Board's project on accounting for derivative instruments and hedging activities was undertaken to enhance the visibility and understanding of those transactions and their effects on financial position and performance. Messrs. Cope and Foster believe that if certain of those effects are reported as items of other comprehensive income, application of this Statement in conjunction with that reporting is likely to do little to achieve that objective. In their view, that is inappropriate, particularly when the potential for significant impact that derivative instruments have on an enterprise's performance is an important concern.

Members of the Financial Accounting Standards Board:

Dennis R. Beresford,
  Chairman
Joseph V. Anania

Anthony T. Cope
John M. Foster
Gaylen N. Larson

James J. Leisenring
Gerhard G. Mueller

Appendix A

BACKGROUND INFORMATION AND BASIS FOR CONCLUSIONS

CONTENTS

Appendix A

BACKGROUND INFORMATION AND BASIS FOR CONCLUSIONS

Introduction

35. This appendix summarizes considerations that were deemed significant by Board members in reaching the conclusions in this Statement. It includes reasons for accepting certain approaches and rejecting others. Individual Board members gave greater weight to some factors than to others.

Background Information

36. The term *comprehensive income* was first introduced in Concepts Statement 3, which was issued in December 1980. However, the term comprehensive income was used to communicate the same notion as *earnings* in FASB Concepts Statement No. 1, *Objectives of Financial Reporting by Business Enterprises,* which was issued in November 1978.[7] The Board decided to use comprehensive income rather than earnings in Concepts Statement 3 because it wanted to reserve earnings for possible use to designate a different concept that was narrower than comprehensive income.

37. In Concepts Statement 5, the Board concluded that comprehensive income and its components should be reported as part of a full set of financial statements for a period. The Board also described earnings as part of comprehensive income in that Concepts Statement, indicating that earnings was narrower than comprehensive income, and provided illustrations of possible differences between earnings and comprehensive income. Earnings was described as being similar to net income in current practice, except for cumulative effects of changes in accounting principles, which are included in present net income but are excluded from earnings.

38. In December 1985, Concepts Statement 6 superseded Concepts Statement 3, expanding the scope to encompass not-for-profit organizations. Concepts Statement 6 does not alter the definition of comprehensive income provided in Concepts Statement 3.

39. Prior to the issuance of this Statement, the Board had not required that comprehensive income and its components be reported as part of a full set of financial statements. However, several accounting standards required that certain items that qualify as components of comprehensive income bypass a statement of income and be reported in a balance within a separate component of equity in a statement of financial position. Those items are:

a. Foreign currency translation adjustments (Statement 52, paragraph 13)
b. Gains and losses on foreign currency transactions that are designated as, and are effective as, economic hedges of a net investment in a foreign entity, commencing as of the designation date (Statement 52, paragraph 20(a))
c. Gains and losses on intercompany foreign currency transactions that are of a long-term-investment nature (that is, settlement is not planned or anticipated in the foreseeable future), when the entities to the transaction are consolidated, combined, or accounted for by the equity method in the reporting enterprise's financial statements (Statement 52, paragraph 20(b))
d. A change in the market value of a futures contract that qualifies as a hedge of an asset reported at fair value pursuant to Statement 115 (Statement 80, paragraph 5)
e. A net loss recognized pursuant to Statement 87 as an additional pension liability not yet recognized as net periodic pension cost (Statement 87, paragraph 37)
f. Unrealized holding gains and losses on available-for-sale securities (Statement 115, paragraph 13)
g. Unrealized holding gains and losses that result from a debt security being transferred into the available-for-sale category from the held-to-maturity category (Statement 115, paragraph 15(c))
h. Subsequent decreases (if not an other-than-temporary impairment) or increases in the fair value of available-for-sale securities previously written down as impaired (Statement 115, paragraph 16).

40. Users of financial statements expressed concerns about the practice of reporting some comprehensive

---

[7]Comprehensive income also is the concept that was referred to as earnings in other conceptual framework documents: *Tentative Conclusions on Objectives of Financial Statements of Business Enterprises* (December 1976), FASB Discussion Memorandum, *Conceptual Framework for Financial Accounting and Reporting: Elements of Financial Statements and Their Measurement* (December 1976), FASB Exposure Draft, *Objectives of Financial Reporting and Elements of Financial Statements of Business Enterprises* (December 1977), and FASB Discussion Memorandum, *Reporting Earnings* (July 1979).

income items directly within a balance shown as a separate component of equity. Among those expressing concerns was the Association for Investment Management and Research (AIMR). In its 1993 report, *Financial Reporting in the 1990s and Beyond,* the AIMR urged the Board to implement the concept of comprehensive income for several reasons. Two of those reasons were to discontinue the practice of taking certain items of comprehensive income directly to equity and to provide a vehicle for addressing future accounting issues, such as the display of unrealized gains and losses associated with financial instruments. In that report, the AIMR noted that it has long supported the all-inclusive income concept.

41, The Accounting Policy Committee of the Robert Morris Associates also indicated support for what it referred to as an all-inclusive income statement at a 1995 meeting with the Board by stating that "net income should include the effect of *all* of the current period's economic transactions and other activity of the entity."

42. There is also international precedent for moving toward an all-inclusive income concept. In 1992, the United Kingdom Accounting Standards Board (ASB) issued Financial Reporting Standard (FRS) 3, *Reporting Financial Performance.* That standard introduced a "statement of total recognized gains and losses" as a supplement to the "profit and loss account," which is equivalent to the U.S. income statement. The amount for "recognized gains and losses relating to the year" in the statement of total recognized gains and losses is analogous to comprehensive income.

43. Largely in response to the precedent set by the ASB, other international standard setters have focused attention on reporting financial performance. As part of its efforts to promote international harmonization, the Board discussed reporting comprehensive income with the ASB as well as with standard setters from the International Accounting Standards Committee (IASC), the Canadian Institute of Chartered Accountants, the Australian Accounting Research Foundation, and the New Zealand Society of Accountants.

44. In July 1996, the IASC issued an Exposure Draft, *Presentation of Financial Statements,* which included a proposed requirement for a new primary financial statement referred to as a "statement of nonowner movements in equity." The purpose of that statement would be to highlight more prominently gains and losses, such as those arising from revaluations and deferred exchange differences, that are not reported in the income statement under existing IASC standards.[8] The IASC's proposed requirement is similar in concept to this Statement's requirement for reporting comprehensive income and the ASB's requirement for a statement of total recognized gains and losses.

45. In addition to users' concerns about reporting comprehensive income items in equity and the desire for international harmonization, the project on reporting comprehensive income became more urgent because of the increasing use of separate components in equity for certain comprehensive income items. In that regard, a recent motivating factor for adding the comprehensive income project to the Board's technical agenda was the Board's financial instruments project, which is expected to result in additional comprehensive income items.

Financial Instruments Project

46. Many financial instruments are "off-balance-sheet." In the derivatives and hedging portion of the financial instruments project, the Board has proposed that all derivative instruments should be recognized and measured at fair value. Moreover, Board members believe that most, if not all, financial instruments ultimately should be recognized and measured at fair value because fair values generally are more decision useful (that is, more relevant), more understandable, and more practical to use than cost or cost-based measures.

47. The use of fair values to measure financial instruments necessarily raises questions about how the resulting gains and losses should be reported. Certain constituents expressed concern that using fair values will (a) cause more gains and losses to be recognized than currently are recognized and (b) increase the volatility of reported net income.

48. While measuring financial instruments at fair value results in recognizing gains and losses on those

---

[8]In redeliberations of the IASC Exposure Draft, the proposed requirement for a separate statement of nonowner movements in equity has been modified. As of April 1997, the IASC tentatively decided to require that an enterprise present, as a separate component of its financial statements, a statement showing (a) the net profit or loss for the period, (b) each item of income and expenses and gains and losses which, as required by other standards, are recognized directly in equity, and the total of those items, (c) the total of both item (a) and item (b) above, and (d) the cumulative effect of changes in accounting policy and the correction of fundamental errors.

instruments, it does not necessarily follow that those gains and losses must be reported in the income statement as part of net income. The Board believes that it is appropriate and consistent with the definition of comprehensive income provided in the Concepts Statements to include some gains and losses in net income and to exclude others from net income and report them as part of comprehensive income outside net income. Furthermore, reporting separately gains and losses in a financial statement would make those gains and losses more transparent than if they were only included within the equity section of a statement of financial position.

49. In response to the concerns discussed in paragraphs 40-48, the Board added a project on reporting comprehensive income to its agenda in September 1995. The Board's objective was to issue a Statement that requires that an enterprise report all components of comprehensive income in a financial statement that is displayed with the same prominence as other financial statements that constitute a full set.

50. An FASB Exposure Draft, *Reporting Comprehensive Income,* was issued in June 1996. The Board received 281 comment letters on the Exposure Draft, and 22 individuals and organizations presented their views at a public hearing held in November 1996.[9] In addition, the Board discussed the Exposure Draft in meetings with constituents, the Financial Instruments Task Force, and the Financial Accounting Standards Advisory Council. The comments from those groups, comment letters, and public hearing testimony were considered by the Board during its redeliberations of the issues addressed by the Exposure Draft at public meetings held in 1997. This Statement is a result of those Board meetings and redeliberations.

Benefits and Costs

51. In accomplishing its mission, the Board follows certain precepts, including the precept to promulgate standards only when the expected benefits of the information exceed the perceived costs. The Board endeavors to determine that a standard will fill a significant need and that the costs imposed to meet that standard, as compared to other alternatives, are justified in relation to the overall benefits of the resulting information.

52. Based on the recommendations by users of financial statements, the increasing use of separate accounts in equity for certain comprehensive income items, and issues arising in the financial instruments project, the Board concluded that a standard on reporting comprehensive income was needed. This Statement should help facilitate a better understanding of an enterprise's financial activities by users of financial statements because it will result in enhanced comparability within and between enterprises by providing more consistency as to how the balances of components of other comprehensive income and changes in them are presented in financial statements. Moreover, this Statement provides a method for reporting comprehensive income that should prove helpful in addressing and resolving issues that potentially include items of comprehensive income now and in the future. Because enterprises already accumulate information about components of what this Statement identifies as other comprehensive income and report that information in a statement of financial position or in notes accompanying it, the Board determined that there would be little incremental cost associated with the requirements of this Statement beyond the cost of understanding its requirements and deciding how to apply them.

Conclusions on Basic Issues

Scope

53. The Board decided to limit the project's scope to issues of reporting and display of comprehensive income so that it could complete the project in a timely manner. The Board concluded that timely completion was important because of the project's relationship to the project on accounting for derivatives and hedging activities.

54. Although the scope of the project was limited to issues of reporting and display, the Board recognizes that other more conceptual issues are involved in reporting comprehensive income. Such issues include questions about when components of comprehensive income should be recognized in financial statements and how those components should be measured. In addition, there are conceptual questions about the characteristics of items that generally accepted accounting principles require to be included in net income versus the characteristics of items that this Statement identifies as items that are to be included in comprehensive income outside net income. Furthermore, there are several items that generally accepted

---

[9]The public hearings on the comprehensive income Exposure Draft and the June 1996 FASB Exposure Draft, *Accounting for Derivative and Similar Financial Instruments and for Hedging Activities,* were held jointly.

accounting principles require to be recognized as direct adjustments to paid-in capital or other equity accounts that this Statement does not identify as being part of comprehensive income. (Refer to paragraphs 108-119.) The Board expects to consider those types of issues in one or more broader-scope projects related to reporting comprehensive income.

55. The Board considered whether not-for-profit organizations should be permitted to follow the provisions of this Statement and decided that those organizations should continue to follow the requirements of Statement 117. Because Statement 117 requires that those organizations report the change in net assets for a period in a statement of activities, those organizations already are displaying the equivalent of comprehensive income.

Issues Considered

56. The issues considered in this project were organized under the following general questions: (a) whether comprehensive income should be reported, (b) whether cumulative accounting adjustments should be included in comprehensive income, (c) how components of comprehensive income should be classified for display, (d) whether comprehensive income and its components should be displayed in one or two statements of financial performance, and (e) whether components of other comprehensive income should be displayed before or after their related tax effects.

Reporting of comprehensive income

57. The Board considered the following issues about reporting comprehensive income: (a) whether all items that are or will be recognized under current and future accounting standards as items of comprehensive income should be reported in a statement of financial performance, (b) whether a total amount for comprehensive income should be displayed, (c) how the total amount of comprehensive income should be labeled or described, and (d) whether a per-share amount for comprehensive income should be displayed.

Reporting all items of comprehensive income in a statement of financial performance

58. The Exposure Draft proposed that changes in the accumulated balances of income items currently required to be reported directly in a separate component of equity in a statement of financial position (un-

realized gains and losses on available-for-sale-securities, minimum pension liability adjustments, and translation gains and losses) should instead be reported in a statement of financial performance. In deliberations leading to the Exposure Draft, the Board noted that those items would be included in a statement of financial performance under the all-inclusive income concept.

59. Some respondents to the Exposure Draft stated that information about the components of other comprehensive income already was available elsewhere in the financial statements and that it was unnecessary for the Board to require that information to be reported separately and aggregated into a measure of comprehensive income. Other respondents agreed that the components of other comprehensive income should be displayed in a more transparent manner. However, a majority of those respondents indicated that until the Board addresses the conceptual issues discussed in paragraph 54, it was premature for the Board to require that the components be reported in a statement of financial performance.

60. Most respondents to the Exposure Draft asserted that the requirement to report comprehensive income and its components in a statement of financial performance would result in confusion. Much of that confusion would stem from reporting two financial performance measures (net income and comprehensive income) and users' inability to determine which measure was the appropriate one for investment decisions, credit decisions, or capital resource allocation. Many of those respondents argued that the items identified as other comprehensive income were not performance related and that it would be not only confusing but also misleading to require that those items be included in a performance statement. Finally, some respondents indicated that comprehensive income would be volatile from period to period and that that volatility would be related to market forces beyond the control of management. In their view, therefore, it would be inappropriate to highlight that volatility in a statement of financial performance. Other respondents said that comprehensive income was more a measure of entity performance than it was of management performance and that it was therefore incorrect to argue that it should not be characterized as a performance measure because of management's inability to control the market forces that could result in that measure being volatile from period to period.

61. Many respondents suggested that the Board could achieve the desired transparency for the components of other comprehensive income by requiring that they be displayed in an expanded statement of changes in equity or in a note to the financial statements. Respondents said that either of those types of display would be more acceptable than display in a performance statement because the components of other comprehensive income would not be characterized as being performance related.

62. In response to constituents' concerns about the requirement in the Exposure Draft to report comprehensive income and its components in a statement of financial performance, the Board considered three additional approaches in its redeliberations. The first approach would require disclosure of comprehensive income and its components in a note to the financial statements. The second approach would require the display of comprehensive income and its components in a statement of changes in equity. The third approach would require the reporting of comprehensive income and its components in a financial statement that is displayed with the same prominence as other financial statements, thereby permitting an enterprise to report the components of comprehensive income in one or two statements of financial performance as proposed by the Exposure Draft or in a statement of changes in equity if that statement was presented as a financial statement.

63. The Board decided against permitting an enterprise to disclose comprehensive income and its components in a note to the financial statements. The Board acknowledged that it could justify note disclosure because it would provide important information in the interim while the conceptual issues surrounding comprehensive income reporting were studied in more depth. However, the Board decided that such disclosure would be inconsistent with the Concepts Statements, which both define comprehensive income and call for the reporting of it as part of a full set of financial statements. The Board also agreed that only disclosure of comprehensive income and its components was inconsistent with one of the objectives of the project, which was to take a first step toward the implementation of the concept of comprehensive income by requiring that its components be displayed in a financial statement.

64. The Board also decided against requiring that an enterprise display comprehensive income and its components in a statement of changes in equity. APB Opinion No. 12, *Omnibus Opinion—1967,* requires that an enterprise report changes in stockholders' equity accounts other than retained earnings whenever both financial position and results of operations are presented. However, paragraph 10 of Opinion 12 states that "disclosure of such changes may take the form of separate statements or may be made in the basic financial statements or notes thereto." The Board agreed that it was important for information about other comprehensive income and total comprehensive income to be displayed in a financial statement presented as prominently as other financial statements that constitute a full set of financial statements. Because Opinion 12 permits an enterprise to report changes in equity in a note to the financial statements, the Board agreed that if it required an enterprise to display comprehensive income and its components in a statement of changes in equity that it would first have to implement a requirement for all enterprises to provide such a statement. The Board also acknowledged that the Securities and Exchange Commission requires that public enterprises provide information about changes in equity but, similar to Opinion 12, those requirements permit an enterprise to display that information in a note to the financial statements.[10] The Board noted that some enterprises might not have items of other comprehensive income and decided that it would be burdensome to require that those enterprises provide a statement of changes in equity when the impetus for that requirement did not apply to them. The Board also noted that some enterprises might have only one item of other comprehensive income and that those enterprises might prefer to report that item below net income in a single statement instead of creating a separate statement of changes in equity to report that amount.

65. The Board decided that it could achieve the desired transparency for the components of other comprehensive income and at the same time be responsive to the concerns of its constituents by permitting a choice of displaying comprehensive income and its components (a) in one or two statements of financial performance (as proposed by the Exposure Draft) or (b) in a statement of changes in equity. The Board

---

[10]SEC Regulation S-X, Section 210.3-04, "Changes in Other Stockholders' Equity," states that "an analysis of the changes in each caption of other stockholders' equity presented in the balance sheets shall be given in a note or separate statement. This analysis shall be presented in the form of a reconciliation of the beginning balance to the ending balance for each period for which an income statement is required to be filed with all significant reconciling items described by appropriate captions."

decided that if an enterprise opted to display comprehensive income in a statement of changes in equity, that statement must be presented as part of a full set of financial statements and not in the notes to the financial statements.

66. The Board also decided that until it addresses the conceptual issues surrounding the reporting of comprehensive income, it should not require presentation of comprehensive income as a measure of financial performance. Consequently, the Board agreed to eliminate references to comprehensive income as a performance measure in the standards section of the final Statement. Therefore, this Statement requires that all items that are recognized under accounting standards as components of comprehensive income be reported in a financial statement that is displayed with the same prominence as other financial statements that constitute a full set of financial statements that report financial position, results of operations, and cash flows.

67. The Board decided to encourage an enterprise to report comprehensive income and the components of other comprehensive income in an income statement below the total for net income or in a separate statement of comprehensive income that begins with net income as originally proposed by the Exposure Draft. The Board believes that displaying comprehensive income in an income-statement-type format is more consistent with the Concepts Statements and therefore is conceptually superior to displaying it in a statement of changes in equity. That type of display also is consistent with the all-inclusive income concept. Furthermore, display of comprehensive income in an income-statement-type format provides the most transparency for its components. Also, it may be more practical for an enterprise that has several items of other comprehensive income to display them outside a statement of changes in equity. Finally, display in an income-statement-type format is consistent with the Board's desire to implement a broader-scope project on comprehensive income that ultimately could move toward reporting comprehensive income and its components in a statement of financial performance.

Displaying a total for comprehensive income

68. The Board decided to retain the requirement in the Exposure Draft to display a total amount for comprehensive income in the financial statement in which its components are displayed regardless of whether an enterprise chooses to display those components in an income-statement-type format or in a statement of changes in equity. The Board agreed that that total will demonstrate articulation between an enterprise's financial position at the end of the period and all aspects of its financial activities for the period, thereby enhancing the understandability of the statements. Also, that total will provide enhanced comparability between enterprises by providing a benchmark for users.

Describing the total for comprehensive income

69. The term *comprehensive income* is used consistently in this Statement to describe the total of all components of comprehensive income, including net income. However, the Board decided not to require that an enterprise use that term in financial statements because it traditionally has not specified how particular amounts should be labeled and often has simply required that a "descriptive label" be used. In practice, a variety of terms, such as net income, net earnings, or earnings, are used to describe the total appearing at the bottom of a statement that reports the results of operations.

70. Many respondents to the Exposure Draft indicated that the term comprehensive income should not be used. They said that the term is misleading because the amount is neither "comprehensive" nor "income." Although the Exposure Draft did not require use of the term comprehensive income, its consistent usage throughout the document (and in its title) gave respondents the impression that it was required.

71. The Board discussed whether using the term comprehensive income would be misleading. The Board agreed that comprehensive income is "income" because changes in equity (changes in assets and liabilities) are identified by the Concepts Statements as revenues, expenses, gains, and losses. The Board acknowledged that comprehensive income will never be completely "comprehensive" because there always will be some assets and liabilities that cannot be measured with sufficient reliability. Therefore, those assets and liabilities as well as the changes in them will not be recognized in the financial statements. For example, the internally generated intangible asset often referred to as intellectual capital is not presently measured and recognized in financial statements. The Board agreed that comprehensive income is "comprehensive" to the extent that it includes all recognized changes in equity during a period from transactions and other events and

circumstances from nonowner sources. The Board acknowledged that there are certain changes in equity that have characteristics of comprehensive income but that are not presently included in it. (Refer to paragraphs 108-119.) Those items may be addressed in a broader-scope project on comprehensive income.

72. In considering other terminology that could be used to describe the aggregate total referred to by this Statement as comprehensive income, the Board acknowledged that in paragraph 13 of Concepts Statement 5, the terms *comprehensive income* and *total nonowner changes in equity* are used as synonyms: "A full set of financial statements for a period should show . . . comprehensive income (total nonowner changes in equity) for the period" (footnote reference omitted). In paragraph 40 of that Concepts Statement the Board noted that:

> Just as a variety of terms are used for net income in present practice, the Board anticipates that total nonowner changes in equity, comprehensive loss, and other equivalent terms will be used in future financial statements as names for comprehensive income.

Nonetheless, the term comprehensive income is used consistently throughout the remainder of Concepts Statement 5 and throughout Concepts Statement 6.

73. In its redeliberations, the Board discussed whether it should continue using the term comprehensive income in this Statement. The Board believes that as a result of the Exposure Drafts on comprehensive income and derivatives and hedging, the term comprehensive income has become more familiar and better understood. Although some constituents argued that the items described as other comprehensive income are not "true" gains and losses, they are defined as gains and losses by the Concepts Statements. Therefore, the Board decided that it is appropriate to continue using the term comprehensive income rather than total nonowner changes in equity in this Statement.

74. The Board also reasoned that once it addresses the conceptual issues in a broader-scope project on comprehensive income, it can consider requiring comprehensive income to be reported in a statement of financial performance. If comprehensive income was ultimately to be reported in a statement of financial performance, the term comprehensive income is more descriptive of a performance measure than are

other terms such as total nonowner changes in equity. Therefore, the Board decided that it would be instructional to continue using the term comprehensive income throughout this Statement. However, it decided to clarify that the term comprehensive income is not required and that other terms may be used to describe that amount. The Board decided to make that clarification by including a footnote reference to paragraph 40 of Concepts Statement 5 in this Statement.

Displaying per-share amounts for comprehensive income

75. The Exposure Draft proposed that a public enterprise should display a per-share amount for comprehensive income. The Board thought that it was important that comprehensive income receive appropriate attention and was concerned that it could be perceived as being inferior to measures such as net income if a per-share amount were not required. Moreover, the Board decided that a requirement to display a per-share amount would impose little or no incremental cost on an enterprise.

76. Most respondents were opposed to the requirement for a per-share amount for comprehensive income. They argued that a per-share amount would give comprehensive income more prominence than net income and would result in confusion, especially if analysts quote earnings per share for some enterprises and comprehensive income per share for others. Many respondents suggested that until the Board addresses the conceptual issues involved in reporting comprehensive income (such as when components of comprehensive income should be recognized in financial statements, how those components should be measured, and the criteria for inclusion of those items in net income or in other comprehensive income), it was premature to require a per-share amount for it.

77. The Board decided to eliminate the requirement for a per-share amount for comprehensive income in this Statement. The Board agreed with those respondents that said the conceptual issues involved in reporting comprehensive income should be addressed before requiring a per-share amount. Furthermore, the Board thought that a requirement for a per-share amount was inconsistent with its decisions to (a) permit an enterprise to display comprehensive income and its components in a statement of changes in equity and (b) not require an enterprise to report comprehensive income as a performance measure.

Including cumulative accounting adjustments in comprehensive income

78. In addressing what items should be included in comprehensive income, the Board considered whether the effects of certain accounting adjustments related to earlier periods, such as the principal example in current practice—cumulative effects of changes in accounting principles—should be reported as part of comprehensive income. Revenues, expenses, gains, and losses of the current period—including those that bypass the income statement and go directly to equity—are all clearly part of comprehensive income and were not at issue.

79. The Board considered the definition of comprehensive income in Concepts Statement 5, which states that "comprehensive income is a broad measure of the effects of transactions and other events on an entity, comprising *all recognized changes in equity* (net assets) of the entity during a period . . . except those resulting from investments by owners and distributions to owners" (paragraph 39; footnote reference omitted; emphasis added). Concepts Statement 5 further indicates that comprehensive income includes cumulative accounting adjustments. The Board continues to support that definition and, therefore, decided to include cumulative accounting adjustments as part of comprehensive income.

80. The Board considered two alternatives for displaying cumulative accounting adjustments in financial statements: (a) include cumulative accounting adjustments in comprehensive income by displaying them as part of other comprehensive income and (b) include cumulative accounting adjustments in comprehensive income by continuing to display them as part of net income.

81. The first alternative, display cumulative accounting adjustments as part of other comprehensive income, would have allowed the Board to begin to implement the concept of earnings as described in Concepts Statement 5, because cumulative accounting adjustments would no longer be included in net income. Concepts Statement 5 describes *earnings* as "a measure of performance for a period and to the extent feasible excludes items that are extraneous to that period—items that belong primarily to other periods" (paragraph 34, footnote reference omitted). Earnings, so defined, excludes cumulative effects of changes in accounting principle. Nonetheless, earnings have been included in net income since

Opinion 20. As a result, earnings is similar to, but not necessarily the same as, net income in current practice.

82. The Board committed at the outset to limit the project's scope to display of comprehensive income. The Board's decision to continue to display cumulative accounting adjustments as part of net income resulted more from adherence to that scope commitment than to the merits of the arguments for either alternative.

Display of components of comprehensive income

83. The Board considered two issues related to the display of components of comprehensive income: (a) whether comprehensive income should be divided into two broad display classifications, net income and other comprehensive income, and (b) how other comprehensive income should be classified for display in a financial statement.

Dividing comprehensive income into net income and other comprehensive income

84. The Board decided that comprehensive income should be divided into two broad display classifications, net income and other comprehensive income. The Board reasoned that the division would generally preserve a familiar touchstone for users of financial statements.

85. For similar reasons, the Board also decided not to change the remaining display classifications of net income (that is, continuing operations, discontinued operations, extraordinary items, and cumulative-effect adjustments).

Display classifications for other comprehensive income

86. The Board looked to both the Concepts Statements and current practice in considering how the components of other comprehensive income might be classified for purposes of display. The Concepts Statements provide general guidance about classification, with homogeneity of items being identified as a key factor and the need to combine items that have essentially similar characteristics (and the need to segregate those that do not have similar characteristics) being emphasized.

87. In identifying current practice, the Board considered the results of an FASB staff study of a sample of

financial statements that revealed that most enterprises classify balances of items of other comprehensive income in the equity sections of their statements of financial position according to the accounting standards to which those items relate. Because those accounting standards result in items of comprehensive income that are quite different from one another (for example, the items arising under Statement 52 on foreign currency are quite different from those arising under Statement 87 on pensions), the staff's findings were that existing practice is consistent with the guidance in the Concepts Statements.

88. Based on those considerations, the Board decided that the classification of items of other comprehensive income should be based on the nature of the items. The Board also concluded that the current practice of classifying items according to existing standards generally is appropriate at the present time. However, future standards may result either in additional classifications of other comprehensive income or in additional items within current classifications of other comprehensive income.

89. The Board also considered the need to display reclassification adjustments. Those adjustments are necessary to avoid double counting certain items in comprehensive income. For example, gains realized during the current period and included in net income for that period may have been included in other comprehensive income as unrealized holding gains in the period in which they arose. If they were, they would have been included in comprehensive income in the period in which they were displayed in other comprehensive income and must be offset in the period in which they are displayed in net income.

90. The current-period change in the balance of particular items of other comprehensive income could be displayed gross or net. If reported gross, reclassification adjustments are reported separately from other changes in the balance; thus, the total change is displayed as two amounts. If reported net, reclassification adjustments are combined with other changes in the balance; thus, the total change is displayed as a single amount. Both approaches are illustrated in Appendix B, Format A.

91. The Board decided that an enterprise should use a gross display for classifications of other comprehensive income where it is practicable to ascertain the amount of reclassification adjustments for particular items within that classification. The Board concluded that it should be practicable for an enterprise to calculate reclassification adjustments for securities and other financial instruments and for foreign currency translation items but that it is not practicable for an enterprise to calculate reclassification adjustments for minimum pension liability adjustments. Therefore, an enterprise is required to use a gross display for classifications of other comprehensive income resulting from gains and losses on securities and other financial instruments and for foreign currency items and to use a net display for the classification of other comprehensive income resulting from minimum pension liability adjustments.

92. The Board decided that under a gross display, an enterprise could display reclassification adjustments either as a single section within other comprehensive income or as part of the classification of other comprehensive income to which those adjustments relate (such as foreign currency items or gains and losses on available-for-sale securities). However, if all reclassification adjustments are displayed in a single section within other comprehensive income, they should be descriptively labeled so that they can be traced to their respective classification within other comprehensive income. For example, the reclassification adjustments should be labeled as relating to available-for-sale securities or foreign currency items.

93. The notice for recipients of the Exposure Draft asked if it would be practicable to determine reclassification amounts for (a) gains and losses on available-for-sale securities, (b) foreign currency items, and (c) minimum pension liability adjustments. A majority of the respondents that commented on reclassification adjustments generally agreed that it would be practicable to determine reclassification adjustments for available-for-sale securities and foreign currency items but that it would not be practicable to determine a reclassification adjustment for minimum pension liability adjustments.

94. In response to other comments from constituents about reclassification adjustments, the Board decided to (a) include an example illustrating the calculation of reclassification adjustments for available-for-sale securities, (b) clarify that the requirement for a reclassification amount for foreign currency translation adjustments is limited to translation gains and losses realized upon sale or complete or substantially complete liquidation of an investment in a foreign entity, (c) encourage, but not require, reclassification adjustments for earlier period financial statements presented for comparison to the first period in which

this Statement is adopted, and (d) permit an enterprise to display reclassification adjustments on the face of the financial statement where comprehensive income is reported or in a note to the financial statements. Therefore, for all classifications of other comprehensive income other than minimum pension liability adjustments, an enterprise may either (1) use a gross display on the face of the financial statement or (2) use a net display on the face of the financial statement and disclose the gross changes in the notes to the financial statements.

95. The Board also decided that an enterprise should display the accumulated balance of other comprehensive income in the equity section of the statement of financial position separately from retained earnings and additional paid-in capital and use a descriptive title such as *accumulated other comprehensive income* for that separate component of equity. So that users of financial statements are able to trace the component of other comprehensive income displayed in a financial statement to its corresponding balance, the Board decided that an enterprise should disclose accumulated balances for each classification in that separate component of equity on the face of a statement of financial position, in a statement of changes in equity, or in notes to the financial statements. Each display classification should correspond to display classifications used elsewhere in the same set of financial statements for components of other comprehensive income.

Display of comprehensive income in one or two statements of financial performance

96. The Exposure Draft proposed that an enterprise should be required to display the components of comprehensive income in either one or two statements of financial performance. In addressing whether comprehensive income should be displayed in one or two statements of financial performance, the Board noted that accounting standards in the United Kingdom require that the equivalent to comprehensive income be displayed in two statements. The Board concluded that a two-statement approach might be preferred by many constituents. However, some enterprises with few items of other comprehensive income might prefer to display comprehensive income by means of a single statement and they should not be prohibited from doing so.

97. Respondents to the Exposure Draft provided mixed views about whether the Board should permit a choice of displaying comprehensive income in one

statement or two statements of financial performance. Of the respondents that agreed with the Board's decision to permit a choice of one or two statements, some stated that the preparer should be allowed to decide which format best depicts the enterprise's other comprehensive income items. Most of the respondents that disagreed with the Board's decision to permit a choice of one or two statements indicated that the Board should mandate the two-statement approach because that type of display could alleviate confusion by clearly distinguishing between net income and comprehensive income. Based on comments from constituents, the Board found no compelling reason to eliminate either the one-statement approach or the two-statement approach for those enterprises that choose to display comprehensive income in an income-statement-type format.

98. The Board also decided that an enterprise should use a "reconciled" format for reporting comprehensive income whereby the components of other comprehensive income are the reconciling amounts between net income and comprehensive income. That format makes the relationship between net income and comprehensive income more apparent and might better facilitate the transition to reporting comprehensive income.

99. Under a reconciled format, an enterprise that chooses to display comprehensive income in an income-statement-type format by using two statements should begin the second statement with net income, the bottom line of the first statement. An enterprise that chooses to display comprehensive income in an income-statement-type format by using one statement should include net income as a subtotal within that statement. An enterprise that chooses to display comprehensive income in a statement of changes in equity should display net income in that statement in such a way that it can be added to the components of other comprehensive income to arrive at total comprehensive income. Appendix B includes illustrations of a one-statement and two-statement approach as well as two illustrations of a statement-of-changes-in-equity approach.

Display of related tax effects

100. The Board had two competing objectives in considering whether the components of other comprehensive income should be displayed before or after their related tax effects. The first objective was to

facilitate the traceability of reclassification adjustments from other comprehensive income to net income. Because the corresponding net income components generally are displayed before tax, to achieve that objective, reclassification adjustments must be displayed before tax and, consequently, other comprehensive income items also must be displayed before tax in a financial statement.

101. The second objective was to show clearly how other comprehensive income items change the accumulated balance in equity. Because accumulated other comprehensive income is displayed in the equity section of a statement of financial position net of tax, to achieve that objective, it is necessary to display the changes that are incorporated into that balance net of tax.

102. Some Board members were more concerned about the traceability of reclassification adjustments from other comprehensive income to net income than they were about the transfer of other comprehensive income items to their accumulated balance in equity. Therefore, they favored a display whereby an enterprise would show all components of other comprehensive income on a before-tax basis and display the tax effects of those items on one line, similar to the way in which the tax effects for income from continuing operations are displayed.

103. Other Board members thought that a net-of-tax display would be acceptable as long as adequate disclosure of the related tax effects was provided so that before-tax amounts could be ascertained. Furthermore, because of its decision to permit an enterprise to display comprehensive income and its components in a statement of changes in equity, the Board thought that a net-of-tax display of the components of other comprehensive income would be more practical in that statement because other items in that statement are displayed net of related tax effects.

104. The Board concluded that regardless of whether a before-tax or net-of-tax display was used, adequate disclosure of the amount of income tax expense or benefit allocated separately to individual components of other comprehensive income should be provided. Furthermore, the Board concluded that the tax disclosure provisions should be an integral part of the comprehensive income standard.

105. The Board decided that an enterprise should be permitted a choice of whether to display components of other comprehensive income on a before-tax basis

or on a net-of-tax basis. Both display formats provide adequate information as long as disclosures of the related tax effects are provided.

Conclusions on Other Issues

Including Prior-Period Adjustments in Comprehensive Income

106. The Board considered whether items accounted for as prior-period adjustments should be included in comprehensive income of the current period. Opinion 9, as amended by FASB Statement No. 16, *Prior Period Adjustments,* requires that prior-period adjustments be reflected as retroactive restatements of the amounts of net income (and the components thereof) and retained earnings balances (as well as other affected balances) for all financial statements presented for comparative purposes. In single-period financial statements, prior-period adjustments are reflected as adjustments of the opening balance of retained earnings. The Board decided that because of the requirement for retroactive restatement of earlier period financial statements, items accounted for as prior-period adjustments are effectively included in comprehensive income of earlier periods and, therefore, should not be displayed in comprehensive income of the current period.

Statement of Cash Flows Reporting

107. The Board considered whether the operating section of an indirect-method statement of cash flows or the reconciliation provided with the operating section of a direct-method statement of cash flows should begin with comprehensive income instead of net income as is required by FASB Statement No. 95, *Statement of Cash Flows.* When items of other comprehensive income are noncash items, they would become additional reconciling items in arriving at cash flows from operating activities and would add additional items to the statement of cash flows without adding information content. Thus, the Board decided not to amend Statement 95.

Other Items Reported in Equity

108. Certain items are presently recorded in equity that some respondents to the Exposure Draft thought should be considered as items of other comprehensive income. Those items are discussed below.

Deferred compensation expense and unearned ESOP shares

109. The Board considered whether unearned or deferred compensation expense, which is shown as a separate reduction of shareholders' equity pursuant to APB Opinion No. 25, *Accounting for Stock Issued to Employees,* should be included as an item of other comprehensive income. Paragraph 14 of Opinion 25 requires recognition of unearned compensation as a separate reduction of shareholders' equity if stock is issued in a plan before some or all of the services are performed by the employee. According to Opinion 25, in the subsequent periods in which the employee performs services to the employer, the employer is required to reduce the unearned compensation amount in shareholders' equity and recognize compensation expense for a corresponding amount. Therefore, those transactions have both equity and expense characteristics.

110. The Board also considered whether a reduction of shareholders' equity related to employee stock ownership plans (ESOPs) should be included as an item of other comprehensive income. AICPA Statements of Position 76-3, *Accounting Practices for Certain Employee Stock Ownership Plans,* and 93-6, *Employers' Accounting for Employee Stock Ownership Plans,* provide guidance on accounting for three types of ESOPs: leveraged, nonleveraged, and pension reversion.[11] The accounting for a leveraged ESOP results in a direct reduction to shareholders' equity in the form of a debit to unearned ESOP shares both when an employer issues shares or sells treasury shares to an ESOP and when a leveraged ESOP buys outstanding shares of the employer's stock on the open market. As ESOP shares are committed to be released (SOP 93-6) or are released (SOP 76-3), unearned ESOP shares are credited and, depending on the purpose for which the shares are released, (a) compensation cost, (b) dividends payable, or (c) compensation liabilities are debited. Transactions in which unearned ESOP shares are credited and compensation cost is debited have both equity and expense characteristics.

111. The Board agreed that it could be argued that the direct reductions to shareholders' equity under Opinion 25 and SOP 93-6 that will eventually be recognized as compensation expense are items of other comprehensive income. However, because those transactions involve the company's own stock, an argument also could be made that those are transactions with owners and hence are not other comprehensive income. In other words, those types of transactions have both equity (transaction with owners) characteristics and expense (comprehensive income) characteristics.

112. The Board concluded that it was beyond the scope of the project to determine whether deferred compensation expense and reductions to equity related to ESOPs were items of other comprehensive income. Therefore, until it makes a definitive decision about those items in a broader-scope project on comprehensive income, those transactions are to be considered as equity transactions and are not to be included as other comprehensive income.

Taxes not payable in cash

113. A reorganized enterprise may suffer net operating losses prior to reorganization that provide it with significant tax advantages going forward. SOP 90-7, *Financial Reporting by Entities in Reorganization Under the Bankruptcy Code,* requires that a reorganized enterprise record a "full tax rate" on its pretax income although its actual cash taxes paid are minimal because of those net operating loss carryforwards. "Taxes not payable in cash" are reported in the income statement as an expense with a corresponding increase to paid-in capital in shareholders' equity.[12]

114. One respondent to the Exposure Draft contended that the amount credited to paid-in capital for taxes not payable in cash represented a "significant economic or cash flow benefit" and "is a change in equity from nonowner sources." Therefore, that respondent suggested that that amount should be included as an item of other comprehensive income.

115. The Board agreed that the credit to paid-in capital resulting from taxes not payable in cash is not a transaction with an owner. However, the Board decided that that credit derives from the accounting required upon reorganization that results in adjustments to equity accounts based on reorganization

---

[11]SOP 93-6 superseded SOP 76-3 and is required for ESOP shares acquired after December 31, 1992. Employers are permitted, but not required, to apply the provisions of SOP 93-6 to shares purchased by ESOPs on or before December 31, 1992, that have not been committed to be released as of the beginning of the year of adoption.

[12]Under SOP 90-7, "benefits realized from preconfirmation net operating loss carryforwards should first reduce reorganization values in excess of amounts allocable to identifiable assets and other intangibles until exhausted and thereafter be reported as a direct addition to paid-in capital."

value. Therefore, although taxes not payable in cash is not a transaction with an owner, it does not qualify as comprehensive income because the credit to paid-in capital stems from transactions and accounting that took place upon reorganization. In effect, the credit to paid-in capital for taxes not payable in cash adjusts transactions that were recorded in equity in an earlier period and does not result from the current-period debit to income tax expense. Therefore, the Board decided that taxes not payable in cash should not be included as an item of other comprehensive income. In a broader-scope project, the Board may consider whether the initial accounting upon reorganization that results in adjustments to equity accounts based on reorganization value should result in the recognition of comprehensive income. If so, that would ultimately affect the reporting of taxes not payable in cash as part of comprehensive income.

Gains and losses resulting from contracts that are indexed to a company's shares and ultimately settled in cash

116. One respondent to the Exposure Draft indicated that the Board should consider whether a gain or loss arising from a contract that is indexed to a company's shares and ultimately settled in cash should be considered as an item of other comprehensive income. EITF Issue No. 94-7, "Accounting for Financial Instruments Indexed to, and Potentially Settled in, a Company's Own Stock,"[13] addresses four types of freestanding contracts that a company may enter into that are indexed to, and sometimes settled in, its own shares: (a) a forward sale contract, (b) a forward purchase contract, (c) a purchased put option, and (d) a purchased call option. Those contracts may be settled by physical settlement, net share settlement, or net cash settlement.

117. Issue 94-7 indicates that contracts that give the company a choice of net cash settlement or settlement in its own shares are equity instruments and should be measured initially at fair value. If such contracts are ultimately settled in cash, the amount of cash paid or received should be an adjustment to contributed capital. The Board considered whether the amount of cash paid or received (which represents a loss or gain on the contract) should be included as an item of other comprehensive income.

118. In Issue 94-7, the Emerging Issues Task Force reached a consensus that contracts that give the company a choice of net cash settlement or settlement in its own shares are equity instruments. Comprehensive income excludes all changes in equity resulting from investments by owners. Therefore, the Board decided that until it addresses that issue in a broader-scope project, a net cash settlement resulting from a change in value of such a contract should be treated as a change in value of an equity instrument and should not be considered as an item of comprehensive income.

Other paid-in capital transactions not addressed

119. The Board recognizes that there may be other transactions that are reported as direct adjustments to paid-in capital or other equity accounts that have characteristics similar to items that the Board has identified as other comprehensive income. Instead of addressing those transactions on a piecemeal basis, the Board decided that transactions required by generally accepted accounting principles to be recognized in paid-in capital or other similar nonincome equity accounts are not to be displayed as other comprehensive income. However, the Board may collectively address those types of transactions in a broader-scope project on comprehensive income.

Display of Other Comprehensive Income under the Equity Method of Accounting

120. Under APB Opinion No. 18, *The Equity Method of Accounting for Investments in Common Stock,* an investor records its proportionate share of the investee's net income (net loss) as investment income along with a corresponding increase (decrease) to the investment account. Several respondents to the Exposure Draft asked the Board to address the question of how an investor should record its proportionate share of the investee's other comprehensive income.

121. Paragraph 19(e) of Opinion 18 states that a transaction of an investee of a capital nature that affects the investor's share of stockholders' equity of the investee should be accounted for as if the investee were a consolidated subsidiary. Therefore, an investor records its proportionate share of the investee's equity adjustments for other comprehensive income

---

[13]Issue 94-7 was combined with and codified in EITF Issue No. 96-13, "Accounting for Sales of Options or Warrants on Issuer's Stock with Various Forms of Settlement."

(unrealized gains and losses on available-for-sale securities, minimum pension liability adjustments, and foreign currency items) as increases or decreases to the investment account with corresponding adjustments in equity. Under this Statement, an enterprise may elect to display other comprehensive income in an income-statement-type format (below net income or in a separate statement beginning with net income) or in a statement-of-changes-in-equity format.

122. The Board decided that the format in which an investee displays other comprehensive income should not impact how an investor displays its proportionate share of those amounts. Therefore, regardless of how an investee chooses to display other comprehensive income, an investor should be permitted to combine its proportionate share of those amounts with its own other comprehensive income items and display the aggregate of those amounts in an income-statement-type format or in a statement of changes in equity.

Other Comprehensive Income of Subsidiaries

123. The October 1995 FASB Exposure Draft of a proposed Statement, *Consolidated Financial Statements: Policy and Procedures,* would require that a portion of the net income or loss of a subsidiary that is not wholly owned be attributed to the noncontrolling interest (minority interest) on the basis of its proportionate interest in the subsidiary's net income or loss. The net income attributable to the noncontrolling interest would be deducted from consolidated net income to arrive at an amount called *net income attributable to the controlling interest.* If that Statement is finalized as proposed, the Board will have to determine whether other comprehensive income will be attributed to the noncontrolling and controlling interests on the same basis as items of net income and how the amounts attributed to those interests will be displayed.

Interim-Period Reporting

124. The Exposure Draft proposed that a publicly traded enterprise should be required to report an amount for total comprehensive income in condensed financial statements of interim periods issued to shareholders. In its redeliberations, the Board acknowledged that requiring information about total comprehensive income without requiring information about its components might result in a limited understanding of an enterprise's activities and considered whether it also should require a publicly

traded enterprise to report the components of other comprehensive income at interim periods.

125. The Board was concerned that adding a requirement for interim-period financial information about the components of other comprehensive income might create a disincentive for voluntary reporting of interim financial information, particularly for those enterprises that disagree with the annual reporting of comprehensive income. The Board decided that if there is a significant difference between total comprehensive income and net income in interim periods, an enterprise would be inclined to explain that difference by disclosing the components. Furthermore, the Board decided that it should not alter the Exposure Draft's interim-period reporting requirements by mandating additional information. Therefore, the Board decided to retain the requirement for a publicly traded enterprise to report total comprehensive income in condensed financial statements of interim periods issued to shareholders.

Effective Date and Transition

126. The Board proposed in the Exposure Draft that this Statement should be effective for fiscal years beginning after December 15, 1996, for all enterprises. That effective date was established under the presumption that a Statement would be issued in the first quarter of 1997. Because the Statement was not issued until late in the second quarter of 1997, the Board decided to postpone the effective date until fiscal years beginning after December 15, 1997. In deciding on that effective date, the Board agreed that the costs and start-up time associated with implementing this Statement should be minimal and that, with the exception of reclassification adjustments, an enterprise will only be displaying information currently available in a different format.

127. The Board also decided to permit an enterprise, for fiscal years beginning prior to December 16, 1997, initially to apply the provisions of this Statement for a fiscal year for which annual financial statements have not previously been issued. If the Statement is adopted prior to the effective date and during an interim period other than the first interim period, all prior interim periods of that fiscal year must be reclassified.

128. The Board decided that an enterprise should be required to apply the provisions of this Statement to comparative financial statements provided for earlier periods to make them comparable to the financial

statements for the current period. An enterprise should not encounter difficulties in reclassifying earlier periods' financial statements because the information required to be displayed by this Statement previously was displayed in the statement of changes in equity, the equity section of the statement of financial position, or in notes to the financial statements. The Board decided not to require, but to encourage, an enterprise to display reclassification adjustments for earlier period financial statements presented for comparison to the first period in which this Statement is adopted.

Appendix B

ILLUSTRATIVE EXAMPLES

129. This appendix provides illustrations of reporting formats for comprehensive income, required disclosures, and a corresponding statement of financial position. The illustrations are intended as examples only; they illustrate some recommended formats. Other formats or levels of detail may be appropriate for certain circumstances. An enterprise is encouraged to provide information in ways that are most understandable to investors, creditors, and other

external users of financial statements. For simplicity, the illustrations provide information only for a single period; however, the Board realizes that most enterprises are required to provide comparative financial statements.

130. Brackets are used to highlight certain basic totals that must be displayed in financial statements to comply with the provisions of this Statement. This Statement requires not only displaying those certain basic totals but also reporting components of those aggregates. For example, it requires reporting information about unrealized gains and losses on available-for-sale securities, foreign currency items, and minimum pension liability adjustments.

131. The illustrations use the term *comprehensive income* to label the total of all components of comprehensive income, including net income. The illustrations use the term *other comprehensive income* to label revenues, expenses, gains, and losses that are included in comprehensive income but excluded from net income. This Statement does not require that an enterprise use those terms in its financial statements. Other equivalent terms, such as *total non-owner changes in equity,* can be used as labels for what this Statement refers to as comprehensive income.

Format A: One-Statement Approach

Enterprise
Statement of Income and Comprehensive Income
Year Ended December 31, 19X9

Revenues		$140,000
Expenses		(25,000)
Other gains and losses		8,000
Gain on sale of securities		2,000
Income from operations before tax		125,000
Income tax expense		(31,250)
Income before extraordinary item and cumulative effect of accounting change		93,750
Extraordinary item, net of tax		(28,000)
Income before cumulative effect of accounting change		65,750
Cumulative effect of accounting change, net of tax		(2,500)
[Net income		63,250]
Other comprehensive income, net of tax:		
Foreign currency translation adjustments[a]		8,000
Unrealized gains on securities:[b]		
Unrealized holding gains arising during period	$13,000	
Less: reclassification adjustment for gains included in net income	(1,500)	11,500
Minimum pension liability adjustment[c]		(2,500)
Other comprehensive income		17,000
[Comprehensive income		$ 80,250]

Alternatively, components of other comprehensive income could be displayed before tax with one amount shown for the aggregate income tax expense or benefit:

Other comprehensive income, before tax:		
Foreign currency translation adjustments[a]		$ 10,666
Unrealized gains on securities:[b]		
Unrealized holding gains arising during period	$17,333	
Less: reclassification adjustment for gains included in net income	(2,000)	15,333
Minimum pension liability adjustment[c]		(3,333)
Other comprehensive income, before tax		22,666
[Income tax expense related to items of other comprehensive income		(5,666)]
Other comprehensive income, net of tax		$ 17,000

---

[a] It is assumed that there was no sale or liquidation of an investment in a foreign entity. Therefore, there is no reclassification adjustment for this period.

[b] This illustrates the gross display. Alternatively, a net display can be used, with disclosure of the gross amounts (current-period gain and reclassification adjustment) in the notes to the financial statements.

[c] This illustrates the required net display for this classification.

Format B: Two-Statement Approach

Enterprise
Statement of Income
Year Ended December 31, 19X9

Revenues	$140,000
Expenses	(25,000)
Other gains and losses	8,000
Gain on sale of securities	2,000
Income from operations before tax	125,000
Income tax expense	(31,250)
Income before extraordinary item and cumulative effect of accounting change	93,750
Extraordinary item, net of tax	(28,000)
Income before cumulative effect of accounting change	65,750
Cumulative effect of accounting change, net of tax	(2,500)
[Net income	$ 63,250]

Enterprise
Statement of Comprehensive Income
Year Ended December 31, 19X9

[Net income		$63,250]
Other comprehensive income, net of tax:		
Foreign currency translation adjustments[a]		8,000
Unrealized gains on securities:[b]		
Unrealized holding gains arising during period	$13,000	
Less: reclassification adjustment for gains included in net income	(1,500)	11,500
Minimum pension liability adjustment[c]		(2,500)
Other comprehensive income		17,000
[Comprehensive income		$80,250]

Alternatively, components of other comprehensive income could be displayed before tax with one amount shown for the aggregate income tax expense or benefit as illustrated in Format A.

---

[a]It is assumed that there was no sale or liquidation of an investment in a foreign entity. Therefore, there is no reclassification adjustment for this period.

[b]This illustrates the gross display. Alternatively, a net display can be used, with disclosure of the gross amounts (current-period gain and reclassification adjustment) in the notes to the financial statements.

[c]This illustrates the required net display for this classification.

Format C: Statement-of-Changes-in-Equity Approach (Alternative 1)

Enterprise
Statement of Changes in Equity
Year Ended December 31, 19X9

	Total	Comprehensive Income[a]	Retained Earnings	Accumulated Other Comprehensive Income	Common Stock	Paid-in Capital
Beginning balance	$563,500		$ 88,500	$25,000	$150,000	$300,000
Comprehensive income						
Net income	63,250	$63,250	63,250			
Other comprehensive income, net of tax						
Unrealized gains on securities, net of reclassification adjustment (see disclosure)	11,500	11,500				
Foreign currency translation adjustments	8,000	8,000				
Minimum pension liability adjustment	(2,500)	(2,500)				
Other comprehensive income		17,000		17,000		
Comprehensive income		$80,250				
Common stock issued	150,000				50,000	100,000
Dividends declared on common stock	(10,000)		(10,000)			
Ending balance	$783,750		$141,750	$42,000	$200,000	$400,000

Disclosure of reclassification amount:[b]

Unrealized holding gains arising during period	$13,000
Less: reclassification adjustment for gains included in net income	(1,500)
Net unrealized gains on securities	$11,500

[a] Alternatively, an enterprise can omit the separate column labeled "Comprehensive Income" by displaying an aggregate amount for comprehensive income ($80,250) in the "Total" column.
[b] It is assumed that there was no sale or liquidation of an investment in a foreign entity. Therefore, there is no reclassification adjustment for this period.

Format D: Statement-of-Changes-in-Equity Approach (Alternative 2)

Enterprise
Statement of Changes in Equity
Year Ended December 31, 19X9

Retained earnings		
Balance at January 1	$ 88,500	
Net income	63,250	[$ 63,250]
Dividends declared on common stock	(10,000)	
Balance at December 31	141,750	
Accumulated other comprehensive income[a]		
Balance at January 1	25,000	
Unrealized gains on securities, net of reclassification adjustment (see disclosure)		11,500
Foreign currency translation adjustments		8,000
Minimum pension liability adjustment		(2,500)
Other comprehensive income	17,000	17,000
Comprehensive income		[$ 80,250]
Balance at December 31	42,000	
Common stock		
Balance at January 1	150,000	
Shares issued	50,000	
Balance at December 31	200,000	
Paid-in capital		
Balance at January 1	300,000	
Common stock issued	100,000	
Balance at December 31	400,000	
Total equity	$783,750	

Disclosure of reclassification amount:[b]

Unrealized holding gains arising during period	$ 13,000
Less: reclassification adjustment for gains included in net income	(1,500)
Net unrealized gains on securities	$ 11,500

---
[a]All items of other comprehensive income are displayed net of tax.

[b]It is assumed that there was no sale or liquidation of an investment in a foreign entity. Therefore, there is no reclassification adjustment for this period.

All Formats: Required Disclosure of Related Tax Effects Allocated to Each Component of Other Comprehensive Income

Enterprise
Notes to Financial Statements
Year Ended December 31, 19X9

	Before-Tax Amount	Tax (Expense) or Benefit	Net-of-Tax Amount
Foreign currency translation adjustments	$10,666	$(2,666)	$ 8,000
Unrealized gains on securities:			
Unrealized holding gains arising during period	17,333	(4,333)	13,000
Less: reclassification adjustment for gains realized in net income	(2,000)	500	(1,500)
Net unrealized gains	15,333	(3,833)	11,500
Minimum pension liability adjustment	(3,333)	833	(2,500)
Other comprehensive income	$22,666	$(5,666)	$17,000

Alternatively, the tax amounts for each component can be displayed parenthetically on the face of the financial statement in which comprehensive income is reported.

All Formats: Disclosure of Accumulated Other Comprehensive Income Balances

Enterprise
Notes to Financial Statements
Year Ended December 31, 19X9

	Foreign Currency Items	Unrealized Gains on Securities	Minimum Pension Liability Adjustment	Accumulated Other Comprehensive Income
Beginning balance	$ (500)	$25,500	$ 0	$25,000
Current-period change	8,000	11,500	(2,500)	17,000
Ending balance	$7,500	$37,000	$(2,500)	$42,000

Alternatively, the balances of each classification within accumulated other comprehensive income can be displayed in a statement of changes in equity or in a statement of financial position.

All Formats: Accompanying Statement of Financial Position

Enterprise
Statement of Financial Position
December 31, 19X9

Assets:
Cash	$ 150,000
Accounts receivable	175,000
Available-for-sale securities	112,000
Plant and equipment	985,000
Total assets	$1,422,000

Liabilities:
Accounts payable	$ 112,500
Accrued liabilities	79,250
Pension liability	128,000
Notes payable	318,500
Total liabilities	$ 638,250

Equity:
Common stock	$ 200,000
Paid-in capital	400,000
Retained earnings	141,750
[Accumulated other comprehensive income	42,000]
Total equity	783,750
Total liabilities and equity	$1,422,000

Appendix C

ILLUSTRATIVE EXAMPLES OF THE DETERMINATION OF RECLASSIFICATION ADJUSTMENTS

132. This Statement requires that an enterprise determine reclassification adjustments for each classification of other comprehensive income, except minimum pension liability adjustments. An enterprise may display reclassification adjustments on the face of the financial statement in which comprehensive income is reported, or it may disclose reclassification adjustments in the notes to the financial statements.

133. This appendix provides illustrations of the calculation of reclassification adjustments for Statement 115 available-for-sale securities. Illustration 1 is of available-for-sale equity securities, and Illustration 2 is of available-for-sale debt securities. The illustrations are intended as examples only; they do not represent actual situations.

134. Illustrations 1 and 2 involve a nonpublic enterprise that follows the practice of recognizing all unrealized gains and losses on available-for-sale securities in other comprehensive income before recognizing them as realized gains and losses in net income. Therefore, the before-tax amount of the reclassification adjustment recognized in other comprehensive income is equal to, but opposite in sign from, the amount of the realized gain or loss recognized in net income.

Illustration 1: Statement 115 Available-for-Sale Equity Securities

135. The available-for-sale equity securities in this illustration appreciate in fair value. On December 31, 1997, Enterprise purchased 1,000 shares of equity securities at $10 per share, which it classified

as available for sale. The fair value of the securities at December 31, 1998 and December 31, 1999 was $12 and $15, respectively. There were no dividends declared on the securities that were sold on December 31, 1999. A tax rate of 30 percent is assumed.

Calculation of Holding Gains

	Before Tax	Income Tax	Net of Tax
Holding gains recognized in other comprehensive income:			
Year ended December 31, 1998	$2,000	$ 600	$1,400
Year ended December 31, 1999	3,000	900	2,100
Total gain	$5,000	$1,500	$3,500

Amounts Reported in Net Income and Other Comprehensive Income for the Years Ended December 31, 1998 and December 31, 1999

	1998	1999
Net income:		
Gain on sale of securities		$ 5,000
Income tax expense		(1,500)
Net gain realized in net income		3,500
Other comprehensive income:		
Holding gain arising during period, net of tax	$1,400	2,100
Reclassification adjustment, net of tax	0	(3,500)
Net gain (loss) recognized in other comprehensive income	1,400	(1,400)
Total impact on comprehensive income	$1,400	$ 2,100

Illustration 2: Statement 115 Available-for-Sale Debt Securities

136. The available-for-sale interest-bearing debt securities (bonds) in this illustration were purchased at a premium to yield 6.5 percent. Interest income is included in net income based on the historical yield, and the bonds decline in fair value during the first two years in which they are held.

137. On December 31, 1995, registration of Micki Inc.'s 8-year, 8 percent debentures, interest payable annually, became effective and the entire issue of $10,000,000 was sold at par. At the end of each of the next four years, the closing prices and the related market interest rates to maturity were as follows:

December 31	Price ($000)	Yield (%)
1996	$102.6	7.5
1997	107.3	6.5
1998	96.1	9.0
1999	92.2	10.5

138. On December 31, 1997, Enterprise purchased $1,000,000 of Micki Inc.'s bonds on the open market at 107.3 and classified them as available for sale. Enterprise continued to hold the bonds until December 31, 1999, at which time they were sold at 92.2. Enterprise prepared the following schedules in relation to the bonds:

Cost-Based Carrying Amount, Interest Income, and Premium Amortization

Year	(a) Beginning Carrying Value	(b) Cash Interest Received [8% × par]	(c) Interest Income [(a) × 6.5%]	(d) Premium Amortization [(b) – (c)]	(e) Ending Carrying Value [(a) – (d)]
1997					$1,073,000
1998	$1,073,000	$80,000	$69,745	$10,255	1,062,745
1999	1,062,745	80,000	69,078	10,922	1,051,823

Calculation of Before-Tax Holding Loss

Year Ended 12/31	(a) Ending Carrying Value	(b) Ending Fair Value	(c) Change in Fair Value	(d) Premium Amortization	(e) Holding Loss [(c) + (d)]
1997	$1,073,000	$1,073,000	$ 0		
1998	1,062,745	961,000	(112,000)	$10,255	$(101,745)
1999	1,051,823	922,000	(39,000)	10,922	(28,078)

Net-of-Tax Holding Losses
(Assume a Tax Rate of 30 Percent)

	Before Tax	Income Tax	Net of Tax
Holding losses recognized in other comprehensive income:			
Year ended December 31, 1998	$(101,745)	$30,523	$(71,222)
Year ended December 31, 1999	(28,078)	8,423	(19,655)
Total loss	$(129,823)	$38,946	$(90,877)

Amounts Reported in Net Income and Other Comprehensive Income
for the Years Ended December 31, 1998 and December 31, 1999

	1998	1999
Net income:		
Interest income	$ 69,745	$ 69,078
Loss on sale of bonds		(129,823)
Income tax (expense) benefit	(20,923)	18,223
Amounts realized in net income	48,822	(42,522)
Other comprehensive income (OCI):		
Holding loss arising during period, net of tax	(71,222)	(19,655)
Reclassification adjustment, net of tax		90,877
Net (loss) gain recognized in other comprehensive income	(71,222)	71,222
Total impact on comprehensive income	$(22,400)	$ 28,700

139. The following before-tax entries would be made to record the purchase, accrue interest (using the effective interest method based on cost), recognize the change in fair value, and record the sale:

December 31, 1997:

Investment in bonds	$1,073,000	
Cash		$1,073,000

To record purchase of bond

December 31, 1998:

Cash	80,000	
Investment in bonds		10,255
Interest income (to earnings)		69,745

To record interest income on the bond, amortize the premium, and record cash received

Unrealized holding loss (to OCI)	101,745	
Investment in bonds		101,745

To adjust carrying amount of bond to fair value

Accumulated OCI	101,745	
Unrealized holding loss		101,745
Interest income	69,745	
Retained earnings		69,745

To close nominal accounts to real accounts at year-end

December 31, 1999:

Cash	80,000	
Investment in bonds		10,922
Interest income (to earnings)		69,078

To record interest income on the bond, amortize the premium, and record cash received

Unrealized holding loss (to OCI)	28,078	
Investment in bonds		28,078

To adjust carrying amount of bond to fair value

Accumulated OCI	28,078	
Unrealized holding loss		28,078

To close nominal account to real account at year-end

Cash	922,000	
Loss on sale of securities (to earnings)	129,823	
Investment in bonds		922,000
Reclassification adjustment (to OCI)		129,823

To record sale of bond

Reclassification adjustment	129,823	
Accumulated OCI		129,823
Retained earnings	60,745	
Interest income	69,078	
Loss on sale of securities		129,823

To close nominal accounts to real accounts at year-end

FAS131

Statement of Financial Accounting Standards No. 131
Disclosures about Segments of an Enterprise
and Related Information

STATUS

Issued: June 1997

Effective Date: For fiscal years beginning after December 15, 1997

Affects: Amends ARB 43, Chapter 12, paragraph 5
      Supersedes ARB 43, Chapter 12, paragraph 6
      Supersedes ARB 51, paragraph 19
      Amends APB 28, paragraph 30
      Supersedes FAS 14
      Supersedes FAS 18
      Supersedes FAS 21
      Supersedes FAS 24
      Supersedes FAS 30
      Amends FAS 51, footnote 3
      Supersedes FAS 69, paragraph 8(c) and footnote 4
      Amends FAS 69, footnote 7
      Supersedes FAS 94, paragraph 14
      Amends FTB 79-4, paragraphs 1 and 3
      Supersedes FTB 79-4, paragraph 2
      Amends FTB 79-5, paragraphs 1 and 2
      Supersedes FTB 79-8

Affected by: Paragraphs 18, 25, 27, 28, 33, and 123 amended by FAS 135

Other Interpretive Release: FASB *Highlights,* "Segment Information: Guidance on Applying
      Statement 131," December 1998

Issues Discussed by FASB Emerging Issues Task Force (EITF)

  Affects: No EITF Issues

  Interpreted by: Paragraphs 18, 27, and 28 interpreted by EITF Topic No. D-70

  Related Issues: No EITF Issues

SUMMARY

    This Statement establishes standards for the way that public business enterprises report information about operating segments in annual financial statements and requires that those enterprises report selected information about operating segments in interim financial reports issued to shareholders. It also establishes standards for related disclosures about products and services, geographic areas, and major customers. This Statement supersedes FASB Statement No. 14, *Financial Reporting for Segments of a Business Enterprise,* but retains the requirement to report information about major customers. It amends FASB Statement No. 94, *Consolidation of All Majority-Owned Subsidiaries,* to remove the special disclosure requirements for previously unconsolidated subsidiaries. This Statement does not apply to nonpublic business enterprises or to not-for-profit organizations.

This Statement requires that a public business enterprise report financial and descriptive information about its reportable operating segments. Operating segments are components of an enterprise about which separate financial information is available that is evaluated regularly by the chief operating decision maker in deciding how to allocate resources and in assessing performance. Generally, financial information is required to be reported on the basis that it is used internally for evaluating segment performance and deciding how to allocate resources to segments.

This Statement requires that a public business enterprise report a measure of segment profit or loss, certain specific revenue and expense items, and segment assets. It requires reconciliations of total segment revenues, total segment profit or loss, total segment assets, and other amounts disclosed for segments to corresponding amounts in the enterprise's general-purpose financial statements. It requires that all public business enterprises report information about the revenues derived from the enterprise's products or services (or groups of similar products and services), about the countries in which the enterprise earns revenues and holds assets, and about major customers regardless of whether that information is used in making operating decisions. However, this Statement does not require an enterprise to report information that is not prepared for internal use if reporting it would be impracticable.

This Statement also requires that a public business enterprise report descriptive information about the way that the operating segments were determined, the products and services provided by the operating segments, differences between the measurements used in reporting segment information and those used in the enterprise's general-purpose financial statements, and changes in the measurement of segment amounts from period to period.

This Statement is effective for financial statements for periods beginning after December 15, 1997. In the initial year of application, comparative information for earlier years is to be restated. This Statement need not be applied to interim financial statements in the initial year of its application, but comparative information for interim periods in the initial year of application is to be reported in financial statements for interim periods in the second year of application.

Statement of Financial Accounting Standards No. 131

Disclosures about Segments of an Enterprise and Related Information

CONTENTS

INTRODUCTION

1. This Statement requires that public business enterprises[1] report certain information about operating segments in complete sets of financial statements of the enterprise and in condensed financial statements of interim periods issued to shareholders. It also requires that public business enterprises report certain information about their products and services, the geographic areas in which they operate, and their major customers. The Board and the Accounting Standards Board (AcSB) of the Canadian Institute of Chartered Accountants (CICA) cooperated in developing revised standards for reporting information about segments, and the two boards reached the same conclusions.

2. This Statement supersedes FASB Statements No. 14, *Financial Reporting for Segments of a Business Enterprise,* No. 18, *Financial Reporting for Segments of a Business Enterprise—Interim Financial Statements,* No. 24, *Reporting Segment Information in Financial Statements That Are Presented in Another Enterprise's Financial Report,* and No. 30, *Disclosure of Information about Major Customers.* It amends FASB Statement No. 94, *Consolidation of*

---

[1] For convenience, the term *enterprise* is used throughout this Statement to mean public business enterprise unless otherwise stated.

All Majority-Owned Subsidiaries, to eliminate the requirement to disclose additional information about subsidiaries that were not consolidated prior to the effective date of Statement 94. It also amends APB Opinion No. 28, *Interim Financial Reporting,* to require disclosure of selected information about operating segments in interim financial reports to shareholders. Appendix C includes a list of amendments to existing pronouncements.

Objective and Basic Principles

3. The objective of requiring disclosures about segments of an enterprise and related information is to provide information about the different types of business activities in which an enterprise engages and the different economic environments in which it operates to help users of financial statements:

a. Better understand the enterprise's performance
b. Better assess its prospects for future net cash flows
c. Make more informed judgments about the enterprise as a whole.

That objective is consistent with the objectives of general-purpose financial reporting.

4. An enterprise might meet that objective by providing complete sets of financial statements that are disaggregated in several different ways, for example, by products and services, by geography, by legal entity, or by type of customer. However, it is not feasible to provide all of that information in every set of financial statements. This Statement requires that general-purpose financial statements include selected information reported on a single basis of segmentation. The method the Board chose for determining what information to report is referred to as the management approach. The management approach is based on the way that management organizes the segments within the enterprise for making operating decisions and assessing performance. Consequently, the segments are evident from the structure of the enterprise's internal organization, and financial statement preparers should be able to provide the required information in a cost-effective and timely manner.

5. The management approach facilitates consistent descriptions of an enterprise in its annual report and various other published information. It focuses on financial information that an enterprise's decision makers use to make decisions about the enterprise's operating matters. The components that management establishes for that purpose are called *operating segments.*

6. This Statement requires that an enterprise report a measure of segment profit or loss and certain items included in determining segment profit or loss, segment assets, and certain related items. It does not require that an enterprise report segment cash flow. However, paragraphs 27 and 28 require that an enterprise report certain items that may provide an indication of the cash-generating ability or cash requirements of an enterprise's operating segments.

7. To provide some comparability between enterprises, this Statement requires that an enterprise report certain information about the revenues that it derives from each of its products and services (or groups of similar products and services) and about the countries in which it earns revenues and holds assets, regardless of how the enterprise is organized. As a consequence, some enterprises are likely to be required to provide limited information that may not be used for making operating decisions and assessing performance.

8. Nothing in this Statement is intended to discourage an enterprise from reporting additional information specific to that enterprise or to a particular line of business that may contribute to an understanding of the enterprise.

STANDARDS OF FINANCIAL ACCOUNTING AND REPORTING

Scope

9. This Statement applies to public business enterprises. Public business enterprises are those business enterprises that have issued debt or equity securities that are traded in a public market (a domestic or foreign stock exchange or an over-the-counter market, including local or regional markets), that are required to file financial statements with the Securities and Exchange Commission, or that provide financial statements for the purpose of issuing any class of securities in a public market. This Statement does not apply to parent enterprises, subsidiaries, joint ventures, or investees accounted for by the equity method if those enterprises' "separate company" statements also are consolidated or combined in a complete set of financial statements and both the separate company statements and the consolidated or combined statements are included in the same financial report. However, this Statement does apply to those enterprises if they are public enterprises and their financial statements are issued separately. This

Statement also does not apply to not-for-profit organizations or to nonpublic enterprises. Entities other than public business enterprises are encouraged to provide the disclosures described in this Statement.

Operating Segments

Definition

10. An *operating segment* is a component of an enterprise:

a. That engages in business activities from which it may earn revenues and incur expenses (including revenues and expenses relating to transactions with other components of the same enterprise),
b. Whose operating results are regularly reviewed by the enterprise's chief operating decision maker to make decisions about resources to be allocated to the segment and assess its performance, and
c. For which discrete financial information is available.

An operating segment may engage in business activities for which it has yet to earn revenues, for example, start-up operations may be operating segments before earning revenues.

11. Not every part of an enterprise is necessarily an operating segment or part of an operating segment. For example, a corporate headquarters or certain functional departments may not earn revenues or may earn revenues that are only incidental to the activities of the enterprise and would not be operating segments. For purposes of this Statement, an enterprise's pension and other postretirement benefit plans are not considered operating segments.

12. The term *chief operating decision maker* identifies a function, not necessarily a manager with a specific title. That function is to allocate resources to and assess the performance of the segments of an enterprise. Often the chief operating decision maker of an enterprise is its chief executive officer or chief operating officer, but it may be a group consisting of, for example, the enterprise's president, executive vice presidents, and others.

13. For many enterprises, the three characteristics of operating segments described in paragraph 10 clearly identify a single set of operating segments. However, an enterprise may produce reports in which its business activities are presented in a variety of different ways. If the chief operating decision maker uses more than one set of segment information, other factors may identify a single set of components as constituting an enterprise's operating segments, including the nature of the business activities of each component, the existence of managers responsible for them, and information presented to the board of directors.

14. Generally, an operating segment has a *segment manager* who is directly accountable to and maintains regular contact with the chief operating decision maker to discuss operating activities, financial results, forecasts, or plans for the segment. The term segment manager identifies a function, not necessarily a manager with a specific title. The chief operating decision maker also may be the segment manager for certain operating segments. A single manager may be the segment manager for more than one operating segment. If the characteristics in paragraph 10 apply to more than one set of components of an organization but there is only one set for which segment managers are held responsible, that set of components constitutes the operating segments.

15. The characteristics in paragraph 10 may apply to two or more overlapping sets of components for which managers are held responsible. That structure is sometimes referred to as a matrix form of organization. For example, in some enterprises, certain managers are responsible for different product and service lines worldwide, while other managers are responsible for specific geographic areas. The chief operating decision maker regularly reviews the operating results of both sets of components, and financial information is available for both. In that situation, the components based on products and services would constitute the operating segments.

Reportable Segments

16. An enterprise shall report separately information about each operating segment that (a) has been identified in accordance with paragraphs 10-15 or that results from aggregating two or more of those segments in accordance with paragraph 17 and (b) exceeds the quantitative thresholds in paragraph 18. Paragraphs 19-24 specify other situations in which separate information about an operating segment shall be reported. Appendix B includes a diagram that illustrates how to apply the main provisions in this Statement for identifying reportable operating segments.

Aggregation criteria

17. Operating segments often exhibit similar long-term financial performance if they have similar economic characteristics. For example, similar long-term average gross margins for two operating segments would be expected if their economic characteristics were similar. Two or more operating segments may be aggregated into a single operating segment if aggregation is consistent with the objective and basic principles of this Statement, if the segments have similar economic characteristics, and if the segments are similar in each of the following areas:

a. The nature of the products and services
b. The nature of the production processes
c. The type or class of customer for their products and services
d. The methods used to distribute their products or provide their services
e. If applicable, the nature of the regulatory environment, for example, banking, insurance, or public utilities.

Quantitative thresholds

18. An enterprise shall report separately information about an operating segment that meets any of the following quantitative thresholds:

a. Its reported revenue, including both sales to external customers and intersegment sales or transfers, is 10 percent or more of the combined revenue, internal and external, of all reported operating segments.
b. The absolute amount of its reported profit or loss is 10 percent or more of the greater, in absolute amount, of (1) the combined reported profit of all operating segments that did not report a loss or (2) the combined reported loss of all operating segments that did report a loss.
c. Its assets are 10 percent or more of the combined assets of all operating segments.

Information about operating segments that do not meet any of the quantitative thresholds may be disclosed separately.

19. An enterprise may combine information about operating segments that do not meet the quantitative thresholds with information about other operating segments that do not meet the quantitative thresholds to produce a reportable segment only if the operating segments share a majority of the aggregation criteria listed in paragraph 17.

20. If total of external revenue reported by operating segments constitutes less than 75 percent of total consolidated revenue, additional operating segments shall be identified as reportable segments (even if they do not meet the criteria in paragraph 18) until at least 75 percent of total consolidated revenue is included in reportable segments.

21. Information about other business activities and operating segments that are not reportable shall be combined and disclosed in an "all other" category separate from other reconciling items in the reconciliations required by paragraph 32. The sources of the revenue included in the "all other" category shall be described.

22. If management judges an operating segment identified as a reportable segment in the immediately preceding period to be of continuing significance, information about that segment shall continue to be reported separately in the current period even if it no longer meets the criteria for reportability in paragraph 18.

23. If an operating segment is identified as a reportable segment in the current period due to the quantitative thresholds, prior-period segment data presented for comparative purposes shall be restated to reflect the newly reportable segment as a separate segment even if that segment did not satisfy the criteria for reportability in paragraph 18 in the prior period unless it is impracticable to do so. For purposes of this Statement, information is impracticable to present if the necessary information is not available and the cost to develop it would be excessive.

24. There may be a practical limit to the number of reportable segments that an enterprise separately discloses beyond which segment information may become overly detailed. Although no precise limit has been determined, as the number of segments that are reportable in accordance with paragraphs 18-23 increases above 10, the enterprise should consider whether a practical limit has been reached.

Disclosures

25. An enterprise shall disclose the following:

a. General information as described in paragraph 26

b. Information about reported segment profit or loss, including certain revenues and expenses included in reported segment profit or loss, segment assets, and the basis of measurement, as described in paragraphs 27-31
c. Reconciliations of the totals of segment revenues, reported profit or loss, assets, and other significant items to corresponding enterprise amounts as described in paragraph 32
d. Interim period information as described in paragraph 33.

If complete sets of financial statements are provided for more than one period, the information required by this Statement shall be reported for each period presented. Previously reported information for prior periods shall be restated as described in paragraphs 34 and 35.

General information

26. An enterprise shall disclose the following general information:

a. Factors used to identify the enterprise's reportable segments, including the basis of organization (for example, whether management has chosen to organize the enterprise around differences in products and services, geographic areas, regulatory environments, or a combination of factors and whether operating segments have been aggregated)
b. Types of products and services from which each reportable segment derives its revenues.

Information about profit or loss and assets

27. An enterprise shall report a measure of profit or loss and total assets for each reportable segment. An enterprise also shall disclose the following about each reportable segment if the specified amounts are included in the measure of segment profit or loss reviewed by the chief operating decision maker:

a. Revenues from external customers
b. Revenues from transactions with other operating segments of the same enterprise
c. Interest revenue
d. Interest expense
e. Depreciation, depletion, and amortization expense
f. Unusual items as described in paragraph 26 of APB Opinion No. 30, *Reporting the Results of Operations—Reporting the Effects of Disposal of a Segment of a Business, and Extraordinary, Unusual and Infrequently Occurring Events and Transactions*
g. Equity in the net income of investees accounted for by the equity method
h. Income tax expense or benefit
i. Extraordinary items
j. Significant noncash items other than depreciation, depletion, and amortization expense.

An enterprise shall report interest revenue separately from interest expense for each reportable segment unless a majority of the segment's revenues are from interest and the chief operating decision maker relies primarily on net interest revenue to assess the performance of the segment and make decisions about resources to be allocated to the segment. In that situation, an enterprise may report that segment's interest revenue net of its interest expense and disclose that it has done so.

28. An enterprise shall disclose the following about each reportable segment if the specified amounts are included in the determination of segment assets reviewed by the chief operating decision maker:

a. The amount of investment in equity method investees
b. Total expenditures for additions to long-lived assets other than financial instruments, long-term customer relationships of a financial institution, mortgage and other servicing rights, deferred policy acquisition costs, and deferred tax assets.

Measurement

29. The amount of each segment item reported shall be the measure reported to the chief operating decision maker for purposes of making decisions about allocating resources to the segment and assessing its performance. Adjustments and eliminations made in preparing an enterprise's general-purpose financial statements and allocations of revenues, expenses, and gains or losses shall be included in determining reported segment profit or loss only if they are included in the measure of the segment's profit or loss that is used by the chief operating decision maker. Similarly, only those assets that are included in the measure of the segment's assets that is used by the chief operating decision maker shall be reported for that segment. If amounts are allocated to reported segment profit or loss or assets, those amounts shall be allocated on a reasonable basis.

30. If the chief operating decision maker uses only one measure of a segment's profit or loss and only one measure of a segment's assets in assessing segment performance and deciding how to allocate resources, segment profit or loss and assets shall be reported at those measures. If the chief operating decision maker uses more than one measure of a segment's profit or loss and more than one measure of a segment's assets, the reported measures shall be those that management believes are determined in accordance with the measurement principles most consistent with those used in measuring the corresponding amounts in the enterprise's consolidated financial statements.

31. An enterprise shall provide an explanation of the measurements of segment profit or loss and segment assets for each reportable segment. At a minimum, an enterprise shall disclose the following:

a. The basis of accounting for any transactions between reportable segments.
b. The nature of any differences between the measurements of the reportable segments' profits or losses and the enterprise's consolidated income before income taxes, extraordinary items, discontinued operations, and the cumulative effect of changes in accounting principles (if not apparent from the reconciliations described in paragraph 32). Those differences could include accounting policies and policies for allocation of centrally incurred costs that are necessary for an understanding of the reported segment information.
c. The nature of any differences between the measurements of the reportable segments' assets and the enterprise's consolidated assets (if not apparent from the reconciliations described in paragraph 32). Those differences could include accounting policies and policies for allocation of jointly used assets that are necessary for an understanding of the reported segment information.
d. The nature of any changes from prior periods in the measurement methods used to determine reported segment profit or loss and the effect, if any, of those changes on the measure of segment profit or loss.
e. The nature and effect of any asymmetrical allocations to segments. For example, an enterprise might allocate depreciation expense to a segment without allocating the related depreciable assets to that segment.

Reconciliations

32. An enterprise shall provide reconciliations of all of the following:

a. The total of the reportable segments' revenues to the enterprise's consolidated revenues.
b. The total of the reportable segments' measures of profit or loss to the enterprise's consolidated income before income taxes, extraordinary items, discontinued operations, and the cumulative effect of changes in accounting principles. However, if an enterprise allocates items such as income taxes and extraordinary items to segments, the enterprise may choose to reconcile the total of the segments' measures of profit or loss to consolidated income after those items.
c. The total of the reportable segments' assets to the enterprise's consolidated assets.
d. The total of the reportable segments' amounts for every other significant item of information disclosed to the corresponding consolidated amount. For example, an enterprise may choose to disclose liabilities for its reportable segments, in which case the enterprise would reconcile the total of reportable segments' liabilities for each segment to the enterprise's consolidated liabilities if the segment liabilities are significant.

All significant reconciling items shall be separately identified and described. For example, the amount of each significant adjustment to reconcile accounting methods used in determining segment profit or loss to the enterprise's consolidated amounts shall be separately identified and described.

Interim period information

33. An enterprise shall disclose the following about each reportable segment in condensed financial statements of interim periods issued to shareholders:

a. Revenues from external customers
b. Intersegment revenues
c. A measure of segment profit or loss
d. Total assets for which there has been a material change from the amount disclosed in the last annual report
e. A description of differences from the last annual report in the basis of segmentation or in the basis of measurement of segment profit or loss
f. A reconciliation of the total of the reportable segments' measures of profit or loss to the enterprise's consolidated income before income taxes,

extraordinary items, discontinued operations, and the cumulative effect of changes in accounting principles. However, if an enterprise allocates items such as income taxes and extraordinary items to segments, the enterprise may choose to reconcile the total of the segments' measures of profit or loss to consolidated income after those items. Significant reconciling items shall be separately identified and described in that reconciliation.

Restatement of previously reported information

34. If an enterprise changes the structure of its internal organization in a manner that causes the composition of its reportable segments to change, the corresponding information for earlier periods, including interim periods, shall be restated unless it is impracticable to do so. Accordingly, an enterprise shall restate those individual items of disclosure that it can practicably restate but need not restate those individual items, if any, that it cannot practicably restate. Following a change in the composition of its reportable segments, an enterprise shall disclose whether it has restated the corresponding items of segment information for earlier periods.

35. If an enterprise has changed the structure of its internal organization in a manner that causes the composition of its reportable segments to change and if segment information for earlier periods, including interim periods, is not restated to reflect the change, the enterprise shall disclose in the year in which the change occurs segment information for the current period under both the old basis and the new basis of segmentation unless it is impracticable to do so.

Enterprise-Wide Disclosures

36. Paragraphs 37-39 apply to all enterprises subject to this Statement including those enterprises that have a single reportable segment. Some enterprises' business activities are not organized on the basis of differences in related products and services or differences in geographic areas of operations. That is, an enterprise's segments may report revenues from a broad range of essentially different products and services, or more than one of its reportable segments may provide essentially the same products and services. Similarly, an enterprise's segments may hold assets in different geographic areas and report revenues from customers in different geographic areas, or more than one of its segments may operate in the same geographic area. Information required by para-

graphs 37-39 need be provided only if it is not provided as part of the reportable operating segment information required by this Statement.

Information about Products and Services

37. An enterprise shall report the revenues from external customers for each product and service or each group of similar products and services unless it is impracticable to do so. The amounts of revenues reported shall be based on the financial information used to produce the enterprise's general-purpose financial statements. If providing the information is impracticable, that fact shall be disclosed.

Information about Geographic Areas

38. An enterprise shall report the following geographic information unless it is impracticable to do so:

a. Revenues from external customers (1) attributed to the enterprise's country of domicile and (2) attributed to all foreign countries in total from which the enterprise derives revenues. If revenues from external customers attributed to an individual foreign country are material, those revenues shall be disclosed separately. An enterprise shall disclose the basis for attributing revenues from external customers to individual countries.

b. Long-lived assets other than financial instruments, long-term customer relationships of a financial institution, mortgage and other servicing rights, deferred policy acquisition costs, and deferred tax assets (1) located in the enterprise's country of domicile and (2) located in all foreign countries in total in which the enterprise holds assets. If assets in an individual foreign country are material, those assets shall be disclosed separately.

The amounts reported shall be based on the financial information that is used to produce the general-purpose financial statements. If providing the geographic information is impracticable, that fact shall be disclosed. An enterprise may wish to provide, in addition to the information required by this paragraph, subtotals of geographic information about groups of countries.

Information about Major Customers

39. An enterprise shall provide information about the extent of its reliance on its major customers. If revenues from transactions with a single external

customer amount to 10 percent or more of an enterprise's revenues, the enterprise shall disclose that fact, the total amount of revenues from each such customer, and the identity of the segment or segments reporting the revenues. The enterprise need not disclose the identity of a major customer or the amount of revenues that each segment reports from that customer. For purposes of this Statement, a group of entities known to a reporting enterprise to be under common control shall be considered as a single customer, and the federal government, a state government, a local government (for example, a county or municipality), or a foreign government each shall be considered as a single customer.

Effective Date and Transition

40. This Statement shall be effective for fiscal years beginning after December 15, 1997. Earlier application is encouraged. Segment information for earlier years that is reported with corresponding information for the initial year of application shall be restated to conform to the requirements of this Statement unless it is impracticable to do so. This Statement need not be applied to interim financial statements in the initial year of its application, but comparative information for interim periods in the initial year of application shall be reported in financial statements for interim periods in the second year of application.

The provisions of this Statement need not be applied to immaterial items.

This Statement was adopted by the affirmative votes of six members of the Financial Accounting Standards Board. Mr. Leisenring dissented.

Mr. Leisenring dissents from the issuance of this Statement because it does not define segment profit or loss and does not require that whatever measure of profit or loss is reported be consistent with the attribution of assets to reportable segments.

By not defining segment profit or loss, this Statement allows any measure of performance to be displayed as segment profit or loss as long as that measure is reviewed by the chief operating decision maker. Items of revenue and expense directly attributable to a given segment need not be included in the reported operating results of that segment, and no allocation of items not directly attributable to a given segment is required. As a consequence, an item that results directly from one segment's activities can be excluded from that segment's profit or loss. Mr. Leisenring believes that, minimally, this Statement should require that amounts directly incurred by or directly attributable to a segment be included in that segment's profit or loss and that assets identified with a particular segment be consistent with the measurement of that segment's profit or loss.

Mr. Leisenring supports trying to assist users as described in paragraph 3 of this Statement but believes it is very unlikely that that will be accomplished, even with the required disclosures and reconciliation to the entity's annual financial statements, because of the failure to define profit or loss and to impose any attribution or allocation requirements for the measure of profit or loss.

Mr. Leisenring supports the management approach for defining reportable segments and supports requiring disclosure of selected segment information in condensed financial statements of interim periods issued to shareholders. Mr. Leisenring believes, however, that the definitions of revenues, operating profit or loss, and identifiable assets in paragraph 10 of Statement 14 should be retained in this Statement and applied to segments identified by the management approach. Without retaining those definitions or some other agreed-to definition of segment profit or loss, Mr. Leisenring believes that the objective of presenting segment information would more likely be met by retaining the requirements of Statement 14 and amending that Statement to define segments and require disclosure of interim segment information consistent with the provisions of this Statement.

Members of the Financial Accounting Standards Board:

Dennis R. Beresford, *Chairman*	Anthony T. Cope	James J. Leisenring
	John M. Foster	Gerhard G. Mueller
Joseph V. Anania	Gaylen N. Larson	

Appendix A

BACKGROUND INFORMATION AND BASIS FOR CONCLUSIONS

CONTENTS

Appendix A

BACKGROUND INFORMATION AND BASIS FOR CONCLUSIONS

Introduction

41. This appendix summarizes considerations that were deemed significant by Board members in reaching the conclusions in this Statement. It includes reasons for accepting certain approaches and rejecting others. Individual Board members gave greater weight to some factors than to others.

Background Information

42. FASB Statement No. 14, *Financial Reporting for Segments of a Business Enterprise,* was issued in 1976. That Statement required that business enterprises report segment information on two bases: by industry and by geographic area. It also required disclosure of information about export sales and major customers.

43. The Board concluded at the time it issued Statement 14 that information about components of an enterprise, the products and services that it offers, its foreign operations, and its major customers is useful for understanding and making decisions about the enterprise as a whole. Financial statement users observe that the evaluation of the prospects for future cash flows is the central element of investment and lending decisions. The evaluation of prospects requires assessment of the uncertainty that surrounds both the timing and the amount of the expected cash flows to the enterprise, which in turn affect potential cash flows to the investor or creditor. Users also observe that uncertainty results in part from factors related to the products and services an enterprise offers and the geographic areas in which it operates.

44. In its 1993 position paper, *Financial Reporting in the 1990s and Beyond,* the Association for Investment Management and Research (AIMR) said:

> [Segment data] is vital, essential, fundamental, indispensable, and integral to the investment analysis process. Analysts need to know and understand how the various components of a multifaceted enterprise behave economically. One weak member of the group is analogous to a section of blight on a piece of fruit; it has the potential to spread rot over the entirety. Even in the absence of weakness, different segments will generate dissimilar streams of cash flows to which are attached disparate risks and which bring about unique values. Thus, without disaggregation, there is no sensible way to predict the overall amounts, timing, or risks of a complete enterprise's future cash flows. There is little dispute over the analytic usefulness of disaggregated financial data. [pages 59 and 60]

45. Over the years, financial analysts consistently requested that financial statement data be disaggregated to a much greater degree than it is in current practice. Many analysts said that they found Statement 14 helpful but inadequate. In its 1993 position paper, the AIMR emphasized that:

> There is no disagreement among AIMR members that segment information is totally vital to their work. There also is general agreement among them that the current segment reporting standard, Financial Accounting Standard No. 14, is inadequate. Recent work by a subcommittee of the [Financial Accounting Policy Committee] has confirmed that a substantial majority of analysts seek and, when it is available, use quarterly segment data. [page 5]

46. The Canadian Institute of Chartered Accountants (CICA) published a Research Study, *Financial Reporting for Segments,* in August 1992. An FASB Research Report, *Reporting Disaggregated Information,* was published in February 1993. In March 1993, the FASB and the Accounting Standards Board (AcSB) of the CICA agreed to pursue their projects jointly.

47. In May 1993, the FASB and the AcSB jointly issued an Invitation to Comment, *Reporting Disaggregated Information by Business Enterprises.* That Invitation to Comment identified certain issues related to disclosure of information about segments, solicited comments on those issues, and asked readers to identify additional issues. The boards received 129 comment letters from U.S. and Canadian respondents.

48. In late 1993, the FASB and the AcSB formed the Disaggregated Disclosures Advisory Group to advise and otherwise support the two boards in their efforts to improve disaggregated disclosures. The members of the group included financial statement issuers, auditors, financial analysts, and academics from both the United States and Canada. In January 1994, the FASB and the AcSB began discussing changes to Statement 14 and *CICA Handbook* Section 1700, "Segmented Information." The two boards met with and otherwise actively solicited the views of analysts and preparers of financial statements about possible improvements to the current segment reporting requirements. FASB and AcSB members and staff also discussed disaggregated disclosures at meetings of several groups of analysts, including the AIMR's Financial Accounting Policy Committee.

49. In 1991, the AICPA formed the Special Committee on Financial Reporting (the Special Committee) to make recommendations to improve the relevance and usefulness of business reporting. The Special Committee, which comprised financial statement auditors and preparers, established focus groups of credit analysts and equity analysts to assist in formulating its recommendations. The Special Committee issued its report, *Improving Business Reporting— A Customer Focus,* in 1994. That report listed improvements in disclosures of business segment information as its first recommendation and included the following commentary:

> . . . for users analyzing a company involved in diverse businesses, financial information about business segments often is as important as information about the company as a whole. Users suggest that standard setters assign the highest priority to improving segment reporting because of its importance to their work and the perceived problems with current reporting of segment information. [page 68]

50. The report of the Special Committee listed the following as among the most important improvements needed:

a. Disclosure of segment information in interim financial reports

b. Greater number of segments for some enterprises
c. More information about segments
d. Segmentation that corresponds to internal management reports
e. Consistency of segment information with other parts of an annual report.

Similar recommendations had been made in each of the last 20 years in evaluations of corporate reporting conducted by the AIMR.

51. The two boards reached tentative conclusions about an approach to segment reporting that was substantially different from the approach in Statement 14 and Section 1700. Key characteristics of the new approach were that (a) information would be provided about segments of the enterprise that corresponded to the structure of the enterprise's internal organization, that is, about the divisions, departments, subsidiaries, or other internal units that the chief operating decision maker uses to make operating decisions and to assess an enterprise's performance, (b) specific amounts would be allocated to segments only if they were allocated in reports used by the chief operating decision maker for evaluation of segment performance, and (c) accounting policies used to produce the disaggregated information would be the same as those used in the reports used by the chief operating decision maker in allocating resources and assessing segment performance.

52. In February 1995, the staffs of the FASB and the CICA distributed a paper, "Tentative Conclusions on Financial Reporting for Segments" (Tentative Conclusions), to selected securities analysts, the FASB Task Force on Consolidations and Related Matters, the Disaggregated Disclosures Advisory Group, the FASB's Emerging Issues Task Force, the Financial Accounting Standards Advisory Council, the AcSB's list of Associates,[2] and members of representative organizations that regularly work with the boards. The paper also was announced in FASB and CICA publications and was sent to anyone who requested a copy. Board and staff members discussed the Tentative Conclusions with various analyst and preparer groups. Approximately 80 comment letters were received from U.S. and Canadian respondents.

53. In January 1996, the FASB and the AcSB issued virtually identical Exposure Drafts, *Reporting Disaggregated Information about a Business Enterprise.*

The FASB received 221 comment letters and the AcSB received 73 comment letters in response to the Exposure Drafts. A field test of the proposals was conducted in March 1996. A public meeting was held in Toronto in October 1996 to discuss results and concerns with field test participants. Other interested parties attended a public meeting in Norwalk in October 1996 to discuss their concerns about the proposals in the Exposure Drafts. The FASB decided that it could reach an informed decision on the project without holding a public hearing.

54. The FASB and the AcSB exchanged information during the course of redeliberating the proposals in their respective Exposure Drafts. AcSB members and CICA staff attended FASB meetings, and FASB members and staff attended AcSB meetings in late 1996 and in 1997 to discuss the issues raised by respondents. Both boards reached agreement on all of the substantive issues to achieve virtually identical standards for segment reporting in the United States and Canada. Members of the Segment Disclosures Advisory Group (formerly the Disaggregated Disclosures Advisory Group) discussed a draft of the standards section in March 1997.

55. The International Accounting Standards Committee (IASC) issued an Exposure Draft of a proposed International Accounting Standard that would replace International Accounting Standard IAS 14, *Reporting Financial Information by Segment,* in December 1995. Although many of its provisions are similar to those of the FASB and AcSB Exposure Drafts, the IASC's proposal is based on different objectives and is different from those Exposure Drafts. A member of the IASC Segments Steering Committee participated in FASB meetings during the redeliberations of the Exposure Draft, and members of the FASB participated in meetings of the IASC Segments Steering Committee. Many of the respondents to the Exposure Drafts encouraged the FASB and the AcSB to work closely with the IASC to achieve similar standards for segment reporting. The IASC expects to issue a standard on segment reporting later in 1997. Although there likely will be differences between the IASC's requirements for segment reporting and those of this Statement, the boards expect that it will be possible to prepare one set of segment information that complies with both the IASC requirements and those of this Statement.

---

[2]Associates are individuals and organizations with a particular interest in financial reporting issues that have volunteered to provide an outside reaction to AcSB positions at an early stage in the AcSB's deliberations.

56. This Statement addresses the following key issues:

a. What is the appropriate basis for defining segments?
b. What accounting principles and allocations should be used?
c. What specific items of information should be reported?
d. Should segment information be reported in condensed financial statements for interim periods?

Defining Operating Segments of an Enterprise

57. The Board concluded that the *industry approach* to segment disclosures in Statement 14 was not providing the information required by financial statement users and that disclosure of disaggregated information should be based on operating segments. This Statement defines an operating segment as a component of an enterprise (a) that engages in business activities from which it may earn revenues and incur expenses, (b) whose operating results are regularly reviewed by the enterprise's chief operating decision maker to make decisions about resources to be allocated to the segment and to assess its performance, and (c) for which discrete financial information is available.

58. The AIMR's 1993 position paper and the report of the AICPA Special Committee criticized Statement 14's industry segment approach to reporting segment information. The AIMR's position paper included the following:

> FAS 14 requires disclosure of line-of-business information classified by "industry segment." Its definition of segment is necessarily imprecise, recognizing that there are numerous practical problems in applying that definition to different business entities operating under disparate circumstances. That weakness in FAS 14 has been exploited by many enterprises to suit their own financial reporting purposes. As a result, we have seen one of the ten largest firms in the country report all of its operations as being in a single, very broadly defined industry segment. [page 60]

The report of the Special Committee said that "[financial statement users] believe that many companies define industry segments too broadly for business reporting and thus report on too few industry segments" (page 69).

59. The report of the AICPA Special Committee also said that ". . . the primary means to improving industry segment reporting should be to align business reporting with internal reporting" (page 69), and the AIMR's 1993 position paper recommended that:

> . . . priority should be given to the production and dissemination of financial data that reflects and reports sensibly the operations of specific enterprises. If we could obtain reports showing the details of how an individual business firm is organized and managed, we would assume more responsibility for making meaningful comparisons of those data to the unlike data of other firms that conduct their business differently. [pages 60 and 61]

Almost all of the users and many other constituents who responded to the Exposure Draft or who met with Board and staff members agreed that defining segments based on the structure of an enterprise's internal organization would result in improved information. They said that not only would enterprises be likely to report more detailed information but knowledge of the structure of an enterprise's internal organization is valuable in itself because it highlights the risks and opportunities that management believes are important.

60. Segments based on the structure of an enterprise's internal organization have at least three other significant advantages. First, an ability to see an enterprise "through the eyes of management" enhances a user's ability to predict actions or reactions of management that can significantly affect the enterprise's prospects for future cash flows. Second, because information about those segments is generated for management's use, the incremental cost of providing information for external reporting should be relatively low. Third, practice has demonstrated that the term *industry* is subjective. Segments based on an existing internal structure should be less subjective.

61. The AIMR and other users have commented that segment information is more useful if it is consistent with explanatory information provided elsewhere in the annual report. They note that the business review section and the chairman's letter in an annual report frequently discuss the enterprise's operations on a basis different from that of the segment information in the notes to the financial statements and the management's discussion and analysis section, which is required by SEC rules to correspond to the segment

information provided to comply with Statement 14. That appears to occur if the enterprise is not managed in a way that corresponds to the way it defines segments under the requirements of Statement 14. Segmentation based on the structure of an enterprise's internal organization should facilitate consistent discussion of segment financial results throughout an enterprise's annual report.

62. Some respondents to the Exposure Draft opposed the Board's approach for several reasons. Segments based on the structure of an enterprise's internal organization may not be comparable between enterprises that engage in similar activities and may not be comparable from year to year for an individual enterprise. In addition, an enterprise may not be organized based on products and services or geographic areas, and thus the enterprise's segments may not be susceptible to analysis using macroeconomic models. Finally, some asserted that because enterprises are organized strategically, the information that would be reported may be competitively harmful to the reporting enterprise.

63. The Board acknowledges that comparability of accounting information is important. The summary of principal conclusions in FASB Concepts Statement No. 2, *Qualitative Characteristics of Accounting Information,* says: "Comparability between enterprises and consistency in the application of methods over time increases the informational value of comparisons of relative economic opportunities or performance. The significance of information, especially quantitative information, depends to a great extent on the user's ability to relate it to some benchmark." However, Concepts Statement 2 also notes a danger:

> Improving comparability may destroy or weaken relevance or reliability if, to secure comparability between two measures, one of them has to be obtained by a method yielding less relevant or less reliable information. Historically, extreme examples of this have been provided in some European countries in which the use of standardized charts of accounts has been made mandatory in the interest of interfirm comparability but at the expense of relevance and often reliability as well. That kind of uniformity may even adversely affect comparability of information if it conceals real differences between enterprises. [paragraph 116]

64. The Board was concerned that segments defined using the approach in Statement 14 may appear to be more comparable between enterprises than they actually are. Statement 14 included the following:

> Information prepared in conformity with [Statement 14] may be of limited usefulness for comparing an industry segment of one enterprise with a similar industry segment of another enterprise (i.e., for interenterprise comparison). Interenterprise comparison of industry segments would require a fairly detailed prescription of the basis or bases of disaggregation to be followed by all enterprises, as well as specification of the basis of accounting for intersegment transfers and methods of allocating costs common to two or more segments. [paragraph 76]

65. Statement 14 explained why the Board chose not to develop a detailed prescription of the bases of disaggregation:

> . . . differences among enterprises in the nature of their operations and in the extent to which components of the enterprise share common facilities, equipment, materials and supplies, or labor force make unworkable the prescription of highly detailed rules and procedures that must be followed by all enterprises. Moreover, . . . differences in the accounting systems of business enterprises are a practical constraint on the degree of specificity with which standards of financial accounting and reporting for disaggregated information can be established. [paragraph 74]

Those same considerations persuaded the Board not to adopt more specific requirements in this Statement. Both relevance and comparability will not be achievable in all cases, and relevance should be the overriding concern.

66. The AICPA Special Committee, some respondents to the Exposure Draft, and other constituents recommended that the Board require that an enterprise use an alternative method of segmentation for external reporting if its internal organization is not based on differences in products and services or geography. Some specifically recommended adoption of the proposal in the IASC Exposure Draft that was commonly referred to as a "safety net." The IASC Exposure Draft approach to identifying primary and secondary operating segments calls for review of

management's organization of segments, but both primary and secondary segments are required to be defined either on the basis of related products and services or on the basis of geography. That is, regardless of management's organization, segments must be grouped either by related products and services or by geographic areas, and one set must be presented as primary segments and the other as secondary segments.

67. The Board recognizes that an enterprise may not be divided into components with similar products and services or geographic areas for internal purposes and that some users of financial statements have expressed a desire for information organized on those bases. However, instead of an alternative method of segmentation, which would call for multiple sets of segment information in many circumstances, the Board chose to require disclosure of additional information about products and services and about geographic areas of operations for the enterprise as a whole if the basic segment disclosures do not provide it.

68. One reason for not prescribing segmentation along bases of only related products and services or geography is that it is difficult to define clearly the circumstances in which an alternative method that differs from the management approach would be applied consistently. An enterprise with a relatively narrow product line may not consider two products to be similar, while an enterprise with a broad product line may consider those same two products to be similar. For example, a highly diversified enterprise may consider all consumer products to be similar if it has other businesses such as financial services and road construction. However, an enterprise that sells only consumer products might consider razor blades to be different from toasters.

69. A second reason for rejecting that approach is that an alternative method of segmentation would increase the cost to some enterprises to prepare the information. A management approach to defining segments allows enterprises to present the information that they use internally and facilitates consistent descriptions of the components of an enterprise from one part of the annual report to another. An enterprise could be organized by its products and services, geography, a mixture of both products and services and geography, or other bases, such as customer type, and the segment information required by this Statement would be consistent with that method of organization. Furthermore, the enterprise-wide disclosures

about products and services will provide information about the total revenues from related products and services, and the enterprise-wide disclosures about geography will provide information about the revenues and assets of an enterprise both inside and outside its home country. If material, individual foreign country information also is required.

70. The Board recognizes that some enterprises organize their segments on more than one basis. Other enterprises may produce reports in which their activities are presented in a variety of ways. In those situations, reportable segments are to be determined based on a review of other factors to identify the enterprise's operating segments, including the nature of the activities of each component, the existence of managers responsible for them, and the information provided to the board of directors. In many enterprises, only one set of data is provided to the board of directors. That set of data generally is indicative of how management views the enterprise's activities.

Reportable Segments

71. The Board included a notion of reportable segments, a subset of operating segments, in this Statement by defining aggregation criteria and quantitative thresholds for determining which operating segments should be reported separately in the financial statements.

72. A so-called pure management approach to segment reporting might require that an enterprise report all of the information that is reviewed by the chief operating decision maker to make decisions about resource allocations and to assess the performance of the enterprise. However, that level of detail may not be useful to readers of external financial statements, and it also may be cumbersome for an enterprise to present. Therefore, this Statement uses a modified management approach that includes both aggregation criteria and quantitative thresholds for determining reportable operating segments. However, an enterprise need not aggregate similar segments, and it may present segments that fall below the quantitative thresholds.

Aggregation of Similar Operating Segments

73. The Board believes that separate reporting of segment information will not add significantly to an investor's understanding of an enterprise if its operating segments have characteristics so similar that they can be expected to have essentially the same future

prospects. The Board concluded that although information about each segment may be available, in those circumstances the benefit would be insufficient to justify its disclosure. For example, a retail chain may have 10 stores that individually meet the definition of an operating segment, but each store may be essentially the same as the others.

74. Most respondents commented on the aggregation criteria in the Exposure Draft. Many said that the criteria were unreasonably strict, to the extent that nearly identical segments might not qualify for aggregation. Some respondents linked their concerns about competitive harm and too many segments directly to the aggregation criteria, indicating that a relaxation of the criteria would significantly reduce those concerns. To better convey its intent, the Board revised the wording of the aggregation criteria and the introduction to them. However, the Board rejected recommendations that the criteria be indicators rather than tests and that the guidance require only the expectation of similar long-term performance of segments to justify aggregation because those changes might result in a level of aggregation that would cause a loss of potentially valuable information. For the same reason, the Board also rejected suggestions that segments need be similar in only a majority of the characteristics in paragraph 17 to justify aggregation. The Board recognizes that determining when two segments are sufficiently similar to justify aggregating them is difficult and subjective. However, the Board notes that one of the reasons that the information provided under Statement 14 did not satisfy financial statement users' needs is that segments with different characteristics in important areas were at times aggregated.

Quantitative Thresholds

75. In developing the Exposure Draft, the Board had concluded that quantitative criteria might interfere with the determination of operating segments and, if anything, might unnecessarily reduce the number of segments disclosed. Respondents to the Exposure Draft and others urged the Board to include quantitative criteria for determining which segments to report because they said that some enterprises would be required to report too many segments unless specific quantitative guidelines allowed them to omit small segments. Some respondents said that the Exposure Draft would have required disclosure of as many as 25 operating segments, which was not a result anticipated by the Board in its deliberations preceding the Exposure Draft. Others said that enterprises would report information that was too highly aggregated unless quantitative guidelines prevented it. The Board decided that the addition of quantitative thresholds would be a practical way to address respondents' concerns about competitive harm and proliferation of segments without fundamentally changing the management approach to segment definition.

76. Similar to the requirements in Statement 14, the Board decided to require that any operating segment that constitutes 10 percent or more of reported revenues, assets, or profit or loss be reported separately and that reportable segments account for at least 75 percent of an enterprise's external revenues. The Board decided to retain that guidance for the quantitative thresholds because it can be objectively applied and because preparers and users of financial statements already understand it.

77. Inclusion of quantitative thresholds similar to those in Statement 14 necessitates guidance on how to report operating segments that do not meet the thresholds. The Board concluded that enterprises should be permitted to aggregate information about operating segments that do not meet the thresholds with information about other operating segments that do not meet the thresholds if a majority of the aggregation criteria in paragraph 17 are met. That is a more liberal aggregation provision than that for individually material operating segments, but it prohibits aggregation of segments that are dissimilar.

78. Paragraph 125 of Concepts Statement 2 states that ". . . magnitude by itself, without regard to the nature of the item and the circumstances in which the judgment has to be made, will not generally be a sufficient basis for a materiality judgment." That guidance applies to segment information. An understanding of the material segments of an enterprise is important for understanding the enterprise as a whole, and individual items of segment information are important for understanding the segments. Thus, an item of segment information that, if omitted, would change a user's decision about that segment so significantly that it would change the user's decision about the enterprise as a whole is material even though an item of a similar magnitude might not be considered material if it were omitted from the consolidated financial statements. Therefore, enterprises are encouraged to report information about segments that do not meet the quantitative thresholds if management believes that it is material. Those who are familiar with the particular circumstances of each enterprise must decide what constitutes *material*.

Vertically Integrated Enterprises

79. The Board concluded that the definition of an operating segment should include components of an enterprise that sell primarily or exclusively to other operating segments of the enterprise if the enterprise is managed that way. Information about the components engaged in each stage of production is particularly important for understanding vertically integrated enterprises in certain businesses, for example, oil and gas enterprises. Different activities within the enterprise may have significantly different prospects for future cash flows, and users of financial statements have asserted that they need to know results of each operation.

80. Some respondents to the Exposure Draft opposed the requirement to report vertically integrated segments separately. They said that the segment results may not be comparable between enterprises and that transfer prices are not sufficiently reliable for external reporting purposes. The Board considered an approach that would have required separate reporting of vertically integrated segments only if transfer prices were based on quoted market prices and if there was no basis for combining the selling segment and the buying segment. However, that would have been a significant departure from the management approach to defining segments. The Board also was concerned that the criteria would be unworkable. Therefore, the Board decided to retain the Exposure Draft's provisions for vertically integrated segments.

Accounting Principles and Allocations

81. The Board decided that the information to be reported about each segment should be measured on the same basis as the information used by the chief operating decision maker for purposes of allocating resources to segments and assessing segments' performance. That is a management approach to measuring segment information as proposed in the Exposure Draft. The Board does not think that a separate measure of segment profit or loss or assets should have to be developed solely for the purpose of disclosing segment information. For example, an enterprise that accounts for inventory using a specialized valuation method for internal purposes should not be required to restate inventory amounts for each segment, and an enterprise that accounts for pension expense only on a consolidated basis should not be required to allocate pension expense to each operating segment.

82. The report of the AICPA Special Committee said that the Board "should allow companies to report a statistic on the same basis it is reported for internal purposes, if the statistic is reported internally. The usefulness of information prepared only for [external] reporting is questionable. Users want to understand management's perspective on the company and the implications of key statistics." It also said that "key statistics to be reported [should] be limited to statistics a company has available . . ." (page 72).

83. Respondents to the Exposure Draft had mixed reactions to its measurement guidance. Very few suggested that the Board require allocations solely for external reporting purposes. Most agreed that allocations are inherently arbitrary and may not be meaningful if they are not used for management purposes. No respondents suggested that intersegment transfers should be reported on any basis other than that used internally. However, some respondents recommended that information about each segment be provided based on the accounting principles used in the enterprise's general-purpose financial statements. Some observed that unadjusted information from internal sources would not necessarily comply with generally accepted accounting principles and, for that reason, might be difficult for users to understand. Other respondents argued that comparability between enterprises would be improved if the segment information were provided on the basis of generally accepted accounting principles. Finally, a few questioned the verifiability of the information.

84. The Board decided not to require that segment information be provided in accordance with the same generally accepted accounting principles used to prepare the consolidated financial statements for several reasons. Preparing segment information in accordance with the generally accepted accounting principles used at the consolidated level would be difficult because some generally accepted accounting principles are not intended to apply at a segment level. Examples include allocation of the cost of an acquisition to individual assets and liabilities of a subsidiary using the purchase method of accounting, accounting for the cost of enterprise-wide employee benefit plans, accounting for income taxes in an enterprise that files a consolidated income tax return, and accounting for inventory on a last-in, first-out basis if the pools include items in more than one segment. In addition, there are no generally accepted accounting principles for allocating joint costs, jointly used assets, or jointly incurred liabilities to segments

or for pricing intersegment transfers. As a consequence, it generally is not feasible to present segment profitability in accordance with generally accepted accounting principles.

85. The Board recognizes that segment information is subject to certain limitations and that some of that information may not be susceptible to the same degree of verifiability as some other financial information. However, verifiability is not the only important qualitative characteristic of accounting information. Verifiability is a component of reliability, which is one of two characteristics that contribute to the usefulness of accounting information. The other is relevance, which is equally important. Concepts Statement 2 states:

> Although financial information must be both relevant and reliable to be useful, information may possess both characteristics to varying degrees. It may be possible to trade relevance for reliability or vice versa, though not to the point of dispensing with one of them altogether. . . . trade-offs between characteristics may be necessary or beneficial.
>
> In a particular situation, the importance attached to relevance in relation to the importance of other decision specific qualities of accounting information (for example, reliability) will be different for different information users, and their willingness to trade one quality for another will also differ. [paragraphs 42 and 45]

86. It is apparent that users are willing to trade a degree of reliability in segment information for more relevant information. The AIMR's 1993 position paper states:

> Analysts need financial statements structured so as to be consistent with how the business is organized and managed. That means that two different companies in the same industry may have to report segment data differently because they are structured differently themselves. [page 20]

But, as previously noted, the position paper says that, under those circumstances, analysts "would assume more responsibility for making meaningful comparisons of those data to the unlike data of other firms that conduct their business differently" (page 61).

87. The Board believes that the information required by this Statement meets the objective of reliability of which both representational faithfulness and verifiability are components. An auditor can determine whether the information reported in the notes to the financial statements came from the required source by reviewing management reports or minutes from meetings of the board of directors. The information is not required to be provided on a specified basis, but the enterprise is required to explain the basis on which it is provided and to reconcile the segment information to consolidated enterprise totals. Adequate explanation and an appropriate reconciliation will enable a user to understand the information and its limitations in the context of the enterprise's financial statements. The auditor can test both the explanation of segment amounts and the reconciliations to consolidated totals. Furthermore, because management uses that information in its decision-making processes, that information is likely to be highly reliable. The information provided to comply with Statement 14 was more difficult to verify in many situations and was less reliable. Because it was prepared solely for external reporting purposes, it required allocations that may have been arbitrary, and it was based on accounting principles that may have been difficult to apply at the segment level.

88. Paragraph 29 requires amounts allocated to a segment to be allocated on a reasonable basis. However, the Board believes that the potential increased reliability that might have been achieved by requiring allocation of consolidated amounts is illusory because expenses incurred at the consolidated level could be allocated to segments in a variety of ways that could be considered "reasonable." For example, an enterprise could use either the number of employees in each segment or the segment's total salary expense in relation to the consolidated amounts as a basis for allocating pension expense to segments. Those two approaches to allocation could result in significantly different measures of segment profit or loss. However, both the number of employees and the total salary expense might be reasonable bases on which to allocate total pension expense. In contrast, it would not seem reasonable for an enterprise to allocate pension expense to a segment that had no employees eligible for the pension plan. Because of the potential for misleading information that may result from such allocations, the Board decided that it is appropriate for this Statement to require that amounts allocated to a segment be allocated on a reasonable basis.

89. The Board also considered explicitly requiring that revenues and expenses directly incurred by or directly attributable to an operating segment be reported by that segment. However, it decided that, in some cases, whether an item of revenue or expense is attributable to an operating segment is a matter of judgment. Further, such an explicit requirement would be an additional modification of the management approach to measurement. While the Board decided not to include an explicit requirement, it believes that many items of revenue or expense clearly relate to a particular segment and that it would be unlikely that the information used by management would omit those items.

90. To assist users of financial statements in understanding segment disclosures, this Statement requires that enterprises provide sufficient explanation of the basis on which the information was prepared. That disclosure must include any differences in the basis of measurement between the consolidated amounts and the segment amounts. It also must indicate whether allocations of items were made symmetrically. An enterprise may allocate an expense to a segment without allocating the related asset; however, disclosure of that fact is required. Enterprises also are required to reconcile to the consolidated totals in the enterprise's financial statements the totals of reportable segment assets, segment revenues, segment profit or loss, and any other significant segment information that is disclosed.

91. In addition, the advantages of reporting unadjusted management information are significant. That practice is consistent with defining segments based on the structure of the enterprise's internal organization. It imposes little incremental cost on the enterprise and requires little incremental time to prepare. Thus, the enterprise can more easily report segment information in condensed financial statements for interim periods and can report more information about each segment in annual financial statements. Information used by management also highlights for a user of financial statements the risks and opportunities that management considers important.

Information to Be Disclosed about Segments

92. The items of information about each reportable operating segment that must be disclosed as described in paragraphs 25-31 represent a balance between the needs of users of financial statements who may want a complete set of financial statements for each segment and the costs to preparers who may prefer not to disclose any segment information. Statement 14 required disclosure of internal and external revenues; profit or loss; depreciation, depletion, and amortization expense; and unusual items as defined in APB Opinion No. 30, *Reporting the Results of Operations—Reporting the Effects of Disposal of a Segment of a Business, and Extraordinary, Unusual and Infrequently Occurring Events and Transactions,* for each segment. Statement 14 also required disclosure of total assets, equity in the net income of investees accounted for by the equity method, the amount of investment in equity method investees, and total expenditures for additions to long-lived assets. Some respondents to the Exposure Draft objected to disclosing any information that was not required by Statement 14, while others recommended disclosure of additional items that are not required by this Statement. This Statement calls for the following additional disclosures only if the items are included in the measure of segment profit or loss that is reviewed by the chief operating decision maker: significant noncash items, interest revenue, interest expense, and income tax expense.

93. Some respondents to the Exposure Draft expressed concern that the proposals would increase the sheer volume of information compared to what was required to be reported under Statement 14. The Board considers that concern to be overstated for several reasons. Although this Statement requires disclosure of more information about an individual operating segment than Statement 14 required for an industry segment, this Statement requires disclosure of information about only one type of segment—reportable operating segments—while Statement 14 required information about two types of segments—industry segments and geographic segments. Moreover, Statement 14 required that many enterprises create information solely for external reporting, while almost all of the segment information that this Statement requires is already available in management reports. The Board recognizes, however, that some enterprises may find it necessary to create the enterprise-wide information about products and services, geographic areas, and major customers required by paragraphs 36-39.

94. The Board decided to require disclosure of significant noncash items included in the measure of segment profit or loss and information about total expenditures for additions to long-lived segment assets (other than financial instruments, long-term customer relationships of a financial institution, mortgage and other servicing rights, deferred policy acquisition

costs, and deferred tax assets) if that information is reported internally because it improves financial statement users' abilities to estimate cash-generating potential and cash requirements of operating segments. As an alternative, the Board considered requiring disclosure of operating cash flow for each operating segment. However, many respondents said that disclosing operating cash flow in accordance with FASB Statement No. 95, *Statement of Cash Flows,* would require that they gather and process information solely for external reporting purposes. They said that management often evaluates cash generated or required by segments in ways other than by calculating operating cash flow in accordance with Statement 95. For that reason, the Board decided not to require disclosure of cash flow by segment.

95. Disclosure of interest revenue and interest expense included in reported segment profit or loss is intended to provide information about the financing activities of a segment. The Exposure Draft proposed that an enterprise disclose gross interest revenue and gross interest expense for all segments in which reported profit or loss includes those items. Some respondents said that financial services segments generally are managed based on net interest revenue, or the "spread," and that management looks only to that data in its decision-making process. Therefore those segments should be required to disclose only the net amount and not both gross interest revenue and expense. Those respondents noted that requiring disclosure of both gross amounts would be analogous to requiring nonfinancial services segments to disclose both sales and cost of sales. The Board decided that segments that derive a majority of revenue from interest should be permitted to disclose net interest revenue instead of gross interest revenue and gross interest expense if management finds that amount to be more relevant in managing the segment. Information about interest is most important if a single segment comprises a mix of financial and nonfinancial operations. If a segment is primarily a financial operation, interest revenue probably constitutes most of segment revenues and interest expense will constitute most of the difference between reported segment revenues and reported segment profit or loss. If the segment has no financial operations or only immaterial financial operations, no information about interest is required.

96. The Board decided not to require the disclosure of segment liabilities. The Exposure Draft proposed that an enterprise disclose segment liabilities because the Board believed that liabilities are an important

disclosure for understanding the financing activities of a segment. The Board also noted that the requirement in FASB Statement No. 94, *Consolidation of All Majority-Owned Subsidiaries,* to disclose assets, liabilities, and profit or loss about previously unconsolidated subsidiaries was continued from APB Opinion No. 18, *The Equity Method of Accounting for Investments in Common Stock,* pending completion of the project on disaggregated disclosures. However, in commenting on the disclosures that should be required by this Statement, many respondents said that liabilities are incurred centrally and that enterprises often do not allocate those amounts to segments. The Board concluded that the value of information about segment liabilities in assessing the performance of the segments of an enterprise was limited.

97. The Board decided not to require disclosure of research and development expense included in the measure of segment profit or loss. The Exposure Draft would have required that disclosure to provide financial statement users with information about the operating segments in which an enterprise is focusing its product development efforts. Disclosure of research and development expense was requested by a number of financial statement users and was specifically requested in both the report of the AICPA's Special Committee and the AIMR's 1993 position paper. However, respondents said that disclosing research and development expense by segment may result in competitive harm by providing competitors with early insight into the strategic plans of an enterprise. Other respondents observed that research and development is only one of a number of items that indicate where an enterprise is focusing its efforts and that it is much more significant in some enterprises than in others. For example, costs of employee training and advertising were cited as items that often are more important to some enterprises than research and development, calling into question the relevance of disclosing only research and development expense. Additionally, many respondents said that research and development expense often is incurred centrally and not allocated to segments. The Board therefore decided not to require the disclosure of research and development expense by segment.

Interim Period Information

98. This Statement requires disclosure of limited segment information in condensed financial statements that are included in quarterly reports to shareholders, as was proposed in the Exposure Draft.

Statement 14 did not apply to those condensed financial statements because of the expense and the time required for producing segment information under Statement 14. A few respondents to the Exposure Draft said that reporting segment information in interim financial statements would be unnecessarily burdensome. However, users contended that, to be timely, segment information is needed more often than annually and that the difficulties of preparing it on an interim basis could be overcome by an approach like the one in this Statement. Managers of many enterprises agree and have voluntarily provided segment information for interim periods.

99. The Board decided that the condensed financial statements in interim reports issued to shareholders should include disclosure of segment revenues from external customers, intersegment revenues, a measure of segment profit or loss, material changes in segment assets, differences in the basis of segmentation or the way segment profit or loss was measured in the previous annual period, and a reconciliation to the enterprise's total profit or loss. That decision is a compromise between the needs of users who want the same segment information for interim periods as that required in annual financial statements and the costs to preparers who must report the information. Users will have some key information on a timely basis. Enterprises should not incur significant incremental costs to provide the information because it is based on information that is used internally and therefore already available.

Restatement of Previously Reported Information

100. The Board decided to require restatement of previously reported segment information following a change in the composition of an enterprise's segments unless it is impracticable to do so. Changes in the composition of segments interrupt trends, and trend analysis is important to users of financial statements. Some financial statement issuers have said that their policy is to restate one or more prior years for internal trend analysis. Many reorganizations result in discrete profit centers' being reassigned from one segment to another and lead to relatively simple restatements. However, if an enterprise undergoes a fundamental reorganization, restatement may be very difficult and expensive. The Board concluded that in those situations restatement may be impracticable and, therefore, should not be required. However, if an enterprise does not restate its segment information, the enterprise is required to provide current-period segment information on both the old and new bases

of segmentation in the year in which the change occurs unless it is impracticable to do so.

Enterprise-Wide Disclosures

101. Paragraphs 36-39 require disclosure of information about an enterprise's products and services, geographic areas, and major customers, regardless of the enterprise's organization. The required disclosures need be provided only if they are not included as part of the disclosures about segments. The Exposure Draft proposed requiring additional disclosures about products and services and geographic areas *by segment*. Many respondents said that that proposal would have resulted in disclosure of excessive amounts of information. Some enterprises providing a variety of products and services throughout many countries, for example, would have been required to present a large quantity of information that would have been time-consuming to prepare and of questionable benefit to most financial statement users. The Board decided that additional disclosures provided on an enterprise-wide basis rather than on a segment basis would be appropriate and not unduly burdensome. The Board also agreed that those enterprise-wide disclosures are appropriate for all enterprises including those that have a single operating segment if the enterprise offers a range of products and services, derives revenues from customers in more than one country, or both.

102. Based on reviews of published information about public enterprises, discussions with constituents, and a field test of the Exposure Draft, the Board believes that most enterprises are organized by products and services or by geography and will report one or both of those types of information in their reportable operating segment disclosures. However, some enterprises will be required by paragraphs 36-39 to report additional information because the enterprise-wide disclosures are required for all enterprises, even those that have a single reportable segment.

Information about Products and Services

103. This Statement requires that enterprises report revenues from external customers for each product and service or each group of similar products and services for the enterprise as a whole. Analysts said that an analysis of trends in revenues from products and services is important in assessing both past performance and prospects for future growth. Those

trends can be compared to benchmarks such as industry statistics or information reported by competitors. Information about the assets that are used to produce specific products and deliver specific services also might be useful. However, in many enterprises, assets are not dedicated to specific products and services and reporting assets by products and services would require arbitrary allocations.

Information about Geographic Areas

104. This Statement requires disclosure of information about both revenues and assets by geographic area. Analysts said that information about revenues from customers in different geographic areas assists them in understanding concentrations of risks due to negative changes in economic conditions and prospects for growth due to positive economic changes. They said that information about assets located in different areas assists them in understanding concentrations of risks (for example, political risks such as expropriation).

105. Statement 14 requires disclosure of geographic information by geographic region, whereas this Statement requires disclosure of individually material countries as well as information for the enterprise's country of domicile and all foreign countries in the aggregate. This Statement's approach has two significant benefits. First, it will reduce the burden on preparers of financial statements because most enterprises are likely to have material operations in only a few countries or perhaps only in their country of domicile. Second, and more important, it will provide information that is more useful in assessing the impact of concentrations of risk. Information disclosed by country is more useful because it is easier to interpret. Countries in contiguous areas often experience different rates of growth and other differences in economic conditions. Under the requirements of Statement 14, enterprises often reported information about broad geographic areas that included groupings such as Europe, Africa, and the Middle East. Analysts and others have questioned the usefulness of that type of broad disclosure.

106. Respondents to the Exposure Draft questioned how revenues should be allocated to individual countries. For example, guidance was requested for situations in which products are shipped to one location but the customer resides in another location. The Board decided to provide flexibility concerning the basis on which enterprises attribute revenues to individual countries rather than requiring that revenues be attributed to countries according to the location of customers. The Board also decided to require that enterprises disclose the basis they have adopted for attributing revenues to countries to permit financial statement users to understand the geographic information provided.

107. As a result of its decision to require geographic information on an enterprise-wide basis, the Board decided not to require disclosure of capital expenditures on certain long-lived assets by geographic area. Such information on an enterprise-wide basis is not necessarily helpful in forecasting future cash flows of operating segments.

Information about Major Customers

108. The Board decided to retain the requirement in Statement 14, as amended by FASB Statement No. 30, *Disclosure of Information about Major Customers,* to report information about major customers because major customers of an enterprise represent a significant concentration of risk. The 10 percent threshold is arbitrary; however, it has been accepted practice since Statement 14 was issued, and few have suggested changing it.

Competitive Harm

109. A number of respondents to the Exposure Draft noted the potential for competitive harm as a result of disclosing segment information in accordance with this Statement. The Board considered adopting special provisions to reduce the potential for competitive harm from certain segment information but decided against it. In the Invitation to Comment, the Tentative Conclusions, and the Exposure Draft, the Board asked constituents for specific illustrations of competitive harm that has resulted from disclosing segment information. Some respondents said that public enterprises may be at a disadvantage to nonpublic enterprises or foreign competitors that do not have to disclose segment information. Other respondents suggested that information about narrowly defined segments may put an enterprise at a disadvantage in price negotiations with customers or in competitive bid situations.

110. Some respondents said that if a competitive disadvantage exists, it is a consequence of an obligation that enterprises have accepted to gain greater access to capital markets, which gives them certain advantages over nonpublic enterprises and many foreign enterprises. Other respondents said that enterprises

are not likely to suffer competitive harm because most competitors have other sources of more detailed information about an enterprise than that disclosed in the financial statements. In addition, the information that is required to be disclosed about an operating segment is no more detailed or specific than the information typically provided by a smaller enterprise with a single operation.

111. The Board was sympathetic to specific concerns raised by certain constituents; however, it decided that a competitive-harm exemption was inappropriate because it would provide a means for broad noncompliance with this Statement. Some form of relief for single-product or single-service segments was explored; however, there are many enterprises that produce a single product or a single service that are required to issue general-purpose financial statements. Those statements would include the same information that would be reported by single-product or single-service segments of an enterprise. The Board concluded that it was not necessary to provide an exemption for single-product or single-service segments because enterprises that produce a single product or service that are required to issue general-purpose financial statements have that same exposure to competitive harm. The Board noted that concerns about competitive harm were addressed to the extent feasible by four changes made during redeliberations: (a) modifying the aggregation criteria, (b) adding quantitative materiality thresholds for identifying reportable segments, (c) eliminating the requirements to disclose research and development expense and liabilities by segment, and (d) changing the second-level disclosure requirements about products and services and geography from a segment basis to an enterprise-wide basis.

Cost-Benefit Considerations

112. One of the precepts of the Board's mission is to promulgate standards only if the expected benefits of the resulting information exceed the perceived costs. The Board strives to determine that a proposed standard will fill a significant need and that the costs incurred to satisfy that need, as compared with other alternatives, are justified in relation to the overall benefits of the resulting information. The Board concluded that the benefits that will result from this Statement will exceed the related costs.

113. The Board believes that the primary benefits of this Statement are that enterprises will report segment information in interim financial reports, some enter-

prises will report a greater number of segments, most enterprises will report more items of information about each segment, enterprises will report segments that correspond to internal management reports, and enterprises will report segment information that will be more consistent with other parts of their annual reports.

114. This Statement will reduce the cost of providing disaggregated information for many enterprises. Statement 14 required that enterprises define segments by both industry and by geographical area, ways that often did not match the way that information was used internally. Even if the reported segments aligned with the internal organization, the information required was often created solely for external reporting because Statement 14 required certain allocations of costs, prohibited other cost allocations, and required allocations of assets to segments. This Statement requires that information about operating segments be provided on the same basis that it is used internally. The Board believes that most of the enterprise-wide disclosures in this Statement about products and services, geography, and major customers typically are provided in current financial statements or can be prepared with minimal incremental cost.

Applicability to Nonpublic Enterprises and Not-for-Profit Organizations

115. The Board decided to continue to exempt nonpublic enterprises from the requirement to report segment information. Few users of nonpublic enterprises' financial statements have requested that the Board require that those enterprises provide segment information.

116. At the time the Board began considering improvements to disclosures about segment information, FASB Statement No. 117, *Financial Statements of Not-for-Profit Organizations,* had not been issued and there were no effective standards for consolidated financial statements of not-for-profit organizations. Most not-for-profit organizations provided financial information for each of their funds, which is a form of disaggregated information. The situation in Canada was similar. Thus, when the two boards agreed to pursue a joint project, they decided to limit the scope to public business enterprises.

117. The Board provided for a limited form of disaggregated information in paragraph 26 of Statement 117, which requires disclosure of expense by

functional classification. However, the Board acknowledges that the application of that Statement may increase the need for disaggregated information about not-for-profit organizations. A final Statement expected to result from the FASB Exposure Draft, *Consolidated Financial Statements: Policy and Procedures,* also may increase that need by requiring aggregation of information about more entities in the financial statements of not-for-profit organizations.

118. The general approach of providing information based on the structure of an enterprise's internal organization may be appropriate for not-for-profit organizations. However, the Board decided not to add not-for-profit organizations to the scope of this Statement. Users of financial statements of not-for-profit organizations have not urged the Board to include those organizations, perhaps because they have not yet seen the effects of Statement 117 and the Exposure Draft on consolidations. Furthermore, the term *not-for-profit organizations* applies to a wide variety of entities, some of which are similar to business enterprises and some of which are very different. There are likely to be unique characteristics of some of those entities or special user needs that require special provisions, which the Board has not studied. In addition, the AcSB has recently adopted standards for reporting by not-for-profit organizations that are different from Statement 117. In the interest of completing this joint project in a timely manner, the Board decided not to undertake the research and deliberations that would be necessary to adapt the requirements of this Statement to not-for-profit organizations at this time. Few respondents to the Exposure Draft disagreed with the Board's position.

Effective Date and Transition

119. The Board concluded that this Statement should be effective for financial statements issued for fiscal years beginning after December 15, 1997. In developing the Exposure Draft, the Board had decided on an effective date of December 15, 1996. The Board believed that that time frame was reasonable because almost all of the information that this Statement requires is generated by systems already in place within an enterprise and a final Statement was expected to be issued before the end of 1996. However, respondents said that some enterprises may

need more time to comply with the requirements of this Statement than would have been provided under the Exposure Draft.

120. The Board also decided not to require that segment information be reported in financial statements for interim periods in the initial year of application. Some of the information that is required to be reported for interim periods is based on information that would have been reported in the most recent annual financial statements. Without a full set of segment information to use as a comparison and to provide an understanding of the basis on which it is provided, interim information would not be as meaningful.

Appendix B

ILLUSTRATIVE GUIDANCE

121. This appendix provides specific examples that illustrate the disclosures that are required by this Statement and provides a diagram for identifying reportable operating segments. The formats in the illustrations are not requirements. The Board encourages a format that provides the information in the most understandable manner in the specific circumstances. The following illustrations are for a single hypothetical enterprise referred to as Diversified Company.

122. The following is an illustration of the disclosure of descriptive information about an enterprise's reportable segments. (References to paragraphs in which the relevant requirements appear are given in parentheses.)

Description of the types of products and services from which each reportable segment derives its revenues (paragraph 26(b))

Diversified Company has five reportable segments: auto parts, motor vessels, software, electronics, and finance. The auto parts segment produces replacement parts for sale to auto parts retailers. The motor vessels segment produces small motor vessels to serve the offshore oil industry and similar businesses. The software segment produces application software for sale to computer manufacturers and retailers. The electronics segment produces integrated circuits and related products for sale to computer manufacturers. The finance segment is responsible for portions of the company's financial operations including financing customer purchases of products from other segments and real estate lending operations in several states.

Measurement of segment profit or loss and segment assets (paragraph 31)

The accounting policies of the segments are the same as those described in the summary of significant accounting policies except that pension expense for each segment is recognized and measured on the basis of cash payments to the pension plan. Diversified Company evaluates performance based on profit or loss from operations before income taxes not including nonrecurring gains and losses and foreign exchange gains and losses.

Diversified Company accounts for intersegment sales and transfers as if the sales or transfers were to third parties, that is, at current market prices.

Factors management used to identify the enterprise's reportable segments (paragraph 26(a))

Diversified Company's reportable segments are strategic business units that offer different products and services. They are managed separately because each business requires different technology and marketing strategies. Most of the businesses were acquired as a unit, and the management at the time of the acquisition was retained.

123. The following table illustrates a suggested format for presenting information about reported segment profit or loss and segment assets (paragraphs 27 and 28). The same type of information is required for each year for which a complete set of financial statements is presented. Diversified Company does not allocate income taxes or unusual items to segments. In addition, not all segments have significant noncash items other than depreciation and amortization in reported profit or loss. The amounts in this illustration are assumed to be the amounts in reports used by the chief operating decision maker.

	Auto Parts	Motor Vessels	Software	Electronics	Finance	All Other	Totals
Revenues from external customers	$3,000	$5,000	$9,500	$12,000	$ 5,000	$1,000[a]	$35,500
Intersegment revenues	—	—	3,000	1,500	—	—	4,500
Interest revenue	450	800	1,000	1,500	—	—	3,750
Interest expense	350	600	700	1,100	—	—	2,750
Net interest revenue[b]	—	—	—	—	1,000	—	1,000
Depreciation and amortization	200	100	50	1,500	1,100	—	2,950
Segment profit	200	70	900	2,300	500	100	4,070
Other significant noncash items:							
Cost in excess of billings on long-term contracts	—	200	—	—	—	—	200
Segment assets	2,000	5,000	3,000	12,000	57,000	2,000	81,000
Expenditures for segment assets	300	700	500	800	600	—	2,900

---

[a]Revenue from segments below the quantitative thresholds are attributable to four operating segments of Diversified Company. Those segments include a small real estate business, an electronics equipment rental business, a software consulting practice, and a warehouse leasing operation. None of those segments has ever met any of the quantitative thresholds for determining reportable segments.

[b]The finance segment derives a majority of its revenue from interest. In addition, management primarily relies on net interest revenue, not the gross revenue and expense amounts, in managing that segment. Therefore, as permitted by paragraph 27, only the net amount is disclosed.

124. The following are illustrations of reconciliations of reportable segment revenues, profit or loss, and assets, to the enterprise's consolidated totals (paragraphs 32(a), 32(b), and 32(c)). Reconciliations also are required to be shown for every other significant item of information disclosed (paragraph 32(d)). For example, if Diversified Company disclosed segment liabilities, they are required to be reconciled to total consolidated liabilities. The enterprise's financial statements are assumed not to include discontinued operations or the cumulative effect of a change in accounting principles. As discussed in the illustration in paragraph 122, the enterprise recognizes and measures pension expense of its segments based on cash payments to the pension plan, and it does not allocate certain items to its segments.

Revenues

Total revenues for reportable segments	$39,000
Other revenues	1,000
Elimination of intersegment revenues	(4,500)
Total consolidated revenues	$35,500

Profit or Loss

Total profit or loss for reportable segments	$ 3,970
Other profit or loss	100
Elimination of intersegment profits	(500)
Unallocated amounts:	
Litigation settlement received	500
Other corporate expenses	(750)
Adjustment to pension expense in consolidation	(250)
Income before income taxes and extraordinary items	$ 3,070

Assets

Total assets for reportable segments	$79,000
Other assets	2,000
Elimination of receivables from corporate headquarters	(1,000)
Goodwill not allocated to segments	4,000
Other unallocated amounts	1,000
Consolidated total	$85,000

Other Significant Items

	Segment Totals	Adjustments	Consolidated Totals
Interest revenue	$3,750	$ 75	$3,825
Interest expense	2,750	(50)	2,700
Net interest revenue (finance segment only)	1,000	—	1,000
Expenditures for assets	2,900	1,000	3,900
Depreciation and amortization	2,950	—	2,950
Cost in excess of billing on long-term contracts	200	—	200

The reconciling item to adjust expenditures for assets is the amount of expenses incurred for the corporate headquarters building, which is not included in segment information. None of the other adjustments are significant.

125. The following illustrates the geographic information required by paragraph 38. (Because Diversified Company's segments are based on differences in products and services, no additional disclosures of revenue information about products and services are required (paragraph 37)).

126. The following is an illustration of the information about major customers required by paragraph 39. Neither the identity of the customer nor the amount of revenues for each operating segment is required.

Revenues from one customer of Diversified Company's software and electronics segments represents approximately $5,000 of the company's consolidated revenues.

Geographic Information

	Revenues[a]	Long-Lived Assets
United States	$19,000	$11,000
Canada	4,200	—
Taiwan	3,400	6,500
Japan	2,900	3,500
Other foreign countries	6,000	3,000
Total	$35,500	$24,000

[a]Revenues are attributed to countries based on location of customer.

Diagram for Identifying Reportable Operating Segments

127. The following diagram illustrates how to apply the main provisions for identifying reportable operating segments as defined in this Statement. The diagram is a visual supplement to the written standards section. It should not be interpreted to alter any requirements of this Statement nor should it be considered a substitute for the requirements.

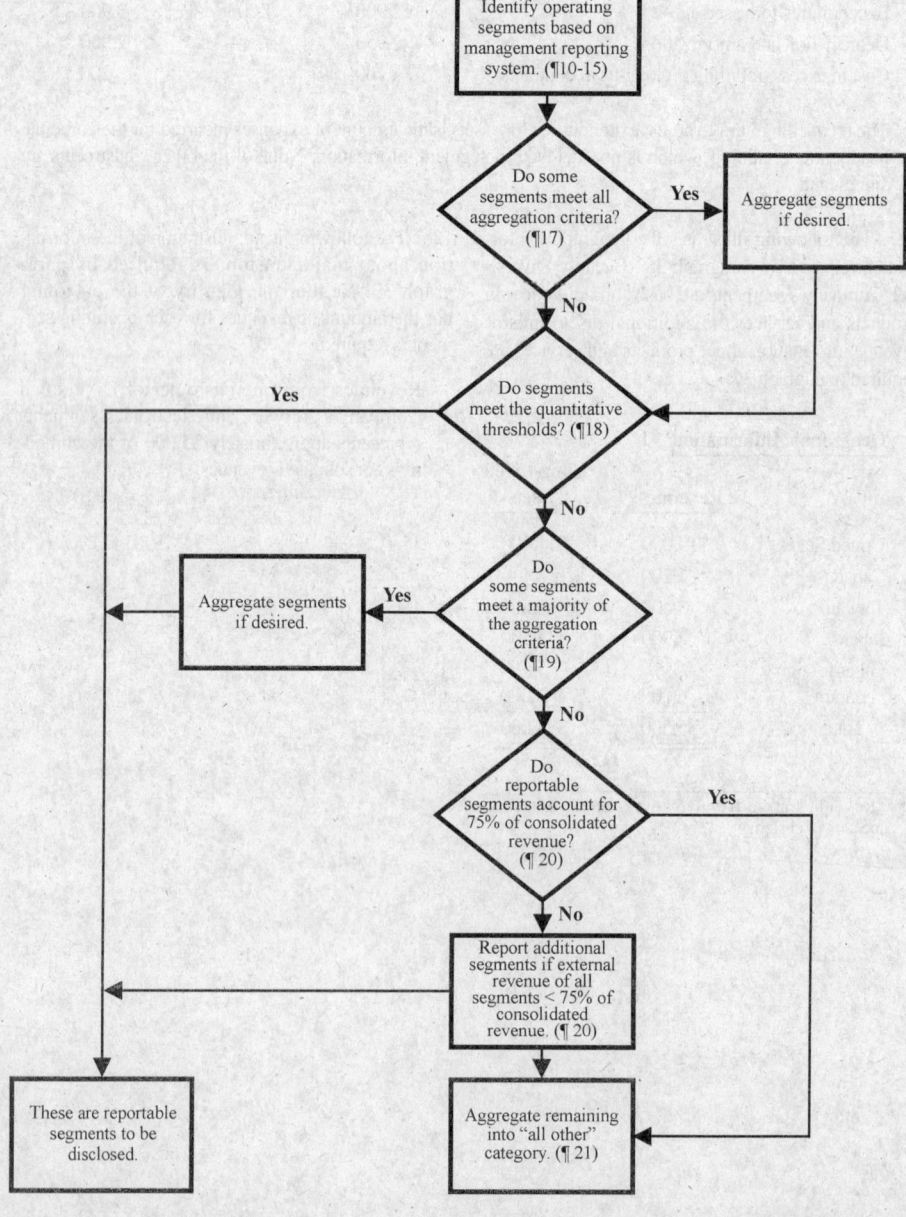

Appendix C

AMENDMENTS TO EXISTING PRONOUNCEMENTS

128. This Statement supersedes the following pronouncements:

a. FASB Statement No. 14, *Financial Reporting for Segments of a Business Enterprise*
b. FASB Statement No. 18, *Financial Reporting for Segments of a Business Enterprise—Interim Financial Statements*
c. FASB Statement No. 21, *Suspension of the Reporting of Earnings per Share and Segment Information by Nonpublic Enterprises*
d. FASB Statement No. 24, *Reporting Segment Information in Financial Statements That Are Presented in Another Enterprise's Financial Report*
e. FASB Statement No. 30, *Disclosure of Information about Major Customers*
f. FASB Technical Bulletin No. 79-8, *Applicability of FASB Statements 21 and 33 to Certain Brokers and Dealers in Securities.*

129. ARB No. 43, Chapter 12, "Foreign Operations and Foreign Exchange," is amended as follows:

a. The following is added at the end of paragraph 5:

FASB Statement No. 131, *Disclosures about Segments of an Enterprise and Related Information,* discusses the requirements for reporting revenues from foreign operations.

b. Paragraph 6 is replaced by the following:

Statement 131 discusses the requirements for reporting assets located outside the United States.

130. Paragraph 19 of ARB No. 51, *Consolidated Financial Statements,* as amended by FASB Statement No. 94, *Consolidation of All Majority-Owned Subsidiaries,* is deleted.

131. The following is added to the listing in paragraph 30 of APB Opinion No. 28, *Interim Financial Reporting:*

i. The following information about reportable operating segments determined according to

the provisions of FASB Statement No. 131, *Disclosures about Segments of an Enterprise and Related Information,* including provisions related to restatement of segment information in previously issued financial statements:

(1) Revenues from external customers
(2) Intersegment revenues
(3) A measure of segment profit or loss
(4) Total assets for which there has been a material change from the amount disclosed in the last annual report
(5) A description of differences from the last annual report in the basis of segmentation or in the measurement of segment profit or loss
(6) A reconciliation of the total of the reportable segments' measures of profit or loss to the enterprise's consolidated income before income taxes, extraordinary items, discontinued operations, and the cumulative effect of changes in accounting principles. However, if, for example, an enterprise allocates items such as income taxes and extraordinary items to segments, the enterprise may choose to reconcile the total of the segments' measures of profit or loss to consolidated income after those items. Significant reconciling items shall be separately identified and described in that reconciliation.

132. In footnote 3 to paragraph 5 of FASB Statement No. 51, *Financial Reporting by Cable Television Companies,* the reference to Statement 14 is replaced by a reference to FASB Statement No. 131, *Disclosures about Segments of an Enterprise and Related Information.*

133. FASB Statement No. 69, *Disclosures about Oil and Gas Producing Activities,* is amended as follows:

a. Footnote 4 to paragraph 8(a) is replaced by the following:

For purposes of this Statement, an industry segment is a component of an enterprise engaged in providing a product or service or a group of related products or services primarily to external customers (that is, customers outside the enterprise) for a profit.

b. Paragraph 8(c) is replaced by the following:

The identifiable assets of oil- and gas-producing activities (tangible and intangible enterprise assets that are used by oil- and gas-producing activities, including an allocated portion of assets used jointly with other operations) are 10 percent or more of the assets of the enterprise, excluding assets used exclusively for general corporate purposes.

c. The second sentence of footnote 7 to paragraph 24 is replaced by the following:

If oil- and gas-producing activities constitute an operating segment, as discussed in paragraphs 10-24 of FASB Statement No. 131, *Disclosures about Segments of an Enterprise and Related Information,* information about the results of operations required by paragraphs 24-29 of this Statement may be included with segment information disclosed elsewhere in the financial report.

134. Paragraph 14 of Statement 94 is deleted.

135. FASB Technical Bulletin No. 79-4, *Segment Reporting of Puerto Rican Operations,* is amended as follows:

a. In paragraph 1, *paragraphs 31-38 of Statement 14* is replaced by *paragraph 38 of FASB Statement No. 131, Disclosures about Segments of an Enterprise and Related Information.*

b. Paragraph 2 is replaced by the following:

Paragraph 38 of Statement 131 requires that certain enterprises disclose information about an enterprise's revenues from customers outside their country of domicile and assets located outside their country of domicile.

c. In paragraph 3, the first sentence and the phrase *Based on those guidelines* in the second sentence are deleted.

136. In FASB Technical Bulletin No. 79-5, *Meaning of the Term "Customer" as It Applies to Health Care Facilities under FASB Statement No. 14,* references to paragraph 39 of Statement 14 are replaced by references to paragraph 39 of FASB Statement No. 131, *Disclosures about Segments of an Enterprise and Related Information.*

Statement of Financial Accounting Standards No. 132 Employers' Disclosures about Pensions and Other Postretirement Benefits

an amendment of FASB Statements No. 87, 88, and 106

STATUS

Issued: February 1998

Effective Date: For fiscal years beginning after December 15, 1997

Affects: Supersedes FAS 87, paragraphs 54, 56, 65, and 69 and Illustration 6
Supersedes FAS 88, paragraph 17
Supersedes FAS 106, paragraphs 74, 77, 78, 82, 106, and 479 through 483

Affected by: Paragraphs 12(b) and 63 amended by FAS 135
Paragraphs 12(d) and 14(e) superseded by FAS 135

SUMMARY

This Statement revises employers' disclosures about pension and other postretirement benefit plans. It does not change the measurement or recognition of those plans. It standardizes the disclosure requirements for pensions and other postretirement benefits to the extent practicable, requires additional information on changes in the benefit obligations and fair values of plan assets that will facilitate financial analysis, and eliminates certain disclosures that are no longer as useful as they were when FASB Statements No. 87, *Employers' Accounting for Pensions*, No. 88, *Employers' Accounting for Settlements and Curtailments of Defined Benefit Pension Plans and for Termination Benefits*, and No. 106, *Employers' Accounting for Postretirement Benefits Other Than Pensions*, were issued. The Statement suggests combined formats for presentation of pension and other postretirement benefit disclosures. The Statement also permits reduced disclosures for nonpublic entities.

This Statement is effective for fiscal years beginning after December 15, 1997. Earlier application is encouraged. Restatement of disclosures for earlier periods provided for comparative purposes is required unless the information is not readily available, in which case the notes to the financial statements should include all available information and a description of the information not available.

Statement of Financial Accounting Standards No. 132

Employers' Disclosures about Pensions and Other Postretirement Benefits

an amendment of FASB Statements No. 87, 88, and 106

CONTENTS

INTRODUCTION

1. The Board added a project on effectiveness of disclosures about pensions and other postretirement benefits to its technical agenda in October 1996 in response to concerns about disclosure discussed in the 1994 report of the AICPA Special Committee on Financial Reporting, *Improving Business Reporting—A Customer Focus,* and the July 1995 FASB Prospectus, *Disclosure Effectiveness.* The project's objective was twofold: (a) to improve disclosures about pensions and other postretirement benefits and (b) to determine whether any of the approaches undertaken to improve those disclosures might apply to other accounting topics.

2. Although current disclosure requirements for pensions and other postretirement benefits are extensive, many users of financial statements told the Board in their responses to the Prospectus that the information provided only partly met their needs. Most of those users wanted information that would assist them in (a) evaluating the employer's obligation under pension and other postretirement benefit plans and the effects on the employer's prospects for future cash flows, (b) analyzing the quality of currently reported net income, and (c) estimating future reported net income. The Board concluded that disclosures about pensions and other postretirement benefits could be improved to provide information that is more comparable, understandable, and concise and that would better serve users' needs.

3. This Statement standardizes the disclosure requirements for pensions and other postretirement benefits to the extent practicable. Appendix A contains background information and the basis for the Board's conclusions. Appendix B contains illustrations of suggested formats for presenting the required disclosures.

STANDARDS OF FINANCIAL ACCOUNTING AND REPORTING

Scope

4. This Statement supersedes the disclosure requirements in FASB Statements No. 87, *Employers' Accounting for Pensions,* No. 88, *Employers' Accounting for Settlements and Curtailments of Defined*

Benefit Pension Plans and for Termination Benefits, and No. 106, *Employers' Accounting for Postretirement Benefits Other Than Pensions.*[1] This Statement addresses disclosure only. It does not address measurement or recognition. Information required to be disclosed about pensions and other postretirement benefits shall not be combined except as permitted by paragraph 10 of this Statement.

Disclosures about Pensions and Other Postretirement Benefits

5. An employer that sponsors one or more defined benefit pension plans or one or more defined benefit postretirement plans shall provide the following information:

a. A reconciliation of beginning and ending balances of the benefit obligation[2] showing separately, if applicable, the effects during the period attributable to each of the following: service cost, interest cost, contributions by plan participants, actuarial gains and losses, foreign currency exchange rate changes,[3] benefits paid, plan amendments, business combinations, divestitures, curtailments, settlements, and special termination benefits

b. A reconciliation of beginning and ending balances of the fair value of plan assets showing separately, if applicable, the effects during the period attributable to each of the following: actual return on plan assets, foreign currency exchange rate changes,[4] contributions by the employer, contributions by plan participants, benefits paid, business combinations, divestitures, and settlements

c. The funded status of the plans, the amounts not recognized in the statement of financial position, and the amounts recognized in the statement of financial position, including:

   (1) The amount of any unamortized prior service cost

   (2) The amount of any unrecognized net gain or loss (including asset gains and losses not yet reflected in market-related value)

   (3) The amount of any remaining unamortized, unrecognized net obligation or net asset exist-

ing at the initial date of application of Statement 87 or 106

   (4) The net pension or other postretirement benefit prepaid assets or accrued liabilities

   (5) Any intangible asset and the amount of accumulated other comprehensive income recognized pursuant to paragraph 37 of Statement 87, as amended

d. The amount of net periodic benefit cost recognized, showing separately the service cost component, the interest cost component, the expected return on plan assets for the period, the amortization of the unrecognized transition obligation or transition asset, the amount of recognized gains and losses, the amount of prior service cost recognized, and the amount of gain or loss recognized due to a settlement or curtailment

e. The amount included within other comprehensive income for the period arising from a change in the additional minimum pension liability recognized pursuant to paragraph 37 of Statement 87, as amended

f. On a weighted-average basis, the following assumptions used in the accounting for the plans: assumed discount rate, rate of compensation increase (for pay-related plans), and expected long-term rate of return on plan assets

g. The assumed health care cost trend rate(s) for the next year used to measure the expected cost of benefits covered by the plan (gross eligible charges) and a general description of the direction and pattern of change in the assumed trend rates thereafter, together with the ultimate trend rate(s) and when that rate is expected to be achieved

h. The effect of a one-percentage-point increase and the effect of a one-percentage-point decrease in the assumed health care cost trend rates on (1) the aggregate of the service and interest cost components of net periodic postretirement health care benefit cost and (2) the accumulated postretirement benefit obligation for health care benefits (For purposes of this disclosure, all other assumptions shall be held constant, and the effects shall be measured based on the substantive plan that is the basis for the accounting.)

---

[1]Existing requirements related to withdrawal from multiemployer plans contained in paragraph 70 of Statement 87 and paragraph 83 of Statement 106 are carried forward unchanged and included in paragraph 11 of this Statement.

[2]For defined benefit pension plans, the benefit obligation is the projected benefit obligation—the actuarial present value as of a date of all benefits attributed by the pension benefit formula to employee service rendered prior to that date. For defined benefit postretirement plans, the benefit obligation is the accumulated postretirement benefit obligation—the actuarial present value of benefits attributed to employee service rendered to a particular date.

[3]The effects of foreign currency exchange rate changes that are to be disclosed are those applicable to plans of a foreign operation whose functional currency is not the reporting currency pursuant to FASB Statement No. 52, *Foreign Currency Translation.*

[4] Refer to footnote 3.

i. If applicable, the amounts and types of securities of the employer and related parties included in plan assets, the approximate amount of future annual benefits of plan participants covered by insurance contracts issued by the employer or related parties, and any significant transactions between the employer or related parties and the plan during the period

j. If applicable, any alternative amortization method used to amortize prior service amounts or unrecognized net gains and losses pursuant to paragraphs 26 and 33 of Statement 87 or paragraphs 53 and 60 of Statement 106

k. If applicable, any substantive commitment, such as past practice or a history of regular benefit increases, used as the basis for accounting for the benefit obligation

l. If applicable, the cost of providing special or contractual termination benefits recognized during the period and a description of the nature of the event

m. An explanation of any significant change in the benefit obligation or plan assets not otherwise apparent in the other disclosures required by this Statement.

Amounts related to the employer's results of operations shall be disclosed for each period for which an income statement is presented. Amounts related to the employer's statement of financial position shall be disclosed for each balance sheet presented.

Employers with Two or More Plans

6. The disclosures required by this Statement may be aggregated for all of an employer's defined benefit pension plans and may be aggregated for all of an employer's defined benefit postretirement plans or may be disaggregated in groups if that is considered to provide the most useful information or is otherwise required by paragraph 7. Disclosures about pension plans with assets in excess of the accumulated benefit obligation generally may be aggregated with disclosures about pension plans with accumulated benefit obligations in excess of assets. The same aggregation is permitted for postretirement plans. However, if those disclosures are combined, an employer shall disclose the aggregate benefit obligation and aggregate fair value of plan assets for plans with benefit obligations in excess of plan assets. The aggregate pension accumulated benefit obligation and aggregate fair value of plan assets for pension plans with accumulated benefit obligations in excess of plan assets also shall be disclosed. Disclosure of amounts recognized in the statement of financial position shall present prepaid benefit costs and accrued benefit liabilities separately.

7. An employer may combine disclosures about pension or postretirement benefit plans outside the United States with those for U.S. plans unless the benefit obligations of the plans outside the United States are significant relative to the total benefit obligation and those plans use significantly different assumptions.

Reduced Disclosure Requirements for Nonpublic Entities

8. A nonpublic entity[5] may elect to disclose the following for its pension and other postretirement benefit plans in lieu of the disclosures required by paragraph 5 of this Statement:

a. The benefit obligation, fair value of plan assets, and funded status of the plan

b. Employer contributions, participant contributions, and benefits paid

c. The amounts recognized in the statement of financial position, including the net pension and other postretirement benefit prepaid assets or accrued liabilities and any intangible asset and the amount of accumulated other comprehensive income recognized pursuant to paragraph 37 of Statement 87, as amended

d. The amount of net periodic benefit cost recognized and the amount included within other comprehensive income arising from a change in the minimum pension liability recognized pursuant to paragraph 37 of Statement 87, as amended

e. On a weighted-average basis, the following assumptions used in the accounting for the plans: assumed discount rate, rate of compensation increase (for pay-related plans), and expected long-term rate of return on plan assets

f. The assumed health care cost trend rate(s) for the next year used to measure the expected cost of benefits covered by the plan (gross eligible

---

[5]A nonpublic entity is any entity other than one (a) whose debt or equity securities trade in a public market either on a stock exchange (domestic or foreign) or in the over-the-counter market, including securities quoted only locally or regionally, (b) that makes a filing with a regulatory agency in preparation for the sale of any class of debt or equity securities in a public market, or (c) that is controlled by an entity covered by (a) or (b).

charges) and a general description of the direction and pattern of change in the assumed trend rates thereafter, together with the ultimate trend rate(s) and when that rate is expected to be achieved

g. If applicable, the amounts and types of securities of the employer and related parties included in plan assets, the approximate amount of future annual benefits of plan participants covered by insurance contracts issued by the employer or related parties, and any significant transactions between the employer or related parties and the plan during the period

h. The nature and effect of significant nonroutine events, such as amendments, combinations, divestitures, curtailments, and settlements.

Defined Contribution Plans

9. An employer shall disclose the amount of cost recognized for defined contribution pension or other postretirement benefit plans during the period separately from the amount of cost recognized for defined benefit plans. The disclosures shall include a description of the nature and effect of any significant changes during the period affecting comparability, such as a change in the rate of employer contributions, a business combination, or a divestiture.

Multiemployer Plans

10. An employer shall disclose the amount of contributions to multiemployer plans during the period. An employer may disclose total contributions to multiemployer plans without disaggregating the amounts attributable to pensions and other postretirement benefits. The disclosures shall include a description of the nature and effect of any changes affecting comparability, such as a change in the rate of employer contributions, a business combination, or a divestiture.

11. Paragraph 70 of Statement 87 and paragraph 83 of Statement 106 are carried forward without reconsideration. Paragraphs 70 and 83 read as follows:

In some situations, withdrawal from a multiemployer plan may result in an employer's having an obligation to the plan for a portion of its unfunded benefit obligations. If withdrawal under circumstances that would give rise to an obligation is either probable or

reasonably possible, the provisions of FASB Statement No. 5, *Accounting for Contingencies,* shall apply.

In some situations, withdrawal from a multiemployer plan may result in an employer's having an obligation to the plan for a portion of the plan's unfunded accumulated postretirement benefit obligation. If it is either probable or reasonably possible that (a) an employer would withdraw from the plan under circumstances that would give rise to an obligation or (b) an employer's contribution to the fund would be increased during the remainder of the contract period to make up a shortfall in the funds necessary to maintain the negotiated level of benefit coverage (a "maintenance of benefits" clause), the employer shall apply the provisions of FASB Statement No. 5, *Accounting for Contingencies.*

Amendments to Existing Pronouncements

12. FASB Statement No. 87, *Employers' Accounting for Pensions,* is amended as follows:

a. Paragraph 54 is replaced by the following:

Refer to paragraphs 5 and 8 of FASB Statement No.132, *Employers' Disclosures about Pensions and Other Postretirement Benefits.*

b. Paragraphs 55 and 56 are replaced by the following:

Refer to paragraphs 6 and 7 of Statement 132.

c. Paragraph 65 is replaced by the following:

Refer to paragraph 9 of Statement 132.

d. Paragraph 66 is replaced by the following:

Refer to paragraphs 5 and 8 of Statement 132.

e. Paragraph 69 is replaced by the following:

Refer to paragraph 10 of Statement 132.

13. Paragraph 17 of FASB Statement No. 88, *Employers' Accounting for Settlements and Curtailments of Defined Benefit Pension Plans and for Termination Benefits*, is replaced by the following:

> Refer to paragraphs 5(a), 5(b), 5(d), 5(l), and 8(h) of FASB Statement No. 132, *Employers' Disclosures about Pensions and Other Postretirement Benefits*.

14. FASB Statement No. 106, *Employers' Accounting for Postretirement Benefits Other Than Pensions*, is amended as follows:

a. Paragraph 74 is replaced by the following:

> Refer to paragraphs 5 and 8 of FASB Statement No. 132, *Employers' Disclosures about Pensions and Other Postretirement Benefits*.

b. Paragraphs 77 and 78 are replaced by the following:

> Refer to paragraphs 6 and 7 of Statement 132.

c. Paragraph 82 is replaced by the following:

> Refer to paragraph 10 of Statement 132.

d. Paragraph 106 is replaced by the following:

> Refer to paragraph 9 of Statement 132.

e. Paragraph 107 is replaced by the following:

> Refer to paragraphs 5 and 8 of Statement 132.

Effective Date

15. This Statement shall be effective for fiscal years beginning after December 15, 1997. Earlier application is encouraged. Restatement of disclosures for earlier periods provided for comparative purposes is required unless the information is not readily available, in which case the notes to the financial statements shall include all available information and a description of the information not available.

> **The provisions of this Statement need not be applied to immaterial items.**

This Statement was adopted by the unanimous vote of the seven members of the Financial Accounting Standards Board:

Edmund L. Jenkins, *Chairman*	Anthony T. Cope	James J. Leisenring
	John M. Foster	Gerhard G. Mueller
Joseph V. Anania	Gaylen N. Larson	

Appendix A

BACKGROUND INFORMATION AND BASIS FOR CONCLUSIONS

CONTENTS

Appendix A

BACKGROUND INFORMATION AND BASIS FOR CONCLUSIONS

Introduction

16. This appendix summarizes considerations that were deemed significant by Board members in reaching the conclusions in this Statement. It includes reasons for accepting certain approaches and rejecting others. Individual Board members gave greater weight to some factors than to others. The Board concluded that it could reach an informed decision on the basis of existing information without a public hearing.

17. The AICPA Special Committee on Financial Reporting (Special Committee) issued a report, *Improving Business Reporting—A Customer Focus,* in December 1994. In that report, the Special Committee recommended that "standard setters should search for and eliminate less relevant disclosures." The Special Committee also noted that many users indicated that "they would be willing to give up less important disclosures to make room for more important information."

18. Disclosure effectiveness has been a concern of the Board for some time. FASB documents that have addressed this issue include the 1980 Invitation to Comment, *Financial Statements and Other Means of Financial Reporting,* and the 1981 Exposure Draft, *Reporting Income, Cash Flows, and Financial Position of Business Enterprises.* Board members and FASB staff have written numerous articles on the topic. In addition, disclosure effectiveness was discussed at an April 1995 Financial Accounting Standards Advisory Council (FASAC) meeting and at several liaison meetings during 1995.

19. The Board issued a Prospectus, *Disclosure Effectiveness,* in July 1995. The Prospectus asked readers to consider possible changes to disclosure requirements consistent with one or both of two objectives: to reduce the cost of preparing and disseminating disclosures while providing users with information they need and to eliminate disclosures that are not useful for decision making. The Prospectus also encouraged further research and discussion on improving the effectiveness of financial reporting.

20. The Board received 71 letters in response to the Prospectus. Respondents generally supported a project to improve disclosure effectiveness, and many respondents suggested that pensions, other postretirement benefits, income taxes, and leases were topics that required specific attention. Several respondents suggested that the Board develop a framework for disclosure.

21. At the January 1996 FASAC meeting, several Council members suggested that the Board take an inductive approach to disclosure effectiveness, beginning by evaluating the requirements for disclosure about pensions and other postretirement benefits. A working group of FASAC members was formed to follow up on that suggestion. That group prepared a proposal that was discussed at the July 1996 FASAC meeting and in August 1996 at a public Board meeting with representatives of the Financial Executives Institute, the Association for Investment Management and Research, and other interested parties.

A Conceptual Framework for Disclosure

22. Some participants in the August 1996 meeting did not favor proceeding with a project before defining the general objectives of disclosure. The Board considered developing a framework for disclosure based on FASB Concepts Statement No. 1, *Objectives of Financial Reporting by Business Enterprises,* and a review of published studies but concluded that not enough information was available to formulate a framework at that time. In October 1996, the Board decided to proceed with an inductive approach to disclosure by initiating a project to examine pensions and other postretirement benefits to determine whether disclosures in that specific area could be improved, and, if so, whether any of the approaches undertaken could be applied to other accounting topics.

23. In June 1997, the Board issued an Exposure Draft, *Employers' Disclosures about Pensions and Other Postretirement Benefits.* The Board received 90 comment letters in response to that Exposure Draft. Most respondents supported the Board's goal of improving disclosure effectiveness and generally stated that the revised disclosures proposed in the Exposure Draft were an improvement over those required by Statements 87 and 106. A few respondents noted that they were able to easily apply the requirements of the Exposure Draft to their prior year's pension and other postretirement benefits note disclosures and that the requirements resulted in more understandable disclosure.

General Considerations

24. Discussions with certain users of financial statements indicated that the disclosures required by Statements 87 and 106, although extensive, did not provide sufficient information to understand the changes in the benefit obligation or to analyze the quality of earnings. This Statement is intended to enhance the utility of the information disclosed.

25. As a result of those discussions, the Board identified two distinct sets of information used by analysts. Some requested information that enabled them to analyze the benefit obligation, fair value of plan assets, and changes in both during the period, including unrecognized gains and losses. The Board stated in Statement 87 that it believed that "it would be conceptually appropriate and preferable to recognize a net pension liability or asset measured as the difference between the projected benefit obligation and plan assets, either with no delay in recognition of gains and losses, or perhaps with gains and losses reported currently in comprehensive income but not in earnings" (paragraph 107). However, because Statement 87 did not require that accounting, the Board decided that this Statement should require disclosure of additional information about the changes in the benefit obligation and the fair value of plan assets during the period, including unrecognized gains and losses.

26. The second set of information was most often requested by those analysts who follow publicly traded companies. Those users stated that they needed information about the quality of current earnings, including recognized and unrecognized amounts, that is useful in forecasting earnings for future periods in an effective and efficient manner.

27. This Statement standardizes the disclosure requirements of Statements 87 and 106 to the extent practicable so that the required information should be

easier to prepare and easier to understand. This Statement also suggests a parallel format for presenting information about pensions and other postretirement benefits in a more understandable manner.

Benefits and Costs

28. Most or all of the additional information required by this Statement should be already available in actuarial or accounting calculations used to account for an employer's pension and other postretirement benefit plans. The Board believes that standardizing the format of the disclosures and eliminating some of the current requirements may reduce preparation time. The benefits to users are in the form of additional relevant amounts and reduced time and effort required to read and understand the pension and other postretirement benefit notes to the financial statements.

Specific Disclosure Requirements

Benefit Obligation and Fair Value of Plan Assets

29. The Board concluded in Statements 87 and 106 that disclosure of the benefit obligation and fair value of plan assets is essential to an understanding of the economics of the employer's benefit plans and that disclosure of the fair value of plan assets is useful in assessing management's stewardship responsibilities for efficient use of those assets.

30. Because the obligation and plan assets are offset in determining the amounts recognized in the statement of financial position and offsetting of assets and liabilities generally is not appropriate unless a right of offset exists,[6] disclosure of the amounts offset provides essential information about future economic benefits and sacrifices.

Explanation of the Changes in the Benefit Obligation and the Fair Value of Plan Assets

31. This Statement amends Statements 87 and 106 to include disclosure of the changes in the benefit obligation and plan assets during the period, including the effects of economic events during the period (including amendments, combinations, divestitures, curtailments, and settlements). Statement 87 required disclosure of the nature and effect of significant matters affecting comparability of information for all pe-

riods presented. Statement 106 required the same disclosure but specifically referred to business combinations or divestitures. In practice, those requirements have not resulted in the anticipated level of disclosure. The Board believes that an explanation of the changes in the benefit obligation and fair value of plan assets in the form of a reconciliation of the beginning and ending balances will provide a format for more complete disclosure that also should be more understandable to users of financial statements.

32. Disclosure of the benefit obligation, fair value of plan assets, and changes in them during the period is consistent with the Board's conceptual framework, which states that "financial reporting should provide information about the economic resources of an enterprise, the claims to those resources (obligations of the enterprise to transfer resources to other entities and owners' equity), and the effects of transactions, events, and circumstances that change resources and claims to those resources" (Concepts Statement 1, paragraph 40; footnote reference omitted).

Reconciliation of the Funded Status with the Amounts Recognized in the Financial Statements

33. Both Statement 87 and Statement 106 require a reconciliation of the funded status of the plan with the amounts recognized in the financial statements. The Board considered eliminating those requirements but decided to retain them in this Statement after financial analysts commented that information about unamortized balances of prior service cost and transition amounts is useful in assessing current earnings and forecasting future amortization. The Board also concluded, as it did in Statement 87, that the amount recognized in the financial statements as a net benefit liability or asset does not reflect fully the underlying financial status of the plan and that a reconciliation of the amounts is essential to an understanding of the relationship between the accounting methodology and the funded status of the plan. For those reasons the Board decided to retain disclosure of the unrecognized amounts, including unamortized prior service cost, unamortized transition amounts, and unrecognized gains and losses.

34. If an additional minimum liability is recognized, the reconciliation includes disclosure of any amount recognized as an intangible asset or included in accumulated other comprehensive income. The format

---

[6]Refer to APB Opinion No. 10, *Omnibus Opinion—1966,* paragraph 7.

recommended in Statement 87 disclosed those amounts as an additional minimum liability. The format that is illustrated in this Statement includes all amounts recognized.

Components of Net Periodic Benefit Cost

35. The Exposure Draft proposed eliminating the requirement in Statements 87 and 106 to disclose the components of net periodic benefit cost. Several respondents suggested that that disclosure be retained to provide greater visibility of the amounts included in the employer's results of operations. In addition, certain users, primarily equity analysts, stated that information included in that disclosure was useful in forecasting an employer's net income. In response to those concerns, the Board decided to retain the requirement in Statements 87 and 106 to disclose the components of net periodic benefit cost and to add disclosures about the expected return on plan assets, the amortization of the transition obligation or asset, and the recognition of gains and losses.

Employers with Two or More Plans

36. Both Statement 87 and Statement 106 required additional disclosure of certain benefit plan information if an employer has plans with benefit obligations in excess of plan assets and plans with assets in excess of benefit obligations. Statement 87 required separate schedules reconciling the funded status of the plan with amounts reported in the employer's statement of financial position for plans with assets in excess of accumulated pension benefit obligations and plans with accumulated pension benefit obligations in excess of plan assets. Statement 106 required separate disclosure of the aggregate plan assets and the aggregate benefit obligation of underfunded plans. The Board decided to change the requirements for pension plans to parallel those for other postretirement benefit plans because those requirements are less complex and provide satisfactory information about the financial position of an employer's plans. The Board decided to retain disclosure of the accumulated pension benefit obligation for pension plans with accumulated benefit obligations in excess of plan assets because that disclosure is useful to regulators and other users of financial information. The Board included a requirement to disclose separately amounts recognized as prepaid benefit costs and accrued benefit costs so that users could determine the amounts included in the statement of financial position.

37. Some respondents to the Exposure Draft, including preparers, disagreed with the Board's decision to permit aggregation of disclosures about plans with different characteristics. They stated that users of financial statements could draw incorrect conclusions about an employer's funding policies or that employers would be able to offset underfunded plans with well-funded plans. The Board decided that permitting the aggregation of disclosures about multiple plans will simplify disclosure and will conform disclosures about pensions to those about other postretirement plans while continuing to provide users with sufficient information about the employer's plans. The Board also noted that, while aggregation of disclosures about plans is permitted by this Statement, an employer may disclose additional disaggregated information if the employer believes doing so provides more meaningful information.

Foreign Plans

38. Statement 87 specified that disclosures about plans outside the United States should not be combined with those about U.S. plans unless those plans use similar assumptions. Statement 106 required separate presentation for foreign plans if the benefit obligations are significant relative to the total benefit obligation for all plans. The Board decided to harmonize those disclosures with this Statement. Accordingly, the Board decided that disclosures about U.S. plans may be combined with those about foreign plans unless the benefit obligations of the foreign plans are significant relative to the employer's total benefit obligation and those plans use significantly different assumptions.

39. Some respondents to the Exposure Draft noted that some foreign plans typically are not funded because there are no tax advantages to funding plans in those jurisdictions. Those respondents suggested that the benefit obligation related to foreign plans be disclosed separately because combining disclosures about foreign and U.S. plans might be misleading. The Board believes that the requirements of paragraph 6 of this Statement will adequately inform users about the presence of underfunded plans. The Board also decided that whether aggregation of disclosures about underfunded plans was appropriate should not depend on whether the plans are located within the United States or abroad.

Assumed Health Care Cost Trend Rates

40. Statement 106 requires disclosure of the assumed health care cost trend rate for the next year

used to measure the expected cost of benefits covered by the plan (gross eligible charges) and a general description of the direction and pattern of change in assumed trend rates thereafter, together with the ultimate trend rate and when that rate was expected to be achieved. All other requirements for disclosure of plan assumptions in Statements 87 and 106 call for disclosure of weighted-average rates. The Exposure Draft that led to Statement 106 proposed disclosure of a weighted average of the assumed health care cost trend rates, but in its deliberations the Board decided that a weighted-average rate can mask differences in an employer's assumptions about year-by-year health care cost trend rates. In the Exposure Draft that led to this Statement, the Board reconsidered the disclosure requirement for assumed health care cost trend rates and decided that disclosure of a weighted-average rate would provide for better comparability among entities and with other assumptions that are disclosed on a weighted-average basis.

41. Some respondents to the Exposure Draft stated that the cost of calculating that disclosure could be significant and argued that the increased cost was not justified in the circumstances. Others reiterated the comments made prior to the issuance of Statement 106 about the potential for the use of a weighted-average rate to mask differences in year-by-year health care cost assumptions. Although some Board members continue to believe that disclosure of the weighted-average rate is more effective, the Board ultimately decided that the disclosures about health care cost trend rate assumptions in Statement 106 provide satisfactory information and that disclosure of a weighted-average measure should not be required, primarily because of respondents' assertions about the incremental cost to provide that information.

The Effects of a One-Percentage-Point Change in the Assumed Health Care Cost Trend Rates

42. Statement 106 requires disclosure of the effects of a one-percentage-point increase in the assumed health care cost trend rates for each future year on (a) the aggregate of the service and interest cost components of net periodic postretirement health care benefit cost and (b) the accumulated postretirement benefit obligation for health care benefits. The Board decided to retain the sensitivity analysis disclosure in Statement 106 and, in addition, to require disclosure of the effects of a one-percentage-point decrease in the assumed health care cost trend rates on (a) the aggregate of the service and interest cost components of

net periodic postretirement health care benefit cost and (b) the accumulated postretirement benefit obligation for health care benefits. Most respondents to the Exposure Draft commented on that additional disclosure requirement. The majority stated that the effects of a one-percentage-point decrease should not be required, and many respondents opposed any sensitivity information.

43. Some Board members questioned the usefulness of a disclosure that focuses on the effects of a change in a single assumption underlying the calculation of the benefit obligation. They noted that calculating the accumulated postretirement benefit obligation requires numerous assumptions and estimates. Changes in certain of those assumptions and estimates may have a much more significant effect on the employer's obligation than changes in the assumed heath care cost trend rates. Moreover, those Board members noted that many assumptions and estimates underlie an entity's financial statements and that one should not focus on the change in a single factor to the exclusion of others that may be equally or more important. Those Board members advocated eliminating the sensitivity analysis as described in the Exposure Draft in favor of examining outside of this project the broader issue of disclosures about risks and uncertainties.

44. Those Board members also noted that the disclosure of a one-percentage-point increase required by Statement 106 was included in that Statement because, at the time, ". . . users [were] considerably less familiar with postretirement health care measurements than with pension measurements and with the subjectivity of the health care cost trend rate and the significant effect that assumption may have on measurement of the postretirement health care obligation" (paragraph 355). Those Board members believe that users are now sufficiently familiar with the effects of changes in health care trend rates on the postretirement health care obligation and, therefore, this disclosure is no longer useful. Accordingly, they expressed strong reservations about retaining it in this Statement.

45. However, a majority of the Board concluded that disclosure of the effects of a one-percentage-point increase and a one-percentage-point decrease in the assumed health care cost trend rate provides useful information to users of financial statements. As previously stated in Statement 106, requiring ". . . sensitivity information will assist users in assessing the comparability of information reported by

different employers as well as the extent to which future changes in assumptions or actual experience different from that assumed may affect the measurement of the obligation and cost. In addition, the sensitivity information may assist users in understanding the relative significance of an employer's cost-sharing policy as encompassed by the employer's substantive plan" (paragraph 354). The Board concluded that those considerations remain relevant today. It noted that sensitivity disclosures are consistent with the recommendations of the AICPA Special Committee for improved disclosure about the uncertainty inherent in the measurement of certain assets and liabilities. Some Board members also noted that the effects of a one-percentage-point change in a plan's assumed health care cost trend rate would be difficult to assess because the way in which health care cost assumptions interact with caps, cost-sharing provisions, and other factors in the plan precludes reasonable estimates of the effects of those changes. The effects of changes in other assumptions, such as the weighted-average discount rate, can be more easily approximated.

46. The Board decided to retain the requirement to disclose the effects of both an increase and a decrease in the assumed health care cost trend rates because the effects of an increase and a decrease are not necessarily symmetrical for a plan due to the way in which health care cost assumptions interact with caps or other cost-sharing provisions and for other reasons. In addition, because the growth in the rate of health care costs has decreased for many plans since the issuance of Statement 106, disclosure of the effects of a decrease in the assumed health care cost trend rates may provide more relevant information than the effects of an increase.

Related Party Transactions

47. Both Statement 87 and Statement 106 required disclosure of the amounts and types of securities of the employer and related parties included in plan assets and the approximate amount of future annual benefits of plan participants covered by insurance contracts issued by the employer or related parties. The Board decided to retain those disclosure requirements in this Statement. The Board also decided to require added disclosures about any significant transactions between the plan and the employer during the period, including noncash transactions, because of the relevance of information about related

party transactions, as described in the basis for conclusions to FASB Statement No. 57, *Related Party Disclosures.*

Other Disclosures Considered

Concentrations of Market Risk

48. The Board considered whether an employer should disclose concentrations of market risk in plan assets. FASB Statement No. 124, *Accounting for Certain Investments Held by Not-for-Profit Organizations,* requires disclosure of the nature of and carrying amount for each individual investment or group of investments that represents a significant concentration of market risk. The Board concluded that disclosures needed about plan assets differ from those about investments held by not-for-profit organizations because trustees of benefit plans are usually constrained to follow policies for the sole benefit of the plan beneficiaries, whereas fund managers of not-for-profit organizations may be constrained only by donor restrictions. Also, provisions of the Employee Retirement Income Security Act generally require that plan trustees diversify plan investments. Consequently, the usefulness of that disclosure requirement for U.S. plans could be limited.

49. Several respondents to the Exposure Draft asked that the Board also consider requiring disclosure of the composition of plan assets as a means of enabling users to assess concentrations of risk in the plan's portfolio. The Board noted that disclosure of the type of information about plan assets that would be required to enable the user to identify and assess concentrations of risk would be extensive, in certain circumstances requiring disclosure about individual securities. The Board decided that requiring extensive disclosures about the composition of plan assets in the employer's financial statements would add significant complexity to the disclosure and was generally inconsistent with its objective of promoting more effective disclosure.

Components of the Benefit Obligation

50. Statements 87 and 106 required disclosure of several components of the benefit obligation. Statement 87 required disclosure of the accumulated pension benefit obligation and the vested pension benefit obligation. Statement 106 required disclosure of the portions of the plan obligation attributable to retirees, other fully eligible plan participants, and other active plan participants.

51. Disclosure of the accumulated pension benefit obligation and vested pension benefit obligation was considered relevant when Statement 87 was issued because there was less agreement at that time as to the best measure of the pension benefit obligation. Some respondents to the Exposure Draft that led to Statement 87 would have limited the recognized liability to the vested pension benefit obligation. In the deliberations preceding the issuance of Statement 87, the Board considered a minimum liability based on the vested pension benefit obligation but concluded that the time at which benefits vest should not be the primary point for recognition of either cost or liabilities. The disclosure requirements of Statement 106 for the portion attributable to retirees, other fully eligible plan participants, and other active plan participants are proxies for disclosure of the vested and nonvested benefit obligation for other postretirement benefit obligations.

52. The Board decided to eliminate the requirement to disclose (a) accumulated pension benefit obligations for plans with assets that exceed that amount, (b) vested pension benefit obligations, and (c) the portions of other postretirement benefit plan obligations attributable to retirees, other fully eligible plan participants, and other active plan participants. None of those amounts are used to forecast pension or other postretirement benefit costs or obligations, and, therefore, those amounts have limited relevance to users of financial statements. The Board decided to retain disclosure of the accumulated pension benefit obligation for plans with accumulated pension benefit obligations in excess of plan assets because that component is used to determine the minimum liability and may be relevant to users of financial statements.

General Descriptive Information

53. Both Statement 87 and Statement 106 required disclosure of general descriptive information about the employer's benefit plans, including employee groups covered, type of benefit formula, funding policy, types of assets held, and significant nonbenefit liabilities, if any. This Statement does not require that disclosure because the Board believes it provides only limited useful information to users of financial statements due to the general nature of the information provided, particularly after aggregating information about multiple plans with different characteristics. In lieu of that disclosure, this Statement requires disclosure of significant events occurring during the period that are otherwise not apparent in the disclo-

sures, as that information is more relevant to users of financial statements. Several respondents to the Exposure Draft stated that the description of the plan required by Statements 87 and 106 can provide useful information about the plan. The Board therefore encourages an employer to provide a description of its plans if such a description would provide meaningful information, such as when the employer sponsors only a single plan.

Materiality

54. The Board considered whether this Statement should include a materiality threshold for requiring certain disclosures about pension and other postretirement benefit plans. Materiality and relevance are both defined in terms of what influences or makes a difference to a decision maker. The Board's position is that "no general standards of materiality could be formulated to take into account all the considerations that enter into an experienced human judgment," but that quantitative materiality criteria may be given by the Board in specific standards, as appropriate (FASB Concepts Statement No. 2, *Qualitative Characteristics of Accounting Information,* paragraph 131).

55. The Board considered implementing materiality thresholds for pension and other postretirement benefit disclosures, including thresholds based on the gross obligations for plan benefits and the employer's assets, equity, revenues, or net income. Each measure had disadvantages. Because a materiality threshold should take into account the information most likely to influence or make a difference to a decision maker, net income appeared to be the most relevant element for publicly traded companies. Some analysts use information about current benefit costs and the funded status of the plan to assess the quality of current earnings and the employer's financial condition. They also use that information to prepare their forecasts of future earnings, measuring the impact on net income as precisely as possible. The Board concluded that a precise threshold in terms of net income was not practicable because of the natural volatility of net income and the resulting difficulty in making materiality judgments with a relatively simple materiality rule. Therefore, this Statement does not include a materiality threshold. However, that does not imply that the provisions of this Statement must be applied to immaterial items. Some entities may determine that some or all pension or other postretirement benefit disclosures are not material after evaluation of all the relevant facts and circumstances.

Nonpublic Entities

56. The *Report of the Committee on Generally Accepted Accounting Principles for Smaller and/or Closely Held Businesses,* issued by the AICPA in August 1976, observed that some disclosures merely provide additional or analytical data and may not be appropriate for all entities. The Committee also observed, however, that analytical data may be appropriate in certain circumstances for certain types of entities.

57. Before issuing the Exposure Draft, the Board had asked certain users of financial statements of nonpublic entities to comment on the usefulness of current and proposed disclosure requirements. Those users observed that they did not require the same level of precision in assessing benefit costs and net income when analyzing the financial statements of nonpublic entities but that they did rely on information about the benefit obligations, assets, and cash flows. Based on the input of those users, the Board concluded that a reduced disclosure set would be appropriate for nonpublic entities. The Board determined that a nonpublic entity should, at a minimum, provide the same information about the benefit obligations, plan assets, recognized assets or liabilities, cash flows, benefit costs, actuarial assumptions, and related party transactions as required for a public entity.

58. The Exposure Draft would have required that a nonpublic entity disclose all of the information in paragraph 5 if total unrecognized pension and other postretirement benefit amounts exceeded 5 percent of equity (or unrestricted net assets). Many respondents objected to that provision out of concern that it might be viewed as the establishment of a materiality standard that could be applied in other circumstances. The Board decided not to require that disclosure but, rather, to provide for reduced disclosures for all nonpublic entities. The Board concluded that introducing a specific threshold was therefore unnecessary.

59. However, because nonpublic entities are not required to provide a reconciliation of the benefit obligation or the fair value of plan assets under the provisions of this Statement, the Board decided to require disclosure of information about the effects of significant nonroutine events during the period, such as amendments, combinations, divestitures, curtailments, and settlements, whenever those events occur. The Board believes that that disclosure is necessary for users of financial statements to understand the effects of those changes that otherwise might not be apparent. Even though this Statement permits reduced disclosures for nonpublic entities, the Board concluded that the incremental information required by paragraph 5 improves understanding and, therefore, encourages those entities to disclose that information.

Effective Date and Transition

60. This Statement is effective for fiscal years beginning after December 15, 1997. Earlier application is encouraged. The Board decided that the disclosures required by this Statement should be provided for earlier periods presented for comparative purposes, unless that information is not readily available. The Board believes that application of this Statement should not impose a hardship on most preparers of financial statements because the systems necessary to provide most, if not all, of the required disclosures are already in place. For that reason, disclosure of comparable prior-year information should not be difficult for most entities.

Appendix B

ILLUSTRATIONS

61. This appendix provides examples that illustrate a parallel format for presenting pension and other postretirement benefit disclosures in a single note to the financial statements. The items presented in these examples have been included for illustrative purposes. However, items may be combined if individually immaterial. The illustrations in this appendix supersede Illustration 6 in Statement 87 and Illustration 7 in Statement 106.

Illustration 1—Disclosures about Pension and Other Postretirement Benefit Plans

62. The following illustrates the 20X2 financial statement disclosures for an employer (Company A) with multiple defined benefit pension and other post-retirement benefit plans. There is no additional minimum pension liability required to be recognized. During 20X2, the employer had an acquisition and made amendments to the plans.

	Pension Benefits		Other Benefits	
	20X2	20X1	20X2	20X1
Change in benefit obligation				
Benefit obligation at beginning of year	$1,266	$1,200	$ 738	$ 700
Service cost	76	72	36	32
Interest cost	114	108	65	63
Plan participants' contributions			20	13
Amendments	120		75	
Actuarial gain	(25)		(24)	
Acquisition	900		600	
Benefits paid	(125)	(114)	(90)	(70)
Benefit obligation at end of year	2,326	1,266	1,420	738
Change in plan assets				
Fair value of plan assets at beginning of year	1,068	880	206	87
Actual return on plan assets	29	188	(3)	24
Acquisition	1,000		25	
Employer contribution	75	114	171	152
Plan participants' contributions			20	13
Benefits paid	(125)	(114)	(90)	(70)
Fair value of plan assets at end of year	2,047	1,068	329	206
Funded status	(279)	(198)	(1,091)	(532)
Unrecognized net actuarial loss	83	38	59	60
Unrecognized prior service cost	260	160	585	540
Prepaid (accrued) benefit cost	$ 64	$ 0	$ (447)	$ 68

	Pension Benefits		Other Benefits	
	20X2	20X1	20X2	20X1
Weighted-average assumptions as of December 31				
Discount rate	9.25%	9.00%	9.00%	9.00%
Expected return on plan assets	10.00	10.00	10.00	10.00
Rate of compensation increase	5.00	5.00		

For measurement purposes, a 10 percent annual rate of increase in the per capita cost of covered health care benefits was assumed for 20X3. The rate was assumed to decrease gradually to 4 percent for 20X9 and remain at that level thereafter.

	Pension Benefits		Other Benefits	
	20X2	**20X1**	**20X2**	**20X1**
Components of net periodic benefit cost				
Service cost	$ 76	$ 72	$ 36	$ 32
Interest cost	114	108	65	63
Expected return on plan assets	(107)	(88)	(21)	(9)
Amortization of prior service cost	20	20	30	30
Recognized net actuarial loss	8	2	1	1
Net periodic benefit cost	$ 111	$114	$111	$117

Company A acquired FV Industries on December 31, 20X2, including its pension and postretirement benefit plans. The company's plans were amended on December 31, 20X2, to establish parity with the benefits provided by FV Industries.

The company has multiple nonpension postretirement benefit plans. The health care plans are contributory, with participants' contributions adjusted annually; the life insurance plans are noncontributory. The accounting for the health care plans anticipates future cost-sharing changes to the written plan that are consistent with the company's expressed intent to increase retiree contributions each year by 50 percent of the excess of the expected general inflation rate over 6 percent. On December 31, 20X2, the company amended its postretirement health care plans to provide long-term care coverage.

Assumed health care cost trend rates have a significant effect on the amounts reported for the health care plans. A one-percentage-point change in assumed health care cost trend rates would have the following effects:

	1-Percentage-Point Increase	1-Percentage-Point Decrease
Effect on total of service and interest cost components	$ 22	$ (20)
Effect on postretirement benefit obligation	173	(156)

Illustration 2—Disclosures for an Employer That Recognizes a Minimum Liability

63. The following illustrates the 20X2 financial statement disclosures if an employer (Company B) has multiple benefit plans including one pension plan for which the employer must recognize an additional minimum liability in accordance with the provisions of paragraph 36 of Statement 87. As of December 31, 20X2, the assumptions are as follows:

- The accrued pension benefit cost for the underfunded plan is $89.

- The minimum liability is $153; thus, the additional minimum liability is $64. The additional minimum liability was $53 in the prior year.
- The total unrecognized transition obligation for the underfunded plan is $50.
- The entry to record the change in the additional minimum liability for the period is:

Other comprehensive income	14
Intangible asset	3
Accrued pension benefit cost	11

	Pension Benefits		Other Benefits	
	20X2	**20X1**	**20X2**	**20X1**
Change in benefit obligation				
Benefit obligation at beginning of year	$1,266	$1,200	$ 738	$ 700
Service cost	76	72	36	32
Interest cost	114	108	65	63
Plan participants' contributions			20	13
Amendments	(20)			
Actuarial gain	(25)		(24)	
Benefits paid	(125)	(114)	(90)	(70)
Benefit obligation at end of year	1,286	1,266	745	738
Change in plan assets				
Fair value of plan assets at beginning of year	1,156	968	206	87
Actual return on plan assets	29	188	(3)	24
Employer contribution	139	114	171	152
Plan participants' contributions			20	13
Benefits paid	(125)	(114)	(90)	(70)
Fair value of plan assets at end of year	1,199	1,156	304	206
Funded status	(87)	(110)	(441)	(532)
Unrecognized actuarial loss	83	38	59	60
Unrecognized prior service cost	170	225	510	540
Net amount recognized	$ 166	$ 153	$ 128	$ 68
Amounts recognized in the statement of financial position consist of:				
Prepaid benefit cost	$ 255	$ 227	$ 128	$ 68
Accrued benefit liability	(153)	(127)		
Intangible asset	50	53		
Accumulated other comprehensive income	14			
Net amount recognized	$ 166	$ 153	$ 128	$ 68

	Pension Benefits		Other Benefits	
	20X2	**20X1**	**20X2**	**20X1**
Weighted-average assumptions as of December 31				
Discount rate	9.25%	9.00%	9.00%	9.00%
Expected return on plan assets	10.00	10.00	10.00	10.00
Rate of compensation increase	5.00	5.00		

For measurement purposes, a 10 percent annual rate of increase in the per capita cost of covered health care benefits was assumed for 20X3. The rate was assumed to decrease gradually to 4 percent for 20X9 and remain at that level thereafter.

	Pension Benefits		Other Benefits	
	20X2	**20X1**	**20X2**	**20X1**
Components of net periodic benefit cost				
Service cost	$ 76	$ 72	$ 36	$ 32
Interest cost	114	108	65	63
Expected return on plan assets	(116)	(97)	(21)	(9)
Amortization of prior service cost	35	35	30	30
Recognized actuarial loss	17	11	1	1
Net periodic benefit cost	$ 126	$129	$111	$117

The projected benefit obligation, accumulated benefit obligation, and fair value of plan assets for the pension plan with accumulated benefit obligations in excess of plan assets were $263, $237, and $84, respectively, as of December 31, 20X2, and $247, $222, and $95, respectively, as of December 31, 20X1.

Company B has multiple nonpension postretirement benefit plans. The health care plan is contributory with participants' contributions adjusted annually; the life insurance plan is noncontributory. The accounting for the health care plan anticipates future cost-sharing changes to the written plan that are consistent with the company's expressed intent to increase retiree contributions each year by 50 percent of the excess of the expected general inflation rate over 6 percent. On December 31, 20X2, the company amended its postretirement health care plan to provide long-term-care coverage and amended its pension plan to change the benefit formula.

Assumed health care cost trend rates have a significant effect on the amounts reported for the health care plan. A one-percentage-point change in assumed health care cost trend rates would have the following effects:

	1-Percentage-Point Increase	1-Percentage-Point Decrease
Effect on total of service and interest cost components	$11	$(10)
Effect on postretirement benefit obligation	89	(80)

Illustration 3—Alternative Disclosure for a Nonpublic Entity

64. The following illustrates the 20X2 financial statement disclosures that could be provided by Company A if it were a nonpublic entity.

	Pension Benefits		Other Benefits	
	20X2	**20X1**	**20X2**	**20X1**
Benefit obligation at December 31	$2,326	$1,266	$ 1,420	$ 738
Fair value of plan assets at December 31	2,047	1,068	329	206
Funded status	$ (279)	$ (198)	$(1,091)	$(532)
Prepaid (accrued) benefit cost recognized in the statement of financial position	$ 64	$ 0	$ (447)	$ 68

	Pension Benefits		Other Benefits	
	20X2	**20X1**	**20X2**	**20X1**
Weighted-average assumptions as of December 31				
Discount rate	9.25%	9.00%	9.00%	9.00%
Expected return on plan assets	10.00	10.00	10.00	10.00
Rate of compensation increase	5.00	5.00		

For measurement purposes, a 10 percent annual rate of increase in the per capita cost of covered health care benefits was assumed for 20X3. The rate was assumed to decrease gradually to 4 percent for 20X9 and remain at that level thereafter.

	Pension Benefits		Other Benefits	
	20X2	**20X1**	**20X2**	**20X1**
Benefit cost	$111	$114	$111	$117
Employer contribution	75	114	171	152
Plan participants' contributions			20	13
Benefits paid	125	114	90	70

The company acquired FV Industries on December 31, 20X2, increasing the pension benefit obligation by $900 and pension plan assets by $1,000 and increasing the other postretirement benefit obligation by $600 and related plan assets by $25. Amendments during the year to the company's plans increased the pension benefit obligation by $120 and the other postretirement benefit obligation by $75.

FAS133

Statement of Financial Accounting Standards No. 133
Accounting for Derivative Instruments
and Hedging Activities

STATUS

Issued: June 1998

Effective Date: For all fiscal quarters of all fiscal years beginning after June 15, 1999 (Deferred to all fiscal quarters of all fiscal years beginning after June 15, 2000 by FAS 137)

Affects: Amends ARB 43, Chapter 4, paragraph 8
Amends FAS 52 by adding paragraph 14A before paragraph 15
Amends FAS 52, paragraphs 15, 16, 30, 31(b), and 162
Supersedes FAS 52, paragraphs 17 through 19 and 21
Amends FAS 60, paragraphs 46 and 50
Amends FAS 65, paragraphs 4 and 9(a)
Supersedes FAS 65, paragraph 9(b)(1)
Supersedes FAS 80
Amends FAS 95, footnote 4
Supersedes FAS 105
Supersedes FAS 107, paragraph 4
Amends FAS 107, paragraphs 10, 13, and 31
Amends FAS 107 by adding paragraphs 15A through 15D after paragraph 15
Amends FAS 113, paragraph 28
Amends FAS 115, paragraphs 4, 13, 15(b), 16, 19 through 22, 115, and 137
Supersedes FAS 119
Amends FAS 124, paragraphs 3, 5, 6, and 112 and footnote 6
Amends FAS 125, paragraphs 4, 14, 31, and 243
Supersedes FAS 126, paragraph 2(c)
Supersedes FTB 79-19, paragraph 6

Affected by: Paragraphs 10(b), 33, 36(b), 40(a), 52(b), 68(l), 155, and 197 superseded by FAS 138
Paragraphs 10(f) and 56 and footnote 9 amended by FAS 140
Paragraphs 11(c) and 29(f) amended by FAS 141
Paragraphs 12, 21(c)(1), 21(d), 21(f), 21(f)(2) through 21(f)(4), 29(d), 29(e), 29(g)(2), 29(h), 29(h)(1) through 29(h)(4), 30, 36, 36(a), 37, 38, 40, 40(b), 42, and 45(b)(4) amended by FAS 138
Paragraph 36A added after paragraph 36, paragraph 37A added after paragraph 37, and paragraphs 40A through 40C added after paragraph 40 by FAS 138
Paragraph 48 amended by FAS 137
Paragraph 50 superseded by FAS 137
Paragraphs 54, 58(b), 58(c)(2), 61(d), 61(e), 68, 68(b), 90, 115, 134, 161, 169, 200, and 540 and footnotes 14 and 19 amended by FAS 138
Paragraph 59(e) amended by FAS 140 and FAS 145
Paragraphs 120A through 120D added after paragraph 120 by FAS 138

Issues Discussed by FASB Emerging Issues Task Force (EITF)

Affects: Nullifies EITF Issues No. 84-14, 84-36, 86-34, 87-2, 87-26, 91-1, and 95-2 and Topics No. D-16, D-22, and D-64

Partially nullifies EITF Issues No. 84-4, 84-5, 84-7, 85-9, 85-20, 85-25, 85-27, 85-29, 86-15, 86-21, 86-28, 88-8, 88-9, 88-18, 89-11, 90-17, 90-19, 91-6, 92-2, 96-11, 96-12, 96-15, 96-17, 97-7, 98-5, and 98-10 and Topic No. D-50

Resolves EITF Issues No. 84-31, 86-26, 87-1, 91-4, 93-10, and 95-11

Partially resolves EITF Issues No. 84-7, 84-20, 85-9, 85-23, 86-28, 88-8, and 90-22

Interpreted by: Paragraph 11(a) interpreted by EITF Issues No. 99-1 and 01-6

Paragraphs 20(a), 28(a), 30(b), and 62 interpreted by EITF Topic No. D-102

Related Issues: EITF Issues No. 86-25, 97-8, 97-15, 98-10, 98-12, 99-2, 99-7, 99-8, 99-9, 00-4, 00-6, 00-8, 00-9, 00-17, 00-18, 00-19, 01-11, 01-12, 02-2, and 02-8 and Topics No. D-51, D-71, D-73, and D-98

SUMMARY

This Statement establishes accounting and reporting standards for derivative instruments, including certain derivative instruments embedded in other contracts, (collectively referred to as derivatives) and for hedging activities. It requires that an entity recognize all derivatives as either assets or liabilities in the statement of financial position and measure those instruments at fair value. If certain conditions are met, a derivative may be specifically designated as (a) a hedge of the exposure to changes in the fair value of a recognized asset or liability or an unrecognized firm commitment, (b) a hedge of the exposure to variable cash flows of a forecasted transaction, or (c) a hedge of the foreign currency exposure of a net investment in a foreign operation, an unrecognized firm commitment, an available-for-sale security, or a foreign-currency-denominated forecasted transaction.

The accounting for changes in the fair value of a derivative (that is, gains and losses) depends on the intended use of the derivative and the resulting designation.

- For a derivative designated as hedging the exposure to changes in the fair value of a recognized asset or liability or a firm commitment (referred to as a fair value hedge), the gain or loss is recognized in earnings in the period of change together with the offsetting loss or gain on the hedged item attributable to the risk being hedged. The effect of that accounting is to reflect in earnings the extent to which the hedge is not effective in achieving offsetting changes in fair value.
- For a derivative designated as hedging the exposure to variable cash flows of a forecasted transaction (referred to as a cash flow hedge), the effective portion of the derivative's gain or loss is initially reported as a component of other comprehensive income (outside earnings) and subsequently reclassified into earnings when the forecasted transaction affects earnings. The ineffective portion of the gain or loss is reported in earnings immediately.
- For a derivative designated as hedging the foreign currency exposure of a net investment in a foreign operation, the gain or loss is reported in other comprehensive income (outside earnings) as part of the cumulative translation adjustment. The accounting for a fair value hedge described above applies to a derivative designated as a hedge of the foreign currency exposure of an unrecognized firm commitment or an available-for-sale security. Similarly, the accounting for a cash flow hedge described above applies to a derivative designated as a hedge of the foreign currency exposure of a foreign-currency-denominated forecasted transaction.
- For a derivative not designated as a hedging instrument, the gain or loss is recognized in earnings in the period of change.

Under this Statement, an entity that elects to apply hedge accounting is required to establish at the inception of the hedge the method it will use for assessing the effectiveness of the hedging derivative and the measurement approach for determining the ineffective aspect of the hedge. Those methods must be consistent with the entity's approach to managing risk.

This Statement applies to all entities. A not-for-profit organization should recognize the change in fair value of all derivatives as a change in net assets in the period of change. In a fair value hedge, the changes in the fair value of the hedged item attributable to the risk being hedged also are recognized. However, because of the format of their statement of financial performance, not-for-profit organizations are not permitted special hedge accounting for derivatives used to hedge forecasted transactions. This Statement does not address how a not-for-profit organization should determine the components of an operating measure if one is presented.

This Statement precludes designating a nonderivative financial instrument as a hedge of an asset, liability, unrecognized firm commitment, or forecasted transaction except that a nonderivative instrument denominated in a foreign currency may be designated as a hedge of the foreign currency exposure of an unrecognized firm commitment denominated in a foreign currency or a net investment in a foreign operation.

This Statement amends FASB Statement No. 52, *Foreign Currency Translation,* to permit special accounting for a hedge of a foreign currency forecasted transaction with a derivative. It supersedes FASB Statements No. 80, *Accounting for Futures Contracts,* No. 105, *Disclosure of Information about Financial Instruments with Off-Balance-Sheet Risk and Financial Instruments with Concentrations of Credit Risk,* and No. 119, *Disclosure about Derivative Financial Instruments and Fair Value of Financial Instruments.* It amends FASB Statement No. 107, *Disclosures about Fair Value of Financial Instruments,* to include in Statement 107 the disclosure provisions about concentrations of credit risk from Statement 105. This Statement also nullifies or modifies the consensuses reached in a number of issues addressed by the Emerging Issues Task Force.

This Statement is effective for all fiscal quarters of fiscal years beginning after June 15, 1999. Initial application of this Statement should be as of the beginning of an entity's fiscal quarter; on that date, hedging relationships must be designated anew and documented pursuant to the provisions of this Statement. Earlier application of all of the provisions of this Statement is encouraged, but it is permitted only as of the beginning of any fiscal quarter that begins after issuance of this Statement. This Statement should not be applied retroactively to financial statements of prior periods.

Statement of Financial Accounting Standards No. 133

Accounting for Derivative Instruments and Hedging Activities

CONTENTS

INTRODUCTION

1. This Statement addresses the accounting for **derivative instruments,**[1] including certain derivative instruments embedded in other contracts, and hedging activities.

2. Prior to this Statement, hedging activities related to changes in foreign exchange rates were addressed in FASB Statement No. 52, *Foreign Currency Translation.* FASB Statement No. 80, *Accounting for Futures Contracts,* addressed the use of futures contracts in other hedging activities. Those Statements addressed only certain derivative instruments and differed in the criteria required for hedge accounting. In addition, the Emerging Issues Task Force (EITF) addressed the accounting for various hedging activities in a number of issues.

3. In developing the standards in this Statement, the Board concluded that the following four fundamental decisions should serve as cornerstones underlying those standards:

a. Derivative instruments represent rights or obligations that meet the definitions of assets or liabilities and should be reported in financial statements.
b. **Fair value** is the most relevant measure for **financial instruments** and the only relevant measure for derivative instruments. Derivative instruments should be measured at fair value, and adjustments to the carrying amount of hedged items should reflect changes in their fair value (that is, gains or losses) that are attributable to the risk being hedged and that arise while the hedge is in effect.
c. Only items that are assets or liabilities should be reported as such in financial statements.
d. Special accounting for items designated as being hedged should be provided only for qualifying items. One aspect of qualification should be an assessment of the expectation of effective offsetting changes in fair values or cash flows during the term of the hedge for the risk being hedged.

Those fundamental decisions are discussed individually in paragraphs 217–231 of Appendix C.

4. This Statement standardizes the accounting for derivative instruments, including certain derivative instruments embedded in other contracts, by requiring that an entity recognize those items as assets or liabilities in the statement of financial position and measure them at fair value. If certain conditions are met, an entity may elect to designate a derivative instrument as follows:

a. A hedge of the exposure to changes in the fair value of a recognized asset or liability, or of an unrecognized **firm commitment,**[2] that are attributable to a particular risk (referred to as a fair value hedge)
b. A hedge of the exposure to variability in the cash flows of a recognized asset or liability, or of a **forecasted transaction,** that is attributable to a particular risk (referred to as a cash flow hedge)
c. A hedge of the foreign currency exposure of (1) an unrecognized firm commitment (a foreign currency fair value hedge), (2) an available-for-sale security (a foreign currency fair value hedge), (3) a forecasted transaction (a foreign currency cash flow hedge), or (4) a net investment in a foreign operation.

This Statement generally provides for matching the timing of gain or loss recognition on the hedging instrument with the recognition of (a) the changes in the fair value of the hedged asset or liability that are attributable to the hedged risk or (b) the earnings effect of the hedged forecasted transaction. Appendix A provides guidance on identifying derivative instruments subject to the scope of this Statement and on assessing hedge effectiveness and is an integral part of the standards provided in this Statement. Appendix B contains examples that illustrate application of this Statement. Appendix C contains background information and the basis for the Board's conclusions. Appendix D lists the accounting pronouncements superseded or amended by this Statement. Appendix E provides a diagram for determining whether a contract is a freestanding derivative subject to the scope of this Statement.

[1] Words defined in Appendix F, the glossary, are set in **boldface type** the first time they appear.

[2] An unrecognized firm commitment can be viewed as an executory contract that represents both a right and an obligation. When a previously unrecognized firm commitment that is designated as a hedged item is accounted for in accordance with this Statement, an asset or a liability is recognized and reported in the statement of financial position related to the recognition of the gain or loss on the firm commitment. Consequently, subsequent references to an asset or a liability in this Statement include a firm commitment.

STANDARDS OF FINANCIAL ACCOUNTING AND REPORTING

Scope and Definition

5. This Statement applies to all entities. Some entities, such as not-for-profit organizations and defined benefit pension plans, do not report earnings as a separate caption in a statement of financial performance. The application of this Statement to those entities is set forth in paragraph 43.

Derivative Instruments

6. A derivative instrument is a financial instrument or other contract with all three of the following characteristics:

a. It has (1) one or more **underlyings** and (2) one or more **notional amounts**[3] or payment provisions or both. Those terms determine the amount of the settlement or settlements, and, in some cases, whether or not a settlement is required.[4]

b. It requires no initial net investment or an initial net investment that is smaller than would be required for other types of contracts that would be expected to have a similar response to changes in market factors.

c. Its terms require or permit net settlement, it can readily be settled net by a means outside the contract, or it provides for delivery of an asset that puts the recipient in a position not substantially different from net settlement.

7. *Underlying, notional amount, and payment provision.* An underlying is a specified interest rate, security price, commodity price, foreign exchange rate, index of prices or rates, or other variable. An underlying may be a price or rate of an asset or liability but is not the asset or liability itself. A notional amount is a number of currency units, shares, bushels, pounds, or other units specified in the contract. The settlement of a derivative instrument with a notional amount is determined by interaction of that notional amount with the underlying. The interaction may be simple multiplication, or it may involve a formula with leverage factors or other constants. A payment provision specifies a fixed or determinable settlement to be made if the underlying behaves in a specified manner.

8. *Initial net investment.* Many derivative instruments require no initial net investment. Some require an initial net investment as compensation for time value (for example, a premium on an option) or for terms that are more or less favorable than market conditions (for example, a premium on a forward purchase contract with a price less than the current forward price). Others require a mutual exchange of currencies or other assets at inception, in which case the net investment is the difference in the fair values of the assets exchanged. A derivative instrument does not require an initial net investment in the contract that is equal to the notional amount (or the notional amount plus a premium or minus a discount) or that is determined by applying the notional amount to the underlying.

9. *Net settlement.* A contract fits the description in paragraph 6(c) if its settlement provisions meet one of the following criteria:

a. Neither party is required to deliver an asset that is associated with the underlying or that has a principal amount, stated amount, face value, number of shares, or other denomination that is equal to the notional amount (or the notional amount plus a premium or minus a discount). For example, most interest rate swaps do not require that either party deliver interest-bearing assets with a principal amount equal to the notional amount of the contract.

b. One of the parties is required to deliver an asset of the type described in paragraph 9(a), but there is a market mechanism that facilitates net settlement, for example, an exchange that offers a ready opportunity to sell the contract or to enter into an offsetting contract.

c. One of the parties is required to deliver an asset of the type described in paragraph 9(a), but that asset

---

[3]Sometimes other names are used. For example, the notional amount is called a face amount in some contracts.

[4]The terms *underlying, notional amount, payment provision,* and *settlement* are intended to include the plural forms in the remainder of this Statement. Including both the singular and plural forms used in this paragraph is more accurate but much more awkward and impairs the readability.

is readily convertible to cash[5] or is itself a derivative instrument. An example of that type of contract is a forward contract that requires delivery of an exchange-traded equity security. Even though the number of shares to be delivered is the same as the notional amount of the contract and the price of the shares is the underlying, an exchange-traded security is readily convertible to cash. Another example is a swaption—an option to require delivery of a swap contract, which is a derivative.

Derivative instruments embedded in other contracts are addressed in paragraphs 12–16.

10. Notwithstanding the conditions in paragraphs 6–9, the following contracts are not subject to the requirements of this Statement:

a. *"Regular-way" security trades.* Regular-way security trades are contracts with no net settlement provision and no market mechanism to facilitate net settlement (as described in paragraphs 9(a) and 9(b)). They provide for delivery of a security within the time generally established by regulations or conventions in the marketplace or exchange in which the transaction is being executed.

b. *Normal purchases and normal sales.* Normal purchases and normal sales are contracts with no net settlement provision and no market mechanism to facilitate net settlement (as described in paragraphs 9(a) and 9(b)). They provide for the purchase or sale of something other than a financial instrument or derivative instrument that will be delivered in quantities expected to be used or sold by the reporting entity over a reasonable period in the normal course of business.

c. *Certain insurance contracts.* Generally, contracts of the type that are within the scope of FASB Statements No. 60, *Accounting and Reporting by Insurance Enterprises,* No. 97, *Accounting and Reporting by Insurance Enterprises for Certain Long-Duration Contracts and for Realized Gains and Losses from the Sale of Investments,* and No. 113, *Accounting and Reporting for Reinsurance of Short-Duration and Long-Duration Contracts,* are not subject to the requirements of this Statement whether or not they are written by in-

surance enterprises. That is, a contract is not subject to the requirements of this Statement if it entitles the holder to be compensated only if, as a result of an identifiable insurable event (other than a change in price), the holder incurs a liability or there is an adverse change in the value of a specific asset or liability for which the holder is at risk. The following types of contracts written by insurance enterprises or held by the insureds are not subject to the requirements of this Statement for the reasons given:

(1) *Traditional life insurance contracts.* The payment of death benefits is the result of an identifiable insurable event (death of the insured) instead of changes in a variable.

(2) *Traditional property and casualty contracts.* The payment of benefits is the result of an identifiable insurable event (for example, theft or fire) instead of changes in a variable.

However, insurance enterprises enter into other types of contracts that may be subject to the provisions of this Statement. In addition, some contracts with insurance or other enterprises combine derivative instruments, as defined in this Statement, with other insurance products or nonderivative contracts, for example, indexed annuity contracts, variable life insurance contracts, and property and casualty contracts that combine traditional coverages with foreign currency options. Contracts that consist of both derivative portions and nonderivative portions are addressed in paragraph 12.

d. *Certain financial guarantee contracts.* Financial guarantee contracts are not subject to this Statement if they provide for payments to be made only to reimburse the guaranteed party for a loss incurred because the debtor fails to pay when payment is due, which is an identifiable insurable event. In contrast, financial guarantee contracts are subject to this Statement if they provide for payments to be made in response to changes in an underlying (for example, a decrease in a specified debtor's creditworthiness).

e. *Certain contracts that are not traded on an exchange.* Contracts that are not exchange-traded

---

[5]FASB Concepts Statement No. 5, *Recognition and Measurement in Financial Statements of Business Enterprises,* states that assets that are readily convertible to cash "have (i) interchangeable (fungible) units and (ii) quoted prices available in an active market that can rapidly absorb the quantity held by the entity without significantly affecting the price" (paragraph 83(a)). For contracts that involve multiple deliveries of the asset, the phrase *in an active market that can rapidly absorb the quantity held by the entity* should be applied separately to the expected quantity in each delivery.

are not subject to the requirements of this Statement if the underlying on which the settlement is based is one of the following:

(1) A climatic or geological variable or other physical variable

(2) The price or value of (a) a nonfinancial asset of one of the parties to the contract provided that the asset is not readily convertible to cash or (b) a nonfinancial liability of one of the parties to the contract provided that the liability does not require delivery of an asset that is readily convertible to cash

(3) Specified volumes of sales or service revenues of one of the parties to the contract.

If a contract has more than one underlying and some, but not all, of them qualify for one of the exceptions in paragraphs 10(e)(1), 10(e)(2), and 10(e)(3), the application of this Statement to that contract depends on its predominant characteristics. That is, the contract is subject to the requirements of this Statement if all of its underlyings, considered in combination, behave in a manner that is highly correlated with the behavior of any of the component variables that do not qualify for an exception.

f. *Derivatives that serve as impediments to sales accounting.* A derivative instrument (whether freestanding or embedded in another contract) whose existence serves as an impediment to recognizing a related contract as a sale by one party or a purchase by the counterparty is not subject to this Statement. For example, the existence of a guarantee of the residual value of a leased asset by the lessor may be an impediment to treating a contract as a sales-type lease, in which case the contract would be treated by the lessor as an operating lease. Another example is the existence of a call option enabling a transferor to repurchase transferred assets that is an impediment to sales accounting under FASB Statement No. 125, *Accounting for Transfers and Servicing of Financial Assets and Extinguishments of Liabilities*.

11. Notwithstanding the conditions of paragraphs 6–10, the reporting entity shall *not* consider the following contracts to be derivative instruments for purposes of this Statement:

a. Contracts issued or held by that reporting entity that are both (1) indexed to its own stock and (2) classified in stockholders' equity in its statement of financial position

b. Contracts issued by the entity in connection with stock-based compensation arrangements addressed in FASB Statement No. 123, *Accounting for Stock-Based Compensation*

c. Contracts issued by the entity as contingent consideration from a business combination. The accounting for contingent consideration issued in a business combination is addressed in APB Opinion No. 16, *Business Combinations*. In applying this paragraph, the issuer is considered to be the entity that is accounting for the combination using the purchase method.

In contrast, the above exceptions do not apply to the counterparty in those contracts. In addition, a contract that an entity either can or must settle by issuing its own equity instruments but that is indexed in part or in full to something other than its own stock can be a derivative instrument for the issuer under paragraphs 6–10, in which case it would be accounted for as a liability or an asset in accordance with the requirements of this Statement.

Embedded Derivative Instruments

12. Contracts that do not in their entirety meet the definition of a derivative instrument (refer to paragraphs 6–9), such as bonds, insurance policies, and leases, may contain "embedded" derivative instruments—implicit or explicit terms that affect some or all of the cash flows or the value of other exchanges required by the contract in a manner similar to a derivative instrument. The effect of embedding a derivative instrument in another type of contract ("the host contract") is that some or all of the cash flows or other exchanges that otherwise would be required by the contract, whether unconditional or contingent upon the occurrence of a specified event, will be modified based on one or more underlyings. An embedded derivative instrument shall be separated from the host contract and accounted for as a derivative instrument pursuant to this Statement if and only if all of the following criteria are met:

a. The economic characteristics and risks of the embedded derivative instrument are not clearly and closely related to the economic characteristics and risks of the host contract. Additional guidance on applying this criterion to various contracts containing embedded derivative instruments is included in Appendix A of this Statement.

b. The contract ("the hybrid instrument") that embodies both the embedded derivative instrument and the host contract is not remeasured at fair value under otherwise applicable generally accepted accounting principles with changes in fair value reported in earnings as they occur.

c. A separate instrument with the same terms as the embedded derivative instrument would, pursuant to paragraphs 6–11, be a derivative instrument subject to the requirements of this Statement. (The initial net investment for the hybrid instrument shall not be considered to be the initial net investment for the embedded derivative.)

13. For purposes of applying the provisions of paragraph 12, an embedded derivative instrument in which the underlying is an interest rate or interest rate index[6] that alters net interest payments that otherwise would be paid or received on an interest-bearing host contract is considered to be clearly and closely related to the host contract unless either of the following conditions exist:

a. The hybrid instrument can contractually be settled in such a way that the investor (holder) would not recover *substantially all* of its initial recorded investment.
b. The embedded derivative could at least double the investor's initial rate of return on the host contract and could also result in a rate of return that is at least twice what otherwise would be the market return for a contract that has the same terms as the host contract and that involves a debtor with a similar credit quality.

Even though the above conditions focus on the investor's rate of return and the investor's recovery of its investment, the existence of either of those conditions would result in the embedded derivative instrument not being considered clearly and closely related to the host contract by both parties to the hybrid instrument. Because the existence of those conditions is assessed at the date that the hybrid instrument is acquired (or incurred) by the reporting entity, the acquirer of a hybrid instrument in the secondary market could potentially reach a different conclusion than could the issuer of the hybrid instrument due to applying the conditions in this paragraph at different points in time.

14. However, interest-only strips and principal-only strips are not subject to the requirements of this Statement provided they (a) initially resulted from separating the rights to receive contractual cash flows of a financial instrument that, in and of itself, did not contain an embedded derivative that otherwise would have been accounted for separately as a derivative pursuant to the provisions of paragraphs 12 and 13 and (b) do not incorporate any terms not present in the original financial instrument described above.

15. An embedded foreign currency derivative instrument shall *not* be separated from the host contract and considered a derivative instrument under paragraph 12 if the host contract is not a financial instrument and it requires payment(s) denominated in (a) the currency of the primary economic environment in which any substantial party to that contract operates (that is, its functional currency) or (b) the currency in which the price of the related good or service that is acquired or delivered is routinely denominated in international commerce (for example, the U.S. dollar for crude oil transactions). Unsettled foreign currency transactions, including financial instruments, that are monetary items and have their principal payments, interest payments, or both denominated in a foreign currency are subject to the requirement in Statement 52 to recognize any foreign currency transaction gain or loss in earnings and shall not be considered to contain embedded foreign currency derivative instruments under this Statement. The same proscription applies to available-for-sale or trading securities that have cash flows denominated in a foreign currency.

16. In subsequent provisions of this Statement, both (a) a derivative instrument included within the scope of this Statement by paragraphs 6–11 and (b) an embedded derivative instrument that has been separated from a host contract as required by paragraph 12 are collectively referred to as derivative instruments. If an embedded derivative instrument is separated from its host contract, the host contract shall be accounted for based on generally accepted accounting principles applicable to instruments of that type that do not contain embedded derivative instruments. If an entity cannot reliably identify and measure the embedded derivative instrument that paragraph 12 requires be separated from the host contract, the entire contract shall be measured at fair value with gain or loss recognized in earnings, but it may not be designated as a hedging instrument pursuant to this Statement.

---

[6]Examples are an interest rate cap or an interest rate collar. An embedded derivative instrument that alters net interest payments based on changes in a stock price index (or another non-interest-rate index) is not addressed in paragraph 13.

**Recognition of Derivatives and Measurement
of Derivatives and Hedged Items**

17. An entity shall recognize all of its derivative instruments in its statement of financial position as either assets or liabilities depending on the rights or obligations under the contracts. All derivative
instruments shall be measured at fair value. The guidance in FASB Statement No. 107, *Disclosures about
Fair Value of Financial Instruments,* as amended,
shall apply in determining the fair value of a financial
instrument (derivative or hedged item). If expected
future cash flows are used to estimate fair value,
those expected cash flows shall be the best estimate
based on reasonable and supportable assumptions
and projections. All available evidence shall be considered in developing estimates of expected future
cash flows. The weight given to the evidence shall be
commensurate with the extent to which the evidence
can be verified objectively. If a range is estimated for
either the amount or the timing of possible cash
flows, the likelihood of possible outcomes shall be
considered in determining the best estimate of future
cash flows.

18. The accounting for changes in the fair value (that
is, gains or losses) of a derivative depends on
whether it has been designated and qualifies as part
of a hedging relationship and, if so, on the reason for
holding it. Either all or a proportion of a derivative
may be designated as the hedging instrument. The
proportion must be expressed as a percentage of the
entire derivative so that the profile of risk exposures
in the hedging portion of the derivative is the same as
that in the entire derivative. (Thus, an entity is prohibited from separating a compound derivative into
components representing different risks and designating any such component as the hedging instrument, except as permitted at the date of initial application by the transition provisions in paragraph 49.)
Subsequent references in this Statement to a derivative as a hedging instrument include the use of only a
proportion of a derivative as a hedging instrument.
Two or more derivatives, or proportions thereof, may
also be viewed in combination and jointly designated
as the hedging instrument. Gains and losses on derivative instruments are accounted for as follows:

a. *No hedging designation.* The gain or loss on
   a derivative instrument not designated as a hedging instrument shall be recognized currently
   in earnings.

b. *Fair value hedge.* The gain or loss on a derivative
   instrument designated and qualifying as a fair
   value hedging instrument as well as the offsetting
   loss or gain on the hedged item attributable to the
   hedged risk shall be recognized currently in earnings in the same accounting period, as provided in
   paragraphs 22 and 23.

c. *Cash flow hedge.* The effective portion of the gain
   or loss on a derivative instrument designated and
   qualifying as a cash flow hedging instrument shall
   be reported as a component of other **comprehensive income** (outside earnings) and reclassified
   into earnings in the same period or periods during
   which the hedged forecasted transaction affects
   earnings, as provided in paragraphs 30 and 31.
   The remaining gain or loss on the derivative instrument, if any, shall be recognized currently in
   earnings, as provided in paragraph 30.

d. *Foreign currency hedge.* The gain or loss on a derivative instrument or nonderivative financial instrument designated and qualifying as a foreign
   currency hedging instrument shall be accounted
   for as follows:

   (1) The gain or loss on the hedging derivative or
       nonderivative instrument in a hedge of a
       foreign-currency-denominated firm commit-
       ment and the offsetting loss or gain on the
       hedged firm commitment shall be recognized
       currently in earnings in the same accounting
       period, as provided in paragraph 37.

   (2) The gain or loss on the hedging derivative
       instrument in a hedge of an available-for-sale
       security and the offsetting loss or gain on
       the hedged available-for-sale security shall
       be recognized currently in earnings in the
       same accounting period, as provided in
       paragraph 38.

   (3) The effective portion of the gain or loss on the
       hedging derivative instrument in a hedge of a
       forecasted foreign-currency-denominated
       transaction shall be reported as a component
       of other comprehensive income (outside
       earnings) and reclassified into earnings in the
       same period or periods during which the
       hedged forecasted transaction affects
       earnings, as provided in paragraph 41. The
       remaining gain or loss on the hedging instru-
       ment shall be recognized currently in
       earnings.

   (4) The gain or loss on the hedging derivative or
       nonderivative instrument in a hedge of a net

investment in a foreign operation shall be reported in other comprehensive income (outside earnings) as part of the cumulative translation adjustment to the extent it is effective as a hedge, as provided in paragraph 42.

19. In this Statement, the *change in the fair value* of an entire financial asset or liability for a period refers to the difference between its fair value at the beginning of the period (or acquisition date) and the end of the period adjusted to exclude (a) changes in fair value due to the passage of time and (b) changes in fair value related to any payments received or made, such as in partially recovering the asset or partially settling the liability.

Fair Value Hedges

General

20. An entity may designate a derivative instrument as hedging the exposure to changes in the fair value of an asset or a liability or an identified portion thereof ("hedged item") that is attributable to a particular risk. Designated hedging instruments and hedged items qualify for fair value hedge accounting if all of the following criteria and those in paragraph 21 are met:

a. At inception of the hedge, there is formal documentation of the hedging relationship and the entity's risk management objective and strategy for undertaking the hedge, including identification of the hedging instrument, the hedged item, the nature of the risk being hedged, and how the hedging instrument's effectiveness in offsetting the exposure to changes in the hedged item's fair value attributable to the hedged risk will be assessed. There must be a reasonable basis for how the entity plans to assess the hedging instrument's effectiveness.
   (1) For a fair value hedge of a firm commitment, the entity's formal documentation at the inception of the hedge must include a reasonable method for recognizing in earnings the asset or liability representing the gain or loss on the hedged firm commitment.
   (2) An entity's defined risk management strategy for a particular hedging relationship may

exclude certain components of a specific hedging derivative's change in fair value, such as time value, from the assessment of hedge effectiveness, as discussed in paragraph 63 in Section 2 of Appendix A.

b. Both at inception of the hedge and on an ongoing basis, the hedging relationship is expected to be highly effective in achieving offsetting changes in fair value attributable to the hedged risk during the period that the hedge is designated. An assessment of effectiveness is required whenever financial statements or earnings are reported, and at least every three months. If the hedging instrument (such as an at-the-money option contract) provides only one-sided offset of the hedged risk, the increases (or decreases) in the fair value of the hedging instrument must be expected to be highly effective in offsetting the decreases (or increases) in the fair value of the hedged item. All assessments of effectiveness shall be consistent with the risk management strategy documented for that particular hedging relationship (in accordance with paragraph 20(a) above).

c. If a written option is designated as hedging a recognized asset or liability, the combination of the hedged item and the written option provides at least as much potential for gains as a result of a favorable change in the fair value of the combined instruments[7] as exposure to losses from an unfavorable change in their combined fair value. That test is met if all possible percentage favorable changes in the underlying (from zero percent to 100 percent) would provide at least as much gain as the loss that would be incurred from an unfavorable change in the underlying of the same percentage.
   (1) A combination of options (for example, an interest rate collar) entered into contemporaneously shall be considered a written option if either at inception or over the life of the contracts a net premium is received in cash or as a favorable rate or other term. (Thus, a collar can be designated as a hedging instrument in a fair value hedge without regard to the test in paragraph 20(c) unless a net premium is received.) Furthermore, a derivative instrument that results from combining a written option

---

[7]The reference to *combined instruments* refers to the written option and the hedged item, such as an embedded purchased option.

and any other nonoption derivative shall be considered a written option.

A nonderivative instrument, such as a Treasury note, shall not be designated as a hedging instrument, except as provided in paragraphs 37 and 42 of this Statement.

The hedged item

21. An asset or a liability is eligible for designation as a hedged item in a fair value hedge if all of the following criteria are met:

a. The hedged item is specifically identified as either all or a specific portion of a recognized asset or liability or of an unrecognized firm commitment.[8] The hedged item is a single asset or liability (or a specific portion thereof) or is a portfolio of similar assets or a portfolio of similar liabilities (or a specific portion thereof).

   (1) If similar assets or similar liabilities are aggregated and hedged as a portfolio, the individual assets or individual liabilities must share the risk exposure for which they are designated as being hedged. The change in fair value attributable to the hedged risk for each individual item in a hedged portfolio must be expected to respond in a generally proportionate manner to the overall change in fair value of the aggregate portfolio attributable to the hedged risk. That is, if the change in fair value of a hedged portfolio attributable to the hedged risk was 10 percent during a reporting period, the change in the fair values attributable to the hedged risk for each item constituting the portfolio should be expected to be within a fairly narrow range, such as 9 percent to 11 percent. In contrast, an expectation that the change in fair value attributable to the hedged risk for individual items in the portfolio would range from 7 percent to 13 percent would be inconsistent with this provision. In aggregating loans in a portfolio to be hedged, an entity may choose to consider some of the following characteristics, as appropriate: loan type, loan size, nature and location of collat-

eral, interest rate type (fixed or variable) and the coupon interest rate (if fixed), scheduled maturity, prepayment history of the loans (if seasoned), and expected prepayment performance in varying interest rate scenarios.[9]

   (2) If the hedged item is a specific portion of an asset or liability (or of a portfolio of similar assets or a portfolio of similar liabilities), the hedged item is one of the following:

   (a) A percentage of the entire asset or liability (or of the entire portfolio)

   (b) One or more selected contractual cash flows (such as the portion of the asset or liability representing the present value of the interest payments in the first two years of a four-year debt instrument)

   (c) A put option, a call option, an interest rate cap, or an interest rate floor embedded in an existing asset or liability that is not an embedded derivative accounted for separately pursuant to paragraph 12 of this Statement

   (d) The residual value in a lessor's net investment in a direct financing or sales-type lease.

   If the entire asset or liability is an instrument with variable cash flows, the hedged item cannot be deemed to be an implicit fixed-to-variable swap (or similar instrument) perceived to be embedded in a host contract with fixed cash flows.

b. The hedged item presents an exposure to changes in fair value attributable to the hedged risk that could affect reported earnings. The reference to affecting reported earnings does not apply to an entity that does not report earnings as a separate caption in a statement of financial performance, such as a not-for-profit organization, as discussed in paragraph 43.

c. The hedged item is not (1) an asset or liability that is remeasured with the changes in fair value attributable to the hedged risk reported currently in earnings (for example, if foreign exchange risk is hedged, a foreign-currency-denominated asset for

---

[8]A firm commitment that represents an asset or liability that a specific accounting standard prohibits recognizing (such as a noncancelable operating lease or an unrecognized mortgage servicing right) may nevertheless be designated as the hedged item in a fair value hedge. A mortgage banker's unrecognized "interest rate lock commitment" (IRLC) does not qualify as a firm commitment (because as an option it does not obligate both parties) and thus is not eligible for fair value hedge accounting as the hedged item. (However, a mortgage banker's "forward sale commitments," which are derivatives that lock in the prices at which the mortgage loans will be sold to investors, may qualify as hedging instruments in cash flow hedges of the forecasted sales of mortgage loans.)

[9]Mortgage bankers and other servicers of financial assets that designate a hedged portfolio by aggregating servicing rights within one or more risk strata used under paragraph 37(g) of Statement 125 would not necessarily comply with the requirement in this paragraph for portfolios of similar assets. The risk stratum under paragraph 37(g) of Statement 125 can be based on any predominant risk characteristic, including date of origination or geographic location.

which a foreign currency transaction gain or loss is recognized in earnings), (2) an investment accounted for by the equity method in accordance with the requirements of APB Opinion No. 18, *The Equity Method of Accounting for Investments in Common Stock,* (3) a minority interest in one or more consolidated subsidiaries, (4) an equity investment in a consolidated subsidiary, (5) a firm commitment either to enter into a business combination or to acquire or dispose of a subsidiary, a minority interest, or an equity method investee, or (6) an equity instrument issued by the entity and classified in stockholders' equity in the statement of financial position.

d. If the hedged item is all or a portion of a debt security (or a portfolio of similar debt securities) that is classified as held-to-maturity in accordance with FASB Statement No. 115, *Accounting for Certain Investments in Debt and Equity Securities,* the designated risk being hedged is the risk of changes in its fair value attributable to changes in the obligor's creditworthiness or if the hedged item is an option component of a held-to-maturity security that permits its prepayment, the designated risk being hedged is the risk of changes in the entire fair value of that option component. (The designated hedged risk for a held-to-maturity security may not be the risk of changes in its fair value attributable to changes in market interest rates or foreign exchange rates. If the hedged item is other than an option component that permits its prepayment, the designated hedged risk also may not be the risk of changes in its overall fair value.)

e. If the hedged item is a nonfinancial asset or liability (other than a recognized loan servicing right or a nonfinancial firm commitment with financial components), the designated risk being hedged is the risk of changes in the fair value of the entire hedged asset or liability (reflecting its actual location if a physical asset). That is, the price risk of a similar asset in a different location or of a major ingredient may not be the hedged risk. Thus, in hedging the exposure to changes in the fair value of gasoline, an entity may not designate the risk of changes in the price of crude oil as the risk being hedged for purposes of determining effectiveness of the fair value hedge of gasoline.

f. If the hedged item is a financial asset or liability, a recognized loan servicing right, or a nonfinancial firm commitment with financial components, the designated risk being hedged is (1) the risk of changes in the overall fair value of the entire

hedged item, (2) the risk of changes in its fair value attributable to changes in market interest rates, (3) the risk of changes in its fair value attributable to changes in the related foreign currency exchange rates (refer to paragraphs 37 and 38), or (4) the risk of changes in its fair value attributable to changes in the obligor's creditworthiness. If the risk designated as being hedged is not the risk in paragraph 21(f)(1) above, two or more of the other risks (market interest rate risk, foreign currency exchange risk, and credit risk) may simultaneously be designated as being hedged. An entity may not simply designate prepayment risk as the risk being hedged for a financial asset. However, it can designate the option component of a prepayable instrument as the hedged item in a fair value hedge of the entity's exposure to changes in the fair value of that "prepayment" option, perhaps thereby achieving the objective of its desire to hedge prepayment risk. The effect of an embedded derivative of the same risk class must be considered in designating a hedge of an individual risk. For example, the effect of an embedded prepayment option must be considered in designating a hedge of market interest rate risk.

22. Gains and losses on a qualifying fair value hedge shall be accounted for as follows:

a. The gain or loss on the hedging instrument shall be recognized currently in earnings.

b. The gain or loss (that is, the change in fair value) on the hedged item attributable to the hedged risk shall adjust the carrying amount of the hedged item and be recognized currently in earnings.

If the fair value hedge is fully effective, the gain or loss on the hedging instrument, adjusted for the component, if any, of that gain or loss that is excluded from the assessment of effectiveness under the entity's defined risk management strategy for that particular hedging relationship (as discussed in paragraph 63 in Section 2 of Appendix A), would exactly offset the loss or gain on the hedged item attributable to the hedged risk. Any difference that does arise would be the effect of hedge ineffectiveness, which consequently is recognized currently in earnings. The measurement of hedge ineffectiveness for a particular hedging relationship shall be consistent with the entity's risk management strategy and the method of assessing hedge effectiveness that was documented at the inception of the hedging relationship, as discussed in paragraph 20(a). Nevertheless, the amount of hedge ineffectiveness recognized in earnings is based on the extent to which exact offset is not achieved. Although a hedging relationship must comply with an entity's established policy range of what is considered "highly effective" pursuant to paragraph 20(b) in order for that relationship to qualify for hedge accounting, that compliance does not assure zero ineffectiveness. Section 2 of Appendix A illustrates assessing hedge effectiveness and measuring hedge ineffectiveness. Any hedge ineffectiveness directly affects earnings because there will be no offsetting adjustment of a hedged item's carrying amount for the ineffective aspect of the gain or loss on the related hedging instrument.

23. If a hedged item is otherwise measured at fair value with changes in fair value reported in other comprehensive income (such as an available-for-sale security), the adjustment of the hedged item's carrying amount discussed in paragraph 22 shall be recognized in earnings rather than in other comprehensive income in order to offset the gain or loss on the hedging instrument.

24. The adjustment of the carrying amount of a hedged asset or liability required by paragraph 22 shall be accounted for in the same manner as other components of the carrying amount of that asset or liability. For example, an adjustment of the carrying amount of a hedged asset held for sale (such as inventory) would remain part of the carrying amount of that asset until the asset is sold, at which point the entire carrying amount of the hedged asset would be recognized as the cost of the item sold in determining earnings. An adjustment of the carrying amount of a hedged interest-bearing financial instrument shall be amortized to earnings; amortization shall begin no later than when the hedged item ceases to be adjusted for changes in its fair value attributable to the risk being hedged.

25. An entity shall discontinue prospectively the accounting specified in paragraphs 22 and 23 for an existing hedge if any one of the following occurs:

a. Any criterion in paragraphs 20 and 21 is no longer met.
b. The derivative expires or is sold, terminated, or exercised.
c. The entity removes the designation of the fair value hedge.

In those circumstances, the entity may elect to designate prospectively a new hedging relationship with a different hedging instrument or, in the circumstances described in paragraphs 25(a) and 25(c) above, a different hedged item or a hedged transaction if the hedging relationship meets the criteria specified in paragraphs 20 and 21 for a fair value hedge or paragraphs 28 and 29 for a cash flow hedge.

26. In general, if a periodic assessment indicates noncompliance with the effectiveness criterion in paragraph 20(b), an entity shall not recognize the adjustment of the carrying amount of the hedged item described in paragraphs 22 and 23 after the last date on which compliance with the effectiveness criterion was established. However, if the event or change in circumstances that caused the hedging relationship to fail the effectiveness criterion can be identified, the entity shall recognize in earnings the changes in the hedged item's fair value attributable to the risk being hedged that occurred prior to that event or change in circumstances. If a fair value hedge of a firm commitment is discontinued because the hedged item no longer meets the definition of a firm commitment, the entity shall derecognize any asset or liability previously recognized pursuant to paragraph 22 (as a result of an adjustment to the carrying amount for the firm commitment) and recognize a corresponding loss or gain currently in earnings.

Impairment

27. An asset or liability that has been designated as being hedged and accounted for pursuant to paragraphs 22–24 remains subject to the applicable requirements in generally accepted accounting principles for assessing impairment for that type of asset or for recognizing an increased obligation for that type of liability. Those impairment requirements shall be applied after hedge accounting has been applied for the period and the carrying amount of the hedged asset or liability has been adjusted pursuant to paragraph 22 of this Statement. Because the hedging instrument is recognized separately as an asset or liability, its fair value or expected cash flows shall not be considered in applying those impairment requirements to the hedged asset or liability.

Cash Flow Hedges

General

28. An entity may designate a derivative instrument as hedging the exposure to variability in expected future cash flows that is attributable to a particular risk. That exposure may be associated with an existing

recognized asset or liability (such as all or certain future interest payments on variable-rate debt) or a forecasted transaction (such as a forecasted purchase or sale).[10] Designated hedging instruments and hedged items or transactions qualify for cash flow hedge accounting if all of the following criteria and those in paragraph 29 are met:

a. At inception of the hedge, there is formal documentation of the hedging relationship and the entity's risk management objective and strategy for undertaking the hedge, including identification of the hedging instrument, the hedged transaction, the nature of the risk being hedged, and how the hedging instrument's effectiveness in hedging the exposure to the hedged transaction's variability in cash flows attributable to the hedged risk will be assessed. There must be a reasonable basis for how the entity plans to assess the hedging instrument's effectiveness.

(1) An entity's defined risk management strategy for a particular hedging relationship may exclude certain components of a specific hedging derivative's change in fair value from the assessment of hedge effectiveness, as discussed in paragraph 63 in Section 2 of Appendix A.

(2) Documentation shall include all relevant details, including the date on or period within which the forecasted transaction is expected to occur, the specific nature of asset or liability involved (if any), and the expected currency amount or quantity of the forecasted transaction.

(a) The phrase *expected currency amount* refers to hedges of foreign currency exchange risk and requires specification of the exact amount of foreign currency being hedged.

(b) The phrase *expected . . . quantity* refers to hedges of other risks and requires specification of the physical quantity (that is, the number of items or units of measure) encompassed by the hedged forecasted transaction. If a forecasted sale or purchase is being hedged for price risk, the hedged transaction cannot be specified solely in terms of expected currency amounts, nor can it be specified as a percentage of sales or purchases during a pe-

riod. The current price of a forecasted transaction also should be identified to satisfy the criterion in paragraph 28(b) for offsetting cash flows.

The hedged forecasted transaction shall be described with sufficient specificity so that when a transaction occurs, it is clear whether that transaction is or is not the hedged transaction. Thus, the forecasted transaction could be identified as the sale of either the first 15,000 units of a specific product sold during a specified 3-month period or the first 5,000 units of a specific product sold in each of 3 specific months, but it could not be identified as the sale of the last 15,000 units of that product sold during a 3-month period (because the last 15,000 units cannot be identified when they occur, but only when the period has ended).

b. Both at inception of the hedge and on an ongoing basis, the hedging relationship is expected to be highly effective in achieving offsetting cash flows attributable to the hedged risk during the term of the hedge, except as indicated in paragraph 28(d) below. An assessment of effectiveness is required whenever financial statements or earnings are reported, and at least every three months. If the hedging instrument, such as an at-the-money option contract, provides only one-sided offset against the hedged risk, the cash inflows (outflows) from the hedging instrument must be expected to be highly effective in offsetting the corresponding change in the cash outflows or inflows of the hedged transaction. All assessments of effectiveness shall be consistent with the originally documented risk management strategy for that particular hedging relationship.

c. If a written option is designated as hedging the variability in cash flows for a recognized asset or liability, the combination of the hedged item and the written option provides at least as much potential for favorable cash flows as exposure to unfavorable cash flows. That test is met if all possible percentage favorable changes in the underlying (from zero percent to 100 percent) would provide at least as much favorable cash flows as the unfavorable cash flows that would be incurred from an unfavorable change in the underlying of the same percentage. (Refer to paragraph 20(c)(1).)

---

[10]For purposes of paragraphs 28–35, the individual cash flows related to a recognized asset or liability and the cash flows related to a forecasted transaction are both referred to as a *forecasted transaction* or *hedged transaction*.

d. If a hedging instrument is used to modify the interest receipts or payments associated with a recognized financial asset or liability from one variable rate to another variable rate, the hedging instrument must be a link between an existing designated asset (or group of similar assets) with variable cash flows and an existing designated liability (or group of similar liabilities) with variable cash flows and be highly effective at achieving offsetting cash flows. A link exists if the basis (that is, the rate index on which the interest rate is based) of one leg of an interest rate swap is the same as the basis of the interest receipts for the designated asset and the basis of the other leg of the swap is the same as the basis of the interest payments for the designated liability. In this situation, the criterion in the first sentence in paragraph 29(a) is applied separately to the designated asset and the designated liability.

A nonderivative instrument, such as a Treasury note, shall not be designated as a hedging instrument for a cash flow hedge.

The hedged forecasted transaction

29. A forecasted transaction is eligible for designation as a hedged transaction in a cash flow hedge if all of the following additional criteria are met:

a. The forecasted transaction is specifically identified as a single transaction or a group of individual transactions. If the hedged transaction is a group of individual transactions, those individual transactions must share the same risk exposure for which they are designated as being hedged. Thus, a forecasted purchase and a forecasted sale cannot both be included in the same group of individual transactions that constitute the hedged transaction.
b. The occurrence of the forecasted transaction is probable.
c. The forecasted transaction is a transaction with a party external to the reporting entity (except as permitted by paragraph 40) and presents an exposure to variations in cash flows for the hedged risk that could affect reported earnings.
d. The forecasted transaction is not the acquisition of an asset or incurrence of a liability that will subsequently be remeasured with changes in fair value attributable to the hedged risk reported currently in earnings (for example, if foreign exchange risk is hedged, the forecasted acquisition of a foreign-currency-denominated asset for

which a foreign currency transaction gain or loss will be recognized in earnings). However, forecasted sales on credit and the forecasted accrual of royalties on probable future sales by third-party licensees are not considered the forecasted acquisition of a receivable. If the forecasted transaction relates to a recognized asset or liability, the asset or liability is not remeasured with changes in fair value attributable to the hedged risk reported currently in earnings.
e. If the variable cash flows of the forecasted transaction relate to a debt security that is classified as held-to-maturity under Statement 115, the risk being hedged is the risk of changes in its cash flows attributable to default or changes in the obligor's creditworthiness. For those variable cash flows, the risk being hedged cannot be the risk of changes in its cash flows attributable to changes in market interest rates.
f. The forecasted transaction does not involve a business combination subject to the provisions of Opinion 16 and is not a transaction (such as a forecasted purchase, sale, or dividend) involving (1) a parent company's interests in consolidated subsidiaries, (2) a minority interest in a consolidated subsidiary, (3) an equity-method investment, or (4) an entity's own equity instruments.
g. If the hedged transaction is the forecasted purchase or sale of a nonfinancial asset, the designated risk being hedged is (1) the risk of changes in the functional-currency-equivalent cash flows attributable to changes in the related foreign currency exchange rates or (2) the risk of changes in the cash flows relating to all changes in the purchase price or sales price of the asset (reflecting its actual location if a physical asset), not the risk of changes in the cash flows relating to the purchase or sale of a similar asset in a different location or of a major ingredient. Thus, for example, in hedging the exposure to changes in the cash flows relating to the purchase of its bronze bar inventory, an entity may not designate the risk of changes in the cash flows relating to purchasing the copper component in bronze as the risk being hedged for purposes of assessing offset as required by paragraph 28(b).
h. If the hedged transaction is the forecasted purchase or sale of a financial asset or liability or the variable cash inflow or outflow of an existing financial asset or liability, the designated risk being hedged is (1) the risk of changes in the cash flows of the entire asset or liability, such as those relating to all changes in the purchase price or sales

price (regardless of whether that price and the related cash flows are stated in the entity's functional currency or a foreign currency), (2) the risk of changes in its cash flows attributable to changes in market interest rates, (3) the risk of changes in the functional-currency-equivalent cash flows attributable to changes in the related foreign currency exchange rates (refer to paragraph 40), or (4) the risk of changes in its cash flows attributable to default or changes in the obligor's creditworthiness. Two or more of the above risks may be designated simultaneously as being hedged. An entity may not designate prepayment risk as the risk being hedged (refer to paragraph 21(f)).

30. The effective portion of the gain or loss on a derivative designated as a cash flow hedge is reported in other comprehensive income, and the ineffective portion is reported in earnings. More specifically, a qualifying cash flow hedge shall be accounted for as follows:

a. If an entity's defined risk management strategy for a particular hedging relationship excludes a specific component of the gain or loss, or related cash flows, on the hedging derivative from the assessment of hedge effectiveness (as discussed in paragraph 63 in Section 2 of Appendix A), that excluded component of the gain or loss shall be recognized currently in earnings. For example, if the effectiveness of a hedge with an option contract is assessed based on changes in the option's intrinsic value, the changes in the option's time value would be recognized in earnings. Time value is equal to the fair value of the option less its intrinsic value.

b. Accumulated other comprehensive income associated with the hedged transaction shall be adjusted to a balance that reflects the *lesser* of the following (in absolute amounts):

   (1) The cumulative gain or loss on the derivative from inception of the hedge less (a) the excluded component discussed in paragraph 30(a) above and (b) the derivative's gains or losses previously reclassified from accumulated other comprehensive income into earnings pursuant to paragraph 31

   (2) The portion of the cumulative gain or loss on the derivative necessary to offset the cumulative change in expected future cash flows on the hedged transaction from inception of the hedge less the derivative's gains or losses previously reclassified from accumulated other comprehensive income into earnings pursuant to paragraph 31.

   That adjustment of accumulated other comprehensive income shall incorporate recognition in other comprehensive income of part or all of the gain or loss on the hedging derivative, as necessary.

c. A gain or loss shall be recognized in earnings, as necessary, for any remaining gain or loss on the hedging derivative or to adjust other comprehensive income to the balance specified in paragraph 30(b) above.

Section 2 of Appendix A illustrates assessing hedge effectiveness and measuring hedge ineffectiveness. Examples 6 and 9 of Section 1 of Appendix B illustrate the application of this paragraph.

31. Amounts in accumulated other comprehensive income shall be reclassified into earnings in the same period or periods during which the hedged forecasted transaction affects earnings (for example, when a forecasted sale actually occurs). If the hedged transaction results in the acquisition of an asset or the incurrence of a liability, the gains and losses in accumulated other comprehensive income shall be reclassified into earnings in the same period or periods during which the asset acquired or liability incurred affects earnings (such as in the periods that depreciation expense, interest expense, or cost of sales is recognized). However, if an entity expects at any time that continued reporting of a loss in accumulated other comprehensive income would lead to recognizing a net loss on the combination of the hedging instrument and the hedged transaction (and related asset acquired or liability incurred) in one or more future periods, a loss shall be reclassified immediately into earnings for the amount that is not expected to be recovered. For example, a loss shall be reported in earnings for a derivative that is designated as hedging the forecasted purchase of inventory to the extent that the cost basis of the inventory plus the related amount reported in accumulated other comprehensive income exceeds the amount expected to be recovered through sales of that inventory. (Impairment guidance is provided in paragraphs 34 and 35.)

32. An entity shall discontinue prospectively the accounting specified in paragraphs 30 and 31 for an existing hedge if any one of the following occurs:

a. Any criterion in paragraphs 28 and 29 is no longer met.

b. The derivative expires or is sold, terminated, or exercised.
c. The entity removes the designation of the cash flow hedge.

In those circumstances, the net gain or loss shall remain in accumulated other comprehensive income and be reclassified into earnings as specified in paragraph 31. Furthermore, the entity may elect to designate prospectively a new hedging relationship with a different hedging instrument or, in the circumstances described in paragraphs 32(a) and 32(c), a different hedged transaction or a hedged item if the hedging relationship meets the criteria specified in paragraphs 28 and 29 for a cash flow hedge or paragraphs 20 and 21 for a fair value hedge.

33. If a cash flow hedge is discontinued because it is probable that the original forecasted transaction will not occur, the net gain or loss in accumulated other comprehensive income shall be immediately reclassified into earnings.

34. Existing requirements in generally accepted accounting principles for assessing asset impairment or recognizing an increased obligation apply to an asset or liability that gives rise to variable cash flows (such as a variable-rate financial instrument), for which the variable cash flows (the forecasted transactions) have been designated as being hedged and accounted for pursuant to paragraphs 30 and 31. Those impairment requirements shall be applied each period after hedge accounting has been applied for the period, pursuant to paragraphs 30 and 31 of this Statement. The fair value or expected cash flows of a hedging instrument shall not be considered in applying those requirements. The gain or loss on the hedging instrument in accumulated other comprehensive income shall, however, be accounted for as discussed in paragraph 31.

35. If, under existing requirements in generally accepted accounting principles, an impairment loss is recognized on an asset or an additional obligation is recognized on a liability to which a hedged forecasted transaction relates, any offsetting net gain related to that transaction in accumulated other comprehensive income shall be reclassified immediately into earnings. Similarly, if a recovery is recognized on the asset or liability to which the forecasted transaction relates, any offsetting net loss that has been accumulated in other comprehensive income shall be reclassified immediately into earnings.

Foreign Currency Hedges

36. Consistent with the functional currency concept in Statement 52, an entity may designate the following types of hedges of foreign currency exposure, as specified in paragraphs 37-42:

a. A fair value hedge of an unrecognized firm commitment or an available-for-sale security
b. A cash flow hedge of a forecasted foreign-currency-denominated transaction or a forecasted intercompany foreign-currency-denominated transaction
c. A hedge of a net investment in a foreign operation.

The criterion in paragraph 21(c)(1) requires that a recognized asset or liability that may give rise to a foreign currency transaction gain or loss under Statement 52 (such as a foreign-currency-denominated receivable or payable) not be the hedged item in a foreign currency fair value or cash flow hedge because it is remeasured with the changes in the carrying amount attributable to what would be the hedged risk (an exchange rate change) reported currently in earnings. Similarly, the criterion in paragraph 29(d) requires that the forecasted acquisition of an asset or the incurrence of a liability that may give rise to a foreign currency transaction gain or loss under Statement 52 not be the hedged item in a foreign currency cash flow hedge because, subsequent to acquisition or incurrence, the asset or liability will be remeasured with changes in the carrying amount attributable to what would be the hedged risk reported currently in earnings. A foreign currency derivative instrument that has been entered into with another member of a consolidated group can be a hedging instrument in the consolidated financial statements only if that other member has entered into an offsetting contract with an unrelated third party to hedge the exposure it acquired from issuing the derivative instrument to the affiliate that initiated the hedge.

Foreign currency fair value hedges

37. *Unrecognized firm commitment.* A derivative instrument or a nonderivative financial instrument[11] that may give rise to a foreign currency transaction gain or loss under Statement 52 can be designated as hedging changes in the fair value of an unrecognized firm commitment, or a specific portion thereof, attributable to foreign currency exchange rates. The designated hedging relationship qualifies for the accounting specified in paragraphs 22–27 if all the fair value hedge criteria in paragraphs 20 and 21 are met.

38. *Available-for-sale security.* A nonderivative financial instrument shall not be designated as the hedging instrument in a fair value hedge of the foreign currency exposure of an available-for-sale security. A derivative instrument can be designated as hedging the changes in the fair value of an available-for-sale *debt* security (or a specific portion thereof) attributable to changes in foreign currency exchange rates. The designated hedging relationship qualifies for the accounting specified in paragraphs 22–27 if all the fair value hedge criteria in paragraphs 20 and 21 are met. An available-for-sale *equity* security can be hedged for changes in the fair value attributable to changes in foreign currency exchange rates and qualify for the accounting specified in paragraphs 22–27 only if the fair value hedge criteria in paragraphs 20 and 21 are met and the following two conditions are satisfied:

a. The security is not traded on an exchange (or other established marketplace) on which trades are denominated in the investor's functional currency.
b. Dividends or other cash flows to holders of the security are all denominated in the same foreign currency as the currency expected to be received upon sale of the security.

The change in fair value of the hedged available-for-sale equity security attributable to foreign exchange risk is reported in earnings pursuant to paragraph 23 and not in other comprehensive income.

39. Gains and losses on a qualifying foreign currency fair value hedge shall be accounted for as specified in paragraphs 22–27. The gain or loss on a nonderivative hedging instrument attributable to foreign currency risk is the foreign currency transaction gain or loss as determined under Statement 52.[12] That foreign currency transaction gain or loss shall be recognized currently in earnings along with the change in the carrying amount of the hedged firm commitment.

Foreign currency cash flow hedges

40. A nonderivative financial instrument shall not be designated as a hedging instrument in a foreign currency cash flow hedge. A derivative instrument designated as hedging the foreign currency exposure to variability in the functional-currency-equivalent cash flows associated with either a forecasted foreign-currency-denominated transaction (for example, a forecasted export sale to an unaffiliated entity with the price to be denominated in a foreign currency) or a forecasted intercompany foreign-currency-denominated transaction (for example, a forecasted sale to a foreign subsidiary or a forecasted royalty from a foreign subsidiary) qualifies for hedge accounting if all of the following criteria are met:

a. The operating unit that has the foreign currency exposure is a party to the hedging instrument (which can be an instrument between a parent company and its subsidiary—refer to paragraph 36).
b. The hedged transaction is denominated in a currency other than that unit's functional currency.
c. All of the criteria in paragraphs 28 and 29 are met, except for the criterion in paragraph 29(c) that requires that the forecasted transaction be with a party external to the reporting entity.
d. If the hedged transaction is a group of individual forecasted foreign-currency-denominated transactions, a forecasted inflow of a foreign currency and a forecasted outflow of the foreign currency cannot both be included in the same group.

41. A qualifying foreign currency cash flow hedge shall be accounted for as specified in paragraphs 30–35.

---

[11]The carrying basis for a nonderivative financial instrument that gives rise to a foreign currency transaction gain or loss under Statement 52 is not addressed by this Statement.

[12]The foreign currency transaction gain or loss on a hedging instrument is determined, consistent with paragraph 15 of Statement 52, as the increase or decrease in functional currency cash flows attributable to the change in spot exchange rates between the functional currency and the currency in which the hedging instrument is denominated.

*Hedges of the foreign currency exposure of a
net investment in a foreign operation*

42. A derivative instrument or a nonderivative financial instrument that may give rise to a foreign currency transaction gain or loss under Statement 52 can be designated as hedging the foreign currency exposure of a net investment in a foreign operation. The gain or loss on a hedging derivative instrument (or the foreign currency transaction gain or loss on the nonderivative hedging instrument) that is designated as, and is effective as, an economic hedge of the net investment in a foreign operation shall be reported in the same manner as a translation adjustment to the extent it is effective as a hedge. The hedged net investment shall be accounted for consistent with Statement 52; the provisions of this Statement for recognizing the gain or loss on assets designated as being hedged in a fair value hedge do not apply to the hedge of a net investment in a foreign operation.

**Accounting by Not-for-Profit Organizations and
Other Entities That Do Not Report Earnings**

43. An entity that does not report earnings as a separate caption in a statement of financial performance (for example, a not-for-profit organization or a defined benefit pension plan) shall recognize the gain or loss on a hedging instrument and a nonhedging derivative instrument as a change in net assets in the period of change unless the hedging instrument is designated as a hedge of the foreign currency exposure of a net investment in a foreign operation. In that case, the provisions of paragraph 42 of this Statement shall be applied. Entities that do not report earnings shall recognize the changes in the carrying amount of the hedged item pursuant to paragraph 22 in a fair value hedge as a change in net assets in the period of change. Those entities are not permitted to use cash flow hedge accounting because they do not report earnings separately. Consistent with the provisions of FASB Statement No. 117, *Financial Statements of Not-for-Profit Organizations,* this Statement does not prescribe how a not-for-profit organization should determine the components of an operating measure, if one is presented.

Disclosures

44. An entity that holds or issues derivative instruments (or nonderivative instruments that are designated and qualify as hedging instruments pursuant to paragraphs 37 and 42) shall disclose its objectives for holding or issuing those instruments, the context needed to understand those objectives, and its strategies for achieving those objectives. The description shall distinguish between derivative instruments (and nonderivative instruments) designated as fair value hedging instruments, derivative instruments designated as cash flow hedging instruments, derivative instruments (and nonderivative instruments) designated as hedging instruments for hedges of the foreign currency exposure of a net investment in a foreign operation, and all other derivatives. The description also shall indicate the entity's risk management policy for each of those types of hedges, including a description of the items or transactions for which risks are hedged. For derivative instruments not designated as hedging instruments, the description shall indicate the purpose of the derivative activity. Qualitative disclosures about an entity's objectives and strategies for using derivative instruments may be more meaningful if such objectives and strategies are described in the context of an entity's overall risk management profile. If appropriate, an entity is encouraged, but not required, to provide such additional qualitative disclosures.

45. An entity's disclosures for every reporting period for which a complete set of financial statements is presented also shall include the following:

Fair value hedges

a. For derivative instruments, as well as nonderivative instruments that may give rise to foreign currency transaction gains or losses under Statement 52, that have been designated and have qualified as fair value hedging instruments and for the related hedged items:
    (1) The net gain or loss recognized in earnings during the reporting period representing (a) the amount of the hedges' ineffectiveness and (b) the component of the derivative instruments' gain or loss, if any, excluded from the assessment of hedge effectiveness, and a description of where the net gain or loss is reported in the statement of income or other statement of financial performance
    (2) The amount of net gain or loss recognized in earnings when a hedged firm commitment no longer qualifies as a fair value hedge.

Cash flow hedges

b. For derivative instruments that have been designated and have qualified as cash flow hedging instruments and for the related hedged transactions:

(1) The net gain or loss recognized in earnings during the reporting period representing (a) the amount of the hedges' ineffectiveness and (b) the component of the derivative instruments' gain or loss, if any, excluded from the assessment of hedge effectiveness, and a description of where the net gain or loss is reported in the statement of income or other statement of financial performance

(2) A description of the transactions or other events that will result in the reclassification into earnings of gains and losses that are reported in accumulated other comprehensive income, and the estimated net amount of the existing gains or losses at the reporting date that is expected to be reclassified into earnings within the next 12 months

(3) The maximum length of time over which the entity is hedging its exposure to the variability in future cash flows for forecasted transactions excluding those forecasted transactions related to the payment of variable interest on existing financial instruments

(4) The amount of gains and losses reclassified into earnings as a result of the discontinuance of cash flow hedges because it is probable that the original forecasted transactions will not occur.

Hedges of the net investment in a foreign operation

c. For derivative instruments, as well as non-derivative instruments that may give rise to foreign currency transaction gains or losses under Statement 52, that have been designated and have qualified as hedging instruments for hedges of the foreign currency exposure of a net investment in a foreign operation, the net amount of gains or losses included in the cumulative translation adjustment during the reporting period.

The quantitative disclosures about derivative instruments may be more useful, and less likely to be perceived to be out of context or otherwise misunderstood, if similar information is disclosed about other financial instruments or nonfinancial assets and liabilities to which the derivative instruments are related by activity. Accordingly, in those situations, an entity is encouraged, but not required, to present a more complete picture of its activities by disclosing that information.

Reporting Changes in the Components of Comprehensive Income

46. An entity shall display as a separate classification within other comprehensive income the net gain or loss on derivative instruments designated and qualifying as cash flow hedging instruments that are reported in comprehensive income pursuant to paragraphs 30 and 41.

47. As part of the disclosures of accumulated other comprehensive income, pursuant to paragraph 26 of FASB Statement No. 130, *Reporting Comprehensive Income,* an entity shall separately disclose the beginning and ending accumulated derivative gain or loss, the related net change associated with current period hedging transactions, and the net amount of any reclassification into earnings.

Effective Date and Transition

48. This Statement shall be effective for all fiscal quarters of all fiscal years beginning after June 15, 1999. Initial application of this Statement shall be as of the beginning of an entity's fiscal quarter; on that date, hedging relationships shall be designated anew and documented pursuant to the provisions of this Statement. Earlier application of all of the provisions of this Statement is encouraged but is permitted only as of the beginning of any fiscal quarter that begins after issuance of this Statement. Earlier application of selected provisions of this Statement is not permitted. This Statement shall not be applied retroactively to financial statements of prior periods.

49. At the date of initial application, an entity shall recognize all freestanding derivative instruments (that is, derivative instruments other than embedded derivative instruments) in the statement of financial position as either assets or liabilities and measure them at fair value, pursuant to paragraph 17.[13] The difference between a derivative's previous carrying amount and its fair value shall be reported as a transition adjustment, as discussed in paragraph 52. The entity also shall recognize offsetting gains and losses on hedged assets, liabilities, and firm commitments

---

[13]For a compound derivative that has a foreign currency exchange risk component (such as a foreign currency interest rate swap), an entity is permitted at the date of initial application to separate the compound derivative into two parts: the foreign currency derivative and the remaining derivative. Each of them would thereafter be accounted for at fair value, with an overall limit that the sum of their fair values could not exceed the fair value of the compound derivative. An entity may not separate a compound derivative into components representing different risks after the date of initial application.

by adjusting their carrying amounts at that date, as discussed in paragraph 52(b). Any gains or losses on derivative instruments that are reported independently as deferred gains or losses (that is, liabilities or assets) in the statement of financial position at the date of initial application shall be derecognized from that statement; that derecognition also shall be reported as transition adjustments as indicated in paragraph 52. Any gains or losses on derivative instruments reported in other comprehensive income at the date of initial application because the derivative instruments were hedging the fair value exposure of available-for-sale securities also shall be reported as transition adjustments; the offsetting losses and gains on the securities shall be accounted for pursuant to paragraph 52(b). Any gain or loss on a derivative instrument reported in accumulated other comprehensive income at the date of initial application because the derivative instrument was hedging the *variable cash flow exposure* of a forecasted (anticipated) transaction related to an available-for-sale security shall remain in accumulated other comprehensive income and shall *not* be reported as a transition adjustment. The accounting for any gains and losses on derivative instruments that arose prior to the initial application of the Statement and that were previously added to the carrying amount of recognized hedged assets or liabilities is not affected by this Statement. Those gains and losses shall not be included in the transition adjustment.

50. At the date of initial application, an entity also shall recognize as an asset or liability in the statement of financial position any embedded derivative instrument that is required pursuant to paragraphs 12–16 to be separated from its host contract if the hybrid instrument in which it is embedded was issued, acquired, or substantively modified by the entity after December 31, 1997. For all of its hybrid instruments that exist at the date of initial application and were issued or acquired before January 1, 1998 and not substantively modified thereafter, an entity may choose either (a) not to apply this Statement to any of those hybrid instruments or (b) to recognize as assets or liabilities all the derivative instruments embedded in those hybrid instruments that would be required pursuant to paragraphs 12–16 to be separated from their host contracts. That choice is not permitted to be applied to only some of an entity's individual hybrid instruments and must be applied on an all-or-none basis.

51. If an embedded derivative instrument is to be separated from its host contract in conjunction with

the initial application of this Statement, the entity shall consider the following in determining the related transition adjustment:

a. The carrying amount of the host contract at the date of initial application shall be based on its fair value on the date that the hybrid instrument was issued or acquired by the entity and shall reflect appropriate adjustments for subsequent activity, such as subsequent cash receipts or payments and the amortization of any premium or discount on the host contract arising from the separation of the embedded derivative.

b. The carrying amount of the embedded derivative instrument at the date of initial application shall be its fair value.

c. The transition adjustment shall be the difference at the date of initial application between (1) the previous carrying amount of the hybrid instrument and (2) the sum of the new net carrying amount of the host contract and the fair value of the embedded derivative instrument. The entity shall not retroactively designate a hedging relationship that could have been made had the embedded derivative instrument initially been accounted for separate from the host contract.

52. The transition adjustments resulting from adopting this Statement shall be reported in net income or other comprehensive income, as appropriate, as the effect of a change in accounting principle and presented in a manner similar to the cumulative effect of a change in accounting principle as described in paragraph 20 of APB Opinion No. 20, *Accounting Changes*. Whether a transition adjustment related to a specific derivative instrument is reported in net income, reported in other comprehensive income, or allocated between both is based on the hedging relationships, if any, that had existed for that derivative instrument and that were the basis for accounting under generally accepted accounting principles before the date of initial application of this Statement.

a. If the transition adjustment relates to a derivative instrument that had been designated in a hedging relationship that addressed the variable cash flow exposure of a forecasted (anticipated) transaction, the transition adjustment shall be reported as a cumulative-effect-type adjustment of accumulated other comprehensive income.

b. If the transition adjustment relates to a derivative instrument that had been designated in a hedging relationship that addressed the fair value exposure of an asset, a liability, or a firm commitment, the transition adjustment for the derivative shall be reported as a cumulative-effect-type adjustment of net income. Concurrently, any gain or loss on the hedged item (that is, difference between the hedged item's fair value and its carrying amount) shall be recognized as an adjustment of the hedged item's carrying amount at the date of initial application, but only to the extent of an offsetting transition adjustment for the derivative. That adjustment of the hedged item's carrying amount shall also be reported as a cumulative-effect-type adjustment of net income. The transition adjustment related to the gain or loss reported in accumulated other comprehensive income on a derivative instrument that hedged an available-for-sale security, together with the loss or gain on the related security (to the extent of an offsetting transition adjustment for the derivative instrument), shall be reclassified to earnings as a cumulative-effect-type adjustment of both net income and accumulated other comprehensive income.

c. If a derivative instrument had been designated in multiple hedging relationships that addressed both the fair value exposure of an asset or a liability and the variable cash flow exposure of a forecasted (anticipated) transaction, the transition adjustment for the derivative shall be allocated between the cumulative-effect-type adjustment of net income and the cumulative-effect-type adjustment of accumulated other comprehensive income and shall be reported as discussed in paragraphs 52(a) and 52(b) above. Concurrently, any gain or loss on the hedged item shall be accounted for at the date of initial application as discussed in paragraph 52(b) above.

d. Other transition adjustments not encompassed by paragraphs 52(a), 52(b), and 52(c) above shall be reported as part of the cumulative-effect-type adjustment of net income.

53. Any transition adjustment reported as a cumulative-effect-type adjustment of accumulated other comprehensive income shall be subsequently reclassified into earnings in a manner consistent with paragraph 31. For those amounts, an entity shall disclose separately in the year of initial application the amount of gains and losses reported in accumulated other comprehensive income and associated with the transition adjustment that are being reclassified into earnings during the 12 months following the date of initial application.

54. At the date of initial application, an entity may transfer any held-to-maturity security into the available-for-sale category or the trading category. An entity will then be able in the future to designate a security transferred into the available-for-sale category as the hedged item, or its variable interest payments as the cash flow hedged transactions, in a hedge of the exposure to changes in market interest rates, changes in foreign currency exchange rates, or changes in its overall fair value. (Paragraph 21(d) precludes a held-to-maturity security from being designated as the hedged item in a fair value hedge of market interest rate risk or the risk of changes in its overall fair value. Paragraph 29(e) similarly precludes the variable cash flows of a held-to-maturity security from being designated as the hedged transaction in a cash flow hedge of market interest rate risk.) The unrealized holding gain or loss on a held-to-maturity security transferred to another category at the date of initial application shall be reported in net income or accumulated other comprehensive income consistent with the requirements of paragraphs 15(b) and 15(c) of Statement 115 and reported with the other transition adjustments discussed in paragraph 52 of this Statement. Such transfers from the held-to-maturity category at the date of initial adoption shall not call into question an entity's intent to hold other debt securities to maturity in the future.[14]

55. At the date of initial application, an entity may transfer any available-for-sale security into the trading category. After any related transition adjustments from initially applying this Statement have been recognized, the unrealized holding gain or loss remaining in accumulated other comprehensive income for any transferred security at the date of initial application shall be reclassified into earnings (but not reported as part of the cumulative-effect-type adjustment for the transition adjustments), consistent with

---

[14]EITF Topic No. D-51, "The Applicability of FASB Statement No. 115 to Desecuritizations of Financial Assets," indicates that certain financial assets received or retained in a desecuritization must be held to maturity to avoid calling into question the entity's intent to hold other debt securities to maturity in the future. In conjunction with the initial adoption of this Statement, the held-to-maturity restriction on those financial assets held on the date of initial application is removed, and those financial assets that had been received or retained in a previous desecuritization are available in the future to be designated as the hedged item, or their variable interest payments as the hedged transaction, in a hedge of the exposure to changes in market interest rates. Consequently, the sale of those financial assets before maturity would not call into question the entity's intent to hold other debt securities to maturity in the future.

paragraph 15(b) of Statement 115. If a derivative instrument had been hedging the variable cash flow exposure of a forecasted transaction related to an available-for-sale security that is transferred into the trading category at the date of initial application and the entity had reported a gain or loss on that derivative instrument in other comprehensive income (consistent with paragraph 115 of Statement 115), the entity also shall reclassify those derivative gains and losses into earnings (but not report them as part of the cumulative-effect-type adjustment for the transition adjustments).

56. At the date of initial application, mortgage bankers and other servicers of financial assets may choose to restratify their servicing rights pursuant to paragraph 37(g) of Statement 125 in a manner that would enable individual strata to comply with the requirements of this Statement regarding what constitutes "a portfolio of similar assets." As noted in footnote 9 of this Statement, mortgage bankers and other servicers of financial assets that designate a hedged portfolio by aggregating servicing rights within one or more risk strata used under paragraph 37(g) of Statement 125 would not necessarily comply with the requirement in paragraph 21(a) of this Statement for portfolios of similar assets, since the risk stratum under paragraph 37(g) of Statement 125 can be based on any predominant risk characteristic, including date of origination or geographic location. The restratification of servicing rights is a change in the application of an accounting principle, and the effect of that change as of the initial application of this Statement shall be reported as part of the cumulative-effect-type adjustment for the transition adjustments.

> **The provisions of this Statement need**
> **not be applied to immaterial items.**

This Statement was adopted by the unanimous vote of the seven members of the Financial Accounting Standards Board:

Edmund L. Jenkins,	Anthony T. Cope	James J. Leisenring
Chairman	John M. Foster	Gerhard G. Mueller
Joseph V. Anania	Gaylen N. Larson	

Appendix A

IMPLEMENTATION GUIDANCE

Section 1: Scope and Definition

Application of Paragraphs 6–11

57. The following discussion further explains the three characteristics of a derivative instrument discussed in paragraphs 6–9.

a. *Underlying.* An underlying is a variable that, along with either a notional amount or a payment provision, determines the settlement of a derivative. An underlying usually is one or a combination of the following:

(1) A security price or security price index
(2) A commodity price or commodity price index
(3) An interest rate or interest rate index
(4) A credit rating or credit index
(5) An exchange rate or exchange rate index

(6) An insurance index or catastrophe loss index
(7) A climatic or geological condition (such as temperature, earthquake severity, or rainfall), another physical variable, or a related index.

However, an underlying may be any variable whose changes are observable or otherwise objectively verifiable. Paragraph 10(e) specifically excludes a contract with settlement based on certain variables unless the contract is exchange-traded. A contract based on any variable that is not specifically excluded is subject to the requirements of this Statement if it has the other two characteristics identified in paragraph 6 (which also are discussed in paragraphs 57(b) and 57(c) below).

b. *Initial net investment.* A derivative requires no initial net investment or a smaller initial net investment than other types of contracts that have a similar response to changes in market factors. For example, entering into a commodity futures contract generally requires no net investment, while purchasing the same commodity requires an initial net investment equal to its market price. However, both contracts reflect changes in the price of the commodity in the same way (that is, similar gains or losses will be incurred). A swap or forward contract also generally does not require an initial net investment unless the terms favor one party over the other. An option generally requires that one party make an initial net investment (a premium) because that party has the rights under the contract and the other party has the obligations. The phrase *initial net investment* is stated from the perspective of only one party to the contract, but it determines the application of the Statement for both parties.[15]

c. *Net settlement.* A contract that meets any one of the following criteria has the characteristic described as net settlement:

(1) Its terms implicitly or explicitly require or permit net settlement. For example, a penalty for nonperformance in a purchase order is a net settlement provision if the amount of the penalty is based on changes in the price of the items that are the subject of the contract. Net settlement may be made in cash or by delivery of any other asset, whether or not it is readily convertible to cash. A fixed penalty for nonperformance is not a net settlement provision.

(2) There is an established market mechanism that facilitates net settlement outside the contract. The term *market mechanism* is to be interpreted broadly. Any institutional arrangement or other agreement that enables either party to be relieved of all rights and obligations under the contract and to liquidate its net position without incurring a significant transaction cost is considered net settlement.

(3) It requires delivery of an asset that is readily convertible to cash. The definition of *readily convertible to cash* in FASB Concepts Statement No. 5, *Recognition and Measurement in Financial Statements of Business Enterprises,* includes, for example, a security or commodity traded in an active market and a unit of foreign currency that is readily convertible into the functional currency of the reporting entity. A security that is publicly traded but for which the market is not very active is readily

convertible to cash if the number of shares or other units of the security to be exchanged is small relative to the daily transaction volume. That same security would not be readily convertible if the number of shares to be exchanged is large relative to the daily transaction volume. The ability to use a security that is not publicly traded or an agricultural or mineral product without an active market as collateral in a borrowing does not, in and of itself, mean that the security or the commodity is readily convertible to cash.

58. The following discussion further explains some of the exceptions discussed in paragraph 10.

a. *"Regular-way" security trades.* The exception in paragraph 10(a) applies only to a contract that requires delivery of securities that are readily convertible to cash.[16] To qualify, a contract must require delivery of such a security within the period of time after the trade date that is customary in the market in which the trade takes place. For example, a contract to purchase or sell a publicly traded equity security in the United States customarily requires settlement within three business days. If a contract for purchase of that type of security requires settlement in three business days, the regular-way exception applies, but if the contract requires settlement in five days, the regular-way exception does not apply. This Statement does not change whether an entity recognizes regular-way security trades on the trade date or the settlement date. However, trades that do not qualify for the regular-way exception are subject to the requirements of this Statement regardless of the method an entity uses to report its security trades.

b. *Normal purchases and normal sales.* The exception in paragraph 10(b) applies only to a contract that requires future delivery of assets (other than financial instruments or derivative instruments) that are readily convertible to cash[17] and only if there is no market mechanism to facilitate net settlement outside the contract. To qualify for the

---

[15]Even though a contract may be a derivative as described in paragraphs 6–10 for both parties, the exceptions in paragraph 11 apply only to the issuer of the contract and will result in different reporting by the two parties. The exception in paragraph 10(b) also may apply to one of the parties but not the other.

[16]Contracts that require delivery of securities that are not readily convertible to cash are not subject to the requirements of this Statement unless there is a market mechanism outside the contract to facilitate net settlement.

[17]Contracts that require delivery of assets that are not readily convertible to cash are not subject to the requirements of this Statement unless there is a market mechanism outside the contract to facilitate net settlement.

exception, a contract's terms also must be consistent with the terms of an entity's normal purchases or normal sales, that is, the quantity purchased or sold must be reasonable in relation to the entity's business needs. Determining whether or not the terms are consistent will require judgment. In making those judgments, an entity should consider all relevant factors, such as (1) the quantities provided under the contract and the entity's need for the related assets, (2) the locations to which delivery of the items will be made, (3) the period of time between entering into the contract and delivery, and (4) the entity's prior practices with regard to such contracts. Evidence such as past trends, expected future demand, other contracts for delivery of similar items, an entity's and industry's customs for acquiring and storing the related commodities, and an entity's operating locations should help in identifying contracts that qualify as normal purchases or normal sales.

c. *Certain contracts that are not traded on an exchange.* A contract that is not traded on an exchange is not subject to the requirements of this Statement if the underlying is:

  (1) A climatic or geological variable or other physical variable. Climatic, geological, and other physical variables include things like the number of inches of rainfall or snow in a particular area and the severity of an earthquake as measured by the Richter scale.

  (2) The price or value of (a) a nonfinancial asset of one of the parties to the contract unless that asset is readily convertible to cash or (b) a nonfinancial liability of one of the parties to the contract unless that liability requires delivery of an asset that is readily convertible to cash.

  (3) Specified volumes of sales or service revenues by one of the parties. That exception is intended to apply to contracts with settlements based on the volume of items sold or services rendered, for example, royalty agreements. It is not intended to apply to contracts based on changes in sales or revenues due to changes in market prices.

If a contract's underlying is the combination of two or more variables, and one or more would not qualify for one of the exceptions above, the application of this Statement to that contract depends on the predominant characteristics of the combined variable. The contract is subject to the requirements of this Statement if the changes in its combined underlying are highly correlated with changes in one of the component variables that would not qualify for an exception.

59. The following discussion illustrates the application of paragraphs 6–11 in several situations.

a. *Forward purchases or sales of to-be-announced securities or securities when-issued, as-issued, or if-issued.* A contract for the purchase and sale of a security when, as, or if issued or to be announced is excluded from the requirements of this Statement as a regular-way security trade if (1) there is no other way to purchase or sell that security and (2) settlement will occur within the shortest period possible for that security.

b. *Credit-indexed contracts (often referred to as credit derivatives).* Many different types of contracts are indexed to the creditworthiness of a specified entity or group of entities, but not all of them are derivative instruments. Credit-indexed contracts that have certain characteristics described in paragraph 10(d) are guarantees and are not subject to the requirements of this Statement. Credit-indexed contracts that do not have the characteristics necessary to qualify for the exception in paragraph 10(d) are subject to the requirements of this Statement. One example of the latter is a credit-indexed contract that requires a payment due to changes in the creditworthiness of a specified entity even if neither party incurs a loss due to the change (other than a loss caused by the payment under the credit-indexed contract).

c. *Take-or-pay contracts.* Under a take-or-pay contract, an entity agrees to pay a specified price for a specified quantity of a product whether or not it takes delivery. Whether a take-or-pay contract is subject to this Statement depends on its terms. For example, if the product to be delivered is not readily convertible to cash and there is no net settlement option, the contract fails to meet the criterion in paragraph 6(c) and is not subject to the requirements of this Statement. However, a contract that meets all of the following conditions is subject to the requirements of this Statement: (1) the product to be delivered is readily convertible to cash, (2) the contract does not qualify for the normal purchases and normal sales exception in paragraph 10(b), and (3) little or no initial net investment in the contract is required.

d. *Short sales (sales of borrowed securities).*[18] Short sales typically involve the following activities:

   (1) Selling a security (by the short seller to the purchaser)

   (2) Borrowing a security (by the short seller from the lender)

   (3) Delivering the borrowed security (by the short seller to the purchaser)

   (4) Purchasing a security (by the short seller from the market)

   (5) Delivering the purchased security (by the short seller to the lender).

Those five activities involve three separate contracts. A contract that distinguishes a short sale involves activities (2) and (5), borrowing a security and replacing it by delivering an identical security. Such a contract has two of the three characteristics of a derivative instrument. The settlement is based on an underlying (the price of the security) and a notional amount (the face amount of the security or the number of shares), and the settlement is made by delivery of a security that is readily convertible to cash. However, the other characteristic, little or no initial net investment, is not present. The borrowed security is the lender's initial net investment in the contract. Consequently, the contract relating to activities (2) and (5) is not a derivative instrument. The other two contracts (one for activities (1) and (3) and the other for activity (4)) are routine and do not generally involve derivative instruments. However, if a forward purchase or sale is involved, and the contract does not qualify for the exception in paragraph 10(a), it is subject to the requirements of this Statement.

e. *Repurchase agreements and "wash sales"* (accounted for as sales as described in paragraphs 68 and 69 of Statement 125). A transfer of financial assets accounted for as a sale under Statement 125 in which the transferor is both obligated and entitled to repurchase the transferred asset at a fixed or determinable price contains two separate features, one of which may be a derivative. The initial exchange of financial assets for cash is a sale-purchase transaction—generally not a transaction that involves a derivative instrument. However, the accompanying forward contract that gives the transferor the right and obligation to repurchase the transferred asset involves an underlying and a notional amount (the price of the security and its denomination), and it does not require an initial

net investment in the contract. Consequently, if the forward contract requires delivery of a security that is readily convertible to cash or otherwise meets the net settlement criterion in paragraph 9, it is subject to the requirements of this Statement.

Application of the Clearly-and-Closely-Related Criterion in Paragraphs 12–16

60. In discussing whether a hybrid instrument contains an embedded derivative instrument (also simply referred to as an *embedded derivative*) that warrants separate accounting, paragraph 12 focuses on whether the economic characteristics and risks of the embedded derivative are clearly and closely related to the economic characteristics and risks of the host contract. If the host contract encompasses a residual interest in an entity, then its economic characteristics and risks should be considered that of an equity instrument and an embedded derivative would need to possess principally equity characteristics (related to the same entity) to be considered clearly and closely related to the host contract. However, most commonly, a financial instrument host contract will not embody a claim to the residual interest in an entity and, thus, the economic characteristics and risks of the host contract should be considered that of a debt instrument. For example, even though the overall hybrid instrument that provides for repayment of principal may include a return based on the market price (the underlying as defined in this Statement) of XYZ Corporation common stock, the host contract does not involve any existing or potential residual interest rights (that is, rights of ownership) and thus would not be an equity instrument. The host contract would instead be considered a debt instrument, and the embedded derivative that incorporates the equity-based return would not be clearly and closely related to the host contract. If the embedded derivative is considered *not* to be clearly and closely related to the host contract, the embedded derivative must be separated from the host contract and accounted for as a derivative instrument *by both parties* to the hybrid instrument, except as provided by paragraph 11(a).

61. The following guidance is relevant in deciding whether the economic characteristics and risks of the embedded derivative are clearly and closely related to the economic characteristics and risks of the host contract.

---

[18]This discussion applies only to short sales with the characteristics described here. Some groups of transactions that are referred to as short sales may have different characteristics. If so, a different analysis would be appropriate, and other derivative instruments may be involved.

a. *Interest rate indexes.* An embedded derivative in which the underlying is an interest rate or interest rate index and a host contract that is considered a debt instrument are considered to be clearly and closely related unless, as discussed in paragraph 13, the embedded derivative contains a provision that (1) permits any possibility whatsoever that the investor's (or creditor's) undiscounted net cash inflows over the life of the instrument would not recover substantially all of its initial recorded investment in the hybrid instrument under its contractual terms or (2) could under any possibility whatsoever at least double the investor's initial rate of return on the host contract and also result in a rate of return that is at least twice what otherwise would be the market return for a contract that has the same terms as the host contract and that involves a debtor with a similar credit quality. The requirement to separate the embedded derivative from the host contract applies to *both parties* to the hybrid instrument even though the above tests focus on the investor's net cash inflows. Plain-vanilla servicing rights, which involve an obligation to perform servicing and the right to receive fees for performing that servicing, do not contain an embedded derivative that would be separated from those servicing rights and accounted for as a derivative.

b. *Inflation-indexed interest payments.* The interest rate and the rate of inflation in the economic environment for the currency in which a debt instrument is denominated are considered to be clearly and closely related. Thus, nonleveraged inflation-indexed contracts (debt instruments, capitalized lease obligations, pension obligations, and so forth) would *not* have the inflation-related embedded derivative separated from the host contract.

c. *Credit-sensitive payments.* The creditworthiness of the debtor and the interest rate on a debt instrument are considered to be clearly and closely related. Thus, for debt instruments that have the interest rate reset in the event of (1) default (such as violation of a credit-risk-related covenant), (2) a change in the debtor's published credit rating, or (3) a change in the debtor's creditworthiness indicated by a change in its spread over Treasury bonds, the related embedded derivative would *not* be separated from the host contract.

d. *Calls and puts on debt instruments.* Call options (or put options) that can accelerate the repayment of principal on a debt instrument are considered to be clearly and closely related to a debt instrument that requires principal repayments unless both (1) the debt involves a substantial premium or discount (which is common with zero-coupon bonds) and (2) the put or call option is only contingently exercisable. Thus, if a substantial premium or discount is not involved, embedded calls and puts (including contingent call or put options that are not exercisable unless an event of default occurs) would *not* be separated from the host contract. However, for contingently exercisable calls and puts to be considered clearly and closely related, they can be indexed only to interest rates or credit risk, not some extraneous event or factor. In contrast, call options (or put options) that do not accelerate the repayment of principal on a debt instrument but instead require a cash settlement that is equal to the price of the option at the date of exercise would *not* be considered to be clearly and closely related to the debt instrument in which it is embedded and would be separated from the host contract. In certain unusual situations, a put or call option may have been subsequently added to a debt instrument in a manner that causes the investor (creditor) to be exposed to performance risk (default risk) by different parties for the embedded option and the host debt instrument, respectively. In those unusual situations, the embedded option and the host debt instrument are *not* clearly and closely related.

e. *Calls and puts on equity instruments.* A put option that enables the holder to require the issuer of an equity instrument to reacquire that equity instrument for cash or other assets is *not* clearly and closely related to that equity instrument. Thus, such a put option embedded in the equity instrument to which it relates should be separated from the host contract by the holder of the equity instrument. That put option also should be separated from the host contract by the issuer of the equity instrument except in those cases in which the put option is not considered to be a derivative instrument pursuant to paragraph 11(a) because it is classified in stockholders' equity. A purchased call option that enables the issuer of an equity instrument (such as common stock) to reacquire that equity instrument would not be considered to be a derivative instrument by the issuer of the equity instrument pursuant to paragraph 11(a). Thus, if the call option were embedded in the related equity instrument, it would not be separated from the host contract by the issuer. However, for the holder of the related equity instrument, the embedded written call option would *not* be considered to be clearly and closely related to the equity instrument and should be separated from the host contract.

f. *Floors, caps, and collars.* Floors or caps (or collars, which are combinations of caps and floors) on interest rates and the interest rate on a debt instrument are considered to be clearly and closely related, provided the cap is at or above the current market price (or rate) and the floor is at or below the current market price (or rate) at issuance of the instrument. Thus, the derivative embedded in a variable-rate debt instrument that has a floor on the interest rate (that is, the floor option) would not be separated from the host contract and accounted for separately even though, in a falling interest rate environment, the debt instrument may have a return to the investor that is a significant amount above the market return of a debt instrument without the floor provision (refer to paragraph 13(b)).

g. *Term-extending options.* An embedded derivative provision that either (1) unilaterally enables one party to extend significantly the remaining term to maturity or (2) automatically extends significantly the remaining term triggered by specific events or conditions is *not* clearly and closely related to the interest rate on a debt instrument unless the interest rate is concurrently reset to the approximate current market rate for the extended term and the debt instrument initially involved no significant discount. Thus, if there is no reset of interest rates, the embedded derivative must be separated from the host contract and accounted for as a derivative instrument. That is, a term-extending option cannot be used to circumvent the restriction in paragraph 61(a) regarding the investor's not recovering substantially all of its initial recorded investment.

h. *Equity-indexed interest payments.* The changes in fair value of an equity interest and the interest yield on a debt instrument are *not* clearly and closely related. Thus, an equity-related derivative embedded in an equity-indexed debt instrument (whether based on the price of a specific common stock or on an index that is based on a basket of equity instruments) must be separated from the host contract and accounted for as a derivative instrument.

i. *Commodity-indexed interest or principal payments.* The changes in fair value of a commodity (or other asset) and the interest yield on a debt instrument are *not* clearly and closely related. Thus, a commodity-related derivative embedded in a commodity-indexed debt instrument must be separated from the noncommodity host contract and accounted for as a derivative instrument.

j. *Indexed rentals:*

(1) *Inflation-indexed rentals.* Rentals for the use of leased assets and adjustments for inflation on similar property are considered to be clearly and closely related. Thus, unless a significant leverage factor is involved, the inflation-related derivative embedded in an inflation-indexed lease contract would *not* be separated from the host contract.

(2) *Contingent rentals based on related sales.* Lease contracts that include contingent rentals based on certain sales of the lessee would *not* have the contingent-rental-related embedded derivative separated from the host contract because, under paragraph 10(e)(3), a non-exchange-traded contract whose underlying is specified volumes of sales by one of the parties to the contract would not be subject to the requirements of this Statement.

(3) *Contingent rentals based on a variable interest rate.* The obligation to make future payments for the use of leased assets and the adjustment of those payments to reflect changes in a variable-interest-rate index are considered to be clearly and closely related. Thus, lease contracts that include contingent rentals based on changes in the prime rate would *not* have the contingent-rental-related embedded derivative separated from the host contract.

k. *Convertible debt.* The changes in fair value of an equity interest and the interest rates on a debt instrument are not clearly and closely related. Thus, for a debt security that is convertible into a specified number of shares of the debtor's common stock or another entity's common stock, the embedded derivative (that is, the conversion option) must be separated from the debt host contract and accounted for as a derivative instrument provided that the conversion option would, as a freestanding instrument, be a derivative instrument subject to the requirements of this Statement. (For example, if the common stock was not readily convertible to cash, a conversion option that requires purchase of the common stock would not be accounted for as a derivative.) That accounting applies only to the holder (investor) if the debt is convertible to the debtor's common stock because, under paragraph 11(a), a separate option with the same terms would not be considered to be a derivative for the issuer.

l. *Convertible preferred stock.* Because the changes in fair value of an equity interest and interest rates on a debt instrument are not clearly and closely related, the terms of the preferred stock (other than the conversion option) must be analyzed to determine whether the preferred stock (and thus the potential host contract) is more akin to an equity instrument or a debt instrument. A typical cumulative fixed-rate preferred stock that has a mandatory redemption feature is more akin to debt, whereas cumulative participating perpetual preferred stock is more akin to an equity instrument.

Section 2: Assessment of Hedge Effectiveness

Hedge Effectiveness Requirements of This Statement

62. This Statement requires that an entity define at the time it designates a hedging relationship the method it will use to assess the hedge's effectiveness in achieving offsetting changes in fair value or offsetting cash flows attributable to the risk being hedged. It also requires that an entity use that defined method consistently throughout the hedge period (a) to assess at inception of the hedge and on an ongoing basis whether it expects the hedging relationship to be highly effective in achieving offset and (b) to measure the ineffective part of the hedge. If the entity identifies an improved method and wants to apply that method prospectively, it must discontinue the existing hedging relationship and designate the relationship anew using the improved method. This Statement does not specify a single method for either assessing whether a hedge is expected to be highly effective or measuring hedge ineffectiveness. The appropriateness of a given method of assessing hedge effectiveness can depend on the nature of the risk being hedged and the type of hedging instrument used. Ordinarily, however, an entity should assess effectiveness for similar hedges in a similar manner; use of different methods for similar hedges should be justified.

63. In defining how hedge effectiveness will be assessed, an entity must specify whether it will include in that assessment all of the gain or loss on a hedging instrument. This Statement permits (but does not require) an entity to exclude all or a part of the hedging instrument's time value from the assessment of hedge effectiveness, as follows:

a. If the effectiveness of a hedge with an option contract is assessed based on changes in the option's intrinsic value, the change in the time value of the contract would be excluded from the assessment of hedge effectiveness.

b. If the effectiveness of a hedge with an option contract is assessed based on changes in the option's minimum value, that is, its intrinsic value plus the effect of discounting, the change in the volatility value of the contract would be excluded from the assessment of hedge effectiveness.

c. If the effectiveness of a hedge with a forward or futures contract is assessed based on changes in fair value attributable to changes in spot prices, the change in the fair value of the contract related to the changes in the difference between the spot price and the forward or futures price would be excluded from the assessment of hedge effectiveness.

In each circumstance above, changes in the excluded component would be included currently in earnings, together with any ineffectiveness that results under the defined method of assessing ineffectiveness. As noted in paragraph 62, the effectiveness of similar hedges generally should be assessed similarly; that includes whether a component of the gain or loss on a derivative is excluded in assessing effectiveness. No other components of a gain or loss on the designated hedging instrument may be excluded from the assessment of hedge effectiveness.

64. In assessing the effectiveness of a cash flow hedge, an entity generally will need to consider the time value of money if significant in the circumstances. Considering the effect of the time value of money is especially important if the hedging instrument involves periodic cash settlements. An example of a situation in which an entity likely would reflect the time value of money is a tailing strategy with futures contracts. When using a tailing strategy, an entity adjusts the size or contract amount of futures contracts used in a hedge so that earnings (or expense) from reinvestment (or funding) of daily settlement gains (or losses) on the futures do not distort the results of the hedge. To assess offset of expected cash flows when a tailing strategy has been used, an entity could reflect the time value of money, perhaps by comparing the present value of the hedged forecasted cash flow with the results of the hedging instrument.

65. Whether a hedging relationship qualifies as highly effective sometimes will be easy to assess, and there will be no ineffectiveness to recognize in earnings during the term of the hedge. If the critical terms

of the hedging instrument and of the entire hedged asset or liability (as opposed to selected cash flows) or hedged forecasted transaction are the same, the entity could conclude that changes in fair value or cash flows attributable to the risk being hedged are expected to completely offset at inception and on an ongoing basis. For example, an entity may assume that a hedge of a forecasted purchase of a commodity with a forward contract will be highly effective and that there will be no ineffectiveness to be recognized in earnings if:

a. The forward contract is for purchase of the same quantity of the same commodity at the same time and location as the hedged forecasted purchase.
b. The fair value of the forward contract at inception is zero.
c. Either the change in the discount or premium on the forward contract is excluded from the assessment of effectiveness and included directly in earnings pursuant to paragraph 63 or the change in expected cash flows on the forecasted transaction is based on the forward price for the commodity.

66. Assessing hedge effectiveness and measuring the ineffective part of the hedge, however, can be more complex. For example, hedge ineffectiveness would result from the following circumstances, among others:

a. A difference between the basis of the hedging instrument and the hedged item or hedged transaction (such as a Deutsche mark–based hedging instrument and Dutch guilder–based hedged item), to the extent that those bases do not move in tandem
b. Differences in critical terms of the hedging instrument and hedged item or hedged transaction, such as differences in notional amounts, maturities, quantity, location, or delivery dates.

Ineffectiveness also would result if part of the change in the fair value of a derivative is attributable to a change in the counterparty's creditworthiness.

67. A hedge that meets the effectiveness test specified in paragraphs 20(b) and 28(b) (that is, both at inception and on an ongoing basis, the entity expects the hedge to be highly effective at achieving offsetting changes in fair values or cash flows) also must meet the other hedge accounting criteria to qualify for hedge accounting. If the hedge initially qualifies for hedge accounting, the entity would continue to assess whether the hedge meets the effectiveness test

and also would measure any ineffectiveness during the hedge period. If the hedge fails the effectiveness test at any time (that is, if the entity does not expect the hedge to be highly effective at achieving offsetting changes in fair values or cash flows), the hedge ceases to qualify for hedge accounting. The discussions of measuring hedge ineffectiveness in the examples in the remainder of this section of Appendix A assume that the hedge satisfied all of the criteria for hedge accounting at inception.

Assuming no ineffectiveness in a hedge with an interest rate swap

68. An assumption of no ineffectiveness is especially important in a hedging relationship involving an interest-bearing financial instrument and an interest rate swap because it significantly simplifies the computations necessary to make the accounting entries. An entity may assume no ineffectiveness in a hedging relationship of interest rate risk involving an interest-bearing asset or liability and an interest rate swap if all of the applicable conditions in the following list are met:

Conditions applicable to both fair value hedges and cash flow hedges

a. The notional amount of the swap matches the principal amount of the interest-bearing asset or liability.
b. The fair value of the swap at its inception is zero.
c. The formula for computing net settlements under the interest rate swap is the same for each net settlement. (That is, the fixed rate is the same throughout the term, and the variable rate is based on the same index and includes the same constant adjustment or no adjustment.)
d. The interest-bearing asset or liability is not prepayable.
e. Any other terms in the interest-bearing financial instruments or interest rate swaps are typical of those instruments and do not invalidate the assumption of no ineffectiveness.

Conditions applicable to fair value hedges only

f. The expiration date of the swap matches the maturity date of the interest-bearing asset or liability.
g. There is no floor or ceiling on the variable interest rate of the swap.
h. The interval between repricings of the variable interest rate in the swap is frequent enough to justify an assumption that the variable payment or receipt is at a market rate (generally three to six months or less).

Conditions applicable to cash flow hedges only

i. All interest receipts or payments on the variable-rate asset or liability during the term of the swap are designated as hedged, and no interest payments beyond the term of the swap are designated as hedged.

j. There is no floor or cap on the variable interest rate of the swap unless the variable-rate asset or liability has a floor or cap. In that case, the swap must have a floor or cap on the variable interest rate that is comparable to the floor or cap on the variable-rate asset or liability. (For this purpose, comparable does not necessarily mean equal. For example, if a swap's variable rate is LIBOR and an asset's variable rate is LIBOR plus 2 percent, a 10 percent cap on the swap would be comparable to a 12 percent cap on the asset.)

k. The repricing dates match those of the variable-rate asset or liability.

l. The index on which the variable rate is based matches the index on which the asset or liability's variable rate is based.

69. The fixed rate on a hedged item need not exactly match the fixed rate on a swap designated as a fair value hedge. Nor does the variable rate on an interest-bearing asset or liability need to be the same as the variable rate on a swap designated as a cash flow hedge. A swap's fair value comes from its net settlements. The fixed and variable rates on a swap can be changed without affecting the net settlement if both are changed by the same amount. That is, a swap with a payment based on LIBOR and a receipt based on a fixed rate of 5 percent has the same net settlements and fair value as a swap with a payment based on LIBOR plus 1 percent and a receipt based on a fixed rate of 6 percent.

70. Comparable credit risk at inception is not a condition for assuming no ineffectiveness even though actually achieving perfect offset would require that the same discount rate be used to determine the fair value of the swap and of the hedged item or hedged transaction. To justify using the same discount rate, the credit risk related to both parties to the swap as well as to the debtor on the hedged interest-bearing asset (in a fair value hedge) or the variable-rate asset on which the interest payments are hedged (in a cash flow hedge) would have to be the same. However,

because that complication is caused by the interaction of interest rate risk and credit risk, which are not easily separable, comparable creditworthiness is not considered a necessary condition to assume no ineffectiveness in a hedge of interest rate risk.

After-tax hedging of foreign currency risk

71. Statement 52 permitted hedging of foreign currency risk on an after-tax basis. The portion of the gain or loss on the hedging instrument that exceeded the loss or gain on the hedged item was required to be included as an offset to the related tax effects in the period in which those tax effects are recognized. This Statement continues those provisions.

***Illustrations of Assessing Effectiveness and
Measuring Ineffectiveness***

72. The following examples illustrate some ways in which an entity may assess hedge effectiveness and measures hedge ineffectiveness for specific strategies. The examples are not intended to imply that other reasonable methods are precluded. However, not all possible methods are reasonable or consistent with this Statement. This section also discusses some methods of assessing hedge effectiveness and determining hedge ineffectiveness that are not consistent with this Statement and thus may not be used.

*Example 1: Fair value hedge of natural gas
inventory with futures contracts*

73. Company A has 20,000 MMBTU's of natural gas stored at its location in West Texas. To hedge the fair value exposure of the natural gas, the company sells the equivalent of 20,000 MMBTU's of natural gas futures contracts on a national mercantile exchange. The futures prices are based on delivery of natural gas at the Henry Hub gas collection point in Louisiana.

Assessing the hedge's expected effectiveness

74. The price of Company A's natural gas inventory in West Texas and the price of the natural gas that is the underlying for the futures it sold will differ as a result of regional factors (such as location, pipeline transmission costs, and supply and demand).[19]

---

[19]The use of a hedging instrument with a different underlying basis than the item or transaction being hedged is generally referred to as a *cross-hedge*. The principles for cross-hedges illustrated in this example also apply to hedges involving other risks. For example, the effectiveness of a hedge of market interest rate risk in which one interest rate is used as a surrogate for another interest rate would be evaluated in the same way as the natural gas cross-hedge in this example.

Company A therefore may not automatically assume that the hedge will be highly effective at achieving offsetting changes in fair value, and it cannot assess effectiveness by looking solely to the change in the price of natural gas delivered to the Henry Hub.

75. Both at inception of the hedge and on an ongoing basis, Company A might assess the hedge's expected effectiveness based on the extent of correlation in recent years for periods similar to the term of the futures contracts between the spot prices of natural gas in West Texas and the spot prices at the Henry Hub.[20] If those prices have been and are expected to continue to be highly correlated, Company A might reasonably expect the changes in the fair value of the futures contracts attributable to changes in the spot price of natural gas at the Henry Hub to be highly effective in offsetting the changes in the fair value of its natural gas inventory. In assessing effectiveness during the term of the hedge, Company A must take into account actual changes in spot prices in West Texas and at the Henry Hub.

76. Company A may not assume that the change in the spot price of natural gas located at Henry Hub, Louisiana, is the same as the change in fair value of its West Texas inventory. The physical hedged item is natural gas in West Texas, not natural gas at the Henry Hub. In identifying the price risk that is being hedged, the company also may not assume that its natural gas in West Texas has a Louisiana natural gas "component." Use of a price for natural gas located somewhere other than West Texas to assess the effectiveness of a fair value hedge of natural gas in West Texas would be inconsistent with this Statement and could result in an assumption that a hedge was highly effective when it was not. If the price of natural gas in West Texas is not readily available, Company A might use a price for natural gas located elsewhere as a base for estimating the price of natural gas in West Texas. However, that base price must be adjusted to reflect the effects of factors, such as location, transmission costs, and supply and demand, that would cause the price of natural gas in West Texas to differ from the base price.

Measuring hedge ineffectiveness

77. Consistent with the company's method of assessing whether the hedge is expected to be highly effective, the hedge would be ineffective to the extent

that (a) the actual change in the fair value of the futures contracts attributable to changes in the spot price of natural gas at the Henry Hub did not offset (b) the actual change in the spot price of natural gas in West Texas per MMBTU multiplied by 20,000. That method excludes the change in the fair value of the futures contracts attributable to changes in the difference between the spot price and the forward price of natural gas at the Henry Hub in determining ineffectiveness. The excluded amount would be reported directly in earnings.

Example 2: Fair value hedge of tire inventory with a forward contract

78. Company B manufactures tires. The production of those tires incorporates a variety of physical components, of which rubber and steel are the most significant, as well as labor and overhead. The company hedges its exposure to changes in the fair value of its inventory of 8,000 steel-belted radial tires by entering into a forward contract to sell rubber at a fixed price.

Assessing the hedge's expected effectiveness

79. Company B decides to base its assessment of hedge effectiveness on changes in the fair value of the forward contract attributable to changes in the spot price of rubber. To determine whether the forward contract is expected to be highly effective at offsetting the change in fair value of the tire inventory, Company B could estimate and compare such changes in the fair value of the forward contract and changes in the fair value of the tires (computed as the market price per tire multiplied by 8,000 tires) for different rubber and tire prices. Company B also should consider the extent to which past changes in the spot prices of rubber and tires have been correlated. Because tires are a nonfinancial asset and rubber is only an ingredient in manufacturing them, Company B may not assess hedge effectiveness by looking to the change in the fair value of only the rubber component of the steel-belted radial tires (paragraph 21(e)). Both at inception of the hedge and during its term, the company must base its assessment of hedge effectiveness on changes in the market price of steel-belted radial tires and changes in the fair value of the forward contract attributable to changes in the spot price of rubber.

---

[20]The period of time over which correlation of prices should be assessed would be based on management's judgment in the particular circumstance.

Measuring hedge ineffectiveness

80. It is unlikely that this transaction would be highly effective in achieving offsetting changes in fair value. However, if Company B concludes that the hedge will be highly effective and the hedge otherwise qualifies for hedge accounting, the ineffective part of the hedge would be measured consistent with the company's method of assessing whether the hedge is expected to be highly effective. Based on that method, the hedge would be ineffective to the extent that the actual changes in (a) the fair value of the forward contract attributable to the change in the spot price of rubber and (b) the market price of steel-belted radials multiplied by the number of tires in inventory did not offset. Because Company B bases its assessment of effectiveness on changes in spot prices, the change in the fair value of the forward contract attributable to changes in the difference between the spot and forward price of rubber would be excluded from the measure of effectiveness and reported directly in earnings.

Example 3: Fair value hedge of growing wheat with futures contracts

81. Company C has a tract of land on which it is growing wheat. Historically, Company C has harvested at least 40,000 bushels of wheat from that tract of land. Two months before its expected harvest, the company sells 2-month futures contracts for 40,000 bushels of wheat, which it wants to designate as a fair value hedge of its growing wheat, rather than as a cash flow hedge of the projected sale of the wheat after harvest.

Assessing the hedge's expected effectiveness and measuring ineffectiveness

82. Even though the futures contracts are for the same type of wheat that Company C expects to harvest in two months, the futures contracts and hedged wheat have different bases because the futures contracts are based on fully grown, harvested wheat, while the hedged item is unharvested wheat with two months left in its growing cycle. The company therefore may not automatically assume that the hedge will be highly effective in achieving offsetting changes in fair value.

83. To determine whether the futures contracts are expected to be highly effective in providing offsetting changes in fair value for the growing wheat, Company C would need to estimate and compare the fair value of its growing wheat and of the futures contracts for different levels of wheat prices. Company C may not base its estimate of the value of its growing wheat solely on the current price of wheat because that price is for grown, harvested wheat. The company might, however, use the current price of harvested wheat together with other relevant factors, such as additional production and harvesting costs and the physical condition of the growing wheat, to estimate the current fair value of its growing wheat crop.

84. It is unlikely that wheat futures would be highly effective in offsetting the changes in value of growing wheat. However, if Company C concludes that the hedge qualifies as highly effective, it would use the same method for measuring actual hedge effectiveness that it uses initially and on an ongoing basis to assess whether the hedge is expected to be highly effective. The hedge would be ineffective to the extent that the actual changes in fair value of the futures contract and of the growing wheat crop did not offset.

Example 4: Fair value hedge of equity securities with option contracts

85. Company D holds 10,000 shares of XYZ stock. It purchases put option contracts on 20,000 shares of XYZ stock with a strike price equal to the current price of the stock to hedge its exposure to changes in the fair value of its investment position attributable to changes in the price of XYZ stock. Company D manages the position using a "delta-neutral" strategy. That is, it monitors the option's "delta"—the ratio of changes in the option's price to changes in the price of XYZ stock. As the delta ratio changes, Company D buys or sells put options so that the next change in the fair value of all of the options held can be expected to counterbalance the next change in the value of its investment in XYZ stock. For put options, the delta ratio moves closer to one as the share price of the stock falls and moves closer to zero as the share price rises. The delta ratio also changes as the exercise period decreases, as interest rates change, and as expected volatility changes. Company D designates the put options as a fair value hedge of its investment in XYZ stock.

Assessing the hedge's expected effectiveness and measuring ineffectiveness

86. Because Company D plans to change the number of options that it holds to the extent necessary to

maintain a delta-neutral position, it may not automatically assume that the hedge will be highly effective at achieving offsetting changes in fair value. Also, because the "delta-neutral" hedging strategy is based on expected changes in the option's fair value, the company may not assess effectiveness based on changes in the option's intrinsic value. Instead, Company D would estimate (a) the gain or loss on the option position that would result from various decreases or increases in the market price of XYZ stock and (b) the loss or gain on its investment in XYZ stock for the same market price changes. To assess the effectiveness of the hedge both at inception and on an ongoing basis, the company could compare the respective gains and losses from different market price changes. The ongoing assessment of effectiveness also must consider the actual changes in the fair value of the put options held and of the investment in XYZ stock during the hedge period.

87. Consistent with the company's method of assessing effectiveness, the hedge would be ineffective to the extent that the actual realized and unrealized gains or losses from changes in the fair value of the options held is greater or less than the change in value of the investment in XYZ stock. The underlying for the put option contracts is the market price of XYZ stock. Therefore, if Company D continually monitors the delta ratio and adjusts the number of options held accordingly, the changes in the fair value of the options and of the hedged item may almost completely offset, resulting in only a small amount of ineffectiveness to be recognized in earnings.

Example 5: Fair value hedge of a treasury bond with a put option contract

88. Company E owns a Treasury bond and wants to protect itself against the fair value exposure to declines in the price of the bond. The company purchases an at-the-money put option on a Treasury security with the same terms (remaining maturity, notional amount, and interest rate) as the Treasury bond held and designates the option as a hedge of the fair value exposure of the Treasury bond. Company E plans to hold the put option until it expires.

Assessing the hedge's expected effectiveness and measuring ineffectiveness

89. Because Company E plans to hold the put option (a static hedge) rather than manage the position with a delta-neutral strategy, it could assess whether it expects the hedge to be highly effective at achieving

offsetting changes in fair value by calculating and comparing the changes in the intrinsic value of the option and changes in the price (fair value) of the Treasury bond for different possible market prices. In assessing the expectation of effectiveness on an ongoing basis, the company also must consider the actual changes in the fair value of the Treasury bond and in the intrinsic value of the option during the hedge period.

90. However, because the pertinent critical terms of the option and the bond are the same in this example, the company could expect the changes in value of the bond attributable to changes in market interest rates and changes in the intrinsic value of the option to offset completely during the period that the option is in the money. That is, there will be no ineffectiveness because the company has chosen to exclude changes in the option's time value from the effectiveness test. Because of that choice, Company E must recognize changes in the time value of the option directly in earnings.

Example 6: Fair value hedge of an embedded purchased option with a written option

91. Company F issues five-year, fixed-rate debt with an embedded (purchased) call option and, with a different counterparty, writes a call option to neutralize the call feature in the debt. The embedded call option and the written call option have the same effective notional amount, underlying fixed interest rate, and strike price. (The strike price of the option in the debt usually is referred to as the call price.) The embedded option also can be exercised at the same times as the written option. Company F designates the written option as a fair value hedge of the embedded prepayment option component of the fixed-rate debt.

Assessing the hedge's expected effectiveness and measuring ineffectiveness

92. To assess whether the hedge is expected to be highly effective in achieving offsetting changes in fair value, Company F could estimate and compare the changes in fair values of the two options for different market interest rates. Because this Statement does not permit derivatives, including embedded derivatives whether or not they are required to be accounted for separately, to be separated into components, Company F can only designate a hedge of the entire change in fair value of the embedded purchased call option. The resulting changes in fair value will be included currently in earnings. Changes

in the fair value of the written option also will be included currently in earnings; any ineffectiveness thus will be automatically reflected in earnings. (The hedge is likely to have some ineffectiveness because the premium for the written call option is unlikely to be the same as the premium for the embedded purchased call option.)

Example 7: Cash flow hedge of a forecasted purchase of inventory with a forward contract

93. Company G forecasts the purchase of 500,000 pounds of Brazilian coffee for U.S. dollars in 6 months. It wants to hedge the cash flow exposure associated with changes in the U.S. dollar price of Brazilian coffee. Rather than acquire a derivative based on Brazilian coffee, the company enters into a 6-month forward contract to purchase 500,000 pounds of Colombian coffee for U.S. dollars and designates the forward contract as a cash flow hedge of its forecasted purchase of Brazilian coffee. All other terms of the forward contract and the forecasted purchase, such as delivery locations, are the same.

Assessing the hedge's expected effectiveness and measuring ineffectiveness

94. Company G bases its assessment of hedge effectiveness and measure of ineffectiveness on changes in forward prices, with the resulting gain or loss discounted to reflect the time value of money. Because of the difference in the bases of the forecasted transaction (Brazilian coffee) and forward contract (Colombian coffee), Company G may not assume that the hedge will automatically be highly effective in achieving offsetting cash flows. Both at inception and on an ongoing basis, Company G could assess the effectiveness of the hedge by comparing changes in the expected cash flows from the Colombian coffee forward contract with the expected net change in cash outflows for purchasing the Brazilian coffee for different market prices. (A simpler method that should produce the same results would consider the expected future correlation of the prices of Brazilian and Colombian coffee, based on the correlation of those prices over past six-month periods.)

95. In assessing hedge effectiveness on an ongoing basis, Company G also must consider the extent of offset between the change in expected cash flows on its Colombian coffee contract and the change in expected cash flows for the forecasted purchase of Brazilian coffee. Both changes would be measured on a cumulative basis for actual changes in the forward price of the respective coffees during the hedge period.

96. Because the only difference between the forward contract and forecasted purchase relates to the type of coffee (Colombian versus Brazilian), Company G could consider the changes in the cash flows on a forward contract for Brazilian coffee to be a measure of perfectly offsetting changes in cash flows for its forecasted purchase of Brazilian coffee. For example, for given changes in the U.S. dollar prices of six-month and three-month Brazilian and Colombian contracts, Company G could compute the effect of a change in the price of coffee on the expected cash flows of its forward contract on Colombian coffee and of a forward contract for Brazilian coffee as follows:

	Estimate of Change in Cash Flows	
	Hedging Instrument: **Forward Contract on Colombian Coffee**	*Estimate of Forecasted Transaction:* **Forward Contract on Brazilian Coffee**
Forward price of Colombian and Brazilian coffee:		
At hedge inception—6-month price	$2.54	$2.43
3 months later—3-month price	2.63	2.53
Cumulative change in price—gain	$.09	$.10
× 500,000 pounds of coffee	× 500,000	× 500,000
Estimate of change in cash flows	$45,000	$50,000

97. Using the above amounts, Company G could evaluate effectiveness 3 months into the hedge by comparing the $45,000 change on its Colombian coffee contract with what would have been a perfectly offsetting change in cash flow for its forecasted purchase—the $50,000 change on an otherwise identical forward contract for Brazilian coffee. The hedge would be ineffective to the extent that there was a difference between the changes in the present value of the expected cash flows on (a) the company's Colombian coffee contract and (b) a comparable forward contract for Brazilian coffee (the equivalent of the present value of $5,000 in the numerical example).

Example 8: Cash flow hedge with a basis swap

98. Company H has a 5-year, $100,000 variable-rate asset and a 7-year, $150,000 variable-rate liability. The interest on the asset is payable by the counterparty at the end of each month based on the prime rate as of the first of the month. The interest on the liability is payable by Company H at the end of each month based on LIBOR as of the tenth day of the month (the liability's anniversary date). The company enters into a 5-year interest rate swap to pay interest at the prime rate and receive interest at LIBOR at the end of each month based on a notional amount of $100,000. Both rates are determined as of the first of the month. Company H designates the swap as a hedge of 5 years of interest receipts on the $100,000 variable-rate asset and the first 5 years of interest payments on $100,000 of the variable-rate liability.

Assessing the hedge's expected effectiveness and measuring ineffectiveness

99. Company H may not automatically assume that the hedge always will be highly effective at achieving offsetting changes in cash flows because the reset date on the receive leg of the swap differs from the reset date on the corresponding variable-rate liability. Both at hedge inception and on an ongoing basis, the company's assessment of expected effectiveness could be based on the extent to which changes in LIBOR have occurred during comparable 10-day periods in the past. Company H's ongoing assessment of expected effectiveness and measurement of actual ineffectiveness would be on a cumulative basis and would incorporate the actual interest rate changes to date. The hedge would be ineffective to the extent that the cumulative change in cash flows on the prime leg of the swap did not offset the cumulative change in expected cash flows on the asset, *and*

the cumulative change in cash flows on the LIBOR leg of the swap did not offset the change in expected cash flows on the hedged portion of the liability. The terms of the swap, the asset, and the portion of the liability that is hedged are the same, with the exception of the reset dates on the liability and the receive leg of the swap. Thus, the hedge will only be ineffective to the extent that LIBOR has changed between the first of the month (the reset date for the swap) and the tenth of the month (the reset date for the liability).

Example 9: Cash flow hedge of forecasted sale with a forward contract

100. Company I, a U.S. dollar functional currency company, forecasts the sale of 10,000 units of its principal product in 6 months to French customers for FF500,000 (French francs). The company wants to hedge the cash flow exposure of the French franc sale related to changes in the US$-FF exchange rate. It enters into a 6-month forward contract to exchange the FF500,000 it expects to receive in the forecasted sale for the U.S. dollar equivalent specified in the forward contract and designates the forward contract as a cash flow hedge of the forecasted sale.

Assessing the hedge's expected effectiveness and measuring ineffectiveness

101. Company I chooses to assess hedge effectiveness at inception and during the term of the hedge based on (a) changes in the fair value of the forward contract attributable to changes in the US$-FF spot rate and (b) changes in the present value of the current U.S. dollar equivalent of the forecasted receipt of FF500,000. Because the critical terms of the forward contract and the forecasted transaction are the same, presumably there would be no ineffectiveness unless there is a reduction in the expected sales proceeds from the forecasted sales. Because Company I is assessing effectiveness based on spot rates, it would exclude the change in the fair value of the forward contract attributable to changes in the difference between the forward rate and spot rate from the measure of hedge ineffectiveness and report it directly in earnings.

Example 10: Attempted hedge of a forecasted sale with a written call option

102. Company J forecasts the sale in 9 months of 100 units of product with a current market price of $95 per unit. The company's objective is to sell the upside potential associated with the forecasted sale by writing a call option for a premium. The company

plans to use the premium from the call option as an offset to decreases in future cash inflows from the forecasted sale that will occur if the market price of the product decreases below $95. Accordingly, Company J sells an at-the-money call option on 100 units of product with a strike price of $95 for a premium. The premium represents only the time value of the option. The option is exercisable at any time within nine months.

103. Company J's objective of using the premium from the written call option as an offset to any decrease in future cash inflows would not meet the notion of effectiveness in this Statement. Future changes in the market price of the company's product will not affect the premium that Company J received, which is all related to time value in this example and thus is the maximum amount by which Company J can benefit. That is, the company could not expect the cash flows on the option to increase so that, at different price levels, a decrease in cash flows from the forecasted sale would be offset by an increase in cash flows on the option.

Appendix B

EXAMPLES ILLUSTRATING APPLICATION OF THIS STATEMENT

Section 1: Hedging Relationships

104. This appendix presents examples that illustrate the application of this Statement. The examples do not address all possible uses of derivatives as hedging instruments. For simplicity, commissions and most other transaction costs, initial margin, and income taxes are ignored unless otherwise stated in an example. It is also assumed in each example that there are no changes in creditworthiness that would alter the effectiveness of any of the hedging relationships.

Example 1: Fair Value Hedge of a Commodity Inventory

105. This example illustrates the accounting for a fair value hedge of a commodity inventory. In the first scenario, the terms of the hedging derivative have been negotiated to produce no ineffectiveness in the hedging relationship. In the second scenario,

there is ineffectiveness in the hedging relationship. To simplify the illustration and focus on basic concepts, the derivative in these two scenarios is assumed to have no time value. In practice, a derivative used for a fair value hedge of a commodity would have a time value that would change over the term of the hedging relationship. The changes in that time value would be recognized in earnings as they occur, either because they represent ineffectiveness or because they are excluded from the assessment of effectiveness (as discussed in paragraph 63). Other examples in this section illustrate accounting for the time value component of a derivative.

Scenario 1—No ineffectiveness in the hedging relationship

106. ABC Company decides to hedge the risk of changes during the period in the overall fair value of its entire inventory of Commodity A by entering into a derivative contract, Derivative Z. On the first day of period 1, ABC enters into Derivative Z and neither receives nor pays a premium (that is, the fair value at inception is zero). ABC designates the derivative as a hedge of the changes in fair value of the inventory due to changes in the price of Commodity A during period 1. The hedging relationship qualifies for fair value hedge accounting. ABC will assess effectiveness by comparing the entire change in fair value of Derivative Z with the change in the market price of the hedged commodity inventory. ABC expects no ineffectiveness because (a) the notional amount of Derivative Z matches the amount of the hedged inventory (that is, Derivative Z is based on the same number of bushels as the number of bushels of the commodity that ABC designated as hedged) and (b) the underlying of Derivative Z is the price of the same variety and grade of Commodity A as the inventory at the same location.

107. At inception of the hedge, Derivative Z has a fair value of zero and the hedged inventory has a carrying amount of $1,000,000 and a fair value of $1,100,000. On the last day of period 1, the fair value of Derivative Z has increased by $25,000, and the fair value of the inventory has decreased by $25,000. The inventory is sold, and Derivative Z is settled on the last day of period 1. The following table illustrates the accounting for the situation described above.

	Debit (Credit)			
	Cash	Derivative	Inventory	Earnings
Period 1				
Recognize change in fair value of derivative		$ 25,000		$ (25,000)
Recognize change in fair value of inventory			$ (25,000)	25,000
Recognize revenue from sale	$1,075,000			(1,075,000)
Recognize cost of sale of inventory			(975,000)	975,000
Recognize settlement of derivative	25,000	(25,000)		
Total	$1,100,000	$ 0	$(1,000,000)	$ (100,000)

108. If ABC had sold the hedged inventory at the inception of the hedge, its gross profit on that sale would have been $100,000. The above example illustrates that, by hedging the risk of changes in the overall fair value of its inventory, ABC recognized the same gross profit at the end of the hedge period even though the fair value of its inventory decreased by $25,000.

Scenario 2—Ineffectiveness in the hedging relationship

109. No ineffectiveness was recognized in earnings in the above situation because the gain on Derivative Z exactly offsets the loss on the inventory. However, if the terms of Derivative Z did not perfectly match the inventory and its fair value had increased by $22,500 as compared with the decline in fair value of the inventory of $25,000, then ineffectiveness of $2,500 would have been recognized in earnings. The following table illustrates that situation (all other facts are assumed to be the same as in Scenario 1).

	Debit (Credit)			
	Cash	Derivative	Inventory	Earnings
Period 1				
Recognize change in fair value of derivative		$ 22,500		$ (22,500)
Recognize change in fair value of inventory			$ (25,000)	25,000
Recognize revenue from sale	$1,075,000			(1,075,000)
Recognize cost of sale of inventory			(975,000)	975,000
Recognize settlement of derivative	22,500	(22,500)		
Total	$1,097,500	$ 0	$(1,000,000)	$ (97,500)

110. The difference between the effect on earnings in this scenario and the effect on earnings in Scenario 1 is the $2,500 of hedge ineffectiveness.

Example 2: Fair Value Hedge of Fixed-Rate Interest-Bearing Debt

Purpose of the example

111. This example demonstrates the mechanics of reporting an interest rate swap used as a fair value hedge of an interest-bearing liability. It is not intended to demonstrate how to compute the fair value of an interest rate swap or an interest-bearing liability. This example has been simplified by assuming that the interest rate applicable to a payment due at any future date is the same as the rate for a payment due at any other date (that is, the yield curve is flat). Although that is an unrealistic assumption, it makes the amounts used in the example easier to understand without detracting from the purpose of the example.

112. The fair values of the swap in this example are determined using the "zero-coupon method." That method involves computing and summing the present value of each future net settlement that would be required by the contract terms if future spot interest rates match the forward rates implied by the current yield curve. The discount rates used are the spot interest rates implied by the current yield curve for hypothetical zero coupon bonds due on the date of each future net settlement on the swap. The zero-coupon method is not the only acceptable method. Explanations of other acceptable methods of determining the fair value of an interest rate swap can be obtained from various published sources. Fair values also may be available from dealers in interest rate swaps and other derivatives.

113. In this example, the term and notional amount of the interest rate swap match the term and principal amount of the interest-bearing liability being hedged. The fixed and variable interest rates used to determine the net settlements on the swap match the current yield curve, and the sum of the present values of the expected net settlements is zero at inception. Thus, paragraph 68 of this Statement permits the re-porting entity to assume that there will be no ineffectiveness. Assessment of effectiveness at one of the swap's repricing dates would confirm the validity of that assumption.

114. A shortcut method can be used to produce the same reporting results as the method illustrated in this example. This shortcut is only appropriate for a fair value hedge of a fixed-rate asset or liability using an interest rate swap and only if the assumption of no ineffectiveness is appropriate.[21] The steps in the shortcut method are as follows:

a. Determine the difference between the fixed rate to be received on the swap and the fixed rate to be paid on the bonds.
b. Combine that difference with the variable rate to be paid on the swap.
c. Compute and recognize interest expense using that combined rate and the fixed-rate liability's principal amount. (Amortization of any purchase premium or discount on the liability also must be considered, although that complication is not incorporated in this example.)
d. Determine the fair value of the interest rate swap.
e. Adjust the carrying amount of the swap to its fair value and adjust the carrying amount of the liability by an offsetting amount.

Amounts determined using the shortcut method and the facts in this example will match the amounts in paragraph 117 even though the shortcut does not involve explicitly amortizing the hedge accounting adjustments on the debt. That is, the quarterly adjustments of the debt and explicit amortization of previous adjustments will have the same net effect on earnings as the shortcut method.

Assumptions

115. On July 1, 20X1, ABC Company borrows $1,000,000 to be repaid on June 30, 20X3. On that same date, ABC also enters into a two-year receive-fixed, pay-variable interest rate swap. ABC designates the interest rate swap as a hedge of the changes in the fair value of the fixed-rate debt attributable to changes in market interest rates. The terms of the interest rate swap and the debt are as follows:

---

[21]A slightly different shortcut method for interest rate swaps used as cash flow hedges is illustrated in Example 5.

	Interest Rate Swap	**Fixed-Rate Debt**
Trade date and borrowing date*	July 1, 20X1	July 1, 20X1
Termination date and maturity date	June 30, 20X3	June 30, 20X3
Notional amount and principal amount	$1,000,000	$1,000,000
Fixed interest rate*	6.41%	6.41%
Variable interest rate	3-month US$ LIBOR	Not applicable
Settlement dates and interest payment dates*	End of each calendar quarter	End of each calendar quarter
Reset dates	End of each calendar quarter through March 31, 20X3	Not applicable

---

*These terms need not match for the assumption of no ineffectiveness to be appropriate. (Refer to paragraphs 68 and 69.)

116. The US$ LIBOR rates that are in effect at inception of the hedging relationship and at each of the quarterly reset dates are assumed to be as follows:

Reset Date	**3-Month LIBOR Rate**
7/1/X1	6.41%
9/30/X1	6.48%
12/31/X1	6.41%
3/31/X2	6.32%
6/30/X2	7.60%
9/30/X2	7.71%
12/31/X2	7.82%
3/31/X3	7.42%

Amounts to be reported

117. The following table summarizes the fair values of the debt and the swap at each quarter end, the details of the changes in the fair values during each quarter (including accrual and payment of interest, the effect of changes in rates, and level-yield amortization of hedge accounting adjustments), the expense for each quarter, and the net cash payments for each quarter. The calculations of fair value of both the debt and the swap are made using LIBOR. (A discussion of the appropriate discount rate appears in paragraph 70.)

	Fixed-Rate Debt	Interest Rate Swap	Expense	Net Payment
July 1, 20X1	$(1,000,000)	$ 0		
Interest accrued	(16,025)	0	$(16,025)	
Payments (receipts)	16,025	0		$ 16,025
Effect of change in rates	1,149	(1,149)	0	
September 30, 20X1	(998,851)	(1,149)	$(16,025)	$ 16,025
Interest accrued	(16,025)	(19)	$(16,044)	
Payments (receipts)	16,025	175		$ 16,200
Amortization of basis adjustments	(156)	0	(156)	
Effect of change in rates	(993)	993	0	
December 31, 20X1	(1,000,000)	0	$(16,200)	$ 16,200
Interest accrued	(16,025)	0	$(16,025)	
Payments (receipts)	16,025	0		$ 16,025
Amortization of basis adjustments	0	0	0	
Effect of change in rates	(1,074)	1,074	0	
March 31, 20X2	(1,001,074)	1,074	$(16,025)	$ 16,025
Interest accrued	(16,025)	17	$(16,008)	
Payments (receipts)	16,025	(225)		$ 15,800
Amortization of basis adjustments	208	0	208	
Effect of change in rates	12,221	(12,221)	0	
June 30, 20X2	(988,645)	(11,355)	$(15,800)	$ 15,800
Interest accrued	(16,025)	(216)	$(16,241)	
Payments (receipts)	16,025	2,975		$ 19,000
Amortization of basis adjustments	(2,759)	0	(2,759)	
Effect of change in rates	789	(789)	0	
September 30, 20X2	(990,615)	(9,385)	$(19,000)	$ 19,000
Interest accrued	(16,025)	(181)	$(16,206)	
Payments (receipts)	16,025	3,250		$ 19,275
Amortization of basis adjustments	(3,069)	0	(3,069)	
Effect of change in rates	532	(532)	0	
December 31, 20X2	(993,152)	(6,848)	$(19,275)	$ 19,275
Interest accrued	(16,025)	(134)	$(16,159)	
Payments (receipts)	16,025	3,525		$ 19,550
Amortization of basis adjustments	(3,391)	0	(3,391)	
Effect of change in rates	(978)	978	0	
March 31, 20X3	(997,521)	(2,479)	$(19,550)	$ 19,550
Interest accrued	(16,025)	(46)	$(16,071)	
Payments (receipts)	1,016,025	2,525		$1,018,550
Amortization of basis adjustments	(2,479)	0	(2,479)	
June 30, 20X3	$ 0	$ 0	$(18,550)	$1,018,550

118. The table demonstrates two important points that explain why the shortcut method described in paragraph 114 produces the same results as the computation in the above table when there is no ineffectiveness in the hedging relationship.

a. In every quarter, the effect of changes in rates on the swap completely offsets the effect of changes in rates on the debt. That is as expected because there is no ineffectiveness.

b. In every quarter except the last when the principal is repaid, the expense equals the cash payment.

119. The following table illustrates the computation of interest expense using the shortcut method described in paragraph 114. The results are the same as the results computed in the above table.

Quarter Ended	(a) Difference between Fixed Rates	(b) Variable Rate on Swap	(c) Sum (a) + (b)	(d) Debt's Principal Amount	(e) Interest Expense ((c) × (d))/4
September 30, 20X1	0.00%	6.41%	6.41%	$1,000,000	$16,025
December 31, 20X1	0.00%	6.48%	6.48%	1,000,000	16,200
March 31, 20X2	0.00%	6.41%	6.41%	1,000,000	16,025
June 30, 20X2	0.00%	6.32%	6.32%	1,000,000	15,800
September 30, 20X2	0.00%	7.60%	7.60%	1,000,000	19,000
December 31, 20X2	0.00%	7.71%	7.71%	1,000,000	19,275
March 31, 20X3	0.00%	7.82%	7.82%	1,000,000	19,550
June 30, 20X3	0.00%	7.42%	7.42%	1,000,000	18,550

120. As stated in the introduction to this example, a flat yield curve is assumed for simplicity. An upward-sloping yield curve would have made the computations more complex. Paragraph 116 would have shown different interest rates for each quarterly repricing date, and the present value of each future payment would have been computed using a different rate (as described in paragraph 112). However, the basic principles are the same. As long as there is no ineffectiveness in the hedging relationship, the shortcut method is appropriate.

Example 3: Fair Value Hedge—Using a Forward Contract to Purchase Foreign Currency to Hedge a Firm Commitment Denominated in a Different Foreign Currency

121. This example illustrates a fair value hedge of a firm commitment to purchase an asset for a price denominated in a foreign currency. In this example, the hedging instrument and the firm commitment are denominated in different foreign currencies. Conse-quently, the hedge is not perfectly effective, and ineffectiveness is recognized immediately in earnings. (The entity in the example could have designed a hedge with no ineffectiveness by using a hedging instrument denominated in the same foreign currency as the firm commitment with terms that match the appropriate terms in the firm commitment.)

122. MNO Company's functional currency is the U.S. dollar. On February 3, 20X7, MNO enters into a firm commitment to purchase a machine for delivery on May 1, 20X7. The price of the machine will be 270,000 Dutch guilders (Df1270,000). Also on February 3, 20X7, MNO enters into a forward contract to purchase 240,000 Deutsche marks (DM240,000) on May 1, 20X7. MNO will pay $0.6125 per DM1 (a total of $147,000), which is the current forward rate for an exchange on May 1, 20X7. MNO designates the forward contract as a hedge of its risk of changes in the fair value of the firm commitment resulting from changes in the U.S. dollar–Dutch guilder forward exchange rate.

123. MNO will assess effectiveness by comparing the overall changes in the fair value of the forward contract to the changes in fair value in U.S. dollars of the firm commitment due to changes in U.S. dollar–Dutch guilder forward exchange rates. MNO expects the forward contract to be highly effective as a hedge because:

a. DM240,000 is approximately equal to Dfl270,000 at the May 1, 20X1 forward exchange rate in effect on February 3, 20X7.
b. Settlement of the forward contract and the firm commitment will occur on the same date.
c. In recent years, changes in the value in U.S. dollars of Deutsche marks over three-month periods have been highly correlated with changes in the

value in U.S. dollars of Dutch guilders over those same periods.

Ineffectiveness will result from the difference between changes in the U.S. dollar equivalent of DM240,000 (the notional amount of the forward contract) and changes in the U.S. dollar equivalent of Dfl270,000 (the amount to be paid for the machine). The difference between the spot rate and the forward exchange rate is not excluded from the hedging relationship because changes in the fair value of the firm commitment are being measured using forward exchange rates.[22]

124. The forward exchange rates in effect on certain key dates are assumed to be as follows:

Date	$-DM Forward Exchange Rate for Settlement on 5/1/X7	$-Dfl Forward Exchange Rate for Settlement on 5/1/X7
Inception of the hedge—2/3/X7	$0.6125 = DM1	$0.5454 = Dfl1
Quarter end—3/31/X7	$0.5983 = DM1	$0.5317 = Dfl1
Machine purchase—5/1/X7	$0.5777 = DM1	$0.5137 = Dfl1

125. The U.S. dollar equivalent and changes in the U.S. dollar equivalent of the forward contract and the firm commitment, the changes in fair value of the forward contract and the firm commitment, and the ineffectiveness of the hedge on those same key dates are shown in the following table. A 6 percent discount rate is used in this example.

[22]If the hedged item were a foreign-currency-denominated available-for-sale security instead of a firm commitment, Statement 52 would have required its carrying value to be measured using the spot exchange rate. Therefore, the spot-forward difference would have been recognized immediately in earnings either because it represented ineffectiveness or because it was excluded from the assessment of effectiveness.

	2/3/X7	3/31/X7	5/1/X7
Forward contract			
$-DM forward exchange rate for settlement on May 1, 20X7	$ 0.6125	$ 0.5983	$ 0.5777
Units of currency (DM)	× 240,000	× 240,000	× 240,000
Forward price of DM240,000 in dollars	147,000	143,592	138,648
Contract price in dollars	(147,000)	(147,000)	(147,000)
Difference	$ 0	$ (3,408)	$ (8,352)
Fair value (present value of the difference)	$ 0	$ (3,391)	$ (8,352)
Change in fair value during the period		$ (3,391)	$ (4,961)
Firm commitment			
$-Dfl forward exchange rate for settlement on May 1, 20X7	$ 0.5454	$ 0.5317	$ 0.5137
Units of currency (Dfl)	× 270,000	× 270,000	× 270,000
Forward price of Dfl270,000 in dollars	(147,258)	(143,559)	(138,699)
Initial forward price in dollars	147,258	147,258	147,258
Difference	$ 0	$ 3,699	$ 8,559
Fair value (present value of the difference)	$ 0	$ 3,681	$ 8,559
Change in fair value during the period		$ 3,681	$ 4,878
Hedge ineffectiveness (difference between changes in fair values of the forward contract denominated in Deutsche marks and the firm commitment denominated in Dutch guilders)		$ 290	$ (83)

This Statement requires that MNO recognize immediately in earnings all changes in fair values of the forward contract. Because MNO is hedging the risk of changes in fair value of the firm commitment attributable to changes in the forward exchange rates, this Statement also requires recognizing those changes immediately in earnings.

126. On May 1, 20X7, MNO fulfills the firm commitment to purchase the machine and settles the forward contract. The entries illustrating fair value hedge accounting for the hedging relationship and the purchase of the machine are summarized below.

		Debit (Credit)			
	Cash	**Firm Commitment**	**Forward Contract**	**Machine**	**Earnings**
March 31, 20X7					
Recognize change in fair value of firm commitment		$ 3,681			$(3,681)
Recognize change in fair value of forward contract			$(3,391)		3,391
					(290)
April 30, 20X7					
Recognize change in fair value of firm commitment		4,878			(4,878)
Recognize change in fair value of forward contract			(4,961)		4,961
					83
May 1, 20X7					
Recognize settlement of forward contract	$ (8,352)		8,352		
Recognize purchase of machine	(138,699)	(8,559)		$147,258	
Total	$(147,051)	$ 0	$ 0	$147,258	$ (207)

Note: To simplify this example and focus on the effects of the hedging relationship, other amounts that would be involved in the purchase of the machine by MNO (for example, shipping costs and installation costs) have been ignored.

The effect of the hedge is to recognize the machine at its price in Dutch guilders (Df1270,000) translated at the forward rate in effect at the inception of the hedge ($0.5454 per Df11).

Example 4: Cash Flow Hedge of the Forecasted Sale of a Commodity Inventory

127. This example illustrates the accounting for a cash flow hedge of a forecasted sale of a commodity. The terms of the hedging derivative have been negotiated to match the terms of the forecasted transaction. Thus, there is no ineffectiveness. The assumptions in this example are similar to those in Example 1, including the assumption that there is no time value in the derivative. However, the entity has chosen to hedge the variability of the cash flows from the forecasted sale of the commodity instead of the changes in its fair value.

128. ABC Company decides to hedge the risk of changes in its cash flows relating to a forecasted sale of 100,000 bushels of Commodity A by entering into a derivative contract, Derivative Z. ABC expects to sell the 100,000 bushels of Commodity A on the last day of period 1. On the first day of period 1, ABC en-

ters into Derivative Z and designates it as a cash flow hedge of the forecasted sale. ABC neither pays nor receives a premium on Derivative Z (that is, its fair value is zero). The hedging relationship qualifies for cash flow hedge accounting. ABC expects that there will be no ineffectiveness from the hedge because (a) the notional amount of Derivative Z is 100,000 bushels and the forecasted sale is for 100,000 bushels, (b) the underlying of Derivative Z is the price of the same variety and grade of Commodity A that ABC expects to sell (assuming delivery to ABC's selling point), and (c) the settlement date of Derivative Z is the last day of period 1 and the forecasted sale is expected to occur on the last day of period 1.

129. At inception of the hedge, the expected sales price of 100,000 bushels of Commodity A is $1,100,000. On the last day of period 1, the fair value of Derivative Z has increased by $25,000, and the expected sales price of 100,000 bushels of Commodity A has decreased by $25,000. Both the sale of 100,000 bushels of Commodity A and the settlement of Derivative Z occur on the last day of period 1. The following table illustrates the accounting, including the net impact on earnings and other comprehensive income (OCI), for the situation described above.

		Debit (Credit)		
	Cash	Derivative	OCI	Earnings
Recognize change in fair value of derivative		$ 25,000	$(25,000)	
Recognize revenue from sale	$1,075,000			$(1,075,000)
Recognize settlement of derivative	25,000	(25,000)		
Reclassify change in fair value of derivative to earnings			25,000	(25,000)
Total	$1,100,000	$ 0	$ 0	$(1,100,000)

130. At the inception of the hedge, ABC anticipated that it would receive $1,100,000 from the sale of 100,000 bushels of Commodity A. The above example illustrates that by hedging the risk of changes in its cash flows relating to the forecasted sale of 100,000 bushels of Commodity A, ABC still received a total of $1,100,000 in cash flows even though the sales price of Commodity A declined during the period.

Example 5: Cash Flow Hedge of Variable-Rate Interest-Bearing Asset

Purpose of the example

131. This example demonstrates the mechanics of accounting for an interest rate swap used as a cash flow hedge of variable interest receipts. It is not intended to demonstrate how to compute the fair value of an interest rate swap. As in Example 2, the zero-coupon method[23] is used to determine the fair values. (Unlike Example 2, the yield curve in this example is assumed to be upward sloping, that is, interest rates are higher for payments due further into the future). In this example, the term, notional amount, and repricing date of the interest rate swap match the term, repricing date, and principal amount of the interest-bearing asset on which the hedged interest receipts are due. The swap terms are "at the market" (as described in paragraphs 68 and 69), so it has a zero value at inception. Thus, the reporting entity is permitted to assume that there will be no ineffectiveness.

132. A shortcut method can be used to produce the same reporting results as the method illustrated in this example. This shortcut is only appropriate if the assumption of no ineffectiveness applies for an inter-

est rate swap used as a cash flow hedge of interest receipts on a variable-rate asset (or interest payments on a variable-rate liability). The steps in the shortcut method are as follows:[24]

a. Determine the difference between the variable rate to be paid on the swap and the variable rate to be received on the bonds.
b. Combine that difference with the fixed rate to be received on the swap.
c. Compute and recognize interest income using that combined rate and the variable-rate asset's principal amount. (Amortization of any purchase premium or discount on the asset must also be considered, although that complication is not incorporated in this example.)
d. Determine the fair value of the interest rate swap.
e. Adjust the carrying amount of the swap to its fair value and adjust other comprehensive income by an offsetting amount.

Background and assumptions

133. On July 1, 20X1, XYZ Company invests $10,000,000 in variable-rate corporate bonds that pay interest quarterly at a rate equal to the 3-month US$ LIBOR rate plus 2.25 percent. The $10,000,000 principal will be repaid on June 30, 20X3.

134. Also on July 1, 20X1, XYZ enters into a two-year receive-fixed, pay-variable interest rate swap and designates it as a cash flow hedge of the variable-rate interest receipts on the corporate bonds. The risk designated as being hedged is the risk of changes in cash flows attributable to changes in market interest rates. The terms of the interest rate swap and the corporate bonds are shown below.

[23]Paragraph 112 discusses the zero-coupon method.
[24]A slightly different shortcut method for interest rate swaps used as fair value hedges is illustrated in Example 2.

	Interest Rate Swap	**Corporate Bonds**
Trade date and borrowing date*[*]	July 1, 20X1	July 1, 20X1
Termination date	June 30, 20X3	June 30, 20X3
Notional amount	$10,000,000	$10,000,000
Fixed interest rate	6.65%	Not applicable
Variable interest rate[†]	3-month US$ LIBOR	3-month US$ LIBORF + 2.25%
Settlement dates and interest payment dates*	End of each calendar quarter	End of each calendar quarter
Reset dates	End of each calendar quarter through March 31, 20X3	End of each calendar quarter through March 31, 20X3

---

[*]These terms need not match for the assumption of no ineffectiveness to be appropriate. (Refer to paragraphs 68 and 69.)

[†]Only the interest rate basis (for example, LIBOR) must match. The spread over LIBOR does not invalidate the assumption of no ineffectiveness.

135. Because the conditions described in paragraph 68 are met, XYZ is permitted to assume that there is no ineffectiveness in the hedging relationship and to recognize in other comprehensive income the entire change in the fair value of the swap.

136. The three-month US$ LIBOR rates in effect at the inception of the hedging relationship and at each of the quarterly reset dates are assumed to be as follows:

Reset Date	3-Month LIBOR Rate
7/1/X1	5.56%
9/30/X1	5.63%
12/31/X1	5.56%
3/31/X2	5.47%
6/30/X2	6.75%
9/30/X2	6.86%
12/31/X2	6.97%
3/31/X3	6.57%

Amounts to be reported

137. XYZ must reclassify to earnings the amount in accumulated other comprehensive income as each interest receipt affects earnings. In determining the amounts to reclassify each quarter, it is important to recognize that the interest rate swap does not hedge the bonds. Instead, it hedges the eight variable interest payments to be received. That is, each of the eight quarterly settlements on the swap is associated with an interest payment to be received on the bonds. Under the zero-coupon method discussed in paragraph 131, the present value of each quarterly settlement is computed separately. Because each payment occurs at a different point on the yield curve, a different interest rate must be used to determine its present value. As each individual interest receipt on the bonds is recognized in earnings, the fair value of the related quarterly settlement on the swap is reclassified to earnings. The fair values and changes in fair values of the interest rate swap and the effects on earnings and other comprehensive income (OCI) for each quarter are as follows:

	Swap Debit (Credit)	OCI Debit (Credit)	Earnings Debit (Credit)	Cash Debit (Credit)
July 1, 20X1	$ 0			
Interest accrued	0			
Payment (receipt)	(27,250)			$27,250
Effect of change in rates	52,100	$ (52,100)		
Reclassification to earnings		27,250	$(27,250)	
September 30, 20X1	24,850	(24,850)	$(27,250)	$27,250
Interest accrued	330	(330)		
Payment (receipt)	(25,500)			$25,500
Effect of change in rates	74,120	(74,120)		
Reclassification to earnings		25,500	$(25,500)	
December 31, 20X1	73,800	(73,800)	$(25,500)	$25,500
Interest accrued	1,210	(1,210)		
Payment (receipt)	(27,250)			$27,250
Effect of change in rates	38,150	(38,150)		
Reclassification to earnings		27,250	$(27,250)	
March 31, 20X2	85,910	(85,910)	$(27,250)	$27,250
Interest accrued	1,380	(1,380)		
Payment (receipt)	(29,500)			$29,500
Effect of change in rates	(100,610)	100,610		
Reclassification to earnings		29,500	$(29,500)	
June 30, 20X2	(42,820)	42,820	$(29,500)	$29,500
Interest accrued	(870)	870		
Payment (receipt)	2,500			$ (2,500)
Effect of change in rates	8,030	(8,030)		
Reclassification to earnings		(2,500)	$ 2,500	
September 30, 20X2	(33,160)	33,160	$ 2,500	$ (2,500)
Interest accrued	(670)	670		
Payment (receipt)	5,250			$ (5,250)
Effect of change in rates	6,730	(6,730)		
Reclassification to earnings		(5,250)	$ 5,250	
December 31, 20X2	(21,850)	21,850	$ 5,250	$ (5,250)
Interest accrued	(440)	440		
Payment (receipt)	8,000			$ (8,000)
Effect of change in rates	16,250	(16,250)		
Reclassification to earnings		(8,000)	$ 8,000	
March 31, 20X3	1,960	(1,960)	$ 8,000	$ (8,000)
Interest accrued	40	(40)		
Payment (receipt)	(2,000)			$ 2,000
Reclassification to earnings		2,000	$ (2,000)	
June 30, 20X3	$ 0	$ 0	$ (2,000)	$ 2,000

138. The table shows that, in each quarter, the net cash receipt or payment on the swap equals the income or expense to be recorded. The net effect on earnings of the interest on the bonds and the reclassification of gains or losses on the swap is shown below.

		Earnings	
For the Quarter Ending	Interest on Bonds	Gains (Losses) Reclassified from OCI	Net Effect
9/30/X1	$ 195,250	$27,250	$ 222,500
12/31/X1	197,000	25,500	222,500
3/31/X2	195,250	27,250	222,500
6/30/X2	193,000	29,500	222,500
9/30/X2	225,000	(2,500)	222,500
12/31/X2	227,750	(5,250)	222,500
3/31/X3	230,500	(8,000)	222,500
6/30/X3	220,500	2,000	222,500
Totals	$1,684,250	$95,750	$1,780,000

139. In this example, the shortcut method described in paragraph 132 works as follows. The difference between the variable rate on the swap and the variable rate on the asset is a net receipt of 2.25 percent. That rate combined with the 6.65 percent fixed rate received on the swap is 8.9 percent. The computed interest income is $890,000 per year or $222,500 per quarter, which is the same as the amount in the table in paragraph 138.

Example 6: Accounting for a Derivative's Gain or Loss in a Cash Flow Hedge—Effectiveness Based on the Entire Change in the Derivative's Fair Value

140. This example has been designed to illustrate application of the guidance for cash flow hedges described in paragraph 30 of this Statement. At the beginning of period 1, XYZ Company enters into a qualifying cash flow hedge of a transaction forecasted to occur early in period 6. XYZ's documented policy is to assess hedge effectiveness by comparing the changes in present value of the expected future cash flows on the forecasted transaction to all of the hedging derivative's gain or loss (that is, no time value component will be excluded as discussed in paragraph 63). In this hedging relationship, XYZ has designated changes in cash flows related to the forecasted transaction attributable to any cause as the hedged risk.

141. The following table includes the assumptions for this example and details the steps necessary to account for a cash flow hedge that is not perfectly effective.

	Fair Value of Derivative Increase (Decrease)		Present Value of Expected Future Cash Flows on Hedged Transaction Increase (Decrease)			
	(A)	(B)	(C)	(D)	(E)	(F)
Period	Change during the Period	Cumulative Change	Change during the Period	Cumulative Change	Lesser of the Two Cumulative Changes	Adjustment to OCI
1	$ 100	$100	$ (96)	$ (96)	$ 96	$ 96
2	94	194	(101)	(197)	194	98
3	(162)	32	160	(37)	32	(162)
4	(101)	(69)	103	66	(66)	(98)
5	30	(39)	(32)	34	(34)	32

Step 1: Determine the change in fair value of the derivative and the change in present value of the cash flows on the hedged transaction (columns A and C).

Step 2: Determine the cumulative changes in fair value of the derivative and the cumulative changes in present value of the cash flows on the hedged transaction (columns B and D).

Step 3: Determine the lesser of the absolute values of the two amounts in Step 2 (column E).

Step 4: Determine the change during the period in the lesser of the absolute values (column F).

Step 5: Adjust the derivative to reflect its change in fair value and adjust other comprehensive income by the amount determined in Step 4. Balance the entry, if necessary, with an adjustment to earnings.

142. The following are the entries required to account for the above cash flow hedge.

		Debit (Credit)		
Period	Description	Derivative	Earnings	OCI
1	Adjust derivative to fair value and OCI by the calculated amount	$ 100	$(4)	$ (96)
2	Adjust derivative to fair value and OCI by the calculated amount	94	4	(98)
3	Adjust derivative to fair value and OCI by the calculated amount	(162)	0	162
4	Adjust derivative to fair value and OCI by the calculated amount	(101)	3	98
5	Adjust derivative to fair value and OCI by the calculated amount	30	2	(32)

143. The following table reconciles the beginning and ending balances in accumulated other comprehensive income.

	Accumulated Other Comprehensive Income—Debit (Credit)			
Period	Beginning Balance	Change in Fair Value	Reclassification	Ending Balance
1	$ 0	$ (96)	$ 0	$ (96)
2	(96)	(94)	(4)	(194)
3	(194)	162	0	(32)
4	(32)	98	0	66
5	66	(30)	(2)	34

The reclassification column relates to re-classifications between earnings and other comprehensive income. In period 2, the $(4) in that column relates to the prior period's derivative gain that was previously recognized in earnings. That amount is reclassified to other comprehensive income in period 2 because the cumulative gain on the derivative is less than the amount necessary to offset the cumulative change in the present value of expected future cash flows on the hedged transaction. In period 5, the $(2) in the reclassification column relates to the derivative loss that was recognized in other comprehensive income in a prior period. At the end of period 4, the derivative's cumulative loss of $69 was greater in absolute terms than the $66 increase in the present value of expected future cash flows on the hedged transaction. That $3 excess had been recognized in earnings during period 4. In period 5, the value of the derivative increased (and reduced the cumulative loss) by $30. The present value of the expected cash flows on the hedged transaction decreased (and reduced the cumulative increase) by $32. The gain on the derivative in period 5 was $2 smaller, in absolute terms, than the decrease in the present value of the expected cash flows on the hedged transaction. Consequently, the entire gain on the derivative is recognized in other comprehensive income. In addition, in absolute terms, the $3 cumulative excess of the loss on the derivative over the increase in the present value of the expected cash flows on the hedged transaction (which had previously been recognized in earnings) increased to $5. As a result, $2 is reclassified from other comprehensive income to earnings so that the $5 cumulative excess has been recognized in earnings.

Example 7: Designation and Discontinuance of a Cash Flow Hedge of the Forecasted Purchase of Inventory

144. This example illustrates the effect on earnings and other comprehensive income of discontinuing a cash flow hedge by dedesignating the hedging derivative before the variability of the cash flows from the hedged forecasted transaction has been eliminated. It also discusses the effect that the location of a physical asset has on the effectiveness of a hedging relationship.

145. On February 3, 20X1, JKL Company forecasts the purchase of 100,000 bushels of corn on May 20, 20X1. It expects to sell finished products produced from the corn on May 31, 20X1. On February 3, 20X1, JKL enters into 20 futures contracts, each for the purchase of 5,000 bushels of corn on May 20, 20X1 (100,000 in total) and immediately designates those contracts as a hedge of the forecasted purchase of corn.

146. JKL chooses to assess effectiveness by comparing the entire change in fair value of the futures contracts to changes in the cash flows on the forecasted transaction. JKL estimates its cash flows on the forecasted transaction based on the futures price of corn adjusted for the difference between the cost of corn delivered to Chicago and the cost of corn delivered to Minneapolis. JKL does not choose to use a tailing strategy (as described in paragraph 64). JKL expects changes in fair value of the futures contracts to be highly effective at offsetting changes in the expected cash outflows for the forecasted purchase of corn because (a) the futures contracts are for the same variety and grade of corn that JKL plans to purchase

and (b) on May 20, 20X1, the futures price for delivery on May 20, 20X1 will be equal to the spot price (because futures prices and spot prices converge as the delivery date approaches). However, the hedge may not be perfectly effective. JKL will purchase corn for delivery to its production facilities in Minneapolis, but the price of the futures contracts is based on delivery of corn to Chicago. If the difference between the price of corn delivered to Chicago and the price of corn delivered to Minneapolis changes during the period of the hedge, the effect of that change will be included currently in earnings according to the provisions of paragraph 30 of this Statement.

147. On February 3, 20X1, the futures price of corn for delivery to Chicago on May 20, 20X1 is $2.6875 per bushel resulting in a total price of $268,750 for 100,000 bushels.

148. On May 1, 20X1, JKL dedesignates the related futures contracts and closes them out by entering into offsetting contracts on the same exchange. As of that date, JKL had recognized in accumulated other comprehensive income gains on the futures contracts of $26,250. JKL still plans to purchase 100,000 bushels of corn on May 20, 20X1. Consequently, the gains that occurred prior to dedesignation will remain in other comprehensive income until the finished product is sold. If JKL had not closed out the futures contracts when it dedesignated them, any further gains or losses would have been recognized in earnings.

149. On May 20, 20X1, JKL purchases 100,000 bushels of corn, and on May 31, 20X1, JKL sells the finished product.

150. The futures prices of corn that are in effect on key dates are assumed to be as follows:

Date	Futures Price per Bushel for Delivery to Chicago on May 20, 20X1	Futures Price Adjusted for Delivery to Minneapolis on May 20, 20X1
Inception of hedging relationship—February 3, 20X1	$2.6875	$2.7375
End of quarter—March 31, 20X1	3.1000	3.1500
Discontinue hedge—May 1, 20X1	2.9500	3.0000
Purchase of corn—May 20, 20X1	2.8500	2.9000

151. The changes in fair value of the futures contracts between inception (February 3, 20X1) and discontinuation (May 1, 20X1) of the hedge are as follows:

	February 3– March 31, 20X1	April 1– May 1, 20X1
Futures price at beginning of period	$ 2.6875	$ 3.1000
Futures price at end of period	3.1000	2.9500
Change in price per bushel	0.4125	(0.1500)
Bushels under contract (20 contracts @ 5,000 bushels each)	× 100,000	× 100,000
Change in fair value—gain (loss)	$ 41,250	$ (15,000)

152. The following table displays the entries to recognize the effects of (a) entering into futures contracts as a hedge of the forecasted purchase of corn, (b) dedesignating and closing out the futures contracts, (c) completing the forecasted purchase of corn, and (d) selling the finished products produced from the corn. Because the difference in prices between corn delivered to Chicago and corn delivered to Minneapolis ($.05 per bushel, as illustrated in paragraph 150) did not change during the period of the hedge, no ineffectiveness is recognized in earnings. If that difference had changed, the resulting ineffectiveness would have been recognized immediately in earnings.

	Cash	Inventory	OCI	Earnings
March 31, 20X1 (end of quarter)				
Recognize change in fair value of futures contracts	$ 41,250		$(41,250)	
May 1, 20X1 (discontinue hedge)				
Recognize change in fair value of futures contracts	(15,000)		15,000	
May 20, 20X1				
Recognize purchase of corn	(290,000)	$ 290,000		
May 31, 20X1				
Recognize cost of sale of product		(290,000)		$290,000
Reclassify changes in fair value of futures contracts to earnings			26,250	(26,250)
Total	$(263,750)	$ 0	$ 0	$263,750

Note: To simplify this example and focus on the effects of the hedging relationship, the margin account with the clearinghouse and certain amounts that would be involved in a sale of JKL's inventory (for example, additional costs of production, selling costs, and sales revenue) have been ignored.

The effect of the hedging strategy is that the cost of the corn recognized in earnings when the finished product was sold was $263,750. If the hedging relationship had not been discontinued early, the cost recognized in earnings would have been $273,750, which was the futures price of the corn, adjusted for delivery to Minneapolis, at the inception of the hedge. Without the strategy, JKL would have recognized $290,000, which was the price of corn delivered to Minneapolis at the time it was purchased.

Example 8: Changes in a Cash Flow Hedge of Forecasted Interest Payments with an Interest Rate Swap

Background

153. This example describes the effects on earnings and other comprehensive income of certain changes in a cash flow hedging relationship. It presents two different scenarios. In the first, the variability of the hedged interest payments is eliminated before the hedging derivative expires. In the second, the interest rate index that is the basis for the hedged interest payments is changed to a different index before the hedging derivative expires.

154. MNO Company enters into an interest rate swap (Swap 1) and designates it as a hedge of the variable interest payments on a series of $5 million notes with 90-day terms. MNO plans to continue is-

suing new 90-day notes over the next five years as each outstanding note matures. The interest on each note will be determined based on LIBOR at the time each note is issued. Swap 1 requires a settlement every 90 days, and the variable interest rate is reset immediately following each payment. MNO pays a fixed rate of interest (6.5 percent) and receives interest at LIBOR. MNO neither pays nor receives a premium at the inception of Swap 1. The notional amount of the contract is $5 million, and it expires in 5 years.

155. Because Swap 1 meets all of the conditions discussed in paragraph 68, MNO is permitted to assume that there will be no ineffectiveness in the hedging relationship and to use the shortcut method illustrated in Example 2.

Scenario 1—Two undesignated interest rate swaps

156. At the end of the second year of the 5-year hedging relationship, MNO discontinues its practice of issuing 90-day notes. Instead, MNO issues a 3-year, $5 million note with a fixed rate of interest (7.25 percent). Because the interest rate on the three-year note is fixed, the variability of the future interest payments has been eliminated. Thus, Swap 1 no longer qualifies for cash flow hedge accounting. However, the net gain or loss on Swap 1 in accumulated other comprehensive income is not reclassified to earnings immediately. Immediate reclassification

is required (and permitted) only if it becomes probable that the hedged transactions (future interest payments) will not occur. The variability of the payments has been eliminated, but it still is probable that they will occur. Thus, those gains or losses will continue to be reclassified from accumulated other comprehensive income to earnings as the interest payments affect earnings (as required by paragraph 31).[25]

157. Rather than liquidate the pay-fixed, receive-variable Swap 1, MNO enters into a pay-variable, receive-fixed interest rate swap (Swap 2) with a 3-year term and a notional amount of $5 million. MNO neither pays nor receives a premium. Like Swap 1, Swap 2 requires a settlement every 90 days and reprices immediately following each settlement. The relationship between 90-day interest rates and longer term rates has changed since MNO entered into Swap 1 (that is, the shape of the yield curve is different). As a result, Swap 2 has different terms and its settlements do not exactly offset the settlements on Swap 1. Under the terms of Swap 2, MNO will receive a fixed rate of 7.25 percent and pay interest at LIBOR.

158. The two swaps are not designated as hedging instruments and are reported at fair value. The changes in fair value are reported immediately in earnings and offset each other to a significant degree.

Scenario 2—Two interest rate swaps designated as a hedge of future variable interest payments

159. At the end of the second year of the 5-year hedging relationship, MNO discontinues its practice of issuing 90-day notes and issues a 3-year, $5 million note with a rate of interest that adjusts every 90 days to the prime rate quoted on that day. Swap 1 is no longer effective as a cash flow hedge because the receive-variable rate on the swap is LIBOR, and the prime rate and LIBOR are expected to change differently. Thus, the cash flows from the swap will not effectively offset changes in cash flows from the three-year note.

160. The net gain or loss on Swap 1 in accumulated other comprehensive income as of the date MNO issues the three-year note is not reclassified into earnings immediately. Immediate reclassification would

be required only if it becomes probable that the hedged transactions (future interest payments) will not occur. The expected amounts of those payments have changed (because they will be based on prime instead of LIBOR, as originally expected), but it still is probable that the payments will occur. Thus, those gains or losses will continue to be reclassified to earnings as the interest payments affect earnings.

161. Rather than liquidate Swap 1 and obtain a separate derivative to hedge the variability of the prime-rate-based interest payments, MNO enters into a pay-LIBOR, receive-prime basis swap. The basis swap has a $5 million notional amount and a 3-year term and requires a settlement every 90 days. MNO designates Swap 1 and the basis swap in combination as the hedging instrument in a cash flow hedge of the variable interest payments on the three-year note. On the three-year note, MNO pays interest at prime. On the basis swap, MNO receives interest at prime and pays interest at LIBOR. On Swap 1, MNO receives interest at LIBOR and pays interest at 6.5 percent. Together, the cash flows from the two derivatives are effective at offsetting changes in the interest payments on the three-year note. Changes in fair values of the two swaps are recognized in other comprehensive income and are reclassified to earnings when the hedged forecasted transactions (the variable interest payments) affect earnings (as required by paragraph 31). Because the two swaps in combination meet the conditions discussed in paragraph 68, MNO is permitted to assume no ineffectiveness and use the shortcut method illustrated in Example 5.

Example 9: Accounting for a Derivative's Gain or Loss in a Cash Flow Hedge—Effectiveness Based on Changes in Intrinsic Value

162. This example illustrates application of the accounting guidance for cash flow hedges described in paragraph 30 of this Statement. At the beginning of period 1, XYZ Company purchases for $9.25 an at-the-money call option on 1 unit of Commodity X with a strike price of $125.00 to hedge a purchase of 1 unit of that commodity projected to occur early in period 5. XYZ's documented policy is to assess hedge effectiveness by comparing changes in cash flows on the hedged transaction (based on changes in the spot price) with changes in the option contract's intrinsic value. Because the hedging instrument is a purchased call option, its intrinsic value

---

[25] If the term of the fixed rate note had been longer than three years, the amounts in accumulated other comprehensive income still would have been reclassified into earnings over the next three years, which was the term of the designated hedging relationship.

cannot be less than zero. If the price of the commodity is less than the option's strike price, the option is out-of-the-money. Its intrinsic value cannot decrease further regardless of how far the commodity price falls, and the intrinsic value will not increase until the commodity price increases to exceed the strike price. Thus, changes in cash flows from the option due to changes in its intrinsic value will offset changes in cash flows on the forecasted purchase

only when the option is in-the-money or at-the-money. That phenomenon is demonstrated in period 3 in the following table when the commodity price declines by $1.25. Because the commodity price is $.75 below the option's strike price, the option's intrinsic value declines by only $.50 (to zero). The effect reverses in period 4 when the commodity price increases by $6.50 and the option's intrinsic value increases by $5.75.

	Period 1	Period 2	Period 3	Period 4
Assumptions				
Ending market price of Commodity X	$127.25	$125.50	$124.25	$130.75
Ending fair value of option:				
Time value	$ 7.50	$ 5.50	$ 3.00	$ 0.00
Intrinsic value	2.25	0.50	0.00	5.75
Total	$ 9.75	$ 6.00	$ 3.00	$ 5.75
Change in time value	$ (1.75)	$ (2.00)	$ (2.50)	$ (3.00)
Change in intrinsic value	2.25	(1.75)	(0.50)	5.75
Total current-period gain (loss) on derivative	$ 0.50	$ (3.75)	$ (3.00)	$ 2.75
Gain (loss) on derivative, adjusted to remove the component excluded from effectiveness test:				
For the current period	$ 2.25	$ (1.75)	$ (0.50)	$ 5.75
Cumulative	2.25	0.50	0.00	5.75
Change in expected future cash flows on hedged transaction:				
For the current period	(2.25)	1.75	1.25	(6.50)
Cumulative	(2.25)	(0.50)	0.75	(5.75)
Balance to be reflected in accumulated other comprehensive income (paragraph 30(b))				
Lesser (in absolute amounts) of derivative's cumulative gain (loss) or amount necessary to offset the cumulative change in expected future cash flows on hedged transaction	$ 2.25	$ 0.50	$ 0.00	$ 5.75

163. The following are the entries required to account for the above cash flow hedge. The steps involved in determining the amounts are the same as in Example 6.

| | | Debit (Credit) | | |
| | | Derivative | Earnings | OCI |
Period	Description			
1	Adjust derivative to fair value and OCI by the calculated amount	$ 0.50	$1.75	$(2.25)
2	Adjust derivative to fair value and OCI by the calculated amount	(3.75)	2.00	1.75
3	Adjust derivative to fair value and OCI by the calculated amount	(3.00)	2.50	0.50
4	Adjust derivative to fair value and OCI by the calculated amount	2.75	3.00	(5.75)

164. The following table reconciles the beginning and ending balances in accumulated other comprehensive income.

| | Accumulated Other Comprehensive Income—Debit (Credit) | | |
Period	Beginning Balance	Change in Intrinsic Value	Ending Balance
1	$ 0.00	$(2.25)	$(2.25)
2	(2.25)	1.75	(0.50)
3	(0.50)	0.50	0.00
4	0.00	(5.75)	(5.75)

The amount reflected in earnings relates to the component excluded from the effectiveness test, that is, the time value component. No reclassifications between other comprehensive income and earnings of the type illustrated in Example 6 are required because no hedge ineffectiveness is illustrated in this example. (The change in cash flows from the hedged transaction was not fully offset in period 3. However, that is not considered ineffectiveness. As described in paragraph 20(b), a purchased call option is considered effective if it provides one-sided offset.)

Example 10: Cash Flow Hedge of the Foreign Currency Exposure in a Royalty Arrangement

165. This example illustrates the accounting for a hedging relationship involving a single hedging derivative and three separate forecasted trans-actions. The three transactions occur on three separate dates, but the payment on receivables related to all three occurs on the same date. The settlement of the hedging derivative will occur on the date the receivable is paid.

166. DEF Company's functional currency is the U.S. dollar. ZYX's functional currency is the Deutsche mark (DM). Effective January 1, 20X1, DEF enters into a royalty agreement with ZYX Company that gives ZYX the right to use DEF's technology in manufacturing Product X. On April 30, 20X1, ZYX will pay DEF a royalty of DM1 million for each unit of Product X sold by that date. DEF expects ZYX to sell one unit of Product X on January 31, one on February 28, and one on March 31. The forecasted royalty is probable because ZYX has identified a demand for Product X and no other supplier has the capacity to fill that demand.

167. Also on January 1, 20X1, DEF enters into a forward contract to sell DM3 million on April 30, 20X1 for a price equal to the forward price of $0.6057 per Deutsche mark. DEF designates the forward contract as a hedge of the risk of changes in its functional-currency-equivalent cash flows attributable to changes in the Deutsche mark–U.S. dollar exchange rates related to the forecasted receipt of DM3 million from the royalty agreement. The spot price and forward price of Deutsche marks at January 1, 20X1 and the U.S. dollar equivalent of DM3 million at those prices are assumed to be as follows:

Prices at January 1, 20X1	$ per DM	$ Equivalent of DM3 Million
Spot price	$0.6019	$1,805,700
4-month forward price	0.6057	1,817,100

168. DEF will exclude from its assessment of effectiveness the portion of the fair value of the forward contract attributable to the spot-forward difference (the difference between the spot exchange rate and the forward exchange rate). That is, DEF will recognize changes in that portion of the derivative's fair value in earnings but will not consider those changes to represent ineffectiveness. DEF will estimate the cash flows on the forecasted transactions based on the current spot exchange rate and will discount that amount. Thus, DEF will assess effectiveness by comparing (a) changes in the fair value of the forward contract attributable to changes in the dollar spot price of Deutsche marks and (b) changes in the present value of the forecasted cash flows based on the current spot exchange rate. Those two changes will exactly offset because the currency and the notional amount of the forward contract match the currency and the total of the expected foreign currency amounts of the forecasted transactions. Thus, if DEF dedesignates a proportion of the forward contract each time a royalty is earned (as described in the following paragraph), the hedging relationship will meet the "highly effective" criterion.

169. As each royalty is earned, DEF recognizes a receivable and royalty income. The forecasted

transaction (the earning of royalty income) has occurred. The receivable is an asset, not a forecasted transaction, and is not eligible for cash flow hedge accounting. Nor is it eligible for fair value hedge accounting of the foreign exchange risk because changes in the receivable's fair value due to exchange rate changes are recognized immediately in earnings. (Paragraph 21(c) prohibits hedge accounting in that situation.) Consequently, DEF will dedesignate a proportion of the forward contract corresponding to the earned royalty. As the royalty is recognized in earnings and each proportion of the derivative is dedesignated, the related derivative gain or loss in accumulated other comprehensive income is reclassified into earnings. After that date, any gain or loss on the dedesignated proportion of the derivative and any transaction loss or gain on the royalty receivable[26] will be recognized in earnings and will substantially offset each other.

170. The spot prices and forward prices for settlement on April 30, 20X1 in effect at inception of the hedge (January 1, 20X1) and at the end of each month between inception and April 30, 20X1 are assumed to be as follows:

	$ per DM	
	Spot Price	Forward Price for Settlement on 4/30/X1
January 1	$0.6019	$0.6057
January 31	0.5970	0.6000
February 28	0.5909	0.5926
March 31	0.5847	0.5855
April 30	0.5729	0.5729

171. The changes in fair value of the forward contract that are recognized each month in earnings and other comprehensive income are shown in the following table. The fair value of the forward is the present value of the difference between the U.S. dollars to be received on the forward ($1,817,100) and the U.S. dollar equivalent of DM3 million based on the current forward rate. A 6 percent discount rate is used in this example.

---

[26]Statement 52 requires immediate recognition in earnings of any foreign currency transaction gain or loss on a foreign-currency-denominated receivable that is not designated as a hedging instrument. Therefore, the effect of changes in spot prices on the royalty receivable must be recognized immediately in earnings.

	Debit (Credit)		
	Forward Contract	**Earnings**	**OCI**
Fair value on January 1	$ 0		
Period ended January 31:			
Change in spot-forward difference	2,364	$ (2,364)	
Change in fair value of dedesignated proportion	0	0	
Change in fair value of designated proportion	14,482		$(14,482)
Reclassification of gain	0	(4,827)	4,827
Fair value on January 31	16,846		
Period ended February 28:			
Change in spot-forward difference	3,873	(3,873)	
Change in fair value of dedesignated proportion	6,063	(6,063)	
Change in fair value of designated proportion	12,127		(12,127)
Reclassification of gain	0	(10,891)	10,891
Fair value on February 28	38,909		
Period ended March 31:			
Change in spot-forward difference	2,718	(2,718)	
Change in fair value of dedesignated proportion	12,458	(12,458)	
Change in fair value of designated proportion	6,213		(6,213)
Reclassification of gain	0	(17,104)	17,104
Fair value on March 31	60,298		
Period ended April 30:			
Change in spot-forward difference	2,445	(2,445)	
Change in fair value of dedesignated proportion	35,657	(35,657)	
Change in fair value of designated proportion	0		0
Fair value on April 30	$98,400		
Cumulative effect		$(98,400)	$ 0

172. The effect on earnings of the royalty agreement and hedging relationship illustrated in this example is summarized by month in the following table.

	Amounts Recognized in Earnings Related to					
	Receivable			Forward Contract		
Period Ended	$ Equivalent of DM1 Million Royalty	Foreign Currency Transaction Gain (Loss)	Amount Attributable to the Dedesignated Proportion	Reclassifications from OCI	Amount Attributable to the Difference between the Spot and Forward Rates	Total Amount Reported in Earnings
January 31	$ 597,000	$ 0	$ 0	$ 4,827	$ 2,364	$ 604,191
February 28	590,900	(6,100)	6,063	10,891	3,873	605,627
March 31	584,700	(12,400)	12,458	17,104	2,718	604,580
April 30	0	(35,400)	35,657	0	2,445	2,702
	$1,772,600	$(53,900)	$54,178	$32,822	$11,400	$1,817,100

$98,400

Example 11: Reporting Cash Flow Hedges in Comprehensive Income and Accumulated Other Comprehensive Income

173. TUV Company's cash flow hedge transactions following adoption of this Statement through the end of 20X4 are as follows:

a. It continually purchases pork belly futures contracts to hedge its anticipated purchases of pork belly inventory.

b. In 20X2, it entered into a Deutsche mark forward exchange contract to hedge the foreign currency risk associated with the expected purchase of a pork belly processing machine with a five-year life that it bought from a vendor in Germany at the end of 20X2.

c. In 20X2, it entered into a 10-year interest rate swap concurrent with the issuance of 10-year variable rate debt (cash flow hedge of future variable interest payments).

d. In January 20X4, it entered into a two-year French franc forward exchange contract to hedge a forecasted export sale (denominated in French francs, expected to occur in December 20X5) of hot dogs to a large customer in France. In June 20X4, it closed the forward contract, but the forecasted transaction is still expected to occur.

174. The following table reconciles the beginning and ending accumulated other comprehensive income balances for 20X4. It supports the comprehensive income display and disclosures that are required under Statement 130, as amended by this Statement. It is assumed that there are no other amounts in accumulated other comprehensive income. The after-tax amounts assume a 30 percent effective tax rate.

	Other Comprehensive Income—Debit (Credit)			
	Accumulated Other Comprehensive Income as of 1/1/X4	Changes in Fair Value Recognized in 20X4	Reclassification Adjustments	Accumulated Other Comprehensive Income as of 12/31/X4
Derivatives designated as hedges of:				
Inventory purchases	$230	$ 85	$(270)	$ 45
Equipment purchase	120		(30)	90
Variable interest rate payments	(40)	10	5	(25)
Export sale	0	(50)	0	(50)
Before-tax totals	$310	$ 45	$(295)	$ 60
After-tax totals	$217	$ 32	$(207)	$ 42

175. The following table illustrates an acceptable method, under the provisions of Statement 130 as amended by this Statement, of reporting the transactions described in paragraphs 173 and 174 in earnings, comprehensive income, and shareholders' equity.

Effect of Selected Items on Earnings and Comprehensive Income
Year Ended December 31, 20X4

	Debit (Credit)	
Effect on earnings before taxes:		
Cost of goods sold	$ 270	
Depreciation	30	
Interest	(5)	
Total	295	
Income tax effect	(88)*	
Effect on earnings after taxes		$ 207
Other comprehensive income, net of tax:		
Cash flow hedges:		
Net derivative losses, net of tax effect of $13	32	
Reclassification adjustments, net of tax effect of $88	(207)	
Net change		(175)
Effect on total comprehensive income		$ 32

---

*This example assumes that it is appropriate under the circumstances, in accordance with FASB Statement No. 109, *Accounting for Income Taxes,* to recognize the related income tax benefit in the current year.

**Effect of Selected Items on
Shareholders' Equity
Year Ended December 31, 20X4
Debit (Credit)**

Accumulated other comprehensive
income:

Balance on December 31, 20X3	$ 217
Net change during the year related to cash flow hedges	(175)
Balance on December 31, 20X4	$ 42

Section 2: Examples Illustrating Application of the Clearly-and-Closely-Related Criterion to Derivative Instruments Embedded in Hybrid Instruments

176. The following examples discuss instruments that contain a variety of embedded derivative instruments. They illustrate how the provisions of paragraphs 12–16 of this Statement would be applied to contracts with the described terms. If the terms of a contract are different from the described terms, the application of this Statement by either party to the contract may be affected. The illustrative instruments and related assumptions in Examples 12–27 are based on examples in Exhibit 96-12A of EITF Issue No. 96-12, "Recognition of Interest Income and Balance Sheet Classification of Structured Notes."

177. Specifically, each example (a) provides a brief discussion of the terms of an instrument that contains an embedded derivative and (b) analyzes the instrument (as of the date of inception) in relation to the provisions of paragraphs 12–16 that require an embedded derivative to be accounted for according to this Statement if it is not clearly and closely related to the host contract. Unless otherwise stated, the examples are based on the assumptions (1) that if the embedded derivative and host portions of the contract are not clearly and closely related, a separate instrument with the same terms as the embedded derivative would meet the scope requirements in paragraphs 6–11 and (2) that the contract is not remeasured at fair value under otherwise applicable generally accepted accounting principles with changes in fair value currently included in earnings.

178. **Example 12: Inverse Floater.** A bond with a coupon rate of interest that varies inversely with changes in specified general interest rate levels or indexes (for example, LIBOR).

Example: Coupon = 5.25 percent for 3 months to July 1994; thereafter at 8.75 percent – 6-month US$ LIBOR to January 1995. "Stepping" option allows for spread and caps to step semiannually to maturity.

Scope Application: An inverse floater contains an embedded derivative (a fixed-for-floating interest rate swap) that is referenced to an interest rate index (in this example, LIBOR) that alters net interest payments that otherwise would be paid by the debtor or received by the investor on an interest-bearing host contract. If the embedded derivative could potentially result in the investor's not recovering substantially all of its initial recorded investment in the bond (that is, if the inverse floater contains no floor to prevent any erosion of principal due to a negative interest rate), the embedded derivative is not considered to be clearly and closely related to the host contract (refer to paragraph 13(a)). In that case, the embedded derivative should be separated from the host contract and accounted for by both parties pursuant to the provisions of this Statement. (In this example, there appears to be no possibility of the embedded derivative increasing the investor's rate of return on the host contract to an amount that is at least double the initial rate of return on the host contract [refer to paragraph 13(b)].) In contrast, if the embedded derivative could not potentially result in the investor's failing to recover substantially all of its initial recorded investment in the bond, the embedded derivative is considered to be clearly and closely related to the host contract and separate accounting for the derivative is neither required nor permitted.

179. **Example 13: Levered Inverse Floater.** A bond with a coupon that varies indirectly with changes in general interest rate levels and applies a multiplier (greater than 1.00) to the specified index in its calculation of interest.

Example: Accrues at 6 percent to June 1994; thereafter at 14.55 percent – (2.5 × 3-month US$ LIBOR).

Scope Application: A levered inverse floater can be viewed as an inverse floater in which the embedded interest rate swap is leveraged. Similar to Example 12, the embedded derivative would not be clearly and closely related to the host contract if it potentially could result in the investor's not recovering substantially all of its initial recorded investment in the bond (refer to paragraph 13(a)) because there is no floor to the interest rate. In that case, the embedded derivative (the leveraged interest rate swap) should be separated from the host contract and accounted for by both parties pursuant to the provisions of this Statement. In contrast, if an embedded derivative could not potentially result in the investor's failing to recover substantially all of its initial recorded investment in the bond and if there was no possibility of the embedded derivative increasing the investor's rate of return on the host contract to an amount that is at least double the initial rate of return on the host contract (refer to paragraph 13(b)), the embedded derivative is considered to be clearly and closely related to the host contract and no separate accounting for the derivative is required or permitted.

180. **Example 14: Delevered Floater.** A bond with a coupon rate of interest that lags overall movements in specified general interest rate levels or indices.

Example: Coupon = $(.5 \times 10$-year constant maturity treasuries (CMT)) + 1.25 percent.

Scope Application: A delevered floater may be viewed as containing an embedded derivative (a deleveraged swap or a series of forward agreements) that is referenced to an interest rate index (for example, 50 percent of 10-year CMT) that alters net interest payments that otherwise would be paid or received on an interest-bearing host contract but could not potentially result in the investor's failing to recover substantially all of its initial recorded investment in the bond (refer to paragraph 13(a)). (In this example, there appears to be no possibility of the embedded derivative increasing the investor's rate of return on the host contract to an amount that is at least double the initial rate of return on the host contract [refer to paragraph 13(b)].) The embedded derivative is considered to be clearly and closely related to the host contract as described in paragraph 13 of this Statement. Therefore, the embedded derivative should *not* be separated from the host contract.

181. **Example 15: Range Floater.** A bond with a coupon that depends on the *number of days* that a reference rate stays within a preestablished collar; otherwise, the bond pays either zero percent interest or a below-market rate.

Example: Standard range floater—The investor receives 5.5 percent on *each day* that 3-month

US$ LIBOR is between 3 percent and 4 percent, with the upper limit increasing annually after a specified date. The coupon will be equal to zero percent for each day that 3-month US$ LIBOR is *outside* that range.

Scope Application: A range floater may be viewed as containing embedded derivatives (two written conditional exchange option contracts with notional amounts equal to the par value of the fixed-rate instrument) that are referenced to an interest rate index (in this example, LIBOR) that alter net interest payments that otherwise would be paid by the debtor or received by the investor on an interest-bearing host contract but could not potentially result in the investor's failing to recover substantially all of its initial recorded investment in the bond (refer to paragraph 13(a)). In this example, there appears to be no possibility of increasing the investor's rate of return on the host contract to an amount that is at least double the initial rate of return on the host contract (refer to paragraph 13(b)). The embedded derivatives are considered to be clearly and closely related to the host contract as described in paragraph 13 of this Statement. Therefore, the embedded derivatives should *not* be separated from the host contract.

182. **Example 16: Ratchet Floater.** A bond that pays a floating rate of interest and has an adjustable cap, adjustable floor, or both that move in sync with each new reset rate.

Example: Coupon = 3-month US$ LIBOR + 50 basis points. In addition to having a lifetime cap of 7.25 percent, the coupon will be collared each period between the previous coupon and the previous coupon plus 25 basis points.

Scope Application: A ratchet floater may be viewed as containing embedded derivatives (combinations of purchased and written options that create changing caps and floors) that are referenced to an interest rate index (in this example, LIBOR) that alter net interest payments that otherwise would be paid by the debtor or received by the investor on an interest-bearing host contract but could not potentially result in the investor's failing to recover substantially all of its initial recorded investment in the bond (refer to paragraph 13(a)). In this example, there appears to be no possibility of increasing the investor's rate of return on the host contract to an amount that is at least double the initial rate of return on the host contract (refer to paragraph 13(b)). The embedded derivatives are considered to be clearly and closely related to the host contract as described in paragraph 13 of this Statement. Therefore, the embedded derivatives should *not* be separated from the host contract.

183. **Example 17: Fixed-to-Floating Note.** A bond that pays a varying coupon (first-year coupon is fixed; second- and third-year coupons are based on LIBOR, Treasury bills, or prime rate).

Scope Application: A fixed-to-floating note may be viewed as containing an embedded derivative (a forward-starting interest rate swap) that is referenced to an interest rate index (such as LIBOR) that alters net interest payments that otherwise would be paid by the debtor or received by the investor on an interest-bearing host instrument but could not potentially result in the investor's failing to recover substantially all of its initial recorded investment in the bond (refer to paragraph 13(a)). Likewise, there is no possibility of increasing the investor's rate of return on the host contract to an amount that is both at least double the initial rate of return on the host contract and at least twice what otherwise would be the market return for a contract that has the same terms as the host contract and that involves a debtor with a similar credit quality (refer to paragraph 13(b)). The embedded derivative is considered to be clearly and closely related to the host contract as described in paragraph 13 of this Statement. Therefore, the embedded derivative should *not* be separated from the host contract.

184. **Example 18: Indexed Amortizing Note.** A bond that repays principal based on a predetermined amortization schedule or target value. The amortization is linked to changes in a specific mortgage-backed security index or interest rate index. The maturity of the bond changes as the related index changes. This instrument includes a varying maturity. (It is assumed for this example that the bond's terms could not potentially result in the investor's failing to recover substantially all of its initial recorded investment in the bond [refer to paragraph 13(a)] nor is there the possibility of increasing the investor's rate of return on the host contract to an amount that is both at least double the initial rate of return on the host contract and at least twice what otherwise would be the market return for a contract that has the same terms as the host contract and that

involves a debtor with a similar credit quality [refer to paragraph 13(b)].)

Scope Application: An indexed amortizing note can be viewed as a fixed-rate amortizing note combined with a conditional exchange option contract that requires partial or total "early" payment of the note based on changes in a specific mortgage-backed security index or a specified change in an interest rate index. Because the requirement to prepay is ultimately tied to changing interest rates, the embedded derivative is considered to be clearly and closely related to a fixed-rate note. Therefore, the embedded derivative should *not* be separated from the host contract.

185. **Example 19: Equity-Indexed Note.** A bond for which the return of interest, principal, or both is tied to a specified equity security or index (for example, the Standard and Poor's 500 [S&P 500] index). This instrument may contain a fixed or varying coupon rate and may place all or a portion of principal at risk.

Scope Application: An equity-indexed note essentially combines an interest-bearing instrument with a series of forward exchange contracts or option contracts. Often, a portion of the coupon interest rate is, in effect, used to purchase options that provide some form of floor on the potential loss of principal that would result from a decline in the referenced equity index. Because forward or option contracts for which the underlying is an equity index are not clearly and closely related to an investment in an interest-bearing note, those embedded derivatives should be separated from the host contract and accounted for by both parties pursuant to the provisions of this Statement.

186. **Example 20: Variable Principal Redemption Bond.** A bond whose principal redemption value at maturity depends on the change in an underlying index over a predetermined observation period. A typical example would be a bond that guarantees a minimum par redemption value of 100 percent and provides the potential for a supplemental principal payment at maturity as compensation for the below-market rate of interest offered with the instrument.

Example: A supplemental principal payment will be paid to the investor, at maturity, if the final S&P 500 closing value (determined at a specified date) is less than its initial value at date of issuance *and* the 10-year CMT is greater than 2 percent as of a specified date. In all cases, the minimum principal redemption will be 100 percent of par.

Scope Application: A variable principal redemption bond essentially combines an interest-bearing investment with an option that is purchased with a portion of the bond's coupon interest payments. Because the embedded option entitling the investor to an additional return is partially contingent on the S&P 500 index closing above a specified amount, it is not clearly and closely related to an investment in a debt instrument. Therefore, the embedded option should be separated from the host contract and accounted for by both parties pursuant to the provisions of this Statement.

187. **Example 21: Crude Oil Knock-in Note.** A bond that has a 1 percent coupon and guarantees repayment of principal with upside potential based on the strength of the oil market.

Scope Application: A crude oil knock-in note essentially combines an interest-bearing instrument with a series of option contracts. A significant portion of the coupon interest rate is, in effect, used to purchase options that provide the investor with potential gains resulting from increases in specified crude oil prices. Because the option contracts are indexed to the price of crude oil, they are not clearly and closely related to an investment in an interest-bearing note. Therefore, the embedded option contract should be separated from the host contract and accounted for by both parties pursuant to the provisions of this Statement.

188. **Example 22: Gold-Linked Bull Note.** A bond that has a fixed 3 percent coupon and guarantees repayment of principal with upside potential if the price of gold increases.

Scope Application: A gold-linked bull note can be viewed as combining an interest-bearing instrument with a series of option contracts. A portion of the coupon interest rate is, in effect, used to purchase call options that provide the investor with potential gains resulting from increases in gold prices. Because the option contracts are indexed to the price of gold, they are not clearly and closely related to an investment in an interest-bearing note. Therefore, the embedded option contracts should be separated from the

host contract and accounted for by both parties pursuant to the provisions of this Statement.

189. **Example 23: Step-up Bond.** A bond that provides an introductory above-market yield and steps up to a new coupon, which will be below then-current market rates or, alternatively, the bond may be called in lieu of the step-up in the coupon rate.

Scope Application: A step-up bond can be viewed as a fixed-rate bond with an embedded call option and a changing interest rate feature. The bond pays an initial above-market interest rate to compensate for the call option and the future below-market rate (that is, below the forward yield curve, as determined at issuance based on the existing upward-sloping yield curve). Because the call option is related to changes in interest rates, it is clearly and closely related to an investment in a fixed-rate bond. Therefore, the embedded derivatives should *not* be separated from the host contract.

190. **Example 24: Credit-Sensitive Bond.** A bond that has a coupon rate of interest that resets based on changes in the issuer's credit rating.

Scope Application: A credit-sensitive bond can be viewed as combining a fixed-rate bond with a conditional exchange contract (or an option) that entitles the investor to a higher rate of interest if the credit rating of the issuer declines. Because the creditworthiness of the debtor and the interest rate on a debt instrument are clearly and closely related, the embedded derivative should *not* be separated from the host contract.

191. **Example 25: Inflation Bond.** A bond with a contractual principal amount that is indexed to the inflation rate but cannot decrease below par; the coupon rate is typically below that of traditional bonds of similar maturity.

Scope Application: An inflation bond can be viewed as a fixed-rate bond for which a portion of the coupon interest rate has been exchanged for a conditional exchange contract (or option) indexed to the consumer price index, or other index of inflation in the economic environment for the currency in which the bond is denominated, that entitles the investor to payment of additional principal based on increases in the referenced index. Such rates of inflation and interest rates on the debt instrument are considered to be clearly and closely related. Therefore, the embedded derivative should *not* be separated from the host contract.

192. **Example 26: Disaster Bond.** A bond that pays a coupon above that of an otherwise comparable traditional bond; however, all or a substantial portion of the principal amount is subject to loss if a specified disaster experience occurs.

Scope Application: A disaster bond can be viewed as a fixed-rate bond combined with a conditional exchange contract (an option). The investor receives an additional coupon interest payment in return for giving the issuer an option indexed to industry loss experience on a specified disaster. Because the option contract is indexed to the specified disaster experience, it cannot be viewed as being clearly and closely related to an investment in a fixed-rate bond. Therefore, the embedded derivative should be separated from the host contract and accounted for by both parties pursuant to the provisions of this Statement.

However, if the "embedded derivative" entitles the holder of the option (that is, the issuer of the disaster bond) to be compensated only for changes in the value of specified assets or liabilities for which the holder is at risk (including the liability for insurance claims payable due to the specified disaster) as a result of an identified insurable event (refer to paragraph 10(c)(2)), a separate instrument with the same terms as the "embedded derivative" would *not* meet the Statement's definition of a derivative in paragraphs 6–11. In that circumstance, because the criterion in paragraph 12(c) would not be met, there is no embedded derivative to be separated from the host contract, and the disaster bond would not be subject to the requirements of this Statement. The investor is essentially providing a form of insurance or reinsurance coverage to the issuer.

193. **Example 27: Specific Equity-Linked Bond.** A bond that pays a coupon slightly below that of traditional bonds of similar maturity; however, the principal amount is linked to the stock market performance of an equity investee of the issuer. The issuer may settle the obligation by delivering the shares of the equity investee or may deliver the equivalent fair value in cash.

Scope Application: A specific equity-linked bond can be viewed as combining an interest-bearing

instrument with, depending on its terms, a series of forward exchange contracts or option contracts based on an equity instrument. Often, a portion of the coupon interest rate is used to purchase options that provide some form of floor on the loss of principal due to a decline in the price of the referenced equity instrument. The forward or option contracts do not qualify for the exception in paragraph 10(e)(2) because the shares in the equity investee owned by the issuer meet the definition of a *financial instrument*. Because forward or option contracts for which the underlying is the price of a specific equity instrument are not clearly and closely related to an investment in an interest-bearing note, the embedded derivative should be separated from the host contract and accounted for by both parties pursuant to the provisions of this Statement.

194. **Example 28: Dual Currency Bond.** A bond providing for repayment of principal in U.S. dollars and periodic interest payments denominated in a foreign currency. In this example, a U.S. entity with the dollar as its functional currency is borrowing funds from an independent party with those repayment terms as described.

Scope Application: Because the portion of this instrument relating to the periodic interest payments denominated in a foreign currency is subject to the requirement in Statement 52 to recognize the foreign currency transaction gain or loss in earnings, the instrument should not be considered as containing an embedded foreign currency derivative instrument pursuant to paragraph 15 of this Statement. In this example, the U.S. entity has the dollar as the functional currency and is making interest payments in a foreign currency. Remeasurement of the liability is required using future equivalent dollar interest payments determined by the current spot exchange rate and discounted at the historical effective interest rate.

195. **Example 29: Short-Term Loan with a Foreign Currency Option.** A U.S. lender issues a loan at an above-market interest rate. The loan is made in U.S. dollars, the borrower's functional currency, and the borrower has the option to repay the loan in U.S. dollars or in a fixed amount of a specified foreign currency.

Scope Application: This instrument can be viewed as combining a loan at prevailing market interest rates and a foreign currency option. The lender has written a foreign currency option exposing it to changes in foreign currency exchange rates during the outstanding period of the loan. The premium for the option has been paid as part of the interest rate. Because the borrower has the option to repay the loan in U.S. dollars or in a fixed amount of a specified foreign currency, the provisions of paragraph 15 are not relevant to this example. Paragraph 15 addresses foreign-currency-denominated interest or principal payments but does not apply to foreign currency options. Because a foreign currency option is not clearly and closely related to issuing a loan, the embedded option should be separated from the host contract and accounted for by both parties pursuant to the provisions of this Statement. In contrast, if both the principal payment and the interest payments on the loan had been payable only in a fixed amount of a specified foreign currency, there would be no embedded foreign currency derivative pursuant to this Statement.

196. Example 30: Lease Payment in Foreign Currency. A U.S. company's operating lease with a Japanese lessor is payable in yen. The functional currency of the U.S. company is the U.S. dollar.

Scope Application: Paragraph 15(a) provides that contracts, other than financial instruments, that specify payments denominated in the currency of the primary economic environment in which any substantial party to that contract operates shall *not* be separated from the host contract and considered a derivative instrument for purposes of this Statement. Using available information about the lessor and its operations, the U.S. company may decide it is reasonable to conclude that the yen would be the currency of the primary economic environment in which the Japanese lessor operates, consistent with the functional currency notion in Statement 52. (That decision can be based on available information and reasonable assumptions about the counterparty; representations from the counterparty are not required.) Thus, the lease should *not* be viewed as containing an embedded swap converting U.S. dollar lease payments to yen. Alternatively, if the lease payments are specified in a currency seemingly unrelated to each party's functional currency, such as drachmas (assuming the leased property is not in Greece), the embedded foreign currency swap should be separated from the host contract and accounted for as a derivative for pur-

poses of this Statement because the provisions of paragraph 15 would not apply and a separate instrument with the same terms would meet the definition of a derivative instrument in paragraphs 6–11.

197. Example 31: Certain Purchases in a Foreign Currency. A U.S. company enters into a contract to purchase corn from a local American supplier in six months for yen; the yen is the functional currency of neither party to the transaction. The corn is expected to be delivered and used over a reasonable period in the normal course of business.

Scope Application: Paragraph 10(b) excludes contracts that require future delivery of commodities that are readily convertible to cash from the accounting for derivatives if the commodities will be delivered in quantities expected to be used or sold by the reporting entity over a reasonable period in the normal course of business. However, the corn purchase contract must be examined to determine whether it contains an embedded derivative that warrants separate accounting. The corn purchase contract can be viewed as a forward contract for the purchase of corn and an embedded foreign currency swap from the purchaser's functional currency (the U.S. dollar) to yen. Because the yen is the functional currency of neither party to the transaction and the purchase of corn is transacted internationally in many different currencies, the contract does not qualify for the exception in paragraph 15 that precludes separating the embedded foreign currency derivative from the host contract. The embedded foreign currency swap should be separated from the host contract and accounted for as a derivative for purposes of this Statement because a separate instrument with the same terms would meet the definition of a derivative instrument in paragraphs 6–11.

198. Example 32: Participating Mortgage. A mortgage in which the investor receives a below-market interest rate and is entitled to participate in the appreciation in the market value of the project that is financed by the mortgage upon sale of the project, at a deemed sale date, or at the maturity or refinancing of the loan. The mortgagor must continue to own the project over the term of the mortgage.

Scope Application: This instrument has a provision that entitles the investor to participate in the appreciation of the referenced real estate (the "project"). However, a separate contract with the same terms would be excluded by the exception in paragraph 10(e)(2) because settlement is based on the value of a nonfinancial asset of one of the parties that is not readily convertible to cash. (This Statement does not modify the guidance in AICPA Statement of Position 97-1, *Accounting by Participating Mortgage Loan Borrowers.*)

199. **Example 33: Convertible Debt.** An investor receives a below-market interest rate and receives the option to convert its debt instrument into the equity of the issuer at an established conversion rate. The terms of the conversion require that the issuer deliver shares of stock to the investor.

Scope Application: This instrument essentially contains a call option on the issuer's stock. Under the provisions of this Statement, the accounting by the issuer and investor can differ. The issuer's accounting depends on whether a separate instrument with the same terms as the embedded written option would be a derivative instrument pursuant to paragraphs 6–11 of this Statement. Because the option is indexed to the issuer's own stock and a separate instrument with the same terms would be classified in stockholders' equity in the statement of financial position, the written option is not considered to be a derivative instrument for the issuer under paragraph 11(a) and should *not* be separated from the host contract.

In contrast, if the terms of the conversion allow for a cash settlement rather than delivery of the issuer's shares at the investor's option, the exception in paragraph 11(a) for the issuer does not apply because the contract would not be classified in stockholders' equity in the issuer's statement of financial position. In that case, the issuer should separate the embedded derivative from the host contract and account for it pursuant to the provisions of this Statement because (a) an option based on the entity's stock price is not clearly and closely related to an interest-bearing debt instrument and (b) the option would not be considered an equity instrument of the issuer.

Similarly, if the convertible debt is indexed to another entity's publicly traded common stock, the issuer should separate the embedded derivative from the host contract and account for it pursuant to the provisions of this Statement because (a) an option based on another entity's stock price is not clearly and closely related to an investment in an interest-bearing note and (b) the option would not be considered an equity instrument of the issuer.

The exception in paragraph 11 does not apply to the investor's accounting. Therefore, in both cases described above, the investor should separate the embedded option contract from the host contract and account for the embedded option contract pursuant to the provisions of this Statement because the option contract is based on the price of another entity's equity instrument and thus is not clearly and closely related to an investment in an interest-bearing note. However, if the terms of conversion do not allow for a cash settlement and if the common stock delivered upon conversion is privately held (that is, is not readily convertible to cash), the embedded derivative would not be separated from the host contract because it would not meet the criteria in paragraph 9.

200. **Example 34: Variable Annuity Products.** These products are investment contracts as contemplated in Statements 60 and 97. Similar to variable life insurance products, policyholders direct their investment account asset mix among a variety of mutual funds composed of equities, bonds, or both, and assume the risks and rewards of investment performance. The funds are generally maintained in separate accounts by the insurance company. Contract terms provide that if the policyholder dies, the greater of the account market value or a minimum death benefit guarantee will be paid. The minimum death benefit guarantee is generally limited to a return of premium plus a minimum return (such as 3 or 4 percent); this life insurance feature represents the fundamental difference from the life insurance contracts that include significant (rather than minimal) levels of life insurance. The investment account may have various payment alternatives at the end of the accumulation period. One alternative is the right to purchase a life annuity at a fixed price determined at the initiation of the contract.

Scope Application: Variable annuity product structures as contemplated in Statement 97 are generally not subject to the scope of this Statement (except for payment options at the end of the accumulation period), as follows:

- *Death benefit component.* Paragraph 10(c)(1) excludes a death benefit from the scope of this Statement because the payment of the death benefit is the result of an identifiable insurable event instead of changes in an underlying. The death benefit in this example is limited to the floor guarantee of the investment account, calculated as the premiums paid into the investment account plus a guaranteed rate of return, less the account market value. Statement 60 remains the applicable guidance for the insurance-related liability accounting.

- *Investment component.* The policyholder directs certain premium investments in the investment account that includes equities, bonds, or both, which are held in separate accounts that are owned by the policyholder and separate from the insurer's general account assets. This component is viewed as a direct investment because the policyholder directs and owns these investments. This component is not a derivative because the policyholder has invested the premiums in acquiring those investments. Furthermore, any embedded derivatives within those investments should not be separated from the host contract by the insurer because the separate account assets are already marked-to-market under Statement 60. In contrast, if the product were an equity-index-based interest annuity (rather than a variable annuity), the investment component would not be viewed as a direct investment because the policyholder does not own those investments, which are assets recorded in the general account of the insurance company. As a result, the host contract would be a debt instrument, and the equity-index-based derivative should be separated and accounted for as a derivative instrument.

- *Investment account surrender right at market value.* Because this right is exercised only at the fund market value (without the insurer's floor guarantee) and relates to an investment owned by the insured, this right is not within the scope of this Statement.

- *Payment alternatives at the end of the accumulation period.* Payment alternatives are options subject to the requirements of this Statement if interest rates or other underlying variables affect the value.

Section 3: Examples Illustrating Application of the Transition Provisions

201. Assume that at December 31, 1999, a calendar-year entity has the following derivatives and hedging relationships in place (for simplicity, income tax effects are ignored):

Before Transition Adjustment—December 31, 1999

| (a) Item | Asset (Liability) | | (d) GAAP Classification prior to Transition | (e) Previous Hedge Resembles | (f) Assumed Post-Transition-Date Accounting under This Statement |
	(b) Carrying Amount	(c) Fair Value			
A.					
Forward contract	$ 0	$(1,500)	Hedges existing inventory (though fair value changes have not been recognized)	Fair value hedge	Fair value hedge of inventory
Inventory	5,000	6,400	Hedged by forward contract		

2167

Before Transition Adjustment—December 31, 1999 (continued)

| (a) Item | Asset (Liability) | | (d) GAAP Classification prior to Transition | (e) Previous Hedge Resembles | (f) Assumed Post-Transition-Date Accounting under This Statement |
	(b) Carrying Amount	(c) Fair Value			
B.					
Interest rate swap	0	180	Hedges fixed-rate bond		Would not qualify as a hedge of the held-to-maturity security—account for swap as a nonhedging derivative*
Fixed-rate bond (classified as held-to-maturity)	1,000	800	Hedged by interest rate swap	Fair value hedge	

*Prior to the effective date of Statement 133, generally accepted accounting principles did not prohibit hedge accounting for a hedge of the interest rate risk in a held-to-maturity security. Thus, transition adjustments may be necessary for hedges of that type because that type of hedging relationship will no longer qualify for hedge accounting under the provisions of this Statement. At the date of initial application, an entity may reclassify any held-to-maturity security into the available-for-sale or trading category (refer to paragraph 54).

C.				
Interest rate swap	0	(350)		Fair value hedge
Fixed-rate bond (classified as available-for-sale)	1,000	1,000	Hedged by interest rate swap (cost basis is $650; unrealized holding gain is $350)	
Other comprehensive income (Statement 115)	(350)	N/A		
				Fair value hedge of the fixed-rate bond
D.				
Foreign currency forward contract	1,000	1,200	Hedges firm purchase commitment	Fair value hedge
Deferred credit	(1,000)	N/A	Deferred gain related to foreign currency forward contract	
Firm commitment to pay foreign currency to purchase machinery	0	(1,200)	Hedged by foreign currency forward contract	Fair value hedge of the firm commitment

Before Transition Adjustment—December 31, 1999 (continued)

(a) Item	(b) Carrying Amount	(c) Fair Value	(d) GAAP Classification prior to Transition	(e) Previous Hedge Resembles	(f) Assumed Post-Transition-Date Accounting under This Statement
E. Swap (no longer held) Deferred credit	(1,000)	N/A	Swap that was hedging a probable forecasted transaction was terminated prior to 12/31/99 and the related gain was deferred	Cash flow hedge	Since the swap is no longer held, there is no new designation
F. 2-year forward contract	0	1,000	Hedges a probable forecasted transaction projected to occur in 1 year	Cash flow hedge	Forward could possibly qualify as a hedging instrument
G. 6-month futures contract (cash settled daily)	0	0	Hedges a probable forecasted transaction projected to occur in 6 months	Cash flow hedge	Cash flow hedge
Deferred debit	500	N/A	Deferred loss related to futures contract		N/A

Note: Columns (b) and (c) are under the heading "Asset (Liability)".

202. To determine transition accounting, existing hedge relationships must be identified as either a fair value *type* of hedge or a cash flow *type* of hedge as identified pursuant to this Statement. They do not have to meet the hedge criteria of this Statement. That identification is indicated in column (e) of the above table.

203. At transition, an entity has an opportunity to redesignate hedging relationships. This example makes certain assumptions regarding post-transition-date accounting pursuant to this Statement as indicated in column (f) of the above table that cannot necessarily be determined from the information provided in this example. The appropriate conditions in this Statement must be met to continue hedge accounting for periods subsequent to transition. However, determining whether a potential hedging relationship meets the conditions of this Statement does not impact the transition accounting. For purposes of determining transition adjustments, existing hedging relationships are categorized as fair value or cash flow hedges based on their general characteristics, without assessing whether all of the applicable conditions would be met.

204. After applying the transition provisions, the above items would be reflected in the financial statements as follows:

After Transition Adjustment—January 1, 2000 (continued)

	Statement of Financial Position		Income Statement	
Item	Asset (Liability)	Other Comprehensive Income	Transition Adjustment Gain (Loss)	Explanation of Accounting at Transition
A.				
Forward contract	$(1,500)	N/A	$(1,500)	Adjust to fair value by recognizing $1,500 loss as a transition adjustment
Inventory	6,400	N/A	1,400	Recognize offsetting $1,400 gain as a transition adjustment*
Net impact			$ (100)	
B.				
Interest rate swap	180	N/A	$ 180	Adjust to fair value by recognizing $180 gain as a transition adjustment
Fixed-rate bond (classified as held-to-maturity)	820	N/A	(180)	Recognize offsetting $180 loss as a transition adjustment
Net impact			$ 0	

*The transition adjustment for the gain on the hedged inventory is limited to the amount that is offset by the loss on the hedging derivative. The entire $1,400 gain is recognized in this example because it is less than the $1,500 loss on the derivative. If the inventory gain had been more than $1,500, only $1,500 would have been recognized as a transition adjustment.

C.

Interest rate swap	(350)	N/A	$ (350)	Adjust to fair value by recognizing a $350 loss as a transition adjustment
Fixed-rate bond (classified as available-for-sale)	1,000	N/A	—	Remove offsetting $350 gain previously reported in OCI (Statement 115) and recognize as a transition adjustment
Other comprehensive income (OCI)	N/A	—	350	
Net impact			$ 0	

D.

Foreign currency forward contract	1,200	N/A	$ 200	Adjust to fair value by recognizing $200 gain as a transition adjustment
Deferred credit	0	N/A	1,000	Remove deferred credit and recognize as a transition adjustment
Firm commitment to pay foreign currency to purchase machinery	(1,200)	N/A	(1,200)	Recognize offsetting $1,200 loss as a transition adjustment
Net impact			$ 0	

After Transition Adjustment—January 1, 2000 (continued)

	Statement of Financial Position		Income Statement	
Item	Asset (Liability)	Other Comprehensive Income	Transition Adjustment Gain (Loss)	Explanation of Accounting at Transition
E. Terminated swap	—	$ —	—	No asset exists for the terminated swap
Deferred credit	—	N/A	—	Remove the deferred credit and recognize in OCI—to be reclassified into earnings consistent with the earnings effect of the hedged forecasted transaction
OCI	N/A	$(1,000)	—	
Net impact			$ 0	
F. Forward contract	1,000	(1,000)	$ 0	Adjust to fair value by recognizing $1,000 gain in OCI—to be reclassified into earnings consistent with the earnings effect of the hedged forecasted transaction

G.

Futures contract	0	N/A	Asset already reported at fair value—no adjustment necessary
Deferred debit	—	N/A	
OCI	N/A	500	Remove deferred debit and recognize in OCI—to be reclassified into earnings consistent with the earnings effect of the hedged forecasted transaction
Net impact	$ 0		

205. In the initial year of application, an entity would also disclose the amounts of deferred gains and losses included in other comprehensive income that are expected to be reclassified into earnings within the next 12 months.

Appendix C

BACKGROUND INFORMATION AND BASIS FOR CONCLUSIONS

CONTENTS

Appendix C

BACKGROUND INFORMATION AND BASIS FOR CONCLUSIONS

Introduction

206. This appendix summarizes considerations that Board members deemed significant in reaching the conclusions in this Statement. It includes reasons for accepting certain views and rejecting others. Individual Board members gave greater weight to some factors than to others.

Background Information

207. The Board is addressing the accounting for derivative instruments[27] and hedging activities as part of its broad project on financial instruments. That project was added to the Board's agenda in 1986 to address financial reporting issues that were arising, or that were given a new sense of urgency, as a result of financial innovation. The project initially focused on disclosures and resulted in the issuance of FASB Statements No. 105, *Disclosure of Information about Financial Instruments with Off-Balance-Sheet Risk and Financial Instruments with Concentrations of Credit Risk,* in March 1990, and No. 107, *Disclosures about Fair Value of Financial Instruments,* in December 1991. This Statement supersedes Statement 105 and amends Statement 107.

208. An FASB staff-authored Research Report, *Hedge Accounting: An Exploratory Study of the Underlying Issues,* was published in September 1991.[28] An FASB Discussion Memorandum, *Recognition and Measurement of Financial Instruments,* was issued in November 1991 as a basis for considering the

---

[27]The terms *derivative instrument* and *derivative* are used interchangeably in this appendix.

[28]Harold Bierman, Jr., L. Todd Johnson, and D. Scott Peterson, FASB Research Report, *Hedge Accounting: An Exploratory Study of the Underlying Issues.*

financial accounting and reporting issues of recognition and measurement raised by financial instruments. The recognition and measurement phase of the financial instruments project, which began with the issuance of that Discussion Memorandum, resulted in the issuance of FASB Statements No. 114, *Accounting by Creditors for Impairment of a Loan,* and No. 115, *Accounting for Certain Investments in Debt and Equity Securities,* in May 1993, FASB Statement No. 118, *Accounting by Creditors for Impairment of a Loan—Income Recognition and Disclosures,* in October 1994, and FASB Statement No. 125, *Accounting for Transfers and Servicing of Financial Assets and Extinguishments of Liabilities,* in June 1996.

209. Concern about financial reporting for derivative instruments and hedging activities is an international phenomenon. In October 1995, an FASB staff-authored Special Report, *Major Issues Related to Hedge Accounting,* was published jointly with representatives of the accounting standards-setting bodies of the United Kingdom, Canada, and Australia and the International Accounting Standards Committee.[29] That Special Report discusses many of the issues that needed to be resolved in developing a hedge accounting model.

210. The Board began deliberating issues relating to derivatives and hedging activities in January 1992. From then until June 1996, the Board held 100 public meetings to discuss various issues and proposed accounting approaches, including 74 Board meetings, 10 meetings with members of the Financial Accounting Standards Advisory Council, 7 meetings with members of the Financial Instruments Task Force and its subgroup on hedging, and 9 meetings with outside representatives. In addition, individual Board members and staff visited numerous companies in a variety of fields and participated in meetings with different representational groups, both nationally and internationally, to explore how different entities manage risk and how those risk management activities should be accounted for.

211. In June 1993, the Board issued a report, "A Report on Deliberations, Including Tentative Conclusions on Certain Issues, related to Accounting for Hedging and Other Risk-adjusting Activities." That report included background information about the Board's deliberations and some tentative conclusions on accounting for derivatives and hedging activities. It also solicited comments from constituents and provided the basis for two public meetings in September 1993.

212. Concern has grown about the accounting and disclosure requirements for derivatives and hedging activities as the extent of use and the complexity of derivatives and hedging activities have rapidly increased in recent years. Changes in global financial markets and related financial innovations have led to the development of new derivatives used to manage exposures to risk, including interest rate, foreign exchange, price, and credit risks. Many believe that accounting standards have not kept pace with those changes. Derivatives can be useful risk management tools, and some believe that the inadequacy of financial reporting may have discouraged their use by contributing to an atmosphere of uncertainty. Concern about inadequate financial reporting also was heightened by the publicity surrounding large derivative losses at a few companies. As a result, the Securities and Exchange Commission, members of Congress, and others urged the Board to deal expeditiously with reporting problems in this area. For example, a report of the General Accounting Office prepared for Congress in 1994 recommended, among other things, that the FASB "proceed expeditiously to develop and issue an exposure draft that provides comprehensive, consistent accounting rules for derivative products. . . ."[30] In addition, some users of financial statements asked for improved disclosures and accounting for derivatives and hedging. For example, one of the recommendations in the December 1994 report published by the AICPA Special Committee on Financial Reporting, *Improving Business Reporting—A Customer Focus,* was to address the disclosures and accounting for innovative financial instruments.

213. Because of the urgency of improved financial information about derivatives and related activities, the Board decided, in December 1993, to redirect some of its efforts toward enhanced disclosures and, in October 1994, issued FASB Statement No. 119, *Disclosure about Derivative Financial Instruments*

---

[29]Jane B. Adams and Corliss J. Montesi, FASB Special Report, *Major Issues Related to Hedge Accounting.*

[30]United States General Accounting Office, Report to Congressional Requesters, *Financial Derivatives: Actions Needed to Protect the Financial System,* May 1994, 16.

and Fair Value of Financial Instruments. This Statement supersedes Statement 119.

214. In June 1996, the Board issued an Exposure Draft, *Accounting for Derivative and Similar Financial Instruments and for Hedging Activities.* Approximately 300 organizations and individuals responded to the Exposure Draft, some with multiple letters. In November 1996, 36 individuals and organizations presented their views at 4 days of public hearings. In addition, six enterprises participated in a limited field test of the provisions of the Exposure Draft. In December 1996, the Board's Financial Instruments Task Force met to discuss the issues raised during the comment letter process and during the public hearings. The Board considered the comments and field test results during its re-deliberations of the issues addressed by the Exposure Draft in 21 public meetings in the first 7 months of 1997. The Financial Instruments Task Force met again with the Board in April 1997 and discussed, among other things, proposed changes to the Exposure Draft reflected in a draft of a Statement. As a consequence of the comments received, the Board made certain changes to the proposals in the Exposure Draft.

215. In August 1997, a draft of the standards section of this Statement and related examples was made available to the Financial Instruments Task Force and other interested parties for comment on its clarity and operationality. The Board received approximately 150 comment letters on that draft and discussed those comments in 10 open Board meetings. Those comments also led to changes to the requirements, intended to make the Statement clearer and more operational.

216. This Statement is an additional step in the Board's project on financial instruments and is intended to address the immediate problems about the recognition and measurement of derivatives while the Board's vision of having all financial instruments measured at fair value in the statement of financial position is pursued. Certain provisions of this Statement will be reconsidered as the Board continues to address the issues in its broad project on financial instruments.

Fundamental Decisions Underlying the Statement

217. The Board made four fundamental decisions about how to account for derivatives and hedging activities; those decisions became the cornerstones of this Statement:

a. Derivative instruments represent rights or obligations that meet the definitions of assets or liabilities and should be reported in financial statements.
b. Fair value is the most relevant measure for financial instruments and the only relevant measure for derivative instruments. Derivative instruments should be measured at fair value, and adjustments to the carrying amounts of hedged items should reflect changes in their fair value (that is, gains or losses) that are attributable to the risk being hedged and that arise while the hedge is in effect.
c. Only items that are assets or liabilities should be reported as such in financial statements.
d. Special accounting for items designated as being hedged should be provided only for qualifying items. One aspect of qualification should be an assessment of the expectation of effective offsetting changes in fair values or cash flows during the term of the hedge for the risk being hedged.

218. *Derivative instruments represent rights or obligations that meet the definitions of assets or liabilities and should be reported in financial statements.* Derivatives are assets or liabilities because they represent rights or obligations. FASB Concepts Statement No. 6, *Elements of Financial Statements,* describes the characteristics of assets and liabilities as follows:

> An asset has three essential characteristics: (a) it embodies a probable future benefit that involves a capacity, singly or in combination with other assets, to contribute directly or indirectly to future net cash inflows, (b) a particular entity can obtain the benefit and control others' access to it, and (c) the transaction or other event giving rise to the entity's right to or control of the benefit has already occurred. . . .
> A liability has three essential characteristics: (a) it embodies a present duty or responsibility to one or more other entities that entails settlement by probable future transfer or use of assets at a specified or determinable date, on occurrence of a specified event, or on

demand, (b) the duty or responsibility obligates a particular entity, leaving it little or no discretion to avoid the future sacrifice, and (c) the transaction or other event obligating the entity has already happened. [paragraphs 26 and 36]

219. The ability to settle a derivative in a gain position by receiving cash, another financial asset, or a nonfinancial asset is evidence of a right to a future economic benefit and is compelling evidence that the instrument is an asset. Similarly, the payment of cash, a financial asset, or a nonfinancial asset that is required to settle a derivative in a loss position is evidence of a duty to sacrifice assets in the future and indicates that the instrument is a liability. The Board believes that recognizing those assets and liabilities will make financial statements more complete and more informative. Before the issuance of this Statement, many derivatives were "off-balance-sheet" because, unlike conventional financial instruments such as stocks, bonds, and loans, derivatives often reflect at their inception only a mutual exchange of promises with little or no transfer of tangible consideration.

220. *Fair value is the most relevant measure for financial instruments and the only relevant measure for derivative instruments. Derivative instruments should be measured at fair value, and adjustments to the carrying amounts of hedged items should reflect changes in their fair value (that is, gains or losses) that are attributable to the risk being hedged and that arise while the hedge is in effect.* In 1991, with the issuance of Statement 107, the Board concluded that disclosure of fair value information about financial instruments is useful to present and potential investors, creditors, and other users of financial statements in making rational investment, credit, and other decisions. Statement 107 describes the Board's rationale:

Fair values of financial instruments depict the market's assessment of the present value of net future cash flows directly or indirectly embodied in them, discounted to reflect both current interest rates and the market's assessment of the risk that the cash flows will not occur. Investors and creditors are interested in predicting the amount, timing, and uncertainty of future net cash inflows to an entity, as those are the primary sources of future cash flows from the entity to them. Periodic information about the fair value of an entity's financial instruments under current conditions and expectations should help those us-

ers both in making their own predictions and in confirming or correcting their earlier expectations.

Information about fair value better enables investors, creditors, and other users to assess the consequences of an entity's investment and financing strategies, that is, to assess its performance. For example, information about fair value shows the effects of a decision to borrow using fixed-rate rather than floating-rate financial instruments or of a decision to invest in long-term rather than short-term instruments. Also, in a dynamic economy, information about fair value permits continuous reassessment of earlier decisions in light of current circumstances. [paragraphs 40 and 41]

221. The Board believes fair values for financial assets and liabilities provide more relevant and understandable information than cost or cost-based measures. In particular, the Board believes that fair value is more relevant to financial statement users than cost for assessing the liquidity or solvency of an entity because fair value reflects the current cash equivalent of the entity's financial instruments rather than the price of a past transaction. With the passage of time, historical prices become irrelevant in assessing present liquidity or solvency.

222. The Board also believes fair value measurement is practical for most financial assets and liabilities. Fair value measurements can be observed in markets or estimated by reference to markets for similar instruments. If market information is not available, fair value can be estimated using other measurement techniques, such as discounted cash flow analyses and option or other pricing models, among others.

223. The Board believes fair value is the *only* relevant measurement attribute for derivatives. Amortized cost is not a relevant measure for derivatives because the historical cost of a derivative often is zero, yet a derivative generally can be settled or sold at any time for an amount equivalent to its fair value. Statement 115 provides reasoning for the belief that amortized cost may be relevant for debt securities that will be held to maturity. In the absence of default, that cost will be realized at maturity, and any interim unrealized gains or losses will reverse. That reasoning does not hold for derivatives or for other financial instruments. The volatility of derivatives' fair values and the irrelevance of amortized cost for derivatives

convinced the Board that fair value is the only relevant measure for derivatives and that all derivatives should be reported in financial statements at fair value. (The latter part of the Board's second fundamental decision, which deals with the mechanics of hedge accounting, is discussed in paragraphs 362 and 363.)

224. Some of the Board's constituents contend that reporting derivatives at fair value will not result in more useful information than results from present practice. Some also say that reporting derivatives at fair value will result in reported gains or losses and increases or decreases in reported equity that are "artificial" because they do not reflect economic benefits or detriments. Some of those concerns are based in part on concerns about using different measurement attributes for derivatives and for other financial instruments. The Board agrees that financial statements would be even more useful if all financial instruments were reported at fair value, and that is its long-term goal. However, some of the arguments against reporting derivatives at fair value are made in the context of assertions that fair value measurements do not provide useful information for either derivatives or other instruments. The following simple example illustrates why the Board does not agree with that view.

225. Bank A and Bank B have identical financial positions at December 31, 20X1, as follows:

Loans	$10 billion	Liabilities	$9 billion
		Equity	1 billion
		Total liabilities	
Total assets	$10 billion	and equity	$10 billion

Both banks' assets consist entirely of variable-rate loans. Both also have fixed-rate debt at 9 percent.

226. In January of 20X2, Bank A becomes concerned that market interest rates will fall below the current level of 10 percent, and it therefore enters into a pay-variable, receive-fixed-at-10-percent interest rate swap. Bank B, on the other hand, chooses not to hedge its variable-rate loans. Bank A's swap will reprice every three months, beginning on April 15, 20X2. By March 31, 20X2, interest rates have fallen significantly, and the fair value of Bank A's swap is $1 billion.

227. For simplicity, the example assumes that each bank's interest income for the first quarter of 20X2 was exactly offset by expenses so that both had earnings of zero. The effects of deferred taxes also are ignored. Thus, if the change in fair value of Bank A's interest rate swap is excluded from its financial statements, as was general practice before this Statement, both banks' balance sheets at March 31, 20X2 would continue to appear as presented in paragraph 225. However, the two banks are not in the same economic position—Bank A has a $1 billion asset that Bank B does not.

228. The following statement of financial position, which reflects the requirements of this Statement if Bank A accounts for the swap as a cash flow hedge, better reflects Bank A's economic position at March 31, 20X2:

Loans	$10 billion	Liabilities	$9 billion
Interest rate		Equity:	
swap	1 billion	Beginning equity	1 billion
		Gain on swap	1 billion
		Total equity	2 billion
		Total liabilities	
Total assets	$11 billion	and equity	$11 billion

Bank A's statement of comprehensive income for the quarter ending March 31, 20X2 will report a gain of $1 billion. Bank B's comprehensive income for the same period will be reported as zero. Under previous accounting for swaps, Bank A would only accrue periodic cash receipts or payments on the swap as the swap reprices and those receipts or payments become due. In contrast, the financial statements of Banks A and B at March 31, 20X2 presented in accordance with this Statement signal to investors and creditors that the future reported earnings and cash flows of the banks will be different. If interest rates remain below 10 percent during the remainder of the term of the loans, Bank A will report higher earnings and will receive higher cash inflows than Bank B. Indeed, whatever happens to interest rates in the future, the two banks are likely to be affected differently. Under previous reporting practices for interest rate swaps and many other derivatives, Bank A and Bank B would have looked exactly alike at March 31, 20X2. However, the two banks are not in the same economic position at March 31, 20X2, and Bank A's increase in reported equity reflects the real difference in the position of the two banks. That increase in equity is by no means "artificial."

229. *Only items that are assets or liabilities should be reported as such in financial statements.* Derivatives are assets or liabilities, and the Board decided that they should be reported in financial statements (fundamental decision 1) and measured at fair value (fundamental decision 2). If derivatives are measured at fair value, the losses or gains that result from changes in their fair values must be reported in the financial statements. However, those losses or gains are not separate assets or liabilities because they have none of the essential characteristics of assets or liabilities as described in paragraph 218. The act of designating a derivative as a hedging instrument does not convert a subsequent loss or gain into an asset or a liability. A loss is not an asset because no future economic benefit is associated with it. The loss cannot be exchanged for cash, a financial asset, or a nonfinancial asset used to produce something of value, or used to settle liabilities. Similarly, a gain is not a liability because no obligation exists to sacrifice assets in the future. Consequently, the Board concluded that losses or gains on derivatives should not be reported as assets or liabilities in a statement of financial position.

230. *Special accounting for items designated as being hedged should be provided only for qualifying items. One aspect of qualification should be an as-*sessment of the expectation of effective offsetting changes in fair values or cash flows during the term of the hedge for the risk being hedged. Because hedge accounting is elective and relies on management's intent, it should be limited to transactions that meet reasonable criteria. The Board concluded that hedge accounting should not be permitted in all cases in which an entity might assert that a relationship exists between items or transactions. A primary purpose of hedge accounting is to link items or transactions whose changes in fair values or cash flows are expected to offset each other. The Board therefore decided that one of the criteria for qualification for hedge accounting should focus on the extent to which offsetting changes in fair values or cash flows on the derivative and the hedged item or transaction during the term of the hedge are expected and ultimately achieved.

231. The offset criterion precludes hedge accounting for certain risk management techniques, such as hedges of strategic risk. For example, a U.S. manufacturer, with no export business, that designates a forward contract to buy U.S. dollars for Japanese yen as a hedge of its U.S. dollar sales would fail the requirement that the cash flows of the derivative are expected to be highly effective in achieving offsetting cash flows on the hedged transaction. A weakened yen might allow a competitor to sell goods imported from Japan more cheaply, undercutting the domestic manufacturer's prices and reducing its sales volume and revenues. However, it would be difficult for the U.S. manufacturer to expect a high degree of offset between a decline in U.S. sales revenue due to increased competition and cash inflows on a foreign currency derivative. Any relationship between the exposure and the "hedging" derivative typically would be quite indirect, would depend on price elasticities, and would be only one of many factors influencing future results. In addition, the risk that a desired or expected number of transactions will not occur, that is, the potential absence of a transaction, is not a hedgeable risk under this Statement. Hedge accounting in this Statement is limited to the direct effects of price changes of various kinds (commodity prices, interest rates, and so on) on fair values of assets and liabilities and the cash flows from transactions, including qualifying forecasted transactions.

Benefits and Costs of This Statement

232. In accomplishing its mission, the Board follows certain precepts, including the precept to promulgate standards only when the expected

benefits of the information exceed the perceived cost. The Board works to determine that a proposed standard will fill a significant need and that the costs imposed to meet the standard, as compared to other alternatives, are justified in relation to the overall benefits of the resulting information.

Problems with Previous Accounting and Reporting Practices

233. The first step in considering whether the benefits of a new accounting standard will justify the related costs is to identify the problems in the existing accounting guidance that a new standard seeks to resolve. The problems with previous accounting and reporting practices for derivatives and hedging activities are discussed below.

234. *The effects of derivatives were not transparent in the basic financial statements.* Under the varied accounting practices that existed before the issuance of this Statement, some derivatives were recognized in financial statements, others were not. If recognized in financial statements, some realized and unrealized gains and losses on derivatives were deferred from earnings recognition and reported as part of the carrying amount (or "basis") of a related item or as if they were freestanding assets and liabilities. Users of financial statements found it difficult to determine what an entity had or had not done with derivatives and the related effects because the basic financial statements often did not report the rights or obligations associated with derivative instruments.

235. *The accounting guidance for derivative instruments and hedging activities was incomplete.* Before the issuance of this Statement, accounting standards specifically addressed only a few types of derivatives. Statement 52 addressed foreign exchange forward contracts, and Statement 80 addressed exchange-traded futures contracts. Only those two Statements specifically provided for "hedge accounting." That is, only those Statements provided special accounting to permit a gain or loss on a derivative to be deferred beyond the period in which it otherwise would be recognized in earnings because it was designated as a hedging instrument. The EITF addressed the accounting for some derivatives and for some hedging activities not covered in either Statement 52 or Statement 80. However, that effort was on an ad hoc basis and gaps remained in the authoritative literature. Accounting practice filled some gaps on specific issues, such as with "synthetic instrument accounting" as described in paragraph 349, but without

commonly understood limitations on the appropriate use of that accounting. The result was that (a) many derivative instruments were carried "off-balance-sheet" regardless of whether they were formally part of a hedging strategy, (b) practices were inconsistent among entities, and (c) users of financial reports had inadequate information.

236. *The accounting guidance for derivative instruments and hedging activities was inconsistent.* Under previous accounting guidance, the required accounting treatment differed depending on the type of instrument used in a hedge and the type of risk being hedged. For example, an instrument hedging an anticipated transaction may have qualified for special accounting if it was a purchased option with certain characteristics or an interest rate futures contract, but not if it was a foreign currency forward or futures contract. Derivatives also were measured differently under previous standards—futures contracts were reported at fair value, foreign currency forward contracts were reported at amounts that reflected changes in foreign exchange spot rates but not changes in forward rates and that were not discounted for the time value of money, and other derivatives often were unrecognized or were reported at nominal amounts not closely related to the fair value of the derivatives (for example, reported at the net cash due that period). Accounting standards also were inconsistent on whether qualification for hedge accounting was based on risk assessment at an entity-wide or an individual-transaction level.

237. *The accounting guidance for derivatives and hedging was difficult to apply.* The lack of a single, comprehensive approach to accounting for derivatives and hedging made the accounting guidance difficult to apply. The incompleteness of FASB Statements on derivatives and hedging forced entities to look to a variety of different sources, including the numerous EITF issues and nonauthoritative literature, to determine how to account for specific instruments or transactions. Because there often was nothing directly on point, entities analogized to other existing guidance. Different sources of analogy often conflicted, and a wide range of answers sometimes was deemed supportable, but those answers often were subject to later challenge.

This Statement Mitigates Those Problems

238. This Statement mitigates those four problems. It increases the visibility, comparability, and understandability of the risks associated with derivatives

by requiring that all derivatives be reported as assets or liabilities and measured at fair value. It reduces the inconsistency, incompleteness, and difficulty of applying previous accounting guidance and practice by providing comprehensive guidance for all derivatives and hedging activities. The comprehensive guidance in this Statement also eliminates some accounting practices, such as "synthetic instrument accounting," that had evolved beyond the authoritative literature.

239. In addition to mitigating the previous problems, this Statement accommodates a range of hedge accounting practices by (a) permitting hedge accounting for most derivative instruments, (b) permitting hedge accounting for cash flow hedges of forecasted transactions for specified risks, and (c) eliminating the requirement in Statement 80 that an entity demonstrate risk reduction on an entity-wide basis to qualify for hedge accounting. The combination of accommodating a range of hedge accounting practices and removing the uncertainty about the accounting requirements for certain strategies should facilitate, and may actually increase, entities' use of derivatives to manage risks.

240. The benefits of improving financial reporting for derivatives and hedging activities come at a cost. Even though much of the information needed to implement this Statement is substantially the same as was required for prior accounting standards for many hedges, and therefore should be available, many entities will incur one-time costs for requisite systems changes. But the benefits of more credible and more understandable information will be ongoing.

241. The Board believes that accounting requirements should be neutral and should not encourage or discourage the use of particular types of contracts. That desire for neutrality must be balanced with the need to reflect substantive economic differences between different instruments. This Statement is the product of a series of many compromises made by the Board to improve financial reporting for derivatives and hedging activities while giving consideration to cost-benefit issues, as well as current practice. The Board believes that most hedging strategies for which hedge accounting is available in current practice have been reasonably accommodated. The Board recognizes that this Statement does not provide special accounting that accommodates some risk management strategies that certain entities wish to use, such as hedging a portfolio of dissimilar items. However, this Statement clarifies and accommodates hedge accounting for more types of deriva-

tives and different views of risk, and provides more consistent accounting for hedges of forecasted transactions than did the limited guidance that existed before this Statement.

242. Some constituents have said that the requirements of this Statement are more complex than existing guidance. The Board disagrees. It believes that compliance with previous guidance was more complex because the lack of a single, comprehensive framework forced entities to analogize to different and often conflicting sources of guidance. The Board also believes that some constituents' assertions about increased complexity may have been influenced by some entities' relatively lax compliance with previous guidance. For example, the Board understands that not all entities complied with Statement 80's entity-wide risk reduction criterion to qualify for hedge accounting, and that also may have been true for requirements for hedging a portfolio of dissimilar items. The Board also notes that some of the more complex requirements of this Statement, such as reporting the gain or loss on a cash flow hedge in earnings in the periods in which the hedged transaction affects earnings, are a direct result of the Board's efforts to accommodate respondents' wishes.

243. The Board took several steps to minimize the incremental costs of the accounting and disclosure requirements of this Statement. For example, this Statement relies on the valuation guidance provided in Statement 107, which most entities have been applying for several years. The Board also decided not to continue the previously required assessment of risk at an entity-wide level, which constituents said is very difficult and costly to make. This Statement also reduces the disclosure requirements that previously were required for derivatives. Some of the previous disclosure requirements for derivatives were intended to partially compensate for inadequate accounting; improving the information provided in the basic financial statements makes possible a reduction in such disclosures.

Scope and Definition

244. As already discussed, the Board decided that derivative instruments should be measured at fair value. The Board also decided that accounting for gains or losses that result from measuring derivatives at fair value should depend on whether or not the derivative instrument is designated and qualifies as a hedging instrument. Those decisions require that the Board clearly identify (a) those instruments to

which this Statement applies and (b) the criteria that must be met for a relationship to qualify for hedge accounting.

245. The Board decided that this Statement should apply to many, but not all, instruments that are often described as derivatives. In reaching that decision, the Board observed that prior accounting standards did not clearly distinguish derivative instruments from other financial and nonfinancial instruments. Financial statement preparers, users, and other interested parties often have trouble clearly distinguishing between instruments that are commonly considered derivatives and other instruments. Accordingly, they often do not agree on whether certain instruments are derivatives. This Statement defines derivative instruments based on their characteristics; the resulting definition may not always coincide with what some market participants consider to be derivatives.

Why Hedging Instruments Are Limited to Derivatives

246. This Statement limits hedge accounting to those relationships in which derivative instruments and certain foreign-currency-denominated nonderivative instruments are designated as hedging instruments and the necessary qualifying criteria are met. The Board recognizes that there may be valid reasons for entering into transactions intended to be hedges using nonderivative instruments, but the Board continues to believe that permitting nonderivative instruments to be designated as hedging instruments would be inappropriate.

247. Achieving the Board's long-term objective of having all financial instruments—both derivative and nonderivative—measured at fair value would eliminate the need for hedge accounting for the risks inherent in existing financial instruments. Both the hedging instrument and the hedged item would be measured at fair value. Accounting for the gains and losses on each in the same way would leave no measurement anomalies to which to apply hedge accounting. As further discussed in paragraphs 326 and 327, the Board considers hedge accounting for forecasted transactions to be inappropriate from a conceptual perspective. In practice, hedge accounting for forecasted (anticipated) transactions has been limited to derivatives, and the Board does not think it would be appropriate to extend hedge accounting for what is not a conceptually defensible practice to nonderivative instruments. To include nonderivative financial instruments, other than in circumstances already permitted by existing accounting pronouncements, as hedging instruments also would add complexity and delay issuing guidance on accounting for derivative instruments. The Board therefore decided to limit hedge accounting to derivatives. Consequently, items such as securities, trade receivables and payables, and deposit liabilities at banks may not be designated as hedging instruments except that, consistent with existing provisions in Statement 52, nonderivative instruments that give rise to transaction gains or losses may be designated as hedges of certain foreign currency exposures.

Defining Characteristics of a Derivative Instrument

248. The Board considered defining a *derivative instrument* in this Statement by merely referencing those instruments commonly understood to be derivatives. That would be similar to the method used in paragraph 5 of Statement 119, which said that "... a *derivative financial instrument* is a futures, forward, swap, or option contract, or other financial instrument with similar characteristics." However, the expansion of financial markets and continued development of innovative financial instruments and other contracts could ultimately render obsolete a definition based solely on examples. Currently, contracts often referred to as derivatives have characteristics similar to other contracts that often are *not* considered to be derivative instruments. For example, purchase orders for certain raw materials have many similarities to forward contracts that are referenced to those same raw materials. The Board is concerned that the existing distinctions between many types of contracts are likely to become even more blurred as new innovative instruments are developed. Therefore, to distinguish between similar contracts and to deal with new instruments that may be developed in the future, this Statement provides a definition of derivative instruments based on distinguishing characteristics rather than merely referring to classes of instruments or titles used to describe them.

249. For purposes of this Statement, a derivative instrument is a financial instrument or other contract that has all three of the following characteristics:

a. It has (1) one or more underlyings and (2) one or more notional amounts or payment provisions or both.
b. It requires no initial net investment or an initial net investment that is smaller than would be required

for other types of contracts that would be expected to have a similar response to changes in market factors.

c. Its terms require or permit net settlement, it can readily be settled net by a means outside the contract, or it provides for delivery of an asset that puts the recipient in a position not substantially different from net settlement.

The Board believes those three characteristics capture the essence of instruments, such as futures and options, that have long been considered derivatives and instruments that are sufficiently similar to those traditional derivatives that they should be accounted for similarly. The following paragraphs discuss each characteristic in more depth. Section 1 of Appendix A provides additional discussion of the three characteristics of a derivative instrument.

Underlyings and notional amounts or payment provisions

250. Derivative instruments typically permit the parties to participate in some or all of the effects of changes in a referenced price, rate, or other variable, which is referred to as the *underlying,* for example, an interest rate or equity index or the price of a specific security, commodity, or currency. As the term is used in this Statement, a referenced asset or liability, if any, is not itself the *underlying* of a derivative contract. Instead, the *price* or *rate* of the associated asset or liability, which is used to determine the settlement amount of the derivative instrument, is the underlying.

251. By itself, an underlying cannot determine the value or settlement of a derivative. Most derivatives also refer to a *notional amount,* which is a number of units specified in the contract. The multiplication or other arithmetical interaction of the notional amount and the underlying determines the settlement of the derivative. However, rather than referring to a notional amount, some derivatives instead contain a *payment provision* that requires settlement if an underlying changes in a specified way. For example, a derivative might require a specified payment if a referenced interest rate increases by 300 basis points. Reference to either a notional amount or a payment provision is needed to compute the contract's periodic settlements and resulting changes in fair value.

252. In concept, any observable variable, including physical as well as financial variables, may be the underlying for a derivative instrument. For example, a contract might specify a payment to be made if it rains more than one inch on a specified day. However, throughout the project that led to this Statement, discussion focused on more traditional derivatives for which the underlying is some form of price, including an interest rate or exchange rate. For example, paragraph 6 of the Exposure Draft referred to "a rate, an index of prices, or another market indicator" in describing an underlying. Relatively late in the process that led to this Statement, the Board considered expanding its scope to include all derivatives based on physical variables but decided not to do so. It was concerned that constituents had not had sufficient opportunity to consider the implications and potential measurement difficulties of including contracts based on physical variables. The Board believes many contracts for which the underlying is a physical variable are currently accounted for as insurance contracts, and it considers that accounting to be adequate for now. However, the Board decided that any derivative instrument that is traded on an exchange, including one based on a physical variable, should be subject to the requirements of this Statement. Accordingly, any derivative based on a physical variable that eventually becomes exchange traded will automatically become subject to the requirements of this Statement. The Board does not believe that measurement or other implementation problems exist for exchange-traded instruments.

253. This Statement also excludes from its scope a derivative instrument for which the underlying is the price or value of a nonfinancial asset of one of the parties to the contract provided that the asset is not readily convertible to cash. Similarly excluded is a derivative instrument for which the underlying is the price or value of a nonfinancial liability of one of the parties to the contract provided that the liability does not require delivery of an asset that is not readily convertible to cash. A contract for which the underlying is specified volumes of sales or service revenues by one of the parties also is excluded. Many such contracts are insurance contracts. An example is a contract based on the condition or value of a building. Others contain an element of compensation for service or for use of another entity's asset. An example is a royalty agreement based on sales of a particular product.

254. Because a derivative may have an underlying that is a combination of variables, the Board added a requirement to clarify the application of

paragraph 10(e). Some of the variables in an underlying that is a combination of variables may be subject to the exceptions in paragraph 10(e) and others may not. The Board did not intend for all contracts with those types of underlyings to be excluded automatically from the scope of this Statement. A contract with a combined underlying is subject to the requirements of this Statement if its settlement is expected to change in a way that is highly correlated with the way it would change if it was based on an underlying that would not be eligible for one of the exceptions in paragraph 10(e).

Initial investment in the contract

255. The second characteristic of a derivative instrument refers to the relative amount of the initial net investment in the contract. Providing the opportunity to participate in the price changes of an underlying without actually having to own an associated asset or owe an associated liability is the basic feature that distinguishes most traditional derivative instruments from nonderivative instruments. Therefore, the Board decided that a contract that at inception requires the holder or writer to invest or receive an amount approximating the notional amount of the contract is not a derivative instrument. The following example illustrates that fundamental difference between a derivative instrument and a nonderivative instrument.

256. A party that wishes to participate in the changes in the fair value of 10,000 shares of a specific marketable equity security can, of course, do so by purchasing 10,000 shares of that security. Alternatively, the party may enter into a forward purchase contract with a notional amount of 10,000 shares of that security and an underlying that is the price of that security. Purchasing the shares would require an initial investment equal to the current price for 10,000 shares and would result in benefits such as the receipt of dividends (if any) and the ability to vote the shares. A simple forward contract entered into at the current forward price for 10,000 shares of the equity instrument would not require an initial investment equal to the notional amount but would offer the same opportunity to benefit or lose from changes in the price of that security.

257. Some respondents to the Exposure Draft suggested that the definition of a derivative instrument should include contracts that require gross exchanges of currencies (for example, currency swaps that require an exchange of different currencies at both in-

ception and maturity). They noted that those contracts are commonly viewed as derivatives, are used in the same manner as derivatives, and therefore should be included in the definition of a derivative instrument. The Board agreed and notes that this Statement's definition of a derivative instrument, as revised from the Exposure Draft, explicitly includes such currency swaps. The Board observes that the initial exchange of currencies of equal fair values in those arrangements does not constitute an initial net *investment* in the contract. Instead, it is the exchange of one kind of *cash* for another kind of *cash* of equal value. The balance of the agreement, a forward contract that obligates and entitles both parties to exchange specified currencies, on specified dates, at specified prices, is a derivative instrument.

258. Paragraphs 6–11 of this Statement address only those contracts that in their entirety are derivative instruments. A contract that requires a relatively large initial net investment may include one or more embedded derivative instruments. The Board's conclusions on embedded derivatives are discussed in paragraphs 293–311.

Net settlement

259. The third distinguishing characteristic of a derivative instrument as defined in this Statement is that it can be readily settled with only a net delivery of assets. Therefore, a derivative contract must meet one of the following criteria:

a. It does not require either party to deliver an asset that is associated with its underlying or that has a principal amount, stated amount, face value, number of shares, or other denomination that is equal to the notional amount (or the notional amount plus a premium or minus a discount).
b. It requires one of the parties to deliver such an asset, but there is a market mechanism that facilitates net settlement.
c. It requires one of the parties to deliver such an asset, but that asset either is readily convertible to cash or is itself a derivative instrument.

260. The Exposure Draft proposed that derivative instruments be distinguished from other instruments by determining whether (a) the holder could settle the contract with only a net cash payment, either by its contractual terms or by custom, and (b) the net payment was determined by reference to changes in the

underlying.[31] Under the Exposure Draft, a contract that required ownership or delivery of an asset associated with the underlying would have been a derivative instrument if a mechanism existed in the market to enter into a closing contract with only a net settlement or if the contract was customarily settled with only a net cash payment based on changes in the underlying. The Board focused in the Exposure Draft on whether there is a mechanism in the market for net settlement because it observed that many derivative instruments are actively traded and can be closed or settled before the contract's expiration or maturity by net settlement in active markets. The Board included the requirement for customary settlement in the Exposure Draft for two reasons: (a) to prevent circumvention of the requirements of this Statement by including nonsubstantive delivery provisions in a contract that otherwise would be considered a derivative and (b) to include in the definition of a derivative all contracts that are typically settled net even if the ability to settle net is not an explicit feature of the contract.

261. Several respondents to the Exposure Draft requested clarification of its net settlement provisions. Respondents observed that the phrase *mechanism in the market* was unclear and could lead to different interpretations in practice. They asked whether *only* an organized exchange would constitute the type of market mechanism that the Board had in mind, or whether a willingness of market participants to enter into such a contract in the over-the-counter or other markets would require that the contract be viewed as a derivative instrument. This Statement responds to those questions by indicating in paragraph 57(c)(2) that the Board intends *market mechanism* to be interpreted broadly to include any institutional arrangement or side agreement that permits either party to be relieved of all rights and obligations under the contract and to liquidate its net position without incurring a significant transaction cost.

262. Respondents also questioned whether *customary* referred to the customs of the reporting entity or the customs of the marketplace. They said that it would be difficult to discern the custom of the marketplace for a non-exchange-traded instrument for which settlement information is not publicly available. They also observed that market customs vary by industry and over time. A criterion based on such customs therefore might lead to different answers at

different points in time (for example, customs that currently require gross settlement might subsequently change) and for different participants to the contracts (for example, a bank might customarily settle a certain type of contract with only a net payment of cash, while a manufacturing entity might customarily settle the same type of contract by delivering the assets associated with the underlying). The definition of a derivative in this Statement does not refer to customary settlement. The Board decided that the provisions of paragraph 9 would achieve the objective of the Exposure Draft.

263. During its redeliberations, the Board discussed whether the definition of a derivative instrument should depend on whether net settlement occurs in cash or for another asset. The Board also discussed whether this Statement should apply to a derivative instrument in which at least one of the items to be exchanged in the future is something other than a financial instrument. The Board decided that the medium of exchange used in the net settlement of a derivative contract should not determine whether the instrument is within the scope of this Statement. A contract that can readily be settled net, whether the settlement is for cash or another asset, should be within the scope of this Statement. As a result of that decision, the Board also decided to delete *financial* from the term *derivative financial instruments* in describing the instruments that are within the scope of this Statement.

Assets that are readily convertible to cash

264. The Board decided that a contract that requires delivery of an asset associated with the underlying in a denomination equal to the notional amount should qualify as a derivative instrument if the asset is readily convertible to cash. (Paragraphs 271and 272 and 275 and 276, respectively, discuss two exceptions to that provision.) As indicated in footnote 5, the term *readily convertible to cash* refers to assets that "have (i) interchangeable (fungible) units and (ii) quoted prices available in an active market that can rapidly absorb the quantity held by the entity without significantly affecting the price."

265. Net settlement is an important characteristic that distinguishes a derivative from a nonderivative because it permits a contract to be settled without either party's accepting the risks and costs customarily associated with owning and delivering the asset associated with the underlying (for example, storage,

---

[31]The term *underlying* as used in the Exposure Draft encompassed the asset or liability, the price of which was the underlying for the contract.

maintenance, and resale). However, if the assets to be exchanged or delivered are themselves readily convertible to cash, those risks are minimal or nonexistent. Thus, the parties generally should be indifferent as to whether they exchange cash or the assets associated with the underlying. The Board recognizes that determining whether assets are readily convertible to cash will require judgment and sometimes will lead to different applications in practice. However, the Board believes that the use of *readily convertible to cash* permits an appropriate amount of flexibility and describes an important characteristic of the derivative instruments addressed by this Statement.

266. The Board considered using the idea of *readily obtainable elsewhere* as is used in Statement 125 to determine whether a derivative instrument that requires that the holder or writer own or deliver the asset or liability that is associated with the underlying is within the scope of this Statement. However, the Board noted that readily obtainable elsewhere relates to the availability of an asset; not necessarily its liquidity. The Board decided that *readily convertible to cash* is the appropriate criterion because it addresses whether the asset can be converted to cash with little effort, not just whether the asset is readily available in the marketplace.

Commodity Contracts

267. Statements 105, 107, and 119 did not address commodity-based contracts because those contracts require or permit future delivery of an item that is not a financial instrument. Statement 105 explained that for a commodity-based contract "... the future economic benefit is receipt of goods or services instead of a right to receive cash or an ownership interest in an entity and the economic sacrifice is delivery of goods or services instead of an obligation to deliver cash or an ownership interest in an entity" (paragraph 32). Some respondents to the Exposure Draft that preceded Statement 119 suggested that the scope be expanded to include commodity-based contracts. The Board decided not to expand the scope at that time principally because of that project's accelerated timetable.

268. The Exposure Draft proposed that the definition of *derivative* include only *financial instruments.* Nevertheless, the Exposure Draft would have included certain commodity contracts because they often have many of the same characteristics as other derivative contracts. They often are used interchangeably with other derivatives, and they present

risks similar to other derivatives. The Board initially proposed to resolve that apparent conflict by amending the definition of *financial instrument* in Statement 107 to include contracts that permit a choice of settlement by delivering either a commodity or cash. As discussed in paragraph 263, the Board decided to change the scope of this Statement to address the accounting for *derivative instruments* rather than just derivative *financial* instruments. Therefore, it was not necessary to amend the definition of a financial instrument in Statement 107 to include certain commodity-based contracts in the scope of this Statement.

269. Changing the scope of this Statement from derivative *financial* instruments to derivative instruments results in including some contracts that settle net for a commodity or other nonfinancial asset. The Board believes that including commodity-based contracts with the essential characteristics of a derivative instrument within the scope of this Statement will help to avoid accounting anomalies that result from measuring similar contracts differently. The Board also believes that including those commodity-based contracts in this Statement will provide worthwhile information to financial statement users and will resolve concerns raised by some respondents to the Exposure Drafts that preceded Statements 107 and 119.

270. The Exposure Draft would have included only commodity-based contracts that permitted net cash settlement, either by their contractual terms or by custom. For the reasons discussed in paragraphs 264–266, the Board decided, instead, to include a contract that requires delivery of an asset associated with the underlying if that asset is readily convertible to cash (for example, gold, silver, corn, and wheat). Different accounting will result depending on whether or not the assets associated with the underlying for a contract are readily convertible to cash. The Board considers that difference to be appropriate because contracts that settle net or by delivering assets readily convertible to cash provide different benefits and pose different risks than those that require exchange of cash or other assets for an asset that is not readily convertible to cash.

Normal purchases and normal sales

271. The Board decided that contracts that require delivery of nonfinancial assets that are readily convertible to cash need not be accounted for as derivative instruments under this Statement if the assets

constitute *normal purchases* or *normal sales* of the reporting entity unless those contracts can readily be settled net. The Board believes contracts for the acquisition of assets in quantities that the entity expects to use or sell over a reasonable period in the normal course of business are not unlike binding purchase orders or other similar contracts to which this Statement does not apply. The Board notes that the normal purchases and normal sales exemption is necessary only for contracts based on assets that are readily convertible to cash.

272. The Board understands that the normal purchases and normal sales provision sometimes will result in different parties to a contract reaching different conclusions about whether the contract is required to be accounted for as a derivative instrument. For example, the contract may be for ordinary sales by one party (and therefore not a derivative instrument) but not for ordinary purchases by the counterparty (and therefore a derivative instrument). The Board considered requiring both parties to account for a contract as a derivative instrument if the purchases or sales by either party were other than ordinary in the normal course of business. However, that approach would have required that one party to the contract determine the circumstances of the other party to that same contract. Although the Board believes that the accounting by both parties to a contract generally should be symmetrical, it decided that symmetry would be impractical in this instance and that a potential asymmetrical result is acceptable.

Financial Instruments

273. Some contracts require the holder or writer to deliver a financial asset or liability that is associated with the underlying and that has a denomination equal to the notional amount of the contract. Determining whether those contracts are derivative instruments depends, at least in part, on whether the related financial assets or liabilities are readily convertible to cash.

Trade date versus settlement date accounting

274. Existing accounting practice is inconsistent about the timing of recognition of transfers of various financial instruments. Some transfers of securities are recognized as of the date of trade (often referred to as trade date accounting). Other transfers are recognized as of the date the financial instrument is actually transferred and the transaction is settled (often referred to as settlement date accounting). During the period between trade and settlement dates, the parties essentially have entered into a forward contract that might meet the definition of a derivative if the financial instrument is readily convertible to cash. Requiring that all forward contracts for purchases and sales of financial instruments that are readily convertible to cash be accounted for as derivatives would effectively require settlement date accounting for all such transactions. Resolving the issue of trade date versus settlement date accounting was not an objective of the project that led to this Statement. Therefore, the Board decided to explicitly exclude forward contracts for "regular-way" security trades from the scope of this Statement.

Regular-way security trades

275. Regular-way security trades are those that are completed (or settled) within the time period generally established by regulations and conventions in the marketplace or by the exchange on which the transaction is being executed. The notion of a regular-way security trade is based on marketplace regulations or conventions rather than on the normal practices of an individual entity. For example, if it is either required or customary for certain securities on a specified exchange to settle within three days, a contract that requires settlement in more than three days is not a regular-way security trade even if the entity customarily enters into contracts to purchase such securities more than three days forward. The Board considered other approaches that focused on reasonable settlement periods or customary settlement periods for the specific parties to a transfer. The Board decided that those approaches were inferior because they lacked the consistency and discipline that are provided by focusing on regular-way security trades. The Board also believes that participants can reasonably determine settlement periods required by the regulations or conventions of an active marketplace. Regulations or conventions may be more difficult to determine for foreign or less active exchanges. However, the provisions in paragraph 10(a) apply only if the holder or writer of the contract is required to deliver assets that are readily convertible to cash. Therefore, the regulations or conventions of the marketplace should be reasonably apparent because the related market must be active enough to rapidly absorb the quantities involved without significantly affecting the price.

276. The Board considered limiting the exclusion for regular-way security trades to purchases or sales of *existing* securities. A forward contract for a regular-way trade of an existing security entitles the

purchaser to receive and requires the seller to deliver a specific security. The delay is a matter of market regulations and conventions for delivery. In contrast, a forward contract for a when-issued or other security that does not yet exist does not entitle or obligate the parties to exchange a specific security. Instead, it entitles the issuer and holder to participate in price changes that occur before the security is issued. For that reason, the Board would have preferred that a forward contract on a security that does not yet exist be subject to the requirements of this Statement. However, the Board was concerned that including, for example, to-be-announced (TBA) Government National Mortgage Association (GNMA) forward contracts and other forward contracts for when-issued securities within the scope of this Statement might subject some entities to potentially burdensome regulatory requirements for transactions in derivatives. On balance, the Board decided to extend the regular-way exemption to purchases and sales of when-issued and TBA securities. However, the exemption applies only if (a) there is no other way to purchase or sell the security and (b) the trade will settle within the shortest period permitted for the security.

Insurance contracts

277. The Exposure Draft explicitly excluded insurance contracts, as defined in Statements 60, 97, and 113, from its definition of a derivative financial instrument. The insurance contracts described in those Statements also were excluded from the scope of Statement 107, which states:

> The Board concluded that disclosures about fair value should not be required for insurance contracts. . . . The Board believes that definitional and valuation difficulties are present to a certain extent in those contracts and obligations, and that further consideration is required before decisions can be made about whether to apply the definition to components of those contracts and whether to require disclosures about fair value for the financial components. [paragraph 74]

278. During the deliberations before issuance of the Exposure Draft, the Board decided to specifically preclude an insurance contract from qualifying as a derivative because it believed definitional and valuation difficulties still existed. The Exposure Draft observed that the insurance industry and the accounting and actuarial professions have not reached a common understanding about how to estimate the fair value of insurance contracts. Developing measurement guidance for them might have delayed the issuance of guidance on accounting for derivatives. The Board intends to reconsider the accounting for insurance contracts in other phases of its financial instruments project.

279. Although the term *insurance contract* is frequently used in Statements 60, 97, and 113, it is not clearly defined in those or other accounting pronouncements. As a result, the Exposure Draft's provision that insurance contracts and reinsurance contracts generally are not derivative instruments may not have been workable. The Board was concerned that the phrase *insurance contracts* might be interpreted quite broadly to encompass most agreements or contracts issued by insurance enterprises as part of their ongoing operations.

280. The accounting provisions for insurance contracts in Statements 60, 97, and 113 are significantly different from the accounting provisions for derivative instruments in this Statement. The Board was concerned that contracts that are substantially the same as other derivative instruments might, instead, be accounted for as insurance contracts. The Board therefore decided to eliminate the Exposure Draft's proposed scope exclusion for insurance contracts and, instead, require that those contracts be included in or excluded from the scope of this Statement based on their characteristics.

281. Insurance contracts often have some of the same characteristics as derivative instruments that are within the scope of this Statement. Often, however, they lack one or more of those characteristics. As a result, most traditional insurance contracts will not be derivative instruments as defined in this Statement. They will be excluded from that definition because they entitle the holder to compensation only if, as a result of an identifiable insurable event (other than a change in price), the holder incurs a liability or there is an adverse change in the value of a specific asset or liability for which the holder is at risk. However, contracts that in their entirety meet this Statement's definition of a derivative instrument, whether issued by an insurance enterprise or another type of enterprise, must be accounted for as such. The Board does not believe that a decision on whether a contract must be accounted for as a derivative should depend on the identity of the issuer. To help in applying the provisions of this Statement, paragraph 10(c) provides some examples illustrating the application of the definition to insurance contracts.

282. The Board acknowledges that many of the problems with determining the fair value of traditional insurance liabilities are still unresolved. The Board notes, however, that many of the issues of how to measure the fair value of insurance contracts do not apply to instruments issued by insurance enterprises that, in their entirety, qualify as derivative instruments under this Statement. Instead, the methods for estimating the fair values of those contracts should be similar to the methods used for derivative instruments with similar characteristics issued by other types of enterprises.

283. Although many contracts issued by insurance enterprises will not, in their entirety, meet the definition of a derivative instrument, some may include embedded derivatives that are required by this Statement to be accounted for separately from the host contract. Contracts that may include embedded derivatives include, but are not limited to, annuity contracts that promise the policyholder a return based on selected changes in the S&P 500 index, variable life and annuity contracts, and property and casualty contracts that combine protection for property damage and changes in foreign currency exchange rates. Section 2 of Appendix B provides additional guidance on insurance contracts with embedded derivative instruments.

*Exception for derivatives that serve as
impediments to recognition of a sale*

284. The existence of certain derivatives affects the accounting for the transfer of an asset or a pool of assets. For example, a call option that enables a transferor to repurchase transferred financial assets that are not readily available would prevent accounting for that transfer as a sale. The consequence is that to recognize the call option would be to count the same thing twice. The holder of the option already recognizes in its financial statements the assets that it has the option to purchase. Thus those types of derivatives are excluded from the scope of this Statement.

*Exception for instruments classified in
stockholders' equity*

285. As noted in paragraph 3(a) of this Statement, derivative instruments are assets or liabilities. Consequently, items appropriately classified in stockholders' equity in an entity's statement of financial position are not within the scope of this Statement. The Board decided to clarify that point by explicitly excluding from the scope of this Statement the accounting for such equity instruments.

286. The Board considered whether this Statement also should exclude instruments that an entity either can or must settle by issuing its own stock but that are indexed to something else. For example, the Board discussed whether an instrument that requires settlement in the issuer's or holder's common stock but that is indexed to changes in the S&P 500 index should be excluded from the scope of this Statement. The Board currently has a project on its agenda that considers whether certain instruments are equity or liabilities. That project will address the issue of whether instruments to be settled in the entity's stock but indexed to something other than its stock are liabilities or equity. The Board will reconsider the application of this Statement to such contracts as necessary when that project is completed. Until that time, contracts that provide for settlement in shares of an entity's stock but that are indexed in part or in full to something other than the entity's stock are to be accounted for as derivative instruments if the contracts satisfy the criteria in paragraphs 6–10 of this Statement. Those contracts are to be classified as assets or liabilities and not as part of stockholders' equity.

Stock-based compensation contracts

287. Paragraph 11(b) of this Statement excludes the issuer's accounting for derivative instruments issued in connection with stock-based compensation arrangements addressed in FASB Statement No. 123, *Accounting for Stock-Based Compensation.* Many such instruments would be excluded by paragraph 11(a) because they are classified in stockholders' equity. However, Statement 123 also addresses stock-based compensation arrangements that are derivatives and that qualify as a liability of the issuer. The Board decided that the issuer's accounting for those contracts is adequately addressed by Statement 123. As with the other exclusions in paragraph 11, the holder's accounting for a derivative instrument in a compensation arrangement addressed by Statement 123 is subject to this Statement.

*Contingent consideration in a business
combination*

288. Opinion 16 addresses the purchaser's (issuer's) accounting for contingent consideration provided in a purchase business combination. The effect of a contingent consideration arrangement on the accounting for a business combination often is significant and depends on the terms and conditions of both the business combination and the contingent consideration

arrangement. Although contingent consideration arrangements may share at least some of the characteristics of derivative instruments addressed by this Statement, the Board decided that without further study it would be inappropriate to change the accounting for them by the entity that accounts for the business combination. The Board currently has a project on its agenda to reconsider the accounting for business combinations. It will consider this issue as part of that project.

289. This Statement does apply to contracts that are similar to, but not accounted for as, contingent consideration under the provisions of Opinion 16 if those contracts satisfy the scope provisions either for a derivative instrument (paragraphs 6–10) or for a contract with an embedded derivative instrument (paragraphs 12–16). In addition, this Statement applies to a seller's (holder's) accounting for contingent consideration that meets its definition of a derivative. For example, assume that a purchaser of a business issues to the seller a freestanding financial instrument (as addressed in EITF Issue No. 97-8, "Accounting for Contingent Consideration Issued in a Purchase Business Combination") that provides contingent consideration in a purchase business combination under Opinion 16. That freestanding instrument is assumed to meet this Statement's definition of a derivative instrument. The purchaser's accounting for the instrument is explicitly excluded from the scope of this Statement, but the seller who receives the instrument must account for it according to the requirements of this Statement.

Application to specific contracts

290. Several respondents to the Exposure Draft asked the Board for specific guidance about whether some contracts meet the definition of a derivative instrument, including sales of securities not yet owned ("short sales"), take-or-pay contracts, and contracts with liquidating damages or other termination clauses. The Board cannot definitively state whether those types of contracts will always (or never) meet the definition because their terms and related customary practices vary. In addition, the terms of the contracts or customary practices may change over time, thereby affecting the determination of whether a particular type of contract meets the definition of a derivative instrument. Appendix A provides examples illustrating how the definition of a derivative instrument applies to certain specific situations.

The Scope of Statement 119

291. This Statement's definition of derivative contracts excludes certain contracts that were included in the scope of Statement 119. For example, a loan commitment would be excluded if it (a) requires the holder to deliver a promissory note that would not be readily convertible to cash and (b) cannot readily be settled net. Other conditional and executory contracts that were included in the scope of Statement 119 may not qualify as derivative instruments under the definition in this Statement. The Board decided that some change in scope from Statement 119 is an appropriate consequence of defining derivative instruments based on their primary characteristics.

292. This Statement supersedes Statement 119. Therefore, one result of excluding instruments that were included in the scope of Statement 119 from the scope of this Statement is that some disclosures previously required for those excluded contracts will no longer be required. The Board considers that result to be acceptable. Moreover, Statement 107 continues to require disclosure of the fair value of all financial instruments by the entities to which it applies.

Embedded Derivatives

293. The Board considers it important that an entity not be able to avoid the recognition and measurement requirements of this Statement merely by embedding a derivative instrument in a nonderivative financial instrument or other contract. Therefore, certain embedded derivatives are included in the scope of this Statement if they would be subject to the Statement on a freestanding basis. However, the Board also decided that some derivatives embedded in host contracts, such as many of the prepayment or call options frequently included as part of mortgage loans and other debt instruments, should be excluded from the scope of this Statement.

Approaches considered

294. The Board considered a number of approaches for determining which contracts with embedded derivatives should be included in the scope of this Statement. Some approaches focused either on an instrument's yield or on its predominant characteristics. The Board decided that those approaches would likely include callable or prepayable debt and perhaps other instruments that often are not thought of as including an embedded derivative, even though they do. The Board also was concerned about the operationality of those approaches.

295. The scope of the Exposure Draft included a contract with both nonderivative and derivative characteristics if some or all of its contractually required cash flows were determined by reference to changes in one or more underlyings in a manner that multiplied or otherwise exacerbated the effect of those changes. That scope was intended to incorporate embedded forwards, swaps, and options with a notional amount that was greater than the face value of the "host" contract or that otherwise "leveraged" the effect of changes in one or more underlyings. Numerous respondents to the Exposure Draft asked for clarification of the phrase *multiplies or otherwise exacerbates* and said that they did not understand why certain instruments were included in the scope of the Exposure Draft while others were not.

296. The Board agreed with respondents that the approach in the Exposure Draft was difficult to apply in a consistent manner. The Board also concluded that the Exposure Draft inappropriately excluded some instruments from its scope and inappropriately included others. For example, an instrument that paid a simple multiple of a market interest rate (for example, 120 percent of U.S. dollar LIBOR) might be considered to have an embedded derivative that requires separate accounting. In contrast, a structured note that paid a return based on 100 percent of the appreciation in the fair value of an equity instrument would not be considered to have an embedded derivative that requires separate accounting.

297. Some respondents to the Exposure Draft suggested that all financial instruments with embedded derivatives be excluded from the scope of this Statement because existing accounting standards for nonderivative instruments provide adequate guidance for those compound financial instruments. The Board rejected that suggestion for three reasons. First, applying existing accounting standards for nonderivative instruments would not necessarily achieve the Board's goal of increasing the transparency of derivatives in the financial statements. For example, existing guidance for the issuer's accounting for indexed debt instruments is incomplete and would not necessarily result in recognition of changes in the fair value of the embedded derivative in either the balance sheet or the income statement. Second, a derivative can be embedded in a contract other than a financial instrument, such as a purchase order. The existing accounting pronouncements for such contracts do not adequately address the accounting for embedded derivatives in those contracts. Third, excluding all compound instruments from its scope

would make it possible to circumvent the provisions of this Statement. One apparent reason that structured notes have become prevalent is that combining various features of derivative and nonderivative instruments produces different accounting results than accounting for each component separately, and participants in transactions involving structured notes sometimes considered the accounting results attractive. Excluding all instruments that embed derivative instruments in nonderivative host contracts from the scope of this Statement would likely increase the incentive to combine those instruments to avoid accounting for derivative instruments according to the provisions of this Statement.

298. Under the approach in the Exposure Draft, contracts designed to result in a rate of return that differs in a nontrivial way from the change in price that would be realized from a direct investment (or obligation) in the referenced asset(s) or other item(s) of an amount comparable to the notional amount or par value of the contract would have been accounted for as derivative instruments. Clarifying the phrase *multiplies or otherwise exacerbates* would have addressed some of the problems raised by respondents to the Exposure Draft, but it still would have focused solely on whether the derivative feature resulted in a meaningful amount of positive or negative leverage. It would not have addressed whether the derivative component and host contract are of the type generally expected to be combined. The results still seemed counterintuitive in that an instrument that paid interest of 120 percent of LIBOR (assuming that 120 percent was not deemed to be a trivial amount of leverage) would be accounted for as a derivative instrument, but a note indexed to 100 percent of the S&P 500 index would not.

Accounting for embedded derivatives separately from the host contract

299. The Exposure Draft would have required that both a host contract and an embedded derivative feature, *together,* be accounted for as a derivative instrument if prescribed criteria were met. As a result, some contracts with embedded derivative features would have been accounted for like derivatives and could have been designated as hedging instruments. Some respondents to the Exposure Draft were concerned that its approach would permit an entity to use a cash instrument as a hedging instrument, which was generally precluded by the Exposure Draft, simply by embedding an insignificant leverage factor in

the interest formula. The Board agreed with those respondents and decided that (a) it was inappropriate to treat instruments that include both nonderivative and derivative components entirely as derivative instruments and (b) nonderivative instruments should only be eligible as hedging instruments in selected circumstances.

300. For several reasons, the Board decided to change the accounting for instruments with embedded derivatives. Most importantly, accounting for the entire instrument as a derivative or nonderivative is inconsistent with the accounting for hedged items required by this Statement. For a fair value hedge, the Exposure Draft would have required that all or a proportionate part of the total changes in fair value of a hedged item be recognized. However, this Statement requires recognizing at its fair value only the portion or proportion of a hedged item attributable to the risk being hedged. That change to a "separation-by-risk" approach is consistent with accounting for a derivative separately from the host contract in which it is embedded. Accounting for the derivative separately from the host contract also is more consistent with the objective of measuring derivative instruments at fair value and does not result in measuring derivative instruments differently simply because they are combined with other instruments.

301. The Board recognizes that there may be circumstances in which an embedded derivative cannot be reliably identified and measured for separation from the host contract. In those circumstances, this Statement requires that the entire contract, including both its derivative and nonderivative portions, be measured at fair value with changes in fair value recognized currently in earnings. The Board expects that an entity that enters into sophisticated investment and funding strategies such as structured notes or other contracts with embedded derivatives will be able to obtain the information necessary to reliably identify and measure the separate components. Accordingly, the Board believes it should be unusual that an entity would conclude that it cannot reliably separate an embedded derivative from its host contract.

302. Instruments that include embedded derivatives that are not accounted for separately from the host contract because the entity is unable to reliably identify and measure the derivative may not be designated as hedging instruments. That prohibition applies to the entire contract, as well as any portion of it, and addresses some of respondents' concerns about designating nonderivative instruments as hedging instruments. Prohibiting an entire contract with an embedded derivative from being designated as a hedging instrument will avoid the inappropriate use of nonderivative instruments as hedging instruments. It also should serve as an incentive to identify and separate derivative features from their host contracts.

303. Measuring an embedded derivative separately from its host contract will require judgment, and sometimes such measurements may be difficult. The Board considered providing specific guidelines for making such measurements but decided that such guidance could be unduly restrictive and could not address all relevant concerns. Instead, the Board decided only to clarify that the objective is to estimate the fair value of the derivative features separately from the fair value of the nonderivative portions of the contract. Estimates of fair value should reflect all relevant features of each component and their effect on a current exchange between willing parties. For example, an embedded purchased option that expires if the contract in which it is embedded is prepaid would have a different value than an option whose term is a specified period that is not subject to truncation.

The clearly-and-closely-related approach

304. This Statement requires that an embedded derivative be accounted for separately from a nonderivative host contract if (a) the derivative, considered on a freestanding basis, would be accounted for as a derivative instrument under this Statement and (b) the economic characteristics of the derivative and the host contract are not *clearly and closely related* to one another. The first of those criteria ensures that only derivative instruments as defined by, and subject to the requirements of, this Statement are accounted for separately. For example, the issuer would not account separately for an option embedded in a hybrid instrument if, on a freestanding basis, that option would be an equity instrument of the entity that is properly classified in stockholders' equity. Whether the issuer should account separately for an equity instrument embedded in an asset or a liability is an issue in the Board's project on liabilities and equity.

305. The second criterion listed in paragraph 304 focuses on whether an embedded derivative bears a close economic relationship to the host contract. As a practical matter, the Board decided that not all embedded derivative features should be required to be accounted for separately from the host contract.

Many hybrid instruments with embedded derivatives that bear a close economic relationship to the host contract were developed many years ago, for reasons that clearly were not based on achieving a desired accounting result. Prepayable mortgages and other prepayable debt instruments are examples of such familiar compound instruments with embedded derivatives. The accounting for those types of hybrid instruments is well established and generally has not been questioned. However, other embedded derivatives, such as an equity- or commodity-linked return included in a debt instrument that may cause the value of the instrument to vary inversely with changes in interest rates, do not bear a close economic relationship to the host contract. Even though conceptually all embedded derivatives should be accounted for separately, the Board decided, as a practical accommodation, that only an embedded derivative that is not considered to be clearly and closely related to its host contract should be accounted for separately.

306. The Board expects the clearly-and-closely-related approach to affect a significant number and wide variety of structured notes and other contracts that include embedded derivatives. Applying the approach will require judgment, which may lead to different accounting for similar instruments. To reduce that possibility, Appendix B provides examples illustrating how to apply the approach.

307. The clearly-and-closely-related approach sometimes will result in different accounting by the parties to a contract. For example, the issuer of convertible debt would not account for the embedded derivative feature separately from the host contract if the derivative component, on a freestanding basis, would not be subject to the requirements of this Statement because of the exclusion in paragraph 11(a). However, an investor in the convertible debt instrument would not be afforded that exclusion and would be required to account for the conversion feature separately from the host contract if the criteria in paragraph 12 are met.

308. The holder and issuer of an equity instrument with an embedded put, such as puttable common stock, would not, however, necessarily treat the embedded derivative differently. A put option embedded in an equity security has the potential to convert the equity security to cash or another asset, and conversion to cash according to the terms of the instrument is not a usual characteristic of an equity security. Accordingly, a put option embedded in an equity security is not clearly and closely related to the host contract if exercise of the put option would result in the payment of cash or delivery of another asset by the issuer of a security (except in those circumstances in which the put option is not considered to be a derivative pursuant to paragraph 11(a) because it is classified in shareholders' equity). Because the embedded put is more closely related to a liability than an equity security, both the issuer and the holder would account for it separately if the criteria in paragraph 12 are met. However, if exercise of the put would result in the issuance of additional equity instruments rather than paying cash or delivering another asset, the put is considered to be clearly and closely related to the equity security.

309. Paragraphs 13–15 of this Statement discuss some common relationships between interest rate features and host contracts, and foreign currency exchange rate features and host contracts. That guidance is provided to simplify the analysis of whether some of the more common types of contracts include embedded derivatives that require separate accounting. Paragraph 13 clarifies that most interest-bearing instruments that include derivative features that serve only to alter net interest payments that otherwise would be made on an interest-bearing host contract are considered to be clearly and closely related to the host contract. However, an embedded derivative that affects interest rates in such a way that the investor might not recover substantially all of its initial recorded investment is not considered to be clearly and closely related to the host contract and therefore should be accounted for separately. Similarly, an embedded derivative that could at least double the investor's initial rate of return on the host contract and also could result in a rate of return that is at least twice what otherwise would be the market return for a contract that has the same terms as the host contract and that involves a debtor with similar credit quality is not considered to be clearly and closely related and should be accounted for separately. The test for separate accounting pursuant to paragraph 13 should be applied based on what is possible under the contractual terms and not on a probability basis. For example, an embedded derivative that could under any circumstances result in the hybrid instrument's being settled in such a way that the holder does not recover substantially all of its initial recorded investment would not be considered to be clearly and closely related to the host contract even though the possibility that such a situation would occur is remote.

310. The Board recognizes that the provisions of paragraph 13(a) might raise the question of whether an interest-only strip is subject to the provisions of this Statement because the holder of an interest-only strip may not recover substantially all of its initial recorded investment. The Board notes that accounting for interest-only and principal-only strips is related to issues concerning accounting for retained interests in securitizations that the Board is currently reconsidering in conjunction with the implementation of Statement 125. Accordingly, the Board decided to exclude from the scope of this Statement interest-only and principal-only strips that meet the criteria in paragraph 14 and further consider the accounting for them in conjunction with its consideration of accounting for retained interests in securitizations.

311. Paragraph 15 provides that an embedded foreign currency derivative is not to be separated from the host contract and considered a derivative pursuant to paragraph 12 if the host contract is not a financial instrument and specifies payments denominated in either of the following currencies:

a. The currency of the primary economic environment in which any substantial party to the contract operates (that is, its functional currency)
b. The currency in which the price of the related good or service is routinely denominated in international commerce (such as the U.S. dollar for crude oil transactions).

For example, a lease of U.S. real estate with payments denominated in Deutsche marks contains an embedded derivative that should be viewed as clearly and closely related to the host lease contract and thus does not require separate accounting if the Deutsche mark is the functional currency of at least one substantial party to the lease. The Board decided that it was important that the payments be denominated in the functional currency of at least one *substantial* party to the transaction to ensure that the foreign currency is integral to the arrangement and thus considered to be clearly and closely related to the terms of the lease. A contract with payments denominated in a currency that is not the functional currency of any substantial party to that contract includes an embedded derivative that is not considered to be clearly and closely related to the host contract and should be accounted for separately under the provisions of this Statement. The second exclusion in paragraph 15 also permits contractual payments to be denominated

in the currency in which the price of the related commodity or service is routinely stated in international commerce without requiring separate accounting for an embedded derivative. The Board decided that it would be appropriate to consider the currency in which contracts for a given commodity are routinely denominated to be clearly and closely related to those contracts, regardless of the functional currency of the parties to that contract.

Fair Value Measurement Guidance

312. The definition of fair value in this Statement is derived from paragraphs 42–44 of Statement 125. The definition originated in paragraphs 5, 6, and 18–29 of Statement 107.

313. This Statement refers to Statement 107 for guidance in applying the definition of fair value. Some respondents to the Exposure Draft asked either for additional guidance on estimating the fair value of financial instruments or for amendments of part of the guidance in Statement 107. They said that the guidance in Statement 107 is not robust enough for recognition purposes (as opposed to disclosure) and allows too much variability in the estimates of fair value, especially for items not traded on a public exchange. The Board decided for several reasons to retain the guidance provided by Statement 107. Statement 107 has been in effect for several years, and entities are familiar with its measurement guidance. In addition, Board members were concerned that reevaluating and making the fair value guidance more prescriptive would significantly delay issuance of this Statement. On balance, the Board decided that the measurement guidance in Statement 107 is sufficient for use in applying this Statement. The Board will consider measurement issues and likely provide additional guidance or change Statement 107's guidance in some areas, perhaps including the areas discussed in the following paragraphs in the course of its project on the fair value measurement of financial instruments.

314. Respondents to the Exposure Draft also provided comments on specific measurement issues, focusing on the following three areas: (a) consideration of a discount or premium in the valuation of a large position, (b) consideration of changes in creditworthiness in valuing a debtor's liabilities, and (c) the valuation of deposit liabilities. Those areas are discussed below.

Consideration of a Discount or Premium in the Valuation of a Large Position

315. Consistent with Statement 107, the definition of fair value in this Statement precludes an entity from using a "blockage" factor (that is, a premium or discount based on the relative size of the position held, such as a large proportion of the total trading units of an instrument) in determining the fair value of a large block of financial instruments. The definition of fair value requires that fair value be determined as the product of the number of trading units of an asset times a quoted market price if available. Statement 107 further clarifies the issue:

> Under the definition of fair value in paragraph 5, the quoted price for a single trading unit in the most active market is the basis for determining market price and reporting fair value. This is the case even if placing orders to sell all of an entity's holdings of an asset or to buy back all of a liability might affect the price, or if a market's normal volume for one day might not be sufficient to absorb the quantity held or owed by an entity. [paragraph 6]

Some respondents to the Exposure Draft indicated that the guidance in Statement 107 (and implicitly the definition of *fair value* in this Statement) should be revised to require or permit consideration of a discount in valuing a large asset position. They asserted that an entity that holds a relatively large amount (compared with average trading volume) of a traded asset and liquidates the entire amount at one time likely would receive an amount less than the quoted market price. Although respondents generally focused on a discount, holding a relatively large amount of an asset might sometimes result in a premium over the market price for a single trading unit. The Board currently believes that the use of a blockage factor would lessen the reliability and comparability of reported estimates of fair value.

Valuation of Liabilities

316. Some respondents to the Exposure Draft noted that Statement 107 permits an entity to choose whether to consider changes in its own creditworthiness in determining the fair value of its debt and asked for further guidance on that issue. The definition of fair value in Statement 125 says that in measuring liabilities at fair value by discounting estimated future cash flows, an objective is to use discount rates at which those liabilities could be settled in an arm's-length transaction. However, the FASB's pronouncements to date have not broadly addressed whether changes in a debtor's creditworthiness after incurrence of a liability should be reflected in measuring its fair value. Pending resolution of the broad issue of the effect of a debtor's creditworthiness on the fair value of its liabilities, the Board decided to use the definition in Statement 125 but not to provide additional guidance on reflecting the effects of changes in creditworthiness.

Valuation of deposit liabilities

317. The guidance in Statement 107 precludes an entity from reflecting a long-term relationship with depositors, commonly known as a core deposit intangible, in determining the fair value of a deposit liability. Paragraph 12 of Statement 107 states, in part:

> In estimating the fair value of deposit liabilities, a financial entity shall not take into account the value of its long-term relationships with depositors, commonly known as core deposit intangibles, which are separate intangible assets, not financial instruments. For deposit liabilities with no defined maturities, the fair value to be disclosed under this Statement is the amount payable on demand at the reporting date.

Some respondents to the Exposure Draft requested that this Statement permit the fair value of deposit liabilities to reflect the effect of the core deposit intangible. The Board decided to make no change to the guidance in Statement 107 on that issue because it will be addressed as part of the Board's current project on measuring financial instruments at fair value. Issues of whether the fair values of certain liabilities (or assets) should reflect their values as if they were settled immediately or whether they should be based on their expected settlement dates, as well as issues of whether or when it would be appropriate to measure portfolios of assets or liabilities rather than individual items in those portfolios, are central to that project.

Other Fair Value Measurement Guidance

318. Statement 107 requires disclosure of the fair value of financial instruments "for which it is *practicable* to estimate that value" (emphasis added). Unlike Statement 107, this Statement provides no *practicability* exception that would permit

an entity to avoid the required fair value measurements. The Board believes that prudent risk management generally would require an entity to measure the fair value of any derivative that it holds as well as any item (or the portion of the item attributable to the identified risk) designated as being hedged in a fair value hedge.

319. This Statement requires that in measuring the change in fair value of a forward contract by discounting future cash flows, the estimate of future cash flows be based on changes in forward rates rather than spot rates. Thus, the gain or loss on, for example, a foreign currency forward contract would be based on the change in the forward rate, discounted to reflect the time value of money until the settlement date. The Board notes that the accounting literature in effect before the issuance of this Statement discusses different methods of estimating the value of a foreign currency forward contract. The Board decided that the valuation of a foreign currency forward contract should consider that (a) currencies will be exchanged at a future date, (b) relative interest rates determine the difference between spot and forward rates, and (c) valuation is affected by the time value of money. The net present value technique is the only method that considers all three items as well as the current settlement of present gains or losses that arise from changes in the spot rate.

Demand for Hedge Accounting

320. The Report on Deliberations describes hedge accounting as a "special accounting treatment that alters the normal accounting for one or more components of a hedge so that counterbalancing changes in the fair values of hedged items and hedging instruments, from the date the hedge is established, are not included in earnings in different periods" (paragraph 28). Demand for special accounting for hedges of the fair value exposure associated with assets and liabilities arises, in part, because of accounting anomalies—that is, differences in the way hedged items and hedging instruments are recognized and measured. Recognition anomalies arise because some assets and liabilities are recognized in the statement of financial position, while others, such as many firm commitments, are not. Measurement anomalies arise because existing accounting standards use different measurement attributes for different assets and liabilities. Some assets and liabilities are measured based on historical costs, others are measured based on current values, and still others are measured at the lower of cost or market value, which

is a combination of historical costs and current values. Accounting recognition and measurement decisions generally have been made independently for each kind of asset or liability without considering relationships with other assets or liabilities. Hedge accounting for assets and liabilities initially arose as a means of compensating for situations in which measurement anomalies between a hedged item and hedging instrument result in recognizing offsetting gains and losses in earnings in different periods.

Hedges of Fair Value Exposures

321. For hedges of fair value exposures, this Statement provides for certain gains and losses on designated assets and liabilities to be recognized in earnings in the same period as the losses and gains on the related derivative hedging instrument. Accounting for all financial instruments at fair value with all changes in fair value recognized similarly, such as in earnings, would eliminate the need for special accounting to accommodate the current mixed-attribute measurement model for fair value hedges of financial assets and liabilities. Fair value accounting for all financial instruments would not, however, affect either the perceived need for special accounting for fair value hedges of nonfinancial assets and liabilities or constituents' desire for special accounting for cash flow hedges of forecasted transactions.

Hedges of Cash Flow Exposures

322. Although accounting anomalies do not exist for cash flow hedges of forecasted transactions, many constituents want special accounting for transactions designed to manage cash flow risk associated with forecasted transactions. Entities often hedge the cash flow risk of forecasted transactions by using a derivative to "lock in" or "fix" the price of the future transaction, or to mitigate the cash flow risk for a certain period of time. They want to recognize the gain or loss on the derivative hedging instrument in earnings in the period or periods in which the forecasted transaction will affect earnings. If the hedging instrument is held until the forecasted transaction occurs, that accounting would base the earnings effect of the transaction on the "fixed price."

323. Some constituents suggested that there is little distinction between forecasted transactions and firm commitments and, consequently, that hedges of forecasted transactions should be accounted for in the same way as hedges of firm commitments. They said that (a) some forecasted transactions may be as

probable as, if not more probable than, some firm commitments, (b) it is often difficult to distinguish between forecasted transactions and firm commitments, and (c) entities do not view forecasted transactions and firm commitments separately for risk management purposes.

324. The Board believes there are several differences between firm commitments and forecasted transactions, irrespective of the probability of occurrence, that make it possible to distinguish between them. Firm commitments and forecasted transactions create different exposures to risk. Firm commitments are fixed-price contracts that expose an entity to a risk of a change in fair value. For example, an increase in the market price of a commodity will not affect the cash to be paid to purchase that commodity under a firmly committed contract; however, it will affect the value of that contract. In contrast, forecasted transactions do not have a fixed price and do expose an entity to a risk of a change in the cash to be paid to purchase the commodity in the future. Because firm commitments and forecasted transactions give rise to different exposures, different hedging strategies must be used. For example, an entity that hedges a firm commitment to purchase an item (a long position) would generally enter into a derivative to "undo" that fixed price (such as an offsetting short position). In contrast, an entity that hedges a forecasted purchase of an item would generally enter into a derivative (such as a contract to purchase the item—a long position) to "fix" the price.

325. Although many firm commitments are not recognized in financial statements, they qualify as assets or liabilities with determinable values, which makes them different from forecasted transactions. The value of a firm commitment is equal to the unrealized gain or loss on the commitment. In contrast, a forecasted transaction has no value and cannot give rise to a gain or loss. Regardless of their probability of occurrence, forecasted transactions are not present rights or obligations of the entity.

326. The Board recognizes that hedging is used to cope with uncertainty about the future and that the risks associated with forecasted transactions may appear to be similar to those associated with assets and liabilities, including firm commitments. However, the fundamental purpose of financial statements is to present relevant measures of *existing* assets and liabilities and changes in them. The Board believes there is no conceptual justification for providing special accounting for the effects of transactions that

have already occurred based solely on management's assertions about other transactions expected to occur in the future. The Board believes it would be conceptually preferable to provide descriptive information about intended links between current and forecasted future transactions in accompanying notes than to let those intended links directly affect the financial statements. As indicated by the Board's third fundamental decision, deferring a derivative gain or loss as a separate asset or liability in the statement of financial position is conceptually inappropriate because the gain or loss neither is itself a liability or an asset nor is it associated with the measurement of another existing asset or liability.

327. To the extent that hedge accounting is justifiable conceptually, it is for the purpose of dealing with anomalies caused by the mixed-attribute accounting model. The lack of an associated asset, liability, gain, or loss to be recognized in the financial statements means that there are no measurement anomalies for a forecasted transaction. Gains and losses on derivative instruments designated as hedges of forecasted transactions can be distinguished from gains and losses on other derivatives only on the basis of management intent. That makes hedge accounting for forecasted transactions problematic from a practical, as well as a conceptual, perspective. Furthermore, it generally is more difficult to assess the effectiveness of a hedge of a forecasted transaction than of a hedge of an existing asset or liability, because a forecasted transaction reflects expectations and intent, not measurable present rights or obligations.

328. Regardless of those conceptual and practical questions, the Board decided to accommodate certain hedges of forecasted transactions because of the current widespread use of and demand for special accounting for forecasted transactions. However, because the Board does not consider hedge accounting for forecasted transactions to be conceptually supportable, the Board chose to impose limits on that accounting, as discussed further in paragraphs 382 and 383.

329. This Statement provides for gains and losses on derivatives designated as cash flow hedges of forecasted transactions to be initially recognized in other comprehensive income and reclassified into earnings in the period(s) that the forecasted transaction affects earnings. As the Board pursues its long-term objective of measuring all financial instruments at fair value in the statement of financial position, it will reconsider whether special accounting for hedges of

forecasted transactions should continue to be permitted. Special accounting for hedges of forecasted financial instrument transactions would serve no purpose if all financial instruments were measured at fair value both at initial recognition and subsequently, with changes in fair value reported in earnings. This Statement consequently prohibits hedge accounting for the acquisition or incurrence of financial instruments that will be subsequently measured at fair value, with changes in fair value reported in earnings.

Hedge Accounting Approaches Considered

330. Over its six years of deliberations, the Board considered four broad approaches, and combinations of those approaches, in addition to the one proposed in the Exposure Draft, as a way to resolve issues related to hedge accounting. Those four broad approaches are discussed below. The hedge accounting approach proposed in the Exposure Draft is discussed in conjunction with the hedge accounting adopted in this Statement (which is discussed beginning at paragraph 351).

Measure All Financial Instruments at Fair Value

331. Consistent with its conclusion that fair value is the most relevant measure for all financial instruments, the Board considered measuring all financial instruments at fair value. Using that single measurement attribute for initial recognition and subsequent measurement would have resolved problems caused by the current mixed-attribute measurement model, at least for financial instruments, and would have been relatively simple and more readily understandable to financial statement users. It also would have increased comparability for identical balance sheet positions between entities, and it would have obviated the need for special accounting for hedges of financial instruments.

332. Several respondents to the Exposure Draft said that fair value measurement should be expanded to all financial instruments, and a few respondents suggested expanding fair value measurement to all assets and liabilities. Some respondents said that it is inconsistent or inappropriate to expand fair value measurement to derivatives before it is expanded to all financial instruments. Other respondents said that fair value measurement for all financial instruments is not a desirable goal.

333. The Board believes changing the accounting model so that all financial instruments are measured

at fair value in the statement of financial position is the superior conceptual solution to hedging issues. However, the Board decided that it was not appropriate at this time to require fair value measurement for all financial instruments. Board members decided that they must first deliberate and reach agreement on conceptual and practical issues related to the valuation of certain financial instruments, including liabilities, and portfolios of financial instruments. The Board is pursuing issues related to fair value measurement of all financial assets and liabilities in a separate project.

334. The Board is committed to work diligently toward resolving, in a timely manner, the conceptual and practical issues related to determining the fair values of financial instruments and portfolios of financial instruments. Techniques for refining the measurement of the fair values of all financial instruments continue to develop at a rapid pace, and the Board believes that all financial instruments should be carried in the statement of financial position at fair value when the conceptual and measurement issues are resolved. For now, the Board believes it is a significant improvement in financial reporting that this Statement requires that all derivatives be measured at fair value in the statement of financial position.

Mark-to-Fair-Value Hedge Accounting

335. Having concluded that its long-term objective of measuring all financial instruments at fair value was not attainable at this time, the Board decided that it needed to permit some form of hedge accounting. One alternative, termed mark-to-fair-value hedge accounting, would have required that an entity measure both the derivative and the hedged item at fair value and report the changes in the fair value of both items in earnings as they occur. Similar to measuring all financial instruments at fair value, that approach would have accommodated a wide variety of risk management strategies and would have overcome the problems attributable to the mixed-attribute measurement model by using a common measurement attribute for both the derivative and the hedged item. Additionally, that approach would have been relatively easy for entities to apply and for financial statement users to understand because hedged items would be reported at fair value and the net ineffectiveness of a hedge would be reported in earnings. There would have been no need to specify which risks could be separately hedged or how to reflect basis risk. However, like measuring all financial instruments at fair value, mark-to-fair-value hedge accounting

would not have addressed constituents' desire for special accounting for cash flow hedges of forecasted transactions.

336. Although the Board liked the idea of extending fair value measurement by marking hedged items to fair value with changes in fair value reported in earnings, it ultimately decided not to adopt mark-to-fair-value hedge accounting for two main reasons. First, measuring hedged items at fair value would have recognized, at the inception of a hedge, unrealized gains and losses on the hedged item that occurred before the hedge period ("preexisting" gains and losses). The Board believes that preexisting gains and losses on the hedged item are unrelated to the hedge and should not provide earnings offset for derivative gains and losses (consistent with its second fundamental decision [paragraphs 220–228]). Recognizing those gains and losses at the inception of a hedge would result in recognizing a gain or loss simply because the hedged item was designated as part of a hedge. That ability to selectively recognize preexisting gains and losses caused some Board members to reject the mark-to-fair-value approach.

337. Another reason the Board rejected that approach is that constituents objected to its effect on earnings—that is, earnings would have reflected changes in the fair value of a hedged item unrelated to the risk being hedged. For example, a hedge of one risk (such as interest rate risk) could have caused recognition in earnings of gains and losses from another risk (such as credit risk) because the mark-to-fair-value approach would have required recognition of the full change in fair value of the hedged item, including the changes in fair value attributable to risk components *not* being hedged. The hedge accounting approach proposed in the Exposure Draft also could have resulted in recognition of the change in fair value of a hedged item attributable to risk components not being hedged. However, the approach in the Exposure Draft would have (a) limited how much of those fair value changes were recognized in earnings and (b) prevented the change in the fair value of the hedged item that is not offset by the change in fair value on the hedging instrument from being recognized in earnings.

Comprehensive Income Approach

338. The Board considered another hedge accounting approach, referred to as the comprehensive income approach, that would have required that derivatives be measured at fair value and classified in one of two categories, *trading* or *risk management*. Gains and losses on derivatives classified as trading would be recognized in earnings in the periods in which they occur. Unrealized gains and losses on risk management derivatives would be reported as a component of other comprehensive income until realized. Realized gains and losses on risk management derivatives would be reported in earnings.

339. That approach would have been relatively easy to apply, it would have made derivatives and related risks transparent, and it would have accommodated some risk management strategies. Hedges of assets, liabilities, and some forecasted transactions would have been accommodated if the duration of the derivative was structured by management to achieve recognition, in the desired period, of any realized gains or losses. Also, because the approach would not have permitted deferral of derivative gains or losses as liabilities or assets, it would not have violated the fundamental decision that only assets and liabilities should be reported as such.

340. The Board rejected the comprehensive income approach for three main reasons. First, the Board does not believe that the distinction between realized and unrealized gains and losses that is the basis for the comprehensive income approach is relevant for financial instruments. The Board acknowledges that the current accounting model often distinguishes between realized and unrealized gains and losses. That distinction, however, is inappropriate for financial instruments. The occurrence of gains and losses on financial instruments—not the act of selling or settling them—affects an entity's economic position and thus should affect its reported financial performance. The Board is concerned that the comprehensive income approach would provide an opportunity for an entity to manage its reported earnings, per-share amounts, and other comprehensive income. Financial instruments generally are liquid, and an entity can easily sell or settle a financial instrument, realize a gain or loss, and maintain the same economic position as before the sale by reacquiring the same or a similar instrument.

341. Second, under the comprehensive income approach, offsetting gains and losses often would not have been reported in earnings at the same time. For example, if an entity used a series of short-term derivatives as a fair value hedge of a long-term fixed-rate loan, the gains and losses on the derivatives would have been recognized in earnings over the life of the loan each time an individual derivative expired

or was terminated. However, the offsetting unrealized losses and gains on the loan would not have been recognized in those same periods. Similarly, offsetting gains and losses on a derivative and a nonfinancial asset or liability would have been recognized together in earnings only if both transactions were specially structured to be realized in the same period. The Board decided on the approach in this Statement, in part, because offsetting gains and losses on fair value hedges would be recognized in earnings in the same period.

342. The third reason the Board did not adopt the comprehensive income approach is that all unrealized gains and losses on derivatives classified as risk management would have been reported in other comprehensive income without offsetting losses or gains, if any, on the hedged item. Thus, the resulting other comprehensive income could have implied a change in net assets when net assets did not change or when they changed in the opposite direction. For example, a $1,000 increase in the fair value of a derivative would have increased other comprehensive income and the carrying amount of the derivative by $1,000. If there was also an offsetting $1,000 loss on the hedged asset or liability, which would not have been reflected in other comprehensive income, the change in other comprehensive income would have implied that net assets had increased by $1,000 when there had been no real change.

343. The hedge accounting approach in this Statement also may result in reporting some derivative gains and losses in other comprehensive income. However, the Board notes that the approach in this Statement limits the amounts reported in other comprehensive income to gains and losses on derivatives designated as hedges of cash flow exposures. The transactions that will give rise to cash flow exposures do not provide offsetting changes in fair value when the related price or rate changes. Consequently, the gains and losses reported in other comprehensive income under this Statement are a faithful representation of the actual volatility of comprehensive income. The Board's reasoning for recognizing in other comprehensive income gains and losses on derivatives designated as hedges of cash flow exposures is further discussed in paragraph 377.

344. Only a few respondents to the Exposure Draft advocated the comprehensive income approach. Although they did not specifically comment on that approach, many respondents objected to recognizing derivative gains and losses in earnings in a

period other than the one in which the hedged item affects earnings. Some opposed reporting derivative gains and losses in other comprehensive income because of the potential for volatility in reported stockholders' equity or net assets, which they considered undesirable.

Full-Deferral Hedge Accounting

345. The Board considered maintaining the approach outlined in Statement 80. Statement 80 permitted deferral of the entire change in the fair value of a derivative used as a hedging instrument by adjusting the basis of a hedged asset or liability, or by recognizing a separate liability or asset associated with a hedge of an unrecognized firm commitment or a forecasted transaction, if the appropriate hedge criteria were met. Many respondents to the Exposure Draft advocated a full-deferral approach. They noted that a full-deferral approach would have been familiar to entities that have applied hedge accounting in the past. That approach also would have provided a mechanism to moderate the earnings "mismatch" that is attributable to the mixed-attribute measurement model. By deferring the earnings recognition of a derivative's gain or loss until the loss or gain on the hedged item has been recognized, offsetting gains or losses on the derivative and hedged item would be recognized in earnings at the same time.

346. However, the full-deferral approach goes beyond correcting for the anomalies created by using different attributes to measure assets and liabilities. The Board rejected that approach for three reasons. First, full-deferral hedge accounting inappropriately permits gains or losses on derivatives designated as hedging the cash flow exposure of forecasted transactions to be reported as separate liabilities or assets in the statement of financial position. Those gains and losses do not represent probable future sacrifices or benefits, which are necessary characteristics of liabilities and assets. Thus, reporting deferred gains or losses as separate liabilities or assets is inconsistent with the Board's conceptual framework.

347. Second, a full-deferral approach is inconsistent with the Board's long-term goal of reporting all financial instruments at fair value in the statement of financial position. For fair value hedges, a full-deferral approach could only have been described as deferring the derivative gain or loss as an adjustment of the basis of the hedged item. For a cash flow hedge of a forecasted purchase of an asset or incurrence of an obligation, a full-deferral approach would have resulted in systematically adjusting the initial carrying

amount of the acquired asset or incurred liability away from its fair value.

348. Finally, the full-deferral approach permits a derivative's gain or loss for a period to be deferred regardless of whether there is a completely offsetting decrease or increase in the fair value of the hedged item for that period. The Board believes it is inappropriate to treat that portion of a hedge that does not achieve its objective as if it had been effective.

Synthetic Instrument Accounting

349. A number of respondents to the Exposure Draft suggested that a different kind of special accounting be provided for "synthetic instrument" strategies. Synthetic instrument accounting, which evolved in practice, views two or more distinct financial instruments (generally a cash instrument and a derivative instrument) as having synthetically created another single cash instrument. The objective of synthetic instrument accounting is to present those multiple instruments in the financial statements as if they were the single instrument that the entity sought to create. Some respondents to the Exposure Draft advocated a synthetic instrument accounting approach for interest rate swaps that are used to modify the interest receipts or payments associated with a hedged financial instrument. That approach, which its advocates also refer to as "the accrual approach," would require the accrual of only the most imminent net cash settlement on the swap. It would not require recognition of the swap itself in the financial statements.

350. The Board decided not to allow synthetic instrument accounting because to do so would be inconsistent with (a) the fundamental decision to report all derivatives in the financial statements, (b) the fundamental decision to measure all derivatives at fair value, (c) the Board's objective to increase the transparency of derivatives and derivative activities, and (d) the Board's objective of providing consistent accounting for all derivative instruments and for all hedging strategies. Synthetic instrument accounting also is not conceptually defensible because it results in netting assets against liabilities (or vice versa) for no reason other than an asserted "connection" between the netted items.

Hedge Accounting in This Statement

351. The hedge accounting approach in this Statement combines elements from each of the approaches considered by the Board. The Board believes the approach in this Statement is consistent with all four of its fundamental decisions and is a significant improvement in financial reporting. It is also more consistent than the approach in the Exposure Draft with what many respondents said was necessary to accommodate their risk management strategies.

352. Some respondents suggested that the financial statement results of applying this Statement will not reflect what they perceive to be the economics of certain hedging and risk management activities. However, there is little agreement about just what the "economics" of hedging and risk management activities are. Because entities have different and often conflicting views of risk and manage risk differently, the Board does not think that a single approach to hedge accounting could fully reflect the hedging and risk management strategies of all entities. The Board also believes that some aspects of "risk management" are hard to distinguish from speculation or "position taking" and that speculative activities should not be afforded special accounting. Thus, providing hedge accounting to the whole range of activities undertaken by some under the broad heading of "risk management" would be inconsistent with improving the usefulness and understandability of financial reporting.

Exposures to Changes in Fair Value or Changes in Cash Flow

353. The accounting prescribed by this Statement is based on two types of risk exposures. One reflects the possibility that a change in price will result in a change in the fair value of a particular asset or liability—a *fair value exposure*. The other reflects the possibility that a change in price will result in variability in expected future cash flows—a *cash flow exposure*.

354. Fair value exposures arise from existing assets or liabilities, including firm commitments. Fixed-rate financial assets and liabilities, for example, have a fair value exposure to changes in market rates of interest and changes in credit quality. Nonfinancial assets and liabilities, on the other hand, have a fair value exposure to changes in the market price of a particular item or commodity. Some assets and liabilities have fair value exposures arising from more than one type of risk.

355. Some cash flow exposures relate to forecasted transactions. For example, a change in the market

price of an asset will change the expected cash out-flows for a future purchase of the asset and may affect the subsequent earnings impact from its use or sale. Similarly, a change in market interest rates will change the expected cash flows for the future interest payments resulting from the forecasted issuance of fixed-rate debt (for which the interest rate has not yet been fixed). Other cash flow exposures relate to existing assets and liabilities. For example, a change in market interest rates will affect the future cash receipts or payments associated with a variable-rate financial asset or liability.

356. Fair value exposures and cash flow exposures often are mutually exclusive, and hedging to reduce one exposure generally increases the other. For example, hedging the variability of interest receipts on a variable-rate loan with a receive-fixed, pay-variable swap "fixes" the interest receipts on the loan and eliminates the exposure to risk of a change in cash flows, but it creates an exposure to the risk of a change in the fair value of the swap. The net cash flows on the loan and the swap will not change (or will change minimally) with market rates of interest, but the combined fair value of the loan and the swap will fluctuate. Additionally, the changes in the fair value of an asset or liability are inseparable from its expected cash flows because those cash flows are a major factor in determining fair value.

Hedge Accounting in This Statement and Risk Reduction

357. The Board believes that entity-wide risk reduction should be a criterion for hedge accounting; it therefore would have preferred to require an entity to demonstrate that a derivative reduces the risk to the entity as a criterion for hedge accounting. However, requiring that a derivative contribute to entity-wide risk reduction would necessitate a single, restrictive definition of risk, such as *either* fair value risk *or* cash flow risk. Actions to mitigate the risk of a change in fair value generally exacerbate the variability of cash flows. Likewise, actions to mitigate the variability of cash flows of existing assets and liabilities necessitate "fixing" cash flows, which in turn generally exacerbates an entity's exposure to changes in fair value. Because this Statement provides hedge accounting for both fair value risk and cash flow risk, an objective assessment of entity-wide risk reduction would be mechanically impossible in most situations. Therefore, the Board did not continue the requirement in Statement 80 that a hedging transaction must

contribute to reducing risk at the entity-wide level to qualify for hedge accounting.

358. As discussed in paragraph 322, a hedge of a forecasted transaction can be described as "fixing" the price of the item involved in the transaction if the hedging instrument is held until the hedged transaction occurs. "Fixing" the price of an expected future transaction is a form of risk management on an individual-transaction basis. The Exposure Draft would have provided cash flow hedge accounting only for derivative instruments with a contractual maturity or repricing date that was on or about the date of the hedged forecasted transaction. However, as discussed further in paragraph 468, the Board removed that criterion for cash flow hedge accounting principally because of respondents' objections to it. This Statement also places no limitations on an entity's ability to prospectively designate, dedesignate, and redesignate a qualifying hedge of the same forecasted transaction. The result of those provisions is that this Statement permits an entity to exclude derivative gains or losses from earnings and recognize them in other comprehensive income even if its objective is to achieve a desired level of risk based on its view of the market rather than to reduce risk. If an entity enters into and then discontinues a derivative transaction designated as a hedge of a forecasted transaction for which the exposure has not changed, one of those actions—either the hedge or the discontinuance of it—must increase, rather than reduce, risk.

359. The considerations just discussed, together with the intense focus on the part of many investors on earnings as a measure of entity performance, lead some Board members to prefer that the gain or loss on a derivative designated as a hedge of a forecasted transaction but not intended to be held until the transaction occurs be recognized directly in earnings. However, those Board members also consider comprehensive income to be a measure of an entity's financial performance that is at least as, if not more, important as earnings. Consequently, those Board members found it acceptable to recognize in other comprehensive income the gain or loss on a derivative designated as a hedge of a forecasted transaction, regardless of whether that derivative is held until the hedged transaction occurs. Those Board members observe, however, that recognizing such gains and losses in other comprehensive income rather than in earnings creates additional pressure concerning the method and prominence of the display of both the

items in other comprehensive income and total comprehensive income.

A Compound Derivative May Not Be Separated into Risk Components

360. The Exposure Draft would have prohibited separating a derivative into either separate *proportions* or separate *portions* and designating any component as a hedging instrument or designating different components as hedges of different exposures. Some respondents objected to both prohibitions. They said that either a pro rata part of a derivative, such as 60 percent, or a portion of a derivative, such as the portion of the change in value of a combined interest rate and currency swap deemed to be attributable to changes in interest rates, should qualify for separate designation as a hedging instrument. The Board decided to permit designation of a pro rata part of a derivative as a hedge. Example 10 in Appendix B illustrates that situation.

361. The Board decided to retain the prohibition against separating a compound derivative into components representing different risks. This Statement permits separation of a hedged item or transaction by risk and also places the burden on management to design an appropriate effectiveness test, including a means of measuring the change in fair value or cash flows attributable to the risk being hedged. In view of those requirements, the Board decided that it was especially important that, to the extent possible, the gain or loss on the derivative be an objectively determined market-based amount rather than an amount "separated out" of an overall gain or loss on the derivative as a whole. Otherwise, even for a derivative for which a quoted price is available, the effectiveness test would compare two computed amounts of gain or loss deemed to be "attributable to the risk being hedged" with no tie to a total gain or loss separately observable in the market, which would make the effectiveness test less meaningful. To permit that would have required that the Board provide guidance on how to compute the fair value of the "synthetic" derivative that is separated out of a compound derivative, both at inception and during the term of the hedge. That would have added complexity to the requirements in this Statement without, in the Board's view, adding offsetting benefits to justify the additional complexity. However, the Board decided to permit separation of the foreign currency component of a compound derivative at the date of initial application of this Statement, as discussed in paragraph 524.

Fair Value Hedges

362. As discussed in paragraph 320, the demand for special accounting for hedges of existing assets and liabilities, including unrecognized firm commitments, arises because of differences in the way derivatives and hedged assets and liabilities are measured. This Statement requires derivatives designated as part of a fair value hedge to be measured at fair value with changes in fair value reported in earnings as they occur. Without special accounting, the gain or loss on a derivative that hedges an item not measured at fair value would be reported in earnings without also reporting the potentially offsetting loss or gain on the item being hedged. Those who engage in hedging transactions do not consider that result to appropriately reflect the relationship between a derivative and hedged item or how they manage risk. Accordingly, this Statement permits gains and losses on designated assets and liabilities to be recognized in earnings in the same period as the losses and gains on related derivative hedging instruments.

Accelerated recognition of the gain or loss on a hedged item

363. Similar to the Exposure Draft, this Statement (a) requires that the gains or losses on a derivative used as a fair value hedging instrument be recognized in earnings as they occur and (b) permits earnings offset by accelerating the recognition of the offsetting losses or gains attributable to the risk being hedged and adjusting the carrying amount of the hedged item accordingly. That notion is consistent with part of the Board's second fundamental decision, namely, that adjustments to the carrying amount of hedged items should reflect offsetting changes in their fair value arising while the hedge is in effect. This Statement modifies the proposals in the Exposure Draft for recognizing the gains and losses on the hedged item in two ways, which are explained below.

Attributable to the risk being hedged

364. The Exposure Draft proposed that the gain or loss on the hedged item that would be recognized under fair value hedge accounting incorporate all risk factors and, therefore, reflect the full change in fair value of the hedged item to the extent of an offsetting gain or loss on the hedging instrument. That focus was intended to prevent a hedged asset or liability from being adjusted farther away from its fair value than it was at inception of the hedge. For example, if the fair value of a hedged asset increased due to a

change in interest rates but simultaneously decreased due to a change in credit quality, the Exposure Draft would have prevented an entity that was hedging only interest rate risk from accelerating recognition of the interest rate gain without also effectively accelerating the credit quality loss. Accelerating only the interest rate gain would adjust the hedged asset away from its fair value.

365. Respondents to the Exposure Draft opposed the proposed approach for the very reason that the Board originally favored it—the approach would not have segregated the sources of the change in a hedged item's fair value. Respondents focused on the earnings impact and expressed concern about recognizing in earnings the fair value changes on the hedged item related to an unhedged risk. They said that recognizing the changes in fair value of the hedged item attributable to all risks would cause unrepresentative earnings volatility and would be misleading in reflecting the results of the entity's hedging activities.

366. The Board believes that the earnings effect of the approach proposed in the Exposure Draft would have reflected an exacerbation of the mixed-attribute measurement model, rather than "unrepresentative earnings volatility." However, because of the concerns expressed by respondents, the Board reconsidered the proposed requirements. The Board generally focuses on the appropriate recognition and measurement of assets and liabilities in developing accounting standards. However, the principal purpose of providing special accounting for hedging activities is to mitigate the effects on earnings of different existing recognition and measurement attributes. Consequently, in this instance, the Board found the focus of respondents on the earnings impact of the approach to hedge accounting to be persuasive and decided to modify the Exposure Draft to focus on the risk being hedged. The Board decided to adopt an approach that accelerates the earnings recognition of the portion of the hedged item's gain or loss attributable to the risk being hedged for the following reasons:

a. It provides the matching of gains and losses on the hedging instrument and the hedged item that respondents desire.
b. It accounts for all or a portion of the change in fair value of the hedged item, and, consequently, it is not inconsistent with the Board's long-term objective of measuring all financial instruments at fair value.

Entire gain or loss attributable to risk being hedged

367. The Exposure Draft proposed that the gain or loss on the hedged item be recognized in earnings only to the extent that it provided offset for the loss or gain on the hedging instrument. Under that proposal, earnings would have reflected hedge ineffectiveness to the extent that the derivative gain or loss exceeded an offsetting loss or gain on the hedged item. It would not have reflected hedge ineffectiveness to the extent that the gain or loss on the derivative was less than the loss or gain on the hedged item. For example, ineffectiveness of $10 would have been recognized if the gain on the derivative was $100 and the corresponding loss on the hedged item was $90, but not if the gain on the derivative was $90 and the loss on the hedged item was $100. The Board would have preferred to reflect all hedge ineffectiveness in earnings. However, the Exposure Draft did not propose that the excess gain or loss on the hedged item be reflected in earnings because that could have resulted in reporting in earnings a gain or loss on the hedged item attributable to changes in unhedged risks.

368. When the Board modified the Exposure Draft to focus only on the gain or loss on the hedged item attributable to the risk being hedged, it decided to report all hedge ineffectiveness in earnings. Recognizing the hedged item's gain or loss due only to the hedged risk will not result in earnings recognition of gains or losses related to unhedged risks.

Measurement of hedged item's gain or loss

369. In this Statement, the gain or loss on the hedged item that is accelerated and recognized in earnings is the portion of the gain or loss that is attributable to the risk being hedged. Although the Board considered several approaches to measuring the gain or loss attributable to the risk being hedged, it decided not to provide detailed guidance on how that gain or loss should be measured. The Board believes that the appropriate measurement of the gain or loss on a hedged item may depend on how an entity manages the hedged risk. Consistent with its decision to require an entity to define at inception how it will assess hedge effectiveness, the Board decided that an entity also should define at inception how it will measure the gain or loss on a hedged item attributable to the risk being hedged. The measurement of that gain or loss should be consistent with the entity's approach to managing risk, assessing hedge effectiveness, and determining hedge ineffectiveness. It

follows that the gain or loss on the hedged item attributable to the risk being hedged can be based on the loss or gain on the derivative, adjusted in certain ways that will be identified during the assessment of hedge effectiveness. Both Section 2 of Appendix A and Appendix B discuss and illustrate situations in which the gain or loss on a hedging derivative must be adjusted to measure the loss or gain on the hedged item.

The exposure draft's exception for certain firm commitments

370. The Exposure Draft proposed a specific exception for a derivative that hedges the foreign currency exposure of a firm commitment to purchase a nonfinancial asset for a fixed amount of foreign currency. That exception would have permitted an entity to consider separately the financial aspect and the nonfinancial aspect of the firm commitment for purposes of designating the hedged item and thus to record the purchased asset at a fixed-dollar (or other functional currency) equivalent of the foreign currency price. The exception is no longer necessary because this Statement permits separate consideration of financial and nonfinancial risks for all fair value hedges of firm commitments.

Cash Flow Hedges

371. As discussed in paragraphs 322–329, the Board decided to permit hedge accounting for certain hedges of forecasted transactions because of the widespread use of and demand for that accounting. The "need" for special accounting for cash flow hedges arises because the hedged transactions are recognized in periods after the one in which a change in the fair value of the derivative occurs and is recognized. Without special accounting, gains and losses on derivatives would be reported in a period different from the earnings impact of the hedged transaction or the related asset acquired or liability incurred.

372. In developing a hedge accounting approach for hedges of cash flow exposures, the Board identified four objectives: (a) to avoid the recognition of the gain or loss on a derivative hedging instrument as a liability or an asset, (b) to make gains and losses not yet recognized in earnings visible, (c) to reflect hedge ineffectiveness, and (d) to limit the use of hedge accounting for cash flow hedges.

First two objectives—avoid conceptual difficulties and increase visibility

373. The Board believes that recognizing gains or losses on derivatives in other comprehensive income, rather than as liabilities or assets, best meets the first two objectives. Many respondents to the Exposure Draft objected to that approach because of the potential for volatility in reported equity. Instead, they advocated reporting a derivative's gain or loss as a freestanding liability or asset. The Board did not change its decision for several reasons. First, the Board believes that reporting a derivative's gain or loss as a liability or an asset is inappropriate and misleading because a gain is not a liability and a loss is not an asset. Second, the Board believes the volatility in other comprehensive income that results from gains and losses on derivatives that hedge cash flow exposures properly reflects what occurred during the hedge period. There are no gains or losses to offset the losses or gains on the derivatives that are reported in other comprehensive income because the hedged transaction has not yet occurred. Third, the Board believes the advantages of reporting all derivatives at fair value, together with recognizing gains and losses on derivatives that hedge cash flow exposures in other comprehensive income, outweigh any perceived disadvantages of potential equity volatility.

Third and fourth objectives—reflect ineffectiveness and impose limitations

374. The Board proposed in the Exposure Draft that the best way to meet the last two objectives (reflect ineffectiveness and impose limitations) would be to reclassify a gain or loss on a derivative designated as a hedging instrument into earnings on the projected date of the hedged forecasted transaction. Effectiveness thus would have been reflected at the date the forecasted transaction was projected to occur. In addition, there would have been little, if any, opportunity for earnings management because gains and losses would not have been reclassified into earnings when realized, when a forecasted transaction actually occurs, or when a forecasted transaction's occurrence is no longer considered probable. The Exposure Draft explained that requiring recognition at the date the forecasted transaction is initially expected to occur emphasizes the importance of carefully evaluating and forecasting future transactions before designating them as being hedged with specific derivatives.

375. Respondents generally opposed the approach in the Exposure Draft because it often would not have matched the derivative gain or loss with the earnings effect of the forecasted transaction, thereby making earnings appear volatile. Respondents generally advocated recognizing a derivative gain or loss in earnings in the same period or periods as the earnings effect of (a) the forecasted transaction (such as a forecasted sale) or (b) the subsequent accounting for the asset acquired or liability incurred in conjunction with the forecasted transaction. To accomplish that result, many respondents advocated deferring the gain or loss on the derivative beyond the date of the forecasted transaction as an adjustment of the basis of the asset acquired or liability incurred in the forecasted transaction.

376. The Board considered two approaches that would have provided basis adjustment for assets acquired or liabilities incurred in conjunction with a forecasted transaction. One approach would have initially deferred a derivative gain or loss as a separate (freestanding) liability or asset and later reported it as an adjustment of the basis of the acquired asset or incurred liability when it was recorded. The Board rejected that approach because a deferred loss is not an asset and a deferred gain is not a liability; reporting them as if they were would be misleading. The other approach would have initially recognized the derivative gain or loss in other comprehensive income and later reported it as an adjustment of the basis of the acquired asset or incurred liability when it was recorded. The Board rejected that approach because it would have distorted reported periodic comprehensive income. For example, removing a gain from other comprehensive income and reporting it as an adjustment of the basis of an acquired asset would result in a decrease in periodic comprehensive income (and total stockholders' equity) caused simply by the acquisition of an asset at its fair value—a transaction that should have no effect on comprehensive income. Additionally, both approaches would have systematically measured the acquired asset or incurred liability at an amount other than fair value at the date of initial recognition. That is, the adjustment would have moved the initial carrying amount of the acquired asset or incurred liability away from its fair value.

377. The Board decided to require that the gain or loss on a derivative be reported initially in other comprehensive income and reclassified into earnings when the forecasted transaction affects earnings. That requirement avoids the problems caused by adjusting the basis of an acquired asset or incurred liability and

provides the same earnings impact. The approach in this Statement, for example, provides for (a) recognizing the gain or loss on a derivative that hedged a forecasted purchase of a machine in the same periods as the depreciation expense on the machine and (b) recognizing the gain or loss on a derivative that hedged a forecasted purchase of inventory when the cost of that inventory is reflected in cost of sales.

378. The Board was concerned that recognizing all derivative gains and losses in other comprehensive income and reclassifying them into earnings in the future, perhaps spread out over a number of years, would not meet its third objective of reflecting hedge ineffectiveness, if any. The Board therefore decided to require that, in general, the ineffective part of a cash flow hedge be immediately recognized in earnings.

Measure of hedge ineffectiveness

379. The Board believes that, in principle, earnings should reflect (a) the component of a derivative gain or loss that is excluded from the defined assessment of hedge effectiveness and (b) any hedge ineffectiveness. However, the Board had concerns about the effect of that approach on other comprehensive income and earnings for a period in which the change in the present value of the future expected cash flows on the hedged transaction exceeds the change in the present value of the expected cash flows on the derivative. In that circumstance, the result would be to defer in other comprehensive income a nonexistent gain or loss on the derivative and to recognize in earnings an offsetting nonexistent loss or gain. For example, if the derivative hedging instrument had a $50 loss for a period in which the change in the present value of the expected cash flows on the hedged transaction was a $55 gain, an approach that reflected all hedge ineffectiveness in earnings would result in reflecting a $55 loss in other comprehensive income and reporting a $5 gain in earnings.

380. To avoid that result, the Board decided that only ineffectiveness due to excess expected cash flows on the derivative should be reflected in earnings. The Board discussed whether that approach should be applied period by period or cumulatively and decided that the ineffectiveness of a cash flow hedge should be determined on a cumulative basis since the inception of the hedge.

381. To illustrate the difference between the period-by-period and cumulative approaches, consider a derivative that had gains (expected cash inflows) of $75

in period 1 and $70 in period 2. The derivative hedges a forecasted transaction for which expected cash outflows increased by $70 and $75 in the same periods, respectively. At the end of period 2, the changes in expected cash flows on the hedge are completely offsetting on a cumulative basis. That is, the derivative has expected cash inflows of $145 and the hedged transaction has an offsetting increase in expected cash outflows of $145. If hedge ineffectiveness is measured and accounted for on a cumulative basis, the $5 excess derivative gain reported in earnings in period 1 would be reversed in period 2. At the end of period 2, retained earnings would reflect zero gain or loss, and comprehensive income would reflect $145 of derivative gain. However, measuring and accounting for hedge ineffectiveness on a period-by-period basis would give a different result because earnings and comprehensive income would be affected for the $5 excess derivative gain in period 1 but not the $5 excess hedged transaction loss in period 2. As a result, at the end of period 2, retained earnings would reflect a $5 gain, even though actual ineffectiveness since hedge inception was a zero gain or loss. Other comprehensive income would reflect a gain of $140, even though the derivative's actual effectiveness since the inception of the hedge was a gain of $145. Thus, in a situation like the one illustrated, retained earnings under the cumulative approach will more accurately reflect total hedge ineffectiveness since the inception of the hedge, and comprehensive income will more accurately reflect total hedge effectiveness for the hedge period. The Board rejected a period-by-period approach because, under that approach, retained earnings would not reflect total hedge ineffectiveness, and comprehensive income would not reflect total hedge effectiveness. Section 2 of Appendix A provides some examples of how the ineffective portion of a derivative gain or loss might be estimated, and Section 1 of Appendix B further illustrates application of the cumulative approach.

Limitations on cash flow hedges

382. Because hedge accounting for forecasted transactions is not conceptually supportable and is not necessary to compensate for recognition or measurement anomalies, the Board decided that this Statement should provide only limited hedge accounting for hedges of forecasted transactions (the Board's fourth objective). In the Exposure Draft, the Board concluded that the best way to limit hedge accounting for a hedge of a forecasted transaction was to require that the gain or loss on a derivative that hedges

a forecasted transaction be reclassified into earnings on the projected date of the forecasted transaction and to limit hedge accounting to the life of the hedging instrument. In formulating this Statement, the Board decided that, because of current practice, it was acceptable to provide for an earnings effect that is more consistent with the entity's objective in entering into a hedge. Consequently, the Board decided to provide limitations on hedges of forecasted transactions through the criteria for qualification for cash flow hedge accounting. The Board believes the criteria discussed in paragraphs 458–473 provide sufficient limitations.

383. The Board also considered limiting hedge accounting for hedges of cash flow exposures based on pragmatic, but arbitrary, limitations. The pragmatic approaches that were considered included limitations based on the length of time until the expected occurrence of the forecasted transaction, the amount of the gain or loss reflected in other comprehensive income, and specific linkage to existing assets or liabilities. For example, a limitation might have required that cash flows occur within five years to qualify as hedgeable. The Board decided that it was more appropriate to rely on specified criteria for cash flow hedges than to apply arbitrary, pragmatic limitations.

General Criteria to Qualify for Designation as a Hedge

384. This Statement requires that certain criteria be met for a hedge to qualify for hedge accounting. The criteria are intended to ensure that hedge accounting is used in a reasonably consistent manner for transactions and exposures that qualify as hedgeable pursuant to this Statement. The criteria discussed in this section are required for both fair value hedges and cash flow hedges. Criteria that are unique to either fair value hedges or cash flow hedges are discussed separately.

Designation, Documentation, and Risk Management

385. The Board decided that concurrent designation and documentation of a hedge is critical; without it, an entity could retroactively identify a hedged item, a hedged transaction, or a method of measuring effectiveness to achieve a desired accounting result. The Board also decided that identifying the nature of the risk being hedged and using a hedging derivative consistent with an entity's established policy for risk

management are essential components of risk management and are necessary to add verifiability to the hedge accounting model.

Highly Effective in Achieving Offsetting Changes in Fair Values or Cash Flows

386. To qualify for hedge accounting, this Statement requires that an entity must expect a hedging relationship to be highly effective in achieving offsetting changes in fair value or cash flows for the risk being hedged. That requirement is consistent with the Board's fourth fundamental decision, which is that one aspect of qualification for special hedge accounting should be an assessment of the effectiveness of a derivative in offsetting the entity's exposure to changes in fair value or variability of cash flows. This Statement does not specify how effectiveness should be assessed; assessment of effectiveness should be based on the objective of management's risk management strategy. However, this Statement does require that the method of assessing effectiveness be reasonable and that the same method be used for similar hedges unless different methods are explicitly justified. The Board considers it essential that an entity document at the inception of the hedge how effectiveness will be assessed for each hedge and then apply that effectiveness test on a consistent basis for the duration of the designated hedge. However, if an entity identifies an improved method for assessing effectiveness, it may discontinue the existing hedging relationship and then designate and document a new hedging relationship using the improved method prospectively.

387. In formulating this Statement, the Board would have preferred specific effectiveness tests for fair value hedges and for cash flow hedges to (a) provide limitations on hedge accounting, (b) result in consistent application of hedge accounting guidance, and (c) increase the comparability of financial statements. The Exposure Draft therefore proposed specific effectiveness tests that would have required an expectation that the changes in fair value or net cash flows of the derivative would "offset substantially all" of the changes in fair value of the hedged item or the variability of cash flows of the hedged transaction attributable to the risk being hedged. Those proposed offset tests were intended to be similar to, though more stringent than, the related requirements of Statement 80:

> At the inception of the hedge and throughout the hedge period, high correlation of

changes in (1) the market value of the futures contract(s) and (2) the fair value of, or interest income or expense associated with, the hedged item(s) shall be probable so that the results of the futures contract(s) will substantially offset the effects of price or interest rate changes on the exposed item(s). [Paragraph 4(b); footnote reference omitted.]

388. Respondents to the Exposure Draft commented that the proposed effectiveness tests for fair value and cash flow hedges would have precluded certain risk management strategies from qualifying for hedge accounting because those tests were based on singular objectives for fair value and cash flow hedges. For example, the effectiveness tests in the Exposure Draft would have prohibited delta-neutral hedging strategies, partial-term hedging strategies, rollover hedging strategies, and hedging based on changes in the intrinsic value of options. Respondents also noted that risk management objectives and strategies differ between entities as well as between different types of hedges within an entity. Based on those concerns, the Board reconsidered the effectiveness tests proposed in the Exposure Draft.

389. The Board attempted to develop a workable effectiveness test that would appropriately deal with the variety of risk management objectives and strategies that exist in practice. It ultimately decided to remove the specific effectiveness tests and, instead, to require that a hedge be expected to be highly effective in achieving offsetting changes in either fair value or cash flows, consistent with an entity's documented risk management objectives and strategy. The Board intends "highly effective" to be essentially the same as the notion of "high correlation" in Statement 80.

390. Because that modification places more emphasis on each entity's approach to risk management, the Board decided to require an expanded description and documentation of an entity's risk management objectives and strategy, including how a derivative's effectiveness in hedging an exposure will be assessed. It also decided that the description of how an entity plans to assess effectiveness must (a) include identification of whether all of the gain or loss on the derivative hedging instrument will be included in the assessment and (b) have a reasonable basis. Those limitations, along with examples of different ways to assess hedge effectiveness in a variety of circumstances, are discussed in Section 2 of Appendix A. The Board may need to revisit the idea of more specific effectiveness tests if an

evaluation of the application of this Statement indicates either too great a disparity in the techniques used for assessing effectiveness or widespread abuse of the flexibility provided.

Basis swaps

391. Basis swaps are derivative instruments that are used to modify the receipts or payments associated with a recognized, variable-rate asset or liability from one variable amount to another variable amount. They do not eliminate the variability of cash flows; instead, they change the basis or index of variability. The Exposure Draft would have required that an entity expect the net cash flows of a derivative to "offset substantially all" of the variability of cash flows associated with the asset or liability to qualify for cash flow hedge accounting. That requirement would have precluded basis swaps from qualifying as hedging instruments.

392. Some respondents to the Exposure Draft criticized its prohibition of hedge accounting for basis swaps. They commented that it should not matter whether an interest rate swap, for example, is used to change the interest receipts or payments associated with a hedged asset or liability from fixed to variable, variable to fixed, or variable to variable. They noted that the fair value and cash flow criteria accommodated only fixed-to-variable and variable-to-fixed swaps. Additionally, some respondents commented that basis swaps should be eligible for hedge accounting treatment because they are an effective means of creating comparable asset-liability positions. For example, if an entity holds a variable-rate, LIBOR-based asset and a variable-rate, prime-based liability, an easy way to match that asset and liability position is to "swap" either the LIBOR asset to prime or the prime liability to LIBOR.

393. Many respondents advocating the use of basis swaps as hedging instruments suggested accommodating basis swaps by accounting for all swaps on a synthetic instrument basis. For the reasons discussed in paragraphs 349 and 350, the Board decided not to provide special accounting based on the creation of synthetic instruments. The Board recognizes, however, that basis swaps can provide offsetting cash flows when they are used to hedge a combined asset-liability position in which the asset and liability have different rate bases. For that reason, this Statement provides an exception for a basis swap that is highly effective as a link between an asset (or group of similar assets) with variable cash flows and a liability (or a group of similar liabilities) with variable cash flows.

394. Some respondents to the Task Force Draft objected to what they saw as stricter requirements for a basis swap to qualify for hedge accounting than for other derivatives. They noted that to qualify for hedge accounting, other strategies need not link an asset and a liability. The Board notes that the requirement that a basis swap link the cash flows of an asset and a liability is necessary for a basis swap to qualify under the general criterion that a derivative must provide offsetting cash flows to an exposure to qualify for cash flow hedge accounting. That is, one leg of the basis swap that links an asset and a liability will provide offsetting cash flows for the asset, and the other leg will provide offsetting cash flows for the liability. Thus, the criteria for basis swaps are essentially the same as—not stricter than—the criteria for other strategies to qualify for hedge accounting.

395. To ensure that a basis swap does, in fact, result in offsetting cash flows, this Statement also requires that the basis of one leg of the swap be the same as the basis of the identified asset and that the basis of the other leg of the swap be the same as the basis of the identified liability. Some respondents to the Task Force Draft suggested that the only requirement should be that one leg of the basis swap be highly effective in offsetting the variable cash flows of the asset and the other leg be highly effective in offsetting the variable cash flows of the liability. The Board noted that such a provision could have an additive effect if neither leg is entirely effective. The sum of the two amounts of ineffectiveness might not satisfy the effectiveness test that other derivatives must meet to qualify for hedge accounting. The Board therefore decided to retain the requirement that the basis of one leg of the basis swap be the same as that of a recognized asset and that the basis of the other leg be the same as that of a recognized liability. Section 2 of Appendix A provides an example of assessing the effectiveness of a hedge with a basis swap.

Written options

396. A written option exposes its writer to the possibility of unlimited loss but limits the gain to the amount of premium received. The Board is concerned about permitting written options to be designated as hedging instruments because a written option serves only to reduce the potential for gain in the

hedged item or hedged transaction. It leaves the potential for loss on the hedged item or hedged transaction unchanged except for the amount of premium received on the written option. Consequently, on a net basis, an entity may be worse off as a result of trying to hedge with a written option. Because of those concerns, the Exposure Draft proposed prohibiting a written option from being eligible for designation as a hedging instrument.

397. Respondents to the Exposure Draft objected to categorically prohibiting written options from being designated as hedging instruments. A number of respondents specifically referred to the use of a written option to hedge the call option feature in a debt instrument. They explained that it may be more cost-effective to issue fixed-rate, callable debt and simultaneously enter into a receive-fixed, pay-variable interest rate swap with an embedded written call option than to directly issue variable-rate, noncallable debt. The Board agreed that hedge accounting should be available for that use of written options. Consequently, this Statement permits designation of a written option as hedging the purchased option embedded in a financial instrument. The Board notes that if the option features in both instruments are exactly opposite, any gains or losses on the two options generally will offset. Section 2 of Appendix A includes an example illustrating such a strategy.

398. The requirements in this Statement for hedge accounting for strategies that use written options are based on symmetry of the gain and loss potential of the combined hedged position. To qualify for hedge accounting, either the upside and downside potential of the net position must be symmetrical or the upside potential must be greater than the downside potential. That is, the combination of the hedged item and the written option must result in a position that provides at least as much potential for gains (or favorable cash flows) as exposure to losses (or unfavorable cash flows). Evaluation of the combined position's relative potential for gains and losses is based on the effect of a favorable or unfavorable change in price of a given percentage. For example, a 25 percent favorable change in the fair value of the hedged item must provide a gain on the combined position that is at least as large as the loss on that combined position that would result from a 25 percent unfavorable change in the fair value of the hedged item.

399. This Statement does not permit hedge accounting for "covered call" strategies—strategies in which an entity writes an option on an asset that it owns (unless that asset is a call option that is embedded in another instrument). In that strategy, any loss on the written option will be covered by the gain on the owned asset. However, a covered call strategy will not qualify for hedge accounting because the risk profile of the combined position is asymmetrical (the exposure to losses is greater than the potential for gains). In contrast, the risk profile of the asset alone is "symmetrical or better" (the potential for gains is at least as great as the exposure to losses).

400. The symmetry requirement for hedges with written options described in paragraph 398 is intended to preclude a written option that is used to sell a portion of the gain potential on an asset or liability from being eligible for hedge accounting. For example, assume that an entity has an investment in equity securities that have a current fair value of $150 per share. To sell some, but not all, of the upside potential of those securities, the entity writes a call option contract to sell the securities for $150 per share and purchases a call option contract to buy the same securities at $160 per share. On a net basis, the entity still has *unlimited* upside potential because there are infinite possible outcomes above $160 per share, but its downside risk is limited to $150 per share. Without the requirement to compare increases and decreases of comparable percentages, an entity could assert that its written option strategy warrants hedge accounting because, after entering into the written and purchased option contracts, there is still more potential for gains than for losses from its combined position in the equity securities and option contracts. The Board decided that hedge accounting should not be available for a transaction that merely "sells" part of the potential for gain from an existing asset.

401. This Statement does not require that a written option be entered into at the same time the hedged item is issued or acquired because the combined position is the same regardless of when the position originated (assuming, of course, that the price of the hedged item is the same as the underlying for the option at the time the hedge is entered into). In addition, the Board decided not to limit the items that may be hedged with written options to financial instruments. The Board decided that this Statement's provisions for hedging with written options should accommodate similar risk management strategies regardless of the nature of the asset or liability that is the hedged item.

*Exposures to Changes in Fair Value or Cash
Flows That Could Affect Reported Earnings*

402. This Statement requires that a hedged item or
hedged forecasted transaction embody an exposure
to changes in fair value or variations in cash flow, for
the risk being hedged, that could affect reported earnings. That is, a change in the fair value of a hedged
item or variation in the cash flow of a hedged forecasted transaction attributable to the risk being
hedged must have the potential to change the amount
that could be recognized in earnings. For example,
the future sale of an asset or settlement of a liability
that exposes an entity to the risk of a change in fair
value may result in recognizing a gain or loss in earnings when the sale or settlement occurs. Changes in
market price could change the amount for which the
asset or liability could be sold or settled and, consequently, change the amount of gain or loss recognized. Forecasted transactions that expose an entity
to cash flow risk have the potential to affect reported
earnings because the amount of related revenue or
expense may differ depending on the price eventually
paid or received. Thus, an entity could designate the
forecasted sale of a product at the market price at the
date of sale as a hedged transaction because revenue
will be recorded at that future sales price.

403. Some respondents to the Exposure Draft asked
the Board to permit some transactions that create an
exposure to variability in cash flows to qualify as
hedgeable transactions even though they could not
affect reported earnings. They asserted that hedges of
those transactions successfully reduce an entity's
cash flow exposure. The Board decided to retain the
criterion of an earnings exposure because the objective of hedge accounting is to allow the gain or loss
on a hedging instrument and the loss or gain on a designated hedged item or transaction to be recognized
in earnings at the same time. Moreover, without an
earnings exposure, there would be no way to determine the period in which the derivative gain or loss
should be included in earnings to comply with this
Statement.

404. The earnings exposure criterion specifically
precludes hedge accounting for derivatives used to
hedge (a) transactions with stockholders as stockholders, such as projected purchases of treasury stock
or payments of dividends, (b) intercompany transactions (except for foreign-currency-denominated forecasted intercompany transactions, which are discussed in paragraphs 482–487) between entities
included in consolidated financial statements, and

(c) the price of stock expected to be issued pursuant
to a stock option plan for which recognized compensation expense is not based on changes in stock
prices after the date of grant. However, intercompany
transactions may present an earnings exposure for a
subsidiary in its freestanding financial statements; a
hedge of an intercompany transaction would be eligible for hedge accounting for purposes of those
statements.

*The Hedged Item or Transaction Is Not
Remeasured through Earnings for
the Hedged Risk*

405. Special hedge accounting is not necessary if
both the hedged item and the hedging instrument are
measured at fair value with changes in fair value reported in earnings as they occur because offsetting
gains and losses will be recognized in earnings together. The Board therefore decided to specifically
prohibit hedge accounting if the related asset or liability is, or will be, measured at fair value, with
changes in fair value reported in earnings when they
occur. That prohibition results from the Board's belief that a standard on hedge accounting should not
provide the opportunity to change the accounting for
an asset or liability that would otherwise be reported
at fair value with changes in fair value reported in
earnings. Thus, for a fair value hedge, the prohibition
is intended to prevent an entity from recognizing
only the change in fair value of the hedged item attributable to the risk being hedged rather than its entire change in fair value. For a cash flow hedge, the
prohibition is intended to prevent an entity from reflecting a derivative's gain or loss in accumulated
other comprehensive income when the related asset
or liability will be measured at fair value upon acquisition or incurrence.

406. The Exposure Draft would have excluded from
its scope all of the assets and liabilities of an entity
that follows specialized industry practice under
which it measures substantially all of its assets at fair
value and recognizes changes in those fair values in
earnings. That exclusion was aimed at preventing
those entities from avoiding fair value accounting.
Respondents to the Exposure Draft noted that exclusion also would have prohibited those entities from
applying hedge accounting to hedged assets or liabilities that are not measured at fair value, such as
long-term debt. The Board decided to remove the exclusion and instead focus on assets and liabilities
that are reported at fair value because that approach
would (a) be consistent with the notion that

eligibility for hedge accounting should be based on the criteria in this Statement, (b) provide consistent fair value accounting for all derivatives, and (c) be responsive to the concerns of constituents.

407. The criteria in this Statement also preclude hedge accounting for an asset or a liability that is remeasured for changes in price attributable to the risk being hedged, with those changes in value reported currently in earnings. The criteria therefore preclude fair value or cash flow hedge accounting for foreign currency risk associated with any asset or liability that is denominated in a foreign currency and remeasured into the functional currency under Statement 52. The Board believes that special accounting is neither appropriate nor necessary in that situation because the transaction gain or loss on the foreign-currency-denominated asset or liability will be reported in earnings along with the gain or loss on the undesignated derivative. The criteria also preclude a cash flow hedge of the forecasted acquisition or incurrence of an item that will be denominated in a foreign currency and remeasured into the functional currency each period after acquisition or incurrence. However, the criteria do not preclude a cash flow hedge of the foreign currency exposure associated with the forecasted purchase of a nonmonetary item for a foreign currency, even if the purchase will be on credit, because nonmonetary items are not subsequently remeasured into an entity's functional currency. Nor do the criteria preclude hedging the forecasted sale of a nonmonetary asset for a foreign currency, even if the sale will be on credit.

Risks That May Be Designated as Being Hedged

408. The Board recognizes that entities are commonly exposed to a variety of risks in the course of their activities, including interest rate, foreign exchange, market price, credit, liquidity, theft, weather, health, catastrophe, competitive, and business cycle risks. The Exposure Draft did not propose detailed guidance on what risks could be designated as being hedged, other than to note in the basis for conclusions that special hedge accounting for certain risk management transactions, such as hedges of strategic risk, would be precluded. In redeliberating the issue of risk, the Board reaffirmed that hedge accounting cannot be provided for all possible risks and decided to be more specific about the risks for which hedge accounting is available.

409. Because this Statement, unlike the Exposure Draft, bases the accounting for a hedged item in a fair value hedge on changes in fair value attributable to the risk being hedged, the Board decided that it needed to limit the types of risks that could be designated as being hedged. The absence of limits could make meaningless the notion of hedge effectiveness by ignoring the consequence of basis or other differences between the hedged item or transaction and the hedging instrument in assessing the initial and continuing qualification for hedge accounting.

410. For example, an entity using a LIBOR-based interest rate futures contract as a hedge of a prime-based asset might assert that the risk being hedged is the fair value exposure of the prime-based asset to changes in LIBOR. Because that designation would ignore the basis difference between the prime-based hedged asset and the LIBOR-based derivative hedging instrument, it could result in asserted "automatic" compliance with the effectiveness criterion. That type of designation might also lead an entity to assert that the amount of the change in the hedged item's fair value attributable to the hedged risk corresponds to the change in the fair value of the hedging derivative and, therefore, to erroneously conclude that the derivative's change in fair value could be used as a surrogate for changes in the fair value of the hedged item attributable to the hedged risk. Such a designation also would remove any possibility that actual ineffectiveness of a hedge would be measured and reflected in earnings in the period in which it occurs.

Financial assets and liabilities

411. For financial instruments, this Statement specifies that hedge accounting is permitted for hedges of changes in fair value or variability of future cash flows that result from changes in four types of risk. As indicated in paragraph 21(f), those four risks also apply to fair value hedges of firm commitments with financial components.

a. *Market price risk.* A fair value hedge focuses on the exposure to changes in the fair value of the entire hedged item. The definition of *fair value* requires that the fair value of a hedged item be based on a quoted market price in an active market, if available. Similarly, a cash flow hedge focuses on variations in cash flows, for example, the cash flows stemming from the purchase or sale of an asset, which obviously are affected by changes in the market price of the item. The Board therefore concluded that the market price risk of the entire hedged item (that is, the risk of changes in the fair value of the entire hedged item) should be eligible for designation as the hedged risk in a fair value hedge. Likewise, variable cash flows stemming from changes in the market price of the entire item are eligible for designation as the hedged risk in a cash flow hedge.

b. *Market interest rate risk.* For financial assets and liabilities, changes in market interest rates may affect the right to receive (or obligation to pay or transfer) cash or other financial instruments in the future or the fair value of that right (or obligation). The time value of money is a broadly accepted concept that is incorporated in generally accepted accounting principles (for example, in APB Opinion No. 21, *Interest on Receivables and Payables,* and FASB Statement No. 91, *Accounting for Nonrefundable Fees and Costs Associated with Originating or Acquiring Loans and Initial Direct Costs of Leases*). Because the marketplace has developed techniques to delineate and extract interest rate risk from financial instruments, the Board decided that the risk that changes in market interest rates will affect the fair value or cash flows of the hedged item warrants being identified as a risk that may be designated as being hedged.

c. *Foreign exchange risk.* The fair value (expressed in the entity's functional currency) of an asset such as a foreign debt or equity security that is classified as available for sale, as well as the fair value of the financial component of a firm commitment that is denominated in a currency other than the entity's functional currency, generally is exposed to changes in foreign exchange rates. Similarly, the cash flows of a forecasted transaction generally are exposed to changes in foreign exchange rates if the transaction will be denominated in a foreign currency. Statement 52 specifies special accounting for reflecting the effects of changes in foreign exchange rates, and this Statement continues much of that accounting. The Board therefore decided that the risk of changes in foreign exchange rates on the fair value of certain hedged items and on the cash flows of hedged transactions warrants being identified as a risk that may be designated as being hedged.

d. *Default (credit) risk.* A financial asset embodies a right to receive cash or another financial instrument from a counterparty. A financial asset thus embodies a risk that the counterparty will fail to perform according to the terms of the contract; that risk generally is referred to as credit risk. Because that risk affects the fair value of a financial asset, as well as the related cash flows, the Board

decided that the risk of the counterparty's default on its obligation is a risk that may be designated as being hedged.

Focusing on those four risks is consistent with the belief that the largest amount of present hedging activity is aimed at protecting against market price, credit, foreign exchange, or interest rate risk. Those also were the risks generally accommodated by special hedge accounting before this Statement. Focusing on those four risks also is consistent with responses to the Exposure Draft. Although the notice for recipients did not ask respondents to comment on the type of risks that should be eligible for hedge accounting, respondents generally discussed hedging transactions in terms of those four risks.

412. This Statement also focuses on those four specified risks because a change in the price associated with one of those risks ordinarily will directly affect the fair value of an asset or liability or the cash flows of a future transaction in a determinable or predictable manner. Price changes associated with other risks may not be as direct. For example, price changes associated with "strategic risk" exposures do not have a direct impact on the fair value of a hedged item or cash flow of a forecasted transaction and thus may not be designated as the risk being hedged. Strategic hedges are described in paragraph 231.

413. This Statement does not permit designating a subcomponent of market price, market interest rate, foreign exchange, or credit risk as the risk being hedged. However, some of those subcomponents may be embodied in a separable portion of a financial instrument. For example, prepayment risk is a subcomponent of market interest rate risk, but the prepayment risk in a financial asset stems from the embedded written call option. An entity may hedge prepayment risk by separately designating a hedge of the embedded call option. Even though this Statement does not require an embedded prepayment option to be accounted for separately because it is deemed to be clearly and closely related to the host contract, that embedded call option still is a derivative. Because this Statement does not permit a compound derivative to be separated into risk components for hedge accounting purposes, only the market price risk of the entire option qualifies as the hedged risk. Hedge effectiveness therefore must be measured based on changes in the fair value of the option.

414. Measuring the effectiveness of a fair value hedge requires determining whether a gain or loss on

a hedging derivative offsets the loss or gain in the value of the hedged item that is attributable to the risk being hedged. Once the change in the value of a hedged item attributable to a particular risk has been offset by the change in value of a hedging derivative, a second, identical derivative cannot also be an effective hedge of that same risk. Similarly, an embedded derivative in a hedged item will modify the nature of the risk to which that item is exposed. Thus, all embedded derivatives relating to the same risk class (that is, market prices, market interest rates, foreign exchange rates, or credit) in a hedged item must be considered together in assessing the effectiveness of an additional (freestanding) derivative as the hedging instrument.

415. For example, an entity might enter into a firm commitment to purchase an asset for 1,000,000 Deutsche marks (DM), with a provision that caps the U.S. dollar equivalent price at $600,000. A hedge of the foreign currency risk in that commitment cannot be effective unless it takes into account the effect of the cap. Similarly, a hedge of the effect on the holder of changes in market interest rates on the unconditional receivable component of a prepayable bond cannot ignore the effect of the embedded prepayment option. To disregard the effects of embedded derivatives related to the same risk class could result in a designated hedge that is not effective at achieving offsetting changes in fair value attributable to the risk being hedged.

Nonfinancial assets and liabilities

416. The Board decided to limit fair value and cash flow hedge accounting for hedges of nonfinancial assets and liabilities (other than recognized loan servicing rights and nonfinancial firm commitments with financial components) to hedges of the risk of changes in the market price of the *entire* hedged item in a fair value hedge or the *entire* asset to be acquired or sold in a hedged forecasted transaction, with one exception. The risk of changes in the functional-currency-equivalent cash flows attributable to changes in foreign exchange rates may be separately hedged in a cash flow hedge of the forecasted purchase or sale of a nonfinancial item. The Board decided not to permit the market price risk of only a principal ingredient or other component of a nonfinancial hedged item to be designated as the risk being hedged because changes in the price of an ingredient or component of a nonfinancial item generally do not have a predictable, separately measurable effect on the price of the item that is comparable to the effect of, say, a change in market interest rates on the price of a bond.

417. For example, if an entity wishes to enter into a cash flow hedge of the variability in cash inflows from selling tires, the market price risk of rubber alone could not be designated as the risk being hedged. There is no mechanism in the market for tires to directly relate the amount or quality of rubber in a tire to the price of the tire. Similarly, if a derivative is used in a fair value hedge to hedge the exposure to changes in the fair value of tires held in inventory, the entity could not designate the market price of rubber as the hedged risk even though rubber is a component of the tires. The fair value of the tire inventory is based on the market price of tires, not rubber, even though the price of rubber may have an effect on the fair value of the tires. Permitting an entity to designate the market price of rubber as the risk being hedged would ignore other components of the price of the tires, such as steel and labor. It also could result in automatic compliance with the effectiveness test even though the price of rubber may not be highly correlated with the market price of tires. As discussed in the effectiveness examples in Section 2 of Appendix A, the use of a rubber-based derivative as a fair value hedge of the tire inventory or a cash flow hedge of its sale or purchase may qualify for hedge accounting. To do so, however, the entire change in the fair value of the derivative and the entire change in the fair value of the hedged item must be expected to be highly effective at offsetting each other, and all of the remaining hedge criteria must be met. Any ineffectiveness must be included currently in earnings.

418. Some respondents to the Task Force Draft objected to this Statement's different provisions about risks that may be hedged in financial versus nonfinancial items. They asserted that an entity also should be permitted to separate a nonfinancial item into its principal components for hedge accounting purposes. The Board considers those differing requirements to be an appropriate consequence of the nature of the items being hedged.

419. For example, the effect of changes in market interest rates qualifies for designation as the hedged risk in a financial item but not in a nonfinancial item. An increase in market interest rates will result in a decrease in the fair value of a fixed-rate financial asset because the market rate of interest directly affects the present value computation of the item's future cash

flows. Similarly, an increase in market interest rates will result in an increase in the cash flows of a variable-rate financial asset. For both fixed- and variable-rate financial assets, the effect of a change in market interest rates is not only direct but also predictable and separately determinable. For instance, holding factors like credit risk constant, it is relatively easy to calculate the effect of a 100-basis-point increase in market interest rates on the market price of a fixed-rate bond with a specified interest rate and specified time to maturity. It is even easier to determine the effect of a 100-basis-point increase in interest rates on the cash flows stemming from a variable-rate bond. In contrast, although an increase of 100 basis points in market interest rates may affect the market price of a residential building, techniques do not currently exist to isolate and predict that effect.

420. The effect of changes in interest rates on the market price of residential real estate is much less direct than the effect of interest rate changes on financial items. Interest rates may indirectly affect the market price of a single-family house because of the effect of a change in market interest rates on consumer buying behavior or rental rates. For example, an increase in market interest rates may lead to decreased consumer demand for real estate mortgage loans and, in turn, for real estate purchases. Enticing consumers to purchase real estate in a higher interest-rate environment may necessitate lower prices. However, a myriad of other factors may affect the price of residential real estate, and any effect of interest rates is not predictable, immediate, or subject to isolation.

421. Unlike a change in market interest rates, it may be possible to isolate the effect of a change in foreign exchange rates on the functional currency cash flows stemming from a nonfinancial item. For example, an entity with a U.S. dollar functional currency owns residential real estate located in France with a market price of FF5,000,000. If the price of residential real estate in France and the U.S. dollar–French franc exchange rate are not correlated, an increase of $0.01 in the value of the franc will increase the U.S. dollar equivalent of the sales price of the real estate by $50,000 (FF5,000,000 × 0.01). This Statement thus permits the effect of changes in foreign exchange rates to be designated as the hedged risk in a cash flow hedge of a forecasted transaction involving a nonfinancial item.

Simultaneous Hedges of Fair Value and Cash Flow Exposures

422. The Exposure Draft would have prohibited the simultaneous designation of an asset or liability as a fair value hedged item and that asset's or liability's cash flows as a hedged forecasted transaction. The Board had previously concluded that, in certain circumstances, if an entity were permitted to apply hedge accounting at the same time for hedges of both the fair value and the cash flow variability of a single item, the results would be questionable because the entity may be hedging some (if not all) of the same cash flows twice. For example, simultaneous hedging of both the fair value of 1,000 barrels of existing crude oil inventory in a fair value hedge and the forecasted sale of refined oil from those 1,000 barrels of oil in a cash flow hedge would change the nature of the entity's exposure to oil price movements. The two hedges would take the entity from a net long position to a net short position; together they would not necessarily neutralize risk.

423. The Board decided to remove the restriction on simultaneous fair value and cash flow hedges. That change was made, in part, because of the change to base both the assessment of hedge effectiveness and hedge accounting on the change in fair value or cash flows attributable to the risk being hedged. The Board believes this Statement can accommodate simultaneous fair value and cash flow hedging in certain situations if different risk exposures are being hedged because hedge accounting in this Statement accounts for each risk exposure separately. For example, an entity might designate both a cash flow hedge of the interest rate risk associated with a variable-rate financial asset and a fair value hedge of the credit risk on that asset.

424. Removing the restriction on simultaneous fair value and cash flow hedges is not, however, intended to permit simultaneous hedges of the same risk, such as credit risk or market price risk, with both a fair value hedge and a cash flow hedge. For example, the Board does not consider the simultaneous hedge of the fair value of crude oil and the cash flows from selling a product made from that oil described in paragraph 422 to be consistent with the requirements of this Statement because the crude oil and the refined product do not present separate earnings exposures. The entity cannot sell both the crude oil and a refined product made from the same oil—it can only do one or the other. Regardless of how it intends to

use the crude oil, the entity can choose to hedge its exposure to changes in the price of a specific amount of crude oil as either a fair value exposure or a cash flow exposure, but not as both.

425. Some respondents to the Exposure Draft opposed the prohibition on simultaneous hedges because it would preclude swapping foreign-currency-denominated variable-rate debt to U.S. dollar fixed-rate debt. That strategy was not eligible for hedge accounting under the Exposure Draft because the variable interest rate exposure is a cash flow exposure and the foreign currency exposure was deemed to be a fair value exposure. Even though this Statement no longer includes a restriction on simultaneous hedges, the foreign currency aspect of that strategy is not hedgeable under this Statement because the debt will be remeasured into the entity's functional currency under Statement 52, with the related transaction gain or loss reported in earnings. An entity might, however, be able to achieve income statement results similar to hedge accounting using separate interest rate and foreign currency derivatives and designating only the interest rate derivative as a hedging instrument. Income statement offset would be achieved for the foreign currency aspect because the change in fair value of the undesignated foreign currency derivatives will flow through earnings along with the remeasurement of the debt into the functional currency.

Prohibition against Hedge Accounting for Hedges of Interest Rate Risk of Debt Securities Classified as Held-to-Maturity

426. This Statement prohibits hedge accounting for a fair value or cash flow hedge of the interest rate risk associated with a debt security classified as held-to-maturity pursuant to Statement 115. During the deliberations that preceded issuance of Statement 115, the Board considered whether such a debt security could be designated as being hedged for hedge accounting purposes. Although the Board's view at that time was that hedging debt securities classified as held-to-maturity is inconsistent with the basis for that classification, Statement 115 did not restrict hedge accounting of those securities because constituents argued that the appropriateness of such restrictions should be considered in the Board's project on hedging.

427. The Exposure Draft proposed prohibiting a held-to-maturity debt security from being designated as a hedged item, regardless of the risk being hedged.

The Exposure Draft explained the Board's belief that designating a derivative as a hedge of the changes in fair value, or variations in cash flow, of a debt security that is classified as held-to-maturity contradicts the notion of that classification. Respondents to the Exposure Draft objected to the proposed exclusion, asserting the following: (a) hedging a held-to-maturity security does not conflict with an asserted intent to hold that security to maturity, (b) a held-to-maturity security contributes to interest rate risk if it is funded with shorter term liabilities, and (c) prohibiting hedge accounting for a hedge of a held-to-maturity security is inconsistent with permitting hedge accounting for other fixed-rate assets and liabilities that are being held to maturity.

428. The Board continues to believe that providing hedge accounting for a held-to-maturity security conflicts with the notion underlying the held-to-maturity classification in Statement 115 if the risk being hedged is the risk of changes in the fair value of the entire hedged item or is otherwise related to interest rate risk. The Board believes an entity's decision to classify a security as held-to-maturity implies that future decisions about continuing to hold that security will not be affected by changes in market interest rates. The decision to classify a security as held-to-maturity is consistent with the view that a change in fair value or cash flow stemming from a change in market interest rates is not relevant for that security. In addition, fair value hedge accounting effectively alters the traditional income recognition pattern for that debt security by accelerating gains and losses on the security during the term of the hedge into earnings, with subsequent amortization of the related premium or discount over the period until maturity. That accounting changes the measurement attribute of the security away from amortized historical cost. The Board also notes that the rollover of a shorter term liability that funds a held-to-maturity security may be eligible for hedge accounting. The Board therefore decided to prohibit both a fixed-rate held-to-maturity debt security from being designated as a hedged item in a fair value hedge and the variable interest receipts on a variable-rate held-to-maturity security from being designated as hedged forecasted transactions in a cash flow hedge if the risk being hedged includes changes in market interest rates.

429. The Board does not consider it inconsistent to prohibit hedge accounting for a hedge of market interest rate risk in a held-to-maturity debt security while permitting it for hedges of other items that an

entity may be holding to maturity. Only held-to-maturity debt securities receive special accounting (that is, being measured at amortized cost when they otherwise would be required to be measured at fair value) as a result of an asserted intent to hold them to maturity.

430. The Board modified the Exposure Draft to permit hedge accounting for hedges of credit risk on held-to-maturity debt securities. It decided that hedging the credit risk of a held-to-maturity debt security is not inconsistent with Statement 115 because that Statement allows a sale or transfer of a held-to-maturity debt security in response to a significant deterioration in credit quality.

431. Some respondents to the Task Force Draft said that a hedge of the prepayment risk in a held-to-maturity debt security should be permitted because it does not contradict the entity's stated intention to hold the instrument to maturity. The Board agreed that in designating a security as held-to-maturity, an entity declares its intention not to voluntarily sell the security as a result of changes in market interest rates, and "selling" a security in response to the exercise of a call option is not a voluntary sale. Accordingly, the Board decided to permit designating the embedded written prepayment option in a held-to-maturity security as the hedged item. Although prepayment risk is a subcomponent of market interest rate risk, the Board notes that prepayments, especially of mortgages, occur for reasons other than changes in interest rates. The Board therefore does not consider it inconsistent to permit hedging of prepayment risk but not interest rate risk in a held-to-maturity security.

Additional Qualifying Criteria for Fair Value Hedges

Specific Identification

432. This Statement requires specific identification of the hedged item. The hedged item must be (a) an entire recognized asset or liability, or an unrecognized firm commitment, (b) a portfolio of similar assets or similar liabilities, or (c) a specific portion of a recognized asset or liability, unrecognized firm commitment, or portfolio of similar items. If an entity hedges a specified portion of a portfolio of similar assets or similar liabilities, that portion should relate to every item in the portfolio. If an entity wishes to

hedge only certain similar items in a portfolio, it should first identify a smaller portfolio of only the items to be hedged.

433. The Exposure Draft would not have permitted designation of a portion of an asset or a liability as a hedged item. Under the Exposure Draft, those items could only have been hedged in their entirety or on a percentage basis. Some respondents to the Exposure Draft objected to that limitation because it precluded identification of only selected contractual cash flows as the item being hedged (referred to as partial-term hedging for a debt security). For example, it would have prohibited identification of the interest payments for the first two years of a four-year fixed-rate debt instrument as the hedged item and, therefore, would have precluded hedge accounting for a hedge of that debt with a two-year interest rate swap.

434. The Board was reluctant to permit identification of a selected portion (rather than proportion) of an asset or liability as the hedged item because it believes that, in many cases, partial-term hedge transactions would fail to meet the offset requirement. For example, the changes in the fair value of a two-year interest rate swap cannot be expected to offset the changes in fair value attributable to changes in market interest rates of a four-year fixed-rate debt instrument. For offset to be expected, a principal repayment on the debt (equal to the notional amount on the swap) would need to be expected at the end of year two. The Board decided to remove the prohibition against partial-term hedging and other designations of a portion of an asset or liability to be consistent with the modification to the Exposure Draft to require an entity to define how the expectation of offsetting changes in fair value or cash flows would be assessed. However, removal of that criterion does not necessarily result in qualification for hedge accounting for partial-term or other hedges of part of an asset or a liability.

435. The criterion in paragraph 21(a) that permits a hedged item in a fair value hedge to be a designated portion of an asset or liability (or a portfolio of similar assets or similar liabilities) makes the following eligible for designation as a hedged item:

a. A percentage of the entire asset or liability (or of the entire portfolio)
b. One or more selected contractual cash flows (such

as the asset or liability representing the interest payments in the first two years of a four-year debt instrument)[32]

c. A put option, a call option, an interest rate cap, or an interest rate floor embedded in an existing asset or liability that is not an embedded derivative accounted for separately under this Statement

d. The residual value in a lessor's net investment in a direct-financing or sales-type lease.

If the entire asset or liability is a variable-rate instrument, the hedged item cannot be a fixed-to-variable interest rate swap (or similar instrument) perceived to be embedded in a fixed-rate host contract. The Board does not intend for an entity to be able to use the provision that a hedged item may be a portion of an asset or liability to justify hedging a contractual provision that creates variability in future cash flows as a fair value hedge rather than as a cash flow hedge. In addition, all other criteria, including the criterion that requires a hedge to be expected to be highly effective at achieving offset, must still be met for items such as the above to be designated and to qualify for hedge accounting.

436. As discussed in paragraphs 414 and 415, in designating a hedge of a component of an asset or liability, an entity must consider the effect of any derivatives embedded in that asset or liability related to the same risk class. To disregard the effects of an embedded derivative related to the same risk class could result in a designated hedge that is not effective at achieving offsetting changes in fair value or cash flows. The same unacceptable result would occur if a freestanding derivative that was accounted for as hedging a particular item was ignored in considering whether another derivative would qualify as a hedge of the same risk in that item.

Recognized Asset or Liability or Unrecognized Firm Commitment

437. This Statement requires that the item designated as hedged in a fair value hedge be a recognized asset or liability or an unrecognized firm commitment. The Board decided that an unrecognized asset or liability that does not embody a firm commitment should not be eligible for designation as a hedged item because applying fair value hedge accounting to such an unrecognized asset or liability would result in recognizing a portion of it. For example, fair value

hedge accounting for an unrecognized intangible asset, such as an internally generated core deposit intangible, would have the effect of recognizing the change in the present value of the intangible asset. The Board believes a change to require or permit recognition of certain intangible assets or potential liabilities that are not now recognized should be made only after careful consideration of the related conceptual and practical issues rather than being a by-product of hedge accounting.

438. This Statement permits an unrecognized firm commitment, including one that is embodied in an unrecognized asset or liability such as an operating lease with substantial cancellation penalties, to be designated as the hedged item in a fair value hedge. The Board recognizes that permitting certain such firm commitments to be designated as hedged items may be viewed as inconsistent with not permitting other unrecognized assets and liabilities to be hedged items. The Board considered limiting the firm commitments that can be hedged items, for example, to those for which there is no explicit authoritative accounting requirement that precludes recognition of the related asset or liability. However, the Board was unable to identify a specific limitation that would be both workable and equitable. Moreover, the Board notes that a firm commitment as defined in this Statement must have a fixed price and a disincentive for nonperformance sufficiently large to make performance probable (discussed further in paragraphs 440 and 441), which makes hedging a firm commitment less problematic than hedging an unrecognized item such as an internally generated intangible asset. Accordingly, with the limited exceptions discussed in paragraphs 455 and 456, the Board decided to permit all firm commitments as defined in this Statement to qualify as hedged items in fair value hedges.

439. This Statement requires that hedge accounting adjustments to the carrying amount of hedged assets and liabilities be subsequently reported in earnings in the same manner as other adjustments of the carrying amount of the hedged item. For example, gains and losses on an interest-bearing debt instrument that are attributable to interest rate risk generally would be amortized over the life of the instrument as a yield adjustment. For some unrecognized firm commitments, such as a firm commitment to purchase inventory, the nature of the hedged item will clearly

---

[32]However, as noted in paragraph 434, it likely will be difficult to find a derivative that will be effective as a fair value hedge of selected cash flows.

specify a basis for recognizing hedge accounting adjustments in income. For others, such as the operating lease discussed in paragraph 438, there will be no obvious pattern of income recognition for hedge accounting adjustments. This Statement requires that an entity specify as part of its initial hedge designation how hedge accounting adjustments will be subsequently recognized in income. The Board believes that such designation at inception of a hedge is consistent with other provisions in this Statement that prohibit retroactive decisions after the results of a hedge are known.

Definition of a firm commitment

440. Because this Statement provides fair value hedge accounting for hedges of unrecognized firm commitments, a definition of *firm commitment* is necessary. For purposes of this Statement, a firm commitment is defined as:

> An agreement with an unrelated party, binding on both parties and usually legally enforceable, with the following characteristics:
>
> a. The agreement specifies all significant terms, including the quantity to be exchanged, the fixed price, and the timing of the transaction. The fixed price may be expressed as a specified amount of an entity's functional currency or of a foreign currency. It also may be expressed as a specified interest rate or specified effective yield.
> b. The agreement includes a disincentive for nonperformance that is sufficiently large to make performance probable.

That definition is based on the definition of a firm commitment in Statements 52 and 80.

441. Some respondents to the Exposure Draft focused more on the "probability" aspect of the definition than on the requirements that the agreement be binding on both parties and that it specify the significant terms of the transaction, including the price. For example, some respondents wanted to treat as a firm commitment for hedge accounting purposes a group of contracts that are binding on one party but not on the other. They said that if the entity is a party to a sufficient number of those contracts, sufficient evidence would be available to permit a reasonable estimate of the number of transactions that would be

consummated under the agreements. The Board notes that an agreement that is binding on one party but not on the other is an option rather than a firm commitment. In developing hedge accounting requirements, the Board believes that the fundamental nature of a financial instrument should not be ignored.

442. The definition of a firm commitment in this Statement requires that the fixed price be specified in terms of a currency (or an interest rate) rather than an index or in terms of the price or a number of units of an asset other than a currency, such as ounces of gold. A price that varies with the market price of the item that is the subject of the firm commitment cannot qualify as a "fixed" price. For example, a price that is specified in terms of ounces of gold would not be a fixed price if the market price of the item to be purchased or sold under the firm commitment varied with the price of gold. To avoid such a situation, the Board decided that it was necessary to require that the fixed price in a firm commitment be specified in terms of a currency or a rate. A similar situation can exist for a firm commitment that is denominated in a foreign currency if the price of the item to be purchased or sold varies with changes in exchange rates. The Board accepted that possibility because it had been accepted under Statement 52, and it did not want to undertake a complete reconsideration of the hedging provisions of that Statement at this time. Therefore, the price may be specified in any currency—it need not be in the entity's functional currency.

Single Asset or Liability or a Portfolio of Similar Assets or Similar Liabilities

443. This Statement retains the provision from the Exposure Draft that prohibits a portfolio of dissimilar items from being designated as a hedged item. Many respondents said that hedge accounting should be extended to hedges of portfolios of dissimilar items (often called *macro hedges*) because macro hedging is an effective and efficient way to manage risk. To qualify for designation as a hedged item on an aggregate rather than individual basis, the Exposure Draft would have required that individual items in a portfolio of similar assets or liabilities be expected to respond to changes in a market variable in an equivalent way. The Exposure Draft also included a list of specific characteristics to be considered in determining whether items were sufficiently similar to qualify for hedging as a portfolio. Respondents said that, taken together, the list of characteristics and the

"equivalent way" requirement would have meant that individual items could qualify as "similar" only if they were virtually identical.

444. To deal with the concerns of respondents, the Board modified the Exposure Draft in two ways. First, the Board deleted the requirement that the value of all items in a portfolio respond in an equivalent way to changes in a market variable. Instead, this Statement requires that the items in a portfolio share the risk exposure for which they are designated as being hedged and that the fair values of individual items attributable to the hedged risk be expected to respond proportionately to the total change in fair value of the hedged portfolio. The Board intends *proportionately* to be interpreted strictly, but the term does not mean *identically*. For example, a group of assets would not be considered to respond proportionately to a change in interest rates if a 100-basis-point increase in interest rates is expected to result in percentage decreases in the fair values of the individual items ranging from 7 percent to 13 percent. However, percentage decreases within a range of 9 percent to 11 percent could be considered proportionate if that change in interest rates reduced the fair value of the portfolio by 10 percent.

445. The second way in which the Board modified the Exposure Draft was to delete the requirement to consider all specified risk characteristics of the items in a portfolio. The Board considered completely deleting the list of risk characteristics included in the Exposure Draft, and the Task Force Draft did not include that list. However, respondents to that draft asked for additional guidance on how to determine whether individual assets or liabilities qualify as "similar." In response to those requests, the Board decided to reinstate the list of characteristics from the Exposure Draft. The Board intends the list to be only an indication of factors that an entity may find helpful.

446. Those two changes are consistent with other changes to the Exposure Draft to focus on the risk being hedged and to rely on management to define how effectiveness will be assessed. It is the responsibility of management to appropriately assess the similarity of hedged items and to determine whether the derivative and a group of hedged items will be highly effective at achieving offset. Those changes to the Exposure Draft do not, however, permit aggregation of dissimilar items. Although the Board recognizes that certain entities are increasingly disposed toward managing specific risks within portfolios of

assets and liabilities, it decided to retain the prohibition of hedge accounting for a hedge of a portfolio of dissimilar items for the reasons discussed in the following paragraphs.

447. Hedge accounting adjustments that result from application of this Statement must be allocated to individual items in a hedged portfolio to determine the carrying amount of an individual item in various circumstances, including (a) upon sale or settlement of the item (to compute the gain or loss), (b) upon discontinuance of a hedging relationship (to determine the new carrying amount that will be the basis for subsequent accounting), and (c) when other generally accepted accounting principles require assessing that item for impairment. The Board decided that a hedge accounting approach that adjusts the basis of the hedged item could not accommodate a portfolio of dissimilar items (macro hedging) because of the difficulties of allocating hedge accounting adjustments to dissimilar hedged items. It would be difficult, if not impossible, to allocate derivative gains and losses to a group of items if their values respond differently (both in direction and in amount) to a change in the risk being hedged, such as market interest rate risk. For example, some components of a portfolio of dissimilar items may increase in value while other components decrease in value as a result of a given price change. Those allocation difficulties are exacerbated if the items to be hedged represent different exposures, that is, a fair value risk and a cash flow risk, because a single exposure to risk must be chosen to provide a basis on which to allocate a net amount to multiple hedged items.

448. The Board considered alternative approaches that would require amortizing the hedge accounting adjustments to earnings based on the average holding period, average maturity or duration of the items in the hedged portfolio, or in some other manner that would not allocate adjustments to the individual items in the hedged portfolio. The Board rejected those approaches because determining the carrying amount for an individual item when it is (a) impaired or (b) sold, settled, or otherwise removed from the hedged portfolio would ignore its related hedge accounting adjustment, if any. Additionally, it was not clear how those approaches would work for certain portfolios, such as a portfolio of equity securities.

449. Advocates of macro hedging generally believe that it is a more effective and efficient way of managing an entity's risk than hedging on an individual-item basis. Macro hedging seems to imply a notion

of entity-wide risk reduction. The Board also believes that permitting hedge accounting for a portfolio of dissimilar items would be appropriate only if risk were required to be assessed on an entity-wide basis. As discussed in paragraph 357, the Board decided not to include entity-wide risk reduction as a criterion for hedge accounting.

450. Although this Statement does not accommodate designating a portfolio of dissimilar items as a hedged item, the Board believes that its requirements are consistent with (a) the hedge accounting guidance that was in Statements 52 and 80, (b) what the Board generally understands to have been current practice in accounting for hedges not addressed by those Statements, and (c) what has been required by the SEC staff. The Board's ultimate goal of requiring that all financial instruments be measured at fair value when the conceptual and measurement issues are resolved would better accommodate risk management for those items on a portfolio basis. Measuring all financial instruments at fair value with all gains or losses recognized in earnings would, without accounting complexity, faithfully represent the results of operations of entities using sophisticated risk management techniques for hedging on a portfolio basis.

*Items the Exposure Draft Prohibited from
Designation as Hedged Items in
Fair Value Hedges*

451. The Exposure Draft proposed to prohibit the following from being designated as a hedged item in a fair value hedge:

a. Oil or gas that has not yet been produced, unmined mineral ore, an agricultural product in process of growing, and similar items
b. An intangible asset
c. An investment accounted for by the equity method
d. Mortgage servicing rights not recognized as assets in accordance with FASB Statement No. 122, *Accounting for Mortgage Servicing Rights*
e. A lease, as defined in FASB Statement No. 13, *Accounting for Leases*
f. A liability for insurance contracts written, as defined and discussed in FASB Statements No. 60, *Accounting and Reporting by Insurance Enterprises,* No. 97, *Accounting and Reporting by Insurance Enterprises for Certain Long-Duration Contracts and for Realized Gains and Losses from the Sale of Investments,* and No. 113, *Accounting and Reporting for Reinsurance of Short-Duration and Long-Duration Contracts,* except for a financial guarantee.

The Board proposed those exclusions, in part, because of concerns about the reliability of available measures of fair values for those items. However, this Statement focuses on changes in the fair value of a hedged item attributable to the risk being hedged, rather than the entire change in the fair value of a hedged item. That shift in focus somewhat mitigated the Board's concerns about determining changes in fair value for those hedged items. The Board agrees with respondents to the Exposure Draft that eligibility for designation as a hedged item should rely on the fair value hedge criteria. Consequently, the Board decided to remove the prohibitions proposed in the Exposure Draft, some of which are discussed further in the following paragraphs. The Board notes, however, that some intangible assets would fail to qualify for hedge accounting because they are neither recognized assets nor firm commitments and would not meet the criterion that requires that the hedged item embody an exposure that could affect reported earnings.

*Oil or gas that has not been produced and
similar items*

452. The Board decided to permit designating as a hedged item in a fair value hedge oil or gas that has not been produced, unmined mineral ore, agricultural products in process of growing, and similar items. In reconsidering whether to specifically prohibit such items from hedge accounting, the Board addressed issues such as (a) whether the costs capitalized to extract, harvest, or mine those items would qualify as a "recognized" asset (one of the criteria for a fair value hedge), (b) whether the amounts recognized for those items bear a close relationship to their fair values, and (c) whether the offset test could ever be met because, for example, extracting and otherwise turning unproduced oil or gas into a salable product would require significant costs. The unproduced oil or gas thus is a different asset from the product upon which a forward sales contract would be based. The Board also considered limiting qualification as a "recognized asset or liability" to those assets and liabilities whose initial recorded amounts represent their fair value at acquisition or incurrence.

453. The Board ultimately decided that hedge accounting qualification for oil or gas that has not been produced, unmined mineral ore, agricultural products in process of growing, and similar items should be

consistent—that is, all of them should be either eligible or ineligible for designation as a hedged item. It decided that such items should be eligible for designation, subject to the other criteria for hedge accounting. However, the Board has significant reservations about how the fair value of such items would be determined and how the effectiveness of a fair value hedge of such items would be assessed. It notes that oil or gas that has not yet been produced, unmined mineral ore, agricultural products in the process of growing, and similar items are not final, salable products. Consequently, a derivative based on a final, salable product has a different basis than the hedged item and may not be highly effective at providing offsetting changes in fair value. It would be more likely that such a derivative would be highly effective at providing offsetting cash flows for the forecasted sale of a product made from oil in the ground, for example. Section 2 of Appendix A provides additional discussion and examples on assessing offset for agricultural products in the process of growing and similar items.

Leases

454. In developing the Exposure Draft, the Board had concerns about the consistency of permitting fair value hedge accounting of a specific risk inherent in a lessor's net investment in a direct financing, sales-type, or leveraged lease (for example, the interest rate risk associated with the minimum lease payments but not the unguaranteed residual value). Under Statement 13, the unguaranteed residual value is viewed simply as a final payment on which income is earned during the lease term. The Board ultimately decided to make all recognized assets and liabilities and unrecognized firm commitments related to leases eligible for designation as hedged items in fair value hedges because it believes that the modification to the Exposure Draft to permit designation of a portion of an item as being hedged would enable a lessor to split out the residual value from its net investment in identifying the hedged item. However, an entity may not designate an operating lease that does not qualify under this Statement's definition of a firm commitment as a hedged item in a fair value hedge because a hedged item must be either a recognized asset or liability or a firm commitment as defined in this Statement.

Investment accounted for by the equity method

455. The Board decided to retain the prohibition in the Exposure Draft from designating an investment

accounted for by the equity method as a hedged item to avoid conflicts with the existing accounting requirements for that item. Providing fair value hedge accounting for an equity method investment conflicts with the notion underlying APB Opinion No. 18, *The Equity Method of Accounting for Investments in Common Stock*. Opinion 18 requires an investor in common stock and corporate joint ventures to apply the equity method of accounting when the investor has the ability to exercise significant influence over the operating and financial policies of the investee. Under the equity method of accounting, the investor generally records its share of the investee's earnings or losses from its investment. It does not account for changes in the price of the common stock, which would become part of the basis of an equity method investment under fair value hedge accounting. Changes in the earnings of an equity method investee presumably would affect the fair value of its common stock. Applying fair value hedge accounting to an equity method investment thus could result in some amount of double counting of the investor's share of the investee's earnings. The Board believes that result would be inappropriate. In addition to those conceptual issues, the Board was concerned that it would be difficult to develop a method of implementing fair value hedge accounting, including measuring hedge ineffectiveness, for equity method investments and that the results of any method would be difficult to understand. For similar reasons, this Statement also prohibits fair value hedge accounting for an unrecognized firm commitment to acquire or dispose of an investment accounted for by the equity method.

Other exclusions

456. For reasons similar to those discussed above, the Board also decided to specifically prohibit designation of (a) a minority interest in one or more consolidated subsidiaries and (b) an equity investment in a consolidated subsidiary as the hedged item in a fair value hedge. Those assets do not qualify for designation as a hedged item in a fair value hedge, and a forecasted transaction to acquire or sell them does not qualify as a hedged transaction in a cash flow hedge. Thus, a firm commitment to acquire or sell one of them also does not qualify as a hedged item in a fair value hedge. For the same reason, a firm commitment to enter into a business combination does not qualify as a hedged item in a fair value hedge.

457. This Statement also specifically prohibits an equity instrument classified by an entity in its stockholders' equity in the statement of financial position

from being designated as a hedged item. That prohibition is consistent with the requirements that (a) a hedged item be a recognized asset or liability and (b) the hedged item present an exposure to changes in fair value that could affect reported earnings. That prohibition does not, of course, apply to the holder of an equity instrument. Paragraph 286 discusses the application of this Statement to obligations (or rights) that may be settled in an entity's own stock but that are indexed to something other than that stock.

Additional Qualifying Criteria for Cash Flow Hedges

Specific Identification

458. To qualify for cash flow hedge accounting, this Statement requires that an entity specifically identify the forecasted transaction that gives rise to the cash flow exposure. That information is necessary to (a) assess the likelihood that the transaction will occur, (b) determine if the cumulative cash flows of the designated derivative are expected to be highly effective at offsetting the change in expected cash flow of the forecasted transaction attributable to the risk being hedged, and (c) assess the hedge's effectiveness on an ongoing basis. The expected market price of the transaction, both at inception of the hedge and subsequently, is necessary information to determine the change in expected cash flows. Because the circumstances of each entity and transaction are different, the information needed to assess the expected offset may vary.

Single Transaction or Group of Individual Transactions

459. The Exposure Draft would have required that an entity be able to predict the date on which a forecasted transaction will occur for it to qualify for cash flow hedge accounting. The Exposure Draft also would have required the gain or loss on a derivative that hedges a forecasted transaction to be reclassified into earnings on the date that the forecasted transaction was expected to occur. This Statement instead requires the gain or loss on a hedge of a forecasted transaction to be reclassified into earnings in the same period(s) that the hedged transaction affects earnings. That change makes it less important for an entity to be able to predict the exact date on which a hedged forecasted transaction will occur. The Board decided to require an entity to identify the hedged forecasted transaction with sufficient specificity to make it clear whether a particular transaction is a

hedged transaction when it occurs. An entity should not be able to choose when to reclassify into earnings a gain or loss on a hedging instrument in accumulated other comprehensive income after the gain or loss has occurred by asserting that the instrument hedges a transaction that has or has not yet occurred. However, the Board does not consider it necessary to require that an entity be able to specify at the time of entering into a hedge the date on which the hedged forecasted transaction will occur to prevent such after-the-fact designation.

460. The following example illustrates the requirement for specific identification of the hedged transaction. Company A determines with a high degree of probability that it will issue $5,000,000 of fixed-rate bonds with a 5-year maturity sometime during the next 6 months, but it cannot predict exactly when the debt issuance will occur. That situation might occur, for example, if the funds from the debt issuance are needed to finance a major project to which Company A is already committed but the precise timing of which has not yet been determined. To qualify for cash flow hedge accounting, Company A might identify the hedged forecasted transaction as, for example, the first issuance of five-year, fixed-rate bonds that occurs during the next six months.

461. The Board understands that it sometimes will be impractical (perhaps impossible) and not cost-effective for an entity to identify each individual transaction that is being hedged. An example is a group of sales or purchases over a period of time to or from one or more parties. The Board decided that an entity should be permitted to aggregate individual forecasted transactions for hedging purposes in some circumstances. As for a hedge of a single forecasted transaction, an entity must identify the hedged transactions with sufficient specificity that it is possible to determine which transactions are hedged transactions when they occur. For example, an entity that expects to sell at least 300,000 units of a particular product in its next fiscal quarter might designate the sales of the first 300,000 units as the hedged transactions. Alternatively, it might designate the first 100,000 sales in each month as the hedged transactions. It could not, however, simply designate any sales of 300,000 units during the quarter as the hedged transaction because it then would be impossible to determine whether the first sales transaction of the quarter was a hedged transaction. Similarly, an entity could not designate the last 300,000 sales of the quarter as the hedged transaction because it would not be possible to determine whether sales early in the quarter were hedged or not.

462. To qualify for hedging as a group rather than individually, the aggregated transactions must share the risk exposure for which they are being hedged. If a forecasted transaction does not share the risk exposure for which the group of items is being hedged, it should not be part of the group being hedged. The Board considers that requirement to be necessary to ensure that a single derivative will be effective as a hedge of the aggregated transactions. To illustrate, under the guidance in this Statement, a single derivative of appropriate size could be designated as hedging a given amount of aggregated forecasted transactions such as the following:

a. Forecasted sales of a particular product to numerous customers within a specified time period, such as a month, a quarter, or a year
b. Forecasted purchases of a particular product from the same or different vendors at different dates within a specified time period
c. Forecasted interest payments on several variable-rate debt instruments within a specified time period.

However, the transactions in each group must share the risk exposure for which they are being hedged. For example, the interest payments in group (c) above must vary with the same index to qualify for hedging with a single derivative. In addition, a forecasted purchase and a forecasted sale cannot both be included in the same group of individual transactions. Although they may be based on the same underlying, they have opposite exposures.

Probability of a Forecasted Transaction

463. The Board concluded that, similar to Statement 80, changes in the fair value of a derivative should be excluded from current earnings only if the related forecasted transaction is probable. An assessment of the likelihood that a forecasted transaction will take place should not be based solely on management's intent because intent is not verifiable. The transaction's probability should be supported by observable facts and the attendant circumstances. Consideration should be given to the following circumstances in assessing the likelihood that a transaction will occur:

a. The frequency of similar past transactions
b. The financial and operational ability of the entity to carry out the transaction
c. Substantial commitments of resources to a particular activity (for example, a manufacturing

facility that can be used in the short run only to process a particular type of commodity)
d. The extent of loss or disruption of operations that could result if the transaction does not occur
e. The likelihood that transactions with substantially different characteristics might be used to achieve the same business purpose (for example, an entity that intends to raise cash may have several ways of doing so, ranging from a short-term bank loan to a common stock offering).

464. The term *probable* is used in this Statement consistent with its use in paragraph 3 of FASB Statement No. 5, *Accounting for Contingencies,* which defines *probable* as an area within a range of the likelihood that a future event or events will occur confirming the fact of the loss. That range is from probable to remote, as follows:

Probable. The future event or events are likely to occur.
Reasonably possible. The chance of the future event or events occurring is more than remote but less than likely.
Remote. The chance of the future event or events occurring is slight.

The term *probable* requires a significantly greater likelihood of occurrence than the phrase *more likely than not.*

465. In addition, the Board believes that both the length of time until a forecasted transaction is projected to occur and the quantity of the forecasted transaction are considerations in determining probability. Other factors being equal, the more distant a forecasted transaction is, the less likely it is that the transaction would be considered probable and the stronger the evidence that would be needed to support an assertion that it is probable. For example, a transaction forecasted to occur in five years may be less likely than a transaction forecasted to occur in one year. However, forecasted interest payments for the next 20 years on variable-rate debt typically would be probable if supported by an existing contract. Additionally, other factors being equal, the greater the physical quantity or future value of a forecasted transaction, the less likely it is that the transaction would be considered probable and the stronger the evidence that would be required to support an assertion that it is probable. For example, less evidence generally would be needed to support forecasted sales of 100,000 units in a particular month than would be needed to support forecasted sales of

950,000 units in that month by an entity, even if its sales have averaged 950,000 units per month for the past 3 months.

Contractual Maturity

466. When an entity enters into a hedge that uses a derivative with a maturity that extends approximately to the date the forecasted transaction is expected to occur, the derivative "locks in" a price or rate for the entire term of the hedge, provided that the hedging instrument is held to its maturity. Consistent with that view, the Exposure Draft proposed that, to qualify for hedge accounting, the contractual maturity or repricing date of the derivative must be on or about the same date as the projected date of the hedged forecasted transaction.

467. Respondents to the Exposure Draft objected to that requirement because it would have precluded rollover strategies and hedges of a portion of the term of a forecasted transaction from qualifying for hedge accounting. A rollover strategy involves establishing over time a series of short-term futures, options, or both in consecutive contract months to hedge a forecasted transaction. In a rollover strategy, the complete series of derivatives is not acquired at the inception of the hedge; rather, short-term derivatives are initially acquired as part of a plan to replace maturing derivatives with successive new short-term hedging derivatives. The Exposure Draft explained the Board's belief that, even though an entity may ultimately achieve the same or similar result with a series of short-term contracts, a single short-term derivative by itself does not lock in a price or rate for the period until the forecasted transaction is expected to occur.

468. The Board decided to remove the maturity criterion and thus to permit hedge accounting for rollover strategies. Respondents asserted that those strategies are a common, cost-effective, risk management practice that may achieve results similar to the results of using a single long-term derivative as the hedging instrument. Although the Board notes that a rollover strategy or other hedge using a derivative that does not extend to the transaction date does not necessarily "fix" the price of a forecasted transaction, it decided to accede to respondents' requests to permit hedge accounting for rollover strategies. The Board also decided that removing the maturity criterion was acceptable because it makes the qualifying requirements for fair value and cash flow hedge accounting more consistent. Prohibiting hedges of a portion of a forecasted transaction term from qualifying for cash flow hedge accounting would have been inconsistent with permitting fair value hedge accounting for hedges of a portion of the life of a hedged asset or liability.

Transaction with External Third Party

469. The Exposure Draft proposed that, to qualify for hedge accounting, a hedged forecasted exposure must be a *transaction*, which Concepts Statement 6 defines as an external event involving transfer of something of value (future economic benefit) between two (or more) entities. That definition was intended to clearly distinguish a transaction from an internal cost allocation or an event that happens within an entity. The Exposure Draft explained that the Board considers hedge accounting to be appropriate only when there is a hedgeable risk arising from a transaction with an external party. Accounting allocations and intercompany transactions, in and of themselves, do not give rise to economic exposure.

470. A number of respondents to the Exposure Draft objected to the requirement that a hedgeable transaction be with an external party because it prohibited an intercompany transaction, including one denominated in a foreign currency, from being designated as a forecasted transaction and afforded hedge accounting.

471. Although the requirements of this Statement are not described in terms of the Concepts Statement 6 definition of a *transaction*, the requirements for hedges of other than foreign currency risk are the same as in the Exposure Draft. As discussed in paragraphs 482–487, the Board decided to accommodate cash flow hedges of the foreign currency risk in forecasted intercompany foreign currency transactions. However, for other than foreign currency hedges, this Statement requires that a forecasted transaction be with a party external to the reporting entity to qualify as a hedged transaction, which is consistent with the Exposure Draft. Therefore, depreciation expense, cost of sales, and similar internal accounting allocations do not qualify as hedgeable forecasted transactions. Forecasted transactions between members of a consolidated entity, except for intercompany transactions denominated in a foreign currency, are not hedgeable transactions except for purposes of separate stand-alone subsidiary financial statements. Thus, a consolidated entity cannot apply hedge accounting to forecasted intercompany transactions, unless the risk being hedged is a foreign currency exposure. A subsidiary could, however, apply

hedge accounting to a hedge of a forecasted inter-company transaction in its separate, stand-alone financial statements because those transactions are with a party "external to" the reporting entity in those stand-alone statements.

Forecasted Transactions Prohibited from Designation as the Hedged Item in a Cash Flow Hedge

472. This Statement prohibits cash flow hedge accounting for forecasted transactions involving (a) an entity's interests in consolidated subsidiaries, (b) minority interests in consolidated subsidiaries, (c) investments accounted for by the equity method, or (d) an entity's own equity instruments classified in stockholders' equity. The reasons for those prohibitions are similar to those for prohibiting the same items from being hedged items in fair value hedges, as discussed in paragraphs 455–457. In addition, the Board noted that implementing cash flow hedge accounting for those items could present significant practical and conceptual problems, such as determining when to transfer to earnings amounts accumulated in other comprehensive income. Finally, certain of those items, such as issuances and repurchases of an entity's own equity instruments, would not qualify for hedge accounting because they do not present a cash flow risk that could affect earnings.

473. Prohibiting the forecasted purchase of a consolidated subsidiary from being the hedged item in a cash flow hedge effectively prohibits cash flow hedge accounting for a forecasted business combination to be accounted for as a purchase, and paragraph 29(f) of this Statement makes that prohibition explicit. The Board noted that the current accounting for a business combination is based on considering the combination as a discrete event at the consummation date. Applying cash flow hedge accounting to a forecasted business combination would be inconsistent with that current accounting. It also would be, at best, difficult to determine when to reclassify the gain or loss on the hedging derivative to earnings.

Foreign Currency Hedges

474. The Board's objectives in providing hedge accounting for hedges of foreign currency exposures are the following:

a. To continue to permit hedge accounting for the types of hedged items and hedging instruments that were permitted hedge accounting under Statement 52

b. To increase the consistency of hedge accounting guidance for foreign currency hedges and other types of hedges by broadening the scope of foreign currency hedges that are eligible for hedge accounting, as necessary.

Carried Forward from Statement 52

475. Because the scope of this project did not include a comprehensive reconsideration of accounting for foreign currency translation, this Statement makes two exceptions to retain certain provisions of Statement 52. The Board decided to make those exceptions to the hedge accounting requirements in this Statement because of the accounting anomalies that otherwise would be created by this Statement and the existing guidance in Statement 52.

476. Although the Board decided not to extend hedge accounting to nonderivative instruments used as hedging instruments, as discussed in paragraphs 246 and 247, it decided to permit an entity to designate a nonderivative financial instrument denominated in a foreign currency as a hedge of a firm commitment. It did so for practical reasons. The Board understands that such hedges are extensively used in practice, and it does not think constituents would understand why that practice should be prohibited now, given the acceptance of it in Statement 52.

477. This Statement also makes an exception to permit an entity to designate a financial instrument denominated in a foreign currency (derivative or nonderivative) as a hedge of the foreign currency exposure of a net investment in a foreign operation. Net investment hedges are subject only to the criteria in paragraph 20 of Statement 52. The net investment in a foreign operation can be viewed as a portfolio of dissimilar assets and liabilities that would not meet the criterion in this Statement that the hedged item be a single item or a group of similar items. Alternatively, it can be viewed as part of the fair value of the parent's investment account. Under either view, without a specific exception, the net investment in a foreign operation would not qualify for hedging under this Statement. The Board decided, however, that it was acceptable to retain the current provisions of Statement 52 in that area. The Board also notes that, unlike other hedges of portfolios of dissimilar items, hedge accounting for the net investment in a foreign operation has been explicitly permitted by the authoritative literature.

478. The Exposure Draft would have retained the approach required by paragraph 20 of Statement 52

for measuring the effective portion of a foreign currency forward contract that is designated as a hedge of the net investment in a foreign operation. The resulting difference between the effective portion and the change in fair value of the hedging derivative would have been reported currently in earnings. The approach in Statement 52 was appropriate given how forward contracts were measured under that Statement. Unlike Statement 52, this Statement requires that forward contracts be measured at fair value, which incorporates discounting future cash flows. Accordingly, the Exposure Draft's requirements would have always produced an amount to be recognized in earnings that would have been of opposite sign to the effective portion recognized in the cumulative translation adjustment component of other comprehensive income. That amount could have been explained only in terms of the arithmetic process that produced it. The Board therefore decided that the effective portion of a forward contract that is a hedge of a net investment should be determined not by looking only to changes in spot rates but should include the effects of discounting in the same way as for forward contracts used in other foreign currency hedges.

Fair value hedges of foreign currency risk in available-for-sale securities

479. This Statement permits the portion of the change in value of foreign-currency-denominated debt securities and certain foreign marketable equity securities classified as available-for-sale that is attributable to foreign exchange risk to qualify for fair value hedge accounting. The requirements of this Statement in that area are generally consistent with the provisions of EITF Issues No. 96-15, "Accounting for the Effects of Changes in Foreign Currency Exchange Rates on Foreign-Currency-Denominated Available-for-Sale Debt Securities," and No. 97-7, "Accounting for Hedges of the Foreign Currency Risk Inherent in an Available-for-Sale Marketable Equity Security." However, unlike those EITF Issues, this Statement does not permit a nonderivative instrument to be used as the hedging instrument in a hedge of an available-for-sale security.

480. Foreign available-for-sale debt securities give rise to hedgeable foreign exchange risk because they embody cash flows denominated in a foreign currency. The cash flows embodied in an investment in a marketable equity security, on the other hand, are not inherently "denominated" in a particular currency. Therefore, both the EITF and the Board concluded

that a marketable equity security has hedgeable foreign exchange risk only if both of the following criteria are met:

a. The marketable equity security (or an instrument that represents an interest in it, such as an American Depository Receipt) is not traded on an exchange (or other established marketplace) on which trades are denominated in the investor's functional currency.
b. The dividends or other cash flows to be received by the investor are all denominated in the same foreign currency as the currency expected to be received upon sale of the security.

Regardless of the country in which the issuer of an equity security is domiciled, that security presents no discernible foreign exchange risk to a holder who may trade the security for a price denominated in its functional currency. For example, for an investor with a U.S. dollar functional currency, its foreign exchange risk related to the equity securities of a multinational company domiciled in Italy that trade on a U.S. exchange is essentially the same as its foreign exchange risk in the equity securities of a U.S. company with significant foreign operations in Italy. In both situations, the investor's foreign exchange risk is indirect and not reliably measurable. The operations of the issuer rather than the prices in which trades in its equity securities are denominated are the source of the investor's foreign exchange risk.

Broadening of Statement 52

481. Unlike Statement 52, this Statement permits hedge accounting for hedges of forecasted foreign currency transactions, including intercompany transactions. Because this Statement permits hedge accounting for hedges of forecasted interest rate, credit, and market price exposures, the Board considered it appropriate to include foreign currency exposures as well. Forecasted intercompany foreign currency transactions are discussed in the following paragraphs.

Forecasted intercompany foreign currency transactions

482. This Statement permits an entity to designate the foreign currency exposure of a forecasted foreign-currency-denominated intercompany transaction as a hedged transaction in a cash flow hedge.

The Exposure Draft proposed that, in general, forecasted transactions between members of a consolidated group would not qualify as hedgeable exposures in the consolidated financial statements. However, if costs are incurred in one currency and the third-party revenues for recovering those costs are generated in another currency, the Exposure Draft would have permitted the entity that incurred the costs to designate the forecasted third-party revenues as a hedged transaction. The Exposure Draft would have required a direct, substantive relationship between the costs incurred and the recovery of those costs from the outside third party. For example, the Exposure Draft would have permitted an English subsidiary that incurs manufacturing costs in pounds sterling to hedge the ultimate sale of that product for French francs by its affiliated French subsidiary to an unrelated third party. The Board proposed that exception because it considered those transactions to be, in substance, direct foreign export sales.

483. A number of respondents said that the guidance provided in the Exposure Draft was unduly restrictive because forecasted intercompany royalties and licensing fees, which are based on third-party sales and remitted from foreign subsidiaries to a parent company, would not be afforded cash flow hedge accounting. Respondents also took exception to the requirement that there be a "direct, substantive relationship" between costs incurred and recovery of those costs.

484. The Board decided to remove the restrictions on hedge accounting for hedges of forecasted intercompany foreign currency transactions because, pursuant to Statement 52 as amended by this Statement, an intercompany transaction that is denominated in a currency other than the entity's functional currency gives rise to a transaction gain or loss if exchange rates change. A forecasted intercompany transaction that is expected to be denominated in a foreign currency can be viewed as giving rise to the same kind of foreign currency risk. Therefore, pursuant to this Statement, a forecasted intercompany transaction that presents an exposure to foreign currency risk and that otherwise satisfies the criteria for a foreign currency cash flow hedge is eligible for designation as a hedged transaction.

485. As with other hedges of forecasted transactions, amounts accumulated in other comprehensive income for a forecasted foreign currency transaction are to be recognized in earnings in the same period or periods that the hedged transaction affects earnings.

Because an intercompany dividend does not affect earnings, a forecasted intercompany dividend cannot qualify as a hedgeable forecasted transaction. In essence, a hedge of a forecasted intercompany dividend expected to be paid from future earnings is a hedge of those future earnings. This Statement prohibits hedge accounting for hedges of future earnings.

486. The Board also made an exception for forecasted intercompany foreign currency transactions because hedging foreign currency intercompany cash flows with foreign currency options is a common practice among multinational companies—a practice that was permitted in specified circumstances under EITF Issue No. 91-1, "Hedging Intercompany Foreign Currency Risks." This Statement modifies Issue 91-1 to permit hedge accounting for intercompany transactions using other derivatives, such as forward contracts, as the hedging instrument and expands the situations in which hedge accounting may be applied because the Board believes the accounting for all derivative instruments should be the same.

487. For a hedge of a forecasted foreign currency transaction to qualify for hedge accounting, this Statement requires that the component of the entity that has the foreign currency exposure be a party to the hedging transaction. That requirement is necessary because, under the functional currency approach in Statement 52, all foreign currency exposures exist only in relation to an entity's functional currency. Thus, for example, a U.S. parent company cannot directly hedge the foreign currency risk in its French franc subsidiary's U.S.-dollar-denominated export sales because the U.S. parent has no exposure to exchange risk for dollar-denominated sales. However, one component of a consolidated entity, such as a central treasury operation, can effectively take on another component's exchange risk by means of an intercompany transaction. For example, the U.S. parent (or a centralized treasury operation with a U.S. dollar functional currency) might enter into a forward contract to buy dollars from its French subsidiary in exchange for francs. The French subsidiary could designate that intercompany forward contract (in which the French subsidiary sells dollars for francs) as a hedge of its forecasted U.S.-dollar-denominated sales. The U.S. parent then would enter into a sell dollars–buy francs forward contract with an unaffiliated third party to offset its foreign exchange risk on the intercompany forward contract. That third-party transaction is required for the previous intercompany arrangement to qualify in the consolidated financial statements as a hedge of the

French subsidiary's forecasted dollar sales. (As noted in paragraph 471, a parent company is a "third party" in a subsidiary's separate financial statements. Thus, the French subsidiary could designate the intercompany derivative as a hedge of its U.S. dollar sales in its stand-alone financial statements regardless of whether the parent has entered into an offsetting contract with an outside party.)

Discontinuing Hedge Accounting

488. This Statement requires that an entity discontinue hedge accounting prospectively if the qualifying criteria are no longer met; if a derivative expires or is sold, terminated, or exercised; or if the entity removes the designation of the hedge. The Board believes hedge accounting is no longer appropriate in those circumstances. This Statement also requires certain modifications to hedge accounting for the interim reporting period in which a discontinuance occurs in circumstances discussed below.

Discontinuing Fair Value Hedge Accounting

489. The Board is concerned that a fair value hedge that no longer qualifies as being highly effective at achieving offsetting changes in fair value for the risk being hedged may continue to receive hedge accounting simply because an entity fails to assess compliance with that effectiveness criterion on a sufficiently frequent basis. If an entity determines at the end of a period that a hedge is no longer effective, it is likely that it was also ineffective during a portion of that period. To minimize the possibility of providing hedge accounting for hedges that do not qualify as highly effective, the Board decided that fair value hedge accounting should not be provided from the point at which the hedge ceased to qualify. It believes that an entity will be able to determine the point at which a hedge became ineffective if it assesses compliance with the effectiveness criterion at the inception of the hedge, on a recurring basis, and whenever something happens that could affect the hedging relationship. The Board believes that immediate evaluation of the effect of relevant changes in circumstances on a hedge's qualification for hedge accounting should be an integral aspect of an ongoing assessment of compliance.

490. The Board expects that entities entering into hedging transactions that do not qualify for an assumption of automatic effectiveness and zero ineffectiveness under the criteria discussed in Appendix A will monitor hedge effectiveness frequently—often

daily. However, the Board recognizes that it may not be cost-effective for some entities to assess compliance with the effectiveness criterion on a daily or weekly basis. It therefore decided that compliance should be assessed no less frequently than quarterly. However, if the event or change in circumstances that caused the hedging relationship to cease to qualify cannot be identified, the entity is prohibited from applying hedge accounting from the date at which compliance was last assessed and satisfied. Otherwise, a hedging relationship that does not satisfy the conditions for fair value hedge accounting might nevertheless receive such accounting.

491. For hedges of firm commitments, the Board decided that if hedge accounting is discontinued because the hedged item no longer meets the definition of a firm commitment, an entity should derecognize any previously recognized asset or liability and recognize a corresponding loss or gain in earnings. That accounting is appropriate because the asset or liability that represented the value of the firm commitment no longer exists if the hedged transaction no longer qualifies as a firm commitment, for example, because performance is no longer probable. The Board believes those circumstances should be rare. A pattern of discontinuing hedge accounting and derecognizing firm commitments would call into question the "firmness" of future hedged firm commitments and the entity's accounting for future hedges of firm commitments.

Discontinuing Cash Flow Hedge Accounting

492. The Exposure Draft proposed that if cash flow hedge accounting is discontinued, the derivative gain or loss accumulated in other comprehensive income to the date of discontinuance would be recognized in earnings on the originally projected date of the hedged forecasted transaction. That proposed requirement was intended to instill discipline in the accounting for cash flow hedges and reduce the possibility for managing earnings. Respondents to the Exposure Draft disagreed with that provision as it related to discontinuances that resulted from a change in probability. They said that gains and losses previously recognized in other comprehensive income should be reclassified into earnings on the date it is decided that the forecasted transaction is no longer considered probable.

493. The Board considers it inappropriate to defer a gain or loss on a derivative that arises after a hedged forecasted transaction is deemed no longer

probable. However, if the occurrence of the forecasted transaction is still reasonably possible, the Board considers it appropriate to continue to include in accumulated other comprehensive income the gain or loss that arose before the date the forecasted transaction is deemed no longer probable. The Board also was concerned that requiring a gain or loss in accumulated other comprehensive income to be reported in earnings when a forecasted transaction is no longer probable but still is reasonably possible (paragraph 464 describes the range of probability) would provide an entity with the opportunity to manage earnings by changing its estimate of probability. For those reasons, the Board decided to require earnings recognition of a related gain or loss in accumulated other comprehensive income only when an entity determines it is probable that the transaction will *not* occur.

494. A pattern of determining that hedged forecasted transactions probably will not occur would call into question both an entity's ability to accurately predict forecasted transactions and the propriety of using hedge accounting in the future for similar forecasted transactions.

Interaction with Standards on Impairment

495. A hedged item may be reported at fair value as a consequence of applying the provisions of this Statement. That would occur if the carrying amount of the hedged item equaled its fair value at the inception of a hedge and all changes in the fair value of a hedged item were recognized as a result of hedge accounting. However, that is not the same as continuous measurement at fair value. Therefore, accounting for changes in the fair value of a hedged item attributable to the risk being hedged does not exempt the hedged item from accounting provisions of other Statements that apply to assets or liabilities that are not measured at fair value. For example, a loan that is designated as a hedged item but is not otherwise measured at fair value or lower of cost or market value is subject to the impairment provisions of Statement 114.

496. Respondents to the Exposure Draft questioned whether the carrying amount of a derivative should be considered in assessing impairment of a related asset or liability, if any. (In this Statement, the term *impairment* includes the recognition of an increase in a liability as well as a decrease in an asset.) The related asset or liability would be either an existing asset or liability or an asset or liability that was acquired or incurred as a result of a hedged forecasted transaction.

497. The Board decided that it would be inappropriate to consider the carrying amount of a derivative hedging instrument in an assessment of impairment of a related asset or liability in either a fair value hedge or a cash flow hedge. To do so would be inconsistent with the fact that the derivative is a separate asset or liability.

498. This Statement provides that a derivative gain or loss recognized in accumulated other comprehensive income as a hedge of a variable cash flow on a forecasted transaction is to be reclassified into earnings in the same period or periods as the offsetting loss or gain on the hedged item. For example, a derivative gain that arose from a cash flow hedge of a purchase of equipment used in operations is to be included in earnings in the same periods that depreciation on the equipment is recognized. The net effect on earnings should be the same as if the derivative gain or loss had been included in the basis of the asset or liability to which the hedged forecasted transaction relates. To be consistent with that provision, the Board decided that a derivative gain that offsets part or all of an impairment loss on a related asset or liability should be reclassified into earnings in the period that an impairment loss is recognized. Similarly, a related derivative loss, if any, in accumulated other comprehensive income should be reclassified into earnings in the same period that a recovery of a previous impairment loss is recognized. The Board decided that the reason that a loss or gain on a hedged asset or liability is recognized in income—for example, whether through an ordinary depreciation charge or an impairment write-down—should not affect the reclassification into earnings of a related offsetting gain or loss in accumulated other comprehensive income.

Current Earnings Recognition of Certain Derivative Losses

499. The Board sees no justification for delaying recognition in earnings of a derivative loss that the entity does not expect to recover through revenues related to the hedged transaction. Accordingly, this Statement prohibits continuing to report a loss in accumulated other comprehensive income if the entity expects that doing so would lead to recognizing a net loss on the combined hedging instrument and the hedged transaction in a future period(s). For example, a loss on a derivative designated as a hedge of

the forecasted purchase of inventory should be recognized in earnings immediately to the extent that the loss is not expected to be recovered through future sales of the inventory. Statements 52 and 80 included the same requirement.

Accounting by Not-for-Profit Organizations and Other Entities That Do Not Report Earnings

500. This Statement applies to all entities, including not-for-profit organizations, defined benefit pension plans, and other entities that do not report earnings as a separate caption in a statement of financial performance. For example, a not-for-profit entity reports the total change in net assets during a period, which is analogous to total comprehensive income for a business enterprise. The Exposure Draft indicated that cash flow hedge accounting would not be available to an entity that does not report earnings. A few respondents objected to what they interpreted as the Exposure Draft's unequal treatment of not-for-profit and other entities that do not report earnings. They did not consider it fair to deny those entities access to hedge accounting for hedges of forecasted transactions.

501. The effect of cash flow hedge accounting is to report a derivative gain or loss in other comprehensive income—that is, outside earnings—in the period in which it occurs and then to reclassify that gain or loss into earnings in a later period. It thus would be mechanically impossible for an entity that only reports an amount comparable to total comprehensive income to apply cash flow hedge accounting. For this Statement to permit a not-for-profit entity, for example, to apply cash flow hedge accounting, the Board would first have to define a subcomponent of the total change in net assets during a period that would be analogous to earnings for a business enterprise. Neither Concepts Statement 6 nor Statement 117 defines such a measure of operating performance for a not-for-profit entity, and an attempt to define that measure was beyond the scope of the project that led to this Statement. Accordingly, the Board decided to retain the provision that cash flow hedge accounting is not available to a not-for-profit or other entity that does not report earnings as a separate caption in a statement of financial performance.

Disclosures

502. This Statement supersedes Statements 105 and 119, both of which provided disclosure guidance for derivatives and financial instruments. Consistent with its objective of making the guidance on financial reporting related to derivatives easier to use, the Board decided that this Statement should provide comprehensive disclosure guidance, as well as recognition and measurement guidance, for derivatives. This Statement therefore carries forward from Statement 119 the requirement for disclosure of a description of the objectives, context, and strategies for holding or issuing derivatives. The purpose of that disclosure is to "help investors and creditors understand what an entity is trying to accomplish with its derivatives" (Statement 119, paragraph 58). The Board also decided to require additional qualitative disclosures describing an entity's risk management policy and the items or transactions and the risks being hedged for each type of hedge. The Board believes the qualitative disclosures are necessary to assist investors, creditors, and other users of financial statements in understanding the nature of an entity's derivative activities and in evaluating the success of those activities, their importance to the entity, and their effect on the entity's financial statements. Many respondents to the Exposure Draft supported the qualitative disclosures.

503. This Statement modifies some of the disclosure requirements from the Exposure Draft, mostly as a result of changes to the accounting requirements proposed in the Exposure Draft. Notwithstanding the modifications, the Board decided to retain many of the disclosure requirements in the Exposure Draft given the extent of use and complexity of derivatives and hedging activities and because many users of financial statements have asked for improved disclosures.

504. A few respondents to the Task Force Draft suggested that both the qualitative and the quantitative disclosures should distinguish between derivatives used for risk management based on the type of risk (for example, interest rate risk, foreign currency risk, or credit risk) being hedged rather than based on accounting designations (for example, fair value hedges versus cash flow hedges). Those respondents said that disclosures organized in that manner, perhaps including even narrower distinctions such as the type of asset or liability that is hedged, would better aid the financial statement user in understanding an entity's success in managing the different types of risk that it encounters.

505. The Board agreed that disclosures presented in a manner that distinguishes between the nature of the risk being hedged would provide useful information that would help users understand management's risk management strategies. However, the Board decided

not to require that disclosures about derivative instruments be organized in the manner suggested by those respondents. The Board made that decision somewhat reluctantly, based primarily on its concern that it could not require such disclosures without additional study and that such a requirement would necessitate a greater level of detail than the disclosures required by this Statement. Distinguishing between derivatives based on their accounting designation, as this Statement requires, helps users understand the information provided in the financial statements. Information about derivatives used in fair value hedges, cash flow hedges, hedges of the net investment in a foreign operation, and for other purposes likely would be needed even if the disclosures distinguished between derivatives based on the type of risk being hedged. The result could be a rather complicated multilevel set of disclosures. The Board also notes that this Statement requires disclosures about the risks that management hedges with derivatives as part of the description of the "context needed" to understand the entity's objectives for holding or issuing those instruments. The Board encourages companies to experiment with ways in which disclosures about derivative instruments, including how the gains and losses on them relate to other exposures of the entity, might be presented to make them more understandable and useful.

506. In response to comments about the volume of the proposed disclosure requirements in both the Exposure Draft and the Task Force Draft, the Board reconsidered the costs and benefits of the proposed disclosures. In reconsidering the proposed disclosures, the Board concluded that by eliminating certain of the requirements, it could reduce the cost of applying the Statement without a significant reduction in the benefits to users. Consequently, the following proposed disclosures were eliminated:

a. Amount of gains and losses on hedged items and on related derivatives recognized in earnings for fair value hedges
b. Description of where in the financial statements hedged items and the gains and losses on those hedged items are reported
c. Cumulative net unamortized amount of gains and losses included in the carrying amount of hedged items
d. Separate amounts for the reporting period of hedging gains and hedging losses on derivatives not recognized in earnings for cash flow hedges
e. Description of where derivatives related to cash flow hedges are reported in the statement of financial position
f. Separate amounts for the reporting period of gains and losses on the cash flow hedging instrument
g. Amount of gains and losses recognized during the period on derivatives not designated as hedges
h. Beginning and ending balances in accumulated other comprehensive income for accumulated derivative gains and losses, and the related current period changes, separately for the following two categories: (1) gains and losses related to forecasted transactions for which the variability of hedged future cash flows has ceased and (2) gains and losses related to forecasted transactions for which that variability has not ceased
i. Description of where gains and losses on derivatives not designated as hedges are reported in the statement of income or other statement of financial performance.

In addition, the Board replaced some of the remaining proposed disclosures requiring separate amounts of *gains and losses* with disclosures requiring the amount of *net gain or loss.*

507. The Board also modified the disclosure requirements as a result of changes to the accounting for fair value and cash flow hedges. Those modifications include:

Modification to Hedge Accounting	Resulting Modification to Disclosure
a. Require an entity to determine how to assess hedge effectiveness and to report all hedge ineffectiveness in earnings.	Add a requirement to disclose the net amount of hedge ineffectiveness recognized in earnings and the component of the derivative's gain or loss excluded from the assessment of hedge effectiveness and included directly in earnings.
b. Require gains and losses included in accumulated other comprehensive income to be reclassified into earnings when the forecasted transaction affects earnings.	Replace proposed disclosure of designated reporting periods in which forecasted transactions are expected to occur and the amounts to be reclassified into earnings in those periods with a description of the transactions or other events that will result in reclassification into earnings of gains and losses that are reported in accumulated other comprehensive income and the estimated net amount of existing gains or losses at the reporting date that is expected to be reclassified into earnings within the next 12 months.
c. Require gain or loss included in accumulated other comprehensive income to be reclassified into earnings when it is probable that a hedged forecasted transaction will not occur.	Require disclosure of gross gains and losses reclassified into earnings as a result of the discontinuance of cash flow hedges because it is probable that the forecasted transactions will not occur.

508. Certain respondents were concerned that some of the cash flow hedge disclosures would reveal proprietary information that could be used by competitors and market participants, putting the disclosing entity at a competitive disadvantage. The Board carefully considered those concerns and decided that the ability of traders and competitors to use the cash flow hedge disclosures to determine an entity's competitively sensitive positions would be significantly limited by an entity's ability to designate and dedesignate derivative instruments as cash flow hedges during the reporting period, the aggregate nature of the cash flow hedging disclosures, and the timing and frequency of those disclosures. Notwithstanding that conclusion, the Board notes that the following modifications to the disclosures proposed in the Exposure Draft and the Task Force Draft are directly responsive to the competitive harm concerns raised by some respondents:

a. Elimination of the proposed disclosure of the separate amounts for the reporting period of hedging gains and hedging losses on the derivatives not recognized in earnings

b. Replacement of the proposed disclosure of the designated reporting periods in which the forecasted transactions are expected to occur and the amounts of gains and losses to be reclassified to earnings in those periods with a description of the transactions or other events that will result in the reclassification into earnings of gains and losses that are reported in accumulated other comprehensive income, and the estimated net amount of the existing gains or losses at the reporting date that is expected to be reclassified into earnings within the next 12 months

c. Elimination of the proposed disclosure of the separate amounts for the reporting period of gains and losses on the cash flow hedging instruments

d. Elimination of the proposed disclosure of the beginning and ending balances in accumulated other comprehensive income for accumulated derivative gains and losses, and the related current period changes, separately for the following two categories: gains and losses related to forecasted transactions for which the variability of hedged future cash flows has ceased and gains and losses

related to forecasted transactions for which the variability of hedged future cash flows has not ceased
e. Replacement of some of the remaining proposed disclosures of separate amounts of *gains and losses* with disclosure of the amount of *net gain or loss*.

The Board believes the required cash flow hedge disclosures, as modified, provide necessary information in helping financial statement users assess the effect on the financial statements of an entity's cash flow hedge strategies.

509. This Statement also amends Statement 107 to carry forward the provision in Statement 119 that encourages disclosure of quantitative information about market risk. That provision has been revised to clarify that it applies to all financial instruments—not just to derivatives. The Board believes that disclosure will provide useful information to users of financial statements about the overall market risk of an entity's financial instruments. The Board is encouraging, rather than requiring, that information because it continues to believe that ". . . the continuing evolution of approaches to risk management limits the ability to clearly define the most useful approach to disclosing quantitative information about market risks" (Statement 119, paragraph 72). The Board observes that the SEC issued final rules[33] in January 1997 that require certain registrants to make quantitative disclosures of market risk similar to those encouraged by Statement 119.

510. The Board decided that disclosures about concentrations of credit risk previously included in Statement 105 should continue to be required because a number of constituents, including some regulators, have commented on their usefulness. The purpose of those disclosures is to allow "investors, creditors, and other users to make their own assessments of the credit risk associated with the area of concentration" (Statement 105, paragraph 100). The Board decided to modify the disclosure about concentrations of credit risk to require that the amount disclosed be based on the gross fair value of the financial instruments rather than the "amount of the accounting loss" (described in Statement 105, paragraph 20(b)). Preparers found "the amount of the accounting loss" to be confusing, and users of financial statements

have stated that fair value information provides a better indication of the credit exposure arising from financial instruments. The disclosure was also modified to require information about an entity's master netting arrangements and their effect on the maximum amount of loss due to credit risk. The Board believes that information provides users with important insight into the potential impact of those arrangements on concentrations of credit risk of an entity.

511. The Board considered either leaving the disclosures about concentrations of credit risk in Statement 105 or including them in this Statement. The Board decided not to retain them in Statement 105 because this Statement supersedes all other guidance in that Statement. The Board decided not to include those disclosures in this Statement because they refer to all financial instruments and this Statement addresses derivative instruments. The Board decided instead to amend Statement 107 to include those disclosures so that all disclosure requirements that apply to all financial instruments will be available in one place.

512. Certain other requirements from Statements 105 and 119 have been deleted, including disclosure of the "face or contract amount" for all derivative financial instruments held at the balance sheet date (Statement 105, paragraph 17, and Statement 119, paragraph 8). The Board originally required that disclosure, in part, to provide users with "information [that] conveys some of the same information provided by amounts recognized for on-balance-sheet instruments" (Statement 105, paragraph 89). That disclosure also provided an indication "of the volume of derivative activity" (Statement 119, paragraph 79). This Statement's requirement that all derivatives be recognized in the statement of financial position at fair value lessens the usefulness of the disclosure of the face or contract amount. For example, reporting all derivatives as assets or liabilities in the statement of financial position will provide an indication of the use of derivatives. More important, although the face or contract amount of derivative instruments held provides some indication of derivatives activity, their usefulness for that purpose may be suspect given that some derivatives are commonly neutralized either by canceling the original derivative—which lowers the reported amount—or by acquiring or issuing an offsetting derivative—which increases the reported amount.

[33]SEC Final Rules, *Disclosure of Accounting Policies for Derivative Financial Instruments and Derivative Commodity Instruments and Disclosure of Quantitative and Qualitative Information about Market Risk Inherent in Derivative Financial Instruments, Other Financial Instruments, and Derivative Commodity Instruments.*

The Exposure Draft would have required the disclosure only when necessary to enable investors and creditors to understand what an entity is trying to accomplish with its derivatives. Some respondents were concerned that provision would not have been operational. The Board agreed and decided that disclosure of the face or contract amount should no longer be required.

513. Also deleted is the requirement to disclose the average fair value of derivative financial instruments held for trading purposes (Statement 119, paragraph 10(a)). The Board originally required that disclosure to provide users "with a better indication of the level of risk assumed by an entity when holding or issuing derivative financial instruments for *trading purposes*" (Statement 119, paragraph 50). The Board had noted that "trading positions typically fluctuate, and the ending balance may not always be representative of the range of balances and related risks that an entity has assumed during a period" (Statement 119, paragraph 50). The Board had also indicated that it did not extend the disclosure to derivatives used for other than trading purposes because "the necessary data may be less likely to be available for derivative financial instruments held or issued for purposes other than trading" (Statement 119, paragraph 54). Because this Statement eliminates the distinction between derivatives held for *trading purposes* and those held for *purposes other than trading* and because of the Board's continuing concerns about the availability of that information, particularly for nonfinancial entities, the Board decided to eliminate that disclosure.

Effective Date and Transition

514. This Statement is effective for fiscal years beginning after June 15, 1999. Recognizing derivatives as assets and liabilities and measuring them at fair value is a primary objective of this Statement, and the Board considers it important to achieve the objective as early as is reasonably possible following the issuance of this Statement. However, many respondents indicated that they would need more than a year following the issuance of this Statement to make the systems changes necessary to implement it. The Board notes that an effective date of years beginning after June 15, 1999 will provide an implementation period of at least a year for all entities. That should be adequate time for entities to assimilate and develop the information required by this Statement. The Board also decided to permit an entity to adopt the provisions of this Statement as of the beginning of any fiscal quarter that begins after issuance of this Statement. The Board recognizes that the financial statements of an entity that adopts this Statement during a fiscal year will be based on differing measurement principles and hedge accounting requirements for derivative instruments. The Board decided that the urgency of providing improved information about derivatives outweighed concerns about the resulting potential lack of consistency within that year's financial statements.

515. Because hedge accounting is based on an entity's intent at the time a hedging relationship is established, the Board decided that retroactive application of the provisions of this Statement was not appropriate. Accordingly, changes in the fair value of derivatives that arose before initial application of this Statement and were previously recognized in net income, added to the carrying amount of hedged assets or liabilities, or included in other comprehensive income as part of a hedge of a net investment in a foreign entity are not to be included in transition adjustments. However, the Board decided that hedging relationships that existed before the date of initial application are relevant in determining other transition adjustments. Basing the transition adjustments on past hedging relationships also should prevent an entity from selectively affecting the transition adjustments by changing previously designated hedging relationships.

516. The Board considered whether past changes in the fair values of derivatives that were deferred as separate assets or liabilities in the statement of financial position rather than being added to the carrying amount of hedged assets or liabilities, such as those related to hedged forecasted transactions, should continue to be deferred at the date of initial application. Continued deferral of those gains and losses would be consistent with the continued deferral of amounts that were previously added to the carrying amount of hedged assets or liabilities. However, separately deferred losses and gains do not represent assets or liabilities and thus are different from amounts that adjusted the basis of an asset or liability or otherwise represent assets or liabilities. Continuing to report them in the statement of financial position would be inconsistent with the Board's fundamental decision to recognize in the statement of financial position only items that are assets or liabilities (paragraph 229). The Board concluded that gains and losses separately characterized as liabilities and assets in the statement of financial position should be removed

and reported in a manner consistent with the requirements of this Statement.

517. The adjustments to recognize all derivatives as assets or liabilities at fair value and to reverse certain deferred gains and losses will affect net income or other comprehensive income at the date of initial application. Consequently, the Board decided also to require that an entity recognize concurrently the effect of any preexisting offsetting differences between the carrying amount and the fair value of hedged items; that is, differences that arose before the date of initial application. The Board noted that reporting offsetting unrealized gains and losses on hedged items is consistent with the notion in this Statement of accelerating gains and losses on hedged items to provide income statement offset.

Transition Provisions for Embedded Derivatives

518. Paragraphs 12–16 of this Statement require that certain embedded derivatives be separated from their host contracts and accounted for as derivative instruments under this Statement. The Board considered how that requirement for separate accounting should apply to hybrid instruments outstanding at the date of initial application of this Statement. In considering that issue, the Board first considered two alternative ways in which an embedded derivative could be separated from the host contract after the date of acquisition or issuance:

a. Based on the fair values of the embedded derivative and the host contract at the date of initial application
b. Based on the fair values of the embedded derivative and the host contract at the date of initial acquisition or issuance.

The choice between those two methods determines the carrying amount of the host contract after separation of the embedded derivative. It also significantly affects the difficulty of obtaining the necessary information needed to separate an embedded derivative from the host contract after the date of initial acquisition or incurrence.

519. Separating a hybrid instrument into its host contract and its embedded derivative based on fair values at the date of initial adoption would be the simpler method. Under that method, the fair value of all of an entity's host contracts and embedded derivatives would be determined as of the same date, based on information current as of that date. In contrast,

basing the separation of an embedded derivative on fair values at the date a hybrid instrument was acquired or incurred would necessitate calculations as of multiple past dates. For an entity with many hybrid instruments, some of which may have been initiated a decade or more in the past, separation based on fair values at dates of acquisition or incurrence could be a significant effort.

520. Although separation based on fair values at the date of initial application of this Statement would be the easier method, its results could be questionable. Many host contracts will be interest-bearing financial instruments, and separating the value of their embedded derivatives will affect both the carrying amounts of the host contracts and their effective interest rates. Determining the carrying amount of such a host contract based on the value of an embedded derivative at a date significantly later than acquisition or issuance of the instrument could result in a substantial discount or premium to be amortized as an adjustment of interest income or expense. For example, several years before it adopts this Statement, an entity might have purchased an equity-indexed note in which the principal is linked to the S&P 500 index. If the S&P 500 index is, say, 60 percent higher on July 1, 1999 when the entity adopts this Statement than it was at the date the note was acquired and the embedded derivative is separated on that basis, the carrying amount of the host contract would be artificially low, resulting in an artificially high reported interest yield. In contrast, separation based on fair values at the date the equity-indexed note was acquired would result in carrying amounts for both components that are determined on the same basis, and the carrying amount for the host contract need not compensate for subsequent changes in the value of the embedded derivative.

521. For the reasons just discussed, the Board decided that separation of a hybrid instrument into its host contract and embedded derivative instrument should be based on fair values at the date the instrument was acquired or issued. Having made that decision, the Board decided it was not feasible to require entities to apply the requirements of paragraphs 12–16 of this Statement to all hybrid instruments held or owed at the date of initial adoption. However, the Board also did not want to provide an entity with the opportunity to embed numerous derivatives in hybrid instruments during the year or two before the effective date of this Statement for the purpose of avoiding its requirements. Therefore, this Statement requires that a hybrid instrument acquired

or issued after December 31, 1997 be separated into its host contract and embedded derivative. For instruments acquired or issued after that date, separation on the basis of fair values at the date of acquisition or issuance should not be unduly burdensome.

522. The Board also considered whether an entity should be permitted to separate hybrid instruments acquired or issued before January 1, 1998 into their host contracts and derivative components if it wishes to do so. That alternative might be provided on either an individual instrument or an entity-wide basis. The Board recognizes that an entity might wish to separate the embedded derivative from a hybrid instrument and designate it as a hedging instrument. However, the Board was concerned that providing a choice on an instrument-by-instrument basis might have unintended consequences, such as separate accounting only for those embedded derivatives that are in a loss position at the date of initial adoption. The Board therefore decided to provide an entity the choice of separating out the embedded derivatives of existing hybrid instruments, but only on an all-or-none basis. The Board also believes that providing the choice only on an entity-wide basis will make it easier for users of financial statements to understand the effects of an entity's choices in transition and the resulting financial information.

Transition Provisions for Compound Derivatives

523. This Statement prohibits separation of a compound derivative instrument into its components for hedge accounting purposes (paragraph 18). The Board does not consider that prohibition to be unduly burdensome on an ongoing basis. To qualify for hedge accounting, an entity will simply need to obtain separate derivative instruments in some situations in which compound derivatives may have been used in the past. However, the Board recognizes that an entity may have entered into long-term derivative instruments combining, for example, foreign exchange and interest rate components before it knew that only separate derivatives would qualify for hedge accounting. The Board therefore considered whether this Statement should include special transition provisions for compound derivatives entered into before the date of initial adoption.

524. The Board understands that many hedging relationships in which compound derivatives were used involved hybrid instruments. For example, an entity may have entered into an interest rate swap with an embedded equity option to hedge outstanding debt with an embedded equity feature, such as a bond

whose principal amount increases with specified percentage increases in the S&P 500 index. The Board believes that its decision not to require separate accounting for the derivative features of hybrid instruments acquired or issued before January 1, 1998 significantly reduces the need to permit compound derivatives outstanding at the date of initial adoption to be separated into dissimilar components. However, this Statement prohibits hedge accounting for the foreign exchange risk in instruments that are remeasured with changes in carrying amounts attributable to changes in foreign exchange rates included currently in earnings. A similar prohibition applies to cash flow hedges of the future acquisition or incurrence of instruments that will be remeasured with changes in carrying value attributable to changes in foreign exchange rates included in current earnings. Thus, a compound derivative that includes a foreign exchange component rarely will qualify for use as a hedging instrument under this Statement. The Board therefore decided to permit only the foreign exchange component of a compound derivative entered into before this Statement is adopted to be separated for accounting purposes. Thus, for example, a derivative that combines a foreign currency forward contract with an interest rate swap may be separated into its components at the date of initial adoption based on the fair values of the components at that date. In contrast, a combined interest rate swap and equity option may not be separated into its components.

Appendix D

AMENDMENTS TO EXISTING PRONOUNCEMENTS

525. This Statement supersedes the following pronouncements:

a. FASB Statement No. 80, *Accounting for Futures Contracts*
b. FASB Statement No. 105, *Disclosure of Information about Financial Instruments with Off-Balance-Sheet Risk and Financial Instruments with Concentrations of Credit Risk*
c. FASB Statement No. 119, *Disclosure about Derivative Financial Instruments and Fair Value of Financial Instruments.*

526. In paragraph 8 of Chapter 4, "Inventory Pricing," of ARB No. 43, *Restatement and Revision of Accounting Research Bulletins,* the following is inserted after the fourth sentence:

(If inventory has been the hedged item in a fair value hedge, the inventory's "cost" basis used in the cost-or-market-whichever-is-lower accounting shall reflect the effect of the adjustments of its carrying amount made pursuant to paragraph 22(b) of FASB Statement No. 133, *Accounting for Derivative Instruments and Hedging Activities.*)

527. FASB Statement No. 52, *Foreign Currency Translation,* is amended as follows:

a. The following paragraph is inserted after the heading *Foreign Currency Transactions* and before paragraph 15:

14A. FASB Statement No. 133, *Accounting for Derivative Instruments and Hedging Activities,* addresses the accounting for free-standing foreign currency derivatives and certain foreign currency derivatives embedded in other instruments. This Statement does not address the accounting for derivative instruments.

b. In the last sentence of paragraph 15, *paragraphs 20 and 21* is replaced by *paragraph 20* and *and foreign currency commitments* is deleted.

c. In the first sentence of paragraph 16, *forward exchange contracts (paragraphs 17–19)* is replaced by *derivative instruments (Statement 133).*

d. Paragraphs 17–19 and the heading preceding paragraph 17 are deleted.

e. Paragraph 21 is replaced by the following:

Hedges of Firm Commitments

The accounting for a gain or loss on a foreign currency transaction that is intended to hedge an identifiable foreign currency commitment (for example, an agreement to purchase or sell equipment) is addressed by paragraph 37 of Statement 133.

f. In the second sentence of paragraph 30, *forward contracts determined in conformity with the requirements of paragraphs 18 and 19 shall be considered transaction gains or losses* is replaced by *derivative instruments shall comply with paragraph 45 of Statement 133.*

g. The following sentence is added at the end of paragraph 31(b):

(Paragraph 45(c) of Statement 133 specifies additional disclosures for instruments designated as hedges of the foreign currency exposure of a net investment in a foreign operation.)

h. The definitions of *currency swaps, discount or premium on a forward contract, forward exchange contract,* and *forward rate* in paragraph 162, the glossary, are deleted.

528. FASB Statement No. 60, *Accounting and Reporting by Insurance Enterprises,* is amended as follows:

a. Paragraph 46, as amended by FASB Statements No. 115, *Accounting for Certain Investments in Debt and Equity Securities,* and No. 124, *Accounting for Certain Investments Held by Not-for-Profit Organizations,* is amended as follows:

(1) The phrase *except as indicated in the following sentence* is added to the end of the second sentence.

(2) The following sentence is added after the second sentence:

All or a portion of the unrealized gain or loss of a security that is designated as being hedged in a fair value hedge shall be recognized in earnings during the period of the hedge, pursuant to paragraph 22 of FASB Statement No. 133, *Accounting for Derivative Instruments and Hedging Activities.*

b. In the first sentence of paragraph 50, as amended by FASB Statement No. 97, *Accounting and Reporting by Insurance Enterprises for Certain Long-Duration Contracts and for Realized Gains and Losses from the Sale of Investments,* and Statement 115, *as hedges as described in FASB Statements No. 52, Foreign Currency Translation, and No. 80, Accounting for Futures Contracts* is replaced by *as either hedges of net investments in foreign operations or cash flow hedges as described in Statement 133.*

529. FASB Statement No. 65, *Accounting for Certain Mortgage Banking Activities,* is amended as follows:

a. The following sentence is added after the first sentence of paragraph 4, as amended by Statements 115 and 124:

> If a mortgage loan has been the hedged item in a fair value hedge, the loan's "cost" basis used in lower-of-cost-or-market accounting shall reflect the effect of the adjustments of its carrying amount made pursuant to paragraph 22(b) of FASB Statement No. 133, *Accounting for Derivative Instruments and Hedging Activities.*

b. In the first sentence of paragraph 9(a), as amended by Statement 115 and FASB Statement No. 125, *Accounting for Transfers and Servicing of Financial Assets and Extinguishments of Liabilities,* the phrase *commitment prices* is replaced by *fair values.*

c. The last sentence of paragraph 9(a), which was added by Statement 115, is deleted.

d. Paragraph 9(b)(1) is deleted.

530. In the third sentence of footnote 4 of FASB Statement No. 95, *Statement of Cash Flows,* as amended by FASB Statement No. 104, *Statement of Cash Flows—Net Reporting of Certain Cash Receipts and Cash Payments and Classification of Cash Flows from Hedging Transactions,* the phrase *futures contracts, forward contracts, option contracts, or swap contracts that are accounted for as hedges of identifiable transactions or events (for example, a cash payment from a futures contract that hedges a purchase or sale of inventory), including anticipatory hedges,* is replaced by *derivative instruments that are accounted for as fair value hedges or cash flow hedges under FASB Statement No. 133, Accounting for Derivative Instruments and Hedging Activities.* In the last sentence of footnote 4, *identifiable transaction or event* is replaced by *asset, liability, firm commitment, or forecasted transaction.*

531. FASB Statement No. 107, *Disclosures about Fair Value of Financial Instruments,* is amended as follows:

a. Paragraph 4 is deleted.

b. The last sentence of paragraph 10, which was added by Statement 119, is deleted.

c. The paragraph added by Statement 119 after paragraph 13 is replaced by the following; the related footnote is deleted:

> In disclosing the fair value of a financial instrument, an entity shall not net that fair value with the fair value of other financial instruments—even if those financial instruments are of the same class or are otherwise considered to be related, for example, by a risk management strategy—except to the extent that the offsetting of carrying amounts in the statement of financial position is permitted under the general principle in paragraphs 5 and 6 of FASB Interpretation No. 39, *Offsetting of Amounts Related to Certain Contracts,* or the exceptions for master netting arrangements in paragraph 10 of Interpretation 39 and for amounts related to certain repurchase and reverse repurchase agreements in paragraphs 3 and 4 of FASB Interpretation No. 41, *Offsetting of Amounts Related to Certain Repurchase and Reverse Repurchase Agreements.*

d. The following paragraphs, with related headings and footnotes, are added after paragraph 15:

Disclosure about Concentrations of Credit Risk of All Financial Instruments

15A. Except as indicated in paragraph 15B, an entity shall disclose all significant concentrations of credit risk arising from *all* financial instruments, whether from an individual counterparty or groups of counterparties. *Group concentrations* of credit risk exist if a number of counterparties are engaged in similar activities and have similar economic characteristics that would cause their ability to meet contractual obligations to be similarly affected by changes in economic or other conditions. The following shall be disclosed about each significant concentration:

a. Information about the (shared) activity, region, or economic characteristic that identifies the concentration

b. The maximum amount of loss due to credit risk that, based on the gross fair value of the financial instrument, the entity would incur if parties to the financial instruments that make up the concentration failed completely to perform according to the terms of the contracts and the collateral or other security, if any, for the amount due proved to be of no value to the entity

c. The entity's policy of requiring collateral or

other security to support financial instruments subject to credit risk, information about the entity's access to that collateral or other security, and the nature and a brief description of the collateral or other security supporting those financial instruments

d. The entity's policy of entering into master netting arrangements to mitigate the credit risk of financial instruments, information about the arrangements for which the entity is a party, and a brief description of the terms of those arrangements, including the extent to which they would reduce the entity's maximum amount of loss due to credit risk.

15B. The requirements of the preceding paragraph do not apply to the following financial instruments, whether written or held:

a. Financial instruments of a pension plan, including plan assets, when subject to the accounting and reporting requirements of Statement 87*

b. The financial instruments described in paragraphs 8(a), 8(c), 8(e), and 8(f) of this Statement, as amended by FASB Statements No. 112, *Employers' Accounting for Postemployment Benefits,* No. 123, *Accounting for Stock-Based Compensation,* and 125, except for reinsurance receivables and prepaid reinsurance premiums.

Encouraged Disclosure about Market Risk of All Financial Instruments

15C. An entity is encouraged, but not required, to disclose quantitative information about the market risks of financial instruments that is consistent with the way it manages or adjusts those risks.

15D. Appropriate ways of reporting the quantitative information encouraged in paragraph 15C will differ for different entities and will likely evolve over time as management approaches and measurement techniques evolve. Possibilities include disclosing (a) more details about current positions and perhaps activity during the period, (b) the hypothetical effects on comprehensive income (or net assets), or annual income, of several possible changes in market prices, (c) a gap analysis of interest rate repricing or maturity dates, (d) the duration of the financial instruments, or (e) the entity's value at risk from derivatives and from other positions at the end of the reporting period and the average value at risk during the year. This list is not exhaustive, and an entity is encouraged to develop other ways of reporting quantitative information.

---

*Financial instruments of a pension plan, other than the obligations for pension benefits, when subject to the accounting and reporting requirements of FASB Statement No. 35, *Accounting and Reporting by Defined Benefit Pension Plans,* are subject to the requirements of paragraph 15A.

e. Example 1 in paragraph 31 is amended as follows:

(1) The following heading and sentence are deleted from illustrative Note V:

Interest rate swap agreements

The fair value of interest rate swaps (used for hedging purposes) is the estimated amount that the Bank would receive or pay to terminate the swap agreements at the reporting date, taking into account current interest rates and the current creditworthiness of the swap counterparties.

(2) In the table, the subheading *Interest rate swaps* and the two following related lines (*In a net receivable position* and *In a net payable position*) are deleted. In the second sentence of the related footnote *, *Interest rate swaps and* is deleted.

532. This Statement carries forward the following amendments that Statement 119 made to Statement 107:

a. In paragraph 10, the following footnote is added after *either in the body of the financial statements or in the accompanying notes*:

*If disclosed in more than a single note, one of the notes shall include a summary table. The summary table shall contain the fair value and related carrying amounts and cross-references to the location(s) of the remaining disclosures required by this Statement, as amended.

b. In paragraph 10, the following is added after the first sentence:

Fair value disclosed in the notes shall be presented together with the related carrying amount in a form that makes it clear whether the fair value and carrying amount represent assets or liabilities and how the carrying amounts relate to what is reported in the statement of financial position.

533. In paragraph 28 of FASB Statement No. 113, *Accounting and Reporting for Reinsurance of Short-Duration and Long-Duration Contracts,* the phrase *FASB Statement No. 105, Disclosure of Information about Financial Instruments with Off-Balance-Sheet Risk and Financial Instruments with Concentrations of Credit Risk* is replaced by *paragraph 15A of FASB Statement No. 107, Disclosures about Fair Value of Financial Instruments, as amended by FASB Statement No. 133, Accounting for Derivative Instruments and Hedging Activities.*

534. FASB Statement No. 115, *Accounting for Certain Investments in Debt and Equity Securities,* is amended as follows:

a. The following sentence is added at the end of paragraph 4, as amended by Statement 124:

> This Statement does not apply to investments in derivative instruments that are subject to the requirements of FASB Statement No. 133, *Accounting for Derivative Instruments and Hedging Activities.* If an investment would otherwise be in the scope of this Statement and it has within it an embedded derivative that is subject to Statement 133, the host instrument (as described in Statement 133) remains within the scope of this Statement. A transaction gain or loss on a held-to-maturity foreign-currency-denominated debt security shall be accounted for pursuant to FASB Statement No. 52, *Foreign Currency Translation.*

b. Paragraph 13, as amended by FASB Statement No. 130, *Reporting Comprehensive Income,* is amended as follows:

(1) The phrase *until realized except as indicated in the following sentence* is added to the end of the second sentence.

(2) The following sentence is added after the second sentence:

> All or a portion of the unrealized holding

gain and loss of an available-for-sale security that is designated as being hedged in a fair value hedge shall be recognized in earnings during the period of the hedge, pursuant to paragraph 22 of Statement 133.

c. In paragraph 15(b), *portion of the* is inserted before *unrealized,* and *that has not been previously recognized in earnings* is added after *transfer.*

d. In paragraph 16, the following is inserted after the first sentence:

> (If a security has been the hedged item in a fair value hedge, the security's "amortized cost basis" shall reflect the effect of the adjustments of its carrying amount made pursuant to paragraph 22(b) of Statement 133.)

e. The first sentence of paragraph 19 is replaced by the following two sentences:

> For securities classified as available-for-sale, all reporting enterprises shall disclose the aggregate fair value, the total gains for securities with net gains in accumulated other comprehensive income, and the total losses for securities with net losses in accumulated other comprehensive income, by major security type as of each date for which a statement of financial position is presented. For securities classified as held-to-maturity, all reporting enterprises shall disclose the aggregate fair value, gross unrecognized holding gains, gross unrecognized holding losses, the net carrying amount, and the gross gains and losses in accumulated other comprehensive income for any derivatives that hedged the forecasted acquisition of the held-to-maturity securities, by major security type as of each date for which a statement of financial position is presented.

f. In the third sentence in paragraph 20, *amortized cost* is replaced by *net carrying amount (if different from fair value).*

g. Paragraph 21 is amended as follows:

(1) In paragraph 21(a), *on those sales* is replaced by *that have been included in earnings as a result of those sales*

(2) In paragraph 21(b), *cost was determined in*

computing realized gain or loss is replaced by the cost of a security sold or the amount reclassified out of accumulated other comprehensive income into earnings was determined

(3) Paragraph 21(d) is replaced by the following:

The amount of the net unrealized holding gain or loss on available-for-sale securities for the period that has been included in accumulated other comprehensive income and the amount of gains and losses reclassified out of accumulated other comprehensive income into earnings for the period

(4) Paragraph 21(e) is replaced by *The portion of trading gains and losses for the period that relates to trading securities still held at the reporting date.*

h. In the first sentence of paragraph 22, *amortized cost* is replaced by *net carrying* and *the net gain or loss in accumulated other comprehensive income for any derivative that hedged the forecasted acquisition of the held-to-maturity security,* is added immediately preceding *the related realized.*

i. The last four sentences of paragraph 115 are deleted.

j. The definition of *fair value* in paragraph 137, the glossary, is replaced by the following:

The amount at which an asset could be bought or sold in a current transaction between willing parties, that is, other than in a forced or liquidation sale. Quoted market prices in active markets are the best evidence of fair value and should be used as the basis for the measurement, if available. If a quoted market price is available, the fair value is the product of the number of trading units times that market price. If a quoted market price is not available, the estimate of fair value should be based on the best information available in the circumstances. The estimate of fair value should consider prices for similar assets and the results of valuation techniques to the extent available in the circumstances. Examples of valuation techniques include the present value of estimated expected future cash flows using a discount rate commensurate with the risks in-

volved, option-pricing models, matrix pricing, option-adjusted spread models, and fundamental analysis. Valuation techniques for measuring assets should be consistent with the objective of measuring fair value. Those techniques should incorporate assumptions that market participants would use in their estimates of values, including assumptions about interest rates, default, prepayment, and volatility.

535. FASB Statement No. 124, *Accounting for Certain Investments Held by Not-for-Profit Organizations,* is amended as follows:

a. In paragraph 3, *except as noted in paragraph 5* is added to the end of the first sentence.

b. The following is added to the end of paragraph 5:

This Statement also does not apply to investments in derivative instruments that are subject to the requirements of FASB Statement No. 133, *Accounting for Derivative Instruments and Hedging Activities.* If an investment would otherwise be in the scope of this Statement and it has within it an embedded derivative that is subject to Statement 133, the host instrument (as described in Statement 133) remains within the scope of this Statement.

c. In the second sentence of paragraph 6, *No. 105, Disclosure of Information about Financial Instruments with Off-Balance-Sheet Risk and Financial Instruments with Concentrations of Credit Risk,* and *No. 119, Disclosure about Derivative Financial Instruments and Fair Value of Financial Instruments* are deleted and *No. 133, Accounting for Derivative Instruments and Hedging Activities,* is added to the end of the sentence.

d. In footnote 6 of paragraph 16, *Paragraph 20 of Statement 105* is replaced by *Paragraph 15A of Statement 107, as amended by Statement 133.*

e. The definition of *fair value* in paragraph 112, the glossary, is replaced by the following:

The amount at which an asset could be bought or sold in a current transaction between willing parties, that is, other than in a forced or liquidation sale. Quoted market prices in active markets are the best evidence of fair value and should be used as the basis for the measurement, if available. If a quoted market price is available, the fair value is the product of the number of trading units times that market price. If a quoted market price is not available, the estimate of fair value should be based on the best information available in the circumstances. The estimate of fair value should consider prices for similar assets and the results of valuation techniques to the extent available in the circumstances. Examples of valuation techniques include the present value of estimated expected future cash flows using a discount rate commensurate with the risks involved, option-pricing models, matrix pricing, option-adjusted spread models, and fundamental analysis. Valuation techniques for measuring assets should be consistent with the objective of measuring fair value. Those techniques should incorporate assumptions that market participants would use in their estimates of values, including assumptions about interest rates, default, prepayment, and volatility.

536. FASB Statement No. 125, *Accounting for Transfers and Servicing of Financial Assets and Extinguishments of Liabilities,* is amended as follows:

a. In paragraph 4, *and that are not within the scope of FASB Statement No. 133, Accounting for Derivative Instruments and Hedging Activities* is added to the end of the second sentence.

b. In paragraph 14, *Except for instruments that are within the scope of Statement 133* is added to the beginning of the first sentence.

c. In the fourth sentence of paragraph 31, *derivative financial instrument* is replaced by *derivative instrument.*

d. In paragraph 243, the glossary, the definition of *derivative financial instrument* is replaced by:

Derivative instrument
Refer to paragraphs 6–9 in FASB Statement No. 133, *Accounting for Derivative Instruments and Hedging Activities.*

537. Paragraph 2(c) of FASB Statement No. 126, *Exemption from Certain Required Disclosures about*

Financial Instruments for Certain Nonpublic Entities, is replaced by the following:

The entity has no instrument that, in whole or in part, is accounted for as a derivative instrument under FASB Statement No. 133, *Accounting for Derivative Instruments and Hedging Activities,* during the reporting period.

538. Paragraph 6 of FASB Technical Bulletin No. 79-19, *Investor's Accounting for Unrealized Losses on Marketable Securities Owned by an Equity Method Investee,* as amended by FASB Statement No. 115, *Accounting for Certain Investments in Debt and Equity Securities,* is replaced by the following:

If an investee that is accounted for by the equity method is required to include unrealized holding gains and losses on investments in debt and equity securities in other comprehensive income pursuant to the provisions of FASB Statement No. 115, *Accounting for Certain Investments in Debt and Equity Securities,* as amended by FASB Statement No. 133, *Accounting for Derivative Instruments and Hedging Activities,* the investor shall adjust its investment in that investee by its proportionate share of the unrealized gains and losses and a like amount shall be included in its other comprehensive income.

Appendix E

DIAGRAM FOR DETERMINING WHETHER A CONTRACT IS A FREESTANDING DERIVATIVE SUBJECT TO THE SCOPE OF THIS STATEMENT

539. The following diagram depicts the process for determining whether a freestanding contract is within the scope of this Statement. The diagram is a visual supplement to the written standards section. It should not be interpreted to alter any requirements of this Statement nor should it be considered a substitute for the requirements. The relevant paragraphs in the standards section and Appendix A are identified in the parenthetical note after the question.

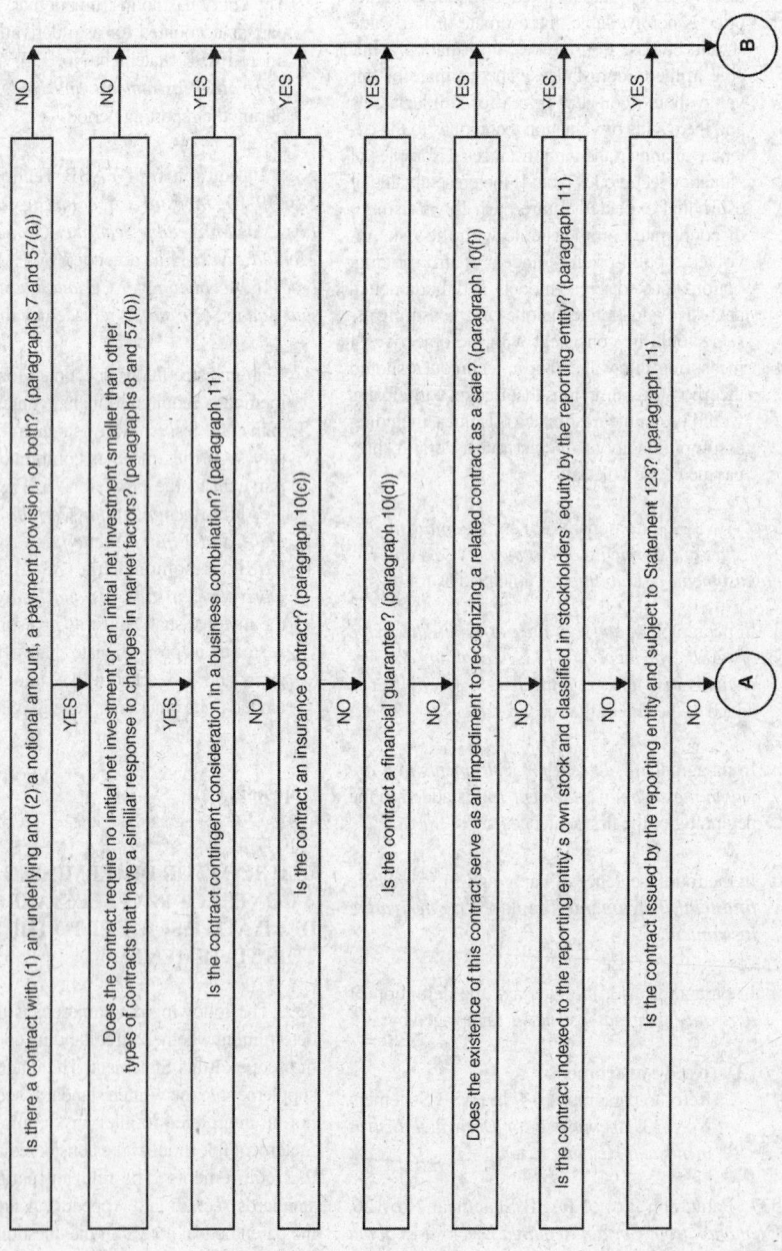

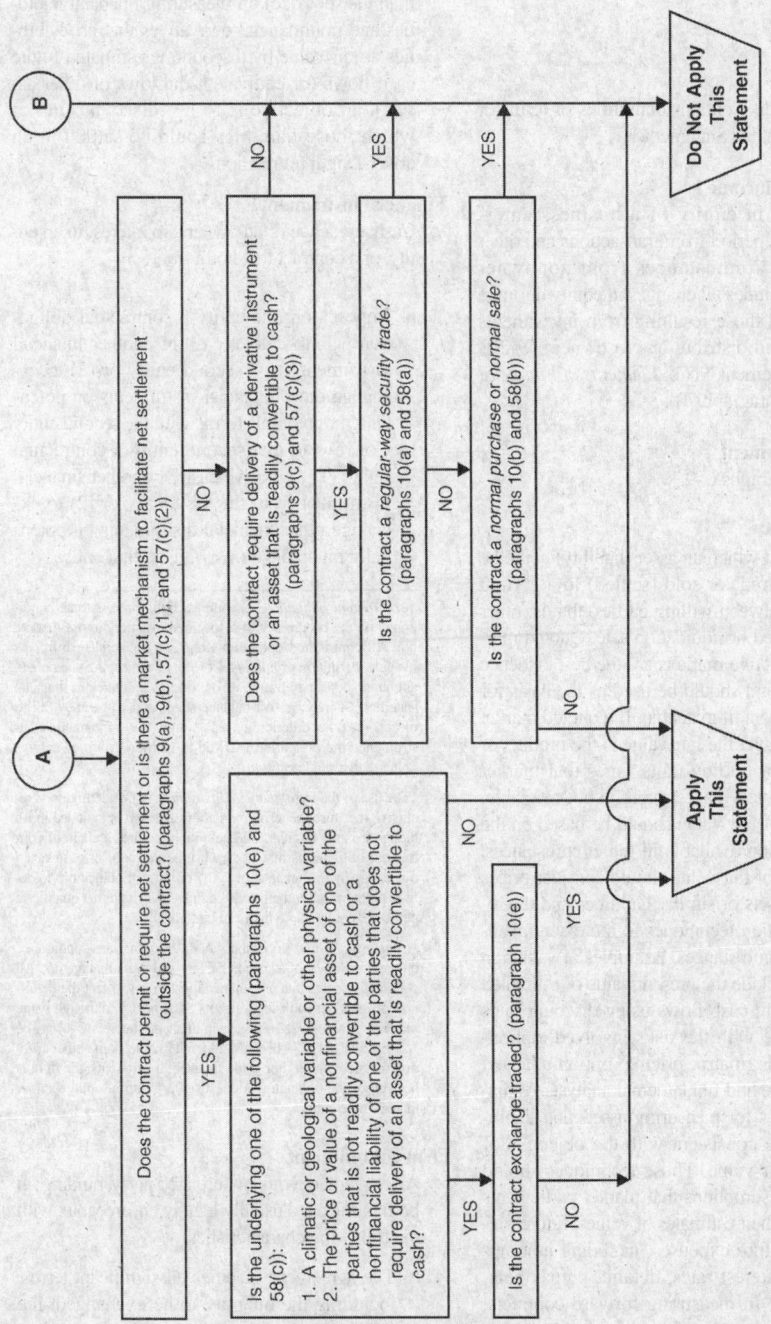

A

Does the contract permit or require net settlement or is there a market mechanism to facilitate net settlement outside the contract? (paragraphs 9(a), 9(b), 57(c)(1), and 57(c)(2))

YES

Is the underlying one of the following (paragraphs 10(e) and 58(c)):

1. A climatic or geological variable or other physical variable?
2. The price or value of a nonfinancial asset of one of the parties that is not readily convertible to cash or a nonfinancial liability of one of the parties that does not require delivery of an asset that is readily convertible to cash?

YES   NO

Is the contract exchange-traded? (paragraph 10(e))

YES   NO

NO

Does the contract require delivery of a derivative instrument or an asset that is readily convertible to cash? (paragraphs 9(c) and 57(c)(3))

NO   YES

Is the contract a *regular-way security trade?* (paragraphs 10(a) and 58(a))

NO   YES

Is the contract a *normal purchase or normal sale?* (paragraphs 10(b) and 58(b))

NO   YES

B

Do Not Apply This Statement

Apply This Statement

Appendix F

GLOSSARY

540. This appendix contains definitions of terms or phrases as used in this Statement.

Comprehensive income

The change in equity of a business enterprise during a period from transactions and other events and circumstances from nonowner sources. It includes all changes in equity during a period except those resulting from investments by owners and distributions to owners (FASB Concepts Statement No. 6, *Elements of Financial Statements,* paragraph 70).

Derivative instrument

Refer to paragraphs 6–9.

Fair value

The amount at which an asset (liability) could be bought (incurred) or sold (settled) in a current transaction between willing parties, that is, other than in a forced or liquidation sale. Quoted market prices in active markets are the best evidence of fair value and should be used as the basis for the measurement, if available. If a quoted market price is available, the fair value is the product of the number of trading units times that market price. If a quoted market price is not available, the estimate of fair value should be based on the best information available in the circumstances. The estimate of fair value should consider prices for similar assets or similar liabilities and the results of valuation techniques to the extent available in the circumstances. Examples of valuation techniques include the present value of estimated expected future cash flows using discount rates commensurate with the risks involved, option-pricing models, matrix pricing, option-adjusted spread models, and fundamental analysis. Valuation techniques for measuring assets and liabilities should be consistent with the objective of measuring fair value. Those techniques should incorporate assumptions that market participants would use in their estimates of values, future revenues, and future expenses, including assumptions about interest rates, default, prepayment, and volatility. In measuring forward contracts, such as foreign currency forward contracts, at fair value by discounting estimated future cash flows, an entity should base the estimate of future cash

flows on the changes in the forward rate (rather than the spot rate). In measuring financial liabilities and nonfinancial derivatives that are liabilities at fair value by discounting estimated future cash flows (or equivalent outflows of other assets), an objective is to use discount rates at which those liabilities could be settled in an arm's-length transaction.

Financial instrument

Cash, evidence of an ownership interest in an entity, or a contract that both:

a. Imposes on one entity a contractual obligation* (1) to deliver cash or another financial instrument[†] to a second entity or (2) to exchange other financial instruments on potentially unfavorable terms with the second entity
b. Conveys to that second entity a contractual right[‡] (1) to receive cash or another financial instrument from the first entity or (2) to exchange other financial instruments on potentially favorable terms with the first entity.

Contractual obligations encompass both those that are conditioned on the occurrence of a specified event and those that are not. All contractual obligations that are financial instruments meet the definition of *liability* set forth in Concepts Statement 6, although some may not be recognized as liabilities in financial statements—may be "off-balance-sheet"—because they fail to meet some other criterion for recognition. For some financial instruments, the obligation is owed to or by a group of entities rather than a single entity.

[†]The use of the term *financial instrument* in this definition is recursive (because the term *financial instrument* is included in it), though it is not circular. The definition requires a chain of contractual obligations that ends with the delivery of cash or an ownership interest in an entity. Any number of obligations to deliver financial instruments can be links in a chain that qualifies a particular contract as a financial instrument.

[‡]*Contractual rights* encompass both those that are conditioned on the occurrence of a specified event and those that are not. All contractual rights that are financial instruments meet the definition of *asset* set forth in Concepts Statement 6, although some may not be recognized as assets in financial statements—may be "off-balance-sheet"—because they fail to meet some other criterion for recognition. For some financial instruments, the right is held by or the obligation is due from a group of entities rather than a single entity.

Firm commitment

An agreement with an unrelated party, binding on both parties and usually legally enforceable, with the following characteristics:

a. The agreement specifies all significant terms, including the quantity to be exchanged, the fixed price, and the timing of the transaction. The fixed price may be expressed as a specified amount of an entity's functional currency or of a foreign currency. It may also be expressed as a specified interest rate or specified effective yield.

b. The agreement includes a disincentive for nonperformance that is sufficiently large to make performance probable.

Forecasted transaction

A transaction that is expected to occur for which there is no firm commitment. Because no transaction or event has yet occurred and the transaction or event when it occurs will be at the prevailing market price, a forecasted transaction does not give an entity any present rights to future benefits or a present obligation for future sacrifices.

Notional amount

A number of currency units, shares, bushels, pounds, or other units specified in a derivative instrument.

Underlying

A specified interest rate, security price, commodity price, foreign exchange rate, index of prices or rates, or other variable. An underlying may be a price or rate of an asset or liability but is not the asset or liability itself.

Statement of Financial Accounting Standards No. 134
Accounting for Mortgage-Backed Securities Retained after the Securitization of Mortgage Loans Held for Sale by a Mortgage Banking Enterprise

an amendment of FASB Statement No. 65

STATUS

Issued: October 1998

Effective Date: For the first fiscal quarter beginning after December 15, 1998

Affects: Amends FAS 65, paragraphs 4 and 6
　　　　Amends FAS 115, paragraph 12(a)

Affected by: No other pronouncements

Accounting for Mortgage-Backed Securities Retained **FAS134**
after the Securitization of Mortgage Loans Held for Sale
by a Mortgage Banking Enterprise

Statement of Financial Accounting Standards No. 134

Accounting for Mortgage-Backed Securities Retained after the Securitization of Mortgage Loans Held for Sale by a Mortgage Banking Enterprise

an amendment of FASB Statement No. 65

CONTENTS

INTRODUCTION

1. FASB Statement No. 65, *Accounting for Certain Mortgage Banking Activities,* establishes accounting and reporting standards for certain activities of mortgage banking enterprises and other enterprises that conduct operations that are substantially similar to the primary operations of a mortgage banking enterprise.

2. Statement 65, as amended by FASB Statements No. 115, *Accounting for Certain Investments in Debt and Equity Securities,* and No. 125, *Accounting for Transfers and Servicing of Financial Assets and Extinguishments of Liabilities,* requires that after the securitization of a mortgage loan held for sale, an entity engaged in mortgage banking activities classify the resulting mortgage-backed security as a trading security. This Statement further amends Statement 65 to require that after the securitization of mortgage loans held for sale, an entity engaged in mortgage banking activities classify the resulting mortgage-backed securities or other retained interests based on its ability and intent to sell or hold those investments. This Statement conforms the subsequent accounting for securities retained after the securitization of mortgage loans by a mortgage banking enterprise with the subsequent accounting for securities retained after the securitization of other types of assets by a non-mortgage banking enterprise.

STANDARDS OF FINANCIAL ACCOUNTING AND REPORTING

Amendment to Statement 65

3. The second sentence of paragraph 6 of Statement 65, which was added by Statement 115 and amended by Statement 125, is deleted. The following is added to the end of paragraph 6:

> After the securitization of a mortgage loan held for sale, any retained mortgage-backed securities shall be classified in accordance with the provisions of Statement 115. However, a mortgage banking enterprise must classify as trading any retained mortgage-backed securities that it commits to sell before or during the securitization process.

4. The fifth sentence of paragraph 4 of Statement 65, as amended by Statement 115, FASB Statement No. 124, *Accounting for Certain Investments Held by Not-for-Profit Organizations,* and FASB Statement No. 133, *Accounting for Derivative Instruments and Hedging Activities,* is deleted.

Amendment to Statement 115

5. The third and fourth sentences of paragraph 12(a) of Statement 115 are deleted.

Effective Date and Transition

6. This Statement shall be effective for the first fiscal quarter beginning after December 15, 1998. Early application is encouraged and is permitted as of the issuance of this Statement. On the date this Statement is initially applied, an enterprise may reclassify mortgage-backed securities and other beneficial interests retained after the securitization of mortgage loans held for sale from the trading category, except for those with sales commitments in place.[1] Those securities and other interests shall be classified based on the entity's ability and intent, on the date this Statement is initially applied, to hold those investments. Transfers from the trading category that result from implementing this Statement shall be accounted for in accordance with paragraph 15(a) of Statement 115.

> **The provisions of this Statement need not be applied to immaterial items.**

This Statement was adopted by the unanimous vote of the seven members of the Financial Accounting Standards Board:

Edmund L. Jenkins,	Anthony T. Cope	James J. Leisenring
Chairman	John M. Foster	Gerhard G. Mueller
Joseph V. Anania	Gaylen N. Larson	

Appendix

BACKGROUND INFORMATION AND BASIS FOR CONCLUSIONS

Background Information

7. Prior to its amendment by Statements 115 and 125, Statement 65 required that mortgage loans and mortgage-backed securities be classified as either held for sale or long-term investments. Mortgage loans and mortgage-backed securities held for sale were reported at the lower of cost or market value. Statement 65 permitted an enterprise to transfer loans or mortgage-backed securities from a held-for-sale to a long-term investment category if the enterprise had both the ability and the intent to hold those loans or securities for the foreseeable future or until maturity.

8. Statement 115 did not allow for debt or marketable equity securities to be measured at the lower of cost or market and amended Statement 65 to require that "the securitization of a mortgage loan held for sale shall be accounted for as the sale of the mortgage loan and the purchase of a mortgage-backed security classified as a trading security at fair value" (paragraph 128(c)). Statement 125 amended Statement 115 and required that "after the securitization of a mortgage loan held for sale, the mortgage-backed security shall be classified as a trading security" (paragraph 237(a)). As a result, Statement 65, as amended, required that an enterprise engaged in mortgage banking activities classify all mortgage-backed securities retained after the securitization of mortgage loans held for sale as trading under Statement 115, regardless of whether the enterprise intended to sell those securities or hold them as long-term investments. Therefore, all unrealized gains or losses on those securities were recognized currently in earnings.

Decision to Amend Statement 65

9. In March 1997, the Mortgage Bankers Association of America (MBAA) asked the Board to reconsider the accounting for securities retained after the securitization of mortgage loans held for sale. The MBAA explained that an enterprise engaged in mortgage banking activities was required to classify those securities exclusively as trading. The MBAA observed that a nonmortgage banking enterprise engaged in the securitization of other types of assets was able to classify the retained securities as trading, available-for-sale, or held-to-maturity under Statement 115.

---

[1]Mortgage-backed securities and other beneficial interests may be reclassified from the trading category when initially applying this Statement without regard for the provisions in paragraph 15 of Statement 115, which states that "given the nature of a trading security, transfers into or from the trading category . . . should be rare."

Accounting for Mortgage-Backed Securities Retained **FAS134**
after the Securitization of Mortgage Loans Held for Sale
by a Mortgage Banking Enterprise

10. The Board believes that the fair value of financial assets and liabilities provides more relevant and understandable information than cost or cost-based measures and has a project on its agenda to consider measuring all financial instruments at fair value. The Board, therefore, considered rejecting the MBAA's request to amend Statement 65 and, instead, addressing the issues as part of its fair value project. However, because the requirements for entities engaged in mortgage banking activities were more stringent than for other entities and it is expected to be several years before a standard addressing the fair value of all financial instruments is effective, the Board decided to address the concerns of the MBAA through an amendment of Statement 65. The Board decided that Statement 65 should be amended to require that an enterprise engaged in mortgage banking activities classify mortgage-backed securities retained after the securitization of mortgage loans held for sale based on its ability and intent to sell or hold those investments. The Board based its decision on several factors, including the concerns of the MBAA.

11. First, an enterprise engaged in mortgage banking activities frequently does not plan to sell all securities or other retained interests resulting from the securitization of mortgage loans held for sale. The enterprise may retain some of those beneficial interests as long-term investments because they are illiquid and difficult to sell. Those beneficial interests also may be retained because the enterprise decides, for a variety of reasons, to maintain a financial interest in the mortgage loans that it originates.

12. Second, some enterprises do not engage in mortgage banking but their activities are similar to those of a mortgage banking enterprise. Because the receivables they originate, transfer, and service are not *mortgages,* their activities are not within the scope of Statement 65. Those enterprises, unlike mortgage banking enterprises, are not required to classify securities retained after the securitization of their receivables as trading. They may, instead, choose to classify their retained securities as available-for-sale and, in some cases, held-to-maturity under Statement 115. The Board considered requiring that those enterprises classify securities retained after securitizing non-mortgage receivables as trading. While that approach would result in greater consistency among enterprises engaged in similar activities, it would require that the scope of this project be expanded signifi-

cantly. The Board decided against that approach and chose, instead, to amend Statement 65. This approach provides a "level playing field" among enterprises engaged in similar activities while addressing only mortgage banking activities at this time.

13. Third, allowing an enterprise to classify retained securities based on its ability and intent to sell or hold those investments is consistent with the approach in Statement 115. While Statement 115 restricts the ability to classify debt securities as held-to-maturity, it permits an enterprise to choose the appropriate classification based on the enterprise's ability and intent to sell or hold the securities. This Statement allows an enterprise engaged in mortgage banking activities an opportunity to choose the appropriate classification for its retained securities, rather than requiring a trading classification in all cases.

14. In April 1998, the Board issued an Exposure Draft, *Accounting for Mortgage-Backed Securities and Certain Other Interests Retained after the Securitization of Mortgage Loans Held for Sale by a Mortgage Banking Enterprise,* for a 45-day comment period. Twenty-five organizations and individuals responded to the Exposure Draft. In August 1998, the Board discussed the issues raised in the comment letters in a public Board meeting. The Board concluded that it could reach an informed decision on the basis of existing information without a public hearing.

The Approach in This Statement

15. The Exposure Draft proposed that an enterprise decide whether securities and other beneficial interests that are retained after the securitization of mortgage loans held for sale would, themselves, be held for sale to determine their proper classification. Retained securities that the enterprise holds for sale would have been classified in the trading category, with changes in their fair value recognized currently in earnings. Other retained nonsecurity beneficial interests that the enterprise holds for sale would have been accounted for like securities and also classified as trading. The Board reasoned that a mortgage banking enterprise should use the same criteria to identify retained securities intended to be sold as it uses to identify loans intended to be sold. That approach would primarily ensure that losses on retained securities and other beneficial interests intended to be sold would be recognized currently in earnings.

Accounting for Retained Securities

16. Many respondents commented that the approach in the Exposure Draft was complex and did not completely level the playing field between a mortgage banking enterprise and a nonmortgage banking enterprise engaged in securitization activities. Those respondents indicated that the accounting for securities retained after the securitization of mortgage loans should be the same as the accounting for securities retained after the securitization of other types of assets. The Board agreed with those respondents and decided to require that retained securities be accounted for in accordance with Statement 115.

17. The Board was concerned that because the term *trading* is not defined precisely in Statement 115, a mortgage banking enterprise could avoid a trading classification for retained securities it had committed to sell. That might occur because the settlement periods for the retained securities of a mortgage banking enterprise may be longer than the typical settlement periods for other types of securities classified as trading in paragraph 12(a) of Statement 115. The Board decided to require a trading classification for any retained securities that a mortgage banking enterprise commits to sell before or during the securitization process.

Accounting for Other Beneficial Interests

18. Statement 115's amendment of Statement 65 addressed only the accounting for *securities* that are retained as beneficial interests. The Exposure Draft proposed that retained nonsecurity interests that are held for sale also be classified as trading. Several respondents to the Exposure Draft observed that paragraph 4 of Statement 65 provides applicable guidance for those other beneficial interests and that other enterprises that securitize loans are not required to classify nonsecurity interests as trading. Because the objective of this project was to conform, as nearly as possible, the accounting for all securitizations of loans, the Board agreed and deleted that requirement. This Statement also does not address the accounting for other beneficial interests that are not held for sale. The Board observes that paragraph 6 of Statement 65 provides applicable guidance. Some of those other retained beneficial interests, however, are subject to the provisions of paragraph 14 of Statement 125 and, therefore, must be measured like investments in debt securities classified as available-for-sale or trading under Statement 115.

Classifying Retained Securities as Held-to-Maturity

19. The Board considered restricting the potential categories to trading or available-for-sale for retained securities but decided that that restriction was unjustified. Some observed that permitting an enterprise engaged in mortgage banking activities to classify retained securities as held-to-maturity was undesirable and incompatible with the Board's project to consider measuring all financial instruments at fair value. However, others observed that nonmortgage banking enterprises may choose to classify debt securities as held-to-maturity if all of the necessary provisions of Statement 115 are met. The Board decided that it is beyond the scope of this Statement to reconsider whether Statement 115 should continue to permit historical cost accounting for some securities. Therefore, the Board decided to permit an enterprise engaged in mortgage banking activities to apply the same intent-based accounting that is applied by other enterprises. Therefore, any sales or transfers of retained securities that are classified as held-to-maturity for reasons other than those in paragraphs 8 and 11 of Statement 115 would call into question an enterprise's ability and intent to hold other debt securities to maturity in the future.

20. The Board expects that many mortgage-backed securities retained after the securitization of mortgage loans held for sale would not be classified as held-to-maturity under Statement 115, as amended by Statement 125. Specifically, the Board notes that paragraph 7 of Statement 115 was amended by Statement 125 to require that "a security may not be classified as held-to-maturity if that security can contractually be prepaid or otherwise settled in such a way that the holder of the security would not recover substantially all of its recorded investment." Likewise, paragraph 14 of Statement 125 requires that "interest-only strips, loans, other receivables, or retained interests in securitizations that can contractually be prepaid or otherwise settled in such a way that the holder would not recover substantially all of its recorded investment shall be subsequently measured like investments in debt securities classified as available-for-sale or trading under Statement 115, as amended by this Statement" (references omitted). However, retained beneficial interests that meet the definition of a derivative or that contain embedded derivative instruments must be accounted for in accordance with Statement 133 upon its adoption. Paragraph 14 of Statement 133 provides an exception for certain interest-only and principal-only strips.

Accounting for Mortgage-Backed Securities Retained **FAS134**
after the Securitization of Mortgage Loans Held for Sale
by a Mortgage Banking Enterprise

Transition

21. The Board decided to permit an enterprise a one-time opportunity to reclassify mortgage-backed securities and other beneficial interests from the trading category, without regard to the restriction in paragraph 15 of Statement 115. That opportunity is available only on the date that this Statement is initially applied. Transfers from the trading category that result from implementing this Statement should be accounted for in accordance with paragraph 15(a) of Statement 115, that is, the unrealized gain or loss at the date of transfer will have already been recognized in earnings and should not be reversed. While this Statement does not address the accounting for other retained beneficial interests, some mortgage banking enterprises may have classified all of the interests that were measured like securities in accordance with paragraph 14 of Statement 125 as trading. Accordingly, some of those other retained beneficial interests may be eligible for transfer into the available-for-sale category when implementing this Statement. An enterprise engaged in mortgage banking activities often holds other securities unrelated to those retained after the securitization of mortgage loans previously held for sale by that enterprise. Statement 65 did *not* require that those securities be classified as trading, and they should already be classified in one of the three categories required by Statement 115. Therefore, the transition provisions of this Statement do *not* apply to those investments.

Statement of Financial Accounting Standards No. 135
Rescission of FASB Statement No. 75
and Technical Corrections

STATUS

Issued: February 1999

Effective Date: For financial statements issued for fiscal years ending after February 15, 1999

Affects: Supersedes ARB 43, Chapter 1A, paragraph 4
   Amends ARB 43, Chapter 3A, paragraph 9
   Amends APB 6, paragraph 12(b)
   Amends APB 16, paragraph 88(a)
   Amends APB 17, paragraph 31
   Amends APB 28, paragraphs 30, 31, and 33
   Amends AIN-APB 30, Interpretation No. 1
   Amends FAS 3, paragraph 14
   Supersedes FAS 13, paragraph 20
   Amends FAS 15, paragraph 4
   Amends FAS 35, paragraph 2
   Amends FAS 43, paragraph 2
   Amends FAS 52, paragraphs 24, 26, 31, 34, and 46
   Amends FAS 60, paragraph 46
   Amends FAS 66, footnote 34
   Supersedes FAS 71, footnote 3
   Supersedes FAS 75
   Amends FAS 87, paragraphs 49 and 66 and Illustration 4
   Supersedes FAS 87, footnote 13
   Amends FAS 89, paragraph 8(b)
   Amends FAS 93, footnote 1
   Amends FAS 102, footnote 3
   Amends FAS 106, paragraphs 65, 103, 107, 392, 417, and 461
   Supersedes FAS 106, paragraphs 464, 467, and 471 and footnote 23
   Amends FAS 109, paragraph 276
   Amends FAS 115, paragraph 7 and footnote 4
   Supersedes FAS 115, paragraph 17
   Amends FAS 123, paragraphs 49, 358, and 359
   Amends FAS 128, paragraph 28
   Amends FAS 130, paragraph 27
   Amends FAS 131, paragraphs 18, 25, 27, 28, 33, and 123
   Amends FAS 132, paragraphs 12(b) and 63
   Supersedes FAS 132, paragraphs 12(d) and 14(e)
   Amends FIN 18, footnote 8
   Supersedes FIN 27, footnote 3
   Amends FIN 39, paragraph 7
   Amends FIN 40, paragraph 5
   Amends FTB 79-5, paragraph 3

Affected by: Paragraphs 4(p)(1), 4(p)(7), and 4(r)(2) superseded by FAS 145
   Paragraph 5(c) amended by FAS 145

Issues Discussed by FASB Emerging Issues Task Force (EITF)

Affects: No EITF Issues

Interpreted by: No EITF Issues

Related Issue: EITF Topic No. D-92

SUMMARY

This Statement rescinds FASB Statement No. 75, *Deferral of the Effective Date of Certain Accounting Requirements for Pension Plans of State and Local Governmental Units*. GASB Statement No. 25, *Financial Reporting for Defined Benefit Pension Plans and Note Disclosures for Defined Contribution Plans*, was issued November 1994, and establishes financial reporting standards for defined benefit pension plans and for the notes to the financial statements of defined contribution plans of state and local governmental entities. Statement 75 is, therefore, no longer needed. This Statement also amends FASB Statement No. 35, *Accounting and Reporting by Defined Benefit Pension Plans*, to exclude from its scope plans that are sponsored by and provide benefits for the employees of one or more state or local governmental units.

This Statement also amends other existing authoritative literature to make various technical corrections, clarify meanings, or describe applicability under changed conditions.

This Statement is effective for financial statements issued for fiscal years ending after February 15, 1999. Earlier application is encouraged.

Statement of Financial Accounting Standards No. 135

Rescission of FASB Statement No. 75 and Technical Corrections

CONTENTS

INTRODUCTION

Rescission of Statement 75

1. FASB Statement No. 75, *Deferral of the Effective Date of Certain Accounting Requirements for Pension Plans of State and Local Governmental Units,* indefinitely deferred the effective date of FASB Statement No. 35, *Accounting and Reporting by Defined Benefit Pension Plans,* for plans that are sponsored by and provide benefits for the employees of one or more state or local governmental units. In November 1994, the Governmental Accounting Standards Board issued GASB Statement No. 25, *Financial Reporting for Defined Benefit Pension Plans and Note Disclosures for Defined Contribution Plans,* which establishes financial reporting standards for defined benefit pension plans and for the notes to the financial statements of defined contribution plans of state and local governmental entities. With the issuance of GASB Statement 25, the provisions of Statement 35, as deferred indefinitely by Statement 75, are no longer applicable for plans that are sponsored by and provide benefits for the employees of one or more state or local governmental units.

Technical Corrections

2. When the Board issues a pronouncement that contains amendments to prior pronouncements, the proposed amendments are reviewed by the Board and exposed for comment as part of the due process procedures. Over the years, the FASB staff and various constituents have identified instances where additional amendments should have been made explicit in certain pronouncements. Although, in general, those "effective" amendments have been appro-

priately indicated in the various editions of the FASB's *Original Pronouncements* and *Current Text* publications, those effective amendments were not subjected to the Board's review and due process procedures. This Statement identifies those effective amendments and establishes them as Board-approved amendments. In addition, this Statement amends existing authoritative literature to (a) correct references to AICPA guidance that has been revised or superseded since the issuance of that literature, (b) extend certain provisions to reflect established practice, and (c) eliminate inconsistencies in existing pronouncements.

STANDARDS OF FINANCIAL ACCOUNTING AND REPORTING

Rescission of Statement 75

3. This Statement rescinds FASB Statement No. 75, *Deferral of the Effective Date of Certain Accounting Requirements for Pension Plans of State and Local Governmental Units.*

Technical Corrections

4. This Statement amends the following pronouncements to make technical corrections to existing authoritative literature:

a. Accounting Research Bulletin No. 43, *Restatement and Revision of Accounting Research Bulletins.*

   (1) Paragraph 4 of Chapter 1A, "Prior Opinions—Rules Adopted by Membership," is deleted (to reflect current established prac-

tice that it is no longer acceptable to show stock of a corporation held in its own treasury as an asset).

(2) Paragraph 9 of Chapter 3A, "Working Capital—Current Assets and Current Liabilities," is amended as follows (effectively amended by FASB Statement No. 115, *Accounting for Certain Investments in Debt and Equity Securities*):

(a) In the third sentence, *marketable securities and* is deleted.

(b) The fourth sentence is deleted.

(c) In the sixth sentence, *for temporary investments, their market value at the balance-sheet date, and* is deleted.

b. APB Opinion No. 6, *Status of Accounting Research Bulletins.* In the first sentence of paragraph 12(b), *,or in some circumstances may be shown as an asset in accordance with paragraph 4 of Chapter 1A of ARB 43* is deleted (to reflect current established practice that it is no longer acceptable to show/stock of a corporation held in its own treasury as an asset).

c. APB Opinion No. 16, *Business Combinations.* In paragraph 88(a), *net realizable values* is replaced by *fair values* (effectively amended by Statement 115).

d. APB Opinion No. 17, *Intangible Assets.* In the third sentence of paragraph 31, *(APB Opinion No. 9, paragraph 21)* is deleted, and in the fourth and fifth sentences of paragraph 31, *extraordinary* is replaced by *unusual* (effectively amended by APB Opinion No. 30, *Reporting the Results of Operations—Reporting the Effects of Disposal of a Segment of a Business, and Extraordinary, Unusual and Infrequently Occurring Events and Transactions*).

e. APB Opinion No. 28, *Interim Financial Reporting.* The following changes are made to clarify the requirements for interim reporting:

(1) In the first and fourth sentences of paragraph 30, *to their securityholders* is deleted.

(2) In the second sentence of paragraph 30, *securityholders with* is deleted.

(3) In the first sentence of paragraph 31, *securityholders* is replaced by *users of the interim financial information.*

(4) In the first sentence of paragraph 33, *securityholders* is replaced by *users of the interim financial information.*

f. AICPA Accounting Interpretation 1, "Illustration of the Application of APB Opinion No. 30." Example (12) is deleted (effectively superseded by Statement 115).

g. FASB Statement No. 3, *Reporting Accounting Changes in Interim Financial Statements.* In paragraph 14, *to its securityholders* is deleted (to clarify the requirements for interim reporting).

h. FASB Statement No. 13, *Accounting for Leases.* Paragraph 20, as amended by FASB Statement No. 77, *Reporting by Transferors for Transfers of Receivables with Recourse,* and FASB Statement No. 125, *Accounting for Transfers and Servicing of Financial Assets and Extinguishments of Liabilities,* is replaced by the following (to revise the amendment made by Statement 125):

The sale or assignment of a lease or of property subject to a lease that was accounted for as a sales-type lease or direct financing lease shall not negate the original accounting treatment accorded the lease. Any transfer of minimum lease payments or guaranteed residual values subject to a sales-type lease or direct financing lease shall be accounted for in accordance with FASB Statement No. 125, *Accounting for Transfers and Servicing of Financial Assets and Extinguishments of Liabilities.* However, transfers of unguaranteed residual values are not subject to the provisions of Statement 125.

i. FASB Statement No. 15, *Accounting by Debtors and Creditors for Troubled Debt Restructurings.* In the second sentence of paragraph 4, *investing in debt securities that were previously issued,* is deleted (effectively amended by Statement 115).

j. FASB Statement No. 35, *Accounting and Reporting by Defined Benefit Pension Plans.* In the first sentence of paragraph 2, *,including state and local governments,* is deleted (to amend the scope of Statement 35 to reflect the issuance of GASB Statement 25).

k. FASB Statement No. 43, *Accounting for Compensated Absences,* as amended by FASB Statement No. 112, *Employers' Accounting for Postemployment Benefits.* In the last sentence of paragraph 2, *or a portion of a line of business* is deleted (effectively amended by FASB Statement No. 121, *Accounting for the Impairment of Long-Lived Assets and for Long-Lived Assets to Be Disposed Of*).

l. FASB Statement No. 52, *Foreign Currency Translation.*

(1) In paragraph 24, *a separate component of equity* in the second sentence and *that separate component of equity* in the last sentence are replaced by *other comprehensive income* (effectively amended by FASB Statement No. 130, *Reporting Comprehensive Income*).

(2) In the last sentence of paragraph 26, *(ARB 43, Chapter 12, paragraph 8)* is deleted (effectively amended by paragraph 16 of FASB Statement No. 94, *Consolidation of All Majority-Owned Subsidiaries,* which deleted ARB 43, Chapter 12, paragraph 8).

(3) In the first sentence of paragraph 31, *separate component of equity for cumulative* is replaced by *accumulated amount of* and *reported in equity* is inserted after *translation adjustments* (effectively amended by Statement 130).

(4) In the first sentence of paragraph 34, *as the opening balance of the cumulative translation adjustments component of equity* is replaced by *in other comprehensive income* (effectively amended by Statement 130).

(5) In the last sentence of paragraph 46, *the cumulative translation adjustments component of equity* is replaced by *other comprehensive income* (effectively amended by Statement 130).

m. FASB Statement No. 60, *Accounting and Reporting by Insurance Enterprises.* In the second sentence of paragraph 46, as amended by Statement 115 and FASB Statement No. 124, *Accounting for Certain Investments Held by Not-for-Profit Organizations,* the phrase *a separate component of equity* is replaced by *other comprehensive income* (effectively amended by Statement 130).

n. FASB Statement No. 66, *Accounting for Sales of Real Estate.* In footnote 34 to paragraph 101, letter *(a)* and *or (b) a right-to-use time-sharing interest that is a sales-type lease as defined in Statement 13, as amended and interpreted* are deleted (to reflect amendments made to Statement 13 by FASB Statement No. 98, *Accounting for Leases;* Statement 98 amends Statement 13 to prohibit a lease involving real estate from being classified as a sales-type lease unless the lease transfers ownership of the property to the lessee by the end of the lease term; therefore, a right-to-use time-sharing interest would not meet this requirement).

o. FASB Statement No. 71, *Accounting for the Effects of Certain Types of Regulation.* Footnote 3 to paragraph 5(a) is replaced by the following (to update the scope of Statement 71 to reflect both the existence of the GASB as well as the appropriate literature to be followed):

GASB Statement No. 20, *Accounting and Financial Reporting for Proprietary Funds and Other Governmental Entities That Use Proprietary Fund Accounting,* paragraph 9, provides that state and local proprietary activities that meet the criteria of paragraph 5 may apply this FASB Statement and related pronouncements (including FASB Statements No. 90, *Regulated Enterprises—Accounting for Abandonments and Disallowances of Plant Costs,* No. 92, *Regulated Enterprises—Accounting for Phase-in Plans,* and No. 101, *Regulated Enterprises—Accounting for the Discontinuation of Application of FASB Statement No. 71*) that were issued on or before November 30, 1989. Amendments of FASB pronouncements related to regulated operations issued after that date are subject to the provisions of GASB Statement 20, paragraph 7.

p. FASB Statement No. 87, *Employers' Accounting for Pensions.* The following changes are made to revise the amendments made by FASB Statement No. 132, *Employers' Disclosures about Pensions and Other Postretirement Benefits:*

(1) In paragraph 34, *(a) the difference between the actual return on plan assets and the expected return on plan assets and (b)* is deleted.

(2) In the first sentence of paragraph 49, *paragraph 54* is replaced by *paragraphs 5 and 8 of FASB Statement No. 132, Employers' Disclosures about Pensions and Other Post-retirement Benefits.*

(3) Footnote 13 to paragraph 54(b) is deleted.

(4) Paragraph 55, deleted by Statement 132, is reinstated.

(5) Paragraph 66, deleted by Statement 132, is reinstated. In the last sentence of that paragraph, *and disclosure requirements shall be determined in accordance with the provisions of this Statement applicable to a defined benefit plan* is replaced by *requirements shall be determined in accordance with the provisions of this Statement applicable to a defined benefit plan and the disclosure requirements shall be determined in accordance with the provisions of paragraphs 5 and 8 of Statement 132.*

(6) In Illustration 4 in paragraph 261, the disclosures for the years 1987, 1988, and 1989 and the related footnotes are deleted. (Appendix B of Statement 132 provides examples that illustrate the revised required disclosures.)

(7) In the first sentence of the definition of *Gain or loss component (of net periodic pension cost)* in paragraph 264 (the glossary), *The sum of (a) the difference between the actual return on plan assets and the expected return on plan assets and (b)* is deleted.

q. FASB Statement No. 89, *Financial Reporting and Changing Prices.* In paragraph 8(b), *(currently 1967)* is replaced by *(currently 1982–1984)* (to bring the measurement guidance up to date).

r. FASB Statement No. 106, *Employers' Accounting for Postretirement Benefits Other Than Pensions.*

(1) In the first sentence of paragraph 103, *or a portion of a line of business* is deleted (effectively amended by Statement 121).

(2) The following changes are made to revise the amendments made by Statement 132:

(a) In paragraph 62, *the difference between the actual return on plan assets and the expected return on plan assets, (b) any gain or loss immediately recognized or the amortization of the unrecognized net gain or loss from previous periods, and (c)* is replaced by *any gain or loss immediately recognized or the amortization of the unrecognized net gain or loss from previous periods and (b).*

(b) In the first sentence of paragraph 65, *paragraph 74* is replaced by *paragraphs 5 and 8 of FASB Statement No. 132, Employers' Disclosures about Pensions and Other Post-retirement Benefits.*

(c) Footnote 23 to paragraph 74(b) is deleted.

(d) Paragraph 107, deleted by Statement 132, is reinstated. In the last sentence of that paragraph *and disclosure requirements shall be determined in accordance with the provisions of this Statement applicable to a defined benefit plan* is replaced by *requirements shall be determined in accordance with the provisions of this Statement applicable to a defined benefit plan and the disclosure requirements shall be determined in accordance with the provisions of paragraphs 5 and 8 of Statement 132.*

(e) The fourth sentence of paragraph 392 is deleted.

(f) In the third sentence of paragraph 417, *paragraph 74(c)* is replaced by *paragraph 5(c) of Statement 132.*

(g) In the first sentence of paragraph 461, *paragraph 74(b)* is replaced by *paragraph 5(d) of Statement 132.*

(h) Paragraph 464 and the related footnotes are replaced by the following:

The 1994 financial statements include the following disclosure of the components of net periodic postretirement benefit cost:

Service cost	$ 320,000
Interest cost	630,000
Expected return on plan assets	(87,000)
Amortization of transition obligation	300,000
Recognized net actuarial loss	5,000
Net periodic postretirement benefit cost	$1,168,000

(i) Paragraph 467 and the related footnotes are replaced by the following:

The 1995 financial statements include the following disclosure of the components of net periodic postretirement benefit cost:

Service cost	$ 360,000
Interest cost	652,500
Expected return on plan assets	(193,700)
Amortization of transition obligation	300,000
Net periodic postretirement benefit cost	$1,118,800

(j) Paragraph 471, its heading, and the related footnotes are deleted.

s. FASB Statement No. 109, *Accounting for Income Taxes*. Paragraph 276 is amended as follows (effectively amended by Statement 130):

(1) In the first sentence, *or to other comprehensive income* is inserted after *equity*.

(2) In the second sentence, *directly to shareholders' equity* is replaced by *to other comprehensive income*.

(3) In subparagraph (c), *charged to the cumulative translation adjustment account* is replaced by *reported in other comprehensive income and accumulated*.

(4) In subparagraph (f), *credited directly to the cumulative translation adjustment account* is replaced by *reported in other comprehensive income and accumulated*.

t. FASB Statement No. 115, *Accounting for Certain Investments in Debt and Equity Securities*.

(1) The following sentence is added to the end of paragraph 7, as amended by FASB State-ment 125 (effectively amended by FASB Statement No. 133, *Accounting for Derivative Instruments and Hedging Activities*):

A debt security with those characteristics should be evaluated in accordance with paragraphs 12–16 of Statement 133 to determine whether it contains an embedded derivative that must be accounted for separately.

(2) Paragraph 17 is replaced by the following (to supersede the requirement that all trading securities be classified as current assets):

An enterprise that presents a classified statement of financial position shall report individual held-to-maturity securities, individual available-for-sale securities, and individual trading securities as either current or noncurrent, as appropriate, under the provisions of ARB No. 43, Chapter 3A, "Working Capital—Current Assets and Current Liabilities."[5]

u. FASB Statement No. 123, *Accounting for Stock-Based Compensation*. The following changes are made to clarify the amendments made by FASB Statement No. 128, *Earnings per Share:*

(1) In the last sentence of paragraph 49, as amended by Statement 128, *or forfeited* is inserted after *granted.*

(2) The following is inserted at the beginning of paragraph 358, as amended by Statement 128:

> Under paragraph 28 of this Statement, an entity has the choice of estimating forfeitures in advance or recognizing forfeitures as they occur. However, the weighted-average number of options outstanding, rather than the number of options expected to vest, would be used in computing diluted EPS. In addition, the average net unrecognized compensation cost would include the options not expected to vest.

(3) In paragraph 359, as amended by Statement 128, *all* is replaced by *the weighted-average number of.*

v. FASB Statement No. 128, *Earnings per Share*. In paragraph 28, the first sentence is replaced by the following (to clarify the effect of dilutive securities):

> Dilutive securities that are issued during a period and dilutive convertible securities for which conversion options lapse, for which preferred stock is redeemed, or for which related debt is extinguished during a period shall be included in the denominator of diluted EPS for the period that they were outstanding.

w. FASB Statement No. 130, *Reporting Comprehensive Income*. In the last sentence of paragraph 27, *issued to shareholders* is deleted (to clarify the requirements for interim reporting).

x. FASB Statement No. 131, *Disclosures about Segments of an Enterprise and Related Information.*

(1) In paragraph 18:

(a) In subparagraph (a), *reported* preceding *operating segments* is deleted (to clarify that the test is applied to the total revenues of all operating segments).

(b) The last sentence is replaced with the following (to clarify the requirements for reporting operating segments):

> Operating segments that do not meet any of the quantitative thresholds may be considered reportable, and separately disclosed, if management believes that information about the segment would be useful to readers of the financial statements.

(2) In paragraph 25 (to clarify the requirements for periods for which segment information is required):

(a) In the first sentence, *for each period for which an income statement is presented* is inserted after *following.*

(b) The penultimate sentence of that paragraph is replaced with the following:

> However, reconciliations of balance sheet amounts for reportable segments to consolidated balance sheet amounts are required only for each year for which a balance sheet is presented.

(3) In the second sentence of paragraph 27, *(a)* is inserted after *specified amounts* and *or (b) are otherwise regularly provided to the chief operating decision maker, even if not included in that measure of segment profit or loss* is inserted before the colon (to clarify the circumstances under which the items identified by that paragraph are required to be disclosed).

(4) In the first sentence of paragraph 28, *(a)* is inserted after *specified amounts* and *or (b) are otherwise regularly provided to the chief operating decision maker, even if not included in the determination of segment assets* is inserted before the colon (to clarify the circumstances under which the items identified by that paragraph are required to be disclosed).

(5) In the first sentence of paragraph 33, *issued to shareholders* is deleted (to clarify the requirements for interim reporting).

(6) In the second sentence of paragraph 123, *a complete set of financial statements* is replaced by *an income statement* (to clarify the requirements for periods for which segment information is required).

y. FASB Statement No. 132, *Employers' Disclosures about Pensions and Other Postretirement Benefits*. The following changes are made to revise the amendments made by Statement 132:

(1) In paragraph 12(b), *Paragraphs 55 and 56 are* is replaced by *Paragraph 56 is*.

(2) Paragraphs 12(d) and 14(e) are deleted.

(3) In the third bullet of paragraph 63, *transition obligation* is replaced by *prior service cost.*

z. FASB Interpretation No. 18, *Accounting for Income Taxes in Interim Periods*. In footnote 8 to paragraph 9, *realization of the tax benefit is not assured* is replaced by *it is more likely than not that the tax benefit will not be realized* (effectively amended by Statement 109).

aa. FASB Interpretation No. 27, *Accounting for a Loss on a Sublease*. Footnote 3 to paragraph 3 is deleted (effectively superseded by Statement 121).

bb. FASB Interpretation No. 40, *Applicability of Generally Accepted Accounting Principles to Mutual Life Insurance and Other Enterprises*. The last sentence of paragraph 5 is deleted (effectively amended by paragraph 4 of FASB Statement No. 120, *Accounting and Reporting by Mutual Life Insurance Enterprises and by Insurance Enterprises for Certain Long-Duration Participating Contracts*).

cc. FASB Technical Bulletin No. 79-5, *Meaning of the Term "Customer" as It Applies to Health Care Facilities under FASB Statement No. 14*. In the first sentence of paragraph 3, *Statement 14* is replaced by *Statement 131* (effectively amended by Statement 131, which supersedes

FASB Statement No. 14, *Financial Reporting for Segments of a Business Enterprise*).

5. This Statement amends the following pronouncements to delete or amend references to AICPA pronouncements that have been revised or superseded:

a. FASB Statement No. 93, *Recognition of Depreciation by Not-for-Profit Organizations*. In footnote 1 to paragraph 1, *Hospital Audit Guide (1972), Audits of Colleges and Universities (1973), Audits of Voluntary Health and Welfare Organizations (1974), and Statement of Position 78-10, Accounting Principles and Reporting Practices for Certain Nonprofit Organizations (1978)* is replaced by *Health Care Organizations and Not-for-Profit Organizations*.

b. FASB Statement No. 102, *Statement of Cash Flows—Exemption of Certain Enterprises and Classification of Cash Flows from Certain Securities Acquired for Resale*. In footnote 3 to paragraph 8, *Industry Audit Guide, Audits of Banks* is replaced by *Audit and Accounting Guide, Banks and Savings Institutions*.

c. FASB Statement No. 115, *Accounting for Certain Investments in Debt and Equity Securities*. In footnote 4 to paragraph 16, *AICPA Auditing Interpretation, Evidential Matter for the Carrying Amount of Marketable Securities, which was issued in 1975 and incorporated in Statement on Auditing Standards No. 1, Codification of Auditing Standards and Procedures, as Interpretation 20* is replaced by *AICPA Statement on Auditing Standards No. 81, Auditing Investments*.

d. FASB Interpretation No. 39, *Offsetting of Amounts Related to Certain Contracts*. In paragraph 7, *Industry Audit Guide, Audits of Banks* is replaced by *Audit and Accounting Guide, Banks and Savings Institutions*.

Effective Date and Transition

6. This Statement is effective for financial statements issued for fiscal years ending after February 15, 1999. Earlier application is encouraged.

> The provisions of this Statement need
> not be applied to immaterial items.

*This Statement was adopted by the unanimous vote of the seven members of the Financial Accounting
Standards Board:*

Edmund L. Jenkins, *Chairman* Joseph V. Anania	Anthony T. Cope John M. Foster Gaylen N. Larson	James J. Leisenring Gerhard G. Mueller

Appendix

BACKGROUND INFORMATION AND
BASIS FOR CONCLUSIONS

Rescission of Statement 75

7. Statement 35 was issued in March 1980 and defines generally accepted accounting principles for general-purpose external financial reports of defined benefit pension plans. It was intended to apply both to plans in the private sector and to plans sponsored by state and local governmental units. As originally issued, Statement 35 was to be effective for plan years beginning after December 15, 1980.

8. In April 1982, the Board issued FASB Statement No. 59, *Deferral of the Effective Date of Certain Accounting Requirements for Pension Plans of State and Local Governmental Units*. That Statement amended Statement 35 by deferring its applicability until plan years beginning after June 15, 1982, for plans that are sponsored by and provide benefits for the employees of one or more state or local governmental units.

9. In November 1982, the Financial Accounting Foundation (FAF) reached agreement with the Municipal Finance Officers Association, the National Association of State Auditors, Comptrollers and Treasurers, and the American Institute of Certified Public Accountants regarding the establishment of a Governmental Accounting Standards Board (GASB).

10. In November 1983, the Board issued Statement 75. Statement 75 indefinitely deferred the effective date of Statement 35 for plans that are sponsored by and provide benefits for the employees of one or more state or local governmental units. The Board believed that while discussions relating to the formation and operation of the GASB were in progress,

those efforts should not be impaired by the imposition of a new standard (that is, Statement 35) or by the existence of differing standards issued by different bodies.

11. The GASB was organized in 1984 by the FAF to establish standards of financial accounting and reporting for state and local governmental entities. Its standards guide the preparation of external financial reports of those entities.

12. In June 1984, the GASB placed on its agenda a project on pension accounting and financial reporting for plans and participating employers. In July 1984, the GASB issued GASB Statement No. 1, *Authoritative Status of NCGA Pronouncements and AICPA Industry Audit Guide*. In that Statement, the GASB identified three pronouncements (one of which was Statement 35) as sources of acceptable accounting and reporting principles for pension plans and employers, pending issuance of a GASB Statement or Statements on pensions.

13. In November 1986, the GASB issued GASB Statement No. 5, *Disclosure of Pension Information by Public Employee Retirement Systems and State and Local Governmental Employers*. GASB Statement 5 superseded all previous authoritative guidance on pension note disclosures but continued to recognize the pronouncements, as amended, previously identified (including Statement 35) as sources of guidance for pension recognition, measurement, and display, pending issuance of a future GASB Statement or Statements.

14. In July 1990, the GASB began deliberations on pension plan reporting issues. An Exposure Draft, *Financial Reporting for Defined Benefit Pension Plans and Note Disclosures for Defined Contribution Plans,* was released for comment in 1994, and the final Statement (GASB Statement 25) was issued in November 1994.

15. GASB Statement 25 establishes financial reporting standards for defined benefit pension plans and

for the notes to the financial statements of defined contribution plans of state and local governmental entities. Financial reporting standards for post-employment healthcare plans administered by defined benefit pension plans and for the pension expenditure/expense of employers are included, respectively, in GASB Statements No. 26, *Financial Reporting for Postemployment Healthcare Plans Administered by Defined Benefit Pension Plans,* and No. 27, *Accounting for Pensions by State and Local Governmental Employers.* The requirements of GASB Statement 25 are effective for periods beginning after June 15, 1996. Accordingly, Statement 75 is no longer necessary.

Technical Corrections

16. At the time a pronouncement is developed by the Board, part of the process requires that a determination be made of the effect this new guidance will have on existing authoritative accounting pronouncements. If there is an effect, then the new pronouncement should amend or supersede the existing authoritative literature in detail so that there is (a) no doubt about what the amendment changes and (b) no conflict between the requirements of prior pronouncements and the requirements of the new pronouncement.

17. However, sometimes certain detailed amendments that could have been explicitly made to the authoritative literature were omitted because, for example, they were overlooked when the new pronouncement was prepared. As those omissions were discovered by the FASB staff or members of the accounting profession, corrections were made to the various editions of the FASB's *Current Text* through effective amendments, and the locations of those amendments were appropriately indicated in the *Original Pronouncements.* However, those effective technical amendments have not been subjected to the Board's usual due process procedures. The Board decided to take this opportunity to identify those effective amendments and issue them as Board-approved amendments.

18. When the Board first issued a standard to make technical corrections (FASB Statement No. 111, *Rescission of FASB Statement No. 32 and Technical Corrections,* in November 1992) the Board considered what parts of previously issued pronouncements to amend and decided that only the official guidance sections should be amended. The Board continues to believe that only the official guidance

sections should be amended. In other words, the Board believes that the introduction, background information, and basis for conclusions paragraphs provide historical information that should not be amended or superseded unless the entire pronouncement is superseded. Those paragraphs are considered historical because they document the circumstances surrounding the development of a pronouncement. For example, they record (a) the reasons why the accounting requirements were considered to be necessary at that time, (b) what alternative guidance was considered, and (c) what the public comments were regarding the proposed requirements and how those comments were resolved.

19. In addition to the accounting guidance and historical paragraphs, a pronouncement sometimes contains other paragraphs or appendixes. Those paragraphs or appendixes are ones that (a) state the scope of the pronouncement, (b) indicate substantive amendments to other existing pronouncements, (c) present examples or illustrations of application of the requirements of the pronouncement, and (d) present a glossary of the terms used in the pronouncement. The Board believes that the content of those various paragraphs and appendixes does provide part of the accounting guidance of the pronouncement and should be amended if the pronouncement is amended by a subsequent pronouncement. The Board has further decided that when a pronouncement is superseded, the amendments made by that superseded pronouncement remain in effect unless they are explicitly amended. Thus, if a paragraph (or part of one) is deleted without any replacement text, the deletion would still stand. If the Board decides to undo the deletion, then the new (superseding) Statement must explicitly add back the deleted text. However, if a superseded document either (a) has superseded text in a previous standard by replacing it with new text or (b) has added text to a previous standard, the new (superseding) Statement must either (1) explicitly repeat the amendment from the superseded document that added text or replaced text (for example, refer to paragraph 238 of Statement 125 and paragraph 532 of Statement 133) or (2) explicitly delete text that was added or replaced by the superseded document (for example, refer to paragraph 237(h) of Statement 125 and paragraph 531(b) of Statement 133).

20. Some of the technical corrections in this Statement are not the direct result of effective amendments by new standards. That is, some amendments

have been made to extend certain provisions to reflect established practice or clarify inconsistencies in existing pronouncements. For example:

a. Prior to being superseded by the Accounting Principles Board, the Committee on Accounting Procedure and the Committee on Terminology of the AICPA issued a series of Accounting Research Bulletins between 1939 and 1953. In 1953, the Committee on Accounting Procedure restated and revised the first 42 Bulletins. The purpose of the restatement (codified into ARB 43) was to eliminate what was no longer applicable, to condense and clarify required revisions, and to arrange the retained material by subjects rather than in the order of issuance. In 1953, practice permitted the accounting, in some circumstances, for stock of a corporation held in its own treasury as an asset. In EITF Issue No. 97-14, "Accounting for Deferred Compensation Arrangements Where Amounts Earned Are Held in a Rabbi Trust and Invested," the Emerging Issues Task Force reached a consensus that company shares held by a rabbi trust should be treated as treasury stock in the employer's financial statements. In connection with that Issue, the staff of the Securities and Exchange Commission (SEC) nullified its previously stated position that asset classification may be appropriate if the shares repurchased are expected to be reissued promptly (within one year) under existing stock plans. The Board also believes that it is no longer acceptable to show stock of a corporation held in its own treasury as an asset. One constituent notified the Board that that position may conflict with a provision in paragraph 13 of Opinion 6, which states:

> Laws of some states govern the circumstances under which a corporation may acquire its own stock and prescribe the accounting treatment therefor. Where such requirements are at variance with paragraph 12, the accounting should conform to the applicable law.

The Board considered the point and observed that that reference is not specific to classifying treasury stock as an asset. Furthermore, several Board members expressed concern about that sentence being applied too broadly.

b. Paragraph 21 of APB Opinion No. 9, *Reporting the Results of Operations,* provided criteria for the determination of extraordinary items. Examples

of extraordinary items included "the write-off of goodwill due to unusual events or developments within the period." Paragraph 31 of Opinion 17 provides that a loss resulting from a reduction in the unamortized cost of intangible assets does "not necessarily justify an extraordinary charge to income" and that "the reason for an extraordinary deduction should be disclosed." In June 1973 (three years after Opinion 17 was issued), Opinion 30 was issued which supersedes the criteria in Opinion 9 for the determination of extraordinary items. Paragraph 23 of Opinion 30 states that "certain gains and losses should not be reported as extraordinary items because they are usual in nature or may be expected to recur as a consequence of customary and continuing business activities. Examples include: (a) write-down or write-off of . . . other intangible assets." Paragraph 26 of Opinion 30, however, provides the following guidance on disclosure of unusual or infrequently occurring items: "A material event or transaction that is unusual in nature or occurs infrequently but not both, and therefore does not meet both criteria for classification as an extraordinary item, should be reported as a separate component of income from continuing operations." The Board observes that Opinion 17 was never amended to reflect the provisions of Opinion 9 that were superseded by Opinion 30 in that the write-down or write-off of intangibles may be an unusual item but may not be an extraordinary item. Accordingly, that change is being made at this time.

c. Paragraph 1 of Opinion 28 states that "the purpose of this Opinion is to clarify the application of accounting principles and reporting practices to interim financial information, including interim financial statements and summarized interim financial data of publicly traded companies issued for external reporting purposes." The specific requirements for interim disclosures found in Opinion 28 and various other pronouncements refer to the applicability of such requirements to financial information *issued to an enterprise's shareholders or securityholders.* Some have suggested that the interim disclosure requirements of those standards are not applicable to quarterly financial information reported pursuant to the Securities Exchange Act of 1934 on Forms 10-Q or 10-QSB, which generally are not issued to shareholders or securityholders. The interim disclosure requirements have been amended to clarify that the requirements are intended to be applied to interim financial reporting, including interim financial statements and summarized interim financial data of publicly traded companies issued for external reporting purposes.

d. Example (12) of the Accounting Interpretation of Opinion 30, provides as an example of a transaction that would meet both criteria of being unusual in nature and infrequent of occurrence a situation in which a company sells a block of common stock of a publicly traded company. The block of shares, which represents less than 10 percent of the publicly held company, is the only security investment the company has ever owned. The Board acknowledges that it would be a very rare situation for an entity to ever own (and intend to ever own) just one security investment. However, were that situation to arise, the Board believes that in accordance with Statement 115, it would no longer be acceptable to report the realized gain or loss on the sale of such a security as an extraordinary item when the unrealized gains or losses are reported in other comprehensive income or income from operations, as applicable.

e. The SEC, in Regulation S-X, requires that for public companies segment information required by Statement 14 must be provided for each year for which an audited statement of income is presented. As originally issued, Statement 131 requires segment information to be provided for each year for which a complete set of financial statements is presented. Because Statement 131 is applicable to only public companies, and the SEC will continue to require that segment information be presented for each year for which an audited statement of income is presented, the Board believes that amending Statement 131 to conform the reporting requirements is appropriate.

f. Paragraphs 27 and 28 of Statement 131 require disclosure of certain specified amounts relating to segment profit or loss and assets. The introductory language of those paragraphs states that disclosure of the specified amounts is required if the specified amounts are included in the measure of segment profit or loss (or in the determination of segment assets) reviewed by the chief operating decision maker. The first sentence of paragraph 29 further states that "the amount of each segment item reported shall be the measure reported to the chief operating decision maker for purposes of making decisions about allocating resources to the segment and assessing its performance." In May 1998, the FASB staff made an announcement at an EITF meeting (refer to EITF Topic No. D-70, "Questions Related to the Implementation of FASB Statement No. 131") that indicates the staff response to a technical inquiry relating to the requirements of paragraph 27. Specifically, the staff responded that if the items specified in paragraph 27 (and in paragraph 28) are provided to the chief operating decision maker for purposes of evaluating segment performance, then disclosure of such items is required even if such items are not included in the measure of segment profit or loss (or in the determination of segment assets) that is reviewed by the chief operating decision maker. The Board agreed with the staff's conclusion that the introductory language of paragraphs 27 and 28 should be considered together with the measurement guidance provided in paragraphs 29–31 and that as part of this project to make technical corrections, the introductory language of paragraphs 27 and 28 should be amended.

Comments on Exposure Draft

21. The Board issued an Exposure Draft, *Amendment to FASB Statement No. 66, Rescission of FASB Statement No. 75, and Technical Corrections,* for comment on October 13, 1998, and received nine letters of comment. Many of the respondents expressed concern about an amendment to Statement 66 that was proposed in the Exposure Draft. Subsequent to the issuance of the Exposure Draft, the Board decided to exclude that proposed amendment from this project because of the complexity of some of the issues that were raised in the comment letters. That issue will be addressed separately by the Board.

22. A majority of respondents agreed with the technical corrections proposed in the Exposure Draft. Several respondents indicated support for the practice of making needed technical corrections when they are identified and then formally issuing those corrections as Board-approved amendments after due process. A few respondents had suggestions for additional amendments and technical corrections. Some of those suggested amendments are included in this Statement.

Statement of Financial Accounting Standards No. 136
Transfers of Assets to a Not-for-Profit Organization or Charitable Trust That Raises or Holds Contributions for Others

STATUS

Issued: June 1999

Effective Date: For financial statements issued for fiscal periods beginning after December 15, 1999; paragraph 12 continues to be effective for fiscal years ending after September 15, 1996

Affects: Supersedes FIN 42

Affected by: Footnote 5 amended by FAS 140

SUMMARY

This Statement establishes standards for transactions in which an entity—the *donor*—makes a contribution by transferring assets to a not-for-profit organization or charitable trust—the *recipient organization*—that accepts the assets from the donor and agrees to use those assets on behalf of or transfer those assets, the return on investment of those assets, or both to another entity—the *beneficiary*—that is specified by the donor. It also establishes standards for transactions that take place in a similar manner but are not contributions because the transfers are revocable, repayable, or reciprocal.

This Statement requires a recipient organization that accepts cash or other financial assets from a donor and agrees to use those assets on behalf of or transfer those assets, the return on investment of those assets, or both to a specified unaffiliated beneficiary to recognize the fair value of those assets as a liability to the specified beneficiary concurrent with recognition of the assets received from the donor. However, if the donor explicitly grants the recipient organization variance power or if the recipient organization and the specified beneficiary are financially interrelated organizations, the recipient organization is required to recognize the fair value of any assets it receives as a contribution received. Not-for-profit organizations are financially interrelated if (a) one organization has the ability to influence the operating and financial decisions of the other and (b) one organization has an ongoing economic interest in the net assets of the other.

This Statement does not establish standards for a trustee's reporting of assets held on behalf of specified beneficiaries, but it does establish standards for a beneficiary's reporting of its rights to assets held in a charitable trust.

This Statement requires that a specified beneficiary recognize its rights to the assets held by a recipient organization as an asset unless the donor has explicitly granted the recipient organization variance power. Those rights are either an interest in the net assets of the recipient organization, a beneficial interest, or a receivable. If the beneficiary and the recipient organization are financially interrelated organizations, the beneficiary is required to recognize its interest in the net assets of the recipient organization and adjust that interest for its share of the change in net assets of the recipient organization. If the beneficiary has an unconditional right to receive all or a portion of the specified cash flows from a charitable trust or other identifiable pool of assets, the beneficiary is required to recognize that beneficial interest, measuring and subsequently remeasuring it at fair value, using a valuation technique such as the present value of the estimated expected future cash flows. If the recipient organization is explicitly granted variance power, the specified beneficiary does not recognize its potential for future distributions from the assets held by the recipient organization. In all other cases, a beneficiary recognizes its rights as a receivable.

This Statement describes four circumstances in which a transfer of assets to a recipient organization is accounted for as a liability by the recipient organization and as an asset by the resource provider because the transfer is revocable or reciprocal. Those four circumstances are if (a) the transfer is subject to the resource provider's unilateral right to redirect the use of the assets to another beneficiary, (b) the transfer is accompanied by the resource provider's conditional promise to give or is otherwise revocable or repayable, (c) the resource provider controls the recipient organization and specifies an unaffiliated beneficiary, or (d) the resource provider specifies itself or its affiliate as the beneficiary and the transfer is not an equity transaction. If the transfer is an equity transaction and the resource provider specifies itself as beneficiary, it records an interest in the net assets of the recipient organization (or an increase in a previously recognized interest). If the resource provider specifies an affiliate as beneficiary, the resource provider records an equity transaction as a separate line item in its statement of activities, and the affiliate named as beneficiary records an interest in the net assets of the recipient organization. The recipient organization records an equity transaction as a separate line item in its statement of activities.

This Statement requires certain disclosures if a not-for-profit organization transfers assets to a recipient organization and specifies itself or its affiliate as the beneficiary or if it includes in its financial statements a ratio of fundraising expenses to amounts raised.

This Statement incorporates without reconsideration the guidance in FASB Interpretation No. 42, *Accounting for Transfers of Assets in Which a Not-for-Profit Organization Is Granted Variance Power,* and supersedes that Interpretation.

This Statement is effective for financial statements issued for fiscal periods beginning after December 15, 1999, except for the provisions incorporated from Interpretation 42, which continue to be effective for fiscal years ending after September 15, 1996. Earlier application is encouraged. This Statement may be applied either by restating the financial statements of all years presented or by recognizing the cumulative effect of the change in accounting principle in the year of the change.

Transfers of Assets to a Not-for-Profit
Organization or Charitable Trust That Raises
or Holds Contributions for Others

FAS136

Statement of Financial Accounting Standards No. 136

Transfers of Assets to a Not-for-Profit Organization or Charitable Trust That Raises or Holds Contributions for Others

CONTENTS

INTRODUCTION

1. Paragraph 4 of FASB Statement No. 116, *Accounting for Contributions Received and Contributions Made,* states, "This Statement does not apply to transfers of assets in which the reporting entity acts as an agent, trustee, or intermediary, rather than as a donor or donee." The Board was asked how to differentiate situations in which a not-for-profit organization acts as an agent, trustee, or intermediary from situations in which a not-for-profit organization acts as a donor and a donee. The Board was told that those determinations are especially difficult if, as part of its charitable mission, an organization solicits and collects cash, products, or services and distributes those assets, the return on investment of those assets, or both to other organizations.

2. The Board also was asked how an organization that has that mission should report receipts and dis-bursements of assets if those transfers are not its contributions as defined in Statement 116. Additionally, some organizations asked whether a beneficiary should report its rights to the assets held by a recipient organization and, if so, how those rights should be reported.

STANDARDS OF FINANCIAL ACCOUNTING AND REPORTING

Scope

3. Paragraphs 8–16 of this Statement apply to transactions in which an entity—the *donor*—makes a contribution by transferring assets to a not-for-profit organization or charitable trust—the *recipient organization*—that accepts the assets from the donor and agrees to use those assets on behalf of or transfer those assets, the return on investment of those assets,

or both to an unaffiliated[1] entity—the *beneficiary*—that is specified by the donor.[2]

4. Paragraphs 17–19 of this Statement apply to transactions that take place in a similar manner but are not contributions for one of the following reasons:

a. The entity that transfers the assets to the recipient organization—the *resource provider*[3]—is related to the beneficiary in a way that causes the transfer to be reciprocal.
b. Conditions imposed by the resource provider or the relationships between the parties make the transfer of assets to the recipient organization revocable or repayable.

5. Paragraph 20 of this Statement applies to all not-for-profit organizations that disclose a ratio of fund-raising expenses to amounts raised, including organizations that are not involved in transfers of the types described in paragraphs 3 and 4.

6. This Statement applies to transfers of cash and other assets, including the assets described in paragraph 5 of Statement 116: "securities, land, buildings, use of facilities or utilities, materials and supplies, intangible assets, services, and unconditional promises to give those items in the future."

7. This Statement supersedes FASB Interpretation No. 42, *Accounting for Transfers of Assets in Which a Not-for-Profit Organization Is Granted Variance Power*. Paragraph 2 of Interpretation 42 is carried forward without reconsideration in paragraph 12 of this Statement.

Intermediary

8. Although in general usage the term *intermediary* encompasses a broad range of situations in which an organization acts between two or more other parties, use of the term in paragraph 4 of Statement 116 is more narrow and specific. The term is used to refer to situations in which a recipient organization acts as a facilitator for the transfer of assets between a potential donor and a potential beneficiary (donee) but is neither an agent or trustee nor a donee and donor as contemplated by Statement 116.[4] If an intermediary receives cash or other financial assets,[5] it shall recognize its liability to the specified beneficiary concurrent with its recognition of the assets received from the donor. Both the liability and the assets shall be measured at the fair value of the assets received. If an intermediary receives nonfinancial assets, it is permitted, but not required, to recognize its liability and those assets provided that the intermediary reports consistently from period to period and discloses its accounting policy.

Trustee

9. A recipient organization acts as a *trustee* if it has a duty to hold and manage assets for the benefit of a specified beneficiary in accordance with a charitable trust agreement. This Statement does not establish standards for a trustee's reporting of assets held on behalf of a specified beneficiary, but paragraphs 15 and 16 establish standards for the beneficiary's reporting of its rights to trust assets—its beneficial interest in the charitable trust.

Agent

10. An *agent* acts for and on behalf of another. Although the term *agency* has a legal definition, the term is used in this Statement with a broader meaning to encompass not only legal agency, but also the relationships described in this Statement. A recipient organization acts as an agent for and on behalf of a donor if it receives assets from the donor and agrees

---

[1] FASB Statement No. 57, *Related Party Disclosures,* defines *affiliate* as "a party that, directly or indirectly through one or more intermediaries, controls, is controlled by, or is under common control with an enterprise" (paragraph 24(a)). Thus, an *unaffiliated* beneficiary is a beneficiary other than the donor or its affiliate.

[2] In some cases, the donor, recipient organization, or beneficiary is a governmental entity. This Statement and other pronouncements of the Financial Accounting Standards Board do not apply to governmental entities unless the Governmental Accounting Standards Board issues a pronouncement that makes them applicable.

[3] If the transfer of assets is not a contribution or not yet a contribution, this Statement uses the term resource provider rather than the term donor to refer to the entity that transfers the assets to the recipient organization.

[4] Example 4 of Statement 116 (paragraph 180) illustrates the use of the term intermediary. In that example, the organization facilitates a contribution between a potential donor, a lawyer willing to provide free legal services, and a potential donee, an individual in need of free legal services. The organization is not itself a donee and donor, nor is it a recipient of the services provided by the donor (lawyer) to the donee (individual).

[5] FASB Statement No. 125, *Accounting for Transfers and Servicing of Financial Assets and Extinguishments of Liabilities,* defines *financial asset* as "cash, evidence of an ownership interest in an entity, or a contract that conveys to a second entity a contractual right (a) to receive cash or another financial instrument from a first entity or (b) to exchange other financial instruments on potentially favorable terms with the first entity" (paragraph 243).

Transfers of Assets to a Not-for-Profit
Organization or Charitable Trust That Raises
or Holds Contributions for Others   **FAS136**

to use those assets on behalf of or transfer those assets, the return on investment of those assets, or both to a specified beneficiary. A recipient organization acts as an agent for and on behalf of a beneficiary if it agrees to solicit assets from potential donors specifically for the beneficiary's use and to distribute those assets to the beneficiary. A recipient organization also acts as an agent if a beneficiary can compel the organization to make distributions to it or on its behalf.

11. Except as described in paragraphs 12 and 14 of this Statement, a recipient organization that accepts assets from a donor and agrees to use those assets on behalf of or transfer those assets, the return on investment of those assets, or both to a specified beneficiary is not a donee. It shall recognize its liability to the specified beneficiary concurrent with its recognition of cash or other financial assets received from the donor. Both the liability and the assets shall be measured at the fair value of the assets received. Except as described in paragraphs 12 and 14 of this Statement, a recipient organization that receives nonfinancial assets is permitted, but not required, to recognize its liability and those assets provided that the organization reports consistently from period to period and discloses its accounting policy.

12. A recipient organization that is directed by a donor to distribute the transferred assets, the return on investment of those assets, or both to a specified unaffiliated beneficiary acts as a donee, rather than an agent, trustee, or intermediary, if the donor explicitly grants the recipient organization variance power—that is, the unilateral power to redirect the use of the transferred assets to another beneficiary. In that situation, *explicitly grants* means that the recipient organization's unilateral power to redirect the use of the assets is explicitly referred to in the instrument transferring the assets, and *unilateral power* means that the recipient organization can override the donor's instructions without approval from the donor, specified beneficiary, or any other interested party.

Financially Interrelated Organizations

13. The recipient organization and the specified beneficiary are *financially interrelated organizations* if the relationship between them has both of the following characteristics:

a. One organization has the ability to influence the operating and financial decisions of the other. The ability to exercise that influence may be demonstrated in several ways:

(1) The organizations are affiliates.
(2) One organization has considerable representation on the governing board of the other organization.
(3) The charter or bylaws of one organization limit its activities to those that are beneficial to the other organization.
(4) An agreement between the organizations allows one organization to actively participate in policymaking processes of the other, such as setting organizational priorities, budgets, and management compensation.

b. One organization has an ongoing economic interest in the net assets of the other. If the specified beneficiary has an ongoing economic interest in the net assets of the recipient organization, the beneficiary's rights to the assets held by the recipient organization are residual rights; that is, the value of those rights increases or decreases as a result of the investment, fundraising, operating, and other activities of the recipient organization. Alternatively, but less common, a recipient organization may have an ongoing economic interest in the net assets of the specified beneficiary. If so, the recipient organization's rights are residual rights, and their value changes as a result of the operations of the beneficiary.

14. If a recipient organization and a specified beneficiary are financially interrelated organizations and the recipient organization is not a trustee, the recipient organization shall recognize a contribution received when it receives assets (financial or nonfinancial) from the donor that are specified for the beneficiary. For example, a foundation that exists to raise, hold, and invest assets for the specified beneficiary or for a group of affiliates of which the specified beneficiary is a member generally is financially interrelated with the organization or organizations it supports and recognizes contribution revenue when it receives assets from the donor.

Beneficiary

15. A specified beneficiary shall recognize its rights to the assets (financial or nonfinancial) held by a recipient organization as an asset unless the recipient organization is explicitly granted variance power. Those rights are either an interest in the net assets of the recipient organization, a beneficial interest, or a receivable. If the beneficiary and the recipient organization are financially interrelated organizations, the beneficiary shall recognize its interest in the net

assets of the recipient organization and adjust that interest for its share of the change in net assets of the recipient organization.[6] If the beneficiary has an unconditional right to receive all or a portion of the specified cash flows from a charitable trust or other identifiable pool of assets, the beneficiary shall recognize that beneficial interest, measuring and subsequently remeasuring it at fair value, using a valuation technique such as the present value of the estimated expected future cash flows. In all other cases, a beneficiary shall recognize its rights to the assets held by a recipient organization as a receivable and contribution revenue in accordance with the provisions of Statement 116 for unconditional promises to give.[7]

16. If the donor explicitly grants a recipient organization variance power, the specified unaffiliated beneficiary shall not recognize its potential for future distributions from the assets held by the recipient organization.

Transfers of Assets That Are Not Contributions

17. A transfer of assets to a recipient organization is not a contribution and shall be accounted for as an asset by the resource provider and as a liability by the recipient organization if one or more of the following conditions is present:

a. The transfer is subject to the resource provider's unilateral right to redirect the use of the assets to another beneficiary.
b. The transfer is accompanied by the resource provider's conditional promise to give or is otherwise revocable or repayable.
c. The resource provider controls the recipient organization and specifies an unaffiliated beneficiary.
d. The resource provider specifies itself or its affiliate as the beneficiary and the transfer is not an equity transaction (paragraph 18).

18. A transfer of assets to a recipient organization is an equity transaction if all of the following conditions are present:

a. The resource provider specifies itself or its affiliate as the beneficiary.
b. The resource provider and the recipient organization are financially interrelated organizations.
c. Neither the resource provider nor its affiliate expects payment of the transferred assets, although payment of investment return on the transferred assets may be expected.

If a resource provider specifies itself as beneficiary, it shall report an equity transaction as an interest in the net assets of the recipient organization (or as an increase in a previously recognized interest). If a resource provider specifies an affiliate as beneficiary, the resource provider shall report an equity transaction as a separate line in its statement of activities, and the affiliate named as beneficiary shall report an interest in the net assets of the recipient organization. A recipient organization shall report an equity transaction as a separate line item in its statement of activities.

Disclosures

19. If a not-for-profit organization transfers assets to a recipient organization and specifies itself or its affiliate as the beneficiary, it shall disclose the following information for each period for which a statement of financial position is presented:

a. The identity of the recipient organization to which the transfer was made
b. Whether variance power was granted to the recipient organization and, if so, a description of the terms of the variance power
c. The terms under which amounts will be distributed to the resource provider or its affiliate
d. The aggregate amount recognized in the statement of financial position for those transfers and

---

[6]Recognizing an interest in the net assets of the recipient organization and adjusting that interest for a share of the change in net assets of the recipient organization is similar to the equity method, which is described in APB Opinion No. 18, *The Equity Method of Accounting for Investments in Common Stock*. If the beneficiary and the recipient organization are included in consolidated financial statements, the beneficiary's interest in the net assets of the recipient organization would be eliminated in accordance with paragraph 6 of Accounting Research Bulletin No. 51, *Consolidated Financial Statements*.

[7]For an unconditional promise to give to be recognized in financial statements, paragraph 6 of Statement 116 states, "... there must be sufficient evidence in the form of verifiable documentation that a promise was made and received." Paragraph 15 of Statement 116 states, "Receipts of unconditional promises to give with payments due in future periods shall be reported as restricted support unless explicit donor stipulations or circumstances surrounding the receipt of a promise make clear that the donor intended it to be used to support activities of the current period." Paragraph 20 of Statement 116 states, "The present value of estimated future cash flows using a discount rate commensurate with the risks involved is an appropriate measure of fair value of unconditional promises to give cash" (footnote reference omitted).

*Transfers of Assets to a Not-for-Profit
Organization or Charitable Trust That Raises
or Holds Contributions for Others*   **FAS136**

whether that amount is recorded as an interest in the net assets of the recipient organization or as another asset (for example, as a beneficial interest in assets held by others or a refundable advance).

20. If a not-for-profit organization discloses in its financial statements a ratio of fundraising expenses to amounts raised, it also shall disclose how it computes that ratio.

EFFECTIVE DATE AND TRANSITION

21. Except for the provisions of paragraph 12, the provisions of this Statement shall be effective for financial statements issued for fiscal periods beginning after December 15, 1999. Earlier application is encouraged. The provisions of paragraph 12, which are carried forward from Interpretation 42, shall continue

to be effective for fiscal years ending after September 15, 1996. Unless this Statement is applied retroactively under the provisions of paragraph 22, the effect of initially applying this Statement shall be reported as the effect of a change in accounting principle in a manner similar to the cumulative effect of a change in accounting principle (APB Opinion No. 20, *Accounting Changes,* paragraph 19). The amount of cumulative effect shall be based on a retroactive computation.

22. This Statement may be applied retroactively by restating opening net assets for the earliest year presented or for the year in which this Statement is first applied if no prior years are presented. In the period in which this Statement is first applied, an entity shall disclose the nature of any restatement and its effect on the change in net assets and each class of net assets for each period presented.

> **The provisions of this Statement need
> not be applied to immaterial items.**

This Statement was adopted by the unanimous vote of the seven members of the Financial Accounting Standards Board:

Edmund L. Jenkins, *Chairman*	Anthony T. Cope	James J. Leisenring
	John M. Foster	Gerhard G. Mueller
Joseph V. Anania	Gaylen N. Larson	

Appendix A

ILLUSTRATIVE GUIDANCE

Introduction

23. This appendix provides a diagram to assist entities in the application of this Statement and examples that illustrate the application of the standards in specific situations. The diagram is a visual supplement to the written standards section. It should not be interpreted to alter any requirements of this Statement, nor should it be considered a substitute for those requirements. The relevant paragraphs of the standards section of this Statement and of FASB Statement No. 116, *Accounting for Contributions Received and Contributions Made,* are identified in the parenthetical notes. The

examples do not address all possible situations or applications of this Statement.

Diagram

24. The diagram depicts the process for determining the appropriate accounting for a transfer of assets from a donor to a recipient organization that accepts the assets and agrees to use those assets on behalf of a beneficiary specified by the donor or transfer those assets, the return on investment of those assets, or both to a beneficiary specified by the donor. (For additional information about how a beneficiary is specified, refer to paragraphs 68 and 69.) The diagram also depicts the process for determining the appropriate accounting for a transfer from a resource provider that takes place in a similar manner but is not a contribution because the transfer is revocable, repayable, or reciprocal.

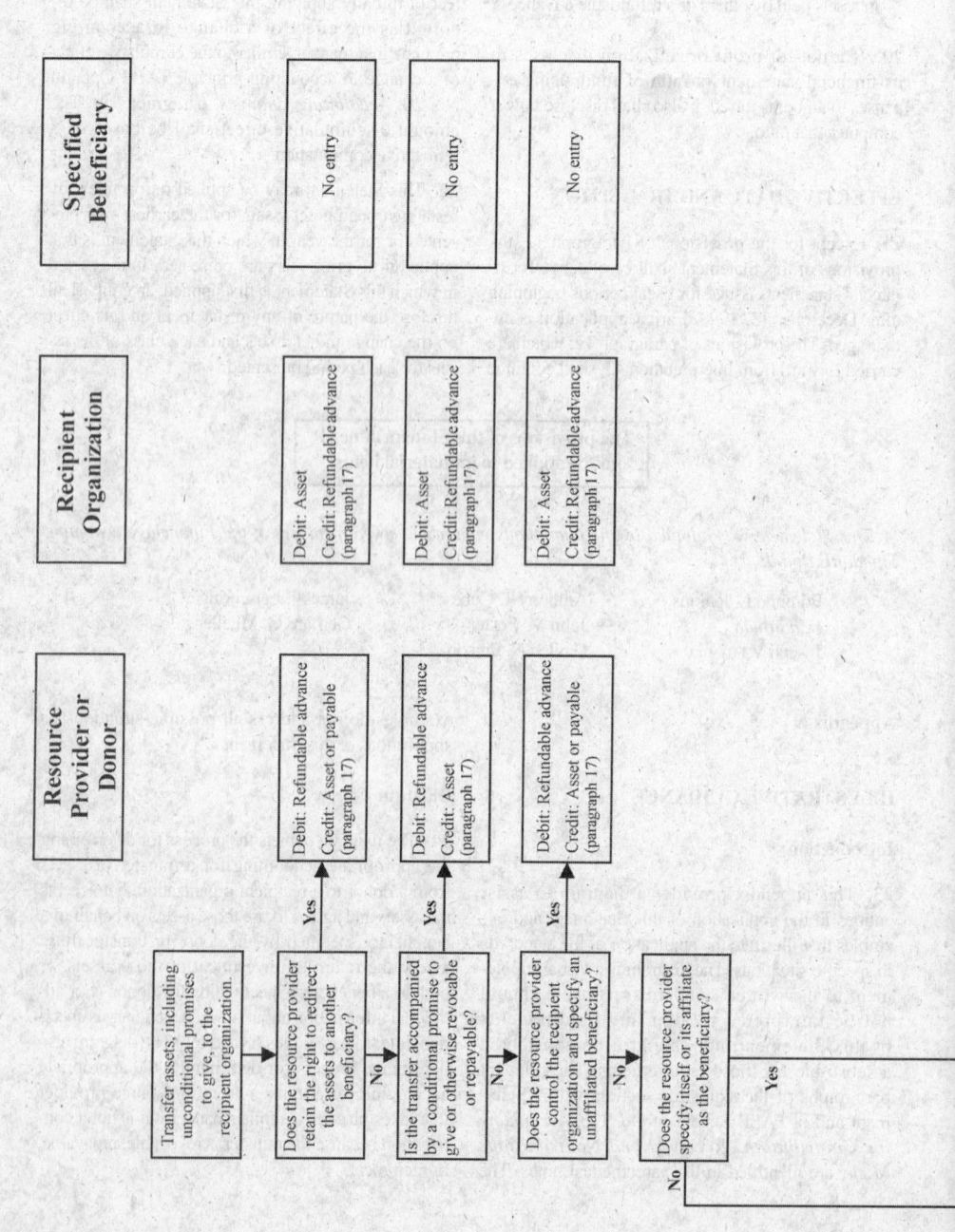

*Transfers of Assets to a Not-for-Profit
Organization or Charitable Trust That Raises
or Holds Contributions for Others* **FAS136**

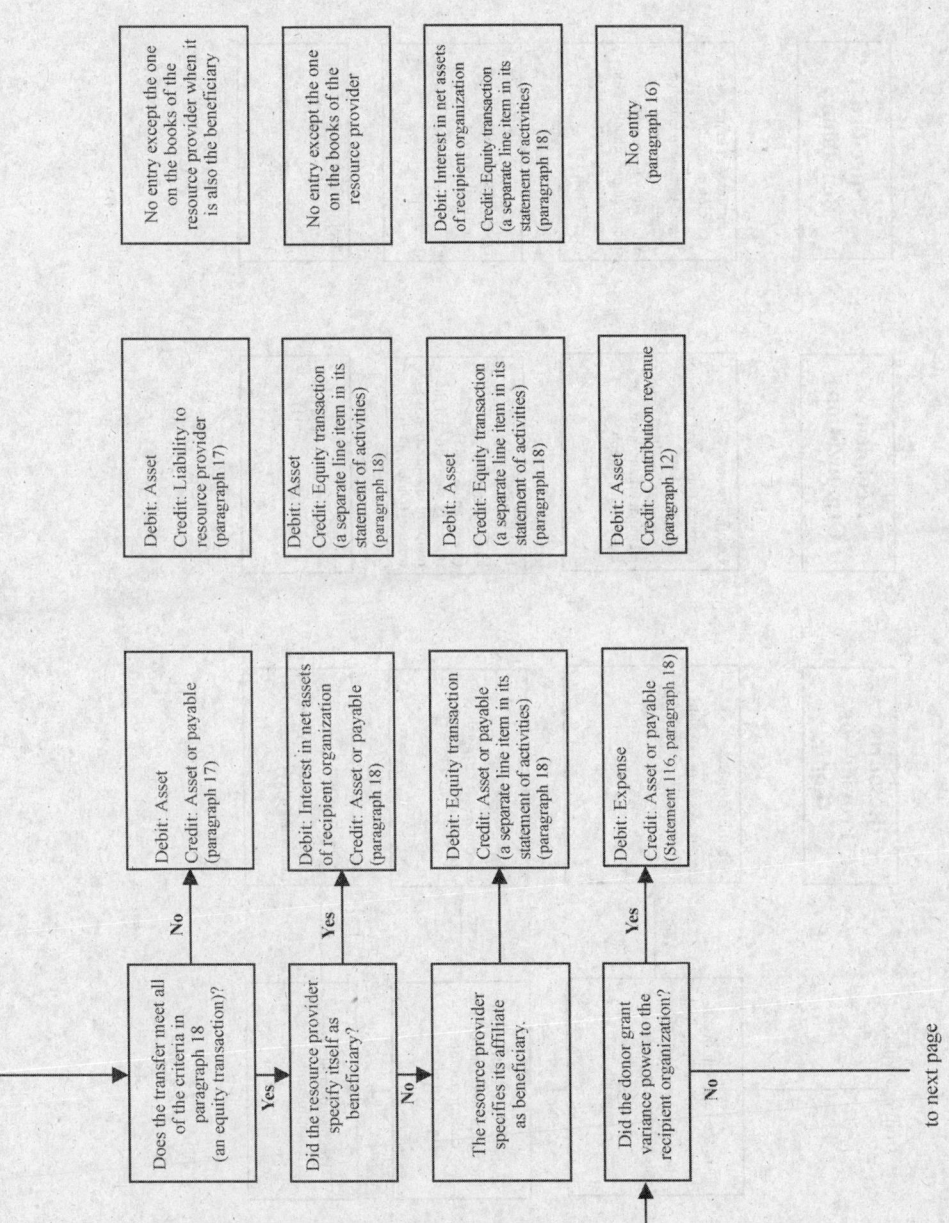

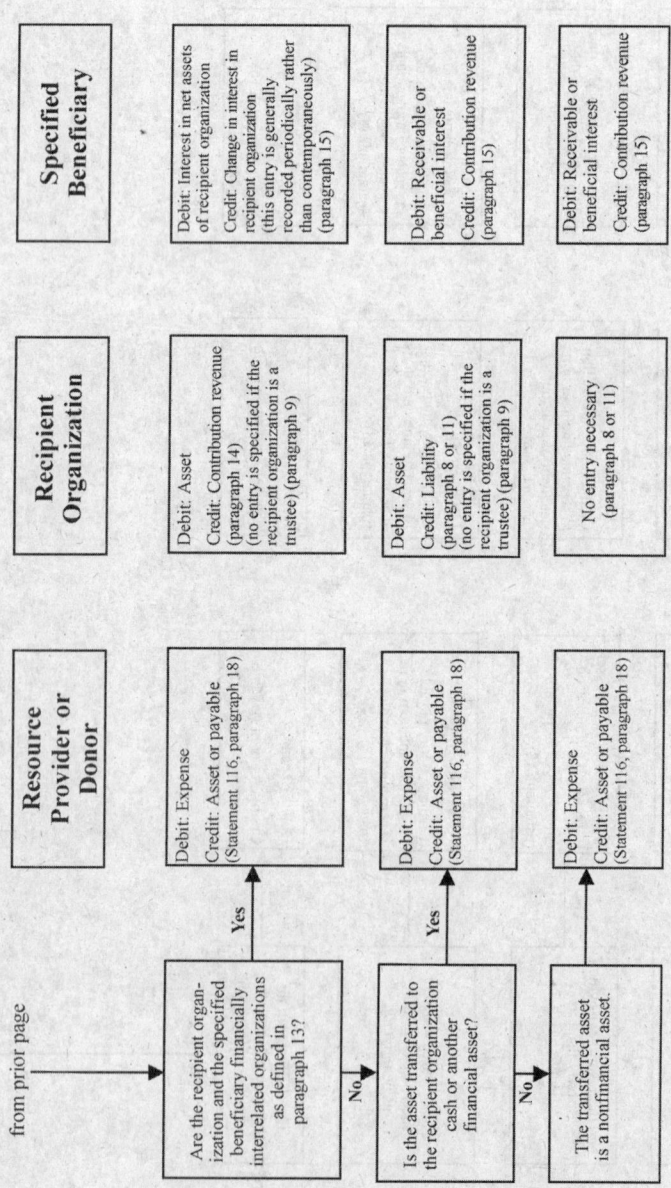

Transfers of Assets to a Not-for-Profit   **FAS136**
Organization or Charitable Trust That Raises
or Holds Contributions for Others

Example 1—Gifts to a Federated Fundraising Organization

25. Federated Fundraising Organization provides three choices to donors in its annual workplace campaign. Donors can give without restriction, direct their gifts to one of four community needs identified by Federated Fundraising Organization, or specify that their gifts be transferred to an organization of their choice. The campaign literature informs donors that if they choose to specify an organization to which their gift should be transferred, the organization must be a social welfare organization within the community that has tax-exempt status under Internal Revenue Code Section 501(c)(3). The campaign literature also provides a schedule of the administrative fees that will be deducted from all gifts that are to be transferred to the donor's chosen organization.

26. Federated Fundraising Organization would recognize the fair values of the unrestricted gifts as contribution revenue that increases unrestricted net assets. It would recognize the fair values of the gifts targeted to the four specified community needs as contribution revenue that increases temporarily restricted net assets. It would recognize the fair values of gifts that are to be transferred to organizations chosen by the donors as increases in its assets and as liabilities to those specified beneficiaries (paragraph 11). However, if some of the gifts that are intended for specified beneficiaries are gifts of nonfinancial assets, Federated Fundraising Organization would recognize those nonfinancial assets and its liability to transfer them to the specified beneficiaries if that were its policy; otherwise, it would recognize neither the nonfinancial assets nor a liability (paragraph 11). Federated Fundraising Organization would recognize as revenue the administrative fees withheld from amounts to be transferred to the donors' chosen organizations.

27. The organizations chosen by the donors would recognize the fair value of the transferred assets as contribution revenue in accordance with the provisions of Statement 116 for unconditional promises to give (paragraph 15). Thus, the revenue would increase temporarily restricted net assets unless the donor specified a permanent restriction or it was clear that the donor intended the gift to support activities of the current period (Statement 116, paragraph 15). In accordance with paragraph 24 of FASB Statement No. 117, *Financial Statements of Not-for-Profit Organizations,* the beneficiaries would report the gross amounts of the gifts as contribution revenue and the administrative fees withheld by Federated Fundraising Organization as expenses. The net amount would be recognized as a receivable (paragraph 15).

28. Instead of conducting the campaign as described above, Federated Fundraising Organization's campaign literature, including the form that donors use to specify a beneficiary, clearly states that if donors choose to give and specify a beneficiary, the allocation committee has the authority to redirect their gifts if the committee perceives needs elsewhere in the community that are greater. By giving under those terms, donors explicitly grant Federated Fundraising Organization variance power. Thus, Federated Fundraising Organization would recognize an unrestricted contribution (paragraph 12), and the specified beneficiaries would be precluded from recognizing their potential for future distributions from the assets (paragraph 16).

Example 2—Gifts to a Community Foundation for the Benefit of a Not-for-Profit Organization

29. The governing board of City Botanical Society decides to raise funds to build an endowment. The governing board signs an agreement to establish a fund at Community Foundation. Community Foundation and City Botanical Society are not financially interrelated organizations. City Botanical Society solicits gifts to the fund. The campaign materials inform donors that the endowment will be owned and held by Community Foundation. The materials explain that the gifts will be invested and that the return from their investment will be distributed to City Botanical Society, subject to Community Foundation's spending policy and to Community Foundation's right to redirect the return to another beneficiary without the approval of the donor, City Botanical Society, or any other party if distributions to City Botanical Society become unnecessary, impossible, or inconsistent with the needs of the community. The donor-response card also clearly describes Community Foundation's right to redirect the return of the fund. The campaign materials indicate that donors should send their contributions to Community Foundation using a preaddressed envelope included for that purpose.

30. Community Foundation would recognize the fair value of gifts received as assets and as contribution revenue. The donors explicitly granted variance power by using a donor-response card that clearly states that gifts are subject to Community Foundation's unilateral power to redirect the return to another beneficiary (paragraph 12).

31. City Botanical Society is precluded from recognizing its potential rights to the assets held by Community Foundation because the donors explicitly granted variance power (paragraph 16). City Botanical Society would recognize only its annual grants from Community Foundation as contributions.

32. Whether a donor intended to make a contribution to Community Foundation may not be clear if the donor responds to the campaign materials by sending a contribution and the donor-response card directly to City Botanical Society. City Botanical Society could resolve the ambiguity by a review of the facts and circumstances surrounding the gift, communications with the donor, or both. If it is ultimately determined that the donor intended to make a gift to the fund owned and held by Community Foundation and to explicitly grant variance power, City Botanical Society would be an agent responsible for transferring that gift to Community Foundation (paragraph 11).

Example 3—Cash Transfer from a Not-for-Profit Organization to Another Not-for-Profit Organization for the Benefit of an Individual

33. Local Church transfers cash to Seminary and instructs Seminary to use the money to grant a scholarship to Individual, who is a parishioner of Local Church.

34. Seminary would recognize the cash and a liability to Individual in the same amount because it merely is facilitating the cash transfer from Local Church to Individual (paragraph 8).

Example 4—Assets Transferred from an Individual to a Bank to Establish a Charitable Trust for the Benefit of a Not-for-Profit Organization

35. Individual transfers assets to National Bank to establish an irrevocable charitable trust for the sole benefit of Museum. National Bank will serve as trustee. Individual sets forth in the trust agreement the policies that direct the economic activities of the trust. The trust term is five years. Each year, the income received on the investments of the trust will be distributed to Museum. At the end of year 5, the corpus of the trust (original assets and net appreciation on those assets) will be paid to Museum.

36. This Statement does not establish standards for the trustee, National Bank (paragraph 9). Because

Museum is unable to influence the operating or financial decisions of the trustee, Museum and National Bank are not financially interrelated organizations (paragraph 13(a)). Therefore, Museum would recognize its asset (a beneficial interest in the trust) and contribution revenue that increases temporarily restricted net assets (paragraph 15). Museum would measure its beneficial interest at fair value, using a valuation technique such as the present value of the estimated expected future cash receipts from the trust's assets (paragraph 15). That value generally can be measured by the fair value of the assets contributed to the trust.

Example 5—Gift of Nonfinancial Assets to an Institutionally Related Foundation

37. Corporation sends dental supplies to University Foundation to be used by students in University's dental clinic. University Foundation's bylaws state that it is organized for the purpose of stimulating voluntary financial support from alumni and other donors for the benefit of University, especially for addressing the long-term academic priorities of University. As with most gifts it receives, University Foundation can choose the timing of the distribution to University and can place additional limitations on the distribution if those limitations are consistent with Corporation's restrictions. University does not control University Foundation.

38. University Foundation recognizes the fair value of the dental supplies (nonfinancial assets) as an increase in assets and as contribution revenue that increases temporarily restricted net assets because University and University Foundation are financially interrelated organizations (paragraph 14). University can influence the financial and operating decisions of University Foundation because the bylaws of University Foundation limit its activities to those that benefit University (paragraph 13(a)). University has an ongoing economic interest in the net assets of University Foundation because the results of University Foundation's activities accrue to the benefit of University (paragraph 13(b)). When University Foundation distributes the dental supplies to University, it reduces its assets and recognizes an expense and the expiration of the restriction.

39. Periodically, in conjunction with preparing its financial statements, University recognizes the change in its interest in the net assets of University Foundation, which would include the gift of nonfinancial assets received by the foundation (paragraph 15). Because payments from University Foundation are due

Transfers of Assets to a Not-for-Profit **FAS136**
Organization or Charitable Trust That Raises
or Holds Contributions for Others

in future periods, the increase (or decrease) in University's interest would be classified as a change in temporarily restricted net assets unless donors placed permanent restrictions on their gifts (footnote 6 to paragraph 15). When the dental supplies and other assets are distributed to it, University would recognize the assets received and decrease its interest in the net assets of University Foundation.[8]

40. If, instead, University controlled University Foundation, University would be able to access at will any assets held by University Foundation. Implying a time restriction on the gifts held by University Foundation would be inappropriate. When recognizing the change in its interest in University Foundation, University would report the resulting net assets in the same net asset classifications as University Foundation.

Example 6—Cash Gift to a Healthcare Foundation That Supports Three Affiliated Organizations

41. Corporation transfers cash to Healthcare Foundation and requests that Healthcare Foundation use the gift to provide healthcare benefits to the community. Healthcare Foundation's bylaws state that it is organized for the purpose of stimulating voluntary financial support from donors for the benefit of Hospital, Nursing Home, and Walk-in Clinic, all of which are located in the community. Hospital, Nursing Home, Walk-in Clinic, and Healthcare Foundation are affiliates that are controlled by Healthcare System.

42. Healthcare Foundation would recognize cash and contribution revenue that increases unrestricted net assets because Corporation did not specify a beneficiary for its gift. Healthcare Foundation can choose how to distribute the gift among the three affiliates (paragraph 69).

43. Periodically, in conjunction with preparing their financial statements, Hospital, Nursing Home, and Walk-in Clinic recognize the changes in their interests in the net assets of Healthcare Foundation (paragraph 15). When measuring its interest in Healthcare Foundation, each affiliate would include only the net assets of Healthcare Foundation that are restricted to

that affiliate's use. None of them would include in their individual interest the net assets resulting from the gift received from Corporation because Healthcare Foundation can choose how to distribute the gift among the three affiliates. Healthcare System would include the net assets resulting from the gift received from Corporation, as well as other changes in the net assets of Healthcare Foundation, in its interest in the net assets of the foundation.[9]

44. If Healthcare Foundation, Hospital, Nursing Home, and Walk-in Clinic entered into an agreement that specified how unrestricted gifts to Healthcare Foundation should be divided, each affiliate would also include its share of Healthcare Foundation's unrestricted net assets, computed in accordance with that agreement, when it measured its interest in Healthcare Foundation. Similarly, if Healthcare System directed that unrestricted gifts to Healthcare Foundation be distributed to the three affiliates in accordance with a specified formula, each affiliate would include its share of unrestricted net assets, computed in accordance with that formula, when it measured its interest in Healthcare Foundation.

45. If Corporation had specified that its gift be used for the benefit of Walk-in Clinic rather than giving without restriction, Healthcare Foundation would recognize contribution revenue that increases temporarily restricted net assets because Hospital, Nursing Home, Walk-in Clinic, and Healthcare Foundation are financially interrelated organizations (paragraph 14). Their relationship meets both requirements of paragraph 13. Hospital, Nursing Home, and Walk-in Clinic can influence the financial and operating decisions of Healthcare Foundation because all four organizations are under common control and the bylaws of Healthcare Foundation limit its activities to support of its three affiliates (paragraph 13(a)). Hospital, Nursing Home, and Walk-in Clinic each have an ongoing economic interest in the net assets of Healthcare Foundation because their rights to the assets held by Healthcare Foundation are residual rights in an ongoing relationship (paragraph 13(b)). Walk-in Clinic would include the net assets resulting from the gift received from Corporation in its interest in the net assets of Healthcare Foundation.

---

[8]The provisions of this Statement do not apply to University if University is a governmental entity. The Governmental Accounting Standards Board sets standards for those entities.

[9]An interest in the net assets of an affiliate would be eliminated if that affiliate were included in the consolidated financial statements of the interest holder.

Example 7—Cash Gift to a Foundation That Supports Two Unaffiliated Not-for-Profit Organizations

46. Individual transfers cash to Arts Foundation and specifies that the money be used to support the expenses of the ballet. Arts Foundation's bylaws state that it is organized for the purpose of stimulating voluntary financial support from donors for the benefit of Community Ballet and Community Theater. At the time Arts Foundation was created, the three organizations entered into an agreement that specifies that if a donor does not specify the organization to which the gift should be transferred, the gift will be split equally between Community Ballet and Community Theater. The agreement also specifies that (a) representatives from the three organizations will meet annually and determine campaign priorities for the next year and (b) the costs of operating Arts Foundation will be equally split between Community Ballet and Community Theater. Arts Foundation is not controlled by Community Ballet, Community Theater, or Individual.

47. Arts Foundation would report assets and contribution revenue that increases temporarily restricted net assets because Community Ballet and Arts Foundation are financially interrelated organizations (paragraph 14). Community Ballet has the ability to influence the operating and financial decisions of Arts Foundation because the agreement allows Community Ballet to participate in the policymaking processes of Arts Foundation (paragraph 13(a)). The agreement also establishes Community Ballet's rights as residual rights because it specifies how the revenues and expenses of Arts Foundation will be shared (paragraph 13(b)). When Arts Foundation distributes assets to Community Ballet, it reduces its assets and recognizes an expense.

48. Periodically, in conjunction with preparing their financial statements, Community Ballet and Community Theater recognize the changes in their interests in the net assets of Arts Foundation (paragraph 15). Community Ballet would include the net assets resulting from the gift received from Individual in its interest in the net assets of Arts Foundation because Individual specified that the gift be used to support the ballet and Arts Foundation's bylaws limit it to supporting Community Ballet. Community Ballet would also include in its interest all other gifts restricted to its benefit and its share of unrestricted net assets. Because payments from Arts Foundation are due in future periods, the increase (or decrease) in

Community Ballet's interest would be classified as a change in temporarily restricted net assets unless donors placed permanent restrictions on their gifts (footnote 6 to paragraph 15). When assets are distributed to Community Ballet, it recognizes the assets received and decreases its interest in the net assets of Arts Foundation.

49. In contrast to this example, some foundations and associations raise contributions for a large number of unaffiliated not-for-profit organizations (often referred to as member organizations). By virtue of their numbers, those member organizations generally do not individually influence the operating and financial decisions of the foundation (or association). Thus, any one member organization and the foundation (or association) are not financially interrelated organizations (paragraph 13(a)). Because the organizations are not financially interrelated, the foundation (or association) recognizes a liability if a donor to the foundation (or association) specifies that the gift should be transferred to a particular member organization (paragraph 11). The specified member organization would recognize a receivable and contribution revenue that increases temporarily restricted net assets unless the donor specified a permanent restriction or it was clear that the donor intended the gift to support activities of the current period (paragraph 15 and footnote 6).

Example 8—Gift of a Nonfinancial Asset to a Federated Fundraising Organization for Transfer to Another Not-for-Profit Organization

50. Individual transfers a car to Federated Fundraising Organization and requests that the car be transferred to Local Daycare Center. Individual specifies that Federated Fundraising Organization may use the car for one year before transferring it to Local Daycare Center. Local Daycare Center is a member organization of Federated Fundraising Organization, but that status does not confer any ability to actively participate in the policymaking processes of Federated Fundraising Organization.

51. Because Federated Fundraising Organization and Local Daycare Center are not financially interrelated organizations, Federated Fundraising Organization would recognize the car as an asset and a liability to Local Daycare Center if its policy were to recognize nonfinancial assets; otherwise, it would recognize neither the nonfinancial assets nor a liability (paragraph 11). If, instead of refusing the gift of the use of the car, Federated Fundraising Organization decides to use it for a year before transfer-

Transfers of Assets to a Not-for-Profit   **FAS136**
Organization or Charitable Trust That Raises
or Holds Contributions for Others

ring it to Local Daycare Center, Federated Fundraising Organization would recognize the fair value of the gift of one-year's use of the car in accordance with paragraph 8 of Statement 116. (The use of a car is a contributed asset and not a contributed service.)

52. Local Daycare Center would recognize a receivable and contribution revenue that increases temporarily restricted net assets (paragraph 15). It would measure the contribution received at the fair value of the car; however, if Federated Fundraising Organization chooses to use the car for a year before transferring it, the fair value would be reduced accordingly.

Example 9—Transfer of Assets from a Not-for-Profit Organization to a Community Foundation to Establish an Endowment for the Benefit of the Not-for-Profit Organization

53. Symphony Orchestra receives a large unrestricted gift of securities from Individual. Because it has no investment expertise, Symphony Orchestra transfers the securities to Community Foundation to establish an endowment fund. The agreement between Symphony Orchestra and Community Foundation states that the transfer is irrevocable and that the transferred assets will not be returned to Symphony Orchestra. However, Community Foundation will make annual distributions of the income earned on the endowment fund, subject to Community Foundation's spending policy. The agreement also permits Community Foundation to substitute another beneficiary in the place of Symphony Orchestra if Symphony Orchestra ceases to exist or if the governing board of Community Foundation votes that support of Symphony Orchestra (a) is no longer necessary or (b) is inconsistent with the needs of the community. (That is, Symphony Orchestra explicitly grants variance power to Community Foundation.) The agreement does not permit either organization to appoint members to the other organization's governing board or otherwise participate in the policy-making processes of the other.

54. Community Foundation would recognize the fair value of the transferred securities as an increase in investments and a liability to Symphony Orchestra because Symphony Orchestra transferred assets to Community Foundation and specified itself as beneficiary (paragraph 17(d)). The transfer is not an equity transaction because Community Foundation and Symphony Orchestra are not financially interrelated organizations (paragraph 18(b)). Sym-

phony Orchestra is unable to influence the operating or financial decisions of Community Foundation (paragraph 13(a)).

55. Symphony Orchestra would recognize the fair value of the gift of securities from Individual as contribution revenue. When it transfers the securities to Community Foundation, it would recognize the transfer as a decrease in investments and an increase in an asset, for example, as a beneficial interest in assets held by Community Foundation (paragraph 17(d)). Also, Symphony Orchestra would disclose in its financial statements the identity of Community Foundation, the terms under which Community Foundation will distribute amounts to Symphony Orchestra, a description of the variance power granted to Community Foundation, and the aggregate amount reported in the statement of financial position and how that amount is described (paragraph 19).

56. In this example, Symphony Orchestra would recognize an asset and Community Foundation would recognize a liability because the transaction is deemed to be reciprocal (paragraph 96). Symphony Orchestra transfers its securities to Community Foundation in exchange for future distributions. Community Foundation, by its acceptance of the transfer, agrees that at the time of the transfer distributions to Symphony Orchestra are capable of fulfillment and consistent with the foundation's mission. Although the value of those future distributions may not be commensurate with the value of the securities given up (because Symphony Orchestra is at risk of cessation of the distributions), the transaction is accounted for as though those values are commensurate. In comparison, the donors to Community Foundation in Example 2 explicitly grant variance power to Community Foundation in a nonreciprocal transfer. In that example, it is clear that the donors have made a contribution because they retain no beneficial interests in the transferred assets. Because the donors in Example 2 explicitly grant variance power to Community Foundation, it, rather than City Botanical Society, is the recipient of that contribution.

Example 10—Transfer of Investments from a Not-for-Profit Organization to a Foundation It Creates to Hold Those Assets

57. The governing board of Private Elementary School creates a foundation to hold and manage the school's investments. It transfers its investment portfolio to the newly created PES Foundation. An agreement between Private Elementary School and PES

Foundation allows the school to request distributions from both the original investments and the return on those investments, subject to approval by the governing board of PES Foundation, which will not be unreasonably withheld. The agreement also permits Private Elementary School to transfer additional investments in the future.

58. PES Foundation would recognize the fair value of the investments as assets and a liability to Private Elementary School because Private Elementary School transferred assets to PES Foundation and specified itself as beneficiary (paragraph 17(d)). The transfer of assets is not an equity transaction because Private Elementary School expects repayment of the transferred assets, and thus the transaction does not meet the criterion in paragraph 18(c).

59. Private Elementary School would decrease its investments and recognize another asset, for example, a beneficial interest in assets held by PES Foundation (paragraph 17(d)). Also, Private Elementary School would disclose in its financial statements the identity of PES Foundation, the terms of the agreement under which it can receive future distributions, including the fact that the distributions are not subject to variance power, and the aggregate amount reported in the statement of financial position and how that amount is described (paragraph 19).

Appendix B

BACKGROUND INFORMATION AND BASIS FOR CONCLUSIONS

CONTENTS

Transfers of Assets to a Not-for-Profit **FAS136**
Organization or Charitable Trust That Raises
or Holds Contributions for Others

Appendix B

BACKGROUND INFORMATION AND BASIS FOR CONCLUSIONS

Introduction

60. This appendix summarizes considerations that Board members deemed significant in reaching the conclusions in this Statement. It includes reasons for accepting certain approaches and rejecting others. Individual Board members gave greater weight to some factors than to others.

Background Information

61. The Board issued FASB Statement No. 116, *Accounting for Contributions Received and Contributions Made,* in June 1993. In May 1995, at the request of several community foundations and other interested parties, the Board decided to provide an interpretation of paragraph 4 of Statement 116 to address whether a transfer of assets from a donor to a community foundation is a contribution received by the community foundation if the donor (a) directs the foundation to distribute the transferred assets, the return on investment of those assets, or both to a specified beneficiary and (b) grants the foundation variance power to redirect the use of the transferred assets away from the specified beneficiary.

62. Subsequently, other not-for-profit organizations, including federated fundraising organizations and institutionally related foundations, asked the Board to expand the scope of the project to describe the circumstances in which they could report contributions received for transfers of assets that ultimately would be transferred to another organization. Some organizations, particularly federated fundraising organizations and institutionally related foundations, said that if paragraph 4 of Statement 116 were interpreted in a broad way, many or most of their current activities no longer would be accounted for as contributions received and contributions made. They asserted that recording only some of their fundraising activities as contributions received would understate the amounts raised, result in misleading financial statements, and render meaningless many key financial ratios used in the industry. The Board considered the concerns expressed by those organizations and decided to address the applicability of paragraph 4 of Statement 116 for all not-for-profit organizations that receive and distribute assets for charitable purposes.

63. In December 1995, the Board issued an Exposure Draft of a proposed Interpretation, *Transfers of Assets in Which a Not-for-Profit Organization Acts as an Agent, Trustee, or Intermediary.* That Exposure Draft would have clarified the use of the terms *agent, trustee,* and *intermediary* in Statement 116. The Board received 115 comment letters on the Exposure Draft. The Board considered the concerns raised by respondents at several public meetings. In September 1996, the Board issued FASB Interpretation No. 42, *Accounting for Transfers of Assets in Which a Notfor-Profit Organization Is Granted Variance Power,* which had a narrower scope than that of the Exposure Draft. Interpretation 42 clarified that an organization that receives assets acts as a donee and a donor, rather than as an agent, trustee, or intermediary, if the donor specifies an unaffiliated beneficiary or beneficiaries and explicitly grants the recipient organization variance power, that is, grants the unilateral power to redirect the use of the assets away from the specified beneficiary or beneficiaries. With only minor editorial changes, the guidance in that Interpretation is incorporated in paragraph 12 of this Statement.

64. Concurrent with its decision to issue Interpretation 42, the Board also agreed to consider the following three situations in a second phase of the project: (a) accounting by a recipient organization that is not granted variance power, (b) accounting by a beneficiary if a donor transfers assets to a recipient organization and specifies that the assets must be conveyed to the beneficiary or used for its benefit, and (c) accounting for transfers in which the resource provider and the beneficiary are the same party.

65. In July 1998, the Board issued an Exposure Draft of a proposed Statement, *Transfers of Assets involving a Not-for-Profit Organization That Raises or Holds Contributions for Others.* The Board received over 450 comment letters from representatives of over 280 entities. Most respondents commented only on the issue of accounting by agents and intermediaries; the majority of them were federated fundraising organizations. The concerns raised by respondents were considered by the Board at four public meetings. The redeliberation of the issues addressed by this Statement did not result in substantive changes in the proposed requirements; however, disclosure requirements, clarifications, and illustrative guidance were added. The Board concluded that it could reach an informed decision on the basis of existing information without a public hearing.

Basis for Conclusions

66. Paragraph 4 of Statement 116 states that that Statement does not apply in situations in which an organization acts as an agent, trustee, or intermediary between two or more other parties but is not itself a donee and donor. Paragraphs 52–54 and 175 of Statement 116, as well as Examples 2–5 in paragraphs 177–181 of Statement 116, indicate the Board's intentions. Those examples focus on an organization that is both a trustee and a donee (Example 2), an organization that is an agent for the receipt of goods (Example 3), an organization that facilitates a transfer of assets between other parties and is neither a donee nor a donor (Example 4), and an organization that is an intermediary in processing a transfer payment between other parties (Example 5).

Recipient Organizations

Intermediary

67. In general usage, the term intermediary encompasses a broad range of situations in which an organization acts between two or more other parties. In some of those situations, the organization may be both a donee (when it receives a gift) and a donor (when it makes a gift to a beneficiary). In other situations, the organization does not itself receive or make a gift, but it may be a facilitator, conduit, agent, or trustee between a donor and a donee. The use of the term intermediary in paragraph 4 of Statement 116 is not intended to preclude charitable and other not-for-profit organizations from accounting for transfers of assets they receive and transfers of assets they make as contributions if they are donees and donors. Instead, the use of the term intermediary in Statement 116 is narrow and specific and refers to situations in which an organization facilitates the transfer of assets but does not itself receive or make a gift.

Agent and trustee

68. In some agency and some trustee arrangements, a resource provider has not made a gift because it can derive future economic benefit from the transferred assets. In other cases, it is clear that the resource provider is a donor and has made a gift; however, it may not be clear who the donee is because the donor transfers the assets to the recipient organization but specifies another entity as beneficiary of the gift. A donor may specify the beneficiary (a) by name, (b) by stating that all entities that meet a set of donor-defined criteria are beneficiaries, or (c) by actions surrounding the transfer that make clear the identity of the beneficiary, such as by responding to a request from an organization that exists to raise assets for the beneficiary. Because paragraph 53 of Statement 116 states that "the recipient of assets who is an agent or trustee has *little or no discretion* in determining how the assets transferred will be used" (emphasis added), the Board considered whether a recipient organization can recognize a contribution received if its discretion is limited by the donor's specification of a beneficiary.

69. By contrasting three situations, paragraphs 53 and 54 of Statement 116 indicate the Board's view that an organization has discretion sufficient to recognize a contribution received if it can choose the beneficiaries of the assets. Paragraph 53 describes two situations that may be agency transactions: (a) a recipient organization that receives cash that it must disburse to all that meet guidelines specified by the resource provider or return the cash and (b) a recipient organization that receives cash that it must disburse to individuals identified by the resource provider or return the cash. Paragraph 54 contrasts those two situations to a situation in which ",... the resource provider allows the recipient to establish, define, and carry out the programs that disburse the cash, products, or services to the recipient's beneficiaries...." In that latter situation, Statement 116 specifies that "... the recipient generally is involved in receiving and making contributions" (paragraph 54). Thus, if a donor uses broad generalizations to describe beneficiaries or to indicate a field of interest, such as Midwestern flood victims, homeless individuals, or teenaged children, the recipient organization has the ability to choose the beneficiaries of the assets and is a donee.

70. Similarly, the recipient organization has the ability to choose the beneficiaries if neither the language used by the donor nor the representations of the recipient organization cause the donor to believe that it can direct the gift to a specified beneficiary. For example, a recipient organization might request that a donor indicate an organization that best serves the needs of the community and tell the donor that the information will be considered by the allocation committee when it makes its distributions to community organizations. If that request is conveyed in a manner that leads a donor to reasonably conclude that its role is merely to propose a possible allocation, the recipient organization has the discretion to choose the beneficiary of the assets.

Transfers of Assets to a Not-for-Profit **FAS136**
Organization or Charitable Trust That Raises
or Holds Contributions for Others

71. Conversely, if that request is conveyed in a manner that creates a donor's reasonable expectation that the gift will be used for the benefit of or will be transferred to the indicated beneficiary, the recipient organization does not have discretion to choose the beneficiary unless the donor explicitly grants variance power. Paragraph 2 of Interpretation 42 stated that "a recipient organization that is directed by a resource provider to distribute the transferred assets . . . to a specified third-party beneficiary acts as a donee and a donor . . . if the resource provider explicitly grants the recipient organization the unilateral power to redirect the use of the transferred assets to another beneficiary" (footnote reference omitted).

72. The Board considered whether discretion to determine the timing of the distribution to the specified beneficiary, by itself, gives the recipient organization discretion sufficient to recognize a contribution. The Board concluded that that limited discretion is not sufficient. The ability to choose a payment date does not relieve an entity from its obligation to pay.

Meeting the definition of a liability

73. To qualify as a liability of a recipient organization, an agreement to transfer assets to the beneficiary specified by the donor must obligate the recipient organization, leaving it little or no discretion to avoid a future sacrifice of assets without significant penalty. FASB Concepts Statement No. 6, *Elements of Financial Statements,* states, "Liabilities are probable future sacrifices of economic benefits arising from present obligations of a particular entity to transfer assets or provide services to other entities in the future as a result of past transactions or events" (paragraph 35; footnote references omitted).

74. The Board concluded that when a recipient organization accepts assets from a donor and agrees to use them on behalf of or transfer them to a beneficiary specified by the donor, the recipient organization assumes an obligation that meets the definition of a liability unless the donor explicitly grants variance power. The recipient organization represents to the donor that it will deliver the assets, the return on investment of those assets, or both to the beneficiary specified by the donor. The donor relies on that representation and expects the recipient organization to carry out its duties in due course or at the time specified by the donor. Thus, unless the recipient organization explicitly reserves a right to do so, it cannot, at its own discretion, avoid its transfer to the specified beneficiary or make the transfer to a different beneficiary.

The donor has a right to expect that the assets will be transferred to the specified beneficiary in the future, and the recipient organization has a social and moral obligation, and most likely a legal obligation, to make the transfer. Consequently, if it is the donor's understanding that the recipient organization will transfer the contributed assets to its intended beneficiary, that beneficiary, not the recipient organization, has received the contribution.

75. The Board concluded that a representation made to a donor to transfer assets to a specified beneficiary differs from other representations made to donors when accepting gifts, such as representations to use assets in a particular program or to buy a fixed asset. That second type of representation (a donor-imposed restriction) is a fiduciary responsibility, and ". . . a not-for-profit organization's fiduciary responsibility to use assets to provide services to beneficiaries does not itself create a duty of the organization to pay cash, transfer other assets, or provide services to one or more creditors" (Concepts Statement 6, paragraph 57). The donor's identification of a specific beneficiary to which the assets must be transferred differentiates the transaction from time- and purpose-restricted contributions and makes the recipient organization's representation to the donor one that constitutes a present obligation of the recipient organization to another entity.

Meeting the definition of an asset

76. To qualify as an asset of the recipient organization, an asset received from a donor must provide a recipient organization with a future economic benefit that it can control. Concepts Statement 6 states, "Assets are probable future economic benefits obtained or controlled by a particular entity as a result of past transactions or events" (paragraph 25; footnote reference omitted).

77. The Board concluded that a recipient organization should recognize an asset because it has the ability to obtain and control the future economic benefits of the assets transferred to it, albeit temporarily. The recipient organization has an asset because, until it must transfer cash to the beneficiary, it can invest the cash received, use it to pay other liabilities or to purchase goods or services, or otherwise use the cash for its own purposes. Similarly, most financial assets received also can be temporarily used for the recipient organization's own purposes. Those assets should be recognized in the financial statements along with the liability to transfer the assets to the specified beneficiary.

78. However, the nature of nonfinancial assets (for example, land, buildings, use of facilities or utilities, materials and supplies, intangible assets, or services) usually limits the ability of an intermediary or agent to use the assets for its own benefit before it transfers them to the beneficiary. For example, fiduciary responsibilities of the intermediary or agent prevent it from using the assets if they are of a type that could be used up or would diminish in value if used. Also, if the assets are nonfinancial assets, the intermediary or agent is likely to deliver to the beneficiary the same assets that it received from the donor. Thus, any changes in the value of those assets during the holding period would accrue to the beneficiary (rather than the intermediary or agent). Additionally, excluding nonfinancial assets from the recognition requirement also has the practical effect of relieving an intermediary or agent from the burden of obtaining fair values for food, supplies, and similar items that it holds only for a short time.

79. The Board decided to permit, but not require, the recipient organizations described in paragraphs 8 and 11 of this Statement to recognize transferred nonfinancial assets and the liability to transfer those nonfinancial assets to the specified beneficiary. Several respondents to the Exposure Draft commented on reporting nonfinancial assets; half of them agreed with the Board's conclusions. The majority of the respondents that disagreed said that recipient organizations should recognize all nonfinancial assets that they hold. The Board acknowledges that a standard that permits, but does not require, the recognition of nonfinancial assets may result in reporting that excludes some items from the statement of financial position even though they are assets of the recipient organization because it can temporarily obtain some economic benefits from those items. However, a standard that requires recognition of all nonfinancial assets might result in inclusion of items in the statement of financial position that do not meet the definition of an asset in Concepts Statement 6 because the recipient organization does not control any economic benefits from those items; thus, that standard, also, would arguably be flawed. The Board was not convinced that requiring recognition of all nonfinancial assets would be preferable, and it decided to retain the conclusions of the Exposure Draft.

80. The Board considered whether recipient organizations that are trustees of charitable trusts should recognize an asset and a liability for trust assets but decided that this Statement should not establish standards for accounting by trustees. The Board specified two reasons for that decision. First, a recipient organization that is a trustee may not have an asset because a trustee's ability to obtain the benefits of trust assets is usually significantly limited by its fiduciary responsibilities and by the trust agreement. For example, the trust agreement often requires separate identification of trust property, defines permissible investments, and describes allocation of investment return. Second, current financial reporting requirements for trustees that are banks differ from requirements for trustees that are not-for-profit organizations,[10] primarily in the area of whether the trustees include the assets and liabilities of trusts in their own financial statements. A separate project on consolidated financial statements is expected to provide guidance for determining when, if ever, a trustee controls a trust and should include the assets and liabilities of the trust in its consolidated financial statements.

81. Only a few respondents to the Exposure Draft commented on the exclusion of standards for trustees, and none of those respondents indicated that the existing guidance needed improvement. One respondent asked whether the Board intended to exclude certain not-for-profit organizations from the scope of this Statement by its decision to exclude standards for trustees. That respondent explained that in some states not-for-profit organizations are organized under trust law rather than as corporations. Those organizations are not trustees as described in paragraph 9 of this Statement because, under those statutes, they hold assets "in trust" for the community or some other broadly described group, rather than for a specific beneficiary. Thus, those organizations are included within the scope of this Statement.

Transfers in which the donor grants variance power

82. This Statement supersedes Interpretation 42 and incorporates its conclusions without reconsideration. Paragraphs 12–15 of the basis for conclusions of that Interpretation are also incorporated as paragraphs 83–86 of this Statement.

83. The Board concluded that an organization that receives assets has discretion sufficient to recognize a

---

[10]Chapter 6 of the AICPA Audit and Accounting Guide, *Not-for-Profit Organizations,* describes those requirements.

Transfers of Assets to a Not-for-Profit **FAS136**
Organization or Charitable Trust That Raises
or Holds Contributions for Others

contribution received if it can choose the beneficiary of the assets. For example, if a donor instructs a recipient organization to use the assets only within a particular field of interest, the recipient organization has discretion to choose a specific beneficiary and, accordingly, has received a contribution. In interpreting the application of Statement 116 to situations in which a donor specifies an unaffiliated beneficiary, the Board concluded that a recipient organization can choose the beneficiary if the donor explicitly grants the recipient organization variance power, that is, the power to override the donor's instructions without approval by another party.

84. A recipient organization may obtain the power to redirect the use of assets transferred to it through various means, including standard provisions in donor-choice forms or explicit donor stipulation in gift instruments. For example, community foundations may obtain the unilateral power to redirect the use of assets transferred to them through explicit reference to the variance power granted to them by donors in written gift instruments. The variance power may be explicitly referred to in the terms of the gift instrument and further explained in the community foundation's declaration of trust, articles of incorporation, or governing instruments. Variance power, required by the U.S. Treasury Regulations for trust-form community foundations, is described in those Regulations as the power to

> ... modify any restriction or condition on the distribution of funds for any specified charitable purposes or to specified organizations if in the sole judgment of the governing body (without the necessity of the approval of any participating trustee, custodian, or agent), such restriction or condition becomes, in effect, unnecessary, incapable of fulfillment, or inconsistent with the charitable needs of the community or area served. [1.170A–9(e)(11)(v)(B)(1)]

85. Some say that variance power, as described in the U.S. Treasury Regulations, is conditional. They say that until a change in circumstances occurs and the recipient organization exercises its power to redirect the use of the assets transferred by the donor, the recipient organization should not recognize a contribution (or revenue) because it does not control the future economic benefits of the transferred assets. Some also say that organizations use variance power infrequently because use of that power is typically conditioned on a change in circumstances.

86. The Board believes that while variance power, as described in the U.S. Treasury Regulations, has the appearance of being conditional, the asserted "condition" is not effective because (a) the condition can be substantially met solely by a declaration of the governing board of the recipient organization that states that a distribution to a specified beneficiary is unnecessary, incapable of fulfillment, or inconsistent with the charitable needs of the community or organizations being served and (b) the variance power is unilateral—exercise of the power does not require approval from the donor, beneficiary, or any other interested party. The Board concluded that an organization that is explicitly granted variance power has the ability to use assets it receives to further its own purpose—meeting community needs—from the date it accepts the assets. In that situation, the recipient organization should account for receipt of funds by recognizing an asset and corresponding contribution revenue. Respondents to the December 1995 Exposure Draft generally agreed with the Board's conclusion that an organization that is explicitly granted variance power has sufficient discretion to recognize assets and contribution revenue.

87. The Board's conclusions about transactions in which a resource provider grants variance power but specifies itself or its affiliate, rather than a third party, as beneficiary are discussed in paragraph 96.

Beneficiaries

88. The Board considered whether a beneficiary's rights to the assets transferred to a recipient organization should be recognized as an asset of the beneficiary. The Board concluded that the beneficiary should recognize those rights as an asset if the recipient organization is not explicitly granted variance power. Clearly, unless the donor grants variance power, the recipient organization's representation to the donor that it will transfer the assets to the specified beneficiary is evidence of a probable future benefit to that beneficiary. The donor expects that the recipient organization will deliver and that the specified beneficiary will receive the assets it transferred. In addition, the recipient organization has a social and moral obligation, and most likely a legal obligation, to deliver the assets to the beneficiary. That obligation provides the beneficiary with the ability to obtain the future benefit of the assets. (An obligation may not exist if the recipient organization and the specified beneficiary are financially interrelated organizations. Refer to paragraphs 98–104.) Finally, unless

the recipient organization is explicitly granted variance power, the event that gives rise to the beneficiary's rights (the acceptance of the assets from the donor and the representation that they will be transferred to the specified beneficiary) has already occurred.

89. In contrast, the Board concluded that if the recipient organization is explicitly granted variance power, the specified beneficiary does not have a right that meets the criteria for recognition in financial statements. Because variance power is defined as a unilateral power, another beneficiary can be substituted without the permission of the donor, the specified beneficiary, or any other interested party. Thus, the specified beneficiary is unable to control others' access to the future economic benefits of the assets held by the recipient organization. Further, because the recipient organization can change the beneficiary at will, no past event giving rise to a beneficiary's right has occurred and none will occur until the recipient organization promises to give the transferred assets to the specified beneficiary. Thus, the specified beneficiary's potential for future distributions from the assets held by the recipient organization does not meet the definition of an asset.

90. Most respondents to the Exposure Draft that commented about beneficiary reporting agreed with the Board's conclusions. However, several of those that disagreed expressed concerns about the administrative burdens of identifying assets that are held by recipient organizations for the beneficiary. In addition, many respondents that act as recipient organizations expressed concerns about the burden of notifying beneficiaries of the amounts of assets they hold. The Board believes that in most instances recipient organizations tend to raise resources on an ongoing basis for a select group of beneficiaries. Thus, specified beneficiaries generally are aware of the efforts of recipient organizations, and the ongoing relationships between the organizations usually enable the beneficiaries to request and receive the information that they need for the preparation of their annual (or quarterly) financial statements. Although systems may need to be enhanced to gather or provide information on a more timely basis, the Board believes that the basic systems generally are in place.

Relationships between Resource Providers, Recipient Organizations, and Beneficiaries

91. Relationships between two or more of the parties—resource provider (or donor), recipient or-

ganization, and beneficiary—may indicate that a recipient organization's role differs from that of an agent (paragraph 10). The Board decided that to ensure comparable accounting between similar organizations, it was necessary to consider the three specific situations that are discussed in paragraphs 92–104.

Relationship between a resource provider and a recipient organization

92. If a resource provider transfers assets to a recipient organization that it controls and directs that recipient organization to transfer the assets to a specified beneficiary, the resource provider, by virtue of its control over the recipient organization, has the ability to revoke the transfer or to substitute another beneficiary or another purpose for the transferred assets. Because the resource provider retains control of the transferred assets, it has not made a contribution. The Board concluded that until the transferred assets are beyond the control of the resource provider, the transaction should be reported as an asset by the resource provider and a liability by the recipient organization (for example, as a refundable advance).

93. Some respondents to the Exposure Draft asked the Board to provide a definition of control. The Board declined to do so in this Statement. Several definitions of control exist. For the purposes of FASB Statement No. 57, *Related Party Disclosures,* control is defined as "the possession, direct or indirect, of the power to direct or cause the direction of the management and policies of an enterprise through ownership, by contract, or otherwise" (paragraph 24(b)). AICPA Statement of Position 94-3, *Reporting of Related Entities by Not-for-Profit Organizations,* has a similar definition; it defines control as "the direct or indirect ability to determine the direction of management and policies through ownership, contract, or otherwise" (glossary). The guidance in those documents should be considered when determining whether one entity controls another. In February 1999, the Board issued an Exposure Draft, *Consolidated Financial Statements: Purpose and Policy,* which defines control as "the ability of an entity to direct the policies and management that guide the ongoing activities of another entity so as to increase its benefits and limit its losses from that other entity's activities" (paragraph 6(a)). If the provisions of that Exposure Draft are adopted, its definition of control will supersede those in Statement 57 and SOP 94-3.

Transfers of Assets to a Not-for-Profit **FAS136**
Organization or Charitable Trust That Raises
or Holds Contributions for Others

Relationship between a resource provider and a beneficiary

94. The Board decided that if a resource provider and a specified beneficiary are one and the same or if they are affiliates (as defined in Statement 57, paragraph 24(a)), the transfer of assets to the recipient organization differs from one in which a resource provider specifies an unaffiliated beneficiary. If a resource provider and a beneficiary are neither the same nor affiliated, the resource provider retains no future economic benefit in the assets transferred and a contribution has been made. However, if a resource provider specifies itself or its affiliate as the beneficiary, it retains a future economic benefit in the transferred assets. Because the transfer of assets is not a nonreciprocal transfer,[11] a contribution neither has been made by the resource provider nor has been received by the beneficiary. The Board concluded that the transfer should be reported as an exchange of an asset for another asset by the resource provider and as an asset and a liability by the recipient organization or as an equity transaction by both entities.

95. The Exposure Draft used the term *equity transfer* rather than *equity transaction.* Some respondents found the use of that term confusing because the AICPA Audit and Accounting Guide, *Health Care Organizations,* uses the term equity transfer to describe another type of transaction—one in which the transferor receives nothing of immediate economic value; for example, the transferor does not receive a financial interest or ownership. The transaction described in the healthcare organizations Guide may not meet the second of the three criteria in paragraph 18 of this Statement—the requirement that the resource provider and the recipient organization be financially interrelated organizations. Although the organizations meet the first requirement of paragraph 13 of this Statement (because the healthcare organizations Guide requires that the transferor and the transferee be affiliates), they may not meet the second requirement of that paragraph. To avoid confusion, the term in this Statement was changed from equity transfer to equity transaction.

96. If a resource provider transfers assets to a recipient organization and specifies itself or its affiliate as the beneficiary, the Board believes that a presumption that the transfer is reciprocal, and therefore not a contribution, is necessary even if the resource provider explicitly grants the recipient organization variance power. At the time of the transfer, the resource provider expects to receive future distributions because it specifies itself or its affiliate as a beneficiary, and, by its acceptance of the transfer, the recipient organization agrees that distributions to the resource provider or its affiliate are capable of fulfillment and consistent with the recipient organization's mission. The value of those future distributions, however, may not be commensurate with the value of the transferred assets because the resource provider is at risk of cessation of the distributions as a result of its grant of variance power. If the values exchanged are not commensurate, in concept, the transfer is in part a contribution (paragraphs 3 and 51 of Statement 116). The Board decided that presuming that the entire transfer is reciprocal is preferable to requiring that a resource provider compute the contribution portion because that computation would require measuring the risk that the variance power would be exercised. Further, it is not clear whether a not-for-profit organization (resource provider) can grant a recipient organization the legally valid power to redirect the use of the transferred assets to another beneficiary if the not-for-profit organization originally received those assets with donors' restrictions on their use. The recipient organization might redirect the use of the assets in a way that could violate the resource provider's fiduciary responsibilities to its own donors. The Board decided that it is necessary to presume that the resource provider has retained the future economic benefits of the transferred assets.

97. Some respondents also asked about other transfers to affiliates that did not meet the criteria of either paragraph 17 or 18 of this Statement. The answers to those questions are beyond the scope of this Statement. This Statement sets standards only for transfers to a recipient organization that is not the beneficiary of the transferred assets.

Relationship between a recipient organization and a beneficiary

98. The Board decided that if a beneficiary and a recipient organization are financially interrelated organizations, the recipient organization may not have

---

[11]Statement 116 defines *contribution* as "an unconditional transfer of cash or other assets to an entity or a settlement or cancellation of its liabilities in a voluntary nonreciprocal transfer by another entity acting other than as an owner" (paragraph 209). Statement 116 defines *nonreciprocal transfer* as "a transaction in which an entity incurs a liability or transfers an asset to another entity (or receives an asset or cancellation of a liability) without directly receiving (or giving) value in exchange" (paragraph 209).

a liability to deliver the transferred assets, the return on investment of those assets, or both to the beneficiary. Some respondents disagreed and said that a recipient organization should report a liability regardless of its relationship to the beneficiary. The Board concluded that because the beneficiary can influence the operating and financial decisions of the related recipient organization (or alternatively, the recipient organization can influence the operating and financial decisions of the beneficiary), their relationship differs from that of most debtors and creditors. In the absence of a donor's instruction to do otherwise, a related recipient organization often has the discretion to decide whether to transfer the assets to the beneficiary, to invest them and transfer only the investment return, or to spend them for a purpose that directly or indirectly benefits the beneficiary (including payment of the recipient organization's operating expenses). Further, the beneficiary generally does not attempt to compel delivery of the transferred assets if the recipient organization chooses to hold them. The beneficiary and its related recipient organization often have a collective mission—to best provide the philanthropic services of the beneficiary. They cooperate because they are more effective in achieving their missions when they work harmoniously. Thus, the nature of the relationship between the recipient organization and the beneficiary may permit the recipient organization to avoid the delivery of the transferred assets without significant penalty. If that is so, there is no present obligation to transfer assets or provide services in the future and no liability exists.

99. The Board attempted to define a set of criteria for agents, trustees, and intermediaries that would distinguish transactions that create liabilities from those that increase net assets (contribution revenue). It decided that the criteria being developed were overly complex and not operational. Instead, the Board decided that if a recipient organization and a beneficiary are financially interrelated organizations and the recipient organization is not a trustee, the recipient organization should recognize a contribution received, and the beneficiary should recognize its interest in the net assets of the recipient organization and subsequent changes in the value of that interest.

100. In some cases, the relationship between a beneficiary and a recipient organization is characterized by control in addition to an ongoing economic interest in net assets. If existing standards required consolidation whenever there is a control relationship,[12] then a contribution to either the beneficiary or the recipient organization would be a contribution to the consolidated entity and would be reflected in the consolidated financial statements. If the entities were consolidated, the question of whether the contribution should be recognized by the recipient organization or the beneficiary would be relevant only to separately issued financial statements of the controlled entity. The lack of standards requiring consolidation when a control relationship exists was a factor in the Board's decision to specifically address the relationship between the recipient organization and the beneficiary. Several respondents to the Exposure Draft said that the Board should defer establishing standards for financially interrelated organizations until after the completion of the Board's consolidations project. Because the guidance developed in this project is consistent with the proposed guidance in the consolidations project, the Board saw no compelling reason to delay the issuance of this Statement.

101. The Board considered whether special accounting should apply only to relationships between recipient organizations and beneficiaries that are characterized by control but determined that it would be inappropriate to base the approach on a definition of control that is currently under examination in the Board's project on consolidations. Some respondents to the Exposure Draft suggested that the Board could use *significant influence* rather than control as the basis for its approach. However, significant influence is described in APB Opinion No. 18, *The Equity Method of Accounting for Investments in Common Stock,* in terms of ownership of voting shares. Thus, it could not be applied easily and on a consistent basis to relationships between not-for-profit organizations. Instead, the Board chose to describe relationships that demonstrate one organization's ability to influence the operating and financial decisions of the other.

102. The Board also focused on relationships in which a beneficiary's rights to the assets held by the recipient organization are residual rights; that is, the value of those rights increases or decreases as a result of the investment, fundraising, operating, and other

---

[12]Paragraph 12 of SOP 94-3 and Chapter 11 of the healthcare organizations Guide permit but do not require consolidation if a not-for-profit organization controls another organization in which it has an economic interest and its control takes a form other than majority ownership or voting interest. Consolidation of related entities is required only in the circumstances described in paragraphs 10 and 11 of SOP 94-3 and in Chapter 11 of the healthcare organizations Guide.

Transfers of Assets to a Not-for-Profit   **FAS136**
Organization or Charitable Trust That Raises
or Holds Contributions for Others

activities of the recipient organization. Although the beneficiary may not have control of the recipient organization, its interest is essentially equivalent to a parent's residual interest in a subsidiary or an investor's residual interest if the investor has significant influence over the investee's operating and financial policies. In contrast, if a relationship between a beneficiary and a recipient organization is not characterized by an ongoing economic interest of a residual nature, the rights of a beneficiary are fixed or determinable and similar to those of a creditor.

103. The Board concluded that it is appropriate to use a method of accounting that, like the equity method of accounting, recognizes increases or decreases in the economic resources underlying the beneficiary's interest in the periods in which those changes are reflected in the accounts of the recipient organization. That method is appropriate because the cooperative relationship with the recipient organization allows the beneficiary to influence the operating or financial decisions of the recipient organization, and "The equity method tends to be most appropriate if an investment enables the investor to influence the operating or financial decisions of the investee" (Opinion 18, paragraph 12).

104. The Board noted that SOP 94-3 defines and provides examples of economic interest. Chapter 11 of the healthcare organizations Guide has the same definition and examples. Although most of the relationships described in that definition are potentially ongoing economic interests in the net assets, some do not meet the criterion in paragraph 13(b) of this Statement. Only economic interests that are both ongoing and residual interests in the net assets are ongoing economic interests in the net assets.

Disclosures

105. A few respondents to the Exposure Draft suggested that the Board require organizations to disclose the ratio of fundraising expenses to amounts raised. They expressed concern that a recipient organization might appear less efficient if the ratio was computed using contributions rather than total amounts raised as the denominator. The Board observed that not-for-profit organizations do not agree on how fundraising ratios should be computed or whether they should be required in financial statements. Rather than requiring a ratio and prescribing one method of computing it, which might appear to be an endorsement of that ratio as the best measure of fundraising efficiency, the Board decided

that if an organization chooses to include on the face of its statement of activities or in the notes to its financial statements a ratio of fundraising expenses to total amounts raised, it must describe how it computes that ratio.

106. Other respondents to the Exposure Draft suggested that specified beneficiaries should disclose information about legal or donor-imposed restrictions on the availability of assets held for them by recipient organizations. In most cases, the disclosures required by paragraphs 11 and 14 of FASB Statement No. 117, *Financial Statements of Not-for-Profit Organizations,* are sufficient. However, if an organization transfers assets to another and specifies itself or its affiliate as the beneficiary, the users of its financial statements might not be aware of additional limitations imposed by the terms of the agreement with the recipient organization. The Board believes that the disclosures specified in paragraph 19 of this Statement provide information that is useful in assessing management's stewardship and the organization's liquidity and exposure to risk.

107. A few respondents asked whether the disclosure requirements of paragraph 20 of Opinion 18 apply to beneficiaries that report their interests in the net assets of the recipient organization using a method similar to the equity method. The specific terms of those requirements are not particularly relevant because they are expressed in terms of the ownership of common stock of another entity. The Board decided that the disclosure requirements of SOP 94-3 are sufficient to provide the information that users of financial statements are likely to need.

Reporting Results of Fundraising Efforts in the Financial Statements

108. Recipient organizations that solicit and collect cash, products, or services and distribute those assets for charitable purposes have expressed concern that reporting less than 100 percent of the results of their fundraising efforts as contribution revenue would understate the magnitude of their central operations. The Board acknowledges the desire of those organizations to report the results of total campaign efforts to the users of financial statements. However, the Board believes that if a recipient organization is acting as an agent, trustee, or intermediary, the assets received are not its revenue. Although the receipt of the transferred assets is an inflow of assets from activities that constitute the entity's ongoing major or central

operations (and, thus, might seem to meet the definition of revenue in paragraph 78 of Concepts Statement 6), that inflow is accompanied by an offsetting liability to the specified beneficiary. Consequently, the receipt of the transferred assets is not revenue, just as a deposit to an escrow account (which is also an inflow of assets from activities that constitute the entity's major or central operations) is not revenue to the real estate agency that receives it.

109. To the extent that an organization's activities include raising and distributing cash, the total amounts raised and distributed may be evident from a statement of cash flows prepared using the direct method for reporting operating cash flows. In addition, generally accepted accounting principles do not preclude entities from providing supplementary information or additional disclosures. An organization may provide a schedule reflecting fundraising efforts or campaign accomplishments or may disclose total amounts raised on the statement of activities, provided that amounts raised in an agent, trustee, or intermediary capacity are not shown as revenues. The following illustration provides three possible methods of displaying fundraising efforts in the revenue section of the statement of activities. Methods 2 and 3 display the total amounts raised.

An organization raises $6,000 of contributions, $100 of other support, and $4,000 accounted for as agent, trustee, or intermediary transactions because donors have specified beneficiaries without granting variance power. Of the $4,000 accounted for as agent, trustee, or intermediary transactions, the organization pays out $3,600 to specified beneficiaries and retains $400 as its administrative fee.

Method 1

Contributions		$ 6,000
Other support		100
Total support		6,100
Administrative fees retained on amounts designated by donors for specific organizations		400
Total support and revenue		$ 6,500

Method 2

Contributions		$ 6,000
Other support		100
Total support		6,100
Other revenue:		
Amounts designated by donors for specific organizations	$4,000	
Less: Amounts held for or remitted to those organizations	3,600	
Administrative fees retained on amounts designated by donors for specific organizations		400
Total support and revenue		$ 6,500

Method 3

Total amounts raised*	$10,000
Less: Amounts designated by donors for specific organizations	4,000
Total contributions	6,000
Other revenue:	
Other support	100
Administrative fees retained on amounts designated by donors for specific organizations	400
Total support and revenue	$ 6,500

---

*Other terms, such as *campaign results* or *campaign efforts,* may be used.

Transfers of Assets to a Not-for-Profit   **FAS136**
Organization or Charitable Trust That Raises
or Holds Contributions for Others

The Board concluded that each of the methods reports the recipient organization's revenues ($6,500) in a way that is both easily understood by users of the financial statements and representationally faithful.

Effective Date and Transition

110. The Board decided that this Statement should be effective for financial statements issued for fiscal periods beginning after December 15, 1999, except for the provisions of paragraph 12, which already are effective because they are incorporated from Interpretation 42. A few respondents to the Exposure Draft said that organizations might have difficulty implementing this Statement by its proposed effective date, which was for fiscal years beginning after June 15, 1999. The Board believes that the revised effective date provides adequate time for entities to implement this Statement's provisions and for users of financial statements to understand how those provisions affect their analyses. Although the provisions of this Statement must be applied retroactively to appropriately reflect the interests of specified beneficiaries in endowment gifts held on their behalf by recipient organizations, the Board decided that the effect of applying the provisions could be reported either as a cumulative effect of a change in accounting principle or by restatement of prior years' information. The Board encourages earlier application of this Statement.

Statement of Financial Accounting Standards No. 137
Accounting for Derivative Instruments and Hedging Activities—Deferral of the Effective Date of FASB Statement No. 133

an amendment of FASB Statement No. 133

STATUS

Issued: June 1999

Effective Date: June 1999

Affects: Amends FAS 133, paragraph 48
Supersedes FAS 133, paragraph 50

Affected by: No other pronouncements

Accounting for Derivative Instruments and
Hedging Activities—Deferral of the Effective Date
of FASB Statement No. 133

FAS137

Statement of Financial Accounting Standards No. 137

Accounting for Derivative Instruments and Hedging Activities— Deferral of the Effective Date of FASB Statement No. 133

an amendment of FASB Statement No. 133

CONTENTS

INTRODUCTION

1. FASB Statement No. 133, *Accounting for Derivative Instruments and Hedging Activities,* was issued in June 1998. It establishes accounting and reporting standards for derivative instruments, including certain derivative instruments embedded in other contracts (collectively referred to as derivatives), and for hedging activities. As issued, Statement 133 is effective for all fiscal quarters of all fiscal years beginning after June 15, 1999, with earlier application encouraged.

2. The Board received requests to consider delaying the effective date of Statement 133. Entities and their auditors requested more time to study, understand, and implement the provisions of that Statement as they apply to entities' transactions and circumstances. Entities also requested more time to complete information system modifications. The Board concluded that, for the reasons presented in the appendix to this Statement, it is appropriate to defer the effective date of Statement 133. However, the Board continues to encourage early application of Statement 133.

STANDARDS OF FINANCIAL ACCOUNTING AND REPORTING

Amendments to Statement 133

3. Statement 133 is amended as follows:

a. The first sentence of paragraph 48 is replaced by the following:

This Statement shall be effective for all fiscal quarters of all fiscal years beginning after June 15, 2000.

b. Paragraph 50 is replaced by the following:

At the date of initial application, an entity shall choose to either (a) recognize as an asset or liability in the statement of financial position all embedded derivative instruments that are required pursuant to paragraphs 12–16 to be separated from their host contracts or (b) select either January 1, 1998 or January 1, 1999 as a transition date for embedded derivatives. If the entity chooses to select a transition date, it shall recognize as separate assets and liabilities (pursuant to paragraphs 12–16) only those derivatives embedded in hybrid instruments issued, acquired, or substantively modified by the entity on or after the selected transition date. That choice is not permitted to be applied to only some of an entity's individual hybrid instruments and must be applied on an all-or-none basis.

Effective Date

4. This Statement is effective upon issuance. An entity that has already applied the provisions of Statement 133 and has issued interim or annual financial statements reflecting that application may not revert to a previous method of accounting for derivative instruments and hedging activities.

> **The provisions of this Statement need not be applied to immaterial items.**

This Statement was adopted by the affirmative votes of five members of the Financial Accounting Standards Board. Messrs. Cope and Foster dissented.

Messrs. Cope and Foster dissent from the issuance of this Statement. They disagree with the conclusion that the benefits of delay outweigh the advantages of prompt implementation. They are concerned that users of financial statements will continue to be deprived of information that has long been recognized as critical to the investment decision-making process. Lack of transparent recognition and consistent accounting for derivatives and hedging transactions has already led to substantial investor losses that could have been avoided had there been proper accounting and disclosures. As the number and variety of derivative transactions expand, and considering increased market volatility, they believe that, without appropriate accounting and disclosure, the risk of investors and creditors incurring unanticipated losses in the future remains high. Users of financial statements need to know what risk exposures exist or do not ex-

ist. The implementation of Statement 133 will contribute significantly toward meeting that need, and Messrs. Cope and Foster believe that its implementation should not be delayed.

Mr. Cope also believes that, although the provisions of paragraph 3(b) are a logical extension of a decision to defer implementation of the entire standard, the result is a complication and extension of the transition period during which it will be even more difficult for investors to make valid comparisons between entities. That transitional problem would be avoided if the Statement was not deferred.

Mr. Foster also believes that the change in the transition requirements set out in paragraph 3(b) is inappropriate. The Board's constituents have known since June 1998 when Statement 133 was issued that they would be required to account separately for derivatives embedded in complex financial instruments entered into on or after January 1, 1998. Mr. Foster sees no reason to grandfather the accounting for any more embedded derivatives than those that were originally grandfathered by Statement 133.

Members of the Financial Accounting Standards Board:

Edmund L. Jenkins,	Anthony T. Cope	James J. Leisenring
Chairman	John M. Foster	Gerhard G. Mueller
Joseph V. Anania	Gaylen N. Larson	

Appendix

BACKGROUND INFORMATION AND BASIS FOR CONCLUSIONS

5. At the time Statement 133 was issued in June 1998, the Board was aware of the complexities associated with transactions involving derivative instruments and their prevalent use as hedging instruments. Because of that, even before Statement 133 was issued, the Board established the Derivatives Implementation Group (DIG) to assist the FASB in answering questions that companies might face as they began implementing the Statement. Additionally, early on, the FASB developed an educational course on implementing Statement 133, which has been widely used.

6. Despite the anticipatory effort extended by the Board to address implementation issues, some preparers of financial statements and auditors expressed concern about certain challenges they face in applying Statement 133. Those challenges include organization-wide educational efforts and information system modifications.

7. The educational challenges relate mainly to the scope of the Statement and the new approach to recognizing and measuring hedge effectiveness. Statement 133 has a potentially pervasive effect that requires an understanding of technical issues that span several functional areas in some organizations. Constituents expressed concern that they simply have not had enough time to master the new accounting requirements and their implications for derivative and hedging transactions throughout their organizations. In many cases, there may be an unanticipated need to modify existing contracts that currently include embedded derivatives.

8. The Board was informed that the ability to modify or develop information systems in response to Statement 133 is hindered by the level of effort required to modify and test those systems to ensure their proper operation in the year 2000. Constituents reported that those required information systems modifications consumed more resources than expected. In turn, information systems resources were unavailable to ensure compliance with Statement 133. Many companies have imposed moratoriums on information systems changes during the third and fourth quarters of 1999 that will extend through the first quarter of 2000. That has created obstacles that were unanticipated by the Board and constituents when the original effective date of the Statement was selected.

9. The Board believes that the issues identified by constituents regarding the difficulties associated with implementation will prevent many of them from achieving a sound and consistent implementation of Statement 133. The Board was requested to consider different types of deferrals that included rolling effective dates for DIG conclusions and deferring selected provisions of Statement 133 that were of particular concern to some constituents. The Board decided that the simplest and most effective alternative was a complete deferral for a period of one year.

10. With a delayed effective date, the Board remains concerned that users of financial statements will be deprived of information that the Board continues to believe is critical. Nonetheless, the Board believes that the disadvantages associated with immediate implementation, particularly inconsistent application of the standard caused by lack of adequate information systems, outweigh the benefits of requiring immediate implementation. A one-year deferral will allow constituents to overcome the educational and information systems challenges they currently face. The Board believes that the deferral of the effective date of Statement 133 will not only facilitate its adoption but also enhance consistent application of its provisions for the ultimate benefit of users.

11. On May 20, 1999, the Board issued an Exposure Draft, *Accounting for Derivative Instruments and Hedging Activities—Deferral of the Effective Date of FASB Statement No. 133,* which proposed deferring the effective date of Statement 133 for one year. The Board received 77 letters of comment from respondents. There was overwhelming support for the Board's decision to defer the effective date of Statement 133. Two respondents requested that the Board consider deferring the date that differentiates which hybrid instruments in existence at the date of initial application must be analyzed to determine whether the related embedded derivatives are required to be separated from host contracts. The Board concluded that was a reasonable request given the change in the effective date of Statement 133. The Board concluded that it could reach an informed decision on the basis of existing information without a public hearing and that the effective date specified in paragraph 4 is advisable in the circumstances.

Statement of Financial Accounting Standards No. 138
Accounting for Certain Derivative Instruments
and Certain Hedging Activities

an amendment of FASB Statement No. 133

STATUS

Issued: June 2000

Effective Date: For all fiscal quarters of all fiscal years beginning after June 15, 2000

Affects: Supersedes FAS 133, paragraphs 10(b), 33, 36(b), 40(a), 52(b), 68(l), 155, and 197
Amends FAS 133, paragraphs 12, 21(c)(1), 21(d), 21(f), 21(f)(2) through 21(f)(4), 29(d), 29(e), 29(g)(2), 29(h), 29(h)(1) through 29(h)(4), 30, 36, 36(a), 37, 38, 40, 40(b), 42, 45(b)(4), 54, 58(b), 58(c)(2), 61(d), 61(e), 68, 68(b), 68(d), 90, 115, 134, 161, 169, 200, and 540 and footnotes 14 and 19
Amends FAS 133 by adding paragraph 36A after paragraph 36, paragraph 37A after paragraph 37, paragraphs 40A through 40C after paragraph 40, and paragraphs 120A through 120D after paragraph 120

Affected by: No other pronouncements

Issues Discussed by FASB Emerging Issues Task Force (EITF)

Affects: No EITF Issues

Interpreted by: Paragraph 4(a) interpreted by EITF Topic No. D-105

Related Issues: No EITF Issues

Statement of Financial Accounting Standards No. 138

Accounting for Certain Derivative Instruments and Certain Hedging Activities

an amendment of FASB Statement No. 133

CONTENTS

INTRODUCTION

1. FASB Statement No. 133, *Accounting for Derivative Instruments and Hedging Activities,* establishes accounting and reporting standards for derivative instruments, including certain derivative instruments embedded in other contracts, (collectively referred to as derivatives) and for hedging activities. This Statement addresses a limited number of issues causing implementation difficulties for numerous entities that apply Statement 133.

2. This Statement amends the accounting and reporting standards of Statement 133 for certain derivative instruments and certain hedging activities as indicated below.

a. The normal purchases and normal sales exception in paragraph 10(b) may be applied to contracts that implicitly or explicitly permit net settlement, as discussed in paragraphs 9(a) and 57(c)(1), and contracts that have a market mechanism to facilitate net settlement, as discussed in paragraphs 9(b) and 57(c)(2).

b. The specific risks that can be identified as the hedged risk are redefined so that in a hedge of interest rate risk, the risk of changes in the benchmark interest rate[1] would be the hedged risk.

c. Recognized foreign-currency-denominated assets and liabilities for which a foreign currency transaction gain or loss is recognized in earnings under the provisions of paragraph 15 of FASB State-

ment No. 52, *Foreign Currency Translation,* may be the hedged item in fair value hedges or cash flow hedges.

d. Certain intercompany derivatives may be designated as the hedging instruments in cash flow hedges of foreign currency risk in the consolidated financial statements if those intercompany derivatives are offset by unrelated third-party contracts on a net basis.

3. This Statement also amends Statement 133 for decisions made by the Board relating to the Derivatives Implementation Group (DIG) process. Certain decisions arising from the DIG process that required specific amendments to Statement 133 are incorporated in this Statement.

STANDARDS OF FINANCIAL ACCOUNTING AND REPORTING

Amendments to Statement 133

4. Statement 133 is amended as follows:

Amendment Related to Normal Purchases and Normal Sales

a. Paragraph 10(b) is replaced by the following:

> *Normal purchases and normal sales.* Normal purchases and normal sales are contracts that provide for the purchase or sale of something

---

[1]Benchmark interest rate is defined in paragraph 4(jj) of this Statement.

other than a financial instrument or derivative instrument that will be delivered in quantities expected to be used or sold by the reporting entity over a reasonable period in the normal course of business. However, contracts that have a price based on an underlying that is not clearly and closely related to the asset being sold or purchased (such as a price in a contract for the sale of a grain commodity based in part on changes in the S&P index) or that are denominated in a foreign currency that meets neither of the criteria in paragraphs 15(a) and 15(b) shall not be considered normal purchases and normal sales. Contracts that contain net settlement provisions as described in paragraphs 9(a) and 9(b) may qualify for the normal purchases and normal sales exception if it is probable at inception and throughout the term of the individual contract that the contract will not settle net and will result in physical delivery. Net settlement (as described in paragraphs 9(a) and 9(b)) of contracts in a group of contracts similarly designated as normal purchases and normal sales would call into question the classification of all such contracts as normal purchases or normal sales. Contracts that require cash settlements of gains or losses or are otherwise settled net on a periodic basis, including individual contracts that are part of a series of sequential contracts intended to accomplish ultimate acquisition or sale of a commodity, do not qualify for this exception. For contracts that qualify for the normal purchases and normal sales exception, the entity shall document the basis for concluding that it is probable that the contract will result in physical delivery. The documentation requirements can be applied either to groups of similarly designated contracts or to each individual contract.

Amendments to Redefine Interest Rate Risk

b. Paragraph 21 is amended as follows:

(1) The first sentence of subparagraph (d) is replaced by the following:

> If the hedged item is all or a portion of a debt security (or a portfolio of similar debt securities) that is classified as held-to-maturity in accordance with FASB Statement No. 115, *Accounting for Certain Investments in Debt and Equity Securities,* the designated risk being hedged is the risk

of changes in its fair value attributable to credit risk, foreign exchange risk, or both. If the hedged item is an option component of a held-to-maturity security that permits its prepayment, the designated risk being hedged is the risk of changes in the entire fair value of that option component.

(2) In the first parenthetical sentence of subparagraph (d), *changes in market interest rates or foreign exchange rates* is replaced by *interest rate risk.*

(3) In subparagraph (f)(2), *market interest rates* is replaced by *the designated **benchmark interest rate** (referred to as interest rate risk).*

(4) In subparagraph (f)(3), *(refer to paragraphs 37 and 38)* is replaced by *(referred to as foreign exchange risk) (refer to paragraphs 37, 37A, and 38).*

(5) In subparagraph (f)(4), *both* is inserted between *to* and *changes* and *the obligor's creditworthiness* is replaced by *the obligor's creditworthiness and changes in the spread over the benchmark interest rate with respect to the hedged item's credit sector at inception of the hedge (referred to as credit risk).*

(6) In the second sentence of subparagraph (f), *market* is deleted.

(7) In subparagraph (f), the following sentences and footnote are added after the second sentence:

> The benchmark interest rate being hedged in a hedge of interest rate risk must be specifically identified as part of the designation and documentation at the inception of the hedging relationship. Ordinarily, an entity should designate the same benchmark interest rate as the risk being hedged for similar hedges, consistent with paragraph 62; the use of different benchmark interest rates for similar hedges should be rare and must be justified. In calculating the change in the hedged item's fair value attributable to changes in the benchmark interest rate, the estimated cash flows used in calculating fair value must be based on all of the contractual cash flows of the entire hedged item. Excluding some of the

hedged item's contractual cash flows (for example, the portion of the interest coupon in excess of the benchmark interest rate) from the calculation is not permitted.*

---

*The first sentence of paragraph 21(a) that specifically permits the hedged item to be identified as either all or a specific portion of a recognized asset or liability or of an unrecognized firm commitment is not affected by the provisions in this subparagraph.

(8) In the fourth sentence of subparagraph (f), *overall* is inserted between *exposure to changes in the* and *fair value of that.*

(9) In the last sentence of subparagraph (f), *market* is deleted.

c. Paragraph 29 is amended as follows:

(1) In the first sentence of subparagraph (e), *default or changes in the obligor's creditworthiness* is replaced by *credit risk, foreign exchange risk, or both.*

(2) In the last sentence of subparagraph (e), *changes in market interest rates* is replaced by *interest rate risk.*

(3) In the first sentence of subparagraph (h), *(or the interest payments on that financial asset or liability)* is added after *sale of a financial asset or liability.*

(4) In subparagraph (h)(1), *the risk of changes in the cash flows of the entire asset or liability* is replaced by *the risk of overall changes in the hedged cash flows related to the asset or liability.*

(5) In subparagraph (h)(2), *market interest rates* is replaced by *the designated benchmark interest rate (referred to as interest rate risk).*

(6) In subparagraph (h)(3), *(refer to paragraph 40)* is replaced by *(referred to as foreign exchange risk) (refer to paragraphs 40, 40A, 40B, and 40C).*

(7) In subparagraph (h)(4), *default or changes in the obligor's creditworthiness* is replaced by

default, changes in the obligor's creditworthiness, and changes in the spread over the benchmark interest rate with respect to the hedged item's credit sector at inception of the hedge (referred to as credit risk).

(8) In subparagraph (h), the following sentences are added after the second sentence:

The benchmark interest rate being hedged in a hedge of interest rate risk must be specifically identified as part of the designation and documentation at the inception of the hedging relationship. Ordinarily, an entity should designate the same benchmark interest rate as the risk being hedged for similar hedges, consistent with paragraph 62; the use of different benchmark interest rates for similar hedges should be rare and must be justified. In a cash flow hedge of a variable-rate financial asset or liability, either existing or forecasted, the designated risk being hedged cannot be the risk of changes in its cash flows attributable to changes in the specifically identified benchmark interest rate if the cash flows of the hedged transaction are explicitly based on a different index, for example, based on a specific bank's prime rate, which cannot qualify as the benchmark rate. However, the risk designated as being hedged could potentially be the risk of overall changes in the hedged cash flows related to the asset or liability, provided that the other criteria for a cash flow hedge have been met.

d. Paragraph 54 is amended as follows:

(1) In the second sentence, *market interest rates, changes in foreign currency exchange rates,* is replaced by *the designated benchmark interest rate.*

(2) In the third and fourth (parenthetical) sentences, *market* is deleted.

(3) In the penultimate sentence of footnote 14, *market interest rates* is replaced by *interest rate risk.*

e. In the first sentence of paragraph 90, *market* is deleted.

Amendments Related to Hedging Recognized Foreign-Currency-Denominated Assets and Liabilities

f. In paragraph 21(c)(1), *(for example, if foreign exchange risk is hedged, a foreign-currency-denominated asset for which a foreign currency transaction gain or loss is recognized in earnings)* is deleted.

g. Paragraph 29(d) is amended as follows:

(1) In the first sentence, *(for example, if foreign exchange risk is hedged, the forecasted acquisition of a foreign-currency-denominated asset for which a foreign currency transaction gain or loss will be recognized in earnings)* is deleted.

(2) The second sentence is deleted.

h. In paragraph 29(g)(2), *(reflecting its actual location if a physical asset)* is replaced by *reflecting its actual location if a physical asset (regardless of whether that price and the related cash flows are stated in the entity's functional currency or a foreign currency).*

i. The following subparagraph is added after subparagraph (c) of paragraph 30:

d.
In a cash flow hedge of the variability of the functional-currency-equivalent cash flows for a recognized foreign-currency-denominated asset or liability that is remeasured at spot exchange rates under paragraph 15 of Statement 52, an amount that will offset the related transaction gain or loss arising from the remeasurement and adjust earnings for the cost to the purchaser (income to the seller) of the hedging instrument shall be reclassified each period from other comprehensive income to earnings.

j. Paragraph 36 is amended as follows:

(1) In the first sentence, *Consistent with the functional currency concept in Statement 52* is replaced by *If the hedged item is denominated in a foreign currency.*

(2) In subparagraph (a), *an available-for-sale security* is replaced by *a recognized asset or liability (including an available-for-sale security).*

(3) Subparagraph (b) is replaced by the following:

A cash flow hedge of a forecasted transaction, an unrecognized firm commitment, the forecasted functional-currency-equivalent cash flows associated with a recognized asset or liability, or a forecasted intercompany transaction.

(4) The first two sentences following subparagraph (c) are replaced by the following:

The recognition in earnings of the foreign currency transaction gain or loss on a foreign-currency-denominated asset or liability based on changes in the foreign currency spot rate is not considered to be the remeasurement of that asset or liability with changes in fair value attributable to foreign exchange risk recognized in earnings, which is discussed in the criteria in paragraphs 21(c)(1) and 29(d). Thus, those criteria are not impediments to either a foreign currency fair value or cash flow hedge of such a foreign-currency-denominated asset or liability or a foreign currency cash flow hedge of the forecasted acquisition or incurrence of a foreign-currency-denominated asset or liability whose carrying amount will be remeasured at spot exchange rates under paragraph 15 of Statement 52.

k. The following paragraph is added after paragraph 36:

36A. The provisions in paragraph 36 that permit a recognized foreign-currency-denominated asset or liability to be the hedged item in a fair value or cash flow hedge of foreign currency exposure also pertain to a recognized foreign-currency-denominated receivable or payable that results from a hedged forecasted foreign-currency-denominated sale or purchase on credit. An entity may choose to designate a single cash flow hedge that encompasses the variability of functional currency cash flows attributable to foreign exchange risk related to the settlement of the foreign-currency-denominated receivable or payable resulting from a forecasted sale or purchase on credit. Alternatively, an entity may choose to designate a cash flow hedge of the variability of functional currency cash flows attributable to foreign exchange risk related to a forecasted foreign-currency-denominated sale or purchase on credit and then separately designate a foreign currency fair value hedge of the resulting recognized foreign-currency-denominated receivable or payable. In that case, the cash flow hedge would terminate (be dedesignated) when the hedged sale or purchase occurs and the foreign-currency-denominated receivable or payable is recognized. The use of the same foreign currency derivative instrument for both the cash flow hedge and the fair value hedge is not prohibited though some ineffectiveness may result.

l. The following paragraph is added after paragraph 37:

> 37A. *Recognized asset or liability.* A nonderivative financial instrument shall not be designated as the hedging instrument in a fair value hedge of the foreign currency exposure of a recognized asset or liability. A derivative instrument can be designated as hedging the changes in the fair value of a recognized asset or liability (or a specific portion thereof) for which a foreign currency transaction gain or loss is recognized in earnings under the provisions of paragraph 15 of Statement 52. All recognized foreign-currency-denominated assets or liabilities for which a foreign currency transaction gain or loss is recorded in earnings may qualify for the accounting specified in paragraphs 22–27 if all the fair value hedge criteria in paragraphs 20 and 21 and the conditions in paragraphs 40(a) and 40(b) are met.

m. Paragraph 40 is amended as follows:

> (1) The second sentence is replaced by the following:
>
> > A derivative instrument designated as hedging the foreign currency exposure to variability in the functional-currency-equivalent cash flows associated with a forecasted transaction (for example, a fore-

casted export sale to an unaffiliated entity with the price to be denominated in a foreign currency), a recognized asset or liability, an unrecognized firm commitment, or a forecasted intercompany transaction (for example, a forecasted sale to a foreign subsidiary or a forecasted royalty from a foreign subsidiary) qualifies for hedge accounting if all the following criteria are met:

> (2) The following subparagraph is added:
>
> > e. If the hedged item is a recognized foreign-currency-denominated asset or liability, all the variability in the hedged item's functional-currency-equivalent cash flows must be eliminated by the effect of the hedge. (For example, a cash flow hedge cannot be used with a variable-rate foreign-currency-denominated asset or liability and a derivative based solely on changes in exchange rates because the derivative does not eliminate all the variability in the functional currency cash flows.)

Amendments Related to Intercompany Derivatives

n. In the last sentence of paragraph 36, *in a fair value hedge or in a cash flow hedge of a recognized foreign-currency-denominated asset or liability or in a net investment hedge* is added after *can be a hedging instrument.*

o. The following paragraphs are added after paragraph 40:

> 40A. *Internal derivative.* A foreign currency derivative contract that has been entered into with another member of a consolidated group (such as a treasury center) can be a hedging instrument in a foreign currency cash flow hedge of a forecasted borrowing, purchase, or sale or an unrecognized firm commitment in the consolidated financial statements only if the following two conditions are satisfied. (That foreign currency derivative instrument is hereafter in this section referred to as an *internal derivative.*)
>
> a. From the perspective of the member of the consolidated group using the derivative as a hedging instrument (hereafter in this section

referred to as the *hedging affiliate*), the criteria for foreign currency cash flow hedge accounting in paragraph 40 must be satisfied.

b. The member of the consolidated group not using the derivative as a hedging instrument (hereafter in this section referred to as the *issuing affiliate*) must either (1) enter into a derivative contract with an unrelated third party to offset the exposure that results from that internal derivative or (2) if the conditions in paragraph 40B are met, enter into derivative contracts with unrelated third parties that would offset, on a net basis for each foreign currency, the foreign exchange risk arising from multiple internal derivative contracts.

40B. *Offsetting net exposures.* If an issuing affiliate chooses to offset exposure arising from multiple internal derivative contracts on an aggregate or net basis, the derivatives issued to hedging affiliates may qualify as cash flow hedges in the consolidated financial statements only if all of the following conditions are satisfied:

a. The issuing affiliate enters into a derivative contract with an unrelated third party to offset, on a net basis for each foreign currency, the foreign exchange risk arising from multiple internal derivative contracts, and the derivative contract with the unrelated third party generates equal or closely approximating gains and losses when compared with the aggregate or net losses and gains generated by the derivative contracts issued to affiliates.

b. Internal derivatives that are not designated as hedging instruments are excluded from the determination of the foreign currency exposure on a net basis that is offset by the third-party derivative. In addition, nonderivative contracts may not be used as hedging instruments to offset exposures arising from internal derivative contracts.

c. Foreign currency exposure that is offset by a single net third-party contract arises from internal derivative contracts that mature within the same 31-day period and that involve the same currency exposure as the net third-party derivative. The offsetting net third-party derivative related to that group of contracts must offset the aggregate or net exposure to that currency, must mature within the same 31-day period, and must be entered into within 3 business days after the designation of the internal derivatives as hedging instruments.

d. The issuing affiliate tracks the exposure that it acquires from each hedging affiliate and maintains documentation supporting linkage of each internal derivative contract and the offsetting aggregate or net derivative contract with an unrelated third party.

e. The issuing affiliate does not alter or terminate the offsetting derivative with an unrelated third party unless the hedging affiliate initiates that action. If the issuing affiliate does alter or terminate any offsetting third-party derivative (which should be rare), the hedging affiliate must prospectively cease hedge accounting for the internal derivatives that are offset by that third-party derivative.

40C. A member of a consolidated group is not permitted to offset exposures arising from multiple internal derivative contracts on a net basis for foreign currency cash flow exposures related to recognized foreign-currency-denominated assets or liabilities. That prohibition includes situations in which a recognized foreign-currency-denominated asset or liability in a fair value hedge or cash flow hedge results from the occurrence of a specifically identified forecasted transaction initially designated as a cash flow hedge.

Amendments for Certain Interpretations of Statement 133 Cleared by the Board Relating to the Derivatives Implementation Group Process

p. In the second sentence of paragraph 12, *host* is inserted between *would be required by the* and *contract, whether unconditional.*

Amendments to Implement Guidance in Implementation Issue No. G3, "Discontinuation of a Cash Flow Hedge"

q. Paragraph 33 is replaced by the following:

The net derivative gain or loss related to a discontinued cash flow hedge shall continue to be reported in accumulated other comprehensive income unless it is probable that the forecasted transaction will *not* occur by the end of the originally specified time period (as documented at the inception of the hedging relationship) or within an additional two-month period of time thereafter, except as indicated in the following sentence. In rare cases, the existence of extenuating circumstances that are related to the nature of the forecasted transaction and are outside the control or influence of the reporting entity may cause the forecasted transaction to be probable of occurring on a date that is beyond the additional two-month period of time, in which case the net derivative gain or loss related to the discontinued cash flow hedge shall continue to be reported in accumulated other comprehensive income until it is reclassified into earnings pursuant to paragraph 31. If it is probable that the hedged forecasted transaction will not occur either by the end of the originally specified time period or within the additional two-month period of time and the hedged forecasted transaction also does not qualify for the exception described in the preceding sentence, that derivative gain or loss reported in accumulated other comprehensive income shall be reclassified into earnings immediately.

r. The following is added at the end of paragraph 45(b)(4):

> by the end of the originally specified time period or within the additional period of time discussed in paragraph 33.

Amendments to Implement Guidance in Implementation Issue No. H1, "Hedging at the Operating Unit Level"

s. In the last sentence of paragraph 37, *and the conditions in paragraphs 40(a) and 40(b)* is added between *paragraphs 20 and 21* and *are met.*

t. In the third sentence of paragraph 38, *and the conditions in paragraphs 40(a) and 40(b)* is added between *paragraphs 20 and 21* and *are met.*

u. In paragraph 42, *provided the conditions in paragraphs 40(a) and 40(b) are met* is added to the end of the first sentence.

Amendments to Implement Guidance in Implementation Issue No. H2, "Requirement That the Unit with the Exposure Must Be a Party to the Hedge"

v. Paragraph 40 is amended as follows:

(1) Subparagraph (a) is replaced by the following:

> For consolidated financial statements, either (1) the operating unit that has the foreign currency exposure is a party to the hedging instrument or (2) another member of the consolidated group that has the same functional currency as that operating unit (subject to the restrictions in this subparagraph and related footnote) is a party to the hedging instrument. To qualify for applying the guidance in (2) above, there may be no intervening subsidiary with a different functional currency.* (Refer to paragraphs 36, 40A, and 40B for conditions for which an intercompany foreign currency derivative can be the hedging instrument in a cash flow hedge of foreign exchange risk.)

> *For example, if a dollar-functional, second-tier subsidiary has a Euro exposure, the dollar-functional consolidated parent company could designate its U.S. dollar–Euro derivative as a hedge of the second-tier subsidiary's exposure provided that the functional currency of the intervening first-tier subsidiary (that is, the parent of the second-tier subsidiary) is also the U.S. dollar. In contrast, if the functional currency of the intervening first-tier subsidiary was the Japanese yen (thus requiring the financial statements of the second-tier subsidiary to be translated into yen before the yen-denominated financial statements of the first-tier subsidiary are translated into U.S. dollars for consolidation), the consolidated parent company could not designate its U.S. dollar–Euro derivative as a hedge of the second-tier subsidiary's exposure.

(2) In subparagraph (b), *that* is replaced by *the hedging.*

Amendments to the Transition Guidance, the Implementation Guidance in Appendix A of Statement 133, and the Examples in Appendix B of Statement 133

w. Paragraph 52(b) is replaced by the following:

> If the transition adjustment relates to a derivative instrument that had been designated in a hedging relationship that addressed the fair value exposure of an asset, a liability, or a firm commitment, the transition adjustment for the derivative shall be reported as a cumulative-effect-type adjustment of net income. Concurrently, any gain or loss on the hedged item shall be recognized as an adjustment of the hedged item's carrying amount at the date of initial application, but only to the extent of an offsetting transition adjustment

for the derivative. Only for purposes of applying the preceding sentence in determining the hedged item's transition adjustment, the gain or loss on the hedged item may be either (1) the overall gain or loss on the hedged item determined as the difference between the hedged item's fair value and its carrying amount on the date of initial application (that is, not limited to the portion attributable to the hedged risk nor limited to the gain or loss occurring during the period of the preexisting hedging relationship) or (2) the gain or loss on the hedged item attributable to the hedged risk (limited to the hedged risks that can be designated under paragraph 21 of this Statement) during the period of the preexisting hedging relationship. That adjustment of the hedged item's carrying amount shall also be reported as a cumulative-effect-type adjustment of net income. The transition adjustment related to the gain or loss reported in accumulated other comprehensive income on a derivative instrument that hedged an available-for-sale security, together with the loss or gain on the related security (to the extent of an offsetting transition adjustment for the derivative instrument), shall be reclassified to earnings as a cumulative-effect-type adjustment of both net income and accumulated other comprehensive income.

x. Paragraph 58 is amended as follows:

(1) In the first sentence of subparagraph (b), *requires* is replaced by *involves* and *that are readily convertible to cash*[17] *and only if there is no market mechanism to facilitate net settlement outside the contract* and footnote 17 are deleted.

(2) The following sentence is added at the end of subparagraph (b):

Also, in order for a contract that meets the net settlement provisions of paragraphs 9(a) and 57(c)(1) and the market mechanism provisions of paragraphs 9(b) and 57(c)(2) to qualify for the exception, it must be probable at inception and throughout the term of the individual contract that the contract will not settle net and will result in physical delivery.

(3) The following two sentences are added at the end of subparagraph (c)(2):

This exception applies only to nonfinancial assets that are unique and only if a nonfinancial asset related to the underlying is owned by the party that would *not* benefit *under the contract* from an increase in the price or value of the nonfinancial asset. If the contract is a call option contract, the exception applies only if that nonfinancial asset is owned by the party that would not benefit under the contract from an increase in the price or value of the nonfinancial asset above the option's strike price.

y. Paragraph 61 is amended as follows:

(1) The last two sentences of subparagraph (d) are deleted.

(2) In the second sentence of subparagraph (e), *the equity instrument* is replaced by *a publicly traded equity instrument.*

z. Paragraph 68 is amended as follows:

(1) In the second sentence, *an interest-bearing asset or liability* is replaced by *a recognized interest-bearing asset or liability.*

(2) In subparagraph (b), *its inception* is replaced by *the inception of the hedging relationship.*

(3) In subparagraph (d), the following is added at the end of the sentence:

(that is, able to be settled by either party prior to its scheduled maturity), except as indicated in the following sentences. This criterion does not apply to an interest-bearing asset or liability that is prepayable solely due to an embedded call option provided that the hedging interest rate swap contains an embedded mirror-image call option. The call option embedded in the swap is considered a mirror image of the call option embedded in the hedged item if (1) the terms of the two call options match (including matching maturities, strike price, related notional amounts, timing and frequency of payments, and dates on which the instruments may be called) and (2) the entity is the writer of one call option and the holder (or purchaser) of the other call option. Similarly, this criterion does not apply to an interest-bearing asset or liability that is prepayable solely due to an embedded put option provided that the hedging interest rate swap contains an embedded mirror-image put option.

(4) The following subparagraph and footnote are added after subparagraph (d):

> dd. The index on which the variable leg of the swap is based matches the benchmark interest rate designated as the interest rate risk being hedged for that hedging relationship.*

---

*For cash flow hedge situations in which the cash flows of the hedged item and the hedging instrument are based on the same index but that index is not the benchmark interest rate, the shortcut method is not permitted. However, the entity may obtain results similar to results obtained if the shortcut method was permitted.

(5) Subparagraph (l) is deleted.

aa. In the third sentence of footnote 19 to paragraph 74, *market* is deleted.

bb. Paragraph 115 is amended as follows:

(1) In the third sentence, *market interest rates* is replaced by *the designated benchmark interest rate.*

(2) The following sentence is added after the third sentence:

> ABC designates changes in LIBOR swap rates as the benchmark interest rate in hedging interest rate risk.

cc. The following example is added after paragraph 120 and before Example 3:

Example 2A: Fair Value Hedge of the LIBOR Swap Rate in a $100,000 BBB-Quality 5-Year Fixed-Rate Noncallable Note

120A. This example illustrates one method that could be used in determining the hedged item's change in fair value attributable to changes in the benchmark interest rate. Other methods could be used in determining the hedged item's change in fair value attributable to changes in the benchmark interest rate as long as those methods meet the criteria in paragraph 21(f).

120B. On January 1, 20X0, GHI Company issues at par a $100,000 BBB-quality 5-year fixed-rate noncallable debt instrument with an annual 10 percent interest coupon. On that date, the issuer enters into a 5-year interest rate swap based on the LIBOR swap rate and designates it as the hedging instrument in a fair value hedge of the $100,000 liability. Under the terms of the swap, GHI will receive fixed interest at 7 percent and pay variable interest at LIBOR. The variable leg of the swap resets each year on December 31 for the payments due the following year. This example has been simplified by assuming that the interest rate applicable to a payment due at any future date is the same as the rate for a payment at any other date (that is, the yield curve is flat). During the hedge period, the gain or loss on the swap will be recorded in earnings. The example assumes that immediately before the interest rate on the variable leg resets on December 31, 20X0, the LIBOR swap rate increased by 50 basis points to 7.50 percent, and the change in fair value of the swap for the period from January 1 to December 31, 20X0 is a loss in value of $1,675.

Changes in the fair value of the hedged item attributable to the changes in the benchmark interest rate for a specific period

120C. Under this method, the change in a hedged item's fair value attributable to changes in the benchmark interest rate for a specific period is determined as the difference between two present value calculations as of the end of the period that exclude or include, respectively, the effect of the changes in the benchmark interest rate during the period. The discount rates used for those present value calculations would be, respectively, (a) the discount rate equal to the market interest rate for that hedged item at the inception of the hedge adjusted (up or down) for changes in the benchmark rate (designated as the interest rate risk being hedged) from the inception of the hedge to the beginning date of the period for which the change in fair value is being calculated* and (b) the discount rate equal to the market interest rate for that hedged item at the inception of the hedge adjusted (up or down) for changes in the designated benchmark rate from the inception of the hedge to the ending date of the period for which the change in fair value is being calculated. Both present value calculations are computed using the estimated future cash flows for the hedged item (which typically would be its remaining contractual cash flows).

120D. In GHI's quarterly assessments of hedge effectiveness for each of the first three quarters of year 20X0 in this example, there was zero change in the hedged item's fair value attributable to changes in the benchmark inter-

est rate because there was no change in the LIBOR swap rate. However, in the assessment for the fourth quarter 20X0, the discount rate for the beginning of the period is 10 percent (the hedged item's original market interest rate with an adjustment of zero), and the discount rate for the end of the period is 10.50 percent (the hedged item's original market interest rate adjusted for the change during the period in the LIBOR swap rate [+0.50 percent]).

December 31, 20X0

Calculate the present value using the beginning-of-period discount rate of 10 percent:

$10,000pmt, 10%i, 4n, PV =	$ 31,699	(interest payments)
$100,000fv, 10%i, 4n, PV =	68,301	(principal payment)
Total present value	$100,000	

Calculate the present value using the end-of-period discount rate of 10.50 percent (that is, the beginning-of-period discount rate adjusted for the change during the period in the LIBOR swap rate of 50 basis points):

$10,000pmt, 10.50%i, 4n, PV =	$31,359	(interest payments)
$100,000fv, 10.50%i, 4n, PV =	67,073	(principal payment)
Total present value	$98,432	

The change in fair value of the hedged item attributable to the change in the benchmark interest rate is $100,000 – $98,432 = $1,568 (the fair value decrease in the liability is a gain on debt).

When the change in fair value of the hedged item ($1,568 gain) attributable to the risk being hedged is compared with the change in fair value of the hedging instrument ($1,675 loss), ineffectiveness of $107 results. That ineffectiveness will be reported in earnings, because both changes in fair value are recorded in earnings.

---

*This Statement does not provide specific guidance on the discount rate that must be used in the calculation. However, the method chosen by GHI and described in this illustration requires that the discount rate be based on the market interest rate for the hedged item at the inception of the hedging relationship.

---

dd. Paragraph 134 is amended as follows:

  (1) In the second sentence, *market interest rates* is replaced by *the designated benchmark interest rate.*

  (2) The following sentence is added after the second sentence:

    XYZ designates changes in LIBOR swap rates as the benchmark interest rate in hedging interest rate risk.

ee. Paragraph 155 is replaced by the following:

  Because Swap 1 and the hedged forecasted interest payments are based on the same notional amount, have the same reset dates, and are based on the same benchmark interest rate designated under paragraph 29(h), MNO may conclude that there will be no ineffectiveness in the hedging relationship (absent a default by the swap counterparty).

ff. The last sentence of paragraph 161 is deleted.

gg. Paragraph 169 is amended as follows:

(1) In the third sentence, *is not eligible for cash flow hedge accounting* is replaced by *would separately be eligible to be designated as a fair value hedge of foreign exchange risk or continue to be eligible as a cash flow hedge of foreign exchange risk.*

(2) The fourth sentence and the fifth (parenthetical) sentence are deleted.

(3) The sixth sentence is replaced by the following:

Consequently, if the variability of the functional currency cash flows related to the royalty receivable is not being hedged, DEF will dedesignate a proportion of the hedging instrument in the original hedge relationship with respect to the proportion of the forward contract corresponding to the earned royalty.

(4) In the last sentence, *will substantially offset* is replaced by *may substantially offset.*

hh. Paragraph 197 is replaced by the following:

Example 31: Certain Purchases in a Foreign Currency. A U.S. company enters into a contract to purchase corn from a local American supplier in six months for a fixed amount of Japanese yen; the yen is the functional currency of neither party to the transaction. The corn is expected to be delivered and used over a reasonable period in the normal course of business.

Scope Application: Paragraph 10(b) excludes contracts that require future delivery of commodities that are readily convertible to cash from the accounting for derivatives if the commodities will be delivered in quantities expected to be used or sold by the reporting entity over a reasonable period in the normal course of business. However, that paragraph also states that contracts that are denominated in a foreign currency that meets neither of the criteria in paragraphs 15(a) and 15(b) shall not be considered normal purchases and normal sales. Because the Japanese yen is not the functional currency of either party to the con-

tract and the purchase of corn is transacted internationally in many different currencies, the contract does not qualify for the normal purchases and normal sales exception. The contract is a compound derivative comprising a U.S. dollar-denominated forward contract for the purchase of corn and an embedded foreign currency swap from the purchaser's functional currency (the U.S. dollar) to yen. Consistent with the last sentence of footnote 13 to paragraph 49, the compound derivative cannot be separated into its components (representing the foreign currency derivative and the forward commodity contract) and accounted for separately under this Statement.

ii. Paragraph 200 is amended as follows:

(1) The second bullet is amended as follows:

(a) In the first sentence, *owned by the policyholder and separate* is replaced by *distinct.*

(b) The second sentence is deleted.

(c) In the third sentence, *considered* is inserted between *not* and *a derivative,* and *the policyholder has invested the premiums in acquiring those investments* is replaced by *of the unique attributes of traditional variable annuity contracts issued by insurance companies.*

(d) In the penultimate sentence, *traditional* is inserted between *rather than a* and *variable annuity* in the parenthetical phrase, and *not be viewed as a direct investment because the policyholder does not own those investments, which are assets recorded in the general account of the insurance company* is replaced by *contain an embedded derivative (the equity index-based derivative) that meets all the requirements of paragraph 12 of this Statement for separate accounting: (a) the economic characteristics and risks of the embedded derivative would not be clearly and closely related to the economic characteristics and risks of the host contract (that is, the host contract is a debt instrument and the embedded option is equity-indexed), (b) the hybrid instrument would not be remeasured at fair value with changes in fair value reported in earnings as they occur under GAAP, and (c) a separate instrument with the same terms as the embedded derivative instrument would be a derivative instrument pursuant to paragraphs 6–11 of this Statement.*

(e) The last sentence is deleted.

(2) In the third bullet, *an investment owned by the insured* is replaced by *a traditional variable annuity contract issued by an insurance company.*

(3) The following sentences are added to the end of the paragraph after the last bullet:

> The guidance in the second and third bullets above is an exception for traditional variable annuity contracts issued by insurance companies. In determining the accounting for other seemingly similar structures, it would be inappropriate to analogize to the above guidance due to the unique attributes of traditional variable annuity contracts.

Amendments to the Glossary of Statement 133

jj. The following terms and definitions are added to paragraph 540:

Benchmark interest rate
A widely recognized and quoted rate in an active financial market that is broadly indicative of the overall level of interest rates attributable to high-credit-quality obligors in that market. It is a rate that is widely used in a given financial market as an underlying basis for determining the interest rates of individual financial instruments and commonly referenced in interest-rate-related transactions.

In theory, the benchmark interest rate should be a risk-free rate (that is, has no risk of default). In some markets, government borrowing rates may serve as a benchmark. In other markets, the benchmark interest rate may be an interbank offered rate. In the United States, currently only the interest rates on direct Treasury obligations of the U.S. government and, for practical reasons, the LIBOR swap rate are considered to be benchmark interest rates. In each financial market, only the one or two most widely used and quoted rates that meet the above criteria may be considered benchmark interest rates.

LIBOR swap rate
The fixed rate on a single-currency, constant-notional interest rate swap that has its floating-rate leg referenced to the London Interbank Offered Rate (LIBOR) with no additional spread over LIBOR on that floating-rate leg. That fixed rate is the derived rate that would result in the swap having a zero fair value at inception because the present value of fixed cash flows, based on that rate, equate to the present value of the floating cash flows.

Effective Date and Transition

5. For an entity that has not adopted Statement 133 before June 15, 2000, this Statement shall be adopted concurrently with Statement 133 according to the provisions of paragraph 48 of Statement 133.

6. For an entity that has adopted Statement 133 prior to June 15, 2000, this Statement shall be effective for all fiscal quarters beginning after June 15, 2000, in accordance with the following transition provisions.

a. At the date of initial application, an entity may elect to derecognize in the balance sheet any derivative instrument that would qualify under this Statement as a normal purchases or normal sales contract and record a cumulative effect of a change in accounting principle as described in paragraph 20 of APB Opinion No. 20, *Accounting Changes.* The election to derecognize may not be applied to only some of an entity's normal purchases and normal sales contracts and must be applied on an all-or-none basis. That election to derecognize a derivative instrument may be applied retroactively to the beginning of any fiscal quarter for which interim financial information or financial statements have not been issued.

b. At the date of initial application, an entity must dedesignate the market interest rate as the hedged risk in a hedge of interest rate risk. An entity is permitted to designate anew the benchmark interest rate as the hedged risk in a hedge of interest rate risk.

c. At the date of initial application, an entity may designate a recognized foreign-currency-denominated asset or liability as the hedged item in a hedge of foreign exchange risk pursuant to paragraphs 21 and 29 of Statement 133, as amended by this Statement. An entity may also designate intercompany derivatives that meet the requirements in paragraph 4(l) of this Statement (paragraphs 40A and 40B of Statement 133) as hedging instruments in cash flow hedges of foreign exchange risk when those intercompany derivatives have been offset on only a net basis with third-party derivatives. Any designations permitted by this subparagraph shall be made on a prospective basis.

> **The provisions of this Statement need not be applied to immaterial items.**

This Statement was adopted by the affirmative votes of five members of the Financial Accounting Standards Board. Messrs. Foster and Leisenring dissented.

Messrs. Foster and Leisenring dissent from the issuance of this Statement because they believe this Statement does not represent an improvement in financial reporting. The Board concluded in Statement 133, because of anomalies created by a mixed-attribute accounting model, that hedge accounting was appropriate in certain limited circumstances. At the same time, however, it concluded that hedge accounting was appropriate only to the extent that the hedging instrument was effective in offsetting changes in the fair value of the hedged item or the variability of cash flows of the hedged transaction and that any ineffectiveness in achieving that offset should be reflected in earnings. While Statement 133 gave wide latitude to management in determining the method for measuring effectiveness, it is clear that the hedged risk is limited to (a) the risk of changes in the entire hedged item, (b) the risk attributable to changes in market interest rates, (c) the risk attributable to changes in foreign currency exchange rates, and (d) the risk attributable to changes in the obligor's creditworthiness. Those limitations were designed to limit an entity's ability to define the risk being hedged in such a manner as to eliminate or minimize ineffectiveness for accounting purposes. The effect of the provisions in this amendment relating to (1) the interest rate that is permitted to be designated as the hedged risk and (2) permitting the foreign currency risk of foreign-currency-denominated assets and liabilities to be designated as hedges will be to substantially reduce or, in some circumstances, eliminate the amount of hedge ineffectiveness that would otherwise be reflected in earnings. For example, permitting an entity to designate the risk of changes in the LIBOR swap rate curve as the risk being hedged in a fair value hedge when the interest rate of the instrument being hedged is not based on the LIBOR swap rate curve ignores certain effects of basis risk, which, prior to this amendment, would have been appropriately required to be recognized in earnings. Messrs. Foster and Leisenring believe that retreat from Statement 133 is a modification to the basic model of Statement 133, which requires that ineffectiveness of hedging relationships be measured and reported in earnings.

In Statement 133, the Board stated its vision for all financial instruments ultimately to be measured at fair value. If all financial instruments were measured at fair value with changes in fair value recorded currently in earnings, the need for hedge accounting for the risks inherent in existing financial instruments would be eliminated because both the hedging instrument and the hedged item would be measured at fair value. Recognizing and measuring the changes in fair value of all financial instruments using the same criteria and measurement attributes would leave no anomalies related to financial instruments. Consequently, the Board has tentatively concluded in its project on measuring all financial instruments at fair value that all changes in fair value be reflected in earnings. Statement 133 is a step toward achieving the Board's vision because it requires recognizing currently in earnings the amounts for which a hedging instrument is ineffective in offsetting the changes in the fair value of the hedged item or the variability of cash flows of the hedged transaction. Messrs. Foster and Leisenring believe the amendments to Statement 133 referred to in the paragraph above represent steps backward from achieving the Board's vision of reporting all financial instruments at fair value because the result of those amendments is to report the effects of hedging instruments that are not fully effective in offsetting the changes in fair value attributable to the risk being hedged as if they were.

Messrs. Foster and Leisenring believe that even if one accepts the exception that a benchmark interest rate that clearly is not a risk-free rate can be considered to be a risk-free rate, the extension of that exception to permit the benchmark interest rate to be the hedged risk in a financial instrument for which the interest rate is less than the benchmark rate is inappropriate. There can be no risk to an entity for that portion of the credit spread of the benchmark interest rate that is in excess of the credit spread of the hedged item. Yet that exception requires the change in that portion of the credit spread to be recognized in the basis adjustment of the hedged item, so that the ineffectiveness attributable to the portion of the derivative that hedges a nonexistent risk is not recognized. For example, if there is a change during a period in the value of the portion of the credit spread of the LIBOR swap rate (designated hedged risk) that is

in excess of the credit spread of the hedged item, under no circumstances could that change affect the fair value of the hedged item. This Statement, however, mandates that in those circumstances an artificial change in fair value be recognized in the basis of the hedged item.

In this regard, Messrs. Foster and Leisenring observe that permitting the benchmark interest rate to be the hedged risk in a financial instrument that has an interest rate that is less than the benchmark rate creates an anomaly related to the shortcut method. In hedges in which a portion of the derivative is designated as hedging a nonexistent risk (the excess of the benchmark interest rate over the actual interest rate of the hedged item), no ineffectiveness will be recognized when using the shortcut method even though the hedging relationship is clearly not effective. But in certain hedges where there is likely to be little ineffectiveness because the interest rate indexes of the hedged item and the hedging instrument are the same, the shortcut method, in which no ineffectiveness is assumed, is not available.

Members of the Financial Accounting Standards Board:

Edmund L. Jenkins, Chairman
Anthony T. Cope

John M. Foster
Gaylen N. Larson
James J. Leisenring

Gerhard G. Mueller
Edward W. Trott

Appendix A

BACKGROUND INFORMATION AND BASIS FOR CONCLUSIONS

CONTENTS

Appendix A

BACKGROUND INFORMATION AND BASIS FOR CONCLUSIONS

Introduction

7. This appendix summarizes considerations that Board members deemed significant in reaching the conclusions in this Statement. It includes reasons for accepting certain views and rejecting others. Individual Board members gave greater weight to some factors than to others.

Background Information

8. The Board received numerous requests to amend Statement 133. The requests focused mainly on guidance related to specific issues that, if amended, would ease implementation difficulties for a large number of entities. In reviewing those requests, the Board did not discover any new significant information suggesting that the framework of Statement 133 was inappropriate or that major changes should be made. However, after meeting with members of the Derivatives Implementation Group (DIG) in an open meeting, the Board decided to analyze six specific issues, and it developed the following criteria to help in determining which issues, if any, to consider for a possible amendment of Statement 133:

a. Implementation difficulties would be eased for a large number of entities.
b. There would be no conflict with or modifications to the basic model of Statement 133.
c. There would be no delay in the effective date of Statement 133.

9. Of the six issues, the Board determined that it would be appropriate to amend Statement 133 for four of those issues (identified as the normal purchases and normal sales exception, hedging the benchmark interest rate, hedging recognized foreign-currency-denominated debt instruments, and hedging with intercompany derivatives). The Board determined that amending Statement 133 for the remaining two issues (identified as partial-term hedging and purchased option hedges) would conflict with the basic model of Statement 133. The Board also concluded that additional amendments to Statement 133 were warranted to clarify certain provisions of the Statement related to implementation guidance arising

from the DIG process and cleared by the Board and posted on its web site.

10. In March 2000, the Board issued an Exposure Draft, *Accounting for Certain Derivative Instruments and Certain Hedging Activities,* for a 31-day comment period. Eighty-two organizations and individuals responded to the Exposure Draft. The Board considered the comments received during its redeliberations of the issues addressed by the Exposure Draft in three public meetings during April and May 2000. The Board concluded that it could reach informed decisions on the basis of existing information without a public hearing.

Amendments to Statement 133

Normal Purchases and Normal Sales Exception

11. This Statement amends Statement 133 to permit the normal purchases and normal sales exception in paragraph 10(b) of Statement 133 to be applied to certain contracts that meet the net settlement provisions discussed in paragraphs 9(a) and 57(c)(1) and the market mechanism provisions discussed in paragraphs 9(b) and 57(c)(2). The Board received comments that certain contracts, such as purchase orders for which physical delivery was intended and expected in the normal course of business, met the definition of a derivative because of the net settlement provisions in paragraphs 9(a) and 57(c)(1) and the market mechanism provisions in paragraphs 9(b) and 57(c)(2). The Board decided that contracts that require delivery of nonfinancial assets need not be accounted for as derivative instruments under this Statement if the assets constitute normal purchases or normal sales of the reporting entity and the criteria identified in paragraph 4(a) of this Statement were met.

12. The Board believes that the normal purchases and normal sales exception should not be permitted to be applied to contracts that require cash settlements of gains or losses or otherwise settle gains or losses on a periodic basis because those settlements are net settlements. The Board observed that an entity may designate those contracts as a hedged item in an all-in-one hedge, pursuant to Statement 133 Implementation Issue No. G2, "Hedged Transactions That Arise from Gross Settlement of a Derivative ('All in One' Hedges)."

13. Some respondents to the Exposure Draft suggested that a planned series of contracts used in the

normal course of business consistent with recognized industry practice should qualify for the normal purchases and normal sales exception. Some respondents in the electric utility industry suggested that the unplanned netting of transactions with the same counterparty (referred to as a "bookout") should also qualify for the normal purchases and normal sales exception. They also noted that because of changes in circumstances, the bookout procedure is common in the electric utility industry as a scheduling convenience when two utilities happen to have offsetting transactions. The Board rejected both notions because those transactions result in a net settlement of the contract. The normal purchases and normal sales exception only relates to a contract that results in gross delivery of the commodity under that contract.

Hedging the Benchmark Interest Rate

14. This Statement amends Statement 133 to permit a *benchmark interest rate* to be designated as the hedged risk in a hedge of interest rate risk. Statement 133 Implementation Issue No. E1, "Hedging the Risk-Free Interest Rate," provided implementation guidance for Statement 133 that indicated that the hedged risk in a hedge of interest rate risk would be the hedged item's *market interest rate,* defined as the risk-free rate plus the credit sector spread appropriate for that hedged item at the inception of the hedge. Comments received by the Board on Implementation Issue E1 indicated (a) that the concept of market interest rate risk as set forth in Statement 133 differed from the common understanding of interest rate risk by market participants, (b) that the guidance in the Implementation Issue was inconsistent with present hedging activities, and (c) that measuring the change in fair value of the hedged item attributable to changes in credit sector spreads would be difficult because consistent sector spread data are not readily available in the market.

15. The Board decided that, with respect to the separation of interest rate risk and credit risk, the risk of changes in credit sector spread and any credit spread attributable to a specific borrower should be encompassed in credit risk rather than interest rate risk. Under that approach, an entity would be permitted to designate the risk of changes in the risk-free rate as the hedged risk, and any spread above that rate would be deemed to reflect credit risk. The Board concluded that considering all the effects of credit risk together was more understandable and more operational than the distinction between interest rate risk and credit risk in Implementation Issue E1.

16. The Board decided that, in the United States, the interest rate on direct Treasury obligations of the U.S. government provides the best measure of the risk-free rate. Thus, the Board considered defining interest rate risk based only on Treasury rates in the United States. However, the Board decided to make an exception and extend the definition of interest rate risk to include interest rate swap rates based on the London Interbank Offered Rate (LIBOR). The Board had been informed that

a. LIBOR-based interest rate swaps are the most commonly used hedging instruments in the U.S. financial markets in hedges of interest rate risk.
b. There are technical factors (such as supply and demand) that may affect the rates on direct obligations of any single issuer, even the U.S. government.
c. Financial markets consider LIBOR rates as inherently liquid, stable, and a reliable indicator of interest rates and, if the rate for hedging interest rate risk was limited to U.S. Treasury rates, many common hedging relationships using LIBOR-based swaps might not qualify for hedge accounting.

Because the Board decided to permit a rate that is not fully risk-free to be the designated risk in a hedge of interest rate risk, it developed the general notion of *benchmark interest rate* to encompass both risk-free rates and rates based on the LIBOR swap curve in the United States.

17. In deliberations leading up to the Exposure Draft and in response to comments on the Exposure Draft, the Board considered whether other rates, such as the commercial paper rate and the Fed Funds rate, in the U.S. financial markets should be included in the definition of benchmark interest rate and whether those rates should be permitted to be designated as the hedged risk in a hedge of interest rate risk. The Board also considered the notion of defining the benchmark interest rate as the portion of an instrument's overall rate that is used as the underlying basis for pricing a financial instrument. (For example, numerous indexes such as the Fed Funds rate, the Prime rate, the FNMA Par Mortgage rate, and the BMA index are used as the underlying basis for pricing a financial instrument.) The Board rejected both notions and decided that allowing more than two benchmark rates to define interest rate risk was unnecessary and would make the resulting financial statements more

difficult to understand. Therefore, other such indexes may not be used as the benchmark interest rate in the United States.

18. The Board considered the operationality of the definition of the benchmark interest rate in global financial markets. The Board acknowledged that, in some foreign markets, the rate of interest on sovereign debt is considered the benchmark interest rate; that is, market participants consider that rate free of credit risk. However, in other markets, the relevant interbank offered rate may be the best reflection of the benchmark interest rate.

19. The Board determined that any definition of the benchmark interest rate that may be hedged should be flexible enough to withstand potential future developments in financial markets. For example, the Board decided that the current definition would result in the ability to replace the LIBOR swap rate with a more relevant benchmark interest rate should changes in the financial markets render the use of LIBOR swap rates obsolete.

20. Respondents to the Exposure Draft indicated that the Board should revise the proposed amendments to paragraphs 21(f) and 29(h) that stated that the benchmark interest rate being hedged in a hedge of interest rate risk should not reflect greater credit risk than is inherent in the hedged item. They said that many financial instruments are priced based on a positive or negative credit spread to the benchmark rate and that interest rate risk is managed based on the benchmark rate, regardless of whether the rate inherent in the instrument is above or below the benchmark rate. The Board rejected the notion of the existence of negative credit risk, but on an exception basis it decided to remove the prohibition that the benchmark interest rate being hedged in a hedge of interest rate risk should not reflect greater credit risk than is inherent in the hedged item. Thus, the benchmark interest rate can be the designated hedged risk in a hedge of interest rate risk regardless of the credit risk inherent in the hedged item (for example, the LIBOR swap rate could be the designated hedged risk in an AAA-rated security even if the overall market interest rate of the instrument is less than the LIBOR swap rate).

21. This Statement requires that in a cash flow hedge of a variable-rate financial asset or liability, either existing or forecasted, the designated risk being hedged cannot be the risk of changes in its cash flows attributable to changes in the benchmark interest rate if the cash flows of the hedged transaction are explicitly based on a different index. The effectiveness of a cash flow hedge of the variability in interest payments of a variable-rate financial asset or liability, either existing or forecasted, is affected by the interest rate index on which the variability is based and the extent to which the hedging instrument provides offset. Changes in credit sector spreads embodied within the interest rate index on which the variability is based do not affect the assessment and measurement of hedge effectiveness if both the cash flows on the hedging instrument and the hedged cash flows of the existing financial asset or liability or the variable-rate financial asset or liability that is forecasted to be acquired or issued are based on the same index. However, if the cash flows on the hedging instrument and the hedged cash flows of the existing financial asset or liability or the variable-rate financial asset or liability that is forecasted to be acquired or issued are based on different indexes, the basis difference between those indexes would affect the assessment and measurement of hedge effectiveness.

Shortcut method

22. Because the shortcut method applies to hedges of interest rate risk with the use of an interest rate swap, the decision to redefine interest rate risk necessitated that the Board address the effect on the shortcut method for fair value hedges and cash flow hedges. For fair value hedges, an assumption of no ineffectiveness, an important premise of the shortcut method, is invalidated when the interest rate index embodied in the variable leg of the interest rate swap is different from the benchmark interest rate being hedged. In situations in which the interest rate index embodied in the variable leg of the swap has greater credit risk than that embodied in the benchmark interest rate, the effect of the change in the swap's credit sector spread over that in the benchmark interest rate would represent hedge ineffectiveness because it relates to an *unhedged* risk (credit risk) rather than to the hedged risk (interest rate risk). In situations in which the interest rate index embodied in the variable leg of the swap has less credit risk than that embodied in the benchmark interest rate, the effect of the change in a certain portion of the hedged item's spread over the swap interest rate would also represent hedge ineffectiveness. The Board decided that in order for an entity to comply with an assumption of no ineffectiveness, the index on which the variable leg of the swap is based should match the benchmark interest rate designated as the interest rate risk being hedged for the hedging relationship.

23. For cash flow hedges of an existing variable-rate financial asset or liability, the designated risk being hedged cannot be the risk of changes in its cash flows attributable to changes in the benchmark interest rate if the cash flows of the hedged item are explicitly based on a different index. In those situations, because the risk of changes in the benchmark interest rate (that is, interest rate risk) cannot be the designated risk being hedged, the shortcut method cannot be applied. The Board's decision to require that the index on which the variable leg of the swap is based match the benchmark interest rate designated as the interest rate risk being hedged for the hedging relationship also ensures that the shortcut method is applied only to interest rate risk hedges. The Board's decision precludes use of the shortcut method in situations in which the cash flows of the hedged item and the hedging instrument are based on the same index but that index is not the designated benchmark interest rate. The Board noted, however, that in some of those situations, an entity easily could determine that the hedge is perfectly effective. The shortcut method would be permitted for cash flow hedges in situations in which the cash flows of the hedged item and the hedging instrument are based on the same index and that index is the designated benchmark interest rate.

Determining the change in a hedged item's fair value attributable to changes in the benchmark interest rate

24. This Statement provides limited guidance on how the change in a hedged item's fair value attributable to changes in the designated benchmark interest rate should be determined. The Board decided that in calculating the change in the hedged item's fair value attributable to changes in the designated benchmark interest rate, the estimated cash flows used must be based on all of the contractual cash flows of the entire hedged item. That guidance does not mandate the use of any one method, but it precludes the use of a method that excludes some of the hedged item's contractual cash flows (such as the portion of interest payments attributable to the obligor's credit risk above the benchmark rate) from the calculation. The Board concluded that excluding some of the hedged item's contractual cash flows would introduce a new approach to bifurcation of a hedged item that does not currently exist in the Statement 133 hedging model.

Hedging Recognized Foreign-Currency-Denominated Assets or Liabilities

25. This Statement amends Statement 133 to allow a recognized foreign-currency-denominated asset or liability to be the hedged item in a fair value or cash flow hedge. Statement 133 precluded hedge accounting for an asset or liability that is remeasured for changes in price attributable to the risk being hedged when those changes are reported currently in earnings. Statement 133 also precluded fair value or cash flow hedge accounting for foreign currency risk associated with any asset or liability that is denominated in a foreign currency and remeasured into the functional currency under FASB Statement No. 52, *Foreign Currency Translation.* The Board received requests to remove the preclusion for any asset or liability denominated in a foreign currency because, even though the transaction gain or loss on the undesignated asset or liability and the change in fair value of the undesignated derivative were reported currently in earnings, different measurement criteria were used for each instrument, which created volatility in earnings.

26. The Exposure Draft proposed an exception to the general principle to permit both fair value hedges and cash flow hedges of foreign-currency-denominated debt instruments. The exception was applicable to foreign-currency-denominated debt instruments that were either held (assets) or owed (liabilities) and included instruments such as bonds, loans, receivables, and payables. The Board initially decided to limit the hedged items to debt instruments because of uncertainty related to the types of instruments that could possibly be included in the scope if all recognized foreign-currency-denominated assets or liabilities were permitted to be hedged. Respondents to the Exposure Draft requested that the Board expand the scope of the allowable hedged items beyond debt instruments. They noted that the concerns expressed by the Board could be mitigated if the determination of the eligibility of a hedged item was based on whether the item gives rise to a transaction gain or loss under paragraph 15 of Statement 52. The Board concluded that basing the eligibility of the hedged item on the guidance in paragraph 15 of Statement 52 would mitigate the scope concerns. Therefore, the Board decided to permit all recognized foreign-currency-denominated assets and liabilities for which a foreign currency transaction gain or loss is recognized in earnings to be hedged items.

27. Designated hedging instruments and hedged items qualify for fair value hedge accounting and cash flow hedge accounting under this Statement only if all of the criteria in Statement 133 for fair value hedge accounting and cash flow hedge accounting are met. The Board concluded that fair value hedges could be used for all recognized foreign-currency-denominated asset or liability hedging situations and that cash flow hedges could be used for recognized foreign-currency-denominated asset or liability hedging situations in which all of the variability in the functional-currency-equivalent cash flows are eliminated by the effect of the hedge. Remeasurement of the foreign-currency-denominated assets and liabilities will continue to be based on the guidance in Statement 52, which requires remeasurement based on spot exchange rates, regardless of whether a fair value hedging relationship or a cash flow hedging relationship exists.

28. The Board decided to permit cash flow hedge accounting for recognized foreign-currency-denominated assets and liabilities because it believes that the effects on earnings related to the use of different measurement criteria for the hedged transaction and the hedging instrument will be eliminated. The transaction gain or loss arising from the remeasurement of the foreign-currency-denominated asset or liability would be offset by a related amount reclassified each period from other comprehensive income to earnings. The Board believes that is consistent with the principal purpose of providing special hedge accounting to mitigate the effects on earnings of different existing measurement criteria.

29. The Board's decision to permit fair value hedge accounting for assets and liabilities denominated in a foreign currency relates to the ability of an entity to designate a compound derivative as a hedging instrument in a hedge of both interest rate risk and foreign exchange rate risk. An entity's ability to use a compound derivative would achieve the same result that would be achieved prior to this amendment with the use of an interest rate derivative as a qualifying hedging instrument to hedge interest rate risk and an undesignated foreign currency derivative to hedge exchange rate risk. Permitting use of a compound derivative in a fair value hedge of interest rate risk and foreign exchange risk would result in the value of the foreign currency asset or liability being adjusted for changes in fair value attributable to changes in foreign interest rates before remeasurement at the spot exchange rate. The ability to adjust the foreign currency asset or liability for changes in

foreign interest rates effectively eliminates any difference recognized currently in earnings related to the use of different measurement criteria for the hedged item and the hedging instrument. The Board concluded that in the situations in which fair value hedges would be used, remeasurement of the foreign-currency-denominated asset or liability based on the spot exchange rate would result in the same functional currency value that would result if the instrument was remeasured based on the forward exchange rate.

Hedging with Intercompany Derivatives

30. Paragraph 36 of Statement 133 permits a derivative instrument entered into with another member of the consolidated group to qualify as a foreign currency hedging instrument in the consolidated financial statements only if the member of the consolidated group has entered into an individual offsetting derivative contract with an unrelated third party. Constituents requested that Statement 133 be amended to permit derivative instruments entered into with a member of the consolidated group to qualify as hedging instruments in the consolidated financial statements if those internal derivatives are offset by unrelated third-party contracts on a net basis.

31. Constituents requested that those amendments continue to reflect the practice employed by many organizations of managing risk on a centralized basis. That practice involves transferring risk exposures assumed by various affiliates to a treasury center through internal derivative contracts, which are designated as hedging instruments by the affiliates. The risk exposures assumed by the treasury center by issuing internal derivative contracts to affiliates are offset on a net basis, rather than individually, by contracts with unrelated third parties. In the original deliberations leading to the issuance of Statement 133, the Board determined that the functional currency concepts of Statement 52 necessitated that the operating unit that has exposure to foreign exchange risk be a party to the hedging instrument. That foreign exchange risk exists because the currency in which a transaction is denominated is different from the operating unit's functional currency. The Board also recognized the prevalent use of treasury center operations to centrally manage foreign exchange risk. Because of those factors, the Board decided in its original deliberations of Statement 133 to permit the designation of a derivative issued by a

member of the consolidated group as a foreign currency hedging instrument in the consolidated financial statements, provided that the internal derivative was offset on a one-to-one basis with a third party. Constituents said that while paragraph 36 of Statement 133 permits both the designation of internal derivatives as hedges of foreign exchange risk and the use of a treasury center, the requirement to individually offset each internal derivative with a third-party contract negates the efficiency and cost savings provided by a treasury center.

32. In considering the requests for amendment, the Board observed that a fundamental justification for the application of hedge accounting to internal derivative contracts in consolidated financial statements under paragraph 36 of Statement 133 is the existence of an individual offsetting third-party derivative contract that supports each internal derivative. Further, the practice of offsetting multiple internal derivatives with a net third-party contract appears to portray the nonderivative hedged items in various affiliates functioning as hedges of one another. The Board also observed that applying hedge accounting to internal derivatives that are offset on a net basis by a third-party derivative contract could be viewed as macro hedging—using a single derivative to hedge a dissimilar portfolio of assets *and* liabilities—which is not permitted under Statement 133. However, the Board acknowledged that this practice differs from macro hedging because internal derivative contracts establish individual hedging relationships that can be linked to the net third-party contract.

33. In addition, the Board concluded that applying hedge accounting in the consolidated financial statements under Statement 133 to internal derivatives that are offset on a net basis by third-party contracts would conflict with basic consolidation procedures required by paragraph 6 of ARB No. 51, *Consolidated Financial Statements*. The Board determined that such a conflict exists because certain effects related to intercompany balances arising from the application of hedge accounting to internal derivative contracts would not be eliminated in consolidation. For example, for fair value hedges, the adjustment to the carrying amount of the hedged item, as determined by the change in fair value of the hedged item attributable to the hedged risk, results from applying hedge accounting to internal derivatives and would not be eliminated in consolidation. For cash flow hedges, amounts recorded in other comprehensive income, and the timing of reclassification of those amounts into earnings, similarly result from applying

hedge accounting to internal derivatives and would not be eliminated in consolidation. For those reasons, the Board determined that, as a general rule, derivatives entered into with a member of the consolidated group should not qualify as hedging instruments in the consolidated financial statements if those internal derivatives are not offset by unrelated third-party contracts on an individual basis.

34. Notwithstanding, the Board decided to permit a limited exception for internal derivatives designated as foreign currency cash flow hedges of forecasted borrowings, purchases, or sales denominated in foreign currency or unrecognized firm commitments, subject to meeting certain criteria. For foreign currency cash flow hedges of those items, the Board decided to permit internal derivatives designated as hedging instruments to be offset on a net basis, rather than individually, by third-party derivative contracts. The Board believes that exception for those foreign currency cash flow hedges is not sufficiently different from the accounting for certain foreign currency items provided for in existing accounting literature.

35. The Board decided that that exception should not be extended to internal derivatives designated either as foreign currency fair value hedges or foreign currency cash flow hedges of recognized foreign-currency-denominated assets or liabilities (as permitted by paragraphs 36(a) and 36(b) of Statement 133, as amended by this Statement). That is, in order to apply hedge accounting to internal derivatives designated as hedges of those hedged items in the consolidated financial statements, the internal derivatives must be offset by third-party contracts on an individual basis rather than on a net basis. In reaching that conclusion, the Board reasoned that permitting internal derivatives that hedge recognized foreign-currency-denominated assets or liabilities in foreign currency fair value or cash flow hedges to be offset on a net basis would result in the consolidated financial statements reflecting those nonderivative hedged items effectively functioning as hedging instruments in hedges of other foreign-currency-denominated assets or liabilities, forecasted borrowings, purchases, or sales or unrecognized firm commitments in various affiliates. The Board decided not to change the prohibition against using a nonderivative instrument as the hedging instrument in a foreign currency cash flow hedge.

36. The Board also decided not to permit internal derivative contracts to be designated as hedging instruments in the consolidated financial statements in fair

value or cash flow hedges of interest rate risk, credit risk, or the risk of changes in overall fair value or cash flows. The Board observed that the requirement that the operating unit that has exposure to risk be a party to the hedging instrument exists only for hedges of foreign exchange risk but not for hedges of risks other than foreign exchange risk. Further, even if internal derivative contracts were permitted to be designated as hedging instruments in the consolidated financial statements in a hedge of interest rate risk, credit risk, or the risk of changes in overall fair value or cash flows, permitting those internal derivatives to be offset on a net basis by a third-party derivative would create a new anomaly with respect to the application of consolidation procedures. However, in hedging interest rate risk, credit risk, or the risk of changes in overall fair value or cash flows, an entity may use internal derivatives as hedging instruments in separate company financial statements.

Amendments to the Transition Provisions and the Examples in Appendix B

37. This Statement amends the transition provisions in paragraph 52(b) of Statement 133 for determining the transition adjustment for the hedged item designated in a preexisting fair-value-type hedging relationship. The Board received comments that the requirements that the overall gain or loss on the hedged item determined based on the difference between the hedged item's fair value and its carrying amount on the date of initial application could result in recognizing the effect of unhedged risks in that transition adjustment. As a result, the Board decided to also allow the determination of the hedged item's transition adjustment to be based on the change in the hedged item's fair value attributable to the hedged risk (limited to the hedged risks that can be designated under paragraph 21 of Statement 133) during the period of the preexisting hedging relationship.

38. This Statement also deletes the last sentence of paragraph 161 because the hedging instrument in Example 8 does not meet the criterion in paragraph 68(b) to qualify for the shortcut method. The hedging instrument does not have fair value of zero at inception of the hedging relationship.

39. Paragraph 155 is also amended because Swap 1 in Example 8 does not qualify for the shortcut method. The swap is designated in a hedge of a series of forecasted interest payments, only one of which relates to a recognized interest-bearing liability; the remainder relate to a forecasted borrowing. The shortcut method is limited to either a fair value or cash flow hedging relationship of interest rate risk involving an existing recognized interest-bearing asset or liability and an interest rate swap. Thus, a cash flow hedge of the variability in interest on a probable forecasted lending or borrowing is not eligible for the shortcut method.

Appendix B

AMENDED PARAGRAPHS OF STATEMENT 133 MARKED TO SHOW CHANGES MADE BY THIS STATEMENT

40. This appendix contains paragraphs of Statement 133 marked to integrate changes from this amendment. The Board plans to issue an amended version of Statement 133 that includes the standards section, the implementation guidance (including examples), and the glossary.

> 10b. *Normal purchases and normal sales.* Normal purchases and normal sales are contracts that provide for the purchase or sale of something other than a financial instrument or derivative instrument that will be delivered in quantities expected to be used or sold by the reporting entity over a reasonable period in the normal course of business. However, contracts that have a price based on an underlying that is not clearly and closely related to the asset being sold or purchased (such as a price in a contract for the sale of a grain commodity based in part on changes in the S&P index) or that are denominated in a foreign currency that meets neither of the criteria in paragraphs 15(a) and 15(b) shall not be considered normal purchases and normal sales. Contracts that contain net settlement provisions as described in paragraphs 9(a) and 9(b) may qualify for the normal purchases and normal sales exception if it is probable at inception and throughout the term of the individual contract that the contract will not settle net and will result in physical delivery. Net settlement (as described in paragraphs 9(a) and 9(b)) of contracts in a group of contracts similarly designated as normal purchases and normal sales would call into question the classification of all such contracts as normal purchases or normal sales. Contracts that require cash settlements of gains or losses or are otherwise settled net on a periodic basis, including individual contracts that are part of a series of sequential contracts intended to accomplish ultimate acquisition or sale of a commodity, do not qualify for this exception. For contracts that qualify for the normal purchases and normal sales exception, the entity shall document the basis for concluding that it is probable that the contract will result in physical delivery. The documentation requirements can be applied either to groups of similarly designated contracts or to each individual contract.~~with no net settlement provision and no market mechanism to facilitate net settlement (as described in paragraphs 9(a) and 9(b)). They provide for the purchase or sale of something other than a financial instrument or derivative instrument that will be delivered in quantities expected to be used or sold by the reporting entity over a reasonable period in the normal course of business.~~

12. Contracts that do not in their entirety meet the definition of a derivative instrument (refer to paragraphs 6–9), such as bonds, insurance policies, and leases, may contain "embedded" derivative instruments—implicit or explicit terms that affect some or all of the cash flows or the value of other exchanges required by the contract in a manner similar to a derivative instrument. The effect of embedding a derivative instrument in another type of contract ("the host contract") is that some or all of the cash flows or other exchanges that otherwise would be required by the host contract, whether unconditional or contingent upon the occurrence of a specified event, will be modified based on one or more underlyings. An embedded derivative instrument shall be separated from the host contract and accounted for as a derivative instrument pursuant to this Statement if and only if all of the following criteria are met:

   a. The economic characteristics and risks of the embedded derivative instrument are not clearly and closely related to the economic characteristics and risks of the host contract. Additional guidance on applying this criterion to various contracts containing embedded derivative instruments is included in Appendix A of this Statement.
   b. The contract ("the hybrid instrument") that embodies both the embedded derivative instrument and the host contract is not remeasured at fair value under otherwise applicable generally accepted accounting principles with changes in fair value reported in earnings as they occur.
   c. A separate instrument with the same terms as the embedded derivative instrument would, pursuant to paragraphs 6–11, be a derivative instrument subject to the requirements of this Statement. (The

initial net investment for the hybrid instrument shall not be considered to be the initial net investment for the embedded derivative.)

Fair Value Hedges

The hedged item

21(c). The hedged item is not (1) an asset or liability that is remeasured with the changes in fair value attributable to the hedged risk reported currently in earnings ~~(for example, if foreign exchange risk is hedged, a foreign-currency-denominated asset for which a foreign currency transaction gain or loss is recognized in earnings)~~, (2) an investment accounted for by the equity method in accordance with the requirements of APB Opinion No. 18, *The Equity Method of Accounting for Investments in Common Stock,* (3) a minority interest in one or more consolidated subsidiaries, (4) an equity investment in a consolidated subsidiary, (5) a firm commitment either to enter into a business combination or to acquire or dispose of a subsidiary, a minority interest, or an equity method investee, or (6) an equity instrument issued by the entity and classified in stockholders' equity in the statement of financial position.

21(d). If the hedged item is all or a portion of a debt security (or a portfolio of similar debt securities) that is classified as held-to-maturity in accordance with FASB Statement No. 115, *Accounting for Certain Investments in Debt and Equity Securities,* the designated risk being hedged is the risk of changes in its fair value attributable to credit risk, foreign exchange risk, or both. If the hedged item is an option component of a held-to-maturity security that permits its prepayment, the designated risk being hedged is the risk of changes in the entire fair value of that option component. ~~the risk of changes in its fair value attributable to changes in the obligor's creditworthiness or if the hedged item is an option component of a held-to-maturity security that permits its prepayment, the designated risk being hedged is the risk of changes in the entire fair value of that option component.~~ (The designated hedged risk for a held-to-maturity security may not be the risk of changes in its fair value attributable to interest rate risk ~~changes in market interest rates or foreign exchange rates~~. If the hedged item is other than an option component that permits its prepayment, the designated hedged risk also may not be the risk of changes in its overall fair value.)

21(f). If the hedged item is a financial asset or liability, a recognized loan servicing right, or a nonfinancial firm commitment with financial components, the designated risk being hedged is
   (1) the risk of changes in the overall fair value of the entire hedged item,
   (2) the risk of changes in its fair value attributable to changes in the designated benchmark interest rate (referred to as interest rate risk) ~~market interest rates~~,
   (3) the risk of changes in its fair value attributable to changes in the related foreign currency exchange rates (referred to as foreign exchange risk) (refer to paragraphs 37, 37A, and 38) ~~(refer to paragraphs 37 and 38)~~, or
   (4) the risk of changes in its fair value attributable to both changes in the obligor's creditworthiness and changes in the spread over the benchmark interest rate with respect to the hedged item's credit sector at inception of the hedge (referred to as credit risk) ~~the obligor's creditworthiness~~.
If the risk designated as being hedged is not the risk in paragraph 21(f)(1) above, two or more of the other risks (~~market~~ interest rate risk, foreign currency exchange risk, and credit risk) may simultaneously be designated as being hedged. The benchmark interest rate being hedged in a hedge of interest rate risk must be specifically identified as part of the designation and documentation at the inception of the hedging relationship. Ordinarily, an entity should designate the same benchmark interest rate as the risk being hedged for similar hedges, consistent with paragraph 62; the use of different benchmark interest rates for similar hedges should be rare and must be justified. In calculating the change in the hedged item's fair value attributable to changes in the benchmark interest rate, the estimated cash flows used in calculating fair value

must be based on all of the contractual cash flows of the entire hedged item. Excluding some of the hedged item's contractual cash flows (for example, the portion of the interest coupon in excess of the benchmark interest rate) from the calculation is not permitted.* An entity may not simply designate prepayment risk as the risk being hedged for a financial asset. However, it can designate the option component of a prepayable instrument as the hedged item in a fair value hedge of the entity's exposure to changes in the overall fair value of that "prepayment" option, perhaps thereby achieving the objective of its desire to hedge prepayment risk. The effect of an embedded derivative of the same risk class must be considered in designating a hedge of an individual risk. For example, the effect of an embedded prepayment option must be considered in designating a hedge of ~~market~~ interest rate risk.

---

*The first sentence of paragraph 21(a) that specifically permits the hedged item to be identified as either all or a specific portion of a recognized asset or liability or of an unrecognized firm commitment is not affected by the provisions in this subparagraph.

Cash Flow Hedges

The hedged forecasted transaction

29(d). The forecasted transaction is not the acquisition of an asset or incurrence of a liability that will subsequently be remeasured with changes in fair value attributable to the hedged risk reported currently in earnings ~~(for example, if foreign exchange risk is hedged, the forecasted acquisition of a foreign-currency-denominated asset for which a foreign currency transaction gain or loss will be recognized in earnings). However, forecasted sales on credit and the forecasted accrual of royalties on probable future sales by third-party licensees are not considered the forecasted acquisition of a receivable~~. If the forecasted transaction relates to a recognized asset or liability, the asset or liability is not remeasured with changes in fair value attributable to the hedged risk reported currently in earnings.

29(e). If the variable cash flows of the forecasted transaction relate to a debt security that is classified as held-to-maturity under Statement 115, the risk being hedged is the risk of changes in its cash flows attributable to credit risk, foreign exchange risk, or both~~default or changes in the obligor's creditworthiness~~. For those variable cash flows, the risk being hedged cannot be the risk of changes in its cash flows attributable to interest rate risk~~changes in market interest rates~~.

29(g)(2). the risk of changes in the cash flows relating to all changes in the purchase price or sales price of the asset ~~(reflecting its actual location if a physical asset)~~ (regardless of whether that price and the related cash flows are stated in the entity's functional currency or a foreign currency), not the risk of changes in the cash flows relating to the purchase or sale of a similar asset in a different location or of a major ingredient. Thus, for example, in hedging the exposure to changes in the cash flows relating to the purchase of its bronze bar inventory, an entity may not designate the risk of changes in the cash flows relating to purchasing the copper component in bronze as the risk being hedged for purposes of assessing offset as required by paragraph 28(b).

29(h). If the hedged transaction is the forecasted purchase or sale of a financial asset or liability (or the interest payments on that financial asset or liability) or the variable cash inflow or outflow of an existing financial asset or liability, the designated risk being hedged is
 (1) the risk of overall changes in the hedged cash flows ~~of~~related to the ~~entire~~ asset or liability, such as those relating to all changes in the purchase price or sales price (regardless of whether that price and the related cash flows are stated in the entity's functional currency or a foreign currency),
 (2) the risk of changes in its cash flows attributable to changes in the designated benchmark interest rate (referred to as interest rate risk)~~market interest rates~~,

(3) the risk of changes in the functional-currency-equivalent cash flows attributable to changes in the related foreign currency exchange rates (referred to as foreign exchange risk) (refer to paragraphs 40, 40A, 40B, and 40C)(refer to paragraph 40), or

(4) the risk of changes in its cash flows attributable to default, changes in the obligor's credit-worthiness, and changes in the spread over the benchmark interest rate with respect to the hedged item's credit sector at inception of the hedge (referred to as credit risk)default or changes in the obligor's creditworthiness.

Two or more of the above risks may be designated simultaneously as being hedged. The bench-mark interest rate being hedged in a hedge of interest rate risk must be specifically identified as part of the designation and documentation at the inception of the hedging relationship. Ordi-narily, an entity should designate the same benchmark interest rate as the risk being hedged for similar hedges, consistent with paragraph 62; the use of different benchmark interest rates for similar hedges should be rare and must be justified. In a cash flow hedge of a variable-rate finan-cial asset or liability, either existing or forecasted, the designated risk being hedged cannot be the risk of changes in its cash flows attributable to changes in the specifically identified benchmark interest rate if the cash flows of the hedged transaction are explicitly based on a different index, for example, based on a specific bank's prime rate, which cannot qualify as the benchmark rate. However, the risk designated as being hedged could potentially be the risk of overall changes in the hedged cash flows related to the asset or liability, provided that the other criteria for a cash flow hedge have been met. An entity may not designate prepayment risk as the risk being hedged (refer to paragraph 21(f)).

30. The effective portion of the gain or loss on a derivative designated as a cash flow hedge is reported in other comprehensive income, and the ineffective portion is reported in earnings. More specifically, a qualifying cash flow hedge shall be accounted for as follows:

a. If an entity's defined risk management strategy for a particular hedging relationship excludes a spe-cific component of the gain or loss, or related cash flows, on the hedging derivative from the assess-ment of hedge effectiveness (as discussed in paragraph 63 in Section 2 of Appendix A), that ex-cluded component of the gain or loss shall be recognized currently in earnings. For example, if the effectiveness of a hedge with an option contract is assessed based on changes in the option's intrin-sic value, the changes in the option's time value would be recognized in earnings. Time value is equal to the fair value of the option less its intrinsic value.

b. Accumulated other comprehensive income associated with the hedged transaction shall be adjusted to a balance that reflects the *lesser* of the following (in absolute amounts):

(1) The cumulative gain or loss on the derivative from inception of the hedge less (a) the excluded component discussed in paragraph 30(a) above and (b) the derivative's gains or losses previ-ously reclassified from accumulated other comprehensive income into earnings pursuant to paragraph 31

(2) The portion of the cumulative gain or loss on the derivative necessary to offset the cumulative change in expected future cash flows on the hedged transaction from inception of the hedge less the derivative's gains or losses previously reclassified from accumulated other comprehen-sive income into earnings pursuant to paragraph 31.

That adjustment of accumulated other comprehensive income shall incorporate recognition in other comprehensive income of part or all of the gain or loss on the hedging derivative, as necessary.

c. A gain or loss shall be recognized in earnings, as necessary, for any remaining gain or loss on the hedging derivative or to adjust other comprehensive income to the balance specified in para-graph 30(b) above.

d. In a cash flow hedge of the variability of the functional-currency-equivalent cash flows for a recog-nized foreign-currency-denominated asset or liability that is remeasured at spot exchange rates un-der paragraph 15 of Statement 52, an amount that will offset the related transaction gain or loss aris-ing from the remeasurement and adjust earnings for the cost to the purchaser (income to the seller) of the hedging instrument shall be reclassified each period from other comprehensive income to earnings.

Section 2 of Appendix A illustrates assessing hedge effectiveness and measuring hedge ineffectiveness. Examples 6 and 9 of Section 1 of Appendix B illustrate the application of this paragraph.

33. The net derivative gain or loss related to a discontinued cash flow hedge shall continue to be reported in accumulated other comprehensive income unless it is probable that the forecasted transaction will *not* occur by the end of the originally specified time period (as documented at the inception of the hedging relationship) or within an additional two-month period of time thereafter, except as indicated in the following sentence. In rare cases, the existence of extenuating circumstances that are related to the nature of the forecasted transaction and are outside the control or influence of the reporting entity may cause the forecasted transaction to be probable of occurring on a date that is beyond the additional two-month period of time, in which case the net derivative gain or loss related to the discontinued cash flow hedge shall continue to be reported in accumulated other comprehensive income until it is reclassified into earnings pursuant to paragraph 31. If it is probable that the hedged forecasted transaction will not occur either by the end of the originally specified time period or within the additional two-month period of time and the hedged forecasted transaction also does not qualify for the exception described in the preceding sentence, that derivative gain or loss reported in accumulated other comprehensive income shall be reclassified into earnings immediately.~~If a cash flow hedge is discontinued because it is probable that the original forecasted transaction will not occur, the net gain or loss in accumulated other comprehensive income shall be immediately reclassified into earnings.~~

Foreign Currency Hedges

36. ~~Consistent with the functional currency concept in Statement 52~~If the hedged item is denominated in a foreign currency, an entity may designate the following types of hedges of foreign currency exposure, as specified in paragraphs 37–42:

a. A fair value hedge of an unrecognized firm commitment or a recognized asset or liability (including an available-for-sale security)
b. A cash flow hedge of a forecasted ~~foreign-currency-denominated~~ transaction, an unrecognized firm commitment, the forecasted functional-currency-equivalent cash flows associated with a recognized asset or liability, or a forecasted intercompany ~~foreign-currency-denominated~~ transaction
c. A hedge of a net investment in a foreign operation.

The recognition in earnings of the foreign currency transaction gain or loss on a foreign-currency-denominated asset or liability based on changes in the foreign currency spot rate is not considered to be the remeasurement of that asset or liability with changes in fair value attributable to foreign exchange risk recognized in earnings, which is discussed in the criteria~~The criterion~~ in paragraphs 21(c)(1) and 29(d).~~requires that a recognized asset or liability that may give rise to a foreign currency transaction gain or loss under Statement 52 (such as a foreign-currency-denominated receivable or payable) not be the hedged item in a foreign currency fair value or cash flow hedge because it is remeasured with the changes in the carrying amount attributable to what would be the hedged risk (an exchange rate change) reported currently in earnings.~~ Thus, those criteria are not impediments to either a foreign currency fair value or cash flow hedge of such a foreign-currency-denominated asset or liability or a foreign currency cash flow hedge of the forecasted acquisition or incurrence of a foreign-currency-denominated asset or liability whose carrying amount will be remeasured at spot exchange rates under paragraph 15 of Statement 52.~~Similarly, the criterion in paragraph 29(d) requires that the forecasted acquisition of an asset or the incurrence of a liability that may give rise to a foreign currency transaction gain or loss under Statement 52 not be the hedged item in a foreign currency cash flow hedge because, subsequent to acquisition or incurrence, the asset or liability will be remeasured with changes in the carrying amount attributable to what would be the hedged risk reported currently in earnings.~~ A foreign currency derivative instrument that has been entered into with another member of a consolidated group can be a hedging instrument in a fair value hedge or in a cash flow hedge of a recognized foreign-currency-denominated asset or liability or in a net investment hedge in the consolidated financial statements only if that other member has entered into an offsetting contract with an unrelated third party to hedge the exposure it acquired from issuing the derivative instrument to the affiliate that initiated the hedge.

36A. The provisions in paragraph 36 that permit a recognized foreign-currency-denominated asset or liability to be the hedged item in a fair value or cash flow hedge of foreign currency exposure also pertain to a recognized foreign-currency-denominated receivable or payable that results from a hedged forecasted foreign-currency-denominated sale or purchase on credit. An entity may choose to designate a single cash flow hedge that encompasses the variability of functional currency cash flows attributable to foreign exchange risk related to the settlement of the foreign-currency-denominated receivable or payable resulting from a forecasted sale or purchase on credit. Alternatively, an entity may choose to designate a cash flow hedge of the variability of functional currency cash flows attributable to foreign exchange risk related to a forecasted foreign-currency-denominated sale or purchase on credit and then separately designate a foreign currency fair value hedge of the resulting recognized foreign-currency-denominated receivable or payable. In that case, the cash flow hedge would terminate (be dedesignated) when the hedged sale or purchase occurs and the foreign-currency-denominated receivable or payable is recognized. The use of the same foreign currency derivative instrument for both the cash flow hedge and the fair value hedge is not prohibited though some ineffectiveness may result.

Foreign currency fair value hedges

37. *Unrecognized firm commitment.* A derivative instrument or a nonderivative financial instrument[11] that may give rise to a foreign currency transaction gain or loss under Statement 52 can be designated as hedging changes in the fair value of an unrecognized firm commitment, or a specific portion thereof, attributable to foreign currency exchange rates. The designated hedging relationship qualifies for the accounting specified in paragraphs 22–27 if all the fair value hedge criteria in paragraphs 20 and 21 and the conditions in paragraphs 40(a) and 40(b) are met.

37A. *Recognized asset or liability.* A nonderivative financial instrument shall not be designated as the hedging instrument in a fair value hedge of the foreign currency exposure of a recognized asset or liability. A derivative instrument can be designated as hedging the changes in the fair value of a recognized asset or liability (or a specific portion thereof) for which a foreign currency transaction gain or loss is recognized in earnings under the provisions of paragraph 15 of Statement 52. All recognized foreign-currency-denominated assets or liabilities for which a foreign currency transaction gain or loss is recorded in earnings may qualify for the accounting specified in paragraphs 22–27 if all the fair value hedge criteria in paragraphs 20 and 21 and the conditions in paragraphs 40(a) and 40(b) are met.

38. *Available-for-sale security.* A nonderivative financial instrument shall not be designated as the hedging instrument in a fair value hedge of the foreign currency exposure of an available-for-sale security. A derivative instrument can be designated as hedging the changes in the fair value of an available-for-sale *debt* security (or a specific portion thereof) attributable to changes in foreign currency exchange rates. The designated hedging relationship qualifies for the accounting specified in paragraphs 22–27 if all the fair value hedge criteria in paragraphs 20 and 21 and the conditions in paragraphs 40(a) and 40(b) are met. An available-for-sale *equity* security can be hedged for changes in the fair value attributable to changes in foreign currency exchange rates and qualify for the accounting specified in paragraphs 22–27 only if the fair value hedge criteria in paragraphs 20 and 21 are met and the following two conditions are satisfied:

a. The security is not traded on an exchange (or other established marketplace) on which trades are denominated in the investor's functional currency.
b. Dividends or other cash flows to holders of the security are all denominated in the same foreign currency as the currency expected to be received upon sale of the security.

The change in fair value of the hedged available-for-sale equity security attributable to foreign exchange risk is reported in earnings pursuant to paragraph 23 and not in other comprehensive income.

Foreign currency cash flow hedges

40. A nonderivative financial instrument shall not be designated as a hedging instrument in a foreign currency cash flow hedge. A derivative instrument designated as hedging the foreign currency exposure to variability in the functional-currency-equivalent cash flows associated with ~~either~~ a forecasted ~~foreign-currency-denominated~~ transaction (for example, a forecasted export sale to an unaffiliated entity with the price to be denominated in a foreign currency), a recognized asset or liability, an unrecognized firm commitment, or a forecasted intercompany ~~foreign-currency-denominated~~ transaction (for example, a forecasted sale to a foreign subsidiary or a forecasted royalty from a foreign subsidiary) qualifies for hedge accounting if all ~~of~~ the following criteria are met:

a. For consolidated financial statements, either (1) the operating unit that has the foreign currency exposure is a party to the hedging instrument or (2) another member of the consolidated group that has the same functional currency as that operating unit (subject to the restrictions in this subparagraph and related footnote) is a party to the hedging instrument. To qualify for applying the guidance in (2) above, there may be no intervening subsidiary with a different functional currency.* (Refer to paragraphs 36, 40A, and 40B for conditions for which an intercompany foreign currency derivative can be the hedging instrument in a cash flow hedge of foreign exchange risk.) ~~The operating unit that has the foreign currency exposure is a party to the hedging instrument (which can be an instrument between a parent company and its subsidiary—refer to paragraph 36).~~
b. The hedged transaction is denominated in a currency other than ~~that~~ the hedging unit's functional currency.
c. All of the criteria in paragraphs 28 and 29 are met, except for the criterion in paragraph 29(c) that requires that the forecasted transaction be with a party external to the reporting entity.
d. If the hedged transaction is a group of individual forecasted foreign-currency-denominated transactions, a forecasted inflow of a foreign currency and a forecasted outflow of the foreign currency cannot both be included in the same group.
e. If the hedged item is a recognized foreign-currency-denominated asset or liability, all the variability in the hedged item's functional-currency-equivalent cash flows must be eliminated by the effect of the hedge. (For example, a cash flow hedge cannot be used with a variable-rate foreign-currency-denominated asset or liability and a derivative based solely on changes in exchange rates because the derivative does not eliminate all the variability in the functional currency cash flows.)

40A. *Internal derivative.* A foreign currency derivative contract that has been entered into with another member of a consolidated group (such as a treasury center) can be a hedging instrument in a foreign currency cash flow hedge of a forecasted borrowing, purchase, or sale or an unrecognized firm commitment in the consolidated financial statements only if the following two conditions are satisfied. (That foreign currency derivative instrument is hereafter in this section referred to as an *internal derivative.*)

a. From the perspective of the member of the consolidated group using the derivative as a hedging instrument (hereafter in this section referred to as the *hedging affiliate*), the criteria for foreign currency cash flow hedge accounting in paragraph 40 must be satisfied.

---

*For example, if a dollar-functional, second-tier subsidiary has a Euro exposure, the dollar-functional consolidated parent company could designate its U.S. dollar–Euro derivative as a hedge of the second-tier subsidiary's exposure provided that the functional currency of the intervening first-tier subsidiary (that is, the parent of the second-tier subsidiary) is also the U.S. dollar. In contrast, if the functional currency of the intervening first-tier subsidiary was the Japanese yen (thus requiring the financial statements of the second-tier subsidiary to be translated into yen before the yen-denominated financial statements of the first-tier subsidiary are translated into U.S. dollars for consolidation), the consolidated parent company could not designate its U.S. dollar–Euro derivative as a hedge of the second-tier subsidiary's exposure.

b. The member of the consolidated group not using the derivative as a hedging instrument (hereafter in this section referred to as the *issuing affiliate*) must either (1) enter into a derivative contract with an unrelated third party to offset the exposure that results from that internal derivative or (2) if the conditions in paragraph 40B are met, enter into derivative contracts with unrelated third parties that would offset, on a net basis for each foreign currency, the foreign exchange risk arising from multiple internal derivative contracts.

40B. *Offsetting net exposures.* If an issuing affiliate chooses to offset exposure arising from multiple internal derivative contracts on an aggregate or net basis, the derivatives issued to hedging affiliates may qualify as cash flow hedges in the consolidated financial statements only if all of the following conditions are satisfied:

a. The issuing affiliate enters into a derivative contract with an unrelated third party to offset, on a net basis for each foreign currency, the foreign exchange risk arising from multiple internal derivative contracts, and the derivative contract with the unrelated third party generates equal or closely approximating gains and losses when compared with the aggregate or net losses and gains generated by the derivative contracts issued to affiliates.
b. Internal derivatives that are not designated as hedging instruments are excluded from the determination of the foreign currency exposure on a net basis that is offset by the third-party derivative. In addition, nonderivative contracts may not be used as hedging instruments to offset exposures arising from internal derivative contracts.
c. Foreign currency exposure that is offset by a single net third-party contract arises from internal derivative contracts that mature within the same 31-day period and that involve the same currency exposure as the net third-party derivative. The offsetting net third-party derivative related to that group of contracts must offset the aggregate or net exposure to that currency, must mature within the same 31-day period, and must be entered into within 3 business days after the designation of the internal derivatives as hedging instruments.
d. The issuing affiliate tracks the exposure that it acquires from each hedging affiliate and maintains documentation supporting linkage of each internal derivative contract and the offsetting aggregate or net derivative contract with an unrelated third party.
e. The issuing affiliate does not alter or terminate the offsetting derivative with an unrelated third party unless the hedging affiliate initiates that action. If the issuing affiliate does alter or terminate the offsetting third-party derivative (which should be rare), the hedging affiliate must prospectively cease hedge accounting for the internal derivatives that are offset by that third-party derivative.

40C. A member of a consolidated group is not permitted to offset exposures arising from multiple internal derivative contracts on a net basis for foreign currency cash flow exposures related to recognized foreign-currency-denominated assets or liabilities. That prohibition includes situations in which a recognized foreign-currency-denominated asset or liability in a fair value hedge or cash flow hedge results from the occurrence of a specifically identified forecasted transaction initially designated as a cash flow hedge.

42. A derivative instrument or a nonderivative financial instrument that may give rise to a foreign currency transaction gain or loss under Statement 52 can be designated as hedging the foreign currency exposure of a net investment in a foreign operation provided the conditions in paragraphs 40(a) and 40(b) are met. The gain or loss on a hedging derivative instrument (or the foreign currency transaction gain or loss on the nonderivative hedging instrument) that is designated as, and is effective as, an economic hedge of the net investment in a foreign operation shall be reported in the same manner as a translation adjustment to the extent it is effective as a hedge. The hedged net investment shall be accounted for consistent with Statement 52; the provisions of this Statement for recognizing the gain or loss on assets designated as being hedged in a fair value hedge do not apply to the hedge of a net investment in a foreign operation.

45. An entity's disclosures for every reporting period for which a complete set of financial statements is presented also shall include the following: . . .

Cash flow hedges

b. For derivative instruments that have been designated and have qualified as cash flow hedging instruments and for the related hedged transactions:

(1) The net gain or loss recognized in earnings during the reporting period representing (a) the amount of the hedges' ineffectiveness and (b) the component of the derivative instruments' gain or loss, if any, excluded from the assessment of hedge effectiveness, and a description of where the net gain or loss is reported in the statement of income or other statement of financial performance

(2) A description of the transactions or other events that will result in the reclassification into earnings of gains and losses that are reported in accumulated other comprehensive income, and the estimated net amount of the existing gains or losses at the reporting date that is expected to be reclassified into earnings within the next 12 months

(3) The maximum length of time over which the entity is hedging its exposure to the variability in future cash flows for forecasted transactions excluding those forecasted transactions related to the payment of variable interest on existing financial instruments

(4) The amount of gains and losses reclassified into earnings as a result of the discontinuance of cash flow hedges because it is probable that the original forecasted transactions will not occur by the end of the originally specified time period or within the additional period of time discussed in paragraph 33.

Effective Date and Transition

52(b). If the transition adjustment relates to a derivative instrument that had been designated in a hedging relationship that addressed the fair value exposure of an asset, a liability, or a firm commitment, the transition adjustment for the derivative shall be reported as a cumulative-effect-type adjustment of net income. Concurrently, any gain or loss on the hedged item (that is, difference between the hedged item's fair value and its carrying amount) shall be recognized as an adjustment of the hedged item's carrying amount at the date of initial application, but only to the extent of an offsetting transition adjustment for the derivative. Only for purposes of applying the preceding sentence in determining the hedged item's transition adjustment, the gain or loss on the hedged item may be either (1) the overall gain or loss on the hedged item determined as the difference between the hedged item's fair value and its carrying amount on the date of initial application (that is, not limited to the portion attributable to the hedged risk nor limited to the gain or loss occurring during the period of the preexisting hedging relationship) or (2) the gain or loss on the hedged item attributable to the hedged risk (limited to the hedged risks that can be designated under paragraph 21 of this Statement) during the period of the preexisting hedging relationship. That adjustment of the hedged item's carrying amount shall also be reported as a cumulative-effect-type adjustment of net income. The transition adjustment related to the gain or loss reported in accumulated other comprehensive income on a derivative instrument that hedged an available-for-sale security, together with the loss or gain on the related security (to the extent of an offsetting transition adjustment for the derivative instrument), shall be reclassified to earnings as a cumulative-effect-type adjustment of both net income and accumulated other comprehensive income.

54. At the date of initial application, an entity may transfer any held-to-maturity security into the available-for-sale category or the trading category. An entity will then be able in the future to designate a security transferred into the available-for-sale category as the hedged item, or its variable interest payments as the cash flow hedged transactions, in a hedge of the exposure to changes in the designated benchmark interest rate market interest rates, changes in foreign currency exchange rates, or changes in its overall fair value. (Paragraph 21(d) precludes a held-to-maturity security from being designated as the hedged item in a fair value hedge of market interest rate risk or the risk of changes in its overall fair value. Paragraph 29(e) similarly precludes the variable cash flows of a held-to-maturity security from being designated as the hedged transaction in a cash flow hedge of market interest rate risk.) The unrealized holding gain or loss on a held-to-maturity security transferred to another category at the date of

initial application shall be reported in net income or accumulated other comprehensive income consistent with the requirements of paragraphs 15(b) and 15(c) of Statement 115 and reported with the other transition adjustments discussed in paragraph 52 of this Statement. Such transfers from the held-to-maturity category at the date of initial adoption shall not call into question an entity's intent to hold other debt securities to maturity in the future.[14]

---

[14] EITF Topic No. D-51, "The Applicability of FASB Statement No. 115 to Desecuritizations of Financial Assets," indicates that certain financial assets received or retained in a desecuritization must be held to maturity to avoid calling into question the entity's intent to hold other debt securities to maturity in the future. In conjunction with the initial adoption of this Statement, the held-to-maturity restriction on those financial assets held on the date of initial application is removed, and those financial assets that had been received or retained in a previous desecuritization are available in the future to be designated as the hedged item, or their variable interest payments as the hedged transaction, in a hedge of the exposure to changes in interest rate risk~~market interest rates~~. Consequently, the sale of those financial assets before maturity would not call into question the entity's intent to hold other debt securities to maturity in the future.

Appendix A—Implementation Guidance

58. The following discussion further explains some of the exceptions discussed in paragraph 10.

a. *"Regular-way" security trades.* The exception in paragraph 10(a) applies only to a contract that requires delivery of securities that are readily convertible to cash.[16] To qualify, a contract must require delivery of such a security within the period of time after the trade date that is customary in the market in which the trade takes place. For example, a contract to purchase or sell a publicly traded equity security in the United States customarily requires settlement within three business days. If a contract for purchase of that type of security requires settlement in three business days, the regular-way exception applies, but if the contract requires settlement in five days, the regular-way exception does not apply. This Statement does not change whether an entity recognizes regular-way security trades on the trade date or the settlement date. However, trades that do not qualify for the regular-way exception are subject to the requirements of this Statement regardless of the method an entity uses to report its security trades.

b. *Normal purchases and normal sales.* The exception in paragraph 10(b) applies only to a contract that ~~requires~~involves future delivery of assets (other than financial instruments or derivative instruments)~~that are readily convertible to cash[17] and only if there is no market mechanism to facilitate net settlement outside the contract~~. To qualify for the exception, a contract's terms also must be consistent with the terms of an entity's normal purchases or normal sales, that is, the quantity purchased or sold must be reasonable in relation to the entity's business needs. Determining whether or not the terms are consistent will require judgment. In making those judgments, an entity should consider all relevant factors, such as (1) the quantities provided under the contract and the entity's need for the related assets, (2) the locations to which delivery of the items will be made, (3) the period of time between entering into the contract and delivery, and (4) the entity's prior practices with regard to such contracts. Evidence such as past trends, expected future demand, other contracts for delivery of similar items, an entity's and industry's customs for acquiring and storing the related commodities, and an entity's operating locations should help in identifying contracts that qualify as normal purchases or normal sales. Also, in order for a contract that meets the net settlement provisions of paragraphs 9(a) and 57(c)(1) and the market mechanism provisions of paragraphs 9(b) and 57(c)(2) to qualify for the exception, it must be probable at inception and throughout the term of the individual contract that the contract will not settle net and will result in physical delivery.

c. *Certain contracts that are not traded on an exchange.* A contract that is not traded on an exchange is not subject to the requirements of this Statement if the underlying is:

   (1) A climatic or geological variable or other physical variable. Climatic, geological, and other physical variables include things like the number of inches of rainfall or snow in a particular area and the severity of an earthquake as measured by the Richter scale.

---

[17] ~~Contracts that require delivery of assets that are not readily convertible to cash are not subject to the requirements of this Statement unless there is a market mechanism outside the contract to facilitate net settlement.~~

(2) The price or value of (a) a nonfinancial asset of one of the parties to the contract unless that asset is readily convertible to cash or (b) a nonfinancial liability of one of the parties to the contract unless that liability requires delivery of an asset that is readily convertible to cash. This exception applies only to nonfinancial assets that are unique and only if a nonfinancial asset related to the underlying is owned by the party that would *not* benefit *under the contract* from an increase in the price or value of the nonfinancial asset. If the contract is a call option contract, the exception applies only if that nonfinancial asset is owned by the party that would not benefit under the contract from an increase in the price or value of the nonfinancial asset above the option's strike price.

(3) Specified volumes of sales or service revenues by one of the parties. That exception is intended to apply to contracts with settlements based on the volume of items sold or services rendered, for example, royalty agreements. It is not intended to apply to contracts based on changes in sales or revenues due to changes in market prices.

If a contract's underlying is the combination of two or more variables, and one or more would not qualify for one of the exceptions above, the application of this Statement to that contract depends on the predominant characteristics of the combined variable. The contract is subject to the requirements of this Statement if the changes in its combined underlying are highly correlated with changes in one of the component variables that would not qualify for an exception.

61(d). *Calls and puts on debt instruments.* Call options (or put options) that can accelerate the repayment of principal on a debt instrument are considered to be clearly and closely related to a debt instrument that requires principal repayments unless both (1) the debt involves a substantial premium or discount (which is common with zero-coupon bonds) and (2) the put or call option is only contingently exercisable. Thus, if a substantial premium or discount is not involved, embedded calls and puts (including contingent call or put options that are not exercisable unless an event of default occurs) would *not* be separated from the host contract. However, for contingently exercisable calls and puts to be considered clearly and closely related, they can be indexed only to interest rates or credit risk, not some extraneous event or factor. In contrast, call options (or put options) that do not accelerate the repayment of principal on a debt instrument but instead require a cash settlement that is equal to the price of the option at the date of exercise would *not* be considered to be clearly and closely related to the debt instrument in which it is embedded and would be separated from the host contract. ~~In certain unusual situations, a put or call option may have been subsequently added to a debt instrument in a manner that causes the investor (creditor) to be exposed to performance risk (default risk) by different parties for the embedded option and the host debt instrument, respectively. In those unusual situations, the embedded option and the host debt instrument are *not* clearly and closely related.~~

61(e). *Calls and puts on equity instruments.* A put option that enables the holder to require the issuer of an equity instrument to reacquire that equity instrument for cash or other assets is *not* clearly and closely related to that equity instrument. Thus, such a put option embedded in a publicly traded ~~the~~ equity instrument to which it relates should be separated from the host contract by the holder of the equity instrument. That put option also should be separated from the host contract by the issuer of the equity instrument except in those cases in which the put option is not considered to be a derivative instrument pursuant to paragraph 11(a) because it is classified in stockholders' equity. A purchased call option that enables the issuer of an equity instrument (such as common stock) to reacquire that equity instrument would not be considered to be a derivative instrument by the issuer of the equity instrument pursuant to paragraph 11(a). Thus, if the call option were embedded in the related equity instrument, it would not be separated from the host contract by the issuer. However, for the holder of the related equity instrument, the embedded written call option would *not* be considered to be clearly and closely related to the equity instrument and should be separated from the host contract.

68. An assumption of no ineffectiveness is especially important in a hedging relationship involving an interest-bearing financial instrument and an interest rate swap because it significantly simplifies the computations necessary to make the accounting entries. An entity may assume no ineffectiveness in a

hedging relationship of interest rate risk involving a recognized~~an~~ interest-bearing asset or liability and an interest rate swap if all of the applicable conditions in the following list are met:

Conditions applicable to both fair value hedges and cash flow hedges

a. The notional amount of the swap matches the principal amount of the interest-bearing asset or liability.
b. The fair value of the swap at the inception of the hedging relationship~~its inception~~ is zero.
c. The formula for computing net settlements under the interest rate swap is the same for each net settlement. (That is, the fixed rate is the same throughout the term, and the variable rate is based on the same index and includes the same constant adjustment or no adjustment.)
d. The interest-bearing asset or liability is not prepayable (that is, able to be settled by either party prior to its scheduled maturity), except as indicated in the following sentences. This criterion does not apply to an interest-bearing asset or liability that is prepayable solely due to an embedded call option provided that the hedging interest rate swap contains an embedded mirror-image call option. The call option embedded in the swap is considered a mirror image of the call option embedded in the hedged item if (1) the terms of the two call options match (including matching maturities, strike price, related notional amounts, timing and frequency of payments, and dates on which the instruments may be called) and (2) the entity is the writer of one call option and the holder (or purchaser) of the other call option. Similarly, this criterion does not apply to an interest-bearing asset or liability that is prepayable solely due to an embedded put option provided that the hedging interest rate swap contains an embedded mirror-image put option.
dd. The index on which the variable leg of the swap is based matches the benchmark interest rate designated as the interest rate risk being hedged for that hedging relationship.*
e. Any other terms in the interest-bearing financial instruments or interest rate swaps are typical of those instruments and do not invalidate the assumption of no ineffectiveness.

Conditions applicable to fair value hedges only

f. The expiration date of the swap matches the maturity date of the interest-bearing asset or liability.
g. There is no floor or ceiling on the variable interest rate of the swap.
h. The interval between repricings of the variable interest rate in the swap is frequent enough to justify an assumption that the variable payment or receipt is at a market rate (generally three to six months or less).

Conditions applicable to cash flow hedges only

i. All interest receipts or payments on the variable-rate asset or liability during the term of the swap are designated as hedged, and no interest payments beyond the term of the swap are designated as hedged.
j. There is no floor or cap on the variable interest rate of the swap unless the variable-rate asset or liability has a floor or cap. In that case, the swap must have a floor or cap on the variable interest rate that is comparable to the floor or cap on the variable-rate asset or liability. (For this purpose, comparable does not necessarily mean equal. For example, if a swap's variable rate is LIBOR and an asset's variable rate is LIBOR plus 2 percent, a 10 percent cap on the swap would be comparable to a 12 percent cap on the asset.)
k. The repricing dates match those of the variable-rate asset or liability.
l. ~~The index on which the variable rate is based matches the index on which the asset or liability's variable rate is based.~~

---

*For cash flow hedge situations in which the cash flows of the hedged item and the hedging instrument are based on the same index but that index is not the benchmark interest rate, the shortcut method is not permitted. However, the entity may obtain results similar to results obtained if the shortcut method was permitted.

[19]The use of a hedging instrument with a different underlying basis than the item or transaction being hedged is generally referred to as a *cross-hedge.* The principles for cross-hedges illustrated in this example also apply to hedges involving other risks. For example, the effectiveness of a hedge of ~~market~~ interest rate risk in which one interest rate is used as a surrogate for another interest rate would be evaluated in the same way as the natural gas cross-hedge in this example.

[Paragraph 74 to which this footnote relates has not been amended by this Statement.]

90. However, because the pertinent critical terms of the option and the bond are the same in this example, the company could expect the changes in value of the bond attributable to changes in ~~market~~ interest rates and changes in the intrinsic value of the option to offset completely during the period that the option is in the money. That is, there will be no ineffectiveness because the company has chosen to exclude changes in the option's time value from the effectiveness test. Because of that choice, Company E must recognize changes in the time value of the option directly in earnings.

Appendix B—Examples

115. On July 1, 20X1, ABC Company borrows $1,000,000 to be repaid on June 30, 20X3. On that same date, ABC also enters into a two-year receive-fixed, pay-variable interest rate swap. ABC designates the interest rate swap as a hedge of the changes in the fair value of the fixed-rate debt attributable to changes in the designated benchmark interest rate~~market interest rates~~. ABC designates changes in LIBOR swap rates as the benchmark interest rate in hedging interest rate risk. The terms of the interest rate swap and the debt are as follows:

	Interest Rate Swap	Fixed-Rate Debt
Trade date and borrowing date*	July 1, 20X1	July 1, 20X1
Termination date and maturity date	June 30, 20X3	June 30, 20X3
Notional amount and principal amount	$1,000,000	$1,000,000
Fixed interest rate*	6.41%	6.41%
Variable interest rate	3-month US$ LIBOR	Not applicable
Settlement dates and interest payment dates*	End of each calendar quarter	End of each calendar quarter
Reset dates	End of each calendar quarter through March 31, 20X3	Not applicable

*These terms need not match for the assumption of no ineffectiveness to be appropriate. (Refer to paragraphs 68 and 69.)

Example 2A: Fair Value Hedge of the LIBOR Swap Rate in a $100,000 BBB-Quality 5-Year Fixed-Rate Noncallable Note

120A. This example illustrates one method that could be used in determining the hedged item's change in fair value attributable to changes in the benchmark interest rate. Other methods could be used in determining the hedged item's change in fair value attributable to changes in the benchmark interest rate as long as those methods meet the criteria in paragraph 21(f).

120B. On January 1, 20X0, GHI Company issues at par a $100,000 BBB-quality 5-year fixed-rate noncallable debt instrument with an annual 10 percent interest coupon. On that date, the issuer enters into a 5-year interest rate swap based on the LIBOR swap rate and designates it as the hedging instrument in a fair value hedge of the $100,000 liability. Under the terms of the swap, GHI will receive fixed interest at 7 percent and pay variable interest at LIBOR. The variable leg of the swap resets each year on December 31 for the payments due the following year. This example has been simplified by assuming that the interest rate applicable to a payment due at any future date is the same as the rate for a payment at any other date (that is, the yield curve is flat). During the hedge period, the gain or loss on the swap will be recorded in earnings. The example assumes that immediately before the interest rate on the variable leg resets on December 31, 20X0, the LIBOR swap rate increased by 50 basis points to 7.50 percent, and the change in fair value of the swap for the period from January 1 to December 31, 20X0 is a loss in value of $1,675.

Changes in the fair value of the hedged item attributable to the changes in the benchmark interest rate for a specific period

120C. Under this method, the change in a hedged item's fair value attributable to changes in the benchmark interest rate for a specific period is determined as the difference between two present value calculations as of the end of the period that exclude or include, respectively, the effect of the changes in the benchmark interest rate during the period. The discount rates used for those present value calculations would be, respectively, (a) the discount rate equal to the market interest rate for that hedged item at the inception of the hedge adjusted (up or down) for changes in the benchmark rate (designated as the interest rate risk being hedged) from the inception of the hedge to the beginning date of the period for which the change in fair value is being calculated* and (b) the discount rate equal to the market interest rate for that hedged item at the inception of the hedge adjusted (up or down) for changes in the designated benchmark rate from the inception of the hedge to the ending date of the period for which the change in fair value is being calculated. Both present value calculations are computed using the estimated future cash flows for the hedged item (which typically would be its remaining contractual cash flows).

120D. In GHI's quarterly assessments of hedge effectiveness for each of the first three quarters of year 20X0 in this example, there was zero change in the hedged item's fair value attributable to changes in the benchmark interest rate because there was no change in the LIBOR swap rate. However, in the assessment for the fourth quarter 20X0, the discount rate for the beginning of the period is 10 percent (the hedged item's original market interest rate with an adjustment of zero), and the discount rate for the end of the period is 10.50 percent (the hedged item's original market interest rate adjusted for the change during the period in the LIBOR swap rate [+0.50 percent]).

December 31, 20X0

Calculate the present value using the beginning-of-period discount rate of 10 percent:

$10,000pmt, 10%i, 4n, PV =	$ 31,699	(interest payments)
$100,000fv, 10%i, 4n, PV =	$ 68,301	(principal payment)
Total present value	$100,000	

Calculate the present value using the end-of-period discount rate of 10.50 percent (that is, the beginning-of-period discount rate adjusted for the change during the period in the LIBOR swap rate of 50 basis points):

$10,000pmt, 10.50%i, 4n, PV =	$31,359	(interest payments)
$100,000fv, 10.50%i, 4n, PV =	$67,073	(principal payment)
Total present value	$98,432	

The change in fair value of the hedged item attributable to the change in the benchmark interest rate is $100,000 – $98,432 = $1,568 (the fair value decrease in the liability is a gain on debt).

---

*This Statement does not provide specific guidance on the discount rate that must be used in the calculation. However, the method chosen by GHI and described in this illustration requires that the discount rate be based on the market interest rate for the hedged item at the inception of the hedging relationship.

When the change in fair value of the hedged item ($1,568 gain) attributable to the risk being hedged is compared with the change in fair value of the hedging instrument ($1,675 loss), ineffectiveness of $107 results. That ineffectiveness will be reported in earnings, because both changes in fair value are recorded in earnings.

134. Also on July 1, 20X1, XYZ enters into a two-year receive-fixed, pay-variable interest rate swap and designates it as a cash flow hedge of the variable-rate interest receipts on the corporate bonds. The risk designated as being hedged is the risk of changes in cash flows attributable to changes in ~~the designated benchmark interest rate~~market interest rates. XYZ designates changes in LIBOR swap rates as the benchmark interest rate in hedging interest rate risk. The terms of the interest rate swap and the corporate bonds are shown below.

	Interest Rate Swap	**Corporate Bonds**
Trade date and borrowing date*	July 1, 20X1	July 1, 20X1
Termination date	June 30, 20X3	June 30, 20X3
Notional amount	$10,000,000	$10,000,000
Fixed interest rate	6.65%	Not applicable
Variable interest rate[†]	3-month US$ LIBOR	3-month US$ LIBOR + 2.25%
Settlement dates and interest payment dates*	End of each calendar quarter	End of each calendar quarter
Reset dates	End of each calendar quarter through March 31, 20X3	End of each calendar quarter through March 31, 20X3

---

*These terms need not match for the assumption of no ineffectiveness to be appropriate. (Refer to paragraphs 68 and 69.)

[†]Only the interest rate basis (for example, LIBOR) must match. The spread over LIBOR does not invalidate the assumption of no ineffectiveness.

155. Because Swap 1 and the hedged forecasted interest payments are based on the same notional amount, have the same reset dates, and are based on the same benchmark interest rate designated under paragraph 29(h)~~meets all of the conditions discussed in paragraph 68~~, MNO may conclude~~is permitted to assume~~ that there will be no ineffectiveness in the hedging relationship ~~and to use the shortcut method illustrated in Example 2~~(absent a default by the swap counterparty).

161. Rather than liquidate Swap 1 and obtain a separate derivative to hedge the variability of the prime-rate-based interest payments, MNO enters into a pay-LIBOR, receive-prime basis swap. The basis swap has a $5 million notional amount and a 3-year term and requires a settlement every 90 days. MNO designates Swap 1 and the basis swap in combination as the hedging instrument in a cash flow hedge of the variable interest payments on the three-year note. On the three-year note, MNO pays interest at prime. On the basis swap, MNO receives interest at prime and pays interest at LIBOR. On Swap 1, MNO receives interest at LIBOR and pays interest at 6.5 percent. Together, the cash flows from the two derivatives are effective at offsetting changes in the interest payments on the three-year note. Changes in fair values of the two swaps are recognized in other comprehensive income and are reclassified to earnings when the hedged forecasted transactions (the variable interest payments) affect earnings (as required by paragraph 31). ~~Because the two swaps in combination meet the conditions discussed in paragraph 68, MNO is permitted to assume no ineffectiveness and use the shortcut method illustrated in Example 5.~~

169. As each royalty is earned, DEF recognizes a receivable and royalty income. The forecasted transaction (the earning of royalty income) has occurred. The receivable is an asset, not a forecasted transaction, and would separately be eligible to be designated as a fair value hedge of foreign exchange risk or

continue to be eligible as a cash flow hedge of foreign exchange risk~~is not eligible for cash flow hedge accounting. Nor is it eligible for fair value hedge accounting of the foreign exchange risk because changes in the receivable's fair value due to exchange rate changes are recognized immediately in earnings. (Paragraph 21(c) prohibits hedge accounting in that situation.)~~ Consequently, if the variability of the functional currency cash flows related to the royalty receivable is not being hedged, DEF will dedesignate a proportion of the hedging instrument in the original hedge relationship with respect to the proportion of the forward contract corresponding to the earned royalty. As the royalty is recognized in earnings and each proportion of the derivative is dedesignated, the related derivative gain or loss in accumulated other comprehensive income is reclassified into earnings. After that date, any gain or loss on the dedesignated proportion of the derivative and any transaction loss or gain on the royalty receivable[26] will be recognized in earnings and may~~will~~ substantially offset each other.

197. **Example 31: Certain Purchases in a Foreign Currency.** A U.S. company enters into a contract to purchase corn from a local American supplier in six months for a fixed amount of Japanese yen; the yen is the functional currency of neither party to the transaction. The corn is expected to be delivered and used over a reasonable period in the normal course of business.

Scope Application: Paragraph 10(b) excludes contracts that require future delivery of commodities that are readily convertible to cash from the accounting for derivatives if the commodities will be delivered in quantities expected to be used or sold by the reporting entity over a reasonable period in the normal course of business. However, that paragraph also states that contracts that are denominated in a foreign currency that meets neither of the criteria in paragraphs 15(a) and 15(b) shall not be considered normal purchases and normal sales.~~the corn purchase contract must be examined to determine whether it contains an embedded derivative that warrants separate accounting.~~ Because the Japanese yen is not the functional currency of either party to the contract and the purchase of corn is transacted internationally in many different currencies, the contract does not qualify for the normal purchases and normal sales exception. The contract is a compound derivative comprising~~The corn purchase contract can be viewed as~~ a U.S. dollar-denominated forward contract for the purchase of corn and an embedded foreign currency swap from the purchaser's functional currency (the U.S. dollar) to yen. Consistent with the last sentence of footnote 13 to paragraph 49, the compound derivative cannot be separated into its components (representing the foreign currency derivative and the forward commodity contract) and accounted for separately under this Statement.~~Because the yen is the functional currency of neither party to the transaction and the purchase of corn is transacted internationally in many different currencies, the contract does not qualify for the exception in paragraph 15 that precludes separating the embedded foreign currency derivative from the host contract. The embedded foreign currency swap should be separated from the host contract and accounted for as a derivative for purposes of this Statement because a separate instrument with the same terms would meet the definition of a derivative instrument in paragraphs 6-11.~~

200. **Example 34: Variable Annuity Products.** These products are investment contracts as contemplated in Statements 60 and 97. Similar to variable life insurance products, policyholders direct their investment account asset mix among a variety of mutual funds composed of equities, bonds, or both, and assume the risks and rewards of investment performance. The funds are generally maintained in separate accounts by the insurance company. Contract terms provide that if the policyholder dies, the greater of the account market value or a minimum death benefit guarantee will be paid. The minimum death benefit guarantee is generally limited to a return of premium plus a minimum return (such as 3 or 4 percent); this life insurance feature represents the fundamental difference from the life insurance contracts that include significant (rather than minimal) levels of life insurance. The investment account may have various payment alternatives at the end of the accumulation period. One alternative is the right to purchase a life annuity at a fixed price determined at the initiation of the contract.

Scope Application: Variable annuity product structures as contemplated in Statement 97 are generally not subject to the scope of this Statement (except for payment options at the end of the accumulation period), as follows:

- *Death benefit component.* Paragraph 10(c)(1) excludes a death benefit from the scope of this Statement because the payment of the death benefit is the result of an identifiable insurable event instead of changes in an underlying. The death benefit in this example is limited to the floor guarantee of the investment account, calculated as the premiums paid into the investment account plus a guaranteed rate of return, less the account market value. Statement 60 remains the applicable guidance for the insurance-related liability accounting.
- *Investment component.* The policyholder directs certain premium investments in the investment account that includes equities, bonds, or both, which are held in separate accounts that are distinct~~owned by the policyholder and separate~~ from the insurer's general account assets. ~~This component is viewed as a direct investment because the policyholder directs and owns these investments.~~ This component is not considered a derivative because of the unique attributes of traditional variable annuity contracts issued by insurance companies~~the policyholder has invested the premiums in acquiring those investments~~. Furthermore, any embedded derivatives within those investments should not be separated from the host contract by the insurer because the separate account assets are already marked-to-market under Statement 60. In contrast, if the product were an equity-index-based interest annuity (rather than a traditional variable annuity), the investment component would contain an embedded derivative (the equity index-based derivative) that meets all the requirements of paragraph 12 of this Statement for separate accounting: (a) the economic characteristics and risks of the embedded derivative would not be clearly and closely related to the economic characteristics and risks of the host contract (that is, the host contract is a debt instrument and the embedded option is equity-indexed), (b) the hybrid instrument would not be remeasured at fair value with changes in fair value reported in earnings as they occur under GAAP, and (c) a separate instrument with the same terms as the embedded derivative instrument would be a derivative instrument pursuant to paragraphs 6–11 of this Statement.~~not be viewed as a direct investment because the policyholder does not own those investments, which are assets recorded in the general account of the insurance company. As a result, the host contract would be a debt instrument, and the equity-index-based derivative should be separated and accounted for as a derivative instrument.~~
- *Investment account surrender right at market value.* Because this right is exercised only at the fund market value (without the insurer's floor guarantee) and relates to a traditional variable annuity contract issued by an insurance company~~an investment owned by the insured~~, this right is not within the scope of this Statement.
- *Payment alternatives at the end of the accumulation period.* Payment alternatives are options subject to the requirements of this Statement if interest rates or other underlying variables affect the value.

The guidance in the second and third bullets above is an exception for traditional variable annuity contracts issued by insurance companies. In determining the accounting for other seemingly similar structures, it would be inappropriate to analogize to the above guidance due to the unique attributes of traditional variable annuity contracts.

Appendix F—Glossary

540. This appendix contains definitions of terms or phrases as used in this Statement.

Benchmark interest rate

A widely recognized and quoted rate in an active financial market that is broadly indicative of the overall level of interest rates attributable to high-credit-quality obligors in that market. It is a rate that is widely used in a given financial market as an underlying basis for determining the interest rates of individual financial instruments and commonly referenced in interest-rate-related transactions.

In theory, the benchmark interest rate should be a risk-free rate (that is, has no risk of default). In some markets, government borrowing rates may serve as a benchmark. In other markets, the benchmark interest rate may be an interbank offered rate. In the United States, currently only the interest rates on direct Treasury obligations of the U.S. government and, for practical reasons, the LIBOR swap rate are considered to be benchmark interest rates. In each financial market, only the one or two most widely used and quoted rates that meet the above criteria may be considered benchmark interest rates.

Comprehensive income

The change in equity of a business enterprise during a period from transactions and other events and circumstances from nonowner sources. It includes all changes in equity during a period except those resulting from investments by owners and distributions to owners (FASB Concepts Statement No. 6, *Elements of Financial Statements,* paragraph 70).

Derivative instrument

Refer to paragraphs 6–9.

Fair value

The amount at which an asset (liability) could be bought (incurred) or sold (settled) in a current transaction between willing parties, that is, other than in a forced or liquidation sale. Quoted market prices in active markets are the best evidence of fair value and should be used as the basis for the measurement, if available. If a quoted market price is available, the fair value is the product of the number of trading units times that market price. If a quoted market price is not available, the estimate of fair value should be based on the best information available in the circumstances. The estimate of fair value should consider prices for similar assets or similar liabilities and the results of valuation techniques to the extent available in the circumstances. Examples of valuation techniques include the present value of estimated expected future cash flows using discount rates commensurate with the risks involved, option-pricing models, matrix pricing, option-adjusted spread models, and fundamental analysis. Valuation techniques for measuring assets and liabilities should be consistent with the objective of measuring fair value. Those techniques should incorporate assumptions that market participants would use in their estimates of values, future revenues, and future expenses, including assumptions about interest rates, default, prepayment, and volatility. In measuring forward contracts, such as foreign currency forward contracts, at fair value by discounting estimated future cash flows, an entity should base the estimate of future cash flows on the changes in the forward rate (rather than the spot rate). In measuring financial liabilities and nonfinancial derivatives that are liabilities at fair value by discounting estimated future cash flows (or equivalent outflows of other assets), an objective is to use discount rates at which those liabilities could be settled in an arm's-length transaction.

Financial instrument

Cash, evidence of an ownership interest in an entity, or a contract that both:

a. Imposes on one entity a contractual obligation* (1) to deliver cash or another financial instrument[†] to a second entity or (2) to exchange other financial instruments on potentially unfavorable terms with the second entity

b. Conveys to that second entity a contractual right[‡] (1) to receive cash or another financial instrument from the first entity or (2) to exchange other financial instruments on potentially favorable terms with the first entity.

Firm commitment

An agreement with an unrelated party, binding on both parties and usually legally enforceable, with the following characteristics:

a. The agreement specifies all significant terms, including the quantity to be exchanged, the fixed price, and the timing of the transaction. The fixed price may be expressed as a specified amount of an entity's functional currency or of a foreign currency. It may also be expressed as a specified interest rate or specified effective yield.

b. The agreement includes a disincentive for nonperformance that is sufficiently large to make performance probable.

Forecasted transaction

A transaction that is expected to occur for which there is no firm commitment. Because no transaction or event has yet occurred and the transaction or event when it occurs will be at the prevailing market price, a forecasted transaction does not give an entity any present rights to future benefits or a present obligation for future sacrifices.

LIBOR swap rate

The fixed rate on a single-currency, constant-notional interest rate swap that has its floating-rate leg referenced to the London Interbank Offered Rate (LIBOR) with no additional spread over LIBOR on that floating-rate leg. That fixed rate is the derived rate that would result in the swap having a zero fair value at inception because the present value of fixed cash flows, based on that rate, equate to the present value of the floating cash flows.

Notional amount

A number of currency units, shares, bushels, pounds, or other units specified in a derivative instrument.

Underlying

A specified interest rate, security price, commodity price, foreign exchange rate, index of prices or rates, or other variable. An underlying may be a price or rate of an asset or liability but is not the asset or liability itself.

Contractual obligations encompass both those that are conditioned on the occurrence of a specified event and those that are not. All contractual obligations that are financial instruments meet the definition of *liability* set forth in Concepts Statement 6, although some may not be recognized as liabilities in financial statements—may be "off-balance-sheet"—because they fail to meet some other criterion for recognition. For some financial instruments, the obligation is owed to or by a group of entities rather than a single entity.

[†]The use of the term *financial instrument* in this definition is recursive (because the term *financial instrument* is included in it), though it is not circular. The definition requires a chain of contractual obligations that ends with the delivery of cash or an ownership interest in an entity. Any number of obligations to deliver financial instruments can be links in a chain that qualifies a particular contract as a financial instrument.

[‡]*Contractual rights* encompass both those that are conditioned on the occurrence of a specified event and those that are not. All contractual rights that are financial instruments meet the definition of *asset* set forth in Concepts Statement 6, although some may not be recognized as assets in financial statements—may be "off-balance-sheet"—because they fail to meet some other criterion for recognition. For some financial instruments, the right is held by or the obligation is due from a group of entities rather than a single entity.

Statement of Financial Accounting Standards No. 139
Rescission of FASB Statement No. 53 and amendments to FASB Statements No. 63, 89, and 121

STATUS

Issued: June 2000

Effective Date: For financial statements for fiscal years beginning after December 15, 2000

Affects: Supersedes FAS 53
  Amends FAS 63, paragraph 1
  Amends FAS 63 by adding paragraph 1A after paragraph 1
  Amends FAS 89, paragraph 44
  Amends FAS 121, paragraphs 3(b) and 147

Affected by: No other pronouncements

SUMMARY

This Statement rescinds FASB Statement No. 53, *Financial Reporting by Producers and Distributors of Motion Picture Films.* An entity that previously was subject to the requirements of Statement 53 shall follow the guidance in AICPA Statement of Position 00-2, *Accounting by Producers or Distributors of Films.* This Statement also amends FASB Statements No. 63, *Financial Reporting by Broadcasters,* No. 89, *Financial Reporting and Changing Prices,* and No. 121, *Accounting for the Impairment of Long-Lived Assets and for Long-Lived Assets to Be Disposed Of.*

This Statement is effective for financial statements for fiscal years beginning after December 15, 2000. Earlier application is permitted only upon early adoption of the Statement of Position.

Statement of Financial Accounting Standards No. 139

Rescission of FASB Statement No. 53 and amendments to FASB Statements No. 63, 89, and 121

CONTENTS

INTRODUCTION

1. FASB Statement No. 53, *Financial Reporting by Producers and Distributors of Motion Picture Films,* was issued in 1981. Statement 53 extracted specialized accounting and reporting principles and practices from the AICPA Industry Accounting Guide, *Accounting for Motion Picture Films,* and AICPA Statement of Position 79-4, *Accounting for Motion Picture Films.* It also established financial accounting and reporting standards for producers or distributors of motion picture films.

2. Since the issuance of Statement 53, extensive changes have occurred in the film industry. Through 1981, the majority of a film's revenue resulted from distribution to movie theaters and free television. Since that time, numerous additional forms of exploitation (such as home video, satellite and cable television, and pay-per-view television) have come into existence, and international revenue has increased in significance. Concurrent with those changes, significant variations in the application of Statement 53 arose.

3. In 1995, in response to concerns raised by constituents, the Board asked the Accounting Standards Executive Committee (AcSEC) of the AICPA to develop a Statement of Position providing guidance on the accounting and reporting requirements for producers or distributors of motion picture films. In response to that request, AcSEC developed AICPA Statement of Position 00-2, *Accounting by Producers or Distributors of Films.* An entity that is a producer

or distributor of films and that previously applied Statement 53 is now required to follow the guidance in SOP 00-2. This Statement and SOP 00-2 are effective for fiscal years beginning after December 15, 2000.

STANDARDS OF FINANCIAL ACCOUNTING AND REPORTING

Rescission of Statement 53

4. This Statement rescinds FASB Statement No. 53, *Financial Reporting by Producers and Distributors of Motion Picture Films.*

Amendments to Existing Pronouncements

5. FASB Statement No. 63, *Financial Reporting by Broadcasters,* is amended as follows:

a. The following is inserted before the last sentence of paragraph 1:

> In June 2000, AICPA Statement of Position 00-2, *Accounting by Producers or Distributors of Films,* was issued and is applicable to all producers or distributors that own or hold rights to distribute or exploit films.

b. The following paragraph is added after the caption *Standards of Financial Accounting and Reporting* and before the caption *License Agreements for Program Material:*

A broadcaster shall apply the guidance in SOP 00-2 if it owns the film (program material) that is shown on its cable, network, or local television outlets.

6. In paragraph 44 of FASB Statement No. 89, *Financial Reporting and Changing Prices,* the definition of *motion picture films* is replaced by the following:

All types of film, including feature films, television specials, television series, or similar products (including animated films and television programming) that are sold, licensed, or exhibited, whether produced on film, video tape, digital, or other video recording format.

7. FASB Statement No. 121, *Accounting for the Impairment of Long-Lived Assets and for Long-Lived Assets to Be Disposed Of,* is amended as follows:

a. Paragraph 3(b) is replaced by *AICPA Statement of Position 00-2, Accounting by Producers or Distributors of Films.*

b. In the table following paragraph 147, the reference to Statement 53 is deleted and the following is added to the table.

FASB Statement No. 139, *Rescission of FASB Statement 53 and amendments to FASB Statements No. 63, 89, and 121**

---

*In June 2000, AICPA Statement of Position 00-2, *Accounting by Producers or Distributors of Films,* was issued. Motion picture films are subject to the impairment guidance in paragraphs 43–47 of SOP 00-2.

EFFECTIVE DATE AND TRANSITION

8. This Statement shall be effective for financial statements for fiscal years beginning after December 15, 2000. Earlier application is permitted only upon early adoption of SOP 00-2.

The provisions of this Statement need not be applied to immaterial items.

This Statement was adopted by the unanimous vote of the seven members of the Financial Accounting Standards Board:

Edmund L. Jenkins,	John M. Foster	Gerhard G. Mueller
Chairman	Gaylen N. Larson	Edward W. Trott
Anthony T. Cope	James J. Leisenring	

Appendix

BACKGROUND INFORMATION AND BASIS FOR CONCLUSIONS

9. This appendix summarizes considerations that Board members deemed significant in reaching the conclusions in this Statement.

10. Statement 53 was issued in December 1981 as part of the process of extracting specialized accounting and reporting principles and practices from AICPA Statements of Position and Guides on accounting and auditing matters and issuing them in FASB Statements after appropriate due process. Statement 53 established the financial accounting

and reporting standards for producers or distributors of motion picture films.

11. The Entertainment and Sports Industry Committee of the California Society of Certified Public Accountants (the Committee) submitted a letter dated September 15, 1994, to the FASB requesting that the Board reconsider certain provisions of Statement 53. The Committee's letter included a White Paper containing the recommendations of the Committee's FAS 53 Task Force to revise Statement 53. The Committee's request was endorsed by AcSEC in a letter dated September 27, 1994, to the FASB.

12. According to the September 15, 1994 letter, the Committee formed the FAS 53 Task Force because of concerns relating to the following issues:

a. Statement 53 did not address the extensive changes that have occurred in the industry since its issuance. When Statement 53 was issued, most of a film's revenue came from distribution to U.S. movie theaters. At present, the industry has additional forms of distribution (videocassettes, satellite and cable television, CD-ROM, laser and digital video discs [DVD], and pay-per-view television, plus licensing revenues from products tied to the film) that did not exist or were not significant when Statement 53 was issued. The industry now also distributes to new emerging international markets (for example, eastern Europe and China).

b. Application of Statement 53 varied significantly within the industry.

c. The validity and accuracy of financial statements issued by companies in the motion picture industry were questioned after certain business failures.

13. In response to those concerns, the Board requested in July 1995 that AcSEC undertake a project to reconsider the accounting and financial reporting for the motion picture industry. The Board considered adding the project to its own agenda because certain Board members at that time believed that "maintenance" of an FASB Statement was the Board's responsibility. However, the Board ultimately decided that AcSEC was better suited to address the needs of that specific industry. The Board indicated that it would either amend or rescind Statement 53 depending on the outcome of AcSEC's project.

14. The Board concluded that it should rescind Statement 53 based on the results of the AcSEC project to develop guidance on the accounting and financial reporting requirements for producers or distributors of motion picture films. The Board believes that (a) there is a need for the guidance, (b) the guidance will improve practice, and (c) the benefits will exceed the cost of implementation.

Comments on Exposure Drafts

15. The FASB Exposure Draft, *Rescission of FASB Statement No. 53,* and the Exposure Draft of the proposed AICPA Statement of Position, *Accounting by Producers and Distributors of Films,* were issued for comment on October 16, 1998. Twenty-eight organizations commented on those Exposure Drafts. The notice to respondents of the proposed SOP indicated that it was only necessary to send one letter to the AICPA commenting on both of the Exposure Drafts. However, 10 of those 28 organizations sent separate letters to the FASB, and those additional letters were primarily from respondents that did not support the issuance of the proposed SOP. As a result, many of those letters did not support the Board's rescinding Statement 53. The basis for conclusions in SOP 00-2 discusses AcSEC's resolution of matters raised in the comment letters. The Board held two public meetings with representatives of AcSEC and reviewed the issues raised in the comment letters. The Board believes that AcSEC responded to those issues in an acceptable manner.

Amendment of Statement 63

16. The Board decided to amend FASB Statement No. 63, *Financial Reporting by Broadcasters,* to clarify that the requirements of SOP 00-2 apply to a film owned by a broadcaster. Previously, Statement 63 only addressed licensing agreements.

Statement of Financial Accounting Standards No. 140
Accounting for Transfers and Servicing of Financial Assets and Extinguishments of Liabilities

a replacement of FASB Statement No. 125

STATUS

Issued: September 2000

Effective Date: For transfers and servicing of financial assets and extinguishments of liabilities occurring after March 31, 2001 and for disclosures relating to securitization transactions and collateral for fiscal years after December 15, 2000

Affects: Supersedes APB 26, paragraph 3(a)
Supersedes FAS 13, paragraph 20
Amends FAS 22, footnote 1
Amends FAS 65, paragraphs 1, 9(a), 10, 15, 34
Supersedes FAS 65, paragraphs 8, 11, 16 through 19, 30, and the paragraphs added after paragraph 30 by FAS 122 and footnotes 4 and 6
Supersedes FAS 76
Supersedes FAS 77
Amends FAS 107, paragraph 28
Supersedes FAS 107, paragraph 8(b)
Amends FAS 115, paragraph 7
Supersedes FAS 122
Supersedes FAS 125
Supersedes FAS 127
Amends FAS 133, paragraphs 10(f), 56, 59(e), and footnote 9
Amends FAS 136, footnote 5
Amends FIN 43, footnote 2
Supersedes FTB 84-4
Supersedes FTB 85-2
Supersedes FTB 86-2, paragraph 12
Supersedes FTB 87-3, paragraphs 1 through 7 and 9

Affected by: Paragraph 19 amended by FTB 01-1
Paragraph 24 superseded by FTB 01-1

Other Interpretive Pronouncement: FTB 01-1

Other Interpretive Release: FASB Special Report, *A Guide to Implementation of Statement 140 on Accounting for Transfers and Servicing of Financial Assets and Extinguishments of Liabilities: Questions and Answers*

Issues Discussed by FASB Emerging Issues Task Force (EITF)

Affects: Nullifies EITF Issues No. 86-24, 86-39, 90-2, 94-9, 96-20, and 97-6 and Topics No. D-13, D-48, and D-75
Partially nullifies EITF Issues No. 84-5, 85-25, 85-40, 86-38, 87-30, 88-17, 88-20, 88-22, 89-2, 89-4, 92-2, and 96-10
Resolves EITF Issues No. 84-21, 84-26, 85-26, 85-30, 85-34, 87-25, and 94-4 and Topic No. D-67
Partially resolves EITF Issues No. 84-20, 84-30, 87-18, 87-20, 87-30, 88-11, and 92-2 and Topic No. D-14

Interpreted by: Paragraph 9 interpreted by EITF Topics No. D-51, D-65, and D-99
               Paragraph 9(a) interpreted by EITF Topic No. D-94
               Paragraph 10 interpreted by EITF Issue No. 98-15
               Paragraph 11 interpreted by EITF Topic No. D-69
               Paragraph 16 interpreted by EITF Issues No. 96-19 and 98-14
               Paragraph 17 interpreted by EITF Topic No. D-65
               Paragraph 17(e)(2) interpreted by EITF Topic No. D-69
               Paragraphs 24, 27, and 28 interpreted by EITF Topic No. D-94
               Paragraphs 35, 37, and 41 through 44 interpreted by EITF Topic No. D-99
               Paragraphs 47 and 49 interpreted by EITF Topic No. D-65
               Paragraph 61 interpreted by EITF Topic No. D-99
               Paragraph 69 interpreted by EITF Topic No. D-69
               Paragraphs 80 through 84 interpreted by EITF Topic No. D-94

Related Issues: EITF Issues No. 84-15, 85-13, 86-8, 86-36, 87-34, 88-18, 90-18, 90-19, 90-21, 95-5, 97-3, 97-14, 98-8, 98-12, 99-8, 00-9, 00-17, 01-2, and 02-2 and Topics No. D-63 and D-66

SUMMARY

This Statement replaces FASB Statement No. 125, *Accounting for Transfers and Servicing of Financial Assets and Extinguishments of Liabilities*. It revises the standards for accounting for securitizations and other transfers of financial assets and collateral and requires certain disclosures, but it carries over most of Statement 125's provisions without reconsideration.

This Statement provides accounting and reporting standards for transfers and servicing of financial assets and extinguishments of liabilities. Those standards are based on consistent application of a *financial-components approach* that focuses on control. Under that approach, after a transfer of financial assets, an entity recognizes the financial and servicing assets it controls and the liabilities it has incurred, derecognizes financial assets when control has been surrendered, and derecognizes liabilities when extinguished. This Statement provides consistent standards for distinguishing transfers of financial assets that are sales from transfers that are secured borrowings.

A transfer of financial assets in which the transferor surrenders control over those assets is accounted for as a sale to the extent that consideration other than beneficial interests in the transferred assets is received in exchange. The transferor has surrendered control over transferred assets if and only if all of the following conditions are met:

a. The transferred assets have been isolated from the transferor—put presumptively beyond the reach of the transferor and its creditors, even in bankruptcy or other receivership.
b. Each transferee (or, if the transferee is a qualifying special-purpose entity (SPE), each holder of its beneficial interests) has the right to pledge or exchange the assets (or beneficial interests) it received, and no condition both constrains the transferee (or holder) from taking advantage of its right to pledge or exchange and provides more than a trivial benefit to the transferor.
c. The transferor does not maintain effective control over the transferred assets through either (1) an agreement that both entitles and obligates the transferor to repurchase or redeem them before their maturity or (2) the ability to unilaterally cause the holder to return specific assets, other than through a cleanup call.

This Statement requires that liabilities and derivatives incurred or obtained by transferors as part of a transfer of financial assets be initially measured at fair value, if practicable. It also requires that servicing assets and other retained interests in the transferred assets be measured by allocating the previous carrying amount between the assets sold, if any, and retained interests, if any, based on their relative fair values at the date of the transfer.

This Statement requires that servicing assets and liabilities be subsequently measured by (a) amortization in proportion to and over the period of estimated net servicing income or loss and (b) assessment for asset impairment or increased obligation based on their fair values.

This Statement requires that a liability be derecognized if and only if either (a) the debtor pays the creditor and is relieved of its obligation for the liability or (b) the debtor is legally released from being the primary obligor under the liability either judicially or by the creditor. Therefore, a liability is not considered extinguished by an in-substance defeasance.

This Statement provides implementation guidance for assessing isolation of transferred assets, conditions that constrain a transferee, conditions for an entity to be a qualifying SPE, accounting for transfers of partial interests, measurement of retained interests, servicing of financial assets, securitizations, transfers of sales-type and direct financing lease receivables, securities lending transactions, repurchase agreements including "dollar rolls," "wash sales," loan syndications and participations, risk participations in banker's acceptances, factoring arrangements, transfers of receivables with recourse, and extinguishments of liabilities. This Statement also provides guidance about whether a transferor has retained effective control over assets transferred to qualifying SPEs through removal-of-accounts provisions, liquidation provisions, or other arrangements.

This Statement requires a debtor to (a) reclassify financial assets pledged as collateral and report those assets in its statement of financial position separately from other assets not so encumbered if the secured party has the right by contract or custom to sell or repledge the collateral and (b) disclose assets pledged as collateral that have not been reclassified and separately reported in the statement of financial position. This Statement also requires a secured party to disclose information about collateral that it has accepted and is permitted by contract or custom to sell or repledge. The required disclosure includes the fair value at the end of the period of that collateral, and of the portion of that collateral that it has sold or repledged, and information about the sources and uses of that collateral.

This Statement requires an entity that has securitized financial assets to disclose information about accounting policies, volume, cash flows, key assumptions made in determining fair values of retained interests, and sensitivity of those fair values to changes in key assumptions. It also requires that entities that securitize assets disclose for the securitized assets and any other financial assets it manages together with them (a) the total principal amount outstanding, the portion that has been derecognized, and the portion that continues to be recognized in each category reported in the statement of financial position, at the end of the period; (b) delinquencies at the end of the period; and (c) credit losses during the period.

In addition to replacing Statement 125 and rescinding FASB Statement No. 127, *Deferral of the Effective Date of Certain Provisions of FASB Statement No. 125,* this Statement carries forward the actions taken by Statement 125. Statement 125 superseded FASB Statements No. 76, *Extinguishment of Debt,* and No. 77, *Reporting by Transferors for Transfers of Receivables with Recourse.* Statement 125 amended FASB Statement No. 115, *Accounting for Certain Investments in Debt and Equity Securities,* to clarify that a debt security may not be classified as held-to-maturity if it can be prepaid or otherwise settled in such a way that the holder of the security would not recover substantially all of its recorded investment. Statement 125 amended and extended to all servicing assets and liabilities the accounting standards for mortgage servicing rights now in FASB Statement No. 65, *Accounting for Certain Mortgage Banking Activities,* and superseded FASB Statement No. 122, *Accounting for Mortgage Servicing Rights.* Statement 125 also superseded FASB Technical Bulletins No. 84-4, *In-Substance Defeasance of Debt,* and No. 85-2, *Accounting for Collateralized Mortgage Obligations (CMOs),* and amended FASB Technical Bulletin No. 87-3, *Accounting for Mortgage Servicing Fees and Rights.*

Statement 125 was effective for transfers and servicing of financial assets and extinguishments of liabilities occurring after December 31, 1996, and on or before March 31, 2001, except for certain provisions. Statement 127 deferred until December 31, 1997, the effective date (a) of paragraph 15 of Statement 125 and (b) for repurchase agreement, dollar-roll, securities lending, and similar transactions, of paragraphs 9–12 and 237(b) of Statement 125.

This Statement is effective for transfers and servicing of financial assets and extinguishments of liabilities occurring after March 31, 2001. This Statement is effective for recognition and reclassification of collateral and for disclosures relating to securitization transactions and collateral for fiscal years ending after December 15, 2000. Disclosures about securitization and collateral accepted need not be reported for periods ending on or before December 15, 2000, for which financial statements are presented for comparative purposes.

This Statement is to be applied prospectively with certain exceptions. Other than those exceptions, earlier or retroactive application of its accounting provisions is not permitted.

Statement of Financial Accounting Standards No. 140

Accounting for Transfers and Servicing of Financial Assets and Extinguishments of Liabilities

a replacement of FASB Statement No. 125

CONTENTS

INTRODUCTION AND SCOPE

1. The Board added a project on financial instruments and off-balance-sheet financing to its agenda in May 1986. The project is intended to develop standards to aid in resolving existing financial accounting and reporting issues and other issues likely to arise in the future about various financial instruments and related transactions. The November 1991 FASB Discussion Memorandum, *Recognition and Measurement of Financial Instruments,* describes the issues to be considered. This Statement focuses on the issues of accounting for **transfers**[1] and servicing of **financial assets** and extinguishments of liabilities.

2. Transfers of financial assets take many forms. Accounting for transfers in which the **transferor** has no continuing involvement with the transferred assets or with the **transferee** has not been controversial. However, transfers of financial assets often occur in which the transferor has some continuing involvement either with the assets transferred or with the transferee. Examples of continuing involvement are **recourse,** servicing, agreements to reacquire, options written or held, and pledges of **collateral.** Transfers of financial assets with continuing involvement raise issues about the circumstances under which the transfers should be considered as sales of all or part of the assets or as secured borrowings and about how transferors and transferees should account for sales and secured borrowings. This Statement establishes standards for resolving those issues.

3. An entity may settle a liability by transferring assets to the creditor or otherwise obtaining an unconditional release. Alternatively, an entity may enter into other arrangements designed to set aside assets dedicated to eventually settling a liability. Accounting for those arrangements has raised issues about when a liability should be considered extinguished. This Statement establishes standards for resolving those issues.

---

[1] Terms defined in Appendix E, the glossary, are set in **boldface type** the first time they appear.

4. This Statement does not address transfers of custody of financial assets for safekeeping, contributions,[2] transfers of ownership interests that are in substance sales of real estate, exchanges of equity method investments for similar productive assets, or investments by owners or distributions to owners of a business enterprise. This Statement does not address subsequent measurement of assets and liabilities, except for (a) **servicing assets** and **servicing liabilities** and (b) **interest-only strips,** securities, retained interests in securitizations, loans, other receivables, or other financial assets that can contractually be prepaid or otherwise settled in such a way that the holder would not recover substantially all of its recorded investment and that are not within the scope of FASB Statement No. 133, *Accounting for Derivative Instruments and Hedging Activities.* This Statement does not change the accounting for employee benefits subject to the provisions of FASB Statement No. 87, *Employers' Accounting for Pensions,* No. 88, *Employers' Accounting for Settlements and Curtailments of Defined Benefit Pension Plans and for Termination Benefits,* or No. 106, *Employers' Accounting for Postretirement Benefits Other Than Pensions.* This Statement does not change the provisions relating to leveraged leases in FASB Statement No. 13, *Accounting for Leases,* or money-over-money and wrap lease transactions involving nonrecourse debt subject to the provisions of FASB Technical Bulletin No. 88-1, *Issues Relating to Accounting for Leases.* This Statement does not address transfers of nonfinancial assets, for example, servicing assets, or transfers of unrecognized financial assets, for example, minimum lease payments to be received under operating leases.

5. The Board concluded that an objective in accounting for transfers of financial assets is for each entity that is a party to the transaction to recognize only assets it controls and liabilities it has incurred, to **derecognize** assets only when control has been surrendered, and to derecognize liabilities only when they have been extinguished. Sales and other transfers frequently result in a disaggregation of financial assets and liabilities into components, which become separate assets and liabilities. For example, if an entity sells a portion of a financial asset it owns, the portion retained becomes an asset separate from the portion sold and from the assets obtained in exchange.

6. The Board concluded that another objective is that recognition of financial assets and liabilities should not be affected by the sequence of transactions that result in their acquisition or incurrence unless the effect of those transactions is to maintain effective control over a transferred financial asset. For example, if a transferor sells financial assets it owns and at the same time writes an "at-the-money" put option (such as a guarantee or recourse obligation) on those assets, it should recognize the put obligation in the same manner as would another unrelated entity that writes an identical put option on assets it never owned. Similarly, a creditor may release a debtor on the condition that a third party assumes the obligation and that the original debtor becomes secondarily liable. In those circumstances, the original debtor becomes a guarantor and should recognize a guarantee obligation in the same manner as would a third-party guarantor that had never been primarily liable to that creditor, whether or not explicit consideration was paid for that guarantee. However, certain agreements to repurchase or redeem transferred assets maintain effective control over those assets and should therefore be accounted for differently than agreements to acquire assets never owned.

7. Before FASB Statement No. 125, *Accounting for Transfers and Servicing of Financial Assets and Extinguishments of Liabilities,* accounting standards generally required that a transferor account for financial assets transferred as an inseparable unit that had been either entirely sold or entirely retained. Those standards were difficult to apply and produced inconsistent and arbitrary results. For example, whether a transfer "purported to be a sale" was sufficient to determine whether the transfer was accounted for and reported as a sale of receivables under one accounting standard or as a secured borrowing under another. After studying many of the complex developments that have occurred in financial markets during recent years, the Board concluded that previous approaches that viewed each financial asset as an indivisible unit do not provide an appropriate basis for developing consistent and operational standards for dealing with transfers and servicing of financial assets and extinguishments of liabilities. To address those issues adequately and consistently, the Board decided to adopt as the basis for this Statement a *financial-components approach* that focuses on control and recognizes that

---

[2]Contributions—unconditional nonreciprocal transfers of assets—are addressed in FASB Statement No. 116, *Accounting for Contributions Received and Contributions Made.*

financial assets and liabilities can be divided into a variety of components.

8. The Board issued Statement 125 in June 1996. After the issuance of that Statement, several parties called for reconsideration or clarification of certain provisions. Matters the Board was asked to reconsider or clarify included:

a. Circumstances in which a special-purpose entity (SPE) can be considered qualifying
b. Circumstances in which the assets held by a qualifying SPE should appear in the consolidated financial statements of the transferor
c. Whether sale accounting is precluded if the transferor holds a right to repurchase transferred assets that is attached to, is embedded in, or is otherwise transferable with the financial assets
d. Circumstances in which sale accounting is precluded if transferred financial assets can be removed from an SPE by the transferor (for example, under a removal-of-accounts provision (ROAP))
e. Whether arrangements that obligate, but do not entitle, a transferor to repurchase or redeem transferred financial assets should affect the accounting for those transfers
f. The impact of the powers of the Federal Deposit Insurance Corporation (FDIC) on isolation of assets transferred by financial institutions
g. Whether transfers of financial assets measured using the equity method of accounting should continue to be included in the scope of Statement 125
h. Whether disclosures should be enhanced to provide more information about assumptions used to determine the fair value of retained interests and the gain or loss on financial assets sold in securitizations
i. The accounting for and disclosure about collateral that can be sold or repledged.

The Board concluded that those requests to reconsider certain provisions of Statement 125 were appropriate and added a project to amend Statement 125 to its agenda in March 1997. This Statement is the result. To present the amended accounting standards for transfers of financial assets more clearly, this Statement replaces Statement 125. However, most of the provisions of Statement 125 have been carried forward without reconsideration.

STANDARDS OF FINANCIAL ACCOUNTING AND REPORTING

Accounting for Transfers and Servicing of Financial Assets

9. A transfer of financial assets (or all or a portion of a financial asset) in which the transferor surrenders control over those financial assets shall be accounted for as a sale to the extent that consideration other than **beneficial interests** in the transferred assets is received in exchange. The transferor has surrendered control over transferred assets if and only if *all of the following conditions* are met:

a. The transferred assets have been isolated from the transferor—put presumptively beyond the reach of the transferor and its creditors, even in bankruptcy or other receivership (paragraphs 27 and 28).
b. Each transferee (or, if the transferee is a qualifying SPE (paragraph 35), each holder of its beneficial interests) has the right to pledge or exchange the assets (or beneficial interests) it received, and no condition both constrains the transferee (or holder) from taking advantage of its right to pledge or exchange and provides more than a trivial benefit to the transferor (paragraphs 29–34).
c. The transferor does not maintain effective control over the transferred assets through either (1) an agreement that both entitles and obligates the transferor to repurchase or redeem them before their maturity (paragraphs 47–49) or (2) the ability to unilaterally cause the holder to return specific assets, other than through a **cleanup call** (paragraphs 50–54).

10. Upon completion of any transfer of financial assets, the transferor shall:

a. Continue to carry in its statement of financial position any retained interest in the transferred assets, including, if applicable, servicing assets (paragraphs 61–67), beneficial interests in assets transferred to a qualifying SPE in a **securitization** (paragraphs 73–84), and retained **undivided interests** (paragraphs 58 and 59)
b. Allocate the previous carrying amount between the assets sold, if any, and the retained interests, if any, based on their relative **fair values** at the date of transfer (paragraphs 56–60).

Accounting for Transfers and Servicing of
Financial Assets and Extinguishments of Liabilities
FAS140

11. Upon completion[3] of a transfer of assets that satisfies the conditions to be accounted for as a sale (paragraph 9), the transferor (**seller**) shall:

a. Derecognize all assets sold
b. Recognize all assets obtained and liabilities incurred in consideration as **proceeds** of the sale, including cash, put or call options held or written (for example, guarantee or recourse obligations), forward commitments (for example, commitments to deliver additional receivables during the revolving periods of some securitizations), swaps (for example, provisions that convert interest rates from fixed to variable), and servicing liabilities, if applicable (paragraphs 56, 57, and 61–67)
c. Initially measure at fair value assets obtained and liabilities incurred in a sale (paragraphs 68–70) or, if it is not practicable to estimate the fair value of an asset or a liability, apply alternative measures (paragraphs 71 and 72)
d. Recognize in earnings any gain or loss on the sale.

The transferee shall recognize all assets obtained and any liabilities incurred and initially measure them at fair value (in aggregate, presumptively the price paid).

12. If a transfer of financial assets in exchange for cash or other consideration (other than beneficial interests in the transferred assets) does not meet the criteria for a sale in paragraph 9, the transferor and transferee shall account for the transfer as a secured borrowing with pledge of collateral (paragraph 15).

Recognition and Measurement of Servicing Assets and Liabilities

13. Each time an entity undertakes an obligation to service financial assets it shall recognize either a servicing asset or a servicing liability for that servicing contract, unless it transfers the assets to a qualifying SPE in a **guaranteed mortgage securitization,** retains all of the resulting securities, and classifies them as debt securities held-to-maturity in accordance with FASB Statement No. 115, *Accounting for Certain Investments in Debt and Equity Securities.* If the servicing asset or liability was purchased or assumed rather than undertaken in a sale or

securitization of the financial assets being serviced, it shall be measured initially at its fair value, presumptively the price paid. A servicing asset or liability shall be amortized in proportion to and over the period of estimated net servicing income (if servicing revenues exceed servicing costs) or net servicing loss (if servicing costs exceed servicing revenues). A servicing asset or liability shall be assessed for impairment or increased obligation based on its fair value (paragraphs 61–64).

Financial Assets Subject to Prepayment

14. Interest-only strips, retained interests in securitizations, loans, other receivables, or other financial assets that can contractually be prepaid or otherwise settled in such a way that the holder would not recover substantially all of its recorded investment, except for instruments that are within the scope of Statement 133, shall be subsequently measured like investments in debt securities classified as available-for-sale or trading under Statement 115, as amended (paragraph 362).

Secured Borrowings and Collateral

15. A debtor may grant a **security interest** in certain assets to a lender (the secured party) to serve as collateral for its obligation under a borrowing, with or without recourse to other assets of the debtor. An obligor under other kinds of current or potential obligations, for example, interest rate swaps, also may grant a security interest in certain assets to a secured party. If collateral is transferred to the secured party, the custodial arrangement is commonly referred to as a pledge. Secured parties sometimes are permitted to sell or repledge (or otherwise transfer) collateral held under a pledge. The same relationships occur, under different names, in transfers documented as sales that are accounted for as secured borrowings (paragraph 12). The accounting for noncash[4] collateral by the debtor (or obligor) and the secured party depends on whether the secured party has the right to sell or repledge the collateral and on whether the debtor has defaulted.

a. If the secured party (transferee) has the right by contract or custom to sell or repledge the collateral, then the debtor (transferor) shall reclassify

---

[3]Although a transfer of securities may not be considered to have reached completion until the settlement date, this Statement does not modify other generally accepted accounting principles, including FASB Statement No. 35, *Accounting and Reporting by Defined Benefit Pension Plans,* and AICPA Statements of Position and audit and accounting Guides for certain industries, that require accounting at the trade date for certain contracts to purchase or sell securities.

[4]Cash "collateral," sometimes used, for example, in securities lending transactions (paragraphs 91–95), shall be derecognized by the payer and recognized by the recipient, not as collateral, but rather as proceeds of either a sale or a borrowing.

that asset and report that asset in its statement of financial position separately (for example, as security pledged to creditors) from other assets not so encumbered.

b. If the secured party (transferee) sells collateral pledged to it, it shall recognize the proceeds from the sale and its obligation to return the collateral. The sale of the collateral is a transfer subject to the provisions of this Statement.

c. If the debtor (transferor) defaults under the terms of the secured contract and is no longer entitled to redeem the pledged asset, it shall derecognize the pledged asset, and the secured party (transferee) shall recognize the collateral as its asset initially measured at fair value or, if it has already sold the collateral, derecognize its obligation to return the collateral.

d. Except as provided in paragraph 15(c), the debtor (transferor) shall continue to carry the collateral as its asset, and the secured party (transferee) shall not recognize the pledged asset.

Extinguishments of Liabilities

16. A debtor shall derecognize a liability if and only if it has been extinguished. A liability has been extinguished if either of the following conditions is met:

a. The debtor pays the creditor and is relieved of its obligation for the liability. Paying the creditor includes delivery of cash, other financial assets, goods, or services or reacquisition by the debtor of its outstanding debt securities whether the securities are canceled or held as so-called treasury bonds.

b. The debtor is legally released[5] from being the primary obligor under the liability, either judicially or by the creditor.

Disclosures

17. An entity shall disclose the following:

a. For collateral:
  (1) If the entity has entered into repurchase agreements or securities lending transactions, its policy for requiring collateral or other security
  (2) If the entity has pledged any of its assets as collateral that are not reclassified and separately reported in the statement of financial

position pursuant to paragraph 15(a), the carrying amount and classification of those assets as of the date of the latest statement of financial position presented
  (3) If the entity has accepted collateral that it is permitted by contract or custom to sell or repledge, the fair value as of the date of each statement of financial position presented of that collateral and of the portion of that collateral that it has sold or repledged, and information about the sources and uses of that collateral

b. If debt was considered to be extinguished by in-substance defeasance under the provisions of FASB Statement No. 76, *Extinguishment of Debt,* prior to the effective date of Statement 125,[6] a general description of the transaction and the amount of debt that is considered extinguished at the end of the period so long as that debt remains outstanding

c. If assets are set aside after the effective date of Statement 125 solely for satisfying scheduled payments of a specific obligation, a description of the nature of restrictions placed on those assets

d. If it is not practicable to estimate the fair value of certain assets obtained or liabilities incurred in transfers of financial assets during the period, a description of those items and the reasons why it is not practicable to estimate their fair value

e. For all servicing assets and servicing liabilities:
  (1) The amounts of servicing assets or liabilities recognized and amortized during the period
  (2) The fair value of recognized servicing assets and liabilities for which it is practicable to estimate that value and the method and significant assumptions used to estimate the fair value
  (3) The risk characteristics of the underlying financial assets used to stratify recognized servicing assets for purposes of measuring impairment in accordance with paragraph 63
  (4) The activity in any valuation allowance for impairment of recognized servicing assets—including beginning and ending balances, aggregate additions charged and reductions credited to operations, and aggregate direct write-downs charged against the allow-

---

[5]If nonrecourse debt (such as certain mortgage loans) is assumed by a third party in conjunction with the sale of an asset that serves as sole collateral for that debt, the sale and related assumption effectively accomplish a legal release of the seller-debtor for purposes of applying this Statement.

[6]Refer to footnote 11 to paragraph 19.

Accounting for Transfers and Servicing of
Financial Assets and Extinguishments of Liabilities
FAS140

ances—for each period for which results of operations are presented.

f. If the entity has securitized financial assets during any period presented and accounts for that transfer as a sale, for each major asset type (for example, mortgage loans, credit card receivables, and automobile loans):

  (1) Its accounting policies for initially measuring the retained interests, if any, including the methodology (whether quoted market price, prices based on sales of similar assets and liabilities, or prices based on valuation techniques) used in determining their fair value (paragraphs 68–70)

  (2) The characteristics of securitizations (a description of the transferor's continuing involvement with the transferred assets, including, but not limited to, servicing, recourse, and restrictions on retained interests) and the gain or loss from sale of financial assets in securitizations

  (3) The key assumptions[7] used in measuring the fair value of retained interests at the time of securitization (including, at a minimum, quantitative information about discount rates, expected prepayments including the expected weighted-average life of prepayable financial assets,[8] and anticipated credit losses, if applicable)

  (4) Cash flows between the securitization SPE and the transferor, unless reported separately elsewhere in the financial statements or notes (including proceeds from new securitizations, proceeds from collections reinvested in revolving-period securitizations, purchases of delinquent or foreclosed loans, servicing fees, and cash flows received on interests retained)

g. If the entity has retained interests in securitized financial assets at the date of the latest statement of financial position presented, for each major asset type (for example, mortgage loans, credit card receivables, and automobile loans):

  (1) Its accounting policies for subsequently measuring those retained interests, including the methodology (whether quoted market price, prices based on sales of similar assets

and liabilities, or prices based on valuation techniques) used in determining their fair value (paragraphs 68–70)

  (2) The key assumptions used in subsequently measuring the fair value of those interests (including, at a minimum, quantitative information about discount rates, expected prepayments including the expected weighted-average life of prepayable financial assets, and anticipated credit losses, including expected static pool losses,[9] if applicable)

  (3) A sensitivity analysis or stress test showing the hypothetical effect on the fair value of those interests of two or more unfavorable variations from the expected levels for each key assumption that is reported under (2) above independently from any change in another key assumption, and a description of the objectives, methodology, and limitations of the sensitivity analysis or stress test

  (4) For the securitized assets and any other financial assets that it manages together with them:[10]

    (a) The total principal amount outstanding, the portion that has been derecognized, and the portion that continues to be recognized in each category reported in the statement of financial position, at the end of the period

    (b) Delinquencies at the end of the period

    (c) Credit losses, net of recoveries, during the period

    Disclosure of average balances during the period is encouraged, but not required.

Implementation Guidance

18. Appendix A describes certain provisions of this Statement in more detail and describes their application to certain types of transactions. Appendix A is an integral part of the standards provided in this Statement.

Effective Date and Transition

19. Except as provided in paragraphs 20–25, this Statement shall be effective for transfers and servicing of financial assets and extinguishments

---

[7]If an entity has made multiple securitizations of the same major asset type during a period, it may disclose the range of assumptions.

[8]The weighted-average life of prepayable assets in periods (for example, months or years) can be calculated by multiplying the principal collections expected in each future period by the number of periods until that future period, summing those products, and dividing the sum by the initial principal balance.

[9]Expected static pool losses can be calculated by summing the actual and projected future credit losses and dividing the sum by the original balance of the pool of assets.

[10]Excluding securitized assets that an entity continues to service but with which it has no other continuing involvement.

of liabilities occurring after March 31, 2001. This Statement shall be applied prospectively,[11] except as provided in paragraphs 20, 21, 23, and 24. Earlier or retroactive application of this Statement is not permitted.

20. For each servicing contract in existence before January 1, 1997, previously recognized servicing rights and "excess servicing" receivables that do not exceed **contractually specified servicing fees** shall be combined, net of any previously recognized servicing obligations under that contract, as a servicing asset or liability. Previously recognized servicing receivables that exceed contractually specified servicing fees shall be reclassified as interest-only strips receivable. Thereafter, the subsequent measurement provisions of this Statement shall be applied to the servicing assets or liabilities for those servicing contracts (paragraph 63) and to the interest-only strips receivable (paragraph 14).

21. The provisions of paragraph 14 and the amendment to Statement 115 (paragraph 362) shall be effective for financial assets held on or acquired after January 1, 1997.

22. Paragraphs 17(f) and 17(g) shall be effective for financial statements for fiscal years ending after December 15, 2000. The information required to be disclosed about securitizations of financial assets during the period that are accounted for as sales need not be reported for periods ending on or before December 15, 2000, for which an income statement is presented for comparative purposes.

23. Collateral previously recognized in financial statements in accordance with the requirements of paragraphs 15(a)(ii) and 15(b) of Statement 125 that is no longer to be recognized in accordance with paragraph 15 of this Statement shall no longer be rec-

ognized in financial statements for fiscal years ending after December 15, 2000, and financial statements for previous periods presented for comparative purposes shall be restated accordingly. The requirements for reclassification of certain assets in paragraph 15(a) of this Statement and for disclosure about collateral pledged and accepted in paragraphs 17(a)(2) and 17(a)(3) shall be effective for financial statements for fiscal years ending after December 15, 2000; that information need not be reported for periods ending on or before December 15, 2000, for which a statement of financial position is presented for comparative purposes.

24. Assets transferred on or before March 31, 2001, and transfers of assets after that date required by commitments made before that date to transferees or beneficial interest holders (BIHs) other than the transferor, its affiliates,[12] or its **agents** shall continue to be accounted for under the previous accounting standards for transfers of assets that applied when the transferor made or committed to those transfers. Transfers of assets after that date, unless required by commitments made before that date to transferees or BIHs unrelated to the transferor, shall be subject to all the provisions of this Statement.

25. A formerly qualifying SPE that fails to meet one or more conditions for being a qualifying SPE under this Statement shall continue to be considered a qualifying SPE if it maintains its qualifying status under previous accounting standards, does not issue new beneficial interests after the effective date, and does not receive assets it was not committed to receive (through a commitment to BIHs unrelated to the transferor) before the effective date. Otherwise, the formerly qualifying SPE and assets transferred to it shall be subject to other consolidation policy standards and guidance and to all the provisions of this Statement.

The provisions of this Statement need not be applied to immaterial items.

---

[11]Statement 125 applies to transfers and servicing of financial assets and extinguishments of liabilities occurring after December 31, 1996 (after December 31, 1997, for transfers affected by FASB Statement No. 127, *Deferral of the Effective Date of Certain Provisions of FASB Statement No. 125*) and on or before March 31, 2001. Statement 127 deferred until December 31, 1997, the effective date (a) of paragraph 15 of Statement 125 and (b) for repurchase agreement, dollar-roll, securities lending, and similar transactions, of paragraphs 9–12 and 237(b) of Statement 125.

[12]In this Statement, the term *affiliate* is used in the same sense as it is used in FASB Statement No. 57, *Related Party Disclosures*.

This Statement was adopted by the affirmative votes of five members of the Financial Accounting Standards Board. Mr. Crooch abstained. Mr. Foster dissented.

Mr. Foster dissents from the issuance of this Statement *[Statement 140]* because he believes its amendments to Statement 125 negate the rationale in that Statement *[Statement 125]* that underlies the accounting for transfers of financial assets to certain qualifying SPEs. Furthermore, he believes the amendments made by this Statement to the accounting for collateral conflict with the underlying concept that an entity recognizes assets that it controls.

A principal requirement for transfers of financial assets to be accounted for as sales pursuant to Statement 125 is that the transferor surrenders control of those assets. The Board reasoned that in most situations, excepting transactions involving repurchase agreements and similarly structured arrangements, the transferor had not surrendered control unless the transferee had unconstrained rights to pledge or exchange the transferred assets. However, if that criterion was applied to securitization transactions, very few would be accounted for as sales, because, in those transactions, SPEs to which the financial assets have been transferred are generally limited by their governing documents in their ability to pledge or exchange the transferred assets. The Board believes that many securitization transactions are, in substance, sales. Consequently, the Board developed a separate rationale for determining which transfers to SPEs (which are primarily securitization transactions) could qualify as sales.

In securitization transactions, assets are transferred to an SPE, which holds the assets on behalf of the BIHs. As discussed in paragraph 173 of this Statement, the Board developed a notion that in a qualifying SPE, the BIHs are the ultimate holders of the transferred assets. That notion is based on the premise that because the powers of a qualifying SPE are essentially limited to holding the transferred assets and collecting and distributing the cash flows that arise from the transferred assets, the BIHs effectively have undivided interests in the transferred assets. The Board observed that "the effect of establishing the qualifying SPE is to merge the contractual rights in the transferred assets and to *allocate undivided interests in them*—the beneficial interests" (Statement 125, paragraph 127; paragraph 173 of this Statement; emphasis added). Accordingly, the Board concluded that if the BIHs can pledge or exchange their beneficial interests without constraint (and if the

other criteria in paragraph 9 are met), the transferor has surrendered control over the transferred assets.

Mr. Foster believes it is clear that if an SPE can pledge or exchange its assets, the BIHs do not have undivided interests in the assets initially transferred to that SPE. Rather, they have undivided interests in an undefined pool of assets, and having the ability to freely pledge or exchange their beneficial interests is not tantamount to being able to transfer undivided interests in those assets that were transferred to the SPE. It is the ability to pledge or exchange undivided interests in the transferred assets that underlies the conclusion that transfers of financial assets to qualifying SPEs be accounted for as sales. For that conclusion to be valid, Mr. Foster believes qualifying SPEs should not be permitted to pledge or exchange assets under any circumstances and particularly so when the exchanges occur at the behest and on behalf of the transferor/servicer. When transferred assets can be pledged or exchanged by the SPE, the ability of BIHs to transfer their beneficial interests in the SPE has no bearing on whether the transferor has surrendered control over those assets. Yet, this Statement offers no other rationale for why control over assets transferred to an SPE having the expanded powers provided by this amendment is considered to be surrendered.

Mr. Foster dissented from the issuance of Statement 125 (see previous dissent included below) in part because he believes that in securitizations having a revolving-period agreement, effective control over the assets has not been surrendered. He believes the existence of and the need for ROAPs that enable the transferor to reclaim specific transferred receivables in securitizations having a revolving-period agreement are further evidence that the receivables transferred in those securitizations continue to be effectively controlled by the transferor and that those securitization transactions are, therefore, secured borrowings. (He notes that, in addition to the transferor's ability to reclaim specific receivables from the SPE, the transferor generally continues to collect the cash from the transferred receivables, commingles that cash with its own cash, invests the cash for its own benefit, and uses the cash to buy additional receivables from itself that it selects. Furthermore, the transferor, within fairly wide latitude, has the power to change the interest rate on already transferred receivables.)

Statement 125, prior to amendment by this Statement, provides that for a sale to occur a transferor of financial assets to a qualifying SPE cannot maintain effective control over those assets. That notion that a transferor cannot recognize a sale if it maintains effective control through an option to reclaim the transferred assets is carried forward in this Statement in paragraph 9(c)(2). However, the notion is modified in this Statement to make a distinction between call options that are unilaterally exercisable by the transferor and options for which the exercise by the transferor is conditioned upon an event outside its control. The effect of this modification is that if the transferor can only reclaim the receivable upon the occurrence of an event outside its control, it is not considered to have retained effective control. Mr. Foster believes that effective control is maintained by any option to reclaim transferred assets that is held by the transferor, but even more so in the case where the transferor holds a call on a specific receivable transferred to an SPE for which it has previously issued a call on that same receivable to another party (such as in the case of an affinity relationship described in paragraph 87(c)). In that case, the transferor has already promised that if that other party calls the receivable, it will deliver it. Consequently, if it transfers the receivable, it must control it through a ROAP that enables it to reclaim it—the transferor cannot surrender control of the receivable because it would be unable to perform in the event that specific receivable is called by that other party. Mr. Foster does not understand why control is deemed to have been surrendered in circumstances that *require* that a transferor have the ability to reclaim a transferred receivable when control is deemed not to have been surrendered in circumstances that enable a transferor to reclaim transferred receivables at its discretion.

A fundamental tenet of Statement 125 is that a transferor has surrendered control over an asset only if the transferee can exchange or pledge that transferred asset. The transferee then can control the asset, because it is free to sell, pledge, or do anything else it desires with the asset.[13] An entity that holds collateral in the form of a financial asset that it can pledge or exchange likewise can control that collateral. Statement 125, prior to amendment by this Statement, required that an entity that holds collateral that can be sold or repledged recognize that collateral as its asset unless the transferor can redeem the pledged collateral on short notice. This Statement amends Statement 125 to require that collateral not be recognized by the entity that holds it, even in circumstances in which it can be sold or repledged. Only after cash is received in exchange for collateral that is subsequently sold is the fact that the holder of the collateral had an asset acknowledged. Mr. Foster believes that the amendment related to collateral also is inconsistent with the concepts underlying Statement 125.

Members of the Financial Accounting Standards Board:

Edmund L. Jenkins,	G. Michael Crooch	Gerhard G. Mueller
Chairman	John M. Foster	Edward W. Trott
Anthony T. Cope	Gaylen N. Larson	

Statement 125 was adopted in June 1996 by the affirmative votes of six members of the Financial Accounting Standards Board. Mr. Foster dissented.

Mr. Foster dissents from the issuance of Statement 125 because he believes that the notion of effective control that is applied to repurchase agreements, including dollar rolls, and securities lending transactions should be applied consistently to other transfers of financial assets, including securitization transactions. Furthermore, he believes that in those instances where the financial-components approach is applied, all rights (assets) and obligations (liabilities) that are recognized by the transferor after a sale or securitization has occurred should be measured at fair value.

Under paragraphs 9(a) and 9(b) of Statement 125, control is deemed to have been surrendered if the transferred assets have been legally isolated from the transferor and the transferee has the right to pledge or exchange the transferred assets. That notion of control is the cornerstone of the financial-components

---

[13]The Board crafted an exception to this principle so that repurchase agreements, securities lending transactions, and similarly structured transactions would not be accounted for as sales.

approach. However, the Board considered that approach inappropriate to account for certain transactions, such as those involving repurchase agreements, including dollar rolls, and securities lending transactions, where legal control over the assets has been surrendered, but where the Board believes that effective control still exists. For those transactions, paragraph 9(c) of Statement 125 was specifically crafted to override the criteria for transfers of legal control in paragraphs 9(a) and 9(b) of Statement 125. Paragraph 9(c), however, was designed to provide an exception only for certain transactions resulting in inconsistent application of the control notion: one set of transfers of financial assets—securitizations—is accounted for using a narrow, legal definition of control while others are accounted for using a broad notion of effective control. Mr. Foster favors an approach that encompasses the broader notion of effective control. He questions why, if the financial-components approach is inappropriate to account for all transfers of financial assets, it is appropriate to apply it to securitizations. He believes that if the entirety of the arrangement is considered, certain securitization transactions, such as those having a revolving-period agreement, also result in effective control being retained by the transferor and accordingly those transactions should be accounted for as secured borrowings.

In securitizations having a revolving-period agreement, which are described in paragraphs 130–133 of Statement 125 [paragraphs 192–195 of this Statement], the transferor generally continues to collect the cash from the transferred receivables, commingles that cash with its own cash, invests the cash for its own benefit, and uses the cash to buy additional receivables from itself that it selects. As a result of those features, the future benefits of the receivables (the cash flows to be received from them) that inure to the transferor are little different, if at all, from the future benefits that the transferor would obtain from receivables that it holds for its own account. Mr. Foster believes that in those transactions effective control of the receivables has not been surrendered and that the transferred receivables continue to be assets of the transferor.

Paragraph 26 of FASB Concepts Statement No. 6, *Elements of Financial Statements,* states, "An asset has three essential characteristics: (a) it embodies a probable future benefit that involves a capacity, singly or in combination with other assets, to contribute directly or indirectly to future net cash inflows, (b) a particular entity can obtain the benefit and control others' access to it, and (c) the transaction or other event giving rise to the entity's right to or control of

the benefit has already occurred." Mr. Foster believes that in securitizations having revolving-period agreements, the transferred receivables meet each of those criteria from the perspective of the transferor. The transferred receivables directly or indirectly contribute to the transferor's cash inflows—it generally receives and retains all of the cash inflows during the term of the arrangement subject only to payment of what amounts to interest on the investment of the holders of beneficial interests—and the transferor can and does obtain and control others' access to both the receivables and the cash inflows by its structuring of the transaction and retention of most of the cash flows until termination of the arrangement. Paragraph 131 of Statement 125 [paragraph 193 of this Statement] asserts that the cash obtained by the transferor in those securitizations is received in exchange for new receivables and is not obtained as a benefit attributable to its previous ownership of the transferred receivables. In substance, however, the transfer of new receivables is little different from the substitution of collateral prevalent in many secured loan arrangements. In short, the transferred receivables have all of the attributes of assets controlled by the transferor.

As described below, the principal criteria cited in the basis for conclusions for treating repurchase agreements and securities lending transactions as secured borrowings apply equally to many securitizations, particularly those having a revolving-period agreement.

The inability of the transferor in a transfer with a revolving-period agreement to sell new receivables elsewhere because it has contracted to sell those new receivables on prearranged terms at times that it does not determine or have much influence over is asserted to be significant in paragraph 131 of Statement 125 [paragraph 193 of this Statement]. However, within fairly wide latitude, the transferor in those circumstances has retained the right to change the interest rate (the price) on both the previously transferred receivables and receivables to be transferred in the future. Mr. Foster believes that that right substantially diminishes any disadvantage of not being able to sell the receivables elsewhere and substantially negates any effect, favorable or onerous, on the transferor as a result of changes in market conditions as asserted in paragraph 50 of Statement 125 [paragraph 76 of this Statement]. In fact, any effects on the transferor result solely from having financed the receivables at whatever rate is paid the beneficial owners of the securities. Furthermore, the transferor of assets transferred under repurchase agreements or in securities lending transactions cannot sell those assets elsewhere.

Two reasons advanced in support of the treatment of repurchase agreements and securities lending transactions as secured borrowings are that (a) those transactions are difficult to characterize because they have attributes of both borrowings and sales and (b) supporting arguments can be found for accounting for those transactions as borrowings or sales. Those two reasons are equally applicable to securitization transactions having a revolving-period agreement—they are treated as sales for purposes of marketing to investors and as borrowings for tax purposes, and legal opinions and the prospectuses for those transactions acknowledge that their treatment as sales may not be sustained in a legal dispute.

The only supporting arguments cited for the treatment of repurchase agreements and securities lending transactions as secured borrowings that are not equally applicable to certain securitizations are that (a) forward contracts that are fully secured should be treated differently than those that are unsecured and (b) making a change in existing accounting practice would have a substantial impact on the reported financial position of certain entities and on the markets in which they participate. Mr. Foster does not believe that the existence of security in support of a transaction should determine its accounting treatment and notes that extension of the reasoning in paragraph 141 of Statement 125 [paragraph 207 of this Statement] would lead to lenders not recognizing loans receivable that are unsecured. While it may be necessary to consider prior accounting treatment and the effect a change in accounting practice would have on certain entities, Mr. Foster believes that those factors should carry relatively little weight in determining what is an appropriate accounting standard.

Paragraph 18 of Opinion 29 states, "The Board concludes that in general accounting for nonmonetary transactions should be based on the fair values of the assets (or services) involved which is the same basis as that used in monetary transactions. Thus, the cost of a nonmonetary asset acquired in exchange for another nonmonetary asset is the fair value of the asset surrendered to obtain it . . ." (footnote reference omitted). The conclusion embodied in that language is that the accounting for both monetary and nonmonetary transactions acquired in an exchange should be based on the fair values of the assets (or services) involved. Mr. Foster believes that in securitization transactions in which control is deemed under this Statement to be surrendered and in partial sales of financial assets, assets (or rights) are surrendered in exchange for cash and other rights and obligations, all of which are new.[14] The new assets (rights) received are part of the proceeds of the exchange, and any liabilities (obligations) incurred are a reduction of the proceeds. As such, those new assets and liabilities should be measured at their fair values as they are in all other exchange transactions.

Statement 125 contends that in those transactions certain components of the original assets have not been exchanged. If that is one's view, however, it is clear that a transaction of sufficient significance to result in the derecognition of assets has occurred. Furthermore, the event of securitization results in a change in the form and value of assets—securities are generally more easily sold or used as collateral and thus are more valuable than receivables. Mr. Foster believes that a securitization transaction, like the initial recognition of an asset or liability and derecognition of assets and liabilities where it is clear an exchange has occurred, is also sufficiently significant that the resulting, or remaining components of, assets and liabilities should be recorded at fair value.

Mr. Foster also notes, as described in paragraphs 182–184 of Statement 125 [paragraphs 271–273 of this Statement], that the distinctions made in paragraphs 10 and 11 between (a) assets retained and (b) assets obtained and liabilities incurred are arbitrary. For example, one could easily argue that beneficial interests acquired in a transfer of receivables have different rights and obligations than the receivables and accordingly should be accounted for not as retained assets, but as new and different assets, and, arguably, the rights inherent in derivatives arising in a securitization transaction, which are considered new rights (assets) in Statement 125, were embedded, albeit in an obscure form, in the transferred assets and could be as readily identified as retained portions of them. That the Board needed to make those distinctions arbitrarily begs for a consistent measurement attribute—fair value—for all of the rights and obligations held by the transferor subsequent to the transfer.

---

[14]In the case of a partial sale of a financial asset, the transferor generally has reduced the marketability of the asset because it can no longer sell the entire asset—it can only sell part of that asset. Consequently, the partial interest in the original asset has different rights and privileges than those embodied in the original asset and, therefore, is a new asset—different from the original asset.

Appendix A

IMPLEMENTATION GUIDANCE

CONTENTS

Appendix A

IMPLEMENTATION GUIDANCE

Introduction

26. This appendix describes certain provisions of this Statement in more detail and describes how they apply to certain types of transactions. This appendix discusses generalized situations. Facts and circumstances and specific contracts need to be considered carefully in applying this Statement. This appendix is an integral part of the standards provided in this Statement.

Isolation beyond the Reach of the Transferor and Its Creditors

27. The nature and extent of supporting evidence required for an assertion in financial statements that transferred financial assets have been isolated—put presumptively beyond the reach of the transferor and its creditors, either by a single transaction or a series of transactions taken as a whole—depend on the facts and circumstances. All available evidence that either supports or questions an assertion shall be considered. That consideration includes making judgments about whether the contract or circumstances permit the transferor to revoke the transfer. It also may include making judgments about the kind of bankruptcy or other receivership into which a transferor or SPE might be placed, whether a transfer of financial assets would likely be deemed a true sale at law, whether the transferor is affiliated with the transferee, and other factors pertinent under applicable law. Derecognition of transferred assets is appropriate only if the available evidence provides reasonable assurance that the transferred assets would be beyond the reach of the powers of a bankruptcy trustee or other receiver for the transferor or any **consolidated affiliate of the transferor** that is not a special-purpose corporation or other entity designed to make remote the possibility that it would enter bankruptcy or other receivership (paragraph 83(c)).

28. Whether securitizations isolate transferred assets may depend on such factors as whether the securitization is accomplished in one step or two steps (paragraphs 80–84). Many common financial transactions, for example, typical repurchase agreements and securities lending transactions, isolate transferred assets from the transferor, although they may not meet the other criteria for surrender of control.

Conditions That Constrain a Transferee

29. Sale accounting is allowed under paragraph 9(b) only if each transferee has the right to pledge, or the right to exchange, the transferred assets or beneficial interests it received, but constraints on that right also matter. Many transferor-imposed or other conditions on a transferee's right to pledge or exchange a transferred asset both constrain a transferee from pledging or exchanging the transferred assets and, through that constraint, provide more than a trivial benefit to the transferor. For example, a provision in the transfer contract that prohibits selling or pledging a transferred loan receivable not only constrains the transferee but also provides the transferor with the more-than-trivial benefits of knowing who has the asset, a prerequisite to repurchasing the asset, and of being able to block the asset from finding its way into the hands of a competitor for the loan customer's business or someone that the loan customer might consider an undesirable creditor. Transferor-imposed contractual constraints that narrowly limit timing or terms, for example, allowing a transferee to pledge only on the day assets are obtained or only on terms agreed with the transferor, also constrain the transferee and presumptively provide the transferor with more-than-trivial benefits.

30. However, some conditions do not constrain a transferee from pledging or exchanging the asset and therefore do not preclude a transfer subject to such a condition from being accounted for as a sale. For example, a transferor's right of first refusal on the occurrence of a bona fide offer to the transferee from a third party presumptively would not constrain a transferee, because that right in itself does not enable

the transferor to compel the transferee to sell the assets and the transferee would be in a position to receive the sum offered by exchanging the asset, albeit possibly from the transferor rather than the third party. Further examples of conditions that presumptively would not constrain a transferee include (a) a requirement to obtain the transferor's permission to sell or pledge that is not to be unreasonably withheld, (b) a prohibition on sale to the transferor's competitor if other potential willing buyers exist, (c) a regulatory limitation such as on the number or nature of eligible transferees (as in the case of securities issued under Securities Act Rule 144A or debt placed privately), and (d) illiquidity, for example, the absence of an active market. Judgment is required to assess the significance of some conditions. For example, a prohibition on sale to the transferor's competitor would be a significant constraint if that competitor were the only potential willing buyer other than the transferor.

31. A condition imposed by a transferor that constrains the transferee presumptively provides more than a trivial benefit to the transferor. A condition *not* imposed by the transferor that constrains the transferee may or may not provide more than a trivial benefit to the transferor. For example, if the transferor refrains from imposing its usual contractual constraint on a specific transfer because it knows an equivalent constraint is already imposed on the transferee by a third party, it presumptively benefits more than trivially from that constraint. However, the transferor cannot benefit from a constraint if it is unaware at the time of the transfer that the transferee is constrained.

Transferor's Rights or Obligations to Reacquire Transferred Assets

32. Some rights or obligations to reacquire transferred assets both constrain the transferee and provide more than a trivial benefit to the transferor, thus precluding sale accounting under paragraph 9(b). For example, a **freestanding call** option written by a transferee to the transferor benefits the transferor and, if the transferred assets are not readily obtainable in the marketplace, is likely to constrain a transferee because it might have to default if the call was exercised and it had exchanged or pledged the assets. A freestanding forward purchase-sale contract between

the transferor and the transferee on transferred assets not readily obtainable in the marketplace would benefit the transferor and is likely to constrain a transferee in much the same manner. Judgment is necessary to assess constraint and benefit. For example, put options written to the transferee generally do not constrain it, but a put option on a not-readily-obtainable asset may benefit the transferor and effectively constrain the transferee if the option is sufficiently deep-in-the-money when it is written that it is probable that the transferee will exercise it and the transferor will reacquire the transferred asset. In contrast, a sufficiently out-of-the-money call option held by the transferor may not constrain a transferee if it is probable when the option is written that it will not be exercised. Freestanding rights to reacquire transferred assets that are readily obtainable presumptively do not constrain the transferee from exchanging or pledging them and thus do not preclude sale accounting under paragraph 9(b).

33. Other rights or obligations to reacquire transferred assets, regardless of whether they constrain the transferee, may result in the transferor's maintaining effective control over the transferred assets, as discussed in paragraphs 50–54, thus precluding sale accounting under paragraph 9(c)(2).[15]

Conditions That Constrain a Holder of Beneficial Interests in a Qualifying SPE

34. The considerations in paragraphs 29–32, about conditions that may or may not constrain a transferee that is not a qualifying SPE from pledging or exchanging the transferred assets, also extend to conditions that may or may not constrain a BIH from pledging or exchanging its beneficial interests in assets transferred to a qualifying SPE. For example, if BIHs agree to sell their beneficial interests in a qualifying SPE back to the transferor upon request at the price paid plus a stated return, that arrangement clearly conveys more than a trivial benefit to the transferor; sale accounting for the transfer to the qualifying SPE would be precluded if that agreement constrained a BIH from exchanging or pledging its beneficial interest.

---

[15]And it is necessary to consider the overall effect of related rights and obligations in assessing such matters as whether a transferee is constrained or a transferor has maintained effective control. For example, if the transferor or its affiliate or agent is the servicer for the transferred asset and is empowered to decide to put the asset up for sale, and has the right of first refusal, that combination would place the transferor in position to unilaterally cause the return of a specific transferred asset and thus maintain the transferor's effective control of the transferred asset as discussed in paragraphs 9(c)(2) and 50.

Qualifying SPE

35. A qualifying SPE[16] is a trust or other legal vehicle that meets *all* of the following conditions:

a. It is demonstrably distinct from the transferor (paragraph 36).

b. Its permitted activities (1) are significantly limited, (2) were entirely specified in the legal documents that established the SPE or created the beneficial interests in the transferred assets that it holds, and (3) may be significantly changed only with the approval of the holders of at least a majority of the beneficial interests held by entities other than any transferor, its affiliates, and its agents (paragraphs 37 and 38).

c. It may hold only:

(1) Financial assets transferred to it that are passive in nature (paragraph 39)

(2) Passive **derivative financial instruments** that pertain to beneficial interests (other than another derivative financial instrument) issued or sold to parties other than the transferor, its affiliates, or its agents (paragraphs 39 and 40)

(3) Financial assets (for example, guarantees or rights to collateral) that would reimburse it if others were to fail to adequately service financial assets transferred to it or to timely pay obligations due to it and that it entered into when it was established, when assets were transferred to it, or when beneficial interests (other than derivative financial instruments) were issued by the SPE

(4) Servicing rights related to financial assets that it holds

(5) Temporarily, nonfinancial assets obtained in connection with the collection of financial assets that it holds (paragraph 41)

(6) Cash collected from assets that it holds and investments purchased with that cash pending distribution to holders of beneficial interests that are appropriate for that purpose (that is, money-market or other relatively risk-free instruments without

options and with maturities no later than the expected distribution date).

d. If it can sell or otherwise dispose of noncash financial assets, it can do so only in automatic response to one of the following conditions:

(1) Occurrence of an event or circumstance that (a) is specified in the legal documents that established the SPE or created the beneficial interests in the transferred assets that it holds; (b) is outside the control of the transferor, its affiliates, or its agents; and (c) causes, or is expected at the date of transfer to cause, the fair value of those financial assets to decline by a specified degree below the fair value of those assets when the SPE obtained them (paragraphs 42 and 43)

(2) Exercise by a BIH (other than the transferor, its affiliates, or its agents) of a right to put that holder's beneficial interest back to the SPE (paragraph 44)

(3) Exercise by the transferor of a call or ROAP specified in the legal documents that established the SPE, transferred assets to the SPE, or created the beneficial interests in the transferred assets that it holds (paragraphs 51–54 and 85–88)

(4) Termination of the SPE or maturity of the beneficial interests in those financial assets on a fixed or determinable date that is specified at inception (paragraph 45).

Need to Be Demonstrably Distinct from the Transferor

36. A qualifying SPE is demonstrably distinct from the transferor only if it cannot be unilaterally dissolved by any transferor, its affiliates, or its agents and either (a) at least 10 percent of the fair value of its beneficial interests is held by parties other than any transferor, its affiliates, or its agents or (b) the transfer is a guaranteed mortgage securitization.[17] An ability to unilaterally dissolve an SPE can take many forms, including but not limited to holding sufficient beneficial interests to demand that the trustee dissolve the SPE, the right to call all the assets transferred to the

---

[16]The description of a qualifying SPE is restrictive. The accounting for qualifying SPEs and transfers of financial assets to them should not be extended to any entity that does not currently satisfy all of the conditions articulated in this paragraph.

[17]An effect of that provision, in conjunction with paragraph 46, is that mortgage-backed securities retained in a guaranteed mortgage securitization in which the SPE meets all conditions for being a qualifying SPE are classified in the financial statements of the transferor as securities that are subsequently measured under Statement 115.

SPE, and a right to call or a prepayment privilege on the beneficial interests held by other parties.

Limits on Permitted Activities

37. The powers of the SPE must be limited to those activities allowed by paragraph 35 for it to be a qualifying SPE. Many kinds of entities are not so limited. For example, any bank, insurance company, pension plan, or investment company has powers that cannot be sufficiently limited for it to be a qualifying SPE.

38. The BIHs other than any transferor, its affiliates, or its agents may have the ability to change the powers of a qualifying SPE. If the powers of a previously qualifying SPE are changed so that the SPE is no longer qualifying, unless the conditions in paragraph 9(b) are then met by the SPE itself and the conditions in paragraphs 9(a) and 9(c) continue to be met, that change would bring the transferred assets held in the SPE back under the control of the transferor (paragraph 55).

Limits on What a Qualifying SPE May Hold

39. A financial asset or derivative financial instrument is passive only if holding the asset or instrument does not involve its holder in making decisions other than the decisions inherent in servicing (paragraph 61). An equity instrument is not passive if the qualifying SPE can exercise the voting rights and is permitted to choose how to vote. Investments are not passive if through them, either in themselves or in combination with other investments or rights, the SPE or any related entity, such as the transferor, its affiliates, or its agents, is able to exercise control or significant influence (as defined in generally accepted accounting principles for consolidation policy and for the equity method, respectively) over the investee. A derivative financial instrument is not passive if, for example, it includes an option allowing the SPE to choose to call or put other financial instruments; but other derivative financial instruments can be passive, for example, interest rate caps and swaps and forward contracts. Derivative financial instruments that result in liabilities, like other liabilities of a qualifying SPE, are a kind of beneficial interest in the qualifying SPE's assets.

40. A derivative financial instrument pertains to beneficial interests (other than another derivative financial instrument) issued only if it:

a. Is entered into (1) when the beneficial interests are issued by the qualifying SPE to parties other than the transferor, its affiliates, or its agents or sold to such other parties after being issued by the qualifying SPE to the transferor, its affiliates, or its agents or (2) when a passive derivative financial instrument needs to be replaced upon occurrence of an event or circumstance (specified in the legal documents that established the SPE or created the beneficial interests in the transferred assets that it holds) outside the control of the transferor, its affiliates, or its agents, for example, when the counterparty to the derivative defaults or is downgraded below a specified threshold

b. Has a notional amount that does not initially exceed the amount of those beneficial interests and is not expected to exceed them subsequently

c. Has characteristics that relate to, and partly or fully but not excessively counteract, some risk associated with those beneficial interests or the related transferred assets.

41. A qualifying SPE may hold nonfinancial assets other than servicing rights only temporarily and only if those nonfinancial assets result from collecting the transferred financial assets. For example, a qualifying SPE could be permitted to temporarily hold foreclosed nonfinancial collateral. In contrast, an entity cannot be a qualifying SPE if, for example, it receives from a transferor significant secured financial assets likely to default with the expectation that it will foreclose on and profitably manage the securing nonfinancial assets. A qualifying SPE also may hold the residual value of a sales-type or a direct financing lease only to the extent that it is guaranteed at the inception of the lease either by the lessee or by a third party financially capable of discharging the obligations that may arise from the guarantee (paragraph 89).

Limits on Sales or Other Dispositions of Assets

42. Examples of requirements to sell, exchange, put, or distribute (hereinafter referred to collectively as dispose of) noncash financial assets that *are* permitted activities of a qualifying SPE—because they respond automatically to the occurrence of an event or circumstance that (a) is specified in the legal documents that established the SPE or created the beneficial interests in the transferred assets that it holds; (b) is outside the control of the transferor, its affiliates, or its agents; and (c) causes, or is expected to cause, the fair value of those assets to decline by a specified degree below the fair value of those assets when the qualifying SPE obtained

them—include requirements to dispose of transferred assets in response to:

a. A failure to properly service transferred assets that could result in the loss of a substantial third-party credit guarantee
b. A default by the obligor
c. A downgrade by a major rating agency of the transferred assets or of the underlying obligor to a rating below a specified minimum rating
d. The involuntary insolvency of the transferor
e. A decline in the fair value of the transferred assets to a specified value less than their fair value at the time they were transferred to the SPE.

43. The following are examples of powers or requirements to dispose of noncash financial assets that *are not* permitted activities of a qualifying SPE, because they do not respond automatically to the occurrence of a specified event or circumstance outside the control of the transferor, its affiliates, or its agents that causes, or is expected to cause, the fair value of those transferred assets to decline by a specified degree below the fair value of those assets when the SPE obtained them:

a. A power that allows an SPE to choose to either dispose of transferred assets or hold them in response to a default, a downgrade, a decline in fair value, or a servicing failure
b. A requirement to dispose of marketable equity securities upon a specified decline from their "highest fair value" if that power could result in disposing of the asset in exchange for an amount that is more than the fair value of those assets at the time they were transferred to the SPE
c. A requirement to dispose of transferred assets in response to the violation of a nonsubstantive contractual provision (that is, a provision for which there is not a sufficiently large disincentive to ensure performance).

44. A qualifying SPE may dispose of transferred assets automatically to the extent necessary to comply with the exercise by a BIH (other than the transferor, its affiliates, or its agents) of its right to put beneficial interests back to the SPE in exchange for:

a. A full or partial distribution of those assets
b. Cash (which may require that the SPE dispose of

those assets or issue beneficial interests to generate cash to fund settlement of the put)
c. New beneficial interests in those assets.

45. A qualifying SPE may have the power to dispose of assets to a party other than the transferor, its affiliate, or its agent on termination of the SPE or maturity of the beneficial interests, but only automatically on fixed or determinable dates that are specified at inception. For example, if an SPE is required to dispose of long-term mortgage loans and terminate itself at the earlier of (a) the specified maturity of beneficial interests in those mortgage loans or (b) the date of prepayment of a specified amount of the transferred mortgage loans, the termination date is a fixed or determinable date that was specified at inception. In contrast, if that SPE has the power to dispose of transferred assets on two specified dates and the SPE can decide which transferred assets to sell on each date, the termination date is *not* a fixed or determinable date that was specified at inception.

Qualifying SPEs and Consolidated Financial Statements

46. A qualifying SPE shall not be consolidated in the financial statements of a transferor or its affiliates.

Maintaining Effective Control over Transferred Assets

Agreement to Repurchase or Redeem Transferred Assets

47. An agreement that both entitles and obligates the transferor to repurchase or redeem transferred assets from the transferee maintains the transferor's effective control over those assets under paragraph 9(c)(1), and the transfer is therefore to be accounted for as a secured borrowing, if and only if all of the following conditions are met:

a. The assets to be repurchased or redeemed are the same or substantially the same as those transferred (paragraph 48).
b. The transferor is able to repurchase or redeem them on substantially the agreed terms, even in the event of default by the transferee (paragraph 49).
c. The agreement is to repurchase or redeem them before maturity, at a fixed or determinable price.

Accounting for Transfers and Servicing of
Financial Assets and Extinguishments of Liabilities
FAS140

d. The agreement is entered into concurrently with the transfer.

48. To be substantially the same,[18] the asset that was transferred and the asset that is to be repurchased or redeemed need to have all of the following characteristics:

a. The same primary obligor (except for debt guaranteed by a sovereign government, central bank, government-sponsored enterprise or agency thereof, in which case the guarantor and the terms of the guarantee must be the same)
b. Identical form and type so as to provide the same risks and rights
c. The same maturity (or in the case of mortgage-backed pass-through and pay-through securities, similar remaining weighted-average maturities that result in approximately the same market yield)
d. Identical contractual interest rates
e. Similar assets as collateral
f. The same aggregate unpaid principal amount or principal amounts within accepted "good delivery" standards for the type of security involved.

49. To be able to repurchase or redeem assets on substantially the agreed terms, even in the event of default by the transferee, a transferor must at all times during the contract term have obtained cash or other collateral sufficient to fund substantially all of the cost of purchasing replacement assets from others.

Ability to Unilaterally Cause the Return of Specific Transferred Assets

50. Some rights to reacquire transferred assets (or to acquire beneficial interests in transferred assets held by a qualifying SPE), regardless of whether they constrain the transferee, may result in the transferor's maintaining effective control over the transferred assets through the **unilateral ability** to cause the return of specific transferred assets. Such rights preclude sale accounting under paragraph 9(c)(2). For example, an **attached call** in itself would not constrain a transferee who is able, by exchanging or pledging the asset subject to that call, to obtain substantially all of its economic benefits. An attached call could result, however, in the transferor's maintaining effective control over the transferred asset(s) because the attached call gives the transferor the ability to unilaterally cause whoever holds that specific asset to re-

turn it. In contrast, transfers of financial assets subject to calls embedded by the issuers of the financial instruments, for example, callable bonds or prepayable mortgage loans, do not preclude sale accounting. Such an **embedded call** does not result in the transferor's maintaining effective control, because it is the issuer rather than the transferor who holds the call.

51. If the transferee is a qualifying SPE, it has met the conditions in paragraph 35(d) and therefore must be constrained from choosing to exchange or pledge the transferred assets. In that circumstance, any call held by the transferor is effectively attached to the assets and could—depending on the price and other terms of the call—maintain the transferor's effective control over transferred assets through the ability to unilaterally cause the transferee to return specific assets. For example, a transferor's unilateral ability to cause a qualifying SPE to return to the transferor or otherwise dispose of specific transferred assets at will or, for example, in response to its decision to exit a market or a particular activity, could provide the transferor with effective control over the transferred assets.

52. A call that is attached to transferred assets maintains the transferor's effective control over those assets if, under its price and other terms, the call conveys more than a trivial benefit to the transferor. Similarly, any unilateral right to reclaim specific assets transferred to a qualifying SPE maintains the transferor's effective control over those assets if the right conveys more than a trivial benefit to the transferor. A call or other right conveys more than a trivial benefit if the price to be paid is fixed, determinable, or otherwise potentially advantageous, unless because that price is so far out of the money or for other reasons it is probable when the option is written that the transferor will not exercise it. Thus, for example, a call on specific assets transferred to a qualifying SPE at a price fixed at their principal amount maintains the transferor's effective control over the assets subject to that call. Effective control over transferred assets can be present even if the right to reclaim is indirect. For example, if an embedded call allows a transferor to buy back the beneficial interests of a qualifying SPE at a fixed price, then the transferor remains in effective control of the assets underlying those beneficial interests. A cleanup call, however, is permitted as an exception to that general principle.

---

[18]In this Statement, the term *substantially the same* is used consistently with the usage of that term in the AICPA Statement of Position 90-3, *Definition of the Term Substantially the Same for Holders of Debt Instruments, as Used in Certain Audit Guides and a Statement of Position.*

53. A right to reclaim specific transferred assets by paying their fair value when reclaimed generally does not maintain effective control, because it does not convey a more than trivial benefit to the transferor. However, a transferor has maintained effective control if it has such a right and also holds the residual interest in the transferred assets. For example, if a transferor can reclaim such assets at termination of the qualifying SPE by purchasing them in an auction, and thus at what might appear to be fair value, then sale accounting for the assets it can reclaim would be precluded. Such circumstances provide the transferor with a more than trivial benefit and effective control over the assets, because it can pay any price it chooses in the auction and recover any excess paid over fair value through its residual interest.

54. A transferor that has a right to reacquire transferred assets from a qualifying SPE does not maintain effective control if the reclaimed assets would be randomly selected and the amount of the assets reacquired is sufficiently limited (paragraph 87(a)), because that would not be a right to reacquire *specific* assets. Nor does a transferor maintain effective control through an obligation to reacquire transferred assets from a qualifying SPE if the transfer could occur only after a specified failure of the servicer to properly service the transferred assets that could result in the loss of a third-party guarantee (paragraph 42(a)) or only after a BIH other than the transferor, its affiliate, or its agent requires a qualifying SPE to repurchase that beneficial interest (paragraph 44(b)), because the transferor could not cause that reacquisition *unilaterally.*

Changes That Result in the Transferor's Regaining Control of Assets Sold

55. A change in law, status of the transferee as a qualifying SPE, or other circumstance may result in the transferor's regaining control of assets previously accounted for appropriately as having been sold, because one or more of the conditions in paragraph 9 are no longer met. Such a change, unless it arises solely from either the initial application of this Statement or a change in market prices (for example, an increase in price that moves into-the-money a freestanding call that was originally sufficiently out-of-the-money that it was judged not to constrain the

transferee), is accounted for in the same manner as a purchase of the assets from the former transferee(s) in exchange for liabilities assumed (paragraph 11). After that change, the transferor recognizes in its financial statements those assets together with liabilities to the former transferee(s) or BIHs in those assets (paragraph 38). The transferor initially measures those assets and liabilities at fair value on the date of the change, as if the transferor purchased the assets and assumed the liabilities on that date. The former transferee would derecognize the assets on that date, as if it had sold the assets in exchange for a receivable from the transferor.

Measurement of Interests Held after a Transfer of Financial Assets

Assets Obtained and Liabilities Incurred as Proceeds

56. The proceeds from a sale of financial assets consist of the cash and any other assets obtained in the transfer less any liabilities incurred. Any asset obtained that is not an interest in the transferred asset is part of the proceeds from the sale. Any liability incurred, even if it is related to the transferred assets, is a reduction of the proceeds. Any derivative financial instrument entered into concurrently with a transfer of financial assets is either an asset obtained or a liability incurred and part of the proceeds received in the transfer. All proceeds and reductions of proceeds from a sale shall be initially measured at fair value, if practicable.

Illustration—Recording Transfers with Proceeds of Cash, Derivatives, and Other Liabilities

57. Company A sells loans with a fair value of $1,100 and a carrying amount of $1,000. Company A retains no servicing responsibilities but obtains an option to purchase from the transferee loans similar to the loans sold (which are readily obtainable in the marketplace) and assumes a limited recourse obligation to repurchase delinquent loans.

Company A agrees to provide the transferee a return at a floating rate of interest even though the contractual terms of the loan are fixed rate in nature (that provision is effectively an interest rate swap).

Fair Values

Cash proceeds	$1,050
Interest rate swap	40
Call option	70
Recourse obligation	60

Net Proceeds

Cash received	$1,050
Plus: Call option	70
Interest rate swap	40
Less: Recourse obligation	(60)
Net proceeds	$1,100

Gain on Sale

Net proceeds	$1,100
Carrying amount of loans sold	1,000
Gain on sale	$ 100

Journal Entry

Cash	1,050	
Interest rate swap	40	
Call option	70	
Loans		1,000
Recourse obligation		60
Gain on sale		100
To record transfer		

Retained Interests

58. Other interests in transferred assets—those that are not part of the proceeds of the transfer—are retained interests over which the transferor has not relinquished control. They shall be measured at the date of the transfer by allocating the previous carrying amount between the assets sold, if any, and the retained interests, based on their relative fair values. Allocation procedures shall be applied to all transfers in which interests are retained, even those that do not qualify as sales. Examples of retained interests include securities backed by the transferred assets, undivided interests, servicing assets, and cash reserve accounts and residual interests in securitization trusts. If a transferor cannot determine whether an asset is a retained interest or proceeds from the sale, the asset shall be treated as proceeds from the sale and accounted for in accordance with paragraph 56.

59. If the retained interests are subordinated to more senior interests held by others, that subordination may concentrate into the retained interests most of the risks inherent in the transferred assets and shall be taken into consideration in estimating the fair value of the retained interests. For example, if the amount of the gain recognized, after allocation, on a securitization with a subordinated retained interest is greater than the gain would have been had the entire asset been sold, the transferor needs to be able to identify why that can occur. Otherwise, it is likely that the impact of the retained interest being subordinate to a senior interest has not been adequately considered in the determination of the fair value of the subordinated retained interest.

Illustration—Recording Transfers of Partial Interests

60. Company B sells a pro rata nine-tenths interest in loans with a fair value of $1,100 and a carrying amount of $1,000. There is no servicing asset or liability, because Company B estimates that the **benefits of servicing** are just adequate to compensate it for its servicing responsibilities.

Fair Values

Cash proceeds for nine-tenths interest sold	$990
One-tenth interest retained [($990 ÷ $\frac{9}{10}$) × $\frac{1}{10}$]	110

Carrying Amount Based on Relative Fair Values

	Fair Value	Percentage of Total Fair Value	Allocated Carrying Amount
Nine-tenths interest sold	$ 990	90	$ 900
One-tenth interest retained	110	10	100
Total	$1,100	100	$1,000

Gain on Sale

Net proceeds	$990
Carrying amount of loans sold	900
Gain on sale	$ 90

Journal Entry

Cash	990	
Loans		900
Gain on sale		90
To record transfer		

Servicing Assets and Liabilities

61. Servicing of mortgage loans, credit card receivables, or other financial assets commonly includes, but is not limited to, collecting principal, interest, and escrow payments from borrowers; paying taxes and insurance from escrowed funds; monitoring delinquencies; executing foreclosure if necessary; temporarily investing funds pending distribution; remitting fees to guarantors, trustees, and others providing services; and accounting for and remitting principal and interest payments to the holders of beneficial interests in the financial assets. Servicing is inherent in all financial assets; it becomes a distinct asset or liability only when contractually separated from the underlying assets by sale or securitization of the assets with servicing retained or separate purchase or assumption of the servicing.

62. An entity that undertakes a contract to service financial assets shall recognize either a servicing asset or a servicing liability, with only one exception. (That exception is if the transferor transfers the assets in a guaranteed mortgage securitization, retains all of the resulting securities, and classifies them as debt securities held-to-maturity in accordance with Statement 115, in which case the servicing asset or liability may be reported together with the asset being serviced.) Each sale or securitization with servicing retained or separate purchase or assumption of servicing results in a servicing contract. A servicer of financial assets commonly receives the benefits of servicing—revenues from contractually specified servicing fees, late charges, and other ancillary sources, including "float," all of which it is entitled to receive only if it performs the servicing—and incurs the costs of servicing the assets. Each servicing contract results in a servicing asset or servicing liability. Typically, the benefits of servicing are expected to be more than **adequate compensation** to a servicer for performing the servicing, and the contract results in a servicing asset. However, if the benefits of servicing are not expected to adequately compensate a servicer for performing the servicing, the contract results in a servicing liability. (A servicing asset may

become a servicing liability, or vice versa, if circumstances change, and the initial measure for servicing may be zero if the benefits of servicing are just adequate to compensate the servicer for its servicing responsibilities.)

63. A servicer that recognizes a servicing asset or servicing liability shall account for the contract to service financial assets separately from those assets, as follows:

a. Report servicing assets separately from servicing liabilities in the statement of financial position (paragraph 13).
b. Initially measure servicing assets retained in a sale or securitization of the assets being serviced at their allocated previous carrying amount based on relative fair values, if practicable, at the date of the sale or securitization (paragraphs 10, 58–60, and 68–72).
c. Initially measure servicing assets purchased or servicing liabilities assumed at fair value (paragraph 13).
d. Initially measure servicing liabilities undertaken in a sale or securitization at fair value, if practicable (paragraphs 11(b), 11(c), and 68–72).
e. Account separately for rights to future interest income from the serviced assets that exceeds contractually specified servicing fees. Those rights are not servicing assets; they are financial assets, effectively interest-only strips to be accounted for in accordance with paragraph 14 of this Statement.
f. Subsequently measure servicing assets by amortizing the amount recognized in proportion to and over the period of estimated net servicing income—the excess of servicing revenues over servicing costs (paragraph 13).
g. Subsequently evaluate and measure impairment of servicing assets as follows:
  (1) Stratify servicing assets based on one or more of the predominant risk characteristics of the underlying financial assets. Those characteristics may include financial asset type,[19] size, interest rate, date of origination, term, and geographic location.
  (2) Recognize impairment through a valuation allowance for an individual stratum. The amount of impairment recognized shall be the amount by which the carrying amount of servicing assets for a stratum exceeds their

fair value. The fair value of servicing assets that have not been recognized shall not be used in the evaluation of impairment.
  (3) Adjust the valuation allowance to reflect changes in the measurement of impairment subsequent to the initial measurement of impairment. Fair value in excess of the carrying amount of servicing assets for that stratum, however, shall not be recognized. This Statement does not address when an entity should record a direct write-down of recognized servicing assets (paragraph 13).
h. Subsequently measure servicing liabilities by amortizing the amount recognized in proportion to and over the period of estimated net servicing loss—the excess of servicing costs over servicing revenues. However, if subsequent events have increased the fair value of the liability above the carrying amount, for example, because of significant changes in the amount or timing of actual or expected future cash flows from the cash flows previously projected, the servicer shall revise its earlier estimates and recognize the increased obligation as a loss in earnings (paragraph 13).

64. As indicated above, transferors sometimes agree to take on servicing responsibilities when the future benefits of servicing are not expected to adequately compensate them for performing that servicing. In that circumstance, the result is a servicing liability rather than a servicing asset. For example, if in the transaction illustrated in paragraph 57 the transferor had agreed to service the loans without explicit compensation and it estimated the fair value of that servicing obligation at $50, net proceeds would be reduced to $1,050, gain on sale would be reduced to $50, and the transferor would report a servicing liability of $50.

Illustration—Sale of Receivables with Servicing Retained

65. Company C originates $1,000 of loans that yield 10 percent interest income for their estimated lives of 9 years. Company C sells the $1,000 principal plus the right to receive interest income of 8 percent to another entity for $1,000. Company C will

---

[19]For example, for mortgage loans, financial asset type refers to the various conventional or government guaranteed or insured mortgage loans and adjustable-rate or fixed-rate mortgage loans.

continue to service the loans, and the contract stipulates that its compensation for performing the servicing is the right to receive half of the interest income not sold. The remaining half of the interest income not sold is considered an interest-only strip receivable. At the date of the transfer, the fair value of the loans, including servicing, is $1,100. The fair value of the servicing asset is $40.

Fair Values

Cash proceeds	$1,000
Servicing asset	40
Interest-only strip receivable	60

Carrying Amount Based on Relative Fair Values

	Fair Value	Percentage of Total Fair Value	Allocated Carrying Amount
Loans sold	$1,000	91.0	$ 910
Servicing asset	40	3.6	36
Interest-only strip receivable	60	5.4	54
Total	$1,100	100.0	$1,000

Gain on Sale

Net proceeds	$1,000
Carrying amount of loans sold	910
Gain on sale	$ 90

Journal Entries

Cash	1,000	
Loans		910
Gain on sale		90
To record transfer		

Servicing asset	36	
Interest-only strip receivable	54	
Loans		90
To record servicing asset and interest-only strip receivable		

Interest-only strip receivable	6	
Equity		6
To begin to subsequently measure interest-only strip receivable like an available-for-sale security (paragraph 14)		

66. The previous illustration demonstrates how a transferor would account for a simple sale or securitization in which servicing is retained. Company C might instead transfer the financial assets to a corporation or a trust that is a qualifying SPE. The qualifying SPE then securitizes the loans by selling beneficial interests to the public. The qualifying SPE pays the cash proceeds to the original transferor, which accounts for the transfer as a sale and derecognizes the financial assets assuming that the criteria in paragraph 9 are met. Securitizations often combine the elements shown in paragraphs 57, 60, and 65, as illustrated below.

Illustration—Recording Transfers of Partial Interests with Proceeds of Cash, Derivatives, Other Liabilities, and Servicing

67. Company D originates $1,000 of prepayable loans that yield 10 percent interest income for their 9-year expected lives. Company D sells nine-tenths of the principal plus interest of 8 percent to another entity. Company D will continue to service the loans, and the contract stipulates that its compensation for performing the servicing is the 2 percent of the interest income not sold. Company D obtains an option to purchase from the transferee loans similar to the loans sold (which are readily obtainable in the marketplace) and incurs a limited recourse obligation to repurchase delinquent loans.

Fair Values

Cash proceeds	$900
Call option	70
Recourse obligation	60
Servicing asset	90
One-tenth interest retained	100

Net Proceeds

Cash received	$900
Plus: Call option	70
Less: Recourse obligation	(60)
Net proceeds	$910

Carrying Amount Based on Relative Fair Values

	Fair Value	Percentage of Total Fair Value	Allocated Carrying Amount
Interest sold	$ 910	83	$ 830
Servicing asset	90	8	80
One-tenth interest retained	100	9	90
Total	$1,100	100	$1,000

Gain on Sale

Net proceeds	$910
Carrying amount of loans sold	830
Gain on sale	$ 80

Journal Entries

Cash	900	
Call option	70	
Loans		830
Recourse obligation		60
Gain on sale		80
To record transfer		
Servicing asset	80	
Loans		80
To record servicing asset		

At the time of the transfer, Company D reports its one-tenth retained interest in the loans at its allocated carrying amount of $90.

Fair Value

68. The fair value of an asset (or liability) is the amount at which that asset (or liability) could be bought (or incurred) or sold (or settled) in a current transaction between willing parties, that is, other than in a forced or liquidation sale. Quoted market prices in active markets are the best evidence of fair value and shall be used as the basis for the measurement, if available. If a quoted market price is available, the fair value is the product of the number of trading units times that market price.

69. If quoted market prices are not available, the estimate of fair value shall be based on the best information available in the circumstances. The estimate of fair value shall consider prices for similar assets and liabilities and the results of valuation techniques to the extent available in the circumstances. Examples of valuation techniques include the present value of estimated future cash flows,[20] option-pricing models, matrix pricing, option-adjusted spread models, and fundamental analysis.

Valuation techniques for measuring financial assets and liabilities and servicing assets and liabilities shall be consistent with the objective of measuring fair value. Those techniques shall incorporate assumptions that market participants would use in their estimates of values, future revenues, and future expenses, including assumptions about interest rates, default, prepayment, and volatility.[21] In measuring **financial liabilities** and servicing liabilities at fair value, the objective is to estimate the value of the assets required currently to (a) settle the liability with the holder or (b) transfer a liability to an entity of comparable credit standing.

70. Estimates of expected future cash flows, if used to estimate fair value, shall be based on reasonable and supportable assumptions and projections. All available evidence shall be considered in developing estimates of expected future cash flows. The weight given to the evidence shall be commensurate with the extent to which the evidence can be verified objectively. If a range is estimated for either the amount or timing of possible cash flows, the likelihood of possible outcomes shall be considered either directly, if applying an expected cash flow approach, or indirectly through the risk-adjusted discount rate, if determining the best estimate of future cash flows.

---

[20]FASB Concepts Statement No. 7, *Using Cash Flow Information and Present Value in Accounting Measurements*, discusses the use of present value techniques in measuring the fair value of an asset (or liability) in paragraphs 42–54 and 75–88. The Board believes that an expected present value technique is superior to traditional "best estimate" techniques, especially in situations in which the timing or amount of estimated cash flows is uncertain, as is often the case for retained interests in transferred financial assets. Concepts Statement 7 also discusses in paragraph 44 the steps needed to complete a proper search for the "rate commensurate with the risk" in applying the traditional technique.

[21]The timing and amount of future cash flows for retained interests in securitizations are commonly uncertain, especially if those interests are subordinate to more senior beneficial interests. Applying the present value approach depends heavily on assumptions about default and prepayment of all the assets securitized, because of the implicit credit or prepayment risk enhancement arising from the subordination.

If It Is Not Practicable to Estimate Fair Values

71. If it is not practicable to estimate the fair values of assets, the transferor shall record those assets at zero. If it is not practicable to estimate the fair values of liabilities, the transferor shall recognize no gain on the transaction and shall record those liabilities at the greater of:

a. The excess, if any, of (1) the fair values of assets obtained less the fair values of other liabilities incurred, over (2) the sum of the carrying values of the assets transferred

b. The amount that would be recognized in accordance with FASB Statement No. 5, *Accounting for Contingencies,* as interpreted by FASB Interpretation No. 14, *Reasonable Estimation of the Amount of a Loss.*

Illustration—Recording Transfers If It Is Not Practicable to Estimate a Fair Value

72. Company E sells loans with a carrying amount of $1,000 to another entity for cash plus a call option to purchase loans similar to the loans sold (which are readily obtainable in the marketplace) and incurs a limited recourse obligation to repurchase any delinquent loans. Company E undertakes to service the transferred assets for the other entity. In Case 1, Company E finds it impracticable to estimate the fair value of the servicing contract, although it is confident that servicing revenues will be more than adequate compensation for performing the servicing. In Case 2, Company E finds it impracticable to estimate the fair value of the recourse obligation.

Fair Values	Case1	Case2
Cash proceeds	$1,050	$1,050
Servicing asset	XX*	40
Call option	70	70
Recourse obligation	60	XX*
Fair value of loans transferred	1,100	1,100

*Not practicable to estimate fair value.

Net Proceeds	Case 1	Case 2
Cash received	$1,050	$1,050
Plus: Call option	70	70
Less: Recourse obligation	(60)	XX
Net proceeds	$1,060	$1,120

Carrying Amount Based on Relative Fair Values (Case 1)

	Fair Value	Percentage of Total Fair Value	Allocated Carrying Amount
Loans sold	$1,060	100	$1,000
Servicing asset	0	0	0
Total	$1,060	100	$1,000

Carrying Amount Based on Relative Fair Values (Case 2)

	Fair Value	Percentage of Total Fair Value	Allocated Carrying Amount
Loans sold	$1,120	97	$ 970
Servicing asset	40	3	30
Total	$1,160	100	$1,000

Journal Entries	Case 1		Case 2
Cash	1,050		1,050
Servicing asset	0*		30
Call option	70		70
Loans		1,000	1,000
Recourse obligation		60	150[†]
Gain on sale		60	0
To record transfer			

*Assets shall be recorded at zero if an estimate of the fair value of the assets is not practicable.

[†]The amount recorded as a liability in this example equals the sum of the known assets less the fair value of the known liabilities, that is, the amount that results in no gain or loss.

Securitizations

73. Financial assets such as mortgage loans, automobile loans, trade receivables, credit card receivables, and other revolving charge accounts are assets commonly transferred in securitizations. Securitizations of mortgage loans may include pools of single-family residential mortgages or other types of real estate mortgage loans, for example, multifamily residential mortgages and commercial property mortgages. Securitizations of loans secured by chattel mortgages on automotive vehicles as well as other equipment (including direct financing or sales-type leases) also are common. Both financial and nonfinancial assets can be securitized; life insurance policy loans, patent and copyright royalties, and even taxi medallions also have been securitized. But securitizations of nonfinancial assets are outside the scope of this Statement.

74. An originator of a typical securitization (the transferor) transfers a portfolio of financial assets to an SPE, commonly a trust. In "pass-through" and "pay-through" securitizations, receivables are transferred to the SPE at the inception of the securitization, and no further transfers are made; all cash collections are paid to the holders of beneficial interests in the SPE. In "revolving-period" securitizations, receivables are transferred at the inception and also periodically (daily or monthly) thereafter for a defined period (commonly three to eight years), referred to as the revolving period. During the revolving period, the SPE uses most of the cash collections to purchase additional receivables from the transferor on prearranged terms.

75. Beneficial interests in the SPE are sold to investors and the proceeds are used to pay the transferor for the assets transferred. Those beneficial interests may comprise either a single class having equity characteristics or multiple classes of interests, some having debt characteristics and others having equity characteristics. The cash collected from the portfolio is distributed to the investors and others as specified by the legal documents that established the SPE.

76. Pass-through, pay-through, and revolving-period securitizations that meet the criteria in paragraph 9 qualify for sale accounting under this Statement. All financial assets obtained or retained and liabilities incurred by the originator of a securitization that qualifies as a sale shall be recognized and measured as provided in paragraph 11; that includes the implicit forward contract to sell new receivables during a revolving period, which may become valuable or onerous to the transferor as interest rates and other market conditions change.

Revolving-Period Securitizations

77. The value of the forward contract implicit in a revolving-period securitization arises from the difference between the agreed-upon rate of return to investors on their beneficial interests in the trust and current market rates of return on similar investments. For example, if the agreed-upon annual rate of return to investors in a trust is 6 percent, and later market rates of return for those investments increased to 7 percent, the forward contract's value to the transferor (and burden to the investors) would approximate the present value of 1 percent of the amount of the investment for each year remaining in the revolving structure after the receivables already transferred have been collected. If a forward contract to sell receivables is entered into at the market rate, its value at inception may be zero. Changes in the fair value of the forward contract are likely to be greater if the investors receive a fixed rate than if the investors receive a rate that varies based on changes in market rates.

78. Gain or loss recognition for revolving-period receivables sold to a securitization trust is limited to receivables that exist and have been sold. Recognition of servicing assets or liabilities for revolving-period receivables is similarly limited to the servicing for the receivables that exist and have been transferred. As new receivables are sold, rights to service them become assets or liabilities and are recognized.

79. Revolving-period securitizations may use either a discrete trust, used for a single securitization, or a master trust, used for many securitizations. To achieve another securitization using an existing master trust, a transferor first transfers additional receivables to the trust and then sells additional ownership interests in the trust to investors. Adding receivables to a master trust, in itself, is neither a sale nor a secured borrowing under paragraph 9, because that transfer only increases the transferor's beneficial interest in the trust's assets. A sale or secured borrowing does not occur until the transferor receives consideration other than beneficial interests in the transferred assets. Transfers that result in an exchange of cash, that is, either transfers that in essence replace previously transferred receivables that have been collected or sales of beneficial interests to outside investors, are transfers in exchange for consideration other than beneficial interests in the transferred assets and thus are accounted for as sales (if they satisfy all the criteria in paragraph 9) or as secured borrowings.

Isolation of Transferred Assets in Securitizations

80. A securitization carried out in one transfer or a series of transfers may or may not isolate the transferred assets beyond the reach of the transferor and its creditors. Whether it does depends on the structure of the securitization transaction taken as a whole, considering such factors as the type and extent of further involvement in arrangements to protect investors from credit and interest rate risks, the availability of other assets, and the powers of bankruptcy courts or other receivers.

81. In certain securitizations, a corporation that, if it failed, would be subject to the U.S. Bankruptcy Code transfers financial assets to a special-purpose trust in exchange for cash. The trust raises that cash by issuing to investors beneficial interests that pass through all cash received from the financial assets, and the transferor has no further involvement with the trust or the transferred assets. The Board understands that those securitizations generally would be judged as having isolated the assets, because in the absence of any continuing involvement there would be reasonable assurance that the transfer would be found to be a true sale at law that places the assets beyond the reach of the transferor and its creditors, even in bankruptcy or other receivership.

82. In other securitizations, a similar corporation transfers financial assets to an SPE in exchange for cash and beneficial interests in the transferred assets. That entity raises the cash by issuing to investors commercial paper that gives them a senior interest in cash received from the financial assets. The beneficial interests retained by the transferring corporation represent a junior interest to be reduced by any credit losses on the financial assets in trust. The commercial paper interests are highly rated by credit rating agencies only if both (a) the credit enhancement from the junior interest is sufficient and (b) the transferor is highly rated. Depending on facts and circumstances, the Board understands that those "single-step" securitizations often would be judged in the United States as not having isolated the assets, because the nature of the continuing involvement may make it difficult to obtain reasonable assurance that the transfer would be found to be a true sale at law that places the assets beyond the reach of the transferor and its creditors in U.S. bankruptcy (paragraph 113). If the transferor fell into bankruptcy and the transfer was found not to be a true sale at law, investors in the transferred assets might be subjected to an automatic stay that would delay payments due them, and they

might have to share in bankruptcy expenses and suffer further losses if the transfer was recharacterized as a secured loan.

83. Still other securitizations use two transfers intended to isolate transferred assets beyond the reach of the transferor and its creditors, even in bankruptcy. In those "two-step" structures:

a. First, the corporation transfers financial assets to a special-purpose corporation that, although wholly owned, is so designed that the possibility that the transferor or its creditors could reclaim the assets is remote. This first transfer is designed to be judged to be a true sale at law, in part because the transferor does not provide "excessive" credit or yield protection to the special-purpose corporation, and the Board understands that transferred assets are likely to be judged beyond the reach of the transferor or the transferor's creditors even in bankruptcy.

b. Second, the special-purpose corporation transfers the assets to a trust or other legal vehicle with a sufficient increase in the credit or yield protection on the second transfer (provided by a junior retained beneficial interest or other means) to merit the high credit rating sought by third-party investors who buy senior beneficial interests in the trust. Because of that aspect of its design, that second transfer might not be judged to be a true sale at law and, thus, the transferred assets could at least in theory be reached by a bankruptcy trustee for the special-purpose corporation.

c. However, the special-purpose corporation is designed to make remote the possibility that it would enter bankruptcy, either by itself or by substantive consolidation into a bankruptcy of its parent should that occur. For example, its charter forbids it from undertaking any other business or incurring any liabilities, so that there can be no creditors to petition to place it in bankruptcy. Furthermore, its dedication to a single purpose is intended to make it extremely unlikely, even if it somehow entered bankruptcy, that a receiver under the U.S. Bankruptcy Code could reclaim the transferred assets because it has no other assets to substitute for the transferred assets.

The Board understands that the "two-step" securitizations described above, taken as a whole, generally would be judged under present U.S. law as having isolated the assets beyond the reach of the transferor and its creditors, even in bankruptcy or other receivership.

84. The powers of receivers for entities not subject to the U.S. Bankruptcy Code (for example, banks subject to receivership by the FDIC) vary considerably, and therefore some receivers may be able to reach financial assets transferred under a particular arrangement and others may not. A securitization may isolate transferred assets from a transferor subject to such a receiver and its creditors even though it is accomplished by only one transfer directly to an SPE that issues beneficial interests to investors and the transferor provides credit or yield protection. For entities that are subject to other possible bankruptcy, conservatorship, or other receivership procedures in the United States or other jurisdictions, judgments about whether transferred assets have been isolated need to be made in relation to the powers of bankruptcy courts or trustees, conservators, or receivers in those jurisdictions.

Removal-of-Accounts Provisions

85. Many transfers of financial assets in securitizations empower the transferor to reclaim assets subject to certain restrictions. Such a power is sometimes called a removal-of-accounts provision (ROAP). Whether a ROAP precludes sale accounting depends on whether the ROAP results in the transferor's maintaining effective control over specific transferred assets (paragraphs 9(c)(2) and 51–54).

86. The following are examples of ROAPs that preclude transfers from being accounted for as sales:

a. An unconditional ROAP or repurchase agreement that allows the transferor to specify the assets that may be removed, because such a provision allows the transferor unilaterally to remove specific assets

b. A ROAP conditioned on a transferor's decision to exit some portion of its business, because whether it can be triggered by canceling an affinity relationship, spinning off a business segment, or accepting a third party's bid to purchase a specified (for example, geographic) portion of the transferor's business, such a provision allows the transferor unilaterally to remove specific assets.

87. The following are examples of ROAPs that *do not* preclude transfers from being accounted for as sales:

a. A ROAP for random removal of excess assets, if the ROAP is sufficiently limited so that the transferor cannot remove specific transferred assets, for example, by limiting removals to the amount of the transferor's retained interest and to one removal per month

b. A ROAP for defaulted receivables, because the removal would be allowed only after a third party's action (default) and could not be caused unilaterally by the transferor

c. A ROAP conditioned on a third-party cancellation, or expiration without renewal, of an affinity or private-label arrangement, because the removal would be allowed only after a third party's action (cancellation) or decision not to act (expiration) and could not be caused unilaterally by the transferor.

88. A ROAP that can be exercised only in response to a third party's action that has not yet occurred does not maintain the transferor's effective control over assets potentially subject to that ROAP. However, when a third party's action (such as default or cancellation) or decision not to act (expiration) occurs that allows removal of assets to be initiated solely by the transferor, the transferor must recognize any assets subject to the ROAP, whether the ROAP is exercised or not. If the ROAP is exercised, the assets are recognized because the transferor has reclaimed the assets. If the ROAP is not exercised, the assets are recognized because the transferor now can unilaterally cause the qualifying SPE to return those specific assets and, therefore, the transferor once again has effective control over those transferred assets (paragraph 55).

Sales-Type and Direct Financing Lease Receivables

89. Sales-type and direct financing receivables secured by leased equipment, referred to as gross investment in lease receivables, are made up of two components: minimum lease payments and residual values. Minimum lease payments are requirements for lessees to pay cash to lessors and meet the definition of a financial asset. Thus, transfers of minimum

lease payments are subject to the requirements of this Statement. Residual values represent the lessor's estimate of the "salvage" value of the leased equipment at the end of the lease term and may be either guaranteed or unguaranteed; residual values meet the definition of financial assets *to the extent that they are guaranteed at the inception of the lease.* Thus, transfers of residual values guaranteed at inception also are subject to the requirements of this Statement. Unguaranteed residual values do not meet the definition of financial assets, nor do residual values guaranteed after inception, and transfers of them are not subject to the requirements of this Statement. Transfers of residual values not guaranteed at inception continue to be subject to Statement 13, as amended. Because residual values guaranteed at inception are financial assets, increases to their estimated value over the life of the related lease are recognized. Entities selling or securitizing lease financing receivables shall allocate the gross investment in receivables between minimum lease payments, residual values guaranteed at inception, and residual values not guaranteed at inception using the individual carrying amounts of those components at the date of transfer. Those entities also shall record a servicing asset or liability in accordance with paragraphs 10 and 13, if appropriate.

Illustration—Recording Transfers of Lease Financing Receivables with Residual Values

90. At the beginning of the second year in a 10-year sales-type lease, Company F sells for $505 a nine-tenths interest in the minimum lease payments and retains a one-tenth interest in the minimum lease payments and a 100 percent interest in the unguaranteed residual value of leased equipment. Company F receives no explicit compensation for servicing, but it estimates that the other benefits of servicing are just adequate to compensate it for its servicing responsibilities and hence initially records no servicing asset or liability. The carrying amounts and related gain computation are as follows:

Carrying Amounts

Minimum lease payments		$ 540
Unearned income related to minimum lease payments		370
Gross investment in minimum lease payments		910
Unguaranteed residual value	$30	
Unearned income related to residual value	60	
Gross investment in residual value		90
Total gross investment in financing lease receivable		$1,000

Gain on Sale

Cash received		$505
Nine-tenths of carrying amount of gross investment in minimum lease payments	$819	
Nine-tenths of carrying amount of unearned income related to minimum lease payments	333	
Net carrying amount of minimum lease payments sold		486
Gain on sale		$ 19

Journal Entry

Cash	505	
Unearned income	333	
Lease receivable		819
Gain on sale		19

To record sale of nine-tenths of the minimum lease payments at the beginning of year 2

Securities Lending Transactions

91. Securities lending transactions are initiated by broker-dealers and other financial institutions that need specific securities to cover a short sale or a customer's failure to deliver securities sold. Transferees ("borrowers") of securities generally are required to provide "collateral" to the transferor ("lender") of securities, commonly cash but sometimes other securities or standby letters of credit, with a value slightly higher than that of the securities "borrowed." If the "collateral" is cash, the transferor typically earns a return by investing that cash at rates higher than the rate paid or "rebated" to the transferee. If the "collateral" is other than cash, the transferor typically receives a fee. Securities custodians or other agents commonly carry out securities lending activities on behalf of clients. Because of the protection of "collateral" (typically valued daily and adjusted frequently for changes in the market price of the securities transferred) and the short terms of the transactions, most securities lending transactions in themselves do not impose significant credit risks on either party. Other risks arise from what the parties to the transaction do with the assets they receive. For example, investments made with cash "collateral" impose market and credit risks on the transferor.

92. In some securities lending transactions, the criteria in paragraph 9 are met, including the effective

control criterion in paragraph 9(c), and consideration other than beneficial interests in the transferred assets is received. Those transactions shall be accounted for (a) by the transferor as a sale of the "loaned" securities for proceeds consisting of the cash "collateral"[22] and a forward repurchase commitment and (b) by the transferee as a purchase of the "borrowed" securities in exchange for the "collateral" and a forward resale commitment. During the term of that agreement, the transferor has surrendered control over the securities transferred and the transferee has obtained control over those securities with the ability to sell or transfer them at will. In that case, creditors of the transferor have a claim only to the "collateral" and the forward repurchase commitment.

93. However, many securities lending transactions are accompanied by an agreement that entitles and obligates the transferor to repurchase or redeem the transferred assets before their maturity under which the transferor maintains effective control over those assets (paragraphs 47–49). Those transactions shall be accounted for as secured borrowings, in which cash (or securities that the holder is permitted by contract or custom to sell or repledge) received as "collateral" is considered the amount borrowed, the securities "loaned" are considered pledged as collateral against the cash borrowed and reclassified as set forth in paragraph 15(a), and any "rebate" paid to the

[22]If the "collateral" in a transaction that meets the criteria in paragraph 9 is a financial asset that the holder is permitted by contract or custom to sell or repledge, that financial asset is proceeds of the sale of the "loaned" securities. To the extent that the "collateral" consists of letters of credit or other financial instruments that the holder is not permitted by contract or custom to sell or repledge, a securities lending transaction does not satisfy the sale criteria and is accounted for as a loan of securities by the transferor to the transferee.

Accounting for Transfers and Servicing of
Financial Assets and Extinguishments of Liabilities
FAS140

transferee of securities is interest on the cash the transferor is considered to have borrowed.

94. The transferor of securities being "loaned" accounts for cash received in the same way whether the transfer is accounted for as a sale or a secured borrowing. The cash received shall be recognized as the transferor's asset—as shall investments made with that cash, even if made by agents or in pools with other securities lenders—along with the obligation to return the cash. If securities that may be sold or repledged are received, the transferor of the securities

being "loaned" accounts for those securities in the same way as it would account for cash received.

Illustration—Securities Lending Transaction Treated as a Secured Borrowing

95. The following example illustrates the accounting for a securities lending transaction treated as a secured borrowing, in which the securities borrower sells the securities upon receipt and later buys similar securities to return to the securities lender:

Facts

Transferor's carrying amount and fair value of security loaned	$1,000
Cash "collateral"	1,020
Transferor's return from investing cash collateral at a 5 percent annual rate	5
Transferor's rebate to the securities borrower at a 4 percent annual rate	4

For simplicity, the fair value of the security is assumed not to change during the 35-day term of the transaction.

Journal Entries for the Transferor

At inception:

Cash	1,020	
Payable under securities loan agreements		1,020
To record the receipt of cash collateral		

Securities pledged to creditors	1,000	
Securities		1,000
To reclassify loaned securities that the secured party has the right to sell or repledge		

Money market instrument	1,020	
Cash		1,020
To record investment of cash collateral		

At conclusion:

Cash	1,025	
Interest		5
Money market instrument		1,020
To record results of investment		

Securities	1,000	
Securities pledged to creditors		1,000
To record return of security		

Payable under securities loan agreements	1,020	
Interest ("rebate")	4	
Cash		1,024
To record repayment of cash collateral plus interest		

Journal Entries for the Transferee

At inception:

Receivable under securities loan agreements	1,020	
Cash		1,020
To record transfer of cash collateral		

Cash	1,000	
Obligation to return borrowed securities		1,000
To record sale of borrowed securities to a third party and the resulting obligation to return securities that it no longer holds		

At conclusion:

Obligation to return borrowed securities	1,000	
Cash		1,000
To record the repurchase of securities borrowed		

Cash	1,024	
Receivable under securities loan agreements		1,020
Interest revenue ("rebate")		4
To record the receipt of cash collateral and rebate interest		

Repurchase Agreements and "Wash Sales"

96. Government securities dealers, banks, other financial institutions, and corporate investors commonly use repurchase agreements to obtain or use short-term funds. Under those agreements, the transferor ("repo party") transfers a security to a transferee ("repo counterparty" or "reverse party") in exchange for cash[23] and concurrently agrees to reacquire that security at a future date for an amount equal to the cash exchanged plus a stipulated "interest" factor.

97. Repurchase agreements can be effected in a variety of ways. Some repurchase agreements are similar to securities lending transactions in that the transferee has the right to sell or repledge the securities to a third party during the term of the repurchase agreement. In other repurchase agreements, the transferee does not have the right to sell or repledge the securities during the term of the repurchase agreement. For example, in a tri-party repurchase agreement, the transferor transfers securities to an independent third-party custodian that holds the securities during the term of the repurchase agreement. Also, many repurchase agreements are for short terms, often overnight, or have indefinite terms that allow either party to terminate the arrangement on short notice. However, other repurchase agreements are for longer terms, sometimes until the maturity of the transferred asset. Some repurchase agreements call for repurchase of securities that need not be identical to the securities transferred.

98. If the criteria in paragraph 9 are met, including the criterion in paragraph 9(c)(1), the transferor shall account for the repurchase agreement as a sale of financial assets and a forward repurchase commitment, and the transferee shall account for the agreement as a purchase of financial assets and a forward resale commitment. Other transfers that are accompanied by an agreement to repurchase the transferred assets that shall be accounted for as sales include transfers with agreements to repurchase at maturity and transfers with repurchase agreements in which the transferee has not obtained collateral sufficient to fund substantially all of the cost of purchasing replacement assets.

---

[23]Instead of cash, other securities or letters of credit sometimes are exchanged. Those transactions are accounted for in the same manner as securities lending transactions (paragraphs 92–94).

Accounting for Transfers and Servicing of
Financial Assets and Extinguishments of Liabilities
FAS140

99. Furthermore, "wash sales" that previously were not recognized if the same financial asset was purchased soon before or after the sale shall be accounted for as sales under this Statement. Unless there is a concurrent contract to repurchase or redeem the transferred financial assets from the transferee, the transferor does not maintain effective control over the transferred assets.

100. As with securities lending transactions, under many agreements to repurchase transferred assets before their maturity the transferor maintains effective control over those assets. Repurchase agreements that do not meet all the criteria in paragraph 9 shall be treated as secured borrowings. Fixed-coupon and dollar-roll repurchase agreements, and other contracts under which the securities to be repurchased need not be the same as the securities sold, qualify as borrowings if the return of substantially the same (paragraph 48) securities as those concurrently transferred is assured. Therefore, those transactions shall be accounted for as secured borrowings by both parties to the transfer.

101. If a transferor has transferred securities to an independent third-party custodian, or to a transferee, under conditions that preclude the transferee from selling or repledging the assets during the term of the repurchase agreement (as in most tri-party repurchase agreements), the transferor has not surrendered control over those assets.

Loan Syndications

102. Borrowers often borrow amounts greater than any one lender is willing to lend. Therefore, it is common for groups of lenders to jointly fund those loans. That may be accomplished by a syndication under which several lenders share in lending to a single borrower, but each lender loans a specific amount to the borrower and has the right to repayment from the borrower.

103. A loan syndication is not a transfer of financial assets. Each lender in the syndication shall account for the amounts it is owed by the borrower. Repayments by the borrower may be made to a lead lender that then distributes the collections to the other lenders of the syndicate. In those circumstances, the lead lender is simply functioning as a servicer and, therefore, shall not recognize the aggregate loan as an asset.

Loan Participations

104. Groups of banks or other entities also may jointly fund large borrowings through loan participa-

tions in which a single lender makes a large loan to a borrower and subsequently transfers undivided interests in the loan to other entities.

105. Transfers by the originating lender may take the legal form of either assignments or participations. The transfers are usually on a nonrecourse basis, and the transferor ("originating lender") continues to service the loan. The transferee ("participating entity") may or may not have the right to sell or transfer its participation during the term of the loan, depending upon the terms of the participation agreement.

106. If the loan participation agreement gives the transferee the right to pledge or exchange those participations and the other criteria in paragraph 9 are met, the transfers to the transferee shall be accounted for by the transferor as sales of financial assets. A transferor's right of first refusal on a bona fide offer from a third party, a requirement to obtain the transferor's permission that shall not be unreasonably withheld, or a prohibition on sale to the transferor's competitor if other potential willing buyers exist is a limitation on the transferee's rights but presumptively does not constrain a transferee from exercising its right to pledge or exchange. However, if the loan participation agreement constrains the transferees from pledging or exchanging their participations, the transferor presumptively receives a more than trivial benefit, has not relinquished control over the loan, and shall account for the transfers as secured borrowings.

Banker's Acceptances and Risk Participations in Them

107. Banker's acceptances provide a way for a bank to finance a customer's purchase of goods from a vendor for periods usually not exceeding six months. Under an agreement between the bank, the customer, and the vendor, the bank agrees to pay the customer's liability to the vendor upon presentation of specified documents that provide evidence of delivery and acceptance of the purchased goods. The principal document is a draft or bill of exchange drawn by the customer that the bank stamps to signify its "acceptance" of the liability to make payment on the draft on its due date.

108. Once the bank accepts a draft, the customer is liable to repay the bank at the time the draft matures. The bank recognizes a receivable from the customer and a liability for the acceptance it has issued to the

vendor. The accepted draft becomes a negotiable financial instrument. The vendor typically sells the accepted draft at a discount either to the accepting bank or in the marketplace.

109. A risk participation is a contract between the accepting bank and a participating bank in which the participating bank agrees, in exchange for a fee, to reimburse the accepting bank in the event that the accepting bank's customer fails to honor its liability to the accepting bank in connection with the banker's acceptance. The participating bank becomes a guarantor of the credit of the accepting bank's customer.

110. An accepting bank that obtains a risk participation shall not derecognize the liability for the banker's acceptance, because the accepting bank is still primarily liable to the holder of the banker's accept-ance even though it benefits from a guarantee of reimbursement by a participating bank. The accepting bank shall not derecognize the receivable from the customer because it has not transferred the receivable: it controls the benefits inherent in that receivable and it is still entitled to receive payment from the customer. The accepting bank shall, however, record the guarantee purchased, and the participating bank shall record a liability for the guarantee issued.

Illustration—Banker's Acceptance with a Risk Participation

111. An accepting bank assumes a liability to pay a customer's vendor and obtains a risk participation from another bank. The details of the banker's acceptance are provided below:

Facts

Face value of the draft provided to vendor	$1,000
Term of the draft provided to vendor	90 days
Commission with an annual rate of 10 percent	25
Fee paid for risk participation	10

Journal Entries for Accepting Bank

At issuance of acceptance:

Receivable from customer	1,000	
Cash	25	
Time draft payable to vendor		1,000
Deferred acceptance commission revenue		25

At purchase of risk participation from a participating bank:

Guarantee purchased	10	
Cash		10

Upon presentation of the accepted time draft:

Time draft payable to vendor	1,000	
Deferred acceptance commission revenue	25	
Cash		1,000
Acceptance commission revenue		25

Upon collection from the customer (or the participating bank, if the customer defaults):

Cash	1,000	
Guarantee expense	10	
Receivable from customer		1,000
Guarantee purchased		10

Journal Entries for Participating Bank

Upon issuing the risk participation:

Cash	10	
Guarantee liability		10

Upon payment by the customer to the accepting bank:

Guarantee liability	10	
Guarantee revenue		10

OR:

In the event of total default by the customer:

Guarantee loss	990	
Guarantee liability	10	
Cash (paid to accepting bank)		1,000

Factoring Arrangements

112. Factoring arrangements are a means of discounting accounts receivable on a nonrecourse, notification basis. Accounts receivable are sold outright, usually to a transferee (the factor) that assumes the full risk of collection, without recourse to the transferor in the event of a loss. Debtors are directed to send payments to the transferee. Factoring arrangements that meet the criteria in paragraph 9 shall be accounted for as sales of financial assets because the transferor surrenders control over the receivables to the factor.

Transfers of Receivables with Recourse

113. In a transfer of receivables with recourse, the transferor provides the transferee with full or limited recourse. The transferor is obligated under the terms of the recourse provision to make payments to the transferee or to repurchase receivables sold under certain circumstances, typically for defaults up to a specified percentage. The effect of a recourse provision on the application of paragraph 9 may vary by jurisdiction. In some jurisdictions, transfers with full recourse may not place transferred assets beyond the reach of the transferor and its creditors, but transfers with limited recourse may. A transfer of receivables with recourse shall be accounted for as a sale, with the proceeds of the sale reduced by the fair value of the recourse obligation, if the criteria in paragraph 9 are met. Otherwise, a transfer of receivables with recourse shall be accounted for as a secured borrowing.

Extinguishments of Liabilities

114. If a creditor releases a debtor from primary obligation on the condition that a third party assumes the obligation and that the original debtor becomes secondarily liable, that release extinguishes the original debtor's liability. However, in those circumstances, whether or not explicit consideration was paid for that guarantee, the original debtor becomes a guarantor. As a guarantor, it shall recognize a guarantee obligation in the same manner as would a guarantor that had never been primarily liable to that creditor, with due regard for the likelihood that the third party will carry out its obligations. The guarantee obligation shall be initially measured at fair value, and that amount reduces the gain or increases the loss recognized on extinguishment.

Appendix B

BACKGROUND INFORMATION AND BASIS FOR CONCLUSIONS

CONTENTS

Appendix B

BACKGROUND INFORMATION AND BASIS FOR CONCLUSIONS

Introduction

115. This appendix summarizes considerations that were deemed significant by Board members in reaching the conclusions in this Statement. It also summarizes the considerations that were deemed significant by Board members in reaching the conclusions in Statement 125. Most of those conclusions and considerations are carried forward without reconsideration. It includes reasons for accepting certain approaches and rejecting others. Individual Board members gave greater weight to some factors than to others.

Background to Statement 125

116. In recent years, transfers of financial assets in which the transferor has some continuing involvement with the transferred assets or with the transferee have grown in volume, variety, and complexity. Those transfers raise the issues of whether transferred financial assets should be considered to be sold and a related gain or loss recorded, whether the assets should be considered to be collateral for borrowings, or whether the transfer should not be recognized.

117. A transferor may sell financial assets and receive in exchange cash or other assets that are unrelated to the assets sold so that the transferor has no continuing involvement with the assets sold. Alternatively, an entity may borrow money and pledge financial assets as collateral, or a transferor may engage in any of a variety of transactions that transfer financial assets to another entity with the transferor having some continuing involvement with the assets transferred. Examples of continuing involvement are recourse or guarantee obligations, servicing, agreements to repurchase or redeem, retained subordinated interests, and put or call options on the assets transferred.

118. Many transactions disaggregate financial assets into separate components by creating undivided interests in pools of financial assets that frequently reflect multiple participations (often referred to as tranches) in a single pool. The components created may later be recombined to restore the original assets or may be combined with other financial assets to create still different assets.

119. An entity also may enter into transactions that change the characteristics of an asset that the entity continues to hold. An entity may sell part of an asset, or an undivided interest in the asset, and retain part of the asset. In some cases, it was not always clear what the accounting should have been.

120. An entity may settle a liability by transferring assets to a creditor and obtaining an unconditional release from the obligation. Alternatively, an entity may arrange for others to settle or set aside assets to settle a liability later. Those alternative arrangements have raised issues about when a liability is extinguished.

121. The Board previously provided guidance for two specific types of transfers of financial assets in FASB Statement No. 77, *Reporting by Transferors for Transfers of Receivables with Recourse,* and in FASB Technical Bulletin No. 85-2, *Accounting for*

Collateralized Mortgage Obligations (CMOs). Confusion and inconsistency in accounting practices developed because the provisions of those two pronouncements provided seemingly conflicting guidance. In practice, if an entity sold financial assets to an SPE that issued debt securities, the guidance under Technical Bulletin 85-2 would be applied, and if any of those securities were obtained by the seller, the transaction would be accounted for as a borrowing. However, if the interests issued by the SPE were designated as participations instead of debt securities, the guidance in Statement 77 would be applied, and the transaction would be accounted for as a sale even if the seller retained recourse on some of the participations. Further, accounting for other types of transfers, whether developed by analogy to Statement 77 or Technical Bulletin 85-2, in industry practices codified in various AICPA audit and accounting Guides, in consensuses of the Emerging Issues Task Force (EITF), or in other ways, added to the confusion and inconsistency.

122. FASB Statement No. 76, *Extinguishment of Debt,* established accounting practices that (a) treat liabilities that are not fully settled as if they had been extinguished and (b) derecognize assets transferred to a trust even though the assets continue to benefit the transferor. Some criticized Statement 76 as being inconsistent with Statement 77; others disagreed.

123. The Board decided that it was necessary to reconsider Statements 76 and 77, Technical Bulletin 85-2, and other guidance and to develop new standards for transfers of financial assets and extinguishments of liabilities.

124. The Board added a project to its agenda in May 1986 to address those and other problems in accounting for financial instruments and off-balance-sheet financing. Statement 125 and this Statement, as part of that project, focus on accounting for transfers and servicing of financial assets and extinguishments of liabilities. The Financial Instruments Task Force, which was formed in January 1989, assisted in the preparation of a Discussion Memorandum on those issues and advised the Board in its deliberations. The FASB Discussion Memorandum, *Recognition and Measurement of Financial Instruments,* was issued in November 1991. The Board received 96 comment letters on the Discussion Memorandum. During 1994 and 1995, the Board discussed issues about transfers and servicing of financial assets and extinguishments of liabilities at numerous public meetings. The Financial Instruments Task Force reviewed drafts of the proposed Statement and discussed it with the Board at a public meeting in February 1995. The Financial Accounting Standards Advisory Council discussed a draft of the proposed Statement and advised the Board at public meetings. The Board also received requests from constituents to discuss issues about credit card securitizations and securities lending transactions and repurchase agreements. The Board met with constituents interested in those issues at public meetings in November 1994 and April 1995.

125. In October 1995, the Board issued an Exposure Draft, *Accounting for Transfers and Servicing of Financial Assets and Extinguishments of Liabilities.* The Board received 112 comment letters on the Exposure Draft, and 24 individuals and organizations presented their views at a public hearing held in February 1996. In addition, 10 enterprises participated in limited field-testing of the provisions of the Exposure Draft. The comments and test results were considered by the Board during its redeliberations of the issues addressed by the Exposure Draft in public meetings in 1996. The Financial Instruments Task Force reviewed a draft of the final Statement. Statement 125 was a result of those Board meetings and deliberations.

Background to This Statement

126. Statement 125 was issued in June 1996 and as issued was effective for transfers and servicing of financial assets and extinguishments of liabilities occurring after December 31, 1996. In December 1996, the Board considered constituents' concerns about their ability to apply certain provisions of Statement 125 by that date, including (a) making the changes to information and accounting systems needed to apply the newly established accounting requirements and (b) effectively tracking supporting data. The Board noted those concerns and issued Statement 127 to defer for one year the effective date of paragraph 15 (addressing secured borrowings and collateral) for all transactions and paragraphs 9–12 (addressing transfers of financial assets) only for transfers of financial assets that are part of repurchase agreement, dollar-roll, securities lending, and similar transactions.

127. In December 1996, after considering other constituent concerns, the Board added to its agenda a project to interpret or possibly amend Statement 125. The project initially focused on the effect of EITF Issue No. 90-18, "Effect of a 'Removal of Accounts'

Provision on the Accounting for a Credit Card Securitization," on accounting for credit card securitizations under Statement 125 and whether a removal-of-accounts provision (ROAP) maintains a transferor's effective control over transferred assets by entitling it to repurchase or redeem transferred assets that are not readily obtainable. The Board subsequently decided that the project also should consider several other issues concerning whether transfers of financial assets are accounted for as sales, including (a) the impact on isolation of transferred assets of the powers of the FDIC as receiver for a failed institution, (b) a transferee's right to sell or pledge transferred assets and the effect of conditions that constrain the transferee, (c) circumstances in which an SPE with some ability to sell transferred financial assets can be considered qualifying under the criteria in paragraph 26 of Statement 125, (d) the conditions for deciding whether assets transferred to a qualifying SPE and beneficial interests in those assets should appear in the consolidated financial statements of the transferor, and (e) a transferor's right to call a transferred financial asset that is not readily obtainable. In response to other concerns expressed by constituents, the Board also decided to consider (1) possible changes to the collateral provisions of paragraph 15 of Statement 125, (2) possible enhanced disclosures for securitizations involving financial assets, and (3) possible exclusion of transfers of financial assets measured using the equity method of accounting from the scope of Statement 125. The Board concluded that resolution of those issues would require an amendment, rather than an interpretation, of Statement 125.

128. In June 1999, the Board issued an Exposure Draft, *Accounting for Transfers of Financial Assets.* The Board received 40 comment letters on the Exposure Draft. In addition, four enterprises and members of the Bond Market Association participated in limited field-testing of certain provisions of the Exposure Draft. The comment letters and test results were considered by the Board during its redeliberations of the issues addressed by the Exposure Draft in 16 public meetings in 1999 and 2000. The Board concluded that it could reach an informed decision on the basis of existing information without a public hearing. The Board decided to issue a final Statement that replaces, rather than amends, Statement 125 after some commentators suggested that that would improve the readability and usefulness of the Statement. The Financial Instruments Task Force and other interested parties reviewed a draft of the final Statement for

clarity and operationality. This Statement is a result of those Board meetings and deliberations.

Benefits and Costs

129. The Board's mission statement charges the Board to determine that a proposed standard will fill a significant need and that the costs it imposes will be justified in relation to the overall benefits.

130. Previous practices in accounting for transfers of financial assets were inconsistent about the circumstances that distinguish sales from secured borrowings. The result was confusion on the part of both users and preparers of financial statements. Statement 125 and this Statement eliminate that inconsistency and reduce that confusion by distinguishing sales from secured borrowings based on the underlying contractual commitments and customs that determine substance. Much of the information needed to implement the accounting required by Statement 125 and carried forward without reconsideration in this Statement is substantially the same as that required for previous accounting and, therefore, should be available. Some of the information may not have been collected in accounting systems but is commonly obtained by sellers and buyers for use in negotiating transactions. Although there will be one-time costs for systems changes needed to apply the accounting required by this Statement, the benefits in terms of more credible, consistent, and understandable information will be ongoing.

131. In addition, in developing Statement 125 and this Statement, the Board considered how the costs incurred to implement their requirements could be minimized by, for example, (a) not requiring retroactive application of the initial measurement provisions of Statement 125 to existing servicing rights and excess servicing receivables, (b) carrying over without change the subsequent measurement (amortization and impairment) provisions of FASB Statement No. 122, *Accounting for Mortgage Servicing Rights,* (c) not requiring allocation of previous carrying amounts of assets partially sold based on relative fair values at acquisition, but rather at the date of transfer, and (d) eliminating the requirement to recognize collateral because the limited benefits do not justify the burden of preparing the information. This Statement requires additional disclosures for securitizations, because events since the issuance of Statement 125 convinced the Board that the need of investors and creditors for better information justifies the costs other entities will incur in developing and reporting that information. Furthermore, many of those

disclosures are already being made voluntarily by some entities. The Board is confident that the benefits derived from the accounting and disclosure required by Statement 125 and this Statement will outweigh the costs of implementation.

Approaches Considered in Developing Statement 125

132. The Board noted that the most difficult questions about accounting for transfers of financial assets concern the circumstances in which it is appropriate to remove previously recognized financial assets from the statement of financial position and to recognize gain or loss. One familiar approach to those questions views each financial asset as a unit that should not be derecognized until the risks and rewards that are embodied in that asset have been surrendered. Variations on that approach attempt to choose which risks and rewards are most critical and whether all or some major portion of those risks and rewards must be surrendered to allow derecognition.

133. In addition to reviewing U.S. accounting literature, the Board reviewed the approach described by the International Accounting Standards Committee (IASC) in its proposed International Accounting Standard, *Financial Instruments,* Exposure Draft E40 (1992), later revised as Exposure Draft E48 (1994). In E40, derecognition of financial assets and liabilities would have been permitted only upon the transfer to others of the underlying risks and rewards, presumably all risks and rewards. That approach could have resulted in an entity's continuing to recognize assets even though it had surrendered control over the assets to a successor entity. The approach in E40 was similar to that taken in Technical Bulletin 85-2. The Board concluded that the approaches proposed in E40 and provided in Technical Bulletin 85-2 were unsatisfactory because the result does not faithfully represent the effects of the transfer of assets and because of the potential for inconsistencies.

134. In response to comments received on E40, the IASC proposal was revised in E48 to require the transfer of *substantially all* risks and rewards. That modification did not overcome the inconsistency noted in paragraphs 130 and 133 of this Statement and would have added the prospect of difficulties in application because of the need to identify, measure, and weigh in the balance each of possibly many and varied risks and rewards embodied in a particular financial asset. The number of different risks and rewards would have varied depending on the definitions used. Questions would have arisen about whether each identified risk and reward should be substantially surrendered to allow derecognition, whether all risks should be aggregated separately from all rewards, and whether risks and rewards should somehow be offset and then combined for evaluation. That modification also might have led to wide variations in practice depending on how various entities interpreted *substantially all* in the necessarily subjective evaluation of the aggregated, offset, and combined risks and rewards. Moreover, viewing each financial asset as an indivisible unit is contrary to the growing practice in financial markets of disaggregating individual financial assets or pools of financial assets into components. The IASC was still studying that issue in its financial instruments project when Statement 125 was issued.

135. In March 1997, the IASC issued jointly with the Canadian Institute of Chartered Accountants a comprehensive Discussion Paper, *Accounting for Financial Assets and Financial Liabilities.* Later in 1997, the IASC Board decided to pursue its financial instruments project along two paths. It joined with national standard setters, including the FASB, in a Joint Working Group to develop, integrate, and harmonize international accounting standards on financial instruments, building on the March 1997 Joint Discussion Paper. At the same time, the IASC decided to complete an interim international standard to serve until the integrated comprehensive standard is completed. In December 1998, the IASC issued that interim standard, IAS 39, *Financial Instruments: Recognition and Measurement.* The provisions for derecognition of a financial asset in that interim standard continue to focus on whether the transferor has retained, or the transferee has taken on, substantially all of the risks and rewards of ownership. The Joint Working Group has reached tentative conclusions on issues about transfers of financial assets that resemble the conclusions in Statement 125 in some respects, with less focus on risks and rewards, but that differ significantly in other respects. However, that group has yet to reach conclusions on certain issues and its work is still in progress. The tentative conclusions have not yet been exposed for public comment. Because (a) the comprehensive international project is still in that early stage, (b) the project has a broad scope including many other issues likely to prove controversial, and (c) the FASB project to amend Statement 125 was limited in scope and urgently needed, the Board did not consider in this project whether to replace the fundamental principles of Statement 125 with the principles being developed

internationally. The Board plans to join the other members of the Joint Working Group in circulating that group's document for public comment, after which the Board expects to consider what further steps it should take.

136. In developing Statement 125, the Board noted that application of a risks-and-rewards approach for derecognizing financial assets would be highly dependent on the sequence of transactions leading to their acquisition. For example, if Entity A initially acquired an undivided subordinated interest in a pool of financial assets, it would recognize that subordinated interest as a single asset. If, on the other hand, Entity B initially acquired a pool of financial assets identical to the pool in which Entity A participates, then sold a senior interest in the pool and continued to hold a subordinated interest identical to the undivided interest held by Entity A, Entity B might be judged under a risks-and-rewards approach to have retained substantially all the risks of the entire pool. Thus, Entity B would carry in its statement of financial position the entire pool of financial assets as well as an obligation equal to the proceeds from the sale of the undivided senior interest, while Entity A would report its identical position quite differently. Those accounting results would disregard one of the fundamental tenets of the Board's conceptual framework; that is, ". . . accountants must not disguise real differences nor create false differences."[24]

137. The Board also considered the approach required by the United Kingdom's Accounting Standards Board in Financial Reporting Standard No. 5, *Reporting the Substance of Transactions,* a variation of the risks-and-rewards approach that requires the surrender of substantially all risks and rewards for derecognition of financial assets but permits, in limited circumstances, the use of a *linked presentation.* Use of the linked presentation is restricted to circumstances in which an entity borrows funds to be repaid from the proceeds of pledged financial assets, any excess proceeds go to the borrower, and the lender has no recourse to other assets of the borrower. In those circumstances, the pledged assets remain on the borrower's statement of financial position, but the unpaid borrowing is reported as a deduction from the pledged assets rather than as a liability; no gain or loss is recognized. That approach had some appeal to the Board because it would have highlighted significant information about transactions that many believe have characteristics of both sales and secured

borrowings. The Board observed, however, that the linked presentation would not have dealt with many of the problems created by the risks-and-rewards approach. Further, the Board concluded that it is not appropriate for an entity to offset restricted assets against a liability or to derecognize a liability merely because assets are dedicated to its repayment, as discussed in paragraphs 309–312.

138. Statement 77 based the determination of whether to derecognize receivables on transfer of control instead of on evaluation of risks and rewards. Statement 125 and this Statement take a similar approach. However, Statement 77 was narrowly focused on sales of receivables with recourse and did not address other transfers of financial assets. Also, the derecognition of receivables under that Statement could depend on the sequence of transactions that led to their acquisition or on whether any options were involved. The Board concluded that simply superseding Technical Bulletin 85-2 and allowing Statement 77 to remain in effect would not have dealt adequately with the issues about transfers of financial assets.

139. Statement 76 followed a risks-and-rewards approach in requiring that (a) it be probable that a debtor would not be required to make future payments with respect to the debt under any guarantees and (b) an in-substance defeasance trust be restricted to owning only monetary assets that are risk free with cash flows that approximately coincide, as to timing and amount, with the scheduled interest and principal payments on the debt being extinguished. The Board concluded that that approach was inconsistent with the financial-components approach that focuses on control developed in this Statement (paragraphs 309–312). As a result, the Board decided to supersede Statement 76 but to carry forward those of its criteria that could be modified to conform to the financial-components approach.

140. The considerations discussed in paragraphs 132–139 led the Board to seek an alternative to the risks-and-rewards approach and variations to that approach.

Objectives of the Financial-Components Approach

141. The Board concluded in Statement 125 that it was necessary to develop an approach that would be

---

[24]FASB Concepts Statement No. 2, *Qualitative Characteristics of Accounting Information,* par. 119.

responsive to current developments in the financial
markets to achieve consistent accounting for transfers and servicing of financial assets and extinguishments of liabilities. That approach—the financial-
components approach—is designed to:

a. Be consistent with the way participants in the financial markets deal with financial assets, including the combination and separation of components of those assets
b. Reflect the economic consequences of contractual
provisions underlying financial assets and liabilities
c. Conform to the FASB conceptual framework.

142. The approach analyzes a transfer of a financial
asset by examining the component assets (controlled
economic benefits) and liabilities (present obligations
for probable future sacrifices of economic benefits)
that exist after the transfer. Each party to the transfer
recognizes the assets and liabilities that it controls after the transfer and no longer recognizes the assets
and liabilities that were surrendered or extinguished
in the transfer. That approach has some antecedents
in existing accounting guidance, for example, in
EITF Issue No. 88-11, "Allocation of Recorded Investment When a Loan or Part of a Loan Is Sold."
The Board identified the concepts set forth in paragraphs 143–145 as an appropriate basis for the
financial-components approach.

**Conceptual Basis for the Financial-Components
Approach**

143. FASB Concepts Statement No. 6, *Elements of
Financial Statements,* states the following about assets:

> Assets are probable future economic ben-
> efits obtained or controlled by a particular en-
> tity as a result of past transactions or events.
> [Paragraph 25, footnote reference omitted.]
> *Every asset is an asset of some entity;
> moreover, no asset can simultaneously be an
> asset of more than one entity,* although a par-
> ticular physical thing or other agent [for ex-
> ample, contractual rights and obligations] that
> provides future economic benefit may pro-
> vide separate benefits to two or more entities
> at the same time. . . . To have an asset, an en-
> tity must control future economic benefit to
> the extent that it can benefit from the asset
> and generally can deny or regulate access to
> that benefit by others, for example, by permit-
> ting access only at a price.

Thus, *an asset of an entity is the future
economic benefit that the entity can control
and thus can, within limits set by the nature of
the benefit or the entity's right to it, use as it
pleases.* The entity having an asset is the one
that can exchange it, use it to produce goods
or services, exact a price for others' use of it,
use it to settle liabilities, hold it, or perhaps
distribute it to owners.

The definition of assets focuses primarily
on the future economic benefit to which an
entity has access and only secondarily on the
physical things and other agents that provide
future economic benefits. *Many physical
things and other agents are in effect bundles
of future economic benefits that can be unbundled in various ways, and two or more entities may have different future economic benefits from the same agent at the same time or
the same continuing future economic benefit
at different times.* For example, two or more
entities may have undivided interests in a parcel of land. Each has a right to future economic benefit that may qualify as an asset under the definition in paragraph 25, even
though the right of each is subject at least to
some extent to the rights of the other(s). Or,
one entity may have the right to the interest
from an investment, while another has the
right to the principal. [Paragraphs 183–185;
emphasis added.]

144. Concepts Statement 6 states the following
about liabilities:

> Liabilities are probable future sacrifices of
> economic benefits arising from present obli-
> gations of a particular entity to transfer assets
> or provide services to other entities in the fu-
> ture as a result of past transactions or events.
> [Paragraph 35, footnote references omitted.]
> Most liabilities are obligations of only one
> entity at a time. Some liabilities are shared—
> for example, two or more entities may be
> "jointly and severally liable" for a debt or for
> the unsatisfied liabilities of a partnership. But
> most liabilities bind a single entity, and those
> that bind two or more entities are commonly
> ranked rather than shared. For example, *a
> primary debtor and a guarantor may both
> be obligated for a debt, but they do not
> have the same obligation—the guarantor
> must pay only if the primary debtor defaults*

Accounting for Transfers and Servicing of
Financial Assets and Extinguishments of Liabilities
FAS140

and thus has a contingent or secondary obligation, which ranks lower than that of the primary debtor.

Secondary, and perhaps even lower ranked, obligations may qualify as liabilities under the definition in paragraph 35, but recognition considerations are highly significant in deciding whether they should formally be included in financial statements because of the effects of uncertainty (paragraphs 44–48). For example, the probability that a secondary or lower ranked obligation will actually have to be paid must be assessed to apply the definition. [Paragraphs 204 and 205; emphasis added.]

145. Financial assets and liabilities are assets and liabilities that qualify as financial instruments as defined in paragraph 3 of FASB Statement No. 107, *Disclosures about Fair Value of Financial Instruments:*

A financial instrument is defined as cash, evidence of an ownership interest in an entity, or a contract that both:

a. Imposes on one entity a contractual obligation (1) to deliver cash or another financial instrument to a second entity or (2) to exchange other financial instruments on potentially unfavorable terms with the second entity

b. Conveys to that second entity a contractual right (1) to receive cash or another financial instrument from the first entity or (2) to exchange other financial instruments on potentially favorable terms with the first entity. [Footnote references omitted.]

146. Based on the concepts and definitions cited in paragraphs 143–145, the Board concluded that the key to applying the financial-components approach can be summarized as follows:

a. The economic benefits provided by a financial asset (generally, the right to future cash flows) are derived from the contractual provisions that underlie that asset, and the entity that controls those benefits should recognize them as its asset.

b. A financial asset should be considered sold and therefore should be derecognized if it is transferred and control is surrendered.

c. A transferred financial asset should be considered pledged as collateral to secure an obligation of the transferor (and therefore should not be derecognized) if the transferor has not surrendered control of the financial asset.

d. Each liability should be recognized by the entity that is primarily liable and, accordingly, an entity that guarantees another entity's obligation should recognize only its obligation to perform on the guarantee.

e. The recognition of financial assets and liabilities should not be affected by the sequence of transactions that led to their existence unless as a result of those transactions the transferor maintains effective control over a transferred asset.

f. Transferors and transferees should account symmetrically for transfers of financial assets.

147. Most respondents to the Exposure Draft of Statement 125 generally supported the financial-components approach, especially as it applies to securitization transactions.

148. The concepts underlying the financial-components approach could be applied by analogy to accounting for transfers of nonfinancial assets and thus could result in accounting that differs significantly from that required by existing standards and practices. However, the Board believes that financial and nonfinancial assets have significantly different characteristics, and it is not clear to what extent the financial-components approach is applicable to nonfinancial assets. Nonfinancial assets have a variety of operational uses, and management skill plays a considerable role in obtaining the greatest value from those assets. In contrast, financial assets have no operational use. They may facilitate operations, and financial assets may be the principal "product" offered by some entities. However, the promise embodied in a financial asset is governed by contract. Once the contract is established, management skill plays a limited role in the entity's ability to realize the value of the instrument. Furthermore, the Board believes that attempting to extend Statement 125 and this Statement to transfers of nonfinancial assets would unduly delay resolving the issues for transfers of financial assets, because of the significant differences between financial assets and nonfinancial assets and because of the significant unresolved recognition and measurement issues posed by those differences. For those reasons, the Board concluded that existing accounting practices for transfers of nonfinancial assets should not be changed at this time. The Board further concluded that transfers of servicing assets and transfers of property subject to operating leases are not

within the scope of Statement 125 and this Statement because they are nonfinancial assets.

149. The following paragraphs discuss the application of the concepts and principles described in paragraphs 143–148, both as the concepts and principles were applied initially in Statement 125 and as they are, in some cases, applied differently in this Statement. First, circumstances that require derecognition of transferred assets and recognition of assets and liabilities received in exchange are discussed in the paragraphs about sales of financial assets, transfers to SPEs, and other transfers (paragraphs 150–264). Then, the measurement of assets controlled and liabilities incurred (paragraphs 265–305) and subsequent measurement (paragraphs 306–308) are discussed. Finally, extinguishments of liabilities are discussed (paragraphs 309–315).

Sales of Financial Assets

150. If an entity transfers financial assets, surrenders control of those assets to a successor entity, and has no continuing involvement with those assets, accounting for the transaction as a sale and derecognizing the assets and recognizing the related gain or loss is not controversial. However, accounting for transfers of financial assets has been controversial and inconsistent in circumstances in which an entity transfers only a partial interest in a financial asset or has some other continuing involvement with the transferred asset or the transferee.

151. Under the financial-components approach, the accounting for a transfer is based on whether a transferor surrenders control of financial assets. Paragraph 3 of Statement 77 states, "This Statement establishes standards of financial accounting and reporting by transferors for transfers of receivables with recourse that *purport to be sales* of receivables" (emphasis added). The Board believes that, while it may have some significance at law, a more exacting test than whether a transaction purports to be a sale is needed to conclude that control has been surrendered in a manner that is consistent with the definitions in Concepts Statement 6. The Board concluded that a sale occurs only if control has been surrendered to another entity or group of entities and that surrender of control depends on whether (a) transferred assets have been isolated from the transferor, (b) transferees have obtained the right to pledge or exchange either the transferred assets or beneficial interests in the transferred assets, and (c) the transferor does not maintain effective control

over the transferred assets through an agreement to repurchase or redeem them before their maturity or through the ability to unilaterally cause the holder to return specific assets.

Isolation beyond the Reach of the Transferor, Even in Bankruptcy or Other Receivership

152. The Board developed its criterion that transferred assets must be isolated—put presumptively beyond the reach of the transferor and its creditors, even in bankruptcy or other receivership (paragraph 9(a))—in large part with reference to securitization practices. Credit rating agencies and investors in securitized assets pay close attention to (a) the possibility of bankruptcy or other receivership of the transferor, its affiliates, or the SPE, even though that possibility may seem unlikely given the present credit standing of the transferor, and (b) what might happen in such a receivership, because those are major areas of risk for them. If certain receivers can reclaim securitized assets, investors will suffer a delay in payments due them and may be forced to accept a pro rata settlement. Credit rating agencies and investors commonly demand transaction structures that minimize those possibilities and sometimes seek assurances from attorneys about whether entities can be forced into receivership, what the powers of a receiver might be, and whether the transaction structure would withstand receivers' attempts to reach the securitized assets in ways that would harm investors. Unsatisfactory structures or assurances commonly result in credit ratings that are no higher than those for the transferor's liabilities and in lower prices for transferred assets.

153. Because legal isolation of transferred assets has substance, the Board decided that it could and should serve as an important part of the basis for determining whether a sale should be recognized. Some constituents expressed concern about the feasibility of an accounting standard based on those legal considerations, but the Board concluded that having to consider only the evidence available should make that requirement workable.

154. Respondents to the Exposure Draft of Statement 125 raised several questions about the application of the isolation criterion in paragraph 9(a) to existing securitization structures. The questions included whether it was necessary to consider separately the accounting by the first-tier SPE, whose transfer to the second-tier trust taken by itself might not satisfy the isolation test. After considering

those comments and consulting with respondents who specialize in the structure of securitization transactions, the Board concluded that related language in Appendix A should be revised to explain that that criterion can be satisfied either by a single transaction or by a series of transactions considered as a whole. As discussed in paragraphs 80–84, the Board understands that the series of transactions in a typical two-tier structure taken as a whole may satisfy the isolation test because the design of the structure achieves isolation.

155. The Board understands that a one-tier structure with significant continuing involvement by a transferor subject to the U.S. Bankruptcy Code might not satisfy the isolation test, because a trustee in bankruptcy has substantial powers that could alter amounts that investors might receive and thus it may be difficult to conclude that control has been relinquished. Some respondents argued that a one-tier structure with continuing involvement generally should be adequate if the transferor's credit rating is sufficiently high that the chance of sudden bankruptcy is remote. The Board did not accept that view because isolation should not depend on the credit standing of the transferor.

156. Some constituents questioned whether the term *affiliates* was used in Statement 125 in the same sense as it was used in FASB Statement No. 57, *Related Party Disclosures,* or more narrowly. Their concerns included, for example, how the meaning of that term might affect whether a transfer from a subsidiary to a sister subsidiary, which would be eliminated in the consolidated financial statements of their common parent, could ever qualify as a sale in the separate financial statements of the transferring subsidiary. The Board chose to clarify that matter by (a) revising the discussion in paragraph 27 of this Statement to emphasize that whether a transfer has isolated the transferred assets can depend on which financial statements are being presented and (b) introducing the term *consolidated affiliate of the transferor* where the Board intended a narrower sense than *affiliate* as used in Statement 57.

If the FDIC is receiver

157. During the deliberations leading up to the issuance of Statement 125, constituents asked the Board to explain how the criterion in paragraph 9(a) applied to transfers by institutions subject to possible receivership by the FDIC, in view of the limited, special powers of the FDIC to repudiate certain contracts.

The Board's understanding at the time Statement 125 was issued was that financial assets transferred by a U.S. bank were not subject to an automatic stay under FDIC receivership and that the receiver could only obtain those assets if it makes the investors whole, that is, by paying them compensation equivalent to all the economic benefits embodied in the transferred assets (principal and interest earned to date). Based on that understanding, the Board concluded, as explained in paragraphs 58 and 121 of Statement 125, that those limited powers appeared insufficient to place transferred assets within reach of the receiver and, therefore, assets transferred subject to those powers could be considered isolated from their transferor.

158. In implementing Statement 125, the Board's earlier understanding of the powers of the FDIC, as explained in paragraphs 58 and 121 of Statement 125, was called into question. During 1998, the Board learned the following from attorneys specializing in FDIC matters and from members of the FDIC staff:

a. The FDIC's practice in repudiating contracts has most often been to pay principal and interest *to date of payment,* unless the assets have been fraudulently conveyed or conveyed to an affiliate under improper circumstances. However, the FDIC has the power to repudiate contracts that it characterizes as secured borrowings and, thereby, reclaim transferred assets by paying principal and interest *to the date of receivership,* which may be as many as 180 days before the date of payment.

b. Relevant statutes require, in the case of certain repurchase agreements and similar contracts characterized as *qualified financial contracts,* that the FDIC pay all reasonably expected damages to repudiate those contracts. Therefore, the FDIC has to pay at least principal and interest to *date of payment* on those contracts.

c. Attorneys generally have been unable to provide opinions sufficient to satisfy preparers and auditors that many kinds of transfers of financial assets by financial institutions subject to the powers of the FDIC have isolated those assets. It is unclear in which circumstances attorneys might be able to provide such opinions for certain other transfers of financial assets by those institutions.

159. Based on that new information, the Board decided that this issue required reconsideration. The

Board considered whether the FDIC's powers to reclaim transferred assets by paying principal and interest to date of receivership were still limited enough that transferred assets potentially subject to those powers could be considered isolated. The Board rejected the possibility of modifying the observations in paragraphs 58 and 121 of Statement 125 to indicate that a receiver's right to reclaim transferred assets by paying principal and interest *to date of receivership* does not preclude sale accounting because that would selectively weaken the standard of isolation and impair comparability across industries. Instead, the Board decided that any discussion about the FDIC's powers should simply reiterate, perhaps more clearly, that transferred financial assets subject to the limited power of a receiver to reclaim them could be considered isolated only if the receiver would have to pay at least principal and interest *to date of payment.*

160. After that decision, representatives of the FDIC, the Auditing Standards Board of the AICPA, banks, and the securities bar discussed what actions, if any, the FDIC could take that would alleviate those legal, auditing, and accounting difficulties. In July 2000, the FDIC adopted, after public comment and other due process, a final rule, *Treatment by the Federal Deposit Insurance Corporation as Conservator or Receiver of Financial Assets Transferred by an Insured Depository Institution in Connection with a Securitization or Participation.* That final rule modifies the FDIC's powers so that, subject to certain conditions, it shall not recover, reclaim, or recharacterize as property of the institution or the receivership any financial assets transferred by an insured depository institution in connection with a securitization or participation. The final rule also states that the FDIC may repeal or amend that final rule but that any such repeal or amendment would not apply to any transfers of financial assets made in connection with a securitization or participation that was in effect before such repeal or amendment. In view of that final rule and after consultation with other affected parties, the Board concluded that specific guidance about the effect of the FDIC's powers as receiver on the isolation of transferred assets would no longer be needed. Therefore, this Statement removes that specific guidance.

Transferee's Rights to Pledge or Exchange

161. The second criterion (paragraph 9(b)) for a transfer to be a sale focuses on whether the transferee has the right to pledge or exchange the transferred assets. That criterion is consistent with the idea that the entity that has an asset is the one that can use it in the various ways set forth in Concepts Statement 6, paragraph 184 (quoted in paragraph 143 of this Statement). A transferee may be able to use a transferred asset in some of those ways but not in others. Therefore, establishing criteria for determining whether control has been relinquished to a transferee necessarily depends in part on identifying which ways of using the kind of asset transferred are the decisive ones. In the case of transfers of financial assets, the transferee holds the assets, but that is not necessarily decisive because the economic benefits of financial assets consist primarily of future cash inflows. The Board concluded that the ways of using assets that are important in determining whether a transferee holding a financial asset controls it are the ability to exchange it or pledge it as collateral and thus obtain all or most of the cash inflows that are the primary economic benefits of financial assets. As discussed in paragraph 173, if the transferee is a qualifying SPE, the ultimate holders of the assets are the beneficial interest holders (BIHs), and the important rights concern their ability to exchange or pledge their interests.

162. The Exposure Draft of Statement 125 proposed that a transferee be required to have the right—free of transferor-imposed conditions—to pledge or exchange the transferred assets for a transfer to qualify as a sale. Respondents to the Exposure Draft observed that some transferor-imposed conditions may not indicate that the transferor retains control over the assets transferred. The respondents suggested that some conditions are imposed for business or competitive purposes, not to keep control over future economic benefits of the transferred assets, and that those conditions should not preclude a transfer from being accounted for as a sale. Other respondents noted that not all conditions that might limit a transferee's ability to take advantage of a right to pledge or exchange transferred assets were necessarily imposed by the transferor. The Board decided that the criterion should not be restricted to being transferor imposed and that some conditions, described in paragraph 25 of Statement 125, should not disqualify a transaction, so long as those conditions do not constrain the transferee from taking advantage of its right to pledge or exchange the transferred assets.

163. In implementing Statement 125, two issues emerged relating to its second criterion for recognizing a transfer of financial assets as a sale (paragraph 9(b)(1) of Statement 125). The first issue was what types of constraints on the transferee's right to

Accounting for Transfers and Servicing of
Financial Assets and Extinguishments of Liabilities
FAS140

pledge or exchange transferred assets preclude sale accounting. The second issue was whether a transferee must obtain *either* the right to pledge transferred assets *or* the right to exchange them or whether a transferee must obtain *both* rights for the transfer to qualify for sale accounting.

164. The Board questioned whether sale accounting should be precluded because of a constraint on the transferee's ability to sell or pledge that does not benefit the transferor. The Board concluded that unless the constraint provides more than a trivial benefit to the transferor, it does not affect whether the transferor has surrendered control and, therefore, there is little reason for the transferor to continue recognizing the transferred asset. Consequently, such constraints should not preclude sale accounting.

165. Whether a constraint is of more than trivial benefit to the transferor may not always be clear. The Board reasoned that transferors incur costs if they impose constraints, since transferees presumably pay less than they would pay to obtain the asset without constraint. Transferors presumably incur those costs for good reasons. The Board therefore concluded that, absent evidence to the contrary, imposition of a constraint by a transferor results in a more than trivial benefit to the transferor.

166. However, it is not so clear whether conditions not imposed by the transferor constrain the transferee *and* benefit the transferor. The Board considered four possibilities. First, Statement 125 could have been left unchanged, and therefore it would have continued to preclude sale accounting if any condition constrained the transferee, even if the transferor did not somehow benefit. The Board rejected that first possibility because transferred assets from which the transferor can obtain no further benefits are no longer its assets and should be removed from its statement of financial position. Second, the Board could have returned to the provisions proposed in the Exposure Draft of Statement 125, under which conditions not imposed by the transferor that constrain the transferee have no effect on the accounting. The Board rejected that second possibility because it would have excluded from the transferor's statement of financial position some assets from which, through the constraint, it still can obtain future benefits. Third, the Board could have precluded sale accounting for conditions not imposed by the transferor that constrain the transferee, unless the transferor has no continuing involvement with the transferred assets. The Board rejected that third possibility, even though it avoided

the problems of the first two possibilities, because it seemed in conflict with the financial-components approach and would have required resolving numerous issues including whether some types of continuing involvement are so minor that they should not preclude sale accounting. The fourth possibility, which the Board adopted because it avoided the problems of the other three possibilities, was to preclude sale accounting for conditions not imposed by the transferor that constrain the transferee only if the constraint is known to the transferor and it is evident that the transferor, directly or indirectly, obtains a more than trivial benefit from those constraints. While some respondents to the Exposure Draft for this Statement raised issues about the difficulty in making judgments about whether a transferor is aware of a constraint and whether a benefit to the transferor is more than trivial, the Board concluded that the fourth possibility is nonetheless the best of the alternatives and reaffirmed that conclusion.

167. As discussed in paragraphs 32 and 33, assessing whether an option to reacquire a transferred asset constrains a transferee's apparent right to pledge or exchange transferred assets requires judgment. Despite the challenges of making such judgments in practice, the Board concluded that some options do constrain a transferee and benefit a transferor so that a transferor remained in control, and others do not. Whether they do or do not can only be assessed after considering all the relevant facts and circumstances. The Board reasoned that if, for example, a call option is sufficiently deep-in-the-money, the transferee would be more likely to have to hold the assets to comply with a potential exercise of the call. Conversely, even though it technically conveys no right to a transferor, a put option written by the transferor to the transferee on assets not readily obtainable elsewhere might constrain a transferee if, for example, it is sufficiently deep-in-the-money that it would be imprudent for the transferee to sell the assets for the market price rather than holding it to get the much higher put price from the transferor. The Board concluded that that assessment of whether an option constrains a transferee need only be made at the date of transfer because it was impractical to require that the transferor reevaluate the written call or put option after the transfer date, and if prices changed sufficiently that a call that did not initially constrain the transferee subsequently went into-the-money, it might not matter because the transferee might already have sold the transferred assets.

168. Paragraph 9(b)(1) of Statement 125 established a criterion that, for sale treatment, the transferee be able to pledge *or* exchange the transferred assets. Some constituents found that criterion ambiguous for (a) certain transfers after which transferees have the right to pledge the transferred assets but not to exchange them and (b) other transfers after which the transferees are permitted to exchange transferred assets but not to pledge them. Some constituents contended that because the implementation guidance in paragraph 25 of Statement 125 included no mention of pledging in its examples of when a transferee is constrained, the Board must have meant that the test of paragraph 9(b)(1) could be failed exclusively by lack of the unconstrained right to exchange the asset, implying that the transferee must have both the right to pledge and the right to exchange to qualify for sale treatment under that criterion. The Board intended that the *or* in that test should be inclusive, indicating in paragraph 122 of Statement 125 (and carried forward in paragraph 161 of this Statement) that the ability to obtain all or most of the cash inflows that are the primary economic benefits of a financial asset, whether by exchanging it or pledging it as collateral, is what is important in determining whether a transferee controls a financial asset.

169. The Board revisited the "exchange *or* pledge" question and again in developing this Statement concluded that the criterion in paragraph 9(b) is inclusive: it is the ability to obtain all or most of the cash inflows, *either* by exchanging the transferred asset *or* by pledging it as collateral. The Board was concerned that requiring both the ability to pledge and the ability to exchange would, for example, permit some transferors to opt out of sale accounting by simply adding a prohibition—unimportant to that transferee—against pledging the asset.

Settlement Date and Trade Date Accounting

170. Many transfers of financial assets have been recognized at the settlement date. During its redeliberations of Statement 125, the Board discussed the implications of that Statement on trade date accounting for certain securities transactions and concluded that Statement 125 did not set out to address that issue. Therefore, the Board decided that Statement 125 should not modify generally accepted accounting principles, including FASB Statement No. 35, *Accounting and Reporting by Defined Benefit Pension Plans,* and AICPA Statements of Position and audit and accounting Guides for certain industries, that require accounting at the trade date for certain contracts

to purchase or sell securities. That decision is carried forward without reconsideration in this Statement.

Transfers to Qualifying SPEs, including Securitizations

171. Many transfers of financial assets are to qualifying SPEs of the type described in paragraph 26 of Statement 125 (paragraph 35 of this Statement). After those transfers, the qualifying SPE holds legal title to the transferred assets but does not have the right to pledge or exchange the transferred assets free of constraints. Rather, the activities of the qualifying SPE are limited to carrying out the provisions of the legal documents that established it. One significant purpose of those limitations on activities often is to make remote the possibility that a qualifying SPE could enter bankruptcy or other receivership, even if the transferor were to enter receivership.

172. Some commentators asked whether the qualifying SPE criteria apply to entities formed for purposes other than transfers of financial assets. The Board decided that the description of a qualifying SPE in paragraph 26 of Statement 125 should be restrictive. Transfers to entities that meet all of the conditions in paragraph 26 of Statement 125 may qualify for sale accounting under paragraph 9 of Statement 125. Other entities with some similar characteristics also might be broadly described as "special-purpose." For example, an entity might be formed for the purpose of holding specific nonfinancial assets and liabilities or carrying on particular commercial activities. The Board decided that those entities are not qualifying SPEs under Statement 125 nor under this Statement and that the accounting for transfers of financial assets to SPEs should not be extended to transfers to any entity that does not satisfy all of the conditions in paragraph 26 of Statement 125 (paragraph 35 of this Statement).

173. Qualifying SPEs issue beneficial interests of various kinds—variously characterized as debt, participations, residual interests, and otherwise—as required by the provisions of those agreements. Holders of beneficial interests in the qualifying SPE have the right to pledge or exchange those interests but do not control the individual assets held by the qualifying SPE. The effect of establishing the qualifying SPE is to merge the contractual rights in the transferred assets and to allocate undivided interests in them—the beneficial interests. Therefore, the right of holders to pledge or exchange those beneficial interests is the counterpart of the right of a transferee to pledge or exchange the transferred assets themselves.

174. Sometimes financial assets, especially mortgage loans, are securitized and the transferor retains all of the beneficial interests in the qualifying SPE as securities. The objective is to increase financial flexibility because securities are more liquid and can more readily be sold or pledged as collateral to secure borrowings. In some cases, securitization may reduce regulatory capital requirements. The Board concluded that transfers of financial assets to a qualifying SPE, including securitizations, should qualify as sales only to the extent that consideration other than beneficial interests in the transferred assets is received.

The Conditions for a Qualifying SPE

175. One condition for sale accounting in Statement 125 was that the transferee must obtain "the right—free of conditions that constrain it from taking advantage of that right . . .—to pledge or exchange the transferred assets" (Statement 125, paragraph 9(b)(1)). In developing that criterion, the Board reasoned that the transferee's ability to control the transferred financial assets provides strong evidence that the transferor has surrendered control. However, one principal objective of Statement 125 was to address the accounting for securitization transactions; the Board recognized that often the transferee in a securitization is a trust, corporation, or other legal vehicle (an SPE) that can engage in only limited activities and, therefore, is typically constrained from pledging or exchanging the transferred asset. The Board decided that some transfers to SPEs should qualify for sale accounting and, therefore, developed in Statement 125 the idea of a qualifying SPE.

176. Under Statement 125, a trust, corporation, or other legal vehicle that has a standing at law distinct from the transferor and whose activities are permanently limited by the legal documents establishing it to those identified in paragraph 26 of Statement 125 (and reconsidered in this Statement in paragraph 35) is a qualifying SPE. The Board observed that "the effect of establishing the qualifying special-purpose entity is to merge the contractual rights in the transferred assets and to allocate undivided interests in them—the beneficial interests" (Statement 125, paragraph 127). The Board reached that conclusion in part because a qualifying SPE "does not have the right to pledge or exchange the transferred assets" (paragraph 125 of Statement 125, reconsidered in this Statement in paragraph 171), a right that would involve its acting as an operating entity. Therefore, the Board observed that if the transferee is a qualify-ing SPE, the assets are legally owned by the trustee on behalf of those parties having a beneficial interest in the assets, and the right of those BIHs to pledge or exchange their beneficial interests is the counterpart of the right of an ordinary transferee (for example, an entity other than a qualifying SPE) to pledge or exchange the transferred assets themselves.

177. When Statement 125 was issued, the Board's understanding was that the activities of most SPEs used in securitization transactions were limited to those identified in paragraph 26 of Statement 125. After Statement 125 was issued, commentators expressed concern that many SPEs that are transferees in securitization transactions have more and different powers than those described in that paragraph.

178. In response to that concern, the FASB staff developed an announcement issued as EITF Topic No. D-66, "Effect of a Special-Purpose Entity's Powers to Sell, Exchange, Repledge, or Distribute Transferred Financial Assets under FASB Statement No. 125," in January 1998. While the FASB staff was developing that announcement, it became apparent that some SPEs engage in activities such as selling transferred assets and refinancing or reselling the rights to transferred financial assets. While the Board did not object to the issuance of Topic D-66 as an interim step, the Board recognized that it raised significant issues that warranted consideration as part of its project to amend Statement 125.

179. In 1998 and 1999, the Board reconsidered how it could better distinguish between qualifying SPEs, transfers to which fell under paragraph 9(b)(2) of Statement 125, and other entities, transfers to which fell under paragraph 9(b)(1) of Statement 125. The Board reviewed the various powers held and activities engaged in by SPEs whose primary purpose is limited to passively holding financial assets on behalf of BIHs in those assets. The Board concluded that some powers and activities are appropriate or even necessary to support that primary purpose, while other powers and activities are unnecessary or even inappropriate for that purpose. The Board developed a revised notion of *qualifying SPE* based on that conclusion. The Board identified four conditions necessary for an SPE to be a qualifying SPE under this Statement. Those conditions must be present in order for it to be appropriate to look through the qualifying SPE to the BIHs and their ability to pledge or exchange their interests to determine sale accounting.

Need to be demonstrably distinct from the transferor

180. The first condition is that a qualifying SPE must be demonstrably distinct from the transferor. One of the original conditions for being a qualifying SPE in Statement 125, carried over in the Exposure Draft for this Statement, required a qualifying SPE to have distinct standing at law. Commentators urged the Board to replace that notion with the requirement that the transferor not be able to unilaterally dissolve an SPE as a condition for qualifying status. Those commentators argued that (a) *distinct standing at law* does not seem to have a uniform meaning that could be an acceptable basis upon which to build a standard, (b) distinct standing at law is possible without a third-party investor and could be achieved in some cases by simply pledging collateral, (c) a standard that enables accountants to determine, through analyzing the provisions of a trust agreement, whether or not the termination and dissolution of the trust are within the control of the transferor would be preferable, and (d) attorneys cannot opine on the concept of "distinct standing at law" by using case law or legal references because it is not an established legal concept. In lieu of *distinct standing at law,* some commentators suggested that the Board develop a notion based on the premise that no accounting recognition should be given to a transaction with an SPE unless a third party is involved. A number of constituents went further to suggest that there be some minimum level of outside beneficial interests.

181. The Board considered those suggestions and concluded that requiring that a qualifying SPE have a minimum level of outside beneficial interests is a useful concept. The Board reasoned that a required minimum outside beneficial interest is consistent with the idea that an ownership interest has been transferred and gave substance to the qualifying SPE's limitations in that another party is relying on those limitations. But to be operational, it was necessary to determine the minimum percentage of outside beneficial interests. After considering the characteristics of common securitization SPEs, the Board chose not to set a high minimum percentage, in part because, while most common securitization SPEs have outside interests in excess of two-thirds much of the time, they do not maintain that level during ramp-up and wind-down phases or, in some cases, during seasonal variations in the levels of assets in the trust. The Board concluded that its objective in requiring a minimum outside beneficial interest is to establish that the qualifying SPE is demonstrably distinct from

the transferor. The Board decided that if at least 10 percent of the interests in the transferred assets (or 10 percent of the interests in a series in the master trust) were currently held by third parties and if the transferor could not unilaterally dissolve the SPE, that is sufficient evidence to demonstrate that the SPE is demonstrably distinct from the transferor, its affiliates, or its agents. The Board settled on the 10 percent level, not because it was grounded in any particular literature, but because it appeared sufficient to demonstrate that the transferee is distinct from the transferor.

182. In connection with its discussion of minimum outside beneficial interest, the Board was asked whether a guarantee, if it is the only outside beneficial interest and worth less than 10 percent of the total value of the securitization, was sufficient to demonstrate that an SPE was distinct from the transferor. Some commentators mentioned "swap-and-hold" securitizations, in which the transferor takes back and retains all the mortgage-backed securities. The Board decided to make an exception to the 10 percent minimum for what this Statement refers to as a *guaranteed mortgage securitization,* a securitization of mortgage loans that is within the scope of FASB Statement No. 65, *Accounting for Certain Mortgage Banking Activities,* as amended, and includes a substantive guarantee by a third party. While a substantive guarantee by a third party clearly can have significant impact on the value and liquidity of the interests retained in guaranteed mortgage securitizations, which is consistent with the conclusion that the SPE is demonstrably distinct from the transferor, that impact is not the primary reason for this exception. Instead, the Board made that exception primarily in view of the long history of specialized accounting for mortgage banking activities, including its recent reconsideration of the measurement of retained mortgage-backed securities in FASB Statement No. 134, *Accounting for Mortgage-Backed Securities Retained after the Securitization of Mortgage Loans Held for Sale by a Mortgage Banking Enterprise.*

183. The Board considered extending that exception to other kinds of securitizations, for example, securitizations using nonqualifying SPEs or securitizations of assets that do not arise from mortgage banking activities, but decided that that exception should not be extended, even by analogy in practice. That resolves an issue that was the subject of proposed FASB Technical Bulletin 99-a, *Classification and Measurement*

of Financial Assets Securitized Using a Special-Purpose Entity, issued for comment on August 11, 1999, but not issued in final form.

Limits on permitted activities

184. The second condition is that the permitted activities of a qualifying SPE are significantly limited, were entirely specified in the legal documents that established the SPE or that created the beneficial interests in the transferred assets that it holds, and may be significantly changed only with the approval of at least a majority of the beneficial interests held by entities other than the transferor, its affiliates, or its agents. In Statement 125, the Board required that a qualifying SPE's powers be permanently limited, in part so that a transferor could not treat as sold assets it had seemingly relinquished if it could still control them by changing the SPE's rules specifying required or permitted activities. However, the Board later learned that limitations on entities in certain forms, including many corporation or partnership forms sometimes used for SPEs, cannot be permanent. Rather than effectively precluding sale treatment for transfers to such SPEs, the Board instead chose to modify this condition to allow for the impermanence of limitations but still limit the ability of the transferor to modify the structure. Consequently, the second condition allows changes to the structure only with the approval of a majority of third-party BIHs that, presumably, would be reluctant to make changes that would adversely affect their interests.

Limits on the assets it can hold

185. The third condition is that a qualifying SPE must be limited as to the assets it can hold. That is in keeping with the Board's view that a qualifying SPE is not an ordinary business but rather a vehicle for indirect ownership by the BIHs of the assets held by the qualifying SPE. The principal type of assets that a qualifying SPE can hold are financial assets transferred to it. The Board concluded that it would be inconsistent with a qualifying SPE's limited purpose for it to actively purchase its principal assets in the marketplace; instead, the SPE should passively accept those assets transferred to it. The Board also concluded that it would be inconsistent for a qualifying SPE to hold assets that are not passive, because holding nonpassive assets involves making decisions and decision-making is not consistent with the notion of only having passive custody of assets for the benefit of BIHs. Thus, the Board did not allow a qualifying SPE to hold investments large enough either in

themselves or in combination with other investments to enable it or any related entity to exercise control or significant influence over an investee. For the same reasons, the Board did not allow a qualifying SPE to hold equity securities that have voting rights attached unless the SPE has no ability to exercise the voting rights or choose how to vote.

186. The Exposure Draft of this Statement proposed that in addition to financial assets transferred to it, a qualifying SPE be permitted to hold five other types of assets: (a) derivative instruments entered into at the same time that financial assets were transferred to the SPE or beneficial interests (other than derivatives) were created, (b) rights to service its financial assets, (c) financial assets that would reimburse it if others were to fail to adequately service its financial assets or to timely pay obligations due on those financial assets, (d) temporarily, nonfinancial assets received in connection with collection of its financial assets, and (e) cash collected from its financial instruments and certain investments purchased with that cash pending distribution. Constituents pointed out that SPEs used in securitizations were commonly permitted to hold those types of assets. The Board decided to permit a qualifying SPE to hold those types of assets because they are inherent in financial assets, are necessary in connection with fiduciary responsibilities to BIHs, or are held only temporarily as a result of collecting or attempting to collect some of the financial assets the qualifying SPE previously held. The Board decided that only those types of assets can be held because holding other types of assets is inconsistent with the qualifying SPE's principal purpose of passively conveying indirect ownership of transferred financial assets to BIHs.

187. The concerns of respondents to the Exposure Draft of this Statement as to the types of assets that a qualifying SPE can hold focused on the proposed limitations on derivative instruments. Specifically, respondents were concerned whether allowing a qualifying SPE to enter into a derivative instrument avoids accounting requirements under FASB Statement No. 133, *Accounting for Derivative Instruments and Hedging Activities,* and whether a large derivative instrument could be put into or entered into by a qualifying SPE that held only a small amount of other financial assets. They also were concerned that some derivative instruments require too many decision-making abilities to be held by a qualifying SPE. The Board decided to limit the notional amount of derivative instruments that a qualifying SPE could enter into. The Board decided that the limit should

comprehend only derivative instruments that pertain to outside beneficial interests—those issued by the qualifying SPE to parties other than the transferor, its affiliates, or its agents or sold to such other parties after being issued by the qualifying SPE to the transferor, its affiliates, or its agents. The Board noted that if the transferor wanted to enter into derivative instruments pertaining to the beneficial interests it holds, it could accomplish that by entering into such derivative instruments on its own behalf, which would be accounted for under Statement 133.

188. Several other issues arose concerning derivative instruments in qualifying SPEs. The Board considered requiring that the derivative instruments qualify as a fair value or cash flow hedge of the qualifying SPE's assets or beneficial interests under Statement 133. The Board rejected that approach after considering the various purposes for which securitizations and other qualifying SPE activities are formed. The Board, however, still wanted to ensure that the derivative instrument *pertains* to outside beneficial interests. Therefore, the Board decided that for a qualifying SPE, a derivative instrument should have a notional amount not exceeding the amount of those beneficial interests. Because leverage can make a derivative instrument more powerful than its notional amount indicates, the Board decided that a derivative instrument should have characteristics that relate to and partly or fully (but not excessively) counteract some risk associated with those beneficial interests or the related transferred assets. The Board also decided, consistent with its decisions on equity instruments, that qualifying SPEs should hold only derivative instruments that do not require active decisions. The Board further decided, in keeping with limiting qualifying SPEs to holding financial assets, that the only derivative instruments they can hold are those that are financial instruments—*derivative financial instruments.*

Limits on sales or other dispositions of assets

189. The fourth condition is that if a qualifying SPE has powers to sell or otherwise dispose of[25] its assets those powers must be limited in specified ways. After considering what the FASB staff had learned in developing its announcement on Topic D-66, the Board concluded, in contrast to its conclusion in Statement 125, that a qualifying SPE should not be entirely prohibited from disposing of assets. The Board

considered that, in many securitizations, the trustee or management of the SPE (under fiduciary duties to protect the interests of *all* parties to the structure) is required to dispose of assets in response to adverse events specified in the legal documents that established the SPE or created its beneficial interests in the transferred assets, that are outside the control of the transferor, its affiliates, or its agents. Also, in some securitizations, the SPE is required to dispose of assets, if necessary, to repurchase or redeem beneficial interests at the option of BIHs other than the transferor and its affiliates. In other securitizations, the transferor has the right to remove assets from the SPE under ROAPs or call provisions (discussed further in paragraphs 231–236). And in some securitizations, the SPE is required to liquidate itself or otherwise dispose of its assets on a date set at inception. The Board reasoned that in all four of those situations, the disposal is forced on the SPE. That is, in none of those situations does the SPE or its agents have the power to choose whether the SPE disposes of specific assets or when that disposal occurs. The Board therefore concluded that a qualifying SPE's powers to dispose of assets should be limited to those four narrowly defined circumstances. Constituents generally supported allowing disposal of assets in those circumstances, although some suggested that disposal of transferred assets also be allowed in response to a specified adverse event, without having to wait for it to cause a specified decline in fair value, if it is the type of event that would reasonably be expected at the outset to cause such a decline and that event is identified in the documents establishing the SPE. The Board adopted that suggestion.

190. The Board reasoned that an SPE that has the power to choose whether to dispose of its assets, even in limited circumstances, has much of the same ability to manage its assets as an ordinary entity. In those situations, the Board concluded that the SPE is not simply acting like a custodian, passively holding assets on behalf of the BIHs, and consequently it should not be a qualifying SPE. Some constituents argued that a qualifying SPE or its servicer should be allowed to exercise at least what constituents termed a *commercially reasonable and customary amount of discretion* in deciding whether to dispose of assets in the specified circumstances. Some constituents argued that allowing a qualifying SPE only to have provisions that require disposal without choice raises

---

[25]The term *dispose of* is used to collectively refer to the SPE's ability to sell, exchange, put, or distribute its assets.

the risks of forcing a disposal at a bad time or that allowing no discretion conflicts with the fiduciary duties of the SPE's trustee or servicer. The Board acknowledged the concerns that underlie those views but did not change that provision, reasoning that a qualifying SPE with that flexibility should not be considered to be a passive conduit through which its BIHs own portions of its assets, as opposed to owning shares or obligations in an ordinary business enterprise.

191. The Board considered but rejected a general condition that would permit a qualifying SPE to sell assets as long as the sales were made "to avoid losses." Such a condition would have allowed an SPE to have powers to sell as long as the primary objective was not to realize gains or maximize return, a concept introduced in Topic D-66. The Board rejected it because it would have given the trustee, servicer, or transferor considerable discretion in choosing whether or not the SPE should sell if a loss was threatened. Such discretion is more in keeping with being an ordinary business that manages its own assets than with being a passive repository of assets on behalf of others. The Board did, however, choose to retain some notion of selling to avoid losses in paragraph 42 of this Statement. That paragraph describes circumstances specified at the inception of the qualifying SPE in which the qualifying SPE is required to sell transferred assets that have declined (or are expected to decline) below their fair value at the date of transfer into the qualifying SPE. The Board also considered but rejected requiring that a qualifying SPE derive no more than an insignificant value from collecting or otherwise preserving the assets it holds. The Board reasoned that while some financial assets need more servicing efforts than do others, the amount of effort expended in servicing an asset does not justify different accounting.

Securitizations with Revolving-Period Features

192. As noted in paragraph 74, in some securitizations, short-term receivables are transferred to an SPE, and the SPE then issues long-term beneficial interests. Collections from transferred receivables are used to purchase additional receivables during a defined period called the revolving period. Thereafter, the collections are used to redeem beneficial interests in due course. Some have questioned the propriety of sales treatment in those securitizations because much of the cash collected during the revolving period is returned to the transferor. The Board decided that sales treatment is appropriate for transfers with

revolving-period features because the transferor surrenders control of the assets transferred. While the revolving-period agreement requires that the transferor sell receivables to the trust in exchange for cash on prearranged terms, sales of additional receivables during the revolving period are separate transactions from the original sale.

193. The transferor in a transfer with a revolving-period agreement, such as a credit card securitization, must sell receivables to the securitization trust on prearranged terms. The transferor can perhaps predict the timing of transfers, but the actual timing depends primarily on borrower behavior. If not bound by that contract, the transferor could sell its new receivables elsewhere, possibly on better terms. The transferor obtains the cash as proceeds in exchange for new receivables transferred under the revolving-period agreement, not as benefits from its previous ownership of the receivables or its residual interest in the securitization trust.

194. The revolving-period agreement is an implicit forward contract, with rights and obligations on both sides. The transferor has little or no discretion to avoid its obligations under the revolving-period agreement and would suffer adverse consequences for failure to deliver receivables to the trust during the revolving period. For example, if the transferor were to take deliberate actions to avoid its obligations to sell receivables by triggering the agreement's "early amortization" provisions, the transferor would be exposed to litigation for not honoring its commitment. The transferor also could suffer if it later tried to sell its receivables in the securitization market: the transferor would probably have to offer wary investors a higher return. Deliberate early termination by the transferor is rare in practice because of those adverse consequences. Similarly, the securitization trust and investors cannot avoid the obligation to purchase additional receivables. For those reasons, the revolving-period agreement does not provide control over receivables previously sold but rather is an implicit forward contract for future sales of receivables.

195. Some respondents to the Exposure Draft of Statement 125 proposed that existing revolving-period securitizations should continue to apply previous accounting standards for all transfers into an existing trust after the effective date of Statement 125. Several respondents asked about the effect of the provisions of Statement 125 on transfers into a master trust that is used for a series of securitizations. They pointed out that it would be difficult to change the

present structure of those trusts in response to new accounting standards. Others observed that because master trusts have very long or indefinite lives, "grandfathering" transfers to existing trusts would result in noncomparable financial statements for a long time to come. After considering those arguments, the Board decided to retain the proposed requirement that Statement 125 apply to all transfers of assets after its effective date, in order to minimize the noncomparability caused by the transition. For similar reasons, the Board adopted the same requirement in this Statement. (Paragraph 341 discusses transition provisions relating to qualifying SPEs that would no longer qualify under current guidance in this Statement.) Separately, in response to constituents' questions, the Board also clarified in paragraph 79 that a transfer into a master trust in exchange for beneficial interests is neither a sale nor a secured borrowing under the provisions of paragraph 9.

Qualifying SPEs and Consolidated Financial Statements

196. Statement 125 did not address whether a transferor should consolidate a qualifying SPE. In that Statement, the Board acknowledged that consolidation of SPEs was an issue that merited further consideration and that it would deliberate that issue in its current project on consolidated financial statements. Because the Board had not yet issued a new Statement on consolidation policy,[26] constituents were concerned about whether assets sold to a qualifying SPE might still be shown in the consolidated financial statements of the transferor and requested additional guidance on that issue. In September 1996, the EITF discussed Issue No. 96-20, "Impact of FASB Statement No. 125 on Consolidation of Special-Purpose Entities." The EITF reached a consensus that the Statement 125 definition of control should be applied in assessing whether an SPE should be consolidated, but only if all assets in the qualifying SPE are financial assets and are not the result of a structured transaction that has the effect of converting nonfinancial assets into financial assets or recognizing previously unrecognized financial assets. In all other circumstances, the EITF stated that the transferor should continue to apply the criteria of EITF Topic No. D-14, "Transactions involving Special-Purpose Entities," and EITF Issue No. 90-15, "Impact of Nonsubstantive Lessors, Residual Value

Guarantees, and Other Provisions in Leasing Transactions," as appropriate. The Board indicated at that time that it planned to include further guidance on consolidating qualifying SPEs either in the Statement on consolidation policy or in this Statement.

197. The Board considered resolving the qualifying SPE consolidation issue by making an exception to present and perhaps future consolidation standards to exempt from ordinary consolidation policies entities whose assets are all or almost all financial assets. That exception arguably could be justified because financial assets are different from other assets and entities that hold little else should be treated differently. While that alternative would have resolved the immediate issue, the Board rejected it because it would have prejudged a significant issue in the separate project on consolidation policy, without having sufficiently examined the ramifications of an exception to consolidation.

198. Instead, the Board reasoned that the event that warrants derecognition of assets transferred to a qualifying SPE is the issuance of beneficial interests in the transferred assets to third-party BIHs in exchange for cash or other assets. That reasoning is consistent with paragraphs 9 and 79 of this Statement (paragraphs 9 and 53 of Statement 125). Paragraph 9 states that "a transfer of financial assets . . . in which the transferor surrenders control over those financial assets shall be accounted for as a sale *to the extent that consideration other than beneficial interests in the transferred assets* is received in exchange" (emphasis added). Paragraph 79 states that "adding receivables to a master trust, in itself, is neither a sale nor a secured borrowing under paragraph 9, because that transfer only increases the transferor's beneficial interest in the trust's assets. A sale or secured borrowing does not occur *until the transferor receives consideration other than beneficial interests in the transferred assets*" (emphasis added). Once beneficial interests are issued to BIHs other than the transferor or its affiliates in exchange for consideration, the economic benefits of all the assets held in a qualifying SPE are divided among and controlled by the BIHs, not by the transferor whose assets they once were and not by the qualifying SPE or the trustee that may be the legal owner. Once the assets are legally isolated and beneficial interests in those assets are issued, the qualifying SPE is in the position of a custodian holding the underlying assets for the BIHs. Assets held in

---

[26]An Exposure Draft, *Consolidated Financial Statements: Purpose and Policy,* was issued in February 1999, with a comment period that ended May 24, 1999. That Exposure Draft has not yet resulted in a final Statement.

a qualifying SPE are therefore effectively the assets of its BIHs. Accordingly, the Board proposed in the Exposure Draft of this Statement that assets sold to a qualifying SPE should not be recognized as assets and that related beneficial interests should not be recognized as liabilities in consolidated or other financial statements of a transferor, servicer, or sponsor of the SPE.

199. Constituents urged the Board to retain that provision. They argued that it would be unreasonable to grant sale treatment to a transferor for a transfer of assets to a qualifying SPE and issuance of beneficial interests to third-party BIHs, which acknowledges that such assets have been effectively sold to third parties, and then to require that a qualifying SPE be consolidated in the financial statements of the transferor with the sale effectively eliminated in consolidation. The Board accepted that reasoning, in view of the criteria for sale treatment in paragraph 9 and the characteristics of entities that meet the conditions established by this Statement to be qualifying SPEs. However, the Board concluded that this Statement's special guidance for consolidation of qualifying SPEs should focus only on the consolidated financial statements of the transferor and its affiliates because, unless it is an affiliate of the transferor, a servicer, sponsor, agent, or other BIH of a qualifying SPE did not transfer the assets and record a sale. This Statement therefore provides that a qualifying SPE should not be consolidated in the financial statements of a transferor and its affiliates. The Board has tentatively decided that the scope of the planned Statement on consolidation policy will exclude that issue; however, any entity that is not a transferor of assets to a qualifying SPE, or an affiliate of the transferor, needs to consider other existing or future generally accepted accounting principles on consolidation policy to determine whether it is required to consolidate a qualifying SPE in the financial statements being presented.

Arrangements That Arguably Maintain a Transferor's Effective Control over Transferred Assets

Repurchase Agreements and Securities Lending Transactions

200. The Exposure Draft of Statement 125 proposed that transfers of financial assets with repurchase commitments, such as repurchase agreements and securi-

ties lending transactions, should qualify as secured borrowings only if the transfer was *assuredly temporary*—the period until repurchase is less than three months or the period is indefinite but the contracts are repriced daily at overnight market rates and can be terminated by either party on short notice. It also proposed that the assets to be repurchased had to be the same (for example, U.S. securities having the same CUSIP number) as those transferred. Respondents generally disagreed with those provisions of the Exposure Draft of Statement 125 about those transactions, and the Board changed the provisions in its redeliberations.

Legal and economic ambiguity of these transactions

201. Repurchase agreements and securities lending transactions are difficult to characterize because those transactions are ambiguous: they have attributes of both sales and secured borrowings. Repurchase agreements typically are documented as sales with forward purchase contracts and generally are treated as sales in bankruptcy law and receivers' procedures, but as borrowings in tax law, under court decisions that cite numerous economic and other factors. Repurchase agreements are commonly characterized by market participants as secured borrowings, even though one reason that repurchase agreements arose is that selling and then buying back securities, rather than borrowing with those securities as collateral, allow many government agencies, banks, and other active participants in the repurchase agreement market to stay "within investment and borrowing parameters that delineate what they may or may not do."[27] Securities loans are commonly documented as loans of securities collateralized by cash or by other securities or by letters of credit, but the "borrowed" securities are invariably sold, free of any conditions, by the "borrowers," to fulfill obligations under short sales or customers' failure to deliver securities they have sold; securities loans are generally treated as sales under U.S. bankruptcy and tax laws (but only as they relate to income distributions).

202. Previous accounting practice generally has treated repurchase agreements as secured borrowings, although "repos-to-maturity" and certain other longer term repurchase agreements have been treated as sales. Previous accounting practice has not recognized some securities lending transactions, because

---

[27]Marcia Stigum, *The Repo and Reverse Markets* (Homewood, Ill.: Dow Jones-Irwin, 1989), 313.

the transactions were executed by an entity's custodian or other agent, and has treated others as secured borrowings. Supporting arguments exist for accounting for both kinds of transactions as borrowings, both kinds as sales, or some as borrowings and others as sales.

203. The American Law Institute[28] describes the legal status of a securities lending transaction as follows:

> The securities lender does not retain any property interest in the securities that are delivered to the borrower. The transaction is an outright transfer in which the borrower obtains full title . . . the borrower needs the securities to transfer them to someone else . . . if the securities borrower defaults on its redelivery obligation, the securities lender has no property interest in the original securities that could be asserted against any person to whom the securities borrower may have transferred them. . . . The securities lender's protection is its right to foreclose on the collateral given to secure the borrower's redelivery obligation. Perhaps the best way to understand securities lending is to note that the word "loan" in securities lending transactions is used in the sense it carries in loans of money, as distinguished from loans of specific identifiable chattels. Someone who lends money does not retain any property interest in the money that is handed over to the borrower.

204. While that description focuses on securities lending, much of it appears applicable to repurchase agreements as well. If judged by the criteria in paragraphs 9(a) and 9(b) and the legal reasoning in paragraph 203, financial assets transferred under typical repurchase or securities lending agreements would qualify for derecognition as having been sold for proceeds consisting of cash and a forward purchase contract. During the term of the agreement, the transferred assets are isolated from the transferor, are placed in the hands of a transferee that can—and typically does—obtain their benefits by selling or pledging them, and are readily obtainable in the market.

205. The Board considered requiring sales treatment for all of those transactions. The Board also considered an approach that would have recognized the effects of the transaction in the statement of financial position (recognizing the proceeds received as cash or securities and a forward purchase contract) without characterizing the transaction as a sale. The Board ultimately decided, for both conceptual and practical reasons, that secured borrowing treatment should be retained for most of those transactions.

206. In concept, having a forward purchase contract—a right and obligation to buy an asset—is not the same as owning that asset. Dividends or interest on securities are paid by the issuer to the current security holder, that is, to whoever may now hold the securities transferred in the repurchase agreement or loan, while the transferor has at most only the contractual right to receive—from the transferee—payments in lieu of dividends or interest. In addition, the voting rights reside not with the transferor but with the current security holder, because those rights generally cannot be contractually released.

207. However, the commitments entered into in a repurchase or securities lending agreement are more extensive than a common forward purchase contract. The transferor has agreed to repurchase the security, often in as little as a day, at a fixed price that differs from the sale price by an amount that is essentially interest on the cash transferred. The transferor also commonly receives payments in lieu of interest or dividends and has protection of collateral that is valued daily and adjusted frequently for changes in the market value of the transferred asset—collateral that the transferor is entitled to use to purchase replacement securities should the transferee default, even in the event of bankruptcy or other receivership. Those arrangements are not typical of forward purchase contracts and suggest that having a repurchase agreement or securities lending contract to repurchase a transferred asset before its maturity is much like still owning that asset.

208. Practically, participants in the very large markets for repurchase agreements and securities lending transactions are, for the most part, unaccustomed to treating those transactions as sales, and a change to sale treatment would have a substantial impact on their reported financial position. Given the difficulty in characterizing those ambiguous transactions, the

---

[28]*Uniform Commercial Code, Revised Article 8, Investment Securities,* Proposed Final Draft (Philadelphia: American Law Institute, 1994), 18 and 19.

decision to treat all of those transactions as sales would be a close call, and the Board was not convinced that the benefits of a change based on that close call would justify the costs.

209. The Exposure Draft of Statement 125 proposed that transfers of financial assets with repurchase commitments, such as repurchase agreements and securities lending transactions, should be accounted for as secured borrowings if the transfers were assuredly temporary, and as sales if the transfers were not assuredly temporary. As proposed, to be assuredly temporary, the period until repurchase would have had to be short enough not to diminish assurance that the contract and arrangements backing it up would prove effective, that is, with maturities either under three months or indefinite and terminable by either party on short notice. Also, to be assuredly temporary, the entity would have had to be entitled and obligated to repurchase the same assets. After considering comment letters and testimony at the public hearing, the Board decided to change both of those proposed requirements.

The period until repurchase

210. The Exposure Draft of Statement 125 proposed that transfers of financial assets should qualify as borrowings if the period until repurchase is less than three months or the period is indefinite but the contracts are repriced daily at overnight market rates and can be terminated by either party on short notice. A three-month limit was arbitrary, but based on its initial inquiries, the Board tentatively concluded that three months would be a clear and workable time limit that should not present difficulty, because it understood that most repurchase agreements and securities loans are for periods much shorter than three months or are indefinite, and almost all of the others are for periods much longer than three months.

211. Respondents generally disagreed with that provision of the Exposure Draft of Statement 125. They argued that the arbitrary three-month limit would not be effective and that entities could alter the accounting for a transfer by adding or subtracting one or two days to or from the term of the agreement. While some offered other arbitrary time limits, many respondents argued that all transfers accompanied by a forward contract to repurchase the transferred assets before maturity should be accounted for as secured borrowings. In their view, most repurchase agreements represent a temporary transfer of only some elements of control over the transferred assets.

212. After considering those comments, the Board decided to remove the proposed requirement that the period until repurchase be less than three months. Board members concluded that any distinction based on the specified time until repurchase would not be workable. As outlined in paragraph 207, the elements of control by the transferee over assets obtained in a typical securities lending or repurchase agreement are both temporary and limited. The Board concluded that the contractual obligation and right to repurchase an asset before its maturity effectively bind the asset transferred back to the transferor.

213. Some respondents suggested a distinction based on a different time period, or on the proportion of the life of the asset transferred, but the Board rejected those possibilities. Any other time period would have the same faults as the three-month limit proposed in that Exposure Draft: it would be arbitrary, with no meaningful distinction between transactions just on one side of the limit and those just on the other side. Similarly, the Board concluded that the only meaningful distinction based on required repurchase at some proportion of the life of the assets transferred is between a "repo-to-maturity," in which the typical settlement is a net cash payment, and a repurchase before maturity, in which the portion of the asset that remains outstanding is indeed reacquired in an exchange.

Substantially the same assets

214. The Exposure Draft of Statement 125 proposed that a repurchase agreement would have to require return of the same asset (for example, U.S. securities having the same CUSIP number) for the transfer to be treated as a borrowing. In that Exposure Draft, the Board reasoned that agreements to acquire securities that—while perhaps similar—are not the same as those transferred do not maintain any kind of control over the transferred securities. Most repurchase agreements require return of the same asset. Some are less rigid. For example, some mortgage-backed instruments are transferred in a class of repurchase agreements known as *dollar rolls*. There are several procedural differences between dollar-roll transactions and ordinary repurchase agreements. However, the most significant difference is the agreement that assets returned need not be the same as those transferred. Instead, the transferor agrees to accept back assets with characteristics that are substantially the same within limits established by the market.

215. While a few respondents supported the reasoning in the Exposure Draft of Statement 125, most did

not. Respondents argued that the economic differences between the assets initially transferred and assets to be reacquired under a dollar-roll transaction that meets the existing accounting criteria for being substantially the same are, as the term implies, not substantial and should not result in an accounting difference. They argued that existing accounting guidance found in AICPA Statement of Position 90-3, *Definition of the Term Substantially the Same for Holders of Debt Instruments, as Used in Certain Audit Guides and a Statement of Position,* has proven adequate to constrain the characteristics of assets that are to be reacquired. After redeliberation, the Board accepted those arguments and decided that if the assets to be repurchased are the same or substantially the same as those concurrently transferred, the transaction should be accounted for as a secured borrowing. The Board also decided to incorporate the definition in SOP 90-3 in this Statement (carried forward without reconsideration). The Board noted that not all contracts in the dollar-roll market require that the securities involved have all of the characteristics of "substantially the same." If the contract does not require that, the transferor does not maintain effective control.

The importance of the right and obligation to repurchase, collateral, and symmetry

216. The Board based its decisions about agreements that maintain effective control over transferred assets in part on observation of contracts and practices that prevail in the repurchase agreement and securities lending markets. Concerns of market participants about risk of default by the parties to the contract, rights at law in the event of default, and credit risk of transferred assets, among other factors, have led to several contractual features intended to assure that the transferors indeed maintain effective control.

217. The Board decided that to maintain effective control, the transferor must have *both* the contractual right *and* the contractual obligation to reacquire securities that are identical to or substantially the same as those concurrently transferred. Transfers that include only the right to reacquire, at the option of the transferor or upon certain conditions, or only the obligation to reacquire, at the option of the transferee or upon certain conditions, generally do not maintain the transferor's control, because the option might not be exercised or the conditions might not occur. Similarly, expectations of reacquiring the same securities without any contractual commitments, as in "wash sales," provide no control over the transferred securities.

218. The Board also decided that the transferor's right to repurchase is not assured unless it is protected by obtaining collateral sufficient to fund substantially all of the cost of purchasing identical replacement securities during the term of the contract so that it has received the means to replace the assets even if the transferee defaults. Judgment is needed to interpret the term *substantially all* and other aspects of the criterion that the terms of a repurchase agreement do not maintain effective control over the transferred asset. However, arrangements to repurchase or lend readily obtainable securities, typically with as much as 98 percent collateralization (for entities agreeing to repurchase) or as little as 102 percent overcollateralization (for securities lenders), valued daily and adjusted up or down frequently for changes in the market price of the security transferred and with clear powers to use that collateral quickly in the event of default, typically fall clearly within that guideline. The Board believes that other collateral arrangements typically fall well outside that guideline.

219. Some commentators argued for a continuation of previous asymmetrical practices in accounting for dollar rolls. In previous practice, transferors have accounted for dollar-roll agreements as borrowing transactions, while dealers who receive the transferred assets have accounted for them as purchases. The Board observed that the same transaction cannot in concept or simple logic be a borrowing-lending arrangement to the transferor and a purchase-sale transaction to the transferee. The Exposure Draft of Statement 125 would have resolved that asymmetry by requiring that transferors account for the transactions as sales. In response to commentators' concerns about transferors' accounting, Statement 125 and this Statement instead call for transferors to account for qualifying dollar-roll transactions as secured borrowings and requires that dealers account for the same transactions as secured loans.

Other Arrangements to Reclaim Transferred Assets

220. The Board considered whether to allow sale treatment if a transferor of financial assets concurrently acquires from the transferee a call option on the assets sold. Some questioned under what conditions the transferor that holds a call option has surrendered control of the assets to the transferee. Some believe that an entity that holds an option to acquire a financial asset controls that asset. However, the

holder of a call option does not receive interest or dividends generated by the asset, cannot exercise any voting rights inherent in the asset, may not be aware of the location or present custody of the asset, and is not able to sell the asset and deliver it without first exercising the call. And it may never exercise the call. If an entity that holds a call option on an asset controls that asset, then it follows that the entity should recognize the asset under the call option at the time the call option is acquired. However, two parties would then recognize the same asset—the entity that holds the call option and either the writer of the call option or the party from whom the writer plans to acquire the asset if the call is exercised. Therefore, others believe that a call option never conveys effective control over a transferred asset. The Board concluded that whether a transferor maintains effective control over a transferred asset through an option to reacquire it depends on the nature of the asset and the terms of that option.

221. The Board concluded in Statement 125 that sale treatment should not be precluded in instances in which the transferor simultaneously obtains a call option on the asset sold, provided that the asset is readily obtainable. The writer of a call option on a financial asset may choose not to own the asset under the call option if it is readily obtainable; it may instead plan to acquire that asset if the call is exercised and delivery is demanded. In those circumstances, it is realistic to assume that the transferee can sell or repledge the asset to a third party and, at the same time, in good faith write a call option on that asset.

222. The Board concluded in Statement 125 that a sale should not be recognized in instances in which the transferor simultaneously obtains a call on a transferred asset that is not readily obtainable. The resulting accounting treatment of an option on a not-readily-obtainable asset that is obtained as part of a transfer of financial assets is different from the accounting treatment generally accorded to the same option that is purchased for cash. From the transferor's viewpoint, that difference in accounting treatment between an option purchased and an option obtained as part of a transfer of assets conflicts with the principle that the recognition of financial assets and liabilities should not be affected by the sequence of transactions that led to their existence. However, as noted in paragraph 25 of Statement 125, if the option is a component of a transfer of financial assets, and it does not constrain the transferee from selling or repledging the asset, that should not preclude the transfer from being accounted for as a sale. If the exist-

ence of an option constrains the transferee from selling or repledging the transferred asset (because the asset is not readily obtainable to satisfy the option if exercised), then the transferor has not relinquished effective control over the asset and thus should not derecognize it.

223. The Board reached a somewhat different conclusion in this Statement. The Board began its work on this Statement by considering the impact of Statement 125 on Issue 90-18. In particular, the concern was whether certain ROAPs maintain the transferor's effective control over the transferred assets through an agreement to repurchase or redeem transferred financial assets that are not readily obtainable and thus preclude sale treatment under paragraph 9(c)(2) of Statement 125. Initial Board discussions focused on the various circumstances under which transferors can remove transferred assets from securitization trusts and on the nature of the assets in question.

224. In those discussions, the Board noted that assets substantially the same as the credit card receivables in a particular securitization trust are readily obtainable only from within the trust itself or from the transferor, arguably indicating that such transfers fail to satisfy the criterion for sale treatment in paragraph 9(c)(2) of Statement 125 and therefore should be accounted for as secured borrowings. In developing this Statement, the Board concluded that after a securitization that isolates assets transferred into a qualifying SPE, the assets being accounted for in a securitization are not the underlying transferred assets but rather the beneficial interests in those assets that were sold to third-party investors or retained by the transferor. Therefore, for qualifying SPEs, the pertinent criterion is whether the transferor has a right to redeem the beneficial interests that constrain the BIHs from exchanging or pledging those interests, a matter already dealt with in a separate criterion (paragraph 9(b) of this Statement).

225. The Board concluded in this Statement that whether the transferor maintains control over assets transferred to a qualifying SPE does not depend entirely on whether those assets were readily obtainable. Rather, whether the transferor maintains control depends on whether it can unilaterally cause the return of specific transferred assets (for example, an asset with a certain certificate number) held in the qualifying SPE. That led to the criterion in paragraph 9(c) of this Statement, as discussed in paragraphs 231–236.

Rights to repurchase or redeem assets from transferees that are not qualifying SPEs

226. The Board also discussed in developing this Statement whether it should continue to include an explicit criterion, like that in paragraph 9(c)(2) of Statement 125, that would preclude sale treatment for transfers of not-readily-obtainable assets to transferees that are *not* qualifying SPEs if the transferor has the right to repurchase or redeem those assets. Some constituents suggested that transfers in which the transferor has a call provision entitling it to repurchase the transferred assets should not be accounted for as sales, particularly if the assets are not readily obtainable, because the transferor is able to use the call to get back the same assets it transferred or similar assets. Those constituents argue that the transferee's ability or inability to exchange or pledge the assets should not determine whether the transfer is a sale.

227. The Board reviewed its reasoning in Statement 125, paragraph 156, and again concluded that a call provision or other right to repurchase or redeem should preclude sale accounting if (a) the existence of that right constrains the transferee from exchanging or pledging the assets or (b) the rights to reacquire transferred assets result in the transferor's maintaining effective control over the transferred assets. The Board continues to support the fundamental principle of symmetry in Statement 125: for a transfer to be a sale, the transferor must relinquish control and the transferee must be in control, so that the criteria need to look to the position of both parties.

228. The Board reasoned that if the transferee is able, notwithstanding the transferor's right to repurchase or redeem, to pledge or exchange the transferred assets and thereby obtain substantially all of the cash flows embodied in them, then the transferor's right to repurchase or redeem does not give it effective control over the assets and should not preclude sale accounting, except in the circumstances described in paragraph 9(c) of Statement 125 and this Statement. The Board agreed that a transferee is not constrained if it can subsequently pledge or exchange transferred assets subject to an attached or embedded call, even if the assets are not readily obtainable. The Board also agreed that the transferee is not constrained by a freestanding call if it can redeem or repurchase the assets it has sold or repledged from the subsequent transferee or obtain them elsewhere when the call is exercised. In light of that set of decisions, the Exposure Draft to this Statement concluded that

the condition in paragraph 9(c)(2) of Statement 125 should no longer be required because (a) it is redundant for transfers to entities other than qualifying SPEs and (b) it is unnecessary for transfers to qualifying SPEs as discussed in paragraphs 224 and 225.

229. Some respondents to the Exposure Draft of this Statement suggested that the Board reconsider whether a call on not-readily-obtainable assets should preclude sale accounting, expressing particular concern about the accounting for attached calls. They argued that the transferor is in the same economic position and therefore indifferent to whether the call is freestanding or attached, because it can reassume control over the assets in either case. In redeliberations, the Board concluded that a freestanding call leaves both the transferor and the transferee in a different economic position than does an attached call. A freestanding call may constrain the transferee from disposing of a transferred asset, out of concern that it could not be replaced should the transferor exercise its call. If the transferee is constrained, the transferor's control over the asset is maintained because the transferee is not only obligated to deliver the asset but has on hand the very asset that was transferred. However, if the transferee is not constrained by a freestanding call (for example, because the asset is readily obtainable), the call gives the transferor no remaining connection with the transferred asset. The transferor's only asset under a nonconstraining freestanding call is the transferee's promise to find an asset sufficiently like the transferred asset to satisfy the transferor should it exercise its call. In contrast, a call attached to the asset does not constrain the transferee from disposing of the asset, subject to that call, even if the asset is not readily obtainable. However, an attached call maintains the transferor's connection with the transferred asset, because exercise of the call brings back that very asset from whoever now holds it. The Board concluded that those different economic positions call for different accounting.

230. The Board considered two approaches for resolving this difficulty. The first would have reinstated the wording in paragraph 9(c)(2) of Statement 125. The Board rejected that approach because some calls on not-readily-obtainable assets (for example, certain conditional calls or out-of-the-money calls) do not necessarily constrain transferees or benefit transferors, making it difficult to conclude that they give a transferor effective control over the assets, and because that approach would be difficult to

reconcile with the accounting for ROAPs (para-graphs 231–236). The other approach, which the Board adopted because it avoided those difficulties, was to revise paragraph 9(c)(2) to preclude sale accounting if the transferor maintains effective control through a call option or other right that gives it the ability to unilaterally cause the transferee to return specific transferred assets, and to clarify in para-graphs 50–54 the kinds of rights that do and do not maintain effective control. The Board continues to believe that an option to acquire assets, even assets previously owned, is not the same as owning those assets, unless that option conveys effective control over the assets.

Rights to unilaterally reclaim specific assets transferred to qualifying SPEs

231. The Board concluded in Statement 125 that sale treatment is inappropriate for transfers to a quali-fying SPE of assets that the transferor is in a position to reclaim. The Board did not change its view in de-veloping this Statement. However, the Board decided to change the way that view is carried out in the standards. Statement 125 excluded the ability to re-turn assets to the transferor from the list of activities that a qualifying SPE was permitted to engage in. Therefore, an SPE that was permitted to return assets to the transferor could not be a qualifying SPE under Statement 125 as originally interpreted. (The staff an-nouncement in Topic D-66 later did permit qualify-ing SPEs to have certain powers to return assets to the transferor, its affiliates, or its agents.) Rather than disqualify SPEs because the transferor has the unilat-eral ability to cause the SPE to return specified assets, this Statement instead provides that transfers of as-sets to qualifying SPEs are not sales if the transferor through that ability retains effective control over specific transferred assets.

232. The Board chose to preclude sale accounting if the transferor has any ability to unilaterally reclaim specific transferred assets from a qualifying SPE on terms that are potentially advantageous to the transferor—whether through a ROAP, the ability to cause the liquidation of the entity, a call option, for-ward purchase contract, or other means—because, in those circumstances, the transferor would effectively control the transferred assets. The transferor main-tains effective control by being able to initiate action to reclaim specific assets with the knowledge that the qualifying SPE cannot sell or distribute the assets be-cause of restrictions placed on it.

233. The Board's decision precludes sale accounting for transfers of financial assets subject to an uncondi-tional ROAP or repurchase agreement that allows the transferor to specify the assets removed. It also pre-cludes sale accounting for transfers of financial assets subject to a ROAP in response to a transferor's deci-sion to exit some portion of its business. The Board reached that conclusion because such provisions allow the transferor to unilaterally remove specified assets from the qualifying SPE, which demonstrates that the transferor retains effective control over the assets.

234. The Board did decide to allow sale accounting for transfers subject to certain other types of ROAPs that are commonly found in securitization structures. For example, it permitted sale treatment for transfers subject to a ROAP that allows the transferor to re-move specific financial assets after a third-party can-cellation, or expiration without renewal, of an affinity or private-label arrangement on the grounds that the removal would be allowed only after a third party's action (cancellation) or decision not to act (expira-tion) and could not be initiated *unilaterally* by the transferor. In reaching that conclusion, the Board ac-knowledged that the transferor may, through its ac-tion or inaction, sometimes instigate the third-party cancellation or expiration of an affinity or private-label arrangement but noted that it would be unwork-able to base the accounting on identifying which en-tity was the main instigator and unreasonable to deny sale treatment just because removal of accounts could be required by a cancellation or nonrenewal that the transferor was powerless to avoid. The Board's decision also does not preclude sale account-ing because of a ROAP that allows the transferor to randomly remove transferred assets at its discretion, but only if the ROAP is sufficiently limited so that it does not allow the transferor to remove *specific* transferred assets.

235. This Statement also precludes sale accounting if the transferor of financial assets to a qualifying SPE has the ability to unilaterally take back specific transferred assets through the liquidation of the en-tity, a call option, forward purchase contract, or other means. The Board's reasoning behind this more gen-eral principle is the same as for ROAPs. For ex-ample, the Board concluded that a transferor has maintained effective control over specific transferred assets if (a) the transferor or its affiliates may reclaim the transferred assets, for example, at termination of the qualifying SPE or at maturity or redemption of the beneficial interests *and* (b) either the price the

transferor is to pay is fixed or determinable or the transferor holds the residual interest in the transferred assets, because those abilities provide the transferor with effective control over the assets. In the latter circumstance, the transferor that holds the residual interest could pay any price it wished to buy back the assets in a public auction, for example, because it would get back any excess paid over fair value via its residual interest.

236. For the same practical reasons as those in Statement 125, the Board chose to continue to allow a cleanup call and, in response to constituents' requests, changed the definition of *cleanup call* to allow the servicer, which may be the transferor, to hold a cleanup call as Statement 77 had done. In reaching this decision, the Board considered but rejected the notion that parties other than the servicer could hold the option, because only the servicer is burdened when the amount of outstanding assets falls to a level at which the cost of servicing the assets becomes burdensome—the defining condition of a cleanup call—and any other party would be motivated by some other incentive in exercising a call. The Board permitted a cleanup call on beneficial interests in the transferred assets because the same sort of burdensome costs in relation to benefits may arise when the remaining assets or beneficial interests fall to a small portion of their original level.

Collateral

Accounting for Collateral under Statement 125

237. The Exposure Draft of Statement 125 proposed that for transactions involving collateral, including securities lending transactions and repurchase agreements, secured parties should recognize all cash collateral received as well as all other financial instruments received as collateral that they have the ability by contract or custom to sell or repledge prior to the debtor's default, because they have important rights over that collateral. Secured parties in those positions are entitled and able to use the cash received as collateral, or the cash they can obtain by selling or repledging other collateral, for their own purposes. Therefore, in the Exposure Draft of Statement 125, the Board concluded that that collateral is the secured party's asset, along with an obligation to return the collateral that is the secured party's liability, and reasoned that if that collateral was permitted to be excluded from the statement of financial position, assets that secured parties can use to generate income would not be recognized. Reporting income but not

the assets that generate it could understate a secured party's assets (and liabilities) as well as overstate its return on assets. In contrast, noncash collateral that secured parties are not able to sell or repledge cannot be used to generate cash or otherwise benefit the secured party (other than by reducing the credit risk on the financial asset it secures, an effect already recognized in measuring that financial asset) and is not the secured party's asset.

238. The Board noted that the accounting proposed was consistent with Governmental Accounting Standards Board (GASB) Statement No. 28, *Accounting and Financial Reporting for Securities Lending Transactions,* which was issued in May 1995. GASB Statement 28 also requires, for reasons similar to those noted in Statement 125, that securities lenders record noncash collateral if the contract specifically allows the governmental entity to pledge or sell the collateral before a debtor defaults.

239. Many respondents to the Exposure Draft of Statement 125 objected to recognition of collateral because they contended that the proposed accounting would result in the same asset being recognized by two entities. As discussed in paragraph 259 of this Statement (carried forward from paragraph 172 of Statement 125), while the secured party reports the security as its asset, the transferor reports a different asset, a receivable for the return of the collateral from the secured party. Respondents also argued that recognizing the collateral implies that the secured party expects all the benefits of that asset, whereas it typically is not entitled to retain dividends, interest, or benefits from appreciation. Respondents who objected to recognizing collateral generally preferred that secured parties disclose collateral received. Other respondents suggested that it was not clear that the proposed collateral provisions applied not only to a secured borrowing but also to collateral pledged in all other kinds of transactions.

240. The Board reconsidered the provisions of the Exposure Draft of Statement 125 in light of those comments. To improve clarity and refine its conclusions, the Board focused on four types of collateral that a secured party arguably should recognize as its assets: (a) cash collateral, (b) collateral securing obligations in default, (c) other collateral that the secured party has sold or repledged, and (d) other collateral that the secured party can sell or repledge.

Cash collateral

241. Some respondents objected to recording any asset received as collateral, even cash, on the grounds that it remains the asset of the party posting it as collateral and is therefore not the secured party's asset. Other respondents agreed that cash collateral should be recognized because transfers of financial assets in exchange for cash collateral cannot be distinguished from borrowing cash and because cash is fungible. It is therefore impossible to determine whether it has been used by the secured party. The Board concluded for the latter reason that all cash collateral should be recorded as an asset by the party receiving it, together with a liability for the obligation to return it to the payer, whose asset is a receivable.

Collateral securing obligations in default

242. Many respondents pointed out that collateral securing an obligation becomes the property of the secured party upon default on the secured obligation. A respondent argued differently, maintaining that a defaulting debtor does not relinquish control over the collateral until it no longer has an opportunity to redeem the collateral by curing the default. The Board agreed in Statement 125 that the secured party should recognize collateral, to the extent it has not already recognized the collateral, if the debtor defaults and is no longer entitled to redeem it.

Other collateral that the secured party has sold or repledged

243. Some respondents to the Exposure Draft of Statement 125 who agreed that cash collateral should be recognized argued that the secured party should not recognize other collateral unless the debtor had defaulted, no matter what powers it has over that collateral, again because in their view the transferred assets remain the assets of the transferor. Others argued that while it may make sense for the secured party to recognize an obligation if collateral is sold, as is common practice in some industries, it is not common practice for broker-dealers and others to recognize an asset and a liability when they repledge collateral. Respondents from the broker-dealer community noted that they regularly repledge substantial amounts of collateral in conjunction with loans secured by customer margin balances and "borrow versus pledge" matched securities transactions and that that collateral activity has not been recognized under previous practice, although it has been disclosed. After considering those arguments, the Board concluded that collateral should be considered for recognition when it is sold or repledged, because the ability to pledge or exchange an asset is the benefit that the Board determined constitutes control over a financial asset, as set forth in paragraph 9(b) and discussed in paragraphs 161 and 162 of this Statement.

244. One respondent observed that the documentation supporting some transactions preserves the transferor's legal right to redeem its collateral, even though the transferee has repledged the assets to a third entity. In those instances, should the transferee default, the transferor has rights to redeem its collateral directly from the third entity to which the initial transferee repledged it. The respondent argued that a transferee with that right has not surrendered control over the assets. The Board agreed with that reasoning and adopted it. Because the status of the right to redeem may not always be clear, the Board chose to implement it by requiring recognition of collateral by the secured party if it sells or repledges collateral on terms that do not enable it to repurchase or redeem the collateral from the transferor on short notice. One result is that broker-dealers and others who obtain financial assets in reverse repurchase agreements, securities loans, or as collateral for loans and then sell or repledge those assets will in some cases recognize under Statement 125 assets and liabilities that previously went unrecognized. The Board noted that obligations to return to the transferor assets borrowed and then sold have sometimes been effectively recognized as part of a liability for securities sold but not yet purchased, and it did not require any change in that practice.

Other collateral that the secured party can sell or repledge

245. The Exposure Draft of Statement 125 called for recognition of collateral that the secured party can repledge or exchange but has not yet used. Some argued that secured parties should not be required to recognize any unused collateral, reasoning that the collateral and related obligation do not meet the definition of an asset or a liability of the secured party. They contended that to be considered an asset of the secured party the collateral must embody a probable future economic benefit that contributes directly or indirectly to future net cash inflows and that in the case of many kinds of collateral, there is only a possible benefit that has not been realized until that collateral is sold or repledged. The Board disagreed, noting that collateral that can be sold or repledged has a capacity to contribute directly to future cash

inflows—from a sale or secured borrowing—and that the obligation to return the collateral when reclaimed will require a future economic sacrifice—the relinquishing of control. The Board also observed that broker-dealers and others are able to benefit from collateral in various ways and that the right to benefit from the use of a financial asset is, in itself, an asset.

246. A respondent to the Exposure Draft of Statement 125 pointed out that the right to repledge or exchange is significantly constrained if the transferor has the right and ability to redeem the collateral on short notice, for example, by substituting other collateral or terminating the contract on short notice, and thereby demand the return of the particular security pledged as collateral. The Board agreed, reasoning that a transferor that can redeem its pledged collateral on short notice has not surrendered control of the transferred assets. The transferee would be able to use the transferred assets in certain ways to earn a return during the period of the agreement, but the value of its asset may be very limited because of the transferor's rights to substitute or cancel.

247. In developing the Exposure Draft of Statement 125, the Board considered an approach that would have recorded only the net value of the specific rights that the secured party has over the collateral. That approach might have been consistent with the financial-components approach, and several respondents asked the Board to consider it. However, no one, including the Board, was able to identify a method that the Board judged to be sound for separating the collateral into components.

248. Another possibility considered would have been to recognize the transfer of control over the collateral and for the two parties each to report their mutual rights and obligations under the contract net, that is, for the debtor to net its receivable for the transferred security against its obligation under the secured borrowing and for the secured creditor to net its obligation to return the security against its secured loan receivable. The only change to the statement of financial position would have been the difference in carrying amounts, if any, with a note disclosing the details. That approach is different from present practice in its details but would have produced similar total assets and liabilities. It arguably would have been more consistent with the financial-components approach that focuses on control and would have simplified the accounting. While this approach appealed to some Board members, the Board ultimately rejected it. The approach would have been inconsistent

with other pronouncements that govern offsetting, because in this case there is no intent to settle net.

249. After considering comments and testimony on those matters, the Board decided in Statement 125 that financial assets transferred as collateral in a secured borrowing should be recognized by the secured party as an asset with a corresponding liability for the obligation to return the collateral if the secured party was permitted by contract or custom to sell or repledge the collateral and the transferor did not have the right and ability to redeem the collateral on short notice, for example, by substituting other collateral or terminating the contract.

Accounting for Collateral under This Statement

250. After the issuance of Statement 125, implementation issues emerged in applying the requirements for accounting for collateral in paragraph 15 of that Statement. Those issues focused on whether the secured party is constrained from taking advantage of the right to sell or repledge collateral. The notion of constraint was expressed in paragraph 15(a)(2) of Statement 125, which required determining whether the debtor has the right and ability to redeem the collateral on short notice, for example, by substituting other collateral or terminating the contract. In developing Statement 125, the Board assumed that the debtor's right to redeem the collateral on short notice would significantly constrain the secured party from realizing a substantial portion of the value from the collateral and that that constraint would benefit the debtor. While a secured party subject to that constraint might use the collateral in certain ways to earn a return during the period of the agreement, the value of its asset seemed to be very limited because of the debtor's right to demand the return of the particular security pledged as collateral on short notice.

251. However, the Board learned that paragraph 15 had been interpreted by constituents to indicate that collateral is not required to be recorded as an asset by a secured party if the debtor has the right to substitute other collateral or terminate the agreement on short notice, even if that right to substitute or terminate does not constrain the secured party from selling or repledging the collateral and therefore realizing all or most of its value. Because paragraph 15 did not explicitly require the secured party to consider factors beyond the existence of the debtor's right to substitute the collateral or terminate the contract on short notice in determining whether the ability of a secured party to obtain a benefit from the collateral is significantly constrained, some secured parties may not

have recognized as assets collateral pledged under contracts even if the debtor's right may not have imposed a significant constraint. The result of those differing interpretations was lack of comparability between entities.

252. The Board decided to address this issue by reconsidering the accounting model for transfers of collateral. The Board proposed in the Exposure Draft of this Statement to require that the secured party record the fair value of the right to sell or repledge collateral in all transactions in which the secured party receives that right. The fair value of that right would have been symmetrically derecognized by the debtor.

253. Under that approach, the nature of the right to sell or repledge would have been viewed as the secured party's opportunity to use that asset to generate income during the period that it is available to the secured party. That right represents only a portion of the rights associated with the collateral. Not recording the full value of the collateral is consistent with the Board's conclusion that the secured party does not obtain enough control to cause the transferor to derecognize the assets but that the secured party does obtain some rights to the collateral.

254. The Board also decided at that time that if a secured party has exercised its right to sell or repledge the collateral, it has and should recognize a liability to the transferor. The Board concluded that if the secured party has sold another entity's asset, the best measure of that liability is what it would have to sacrifice now to settle the liability—by obtaining a similar asset in the market to deliver to the debtor—which is the fair value of the pledged asset. Extending that reasoning, the Board concluded in the Exposure Draft of this Statement that the best measure of the secured party's liability if it has repledged the collateral is what it would have to sacrifice now to settle its obligation—either by redeeming the repledged asset early or by borrowing in the market a similar asset to deliver to the debtor—which is the fair value of the right to sell or repledge.

255. Constituents expressed concern about whether the approach proposed in the Exposure Draft of this Statement was operational. Some members of the Bond Market Association also questioned the operationality of the approach and conducted a limited field test. At a Board meeting to discuss the results of the field test, representatives of that association voiced three concerns about the "value-of-the-rights"

approach. First, the value of the right was not priced in the marketplace, so it was necessary to estimate the fair value of the right indirectly by measuring the difference between the unsecured rate and the secured rate for each transaction category multiplied by the duration and the notional amount. Second, there were a number of ways to calculate that estimate. Third, it was necessary to assume durations for open transactions, because there is no termination date on open transactions, and there was little evidence to support the assumptions as to how long the transaction would be open. Participants in the field test argued that subsequent accounting at fair value would be difficult but that disclosure of the gross amount of the collateral instead would convey useful information that would be less difficult to obtain.

256. After considering the results of that field test and other comments, the Board decided that while the value-of-the-rights approach was conceptually the best of the alternatives it had discussed, the cost of measuring the value of the right to use collateral outweighed the benefit of the generally immaterial result of the measurement. In addition, some Board members expressed concern that the right under consideration (the financial component of the asset no longer held by the debtor) in that approach was not the same as the debtor's right to reclaim the pledged asset.

257. The Board adopted an alternative approach that requires the debtor to reclassify, in its statement of financial position, financial assets pledged that the secured party has the right to sell or repledge. That alternative carries over, and extends, a requirement in Statement 125 that applied only to collateral that the debtor did not have the right to redeem on short notice. The Board considers separate classification of pledged receivables in the statement of financial position to be necessary once those assets are pledged to a party who has the right to, and commonly does, sell or repledge them, because those financial assets pledged are effectively only receivables from the secured party and should not be reported in a way that suggests that the debtor still holds them. The Board considered requiring that the secured party recognize all such collateral as its assets but concluded that was inappropriate for the reasons cited in developing the value-of-the-rights approach. The Board carried over the requirement in Statement 125 that the secured party recognize its obligation to return collateral that it has sold to other parties, which had not been questioned by commentators. The Board also carried

over, in paragraphs 92–94 of this Statement, the requirement to recognize cash "collateral" or securities received as "collateral" that a securities lender is permitted to sell or repledge, because the Board considers them to be, not collateral, but the proceeds of either a sale of the "loaned" securities or a borrowing secured by them.

Security Interests, Custodial Arrangements, Contributions, and Other Transfers That Do Not Qualify as Sales

258. The Board concluded that a borrower that grants a security interest in financial assets should not derecognize the financial assets during the term of the secured obligation. Although the borrower's rights to those assets are restricted because it cannot sell them until the borrowing is repaid, it has not surrendered control if the lender cannot sell or repledge the assets unless the borrower defaults. That assets subject to a security interest have been pledged, and are therefore collateral in the possession of the lender or the lender's agent, does not affect recognition by the debtor because effective control over those assets remains with the debtor in the absence of default under the terms of the borrowing.

259. To maintain symmetry in the accounting of secured parties and debtors (paragraphs 237–257), the Board decided that debtors should reclassify in their statements of financial position collateral that has been put into the hands of a secured party that is permitted by contract or custom to sell or repledge it. That reclassification avoids a situation in which two or more entities report the same assets as if both held them (as could occur under previous accounting practices).

260. Under previous practice, financial assets transferred to another party for safekeeping or custody continue to be carried as assets by the transferor. The only consideration exchanged in those transfers is, perhaps, payment of a fee by the transferor to the custodian for the custodial services. The custodian does not control the assets but must follow the transferor's instructions. The Board concluded that existing practice should continue and that this Statement need not deal with transfers of custody for safekeeping.

261. Some transfers of financial assets are unconditional nonreciprocal transfers that are contributions. The Board did not address them in Statement 125 and this Statement because accounting for contributions is addressed in FASB Statement No. 116, *Accounting for Contributions Received and Contributions Made.*

262. Some transfers of financial assets will fail to meet the criteria specified in paragraph 9 to be accounted for as sales even though they might be structured as and purport to be sales. The Board concluded that those transfers should be accounted for as secured borrowings.

Scope and Definition

263. In developing this Statement, the Board chose to exclude from its scope transfers of investments in financial assets that are in substance the sale of real estate and exchanges of equity method investments for similar productive assets. Those transactions were excluded because, as the EITF noted in its Issues No. 98-7, "Accounting for Exchanges of Similar Equity Method Investments," and No. 98-8, "Accounting for Transfers of Investments That Are in Substance Real Estate," there were inadvertent overlaps in scope between Statement 125 and other accounting standards issued previously. Under APB Opinion No. 29, *Accounting for Nonmonetary Transactions,* exchanges of similar productive assets, including equity investments accounted for under the equity method, are accounted for based on the recorded amount of the asset relinquished. Under FASB Statement No. 66, *Accounting for Sales of Real Estate,* the sale of stock in enterprises with substantial real estate or of interests in certain partnerships are examples of transactions that are in substance the sale of real estate, and sales of real estate are accounted for differently from the accounting for transfers of financial assets under Statement 125. The Board's decision affirms the consensuses in Issues 98-7 and 98-8. The Board also considered removing from the scope of this Statement all other transfers of equity interests accounted for under the equity method but decided against that because no other pronouncements of the FASB or its predecessors provide accounting standards for such transactions.

264. Statement 125 amended earlier leasing pronouncements to require the residual value of an asset leased in a sales-type or direct financing lease to be classified as a financial asset, and the increase in its estimated value to be recognized over the remaining lease term, *to the extent that the residual value is guaranteed* by any party. In response to a constituent's comment that practice in interpreting that guidance was diverse, the Board decided to amend that guidance, in paragraphs 89 and 352 of this Statement, to clarify that a residual value of a leased asset

is a financial asset only to the extent of a guarantee obtained (whether from a third party or the lessee) *at inception of the lease.* The Board considered several alternatives. It rejected financial instrument classification for all guaranteed residual values (whether guaranteed at inception or later) because the Board views a guarantee obtained after lease inception as a contract separate from the lease. The Board rejected restricting that classification only to residual values guaranteed by the lessee because it was convinced by constituents that it did not matter who guaranteed the residual value and that securitizations of leases commonly involve a third-party guarantee. The Board also accepted that it was important for securitization purposes to allow a guarantee at inception to change the nature of a residual value to a financial asset so that it could be held by a qualifying SPE. Constituents noted that unless the qualifying SPE holds the residual interests as well as the guarantee and the lease receivables, concern may arise that the party holding the residual interests could nullify the lease contract in receivership.

Measurement under the Financial-Components Approach

265. Following a transfer of financial assets that qualifies as a sale, assets retained or obtained and liabilities incurred by the transferor could at first be measured at either (a) fair value at the date of the transfer or (b) an allocated portion of the transferor's carrying amount for the assets transferred.

266. The usual initial measure of assets and liabilities is the price in an exchange transaction or the equivalent fair value. Paragraph 88 of FASB Concepts Statement No. 5, *Recognition and Measurement in Financial Statements of Business Enterprises,* states:

   Initial recognition of assets acquired and liabilities incurred generally involves measurement based on current exchange prices at the date of recognition. Once an asset or a liability is recognized, it continues to be measured at the amount initially recognized until an event that changes the asset or liability or its amount occurs and meets the recognition criteria.

267. In Opinion 29, the Accounting Principles Board, in prescribing the basis for measurement of assets received in nonmonetary exchanges, states:

   . . . in general accounting for nonmonetary transactions should be based on the fair

values of the assets (or services) involved which is the same basis as that used in monetary transactions. [Paragraph 18, footnote reference omitted.]

268. The Board believes that those concepts should be applied to new interests obtained or incurred in transfers of financial assets. At issue is whether the financial assets controlled and liabilities incurred in a transfer of financial assets that qualifies as a sale are new to the transferor and thus are part of the proceeds from the transfer, subject to initial measurement using the concepts summarized in paragraphs 266 and 267, or instead are retained beneficial interests over which the transferor has not surrendered control that need not be subject to new measurement under those concepts. The Board concluded that the answer depends on the type of financial instrument or other interest held or incurred.

269. The Board decided that a distinction can and should be made between new assets and liabilities that are part of the proceeds from the transfer and continuing interests in retained assets held in a new form. Cash received as proceeds for assets sold has no continuing connection with those assets and is clearly a new asset. Unrelated assets obtained also are clearly new assets, for example, a government bond received in exchange for transferred accounts receivable. Any asset received that is not an interest in the transferred asset is new to the transferor and thus is part of the proceeds from the sale. Any liability incurred, even if it is related to the transferred assets, is an obligation that is new to the transferor and thus a reduction of proceeds. Therefore, all of those new assets and liabilities should be initially measured at fair value. The issue becomes more challenging for assets controlled after a sale that are related to the assets sold.

Measuring Liabilities and Derivative Financial Instruments Related to Assets Sold at Fair Value

270. An entity that sells a financial asset may incur liabilities that are related to the assets sold. A common example of a liability incurred by the transferor is a recourse or guarantee obligation. Certain risks, such as recourse or guarantees, are inherent in the original financial asset before it is transferred, which might seem to support carrying over the prior carrying amount. However, before the transfer, the transferor has no obligation to another party; after the transfer, it does. The Board concluded that liabilities

incurred in a transfer of financial assets are therefore new and should be initially measured at fair value.

271. An entity that sells a financial asset may enter into derivative financial instrument contracts that are related to the assets sold, for example, options, forwards, or swaps. One example is an option that allows purchasers of receivables to put them back to the transferor, which is similar to a recourse obligation. Another example is a repurchase commitment held by the seller in a repurchase agreement that is accounted for as a sale,[29] which is a kind of forward contract. A third example is an agreement similar to an interest rate swap in which the transferor receives from a securitization trust the fixed interest amounts due on securitized receivables and pays the trust variable amounts based on a floating interest rate index. A party to an option or a forward purchase or sale commitment generally does not recognize the acquisition or disposition of the underlying assets referenced in the contract until and unless delivery occurs. A party to a swap recognizes the net present value of amounts receivable or payable under the swap rather than the full notional amount of the contract. Options, forward commitments, swaps, and other derivative contracts are financial assets or liabilities separate and distinct from the underlying asset. For that reason and because of the practical need to make a workable distinction, the Board concluded that derivative financial instruments entered into by a seller in an exchange for a financial asset are newly created in the transaction and should be considered part of the proceeds and initially measured at fair value at the date of exchange.

272. Respondents to the Exposure Draft of Statement 125 asked the Board to provide more detailed guidance on how they should differentiate between an asset or liability that is part of the proceeds of a transfer and a retained interest in transferred assets. The Board acknowledges that, at the margin, it may be difficult to distinguish between a retained interest in the asset transferred and a newly created asset. The Board believes that it is impractical to provide detailed guidance that would cover all possibilities. A careful examination of cash flows, risks, and other provisions should provide a basis for resolving most questions. However, the Board agreed that it would be helpful to provide guidance if an entity cannot determine how to classify an instrument and decided that in that case the instrument should be considered

to be a new asset and thus part of the proceeds of the sale initially measured at fair value.

Measuring Retained Interests in Assets Sold at Allocated Previous Carrying Amount

273. The Board decided that all other interests in the transferred financial assets held after a securitization or other transfer of financial assets should be measured at their previous carrying amount, allocated between the assets sold, if any, and the retained interests, if any, based on their relative fair values at the date of the transfer. Retained interests in the transferred assets continue to be assets of the transferor, albeit assets of a different kind, because they never left the possession of the transferor and, thus, a surrender of control cannot have occurred. Therefore, the retained interests should continue to be carried at their allocated previous carrying amount, with no gain or loss recognized. Defining this category as the residual set of interests in transferred instruments held after the transfer (those interests that are neither derivatives nor liabilities of the transferor) establishes a clearer distinction between assets and liabilities that are part of the proceeds of the transfer and retained interests.

Other Alternatives Considered

274. In developing the Exposure Draft of Statement 125, the Board considered several alternative measurement approaches including (a) measuring all assets held after a securitization or sale of a partial undivided interest (either a pro rata interest or a nonproportional interest) initially at fair value, (b) measuring interests held after a securitization at fair value and measuring retained undivided interests at allocated previous carrying amounts, and (c) measuring all interests in transferred financial assets held after a transfer at their allocated previous carrying amounts. Some respondents to that Exposure Draft supported each of those approaches. However, most respondents agreed with the Board's reasoning that a retained interest in a transferred asset represents continuing control over a previous asset, albeit in different form, and thus should not be remeasured at fair value. Most respondents also accepted the approach proposed in the Exposure Draft of Statement 125 as workable.

275. Another possibility that was rejected by the Board was to allocate the carrying amount between the portion of an asset sold and the portion of an asset

---

[29]Accounting for repurchase agreements is discussed in paragraphs 96–101.

retained based on relative fair values at the date the receivable was originated or acquired by the transferor, adjusted for payments and other activity from the date of acquisition to the date of transfer. The consensus reached in EITF Issue No. 88-11, "Allocation of Recorded Investment When a Loan or Part of a Loan Is Sold," required use of that acquisition date method unless it is not practical, in which case the allocation should be based on relative fair values at the date of sale. In its deliberations of Statement 125 and this Statement, the Board decided to require allocation based on fair values at the date of sale or securitization because it is more representative of the asset's value, and the cost of re-creating the information from the date of acquisition would exceed the perceived benefits. The Board decided that the acquisition date method was not clearly superior in concept to an allocation based on fair values at the date of sale or securitization and, based in part on practices under that consensus, that that method was so often impractical because of recordkeeping difficulties that it was not useful as a general principle. No other possible methods of allocation appeared likely to produce results that were significantly more relevant.

Servicing Assets and Servicing Liabilities

276. Previously, net "mortgage servicing rights" were recognized as assets, and those rights were accounted for in accordance with FASB Statements No. 65, *Accounting for Certain Mortgage Banking Activities,* No. 91, *Accounting for Nonrefundable Fees and Costs Associated with Originating or Acquiring Loans and Initial Direct Costs of Leases,* No. 115, *Accounting for Certain Investments in Debt and Equity Securities,* and No. 122, *Accounting for Mortgage Servicing Rights.* The amount recognized as net mortgage servicing rights was based on the fair value of certain expected cash inflows net of expected cash outflows. The expected cash inflows—future servicing revenues—included a normal servicing fee,[30] expected late charges, and other ancillary revenues. The expected cash outflows—future servicing costs—included various costs of performing the servicing. A separate "excess servicing fee receivable" was recognized if the servicer expected to receive cash flows in excess of a normal servicing fee, and a liability was recognized if the servicer expected to receive less than a normal servicing

fee or if the entity's servicing costs were expected to exceed normal costs. The servicing rights asset was subsequently measured by amortization and assessment for impairment based on its fair value. That set of procedures has been called the mortgage servicing method.

277. Servicing assets and obligations for other assets sold or securitized were either accounted for like mortgage servicing or, more commonly, remained unrecognized until amounts were received and services were provided. Attempts have been made in practice to extend the mortgage servicing method to the servicing of other financial assets. However, identifying a normal servicing fee and other aspects of the mortgage servicing method have been difficult and disparate practices have resulted. The Board concluded it was necessary to address in this project accounting for servicing of all kinds of financial assets.

278. In October 1993, the Board decided to reconsider the accounting for mortgage servicing activities established in Statement 65. The primary thrust of that project was to resolve differences in the accounting for purchased versus originated mortgage servicing. Statement 122 was the result of that effort. In February 1995, the Board decided that accounting for excess mortgage servicing receivables and other servicing issues should be dealt with, to the extent necessary, not in that project but rather in this one, because those issues largely arise in transfers of financial assets and possible answers are necessarily interrelated. The Board considered alternative methods of accounting for servicing (the mortgage servicing method required by Statement 65, as amended by Statement 122, as well as a gross method and a right or obligation method) and chose a method that combines the best features of the mortgage servicing method and other possible methods.

Alternatives to the Mortgage Servicing Method

279. The mortgage servicing method described in paragraph 276 was required by Statement 65, as amended by Statement 122, for mortgage servicing rights. While that method was familiar to mortgage servicers and had certain advantages over other methods, the distinction between normal and excess servicing and other complexities of the method made it difficult to apply for some other kinds of servicing.

---

[30]Statement 65 defined a current (normal) servicing fee rate as "a servicing fee rate that is representative of servicing fee rates most commonly used in comparable servicing agreements covering similar types of mortgage loans." FASB Technical Bulletin No. 87-3, *Accounting for Mortgage Servicing Fees and Rights,* clarified what rate a seller-servicer should use as a servicing fee rate as described in Statement 65.

280. The Board considered a gross method that would have required that a servicer recognize both a servicing receivable asset consisting of expected future servicing revenues and a servicing obligation liability for the servicing work to be performed. The Board decided that it was questionable whether a receivable for servicing not yet rendered met the definition of an asset and that, given the conceptual questions, that method did not merit the large change in practice that it would have required.

281. The Board also considered a right or obligation method that would have recognized a single item, commonly an asset but occasionally a liability, for each servicing contract. That asset or liability would have been the net of the gross asset and liability that would have been reported separately under the gross approach. The resulting asset would have been subsequently measured like an interest-only strip, that is, at fair value with unrealized gains and losses recognized in equity if available-for-sale. Some respondents suggested that servicing rights should be subsequently measured in that way, because reporting servicing rights at fair value would be more useful to investors and other financial statement users than the historical cost amortization and impairment methods of the mortgage servicing approach. Furthermore, under an approach like that in Statement 115, unrealized gains and losses would not have been recognized in earnings, but rather in a separate component of shareholders' equity.

282. The Board considered the right or obligation method well suited in several respects to the range of mortgage and other servicing contracts that now exist or might arise. However, the Board did not choose that method in part for the practical reason of avoiding an early change from the recently adopted provisions of Statement 122. Instead, the Board chose to combine the best features of that method—the simplicity of reporting only a single asset or liability for each servicing contract and not having to distinguish between normal and excess servicing—with the best features of the mortgage servicing method.

Recognition and Measurement of Servicing Assets and Servicing Liabilities

283. The method adopted in Statement 125 carries forward the amortization and impairment provisions that were required under the mortgage servicing method in Statements 65 and 122 and that method was not reconsidered in this Statement. The Board considers those subsequent measurement provisions

workable. However, changes to the mortgage servicing method are necessary to adapt the accounting for mortgage servicing to all servicing assets and servicing liabilities, to reduce complexities for financial statement preparers and users, and to be compatible with the other recognition and initial measurement principles in Statement 125 and this Statement.

284. One change is the elimination of the distinction between normal and excess servicing. The Board decided that that distinction has been too difficult to make except in markets as liquid as the market for residential mortgage servicing. The Board considered two ways in which normal and excess servicing might be retained in accounting for those liquid markets.

285. One way would have been to leave in place the accounting for servicing of mortgages as required in Statement 65, as amended by Statement 122, while using a different method that was not dependent on determining a normal servicing fee for all other servicing. However, the Board concluded that comparability of financial statements would have suffered if the accounting for essentially similar servicing activities differed depending on the type of asset serviced. Another way would have been to revise the definition of normal servicing fee rates so that servicers could determine a normal servicing fee rate in the absence of a developed secondary market for servicing. That change would have provided servicers of other types of loans or receivables (such as auto loans and credit card balances) with an opportunity to establish normal servicing rates and apply the mortgage servicing method to other servicing rights, rather than be subject to recognizing less gain or more loss on the sale of receivables because normal servicing was unknown. The Board considered that method but concluded that that alternative might result in continuing questions about what are normal servicing fees for different types of servicing.

286. The Board also noted that the distinction between normal and excess servicing, even in liquid markets, is no longer relevant for financial reporting because under current market practices, excess and normal servicing assets, which arise from a single contract, generally cannot be sold separately after the sale or securitization of the underlying financial assets. The excess servicing receivable, like normal servicing, will be collected only if the servicing work is performed satisfactorily. In addition, accounting based on that distinction is unduly complex and often

results in several assets and liabilities being recognized for one servicing contract. While excess servicing continues to resemble an interest-only strip in some respects, the Board concluded in light of the lessened distinction between normal and excess servicing that it is more useful to account for all servicing assets and servicing liabilities in a similar manner.

287. The Board chose instead to distinguish only between the benefits of servicing—amounts that will be received only if the servicing work is performed to the satisfaction of the assets' owner or trustee—and other amounts retained after a securitization or other transfer of financial assets. A consequence of that method is that interest-only strips retained in securitizations, which do not depend on the servicing work being performed satisfactorily, are subsequently measured differently from servicing assets that arise from the same securitizations. That difference in accounting could lead transferors that retain an interest in transferred assets to select a stated servicing fee that results in larger servicing assets and lower retained interests (or vice versa) with an eye to subsequent accounting. The Board believes, however, that the potential accounting incentives for selecting a higher or lower stated servicing fee largely will counterbalance each other.

288. Most respondents agreed with the Board's decision to eliminate the distinction between excess and normal servicing. Some respondents to the Exposure Draft of Statement 125 asked for further explanation of the new terms it used for accounting for servicing and about how they differed from the terminology of the mortgage servicing approach used in prior pronouncements. In response, Statement 125 defines the terms *adequate compensation* for servicing, *benefits of servicing,* and *contractually specified servicing fees.* Those definitions and the discussion of them are carried forward without reconsideration in the glossary and in paragraphs 61–64 of this Statement.

289. The Exposure Draft of Statement 125 proposed that an entity account for all servicing assets in the same manner because rights to service financial assets, while they may differ in the particulars of the servicing, in the extent of compensation, and in liquidity, are in essence the same. As with other retained interests in transferred assets, valid arguments can be made for measuring servicing assets either at allocated previous carrying amount or at fair value. However, the Board saw no reason to treat retained servicing assets differently than other re-

tained interests and therefore decided that they should be initially measured at allocated previous carrying amount.

290. For similar reasons, the Board viewed servicing liabilities as new obligations arising from a transfer and decided to account for them like other liabilities incurred upon sale or securitization, at fair value.

291. Some respondents questioned how to apply the transition provisions to servicing rights and excess servicing receivables in existence as of the effective date of Statement 125. The Board retained paragraph 20 of Statement 125 without reconsideration in this Statement. Paragraph 25 does not permit retroactive application of Statement 125 to (a) ensure comparability between entities and (b) clarify how Statement 125 should be applied to previous balances.

Financial Assets Subject to Prepayment

292. Paragraph 362 of this Statement carries forward without reconsideration from Statement 125 the amendment to Statement 115 to eliminate the use of the *held-to-maturity* category for securities subject to substantial prepayment risk, thereby requiring that they be classified as either available-for-sale or trading and subsequently measured at fair value. Paragraph 14 extends that measurement principle to interest-only strips, loans, other receivables, and retained interests in securitizations subject to substantial prepayment risk.

293. The justification for using historical-cost-based measurement for debt securities classified as held-to-maturity is that no matter how market interest rates fluctuate, the holder will recover its recorded investment and thus realize no gains or losses when the issuer pays the amount promised at maturity. The same argument is used to justify historical-cost-based measurement for other receivables not held for sale. That justification does not extend to receivables purchased at a substantial premium over the amount at which they can be prepaid, and it does not apply to instruments whose payments derive from prepayable receivables but have no principal balance, as demonstrated by large losses realized in recent years by many holders of interest-only strips and other mortgage derivatives. As a result, the Board concluded that those receivables must be subsequently measured at fair value with gains or losses being recognized either in earnings (if classified as trading) or in a separate component of shareholders' equity (if classified as available-for-sale). The Board, by deciding

that a receivable may not be classified as held-to-maturity if it can be prepaid or otherwise settled in such a way that the holder of the asset would not recover *substantially all* of its recorded investment, left room for judgment, so that investments in mortgage-backed securities or callable securities purchased at an insubstantial premium, for example, are not necessarily disallowed from being classified as held-to-maturity.

294. Some respondents to the Exposure Draft of Statement 125 agreed with the Board's conclusions about financial assets subject to prepayment when applied to interest-only strips but questioned the application of those conclusions to loans, other receivables, and retained interests in securitizations. They maintained that the nature of the instrument and management's intent should govern classification rather than actions that a borrower might take under the contract.

295. The Board did not agree with those arguments. A lender that holds a portfolio of prepayable loans or bonds at par will realize the carrying amount of its investment if the borrowers prepay. However, if the lender originated or acquired those loans or bonds at a substantial premium to par, it may lose some or all of that premium and thus not recover a substantial portion of its recorded investment if borrowers prepay. The potential loss is less drastic for premium loans or bonds than for interest-only strips, but it can still be substantial. The Board concluded that the rationale outlined in paragraph 293 extends to any situation in which a lender would not recover substantially all of its recorded investment if borrowers were to exercise prepayment or other rights granted to them under the contracts. The Board also concluded that the provisions of paragraph 14 do not apply to situations in which events that are not the result of contractual provisions, for example, borrower default or changes in the value of an instrument's denominated currency relative to the entity's functional currency, cause the holder not to recover substantially all of its recorded investment.

296. Other respondents asked that the Board clarify the term *substantially all*. Some suggested that the Board use the 90 percent test found in APB Opinion No. 16, *Business Combinations*. Although applying the term *substantially all* requires judgment about how close to 100 percent is close enough, the Board

decided to leave the language of paragraphs 14 and 362 unchanged rather than to require a specific percentage test that would be inherently arbitrary.

Fair Value

297. The Board decided to include an approach for measuring fair value that would be broadly applicable. The definition of fair value in paragraphs 68–70 is consistent with that included in other recent Statements.[31] The Board found no compelling reason to redefine *fair value* under the financial-components approach.

298. Many of the assets and liabilities held after a sale by a transferor with continuing involvement are not traded regularly. Because quoted market values would not be available for those assets and liabilities, fair values would need to be determined by other means in applying the financial-components approach. There was concern that, in some cases, the best estimate of fair value would not be sufficiently reliable to justify recognition in earnings of a gain following a sale of financial assets with continuing involvement, because errors in the estimate of asset value or liability value might result in recording a nonexistent gain. The Board considered requiring that fair value be verifiable to achieve a higher degree of reliability to justify recognition in earnings of a gain following a sale of financial assets with continuing involvement. However, to promote consistency between its Statements, the Board decided not to introduce a new notion of fair value based on reliability.

299. The Exposure Draft of Statement 125 proposed that gain recognition following a sale with continuing involvement should be allowed only to the extent that it is practicable to estimate fair values for assets obtained and liabilities incurred in sales with continuing involvement. To accomplish that, the Board concluded that if it is not practicable to estimate their fair values, assets should be measured at zero and liabilities at the greater of the amount called for under FASB Statement No. 5, *Accounting for Contingencies,* as interpreted by FASB Interpretation No. 14, *Reasonable Estimation of the Amount of a Loss,* or the excess, if any, of the fair value of the assets obtained less the fair value of the other liabilities incurred over the sum of the carrying values of the assets transferred. That requirement was intended to

---

[31]FASB Statement No. 121, *Accounting for the Impairment of Long-Lived Assets and for Long-Lived Assets to Be Disposed Of,* par. 7, Statement 122, par. 3(f), and Statement No. 133, *Accounting for Derivative Instruments and Hedging Activities,* par. 540.

prevent recognition of nonexistent gains through underestimating liabilities. The Board considered whether the practicability exception should be extended to the transferee's accounting and decided not to allow such an exception. The Board concluded that because the transferee is the purchaser of the assets, it should be able to value all assets and any liabilities it purchased or incurred, presumptively based on the purchase price paid. In addition, because the transferee recognizes no gain or loss on the transfer, there is no possibility of recognizing a nonexistent gain.

300. Respondents to the Exposure Draft of Statement 125 asked the Board to clarify the meaning of the term *practicable,* especially in relation to the use of the same term in Statement 107. The comment letters also revealed a considerable range of interpretation of that provision among respondents. Some suggested that the provision would apply to all but the most common transactions. Others suggested that the provision would seldom apply and alluded to the relatively few entities that have used the practicability exception in Statement 107.

301. Because no practicability exception is used, for example, in Statement 133, the Board considered whether to expand the discussion of practicability, or to remove it from Statement 125 and this Statement. The Board ultimately concluded that the practicability provisions should remain unchanged in this Statement for the reasons noted in paragraphs 298 and 299.

302. Other respondents to the Exposure Draft of Statement 125 suggested that there should be a limit on the amount of gain that can be recognized in a transfer of financial assets. Several suggested the limitation found in Issue 88-11. In that Issue, the task force reached a consensus that "the amount of any gain recognized when a portion of a loan is sold should not exceed the gain that would be recognized if the entire loan was sold." Respondents maintained that a limitation would meet the Board's objective of preventing recognition of nonexistent gains through underestimating liabilities.

303. The Board rejected the suggested limitation for several reasons. First, it was not clear that the limitation in Issue 88-11 could have been applied across a wide range of transactions. The limitation presumes that a market price exists for transfers of whole assets, but one reason that securitization transactions take place is because sometimes no market exists for the whole assets being securitized. Second, the limitation would have required that accountants ignore the added value that many maintain is created when assets are divided into their several parts. Third, the use of relative fair values at the date of transfer, rather than relative fair values on initial acquisition as in Issue 88-11, would have mitigated many of the concerns that appear to have prompted the task force to adopt a limitation. Finally, the Board was concerned that a gain limitation might have obscured the need to consider whether the transaction gives rise to a loss.

304. In its deliberations of this Statement, the Board considered constituents' concerns that retained interests were not being appropriately valued in certain securitizations. One constituent suggested that, under the relative-fair-value allocation method required by paragraph 10 of Statement 125, transferors were allocating too much to the relatively low-risk senior interests that have been sold, whereas the bulk of the profit from lending and selling loans ought to be attributed to realizing the value of the high-risk subordinated interests, which typically have not yet been sold. The Board again considered limiting the amount of the gain, as discussed prior to Statement 125, but rejected that limitation for the same reasons cited in paragraph 303.

305. The Board recognizes that risk assumed in connection with subordinated retained interests will affect the expected cash flows or discount rate used to value the retained interests and agreed with constituents' concern that risk has not always been adequately taken into account. To the extent that risk is not adequately taken into account, subordinated retained interests are overvalued and consequently the gain calculated is higher (or loss is lower) than it should be. However, the Board does not believe that concerns about failure to reasonably estimate the fair value of the various items created in a securitization can be eliminated by an arbitrary ceiling. Instead, the Board believes those responsible for financial statements need to exercise care in applying this Statement, and, as discussed in paragraph 59, should be able to identify the reasons for gains on securitization. For the same reasons, as discussed in paragraphs 323–332, the Board also decided in this Statement to require disclosure about the key assumptions made in valuing retained interests.

Subsequent Measurement

306. The provisions of Statement 125 that were carried forward without reconsideration in this Statement focus principally on the initial recognition and

measurement of assets and liabilities that result from transfers of financial assets. This Statement does not address subsequent measurement except for servicing assets and servicing liabilities and financial assets subject to prepayment that were also addressed in Statement 125.

307. Several respondents to the Exposure Draft of Statement 125 also asked the Board to include guidance about subsequent measurement. They observed that the financial-components approach leads to recognition of assets and liabilities that were not recognized under previous standards. They also observed that accountants who draw analogies to existing accounting practices may find a variety of equally plausible approaches to subsequent measurement.

308. The Board is sensitive to concerns about subsequent measurement, especially to the possibility of emerging diversity in practice. However, attempting to address subsequent measurement would have expanded significantly the scope of this project. In addition, any guidance on subsequent measurement in this project would have applied only to assets and liabilities that emerge from a transfer of financial assets. Accounting for similar assets and liabilities not connected with a transfer of financial assets would have continued to follow existing practice; if so, diversity would have continued to exist. On balance, the Board concluded that it was better to complete this project without providing guidance on subsequent measurement and leave reconsideration of existing standards and practices for subsequent measurement for future segments of the Board's financial instruments project or other projects.

Extinguishments of Liabilities

309. Statement 76 required that a debtor treat a liability as if extinguished if it completed an in-substance defeasance. Under that Statement, a debtor derecognized a liability if it transferred essentially risk-free assets to an irrevocable defeasance trust and the cash flows from those assets approximated the scheduled interest and principal payments of the debt that was being extinguished. Under that Statement, the debtor also derecognized the assets that were set aside in the trust.

310. Derecognition of liabilities after an in-substance defeasance has been controversial. A number of respondents to the Exposure Drafts that led to Statement 76 and subsequent Board requests for comment have criticized the transactions as having insufficient economic substance to justify derecognition or gain recognition. Researchers and analysts have demonstrated that in-substance defeasance transactions conducted after interest rates have risen, which resulted in an accounting gain under Statement 76, have economic impact; those transactions constitute an economic loss to shareholders.[32] That research and analysis suggest that derecognition of liabilities and recognition of a gain in those circumstances may not be representationally faithful.

311. Under the financial-components approach, an in-substance defeasance transaction does not meet the derecognition criteria for either the liability or the asset. The transaction lacks the following critical characteristics:

a. The debtor is not released from the debt by putting assets in the trust; if the assets in the trust prove insufficient, for example, because a default by the debtor accelerates its debt, the debtor must make up the difference.
b. The lender is not limited to the cash flows from the assets in trust.
c. The lender does not have the ability to dispose of the assets at will or to terminate the trust.
d. If the assets in the trust exceed what is necessary to meet scheduled principal and interest payments, the transferor can remove the assets.
e. Neither the lender nor any of its representatives is a contractual party to establishing the defeasance trust, as holders of interests in a qualifying SPE or their representatives would be.
f. The debtor does not surrender control of the benefits of the assets because those assets are still being used for the debtor's benefit, to extinguish its debt, and because no asset can be an asset of more than one entity, those benefits must still be the debtor's assets.

312. The Board concluded that the previous treatment of in-substance defeasance was inconsistent

---

[32]The research referred to includes John R. M. Hand, Patricia J. Hughes, and Stephan E. Sefcik, "In-Substance Defeasances: Security Price Reactions and Motivations," *Journal of Accounting and Economics* (May 1990): 47–89; Judy Beckman, J. Ralph Byington, and Paul Munter, "Extinguishment of Debt by In-Substance Defeasance: Managerial Perspectives," *Journal of Corporate Accounting and Finance* (Winter 1989/90): 167–174; Bruce R. Gaumnitz and Joel E. Thompson, "In-Substance Defeasance: Costs, Yes; Benefits, No," *Journal of Accountancy* (March 1987): 102–105; and Abraham M. Stanger, "Accounting Developments: In-Substance Defeasance—Reality or Illusion?" *The Corporation Law Review* (Summer 1984): 274–277.

with the derecognition criteria of the financial-components approach and that the provisions on in-substance defeasance in Statement 76 should be superseded by Statement 125. Respondents to the Exposure Draft of Statement 125 generally accepted that change, although some disagreed, citing arguments similar to those made in Statement 76 and refuted, in the Board's view, by the critical characteristics cited in paragraph 311.

313. Paragraph 3(a) of Statement 76 required derecognition of the transferred assets and the liability by the debtor if a debtor transfers assets to its creditor in exchange for a release from all further obligation under the liability. That provision has not been controversial and is consistent with the financial-components approach. Accordingly, paragraph 3(a) of Statement 76 was incorporated substantially unchanged as paragraph 16(a) of this Statement.

314. Paragraph 3(b) of Statement 76 stated, "The debtor is legally released from being the primary obligor under the debt either judicially or by the creditor *and it is probable that the debtor will not be required to make future payments with respect to that debt under any guarantees*" (emphasis added; footnote references omitted). Except for the italicized portion, paragraph 3(b) was carried forward without reconsideration as paragraph 16(b) of this Statement. Some respondents to the Exposure Draft of Statement 125 disagreed with that change, arguing that the revised provision was too lenient in that it might allow, for example, derecognition of liabilities and inappropriate gain recognition when entities are replaced as primary obligor by entities with little economic substance. However, the italicized phrase is omitted from Statement 125 and this Statement because it is contrary to the financial-components approach. If an entity is released from being a primary obligor and becomes a secondary obligor and thus effectively a guarantor of that liability, it should recognize that guarantee in the same manner as a third-party guarantor that was never the primary obligor. The Board noted, however, that concerns about inappropriate gains are unwarranted: if an entity with little substance were to become a primary obligor, a guarantor of that obligation would have to recognize a liability almost as great as if it were the primary obligor. To emphasize those matters, the Board included a discussion of the secondary obligor's liability in Appendix A.

315. The Board concluded that the basic principle that liabilities should be derecognized only if the

debtor pays the creditor or is legally released from its obligation applies not just to debt securities but to all liabilities. Accordingly, Statement 125 and this Statement broaden the scope of paragraphs 3(a) and 3(b) of Statement 76 to include all liabilities not excluded from Statement 125 and this Statement's scope by paragraph 4 and to delete the reference to sales in the public market.

Disclosures

316. The Board decided that Statement 125 should continue to require disclosure of debt defeased in accordance with Statement 76 before the effective date of Statement 125 because Statement 125 does not change the accounting for those defeasance transactions. The Board also decided to require that an entity disclose assets restricted to the repayment of particular debt obligations, for example, in in-substance defeasance transactions after Statement 125 becomes effective, because while that restriction is insufficient cause to derecognize the assets, that information is useful in determining what resources are unavailable to general creditors and for general operations. The Board decided that an entity should disclose its policies for requiring collateral or other securities in repurchase agreements and securities lending transactions accounted for as borrowings. The Board believes that that information is useful for assessing the amount of risk that an entity assumes in repurchase agreements and securities lending transactions, which appears to vary considerably in practice.

317. The Board also decided to carry forward the disclosures required by Statement 122 and extend them to all servicing rights, because those disclosures provide information financial statement users need to make independent judgments about the value of servicing rights and obligations and the related risks.

318. In addition, the Board decided to require that an entity describe items for which it is impracticable to measure their fair value and disclose why the fair value of an asset obtained or liability incurred could not be estimated, despite the concerns of some Board members that this requirement was unnecessary and might lead to uninformative disclosures.

Disclosures about Collateral

319. In connection with the issuance of Statement 125, the Board decided to require entities to disclose their policies for requiring collateral or other security for securities lending transactions and repurchase agreements to inform users about the

credit risk that entities assume in those transactions, because there appeared to be significant variation in practice. Commentators did not object to that disclosure, which is carried forward without substantial change in this Statement.

320. After it decided to remove certain of Statement 125's recognition requirements for collateral, the Board decided that further disclosures about the value of collateral are appropriate. It chose to require disclosure of (a) the fair value of collateral accepted that could be sold or repledged and (b) the portion of that collateral that had been sold or repledged. The Board considers that information relevant for investors and creditors who wish to understand the scale of collateralized transactions, the extent to which that collateral is used, or the relationship between income from use of collateral and the amount of collateral used and available for use. In considering the costs of preparing that information, the Board determined that similar information is already maintained for other purposes by entities that accept large amounts of collateral. The Board believes that that information could be developed by other entities at a moderate cost well justified by the value of the information. Commentators generally favored that disclosure instead of the proposal to account for the value of rights to use collateral. After the Board decided in its redeliberations that collateral should not be accounted for under the value-of-the-rights approach or recognized as an asset by secured parties, it concluded that those disclosures are necessary to indicate the extent of collateral available to the secured party and the usage of that resource, and required them in this Statement.

321. In the Exposure Draft of Statement 125, the Board did not propose additional disclosures by entities that pledge their assets, largely because disclosure of assets pledged as security is already required under paragraphs 18 and 19 of Statement 5. After the Board decided in its redeliberations that collateral should not be accounted for under the value-of-the-rights approach, as discussed in paragraphs 255 and 256, it chose to refine the general requirement from Statement 5, to avoid redundant information. Specifically, this Statement requires an entity that pledges any assets as collateral that the secured party *cannot* sell or repledge to disclose the carrying amount and classification of those assets. Collateral that a secured party can sell or repledge is already reclassified and separately reported in the statement of financial position pursuant to paragraph 15(a).

322. In the redeliberations of this Statement, the Board considered two other alternatives for disclos-

ing collateral. The first alternative was to require disclosure of the value of the right to use collateral, in place of recognition of that value in the financial statements. The Board concluded, based in part on the results of the informal field test, that the cost of computing and disclosing the value of the right to use the collateral would exceed its benefits. The second alternative would have required the disclosure of earnings generated by secured parties from the use of pledged collateral. Additional research on the feasibility of that alternative uncovered a potential for inconsistency in disclosures across firms that could result in lack of comparability. In addition, the Board accepted arguments that information about earnings generated from the use of collateral is not currently isolated for management or reporting purposes and therefore new systems would have been needed to be developed by the larger firms to generate that information for disclosure. Because it appeared doubtful that the value of this information would justify the cost of extensive systems changes, the Board rejected that alternative.

Disclosures about Securitizations

323. During the deliberations leading to Statement 125, the Board considered whether additional disclosures were necessary in the context of that Statement or whether current standards provide adequate disclosure of interests retained in a transfer of financial assets. The Board concluded then that sufficient requirements were in place (for example, in FASB Statement No. 95, *Statement of Cash Flows,* and other pronouncements) for transfers and servicing of financial assets, extinguishments of liabilities, and the resulting components of those transfers and extinguishments and that the potential benefits of requiring additional disclosures did not appear to justify the costs involved.

324. Since Statement 125 became effective, however, a number of entities that securitize financial assets have materially restated gains recognized in earlier financial statements or have materially changed estimates of the fair value of their retained interests. Those restatements led some to contend that gain or loss recognition should not be permitted for securitizations in which significant interests are retained by the transferor and others to demand additional disclosures. The Board rejected suggestions that gain or loss recognition is inappropriate for transfers of financial assets that qualify as sales, though it observed that Statement 125 and this Statement do have procedures to be followed if it is impracticable to measure

the fair value of retained interests. However, the Board did agree to consider whether, in light of those developments, the benefits of further disclosure might indeed justify the costs involved.

325. Members of the Board and staff met with analysts, investors, and preparers during 1998 to learn more about the type of information that financial statement users need to adequately assess the amounts of risks involved in securitization transactions and the availability of that information. Some analysts and investors called for increased disclosure about key assumptions because they believe that the current disclosures are inadequate and sometimes misleading. They contend that assumptions about interest rates, prepayments, and losses are especially important in assessing whether the projected future earnings of an entity are attainable and whether write-downs of retained interests or other unfavorable events will occur.

326. Based on those discussions and the concerns voiced, the Board concluded that disclosures about securitization transactions needed to be enhanced. Preparers of financial statements from the financial services industry told Board members and staff that they already prepare and disclose much of the information that financial statement users want, in documents required to be filed with the SEC, in electronic information media in connection with publicly offered securitizations, or in data voluntarily provided on an entity-wide basis. They suggested that summary disclosures (disaggregated on a product-by-product basis) provided in financial statements or in the management discussion and analysis (MD&A) could offer investors and analysts the information that they need to assess both the level of risk and the impact that securitizations have on an entity's overall earnings.

327. The Board decided that enhanced disclosures should focus on two aspects of securitizations: the results of securitization transactions entered into during the period and the valuation of retained interests in past securitizations that are still outstanding at the end of the period.

328. The Board concluded that, at a minimum, financial statements should provide, for all securitizations entered into during the period, a description of (a) the transferor's accounting policies for initially measuring interests retained in a securitization; (b) the characteristics of securitizations entered into, and gain or loss from securitizations of financial as-

sets during the year by major type of asset; (c) quantitative information about key assumptions used to value interests retained at the time of securitization that affect the amount of income recognized during the period; and (d) cash flows between the securitization SPE and the transferor. The Board concluded that under those requirements, financial statement users would receive information that would assist them in assessing the effect of securitization transactions on the results of operations and cash flows and be useful in assessing the valuation of interest-only strips, subordinated tranches, servicing, cash reserve accounts, and other interests retained in the securitization. The Board chose to require disclosures by major class of asset securitized because prepayment, credit loss, and interest rates vary so widely between major classes that aggregating data across those classes would obscure useful information. The Board decided to require information about weighted-average life so that disclosures of prepayment assumptions would be more comparable if different companies use different calculation methods. While other disclosures were suggested, the Board concluded that the problems associated with restatements and inappropriate assumptions could be best highlighted by the disclosures it selected and that the cost of further disclosures might outweigh the benefits of requiring those disclosures.

329. Some commentators suggested that certain of the proposed required disclosures about cash flows between the securitization SPE and the transferor might be redundant with information already disclosed elsewhere; for example, the proceeds from securitization might already be reported in cash flow statements. Other constituents pointed out that that information is not always apparent in cash flow statements, perhaps because it is aggregated with other information. The Board agreed with both groups. To avoid requiring any redundancy, the Board revised its proposed requirement to require disclosure of cash flows between the securitization SPE and the transferor, unless that information is reported separately elsewhere in the financial statements or notes.

330. For retained interests outstanding at the end of the period, the Board concluded that three types of disclosures would be useful in assessing their valuation. Those disclosures include (a) the accounting policies for measuring retained interests at the end of the period being reported on, including the methodology used in determining or estimating their fair value; (b) quantitative information about key assumptions used in valuing those retained interests; and (c) a sensitivity analysis or stress test that would quantify the effect that unfavorable variations from

the expected levels of interest rates, prepayment patterns, credit losses, or other key assumptions would have on the estimates of fair value of the retained interests. The Board decided to require static pool information so that disclosures of credit loss assumptions would be more comparable if different entities use different calculation methods. The Board concluded that sensitivity information would provide users of financial statements with a means of comparing their estimates of the market's performance with the entity's estimates, seeing the pro forma effects of changes in assumptions on the financial statements, and assessing the potential effect of a future change in market conditions on the value of the entity's retained interests. The Board chose to require disclosure of the impact of two or more pessimistic variations for each key assumption so that the results would indicate whether the valuation had a linear relationship to the assumption. The Board chose not to specify any particular changes in assumptions so that companies could select the changes that best portray the sensitivity of estimates of fair value.

331. Some commentators supported the proposed disclosures and asked for additional information. One request that the Board adopted was to require disclosure of the total financial assets managed by securitizers from loans sold as well as those that remain on the statement of financial position, with the goal of highlighting a source of risks (and benefits) to securitizers through their retained interests. The Board chose to specifically exclude from this disclosure securitized assets that an entity continues to service but with which it has no other continuing involvement. The Board reasoned that a disclosure of the total financial assets managed by securitizers, including loans sold as well as those that remain on the statement of financial position, would not only be useful but would also be economical for many securitizers to produce because many already report that in the MD&A or in voluntary disclosures. The Board discussed, but decided against, requiring disclosure of average balances of managed assets outstanding for the year, partly because current GAAP does not require disclosures of other average balances; it decided to encourage that disclosure, however, in part, because it provides a useful base for comparison of credit losses for the year.

332. Some commentators suggested that this Statement include a specific materiality threshold below which certain disclosures for securitization transactions would not be required. The Board chose not to do that. Materiality and relevance are both defined in

terms of what influences or makes a difference to a decision maker. The Board's position is that " . . . no general standards of materiality could be formulated to take into account all the considerations that enter into an experienced human judgment," but that quantitative materiality criteria may be given by the Board in specific standards, as appropriate (FASB Concepts Statement No. 2, *Qualitative Characteristics of Accounting Information,* paragraph 131). The Board has only rarely given quantitative materiality criteria in specific standards. The one recent example is the 10 percent threshold for reported segments in FASB Statement No. 131, *Disclosures about Segments of an Enterprise and Related Information,* which the Board retained from an earlier Statement "because it can be objectively applied and because preparers and users of financial statements already understand it" (paragraph 76). The latter reason does not apply in this Statement, and the Board identified no persuasive reason to take its place. Therefore, this Statement does not include a materiality threshold. However, that conclusion does not imply that the provisions of this Statement must be applied to immaterial items. Some entities may determine that some or all disclosures about securitization transactions are not material after an evaluation of all the relevant facts and circumstances.

Effective Date and Transition for Statement 125

333. The Board proposed that Statement 125 should be effective for transfers and servicing of financial assets and extinguishments of liabilities occurring after December 31, 1996, and the Board did not change that effective date in the final Statement. While many respondents accepted and some even urged adoption on that date, some respondents expressed concern about the ability to carry out certain of Statement 125's provisions by that date, including systems changes needed to keep track of supporting data efficiently. The Board concluded that some of those concerns should be ameliorated by the effects of changes from the Exposure Draft on the accounting for repurchase agreements, securities lending, loan participations, and collateral, and that in other cases data adequate for external financial reporting could be obtained in other ways while systems changes were being completed. After Statement 125 was issued, representatives from various enterprises, particularly those representing brokers and dealers in securities, continued to express to the Board concerns about the effective date of Statement 125 for those types of

transactions (repurchase agreements, securities lending, loan participations, and collateral). Those representatives convinced the Board that for those types of transactions, substantial changes to information systems and accounting processes were essential for brokers and dealers in securities and other enterprises to comply with Statement 125 and that those changes would make it extremely difficult, if not impossible, for affected enterprises to account for those transfers of financial assets and apply the secured borrowing and collateral provisions of Statement 125 as soon as January 1, 1997. The Board appreciated the concerns expressed by those enterprises that attempting to account for those types of transactions manually until appropriate modifications could be made to information systems and accounting processes might lead to a significant temporary deterioration in the financial controls and quality of financial information of the affected enterprises. In November 1996, the Board decided to defer for one year the effective date (a) of paragraph 15 and (b) for repurchase agreement, dollar-roll, securities lending, and similar transactions, of paragraphs 9–12 and 237(b) of Statement 125. For those types of transfers, Statement 125 became effective for transfers occurring after December 31, 1997.

334. The Exposure Draft of Statement 125 proposed that the Statement should be applied prospectively to achieve consistency in accounting for transfers of financial assets. That requirement was also meant to ensure that all entities entering into a given transaction report that transaction under the same guidance. If entities were permitted to implement early or implement at the beginning of fiscal years that did not coincide, opportunities might arise to structure transactions in ways that result in the same assets and liabilities being reported in the financial statements of both parties or in the financial statements of neither party. The Board found that possibility undesirable. Most respondents to the Exposure Draft of Statement 125 generally accepted that conclusion.

335. The Board also decided that retroactive implementation for all entities was not feasible and that allowing voluntary retroactive implementation was unwise because it would impair comparability of financial statements by permitting disparate accounting treatment for similar transactions reported in previous periods. The Board concluded that those considerations outweighed the lack of consistency within an entity's financial statements for transactions occurring before and after the effective date of Statement 125. In addition, the Board concluded that the benefits of retroactive application of the provisions of Statement 125 would not justify the considerable cost of doing that. Respondents generally accepted that conclusion.

Effective Date and Transition for This Statement

336. The Board decided that the accounting provisions of this Statement that are changed from or in addition to those in Statement 125 should be applied prospectively to transfers of financial assets occurring after March 31, 2001, except for the provisions relating to collateral. That transaction-based prospective approach is the same as that used in Statement 125 and was adopted in this Statement for the same reason: to achieve consistency in accounting for transfers of financial assets and to ensure that all entities entering into a given transaction report that transaction under the same guidance. Retroactive implementation for all entities was not feasible, and allowing voluntary retroactive implementation was unwise because it would impair comparability of financial statements by permitting disparate accounting treatment for similar transactions reported in previous periods.

337. The Board initially considered making this Statement effective for transfers occurring after December 31, 2000. Adopting the accounting provisions of this Statement at the beginning of a calendar year would simplify the transition for preparers and users of the financial statements of a majority of larger U.S. enterprises, which use the calendar year as their fiscal year. However, after considering constituents' comments, the Board concluded that an effective date that soon would be inappropriate. The Board also concluded that a one-year postponement in effective date would unduly delay necessary improvements in financial reporting. Instead, the Board decided that entities would be in a better position to implement this Statement if it were effective for transfers occurring after March 31, 2001, six months after issuance. The Board concluded that that interval should allow constituents the time needed to assess the standards, consider the effect of EITF issues and other implementation guidance, negotiate new contractual arrangements, and revise their accounting systems to conform to the amendment.

338. The Board believes that the disclosure requirements of this Statement for securitization transactions should be implemented as early as possible, in view of concerns that markets for securitized assets and other securities of the issuers of securitized assets

have been adversely affected by the lack of sufficient and comparable information. In addition, constituents informed the Board that many entities that securitize assets use the kind of information required to be disclosed under this Statement to manage internally. Therefore, for many entities, the cost and time to aggregate the data for disclosure in financial statements should be minimal. For those reasons, the Board concluded that securitization disclosures mandated by this Statement could be required for financial statements for fiscal years ending after December 15, 2000. The Board also decided that disclosures required for securitization transactions that have occurred during the period that are accounted for as sales should be made for each year for which an income statement is presented for comparative purposes, so that investors and creditors can better understand the effects of the key assumptions on those income statements. However, in response to comments from constituents, the Board chose not to require that those disclosures be reported for periods ending on or before December 15, 2000, for which an income statement is presented for comparative purposes. The Board reasoned that those disclosures should be required only prospectively because they might be difficult to develop for prior years, especially if securitzations are not the company's core business.

339. For the reasons cited above, the Board decided that disclosures about the assumptions used in valuing the retained interests remaining at the end of the period and the sensitivity of those assumptions need not be required for earlier periods in comparative financial statements, as that information is relevant primarily as of the latest statement of financial position.

340. In light of the Board's decision not to require that collateral be accounted for under the value-of-the-rights approach, the Board decided that collateral that was previously recognized by secured parties in accordance with paragraphs 15(a)(ii) and 15(b) of Statement 125 should not continue to be recognized in financial statements for fiscal years ending after December 15, 2000, and that financial statements for earlier periods presented for comparative purposes should be restated accordingly. The Board concluded that (a) to do so would improve comparability between entities and consistency between periods in recognized amounts and (b) the amount of collateral that would be reported on future statements of financial position would soon become minimal given the short average time that much pledged collateral is held. The Board had originally proposed in the Expo-

sure Draft of this Statement that disclosure requirements for collateral should first be required in financial statements prepared for fiscal years ending after December 15, 2001, because of the relationship between the disclosures about collateral and the proposed accounting provisions that would not have been effective until January 1, 2001. However, in keeping with its decision to require that the asset and liability accounts currently being reported for collateral be removed from the statement of financial position for fiscal years ending after December 15, 2000, the Board decided to require the same effective date for disclosures about collateral. The Board reasoned that those disclosures should be required only prospectively because they might be difficult to develop for prior years.

341. The Board also considered the effect of applying this Statement on previously transferred assets and previously qualifying SPEs in light of constituents' arguments that changing the requirements for a qualifying SPE without some transition relief would result in (a) assets that were previously recorded as having been sold to previously qualifying SPEs suddenly reappearing in the financial statements of the transferor solely because the SPEs could not meet the revised standards for qualifying SPEs and (b) future transfers that were required under previous commitments to unrelated transferees or BIHs having to be accounted for as secured borrowings. The Board discussed the validity of constituents' concerns that changes in the requirements would (1) cause an unexpected build-up of assets on the transferor's balance sheet, (2) conflict with transition guidance in paragraph 55 of this Statement, (3) result in significant costs to restructure existing qualifying SPEs if that could be done at all, (4) result in partial consolidation of transferred assets, and (5) cause certain transfers subject to the new conditions for ROAPs to no longer be accounted for as sales. The Board decided to ameliorate what it judged to be the more onerous of those concerns by permitting formerly qualifying SPEs to continue to apply the requirements of Statement 125 but limiting that "grandfathering" to entities just carrying out previous commitments made to unrelated BIHs, and at the same time complying with previous standards. The Board did not extend that transition relief to SPEs that engage in new transactions, such as taking in new assets not already committed to or issuing new beneficial interests, because the Board wanted to minimize the

length of the period of noncomparability that that transition provision will cause.

Appendix C

ILLUSTRATIVE GUIDANCE

342. This appendix provides specific examples that illustrate the disclosures that are required by this Statement. The formats in the illustrations are not required by the Statement. The Board encourages entities to use a format that displays the information in the most understandable manner in the specific circumstances. References to paragraphs of this Statement in which the relevant requirements appear are given in parentheses.

343. The first example illustrates the disclosure of accounting policies for retained interests. In particular, it describes the accounting policies for (a) initial measurement (paragraph 17(f)(1)) and (b) subsequent measurement (paragraph 17(g)(1)), including determination of fair value.

NOTE X—SUMMARY OF SIGNIFICANT ACCOUNTING POLICIES

Receivable Sales

When the Company sells receivables in securitizations of automobile loans, credit card loans, and residential mortgage loans, it retains interest-only strips, one or more subordinated tranches, servicing rights, and in some cases a cash reserve account, all of which are retained interests in the securitized receivables. Gain or loss on sale of the receivables depends in part on the previous carrying amount of the financial assets involved in the transfer, allocated between the assets sold and the retained interests based on their relative fair value at the date of transfer. To obtain fair values, quoted market prices are used if available. However, quotes are generally not available for retained interests, so the Company generally estimates fair value based on the present value of

future expected cash flows estimated using management's best estimates of the key assumptions—credit losses, prepayment speeds, forward yield curves, and discount rates commensurate with the risks involved.

344. In addition to the disclosure of assumptions used in determining the values of retained interests at the time of securitization that are presented in paragraph 343, this Statement also requires similar disclosures at the end of the latest period being presented. The following example illustrates disclosures about the characteristics of securitizations and gain or loss from securitizations and other sales by major type of asset (paragraph 17(f)(2)).

NOTE Y—SALES OF RECEIVABLES

During 20X2 and 20X1, the Company sold automobile loans, residential mortgage loans, and credit card loans in securitization transactions. In all those securitizations, the Company retained servicing responsibilities and subordinated interests. The Company receives annual servicing fees approximating 0.5 percent (for mortgage loans), 2 percent (for credit card loans), and 1.5 percent (for automobile loans) of the outstanding balance and rights to future cash flows arising after the investors in the securitization trust have received the return for which they contracted. The investors and the securitization trusts have no recourse to the Company's other assets for failure of debtors to pay when due. The Company's retained interests are subordinate to investor's interests. Their value is subject to credit, prepayment, and interest rate risks on the transferred financial assets.

In 20X2, the Company recognized pretax gains of $22.3 million on the securitization of the automobile loans, $30.2 million on the securitization of credit card loans, and $25.6 million on the securitization of residential mortgage loans.

In 20X1, the Company recognized pretax gains of $16.9, $21.4, and $15.0 million on the securitization of the automobile loans, credit card loans, and residential mortgage loans, respectively.

FAS140   *FASB Statement of Standards*

345. The following is an illustration of the quantitative information about key assumptions used in measuring retained interests at the date of sale or securitization for each financial period presented (paragraph 17(f)(3)).

Key economic assumptions used in measuring the retained interests at the date of securitization resulting from securitizations completed during the year were as follows (rates* per annum):

20X2

	Automobile Loans	Credit Card Loans	Residential Mortgage Loans Fixed-Rate	Residential Mortgage Loans Adjustable†
Prepayment speed	1.00%	15.0%	10.00%	8.0%
Weighted-average life (in years)[33]	1.8	0.4	7.2	6.5
Expected credit losses	3.10–3.40%	6.10%	1.25%	1.30%
Residual cash flows discounted at	12.0–13.0%	12.00%	10.00%	8.50%
Variable returns to transferees	Forward Eurodollar yield curve plus contractual spread over LIBOR ranging from 30 to 80 basis points		Not applicable	

20X1

	Automobile Loans	Credit Card Loans	Residential Mortgage Loans Fixed-Rate	Residential Mortgage Loans Adjustable†
Prepayment speed	1.00%	12.85%	8.00%	6.00%
Weighted-average life (in years)[33]	1.8	0.4	8.5	7.2
Expected credit losses	3.50–3.80%	5.30%	1.25%	2.10%
Residual cash flows discounted at	13.00–13.50%	13.00%	11.75%	11.00%
Variable returns to transferees	Forward Eurodollar yield curve plus contractual spread over LIBOR ranging from 28 to 70 basis points		Not applicable	

Notes:

*Weighted-average rates for securitizations entered into during the period for securitizations of loans with similar characteristics.

†Rates for these loans are adjusted based on an index (for most loans, the 1-year Treasury note rate plus 2.75 percent). Contract terms vary, but for most loans, the rate is adjusted every 12 months by no more than 2 percent.

---

[33]The weighted-average life in periods (for example, months or years) of prepayable assets is calculated by summing the product of (a) the sum of the principal collections expected in each future period times (b) the number of periods until collection, and then dividing that total by (c) the initial principal balance.

2432

346. The following is an illustration that combines disclosure of the key assumptions used in valuing retained interests at the end of the latest period (paragraph 17(g)(2)) and the hypothetical effect on current fair value of two or more pessimistic variations from the expected levels for each of the key assumptions (paragraph 17(g)(3)).

At December 31, 20X2, key economic assumptions and the sensitivity of the current fair value of residual cash flows to immediate 10 percent and 20 percent adverse changes in those assumptions are as follows ($ in millions):

	Automobile Loans	Credit Card Loans	Residential Mortgage Loans	
			Fixed-Rate	Adjustable
Carrying amount/fair value of retained interests	$15.6	$21.25	$12.0	$13.3
Weighted-average life (in years)[34]	1.7	0.4	6.5	6.1
Prepayment speed assumption (annual rate)	**1.3%**	**15.0%**	**11.5%**	**9.3%**
Impact on fair value of 10% adverse change	*$0.3*	*$1.6*	*$3.3*	*$2.6*
Impact on fair value of 20% adverse change	*$0.7*	*$3.0*	*$7.8*	*$6.0*
Expected credit losses (annual rate)	**3.0%**	**6.1%**	**0.9%**	**1.8%**
Impact on fair value of 10% adverse change	*$4.2*	*$3.2*	*$1.1*	*$1.2*
Impact on fair value of 20% adverse change	*$8.4*	*$6.5*	*$2.2*	*$3.0*
Residual cash flows discount rate (annual)	**14.0%**	**14.0%**	**12.0%**	**9.0%**
Impact on fair value of 10% adverse change	*$1.0*	*$0.1*	*$0.6*	*$0.5*
Impact on fair value of 20% adverse change	*$1.8*	*$0.1*	*$0.9*	*$0.9*
Interest rates on variable and adjustable contracts	Forward Eurodollar yield curve plus contracted spread			
Impact on fair value of 10% adverse change	*$1.5*	*$4.0*	*$0.4*	*$1.5*
Impact on fair value of 20% adverse change	*$2.5*	*$8.1*	*$0.7*	*$3.8*

These sensitivities are hypothetical and should be used with caution. As the figures indicate, changes in fair value based on a 10 percent variation in assumptions generally cannot be extrapolated because the relationship of the change in assumption to the change in fair value may not be linear. Also, in this table, the effect of a variation in a particular assumption on the fair value of the retained interest is calculated without changing any other assumption; in reality, changes in one factor may result in changes in another (for example, increases in market interest rates may result in lower prepayments and increased credit losses), which might magnify or counteract the sensitivities.

---

[34]Footnote 8, paragraph 17(f)(3), describes how weighted-average life can be calculated.

347. The following is an illustration of disclosure of expected static pool credit losses (paragraph 17(g)(2)).

	Automobile Loans Securitized in		
Actual and Projected Credit Losses (%) as of:	**20X0**	**20X1**	**20X2**
December 31, 20X2	5.0	5.9	5.1
December 31, 20X1	5.1	5.0	
December 31, 20X0	4.5		

Note: Static pool losses are calculated by summing the actual and projected future credit losses and dividing them by the original balance of each pool of assets. The amount shown here for each year is a weighted average for all securitizations during the period.

348. The following is an illustration of the disclosure of cash flows between the securitization SPE and the transferor (paragraph 17(f)(4)).

The table below summarizes certain cash flows received from and paid to securitization trusts ($ in millions):

	Year Ended December 31	
	20X2	**20X1**
Proceeds from new securitizations	$1,413	$ 971
Proceeds from collections reinvested in previous credit card securitizations	3,150	2,565
Servicing fees received	23	19
Other cash flows received on retained interests*	81	52
Purchases of delinquent or foreclosed assets	(45)	(25)
Servicing advances	(102)	(73)
Repayments of servicing advances	90	63

Note:
*This amount represents total cash flows received from retained interests by the transferor other than servicing fees. Other cash flows include, for example, all cash flows from interest-only strips and cash above the minimum required level in cash collateral accounts.

349. The following illustration presents quantitative information about delinquencies, net credit losses, and components of securitized financial assets and other assets managed together with them ($ in millions):

Type of Loan	Total Principal Amount of Loans		Principal Amount of Loans 60 Days or More Past Due*		Average Balances[35]		Net Credit Losses[†]	
	At December 31		At December 31		During the Year		During the Year	
	20X2	20X1	20X2	20X1	20X2	20X1	20X2	20X1
Automobile loans	$ 830	$ 488	$42.3	$26.8	$ 720	$ 370	$21.6	$12.6
Residential mortgage loans (fixed-rate)	482	302	5.8	3.6	470	270	5.6	3.2
Residential mortgage loans (adjustable)	544	341	7.1	6.8	520	300	6.2	6.0
Credit card loans	300	250	15	12.5	350	300	16	15
Total loans managed or securitized[‡]	2,156	1,381	$70.2	$49.7	2,060	1,240	$49.4	$36.8
Less:								
Loans securitized[§]	1,485	905			1,368	752		
Loans held for sale or securitization	19	11			17	9		
Loans held in portfolio[36]	$ 652	$ 465			$ 675	$ 479		

Notes:

*Loans 60 days or more past due are based on end of period total loans.

†Net credit losses are charge-offs and are based on total loans outstanding.

‡Owned and securitized loans are customer loans, credit card loans, mortgage loans, auto loans, and other loans, as applicable, in which the transferor retains a subordinate interest or retains any risk of loss (for example, 10 percent recourse).

§Represents the principal amount of the loan. Interest-only strips and servicing rights (or other retained interests) held for securitized assets are excluded from this table because they are recognized separately.

35This disclosure is optional.

36Loans held in portfolio are reported separately from loans held for securitization because they are measured differently.

Appendix D

AMENDMENTS TO EXISTING PRONOUNCEMENTS

350. This Statement replaces FASB Statement No. 125, *Accounting for Transfers and Servicing of Financial Assets and Extinguishments of Liabilities,* and rescinds FASB Statement No. 127, *Deferral of the Effective Date of Certain Provisions of FASB Statement No. 125.*

351. This Statement also carries forward the following supersessions that were made by Statement 125:

a. FASB Statement No. 76, *Extinguishment of Debt*
b. FASB Statement No. 77, *Reporting by Transferors for Transfers of Receivables with Recourse*
c. FASB Statement No. 122, *Accounting for Mortgage Servicing Rights*
d. FASB Technical Bulletin No. 84-4, *In-Substance Defeasance of Debt*
e. FASB Technical Bulletin No. 85-2, *Accounting for Collateralized Mortgage Obligations (CMOs).*

352. Paragraph 20 of FASB Statement No. 13, *Accounting for Leases,* as amended by Statements 77 and 125, and FASB Statement No. 135, *Rescission of FASB Statement No. 75 and Technical Corrections,* is replaced by the following:

> The sale or assignment of a lease or of property subject to a lease that was accounted for as a sales-type lease or direct financing lease shall not negate the original accounting treatment accorded the lease. Any transfer of minimum lease payments under, or residual values that are guaranteed at the inception of, a sales-type lease or direct financing lease shall be accounted for in accordance with FASB Statement No. 140, *Accounting for Transfers and Servicing of Financial Assets and Extinguishments of Liabilities.* However, transfers of unguaranteed residual values and residual values that are guaranteed after the inception of the lease are not subject to the provisions of Statement 140.

353. FASB Statement No. 133, *Accounting for Derivative Instruments and Hedging Activities,* is amended as follows:

a. In the last sentence of paragraph 10(f), *FASB Statement No. 125, Accounting for Transfers and Servicing of Financial Assets and Extinguishments of Liabilities* is replaced by *FASB Statement No. 140, Accounting for Transfers and Servicing of Financial Assets and Extinguishments of Liabilities.*
b. In both sentences of footnote 9 to paragraph 21, *paragraph 37(g) of Statement 125* is replaced by *paragraph 63(g) of Statement 140.*
c. In the first and second sentences of paragraph 56, *paragraph 37(g) of Statement 125* is replaced by *paragraph 63(g) of Statement 140.*
d. In the first sentence of paragraph 59(e), *paragraphs 68 and 69 of Statement 125* is replaced by *paragraphs 98 and 99 of Statement 140.*

354. In footnote 5 to paragraph 8 of FASB Statement No. 136, *Transfers of Assets to a Not-for-Profit Organization or Charitable Trust That Raises or Holds Contributions for Others,* the reference to *FASB Statement No. 125, Accounting for Transfers and Servicing of Financial Assets and Extinguishments of Liabilities* is replaced by *FASB Statement No. 140, Accounting for Transfers and Servicing of Financial Assets and Extinguishments of Liabilities* and *(paragraph 243)* is replaced by *(paragraph 364).*

355. In footnote 2 to paragraph 3 of FASB Interpretation No. 43, *Real Estate Sales,* the reference to *FASB Statement No. 125, Accounting for Transfers and Servicing of Financial Assets and Extinguishments of Liabilities* is replaced by *FASB Statement No. 140, Accounting for Transfers and Servicing of Financial Assets and Extinguishments of Liabilities.*

356. Paragraph 12 of FASB Technical Bulletin No. 86-2, *Accounting for an Interest in the Residual Value of a Leased Asset: Acquired by a Third Party or Retained by a Lessor That Sells the Related Minimum Rental Payments,* as amended by Statement 125, is replaced by the following:

> Yes. A residual value of a leased asset is a financial asset to the extent guaranteed at the inception of the lease. Accordingly, increases to its estimated value over the remaining lease term should be recognized.

Amendments and Deletions Made by Statement 125 Carried Forward in This Statement with Minor Changes

357. Paragraph 3(a) of APB Opinion No. 26, *Early Extinguishment of Debt,* as amended by Statement 76, is replaced by the following:

> *Extinguishment of liabilities.* FASB Statement No. 140, *Accounting for Transfers and Servicing of Financial Assets and Extinguishments of Liabilities,* defines transactions that the debtor shall recognize as an extinguishment of a liability.

358. The last sentence of footnote 1 to paragraph 1 of FASB Statement No. 22, *Changes in the Provisions of Lease Agreements Resulting from Refundings of Tax-Exempt Debt,* as amended by Statement 76 is deleted.

359. FASB Statement No. 65, *Accounting for Certain Mortgage Banking Activities,* is amended as follows:

a. Paragraph 8, as amended by FASB Statement No. 115, *Accounting for Certain Investments in Debt and Equity Securities,* is deleted.

b. The last sentence of paragraph 9(a) prior to the amendment by Statement 115 is deleted.

c. In paragraph 10, *(paragraphs 16 through 19)* is deleted and replaced by *(paragraph 13 of FASB Statement No. 140, Accounting for Transfers and Servicing of Financial Assets and Extinguishments of Liabilities).*

d. Paragraph 11 and footnote 4 are deleted.

e. In paragraph 15, the reference to paragraph 18 (as amended by FASB StatementNo. 122, *Accounting for Mortgage Servicing Rights*) is deleted, and the following is added to the end of paragraph 15 replacing the sentence added by Statement 122:

> The rate used to determine the present value shall be an appropriate long-term interest rate. For this purpose, estimates of future servicing revenue shall include expected late charges and other ancillary revenue. Estimates of expected future servicing costs shall include direct costs associated with performing the servicing function and appropriate allocations of other costs. Estimated future servicing costs may be determined on an incremental cost basis. The amount capitalized shall be amortized in proportion to, and over the period of, estimated net servicing income—the excess of servicing revenues over servicing costs.

f. Paragraphs 16–19 and 30 and footnote 6, as amended by Statement 122, are deleted.

g. The three paragraphs added by Statement 122 after paragraph 30 are deleted.

h. In paragraph 34, the terms *current (normal) servicing fee rate* and *servicing* and their definitions are deleted.

360. This Statement carries forward the following amendments that Statement 122 made to Statement 65:

a. In the first sentence of paragraph 1, *origination or acquisition* is replaced by *purchase or acquisition.*

b. In the first sentence of paragraph 10, *of existing* is replaced by *or origination of.*

361. FASB Statement No. 107, *Disclosures about Fair Value of Financial Instruments,* is amended as follows:

a. Paragraph 8(b) is replaced by the following:

> Substantively extinguished debt subject to the disclosure requirements of FASB Statement No. 140, *Accounting for Transfers and Servicing of Financial Assets and Extinguishments of Liabilities*

b. In the last sentence of paragraph 28, , *or the rate that an entity would have to pay to acquire essentially risk-free assets to extinguish the obligation in accordance with the requirements of Statement 76* is deleted.

362. The following sentence is added after the first sentence of paragraph 7 of Statement 115 as amended by FASB Statement No. 135, *Rescission of FASB Statement No. 75 and Technical Corrections:*

> A security may not be classified as held-to-maturity if that security can contractually be prepaid or otherwise settled in such a way that the

holder of the security would not recover substantially all of its recorded investment.

363. FASB Technical Bulletin No. 87-3, *Accounting for Mortgage Servicing Fees and Rights,* is amended as follows:

a. Paragraphs 1–7 are deleted.

b. Paragraph 9, as amended by Statement 122, is replaced by the following:

An enterprise may acquire servicing assets or liabilities by purchasing or originating financial assets with servicing rights retained or by purchasing the servicing rights separately. Servicing assets and liabilities are amortized in proportion to, and over the period of, estimated net servicing income—the excess of servicing revenues over servicing costs.

Appendix E

GLOSSARY

364. This appendix defines terms used in this Statement.

Adequate compensation
The amount of benefits of servicing that would fairly compensate a substitute servicer should one be required, which includes the profit that would be demanded in the marketplace.

Agent
A party that acts for and on behalf of another party. For example, a third-party intermediary is an agent of the transferor if it acts on behalf of the transferor.

Attached call
A call option held by the transferor of a financial asset that becomes part of and is traded with the underlying instrument. Rather than being an obligation of the transferee, an attached call is traded with and diminishes the value of the underlying instrument transferred subject to that call.

Beneficial interests
Rights to receive all or portions of specified cash inflows to a trust or other entity, including senior and subordinated shares of interest, principal, or other cash inflows to be "passed-through" or "paid-through," premiums due to guarantors, commercial paper obligations, and residual interests, whether in the form of debt or equity.

Benefits of servicing
Revenues from contractually specified servicing fees, late charges, and other ancillary sources, including "float."

Cleanup call
An option held by the servicer or its affiliate, which may be the transferor, to purchase the remaining transferred financial assets, or the remaining beneficial interests not held by the transferor, its affiliates, or its agents in a qualifying SPE (or in a series of beneficial interests in transferred assets within a qualifying SPE), if the amount of outstanding assets or beneficial interests falls to a level at which the cost of servicing those assets or beneficial interests becomes burdensome in relation to the benefits of servicing.

Collateral
Personal or real property in which a security interest has been given.

Consolidated affiliate of the transferor
An entity whose assets and liabilities are included with those of the transferor in the consolidated, combined, or other financial statements being presented.

Contractually specified servicing fees
All amounts that, per contract, are due to the servicer in exchange for servicing the financial asset and would no longer be received by a servicer if the beneficial owners of the serviced assets (or their trustees or agents) were to exercise their actual or potential authority under the contract to shift the servicing to another servicer. Depending on the servicing contract, those fees may include some or all of the difference between the interest rate collectible on the asset being serviced and the rate to be paid to the beneficial owners of those assets.

Derecognize
Remove previously recognized assets or liabilities from the statement of financial position.

2438

Derivative financial instrument

A derivative instrument (as defined in Statement 133) that is a financial instrument (refer to Statement 107, paragraph 3).

Embedded call

A call option held by the issuer of a financial instrument that is part of and trades with the underlying instrument. For example, a bond may allow the issuer to call it by posting a public notice well before its stated maturity that asks the current holder to submit it for early redemption and provides that interest ceases to accrue on the bond after the early redemption date. Rather than being an obligation of the initial purchaser of the bond, an embedded call trades with and diminishes the value of the underlying bond.

Fair value

Refer to paragraphs 68–70.

Financial asset

Cash, evidence of an ownership interest in an entity, or a contract that conveys to a second entity a contractual right (a) to receive cash or another financial instrument from a first entity or (b) to exchange other financial instruments on potentially favorable terms with the first entity (Statement 107, paragraph 3(b)).

Financial liability

A contract that imposes on one entity a contractual obligation (a) to deliver cash or another financial instrument to a second entity or (b) to exchange other financial instruments on potentially unfavorable terms with the second entity (Statement 107, paragraph 3(a)).

Freestanding call

A call that is neither embedded in nor attached to an asset subject to that call.

Guaranteed mortgage securitization

A securitization of mortgage loans that is within the scope of FASB Statement No. 65, *Accounting for Certain Mortgage Banking Activities,* as amended, and includes a substantive guarantee by a third party.

Interest-only strip

A contractual right to receive some or all of the interest due on a bond, mortgage loan, collateralized mortgage obligation, or other interest-bearing financial asset.

Proceeds

Cash, derivatives, or other assets that are obtained in a transfer of financial assets, less any liabilities incurred.

Recourse

The right of a transferee of receivables to receive payment from the transferor of those receivables for (a) failure of debtors to pay when due, (b) the effects of prepayments, or (c) adjustments resulting from defects in the eligibility of the transferred receivables.

Securitization

The process by which financial assets are transformed into securities.

Security interest

A form of interest in property that provides that upon default of the obligation for which the security interest is given, the property may be sold in order to satisfy that obligation.

Seller

A transferor that relinquishes control over financial assets by transferring them to a transferee in exchange for consideration.

Servicing asset

A contract to service financial assets under which the estimated future revenues from contractually specified servicing fees, late charges, and other ancillary revenues are expected to more than adequately compensate the servicer for performing the servicing. A servicing contract is either (a) undertaken in conjunction with selling or securitizing the financial assets being serviced or (b) purchased or assumed separately.

Servicing liability

A contract to service financial assets under which the estimated future revenues from contractually specified servicing fees, late charges, and other ancillary revenues are not expected to adequately compensate the servicer for performing the servicing.

Transfer

The conveyance of a noncash financial asset by and to someone other than the issuer of that financial asset. Thus, a transfer includes selling a receivable, putting it into a securitization trust, or posting it as collateral but excludes the origination of that receivable, the settlement of that receivable, or the restructuring of that receivable into a security in a troubled debt restructuring.

Transferee

An entity that receives a financial asset, a portion of a financial asset, or a group of financial assets from a transferor.

Transferor

An entity that transfers a financial asset, a portion of a financial asset, or a group of financial assets that it controls to another entity.

Undivided interest

Partial legal or beneficial ownership of an asset as a tenant in common with others. The proportion owned may be pro rata, for example, the right to receive 50 percent of all cash flows from a security, or non–pro rata, for example, the right to receive the interest from a security while another has the right to the principal.

Unilateral ability

A capacity for action not dependent on the actions (or failure to act) of any other party.

Statement of Financial Accounting Standards No. 141
Business Combinations

STATUS

Issued: June 2001

Effective Date: For all business combinations initiated after June 30, 2001

Affects: Supersedes APB 16
       Amends APB 20, paragraphs 12 and 35
       Amends APB 28, paragraph 21
       Amends APB 29, paragraph 4(a)
       Amends APB 30, paragraphs 7 and 20
       Supersedes AIN-APB 16
       Supersedes FAS 10
       Amends FAS 15, footnotes 5, 6, and 16
       Amends FAS 16, footnote 6
       Supersedes FAS 38
       Amends FAS 44, paragraph 4
       Amends FAS 45, paragraph 19
       Amends FAS 72, paragraphs 4, 8, 9, and 14
       Supersedes FAS 72, footnote 1
       Supersedes FAS 79
       Amends FAS 87, paragraph 74 and Illustration 7
       Amends FAS 95, paragraph 134(g)
       Amends FAS 106, paragraphs 86 and 444
       Amends FAS 109, paragraphs 11(h), 13, 30, 36(d), 259, and 270
       Amends FAS 123, paragraphs 8 and 36
       Amends FAS 128, paragraph 59
       Amends FAS 133, paragraphs 11(c) and 29(f)
       Amends FIN 4, paragraph 4
       Amends FIN 9, paragraphs 4, 5, 7, and 8
       Supersedes FIN 9, paragraph 6
       Amends FIN 21, paragraphs 13, 15, 16, and 19 and footnote 4
       Supersedes FIN 21, paragraph 14
       Supersedes FIN 44, paragraphs 81 and 82
       Amends FIN 44, paragraphs 83 and 84
       Amends FTB 84-1, paragraph 6
       Amends FTB 85-5, paragraphs 1 through 4, 6, and 7
       Supersedes FTB 85-5, paragraphs 13 through 24

Affected by: Paragraphs 46 and E5 and footnote 25 amended by FAS 145
       Paragraph E10 superseded by FAS 145
       Footnote 18 superseded by FAS 145

Issues Discussed by FASB Emerging Issues Task Force (EITF)

Affects: Nullifies EITF Issues No. 85-14, 86-10, 86-31, 87-15, 87-16, 87-27, 88-26, 88-27, 95-12, 96-8, 97-9, 99-6, and 99-18 and Topics No. D-19, D-40, and D-59
       Partially nullifies EITF Issues No. 87-21, 91-5, 95-14, 97-2, 99-7, and 00-23
       Resolves EITF Issues No. 84-22, 90-10, 93-2, and 96-23
       Partially resolves EITF Issue No. 98-3

Interpreted by: Paragraphs 4 through 7 and 16 through 18 interpreted by EITF Issue No. 90-13
Paragraph 20 interpreted by EITF Issues No. 88-16 and 95-3
Paragraph 21 interpreted by EITF Issue No. 88-16
Paragraph 22 interpreted by EITF Issues No. 88-16 and 99-12
Paragraphs 23 and 24 interpreted by EITF Issue No. 88-16
Paragraphs 25 through 27 interpreted by EITF Issues No. 97-8 and 97-15
Paragraph 28 interpreted by EITF Issues No. 95-8 and 97-15
Paragraphs 29 through 31 interpreted by EITF Issue No. 97-15
Paragraph 34 interpreted by EITF Issue No. 95-8
Paragraph 36 interpreted by EITF Issues No. 85-41, 87-11, 90-6, 90-12, 95-3, and 98-1
Paragraph 37 interpreted by EITF Issues No. 85-41, 88-19, 90-12, 95-3, and 98-1
Paragraph 37(j) interpreted by EITF Issue No. 85-45
Paragraph 40 interpreted by EITF Issues No. 90-6 and 93-7
Paragraph 49 interpreted by EITF Topic No. D-87
Paragraph 61(b) interpreted by EITF Topic No. D-100
Paragraph F1 interpreted by EITF Issue No. 95-3

Related Issues: EITF Issues No. 84-35, 84-39, 85-8, 85-11, 85-42, 85-46, 86-9, 86-14, 90-5, 92-9, 94-2, 95-7, 96-5, 96-7, 96-17, 98-4, 99-15, 00-6, 01-2, and 01-3 and Topics No. D-54, D-84, and D-97

SUMMARY

This Statement addresses financial accounting and reporting for business combinations and supersedes APB Opinion No. 16, *Business Combinations,* and FASB Statement No. 38, *Accounting for Preacquisition Contingencies of Purchased Enterprises.* All business combinations in the scope of this Statement are to be accounted for using one method—the purchase method.

Reasons for Issuing This Statement

Under Opinion 16, business combinations were accounted for using one of two methods, the pooling-of-interests method (pooling method) or the purchase method. Use of the pooling method was required whenever 12 criteria were met; otherwise, the purchase method was to be used. Because those 12 criteria did not distinguish economically dissimilar transactions, similar business combinations were accounted for using different methods that produced dramatically different financial statement results. Consequently:

- Analysts and other users of financial statements indicated that it was difficult to compare the financial results of entities because different methods of accounting for business combinations were used.
- Users of financial statements also indicated a need for better information about intangible assets because those assets are an increasingly important economic resource for many entities and are an increasing proportion of the assets acquired in many business combinations. While the purchase method recognizes all intangible assets acquired in a business combination (either separately or as goodwill), only those intangible assets previously recorded by the acquired entity are recognized when the pooling method is used.
- Company managements indicated that the differences between the pooling and purchase methods of accounting for business combinations affected competition in markets for mergers and acquisitions.

Differences between This Statement and Opinion 16

The provisions of this Statement reflect a fundamentally different approach to accounting for business combinations than was taken in Opinion 16. The single-method approach used in this Statement reflects the conclusion that virtually all business combinations are acquisitions and, thus, all business combinations should be accounted for in the same way that other asset acquisitions are accounted for—based on the values exchanged.

This Statement changes the accounting for business combinations in Opinion 16 in the following significant respects:

- This Statement requires that all business combinations be accounted for by a single method—the purchase method.
- In contrast to Opinion 16, which required separate recognition of intangible assets that can be identified and named, this Statement requires that they be recognized as assets apart from goodwill if they meet one of two criteria—the contractual-legal criterion or the separability criterion. To assist in identifying acquired intangible assets, this Statement also provides an illustrative list of intangible assets that meet either of those criteria.
- In addition to the disclosure requirements in Opinion 16, this Statement requires disclosure of the primary reasons for a business combination and the allocation of the purchase price paid to the assets acquired and liabilities assumed by major balance sheet caption. When the amounts of goodwill and intangible assets acquired are significant in relation to the purchase price paid, disclosure of other information about those assets is required, such as the amount of goodwill by reportable segment and the amount of the purchase price assigned to each major intangible asset class.

This Statement does not change many of the provisions of Opinion 16 and Statement 38 related to the application of the purchase method. For example, this Statement does not fundamentally change the guidance for determining the cost of an acquired entity and allocating that cost to the assets acquired and liabilities assumed, the accounting for contingent consideration, and the accounting for preacquisition contingencies. That guidance is carried forward in this Statement (but was not reconsidered by the Board). Also, this Statement does not change the requirement to write off certain research and development assets acquired in a business combination as required by FASB Interpretation No. 4, *Applicability of FASB Statement No. 2 to Business Combinations Accounted for by the Purchase Method.*

How the Changes in This Statement Improve Financial Reporting

The changes to accounting for business combinations required by this Statement improve financial reporting because the financial statements of entities that engage in business combinations will better reflect the underlying economics of those transactions. In particular, application of this Statement will result in financial statements that:

- *Better reflect the investment made in an acquired entity*—the purchase method records a business combination based on the values exchanged, thus, users are provided information about the total purchase price paid to acquire another entity, which allows for more meaningful evaluation of the subsequent performance of that investment. Similar information is not provided when the pooling method is used.
- *Improve the comparability of reported financial information*—all business combinations are accounted for using a single method, thus, users are able to compare the financial results of entities that engage in business combinations on an apples-to-apples basis. That is because the assets acquired and liabilities assumed in all business combinations are recognized and measured in the same way regardless of the nature of the consideration exchanged for them.
- *Provide more complete financial information*—the explicit criteria for recognition of intangible assets apart from goodwill and the expanded disclosure requirements of this Statement provide more information about the assets acquired and liabilities assumed in business combinations. That additional information should, among other things, provide users with a better understanding of the resources acquired and improve their ability to assess future profitability and cash flows.

Requiring one method of accounting reduces the costs of accounting for business combinations. For example, it eliminates the costs incurred by entities in positioning themselves to meet the criteria for using the pooling method, such as the monetary and nonmonetary costs of taking actions they might not otherwise have taken or refraining from actions they might otherwise have taken.

How the Conclusions in This Statement Relate to the Conceptual Framework

The Board concluded that because virtually all business combinations are acquisitions, requiring one method of accounting for economically similar transactions is consistent with the concepts of representational faithfulness and comparability as discussed in FASB Concepts Statement No. 2, *Qualitative Characteristics of Accounting Information.* In developing this Statement, the Board also concluded that goodwill should be recognized as an asset because it meets the assets definition in FASB Concepts Statement No. 6, *Elements of Financial Statements,* and the asset recognition criteria in FASB Concepts Statement No. 5, *Recognition and Measurement in Financial Statements of Business Enterprises.*

The Board also noted that FASB Concepts Statement No. 1, *Objectives of Financial Reporting by Business Enterprises,* states that financial reporting should provide information that helps in assessing the amounts, timing, and uncertainty of prospective net cash inflows to an entity. The Board noted that because the purchase method records the net assets acquired in a business combination at their fair values, the information provided by that method is more useful in assessing the cash-generating abilities of the net assets acquired than the information provided by the pooling method.

Some of the Board's constituents indicated that the pooling method should be retained for public policy reasons. For example, some argued that eliminating the pooling method would impede consolidation of certain industries, reduce the amount of capital flowing into certain industries, and slow the development of new technology. Concepts Statement 2 states that a necessary and important characteristic of accounting information is neutrality. In the context of business combinations, neutrality means that the accounting standards should neither encourage nor discourage business combinations but rather, provide information about those combinations that is fair and evenhanded. The Board concluded that its public policy goal is to issue accounting standards that result in neutral and representationally faithful financial information and that eliminating the pooling method is consistent with that goal.

The Effective Date of This Statement

The provisions of this Statement apply to all business combinations initiated after June 30, 2001. This Statement also applies to all business combinations accounted for using the purchase method for which the date of acquisition is July 1, 2001, or later.

This Statement does not apply, however, to combinations of two or more not-for-profit organizations, the acquisition of a for-profit business entity by a not-for-profit organization, and combinations of two or more mutual enterprises.

Statement of Financial Accounting Standards No. 141

Business Combinations

CONTENTS

INTRODUCTION

1. This Statement addresses financial accounting and reporting for business combinations. This Statement supersedes APB Opinion No. 16, *Business Combinations,* and amends or supersedes a number of interpretations of that Opinion. However, this Statement carries forward without reconsideration the guidance in Opinion 16 and certain of its amendments and interpretations related to the application of the purchase method of accounting, including (a) guidance in Opinion 16 described as the principles of historical-cost accounting (refer to paragraphs 3–8), (b) determining the cost of an acquired entity (refer to paragraphs 20–34), (c) allocation of the cost of an acquired entity to assets acquired and liabilities assumed (refer to paragraphs 36–38), and (d) determining the date of acquisition (refer to paragraphs 48 and 49). This Statement also supersedes FASB Statement No. 38, *Accounting for Preacquisition Contingencies of Purchased Enterprises,* but carries forward the guidance from that Statement without reconsideration (refer to paragraphs 40 and 41). The guidance carried forward from Opinion 16 and Statement 38 has been quoted, paraphrased, or rephrased as necessary so that it can be understood in the context of this Statement. The original source of that guidance has been noted parenthetically. The Board intends to reconsider some or all of that guidance (as well as related Emerging Issues Task Force [EITF] issues) in another project.

2. Appendix A to this Statement provides implementation guidance on the application of the purchase method of accounting for a business combination and is an integral part of the standards provided in this Statement. Appendix B provides background information and the basis for the Board's conclusions. Appendix C provides illustrations of some of the financial statement disclosures that this Statement requires. Appendix D carries forward without reconsideration certain provisions of Opinion 16 and its interpretations that have been deleted or superseded by this Statement but that continue to be relevant to past transactions that were accounted for using the **pooling-of-interests method.**[1] This Statement amends or supersedes other accounting pronouncements listed in Appendix E, but it does not change the status of the EITF Issues that provide guidance on applying the purchase method. Appendix F provides a glossary of terms as used in this Statement.

STANDARDS OF FINANCIAL ACCOUNTING AND REPORTING

Accounting for Asset Acquisitions— General Concepts

3. The accounting for a business combination follows the concepts normally applicable to the initial recognition and measurement of assets acquired, liabilities assumed or incurred, and equity shares issued, as well as to the subsequent accounting for those items. Those concepts are set forth in paragraphs 4–8. The standards of accounting and reporting for a business combination by the purchase method, which are based on those concepts, are set forth in paragraphs 9–58 (Opinion 16, paragraph 66).

4. *Initial recognition.* Assets are commonly acquired in exchange transactions that trigger the initial recognition of the assets acquired and any liabilities assumed. If the consideration given in exchange for the asset (or net assets) acquired is in the form of assets surrendered (such as cash), the assets surrendered are derecognized at the date of acquisition. If the consideration given is in the form of liabilities incurred or equity interests issued, the liabilities incurred and equity interests issued are initially recognized at the date of acquisition (Opinion 16, paragraph 67).

5. *Initial measurement.* Like other exchange transactions generally, acquisitions are measured on the basis of the **fair values** exchanged. In exchange transactions, the fair values of the net assets acquired and the consideration paid are assumed to be equal, absent evidence to the contrary. Thus, the "cost"[2] of an acquisition to the acquiring entity is equal to the fair values exchanged and no gain or loss is generally recognized. Exceptions to that general condition include (a) the gain or loss that is recognized if the fair value of noncash assets given as consideration differs from their carrying amounts on the acquiring entity's books and (b) the extraordinary gain that is sometimes recognized by the acquiring entity if the fair value of the net assets acquired in a business combination exceeds the cost of the acquired entity (refer to paragraphs 45and 46) (Opinion 16, paragraph 67).

---

[1]Terms defined in Appendix F, the glossary, are set forth in **boldface type** the first time they appear.

[2]Cost is a term that is often used to refer to the amount at which an entity initially recognizes an asset at the date it is acquired, whatever the manner of acquisition.

6. Exchange transactions in which the consideration given is cash are measured by the amount of cash paid. However, if the consideration given is not in the form of cash (that is, in the form of noncash assets, liabilities incurred, or equity interests issued), measurement is based on the fair value of the consideration given or the fair value of the asset (or net assets) acquired, whichever is more clearly evident and, thus, more reliably measurable (Opinion 16, paragraph 67).

7. *Allocating cost.* Acquiring assets in groups requires not only ascertaining the cost of the asset (or net asset) group but also allocating that cost to the individual assets (or individual assets and liabilities) that make up the group. The cost of such a group is determined using the concepts described in paragraphs 5 and 6. A portion of the cost of the group is then assigned to each individual asset (or individual assets and liabilities) acquired on the basis of its fair value. In a business combination, an excess of the cost of the group over the sum of the amounts assigned to the tangible assets, **financial assets,** and separately recognized **intangible assets** acquired less liabilities assumed is evidence of an unidentified intangible asset or assets (Opinion 16, paragraph 68).

8. *Accounting after acquisition.* The nature of an asset and not the manner of its acquisition determines an acquiring entity's subsequent accounting for the asset. The basis for measuring the asset acquired—whether the amount of cash paid, the fair value of an asset received or given up, the fair value of a liability incurred, or the fair value of equity shares issued—has no effect on the subsequent accounting for the asset (Opinion 16, paragraph 69).

Standards of Accounting for Business Combinations

Scope

9. For purposes of applying this Statement, a *business combination* occurs when an entity[3] acquires net assets that constitute a business[4] or acquires equity interests of one or more other entities and obtains control[5] over that entity or entities. This Statement does not address transactions in which control is obtained through means other than an acquisition of net assets or equity interests. For purposes of this Statement, the formation of a joint venture is not a business combination.[6]

10. This Statement applies to combinations involving either incorporated or unincorporated entities. The provisions of this Statement apply equally to a business combination in which (a) one or more entities are merged or become subsidiaries, (b) one entity transfers net assets or its owners transfer their equity interests to another, or (c) all entities transfer net assets or the owners of those entities transfer their equity interests to a newly formed entity (some of which are referred to as roll-up or put-together transactions). All those transactions are business combinations regardless of whether the form of consideration given is cash, other assets, a business or a subsidiary of the entity, debt, common or preferred shares or other equity interests, or a combination of those forms and regardless of whether the former owners of one of the combining entities as a group retain or receive a majority of the voting rights of the combined entity. An exchange of a business for a business also is a business combination.

11. The acquisition of some or all of the noncontrolling interests in a subsidiary is not a business combination. However, paragraph 14 of this Statement specifies the method of accounting for those transactions. The term business combination as used in this Statement also excludes transfers of net assets or exchanges of equity interests between entities under common control. Paragraphs D11–D18 of Appendix D provide examples of those transactions and accounting guidance for them.

12. This Statement does not apply to combinations between **not-for-profit organizations,** nor does it

---

[3]This Statement applies to a business enterprise, a new entity formed to complete a business combination, or a **mutual enterprise**, each of which is referred to herein as an *entity*. That term can refer to any of the various forms in which the participants in a business combination may exist. However, a new entity formed to complete a business combination would not necessarily be the acquiring entity (refer to paragraph 19).

[4]EITF Issue No. 98-3, "Determining Whether a Nonmonetary Transaction Involves Receipt of Productive Assets or of a Business," provides guidance on determining whether an asset group constitutes a business.

[5]Control is generally indicated by "ownership by one company, directly or indirectly, of over fifty percent of the outstanding voting shares of another company" (ARB No. 51, *Consolidated Financial Statements,* paragraph 2, as amended by FASB Statement No. 94, *Consolidation of All Majority-owned Subsidiaries*), although control may exist in other circumstances.

[6]The Board intends to address the accounting for other events or transactions that are similar to a business combination but do not meet this Statement's definition of a business combination and the accounting for joint venture formations in another project.

apply to the acquisition of a for-profit business entity by a not-for-profit organization.[7]

Method of Accounting

13. All business combinations in the scope of this Statement shall be accounted for using the purchase method as described in this Statement and other pronouncements (refer to paragraph A3 of Appendix A).

14. The acquisition of some or all of the noncontrolling interests in a subsidiary—whether acquired by the parent, the subsidiary itself, or another affiliate—shall be accounted for using the purchase method. Paragraphs A5–A7 of Appendix A provide additional accounting guidance for those transactions.[8]

Application of the Purchase Method

Identifying the acquiring entity

15. Application of the purchase method requires the identification of the acquiring entity. All business combinations in the scope of this Statement shall be accounted for using the purchase method. Thus, the acquiring entity shall be identified in all business combinations.

16. In a business combination effected solely through the distribution of cash or other assets or by incurring liabilities, the entity that distributes cash or other assets or incurs liabilities is generally the acquiring entity.

17. In a business combination effected through an exchange of equity interests, the entity that issues the equity interests is generally the acquiring entity. In some business combinations (commonly referred to as reverse acquisitions), however, the acquired entity issues the equity interests. Commonly, the acquiring entity is the larger entity. However, the facts and circumstances surrounding a business combination sometimes indicate that a smaller entity acquires a larger one. In some business combinations, the combined entity assumes the name of the acquired entity. Thus, in identifying the acquiring entity in a combination effected through an exchange of equity interests, all pertinent facts and circumstances shall be considered, in particular:

a. The relative voting rights in the combined entity after the combination—all else being equal, the acquiring entity is the combining entity whose owners as a group retained or received the larger portion of the voting rights in the combined entity. In determining which group of owners retained or received the larger portion of the voting rights, consideration shall be given to the existence of any unusual or special voting arrangements and options, warrants, or convertible securities.

b. The existence of a large minority voting interest in the combined entity when no other owner or organized group of owners has a significant voting interest—all else being equal, the acquiring entity is the combining entity whose single owner or organized group of owners holds the large minority voting interest in the combined entity.

c. The composition of the governing body of the combined entity—all else being equal, the acquiring entity is the combining entity whose owners or governing body has the ability to elect or appoint a voting majority of the governing body of the combined entity.

d. The composition of the senior management of the combined entity—all else being equal, the acquiring entity is the combining entity whose senior management dominates that of the combined entity. Senior management generally consists of the chairman of the board, chief executive officer, chief operating officer, chief financial officer, and those divisional heads reporting directly to them, or the executive committee if one exists.

e. The terms of the exchange of equity securities—all else being equal, the acquiring entity is the combining entity that pays a premium over the market value of the equity securities of the other combining entity or entities.[9]

---

[7]The Board intends to address issues related to the accounting for combinations between not-for-profit organizations and issues related to the accounting for the acquisition of a for-profit business entity by a not-for-profit organization in another project.

[8]The October 2000 FASB Exposure Draft, *Accounting for Financial Instruments with Characteristics of Liabilities, Equity, or Both,* proposes that a noncontrolling interest in a subsidiary be reported in consolidated financial statements as a separate component of equity and that distributions to holders of those noncontrolling interests be recognized as equity distributions. If those proposed provisions are affirmed, the Board will consider those provisions when it reconsiders the accounting for the acquisition of noncontrolling interests in a subsidiary, in particular whether the acquisition of those interests should be accounted for as an equity distribution rather than by the purchase method.

[9]This criterion shall apply only if the equity securities exchanged in a business combination are traded in a public market on either (a) a stock exchange (domestic or foreign) or (b) in an over-the-counter market (including securities quoted only locally or regionally).

18. Some business combinations involve more than two entities. In identifying the acquiring entity in those cases, consideration also shall be given to which combining entity initiated the combination and whether the assets, revenues, and earnings of one of the combining entities significantly exceed those of the others.

19. If a new entity is formed to issue equity interests to effect a business combination, one of the existing combining entities shall be determined to be the acquiring entity on the basis of the evidence available. The guidance in paragraphs 16–18 shall be used in making that determination.

Determining the cost of the acquired entity

20. The same accounting principles shall apply in determining the cost of assets acquired individually, those acquired in a group, and those acquired in a business combination. A cash payment by an acquiring entity shall be used to measure the cost of an acquired entity. Similarly, the fair values of other assets distributed as consideration, such as marketable securities or properties, and the fair values of liabilities incurred by an acquiring entity shall be used to measure the cost of an acquired entity (Opinion 16, paragraph 72).

21. The distinctive characteristics of preferred shares make some preferred share issues similar to debt securities, while others are similar to common shares, with many gradations in between. Those characteristics may affect the determination of the cost of an acquired entity. For example, the fair value of nonvoting, nonconvertible preferred shares that lack characteristics of common shares may be determined by comparing the specified dividend and redemption terms with those of comparable securities and by assessing market factors. Thus, although the principle of recording the fair value of consideration received for shares issued applies to all equity securities, senior as well as common shares, the cost of an entity acquired by issuing senior equity securities may be determined in practice on the same basis as for debt securities (Opinion 16, paragraph 73).

22. The fair value of securities traded in the market is generally more clearly evident than the fair value of an acquired entity (paragraph 6). Thus, the quoted market price of an equity security issued to effect a business combination generally should be used to estimate the fair value of an acquired entity after recognizing possible effects of price fluctuations, quanti-

ties traded, issue costs, and the like. The market price for a reasonable period before and after the date that the terms of the acquisition are agreed to and announced shall be considered in determining the fair value of securities issued (Opinion 16, paragraph 74).

23. If the quoted market price is not the fair value of the equity securities, either preferred or common, the consideration received shall be estimated even though measuring directly the fair values of net assets received is difficult. Both the net assets received, including **goodwill,** and the extent of the adjustment of the quoted market price of the shares issued shall be weighed to determine the amount to be recorded. All aspects of the acquisition, including the negotiations, shall be studied, and independent appraisals may be used as an aid in determining the fair value of securities issued. Consideration other than equity securities distributed to effect an acquisition may provide evidence of the total fair value received (Opinion 16, paragraph 75).

Costs of the business combination

24. The cost of an entity acquired in a business combination includes the direct costs of the business combination. Costs of registering and issuing equity securities shall be recognized as a reduction of the otherwise determinable fair value of the securities. However, indirect and general expenses related to business combinations shall be expensed as incurred (Opinion 16, paragraph 76).

Contingent consideration

25. A business combination agreement may provide for the issuance of additional shares of a security or the transfer of cash or other consideration contingent on specified events or transactions in the future. Some agreements provide that a portion of the consideration be placed in escrow to be distributed or returned to the transferor when specified events occur. Either debt or equity securities may be placed in escrow, and amounts equal to interest or dividends on the securities during the contingency period may be paid to the escrow agent or to the potential security holder (Opinion 16, paragraph 77).

26. Cash and other assets distributed, securities issued unconditionally, and amounts of contingent consideration that are determinable at the date of acquisition shall be included in determining the cost of an acquired entity and recorded at that date. Consideration that is issued or issuable at the expiration of

the contingency period or that is held in escrow pending the outcome of the contingency shall be disclosed but not recorded as a liability or shown as outstanding securities unless the outcome of the contingency is determinable beyond a reasonable doubt (Opinion 16, paragraph 78).

27. The contingent consideration usually should be recorded when the contingency is resolved and consideration is issued or becomes issuable. In general, the issuance of additional securities or distribution of other consideration at resolution of contingencies based on earnings shall result in an additional element of cost of an acquired entity. In contrast, the issuance of additional securities or distribution of other consideration at resolution of contingencies based on security prices shall not change the recorded cost of an acquired entity (Opinion 16, paragraph 79).

Contingency based on earnings

28. Additional consideration may be contingent on maintaining or achieving specified earnings levels in future periods. When the contingency is resolved and additional consideration is distributable, the acquiring entity shall record the fair value of the consideration issued or issuable as an additional cost of the acquired entity[10] (Opinion 16, paragraph 80).

Contingency based on security prices

29. Additional consideration may be contingent on the market price of a specified security issued to effect a business combination. Unless the price of the security at least equals the specified amount on a specified date or dates, the acquiring entity is required to issue additional equity or debt securities or transfer cash or other assets sufficient to make the current value of the total consideration equal to the specified amount. The securities issued unconditionally at the date the combination is consummated shall be recorded at that date at the specified amount (Opinion 16, paragraph 81).

30. The issuance of additional securities or distribution of other consideration upon resolution of a contingency based on security prices shall not affect the cost of the acquired entity, regardless of whether the amount specified is a security price to be maintained or a higher security price to be achieved. When the contingency is resolved and additional consideration is distributable, the acquiring entity shall record the current fair value of the additional consideration issued or issuable. However, the amount previously recorded for securities issued at the date of acquisition shall be simultaneously reduced to the lower current value of those securities. Reducing the value of debt securities previously issued to their later fair value results in recording a discount on debt securities. That discount shall be amortized from the date the additional securities are issued (Opinion 16, paragraph 82).

31. Accounting for contingent consideration based on conditions other than those described shall be inferred from the procedures outlined. For example, if the consideration contingently issuable depends on both future earnings and future security prices, an additional cost of the acquired entity shall be recorded for the additional consideration contingent on earnings, and previously recorded consideration shall be reduced to the current value of the consideration contingent on security prices. Similarly, if the consideration contingently issuable depends on later settlement of a contingency, an increase in the cost of acquired assets, if any, shall be amortized, if applicable, over the remaining useful lives of the assets[11] (Opinion 16, paragraph 83).

Interest or dividends during contingency period

32. Amounts paid to an escrow agent representing interest and dividends on securities held in escrow shall be accounted for according to the accounting for the securities. That is, until the disposition of the securities in escrow is resolved, payments to the escrow agent shall not be recorded as interest expense or dividend distributions. An amount equal to interest and dividends later distributed by the escrow agent to the former shareholders shall be added to the cost of the acquired assets at the date distributed (Opinion 16, paragraph 84).

Tax effect of imputed interest

33. A tax reduction resulting from imputed interest on contingently issuable shares reduces the fair value

---

[10]Paragraph 46 provides guidance on accounting for contingent consideration in a business combination if the fair value of the net assets acquired exceeds the cost of the acquired entity.

[11]Whether an increase in the cost of the acquired assets will be amortized depends on the nature of the asset. Guidance on the subsequent accounting for goodwill and other intangible assets acquired in a business combination is provided in FASB Statement No. 142, *Goodwill and Other Intangible Assets*.

recorded for contingent consideration based on earnings and increases additional capital recorded for contingent consideration based on security prices (Opinion 16, paragraph 85).

Compensation in contingent agreements

34. If the substance of the agreement for contingent consideration is to provide compensation for services or use of property or profit sharing, the additional consideration given shall be recognized as an expense of the appropriate periods (Opinion 16, paragraph 86).

Allocating the cost of an acquired entity to assets acquired and liabilities assumed

35. Following the process described in paragraphs 36–46 (commonly referred to as the purchase price allocation), an acquiring entity shall allocate the cost of an acquired entity to the assets acquired and liabilities assumed based on their estimated fair values at date of acquisition (refer to paragraph 48). Prior to that allocation, the acquiring entity shall (a) review the purchase consideration if other than cash to ensure that it has been valued in accordance with the requirements in paragraphs 20–23 and (b) identify all of the assets acquired and liabilities assumed, including intangible assets that meet the recognition criteria in paragraph 39, regardless of whether they had been recorded in the financial statements of the acquired entity.

36. Among other sources of relevant information, independent appraisals and actuarial or other valuations may be used as an aid in determining the estimated fair values of assets acquired and liabilities assumed. The tax basis of an asset or liability shall not be a factor in determining its estimated fair value (Opinion 16, paragraph 87).

Assets acquired and liabilities assumed, except goodwill

37. The following is general guidance for assigning amounts to assets acquired and liabilities assumed, except goodwill:

a. Marketable securities at fair values
b. Receivables at present values of amounts to be received determined at appropriate current interest rates, less allowances for uncollectibility and collection costs, if necessary
c. Inventories
 (1) Finished goods and merchandise at estimated selling prices less the sum of (a) costs of disposal and (b) a reasonable profit allowance for the selling effort of the acquiring entity
 (2) Work in process at estimated selling prices of finished goods less the sum of (a) costs to complete, (b) costs of disposal, and (c) a reasonable profit allowance for the completing and selling effort of the acquiring entity based on profit for similar finished goods
 (3) Raw materials at current replacement costs
d. Plant and equipment
 (1) To be used, at the current replacement cost for similar capacity[12] unless the expected future use of the assets indicates a lower value to the acquiring entity
 (2) To be sold, at fair value less cost to sell
e. Intangible assets that meet the criteria in paragraph 39 at estimated fair values
f. Other assets, including land, natural resources, and nonmarketable securities, at appraised values
g. Accounts and notes payable, long-term debt, and other claims payable, at present values of amounts to be paid determined at appropriate current interest rates
h. A liability for the projected benefit obligation in excess of plan assets or an asset for plan assets in excess of the projected benefit obligation of a single-employer defined benefit pension plan, at amounts determined in accordance with paragraph 74 of FASB Statement No. 87, *Employers' Accounting for Pensions*
i. A liability for the accumulated postretirement benefit obligation in excess of the fair value of plan assets or an asset for the fair value of the plan assets in excess of the accumulated postretirement benefit obligation of a single-employer defined benefit postretirement plan at amounts determined in accordance with paragraphs 86–88 of FASB Statement No. 106, *Employers' Accounting for Postretirement Benefits Other Than Pensions*
j. Liabilities and accruals—such as accruals for warranties, vacation pay, and deferred compensation—at present values of amounts to be paid determined at appropriate current interest rates
k. Other liabilities and commitments—such as unfavorable leases, contracts, and commitments and

---

[12]Replacement cost may be determined directly if a used-asset market exists for the assets acquired. Otherwise, the replacement cost should be estimated from the replacement cost new less estimated accumulated depreciation.

plant closing expense incident to the acquisition—at present values of amounts to be paid determined at appropriate current interest rates

l. **Preacquisition contingencies** at amounts determined in accordance with paragraph 40 of this Statement (Opinion 16, paragraph 88).

38. An acquiring entity shall not recognize the goodwill previously recorded by an acquired entity, nor shall it recognize the deferred income taxes recorded by an acquired entity before its acquisition. A deferred tax liability or asset shall be recognized for differences between the assigned values and the tax bases of the recognized assets acquired and liabilities assumed in a business combination in accordance with paragraph 30 of FASB Statement No. 109, *Accounting for Income Taxes* (Opinion 16, paragraph 88).

Intangible assets

39. An intangible asset shall be recognized as an asset apart from goodwill if it arises from contractual or other legal rights (regardless of whether those rights are transferable or separable from the acquired entity or from other rights and obligations). If an intangible asset does not arise from contractual or other legal rights, it shall be recognized as an asset apart from goodwill only if it is separable, that is, it is capable of being separated or divided from the acquired entity and sold, transferred, licensed, rented, or exchanged (regardless of whether there is an intent to do so). For purposes of this Statement, however, an intangible asset that cannot be sold, transferred, licensed, rented, or exchanged individually is considered separable if it can be sold, transferred, licensed, rented, or exchanged in combination with a related contract, asset, or liability. For purposes of this Statement, an assembled workforce shall not be recognized as an intangible asset apart from goodwill. Appendix A provides additional guidance relating to the recognition of acquired intangible assets apart from goodwill, including an illustrative list of intangible assets that meet the recognition criteria in this paragraph.

Preacquisition contingencies

40. A preacquisition contingency other than the potential tax effects of (a) temporary differences and carryforwards of an acquired entity that exist at the acquisition date and (b) income tax uncertainties related to the acquisition (for example, an uncertainty related to the tax basis of an acquired asset that will ultimately be agreed to by the taxing authority)[13] shall be included in the purchase price allocation based on an amount determined as follows:

a. If the fair value of the preacquisition contingency can be determined during the **allocation period,** that preacquisition contingency shall be included in the allocation of the purchase price based on that fair value.[14]

b. If the fair value of the preacquisition contingency cannot be determined during the allocation period, that preacquisition contingency shall be included in the allocation of the purchase price based on an amount determined in accordance with the following criteria:

(1) Information available prior to the end of the allocation period indicates that it is probable that an asset existed, a liability had been incurred, or an asset had been impaired at the consummation of the business combination. It is implicit in this condition that it must be probable that one or more future events will occur confirming the existence of the asset, liability, or impairment.

(2) The amount of the asset or liability can be reasonably estimated.

The criteria of this subparagraph shall be applied using the guidance provided in FASB Statement No. 5, *Accounting for Contingencies,* and related FASB Interpretation No. 14, *Reasonable Estimation of the Amount of a Loss,* for application of the similar criteria of paragraph 8 of Statement 5[15] (Statement 38, paragraph 5).

41. After the end of the allocation period, an adjustment that results from a preacquisition contingency

---

[13]Those potential income tax effects shall be accounted for in accordance with the provisions of Statement 109.

[14]For example, if it can be demonstrated that the parties to a business combination agreed to adjust the total consideration by an amount because of a contingency, that amount would be a determined fair value of that contingency.

[15]Interpretation 14 specifies the amount to be accrued if the reasonable estimate of the amount is a range. If some amount within the range appears at the time to be a better estimate than any other amount within the range, that amount is accrued. If no amount within the range is a better estimate than any other amount, however, the minimum amount in the range is accrued.

other than a loss carryforward[16] shall be included in the determination of net income in the period in which the adjustment is determined (Statement 38, paragraph 6).

Research and development assets

42. This Statement does not change the requirement in paragraph 5 of FASB Interpretation No. 4, *Applicability of FASB Statement No. 2 to Business Combinations Accounted for by the Purchase Method,* that the amounts assigned to tangible and intangible assets to be used in a particular research and development project that *have no alternative future use* shall be charged to expense at the acquisition date.

Excess of cost over the fair value of acquired net assets (goodwill)

43. The excess of the cost of an acquired entity over the net of the amounts assigned to assets acquired and liabilities assumed shall be recognized as an asset referred to as goodwill. An acquired intangible asset that does not meet the criteria in paragraph 39 shall be included in the amount recognized as goodwill.

Excess of fair value of acquired net assets over cost

44. In some cases, the sum of the amounts assigned to assets acquired and liabilities assumed will exceed the cost of the acquired entity *(excess over cost* or *excess).* That excess shall be allocated as a pro rata reduction of the amounts that otherwise would have been assigned to all of the acquired assets[17] except (a) financial assets other than investments accounted for by the equity method, (b) assets to be disposed of by sale,[18] (c) deferred tax assets, (d) prepaid assets relating to pension or other postretirement benefit plans, and (e) any other current assets.[19]

45. If any excess remains after reducing to zero the amounts that otherwise would have been assigned to those assets, that remaining excess shall be recognized as an extraordinary gain as described in paragraph 11 of APB Opinion No. 30, *Reporting the Results of Operations—Reporting the Effects of Disposal of a Segment of a Business, and Extraordinary, Unusual and Infrequently Occurring Events and Transactions.* The extraordinary gain shall be recognized in the period in which the business combination is completed unless the combination involves contingent consideration that, if paid or issued, would be recognized as an additional element of cost of the acquired entity (refer to paragraph 46). If an extraordinary gain is recognized before the end of the allocation period, any subsequent adjustments to that extraordinary gain that result from changes to the purchase price allocation shall be recognized as an extraordinary item.

46. If a business combination involves a contingent consideration agreement that might result in recognition of an additional element of cost of the acquired entity when the contingency is resolved (a contingency based on earnings), an amount equal to the lesser of the maximum amount of contingent consideration or the excess shall be recognized as if it was a liability. When the contingency is resolved and the consideration is issued or becomes issuable, any excess of the fair value of the contingent consideration issued or issuable over the amount that was recognized as if it was a liability shall be recognized as an additional cost of the acquired entity. If the amount initially recognized as if it was a liability exceeds the fair value of the consideration issued or issuable, that excess shall be allocated as a pro rata reduction of the amounts assigned to assets acquired in accordance with paragraph 44. Any amount that remains after reducing those assets to zero shall be recognized as an extraordinary gain in accordance with paragraph 45.

Accounting for goodwill and other intangible assets acquired

47. After initial recognition, goodwill and other intangible assets acquired in a business combination

---

[16]Refer to footnote 13.

[17]The acquired assets include research and development assets acquired and charged to expense in accordance with paragraph 5 of Interpretation 4 (refer to paragraph 42).

[18]Assets to be disposed of by sale include assets to be disposed of as that term is used in FASB Statement No. 121, *Accounting for the Impairment of Long-Lived Assets and for Long-Lived Assets to Be Disposed Of,* and assets of a segment of a business being accounted for as a discontinued operation under APB Opinion No. 30, *Reporting the Results of Operations—Reporting the Effects of Disposal of a Segment of a Business, and Extraordinary, Unusual and Infrequently Occurring Events and Transactions.*

[19]Prior to allocation of the excess, if any, the acquiring entity shall reassess whether all acquired assets and assumed liabilities have been identified and recognized and perform remeasurements to verify that the consideration paid, assets acquired, and liabilities assumed have been properly valued (refer to paragraph 35).

shall be accounted for in accordance with the provisions of FASB Statement No. 142, *Goodwill and Other Intangible Assets.*[20]

Date of acquisition

48. The date of acquisition (also referred to as the acquisition date) ordinarily is the date assets are received and other assets are given, liabilities are assumed or incurred, or equity interests are issued. However, the parties may, for convenience, designate as the effective date the end of an accounting period between the dates a business combination is initiated and consummated. The designated date should ordinarily be the acquisition date for accounting purposes if a written agreement provides that effective control of the acquired entity is transferred to the acquiring entity on that date without restrictions except those required to protect the shareholders or other owners of the acquired entity, such as restrictions on significant changes in the operations, permission to pay dividends equal to those regularly paid before the effective date, and the like. Designating an effective date other than the date assets or equity interests are transferred or liabilities are assumed or incurred requires adjusting the cost of an acquired entity and net income otherwise reported to compensate for recognizing income before consideration is transferred. The cost of an acquired entity and net income shall therefore be reduced by imputed interest at an appropriate current rate on assets given, liabilities assumed or incurred, or preferred shares distributed as of the transfer date to acquire the entity (Opinion 16, paragraph 93).

49. The cost of an acquired entity and the amounts assigned to the assets acquired and liabilities assumed shall be determined as of the date of acquisition. The statement of income of an acquiring entity for the period in which a business combination occurs shall include the income of the acquired entity after the date of acquisition by including the revenue and expenses of the acquired entity based on the cost to the acquiring entity (Opinion 16, paragraph 94).

Documentation at date of acquisition

50. The provisions of Statement 142 require that the assets acquired and liabilities assumed in a business combination that meet certain criteria, including goodwill, be assigned to a **reporting unit** as of the date of acquisition. For use in making those assignments, the basis for and method of determining the purchase price of an acquired entity and other related factors (such as the underlying reasons for the acquisition and management's expectations related to dilution, synergies, and other financial measurements) shall be documented at the date of acquisition.

Disclosures in Financial Statements

51. The notes to the financial statements of a combined entity shall disclose the following information in the period in which a material business combination is completed:

a. The name and a brief description of the acquired entity and the percentage of voting equity interests acquired
b. The primary reasons for the acquisition, including a description of the factors that contributed to a purchase price that results in recognition of goodwill
c. The period for which the results of operations of the acquired entity are included in the income statement of the combined entity
d. The cost of the acquired entity and, if applicable, the number of shares of equity interests (such as common shares, preferred shares, or partnership interests) issued or issuable, the value assigned to those interests, and the basis for determining that value
e. A condensed balance sheet disclosing the amount assigned to each major asset and liability caption of the acquired entity at the acquisition date
f. Contingent payments, options, or commitments specified in the acquisition agreement and the accounting treatment that will be followed should any such contingency occur
g. The amount of purchased research and development assets acquired and written off in the period (refer to paragraph 42) and the line item in the income statement in which the amounts written off are aggregated
h. For any purchase price allocation that has not been finalized, that fact and the reasons therefor. In subsequent periods, the nature and amount of any material adjustments made to the initial allocation of the purchase price shall be disclosed.

52. The notes to the financial statements also shall disclose the following information in the period in

[20]As stated in paragraph 8 of Statement 142, the accounting for some acquired intangible assets after initial recognition is prescribed by pronouncements other than Statement 142.

which a material business combination is completed if the amounts assigned to goodwill or to other intangible assets acquired are significant in relation to the total cost of the acquired entity:

a. For intangible assets subject to amortization:[21]
   (1) The total amount assigned and the amount assigned to any major **intangible asset class**
   (2) The amount of any significant **residual value,** in total and by major intangible asset class
   (3) The weighted-average amortization period, in total and by major intangible asset class
b. For intangible assets *not* subject to amortization,[22] the total amount assigned and the amount assigned to any major intangible asset class
c. For goodwill:
   (1) The total amount of goodwill and the amount that is expected to be deductible for tax purposes
   (2) The amount of goodwill by reportable segment (if the combined entity is required to disclose segment information in accordance with FASB Statement No. 131, *Disclosures about Segments of an Enterprise and Related Information*), unless not practicable.[23]

An example of the disclosure requirements in this paragraph and paragraph 51 is provided in illustration 1 in Appendix C.

53. The notes to the financial statements shall disclose the following information if a series of individually immaterial business combinations completed during the period are material in the aggregate:

a. The number of entities acquired and a brief description of those entities
b. The aggregate cost of the acquired entities, the number of equity interests (such as common shares, preferred shares, or partnership interests) issued or issuable, and the value assigned to those interests
c. The aggregate amount of any contingent payments, options, or commitments and the accounting treatment that will be followed should any such contingency occur (if potentially significant in relation to the aggregate cost of the acquired entities)

d. The information described in paragraph 52 if the aggregate amount assigned to goodwill or to other intangible assets acquired is significant in relation to the aggregate cost of the acquired entities.

An example of those disclosure requirements is provided in illustration 2 in Appendix C.

54. If the combined entity is a **public business enterprise,** the notes to the financial statements shall include the following supplemental information on a pro forma basis for the period in which a material business combination occurs (or for the period in which a series of individually immaterial business combinations occur that are material in the aggregate):

a. Results of operations for the current period as though the business combination or combinations had been completed at the beginning of the period, unless the acquisition was at or near the beginning of the period
b. Results of operations for the comparable prior period as though the business combination or combinations had been completed at the beginning of that period if comparative financial statements are presented.

55. At a minimum, the supplemental pro forma information shall display revenue, income before extraordinary items and the cumulative effect of accounting changes, net income, and earnings per share. In determining the pro forma amounts, income taxes, interest expense, preferred share dividends, and depreciation and amortization of assets shall be adjusted to the accounting base recognized for each in recording the combination. Pro forma information related to results of operations of periods prior to the combination shall be limited to the results of operations for the immediately preceding period. Disclosure also shall be made of the nature and amount of any material, nonrecurring items included in the reported pro forma results of operations.

56. In the period in which an extraordinary gain is recognized related to a business combination (paragraphs 45 and 46), the notes to the financial statements shall disclose the information required by paragraph 11 of Opinion 30.

---

[21]Statement 142 provides guidance for determining whether an intangible asset is subject to amortization.

[22]Refer to footnote 21.

[23]For example, it would not be practicable to disclose this information if the assignment of goodwill to reporting units (as required by Statement 142) has not been completed as of the date the financial statements are issued.

57. The notes to the financial statements also shall disclose the information required by paragraphs 51 and 52 if a material business combination is completed after the balance sheet date but before the financial statements are issued (unless not practicable).

Disclosures in Interim Financial Information

58. The summarized interim financial information of a public business enterprise shall disclose the following information if a material business combination is completed during the current year up to the date of the most recent interim statement of financial position presented:

a. The information described in paragraph 51(a)–(d).
b. Supplemental pro forma information that discloses the results of operations for the current interim period and the current year up to the date of the most recent interim statement of financial position presented (and for the corresponding periods in the preceding year) as though the business combination had been completed as of the beginning of the period being reported on. That pro forma information shall display, at a minimum, revenue, income before extraordinary items and the cumulative effect of accounting changes (including those on an interim basis), net income, and earnings per share.
c. The nature and amount of any material, nonrecurring items included in the reported pro forma results of operations.

Effective Date and Transition

59. Except for combinations between two or more mutual enterprises, this Statement shall be effective as follows:

a. The provisions of this Statement shall apply to all business combinations initiated after June 30, 2001. Use of the pooling-of-interests method for those business combinations is prohibited.
b. The provisions of this Statement also shall apply to all business combinations accounted for by the purchase method for which the date of acquisition is July 1, 2001, or later.

The following definition of *initiated* from paragraph 46 of Opinion 16 shall be used in determining the effective date of this Statement:

> A plan of combination is initiated on the earlier of (1) the date that the major terms of a plan, including the ratio of exchange of stock, are announced publicly or otherwise formally made known to the stockholders of any one of the combining companies or (2) the date that stockholders of a combining company are notified in writing of an exchange offer. Therefore, a plan of combination is often initiated even though consummation is subject to the approval of stockholders and others.

Paragraphs D4–D8 of Appendix D provide additional guidance relating to that definition. Any alteration in the terms of the exchange in a plan of combination constitutes initiation of a new plan of combination. Therefore, if the terms of the exchange in a plan of combination initiated on or before June 30, 2001, and in process on June 30, 2001, are altered after that date, the combination shall be accounted for by the purchase method in accordance with this Statement.

60. For combinations between two or more mutual enterprises, this Statement shall not be effective until interpretative guidance related to the application of the purchase method to those transactions is issued.[24]

61. The following transition provisions apply to business combinations for which the acquisition date was before July 1, 2001, that were accounted for using the purchase method:

a. The carrying amount of acquired intangible assets that do not meet the criteria in paragraph 39 for recognition apart from goodwill (and any related deferred tax liabilities if the intangible asset amortization is not deductible for tax purposes) shall be reclassified as goodwill as of the date Statement 142 is initially applied in its entirety.
b. The carrying amount of (1) any recognized intangible assets that meet the recognition criteria in paragraph 39 or (2) any unidentifiable intangible assets recognized in accordance with paragraph 5 of FASB Statement No. 72, *Accounting for Certain Acquisitions of Banking or Thrift Institutions,*

---

[24]The Board intends to consider issues related to the application of the purchase method to combinations between two or more mutual enterprises in a separate project.

that have been included in the amount reported as goodwill (or as goodwill and intangible assets) shall be reclassified and accounted for as an asset apart from goodwill as of the date Statement 142 is initially applied in its entirety.[25]

c. Other than as set forth in (a) and (b), an entity shall not change the amount of the purchase price assigned to the assets acquired and liabilities assumed in a business combination for which the acquisition date was before July 1, 2001.[26]

62. As of the earlier of the first day of the fiscal year beginning after December 15, 2001, or the date Statement 142 is initially applied in its entirety, the amount of any unamortized deferred credit related to an excess over cost arising from (a) a business combination for which the acquisition date was before July 1, 2001, or (b) an investment accounted for by the equity method acquired before July 1, 2001, shall be written off and recognized as the effect of a change in accounting principle. The effect of the accounting change and related income tax effects shall be presented in the income statement between the captions *extraordinary items* and *net income.* The per-share information presented in the income statement shall include the per-share effect of the accounting change.

> **The provisions of this Statement need not be applied to immaterial items.**

This Statement was adopted by the unanimous vote of the six members of the Financial Accounting Standards Board:

Edmund L. Jenkins,
   Chairman

G. Michael Crooch
John M. Foster
Gaylen N. Larsen

Gerhard G. Mueller
Edward W. Trott

Appendix A

IMPLEMENTATION GUIDANCE

Introduction

A1. This appendix provides guidance to assist entities in the application of certain provisions of this Statement and is therefore an integral part of the standards provided in this Statement. This appendix discusses generalized situations. The facts and circumstances of each business combination should be considered carefully in applying this Statement.

A2. This Statement requires that all business combinations be accounted for using the purchase method. As stated in paragraph 1, this Statement carries forward without reconsideration portions of APB Opinion No. 16, *Business Combinations,* that provide guidance related to the application of the purchase method. While this Statement supersedes all of the AICPA Accounting Interpretations of Opinion 16, guidance in several of those interpretations continues to be relevant in applying certain of the provisions of Opinion 16 that are carried forward in this Statement. Therefore, the guidance in those interpretations has been carried forward without reconsideration in paragraphs A5–A9 of this appendix. Because that guidance has been quoted, paraphrased, or rephrased so that it can be understood in the context of this Statement, the original source of the guidance has been noted parenthetically. The Board intends to reconsider some of that guidance in another of its business combinations projects.

A3. This Statement does not supersede other pronouncements that provide guidance on accounting

---

[25]For example, when a business combination was initially recorded, a portion of the acquired entity was assigned to intangible assets that meet the recognition criteria in paragraph 39. Those intangible assets have been included in the amount reported on the statement of financial position as goodwill (or as goodwill and other intangible assets). However, separate general ledger or other accounting records have been maintained for those assets.

[26]This transition provision does not, however, affect the requirement to change the amounts assigned to the assets acquired in a business combination due to (a) the resolution of a consideration contingency based on earnings (paragraph 28) or (b) changes to the purchase price allocation prior to the end of the allocation period (paragraph 40).

for a business combination using the purchase method. Guidance in those pronouncements, which are listed below, shall be considered when applying the provisions of this Statement.

a. FASB Statement No. 72, *Accounting for Certain Acquisitions of Banking or Thrift Institutions*
b. FASB Interpretation No. 4, *Applicability of FASB Statement No. 2 to Business Combinations Accounted for by the Purchase Method*
c. FASB Interpretation No. 9, *Applying APB Opinions No. 16 and 17 When a Savings and Loan Association or a Similar Institution Is Acquired in a Business Combination Accounted for by the Purchase Method*
d. FASB Interpretation No. 21, *Accounting for Leases in a Business Combination*
e. FASB Interpretation No. 44, *Accounting for Certain Transactions involving Stock Compensation* (paragraphs 83–85)
f. FASB Technical Bulletin No. 85-5, *Issues Relating to Accounting for Business Combinations.*

A4. This Statement requires that intangible assets that meet the criteria in paragraph 39 be recognized as assets apart from goodwill. Paragraphs A10–A13 provide examples that illustrate how the guidance in paragraph 39 should be applied to certain generalized situations. Paragraph A14 includes a non-inclusive list of intangible assets that meet the criteria for recognition apart from goodwill.[27] Paragraphs A15–A28 describe some of the intangible assets included on that list and explain how the criteria in paragraph 39 generally apply to them.

Application of Paragraph 14—Accounting for the Acquisition of Some or All of the Noncontrolling Interests in a Subsidiary

A5. Paragraph 14 continues the practice established by Opinion 16 of accounting for the acquisition of noncontrolling interests of a subsidiary (commonly referred to as a minority interest) using the purchase method. Several interpretations of Opinion 16 provide guidance on the accounting for those transactions, and that guidance has been carried forward in paragraphs A6 and A7. The interpretative guidance in Technical Bulletin 85-5 also shall be considered when accounting for those transactions.

A6. Examples of the types of transactions that constitute the acquisition of a minority interest include the following: (a) a parent exchanges its common stock or assets or debt for common stock held by minority stockholders of its subsidiary, (b) the subsidiary buys as treasury stock the common stock held by minority stockholders, or (c) another subsidiary of the parent exchanges its common stock or assets or debt for common stock held by the minority stockholders of an affiliated subsidiary.

A7. Another type of transaction that constitutes the acquisition of a minority interest is a transaction in which a subsidiary exchanges its common stock for the outstanding voting common stock of its parent (usually referred to as a downstream merger). Those transactions shall be accounted for as if the parent had exchanged its common stock for common stock held by minority stockholders of its subsidiary. Whether a parent acquires the minority or a subsidiary acquires its parent, the result is a single stockholder group, including the former minority stockholders, owning the consolidated net assets. The same would be true if a new corporation exchanged its common stock for the common stock of the parent and the common stock of the subsidiary held by minority stockholders (AICPA Accounting Interpretation 26, "Acquisition of Minority Interest," of Opinion 16).

Application of Paragraph 24—Costs of the Business Combination

A8. Paragraph 24 states that the cost of an acquired entity includes the direct costs of the business combination. Those direct costs include "out-of-pocket" or incremental costs directly related to a business combination such as a finder's fee and fees paid to outside consultants for accounting, legal, or engineering investigations or for appraisals. Internal costs associated with a business combination (whether one-time costs or recurring in nature) shall be expensed as incurred. In addition, costs related to unsuccessful negotiations also shall be expensed as incurred (AICPA Accounting Interpretation 33, "Costs of Maintaining an 'Acquisitions' Department," of Opinion 16).

A9. Paragraph 24 also states that costs of registering and issuing equity securities shall be recognized as a reduction of the otherwise determinable fair value of the securities. A publicly held company issuing *unregistered* equity securities in a business combination

---

[27]As described in paragraph A18, some of the intangible assets identified on that list as meeting the separability criterion should not be recognized apart from goodwill if terms of confidentiality or other agreements prohibit the acquiring entity from selling, leasing, or otherwise exchanging the asset.

with an agreement for subsequent registration shall record those securities at the fair value of its registered securities less an estimate of the related registration costs. A liability shall be recognized at the date of acquisition in the amount of the present value of the estimated costs of registration. Any difference between the actual costs of registration and the recorded liability (including imputed interest) shall be recognized as an adjustment to the carrying amount of goodwill. If the securities issued in the business combination are to be included in the registration of a planned future offering of other securities (piggyback registration), only the incremental costs of registering the equity securities issued shall be recognized as a liability at the acquisition date (AICPA Accounting Interpretation 35, "Registration Costs in a Purchase," of Opinion 16).

Application of Paragraph 39—Recognition of Intangible Assets Apart from Goodwill

A10. Paragraph 39 states that an acquired intangible asset shall be recognized as an asset apart from goodwill if it arises from contractual or other legal rights (the contractual-legal criterion). Intangible assets that meet that criterion shall be recognized apart from goodwill even if the asset is not transferable or separable from the acquired entity or from other rights and obligations. For example:

a. An acquired entity leases a manufacturing facility under an operating lease that has terms that are favorable relative to market prices.[28] The lease terms explicitly prohibit transfer of the lease (through either sale or sublease). The value arising from that operating lease contract is an intangible asset that meets the contractual-legal criterion for recognition apart from goodwill, even though the lease contract cannot be sold or otherwise transferred.

b. An acquired entity owns and operates a nuclear power plant. The license to operate that power plant is an intangible asset that meets the contractual-legal criterion for recognition apart from goodwill, even if it cannot be sold or transferred apart from the acquired power plant. This Statement does not preclude an acquiring entity from recognizing the fair value of the operating license and the fair value of the power plant as a single asset for financial reporting purposes if the useful lives of those assets are similar.

c. An acquired entity owns a technology patent. It has licensed that patent to others for their exclusive use outside the United States in exchange for which the entity receives a specified percentage of future non-U.S. revenue. Both the technology patent and the related license agreement meet the contractual-legal criterion for recognition apart from goodwill even if it would not be practical to sell or exchange the patent and the related license agreement apart from one another.

A11. If an acquired intangible asset does *not* arise from contractual or other legal rights, paragraph 39 requires that it be recognized as an asset apart from goodwill only if it is separable—that is, it is capable of being separated or divided from the acquired entity and sold, transferred, licensed, rented, or exchanged (the separability criterion). Exchange transactions provide evidence that an intangible asset is separable from the acquired entity and might provide information that can be used to estimate its fair value. An acquired intangible asset meets the separability criterion if there is evidence of exchange transactions for that type of asset or an asset of a similar type (even if those exchange transactions are infrequent and regardless of whether the acquiring entity is involved in them). For example, customer and subscriber lists are frequently leased and thus meet the separability criterion. Even if an entity believes its customer lists have different characteristics than other customer lists, the fact that customer lists are frequently leased generally means that the acquired entity's customer list meets the separability criterion. Title plant assets also are bought and sold in exchange transactions (either in whole or in part) or are leased, although less frequently than customer lists. Title plant assets also would meet the separability criterion.

A12. An intangible asset that meets the separability criterion shall be recognized apart from goodwill even if the acquiring entity does not intend to sell, lease, or otherwise exchange that asset. The separability criterion is met because the asset is capable of being separated from the acquired entity and sold, transferred, licensed, rented, or otherwise exchanged for something else of value. For example, because an acquired customer list is generally capable of being rented, it meets the separability criterion regardless of whether the acquiring entity intends to rent it.

---

[28]In some cases, the terms of an operating lease might be unfavorable relative to market prices. Paragraph 37(k) of this Statement states that a portion of the purchase price should be assigned to liabilities such as unfavorable leases.

A13. As stated in paragraph 39, an intangible asset that is not separable from the entity individually still meets the separability criterion if it is separable from the acquired entity in combination with a related contract, asset, or liability. For example:

a. Deposit liabilities and related depositor relationship intangible assets are exchanged in observable exchange transactions. Therefore, the depositor relationship intangible asset shall be recognized apart from goodwill.

b. An acquired entity owns a registered trademark, a related secret formula, and unpatented technical expertise used to manufacture the trademarked product. To transfer ownership of a trademark in the United States, the owner is also required to transfer everything else necessary for the new owner to produce a product or service indistinguishable from that produced by the former owner. Because the unpatented technical expertise must be separated from the entity and sold if the related trademark is sold, it meets the separability criterion.

Examples of Intangible Assets That Meet the Criteria for Recognition Apart from Goodwill

A14. The following are examples of intangible assets that meet the criteria for recognition as an asset apart from goodwill. The following illustrative list is not intended to be all-inclusive, thus, an acquired intangible asset might meet the recognition criteria of this Statement but not be included on that list. Assets designated by the symbol (†) are those that would be recognized apart from goodwill because they meet the contractual-legal criterion.[29] Assets designated by the symbol (▲) do not arise from contractual or other legal rights, but shall nonetheless be recognized apart from goodwill because they meet the separability criterion. The determination of whether a specific acquired intangible asset meets the criteria in this Statement for recognition apart from goodwill shall be based on the facts and circumstances of each individual business combination.

a. Marketing-related intangible assets
  (1) Trademarks, tradenames†
  (2) Service marks, collective marks, certification marks†

(3) Trade dress (unique color, shape, or package design)†
(4) Newspaper mastheads†
(5) Internet domain names†
(6) Noncompetition agreements†

b. Customer-related intangible assets
  (1) Customer lists▲
  (2) Order or production backlog†
  (3) Customer contracts and related **customer relationships**†
  (4) Noncontractual customer relationships▲

c. Artistic-related intangible assets
  (1) Plays, operas, ballets†
  (2) Books, magazines, newspapers, other literary works†
  (3) Musical works such as compositions, song lyrics, advertising jingles†
  (4) Pictures, photographs†
  (5) Video and audiovisual material, including motion pictures, music videos, television programs†

d. Contract-based intangible assets
  (1) Licensing, royalty, standstill agreements†
  (2) Advertising, construction, management, service or supply contracts†
  (3) Lease agreements†
  (4) Construction permits†
  (5) Franchise agreements†
  (6) Operating and broadcast rights†
  (7) Use rights such as drilling, water, air, mineral, timber cutting, and route authorities†
  (8) Servicing contracts such as mortgage servicing contracts†
  (9) Employment contracts†

e. Technology-based intangible assets
  (1) Patented technology†
  (2) Computer software and mask works†
  (3) Unpatented technology▲
  (4) Databases, including title plants▲
  (5) Trade secrets, such as secret formulas, processes, recipes.†

Marketing-related intangible assets

A15. Marketing-related intangible assets are those assets that are primarily used in the marketing or promotion of products or services. Trademarks are words, names, symbols, or other devices used in trade to indicate the source of the product and to distinguish it from the products of others. A service

---

[29]The intangible assets designated by the symbol (†) also might meet the separability criterion. However, separability is not a necessary condition for an asset to meet the contractual-legal criterion.

mark identifies and distinguishes the source of a service rather than a product. Collective marks are used to identify the goods or services of members of a group, and certification marks are used to certify the geographic origin or other characteristics of a good or service. In the United States and other countries, trademarks, service marks, collective marks, and certification marks may be protected legally through registration with governmental agencies, continuous use in commerce, or by other means. If registered or otherwise provided legal protection, a trademark or other mark is an intangible asset that meets the contractual-legal criterion for recognition apart from goodwill. Otherwise, a trademark or other mark shall be recognized apart from goodwill only if the separability criterion is met, which would normally be the case.

A16. The terms *brand* and *brand name* often are used as synonyms for trademarks and tradenames. However, the former are general marketing terms that are typically used to refer to a group of complementary assets such as the trademark (or service mark) and its related tradename, formulas, recipes, and technological expertise (which may or may not be patented). This Statement does not preclude an entity from recognizing, as a single asset apart from goodwill, a group of complementary intangible assets commonly referred to as a brand if the assets that make up that group have similar useful lives.

A17. An Internet domain name is a unique alphanumeric name that is used to identify a particular numeric Internet address. Registration of a domain name associates the name with a designated computer on the Internet for the period the registration is in effect. Those registrations are renewable. Registered domain names shall be recognized as an intangible asset apart from goodwill because they meet the contractual-legal criterion.

Customer-related intangible assets

Customer lists

A18. A customer list consists of information about customers such as their name and contact information. A customer list also may be in the form of a database that includes other information about the customers such as their order history and demographic information. A customer list does not generally arise from contractual or other legal rights. However, customer lists are valuable and are frequently leased or exchanged. Therefore, an acquired customer list would meet the separability criterion for recognition

apart from goodwill. An acquired customer list would *not* meet that criterion, however, if the terms of confidentiality or other agreements prohibit an entity from selling, leasing, or otherwise exchanging information about its customers.

Order or production backlog

A19. If an acquired order or production backlog arises from contracts such as purchase or sales orders, it meets the contractual-legal criterion for recognition apart from goodwill (even if the purchase or sales orders were cancelable).

Customer contracts and related customer relationships

A20. If an entity establishes relationships with its customers through contracts, those customer relationships would arise from contractual rights. Therefore, customer contracts and the related customer relationships are intangible assets that meet the contractual-legal criterion. This Statement requires that those intangible assets be recognized as assets apart from goodwill even if confidentiality or other contractual terms prohibit the sale or transfer of the contract separately from the acquired entity.

Noncontractual customer relationships

A21. If a customer relationship does not arise from a contract, this Statement requires that the relationship be recognized as an intangible asset apart from goodwill if it meets the separability criterion. Exchange transactions for the same asset or a similar type of asset provide evidence of separability of a noncontractual customer relationship and might also provide information about exchange prices that should be considered when estimating its fair value. For example, relationships with depositors are frequently exchanged with the related deposits and, thus, meet the criteria for recognition as an intangible asset apart from goodwill.

Artistic-related intangible assets

A22. Artistic-related intangible assets meet the criteria for recognition apart from goodwill if the assets arise from contractual rights or legal rights such as those provided by copyright. In the United States for example, copyrights are granted by the government for the life of the creator plus 50 years. Copyrights can be transferred either in whole through assignments or in part through licensing agreements. In determining the fair value of a copyright intangible asset, consideration shall be given to the existence of any assignments or licenses of the acquired copyright. This Statement does not preclude an acquiring entity from recognizing a copyright intangible asset and any related assignments or license agreements as a single intangible asset for financial reporting purposes if their useful lives are similar.

Contract-based intangible assets

A23. Contract-based intangible assets represent the value of rights that arise from contractual arrangements. Customer contracts (refer to paragraph A20) are one particular type of contract-based intangible asset. Contracts to service financial assets are another. While servicing is inherent in all financial assets, it becomes a distinct asset or liability only when (a) contractually separated from the underlying financial assets by sale or securitization of the assets with servicing retained or (b) through the separate purchase and assumption of the servicing. If mortgage loans, credit card receivables, or other financial assets are acquired in a business combination with servicing retained, this Statement does not require recognition of the inherent servicing rights as an intangible asset because the fair value of the servicing intangible asset is considered in the measurement of the fair value of the acquired financial asset. However, a contract representing an acquired **servicing asset** is an intangible asset that shall be recognized apart from goodwill.

A24. If the terms of a contract give rise to a liability or commitment (which might be the case if the terms of an operating lease or customer contract are unfavorable relative to market prices), that liability or commitment shall be recognized as required by paragraph 37(k) of this Statement.

Technology-based intangible assets

A25. Technology-based intangible assets relate to innovations or technological advances. As stated in paragraphs A26–A28, the future economic benefits of those assets are often protected through contractual or other legal rights. Thus, many technology-based intangible assets meet the contractual-legal criterion for recognition apart from goodwill.

Computer software and mask works

A26. If computer software and program formats are protected legally such as by patent or copyright, they meet the contractual-legal criterion for recognition apart from goodwill. Mask works are software permanently stored on a read-only memory chip as a series of stencils or integrated circuitry. Mask works may be provided legal protection; for example, in the United States mask works qualify for protection under the Semiconductor Chip Protection Act of 1984. Acquired mask works protected under the provisions of that Act or other similar laws or regulations also meet the contractual-legal criterion for recognition apart from goodwill.

Databases, including title plants

A27. Databases are collections of information, often stored in electronic form (such as on computer disks or files). An acquired database that includes original works of authorship is entitled to copyright protection and, if so protected, meets the contractual-legal criterion for recognition apart from goodwill. However, a database often includes information created as a consequence of an entity's normal operations, such as a customer list or specialized information such as a title plant, scientific data, and credit information. Databases that are not protected by copyright can be (and often are) exchanged in their entirety or in part. Alternatively, they can be (and often are) licensed or leased to others. Thus, even if the future economic benefit of a database does not arise from legal rights, it meets the separability criterion for recognition as an asset apart from goodwill.

Trade secrets, such as secret formulas, processes, recipes

A28. A trade secret is "information, including a formula, pattern, compilation, program, device, method, technique, or process, that (1) derives independent economic value, actual or potential, from not being generally known . . . and (2) is the subject of efforts that are reasonable under the circumstances to maintain its secrecy."[30] If the future economic benefit of an acquired trade secret is protected legally, such as by the Uniform Trade Secrets Act or other laws and regulations, that asset meets the contractual-legal criterion for recognition as an asset apart from goodwill. Otherwise, a trade secret would be recognized as an asset apart from goodwill only if the separability criterion was met, which is likely to be the case.

---

[30]Melvin Simensky and Lanning Bryer, *The New Role of Intellectual Property in Commercial Transactions* (New York: John Wiley & Sons, 1998), page 293.

Appendix B

BACKGROUND INFORMATION AND BASIS FOR CONCLUSIONS

CONTENTS

Appendix B

BACKGROUND INFORMATION AND BASIS FOR CONCLUSIONS

Introduction

B1. This appendix summarizes considerations that Board members deemed significant in reaching the conclusions in this Statement. It includes reasons for accepting certain approaches and rejecting others. Individual Board members gave greater weight to some factors than to others. It also summarizes the considerations that were deemed significant in reach-

ing the conclusions in FASB Statement No. 38, *Accounting for Preacquisition Contingencies of Purchased Enterprises*. Those conclusions and considerations are carried forward in this Statement without reconsideration.

Background Information

B2. Prior to the issuance of this Statement, the guidance on accounting for business combinations was provided by APB Opinion No. 16, *Business Combinations*, which the Accounting Principles Board (APB) of the American Institute of Certified Public Accountants (AICPA) issued in 1970. Opinion 16 provided for two methods of accounting for business combinations, the pooling-of-interests method (pooling method) and the purchase method. Those methods were not alternatives or substitutes for one another. Opinion 16 required that the pooling method be used if a business combination met 12 specified conditions; otherwise, the purchase method was to be used.

B3. During the 1970s, the FASB had an active project on its agenda to reconsider the accounting for business combinations and purchased intangible assets. However, the Board later decided to defer consideration of the issues in that project until after it had completed development of its conceptual framework for accounting and reporting. In 1981, the Board removed the inactive business combinations project from its agenda to focus on higher priority projects.

B4. In August 1996, the Board added the current project on accounting for business combinations to its agenda. The objective of this project was to improve the transparency of accounting and reporting of business combinations including the accounting for goodwill and other intangible assets by reconsidering the requirements of Opinion 16 and APB Opinion No. 17, *Intangible Assets* (which also was issued in 1970). In 1999, the Board decided that that objective would best be achieved through several projects focused on specific issues. In the first of those projects, which ended with the concurrent issuance of this Statement and FASB Statement No. 142, *Goodwill and Other Intangible Assets,* the Board reconsidered the methods of accounting for business combinations and the accounting for goodwill and other intangible assets. Another project will address issues associated with the accounting for combinations between not-for-profit organizations, the acquisition of a for-profit entity by a not-for-profit organization, and combinations between mutual enterprises. The Board intends to consider issues related to the accounting for the formation of joint ventures and other new entities, push-down accounting (including spinoffs), and common control transactions in another project. In still another project the Board intends to consider issues related to the provisions of Opinion 16 and Statement 38 that are carried forward in this Statement without reconsideration and other issues related to the application of the purchase method, such as the accounting for step acquisitions.[31]

Reasons the FASB Took on the Project

B5. A principal reason for taking on this project in 1996 was the increase in merger and acquisition activity that brought greater attention to the fact that two transactions that are economically similar may be accounted for by different methods that produce dramatically different financial statement results. Consequently, both the representational faithfulness and the comparability of those financial statements suffer.

B6. Another reason that the Board decided to undertake this project was that many perceived the differences in the pooling and purchase methods to have affected competition in markets for mergers and acquisitions. Entities that could not meet all of the conditions for applying the pooling method believed that they faced an unlevel playing field in competing for targets with entities that could apply that method. That perception and the resulting attempts to expand the application of the pooling method placed considerable tension on the interpretation and application of the provisions of Opinion 16. The volume of inquiries fielded by the staffs of the FASB and Securities and Exchange Commission (SEC) and the auditing profession was evidence of that tension.

B7. The unlevel playing field that was perceived to stem from the application of the pooling and purchase methods extended internationally as well. Cross-border differences in accounting standards for business combinations and the rapidly accelerating movement of capital flows globally heightened the need for accounting standards to be comparable internationally. Promoting international comparability in accounting standards is part of the Board's mission, and many members of the Financial Accounting Standards Advisory Council (FASAC) cited the opportunity to promote greater international comparability in the standards for business combinations as a reason for adding this project to the Board's agenda. (FASAC had consistently ranked a possible project on business combinations as a high priority for a number of years.)

International Cooperation

B8. Largely because of concerns about the perception of an unlevel cross-border playing field with the

---

[31]For example, AICPA Accounting Interpretation 2, "Goodwill in a Step Acquisition," of Opinion 17, stated that when an entity acquires another entity or an investment accounted for by the equity method through a series of purchases (commonly referred to as a step acquisition), the entity should identify the cost of each investment, the fair value of the underlying assets acquired, and the goodwill for each step acquisition.

United States in the accounting standards for business combinations, the Accounting Standards Board (AcSB) of the Canadian Institute of Chartered Accountants (CICA) conducted a business combinations project concurrently with the FASB's project. The goal of that concurrent effort was to establish common standards on business combinations and intangible assets.

B9. The FASB also worked with other members of an international organization of standard-setting bodies with the aim of achieving convergence internationally with respect to the methods of accounting for business combinations. That organization, known as the "Group of 4 plus 1" (G4+1), consisted of the Australian Accounting Standards Board (AASB), the New Zealand Financial Reporting Standards Board (FRSB), the United Kingdom Accounting Standards Board (UK ASB), the AcSB, the FASB, and an observer, the International Accounting Standards Committee (IASC).

Conduct of the FASB's Project

B10. The Board formed a business combinations task force comprising individuals from a number of organizations representing a wide range of the Board's constituents. The first meeting of that task force was held in February 1997. Relevant academic research was reviewed, and the meeting discussion centered on a background paper that addressed the project's scope, the direction the project should take, and how the project should be conducted.

B11. The June 1997 FASB Special Report, *Issues Associated with the FASB Project on Business Combinations,* was based on that background paper and indicated some of the Board's initial decisions about the project's scope, direction, and conduct. The 54 comment letters received in response to that Special Report generally expressed agreement with those decisions.

B12. In 1998, the FASB participated in the development of a G4+1 Position Paper, *Recommendations for Achieving Convergence on the Methods of Accounting for Business Combinations.* That Position Paper considered the pooling method, the purchase method, and the fresh-start method,[32] and concluded

that only the purchase method should be used to account for business combinations.

B13. The Board issued the Position Paper as an FASB Invitation to Comment, *Methods of Accounting for Business Combinations: Recommendations of the G4+1 for Achieving Convergence,* in December 1998, the same date on which other G4+1 member organizations issued similar documents for comment. The FASB received 148 comment letters, the AcSB received 40 letters, the UK ASB received 35 letters, the IASC received 35 letters, the AASB received 5 letters, and the FRSB received 4 letters.

B14. After considering the recommendations of the G4+1 and the responses to the Invitation to Comment, the Board decided that only the purchase method should be used to account for business combinations. The Board also decided that certain changes should be made in how the purchase method should be applied, particularly in the accounting for and financial statement presentation of goodwill and other intangible assets. Those changes were proposed in the September 1999 FASB Exposure Draft, *Business Combinations and Intangible Assets* (1999 Exposure Draft). The Board received 210 comment letters in response to the 1999 Exposure Draft. In February 2000, the Board held 4 days of public hearings, 2 days in San Francisco and 2 days in New York City, at which 43 individuals or organizations presented their views on the 1999 Exposure Draft.

B15. In redeliberating the proposals in the 1999 Exposure Draft, the Board considered changes suggested by various constituents, in particular those related to the accounting for goodwill. During October and November 2000, Board and staff members explored the suggested changes to the accounting for goodwill in field visits with 14 companies. The Board's deliberations resulted in significant changes to the proposed requirements related to goodwill but not to other issues addressed in the 1999 Exposure Draft. In particular, the Board decided that goodwill should no longer be amortized and should be tested for impairment in a manner different from how other assets are tested for impairment. The Board also affirmed the proposal that only the purchase method

---

[32]Under the fresh-start method, the assets and liabilities of the combining entities (regardless of whether they had been recognized in the statements of financial position of those entities) are recognized in the statement of financial position of the combined entity at fair value. The combined entity is treated as a new entity as of the date of the combination and its history commences on that date. The fresh-start method is currently used in practice to account for certain corporate reorganization transactions. As with the purchase method, the fresh-start method can be applied to business combinations that are effected by cash, other assets, debt, equity shares, or a combination thereof.

should be used to account for business combinations. In February 2001, the Board issued a revised Exposure Draft, *Business Combinations and Intangible Assets—Accounting for Goodwill* (2001 Exposure Draft), that proposed changes to the 1999 Exposure Draft with regard to the accounting for goodwill and the initial recognition of intangible assets other than goodwill. The Board received 211 comment letters on the 2001 Exposure Draft.

B16. The Board decided to separate the guidance for business combinations from that for goodwill and other intangible assets and issue that guidance in two final documents, this Statement and Statement 142. Those two Statements parallel and supersede Opinions 16 and 17, respectively. Statement 142 was issued concurrently with this Statement.

B17. The Board also decided that this Statement should supersede Statement 38 and carry forward without reconsideration portions of the guidance in Opinion 16 and that Statement related to the application of the purchase method.

Basis for Conclusions

Definition and Scope

B18. In developing the 1999 Exposure Draft, the Board concluded that because this project is primarily focused on the methods of accounting for business combinations, this Statement should generally retain the definition and scope of Opinion 16. The Board affirmed that conclusion in its redeliberations of the 1999 Exposure Draft.

B19. The 1999 Exposure Draft proposed certain changes to the Opinion 16 definition of a business combination to reflect the Board's conclusion that all two-party business combinations and virtually all other business combinations (other than joint venture formations) are acquisitions. Specifically, the 1999 Exposure Draft proposed that a *business combination* be defined as occurring when one entity acquires all or a portion of the net assets that constitutes a business or equity interests of one or more entities and obtains control over the entity or entities.

B20. Respondents to the 1999 Exposure Draft were asked to comment on that proposed definition, in particular whether it would appear to include or exclude business combinations that were not similarly covered by the Opinion 16 definition. The principal concern expressed by respondents that commented on

that issue related to the proposal that a business combination be defined as occurring when one entity acquires equity interests of another entity and obtains control over that entity. Many of those respondents said that that definition would exclude certain transactions covered by Opinion 16 from the scope of the 1999 Exposure Draft, in particular, transactions in which none of the former shareholder groups of the combining entities obtain control over the combined entity (such as roll-ups, put-togethers, and so-called mergers of equals). During its redeliberations of the 1999 Exposure Draft, the Board concluded that those transactions should be included in the definition of a business combination and in the scope of this Statement. Therefore, paragraph 10 explicitly states that the provisions of this Statement also apply to business combinations in which none of the owners of the combining entities as a group retain or receive a majority of the voting rights of the combined entity. However, the Board acknowledges that some of those business combinations might not be acquisitions, and it intends to consider in another project whether business combinations that are not acquisitions should be accounted for using the fresh-start method rather than the purchase method.

B21. Respondents to the 1999 Exposure Draft suggested that because joint venture formations were to be excluded from the scope of that proposed Statement, the Board should define *joint venture*. The Board concluded that this Statement should not provide that definition. The Board noted that constituents consider the guidance in paragraph 3(d) of APB Opinion No. 18, *The Equity Method of Accounting for Investments in Common Stock,* in assessing whether an entity is a joint venture, and it decided not to change that practice at this time. The Board intends to develop a definition of joint venture as part of its project on accounting for joint venture and other new entity formations.

B22. Respondents to the 1999 Exposure Draft also said that the Board should define the term *business.* The Board observed that in EITF Issue No. 98-3, "Determining Whether a Nonmonetary Transaction Involves Receipt of Productive Assets or of a Business," the EITF reached a consensus on guidance for determining whether a business has been received in an exchange transaction. That guidance discusses the characteristics of a business. The Board concluded that while it was not necessary to define *business* for purposes of this Statement, this Statement should refer to the guidance provided in Issue 98-3.

B23. The Board affirmed the decision it made in developing the 1999 Exposure Draft that this Statement would not address transactions, events, or circumstances that result in one entity obtaining control over another entity through means other than the acquisition of net assets or equity interests. Therefore, this Statement does not change current accounting practice with respect to those transactions. For example, if a previously unconsolidated majority-owned entity is consolidated as a result of control being obtained by the lapse or elimination of participating veto rights that were held by minority stockholders, a new basis for the investment's total carrying amount is not recognized under current practice. Instead, only the display of the majority-owned investment in the consolidated financial statements is changed. The majority-owned entity is consolidated rather than reported as a single investment accounted for by the equity method. That treatment is consistent with the practice for accounting for step acquisitions, in which a parent obtains control of a subsidiary through two or more purchases of the investee-subsidiary's stock. In addition, this Statement does not change the consensuses reached in EITF Issue No. 97-2, "Application of FASB Statement No. 94 and APB Opinion No. 16 to Physician Practice Management Entities and Certain Other Entities with Contractual Management Arrangements." The Board intends to consider the accounting for transactions in which control of an entity is obtained through means other than the acquisition of net assets or equity interests in another project.

B24. The Board acknowledged, as it did prior to issuing the 1999 Exposure Draft, that this Statement does not address many current practice issues, such as accounting for recapitalization transactions or joint venture and other new entity formations and transactions between entities under common control. Those are among the issues that the Board intends to consider in another project.

Methods of Accounting for Business Combinations

B25. In deliberating the methods of accounting for business combinations, the Board carefully considered the analyses of the issues in the G4+1 Position Paper, as well as the conclusions and recommendations that were based on those analyses. The Board also carefully considered the views expressed by respondents to the Invitation to Comment, as well as those of respondents to the corresponding documents of other G4+1 member organizations. In later redeliberating the proposals made in the 1999 Exposure

Draft, the Board also carefully considered the views expressed by respondents to that Exposure Draft, most of which reiterated views expressed by respondents to the Invitation to Comment.

B26. Like the G4+1, the Board considered three possible methods of accounting for business combinations—the pooling method, the purchase method, and the fresh-start method. Also like the G4+1, the Board observed that neither the pooling method nor the fresh-start method could be appropriately used for all business combinations.

B27. In assessing those methods, the Board was mindful of the disadvantages of having more than one method of accounting for business combinations, as evidenced by the experience with Opinion 16 over the past three decades. Among those disadvantages are the incentives for accounting arbitrage that inevitably exist when different methods produce dramatically different financial statement results for economically similar transactions. Another disadvantage is the difficulty in drawing unambiguous and nonarbitrary boundaries between the transactions to which the different accounting methods would apply. Still others include the difficulties and costs associated with applying, auditing, and enforcing the resulting standards. Yet others relate to difficulties with analyzing the information provided by different methods because users commonly do not have the means available to convert from the information provided by one method to that provided by another.

B28. The Board concluded that having more than one method could be justified only if the alternative method (or methods) could be demonstrated to produce information that is more decision useful and if unambiguous and nonarbitrary boundaries could be established that unequivocally distinguish when one method is to be applied rather than another.

Reasons for adopting the purchase method

B29. The Board concluded that the purchase method is the appropriate method of accounting for all business combinations that are acquisitions, as did the G4+1. The purchase method is consistent with how the historical-cost accounting model generally accounts for transactions in which assets are acquired and liabilities are assumed or incurred, and it therefore produces information that is comparable to other accounting information. Under the purchase method, one of the combining entities is viewed as surviving the transaction and is considered the acquiring entity.

The other combining entities that do not survive the combination as independent entities are considered the acquired entities. The purchase method recognizes and measures assets and liabilities in the same way regardless of the nature of the consideration that is exchanged for them. Consequently, users of financial statements are better able to assess the initial costs of the investments made and the subsequent performance of those investments and compare them with the performance of other entities. Moreover, the purchase method is familiar to preparers, auditors, regulators, and users of financial statements.

B30. Respondents to both the Invitation to Comment and the 1999 Exposure Draft generally agreed that most business combinations are acquisitions, and many stated that all combinations involving only two entities are acquisitions. Respondents also agreed that the purchase method is the appropriate method of accounting for business combinations that are acquisitions. However, some qualified their support for the purchase method contingent upon the Board's decisions about certain aspects of applying that method, particularly the accounting for goodwill.

B31. Because the purchase method is the only appropriate method of accounting for business combinations that are acquisitions, the question considered by the Board was whether any combinations are not acquisitions and, if so, whether the pooling method or the fresh-start method should be used to account for them. The Board generally agreed with the analyses and conclusions in the G4+1 Position Paper and concluded that all two-party business combinations other than joint venture formations are acquisitions. Accordingly, the Board decided that one method, the purchase method, should be used to account for all two-party business combinations except joint venture formations.

B32. The Board also concluded that most business combinations involving three or more entities (multi-party combinations) are acquisitions. The Board acknowledged that some multi-party combinations (in particular, those that are commonly referred to as roll-up or put-together transactions) might not be acquisitions; however, it noted that presently those transactions are generally accounted for by the purchase method. The Board decided not to change that practice at this time. Consequently, this Statement requires that the purchase method be used to account for all multi-party combinations, including those that some might not consider to be acquisitions. As discussed in paragraph B4, however, the Board

intends to consider whether joint venture formations and multi-party business combinations that are not acquisitions should be accounted for by the fresh-start method rather than the purchase method.

B33. The Board noted that requiring the use of the purchase method will bring the accounting for business combinations in the United States more in step with how those combinations are accounted for in other jurisdictions because that method is widely or exclusively used in those jurisdictions.

B34. The Board also concluded that identifying the acquiring entity is practicable in all cases, although doing so may be difficult in some instances. In that regard, some respondents to the 1999 Exposure Draft noted that even though identifying an acquirer might sometimes be difficult, an acquirer nonetheless must be identified for U.S. federal income tax purposes.

B35. Paragraphs B36–B85 discuss the bases for the Board's decision to reaffirm its proposal in the 1999 Exposure Draft to reject the pooling method and fresh-start method in favor of the purchase method.

Reasons for rejecting the pooling method

Mergers and acquisitions are similar economically

B36. Many respondents to the Invitation to Comment and the 1999 Exposure Draft argued that mergers (business combinations in which the consideration is in the form of equity interests) should be accounted for differently than acquisitions. They stated that, in mergers, ownership interests are completely or substantially continued, no new capital is invested and no assets are distributed, postcombination ownership interests are proportional to those prior to the combination, and the intention is to have a uniting of commercial strategies going forward. Moreover, no change in control of the entity's assets or liabilities occurs and no earnings process culminates. Those respondents said that a merger should be accounted for in terms of the carrying amounts of the assets and liabilities of the combining entities because unlike acquisitions, in which only the acquiring entity survives the combination, all of the combining entities effectively survive a merger.

B37. A few respondents urged that the pooling method be applied to all business combinations, regardless of the nature of the consideration, and a few others urged that it be applied to all mergers. The

Board is not aware of any jurisdiction in which *all* business combinations are or may be accounted for by the pooling method. In most jurisdictions, use of that method has been limited to mergers. The Board also is not aware of any jurisdiction in which all *mergers* are accounted for by the pooling method. In most jurisdictions that permit use of the pooling method for mergers, many mergers are accounted for by the purchase method. Thus, adoption of the suggestions to broaden the application of the pooling method would move away from rather than toward greater convergence of accounting standards internationally for business combinations. Furthermore, the Board does not believe that the nature of the consideration tendered—equity interests in the case of mergers—should dictate how the net assets acquired should be recorded.

B38. Most respondents that favored retaining the pooling method urged that its application be limited. Some stated that application of the pooling method should be limited to those combinations that meet certain conditions, either the same as those in Opinion 16 or a simpler set. However, many stated that its application should be more restricted than under Opinion 16. They generally urged that its application be limited to "true mergers" or "mergers of equals," which they described as combinations of entities of approximately equal size or those in which an acquirer could not be readily identified. Some added that the combining businesses should be complementary in nature and that the risks and rewards associated with the assets obtained should be similar to those associated with assets given up. Several respondents stated that true mergers or mergers of equals might be accounted for by either the pooling method or the fresh-start method but did not suggest which of those methods might be more appropriate or what the criteria should be for determining which method to apply.

B39. The Board noted that mergers are not transactions between owners as asserted by proponents of the pooling method, but rather that the combining entities themselves are deeply involved in those transactions. The issuance of shares is an investment by owners from the issuing entity's perspective. The net assets of one entity are transferred to another, which issues its shares in exchange, and that transaction should be accounted for on the same basis that would be used to record an investment by owners in the form of cash—that is, on a fair value basis. From the perspective of the acquired entity's shareholders, that transaction is an exchange transaction, a sale on their part and a purchase on the part of the surviving entity. In that regard, the Board observed that the shareholders of the acquired entity typically receive a premium for their shares, which is consistent with being sellers. Furthermore, the acquired entity's shareholders often become relatively more liquid following the exchange by virtue of receiving shares that are more widely and deeply traded than those they gave up (particularly if their shares had been privately held or closely held), which also is consistent with the usual outcome for sellers.

B40. Many respondents agreed with the Board's conclusion that although ownership interests are continued in a merger, they are not the same interests as before the combination. That is because control over precombination assets is reduced by sharing, and shared control over other assets is gained. Thus, not only does control change but also what is controlled changes. Furthermore, the risks and rewards associated with the assets obtained may or may not be similar to those given up, and the combination itself may have either increased or decreased risks and the potential for rewards. Finally, even though "intent" in the form of a uniting of commercial strategies going forward is sometimes cited as a feature of mergers, the Board believes that all business combinations entail some bringing together of commercial strategies and, thus, that feature is not unique to mergers.

B41. Some respondents stated that mergers are virtually identical to acquisitions economically, making them in-substance acquisitions. In that regard, some noted that shares could have been issued for cash and that cash then used to effect the combination, with the end result being the same economically as if shares had been used to effect the combination.

B42. The Board concluded that "true mergers" or "mergers of equals" are nonexistent or so rare as to be virtually nonexistent, and many respondents agreed. Other respondents stated that even if a true merger or merger of equals did occur, it would be so rare that a separate accounting treatment is not warranted. They also stated that developing the criteria necessary to identify those transactions simply would be a continuation of the same problems and potential for abuse evidenced by Opinion 16. The Board agreed, observing that even in those standards set by others that restrict use of the pooling method to true mergers or mergers of equals (such as the AcSB, the UK ASB, and the IASC), there are differences not only in the criteria themselves but in how they are interpreted and applied. The Board further observed that respondents and other constituents were unable to suggest an unambiguous and nonarbitrary boundary for distinguishing true mergers or mergers of equals from other two-party business combinations and concluded that developing such an operational boundary would not be feasible. Moreover, even if those mergers could feasibly be distinguished from other combinations, the Board concluded that it does not follow that such combinations should be accounted for on a carry-over basis. If they were to be accounted for using a method other than the purchase method, the Board believes that a better method would be the fresh-start method.

Information provided is not decision useful

B43. Some proponents of the pooling method argued that the information it provides for some business combinations is more decision useful. They argued that the information is more reliable, in particular, more representationally faithful, than the information that the purchase method would provide if it were applied to those combinations. However, other respondents countered, stating that the information provided by the purchase method is more revealing than that provided by the pooling method. Respondents also noted that the pooling method does not hold management accountable for the investment made and the subsequent performance of that investment. In contrast, the accountability that results from applying the purchase method forces management to examine business combination deals carefully to see that they make sense economically.

B44. The Board observed that an important facet of decision-useful information is information about cash-generating abilities and cash flows generated. As FASB Concepts Statement No. 1, *Objectives of Financial Reporting by Business Enterprises*, states, " . . . financial reporting should provide information to help investors, creditors, and others assess the amounts, timing, and uncertainty of prospective net cash inflows to the related enterprise" (paragraph 37; footnote reference omitted). The Board noted that neither the cash-generating abilities of the combined entity nor its future cash flows generally are affected by the method used to account for the combination. However, fair values reflect the expected cash flows associated with acquired assets and assumed liabilities. Because the pooling method records the net assets acquired at their carrying amounts rather than at their fair values, the information that the pooling

method provides about the cash-generating abilities of those net assets is less useful than that provided by other methods.

B45. The Board also concluded that the information provided by the pooling method is less relevant in terms of completeness, predictive value, and feedback value than the information that is provided by other methods. It also is less reliable because, for example, by recording assets and liabilities at the carrying amounts of predecessor entities, postcombination revenues may be overstated (and expenses understated) as the result of embedded gains that were generated by predecessor entities but not recognized by them. Furthermore, because of variations in when the pooling method is applied, similar combinations may be accounted for by different methods, adversely affecting both representational faithfulness and comparability.

B46. Comparability is another important facet of information that is decision useful. As FASB Concepts Statement No. 2, *Qualitative Characteristics of Accounting Information*, states, "The purpose of comparison is to detect and explain similarities and differences" (paragraph 113). It also notes that "the difficulty in making financial comparisons among enterprises because of the use of different accounting methods has been accepted for many years as the principal reason for the development of accounting standards" (paragraph 112).

B47. Most of the respondents to the Invitation to Comment agreed that differences in the methods of accounting for business combinations and when they are applied make it difficult to compare financial statements.

B48. Respondents to the 1999 Exposure Draft expressed mixed views. Some proponents of the pooling method argued that eliminating it would hinder comparability, describing the purchase method as an "apples and oranges approach" because it measures the net assets of the acquired entity at fair value and those of the acquiring entity at historical cost. However, opponents of the pooling method stated that the purchase method produces results that are comparable with those of entities that grow by acquiring similar assets in a number of smaller purchases that are not business combinations. The Board agreed with those who stated that the purchase method is consistent with how other asset acquisitions are accounted for, and it disagreed with those who described it as an apples-and-oranges approach.

B49. Proponents of the pooling method also argued that the pooling method enhances the comparability of the financial statements of entities that grow though acquisition (a "buy strategy") with those of entities that grow internally (a "build strategy"). They asserted that the pooling method enhances comparability because it avoids recognizing assets on the statement of financial position and related charges to the income statement that the purchase method requires. The Board concluded that comparability between entities that "buy" and those that "build" is a false comparability because the outlays that are made for the assets in question are never accounted for under the pooling method, whereas they are accounted for when the assets are developed internally.

B50. Opponents of the pooling method stated that eliminating that method would enhance the comparability of financial statements of entities that grow by means of acquisitions. After considering all of the views expressed by respondents, the Board agreed with those that stated that comparability of financial information reported by entities that engage in business combinations would be enhanced by eliminating the pooling method.

Inconsistencies across jurisdictions and over time

B51. The Board observed that there are inconsistencies internationally with regard to whether and when the pooling method is applied. In some jurisdictions, its use is prohibited, and in those jurisdictions where its use is not prohibited, it is applied to some—but not all—business combinations in which the consideration is in the form of equity interests, with the particulars varying from jurisdiction to jurisdiction.

B52. The Board also observed that because accounting standards for business combinations in the United States have changed over time, there has been variation over time as to which business combinations qualify for application of the pooling method. For example, Opinion 16 was designed to narrow the application of the pooling method to only those combinations that met 12 stated conditions.

B53. The Board noted that if the pooling method were based on a sound underlying conceptual foundation, there would not be inconsistencies in how that method is applied internationally, nor would there have been changes over time in the transactions that qualify for use of that method in the United States.

B54. The Board observed that the pooling method is used today to account for transactions that are quite different from those it was originally intended to account for. As discussed in the Invitation to Comment's appendix entitled "The History of the Pooling-of-Interests Method in the Jurisdictions of G4+1 Member Organizations," the pooling method in the United States

> . . . has its roots in an approach developed
> for combinations in which a strong degree of
> affiliation existed between the combining
> companies prior to the combination. That approach was gradually extended to a quite different set of combinations, namely those in
> which the combining companies had not
> been part of the same "family" and whose existing relationships—if any—had simply
> been incident to normal business activities,
> such as those with suppliers or customers.
> [page 26]

B55. The Board also observed that early uses of the pooling method occurred in certain regulated industries in which the rates that regulated entities could charge their customers were based on the cost of their assets. Rather than permit those entities to charge higher rates as a result of business combinations, particularly between entities that had been so closely related that the presence of arm's-length bargaining was open to question, regulators held that no new values should be assigned to the assets being combined. That was because no change in substance had occurred from the rate payers' perspective—the net assets being employed before and after the combination were the same. Accordingly, rate regulation issues expanded the use of the pooling method, even to combinations in which the consideration was not in the form of stock.

B56. Although use of the pooling method has spread considerably in the years since its inception, the Board observed that the criteria for its application today bear little or no resemblance to those that would be consistent with its roots.

Inconsistent with historical-cost accounting model

B57. The Board observed that the pooling method is an exception to the general concept that exchange transactions are accounted for in terms of the fair values of the items exchanged. Because the pooling method records the combination in terms of the carrying amounts of the parties to the transaction, it fails to record the investment made in the combination and fails to hold management accountable for that investment and its subsequent performance.

B58. Some proponents of the pooling method asserted that use of that method is consistent with the historical-cost model and that eliminating it would be another step down the road toward a fair value model. They argued that before eliminating the pooling method, the Board should resolve the broad issue of whether to adopt a fair value model in place of the historical-cost model. In the Board's view, regardless of the merits of a fair value model, the pooling method is an aberration that is inconsistent with the historical-cost model. The reason relates to the fundamental role of transactions in accounting.

B59. The Board observed that although the historical-cost model is frequently described as being "transaction based," the fair value model also records all transactions. In both models, the transactions are recorded at the same amounts. The main difference between those models does not relate to whether transactions that the entity engages in are recorded; it lies in what is recorded between transactions.

B60. Under the fair value model, a "truing up" takes place between transactions that involves recognizing nontransactional events and circumstances that affect the entity's assets and liabilities. That "truing up" also involves making end-of-period adjustments that are needed to update the fair values of those assets and liabilities in order to prepare financial statements.

B61. In contrast, under the historical-cost model, entries that are recorded between transactions are not generally aimed at truing-up the measures of the entity's assets and liabilities but rather at allocating or assigning costs to particular accounting periods. To the extent that any truing-up takes place, it generally is limited to recognizing such events as calamities, decreases in the market value of inventories below their cost, and impairments of long-lived assets. Thus, the truing-up is largely left to subsequent transactions that the entity engages in. Therefore, those transactions provide the "reality check" that is needed to validate the historical-cost model, without which its outputs would be suspect. Stated another way, transactions are the essential part of the historical-cost model that provide the reckoning that otherwise might not occur.

B62. The pooling method effectively sidesteps the reckoning that comes with business combination transactions by assuming that those transactions are exchanges between the owners of the combining entities rather than between the entities themselves. That method does not recognize the values exchanged in the records of the combined entity, only the carrying amounts of the predecessor entities. The failure to record those values can adversely affect the reliability of the combined entity's financial statements for years—and even decades—to come. For those reasons, the Board concluded that the pooling method is inconsistent with the historical-cost model.

Consistency with other standards

B63. A few respondents noted that FASB Statement No. 140, *Accounting for Transfers and Servicing of Financial Assets and Extinguishments of Liabilities*, precludes sale accounting for transfers of financial assets when there is continuing involvement of the transferor (such as retaining an ownership interest in the asset purported to be sold). Those respondents argued that if owners of both combining entities in a business combination have a significant degree of continuing involvement in the combined entity, neither owner has "sold" their entity. Therefore, the use of the purchase method for all business combinations may be inconsistent with accounting for certain securitization transactions as set forth in Statement 140. The Board observed, however, that Statement 140 addresses transfers of financial assets and that those transactions are fundamentally different from business combinations. Moreover, the provisions of Statement 140 preclude recognition of a transfer of assets as a sale if the transferor does not surrender control over those assets. In contrast, in a business combination that is effected by cash, control over the net assets of the acquired entity *is* transferred, and in those affected by stock, control over precombination net assets *is* reduced and shared.

Disclosure not an adequate response

B64. In urging that the pooling method be retained, a few respondents to the Invitation to Comment and the 1999 Exposure Draft stated that any perceived problems with having two methods of accounting could be addressed by enhanced disclosures in the notes to the financial statements. However, they generally did not specify what those disclosures should be and how they would help overcome the comparability problems that inevitably result from having two methods.

B65. In developing the 1999 Exposure Draft, the Board considered the matter of enhanced disclosures but doubted the usefulness of almost any disclosures short of disclosing what the results would have been had the purchase method been used to account for the business combination. Even so, providing disclosures that would enable users of financial statements to determine what the results would have been had the transaction been accounted for by the purchase method would be a costly solution that begs the question of why the purchase method was not used to account for the transaction in the first place. Since the respondents to the 1999 Exposure Draft that raised that issue did not provide any information that the Board had not already considered, the Board rejected the addition of enhanced disclosures as a viable alternative.

Not cost beneficial

B66. Some respondents cited cost-benefit considerations as a reason for retaining the pooling method. They argued that the pooling method is a quicker and less expensive way to account for a business combination because it does not require an entity to hire outside appraisers to value assets for accounting purposes.

B67. Other respondents favored eliminating the pooling method for cost-benefit reasons. Some argued that the pooling method causes preparers of financial statements, auditors, regulators, and others to spend unproductive time dealing with what they described as the detailed and somewhat illogical criteria required by Opinion 16 in attempts to have certain business combinations qualify for application of the pooling method. Others noted that using the purchase method of accounting for all business combinations would eliminate the enormous amount of interpretive guidance necessary to accommodate the pooling method. They also stated that the benefits derived from the purchase method as the only method of accounting for business combinations would significantly outweigh any issues that might arise from accounting for the very rare true merger or merger of equals by the purchase method.

B68. The Board addressed cost-benefit considerations in developing the 1999 Exposure Draft and concluded that a single method of accounting is preferable in light of those considerations because having more than one method would lead to higher costs associated with applying, auditing, enforcing, and analyzing the information produced by them. Cost-benefit considerations were thoroughly analyzed at that time and are discussed in paragraphs B225–B234. The Board concluded that those that favor retaining the pooling method on the basis of cost-benefit considerations did not provide any additional information that the Board did not consider previously.

Public policy not served by retention

B69. A number of respondents to the Invitation to Comment and the 1999 Exposure Draft argued that public policy considerations should dominate the Board's decisions. Some argued that eliminating the pooling method would require some investors to adjust to different measures of performance, potentially affecting market valuations adversely in certain industries during the transition period. Others argued that it would impede desirable consolidation in certain industries, reduce the amount of capital flowing into those industries, slow the development of new technology, and adversely affect entrepreneurial culture. Still others argued that eliminating the pooling method would remove a competitive advantage that U.S. companies have in competing with foreign companies for acquisitions and could impose a competitive disadvantage on them. Yet others argued that it would reduce the options available to certain regulatory agencies and possibly require regulated entities to maintain a second set of books. A few argued that elimination of the pooling method, by imposing an accounting hurdle on business combinations, would hinder obtaining the economic advantages afforded by the recently enacted Financial Services Reform Act in the United States that reforms the Glass-Steagall Act of 1933.

B70. Other respondents did not share those views. Some stated that because business combinations are driven by their underlying economics and not accounting considerations, economically sound deals would be completed regardless of the method used to account for them. Others noted that the financial community values business combinations in terms of their fair values rather than book values and, therefore, those transactions should initially be recognized in the financial statements at fair value.

B71. The Board has long held that accounting standards should not be slanted to favor one set of economic interests over another. For example, if accounting standards result in information that favors sellers in capital markets, those standards simultaneously disfavor buyers in those markets. If accounting standards were slanted, they would not be neutral, and the information that they produce would not be neutral. Consequently, financial reporting would not be fair and evenhanded and thus would lose its credibility.

B72. The Board noted that Concepts Statement 2 states that "neutrality means that either in formulating or implementing standards, the primary concern should be the relevance and reliability of the information that results, not the effect that the new rule may have on a particular interest" (paragraph 98). It goes on to explain that:

> Neutrality does not mean "without purpose," nor does it mean that accounting should be without influence on human behavior. Accounting information cannot avoid affecting behavior, nor should it. If it were otherwise, the information would be valueless—by definition, irrelevant—and the effort to produce it would be futile. It is, above all, the predetermination of a desired result, and the consequential selection of information to induce that result, that is the negation of neutrality in accounting. To be neutral, accounting information must report economic activity as faithfully as possible, without coloring the image it communicates for the purpose of influencing behavior in *some particular direction*. [Paragraph 100, emphasis in original.]

B73. Concepts Statement 2 acknowledges the argument that has been made against neutrality in accounting standards—that it may inhibit the FASB from working toward achieving public policy goals. However, the Board noted that that argument raises several issues. One is that there would have to be agreement on what those goals should be. Another is that since goals change with changes in government, questions would arise about the desirability or feasibility of changing accounting standards every time public policy changes. Moreover, to the extent that accounting standards become a means of facilitating or implementing public policy, the ability of those standards to help guide policy and measure its results is unavoidably diminished. For those reasons, the Board concluded that accounting standards should be neutral.

B74. Neutrality is also an essential component of the precepts that the Board follows in the conduct of its activities. One of those precepts, as stated in the FASB's mission statement, is as follows:

> *To be objective in its decision making* and to ensure, insofar as possible, the neutrality of

information resulting from its standards. To be neutral, information must report economic activity as faithfully as possible without coloring the image it communicates for the purpose of influencing behavior in any particular direction. [FASB *Rules of Procedure,* page 3]

B75. In the final analysis, the Board concluded that the accounting standards for business combinations should not seek to encourage or discourage business combinations. Instead, those standards should produce information about those combinations that is fair and evenhanded to those having opposing economic interests. The Board also concluded that those who argue for the pooling method on the basis that they believe that it fosters more combinations are not seeking to have neutral, evenhanded information disseminated.

B76. The Board carefully studied the responses to the 1999 Exposure Draft including those of respondents that favored retaining the pooling method on the basis of what they asserted to be public policy reasons. The information provided by those respondents did not cause the Board to change its view that its public policy goal is to issue accounting standards that result in neutral and representationally faithful financial information and that eliminating the pooling method is consistent with that goal.

Purchase method flaws remedied

B77. A number of respondents to the Invitation to Comment and the 1999 Exposure Draft indicated that the pooling method should be retained because of problems associated with the purchase method, particularly the requirement to recognize goodwill and subsequently amortize it in determining net income. Some argued that goodwill is not an asset and should not be recognized (and thus not amortized). Others argued that goodwill is an asset but not a wasting asset and thus should not be amortized. Still others argued that goodwill may be a wasting asset but that estimates of its useful life are inherently subjective. They argued that goodwill should be written off immediately in determining net income, other comprehensive income, or equity or, alternatively, that it should be assigned an arbitrary life that is both short and uniform and then amortized in determining net income, other comprehensive income, or equity. Yet others noted that reported earnings might be drastically affected by additional noncash charges for depreciation, depletion, and amortization that result from accounting for a business combination by the purchase method. However, most focused on the effects of goodwill amortization.

B78. The Board concluded that the concerns cited about the purchase method did not justify retaining the pooling method, as some had urged, and it affirmed its decision that the pooling method was so fundamentally flawed as to not warrant retention.

B79. For the reasons cited in paragraphs B36–B78, the Board concluded that the pooling method should not be used to account for any business combination.

Reasons for rejecting the fresh-start method

B80. Few of the respondents to the Invitation to Comment and the 1999 Exposure Draft that commented on the fresh-start method supported its use to account for any business combination. And, as noted previously, several respondents to that Exposure Draft stated that mergers of equals could be accounted for by either the pooling method or the fresh-start method but did not indicate which would be more appropriate or suggest criteria for making that determination.

B81. The Board acknowledged that a case can be made for using the fresh-start method to account for business combinations that are not acquisitions, which might be defined as transactions in which an acquiring entity cannot be identified or one in which the acquiring entity is substantially modified by the transaction. Under the fresh-start method, none of the combining entities are viewed as having survived the combination as an independent reporting entity. Rather, the combination is viewed as the transfer of the net assets of the combining entities to a new entity that assumes control over them, and the history of that new entity, by definition, begins with the combination.

B82. The Board noted that under the fresh-start method, the new entity has no history against which to compare itself and it is difficult to compare the results of the new entity with those of its predecessors for periods before the combination. Furthermore, new accounting guidance would have to be developed for implementing the method, and many unsettled aspects (such as whether goodwill should be recognized and how it should be measured) would have to be addressed before it could be applied.

B83. The Board noted that if the fresh-start method were to be applied only to those two-party combina-

tions in which an acquiring entity cannot be identified or the combining entities were equal in all respects, such combinations would be so rare—if they occurred at all—as to not justify the need for a new and separate method. The Board also noted that if the method also were to be applied to two-party combinations in which the acquiring entity is substantially modified, *substantially modified* would have to be defined, which would likely prove to be difficult to do in an unambiguous and nonarbitrary way. Moreover, those two-party combinations would be relatively few in number. Furthermore, the method may offer the potential for accounting arbitrage because the financial statement results it produces are apt to differ significantly from those that the purchase method produces.

B84. The Board concluded that the advantages of using the fresh-start method for two-party combinations such as those discussed in paragraph B81 (primarily enhanced representational faithfulness) were outweighed by the disadvantages of having two methods of accounting (particularly the potential for accounting arbitrage but also the difficulties of drawing unambiguous and nonarbitrary boundaries between the methods). The Board further concluded that an alternative to the purchase method of accounting for those combinations was not needed because it is possible to apply the purchase method to them.

B85. The Board observed that the fresh-start method might be appropriate for certain multi-party combinations. However, as discussed in paragraph B32, the Board noted that those transactions are generally accounted for by the purchase method and it decided not to change that practice at this time. Also as discussed in paragraph B32, the Board intends to consider whether joint venture formations and multi-party business combinations that are not acquisitions should be accounted for by the fresh-start method rather than by the purchase method.

Acquisition of Noncontrolling Interests in a Subsidiary

B86. As it did prior to issuing the 1999 Exposure Draft, the Board concluded that this Statement should continue the practice established in Opinion 16 of accounting for the acquisition of noncontrolling interests in a subsidiary (commonly referred to as minority interests) using the purchase method. The Board intends to consider the accounting for those transactions in another project. The

Board also noted that those deliberations might be affected by conclusions reached in its liabilities and equity project. In the development of the October 2000 FASB Exposure Draft, *Accounting for Financial Instruments with Characteristics of Liabilities, Equity, or Both,* the Board concluded that (a) noncontrolling interests in a subsidiary should be reported in consolidated financial statements as a separate component of equity and (b) distributions to holders of instruments that are classified as equity should be recognized as equity distributions. If the Board affirms those provisions in its redeliberations of that Exposure Draft, it will consider whether the acquisition of a minority interest should be accounted for as an equity distribution rather than by the purchase method.

Application of the Purchase Method

Accounting for asset acquisitions—general concepts

B87. In reaching the conclusion that the purchase method should be used to account for all business combinations, the Board affirmed the basic principles of historical-cost accounting included in paragraphs 66–69 of Opinion 16. Specifically, the Board affirmed that an asset acquisition should be measured on the basis of the values exchanged and that measurement of the values exchanged should be based on the fair value of the consideration given or the fair value of the net assets acquired, whichever is more reliably measurable. The Board also affirmed that when groups of assets are acquired, the value of the asset (or net asset) group as a whole should be allocated to the individual assets (or assets and liabilities) that make up the group on the basis of their fair values. Accordingly, this Statement carries forward from Opinion 16 those general principles; however, those principles have been rephrased as general concepts so that they can be understood in the context of this Statement.

Identifying the acquiring entity

B88. The Board's decision that all business combinations in the scope of this Statement should be accounted for by the purchase method means that the acquiring entity must be identified in every business combination. One of the issues raised in the Invitation to Comment focused on situations in which identifying the acquiring entity is difficult. Most of the respondents that commented on that issue sug-

gested that the Board develop additional criteria for identifying the acquiring entity.

B89. In developing the 1999 Exposure Draft, the Board affirmed the guidance in Opinion 16 that states that in a business combination effected solely through the distribution of cash or other assets or by incurring liabilities, the entity that distributes cash or other assets or assumes or incurs liabilities is the acquiring entity. The Board considered a variety of suggestions made by respondents to the Invitation to Comment on factors that should be considered in applying the purchase method to situations in which the acquiring entity cannot be as readily identified. The guidance proposed in the 1999 Exposure Draft reflected the Board's conclusion that all pertinent facts and circumstances should be considered when identifying the acquiring entity, particularly the relative voting rights in the combined entity after the combination. That proposed guidance stated that in determining which shareholder group retained or received the larger portion of the voting rights in the combined entity, the existence of any unusual or special voting arrangements, and options, warrants, or convertible securities should be considered. The proposed guidance also reflected the Board's conclusion that consideration also should be given to factors related to the composition of the board of directors and senior management of the combined entity and that those factors should be weighted equally with the factors related to voting rights.

B90. The respondents to the 1999 Exposure Draft that commented on the proposed criteria for identifying the acquiring entity generally agreed that they were appropriate. Some of those respondents said that the guidance proposed in that Exposure Draft was an improvement over Opinion 16 because it provided additional factors to consider in determining which shareholder group retained or received the larger share of the voting rights in the combined entity. However, many of the respondents suggested improvements to the proposed criteria and some suggested that the Board consider other criteria.

B91. Several respondents to the 1999 Exposure Draft suggested that the Board retain the presumptive approach in Opinion 16 for identifying the acquiring entity in transactions effected through an exchange of equity interests. That approach presumes that absent evidence to the contrary, the acquiring entity is the combining entity whose owners as a group retain or receive the larger share of the voting rights in the combined entity. Other respondents suggested that the factors to be considered in identifying the acquiring entity should be provided in the form of a hierarchy. Some of those respondents also suggested that the Board provide additional guidance explaining how factors relating to voting rights (unusual special voting arrangements and options, warrants, or convertible securities) would affect the determination of the acquiring entity.

B92. The Board carefully considered those suggestions. However, the Board observed, as it did in developing the 1999 Exposure Draft, that each business combination is unique and, therefore, the facts and circumstances relevant to identifying the acquiring entity in one combination may be less relevant in another. The Board affirmed its conclusion that this Statement should not retain the presumptive approach in Opinion 16 nor provide hierarchical guidance. The Board concluded that doing so would imply that some factors are more important in identifying the acquiring entity than others. However, as suggested by respondents, the Board decided to modify the guidance proposed in the 1999 Exposure Draft to explain how some of the factors influence the identification of the acquiring entity.

B93. In developing the 1999 Exposure Draft, the Board decided not to require consideration of the payment of a premium over the market value of the equity securities acquired as evidence of the identity of the acquiring entity. The Board observed that while that criterion would be a useful indicator, it would be difficult to evaluate when quoted market prices are not available for the equity securities exchanged. A number of respondents to the 1999 Exposure Draft said that the payment of a premium is a strong indicator of the identity of the acquirer. Upon reconsideration, the Board decided that this Statement would include the payment of a premium as a criterion to be considered in identifying the acquirer, but only when the equity securities exchanged in a business combination are traded in a public market.

B94. Some respondents to the Invitation to Comment and the 1999 Exposure Draft suggested that the relative market capitalizations and relative net asset sizes of the combining entities also should be considered when identifying the acquiring entity. The Board noted, however, that entities could engage in various transactions in contemplation of a business combination, such as asset dispositions and treasury stock transactions. Those transactions would result in different market capitalizations and net asset sizes than those that existed before the combination was con-

templated. The Board also noted that assessing relative net assets on the basis of precombination carrying amounts would be inappropriate, while assessing them on the basis of fair values could entail significant cost. Thus, although those factors may in some cases provide evidence as to which entity is the acquiring entity, the Board concluded that consideration of those factors should not be required in all combinations.

B95. In developing the 1999 Exposure Draft, the Board observed that identifying the acquirer might be difficult in some multi-party business combinations, particularly those combinations that might not be acquisitions but are to be accounted for as such under this Statement. In the basis for conclusions to that Exposure Draft, the Board noted that in those circumstances it might be helpful to consider additional factors such as which of the entities initiated the combination and whether the reported amounts of assets, revenues, and earnings of one of the combining entities significantly exceed those of the others. In response to suggestions made by respondents to the 1999 Exposure Draft, the Board decided to include that guidance in the standards section of this Statement.

B96. In addition, as suggested by respondents, the Board decided that this Statement should explicitly state that in some business combinations, such as those described as "reverse acquisitions," the entity that issues the equity interests may not be the acquiring entity for financial reporting purposes.

Determining the cost of the acquired entity and date of acquisition

B97. The Board decided that this Statement would carry forward without reconsideration the provisions of Opinion 16 related to determining the cost of the acquired entity and the date of acquisition. The Board intends to reconsider some or all of that guidance in its separate project focused on issues related to the application of the purchase method.

B98. The Board recognizes that this Statement carries forward from Opinion 16 contradictory guidance about the date that should be used to value equity interests issued to effect a business combination. Paragraph 74 of Opinion 16, carried forward in paragraph 22, states that the market price for a reasonable period before and after the date the terms of the acquisition are agreed to and announced should be considered in determining the fair value of the securities issued. However, paragraph 94 of Opinion 16, carried forward in paragraph 49, states that the cost of an acquired entity should be determined as of the date of acquisition. Paragraph 48 defines that date as the date that assets are received and other assets are given, liabilities are assumed or incurred, or equity interests are issued. The Board decided to defer resolution of that apparent contradiction to its project on issues related to the application of the purchase method. Therefore, this Statement does not change the status of the guidance in EITF Issue No. 99-12, "Determination of the Measurement Date for the Market Price of Acquirer Securities Issued in a Purchase Business Combination," or EITF Topic No. D-87, "Determination of the Measurement Date for Consideration Given by the Acquirer in a Business Combination When That Consideration is Securities Other Than Those Issued by the Acquirer." This Statement also does not change the status of the guidance of other EITF issues interpreting the provisions of Opinion 16 related to determining the cost of the acquired entity.

Allocating the cost of the acquired entity

B99. In developing this Statement, the Board affirmed the basic principle set forth in Opinion 16 that the cost of an asset group should be allocated to the individual assets (or assets and liabilities) that make up the group on the basis of their fair values. However, the Board decided that this project would reconsider several aspects of the Opinion 16 guidance related to the allocation of the cost of an acquired entity in a business combination. As described in paragraphs B101–B146, the Board affirmed the requirement in Opinion 16 that the excess of the cost of an acquired entity over the net of the amounts assigned to assets acquired and liabilities assumed should be recognized as an asset referred to as goodwill. The Board decided to change the requirements in Opinion 16 for determining whether an acquired intangible asset should be recognized as an asset apart from goodwill (refer to paragraphs B147–B170). The Board also reconsidered and decided to change the guidance in Opinion 16 related to the accounting for the excess of the fair value of net assets acquired over the cost of an acquired entity (commonly referred to as negative goodwill) (refer to paragraphs B187–B193).

B100. The Board decided that this Statement should carry forward, without reconsideration, the general guidance in Opinion 16 for assigning amounts to assets acquired and liabilities assumed (paragraph 88 of that Opinion). The Board recognizes that some of that guidance may be inconsistent with the term *fair value* as defined in this Statement. For example, uncertainties about the collectibility of accounts or loans receivable would affect their fair value. If accounts or loans receivable were assigned an amount equal to their fair value, there would be no need to separately recognize an allowance for uncollectible accounts as stated in paragraph 37(b). The Board decided, however, that it would consider those inconsistencies in a separate project on issues related to the application of the purchase method.

Excess of cost over the fair value of acquired net assets (goodwill)

B101. For the reasons described in paragraphs B102–B139, the Board affirmed the conclusion expressed in both the 1999 Exposure Draft and the 2001 Exposure Draft that goodwill meets the assets definition in FASB Concepts Statement No. 6, *Elements of Financial Statements,* and the asset recognition criteria in FASB Concepts Statement No. 5, *Recognition and Measurement in Financial Statements of Business Enterprises.* Most respondents to those Exposure Drafts agreed with that conclusion. Generally, those in agreement said that goodwill is an asset because future benefits are expected from it in conjunction with the future benefits expected from other assets and that the consideration paid is evidence of the existence of that asset. Many of those respondents referred to goodwill as a special type of asset—one that cannot be separated from the other net assets of an entity.

The nature of goodwill

B102. As described in the 1999 Exposure Draft and the 2001 Exposure Draft, the amount that in practice has been recognized as goodwill includes the following six components:

- Component 1—The excess of the fair values over the book values of the acquired entity's net assets at the date of acquisition.
- Component 2—The fair values of other net assets that had not been recognized by the acquired entity at the date of acquisition. They may not have been recognized because they failed to meet the recognition criteria (perhaps because of measurement difficulties), because of a requirement that prohibited their recognition, or because the entity concluded that the costs of recognizing them separately were not justified by the benefits.

- Component 3—The fair value of the "going-concern" element of the acquired entity's existing business. The going-concern element represents the ability of the established business to earn a higher rate of return on an assembled collection of net assets than would be expected if those net assets had to be acquired separately. That value stems from the synergies of the net assets of the business, as well as from other benefits (such as factors related to market imperfections, including the ability to earn monopoly profits and barriers to market entry—either legal or because of transaction costs—by potential competitors).
- Component 4—The fair value of the expected synergies and other benefits from combining the acquiring entity's and acquired entity's net assets and businesses. Those synergies and other benefits are unique to each combination, and different combinations would produce different synergies and, hence, different values.
- Component 5—Overvaluation of the consideration paid by the acquiring entity stemming from errors in valuing the consideration tendered. Although the purchase price in an all-cash transaction would not be subject to measurement error, the same may not necessarily be said of a transaction involving the acquiring entity's equity interests. For example, if the number of common shares being traded daily is small relative to the number of shares issued in the combination, imputing the current market price to all of the shares issued to effect the combination may produce a higher value than those shares would produce if they were sold for cash and the cash then used to effect the combination.
- Component 6—Overpayment or underpayment by the acquiring entity. Overpayment might occur, for example, if the price is driven up in the course of bidding for the acquired entity, while underpayment may occur in the case of a distress sale or fire sale.

B103. The Board continues to believe that the following analysis of those components is useful in understanding the nature of goodwill. The first two components, both of which relate to the acquired entity, conceptually are not part of goodwill. The first component is not an asset in and of itself but instead reflects gains that were not recognized by the acquired entity on its net assets. As such, that component is part of those assets rather than part of goodwill. The second component also is not part of goodwill conceptually; it primarily reflects intangible assets that might be recognized as individual assets.

B104. The fifth and sixth components, both of which relate to the acquiring entity, also are not conceptually part of goodwill. The fifth component is not an asset in and of itself or even part of an asset but, rather, is a measurement error. The sixth component also is not an asset; conceptually it represents a loss (in the case of overpayment) or a gain (in the case of underpayment) to the acquiring entity. Thus, neither of those components is conceptually part of goodwill.

B105. As the Board noted in both the 1999 Exposure Draft and the 2001 Exposure Draft, the third and fourth components *are* conceptually part of goodwill. The third component relates to the acquired entity and reflects the excess assembled value of the acquired entity's net assets. It represents the preexisting goodwill that was either internally generated by the acquired entity or acquired by it in prior business combinations. The fourth component relates to the acquired entity and acquiring entity jointly and reflects the excess assembled value that is created by the combination—the synergies that are expected from combining those businesses. The Board described the third and fourth components collectively as "core goodwill."

B106. Consistent with both the 1999 Exposure Draft and the 2001 Exposure Draft, this Statement calls for efforts to avoid subsuming the first, second, and fifth components of goodwill into the amount initially recognized as goodwill. Specifically, an acquiring entity is required to make every effort to (a) measure the purchase consideration accurately (eliminating or reducing component 5), (b) record the net assets acquired at their fair values rather than their carrying amounts (eliminating or reducing component 1), and (c) recognize all acquired intangible assets meeting the criteria in paragraph 39 of this Statement so that they are not subsumed into the amount initially recognized as goodwill (reducing component 2).

Whether goodwill meets the assets definition

B107. Opinion 16 defined goodwill as the "excess of the cost of the acquired company over the sum of the amounts assigned to identifiable assets acquired less liabilities assumed" (paragraph 87). That definition describes how the cost of goodwill should be calculated rather than explaining what goodwill is or what it represents. As such, it confuses the substance of goodwill with how goodwill is to be measured.

B108. Opinion 16 was adopted in August 1970, at a time when the APB was developing its own definition of assets. However, that definition has been replaced by the FASB's definition, which is the benchmark against which goodwill should be judged.

B109. According to Concepts Statement 6:

> Assets are probable future economic benefits obtained or controlled by a particular entity as a result of past transactions or events. [Paragraph 25; footnote reference omitted.]

The footnote to that paragraph points out that "*probable* is used with its usual general meaning, rather than in a specific accounting or technical sense (such as that in FASB Statement No. 5, *Accounting for Contingencies,* par. 3), and refers to that which can reasonably be expected or believed on the basis of available evidence or logic but is neither certain nor proved. . . ."

B110. Concepts Statement 6 further explains that:

> An asset has three essential characteristics: (a) it embodies a probable future benefit that involves a capacity, singly or in combination with other assets, to contribute directly or indirectly to future net cash inflows, (b) a particular entity can obtain the benefit and control others' access to it, and (c) the transaction or other event giving rise to the entity's right to or control of the benefit has already occurred. [paragraph 26]

Because the question of whether goodwill meets the assets definition depends on whether core goodwill possesses each of those three essential characteristics, the Board considered it in the context of each of those characteristics.

Future Economic Benefit

B111. Concepts Statement 6 states that:

> Future economic benefit is the essence of an asset. . . . An asset has the capacity to serve the entity by being exchanged for something else of value to the entity, by being used to produce something of value to the entity, or by being used to settle its liabilities. [paragraph 172]

The Board noted that goodwill cannot be exchanged for something else of value to the entity, nor can it be used to settle the entity's liabilities. Goodwill also lacks the capacity singly to produce future net cash inflows, although it can—in combination with other assets—produce cash flows. As a result, the future benefit associated with goodwill generally is more nebulous and may be less certain than the benefit that is associated with most other assets.

B112. Concepts Statement 6 states that "the most obvious evidence of future economic benefit is a market price" (paragraph 173). Because goodwill does not have the capacity to contribute directly to future net cash inflows, it is not priced separately in the marketplace, but rather is priced in combination with other assets with which it produces future net cash inflows. That capacity is reflected by the premium that an entity as a whole commands in comparison to the sum of the fair values of its component parts.

B113. The Board concluded that although goodwill is not priced separately, that does not preclude it from having future economic benefit. In that regard, Concepts Statement 6 states that "anything that is commonly bought and sold has future economic benefit, including the individual items that a buyer obtains and is willing to pay for in a 'basket purchase' of several items or in a business combination" (paragraph 173).

B114. The Board observed that the premium associated with goodwill may be reflected in several ways. One way is based on the market capitalization of the acquired entity as a stand-alone entity, with the premium over the sum of the fair values of the identifiable net assets reflecting the "going concern" element of the business. Another way is by the takeover premium, the price that the acquired entity as a whole commands as a target, which often is considerably higher than its market capitalization on a stand-alone basis, and reflects the synergies arising out of the combination.

Control

B115. In addition to having future economic benefit, there must be control over that benefit if goodwill is to meet the definition of assets. The Board concluded that control is provided by means of the acquiring entity's ability to direct the policies and management of the acquired entity.

Past Transaction or Event

B116. The control over future economic benefit must also result from a past transaction or event if goodwill is to meet the definition of assets. The Board concluded that the past transaction or event is the transaction in which the controlling interest was obtained by the acquiring entity.

Opposing Views

B117. Some respondents to the 1999 Exposure Draft and the 2001 Exposure Draft expressed opposing views about whether goodwill meets the assets definition. Some argued that goodwill is not an asset because that conclusion would equate costs with assets. Concepts Statement 6 states that "although an entity normally incurs costs to acquire or use assets, costs incurred are not themselves assets. The essence of an asset is its future economic benefit rather than whether or not it was acquired at a cost" (paragraph 179). It further states that ". . . since an entity commonly obtains assets by incurring costs, incurrence of a cost may be evidence that an entity has acquired one or more assets, but it is not conclusive evidence. . . . The ultimate evidence of the existence of assets is the future economic benefit, not the costs incurred" (paragraph 180). Thus, the Board rejected that argument because it concluded that goodwill has future economic benefit.

B118. Other respondents argued that goodwill does not meet the assets definition because it cannot be sold apart from the business. Under that view, assets that are not cash or contractual claims to cash or services must be capable of being sold separately for cash, and thus exchangeability is an essential characteristic. In that regard, the Board noted that Concepts Statement 6 expressly considers the matter of exchangeability, noting that, in addition to the three essential characteristics described above:

> Assets commonly have other features that help identify them—for example, assets may be acquired at a cost and they may be tangible, exchangeable, or legally enforceable. However, those features are not essential characteristics of assets. Their absence, by itself, is not sufficient to preclude an item's qualifying as an asset. That is, assets may be acquired without cost, they may be intangible, and although not exchangeable they may be usable by the entity in producing or distributing other goods or services. [Paragraph 26; footnote reference omitted.]

B119. Concepts Statement 6 noted that absence of exchangeability of an asset may create recognition and measurement problems, "but it in no way ne-

gates future economic benefit that can be obtained . . ." (footnote 62). Thus, exchangeability is expressly ruled out as an element of the assets definition, and so the Board rejected that argument.

Initial recognition of goodwill as an asset

B120. Paragraph 63 of Concepts Statement 5 contains four fundamental recognition criteria that apply to all recognition decisions:

a. Definitions—The item meets the definition of an element of financial statements.
b. Measurability—It has a relevant attribute measurable with sufficient reliability.
c. Relevance—The information about it has the potential to make a difference in user decisions.
d. Reliability—The information is representationally faithful, verifiable, and neutral.

An item meeting those criteria should be recognized in the financial statements, subject to a cost-benefit constraint and a materiality threshold.

Definition

B121. Based on its analysis, the Board concluded that core goodwill meets the assets definition in Concepts Statement 6, thereby leaving the criteria of measurability, relevance, and reliability to be considered.

Measurability

B122. Because the scope of the business combinations project focuses only on goodwill that is acquired in conjunction with a business combination, the Board noted that the cost incurred in the combination transaction provides the basis for initially measuring goodwill.

B123. The Board questioned whether goodwill should be initially recognized as an asset because of concerns about its measurability, since it is not exchangeable separate from other assets of the entity. The Board's concerns focused on the ability to measure goodwill both initially, based on the combination transaction, and subsequent to that transaction. However, the Board acknowledged that exchangeability is not a criterion of the assets definition in Concepts Statement 6 and that even though assets like goodwill may be more difficult to measure than other assets, measurement would be possible.

B124. The Board also noted that the measurement of goodwill is complicated by the potential that some or all of components 1, 2, 5, or 6 (identified in paragraph B102) might be included. However, the Board concluded that including those components in the measurement of goodwill is preferable to not recording goodwill at all.

B125. The Board further noted that measuring goodwill subsequent to its initial recognition is complicated by difficulties in determining its consumption or decline in value. However, the Board concluded that such difficulties are not unique to goodwill.

B126. The Board concluded that the measurability criterion is met, although not as readily as with many other assets, particularly with respect to measurement after initial recognition.

Relevance

B127. In assessing whether information about goodwill is relevant, the Board considered the views of users as reported by the AICPA Special Committee[33] and as expressed by the Financial Accounting Policy Committee (FAPC) of the Association for Investment Management and Research (AIMR) in its 1993 position paper, *Financial Reporting in the 1990s and Beyond.* The Board observed that users have mixed views about whether goodwill should be recognized as an asset. While some are troubled by the lack of comparability between internally generated goodwill and acquired goodwill that results under present standards, others do not appear to be particularly bothered by it. However, users appear to be reluctant to give up information about the cost of goodwill that is acquired in conjunction with a business combination and measured as part of the transaction price. In the view of the AICPA Special Committee, users want to retain the option of being able to use that information. Similarly, the FAPC stated that the amount paid for goodwill should be reported.

B128. The Board also considered the growing use of "economic value added" (EVA)[34] and similar measures, which increasingly are being employed as means of assessing performance. The Board observed that such measures commonly incorporate goodwill, and in the case of business combinations that are accounted for by the pooling method, an adjustment is commonly made to incorporate a measure of the goodwill that would not be recognized under that method. As a result, the aggregate amount of goodwill is included in the base that is subject to a capital charge that is part of the EVA measure, and management is held accountable for the total investment in the acquired entities.

B129. The Board also considered evidence about the relevance of goodwill that has been provided by a number of recent research studies that empirically examined the relationship between goodwill and the market value of business entities.[35] Those studies generally found a positive relationship between the reported goodwill of entities and their market values, thereby indicating that investors in the markets behave as if they view goodwill as an asset. For those reasons, the Board concluded that the relevance criterion is met.

Reliability

B130. According to Concepts Statement 2, to be reliable, information about an item must be representationally faithful, verifiable, and neutral. It must also be sufficiently faithful in its representation of the underlying resource and sufficiently free of error and bias to be useful to investors, creditors, and others in making decisions. Thus, for an asset to be recognized, information about the existence and amount of an asset must be reliable.

B131. Concepts Statement 2 states that "representational faithfulness is correspondence or agreement between a measure or description and the phenomenon it purports to represent" (paragraph 63). Thus, to the extent that recorded goodwill consists of the

[33]AICPA Special Committee on Financial Reporting, *Improving Business Reporting—A Customer Focus* (New York: AICPA, 1994).

[34]EVA was developed by the consulting firm of Stern Stewart & Company (and is a registered trademark of Stern Stewart) as a financial performance measure that improves management's ability to make decisions that enhance shareholder value.

[35]Refer to, for example, Eli Amir, Trevor S. Harris, and Elizabeth K. Venuti, "A Comparison of the Value-Relevance of U.S. versus Non-U.S. GAAP Accounting Measures Using Form 20-F Reconciliations," *Journal of Accounting Research,* Supplement (1993): 230–264; Mary Barth and Greg Clinch, "International Accounting Differences and Their Relation to Share Prices: Evidence from U.K., Australian and Canadian Firms," *Contemporary Accounting Research* (spring 1996): 135–170; Keith W. Chauvin and Mark Hirschey, "Goodwill, Profitability, and the Market Value of the Firm," *Journal of Accounting and Public Policy* (summer 1994): 159–180; Ross Jennings, John Robinson, Robert B. Thompson, and Linda Duvall, "The Relation between Accounting Goodwill Numbers and Equity Values," *Journal of Business Finance and Accounting* (June 1996): 513–533; and Mark G. McCarthy and Douglas K. Schneider, "Market Perception of Goodwill: Some Empirical Evidence," *Accounting and Business Research* (winter 1995): 69–81.

excess of fair values over book values of the acquired entity's net assets (component 1) or the fair values of unrecorded net assets of the acquired entity (component 2), it is not representationally faithful. However, the Board observed that this Statement contains guidance aimed at minimizing the inclusion of those components in the amount recorded for goodwill. Moreover, any problem that would result from their inclusion is limited to mislabeling items that are all assets of some kind, which is not as serious as labeling expenses or losses as assets, in which case the amount reported for total assets would not be representationally faithful.

B132. Alternatively, recorded goodwill might include overvaluation of the consideration paid by the acquiring entity (component 5) or overpayment by the acquiring entity (component 6). To the extent that goodwill includes those components, it is including items that are not assets at all. Thus, including them in the asset described as goodwill would not be representationally faithful, nor would the amount reported for total assets be representationally faithful because it would include amounts that are not assets. The Board noted that that would constitute a more serious breach of representational faithfulness than would including components 1 or 2.

B133. However, the Board observed that it may be difficult to determine the cost attributable to each item in a basket purchase and that the acquisition cost may be difficult to determine if equity interests were used to acquire the basket of assets. The problem thus is not unique to the accounting for goodwill in conjunction with business combinations, but arises in many other situations as well. That indicates that representational faithfulness or reliability of measurement in accounting is often not an absolute, but rather one of degree.

B134. While there may be difficulties of representational faithfulness in recognizing most or all of an acquisition premium as an asset labeled goodwill for the reasons cited above, the Board observed that there are corresponding difficulties in the alternative of writing it off immediately as an expense or loss. That is because, to the extent that recorded goodwill consists of what conceptually is goodwill (components 3 and 4) and other assets (components 1 and 2), depicting those assets as expenses or losses is not representationally faithful either.

B135. Indeed, to the extent that recorded goodwill consists primarily of core goodwill and other assets,

the Board observed that writing it off as an expense or loss would be less representationally faithful than recognizing it as an asset, particularly at the date of the business combination. Treating an item that primarily is an asset as an expense or loss may be said to reflect bias, which Concepts Statement 2 described as "the tendency of a measure to fall more often on one side than the other of what it represents instead of being equally likely to fall on either side. Bias in accounting measures means a tendency to be consistently too high or too low" (paragraph 77). Accordingly, the Board concluded that the reliability criterion is met.

Opposing Views

B136. Some of the respondents to the 1999 Exposure Draft and the 2001 Exposure Draft argued that goodwill should be written off immediately to earnings, other comprehensive income, or equity on the basis that goodwill does not meet the assets definition or the other criteria for initial recognition. Others argued that writing goodwill off immediately would eliminate much of the difference between the financial statements of entities that grow by acquisitions and those that grow internally and would be preferable to the alternative of capitalizing internally generated goodwill. The Board observed those views in reaching its tentative decision that goodwill should be recognized as an asset and again in certain of the responses to the Invitation to Comment that expressed disagreement with that tentative decision.

B137. In its redeliberations of the 1999 Exposure Draft, the Board affirmed its observation that goodwill does meet the assets definition and the other criteria for initial recognition and, therefore, writing it off immediately to earnings or other comprehensive income would not be representationally faithful. The Board also affirmed its observation that charging it off to equity directly without flowing through earnings or other comprehensive income could only be interpreted conceptually as a distribution to owners.

B138. The Board acknowledged that recognizing only goodwill acquired in a business combination and not goodwill that is generated internally results in differences in financial statements that make comparison more difficult. However, as it did in developing the 1999 Exposure Draft and the 2001 Exposure Draft, the Board concluded that the differences in accounting between acquired goodwill and internally generated goodwill are not unique as they also arise between other assets that are acquired and those that are internally generated.

B139. The Board also observed the potential for accounting arbitrage that might accompany a requirement that goodwill be written off immediately while other components of the acquisition premium could not be similarly written off. That sharply different treatment would provide incentives for entities to allocate more of the premium to goodwill and less to other assets in order to enhance future earnings by avoiding the future charges against earnings related to those assets.

Initial measurement of goodwill

B140. In developing the 1999 Exposure Draft, the Board observed that because goodwill cannot be purchased separately but only as part of business combination transactions, those transactions are necessarily the basis for initially measuring it. As such, difficulties associated with measuring the acquisition cost in those transactions can have a direct effect on the measurement of goodwill.

B141. Difficulties in measuring acquisition costs in a business combination relate largely to the nature of the consideration tendered. Concepts Statement 2 acknowledged that, stating, "The acquisition cost may also be difficult to determine if assets are acquired . . . by issuing stock . . ." (paragraph 65). Although the acquisition costs in all-cash transactions are not difficult to measure, the Board noted the potential for overvaluation (component 5) when the consideration consists wholly or partially of shares of the acquiring entity's stock.

B142. The Board also noted that that difficulty is not unique to the measurement of goodwill, however, and extends to all the net assets acquired in a business combination in which the consideration involves equity interests of the acquiring entity. It also is not unique to business combinations and extends to any transaction in which assets or groups of assets are acquired in exchange for equity interests of the acquiring entity. However, the Board acknowledged that the effects of those difficulties would be more pronounced for goodwill than for other assets and liabilities, since it is measured as a residual of the acquisition cost incurred.

B143. The Board also observed that even if the acquisition cost can be measured without difficulty, difficulties may arise in assigning that cost to the individual net assets acquired in the "basket purchase," including goodwill. Although measuring some items acquired in a basket purchase is less difficult than measuring other items, particularly if they are exchangeable and traded regularly in the marketplace (or otherwise routinely obtained in transactions other than a business combination), that is not the case with goodwill, since it is not exchangeable. However, many other assets acquired in a business combination—especially many intangible assets—are not traded regularly or otherwise routinely obtained in other transactions. As a result, assigning a portion of the cost of the acquisition to goodwill is not necessarily more difficult than it is for those other assets.

B144. Despite those difficulties, the Board believes that knowledgeable users of financial statements can and do understand the limitations inherent in accounting for goodwill. The Board also believes that users are generally familiar with and understand the present requirements in Opinion 16 for initially measuring purchased goodwill.

B145. The Board therefore concluded that the approach to initial measurement of goodwill that is taken in Opinion 16 is appropriate and that no other alternative identified would be a significant improvement. The Board expressed concern about measuring goodwill as a residual but acknowledged that there is no other real measurement alternative, since goodwill is not separable from the entity or exchangeable.

B146. Accordingly, the 1999 Exposure Draft and the 2001 Exposure Draft proposed that goodwill should be measured initially as the excess of the cost of the acquired entity over the fair value of the net assets acquired, consistent with the requirements of Opinion 16. In that regard, the Board noted that acquiring entities should make every effort (a) to measure the purchase consideration accurately, (b) to record the fair values rather than the book values of net assets acquired, and (c) to ensure that all intangible assets not previously recorded are recorded so that those items are not included in what is recognized as goodwill. Few respondents to those Exposure Drafts commented on that requirement or suggested alternative measurement approaches. The Board affirmed that requirement in its redeliberations.

Initial recognition and measurement of intangible assets other than goodwill

Definition of intangible assets

B147. In the deliberations that led to the 1999 Exposure Draft, the Board concluded that the characteristics that distinguish intangible assets from other assets are that they are (a) without physical substance, (b) not financial instruments, and (c) not current assets. The 1999 Exposure Draft defined intangible assets in terms of those characteristics. Several respondents to that Exposure Draft noted that some intangible assets (such as order or production backlogs) are current assets. They observed that some might interpret the proposed definition in the 1999 Exposure Draft as prohibiting recognition of those intangible assets apart from goodwill, which they believed was not the Board's intent. The Board agreed with those respondents and decided that this Statement should define intangible assets more broadly, that is, as assets (not including financial assets) that lack physical substance.

Distinguishing intangible assets from goodwill

B148. At the inception of this project, the Board observed that intangible assets make up an increasing proportion of the assets of many (if not most) entities. The Board also observed that intangible assets acquired in a business combination often were included in the amount recognized as goodwill, despite the provisions in Opinion 16 that required they be recognized apart from goodwill.

B149. For two primary reasons, the Board concluded that this Statement should provide explicit criteria for determining whether an acquired intangible asset should be recognized apart from goodwill. First, the Board affirmed the conclusion it reached prior to issuance of the 1999 Exposure Draft that the decision usefulness of financial statements would be enhanced if intangible assets acquired in a business combination were distinguished from goodwill. As stated in Concepts Statement 5:

> Classification in financial statements facilitates analysis by grouping items with essentially similar characteristics and separating items with essentially different characteristics. Analysis aimed at objectives such as predicting amounts, timing, and uncertainty of future cash flows requires financial information segregated into reasonably homog-

enous groups. For example, components of financial statements that consist of items that have similar characteristics in one or more respects, such as continuity or recurrence, stability, risk, and reliability, are likely to have more predictive value than if their characteristics are dissimilar. [paragraph 20]

B150. Second, for several Board members, having explicit criteria that determine whether an acquired intangible asset should be recognized apart from goodwill was important to their decision that goodwill is an indefinite-lived asset that should no longer be amortized. Absent such criteria, many more finite-lived intangible assets would be included in the amount recognized as goodwill.

B151. In developing the 1999 Exposure Draft, the Board considered various characteristics that might distinguish other intangible assets from goodwill. Based on the Board's conclusion that identifiability is the characteristic that conceptually distinguishes other intangible assets from goodwill, the 1999 Exposure Draft proposed that intangible assets that are identifiable and reliably measurable should be recognized as assets apart from goodwill. Most respondents to the 1999 Exposure Draft agreed that many intangible assets are identifiable and that various intangible assets are reliably measurable. Many of those respondents generally agreed that the proposed recognition criteria would improve the transparency of financial reporting for business combinations—a primary objective of this project. However, respondents' views on the proposed recognition criteria varied. Many of those respondents suggested alternative recognition criteria and many urged the Board to clarify the term *reliably measurable*.

B152. The Board considered those suggestions and decided to modify the proposed recognition criteria to provide a clearer distinction between intangible assets that should be recognized apart from goodwill and those that should be subsumed into goodwill. The 2001 Exposure Draft reflected the Board's conclusion that an intangible asset should be recognized apart from goodwill if it meets the asset recognition criteria in Concepts Statement 5 and if either (a) control over the future economic benefits of the asset results from contractual or other legal rights (the contractual-legal criterion) or (b) the intangible asset is capable of being separated or divided and sold, transferred, licensed, rented, or exchanged (either separately or as part of a group of assets) (the separability criterion). The Board concluded that sufficient information should exist to reliably measure the fair value of that asset if an asset has an underlying contractual or legal basis or if it is capable of being separated from the entity. Thus, the change in the recognition criteria eliminated the need to explicitly include reliably measurable as a recognition criterion or to clarify the meaning of that term.

B153. In developing those recognition criteria, the Board acknowledged that they would result in some finite-lived intangible assets being subsumed into the amount initially recognized as goodwill. The Board concluded, however, that the advantages of the revised criteria (in particular, greater consistency in their application) outweighed the disadvantages of recognizing some finite-lived intangible assets as part of goodwill.

B154. Most of the respondents to the 2001 Exposure Draft that commented on the revised recognition criteria agreed that they were an improvement over the recognition criteria proposed in the 1999 Exposure Draft. However, some of those respondents suggested alternative recognition criteria or made other suggestions. Many of those alternative recognition criteria were similar to the suggestions made by respondents to the 1999 Exposure Draft. Paragraphs B155–B164 describe the Board's reasons for accepting some suggestions made by respondents and rejecting others.

B155. The 2001 Exposure Draft proposed that an intangible asset would need to meet the asset recognition criteria in Concepts Statement 5 in order to be recognized apart from goodwill. Several respondents to that Exposure Draft said that inclusion of that criterion was inconsistent with the Board's stated presumption that an intangible asset that meets the contractual-legal criterion or the separability criterion also would meet the asset recognition criteria. The Board agreed with those respondents that it was not necessary to explicitly state that an intangible asset that meets the recognition criteria in paragraph 39 also meets the asset recognition criteria in Statement 5.

Reasons for the contractual-legal criterion

B156. In considering alternative recognition criteria, the Board observed that in contrast to goodwill, the values of many intangible assets arise from rights conveyed legally by contract, statute, or similar means. For example, franchises are granted to automobile dealers, fast-food outlets, and professional sports teams. Trademarks and service marks may be registered with the government. Contracts are often negotiated with customers or suppliers. Technological innovations are often protected by patent. In contrast, the value of goodwill arises from the collection of assembled assets that make up an acquired entity or the value created by assembling a collection of assets through a business combination, such as the synergies that are expected to result from combining one or more businesses. In developing the 2001 Exposure Draft, the Board concluded that the fact that an intangible asset arises from contractual or other legal rights is an important characteristic that distinguishes many intangible assets from goodwill and, therefore, acquired intangible assets with that characteristic should be recognized as an asset apart from goodwill. The Board affirmed that conclusion in its redeliberations of the 2001 Exposure Draft.

Reasons for the separability criterion

B157. In reconsidering the recognition criteria proposed in the 1999 Exposure Draft, the Board also noted that although some intangible assets do not arise from rights conveyed by contract or other legal means, they are nonetheless capable of being separated from the acquired entity and exchanged for something else of value. Others, like goodwill, cannot be separated from an entity and sold or otherwise transferred. The Board concluded that separability is another important characteristic that distinguishes many intangible assets from goodwill and, therefore, acquired intangible assets with that characteristic should be recognized as assets apart from goodwill. The Board affirmed that conclusion in its redeliberations of the 2001 Exposure Draft.

B158. The 2001 Exposure Draft proposed that an intangible asset that was not separable individually would meet the separability criterion if it could be sold, transferred, licensed, rented, or exchanged along with a group of related assets or liabilities. Some respondents to that Exposure Draft suggested that the Board eliminate that requirement, arguing that unless the asset is separable individually it should be included in the amount recognized as goodwill. Others suggested the Board clarify the meaning of the term *group of related assets,* noting that even goodwill can be separated from the acquired entity if the asset group sold constitutes a business.

B159. As it did prior to issuing the 2001 Exposure Draft, the Board noted that some intangible assets are so closely related to another asset or liability that they are usually sold as a "package" (as is the case with deposit liabilities and the related depositor relationship intangible asset). The Board concluded that if those intangible assets were subsumed into goodwill, gains might be inappropriately recognized if the intangible asset was later sold along with the related asset or obligation. However, the Board agreed that the proposed requirement to recognize an intangible asset separately from goodwill if it could be sold or transferred as part of an asset group was a broader criterion than it had intended. For those reasons, this Statement states that an intangible asset that is not separable individually meets the separability criterion if it can be separated and divided from the entity and sold, transferred, licensed, rented, or exchanged in combination with a related contract, other asset, or liability.

B160. At the suggestion of some respondents to the 2001 Exposure Draft, the Board considered explicitly limiting the separability criterion to intangible assets that are separable *and* that trade in observable exchange transactions. While the Board agreed that exchange transactions provide evidence of an asset's separability, it concluded that those transactions were not necessarily the only evidence of separability. Therefore, the Board concluded that it should not limit the recognition of intangible assets that meet the separability criterion to only those that are traded in observable exchange transactions.

B161. Several respondents to the 2001 Exposure Draft suggested that the separability criterion be modified to require recognition of an intangible asset apart from goodwill only if management of the entity *intends* to sell, lease, or otherwise exchange the asset. The Board rejected that suggestion because it does not believe that the intent to sell or otherwise exchange the asset is the relevant factor that distinguishes some intangible assets from goodwill. Rather, it is the asset's *capability* of being separated from the entity and exchanged for something else of value that is the distinction requiring that it be accounted for separately from goodwill.

Reasons for rejecting other suggested recognition criteria

B162. Some respondents to both the 1999 Exposure Draft and the 2001 Exposure Draft suggested that the Board eliminate the requirement to recognize intangible assets apart from goodwill. Others suggested that all intangible assets with characteristics similar

to goodwill should be included in the amount recorded as goodwill. The Board rejected those suggestions because they would diminish rather than improve the decision usefulness of reported financial information.

B163. Some respondents to the 1999 Exposure Draft and the 2001 Exposure Draft doubted their ability to reliably measure the fair values of many intangible assets. They suggested, therefore, that the only intangible assets that should be recognized apart from goodwill are those that have direct cash flows and those that are bought and sold in observable exchange transactions. The Board rejected that suggestion. The Board noted that in a business combination, the fair value of the asset acquired—the acquired entity—is established through a bargained exchange transaction. This Statement requires allocation of that fair value to individual assets acquired, including financial assets, tangible assets, and intangible assets based on their fair values. During redeliberations of the 2001 Exposure Draft, the Board affirmed its belief that the fair value estimates for intangible assets that meet the recognition criteria in this Statement will be sufficiently reliable for the purpose of that purchase price allocation. The Board acknowledged that the fair value estimates for some intangible assets that meet the recognition criteria might lack the precision of the fair value measurements for other assets. However, the Board also concluded that the financial information that will be provided by recognizing intangible assets at their estimated fair values is more representationally faithful than that which would be provided if those intangible assets were subsumed into goodwill on the basis of measurement difficulties. Moreover, including finite-lived intangible assets in goodwill that is not being amortized would further diminish the representational faithfulness of financial statements.

B164. Some of the Board's constituents believe that an item is not an asset if it is not separable. As it did prior to issuance of the 1999 Exposure Draft and the 2001 Exposure Draft, the Board noted that the assets definition in Concepts Statement 6 does not include separability as a necessary characteristic. Thus, although certain intangible assets meeting the contractual-legal criterion might not be separable, they do meet the assets definition.

Illustrative list of intangible assets

B165. Appendix A of the 1999 Exposure Draft included an illustrative list of identifiable intangible assets that might be acquired in a business combination (some of which did not meet the recognition criteria proposed in the 1999 Exposure Draft). The Board agreed with the respondents to the 2001 Exposure Draft that urged the Board to retain such a list in this Statement. However, because the Board changed the criteria for recognizing intangible assets apart from goodwill and decided to include on the list intangible assets meeting the recognition criteria in this Statement, the list of intangible assets in Appendix A of this Statement differs from the proposed list in the 1999 Exposure Draft. For example, the list in the Exposure Draft included customer base as an identifiable intangible asset. The Board views a customer base as a group of customers that are not known or identifiable to the entity (such as customers of a fastfood franchise). The Board concluded that a customer base does not meet the criteria for recognition apart from goodwill and, therefore, customer base is not included on the list in paragraph A14. The Board similarly concluded that other intangible assets listed in Appendix A of the 1999 Exposure Draft would not generally meet the recognition criteria in this Statement and, thus, those assets also have been excluded from the list in paragraph A14. Examples of those intangible assets include customer service capability, presence in geographic markets or locations, nonunion status or strong labor relations, ongoing training or recruiting programs, outstanding credit ratings and access to capital markets, and favorable government relations.

B166. The Board also removed some of the items included on the proposed list in the 1999 Exposure Draft because they represent asset categories that might include both tangible and intangible assets. For example, many different types of assets might be included in the broad category of research and development assets. Whether a specific research and development asset is an intangible asset depends on the nature of the asset.

B167. The Board noted that the list in paragraph A14 is not all-inclusive. The fact that an intangible asset that was included on the proposed list in the 1999 Exposure Draft is not listed in paragraph A14 does not mean that the intangible asset does not meet the recognition criteria in paragraph 39. The nature of each acquired intangible asset needs to be considered in determining whether the recognition criteria of this Statement are met.

Exceptions to the recognition criteria

Assembled workforce

B168. The Board recognizes that the intellectual capital of an assembled workforce is an important resource of many entities. The Board therefore decided that this Statement should address whether an assembled workforce of at-will employees should be recognized as an intangible asset apart from goodwill.

B169. Some constituents believe there are circumstances under which an assembled workforce could be viewed as meeting either the contractual-legal criterion or the separability criterion for recognition as an asset apart from goodwill. However, the Board decided not to explicitly consider whether and in what circumstances an assembled workforce would meet those criteria. The Board observed that even if an assembled workforce met the criteria for recognition as an intangible asset apart from goodwill, the technique often used to measure the fair value of that asset is replacement cost—the cost to hire and train a comparable assembled workforce. The Board believes that replacement cost is not a representationally faithful measurement of the fair value of the intellectual capital acquired in a business combination. The Board concluded that techniques to measure the value of an assembled workforce and the related intellectual capital with sufficient reliability are not currently available. Consequently, it decided to make an exception to the recognition criteria and require that the fair value of an assembled workforce acquired be included in the amount initially recorded as goodwill, regardless of whether it meets the recognition criteria in paragraph 39.

Acquired research and development assets

B170. The Board also considered whether this Statement should address issues related to the accounting for research and development assets acquired in business combinations. During development of the 1999 Exposure Draft, the Board noted that some of the issues associated with acquired research and development assets are unique to those assets and not directly related to other business combinations issues. The Board concluded that it was not possible to address those issues without considering the issues associated with accounting for research and development costs generally. Consequently, the Board decided not to address them in this Statement. Therefore, neither the 1999 Exposure Draft nor the 2001 Exposure Draft proposed any change to the requirement in paragraph 5 of FASB Interpretation No. 4, *Applicability of FASB Statement No. 2 to Business Combinations Accounted for by the Purchase Method,* that the amounts assigned to tangible and intangible assets to be used in a particular research and development project that *have no alternative future use* be charged to expense at the acquisition date. A few respondents to the 2001 Exposure Draft suggested that the amount of acquired research and development assets be subsumed into the amount recognized as goodwill. In its redeliberations, the Board affirmed its conclusion not to reconsider the guidance in Interpretation 4 at this time. The Board concluded that intangible assets in the scope of that Interpretation should be charged to expense at the acquisition date regardless of whether they meet the criteria in paragraph 39 for recognition apart from goodwill.

Initial measurement of intangible assets

B171. As proposed in the 1999 Exposure Draft and consistent with the requirements of Opinion 16, intangible assets acquired in a business combination and recognized in accordance with paragraph 39 of this Statement should initially be assigned an amount based on their fair values. As noted in paragraph 7 of FASB Concepts Statement No. 7, *Using Cash Flow Information and Present Value in Accounting Measurements,* in recent years the Board has identified fair value as the objective for most measurements at initial recognition. None of the respondents to the 1999 Exposure Draft suggested alternative measurement approaches.

B172. The Board noted that an intangible asset arising from a contractual or other legal rights represents the future cash flows that are expected to result from ownership of that contract or legal right. Its fair value represents the amount at which it could be bought or sold in a current transaction between willing parties, that is, other than in a forced or liquidation sale. For example, the fair value of an order backlog would represent the amount a buyer would be willing to pay to acquire the future cash flows expected to arise from that order backlog.

B173. The Board recognizes that the requirements in this Statement might change current practice with respect to the amounts assigned to some intangible assets, in particular those that arise from contractual

or other legal rights. For example, the Board has been informed that in current practice, the amount assigned to acquired operating lease contracts (when the acquired entity is the lessor) and customer contracts often is based on the amount by which the contract terms are favorable relative to market prices at the date of acquisition. Thus, in some cases, no amount is assigned to lease and other contracts that are "at the money"—that is, when the contract terms reflect market prices at the date of acquisition. The Board observed, however, that such "at the money" contracts are bought and sold in exchange transactions—the purchase and sale of airport gates (an operating lease) within the airline industry and customer contracts in the home security industry are two examples of those exchange transactions. The Board believes that those transactions provide evidence that a contract may have value for reasons other than terms that are favorable relative to market prices. The Board therefore concluded that the amount by which the terms of a contract are favorable relative to market prices would not necessarily represent the fair value of that contract.

B174. Several respondents noted that a present value technique might often be the best available technique with which to estimate the fair value of an acquired intangible asset. Some of those respondents asked whether the estimated cash flows used in applying that technique should be limited to the cash flows expected over the remaining legal or contractual term of the acquired asset. The Board noted that judgment is required in estimating the period and amount of expected cash flows. Those estimates should be consistent with the objective of measuring fair value and, thus, should incorporate assumptions that marketplace participants would use in making estimates of fair value, such as assumptions about future contract renewals and other benefits such as those that might result from acquisition-related synergies. The Board noted that if such information is not available without undue cost and effort, an entity should use its own assumptions. The Board also noted that while many contracts or other rights (including customer contracts) are fixed in duration, past history (and industry practice) often provides evidence that the contracts or rights are generally renewed without substantial cost and effort. For example, although contracts to manage investments of mutual funds are often short-term contracts (one year or less), the Board has been informed that in many (if not most) cases those contracts are continuously renewed. The Board has also been informed that while some legal rights such as trademarks and broadcast licenses have finite legal lives, those rights are renewable and are often renewed without challenge. In cases such as those, the Board believes that estimates of future cash flows used in measuring the fair value of the acquired intangible asset likely would reflect cash flows for periods that extend beyond the remaining term of the acquired contract or legal right. The Board noted that Concepts Statement 7 discusses the essential elements of a present value measurement (paragraph 23), provides examples of circumstances in which an entity's expected cash flows might differ from the market expected cash flows (paragraph 32), and discusses the use of present value techniques in measuring the fair value of an asset or liability (paragraphs 39–54 and 75–88).

Preacquisition contingencies

B175. This Statement carries forward without reconsideration the provisions in Statement 38, as amended, that relate to the accounting for preacquisition contingencies of purchased entities. Specifically, paragraph 40 of this Statement carries forward the requirement in paragraph 5 of Statement 38 that the amount paid for the contingent asset or liability be estimated. Paragraph 41 of this Statement carries forward the requirement in paragraph 6 that after the end of the allocation period, an adjustment that results from a preacquisition contingency other than an income tax loss carryforward should be included in the determination of net income in the period in which the adjustment is determined. Paragraphs 19–21 of the basis for conclusions of Statement 38 explain the approach the Board used in developing that guidance:

> This Statement distinguishes between (a) an amount deemed to have been paid for an item that includes an element of risk and (b) the gain or loss that results from the risk assumed.
>
> Paragraph 5 [carried forward in paragraph 40 of this Statement] requires that the amount paid for the contingent asset or liability be estimated. If its fair value can be determined, that fair value is used as the basis for recording the asset or liability. Otherwise, an amount determined on the basis of criteria drawn from Statement 5 is used as the best available estimate of fair value. In accordance with the rationale of Opinion 16 (which requires that all assets and liabilities of the acquired enterprise, whether recorded or unrecorded, be identified and recorded by the

acquiring enterprise and that only the residual purchase price that cannot be allocated to specific assets and liabilities be allocated to goodwill) this Statement allows a period of time (the "allocation period") for discovery and quantification of preacquisition contingencies.

> Paragraph 6 [carried forward in paragraph 41 of this Statement] requires that subsequent adjustments of the amounts recorded as a part of the purchase allocation be included in the determination of net income in the period in which the adjustments are determined. In contrast to the amounts deemed paid for the asset or liability, those subsequent adjustments are gains or losses that result from the uncertainties and related risks assumed in the purchase.

B176. Paragraph 22 of the basis for conclusions of Statement 38 also explains the differences between the accounting for contingent consideration and the accounting for preacquisition contingencies, as follows.

> The following examples illustrate the relationship of the accounting for contingent consideration to the nature of the agreement and contrast the nature of each agreement with the nature of a preacquisition contingency:
>
> a. If the contingent consideration is based on subsequent earnings, the additional consideration, when determinable, increases the purchase price because the increased value that was purchased has been demonstrated. Additional goodwill was proven to exist by the achievement of the specified level of earnings. In contrast, when an enterprise changes its estimate of a preacquisition contingent liability, there is nothing to indicate that additional value has been created. A payment is expected to be required, but the payment does not demonstrate that an asset exists or is more valuable than before the payment was anticipated.
> b. If the contingent consideration represents payment of amounts withheld to insure against the existence of contingencies, neither the payment of the contingent consideration nor the payment of a liability that results from the contingency with the

funds withheld affects the acquiring enterprise's accounting for the business combination. The escrow is a way of protecting the buyer against risk. The buyer has agreed to pay the amount either to the seller or to a third-party claimant; and thus, the only uncertainty to the buyer is the identity of the payee. The amount of the agreed consideration that is withheld would be recorded as part of the purchase price in the original allocation. In contrast, a change in an estimate of a preacquisition contingency for which the acquiring enterprise assumed responsibility represents a change in the total amount that will be paid out or received by the acquiring enterprise. The buyer assumed the risk and is subject to the results of that risk.

B177. In developing Statement 38, the Board concluded that the provisions of that Statement should not be applied to contingencies that arise from the acquisition and that did not exist prior to the acquisition (such as contingencies related to litigation over the acquisition and the tax effect of the purchase). Paragraph 23 of Statement 38 explains the basis for that conclusion:

A number of respondents to the Exposure Draft questioned whether this Statement should be applied to contingencies that arise from the acquisition and that did not exist prior to the acquisition. Examples provided included litigation over the acquisition and the tax effect of the purchase. The Board concluded that such contingencies are the acquiring enterprise's contingencies, rather than preacquisition contingencies of the acquired enterprise. Accordingly, Statement 16 applies to those contingencies after the initial purchase allocation.

B178. Also in developing Statement 38, the Board considered and rejected an approach that would have made a distinction based on whether contingencies were known to the acquiring entity at the date of the purchase. As was explained in paragraphs 24 and 25 of Statement 38:

Some believe that a distinction should be made based on whether contingencies were known to the acquiring enterprise at the date of the purchase. In their opinion, the initial recorded estimate for contingencies that were identified at the date of the purchase should be an adjustment of the purchase price and its allocation regardless of when that estimate becomes determinable. The acquiring enterprise agreed to assume those identified contingencies as a condition of the purchase, and presumably that assessment was considered directly in arriving at the purchase price; accordingly, they should be accounted for as part of the purchase. On the other hand, the discovery of contingent assets or liabilities that were *not* identified at the date of the purchase should not affect the allocation of a purchase price because unknown contingencies could not enter directly in the determination of the purchase price and discovery of unexpected assets or liabilities should not affect cost assigned to the other assets and liabilities acquired.

The Board rejected the approach outlined in paragraph 24 for a number of reasons, including the following:

a. An approach that would base the allocation of the purchase price on whether an item was known to the acquiring enterprise at the date of the purchase would conflict with the requirements of Opinion 16 for allocation of the cost of an enterprise accounted for by the purchase method. Paragraph 87 of Opinion 16 [carried forward without reconsideration in paragraph 36 of this Statement] requires the acquiring enterprise to assign "a portion of the cost of the acquired company" to "all identifiable assets acquired . . . and liabilities assumed . . . , whether or not shown in the financial statements of the acquired company." The reference to "identifiable" does not indicate an intent to limit the allocation to items that were known at the date of the purchase.
b. A distinction based on whether contingencies were known to the acquiring enterprise at the date of the purchase could be viewed as only partially reflecting the economics of many purchase combinations. Many factors affect the purchase price in a business combination. Known contingencies would be one of those factors. Other factors might include amounts of earnings, demonstrated growth in earnings, and unknown preacquisition contingencies, the

potential existence of which would never-theless enter into an assessment of risk and affect the purchase price.

c. If all preacquisition contingencies that re-sult from a cause that was identified at the date of the purchase were considered part of the purchase consideration, the distinc-tion between an identified contingency and one that was not identified would be vague.

d. A requirement that initial recorded esti-mates for some contingencies be recorded as adjustments of the purchase allocation could discourage an enterprise from recording timely estimates.

B179. In Statement 38, the Board also considered and rejected an approach that would exclude from in-come of the acquiring entity all adjustments that re-sult from preacquisition contingencies. Paragraph 27 of Statement 38 cited the following as the Board's reasons for rejecting that approach:

a. The usual practice in the current accounting environment is for irregularly occurring costs that result from risks assumed by the enterprise to be reflected in income when they occur. The Board did not believe that it should differentiate be-tween risks assumed by purchase and other business risks.

b. The distinction between an adjustment related to a preacquisition contingency and an adjustment that results from current events is not always clear. For example, an enterprise may settle litigation be-cause the cost of a successful defense would ex-ceed the cost of the settlement. The opinion of counsel may be that the case can be successfully defended. In that case, whether the cost of the settlement relates to the preacquisition event that is the stated cause of the litigation or to the current litigious environment is not clear.

B180. As was explained in paragraph 28 of Statement 38, the Board also considered whether all adjustments related to preacquisition contingen-cies should be included in income of the acquired entity in the period in which the adjustments are determined:

[Some] note that Statement 16 requires ac-cruals of estimated losses from loss contin-gencies to be included in income in the period in which they are determined, and they be-lieve that contingencies assumed through

purchase should be accounted for the same as other contingencies. Although the Board gen-erally agreed, it concluded that an "allocation period" was needed to permit adequate time to make reasonable estimates for the purchase allocation required by Opinion 16.

Criteria for amount to be included in purchase allocation

B181. In developing Statement 38, the Board noted that a requirement to recognize contingent assets in the allocation of the purchase price could be viewed as inconsistent with the practice described in para-graph 17(a) of Statement 5 that "contingencies that might result in gains usually are not reflected in the accounts since to do so might be to recognize rev-enue prior to its realization." As discussed in para-graph 30 of Statement 38, "The Board concluded that this usual practice is not applicable to a purchase allo-cation because revenue does not result from such an allocation; rather, the question is whether to allocate amounts paid to identifiable assets that have value or to goodwill."

B182. During the development of Statement 38, the Board considered comments made by constituents that the fair value of a preacquisition contingency can sometimes be determined and that that fair value might not equal the amount determined in accord-ance with the criteria in Statement 5. As explained in paragraphs 32 and 33 of Statement 38, the Board de-cided to permit recording a preacquisition contin-gency based on its fair value if that fair value can be determined:

The Board did not intend to modify the general requirement of paragraph 87 of Opin-ion 16 . . . that the purchase allocation be based on the fair value of the assets acquired and the liabilities assumed. Rather, the crite-ria were provided because fair value of a pre-acquisition contingency usually would not be determinable. Accordingly, the Board added paragraph 5(a) to this Statement, to permit re-cording a preacquisition contingency based on its fair value if that fair value can be deter-mined. Otherwise, paragraph 5(b) requires that the amount recorded be based on the cri-teria included in the Exposure Draft.

Some respondents to the Exposure Draft inquired whether it would be appropriate to base the amount recorded on the present value of the amount determined in accordance with the criteria in paragraph 5(b) because the nature of the resulting amount would be a monetary asset or liability. The Board concluded that it should not specify such a requirement because the timing of payment or receipt of a contingent item seldom would be sufficiently determinable to permit the use of a present value technique on a reasonable basis. However, this Statement does not prohibit the use of a present value if appropriate.

Allocation period

B183. Paragraphs 34–38 of Statement 38 explain the Board's reasons for specifying a time period, referred to as the allocation period, during which estimates of preacquisition contingencies could be included in the purchase price allocation:

Opinion 16 provides the general principles of accounting for a business combination by the purchase method. The acquiring enterprise determines the value of the consideration given to the sellers, the present value of the liabilities assumed, and the value of the assets acquired. The total value of the consideration given and the liabilities assumed is then allocated among the identifiable assets acquired based on their value; and the balance, if any, is allocated to "goodwill."

The Board recognizes that completion of the allocation process that is required by Opinion 16 may sometimes require an extended period of time. For example, appraisals might be required to determine replacement cost of plant and equipment acquired, a discovery period may be needed to identify and value intangible assets acquired, and an actuarial determination may be required to determine the pension liability to be accrued.

If a business combination is consummated toward the end of an acquiring enterprise's fiscal year or the acquired enterprise is very large or unusually complex, the acquiring enterprise may not be able to obtain some of the data required to complete the allocation of the cost of the purchased enterprise for inclusion in its next annual financial report. In that case, a tentative allocation might be made using the values that have been determined and preliminary estimates of the values that have not yet been determined. The portions of the

allocation that relate to the data that were not available subsequently are adjusted to reflect the finally determined amounts, usually by adjusting the preliminary amount with a corresponding adjustment of goodwill.

The Board considered specifying a time period during which estimates of preacquisition contingencies could be recorded as part of the purchase allocation. The Board concluded that it should relate the recording of preacquisition contingencies in the purchase allocation to the nature and process of the allocation, rather than to an arbitrary time limit. However, to indicate the Board's intent that the defined "allocation period" should not be unreasonably extended, paragraph 4(b) notes that the existence of a preacquisition contingency for which an amount cannot be estimated does not, of itself, extend the "allocation period." For example, the existence of litigation for which no estimate can be made in advance of the disposition by a court does not extend the "allocation period." That paragraph also notes that the "allocation period" should usually not exceed one year from the consummation date.

The "allocation period" is intended to differentiate between amounts that are determined as a result of the identification and valuation process required by Opinion 16 for all assets acquired and liabilities assumed and amounts that are determined because information that was not previously obtainable becomes obtainable. Thus, the "allocation period" would continue while the acquiring enterprise's counsel was making an evaluation of a claim, but it would not continue if the counsel's evaluation were complete and resulted in the conclusion that no estimate could be made pending further negotiations with the claimant.

Preacquisition net operating loss carryforwards

B184. Also during development of Statement 38, the Board noted the similarity of preacquisition net operating tax loss carryforwards to the other types of preacquisition contingencies. The Board decided that the accounting for net operating loss carryforwards should not be conformed to the accounting for preacquisition contingencies for those contingencies in the scope of Statement 38.

Recognition of deferred taxes

B185. As proposed in the 2001 Exposure Draft, Statement 142 does not permit amortization of either goodwill or intangible assets with indefinite useful lives. Several respondents to the 2001 Exposure Draft suggested that the Board consider permitting nonrecognition of deferred taxes for the differences between the carrying amount and the tax bases of goodwill and intangible assets that are not amortized (whether those differences exist at the date the assets are initially recognized or arise in future periods). Some of those respondents noted that if goodwill or other intangible assets are not amortized, the related deferred tax liability will remain on the balance sheet until the asset is sold, completely impaired, or otherwise disposed of. In that case, settlement of that deferred tax liability could take an extremely long time. Others argued that the proposed nonrecognition of deferred tax liabilities related to goodwill and intangible assets with indefinite useful lives is analogous to two exceptions to the comprehensive recognition of deferred taxes required by FASB Statement No. 109, *Accounting for Income Taxes*—nonrecognition of deferred U.S. tax liabilities for foreign unremitted earnings and nonrecognition of a deferred tax liability for nondeductible goodwill.

B186. The Board acknowledged that its decision not to amortize goodwill and certain intangible assets creates a situation that did not exist when the Board deliberated Statement 109. However, the same arguments made by respondents to the 2001 Exposure Draft for nonrecognition of deferred tax liabilities related to goodwill and intangible assets with indefinite useful lives also were made at the time Statement 109 was developed. Those arguments were extensively studied and debated, and in the end the Board decided that Statement 109 would require comprehensive recognition of deferred taxes subject only to the limited number of exceptions identified in paragraph 9 of that Statement. In its redeliberations of the 2001 Exposure Draft, the Board concluded that this Statement should not amend Statement 109 to provide more exceptions to comprehensive recognition of deferred taxes.

Excess of the fair value of acquired net assets over cost

B187. In some business combinations, the amounts assigned to the acquired net assets exceed their cost. That excess (commonly referred to as negative goodwill) is referred to herein as the *excess over cost* or

excess. The Board affirmed its belief expressed in both the 1999 Exposure Draft and the 2001 Exposure Draft that substantially all business combinations are exchange transactions in which each party receives and sacrifices commensurate value. Accordingly, an excess rarely would remain if the valuations inherent in the purchase price allocation process were properly performed. The Board affirmed the requirement proposed in both the 1999 Exposure Draft and the 2001 Exposure Draft that if an excess remains after the initial allocation of the purchase price, the acquiring entity shall reassess whether all acquired assets and liabilities assumed have been identified and recognized. In addition, accurate and thorough remeasurements should be performed to verify that the consideration paid and the assets acquired and liabilities assumed have been properly valued.

B188. As expressed in both the 1999 Exposure Draft and the 2001 Exposure Draft, Board members believe that, in most cases, the excess is due to measurement errors in the purchase price allocation. Therefore, the Board affirmed its conclusion that the excess should be used to adjust the amounts initially assigned to certain assets. Based on suggestions made by respondents to the 1999 Exposure Draft and the 2001 Exposure Draft, the Board concluded that the excess should be allocated on a pro rata basis to all acquired assets *except* financial assets other than investments accounted for by the equity method, assets to be disposed of by sale, deferred tax assets, prepaid assets relating to pension or other postretirement benefit plans, and any other current assets. The Board concluded that those assets should be excluded from the allocation of the excess because (with the exception of equity method investments and deferred tax assets) their fair values are generally more certain than those of other assets. The Board also observed that not excluding those assets potentially would result in ordinary gain recognition in the near term as those assets are realized.

B189. As it did prior to issuing the 1999 Exposure Draft and the 2001 Exposure Draft, the Board concluded that any excess remaining after those assets had been reduced to zero should be recognized as an extraordinary gain.

B190. Respondents to both the 1999 Exposure Draft and the 2001 Exposure Draft offered little support for the proposed treatment of the excess—particularly the requirement to record an extraordinary gain (if an excess remained after reducing the amount assigned to certain assets to zero). Respondents asserted that recognizing any gain on a purchase transaction cannot be justified conceptually. They generally favored recognizing the remaining excess as a deferred credit that would be amortized in some manner—as is done in current practice.

B191. A number of respondents also disagreed with the proposed requirement to allocate the excess to specified acquired assets—especially given the emphasis in both Exposure Drafts on initially recording assets and liabilities at their fair value. Most of those respondents suggested that the entire excess should be recognized as a deferred credit. However, a few respondents suggested that the excess should be recognized as a component of equity or as a contingent liability.

B192. While the Board acknowledged the views expressed by those respondents, it affirmed its conclusion that accounting for the excess as an unrecognizable obligation would require recognition of a credit balance that does not meet the definition of a liability in Concepts Statement 6. Moreover, if that credit balance was treated as if it was a liability, that credit balance would be reduced only when, if ever, it was determined that the related outlays had been incurred. Because of the inherent difficulties in making those determinations and because entities would not be permitted to recognize such obligations in other circumstances, the Board affirmed its conclusion that the only practical approach would be to recognize the excess as an extraordinary gain. The Board noted that extraordinary treatment is appropriate to highlight the fact that an excess exists and to reflect the unusual nature and infrequent occurrence of the item. The Board also noted that regardless of how the excess is accounted for, it results in recognition of a gain as a result of the purchase transaction. The only issue is when that gain is recognized—immediately or in future periods.

B193. In developing the 2001 Exposure Draft the Board decided that recognition of the excess as a reduction in the amounts that would otherwise have been assigned to the assets acquired or as an extraordinary gain should be delayed in combinations involving contingent consideration. That is because, while the initial purchase price (excluding the contingent amount) could be below the fair value of the net assets acquired prior to resolution of the contingency (giving rise to an excess over cost), resolution resulting in additional consideration could significantly change that result. Thus, recognizing an extraordinary gain related to that excess when the business

combination is recognized initially could result in recognition of an extraordinary gain that perhaps should not have been recognized and that may be reversed (partially or fully) if and when the contingent consideration is paid or issued. None of the respondents to the 2001 Exposure Draft specifically objected to that view and the Board affirmed it during redeliberations. Thus, this Statement requires that if a business combination involves a consideration contingency that might result in additional cost of the acquired entity, an amount equal to the lesser of the excess or the maximum amount of contingent consideration is to be recognized as if it was a liability until the consideration contingency is resolved.

Documentation at date of acquisition

B194. Statement 142 requires that acquiring entities assign acquired assets (including goodwill) and liabilities to reporting units. In developing the 2001 Exposure Draft, the Board concluded that entities should be required to document certain facts and circumstances surrounding the business combination for use in making those assignments. The proposed documentation requirements included the basis for and method of determining the purchase price and other information such as the reasons for the acquisition and management's expectations related to dilution, synergies, and other financial measurements. None of the respondents to that Exposure Draft commented on those requirements. The Board concluded that those documentation requirements should be retained in this Statement.

Disclosures in Financial Statements

B195. Because a business combination often results in a significant change to an entity's operations, the nature and extent of the information disclosed about the transaction bear on users' abilities to assess the effects of such changes on postacquisition earnings and cash flows. Accordingly, the Board decided that as part of this project, it would assess the usefulness of the disclosure requirements in Opinion 16 for entities that apply the purchase method. As part of that assessment, the Board solicited input from analysts and other users of financial statements on ways to improve the disclosure requirements in Opinion 16. As it did prior to issuing the 1999 Exposure Draft, the Board concluded that the disclosure requirements in Opinion 16 should be retained. The Board then considered whether other information should be disclosed to supplement the information provided under the disclosure requirements in Opinion 16.

B196. In developing the 1999 Exposure Draft the Board concluded that additional disclosures should be required to provide decision-useful information about the net assets acquired in a business combination. Specifically, the Board concluded that additional information should be provided relating to (a) the allocation of the purchase price to assets acquired and liabilities assumed, (b) the nature and amount of intangible assets acquired, and (c) the amount of goodwill recognized.

Disclosure of information about the purchase price allocation and pro forma sales and earnings

B197. In developing the 1999 Exposure Draft, the Board decided to require disclosure of information about the purchase price allocation, specifically, information about the amount of the step-up in assets acquired and liabilities assumed. That Exposure Draft would have required tabular disclosure of the fair values allocated to each of the major balance sheet captions and the related carrying amounts as recognized in the statement of financial position of the acquired entity immediately before its acquisition. Based on input received from analysts, the Board concluded that that information would provide users with a powerful tool for assessing the postacquisition earnings and cash flows of acquiring entities. That input also led the Board to conclude that information about the step-up in the basis of assets acquired and liabilities assumed would be more useful in assessing those postacquisition earnings and cash flows than the pro forma sales and earnings disclosures required by Opinion 16. Consequently, the 1999 Exposure Draft proposed that the pro forma disclosure requirement in Opinion 16 be eliminated.

B198. Respondents' views on the proposed requirement to disclose information about the purchase price allocation were mixed. About half of the respondents that commented on that proposed requirement agreed that the information it would provide would be useful in assessing postacquisition earnings and cash flow of the acquiring entity. The respondents that disagreed with that proposed requirement were primarily opposed to disclosure of information about the carrying amounts of assets acquired and liabilities assumed. They questioned the usefulness of that information, particularly if the financial statements of the acquired entity were not audited or if they were prepared on a basis other than U.S. generally accepted accounting principles. After considering those views, the Board affirmed its conclusion that information about the allocation of the purchase price to major balance sheet captions would be useful in assessing the amount and timing of future cash flows. However, it agreed with those respondents that information about the related carrying amounts might be of limited usefulness. Thus, this Statement requires disclosure of information about the allocation of the purchase price to each major balance sheet caption of the acquired entity but not their related carrying amounts.

B199. Respondents also expressed mixed views about the proposal to eliminate the pro forma sales and earnings disclosures required by Opinion 16. Many of the respondents supported elimination of those disclosure requirements. Those respondents said that the information provided has little value because it is based on hypothetical assumptions and mechanical computations. Respondents that favored retaining those disclosures said that the pro forma information is useful for measuring growth and in assessing whether the synergies expected to result from the combination have been achieved. After considering respondents' views, the Board concluded that the pro forma disclosure requirements in Opinion 16 should be retained in this Statement.

B200. Several users suggested that the Board require disclosure of pro forma sales and earnings information at the reportable segment level because that information would be useful in assessing the amount and timing of future goodwill impairment losses. The Board rejected that suggestion because it concluded that the costs of preparing and disclosing that information would exceed the benefits derived from its use.

B201. The Board noted that FASB Statement No. 79, *Elimination of Certain Disclosures for Business Combinations by Nonpublic Enterprises,* exempts nonpublic entities from the Opinion 16 requirement to disclose supplemental pro forma information. Preparers and attestors of financial statements of nonpublic entities urged the Board to continue that exemption, arguing that the costs of preparing the pro forma information exceed the benefit of providing it. After considering those views, the Board concluded that nonpublic entities should continue to be exempt from the pro forma disclosure requirements of this Statement.

Disclosures related to goodwill

B202. The 1999 Exposure Draft proposed that in the year of acquisition, the notes to financial statements should include a description of the elements that underlie goodwill, the useful life of goodwill and how it was determined, and the amortization method. As a consequence of its decision that goodwill should not be amortized, the Board decided to eliminate the requirement to disclose the useful life of goodwill and the amortization method because they are not applicable under a nonamortization approach. The Board also decided to eliminate the requirement to disclose a description of the elements that underlie goodwill because its purpose was to provide a basis for assessing the appropriateness of the goodwill amortization period.

B203. The Board concluded, however, that information about the amount of goodwill, in particular the amount of goodwill by reportable segment, would be useful in assessing the amount and timing of potential goodwill impairment charges. After considering input from analysts and other users of financial statements, the Board decided that for each material business combination, the notes to the financial statements should disclose (a) the reasons for the acquisition including a description of the factors that led to the payment of a purchase price that resulted in goodwill and (b) the amount of goodwill assigned to each reportable segment.

B204. The Board acknowledged, however, that information about the amount of goodwill by reportable segment is only useful if users also are provided information about performance at that level. The Board decided, therefore, that the requirement to disclose the amount of goodwill by reportable segment should be limited to those entities that are within the scope of FASB Statement No. 131, *Disclosures about Segments of an Enterprise and Related Information.*

B205. Based on input received from analysts and other users, the Board also concluded that information about the amount of goodwill that is expected to be deducted for tax purposes is useful in assessing the amount and timing of future cash flows of the combined entity. The Board therefore decided to require disclosure of that amount if the goodwill initially recognized in a material business combination is significant in relation to the total cost of the acquired entity.

B206. Several respondents to the 2001 Exposure Draft commented on the proposed requirement to disclose goodwill by reportable segment. Half of those respondents agreed with the requirement and half suggested it be eliminated. The Board affirmed

its conclusion that disclosure of that information is useful in estimating the amount and timing of future impairment losses and, thus, concluded that the disclosure requirement should be retained.

B207. Several respondents to the 2001 Exposure Draft suggested that entities be required to provide information about the methods and key assumptions that would be used in measuring the fair value of a reporting unit and the types of events that would likely give rise to a goodwill impairment test. They argued that that information is needed to make informed judgments about the timing and amount of potential future impairment losses. The Board considered similar suggestions during development of the 2001 Exposure Draft. The Board concluded that without access to management's cash flow projections and its methods of estimating those future cash flows, and information about past cash flows or earnings at the reporting unit level, the suggested disclosures would be of little benefit to users in making those judgments. In addition, the Board noted that information about methods and assumptions could be useful only if changes to those methods and assumptions are disclosed almost continuously. The Board affirmed its initial conclusions in its redeliberations of the 2001 Exposure Draft and, therefore, this Statement does not require disclosure of that information.

Disclosure of information about intangible assets other than goodwill

B208. The 1999 Exposure Draft proposed that certain information be disclosed in the notes to the financial statements for each major intangible asset class. The information that would have been required to be disclosed included (a) a description of the assets and the amounts assigned to them at the acquisition date, (b) the key assumptions and methodologies used to determine those amounts, (c) a description of the amortization method, and (d) the weighted-average amortization period. Many respondents to that Exposure Draft commented on the proposed disclosure requirements. Most agreed that additional information about intangible assets acquired would be useful, but many urged the Board to consider reducing the extent of the disclosure requirements. They argued that the cost of providing the information, particularly for entities that complete multiple acquisitions in a single period, would exceed the benefits derived from that information.

B209. After considering the suggestions made by those respondents, the Board affirmed its conclusion that financial statements should provide additional information about acquired intangible assets other than goodwill. However, in view of the changes made to the proposed accounting for intangible assets and the comments made by respondents, the Board revised the disclosure requirements related to acquired intangible assets.

B210. The Board concluded that if the amount assigned to intangible assets is significant in relation to the total cost of an acquired entity, the following information should be disclosed because it is useful in assessing the amount and timing of future cash flows: (a) the total amount assigned to intangible assets subject to amortization and the total amount assigned to those that are not subject to amortization, (b) the amount assigned to each major intangible asset class, and (c) for intangible assets subject to amortization, the weighted-average amortization period in total and for each major intangible asset class. The Board also concluded that disclosure should be made, both in total and for each major intangible asset class, of the amount of any significant residual value assumed.

B211. Although not proposed in the 1999 Exposure Draft, at the suggestion of respondents the Board also decided to require disclosure of the amount of research and development assets acquired and written off at the date of acquisition in accordance with Interpretation 4, as well as the line item in which those write-offs are aggregated.

Other disclosure requirements

B212. The 1999 Exposure Draft proposed disclosure of certain information (as provided for in paragraph 53) if a series of immaterial business combinations were completed in a reporting period that are material in the aggregate. The Board affirmed that requirement, noting that it is consistent with Opinion 16.

B213. In addition, the 1999 Exposure Draft proposed that the information required to be disclosed for a completed business combination would also be disclosed for a material business combination completed after the balance sheet date but before the financial statements are issued (unless disclosure of such information is not practicable). The Board concluded that that disclosure requirement should be retained in this Statement, noting that none of the respondents to the 1999 Exposure Draft commented on that disclosure requirement and that the requirement is consistent with subsequent-events literature within the auditing standards.

Disclosures in Interim Financial Information

B214. Several analysts and other users recommended that the Board consider requiring disclosure of supplemental pro forma sales and earnings information in interim financial information. They argued that that information would be more useful if it was available on a timelier basis. Board members noted that APB Opinion No. 28, *Interim Financial Reporting,* requires disclosures about completed business combinations but does not specify what those disclosures should be. The Board agreed with the suggestion that it amend Opinion 28 to require disclosure of pro forma sales and earnings information in interim financial information.

Effective Date and Transition

Method of accounting for business combinations

B215. The 1999 Exposure Draft proposed that the requirements of this Statement would be effective for business combinations initiated after the date this Statement is issued. A number of respondents to that Exposure Draft suggested the Board consider deferring the effective date for three to six months after issuance to provide time for analysis, interpretation, and implementation of this Statement. The Board affirmed its conclusion that deferral of the effective date would not be necessary because its constituents will have had sufficient time to consider the implications of the Board's decision on planned transactions and because application of the purchase method to all business combinations will not create significant new implementation issues. Thus, the Board concluded that the requirements of this Statement should be applied to business combinations initiated after June 30, 2001. As with the 1999 Exposure Draft, this Statement uses the Opinion 16 definition of initiation date. According to that definition, a business combination is initiated on the earlier of (a) the date that the major terms of a plan are announced publicly or otherwise formally made known or (b) the date that stockholders of a combining entity are notified in writing of an exchange offer.

B216. In reaching its decision on the effective date, the Board noted that business combinations generally are undertaken for strategic and economic considerations that are largely independent of accounting standards. However, the effect of the proposed transaction on postcombination reported earnings commonly is considered by entities in planning and negotiating those transactions. Prospective application for transactions initiated after this Statement is issued therefore avoids situations in which transactions are planned using one accounting standard and accounted for using another.

B217. In developing the 1999 Exposure Draft, the Board concluded that business combinations recorded prior to the issuance of this Statement and business combinations in process when this Statement is issued should be "grandfathered" under Opinion 16. The Board noted that retroactive application of the purchase method to business combinations previously accounted for by the pooling method would have resulted in more comparable financial statements. However, retroactive application would be impractical or burdensome for many entities because the information needed to apply the purchase method may not exist or may no longer be obtainable. Respondents to the 1999 Exposure Draft that addressed that issue supported that decision, and the Board affirmed it in the course of its redeliberations. Several respondents to the 1999 Exposure Draft raised questions related to how the purchase method should be applied to combinations between mutual enterprises. The Board decided to defer the effective date of this Statement with respect to those transactions until interpretative guidance addressing those questions is issued.

Provisions related to the application of the purchase method

B218. This Statement changes certain requirements in Opinion 16 related to the application of the purchase method. Under the transition provisions included in the 1999 Exposure Draft, similar proposed changes would have been effective for business combinations *initiated* after the date that a final Statement was issued. Because amortization of all goodwill will cease upon initial application of Statement 142, Board members concluded that the effective date for the provisions of this Statement related to the application of the purchase method, in particular the criteria for recognition of intangible assets apart from goodwill, should be changed. Therefore, the Board concluded that this Statement should be effective for all business combinations accounted for by the purchase method for which the date of acquisition is July 1, 2001, or later.

Transition

Excess of the fair value of acquired net assets over cost

B219. In developing the 1999 Exposure Draft, the Board concluded that the provisions related to the excess of the fair values of acquired net assets over cost should be applied on a prospective basis because of the operational difficulties that retroactive application would present. The Board reconsidered that decision in developing the 2001 Exposure Draft and decided that as of the beginning of the first fiscal quarter after the date the final Statement is issued, the amount of such excess that is recorded in the statement of financial position as a deferred credit as required by Opinion 16 should be recognized as an extraordinary gain. As suggested by respondents to the 2001 Exposure Draft, the Board concluded that the amount of any excess over cost that is recorded in the statement of financial position as a deferred credit as required by Opinion 16 should be recognized as the effect of a change in accounting principle as of the earlier of either the first day of the fiscal year beginning after December 15, 2001, or the date that Statement 142 is initially applied in its entirety.

Goodwill and other intangible assets

B220. Because this Statement changes the criteria for recognizing intangible assets apart from goodwill, the Board considered whether entities should be required to reassess the intangible assets currently recognized separately in the statement of financial position and possibly reclassify intangible assets that do not meet the new recognition criteria as goodwill and vice versa. For example, some entities may have an assembled workforce recognized as a separate intangible asset, which is not permitted by this Statement. Conversely, some entities may have subsumed into goodwill acquired intangible assets that would be recognized separately under the criteria in this Statement.[36] The Board noted that it would be fairly straightforward to determine whether recognized intangible assets meet the new criteria for recognition apart from goodwill but that it would not be so straightforward to identify intangible assets that meet those criteria that were previously subsumed in goodwill. In developing the 2001 Exposure Draft,

---

[36]Entities might not have adhered strictly to the purchase price allocation requirements in Opinion 16 because Opinion 17 required amortization of all acquired intangible assets and limited the maximum amortization for both goodwill and other intangible assets to 40 years.

the Board concluded that it would not be appropriate to require the reassessment in one direction but not the other.

B221. Several respondents to the 2001 Exposure Draft urged the Board to reconsider those proposed transition provisions, in particular the prohibition against reclassification as goodwill those recognized intangible assets that do not meet the recognition criteria in this Statement. They argued that permitting such reclassifications would improve the comparability of financial statements.

B222. The basis for conclusions to the 2001 Exposure Draft stated that if an entity had aggregated goodwill and intangible assets as one amount for reporting purposes and information exists on how the purchase price was initially allocated between goodwill and other intangible assets, that entity would be required to disaggregate existing intangible assets that meet the recognition criteria in paragraph 39 and report them separately in subsequent statements of financial position. The Board agreed that it should not require disaggregation of that type while prohibiting reclassification of recognized intangible assets that do not meet the criteria for recognition apart from goodwill. Accordingly, the Board decided to retain the disaggregation requirement proposed in the 2001 Exposure Draft and require that entities reclassify as goodwill any recognized intangible assets that do not meet the recognition criteria in paragraph 39.

B223. The Board considered whether the requirement to disaggregate existing intangible assets that meet the recognition criteria from the amount reported as goodwill would affect the recorded deferred tax balances. The Board noted that Statement 109 requires that deferred taxes be provided for differences between the book and tax bases of intangible assets acquired in a business combination. Only goodwill that is not deductible for tax purposes is exempt from that requirement. The Board concluded that the requirement to disaggregate existing intangible assets that were previously included in the amount reported as goodwill would not affect the amount of recorded deferred tax balances, as deferred taxes would have been provided for any differences between the book and tax bases of those assets.

B224. The Board then considered the consequences of reclassifying existing intangible assets as goodwill on recorded deferred tax balances. The Board concluded that when an existing intangible asset is reclassified as goodwill (because it does not meet the recognition criteria in this Statement), it should be considered goodwill for purposes of accounting for income taxes. Thus, if an intangible asset reclassified as goodwill is an asset for which amortization is not deductible for tax purposes, that asset should be considered as nondeductible goodwill that Statement 109 exempts from the requirements for deferred tax recognition. The Board concluded that any deferred tax liabilities associated with those intangible assets should be eliminated through a corresponding reduction in the carrying amount of goodwill. The Board concluded that if an intangible asset that is deductible for tax purposes is reclassified as goodwill under the transition provisions of this Statement, it should be deemed to be deductible goodwill for which recognition of deferred taxes is required. Thus, reclassification of that asset as goodwill would not affect the recorded deferred tax balances.

Benefits and Costs

B225. The mission of the FASB is to establish and improve standards of financial accounting and reporting for the guidance and education of the public, including preparers, auditors, and users of financial information. In fulfilling that mission, the Board endeavors to determine that a proposed standard will fill a significant need and that the costs imposed to meet that standard, as compared with other alternatives, are justified in relation to the overall benefits of the resulting information. Although the costs to implement a new standard may not be borne evenly, investors and creditors—both present and potential—as well as others benefit from improvements in financial reporting, thereby facilitating the functioning of markets for capital and credit and the efficient allocation of resources in the economy.

B226. The Board believes that this Statement will remedy certain significant deficiencies and fill certain significant voids in financial reporting. The requirement to account for all business combinations by the purchase method will provide users of financial statements with information about the cost of those transactions that the pooling method does not provide because that method does not reflect the values exchanged in the business combination transaction. Therefore, users of financial statements will be better able to assess the initial costs of those investments. They also will be better able to assess the subsequent performance of those investments.

B227. Information about assets and liabilities also will be more complete and comparable. Assets acquired and liabilities assumed that were not previously recorded by predecessor entities will be recorded, as they would be if they had been obtained outside a business combination. Moreover, assets and liabilities that are acquired in a business combination will be measured in the same way as those assets and liabilities that are acquired by other means, either individually or in groups. Consequently, financial statement comparability will be enhanced.

B228. The Board observed that intangible assets constitute a growing share of assets for entities generally and are, in fact, most of the assets of some individual entities. However, information about the intangible assets owned by those entities is often incomplete and inadequate. The Board believes that the changes in the criteria for initial recognition of goodwill and other intangible assets acquired in business combinations will result in more information about those assets than was the case previously.

B229. This Statement also will bring the accounting for business combinations in the United States more in step with how those combinations are accounted for outside the United States. The Board observed that widespread use of the pooling method is largely a phenomenon in the United States and that use of that method in other countries around the world is rare in many jurisdictions and prohibited in others. Consequently, investors will be better able to compare the financial statements of U.S. entities that enter business combinations with those of foreign entities that have engaged in business combinations. Furthermore, this Statement will be an important step in the process of achieving greater convergence of cross-border accounting requirements generally, consistent with the Board's mission statement. That, in turn, will reduce costs now borne by preparers, auditors, and users of financial statements alike, as well as facilitate the efficient allocation of capital globally.

B230. The Board believes that preparers and auditors of financial statements domestically also will benefit from this Statement. The existence of two methods of accounting for similar business combinations that produce such dramatically different financial statement results often puts preparers of financial statements under pressure to obtain the accounting treatment that is deemed to have the more favorable effect on the earnings that are reported postcombination. As a result, the Board has been informed that the ability or inability to use the pooling method is perceived by many to affect competition for mergers and acquisitions, including whether those transactions are entered into and the prices that are negotiated for them. However, there are often uncertainties about whether entities can qualify to use the favored method, and those uncertainties can lead to conflicts between preparers, auditors, and regulators in interpreting and applying those qualifying criteria. This Statement removes those uncertainties.

B231. The Board observed that business entities often incur significant costs in seeking to use the pooling method. Those costs are both monetary and nonmonetary as entities try to position themselves to meet the criteria to qualify for use of that method and sometimes take actions that those entities might not otherwise take or refrain from taking actions that they might otherwise take. This Statement removes the need to incur those costs.

B232. The Board believes that the guidance in this Statement is not overly complex. Indeed, it eliminates guidance that many have found to be complex, costly, and arbitrary, and that has been the source of considerable uncertainties and costs in the marketplace. Moreover, this Statement does not introduce a new method of accounting but rather expands the use of an existing method that is familiar, has been widely used, and for which there is a substantial base of experience.

B233. Some argue that the pooling method is less costly to apply than the purchase method and thus a requirement to use only the purchase method will impose costs on preparers. However, as noted above, preparers of financial statements often incur significant costs in attempting to qualify to use the pooling method, and those costs may be greater than the costs incurred in applying the purchase method. Moreover, the use of two methods that produce such dramatically different financial statement outcomes makes it difficult or impossible for users to compare the financial statements of entities that have accounted for their business combinations by different methods. Use of the pooling method also makes it difficult or impossible for users to compare the financial statements of entities that acquire their assets in business combinations accounted for by that method with the financial statements of entities that purchase their assets individually or in groups rather than by means of business combinations. Therefore, the Board believes that this Statement will not impose aggregate costs greater than those that have been borne previously and instead should reduce some costs significantly.

B234. The Board has sought to reduce the costs of applying this Statement and facilitate transition to its requirements by making its provisions with respect to the method to be used to account for business combinations prospective rather than retroactive.

Appendix C

ILLUSTRATIONS

Introduction

C1. This appendix provides illustrations of some of the disclosure requirements of this Statement. The information is presented for illustrative purposes only and, therefore, may not be representative of actual transactions.

Illustration 1—Disclosure of a Material Business Combination in the Year of Acquisition

C2. The following illustrates the disclosures required if a material business combination is completed during the reporting period (paragraphs 51 and 52).

Footnote C: Acquisitions (dollars in thousands)

On June 30, 20X2, Alpha acquired 100 percent of the outstanding common shares of Beta. The results of Beta's operations have been included in the consolidated financial statements since that date. Beta is a provider of data networking products and services in Canada and Mexico. As a result of the acquisition, Alpha is expected to be the leading provider of data networking products and services in those markets. It also expects to reduce costs through economies of scale.

The aggregate purchase price was $9,400, including $7,000 of cash and common stock valued at $2,400. The value of the 100,000 common shares issued was determined based on the average market price of Alpha's common shares over the 2-day period before and after the terms of the acquisition were agreed to and announced.

The following table summarizes the estimated fair values of the assets acquired and liabilities assumed at the date of acquisition. Alpha is in the process of obtaining third-party valuations of certain intangible assets; thus, the allocation of the purchase price is subject to refinement.

At June 30, 20X2 ($000s)	
Current assets	$ 2,400
Property, plant, and equipment	1,500
Intangible assets	4,900
Goodwill	2,200
Total assets acquired	11,000
Current liabilities	(500)
Long-term debt	(1,100)
Total liabilities assumed	(1,600)
Net assets acquired	$ 9,400

Of the $4,900 of acquired intangible assets, $1,400 was assigned to registered trademarks that are not subject to amortization and $1,000 was assigned to research and development assets that were written off at the date of acquisition in accordance with FASB Interpretation No. 4, *Applicability of FASB Statement No. 2 to Business Combinations Accounted for by the Purchase Method.* Those write-offs are included in general and administrative expenses. The remaining $2,500 of acquired intangible assets have a weighted-average useful life of approximately 4 years. The intangible assets that make up that amount include computer software of $1,500 (3-year weighted-average useful life), patents of $800 (7-year weighted-average useful life), and other assets of $200 (5-year weighted-average useful life).

The $2,200 of goodwill was assigned to the technology and communications segments in the amounts of $1,300 and $900, respectively. Of that total amount, $250 is expected to be deductible for tax purposes.

Illustration 2—Disclosures in Year of Acquisition of Several Individually Immaterial Business Combinations That Are Material in the Aggregate

C3. The following illustrates the disclosures required if a series of individually immaterial business combinations are completed during a period that are material in the aggregate (paragraph 53). The illustration assumes that Alpha completed four business combinations, one during each quarter of its fiscal year ending December 31, 20X3.

Footnote C: Acquisitions (dollars in thousands)

In 20X3, Alpha acquired the following 4 entities for a total cost of $1,000, which was paid primarily in cash:

- Omega Consulting, based in Zurich, Switzerland, a leading provider of telecommunications consulting services
- Nittany Systems, based in Toronto, Canada, a producer of digital networking technology
- Sherman Communications, Inc., based in Portland, Oregon, a start-up data networking company
- Blue and White Networks, Inc., based in Atlanta, Georgia, a designer and manufacturer of wireless communications networks.

Goodwill recognized in those transactions amounted to $300, and that amount is expected to be fully deductible for tax purposes. Goodwill was assigned to the communication and technology segments in the amounts of $120 and $180, respectively.

Appendix D

CONTINUING AUTHORITATIVE GUIDANCE

Introduction

D1. APB Opinion No. 16, *Business Combinations,* required that the pooling-of-interests method (pooling method) be used if a business combination met certain criteria. This Statement prohibits the use of the pooling method for business combinations initiated after June 30, 2001. This Statement supersedes Opinion 16 and the AICPA Accounting Interpretations of that Opinion that provide guidance on applying the pooling method. This appendix carries forward, without reconsideration, guidance in Opinion 16 and its interpretations that may be helpful in applying the transition provisions of this Statement and in accounting for past transactions to which the pooling method was applied (paragraphs D4–D10).

D2. Consistent with the provisions of Opinion 16, the provisions of this Statement do not apply to transfers of net assets or exchanges of shares between entities under common control. Guidance in Opinion 16 and an interpretation of that Opinion that has been used in past practice to account for those transactions also is carried forward without reconsideration in this appendix (paragraphs D11–D18).

D3. The following guidance has been quoted, paraphrased, or modified as necessary so that it can be understood in the context of this Statement. The original source of the guidance is noted parenthetically or otherwise. Some of that guidance may be reconsidered by the Board in another project.

Initiation Date of a Business Combination

D4. Paragraph 59 of this Statement carries forward the Opinion 16 definition of *initiated* as it relates to a business combination. Paragraphs D5–D8 carry forward without reconsideration the interpretations of Opinion 16 that provide guidance relating to that definition. That guidance should be considered in applying the transition provisions of this Statement.

D5. A business combination is not initiated until the major terms are set and announced publicly or formally communicated to the shareholders who will tender their shares to the issuing corporation. A corporation may communicate to its own shareholders its intent to make a tender offer or to negotiate the terms of a proposed business combination with another company. However, intent to tender or to negotiate does not constitute "initiation." A business combination is not initiated until the major terms are "set" and announced publicly or formally communicated to shareholders. Paragraph 59 of this Statement defines initiation in terms of two dates. The first date is for the announcement of an exchange offer negotiated between representatives of two (or more) corporations. The second date is for a tender offer made by a corporation directly or by newspaper advertisement to the shareholders of another company. In the second date specified for initiation, a *combining company* refers to the company whose shareholders will tender their shares to the issuing corporation. An *exchange offer* refers to the major terms of a plan including the ratio of exchange (or formula to determine that ratio). A corporation may communicate to its *own* shareholders its intent to make a tender offer or to negotiate the terms of a proposed business combination with another company. However, intent to tender or to negotiate does not constitute initiation (AICPA Accounting Interpretation 2, "Notification to Stockholders," of Opinion 16).

D6. To constitute initiation of a business combination, the actual exchange ratio (1 for 1, 2 for 1, and so forth) of shares need not be known provided that the ratio of exchange is absolutely determinable by objective means in the future. A formula would usually provide such a determination. A formula to determine the exchange ratio might include factors such as earnings for a period of time, market prices of shares at a particular date, average market prices for a period of time, and appraised valuations. The formula may include upper limits, lower limits, or both for the exchange ratio, and the limits may provide for adjustments based on appraised valuations, audits of the financial statements, and so forth. However, to constitute initiation of a business combination, the formula must be announced or communicated to shareholders. Any subsequent changes in the terms of a formula used to initiate a business combination constitute a new plan of combination. That new plan of combination would be accounted for in accordance with the provisions of this Statement (AICPA Accounting Interpretation 1, "Ratio of Exchange," of Opinion 16).

D7. A business combination also may be initiated at the date the shareholders of a closely held company grant an option to exchange shares at a future date to another company. The terms of the grant must require unilateral performance by either party or bilateral performance by both parties in order to constitute initiation of a business combination. Thus, if one company is required to issue shares upon the tendering of shares by the shareholders of another company, or if the shareholders are required to tender their shares upon demand, the date the option is granted is the initiation date. However, an agreement that grants only the right of first refusal *does not* constitute initiation of a business combination. For example, if the shareholders of a closely held company decide to consider entering into a business combination in the future and the shareholders agree to negotiate with one company before negotiating with any other company, a business combination has not been initiated. Neither party may be obligated to perform or to pay damages in the absence of performance (AICPA Accounting Interpretation 29, "Option May Initiate Combination," of Opinion 16).

D8. Termination of a plan of combination prior to shareholder approval has an effect on the initiation date of a business combination. If negotiations of a plan of combination are formally terminated and then are subsequently resumed, the subsequent resumption always constitutes a new plan. Formal announcement of the major terms of the new plan constitutes a new initiation date, even if the terms are the same as the terms of the previously terminated plan. In such circumstances, if the new initiation date falls after June 30, 2001, that combination should be accounted for in accordance with the provisions of this Statement (AICPA Accounting Interpretation 10, "Effect of Termination," of Opinion 16).

Disposition of Assets after a Combination Accounted for Using the Pooling Method

D9. Following a business combination accounted for by the pooling method, the combined entity might dispose of assets of the previously separate entities. Unless those disposals are part of customary business activities of the combined entity, any gain or loss recognized resulting from that disposition might require recognition as an extraordinary item. Recognition as an extraordinary item is warranted because the pooling method of accounting would have been inappropriate if the combined entity had made a commitment or had planned to dispose of a significant part of the assets of one of the combining entities.

D10. The combined entity should recognize the gain or loss resulting from the disposal of a significant part of the assets or a separable segment of the previously separate entities, less applicable income tax effect, as an extraordinary item if (a) the gain or loss is material in relation to the net income of the combined entity and (b) the disposition is within two years after the combination is consummated (Opinion 16, paragraph 60).

Transactions between Entities under Common Control

D11. Consistent with the provisions of Opinion 16, paragraph 11 of this Statement states that the term *business combination* excludes transfers of net assets or exchanges of shares between entities under common control. The following are examples of those types of transactions:

a. An entity charters a newly formed entity and then transfers some or all of its net assets to that newly chartered entity.
b. A parent company transfers the net assets of a wholly owned subsidiary into the parent company and liquidates the subsidiary. That transaction is a change in legal organization but not a change in the reporting entity.
c. A parent company transfers its interest in several partially owned subsidiaries to a new wholly

owned subsidiary. That also is a change in legal organization but not in the reporting entity.

d. A parent company exchanges its ownership interests or the net assets of a wholly owned subsidiary for additional shares issued by the parent's partially owned subsidiary, thereby increasing the parent's percentage of ownership in the partially owned subsidiary but leaving all of the existing minority interest outstanding.

D12. When accounting for a transfer of assets or exchange of shares between entities under common control, the entity that receives the net assets or the equity interests shall initially recognize the assets and liabilities transferred at their carrying amounts in the accounts of the transferring entity at the date of transfer.

D13. The purchase method of accounting shall be applied if the effect of the transfer or exchange described in paragraph D11 is the acquisition of all or a part of the noncontrolling equity interests in a subsidiary (refer to paragraph 14).

Procedural Guidance

D14. Some transfers of net assets or exchanges of shares between entities under common control result in a change in the reporting entity. In practice, the method that many entities have used to account for those transactions is similar to the pooling method. Certain provisions in Opinion 16 relating to application of the pooling method provide a source of continuing guidance on the accounting for transactions between entities under common control. Paragraphs D15–D18 provide procedural guidance that should be considered when preparing financial statements and related disclosures for the entity that receives the net assets.

D15. In some instances, the entity that receives the net assets or equity interests (the receiving entity) and the entity that transferred the net assets or equity interests (the transferring entity) may account for similar assets and liabilities using different accounting methods. In such circumstances, the carrying values of the assets and liabilities transferred may be adjusted to the basis of accounting used by the receiving entity if the change would otherwise have been appropriate. Any such change in accounting method should be applied retroactively, and financial statements presented for prior periods should be restated (Opinion 16, paragraph 52).

D16. The financial statements of the receiving entity should report results of operations for the period in which the transfer occurs as though the transfer of net assets or exchange of equity interests had occurred at the beginning of the period. Results of operations for that period will thus comprise those of the previously separate entities combined from the beginning of the period to the date the transfer is completed and those of the combined operations from that date to the end of the period. By eliminating the effects of intercompany transactions in determining the results of operations for the period before the combination, those results will be on substantially the same basis as the results of operations for the period after the date of combination. The effects of intercompany transactions on current assets, current liabilities, revenue, and cost of sales for periods presented and on retained earnings at the beginning of the periods presented should be eliminated to the extent possible. The nature of and effects on earnings per share of nonrecurring intercompany transactions involving long-term assets and liabilities need not be eliminated but should be disclosed (Opinion 16, paragraph 56).

D17. Similarly, the receiving entity should present the statement of financial position and other financial information as of the beginning of the period as though the assets and liabilities had been transferred at that date. Financial statements and financial information presented for prior years should also be restated to furnish comparative information. All restated financial statements and financial summaries should indicate clearly that financial data of previously separate entities are combined (Opinion 16, paragraph 57).

D18. Notes to financial statements of the receiving entity should disclose the following for the period in which the transfer of assets and liabilities or exchange of equity interests occurred:

a. The name and brief description of the entity included in the reporting entity as a result of the net asset transfer or exchange of equity interests

b. The method of accounting for the transfer of net assets or exchange of equity interests.

Appendix E

AMENDMENTS TO EXISTING PRONOUNCEMENTS

E1. This Statement supersedes the following pronouncements:

a. APB Opinion No. 16, *Business Combinations*
b. All of the AICPA Accounting Interpretations of Opinion 16
c. FASB Statement No. 10, *Extension of "Grandfather" Provisions for Business Combinations*
d. FASB Statement No. 38, *Accounting for Preacquisition Contingencies of Purchased Enterprises*
e. FASB Statement No. 79, *Elimination of Certain Disclosures for Business Combinations by Nonpublic Enterprises.*

E2. APB Opinion No. 20, *Accounting Changes*, is amended as follows:

a. The last sentence of paragraph 12 is deleted.

b. In the last sentence of paragraph 35, *Paragraphs 56 to 65 and 93 to 96 of APB Opinion No. 16, Business Combinations* is replaced by *Paragraphs 51–58 of FASB Statement No. 141, Business Combinations.*

E3. The fourth sentence of paragraph 21 of APB Opinion No. 28, *Interim Financial Reporting*, is amended as follows:

a. The phrase *, business combinations treated for accounting purposes as poolings of interests and acquisition of a significant business* is replaced by *and business combinations.*

b. The following footnote is added to the end of that sentence:

*Disclosures required in interim financial information related to a business combination are set forth in paragraph 58 of FASB Statement No. 141, Business Combinations.

E4. In paragraph 4(a) of APB Opinion No. 29, *Accounting for Nonmonetary Transactions*, the phrase

APB Opinion No. 16, Business Combinations, is replaced by *FASB Statement No. 141, Business Combinations,* and the following footnote is added to the end of that paragraph:

*Paragraph 10 of Statement 141 states that an exchange of a business for a business is a business combination.

E5. APB Opinion No. 30, *Reporting the Results of Operations—Reporting the Effects of Disposal of a Segment of a Business, and Extraordinary, Unusual and Infrequently Occurring Events and Transactions,* is amended as follows:

a. In the third sentence of paragraph 7, *or of APB Opinion No. 16, Business Combinations, paragraph 60,* is deleted.

b. The following sentence is added at the end of paragraph 20:

However, the following items shall be recognized as extraordinary items regardless of whether those criteria are met:

(1) Classifications of gains or losses from extinguishment of debt pursuant to paragraph 8 of FASB Statement No. 4, *Reporting Gains and Losses from Extinguishment of Debt*
(2) The net effect of discontinuing the application of FASB Statement No. 71, *Accounting for the Effects of Certain Types of Regulation,* pursuant to paragraph 6 of FASB Statement No. 101, *Regulated Enterprises—Accounting for the Discontinuation of Application of FASB Statement No. 71*
(3) The remaining excess of fair value of acquired net assets over cost pursuant to paragraphs 45 and 46 of FASB Statement No. 141, *Business Combinations.*

E6. FASB Statement No. 15, *Accounting by Debtors and Creditors for Troubled Debt Restructurings,* is amended as follows:

a. In footnote 5 to paragraph 13, *(See paragraph 67 of APB Opinion No. 16, "Business Combinations.")* is replaced by *(See paragraph 6 of FASB Statement No. 141, Business Combinations.).*

b. In footnote 6 to paragraph 13, *paragraphs 88 and 89 of APB Opinion No. 16* is replaced by *paragraphs 37 and 38 of Statement 141.*

c. In footnote 16 to paragraph 28, *(See paragraph 67 of APB Opinion No. 16.)* is replaced by *(See paragraph 6 of Statement 141.)*.

E7. In the first sentence of footnote 6 to paragraph 12 of FASB Statement No. 16, *Prior Period Adjustments,* the phrase *a change in accounting method permitted by paragraph 52 of APB Opinion No. 16,* is deleted.

E8. In the first sentence of paragraph 4 of FASB Statement No. 44, *Accounting for Intangible Assets of Motor Carriers,* the following footnote is added after *APB Opinion No. 16, Business Combinations*:

> *FASB Statement No. 141, *Business Combinations,* supersedes Opinion 16. However, the guidance from paragraph 88 of Opinion 16 is carried forward in paragraphs 37 and 38 of Statement 141.

E9. Paragraph 19 of FASB Statement No. 45, *Accounting for Franchise Fee Revenue,* is amended as follows:

a. In the first sentence, *APB Opinion No. 16, Business Combinations,* is replaced by *FASB Statement No. 141, Business Combinations,* .

b. The second and third sentences are deleted.

E10. In the first sentence of footnote 3 to paragraph 11 of FASB Statement No. 68, *Research and Development Arrangements,* the phrase *accounted for by the purchase method* is deleted.

E11. FASB Statement No. 72, *Accounting for Certain Acquisitions of Banking or Thrift Institutions,* is amended as follows:

a. The first sentence of paragraph 4 is replaced by the following:

> In a business combination involving the acquisition of a banking or thrift institution, intangible assets acquired that meet the criteria in paragraph 39 of FASB Statement No. 141, *Business Combinations,* shall be recognized as assets apart from goodwill.

b. In the second sentence of paragraph 8, *(paragraphs 87 and 88 of Opinion 16)* is replaced by *(paragraphs 35–39 of Statement 141).*

c. In the first sentence of paragraph 9, *accounted for by the purchase method* is deleted.

E12. FASB Statement No. 87, *Employers' Accounting for Pensions,* is amended as follows:

a. In the first sentence of paragraph 74, *that is accounted for by the purchase method under Opinion 16* is deleted.

b. In the first sentence of Illustration 7—Accounting for a Business Combination, in paragraph 261, *accounted for as a purchase* is deleted.

E13. Paragraph 134(g) of FASB Statement No. 95, *Statement of Cash Flows,* is amended as follows:

a. At the end of the first sentence, *in a business combination* is added.

b. The second sentence is deleted.

E14. FASB Statement No. 106, *Employers' Accounting for Postretirement Benefits Other Than Pensions,* is amended as follows:

a. In the first sentence of paragraph 86, *that is accounted for by the purchase method under Opinion 16* is deleted.

b. In the first sentence of paragraph 444, *and accounts for the business combination as a purchase pursuant to APB Opinion No. 16, Business Combinations* is replaced by *in a business combination.*

E15. FASB Statement No. 109, *Accounting for Income Taxes,* is amended as follows:

a. In the heading to paragraph 11(h), *accounted for by the purchase method* is deleted.

b. In the first sentence of paragraph 11(h), *accounted for as a purchase under APB Opinion No. 16, Business Combinations* is deleted.

c. In the last sentence of paragraph 13, *accounted for by the purchase method* is deleted.

d. In the first sentence of paragraph 30, *"negative goodwill"* is replaced by *excess over cost (also referred to as negative goodwill).*

e. In paragraph 36(d), the following footnote is added to *pooling of interests*:

> *FASB Statement No. 141, *Business Combinations,* prohibits the use of the pooling-of-

interests method for all business combinations initiated after June 30, 2001.

f. In the first sentence of paragraph 259, *accounted for as a purchase under Opinion 16* is deleted.

g. In paragraph 270, the following footnote is added to the end of the first sentence:

> *Statement 141 prohibits the use of the pooling-of-interests method for all business combinations initiated after June 30, 2001.

E16. FASB Statement No. 123, *Accounting for Stock-Based Compensation,* is amended as follows:

a. In the last sentence of paragraph 8, *purchase* is deleted.

b. In the first sentence of paragraph 36, *, except for those made to reflect the terms of the exchange of shares in a business combination accounted for as a pooling of interests,* is deleted.

E17. Paragraph 59 of FASB Statement No. 128, *Earnings per Share,* is amended as follows:

a. In the first sentence, *transaction accounted for as a purchase* is deleted.

b. The second sentence is deleted.

E18. FASB Statement No. 133, *Accounting for Derivative Instruments and Hedging Activities,* is amended as follows:

a. In the second sentence of paragraph 11(c), *APB Opinion No. 16* is replaced by *FASB Statement No. 141.*

b. In paragraph 29(f), *Opinion 16* is replaced by *Statement 141.*

E19. The following footnote is added to the end of the first sentence of paragraph 4 of FASB Interpretation No. 4, *Applicability of FASB Statement No. 2 to Business Combinations Accounted for by the Purchase Method:*

> *Opinion 16 was superseded by FASB Statement No. 141, *Business Combinations.* However, Statement 141 (paragraph 42) does not change the requirement in paragraph 5 of this Interpretation that the amounts assigned to acquired tangible and intangible assets to be used in a particular research and development project that have no

alternative future use be charged to expense at the date of acquisition.

E20. FASB Interpretation No. 9, *Applying APB Opinions No. 16 and 17 When a Savings and Loan Association or a Similar Institution Is Acquired in a Business Combination Accounted for by the Purchase Method,* is amended as follows:

a. Paragraph 4 is amended as follows:

(1) The first sentence of paragraph 4 is replaced by the following:

> *Paragraph 35 of FASB Statement No. 141, Business Combinations,* states that "... an acquiring entity shall allocate the cost of an acquired entity to the assets acquired and liabilities assumed based on their estimated fair values at date of acquisition. ..."

(2) In the last sentence, *APB Opinion No. 16* is replaced by *Statement 141.*

b. Paragraph 5 is amended as follows:

(1) In the first sentence, *Paragraph 88 of APB Opinion No. 16* is replaced by *Paragraph 37 of Statement 141.*

(2) In the second sentence, *paragraph 88(b)* is replaced by *paragraph 37(b).*

c. Paragraph 6 is replaced by the following:

> As described in paragraph 37(e) of Statement 141, acquired intangible assets that meet the criteria in paragraph 39 of that Statement shall be assigned an amount based on their estimated fair values.

d. In the first sentence of paragraph 7, *paragraph 88(g)* is replaced by *paragraph 37(g) of Statement 141.*

e. Paragraph 8, as amended by FASB Statement No. 72, *Accounting for Certain Acquisitions of Banking or Thrift Institutions,* is amended as follows:

(1) The second sentence is replaced by the following:

> If any of those factors meet the criteria in paragraph 39 of Statement 141, the fair

value of that factor shall be recognized as an asset apart from goodwill.

(2) In the third sentence, *amount paid for that separately identified intangible* is replaced by *fair value for that separately recognized intangible asset.*

(3) The fourth sentence is replaced by the following:

> An acquired intangible asset that does not meet the criteria in paragraph 39 of Statement 141 shall be included in the amount recorded as goodwill.

(4) In the fifth and sixth sentences, which were added by Statement 72, *identified intangible assets* is replaced by *separately recognized intangible assets.*

E21. FASB Interpretation No. 21, *Accounting for Leases in a Business Combination,* is amended as follows:

a. In the first sentence of paragraph 13, , *whether accounted for by the purchase method or by the pooling of interests method,* is deleted.

b. Paragraph 14 and the heading preceding it are deleted.

c. Paragraph 15 is amended as follows:

(1) In the first sentence, *that is accounted for by the purchase method* is deleted.

(2) In the second sentence, *paragraph 88 of APB Opinion No. 16* is replaced by *paragraphs 36–39 of FASB Statement No. 141, Business Combinations.*

(3) In the third sentence, *Opinion No. 16* is replaced by *Statement 141.*

d. Paragraph 16 is amended as follows:

(1) In the first sentence, *that is accounted for by the purchase method* is deleted.

(2) In the third sentence, *paragraph 88 of APB Opinion No. 16* is replaced by *paragraphs 37 and 38 of Statement 141.*

e. In footnote 4 to paragraph 18, *paragraph 46(a) of APB Opinion No. 16* is replaced by *paragraph 59 of Statement 141.*

f. In the heading above paragraph 19, *PURCHASE* is replaced by *BUSINESS.*

g. In the first sentence of paragraph 19, *accounted for by the purchase method* is deleted.

E22. FASB Interpretation No. 44, *Accounting for Certain Transactions involving Stock Compensation,* is amended as follows:

a. Paragraphs 81 and 82 are deleted.

b. In the first sentence of paragraph 83, *purchase* is deleted and *APB Opinion No. 16* is replaced by *FASB Statement No. 141.*

c. In the first sentence of paragraph 84, *purchase* is deleted and *Opinion 16* is replaced by *Statement 141.*

E23. In paragraph 6 of FASB Technical Bulletin No. 84-1, *Accounting for Stock Issued to Acquire the Results of a Research and Development Arrangement,* the phrase *paragraph 67 of Opinion 16* is replaced by *paragraphs 4–6 of FASB Statement No. 141, Business Combinations.*

E24. FASB Technical Bulletin No. 85-5, *Issues Relating to Accounting for Business Combinations,* is amended as follows:

a. In paragraph 1, *accounted for by the purchase method* is deleted.

b. Paragraph 2 is amended as follows:

(1) In the first sentence, *accounted for by the purchase method* is deleted.

(2) In the second sentence, *purchase* is deleted.

c. The first sentence of paragraph 3 is replaced by the following:

> Paragraph 24 of FASB Statement No. 141, *Business Combinations,* states that:
>
> > The cost of an entity acquired in a business combination includes the di-

rect costs of the business combination. ... However, indirect and general expenses related to business combinations shall be expensed as incurred.

d. Paragraph 4 is amended as follows:

(1) In the fifth sentence, *Paragraph 88 of Opinion 16 provides* is replaced by *Paragraphs 37 and 38 of Statement 141 provide.*

(2) In the sixth sentence, *Paragraph 88(i) is* replaced by *Paragraph 37(k).*

(3) In the eighth sentence, *paragraph 88(i) is* replaced by *paragraph 37(k).*

e. In the second sentence of paragraph 6, *paragraph 43 of Opinion 16 is replaced by paragraph 14 of Statement 141.*

f. In the last sentence of paragraph 7, *Accounting Interpretation 39 of Opinion 16 is replaced by Paragraph D12 of Statement 141.*

g. Paragraphs 13–24 and the related headings are deleted.

Appendix F

GLOSSARY

F1. This appendix contains definitions of certain terms used in this Statement.

Allocation period
The period that is required to identify and measure the fair value of the assets acquired and the liabilities assumed in a business combination. The allocation period ends when the acquiring entity is no longer waiting for information that it has arranged to obtain and that is known to be available or obtainable. Thus, the existence of a preacquisition contingency for which an asset, a liability, or an impairment of an asset cannot be estimated does not, of itself, extend the allocation period. Although the time required will vary with circumstances, the allocation period should usually not exceed one year from the consummation of a business combination (FASB Statement No. 38,

Accounting for Preacquisition Contingencies of Purchased Enterprises, paragraph 4(b)).

Customer relationship
For purposes of this Statement, a customer relationship exists between an entity and its customer if (a) the entity has information about the customer and has regular contact with the customer and (b) the customer has the ability to make direct contact with the entity. Relationships may arise from contracts (such as supplier contracts and service contracts). However, customer relationships may arise through means other than contracts, such as through regular contact by sales or service representatives.

Fair value
The amount at which an asset (or liability) could be bought (or incurred) or sold (or settled) in a current transaction between willing parties, that is, other than in a forced or liquidation sale.

Financial asset
Cash, evidence of an ownership interest in an entity, or a contract that conveys to a second entity a contractual right (a) to receive cash or another financial instrument from a first entity or (b) to exchange other financial instruments on potentially favorable terms with the first entity (FASB Statement No. 107, *Disclosures about Fair Value of Financial Instruments,* paragraph 3(b)).

Goodwill
The excess of the cost of an acquired entity over the net of the amounts assigned to assets acquired and liabilities assumed. The amount recognized as goodwill includes acquired intangible assets that do not meet the criteria in paragraph 39 for recognition as assets apart from goodwill.

Intangible assets
Assets (not including financial assets) that lack physical substance.

Intangible asset class
A group of intangible assets that are similar, either by their nature or by their use in the operations of an entity.

Mutual enterprise

An entity other than an investor-owned entity that provides dividends, lower costs, or other economic benefits directly and proportionately to its owners, members, or participants. Mutual insurance companies, credit unions, and farm and rural electric cooperatives are examples of mutual enterprises (FASB Concepts Statement No. 4, *Objectives of Financial Reporting by Non-business Organizations,* paragraph 7).

Not-for-profit organization

An entity that possesses the following characteristics that distinguish it from a business enterprise: (a) contributions of significant amounts of resources from resource providers who do not expect commensurate or proportionate pecuniary return, (b) operating purposes other than to provide goods or services at a profit, and (c) absence of ownership interests like those of business enterprises. Not-for-profit organizations have those characteristics in varying degrees (Concepts Statement 4, paragraph 6). Entities that clearly fall outside this definition include all investor-owned entities and mutual enterprises.

Pooling-of-interests method

A method of accounting for business combinations that was required to be used in certain circumstances by APB Opinion No. 16, *Business Combinations.* Under the pooling-of-interests method, the carrying amount of assets and liabilities recognized in the statements of financial position of each combining entity are carried forward to the statement of financial position of the combined entity. No other assets or liabilities are recognized as a result of the combination, and thus the excess of the purchase price over the book value of the net assets acquired (the purchase premium) is not recognized. The income statement of the combined entity for the year of the combination is presented as if the entities had been combined for the full year; all comparative financial statements are presented as if the entities had previously been combined.

Preacquisition contingency

A contingency of an entity that is acquired in a business combination that is in existence before the consummation of the combination. A preacquisition contingency can be a contingent asset, a contingent liability, or a contingent impairment of an asset (Statement 38, paragraph 4(a)).

Public business enterprise

An enterprise that has issued debt or equity securities that are traded in a public market (a domestic or foreign stock exchange or an over-the-counter market, including local or regional markets), that is required to file financial statements with the Securities and Exchange Commission, or that provides financial statements for the purpose of issuing any class of securities in a public market (FASB Statement No. 131, *Disclosures about Segments of an Enterprise and Related Information,* paragraph 9).

Reporting unit

The level of reporting at which goodwill is tested for impairment. A reporting unit is an operating segment or one level below an operating segment (as that term is defined in paragraph 10 of Statement 131) (FASB Statement No. 142, *Goodwill and Other Intangible Assets,* paragraph F1).

Residual value

The estimated fair value of an intangible asset at the end of its useful life to the entity, less any disposal costs.

Servicing asset

A contract to service financial assets under which the estimated future revenues from contractually specified servicing fees, late charges, and other ancillary revenues are expected to more than adequately compensate the servicer for performing the servicing. A servicing contract is either (a) undertaken in conjunction with selling or securitizing the financial assets being serviced or (b) purchased or assumed separately (FASB Statement No. 140, *Accounting for Transfers and Servicing of Financial Assets and Extinguishments of Liabilities,* paragraph 364).

Statement of Financial Accounting Standards No. 142
Goodwill and Other Intangible Assets

STATUS

Issued: June 2001

Effective Date: For fiscal years beginning after December 31, 2001; goodwill acquired in business combinations after June 30, 2001 shall not be amortized

Affects: Supersedes ARB 43, Chapter 5
Supersedes APB 17
Amends APB 18, paragraphs 19(m) and 19(n)
Supersedes APB 18, footnotes 9 and 12
Supersedes AIN-APB 17
Amends FAS 2, paragraph 11(c)
Amends FAS 44, paragraphs 3, 4, and 7
Amends FAS 51, paragraphs 13 and 14
Amends FAS 52, paragraph 48
Amends FAS 68, footnote 3
Supersedes FAS 71, paragraphs 29 and 30
Amends FAS 72, paragraphs 2, 4, 6, and 7
Supersedes FAS 72, footnotes 5 and 6
Amends FAS 121, paragraphs 3, 4, 6, and 147
Supersedes FAS 121, paragraph 12
Amends FIN 9, paragraph 8
Supersedes FIN 9, paragraph 9

Affected by: Paragraph 7 and footnote 22 superseded by FAS 144
Paragraphs 8, 8(i), and 35 amended by FAS 145
Paragraphs 15, 17, 28(f), 29, and Appendix A (Examples 1, 2, 3, 5, and 9) amended by FAS 144
Paragraph D11(a)(2) superseded by FAS 145

Issues Discussed by FASB Emerging Issues Task Force (EITF)

Affects: Partially nullifies EITF Issues No. 85-8, 85-42, 88-20, and 90-6

Interpreted by: Paragraph 10 interpreted by EITF Issue No. 97-13
Paragraphs 17 and 20 interpreted by EITF Issue No. 02-7
Paragraph 30 interpreted by EITF Topic No. D-101
Paragraph 49(b) interpreted by EITF Topic No. D-100

Related Issue: EITF Issues No. 85-41, 88-19, 89-19, 92-9, and 93-1

SUMMARY

This Statement addresses financial accounting and reporting for acquired goodwill and other intangible assets and supersedes APB Opinion No. 17, *Intangible Assets*. It addresses how intangible assets that are acquired individually or with a group of other assets (but not those acquired in a business combination) should be accounted for in financial statements upon their acquisition. This Statement also addresses how goodwill and other intangible assets should be accounted for after they have been initially recognized in the financial statements.

Reasons for Issuing This Statement

Analysts and other users of financial statements, as well as company managements, noted that intangible assets are an increasingly important economic resource for many entities and are an increasing proportion of the assets acquired in many transactions. As a result, better information about intangible assets was needed. Financial statement users also indicated that they did not regard goodwill amortization expense as being useful information in analyzing investments.

Differences between This Statement and Opinion 17

This Statement changes the unit of account for goodwill and takes a very different approach to how goodwill and other intangible assets are accounted for subsequent to their initial recognition. Because goodwill and some intangible assets will no longer be amortized, the reported amounts of goodwill and intangible assets (as well as total assets) will not decrease at the same time and in the same manner as under previous standards. There may be more volatility in reported income than under previous standards because impairment losses are likely to occur irregularly and in varying amounts.

This Statement changes the subsequent accounting for goodwill and other intangible assets in the following significant respects:

- Acquiring entities usually integrate acquired entities into their operations, and thus the acquirers' expectations of benefits from the resulting synergies usually are reflected in the premium that they pay to acquire those entities. However, the transaction-based approach to accounting for goodwill under Opinion 17 treated the acquired entity as if it remained a stand-alone entity rather than being integrated with the acquiring entity; as a result, the portion of the premium related to expected synergies (goodwill) was not accounted for appropriately. This Statement adopts a more aggregate view of goodwill and bases the accounting for goodwill on the units of the combined entity into which an acquired entity is integrated (those units are referred to as reporting units).
- Opinion 17 presumed that goodwill and all other intangible assets were wasting assets (that is, finite lived), and thus the amounts assigned to them should be amortized in determining net income; Opinion 17 also mandated an arbitrary ceiling of 40 years for that amortization. This Statement does not presume that those assets are wasting assets. Instead, goodwill and intangible assets that have indefinite useful lives will not be amortized but rather will be tested at least annually for impairment. Intangible assets that have finite useful lives will continue to be amortized over their useful lives, but without the constraint of an arbitrary ceiling.
- Previous standards provided little guidance about how to determine and measure goodwill impairment; as a result, the accounting for goodwill impairments was not consistent and not comparable and yielded information of questionable usefulness. This Statement provides specific guidance for testing goodwill for impairment. Goodwill will be tested for impairment at least annually using a two-step process that begins with an estimation of the fair value of a reporting unit. The first step is a screen for potential impairment, and the second step measures the amount of impairment, if any. However, if certain criteria are met, the requirement to test goodwill for impairment annually can be satisfied without a remeasurement of the fair value of a reporting unit.
- In addition, this Statement provides specific guidance on testing intangible assets that will not be amortized for impairment and thus removes those intangible assets from the scope of other impairment guidance. Intangible assets that are not amortized will be tested for impairment at least annually by comparing the fair values of those assets with their recorded amounts.
- This Statement requires disclosure of information about goodwill and other intangible assets in the years subsequent to their acquisition that was not previously required. Required disclosures include information about the changes in the carrying amount of goodwill from period to period (in the aggregate and by reportable segment), the carrying amount of intangible assets by major intangible asset class for those assets subject to amortization and for those not subject to amortization, and the estimated intangible asset amortization expense for the next five years.

This Statement carries forward without reconsideration the provisions of Opinion 17 related to the accounting for internally developed intangible assets. This Statement also does not change the requirement to expense the cost of certain acquired research and development assets at the date of acquisition as required by FASB Statement No. 2, *Accounting for Research and Development Costs,* and FASB Interpretation No. 4, *Applicability of FASB Statement No. 2 to Business Combinations Accounted for by the Purchase Method.*

How the Changes in This Statement Improve Financial Reporting

The changes included in this Statement will improve financial reporting because the financial statements of entities that acquire goodwill and other intangible assets will better reflect the underlying economics of those assets. As a result, financial statement users will be better able to understand the investments made in those assets and the subsequent performance of those investments. The enhanced disclosures about goodwill and intangible assets subsequent to their acquisition also will provide users with a better understanding of the expectations about and changes in those assets over time, thereby improving their ability to assess future profitability and cash flows.

How the Conclusions in This Statement Relate to the Conceptual Framework

The Board concluded that amortization of goodwill was not consistent with the concept of representational faithfulness, as discussed in FASB Concepts Statement No. 2, *Qualitative Characteristics of Accounting Information.* The Board concluded that nonamortization of goodwill coupled with impairment testing *is* consistent with that concept. The appropriate balance of both relevance and reliability and costs and benefits also was central to the Board's conclusion that this Statement will improve financial reporting.

This Statement utilizes the guidance in FASB Concepts Statement No. 7, *Using Cash Flow Information and Present Value in Accounting Measurements,* for estimating the fair values used in testing both goodwill and other intangible assets that are not being amortized for impairment.

The Effective Date of This Statement

The provisions of this Statement are required to be applied starting with fiscal years beginning after December 15, 2001. Early application is permitted for entities with fiscal years beginning after March 15, 2001, provided that the first interim financial statements have not previously been issued. This Statement is required to be applied at the beginning of an entity's fiscal year and to be applied to all goodwill and other intangible assets recognized in its financial statements at that date. Impairment losses for goodwill and indefinite-lived intangible assets that arise due to the initial application of this Statement (resulting from a transitional impairment test) are to be reported as resulting from a change in accounting principle.

There are two exceptions to the date at which this Statement becomes effective:

- Goodwill and intangible assets acquired after June 30, 2001, will be subject immediately to the nonamortization and amortization provisions of this Statement.
- The provisions of this Statement will not be applicable to goodwill and other intangible assets arising from combinations between mutual enterprises or to not-for-profit organizations until the Board completes its deliberations with respect to application of the purchase method by those entities.

Statement of Financial Accounting Standards No. 142

Goodwill and Other Intangible Assets

CONTENTS

INTRODUCTION

1. This Statement addresses financial accounting and reporting for intangible assets acquired individually or with a group of other assets (but not those acquired in a business combination) at acquisition. This Statement also addresses financial accounting and reporting for goodwill and other intangible assets subsequent to their acquisition. FASB Statement No. 141, *Business Combinations,* addresses financial accounting and reporting for goodwill and other intangible assets acquired in a business combination at acquisition.[1]

2. This Statement supersedes APB Opinion No. 17, *Intangible Assets;* however, it carries forward without reconsideration the provisions in Opinion 17 related to internally developed intangible assets. The Board did not reconsider those provisions because they were outside the scope of its project on business combinations and acquired intangible assets. The guidance carried forward from Opinion 17 has been quoted, paraphrased, or rephrased as necessary so that it can be understood in the context of this Statement. The original source of that guidance has been noted parenthetically.

3. Appendix A to this Statement provides implementation guidance on how intangible assets should be accounted for in accordance with this Statement. Appendix A is an integral part of the standards provided in this Statement. Appendix B provides background information and the basis for the Board's conclusions. Appendix C provides illustrations of some of the financial statement disclosures that this Statement requires. Appendix D lists other accounting pronouncements superseded or amended by this Statement. Appendix E includes relevant excerpts from FASB Concepts Statement No. 7, *Using Cash Flow Information and Present Value in Accounting Measurements.* Appendix F provides a glossary of terms used in this Statement.

STANDARDS OF FINANCIAL ACCOUNTING AND REPORTING

Scope

4. The initial recognition and measurement provisions of this Statement apply to **intangible assets**[2] acquired individually or with a group of other assets (but not those acquired in a business combination).[3] The remaining provisions of this Statement apply to **goodwill** that an entity[4] recognizes in accordance with Statement 141 and to other intangible assets that an entity acquires, whether individually, with a group of other assets, or in a business combination. While goodwill is an intangible asset, the term *intangible asset* is used in this Statement to refer to an intangible asset other than goodwill.

5. This Statement applies to costs of internally developing goodwill and other unidentifiable intangible assets with indeterminate lives. Some entities capitalize costs incurred to develop identifiable intangible assets, while others expense those costs as incurred. This Statement also applies to costs of internally developing identifiable intangible assets that an entity recognizes as assets (Opinion 17, paragraphs 5 and 6).

6. This Statement applies to goodwill and other intangible assets recognized on the acquisition of some or all of the noncontrolling interests in a subsidiary—whether acquired by the parent, the subsidiary itself, or another affiliate.[5] This Statement, including its transition provisions, applies to amounts recognized as goodwill in applying the equity method of accounting and to the excess reorganization value recognized by entities that adopt fresh-start reporting in accordance with AICPA Statement of Position 90-7, *Financial Reporting by Entities in Reorganization Under the Bankruptcy Code.* That excess reorganization value shall be reported as goodwill and accounted for in the same manner as goodwill.

---

[1]Statement 141 was issued concurrently with this Statement and addresses financial accounting and reporting for business combinations. It supersedes APB Opinion No. 16, *Business Combinations,* and FASB Statement No. 38, *Accounting for Preacquisition Contingencies of Purchased Enterprises.*

[2]Terms defined in Appendix F, the glossary, are set forth in **boldface** type the first time they are used.

[3]Statement 141 addresses the initial recognition and measurement of intangible assets acquired in a business combination.

[4]This Statement applies to a business enterprise, a **mutual enterprise,** and a **not-for-profit organization,** each of which is referred to herein as an *entity.*

[5]Statement 141 requires that the acquisition of some or all of the noncontrolling interests in a subsidiary be accounted for using the purchase method.

7. This Statement amends FASB Statement No. 121, *Accounting for the Impairment of Long-Lived Assets and for Long-Lived Assets to Be Disposed Of,* to exclude from its scope goodwill and intangible assets that are not amortized.

8. Except as described in Appendix D, this. Statement does not change the accounting prescribed in the following pronouncements:

a. FASB Statement No. 2, *Accounting for Research and Development Costs*

b. FASB Statement No. 19, *Financial Accounting and Reporting by Oil and Gas Producing Companies*

c. FASB Statement No. 44, *Accounting for Intangible Assets of Motor Carriers*

d. FASB Statement No. 50, *Financial Reporting in the Record and Music Industry*

e. FASB Statement No. 61, *Accounting for Title Plant*

f. FASB Statement No. 63, *Financial Reporting by Broadcasters*

g. FASB Statement No. 71, *Accounting for the Effects of Certain Types of Regulation* (paragraphs 29 and 30)

h. FASB Statement No. 72, *Accounting for Certain Acquisitions of Banking or Thrift Institutions* (paragraphs 4–7)

i. FASB Statement No. 86, *Accounting for the Costs of Computer Software to Be Sold, Leased, or Otherwise Marketed* (paragraph 7)

j. FASB Statement No. 109, *Accounting for Income Taxes* (a deferred tax asset)

k. FASB Statement No. 140, *Accounting for Transfers and Servicing of Financial Assets and Extinguishments of Liabilities* (a servicing asset or liability)

l. FASB Interpretation No. 4, *Applicability of FASB Statement No. 2 to Business Combinations Accounted for by the Purchase Method.*

Initial Recognition and Measurement of Intangible Assets

9. An intangible asset that is acquired either individually or with a group of other assets (but not those acquired in a business combination) shall be initially recognized and measured based on its **fair value.** General concepts related to the initial measurement of assets acquired in exchange transactions, including intangible assets, are provided in paragraphs 5–7 of Statement 141.[6] The cost of a group of assets acquired in a transaction other than a business combination shall be allocated to the individual assets acquired based on their relative fair values and shall not give rise to goodwill.[7] Intangible assets acquired in a business combination are initially recognized and measured in accordance with Statement 141.[8]

Internally Developed Intangible Assets

10. Costs of internally developing, maintaining, or restoring intangible assets (including goodwill) that are not specifically identifiable, that have indeterminate lives, or that are inherent in a continuing business and related to an entity as a whole, shall be recognized as an expense when incurred (Opinion 17, paragraph 24).

Accounting for Intangible Assets

Determining the Useful Life of an Intangible Asset

11. The accounting for a recognized intangible asset is based on its **useful life** to the reporting entity. An intangible asset with a finite useful life is amortized; an intangible asset with an indefinite useful life is not amortized. The useful life of an intangible asset to an entity is the period over which the asset is expected to contribute directly or indirectly to the future cash flows of that entity.[9] The estimate of the useful life of

---

[6]Although those paragraphs refer to determining the cost of the assets acquired, both paragraph 6 of Statement 141 and paragraph 18 of APB Opinion No. 29, *Accounting for Nonmonetary Transactions,* note that, in general, cost should be measured based on the fair value of the consideration given or the fair value of the net assets acquired, whichever is more reliably measurable.

[7]Statement 141 requires intangible assets acquired in a business combination that do not meet certain criteria to be included in the amount initially recognized as goodwill. Those recognition criteria do not apply to intangible assets acquired in transactions other than business combinations.

[8]Statement 2 and Interpretation 4 require amounts assigned to acquired intangible assets that are to be used in a particular research and development project and that *have no alternative future use* to be charged to expense at the acquisition date. Statement 141 does not change that requirement, nor does this Statement.

[9]The useful life of an intangible asset shall reflect the period over which it will contribute to the cash flows of the reporting entity, not the period of time that it would take that entity to internally develop an intangible asset that would provide similar benefits.

an intangible asset to an entity shall be based on an analysis of all pertinent factors, in particular:

a. The expected use of the asset by the entity
b. The expected useful life of another asset or a group of assets to which the useful life of the intangible asset may relate (such as mineral rights to depleting assets)
c. Any legal, regulatory, or contractual provisions that may limit the useful life
d. Any legal, regulatory, or contractual provisions that enable renewal or extension of the asset's legal or contractual life without substantial cost (provided there is evidence to support renewal or extension and renewal or extension can be accomplished without material modifications of the existing terms and conditions)
e. The effects of obsolescence, demand, competition, and other economic factors (such as the stability of the industry, known technological advances, legislative action that results in an uncertain or changing regulatory environment, and expected changes in distribution channels)
f. The level of maintenance expenditures required to obtain the expected future cash flows from the asset (for example, a material level of required maintenance in relation to the carrying amount of the asset may suggest a very limited useful life).[10]

If no legal, regulatory, contractual, competitive, economic, or other factors limit the useful life of an intangible asset to the reporting entity, the useful life of the asset shall be considered to be indefinite. The term *indefinite* does not mean infinite. Appendix A includes illustrative examples of different intangible assets and how they should be accounted for in accordance with this Statement, including determining whether the useful life of an intangible asset is indefinite.

Intangible Assets Subject to Amortization

12. A recognized intangible asset shall be amortized over its useful life to the reporting entity unless that life is determined to be indefinite. If an intangible asset has a finite useful life, but the precise length of that life is not known, that intangible asset shall be amortized over the best estimate of its useful life. The method of amortization shall reflect the pattern in

which the economic benefits of the intangible asset are consumed or otherwise used up. If that pattern cannot be reliably determined, a straight-line amortization method shall be used. An intangible asset shall not be written down or off in the period of acquisition unless it becomes impaired during that period.[11]

13. The amount of an intangible asset to be amortized shall be the amount initially assigned to that asset less any **residual value.** The residual value of an intangible asset shall be assumed to be zero unless at the end of its useful life to the reporting entity the asset is expected to continue to have a useful life to another entity and (a) the reporting entity has a commitment from a third party to purchase the asset at the end of its useful life or (b) the residual value can be determined by reference to an exchange transaction in an existing market for that asset and that market is expected to exist at the end of the asset's useful life.

14. An entity shall evaluate the remaining useful life of an intangible asset that is being amortized each reporting period to determine whether events and circumstances warrant a revision to the remaining period of amortization. If the estimate of an intangible asset's remaining useful life is changed, the remaining carrying amount of the intangible asset shall be amortized prospectively over that revised remaining useful life. If an intangible asset that is being amortized is subsequently determined to have an indefinite useful life, the asset shall be tested for impairment in accordance with paragraph 17. That intangible asset shall no longer be amortized and shall be accounted for in the same manner as other intangible assets that are not subject to amortization.

Recognition and measurement of an impairment loss

15. An intangible asset that is subject to amortization shall be reviewed for impairment in accordance with Statement 121 by applying the recognition and measurement provisions in paragraphs 4–11 of that Statement. In accordance with Statement 121, an impairment loss shall be recognized if the carrying amount of an intangible asset is not recoverable and its carrying amount exceeds its fair value. After an impairment loss is recognized, the adjusted carrying

---

[10]As in determining the useful life of depreciable tangible assets, regular maintenance may be assumed but enhancements may not.

[11]However, both Statement 2 and Interpretation 4 require amounts assigned to acquired intangible assets that are to be used in a particular research and development project and that have no alternative future use to be charged to expense at the acquisition date.

amount of the intangible asset shall be its new accounting basis. Subsequent reversal of a previously recognized impairment loss is prohibited.

Intangible Assets Not Subject to Amortization

16. If an intangible asset is determined to have an indefinite useful life, it shall not be amortized until its useful life is determined to be no longer indefinite. An entity shall evaluate the remaining useful life of an intangible asset that is not being amortized each reporting period to determine whether events and circumstances continue to support an indefinite useful life. If an intangible asset that is not being amortized is subsequently determined to have a finite useful life, the asset shall be tested for impairment in accordance with paragraph 17. That intangible asset shall then be amortized prospectively over its estimated remaining useful life and accounted for in the same manner as other intangible assets that are subject to amortization.

Recognition and measurement of an impairment loss

17. An intangible asset that is not subject to amortization shall be tested for impairment annually, or more frequently if events or changes in circumstances indicate that the asset might be impaired. (Paragraph 5 of Statement 121 includes examples of impairment indicators.) The impairment test shall consist of a comparison of the fair value of an intangible asset with its carrying amount.[12] If the carrying amount of an intangible asset exceeds its fair value, an impairment loss shall be recognized in an amount equal to that excess. After an impairment loss is recognized, the adjusted carrying amount of the intangible asset shall be its new accounting basis. Subsequent reversal of a previously recognized impairment loss is prohibited.

Accounting for Goodwill

18. Goodwill shall not be amortized. Goodwill shall be tested for impairment at a level of reporting referred to as a reporting unit. (Paragraphs 30–36 provide guidance on determining reporting units.) Impairment is the condition that exists when the carrying amount of goodwill exceeds its implied fair value.[13] The two-step impairment test discussed in paragraphs 19–22 shall be used to identify potential goodwill impairment and measure the amount of a goodwill impairment loss to be recognized (if any).

Recognition and Measurement of an Impairment Loss

19. The first step of the goodwill impairment test, used to identify potential impairment, compares the fair value of a reporting unit with its carrying amount, including goodwill. The guidance in paragraphs 23–25 shall be used to determine the fair value of a reporting unit. If the fair value of a reporting unit exceeds its carrying amount, goodwill of the reporting unit is considered not impaired, thus the second step of the impairment test is unnecessary. If the carrying amount of a reporting unit exceeds its fair value, the second step of the goodwill impairment test shall be performed to measure the amount of impairment loss, if any.

20. The second step of the goodwill impairment test, used to measure the amount of impairment loss, compares the implied fair value of reporting unit goodwill with the carrying amount of that goodwill. The guidance in paragraph 21 shall be used to estimate the implied fair value of goodwill. If the carrying amount of reporting unit goodwill exceeds the implied fair value of that goodwill, an impairment loss shall be recognized in an amount equal to that excess. The loss recognized cannot exceed the carrying amount of goodwill. After a goodwill impairment loss is recognized, the adjusted carrying amount of goodwill shall be its new accounting basis. Subsequent reversal of a previously recognized goodwill impairment loss is prohibited once the measurement of that loss is completed.

21. The implied fair value of goodwill shall be determined in the same manner as the amount of goodwill recognized in a business combination is determined. That is, an entity shall allocate the fair value of a reporting unit to all of the assets and liabilities of that unit (including any unrecognized intangible assets) as if the reporting unit had been acquired in a business combination and the fair value of the reporting

---

[12]The fair value of an intangible asset shall be estimated using the guidance in paragraphs 23–25 (except the guidance specific to estimating the fair value of a **reporting unit**).

[13]The fair value of goodwill can be measured only as a residual and cannot be measured directly. Therefore, this Statement includes a methodology to determine an amount that achieves a reasonable estimate of the value of goodwill for purposes of measuring an impairment loss. That estimate is referred to herein as the *implied fair value of goodwill*.

unit was the price paid to acquire the reporting unit.[14] The excess of the fair value of a reporting unit over the amounts assigned to its assets and liabilities is the implied fair value of goodwill. That allocation process shall be performed only for purposes of testing goodwill for impairment; an entity shall not write up or write down a recognized asset or liability, nor should it recognize a previously unrecognized intangible asset as a result of that allocation process.

22. If the second step of the goodwill impairment test is not complete before the financial statements are issued and a goodwill impairment loss is probable and can be reasonably estimated, the best estimate of that loss shall be recognized in those financial statements.[15] Paragraph 47(c) requires disclosure of the fact that the measurement of the impairment loss is an estimate. Any adjustment to that estimated loss based on the completion of the measurement of the impairment loss shall be recognized in the subsequent reporting period.

Fair value measurements

23. The fair value of an asset (or liability) is the amount at which that asset (or liability) could be bought (or incurred) or sold (or settled) in a current transaction between willing parties, that is, other than in a forced or liquidation sale. Thus, the fair value of a reporting unit refers to the amount at which the unit as a whole could be bought or sold in a current transaction between willing parties. Quoted market prices in active markets are the best evidence of fair value and shall be used as the basis for the measurement, if available. However, the market price of an individual equity security (and thus the market capitalization of a reporting unit with publicly traded equity securities) may not be representative of the fair value of the reporting unit as a whole.[16] The quoted market price of an individual equity security, therefore, need not be the sole measurement basis of the fair value of a reporting unit.

24. If quoted market prices are not available, the estimate of fair value shall be based on the best infor-mation available, including prices for similar assets and liabilities and the results of using other valuation techniques. A present value technique is often the best available technique with which to estimate the fair value of a group of net assets (such as a reporting unit). If a present value technique is used to measure fair value, estimates of future cash flows used in that technique shall be consistent with the objective of measuring fair value. Those cash flow estimates shall incorporate assumptions that marketplace participants would use in their estimates of fair value. If that information is not available without undue cost and effort, an entity may use its own assumptions. Those cash flow estimates shall be based on reasonable and supportable assumptions and shall consider all available evidence. The weight given to the evidence shall be commensurate with the extent to which the evidence can be verified objectively. If a range is estimated for the amounts or timing of possible cash flows, the likelihood of possible outcomes shall be considered. Concepts Statement 7 discusses the essential elements of a present value measurement (paragraph 23), provides examples of circumstances in which an entity's cash flows might differ from the market cash flows (paragraph 32), and discusses the use of present value techniques in measuring the fair value of an asset or a liability (paragraphs 39–54 and 75–88). Appendix E of this Statement incorporates those paragraphs of Concepts Statement 7.

25. In estimating the fair value of a reporting unit, a valuation technique based on multiples of earnings or revenue or a similar performance measure may be used if that technique is consistent with the objective of measuring fair value. Use of multiples of earnings or revenue in determining the fair value of a reporting unit may be appropriate, for example, when the fair value of an entity that has comparable operations and economic characteristics is observable and the relevant multiples of the comparable entity are known. Conversely, use of multiples would not be appropriate in situations in which the operations or activities of an entity for which the multiples are

---

[14]The relevant guidance in paragraphs 35–38 of Statement 141 shall be used in determining how to allocate the fair value of a reporting unit to the assets and liabilities of that unit. Included in that allocation would be research and development assets that meet the criteria in paragraph 32 of this Statement even if Statement 2 or Interpretation 4 would require those assets to be written off to earnings when acquired.

[15]Refer to FASB Statement No. 5, *Accounting for Contingencies.*

[16]Substantial value may arise from the ability to take advantage of synergies and other benefits that flow from control over another entity. Consequently, measuring the fair value of a collection of assets and liabilities that operate together in a controlled entity is different from measuring the fair value of that entity's individual equity securities. An acquiring entity often is willing to pay more for equity securities that give it a controlling interest than an investor would pay for a number of equity securities representing less than a controlling interest. That control premium may cause the fair value of a reporting unit to exceed its market capitalization.

known are not of a comparable nature, scope, or size as the reporting unit for which fair value is being estimated.

When to test goodwill for impairment

26. Goodwill of a reporting unit shall be tested for impairment on an annual basis and between annual tests in certain circumstances (refer to paragraph 28). The annual goodwill impairment test may be performed any time during the fiscal year provided the test is performed at the same time every year. Different reporting units may be tested for impairment at different times.

27. A detailed determination of the fair value of a reporting unit may be carried forward from one year to the next if all of the following criteria have been met:

a. The assets and liabilities that make up the reporting unit have not changed significantly since the most recent fair value determination. (A recent significant acquisition or a reorganization of an entity's segment reporting structure is an example of an event that might significantly change the composition of a reporting unit.)
b. The most recent fair value determination resulted in an amount that exceeded the carrying amount of the reporting unit by a substantial margin.
c. Based on an analysis of events that have occurred and circumstances that have changed since the most recent fair value determination, the likelihood that a current fair value determination would be less than the current carrying amount of the reporting unit is remote.

28. Goodwill of a reporting unit shall be tested for impairment between annual tests if an event occurs or circumstances change that would more likely than not reduce the fair value of a reporting unit below its carrying amount. Examples of such events or circumstances include:

a. A significant adverse change in legal factors or in the business climate

b. An adverse action or assessment by a regulator
c. Unanticipated competition
d. A loss of key personnel
e. A more-likely-than-not expectation that a reporting unit or a significant portion of a reporting unit will be sold or otherwise disposed of
f. The testing for recoverability under Statement 121 of a significant asset group within a reporting unit
g. Recognition of a goodwill impairment loss in the financial statements of a subsidiary that is a component of a reporting unit.

In addition, paragraph 39 requires that goodwill be tested for impairment after a portion of goodwill has been allocated to a business to be disposed of.

29. If goodwill and another asset (or asset group) of a reporting unit are tested for impairment at the same time, the other asset (or asset group) shall be tested for impairment before goodwill. For example, if a significant asset group is to be tested for impairment under Statement 121 (thus potentially requiring a goodwill impairment test), the impairment test for the significant asset group would be performed before the goodwill impairment test. If the asset group was impaired, the impairment loss would be recognized prior to goodwill being tested for impairment.

Reporting unit

30. A reporting unit is an operating segment or one level below an operating segment (referred to as a component).[17] A component of an operating segment is a reporting unit if the component constitutes a business[18] for which discrete financial information is available and segment management[19] regularly reviews the operating results of that component. However, two or more components of an operating segment shall be aggregated and deemed a single reporting unit if the components have similar economic characteristics.[20] An operating segment shall be deemed to be a reporting unit if all of its components are similar, if none of its components is a reporting unit, or if it comprises only a single

---

[17]For purposes of determining reporting units, an operating segment is as defined in paragraph 10 of FASB Statement No. 131, *Disclosures about Segments of an Enterprise and Related Information.*

[18]Emerging Issues Task Force Issue No. 98-3, "Determining Whether a Nonmonetary Transaction Involves Receipt of Productive Assets or of a Business," includes guidance on determining whether an asset group constitutes a business.

[19]Segment management consists of one or more segment managers, as that term is defined in paragraph 14 of Statement 131.

[20]Paragraph 17 of Statement 131 shall be considered in determining if the components of an operating segment have similar economic characteristics.

component. The relevant provisions of Statement 131 and related interpretive literature shall be used to determine the reporting units of an entity.

31. An entity that is not required to report segment information in accordance with Statement 131 is nonetheless required to test goodwill for impairment at the reporting unit level. That entity shall use the guidance in paragraphs 10–15 of Statement 131 to determine its operating segments for purposes of determining its reporting units.

Assigning acquired assets and assumed liabilities to reporting units

32. For the purpose of testing goodwill for impairment, acquired assets and assumed liabilities shall be assigned to a reporting unit as of the acquisition date if both of the following criteria are met:

a. The asset will be employed in or the liability relates to the operations of a reporting unit.
b. The asset or liability will be considered in determining the fair value of the reporting unit.

Assets or liabilities that an entity considers part of its corporate assets or liabilities shall also be assigned to a reporting unit if both of the above criteria are met. Examples of corporate items that may meet those criteria and therefore would be assigned to a reporting unit are environmental liabilities that relate to an existing operating facility of the reporting unit and a pension obligation that would be included in the determination of the fair value of the reporting unit. This provision applies to assets acquired and liabilities assumed in a business combination and to those acquired or assumed individually or with a group of other assets.

33. Some assets or liabilities may be employed in or relate to the operations of multiple reporting units. The methodology used to determine the amount of those assets or liabilities to assign to a reporting unit shall be reasonable and supportable and shall be applied in a consistent manner. For example, assets and liabilities not directly related to a specific reporting unit, but from which the reporting unit benefits, could be allocated according to the benefit received by the different reporting units (or based on the relative fair values of the different reporting units). In the case of pension items, for example, a pro rata allocation based on payroll expense might be used.

Assigning goodwill to reporting units

34. For the purpose of testing goodwill for impairment, *all* goodwill acquired in a business combination shall be assigned to one or more reporting units as of the acquisition date. Goodwill shall be assigned to reporting units of the acquiring entity that are expected to benefit from the synergies of the combination even though other assets or liabilities of the acquired entity may not be assigned to that reporting unit. The total amount of acquired goodwill may be divided among a number of reporting units. The methodology used to determine the amount of goodwill to assign to a reporting unit shall be reasonable and supportable and shall be applied in a consistent manner. In addition, that methodology shall be consistent with the objectives of the process of assigning goodwill to reporting units described in paragraph 35.

35. In concept, the amount of goodwill assigned to a reporting unit would be determined in a manner similar to how the amount of goodwill recognized in a business combination is determined. In essence, the fair value for each reporting unit representing a "purchase price" would be determined, and that purchase price would be allocated to the assets and liabilities of that unit.[21] If the purchase price exceeds the amount assigned to those net assets, that excess would be the goodwill assigned to that reporting unit. However, if goodwill is to be assigned to a reporting unit that has not been assigned any of the assets acquired or liabilities assumed in that acquisition, the amount of goodwill to be assigned to that unit might be determined by applying a "with and without" computation. That is, the difference between the fair value of that reporting unit before the acquisition and its fair value after the acquisition represents the amount of goodwill to be assigned to that reporting unit.

Reorganization of reporting structure

36. When an entity reorganizes its reporting structure in a manner that changes the composition of one or more of its reporting units, the guidance in paragraphs 32 and 33 shall be used to reassign assets and liabilities to the reporting units affected. However,

---

[21]Paragraphs 35–38 of Statement 141 provide guidance on allocating the purchase price to the assets acquired and liabilities assumed in a business combination.

goodwill shall be reassigned to the reporting units affected using a relative fair value allocation approach similar to that used when a portion of a reporting unit is to be disposed of (refer to paragraph 39). For example, if existing reporting unit A is to be integrated with reporting units B, C, and D, goodwill in reporting unit A would be assigned to units B, C, and D based on the relative fair values of the three portions of reporting unit A prior to those portions being integrated with reporting units B, C, and D.

Goodwill impairment testing by a subsidiary

37. All goodwill recognized by a public or non-public subsidiary (subsidiary goodwill) in its separate financial statements that are prepared in accordance with generally accepted accounting principles shall be accounted for in accordance with this Statement. Subsidiary goodwill shall be tested for impairment at the subsidiary level using the subsidiary's reporting units. If a goodwill impairment loss is recognized at the subsidiary level, goodwill of the reporting unit or units (at the higher consolidated level) in which the subsidiary's reporting unit with impaired goodwill resides must be tested for impairment if the event that gave rise to the loss at the subsidiary level would more likely than not reduce the fair value of the reporting unit (at the higher consolidated level) below its carrying amount (refer to paragraph 28(g)). Only if goodwill of that higher-level reporting unit is impaired would a goodwill impairment loss be recognized at the consolidated level.

Goodwill impairment testing when a noncontrolling interest exists

38. Goodwill arising from a business combination with a continuing noncontrolling interest shall be tested for impairment using an approach consistent with the approach used to measure the noncontrolling interest at the acquisition date. (A noncontrolling interest is sometimes referred to as a minority interest.) For example, if goodwill is initially recognized based only on the controlling interest of the parent, the fair value of the reporting unit used in the impairment test should be based on that controlling interest and should not reflect the portion of fair value attributable to the noncontrolling interest. Similarly, the implied fair value of goodwill that is determined in the second step of the impairment test and used to measure the impairment loss should reflect only the parent company's interest in that goodwill.

Disposal of All or a Portion of a Reporting Unit

39. When a reporting unit is to be disposed of in its entirety, goodwill of that reporting unit shall be included in the carrying amount of the reporting unit in determining the gain or loss on disposal.[22] When a portion of a reporting unit that constitutes a business[23] is to be disposed of, goodwill associated with that business shall be included in the carrying amount of the business in determining the gain or loss on disposal. The amount of goodwill to be included in that carrying amount shall be based on the relative fair values of the business to be disposed of and the portion of the reporting unit that will be retained. For example, if a business is being sold for $100 and the fair value of the reporting unit excluding the business being sold is $300, 25 percent of the goodwill residing in the reporting unit would be included in the carrying amount of the business to be sold. However, if the business to be disposed of was never integrated into the reporting unit after its acquisition and thus the benefits of the acquired goodwill were never realized by the rest of the reporting unit, the current carrying amount of that acquired goodwill shall be included in the carrying amount of the business to be disposed of. That situation might occur when the acquired business is operated as a stand-alone entity or when the business is to be disposed of shortly after it is acquired. When only a portion of goodwill is allocated to a business to be disposed of, the goodwill remaining in the portion of the reporting unit to be retained shall be tested for impairment in accordance with paragraphs 19–22 (using its adjusted carrying amount).

Equity Method Investments

40. The portion of the difference between the cost of an investment and the amount of underlying equity in net assets of an equity method investee that is recognized as goodwill in accordance with paragraph 19(b) of APB Opinion No. 18, *The Equity Method of Accounting for Investments in Common*

---

[22]For purposes of this Statement, the terms *disposal* and *disposed of* refer to assets to be disposed of as that term is used in Statement 121 and to assets of a segment of a business being accounted for as a discontinued operation under APB Opinion No. 30, *Reporting the Results of Operations—Reporting the Effects of Disposal of a Segment of a Business and Extraordinary, Unusual and Infrequently Occurring Events and Transactions.*

[23]Refer to footnote 18.

Stock (equity method goodwill) shall not be amortized. However, equity method goodwill shall not be tested for impairment in accordance with this Statement. Equity method investments shall continue to be reviewed for impairment in accordance with paragraph 19(h) of Opinion 18.

Deferred Income Taxes

41. Paragraph 30 of Statement 109 states that deferred income taxes are not recognized for any portion of goodwill for which amortization is not deductible for income tax purposes. Paragraphs 261 and 262 of that Statement provide additional guidance for recognition of deferred income taxes related to goodwill when amortization of goodwill is deductible for tax purposes. This Statement does not change the requirements in Statement 109 for recognition of deferred income taxes related to goodwill and intangible assets.

Financial Statement Presentation

Intangible Assets

42. At a minimum, all intangible assets shall be aggregated and presented as a separate line item in the statement of financial position. However, that requirement does not preclude presentation of individual intangible assets or classes of intangible assets as separate line items. The amortization expense and impairment losses for intangible assets shall be presented in income statement line items within continuing operations as deemed appropriate for each entity. Paragraphs 14 and 16 require that an intangible asset be tested for impairment when it is determined that the asset should no longer be amortized or should begin to be amortized due to a reassessment of its remaining useful life. An impairment loss resulting from that impairment test shall *not* be recognized as a change in accounting principle.

Goodwill

43. The aggregate amount of goodwill shall be presented as a separate line item in the statement of financial position. The aggregate amount of goodwill impairment losses shall be presented as a separate line item in the income statement before the subtotal *income from continuing operations* (or similar caption) unless a goodwill impairment loss is associated with a discontinued operation. A goodwill impairment loss associated with a discontinued operation shall be included (on a net-of-tax basis) within the results of discontinued operations.

Disclosures

44. For intangible assets acquired either individually or with a group of assets, the following information shall be disclosed in the notes to the financial statements in the period of acquisition:

a. For intangible assets subject to amortization:
   (1) The total amount assigned and the amount assigned to any major **intangible asset class**
   (2) The amount of any significant residual value, in total and by major intangible asset class
   (3) The weighted-average amortization period, in total and by major intangible asset class
b. For intangible assets *not* subject to amortization, the total amount assigned and the amount assigned to any major intangible asset class
c. The amount of research and development assets acquired and written off in the period and the line item in the income statement in which the amounts written off are aggregated.

45. The following information shall be disclosed in the financial statements or the notes to the financial statements for each period for which a statement of financial position is presented:

a. For intangible assets subject to amortization:
   (1) The gross carrying amount and accumulated amortization, in total and by major intangible asset class
   (2) The aggregate amortization expense for the period
   (3) The estimated aggregate amortization expense for each of the five succeeding fiscal years
b. For intangible assets *not* subject to amortization, the total carrying amount and the carrying amount for each major intangible asset class
c. The changes in the carrying amount of goodwill during the period including:
   (1) The aggregate amount of goodwill acquired
   (2) The aggregate amount of impairment losses recognized
   (3) The amount of goodwill included in the gain or loss on disposal of all or a portion of a reporting unit.

Entities that report segment information in accordance with Statement 131 shall provide the above information about goodwill in total and for each reportable segment and shall disclose any significant changes in the allocation of goodwill by reportable segment. If any portion of goodwill has not yet been allocated to a reporting unit at the date the financial statements are issued, that unallocated amount and the reasons for not allocating that amount shall be disclosed.

Illustration 1 in Appendix C provides an example of those disclosure requirements.

46. For each impairment loss recognized related to an intangible asset, the following information shall be disclosed in the notes to the financial statements that include the period in which the impairment loss is recognized:

a. A description of the impaired intangible asset and the facts and circumstances leading to the impairment
b. The amount of the impairment loss and the method for determining fair value
c. The caption in the income statement or the statement of activities in which the impairment loss is aggregated
d. If applicable, the segment in which the impaired intangible asset is reported under Statement 131.

47. For each goodwill impairment loss recognized, the following information shall be disclosed in the notes to the financial statements that include the period in which the impairment loss is recognized:

a. A description of the facts and circumstances leading to the impairment
b. The amount of the impairment loss and the method of determining the fair value of the associated reporting unit (whether based on quoted market prices, prices of comparable businesses, a present value or other valuation technique, or a combination thereof)
c. If a recognized impairment loss is an estimate that has not yet been finalized (refer to paragraph 22), that fact and the reasons therefor and, in subsequent periods, the nature and amount of any significant adjustments made to the initial estimate of the impairment loss.

Illustration 1 in Appendix C provides an example of those disclosure requirements.

Effective Date and Transition

48. This Statement shall be effective as follows:

a. All of the provisions of this Statement shall be applied in fiscal years beginning after December 15, 2001, to all goodwill and other intangible assets recognized in an entity's statement of financial position at the beginning of that fiscal year, regardless of when those previously recognized assets were initially recognized. Early application is permitted for entities with fiscal years beginning after March 15, 2001, provided that the first interim financial statements have not been issued previously. In all cases, the provisions of this Statement shall be initially applied at the beginning of a fiscal year. Retroactive application is not permitted. (Refer to paragraphs 53–61 for additional transition provisions.)
b. As described in paragraphs 50 and 51, certain provisions of this Statement shall be applied to goodwill and other acquired intangible assets for which the acquisition date is after June 30, 2001, even if an entity has not adopted this Statement in its entirety.
c. This Statement shall not be applied to previously recognized goodwill and intangible assets acquired in a combination between two or more mutual enterprises, acquired in a combination between not-for-profit organizations, or arising from the acquisition of a for-profit business entity by a not-for-profit organization until interpretive guidance related to the application of the purchase method to those transactions is issued (refer to paragraph 52).[24]

49. Paragraph 61 of Statement 141 includes the following transition provisions related to goodwill and intangible assets acquired in business combinations for which the acquisition date was before July 1, 2001, that were accounted for by the purchase method.

a. The carrying amount of acquired intangible assets that do not meet the criteria in paragraph 39 of Statement 141 for recognition apart from goodwill (and any related deferred tax liabilities if the intangible asset amortization is not deductible for tax purposes) shall be reclassified as goodwill as of the date this Statement is initially applied in its entirety.
b. The carrying amount of (1) any recognized intangible assets that meet the recognition criteria in

paragraph 39 of Statement 141 or (2) any unidentifiable intangible assets recognized in accordance with paragraph 5 of Statement 72 that have been included in the amount reported as goodwill (or as goodwill and intangible assets) shall be reclassified and accounted for as an asset apart from goodwill as of the date this Statement is initially applied in its entirety.[25]

Goodwill and Intangible Assets Acquired after June 30, 2001

50. Goodwill acquired in a business combination for which the acquisition date is after June 30, 2001, shall not be amortized. For example, an entity with a December 31, 2001 fiscal year-end would be required to initially apply the provisions of this Statement on January 1, 2002; if that entity completed a business combination on October 15, 2001, that gave rise to goodwill, it would not amortize the goodwill acquired in that business combination even though it would continue to amortize until January 1, 2002, goodwill that arose from any business combination completed before July 1, 2001. Intangible assets other than goodwill acquired in a business combination or other transaction for which the date of acquisition is after June 30, 2001, shall be amortized or not amortized in accordance with paragraphs 11–14 and 16 of this Statement.

51. Goodwill and intangible assets acquired in a transaction for which the acquisition date is after June 30, 2001, but before the date that this Statement is applied in its entirety (refer to paragraph 48(a)), shall be reviewed for impairment in accordance with Opinion 17 or Statement 121 (as appropriate) until the date that this Statement is applied in its entirety. Similarly, the financial statement presentation and disclosure provisions of this Statement shall not be applied to those assets until this Statement is applied in its entirety.

52. Goodwill and intangible assets acquired in a combination between two or more mutual enterprises, acquired in a combination between not-for-profit organizations, or arising from the acquisition of a for-profit business entity by a not-for-profit organi-

zation for which the acquisition date is after June 30, 2001, shall continue to be accounted for in accordance with Opinion 17 (refer to footnote 24).

Previously Recognized Intangible Assets

53. To apply this Statement to intangible assets acquired in a transaction for which the acquisition date is on or before June 30, 2001, the useful lives of those previously recognized intangible assets shall be reassessed using the guidance in paragraph 11 and the remaining amortization periods adjusted accordingly.[26] That reassessment shall be completed prior to the end of the first interim period of the fiscal year in which this Statement is initially applied. Previously recognized intangible assets deemed to have indefinite useful lives shall be tested for impairment as of the beginning of the fiscal year in which this Statement is initially applied (in accordance with paragraph 17). That transitional intangible asset impairment test shall be completed in the first interim period in which this Statement is initially applied, and any resulting impairment loss shall be recognized as the effect of a change in accounting principle. The effect of the accounting change and related income tax effects shall be presented in the income statement between the captions *extraordinary items* and *net income*. The per-share information presented in the income statement shall include the per-share effect of the accounting change.

Previously Recognized Goodwill

54. At the date this Statement is initially applied, an entity shall establish its reporting units based on its reporting structure at that date and the guidance in paragraphs 30 and 31. Recognized net assets, excluding goodwill, shall be assigned to those reporting units using the guidance in paragraphs 32 and 33. Recognized assets and liabilities that do not relate to a reporting unit, such as an environmental liability for an operation previously disposed of, need not be assigned to a reporting unit. *All* goodwill recognized in an entity's statement of financial position at the date this Statement is initially applied shall be assigned to one or more reporting units. Goodwill shall be assigned in a reasonable and supportable manner. The

---

[25]For example, when a business combination was initially recorded, a portion of the acquired entity was assigned to intangible assets that meet the recognition criteria in paragraph 39 of Statement 141. Those intangible assets have been included in the amount reported on the statement of financial position as goodwill (or as goodwill and other intangible assets). However, separate general ledger or other accounting records have been maintained for those assets.

[26]For example, the amortization period for a previously recognized intangible asset might be increased if its original useful life was estimated to be longer than the 40-year maximum amortization period allowed by Opinion 17.

sources of previously recognized goodwill shall be considered in making that initial assignment as well as the reporting units to which the related acquired net assets were assigned. The guidance in paragraphs 34 and 35 may be useful in assigning goodwill to reporting units upon initial application of this Statement.

55. Goodwill in each reporting unit shall be tested for impairment as of the beginning of the fiscal year in which this Statement is initially applied in its entirety (in accordance with paragraphs 19–21). An entity has six months from the date it initially applies this Statement to complete the first step of that transitional goodwill impairment test. However, the amounts used in the transitional goodwill impairment test shall be measured as of the beginning of the year of initial application. If the carrying amount of the net assets of a reporting unit (including goodwill) exceeds the fair value of that reporting unit, the second step of the transitional goodwill impairment test must be completed as soon as possible, but no later than the end of the year of initial application.

56. An impairment loss recognized as a result of a transitional goodwill impairment test shall be recognized as the effect of a change in accounting principle. The effect of the accounting change and related income tax effects shall be presented in the income statement between the captions *extraordinary items* and *net income*. The per-share information presented in the income statement shall include the per-share effect of the accounting change. Although a transitional impairment loss for goodwill may be measured in other than the first interim reporting period, it shall be recognized in the first interim period irrespective of the period in which it is measured, consistent with paragraph 10 of FASB Statement No. 3, *Reporting Accounting Changes in Interim Financial Statements*. The financial information for the interim periods of the fiscal year that precede the period in which the transitional goodwill impairment loss is measured shall be restated to reflect the accounting change in those periods. The aggregate amount of the accounting change shall be included in restated net income of the first interim period of the year of initial application (and in any year-to-date or last-12-months-to-date financial reports that include the first interim period). Whenever financial information is presented that includes the periods that precede the period in which the transitional goodwill impairment loss is measured, that financial information shall be presented on the restated basis.

57. If events or changes in circumstances indicate that goodwill of a reporting unit might be impaired before completion of the transitional goodwill impairment test, goodwill shall be tested for impairment when the impairment indicator arises (refer to paragraph 28). A goodwill impairment loss that does *not* result from a transitional goodwill impairment test shall not be recognized as the effect of a change in accounting principle; rather it shall be recognized in accordance with paragraph 43.

58. In addition to the transitional goodwill impairment test, an entity shall perform the required annual goodwill impairment test in the year that this Statement is initially applied in its entirety. That is, the transitional goodwill impairment test may not be considered the initial year's annual test unless an entity designates the beginning of its fiscal year as the date for its annual goodwill impairment test.

Equity Method Goodwill

59. Upon initial application of this Statement, the portion of the excess of cost over the underlying equity in net assets of an investee accounted for using the equity method that has been recognized as goodwill shall cease being amortized. However, equity method goodwill shall not be tested for impairment in accordance with this Statement (refer to paragraph 40).

Transitional Disclosures

60. Upon completion of the first step of the transitional goodwill impairment test, the reportable segment or segments in which an impairment loss might have to be recognized and the period in which that potential loss will be measured shall be disclosed in any interim financial information.

61. In the period of initial application and thereafter until goodwill and all other intangible assets have been accounted for in accordance with this Statement in all periods presented, the following information shall be displayed either on the face of the income statement or in the notes to the financial statements: income before extraordinary items and net income for all periods presented adjusted to exclude amortization expense (including any related tax effects) recognized in those periods related to goodwill, intangible assets that are no longer being amortized, any deferred credit related to an excess over cost (amortized in accordance with Opinion 16), and equity method goodwill. The adjusted income before

extraordinary items and net income also shall reflect any adjustments for changes in amortization periods for intangible assets that will continue to be amortized as a result of initially applying this Statement (including any related tax effects). In addition, the notes to the financial statements shall disclose a reconciliation of reported net income to the adjusted net income. Similarly adjusted earnings-per-share amounts for all periods presented may be presented either on the face of the income statement or in the notes to the financial statements. Illustration 2 in Appendix C provides an example of those transitional disclosure requirements.

> **The provisions of this Statement need not be applied to immaterial items.**

This Statement was adopted by the unanimous vote of the six members of the Financial Accounting Standards Board:

Edmund L. Jenkins,	G. Michael Crooch	Gerhard G. Mueller
Chairman	John M. Foster	Edward W. Trott
	Gaylen N. Larson	

Appendix A

IMPLEMENTATION GUIDANCE ON INTANGIBLE ASSETS

A1. This appendix provides guidance on how intangible assets should be accounted for in accordance with paragraphs 11–17 of this Statement and is an integral part of the standards of this Statement. Each of the following examples describes an acquired intangible asset and the facts and circumstances surrounding the determination of its useful life and the subsequent accounting based on that determination. The facts and circumstances unique to each acquired intangible asset need to be considered in making similar determinations.

Example 1

An acquired customer list. A direct-mail marketing company acquired the customer list and expects that it will be able to derive benefit from the information on the acquired customer list for at least one year but for no more than three years.

The customer list would be amortized over 18 months, management's best estimate of its useful life, following the pattern in which the expected benefits will be consumed or otherwise used up. Although the acquiring entity may intend to add customer names and other information to the list in the future, the expected benefits of the acquired customer list relate only to the customers on that list at the date of acqui- sition (a closed-group notion). The customer list would be reviewed for impairment under FASB Statement No. 121, Accounting for the Impairment of Long-Lived Assets and for Long-Lived Assets to Be Disposed Of.

Example 2

An acquired patent that expires in 15 years. The product protected by the patented technology is expected to be a source of cash flows for at least 15 years. The reporting entity has a commitment from a third party to purchase that patent in 5 years for 60 percent of the fair value of the patent at the date it was acquired, and the entity intends to sell the patent in 5 years.

The patent would be amortized over its five-year useful life to the reporting entity following the pattern in which the expected benefits will be consumed or otherwise used up. The amount to be amortized is 40 percent of the patent's fair value at the acquisition date (residual value is 60 percent). The patent would be reviewed for impairment under Statement 121.

Example 3

An acquired copyright that has a remaining legal life of 50 years. An analysis of consumer habits and market trends provides evidence that the copyrighted material will generate cash flows for approximately 30 more years.

The copyright would be amortized over its 30-year estimated useful life following the pattern in which the expected benefits will be consumed or otherwise used up and reviewed for impairment under Statement 121.

Example 4

An acquired broadcast license that expires in five years. The broadcast license is renewable every 10 years if the company provides at least an average level of service to its customers and complies with the applicable Federal Communications Commission (FCC) rules and policies and the FCC Communications Act of 1934. The license may be renewed indefinitely at little cost and was renewed twice prior to its recent acquisition. The acquiring entity intends to renew the license indefinitely, and evidence supports its ability to do so. Historically, there has been no compelling challenge to the license renewal. The technology used in broadcasting is not expected to be replaced by another technology any time in the foreseeable future. Therefore, the cash flows from that license are expected to continue indefinitely.

The broadcast license would be deemed to have an indefinite useful life because cash flows are expected to continue indefinitely. Therefore, the license would not be amortized until its useful life is deemed to be no longer indefinite. The license would be tested for impairment in accordance with paragraph 17 of this Statement.

Example 5

The broadcast license in Example 4. The FCC subsequently decides that it will no longer renew broadcast licenses, but rather will auction those licenses. At the time the FCC decision is made, the broadcast license has three years until it expires. The cash flows from that license are expected to continue until the license expires.

Because the broadcast license can no longer be renewed, its useful life is no longer indefinite. Thus, the acquired license would be tested for impairment in accordance with paragraph 17 of this Statement. The license would then be amortized over its remaining three-year useful life following the pattern in which the expected benefits will be consumed or otherwise used up. Because the license will be subject to amortization, in the future it would be reviewed for impairment under Statement 121.

Example 6

An acquired airline route authority from the United States to the United Kingdom that expires in three years. The route authority may be renewed every five years, and the acquiring entity intends to comply with the applicable rules and regulations surrounding renewal. Route authority renewals are routinely granted at a minimal cost and have historically been renewed when the airline has complied with the applicable rules and regulations. The acquiring entity expects to provide service to the United Kingdom from its hub airports indefinitely and expects that the related supporting infrastructure (airport gates, slots, and terminal facility leases) will remain in place at those airports for as long as it has the route authority. An analysis of demand and cash flows supports those assumptions.

Because the facts and circumstances support the acquiring entity's ability to continue providing air service to the United Kingdom from its U.S. hub airports indefinitely, the intangible asset related to the route authority is considered to have an indefinite useful life. Therefore, the route authority would not be amortized until its useful life is deemed to be no longer indefinite and would be tested for impairment in accordance with paragraph 17 of this Statement.

Example 7

An acquired trademark that is used to identify and distinguish a leading consumer product that has been a market-share leader for the past eight years. The trademark has a remaining legal life of 5 years but is renewable every 10 years at little cost. The acquiring entity intends to continuously renew the trademark, and evidence supports its ability to do so. An analysis of product life cycle studies; market, competitive, and environmental trends; and brand extension opportunities provides evidence that the trademarked product will generate cash flows for the acquiring entity for an indefinite period of time.

The trademark would be deemed to have an indefinite useful life because it is expected to contribute to cash flows indefinitely. Therefore, the trademark would not be amortized until its useful life is no longer indefinite. The trademark would be tested for impairment in accordance with paragraph 17 of this Statement.

Example 8

A trademark that distinguished a leading consumer product that was acquired 10 years ago. When it was acquired, the trademark was considered to have an indefinite useful life because the product was expected to generate cash flows indefinitely. During the annual impairment test of the intangible asset, the entity determines that unexpected competition has entered the market that will reduce future sales of the product. Management estimates that cash flows generated by that consumer product will be 20 percent less for the foreseeable future; however, management expects that the product will continue to generate cash flows indefinitely at those reduced amounts.

As a result of the projected decrease in future cash flows, the entity determines that the estimated fair value of the trademark is less than its carrying amount, and an impairment loss is recognized. Because it is still deemed to have an indefinite useful life, the trademark would continue to not be amortized and would continue to be tested for impairment in accordance with paragraph 17 of this Statement.

Example 9

A trademark for a line of automobiles that was acquired several years ago in an acquisition of an automobile company. The line of automobiles had been produced by the acquired entity for 35 years with numerous new models developed under the trademark. At the acquisition date, the acquiring entity expected to continue to produce that line of automobiles, and an analysis of various economic factors indicated there was no limit to the period of time the trademark would contribute to cash flows. Because cash flows were expected to continue indefinitely, the trademark was not amortized. Management recently decided to phase out production of that automobile line over the next four years.

Because the useful life of that acquired trademark is no longer deemed to be indefinite, the trademark would be tested for impairment in accordance with paragraph 17 of this Statement. The carrying amount of the trademark after adjustment, if any, would then be amortized over its remaining four-year useful life following the pattern in which the expected benefits will be consumed or otherwise used up. Because the trademark will be subject to amortization, in the future it would be reviewed for impairment under Statement 121.

Appendix B

BACKGROUND INFORMATION AND BASIS FOR CONCLUSIONS

CONTENTS

Appendix B

BACKGROUND INFORMATION AND BASIS FOR CONCLUSIONS

Introduction

B1. This appendix summarizes considerations that Board members deemed significant in reaching the conclusions in this Statement. It includes reasons for accepting certain approaches and rejecting others. Individual Board members gave greater weight to some factors than to others.

Background Information

B2. Prior to the issuance of this Statement, the guidance on accounting for goodwill and other intangible assets was provided by APB Opinion No. 17, *Intangible Assets,* which the Accounting Principles Board (APB) of the American Institute of Certified Public Accountants (AICPA) issued in 1970. Opinion 17 required that intangible assets that are acquired in business combination transactions or other transactions be recognized as assets in the financial statements of acquiring entities and that the costs incurred to develop intangible assets that are not specifically identifiable be recognized as expenses in the financial statements of entities incurring those costs. It also required that goodwill and other intangible assets be amortized by systematic charges over the period expected to be benefited by those assets, not to exceed 40 years.

B3. During the 1970s, the FASB had an active project on its agenda to reconsider the accounting for business combinations and purchased intangible assets. However, the Board later decided to defer consideration of the issues in that project until after it completed development of its conceptual framework for accounting and reporting. In 1981, the Board removed the inactive business combinations project from its agenda to focus on higher priority projects.

B4. In August 1996, the Board added the current project on accounting for business combinations to its agenda. The objective of this project was to improve the transparency of accounting and reporting of business combinations, including the accounting for goodwill and other intangible assets, by reconsidering the requirements of Opinion 17 and APB Opinion No. 16, *Business Combinations* (which also was issued in 1970). In 1999, the Board decided that that objective would best be achieved through several projects focused on specific issues. In the first of those projects, which ended with the concurrent issuance of this Statement and FASB Statement No. 141, *Business Combinations,* the Board reconsidered the accounting for goodwill and other intangible assets and the methods of accounting for business combinations. Another project will address issues associated with the accounting for combinations between not-for-profit organizations, the acquisition of a for-profit entity by a not-for-profit organization, and combinations between mutual enterprises. The Board intends to consider issues related to the accounting for the formation of joint ventures and other new entities, push-down accounting (including spinoffs), and common control transactions in another project. In still another project, the Board intends to consider issues related to the provisions of Opinion 16 and FASB Statement No. 38, *Accounting for Preacquisition Contingencies of Purchased Enterprises,* that were carried forward in Statement 141 without reconsideration, and other issues related to the application of the purchase method, such as the accounting for step acquisitions.[27]

Reasons the FASB Took on the Project

B5. A principal reason for taking on this project in 1996 was the increase in merger and acquisition activity that brought greater attention to the fact that two transactions that are economically similar may be accounted for by different methods that produce dramatically different financial statement results. Consequently, both the representational faithfulness and the comparability of those financial statements suffer.

B6. Another reason that the Board decided to undertake this project was that many perceived the differences in the pooling-of-interests method (pooling method) and purchase method to have affected competition in markets for mergers and acquisitions. Entities that could not meet all of the conditions for applying the pooling method believed that they faced an unlevel playing field in competing for targets with entities that could apply that method. That perception and the resulting attempts to expand the application of the pooling method placed considerable tension on the interpretation and application of the provisions of Opinion 16. The volume of inquiries fielded by the staffs of the FASB and Securities and Exchange

Commission (SEC) and the auditing profession was evidence of that tension.

B7. The unlevel playing field that was perceived to stem from the application of the pooling and purchase methods extended internationally as well. Cross-border differences in accounting standards for business combinations and the rapidly accelerating movement of capital flows globally heightened the need for accounting standards to be comparable internationally. Promoting international comparability in accounting standards is part of the Board's mission, and many members of the Financial Accounting Standards Advisory Council (FASAC) cited the opportunity to promote greater international comparability in the standards for business combinations as a reason for adding this project to the Board's agenda. (FASAC had consistently ranked a possible project on business combinations as a high priority for a number of years.)

International Cooperation

B8. Largely because of concerns about the perception of an unlevel cross-border playing field with the United States in the accounting standards for business combinations, the Accounting Standards Board (AcSB) of the Canadian Institute of Chartered Accountants conducted a business combinations project concurrently with the FASB's project. The goal of that concurrent effort was to establish common standards on business combinations and intangible assets.

B9. The FASB also worked with other members of an international organization of standard-setting bodies with the aim of achieving convergence internationally with respect to the methods of accounting for business combinations. That organization, known as the "Group of 4 plus 1" (G4+1), consisted of the Australian Accounting Standards Board, the New Zealand Financial Reporting Standards Board, the United Kingdom Accounting Standards Board (UK ASB), the AcSB, the FASB, and an observer, the International Accounting Standards Committee (IASC).

Conduct of the FASB's Project

B10. The Board formed a business combinations task force comprising individuals from a number of

---

[27]For example, AICPA Accounting Interpretation 2, "Goodwill in a Step Acquisition," of Opinion 17 stated that when an entity acquires another entity or an investment accounted for by the equity method through a series of purchases (commonly referred to as a step acquisition), the entity should identify the cost of each investment, the fair value of the underlying assets acquired, and the goodwill for each step acquisition.

organizations representing a wide range of the Board's constituents. The first meeting of that task force was held in February 1997. Relevant academic research was reviewed, and the meeting discussion centered on a background paper that addressed the project's scope, the direction the project should take, and how the project should be conducted.

B11. The June 1997 FASB Special Report, *Issues Associated with the FASB Project on Business Combinations,* was based on that background paper and indicated some of the Board's initial decisions about the project's scope, direction, and conduct. The 54 comment letters received in response to that Special Report generally expressed agreement with those decisions.

B12. In 1998, the FASB participated in the development of a G4+1 Position Paper, *Recommendations for Achieving Convergence on the Methods of Accounting for Business Combinations.* The Board issued the Position Paper as an FASB Invitation to Comment, *Methods of Accounting for Business Combinations: Recommendations of the G4+1 for Achieving Convergence,* in December 1998, the same date on which other G4+1 member organizations issued similar documents for comment.

B13. After considering the recommendations of the G4+1 and the responses to the Invitation to Comment, the Board decided that only the purchase method should be used to account for business combinations. The Board also decided that certain changes should be made in how the purchase method should be applied, particularly in the accounting for and financial statement presentation of goodwill and other intangible assets. Those changes included limiting the maximum amortization period for goodwill to 20 years, presenting goodwill amortization expense on a net-of-tax basis in the income statement, and not amortizing certain intangible assets. Those changes were proposed in the September 1999 FASB Exposure Draft, *Business Combinations and Intangible Assets* (1999 Exposure Draft). The Board received 210 comment letters in response to that Exposure Draft. In February 2000, the Board held 4 days of public hearings, 2 days in San Francisco and 2 days in New York City, at which 43 individuals or organizations presented their views on the 1999 Exposure Draft.

B14. In redeliberating the proposals in the 1999 Exposure Draft, the Board considered changes suggested by various constituents, in particular those related to the accounting for goodwill. During October and November 2000, Board and staff members explored the suggested changes to the accounting for goodwill in field visits with 14 companies. The Board's deliberations resulted in significant changes to the proposed requirements related to goodwill but not to other issues addressed in the 1999 Exposure Draft. In particular, the Board decided that goodwill should no longer be amortized and should be tested for impairment in a manner different from other assets. The Board also affirmed the proposal that only the purchase method should be used to account for business combinations. In February 2001, the Board issued a revised Exposure Draft, *Business Combinations and Intangible Assets—Accounting for Goodwill* (2001 Exposure Draft), that proposed changes to the 1999 Exposure Draft with regard to the accounting for goodwill and the initial recognition of intangible assets other than goodwill. The Board received 211 comment letters on the 2001 Exposure Draft.

B15. The Board decided to separate the guidance for goodwill and other intangible assets from that for business combinations and issue that guidance in two final documents, this Statement and Statement 141. Those two Statements parallel and supersede Opinions 17 and 16, respectively. Statement 141 was issued concurrently with this Statement.

Scope

B16. This Statement applies to all entities, including mutual enterprises and not-for-profit organizations. The 2001 Exposure Draft excluded from its scope goodwill and other intangible assets acquired in combinations between two or more not-for-profit organizations and goodwill acquired in an acquisition of a for-profit entity by a not-for-profit organization. Rather than exclude goodwill and other intangible assets acquired in those transactions from the scope of this Statement, the Board concluded that it would be more appropriate to include those assets in the scope of this Statement. However, the Board agreed to delay the effective date of this Statement as it applies to not-for-profit organizations and combinations between two or more mutual enterprises until it completes the project on its agenda addressing issues related to combinations of those entities. The Board noted that goodwill and intangible assets acquired in those types of combinations would be accounted for in the same manner as goodwill and intangible assets acquired in business combinations unless distinguishing characteristics or circumstances are identified justifying a different accounting treatment.

B17. This Statement applies to excess reorganization value recognized in accordance with AICPA Statement of Position (SOP) 90-7, *Financial Reporting by Entities in Reorganization Under the Bankruptcy Code.* SOP 90-7 states that the excess reorganization value resulting from reorganization under the Bankruptcy Code is an intangible asset that should be amortized in accordance with Opinion 17, generally over a period substantially less than 40 years. Because this Statement supersedes Opinion 17, respondents to the 2001 Exposure Draft requested that the Board address whether excess reorganization value should be accounted for like goodwill and not be amortized or accounted for like an intangible asset and thus possibly continue to be amortized.

B18. Most respondents stated that excess reorganization value is similar to goodwill and therefore should be accounted for in the same manner as goodwill. The Board agreed with those respondents and concluded that excess reorganization value recognized in accordance with SOP 90-7 should be accounted for as goodwill in accordance with this Statement. The Board decided that the transition provisions in this Statement should apply to previously recognized excess reorganization value that is being accounted for in accordance with Opinion 17.

B19. The Board decided that this Statement should not change the accounting for an unidentifiable intangible asset recognized in an acquisition of a bank or thrift institution that is prescribed in FASB Statement No. 72, *Accounting for Certain Acquisitions of Banking or Thrift Institutions.* The Board noted that Statement 72 does not refer to the unidentifiable intangible asset as goodwill and concluded that it would not be appropriate to account for that intangible asset as if it were goodwill without a full reconsideration of the issues associated with that industry, which is beyond the issues addressed in this Statement.

Intangible Assets

Scope and Definition

B20. The Board initially decided that the focus of this project with respect to intangible assets should be limited to those intangible assets acquired in a business combination. However, the Board acknowledged in the Special Report that it would consider the need to expand the scope to other intangible assets as the project progressed.

B21. The Board observed that the scope of Opinion 17 is not limited to intangible assets acquired in a business combination but rather encompasses intangible assets generally. Other standards, such as Financial Reporting Standard (FRS) 10, *Goodwill and Intangible Assets,* issued by the UK ASB, and International Accounting Standard (IAS) 38, *Intangible Assets,* issued by the IASC, also apply to intangible assets generally.

B22. The Board considered whether to include in the scope of this project all acquired intangible assets rather than only those acquired in a business combination. The Board noted that doing so would have the advantage of treating all acquired intangible assets similarly regardless of whether they were acquired in a business combination or in another transaction. The Board also noted that it might result in greater convergence with the requirements in standards outside the United States.

B23. The Board noted, however, that the guidance in Opinion 17 does not specify how the costs of internally developing specifically identifiable intangible assets that have limited lives should be treated. As a result, those costs may be either recognized as assets and amortized or expensed as incurred. The only provisions of Opinion 17 that relate to such assets are those concerning amortization, which relate to other intangible assets as well. The Board further noted that guidance for certain types of intangible assets, such as computer software, is provided in other standards and that the Board's intent generally was not to amend those standards as part of the business combinations project.

B24. Internally developed intangible assets raise many accounting issues that have little to do with business combinations, so the Board decided not to address them in the business combinations project.[28] However, the Board concluded that the accounting issues associated with intangible assets acquired in transactions other than business combinations are sufficiently similar to those associated with such assets acquired in business combinations and thus decided to address them in this project.

---

[28]Because this Statement supersedes all of Opinion 17, this Statement carries forward the provisions in that Opinion related to internally developed intangible assets. As noted in paragraph 2, the Board has not reconsidered those provisions as they are outside the project's scope.

B25. The Board also noted that research and development costs are excluded from the scope of Opinion 17 by FASB Interpretation No. 4, *Applicability of FASB Statement No. 2 to Business Combinations Accounted for by the Purchase Method,* but not from the scope of Opinion 16. The Board therefore considered issues related to the accounting for research and development assets acquired in business combinations. During the development of the 1999 Exposure Draft, the Board noted that some of the issues associated with research and development assets are unique to those assets and not directly related to other business combinations issues. The Board concluded that it was not possible to address those issues without considering the issues associated with accounting for research and development costs generally. Consequently, the Board decided not to address issues associated with research and development assets in this project.

B26. Statement 141, which supersedes Opinion 16, addresses the initial recognition and measurement of intangible assets, including goodwill, that are acquired in a business combination. This Statement addresses the initial recognition and measurement of intangible assets acquired in transactions other than business combinations, as well as the subsequent recognition and measurement of intangible assets generally.

B27. In the deliberations that led to the 1999 Exposure Draft, the Board concluded that the characteristics that distinguish intangible assets from other assets are that they are (a) without physical substance, (b) not financial instruments, and (c) not current assets. The 1999 Exposure Draft defined intangible assets in terms of those characteristics. Several respondents to that Exposure Draft noted that some intangible assets (such as order or production backlogs) are current assets. They observed that some might interpret that proposed definition as prohibiting recognition of those intangible assets as intangible assets, which they believed was not the Board's intent. The Board agreed with those respondents and decided that this Statement should define intangible assets more broadly, that is, as assets (not including financial assets) that lack physical substance.

Initial Recognition of Intangible Assets Acquired in Transactions Other Than Business Combinations

B28. At the inception of this project, the Board observed that intangible assets make up an increasing proportion of the assets of many (if not most) entities, but despite their importance, those assets often are not recognized as such. Accordingly, the Board concluded in the 1999 Exposure Draft that the decision usefulness of financial statements would be enhanced by the recognition of more intangible assets. The Board affirmed that view in its redeliberations.

B29. The Board noted that, to be recognized, intangible assets acquired in transactions other than business combinations must meet the four fundamental recognition criteria for assets in paragraph 63 of FASB Concepts Statement No. 5, *Recognition and Measurement in Financial Statements of Business Enterprises.* Those criteria are that the item meets the assets definition, it has an attribute that is measurable with sufficient reliability, the information about it is capable of making a difference in user decisions, and the information is representationally faithful, verifiable, and neutral.

B30. The Board observed that bargained exchange transactions that are conducted at arm's length provide reliable evidence about the existence and fair value of acquired intangible assets. Accordingly, the Board concluded that those transactions provide a basis for recognizing those assets in the financial statements of the acquiring entities. The Board also observed that similarly reliable evidence about the existence and fair value of intangible assets that are developed internally is not generally available.

B31. The Board also considered how to distinguish intangible assets from each other. The Board observed that, conceptually, the main reason for distinguishing intangible assets from each other is to enhance the decision usefulness of financial statements. As stated in Concepts Statement 5:

> Classification in financial statements facilitates analysis by grouping items with essentially similar characteristics and separating items with essentially different characteristics. Analysis aimed at objectives such as predicting amounts, timing, and uncertainty of future cash flows requires financial information segregated into reasonably homogenous groups. For example, components of financial statements that consist of items that have similar characteristics in one or more respects, such as continuity or recurrence, stability, risk, and reliability, are likely to have more predictive value than if their characteristics are dissimilar. [paragraph 20]

B32. In the 1999 Exposure Draft, the Board observed that many intangible assets are based on rights that are conveyed legally by contract, statute, or similar means. It also noted that many such assets are exchangeable, as are other intangible assets that are not based on such rights. The Board noted that intangible assets span a spectrum, with intangible assets that are readily exchangeable at one end and others that are "goodwill like" at the other end. In that regard, it noted that exchangeability is a useful basis for distinguishing different types of intangible assets because those that are capable of being sold or otherwise transferred constitute a potential source of funds.

B33. In considering responses to the 1999 Exposure Draft, the Board reconsidered the guidance proposed for the recognition of intangible assets apart from goodwill. As a result, Statement 141 requires that an intangible asset be recognized apart from goodwill if it meets either of two criteria.

B34. Statement 141 requires that an intangible asset be recognized apart from goodwill if it arises from contractual or other legal rights, regardless of whether those rights are transferable or separable from the entity or from other rights and obligations (the contractual-legal criterion). In that regard, the Board observed that the values of many intangible assets arise from rights conveyed legally by contract, statute, or similar means. For example, franchises are granted to automobile dealers, fast-food outlets, and professional sports teams. Trademarks and service marks may be registered with the government. Contracts often are negotiated with customers or suppliers. Technological innovations are often protected by patents. The Board concluded that the fact that an intangible asset arises from contractual or other legal rights is an important characteristic and intangible assets with that characteristic should be recognized apart from goodwill.

B35. Statement 141 also requires that an acquired intangible asset be recognized apart from goodwill if the intangible asset is separable, that is, it is capable of being separated or divided from the entity and sold, transferred, licensed, rented, or exchanged, regardless of whether there is an intent to do so (the separability criterion). The Board noted that some acquired intangible assets may have been developed internally by the acquired entity. The Board noted that although some intangible assets do not arise from rights conveyed by contract or other legal means, they are nonetheless capable of being separated and exchanged for something else of value. Other intangible assets cannot be separated and sold or otherwise transferred. The Board concluded that separability is another important characteristic and, therefore, intangible assets with that characteristic should be recognized apart from goodwill.[29]

B36. The Board observed that the contractual-legal criterion and the separability criterion are the basis for distinguishing between intangible assets and goodwill acquired in business combination transactions and are not applicable to other transactions in which intangible assets are acquired (because goodwill arises only in business combinations or in transactions accounted for like business combinations). However, the Board observed that those criteria may constitute a useful basis for distinguishing between different types of recognized intangible assets that are acquired in other transactions, thereby enhancing the decision usefulness of the financial statements, consistent with paragraph 20 of Concepts Statement 5.

B37. The Board also noted that Statement 141 contains a presumption that an intangible asset that meets the contractual-legal criterion or the separability criterion also would meet the asset recognition criteria in Concepts Statement 5.[30] The Board observed that intangible assets that are acquired individually or with a group of assets in a transaction other than a business combination also may meet the asset recognition criteria in Concepts Statement 5 even though they do not meet either the contractual-legal criterion or the separability criterion (for example, specially-trained employees or a unique manufacturing process related to an acquired manufacturing plant). Such

---

[29]As it did prior to issuing the 2001 Exposure Draft, the Board noted that some intangible assets are so closely related to another asset or liability that they usually are sold as a "package" (as is the case with deposit liabilities and the related depositor relationship intangible asset). The Board concluded that an intangible asset that does not meet the separability criterion individually meets the separability criterion if it can be separated and divided from the entity and sold, transferred, licensed, rented, or exchanged with a related contract, asset, or liability.

[30]Some respondents to both Exposure Drafts doubted their ability to reliably measure the fair values of many intangible assets, particularly those acquired in groups with other assets. The Board noted that the fair values of the assets acquired are established through bargained exchange transactions. The Board acknowledged that the fair value estimates for some intangible assets that meet the recognition criteria might lack the precision of the fair value measurements for other assets. However, the Board also concluded that the financial information that will be provided by recognizing intangible assets at their estimated fair values is more representationally faithful than that which would be provided if those intangible assets were not recognized as intangible assets on the basis of measurement difficulties.

transactions commonly are bargained exchange transactions that are conducted at arm's length, which the Board concluded provides reliable evidence about the existence and fair value of those assets. Thus, those assets should be recognized as intangible assets.

Initial Measurement of Intangible Assets Acquired in Transactions Other Than Business Combinations

B38. Both Statement 141 and this Statement require that acquired intangible assets initially be assigned an amount based on their fair values, which is consistent with the requirements of Opinions 16 and 17 and the proposals of the 1999 Exposure Draft. As noted in paragraph 7 of FASB Concepts Statement No. 7, *Using Cash Flow Information and Present Value in Accounting Measurements,* in recent years the Board has identified fair value as the objective for most measurements at initial recognition. None of the respondents to the 1999 Exposure Draft suggested alternative measurement approaches.

B39. In Statement 141 the Board affirmed the basic principles of historical-cost accounting included in paragraphs 66–69 of Opinion 16. Specifically, the Board affirmed that an asset acquisition should be measured on the basis of the values exchanged and that measurement of the values exchanged should be based on the fair value of the consideration given or the fair value of the net assets acquired, whichever is more reliably measurable. For similar reasons, the Board concluded in this Statement that acquired intangible assets should be initially measured based on their fair values. The Board also agreed that when groups of assets are acquired, the value of the asset (or net asset) group as a whole should be allocated to the individual assets (or assets and liabilities) that make up the group on the basis of their relative fair values.

B40. The Board noted that an intangible asset arising from a contractual or other legal right represents the future cash flows that are expected to result from ownership of that contract or legal right. Fair value represents the amount at which that asset could be bought or sold in a current transaction between willing parties, that is, in other than a forced or liquidation sale. For example, the fair value of an order backlog would represent the amount a buyer would be willing to pay to acquire the future cash flows expected to arise from that order backlog.

B41. The Board recognizes that the requirements of this Statement might change current practice with respect to the amounts assigned to some intangible assets, in particular those that arise from contractual or other legal rights. For example, the Board has been informed that in current practice the amount assigned to acquired operating lease contracts (from the lessor's perspective) and customer contracts often is based on the amount by which the contract terms are favorable relative to market prices at the date of acquisition. Thus, no amount is typically assigned to lease and other contracts that are "at the money"— that is, when the contract terms reflect market prices at the date of acquisition. The Board observed, however, that such "at the money" contracts are bought and sold in exchange transactions—the purchase and sale of airport gates (an operating lease) within the airline industry and customer contracts in the home security industry are two examples of those exchange transactions. The Board believes that those transactions provide evidence that a contract may have value for reasons other than terms that are favorable relative to market prices. The Board therefore concluded that the amount by which the terms of a contract are favorable relative to market prices would not always represent the fair value of that contract.

B42. Several respondents noted that a present value technique might often be the best available technique with which to estimate the fair value of an acquired intangible asset. Some of those respondents asked whether the estimated cash flows used in applying that technique should be limited to the cash flows expected over the remaining legal or contractual term of the acquired asset. The Board noted that judgment is required in estimating the period of expected cash flows. Those estimates should be consistent with the objective of measuring fair value and, thus, should incorporate assumptions that marketplace participants would use in estimating fair value, such as assumptions about contract renewals and other benefits, such as those that might result from acquisition-related synergies.

B43. The Board noted that if such information is not available without undue cost and effort, an entity should use its own assumptions. The Board also noted that while many contracts or other rights (including customer contracts) are fixed in duration, past history (and industry practice) often provides evidence that the contracts or rights generally are renewed without substantial cost and effort. For example, although contracts to manage investments of mutual funds are often short-term contracts (one-year term or less), the Board has been informed that in many (if not most) cases those contracts are continuously renewed. The Board has also been informed that while some legal rights such as trademarks and broadcast licenses have finite legal lives, those rights are renewable and are often renewed without challenge. In those cases, the Board believes that estimates of future cash flows used in measuring the fair value of the acquired intangible asset would reflect cash flows for periods that extend beyond the remaining term of the acquired contract or legal right. The Board noted that Concepts Statement 7 discusses the essential elements of a present value measurement (paragraph 23), provides examples of circumstances in which an entity's expected cash flows might differ from the market cash flows (paragraph 32), and discusses the use of present value techniques in measuring the fair value of an asset or liability (paragraphs 39–54 and 75–88).

Subsequent Recognition and Measurement

Useful lives of intangible assets

B44. The Board observed that the useful lives of intangible assets are related to the expected cash inflows that are associated with those assets. Accordingly, the Board concluded that the amortization periods for intangible assets should generally reflect those useful lives and, by extension, the cash flow streams associated with them. The Board noted that the useful lives and amortization periods of intangible assets should reflect the periods over which those assets will contribute to cash flows, not the period of time that would be required to internally develop those assets.

B45. The Board agreed that the useful life of an intangible asset is indefinite if that life extends beyond the foreseeable horizon—that is, there is no foreseeable limit on the period of time over which it is expected to contribute to the cash flows of the reporting entity. The Board concluded that if an entity performs an analysis of all of the pertinent factors that should be considered in determining the useful life of an intangible asset (such as those in paragraph 11) and finds that there is no limit on the useful life of an intangible asset, that asset should be deemed to have an indefinite useful life.

B46. The Board noted that the cash flows and useful lives of intangible assets that are based on legal rights are constrained by the duration of those legal rights.

Thus, the useful lives of such intangible assets cannot extend beyond the length of their legal rights and may be shorter. Accordingly, the Board concluded that in determining the useful lives of those intangible assets, consideration should be given to the periods that the intangible assets contribute to cash flows, which are subject to the expiration of the legal rights.

B47 The Board observed that legal rights often are conveyed for limited terms that may be renewed, and therefore it considered whether renewals should be assumed in establishing useful lives for those intangible assets. The Board noted that some types of licenses are initially issued for finite periods but renewals are routinely granted with little cost, provided that licensees have complied with the applicable rules and regulations. Such licenses trade at prices that reflect more than the remaining term, thereby indicating that renewal at minimal cost is the general expectation, and thus their useful lives may be indefinite. However, renewals are not assured for other types of licenses, and even if they are renewed, substantial costs may be incurred for their renewal. Because the useful lives of certain intangible assets depend on renewal and on the associated costs, the Board concluded that the useful lives assigned to those assets may reflect renewal only if there is evidence to support renewal without substantial cost.

B48. The Board observed that renewals could result in some of those intangible assets having long or indefinite useful lives. The Board also observed that some assets are based on legal rights that are conveyed in perpetuity rather than for finite terms. As such, those assets may have cash flows associated with them that may be expected to continue for many years or even indefinitely. If the cash flows are expected to continue for a finite period, then the useful life of the asset is limited to that finite period. However, if the cash flows are expected to continue indefinitely, the useful life may be indefinite rather than finite. The Board also observed that intangible assets that are not based on legal rights also may have long or indefinite useful lives. Such assets, for example, may be ones that can be and are bought and sold, thereby providing evidence of their continued existence. Those markets also provide evidence of the fair values of those assets, either directly from transactions in which those assets are exchanged, or indirectly, utilizing models that incorporate transaction prices for similar assets as inputs.

Amortization

Amortization period

B49. The Board observed that Opinion 17 required intangible assets to be amortized over their expected useful lives; however, amortization periods were limited to 40 years. The Board noted that standards elsewhere that address intangible assets are generally similar. However, in some cases, the maximum amortization period is less than 40 years, with 20 years frequently being the presumed or absolute maximum. The Board noted that both FRS 10 and IAS 38 have presumptive maximums of 20 years. However, FRS 10 permits some intangible assets not to be amortized at all, provided that (a) the durability of the asset can be demonstrated[31] and justifies an amortization period longer than 20 years and (b) the asset is capable of continued measurement so that annual impairment reviews can be conducted. IAS 38 requires all intangible assets to be amortized but does not specify a maximum amortization period.

B50. Because of the potential for at least some intangible assets to have long or indefinite useful lives, the Board initially considered whether a maximum amortization period of 20 years should be applied to all of those assets, as it initially had decided with respect to goodwill (in developing the 1999 Exposure Draft). The Board observed that reducing the maximum amortization period for those assets from 40 years to 20 years would be a significant change from the requirements of Opinion 17.

B51. The Board noted in the 1999 Exposure Draft that having the same maximum amortization periods for intangible assets as for goodwill might discourage entities from recognizing more intangible assets apart from goodwill. Not independently recognizing those intangible assets when they exist and can be reliably measured adversely affects the relevance and representational faithfulness of the financial statements. Accordingly, the Board concluded in the 1999 Exposure Draft that setting a maximum amortization period of 20 years for all intangible assets would not have been appropriate.

B52. The Board observed, however, that a 20-year limitation constituted a useful benchmark or hurdle and concluded that it should be a presumptive maxi-

mum. Accordingly, the Board concluded in the 1999 Exposure Draft that intangible assets that have useful lives exceeding 20 years could be amortized over periods exceeding 20 years if they generate clearly identifiable cash flows that are expected to continue for more than 20 years. Support for that amortization period would have been provided by a legal life exceeding 20 years or exchangeability of the asset.

B53. Responses to the 1999 Exposure Draft varied. Some respondents stated that no intangible assets should be amortized; others stated that a presumption about the length of the amortization period was not necessary, nor was a maximum. The Board reaffirmed in this Statement that intangible assets with finite useful lives should be amortized. The Board noted that the revised criteria for an intangible asset to be recognized apart from goodwill (contractual-legal and separability) are similar to the criteria in the 1999 Exposure Draft for overcoming the 20-year useful life presumption. (The 1999 Exposure Draft would have required an intangible asset to have clearly identifiable cash flows in order to overcome that presumption.) The Board noted that the useful life of an intangible asset is defined in this Statement as the period over which an asset is expected to contribute directly or indirectly to future cash flows. The Board therefore concluded that a recognized intangible asset should be amortized over its useful life to the reporting entity and that there should be no limit, presumed or maximum, on that amortization period. However, the Board agreed that an entity is required to periodically evaluate the remaining useful lives of intangible assets and revise the amortization period of an intangible asset if it is determined that the useful life of the asset is longer or shorter than originally estimated.

Amortization method

B54. In considering the methods of amortization, the Board noted that Opinion 17 required that a straight-line method be used to amortize intangible assets unless another method was demonstrated to be more appropriate. However, the Board also noted that circumstances may exist in which another method may be more appropriate, such as in the case of a license that entitles the holder to produce a finite quantity of product. The Board therefore concluded that the amortization method adopted should reflect the pattern

---

[31]Paragraph 20 of FRS 10 notes that durability depends on a number of factors such as the nature of the business, the stability of the industry in which the acquired business operates, typical lifespans of the products to which the goodwill attaches, the extent to which the acquisition overcomes market entry barriers that will continue to exist, and the expected future impact of competition on the business.

in which the asset is consumed if that pattern can be reliably determined, with the straight-line method being used as a default.

Amortizable amount and residual value

B55. The Board noted that some intangible assets could have residual values at the ends of their useful lives to the entity that acquired them. Opinion 17 was silent about the role of residual values in determining the amortizable amount; however, both FRS 10 and IAS 38 address residual values. Thus, the Board concluded that explicit mention should be made of the use of residual values in determining amortizable amounts. Specifically, the Board decided that the residual value of an intangible asset should be assumed to be zero unless the asset's useful life to the reporting entity is less than its useful life generally and reliable evidence is available concerning the residual value. Such evidence should be in the form of either a commitment by a third party to purchase the asset at the end of its useful life or an existing market for the asset that is expected to exist at the end of the asset's useful life. During its redeliberations of the 1999 Exposure Draft, the Board clarified that the residual value is the net amount that an entity expects to obtain for an intangible asset at the end of its useful life to that entity—not at the end of its useful life in general. The Board also clarified that the residual value should be determined net of any costs to dispose of the intangible asset.

Nonamortization

B56. In developing the 1999 Exposure Draft, the Board observed that certain intangible assets may have useful lives that are indefinite and amortizing those assets would not be representationally faithful. However, because most intangible assets have finite useful lives, the Board noted that an assertion of an indefinite useful life should have to meet a high hurdle in terms of evidence to justify nonamortization. In the 1999 Exposure Draft, the Board concluded that the only evidence that would be sufficient to overcome such a hurdle would be that the intangible asset generates cash flows indefinitely and that there is an observable market for it. Examples of such intangible assets might be airport route authorities, certain trademarks, and taxicab medallions.

B57. Respondents to the 1999 Exposure Draft generally supported nonamortization of certain intangible assets; however, some respondents suggested that all intangible assets be amortized (over a maxi-

mum of 20 years). Some respondents noted that the existence of an observable market is not pertinent to the decision as to whether an asset's useful life is finite or indefinite; therefore, an observable market should not be a criterion for nonamortization of intangible assets. The Board affirmed its decision that intangible assets with indefinite useful lives should not be amortized and reconsidered the need for an observable market criterion. The Board observed that in light of the revised criteria for determining which intangible assets are to be recognized apart from goodwill, an observable market might not be necessary to support nonamortization of intangible assets deemed to have indefinite useful lives.

B58. The Board reasoned that an intangible asset that is separable or is subject to contractual or legal-based rights will have an observable market or will have identifiable cash flows associated with it. The Board noted that Concepts Statement 7 (issued after issuance of the 1999 Exposure Draft) provides guidance for using cash flows to determine the fair value of an asset in the absence of an observable market. Because there are different ways to determine fair value, the Board concluded that it was not necessary that there be an observable market for an intangible asset in order for that asset not to be amortized. Therefore, any intangible asset that is determined to have an indefinite useful life should not be amortized until that life is determined to be no longer indefinite.

B59. The Board observed that an indefinite useful life is not necessarily an infinite useful life. As noted in paragraph B45, the useful life of an intangible asset is indefinite if no limit is placed on the end of its useful life to the reporting entity. The Board also observed that indefinite does not mean the same as indeterminate. Thus, even if the precise useful life of a finite-lived intangible asset is not determinable, the intangible asset still would have to be amortized, and the amortization period would reflect the best estimate of the useful life of that asset.

B60. The Board affirmed that an intangible asset like a taxicab medallion may be considered to have an indefinite useful life because the right associated with that asset can be renewed indefinitely at little or no cost. The Board observed that paragraph 11(d) requires an entity to consider the ability to renew or extend a specified limit on an intangible asset's legal or contractual life in determining the length of its useful life to the reporting entity if evidence supports renewal or extension without substantial cost. The

Board noted that whether the cost of renewal is substantial should be determined based on the relationship of the renewal cost to the fair value of the intangible asset at the time it is acquired.

B61. As noted previously, the Board agreed that an entity should periodically evaluate the remaining useful lives of intangible assets. The Board affirmed that when an intangible asset's useful life is no longer considered to be indefinite, such as when unanticipated competition enters the market, the intangible asset must be amortized over the remaining period that it is expected to contribute to cash flows. Similarly, the Board agreed that an intangible asset that initially is deemed to have a finite useful life should cease being amortized if it is subsequently determined to have an indefinite useful life, for example, due to a change in legal requirements.

Reviews for impairment

B62. The Board concluded that intangible assets that are being amortized should continue to be reviewed for impairment in accordance with FASB Statement No. 121, *Accounting for the Impairment of Long-Lived Assets and for Long-Lived Assets to Be Disposed Of.* However, the Board noted that a different approach to impairment reviews was needed for intangible assets that are not being amortized. As the Board observed in conjunction with its consideration of goodwill impairment, nonamortization places heavy reliance on the reviews for impairment. Because the cash flows associated with intangible assets having indefinite useful lives would extend into the future indefinitely, those assets might never fail the undiscounted cash flows recoverability test in Statement 121, even if those cash flows were expected to decrease over time.

B63. Accordingly, the Board decided that the recognition of impairment losses on intangible assets with indefinite useful lives should be based on the fair values of those assets without performing the recoverability test, noting that that would be an exception to Statement 121. However, the impairment losses would be measured as the excess of the carrying amount over fair value, which is consistent with Statement 121.

B64. Because the Board eliminated the observable market criterion for nonamortization of intangible assets, the Board addressed how fair value should be determined for impairment purposes in the absence of an observable market price. When it agreed to

eliminate the observable market criterion, the Board noted that Concepts Statement 7 provides guidance for using cash flows to determine the fair value of an asset in the absence of an observable market. The Board concluded that the fair value measurement guidance included in this Statement that is based on Concepts Statement 7 should be used to determine the fair value of intangible assets for impairment purposes.

B65. The 1999 Exposure Draft required that the fair value of an intangible asset not being amortized be tested for impairment on an annual basis. The Board reaffirmed that requirement after it decided that goodwill should be tested for impairment on an annual basis. The Board also concluded that an intangible asset not being amortized should be tested for impairment whenever events occur or circumstances change between annual tests indicating that the asset might be impaired. The Board agreed that the examples of impairment indicators in paragraph 5 of Statement 121 were appropriate for intangible assets not being amortized.

B66. The Board agreed that when the estimate of the remaining useful life of an intangible asset changes from finite to indefinite or vice versa, the asset should be tested for impairment (in accordance with paragraph 17) prior to the change in the method of accounting for that intangible asset. The Board observed that any resulting impairment loss would be due to a change in accounting estimate and thus, consistent with APB Opinion No. 20, *Accounting Changes,* should be recognized as a change in estimate, not as a change in accounting principle. Therefore, that loss would be presented in the income statement in the same manner as other impairment losses (except a transitional impairment loss).

Goodwill

Initial Recognition and Measurement

B67. Statement 141 addresses the initial recognition and measurement of acquired goodwill. In that Statement, the Board concluded that acquired goodwill meets the assets definition in FASB Concepts Statement No. 6, *Elements of Financial Statements,* and the asset recognition criteria in Concepts Statement 5. In addition, the Board concluded that goodwill should be measured as the excess of the cost of an acquired entity over the sum of the amounts assigned to assets acquired and liabilities assumed. This Statement addresses the recognition and measurement of goodwill subsequent to its acquisition.

Subsequent Recognition and Measurement

B68. The Board considered the following alternatives for accounting for goodwill after it has been initially recognized: (a) write off all or a portion of goodwill immediately, (b) report goodwill as an asset that is amortized over its useful life, (c) report goodwill as an asset that is not amortized but is reviewed for impairment, or (d) report goodwill as an asset, a portion of which is amortized and a portion of which is not amortized (a mixed approach).

Immediate write-off

B69. As explained in Statement 141, the Board concluded that goodwill meets the criteria for recognition of an asset and therefore should not be written off at the date of an acquisition. In discussing whether goodwill should be written off immediately subsequent to its initial recognition, the Board noted that it would be difficult to explain why goodwill is written off immediately after having just been recognized as an asset. If goodwill had been worthless on the date of acquisition, it would not have met the assets definition and would not have been recognized. However, if goodwill had value initially, virtually no event other than a catastrophe could subsequently occur in which it instantaneously became worthless.

B70. Some respondents to both Exposure Drafts argued that goodwill should be written off immediately because of the uncertainties associated with goodwill subsequent to its initial recognition. The Board noted that if the uncertainties associated with goodwill were so great as to mandate its write-off immediately following initial recognition, those same uncertainties should have been present when it was acquired and would have been reflected in the purchase price of the acquired entity. Furthermore, the Board questioned whether an informational purpose would be served if goodwill were to be recognized only momentarily as an asset unless it were in fact only momentarily an asset. The Board additionally noted that difficulties arise in determining the diminution in value of goodwill in subsequent periods but observed that such difficulties are not unique to goodwill. The Board accordingly concluded that immediate write-off subsequent to initial recognition was not justifiable.

A mixture of amortization and nonamortization

B71. Early in the project, the Board concluded that at least part of goodwill may be a nonwasting asset

and thus may have an indefinite useful life. To the extent that recognized goodwill is a composite of several "discernible elements" having different useful lives, the Board concluded that goodwill should in concept be accounted for in such a way as to reflect those lives. That is, ideally, the portion of goodwill that has an indefinite useful life would not be amortized, and the portion of goodwill that has a finite useful life would be amortized over that life. Accordingly, the Board considered what it described as the "discernible-elements approach" as the basis for determining the portion of goodwill that should not be amortized and the amortization period for the portion of goodwill that should be amortized.

B72. The discernible-elements approach may be described broadly as follows. At acquisition, the reasons for paying a premium over the fair value of the acquired entity's identifiable net assets would be identified and documented, with that analysis supporting and justifying the amount of goodwill recorded. The recorded amount of goodwill would be allocated to each of its discernible elements based on that analysis. Those elements would be assessed to determine whether they had finite or indefinite useful lives, based on the length of time that they were expected to contribute to cash flows. The lengths of the finite useful lives also would be determined. The portion of goodwill with a finite useful life would then be amortized over the weighted-average useful life of the discernible elements. The portion of goodwill with an indefinite useful life would not be amortized but would be subject to impairment reviews (if an appropriate impairment test could be developed).

B73. The Board acknowledged, however, that such an approach would involve numerous subjective judgments on the part of entities in identifying discernible elements, allocating the purchase premium to them, and assessing their useful lives. As a result, the Board conducted a field test of its proposed approach in mid-1998. Participants supported the approach conceptually but expressed concerns about the subjective judgments required to apply it and noted that it affords opportunities for manipulation of reported amounts in financial statements. Moreover, comparisons of how those participants applied the approach to prior business combinations demonstrated significant differences, thereby underscoring concerns about its operationality. The Board concluded that the discernible-elements approach was not sufficiently operational to require its use in amortizing goodwill. Because the Board concluded that segregating the parts of goodwill that are wasting and nonwasting is not feasible, it proposed in the 1999 Exposure Draft that all goodwill should continue to be amortized.

Amortization

B74. The 1999 Exposure Draft proposed that goodwill would be amortized over its useful life and that the amortization period would not exceed 20 years. At the time, the Board observed that one argument for amortizing goodwill was that goodwill should be allocated to achieve a proper allocation of its costs to future operations. Another argument was that acquired goodwill is an asset that is consumed and replaced with internally generated goodwill and that the acquired goodwill therefore must be amortized (even though the internally generated goodwill that is replacing it cannot be recognized as an asset). Another argument was that the useful life of goodwill cannot be predicted with a satisfactory level of reliability, nor can the pattern in which goodwill diminishes be known. Hence, in the 1999 Exposure Draft the Board concluded that amortization over an arbitrary period of time was the only practical solution to an intractable problem and was preferable to the alternative of writing off goodwill immediately because that would be even less representationally faithful.

B75. The Board acknowledged that achieving an acceptable level of reliability in the form of representational faithfulness was one of the primary challenges it faced in deliberating the accounting for goodwill. The useful life of goodwill and the pattern in which it diminishes are both difficult to predict, yet its amortization depends on such predictions. As a result, the Board acknowledged that the amount amortized in any given period can be described as only a rough estimate of the decrease in goodwill during that period. However, the Board noted that users of financial statements can be expected to understand such limitations of goodwill amortization.

B76. To assist users in understanding those limitations, the Board concluded in the 1999 Exposure Draft that goodwill amortization expense should be separated from other items on the income statement to make it more transparent. In reaching that conclusion, the Board noted the anomalous accounting between acquired goodwill and internally generated goodwill and that goodwill is different from other assets. The Board concluded that those differences justified displaying charges associated with goodwill (amortization expense and impairment losses)

differently, particularly because goodwill may be a nonwasting asset in part and because measures of its amortization and impairment may be less precise than other measures of income items.

B77. The Board further acknowledged constituents' assertions that many users assess goodwill charges differently than other income items, in some cases eliminating them from their analysis of earnings per share. The Board therefore concluded that a more transparent display would facilitate the analyses of those users but would not impair the analyses of users that do not assess those charges differently. Thus, the 1999 Exposure Draft proposed that goodwill charges be presented on a net-of-tax basis as a separate line item in the income statement. That line item would have been immediately preceded by a required subtotal of income after taxes but before goodwill charges and would have been immediately followed by an appropriately titled subtotal.

B78. Respondents' views on the requirements proposed in the 1999 Exposure Draft varied. Some respondents agreed with the Board that goodwill should be amortized like other assets; others favored not amortizing goodwill but testing it for impairment; still others suggested that goodwill be written off immediately. Many respondents that expressed support for the requirement to amortize goodwill stated that although amortization was not necessarily their first preference, they were willing to accept the proposed requirement given the method proposed in the 1999 Exposure Draft of displaying goodwill amortization in the income statement. Many respondents, however, did not agree with the proposal to place an arbitrary limit of 20 years on the goodwill amortization period. Others expressed the view that 20 years was too long.

Reconsideration of a nonamortization approach

B79. When it issued the 1999 Exposure Draft, the Board acknowledged that not all goodwill declines in value and that goodwill that does decline in value rarely does so on a straight-line basis. Because the Board agreed with respondents who stated that straight-line amortization of goodwill over an arbitrary period does not reflect economic reality and thus does not provide useful information, the Board reconsidered its decision to require amortization of goodwill. The Board reaffirmed its belief that immediate write-off of goodwill was not appropriate and thus focused its reconsideration on nonamortization of goodwill.

B80. As part of its reconsideration of the 1999 Exposure Draft, the Board sought additional input from its constituents. Two groups of constituents met with the Board to discuss their proposed approaches to accounting for goodwill, under which goodwill would not be amortized but would be tested for impairment. Based on those presentations, informal discussion with Board members, and additional research, a general approach to testing goodwill for impairment (general impairment approach) was developed.

B81. During October and November 2000, the Board discussed that general impairment approach with 14 companies in a variety of industries to gather input on how it might be implemented. Those field visits also included a discussion of the methods currently used by companies to value potential acquisitions, analyze the subsequent performance of an acquired business, test goodwill for impairment, and determine the amount of goodwill to write off when an acquired business is subsequently sold or disposed of. Field visit participants offered suggestions to change and improve the general impairment approach. After contemplating and summarizing the findings from those field visits, the Board reconsidered its reasons for concluding in the 1999 Exposure Draft that a nonamortization approach was *not* appropriate for goodwill.

Some portion of goodwill is a wasting asset

B82. The 1999 Exposure Draft noted that, conceptually, at least part of what is recognized as goodwill may have an indefinite useful life that could last as long as the business is considered a going concern. However, the Board concluded that some of what is recognized as goodwill might have a finite useful life partly because goodwill is measured as a residual and may include components (representing assets or components of assets) that are wasting assets and therefore should be amortized. As discussed previously, prior to issuing the 1999 Exposure Draft, the Board considered the discernible-elements approach that would have required amortization of the wasting portion of goodwill and nonamortization of the non-wasting portion (that is, the portion with an indefinite useful life). However, the Board concluded that segregating the portion of recognized goodwill that might not be a wasting asset from the portion that is a wasting asset would not be practicable.

B83. The 1999 Exposure Draft proposed that an intangible asset that could not be reliably measured should be recognized as part of goodwill. The Board

decided to change that proposed treatment to require that only intangible assets that do not have an underlying contractual or other legal basis or are not capable of being separated and sold, transferred, licensed, rented, or exchanged be recognized as part of goodwill. The Board believes that application of those criteria should result in more recognition and reporting uniformity in the intangible assets that are recognized apart from goodwill. In addition, the intangible assets that would be recognized as part of goodwill using the revised criteria generally would be "goodwill like" in nature. The Board concluded that by revising the criteria for separating intangible assets from goodwill, the portion of recognized goodwill that might be wasting would be smaller than it might have been using the criteria in the 1999 Exposure Draft. Thus, Board members viewed nonamortization of all goodwill as more appropriate than it would have been under the 1999 Exposure Draft. However, the Board still needed to overcome its concerns with testing goodwill for impairment and develop an operational impairment test.

Concerns with testing goodwill for impairment

Internally generated goodwill

B84. Unlike many other assets that are tested for impairment, goodwill does not have a set of cash flows uniquely associated with it. Instead, the cash flows associated with acquired goodwill usually are intermingled with those associated with internally generated goodwill and other assets because entities generally enter into business combinations to reduce costs and achieve synergies, which entails integrating the acquired entity with the acquiring entity.

B85. In its reconsideration of the goodwill impairment issue, the Board assessed to what extent it would be appropriate to allow the accounting model to compensate for the fact that acquired goodwill might be replaced by internally generated goodwill. Many respondents noted that the current accounting model does not permit recognition of internally generated intangible assets, including goodwill. They also noted that a good portion of an entity's value may be related to those unrecognized intangible assets. Respondents mentioned the growing disparity between the market capitalization of many entities and their book values as strong evidence of that unrecognized value. Board members concluded that it is appropriate to assume that acquired goodwill is being replaced by internally generated goodwill provided that an entity is able to maintain the overall value of goodwill (for example, by expending resources on advertising and customer service).

Integration of an acquired entity

B86. Prior to issuing the 1999 Exposure Draft, the Board's discussions of goodwill impairment tests generally centered on testing goodwill specific to an acquisition. The Board concluded that keeping track of acquisition-specific goodwill for impairment purposes would be almost impossible once an acquired entity was integrated with the acquiring entity. The Board considered the alternative of testing goodwill at the combined entity (total company) level to be unacceptable. The Board learned in its field visits that synergies occur below the combined entity level and that management is often held accountable for acquisitions at a lower level. In addition, Board members noted that the higher the level of review, the more difficult it would be to develop a robust impairment test and the less confident investors would be with the results of the impairment tests. The Board considered further the fact that an acquired entity often is integrated with a part of the acquiring entity and concluded that, in those cases, goodwill should be tested for impairment in conjunction with more than just the net assets of the acquired entity. The Board concluded that, in most cases, it is appropriate to test goodwill for impairment in the aggregate at a level higher than that of the acquired entity and lower than that of the combined entity. Thus, the 2001 Exposure Draft proposed that goodwill be tested for impairment at a level referred to as a reporting unit. The Board envisioned that a reporting unit generally would be at a level somewhere between a reportable operating segment (as defined in FASB Statement No. 131, *Disclosures about Segments of an Enterprise and Related Information*) and an asset group (as that term is used in Statement 121). (Paragraphs B101–B112 discuss the reporting unit in more detail.)

B87. The Board noted that the anomalies that result from the differences in how acquired goodwill and internally generated goodwill are accounted for also justify a departure from the current model of accounting for goodwill on an acquisition-specific basis subsequent to an acquisition. The Board observed that an entity often has internally generated goodwill and goodwill-like assets that are not recognized on its balance sheet. Thus, it would be infrequent that the value of the actual (recognized and unrecognized) goodwill and goodwill-like assets of an entity would be less than the amount portrayed as goodwill in

its balance sheet even if the value of the goodwill associated with a specific acquisition declined subsequent to its acquisition. This point was significant to some Board members in agreeing to accept a non-amortization approach and depart from the normal acquisition-specific model for testing goodwill for impairment.

Undiscounted cash flows

B88. Prior to issuing the 1999 Exposure Draft, the Board discussed testing goodwill for impairment using an undiscounted cash flow method similar to that required for long-lived assets in Statement 121. The Board concluded at that time that a similar method would not be appropriate for goodwill because the cash flows in question could continue for many years—longer than most other assets.

B89. Another reason the Board ultimately decided against using an undiscounted cash flow method to test goodwill for impairment was that constituents generally agreed with the 1999 Exposure Draft proposal that intangible assets that are not being amortized should not be tested for impairment in accordance with Statement 121 and thus should be excluded from the scope of that Statement. The 1999 Exposure Draft would have required that an intangible asset not being amortized be tested for impairment on an annual basis and that an impairment loss be recognized if the carrying amount of the intangible asset exceeded its fair value. That proposed fair value impairment test would have differed from the impairment test used for all other assets. Thus, the Board decided to continue to pursue an approach that would exclude nonamortized intangible assets—including goodwill—from the scope of Statement 121 and to test for impairment using a fair-value-based approach.

Decision usefulness

B90. During its field visits, the Board learned that, in addition to the many analysts that ignore goodwill amortization expense in their analyses, many entities ignore goodwill amortization expense in measuring operating performance for internal reporting purposes; rather, they hold management responsible for the amount invested in an acquired entity (including goodwill). A number of field visit participants noted, for example, that in measuring return on net assets, management would include goodwill in the denominator (asset base) but would exclude the amortization expense from the numerator (operating earnings).

Thus, Board members acknowledged that not only do many users of financial statements ignore goodwill amortization expense in making investment and credit decisions, entities often do not consider goodwill amortization expense in evaluating the performance of management.

B91. In addition, Board members noted that reported earnings often increase in the period following the final amortization expense of goodwill even though operations may not have changed significantly. Some Board members believe that result is not representationally faithful because that earnings increase arises from the cessation of prior "doubling-up" of expenses related to goodwill, which occurs when the income statement is charged for expiring goodwill (amortization of past outlays for acquired goodwill) at the same time it is charged for current outlays to create goodwill (internally generated goodwill). As a result, reported earnings in those prior periods were decreased in such a way that they did not faithfully reflect the economic changes that occurred in those periods.

Nonamortization in some or all cases

B92. Upon reconsideration of all of those issues, the Board concluded that an acceptable impairment test could be developed based on aggregate goodwill rather than only acquired goodwill and that nonamortization of goodwill coupled with a fair-value-based impairment test would result in more representationally faithful and decision-useful financial information. The Board then considered whether it was appropriate to permit entities to amortize acquired goodwill in certain circumstances, noting that impairment issues would have to be considered regardless of whether goodwill was being amortized.

B93. The Board was doubtful that it could develop operational criteria to identify the circumstances in which goodwill should be amortized. The Board noted that if it were to permit both nonamortization and amortization of goodwill (a variation of the mixed approach), entities effectively would have a free choice as to which method to use to account for goodwill, resulting in a significant potential for noncomparable financial reporting among entities. More important, because the Board concluded that its approach would result in more representationally faithful financial information, to permit goodwill to be amortized would be inappropriate.

B94. The Board also concluded that not amortizing goodwill in all circumstances would provide information that is more useful to investors than adopting a mixed approach under which goodwill would be permitted to be amortized in some circumstances. The Board observed that adopting a nonamortization approach for all goodwill would not mean that goodwill would never be written down or that it would only be written down occasionally in large amounts. Board members noted that if the carrying amount of goodwill of a reporting unit cannot be maintained, the impairment test would accommodate both periodic and irregular write-downs of goodwill to reflect that decline in value. For example, an entity might acquire a mature business that is considered a "cash cow" and is not expected to grow. Specifically, the acquired business is expected to generate cash flows for a limited period of time as it winds down its operations and eventually ceases to operate. The Board acknowledged that if that acquired business were to be operated as a separate reporting unit, that reporting unit would recognize goodwill impairment losses on a regular basis until its goodwill is reduced to zero, presumably when operations cease. Thus, the Board concluded in the 2001 Exposure Draft to depart from the prior view that all goodwill should be amortized and adopted a nonamortization approach for all goodwill.

Nonamortization of goodwill and related impairment tests

B95. Most respondents to the 2001 Exposure Draft agreed with the Board's conclusions on the fundamental aspects of the proposed nonamortization approach. They said that nonamortization of goodwill, coupled with impairment testing and appropriate disclosure, promotes transparency in financial reporting and thus provides useful information to those who rely on financial statements. In addition, respondents noted that not amortizing goodwill is consistent with both how an entity manages its business and how investors view goodwill.

B96. Most respondents that disagreed with the Board's conclusions did so because they consider goodwill to be a wasting asset or because the proposed nonamortization approach in essence allows acquisitive entities to capitalize internally generated goodwill. Respondents argued that effectively capitalizing internally generated goodwill is inconsistent with the general accounting model and introduces an unlevel playing field favoring entities that grow by acquisition rather than internally. Most respondents who disagreed with nonamortization of goodwill suggested that goodwill be amortized over a life of up to 20 years with "below-the-line" income statement presentation, as proposed in the 1999 Exposure Draft.

B97. The Board acknowledged that the proposed impairment test would ensure only that the carrying amount of goodwill of a reporting unit does not exceed the total goodwill (acquired and internally generated) of that unit and thus could be viewed as effectively capitalizing internally generated goodwill. However, acquired goodwill cannot be isolated from internally generated goodwill after the acquired business is integrated with a larger part of the acquiring entity. Moreover, acquired goodwill and goodwill created subsequent to the acquisition cannot be separately identified even if the acquired business is not integrated with other parts of the acquiring entity.

B98. Without the ability to measure internally generated goodwill and factor that measure into the impairment test, the carrying amount of goodwill that is tested for impairment always will be shielded by goodwill internally generated both before and after the acquisition. Thus, the Board was unable to determine a way to apply a nonamortization approach coupled with impairment testing and avoid the possibility of what some describe as "backdoor" capitalization of internally generated goodwill. The Board noted that some consider amortization of goodwill to be unfair to entities whose growth comes largely from acquisitions rather than from internal sources because of the "doubling-up" of expenses that occurs within a specific reporting period as the result of expensing current outlays that generate goodwill (such as advertising and research and development outlays) and concurrently amortizing acquired goodwill. Thus, the Board did not consider it possible to develop a method of accounting for acquired goodwill that all would agree established a level playing field in all circumstances. Accordingly, the Board focused on which method better reflects the economic impact of goodwill on an entity.

B99. The Board reaffirmed its decision that nonamortization of goodwill combined with an adequate impairment test will provide financial information that more faithfully reflects the economic impact of acquired goodwill on the value of an entity than does amortization of goodwill. The Board concluded that the goodwill impairment test prescribed by this Statement will adequately capture goodwill impairment. It thus concluded that nonamortization of goodwill will result in the most useful financial information within the constraints of the current accounting model and available valuation techniques.

B100. Some respondents to the 2001 Exposure Draft stated that while their preference is an impairment-only (nonamortization) model for goodwill, it would be appropriate to amortize goodwill in certain circumstances. Examples include acquisition of a business that is a cash cow, a small business that is unable to devote resources to the impairment test, and acquisitions of high-tech companies. In developing the 2001 Exposure Draft, the Board considered whether a mixed model would be more appropriate than an impairment-only model. At that time, the Board was concerned that unless operational criteria could be developed that would limit amortization of goodwill to specific circumstances, preparers might interpret this Statement as allowing free choice in accounting for goodwill. In addition, the Board was not confident that operational criteria could be developed that would distinguish those circumstances in which amortization would be appropriate from those in which it would *not* be appropriate. The Board noted that allowing some entities to amortize goodwill might impair comparability in financial reporting. For those same reasons, the Board concluded that amortization of goodwill should not be permitted in any circumstance, noting that the impairment test will capture steadily declining goodwill provided that the level of testing is low enough.

Reporting unit

B101. The 2001 Exposure Draft proposed that goodwill be tested for impairment at the reporting unit level. A reporting unit was defined in that Exposure Draft as the lowest level of an entity that is a business and that can be distinguished, physically and operationally and for internal reporting purposes, from the other activities, operations, and assets of the entity. As defined, a reporting unit could be no higher than a reportable operating segment (segment) and would generally be lower than that level of reporting. However, the Board acknowledged that for some entities, a reporting unit would be the same as a segment and that for narrowly focused entities, the entity as a whole might be one reporting unit.

B102. The Board initially considered testing goodwill at the segment level in all cases, based on the presumption that that level generally is the lowest reporting level that captures all of the goodwill of a specific acquisition. However, field visit participants informed the Board that they often allocate goodwill below the segment level—for example, to operating or business unit levels. After considering the views of field visit participants and others, the Board concluded that the Statement should permit some flexibility in the level at which goodwill is tested for impairment and that it should allow the level to differ as appropriate from entity to entity and industry to industry. Board members noted that goodwill by its nature will be associated with the operations of an entity at different levels—possibly different levels within the same overall entity. The Board's intent was that a reporting unit would be the level of internal reporting that reflects the way an entity manages its business or operations and to which goodwill naturally would be associated.

B103. It was important to the Board that the impairment test be performed at a level at which information about the operations of an entity and the assets and liabilities that support those operations are documented for internal reporting purposes (as well as possibly for external reporting purposes). That approach reflects the Board's belief that the information an entity reports for internal use will reflect the way the overall entity is managed. Therefore, the Board did not intend the concept of a reporting unit and the requirement to test goodwill for impairment at that level to create a new internal reporting level. The Board believed that information entities currently generate about their operations, such as cash flows by business unit for planning purposes, would be used in measuring the fair value of a reporting unit. Similarly, information about the underlying assets and liabilities currently reported by an entity, such as a balance sheet for each division, would be used to identify the net assets of a reporting unit.

B104. However, many respondents to the 2001 Exposure Draft interpreted the reporting unit to be a level much lower than the level the Board had intended. Some respondents asserted that an entity could have hundreds or possibly thousands of reporting units. Also, there were differences of opinion about whether the reporting unit as defined in the 2001 Exposure Draft allowed for the flexibility that the Board had intended. Many respondents asserted that they would be required to test goodwill for impairment at a level that had no bearing on how the acquisition was integrated into the acquiring entity or how the overall combined entity was managed.

B105. Most respondents who disagreed with using the reporting unit as defined in the 2001 Exposure Draft suggested that goodwill be tested at the reportable segment level or at the operating segment level (both as defined in Statement 131). Respondents stated that testing goodwill for impairment at a level based on Statement 131 would be more operational and more consistently applied. Respondents observed that public entities currently apply the operating segment concept for financial reporting purposes and have processes in place to identify and accumulate information about operating segments. Thus, the operating segment concept is more easily understood than the proposed reporting unit concept and also takes advantage of the processes currently in place. In addition, respondents noted that segments would be a more manageable level for impairment testing because segments are changed far less often than lower level units. It was also observed that because financial statement users are more familiar with Statement 131, testing goodwill for impairment at the segment level would provide information that financial statement users can relate to other segment information provided in the financial statements.

B106. However, many respondents who suggested that goodwill be tested for impairment at the segment level also suggested that entities be permitted to test goodwill for impairment at a lower "reporting unit" level as long as the entity documented its policy for doing so and applied that policy on a consistent basis. The Board reaffirmed its belief that there should be a common methodology for determining the unit of account (the reporting unit) and that permitting exceptions would raise comparability and unlevel playing field issues.

B107. Because it did not intend the requirement to test goodwill for impairment at the reporting unit level to create a new level of reporting and because of concerns about inconsistent application, the Board reconsidered the definition of a reporting unit proposed in the 2001 Exposure Draft. The Board considered and rejected attempting to revise the reporting unit definition to better describe what the Board originally intended. While revising the definition would allow for the most flexibility in determining the appropriate level at which to test goodwill for impairment, Board members did not think it would be possible to devise a definition that would be interpreted and applied in a consistent manner.

B108. The Board agreed with respondents who suggested that the level of impairment testing should relate to the segment reporting requirements of Statement 131. The Board thus considered requiring goodwill to be tested for impairment at the operating segment level in all instances. An operating segment is defined in Statement 131 (paragraph 10) as a component of an enterprise:

(a) That engages in business activities from which it may earn revenues and incur expenses (including revenues and expenses relating to transactions with other components of the same enterprise),

(b) Whose operating results are regularly reviewed by the enterprise's chief operating decision maker to make decisions about resources to be allocated to the segment and assess its performance, and

(c) For which discrete financial information is available.

B109. The Board concluded that in many cases the operating segment level may be too high a level at which to perform the goodwill impairment test. That conclusion was based on the requests of respondents that the Statement permit entities to test goodwill for impairment below the operating segment level if the entity is able to do so.

B110. Consequently, the Board considered defining a reporting unit to be one reporting level below the operating segment level, which would be the business units or components of an operating segment whose operating results are regularly reviewed by the segment manager. (As described in Statement 131, segment managers are the direct reports of the chief operating decision maker.) Under that approach, reporting units would align with how operating results are regularly reviewed by the segment manager to make decisions about resource allocation and to assess segment performance. That definition also would be similar to what the Board intended the proposed definition of a reporting unit to capture.

B111. The Board concluded that this Statement should retain the term *reporting unit* but should redefine the term using the concepts in Statement 131 so that the concept would be familiar to both preparers and users. However, the Board wanted to retain some flexibility in application of the reporting unit definition such that a reporting unit could vary somewhat from entity to entity and even within an entity, as appropriate under the circumstances. Thus, as defined in this Statement, a component of an operating segment is a reporting unit if the component is a business for which discrete financial information is available and segment management regularly reviews the operating results of that

component. However, the Board acknowledged that even though segment management might review the operating results of a number of business units (components of an operating segment), components with similar economic characteristics should be aggregated into one reporting unit. The Board reasoned that the benefits of goodwill would be shared by components of an operating segment that have similar economic characteristics and that requiring goodwill to be allocated among components with similar economic characteristics would be arbitrary and unnecessary for purposes of impairment testing. Consider an operating segment that consists of four components. Segment management reviews the operating results of each component, all of which are businesses for which discrete financial information is available. If three of those components share similar economic characteristics, the operating segment would consist of two reporting units. The component that has economic characteristics dissimilar from the other components of the operating segment would be its own reporting unit, and the three components with similar economic characteristics would constitute one reporting unit.

B112. Therefore, reporting units will vary depending on the level at which performance of the segment is reviewed, how many businesses the operating segment includes, and the similarity of those businesses. Thus, as in the 2001 Exposure Draft, a reporting unit could be the same as an operating segment, which could be the same as a reportable segment, which could be the same as the entity as a whole (entity level). Board members observed that the revised definition of a reporting unit will yield the same results for many entities as was intended by the reporting unit definition proposed in the 2001 Exposure Draft.

Nonpublic entities

B113. Having decided that the determination of reporting units should be linked to segment reporting in Statement 131, the Board considered whether to make an exception or provide additional guidance for entities that are not required to apply Statement 131. The Board concluded that although nonpublic entities are not required to follow the segment disclosure requirements in Statement 131, those entities should *not* be exempt from testing goodwill for impairment at the reporting unit level. The Board noted that many nonpublic entities have internal reporting systems that currently gather or are capable of gathering the data necessary to test goodwill for impairment at a level below the entity level. As with public entities, the reporting unit level for many nonpublic entities may be the same as the entity level. Thus, nonpublic entities would not be precluded from testing for impairment at the entity level—if in fact that level meets the definition of a reporting unit. The Board believes that the guidance in this Statement and Statement 131 is sufficient for nonpublic entities with more than one reporting unit to test goodwill for impairment at the reporting unit level.

Assigning acquired assets and assumed liabilities to reporting units

B114. The 2001 Exposure Draft proposed that for purposes of testing goodwill for impairment, the assets and liabilities of an acquired entity (including goodwill) that would be used in the operations of a reporting unit or that relate to those operations would have to be assigned to that reporting unit as of the acquisition date. The Board concluded that assigning assets and liabilities to reporting units would be necessary to make the goodwill impairment test that incorporates the values of those net assets operational. The Board noted that to the extent corporate assets or liabilities related to a reporting unit (such as pension and environmental liabilities), those assets and liabilities should be assigned as well.

B115. Respondents to the 2001 Exposure Draft expressed concerns with the requirement to assign goodwill and other assets and liabilities to reporting units. Respondents were particularly concerned with the requirement to assign corporate assets and liabilities to reporting units because of the difficulty, cost, inconsistency of application, and loss of synergies in making what they viewed as subjective and arbitrary allocation decisions. Other respondents disagreed with that requirement, noting that many businesses are best managed with the evaluation and responsibility of corporate assets and liabilities occurring at the overall entity level. Some respondents noted that their concerns would be minimized if goodwill were to be tested for impairment at the segment level instead of the proposed reporting unit level.

B116. The Board noted that the 2001 Exposure Draft would not have required *all* acquired assets and assumed liabilities to be assigned to reporting units, only those that would be employed in or were related to the operations of a unit. The Board concluded that the objective of the assignment process should be to ensure that the assets and liabilities that are assigned to a reporting unit are the same net assets that are considered in determining the fair value of that unit—an "apples-to-apples" comparison. Therefore, to the extent corporate items are reflected in the value of a reporting unit, they should be assigned to the reporting unit. For example, pension liabilities related to active employees would normally be assumed when acquiring a business; thus, that type of liability generally would be considered in determining the fair value of a reporting unit.

B117. The Board agreed that this Statement should clarify that an asset or liability should be assigned to a reporting unit only if it would be considered in determining the fair value of the unit. To do otherwise would not result in an apples-to-apples comparison. The Board confirmed that another objective of the exercise is to assign to a reporting unit all of the assets and liabilities that would be necessary for that reporting unit to operate as a business. Board members noted that it is those net assets that will generate the cash flows used to determine the fair value of a reporting unit.

B118. The Board agreed to retain the general guidance proposed in the 2001 Exposure Draft for determining how to assign assets and liabilities to reporting units. That is, the methodology used to assign assets and liabilities to reporting units should be reasonable, supportable, and applied in a consistent manner. Board members observed that it is possible for a reasonable allocation method to be very general.

Assigning goodwill to reporting units

B119. The 2001 Exposure Draft included limited guidance on how to assign acquired goodwill to reporting units. Respondents to the 2001 Exposure Draft questioned whether an entity would be required to assign goodwill only to the reporting units where the net assets acquired have been assigned and whether it would be possible to have overall "enterprise" goodwill that would not be assigned to any reporting unit. Respondents suggested that enterprise goodwill could be tested for impairment at the total entity level.

B120. The Board affirmed that all goodwill should be allocated to reporting units. Board members observed that if some portion of goodwill is deemed to relate to the entity as a whole, that portion of goodwill should be assigned to all of the reporting units of the entity in a reasonable and supportable manner. The Board also concluded that goodwill should be assigned to the reporting units of the acquiring entity that are expected to benefit from the synergies of the combination even though those units may not be assigned any other assets or any liabilities of the acquired entity.

B121. The Board acknowledged that the requirement in this Statement to assign what some view as corporate assets and liabilities to reporting units could be considered inconsistent with the requirements in Statement 131. For purposes of reporting information about assets by segment, entities are required by Statement 131 to include in reported segment assets only those assets that are included in the measure of the segment's assets that is used by the chief operating decision maker. Thus, goodwill and other assets and liabilities may not be included in reported segment assets. This Statement does not require that goodwill and all other related assets and liabilities assigned to reporting units for purposes of testing goodwill for impairment be reflected in the entity's reported segments. However, even though an asset may not be included in reported segment assets, the asset (or liability) should be allocated to a reporting unit for purposes of testing for impairment if it meets the criteria in paragraph 32 of this Statement. This Statement also requires that the amount of goodwill in each segment be disclosed in the notes to the financial statements.

Reorganization of reporting structure

B122. The 2001 Exposure Draft did not address how goodwill and the other assets and liabilities that make up a reporting unit should be reassigned when an entity reorganizes its reporting structure. The Board concluded that the guidance provided in the Statement for assigning acquired assets and assumed liabilities should be used to reassign assets and liabilities of reporting units that are reorganized. However, this Statement requires goodwill to be reassigned to reorganized reporting units using a relative fair value allocation method similar to that used to determine the amount of goodwill to allocate to a business being disposed of. The Board concluded that reorganizing a reporting unit is similar to selling off a business within that reporting unit; thus, the same allocation methodology should be used.

Recognition and measurement of an impairment loss

B123. In the 2001 Exposure Draft, the Board concluded that a fair-value-based impairment test should estimate the implied fair value of goodwill, which

would be compared with the carrying amount of goodwill to determine whether goodwill is impaired. The Board acknowledged that it is not possible to directly measure the fair value of goodwill, noting that goodwill is measured as a residual amount at acquisition. The Board concluded that a method similar to the method of allocating the purchase price to the net assets acquired could be used to measure the value of goodwill subsequent to its initial recognition. Thus, the Board decided that some measure of net assets of a reporting unit should be subtracted from the fair value of a reporting unit to determine the implied fair value of that reporting unit's goodwill.

B124. The Board then considered how to measure the value of net assets that will be subtracted from the fair value of a reporting unit to determine the implied fair value of goodwill. The Board considered the following alternatives: (a) the fair value of recognized net assets (excluding goodwill), (b) the fair value of *both* recognized *and* unrecognized net assets (excluding goodwill), (c) the book value of recognized net assets (excluding goodwill), and (d) the book value of recognized net assets (excluding goodwill) adjusted for any known differences between book value and fair value. The Board concluded that subtracting the fair value of *both* recognized *and* unrecognized net assets would result in an estimate closest to the implied fair value of goodwill. However, the Board concluded that the cost of identifying the unrecognized net assets and determining their fair values in addition to the costs of determining the fair values of the recognized net assets outweighed the benefits of that alternative.

B125. The Board acknowledged that subtracting the fair value of only *recognized* net assets (excluding goodwill) from the fair value of a reporting unit generally would result in a residual amount that includes more than acquired goodwill. That is, the residual amount also would include the fair value of unrecognized goodwill and other intangible assets that were internally generated both before and after an acquisition and the fair value of any unrecognized goodwill and other intangible assets that were acquired in prior business combinations accounted for by the pooling method, as well as asset "step-ups" in basis that were not recognized. The Board referred to the above amounts as adding "cushion" to the estimate of the implied fair value of goodwill. The Board was not as concerned about the cushion resulting from unrecognized internally generated goodwill as it was about the cushion arising from other unrecognized assets of the reporting unit because the latter confuses different types of assets while the former does not. The Board noted that if the *book value* of recognized net assets was subtracted, the cushion also would include the unrecognized increase (or decrease) in the fair value of the reporting unit's recognized net assets.

B126. The Board concluded that subtracting the fair value of recognized net assets (excluding goodwill) would result in the next best estimate of the implied fair value of goodwill, even though it would include an additional cushion attributable to the fair value of the *unrecognized* net assets. Even though that choice had its associated costs, after considering the remaining two choices—subtracting the book value or adjusted book value of recognized net assets—both of which generally would include even more cushion, the Board decided that subtracting the fair value of recognized net assets would strike an acceptable balance between costs and benefits. Thus, the 2001 Exposure Draft proposed that the implied fair value of reporting unit goodwill be estimated by subtracting the fair value of the recognized net assets of a reporting unit from the fair value of the reporting unit as a whole. If the resulting implied fair value of goodwill were less than the carrying amount of that goodwill, an impairment loss equal to that difference should have been recognized.

B127. While a few respondents to the 2001 Exposure Draft supported the proposed impairment test, most respondents asserted that the proposed test would not be cost-effective. Their concerns related primarily to the requirement to determine the fair value of recognized net assets (in order to estimate the implied fair value of goodwill). Most respondents said that the costs related to estimating the fair value of recognized net assets did not outweigh the benefits associated with having a better estimate of the implied fair value of goodwill to use in the impairment test. Respondents noted that a goodwill impairment test by its very nature will include some level of imprecision.

B128. Respondents suggested a variety of approaches to test goodwill for impairment, including using an approach similar to that in Statement 121 (and the June 2000 FASB Exposure Draft, *Accounting for the Impairment or Disposal of Long-Lived Assets and for Obligations Associated with Disposal Activities,* which would amend Statement 121). Some respondents argued for a Statement 121 approach on the basis of familiarity, reliability, practicality, and consistency. However, the recoverability test in Statement 121 uses undiscounted cash flows,

and the Board again rejected that approach because it results in an unacceptably large cushion in the impairment test.

B129. Very few respondents to the 2001 Exposure Draft took exception to using the fair value of a reporting unit as the starting point for the impairment test or with the conceptual soundness of basing the impairment test on the implied fair value of goodwill. Thus, the Board agreed that it would consider only an approach that began with a determination of the fair value of a reporting unit, and it reaffirmed its conclusion that a fair-value-based impairment model should be used for goodwill. The Board thus sought to develop an approach that would lessen the cost of performing the impairment test.

B130. The suggestion that was provided most often by respondents to reduce the cost of the impairment test was to compare the fair value of a reporting unit with its carrying amount, including goodwill (carrying amount approach). Respondents observed that carrying amounts may be a reasonable proxy for fair values. Under that approach, if the carrying amount of a reporting unit exceeds its fair value, goodwill would be considered impaired, and an impairment loss would be recognized equal to that excess. The carrying amount approach is the least costly of all the suggested approaches because it requires only an estimate of the reporting unit's fair value and not of the fair value of its associated assets and liabilities.

B131. The Board decided not to adopt the carrying amount approach for the dual purpose of (a) identifying situations in which goodwill is impaired and (b) measuring the amount of impairment in the situations identified. The Board noted that comparing the carrying amount of a reporting unit, including goodwill, with the fair value of that unit could not be said to be an estimate of the implied fair value of goodwill. The difference generally would include too much cushion, and that approach also would be inconsistent with the way in which impairments of other assets and asset groups are measured under Statement 121.

B132. Some respondents suggested that the Board adopt a two-step approach if it found the measure of impairment under a carrying amount approach unacceptable. They noted that the comparison of the carrying amount with the fair value of a reporting unit could be the first step—a screen to identify potential goodwill impairment. If the carrying amount of a reporting unit exceeded its fair value, the actual amount of impairment loss could be measured on a different basis.

B133. The Board considered the extent to which adding the carrying amount comparison as a screen to identify potential goodwill impairment would allow possibly significant impairments to go unrecognized. The Board noted that use of that screen would add a cushion to the impairment test proposed in the 2001 Exposure Draft equal to the difference between the carrying amounts of tangible and intangible assets and their fair values—with the greater disparity likely to be in the intangible assets. That cushion would exist, however, only if the value of the intangible assets is being maintained or increased. In that situation, the value of goodwill is most likely also being maintained. That is, the Board observed that the appreciation of intangible assets and the appreciation of goodwill likely are correlated to some extent. The Board observed that the converse is likely also to be true—if the value of goodwill is *not* being maintained, the value of intangible assets probably also is not being maintained, and the value of recognized intangible assets would provide little or no cushion to the impairment test. Thus, using a carrying amount comparison as a screen for potential goodwill impairment likely would not allow as many impairments to go unrecognized as it might at first appear to do.

B134. Thus, the Board concluded that adding a carrying amount comparison to the impairment test would reduce the costs of applying the goodwill impairment test without unduly compromising the integrity of the model. Having decided that a two-step test would be a reasonable response to the cost-benefit challenge posed by its constituents, the Board considered whether to retain the measure of impairment proposed in the 2001 Exposure Draft or whether an improved measure would be feasible.

B135. As noted in paragraph B124, in developing the 2001 Exposure Draft, the Board observed that the best estimate of goodwill impairment would be based on a purchase price allocation approach in which the fair value of both recognized and unrecognized net assets is subtracted from the fair value of a reporting unit to determine the implied fair value of goodwill. Because that method is the same method by which goodwill is initially measured, the resulting reported amount of goodwill (after the impairment charge) would be the best available estimate consistent with the initial measurement of goodwill upon its acquisition. The Board rejected that approach in its deliberations of the 2001 Exposure Draft because it considered the process of identifying unrecognized net assets and determining their fair values to be too costly to require on a relatively frequent basis.

However, the Board reasoned that if the measurement of goodwill impairment was preceded by a less costly screen for potential impairment, the cost of measuring goodwill impairment using a purchase price allocation process would be justifiable. The measurement process would be required relatively infrequently, and it would produce better information in those situations in which there was potential goodwill impairment. Therefore, this Statement requires goodwill impairment to be measured using a purchase price allocation process. That is, if the first step of the goodwill impairment test indicates potential impairment, then the implied fair value of goodwill would be estimated by allocating the already estimated fair value of the reporting unit to all the assets and liabilities associated with that unit, including unrecognized intangible assets.

B136. The Board concluded that this Statement should require that the allocation of the total fair value of the reporting unit to its net assets follow the purchase price allocation guidance in Statement 141. That process is familiar to all entities that would be testing goodwill for impairment because it is the same process the entity would have used to initially measure the goodwill recognized in its financial statements.

When to test goodwill for impairment

B137. After discussions with field visit participants, the Board proposed in the 2001 Exposure Draft that goodwill be tested for impairment whenever events occur or circumstances change indicating potential impairment (an events-and-circumstances approach) and not on an annual basis. The Board acknowledged that management often reviews the operating performance of reporting units on a regular basis; therefore, a requirement for an annual impairment test might be redundant and thus might involve unnecessary time and expense.

B138. The 1999 Exposure Draft included examples of events and circumstances that would give rise to a goodwill impairment test (in addition to the examples in Statement 121). The Board revised those examples to reflect its decision that goodwill should be tested for impairment at the reporting unit level. The 2001 Exposure Draft included the revised examples of events or circumstances that would require an entity to test goodwill in one or more reporting units for impairment (impairment indicators). The Board affirmed that the list of impairment indicators is not meant to be exhaustive and that an individual event, as well as a series of events, might give rise to the need for an impairment test.

B139. Most respondents agreed with the Board's conclusion in the 2001 Exposure Draft to test goodwill for impairment using an events-and-circumstances approach. Most of those respondents stated that such an approach would be cost-effective because it would generally result in testing goodwill for impairment less frequently than once a year and because the fair value of each reporting unit would not have to be determined annually. However, respondents expressed concern that because the proposed list of impairment indicators included events that occur often in the common course of business, goodwill impairment tests would be required more frequently than is feasible. Respondents offered a number of suggestions for ways to reduce the frequency of an impairment test under an events-and-circumstances approach, including requiring the impairment test only if two or more indicators are present and using the indicators as a guide for testing instead of as a mandatory requirement to test for impairment.

B140. Some respondents disagreed with the proposal that goodwill be tested for impairment using only an events-and-circumstances approach, preferring that goodwill be tested for impairment annually. Attestors noted that under an annual approach, they would be able to provide positive assurance about whether goodwill is impaired, rather than negative assurance that no event occurred or circumstance changed that would require an impairment test. Other respondents noted that an annual approach would result in more consistent application and comparable financial statements and would reduce the subjectivity of and second-guessing about the timing of an impairment charge.

B141. The Board noted that although most respondents supported the proposed events-and-circumstances approach, the concerns that were expressed with the list of impairment indicators suggest that such an approach might not be operational. That is, even if the list of impairment indicators was revised, the revised list still might not be applied or interpreted consistently—thereby undermining the integrity of the impairment model itself. Furthermore, if goodwill was tested for impairment on an annual basis, the recognition of an impairment loss would be less dependent on the subjective interpretation of the performance of reporting units. In addition, Board members observed that goodwill impairments generally do not occur suddenly but occur as a result of a series of events that might not be captured by a list of impairment indicators. An annual test would provide a safety net for impairments that arise as the result of a series of events.

B142. A principal reason that the Board concluded not to propose an annual test in the 2001 Exposure Draft was the cost associated with the proposed impairment test. Having decided to reduce the cost of the impairment test by adding a screen for potential impairment and also to decrease in many cases the number of reporting units, the Board observed that the cost of an annual impairment test would be lower than under the 2001 Exposure Draft, thereby making an annual approach more feasible.

B143. The Board acknowledged that an annual test would entail some cost to preparers because fair value determinations will have to be made for each reporting unit. However, for most entities, the most labor-intensive and potentially expensive part of the process relates to assigning goodwill and net assets to reporting units and establishing the model and key assumptions that will be used to measure the fair value of each reporting unit. Board members observed that those costs will be incurred whether goodwill is tested for impairment annually or on an events-and-circumstances basis. Thus, once the initial fair value of each reporting unit has been determined, the incremental costs associated with annual testing generally will be much lower than those one-time costs.

B144. The Board concluded that the incremental cost of an annual impairment test can be justified because of the benefit to users of financial statements in the form of positive assurance that the carrying amount of goodwill is not overstated. Annual testing would also enhance comparability between entities, since every entity would be testing goodwill for impairment with the same frequency.

B145. Integral to the Board's decision that goodwill should be tested for impairment annually was the view that an annual requirement should not call for a "fresh start" effort in determining the fair value of each reporting unit every year. That is, many entities should be able to conclude that the fair value of a reporting unit is greater than its carrying amount without actually recomputing the fair value of the reporting unit. That conclusion could be supported if the last fair value determination exceeded the carrying amount by a substantial margin and nothing had happened since the last fair value determination that would make the likelihood that the current fair value of the reporting unit would be less than its current carrying amount remote. However, if a recent acquisition, divestiture, or reorganization affected a reporting unit, the fair value of the reporting unit would need to be remeasured for purposes of impairment testing.

B146. The Board noted that testing annually for goodwill impairment would not negate the need for management to be aware of events occurring or circumstances changing between annual tests indicating potential impairment. Should there be such an event or circumstance, an entity would be required to test goodwill for impairment at that time and not wait until the next annual test. Board members observed that when an impairment indicator arises toward the end of an interim reporting period, an entity might not be able to complete the goodwill impairment test before its financial statements are issued. The Board concluded that it would be appropriate for an entity to recognize its best estimate of that impairment loss in those circumstances.

Benchmark assessment

B147. The 2001 Exposure Draft proposed that a benchmark assessment be performed in conjunction with most significant acquisitions and in conjunction with a reorganization of an entity's reporting structure. As proposed, a benchmark assessment involved identifying and documenting the goodwill and net assets associated with a reporting unit, the expectations related to the performance of the unit, and the valuation model and key assumptions to be used in measuring the fair value of the reporting unit. In addition, an entity would have been required to measure the fair value of the reporting unit, compare the fair value of the reporting unit with its carrying amount, and possibly test goodwill for impairment. The purpose of the benchmark assessment was to establish a starting point for future goodwill impairment tests.

B148. Most respondents to the 2001 Exposure Draft disagreed with the specific steps of the benchmark assessment, stating that the assessment would be time-consuming, costly to implement and comply with, and in excess of what is necessary to establish a baseline for performing future impairment tests. Most respondents agreed that entities should be required to document expectations, assumptions, and valuation models after an acquisition. However, respondents stated that a determination of the fair value of the unit should not be required unless an impairment indicator is present.

B149. The Board concluded that a requirement to perform a benchmark assessment was no longer necessary because goodwill would be tested for impairment annually and because the first step of the impairment test would be a comparison of the fair value of a reporting unit with its carrying amount. Board members observed that most of the identification and documentation steps inherent in the benchmark assessment would have to be performed subsequent to an acquisition or reorganization and prior to any impairment test regardless of whether this Statement required performance of those steps. However, this Statement does not require that the groundwork for performing an impairment test be completed within a set time period, other than that necessary to perform the transitional goodwill impairment test.

Fair value of a reporting unit

B150. Prior to issuing the 2001 Exposure Draft, the Board considered various valuation methods that could be used in testing goodwill for impairment, including methods based on market capitalization, discounted cash flow, residual income valuation, cash flow return on investment, and economic value added. Board members generally agreed that each of those methods could be used to determine the fair value of a reporting unit and that entities should be permitted to use a valuation method with which they are familiar, providing that the result is consistent with the objective of fair value.

B151. Some respondents to the 2001 Exposure Draft stated that because of the subjectivity inherent in measuring the fair value of a reporting unit, the Board should provide more guidance in this Statement on using present value techniques to estimate fair value. In particular, respondents requested that this Statement provide guidance on how to use cash flows to measure the fair value of a reporting unit. Some respondents suggested that this Statement incorporate the guidance from FRS 11, *Impairment of Fixed Assets and Goodwill,* including growth rate assumptions used in estimating cash flows.

B152. The Board observed that the goodwill impairment test in FRS 11 is focused on acquisition-specific goodwill. Thus, the unit of account in FRS 11 is inconsistent with the use of the reporting unit in this Statement as the unit of account for goodwill impairment testing. The Board concluded that because the restrictions on growth assumptions in FRS 11 could be inconsistent with the requirement to measure the reporting unit at fair value, similar assumptions should *not* be included in this Statement. However, Board members observed that when cash flows are used to estimate fair value, those cash flows should be consistent with the most recent budgets and plans approved by management. As noted previously, one of the reasons the Board decided to test goodwill for impairment at the reporting unit level is that it is generally the level at which information about cash flows is generated for planning purposes. Board members also observed that in estimating cash flows for purposes of determining the fair value of a reporting unit, some consideration should be given to industry trends.

B153. The Board noted that addressing the various issues raised by respondents would require the Board to develop "how to" guidance (including valuation guidance) on using present value techniques to estimate fair value that is beyond the scope of this Statement. The Board reaffirmed that this Statement should explain the objective of the fair value measurement exercise and allow preparers latitude in applying that objective to their specific circumstances based on the guidance in Concepts Statement 7. To assist preparers in applying that guidance, the Board decided to include in Appendix E of this Statement excerpts from Concepts Statement 7 that discuss present value techniques (both expected and traditional) and when those techniques should be used.

B154. The Board reaffirmed its conclusion that if a reporting unit has publicly traded equity securities, the ability of a controlling shareholder to benefit from synergies and other intangible assets that arise from control might cause the fair value of a reporting unit as a whole to exceed its market capitalization. Therefore, in those few instances in which a reporting unit has publicly traded equity securities, the fair value measurement need not be based solely on the quoted market price of an individual share of that security. The Board acknowledges that the assertion in paragraph 23 that the market capitalization of a reporting unit with publicly traded equity securities may not be representative of the fair value of the reporting unit as a whole can be viewed as inconsistent with the definition of fair value in FASB Statements No. 115, *Accounting for Certain Investments in Debt and Equity Securities,* and No. 133, *Accounting for Derivative Instruments and Hedging Activities.* Those Statements maintain that "if a quoted market price is available, the fair value is the product of the number of trading units times that market price." However, the Board decided that measuring the fair value of an en-

tity with a collection of assets and liabilities that operate together to produce cash flows is different from measuring the fair value of that entity's individual equity securities. That decision is supported by the fact that an entity often is willing to pay more for equity securities that give it a controlling interest than an investor would pay for a number of equity securities that represent less than a controlling interest. Thus, consideration of the impact of a control premium when control is known to exist in measuring the fair value of a reporting unit is appropriate, whereas it is not for a noncontrolling position in equity interests.

B155. The Board noted that in most instances quoted market prices for a reporting unit would not be available and thus would not be used to measure the fair value of a reporting unit. The Board concluded that absent a quoted market price, a present value technique might be the best available technique to measure the fair value of a reporting unit. However, the Board agreed that this Statement should not preclude use of valuation techniques other than a present value technique, as long as the resulting measurement is consistent with the objective of fair value. That is, the valuation technique used should capture the five elements outlined in paragraph 23 of Concepts Statement 7 and should result in a valuation that yields results similar to a discounted cash flows method. The Board also noted that, consistent with Concepts Statement 7, the fair value measurement should reflect estimates and expectations that marketplace participants would use in their estimates of fair value whenever that information is available without undue cost and effort. This Statement, like Concepts Statement 7, does not preclude the use of an entity's own estimates, as long as there is no information indicating that marketplace participants would use different assumptions. If such information exists, the entity must adjust its assumptions to incorporate that market information. The Board clarified that use of a valuation technique based on multiples of earnings or revenues or similar performance measures should not be precluded so long as the resulting measurement is consistent with a fair value objective. Use of such multiples may be appropriate when both the fair value and multiple of a comparable entity are available. The Board also agreed that if an acquired entity is a significant portion of a reporting unit (or a reporting unit itself) and the technique used to value the acquisition (determine the purchase price) is consistent with the objective of measuring fair value, the assumptions underlying that valuation should be used in measuring the fair value of the reporting unit. Board members noted that a valuation technique similar to that used to value the acquisition would most likely be used by the entity to determine the fair value of the reporting unit. For example, if the purchase price were based on an expected cash flow model, that cash flow model and related assumptions would be used to measure the fair value of the reporting unit.

Goodwill impairment testing by a subsidiary

B156. Some respondents to the 2001 Exposure Draft raised issues about how goodwill should be tested for impairment when the reporting entity has one or more subsidiaries that prepare separate financial statements in accordance with generally accepted accounting principles (separate GAAP financial statements). They questioned whether goodwill that is reported in the separate GAAP financial statements of a subsidiary (subsidiary goodwill) should be tested for impairment at the subsidiary level (that is, at the level of the subsidiary's reporting units) or at the higher consolidated level (that is, at the level of the parent's reporting unit or units that encompass the subsidiary).

B157. The Board noted that subsidiary goodwill might arise from (a) acquisitions that a subsidiary made prior to its being acquired by the parent, (b) acquisitions that a subsidiary made subsequent to its being acquired by the parent, and (c) goodwill arising from the business combination in which a subsidiary was acquired that the parent company pushed down to the subsidiary's financial statements. Some respondents urged that subsidiary goodwill be tested for impairment only at the reporting units at the higher consolidated level, with any impairment losses recognized being pushed down to the subsidiary. Other respondents urged that subsidiary goodwill be tested for impairment at the subsidiary level, and some also urged that any impairment losses recognized at the subsidiary level also be recognized at (pushed up to) the consolidated level.

B158. Some respondents asked that a distinction be made between the requirements for subsidiaries that are public entities and those that are nonpublic entities. Those respondents suggested that goodwill of a public subsidiary be tested for impairment at the subsidiary level but that goodwill of a nonpublic subsidiary be tested only at the consolidated level, with any impairment losses recognized at the consolidation level being allocated to the subsidiaries. The Board observed that subsidiaries prepare separate GAAP financial statements largely because the information

needs of minority stockholders, creditors, and regulators of those subsidiaries cannot be filled by the GAAP financial statements of the consolidated group. Information that pertains to the consolidated group is not relevant to them because their interests are limited to the subsidiary. Users of subsidiary financial statements therefore should be entitled to expect that the same accounting requirements have been applied regardless of whether the reporting entity in question is a subsidiary of another reporting entity. The Board accordingly concluded that goodwill that is reported on the separate GAAP financial statements of a subsidiary should be tested for impairment at the subsidiary level.

B159. The Board observed that if goodwill impairment testing is performed at the subsidiary level, the question of whether to push down impairment losses from the consolidated level is not pertinent. However, it noted that an impairment loss that is recognized at the subsidiary level may indicate potential goodwill impairment in the reporting unit or units at the consolidated level at which the subsidiary resides. The Board therefore concluded that if an impairment loss is recognized at the subsidiary level, that loss should not be recognized at (pushed up to) the consolidated level; rather, an entity should consider whether an interim impairment test should be performed on goodwill in the reporting unit or units of the parent company in which the subsidiary resides. (Paragraph 28 addresses when an entity should test goodwill for impairment between annual tests.) If testing at the consolidated level leads to an impairment loss, that loss should be recognized at that level separately from the subsidiary's loss. The Board further concluded that the requirements for testing goodwill should be the same for both public and nonpublic subsidiaries because the needs of the users of those subsidiaries' separate GAAP financial statements are the same.

Disposal of all or a portion of a reporting unit

B160. The 1999 Exposure Draft proposed that when goodwill is associated with assets to be sold or otherwise disposed of, some amount of goodwill should be included in the cost of the assets disposed of. The June 2000 impairment Exposure Draft proposed guidance for associating assets to be disposed of with related goodwill. That Exposure Draft proposed that goodwill generally should be allocated to assets to be disposed of on a pro rata basis using the relative fair values of the acquired long-lived assets and intangible assets at the acquisition date. In developing the

2001 Exposure Draft, the Board observed that the guidance proposed in the June 2000 impairment Exposure Draft was based on the current acquisition-specific model of accounting for goodwill subsequent to an acquisition. Thus, the Board considered whether that guidance was appropriate given its fundamental decision to move to a model that considers the reporting unit to be the unit of account for goodwill after an acquisition.

B161. The Board concluded that because the reporting unit is the unit of account for goodwill, goodwill cannot be identified or associated with an asset group at a level lower than the reporting unit, other than in an arbitrary manner. However, the Board realized that when a significant portion of a reporting unit is to be disposed of, it is necessary to determine whether the net assets of the reporting unit that remain after the disposition can support the carrying amount of goodwill. Thus, the 2001 Exposure Draft would have required that goodwill be tested for impairment in those circumstances; however, the assets to be disposed of would not have been included in that test. In that Exposure Draft, if the implied fair value of the reporting unit's goodwill were determined to be less than its carrying amount, the excess of the carrying amount of goodwill over its implied fair value would have been included in the carrying amount of the net assets to be disposed of. The 2001 Exposure Draft also proposed that when a reporting unit is to be disposed of in its entirety, all of that reporting unit's goodwill would be included in the carrying amount of its net assets.

B162. Many respondents to the 2001 Exposure Draft did not agree with the proposed accounting for disposal of a significant portion of a reporting unit because it might distort the calculation of the gain or loss to be recognized on disposal. Those respondents noted that because the proposed goodwill impairment approach may result in capitalization of internally generated goodwill and other unrecognized assets, goodwill associated with the net assets disposed of might not be included in the gain or loss calculation, thus exaggerating any gain or minimizing any loss. Some respondents suggested that some amount of goodwill should always be allocated to the portion of a reporting unit that is sold.

B163. Having redefined the reporting unit to be generally a higher level than that proposed in the 2001 Exposure Draft, the Board assessed whether it would be possible for goodwill to be meaningfully allocated below the reporting unit level. For example, the Board considered how frequently a reporting unit would consist of one or more businesses. The Board acknowledged that if this Statement were to permit or require allocation of goodwill below the reporting unit for disposal accounting purposes, it would be nearly impossible to limit how low that allocation could go.

B164. The Board concluded that it would not be possible to describe the circumstances in which goodwill should be allocated to a portion of a reporting unit being disposed of with sufficient rigor that the guidance would be interpreted and applied consistently. However, the Board acknowledged that when a business is being disposed of, it would be appropriate to presume that some amount of goodwill is associated with that business. Thus, the Board concluded that an allocation should be required only when the net assets being disposed of constitute a business. The Board noted that that would be consistent with recognizing goodwill when a business is acquired.

B165. The Board considered various allocation approaches, recognizing that any allocation approach would be arbitrary. The Board agreed that this Statement should prescribe use of a specific allocation method such that the amount of goodwill allocated to a business to be disposed of would be determined consistently from entity to entity. The Board concluded that a relative-fair-value allocation method would result in a reasonable estimation of the amount of goodwill that might be associated with a business being disposed of and would not be overly complex to apply. Therefore, this Statement requires that when a portion of a reporting unit being disposed of constitutes a business, the amount of goodwill assigned to that business should be based on the relative fair values of the business to be disposed of and the remaining portion of the reporting unit. However, due to the imprecision of any allocation approach, the Board concluded that the goodwill remaining with the reporting unit should be tested for impairment after goodwill has been allocated to the business being sold.

B166. The Board observed that when an acquired business is being disposed of and the benefits of goodwill acquired with that business have not been realized by any portion of the reporting unit other than the acquired business, the carrying amount of that acquired goodwill should be included in the net assets disposed of. Therefore, this Statement requires that the relative-fair-value allocation method *not* be used to allocate goodwill to a business being disposed of if that business was not integrated into the reporting unit after its acquisition. Board members noted that those situations (such as when the acquired business is operated as a stand-alone entity) would be infrequent because some amount of integration generally occurs after an acquisition.

Amendment of Statement 121

B167. This Statement amends Statement 121 to eliminate the requirement that the carrying amount of goodwill associated with a long-lived asset be combined with that asset's carrying value when testing that long-lived asset (or group of assets) for impairment. Goodwill is to be tested for impairment only in accordance with this Statement. The 2001 Exposure Draft proposed that when an asset group being tested for impairment is also a reporting unit, goodwill would be tested for impairment (and any impairment loss recognized) *before* the other long-lived assets are tested for impairment. The Board reconsidered that proposal given its decision to add a step to the impairment test that is based on the carrying amounts of the assets and liabilities of the reporting unit. Board members considered it important that the carrying amount used to identify potential impairment reflect amounts that have already been adjusted for impairment. Thus, this Statement requires goodwill to be tested for impairment *after* all other assets have been tested for impairment when more than one impairment test is required at the same time. The Board clarified that that requirement applies to all assets that are tested for impairment, not just those included in the scope of Statement 121.

B168. The Board observed that in situations in which a reporting unit consists of multiple lower-level asset groups, an event might occur that requires an impairment test of some, but not all, of those asset groups. That same event might or might not require an impairment test of reporting unit goodwill. The Board concluded that because the reporting unit is the unit of account for goodwill, the reporting unit *is* the lowest level with which goodwill can be associated; therefore, goodwill is not associated with a lower-level asset group. Based on that view, the Board decided that reporting unit goodwill should not be allocated to or otherwise associated with a lower-level asset group as previously required by Statement 121. This Statement amends Statement 121 to eliminate that requirement.

Equity method investments

B169. Under APB Opinion No. 18, *The Equity Method of Accounting for Investments in Common Stock,* an investor is required to apply the equity method of accounting if its investment in voting stock gives it the ability to exercise significant influence over operating and financial policies of the investee. The investor's cost and the underlying equity in net assets of the investee often differ, and Opinion 18 requires that that difference be accounted for as if the investee were a consolidated subsidiary. An investor is therefore required to complete a purchase price allocation, which often results in identification of part of the difference as goodwill. (However, that amount is not reported as goodwill in the investor's statement of financial position.) The Board reasoned that goodwill associated with equity method investments (equity method goodwill) should be accounted for in the same manner as goodwill arising from a business combination. Thus, the 2001 Exposure Draft proposed that equity method goodwill should not be amortized.

B170. Equity method investments are reviewed for impairment in accordance with Opinion 18, and it is the equity investment as a whole that is reviewed for impairment, not the underlying net assets. The Board concluded that because equity method goodwill is not separable from the related investment, that goodwill should not be tested for impairment in accordance with this Statement. Thus, the 2001 Exposure Draft proposed that equity method goodwill be exempt from the impairment provisions of this Statement. Respondents generally agreed with the Board's conclusions related to equity method goodwill, and the Board reaffirmed those conclusions.

Deferred Income Taxes

B171. The 2001 Exposure Draft proposed that the requirement in Statement 109, *Accounting for Income Taxes* (paragraphs 30, 262, and 263), to recognize deferred taxes related to goodwill when amortization of goodwill is deductible for tax purposes not be changed. Some respondents to that Exposure Draft, however, objected to recognition of a deferred tax liability related to tax-deductible goodwill.

B172. In a taxable business combination, the purchase price is allocated to the acquired assets and liabilities for tax purposes similarly to the way it is allocated for financial reporting (book) purposes. Because usually there is no temporary difference created at the date of acquisition, no deferred tax liability related to goodwill is recognized at that date. However, taxable temporary differences will arise in the future as goodwill is amortized for tax purposes but not for book purposes. In those circumstances, an excess of the book basis over the tax basis of goodwill is a taxable temporary difference for which a deferred tax liability must be recognized under Statement 109. This issue does not arise for nontaxable business combinations because Statement 109 prohibits recognition of a deferred tax liability related to goodwill when amortization is not deductible for tax purposes.

B173. Respondents to the 2001 Exposure Draft noted that a deferred tax liability would not be settled until some indefinite future period when goodwill is impaired, sold, or otherwise disposed of—all of which are future events that respondents asserted are unlikely to occur. They requested that this Statement amend Statement 109 to require recognition of a deferred tax liability related to tax-deductible goodwill only at such time as a goodwill impairment loss is recognized or goodwill is assigned to a business that is sold or otherwise disposed of.

B174. Board members observed that similar issues exist for intangible assets other than goodwill, because they also could have a book basis with little or no tax basis. Statement 109 requires recognition of a deferred tax liability related to other intangible assets. Like goodwill, absent amortization, the deferred tax liability will remain on the balance sheet until such time as the intangible asset is impaired, sold, or otherwise disposed of.

B175. The Board acknowledged that nonamortization of goodwill and intangible assets with indefinite useful lives was not contemplated when the Board deliberated Statement 109. However, the arguments used by respondents to the 2001 Exposure Draft for nonrecognition of deferred tax liabilities related to goodwill and intangible assets with indefinite useful lives were made at that time and were extensively debated. Statement 109 requires comprehensive recognition of deferred taxes subject only to a limited number of exceptions. Statement 109 continues exceptions for some of the areas addressed by APB Opinion No. 23, *Accounting for Income Taxes—Special Areas,* but prohibits nonrecognition of a deferred tax liability for all analogous types of taxable temporary differences. Therefore, the Board reconfirmed that Statement 109 should not be amended for the purposes of permitting additional exceptions to comprehensive recognition of deferred income taxes.

Financial Statement Presentation

Presentation in Statement of Financial Position

B176. The Board observed that Opinion 17 did not require that goodwill be displayed separately in the statement of financial position and that, in practice, goodwill has been displayed together with other intangible assets. However, the Board agreed that goodwill is unique among assets and that different users of financial statements may assess it differently in their analyses. The Board therefore concluded that goodwill differed sufficiently from other assets and other intangible assets to justify being displayed separately in the statement of financial position.

B177. The Board further observed that intangible assets other than goodwill also differ significantly from other assets and therefore concluded that they also should be displayed in the aggregate separately in the statement of financial position. The Board noted that such a requirement would not preclude separately displaying individual intangible assets or classes of those assets that are material. The Board clarified that an entity should continue to display intangible assets in their proper classification whether that be as a current asset or a noncurrent asset.

B178. The 1999 Exposure Draft proposed that both goodwill and other intangible assets be displayed in the aggregate separately in the statement of financial position, and the 2001 Exposure Draft (which focused only on goodwill) affirmed that display for goodwill. Respondents agreed that separate presentations of those items provide useful information. The Board therefore decided to retain those presentation requirements in this Statement, noting that separating goodwill from other assets in the statement of financial position is even more important under a nonamortization model.

Presentation in the Income Statement

B179. The Board observed that amortization and impairment charges for goodwill and other intangible assets traditionally have been displayed in the income statement among those expenses that are presented on a pretax basis. Moreover, in practice, those charges often have been commingled with other expenses, such as depreciation and amortization or selling and administrative expenses. The Board noted concerns that such commingling can make the analysis of financial statements more difficult. Some respondents urged that the charges for goodwill and other intangible assets be separated from charges for other items, as well as from each other.

B180. Under the 1999 Exposure Draft, goodwill impairment losses would have been combined with goodwill amortization expense and presented on a net-of-tax basis as a separate line item in the income statement. The Board noted that the special income statement treatment proposed in the 1999 Exposure Draft was aimed at making goodwill amortization expense more transparent. Therefore, the special display provisions were designed primarily for goodwill amortization expense—not goodwill impairment losses. The 1999 Exposure Draft also proposed that charges for the amortization or impairment of intangible assets continue to be displayed on a pretax basis in line items as deemed appropriate by the reporting entity, as they traditionally had been displayed.

B181. Some respondents to that Exposure Draft suggested that all of the charges related to the entire premium of the purchase price of an entity over the book value of its net assets (including charges related to the step-up in basis of recorded net assets and the recognition of previously unrecognized assets and liabilities) be afforded a special presentation, similar to that proposed in the 1999 Exposure Draft for goodwill charges. They argued that such a presentation would facilitate the analysis of earnings trends related to the combining entities following the business combination. They also argued that those charges should be accorded similar presentation because (a) goodwill is an intangible asset, (b) the amount recognized as goodwill may include certain intangible assets that cannot be recognized apart from goodwill, and (c) some intangible assets are "goodwill like."

B182. The Board observed that there may have been cases in practice in which much or all of the premium over book value had been assigned to goodwill and thus the amortization charge for goodwill would have included much or all of the charges relating to that premium. However, the Board noted that accounting standards have consistently differentiated goodwill from the premium over book values. Moreover, the Board noted that such a presentation would be akin to those produced by the pooling method, which would conflict with the Board's decision to eliminate that method. The Board further noted that its subsequent adoption of the contractual-legal criterion and separability criterion sharpened the differences between what would be recognized as goodwill and what would be recognized as other intangible assets. The Board therefore rejected sug-

gestions that other charges related to the purchase premium (other than goodwill charges) should be afforded a special presentation.

B183. In developing the 2001 Exposure Draft, the Board discussed whether goodwill impairment losses should be presented in the income statement in the same manner as any other impairment loss (as a component of pretax operating income) or in accordance with the special display provisions proposed in the 1999 Exposure Draft. The 2001 Exposure Draft proposed that a goodwill impairment loss recognized under a nonamortization model be reported in the same manner as an impairment loss recognized on other assets. Respondents to the 2001 Exposure Draft agreed with that proposal. The Board therefore reaffirmed its conclusion that a goodwill impairment loss (other than a transitional goodwill impairment loss) should be reported as a component of income from operations (before income taxes) unless the goodwill impairment loss is associated with a discontinued operation—in which case it would be included within the results of the discontinued operation.

B184. Consistent with its decision that the impairment charges for goodwill should be displayed on a pretax basis like that for charges related to other intangible assets, the Board reaffirmed its conclusion in the 1999 Exposure Draft that the charges related to other intangible assets should continue to be displayed on a pretax basis as a component of income from continuing operations. As noted in paragraph B66, the Board concluded that an impairment loss recognized as the result of a change in the estimate of the remaining useful life of an intangible asset should not be recognized as the effect of a change in accounting principle.

Disclosures

Information about Intangible Assets in the Year of Acquisition

B185. The 1999 Exposure Draft proposed that certain information be disclosed in the notes to the financial statements for each class of intangible asset. The information that would have been required to be disclosed included (a) a description of the intangible assets and the amounts assigned to them at the acquisition date, (b) the key assumptions and methodologies used to determine those amounts, (c) a description of the amortization method, and (d) the weighted-average amortization period. Many respondents to that Exposure Draft commented on the proposed disclosure requirements. Most agreed that additional information about acquired intangible assets would be useful, but many urged the Board to consider reducing the extent of the disclosure requirements. They argued that the cost of providing the information would exceed the benefits derived from it.

B186. After considering the suggestions made by those respondents, the Board reaffirmed its conclusion that financial statements should provide additional information about acquired intangible assets other than goodwill. However, the Board agreed that eliminating certain proposed disclosures would not significantly diminish the decision usefulness of the information provided.

B187. The Board concluded that the following information should be disclosed for use in assessing the amount and timing of future cash inflows: (a) the total amounts assigned to intangible assets subject to amortization and those that are not subject to amortization, (b) the amount assigned to each major class of intangible asset, and (c) the weighted-average amortization period in total and for each major class of asset. The Board also concluded that disclosure should be made of the amount of any significant residual values assumed both in total and for each major class of intangible asset. Although not proposed in the 1999 Exposure Draft, the Board also decided that when an entity acquires research and development assets and writes off those assets at the date of acquisition, it should be required to disclose the amount written off as well as the line item in which that write-off is aggregated.

Information about Intangible Assets Subsequent to an Acquisition

B188. The Board decided to require disclosure of certain information for each class of intangible asset subject to amortization in periods following the acquisition. That information includes the gross carrying amount, amortization method, accumulated amortization, current-period amortization expense, and the estimated aggregate amortization expense for each of the five succeeding fiscal years. The Board noted that presenting that information in tabular form would be a concise way to meet the disclosure requirement. The Board concluded that that disclosure requirement was appropriate, given its decision to permit entities to aggregate the presentation of intangible assets in the statement of financial position.

B189. In addition, the Board concluded that in the years subsequent to an acquisition, entities should disclose by major class information about the total carrying amount of those intangible assets not subject to amortization. That information is useful because those intangible assets are tested for impairment on an annual basis.

Information about Goodwill Subsequent to an Acquisition

B190. In its redeliberations of the 1999 Exposure Draft, the Board reconsidered all of the proposed goodwill disclosure requirements because they were based on a model that would have required amortization of goodwill. The Board consulted with a group of financial statement users before deciding what information about goodwill should be disclosed in the notes to the financial statements if goodwill is to be tested for impairment rather than amortized. The 2001 Exposure Draft proposed that in the years subsequent to an acquisition, entities should disclose information about changes in the carrying amount of goodwill and the reasons for those changes. The Board observed that that information might be concisely disclosed in a tabular format. The 2001 Exposure Draft also proposed that entities presenting segment information in accordance with Statement 131 should disclose information about the changes in the carrying amount of goodwill by segment.

B191. Some respondents stated that the requirement to disclose the changes in the carrying amount of goodwill is not necessary because that information is presented elsewhere in the financial statements. In addition, respondents questioned why the 2001 Exposure Draft would require disclosure of goodwill information at the segment level when Statement 131 does not require disclosure of that information. The Board agreed that if the required information about goodwill is disclosed elsewhere in the financial statements, it would not need to be repeated in the notes. In addition, the Board decided to retain the requirement to disclose information about goodwill by segment, noting that the unit of account used for impairment testing (the reporting unit) is based on the segment reporting structure.

B192. In its discussions about what information should be disclosed when a goodwill impairment loss is recognized, the Board considered the disclosures required by Statement 121 when an impairment loss is recognized for a long-lived asset or group of assets. The 2001 Exposure Draft proposed disclosure of similar information when a goodwill impairment loss is recognized—including the facts and circumstances leading to the impairment of goodwill, such as the events or series of events that gave rise to the impairment test. The Board agreed to retain that requirement in this Statement, noting that it is important for users to understand whether an impairment loss is due to external factors or events that should have been within management's control and whether the loss is related to a recently acquired entity.

B193. The 2001 Exposure Draft proposed that when an impairment loss is recognized, information should be disclosed at the reporting unit level. That information would have included a description of the reporting unit for which the loss is recognized, the adjusted carrying amount of reporting unit goodwill, and the amount of the impairment loss. The Board observed that when an impairment loss is recognized, disclosure of information about goodwill at the reporting unit level would be helpful both in assessing the magnitude of the loss recognized and in assessing the amount of potential future impairment losses.

B194. Most respondents disagreed with that requirement, noting that no other information is provided at the reporting unit level and that disclosing only one piece of information at that level would be both confusing and useless. The Board agreed, further noting that based on the revised definition of a reporting unit, information provided to users about impairment losses at a level below the segment level would not be significantly different from the information available at the segment level. Therefore, the Board concluded that disclosure of general information about an impairment loss and of the segment to which the impaired goodwill relates would be sufficient.

Effective Date and Transition

B195. The 2001 Exposure Draft proposed that all entities initially apply this Statement at the beginning of the first fiscal quarter following its issuance. Based on that proposed effective date, it was estimated that an entity with a fiscal year ending on December 31, 2001, would initially apply this Statement on July 1, 2001. That proposed effective date was based on the Board's conclusion that because nonamortization of goodwill results in financial statements that are more representationally faithful, it would be important for this Statement to become effective as soon as possible after issuance. The Board also noted that for comparability reasons, amortization of all previously recognized goodwill should stop within the same

interim (three month) reporting period following issuance of this Statement.

B196. A number of respondents to the 2001 Exposure Draft indicated a preference for applying this Statement as of the beginning of a fiscal year. Those respondents noted that mid-year implementation of this Statement would hinder comparability of financial statements and cause confusion for financial statement users. Most respondents who suggested changing the effective date to the beginning of a fiscal year suggested that this Statement be effective for fiscal years beginning after its issuance date. Others preferred allowing entities some lead time and suggested that this Statement be effective for fiscal years beginning after December 15, 2001. The Board noted that under either approach the vast majority of entities would be required to initially apply this Statement on or after January 1, 2002—at least six months after the proposed effective date.

Previously Recognized Goodwill

B197. The 2001 Exposure Draft proposed that this Statement apply to goodwill already recognized in an entity's financial statements at the date an entity initially applies this Statement (previously recognized goodwill) as well as to goodwill recognized in its financial statements after that date. Respondents agreed that previously recognized goodwill should no longer be amortized upon initial application of this Statement. The Board reaffirmed that provision, noting that if amortization of previously recognized goodwill were to continue after an entity initially applies this Statement, financial statements would suffer from the noncomparability the Board was concerned about in discussing whether to adopt a mixed approach to account for goodwill. In addition, the Board noted that to be operational the goodwill impairment provisions in this Statement must apply to previously recognized goodwill as well as to goodwill recognized in the future. Most important, the Board concluded that nonamortization of goodwill in conjunction with testing for impairment is the most representationally faithful method of accounting for goodwill and that a nonamortization approach should be applied in all circumstances.

B198. Board members concluded that, for the reasons provided by respondents, this Statement should be applied as of the beginning of a fiscal year and that entities should be provided additional time to prepare for its initial application. Therefore, this Statement is to be applied to previously recognized goodwill and other intangible assets in fiscal years beginning after December 15, 2001, and is to be applied at the beginning of the year of initial application. Retroactive application of this Statement is not permitted. However, the Board did not want to preclude an entity that was prepared to initially apply this Statement sooner than the required effective date from being able to initially apply it earlier than that date. Thus, an entity with a fiscal year beginning after March 15, 2001, may initially apply this Statement as of the beginning of that fiscal year provided its first interim financial statements have not been issued.

B199. However, mutual enterprises and not-for-profit organizations may not apply this Statement until interpretive guidance related to the application of the purchase method by those entities is issued. The Board plans to consider issues related to the application of the purchase method to combinations between two or more mutual enterprises, combinations between not-for-profit organizations, and the acquisition of a for-profit business entity by a not-for-profit organization in a separate project. In the interim, Opinions 16 and 17 continue to apply to those transactions.

B200. Upon initial application of this Statement, an entity will have to establish its reporting units and assign recognized assets and liabilities that meet the criteria in paragraph 32 to those reporting units. The Board concluded that the guidance in this Statement on assigning acquired assets and assumed liabilities to reporting units should be used to make the initial assignment of assets and liabilities to reporting units. Board members noted that recognized assets and liabilities that do not relate to a reporting unit (such as an environmental liability for an operation previously disposed of) should not be allocated to a reporting unit.

B201. Once those reporting units are established, all previously recognized goodwill will have to be assigned to those units—no matter how long ago it was acquired. However, because of the difficulties in reconstructing conditions that existed when past acquisitions were made, the Board concluded that previously recognized goodwill should be assigned based on the current reporting unit structure and not the structure that existed when the goodwill was acquired. However, the Board observed that in making that assignment, an entity should consider the source of previously recognized goodwill and the reporting units to which the related acquired net assets were assigned. Board members noted that the guidance

provided in paragraphs 34 and 35 might also be helpful in assigning previously recognized goodwill to reporting units.

Transitional goodwill impairment test

B202. Having decided that previously recognized goodwill should no longer be amortized upon initial application of this Statement, the Board addressed whether previously recognized goodwill should be tested for impairment concurrent with the cessation of amortization. The Board observed that previously recognized goodwill is currently subject to the limited impairment guidance in Opinion 17 and ARB 43, Chapter 5, "Intangible Assets." Many entities currently test goodwill for impairment on an undiscounted cash flow basis, similar to the method that Statement 121 requires to test long-lived assets for recoverability. Thus, it is possible that previously recognized goodwill that is not considered impaired under current U.S. GAAP would be determined to be impaired if the impairment provisions in this Statement were applied to goodwill at the date an entity initially applied this Statement.

B203. In developing the 2001 Exposure Draft, Board members observed that requiring goodwill in each reporting unit to be tested for impairment upon initial application of this Statement—particularly determining the fair value of the underlying net assets of each reporting unit—would be both costly and difficult. Thus, for cost-benefit reasons the 2001 Exposure Draft proposed that, absent an impairment indicator, previously recognized goodwill should not be tested for impairment upon initial application of this Statement. However, an entity would have been required to perform a transitional benchmark assessment within six months of the date it initially applied this Statement. As part of that transitional benchmark assessment, an entity would have been required to compare the fair value of each reporting unit having goodwill with the carrying amount of its net assets (including goodwill). If the carrying amount of the reporting unit exceeded its fair value, goodwill of that reporting unit would have been required to be tested for impairment.

B204. Most respondents to the 2001 Exposure Draft agreed with the proposed requirement to perform a benchmark assessment on previously recognized goodwill upon initial application of this Statement rather than a full impairment test. However, those respondents stated that entities would need more than the proposed six months to complete the transitional benchmark assessment. Respondents suggested that it would take up to one year for an entity to complete all of the steps of the transitional benchmark assessment.

B205. Recognizing that the step added to the goodwill impairment test to identify potential impairment is the same as the last step of the proposed benchmark assessment (a comparison of the fair value of a reporting unit with its carrying amount), the Board reconsidered its prior decision to not require previously recognized goodwill to be tested for impairment upon initial application of this Statement. Because of the revisions made to the reporting unit definition and goodwill impairment test during its redeliberations of the 2001 Exposure Draft, the Board believes that the revised impairment test will not be as costly or as difficult to apply as the proposed impairment test. Therefore, the Board concluded that previously recognized goodwill *should* be tested for impairment upon initial application of this Statement.

B206. The 2001 Exposure Draft proposed that a goodwill impairment loss recognized as the result of a transitional benchmark assessment (a transitional impairment loss) should be presented as a component of operating income, not as a change in accounting principle. That proposed requirement was based on the Board's belief that it would not be possible to determine the amount of a transitional impairment loss related to current and past reporting periods.

B207. Most respondents disagreed with the Board's conclusion that transitional impairment losses should be recognized in the same manner as all other impairment losses. Those respondents observed that the majority of transitional impairment losses would relate to adoption of the new impairment method and that few, if any, of the losses would relate to current-period losses. Accordingly, respondents asserted that it would be more representationally faithful to depict any transitional impairment losses as stemming from changes in accounting principles rather than as occurring in the current period.

B208. The Board acknowledged that the preponderance of any transitional impairment losses recognized are likely to result from the change in methods and that treating those losses as stemming from changes in accounting principles would be more representationally faithful than treating them as ordinary impairment losses. Therefore, the Board concluded that a transitional impairment loss should be recognized as the effect of a change in accounting principle.

B209. Because the transitional impairment loss is to be reported as a change in accounting principle, the Board considered whether it was necessary to place any parameters around the transitional goodwill impairment test. For example, without parameters, an entity would be permitted to wait until the end of the year of initial application to complete the transitional goodwill impairment test and still report any resulting impairment loss as a change in accounting principle. Board members observed that the reason they decided that a transitional impairment loss should be reported as a change in accounting principle was because most losses would relate primarily to the change in methodology used to test goodwill for impairment. Thus, ideally, the transitional goodwill impairment test should apply to reporting unit goodwill as of the date this Statement is initially applied—not as of any date in the year of initial application.

B210. To address those concerns, the Board concluded that this Statement should require the first step of the transitional goodwill impairment test to be performed within six months of the date the Statement is initially applied. Board members observed that that requirement is similar to the proposed requirement to complete the transitional benchmark assessment within six months of initial application. The purpose of that first step is to identify potential goodwill impairment. The Board noted that because this Statement is not required to be initially applied until at least six months after the date proposed in the 2001 Exposure Draft, entities will have the additional time that respondents to the 2001 Exposure Draft requested to establish reporting units and measure the fair value of those reporting units. The Board concluded that, given the change in the effective date and the change in the definition of a reporting unit, six months is adequate time for preparers to establish their reporting units and develop systems for testing goodwill for impairment at the reporting unit level.

B211. The Board concluded that the fair value of a reporting unit used to identify any potential impairment existing upon initial application of this Statement should be measured as of the beginning of the year in which this Statement is initially applied. Therefore, this Statement requires the amounts used to identify potential impairment (the fair value of a reporting unit and its corresponding carrying amount) to be measured *as of* the first of the year of initial application. The Board noted that specifying an initial measurement date would ensure that transitional goodwill impairment losses would be measured on a consistent basis.

B212. This Statement requires that if the first step of the transitional goodwill impairment test identifies potential impairment, the second step of the impairment test should be completed as soon as possible, but no later than the end of the year of initial application. Regardless of the interim period in which a transitional goodwill impairment loss is measured, the resulting accounting change should be reflected as of the beginning of an entity's fiscal year. The Board observed that this is consistent with the requirements in FASB Statement No. 3, *Reporting Accounting Changes in Interim Financial Statements.*

B213. The Board concluded that because any transitional goodwill impairment loss would be measured as of the first of the year of initial application, an entity should perform the required annual impairment test also in the year of initial application. Otherwise, depending on the measurement date chosen for future annual tests, almost two years could elapse between the transitional goodwill impairment test and the next goodwill impairment test. Notwithstanding the requirement to perform the required annual test in addition to the transitional impairment test, Board members observed that given the provisions in paragraph 27 governing when a detailed determination of the fair value of a reporting unit might not be necessary, it is likely that an entity will not have to recompute the fair value of all its reporting units in the year this Statement is initially applied.

Previously Recognized Intangible Assets

B214. This Statement applies to intangible assets already recognized in an entity's financial statements at the date it initially applies this Statement (previously recognized intangible assets) as well as to intangible assets recognized in its financial statements after that date. The Board concluded that the most representationally faithful method of accounting for intangible assets is to amortize an intangible asset over its useful life with no limit on that amortization period and to not amortize an intangible asset that is deemed to have an indefinite useful life. Thus, upon initial application of this Statement an entity is required to reassess the useful lives of its previously recognized intangible assets using the factors in paragraph 11. As a result of that reassessment, the remaining amortization period for an intangible asset might need to be

adjusted. In addition, a previously recognized intangible asset that is deemed to have an indefinite useful life would cease being amortized.

B215. The Board agreed that recognition of an impairment loss related to an intangible asset that will cease being amortized upon initial application of this Statement should be treated in a manner similar to a transitional goodwill impairment loss. Like goodwill, those intangible assets will be tested for impairment using a different method than had been previously applied to those assets. The Board therefore concluded that an intangible asset that is deemed to have an indefinite useful life should be tested for impairment upon initial application of this Statement and any resulting impairment loss recognized as the effect of a change in accounting principle. The Board clarified that, unlike goodwill, the measurement of that transitional intangible asset impairment loss should be completed in the first interim period in which this Statement is initially applied.

Equity Method Goodwill

B216. In considering the impact this Statement would have on the accounting for equity method investments, Board members noted that Opinion 18 requires entities to allocate the excess of cost over the underlying equity in net assets of an investee accounted for using the equity method to specific accounts of the investee (including intangible assets) and that only the amount remaining after that allocation should be recognized as goodwill (equity method goodwill). The Board clarified that upon initial application of this Statement, the amount previously recognized as equity method goodwill should also cease being amortized.

Transitional Disclosures

B217. As proposed in the 2001 Exposure Draft, many entities would have initially applied this Statement in the middle of their fiscal year. Thus, that Exposure Draft would have required disclosure of income before extraordinary items and net income on a pro forma basis; that is, what those amounts would have been if the amortization and nonamortization provisions for goodwill and other intangible assets had been applied in all periods presented. However, that pro forma information would not have reflected the impact the impairment provisions might have had on prior-period information. The Board reasoned that requiring entities to determine the impact of the impairment provisions on prior periods would not be cost beneficial.

B218. Respondents to the 2001 Exposure Draft were generally supportive of the proposal to present pro forma information, noting that that information would be important for preparing trend analyses and providing comparable information. However, some respondents stated that because a prior-period impairment loss would *not* be adjusted to reflect what it would have been if goodwill had not been amortized, financial statement users will not have a complete picture of what an entity's pattern of goodwill charges would have been under a nonamortization approach. Those respondents suggested that because of that lack of information, pro forma information should *not* be presented in the financial statements.

B219. The Board acknowledged those concerns but concluded that the lack of certain information is an insufficient reason *not* to provide information about what prior earnings may have been if goodwill had not been amortized. However, Board members observed that describing the information to be disclosed as pro forma information might be misleading, since the adjustment to earnings is not all-inclusive. The Board agreed that this Statement should not refer to information as pro forma if in fact it is not. Therefore, this Statement retains the proposed requirements to present (a) prior-period income before extraordinary items and net income adjusted to exclude, among other things, amortization expense related to goodwill and intangible assets that will no longer be amortized and (b) a reconciliation of reported net income to the adjusted net income; however, those adjusted amounts are not to be labeled "pro forma."

Goodwill and Intangible Assets Acquired after June 30, 2001

B220. Because this Statement will not be effective immediately after it is issued as proposed in the 2001 Exposure Draft, the Board considered how an entity should account for goodwill and other intangible assets acquired in transactions completed after this Statement is issued but before an entity initially applies this Statement to previously recognized goodwill and intangible assets. The Board agreed that it was not appropriate to require such goodwill and intangible assets to be accounted for under the current accounting literature. Thus, the Board concluded that goodwill acquired in a business combination completed after June 30, 2001, but before the acquiring entity initially applies this Statement to previously recognized goodwill should not be amortized. However, the Board observed that because this Statement requires goodwill to be tested for impairment at the reporting unit level, the impairment provisions in this Statement cannot be applied to acquisition-specific goodwill. Therefore, an entity may not apply the goodwill impairment provisions to goodwill acquired in a business combination completed after June 30, 2001, until the date that an entity initially applies this Statement to its previously recognized goodwill and intangible assets. For example, an entity with a December 31, 2001 fiscal year-end is required to initially apply this Statement on January 1, 2002, to its previously recognized goodwill. If that entity completed a business combination on October 15, 2001, that gave rise to goodwill, it would not amortize that goodwill even though it would continue to amortize until January 1, 2002, goodwill that arose from business combinations completed before July 1, 2001. The recently acquired goodwill would not be tested for impairment in accordance with this Statement until January 1, 2002. In the interim, the recently acquired goodwill would be tested for impairment in the same manner as previously recognized goodwill.

B221. Similarly, the Board concluded that an intangible asset acquired in a transaction completed after June 30, 2001, but before the acquiring entity initially applies this Statement to previously recognized intangible assets should be accounted for in accordance with the amortization and nonamortization provisions in this Statement related to intangible assets. The impairment provisions in this Statement for intangible assets that are not being amortized differ from the impairment provisions in Chapter 5 of ARB 43, Opinion 17, and Statement 121. Thus, for consistency purposes, the Board concluded that the impairment provisions in this Statement should not apply to intangible assets acquired in a transaction completed after June 30, 2001, until the date that an entity initially applies this Statement to previously recognized goodwill and intangible assets.

Benefits and Costs

B222. The mission of the FASB is to establish and improve standards of financial accounting and reporting for the guidance and education of the public, including preparers, auditors, and users of financial information. In fulfilling that mission, the Board endeavors to determine that a proposed standard will fill a significant need and that the costs imposed to meet that standard, as compared with other alternatives, are justified in relation to the overall benefits of the resulting information. Although the costs to implement a new standard may not be borne evenly, investors and creditors—both present and potential—as well as others, benefit from improvements in financial reporting, thereby facilitating the functioning of markets for capital and credit and the efficient allocation of resources in the economy.

B223. The Board believes that the requirements in this Statement will result in improved financial reporting. The Board observed that intangible assets constitute a growing share of assets for entities generally and are, in fact, most of the assets of some individual entities. However, information about the intangible assets owned by those entities is often incomplete and inadequate. This Statement should lead to the provision of more information about those assets. The Board also believes that the changes in how goodwill and other intangible assets are accounted for subsequent to their acquisition will provide investors with greater transparency with respect to the economic value of goodwill and other acquired intangible assets and the amount and timing of their impact on earnings.

B224. The Board concluded that the benefits of recognizing goodwill charges in the income statement only when goodwill is impaired rather than on a systematic basis over an arbitrary period of time exceed the costs associated with the impairment test required by this Statement. The Board reached several conclusions related to the goodwill impairment test after weighing the costs and benefits of the possible choices. For example, the Board adopted a two-step impairment test that will be less costly to apply than the one-step impairment test proposed in the 2001 Exposure Draft. The step added to the impairment test serves as a screen to identify potential goodwill impairment. If the fair value of a reporting unit exceeds its carrying amount, goodwill is not considered impaired; thus, the more costly step of estimating the implied fair value of goodwill and the amount of impairment loss, if any, is not required. In addition, the Board agreed to revise the definition of a reporting unit proposed in the 2001 Exposure Draft such that it is defined using terminology similar to that in Statement 131—terminology familiar to both preparers and users. Based on that revised definition, an entity may have fewer reporting units than it would have had under the proposed definition.

B225. The Board observed that entities were required to test goodwill for impairment under Opinion 17 and Chapter 5 of ARB 43 and that costs were associated with those impairment tests. Because Opinion 17 and Chapter 5 of ARB 43 included little guidance on how to test goodwill for impairment, entities differed as to how they tested goodwill for impairment. In addition, some or a portion of goodwill was required to be tested for impairment in conjunction with related assets in accordance with Statement 121. Therefore, in some instances goodwill was being tested for impairment under more than one method. This Statement requires that all entities test goodwill for impairment only in accordance with the provisions of this Statement, which will result in financial statements that are more comparable.

B226. Finally, the requirement in this Statement to test previously recognized goodwill for impairment upon initial application of this Statement is similar to the requirement in the 2001 Exposure Draft to perform a transitional benchmark assessment. However, the Board agreed to defer the effective date of this Statement with respect to previously recognized goodwill and intangible assets, thus providing an entity with more time to perform the transitional impairment test than it would have had to perform the transitional benchmark assessment. While this Statement requires goodwill to be tested for impairment on an annual basis beginning with the year in which this Statement is initially applied, the Board agreed that this Statement should provide entities with some relief from having to recompute the fair value of each reporting unit every year.

Appendix C

DISCLOSURE ILLUSTRATIONS

Introduction

C1. This appendix provides illustrations of the financial statement disclosure requirements of this Statement. The information presented in the following examples has been included for illustrative purposes only and, therefore, may not be representative of actual transactions. For simplicity, the illustrative disclosures do not provide all of the background information that would be necessary to arrive at the disclosed information.

Illustration 1—Disclosure Requirements in Periods Subsequent to a Business Combination

C2. In accordance with paragraphs 45 and 47, the following disclosures would be made by Theta Company in its December 31, 20X3 financial statements relating to acquired intangible assets and goodwill. Theta Company has two reporting units with goodwill—Technology and Communications—which also are reportable segments.

Note B: Acquired Intangible Assets

	As of December 31, 20X3	
($000s)	Gross Carrying Amount	Accumulated Amortization
Amortized intangible assets		
Trademark	$1,078	$ (66)
Unpatented technology	475	(380)
Other	90	(30)
Total	$1,643	$(476)
Unamortized intangible assets		
Broadcast licenses	$1,400	
Trademark	600	
Total	$2,000	

Aggregate Amortization Expense:

For year ended 12/31/X3	$319

Estimated Amortization Expense:

For year ended 12/31/X4	$199
For year ended 12/31/X5	$ 74
For year ended 12/31/X6	$ 74
For year ended 12/31/X7	$ 64
For year ended 12/31/X8	$ 54

Note C: Goodwill

The changes in the carrying amount of goodwill for the year ended December 31, 20X3, are as follows:

($000s)	Technology Segment	Communications Segment	Total
Balance as of January 1, 20X3	$1,413	$904	$2,317
Goodwill acquired during year	189	115	304
Impairment losses	—	(46)	(46)
Goodwill written off related to sale of business unit	(484)	—	(484)
Balance as of December 31, 20X3	$1,118	$973	$2,091

The Communications segment is tested for impairment in the third quarter, after the annual forecasting process. Due to an increase in competition in the Texas and Louisiana cable industry, operating profits and cash flows were lower than expected in the fourth quarter of 20X2 and the first and second quarters of 20X3. Based on that trend, the earnings forecast for the next five years was revised. In September 20X3, a goodwill impairment loss of $46 was recognized in the Communications reporting unit. The fair value of that reporting unit was estimated using the expected present value of future cash flows.

Illustration 2—Transitional Disclosures

C3. Paragraph 61 requires disclosure of what reported income before extraordinary items and net income would have been in all periods presented exclusive of amortization expense (including any related tax effects) recognized in those periods related to goodwill, intangible assets that are no longer being amortized, any deferred credit related to an excess over cost, equity method goodwill, and changes in amortization periods for intangible assets that will continue to be amortized (including any related tax effects). Similarly adjusted per-share amounts also are required to be disclosed for all periods presented. Omega Corporation initially applies this Statement on January 1, 2002. The amortization expense and net income of Omega Corporation for the year of initial application and prior two years follow (Omega Corporation recognized no extraordinary items in those years):

	For the Year Ended December 31,		
	20X2	**20X1**	**20X0**
Goodwill amortization	$	$ (40)	$ (40)
Trademark amortization	$	$ (20)	$ (20)
Copyright amortization	$ (9)	$ (12)	$ (12)
Net income	$1,223	$1,450	$1,360

C4. The copyright and the trademark were purchased on January 1, 19X9, and are being amortized on a straight-line basis over 40 years (maximum permitted by APB Opinion No. 17, *Intangible Assets*). Upon initial application of this Statement, Omega Corporation reassesses the useful lives of its intangible assets and determines that the copyright has a remaining useful life of 47 years. Omega Corporation will amortize the remaining balance of $444 related to the copyright over 47 years. The trademark is deemed to have an indefinite useful life because it is expected to generate cash flows indefinitely. Thus, Omega Corporation ceases amortizing the trademark on January 1, 2002.

C5. The following disclosure would be made by Omega Corporation in its December 31, 20X2 financial statements.

Footnote D: Goodwill and Other Intangible Assets—Adoption of Statement 142

	For the Year Ended December 31,		
($000s except for earnings-per-share amounts)	**20X2**	**20X1**	**20X0**
Reported net income	$1,223	$1,450	$1,360
Add back: Goodwill amortization		40	40
Add back: Trademark amortization		20	20
Adjust: Copyright amortization		3	3
Adjusted net income	$1,223	$1,513	$1,423

Footnote D (continued)

($000s except for earnings-per-share amounts)	20X2	20X1	20X0
	For the Year Ended December 31,		
Basic earnings per share:			
Reported net income	$ 2.45	$2.90	$2.72
Goodwill amortization		0.08	0.08
Trademark amortization		0.04	0.04
Copyright amortization		0.01	0.01
Adjusted net income	$ 2.45	$3.03	$2.85
Diluted earnings per share:			
Reported net income	$ 2.23	$2.64	$2.47
Goodwill amortization		0.07	0.07
Trademark amortization		0.04	0.04
Copyright amortization		0.01	0.01
Adjusted net income	$ 2.23	$2.76	$2.59

Appendix D

AMENDMENTS TO EXISTING PRONOUNCEMENTS

D1. This Statement supersedes the following pronouncements:

a. APB Opinion No. 17, *Intangible Assets*
b. Both AICPA Accounting Interpretations of Opinion 17
c. ARB No. 43, Chapter 5, "Intangible Assets."

D2. APB Opinion No. 18, *The Equity Method of Accounting for Investments in Common Stock,* is amended as follows:

a. Footnote 9 to paragraph 19(b) is replaced by the following:

Investors shall not amortize goodwill associated with equity method investments after the date FASB Statement No. 142, *Goodwill and Other Intangible Assets,* is initially applied by the entity in its entirety.

b. The following sentence is added to the end of paragraph 19(m):

If that retroactive adjustment is made on or after the date Statement 142 is initially applied in its entirety, the goodwill related to that investment (including goodwill related to step purchases made prior to the initial application of Statement 142) shall not be amortized in determining the amount of the adjustment.

c. The last sentence of paragraph 19(n) is replaced by the following:

However, if the investor is unable to relate the difference to specific accounts of the investee, the difference shall be recognized as goodwill and not be amortized in accordance with Statement 142.

d. Footnote 12 is deleted.

D3. The heading and first sentence of paragraph 11(c) of FASB Statement No. 2, *Accounting for Research and Development Costs,* are replaced by the following:

Intangible assets purchased from others. The costs of intangible assets that are purchased from others for use in research and development activities and that have alternative future uses (in research and development projects or otherwise) shall be accounted for in accordance with FASB Statement No. 142, *Goodwill and Other Intangible Assets.*

D4. FASB Statement No. 44, *Accounting for Intangible Assets of Motor Carriers,* is amended as follows:

a. In the last sentence of paragraph 3, the two references to *identifiable intangible assets* are replaced by *recognized intangible assets.*

b. Paragraph 4 is amended as follows:

(1) In the first sentence, *identifiable intangible assets* is replaced by *recognized intangible assets* and *paragraphs 24–26 of APB Opinion No. 17, Intangible Assets* is replaced by *paragraphs 9 and 10 of FASB Statement No. 142, Goodwill and Other Intangible Assets.*

(2) In the third sentence, the two references to *identifiable intangibles* are replaced by *recognized intangible assets.*

(3) The last sentence is deleted.

c. The first sentence of paragraph 7 is replaced by the following:

Other recognized intangible assets and goodwill relating to motor carrier operations shall be accounted for in accordance with Statement 142.

D5. FASB Statement No. 51, *Financial Reporting by Cable Television Companies,* is amended as follows:

a. In the first sentence of paragraph 13, *APB Opinion No. 17, Intangible Assets* is replaced by *FASB Statement No. 142, Goodwill and Other Intangible Assets.*

b. Paragraph 14, as amended by FASB Statement No. 121, *Accounting for the Impairment of Long-Lived Assets and Long-Lived Assets to Be Disposed Of,* is amended as follows:

(1) In the first sentence, which was added by Statement 121, *identifiable* is deleted.

(2) The following sentence is added after the first sentence:

Other intangible assets are subject to the provisions of Statement 142.

D6. In the table in paragraph 48 of FASB Statement No. 52, *Foreign Currency Translation,* under the subheading "Examples of revenues and expenses related to nonmonetary items:" *goodwill* is deleted from the line item "Amortization of intangible items such as goodwill, patents, licenses, etc."

D7. The last sentence of footnote 3 to paragraph 11 of FASB Statement No. 68, *Research and Development Arrangements,* is replaced by the following:

The accounting for other recognized intangible assets acquired by the enterprise is specified in FASB Statement No. 142, *Goodwill and Other Intangible Assets.*

D8. FASB Statement No. 71, *Accounting for the Effects of Certain Types of Regulation,* is amended as follows:

a. Paragraph 29 and the heading before it are replaced by the following:

Goodwill

FASB Statement No. 142, *Goodwill and Other Intangible Assets,* states that goodwill shall not be amortized and shall be tested for impairment in accordance with that Statement. For rate-making purposes, a regulator may permit an enterprise to amortize purchased goodwill over a specified period. In other cases, a regulator may direct an enterprise not to amortize goodwill or to write off goodwill.

b. Paragraph 30 is replaced by the following:

If the regulator permits all or a portion of goodwill to be amortized over a specific time period as an allowable cost for rate-making purposes, the regulator's action provides reasonable assurance of the existence of a regulatory asset (paragraph 9). That regulatory asset would then be amortized for financial reporting purposes over the period during which it will be allowed for rate-making purposes. Otherwise, goodwill shall not be amortized and shall be accounted for in accordance with Statement 142.

D9. FASB Statement No. 72, *Accounting for Certain Acquisitions of Banking or Thrift Institutions,* is amended as follows:

a. In the third sentence of paragraph 2, *Opinion 17* is replaced by *FASB Statement No. 142, Goodwill and Other Intangible Assets.*

b. The following sentences are added after the last sentence of paragraph 4:

> An enterprise shall evaluate the periods of amortization continually to determine whether later events and circumstances warrant revised estimates of useful lives. If estimates are changed, the unamortized cost shall be allocated to the increased or reduced number of remaining periods in the revised useful life but not to exceed 40 years after acquisition. Estimation of value and future benefits of an intangible asset may indicate that the unamortized cost should be reduced significantly. However, a single loss year or even a few loss years together do not necessarily justify an unusual charge to income for all or a large part of the unamortized cost of intangible assets. The reason for an unusual deduction shall be disclosed.

c. The first sentence of paragraph 6 is replaced by the following:

> Paragraph 14 of Statement 142 specifies that an entity should evaluate the remaining useful life of an intangible asset that is being amortized each reporting period to determine whether events and circumstances warrant a revision to the remaining period of amortization.

d. In the first sentence of paragraph 7, *For purposes of applying paragraph 32 of Opinion 17,* and related footnote are deleted.

e. Footnote 6 is deleted.

D10. FASB Statement No 121, *Accounting for the Impairment of Long-Lived Assets and for Long-Lived Assets to Be Disposed Of,* is amended as follows:

a. The first sentence of paragraph 3 is replaced by the following:

> This Statement applies to long-lived assets and certain recognized intangible assets (except those not being amortized) to be held and used, and to long-lived assets and certain recognized intangible assets (including those not being amortized) to be disposed of.

b. In paragraph 4, *identifiable intangibles* is replaced by *recognized intangible assets.*

c. In the last sentence of paragraph 6, *and amortization periods* is added after *policies.*

d. Paragraph 12 and the heading before it are deleted.

e. In the table in paragraph 147, the section relating to APB Opinion No. 17 is deleted.

D11. FASB Interpretation No. 9, *Applying APB Opinions No. 16 and 17 When a Savings and Loan Association or a Similar Institution Is Acquired in a Business Combination Accounted for by the Purchase Method,* is amended as follows:

a. Paragraph 8, as amended by Statement 72, is amended as follows:

> (1) In the third sentence, *amortized over its estimated life as specified by APB Opinion No. 17* is replaced by *accounted for in accordance with the provisions of FASB Statement No. 142, Goodwill and Other Intangible Assets.*

> (2) The phrase *and accounted for in accordance with the provisions of Statement 142* is added to the end of the last sentence, which was added by Statement 72.

b. Paragraph 9 is deleted.

Appendix E

EXCERPTS FROM CONCEPTS STATEMENT 7

[Best understood in context of full Concepts Statement]

E1. Paragraph 24 of this Statement states that "a present value technique is often the best available technique with which to estimate the fair value of a group of net assets (such as a reporting unit)." Paragraphs 39–54 and 75–88 of FASB Concepts Statement No. 7, *Using Cash Flow Information and Present Value in Accounting Measurements,* discuss the use of present value techniques in measuring the fair value of an asset or a liability. Those paragraphs of Concepts Statement 7 follow.

The Components of a Present Value Measurement

39. Paragraph 23 describes the following elements that together capture the economic differences between various assets and liabilities:[7]

a. An estimate of the future cash flow, or in more complex cases, series of future cash flows at different times
b. Expectations about possible variations in the amount or timing of those cash flows
c. The time value of money, represented by the risk-free rate of interest
d. The price for bearing the uncertainty inherent in the asset or liability
e. Other, sometimes unidentifiable, factors including illiquidity and market imperfections.

---

[7]The effect of the entity's credit standing on the measurement of its liabilities is discussed in paragraphs 75–88.

40. This Statement contrasts two approaches to computing present value, either of which may be used to estimate the fair value of an asset or a liability, depending on the circumstances. In the expected cash flow approach discussed in this Statement, only the third factor listed in paragraph 39 (the time value of money, represented by the risk-free rate of interest) is included in the discount rate; the other factors cause adjustments in arriving at risk-adjusted expected cash flows. In a traditional approach to present value, adjustments for factors (b)–(e) described in paragraph 39 are embedded in the discount rate.

General Principles

41. The techniques used to estimate future cash flows and interest rates will vary from one situation to another depending on the circumstances surrounding the asset or liability in question. However, certain general principles govern any application of present value techniques in measuring assets or liabilities:

a. To the extent possible, estimated cash flows and interest rates should reflect assumptions about the future events and uncertainties that would be considered in deciding whether to acquire an asset or group of assets in an arm's-length transaction for cash.
b. Interest rates used to discount cash flows should reflect assumptions that are consistent with those inherent in the estimated cash flows. Otherwise, the effect of some assumptions will be double counted or ignored. For example, an interest rate of 12 percent might be applied to contractual cash flows of a loan. That rate reflects expectations about future defaults from loans with particular characteristics. That same 12 percent rate should not be used to discount expected cash flows because those cash flows already reflect assumptions about future defaults.
c. Estimated cash flows and interest rates should be free from both bias and factors unrelated to the asset, liability, or group of assets or liabilities in question. For example, deliberately understating estimated net cash flows to enhance the apparent future profitability of an asset introduces a bias into the measurement.
d. Estimated cash flows or interest rates should reflect the range of possible outcomes rather than a single most-likely, minimum, or maximum possible amount.

Traditional and Expected Cash Flow Approaches to Present Value

42. A present value measurement begins with a set of future cash flows, but existing accounting standards employ a variety of different approaches in specifying cash flow sets. Some applications of present value use contractual cash flows. When contractual cash flows are not available, some applications use an estimate of the single most-likely amount or **best estimate.**

43. Accounting applications of present value have traditionally used a single set of estimated cash flows and a single interest rate, often described as "the rate commensurate with the risk." In effect, although not always by conscious design, the traditional approach assumes that a single interest rate convention can reflect all the expectations about the future cash flows and the appropriate risk premium. The Board expects that accountants

will continue to use the traditional approach for some measurements. In some circumstances, a traditional approach is relatively easy to apply. For assets and liabilities with contractual cash flows, it is consistent with the manner in which marketplace participants describe assets and liabilities, as in "a 12 percent bond."

44. The traditional approach is useful for many measurements, especially those in which comparable assets and liabilities can be observed in the marketplace. However, the Board found that the traditional approach does not provide the tools needed to address some complex measurement problems, including the measurement of nonfinancial assets and liabilities for which no market for the item or a comparable item exists. The traditional approach places most of the emphasis on selection of an interest rate. A proper search for "the rate commensurate with the risk" requires analysis of at least two items—one asset or liability that exists in the marketplace and has an observed interest rate and the asset or liability being measured. The appropriate rate of interest for the cash flows being measured must be inferred from the observable rate of interest in some other asset or liability and, to draw that inference, the characteristics of the cash flows must be similar to those of the asset being measured. Consequently, the measurer must do the following:

a. Identify the set of cash flows that will be discounted.
b. Identify another asset or liability in the marketplace that appears to have similar cash flow characteristics.
c. Compare the cash flow sets from the two items to ensure that they are similar. (For example, are both sets contractual cash flows, or is one contractual and the other an estimated cash flow?)
d. Evaluate whether there is an element in one item that is not present in the other. (For example, is one less liquid than the other?)
e. Evaluate whether both sets of cash flows are likely to behave (vary) in a similar fashion under changing economic conditions.

45. The Board found the expected cash flow approach to be a more effective measurement tool than the traditional approach in many situations. In developing a measurement, the expected cash flow approach uses all expectations about possible cash flows instead of the single most-likely cash flow. For example, a cash flow might be $100, $200, or $300 with probabilities of 10 percent, 60 percent, and 30 percent, respectively. The expected cash flow is $220.[8] The expected cash flow approach thus differs from the traditional approach by focusing on direct analysis of the cash flows in question and on more explicit statements of the assumptions used in the measurement.

---

[8]($100 × .1) + ($200 × .6) + ($300 × .3) = $220. The traditional notion of a best estimate or most-likely amount in this example is $200.

46. The expected cash flow approach also allows use of present value techniques when the timing of cash flows is uncertain. For example, a cash flow of $1,000 may be received in 1 year, 2 years, or 3 years with probabilities of 10 percent, 60 percent, and 30 percent, respectively. The example below shows the computation of **expected present value** in that situation. Again, the expected present value of $892.36 differs from the traditional notion of a best estimate of $902.73 (the 60 percent probability) in this example.[9]

Present value of $1,000 in 1 year at 5%	$952.38	
Probability	10.00%	$ 95.24
Present value of $1,000 in 2 years at 5.25%	$902.73	
Probability	60.00%	541.64
Present value of $1,000 in 3 years at 5.50%	$851.61	
Probability	30.00%	255.48
Expected present value		$892.36

---

[9]Interest rates usually vary with the length of time until settlement, a phenomenon described as the *yield curve.*

47. In the past, accounting standard setters have been reluctant to permit use of present

value techniques beyond the narrow case of "contractual rights to receive money or contractual obligations to pay money on fixed or determinable dates." That phrase, which first appeared in accounting standards in paragraph 2 of Opinion 21, reflects the computational limitations of the traditional approach—a single set of cash flows that can be assigned to specific future dates. The Accounting Principles Board recognized that the amount of cash flows is almost always uncertain and incorporated that uncertainty in the interest rate. However, an interest rate in a traditional present value computation cannot reflect uncertainties in timing. A traditional present value computation, applied to the example above, would require a decision about which of the possible timings of cash flows to use and, accordingly, would not reflect the probabilities of other timings.

48. While many accountants do not routinely use the expected cash flow approach, expected cash flows are inherent in the techniques used in some accounting measurements, like pensions, other postretirement benefits, and some insurance obligations. They are currently allowed, but not required, when measuring the impairment of long-lived assets and estimating the fair value of financial instruments. The use of probabilities is an essential element of the expected cash flow approach, and one that may trouble some accountants. They may question whether assigning probabilities to highly subjective estimates suggests greater precision than, in fact, exists. However, the proper application of the traditional approach (as described in paragraph 44) requires the same estimates and subjectivity without providing the computational transparency of the expected cash flow approach.

49. Many estimates developed in current practice already incorporate the elements of expected cash flows informally. In addition, accountants often face the need to measure an asset or liability using limited information about the probabilities of possible cash flows. For example, an accountant might be confronted with the following situations:

a. The estimated amount falls somewhere between $50 and $250, but no amount in the range is more likely than any other

amount. Based on that limited information, the estimated expected cash flow is $150 [(50 + 250)/2].

b. The estimated amount falls somewhere between $50 and $250, and the most likely amount is $100. However, the probabilities attached to each amount are unknown. Based on that limited information, the estimated expected cash flow is $133.33 [(50 + 100 + 250)/3].

c. The estimated amount will be $50 (10 percent probability), $250 (30 percent probability), or $100 (60 percent probability). Based on that limited information, the estimated expected cash flow is $140 [(50 × .10) + (250 × .30) + (100 × .60)].

50. Those familiar with statistical analysis may recognize the cases above as simple descriptions of (a) *uniform,* (b) *triangular,* and (c) *discrete* distributions.[10] In each case, the estimated expected cash flow is likely to provide a better estimate of fair value than the minimum, most likely, or maximum amount taken alone.

---

[10]The uniform and triangular distributions are *continuous* distributions. For further information about these and other distributions, refer to:

- M. Evans, N. Hastings, and B. Peacock, *Statistical Distributions,* 2d ed. (New York: John Wiley & Sons, Inc., 1993).
- N. Johnson, S. Kotz, and N. Balakrishnan, *Continuous Univariate Distributions,* 2d ed., vol. 2. (New York: John Wiley & Sons, Inc., 1995).

51. Like any accounting measurement, the application of an expected cash flow approach is subject to a cost-benefit constraint. In some cases, an entity may have access to considerable data and may be able to develop many cash flow scenarios. In other cases, an entity may not be able to develop more than general statements about the variability of cash flows without incurring considerable cost. The accounting problem is to balance the cost of obtaining additional information against the additional reliability that information will bring to the measurement. The Board recognizes that judgments about relative costs and benefits vary from one situation to the next and involve financial statement preparers, their auditors, and the needs of financial statement users.

52. Some maintain that expected cash flow techniques are inappropriate for measuring a single item or an item with a limited number of possible outcomes. They offer an example of an asset or liability with two possible outcomes: a 90 percent probability that the cash flow will be $10 and a 10 percent probability that the cash flow will be $1,000. They observe that the expected cash flow in that example is $109[11] and criticize that result as not representing either of the amounts that may ultimately be paid.

---

[11]($10 × .9) + ($1,000 × .1) = $109. For purposes of illustration, this example ignores the time value of money.

53. Assertions like the one just outlined reflect underlying disagreement with the measurement objective. If the objective is accumulation of costs to be incurred, expected cash flows may not produce a representationally faithful estimate of the expected cost. However, this Statement adopts fair value as the measurement objective. The fair value of the asset or liability in this example is not likely to be $10, even though that is the most likely cash flow. Instead, one would expect the fair value to be closer to $109 than to either $10 or $1,000. While this example is a difficult measurement situation, a measurement of $10 does not incorporate the uncertainty of the cash flow in the measurement of the asset or liability. Instead, the uncertain cash flow is presented as if it were a certain cash flow. No rational marketplace participant would sell an asset (or assume a liability) with these characteristics for $10.

54. In recent years, financial institutions and others have developed and implemented a variety of pricing tools designed to estimate the fair value of assets and liabilities. It is not possible here to describe all of the many (often proprietary) pricing models currently in use. However, those tools often build on concepts similar to those outlined in this Statement as well as other developments in modern finance, including option pricing and similar models. For example, the well-known Black-Scholes option pricing model uses the elements of a fair value measurement described in paragraph 23 as appropriate in estimating the fair value of an option. To the extent that a pricing model includes each of the elements of fair value, its use is consistent with this Statement.

Present Value in the Measurement of Liabilities

75. The concepts outlined in this Statement apply to liabilities as well as to assets. However, the measurement of liabilities sometimes involves problems different from those encountered in the measurement of assets and may require different techniques in arriving at fair value. When using present value techniques to estimate the fair value of a liability, the objective is to estimate the value of the assets required currently to (a) settle the liability with the holder or (b) transfer the liability to an entity of comparable credit standing.

76. To estimate the fair value of an entity's notes or bonds payable, accountants attempt to estimate the price at which other entities are willing to hold the entity's liabilities as assets. That process involves the same techniques and computational problems encountered in measuring assets. For example, the proceeds from a loan are the price that a lender paid to hold the borrower's promise of future cash flows as an asset. Similarly, the fair value of a bond payable is the price at which that security trades, as an asset, in the marketplace. As outlined in paragraphs 78–81, this estimate of fair value is consistent with the objective of liability measurement described in the preceding paragraph.

77. On the other hand, some liabilities are owed to a class of individuals who do not usually sell their rights as they might sell other assets. For example, entities often sell products with an accompanying warranty. Buyers of those products rarely have the ability or inclination to sell the warranty separately from the covered asset, but they own a warranty asset nonetheless. Some of an entity's liabilities, like an obligation for environmental cleanup, are not the assets of identifiable individuals. However, such liabilities are

sometimes settled through assumption by a third party. In estimating the fair value of such liabilities accountants attempt to estimate the price that the entity would have to pay a third party to assume the liability.

Credit Standing and Liability Measurement

78. The most relevant measure of a liability always reflects the credit standing of the entity obligated to pay. Those who hold the entity's obligations as assets incorporate the entity's credit standing in determining the prices they are willing to pay. When an entity incurs a liability in exchange for cash, the role of its credit standing is easy to observe. An entity with a strong credit standing will receive more cash, relative to a fixed promise to pay, than an entity with a weak credit standing. For example, if 2 entities both promise to pay $500 in 5 years, the entity with a strong credit standing may receive about $374 in exchange for its promise (a 6 percent interest rate). The entity with a weak credit standing may receive about $284 in exchange for its promise (a 12 percent interest rate). Each entity initially records its respective liability at fair value, which is the amount of proceeds received—an amount that incorporates that entity's credit standing.

79. The effect of an entity's credit standing on the fair value of particular liabilities depends on the ability of the entity to pay and on liability provisions that protect holders. Liabilities that are guaranteed by governmental bodies (for example, many bank deposit liabilities in the United States) may pose little risk of default to the holder. Other liabilities may include sinking-fund requirements or significant collateral. All of those aspects must be considered in estimating the extent to which the entity's credit standing affects the fair value of its liabilities.

80. The role of the entity's credit standing in a settlement transaction is less direct but equally important. A settlement transaction involves three parties—the entity, the parties to whom it is obligated, and a third party. The price of the transaction will reflect the competing interests of each party. For example, suppose Entity A has an obligation to pay $500 to Entity B 3 years hence. Entity A has a poor credit rating and therefore borrows at a 12 percent interest rate.

a. In a settlement transaction, Entity B would never consent to replace Entity A with an entity of lower credit standing. All other things being equal, Entity B might consent to replace Entity A with a borrower of similar credit standing and would probably consent to replace Entity A with a more creditworthy entity.
b. Entity C has a good credit rating and therefore borrows at a 6 percent interest rate. It might willingly assume Entity A's obligation for $420 (the present value at 6 percent). Entity C has no incentive to assume the obligation for less (a higher interest rate) if it can borrow at 6 percent because it can receive $420 for an identical promise to pay $500.
c. However, if Entity A were to borrow the money to pay Entity C, it would have to promise $590 ($420 due in 3 years with accumulated interest at 12 percent).

81. Based on the admittedly simple case outlined above, the fair value of Entity A's liability should be approximately $356 (the present value of $500 in 3 years at 12 percent). The $420 price demanded by Entity C includes the fair value of Entity A's liability ($356) plus the price of an upgrade in the credit quality of the liability. There may be situations in which an entity might pay an additional amount to induce others to enter into a settlement transaction. Those cases are analogous to the purchase of a credit guarantee and, like the purchase of a guarantee, the additional amount represents a separate transaction rather than an element in the fair value of the entity's original liability.

82. The effect of an entity's credit standing on the measurement of its liabilities is usually captured in an adjustment to the interest rate, as illustrated above. This is similar to the traditional approach to incorporating risk and uncertainty in the measurement of assets and is well suited to liabilities with contractual cash flows. An expected cash flow approach may be more effective when measuring the effect of credit standing on other liabilities. For example, a liability may present the entity with a range of possible outflows, ranging

from very low to very high amounts. There may be little chance of default if the amount is low, but a high chance of default if the amount is high. In situations like this, the effect of credit standing may be more effectively incorporated in the computation of expected cash flows.

83. The role of an entity's credit standing in the accounting measurement of its liabilities has been a controversial question among accountants. The entity's credit standing clearly affects the interest rate at which it borrows in the marketplace. The initial proceeds of a loan, therefore, always reflect the entity's credit standing at that time. Similarly, the price at which others buy and sell the entity's loan includes their assessment of the entity's ability to repay. The example in paragraph 80 demonstrates how the entity's credit standing would affect the price it would be required to pay to have another entity assume its liability. However, some have questioned whether an entity's financial statements should reflect the effect of its credit standing (or changes in credit standing).

84. Some suggest that the measurement objective for liabilities is fundamentally different from the measurement objective for assets. In their view, financial statement users are better served by liability measurements that focus on the entity's obligation. They suggest a measurement approach in which financial statements would portray the present value of an obligation such that two entities with the same obligation but different credit standing would report the same carrying amount. Some existing accounting pronouncements take this approach, most notably FASB Statements No. 87, *Employers' Accounting for Pensions,* and No. 106, *Employers' Accounting for Postretirement Benefits Other Than Pensions.*

85. However, there is no convincing rationale for why the initial measurement of some liabilities would necessarily include the effect of credit standing (as in a loan for cash) while others might not (as in a warranty liability or similar item). Similarly, there is no rationale for why, in initial or fresh-start measurement, the recorded amount of a liability should reflect something other than the price that

would exist in the marketplace. Consistent with its conclusions on fair value (refer to paragraph 30), the Board found no rationale for taking a different view in subsequent fresh-start measurements of an existing asset or liability than would pertain to measurements at initial recognition.

86. Some argue that changes in an entity's credit standing are not relevant to users of financial statements. In their view, a fresh-start measurement that reflects changes in credit standing produces accounting results that are confusing. If the measurement includes changes in credit standing, and an entity's credit standing declines, the fresh-start measurement of its liabilities declines. That decline in liabilities is accompanied by an increase in owners' equity, a result that they find counterintuitive. How, they ask, can a bad thing (declining credit standing) produce a good thing (increased owners' equity)?

87. Like all measurements at fair value, fresh-start measurement of liabilities can produce unfamiliar results when compared with reporting the liabilities on an amortized basis. A change in credit standing represents a change in the relative positions of the two classes of claimants (shareholders and creditors) to an entity's assets. If the credit standing diminishes, the fair value of creditors' claims diminishes. The amount of shareholders' residual claim to the entity's assets may appear to increase, but that increase probably is offset by losses that may have occasioned the decline in credit standing. Because shareholders usually cannot be called on to pay a corporation's liabilities, the amount of their residual claims approaches, and is limited by, zero. Thus, a change in the position of borrowers necessarily alters the position of shareholders, and vice versa.

88. The failure to include changes in credit standing in the measurement of a liability ignores economic differences between liabilities. Consider the case of an entity that has two classes of borrowing. Class One was transacted when the entity had a strong credit standing and a correspondingly low interest rate. Class Two is new and was transacted under the entity's current lower credit standing. Both classes trade in the marketplace based

on the entity's current credit standing. If the two liabilities are subject to fresh-start measurement, failing to include changes in the entity's credit standing makes the classes of borrowings seem different—even though the marketplace evaluates the quality of their respective cash flows as similar to one another.

E2. Paragraph 24 of this Statement requires that estimates of future cash flows used in a present value technique be consistent with the objective of measuring fair value. Paragraph 23 of Concepts Statement 7 discusses the essential elements of a present value measurement. That paragraph of Concepts Statement 7 follows.

> 23. A present value measurement that fully captures the economic differences between the five assets described in paragraph 20 would necessarily include the following elements:
>
> a. An estimate of the future cash flow, or in more complex cases, series of future cash flows at different times[2]
> b. Expectations about possible variations in the amount or timing of those cash flows
> c. The time value of money, represented by the risk-free rate of interest
> d. The price for bearing the uncertainty inherent in the asset or liability
> e. Other, sometimes unidentifiable, factors including illiquidity and market imperfections.

---

[2]In complex measurements, such as measurements of liabilities settled by providing services, cash flow estimates necessarily include elements like overhead and profit margins inherent in the price of goods and services.

E3. Paragraph 24 of this Statement requires that estimates of future cash flows used in a present value technique incorporate assumptions that marketplace participants would use in their estimates of fair value. If that information is not available without undue cost and effort, an entity may use its own assumptions. Paragraph 32 of Concepts Statement 7 provides examples of circumstances in which an entity's cash flows (entity assumptions) might differ from the market cash flows (marketplace assumptions). That paragraph of Concepts Statement 7 follows.

> 32. An entity's best estimate of the present value of cash flows will not necessarily equal the fair value of those uncertain cash flows.

There are several reasons why an entity might expect to realize or pay cash flows that differ from those expected by others in the marketplace. Those include:

a. The entity's managers might intend different use or settlement than that anticipated by others. For example, they might intend to operate a property as a bowling alley, even though others in the marketplace consider its highest and best use to be a parking lot.
b. The entity's managers may prefer to accept risk of a liability (like a product warranty) and manage it internally, rather than transferring that liability to another entity.
c. The entity might hold special preferences, like tax or zoning variances, not available to others.
d. The entity might hold information, trade secrets, or processes that allow it to realize (or avoid paying) cash flows that differ from others' expectations.
e. The entity might be able to realize or pay amounts through use of internal resources. For example, an entity that manufactures materials used in particular processes acquires those materials at cost, rather than the market price charged to others. An entity that chooses to satisfy a liability with internal resources may avoid the markup or anticipated profit charged by outside contractors.

Appendix F

GLOSSARY

F1. This appendix contains definitions of certain terms used in this Statement.

Fair value
> The amount at which an asset (or liability) could be bought (or incurred) or sold (or settled) in a current transaction between willing parties, that is, other than in a forced or liquidation sale.

Goodwill
> The excess of the cost of an acquired entity over the net of the amounts assigned to assets acquired and liabilities assumed. The amount recognized as goodwill includes acquired intangible assets

that do not meet the criteria in FASB Statement No. 141, *Business Combinations,* for recognition as an asset apart from goodwill.

Intangible assets

Assets (not including financial assets) that lack
physical substance. (The term *intangible assets* is
used in this Statement to refer to intangible assets
other than goodwill.)

Intangible asset class

A group of intangible assets that are similar, either by their nature or by their use in the operations of an entity.

Mutual enterprise

An entity other than an investor-owned entity that
provides dividends, lower costs, or other economic benefits directly and proportionately to its
owners, members, or participants. Mutual insurance companies, credit unions, and farm and rural electric cooperatives are examples of mutual
enterprises (FASB Concepts Statement No. 4,
*Objectives of Financial Reporting by Nonbusi-
ness Organizations,* paragraph 7).

Not-for-profit organization

An entity that possesses the following characteristics that distinguish it from a business enter-

prise: (a) contributions of significant amounts of
resources from resource providers who do not expect commensurate or proportionate pecuniary
return, (b) operating purposes other than to provide goods or services at a profit, and (c) absence
of ownership interests like those of business enterprises. Not-for-profit organizations have those
characteristics in varying degrees (Concepts
Statement 4, paragraph 6). Entities that clearly
fall outside this definition include all investor-
owned entities and mutual enterprises.

Reporting unit

The level of reporting at which goodwill is tested
for impairment. A reporting unit is an operating
segment or one level below an operating segment
(as that term is defined in paragraph 10 of FASB
Statement No. 131, *Disclosures about Segments
of an Enterprise and Related Information*).

Residual value

The estimated fair value of an intangible asset at
the end of its useful life to an entity, less any disposal costs.

Useful life

The period over which an asset is expected to
contribute directly or indirectly to future cash
flows.

FAS143

Statement of Financial Accounting Standards No. 143
Accounting for Asset Retirement Obligations

STATUS

Issued: June 2001

Effective Date: For financial statements for fiscal years beginning after June 15, 2002

Affects: Supersedes FAS 19, paragraph 37

Affected by: Paragraphs 2 and 12 amended by FAS 144
Footnote 11 superseded by FAS 144

Issues Discussed by FASB Emerging Issues Task Force (EITF)

Affects: No EITF Issues

Interpreted by: No EITF Issues

Related Issues: EITF Issues No. 89-13, 90-8, 95-23, and 02-6

SUMMARY

This Statement addresses financial accounting and reporting for obligations associated with the retirement of tangible long-lived assets and the associated asset retirement costs. This Statement applies to all entities. It applies to legal obligations associated with the retirement of long-lived assets that result from the acquisition, construction, development and (or) the normal operation of a long-lived asset, except for certain obligations of lessees. As used in this Statement, a legal obligation is an obligation that a party is required to settle as a result of an existing or enacted law, statute, ordinance, or written or oral contract or by legal construction of a contract under the doctrine of promissory estoppel. This Statement amends FASB Statement No. 19, *Financial Accounting and Reporting by Oil and Gas Producing Companies.*

Reasons for Issuing This Statement

The Board decided to address the accounting and reporting for asset retirement obligations because:

- Users of financial statements indicated that the diverse accounting practices that have developed for obligations associated with the retirement of tangible long-lived assets make it difficult to compare the financial position and results of operations of companies that have similar obligations but account for them differently.
- Obligations that meet the definition of a liability were not being recognized when those liabilities were incurred or the recognized liabilty was not consistently measured or presented.

Differences between This Statement, Statement 19, and Existing Practice

This Statement requires that the fair value of a liability for an asset retirement obligation be recognized in the period in which it is incurred if a reasonable estimate of fair value can be made. The associated asset retirement costs are capitalized as part of the carrying amount of the long-lived asset. This Statement differs from Statement 19 and current practice in several significant respects.

- Under Statement 19 and most current practice, an amount for an asset retirement obligation was recognized using a cost-accumulation measurement approach. Under this Statement, the amount initially recognized is measured at fair value.

- Under Statement 19 and most current practice, amounts for retirement obligations were not discounted and therefore no accretion expense was recorded in subsequent periods. Under this Statement, the liability is discounted and accretion expense is recognized using the credit-adjusted risk-free interest rate in effect when the liability was initially recognized.
- Under Statement 19, dismantlement and restoration costs were taken into account in determining amortization and depreciation rates. Consequently, many entities recognized asset retirement obligations as a contra-asset. Under this Statement, those obligations are recognized as a liability. Also, under Statement 19 the obligation was recognized over the useful life of the related asset. Under this Statement, the obligation is recognized when the liability is incurred.

Some current practice views a retirement obligation as a contingent liability and applies FASB Statement No. 5, *Accounting for Contingencies,* in determining when to recognize a liability. The measurement objective in this Statement is fair value, which is not compatible with a Statement 5 approach. A fair value measurement accommodates uncertainty in the amount and timing of settlement of the liability, whereas under Statement 5 the recognition decision is based on the level of uncertainty.

This Statement contains disclosure requirements that provide descriptions of asset retirement obligations and reconciliations of changes in the components of those obligations.

How the Changes in This Statement Improve Financial Reporting

Because all asset retirement obligations that fall within the scope of this Statement and their related asset retirement cost will be accounted for consistently, financial statements of different entities will be more comparable. Also,

- Retirement obligations will be recognized when they are incurred and displayed as liabilities. Thus, more information about future cash outflows, leverage, and liquidity will be provided. Also, an initial measurement at fair value will provide relevant information about the liability.
- Because the asset retirement cost is capitalized as part of the asset's carrying amount and subsequently allocated to expense over the asset's useful life, information about the gross investment in long-lived assets will be provided.
- Disclosure requirements contained in this Statement will provide more information about asset retirement obligations.

How the Statement Generally Changes Financial Statements

Because of diverse practice in current accounting for asset retirement obligations, various industries and entities will be affected differently. This Statement will likely have the following effects on current accounting practice:

- Total liabilities generally will increase because more retirement obligations will be recognized. For some entities, obligations will be recognized earlier, and they will be displayed as liabilities rather than as contra-assets. In certain cases, the amount of a recognized liability may be lower than that recognized in current practice because a fair value measurement entails discounting.
- The recognized cost of assets will increase because asset retirement costs will be added to the carrying amount of the long-lived asset. Assets also will increase because assets acquired with an existing retirement obligation will be displayed on a gross rather than on a net basis.
- The amount of expense (accretion expense plus depreciation expense) will be higher in the later years of an asset's life than in earlier years.

How the Conclusions in the Statement Relate to the Conceptual Framework

The Board concluded that all retirement obligations within the scope of this Statement that meet the definition of a liability in FASB Concepts Statement No. 6, *Elements of Financial Statements,* should be recognized as a liability when the recognition criteria in FASB Concepts Statement No. 5, *Recognition and Measurement in Financial Statements of Business Enterprises,* are met.

The Board also decided that the liability for an asset retirement obligation should be initially recognized at its estimated fair value as discussed in FASB Concepts Statement No. 7, *Using Cash Flow Information and Present Value in Accounting Measurements.*

Effective Date

This Statement is effective for financial statements issued for fiscal years beginning after June 15, 2002. Earlier application is encouraged.

Statement of Financial Accounting Standards No. 143

Accounting for Asset Retirement Obligations

CONTENTS

INTRODUCTION

1. Diverse accounting practices have developed for obligations associated with the retirement of tangible long-lived assets. Some entities accrue those obligations ratably over the useful life of the related asset, either as an element of depreciation expense (and accumulated depreciation) or as a liability. Other entities do not recognize liabilities for those obligations until an asset is retired. This Statement establishes accounting standards for recognition and measurement of a liability for an asset retirement obligation and the associated asset retirement cost.[1]

STANDARDS OF FINANCIAL ACCOUNTING AND REPORTING

Scope

2. This Statement applies to all entities. This Statement applies to legal obligations associated with the *retirement*[2] of a tangible long-lived asset that result from the acquisition, construction, or development and (or) the normal operation of a long-lived asset, except as explained in paragraph 17 for certain obligations of lessees. As used in this Statement, a legal obligation is an obligation that a party is required to

---

[1]The term *asset retirement obligation* refers to an obligation associated with the retirement of a tangible long-lived asset. The term *asset retirement cost* refers to the amount capitalized that increases the carrying amount of the long-lived asset when a liability for an asset retirement obligation is recognized.

[2]In this Statement, the term *retirement* is defined as the other-than-temporary removal of a long-lived asset from service. That term encompasses sale, abandonment, recycling, or disposal in some other manner. However, it does not encompass the temporary idling of a long-lived asset.

settle as a result of an existing or enacted law, statute, ordinance, or written or oral contract or by legal construction of a contract under the doctrine of promissory estoppel.[3] This Statement does not apply to obligations that arise solely from a *plan to dispose* of a long-lived asset as that phrase is used in paragraph 15 of FASB Statement No. 121, *Accounting for the Impairment of Long-Lived Assets and for Long-Lived Assets to Be Disposed Of.* An obligation that results from the improper operation of an asset also is not within the scope of this Statement but may be subject to the provisions of AICPA Statement of Position 96-1, *Environmental Remediation Liabilities.*

Initial Recognition and Measurement of a Liability for an Asset Retirement Obligation

3. An entity shall recognize the fair value of a liability for an asset retirement obligation in the period in which it is incurred if a reasonable estimate of fair value can be made.[4] If a reasonable estimate of fair value cannot be made in the period the asset retirement obligation is incurred, the liability shall be recognized when a reasonable estimate of fair value can be made.

4. Paragraph 35 of FASB Concepts Statement No. 6, *Elements of Financial Statements,* defines a liability as follows:

> Liabilities are probable[21] future sacrifices of economic benefits arising from present obligations of a particular entity to transfer assets or provide services to other entities in the future as a result of past transactions or events. [Footnote 22 omitted.]

---

[21] *Probable* is used with its usual general meaning, rather than in a specific accounting or technical sense (such as that in Statement 5, par. 3), and refers to that which can reasonably be expected or believed on the basis of available evidence or logic but is neither certain nor proved (*Webster's New World Dictionary,* p. 1132). Its inclusion in the definition is intended to acknowledge that business and other economic activities occur in an environment characterized by uncertainty in which few outcomes are certain (pars. 44–48).

5. As stated in the above footnote, the definition of a liability in Concepts Statement 6 uses the term *prob-*

able in a different sense than it is used in FASB Statement No. 5, *Accounting for Contingencies.* As used in Statement 5, probable requires a high degree of expectation. The term probable in the definition of a liability, however, is intended to acknowledge that business and other economic activities occur in an environment in which few outcomes are certain.

6. Statement 5 and FASB Concepts Statement No. 7, *Using Cash Flow Information and Present Value in Accounting Measurements,* deal with uncertainty in different ways. Statement 5 deals with uncertainty about whether a loss has been incurred by setting forth criteria to determine when to *recognize* a loss contingency. Concepts Statement 7 addresses measurement of liabilities and provides a *measurement* technique to deal with uncertainties about the amount and timing of the future cash flows necessary to settle the liability. Paragraphs 55–61 of Concepts Statement 7[5] discuss, in detail, the relationship between the fair value measurement objective and expected cash flow approach that is articulated in Concepts Statement 7 and accounting for contingencies under Statement 5. The guidance in Statement 5 and FASB Interpretation No. 14, *Reasonable Estimation of the Amount of a Loss,* are not applicable to a liability for which the objective is to measure that liability at fair value. That is because in Statement 5 uncertainty is used to decide whether to recognize a liability, whereas in Concepts Statement 7 uncertainties in the amount and timing of settlement are incorporated into the fair value measurement of the recognized liability. This Statement requires that all asset retirement obligations within the scope of this Statement be recognized when a reasonable estimate of fair value can be made.

7. The fair value of a liability for an asset retirement obligation is the amount at which that liability could be settled in a current transaction between willing parties, that is, other than in a forced or liquidation transaction. Quoted market prices in active markets are the best evidence of fair value and shall be used as the basis for the measurement, if available. If quoted market prices are not available, the estimate of fair value shall be based on the best information available in the circumstances, including prices for

---

[3] *Black's Law Dictionary,* seventh edition, defines *promissory estoppel* as, "The principle that a promise made without consideration may nonetheless be enforced to prevent injustice if the promisor should have reasonably expected the promisee to rely on the promise and if the promisee did actually rely on the promise to his or her detriment."

[4] If a tangible long-lived asset with an existing asset retirement obligation is acquired, a liability for that obligation shall be recognized at the asset's acquisition date as if that obligation were incurred on that date.

[5] Appendix F incorporates those paragraphs.

similar liabilities and the results of present value (or other valuation) techniques.

8. A present value technique[6] is often the best available technique with which to estimate the fair value of a liability. If a present value technique is used to estimate fair value, estimates of future cash flows used in that technique shall be consistent with the objective of measuring fair value.[7] Concepts Statement 7 discusses two present value techniques: a traditional approach, in which a single set of estimated cash flows and a single interest rate (a rate commensurate with the risk) are used to estimate fair value, and an expected cash flow approach, in which multiple cash flow scenarios that reflect the range of possible outcomes and a credit-adjusted risk-free rate are used to estimate fair value. Although either present value technique could theoretically be used for a fair value measurement, the expected cash flow approach will usually be the only appropriate technique for an asset retirement obligation. As discussed in paragraph 44 of Concepts Statement 7, proper application of a traditional approach entails analysis of at least two liabilities—one that exists in the marketplace and has an observable interest rate and the liability being measured. The appropriate rate of interest for the cash flows being measured must be inferred from the observable rate of interest of some other liability, and to draw that inference the characteristics of the cash flows must be similar to those of the liability being measured. It would be rare, if ever, that there would be an observable rate of interest for a liability that has cash flows similar to an asset retirement obligation being measured. In addition, an asset retirement obligation will usually have uncertainties in both timing and amount. In that circumstance, employing a traditional present value technique, where uncertainty is incorporated into the rate, will be difficult, if not impossible.

9. The cash flows used in estimates of fair value shall incorporate assumptions that marketplace participants would use in their estimates of fair value whenever that information is available without undue cost and effort. Otherwise, an entity may use its own assumptions.[8] Those estimates shall be based on reasonable and supportable assumptions and shall consider all available evidence. The weight given to the evidence shall be commensurate with the extent to which the evidence can be verified objectively. If a range is estimated for the timing or the amount of possible cash flows, the likelihood of possible outcomes shall be considered. An entity, when using the expected cash flow technique, shall discount the estimated cash flows using a credit-adjusted risk-free rate. Thus, the effect of the entity's credit standing is reflected in the discount rate rather than in the estimated cash flows.

10. A liability for an asset retirement obligation may be incurred over more than one reporting period if the events that create the obligation occur over more than one reporting period. Any incremental liability incurred in a subsequent reporting period shall be considered to be an additional layer of the original liability. Each layer shall be initially measured at fair value. For example, the liability for decommissioning a nuclear power plant is incurred as contamination occurs. Each period, as contamination increases, a separate layer shall be measured and recognized.

Recognition and Allocation of an Asset Retirement Cost

11. Upon initial recognition of a liability for an asset retirement obligation, an entity shall capitalize an asset retirement cost by increasing the carrying amount of the related long-lived asset by the same amount as the liability.[9] An entity shall subsequently allocate that asset retirement cost to expense using a systematic and rational method over its useful life. Application of a systematic and rational allocation method does not preclude an entity from capitalizing an amount of asset retirement cost and allocating an equal amount to expense in the same accounting period.[10]

Asset Impairment

12. In applying the provisions of Statement 121,[11] the carrying amount of the asset being tested for

---

[6]Appendix F incorporates paragraphs 39–54 and 75–88 of Concepts Statement 7 that discuss present value techniques.

[7]Appendix F incorporates paragraph 23 of Concepts Statement 7 that discusses the essential elements of a fair value measurement.

[8]Paragraph 32 of Concepts Statement 7 (included in Appendix F) provides reasons why an entity's assumptions may differ from those expected by others in the marketplace.

[9]Capitalized asset retirement costs do not qualify as *expenditures* for purposes of paragraph 16 of FASB Statement No. 34, *Capitalization of Interest Cost.*

[10]For example, assume an entity acquires a long-lived asset with an estimated life of 10 years. As that asset is operated, the entity incurs one-tenth of the liability for an asset retirement obligation each year. Application of a systematic and rational allocation method would not preclude that entity from capitalizing and then expensing one-tenth of the asset retirement costs each year.

[11]The Board is reconsidering the provisions of Statement 121 and has issued an Exposure Draft, *Accounting for the Impairment or Disposal of Long-Lived Assets and for Obligations Associated with Disposal Activities.*

impairment shall include amounts of capitalized asset retirement costs. Estimated future cash flows related to the liability for an asset retirement obligation that has been recognized in the financial statements shall be excluded from (a) the undiscounted cash flows used to test the asset for recoverability and (b) the discounted cash flows used to measure the asset's fair value. If the fair value of the asset is based on a quoted market price and that price considers the costs that will be incurred in retiring that asset, the quoted market price shall be increased by the fair value of the asset retirement obligation for purposes of measuring impairment.

Subsequent Recognition and Measurement

13. In periods subsequent to initial measurement, an entity shall recognize period-to-period changes in the liability for an asset retirement obligation resulting from (a) the passage of time and (b) revisions to either the timing or the amount of the original estimate of undiscounted cash flows. An entity shall measure and incorporate changes due to the passage of time into the carrying amount of the liability before measuring changes resulting from a revision to either the timing or the amount of estimated cash flows.

14. An entity shall measure changes in the liability for an asset retirement obligation due to passage of time by applying an interest method of allocation to the amount of the liability at the beginning of the period.[12] The interest rate used to measure that change shall be the credit-adjusted risk-free rate that existed when the liability, or portion thereof, was initially measured. That amount shall be recognized as an increase in the carrying amount of the liability and as an expense classified as an operating item in the statement of income, hereinafter referred to as *accretion expense.*[13] Accretion expense shall not be considered to be interest cost for purposes of applying FASB Statement No. 34, *Capitalization of Interest Cost.*

15. Changes resulting from revisions to the timing or the amount of the original estimate of undiscounted cash flows shall be recognized as an increase or a decrease in (a) the carrying amount of the liability for an asset retirement obligation and (b) the related asset retirement cost capitalized as part of the carrying

amount of the related long-lived asset. Upward revisions in the amount of undiscounted estimated cash flows shall be discounted using the current credit-adjusted risk-free rate. Downward revisions in the amount of undiscounted estimated cash flows shall be discounted using the credit-adjusted risk-free rate that existed when the original liability was recognized. If an entity cannot identify the prior period to which the downward revision relates, it may use a weighted-average credit-adjusted risk-free rate to discount the downward revision to estimated future cash flows. When asset retirement costs change as a result of a revision to estimated cash flows, an entity shall adjust the amount of asset retirement cost allocated to expense in the period of change if the change affects that period only or in the period of change and future periods if the change affects more than one period as required by APB Opinion No. 20, *Accounting Changes* (paragraph 31), for a change in estimate.

Effects of Funding and Assurance Provisions

16. Providing assurance that an entity will be able to satisfy its asset retirement obligation does not satisfy or extinguish the related liability. Methods of providing assurance include surety bonds, insurance policies, letters of credit, guarantees by other entities, and establishment of trust funds or identification of other assets dedicated to satisfy the asset retirement obligation. The existence of funding and assurance provisions may affect the determination of the credit-adjusted risk-free rate. For a previously recognized asset retirement obligation, changes in funding and assurance provisions have no effect on the initial measurement or accretion of that liability, but may affect the credit-adjusted risk-free rate used to discount upward revisions in undiscounted cash flows for that obligation. Costs associated with complying with funding or assurance provisions are accounted for separately from the asset retirement obligation.

Leasing Transactions

17. This Statement does not apply to obligations of a lessee in connection with leased property, whether imposed by a lease agreement or by a party other than the lessor, that meet the definition of either minimum lease payments or contingent rentals in paragraph 5 of FASB Statement No. 13, *Accounting for*

---

[12]The subsequent measurement provisions require an entity to identify undiscounted estimated cash flows associated with the initial measurement of a liability. Therefore, an entity that obtains an initial measurement of fair value from a market price or from a technique other than the expected cash flow approach described in Concepts Statement 7 must determine the undiscounted cash flows and estimated timing of those cash flows that are embodied in that fair value amount for purposes of applying the subsequent measurement provisions. Appendix E includes an example of the subsequent measurement of a liability that is initially obtained from a market price.

[13]An entity may use any descriptor for accretion expense so long as it conveys the underlying nature of the expense.

Leases.[14] Those obligations shall be accounted for by the lessee in accordance with the requirements of Statement 13 (as amended). However, if obligations of a lessee in connection with leased property, whether imposed by a lease agreement or by a party other than the lessor, meet the provisions in paragraph 2 of this Statement but do not meet the definition of either minimum lease payments or contingent rentals in paragraph 5 of Statement 13, those obligations shall be accounted for by the lessee in accordance with the requirements of this Statement.

18. Obligations of a lessor in connection with leased property that meet the provisions in paragraph 2 of this Statement shall be accounted for by the lessor in accordance with the requirements of this Statement.

Rate-Regulated Entities

19. This Statement applies to rate-regulated entities that meet the criteria for application of FASB Statement No. 71, *Accounting for the Effects of Certain Types of Regulation,* as provided in paragraph 5 of that Statement. Paragraphs 9 and 11 of Statement 71 provide specific conditions that must be met to recognize a regulatory asset and a regulatory liability, respectively.

20. Many rate-regulated entities currently provide for the costs related to the retirement of certain long-lived assets in their financial statements and recover those amounts in rates charged to their customers. Some of those costs result from asset retirement obligations within the scope of this Statement; others result from costs that are not within the scope of this Statement. The amounts charged to customers for the costs related to the retirement of long-lived assets may differ from the period costs recognized in accordance with this Statement and, therefore, may result in a difference in the timing of recognition of period costs for financial reporting and rate-making purposes. An additional recognition timing difference may exist when the costs related to the retirement of long-lived assets are included in amounts charged to customers but liabilities are not recognized in the financial statements. If the requirements of Statement 71 are met, a regulated entity also shall recognize a regulatory asset or liability for differences in the timing of recognition of the period costs associated with asset retirement obligations for financial reporting pursuant to this Statement and rate-making purposes.

21. The capitalized amount of an asset retirement cost shall be included in the assessment of impairment of long-lived assets of a rate-regulated entity just as that cost is included in the assessment of impairment of long-lived assets of any other entity. FASB Statement No. 90, *Regulated Enterprises— Accounting for Abandonments and Disallowances of Plant Costs,* applies to the asset retirement cost related to a long-lived asset of a rate-regulated entity that has been closed or abandoned.

Disclosures

22. An entity shall disclose the following information about its asset retirement obligations:

a. A general description of the asset retirement obligations and the associated long-lived assets
b. The fair value of assets that are legally restricted for purposes of settling asset retirement obligations
c. A reconciliation of the beginning and ending aggregate carrying amount of asset retirement obligations showing separately the changes attributable to (1) liabilities incurred in the current period, (2) liabilities settled in the current period, (3) accretion expense, and (4) revisions in estimated cash flows, whenever there is a significant change in one or more of those four components during the reporting period.

If the fair value of an asset retirement obligation cannot be reasonably estimated, that fact and the reasons therefor shall be disclosed.

Amendment to Existing Pronouncement

23. Paragraph 37 of FASB Statement No. 19, *Financial Accounting and Reporting by Oil and Gas Producing Companies,* is replaced by the following:

> Obligations for dismantlement, restoration, and abandonment costs shall be accounted for in accordance with the provisions of FASB Statement No. 143, *Accounting for Asset Retirement Obligations.* Estimated residual salvage values shall be taken into account in determining amortization and depreciation rates.

Effective Date and Transition

24. This Statement shall be effective for financial statements issued for fiscal years beginning after

---

[14]Paragraph 1 of Statement 13 provides that Statement 13 does not apply to lease agreements concerning the rights to explore for or to exploit natural resources such as oil, gas, minerals, and timber.

June 15, 2002. Earlier application is encouraged. Initial application of this Statement shall be as of the beginning of an entity's fiscal year. If this Statement is adopted prior to the effective date and during an interim period other than the first interim period of a fiscal year, all prior interim periods of that fiscal year shall be restated.

25. Upon initial application of this Statement, an entity shall recognize the following items in its statement of financial position: (a) a liability for any existing asset retirement obligations adjusted for cumulative accretion to the date of adoption of this Statement, (b) an asset retirement cost capitalized as an increase to the carrying amount of the associated long-lived asset, and (c) accumulated depreciation on that capitalized cost. Amounts resulting from initial application of this Statement shall be measured using current (that is, as of the date of adoption of this Statement) information, current assumptions, and current interest rates. The amount recognized as an asset retirement cost shall be measured as of the date the asset retirement obligation was incurred. Cumulative accretion and accumulated depreciation shall be measured for the time period from the date the liability would have been recognized had the provisions of this Statement been in effect to the date of adoption of this Statement. Appendix D provides examples that illustrate application of the transition provisions of this Statement.

26. An entity shall recognize the cumulative effect of initially applying this Statement as a change in accounting principle as described in paragraph 20 of Opinion 20. The amount to be reported as a cumulative-effect adjustment in the statement of operations is the difference between the amounts, if any, recognized in the statement of financial position prior to the application of this Statement (for example, under the provisions of Statement 19) and the net amount that is recognized in the statement of financial position pursuant to paragraph 25.

27. In addition to disclosures required by paragraphs 19(c), 19(d), and 21 of Opinion 20,[15] an entity shall compute on a pro forma basis and disclose in the footnotes to the financial statements for the beginning of the earliest year presented and at the end of all years presented the amount of the liability for asset retirement obligations as if this Statement had been applied during all periods affected. The pro forma amounts of that liability shall be measured using current (that is, as of the date of adoption of this Statement) information, current assumptions, and current interest rates.

28. Lease classification tests performed in accordance with the requirements of Statement 13 at, or subsequent to, the date of initial application of this Statement shall incorporate the requirements of this Statement to the extent applicable.[16] However, leases existing at the date of initial application of this Statement shall not be reclassified to reflect the effects of the requirements of this Statement on the lease classification tests previously performed in accordance with the requirements of Statement 13.

The provisions of this Statement need not be applied to immaterial items.

This Statement was adopted by the unanimous vote of the six members of the Financial Accounting Standards Board.

Edmund L. Jenkins,
Chairman

G. Michael Crooch
John M. Foster
Gaylen N. Larson

Gerhard G. Mueller
Edward W. Trott

---

[15]Opinion 20 requires an entity to disclose the effect of adopting a new accounting principle on income before extraordinary items and on net income (and on the related per-share amounts) of the period of the change. In addition, it requires an entity to compute on a pro forma basis and disclose on the face of the income statements for all periods presented income before extraordinary items and net income (and the related per-share amounts) as if the newly adopted accounting principle had been applied during all periods affected.

[16]For example, the recorded cost of an asset leased by a lessor may be affected by the requirements of this Statement and would potentially affect the application of the classification criterion in paragraph 7(d) of Statement 13.

Appendix A

IMPLEMENTATION GUIDANCE

CONTENTS

Appendix A

IMPLEMENTATION GUIDANCE

Introduction

A1. This appendix describes certain provisions of this Statement in more detail and explains how they apply to certain situations. Facts and circumstances need to be considered carefully in applying this Statement. This appendix is an integral part of the standards of this Statement.

Scope

Legal Obligation

A2. This Statement applies to legal obligations associated with the retirement of a tangible long-lived asset. For purposes of this Statement, a legal obligation can result from (a) a government action, such as a law, statute, or ordinance, (b) an agreement between entities, such as a written or oral contract, or (c) a promise conveyed to a third party that imposes a reasonable expectation of performance upon the promisor under the doctrine of promissory estoppel. *Black's Law Dictionary,* seventh edition, defines

promissory estoppel as, "The principle that a promise made without consideration may nonetheless be enforced to prevent injustice if the promisor should have reasonably expected the promisee to rely on the promise and if the promisee did actually rely on the promise to his or her detriment."

A3. In most cases involving an asset retirement obligation, the determination of whether a legal obligation exists should be unambiguous. However, in situations in which no law, statute, ordinance, or contract exists but an entity makes a promise to a third party (which may include the public at large) about its intention to perform retirement activities, facts and circumstances need to be considered carefully in determining whether that promise has imposed a legal obligation upon the promisor under the doctrine of promissory estoppel. A legal obligation may exist even though no party has taken any formal action. In assessing whether a legal obligation exists, an entity is not permitted to forecast changes in the law or changes in the interpretation of existing laws and regulations. Preparers and their legal advisors are required to evaluate current circumstances to determine whether a legal obligation exists.

A4. For example, assume a company operates a manufacturing facility and has plans to retire it within five years. Members of the local press have begun to publicize the fact that when the company ceases operations at the plant, it plans to abandon the site without demolishing the building and restoring the underlying land. Due to the significant negative publicity and demands by the public that the company commit to dismantling the plant upon retirement, the company's chief executive officer holds a press conference at city hall to announce that the company will demolish the building and restore the underlying land when the company ceases operations at the plant. Although no law, statute, ordinance, or written contract exists requiring the company to perform any demolition or restoration activities, the promise made by the company's chief executive officer may have created a legal obligation under the doctrine of promissory estoppel. In that circumstance, the company's management (and legal counsel, if necessary) would have to evaluate the particular facts and circumstances to determine whether a legal obligation exists.

A5. Contracts between entities may contain an option or a provision that requires one party to the contract to perform retirement activities when an asset is retired. The other party may decide in the future not to exercise the option or to waive the provision to perform retirement activities, or that party may have a history of waiving similar provisions in other contracts. Even if there is an expectation of a waiver or nonenforcement, the contract still imposes a legal obligation. That obligation is included in the scope of this Statement. The likelihood of a waiver or nonenforcement will affect the measurement of the liability.

Issues Associated with the Retirement of a Tangible Long-Lived Asset

A6. In this Statement, the term *retirement* is defined as the other-than-temporary removal of a long-lived asset from service. As used in this Statement, that term encompasses sale, abandonment, or disposal in some other manner. However, it does not encompass the temporary idling of a long-lived asset. After an entity retires an asset, that asset is no longer under the control of that entity, no longer in existence, or no longer capable of being used in the manner for which the asset was originally acquired, constructed, or developed. Activities necessary to prepare an asset for an alternative use are not associated with the retirement of the asset and are not within the scope of this Statement.

A7. Typically, settlement of an asset retirement obligation is not required until the associated asset is retired. However, certain circumstances may exist in which partial settlement of an asset retirement obligation is required or performed before the asset is fully retired. The fact that partial settlement of an obligation is required or performed prior to full retirement of an asset does not remove that obligation from the scope of this Statement.

A8. For example, consider an entity that owns and operates a landfill. Regulations require that that entity perform capping, closure, and post-closure activities. Capping activities involve covering the land with topsoil and planting vegetation. Closure activities include drainage, engineering, and demolition and must be performed prior to commencing the post-closure activities. Post-closure activities, the final retirement activities, include maintaining the landfill once final certification of closure has been received and monitoring the ground and surface water, gas emissions, and air quality. Closure and post-closure activities are performed after the entire landfill ceases receiving waste (that is, after the landfill is retired). However, capping activities are performed as sections of the landfill become full and are effectively retired. The fact that some of the capping activities are performed while the landfill continues to accept waste does not remove the obligation to perform those intermediate capping activities from the scope of this Statement.

A9. Obligations associated with maintenance, rather than retirement, of a long-lived asset are excluded from the scope of this Statement. The cost of a replacement part that is a component of a long-lived asset is not within the scope of this Statement. Any legal obligations that require disposal of the replaced part are within the scope of this Statement.

Obligations Resulting from the Acquisition, Construction, or Development and (or) Normal Operation of an Asset

A10. Paragraph 2 of this Statement limits its scope to those legal obligations that result from the acquisition, construction, or development and (or) the normal operation of a long-lived asset.

A11. Whether an obligation results from the acquisition, construction, or development of a long-lived asset should, in most circumstances, be clear. For example, if an entity acquires a landfill that is already in operation, an obligation to perform capping, closure, and post-closure activities results from the acquisition and assumption of obligations related to past normal operations of the landfill. Additional obligations will be incurred as a result of future operations of the landfill.

A12. Whether an obligation results from the normal operation of a long-lived asset may require judgment. Obligations that result from the normal operation of an asset should be predictable and likely of occurring. For example, consider a company that owns and operates a nuclear power plant. That company has a legal obligation to perform decontamination activities when the plant ceases operations. Contamination, which gives rise to the obligation, is predictable and likely of occurring and is unavoidable as a result of operating the plant. Therefore, the obligation to perform decontamination activities at that plant results from the normal operation of the plant.

A13. An environmental remediation liability that results from the improper operation of a long-lived asset does not fall within the scope of this Statement. Obligations resulting from improper operations do not represent costs that are an integral part of the tangible long-lived asset and therefore should not be accounted for as part of the cost basis of the asset. For example, a certain amount of spillage may be inherent in the normal operations of a fuel storage facility, but a catastrophic accident caused by noncompliance with a company's safety procedures is not. The obligation to clean up after the catastrophic accident does not result from the normal operation of the facility and is not within the scope of this Statement. An environmental remediation liability that results from the normal operation of a long-lived asset and that is associated with the retirement of that asset shall be accounted for under the provisions of this Statement.

Asset Retirement Obligations with Indeterminate Settlement Dates

A14. An asset retirement obligation may result from the acquisition, construction, or development and (or) normal operation of a long-lived asset that has an indeterminate useful life and thereby an indeterminate settlement date for the asset retirement obligation. Uncertainty about the timing of settlement of the asset retirement obligation does not remove that obligation from the scope of this Statement but will affect the measurement of a liability for that obligation (refer to paragraph A16).

Asset Retirement Obligations Related to Component Parts of Larger Systems

A15. An asset retirement obligation may exist for component parts of a larger system. In some circumstances, the retirement of the component parts may be required before the retirement of the larger system to which the component parts belong. For example,

consider an aluminum smelter that owns and operates several kilns lined with a special type of brick. The kilns have a long useful life, but the bricks wear out after approximately five years of use and are replaced on a periodic basis to maintain optimal efficiency of the kilns. Because the bricks become contaminated with hazardous chemicals while in the kiln, a state law requires that when the bricks are removed, they must be disposed of at a special hazardous waste site. The obligation to dispose of those bricks is within the scope of this Statement. The cost of the replacement bricks and their installation are not part of that obligation.

Liability Recognition—Asset Retirement Obligations with Indeterminate Settlement Dates

A16. Instances may occur in which insufficient information to estimate the fair value of an asset retirement obligation is available. For example, if an asset has an indeterminate useful life, sufficient information to estimate a range of potential settlement dates for the obligation might not be available. In such cases, the liability would be initially recognized in the period in which sufficient information exists to estimate a range of potential settlement dates that is needed to employ a present value technique to estimate fair value.

Liability Recognition—Conditional Obligations

A17. A conditional obligation to perform a retirement activity is within the scope of this Statement. For example, if a governmental unit retains the right (an option) to decide whether to require a retirement activity, there is some uncertainty about whether those retirement activities will be required or waived. Regardless of the uncertainty attributable to the option, a legal obligation to stand ready to perform retirement activities still exists, and the governmental unit might require them to be performed. Uncertainty about whether performance will be required does not defer the recognition of a retirement obligation; rather, that uncertainty is factored into the measurement of the fair value of the liability through assignment of probabilities to cash flows. Uncertainty about performance of conditional obligations shall not prevent the determination of a reasonable estimate of fair value.

A18. A past history of nonenforcement of an unambiguous obligation does not defer recognition of a liability, but its measurement is affected by the uncertainty over the requirement to perform retirement activities. Uncertainty about the requirement to perform retirement activities shall not prevent the determination of a reasonable estimate of fair value. Guidance on how to estimate a liability in the presence of uncertainty about a requirement to perform retirement activities is provided in Appendix C.

Initial Measurement of a Liability for an Asset Retirement Obligation

A19. The objective of the initial measurement of a liability for an asset retirement obligation shall be fair value. Quoted market prices are the best representation of fair value. When market prices are not available, the amount of the liability must be estimated using some other measurement technique. The use of an expected present value technique in measuring the fair value of a liability is discussed in Concepts Statement 7.

A20. In estimating the fair value of a liability for an asset retirement obligation using an expected present value technique, an entity shall begin by estimating cash flows that reflect, to the extent possible, a marketplace assessment of the cost and timing of performing the required retirement activities. The measurement objective is to determine the amount a third party[17] would demand to assume the obligation. Considerations in estimating those cash flows include developing and incorporating explicit assumptions, to the extent possible, about all of the following:

a. The costs that a third party would incur in performing the tasks necessary to retire the asset
b. Other amounts that a third party would include in determining the price of settlement, including, for example, inflation, overhead, equipment charges, profit margin, and advances in technology
c. The extent to which the amount of a third party's costs or the timing of its costs would vary under different future scenarios and the relative probabilities of those scenarios
d. The price that a third party would demand and could expect to receive for bearing the uncertainties and unforeseeable circumstances inherent in the obligation, sometimes referred to as a market-risk premium.

It is expected that uncertainties about the amount and timing of future cash flows can be accommodated by using the expected cash flow technique and therefore will not prevent the determination of a reasonable estimate of fair value.

A21. An entity shall discount estimates of future cash flows using an interest rate that equates to a risk-free interest rate adjusted for the effect of its credit standing (a credit-adjusted risk-free rate).[18] The risk-free interest rate is the interest rate on monetary assets that are essentially risk free and that have maturity dates that coincide with the expected timing of the estimated cash flows required to satisfy the asset retirement obligation.[19] Concepts Statement 7 illustrates an adjustment to the risk-free interest rate to reflect the credit standing of the entity, but acknowledges that adjustments for default risk can be reflected in either the discount rate or the estimated cash flows. The Board believes that in most situations, an entity will know the adjustment required to the risk-free interest rate to reflect its credit standing. Consequently, it would be easier and less complex to reflect that adjustment in the discount rate. In addition, because of the requirements in paragraph 15 relating to upward and downward adjustments in cash flow estimates, it is essential to the operationality of this Statement that the credit standing of the entity be reflected in the interest rate. For those reasons, the Board chose to require that the risk-free rate be adjusted for the credit standing of the entity to determine the discount rate.

A22. Where assets with asset retirement obligations are components of a larger group of assets (for example, a number of oil wells that make up an entire oil field operation), aggregation techniques may be necessary to derive a collective asset retirement obligation. This Statement does not preclude the use of estimates and computational shortcuts that are consistent with the fair value measurement objective when computing an aggregate asset retirement obligation for assets that are components of a larger group of assets.

A23. This Statement requires recognition of the fair value of a conditional asset retirement obligation before the event that either requires or waives performance occurs. Uncertainty surrounding conditional

---

[17]In this context, a third party is meant to encompass participants (or hypothetical participants) that provide settlement of asset retirement obligations in a market.

[18]In determining the adjustment for the effect of its credit standing, an entity should consider the effects of all terms, collateral, and existing guarantees that would affect the amount required to settle the liability.

[19]In the United States, the risk-free rate is the rate for zero-coupon U.S. Treasury instruments.

performance of the retirement obligation is factored into its measurement by assessing the likelihood that performance will be required. In situations in which the conditional aspect has only 2 outcomes and there is no information about which outcome is more probable, a 50 percent likelihood for each outcome shall be used until additional information is available. As the time for notification approaches, more information and a better perspective about the ultimate outcome will likely be obtained. Consequently, reassessment of the timing, amount, and probabilities associated with the expected cash flows may change the amount of the liability recognized. If, as time progresses, it becomes apparent that retirement activities will not be required, the liability and the remaining unamortized asset retirement cost are reduced to zero.

A24. In summary, an unambiguous requirement that gives rise to an asset retirement obligation coupled with a low likelihood of required performance still requires recognition of a liability. Uncertainty about the conditional outcome of the obligation is incorporated into the measurement of the fair value of that liability, not the recognition decision.

Subsequent Recognition and Measurement

A25. In periods subsequent to initial measurement, an entity recognizes the effect of the passage of time on the amount of a liability for an asset retirement obligation. A period-to-period increase in the carrying amount of the liability shall be recognized as an operating item (accretion expense) in the statement of income. An equivalent amount is added to the carrying amount of the liability. To calculate accretion expense, an entity shall multiply the beginning of the period liability balance by the credit-adjusted risk-free rate that existed when the liability was initially measured. The liability shall be adjusted for accretion prior to adjusting for revisions in estimated cash flows.

A26. Revisions to a previously recorded asset retirement obligation will result from changes in the assumptions used to estimate the cash flows required to settle the asset retirement obligation, including changes in estimated probabilities, amounts, and timing of the settlement of the asset retirement obligation, as well as changes in the legal requirements of an obligation. Any changes that result in upward revisions to the undiscounted estimated cash flows shall be treated as a new liability and discounted at the current rate. Any downward revisions to the undiscounted estimated cash flows will result in a reduction of the asset retirement obligation. For downward revisions, the amount of the liability to be removed from the existing accrual shall be discounted at the rate that was used at the time the obligation to which the downward revision relates was originally recorded (or the historical weighted-average rate if the year(s) to which the downward revision applies cannot be determined).

A27. Revisions to the asset retirement obligation result in adjustments of capitalized asset retirement costs and will affect subsequent depreciation of the related asset. Such adjustments are depreciated on a prospective basis.

Appendix B

BACKGROUND INFORMATION AND BASIS FOR CONCLUSIONS

CONTENTS

Appendix B

BACKGROUND INFORMATION AND BASIS FOR CONCLUSIONS

Introduction

B1. This appendix summarizes considerations that Board members deemed significant in reaching the conclusions in this Statement. It includes reasons for accepting certain approaches and rejecting others. Individual Board members gave greater weight to some factors than to others.

Background Information

B2. In February 1994, the Edison Electric Institute (EEI) requested that the Board add a project to its agenda to address accounting for removal costs, including the costs of nuclear decommissioning as well as similar costs incurred in other industries. At its April 1994 meeting, the Financial Accounting Standards Advisory Council (FASAC) discussed the advisability of the Board's adding to its agenda a project limited to accounting for the costs of nuclear decommissioning, a broader project on accounting for removal costs including nuclear decommissioning, or an even broader project on environmental costs. At that time, most FASAC members suggested that the Board undertake either a project on accounting for removal costs or a broader project on environmental costs. In June 1994, the Board also met with representatives from the EEI, the oil and gas industry, the

mining industry, and the AICPA Environmental Task Force to discuss the EEI's request.

B3. In June 1994, the Board added a project to its agenda on accounting for the costs of nuclear decommissioning. Shortly thereafter, the Board expanded the scope of the project to include similar closure or removal-type costs in other industries. An FASB Exposure Draft, *Accounting for Certain Liabilities Related to Closure or Removal of Long-Lived Assets* (initial Exposure Draft), was issued on February 7, 1996. The Board received 123 letters of comment.

B4. In October 1997, the Board decided to continue with the closure or removal project by proceeding toward a revised Exposure Draft. The Board decided to change the title of the project to accounting for obligations associated with the retirement of long-lived assets and the project became subsequently known as the asset retirement obligations project. The Board issued a revised Exposure Draft, *Accounting for Obligations Associated with the Retirement of Long-Lived Assets,* in February 2000 and received 50 letters of comment. The Board concluded that it could reach an informed decision on the basis of existing information without a public hearing.

B5. The major objective of the asset retirement obligations project was to provide accounting requirements for the recognition and measurement of liabilities for obligations associated with the retirement of long-lived assets. Another objective was to provide accounting requirements with respect to the recognition of asset retirement costs as well as guidance for the periodic allocation of those costs to results of operations. The key differences between the initial Exposure Draft and the revised Exposure Draft were in the scope and the requirements for initial measurement of a liability for an asset retirement obligation. Specifically, the revised Exposure Draft (a) broadened the scope of the initial Exposure Draft beyond obligations incurred in the acquisition, construction, development, or early operation of a long-lived asset to asset retirement obligations incurred any time during the life of an asset and (b) proposed that an asset retirement obligation be initially measured at fair value. The initial Exposure Draft would have required an initial measurement that reflected the present value of the estimated future cash flows required to satisfy the closure or removal obligation. One key difference between this Statement and the revised Exposure Draft is in the Statement's scope. This Statement applies only to existing legal obligations, including those for which no formal legal action has been taken but that would be considered legal obligations under the doctrine of promissory estoppel.

Benefits and Costs

B6. The mission of the Board is to establish and improve standards of financial accounting and reporting for the guidance and education of the public, including issuers, auditors, and users of financial information. In fulfilling that mission, the Board must determine that a proposed standard will fill a significant need and that the costs it imposes, compared with possible alternatives, will be justified in relation to the overall benefits of the resulting information. The Board's assessment of the costs and benefits of issuing an accounting standard is unavoidably subjective because there is no method to measure objectively the costs to implement an accounting standard or to quantify the value of improved information in financial statements.

B7. Existing accounting practices for asset retirement obligations were inconsistent in the criteria used for recognition, the measurement objective, and the presentation of those obligations in the financial statements. Some entities did not recognize any asset retirement obligations. Some entities that recognized asset retirement obligations displayed them as a contra-asset. As a result, information that was conveyed in the financial statements about those obligations was inconsistent. This Statement eliminates those inconsistencies and requires disclosure of additional relevant information about those obligations in financial statements.

B8. One of the principal costs of applying this Statement is the cost of implementing the requirement to initially measure the liability for an asset retirement obligation using a fair value measurement objective. Most entities will meet that requirement by using an expected present value technique that incorporates various estimates of expected cash flows. The basis for and procedures necessary to perform that type of calculation can be found in FASB Concepts Statement No. 7, *Using Cash Flow Information and Present Value in Accounting Measurements*. Although many entities have developed information to estimate amounts for asset retirement obligations based on some notion of "cost accumulation," that information probably is not consistent with the requirements of this Statement. Some entities may not have developed any information about asset retirement obligations because, prior to this Statement, they were not required to account for that type of obligation in their financial statements. The Board believes that the benefits resulting from the improvements in financial reporting that result from the application of the requirements of this Statement outweigh the costs of implementing it.

Basis for Conclusions

Scope

B9. The scope of the initial Exposure Draft applied to all entities and to obligations for the closure or removal of long-lived assets that possessed all of the following characteristics:

a. The obligation is incurred in the acquisition, construction, development, or early operation of a long-lived asset.
b. The obligation is related to the closure or removal of a long-lived asset and cannot be satisfied until the current operation or use of the asset ceases.
c. The obligation cannot be realistically avoided if the asset is operated for its intended use.

B10. The objective of those characteristics was to limit the obligations included in the scope to those that were similar in nature to nuclear decommissioning costs and that could, therefore, be recognized and measured according to the accounting model that was proposed for decommissioning obligations.[20] Through educational sessions and the comment letters, the Board learned that, in some industries, closure or removal obligations[21] are not incurred in the same pattern as those for decommissioning. Respondents expressed concern that those characteristics could be interpreted to allow many types of closure or removal obligations to fall outside the scope of the initial Exposure Draft.

B11. Many comments related to the intended meaning of *early operation* as used in the first characteristic in paragraph B9. Many respondents indicated that it was unclear whether that phrase could be interpreted to mean that obligations incurred ratably over the operating life of a long-lived asset were not within the scope of the initial Exposure Draft. Others said that that phrase was ambiguous and, therefore, could result in entities within the same industry accounting for the same type of obligation differently depending on how they interpreted the phrase for their particular situation. Some respondents indicated that the Board should define *early operation* by using bright-line conditions or describe that phrase by using specific examples from various industries.

B12. In deliberations leading to the revised Exposure Draft, the Board decided to eliminate the first characteristic, thereby broadening the scope of the project to asset retirement obligations incurred any time during the life of an asset. In making that decision, the Board emphasized that the determination of whether to recognize a liability should be based on the characteristics of the obligation instead of when that obligation arose. Therefore, the Board agreed that it was unnecessary to limit the scope to obligations that were similar in nature to decommissioning obligations. It also decided that the scope should be equally applicable to asset retirement obligations incurred during the operating life of a long-lived asset. In addition, the Board decided that the requirements for (a) a discounted liability measurement and (b) the capitalization of asset retirement costs were applicable regardless of when in the life of an asset a liability is incurred.

B13. Respondents to the initial Exposure Draft indicated that the second characteristic in paragraph B9 was subject to ambiguous interpretation, especially for an obligation that could be partially satisfied over the useful life of a long-lived asset even though it would not be completely satisfied until operation of that asset ceased. Specifically, in that case, one interpretation of the second characteristic is that the portion of the obligation that could be satisfied before the current operation or use of the asset ceases would not fall within the scope of this Statement, while the remaining portion of the obligation would be considered within the scope. An alternative interpretation is that the entire obligation would be considered to be outside the scope of this Statement.

B14. In deliberations leading to the revised Exposure Draft, the Board decided to eliminate the second characteristic. It observed that the nature of asset retirement obligations in various industries is such that the obligations are not necessarily satisfied when the current operation or use of the asset ceases and, in fact, can be settled during operation of the asset or after the operations cease. The Board agreed that the timing of the ultimate settlement of a liability was unrelated to and should not affect its initial recognition in the financial statements provided the obligation is associated with the retirement of a tangible long-lived asset.

B15. The Board retained the essence of the third characteristic in paragraph B9 that limited the obligations included within the scope to those that cannot be realistically avoided if the asset is operated for its intended use. Specifically, paragraph 2 of this Statement limits the obligations included within the scope to those that are unavoidable by an entity as a result of the acquisition, construction, or development and (or) the normal operation of a long-lived asset, except for certain obligations of lessees.

B16. The initial and revised Exposure Drafts included in their scope both legal and constructive obligations. In the basis for conclusions of the initial Exposure Draft, the Board stressed that the identification of constructive obligations will be more difficult than the identification of legal obligations. It noted that judgment would be required to determine if constructive obligations exist. Many respondents to

---

[20]In general, that model required (a) recognition of the amount of a decommissioning obligation as a liability when incurred, (b) measurement of that liability based on discounted future cash flows using a cost-accumulation approach, and (c) capitalization of the decommissioning costs (the offsetting debit) by increasing the cost of the nuclear facility.

[21]Although the nature of *closure or removal obligations* is similar to the nature of *asset retirement obligations,* the former is used to refer to the obligations that were within the scope of the initial Exposure Draft, and the latter is used to refer to the obligations that are within the broader scope of this Statement.

the initial Exposure Draft indicated that more guidance was needed with respect to the identification of constructive obligations. Therefore, in the revised Exposure Draft, the Board focused on the three characteristics of a liability in paragraph 36 of FASB Concepts Statement No. 6, *Elements of Financial Statements,* rather than on the distinction between a legal obligation and a constructive obligation. Nevertheless, many respondents to the revised Exposure Draft addressed the notion of constructive obligations. Many of those respondents stated that without improved guidance for determining whether a constructive obligation exists, inconsistent application of this Statement would likely result. In deliberations of the revised Exposure Draft, the Board conceded that determining when a constructive obligation exists is very subjective. To achieve more consistent application of this Statement, the Board decided that only existing legal obligations, including legal obligations under the doctrine of promissory estoppel, should be included in the scope. Legal obligations, as used in this Statement, encompass both legally enforceable obligations and constructive obligations, as those terms are used in Concepts Statement 6.

B17. In addition to comments about scope-limiting characteristics, respondents expressed uncertainty about whether the scope of the initial Exposure Draft applied to closure and removal obligations for interim property retirements and replacements for component parts of larger systems.[22] The Board believes that there is no conceptual difference between interim property retirements and replacements and those retirements that occur in circumstances in which the retired asset is not replaced. Therefore, any asset retirement obligation associated with the retirement of or the retirement and replacement of a component part of a larger system qualifies for recognition provided that the obligation meets the definition of a liability. The cost of replacement components is excluded.

B18. Some respondents questioned whether asset retirement obligations with indeterminate settlement dates, such as for an oil refinery, were within the scope of the initial Exposure Draft. They suggested that it would be difficult to estimate a retirement obligation because of uncertainty about the timing of retirement.

B19. The Board decided that asset retirement obligations with indeterminate settlement dates should be included within the scope of this Statement. Uncertainty about the timing of the settlement date does not change the fact that an entity has a legal obligation. The Board acknowledged that although there is an obligation, measurement of that obligation might not be possible if literally no information exists about the timing of settlement. However, some information about the timing of the settlement of a retirement obligation will become available as time goes by. The Board decided that an entity should measure and recognize the fair value of an obligation at the point in time when some information is available to develop various assumptions about the potential timing of cash flows.

B20. The Board also clarified the scope of this Statement relative to the scope of AICPA Statement of Position 96-1, *Environmental Remediation Liabilities.* This Statement applies to legal obligations associated with asset retirements. Legal obligations exist as a result of existing or enacted law, statute, ordinance, or written or oral contract or by legal construction of a contract under the doctrine of promissory estoppel. SOP 96-1 applies to environmental remediation liabilities that relate to pollution arising from some past act, generally as a result of the provisions of Superfund, the corrective-action provisions of the Resource Conservation and Recovery Act of 1976, or analogous state and non-U.S. laws and regulations. An environmental remediation liability that results from the normal operation of a long-lived asset and that is associated with the retirement of that asset shall be accounted for under the provisions of this Statement. An environmental remediation liability that results from other than the normal operation of a long-lived asset probably falls within the scope of SOP 96-1.

Recognition of a Liability for an Asset Retirement Obligation

B21. Prior to this Statement, the objective of many accounting practices was not to recognize and measure obligations associated with the retirement of long-lived assets. Rather, the objective was to achieve a particular expense recognition pattern for

---

[22]Examples of interim property retirements and replacements for component parts of larger systems are components of transmission and distribution systems (utility poles), railroad ties, a single oil well that is part of a larger oil field, and aircraft engines. The assets in those examples may or may not have associated retirement obligations.

those obligations over the operating life of the associated long-lived asset. Using that objective, some entities followed an approach whereby they estimated an amount that would satisfy the costs of retiring the asset and accrued a portion of that amount each period as an expense and as a liability. Other entities used that objective and the provision in paragraph 37 of FASB Statement No. 19, *Financial Accounting and Reporting by Oil and Gas Producing Companies,* that allows them to increase periodic depreciation expense by increasing the depreciable base of a long-lived asset for an amount representing estimated asset retirement costs. Under either of those approaches, the amount of liability or accumulated depreciation recognized in a statement of financial position usually differs from the amount of obligation that an entity actually has incurred. In effect, by focusing on an objective of achieving a particular expense recognition pattern, accounting practices developed that disregarded or circumvented the recognition and measurement requirements of FASB Concepts Statements.

B22. Paragraph 37 of Statement 19 states that "estimated dismantlement, restoration, and abandonment costs . . . shall be taken into account in determining amortization and depreciation rates." Application of that paragraph has the effect of accruing an expense irrespective of the requirements for liability recognition in the FASB Concepts Statements. In doing so, it results in recognition of accumulated depreciation that can exceed the historical cost of a long-lived asset. The Board concluded that an entity should be precluded from including an amount for an asset retirement obligation in the depreciable base of a long-lived asset unless that amount also meets the recognition criteria in this Statement. When an entity recognizes a liability for an asset retirement obligation, it also will recognize an increase in the carrying amount of the related long-lived asset. Consequently, depreciation of that asset will not result in the recognition of accumulated depreciation in excess of the historical cost of a long-lived asset.

B23. This Statement applies to legal obligations associated with the retirement of a tangible long-lived asset that result from the acquisition, construction, or development and (or) the normal operation of a long-lived asset, except for certain obligations of lessees. As used in this Statement, a legal obligation is an obligation that a party is required to settle as a result of existing or enacted law, statute, ordinance, written or oral contract or by legal construction under the doctrine of promissory estoppel. The Board believes that using legal obligations as a scope characteristic includes appropriate constructive obligations. An asset retirement obligation encompasses the three characteristics of a liability set forth in paragraphs 36–40 of Concepts Statement 6 as discussed below. Those characteristics are interrelated; however, each characteristic must be present to meet the definition of a liability.

Duty or responsibility

B24. The first characteristic of a liability is that an entity has "a present duty or responsibility to one or more other entities that entails settlement by probable future transfer or use of assets at a specified or determinable date, on occurrence of a specified event, or on demand." A duty or responsibility becomes a *present* duty or responsibility when an obligating event occurs that leaves the entity little or no discretion to avoid a future transfer or use of assets. A present duty or responsibility does not mean that the obligation must be satisfied immediately. Rather, if events or circumstances have occurred that, as discussed below, give an entity little or no discretion to avoid a future transfer or use of assets, that entity has a present duty or responsibility. If an entity is required by current laws, regulations, or contracts to settle an asset retirement obligation upon retirement of the asset, that requirement is a present duty.

B25. In general, a duty or responsibility is created by an entity's promise, on which others are justified in relying, to take a particular course of action (to perform). That performance will entail the future transfer or use of assets. An entity's promise may be:

a. Unconditional or conditional on the occurrence of a specified future event that is or is not within the entity's control
b. Stated in words, either oral or written, or inferred from the entity's past practice, which, absent evidence to the contrary, others can presume that the entity will continue.

B26. Others are justified in relying on an entity to perform as promised if:

a. They or their representatives are the recipient of the entity's promise.
b. They can reasonably expect the entity to perform (that is, the entity's promise is credible).
c. They either will benefit from the entity's performance or will suffer loss or harm from the entity's nonperformance.

B27. In other situations, a duty or responsibility is created by circumstances in which, absent a promise, an entity finds itself bound to perform, and others are justified in relying on the entity to perform.[23] In those circumstances, others are justified in relying on an entity to perform if:

a. They can reasonably expect the entity to perform.
b. They either will benefit from the entity's performance or will suffer loss or harm from the entity's nonperformance.

B28. The reasonable expectation that the entity will perform is inferred from the particular circumstances, and those circumstances bind the entity to the same degree that it would have been bound had it made a promise.

B29. The assessment of whether there is a legal duty or responsibility for an asset retirement obligation is usually quite clear. However, the assessment of whether there is a duty or responsibility resulting, for example, from a past practice or a representation made to another entity, including the public at large, will require judgment, especially with respect to whether others are justified in relying on the entity to perform as promised. Those judgments should be made within the framework of the doctrine of promissory estoppel (refer to paragraph A3). Once an entity determines that a duty or responsibility exists, it will then need to assess whether an obligating event has occurred that leaves it little or no discretion to avoid the future transfer or use of assets. If such an obligating event has occurred, an asset retirement obligation meets the definition of a liability and qualifies for recognition in the financial statements. However, if an obligating event that leaves an entity little or no discretion to avoid the future transfer or use of assets has not occurred, an asset retirement obligation does not meet the definition of a liability and, therefore, should not be recognized in the financial statements.

Little or no discretion to avoid a future transfer or use of assets

B30. The second characteristic of a liability is that "... the duty or responsibility obligates a particular entity, leaving it little or no discretion to avoid the future sacrifice." Paragraph 203 of Concepts Statement 6 elaborates on that characteristic by indicating

that an entity is not obligated to transfer or use assets in the future if it can avoid that transfer or use of assets at its discretion without significant penalty.

Obligating event

B31. The third characteristic of a liability is that "... the transaction or other event obligating the entity has already happened." The definition of a liability distinguishes between present obligations and future obligations of an entity. Only present obligations are liabilities under the definition, and they are liabilities of a particular entity as a result of the occurrence of transactions or other events or circumstances affecting the entity. Identifying the obligating event is often difficult, especially in situations that involve the occurrence of a series of transactions or other events or circumstances affecting the entity. For example, in the case of an asset retirement obligation, a law or an entity's promise may create a duty or responsibility, but that law or promise in and of itself may not be the obligating event that results in an entity's having little or no discretion to avoid a future transfer or use of assets. An entity must look to the nature of the duty or responsibility to assess whether the obligating event has occurred. For example, in the case of a nuclear power facility, an entity assumes responsibility for decontamination of that facility upon receipt of the license to operate it. However, no obligation to decontaminate exists until the facility is operated and contamination occurs. Therefore, the contamination, not the receipt of the license, constitutes the obligating event.

Initial Recognition and Measurement of a Liability

B32. The initial Exposure Draft would have required that a liability for an asset retirement obligation be initially measured at an amount that reflected the present value of the estimated future cash flows required to satisfy the closure or removal obligation. Subsequent to the issuance of the initial Exposure Draft, the Board issued Concepts Statement 7. In that Concepts Statement, the Board concluded that "the only objective of present value, when used in accounting measurements at initial recognition and fresh-start measurements, is to estimate fair value" (paragraph 25). Consequently, in its deliberations leading to the revised Exposure Draft, the Board concluded that the objective for the initial measurement of a liability for an asset retirement obligation is fair

---

[23]For example, an entity that has recently commenced operations in a particular industry may find itself bound to perform by practice that is predominant in that industry. Absent evidence to the contrary, others are justified in relying on the entity to follow that practice.

value, which is the amount that an entity would be required to pay in an active market to settle the asset retirement obligation in a current transaction in circumstances other than a forced settlement. In that context, fair value represents the amount that a willing third party of comparable credit standing would demand and could expect to receive to assume all of the duties, uncertainties, and risks inherent in the entity's obligation.

B33. The revised Exposure Draft proposed that an entity should recognize a liability for an asset retirement obligation in the period in which all of the following criteria are met:

a. The obligation meets the definition of a liability in paragraph 35 of Concepts Statement 6.
b. A future transfer of assets associated with the obligation is probable.
c. The amount of the liability can be reasonably estimated.

B34. The definition of a liability in Concepts Statement 6 uses the term *probable* in a different sense than it is used in FASB Statement No. 5, *Accounting for Contingencies*. As used in Statement 5, probable requires a high degree of expectation. The term probable in the definition of a liability is intended to acknowledge that business and other economic activities occur in an environment characterized by uncertainty in which few outcomes are certain.

B35. Statement 5 and Concepts Statement 7 deal with uncertainty in different ways. Statement 5 deals with uncertainty about whether a loss has been incurred by setting forth criteria to determine when to *recognize* a loss contingency. Concepts Statement 7, on the other hand, addresses measurement of liabilities and provides a *measurement* technique to deal with uncertainty about the amount and timing of the future cash flows necessary to settle the liability. Because of the Board's decision to incorporate probability into the measurement of an asset retirement obligation, the guidance in Statement 5 and FASB Interpretation No. 14, *Reasonable Estimation of the Amount of a Loss,* is not applicable.

B36. The objective of recognizing the fair value of an asset retirement obligation will result in recognition of some asset retirement obligations for which the likelihood of future settlement, although more

than zero, is less than probable from a Statement 5 perspective.[24] A third party would charge a price to assume an uncertain liability even though the likelihood of a future sacrifice is less than probable. Similarly, when the likelihood of a future sacrifice is probable, the price a third party would charge to assume an obligation incorporates expectations about some future events that are less than probable. Thus, this Statement does not retain the criterion (paragraph B33(b)) that a future transfer of assets associated with the obligation is probable for recognition purposes. This Statement does retain the criteria concerning the existence of a liability (paragraph B33(a)) and the ability to make a reasonable estimate of the amount (paragraph B33(c)).

B37. The Board considered two alternatives to fair value for initial measurement of the liability associated with an asset retirement obligation. One alternative was an entity-specific measurement that would attempt to value the liability in the context of a particular entity. An entity-specific measurement is different from a fair value measurement because it substitutes the entity's assumptions for those that marketplace participants make. Therefore, the assumptions used in an entity-specific measurement of a liability would reflect the entity's expected settlement of the liability and the role of the entity's proprietary skills in that settlement.

B38. Another alternative was a cost-accumulation measurement that would attempt to capture the costs (for example, incremental costs) that an entity anticipates it will incur in settling the liability over its expected term. A cost-accumulation measurement is different from an entity-specific measurement because it excludes assumptions related to a risk premium and may exclude overhead and other internal costs. It is different from a fair value measurement because it excludes those assumptions as well as any additional assumptions market participants would make about estimated cash flows, such as a market-based profit margin.

B39. Most respondents to the revised Exposure Draft disagreed with the Board's decision to require that a liability for an asset retirement obligation be initially measured at fair value. In general, those respondents stated that in most cases an entity settles an asset retirement obligation with internal resources rather than by contracting with a third party and,

---

[24]Recognition at fair value of an obligation for which the likelihood of future settlement is less than probable is consistent with the criteria described in FASB Concepts Statement No. 5, *Recognition and Measurement in Financial Statements of Business Enterprises.*

therefore, a fair value measurement objective would not provide a reasonable estimate of the costs that an entity expects to incur to settle an asset retirement obligation. Additionally, those respondents stated that a fair value measurement objective would overstate an entity's assets and liabilities and result in a gain being reported upon the settlement of the obligation. For those reasons, most of those respondents stated that the Board should adopt a cost-accumulation approach.

B40. The Board considered a cost-accumulation approach[25] in its deliberations of Concepts Statement 7. However, the Board observed there were several problems with that approach.

- Cost-accumulation measurements are accounting conventions, not attempts to replicate market transactions. Consequently, it may be difficult to discern the objective of the measurement. For example, is the "cost" based on direct, incremental expenditures or is it a "full-cost" computation that includes an allocation of overhead and fixed costs? Which costs are included in the overhead pool? Lacking a clear measurement objective, any cost accumulation method would inevitably have to be based on rules that are essentially arbitrary.
- Cost-accumulation measurements are inherently intent-driven and thus lack comparability. One entity might expect to settle all of its asset retirement obligations using internal resources. Another might expect to use internal and outsourced resources. Still another might expect to outsource the settlement of all its obligations. All three could describe the resulting measurement as "cost accumulation," but the results would hardly be comparable—each entity would have a different measurement objective for the same liability.
- Cost-accumulation measurements present a "value" on the balance sheet that an entity would not accept in an exchange transaction. A third party would not willingly assume an asset retirement obligation at a price equal to the cost-accumulation measure. That party would include a margin for the risk involved and a profit margin for performing the service.

Of overriding importance, Board members were concerned that identical liabilities (assuming equivalent credit standing) would be measured at different amounts by different entities. The Board believes that the *value* of a liability is the same regardless of how an entity intends to settle the liability (unless the entities have different credit standing) and that the relative efficiency of an entity in settling a liability using internal resources (that is, the entity's profit margin) should be reflected over the course of its settlement and not before.

B41. If an entity elects to settle an asset retirement obligation using its internal resources, the total cash outflows—no more, no less—required to settle the obligation will, at some time, be included in operating results. The *timing* of when those cash outflows are recognized will affect the profitability of different periods, but when all of the costs of settling the liability have been incurred, the cumulative profitability from that transaction over all periods will be determined only by the total of those cash outflows. The real issue is which period or periods should reflect the efficiencies of incurring lower costs than the costs that would be required by the market to settle the liability. The Board believes it is those periods in which the activities necessary to settle the liability are incurred. If the measurement of the liability does not include the full amount of the costs required by the market to settle it, including a normal profit margin, the "profits" will be recognized prematurely.

Recognition and Allocation of Asset Retirement Costs

B42. This Statement requires that upon initial recognition of a liability, an entity capitalizes an asset retirement cost by increasing the carrying amount of the related long-lived asset. The Board believes that asset retirement costs are integral to or are a prerequisite for operating the long-lived asset and noted that current accounting practice includes in the historical-cost basis of an asset all costs that are necessary to prepare the asset for its intended use. Capitalized asset retirement costs are not a separate asset because there is no specific and separate future economic benefit that results from those costs. In other words, the future economic benefit of those costs lies in the productive asset that is used in the entity's operations.

B43. The Board considered whether asset retirement costs should be recognized as a separately identifiable intangible asset. The Board acknowledges that in certain situations an intangible asset, such as the right to operate a long-lived asset, may be acquired

---

[25]A cost-accumulation approach is a measurement that includes some of the costs an entity would incur to construct an asset or settle a liability.

when obligations for asset retirement costs are incurred. However, the intangible asset is not separable from the long-lived asset, and similar intangible assets, such as building and zoning permits, are generally included in the historical cost of the long-lived asset that is acquired or constructed. Furthermore, the acquisition of an intangible asset in exchange for the agreement to incur asset retirement costs does not occur in all situations.

B44. A majority of respondents to the revised Exposure Draft agreed with the requirement to recognize an amount as an increase in the carrying amount of an asset upon initial recognition of a liability for an asset retirement obligation. However, some respondents indicated that the capitalized amount should be separately classified as an intangible asset because, for example, property taxes might increase if it was classified as a plant cost. For the reasons discussed in paragraph B43, the Board decided that such a concern did not warrant special consideration for classification of an asset retirement cost as an intangible asset.

B45. Because the scope of this Statement includes some obligations incurred more or less ratably over the entire life of a long-lived asset, the Board considered whether asset retirement costs associated with those types of obligations should be recognized as an expense of the period rather than capitalized.

B46. The Board could not develop any rationale for distinguishing between which asset retirement costs should be capitalized and which should be recognized as an expense of the period. The Board concluded that whether a cost is incurred upon acquisition or incurred ratably over the life of an asset does not change its underlying nature and its association with the asset. Therefore, the Board decided that an entity should capitalize all asset retirement costs by increasing the carrying amount of the related long-lived asset. The Board decided to couple that provision with a requirement that an entity allocate that cost to expense using a systematic and rational method over periods in which the related asset is expected to provide benefits. Application of a systematic and rational method does not preclude an entity from using an allocation method that would have the effect of capitalizing an amount of cost and allocating an equal amount to expense in the same accounting period. The Board concluded that a requirement for capitalization of an asset retirement cost along with a requirement for the systematic and rational allocation of it to expense achieves the objectives of (a) obtain-

ing a measure of cost that more closely reflects the entity's total investment in the asset and (b) permitting the allocation of that cost, or portions thereof, to expense in the periods in which the related asset is expected to provide benefits.

B47. The Board noted that if the asset for which there is an associated asset retirement obligation were to be sold, the price a buyer would consent to pay for that asset would reflect an estimate of the fair value of the asset retirement obligation. Because that asset retirement obligation meets the definition of a liability, however, the Board believes that reporting it as a liability with a corresponding increase in the carrying amount of the asset for the asset retirement costs, which has the same net effect as incorporating the fair value of the costs to settle the liability in the valuation of the asset, is more representationally faithful and in concert with Concepts Statement 6.

Subsequent Measurement

B48. The Board considered whether to require a *fresh-start approach* or an *interest method of allocation* for subsequent measurement of the liability for an asset retirement obligation. Using a fresh-start approach, the liability would be remeasured at fair value each period, and all changes in that fair value, including those associated with changes in interest rates, would be recognized in the financial statements. Using an interest method of allocation, the liability would not be remeasured at fair value each period. Instead, an accounting convention would be employed to measure period-to-period changes in the liability resulting from the passage of time and revisions to cash flow estimates. Those changes would then be incorporated into a remeasurement of the liability. That convention would not include changes in interest rates in that remeasurement.

B49. The major advantage of a fresh-start approach over an interest method of allocation is that the fresh-start approach results in the liability being carried in the financial statements at fair value at each reporting period. To preserve the advantages of a fair value measurement objective, the Board concluded in Concepts Statement 7 that fair value should be the objective of fresh-start measurements. The major disadvantage of a fair value objective is that it results in a more volatile expense recognition pattern than an interest method of allocation primarily due to the recognition of changes in fair value resulting from period-to-period changes in interest rates. For entities that incur a liability ratably over the life of an asset, a fresh-start approach may be less burdensome to apply than an interest method of allocation because total expected cash flows are all discounted at a current interest rate. While a fresh-start approach and an interest method of allocation both require revised estimates of expected cash flows each period, under a fresh-start approach the estimated cash flows would all be discounted at the current rate. Alternatively, an interest method of allocation requires maintenance of detailed records of expected cash flows because each layer of the liability is discounted by employing a predetermined interest amortization scheme.

B50. In May 1999, some Board members and staff met with industry representatives to discuss the advantages and disadvantages of a fresh-start approach versus an interest method of allocation for subsequent measurement of a liability for an asset retirement obligation. The industry representatives were asked to prepare examples that were used as a basis for providing input to the Board about the accounting results obtained under the two approaches and the complexity or simplicity of one approach compared with the other.

B51. The industry representatives agreed that the major advantages of a fresh-start approach are that it (a) results in the liability for an asset retirement obligation being carried in the financial statements at fair value and (b) is somewhat less burdensome to apply than an interest method of allocation. However, they emphasized that those advantages do not outweigh the overwhelming disadvantage resulting from the volatile expense recognition pattern created by the requirement under the fresh-start approach to recognize period-to-period changes in interest rates through accretion expense. In fact, they stressed that a fresh-start approach could create negative expense recognition in periods of increasing interest rates and that the effects of significant changes in interest rates during a period could, in certain circumstances, result in gains or losses attributable to the change in the measurement of the asset retirement obligation that would overwhelm income from continuing operations.

B52. The Board agreed that, conceptually, a fresh-start approach is preferable to an interest method of allocation for subsequent measurement of a liability for an asset retirement obligation. However, it acknowledged the perceived disadvantage of the volatile expense recognition pattern resulting from the use of the fresh-start approach. The Board decided that it could justify a departure from the conclusions in Concepts Statement 7, in this instance, because of

the volatility a fair value measurement would entail and because the capitalized amount of the associated asset retirement cost would not be measured at fair value in subsequent periods. Until fair value is required for subsequent measurement of more (or all) liabilities, the Board decided that it may be premature to require that type of measurement in this Statement. For those reasons, the Board decided to require an interest method of allocation for subsequent measurement of a liability for an asset retirement obligation.

B53. Subsequent measurement using an interest method of allocation requires that an entity identify undiscounted estimated cash flows associated with the initial fair value measurement of the liability. Therefore, an entity that obtains the initial fair value of a liability for an asset retirement obligation from, for example, a market price, must nonetheless determine the undiscounted cash flows and estimated timing of those cash flows that are embodied in that fair value amount in order to apply the subsequent measurement requirements of this Statement. Appendix E of this Statement includes an example that illustrates a procedure to impute undiscounted cash flows from market prices.

Measurement of changes resulting from revisions to cash flow estimates

B54. The Board considered situations that might give rise to a change in cash flow estimates. Some situations might occur when a new law is enacted that gives rise to previously unrecognized asset retirement obligations. Another situation might be a *change* in a law that changes the expected cash outflows required to settle an asset retirement obligation. Still other situations might arise as a result of changes in technology or inflation assumptions. The Board considered the appropriate discount rate to apply in each of those circumstances. One possible answer would be to apply the current discount rate to a new obligation and use historical discount rates when there is a modification to the previous cash flow estimates. In the course of its discussion, however, the Board realized that it might be difficult to distinguish the changes in cash flows that arise from a new liability from those attributable to a modification to an estimate for an existing liability. For practical reasons, the Board decided that upward revisions in the undiscounted cash flows related to an asset retirement obligation should be discounted at the current credit-adjusted risk-free rate and that downward revisions in the undiscounted cash flows should be discounted using historical discount rates. If an entity cannot identify the period in which the original cash flows were estimated, it may use a weighted-average credit-adjusted risk-free rate to measure a change in the liability resulting from a downward revision to estimated cash flows.

B55. The Board concluded that revisions in estimates of cash flows are refinements of the amount of the asset retirement obligation, and as such are also refinements of the estimated asset retirement costs that result in adjustments to the carrying amounts of the related asset. Therefore, the Board noted that it was not necessary to distinguish revisions in cash flow estimates that arise from changes in assumptions from those revisions that arise from a new liability—both adjust the carrying amount of the related asset.

Measurement of changes in the liability due to the passage of time (accretion expense)

B56. Also for practical reasons, the Board decided that an entity should be required to measure accretion expense on the carrying amount of the liability by using the same credit-adjusted risk-free rate or rates used to initially measure the liability at fair value.

B57. The Board discussed whether it should specify how the amount representing a change in the liability due to the passage of time should be classified in the statement of operations. The revised Exposure Draft proposed that such a change was most appropriately described as interest expense and that, therefore, an entity should be required to classify it as such in its statement of operations. Respondents expressed concern about the classification as interest expense. Some respondents stated that financial statement users view interest expense as a financing cost arising from borrowing and lending transactions. They also stated that classifying the accretion of the liability as interest expense would distort certain financial ratios, hindering some entities' ability to satisfy current debt covenants and to obtain future borrowings. In response to those concerns, the Board decided that the only requirement should be that the period-to-period change in the liability be classified as a separate item in the operating portion of the income statement.

B58. The Board also discussed whether accretion expense on the liability for an asset retirement obligation should qualify for the pool of interest eligible for capitalization under the provisions of paragraph 12 of FASB Statement No. 34, *Capitalization of Interest Cost.* Specifically, paragraph 12 states that "the

amount of interest cost to be capitalized for qualifying assets is intended to be that portion of the interest cost incurred during the assets' acquisition periods that theoretically could have been avoided . . . if expenditures for the assets had not been made." Paragraph 1 of Statement 34 states that "for the purposes of this Statement, *interest cost* includes interest recognized on obligations having explicit interest rates, interest imputed on certain types of payables in accordance with APB Opinion No. 21, *Interest on Receivables and Payables,* and interest related to a capital lease determined in accordance with FASB Statement No. 13, *Accounting for Leases*" (footnote reference omitted). The Board decided that accretion expense on the liability for an asset retirement obligation should not qualify for interest capitalization because it does not qualify as *interest cost* under the provisions of paragraph 1 of Statement 34.

Funding and Assurance Provisions

B59. In some circumstances, an entity is legally required to provide assurance that it will be able to satisfy its asset retirement obligations. That assurance may be accomplished by demonstrating that the financial resources and financial condition of the entity are sufficient to assure that it can meet those obligations. Other commonly used methods of providing assurance include surety bonds, insurance policies, letters of credit, guarantees by other entities, and establishment of trust funds or identification of other funds for satisfying the asset retirement obligations.

B60. The effect of surety bonds, letters of credit, and guarantees is to provide assurance that third parties will provide amounts to satisfy the asset retirement obligations if the entity that has primary responsibility (the obligor) to do so cannot or does not fulfill its obligations. The possibility that a third party will satisfy the asset retirement obligations does not relieve the obligor from its primary responsibility for those obligations. If a third party is required to satisfy asset retirement obligations due to the failure or inability of the obligor to do so directly, the obligor would then have a liability to the third party. Established generally accepted accounting principles require that the entity's financial statements reflect its obligations even if it has obtained surety bonds, letters of credit, or guarantees by others. However, as discussed in paragraph 16 of this Statement, the effects of those provisions should be considered in adjusting the risk-free interest rate for the effect of the entity's credit standing to arrive at the credit-adjusted risk-free rate.

B61. The option of prepaying an asset retirement obligation may exist; however, it would rarely, if ever, be exercised because prepayment would not relieve the entity of its liability for future changes in its asset retirement obligations. Obtaining insurance for asset retirement obligations is currently as rare as prepayment of those obligations. Because of the limited instances, if any, in which prepayment of asset retirement obligations is made or insurance is acquired, the Board decided to address neither topic. However, the Board noted that even if insurance was obtained, the liability would continue to exist.

B62. In evaluating what effect, if any, assets identified to satisfy asset retirement obligations should have on the accounting and reporting of liabilities, the Board considered two approaches that would have resulted in reporting less than the amount of the present liability for an asset retirement obligation. Under one approach, any assets dedicated to satisfy the asset retirement obligation would, for financial reporting purposes, be offset against the liability. Under the other approach, those dedicated assets could be viewed as an extinguishment of the liability in whole or in part.

B63. Paragraph 7 of APB Opinion No. 10, *Omnibus Opinion—1966,* and FASB Interpretation No. 39, *Offsetting of Amounts Related to Certain Contracts,* establish the general criteria for offsetting of amounts in the statement of financial position. Paragraph 50 of Interpretation 39 discusses offsetting of trust funds established for nuclear decommissioning, which is one of the asset retirement obligations within the scope of this Statement. Those trust funds cannot be offset because the right of offset is not enforceable at law and the payees for costs of asset retirement obligations generally have not been identified at the reporting date.

B64. Some have suggested that trust funds established to meet obligations for pensions and other postretirement benefits are similar to the trust funds established for nuclear decommissioning. In FASB Statements No. 87, *Employers' Accounting for Pensions,* and No. 106, *Employers' Accounting for Postretirement Benefits Other Than Pensions,* the Board provided specific requirements to allow offsetting of plan assets in trust funds established for pension benefits and for other postretirement benefits against the related liabilities of those plans. The Board noted that the offsetting provisions in Statements 87 and 106 are exceptions influenced, in part, by then-existing practice. In addition, the offsetting allowed in State-

ments 87 and 106 is one part of an accounting model that also allows for delayed recognition in financial statements of the changes in the values of the plan assets and liabilities. This Statement provides for immediate recognition of changes in estimated cash flows related to asset retirement obligations. Changes in certain assets dedicated to satisfy those obligations that are subject to the provisions of FASB Statement No. 115, *Accounting for Certain Investments in Debt and Equity Securities,* would also be recognized immediately. The Board decided that it should not provide an exception to the general principle for offsetting in this Statement.

B65. FASB Statement No. 140, *Accounting for Transfers and Servicing of Financial Assets and Extinguishments of Liabilities,* requires that a liability be derecognized if and only if either the debtor pays the creditor and is relieved of its obligation for the liability or the debtor is legally released from being the primary obligor under the liability. Therefore, a liability is not considered extinguished by an in-substance defeasance.

Leasing Transactions

B66. The Board considered whether to amend FASB Statement No. 13, *Accounting for Leases,* and related leasing literature to address asset retirement obligations associated with leased property. However, the Board chose not to amend the existing leasing literature for a number of reasons. When the Board undertook this project, it did not have as an objective a revision of the accounting requirements for leasing transactions. The Board realized that a revision of the existing leasing literature to incorporate the requirements of this Statement would be difficult to accomplish in a limited-scope amendment because of the requirements of the leasing literature with respect to present value measurements and certain concepts concerning how payments for the leased property and residual values affect the criteria for lease classification. Because those aspects of the leasing literature are interrelated and fundamental to the lease accounting model, the Board concluded that a wholesale amendment of the existing leasing literature would likely be required in order to conform the pertinent aspects of the lease accounting model to the accounting model in this Statement. The Board agreed that any substantial revision of the existing leasing literature should be addressed in a separate project. The Board also recognized that Statement 13 (as amended) already contains guidance for lessees with respect to certain obligations that meet the provisions in paragraph 2 of this Statement. The Board concluded that by including in the scope of this Statement all lessor obligations in connection with leased property that meet the provisions in paragraph 2 of this Statement and those lessee obligations in connection with leased property that meet the provisions in paragraph 2 of this Statement but do not meet the definition of either minimum lease payments or contingent rentals in paragraph 5 of Statement 13, it could retain substantially the same scope as it originally contemplated for this project without an amendment of the existing leasing literature.

Rate-Regulated Entities

B67. The Board considered how existing rate-making practices for entities subject to FASB Statement No. 71, *Accounting for the Effects of Certain Types of Regulation,* would affect the accounting by those entities for costs related to asset retirement obligations. The way in which those costs are treated for financial reporting purposes and the way in which they are treated for rate-making purposes often differ. The most common differences arise from different estimates by the entity and its regulator of the future cost of asset retirement activities. Those differences may relate to the estimates of the cost of performing asset retirement activities or the assumptions necessary to develop the estimated future cash flows required to satisfy those obligations. In addition, an entity may make revisions to its estimate of the obligation before a regulator considers those revisions in setting the entity's rates.

B68. Statement 71 requires, subject to meeting certain criteria, that the timing of recognition of certain revenues and expenses for financial reporting purposes conform to decisions or probable decisions of regulators responsible for setting the entity's rates. Because the practices of those regulators for allowing costs related to asset retirement activities are well established, the Board did not consider any future changes in those practices. The Board considered specific issues arising from current rate-making practices about the recognition of regulatory assets or liabilities for differences, if any, in the timing of recognition of costs for financial reporting and rate-making purposes. The Board also considered the appropriate method for recognition and measurement of impairment of the capitalized amount of an asset retirement cost for an asset subject to Statement 71.

B69. An entity is responsible for developing timely and reasonably accurate estimates of the cash

flows related to asset retirement obligations. That responsibility is inherent in the preparation of external financial statements and may be a part of the entity's reporting to others in connection with its asset retirement obligations. The regulator that sets the entity's rates has a responsibility to both the entity and its customers to establish rates that are just and reasonable. Sometimes the responsibilities of the regulator and those of the regulated entity conflict, producing differences in the estimated costs related to asset retirement obligations as discussed in paragraph B67. Statement 71, as amended, specifies the general criteria for the recognition of regulatory assets and liabilities that result from differences, if any, in the timing of recognition of costs for financial reporting and rate-making purposes. FASB Statement No. 92, *Regulated Enterprises—Accounting for Phase-in Plans,* establishes more restrictive criteria for the recognition of regulatory assets in certain situations.

B70. The Board considered whether the general principles of Statement 71 should apply or whether specific criteria similar to those in Statement 92 should apply to the recognition of regulatory assets and liabilities that result from the circumstances described in paragraph B67. The Board concluded that judgment would be required in recognizing regulatory assets and liabilities because of the many reasons for differences between the obligations and costs related to asset retirement obligations recognized for financial reporting and those considered for rate-making purposes. Therefore, the Board decided that the general principles in Statement 71 should be applied in recognizing regulatory assets and liabilities for those differences.

B71. The Board also considered the appropriate method for recognition and measurement of impairment of assets that include capitalized asset retirement costs for entities subject to Statement 71. In FASB Statement No. 121, *Accounting for the Impairment of Long-Lived Assets and for Long-Lived Assets to Be Disposed Of,* the Board considered the issues of recognition and measurement of impairment of long-lived assets of rate-regulated entities. The Board concluded that no additional guidance was needed for recognition and impairment of capitalized assets that include capitalized retirement costs for rate-regulated entities.

B72. Paragraph 12 of this Statement requires that capitalized asset retirement costs be included in the assessment of impairment of long-lived assets. In recent years, several nuclear power plants have ceased operations, and the method and timing of their nuclear decommissioning are being considered. Some of those plants reached the end of their expected useful lives, and others closed prior to the end of their expected useful lives. The actual decommissioning may begin immediately after plant closure or it may be deferred until some future time. In either case, the Board decided that FASB Statement No. 90, *Regulated Enterprises—Accounting for Abandonments and Disallowances of Plant Costs,* should apply to asset retirement costs recognized under the provisions of this Statement in the same way that it applies to other costs of closed or abandoned facilities of rate-regulated entities.

B73. Many rate-regulated entities currently provide for the costs related to asset retirement obligations in their financial statements and recover those amounts in rates charged to their customers. Some of those costs relate to asset retirement obligations within the scope of this Statement; others are not within the scope of this Statement and, therefore, cannot be recognized as liabilities under its provisions. The objective of including those amounts in rates currently charged to customers is to allocate costs to customers over the lives of those assets. The amount charged to customers is adjusted periodically to reflect the excess or deficiency of the amounts charged over the amounts incurred for the retirement of long-lived assets. The Board concluded that if asset retirement costs are charged to customers of rate-regulated entities but no liability is recognized, a regulatory liability should be recognized if the requirements of Statement 71 are met.

Disclosures

B74. The Board believes that the financial statement disclosures required by this Statement will provide information that will be useful in understanding the effects of a liability for an asset retirement obligation on a particular entity and that those disclosures can be prepared without encountering undue complexities or significant incremental costs. The Board decided that information about the general nature of an asset retirement obligation and the related long-lived asset is a fundamental and necessary disclosure.

B75. The Board believes that information about assets that are legally restricted for purposes of settling asset retirement obligations is important to financial statement users and should be disclosed.

B76. The Board considered whether it should require disclosure of other measures of a liability for an asset retirement obligation (for example, current cost, future cost, undiscounted expected cash flows, or entity-specific value). Because the Board decided to require the initial measurement of the liability at fair value, it decided that disclosure of other amounts based on other measurement objectives are inappropriate.

B77. The Board believes that a reconciliation showing the changes in the aggregate carrying amount of the asset retirement obligation would sometimes be useful. Components of the change include (a) liabilities incurred in the current period, (b) liabilities settled in the current period, (c) accretion expense, and (d) revisions resulting from changes in expected cash flows. To reduce the burden on preparers, the Board concluded that a reconciliation showing the changes in the asset retirement obligation would be required only when a significant change occurs in one or more of those components during the reporting period.

B78. Some of the disclosures required by this Statement were proposed by the EEI in its request that the Board consider adding a project on removal costs to its agenda. The Board also received input from some users of financial statements indicating that the disclosures required by this Statement would be useful in understanding the asset retirement obligations of an entity.

Effective Date

B79. This Statement is effective for financial statements issued for fiscal years beginning after June 15, 2002. The Board believes that the effective date provides adequate time for an entity that previously had not reported information about an asset retirement obligation to determine whether any such obligation exists. Furthermore, the Board believes that the effective date provides adequate time for all entities with asset retirement obligations to develop the necessary information to apply the requirements of this Statement. The Board encourages early application of this Statement.

Transition

B80. The transition provisions in the initial Exposure Draft would have required an entity to recognize balance sheet amounts for (a) a closure or removal liability adjusted for the cumulative period costs caused by changes in the present value of that liability due to the passage of time, (b) the capitalized costs of closure or removal, and (c) the related accumulated depreciation of the capitalized costs. The difference between those amounts and the amount recognized in the statement of financial position under present practice would have been recognized as a cumulative-effect adjustment in the period in which the Statement was adopted. The initial Exposure Draft would have required that an entity measure transition amounts by applying its provisions as if the initial Exposure Draft had been in effect when the closure or removal obligation was incurred and without the benefit of hindsight. However, if an entity could not make a reasonable approximation of those amounts based solely on information known in previous periods, it could measure those amounts using current information.

B81. Many respondents to the initial Exposure Draft agreed with its recognition provisions (for example, a cumulative-effect adjustment) but disagreed with the requirement to use information from previous periods to measure transition amounts. They stressed that such a requirement was overly complex and unjustified because it would require an entity to use old cost studies, update the asset calculation with newer studies, and use interest rates in effect when the obligations were incurred. Some respondents further indicated that a requirement to use information from previous periods would only result in the *appearance* of accuracy.

Measurement of transition amounts

B82. The Board discussed whether it should retain in this Statement the requirement in the initial Exposure Draft to measure transition amounts by applying the provisions of this Statement based on information available when an obligation was incurred. That requirement would have entailed retroactively measuring the initial fair value of a liability for an asset retirement obligation and using that same amount as a basis for recognizing the amount to be capitalized as part of the cost of the long-lived asset. Those amounts would then have been used to calculate depreciation related to the long-lived asset and accretion expense on the liability. To measure those amounts retroactively, an entity would have been required to determine historical data and assumptions about the economic environment that would have been considered at the date or dates that (a) a liability for an asset retirement obligation was incurred and (b) any subsequent revisions to cash flow estimates were made.

B83. The Board reasoned that although some entities may have data and assumptions in their historical records related to measurements that were already being made (for example, under the provisions of Statement 19), those records may not include sufficient information to retroactively employ the fair value measurement approach required by this Statement. Furthermore, the Board acknowledged that many entities that are required to apply the provisions of this Statement have not been accounting for asset retirement obligations in present practice because they were not required to do so. The Board concluded that it would not only be costly, but also difficult if not impossible, to reconstruct historical data and assumptions without incorporating the benefit of hindsight.

B84. The Board decided that, at transition, an entity should measure the fair value of a liability for an asset retirement obligation and the corresponding capitalized cost at the date the liability was initially incurred using current (that is, as of the date of adoption of this Statement) information, current assumptions, and current interest rates. That initial fair value of the liability and initial capitalized cost should be used as the basis for measuring depreciation expense and accretion expense for the time period from the date the liability was incurred to the date of adoption of this Statement.

Recognition of transition amounts

B85. The Board considered requiring the changes in accounting that result from the application of this Statement to be recognized (a) as the cumulative effect, based on a retroactive computation, of initially applying a new accounting principle, (b) by restating the financial statements of prior periods, or (c) prospectively, for example, over the remaining life of the long-lived asset. The Board also considered two simplified approaches to recognizing the changes in accounting that result from the application of this Statement.

B86. A cumulative-effect approach results in the immediate recognition and measurement of liability, asset, and accumulated depreciation amounts consistent with the provisions of this Statement. The difference between those amounts and any amounts that had been recognized in the statement of financial position prior to application of this Statement are reported as a cumulative-effect adjustment in the income statement of the period in which this Statement is initially applied. Consistent with paragraph 21 of

APB Opinion No. 20, *Accounting Changes,* an entity is required to disclose the pro forma effects of retroactive application for income before extraordinary items and net income (and the related per-share amounts) for all periods presented.

B87. Restatement, like a cumulative-effect approach, results in the immediate recognition and measurement of liability, asset, and accumulated depreciation amounts consistent with the provisions of this Statement. However, restatement differs from a cumulative-effect approach because prior-period financial statements would be restated to conform to the provisions of this Statement. Therefore, in financial statements presented for comparative purposes, financial statement users would be able to assess the impact of this Statement on income statement and balance sheet amounts.

B88. A prospective approach would result in the delayed recognition or adjustment of a liability for an asset retirement obligation as well as corresponding amounts to the long-lived asset and accumulated depreciation measured under the provisions of this Statement. Under a prospective approach, an entity would neither recognize a cumulative-effect adjustment in the income statement of the period in which this Statement is initially applied nor restate financial statements of previous periods affected by this Statement. Instead, all of the income statement effects related to initial application of this Statement would be recognized in future accounting periods.

B89. When compared with either a cumulative-effect approach or restatement, the Board decided that a prospective approach to transition provides the least useful financial statement information because asset retirement obligations that existed prior to the adoption of this Statement would not be reflected in the financial statements upon adoption of this Statement. For that reason, the Board decided against a prospective approach to transition.

B90. The Board discussed whether a cumulative-effect approach and restatement provide equally useful financial statement information. It acknowledged that restatement would provide more useful information because prior-period balance sheet amounts and prior-period income statement amounts would be re-

stated to reflect the provisions of this Statement. However, some rate-regulated entities expressed concern that if restatement resulted in recognition of additional expenses in prior periods, those expenses might not be recovered in current or future rates. The Board decided that a cumulative-effect approach would provide sufficient information if, in addition to disclosure of the pro forma income statement amounts required by paragraphs 19(c), 19(d), and 21 of Opinion 20, an entity also disclosed on a pro forma basis for the beginning of the earliest year presented and for the ends of all years presented the balance sheet amounts for the liability for asset retirement obligations as if this Statement had been applied during all periods affected. Therefore, the Board decided to require a cumulative-effect approach as described in Opinion 20 with additional prior-period balance sheet disclosures.

B91. The Board also considered, but rejected, two simplified approaches to recognition of transition amounts. Both approaches would have required that an entity recognize a liability for an asset retirement obligation at fair value upon initial application of the provisions of this Statement. The difference between the fair value of the obligation and any amount presently recognized in the balance sheet for that obligation would have been recognized as either (a) an increase or a decrease in the associated long-lived asset or (b) a cumulative-effect adjustment in the income statement of the period of initial application of this Statement. Neither of those approaches would have resulted in the recognition of an amount of accumulated depreciation related to an asset retirement cost.

B92. The Board decided that even though the simplified approaches would have been easier to apply than either a cumulative-effect approach or restatement, except for recognition of a liability for an asset retirement obligation at fair value, they would not have provided financial statement information that is consistent with the provisions of this Statement. Furthermore, both of the simplified approaches would have resulted in an arbitrary amount being recognized as either an asset or a cumulative-effect adjustment. The Board agreed that the simplified approaches would have provided less useful financial statement information than either the cumulative-effect approach or restatement.

Appendix C

ILLUSTRATIVE EXAMPLES—RECOGNITION AND MEASUREMENT PROVISIONS

C1. This appendix includes four examples that illustrate the recognition and measurement provisions of this Statement. Example 1 illustrates (a) initial measurement of a liability for an asset retirement obligation using an expected present value technique, (b) subsequent measurement assuming that there are no changes in estimated cash flows, and (c) settlement of the asset retirement obligation liability (ARO liability) at the end of its term. Example 2 is similar to Example 1. However, Example 2 illustrates subsequent measurement of an ARO liability after a change in estimated cash flows. Example 3 highlights the recognition and measurement provisions of this Statement for an ARO liability that is incurred over more than one reporting period. Example 4 illustrates accounting for asset retirement obligations that are conditional and that have a low likelihood of enforcement.

C2. The examples in this appendix and those in Appendixes D and E incorporate simplified assumptions to provide guidance in implementing this Statement. For instance, Examples 1 and 2 relate to the asset retirement obligation associated with an offshore production platform that also would likely have individual wells and production facilities that would have separate asset retirement obligations. Those examples also assume straight-line depreciation, even though, in practice, depreciation would likely be applied using a units-of-production method. Other simplifying assumptions are used throughout the examples.

Example 1

C3. Example 1 depicts an entity that completes construction of and places into service an offshore oil platform on January 1, 2003. The entity is legally required to dismantle and remove the platform at the end of its useful life, which is estimated to be 10 years. Based on the requirements of this Statement, on January 1, 2003, the entity recognizes a liability for an asset retirement obligation and capitalizes an amount for an asset retirement cost. The entity estimates the initial fair value of the liability using an expected present value technique. The significant assumptions used in that estimate of fair value are as follows:

a. Labor costs are based on current marketplace wages required to hire contractors to dismantle and remove offshore oil platforms. The entity assigns probability assessments to a range of cash flow estimates as follows:

Cash Flow Estimate	Probability Assessment	Expected Cash Flows
$100,000	25%	$ 25,000
125,000	50	62,500
175,000	25	43,750
		$131,250

b. The entity estimates allocated overhead and equipment charges using the rate it applies to labor costs for transfer pricing (80 percent). The entity has no reason to believe that its overhead rate differs from those used by contractors in the industry.
c. A contractor typically adds a markup on labor and allocated internal costs to provide a profit margin on the job. The rate used (20 percent) represents the entity's understanding of the profit that contractors in the industry generally earn to dismantle and remove offshore oil platforms.
d. A contractor would typically demand and receive a premium (market risk premium) for bearing the uncertainty and unforeseeable circumstances inherent in "locking in" today's price for a project that will not occur for 10 years. The entity estimates the amount of that premium to be 5 percent of the estimated inflation-adjusted cash flows.
e. The risk-free rate of interest on January 1, 2003, is 5 percent. The entity adjusts that rate by 3.5 percent to reflect the effect of its credit standing. Therefore, the credit-adjusted risk-free rate used to compute expected present value is 8.5 percent.
f. The entity assumes a rate of inflation of 4 percent over the 10-year period.

Example 1 (continued)

C4. On December 31, 2012, the entity settles its asset retirement obligation by using its internal workforce at a cost of $351,000. Assuming no changes during the 10-year period in the cash flows used to estimate the obligation, the entity would recognize a gain of $89,619 on settlement of the obligation:

Labor	$195,000
Allocated overhead and equipment charges (80 percent of labor)	156,000
Total costs incurred	351,000
ARO liability	440,619
Gain on settlement of obligation	$ 89,619

Initial Measurement of the ARO Liability at January 1, 2003

	Expected Cash Flows 1/1/03
Expected labor costs	$131,250
Allocated overhead and equipment charges (.80 × $131,250)	105,000
Contractor's markup [.20 × ($131,250 + $105,000)]	47,250
Expected cash flows before inflation adjustment	283,500
Inflation factor assuming 4 percent rate for 10 years	1.4802
Expected cash flows adjusted for inflation	419,637
Market-risk premium (.05 × $419,637)	20,982
Expected cash flows adjusted for market risk	$440,619
Present value using credit-adjusted risk-free rate of 8.5 percent for 10 years	$194,879

Interest Method of Allocation

Year	Liability Balance 1/1	Accretion	Liability Balance 12/31
2003	$194,879	$16,565	$211,444
2004	211,444	17,973	229,417
2005	229,417	19,500	248,917
2006	248,917	21,158	270,075
2007	270,075	22,956	293,031
2008	293,031	24,908	317,939
2009	317,939	27,025	344,964
2010	344,964	29,322	374,286
2011	374,286	31,814	406,100
2012	406,100	34,519	440,619

Example 1 (continued)

Schedule of Expenses

Year-End	Accretion Expense	Depreciation Expense	Total Expense
2003	$16,565	$19,488	$36,053
2004	17,973	19,488	37,461
2005	19,500	19,488	38,988
2006	21,158	19,488	40,646
2007	22,956	19,488	42,444
2008	24,908	19,488	44,396
2009	27,025	19,488	46,513
2010	29,322	19,488	48,810
2011	31,814	19,488	51,302
2012	34,519	19,488	54,007

Journal Entries

January 1, 2003:

Long-lived asset (asset retirement cost)	194,879	
ARO liability		194,879

To record the initial fair value of the ARO liability

December 31, 2003–2012:

Depreciation expense (asset retirement cost)	19,488	
Accumulated depreciation		19,488

To record straight-line depreciation on the
asset retirement cost

Accretion expense	Per schedule	
ARO liability		Per schedule

To record accretion expense on the ARO liability

December 31, 2012:

ARO liability	440,619	
Wages payable		195,000
Allocated overhead and equipment charges (.80 × $195,000)		156,000
Gain on settlement of ARO liability		89,619

To record settlement of the ARO liability

Example 2

C5. Example 2 is the same as Example 1 with respect to initial measurement of the ARO liability. In this example, the entity's credit standing improves over time, causing the credit-adjusted risk-free rate to decrease by .5 percent to 8 percent at December 31, 2004.

C6. On December 31, 2004, the entity revises its estimate of labor costs to reflect an increase of 10 percent in the marketplace. In addition, it revises the probability assessments related to those labor costs. The change in labor costs results in an upward revision to the undiscounted cash flows; consequently, the incremental cash flows are discounted at the current rate of 8 percent. All other assumptions remain unchanged. The revised estimate of expected cash flows for labor costs is as follows:

Cash Flow Estimate	Probability Assessment	Expected Cash Flows
$110,000	30%	$ 33,000
137,500	45	61,875
192,500	25	48,125
		$143,000

C7. On December 31, 2012, the entity settles its asset retirement obligation by using an outside contractor. It incurs costs of $463,000, resulting in the recognition of a $14,091 gain on settlement of the obligation:

ARO liability	$477,091
Outside contractor	463,000
Gain on settlement of obligation	$ 14,091

Initial Measurement of the ARO Liability at January 1, 2003

	Expected Cash Flows 1/1/03
Expected labor costs	$131,250
Allocated overhead and equipment charges (.80 × $131,250)	105,000
Contractor's markup [.20 × ($131,250 + $105,000)]	47,250
Expected cash flows before inflation adjustment	283,500
Inflation factor assuming 4 percent rate for 10 years	1.4802
Expected cash flows adjusted for inflation	419,637
Market-risk premium (.05 × $419,637)	20,982
Expected cash flows adjusted for market risk	$440,619
Present value using credit-adjusted risk-free rate of 8.5 percent for 10 years	$194,879

Example 2 (continued)

**Subsequent Measurement of the ARO Liability Reflecting
a Change in Labor Cost Estimate as of December 31, 2004**

	Revised Expected Cash Flows 12/31/04
Incremental expected labor costs ($143,000 – $131,250)	$11,750
Allocated overhead and equipment charges (.80 × $11,750)	9,400
Contractor's markup [.20 × ($11,750 + $9,400)]	4,230
Expected cash flows before inflation adjustment	25,380
Inflation factor assuming 4 percent rate for 8 years	1.3686
Expected cash flows adjusted for inflation	34,735
Market-risk premium (.05 × $34,735)	1,737
Expected cash flows adjusted for market risk	$36,472
Present value of incremental liability using credit-adjusted risk-free rate of 8 percent for 8 years	$19,704

Interest Method of Allocation

Year	Liability Balance 1/1	Accretion	Change in Cash Flow Estimate	Liability Balance 12/31
2003	$194,879	$16,565		$211,444
2004	211,444	17,973	$19,704	249,121*
2005	249,121	21,078		270,199
2006	270,199	22,862		293,061
2007	293,061	24,796		317,857
2008	317,857	26,894		344,751
2009	344,751	29,170		373,921
2010	373,921	31,638		405,559
2011	405,559	34,315		439,874
2012	439,874	37,217		477,091

*The remainder of this table is an aggregation of two layers: the original liability, which is accreted at a rate of 8.5%, and the new incremental liability, which is accreted at a rate of 8.0%.

Schedule of Expenses

Year-End	Accretion Expense	Depreciation Expense	Total Expense
2003	$16,565	$19,488	$36,053
2004	17,973	19,488	37,461
2005	21,078	21,951	43,029
2006	22,862	21,951	44,813
2007	24,796	21,951	46,747
2008	26,894	21,951	48,845
2009	29,170	21,951	51,121
2010	31,638	21,951	53,589
2011	34,315	21,951	56,266
2012	37,217	21,951	59,168

Example 2 (continued)

Journal Entries

January 1, 2003:

Long-lived asset (asset retirement cost)	194,879	
ARO liability		194,879

    To record the initial fair value of the ARO liability

December 31, 2003:

Depreciation expense (asset retirement cost)	19,488	
Accumulated depreciation		19,488

    To record straight-line depreciation on the asset
      retirement cost

Accretion expense	16,565	
ARO liability		16,565

    To record accretion expense on the ARO liability

December 31, 2004:

Depreciation expense (asset retirement cost)	19,488	
Accumulated depreciation		19,488

    To record straight-line depreciation on the asset
      retirement cost

Accretion expense	17,973	
ARO liability		17,973

    To record accretion expense on the ARO liability

Long-lived asset (asset retirement cost)	19,704	
ARO liability		19,704

    To record the change in estimated cash flows

December 31, 2005–2012:

Depreciation expense (asset retirement cost)	21,951	
Accumulated depreciation		21,951

    To record straight-line depreciation on the asset retirement
      cost adjusted for the change in cash flow estimate

Accretion expense	Per schedule	
ARO liability		Per schedule

    To record accretion expense on the ARO liability

December 31, 2012:

ARO liability	477,091	
Gain on settlement of ARO liability		14,091
Accounts payable (outside contractor)		463,000

    To record settlement of the ARO liability

Example 3

C8. Example 3 depicts an entity that places a nuclear utility plant into service on December 31, 2003. The entity is legally required to decommission the plant at the end of its useful life, which is estimated to be 20 years. Based on the requirements of this Statement, the entity recognizes a liability for an asset retirement obligation and capitalizes an amount for an asset retirement cost over the life of the plant as contamination occurs. The following schedule reflects the undiscounted expected cash flows and respective credit-adjusted risk-free rates used to measure each portion of the liability through December 31, 2005, at which time the plant is 90 percent contaminated.

Date	Undiscounted Expected Cash Flows	Credit-Adjusted Risk-Free Rate
12/31/03	$23,000	9.0%
12/31/04	1,150	8.5
12/31/05	1,900	9.2

C9. On December 31, 2005, the entity increases by 10 percent its estimate of undiscounted expected cash flows that were used to measure those portions of the liability recognized on December 31, 2003, and December 31, 2004. Because the change results in an upward revision to the undiscounted estimated cash flows, the incremental estimated cash flow is discounted at the current credit-adjusted risk-free rate of 9.2 percent. As a result, $2,300 (10 percent of $23,000) plus $115 (10 percent of $1,150) plus $1,900 (resulting from contamination in 2005), which totals $4,315 of incremental undiscounted cash flows are discounted at the then current credit-adjusted risk-free rate of 9.2 percent and recorded as a liability on December 31, 2005.

	Date Incurred		
	12/31/03	**12/31/04**	**12/31/05**
Initial measurement of the ARO liability:			
Expected cash flows adjusted for market risk	$23,000	$1,150	$1,900
Credit-adjusted risk-free rate	9.00%	8.50%	9.20%
Discount period in years	20	19	18
Expected present value	$4,104	$244	$390
Measurement of revision in expected cash flows occurring on December 31, 2005:			
Revision in expected cash flows (increase of 10 percent) [($23,000 × 10%) + ($1,150 × 10%)]			$2,415
Credit-adjusted risk-free rate			9.20%
Discount period remaining in years			18
Expected present value			$495

Example 3 (continued)

Carrying Amount of Liability Incurred in 2003

Year	Liability Balance 1/1	Accretion (9.0%)	New Liability	Liability Balance 12/31
2003			$4,104	$4,104
2004	$4,104	$369		4,473
2005	4,473	403		4,876

Carrying Amount of Liability Incurred in 2004

Year	Liability Balance 1/1	Accretion (8.5%)	New Liability	Liability Balance 12/31
2004			$ 244	$ 244
2005	$ 244	$21		265

Carrying Amount of Liability Incurred in 2005
Plus Effect of Change in Estimated Cash Flows

Year	Liability Balance 1/1	Accretion (9.2%)	Change in Cash Flow Estimate	New Liability	Liability Balance 12/31
2005			$495	$390	$885

Carrying Amount of Total Liability

Year	Liability Balance 1/1	Accretion	Change in Cash Flow Estimate	New Liability	Total Carrying Amount 12/31
2003				$4,104	$4,104
2004	$4,104	$369		244	4,717
2005	4,717	424	$495	390	6,026

Example 3 (continued)

Journal Entries

December 31, 2003:

Long-lived asset (asset retirement cost)	4,104	
ARO liability		4,104

    To record the initial fair value of the ARO
        liability incurred this period

December 31, 2004:

Depreciation expense ($4,104 ÷ 20)	205	
Accumulated depreciation		205

    To record straight-line depreciation on the
        asset retirement cost

Accretion expense	369	
ARO liability		369

    To record accretion expense on the ARO liability

Long-lived asset (asset retirement cost)	244	
ARO liability		244

    To record the initial fair value of the ARO
        liability incurred this period

December 31, 2005:

Depreciation expense [($4,104 ÷ 20) + ($244 ÷ 19)]	218	
Accumulated depreciation		218

    To record straight-line depreciation on the
        asset retirement cost

Accretion expense	424	
ARO liability		424

    To record accretion expense on the ARO liability

Long-lived asset (asset retirement cost)	495	
ARO liability		495

    To record the change in liability resulting
        from a revision in expected cash flows

Long-lived asset (asset retirement cost)	390	
ARO liability		390

    To record the initial fair value of the ARO
        liability incurred this period

Example 4

C10. Example 4 illustrates a timber lease[26] wherein the lessor has an option to require the lessee to settle an asset retirement obligation. Assume an entity enters into a five-year lease agreement that grants it the right to harvest timber on a tract of land and that agreement grants the lessor an option to require that the lessee reforest the underlying land at the end of the lease term. Based on past history, the lessee believes that the likelihood that the lessor will exercise that option is low. Rather, at the end of the lease, the lessor will likely accept the land without requiring reforestation. The lessee estimates that there is only a 10 percent probability that the lessor will elect to enforce reforestation.

C11. At the end of the first year, 20 percent of the timber has been harvested. The lessee estimates that the fair value of performing reforestation activities in 4 years for the portion of the land that has been harvested will be $300,000. When estimating the fair value of the ARO liability to be recorded, the lessee incorporates the probability that the restoration provisions will not be enforced:

Cash Flow Estimate	Probability Assessment	Expected Cash Flows
$300,000	10%	$30,000
0	90	0
		$30,000

Present value using credit-adjusted risk-free rate of 8.5 percent for 4 years	$21,647

C12. During the term of the lease, the lessee should reassess the likelihood that the lessor will require reforestation. For example, if the lessee subsequently determines that the likelihood of the lessor electing the reforestation option has increased, that change will result in a change in the estimate of future cash flows and be accounted for as illustrated in Example 2.

Appendix D

ILLUSTRATIVE EXAMPLES— TRANSITION PROVISIONS

D1. This appendix includes four examples that illustrate application of the transition provisions assuming that this Statement is adopted on January 1, 2003 (calendar-year-ends 2001 and 2002 are shown for illustration purposes). Therefore, for measurement purposes, the examples use information and assumptions to derive cash flow estimates related to asset retirement obligations at January 1, 2003. Additionally, the January 1, 2003, risk-free rate adjusted for the effect of the entity's credit standing is 8.5 percent.

Example 1

D2. Example 1 depicts an entity that has not been recognizing amounts related to an asset retirement obligation because no requirement existed. Therefore, in Example 1, prior to adoption of this Statement, no amounts are recognized for an asset retirement obligation in the statement of financial position.

D3. In addition to the assumptions described in paragraph D1, other significant assumptions in Example 1 are as follows:

a. The long-lived asset to which the asset retirement obligation relates was acquired on January 1, 1993, and is estimated to have a useful life of 15 years.
b. 100 percent of the asset retirement obligation occurred at acquisition.
c. The entity uses straight-line depreciation.
d. At January 1, 2003, undiscounted expected cash flows that will be required to satisfy the ARO liability in 2008 are $3 million. Discounting at an 8.5 percent credit-adjusted risk-free rate, the present value of the ARO liability at January 1, 1993, is $882,000.

D4. The interest allocation table, amounts measured under the provisions of this Statement, and journal entries to record the transition amounts are shown below (in thousands).

---

[26]FASB Statement No. 13, *Accounting for Leases,* excludes from its scope "lease agreements concerning the rights to explore for or to exploit natural resources such as oil, gas, minerals, and timber" (paragraph 1).

Example 1 (continued)

Interest Allocation Table
(8.5% Credit-Adjusted Risk-Free Rate)

Year	Liability Balance 1/1	Accretion	Liability Balance 12/31
1993	$ 882	$ 75	$ 957
1994	957	81	1,038
1995	1,038	88	1,126
1996	1,126	96	1,222
1997	1,222	104	1,326
1998	1,326	113	1,439
1999	1,439	122	1,561
2000	1,561	133	1,694
2001	1,694	144	1,838
2002	1,838	156	1,994
2003	1,994	170	2,164
2004	2,164	184	2,348
2005	2,348	200	2,548
2006	2,548	217	2,765
2007	2,765	235	3,000

Transition Amounts Required by the Provisions of ARO Statement

	1/1/93–12/31/00	2001	2002
Liability 1/1	$ 882	$1,694	$1,838
Accretion	812	144	156
Liability 12/31	$1,694	$1,838	$1,994
Asset		$ 882	$ 882
Amount capitalized	$ 882	—	—
Asset 12/31	$ 882	$ 882	$ 882
Accumulated depreciation 1/1		$ 472	$ 531
Depreciation expense ($882 ÷ 15)	$ 472*	59	59
Accumulated depreciation 12/31	$ 472	$ 531	$ 590

---

*$59 × 8 = $472

Journal Entry Required at Transition (1/1/03)

Cumulative-effect adjustment	1,702	
Long-lived asset	882	
Accumulated depreciation		590
Liability for an asset retirement obligation		1,994

Example 2

D5. Example 2 depicts an entity that has been recognizing amounts related to an asset retirement obligation under the provisions of Statement 19. Prior to adoption of this Statement, amounts have been recognized in the statement of financial position as accumulated depreciation. The entity would have previously recognized expense in the income statement under the provisions of Statement 19.

D6. Significant assumptions in Example 2 are as follows:

a. The long-lived asset to which the asset retirement obligation relates was acquired on January 1, 1999, and is estimated to have a useful life of 15 years.
b. 100 percent of the asset retirement obligation occurs at acquisition.
c. The entity uses straight-line depreciation.
d. At January 1, 2003, undiscounted expected cash flows that will be required to satisfy the ARO liability in 2014 are $75 million. Discounting at an 8.5 percent credit-adjusted risk-free rate, the present value of the ARO liability at January 1, 1999, is $22.060 million. That is also the amount that would have been capitalized as an increase to the carrying amount of the long-lived asset at acquisition.
e. The estimated (undiscounted) retirement obligation under the provisions of Statement 19 was $67 million. The entity had been accruing that amount on a straight-line basis over 15 years by recognizing an expense and a credit to accumulated depreciation in the amount of $4.467 million per year.

D7. The interest allocation table, amounts measured under the provisions of this Statement, amounts recognized and measured under the provisions of Statement 19, and journal entries to record the transition amounts are shown below (in thousands).

Interest Allocation Table
(8.5% Credit-Adjusted Risk-Free Rate)

Year	Liability Balance 1/1	Accretion	Liability Balance 12/31
1999	$22,060	$1,875	$23,935
2000	23,935	2,035	25,970
2001	25,970	2,207	28,177
2002	28,177	2,395	30,572
2003	30,572	2,599	33,171
2004	33,171	2,820	35,991
2005	35,991	3,059	39,050
2006	39,050	3,319	42,369
2007	42,369	3,601	45,970
2008	45,970	3,907	49,877
2009	49,877	4,240	54,117
2010	54,117	4,600	58,717
2011	58,717	4,991	63,708
2012	63,708	5,415	69,123
2013	69,123	5,877	75,000

Example 2 (continued)

Transition Amounts Required by the Provisions of ARO Statement

	1999	2000	2001	2002
Liability 1/1		$23,935	$25,970	$28,177
Accretion	$ 1,875	2,035	2,207	2,395
Liability incurred	22,060	—	—	—
Liability 12/31	$23,935	$25,970	$28,177	$30,572
Asset 1/1		$22,060	$22,060	$22,060
Amount capitalized	$22,060	—	—	—
Asset 12/31	$22,060	$22,060	$22,060	$22,060
Accumulated depreciation 1/1		$ 1,471	$ 2,942	$ 4,413
Depreciation expense ($22,060 ÷ 15)	$ 1,471	1,471	1,471	1,471
Accumulated depreciation 12/31	$ 1,471	$ 2,942	$ 4,413	$ 5,884

Amounts Recorded under the Provisions of Statement 19

	1999	2000	2001	2002
Accumulated depreciation 1/1		$ 4,467	$ 8,934	$13,401
Accrued expense (estimated costs of $67 million)	$ 4,467	4,467	4,467	4,467
Accumulated depreciation 12/31	$ 4,467	$ 8,934	$13,401	$17,868

Journal Entry Required at Transition (1/1/03)

Accumulated depreciation (Statement 19)	17,868	
Long-lived asset (Statement 143)	22,060	
Accumulated depreciation (Statement 143)		5,884
Liability for an asset retirement obligation (Statement 143)		30,572
Cumulative-effect adjustment		3,472

Example 3

D8. Example 3 depicts an entity that has been recognizing amounts related to an asset retirement obligation under the provisions of Statement 19. The entity incurs 90 percent, 8 percent, and 2 percent of the asset retirement obligation over the first 3 years of the life of the asset, respectively. In Example 2, the entity incurred 100 percent of the asset retirement obligation upon acquisition.

D9. Significant assumptions in Example 3 are as follows:

a. The long-lived asset to which the asset retirement obligation relates was acquired on January 1, 1986, and is estimated to have a useful life of 20 years.

Example 3 (continued)

b. Upon transition to this Statement, the entity has incurred 100 percent of the asset retirement obligation. However, as discussed in paragraph D8, that obligation was incurred over the first three years of the life of the asset.

c. The entity uses straight-line depreciation.

d. At January 1, 2003, undiscounted expected cash flows that will be required to satisfy the ARO liability in 2006 are $250 million. Discounting at an 8.5 percent credit-adjusted risk-free rate, the present value of the ARO liability at January 1, 2003, is $195.726 million.

e. The total estimated (undiscounted) retirement obligation under the provisions of Statement 19 was $220 million. As of January 1, 2003, $186.785 million of that amount had been accrued.

D10. The following table shows (by year) the undiscounted expected cash flows incurred under the provisions of this Statement and the amounts estimated under the provisions of Statement 19 (in thousands).

Date	Percentage of Total Costs Incurred	ARO Statement Undiscounted Expected Cash Flows	Statement 19 Estimated Retirement Costs
1/1/86	90%	$225,000	$198,000
1/1/87	8	20,000	17,600
1/1/88	2	5,000	4,400
	100%	$250,000	$220,000

D11. The interest allocation table, amounts measured under the provisions of this Statement, amounts recognized and measured under the provisions of Statement 19, and journal entries to record the transition amounts are shown below (in thousands).

Interest Allocation Table
(8.5% Credit-Adjusted Risk-Free Rate)

Year	Liability Balance 1/1	Accretion	Liability Balance 12/31
2000	$153,236*	$13,025	$166,261
2001	166,261	14,132	180,393
2002	180,393	15,333	195,726
2003	195,726	16,637	212,363
2004	212,363	18,051	230,414
2005	230,414	19,586	250,000

*$153,236 = present value of $250,000, 8.5%, 6 years.

Example 3 (continued)

Transition Amounts Required by the Provisions of ARO Statement

	2000	2001	2002
Liability 1/1	$153,236	$166,261	$180,393
Accretion	13,025	14,132	15,333
Liability 12/31	$166,261	$180,393	$195,726
Asset 1/1:			
Capitalized 1/1/86 (PV of $225,000, 8.5%, 20 yrs.)	$ 44,014	$ 44,014	$ 44,014
Capitalized 1/1/87 (PV of $20,000, 8.5%, 19 yrs.)	4,245	4,245	4,245
Capitalized 1/1/88 (PV of $5,000, 8.5%, 18 yrs.)	1,151	1,151	1,151
Asset 12/31	$ 49,410	$ 49,410	$ 49,410
Accumulated depreciation 1/1:		$ 36,970	$ 39,458
Capitalized 1/1/86 [($44,014 ÷ 20) × 14]	$ 30,810		
Capitalized 1/1/87 [($4,245 ÷ 19) × 13]	2,904		
Capitalized 1/1/88 [($1,151 ÷ 18) × 12]	768		
Depreciation expense			
[($44,014 ÷ 20) + ($4,245 ÷ 19) + ($1,151 ÷ 18)]	2,488	2,488	2,488
Accumulated depreciation 12/31	$ 36,970	$ 39,458	$ 41,946

Amounts Recorded under the Provisions of Statement 19

	2000	2001	2002
Accumulated depreciation 1/1:		$164,645	$175,715
1/1/86 accrual [($198,000 ÷ 20) × 14]	$138,600		
1/1/87 accrual [($17,600 ÷ 19) × 13]	12,042		
1/1/88 accrual [($4,400 ÷ 18) × 12]	2,933		
Accrued expense			
[($198,000 ÷ 20) + ($17,600 ÷ 19) + ($4,400 ÷ 18)]	11,070	11,070	11,070
Accumulated depreciation 12/31	$164,645	$175,715	$186,785

Journal Entry Required at Transition (1/1/03)

Cumulative-effect adjustment	1,477	
Accumulated depreciation (Statement 19)	186,785	
Long-lived asset (Statement 143)	49,410	
Accumulated depreciation (Statement 143)		41,946
Liability for an asset retirement obligation (Statement 143)		195,726

Example 4

D12. Example 4 illustrates transition accounting for an oil field composed of numerous individual wells that has been in production for several years before adoption of this Statement. In periods prior to the adoption of this Statement, the entity had been recognizing amounts related to an asset retirement obligation under the provisions of Statement 19. Those amounts have been recognized on the balance sheet as a liability.

D13. Additional assumptions related to this example are as follows:

a. The oil field was discovered in 1990. Production started in 1993.
b. The producing platform is a concrete structure that supports 35 individual wells.
c. The estimated reserves at the time of discovery was 465 millions of barrels of oil equivalent (mmboe) with an expected production life of 20 years.

d. At the time of adoption of this Statement, cumulative production at the site is 300 mmboe, and remaining reserves are estimated to be 250 mmboe. (The increase in reserves is due to enhanced recovery methods.)
e. The amount of ARO liability accrued under Statement 19 at the time of adoption of this Statement on January 1, 2003, was $750,000.[27]
f. The estimated undiscounted cash flows for the asset retirement obligation at the estimated date of retirement in 2013 is $1.5 million.

Discounting at an 8.5 percent credit-adjusted risk-free rate, the present value of the asset retirement obligation for the entire operation is $663,428 at January 1, 2003. The discounted amount in 1993 when the field started production is $293,425. That is the amount that would have been capitalized as part of the oil field cost. The amount of that cost that would have been expensed to date using a units-of-production method is computed as follows:

$$(\text{Cumulative production} \div \text{estimated total production}) \times \$293,425 =$$

$$[300 \div (300 + 250)] \times \$293,425 = \underline{\$160,050}$$

The reduction in the liability to be recognized upon transition is ($750,000 − $663,428) $86,572.

Journal Entry Required at Transition (1/1/03)

Liability (Statement 19)	750,000	
Long-lived asset (Statement 143)	293,425	
Cumulative effect adjustment		219,947
Accumulated depreciation (Statement 143)		160,050
Liability for ARO (Statement 143)		663,428

Appendix E

**ILLUSTRATIVE EXAMPLE—
SUBSEQUENT MEASUREMENT OF
A LIABILITY OBTAINED FROM A
MARKET PRICE**

E1. Subsequent to initial measurement, an entity is required to recognize period-to-period changes in an ARO liability resulting from (a) the passage of time

(accretion expense) and (b) revisions in cash flow estimates. To apply the subsequent measurement provisions of this Statement, an entity must identify undiscounted cash flows related to an ARO liability irrespective of how the liability was initially measured. Therefore, if an entity obtains the initial fair value from a market price, it must impute undiscounted cash flows from that price.

E2. This appendix includes an example that illustrates the subsequent measurement of a liability in

---

[27]Because of changes in estimates of both total reserves and retirement costs during the life of the field, the amount of estimated costs to retire an asset that may have been previously recognized in accumulated depreciation may not be determinable using cumulative production data. However, in the absence of more complete information, a shortcut approach that bases an estimate of that amount on cumulative production to date, current reserve estimates, or similar data and the current estimate of the asset retirement obligation is appropriate.

situations where the initial liability is based on a market price. The example assumes that the liability is initially recognized at the end of period 0 when the market price is $300,000 and the entity's credit-adjusted risk-free rate is 8 percent. As required by this Statement, revisions in the timing or the amount of estimated cash flows are assumed to occur at the end of the period after accretion on the beginning balance of the liability is calculated. At the end of each period, the following procedure is used to impute cash flows from the end of period market price, compute the change in that price attributable to revisions in estimated cash flows, and calculate accretion expense.

a. The market price and the credit-adjusted risk-free interest rate are used to impute the undiscounted cash flows embedded in the market price.

b. The undiscounted cash flows from (a) are discounted at the initial credit-adjusted risk-free rate

of 8 percent to arrive at the ending balance of the ARO liability per the provisions of this Statement.

c. The beginning balance of the ARO liability is multiplied by the initial credit-adjusted risk-free rate of 8 percent to arrive at the amount of accretion expense per the provisions of this Statement.

d. The difference between the undiscounted cash flows at the beginning of the period and the undiscounted cash flows at the end of the period represents the revision in cash flow estimates that occurred during the period. If that change is an upward revision to the undiscounted estimated cash flows, it is discounted at the current credit-adjusted risk-free rate. If that change is a downward revision, it is discounted at the historical weighted-average rate because it is not practicable to separately identify the period to which the downward revision relates.

Subsequent Measurement of an ARO Liability
Obtained from a Market Price

	End of Period			
	0	**1**	**2**	**3**
Market assumptions:				
Market price (includes market risk premium)	$ 300,000	$400,000	$ 350,000	$380,000
Current risk-free rate adjusted for entity's credit standing	8.00%	7.00%	7.50%	7.50%
Time period remaining	3	2	1	0
Imputed undiscounted cash flows (market price discounted at market rate)	$ 377,914	$457,960	$ 376,250	$380,000
Change in undiscounted cash flows	377,914	80,046	(81,710)	3,750
Discount rate:				
Current credit-adjusted risk-free rate (for upward revisions)	8.00%	7.00%		
Historical weighted-average credit-adjusted risk-free rate (for downward revisions)			7.83%	
Change in undiscounted cash flows discounted at credit-adjusted risk-free rate (current rate for upward revisions and historical rate for downward revisions)	$300,000	$69,916	$(75,777)	$3,750

Measurement of Liability under Provisions of ARO Statement

Period	Beginning Balance	Accretion (8.0%)	Change in Cash Flows	Ending Balance
0			$300,000	$300,000
1	$300,000	$24,000		324,000
2	324,000	25,920		349,920
3	349,920	27,994		377,914

Period	Beginning Balance	Accretion (7.0%)	Change in Cash Flows	Ending Balance
0				
1			$69,916	$69,916
2	$69,916	$4,894		74,810
3	74,810	5,236		80,046

Period	Beginning Balance	Accretion (7.83%)	Change in Cash Flows	Ending Balance
0				
1				
2			$(75,777)	$(75,777)
3	$(75,777)	$(5,933)		(81,710)

Period	Beginning Balance	Accretion	Change in Cash Flows	Ending Balance
0				
1				
2				
3			$3,750	$3,750

Total

Period	Beginning Balance	Accretion Expense	Change in Cash Flows	Ending Balance
0			$300,000	$300,000
1	$300,000	$24,000	69,916	393,916
2	393,916	30,814	(75,777)	348,953
3	348,953	27,297	3,750	380,000

Appendix F

EXCERPTS FROM CONCEPTS STATEMENT 7

[Best understood in context of full Concepts Statement]

F1. Paragraph 6 of this Statement states that FASB Statement No. 5, *Accounting for Contingencies,* and FASB Concepts Statement No. 7, *Using Cash Flow Information and Present Value in Accounting Measurements,* "deal with uncertainty in different ways. Statement 5 deals with uncertainty about whether a loss has been incurred by setting forth criteria to determine when to *recognize* a loss contingency. Concepts Statement 7 addresses measurement of liabilities and provides a *measurement* technique to deal with uncertainties about the amount and timing of the future cash flows necessary to settle the liability." Paragraphs 55–61 of Concepts Statement 7 discuss the relationship between the fair value measurement objective and expected cash flow approach articulated in Concepts Statement 7 and accounting for contingencies under Statement 5. Those paragraphs of Concepts Statement 7 follow:

Relationship to Accounting Contingencies

55. Some have questioned whether the fair value objective and expected cash flow approach described in this Statement conflict with FASB Statement No. 5, *Accounting for Contingencies,* and FASB Interpretation No. 14, *Reasonable Estimation of the Amount of a Loss.* Statement 5 is primarily directed toward determining whether loss contingencies should be recognized and devotes little attention to measurement beyond the requirement that the amount of a loss can be reasonably estimated. This Statement focuses on the choice of a measurement attribute (fair value) and the application of a measurement technique (present value) rather than the decision to recognize a loss. The decision to recognize an asset or liability (or a change in an existing asset or liability) is different from the decision about a relevant measurement attribute. However, there are unavoidable interactions between accounting recognition and measurement, as discussed in paragraphs 56–61.

56. When using estimated cash flow information, fair value measurements may appear to incorporate elements that could not be recognized under the provisions of Statement 5. For example, the fair value of a loan necessarily incorporates expectations about potential default, whereas under Statement 5, a loss cannot be recognized until it is probable that a loss event has occurred. Expectations about potential default are usually embodied in the interest rate, but they can also be expressed as adjustments to the expected cash flows (refer to Appendix A). Similarly, the amount that a third party would charge to assume an uncertain liability necessarily incorporates expectations about future events that are not probable, as that term is used in Statement 5. However, the use of *probable* in the first recognition criterion of Statement 5 refers to the likelihood that an asset has been impaired or a liability incurred. The term does not reference the individual cash flows or factors that would be considered in estimating the fair value of the asset or liability.

57. The potential for interaction between recognition (Is an asset impaired or does a liability exist?) and measurement (How much is the loss or the liability?) is inescapable. For example, a slight change in the assumptions from paragraphs 52 and 53—replacing a 90 percent probability of $10 with a 90 percent probability of $0—would lead some to a conclusion under Statement 5 that no liability should be recognized. The probable amount of loss described in Statement 5 is $0, but the expected cash flow is $100.[12] On the other hand, if the entity has 10 potential liabilities with those characteristics, and the outcomes are independent of one another, some would conclude that the entity has a probable loss of $1,000. They might argue that 1 of the 10 potential liabilities will probably materialize and that recognizing a loss is consistent with Statement 5. Recognition issues like these are among the most intractable in accounting and are beyond the scope of this Statement.

---

[12]($0 × .9) + ($1,000 × .1) = $100. For purposes of illustration, this example ignores the time value of money.

58. The second recognition criterion in Statement 5 focuses on the ability to estimate the *amount of loss.* When describing liabilities, the *amount of loss* often has been used to describe an estimate of the most likely outcome and the accumulation of cash flows associated with that outcome. However, the estimated costs of ultimately settling a liability

are not the same as the fair value of the liability itself; those costs are only one element in determining the fair value of that liability. As described in paragraph 23, measuring the fair value of an asset or liability entails the estimate of future cash flows, an assessment of their possible variability, the time value of money, and the price that marketplace participants demand for bearing the uncertainty inherent in those cash flows.

59. Once the recognition decision is reached, the amount of loss is sometimes reported through an adjustment to the existing amortization or reporting convention rather than through a fresh-start measurement. For example, FASB Statement No. 114, *Accounting by Creditors for Impairment of a Loan,* determines the amount of loss using a revised estimate of cash flows (which can be determined using an expected-cash-flow approach) and the historical effective interest rate—an adjustment within the amortization convention. (A fresh-start measurement would use the revised estimate of cash flows and a current interest rate.) Amortization and depreciation conventions other than the interest method are beyond the scope of this Statement. Adjustments to the interest method of allocation are discussed in paragraphs 89–100.

60. Other losses are reported through a fresh-start measurement of the asset. In those cases, the measurement principles are consistent with those described in this Statement. As mentioned earlier, Statement 121 is an example of a situation in which fair value is used in a fresh-start measurement to measure the amount of loss.

61. Although Statement 5 does not provide explicit measurement guidance for recognized loss contingencies, Interpretation 14 provides some measurement guidance. Interpretation 14 applies to the situation in which "no amount within the range [of loss] is a better estimate than any other amount" (paragraph 3). In those limited circumstances, the Interpretation prescribes a measurement equal to the minimum value in the range. It was developed to address measurement of losses in situations in which a single most-likely amount is not available. The measurement concepts described in this State-

ment focus on expected cash flows as a tool for measuring fair value and, as outlined earlier, the minimum amount in a range is not consistent with an estimate of fair value.

F2. Paragraph 8 of this Statement states that "a present value technique is often the best available technique with which to estimate the fair value of a liability" (footnote reference omitted). Paragraphs 39–54 and 75–88 of Concepts Statement 7 discuss the use of present value techniques in measuring the fair value of an asset or a liability. Those paragraphs of Concepts Statement 7 follow:

The Components of a Present Value Measurement

39. Paragraph 23 describes the following elements that together capture the economic differences between various assets and liabilities:[7]

a. An estimate of the future cash flow, or in more complex cases, series of future cash flows at different times
b. Expectations about possible variations in the amount or timing of those cash flows
c. The time value of money, represented by the risk-free rate of interest
d. The price for bearing the uncertainty inherent in the asset or liability
e. Other, sometimes unidentifiable, factors including illiquidity and market imperfections.

[7]The effect of the entity's credit standing on the measurement of its liabilities is discussed in paragraphs 75–88.

40. This Statement contrasts two approaches to computing present value, either of which may be used to estimate the fair value of an asset or a liability, depending on the circumstances. In the expected cash flow approach discussed in this Statement, only the third factor listed in paragraph 39 (the time value of money, represented by the risk-free rate of interest) is included in the discount rate; the other factors cause adjustments in arriving at risk-adjusted expected cash flows. In a traditional approach to present value, adjustments for factors (b)–(e) described in paragraph 39 are embedded in the discount rate.

General Principles

41. The techniques used to estimate future cash flows and interest rates will vary from

one situation to another depending on the circumstances surrounding the asset or liability in question. However, certain general principles govern any application of present value techniques in measuring assets or liabilities:

a. To the extent possible, estimated cash flows and interest rates should reflect assumptions about the future events and uncertainties that would be considered in deciding whether to acquire an asset or group of assets in an arm's-length transaction for cash.

b. Interest rates used to discount cash flows should reflect assumptions that are consistent with those inherent in the estimated cash flows. Otherwise, the effect of some assumptions will be double counted or ignored. For example, an interest rate of 12 percent might be applied to contractual cash flows of a loan. That rate reflects expectations about future defaults from loans with particular characteristics. That same 12 percent rate should not be used to discount expected cash flows because those cash flows already reflect assumptions about future defaults.

c. Estimated cash flows and interest rates should be free from both bias and factors unrelated to the asset, liability, or group of assets or liabilities in question. For example, deliberately understating estimated net cash flows to enhance the apparent future profitability of an asset introduces a bias into the measurement.

d. Estimated cash flows or interest rates should reflect the range of possible outcomes rather than a single most-likely, minimum, or maximum possible amount.

Traditional and Expected Cash Flow Approaches to Present Value

42. A present value measurement begins with a set of future cash flows, but existing accounting standards employ a variety of different approaches in specifying cash flow sets. Some applications of present value use contractual cash flows. When contractual cash flows are not available, some applications use an estimate of the single most-likely amount or **best estimate.**

43. Accounting applications of present value have traditionally used a single set of estimated cash flows and a single interest rate, often described as "the rate commensurate with the risk." In effect, although not always by conscious design, the traditional approach

assumes that a single interest rate convention can reflect all the expectations about the future cash flows and the appropriate risk premium. The Board expects that accountants will continue to use the traditional approach for some measurements. In some circumstances, a traditional approach is relatively easy to apply. For assets and liabilities with contractual cash flows, it is consistent with the manner in which marketplace participants describe assets and liabilities, as in "a 12 percent bond."

44. The traditional approach is useful for many measurements, especially those in which comparable assets and liabilities can be observed in the marketplace. However, the Board found that the traditional approach does not provide the tools needed to address some complex measurement problems, including the measurement of nonfinancial assets and liabilities for which no market for the item or a comparable item exists. The traditional approach places most of the emphasis on selection of an interest rate. A proper search for "the rate commensurate with the risk" requires analysis of at least two items—one asset or liability that exists in the marketplace and has an observed interest rate and the asset or liability being measured. The appropriate rate of interest for the cash flows being measured must be inferred from the observable rate of interest in some other asset or liability and, to draw that inference, the characteristics of the cash flows must be similar to those of the asset being measured. Consequently, the measurer must do the following:

a. Identify the set of cash flows that will be discounted.

b. Identify another asset or liability in the marketplace that appears to have similar cash flow characteristics.

c. Compare the cash flow sets from the two items to ensure that they are similar. (For example, are both sets contractual cash flows, or is one contractual and the other an estimated cash flow?)

d. Evaluate whether there is an element in one item that is not present in the other. (For example, is one less liquid than the other?)

e. Evaluate whether both sets of cash flows are likely to behave (vary) in a similar fashion under changing economic conditions.

45. The Board found the expected cash flow approach to be a more effective measurement tool than the traditional approach in many

situations. In developing a measurement, the expected cash flow approach uses all expectations about possible cash flows instead of the single most-likely cash flow. For example, a cash flow might be $100, $200, or $300 with probabilities of 10 percent, 60 percent, and 30 percent, respectively. The expected cash flow is $220.[8] The expected cash flow approach thus differs from the traditional approach by focusing on direct analysis of the cash flows in question and on more explicit statements of the assumptions used in the measurement.

---

[8]($100 × .1) + ($200 × .6) + ($300 × .3) = $220. The traditional notion of a best estimate or most-likely amount in this example is $200.

46. The expected cash flow approach also allows use of present value techniques when the timing of cash flows is uncertain. For example, a cash flow of $1,000 may be received in 1 year, 2 years, or 3 years with probabilities of 10 percent, 60 percent, and 30 percent, respectively. The example below shows the computation of **expected present value** in that situation. Again, the expected present value of $892.36 differs from the traditional notion of a best estimate of $902.73 (the 60 percent probability) in this example.[9]

Present value of $1,000 in		
1 year at 5%	$952.38	
Probability	10.00%	$ 95.24
Present value of $1,000 in		
2 years at 5.25%	$902.73	
Probability	60.00%	541.64
Present value of $1,000 in		
3 years at 5.50%	$851.61	
Probability	30.00%	255.48
Expected present value		$892.36

---

[9]Interest rates usually vary with the length of time until settlement, a phenomenon described as the *yield curve.*

47. In the past, accounting standard setters have been reluctant to permit use of present value techniques beyond the narrow case of "contractual rights to receive money or contractual obligations to pay money on fixed or determinable dates." That phrase, which first appeared in accounting standards in paragraph 2 of Opinion 21, reflects the computational limitations of the traditional approach—a single set of cash flows that can be assigned to specific future dates. The Accounting Principles Board recognized that the amount of cash flows is almost always uncertain and incorporated that uncertainty in the interest rate. However, an interest rate in a traditional present value computation cannot reflect uncertainties in timing. A traditional present value computation, applied to the example above, would require a decision about which of the possible timings of cash flows to use and, accordingly, would not reflect the probabilities of other timings.

48. While many accountants do not routinely use the expected cash flow approach, expected cash flows are inherent in the techniques used in some accounting measurements, like pensions, other postretirement benefits, and some insurance obligations. They are currently allowed, but not required, when measuring the impairment of long-lived assets and estimating the fair value of financial instruments. The use of probabilities is an essential element of the expected cash flow approach, and one that may trouble some accountants. They may question whether assigning probabilities to highly subjective estimates suggests greater precision than, in fact, exists. However, the proper application of the traditional approach (as described in paragraph 44) requires the same estimates and subjectivity without providing the computational transparency of the expected cash flow approach.

49. Many estimates developed in current practice already incorporate the elements of expected cash flows informally. In addition, accountants often face the need to measure an asset or liability using limited information about the probabilities of possible cash flows. For example, an accountant might be confronted with the following situations:

a. The estimated amount falls somewhere between $50 and $250, but no amount in the range is more likely than any other amount. Based on that limited information, the estimated expected cash flow is $150 [(50 + 250)/2].

b. The estimated amount falls somewhere between $50 and $250, and the most likely amount is $100. However, the probabilities attached to each amount are unknown. Based on that limited information, the estimated expected cash flow is $133.33 [(50 + 100 + 250)/3].

c. The estimated amount will be $50 (10 percent probability), $250 (30 percent probability), or $100 (60 percent probability). Based on that limited information, the estimated expected cash flow is $140 [(50 × .10) + (250 × .30) + (100 × .60)].

50. Those familiar with statistical analysis may recognize the cases above as simple descriptions of (a) *uniform,* (b) *triangular,* and (c) *discrete* distributions.[10] In each case, the estimated expected cash flow is likely to provide a better estimate of fair value than the minimum, most likely, or maximum amount taken alone.

---

[10]The uniform and triangular distributions are *continuous* distributions. For further information about these and other distributions, refer to:

- M. Evans, N. Hastings, and B. Peacock, *Statistical Distributions,* 2d ed. (New York: John Wiley & Sons, Inc., 1993).
- N. Johnson, S. Kotz, and N. Balakrishnan, *Continuous Univariate Distributions,* 2d ed., vol. 2. (New York: John Wiley & Sons, Inc., 1995).

51. Like any accounting measurement, the application of an expected cash flow approach is subject to a cost-benefit constraint. In some cases, an entity may have access to considerable data and may be able to develop many cash flow scenarios. In other cases, an entity may not be able to develop more than general statements about the variability of cash flows without incurring considerable cost. The accounting problem is to balance the cost of obtaining additional information against the additional reliability that information will bring to the measurement. The Board recognizes that judgments about relative costs and benefits vary from one situation to the next and involve financial statement preparers, their auditors, and the needs of financial statement users.

52. Some maintain that expected cash flow techniques are inappropriate for measuring a single item or an item with a limited number of possible outcomes. They offer an example of an asset or liability with two possible outcomes: a 90 percent probability that the cash flow will be $10 and a 10 percent probability that the cash flow will be $1,000. They observe that the expected cash flow in that example is $109[11] and criticize that result as not representing either of the amounts that may ultimately be paid.

---

[11]($10 × .9) + ($1,000 × .1) = $109. For purposes of illustration, this example ignores the time value of money.

53. Assertions like the one just outlined reflect underlying disagreement with the measurement objective. If the objective is accumulation of costs to be incurred, expected cash flows may not produce a representationally faithful estimate of the expected cost. However, this Statement adopts fair value as the measurement objective. The fair value of the asset or liability in this example is not likely to be $10, even though that is the most likely cash flow. Instead, one would expect the fair value to be closer to $109 than to either $10 or $1,000. While this example is a difficult measurement situation, a measurement of $10 does not incorporate the uncertainty of the cash flow in the measurement of the asset or liability. Instead, the uncertain cash flow is presented as if it were a certain cash flow. No rational marketplace participant would sell an asset (or assume a liability) with these characteristics for $10.

54. In recent years, financial institutions and others have developed and implemented a variety of pricing tools designed to estimate the fair value of assets and liabilities. It is not possible here to describe all of the many (often proprietary) pricing models currently in use. However, those tools often build on concepts similar to those outlined in this Statement as well as other developments in modern finance, including option pricing and similar models. For example, the well-known Black-Scholes option pricing model uses the elements of a fair value measurement described in paragraph 23 as appropriate in estimating the fair value of an option. To the extent that a pricing model includes each of the elements of fair value, its use is consistent with this Statement.

Present Value in the Measurement of Liabilities

75. The concepts outlined in this Statement apply to liabilities as well as to assets. However, the measurement of liabilities sometimes involves problems different from those encountered in the measurement of assets and may require different techniques in arriving at fair value. When using present value techniques to estimate the fair value of a liability, the objective is to estimate the value of the assets required currently to (a) settle the liability with the holder or (b) transfer the liability to an entity of comparable credit standing.

76. To estimate the fair value of an entity's notes or bonds payable, accountants attempt to estimate the price at which other entities are willing to hold the entity's liabilities as assets. That process involves the same techniques and computational problems encountered in measuring assets. For example, the proceeds from a loan are the price that a lender paid to hold the borrower's promise of future cash flows as an asset. Similarly, the fair value of a bond payable is the price at which that security trades, as an asset, in the marketplace. As outlined in paragraphs 78–81, this estimate of fair value is consistent with the objective of liability measurement described in the preceding paragraph.

77. On the other hand, some liabilities are owed to a class of individuals who do not usually sell their rights as they might sell other assets. For example, entities often sell products with an accompanying warranty. Buyers of those products rarely have the ability or inclination to sell the warranty separately from the covered asset, but they own a warranty asset nonetheless. Some of an entity's liabilities, like an obligation for environmental cleanup, are not the assets of identifiable individuals. However, such liabilities are sometimes settled through assumption by a third party. In estimating the fair value of such liabilities accountants attempt to estimate the price that the entity would have to pay a third party to assume the liability.

Credit Standing and Liability Measurement

78. The most relevant measure of a liability always reflects the credit standing of the entity obligated to pay. Those who hold the entity's obligations as assets incorporate the entity's credit standing in determining the prices they are willing to pay. When an entity incurs a liability in exchange for cash, the role of its credit standing is easy to observe. An entity with a strong credit standing will receive more cash, relative to a fixed promise to pay, than an entity with a weak credit standing. For example, if 2 entities both promise to pay $500 in 5 years, the entity with a strong credit standing may receive about $374 in exchange for its promise (a 6 percent interest rate). The entity with a weak credit standing may receive about $284 in exchange for its promise (a 12 percent interest rate). Each entity initially records its respective liability at fair value, which is the amount of proceeds received—an amount that incorporates that entity's credit standing.

79. The effect of an entity's credit standing on the fair value of particular liabilities depends on the ability of the entity to pay and on liability provisions that protect holders. Liabilities that are guaranteed by governmental bodies (for example, many bank deposit liabilities in the United States) may pose little risk of default to the holder. Other liabilities may include sinking-fund requirements or significant collateral. All of those aspects must be considered in estimating the extent to which the entity's credit standing affects the fair value of its liabilities.

80. The role of the entity's credit standing in a settlement transaction is less direct but equally important. A settlement transaction involves three parties—the entity, the parties to whom it is obligated, and a third party. The price of the transaction will reflect the competing interests of each party. For example, suppose Entity A has an obligation to pay $500 to Entity B 3 years hence. Entity A has a poor credit rating and therefore borrows at a 12 percent interest rate.

a. In a settlement transaction, Entity B would never consent to replace Entity A with an entity of lower credit standing. All other things being equal, Entity B might consent to replace Entity A with a borrower of similar credit standing and would probably consent to replace Entity A with a more creditworthy entity.

b. Entity C has a good credit rating and therefore borrows at a 6 percent interest rate. It might willingly assume Entity A's obligation for $420 (the present value at 6 percent). Entity C has no incentive to assume the obligation for less (a higher interest rate) if it can borrow at 6 percent because it can receive $420 for an identical promise to pay $500.

c. However, if Entity A were to borrow the money to pay Entity C, it would have to promise $590 ($420 due in 3 years with accumulated interest at 12 percent).

81. Based on the admittedly simple case outlined above, the fair value of Entity A's liability should be approximately $356 (the present value of $500 in 3 years at 12 percent). The $420 price demanded by Entity C includes the fair value of Entity A's liability ($356) plus the price of an upgrade in the credit quality of the liability. There may be situations in which an entity might pay an additional amount to induce others to enter into a settlement transaction. Those cases are analogous to the purchase of a credit guarantee and, like the purchase of a guarantee, the additional amount represents a separate transaction rather than an element in the fair value of the entity's original liability.

82. The effect of an entity's credit standing on the measurement of its liabilities is usually captured in an adjustment to the interest rate, as illustrated above. This is similar to the traditional approach to incorporating risk and uncertainty in the measurement of assets and is well suited to liabilities with contractual cash flows. An expected cash flow approach may be more effective when measuring the effect of credit standing on other liabilities. For example, a liability may present the entity with a range of possible outflows, ranging from very low to very high amounts. There may be little chance of default if the amount is low, but a high chance of default if the amount is high. In situations like this, the effect of credit standing may be more effectively incorporated in the computation of expected cash flows.

83. The role of an entity's credit standing in the accounting measurement of its liabilities has been a controversial question among

accountants. The entity's credit standing clearly affects the interest rate at which it borrows in the marketplace. The initial proceeds of a loan, therefore, always reflect the entity's credit standing at that time. Similarly, the price at which others buy and sell the entity's loan includes their assessment of the entity's ability to repay. The example in paragraph 80 demonstrates how the entity's credit standing would affect the price it would be required to pay to have another entity assume its liability. However, some have questioned whether an entity's financial statements should reflect the effect of its credit standing (or changes in credit standing).

84. Some suggest that the measurement objective for liabilities is fundamentally different from the measurement objective for assets. In their view, financial statement users are better served by liability measurements that focus on the entity's obligation. They suggest a measurement approach in which financial statements would portray the present value of an obligation such that two entities with the same obligation but different credit standing would report the same carrying amount. Some existing accounting pronouncements take this approach, most notably FASB Statements No. 87, *Employers' Accounting for Pensions,* and No. 106, *Employers' Accounting for Postretirement Benefits Other Than Pensions.*

85. However, there is no convincing rationale for why the initial measurement of some liabilities would necessarily include the effect of credit standing (as in a loan for cash) while others might not (as in a warranty liability or similar item). Similarly, there is no rationale for why, in initial or fresh-start measurement, the recorded amount of a liability should reflect something other than the price that would exist in the marketplace. Consistent with its conclusions on fair value (refer to paragraph 30), the Board found no rationale for taking a different view in subsequent fresh-start measurements of an existing asset or liability than would pertain to measurements at initial recognition.

86. Some argue that changes in an entity's credit standing are not relevant to users of financial statements. In their view, a fresh-start

measurement that reflects changes in credit standing produces accounting results that are confusing. If the measurement includes changes in credit standing, and an entity's credit standing declines, the fresh-start measurement of its liabilities declines. That decline in liabilities is accompanied by an increase in owners' equity, a result that they find counterintuitive. How, they ask, can a bad thing (declining credit standing) produce a good thing (increased owners' equity)?

87. Like all measurements at fair value, fresh-start measurement of liabilities can produce unfamiliar results when compared with reporting the liabilities on an amortized basis. A change in credit standing represents a change in the relative positions of the two classes of claimants (shareholders and creditors) to an entity's assets. If the credit standing diminishes, the fair value of creditors' claims diminishes. The amount of shareholders' residual claim to the entity's assets may appear to increase, but that increase probably is offset by losses that may have occasioned the decline in credit standing. Because shareholders usually cannot be called on to pay a corporation's liabilities, the amount of their residual claims approaches, and is limited by, zero. Thus, a change in the position of borrowers necessarily alters the position of shareholders, and vice versa.

88. The failure to include changes in credit standing in the measurement of a liability ignores economic differences between liabilities. Consider the case of an entity that has two classes of borrowing. Class One was transacted when the entity had a strong credit standing and a correspondingly low interest rate. Class Two is new and was transacted under the entity's current lower credit standing. Both classes trade in the marketplace based on the entity's current credit standing. If the two liabilities are subject to fresh-start measurement, failing to include changes in the entity's credit standing makes the classes of borrowings seem different—even though the marketplace evaluates the quality of their respective cash flows as similar to one another.

F3. Paragraph 8 of this Statement requires that estimates of future cash flows used in a present value technique be consistent with the objective of measuring fair value. Paragraph 23 of Concepts Statement 7 discusses the essential elements of a fair value measurement. That paragraph of Concepts Statement 7 follows:

> 23. A present value measurement that fully captures the economic differences between the five assets described in paragraph 20 would necessarily include the following elements:
>
> a. An estimate of the future cash flow, or in more complex cases, series of future cash flows at different times[2]
> b. Expectations about possible variations in the amount or timing of those cash flows
> c. The time value of money, represented by the risk-free rate of interest
> d. The price for bearing the uncertainty inherent in the asset or liability
> e. Other, sometimes unidentifiable, factors including illiquidity and market imperfections.

---

[2]In complex measurements, such as measurements of liabilities settled by providing services, cash flow estimates necessarily include elements like overhead and profit margins inherent in the price of goods and services.

F4. Paragraph 9 of this Statement requires that estimates of future cash flows used in a present value technique incorporate assumptions that marketplace participants would use in their estimates of fair value whenever that information is available without undue cost and effort. Paragraph 32 of Concepts Statement 7 provides examples of circumstances in which an entity's cash flows (entity assumptions) might differ from the market cash flows (marketplace assumptions). That paragraph of Concepts Statement 7 follows:

> 32. An entity's best estimate of the present value of cash flows will not necessarily equal the fair value of those uncertain cash flows. There are several reasons why an entity might expect to realize or pay cash flows that differ from those expected by others in the marketplace. Those include:
>
> a. The entity's managers might intend different use or settlement than that anticipated by others. For example, they might intend to operate a property as a bowling alley, even though others in the marketplace consider its highest and best use to be a parking lot.

b. The entity's managers may prefer to accept risk of a liability (like a product warranty) and manage it internally, rather than transferring that liability to another entity.

c. The entity might hold special preferences, like tax or zoning variances, not available to others.

d. The entity might hold information, trade secrets, or processes that allow it to realize (or avoid paying) cash flows that differ from others' expectations.

e. The entity might be able to realize or pay amounts through use of internal resources. For example, an entity that manufactures materials used in particular processes acquires those materials at cost, rather than the market price charged to others. An entity that chooses to satisfy a liability with internal resources may avoid the markup or anticipated profit charged by outside contractors.

Statement of Financial Accounting Standards No. 144
Accounting for the Impairment or Disposal of
Long-Lived Assets

STATUS

Issued: August 2001

Effective Date: For financial statements issued for fiscal years beginning after December 15, 2001 and interim periods within those fiscal years

Affects: Amends ARB 51, paragraph 2
Supersedes ARB 51, paragraph 12
Amends APB 18, paragraph 19(h)
Amends APB 28, paragraphs 21, 30(e), and 31
Amends APB 29, paragraphs 21 and 23
Amends APB 30, paragraphs 3, 11, 23, and 25
Supersedes APB 30, paragraphs 8, 9, and 13 through 18 and footnotes 2 and 5 through 7
Amends AIN-APB 30, Interpretation 1
Amends FAS 15, paragraphs 28 and 33
Supersedes FAS 19, paragraph 44(a)
Amends FAS 19 by adding a paragraph after paragraph 62
Amends FAS 34, paragraph 19
Amends FAS 43, paragraph 2
Amends FAS 51, paragraph 14
Amends FAS 60, paragraph 48
Amends FAS 61, paragraph 6
Amends FAS 66, paragraph 65
Supersedes FAS 66, footnote 5
Amends FAS 67, paragraphs 3, 24, and 28
Supersedes FAS 67, paragraphs 16 and 25
Amends FAS 71, paragraphs 9 and 10 and by adding a paragraph after paragraph 10
Amends FAS 88, paragraphs 6(a) and 57 (Example 3A)
Supersedes FAS 88, paragraphs 8 and 16
Amends FAS 94, paragraph 13
Amends FAS 101, paragraph 6
Amends FAS 106, paragraph 96(a)
Supersedes FAS 106, paragraph 103
Amends FAS 112, paragraph 9
Amends FAS 115, paragraph 8(c)
Amends FAS 117, paragraph 164
Supersedes FAS 121
Amends FAS 123, paragraph 9
Supersedes FAS 141, footnote 18
Supersedes FAS 142, paragraph 7 and footnote 22
Amends FAS 142, paragraphs 15, 17, 28(f), 29, and Appendix A (Examples 1 through 3, 5, and 9)
Amends FAS 143, paragraphs 2 and 12
Supersedes FAS 143, footnote 11
Amends FIN 18, paragraphs 19, 35, and 71
Supersedes FIN 18, footnotes 1 and 20
Supersedes FIN 27, paragraph 3
Amends FIN 39, paragraph 7

Affected by: Paragraphs 5, 45, and D1 amended by FAS 145
Paragraph C7 superseded by FAS 145

FASB Statement of Standards

Issues Discussed by FASB Emerging Issues Task Force (EITF)

   Affects: Nullifies EITF Issues No. 85-36, 87-11, 90-6, 90-16, 95-18, and Topic No. D-45
           Partially nullifies EITF Issue No. 93-4
           Resolves EITF Issues No. 84-28 and 95-21
           Partially resolves EITF Issue No. 01-2

   Interpreted by: Paragraphs 9 and 19 through 21 interpreted by EITF Issue No. 95-23
           Paragraph 43 interpreted by EITF Issues No. 87-24 and 93-17
           Paragraph 51 interpreted by EITF Topic No. D-104

   Related Issues: EITF Issues No. 86-22, 87-4, 87-18, 89-13, 93-11, 94-3, 97-4, 99-14, and 00-26

SUMMARY

This Statement addresses financial accounting and reporting for the impairment or disposal of long-lived assets. This Statement supersedes FASB Statement No. 121, *Accounting for the Impairment of Long-Lived Assets and for Long-Lived Assets to Be Disposed Of,* and the accounting and reporting provisions of APB Opinion No. 30, *Reporting the Results of Operations—Reporting the Effects of Disposal of a Segment of a Business, and Extraordinary, Unusual and Infrequently Occurring Events and Transactions,* for the disposal of a *segment of a business* (as previously defined in that Opinion). This Statement also amends ARB No. 51, *Consolidated Financial Statements,* to eliminate the exception to consolidation for a subsidiary for which control is likely to be temporary.

Reasons for Issuing This Statement

Because Statement 121 did not address the accounting for a segment of a business accounted for as a discontinued operation under Opinion 30, two accounting models existed for long-lived assets to be disposed of. The Board decided to establish a single accounting model, based on the framework established in Statement 121, for long-lived assets to be disposed of by sale. The Board also decided to resolve significant implementation issues related to Statement 121.

Differences between This Statement, Statement 121, and Opinion 30 and Additional Implementation Guidance

Long-Lived Assets to Be Held and Used

This Statement retains the requirements of Statement 121 to (a) recognize an impairment loss only if the carrying amount of a long-lived asset is not recoverable from its undiscounted cash flows and (b) measure an impairment loss as the difference between the carrying amount and fair value of the asset. To resolve implementation issues, this Statement:

- Removes goodwill from its scope and, therefore, eliminates the requirement of Statement 121 to allocate goodwill to long-lived assets to be tested for impairment
- Describes a probability-weighted cash flow estimation approach to deal with situations in which alternative courses of action to recover the carrying amount of a long-lived asset are under consideration or a range is estimated for the amount of possible future cash flows
- Establishes a "primary-asset" approach to determine the cash flow estimation period for a group of assets and liabilities that represents the unit of accounting for a long-lived asset to be held and used.

Long-Lived Assets to Be Disposed Of Other Than by Sale

This Statement requires that a long-lived asset to be abandoned, exchanged for a similar productive asset, or distributed to owners in a spinoff be considered held and used until it is disposed of. To resolve implementation issues, this Statement:

- Requires that the depreciable life of a long-lived asset to be abandoned be revised in accordance with APB Opinion No. 20, *Accounting Changes*
- Amends APB Opinion No. 29, *Accounting for Nonmonetary Transactions,* to require that an impairment loss be recognized at the date a long-lived asset is exchanged for a similar productive asset or distributed to owners in a spinoff if the carrying amount of the asset exceeds its fair value.

Long-Lived Assets to Be Disposed Of by Sale

The accounting model for long-lived assets to be disposed of by sale is used for all long-lived assets, whether previously held and used or newly acquired. That accounting model retains the requirement of Statement 121 to measure a long-lived asset classified as held for sale at the lower of its carrying amount or fair value less cost to sell and to cease depreciation (amortization). Therefore, discontinued operations are no longer measured on a net realizable value basis, and future operating losses are no longer recognized before they occur.

This Statement retains the basic provisions of Opinion 30 for the presentation of discontinued operations in the income statement but broadens that presentation to include a component of an entity (rather than a segment of a business). A component of an entity comprises operations and cash flows that can be clearly distinguished, operationally and for financial reporting purposes, from the rest of the entity. A component of an entity that is classified as held for sale or that has been disposed of is presented as a discontinued operation if the operations and cash flows of the component will be (or have been) eliminated from the ongoing operations of the entity and the entity will not have any significant continuing involvement in the operations of the component.

To resolve implementation issues, this Statement:

- Establishes criteria beyond that previously specified in Statement 121 to determine when a long-lived asset is held for sale, including a group of assets and liabilities that represents the unit of accounting for a long-lived asset classified as held for sale. Among other things, those criteria specify that (a) the asset must be available for immediate sale in its present condition subject only to terms that are usual and customary for sales of such assets and (b) the sale of the asset must be probable, and its transfer expected to qualify for recognition as a completed sale, within one year, with certain exceptions.
- Provides guidance on the accounting for a long-lived asset if the criteria for classification as held for sale are met after the balance sheet date but before issuance of the financial statements. That guidance prohibits retroactive reclassification of the asset as held for sale at the balance sheet date. Therefore, the guidance in EITF Issue No. 95-18, "Accounting and Reporting for a Discontinued Business Segment When the Measurement Date Occurs after the Balance Sheet Date but before the Issuance of Financial Statements," is superseded.
- Provides guidance on the accounting for a long-lived asset classified as held for sale if the asset is reclassified as held and used. The reclassified asset is measured at the lower of its (a) carrying amount before being classified as held for sale, adjusted for any depreciation (amortization) expense that would have been recognized had the asset been continuously classified as held and used, or (b) fair value at the date the asset is reclassified as held and used.

How the Changes in This Statement Improve Financial Reporting

The changes in this Statement improve financial reporting by requiring that one accounting model be used for long-lived assets to be disposed of by sale, whether previously held and used or newly acquired, and by broadening the presentation of discontinued operations to include more disposal transactions. Therefore, the accounting for similar events and circumstances will be the same. Additionally, the information value of reported financial information will be improved. Finally, resolving significant implementation issues will improve compliance with the requirements of this Statement and, therefore, comparability among entities and the representational faithfulness of reported financial information.

How the Conclusions in This Statement Relate to the Conceptual Framework

In reconsidering the use of a measurement approach based on net realizable value, and the accrual of future operating losses required under that approach, the Board used the definition of a liability in FASB Concepts Statement No. 6, *Elements of Financial Statements*. The Board determined that future operating losses do not meet the definition of a liability.

In considering changes to Statement 121, the Board focused on the qualitative characteristics discussed in FASB Concepts Statement No. 2, *Qualitative Characteristics of Accounting Information*. In particular, the Board determined that:

- Broadening the presentation of discontinued operations to include more disposal transactions provides investors, creditors, and others with decision-useful information that is relevant in assessing the effects of disposal transactions on the ongoing operations of an entity
- Eliminating inconsistencies from having two accounting models for long-lived assets to be disposed of by sale improves comparability in financial reporting among entities, enabling users to identify similarities in and differences between two sets of economic events.

This Statement also incorporates the guidance in FASB Concepts Statement No. 7, *Using Cash Flow Information and Present Value in Accounting Measurements,* for using present value techniques to measure fair value.

The Effective Date of This Statement

The provisions of this Statement are effective for financial statements issued for fiscal years beginning after December 15, 2001, and interim periods within those fiscal years, with early application encouraged. The provisions of this Statement generally are to be applied prospectively.

Statement of Financial Accounting Standards No. 144

Accounting for the Impairment or Disposal of Long-Lived Assets

CONTENTS

INTRODUCTION

1. This Statement addresses financial accounting and reporting for the impairment of long-lived assets and for long-lived assets to be disposed of. This Statement supersedes FASB Statement No. 121, *Accounting for the Impairment of Long-Lived Assets and for Long-Lived Assets to Be Disposed Of.* However, this Statement retains the fundamental provisions of Statement 121 for (a) recognition and measurement of the impairment of long-lived assets to be held and used and (b) measurement of long-lived assets to be disposed of by sale.

2. This Statement supersedes the accounting and reporting provisions of APB Opinion No. 30, *Reporting the Results of Operations—Reporting the Effects of Disposal of a Segment of a Business, and Extraordinary, Unusual and Infrequently Occurring Events and Transactions,* for segments of a business to be

disposed of. However, this Statement retains the requirement of Opinion 30 to report discontinued operations separately from continuing operations and extends that reporting to a component of an entity that either has been disposed of (by sale, by abandonment, or in a distribution to owners) or is classified as held for sale. This Statement also amends ARB No. 51, *Consolidated Financial Statements,* to eliminate the exception to consolidation for a temporarily controlled subsidiary.

STANDARDS OF FINANCIAL ACCOUNTING AND REPORTING

Scope

3. Except as indicated in paragraphs 4 and 5, this Statement applies to recognized long-lived assets of an *entity*[1] to be held and used or to be disposed of, including (a) capital leases of lessees, (b) long-lived assets of lessors subject to operating leases, (c) proved oil and gas properties that are being accounted for using the successful-efforts method of accounting,[2] and (d) long-term prepaid assets.[3]

4. If a long-lived asset (or assets) is part of a group that includes other assets and liabilities not covered by this Statement, this Statement applies to the group. In those situations, the unit of accounting for the long-lived asset is its group. For a long-lived asset or assets to be held and used, that group (hereinafter referred to as an *asset group*) represents the lowest level for which identifiable cash flows are largely independent of the cash flows of other groups of assets and liabilities. For a long-lived asset or assets to be disposed of by sale or otherwise, that group (hereinafter referred to as a *disposal group*) represents assets to be disposed of together as a group in a single transaction and liabilities directly associated with those as-

sets that will be transferred in the transaction.[4] This Statement does not change generally accepted accounting principles applicable to those other individual assets (such as accounts receivable and inventory) and liabilities (such as accounts payable, long-term debt, and asset retirement obligations) not covered by this Statement that are included in such groups.

5. This Statement does not apply to (a) goodwill, (b) intangible assets not being amortized, (c) long-term customer relationships of a financial institution, such as core deposit intangibles, credit cardholder intangibles, and servicing assets, (d) financial instruments, including investments in equity securities accounted for under the cost or equity method, (e) deferred policy acquisition costs, (f) deferred tax assets, and (g) unproved oil and gas properties that are being accounted for using the successful-efforts method of accounting. This Statement also does not apply to long-lived assets for which the accounting is prescribed by:

- FASB Statement No. 44, *Accounting for Intangible Assets of Motor Carriers*
- FASB Statement No. 50, *Financial Reporting in the Record and Music Industry*
- FASB Statement No. 63, *Financial Reporting by Broadcasters*
- FASB Statement No. 86, *Accounting for the Costs of Computer Software to Be Sold, Leased, or Otherwise Marketed*
- FASB Statement No. 90, *Regulated Enterprises—Accounting for Abandonments and Disallowances of Plant Costs.*

6. Appendix C lists the accounting pronouncements affected by this Statement. Appendix D shows the status of FASB and Accounting Principles Board (APB) pronouncements that refer to impairment of long-lived assets, including those pronouncements that remain authoritative.[5]

---

[1]This Statement applies to a business enterprise and a not-for-profit organization, each of which is referred to herein as an *entity*.

[2]Accounting requirements for oil and gas properties that are accounted for using the full-cost method of accounting are prescribed by the Securities and Exchange Commission (Regulation S-X, Rule 4-10, "Financial Accounting and Reporting for Oil and Gas Producing Activities Pursuant to the Federal Securities Laws and the Energy Policy and Conservation Act of 1975").

[3]In this Statement, all references to a *long-lived asset* refer to a long-lived asset covered by this Statement.

[4]Examples of such liabilities include, but are not limited to, legal obligations that transfer with a long-lived asset, such as certain environmental obligations, and obligations that, for business reasons, a potential buyer would prefer to settle when assumed as part of a group, such as warranty obligations that relate to an acquired customer base.

[5]This Statement amends only pronouncements of the FASB, the APB, and the Committee on Accounting Procedure. Conforming changes to other literature, including consensuses of the FASB's Emerging Issues Task Force and pronouncements of the American Institute of Certified Public Accountants, may be made subsequently.

Long-Lived Assets to Be Held and Used

Recognition and Measurement of an Impairment Loss

7. For purposes of this Statement, *impairment* is the condition that exists when the carrying amount of a long-lived asset (asset group) exceeds its fair value. An impairment loss shall be recognized only if the carrying amount of a long-lived asset (asset group) is not recoverable and exceeds its fair value. The carrying amount of a long-lived asset (asset group) is not recoverable if it exceeds the sum of the undiscounted cash flows expected to result from the use and eventual disposition of the asset (asset group). That assessment shall be based on the carrying amount of the asset (asset group) at the date it is tested for recoverability, whether in use (paragraph 19) or under development (paragraph 20). An impairment loss shall be measured as the amount by which the carrying amount of a long-lived asset (asset group) exceeds its fair value.

When to test a long-lived asset for recoverability

8. A long-lived asset (asset group) shall be tested for recoverability whenever events or changes in circumstances indicate that its carrying amount may not be recoverable. The following are examples of such events or changes in circumstances:

a. A significant decrease in the market price of a long-lived asset (asset group)
b. A significant adverse change in the extent or manner in which a long-lived asset (asset group) is being used or in its physical condition
c. A significant adverse change in legal factors or in the business climate that could affect the value of a long-lived asset (asset group), including an adverse action or assessment by a regulator
d. An accumulation of costs significantly in excess of the amount originally expected for the acquisition or construction of a long-lived asset (asset group)
e. A current-period operating or cash flow loss combined with a history of operating or cash flow losses or a projection or forecast that demonstrates

continuing losses associated with the use of a long-lived asset (asset group)
f. A current expectation that, *more likely than not,*[6] a long-lived asset (asset group) will be sold or otherwise disposed of significantly before the end of its previously estimated useful life.

9. When a long-lived asset (asset group) is tested for recoverability, it also may be necessary to review depreciation estimates and method as required by APB Opinion No. 20, *Accounting Changes,* or the amortization period as required by FASB Statement No. 142, *Goodwill and Other Intangible Assets.*[7] Any revision to the remaining useful life of a long-lived asset resulting from that review also shall be considered in developing estimates of future cash flows used to test the asset (asset group) for recoverability (paragraph 18). However, any change in the accounting method for the asset resulting from that review shall be made only after applying this Statement.

Grouping long-lived assets to be held and used

10. For purposes of recognition and measurement of an impairment loss, a long-lived asset or assets shall be grouped with other assets and liabilities at the lowest level for which identifiable cash flows are largely independent of the cash flows of other assets and liabilities. However, an impairment loss, if any, that results from applying this Statement shall reduce only the carrying amount of a long-lived asset or assets of the group in accordance with paragraph 14.

11. In limited circumstances, a long-lived asset (for example, a corporate headquarters facility) may not have identifiable cash flows that are largely independent of the cash flows of other assets and liabilities and of other asset groups. In those circumstances, the asset group for that long-lived asset shall include all assets and liabilities of the entity.

12. Goodwill shall be included in an asset group to be tested for impairment under this Statement only if the asset group is or includes a *reporting unit.*[8] Goodwill shall not be included in a lower-level asset group that includes only part of a reporting unit. Estimates

---

[6]The term *more likely than not* refers to a level of likelihood that is more than 50 percent.

[7]Paragraphs 10 and 31–33 of Opinion 20 address the accounting for changes in estimates; paragraphs 23 and 24 of Opinion 20 address the accounting for changes in the method of depreciation. Paragraph 11 of Statement 142 addresses the determination of the useful life of an intangible asset.

[8]The term *reporting unit* is defined in Statement 142 as the same level as or one level below an operating segment (as that term is defined in paragraph 10 of FASB Statement No. 131, *Disclosures about Segments of an Enterprise and Related Information*). Statement 142 requires that goodwill be tested for impairment at the reporting unit level.

of future cash flows used to test that lower-level asset group for recoverability shall not be adjusted for the effect of excluding goodwill from the group.

13. Other than goodwill, the carrying amounts of any assets (such as accounts receivable and inventory) and liabilities (such as accounts payable, long-term debt, and asset retirement obligations) not covered by this Statement that are included in an asset group shall be adjusted in accordance with other applicable generally accepted accounting principles prior to testing the asset group for recoverability.[9]

14. An impairment loss for an asset group shall reduce only the carrying amounts of a long-lived asset or assets of the group. The loss shall be allocated to the long-lived assets of the group on a pro rata basis using the relative carrying amounts of those assets, except that the loss allocated to an individual long-lived asset of the group shall not reduce the carrying amount of that asset below its fair value whenever that fair value is determinable without undue cost and effort. (Example 1 of Appendix A illustrates the allocation of an impairment loss for an asset group.)

New cost basis

15. If an impairment loss is recognized, the adjusted carrying amount of a long-lived asset shall be its new cost basis. For a depreciable long-lived asset, the new cost basis shall be depreciated (amortized) over the remaining useful life of that asset. Restoration of a previously recognized impairment loss is prohibited.

Estimates of future cash flows used to test a long-lived asset for recoverability

16. Estimates of future cash flows used to test the recoverability of a long-lived asset (asset group) shall include only the future cash flows (cash inflows less associated cash outflows) that are directly associated with and that are expected to arise as a direct result of the use and eventual disposition of the asset (asset group). Those estimates shall exclude interest charges that will be recognized as an expense when incurred.

17. Estimates of future cash flows used to test the recoverability of a long-lived asset (asset group) shall incorporate the entity's own assumptions about its use of the asset (asset group) and shall consider all available evidence. The assumptions used in developing those estimates shall be reasonable in relation to the assumptions used in developing other information used by the entity for comparable periods, such as internal budgets and projections, accruals related to incentive compensation plans, or information communicated to others. However, if alternative courses of action to recover the carrying amount of a long-lived asset (asset group) are under consideration or if a range is estimated for the amount of possible future cash flows associated with the likely course of action, the likelihood of those possible outcomes shall be considered. A probability-weighted approach may be useful in considering the likelihood of those possible outcomes. (Example 2 of Appendix A illustrates the use of that approach when alternative courses of action are under consideration.)

18. Estimates of future cash flows used to test the recoverability of a long-lived asset (asset group) shall be made for the remaining useful life of the asset (asset group) to the entity. The remaining useful life of an asset group shall be based on the remaining useful life of the primary asset of the group. For purposes of this Statement, the *primary asset* is the principal long-lived tangible asset being depreciated or intangible asset being amortized that is the most significant component asset from which the asset group derives its cash-flow-generating capacity.[10] Factors that an entity generally should consider in determining whether a long-lived asset is the primary asset of an asset group include the following: (a) whether other assets of the group would have been acquired by the entity without the asset, (b) the level of investment that would be required to replace the asset, and (c) the remaining useful life of the asset relative to other assets of the group. If the primary asset is not the asset of the group with the longest remaining useful life, estimates of future cash flows for the group should assume the sale of the group at the end of the remaining useful life of the primary asset.

19. Estimates of future cash flows used to test the recoverability of a long-lived asset (asset group) that is in use, including a long-lived asset (asset group) for which development is substantially complete, shall be based on the existing service potential of the asset

---

[9]Paragraph 29 of Statement 142 requires that goodwill be tested for impairment only after the carrying amounts of the other assets of the reporting unit, including the long-lived assets covered by this Statement, have been tested for impairment under other applicable accounting pronouncements.

[10]The primary asset of an asset group therefore cannot be land or an intangible asset not being amortized.

(asset group) at the date it is tested. The service potential of a long-lived asset (asset group) encompasses its remaining useful life, cash-flow-generating capacity, and for tangible assets, physical output capacity. Those estimates shall include cash flows associated with future expenditures necessary to maintain the existing service potential of a long-lived asset (asset group), including those that replace the service potential of component parts of a long-lived asset (for example, the roof of a building) and component assets other than the primary asset of an asset group. Those estimates shall exclude cash flows associated with future capital expenditures that would increase the service potential of a long-lived asset (asset group).

20. Estimates of future cash flows used to test the recoverability of a long-lived asset (asset group) that is under development shall be based on the expected service potential of the asset (group) when development is substantially complete. Those estimates shall include cash flows associated with all future expenditures necessary to develop a long-lived asset (asset group), including interest payments that will be capitalized as part of the cost of the asset (asset group).[11]

21. If a long-lived asset that is under development is part of an asset group that is in use, estimates of future cash flows used to test the recoverability of that group shall include the cash flows associated with future expenditures necessary to maintain the existing service potential of the group (paragraph 19) as well as the cash flows associated with all future expenditures necessary to substantially complete the asset that is under development (paragraph 20). (Example 3 of Appendix A illustrates that situation.)

Fair value

22. The fair value of an asset (liability) is the amount at which that asset (liability) could be bought (incurred) or sold (settled) in a current transaction between willing parties, that is, other than in a forced or liquidation sale.[12] Quoted market prices in active markets are the best evidence of fair value and shall be used as the basis for the measurement, if available. However, in many instances, quoted market prices in active markets will not be available for the long-lived

assets (asset groups) covered by this Statement. In those instances, the estimate of fair value shall be based on the best information available, including prices for similar assets (groups) and the results of using other valuation techniques.

23. A present value technique is often the best available valuation technique with which to estimate the fair value of a long-lived asset (asset group). Paragraphs 39–54 of FASB Concepts Statement No. 7, *Using Cash Flow Information and Present Value in Accounting Measurements,* discuss the use of two present value techniques to measure the fair value of an asset (liability).[13] The first is expected present value, in which multiple cash flow scenarios that reflect the range of possible outcomes and a risk-free rate are used to estimate fair value. The second is traditional present value, in which a single set of estimated cash flows and a single interest rate (a rate commensurate with the risk) are used to estimate fair value. Either present value technique can be used for a fair value measurement. However, for long-lived assets (asset groups) that have uncertainties both in timing and amount, an expected present value technique will often be the appropriate technique. (Example 4 of Appendix A illustrates the use of that technique.)

24. If a present value technique is used, estimates of future cash flows shall be consistent with the objective of measuring fair value. Assumptions that marketplace participants would use in their estimates of fair value shall be incorporated whenever that information is available without undue cost and effort.[14] Otherwise, the entity may use its own assumptions.

Reporting and Disclosure

25. An impairment loss recognized for a long-lived asset (asset group) to be held and used shall be included in income from continuing operations before income taxes in the income statement of a business enterprise and in income from continuing operations in the statement of activities of a not-for-profit organization. If a subtotal such as "income from operations" is presented, it shall include the amount of that loss.

---

[11]FASB Statement No. 34, *Capitalization of Interest Cost,* states, "The capitalization period shall end when the asset is substantially complete and ready for its intended use" (paragraph 18).

[12]The fair value of an asset or a disposal group refers to the amount at which the group as a whole could be bought or sold in a current single transaction. Therefore, the fair value of the group would not necessarily equate to the sum of the fair values of the individual assets and liabilities of the group.

[13]Appendix E incorporates those paragraphs of Concepts Statement 7.

[14]Concepts Statement 7 discusses the essential elements of a present value measurement (paragraph 23) and provides reasons why an entity's estimates of cash flows might differ from those used by marketplace participants (paragraph 32). Appendix E incorporates those paragraphs.

26. The following information shall be disclosed in the notes to the financial statements that include the period in which an impairment loss is recognized:

a. A description of the impaired long-lived asset (asset group) and the facts and circumstances leading to the impairment
b. If not separately presented on the face of the statement, the amount of the impairment loss and the caption in the income statement or the statement of activities that includes that loss
c. The method or methods for determining fair value (whether based on a quoted market price, prices for similar assets, or another valuation technique)
d. If applicable, the segment in which the impaired long-lived asset (asset group) is reported under FASB Statement No. 131, *Disclosures about Segments of an Enterprise and Related Information.*

Long-Lived Assets to Be Disposed Of Other Than by Sale

27. A long-lived asset to be disposed of other than by sale (for example, by abandonment, in an exchange for a similar productive long-lived asset, or in a distribution to owners in a spinoff) shall continue to be classified as held and used until it is disposed of. Paragraphs 7–26 shall apply while the asset is classified as held and used. If a long-lived asset is to be abandoned or distributed to owners in a spinoff together with other assets (and liabilities) as a group and that disposal group is a *component of an entity*,[15] paragraphs 41–44 shall apply to the disposal group at the date it is disposed of.

Long-Lived Asset to Be Abandoned

28. For purposes of this Statement, a long-lived asset to be abandoned is disposed of when it ceases to be used. If an entity commits to a plan to abandon a long-lived asset before the end of its previously estimated useful life, depreciation estimates shall be revised in accordance with Opinion 20 to reflect the use of the asset over its shortened useful life (refer to paragraph 9).[16] A long-lived asset that has been temporarily idled shall not be accounted for as if abandoned.

Long-Lived Asset to Be Exchanged for a Similar Productive Long-Lived Asset or to Be Distributed to Owners in a Spinoff

29. For purposes of this Statement, a long-lived asset to be exchanged for a similar productive long-lived asset or to be distributed to owners in a spinoff is disposed of when it is exchanged or distributed. If the asset (asset group) is tested for recoverability while it is classified as held and used, the estimates of future cash flows used in that test shall be based on the use of the asset for its remaining useful life, assuming that the disposal transaction will not occur. In addition to any impairment losses required to be recognized while the asset is classified as held and used, an impairment loss, if any, shall be recognized when the asset is disposed of if the carrying amount of the asset (disposal group) exceeds its fair value.[17]

Long-Lived Assets to Be Disposed Of by Sale

Recognition

30. A long-lived asset (disposal group) to be sold shall be classified as held for sale in the period in which all of the following criteria are met:

a. Management, having the authority to approve the action, commits to a plan to sell the asset (disposal group).
b. The asset (disposal group) is available for immediate sale in its present condition subject only to terms that are usual and customary for sales of such assets (disposal groups). (Examples 5–7 of Appendix A illustrate when that criterion would be met.)
c. An active program to locate a buyer and other actions required to complete the plan to sell the asset (disposal group) have been initiated.

[15]A *component of an entity* is defined in paragraph 41 of this Statement as comprising operations and cash flows that can be clearly distinguished, operationally and for financial reporting purposes, from the rest of the entity.

[16]Because the continued use of a long-lived asset demonstrates the presence of service potential, only in unusual situations would the fair value of a long-lived asset to be abandoned be zero while it is being used. When a long-lived asset ceases to be used, the carrying amount of the asset should equal its salvage value, if any. The salvage value of the asset should not be reduced to an amount less than zero.

[17]The provisions of this paragraph apply to those transactions described in paragraphs 21 and 23 of APB Opinion No. 29, *Accounting for Nonmonetary Transactions*, for which the accounting is based on the recorded amount (after reduction, if appropriate, for an indicated impairment of value) of a long-lived asset exchanged or distributed.

d. The sale of the asset (disposal group) is probable,[18] and transfer of the asset (disposal group) is expected to qualify for recognition as a completed sale, within one year, except as permitted by paragraph 31. (Example 8 of Appendix A illustrates when that criterion would be met.)
e. The asset (disposal group) is being actively marketed for sale at a price that is reasonable in relation to its current fair value.
f. Actions required to complete the plan indicate that it is unlikely that significant changes to the plan will be made or that the plan will be withdrawn.

If at any time the criteria in this paragraph are no longer met (except as permitted by paragraph 31), a long-lived asset (disposal group) classified as held for sale shall be reclassified as held and used in accordance with paragraph 38.

31. Events or circumstances beyond an entity's control may extend the period required to complete the sale of a long-lived asset (disposal group) beyond one year. An exception to the one-year requirement in paragraph 30(d) shall apply in the following situations in which such events or circumstances arise:

a. If at the date an entity commits to a plan to sell a long-lived asset (disposal group) the entity reasonably expects that others (not a buyer) will impose conditions on the transfer of the asset (group) that will extend the period required to complete the sale and (1) actions necessary to respond to those conditions cannot be initiated until after a *firm purchase commitment*[19] is obtained and (2) a firm purchase commitment is probable within one year. (Example 9 of Appendix A illustrates that situation.)
b. If an entity obtains a firm purchase commitment and, as a result, a buyer or others unexpectedly impose conditions on the transfer of a long-lived asset (disposal group) previously classified as held for sale that will extend the period required to complete the sale and (1) actions necessary to respond to the conditions have been or will be

timely initiated and (2) a favorable resolution of the delaying factors is expected. (Example 10 of Appendix A illustrates that situation.)
c. If during the initial one-year period, circumstances arise that previously were considered unlikely and, as a result, a long-lived asset (disposal group) previously classified as held for sale is not sold by the end of that period and (1) during the initial one-year period the entity initiated actions necessary to respond to the change in circumstances, (2) the asset (group) is being actively marketed at a price that is reasonable given the change in circumstances, and (3) the criteria in paragraph 30 are met. (Example 11 of Appendix A illustrates that situation.)

32. A long-lived asset (disposal group) that is newly acquired and that will be sold rather than held and used shall be classified as held for sale at the acquisition date only if the one-year requirement in paragraph 30(d) is met (except as permitted by paragraph 31) and any other criteria in paragraph 30 that are not met at that date are probable of being met within a short period following the acquisition (usually within three months).

33. If the criteria in paragraph 30 are met after the balance sheet date but before issuance of the financial statements, a long-lived asset shall continue to be classified as held and used in those financial statements when issued.[20] The information required by paragraph 47(a) shall be disclosed in the notes to the financial statements. If the asset (asset group) is tested for recoverability (on a held-and-used basis) as of the balance sheet date, the estimates of future cash flows used in that test shall consider the likelihood of possible outcomes that existed at the balance sheet date, including the assessment of the likelihood of the future sale of the asset. That assessment made as of the balance sheet date shall not be revised for a decision to sell the asset after the balance sheet date.[21] An impairment loss, if any, to be recognized shall be measured as the amount by which the carrying

---

[18]The term *probable* is used consistent with the meaning associated with it in paragraph 3(a) of FASB Statement No. 5, *Accounting for Contingencies,* and refers to a future sale that is "likely to occur."

[19]A *firm purchase commitment* is an agreement with an unrelated party, binding on both parties and usually legally enforceable, that (a) specifies all significant terms, including the price and timing of the transaction, and (b) includes a disincentive for nonperformance that is sufficiently large to make performance probable.

[20]Refer to AICPA Statement on Auditing Standards No. 1, *Codification of Auditing Standards and Procedures,* Section 560, "Subsequent Events."

[21]Because it is difficult to separate the benefit of hindsight when assessing conditions that existed at a prior date, it is important that judgments about those conditions, the need to test an asset for recoverability, and the application of a recoverability test be made and documented together with supporting evidence on a timely basis.

amount of the asset (asset group) exceeds its fair value at the balance sheet date.

Measurement

34. A long-lived asset (disposal group) classified as held for sale shall be measured at the lower of its carrying amount or fair value less cost to sell. If the asset (disposal group) is newly acquired, the carrying amount of the asset (disposal group) shall be established based on its fair value less cost to sell at the acquisition date. A long-lived asset shall not be depreciated (amortized) while it is classified as held for sale. Interest and other expenses attributable to the liabilities of a disposal group classified as held for sale shall continue to be accrued.

35. Costs to sell are the incremental direct costs to transact a sale, that is, the costs that result directly from and are essential to a sale transaction and that would not have been incurred by the entity had the decision to sell not been made. Those costs include broker commissions, legal and title transfer fees, and closing costs that must be incurred before legal title can be transferred. Those costs exclude expected future losses associated with the operations of a long-lived asset (disposal group) while it is classified as held for sale.[22] If the sale is expected to occur beyond one year as permitted in limited situations by paragraph 31, the cost to sell shall be discounted.

36. The carrying amounts of any assets that are not covered by this Statement, including goodwill, that are included in a disposal group classified as held for sale shall be adjusted in accordance with other applicable generally accepted accounting principles prior to measuring the fair value less cost to sell of the disposal group.[23]

37. A loss shall be recognized for any initial or subsequent write-down to fair value less cost to sell. A gain shall be recognized for any subsequent increase in fair value less cost to sell, but not in excess of the cumulative loss previously recognized (for a write-down to fair value less cost to sell). The loss or gain shall adjust only the carrying amount of a long-lived asset, whether classified as held for sale individually

or as part of a disposal group. A gain or loss not previously recognized that results from the sale of a long-lived asset (disposal group) shall be recognized at the date of sale.

Changes to a Plan of Sale

38. If circumstances arise that previously were considered unlikely and, as a result, an entity decides not to sell a long-lived asset (disposal group) previously classified as held for sale, the asset (disposal group) shall be reclassified as held and used. A long-lived asset that is reclassified shall be measured individually at the lower of its (a) carrying amount before the asset (disposal group) was classified as held for sale, adjusted for any depreciation (amortization) expense that would have been recognized had the asset (disposal group) been continuously classified as held and used, or (b) fair value at the date of the subsequent decision not to sell.

39. Any required adjustment to the carrying amount of a long-lived asset that is reclassified as held and used shall be included in income from continuing operations in the period of the subsequent decision not to sell. That adjustment shall be reported in the same income statement caption used to report a loss, if any, recognized in accordance with paragraph 45. If a component of an entity is reclassified as held and used, the results of operations of the component previously reported in discontinued operations in accordance with paragraph 43 shall be reclassified and included in income from continuing operations for all periods presented.

40. If an entity removes an individual asset or liability from a disposal group previously classified as held for sale, the remaining assets and liabilities of the disposal group to be sold shall continue to be measured as a group only if the criteria in paragraph 30 are met. Otherwise, the remaining long-lived assets of the group shall be measured individually at the lower of their carrying amounts or fair values less cost to sell at that date. Any long-lived assets that will not be sold shall be reclassified as held and used in accordance with paragraph 38.

---

[22]Expected future operating losses that marketplace participants would not similarly consider in their estimates of the fair value less cost to sell of a long-lived asset (disposal group) classified as held for sale shall not be indirectly recognized as part of an expected loss on the sale by reducing the carrying amount of the asset (disposal group) to an amount less than its current fair value less cost to sell.

[23]Paragraph 39 of Statement 142 provides guidance for allocating goodwill to a lower-level asset group to be disposed of that is part of a reporting unit and that constitutes a business. Goodwill is not included in a lower-level asset group to be disposed of that is part of a reporting unit if it does not constitute a business.

**Reporting Long-Lived Assets and Disposal
Groups to Be Disposed Of**

Reporting Discontinued Operations

41. For purposes of this Statement, a *component of an entity* comprises operations and cash flows that can be clearly distinguished, operationally and for financial reporting purposes, from the rest of the entity. A component of an entity may be a reportable segment or an operating segment (as those terms are defined in paragraph 10 of Statement 131), a reporting unit (as that term is defined in Statement 142), a subsidiary, or an asset group (as that term is defined in paragraph 4).

42. The results of operations of a component of an entity that either has been disposed of or is classified as held for sale shall be reported in discontinued operations in accordance with paragraph 43 if both of the following conditions are met: (a) the operations and cash flows of the component have been (or will be) eliminated from the ongoing operations of the entity as a result of the disposal transaction and (b) the entity will not have any significant continuing involvement in the operations of the component after the disposal transaction. (Examples 12–15 of Appendix A illustrate disposal activities that do or do not qualify for reporting as discontinued operations.)

43. In a period in which a component of an entity either has been disposed of or is classified as held for sale, the income statement of a business enterprise (or statement of activities of a not-for-profit organization) for current and prior periods shall report the results of operations of the component, including any gain or loss recognized in accordance with paragraph 37, in discontinued operations. The results of operations of a component classified as held for sale shall be reported in discontinued operations in the period(s) in which they occur. The results of discontinued operations, less applicable income taxes (benefit), shall be reported as a separate component of income before extraordinary items and the cumulative effect of accounting changes (if applicable). For example, the results of discontinued operations may be reported in the income statement of a business enterprise as follows:

Income from continuing operations before income taxes	$XXXX
Income taxes	XXX
Income from continuing operations[24]	$XXXX
Discontinued operations (Note X)	
Loss from operations of discontinued Component X (including loss on disposal of $XXX)	XXXX
Income tax benefit	XXXX
Loss on discontinued operations	XXXX
Net income	$XXXX

A gain or loss recognized on the disposal shall be disclosed either on the face of the income statement or in the notes to the financial statements (paragraph 47(b)).

44. Adjustments to amounts previously reported in discontinued operations that are directly related to the disposal of a component of an entity in a prior period shall be classified separately in the current period in discontinued operations. The nature and amount of such adjustments shall be disclosed. Examples of circumstances in which those types of adjustments may arise include the following:

a. The resolution of contingencies that arise pursuant to the terms of the disposal transaction, such as the resolution of purchase price adjustments and indemnification issues with the purchaser
b. The resolution of contingencies that arise from and that are directly related to the operations of the component prior to its disposal, such as environmental and product warranty obligations retained by the seller
c. The settlement of employee benefit plan obligations (pension, postemployment benefits other

---

[24]This caption shall be modified appropriately when an entity reports an extraordinary item or the cumulative effect of a change in accounting principle or both in accordance with Opinion 20. If applicable, the presentation of per-share data will need similar modification.

than pensions, and other postemployment benefits), provided that the settlement is directly related to the disposal transaction.[25]

Reporting Disposal Gains or Losses in Continuing Operations

45. A gain or loss recognized for a long-lived asset (disposal group) classified as held for sale that is not a component of an entity shall be included in income from continuing operations before income taxes in the income statement of a business enterprise and in income from continuing operations in the statement of activities of a not-for-profit organization. If a subtotal such as "income from operations" is presented, it shall include the amounts of those gains or losses.

Reporting a Long-Lived Asset or Disposal Group Classified as Held for Sale

46. A long-lived asset classified as held for sale shall be presented separately in the statement of financial position. The assets and liabilities of a disposal group classified as held for sale shall be presented separately in the asset and liability sections, respectively, of the statement of financial position. Those assets and liabilities shall not be offset and presented as a single amount. The major classes of assets and liabilities classified as held for sale shall be separately disclosed either on the face of the statement of financial position or in the notes to financial statements (paragraph 47(a)).

Disclosure

47. The following information shall be disclosed in the notes to the financial statements that cover the period in which a long-lived asset (disposal group) either has been sold or is classified as held for sale:

a. A description of the facts and circumstances leading to the expected disposal, the expected manner and timing of that disposal, and, if not separately presented on the face of the statement, the carrying amount(s) of the major classes of assets and liabilities included as part of a disposal group

b. The gain or loss recognized in accordance with paragraph 37 and if not separately presented on the face of the income statement, the caption in the income statement or the statement of activities that includes that gain or loss

c. If applicable, amounts of revenue and pretax profit or loss reported in discontinued operations

d. If applicable, the segment in which the long-lived asset (disposal group) is reported under Statement 131.

48. If either paragraph 38 or paragraph 40 applies, a description of the facts and circumstances leading to the decision to change the plan to sell the long-lived asset (disposal group) and its effect on the results of operations for the period and any prior periods presented shall be disclosed in the notes to financial statements that include the period of that decision.

Effective Date and Transition

49. Except as specified in paragraphs 50 and 51, the provisions of this Statement shall be effective for financial statements issued for fiscal years beginning after December 15, 2001, and interim periods within those fiscal years. Early application is encouraged. Initial application of this Statement shall be as of the beginning of an entity's fiscal year. That is, if the Statement is initially applied prior to the effective date and during an interim period other than the first interim period, all prior interim periods of that fiscal year shall be restated. Restatement of previously issued annual financial statements is not permitted.[26] However, previously issued statements of financial position presented for comparative purposes shall be reclassified to reflect application of the provisions of paragraph 46 of this Statement for reporting disposal groups classified as held for sale.

50. The provisions of this Statement for long-lived assets (disposal groups) to be disposed of by sale or otherwise (paragraphs 27–45 and paragraphs 47 and 48) shall be effective for disposal activities initiated by an entity's commitment to a plan after the effective date of this Statement or after it is initially applied.

51. Except as provided in the following sentence, long-lived assets (disposal groups) classified as held

---

[25]Paragraph 3 of FASB Statement No. 88, *Employers' Accounting for Settlements and Curtailments of Defined Benefit Pension Plans and for Termination Benefits*, defines *settlement* as "a transaction that (a) is an irrevocable action, (b) relieves the employer (or the plan) of primary responsibility for a pension benefit obligation, and (c) eliminates significant risks related to the obligation and the assets used to effect the settlement." A settlement is directly related to the disposal transaction if there is a demonstrated direct cause-and-effect relationship and the settlement occurs no later than one year following the disposal transaction, unless it is delayed by events or circumstances beyond an entity's control (refer to paragraph 31).

[26]Paragraph 43 requires that when a component of an entity is reported as a discontinued operation, the income statements of prior periods be reclassified to report the results of operations of the component separately. This transition provision does not affect that requirement.

for disposal as a result of disposal activities that were initiated prior to this Statement's initial application shall continue to be accounted for in accordance with the prior pronouncement (Statement 121 or Opinion 30) applicable for that disposal. If the criteria in paragraph 30 of this Statement are not met by the end of the fiscal year in which this Statement is initially applied, the related long-lived assets shall be reclassified as held and used in accordance with paragraph 38 of this Statement.

> **The provisions of this Statement need not be applied to immaterial items.**

This Statement was adopted by the unanimous vote of the six members of the Financial Accounting Standards Board:

Edmund L. Jenkins,
Chairman

G. Michael Crooch
John M. Foster
Gary S. Schieneman

Edward W. Trott
John K. Wulff

Appendix A

IMPLEMENTATION GUIDANCE

Introduction

A1. This appendix illustrates application of some of the provisions of this Statement in certain specific situations. The relevant paragraphs of this Statement are identified in the parenthetical notes. The examples do not address all possible situations or applications of this Statement. This appendix is an integral part of the standards provided in this Statement.

Example 1—Allocating an Impairment Loss

A2. This example illustrates the allocation of an impairment loss to the long-lived assets of an asset group (paragraph 14).

A3. An entity owns a manufacturing facility that together with other assets is tested for recoverability as a group. In addition to long-lived assets (Assets A–D), the asset group includes inventory, which is reported at the lower of cost or market in accordance with ARB No. 43, Chapter 4, "Inventory Pricing," and other current assets and liabilities that are not covered by this Statement. The $2.75 million aggregate carrying amount of the asset group is not recoverable and exceeds its fair value by $600,000. In accordance with paragraph 14, the impairment loss of $600,000 would be allocated as shown below to the long-lived assets of the group.

Asset Group	Carrying Amount	Pro Rata Allocation Factor	Allocation of Impairment (Loss)	Adjusted Carrying Amount
	(in $ 000s)			
Current assets	$ 400	—	—	$ 400
Liabilities	(150)	—	—	(150)
Long-lived assets:				
Asset A	590	24%	$(144)	446
Asset B	780	31	(186)	594
Asset C	950	38	(228)	722
Asset D	180	7	(42)	138
Subtotal—long-lived assets	2,500	100	(600)	1,900
Total	$2,750	100%	$(600)	$2,150

A4. If the fair value of an individual long-lived asset of an asset group is determinable without undue cost and effort and exceeds the adjusted carrying amount of that asset after an impairment loss is allocated initially, the excess impairment loss initially allocated to that asset would be reallocated to the other long-lived assets of the group. For example, if the fair value of Asset C is $822,000, the excess impairment loss of $100,000 initially allocated to that asset (based on its adjusted carrying amount of $722,000) would be reallocated as shown below to the other long-lived assets of the group on a pro rata basis using the relative adjusted carrying amounts of those assets.

Long-Lived Assets of Asset Group	Adjusted Carrying Amount	Pro Rata Reallocation Factor	Reallocation of Excess Impairment (Loss)	Adjusted Carrying Amount after Reallocation
	(in $ 000s)			
Asset A	$ 446	38%	$ (38)	$ 408
Asset B	594	50	(50)	544
Asset D	138	12	(12)	126
Subtotal	1,178	100%	(100)	1,078
Asset C	722		100	822
Total—long-lived assets	$1,900		$ 0	$1,900

Example 2—Probability-Weighted Cash Flows

A5. This example illustrates the use of a probability-weighted approach for developing estimates of future cash flows used to test a long-lived asset for recoverability when alternative courses of action are under consideration (paragraph 17).

A6. At December 31, 20X2, a manufacturing facility with a carrying amount of $48 million is tested for recoverability. At that date, 2 courses of action to recover the carrying amount of the facility are under consideration—sell in 2 years or sell at the end of its remaining useful life of 10 years. The facility has identifiable cash flows that are largely independent of the cash flows of other assets.

A7. The following table shows the range and probability of possible estimated cash flows expected to result from the use and eventual disposition of the facility assuming that (a) it is sold at the end of 2 years or (b) it is sold at the end of 10 years. Among other things, the range of possible estimated cash flows considers future sales levels (volume and price) and associated manufacturing costs in varying scenarios that consider (a) the likelihood that existing customer relationships will continue and (b) future economic (market) conditions. The probability assessments consider all information available without undue cost and effort. Such assessments are by their nature subjective and, in many situations, may be limited to management's best judgment about the probabilities of the best, worst, and most-likely scenarios.

Course of Action	Cash Flow Estimate (Use)	Cash Flow Estimate (Disposition)	Cash Flow Estimate	Probability Assessment	Probability-Weighted Cash Flows
		(in $ millions)			
Sell in 2 years	$ 8	$30	$38	20%	$ 7.6
	11	30	41	50	20.5
	13	30	43	30	12.9
					$41.0

Course of Action	Cash Flow Estimate (Use)	Cash Flow Estimate (Disposition)	Cash Flow Estimate	Probability Assessment	Probability-Weighted Cash Flows
		(in $ millions)			
Sell in 10 years	36	1	37	20%	$ 7.4
	48	1	49	50	24.5
	55	1	56	30	16.8
					$48.7

A8. In computing the future cash flows used to test the facility for recoverability, the entity concludes that there is (a) a 60 percent probability that the facility will be sold at the end of 2 years and (b) a 40 percent probability that the facility will continue to be used for its remaining estimated useful life of 10 years. The following table shows the computation of future cash flows based on the probability of those alternative courses of action.[27] As shown, those future cash flows are $44.1 million (undiscounted). Therefore, the carrying amount of the facility of $48 million would not be recoverable.

Course of Action	Probability-Weighted Cash Flows	Probability Assessment (Course of Action)	Expected Cash Flows
	(in $ millions)		
Sell in 2 years	$41.0	60%	$24.6
Sell in 10 years	48.7	40	19.5
			$44.1

Example 3—Estimates of Future Cash Flows Used to Test an Asset Group for Recoverability

A9. A long-lived asset that is under development may be part of an asset group that is in use. In that situation, estimates of future cash flows used to test the recoverability of that group shall include the cash flows associated with future expenditures necessary to maintain the existing service potential of the group as well as the cash flows associated with future expenditures necessary to substantially complete the asset that is under development (paragraph 21).

A10. An entity engaged in mining and selling phosphate estimates future cash flows from its commercially minable phosphate deposits in order to test the recoverability of the asset group that includes the mine and related long-lived assets (plant and equip-

ment). Deposits from the mined rock must be processed in order to extract the phosphate. As the active mining area expands along the geological structure of the mine, a new processing plant is constructed near the production area. Depending on the size of the mine, extracting the minable deposits may require building numerous processing plants over the life of the mine. In testing the recoverability of the mine and related long-lived assets, the estimates of future cash flows from its commercially minable phosphate deposits would include cash flows associated with future expenditures necessary to build all of the required processing plants.

Example 4—Expected Present Value Technique

A11. This example illustrates the application of an expected present value technique to estimate the fair

[27]The alternatives of whether to sell or use an asset are not necessarily independent of each other. In many situations, after estimating the possible future cash flows relating to those potential courses of action, an entity might select the course of action that results in a significantly higher estimate of possible future cash flows. In that situation, the entity generally would use the estimates of possible future cash flows relating only to that course of action in computing future cash flows.

value of a long-lived asset in the absence of an observable market price (paragraph 23).[28] It is based on the facts provided for the manufacturing facility in Example 2.

A12. Consistent with an objective of measuring fair value, the entity's estimates of future cash flows used to test the manufacturing facility for recoverability in Example 2 are adjusted to incorporate assumptions that, based on available information, marketplace participants would use in their estimates of the fair value of the asset. The net effect of those adjustments

is to increase the entity's estimates of future cash flows (on an undiscounted basis) by approximately 15 percent.[29]

A13. The following table shows by year the range and probability of possible cash flows expected to result from the use and eventual disposition of the facility over its remaining useful life of 10 years (Example 2), adjusted for market assumptions. It also shows by year the computation of expected cash flows.

Year	Total Cash Flow Estimate (Market) (in $ millions)	Probability Assessment	Expected Cash Flows
1	$4.6	20%	$ .9
	6.3	50	3.2
	7.5	30	2.3
			$6.4
2	$4.6	20%	$ .9
	6.3	50	3.2
	7.5	30	2.3
			$6.4
3	$4.3	20%	$ .9
	5.8	50	2.9
	6.7	30	2.0
			$5.8
4	$4.3	20%	$ .9
	5.8	50	2.9
	6.7	30	2.0
			$5.8

---

[28]Present value is the current measure of an estimated future cash inflow, discounted at an interest rate for the number of periods between today and the date of the estimated cash flow. The present value of X in n periods in the future and discounted at interest of i per period is computed using the formula $X/(1+i)^n$. Because all of the risks are considered in the estimates of cash flows, the entity discounts the expected cash flows for each year using the risk-free rate of interest. The risk-free rate of interest is the interest rate on monetary assets that are essentially risk free and that have maturity dates that coincide with the expected timing of the cash flow. In the United States, the risk-free rate is the rate for zero-coupon U.S. Treasury instruments. A yield curve for U.S. Treasury instruments may be used to determine the appropriate risk-free rates of interest.

[29]In this example, a reliable estimate of the market risk premium is not available. Paragraph 62 of FASB Concepts Statement No. 7, *Using Cash Flow Information and Present Value in Accounting Measurements,* explains:

> An estimate of fair value should include the price that marketplace participants are able to receive for bearing the uncertainties in cash flows—the adjustment for risk—if the amount is identifiable, measurable, and significant. An arbitrary adjustment for risk, or one that cannot be evaluated by comparison to marketplace information, introduces an unjustified bias into the measurement. On the other hand, excluding a risk adjustment (if it is apparent that marketplace participants include one) would not produce a measurement that faithfully represents fair value. There are many techniques for estimating a risk adjustment, including matrix pricing, option-adjusted spread models, and fundamental analysis. However, in many cases a reliable estimate of the market risk premium may not be obtainable or the amount may be small relative to potential measurement error in the estimated cash flows. In such situations, the present value of expected cash flows, discounted at a risk-free rate of interest, may be the best available estimate of fair value in the circumstances.

Year	Total Cash Flow Estimate (Market) (in $ millions)	Probability Assessment	Expected Cash Flows
5	$4.0	20%	$ .8
	5.4	50	2.7
	6.4	30	1.9
			$5.4
6	$4.0	20%	$ .8
	5.4	50	2.7
	6.4	30	1.9
			$5.4
7	$3.9	20%	$ .8
	5.1	50	2.6
	5.6	30	1.7
			$5.1
8	$3.9	20%	$ .8
	5.1	50	2.6
	5.6	30	1.7
			$5.1
9	$3.9	20%	$ .8
	5.0	50	2.5
	5.5	30	1.7
			$5.0
10	$4.9	20%	$1.0
	6.0	50	3.0
	6.5	30	2.0
			$6.0

A14. The following table shows the computation of the present value of the expected cash flows; that is, the sum of the present values of the expected cash flows by year, which are calculated by discounting those cash flows at a risk-free rate. As shown, the expected present value is $42.3 million. In accordance with paragraph 7, the entity would recognize an impairment loss of $5.7 million ($48 million less $42.3 million).

Year	Expected Cash Flows	Risk-Free Rate of Interest	Present Value	Expected Present Value
		(in $ millions)		
1	$6.4	5.0%	$6.1	
2	6.4	5.1	5.8	
3	5.8	5.2	5.0	
4	5.8	5.4	4.7	
5	5.4	5.6	4.1	
6	5.4	5.8	3.9	
7	5.1	6.0	3.4	
8	5.1	6.2	3.2	
9	5.0	6.4	2.9	
10	6.0	6.6	3.2	
				$42.3

Examples 5–7—Plan-of-Sale Criterion 30(b)

A15. To qualify for classification as held for sale, a long-lived asset (disposal group) must be available for immediate sale in its present condition subject only to terms that are usual and customary for sales of such assets (disposal groups) (paragraph 30(b)). A long-lived asset (disposal group) is available for immediate sale if an entity currently has the intent and ability to transfer the asset (disposal group) to a buyer in its present condition. Examples 5–7 illustrate situations in which the criterion in paragraph 30(b) would or would not be met.

Example 5

A16. An entity commits to a plan to sell its headquarters building and has initiated actions to locate a buyer.

a. The entity intends to transfer the building to a buyer after it vacates the building. The time necessary to vacate the building is usual and customary for sales of such assets. The criterion in paragraph 30(b) would be met at the plan commitment date.
b. The entity will continue to use the building until construction of a new headquarters building is completed. The entity does not intend to transfer the existing building to a buyer until after construction of the new building is completed (and it vacates the existing building). The delay in the timing of the transfer of the existing building imposed by the entity (seller) demonstrates that the building is not available for immediate sale. The criterion in paragraph 30(b) would not be met until construction of the new building is completed, even if a firm purchase commitment for the future transfer of the existing building is obtained earlier.

Example 6

A17. An entity commits to a plan to sell a manufacturing facility and has initiated actions to locate a buyer. At the plan commitment date, there is a backlog of uncompleted customer orders.

a. The entity intends to sell the manufacturing facility with its operations. Any uncompleted customer orders at the sale date would transfer to the buyer. The transfer of uncompleted customer orders at the sale date will not affect the timing of the transfer of the facility. The criterion in paragraph 30(b) would be met at the plan commitment date.

b. The entity intends to sell the manufacturing facility, but without its operations. The entity does not intend to transfer the facility to a buyer until after it ceases all operations of the facility and eliminates the backlog of uncompleted customer orders. The delay in the timing of the transfer of the facility imposed by the entity (seller) demonstrates that the facility is not available for immediate sale. The criterion in paragraph 30(b) would not be met until the operations of the facility cease, even if a firm purchase commitment for the future transfer of the facility is obtained earlier.

Example 7

A18. An entity acquires through foreclosure a real estate property that it intends to sell.

a. The entity does not intend to transfer the property to a buyer until after it completes renovations to increase its sales value. The delay in the timing of the transfer of the property imposed by the entity (seller) demonstrates that the property is not available for immediate sale. The criterion in paragraph 30(b) would not be met until the renovations are completed.
b. After the renovations are completed and the property is classified as held for sale but before a firm purchase commitment is obtained, the entity becomes aware of environmental damage requiring remediation. The entity still intends to sell the property. However, the entity does not have the ability to transfer the property to a buyer until after the remediation is completed. The delay in the timing of the transfer of the property imposed by others before a firm purchase commitment is obtained demonstrates that the property is not available for immediate sale. The criterion in paragraph 30(b) would not continue to be met. The property would be reclassified as held and used in accordance with paragraph 39.

Example 8—Plan-of-Sale Criterion 30(d)

A19. To qualify for classification as held for sale, the sale of a long-lived asset (disposal group) must be probable, and transfer of the asset (disposal group) must be expected to qualify for recognition as a completed sale, within one year (paragraph 30(d)). That criterion would not be met if, for example:

a. An entity that is a commercial leasing and finance company is holding for sale or lease equipment that has recently come off lease and the ultimate form of a future transaction (sale or lease) has not yet been determined.
b. An entity commits to a plan to "sell" a property that is in use, and the transfer of the property will be accounted for as a sale-leaseback through which the seller-lessee will retain more than a minor portion of the use of the property. The property would continue to be classified as held and used and paragraphs 7–26 would apply.[30]

Examples 9–11—Exceptions to Plan-of-Sale Criterion 30(d)

A20. An exception to the one-year requirement in paragraph 30(d) applies in limited situations in which the period required to complete the sale of a long-lived asset (disposal group) will be (or has been) extended by events or circumstances beyond an entity's control and certain conditions are met (paragraph 31). Examples 9–11 illustrate those situations.

Example 9

A21. An entity in the utility industry commits to a plan to sell a disposal group that represents a significant portion of its regulated operations. The sale will require regulatory approval, which could extend the period required to complete the sale beyond one year. Actions necessary to obtain that approval cannot be initiated until after a buyer is known and a firm purchase commitment is obtained. However, a firm purchase commitment is probable within one year. In that situation, the conditions in paragraph 31(a) for an exception to the one-year requirement in paragraph 30(d) would be met.

Example 10

A22. An entity commits to a plan to sell a manufacturing facility in its present condition and classifies the facility as held for sale at that date. After a firm purchase commitment is obtained, the buyer's inspection of the property identifies environmental damage not previously known to exist. The entity is

---

[30]If at the date of the sale-leaseback the fair value of the property is less than its undepreciated cost, a loss would be recognized immediately up to the amount of the difference between undepreciated cost and fair value in accordance with paragraph 3(c) of FASB Statement No. 28, *Accounting for Sales with Leasebacks*.

required by the buyer to remediate the damage, which will extend the period required to complete the sale beyond one year. However, the entity has initiated actions to remediate the damage, and satisfactory remediation of the damage is probable. In that situation, the conditions in paragraph 31(b) for an exception to the one-year requirement in paragraph 30(d) would be met.

Example 11

A23. An entity commits to a plan to sell a long-lived asset and classifies the asset as held for sale at that date.

a. During the initial one-year period, the market conditions that existed at the date the asset was classified initially as held for sale deteriorate and, as a result, the asset is not sold by the end of that period. During that period, the entity actively solicited but did not receive any reasonable offers to purchase the asset and, in response, reduced the price. The asset continues to be actively marketed at a price that is reasonable given the change in market conditions, and the criteria in paragraph 30 are met. In that situation, the conditions in paragraph 31(c) for an exception to the one-year requirement in paragraph 30(d) would be met. At the end of the initial one-year period, the asset would continue to be classified as held for sale.
b. During the following one-year period, market conditions deteriorate further, and the asset is not sold by the end of that period. The entity believes that the market conditions will improve and has not further reduced the price of the asset. The asset continues to be held for sale, but at a price in excess of its current fair value. In that situation, the absence of a price reduction demonstrates that the asset is not available for immediate sale as required by the criterion in paragraph 30(b). In addition, the criterion in paragraph 30(e) requires that an asset be marketed at a price that is reasonable in relation to its current fair value. Therefore, the conditions in paragraph 31(c) for an exception to the one-year requirement in paragraph 30(d) would not be met. The asset would be reclassified as held and used in accordance with paragraph 38.

Examples 12–15—Reporting Discontinued Operations

A24. The results of operations of a component of an entity that either has been disposed of or is classified as held for sale shall be reported in discontinued operations if (a) the operations and cash flows of the component have been (or will be) eliminated from the ongoing operations of the entity as a result of the disposal transaction and (b) the entity will not have any significant continuing involvement in the operations of the component after the disposal transaction (paragraph 42). Examples 12–15 illustrate disposal activities that do or do not qualify for reporting as discontinued operations.

Example 12

A25. An entity that manufactures and sells consumer products has several product groups, each with different product lines and brands. For that entity, a product group is the lowest level at which the operations and cash flows can be clearly distinguished, operationally and for financial reporting purposes, from the rest of the entity. Therefore, each product group is a component of the entity.

A26. The entity has experienced losses associated with certain brands in its beauty care products group.

a. The entity decides to exit the beauty care business and commits to a plan to sell the product group with its operations. The product group is classified as held for sale at that date. The operations and cash flows of the product group will be eliminated from the ongoing operations of the entity as a result of the sale transaction, and the entity will not have any continuing involvement in the operations of the product group after it is sold. In that situation, the conditions in paragraph 42 for reporting in discontinued operations the operations of the product group while it is classified as held for sale would be met.
b. The entity decides to remain in the beauty care business but will discontinue the brands with which the losses are associated. Because the brands are part of a larger cash-flow-generating product group and, in the aggregate, do not represent a group that on its own is a component of the entity, the conditions in paragraph 42 for reporting in discontinued operations the losses associated with the brands that are discontinued would not be met.

Example 13

A27. An entity that is a franchiser in the quick-service restaurant business also operates company-owned restaurants. For that entity, an individual company-owned restaurant is the lowest level at which the operations and cash flows can be clearly distinguished, operationally and for financial reporting purposes, from the rest of the entity. Therefore, each company-owned restaurant is a component of the entity.

a. The entity has experienced losses on its company-owned restaurants in one region. The entity decides to exit the quick-service restaurant business in that region and commits to a plan to sell the restaurants in that region. The restaurants are classified as held for sale at that date. The operations and cash flows of the restaurants in that region will be eliminated from the ongoing operations of the entity as a result of the sale transaction, and the entity will not have any continuing involvement in the operations of the restaurants after they are sold. In that situation, the conditions in paragraph 42 for reporting in discontinued operations the operations of the restaurants while they are classified as held for sale would be met.

b. Based on its evaluation of the ownership mix of its system-wide restaurants in certain markets, the entity commits to a plan to sell its company-owned restaurants in one region to an existing franchisee. The restaurants are classified as held for sale at that date. Although each company-owned restaurant, on its own, is a component of the entity, through the franchise agreement, the entity will (1) receive franchise fees determined, in part, based on the future revenues of the restaurants and (2) have significant continuing involvement in the operations of the restaurants after they are sold. In that situation, the conditions in paragraph 42 for reporting in discontinued operations the operations of the restaurants would not be met.

Example 14

A28. An entity that manufactures sporting goods has a bicycle division that designs, manufactures, markets, and distributes bicycles. For that entity, the bicycle division is the lowest level at which the operations and cash flows can be clearly distinguished, operationally and for financial reporting purposes, from the rest of the entity. Therefore, the bicycle division is a component of the entity.

A29. The entity has experienced losses in its bicycle division resulting from an increase in manufacturing costs (principally labor costs).

a. The entity decides to exit the bicycle business and commits to a plan to sell the division with its op-

erations. The bicycle division is classified as held for sale at that date. The operations and cash flows of the division will be eliminated from the ongoing operations of the entity as a result of the sale transaction, and the entity will not have any continuing involvement in the operations of the division after it is sold. In that situation, the conditions in paragraph 42 for reporting in discontinued operations the operations of the division while it is classified as held for sale would be met.

b. The entity decides to remain in the bicycle business but will outsource the manufacturing operations and commits to a plan to sell the related manufacturing facility. The facility is classified as held for sale at that date. Because the manufacturing facility is part of a larger cash-flow-generating group (the bicycle division), and on its own is not a component of the entity, the conditions in paragraph 42 for reporting in discontinued operations the operations (losses) of the manufacturing facility would not be met. (Those conditions also would not be met if the manufacturing facility on its own was a component of the entity because the decision to outsource the manufacturing operations of the division will not eliminate the operations and cash flows of the division [and its bicycle business] from the ongoing operations of the entity.)

Example 15

A30. An entity owns and operates retail stores that sell household goods. For that entity, each store is the lowest level at which the operations and cash flows can be clearly distinguished, operationally and for financial reporting purposes, from the rest of the entity. Therefore, each store is a component of the entity.

A31. To expand its retail store operations in one region, the entity decides to close two of its retail stores and open a new "superstore" in that region. The new superstore will continue to sell the household goods previously sold through the two retail stores as well as other related products not previously sold. Although each retail store on its own is a component of the entity, the operations and cash flows from the sale of household goods previously sold through the two retail stores in that region will not be eliminated from the ongoing operations of the entity. In that situation, the conditions in paragraph 42 for reporting in discontinued operations the operations of the stores would not be met.

Appendix B

BACKGROUND INFORMATION AND BASIS FOR CONCLUSIONS

CONTENTS

Appendix B

BACKGROUND INFORMATION AND BASIS FOR CONCLUSIONS

Introduction

B1. This appendix summarizes considerations that Board members deemed significant in reaching the conclusions in this Statement. It includes the reasons for accepting certain approaches and rejecting others. Individual Board members gave greater weight to some factors than to others. This appendix also summarizes the considerations that Board members deemed significant in reaching the conclusions in FASB Statement No. 121, *Accounting for the Impairment of Long-Lived Assets and for Long-Lived Assets to Be Disposed Of,* that are still relevant.

Background

B2. Statement 121, which was issued in 1995, established accounting standards for the impairment of long-lived assets to be held and used, including certain identifiable intangibles and goodwill related to those assets. It also established accounting standards for long-lived assets to be disposed of, including certain identifiable intangibles, that were not covered by APB Opinion No. 30, *Reporting the Results of Operations—Reporting the Effects of Disposal of a Segment of a Business, and Extraordinary, Unusual and Infrequently Occurring Events and Transactions.* Opinion 30 established, among other things, accounting and reporting standards for segments of a business to be disposed of. Paragraph 13 of Opinion 30 defined a segment of a business as "a component of an entity whose activities represent a separate major line of business or class of customer."

B3. After the issuance of Statement 121, significant differences existed in the accounting for long-lived assets to be disposed of covered by that Statement and by Opinion 30. The principal differences related to measurement and presentation.

B4. Under Statement 121, a long-lived asset classified as held for disposal was measured at the lower of its carrying amount or fair value less cost to sell, which excludes expected future operating losses that marketplace participants would not similarly consider in their estimates of the fair value less cost to sell of a long-lived asset classified as held for disposal. The gain or loss recognized on the disposal and any related results of operations were reported in continuing operations and separately disclosed in the notes to the financial statements.

B5. Under Opinion 30, a segment of a business to be disposed of was measured at the lower of its carrying amount or net realizable value, adjusted for expected future operating losses of the segment held for disposal. The accrual of future operating losses as previously required under Opinion 30 generally is inappropriate under the Board's conceptual framework, which was developed after the issuance of Opinion 30. The gain or loss recognized on the disposal and the related results of operations were reported in discontinued operations, separately from continuing operations. Under other accounting pronouncements, the measurement but not reporting requirements of Opinion 30 were extended to certain other disposal transactions.

B6. In Statement 121, the Board acknowledged that inconsistency in accounting for long-lived assets to be disposed of. However, at that time, the Board decided not to expand the scope of that Statement to reconsider the requirements of Opinion 30.

B7. Soon after the issuance of Statement 121, the Emerging Issues Task Force (EITF) and others identified significant issues related to the implementation of that Statement. They asked the Board to address those issues, including:

a. How to apply the provisions for long-lived assets to be held and used to a long-lived asset that an entity expects to sell or otherwise dispose of if the entity has not yet committed to a plan to sell or otherwise dispose of the asset
b. How to determine an "indicated impairment of value" of a long-lived asset to be exchanged for a similar productive long-lived asset or to be distributed to owners
c. What criteria must be met to classify a long-lived asset as held for sale and how to account for the asset if those criteria are met after the balance sheet date but before issuance of the financial statements
d. How to account for a long-lived asset classified as held for sale if the plan to sell the asset changes
e. How to display in the income statement the results of operations while a long-lived asset or a group of long-lived assets with separately identifiable operations is classified as held for sale
f. How to display in the statement of financial position a long-lived asset or a group of long-lived assets and liabilities classified as held for sale.

B8. In August 1996, the Board added this project to its agenda to (a) develop a single accounting model, based on the framework established in Statement 121, for long-lived assets to be disposed of by sale and (b) address significant implementation issues.

B9. In June 2000, the Board issued an Exposure Draft of a proposed Statement, *Accounting for the Impairment or Disposal of Long-Lived Assets and for Obligations Associated with Disposal Activities*. The Board received comment letters from 53 respondents to the Exposure Draft. In January 2001, the Board held a public roundtable meeting with some of those respondents to discuss significant issues raised in comment letters. The Board considered respondents' comments during its redeliberations of the issues addressed by the Exposure Draft in public meetings in 2001.

Scope

B10. Except as discussed in paragraphs B11–B14, this Statement applies to recognized long-lived assets to be held and used or to be disposed of. If a long-lived asset is part of a group that includes other assets and liabilities not covered by this Statement, this Statement applies to its asset group or disposal group, as discussed in paragraph 4 of this Statement.

B11. Long-lived assets excluded from the scope of Statement 121 also are excluded from the scope of this Statement. The Board concluded that the objectives of this project could be achieved without reconsidering the accounting for the impairment or disposal of those long-lived assets. Accordingly, this Statement does not apply to (a) financial assets, (b) long-lived assets for which the accounting is prescribed in other broadly applicable accounting pronouncements (such as deferred tax assets), and (c) long-lived assets for which the accounting is prescribed in accounting pronouncements that apply to certain specialized industries (including the record and music, motion picture, broadcasting, software, and insurance industries).

B12. The scope of Statement 121 included goodwill related to an asset group but not goodwill related to a disposal group. Goodwill not covered by Statement 121 was covered by APB Opinion No. 17, *Intangible Assets*. The Exposure Draft would have included in its scope goodwill related to an asset group, and would have amended Opinion 17 to also include in its scope goodwill related to a disposal group. However, after issuance of the Exposure Draft, the Board decided to reconsider the accounting for goodwill and intangible assets in its project on accounting for business combinations. In that project, the Board decided that goodwill and certain other intangible assets should no longer be amortized and should be tested for impairment in a manner different from how the long-lived assets covered by this Statement are tested for impairment. FASB Statement No. 142, *Goodwill and Other Intangible Assets,* addresses the accounting for the impairment of those assets. It also addresses the allocation of goodwill to a disposal group that constitutes a business. Accordingly, this Statement does not apply to goodwill or to intangible assets not being amortized.

B13. Statement 121 did not address the accounting for obligations associated with the disposal of a long-lived asset (disposal group) or for the results of operations during the holding period of the asset (disposal group). Instead, Statement 121 referred to EITF Issue No. 94-3, "Liability Recognition for Certain Employee Termination Benefits and Other Costs to Exit an Activity (including Certain Costs Incurred in a Restructuring)." Issue 94-3 provides guidance on recognition of liabilities for costs associated with restructuring and related disposal activities, including certain employee termination benefits and lease termination costs. During its deliberations of the Exposure Draft, the Board noted that liabilities are recognized under Issue 94-3 even though some of those items might not meet the definition of a liability set forth in the Board's conceptual framework. Because the types of costs covered by Issue 94-3 often are associated with the disposal of long-lived assets, the Board decided to reconsider the guidance in Issue 94-3 and include obligations associated with a disposal activity in the scope of this project.

B14. The Exposure Draft proposed significant changes to the guidance in Issue 94-3. Many respondents to the Exposure Draft disagreed with those proposed changes. Some of those respondents noted potential inconsistencies between the accounting requirements proposed in the Exposure Draft and the accounting requirements of other existing accounting pronouncements. Other respondents said that the Board should not reconsider the guidance in Issue 94-3 until after it undertakes a full conceptual reconsideration of all liabilities. Yet other respondents said that the Board should not reconsider that guidance at all, noting that SEC Staff Accounting Bulletin No. 100, *Restructuring and Impairment Charges,* now provides additional guidance for applying Issue 94-3. To avoid delaying the issuance of guidance on the accounting for the impairment or disposal of long-lived assets to address those issues, the Board decided to remove obligations associated with a disposal activity from the scope of this Statement. The Board plans to redeliberate those issues addressed by the Exposure Draft in a separate project.

Long-Lived Assets to Be Held and Used

Recognition of an Impairment Loss

B15. This Statement retains the requirement of Statement 121 to recognize an impairment loss only if the carrying amount of a long-lived asset (asset group) is not recoverable from its undiscounted cash flows and exceeds its fair value. In Statement 121, the Board decided for practical reasons to require an undiscounted cash flows recoverability test. In reaching that decision, the Board considered but rejected alternative criteria for recognition of an impairment loss. Specifically, the Board considered (a) an economic (fair value) criterion, (b) a permanence criterion, and (c) a probability criterion. Those criteria were discussed in paragraphs 60–62 of Statement 121:

The economic criterion calls for loss recognition whenever the carrying amount of an asset exceeds the asset's fair value. It is an approach that would require continuous evaluation for impairment of long-lived assets similar to the ongoing lower-of-cost-or-market measurement of inventory. The economic criterion is based on the measurement of the asset. Using the same measure for recognition and measurement assures consistent outcomes for identical fact situations. However, the economic criterion presupposes that a fair value is available for every asset on an ongoing basis. Otherwise, an event or change in circumstance would be needed to determine which assets needed to be measured and in which period. Some respondents to the Discussion Memorandum indicated that the results of a measurement should not be sufficient reason to trigger recognition of an impairment loss. They favored using either the permanence or probability criterion to avoid recognition of write-downs that might result from measurements reflecting only temporary market fluctuations.

The permanence criterion calls for loss recognition when the carrying amount of an asset exceeds the asset's fair value and the condition is judged to be permanent. Some respondents to the Discussion Memorandum indicated that a loss must be permanent rather than temporary before recognition should occur. In their view, a high hurdle for recognition of an impairment loss is necessary to prevent premature write-offs of productive assets. Others stated that requiring the impairment loss to be permanent makes the criterion too restrictive and virtually impossible to apply with any reliability. Still others noted that the permanence criterion is not practical to implement; in their view, requiring management to assess whether a loss is permanent goes beyond management's ability to apply judgment and becomes a requirement for management to predict future events with certainty.

The probability criterion, initially presented in the Issues Paper, calls for loss recognition based on the approach taken in FASB Statement No. 5, *Accounting for Contingencies.* Using that approach, an impairment loss would be recognized when it is deemed probable that the carrying amount of an asset cannot be fully recovered. Some respondents to the Discussion Memorandum stated that assessing the probability that an impairment loss has occurred is preferable to other recognition alternatives because it is already required by Statement 5. Most respondents to the Discussion Memorandum supported the probability criterion because, in their view, it best provides for management judgment.

When to test a long-lived asset for recoverability

B16. This Statement retains the requirement of Statement 121 to test a long-lived asset (asset group) for recoverability whenever events or changes in circumstances indicate that its carrying amount may not be recoverable. Paragraph 57 of Statement 121 discussed the basis for the Board's conclusion:

> The Board concluded . . . that management has the responsibility to consider whether an asset is impaired but that to test each asset each period would be too costly. Existing information and analyses developed for management review of the entity and its operations generally will be the principal evidence needed to determine when an impairment exists. Indicators of impairment, therefore, are useful examples of events or changes in circumstances that suggest that the recoverability of the carrying amount of an asset should be assessed.

B17. Statement 121 provided examples of such events or changes in circumstances. The Board decided to expand those examples, carried forward in paragraph 8 of this Statement, to also refer to a current expectation that a long-lived asset (asset group) will be disposed of significantly before the end of its previously estimated useful life (paragraph 8(f)). The Board reasoned that a current expectation that a long-lived asset (asset group) will be disposed of significantly before the end of its previously estimated useful life might indicate that the carrying amount of the asset (group) is not recoverable.

Estimates of future cash flows used to test a long-lived asset for recoverability

B18. Statement 121 provided general guidance for developing estimates of future cash flows used to estimate the fair value of a long-lived asset (asset group) in the absence of an observable market price.

However, it did not specify whether that guidance also should apply for developing estimates of future cash flows used to test a long-lived asset (asset group) for recoverability. Consequently, in implementing Statement 121, questions emerged about how to develop those estimates.

B19. In considering that issue, the Board noted that in contrast to an objective of measuring fair value, the objective of the undiscounted cash flows recoverability test is to assess the recoverability of a long-lived asset (asset group) in the context of a particular entity. The Board decided that because the objectives of measuring fair value and testing a long-lived asset (asset group) for recoverability are different, this Statement should provide guidance for developing estimates of future cash flows used to test for recoverability. The Board acknowledges that significant judgment is required in developing estimates of future cash flows. However, the Board believes that the level of guidance provided by this Statement is sufficient for meeting the objective of an undiscounted cash flows recoverability test.

B20. The guidance provided by this Statement focuses on (a) the cash flow estimation approach, (b) the cash flow estimation period, and (c) the types of asset-related expenditures that should be considered in developing estimates of future cash flows.

Cash flow estimation approach

B21. The guidance in Statement 121 permitted the use of either a probability-weighted approach or a best-estimate approach in developing estimates of future cash flows used to test for recoverability. Both of those cash flow estimation approaches are discussed in FASB Concepts Statement No. 7, *Using Cash Flow Information and Present Value in Accounting Measurements,* issued in February 2000. A probability-weighted approach refers to the sum of probability-weighted amounts in a range of possible estimated amounts. A best-estimate approach refers to the single most-likely amount in a range of possible estimated amounts. During its deliberations leading to the Exposure Draft, the Board reasoned that because the probability-weighted approach discussed in Concepts Statement 7 incorporates uncertainty in estimates of future cash flows, it would provide a more complete and disciplined estimate of future cash flows than would a best-estimate approach. Therefore, the Exposure Draft would have required, rather than permitted, the use of that approach in developing estimates of future cash flows used to test for recoverability.

B22. Several respondents to the Exposure Draft disagreed with that proposed requirement, stating that, for many entities, a probability-weighted approach would not be practical or cost-beneficial in developing estimates of future cash flows used to test for recoverability. The principal concern expressed by respondents was that in many cases, reliable information about the likelihood of possible outcomes would not be available. They said that the Board should permit the use of either a best-estimate approach or a probability-weighted approach in developing those estimates, as under Statement 121. During its redeliberations of the Exposure Draft, the Board decided not to require the probability-weighted approach in Concepts Statement 7 in developing estimates of future cash flows used to test for recoverability. The Board noted that Concepts Statement 7 expresses a preference for a probability-weighted approach, but that preference is discussed in the context of developing estimates of future cash flows that provide the basis for an accounting measurement (fair value). The Board concluded that because estimates of future cash flows used to test for recoverability, in and of themselves, do not provide the basis for an accounting measurement, the preference for a probability-weighted approach in Concepts Statement 7 need not be extended to those estimates. However, the Board agreed that in situations in which alternative courses of action to recover the carrying amount of a long-lived asset (asset group) are under consideration or in which a range is estimated for the amount of possible future cash flows associated with the likely course of action, a probability-weighted approach may be useful in considering the likelihood of those possible outcomes.

Cash flow estimation period

B23. Statement 121 did not specify the cash flow estimation period for estimates of future cash flows used to test for recoverability. The Board decided that the cash flow estimation period should correspond to the period that a long-lived asset (asset group) is expected to provide service potential to the entity. Accordingly, the cash flow estimation period for a long-lived asset is based on its remaining useful life to the entity. If long-lived assets having different remaining useful lives are grouped, the cash flow estimation period for the asset group is based on the remaining useful life of the primary asset of the group to the entity. The definition of a primary asset proposed in the Exposure Draft limited that asset to a tangible long-lived asset. Several respondents to the Exposure Draft agreed with the primary asset approach for determining the cash flow estimation period for an asset group. However, many said that because intangible assets often are more significant than tangible assets, the Board should expand the definition of a primary asset to include those assets.

B24. The Board initially decided to limit the primary asset to a tangible long-lived asset principally to prohibit an entity from arbitrarily designating as the primary asset goodwill associated with the group. The Board's decision was influenced by the then-existing requirement to amortize goodwill over a period of up to 40 years. However, in view of its subsequent decision in Statement 142 that goodwill should no longer be amortized, the Board decided to broaden the definition of a primary asset to include either a recognized tangible asset being depreciated or an intangible asset being amortized. The Board concluded that because there needs to be some boundaries on the cash flow estimation period for an asset group, indefinite-lived assets, such as land and intangible assets not being amortized, are not eligible to be primary assets. The Board affirmed its conclusion in the Exposure Draft that, for many asset groups, the primary asset will be readily identifiable and that the remaining useful life of that asset to the entity is a reasonable basis for consistently determining the cash flow estimation period for an asset group.

B25. During its deliberations leading to the Exposure Draft, the Board considered but rejected alternative approaches for determining the cash flow estimation period for an asset group. One approach would have limited the estimation period to the shorter of (a) the remaining useful life of the primary asset of the group or (b) 10 years and would have assumed the sale of the group at the end of that shortened period (limited estimation approach). The Board observed that because a limited estimation approach would include estimated disposal values (fair values) in estimates of future cash flows used to test for recoverability, the effect of that approach would be to discount some portion of those cash flows. The Board concluded that a limited estimation approach would be inconsistent with the requirement of this Statement to recognize an impairment loss only if the carrying amount of a long-lived asset (asset group) is not recoverable from its undiscounted future cash flows.

B26. Another approach for determining the cash flow estimation period for an asset group would have used the average of the remaining useful lives of the long-lived assets of the group, weighted based on the relative carrying amounts of those assets (weighted-average approach). The Board acknowledged that for some asset groups, a weighted-average approach could avoid difficulties in identifying the primary asset, but it concluded that for many entities, that approach could be unduly burdensome and result in little, if any, incremental benefit. Some respondents to the Exposure Draft suggested that the Board reconsider a weighted-average approach for entities that use a group composite depreciation method. However, the Board noted that the cost-capitalization approach proposed in the Exposure Draft of a proposed AICPA Statement of Position, *Accounting for Certain Costs and Activities Related to Property, Plant, and Equipment,* issued in June 2001, would effectively eliminate that depreciation method. The Board also believes that the approach for determining the cash flow estimation period should be the same for all entities with long-lived assets covered by this Statement.

Asset-related expenditures for a long-lived asset in use

B27. Statement 121 did not identify the types of asset-related expenditures that should be considered in estimates of future cash flows used to test a long-lived asset (asset group) for recoverability. During its deliberations leading to the Exposure Draft, the Board observed that, as a result, an entity could avoid the write-down of a long-lived asset that is in use by including in those estimates the cash flows (cash outflows and cash inflows) associated with all possible improvements that would be capitalized in future periods. In that case, the recoverability of the long-lived asset (asset group) would be assessed based on its expected future service potential ("as improved"), rather than on its existing service potential ("as is").

B28. The Board decided that a long-lived asset (asset group) that is in use, including a long-lived asset (asset group) for which development is substantially complete, should be tested for recoverability based on its existing service potential at the date of that test. Therefore, estimates of future cash flows used in that test should exclude the cash flows associated with asset-related expenditures that would enhance the existing service potential of a long-lived asset (asset group) that is in use.

B29. The Board decided that estimates of future cash flows used to test for recoverability should include cash flows (including estimated salvage values) associated with asset-related expenditures that replace (a) component parts of a long-lived asset or (b) component assets (other than the primary asset) of an asset group, whether those expenditures would be recognized as an expense or capitalized in future periods. The Board considered an alternative approach that would have excluded the cash flows associated with those expenditures. However, the Board observed that because an asset group could not continue to be used without replacing the component assets of the group, there would be an assumption that the asset of the group would be sold at the end of the remaining useful life of the primary asset. By including the estimated disposal values of those assets (fair values) in estimates of future cash flows used to test for recoverability, the effect of that approach would be to discount some portion of the cash flows. As discussed in paragraph B25, such an approach would be inconsistent with the requirement of this Statement to recognize an impairment loss only if the carrying amount of a long-lived asset (asset group) is not recoverable from its undiscounted future cash flows.

B30. Some respondents to the Exposure Draft noted that if an entity has a plan to improve a long-lived asset (asset group) that is in use, the entity could be required to write down the carrying amount of the asset (asset group) even if it would be recoverable after it is improved. They suggested that the Board permit an exception to the existing service potential requirement for a long-lived asset (asset group) that is in use in that situation. During its redeliberations of the Exposure Draft, the Board decided not to make that exception for the reason discussed in paragraph B27. However, the Board observed that in measuring fair value, if marketplace participants would assume the same improvements to the asset as the entity, the estimates of future cash flows used to measure fair value would include the cash flows (cash outflows and cash inflows) associated with those improvements. Consequently, it is possible that although the carrying amount of the asset (asset group) is not recoverable in its present condition, the fair value of the asset (asset group) could exceed its carrying amount and no impairment would exist.

Asset-related expenditures for a long-lived asset under development

B31. The Board observed that in contrast to a long-lived asset (asset group) that is in use, a long-lived asset (asset group) that is under development will not provide service potential until development is substantially complete. The Board decided that such an asset (asset group) should be tested for recoverability based on its expected service potential. Therefore, estimates of future cash flows used in that test should include the cash flows (cash outflows and cash inflows) associated with all future asset-related expenditures necessary to develop the asset (asset group), whether those expenditures would be recognized as an expense or capitalized in future periods.

B32. In Statement 121, the Board decided that estimates of future cash flows used to test a long-lived asset (asset group) for recoverability should exclude all future interest payments, whether those payments would be recognized as an expense or capitalized in future periods. In this Statement, the Board reconsidered that decision, noting that for a long-lived asset (asset group) that is under development, interest payments during the development period would be capitalized in accordance with paragraph 6 of FASB Statement No. 34, *Capitalization of Interest Cost,* which states:

> The historical cost of acquiring an asset includes the costs necessarily incurred to bring it to the condition and location necessary for its intended use. If an asset requires a period of time in which to carry out the activities necessary to bring it to that condition and location, the interest cost incurred during that period as a result of expenditures for the asset is a part of the historical cost of acquiring the asset. [Footnote references omitted.]

The Board reasoned that for a long-lived asset (asset group) that is under development, there is no difference between interest payments and other asset-related expenditures that would be capitalized in future periods. Therefore, the Board decided that estimates of future cash flows used to test a long-lived asset (asset group) for recoverability should exclude only those interest payments that would be recognized as an expense when incurred.

B33. Some respondents to the Exposure Draft asked the Board to clarify how the service potential requirements of this Statement would apply if a long-lived asset that is under development is part of an asset group that includes other assets that are in use. This Statement clarifies that the estimates of future cash flows used to test such an asset group for recoverability should include the cash flows (cash outflows and cash inflows) associated with (a) future asset-related expenditures necessary to complete the asset that is under development and (b) future asset-related expenditures necessary to maintain the existing service potential of the other assets that are in use.

Measurement of an Impairment Loss

B34. This Statement retains the requirement of Statement 121 to measure an impairment loss for a long-lived asset, including an asset that is subject to nonrecourse debt, as the amount by which the carrying amount of the asset (asset group) exceeds its fair value. Paragraphs 69–72 and 103 and 104 of Statement 121 discussed the basis for the Board's conclusion:

> The Board concluded that a decision to continue to operate rather than sell an impaired asset is economically similar to a decision to invest in that asset and, therefore, the impaired asset should be measured at its fair value. The amount of the impairment loss should be the amount by which the carrying amount of the impaired asset exceeds the fair value of the asset. That fair value then becomes the asset's new cost basis.
>
> When an entity determines that expected future cash flows from using an asset will not result in the recovery of the asset's carrying amount, it must decide whether to sell the asset and use the proceeds for an alternative purpose or to continue to use the impaired asset in its operations. The decision presumably is based on a comparison of expected future cash flows from those alternative courses of action and is essentially a capital investment decision. In either alternative, proceeds from the sale of the impaired asset are considered in the capital investment decision. Consequently, a decision to continue to use the impaired asset is equivalent to a new asset purchase decision, and a new basis of fair value is appropriate.
>
> . . . The Board . . . concluded that the fair value of an impaired asset is the best measure of the cost of continuing to use that asset because it is consistent with management's decision process. Presumably, no entity would

decide to continue to use an asset unless that alternative was expected to produce more in terms of expected future cash flows or service potential than the alternative of selling it and reinvesting the proceeds. The Board also believes that using fair value to measure the amount of an impairment loss is not a departure from the historical cost principle. Rather, it is a consistent application of principles practiced elsewhere in the current system of accounting whenever a cost basis for a newly acquired asset must be determined.

The Board believes that fair value is an easily understood notion. It is the amount at which an asset could be bought or sold in a current transaction between willing parties. The fair value measure is basic to economic theory and is grounded in the reality of the marketplace. Fair value estimates are readily available in published form for many assets, especially machinery and equipment. For some assets, multiple, on-line database services provide up-to-date market price information. Estimates of fair value also are subject to periodic verification whenever assets are exchanged in transactions between willing parties.

The Board considered requests for a limited exception to the fair value measurement for impaired long-lived assets that are subject to nonrecourse debt. Some believe that the nonrecourse provision is effectively a put option for which the borrower has paid a premium. They believe that the impairment loss on an asset subject entirely to nonrecourse debt should be limited to the loss that would occur if the asset were put back to the lender.

The Board decided not to provide an exception for assets subject to nonrecourse debt. The recognition of an impairment loss and the recognition of a gain on the extinguishment of debt are separate events, and each event should be recognized in the period in which it occurs. The Board believes that the recognition of an impairment loss should be based on the measurement of the asset at its fair value and that the existence of nonrecourse debt should not influence that measurement.

Alternative measures of an impairment loss

B35. In Statement 121, the Board considered but rejected measures other than fair value for measuring an impairment loss that could have been achieved within the historical cost framework. Specifically, the Board considered (a) a recoverable cost measure, (b) a recoverable cost including interest measure, and (c) different measures for different impairment losses.

B36. Paragraphs 77–81 of Statement 121 discussed a recoverable cost measure:

> Recoverable cost is measured as the sum of the undiscounted future cash flows expected to be generated over the life of an asset. For example, if an asset has a carrying amount of $1,000,000, a remaining useful life of 5 years, and expected future cash flows over the 5 years of $180,000 per year, the recoverable cost would be $900,000 (5 × $180,000), and the impairment loss would be $100,000 ($1,000,000 – $900,000).

The Board did not adopt recoverable cost as the measure of an impairment loss. Proponents of the recoverable cost measure believe that impairment is the result of the inability to recover the carrying amount of an asset. They do not view the decision to retain an impaired asset as an investment decision; rather, they view the recognition of an impairment loss as an adjustment to the historical cost of the asset. They contend that recoverable cost measured by the sum of the undiscounted expected future cash flows is the appropriate carrying amount for an impaired asset and the amount on which the impairment loss should be determined.

Proponents of the recoverable cost measure do not believe that the fair value of an asset is a relevant measure unless a transaction or other event justifies a new basis for the asset at fair value. They do not view impairment to be such an event.

Some proponents of the recoverable cost measure assert that measuring an impaired asset at either fair value or a discounted present value results in an inappropriate understatement of net income in the period of the impairment and an overstatement of net income in subsequent periods. The Board did not agree with that view. Board members noted that measuring an impaired asset at recoverable cost could result in reported losses in future periods if the entity had incurred debt directly associated with the asset.

Proponents of the recoverable cost measure view interest cost as a period cost that should not be included as part of an impairment loss regardless of whether the interest is an accrual of actual debt costs or the result of discounting expected future cash flows using a debt rate.

B37. Paragraphs 82–85 of Statement 121 discussed a recoverable cost including interest measure:

> Recoverable cost including interest generally is measured as either (a) the sum of the undiscounted expected future cash flows including interest costs on actual debt or (b) the present value of expected future cash flows discounted at some annual rate such as a debt rate. For example, if an asset has a carrying value of $1,000,000, a remaining useful life of 5 years, expected future cash flows (excluding interest) over the 5 years of $180,000 per year, and a debt rate of 6 percent, recoverable cost including interest would be $758,225 (4.21236 × $180,000), and the impairment loss would be $241,775 ($1,000,000 – $758,225).

The Board did not adopt recoverable cost including interest as an appropriate measure of an impairment loss. Proponents of the recoverable cost including interest measure agree that the time value of money should be considered in the measure, but they view the time value of money as an element of cost recovery rather than as an element of fair value. Proponents believe that the measurement objective for an impaired asset should be recoverable cost and not fair value. However, they believe that interest should be included as a carrying cost in determining the recoverable cost. To them, the objective is to recognize the costs (including the time value of money) that are not recoverable as an impairment loss and to measure an impaired asset at the costs that are recoverable.

Because of the difficulties in attempting to associate actual debt with individual assets, proponents of the recoverable cost including interest measure believe that the present value of expected future cash flows using a debt rate such as an incremental borrowing rate is a practical means of achieving their measurement objective. They recognize that an entity that has no debt may be required to discount expected future cash flows. They believe that the initial investment decision would have included consideration of the debt or equity cost of funds.

The Board believes that use of the recoverable cost including interest measure would result in different carrying amounts for essentially the same impaired assets because they are owned by different entities that have different debt capacities. The Board does not believe that discounting expected future cash flows using a debt rate is an appropriate measure for determining the value of those assets.

B38. Paragraph 86 of Statement 121 discussed different measures for different impairment losses:

> The Board also considered but did not adopt an alternative approach that would require different measures for different impairments. At one extreme, an asset might be impaired because depreciation assumptions were not adjusted appropriately. At the other extreme, an asset might be impaired because of a major change in its use. Some believe that the first situation is similar to a depreciation "catch-up" adjustment and that an undiscounted measure should be used. They believe that the second situation is similar to a new investment in an asset with the same intended use and that a fair value measure should be used. The Board was unable to develop a workable distinction between the first and second situations that would support the use of different measures.

Fair value

B39. This Statement retains the hierarchy in Statement 121 for measuring fair value. Because quoted market prices in active markets are the best evidence of fair value, they should be used, if available. Otherwise, the estimate of fair value should be based on the best information available in the circumstances, including prices for similar assets (asset groups) and the results of using other valuation techniques.

B40. The Board acknowledges that in many instances, quoted market prices in active markets will not be available for the long-lived assets (asset groups) covered by this Statement. The Board concluded that for those long-lived assets (asset groups), a present value technique is often the best available valuation technique with which to estimate fair value.

Paragraphs 39–54 of Concepts Statement 7, which are incorporated in Appendix E, discuss the use of two present value techniques—expected present value and traditional present value. During its deliberations leading to the Exposure Draft, the Board concluded that an expected present value technique is superior to a traditional present value technique, especially in situations in which the timing or amount of estimated future cash flows is uncertain. Because such situations often arise for the long-lived assets (asset groups) covered by this Statement, the Exposure Draft set forth the Board's expectation that when using a present value technique, most entities would use expected present value.

B41. Several respondents to the Exposure Draft suggested that the Board provide clearer guidance on whether and, if so, when entities are required to use an expected present value technique versus a traditional present value technique to minimize confusion and inconsistent application of this Statement. During its redeliberations of the Exposure Draft, the Board decided not to specify a requirement for either present value technique. The Board decided that preparers should determine the present value technique best suited to their specific circumstances based on the guidance in Concepts Statement 7. However, the Board noted that a traditional present value technique cannot accommodate uncertainties in the timing of future cash flows. Further, for nonfinancial assets, such as those covered by this Statement, paragraph 44 of Concepts Statement 7 explains:

> The traditional approach is useful for many measurements, especially those in which comparable assets and liabilities can be observed in the marketplace. However, the Board found that the traditional approach does not provide the tools needed to address some complex measurement problems, including the measurement of nonfinancial assets and liabilities for which no market for the item or a comparable item exists. The traditional approach places most of the emphasis on selection of an interest rate. A proper search for "the rate commensurate with the risk" requires analysis of at least two items—one asset or liability that exists in the marketplace and has an observed interest rate and the asset or liability being measured. The appropriate rate of interest for the cash flows being measured must be inferred from the ob-

servable rate of interest in some other asset or liability and, to draw that inference, the characteristics of the cash flows must be similar to those of the asset being measured.

B42. In this Statement, the Board clarified that consistent with the objective of measuring fair value, assumptions that marketplace participants would use in their estimates of fair value should be incorporated in estimates of future cash flows whenever that information is available without undue cost and effort. The Exposure Draft provided examples of circumstances in which an entity's assumptions might differ from marketplace assumptions. During its redeliberations of the Exposure Draft, the Board decided that it was not necessary to include those examples in this Statement, noting that related guidance is provided in paragraphs 23 and 32 of Concepts Statement 7, which are incorporated in Appendix E.

B43. The Board recognizes that there may be practical problems in determining the fair value of certain types of long-lived assets (asset groups) covered by this Statement that do not have observable market prices. Because precise information about the relevant attributes of those assets (asset groups) seldom will be available, judgments, estimates, and projections will be required for estimating fair value. Although the objective of using a present value or other valuation technique is to determine fair value, the Board acknowledges that, in some circumstances, the only information available to estimate fair value without undue cost and effort will be the entity's estimates of future cash flows. Paragraph 38 of Concepts Statement 7 explains:

> As a practical matter, an entity that uses cash flows in accounting measurements often has little or no information about some or all of the assumptions that marketplace participants would use in assessing the fair value of an asset or a liability. In those situations, the entity must necessarily use the information that is available without undue cost and effort in developing cash flow estimates. The use of an entity's own assumptions about future cash flows is compatible with an estimate of fair value, as long as there are no contrary data indicating that marketplace participants would use different assumptions. If such data exist, the entity must adjust its assumptions to incorporate that market information.

Grouping Long-Lived Assets to Be Held and Used

B44. For purposes of recognition and measurement of an impairment loss, this Statement retains the requirement of Statement 121 to group a long-lived asset or assets with other assets and liabilities at the lowest level for which identifiable cash flows are largely independent of the cash flows of other assets and liabilities. In Statement 121, the Board acknowledged that the primary issue underlying the grouping of long-lived assets is when, if ever, it is appropriate to offset unrealized losses on some assets by unrealized gains on other assets. However, the Board concluded that such offsetting is appropriate when a long-lived asset that is not an individual source of cash flows is part of a group of assets that are used together to generate joint cash flows. The Board affirmed that conclusion in this Statement. This Statement establishes that an asset group is the unit of accounting for a long-lived asset while it is classified as held and used.

B45. In Statement 121, the Board also acknowledged that grouping long-lived assets requires significant judgment. In that regard, the Board reviewed a series of cases that demonstrated the subjectivity of grouping issues. Paragraphs 96–98 of Statement 121 stated:

> Varying facts and circumstances introduced in the cases inevitably justified different groupings. Although most respondents to the Discussion Memorandum generally favored grouping at the lowest level for which there are identifiable cash flows for recognition and measurement of an impairment loss, determining that lowest level requires considerable judgment.

> The Board considered a case that illustrated the need for judgment in grouping assets for impairment. In that case, an entity operated a bus company that provided service under contract with a municipality that required minimum service on each of five separate routes. Assets devoted to serving each route and the cash flows from each route were discrete. One of the routes operated at a significant deficit that resulted in the inability to recover the carrying amounts of the dedicated assets. The Board concluded that the five bus routes would be an appropriate level at which to group assets to test for and measure impairment because the entity did not have the option to curtail any one bus route.

> The Board concluded that the grouping issue requires significant management judgment within certain parameters. Those parameters are that the assets should be grouped at the lowest level for which there are cash flows that are identifiable and that those cash flows should be largely independent of the cash flows of other groupings of assets.

B46. In this Statement, as in Statement 121, the Board acknowledges that in limited circumstances, an asset group will include all assets and liabilities of the entity. Paragraphs 99 and 100 of Statement 121 explained:

> Not-for-profit organizations that rely in part on contributions to maintain their assets may need to consider those contributions in determining the appropriate cash flows to compare with the carrying amount of an asset. Some respondents to the Exposure Draft stated that the recognition criteria in paragraph 6 would be problematic for many not-for-profit organizations because it may be difficult, if not impossible, for them to identify expected future cash flows with specific assets or asset groupings. In other cases, expected future cash flows can be identified with asset groups. However, if future unrestricted contributions to the organization as a whole are not considered, the sum of the expected future cash flows may be negative, or positive but less than the carrying amount of the asset. For example, the costs of administering a museum may exceed the admission fees charged, but the organization may fund the cash flow deficit with unrestricted contributions.

> Other respondents indicated that similar difficulties would be experienced by business enterprises. For example, the cost of operating assets such as corporate headquarters or centralized research facilities may be funded by revenue-producing activities at lower levels of the enterprise. Accordingly, in limited circumstances, the lowest level of identifiable cash flows that are largely independent of other asset groups may be the entity level. The Board concluded that the recoverability test in paragraph 6 should be performed at the entity level if an asset does not have identifiable cash flows lower than the entity level. The cash flows used in the recoverability test should be reduced by the carrying amounts of

the entity's other assets that are covered by this Statement to arrive at the cash flows expected to contribute to the recoverability of the asset being tested. Not-for-profit organizations should include unrestricted contributions to the organization as a whole that are a source of funds for the operation of the asset.

B47. Based on the Board's previous decisions discussed in paragraph 100 of Statement 121, the Exposure Draft would have required that estimates of future cash flows for an asset group be adjusted to exclude the portion of those cash flows necessary to recover the carrying amounts of the assets and liabilities of the group not covered by this Statement. However, during its redeliberations of the Exposure Draft, the Board decided to eliminate that requirement, noting that because the unit of accounting for a long-lived asset to be held and used is its asset group, such adjustments are unnecessary.

Goodwill

B48. In Statement 142, the Board decided that because goodwill should no longer be amortized, it should be tested for impairment in a manner different from how the long-lived assets covered by this Statement are tested for impairment. In developing the guidance in Statement 142, the Board decided that the reporting unit (as defined in that Statement) is the unit of measure for goodwill and that all goodwill should be tested for impairment at that level. The Board therefore decided to eliminate the requirement of Statement 121 to include goodwill in an asset group previously acquired in a business combination to be tested for impairment, which the Exposure Draft would have retained. The Board decided that goodwill should be included in such an asset group only if it is or includes a reporting unit. Goodwill should be excluded from such an asset group if it is only part of a reporting unit.

B49. During its redeliberations of the Exposure Draft, the Board considered the effect of excluding goodwill from an asset group that is only part of a reporting unit. The Board observed that although the carrying amount of the asset group would exclude goodwill, the estimates of future cash flows used to test the group for recoverability could include cash flows attributable to goodwill. However, the Board decided that those estimates of future cash flows should not be adjusted for the effect of excluding goodwill. The Board reasoned that because any adjustment likely would be arbitrary, adjusted estimates

of future cash flows would not necessarily provide a better estimate of the cash flows expected to contribute to the recoverability of the group. Further, an additional requirement to determine a goodwill adjustment under this Statement would not be cost beneficial.

Allocation of an impairment loss

B50. Paragraph 12 of Statement 121 specified that "in instances where goodwill is identified with assets that are subject to an impairment loss, the carrying amount of the identified goodwill shall be eliminated before making any reduction of the carrying amounts of impaired long-lived assets and identifiable intangibles." However, it did not specify how the excess, if any, should be allocated to the other assets of the group. The Board observed that if long-lived assets having different depreciable lives are grouped, the method used to allocate the excess impairment loss, if any, to the assets of the group can affect the pattern of income recognition over the succeeding years. To improve the consistency and comparability of reported financial information over time and among entities, the Board decided that this Statement should specify an allocation method.

B51. The Board decided that because other accounting requirements prescribe the accounting for assets and liabilities not covered by this Statement that are included in an asset group, an impairment loss that is determined based on the carrying amount and fair value of an asset group should reduce only the carrying amounts of the long-lived assets of the group. Paragraph 14 of this Statement requires that an impairment loss be allocated to those long-lived assets on a pro rata basis using their relative carrying amounts, provided that the carrying amount of an individual long-lived asset of the group is not reduced to an amount less than its fair value whenever that fair value is determinable without undue cost and effort. The Board concluded that it would be inappropriate to reduce the carrying amount of a long-lived asset to an amount below its fair value. The Board believes that the allocation method for an impairment loss provides a consistent basis for adjusting the carrying amounts of the long-lived assets of an asset group.

Depreciation

B52. This Statement retains the requirement of Statement 121 to consider the need to review depreciation estimates and method for a long-lived asset in accordance with APB Opinion No. 20, *Accounting Changes,* if a long-lived asset is tested for recoverability. This Statement clarifies that any revision to the remaining useful life of a long-lived asset resulting from that review should be considered in developing estimates of future cash flows used to test for recoverability but that any change in the method of accounting for the asset should be made only after applying this Statement. In Statement 121, the Board decided not to expand the scope of that Statement to address depreciation issues. The Board affirmed its initial decisions in Statement 121 and, therefore, this Statement does not prescribe the basis for revisions to depreciation estimates or method, or otherwise address depreciation issues.

Restoration of an Impairment Loss

B53. This Statement retains the prohibition in Statement 121 on the restoration of a previously recognized impairment loss. Paragraph 105 of Statement 121 discussed the basis for the Board's conclusion:

> The Board considered whether to prohibit or require restoration of previously recognized impairment losses. It decided that an impairment loss should result in a new cost basis for the impaired asset. That new cost basis puts the asset on an equal basis with other assets that are not impaired. In the Board's view, the new cost basis should not be adjusted subsequently other than as provided under the current accounting model for prospective changes in the depreciation estimates and method and for further impairment losses. Most respondents to the Exposure Draft agreed with the Board's decision that restoration should be prohibited.

Reporting and Disclosure

B54. Paragraph 25 of this Statement retains the requirements of Statement 121 for reporting an impairment loss recognized for a long-lived asset to be held and used. Paragraph 108 of Statement 121 discussed the basis for the Board's conclusion:

> The Board considered the alternative ways described in the Discussion Memorandum for reporting an impairment loss: reporting the loss as a component of continuing operations, reporting the loss as a special item outside continuing operations, or separate reporting of the loss without specifying the classification in the statement of operations. The Board concluded that an impairment loss should be reported as a component of income from continuing operations before income taxes for entities that present an income statement and in the statement of activities of a not-for-profit organization. If no impairment had occurred, an amount equal to the impairment loss would have been charged to operations over time through the allocation of depreciation or amortization. That depreciation or amortization charge would have been reported as part of continuing operations of a business enterprise or as an expense in the statement of activities of a not-for-profit organization. Further, an asset that is subject to a reduction in its carrying amount due to an impairment loss will continue to be used in operations. The Board concluded that an impairment loss does not have characteristics that warrant special treatment, for instance, as an extraordinary item.

B55. Paragraph 26 of this Statement retains the disclosure requirements of Statement 121 relating to impairment losses. Paragraphs 109 and 94 of Statement 121 discussed the basis for the Board's conclusion:

> The Board believes that financial statements should include information on impairment losses that would be most useful to users. After considering responses to the Exposure Draft, the Board concluded that an entity that recognizes an impairment loss should describe the assets impaired and the facts and circumstances leading to the impairment; disclose the amount of the loss and how fair value was determined; disclose the caption in the income statement or the statement of activities in which the loss is aggregated unless that loss has been presented as a separate caption or reported parenthetically on the face of the statement; and, if applicable, disclose the business segment(s) affected. The Board decided not to require further disclosures, such as the assumptions used to estimate expected future cash flows and the discount rate used when fair value is estimated by discounting expected future cash flows.
>
> Several respondents to the Exposure Draft said that disclosure of the discount rate used

to determine the present value of the estimated expected future cash flows should not be required. The Board decided that disclosure of the discount rate without disclosure of the other assumptions used in estimating expected future cash flows generally would not be meaningful to financial statement users. Therefore, this Statement does not require disclosure of the discount rate.

B56. A few respondents to the Exposure Draft suggested that the Board reconsider its decision in Statement 121 not to require disclosure of the discount rate and other assumptions used in measuring fair value. They said that such disclosures would provide useful information for evaluating impairment write-downs. However, the Board concluded that without access to management's cash flow projections and its methods of estimating those cash flows, the suggested disclosures would not necessarily be useful to users in evaluating impairment write-downs. The Board affirmed its initial conclusions in Statement 121 and, therefore, this Statement does not require disclosure of that information.

Early warning disclosures

B57. This Statement, like Statement 121, does not require early warning disclosures. Paragraphs 110 and 111 of Statement 121 discussed the basis for the Board's conclusion:

> In 1985, the AICPA established a task force to consider the need for improved disclosures about risks and uncertainties that affect companies and the manner in which they do business. In July 1987, the task force published *Report of the Task Force on Risks and Uncertainties,* which concluded that companies should make early warning disclosures in their financial statements. In December 1994, AcSEC issued AICPA Statement of Position 94-6, *Disclosure of Certain Significant Risks and Uncertainties.* That SOP requires entities to include in their financial statements disclosures about (a) the nature of operations, (b) the use of estimates in the preparation of financial statements, (c) certain significant estimates, and (d) current vulnerability due to certain concentrations.
>
> The Board observed that early warning disclosures would be useful for certain potential impairments. However, most respondents to the Exposure Draft said that the

Statement should not require early warning disclosures. The Board observed that SOP 94-6 uses essentially the same events or changes in circumstances as those in paragraph 5 of this Statement to illustrate when disclosures of certain significant estimates should be made for long-lived assets. Therefore, the Board concluded that it was not necessary for this Statement to require early warning disclosures.

Amendment to Statement 15

B58. This Statement carries forward the amendment made by Statement 121 to FASB Statement No. 15, *Accounting by Debtors and Creditors for Troubled Debt Restructurings,* discussed in paragraphs 136–138 of Statement 121:

> In May 1993, the Board issued FASB Statement No. 114, *Accounting by Creditors for Impairment of a Loan,* which requires certain impaired loans to be measured based on the present value of expected future cash flows, discounted at the loan's effective interest rate, or as a practical expedient, at the loan's observable market price or the fair value of the collateral if the impaired loan is collateral dependent. Regardless of the measurement method, a creditor should measure impairment based on the fair value of the collateral when the creditor determines that foreclosure is probable. A creditor should consider estimated costs to sell, on a discounted basis, in the measure of impairment if those costs are expected to reduce the cash flows available to repay or otherwise satisfy the loan.
>
> As suggested by one commentator to the Exposure Draft, the Board decided to amend Statement 15 to make the measurement of long-lived assets that are received in full satisfaction of a receivable and that will be sold consistent with the measurement of other long-lived assets under this Statement. The amendment requires that those assets be measured at fair value less cost to sell. The Board considered amending Statement 15 to address shares of stock or equity interests in long-lived assets that are received in full satisfaction of a receivable and that will be sold, but it determined that those items are outside the scope of this Statement.
>
> Loans and long-lived assets are similar in that both are cash-generating assets that are

subject to impairment. However, inherent differences between monetary and nonmonetary assets have resulted in different accounting treatments for them under the current reporting model.

Amendment to Statement 71

B59. This Statement carries forward the amendment made by Statement 121 to FASB Statement No. 71, *Accounting for the Effects of Certain Types of Regulation,* to apply the provisions of this Statement for long-lived assets to be held and used to all assets of a regulated enterprise except (a) regulatory assets that meet the criteria of paragraph 9 of Statement 71 and (b) costs of recently completed plants that are covered by paragraph 7 of FASB Statement No. 90, *Regulated Enterprises—Accounting for Abandonments and Disallowances of Plant Costs.* Therefore, regulatory assets capitalized as a result of paragraph 9 of Statement 71 should be tested for impairment whenever the criteria of that paragraph are no longer met. Paragraphs 127 and 128 of Statement 121 explained:

> FASB Statement No. 71, *Accounting for the Effects of Certain Types of Regulation,* establishes the accounting model for certain rate-regulated enterprises. Because the rates of rate-regulated enterprises generally are designed to recover the costs of providing regulated services or products, those enterprises are usually able to recover the carrying amounts of their assets. Paragraph 10 of Statement 71 states that when a regulator excludes a cost from rates, "the carrying amount of any related asset shall be reduced to the extent that the asset has been impaired. Whether the asset has been impaired shall be judged the same as for enterprises in general" (footnote reference omitted). Statement 71 does not provide any guidance about when an impairment has, in fact, occurred or about how to measure the amount of the impairment.
>
> The Board considered whether the accounting for the impairment of long-lived assets and identifiable intangibles by rate-regulated enterprises that meet the criteria for applying Statement 71 should be the same as for enterprises in general. In March 1993, the EITF discussed incurred costs capitalized pursuant to the criteria of paragraph 9 of Statement 71. The EITF reached a consensus in EITF Issue No. 93-4, "Accounting for

Regulatory Assets," that a cost that does not meet the asset recognition criteria in paragraph 9 of Statement 71 at the date the cost is incurred should be recognized as a regulatory asset when it does meet those criteria at a later date. The EITF also reached a consensus that the carrying amount of a regulatory asset should be reduced to the extent that the asset has been impaired with impairment judged the same as for enterprises in general; the provisions of [Statement 121] nullify that consensus.

B60. Paragraphs 129–134 of Statement 121 discussed approaches considered and the basis for the Board's conclusion:

> The Board considered several approaches to recognizing and measuring the impairment of long-lived assets and identifiable intangibles of rate-regulated enterprises. One approach the Board considered was to apply paragraph 7 of FASB Statement No. 90, *Regulated Enterprises—Accounting for Abandonments and Disallowances of Plant Costs,* to all assets of a regulated enterprise and not just to costs of recently completed plants. That paragraph requires that an impairment loss be recognized when a disallowance is probable and the amount can be reasonably estimated. If a regulator explicitly disallows a certain dollar amount of plant costs, an impairment loss should be recognized for that amount. If a regulator explicitly but indirectly disallows plant costs (for example, by excluding a return on investment on a portion of plant costs), an impairment loss should be recognized for the effective disallowance by estimating the expected future cash flows that have been disallowed as a result of the regulator's action and then computing the present value of those cash flows. That approach would recognize a probable disallowance as an impairment loss, the amount of the loss would be the discounted value of the expected future cash flows disallowed, and the discount rate would be the same as the rate of return used to estimate the expected future cash flows.
>
> A second approach the Board considered was to supersede paragraph 7 of Statement 90 and apply this Statement's requirements to all plant costs. A disallowance would result in costs being excluded from the rate base. The

recognition and measurement requirements of this Statement would be applied to determine whether an impairment loss would be recognized for financial reporting purposes.

A third approach the Board considered was to apply the general impairment provisions of this Statement to all assets of a regulated enterprise except for disallowances of costs of recently completed plants, which would continue to be covered by paragraph 7 of Statement 90. A disallowance would result in the exclusion of costs from the rate base. That disallowance would result in an impairment loss for financial reporting purposes if the costs disallowed relate to a recently completed plant. If the costs disallowed do not relate to a recently completed plant, the recognition and measurement requirements of this Statement would be applied to determine whether and how much of an impairment loss would be recognized for financial reporting purposes.

A fourth approach the Board considered was to apply the general impairment standard to all assets of a regulated enterprise except (a) regulatory assets that meet the criteria of paragraph 9 of Statement 71 and (b) costs of recently completed plants that are covered by paragraph 7 of Statement 90. Impairment of regulatory assets capitalized as a result of paragraph 9 of Statement 71 would be recognized whenever the criteria of that paragraph are no longer met.

The Board decided that the fourth approach should be used in accounting for the impairment of all assets of a rate-regulated enterprise. The Board amended paragraph 9 of Statement 71 to provide that a rate-regulated enterprise should charge a regulatory asset to earnings if and when that asset no longer meets the criteria in paragraph 9(a) and (b) of that Statement. The Board also amended paragraph 10 of Statement 71 to require that a rate-regulated enterprise recognize an impairment for the amount of costs excluded when a regulator excludes all or part of a cost from rates, even if the regulator allows the rate-regulated enterprise to earn a return on the remaining costs allowed.

The Board believes that because a rate-regulated enterprise is allowed to capitalize costs that enterprises in general would otherwise have charged to expense, the impairment criteria for those assets should be different from enterprises in general. The Board believes that symmetry should exist between the recognition of those assets and the subsequent impairment of those assets. The Board could see no reason that an asset created as a result of regulatory action could not be impaired by the actions of the same regulator. Other assets that are not regulatory assets covered by Statement 71 or recently completed plant costs covered by Statement 90, such as older plants or other nonregulatory assets of a rate-regulated enterprise, would be covered by the general provisions of this Statement.

B61. Paragraph 135 of Statement 121 further clarified the accounting for previously disallowed costs that are subsequently allowed by a regulator:

> The Board decided that previously disallowed costs that are subsequently allowed by a regulator should be recorded as an asset, consistent with the classification that would have resulted had those costs initially been included in allowable costs. Thus, plant costs subsequently allowed should be classified as plant assets, whereas other costs (expenses) subsequently allowed should be classified as regulatory assets. The Board amended Statement 71 to reflect this decision. The Board decided to restore the original classification because there is no economic change to the asset—it is as if the regulator never had disallowed the cost. The Board determined that restoration of cost is allowed for rate-regulated enterprises in this situation, in contrast to other impairment situations, because the event requiring recognition of the impairment resulted from actions of an independent party and not management's own judgment or determination of recoverability.

Long-Lived Assets to Be Disposed Of Other Than by Sale

B62. In Statement 121, the Board decided that the provisions for long-lived assets to be disposed of, including the requirement to cease depreciating (amortizing) a long-lived asset when it is classified as held for disposal, should be applied to all long-lived assets to be disposed of, whether by sale or abandonment. During its deliberations leading to the Exposure Draft, the Board reconsidered that decision, noting that its rationale for not depreciating (amortizing) a long-lived asset to be disposed of by sale does not apply to a long-lived asset to be disposed of other than by sale. Such transactions include the abandonment of a long-lived asset, as well as the exchange of a long-lived asset for a similar productive long-lived asset and the distribution of a long-lived asset to owners in a spinoff (including a pro rata distribution to owners of shares of a subsidiary or other investee company that has been or is being consolidated or that has been or is being accounted for under the equity method) or other form of reorganization or liquidation or in a plan that is in substance the rescission of a prior business combination covered by APB Opinion No. 29, *Accounting for Nonmonetary Transactions.*

B63. Specifically, the Board observed that to the extent the carrying amount of a long-lived asset to be disposed of by abandonment is recoverable, it will be recovered principally through operations, rather than through the disposal transaction. Additionally, the accounting guidance in Opinion 29 for the exchange of a similar productive long-lived asset and for the distribution of a long-lived asset to owners in a spinoff is based on the carrying amount of the asset exchanged or distributed. The Board concluded that the Opinion 29 guidance is more consistent with the accounting for a long-lived asset to be held and used than for a long-lived asset to be sold. Thus, the Board decided that a long-lived asset to be disposed of other than by sale should continue to be classified as held and used and depreciated (amortized) until it is abandoned, exchanged, or distributed.

B64. Some respondents to the Exposure Draft said that there is no conceptual difference between sale and other disposal transactions and that the provisions of this Statement for long-lived assets to be disposed of by sale should be applied to other disposal transactions. During its redeliberations of the Exposure Draft, the Board affirmed its conclusion that a long-lived asset to be disposed of other than by sale should continue to be classified as held and used and depreciated (amortized) until disposed of for the reasons discussed in paragraph B63. Accordingly, paragraphs 7–26 of this Statement, except as modified by paragraph 29, apply to that asset or its asset group as previously determined on a held-and-used basis until it is disposed of. If that asset will be disposed of together with other assets and liabilities as a group and the group is a component of an entity, paragraphs 41–44 of this Statement apply to that disposal group when it is disposed of.

Long-Lived Asset to Be Abandoned

B65. The Board decided that if a long-lived asset that is being used is to be abandoned before the end of its previously estimated useful life, depreciation estimates should be revised in accordance with Opinion 20 to reflect the use of the asset over that shortened period. The Board reasoned that because the continued use of a long-lived asset demonstrates the presence of service potential, the immediate writedown of the asset to zero generally is inappropriate. A few respondents to the Exposure Draft suggested that the Board provide additional guidance for revising those depreciation estimates under Opinion 20. However, the Board decided not to address that issue because depreciation issues are beyond the scope of this Statement.

Long-Lived Asset to Be Exchanged for a Similar Productive Long-Lived Asset or to Be Distributed to Owners in a Spinoff

B66. Under Opinion 29 the accounting for the exchange of a long-lived asset for a similar productive long-lived asset and the distribution of a long-lived asset to owners in a spinoff, is based on the recorded amount, "after reduction, if appropriate, for an indicated impairment of value" of the asset exchanged (paragraph 21) or distributed (paragraph 23). After Statement 121 was issued, questions emerged on how to determine "an indicated impairment of value" of the asset exchanged or distributed. The primary issue was whether to apply an undiscounted cash flows recoverability test and, if so, at what level. The EITF discussed the issue in Issue No. 96-2, "Impairment Recognition When a Nonmonetary Asset Is Exchanged or Is Distributed to Owners and Is Accounted for at the Asset's Recorded Amount," but did not reach a consensus.

B67. The Board did not redeliberate the Opinion 29 guidance for exchanges of similar productive assets or spinoffs. This Statement, however, resolves Issue 96-2 by requiring that an indicated impairment of value of a long-lived asset that is exchanged for a similar productive long-lived asset or distributed to owners in a spinoff be recognized if the carrying amount of the asset (disposal group) exceeds its fair value at the disposal date. The accounting guidance in Opinion 29 for an exchange of similar productive assets and for a distribution to owners in a spinoff is based on recorded amounts and not fair value. The Board concluded that using recorded amounts is more consistent with the accounting for a long-lived asset to be held and used than for a long-lived asset to be sold. For that reason, the Board believes that an undiscounted cash flows recoverability test should apply prior to the disposal date. The estimates of future cash flows used in that test are based on the use of the asset for its remaining useful life, assuming that the disposal transaction will not occur.

B68. The Board acknowledges the view of some respondents to the Exposure Draft that because the exchange of a long-lived asset for a similar productive long-lived asset does not culminate an earning process, an undiscounted cash flows recoverability test should apply up through the disposal date. The Board observed that the distribution of a long-lived asset to owners also does not culminate an earning process. However, the Board concluded that those disposal transactions are significant economic events that should result in recognition of an impairment loss if the carrying amount of the asset (disposal group) exceeds its fair value at the disposal date. The Board decided that because the fair value of the asset (disposal group) will be determined in connection with the decision to dispose, the practical expedient of an undiscounted cash flows recoverability test should not apply at the disposal date.

B69. This Statement amends Opinion 29 to require that an indicated impairment of value of a long-lived asset that is exchanged for a similar productive long-lived asset or distributed to owners in a spinoff be recognized if the carrying amount of the asset (disposal group) exceeds its fair value at the disposal date. It also amends paragraph 44(a) of FASB Statement No. 19, *Financial Accounting and Reporting by Oil and Gas Producing Companies,* to extend that requirement to transactions involving the exchange of proved oil- and gas-producing assets that are being accounted for by the successful-efforts method of accounting.

Long-Lived Assets to Be Disposed Of by Sale

Recognition

Plan-of-sale criteria

B70. As a basis for determining when to classify a long-lived asset (disposal group) as held for sale, Statement 121 required a commitment to a plan to sell the asset (disposal group) but did not specify factors beyond that commitment that should be considered. Consequently, in implementing Statement 121, questions emerged about when to classify a long-

lived asset (disposal group) as held for sale. Because a long-lived asset is not depreciated (amortized) while it is classified as held for sale, those questions raised concerns that an entity could improve its operating results by asserting a commitment to a plan to sell a long-lived asset (disposal group) at a future date. Because of those concerns, the Board decided that this Statement should specify criteria for determining when an entity's commitment to a plan to sell a long-lived asset (disposal group) is sufficient for purposes of classifying the asset (disposal group) as held for sale.

B71. The Board decided that a long-lived asset (disposal group) should be classified as held for sale in the period in which all of the criteria in paragraph 30 are met, except as permitted in limited situations by paragraphs 31 and 32. In developing those criteria, the Board considered the criteria established by Opinion 30 for a measurement date and by Issue 94-3 for a commitment date. Certain of those criteria are incorporated in paragraphs 30(a), (c), and (f) of this Statement. Additional criteria established by this Statement are incorporated in paragraphs 30(b), (d), and (e). The Board concluded, and many respondents agreed, that those criteria should enable entities to determine consistently when to classify assets (disposal groups) as held for sale.

Available for immediate sale

B72. Paragraph 30(b) of this Statement establishes a criterion that to qualify for classification as held for sale, a long-lived asset (disposal group) must be available for immediate sale in its present condition. The Board concluded that an asset (disposal group) is available for immediate sale if an entity currently has the intent and ability to transfer the asset (disposal group) to a buyer in its present condition within a period that is usual and customary for sales of such assets. In developing that criterion, the Board decided not to preclude a long-lived asset (disposal group) from being classified as held for sale while it is being used. The Board reasoned that if a long-lived asset (disposal group) is available for immediate sale, the remaining use of the asset (disposal group) is incidental to its recovery through sale and that the carrying amount of the asset (disposal group) will be recovered principally through sale. The Board also decided not to require a binding agreement for a future sale. The Board concluded that such a requirement would unduly delay reporting the effects of a commitment to a plan to sell a long-lived asset (disposal group).

Maximum one-year holding period

B73. In Statement 121, the Board decided not to limit the holding period for a long-lived asset (disposal group) classified as held for sale, principally to allow for situations in which environmental concerns extend the period required to complete a sale beyond one year. In this Statement, the Board reconsidered that decision, noting that in some other situations, a long-lived asset could, as a result, be inappropriately classified as held for sale and not depreciated (amortized) for an extended period. Consequently, paragraph 30(d) of this Statement establishes a maximum one-year holding period for a long-lived asset (disposal group) classified as held for sale. The Board concluded that for a long-lived asset (disposal group) covered by this Statement, a one-year period is a reasonable period within which to assess the probability of a future sale, noting that the APB previously reached a similar conclusion in Opinion 30 for the disposal of a segment.[31]

B74. Because in some situations events or circumstances might extend the period required to complete the sale of a long-lived asset (disposal group) beyond one year, the Board considered whether and, if so, when to permit an exception to the one-year requirement. The Board decided that a delay in the period required to complete a sale should not preclude a long-lived asset (disposal group) from being classified as held for sale if the delay is caused by events or circumstances beyond an entity's control and there is sufficient evidence that the entity remains committed to its plan to sell the asset (disposal group). The Board decided to permit an exception in such situations. The Board concluded that the usefulness and clarity of financial statements would not be improved by having long-lived assets (disposal groups) moving in and out of the held-for-sale classification.

B75. A few respondents to the Exposure Draft suggested that the Board permit an exception to the one-year requirement in all situations in which a long-lived asset is acquired through foreclosure by incorporating in this Statement the held-for-sale presumption in paragraph 10 of AICPA Statement of Position 92-3, *Accounting for Foreclosed Assets,* which stated:

> Most enterprises do not intend to hold foreclosed assets for the production of income but intend to sell them; in fact, some laws and regulations applicable to financial institutions require the sale of foreclosed assets. Therefore, under this SOP, it is presumed that foreclosed assets are held for sale and not for the production of income.

Those respondents said that in situations in which an entity acquires a long-lived asset through foreclosure, circumstances attendant to the foreclosure often extend the period required to complete the sale beyond one year. The Board concluded that this Statement sufficiently addresses the need for an exception to the one-year requirement for all long-lived assets (disposal groups) covered by this Statement, whether previously held and used or newly acquired. To be consistent with an objective of developing a single accounting model for long-lived assets to be disposed of by sale, the Board decided not to incorporate the held-for-sale presumption in SOP 92-3.

Market price reasonable in relation to current fair value

B76. Paragraph 30(e) of this Statement establishes a criterion that to qualify for classification as held for sale, an entity must be actively marketing a long-lived asset (disposal group) at a price that is reasonable in relation to its current fair value. The Board believes that the price at which a long-lived asset (disposal group) is being marketed is indicative of whether the entity currently has the intent and ability to sell the asset (disposal group). A market price that is reasonable in relation to fair value indicates that the asset (disposal group) is available for immediate sale, whereas a market price in excess of fair value indicates that the asset (disposal group) is not available for immediate sale.

Commitment to a plan to sell a long-lived asset after the balance sheet date but before issuance of financial statements

B77. In implementing Statement 121, questions emerged about the required accounting if an entity commits to a plan to sell a long-lived asset after the balance sheet date but before issuance of the financial statements. Prior to this Statement, Opinion 30 and EITF Issue No. 95-18, "Accounting and Reporting for a Discontinued Business Segment When the Measurement Date Occurs after the Balance Sheet

---

[31]Paragraph 15 of Opinion 30 stated that "in the usual circumstance, it would be expected that the plan of disposal would be carried out within a period of one year from the measurement date. . . ."

Date but before the Issuance of Financial Statements," provided related guidance for a segment of a business (as defined in that Opinion). In an expected loss situation, Opinion 30 required that the financial statements be adjusted if the loss "provides evidence of conditions that existed at the date of such statements and affects estimates inherent in the process of preparing them" (footnote 5). Issue 95-18 later incorporated the presumption that an expected loss is evidence of a loss existing at the balance sheet date, unless the subsequent decision to dispose of the segment results from a discrete and identifiable event that occurs unexpectedly after the balance sheet date.

B78. The Board decided that if an entity commits to a plan to sell a long-lived asset after the balance sheet date but before issuance of the financial statements, the asset should continue to be classified as held and used. The Board concluded that retroactively classifying the asset as held for sale would be inconsistent with having specified criteria for determining when an entity's commitment to a plan to sell a long-lived asset (disposal group) is sufficient for purposes of classifying the asset (disposal group) as held for sale. Similarly, the Board concluded that if the asset (asset group) is tested for recoverability on a held-and-used basis as of the balance sheet date, the estimates of future cash flows used in that test should consider the likelihood of possible outcomes that existed at the balance sheet date, including the assessment of the likelihood of the future sale of the asset. That assessment made as of the balance sheet date should not be revised for a decision to sell the asset after the balance sheet date. Therefore, this Statement nullifies Issue 95-18.

B79. The Board considered the view of some respondents to the Exposure Draft that in an expected loss situation, a requirement to classify the asset as held and used could unduly delay recognition of a loss that existed at the balance sheet date. The Board concluded that, on balance, the benefits of having well-defined criteria for when to classify a long-lived asset as held for sale outweigh that concern, noting that the situation referred to by respondents can arise whenever a long-lived asset is expected to be sold but there is no commitment to a plan of sale. The Board observed that if the plan-of-sale criteria are met after the balance sheet date but before issuance of the financial statements, the entity could be required to perform a recoverability test in accordance with paragraph 8(f). In that situation, application of the recoverability test as well as any fair value assessment would be based on facts and circumstances existing

at the balance sheet date and could result in an impairment adjustment as of the balance sheet date. The Board agreed that if prior to meeting the plan-of-sale criteria the entity had previously tested the asset (asset group) for impairment on a held-and-used basis at the balance sheet date, it would be inappropriate to undertake a new recoverability test.

Measurement

Lower of carrying amount or fair value less cost to sell

B80. This Statement retains the requirement of Statement 121 to measure a long-lived asset (disposal group) classified as held for sale at the lower of its carrying amount or fair value less cost to sell. In contrast to a long-lived asset (asset group) to be held and used, a long-lived asset (disposal group) classified as held for sale will be recovered principally through sale rather than through operations. Therefore, accounting for that asset (disposal group) is a process of valuation rather than allocation. The asset (disposal group) is reported at the lower of its carrying amount or fair value less cost to sell, and fair value less cost to sell is evaluated each period to determine if it has changed. Losses (and gains, as permitted by paragraph 37) are reported as adjustments to the carrying amount of a long-lived asset while it is classified as held for sale.

Cost to sell

B81. The Exposure Draft proposed to retain the requirements of Statement 121 for determining cost to sell. Those requirements were discussed in paragraph 116 of Statement 121, which stated:

> The Board concluded that the cost to sell an asset to be disposed of generally includes the incremental direct costs to transact the sale of the asset. Cost to sell is deducted from the fair value of an asset to be disposed of to arrive at the current value of the estimated net proceeds to be received from the asset's future sale. The Board decided that costs incurred during the holding period to protect or maintain an asset to be disposed of generally are excluded from the cost to sell an asset because those costs usually are not required to be incurred in order to sell the asset. However, the Board believes that costs required to be incurred under the terms of a contract for an asset's sale as a condition of the buyer's

consummation of the sale should be included in determining the cost to sell an asset to be disposed of.

B82. Some respondents to the Exposure Draft noted that those requirements for determining cost to sell did not limit cost to sell to the incremental direct costs to transact a sale. They said that, as a result, cost to sell could be interpreted as including normal operating costs (losses) expected to be incurred while a long-lived asset (disposal group) is classified as held for sale, which they did not believe was consistent with the Board's intent. To convey its intent more clearly, the Board decided to revise those requirements to limit cost to sell in all circumstances to the incremental direct costs to transact the sale. Accordingly, costs that are "required to be incurred under the terms of a contract for an asset's sale as a condition of the buyer's consummation of the sale," as referred to in paragraph 116 of Statement 121, would be excluded. In addition, expected future operating losses that marketplace participants would not similarly consider in their estimates of the fair value less cost to sell of a long-lived asset (disposal group) classified as held for sale also would be excluded. In this Statement, the Board clarified that such losses should not be indirectly recognized as part of an expected loss on sale by reducing the carrying amount of the asset (disposal group) to an amount less than its current fair value less cost to sell. Excluding such losses from the measurement of a long-lived asset (disposal group) classified as held for sale supersedes the net realizable value measurement approach previously required under Opinion 30.

Ceasing depreciation (amortization)

B83. This Statement retains the requirement of Statement 121 to cease depreciating (amortizing) a long-lived asset when it is classified as held for sale and measured at the lower of its carrying amount or fair value less cost to sell. Some respondents disagreed with that requirement as also proposed in the Exposure Draft. They said that not depreciating (amortizing) a long-lived asset that is being used is inconsistent with the basic principle that the cost of a long-lived asset should be allocated over the period during which benefits are obtained from its use. The Board considered that view but affirmed its conclusion in Statement 121 that depreciation accounting is inconsistent with the use of a lower of carrying amount or fair value measure for a long-lived asset classified as

held for sale because, as previously stated, accounting for that asset is a process of valuation rather than allocation.

B84. Some respondents also said that not depreciating (amortizing) a long-lived asset that is being used while it is classified as held for sale hinders the comparability of operating results during that period. They said that the comparability of operating results (reported in both continuing operations and in discontinued operations) between periods is more important than the valuation of the asset while it is classified as held for sale. The Board also considered those concerns but observed that in situations where the carrying amount of the asset (disposal group) is written down to its fair value less cost to sell, continuing to depreciate (amortize) the asset reduces its carrying amount below its fair value less cost to sell. The Board concluded that it would be inappropriate to reduce the carrying amount of the asset to an amount below its fair value. The Board further observed that because fair value less cost to sell is required to be evaluated each period, a subsequent decline in the fair value of the asset while it is classified as held for sale will be appropriately reflected in the period of decline.

Long-lived asset acquired in a purchase business combination

B85. Prior to the issuance of Statement 121, EITF Issue No. 87-11, "Allocation of Purchase Price to Assets to Be Sold," provided guidance on the accounting for a disposal group to be sold that was newly acquired in a purchase business combination, including, but not limited to, a segment of a business covered by Opinion 30. The guidance in Issue 87-11 extended the measurement provisions of Opinion 30 in determining the purchase price allocation under Opinion 16. Accordingly, the disposal group was measured at the lower of its carrying amount or net realizable value, adjusted for future operating losses.

B86. Statement 121 subsequently required that a long-lived asset (disposal group) to be sold other than a segment of a business covered by Opinion 30 be measured at the lower of its carrying amount or fair value less cost to sell. However, it did not nullify Issue 87-11 to reflect that change for a long-lived asset (disposal group) to be sold that was newly acquired in a purchase business combination. Consequently, in implementing Statement 121, questions emerged about the impact of that Statement on Issue 87-11. The primary issue was whether and, if so, how the measurement guidance provided by Issue 87-11 should be applied to a long-lived asset (disposal group) that was newly acquired in a purchase business combination. A related issue was how to account for the results of operations of the asset (disposal group) while it was classified as held for sale and whether future operating losses could be considered in measuring the fair value less cost to sell of the asset (disposal group). The EITF discussed that issue in Issue No. 95-21, "Accounting for Assets to Be Disposed Of Acquired in a Purchase Business Combination," but did not reach a consensus.

B87. This Statement resolves Issue 95-21 by requiring that a long-lived asset (disposal group) classified as held for sale be measured at the lower of its carrying amount or fair value less cost to sell, whether previously held and used or newly acquired. This Statement also requires that the results of operations of a long-lived asset (disposal group) classified as held for sale be recognized in the period in which those operations occur, whether reported in continuing operations or in discontinued operations. Therefore, this Statement nullifies Issue 87-11.

Grouping Assets and Liabilities to Be Sold

B88. During its deliberations leading to the Exposure Draft, the Board noted that long-lived assets often are sold together with other assets and liabilities as a group. The Board observed that, as is the case for long-lived assets to be held and used, measuring assets and liabilities classified as held for sale as a group raises the issue of when, if ever, it is appropriate to offset unrealized losses on some assets (liabilities) with unrealized gains on other assets (liabilities). In addition, because liabilities often can be settled separately from the sale of assets, measuring assets and liabilities classified as held for sale as a group also could permit an entity to achieve a desired result by selectively designating the liabilities to be included in a disposal group. To prevent grouping from being used inappropriately to offset unrealized losses with unrealized gains, the Board initially decided that the plan-of-sale criteria should address when assets and liabilities should be classified as held for sale and measured as a group.

B89. The Exposure Draft proposed a criterion that, to classify assets and liabilities as held for sale as a group, the estimated proceeds expected to result from the sale of the group must exceed those that would result from the sale of the assets of the group individually. The Board reasoned that because estimated proceeds reflect the underlying economics of an expected sale transaction, that criterion would provide evidence of an entity's commitment to a plan to sell assets (and liabilities) as a group. Several respondents to the Exposure Draft disagreed with a criterion based on estimated net proceeds, stating that proceeds alone do not necessarily reflect the total (direct and indirect) economic benefit that may result from the sale of assets (and liabilities) as a group. They said that in many situations, valid reasons may exist to sell assets and liabilities as a group even though the estimated net proceeds expected to result from the sale of that group may be less than those that would result from the sale of the assets individually. They also said that in other situations, particularly those in which several assets are to be sold as a group, a requirement to estimate the net proceeds that would result from the sale of assets individually would be unduly burdensome and costly.

B90. Upon reconsideration, the Board decided to eliminate a criterion based on estimated net proceeds. Instead, the Board decided that assets and liabilities should be classified as held for sale as a group if (a) the assets will be sold as a group in a single transaction and (b) the liabilities are directly related to the assets and will be transferred in that transaction. The Board concluded that if assets and liabilities will be sold as a group in a single transaction, accounting for those assets and liabilities as held for sale as a group is appropriate.

Allocation of a loss

B91. During its deliberations leading to the Exposure Draft, the Board decided that this Statement should provide guidance for allocating a loss recognized for a disposal group classified as held for sale that includes assets and liabilities, principally to facilitate the requirement of this Statement to present those assets and liabilities separately in the asset and liability sections of the statement of financial position. The Exposure Draft proposed that a loss be allocated, first, by adjusting the carrying amounts of the liabilities of the group to their fair values and, then, by adjusting the carrying amounts of the long-lived assets of the group by the remaining amount, if any. The Board reasoned that the fair values of the liabilities included in a disposal group generally would be determinable and that the presentation of those liabilities at their fair values would improve the usefulness of the information provided by the statement of financial position.

B92. Upon further consideration, the Board subsequently decided not to retain that allocation method. Instead, the Board decided that because other accounting pronouncements prescribe the accounting for assets and liabilities not covered by this Statement that are included in a disposal group, a loss recognized for a disposal group classified as held for sale should reduce only the carrying amounts of the long-lived assets of the group. The Board concluded that the allocation method for a loss recognized for a disposal group classified as held for sale provides a reasonable basis for reporting both the assets and liabilities of the disposal group in the statement of financial position.

Changes to a Plan of Sale

Reversal of a decision to sell a long-lived asset classified as held for sale

B93. In implementing Statement 121, questions emerged about the required accounting if an entity subsequently decides not to sell a long-lived asset classified as held for sale. Prior to this Statement, other accounting pronouncements provided related guidance, but only for certain assets. If the asset previously was acquired through foreclosure, SOP 92-3 required that the asset be reclassified as held and used and measured at what would have been its carrying amount had the asset been continuously classified as held and used since the time of foreclosure. If the asset previously was acquired in a purchase business combination, EITF Issue No. 90-6, "Accounting for Certain Events Not Addressed in Issue No. 87-11 Relating to an Acquired Operating Unit to Be Sold," required that the asset be reclassified as held and used and measured as under SOP 92-3 if the subsequent decision not to sell was made within one year. If the asset was a segment accounted for as a discontinued operation under Opinion 30, EITF Issue No. 90-16, "Accounting for Discontinued Operations Subsequently Retained," provided guidance on the reclassification to continuing operations of amounts previously reported in discontinued operations.

B94. The Board decided that a long-lived asset to be reclassified as held and used should be measured at the lower of (a) its fair value at the date of the subsequent decision not to sell or (b) its carrying amount on a held-and-used basis at the date of the decision to sell, adjusted for any depreciation (amortization) expense that would have been recognized had the asset been continuously classified as held and used. Therefore, this Statement nullifies Issues 90-6 and 90-16.

B95. The Board considered but rejected an approach that, based on the guidance in SOP 92-3 and Issue 90-6, would have measured a long-lived asset to be reclassified as held and used at what would have been its carrying amount had the asset been continuously classified as held and used (held-and-used approach). The Board observed that a held-and-used approach could measure an asset previously written down to its fair value less cost to sell at an amount greater than its fair value at the date of the subsequent decision not to sell. That would be the case if, for example, the adjusted carrying amount of the asset is recoverable at the date of the subsequent decision not to sell. The Board concluded that it would be inappropriate to write up the carrying amount of a long-lived asset to an amount greater than its fair value based solely on an undiscounted cash flows recoverability test.

B96. Some respondents to the Exposure Draft suggested that the Board reconsider a held-and-used approach. They said that if the adjusted carrying amount of the asset is recoverable at the date of the subsequent decision not to sell, measuring the asset at its fair value would be inconsistent with the requirements of this Statement for other assets to be held and used, in particular, the requirement to write down the carrying amount of a long-lived asset (asset group) only if it is not recoverable. During its redeliberations of the Exposure Draft, the Board considered that inconsistency but again rejected that approach for the reason discussed in paragraph B95.

Removal of an individual asset or liability from disposal group

B97. In view of its decision that assets and liabilities classified as held for sale should be measured as a group, the Board decided that this Statement should address the accounting if an entity subsequently removes an individual asset or liability from a disposal group previously classified as held for sale. The Board considered situations in which an entity decides not to sell an individual asset of the group, decides to sell an individual asset separately from the group, or settles before its maturity an individual liability of the group.

B98. The Exposure Draft would have required that the remaining long-lived assets of the disposal group be measured individually at the lower of their carrying amounts or fair values less cost to sell whenever an individual asset or liability is removed from the group. Several respondents to the Exposure Draft disagreed with that proposed requirement. They said that in many situations, valid reasons may exist for removing an individual asset or liability from a disposal group that have no bearing on an entity's intent and ability to sell the remaining assets and liabilities as a group. They also said that in other situations, particularly those in which several long-lived assets are included in a disposal group, a requirement to measure those assets individually would be unduly burdensome and costly.

B99. The Board considered those concerns raised by respondents. The Board decided that the remaining long-lived assets of the disposal group should be measured individually at the lower of their fair values less cost to sell only if the plan-of-sale criteria in paragraph 30 are no longer met for that group. The Board concluded that those criteria provide sufficient evidence of a commitment to a plan to sell the remaining assets and liabilities as a group and that continuing to account for those assets and liabilities as held for sale as a group is appropriate. In addition, the Board observed that for some disposal groups, there may not be significant offsetting issues.

Reporting and Disclosure of Long-Lived Assets (Disposal Groups) to Be Disposed Of

Reporting Discontinued Operations

B100. Prior to this Statement, guidance on reporting discontinued operations was provided by Opinion 30, which limited that reporting to the results of operations of a segment of a business to be disposed of. Paragraph 13 of Opinion 30 defined a segment of a business as a "component of an entity whose activities represent a separate major line of business or class of customer." Opinion 30 required that the results of operations of a segment to be disposed of be reported in discontinued operations, separately from continuing operations, in the period in which the measurement date occurred and in prior periods presented.

B101. During its deliberations leading to the Exposure Draft, the Board concluded that reporting discontinued operations separately from continuing operations provides investors, creditors, and others with information that is relevant in assessing the effects of disposal transactions on the ongoing operations of an entity. FASB Concepts Statement No. 1, *Objectives of Financial Reporting by Business Enterprises,* states, ". . . financial reporting should provide information to help investors, creditors, and others assess the amounts, timing, and uncertainty of prospective net cash inflows to the related enterprise" (paragraph 37; footnote reference omitted). FASB Concepts Statement No. 5, *Recognition and Measurement in Financial Statements of Business Enterprises,* further states:

> Classification in financial statements facilitates analysis by grouping items with essentially similar characteristics and separating items with essentially different characteristics. Analysis aimed at objectives such as predicting amounts, timing, and uncertainty of future cash flows requires financial information segregated into reasonably homogenous groups. For example, components of financial statements that consist of items that have similar characteristics in one or more respects, such as continuity or recurrence, stability, risk, and reliability, are likely to have more predictive value than if their characteristics are dissimilar. [paragraph 20]

B102. The Board observed that the Opinion 30 definition of a segment of a business has been effective in distinguishing disposal transactions that are likely to have a significant effect on the ongoing operations of the entity. However, the Board also observed that the disposal of other disposal groups that are not reported separately in discontinued operations because they are not segments of a business covered by Opinion 30 also might have a significant effect on the ongoing operations of the entity. To improve the usefulness of the information provided to users, the Board decided to broaden the reporting of discontinued operations, consistent with the recommendation made by the AICPA Special Committee on Financial Reporting in its 1994 report, *Improving Business Reporting—A Customer Focus,* which states:

> Discontinued operations is defined in current practice as a component of a company whose activities represent a separate major line of business or class of customer. That definition should be broadened to include all significant discontinued operations whose assets and results of operations and activities can be distinguished physically and operationally and for business-reporting purposes. [page 138]

B103. The Exposure Draft proposed to broaden the reporting of discontinued operations to include the results of operations of a significant component of an entity, which was defined as a disposal group with operations and assets that can be clearly distinguished physically, operationally, and for financial reporting purposes from the rest of the entity. However, the Board chose not to define the term *significant* to allow for judgment in determining whether, based on facts and circumstances unique to a particular entity, a disposal transaction should be reported in discontinued operations.

B104. Nearly all of the respondents to the Exposure Draft that commented on the proposed requirements for reporting discontinued operations agreed with the Board's decision to broaden the reporting of discontinued operations. However, many of those respondents said that to promote consistent application of the Statement, the Board should provide additional guidance for determining the significance of a component of an entity. Many respondents also referred to the interaction of the significance notion proposed in the Exposure Draft with the materiality concept discussed in SEC Staff Accounting Bulletin No. 99, *Materiality*. Those respondents asked the Board to clarify whether the criteria for assessing materiality in SAB 99 also should apply in assessing significance.

B105. During its redeliberations of the Exposure Draft, the Board decided to eliminate the significance notion from the definition of a component of an entity. The Board concluded that the requirements for reporting discontinued operations should not focus on whether a component of an entity is significant or otherwise incorporate a quantitative criterion. Instead, the Board concluded that those requirements should focus on whether a component of an entity has operations and cash flows that can be clearly distinguished from the rest of the entity, consistent with its objective of broadening the reporting of discontinued operations.

B106. The Board also decided to eliminate the requirement proposed in the Exposure Draft that assets be eliminated in a disposal transaction as a condition for reporting discontinued operations. The Board observed that the emphasis on assets would preclude a component of an entity from being reported as a discontinued operation unless the disposal transaction involved all of the assets of the component—even if the component is a separate business and was an operating segment under FASB Statement No. 131, *Disclosures about Segments of an Enterprise and Related Information*. The Board also decided to eliminate the Exposure Draft's reference to disposal activities that are incident to the evolution of an entity's business, which would have prohibited those disposal activities from being reported as discontinued operations. As noted by some respondents, many disposal transactions could be viewed as incident to the evolution of an entity's business.

B107. As revised, the requirements for reporting discontinued operations focus on whether a component of an entity has operations and cash flows that can be clearly distinguished from the rest of the entity and whether those operations and cash flows have been (or will be) eliminated from the ongoing operations of the entity in the disposal transaction. Given the emphasis on operations, the Board decided to incorporate as a condition for reporting discontinued operations the requirement that an entity have no significant continuing involvement in the operations of a component after it is disposed of. The Board concluded that it would be inappropriate to report a disposal transaction as a discontinued operation in circumstances in which an entity will have significant continuing involvement in the operations of a component after it is disposed of.

B108. During its deliberations of this Statement, the Board considered but rejected other approaches that would have reported in discontinued operations the results of operations of other asset groups as defined in other existing accounting pronouncements. One approach would have used the definition of an *operating segment* in paragraph 10 of Statement 131. Another approach would have used the definition of a *reporting unit* in Statement 142. Yet another approach would have used the definition of a *business* in EITF Issue No. 98-3, "Determining Whether a Nonmonetary Transaction Involves Receipt of Productive Assets or of a Business." The Board concluded that those approaches would not necessarily broaden the reporting of discontinued operations beyond that previously permitted by Opinion 30.

B109. The Board acknowledges that judgment will be required in distinguishing components of an entity from other disposal groups. However, the Board affirmed its conclusion in the Exposure Draft that, on balance, the advantages of broadening the presentation of discontinued operations (primarily enhanced decision usefulness) outweigh the disadvantages of broadening that presentation (primarily the possibility that the use of inconsistent judgments will affect the comparability of information reported about disposal transactions).

Subsequent adjustments to discontinued operations

B110. This Statement specifies requirements for reporting in discontinued operations adjustments in the current period that are related to the disposal of a component of an entity in a prior period. Those requirements carry forward certain of the provisions of other accounting pronouncements relating to the disposal of an Opinion 30 segment that are still relevant.

B111. Paragraphs 44(a) and (b) of this Statement refer to adjustments relating to the resolution of contingencies that arise pursuant to the terms of the disposal transaction, as well as to those that arise from, and that are directly related to, the operations of a component of an entity prior to its disposal. Paragraph 25 of Opinion 30 specified requirements for reporting in discontinued operations adjustments related to the disposal of a segment of a business that was reported in a prior period. It did not, however, specify the types of adjustments to which that reporting was intended to apply. Paragraph 25 of Opinion 30, as amended by FASB Statement No. 16, *Prior Period Adjustments,* stated:

> Circumstances attendant to disposals of a segment of a business and extraordinary items frequently require estimates, for example, of associated costs and occasionally of associated revenue, based on judgment and evaluation of the facts known at the time of first accounting for the event. Each adjustment in the current period of a loss on disposal of a business segment or of an element of an extraordinary item that was reported in a prior period should be separately disclosed as to year of origin, nature, and amount and classified separately in the current period in the same manner as the original item. If the adjustment is the correction of an error, the provisions of APB Opinion No. 20, *Accounting Changes,* paragraphs 36 and 37 should be applied.

B112. SEC Staff Accounting Bulletin No. 93, *Accounting and Disclosures Relating to Discontinued Operations,* clarified for public enterprises the reporting required by paragraph 25 of Opinion 30 as follows:

> The [SEC] staff believes that the provisions of paragraph 25 apply only to adjustments that are necessary to reflect new information about events that have occurred that

becomes available prior to disposal of the business, to reflect the actual timing and terms of the disposal when it is consummated, and to reflect the resolution of contingencies associated with that business, such as warranties and environmental liabilities retained by the seller.

B113. Paragraph 44(c) of this Statement refers to adjustments (gains or losses) associated with the settlement of employee benefit plan obligations (pension, postemployment benefits other than pensions, and other postemployment benefits). Paragraph 3 of FASB Statement No. 88, *Employers' Accounting for Settlements and Curtailments of Defined Benefit Pension Plans and for Termination Benefits,* defines *settlement* as:

> . . . a transaction that (a) is an irrevocable action, (b) relieves the employer (or the plan) of primary responsibility for a pension benefit obligation, and (c) eliminates significant risks related to the obligation and the assets used to effect the settlement.

B114. In accordance with FASB Statement No. 43, *Accounting for Compensated Absences,* Statement 88, and FASB Statement No. 106, *Employers' Accounting for Postretirement Benefits Other Than Pensions,* as amended by this Statement, settlement gains or losses should be recognized in the period in which the settlement occurs. Such gains or losses should be reported in discontinued operations if the settlement is directly related to the disposal of a component of an entity. The Board concluded that a settlement is directly related to the disposal of a component of an entity if (a) there is a demonstrated cause-and-effect relationship and (b) the settlement occurs no later than one year following the disposal transaction, unless it is delayed by events or circumstances beyond an entity's control.

B115. The requirement that a demonstrated cause-and-effect relationship exist incorporates guidance from Statement 88 related to the disposal of a segment of a business previously covered by Opinion 30. Specifically, the answer to Question 37 in the FASB Special Report, *A Guide to Implementation of Statement 88 on Employers' Accounting for Settlements and Curtailments of Defined Benefit Pension Plans and for Termination Benefits,* clarifies that a cause-and-effect relationship can be demonstrated if, for example, settlement of a pension benefit obligation for those employees affected by the sale is a necessary condition of the sale. It further clarified that "in a disposal of all or a portion of a line of business, the timing of a settlement may be at the discretion of the employer. If the employer simply chooses to settle a pension benefit obligation at the time of the sale, the resulting coincidence of events is not, in and of itself, an indication of a cause-and-effect relationship. . . ." In addition, the Board reasoned that a decision to settle later than one year after the disposal date is unlikely to be a direct consequence of the disposal transaction unless that decision is delayed beyond one year by events and circumstances beyond an entity's control.

Reporting Disposal Gains or Losses in Continuing Operations

B116. This Statement retains the requirements of Statement 121 to report gains or losses recognized on long-lived assets (disposal groups) to be sold that are not components of an entity presented in discontinued operations as a component of income from continuing operations. In Statement 121, the Board concluded that the requirements for reporting gains or losses recognized on long-lived assets (disposal groups) to be sold should be consistent with the requirements for reporting impairment losses recognized on long-lived assets (asset groups) to be held and used. The Board affirmed that conclusion in this Statement.

Reporting Long-Lived Assets (Disposal Groups) Classified as Held for Sale

B117. Under Opinion 30, the assets and liabilities of a segment of a business accounted for as a discontinued operation were permitted to be offset and reported in the statement of financial position "net." Footnote 7 of paragraph 18(d) of Opinion 30 explained:

> Consideration should be given to disclosing this information by segregation in the balance sheet of the net assets and liabilities (current and noncurrent) of the discontinued segment. Only liabilities which will be assumed by others should be designated as liabilities of the discontinued segment.

B118. The Board noted that the reporting previously permitted under Opinion 30 is an exception to the general rule that assets and liabilities should not be offset. Assets and liabilities that an entity expects to transfer to a buyer in connection with the sale of assets do not meet the conditions for offsetting in FASB

Interpretation No. 39, *Offsetting of Amounts Related to Certain Contracts*. Paragraph 5 of Interpretation 39 carries forward from APB Opinion No. 10, *Omnibus Opinion—1966,* the general principle that ". . . the offsetting of assets and liabilities in the balance sheet is improper except where a right of setoff exists." In addition, liabilities that an entity expects to transfer to a potential buyer in a disposal transaction do not qualify for derecognition prior to being assumed by a purchaser (or otherwise settled). Paragraph 42 of Concepts Statement 6 states, "Once incurred, a liability continues as a liability of the entity until the entity settles it, or another event or circumstance discharges it or removes the entity's responsibility to settle it."

B119. The Board decided that the assets and liabilities of a disposal group classified as held for sale should not be offset in the statement of financial position. Accordingly, this Statement eliminates the exception to consolidation for a subsidiary for which control is likely to be temporary in paragraph 2 of ARB No. 51, *Consolidated Financial Statements,* as amended by FASB Statement No. 94, *Consolidation of All Majority-Owned Subsidiaries.* The Board concluded that for any disposal group, information about the nature of both the assets and the liabilities of an asset group classified as held for sale is useful to users. Separately presenting those items in the statement of financial position provides information that is relevant and faithfully reports an entity's assets and its liabilities. Also, it segregates (a) those assets that have been measured at the lower of carrying amount or fair value less cost to sell and are not being depreciated from (b) those assets that are measured on a cost basis and are being depreciated. Therefore, this Statement requires that those assets and liabilities be presented separately in the asset and liability sections of the statement of financial position.

B120. The Board decided not to specify whether assets and liabilities held for sale should be classified as current or noncurrent in the statement of financial position. The Board concluded that because requirements for classifying assets and liabilities as current or noncurrent are provided by other accounting pronouncements, including ARB No. 43, Chapter 3, "Working Capital," further guidance in this Statement is not needed.

Disclosure

B121. The Board concluded that the financial statement disclosures previously required by paragraph 19 of Statement 121 and by paragraph 18 of

Opinion 30 provide information that is useful in understanding the effects of the disposal of a long-lived asset (disposal group), including a component of an entity. In the Exposure Draft, the Board decided to retain those disclosures that were still relevant, including the requirement of Opinion 30 to disclose the proceeds from a disposal transaction. Some respondents to the Exposure Draft stated that disclosure of proceeds is of little value, noting that information about cash proceeds is now provided in the statement of cash flows. The Board agreed and decided to eliminate that requirement.

Amendment to Statement 67

B122. Statement 121 amended FASB Statement No. 67, *Accounting for Costs and Initial Rental Operations of Real Estate Projects,* to apply (a) its provisions for long-lived assets to be held and used to land to be developed and projects under development and (b) its provisions for long-lived assets to be disposed of to all completed real estate projects. At that time, the Board believed that assets under development were similar to long-lived assets to be held and used and that all completed projects were "clearly assets to be disposed of." Paragraphs 124–126 of Statement 121 explained:

> The Exposure Draft proposed amending FASB Statements No. 66, *Accounting for Sales of Real Estate,* and No. 67, *Accounting for Costs and Initial Rental Operations of Real Estate Projects,* to change the lower of carrying amount or net realizable value measure to the lower of carrying amount or fair value less cost to sell measure. The Board initially decided to amend those Statements to conform the measurement of assets subject to those Statements with the measurement of assets to be disposed of.
>
> Some real estate development organizations objected to the proposed amendments in the Exposure Draft. They questioned why the scope of a project on long-lived assets included real estate development. They argued that real estate development assets are more like inventory and, therefore, the lower of carrying amount or net realizable value measure is more relevant. They did not address, however, why that measure would be more appropriate for real estate inventory than the lower of cost or market measure required for inventory under paragraph 4 of ARB No. 43, Chapter 4, "Inventory Pricing."

Others disagreed with the inventory argument, asserting that although real estate development assets will eventually be disposed of, the provisions of the Exposure Draft would have required long-term real estate projects to recognize impairments far too frequently. They said that nearly all long-term projects, regardless of their overall profitability, would become subject to write-downs in their early stages of development, only to be reversed later in the life of the project due to revised estimates of fair value less cost to sell. The Board considered alternative approaches to measuring those real estate assets. The Board decided to apply the provisions of paragraphs 4–7 to land to be developed and projects under development and to apply paragraphs 15–17 to completed projects. The Board believes that assets under development are similar to assets held for use, whereas completed projects are clearly assets to be disposed of.

B123. In this Statement, the Board reconsidered the amendment to Statement 67, noting that a completed real estate project might be held available for occupancy (either for rental or for use in the entity's operations), in which case the asset would be similar to a long-lived asset to be held and used. The Board concluded that the provisions of this Statement for long-lived assets to be held and used should be applied to those real estate assets. Therefore, this Statement revises the previous amendment to Statement 67. The provisions of this Statement for long-lived assets to be held and used should be applied to completed real estate projects to be held available for occupancy. The provisions of this Statement for long-lived assets to be disposed of by sale should be applied to completed real estate projects to be sold.

B124. In implementing Statement 121, questions also emerged about the application of its impairment provisions to rental real estate property to be held and used. The primary issue was whether property-related assets should be grouped together with the real estate property in determining whether to recognize, and in measuring, an impairment loss. Such property-related assets include accrued rent and deferred leasing costs recognized for operating leases in accordance with FASB Statement No. 13, *Accounting for Leases* (paragraph 19 and paragraph 5(m), as amended by FASB Statement No. 91, *Accounting for Nonrefundable Fees and Costs Associated with Originating or Acquiring Loans and Initial Direct*

Costs of Leases), and FASB Technical Bulletin No. 85-3, *Accounting for Operating Leases with Scheduled Rent Increases.* The Board concluded that the provisions of paragraphs 10–14 of this Statement for grouping long-lived assets to be held and used should be applied to those real estate assets.

Benefits and Costs

B125. The mission of the FASB is to establish and improve standards of financial accounting and reporting for the guidance and education of the public, including preparers, auditors, and users of financial information. In fulfilling that mission, the Board endeavors to determine that a proposed standard will fill a significant need and that the costs imposed to meet that standard, as compared with other alternatives, are justified in relation to the overall benefits of the resulting information. Although the costs to implement a new standard may not be borne evenly, investors and creditors—both present and potential—as well as others, benefit from improvements in financial reporting, thereby facilitating the functioning of markets for capital and credit and the efficient allocation of resources in the economy.

B126. The Board determined that the requirements in this Statement will result in improved financial reporting. In Statement 121, the Board determined that the information provided to users of financial statements about long-lived assets could be improved by eliminating inconsistencies in the accounting and reporting of the impairment of those assets, thereby improving comparability in financial reporting. In this Statement, the Board determined that the information provided to users of financial statements about long-lived assets could be further improved by eliminating inconsistencies in the accounting and reporting of the disposal of those assets. As discussed in FASB Concepts Statement No. 2, *Qualitative Characteristics of Accounting Information,* providing comparable financial information enables users to identify similarities in and differences between two sets of economic events.

B127. The Board believes that the incremental costs of implementing this Statement have been minimized principally by retaining certain of the fundamental provisions of Statement 121 that are already in effect, in particular, its recognition and measurement provisions for the impairment of long-lived assets to be held and used and its measurement provisions for long-lived assets classified as held for sale. In addition, the Board decided to eliminate from this Statement certain of the proposals in the Exposure Draft that would have changed those existing requirements. Further, the provisions of this Statement generally are to be applied prospectively. Although there may be one-time costs for changes needed to apply the accounting requirements of this Statement, the benefits from more consistent, comparable, and reliable information will be ongoing. The Board believes that the benefits of this Statement outweigh the costs of implementing it.

Effective Date and Transition

B128. The Board decided, except as follows, to require that this Statement be effective for financial statements issued for fiscal years beginning after December 15, 2001, and interim periods within those fiscal years. The Board decided that the provisions relating to disposal transactions should be effective for disposal transactions initiated by a commitment to a plan after the earlier of the effective date of this Statement or the entity's initial application of this Statement. The Board believes that that effective date provides sufficient time for entities and their auditors to analyze, interpret, and prepare for implementation of the provisions of this Statement.

B129. This Statement requires that impairment losses resulting from the initial application of its provisions for long-lived assets to be held and used be reported in the period in which the recognition criteria are initially applied and met based on facts and circumstances existing at that date. This Statement, like Statement 121, requires consideration of the continuing effect of events or changes in circumstances that occurred prior to the Statement's initial application. The Board recognizes the benefits of comparative financial statements but questions the ability of entities to reconstruct estimates of future cash flows based on assessments of events and circumstances as they existed in prior periods and without the use of hindsight.

B130. This Statement requires prospective application of its provisions for disposal transactions, including its provisions for the presentation of discontinued operations, and prohibits retroactive application.[32] The Board concluded that obtaining or developing the information necessary to apply this Statement retroactively could be burdensome for many entities. In addition, the Board observed that information about disposal transactions generally is disclosed by public enterprises (for example, in management's discussion and analysis and in press releases). Disposal transactions involving a component of an entity that are "grandfathered" under Statement 121 would continue to be reported in continuing operations, while disposal transactions involving a segment of a business that are "grandfathered" under Opinion 30 would continue to be reported in discontinued operations. The Board noted that segregating those disposal transactions would mitigate the effect of having different measurement approaches under Statement 121 and Opinion 30—one based on the fair value less cost to sell and the other based on net realizable value. The Board concluded that prospective application for disposal transactions is the most reasonable and practical transition approach when considered together with the need for consistent transition provisions for disposal transactions and the cost associated with retroactive application.

B131. The Board observed that for long-lived assets (disposal groups) to be sold that meet the criteria for a qualifying plan of sale when this Statement is initially applied, a cumulative-effect adjustment would not require an entity to retroactively derive fair values for those assets to be disposed of. Rather, the adjustment would be based on fair values at the date this Statement is initially applied. The Board concluded, however, that it would be inappropriate to require retroactive application for some, but not all, of the provisions for disposal transactions. The Board expects that, based on the requirements of previous accounting pronouncements that address the accounting for disposal transactions, many disposal transactions that are in process when this Statement is initially applied will be completed within one year. Therefore, prospective application should not have a significant, continuing impact on the comparability and consistency of the financial statements.

B132. The Board observed, however, that in some cases assets that are classified as held for disposal when this Statement is initially applied may not meet the criteria in paragraph 30 by the end of the fiscal year in which the Statement is initially applied. The

Board concluded that it would be inappropriate to allow the accounting for those assets to be "grandfathered" indefinitely. Doing so could impair the comparability and consistency of the financial statements and extend the provisions of Opinion 30 that require the accrual of future operating losses for several reporting periods. Therefore, for a long-lived asset (disposal group) classified as held for disposal when this Statement is initially applied, the asset (disposal group) must be reclassified as held and used in accordance with paragraph 38 if the criteria in paragraph 30 are not met by the end of the fiscal year in which this Statement is initially applied.

B133. This Statement requires reclassification of previously issued statements of financial position included for comparative purposes to reflect application of the reporting provisions in paragraph 46 for long-lived assets and disposal groups, including a temporarily controlled subsidiary, classified as held for sale under Statement 121 (that is, the prohibition of offsetting assets and liabilities). The Board believes that requiring reclassification will improve the comparability of those financial statements. Moreover, because that reporting affects only how the assets and liabilities of disposal groups previously classified as held for sale are displayed, the Board concluded that the information necessary to disaggregate and separately report those assets and liabilities would be available.

Appendix C

AMENDMENTS TO EXISTING PRONOUNCEMENTS

C1. This Statement supersedes FASB Statement No. 121, *Accounting for the Impairment of Long-Lived Assets and for Long-Lived Assets to Be Disposed Of.*

C2. Accounting Research Bulletin No. 51, *Consolidated Financial Statements,* is amended as follows:

a. In the last sentence of paragraph 2, as amended by FASB Statement No. 94, *Consolidation of All Majority-Owned Subsidiaries,* the phrase *is likely to be temporary or if it* is deleted.

b. Paragraph 12 is deleted.

---

[32]The prohibition on retroactive application does not extend to the provisions of this Statement for reporting discontinued operations after this Statement is initially applied.

C3. In paragraphs 21 and the heading preceding it, 30(e), and 31 of APB Opinion No. 28, *Interim Financial Reporting,* all references to *segment of a business* or *segments of a business* are replaced by *component of an entity* or *components of an entity,* respectively.

C4. APB Opinion No. 29, *Accounting for Nonmonetary Transactions,* is amended as follows:

a. The following footnote is added to the end of the first sentence of paragraph 21 and to the first sentence of paragraph 23 after the parenthetical phrase:

> *An indicated impairment of value of a long-lived asset covered by FASB Statement No. 144, *Accounting for the Impairment or Disposal of Long-Lived Assets,* shall be determined in accordance with paragraph 29 of that Statement.

C5. APB Opinion No. 30, *Reporting the Results of Operations—Reporting the Effects of Disposal of a Segment of a Business, and Extraordinary, Unusual and Infrequently Occurring Events and Transactions,* is amended as follows:

a. In paragraph 3, *to specify the accounting and reporting for disposal of a segment of a business, (4)* is deleted.

b. Paragraphs 8 and 9 and footnote 2 are deleted.

c. Paragraph 11 is amended as follows:

(1) The following footnote is added to the first sentence immediately following *discontinued operations*:

> *Paragraphs 41–44 of Statement 144 address the reporting of discontinued operations.

(2) In the second sentence, *segment of a business* is replaced by *component of an entity.*

d. Paragraphs 13–18 and the heading preceding those paragraphs are deleted.

e. Footnotes 5–7 are deleted.

f. Paragraph 23 is amended as follows:

(1) The references to *segment of a business* are replaced by *component of an entity.*

(2) The last sentence is replaced by the following:

> Disposals of a component of an entity shall be accounted for and presented in the income statement in accordance with Statement 144 even though the circumstances of the disposal meet the criteria specified in paragraph 20.

g. Paragraph 25 is amended as follows:

(1) In the first sentence, *disposals of a segment of a business and* is deleted.

(2) In the second sentence, *of a loss on disposal of a business segment or* is deleted.

C6. AICPA Accounting Interpretation 1, "Illustration of the Application of APB Opinion No. 30," is amended as follows:

a. The first question and its interpretation are amended as follows:

(1) The interpretation and first discussion are deleted.

(2) The following interpretation is inserted before the second discussion:

> *Interpretation*—The criteria for extraordinary items classification should be considered. That is:
>
> Does the event or transaction meet both criteria of *unusual nature* and *infrequency of occurrence?*

b. The second question and its interpretation are superseded.

C7. In FASB Statement No. 19, *Financial Accounting and Reporting by Oil and Gas Producing Companies,* paragraph 44(a) is replaced by the following:

> a. A transfer of assets used in oil and gas producing activities related to unproved properties in

exchange for other assets also used in oil and gas producing activities.*

---

*If assets used in oil and gas producing activities related to proved properties are transferred in exchange for other assets also used in oil and gas producing activities, a loss, if any, shall be recognized in accordance with paragraph 29 of FASB Statement No. 144, *Accounting for the Impairment or Disposal of Long-Lived Assets.*

C8. In FASB Statement No. 43, *Accounting for Compensated Absences,* the last sentence of paragraph 2, as added by FASB Statement No. 112, *Employers' Accounting for Postemployment Benefits,* is deleted.

C9. In FASB Statement No. 66, *Accounting for Sales of Real Estate,* the following is added to the end of the second sentence of paragraph 65:

> unless the property has been classified as held for sale in accordance with paragraph 30 of FASB Statement No. 144, *Accounting for the Impairment or Disposal of Long-Lived Assets.*

C10. In FASB Statement No. 67, *Accounting for Costs and Initial Rental Operations of Real Estate Projects,* the first and second sentences of paragraph 24 are replaced by the following:

> The provisions in Statement 144 for long-lived assets to be disposed of by sale shall apply to a real estate project, or parts thereof, that is substantially completed and that is to be sold. The provisions in that Statement for long-lived assets to be held and used shall apply to real estate held for development, including property to be developed in the future as well as that currently under development, and to a real estate project, or parts thereof, that is substantially completed and that is to be held and used (for example, for rental). Determining whether the carrying amounts of real estate projects require recognition of an impairment loss shall be based on an evaluation of individual projects.

C11. FASB Statement No. 88, *Employers' Accounting for Settlements and Curtailments of Defined Benefit Pension Plans and for Termination Benefits,* is amended as follows:

a. In paragraph 6(a), *segment of a business* is replaced by *component of an entity.*

b. Paragraphs 8 and 16 and the heading preceding paragraph 16 are deleted.

c. Paragraph 57 is amended as follows:

(1) In the title of Example 3A, *segment* is replaced by *component.*

(2) In Example 3A, the reference to *segment of its business* is replaced by *component of the entity.*

(3) Footnote d to Example 3A is deleted.

C12. FASB Statement No. 106, *Employers' Accounting for Postretirement Benefits Other Than Pensions,* is amended as follows:

a. In paragraph 96(a), *segment of a business* is replaced by *component of an entity.*

b. Paragraph 103 and the heading preceding it are deleted.

C13. In paragraph 8(c) of FASB Statement No. 115, *Accounting for Certain Investments in Debt and Equity Securities,* the reference to *segment* is replaced by *component of an entity.*

C14. In the last sentence of paragraph 164 of FASB Statement No. 117, *Financial Statements of Not-for-Profit Organizations,* the reference to *a discontinued operating segment* is replaced by *reporting discontinued operations.*

C15. Paragraph 9 of FASB Statement No. 123, *Accounting for Stock-Based Compensation,* is amended as follows:

a. In the first sentence, *with the same meaning as in FASB Statement No. 121, Accounting for the Impairment of Long-Lived Assets and for Long-Lived Assets to Be Disposed Of.* is replaced by *to refer to.*

b. In the second sentence, *Statement 121 says that the fair value of an asset is . . .* is deleted.

c. The reference to *[paragraph 7]* at the end of the quotation is deleted.

C16. Footnote 18 to paragraph 44 of FASB Statement No. 141, *Business Combinations,* is deleted.

C17. FASB Statement No. 142, *Goodwill and Other Intangible Assets,* is amended as follows:

a. Paragraph 7 is deleted.

b. Paragraph 15 is amended as follows:

(1) In the first sentence, *Statement 121* is replaced by *FASB Statement No. 144, Accounting for the Impairment or Disposal of Long-Lived Assets,* and *paragraphs 4–11* are replaced by *paragraphs 7–24.*

(2) In the second sentence, *Statement 121* is replaced by *Statement 144.*

c. The second (parenthetical) sentence of paragraph 17 is replaced by *(Paragraph 8 of Statement 144 includes examples of impairment indicators.).*

d. In paragraph 28(f), *Statement 121* is replaced by *Statement 144.*

e. In the second sentence of paragraph 29, *Statement 121* is replaced by *Statement 144.*

f. Footnote 22 to paragraph 39 is deleted.

g. Appendix A is amended as follows:

(1) In the last sentence of Example 1, *FASB Statement No. 121, Accounting for the Impairment of Long-Lived Assets and for Long-Lived Assets to Be Disposed Of* is replaced by *FASB Statement No. 144, Accounting for the Impairment or Disposal of Long-Lived Assets.*

(2) In Examples 2, 3, 5, and 9, all references to *Statement 121* are replaced by *Statement 144.*

C18. FASB Statement No. 143, *Accounting for Asset Retirement Obligations,* is amended as follows:

a. The fourth sentence of paragraph 2 is replaced by:

This Statement does not apply to obligations that arise solely from a plan to sell or otherwise dispose of a long-lived asset covered by FASB Statement No. 144, *Accounting for the Impairment or Disposal of Long-Lived Assets.*

b. Paragraph 12 is amended as follows:

(1) In the first sentence, *Statement 121* is replaced by *Statement 144.*

(2) Footnote 11 is deleted.

C19. FASB Interpretation No. 18, *Accounting for Income Taxes in Interim Periods,* is amended as follows:

a. Footnote 1 to paragraph 5 is replaced by the following:

The terms used in this definition are described in APB Opinion No. 20, *Accounting Changes,* in APB Opinion No. 30, *Reporting the Results of Operations—Reporting the Effects of Disposal of a Segment of a Business, and Extraordinary, Unusual and Infrequently Occurring Events and Transactions,* and in FASB Statement No. 144, *Accounting for the Impairment or Disposal of Long-Lived Assets.* See paragraph 10 of Opinion 30 for *extraordinary items* and paragraph 26 for *unusual items* and *infrequently occurring items.* See paragraph 20 of Opinion 20 for *cumulative effects of changes in accounting principles.* See paragraphs 41–44 of Statement 144 for *discontinued operations.*

b. Paragraph 19 is amended as follows:

(1) All references to *measurement date* are replaced by *date on which the criteria in paragraph 30 of Statement 144 are met.*

(2) In the first sentence, *both (a)* and *and (b) the gain (or loss) on disposal of discontinued operations (including any provision for operating loss subsequent to the measurement date)* are deleted.

(3) All references to *discontinued segment* are replaced by *discontinued component.*

(4) Footnote 20 is replaced by the following:

The term *discontinued component* refers to the disposal of a component of an entity as described in paragraph 41 of Statement 144.

c. In paragraph 35, the references to *segment of a business* are replaced by *component of an entity.*

d. In paragraph 71, under Discontinued operations, *Division* is replaced by *Component* and *Income* *(loss) on disposal of Division X, including provision of $XXXX for operating losses during phaseout period (less applicable income taxes of $XXXX) is deleted.*

C20. Paragraph 3 of FASB Interpretation No. 27, *Accounting for a Loss on a Sublease,* is deleted.

C21. In paragraph 7 of FASB Interpretation No. 39, *Offsetting of Amounts Related to Certain Contracts,* the reference to *APB Opinion No. 30, Reporting the Results of Operations—Reporting the Effects of Disposal of a Segment of a Business, and Extraordinary, Unusual and Infrequently Occurring Events and Transactions (reporting of discontinued operations)* is deleted.

AMENDMENTS MADE BY STATEMENT 121 CARRIED FORWARD IN THIS STATEMENT WITH MINOR CHANGES

C22. In the first sentence of paragraph 19(h) of APB Opinion No. 18, *The Equity Method of Accounting for Investments in Common Stock,* the phrase *the same as a loss in value of other long-term assets* is deleted.

C23. The last question and its interpretation of AICPA Accounting Interpretation 1, "Illustration of the Application of APB Opinion No. 30," are superseded.

C24. FASB Statement No. 15, *Accounting by Debtors and Creditors for Troubled Debt Restructurings,* is amended as follows:

a. The following sentence is added after the first sentence of paragraph 28:

> A creditor that receives long-lived assets that will be sold from a debtor in full satisfaction of a receivable shall account for those assets at their fair value less cost to sell, as that term is used in paragraph 34 of FASB Statement No. 144, *Accounting for the Impairment or Disposal of Long-Lived Assets.*

b. The last sentence of paragraph 28 is replaced by the following:

> The excess of (i) the recorded investment in the receivable[17] satisfied over (ii) the fair value of assets received (less cost to sell, if required above) is a loss to be recognized. For purposes

of this paragraph, losses, to the extent they are not offset against allowances for uncollectible amounts or other valuation accounts, shall be included in measuring net income for the period.

c. In the second sentence of paragraph 33, *at their fair values* is deleted and *less cost to sell* is inserted after *reduced by the fair value.*

C25. The following new heading and paragraph are added after paragraph 62 of FASB Statement No. 19, *Financial Accounting and Reporting by Oil and Gas Producing Companies:*

Impairment Test for Proved Properties and Capitalized Exploration and Development Cost

> The provisions of FASB Statement No. 144, *Accounting for the Impairment or Disposal of Long-Lived Assets,* are applicable to the costs of an enterprise's wells and related equipment and facilities and the costs of the related proved properties. The impairment provisions relating to unproved properties referred to in paragraphs 12, 27–29, 31(b), 33, 40, 47(g), and 47(h) of this Statement remain applicable to unproved properties.

C26. The following sentence is added to the end of paragraph 19 of FASB Statement No. 34, *Capitalization of Interest Cost:*

> The provisions of FASB Statement No. 144, *Accounting for the Impairment or Disposal of Long-Lived Assets,* apply in recognizing impairment of long-lived assets held for use.

C27. The first two sentences of paragraph 14 of FASB Statement No. 51, *Financial Reporting by Cable Television Companies,* are replaced by the following: **[Note: This amendment does not affect the amendment made by paragraph D5(2) of Statement 142 to refer to other intangible assets subject to the provisions of that Statement.]**

> Capitalized plant and certain intangible assets are subject to the provisions of FASB Statement No. 144, *Accounting for the Impairment or Disposal of Long-Lived Assets.*

C28. Paragraph 48 of FASB Statement No. 60, *Accounting and Reporting by Insurance Enterprises,* is amended as follows:

a. In the first sentence, *and an allowance for any impairment in value* is deleted.

b. In the last sentence, *Changes in the allowance for any impairment in value relating to real estate investments* is replaced by *Reductions in the carrying amount of real estate investments resulting from the application of FASB Statement No. 144, Accounting for the Impairment or Disposal of Long-Lived Assets,*.

C29. FASB Statement No. 61, *Accounting for Title Plant,* is amended as follows:

a. In the first and second sentences of paragraph 6, *value* is replaced by *carrying amount.*

b. The last sentence of paragraph 6 is replaced by the following:

> Those events or changes in circumstances, in addition to the examples in paragraph 8 of FASB Statement No. 144, *Accounting for the Impairment or Disposal of Long-Lived Assets,* indicate that the carrying amount of the capitalized costs may not be recoverable. Accordingly, the provisions of Statement 144 apply.

C30. Footnote 5 to paragraph 21 of FASB Statement No. 66, *Accounting for Sales of Real Estate,* is replaced by the following:

> Paragraph 24 of FASB Statement No. 67, *Accounting for Costs and Initial Rental Operations of Real Estate Projects,* as amended by FASB Statement No. 144, *Accounting for the Impairment or Disposal of Long-Lived Assets,* specifies the accounting for property that is substantially completed and that is to be sold.

C31. FASB Statement No. 67, *Accounting for Costs and Initial Rental Operations of Real Estate Projects,* is amended as follows:

a. In paragraph 3, *costs in excess of estimated net realizable value* is replaced by *reductions in the carrying amounts of real estate assets prescribed by FASB Statement No. 144, Accounting for the Impairment or Disposal of Long-Lived Assets.*

b. Paragraph 16 is deleted.

c. Paragraph 25 is replaced by the following:

> Paragraph 8 of Statement 144 provides examples of events or changes in circumstances

that indicate that the recoverability of the carrying amount of a long-lived asset should be assessed. Insufficient rental demand for a rental project currently under construction is an additional example that indicates that the recoverability of the real estate project should be assessed in accordance with the provisions of Statement 144.

d. In paragraph 28, the term *net realizable value* and its definition are deleted.

C32. FASB Statement No. 71, *Accounting for the Effects of Certain Types of Regulation,* is amended as follows:

a. The following sentence is added to the end of paragraph 9:

> If at any time the incurred cost no longer meets the above criteria, that cost shall be charged to earnings.

b. Paragraph 10 is amended as follows:

(1) The second and third sentences are replaced by:

> If a regulator excludes all or part of a cost from allowable costs, the carrying amount of any asset recognized pursuant to paragraph 9 of this Statement shall be reduced to the extent of the excluded cost.

(2) In the fourth sentence, *the asset has* is replaced by *other assets have* and *and FASB Statement No. 144, Accounting for the Impairment or Disposal of Long-Lived Assets, shall apply* is added to the end of that sentence after the footnote added by FASB Statement No. 90, *Regulated Enterprises—Accounting for Abandonments and Disallowances of Plant Costs.*

c. The following new paragraph is added after paragraph 10:

> If a regulator allows recovery through rates of costs previously excluded from allowable costs, that action shall result in recognition of a new asset. The classification of that asset shall be consistent with the classification that would have resulted had those costs been initially included in allowable costs.

C33. The following phrase is added to the end of the third sentence of paragraph 6 of FASB Statement No. 101, *Regulated Enterprises—Accounting for the Discontinuation of Application of FASB Statement No. 71:*

> , and FASB Statement No. 144, *Accounting for the Impairment or Disposal of Long-Lived Assets,* shall apply, except for the provisions for income statement reporting in paragraphs 25 and 26 of that Statement.

Appendix D

REFERENCES TO PRONOUNCEMENTS

D1. There are many references in the existing authoritative literature to impairment of assets. Appendix C indicates the amendments to pronouncements existing at the date of this Statement. The following table lists FASB and APB pronouncements that refer to impairment of long-lived assets and indicates which of those pronouncements will apply the applicable requirements of this Statement and which will continue to apply some other applicable existing requirement.

Existing Pronouncement	Title	Apply Requirement in This Statement	Apply Existing Requirement	Existing Requirement Paragraph Number
APB Opinion No. 18	*The Equity Method of Accounting for Investments in Common Stock*		X	19(h) (as amended by this Statement)
FASB Statement No. 7	*Accounting and Reporting by Development Stage Enterprises*	X		
FASB Statement No. 13	*Accounting for Leases*			
	• Capital leases of lessees	X		
	• Assets of lessors subject to operating leases	X		
	• Sales-type, direct financing, and leveraged leases of lessors		X	17
FASB Statement No. 19	*Financial Accounting and Reporting by Oil and Gas Producing Companies*			
	• Unproved properties		X	12, 27–29, 31(b), 33, 40, 47(g), 47(h)
	• Proved properties, wells, and related equipment and facilities accounted for using the successful-efforts method of accounting	X		

Existing Pronouncement	Title	Apply Requirement in This Statement	Apply Existing Requirement	Existing Requirement Paragraph Number
FASB Statement No. 28	*Accounting for Sales with Leasebacks*	X	X	3(c)
FASB Statement No. 34	*Capitalization of Interest Cost*	X		
FASB Statement No. 44	*Accounting for Intangible Assets of Motor Carriers*		X	3–7
FASB Statement No. 50	*Financial Reporting in the Record and Music Industry*		X	11, 15
FASB Statement No. 51	*Financial Reporting by Cable Television Companies*			
	• Assets that are being depreciated (amortized)	X		
	• Other intangible assets		X	14
FASB Statement No. 60	*Accounting and Reporting by Insurance Enterprises*			
	• Real estate investments	X		
	• Deferred policy acquisition costs		X	32–37
FASB Statement No. 61	*Accounting for Title Plant*	X		
FASB Statement No. 63	*Financial Reporting by Broadcasters*		X	7

FASB Statement No. 65	Accounting for Certain Mortgage Banking Activities	X		7
FASB Statement No. 67	Accounting for Costs and Initial Rental Operations of Real Estate Projects		X	
FASB Statement No. 71	Accounting for the Effects of Certain Types of Regulation			
	• Rate-regulated assets	X		9, 10 (as amended by this Statement)
	• Other assets		X	
FASB Statement No. 72	Accounting for Certain Acquisitions of Banking or Thrift Institutions	X		4
FASB Statement No. 86	Accounting for the Costs of Computer Software to Be Sold, Leased, or Otherwise Marketed	X		10
FASB Statement No. 90	Regulated Enterprises—Accounting for Abandonments and Disallowances of Plant Costs	X		7
FASB Statement No. 97	Accounting and Reporting by Insurance Enterprises for Certain Long-Duration Contracts and for Realized Gains and Losses from the Sale of Investments	X		25, 27

Existing Pronouncement	Title	Apply Requirement in This Statement	Apply Existing Requirement	Existing Requirement Paragraph Number
FASB Statement No. 101	*Regulated Enterprises—Accounting for the Discontinuation of Application of FASB Statement No. 71*	X		
FASB Statement No. 109	*Accounting for Income Taxes*		X	20–26
FASB Statement No. 114	*Accounting by Creditors for Impairment of a Loan*		X	8–16
FASB Statement No. 115	*Accounting for Certain Investments in Debt and Equity Securities*		X	16
FASB Statement No. 140	*Accounting for Transfers and Servicing of Financial Assets and Extinguishments of Liabilities*		X	13, 63(g)
FASB Statement No. 142	*Goodwill and Other Intangible Assets*			
	• Goodwill and intangible assets not being amortized		X	17, 19–22
	• Intangible assets being amortized	X		

Appendix E

EXCERPTS FROM CONCEPTS STATEMENT 7

[Best understood in context of full Concepts Statement]

E1. Paragraph 23 of this Statement states that "a present value technique is often the best available valuation technique with which to estimate the fair value of a long-lived asset (asset group)." Paragraphs 39–54 and 75–88 of FASB Concepts Statement No. 7, *Using Cash Flow Information and Present Value in Accounting Measurements,* discuss the use of present value techniques in measuring the fair value of an asset or a liability. Those paragraphs of Concepts Statement 7 follow.

The Components of a Present Value Measurement

39. Paragraph 23 describes the following elements that together capture the economic differences between various assets and liabilities:[7]

a. An estimate of the future cash flow, or in more complex cases, series of future cash flows at different times
b. Expectations about possible variations in the amount or timing of those cash flows
c. The time value of money, represented by the risk-free rate of interest
d. The price for bearing the uncertainty inherent in the asset or liability
e. Other, sometimes unidentifiable, factors including illiquidity and market imperfections.

---

[7]The effect of the entity's credit standing on the measurement of its liabilities is discussed in paragraphs 75–88.

40. This Statement contrasts two approaches to computing present value, either of which may be used to estimate the fair value of an asset or a liability, depending on the circumstances. In the expected cash flow approach discussed in this Statement, only the third factor listed in paragraph 39 (the time value of money, represented by the risk-free rate of interest) is included in the discount rate; the other factors cause adjustments in arriving at risk-adjusted expected cash flows. In a traditional approach to present value, adjustments for factors (b)–(e) described in paragraph 39 are embedded in the discount rate.

General Principles

41. The techniques used to estimate future cash flows and interest rates will vary from one situation to another depending on the circumstances surrounding the asset or liability in question. However, certain general principles govern any application of present value techniques in measuring assets or liabilities:

a. To the extent possible, estimated cash flows and interest rates should reflect assumptions about the future events and uncertainties that would be considered in deciding whether to acquire an asset or group of assets in an arm's-length transaction for cash.
b. Interest rates used to discount cash flows should reflect assumptions that are consistent with those inherent in the estimated cash flows. Otherwise, the effect of some assumptions will be double counted or ignored. For example, an interest rate of 12 percent might be applied to contractual cash flows of a loan. That rate reflects expectations about future defaults from loans with particular characteristics. That same 12 percent rate should not be used to discount expected cash flows because those cash flows already reflect assumptions about future defaults.
c. Estimated cash flows and interest rates should be free from both bias and factors unrelated to the asset, liability, or group of assets or liabilities in question. For example, deliberately understating estimated net cash flows to enhance the apparent future profitability of an asset introduces a bias into the measurement.
d. Estimated cash flows or interest rates should reflect the range of possible outcomes rather than a single most-likely, minimum, or maximum possible amount.

Traditional and Expected Cash Flow Approaches to Present Value

42. A present value measurement begins with a set of future cash flows, but existing accounting standards employ a variety of different approaches in specifying cash flow sets. Some applications of present value use contractual cash flows. When contractual cash flows are not available, some applica-

tions use an estimate of the single most-likely amount or **best estimate.**

43. Accounting applications of present value have traditionally used a single set of estimated cash flows and a single interest rate, often described as "the rate commensurate with the risk." In effect, although not always by conscious design, the traditional approach assumes that a single interest rate convention can reflect all the expectations about the future cash flows and the appropriate risk premium. The Board expects that accountants will continue to use the traditional approach for some measurements. In some circumstances, a traditional approach is relatively easy to apply. For assets and liabilities with contractual cash flows, it is consistent with the manner in which marketplace participants describe assets and liabilities, as in "a 12 percent bond."

44. The traditional approach is useful for many measurements, especially those in which comparable assets and liabilities can be observed in the marketplace. However, the Board found that the traditional approach does not provide the tools needed to address some complex measurement problems, including the measurement of nonfinancial assets and liabilities for which no market for the item or a comparable item exists. The traditional approach places most of the emphasis on selection of an interest rate. A proper search for "the rate commensurate with the risk" requires analysis of at least two items—one asset or liability that exists in the marketplace and has an observed interest rate and the asset or liability being measured. The appropriate rate of interest for the cash flows being measured must be inferred from the observable rate of interest in some other asset or liability and, to draw that inference, the characteristics of the cash flows must be similar to those of the asset being measured. Consequently, the measurer must do the following:

a. Identify the set of cash flows that will be discounted.

b. Identify another asset or liability in the marketplace that appears to have similar cash flow characteristics.

c. Compare the cash flow sets from the two items to ensure that they are similar. (For example, are both sets contractual cash flows, or is one contractual and the other an estimated cash flow?)

d. Evaluate whether there is an element in one item that is not present in the other. (For example, is one less liquid than the other?)

e. Evaluate whether both sets of cash flows are likely to behave (vary) in a similar fashion under changing economic conditions.

45. The Board found the expected cash flow approach to be a more effective measurement tool than the traditional approach in many situations. In developing a measurement, the expected cash flow approach uses all expectations about possible cash flows instead of the single most-likely cash flow. For example, a cash flow might be $100, $200, or $300 with probabilities of 10 percent, 60 percent, and 30 percent, respectively. The expected cash flow is $220.[8] The expected cash flow approach thus differs from the traditional approach by focusing on direct analysis of the cash flows in question and on more explicit statements of the assumptions used in the measurement.

---

[8]($100 × .1) + ($200 × .6) + ($300 × .3) = $220. The traditional notion of a best estimate or most-likely amount in this example is $200.

---

46. The expected cash flow approach also allows use of present value techniques when the timing of cash flows is uncertain. For example, a cash flow of $1,000 may be received in 1 year, 2 years, or 3 years with probabilities of 10 percent, 60 percent, and 30 percent, respectively. The example below shows the computation of **expected present value** in that situation. Again, the expected present value of $892.36 differs from the traditional notion of a best estimate of $902.73 (the 60 percent probability) in this example.[9]

---

[9]Interest rates usually vary with the length of time until settlement, a phenomenon described as the *yield curve.*

Present value of $1,000		
in 1 year at 5%	$952.38	
Probability	10.00%	$ 95.24
Present value of $1,000		
in 2 years at 5.25%	$902.73	
Probability	60.00%	541.64
Present value of $1,000		
in 3 years at 5.50%	$851.61	
Probability	30.00%	255.48
Expected present value		$892.36

47. In the past, accounting standard setters have been reluctant to permit use of present value techniques beyond the narrow case of "contractual rights to receive money or contractual obligations to pay money on fixed or determinable dates." That phrase, which first appeared in accounting standards in paragraph 2 of Opinion 21, reflects the computational limitations of the traditional approach—a single set of cash flows that can be assigned to specific future dates. The Accounting Principles Board recognized that the amount of cash flows is almost always uncertain and incorporated that uncertainty in the interest rate. However, an interest rate in a traditional present value computation cannot reflect uncertainties in timing. A traditional present value computation, applied to the example above, would require a decision about which of the possible timings of cash flows to use and, accordingly, would not reflect the probabilities of other timings.

48. While many accountants do not routinely use the expected cash flow approach, expected cash flows are inherent in the techniques used in some accounting measurements, like pensions, other postretirement benefits, and some insurance obligations. They are currently allowed, but not required, when measuring the impairment of long-lived assets and estimating the fair value of financial instruments. The use of probabilities is an essential element of the expected cash flow approach, and one that may trouble some accountants. They may question whether assigning probabilities to highly subjective estimates suggests greater precision than, in fact, exists. However, the proper ap-

plication of the traditional approach (as described in paragraph 44) requires the same estimates and subjectivity without providing the computational transparency of the expected cash flow approach.

49. Many estimates developed in current practice already incorporate the elements of expected cash flows informally. In addition, accountants often face the need to measure an asset or liability using limited information about the probabilities of possible cash flows. For example, an accountant might be confronted with the following situations:

a. The estimated amount falls somewhere between $50 and $250, but no amount in the range is more likely than any other amount. Based on that limited information, the estimated expected cash flow is $150 [(50 + 250)/2].
b. The estimated amount falls somewhere between $50 and $250, and the most likely amount is $100. However, the probabilities attached to each amount are unknown. Based on that limited information, the estimated expected cash flow is $133.33 [(50 + 100 + 250)/3].
c. The estimated amount will be $50 (10 percent probability), $250 (30 percent probability), or $100 (60 percent probability). Based on that limited information, the estimated expected cash flow is $140 [(50 × .10) + (250 × .30) + (100 × .60)].

50. Those familiar with statistical analysis may recognize the cases above as simple descriptions of (a) *uniform,* (b) *triangular,* and (c) *discrete* distributions.[10] In each case, the estimated expected cash flow is likely to provide a better estimate of fair value than the minimum, most likely, or maximum amount taken alone.

---

[10]The uniform and triangular distributions are *continuous* distributions. For further information about these and other distributions, refer to:
- M. Evans, N. Hastings, and B. Peacock, *Statistical Distributions,* 2d ed. (New York: John Wiley & Sons, Inc., 1993).
- N. Johnson, S. Kotz, and N. Balakrishnan, *Continuous Univariate Distributions,* 2d ed., vol. 2. (New York: John Wiley & Sons, Inc., 1995).

51. Like any accounting measurement, the application of an expected cash flow approach is subject to a cost-benefit constraint.

In some cases, an entity may have access to considerable data and may be able to develop many cash flow scenarios. In other cases, an entity may not be able to develop more than general statements about the variability of cash flows without incurring considerable cost. The accounting problem is to balance the cost of obtaining additional information against the additional reliability that information will bring to the measurement. The Board recognizes that judgments about relative costs and benefits vary from one situation to the next and involve financial statement preparers, their auditors, and the needs of financial statement users.

52. Some maintain that expected cash flow techniques are inappropriate for measuring a single item or an item with a limited number of possible outcomes. They offer an example of an asset or liability with two possible outcomes: a 90 percent probability that the cash flow will be $10 and a 10 percent probability that the cash flow will be $1,000. They observe that the expected cash flow in that example is $109[11] and criticize that result as not representing either of the amounts that may ultimately be paid.

---

[11]($10 × .9) + ($1,000 × .1) = $109. For purposes of illustration, this example ignores the time value of money.

53. Assertions like the one just outlined reflect underlying disagreement with the measurement objective. If the objective is accumulation of costs to be incurred, expected cash flows may not produce a representationally faithful estimate of the expected cost. However, this Statement adopts fair value as the measurement objective. The fair value of the asset or liability in this example is not likely to be $10, even though that is the most likely cash flow. Instead, one would expect the fair value to be closer to $109 than to either $10 or $1,000. While this example is a difficult measurement situation, a measurement of $10 does not incorporate the uncertainty of the cash flow in the measurement of the asset or liability. Instead, the uncertain cash flow is presented as if it were a certain cash flow. No rational marketplace participant would sell an asset (or assume a liability) with these characteristics for $10.

54. In recent years, financial institutions and others have developed and implemented a variety of pricing tools designed to estimate the fair value of assets and liabilities. It is not possible here to describe all of the many (often proprietary) pricing models currently in use. However, those tools often build on concepts similar to those outlined in this Statement as well as other developments in modern finance, including option pricing and similar models. For example, the well-known Black-Scholes option pricing model uses the elements of a fair value measurement described in paragraph 23 as appropriate in estimating the fair value of an option. To the extent that a pricing model includes each of the elements of fair value, its use is consistent with this Statement.

Present Value in the Measurement of Liabilities

75. The concepts outlined in this Statement apply to liabilities as well as to assets. However, the measurement of liabilities sometimes involves problems different from those encountered in the measurement of assets and may require different techniques in arriving at fair value. When using present value techniques to estimate the fair value of a liability, the objective is to estimate the value of the assets required currently to (a) settle the liability with the holder or (b) transfer the liability to an entity of comparable credit standing.

76. To estimate the fair value of an entity's notes or bonds payable, accountants attempt to estimate the price at which other entities are willing to hold the entity's liabilities as assets. That process involves the same techniques and computational problems encountered in measuring assets. For example, the proceeds from a loan are the price that a lender paid to hold the borrower's promise of future cash flows as an asset. Similarly, the fair value of a bond payable is the price at which that security trades, as an asset, in the marketplace. As outlined in paragraphs 78–81, this estimate of fair value is consistent with the objective of liability measurement described in the preceding paragraph.

77. On the other hand, some liabilities are owed to a class of individuals who do not

usually sell their rights as they might sell other assets. For example, entities often sell products with an accompanying warranty. Buyers of those products rarely have the ability or inclination to sell the warranty separately from the covered asset, but they own a warranty asset nonetheless. Some of an entity's liabilities, like an obligation for environmental cleanup, are not the assets of identifiable individuals. However, such liabilities are sometimes settled through assumption by a third party. In estimating the fair value of such liabilities accountants attempt to estimate the price that the entity would have to pay a third party to assume the liability.

Credit Standing and Liability Measurement

78. The most relevant measure of a liability always reflects the credit standing of the entity obligated to pay. Those who hold the entity's obligations as assets incorporate the entity's credit standing in determining the prices they are willing to pay. When an entity incurs a liability in exchange for cash, the role of its credit standing is easy to observe. An entity with a strong credit standing will receive more cash, relative to a fixed promise to pay, than an entity with a weak credit standing. For example, if 2 entities both promise to pay $500 in 5 years, the entity with a strong credit standing may receive about $374 in exchange for its promise (a 6 percent interest rate). The entity with a weak credit standing may receive about $284 in exchange for its promise (a 12 percent interest rate). Each entity initially records its respective liability at fair value, which is the amount of proceeds received—an amount that incorporates that entity's credit standing.

79. The effect of an entity's credit standing on the fair value of particular liabilities depends on the ability of the entity to pay and on liability provisions that protect holders. Liabilities that are guaranteed by governmental bodies (for example, many bank deposit liabilities in the United States) may pose little risk of default to the holder. Other liabilities may include sinking-fund requirements or significant collateral. All of those aspects must be considered in estimating the extent to which the entity's credit standing affects the fair value of its liabilities.

80. The role of the entity's credit standing in a settlement transaction is less direct but equally important. A settlement transaction involves three parties—the entity, the parties to whom it is obligated, and a third party. The price of the transaction will reflect the competing interests of each party. For example, suppose Entity A has an obligation to pay $500 to Entity B 3 years hence. Entity A has a poor credit rating and therefore borrows at a 12 percent interest rate.

a. In a settlement transaction, Entity B would never consent to replace Entity A with an entity of lower credit standing. All other things being equal, Entity B might consent to replace Entity A with a borrower of similar credit standing and would probably consent to replace Entity A with a more creditworthy entity.

b. Entity C has a good credit rating and therefore borrows at a 6 percent interest rate. It might willingly assume Entity A's obligation for $420 (the present value at 6 percent). Entity C has no incentive to assume the obligation for less (a higher interest rate) if it can borrow at 6 percent because it can receive $420 for an identical promise to pay $500.

c. However, if Entity A were to borrow the money to pay Entity C, it would have to promise $590 ($420 due in 3 years with accumulated interest at 12 percent).

81. Based on the admittedly simple case outlined above, the fair value of Entity A's liability should be approximately $356 (the present value of $500 in 3 years at 12 percent). The $420 price demanded by Entity C includes the fair value of Entity A's liability ($356) plus the price of an upgrade in the credit quality of the liability. There may be situations in which an entity might pay an additional amount to induce others to enter into a settlement transaction. Those cases are analogous to the purchase of a credit guarantee and, like the purchase of a guarantee, the additional amount represents a separate transaction rather than an element in the fair value of the entity's original liability.

82. The effect of an entity's credit standing on the measurement of its liabilities is usually captured in an adjustment to the interest rate.

as illustrated above. This is similar to the traditional approach to incorporating risk and uncertainty in the measurement of assets and is well suited to liabilities with contractual cash flows. An expected cash flow approach may be more effective when measuring the effect of credit standing on other liabilities. For example, a liability may present the entity with a range of possible outflows, ranging from very low to very high amounts. There may be little chance of default if the amount is low, but a high chance of default if the amount is high. In situations like this, the effect of credit standing may be more effectively incorporated in the computation of expected cash flows.

83. The role of an entity's credit standing in the accounting measurement of its liabilities has been a controversial question among accountants. The entity's credit standing clearly affects the interest rate at which it borrows in the marketplace. The initial proceeds of a loan, therefore, always reflect the entity's credit standing at that time. Similarly, the price at which others buy and sell the entity's loan includes their assessment of the entity's ability to repay. The example in paragraph 80 demonstrates how the entity's credit standing would affect the price it would be required to pay to have another entity assume its liability. However, some have questioned whether an entity's financial statements should reflect the effect of its credit standing (or changes in credit standing).

84. Some suggest that the measurement objective for liabilities is fundamentally different from the measurement objective for assets. In their view, financial statement users are better served by liability measurements that focus on the entity's obligation. They suggest a measurement approach in which financial statements would portray the present value of an obligation such that two entities with the same obligation but different credit standing would report the same carrying amount. Some existing accounting pronouncements take this approach, most notably FASB Statements No. 87, *Employers' Accounting for Pensions,* and No. 106, *Employers' Accounting for Postretirement Benefits Other Than Pensions.*

85. However, there is no convincing rationale for why the initial measurement of some liabilities would necessarily include the effect of credit standing (as in a loan for cash) while others might not (as in a warranty liability or similar item). Similarly, there is no rationale for why, in initial or fresh-start measurement, the recorded amount of a liability should reflect something other than the price that would exist in the marketplace. Consistent with its conclusions on fair value (refer to paragraph 30), the Board found no rationale for taking a different view in subsequent fresh-start measurements of an existing asset or liability than would pertain to measurements at initial recognition.

86. Some argue that changes in an entity's credit standing are not relevant to users of financial statements. In their view, a fresh-start measurement that reflects changes in credit standing produces accounting results that are confusing. If the measurement includes changes in credit standing, and an entity's credit standing declines, the fresh-start measurement of its liabilities declines. That decline in liabilities is accompanied by an increase in owners' equity, a result that they find counterintuitive. How, they ask, can a bad thing (declining credit standing) produce a good thing (increased owners' equity)?

87. Like all measurements at fair value, fresh-start measurement of liabilities can produce unfamiliar results when compared with reporting the liabilities on an amortized basis. A change in credit standing represents a change in the relative positions of the two classes of claimants (shareholders and creditors) to an entity's assets. If the credit standing diminishes, the fair value of creditors' claims diminishes. The amount of shareholders' residual claim to the entity's assets may appear to increase, but that increase probably is offset by losses that may have occasioned the decline in credit standing. Because shareholders usually cannot be called on to pay a corporation's liabilities, the amount of their residual claims approaches, and is limited by, zero. Thus, a change in the position of borrowers necessarily alters the position of shareholders, and vice versa.

88. The failure to include changes in credit standing in the measurement of a liability ignores economic differences between liabilities. Consider the case of an entity that has two classes of borrowing. Class One was transacted when the entity had a strong credit standing and a correspondingly low interest rate. Class Two is new and was transacted under the entity's current lower credit standing. Both classes trade in the marketplace based on the entity's current credit standing. If the two liabilities are subject to fresh-start measurement, failing to include changes in the entity's credit standing makes the classes of borrowings seem different—even though the marketplace evaluates the quality of their respective cash flows as similar to one another.

E2. Paragraph 24 of this Statement requires that estimates of future cash flows used in a present value technique be consistent with the objective of measuring fair value. Paragraph 23 of Concepts Statement 7 discusses the essential elements of a present value measurement. That paragraph of Concepts Statement 7 follows.

23. A present value measurement that fully captures the economic differences between the five assets described in paragraph 20 would necessarily include the following elements:

a. An estimate of the future cash flow, or in more complex cases, series of future cash flows at different times[2]
b. Expectations about possible variations in the amount or timing of those cash flows
c. The time value of money, represented by the risk-free rate of interest
d. The price for bearing the uncertainty inherent in the asset or liability
e. Other, sometimes unidentifiable, factors including illiquidity and market imperfections.

---

[2]In complex measurements, such as measurements of liabilities settled by providing services, cash flow estimates necessarily include elements like overhead and profit margins inherent in the price of goods and services.

E3. Paragraph 24 of this Statement also requires that estimates of future cash flows used in a present value technique incorporate assumptions that marketplace participants would use in their estimates of fair value whenever that information is available without undue cost and effort. Paragraph 32 of Concepts Statement 7 provides examples of circumstances in which an entity's cash flows (entity assumptions) might differ from the market cash flows (marketplace assumptions). That paragraph of Concepts Statement 7 follows.

32. An entity's best estimate of the present value of cash flows will not necessarily equal the fair value of those uncertain cash flows. There are several reasons why an entity might expect to realize or pay cash flows that differ from those expected by others in the marketplace. Those include:

a. The entity's managers might intend different use or settlement than that anticipated by others. For example, they might intend to operate a property as a bowling alley, even though others in the marketplace consider its highest and best use to be a parking lot.
b. The entity's managers may prefer to accept risk of a liability (like a product warranty) and manage it internally, rather than transferring that liability to another entity.
c. The entity might hold special preferences, like tax or zoning variances, not available to others.
d. The entity might hold information, trade secrets, or processes that allow it to realize (or avoid paying) cash flows that differ from others' expectations.
e. The entity might be able to realize or pay amounts through use of internal resources. For example, an entity that manufactures materials used in particular processes acquires those materials at cost, rather than the market price charged to others. An entity that chooses to satisfy a liability with internal resources may avoid the markup or anticipated profit charged by outside contractors.

Statement of Financial Accounting Standards No. 145
Rescission of FASB Statements No. 4, 44, and 64,
Amendment of FASB Statement No. 13,
and Technical Corrections

STATUS

Issued: April 2002

Effective Date: For financial statements issued on or after May 15, 2002

Affects: Amends APB 28, paragraph 21
    Amends APB 30, paragraphs 20 and 26
    Supersedes FAS 4
    Amends FAS 13, paragraph 14(a)
    Supersedes FAS 13, paragraph 38
    Amends FAS 15, paragraphs 13, 15, 17, 25(b), and 25(d)
    Supersedes FAS 15, paragraph 21
    Supersedes FAS 19, paragraph 44
    Amends FAS 22, paragraphs 12(a)(i) and 17
    Supersedes FAS 44
    Supersedes FAS 60, paragraph 12
    Supersedes FAS 64
    Amends FAS 95, paragraphs 15, 16(a), 16(b), 17(a), 17(b), footnote 5, and footnotes added to
      paragraphs 22(a) and 23(a) by FAS 102
    Amends FAS 102, paragraphs 8 and 10(b) through 10(e)
    Amends FAS 115, footnote 4
    Amends FAS 128, paragraph 171
    Amends FAS 133, paragraph 59(e)
    Supersedes FAS 135, paragraphs 4(p)(1), 4(p)(7), 4(r)(2)(a), and 5(c)
    Amends FAS 141, paragraphs 46, E5(b), and footnote 25
    Supersedes FAS 141, paragraph E10
    Amends FAS 142, paragraphs 8, 8(i), and 35
    Supersedes FAS 142, paragraph D11(a)(2)
    Amends FAS 144, paragraphs 5, 45, and D1
    Supersedes FAS 144, paragraph C7
    Amends FIN 21, paragraph 15
    Amends FTB 80-1, paragraphs 3 and 4
    Amends FTB 82-1, paragraph 6

Affected by: No other pronouncements

Issues Discussed by FASB Emerging Issues Task Force (EITF)

  Affects: Partially nullifies EITF Issues No. 90-19 and 00-9

  Interpreted by: No EITF Issues

  Related Issues: EITF Issues No. 86-15, 91-2, 96-19, 98-5, and 01-2

SUMMARY

This Statement rescinds FASB Statement No. 4, *Reporting Gains and Losses from Extinguishment of Debt,* and an amendment of that Statement, FASB Statement No. 64, *Extinguishments of Debt Made to Satisfy Sinking-Fund Requirements.* This Statement also rescinds FASB Statement No. 44, *Accounting for Intangible Assets of Motor Carriers.* This Statement amends FASB Statement No. 13, *Accounting for Leases,* to eliminate an inconsistency between the required accounting for sale-leaseback transactions and the required accounting for certain lease modifications that have economic effects that are similar to sale-leaseback transactions. This Statement also amends other existing authoritative pronouncements to make various technical corrections, clarify meanings, or describe their applicability under changed conditions.

Reasons for Issuing This Statement

When Statement 4 was issued in 1975, the Board noted that the provisions of that Statement represented a "practical and reasonable solution to the question regarding income statement classification of gains or losses from extinguishment of debt until such time as the broader issues involved can be addressed" (paragraph 15). Since the issuance of Statement 4, the use of debt extinguishment has become part of the risk management strategy of many companies, particularly those operating in the secondary lending market. Debt extinguishments used as part of an entity's risk management strategy represent one example of debt extinguishments that do not meet the criteria for classification as extraordinary items in APB Opinion No. 30, *Reporting the Results of Operations—Reporting the Effects of Disposal of a Segment of a Business, and Extraordinary, Unusual and Infrequently Occurring Events and Transactions,* and therefore, should not be classified as extraordinary. Statement 64 amended Statement 4 and is no longer necessary because Statement 4 has been rescinded.

Statement 44 was issued to establish accounting requirements for the effects of transition to the provisions of the Motor Carrier Act of 1980 (Public Law 96-296, 96th Congress, July 1, 1980). Those transitions are completed; therefore, Statement 44 is no longer necessary.

This Statement also amends Statement 13 to require sale-leaseback accounting for certain lease modifications that have economic effects that are similar to sale-leaseback transactions. This Statement also makes various technical corrections to existing pronouncements. Those corrections are not substantive in nature.

How the Changes in This Statement Improve Financial Reporting

Under Statement 4, all gains and losses from extinguishment of debt were required to be aggregated and, if material, classified as an extraordinary item, net of related income tax effect. This Statement eliminates Statement 4 and, thus, the exception to applying Opinion 30 to all gains and losses related to extinguishments of debt (other than extinguishments of debt to satisfy sinking-fund requirements—the exception to application of Statement 4 noted in Statement 64). As a result, gains and losses from extinguishment of debt should be classified as extraordinary items only if they meet the criteria in Opinion 30. Applying the provisions of Opinion 30 will distinguish transactions that are part of an entity's recurring operations from those that are unusual or infrequent or that meet the criteria for classification as an extraordinary item.

Under Statement 13, the required accounting treatment of certain lease modifications that have economic effects similar to sale-leaseback transactions was inconsistent with the required accounting treatment for sale-leaseback transactions. This Statement amends paragraph 14(a) of Statement 13 to require that those lease modifications be accounted for in the same manner as sale-leaseback transactions. This amendment is in accordance with the Board's goal of requiring similar accounting treatment for transactions that have similar economic effects.

Statement of Financial Accounting Standards No. 145

Rescission of FASB Statements No. 4, 44, and 64, Amendment of FASB Statement No. 13, and Technical Corrections

CONTENTS

INTRODUCTION

Statements 4 and 64

1. FASB Statement No. 4, *Reporting Gains and Losses from Extinguishment of Debt,* was issued in 1975. Statement 4 required that gains and losses from extinguishment of debt that were included in the determination of net income be aggregated and, if material, classified as an extraordinary item, net of related income tax effect. Statement 4 also required certain disclosures for those items. At the time Statement 4 was issued, the Board concluded that classifying gains and losses from extinguishment of debt as extraordinary items represented a practical and reasonable solution to the issues regarding income statement classification of those gains or losses. However, the Board indicated that that solution was not intended to be permanent.

2. FASB Statement No. 64, *Extinguishments of Debt Made to Satisfy Sinking-Fund Requirements,* was issued in 1982. That Statement made an exception to the provisions of Statement 4 for certain debt extinguishment transactions.

Statement 44

3. FASB Statement No. 44, *Accounting for Intangible Assets of Motor Carriers,* was issued to establish accounting requirements for the effects of transition to the provisions of the Motor Carrier Act of 1980 (Public Law 96-296, 96th Congress, July 1, 1980). Statement 44 also contained a provision that in the event that intrastate operating rights were to be deregulated, the accounting requirements for the effects of transition to those laws would be in accordance with the provisions of Statement 44. All intrastate operating rights have since been deregulated, and the transition to the provisions of those laws is complete.

Amendment of Statement 13

4. Paragraph 14(a) of FASB Statement No. 13, *Accounting for Leases,* describes the accounting by a lessee for certain lease modifications. If a capital lease is modified in such a way that the change in the lease provisions gives rise to a new agreement classified as an operating lease, paragraph 14(a) requires that the asset and obligation under the lease be

removed, a gain or loss be recognized for the difference, and the new lease agreement thereafter be accounted for as any other operating lease. Several constituents advised the Board that, in their view, if a capital lease is modified as described above, the modification has economic effects that are similar to a sale-leaseback transaction. However, Statement 13 does not require the lessee to account for those lease modifications as sale-leaseback transactions. This Statement requires that capital leases that are modified so that the resulting lease agreement is classified as an operating lease be accounted for under the sale-leaseback provisions of FASB Statement No. 98, *Accounting for Leases: Sale-Leaseback Transactions Involving Real Estate; Sales-Type Leases of Real Estate; Definition of the Lease Term; Initial Direct Costs of Direct Financing Leases,* or paragraphs 2 and 3 of FASB Statement No. 28, *Accounting for Sales with Leasebacks,* as applicable.

Technical Corrections

5. Before the Board issues a pronouncement that contains amendments to existing pronouncements, those amendments are reviewed by the Board. This Statement identifies amendments that should have been made to previously existing pronouncements and formally amends the appropriate pronouncements. In addition, this Statement amends existing authoritative pronouncements to (a) correct references to guidance issued by the American Institute of Certified Public Accountants (AICPA) or the FASB that has been revised or superseded since the issuance of the pronouncement and (b) eliminate inconsistencies in existing pronouncements.

STANDARDS OF FINANCIAL ACCOUNTING AND REPORTING

Rescission of Statements 4, 44, and 64

6. This Statement rescinds the following pronouncements:

a. FASB Statement No. 4, *Reporting Gains and Losses from Extinguishment of Debt*
b. FASB Statement No. 44, *Accounting for Intangible Assets of Motor Carriers*
c. FASB Statement No. 64, *Extinguishments of Debt Made to Satisfy Sinking-Fund Requirements.*

Amendments to Existing Pronouncements to Reflect Rescission of Statements 4, 44, and 64

7. This Statement amends the following pronouncements to reflect the rescission of Statements 4, 44, and 64:

a. APB Opinion No. 30, *Reporting the Results of Operations—Reporting the Effects of Disposal of a Segment of a Business, and Extraordinary, Unusual and Infrequently Occurring Events and Transactions.* In the last sentence of paragraph 20, as amended by FASB Statement No. 141, *Business Combinations,* the phrase *(1) Classifications of gains or losses from extinguishment of debt pursuant to paragraph 8 of FASB Statement No. 4, Reporting Gains and Losses from Extinguishment of Debt* is deleted.

b. FASB Statement No. 15, *Accounting by Debtors and Creditors for Troubled Debt Restructurings.*

(1) In paragraphs 13, 15, and 17, *(see paragraph 21)* is deleted.

(2) Paragraph 21 is deleted.

(3) In paragraph 25(b), *and the related income tax effect (paragraph 21)* is deleted.

(4) In paragraph 25(d), *, net of related income tax effect* is deleted.

c. FASB Statement No. 22, *Changes in the Provisions of Lease Agreements Resulting from Refundings of Tax-Exempt Debt.*

(1) The last sentence of paragraph 12(a)(i) is deleted.

(2) In the last sentence of the example of lessee accounting in paragraph 17, *(The loss shall be classified in accordance with FASB Statement No. 4.)* is deleted.

d. FASB Statement No. 144, *Accounting for the Impairment or Disposal of Long-Lived Assets.*

(1) In the last sentence of paragraph 5, the following is deleted:

• FASB Statement No. 44, *Accounting for Intangible Assets of Motor Carriers*

(2) In the table in paragraph D1, the reference to Statement 44 is deleted.

e. FASB Technical Bulletin No. 80-1, *Early Extinguishment of Debt through Exchange for Common or Preferred Stock.* The third sentence of paragraph 4 is deleted.

Amendment of Statement 13

8. FASB Statement No. 13, *Accounting for Leases.* The last sentence of paragraph 14(a) is replaced by the following:

> If the change in the lease provisions gives rise to a new agreement classified as an operating lease, the transaction shall be accounted for under the sale-leaseback requirements of FASB Statement No. 98, *Accounting for Leases: Sale-Leaseback Transactions Involving Real Estate; Sales-Type Leases of Real Estate; Definition of the Lease Term; Initial Direct Costs of Direct Financing Leases,* or paragraphs 2 and 3 of FASB Statement No. 28, *Accounting for Sales with Leasebacks,* as applicable.

Technical Corrections

9. This Statement amends the following pronouncements to make technical corrections to existing authoritative pronouncements:

a. APB Opinion No. 28, *Interim Financial Reporting.* In the fourth sentence of paragraph 21, as amended by FASB Statement No. 141, *Business Combinations,* the phrase *in a purchase* is deleted.

b. APB Opinion No. 30, *Reporting the Results of Operations—Reporting the Effects of Disposal of a Segment of a Business, and Extraordinary, Unusual and Infrequently Occurring Events and Transactions.* In the fourth sentence of paragraph 26, *or in any manner inconsistent with the provisions of paragraphs 8 and 11 of this Opinion* is deleted.

c. FASB Statement No. 13, *Accounting for Leases.* Paragraph 38 is replaced by the following:

> If the nature of the transaction is such that the original lessee is relieved of the primary obligation under the original lease, as would be the case in transactions of the type described in paragraphs 35(b) and 35(c), the termination of the original lease agreement shall be accounted for as follows:

> a. If the original lease was a capital lease of property other than real estate (including integral equipment), the asset and obligation representing the original lease shall be removed from the accounts, a gain or loss shall be recognized for the difference, and, if the original lessee is secondarily liable, the guarantee obligation shall be recognized in accordance with paragraph 114 of FASB Statement No. 140, *Accounting for Transfers and Servicing of Financial Assets and Extinguishments of Liabilities.* Any consideration paid or received upon termination shall be included in the determination of gain or loss to be recognized.

> b. If the original lease was a capital lease of real estate (including integral equipment), the determination as to whether the asset held under the capital lease and the related obligation may be removed from the balance sheet shall be made in accordance with the requirements of FASB Statement No. 66, *Accounting for Sales of Real Estate.* If the criteria for recognition of a sale in Statement 66 are met, the asset and obligation representing the original lease shall be removed from the accounts and any consideration paid or received upon termination and any guarantee obligation shall be recognized in accordance with the requirements above for property other than real estate. If the transaction results in a gain, that gain may be recognized if the criteria in Statement 66 for recognition of profit by the full accrual method are met. Otherwise, the gain shall be recognized in accordance with one of the other profit recognition methods discussed in Statement 66. Any loss on the transaction shall be recognized immediately.

> c. If the original lease was an operating lease and the original lessee is secondarily liable, the guarantee obligation shall be recognized in accordance with paragraph 114 of Statement 140.

d. FASB Statement No. 19, *Financial Accounting and Reporting by Oil and Gas Producing Companies.* Paragraph 44, as amended by FASB Statement No. 144, *Accounting for the Impairment or Disposal of Long-Lived Assets,* is replaced by the following:

In the following types of conveyances, gain or loss shall not be recognized at the time of the conveyance, except as otherwise provided:

a. A transfer of assets used in oil and gas producing activities (including either proved or unproved properties) in exchange for other assets also used in oil and gas producing activities. However, when proved properties are transferred in exchange for other assets also used in oil and gas producing activities, if an impairment loss is indicated under the provisions of FASB Statement No. 144, *Accounting for the Impairment or Disposal of Long-Lived Assets,* it shall be recognized in accordance with paragraph 29 of Statement 144.

b. A pooling of assets in a joint undertaking intended to find, develop, or produce oil or gas from a particular property or group of properties.

e. FASB Statement No. 60, *Accounting and Reporting by Insurance Enterprises.* Paragraph 12 is deleted.

f. FASB Statement No. 95, *Statement of Cash Flows.*

(1) In the last sentence of paragraph 15, as amended by FASB Statement No. 102, *Statement of Cash Flows—Exemption of Certain Enterprises and Classification of Cash Flows from Certain Securities Acquired for Resale,* the phrase *, and securities that are classified as trading securities as discussed in FASB Statement No. 115, Accounting for Certain Investments in Debt and Equity Securities* is added after *Statement 102.*

(2) The parenthetical comment in paragraphs 16(a) and 17(a), as amended by Statement 102, is replaced by the following:

(other than cash equivalents, certain debt instruments that are acquired specifically for resale as discussed in Statement 102, and securities classified as trading securities as discussed in Statement 115)

(3) The parenthetical comment in paragraphs 16(b) and 17(b), as amended by Statement 102, is replaced by the following:

(other than certain equity instruments carried in a trading account as described in Statement 102 and certain securities classified as trading securities as discussed in Statement 115)

(4) In footnote 5, the following parenthetical comment is added after *debt or equity instruments*:

(other than cash equivalents, certain debt instruments that are acquired specifically for resale as discussed in Statement 102, and securities classified as trading securities as discussed in Statement 115)

(5) In the footnote after *goods* in paragraphs 22(a) and 23(a), added by Statement 102, *, and securities that are classified as trading securities as discussed in Statement 115* is added after *Statement 102.*

g. FASB Statement No. 102, *Statement of Cash Flows—Exemption of Certain Enterprises and Classification of Cash Flows from Certain Securities Acquired for Resale.* Paragraph 8 is amended as follows:

(1) The following sentence is added after the first sentence:

Cash receipts and cash payments resulting from purchases and sales of securities classified as trading securities as discussed in FASB Statement No. 115, *Accounting for Certain Investments in Debt and Equity Securities,* shall be classified as operating cash flows.

(2) In the second sentence, *other* is added before *securities.*

h. FASB Statement No. 115, *Accounting for Certain Investments in Debt and Equity Securities.* In footnote 4 to paragraph 16, as amended by FASB Statement No. 135, *Rescission of FASB Statement No. 75 and Technical Corrections,* the phrase *AICPA Statement on Auditing Standards No. 81, Auditing Investments,* is replaced by *AICPA Statement on Auditing Standards No. 92, Auditing Derivative Instruments, Hedging Activities, and Investments in Securities.*

i. FASB Statement No. 128, *Earnings per Share.* In the first sentence of the definition of *contingent stock agreement* in paragraph 171, *accounted for by the purchase method* is deleted.

j. FASB Statement No. 133, *Accounting for Derivative Instruments and Hedging Activities.* In the second sentence of paragraph 59(e), *Statement 125* is replaced by *Statement 140.*

k. FASB Statement No. 135, *Rescission of FASB Statement No. 75 and Technical Corrections.* Paragraphs 4(p)(1), 4(p)(7), and 4(r)(2)(a) are deleted.

l. FASB Statement No. 141, *Business Combinations.*

(1) In the first sentence of paragraph 46, *prior to the pro rata allocation required by paragraph 44* is added after *excess.*

(2) In the first sentence of footnote 25, *cost of the* is added before *acquired.*

(3) Paragraph E10 is deleted.

m. FASB Statement No. 142, *Goodwill and Other Intangible Assets.*

(1) In paragraph 8(i), *(paragraph 7)* is deleted.

(2) The following is added to the end of paragraph 8:

    m. FASB Interpretation No. 9, *Applying APB Opinions No. 16 and 17 When a Savings and Loan Association or a Similar Institution Is Acquired in a Business Combination Accounted for by the Purchase Method.*

(3) The second and third sentences of paragraph 35 are replaced by the following:

An entity would determine the fair value of the acquired business (or portion thereof) to be included in a reporting unit—in essence a "purchase price" for that business. The entity would then allocate that purchase price to the individual assets acquired and liabilities assumed related to that acquired business (or portion thereof).[21] Any excess purchase price is

the amount of goodwill assigned to that reporting unit.

(4) Paragraph D11(a)(2) is deleted.

n. FASB Statement No. 144, *Accounting for the Impairment or Disposal of Long-Lived Assets.*

(1) In the first sentence of paragraph 5, *that are to be held and used* is added after *amortized.*

(2) In the first sentence of paragraph 45, *for a long-lived asset (disposal group) classified as held for sale* is replaced by *on the sale of a long-lived asset (disposal group).*

(3) Under the column "Existing Requirement Paragraph Number" in the section of the table in paragraph D1 relating to FASB Statement No. 19, *Financial Accounting and Reporting by Oil and Gas Producing Companies,* the numbers *31(b), 33* are replaced by *31, 33, 34.*

o. FASB Interpretation No. 21, *Accounting for Leases in a Business Combination.* In the heading before paragraph 15, **Purchase** is replaced by **Business.**

p. FASB Technical Bulletin No. 80-1, *Early Extinguishment of Debt through Exchange for Common or Preferred Stock.* In the first sentence of paragraph 3, *Statement 15 or Opinion 26* is replaced by *Statement 15, as amended by FASB Statement No. 145, Rescission of FASB Statements No. 4, 44, and 64, Amendment of FASB Statement No. 13, and Technical Corrections; Opinion 26; or APB Opinion No. 30, Reporting the Results of Operations—Reporting the Effects of Disposal of a Segment of a Business, and Extraordinary, Unusual and Infrequently Occurring Events and Transactions.*

q. FASB Technical Bulletin No. 82-1, *Disclosure of the Sale or Purchase of Tax Benefits through Tax Leases.* In the first sentence of paragraph 6, , *as amended by FASB Statement No. 145, Rescission of FASB Statements No. 4, 44, and 64, Amendment of FASB Statement No. 13, and Technical Corrections,* is added after *Opinion 30.*

Effective Date and Transition

10. The provisions of this Statement related to the rescission of Statement 4 shall be applied in fiscal years beginning after May 15, 2002. Any gain or loss on extinguishment of debt that was classified as an extraordinary item in prior periods presented that does not meet the criteria in Opinion 30 for classification as an extraordinary item shall be reclassified. Early application of the provisions of this Statement related to the rescission of Statement 4 is encouraged.

11. The provisions in paragraphs 8 and 9(c) of this Statement related to Statement 13 shall be effective for transactions occurring after May 15, 2002, with early application encouraged. All other provisions of this Statement shall be effective for financial statements issued on or after May 15, 2002, with early application encouraged.

12. Early application of the provisions of this Statement may be as of the beginning of the fiscal year or as of the beginning of the interim period in which this Statement is issued.

> The provisions of this Statement need
> not be applied to immaterial items.

This Statement was adopted by the unanimous vote of the seven members of the Financial Accounting Standards Board:

Edmund L. Jenkins,
Chairman
G. Michael Crooch

John M. Foster
Gary S. Schieneman
Katherine A. Schipper

Edward W. Trott
John K. Wulff

Appendix

BACKGROUND INFORMATION AND BASIS FOR CONCLUSIONS

Introduction

A1. This appendix summarizes considerations that Board members deemed significant in reaching the conclusions in this Statement. It includes reasons for accepting certain approaches and rejecting others. Individual Board members gave greater weight to some factors than to others.

A2. In August 2001, in response to constituent requests, the Board undertook a project to rescind Statement 4. As part of that project, the Board decided to take the opportunity to make various technical corrections to other pronouncements. In November 2001, the Board issued the Exposure Draft, *Rescission of FASB Statements No. 4, 44, and 64 and Technical Corrections.* The Board received 30 letters in response to that Exposure Draft.

A3. In redeliberating the proposed technical corrections of the 2001 Exposure Draft, the Board considered additional amendments and technical corrections suggested by various respondents to the Exposure Draft. The Board decided to include one substantive amendment of Statement 13 and several technical corrections that were suggested by respondents and FASB staff members. In February 2002, the Board issued a limited revised Exposure Draft, *Rescission of FASB Statements No. 4, 44, and 64 and Technical Corrections—Amendment of FASB Statement No. 13,* that proposed that the substantive amendment to Statement 13 be included in this Statement. The Board received 10 letters in response to the 2002 Exposure Draft. The Board concluded that on the basis of existing information it could make an informed decision on the matters addressed in this Statement without a public hearing.

Rescission of Statements 4 and 64

A4. The Board noted that at the time Statement 4 was issued, its requirement to classify all gains and losses associated with extinguishment of debt as extraordinary items was intended to be a temporary measure and that application of the criteria in Opinion 30 would seldom, if ever, require that resulting gains and losses be classified as extraordinary items. The Board noted that Statement 4 dictated the classification of gains and losses from extinguishment of debt and, thus, did not permit a conceptual consideration under the provisions of Opinion 30 of whether an extinguishment of debt is extraordinary in nature.

The Board concurred that debt extinguishments are often routine, recurring transactions and concluded that classifying the associated gains and losses as extraordinary items in all cases is inconsistent with the criteria in Opinion 30. Furthermore, such classification may not provide the most useful information to users of financial statements.

A5. The Board observed that the rescission of Statement 4 would not preclude gains and losses from extinguishment of debt that meet the criteria in Opinion 30 from being classified as extraordinary items. The Board noted that Opinion 30 requires disclosures about material gains and losses associated with debt extinguishments that are unusual or infrequent in nature. Thus, applying the provisions of Opinion 30 would distinguish transactions that are part of an entity's recurring operations from those that are unusual or infrequent or that meet the criteria for classification as extraordinary items. The Board concluded that the rescission of Statement 4 would improve financial reporting by eliminating a requirement to classify a normal and important part of many entities' ongoing activities to manage interest rate risk as an extraordinary item.

A6. Some respondents to the 2001 Exposure Draft suggested that the Statement should prohibit classification of gains and losses associated with the extinguishment of debt as extraordinary items. The Board concurred with the observation made at the time Statement 4 was issued that application of the criteria of Opinion 30 to debt extinguishment transactions would seldom, if ever, result in extraordinary item classification of the resulting gains and losses. However, the Board noted that *prohibiting* extraordinary item classification of gains and losses associated with the extinguishment of debt also would not permit a conceptual consideration under the provisions of Opinion 30 of whether an extinguishment of debt is extraordinary in nature. Thus, the Board decided not to prohibit extraordinary item classification of gains and losses related to the extinguishment of debt.

A7. Some respondents suggested that the Board reconsider the criteria in Opinion 30 for extraordinary item classification. Those respondents noted that the recent consensus reached on EITF Issue No. 01-10, "Accounting for the Impact of the Terrorist Attacks of September 11, 2001," raises questions about the appropriateness of those criteria and of the need for extraordinary item classification in general. The Board decided that reconsideration of the extraordinary item classification criteria is beyond the scope of this project. However, the Board is considering matters of financial statement display in its performance reporting project.

A8. Statement 64 amended Statement 4 to require that gains and losses from extinguishments of debt made to satisfy future sinking-fund requirements meet the criteria in paragraph 20 of Opinion 30 in order to qualify for extraordinary item classification. Because Statement 4 is rescinded, Statement 64 is no longer necessary.

Rescission of Statement 44

A9. The Board noted that Statement 44 was issued to establish accounting requirements for the effects of transition to the provisions of the Motor Carrier Act of 1980. The Board concluded that Statement 44 is no longer needed because transition to the provisions of the Motor Carrier Act of 1980 is complete.

Amendment of Statement 13

A10. Several respondents to the 2001 Exposure Draft suggested that Statement 13 be amended to eliminate an inconsistency between the accounting by lessees for certain lease modification transactions that would require reclassification of a capital lease as an operating lease and the accounting for sale-leaseback transactions required by Statement 28 or 98. The Board concluded that the former transactions have economic effects that are similar to sale-leaseback transactions and that it would be appropriate to amend paragraph 14(a) of Statement 13 to eliminate that inconsistency. However, the Board concluded that that particular amendment is not a technical correction because it is substantive in nature. Because a substantive amendment must be subjected to the Board's due process, the Board decided to issue a limited revised Exposure Draft that would amend paragraph 14(a) of Statement 13.

A11. Most respondents to the 2002 Exposure Draft agreed with the Board's conclusions and the provisions of the proposed Statement. No respondents raised compelling arguments opposing the provisions of the 2002 Exposure Draft; therefore, the Board decided to include its provisions in this Statement.

Technical Corrections

A12. At the time a pronouncement is developed, the Board's due process procedures require determination of the effect of the new standard on existing authoritative accounting pronouncements. The existing authoritative pronouncements should be amended for any such effects thereby eliminating doubt as to what is amended and eliminating conflicts between the requirements of prior pronouncements and the requirements of the new pronouncement. When changes that should have been made as a result of that process are subsequently discovered, those changes are made to the various editions of the FASB's *Current Text,* and those editorial corrections are appropriately indicated in its *Original Pronouncements.* The Board decided to formalize those technical corrections by amending the appropriate pronouncements.

A13. A technical correction is a nonsubstantive amendment to an authoritative pronouncement. The Board concluded that an amendment is not substantive if there is evidence in existing authoritative pronouncements that at the time the pronouncement was issued, the issue addressed by the technical correction had been considered by the Board and the Board had reached a conclusion on the issue. A technical correction reflects the Board's intent on decisions that were previously subjected to the Board's due process but that were overlooked or were not clearly stated at the time a pronouncement was issued. The Board observed that some technical corrections may change current practice.

A14. In November 1992, when the Board first issued a standard to make technical corrections (FASB Statement No. 111, *Rescission of FASB Statement No. 32 and Technical Corrections*), the Board considered what parts of previously issued pronouncements to amend and decided that only the official guidance sections should be amended. The Board continues to believe that only those sections should be amended. In other words, the Board believes that the introduction, background information, and basis for conclusions paragraphs provide historical information that should not be amended or superseded unless the entire pronouncement is superseded. Those paragraphs are considered historical because they document the circumstances surrounding the development of a pronouncement. For example, they record (a) the reasons why the accounting requirements were considered to be necessary at that time, (b) the alternative guidance considered, and (c) public comments on the proposed requirements and how those comments were addressed.

A15. In addition to the accounting guidance and historical paragraphs, a pronouncement sometimes contains other paragraphs or appendixes that (a) state the scope of the pronouncement, (b) indicate substantive

amendments to other existing pronouncements, (c) present examples or illustrations of application of the requirements of the pronouncement, or (d) present a glossary of the terms used in the pronouncement. The Board believes that the content of those various paragraphs and appendixes provides part of the accounting guidance of the pronouncement and should be amended if the pronouncement is amended by a subsequent pronouncement.

A16. Most respondents to the 2001 Exposure Draft agreed that the proposed technical corrections represent nonsubstantive amendments to existing authoritative pronouncements. Several respondents suggested additional technical corrections. The Board considered those suggestions and decided to include in this Statement those that met the criteria established for a technical correction.

Effective Date and Transition

A17. The Board noted that the rescission of Statement 4 represents a change in practice relating to the classification of gains and losses from extinguishment of debt. The 2001 Exposure Draft proposed that the provisions of the Statement related to the rescission of Statement 4 be applied as of the beginning of the fiscal year in which the Statement is issued. The Board reasoned that if the provisions of this Statement related to the rescission of Statement 4 were required to be applied from the beginning of an entity's fiscal year, the financial statements for that year would present the debt extinguishment transactions in that year consistently. Further, the Board noted that it would not be onerous for preparers to determine whether debt extinguishments completed prior to the issuance of this Statement meet the criteria for extraordinary item classification.

A18. Several respondents to the 2001 Exposure Draft commented that the requirement to apply those provisions retroactively to the beginning of the fiscal year could have a negative effect on certain debt covenants. The Board considered those comments and decided to require that entities apply the provisions of this Statement related to the rescission of Statement 4 in fiscal years beginning after the Statement is issued. However, the Board decided to encourage early application of those provisions. In addition, the Board decided to require reclassification of the gains and losses related to debt extinguishments that do not meet the criteria in Opinion 30 for extraordinary item treatment for all prior periods presented in comparative financial statements.

A19. The Board decided that the provisions in paragraphs 8 and 9(c) of this Statement that amend Statement 13 should be applied for transactions entered into after issuance of this Statement, with early application encouraged.

A20. The amendments to make technical corrections to existing pronouncements represent codification of items the Board intended to include within accounting pronouncements that are already in effect. The 2001 Exposure Draft proposed that the provisions of this Statement not related to Statement 4 should be effective upon issuance of the Statement. Respondents asked for clarification of whether those provisions should be effective for financial statements issued after the Statement is issued or for transactions occurring after issuance of the final Statement. The Board decided that, except for the provisions discussed in paragraphs A18 and A19, all provisions of this Statement should be effective for financial statements issued after this Statement is issued, with early application encouraged.

Benefits and Costs

A21. The Board's mission statement charges the Board to determine that a proposed standard will fill a significant need and that the costs it imposes will be justified in relation to the overall benefits. The rescis-sion of Statements 4 and 64 eliminates an exception to general practice relating to how to determine whether certain items should be classified as extraordinary. The criteria for extraordinary item classification are outlined in paragraph 20 of Opinion 30, and entities have been successfully applying those criteria for almost 30 years. The Board believes that the benefits of consistent application of the criteria for extraordinary item classification outweigh any effort required on the part of preparers to apply the criteria of Opinion 30 to debt extinguishment transactions. The rescission of Statement 44 removes a no longer relevant standard from the authoritative literature.

A22. The amendment of Statement 13 affects the accounting by the lessee for certain lease modifications that have economic effects similar to sale-leaseback transactions. The Board believes that that amendment improves financial accounting because similar transactions should be accounted for in a similar manner. Further, the Board believes that applying sale-leaseback accounting to the lease modifications addressed in this Statement would not be costly.

A23. The Board believes that financial reporting is both simplified and improved by eliminating the inconsistent and obsolete reporting requirements of Statements 4, 44, and 64 and by incorporating the amendments and technical corrections in this Statement.

(Refer to Volume III of the *Original Pronouncements*
for the appendixes and topical index.)